Make just one call for all your Ohio practice needs!
1-800-344-5009

- State Code
- Court Rules
- Forms
- Practice Guides
- Practice Treatises

ATTENTION: M. STUEBER, D5-N836

BUSINESS REPLY MAIL
FIRST CLASS MAIL   PERMIT NO. 21   ST. PAUL, MN

POSTAGE WILL BE PAID BY ADDRESSEE

WEST
620 OPPERMAN DRIVE
PO BOX 64833
ST PAUL MN 55164-9752

Baldwin's Ohio Handbook Series

OHIO JUVENILE LAW

**by Paul C. Giannelli
and Patricia McCloud Yeomans**

2004 Edition

THOMSON
✳
WEST

For Customer Assistance Call 1-800-328-4880

Mat #40232321

ISBN # 0-8322-1081-1

For information, please call or write:
West
Cleveland Office
6111 Oak Tree Boulevard
P.O. Box 318063
Cleveland, Ohio 44131
        800/362-4500

Dedication

To Helen and Ben

P.C.G.

To my parents

and

To my mentor, Richard T. Graham

P.M.Y.

Preface

This handbook is designed to provide a concise treatise on Ohio juvenile law. It is also intended as a single convenient source for legal materials most often used in juvenile court proceedings: Revised Code Chapters 2151 and 2152, "Juvenile Courts"; the Rules of Juvenile Procedure (annotated); and the Ohio Rules of Evidence.

This is the fourth edition in which William A. Kurtz's name does not appear on the book. Nevertheless, Bill wrote many of the chapters and was a leading force behind the book.

Although the juvenile courts in Ohio have jurisdiction over a variety of civil and criminal cases, this book focuses mainly on those falling within the court's jurisdiction because of something that a child has done or failed to do (delinquent, unruly, and juvenile traffic offender cases) or something that someone else has done or failed to do (neglected, dependent, and abused child cases). In addition, in Chapter 12, we discuss parental notification of abortion and the juvenile court's jurisdiction over the situation in which a pregnant, unmarried, unemancipated minor female desires an abortion.

Through an analysis of reported and unreported cases and the pertinent statutes and rules, all steps in the juvenile court process are traced—from the assumption of jurisdiction over a child to the termination of that jurisdiction. Where appropriate, reference is also made to the IJA-ABA Standards and the laws of other jurisdictions.

Chapter 2950, which governs sex offender registration, has been amended. First, several new offender categories were created: (1) child-victim oriented offender, (2) habitual child-victim offender, and (3) child-victim predator. These categories reclassify crimes against children that are not committed with a sexual motivation. Automatic reclassification provisions were included for persons previously classified as sex offenders under the old law. Second, new registration classifications were enacted: (1) presumptive registration-exempt sexually oriented offenses and (2) registration-exempt sexually oriented offenses. These provisions exempt certain first-time delinquent offenders from the registration requirements. Third, several crimes were added to the sex offender categories. Fourth, new registration and notification requirements became effective. Fifth, an offender residence limitation was established; a person convicted of a sexually oriented offense or child-victim oriented offense may not reside within 1,000 feet of a school. This provision does not apply to juveniles. Sixth, Internet databases, one for the public and one for law enforcement, were authorized. Seventh, penalties for noncompliance were increased.

Two U.S. Supreme Court cases are noteworthy. In *Yarborough v. Alvarado*, 124 S. Ct. 2140 (2004), the Supreme Court stated that the test to determine whether a person is in "custody" under *Miranda* is an objective test and thus a juvenile's age and experience is not relevant in this context. In addition, the Court jettisoned nearly 25 years of confrontation jurisprudence in *Crawford v. Washington*, 124 S. Ct.

1354, 158 L. Ed. 2d 177, 63 Fed. R. Evid. Serv. 1077 (U.S. 2004). This decision will make it more difficult to admit a certain class of hearsay statements.

This Edition includes Ohio Revised Code provisions current through August 4, 2004, and Ohio Court Rules current through July 1, 2004.

Paul C. Giannelli
Patricia McCloud Yeomans

Cleveland, Ohio
September 2004

Foreword

Unique in Ohio, *Ohio Juvenile Law* is the leading reference for Ohio's juvenile courts, practitioners, and children's advocates. This well-received work offers complete, up-to-date analysis of new developments in a direct style and a handy portable format. Covering the law and practice applicable to delinquents, juvenile traffic offenders, unruly children, and neglected, abused, and dependent children, every phase of a juvenile proceeding, from intake to disposition, is outlined and explained.

The author, Paul C. Giannelli, the Albert J. Weatherhead III and Richard W. Weatherhead Professor of Law at Case Western Reserve University School of Law, is a recognized expert on juvenile law.

The author, Patricia McCloud Yeomans, has been a Magistrate at the Cuyahoga County Court of Common Pleas, Juvenile Division since 1990. She has taught the juvenile law course at Case Western Reserve University School of Law since 2000. She has lectured on juvenile law issues and serves on committees which address juvenile law issues.

For convenient research in or away from the office, *Ohio Juvenile Law* contains the full text of the Ohio Rules of Juvenile Procedure, the Rules of Evidence, and Revised Code Chapters 2151 and 2152, "Juvenile Courts"—reprinted from *Baldwin's Ohio Revised Code, Annotated*. Research aids include a Glossary of technical and legal terms, Tables of Cases and of Laws and Rules, cross references, and a comprehensive Subject Index.

We invite you to visit the Internet home page for West at http://west.thomson.com. While on-line, you can view information on *Ohio Juvenile Law* and other West products.

We gratefully acknowledge the contributions of our editorial and production staffs—particularly Lori Lalak Lee, Esq., David Powers, Mark Knaus, and Diona Shaw—in preparing this 2004 Edition for publication. We have tried to make the book as useful as possible, and we would appreciate your comments and suggestions for improvements to future annual editions.

The Publisher

Cleveland, Ohio
September 2004

Table of Abbreviations

A.	Atlantic Reporter
A.2d	Atlantic Reporter, Second Series
Abs.	Ohio Law Abstract
A.D.2d	Appellate Division Reports, Second Series
Akron L. Rev.	Akron Law Review
A.L.R.2d	American Law Reports Annotated, Second Series
A.L.R.3d	American Law Reports Annotated, Third Series
A.L.R.4th	American Law Reports Annotated, Fourth Series
A.L.R. Fed.	American Law Reports Annotated, Federal
Am.	Amended; Amendment
Am. Bar Assn. Jour.	American Bar Association Journal
Am. Crim. L. Rev.	American Criminal Law Review
Am. Jur.2d	American Jurisprudence, Second Series
Annot.	Annotation
App.	Appellate Court
App. R.	Rules of Appellate Procedure (Ohio)
Ariz.	Arizona Reports
Ariz. App.	Arizona Appeals Reports
Art.	Article
BCDSS	Baltimore City Department of Social Services
Bd.	Board
B.U. L. Rev.	Boston University Law Review
Cal.2d	California Reports, Second Series
Cal.3d	California Reports, Third Series
Cal. App.2d	California Appellate Reports, Second Series
Cal. App.3d	California Appellate Reports, Third Series
Calif. L. Rev.	California Law Review
Cal. Rptr.	California Reporter
Capital L. Rev.	Capital University Law Review
Case W. Res. L. Rev.	Case Western Reserve University Law Review
Cf.	Compare
Ch.	Chapter
Cin. L. Rev.	Cincinnati Law Review
Cir.	Circuit Court
Civ. R.	Rules of Civil Procedure (Ohio)
C.J.S.	Corpus Juris Secundum
Clev. Bar J.	Cleveland Bar Journal
Clev-Mar L. Rev.	Cleveland-Marshall Law Review
Clev. St. L. Rev.	Cleveland State Law Review
Colo.	Colorado Reports
Colum. Hum. Rts. L. Rev.	Columbia Human Rights Law Review
Cornell L. Rev.	Cornell Law Review
C.P.	Common Pleas Court
Crim. R.	Rules of Criminal Procedure (Ohio)
CSB	Children Services Board
CSS	Catholic Social Services
Ct.	Court

D.	Decisions (Ohio)
Dayton L. Rev.	University of Dayton Law Review
D.C.	District Court
Del. Super.	Delaware Superior Court
Dist.	District
DNA	Deoxyribonucleic Acid
D.R.	Disciplinary Rules, Code of Professional Responsibility
DYS	Department of Youth Services
E.C.	Ethical Considerations, Code of Professional Responsibility
Ed.	Edition; Editor
E.D.	Eastern District
eff.	Effective
e.g.	for example
Evid. R.	Ohio Rules of Evidence
ex rel.	ex relatione
F.	Federal Reporter
F.2d	Federal Reporter, Second Series
F.3d	Federal Reporter, Third Series
Fam. Ct.	Family Court
Fam. L. Quar.	Family Law Quarterly, American Bar Association
Fla.	Florida Reports
Fla. App.	Florida Appellate Court Reports
F.R.D.	Federal Rules Decisions
F.Supp.	Federal Supplement
Ga.	Georgia Reports
Ga. App.	Georgia Appeals Reports
GC	General Code of Ohio
Gov. Jud. R.	Supreme Court Rules for the Government of the Judiciary
H	House Bill
Harv. L. Rev.	Harvard Law Review
Hawaii	Hawaii Reports
H.B.	House Bill
Id.	Idem (the same)
Idaho	Idaho Reports
IJA-ABA	Institute of Judicial Administration—American Bar Association
Ill.	Illinois Reports
Ill.2d	Illinois Reports, Second Series
Ill. App.3d	Illinois Appellate Court Reports, Third Series
Ill. Laws	Laws of Illinois
Ind.	Indiana Reports
Ind. App.	Indiana Court of Appeals Reports
Ind. L. Rev.	Indiana Law Review
Iowa L. Rev.	Iowa Law Review
J. Crim. L.	Journal of Criminal Law and Criminology
J. Fam. L., Jour. of Family Law	Journal of Family Law
Juv.	Juvenile Court
Juv. R.	Rules of Juvenile Procedure (Ohio)
Kan.	Kansas Reports
La.	Louisiana Reports

L.Ed.	Lawyers' Edition, United States Supreme Court Reports
L.Ed.2d	Lawyers' Edition, United States Supreme Court Reports, Second Series
LSC	Legislative Service Commission
Mass.	Massachusetts Reports
Md.	Maryland Reports
Md. App.	Maryland Appellate Reports
Me. L. Rev.	Maine Law Review
Mercer L. Rev.	Mercer Law Review
Mich.	Michigan Reports
Mich. App.	Michigan Appeals Reports
Mich. L. Rev.	Michigan Law Review
Minn.	Minnesota Reports
Minn. L. Rev.	Minnesota Law Review
Mo.	Missouri Reports
Mun.	Municipal Court
n.	note
Natl. L. J.	National Law Journal
N.C.	North Carolina Reports
N.C. App.	North Carolina Court of Appeals Reports
NCCD	National Council on Crime and Delinquency
N.C.L. Rev.	North Carolina Law Review
N.D.	Northern District
N.E.	Northeastern Reporter
N.E.2d	Northeastern Reporter, Second Series
Neb.	Nebraska Reports
Nev.	Nevada Reports
N.H.	New Hampshire Reports
N.J.	New Jersey Reports
N.J. Super.	New Jersey Superior Court Reports
N.M.	New Mexico Reports
Nor. Ky. L. Rev.	Northern Kentucky Law Review
N.W.2d	Northwestern Reporter, Second Series
N.W. L. Rev.	Northwestern Law Review
N.Y.2d	New York Reports, Second Series
N.Y. Misc.	New York Miscellaneous Reports
N.Y.S.	New York Supplement
N.Y.S.2d	New York Supplement, Second Series
N.Y.U L. Rev.	New York University Law Review
OAC	Ohio Administrative Code
OAG	Opinions of Attorney General
O.Bar.	Ohio Bar Reports
O.B.R.	Ohio Bar Reports
O. Const.	Ohio Constitution
Ohio App.	Ohio Appellate Reports
Ohio App.2d	Ohio Appellate Reports, Second Series
Ohio App.3d	Ohio Appellate Reports, Third Series
Ohio C.C.(n.s.)	Ohio Circuit Court Reports, New Series
Ohio Cir. Dec.	Ohio Circuit Decisions
Ohio Misc.	Ohio Miscellaneous Reports
Ohio Misc.2d	Ohio Miscellaneous Reports, Second Series
Ohio North. L. Rev.	Ohio Northern University Law Review

Ohio N.P.(n.s.)	Ohio Nisi Prius Reports, New Series
Ohio St.	Ohio State Reports
Ohio St.2d	Ohio State Reports, Second Series
Ohio St.3d	Ohio State Reports, Third Series
Ohio St. L. J.	Ohio State Law Journal
O. Jur.2d	Ohio Jurisprudence, Second Series
O. Jur.3d	Ohio Jurisprudence, Third Series
Okla. Crim.	Oklahoma Criminal Reports
Okla. Crim. App.	Oklahoma Court of Criminal Appeals
O.O.3d	Ohio Opinions, Third Series
Or.	Oregon Reports
Or. App.	Oregon Reports, Court of Appeals
P.	Pacific Reporter
P.2d	Pacific Reporter, Second Series
Pa.	Pennsylvania State Reports
Pa. Super.	Pennsylvania Superior Court Reports
PINS	Persons in Need of Supervision
P.L.	Public Laws
P.R.	Puerto Rico Reports
Prob.	Probate Court
RC	Ohio Revised Code
Rev.	Revision
R.I.	Rhode Island Reports
Rptr.	Reporter
S	Senate Bill
San Diego L. Rev.	San Diego Law Review
S.B.	Senate Bill
S.Ct.	United States Supreme Court Reporter
S.D.	Southern District
S.E.2d	Southeastern Reporter, Second Series
So.2d	Southern Reporter, Second Series
Stan. L. Rev.	Stanford Law Review
St. Mary's L. J.	St. Mary's Law Journal
sub nom	under the name
supp.	supplement
Supreme Court Rev.	Supreme Court Review
S.W.2d	Southwestern Reporter, Second Series
Tenn. Code. Ann.	Tennessee Code Annotated
Tex. Civ. App.	Texas Civil Appeals Reports
Traf. R.	Traffic Rules (Ohio)
U.C.D. L. Rev.	U.C. Davis Law Review
U.S.	United States Supreme Court Reports
U.S.C.	United States Code
U.S.C.A.	United States Code Annotated
U.S. Const.	United States Constitution
Utah	Utah Reports
U. Tol. L. Rev.	University of Toledo Law Review
v.	versus; volume
Va.	Virginia Reports
vol.	volume
Vt.	Vermont Reports
Wash.2d	Washington Reports, Second Series
Wash. App.	Washington Appellate Reports

Table of Abbreviations

W.D. .... Western District
Wh. .... Wharton's Reports (Pennsylvania)
WL .... Westlaw
Wm. & Mary L. Rev. ... William and Mary Law Review
W.R.U. L. Rev. .... Western Reserve University Law Review
W. Va. .... West Virginia Reports
Wyo. Stat. .... Wyoming Statutes

Westlaw® Electronic Research Guide

Coordinating Legal Research with Westlaw

Baldwin's Ohio Handbook Series is an essential aid to legal research. Westlaw provides a vast, online library of over 10,000 collections of documents and services that can supplement research begun in this publication, encompassing:

- Federal and state primary law (statutes, regulations, rules, and case law), including West's editorial enhancements, such as headnotes, Key Number classifications, annotations
- Secondary law resources (texts and treatises published by West and by other publishers, as well as law reviews)
- Legal news
- Directories of attorneys and experts
- Court records and filings
- KeyCite™

Specialized topical subsets of these resources have been created for more than thirty areas of practice.

In addition to legal information, there are general news and reference databases and a broad array of specialized materials frequently useful in connection with legal matters, covering accounting, business, environment, ethics, finance, medicine, social and physical sciences.

This guide will focus on a few aspects of Westlaw use to supplement research begun in this publication, and will direct you to additional sources of assistance.

Databases

A database is a collection of documents with some features in common. It may contain statutes, court decisions, administrative materials, commentaries, news or other information. Each database has a unique identifier, used in many Westlaw commands to select a database of interest. For example, the database containing Ohio cases has the indentifier OH-CS.

The Westlaw Directory is a comprehensive list of databases with information about each database, including the types of documents each contains. The first page of a standard or customized Westlaw Directory is displayed upon signing on to Westlaw, except when prior, saved research is resumed.

A special subdirectory, accessible from the main Westlaw Directory, lists databases applicable to Family Law research.

Databases of potential interest in connection with your research include:

OHFL-CS	Ohio Family Law Cases
FFL-CS	Federal Cases—Family Law
FFL-USCA	U.S. Code Sections—Family Law
FL-TP	Law Reviews, Texts & Journals—Family Law
WLD-FAM	West's Legal Directory—Family
CANJFL	Canadian Journal of Family Law
FAMADVO	Family Advocate (ABA)
FAMLQ	Family Law Quarterly (ABA)
FAMLV-LH	Family and Medical Leave Act—Legislative History (Arnold & Porter)
FAM-RES	Family Resources (DIALOG)
INPADOC	INPADOC/Family and Legal Status (DIALOG)
OTP-INPADOC	ONTAP INPADOC/Family Legal Status (DIALOG)
ULVLJFL	University of Louisville Journal of Family Law (Univ. of Louisville)

For information as to currentness and search tips regarding any Westlaw database, enter the SCOPE feature. It is not necessary to include the identifier to obtain scope information about the currently selected database.

Westlaw Highlights

Use of this publication may be supplemented through the Westlaw Bulletin (WLB), the Westlaw Ohio State Bulletin (WSB-OH) and various Topical Highlights, including Family Law Highlights (WTH-FL). Highlights databases contain summaries of significant judicial, legislative and administrative developments and are updated daily; they are searchable both from an automatic list of recent documents and using general Westlaw search methods for documents accumulated over time. The full text of any judicial decision may be retrieved by using the FIND feature.

Consult the Westlaw Directory for a complete, current listing of highlights databases.

Retrieving Cases Citing This Publication

To retrieve cases citing this publication, sign on to a case law database and enter a query in the following form:

Giannelli /10 "Juvenile Law"

Retrieving a Specific Case

The FIND command can be used to quickly retrieve a case whose citation is known. For example:

FI 612 N.E.2d 1068

Updating Case Law Research

KeyCite™ is an enhanced citator service that integrates all the case law on Westlaw. KeyCite provides direct and negative indirect history for any case within the scope of its coverage, citations to other decisions and secondary materials on Westlaw that have mentioned or discussed the cited case, and a complete integration with West's Key Number System so that you can track a legal issue explored in a case. KeyCite is as current as Westlaw and includes all cases on Westlaw, including unpublished opinions.

Retrieving Statutes, Court Rules and Regulations

Annotated and unannotated versions of the Ohio statutes are searchable on Westlaw (identifiers OH-ST-ANN and OH-ST), as are Ohio court rules (OH-RULES) and Ohio Administrative Code (OH-ADC).

The United States Code and United States Code Annotated are searchable databases on Westlaw (identifiers USC and USCA, respectively), as are federal court rules (US-RULES) and regulations (CFR).

In addition, the FIND command may be used to retrieve specific provisions by citation, obviating the need for database selection or search.

Updating Research in re Statutes, Rules and Regulations

When viewing a statute, rule, or regulation on Westlaw after a search or FIND command, it is easy to update your research. A yellow or red flag symbol or other notation will appear on the screen if relevant amendments, repeals, or other new material is available. Clicking on the flag or notation will display the material.

Documents used to update Ohio statutes are also searchable in Ohio Legislative Service (OH-LEGIS). Those used to update rules are searchable in Ohio Orders (OH-ORDERS).

Documents used to update federal statutes, rules, and regulations are searchable in the United States Public Laws (US-PL), Federal Orders (US-ORDERS) and Federal Register (FR) databases, respectively.

Using Westlaw as a Citator

For research beyond the coverage of any citator service, go directly to the databases (cases, for example) containing citing documents and use standard Westlaw search techniques to retrieve documents citing specific constitutional provisions, statutes, standard jury instructions or other authorities.

Fortunately, the specific portion of a citation is often reasonably distinctive, such as 22:636.1, 301.65, 401(k), 12-21-5, 12052. When it is, a search on that specific portion alone may retrieve applicable documents without any substantial number of inapplicable ones (unless the number happens to be coincidentally popular in another context). Ohio statutes fall into this category.

Similarly, if the citation involves more than one number, such as 42 U.S.C.A. § 1201, a search containing both numbers (e.g., 42 +5 1201) is likely to produce mostly desired information, even though the component numbers are common.

If necessary, the search may be limited in several ways:

A. Switch from a general database to one containing mostly cases within the subject area of the cite being researched;

B. Use a connector (&, /S, /P, etc.) to narrow the search to documents including terms which are highly likely to accompany the correct citation in the context of the issue being researched;

C. Include other citation information in the query. Because of the variety of citation formats used in documents, this option should be used primarily where other options prove insufficient. Below are illustrative queries for any database containing Ohio cases.

Civ.Rule Civ Civil O.R.C.P. R.C.P. /7 56

will retrieve cases citing Civil Procedure Rule 56; and

(appellate /2 procedure rule) App.Proc! App.Rule R.A.P. /7 33

will retrieve cases citing Appellate Procedure Rule 33.

Alternative Retrieval Methods

WIN® (Westlaw Is Natural™) allows you to frame your issue in plain English to retrieve documents:

Can parental rights be terminated due to substance abuse (alcohol alcoholism drug narcotic heroin cocaine)?

Alternatively, retrieval may be focused by use of the Terms and Connectors method:

DI(TERMINAT! /P PARENT! /P RIGHT /P ALCOHOL*** DRUG NARCOTIC SUBSTANCE HEROIN COCAINE)

In databases with Key Numbers, either of the above examples will identify Infants ☞155-158 and ☞178-181 as Key Numbers collecting headnotes relevant to this issue if there are pertinent cases.

As the Key Numbers are affixed to points of law by trained specialists based on conceptual understanding of the case, relevant cases that were not retrieved by either of the language-dependent methods will often be found at a Key Number.

Similarly, citations in retrieved documents (to cases, statutes, rules, etc.) may suggest additional, fruitful research using other Westlaw databases (e.g., annotated statutes, rules) or services (e.g., KeyCite™).

Key Number Search

Frequently, case law research rapidly converges on a few topics, headings and Key Numbers within West's Key Number System that are likely to contain relevant cases. These may be discovered from known, relevant reported cases from any jurisdiction; Library References in West publications; browsing in a digest; or browsing the Key Number System on Westlaw using the JUMP feature or the KEY command.

Once discovered, topics, subheadings or Key Numbers are useful as search terms (in databases containing reported cases) alone or with other search terms, to focus the search within a narrow range of potentially relevant material.

For example, to retrieve cases with at least one headnote classified to Parent and Child ☞2.5, sign on to a case law database and enter

285k2.5 [use with other search terms, if desired]

The topic name (Parent and Child) is replaced by its numerical equivalent (285) and the ☞ by the letter k. A list of topics and their numerical equivalents is in the Westlaw Reference Manual and is displayed in Westlaw when the KEY command is entered.

Other topics of special interest include: Abortion and Birth Control (4), Adoption (17), Children Out-of-Wedlock (76H), Husband and Wife (205), Incest (207), Infants (211), and Marriage (253).

Using JUMP

Westlaw's JUMP feature allows you to move from one document to another or from one part of a document to another, then easily return to your original place, without losing your original result. Opportunities to move in this manner are marked in the text with either blue, underlined text or a JUMP symbol (►). Whenever you see the JUMP symbol, you may move to the place designated by the adjacent reference by using the Tab or arrow keys, or mouse click to position the cursor on the JUMP symbol, then pressing Enter or clicking again with the mouse.

Within the text of a court opinion, JUMP arrows are adjacent to case cites and federal statute cites, and adjacent to parenthesized numbers marking discussions corresponding to headnotes.

On a screen containing the text of a headnote, the JUMP arrows allow movement to the corresponding discussion in the text of the opinion,

► (3)

and allow browsing West's Key Number System beginning at various heading levels:

► 285 PARENT AND CHILD
► 285k13.5 Torts
► 285k13.5(4) Negligent supervision or control of child by parent

General Information

The information provided above illustrates some of the ways Westlaw can complement research using this publication. However, this brief overview illustrates only some of the power of Westlaw. The full range of Westlaw search techniques is available to support your research.

Please consult the Westlaw Reference Manual for additional information or assistance or call West's Reference Attorneys at 1-800-REF-ATTY (1-800-733-2889).

For information about subscribing to Westlaw, please call 1-800-328-9352.

RELATED PRODUCTS FROM WEST

STATUTES, CONSTITUTIONS, AND COURT RULES

Baldwin's Ohio Revised Code Annotated
Baldwin's Ohio Legislative Service Annotated
Ohio Constitution Handbook
Ohio Rules of Court, State and Federal
United States Code Annotated

CASE LAW, REPORTERS, DIGESTS, ATTORNEY GENERAL OPINIONS

Ohio Official Reports
West's Ohio Digest
Ohio Attorney General Opinions
SERB Official Reporter
Federal Reporter
Federal Supplement
West's Supreme Court Reporter

ADMINISTRATIVE LAW

Baldwin's Ohio Administrative Code
**Ohio Administrative Law Handbook
and Agency Directory**
Vierow and Lepp
Baldwin's Ohio Monthly Record
Administrative Law and Practice 2d
Administrative Law: Practice and Procedure

GENERAL LEGAL REFERENCES

Ohio Jurisprudence 3d
American Jurisprudence 2d
American Law Reports
Corpus Juris Secundum

OHIO DATABASES ON WESTLAW

Cases, General & Topical

Statutes & Court Rules

Legislative Service, Bills & Bill Tracking

Administrative & Executive Materials

Public Information, Records & Filings

Baldwin's Ohio Practice Series

Ohio Jurisprudence 3d

Ohio Forms, Legal & Business

Law Reviews, Bar Journals & Legal Periodicals

Newspapers & Periodicals

Miscellany

CD-ROM

Baldwin's Ohio Revised Code Annotated with
Ohio Administrative Code, and
SERB Official Reporter

Ohio Reports

Ohio Unreported Appellate Decisions

Baldwin's Ohio Practice Library

West's Ohio Digest

Ohio Jurisprudence 3d

United States Code Annotated

West's Sixth Circuit Reporter

West's Federal District Court Reporter—Sixth Circuit

West's Supreme Court Reporter

Federal Reporter, 1st, 2d, and 3d Series

Federal Supplement

Federal Rules Decisions

Wright & Miller, Federal Practice and Procedure

Topical CD-ROM Libraries

Ohio Jurisprudence Pleading and Practice Forms

Ohio Criminal Defense Motions
Hennenberg and Reinhart

CIVIL PRACTICE AND PROCEDURE

Baldwin's Ohio Practice, Civil Practice
Klein, Darling, and Terez

Baldwin's Ohio Practice, Civil Practice Laws &
Rules Annotated

Ohio Personal Injury Practice

Trial Handbook for Ohio Lawyers
Markus

CRIMINAL LAW AND PRACTICE

Baldwin's Ohio Practice, Criminal Law 2d
Katz, Giannelli, Blair, and Lipton

Baldwin's Ohio Practice, Statutory Charges
Blair

Ohio Arrest, Search and Seizure
Katz

Baldwin's Ohio Practice, Ohio Criminal Justice
Katz and Giannelli (Eds.) (published in cooperation with the Case
Western Reserve University School of Law)

Ohio Domestic Violence Law
Adrine and Ruden

Ohio Driving Under the Influence Law
Painter

Ohio Felony Sentencing Law
Griffin and Katz

Trial Handbook for Ohio Lawyers
Markus

TRIAL AND APPELLATE PRACTICE

Baldwin's Ohio Practice, Evidence 2d
Giannelli and Snyder

Baldwin's Ohio Practice, Rules of Evidence Handbook
Giannelli and Snyder

Ohio Appellate Practice
Painter

Trial Handbook for Ohio Lawyers
Markus

DOMESTIC RELATIONS AND FAMILY LAW

Baldwin's Ohio Practice, Domestic Relations Law 4th
Sowald and Morganstern

**Baldwin's Ohio Practice, Domestic Relations Laws and
Rules Annotated**

Ohio Domestic Violence Law
Adrine and Ruden

Domestic Relations Journal of Ohio
Morganstern

PROBATE AND JUVENILE LAW

Baldwin's Ohio Practice, Merrick-Rippner Probate Law 6th
Carlin

Ohio Probate Code Annotated

Probate Law Journal of Ohio
Brucken

Ohio Juvenile Law
Giannelli and Yeomans

REAL ESTATE

Ohio Landlord Tenant Law
White

Baldwin's Ohio Practice, Ohio Real Estate Law 3d
Kuehnle and Levey

BUSINESS AND LEGAL

Baldwin's Ohio Practice, Business Organizations
Blackford

Baldwin's Ohio Practice, Business Organizations
Laws & Rules
Ekonomon and Heinle (Eds.)

Ohio Consumer Law
Legal Aid Society of Cleveland, Williams (Ed.)

LEGAL FORMS

Ohio Forms Legal and Business

Ohio Forms and Transactions

Ohio Jurisprudence Pleading and Practice Forms

West's Legal Forms, 2d

TAX LAW

Baldwin's Ohio Tax Law and Rules

LABOR LAW

Ohio Civil Service & Collective Bargaining Laws & Rules
Annotated

Ohio Employment Practices Law
Siegel and Stephen

Ohio Workers' Compensation Law Practice Guide
Wasil, Mastrangelo, and DeRose

Workers' Compensation Journal of Ohio
Harris

GOVERNMENT

Baldwin's Ohio Township Law
Princehorn

Gotherman and Babbit, Ohio Municipal Law
Babbit and Lang

Finley's Ohio Municipal Service
Finley

Ohio Election Laws Annotated

Ohio Planning and Zoning Law
Meck and Pearlman

SCHOOL LAW

Baldwin's Ohio School Law
Hastings, Manoloff, Sheeran, and Stype

Ohio School Law Handbook
Hastings, Manoloff, Sheeran, and Stype

Baldwin's Ohio School Law Journal
Lentz

Lentz School Security
Lentz

United States School Laws and Rules

BUILDING CONSTRUCTION AND CODE ENFORCEMENT

Ohio Building Code and Related Codes

Know Your Code: A Guide to the OBC
The PREVIEW Group, Inc.

Code News
Collins

If you would like to inquire about these West publications or place an order, please call 1–800–344–5009.

West
610 Opperman Drive
Eagan, MN 55123

Visit West on the Internet:
http://west.thomson.com

Summary of Contents

		Page
Detailed Volume Table of Contents		xxix

Text

Chapter 1	History & Philosophy	1
Chapter 2	Age Jurisdiction	21
Chapter 3	Subject Matter Jurisdiction	27
Chapter 4	Delinquent Child Jurisdiction	33
Chapter 5	Serious Youthful Offenders	39
Chapter 6	Sex Offender Law	49
Chapter 7	Juvenile Traffic Offender Jurisdiction	61
Chapter 8	Unruly Child Jurisdiction	63
Chapter 9	Neglected & Abused Child Jurisdiction	69
Chapter 10	Dependent Child Jurisdiction	85
Chapter 11	Temporary & Permanent Custody Agreements	93
Chapter 12	Parental Notification of Abortion	97
Chapter 13	Removal Actions	105
Chapter 14	Investigations	109
Chapter 15	Intake, Diversion, & Mediation	139
Chapter 16	Complaint	147
Chapter 17	Venue	165
Chapter 18	Summons	169
Chapter 19	Detention or Shelter Care	181
Chapter 20	Temporary Orders Pending Hearing	191
Chapter 21	Discovery	195
Chapter 22	Transfer of Jurisdiction	203
Chapter 23	Adjudicatory Hearings	235
Chapter 24	Magistrates	297
Chapter 25	Dispositional Hearings	303
Chapter 26	Dispositional Case Plans	317
Chapter 27	Delinquent Child Dispositions	323
Chapter 28	Juvenile Traffic Offender Dispositions	345
Chapter 29	Unruly Child Dispositions	353
Chapter 30	Abused, Neglected, or Dependent Child Dispositions	357
Chapter 31	Motions for Permanent Custody	381
Chapter 32	Jurisdiction Over Parents and Others	391
Chapter 33	Continuing Jurisdiction	397
Chapter 34	Appeals and Habeas Corpus	409

Chapter 35   Juvenile Court Records   423
Chapter 36   Interstate Agreements   433

Appendices

Appendix A   Ohio Revised Code—Selected
              Provisions   App. A-1
Appendix B   Rules of Juvenile Procedure   App. B-1
Appendix C   Ohio Rules of Evidence   App. C-1
Appendix D   Glossary   App. D-1

Table of Laws and Rules   Tbl of L&R-1

Table of Cases   Tbl of Cases-1

Index   Index-1

Detailed Volume Table of Contents

Chapter 1
History & Philosophy

§ 1:1 History & philosophy—Introduction
§ 1:2 Development of juvenile courts
§ 1:3 1925–1966 developments
§ 1:4 Due process revolution
§ 1:5 Future directions
§ 1:6 Ohio experience
§ 1:7 Juvenile code
§ 1:8 Rules of Juvenile Procedure

Chapter 2
Age Jurisdiction

§ 2:1 Age jurisdiction—Introduction
§ 2:2 Age jurisdiction
§ 2:3 Child subject to adult prosecution
§ 2:4 Mistaken or concealed age
§ 2:5 Proof of age jurisdiction
§ 2:6 Common law infancy defense
§ 2:7 Detention of "children" over the age of 18 years

Chapter 3
Subject Matter Jurisdiction

§ 3:1 Subject matter jurisdiction—Introduction
§ 3:2 Exclusive original jurisdiction
§ 3:3 Concurrent jurisdiction

Chapter 4
Delinquent Child Jurisdiction

§ 4:1 Delinquent child jurisdiction—Introduction
§ 4:2 Delinquent child defined
§ 4:3 Federal penal law
§ 4:4 Ohio penal law
§ 4:5 Truancy
§ 4:6 Court order violations
§ 4:7 Transfer to adult criminal court
§ 4:8 Serious Youthful Offender (SYO)

Chapter 5
Serious Youthful Offenders

§ 5:1   Introduction
§ 5:2   Blended sentences
§ 5:3   SYO charging; preliminary hearing
§ 5:4   SYO venue
§ 5:5   SYO enhancements
§ 5:6   SYO adjudicatory hearing
§ 5:7   Mandatory SYO dispositions
§ 5:8   Discretionary SYO dispositions
§ 5:9   Procedural rights
§ 5:10   Invoking adult sentences
§ 5:11   Invoking adult sentence hearing
§ 5:12   Subsequent procedures
§ 5:13   SYO appeals

Chapter 6
Sex Offender Law

§ 6:1   Introduction
§ 6:2   "Sexually oriented offender" defined
§ 6:3   Registration-exempt sexually oriented offenses
§ 6:4   "Habitual sex offender" defined
§ 6:5   "Sexual predator" defined
§ 6:6   "Child-victim oriented offender" defined
§ 6:7   "Habitual child-victim offender" defined
§ 6:8   "Child-victim predator" defined
§ 6:9   Juvenile offender registrant—Repeat offender classification
§ 6:10   Juvenile offender registrant—Mandatory classification
§ 6:11   Juvenile offender registrant—Discretionary classification
§ 6:12   Dispositional completion hearing
§ 6:13   Petitions for reclassification or declassification
§ 6:14   Registration requirements
§ 6:15   Notification requirements
§ 6:16   Internet dissemination
§ 6:17   Residence limitation

Chapter 7
Juvenile Traffic Offender Jurisdiction

§ 7:1   Juvenile traffic offender jurisdiction—Introduction
§ 7:2   Traffic offenders
§ 7:3   Juvenile traffic violations bureau
§ 7:4   Delinquency compared

Chapter 8
Unruly Child Jurisdiction

§ 8:1   Unruly child jurisdiction—Introduction
§ 8:2   Unruly child defined
§ 8:3   Unruly—Wayward or habitually disobedient

§ 8:4   Unruly—Truancy
§ 8:5   Unruly—Endangering conduct
§ 8:6   Unruly—Status offenses
§ 8:7   Unruly—Miscellaneous conduct

Chapter 9

Neglected & Abused Child Jurisdiction

§ 9:1   Neglected & abused child jurisdiction—Introduction
§ 9:2   Parental rights
§ 9:3   Time of neglect
§ 9:4   Neglected child defined
§ 9:5   Neglect—Abandonment
§ 9:6   Neglect—Inadequate care due to parental fault
§ 9:7   Neglect—Subsistence, education & medical care
§ 9:8   Neglect—Special care for child's mental condition
§ 9:9   Neglect—Illegal placement
§ 9:10   Neglect—Physical or mental injury due to omissions
§ 9:11   Neglect—Out-of-home care neglect
§ 9:12   Abused child defined
§ 9:13   Abused child—Sexual victim
§ 9:14   Abused child—Child endangerment
§ 9:15   Abused child—Physical or mental injury exhibited
§ 9:16   Abused child—Physical or mental injury due to parents
§ 9:17   Abused child—Out-of-home abuse

Chapter 10

Dependent Child Jurisdiction

§ 10:1   Dependent child jurisdiction—Introduction
§ 10:2   Dependent child defined
§ 10:3   Dependency—Homeless, destitute or without adequate care
§ 10:4   Dependency—Inadequate care due to parents' mental or physical condition
§ 10:5   Dependency—Detrimental condition or environment
§ 10:6   Dependency—Danger of abuse of neglect

Chapter 11

Temporary & Permanent Custody Agreements

§ 11:1   Temporary & permanent custody agreements—Introduction
§ 11:2   Jurisdiction for custody agreements
§ 11:3   Temporary custody agreements
§ 11:4   Extension of temporary custody agreements
§ 11:5   Permanent custody agreements
§ 11:6   Parental revocation of permanent surrender

Chapter 12

Parental Notification of Abortion

§ 12:1   Parental notification of abortion—Introduction

§ 12:2   Jurisdictional requirements
§ 12:3   Complaint
§ 12:4   Attorney & guardian ad litem
§ 12:5   Venue
§ 12:6   Summons
§ 12:7   Scheduling the hearing
§ 12:8   Hearing
§ 12:9   Case law
§ 12:10   Appeals

Chapter 13

Removal Actions

§ 13:1   Removal actions—Introduction
§ 13:2   Jurisdictional requirements
§ 13:3   Venue
§ 13:4   Summons and notice
§ 13:5   Hearing
§ 13:6   Case law

Chapter 14

Investigations

§ 14:1   Investigations—Introduction
§ 14:2   Exclusionary rule
§ 14:3   Custody, arrests & stops
§ 14:4   Search & seizure
§ 14:5   Consent searches
§ 14:6   School searches
§ 14:7   Probation searches
§ 14:8   DNA databases
§ 14:9   Confessions—Due process
§ 14:10   Confessions—*Miranda*
§ 14:11   Confessions—Right to counsel
§ 14:12   Identification procedures—Self-incrimination
§ 14:13   Identification procedures—Right to counsel
§ 14:14   Identification procedures—Due process
§ 14:15   Fingerprints & photographs
§ 14:16   Abuse, neglect & dependency investigations
§ 14:17   Child abuse reporting statute

Chapter 15

Intake, Diversion, & Mediation

§ 15:1   Intake, diversion, & mediation—Introduction
§ 15:2   Intake
§ 15:3   Diversion, youth services grant
§ 15:4   Mediation
§ 15:5   Arbitration
§ 15:6   Family & Children First Council—Dispute resolution process

Chapter 16

Complaint

§ 16:1   Complaint—Introduction

§ 16:2   Standing to file complaint
§ 16:3   Basis for complaint
§ 16:4   Time requirements—Custody; detention
§ 16:5   Parental identification
§ 16:6   Oath requirement
§ 16:7   Content of complaint; designating type of case
§ 16:8   Delinquency complaints
§ 16:9   Traffic offender complaints
§ 16:10   Unruly complaints
§ 16:11   Neglect & abuse complaints
§ 16:12   Dependency complaints
§ 16:13   Custody proceedings—Required information
§ 16:14   Permanent & temporary custody complaints; planned permanent living arrangements
§ 16:15   Certification or transfer from another court
§ 16:16   Amendment of complaints
§ 16:17   Objections to complaints

Chapter 17

Venue

§ 17:1   Venue—Introduction
§ 17:2   Proper venue
§ 17:3   Proof of venue
§ 17:4   Transfer of venue

Chapter 18

Summons

§ 18:1   Summons—Introduction
§ 18:2   Issuance of summons: Proper parties
§ 18:3   Summons: Contents and form
§ 18:4   Summons: Methods of service
§ 18:5   Waiver of summons requirements

Chapter 19

Detention or Shelter Care

§ 19:1   Detention or shelter care—Introduction
§ 19:2   Place of detention
§ 19:3   Admissions officer
§ 19:4   Detention hearing: Notice
§ 19:5   Detention hearing
§ 19:6   Standard for detention
§ 19:7   Time requirements
§ 19:8   Motions for release
§ 19:9   Bail
§ 19:10   Rights while detained
§ 19:11   Detention facilities
§ 19:12   Closure of hearing

Chapter 20

Temporary Orders Pending Hearing

§ 20:1   Temporary orders pending hearing—Introduction

§ 20:2   Temporary care orders
§ 20:3   Emergency medical orders
§ 20:4   Required hearings
§ 20:5   Notice of hearing
§ 20:6   Time requirements

Chapter 21
Discovery

§ 21:1   Discovery—Introduction
§ 21:2   Scope of discovery—Rule 24
§ 21:3   Discovery procedure—Rule 24
§ 21:4   Depositions
§ 21:5   Subpoenas
§ 21:6   Social history report
§ 21:7   Court records
§ 21:8   Victim impact statement

Chapter 22
Transfer of Jurisdiction

§ 22:1   Transfer of jurisdiction—Introduction
§ 22:2   Rationale for transfer
§ 22:3   Constitutional issues
§ 22:4   Improper transfer—Lack of jurisdiction
§ 22:5   Transfer age requirement
§ 22:6   Probable cause requirement
§ 22:7   Mandatory transfer
§ 22:8   Discretionary transfer
§ 22:9   Amenability hearing procedures
§ 22:10   Mental examination
§ 22:11   Right to counsel
§ 22:12   Notice
§ 22:13   Rules of evidence
§ 22:14   Self-incrimination
§ 22:15   Access to reports & discovery
§ 22:16   Right to present evidence
§ 22:17   Statement of reasons
§ 22:18   Right to a transcript
§ 22:19   Public hearing—Victims—Gag orders
§ 22:20   Impartial judge
§ 22:21   Retention of jurisdiction
§ 22:22   Transfer of jurisdiction
§ 22:23   Appeals
§ 22:24   Double jeopardy
§ 22:25   Bail
§ 22:26   Motions to suppress

Chapter 23
Adjudicatory Hearings

§ 23:1   Adjudicatory hearings—Introduction
§ 23:2   Constitutional issues

§ 23:3   Right to counsel
§ 23:4   Waiver of right to counsel
§ 23:5   Ineffective assistance of counsel
§ 23:6   Guardian ad litem
§ 23:7   Mental competency
§ 23:8   Pleas
§ 23:9   Uncontested cases
§ 23:10   Jury trials
§ 23:11   Public trials; gag orders
§ 23:12   Right to be present
§ 23:13   Burden of proof
§ 23:14   Rules of evidence
§ 23:15   Evidence—Privileges
§ 23:16   Evidence—Hearsay
§ 23:17   Evidence—Separation of witnesses
§ 23:18   Evidence—Competency of witnesses
§ 23:19   Evidence—Experts
§ 23:20   Evidence—Impeachment
§ 23:21   Evidence—Corroboration rules
§ 23:22   Right of confrontation
§ 23:23   Confrontation—Face-to-face confrontation
§ 23:24   Confrontation—Cross-examination
§ 23:25   Confrontation—Hearsay
§ 23:26   Confrontation—Waiver
§ 23:27   Self-incrimination
§ 23:28   Impartial judge
§ 23:29   Speedy trial
§ 23:30   Right to a transcript
§ 23:31   Double jeopardy
§ 23:32   Juvenile & adult cases—Truancy

Chapter 24

Magistrates

§ 24:1   Magistrates—Introduction
§ 24:2   Qualifications
§ 24:3   Order of reference
§ 24:4   Pretrial orders
§ 24:5   Hearings
§ 24:6   Recording of proceedings
§ 24:7   Magistrate's decision
§ 24:8   Objections
§ 24:9   Court action

Chapter 25

Dispositional Hearings

§ 25:1   Dispositional hearings—Introduction
§ 25:2   Bifurcated hearings
§ 25:3   Judge or magistrate
§ 25:4   Time requirements
§ 25:5   Right to attend dispositional hearing
§ 25:6   Conduct of hearing
§ 25:7   Advisement of rights

§ 25:8   Burden of proof
§ 25:9   Evidence
§ 25:10   Social history & medical examinations
§ 25:11   Victim participation
§ 25:12   Transcripts
§ 25:13   Judgment & records
§ 25:14   Reasonable efforts determination—Abuse, neglect & dependency

Chapter 26

Dispositional Case Plans

§ 26:1   Dispositional case plans—Introduction
§ 26:2   Requirements
§ 26:3   Time requirements for case plans
§ 26:4   Court approval; journalization
§ 26:5   Case plan amendments
§ 26:6   Goals & priorities
§ 26:7   Due process

Chapter 27

Delinquent Child Dispositions

§ 27:1   Delinquent child dispositions—Introduction
§ 27:2   Dispositional alternatives
§ 27:3   Department of Youth Services commitment
§ 27:4   DYS release
§ 27:5   Child protective services
§ 27:6   County or private facility commitment
§ 27:7   Community control sanctions
§ 27:8   Probation
§ 27:9   Drug & alcohol dispositions
§ 27:10   House arrest & electronic monitoring
§ 27:11   Driving privileges
§ 27:12   Fines
§ 27:13   Restitution
§ 27:14   Forfeiture
§ 27:15   Costs & reimbursements
§ 27:16   Truancy dispositions
§ 27:17   Court custody
§ 27:18   "Catch-all" provision
§ 27:19   Plural dispositions
§ 27:20   Victim-mediation

Chapter 28

Juvenile Traffic Offender Dispositions

§ 28:1   Juvenile traffic offender dispositions—Introduction
§ 28:2   Suspension or revocation
§ 28:3   Financial sanctions
§ 28:4   Community control and probation
§ 28:5   Restitution
§ 28:6   Commitment to juvenile facility
§ 28:7   Seat belt law violations

§ 28:8 Revocation of probationary operator's license
§ 28:9 Occupational driving privileges
§ 28:10 Imposition of adult penalties
§ 28:11 Parental orders

Chapter 29

Unruly Child Dispositions

§ 29:1 Unruly child dispositions—Introduction
§ 29:2 Unruly—Dispositional alternatives
§ 29:3 Unruly—Delinquency dispositions
§ 29:4 Unruly—Drug & alcohol cases
§ 29:5 Unruly—Truancy cases

Chapter 30

Abused, Neglected, or Dependent Child Dispositions

§ 30:1 Abused, neglected, or dependent child dispositions—Introduction
§ 30:2 General principles for abuse, neglect and dependency dispositions
§ 30:3 Costs of dispositions
§ 30:4 Dispositional alternatives for abuse, neglect or dependency
§ 30:5 Protective supervision
§ 30:6 Temporary custody
§ 30:7 Legal custody
§ 30:8 Permanent custody—Defined
§ 30:9 Permanent custody—Requirements
§ 30:10 Permanent custody—Parental placement within reasonable time
§ 30:11 Permanent custody—"Best interest" factors
§ 30:12 Permanent custody—Procedural issues
§ 30:13 Planned permanent living arrangement
§ 30:14 Jurisdiction over parents

Chapter 31

Motions for Permanent Custody

§ 31:1 Motions for permanent custody—Introduction
§ 31:2 Filing of motion
§ 31:3 Time requirements for permanent custody motions
§ 31:4 Hearings on permanent custody motions
§ 31:5 Evidence
§ 31:6 Findings
§ 31:7 Foster parents as "psychological parents"
§ 31:8 Implementation of case plan
§ 31:9 Effect on parental rights

Chapter 32

Jurisdiction Over Parents and Others

§ 32:1 Jurisdiction over parents and others—Introduction
§ 32:2 Jurisdiction over parents and others

§ 32:3   Responsibilities to victims and others

Chapter 33

Continuing Jurisdiction

§ 33:1   Continuing jurisdiction—Introduction
§ 33:2   Motions
§ 33:3   Detention
§ 33:4   Abuse, neglect, and dependency proceedings
§ 33:5   Other proceedings
§ 33:6   Revocation of probation
§ 33:7   Suspended commitments
§ 33:8   Contempt
§ 33:9   Department of Youth Services
§ 33:10   Child custody agency commitment—Semiannual administrative review
§ 33:11   Child custody agency commitment—Juvenile court dispositional review

Chapter 34

Appeals and Habeas Corpus

§ 34:1   Appeals and habeas corpus—Introduction
§ 34:2   Types of cases
§ 34:3   Standing
§ 34:4   Final order requirement
§ 34:5   Notice of appeal
§ 34:6   Stay of proceedings
§ 34:7   Appeal bond
§ 34:8   State appeals
§ 34:9   Right to transcript
§ 34:10   Right to counsel
§ 34:11   Effect on further juvenile court proceedings
§ 34:12   Habeas corpus

Chapter 35

Juvenile Court Records

§ 35:1   Juvenile court records—Introduction
§ 35:2   Confidentiality requirement
§ 35:3   Non-juvenile court proceedings
§ 35:4   Expungement and sealing

Chapter 36

Interstate Agreements

§ 36:1   Interstate agreements—Introduction
§ 36:2   Interstate Compact on Juveniles
§ 36:3   Extradition

Appendices

Appendix A Ohio Revised Code—Selected Provisions

Ch. 2151   Juvenile Courts—General Provisions
Ch. 2152   Juvenile Courts—Criminal Provisions

Appendix B Rules of Juvenile Procedure

Rule 1   Scope of rules: applicability; construction; exceptions
Rule 2   Definitions
Rule 3   Waiver of rights
Rule 4   Assitance of counsel; guardian ad litem
Rule 5   [Reserved]
Rule 6   Taking into custody
Rule 7   Detention and shelter care
Rule 8   Filing by electronic means
Rule 9   Intake
Rule 10   Complaint
Rule 11   Transfer to another county
Rule 12   [Reserved]
Rule 13   Temporary disposition; temporary orders; emergency medical and
                    surgical treatment
Rule 14   Termination, extension or modification of temporary custody orders
Rule 15   Process: issuance, form
Rule 16   Process: service
Rule 17   Subpoena
Rule 18   Time
Rule 19   Motions
Rule 20   Service and filing of papers when required subsequent to filing of
                    complaint
Rule 21   Preliminary conferences
Rule 22   Pleadings and motions; defenses and objections
Rule 23   Continuance
Rule 24   Discovery
Rule 25   Depositions
Rule 26   [Reserved]
Rule 27   Hearings: general
Rule 28   [Reserved]
Rule 29   Adjudicatory hearing
Rule 30   Relinquishment of jurisdiction for purposes of criminal prosecution
Rule 31   [Reserved]
Rule 32   Social history; physical examination; mental examination;
                    investigation involving the allocation of parental rights and
                    responsibilities for the care of children
Rule 33   [Reserved]
Rule 34   Dispositional hearing
Rule 35   Proceedings after judgment
Rule 36   Dispositional review
Rule 37   Recording of proceedings
Rule 38   Voluntary surrender of custody
Rule 39   Out of county removal hearings
Rule 40   Magistrates
Rule 41   [Reserved]
Rule 42   Consent to marry
Rule 43   Reference to Ohio Revised Code
Rule 44   Jurisdiction unaffected

Rule 45   Rules by juvenile courts; procedure not otherwise specified
Rule 46   Forms
Rule 47   Effective date
Rule 48   Title

Appendix C Ohio Rules of Evidence

Article I   General Provisions
Article II   Judicial Notice
Article III   Presumptions
Article IV   Relevancy and Its Limits
Article V   Privileges
Article VI   Witnesses
Article VII   Opinions and Expert Testimony
Article VIII Hearsay
Article IX   Authentication and Identification
Article X   Contents of Writings, Recordings and Photographs
Article XI   Miscellaneous Rules

Appendix D Glossary

Chapter 1

History & Philosophy

> **KeyCite®:** Cases and other legal materials listed in KeyCite Scope can be researched through West's KeyCite service on Westlaw®. Use KeyCite to check citations for form, parallel references, prior and later history, and comprehensive citator information, including citations to other decisions and secondary materials.

§ 1:1   History & philosophy—Introduction
§ 1:2   Development of juvenile courts
§ 1:3   1925–1966 developments
§ 1:4   Due process revolution
§ 1:5   Future directions
§ 1:6   Ohio experience
§ 1:7   Juvenile code
§ 1:8   Rules of Juvenile Procedure

§ 1:1   History & philosophy—Introduction

The establishment of the juvenile court system at the turn of the last century was an historic development, one that still provokes controversy a century later. The juvenile court system, unlike most other courts, was based on a specific philosophy. This chapter discusses the various stages through which the juvenile court system has passed, from its early history to the due process revolution of the 1960s to its present status.

The Ohio history is also examined. The concluding sections of this chapter review the principal non-constitutional laws governing the juvenile court system in Ohio: the Juvenile Code and the Rules of Juvenile Procedure.

§ 1:2   Development of juvenile courts

Illinois established the first juvenile court in 1899.[1] The purpose clause of the enabling Act directed that "the care, custody and discipline of a child shall approximate as nearly as may be that which should be given by its parents, and in all cases where it can properly be done the child [shall] be placed in an improved family home and become a member of the family by legal adoption or otherwise."[2]

The Act contained a number of features that influenced the development of the juvenile court system in this country. First, the Act established a separate court for cases involving children under sixteen alleged to be delinquent, dependent, or neglected. A delinquent child was defined as a child under sixteen "who violates any law of this state or any city or village ordinance." Noncriminal misbehavior (e.g., unruliness) was added to the definition of delinquency in 1901.[3] Second, the enabling Act established special procedures for juvenile cases. Third, the Act prohibited the detention of a child under twelve years of age in a jail or police station and required the separation of

---

[Section 1:2]
[1]Illinois Juvenile Court Act of 1899. 1899 Ill. Laws 131.

[2]1899 Ill. Laws 137.

[3]Schultz, The Cycle of Juvenile Court History, 19 Crime & Delinquency 457 (1973).

juveniles and adults when placed in the same institution. Fourth, it provided for probation officers to investigate cases and supervise juveniles placed on probation.

Within six years of the passage of the Illinois Act, thirty states had enacted juvenile court legislation.[4] By 1925 every state but two had a juvenile court.[5] Today, every jurisdiction has a juvenile court system. The Juvenile Justice and Delinquency Prevention Act of 1974[6] governs juvenile court practice in federal courts.[7]

Parens patriae doctrine. The doctrine of parens patriae underlies the philosophy of the juvenile court system.[8] The concept that "the state is the higher or the ultimate parent of all of the dependents within its borders"[9] was used to justify the commitment of children to reform school as early as 1839.[10]

Rehabilitative ideal. The juvenile court movement was based on a distinct philosophy, the keystone of which was rehabilitation. In the words of two early commentators, "Its purpose is not to punish but to save."[11] Commenting on the practice which existed prior to the adoption of the juvenile court, another early authority wrote, "What was lacking was the conception that a child that broke the law was to be dealt with by the state not as a criminal but as a child needing care, education, and protection."[12]

Separate court system. In order to achieve the goal of rehabilitation, the reformers argued for a separate court for children. According to the reformers, the criminal court system had failed to assist the delinquent child.[13] Oriented primarily toward punishment, the criminal court simply did not focus on the proper issue. It "did not ask how he had come to do the particular act which had brought him before the court. It put but one question, 'Has he committed this crime?' It did not inquire, 'What is the best thing to do for this lad?' "[14]

From its inception, this separate court existed as a civil, not criminal, court. Consequently, children subject to its jurisdiction remained unfettered with the stigma of a criminal conviction. To further protect the child, juvenile records were considered confidential, and the court's proceedings remained closed to the public. Moreover, the juvenile court system discarded

---

[4]Paulsen, *Kent v. United States*: The Constitutional Context of Juvenile Cases, 1966 Supreme Court Rev. 167, 169.

[5]President's Commission on Law Enforcement and Administration of Justice, Task Force Report: Juvenile Delinquency and Youth Crime 3 (1967).

[6]18 U.S.C.A. § 5031 to 18 U.S.C.A. § 5042.

[7]See generally Sessions & Bracey, A Synopsis of the Federal Juvenile Delinquency Act, 14 St. Mary's L. J. 509 (1983); Treatment of juvenile alleged to have violated law of United States under Federal Juvenile Delinquency Act, 58 A.L.R. Fed. 232.

[8]"In the branch of civil law that deals with issues of equity, under the medieval English doctrine of *parens patriae*, court sponsors found the appropriate legal precedent to champion their expansive view of juvenile courts as instruments of moral and social uplift." Schlossman, Juvenile Justice: History and Philosophy, in 3 Encyclopedia of Crime and Justice 961, 962 (Kadish ed. 1983).

[9]Mack, The Juvenile Court, 23 Harv. L. Rev. 104 (1909).

[10]Ex parte Crouse, 4 Wh. 9 (Pa. 1839).

[11]Flexner & Oppenheimer, The Legal Aspect of the Juvenile Court 9 (1922) (Children's Bureau Pub. No. 99).

[12]Lou, Juvenile Courts in the United States 18 (1927).

[13]"[T]he reformers generally rejected deterrence and retribution as adequate notions to justify criminal sanctions. A criminal law based on such principles had failed to suppress crime and was cruel to individuals because of its failure to individualize treatment." Paulsen, *Kent v. United States*: The Constitutional Context of Juvenile Cases, 1966 Supreme Court Rev. 167, 169.

[14]Mack, The Juvenile Court, 23 Harv. L. Rev. 104, 107 (1909).

the procedures applicable in criminal cases.[15] Section 5 of the original Illinois Act provided that "the court shall proceed to hear and dispose of the case in a summary manner."[16] The juvenile court judge would act "as a wise and merciful father."[17] Despite the lack of procedural safeguards, the courts repeatedly upheld the constitutionality of juvenile court procedures.[18]

Social science methods. The early reformers also placed great reliance on the methodologies of the social sciences to bring about the rehabilitation of juveniles: "[T]he Juvenile Court is conceived in the spirit of the clinic; it is a kind of laboratory of human behavior."[19] As another early commentator observed:

> The Juvenile Court is conspicuously a response to the modern spirit of social justice. It is perhaps the first legal tribunal where law and science, especially the science of medicine and those sciences which deal with human behavior, such as biology, sociology, and psychology, work side by side. . . . The methods which it uses are those of social case work.[20]

The juvenile court movement was part of a larger progressive reform movement which surfaced at the turn of the century. Child labor and welfare laws and compulsory school attendance laws were other aspects of this development.[21]

Criticisms. Several commentators have attacked the view that the juvenile court movement was the product of a reform effort designed to improve the lot of juveniles. For example, A. M. Platt has written:

> Child saving may be understood as a crusade which served symbolic and ceremonial functions for native, middle-class Americans. The movement was not so much a break with the past as an affirmation of faith in traditional institutions. Parental authority, home education, rural life, and the independence of the family as a social unit were emphasized because they seemed threatened at this time by urbanism and industrialism. The child savers elevated the nuclear family, especially women as stalwarts of the family, and defended the family's right to supervise the socialization of youth.[22]

In a later section of his book, he commented:

> It is inaccurate to regard the child savers as liberal reformers and their opponents as staunch conservatives, for the authoritarian impulse was implicit in the child-saving movement. . . . In effect, only lower-class families were evaluated as to their competence, whereas the propriety of middle-class families was exempt from investigation and recrimination.[23]

---

[15]"The proceedings were divested of almost all features which are attached to a criminal proceeding. . . . In short, the chancery practice was substituted for that of the criminal procedure." Lou, Juvenile Courts in the United States 20 (1927).

[16]1899 Ill. Laws 133.

[17]Mack, The Juvenile Court, 23 Harv. L. Rev. 104, 107 (1909).

[18]E.g., Lindsay v. Lindsay, 257 Ill. 328, 100 N.E. 892 (1913); Ex parte Sharp, 15 Idaho 120, 96 P. 563 (1908); Commonwealth v. Fisher, 213 Pa. 48, 62 A. 198 (1905); Mill v. Brown, 31 Utah 473, 88 P. 609 (1907).

[19]Van Waters, The Socialization of Juvenile Court Procedure, in Hoag & Williams, Crime, Abnormal Minds and the Law 158 (1923).

[20]Lou, Juvenile Courts in the United States 2 (1927).

[21]Feld, The Transformation of the Juvenile Court, 75 Minn. L. Rev. 691, 694 (1991).

[22]Platt, The Child Savers: The Invention of Delinquency 98 (2d ed. 1977).

[23]Platt, The Child Savers: The Invention of Delinquency 98, 135 (2d ed. 1977). See also Fox, Juvenile Justice Reform: An Historical Perspective, 22 Stan. L. Rev. 1187, 1229 (1970):

> In summary, the 1899 Illinois Act (1) restated the belief in the value of coercive predictions, (2) continued nineteenth-century summary trials for children about whom the predictions were to be made, (3) made no improvements in the long-condemned institutional care furnished these same children, (4) codified the view that institutions should, even without badly needed financial help from the legislature, replicate family life, and that foster homes should be found for predelinquents, and (5) reinforced the private sectarian interests, whose role long had been decried by leading child welfare reformers in the area of juvenile care.

Platt's view of the early reformers, however, has not gone unchallenged.[24]

§ 1:3   1925–1966 developments

From the creation of the first juvenile court in 1899 until 1966, the United States Supreme Court never decided a juvenile court case. The Court did consider whether a juvenile's confession was admissible in evidence in two cases during this period,[1] but both cases involved criminal trials. As noted above, by 1925 the juvenile court system was firmly established. One commentary on these years provides the following picture:

> From 1925 until . . . 1966, juvenile courts operated without legal oversight or monitoring. Many would say that juvenile courts in this period were not really courts at all. There was little or no place for law, lawyers, reporters and the usual paraphernalia of courts; this is not at all surprising because the proponents of the Juvenile Court movement had specifically rejected legal institutions as appropriate to the rehabilitation of children.[2]

It would be a mistake, however, to conclude that nothing of significance occurred during this interval. In 1962, New York enacted the Family Court Act. This Act established a separate classification for noncriminal misbehavior—Persons in Need of Supervision (PINS). This classification aimed to distinguish PINS from delinquents, thereby eliminating the stigma attached to the delinquency label for the PINS child.[3] The Act also established a bifurcated hearing procedure, the first stage focusing on the facts of the case and the second on disposition. In addition, a state-financed system of law guardians was established; limits were placed on pretrial detention; and the right to remain silent was recognized.[4] As one court commented, these provisions "are indicative of legislative recognition of the fact that such proceedings, resulting as they do in a loss of personal freedom, are at the very least quasi-criminal in nature."[5]

Thus, there emerged a middle ground between the lack of procedural safeguards characteristic of the early juvenile courts and the rigorous adherence to procedural rights found in adult trials.

Research References
Carlin, Baldwin's Ohio Practice, Merrick-Rippner Probate Law (6th ed.), Ch 104

§ 1:4   Due process revolution

Kent v. United States. In 1966, the United States Supreme Court in *Kent v. United States*[1] examined the juvenile court system for the first time. *Kent* involved proceedings to transfer a child's case from the juvenile court to a criminal court for trial as an adult.[2] The Court's language in *Kent* signaled the end of the era when juvenile courts could be described as "not really

---

[24]See Schultz, The Cycle of Juvenile Court History, 19 Crime & Delinquency 457 (1973). See also Schlossman, Juvenile Justice: History and Philosophy, in 3 Encyclopedia of Crime and Justice 961 (Kadish ed. 1983).

[Section 1:3]

[1]See Gallegos v. Colorado, 370 U.S. 49, 82 S. Ct. 1209, 8 L. Ed. 2d 325, 87 A.L.R.2d 614 (1962); Haley v. State of Ohio, 332 U.S. 596, 68 S. Ct. 302, 92 L. Ed. 224 (1948).

[2]Wadlington, Whitebread, & Davis, Cases and Materials on Children in the Legal System 198 (1983).

[3]IJA-ABA Juvenile Justice Standards, A Summary and Analysis 33 (2d ed. 1982).

[4]Paulsen, The Constitutional Domestication of the Juvenile Court, 1967 Supreme Court Rev. 233, 244.

[5]In re W., 19 N.Y.2d 55, 62, 277 N.Y.S.2d 675, 224 N.E.2d 102 (1966).

[Section 1:4]

[1]Kent v. U.S., 383 U.S. 541, 86 S. Ct. 1045, 16 L. Ed. 2d 84 (1966).

[2]For a further discussion of the transfer process, see Transfer of Jurisdiction Ch 22.

courts." Referring to the doctrine of parens patriae, Justice Fortas wrote, "But the admonition to function in a 'parental' relationship is not an invitation to procedural arbitrariness."[3] Then he stated:

> While there can be no doubt of the original laudable purpose of juvenile courts, studies and critiques in recent years raise serious questions as to whether actual performance measures well enough against theoretical purpose to make tolerable the immunity of the process from the reach of constitutional guaranties applicable to adults. There is much evidence that some juvenile courts . . . lack the personnel, facilities and techniques to perform adequately as representatives of the State in a *parens patriae* capacity, at least with respect to children charged with law violation. There is evidence, in fact, that there may be grounds for concern that the child receives the worst of both worlds: that he gets neither the protections accorded to adults nor the solicitous care and regenerative treatment postulated for children.[4]

Although some of the Court's language indicated that *Kent* involved only an issue of statutory interpretation, the opinion also referred to constitutional principles: "[W]e do hold that the [transfer] hearing must measure up to the essentials of due process and fair treatment."[5]

In re Gault. Any doubts about the Court's intention to apply due process safeguards to juvenile court practice were resolved in *In re Gault*,[6] a decision which changed the nature of juvenile court proceedings. According to the Court, "[N]either the Fourteenth Amendment [due process] nor the Bill of Rights is for adults alone."[7] Soon after *Gault* was decided, one court aptly observed, "The Supreme Court has recently revolutionized the procedural aspects of juvenile court proceedings."[8]

The Court in *Gault* questioned the underpinnings of the juvenile court system. The doctrine of parens patriae, according to the Court, was suspect: "[I]ts meaning is murky and its historic credentials are of dubious relevance."[9] The term delinquent "has come to involve only slightly less stigma than the term 'criminal' applied to adults."[10] The "claim of secrecy . . . is more rhetoric than reality."[11] Incarceration, "whether it is called 'criminal' or 'civil,' " is nevertheless "a deprivation of liberty."[12] The Court went on to hold that in an adjudicatory hearing to determine delinquency, a child has the right to be notified of the charges, the right to be represented by counsel, the right to confront witnesses who testify against him, and the privilege against compelled self-incrimination.[13]

Two further aspects of the Court's opinion are noteworthy. First, the Court did not believe its decision would ruin the juvenile court system: "[T]he observance of due process standards, intelligently and not ruthlessly administered, will not compel the States to abandon or displace any of the substantive benefits of the juvenile process."[14] Second, the Court limited its holding to delinquency proceedings, and then only to the adjudicatory hearing:

> We do not in this opinion consider the impact of these constitutional provi-

---

[3]Kent v. U.S., 383 U.S. 541, 555, 86 S. Ct. 1045, 16 L. Ed. 2d 84 (1966).

[4]Kent v. U.S., 383 U.S. 541, 555–56, 86 S. Ct. 1045, 16 L. Ed. 2d 84 (1966).

[5]Kent v. U.S., 383 U.S. 541, 562, 86 S. Ct. 1045, 16 L. Ed. 2d 84 (1966). For a further discussion of *Kent*, see § 22:3, Constitutional issues.

[6]Application of Gault, 387 U.S. 1, 87 S. Ct. 1428, 18 L. Ed. 2d 527 (1967).

[7]Application of Gault, 387 U.S. 1, 13, 87 S. Ct. 1428, 18 L. Ed. 2d 527 (1967).

[8]Kent v. U. S., 401 F.2d 408, 409 (D.C. Cir. 1968).

[9]Application of Gault, 387 U.S. 1, 16, 87 S. Ct. 1428, 18 L. Ed. 2d 527 (1967).

[10]Application of Gault, 387 U.S. 1, 24, 87 S. Ct. 1428, 18 L. Ed. 2d 527 (1967).

[11]Application of Gault, 387 U.S. 1, 24, 87 S. Ct. 1428, 18 L. Ed. 2d 527 (1967).

[12]Application of Gault, 387 U.S. 1, 50, 87 S. Ct. 1428, 18 L. Ed. 2d 527 (1967).

[13]For a further discussion of *Gault*, see Adjudicatory Hearings Ch 23.

[14]Application of Gault, 387 U.S. 1, 21, 87 S. Ct. 1428, 18 L. Ed. 2d 527 (1967).

sions upon the totality of the relationship of the juvenile and the state. We do not even consider the entire process relating to juvenile "delinquents." For example, we are not here concerned with the procedures or constitutional rights applicable to the pre-judicial stages of the juvenile process, nor do we direct our attention to the post-adjudicative or dispositional process.[15]

Thus, the *Gault* Court, while using broad language, issued a narrow ruling, limited to specified rights at the adjudicatory stage of delinquency cases.[16] Nevertheless, the ramifications of the decision were not so limited. As one court remarked: "[T]he language of [*Gault*] exhibits a spirit that transcends the specific issues there involved."[17] According to one observer, *Gault* "identified two crucial disjunctions between juvenile justice rhetoric and reality: the theory versus practice of rehabilitation, and the differences between the procedural safeguards afforded adults and those available to juveniles."[18]

Reasonable doubt standard. In 1970, the Court returned to the examination of juvenile court procedure. In *In re Winship*,[19] the Court held that the "beyond a reasonable doubt" standard of proof applicable in adult criminal cases also applied in delinquency cases where a child's liberty was at issue. The Court repeated some of the themes articulated in *Gault*. It rejected the civil-criminal label found in juvenile law jurisprudence: "We made clear [in *Gault*] that civil labels and good intentions do not themselves obviate the need for criminal due process safeguards in juvenile courts."[20] Again, the Court stressed that its decision would not destroy the "beneficial aspects of the juvenile process."[21]

Jury trial. The Court's next case, *McKeiver v. Pennsylvania*,[22] considered the right to trial by jury. Unlike its prior decisions, however, the Court declined to extend this constitutional guarantee to juvenile cases. In reviewing its prior decisions, the Court pointed out that it had not held that *"all* rights constitutionally assured to an adult accused of crime also are to be enforced or made available to the juvenile in his delinquency proceeding."[23] In particular, the Court noted that it had yet to hold that a delinquency proceeding was a " 'criminal prosecution,' within the meaning and reach of the Sixth Amendment."[24] Instead, the Court had relied on the more flexible Due Process Clause in its prior cases.

The Court also remarked that in its prior cases it had insisted that its decisions "not spell the doom of the juvenile court system or even deprive it of

---

[15]Application of Gault, 387 U.S. 1, 13, 87 S. Ct. 1428, 18 L. Ed. 2d 527 (1967). On this issue the Court also wrote, "The problems of pre-adjudication treatment of juveniles, and of post-adjudication disposition, are unique to the juvenile process; hence what we hold in this opinion with regard to the procedural requirements at the adjudicatory stage has no necessary applicability to other steps of the juvenile process." Application of Gault, 387 U.S. 1, 31 n.48, 87 S. Ct. 1428, 18 L. Ed. 2d 527 (1967).

[16]See McKeiver v. Pennsylvania, 403 U.S. 528, 538–39, 91 S. Ct. 1976, 29 L. Ed. 2d 647 (1971).

[17]In re Urbasek, 38 Ill. 2d 535, 541, 232 N.E.2d 716 (1967). See also Kemplen v. State of Md., 428 F.2d 169, 172 (4th Cir. 1970).

[18]Feld, The Transformation of the Juvenile Court, 75 Minn. L. Rev. 691, 695 (1991).

[19]In re Winship, 397 U.S. 358, 90 S. Ct. 1068, 25 L. Ed. 2d 368 (1970).

[20]In re Winship, 397 U.S. 358, 365–66, 90 S. Ct. 1068, 25 L. Ed. 2d 368 (1970).

[21]In re Winship, 397 U.S. 358, 366, 90 S. Ct. 1068, 25 L. Ed. 2d 368 (1970). See § 23:13, Burden of proof.

[22]McKeiver v. Pennsylvania, 403 U.S. 528, 91 S. Ct. 1976, 29 L. Ed. 2d 647 (1971).

[23]McKeiver v. Pennsylvania, 403 U.S. 528, 533, 91 S. Ct. 1976, 29 L. Ed. 2d 647 (1971).

[24]McKeiver v. Pennsylvania, 403 U.S. 528, 541, 91 S. Ct. 1976, 29 L. Ed. 2d 647 (1971). The Sixth Amendment provides:

In all criminal prosecutions, the accused shall enjoy the right to a speedy and public trial, by an impartial jury of the State and district wherein the crime shall have been committed, which district shall have been previously ascertained by law, and to be informed of the nature and cause of the accusation; to be confronted with the witnesses against him; to have compulsory process for obtaining witnesses in his favor, and to have the Assistance of Counsel for his defense.

its 'informality, flexibility, or speed.' "[25] These concerns led the Court to conclude that the right to jury trial would adversely affect the juvenile court system. The Court, however, repeated its belief that the "civil-criminal" distinction was not a controlling factor[26] and that the "fond and idealistic hopes of the juvenile court proponents and early reformers of three generations ago have not been realized."[27] Still, the Court was "reluctant to say that, despite disappointments of grave dimensions, [the juvenile court system] still does not hold promise . . . [or] that the system cannot accomplish its rehabilitative goals."[28]

Double jeopardy. The concern that the Court's refusal to recognize the right to jury trial in *McKeiver* might signal an end to its scrutiny of the juvenile court system did not last long. In *Breed v. Jones*,[29] a 1975 decision, the Court held the Double Jeopardy Clause,[30] which protects an individual from being tried twice for the same offense, applicable to juvenile court proceedings: "We believe it is simply too late in the day to conclude . . . that a juvenile is not put in jeopardy at a proceeding whose object is to determine whether he has committed acts that violate a criminal law and whose potential consequences include both the stigma inherent in such a determination and the deprivation of liberty for many years."[31] Again, the Court rejected the civil-criminal distinction.[32] Although the Court did not find double jeopardy violations in two subsequent cases,[33] it also did not back away from its position in *Breed* that the clause applied to juvenile cases.

Confessions. In another delinquency case, the Court considered the applicability of *Miranda v. Arizona*[34] to a juvenile's confession. In *Fare v. Michael C.*,[35] the Court held that a child's request for his probation officer was not an automatic invocation of the Fifth Amendment's privilege against self-incrimination.[36] In *Yarborough v. Alvarado*,[37] the Supreme Court stated that the test to determine whether a person is in "custody" under *Miranda* is an objective test and thus a juvenile's age and experience is not relevant in this context.

Neglect cases. The Supreme Court's initial juvenile court cases dealt with delinquency proceedings, and when the Court granted due process rights in these cases, it carefully limited its holdings to delinquency cases. In the 1980s, however, the Court addressed due process issues in nondelinquency cases. For example, in *Lassiter v. Department of Social Services*,[38] the Court examined the applicability of due process rights in neglect cases. *Lassiter*, however, involved only one type of neglect proceeding—that involving the

---

[25]McKeiver v. Pennsylvania, 403 U.S. 528, 534, 91 S. Ct. 1976, 29 L. Ed. 2d 647 (1971).

[26]McKeiver v. Pennsylvania, 403 U.S. 528, 534, 91 S. Ct. 1976, 29 L. Ed. 2d 647 (1971).

[27]McKeiver v. Pennsylvania, 403 U.S. 528, 543–44, 91 S. Ct. 1976, 29 L. Ed. 2d 647 (1971).

[28]McKeiver v. Pennsylvania, 403 U.S. 528, 547, 91 S. Ct. 1976, 29 L. Ed. 2d 647 (1971). See § 23:10, Jury trials.

[29]Breed v. Jones, 421 U.S. 519, 95 S. Ct. 1779, 44 L. Ed. 2d 346 (1975).

[30]The Fifth Amendment provides that no person shall "be twice put in jeopardy of life or limb" for the same offense.

[31]Breed v. Jones, 421 U.S. 519, 529, 95 S. Ct. 1779, 44 L. Ed. 2d 346 (1975).

[32]Breed v. Jones, 421 U.S. 519, 529, 95 S. Ct. 1779, 44 L. Ed. 2d 346 (1975).

[33]Illinois v. Vitale, 447 U.S. 410, 100 S. Ct. 2260, 65 L. Ed. 2d 228 (1980); Swisher v. Brady, 438 U.S. 204, 98 S. Ct. 2699, 57 L. Ed. 2d 705, 25 Fed. R. Serv. 2d 1463 (1978).

[34]Miranda v. Arizona, 384 U.S. 436, 86 S. Ct. 1602, 16 L. Ed. 2d 694, 10 A.L.R.3d 974 (1966) (The Fifth Amendment requires that, prior to interrogation, a person in custody be informed of the right to remain silent and the right to the presence of counsel.).

[35]Fare v. Michael C., 442 U.S. 707, 99 S. Ct. 2560, 61 L. Ed. 2d 197 (1979).

[36]For a discussion of the admissibility of confessions, see Investigations Ch 14.

[37]Yarborough v. Alvarado, 124 S. Ct. 2140 (U.S. 2004).

[38]Lassiter v. Department of Social Services of Durham County, N. C., 452 U.S. 18, 101 S. Ct. 2153, 68 L. Ed. 2d 640 (1981).

permanent termination of parental rights. Finding a parent's interest in such a proceeding to be "a commanding one,"[39] the Court held that due process may require the appointment of counsel for indigent parents. The *Lassiter* holding requires assessing the right to counsel on a case-by-case basis.

Santosky v. Kramer[40] also involved proceedings to terminate parental custodial rights permanently. The issue before the Court was whether the "preponderance of evidence" standard, the burden of proof applied in civil cases, satisfied due process requirements in termination proceedings. The Court held that it did not: "In parental rights termination proceedings, the private interest affected is commanding; the risk of error from using a preponderance standard is substantial; and the countervailing governmental interest favoring that standard is comparatively slight."[41] Accordingly, the Court held that due process required "clear and convincing" proof in termination proceedings.

In *M.L.B. v. S.L.J.*,[42] the Court reviewed a state statute that required an indigent in a proceeding to terminate parental rights to pay an advance record fee of about $2,352 as a condition for an appeal. The Court ruled that the fee violated the Equal Protection and Due Process Clauses of the Fourteenth Amendment. The Court noted that it had "repeatedly noticed what sets parental status termination decrees apart from mine run civil actions, even from other domestic relations matters such as divorce, paternity, and child custody. . . . To recapitulate, termination decrees 'wor[k] a unique kind of deprivation.' . . . In contrast to matters modifiable at the parties' will or based on changed circumstances, termination adjudications involve the awesome authority of the State 'to destroy permanently all legal recognition of the parental relationship.' . . . We are therefore satisfied that the label 'civil' should not entice us to leave undisturbed the Mississippi courts' disposition of this case."[43]

Baltimore City Department of Social Services v. Bouknight[44] involved a Fifth Amendment challenge to a juvenile court order requiring the production of Bouknight's abused son. The son previously had been adjudicated a child in need of assistance and returned to Bouknight under the supervision of the Baltimore City Department of Social Services [BCDSS]. The juvenile court subsequently granted BCDSS's petition for the child's removal from Bouknight's custody. When the child could not be located, BCDSS feared he might be dead or injured. The juvenile court found her in civil contempt for failing to produce the child. Bouknight argued that the contempt order violated the privilege against self-incrimination.

The Supreme Court rejected this argument. The Fifth Amendment covers only compelled *testimonial* or *communicative* evidence, and, typically, the act of producing evidence, in itself, is not testimonial. Moreover, "a person may not claim the Amendment's protections based upon the incrimination that may result from the contents or nature of the thing demanded."[45] Bouknight asserted that the "act of producing" her son was an implicit communication of her control of him and might aid the state in prosecuting her.

---

[39]Lassiter v. Department of Social Services of Durham County, N. C., 452 U.S. 18, 27, 101 S. Ct. 2153, 68 L. Ed. 2d 640 (1981). See § 23:3, Right to counsel.

[40]Santosky v. Kramer, 455 U.S. 745, 102 S. Ct. 1388, 71 L. Ed. 2d 599 (1982).

[41]Santosky v. Kramer, 455 U.S. 745, 758, 102 S. Ct. 1388, 71 L. Ed. 2d 599 (1982). See § 23:13, Burden of proof. For a discussion of reasonable efforts to place child with parents, see § 25:14, Reasonable efforts determination.

[42]M.L.B. v. S.L.J., 519 U.S. 102, 117 S. Ct. 555, 136 L. Ed. 2d 473 (1996).

[43]M.L.B. v. S.L.J., 519 U.S. 102, 117 S. Ct. 555, 569–70, 136 L. Ed. 2d 473 (1996).

[44]Baltimore City Dept. of Social Services v. Bouknight, 493 U.S. 549, 110 S. Ct. 900, 107 L. Ed. 2d 992, 29 Fed. R. Evid. Serv. 273 (1990).

[45]Baltimore City Dept. of Social Services v. Bouknight, 493 U.S. 549, 555, 110 S. Ct. 900, 107 L. Ed. 2d 992, 29 Fed. R. Evid. Serv. 273 (1990).

The Court acknowledged this argument but ruled that this situation was analogous to the "required records" exception to the Fifth Amendment. This exception applies when "a person assumes control over items that are the legitimate object of the government's noncriminal regulatory powers."[46] Bouknight had accepted the care of her son subject to the custodial order's conditions, one of which was to cooperate with BCDSS. She "submitted to the routine operation of the regulatory system and agreed to hold [her son] in a manner consonant with the State's regulatory interests and subject to inspection by BCDSS."[47] Because the State's interest in the child's well-being was unrelated to criminal law enforcement, the privilege did not apply.

In *Ferguson v. City of Charleston*,[48] the Supreme Court considered the use of a urine test of a mother to determine whether she had taken cocaine. Motivated by an apparent increase in cocaine use by patients receiving prenatal care, the Medical University of South Carolina [MUSC] instituted a policy to identify pregnant patients suspected of drug abuse and began conducting urine tests of hospital obstetric patients pursuant to that policy. Ten obstetric patients who were arrested after testing positive for cocaine sued the City of Charleston, law enforcement officials who developed and enforced the policy, and representatives of MUSC alleging, inter alia, violation of the Fourth Amendment's prohibition against nonconsensual, warrantless, and suspicionless searches. The Supreme Court held that: (1) the urine tests conducted by MUSC were "searches" within the meaning of the Fourth Amendment, and (2) absent patients' consent, the testing and subsequent reporting of positive test results to the police constituted unreasonable searches. The Court found that "[b]ecause the hospital seeks to justify its authority to conduct drug tests and to turn the results over to law enforcement agents without the knowledge or consent of the patients, this case differs from the four previous cases in which we have considered whether comparable drug tests 'fit within the closely guarded category of constitutionally permissible suspicionless searches.' "[49]

Preventive detention. In *Schall v. Martin*,[50] the Court upheld the constitutionality of pretrial preventive detention for accused juvenile delinquents. As in its prior cases, the Court again attempted to "strike a balance—to respect the 'informality' and 'flexibility' that characterize juvenile proceedings . . . and yet to ensure that such proceedings comport with the 'fundamental fairness' demanded by the Due Process Clause."[51] Thus, at the same time the Court wrote that "[t]here is no doubt that the Due Process Clause is applicable in juvenile proceedings,"[52] it also reaffirmed the state's parens patriae interest: "The State has 'a *parens patriae* interest in preserving and promoting the welfare of the child,' . . . which makes a juvenile

---

[46]Baltimore City Dept. of Social Services v. Bouknight, 493 U.S. 549, 558, 110 S. Ct. 900, 107 L. Ed. 2d 992, 29 Fed. R. Evid. Serv. 273 (1990).

In Wilson v. U.S., 221 U.S. 361, 382, 31 S. Ct. 538, 55, 55 L. Ed. 771 (1911), the Court wrote:

[W]here, by virtue of their character and the rules of law applicable to them, the books and papers are held subject to examination by the demanding authority, the custodian has no privilege to refuse production although their contents tend to criminate him. In assuming their custody he has accepted the incident obligation to permit inspection.

[47]Baltimore City Dept. of Social Services v. Bouknight, 493 U.S. 549, 559, 110 S. Ct. 900, 107 L. Ed. 2d 992, 29 Fed. R. Evid. Serv. 273 (1990).

[48]Ferguson v. City of Charleston, 532 U.S. 67, 121 S. Ct. 1281, 149 L. Ed. 2d 205 (2001).

[49]Ferguson v. City of Charleston, 532 U.S. 67, 77, 121 S. Ct. 1281, 149 L. Ed. 2d 205 (2001).

[50]Schall v. Martin, 467 U.S. 253, 104 S. Ct. 2403, 81 L. Ed. 2d 207 (1984).

[51]Schall v. Martin, 467 U.S. 253, 263, 104 S. Ct. 2403, 81 L. Ed. 2d 207 (1984).

[52]Schall v. Martin, 467 U.S. 253, 263, 104 S. Ct. 2403, 81 L. Ed. 2d 207 (1984).

proceeding fundamentally different from an adult criminal trial."[53] Specifically, the Court held that preventive detention served a legitimate state objective and that the procedural safeguards provided—notice, a hearing, counsel, and a statement of reasons—satisfied due process requirements.

School searches. In *New Jersey v. T.L.O.*,[54] the Court considered the constitutionality of a school search. In that case a student was taken to the principal's office for smoking in the lavatory. A search of her purse revealed cigarettes as well as marijuana, a discovery that led to the initiation of delinquency proceedings. Initially, the Court declared the Fourth Amendment applicable to school searches, thereby rejecting the view that school officials were private citizens, acting in loco parentis, and thus not subject to the Fourth Amendment.[55]

Next, the Court focused on the requirements of the Fourth Amendment in the school setting. In this context, the student's legitimate expectations of privacy are balanced against the school's legitimate need to maintain an environment in which learning can take place. The Court found that the warrant and probable cause requirements imposed too high a burden on the proper functioning of school officials. The Court went on to rule that "reasonable suspicion" is the controlling standard in determining the constitutionality of these searches.[56]

In *Vernonia School District 47J v. Acton*,[57] the United States Supreme Court upheld random urinalysis drug testing for public high school students who participated in athletic programs. Based on *T.L.O.* and prior cases upholding drug testing in other contexts,[58] the Court found the drug testing scheme at issue reasonable. "Fourth Amendment rights, no less than First and Fourteenth Amendment, are different in public schools than elsewhere; the 'reasonableness' inquiry cannot disregard the schools' custodial and tutelary responsibility for children."[59]

In *Board of Education v. Earls*,[60] the Court extended the holding in *Vernonia* to permit drug testing of all students participating in competetive, extracurricular activities. The School District's policy was "a reasonable means of furthering [its] important interest in preventing and deterring drug use among its school children."[61]

Related cases. The Court has decided several cases that relate to the juvenile court policy of confidentiality. *Davis v. Alaska*,[62] a criminal case, involved the cross-examination of a prosecution witness regarding his juvenile record. Although the Court recognized the legitimacy of the state's

---

[53]Schall v. Martin, 467 U.S. 253, 263, 104 S. Ct. 2403, 81 L. Ed. 2d 207 (1984). For a discussion of the state's parens patriae interest in unborn children, see § 9:6, Neglect—Subsistence, education & medical care.

[54]New Jersey v. T.L.O., 469 U.S. 325, 105 S. Ct. 733, 83 L. Ed. 2d 720, 21 Ed. Law Rep. 1122 (1985).

[55]New Jersey v. T.L.O., 469 U.S. 325, 336, 105 S. Ct. 733, 83 L. Ed. 2d 720, 21 Ed. Law Rep. 1122 (1985).

[56]New Jersey v. T.L.O., 469 U.S. 325, 341–42, 105 S. Ct. 733, 83 L. Ed. 2d 720, 21 Ed. Law Rep. 1122 (1985). See § 14:6, School searches.

[57]Vernonia School Dist. 47J v. Acton, 515 U.S. 646, 115 S. Ct. 2386, 132 L. Ed. 2d 564, 101 Ed. Law Rep. 37 (1995).

[58]See National Treasury Employees Union v. Von Raab, 489 U.S. 656, 109 S. Ct. 1384, 103 L. Ed. 2d 685 (1989); Skinner v. Railway Labor Executives' Ass'n, 489 U.S. 602, 109 S. Ct. 1402, 103 L. Ed. 2d 639 (1989).

[59]Vernonia School Dist. 47J v. Acton, 515 U.S. 646, 115 S. Ct. 2386, 2392, 132 L. Ed. 2d 564, 101 Ed. Law Rep. 37 (1995).

[60]Board of Education v. Earls, 536 U.S. 822, 122 S. Ct. 2559, 153 L. Ed. 2d 735 (2002) (activities covered included the Academic Team, Future Farmers of America, Future Homemakers of America, band, choir, pom-pom, cheerleading, and athletics).

[61]Board of Education v. Earls, 536 U.S. 822, 838, 122 S. Ct. 2559, 153 L. Ed. 2d 735 (2002).

[62]Davis v. Alaska, 415 U.S. 308, 94 S. Ct. 1105, 39 L. Ed. 2d 347 (1974).

protective policy concerning juveniles, it found that the "State's policy interest in protecting the confidentiality of a juvenile offender's record cannot require yielding of so vital a constitutional right as the effective cross-examination for bias of an adverse witness."[63] In sum, the Sixth Amendment right of confrontation outweighed the state's protective policy, at least under the facts of that case.

Smith v. Daily Mail Publishing Co.[64] involved a conflict between juvenile court confidentiality and the First Amendment's freedom of press guarantee. In *Smith*, two newspapers were indicted for violating a criminal statute that prohibited publication, without court approval, of the name of any person charged as a juvenile offender. The Court held that the state's interest in protecting the child through a policy of confidentiality did not outweigh the significant First Amendment rights involved. The Court, however, also emphasized the limited nature of its decision:

> Our holding in this case is narrow. There is no issue before us of unlawful press access to confidential judicial proceedings . . . ; there is no issue here of privacy or prejudicial pretrial publicity. At issue is simply the power of a state to punish the truthful publication of an alleged juvenile delinquent's name lawfully obtained by a newspaper. The asserted state interest cannot justify the statute's imposition of criminal sanctions on this type of publication.[65]

A prior case, *Oklahoma Publishing Co. v. District Court In and For Oklahoma County*,[66] involved a pretrial order prohibiting the news media from publishing the name or photograph of a child charged as a delinquent for second-degree murder. The child's name was obtained at a detention hearing, which the press was permitted to attend. The Court held that the press could not be prohibited from publishing information lawfully obtained during open court proceedings.

Cross References
§ 9:6, Ch 14, Ch 22, Ch 23, § 25:5, § 35:2
Research References
Carlin, Baldwin's Ohio Practice, Merrick-Rippner Probate Law (6th ed.), Ch 104

§ 1:5 Future directions

There have been many calls for changes in the juvenile court system. In 1967, the year of the *Gault* decision, the Report of the President's Commission on Law Enforcement and Administration of Justice was published. The Report concluded that the reformers' initial hopes for the juvenile court system remained unrealized: "It has not succeeded significantly in rehabilitating delinquent youth . . . or in bringing justice and compassion to the child offender."[1] The Report disagreed with the reformers' view that delinquency was rooted in the individual. According to the Report, "[D]elinquency is not so much an act of individual deviancy as a pattern of behavior produced by a multitude of pervasive societal influences well beyond the reach of the ac-

---

[63]Davis v. Alaska, 415 U.S. 308, 320, 94 S. Ct. 1105, 39 L. Ed. 2d 347 (1974). For a discussion of the right of confrontation, see § 23:22, Right of confrontation. See also § 35:2, Confidentiality requirement.

[64]Smith v. Daily Mail Pub. Co., 443 U.S. 97, 99 S. Ct. 2667, 61 L. Ed. 2d 399 (1979).

[65]Smith v. Daily Mail Pub. Co., 443 U.S. 97, 105–06, 99 S. Ct. 2667, 61 L. Ed. 2d 399 (1979). For a discussion of confidentiality of juvenile court records, see § 35:2, Confidentiality requirement.

[66]Oklahoma Pub. Co. v. District Court In and For Oklahoma County, 430 U.S. 308, 97 S. Ct. 1045, 51 L. Ed. 2d 355 (1977).

[Section 1:5]
[1]President's Commission on Law Enforcement and Administration of Justice, The Challenge of Crime in a Free Society 80 (1967). The Commission published a separate volume on juvenile justice—Task Force Report: Juvenile Delinquency and Youth Crime (1967).

tions of any judge, probation officer, correctional counselor, or psychiatrist."[2] The Report's proposals for reform have been summarized as "diversion, due process, and deinstitutionalization."[3] In short, the state should minimize harm to the child by "interfering in their lives as infrequently and unobtrusively as community safety . . . will allow."[4]

Another reform effort, the Juvenile Justice Project, was sponsored by the Institute of Judicial Administration and the American Bar Association.[5] The Standards published by the Project recommend a number of significant reforms. First, the Standards recommend the abolition of juvenile court jurisdiction over noncriminal misbehavior or status offenses: "A juvenile's acts of misbehavior, ungovernability, or unruliness which do not violate the criminal law should not constitute a ground for asserting juvenile court jurisdiction over the juvenile committing them."[6] This recommendation goes beyond earlier reforms, which called for the deinstitutionalization of status offenders. It is one of several recommendations aimed at limiting juvenile court jurisdiction.

Second, the Standards recommend restrictive criteria for state intervention in neglect cases: "In general, coercive intervention is limited [under the Standards] to situations where the child has suffered, or is likely to suffer, serious harm."[7] Again, this recommendation would limit the reach of juvenile court jurisdiction.

Third, the Standards recommend that delinquency dispositions be determinate and proportional to the seriousness of the offense.[8] The Standards "reject the use of indeterminacy as a governing principle of juvenile sentencing."[9] Indeterminate sentences are based on the theory of rehabilitation, the guiding principle of the early reformers who created the first juvenile courts. Thus, this recommendation represents a significant break with the original juvenile court philosophy.

Fourth, the Standards recommend procedural changes which would enhance the "visibility and accountability of decision making."[10] For example, in delinquency cases the Standards propose public trials[11] and jury trials on request.[12] These recommendations would further reduce the differences between delinquency proceedings and criminal trials.

Moreover, some commentators continue to question the underlying justifications for the juvenile court system, at least in delinquency cases:

> [T]he juvenile court has been effectively criminalized in that its current administrative assumptions and operations are virtually indistinguishable from those of adult criminal courts. At the same time, however, the procedures

---

[2]President's Commission on Law Enforcement and Administration of Justice, The Challenge of Crime in a Free Society 80 (1967). The Commission published a separate volume on juvenile justice—Task Force Report: Juvenile Delinquency and Youth Crime (1967).

[3]Tonry, Juvenile Justice and the National Crime Commissions, in Pursuing Justice for the Child 281, 290–91 (Rosenheim ed. 1976). In 1976, another national crime commission issued its own report on juvenile justice: National Advisory Committee on Criminal Justice Standards and Goals, Juvenile Justice and Delinquency Prevention (1976).

[4]Tonry, Juvenile Justice and the National Crime Commissions, in Pursuing Justice for the Child 281, 291 (Rosenheim ed. 1976).

[5]See IJA-ABA Juvenile Justice Standards, A Summary and Analysis (2d ed. 1982). For symposia on the Standards, see 57 B.U. L. Rev. 617–776 (1977); 52 N.Y.U. L. Rev. 1014–1135 (1977).

[6]IJA-ABA Standards Relating to Noncriminal Misbehavior 23 (1982).

[7]IJA-ABA Standards Relating to Abuse and Neglect 4 (1981).

[8]IJA-ABA Juvenile Justice Standards, A Summary and Analysis 22–23 (2d ed. 1982).

[9]IJA-ABA Standards Relating to Dispositions 26 (1980). See also IJA-ABA Standards Relating to Juvenile Delinquency and Sanctions 41 (1980).

[10]IJA-ABA Standards for Juvenile Justice: A Summary and Analysis 23 (2d ed. 1982).

[11]IJA-ABA Standards Relating to Adjudication 70 (1980).

[12]IJA-ABA Standards Relating to Adjudication 70, 51 (1980).

of the juvenile court often provide protections for juveniles less adequate than those afforded adult criminal defendants. As a result, juveniles receive the worst of both worlds, and the reasons for the very existence of a separate juvenile court are called into question.[13]

The abolitionist movement has gained support in recent years. One commentator has argued that society's current view of adolescence is inconsistent with the turn-of-the-century view that led to the creation of the juvenile court system. Thus, the system lacks a legitimate foundation. Moreover, the lack of procedural safeguards as compared with criminal courts is another reason for abolition.[14]

Those who support the current system acknowledge its shortcomings but argue that the criminal courts are worse.[15]

The Ohio juvenile court system is not without its critics. One commentator, while acknowledging that the reform efforts to date show "a picture of progress toward a better Juvenile Justice System,"[16] advocated further change:

> The litany of judicial abuse has been long and will continue until adequate monitoring of the juvenile court system is accomplished by both appellate courts and the public. Legislation establishing appropriate appellate standards will be needed, as well as legislation opening juvenile courts to the press and public. While open juvenile courts include possible negative potential, some courts, both in Ohio and out-of-state, have been open for years without any adverse effect on the system or the juvenile therein.[17]

§ 1:6 Ohio experience

As early as 1869, the Ohio Supreme Court recognized the state's authority to commit children to reform schools.[1] According to the court, the "authority of the state, as *parens patriae*, to assume the guardianship and education of neglected homeless children, as well as neglected orphans, is unquestioned."[2] "The juvenile court as we know it today did not exist at common law, though it has roots in the common-law doctrine of *parens patriae*, which made the courts of chancery responsible for the protection of infants."[3]

Ohio also became one of the first states to enact juvenile court legislation, establishing the Cuyahoga County Juvenile Court in 1902[4] and extending the system statewide by 1906.[5] This legislation governed juvenile court practice until 1937 when Ohio adopted the Standard Juvenile Court Act.[6] As

---

[13]Feld, Criminalizing Juvenile Justice: Rules of Procedure for the Juvenile Court, 69 Minn. L. Rev. 141, 142 (1984). See also Feld, The Transformation of the Juvenile Court, 75 Minn. L. Rev. 691 (1991).

[14]Ainsworth, Re-Imagining Childhood and Reconstructing the Legal Order: The Case for Abolishing the Juvenile Court, 69 N.C. L. Rev. 1083 (1993).

[15]Rosenberg, Leaving Bad Enough Alone: A Response to the Juvenile Court Abolitionists, 1993 Wis. L. Rev. 163. See also Dawson, The Future of Juvenile Justice: Is It Time to Abolish the System, 81 J. Crim. L. & Criminology (1990).

[16]Willey, The History of Juvenile Law Reform in Ohio Since Gault, 12 Ohio North L. Rev. 469, 471 (1985).

[17]Willey, The History of Juvenile Law Reform in Ohio Since Gault, 12 Ohio North L. Rev. 469, 471 (1985).

[Section 1:6]

[1]Prescott v. State, 19 Ohio St. 184, 1869 WL 42 (1869).

[2]Cincinnati House of Refuge v. Ryan, 37 Ohio St. 197, 204, 1881 WL 85 (1881). See also In re Tailford, 95 Ohio St. 411, 116 N.E. 1086 (1917) (petition denied on authority of *Ryan*); Bleier v. Crouse, 13 Ohio App. 69, 1920 WL 515 (1st Dist. Hamilton County 1920); State ex rel. Fortini v. Hoffman, 12 Ohio App. 341, 1920 WL 502 (1st Dist. Hamilton County 1920).

[3]In re T.R., 52 Ohio St. 3d 6, 556 N.E.2d 439 (1990).

[4]95 Ohio Laws 785 (1902).

[5]97 Ohio Laws 561 (1904); 98 Ohio Laws 314 (1906); 99 Ohio Laws 192 (1908).

[6]See Whitlatch, The Juvenile Court—A Court of Law, 18 W.R.U. L. Rev. 1239 (1967).

in other jurisdictions, the constitutionality of this legislation was upheld by the courts.[7] The right to counsel,[8] the privilege against self-incrimination,[9] trial by jury,[10] and the right to bail[11] were all held inapplicable to juvenile proceedings. The traditional arguments were offered to support these decisions: juvenile proceedings "are civil in nature and not criminal" and are "for the purpose of correction and rehabilitation and not for punishment."[12]

The pre-*Gault* view of the juvenile court system is captured in the following commentary by an Ohio juvenile court judge:

> The doctrine of *parens patriae,* which justifies those procedures in the juvenile court which seem superficially to conflict with the constitutional liberties of the person, requires that the court act as a wise and kindly parent would in dealing with his own children, toward those children who are brought before the court.[13]

Similar language is found in judicial opinions: "The Juvenile Court is wholly beneficent in its purpose. Its objective is to redeem and save erring children and youth."[14] "The philosophy . . . is not to consider the child . . . a criminal but rather to take him in hand for the purpose of protecting him from evil influences. The state thus becomes the *parens patriae* of the child on the theory that he needs protection, care and training."[15] The Ohio Supreme Court wrote: "Motivated by a humanitarian impulse, the law prohibits the use of Juvenile Court proceedings, or of proof developed thereon, against a child in any other court to discredit him or to mark him as one possessing a criminal history."[16]

Even in the post-*Gault* era, the early philosophy sometimes surfaces in the cases. For example, a court of appeals wrote the following in a 1997 decision: "A complaint in juvenile court alleging delinquency does not need to be read as strictly as a criminal indictment. Juvenile court is neither criminal nor penal in nature, but is an administrative police regulation of a corrective nature. . . . Being found a juvenile delinquent is different from being found guilty of a crime in Ohio."[17] In 2000, the Ohio Supreme Court wrote that the "juvenile justice system is grounded in the legal doctrine of *parens patriae*, meaning the state has the power to act as a provider of protection to those unable to care for themselves."[18]

---

[7]E.g., Ex parte Januszewski, 196 F. 123 (C.C.S.D. Ohio 1911); Leonard v. Licker, 3 Ohio App. 377, 26 Ohio C.D. 427, 1914 WL 1176 (5th Dist. Richland County 1914).

[8]Cope v. Campbell, 175 Ohio St. 475, 26 Ohio Op. 2d 88, 196 N.E.2d 457 (1964).

[9]State v. Shardell, 107 Ohio App. 338, 343, 8 Ohio Op. 2d 262, 79 Ohio L. Abs. 534, 153 N.E.2d 510 (8th Dist. Cuyahoga County 1958).

[10]In re Darnell, 173 Ohio St. 335, 19 Ohio Op. 2d 269, 182 N.E.2d 321 (1962).

[11]State ex rel. Peaks v. Allaman, 51 Ohio Op. 321, 66 Ohio L. Abs. 403, 115 N.E.2d 849 (Ct. App. 2d Dist. Montgomery County 1952).

[12]Cope v. Campbell, 175 Ohio St. 475, 477–78, 26 Ohio Op. 2d 88, 196 N.E.2d 457 (1964).

[13]Young, A Synopsis of Ohio Juvenile Court Law, 31 Cin. L. Rev. 131, 136 (1962). See also Harpst, Practice in Cuyahoga County Juvenile Court, 10 Clev.-Mar. L. Rev. 507 (1961).

[14]In re Heist, 11 Ohio Op. 537, 27 Ohio L. Abs. 1, 3 Ohio Supp. 259 (Juv. Ct. 1938).

[15]State v. Shardell, 107 Ohio App. 338, 340, 8 Ohio Op. 2d 262, 79 Ohio L. Abs. 534, 153 N.E.2d 510 (8th Dist. Cuyahoga County 1958).

[16]Malone v. State, 130 Ohio St. 443, 453–54, 5 Ohio Op. 59, 200 N.E. 473 (1936).

[17]In re Good, 118 Ohio App. 3d 371, 692 N.E.2d 1072 (12th Dist. Butler County 1997) (citations omitted).

[18]State v. Hanning, 89 Ohio St. 3d 86, 88, 2000-Ohio-436, 728 N.E.2d 1059 (2000).

§ 1:7 Juvenile code

The above picture changed dramatically after *Gault* was decided in 1967.[1] Major revisions in the Juvenile Code were enacted in 1969.[2] Reform efforts beginning in the 1970s resulted in legislative changes in 1976, 1980, 1981, 1988, and 1995. The changes adopted in 1976,[3] 1980,[4] and 1988[5] dealt primarily with proceedings involving neglected, dependent, and abused children. In order to insure that permanent planning would be made for children in the custody of child-care agencies, provisions were added to the Code requiring these agencies to submit periodic reviews to the juvenile court detailing the efforts which had been made to rehabilitate the family, including a recommendation for the permanent custody of the child.[6] Other amendments mandated the drafting of written case plans specifying the actions required of the parents in order to regain custody of their child, as well as the services and treatment that would be offered by the agency to achieve this goal.[7] Standards governing the procedures and findings required in proceedings involving the termination of parental rights were also adopted.[8]

The legislative changes in 1981[9] had a twofold effect: the deinstitutionalization of unruly children and delinquent-misdemeanants, and the increased control over delinquent-felons through institutionalization for prescribed minimum periods.[10] The powers and duties of the juvenile court and the Department of Youth Services with regard to delinquents were redefined.[11] With the assistance of state subsidies, local communities were given responsibility for developing programs for unruly children and delinquent-misdemeanants, primarily through diversion from the juvenile court to appropriate community agencies.[12] The resources of the state were restricted to delinquent-felons, who were thought to require a more secure setting for treatment and rehabilitation, as well as for the protection of the public.[13]

Because of apparent dissatisfaction with the results of prior legislative efforts,[14] and in order to insure Ohio's compliance with federal mandates,[15] in 1988[16] and 1999[17] the General Assembly enacted comprehensive changes in the laws governing neglect, dependency, and abuse proceedings. These

---

[Section 1:7]

[1]See In re Agler, 19 Ohio St. 2d 70, 48 Ohio Op. 2d 85, 249 N.E.2d 808 (1969) (discussing changes in Ohio law as a result of *Gault*).

[2]See Willey, Ohio's Post-Gault Juvenile Court Law, 3 Akron L. Rev. 152 (1970).

[3]1976 H.B. 156, eff. 1-1-77.

[4]1980 H.B. 695, eff. 10-24-80. See Blank, Reunification Planning for Children in Custody of Ohio's Children Services Boards: What Does the Law Require? 16 Akron L. Rev. 681 (1983); Christoff, Children in Limbo in Ohio: Permanency Planning and the State of the Law, 16 Capital L. Rev. 1 (1986).

[5]1988 S.B. 89, eff. 1-1-89.

[6]RC 2151.416 (former RC 5103.151, amended and recodified by 1988 S.B. 89, eff. 1-1-89). See § 33:9, Department of Youth Services.

[7]RC 2151.412. See § 25:14, Reasonable efforts determination; Dispositional Case Plans Ch 26.

[8]RC 2151.413, RC 2151.414. See § 30:2, General principles for abuse, neglect and dependency dispositions; § 30:12, Permanent custody—Procedural issues.

[9]1981 H.B. 440, eff. 1-1-81.

[10]RC 2152.16 (former RC 2151.355). See Delinquent Child Jurisdiction Ch 4; Unruly Child Jurisdiction Ch 8.

[11]See Delinquent Child Dispositions Ch 27.

[12]RC 5139.34. See § 15:3, Diversion, youth services grant.

[13]For a discussion of amendments proposed in 1977–78, see Willey, The Proposed Ohio Juvenile Code of 1977–78, 39 Ohio St. L. J. 273 (1978).

[14]1976 H.B. 156, eff. 1-1-77; 1980 H.B. 695, eff. 10-24-80.

[15]PL 96-272, Adoption Assistance and Child Welfare Act of 1980.

[16]1988 S.B. 89, eff. 1-1-89.

[17]1998 H.B. 484, eff. 3-18-99.

changes cover a wide variety of procedural and substantive issues which significantly impact the operations of juvenile courts and county departments of job and family services. The overall intent of the legislation is to prevent "foster care drift" by, among other things, establishing maximum time limits under which children may remain in the custody of public and private child care agencies,[18] and increasing the responsibilities of juvenile courts to review and oversee the permanency planning efforts of these agencies.[19]

In response to the perception that the volume of juvenile crime was increasing and the seriousness escalating, in 1995 the General Assembly made several changes in the statutes governing juvenile delinquency proceedings.[20] The most significant changes were reducing the minimum age for transfer to the adult court from fifteen to fourteen,[21] mandating transfer to the adult court under certain circumstances,[22] and increasing the minimum terms of commitment to the Department of Youth Services for certain specified delinquency offenses.[23]

Truancy. In 2000, Senate Bill 181 adopted a new approach for dealing with truancy. A new category of unruly child was created: habitual truant. An "habitual truant" is defined as a child of compulsory school age who is absent without legitimate excuse from the public school the child is supposed to attend for five or more consecutive school days, seven or more school days in one school month, or 12 or more school days in a school year.[24] In addition, a repeat habitual truant becomes a delinquent child.[25]

The 2000 statutory amendments also included a new delinquency category—"chronic truant." A "chronic truant" is defined as a child of compulsory school age who is absent without legitimate excuse from the public school the child is supposed to attend for seven or more consecutive school days, ten or more school days in one school month, or fifteen or more school days in a school year.[26]

Delinquency. Senate Bill 179, based on the Ohio Criminal Sentencing Commission's recommendations,[27] made groundbreaking changes in the treatment of delinquency cases. The bill became effective on January 1, 2002.

First, a new chapter, RC Ch. 2152, was added to the juvenile code for delinquent, traffic offender, and some adult cases. Under this chapter, the overriding purposes of the law are (1) protecting the public interest and safety, (2) holding offenders accountable, (3) restoring victims, (4) rehabilitating offenders, and (5) providing for the care, protection, and mental and physical development of children.[28] These purposes are to be achieved through a system of graduated sanctions and services. In contrast, prior law delineated the purposes as (1) providing for the care, protection, and mental and physical development of children, and (2) protecting the public interest in "removing the consequences of criminal behavior and the taint of criminality" from delinquent children and to substitute a program of supervision, care, and rehabilitation. These purposes were to be achieved in a family environment,

---

[18]RC 2151.353(F), RC 2151.353(G), RC 2151.415. See § 30:5, Protective supervision.

[19]RC 2151.412, RC 2151.416, RC 2151.417, RC 2151.419, RC 5103.15. See § 25:14, Reasonable efforts determination; Dispositional Case Plans Ch 26.

[20]1995 H.B. 1, eff. 1-1-96.

[21]RC 2151.26(B), RC 2151.26(C)(1). See § 22:7, Mandatory transfer; § 22:5, Age requirement; § 22:8, Discretionary transfer.

[22]RC 2151.26(B). See § 22:7, Mandatory transfer.

[23]RC 2152.16. See § 27:3, Department of Youth Services.

[24]RC 2151.011(B)(17).

[25]RC 2152.02(F)(4).

[26]RC 2152.02(F)(5).

[27]See Ohio Criminal Sentencing Commission, A Plan for Juvenile Sentencing in Ohio (Fall 1999).

[28]RC 2152.01(A).

separating the child from parents only when necessary for the child's welfare or public safety.[29] With the deletion of the quoted phrase, these purposes remain for abused, neglected, dependent, and unruly children.

Second, Senate Bill 179 recognized a new category of delinquency—Serious Youthful Offender (SYO), along with blended sentences.[30] Only SYOs are eligible for blended sentences, which contain both a juvenile disposition and an adult criminal sentence. The adult sentence is stayed while the juvenile term is served; the adult portion can be invoked only for specified rule violations after the juvenile turns 14 and after a hearing. SYO classification depends on age, level of felony, and enhancement factors. An SYO disposition may be discretionary or mandatory. Because of the possibility of an adult sentence, greater procedural safeguards—such as grand jury indictment and jury trials—are required.

Third, S.B. 179 provided a new balancing test for determining discretionary bindover, along with the overriding principles under RC 2152.01. The new balancing test specifies factors both "for" and "against" transfer.

The court must consider the following factors (and other relevant factors) in favor of bindover: (1) The victim suffered physical, psychological, or serious economic harm; (2) The victim's physical or mental harm was exacerbated by the victim's physical or mental vulnerability or age; (3) The juvenile's relationship with the victim facilitated the act; (4) The juvenile committed the act for hire or as part of a gang or other organized criminal activity; (5) The juvenile displayed, brandished, indicated, or used a firearm; (6) At the time of the act charged, the juvenile was awaiting adjudication or disposition for delinquency, was under a community sanction, or was on parole for a prior delinquency; (7) The results of previous juvenile sanctions and programs show that rehabilitation will not occur in the juvenile system; (8) The juvenile is emotionally, physically, or psychologically mature enough for transfer; and (9) There is not sufficient time for rehabilitation in the juvenile system.[31]

The court must consider these factors against bindover: (1) The victim induced or facilitated the act charged; (2) The juvenile acted under provocation; (3) The juvenile was not the principal offender or, at the time of the act charged, was under the negative influence or coercion of another; (4) The juvenile did not cause physical harm to any person or property, or have reasonable cause to believe such harm would occur; (5) The juvenile was not previously found delinquent; (6) The child is not emotionally, physically, or psychologically mature enough for transfer; (7) The juvenile is mentally ill or mentally retarded; and (8) There is sufficient time to rehabilitate the child in the juvenile system and the level of security available reasonably assures public safety.[32]

There were numerous other changes.

§ 1:8 Rules of Juvenile Procedure

In 1968, Ohio adopted the Modern Courts Amendment to the Ohio Constitution. Article IV, section 5(B) recognizes the Supreme Court's rulemaking authority. It provides, "The Supreme Court shall prescribe rules governing practice and procedure in all courts of the state, which rules shall not abridge, enlarge, or modify any substantive right. . . . All laws in conflict with such rules shall be of no further force or effect after such rules have

---

[29]RC 2151.01.

[30]See Serious Youthful Offenders Ch 5.

[31]RC 2152.12(D).

[32]RC 2152.12(E).

taken effect."[1] Pursuant to this rulemaking authority, the Court promulgated the Rules of Juvenile Procedure in 1972.[2]

The Court is empowered to promulgate procedural, but not substantive, rules. As one court has commented: "While the Juvenile Rules were enacted pursuant to Article IV of the Ohio Constitution to establish a uniform procedure for the courts of Ohio, they do not affect the jurisdiction of the juvenile courts as established by statute."[3] The line between substance and procedure, however, is a difficult one to draw[4] and may vary depending on the context in which these terms are used.[5] There are several instances in which the Juvenile Code, RC Chapter 2151, and the Juvenile Rules contain provisions that are both substantive and procedural.[6] Moreover, conflicts exist between the Code and the Rules with respect to issues that cannot be easily characterized as either substantive or procedural.[7]

The difficulty in distinguishing between substance and procedure was exacerbated by the extensive revisions made in the Ohio Rules of Juvenile Procedure in 1994.[8] One of the purposes of the rule changes was to conform the rules with statutory changes that resulted from 1988 Senate Bill 89, effective January 1, 1989. This outcome seems to ignore the fact that statutes and rules are intended to govern different legal precepts. Now that the rules employ language almost identical to the statutes on several points of law, the rules have become replete with substantive law. Moreover, whenever the General Assembly decides to amend a statute, as it did in 1996 with the enactment of 1996 House Bill 274 and in 1999 with 1998 House Bill 484, effective March 18, 1999, the corresponding rule will immediately be in conflict

---

[Section 1:8]

[1]See In re Coy, 67 Ohio St. 3d 215, 1993-Ohio-202, 616 N.E.2d 1105 (1993); Rockey v. 84 Lumber Co., 66 Ohio St. 3d 221, 1993-Ohio-174, 611 N.E.2d 789 (1993); see Krause v. State, 31 Ohio St. 2d 132, 60 Ohio Op. 2d 100, 285 N.E.2d 736 (1972). For a discussion of the effect of a statute establishing a procedural principle which is enacted after the promulgation of a supreme court rule on the same subject, see Browne, Civil Rule 1 and the Principle of Primacy: A Guide to the Resolution of Conflicts Between Statutes and the Civil Rules, 5 Ohio North L. Rev. 363 (1978). See also In re Brofford, 83 Ohio App. 3d 869, 615 N.E.2d 1120 (10th Dist. Franklin County 1992); State ex rel. Lamier v. Lamier, 105 Ohio App. 3d 797, 664 N.E.2d 1384 (8th Dist. Cuyahoga County 1995); In re Vickers Children, 14 Ohio App. 3d 201, 470 N.E.2d 438 (12th Dist. Butler County 1983) (Juvenile Rules control over subsequently enacted inconsistent statutes purporting to govern procedural matters.); In re Doe, 57 Ohio Misc. 2d 20, 22, 565 N.E.2d 891 (C.P. 1990).

[2]Juv. R. 47(A).

[3]In re Fleming, 76 Ohio App. 3d 30, 38, 600 N.E.2d 1112 (6th Dist. Lucas County 1991). See also Juv. R. 44.

[4]E.g., State v. Douglas, 20 Ohio St. 3d 34, 485 N.E.2d 711 (1985) (Procedure for determining whether to transfer a child to the adult court for criminal prosecution is governed by RC 2151.26 and Juv. R. 30.); Linger v. Weiss, 57 Ohio St. 2d 97, 11 Ohio Op. 3d 281, 386 N.E.2d 1354 (1979) (Time limits set forth in Juv. R. 29(A) and Juv. R. 34(A) are procedural, not substantive.); In re Therklidsen, 54 Ohio App. 2d 195, 8 Ohio Op. 3d 335, 376 N.E.2d 970 (10th Dist. Franklin County 1977) (Ten-day period of limitation in Juv. R. 29(A) is procedural.); Corona, 1981 WL 4502 (Ohio Ct. App. 8th Dist. Cuyahoga County 1981) (Failure to adhere to the time limits in Juv. R. 29(F) is a procedural irregularity and thus does not affect the court's jurisdiction.); In re Doe, 57 Ohio Misc. 2d 20, 565 N.E.2d 891 (C.P. 1990) (Notice provisions of Juv. R. 15(A) are procedural and control over RC 2151.85(D).). Contra State v. Newton, 1983 WL 6836 (Ohio Ct. App. 6th Dist. Fulton County 1983) (If no detention hearing is held within 72 hours and no adjudicatory hearing is held within 10 days, the complaint must be dismissed.).

See also Giannelli and Snyder, Baldwin's Ohio Practice, Evidence (2d ed.) § 102.5; Note, Substance and Procedure: The Scope of Judicial Rule Making Authority in Ohio, 37 Ohio St. L. J. 364 (1976).

[5]Gregory v. Flowers, 32 Ohio St. 2d 48, 61 Ohio Op. 2d 295, 290 N.E.2d 181 (1972).

[6]See Kameya & Pringle, A Comparative Analysis of Chapter 2151 Ohio Revised Code and the Ohio Rules of Juvenile Procedure (Federation for Community Planning, Cleveland, Ohio, June 19, 1980).

[7]E.g., RC 2151.281 and Juv. R. 4(B) (requirements for appointment of guardian ad litem); RC 2151.314 and Juv. R. 7(F) (time limitations for detention and shelter care decisions).

[8]The 1994 amendments are printed at 69 Ohio St.3d CXLIV (1994).

with the amended statute, necessitating additional rulemaking action from the Supreme Court.

Other conflicts exist between the Juvenile Rules and the Traffic Rules when applied to juvenile traffic offender cases.[9]

Cross References
§ 15:3, Ch 22, Ch 25, Ch 30, Ch 33, § 35:2

---

[9]Pursuant to Juv. R. 1 and Traf. R. 1 and Traf. R. 2, juvenile traffic offender proceedings are governed by both sets of rules. Several conflicts exist, including Juv. R. 7 and Traf. R. 4 (governing the granting of bail as opposed to the standards for detaining children); Juv. R. 15, Juv. R. 16 and Traf. R. 6 (form and service of summons and warrants); Juv. R. 29 and Traf. R. 8(D) (explanation of rights); Juv. R. 27 and Traf. R. 9 (provision for jury trials); Juv. R. 29(C) and Traf. R. 10 (permissible pleas).

Chapter 2
Age Jurisdiction

KeyCite®: Cases and other legal materials listed in KeyCite Scope can be researched through West's KeyCite service on Westlaw®. Use KeyCite to check citations for form, parallel references, prior and later history, and comprehensive citator information, including citations to other decisions and secondary materials.

---

§ 2:1   Age jurisdiction—Introduction
§ 2:2   Age jurisdiction
§ 2:3   Child subject to adult prosecution
§ 2:4   Mistaken or concealed age
§ 2:5   Proof of age jurisdiction
§ 2:6   Common law infancy defense
§ 2:7   Detention of "children" over the age of 18 years

§ 2:1   Age jurisdiction—Introduction

This chapter discusses the age jurisdiction of juvenile courts, including issues concerning mistaken and concealed age as well as proof requirements. Subject matter jurisdiction is discussed in the following chapters.

§ 2:2   Age jurisdiction

The juvenile court's age jurisdiction over delinquent, unruly, neglected, dependent, or abused children or juvenile traffic offenders turns on the definition of the term "child." Generally, under Ohio law, a child is a person who is under age 18.[1]

Based on the common law rule that there is no fraction of a day, the date of birth, and not the hour of birth, controls in computing a person's age.[2]

Neglect, abuse & dependency. It is implicit in the statutes that abuse, neglect, and dependency proceedings must be conducted before the child reaches age 18.[3] With respect to cases in which the child is the victim rather than the offender, an unborn child may be considered a "child" under RC 2151.011 since it is from the point of viability that the state has an interest in the child's care, protection, and development.[4]

Delinquency. If the person violates a law prior to reaching age 18, that person is considered a child irrespective of his or her age at the time the complaint is filed,[5] with some exceptions.[6]

Where a child has committed a delinquent act 10 days before his eigh-

---

[Section 2:2]

[1]RC 2151.011(B)(5). See also Juv. R. 2(D).

[2]State v. Clark, 84 Ohio App. 3d 789, 618 N.E.2d 257 (5th Dist. Stark County 1993).

[3]See RC 2151.353(E)(1), RC 2151.415(E).

[4]In re Ruiz, 27 Ohio Misc. 2d 31, 500 N.E.2d 935 (C.P. 1986). See also Cox v. Court of Common Pleas of Franklin County, Div. of Domestic Relations, Juvenile Branch, 42 Ohio App. 3d 171, 537 N.E.2d 721 (10th Dist. Franklin County 1988), in which the court refused to address the issue of whether a fetus is a "child."

[5]RC 2151.011(B)(6)(b), RC 2151.27(B). See also State ex rel. Heth v. Moloney, 126 Ohio St. 526, 186 N.E. 362 (1933); In re Hennessey, 146 Ohio App. 3d 743, 745, 2001-Ohio-2267, 768 N.E.2d 663 (3d Dist. Mercer County 2001) ("[A] child may have reached the age of eighteen at

teenth birthday, a juvenile court has authority to hold his parents responsible for his support until the age of 21, as he was a "child" within the meaning of RC 2151.011(B)(1).[7]

A juvenile who retains stolen property beyond age 18 may be charged as an adult for receiving stolen property because of "the continuous course of conduct involved in retaining such property."[8]

Marital status. The marital status of a child has no bearing on the jurisdiction of the juvenile court.[9] Thus, the fact that a female under the age of 18 is married does not exempt her from laws pertaining to juveniles,[10] nor does it prevent the prosecution of someone for contributing to her delinquency.[11]

§ 2:3 Child subject to adult prosecution

Child who reaches age 21. Based on 1997 statutory amendments,[1] Ohio law now provides that any child who commits a felony and who is not taken into custody or apprehended for that act until after reaching age 21 is not considered a child "in relation" to that act,[2] and the juvenile court does not have jurisdiction to hear or determine any portion of the case.[3] Under such circumstances, a criminal prosecution must be commenced in adult court as if the person had been age 18 or older when the offense was committed.[4]

Because RC 2152.02(C)(3) applies specifically to felony offenses and because RC 2151.38(A) provides that dispositional orders made by a juvenile court terminate when the child turns age 21, neither the juvenile court nor the adult court would apparently have jurisdiction when, under the above circumstances, the delinquent act is a misdemeanor. Moreover, since the triggering event is the act of taking the child into custody,[5] it is not clear what, if any, court would have jurisdiction if the child is taken into custody for a

---

the time of *disposition* and still be deemed a child, as the statute does not expressly exclude such a finding."); In re DeGeronimo, No. 40089 (8th Dist. Ct. App., Cuyahoga, 6-28-79); In re Davis, 22 Ohio Op. 2d 108, 87 Ohio L. Abs. 222, 179 N.E.2d 198 (Juv. Ct. 1961); RC 2151.358(H); Matter of Campbell, 1997 WL 401546 (Ohio Ct. App. 11th Dist. Lake County 1997).

[6]See § 2:3, Child subject to adult prosecution.

[7]In re Hinko, 84 Ohio App. 3d 89, 616 N.E.2d 515 (8th Dist. Cuyahoga County 1992).

[8]State v. Homer, 78 Ohio App. 3d 477, 478, 605 N.E.2d 426 (11th Dist. Geauga County 1992).

[9]However, pursuant to Juv. R. 2(Y), the child's spouse would be a party to juvenile court proceedings concerning the child.

[10]State v. Wilcox, 26 Ohio N.P. (n.s.) 343, 1926 WL 2503 (Juv. Ct. 1926).

[11]State ex rel. Meng v. Todaro, 161 Ohio St. 348, 53 Ohio Op. 252, 119 N.E.2d 281 (1954). However, RC 2907.01(I) specifically excludes a married juvenile from the purview of the criminal sex offense statutes (RC Ch. 2907) designed to protect juveniles.

[Section 2:3]
[1]1996 H.B. 124, eff. 3-31-97.

[2]RC 2152.02(C)(3).

[3]RC 2151.23(I), RC 2152.12(J).

[4]RC 2151.23(I), RC 2152.12(J). See also State v. Walls, 96 Ohio St. 3d 437, 442, 2002-Ohio-5059, 775 N.E.2d 829 (2002) ("Focusing on the date of Walls's offense, we conclude that the General Assembly intended that the 1997 amendments to R.C. Chapter 2151 apply retrospectively. The 1997 version of R.C. 2151.011(B)(6)(c) changed the definition of 'child' to *exclude* '[a]ny person who, while under eighteen years of age, commits an act that would be a felony if committed by an adult and who is not taken into custody or apprehended for that act until after that person attains twenty-one years of age.' Also effective in 1997, the General Assembly added R.C. 2151.23(I), which declared the juvenile court's lack of jurisdiction over a person 21 years of age who is apprehended for an offense committed prior to the person's 18th birthday. . . . These changes to the statutory scheme effectively removed anyone over 21 years of age from juvenile-court jurisdiction, regardless of the date on which the person allegedly committed the offense. In other words, the statutory amendments made the age of the *offender upon apprehension* the touchstone of determining juvenile-court jurisdiction without regard to whether the alleged offense occurred prior to the amendments' effective date. From these circumstances, we find an express legislative intent that the juvenile statutes apply retroactively.").

[5]RC 2152.02(C)(3).

felony before age 21, but the adjudicatory and dispositional hearings are not commenced or completed until after the child reaches age 21. Prior to the statutory amendments, the case law generally recognized the continuing jurisdiction of juvenile court under such circumstances.[6]

Child who was previously convicted. A 1997 statutory amendment to the definition of child (RC 2151.011(B)(6)(e) and (f))[7] resolved several problems with earlier definitions of the term. As a general rule, any person whose case is transferred for criminal prosecution and who subsequently is convicted of a felony in that case is not considered a "child" in the transferred case,[8] or in a case in which the person is alleged to have committed any offense prior to or subsequent to the transfer.[9] An exception, added in 1997, is that the person is considered a "child" with respect to a subsequent offense for the limited purposes of the filing of a delinquency complaint and the conducting of a preliminary transfer hearing.[10] Prior to the amendment, there was considerable confusion created by 1996 legislative enactments as to the parameters of the term "child" with respect to persons under age 18 who had been convicted in adult criminal prosecutions.[11]

A 1997 amendment to Juvenile Rule 30(A),[12] removing from the rule any reference to minimum age, reconciled a conflict between the rule and statute as to the minimum age at which a child may be transferred for adult prosecution. The statute sets the minimum age at 14.[13]

§ 2:4 Mistaken or concealed age

Under RC 2152.03, proceedings against an arrested child must be initiated in the juvenile court; if the child is taken before an adult court judge, that judge must transfer the case to the appropriate juvenile court. Similarly, RC 2152.12(H) prohibits the prosecution of any person as an adult where the person has committed the offense prior to attaining age 18, unless the person has been transferred to adult court pursuant to law.[1] This statute further provides that the criminal prosecution of a person as an adult based on the mistaken belief that the person was an adult at the time of the offense is a nullity to which jeopardy does not attach.

Despite these statutory provisions, several courts have held that a child who intentionally misrepresents himself to be an adult or does not object to the assumption of jurisdiction by the adult criminal court waives the right to be processed as a child in juvenile court.[2] The rationale is that to hold

---

[6]See In re Cox, 36 Ohio App. 2d 65, 65 Ohio Op. 2d 51, 301 N.E.2d 907 (7th Dist. Mahoning County 1973); In re J.B., 71 Ohio Misc. 2d 63, 654 N.E.2d 216 (C.P. 1995); Matter of McCourt, 1993 WL 327677 (Ohio Ct. App. 7th Dist. Belmont County 1993). But see In re C., 61 Ohio Misc. 2d 610, 614, 580 N.E.2d 1182 (C.P. 1991), which held that the juvenile court did not have jurisdiction because the court did not believe "it was the intent of the legislature for a person, regardless of age when charged, to be forever under the jurisdiction of the juvenile court for acts committed when legally a child."

[7]1996 H.B. 124, eff. 3-31-97, now RC 2152.02(C).

[8]RC 2152.02(C)(4).

[9]RC 2152.02(C)(5). The rule applies to a prior case only if it has not been disposed of by a juvenile court or trial court.

[10]RC 2151.011(B)(6)(f).

[11]See Kurtz & Giannelli, Ohio Juvenile Law § 2.12(B) (1996–97 Edition).

[12]Juv. R. 30(A), eff. 7-1-97.

[13]RC 2152.12(A). See § 22:7, Mandatory transfer, and § 22:8, Discretionary transfer.

[Section 2:4]

[1]See Transfer of Jurisdiction Ch 22.

[2]Hemphill v. Johnson, 31 Ohio App. 2d 241, 60 Ohio Op. 2d 404, 287 N.E.2d 828 (2d Dist. Montgomery County 1972); State v. Peterson, 9 Ohio Misc. 154, 38 Ohio Op. 2d 220, 38 Ohio Op. 2d 245, 223 N.E.2d 838 (Mun. Ct. 1966); Mellott v. Alvis, 109 Ohio App. 486, 12 Ohio Op. 2d 23, 81 Ohio L. Abs. 532, 162 N.E.2d 623 (10th Dist. Franklin County 1959); Harris v. Alvis, 61 Ohio

otherwise would permit the child to lie about his age until the conclusion of the adult proceeding and then choose whether to reveal his correct age depending on the outcome of the prosecution. However, the Ohio Supreme Court subsequently held that the juvenile court's exclusive subject matter jurisdiction over alleged delinquents cannot be waived, and a party's failure to object to the criminal court's subject matter jurisdiction cannot bestow jurisdiction where none exists.[3]

An appellate court has held that the general division of a common pleas court has subject matter jurisdiction over a murder prosecution where the defendant was unsure of his actual birth date but claimed he was not more than age 18 at the time of the offense. Documentary evidence from the county children services board contained two conflicting birth dates almost four years apart, and a bone marrow test indicated that the defendant was approximately 20 years old on the date of the offense.[4]

§ 2:5 Proof of age jurisdiction

Because juvenile courts are statutory courts whose jurisdiction depends on the age of the person before them, a court of appeals in *State v. Mendenhall*[1] held that the prosecution's failure to establish age in delinquency cases before resting its case constitutes a failure to invoke the court's subject matter jurisdiction and must result in a dismissal of the complaint. In *Mendenhall*, which was decided prior to the adoption of the Juvenile Rules, the objection was raised by means of a motion to dismiss following the close of the prosecution's case.

However, later cases hold that age relates to personal jurisdiction rather than subject matter jurisdiction; consequently, any objection to jurisdiction is waived if not raised before the hearing.[2] These courts relied on Juvenile Rule 22(D), which provides that defects in the institution of the proceedings or in the complaint, other than those relating to the jurisdiction of the court or to the charge, must be raised before the hearing or are waived.[3]

Nevertheless, a later court of appeals decision, *In re Auterson*,[4] relied on *Mendenhall* in holding that the trial court should have granted a motion for a judgment of acquittal filed on behalf of a child under Criminal Rule 29, where the prosecution failed to meet its burden of establishing the child's minority.[5] The court reasoned that when the state fails to establish minority, the matter is not within the court's jurisdiction and any judgment rendered is a nullity.

An allegation in the complaint that a child is under the age of 18 is not

---

L. Abs. 311, 104 N.E.2d 182 (Ct. App. 2d Dist. Franklin County 1950); Ex parte Pharr, 10 Ohio App. 395, 1919 WL 870 (1st Dist. Hamilton County 1919); State v. Klingenberger, 113 Ohio St. 418, 3 Ohio L. Abs. 675, 149 N.E. 395 (1925); State v. Tillman, 66 Ohio App. 3d 464, 585 N.E.2d 550 (9th Dist. Lorain County 1990); State v. Soke, 1993 WL 266951 (Ohio Ct. App. 8th Dist. Cuyahoga County 1993); State ex rel. Leis v. Black, 45 Ohio App. 2d 191, 74 Ohio Op. 2d 270, 341 N.E.2d 853 (1st Dist. Hamilton County 1975).

[3]State v. Wilson, 73 Ohio St. 3d 40, 1995-Ohio-217, 652 N.E.2d 196 (1995). See In re Johnson, 106 Ohio App. 3d 38, 665 N.E.2d 247 (1st Dist. Hamilton County 1995). See Subject Matter Jurisdiction Ch 3.

[4]State v. Neguse, 71 Ohio App. 3d 596, 594 N.E.2d 1116 (10th Dist. Franklin County 1991).

[Section 2:5]
[1]State v. Mendenhall, 21 Ohio App. 2d 135, 50 Ohio Op. 2d 227, 255 N.E.2d 307 (11th Dist. Lake County 1969).

[2]In re Fudge, 59 Ohio App. 2d 129, 13 Ohio Op. 3d 176, 392 N.E.2d 1262 (2d Dist. Clark County 1977). See also In re Atwell, Nos. 40667, 40719 (8th Dist. Ct. App., Cuyahoga, 1-17-80).

[3]See also In re McCourt, 1987 WL 15812 (Ohio Ct. App. 9th Dist. Medina County 1987).

[4]Auterson, 1982 WL 6000 (Ohio Ct. App. 12th Dist. Clermont County 1982).

[5]Because Juv. R. 22 seems to control this issue, the court's reliance on the Criminal Rules is questionable.

enough to establish age jurisdiction.[6] However, where the child appears with counsel and the court observes the child to be of tender age, this may constitute sufficient evidence that the subject is a juvenile.[7] In a delinquency hearing where a court clerk asked the subject if he was 17 years old at the time of the alleged offense and the subject answered in the affirmative, age jurisdiction was established.[8] Similarly, where the child's counsel agreed to stipulate that the child was a minor, it was unnecessary to establish his age.[9]

In *In re Burton S.*,[10] the court of appeals rejected the juvenile's argument that the juvenile court lacked jurisdiction over him since the state failed to present evidence of his age. The court reasoned:

> Since the complaint in this case alleged appellant to be a delinquent child, the juvenile court had subject matter jurisdiction. Appellant is not, however, arguing that he was in fact over the age of eighteen. Therefore, he is not challenging the court's subject matter jurisdiction. Rather, he is, in reality, contending that the court had no personal jurisdiction because appellee failed to present evidence at trial of his age. Since appellant failed to challenge personal jurisdiction either in a responsive pleading or a motion prior to his answer, he waived any defense based upon personal jurisdiction. Moreover, because appellant was, in fact, under eighteen at the time of the offense, any such motion would have been denied.[11]

§ 2:6 Common law infancy defense

Because the statutory definition of "child" contains no minimum age requirement, there is some question whether Ohio follows the common law, which makes seven years the minimum age for criminal capacity.[1] This issue has not been directly confronted in any reported Ohio decisions.[2] However, the Ohio Supreme Court in *In re Washington*[3] specifically abolished the common law rule that a child under the age of 14 is rebuttably presumed incapable of committing rape. In distinguishing its holding in *In re Washington* from a prior decision in *In re M.D.*[4] in which the Supreme Court appeared to endorse the rebuttable presumption, the Court stated:

---

[6]State v. Mendenhall, 21 Ohio App. 2d 135, 50 Ohio Op. 2d 227, 255 N.E.2d 307 (11th Dist. Lake County 1969); Auterson, 1982 WL 6000 (Ohio Ct. App. 12th Dist. Clermont County 1982).

[7]In re Fudge, 59 Ohio App. 2d 129, 13 Ohio Op. 3d 176, 392 N.E.2d 1262 (2d Dist. Clark County 1977).

[8]State v. Cunningham, No. 31563 (8th Dist. Ct. App., Cuyahoga, 11-9-72). See also In re Ball, 2003-Ohio-395, 2003 WL 193519 (3rd Dist. Allen County 2003).

[9]State v. Gaida, No. 30423 (8th Dist. Ct. App., Cuyahoga, 3-2-72).

[10]In re Burton S., 136 Ohio App. 3d 386, 736 N.E.2d 928 (6th Dist. Ottawa County 1999).

[11]In re Burton S., 136 Ohio App. 3d 386, 391–92, 736 N.E.2d 928 (6th Dist. Ottawa County 1999). The court also wrote: "Appellant may also be arguing that appellee failed to establish his age which is an essential element to prove a delinquency charge. This argument is basically a sufficiency of the evidence issue. However, in our view, once a trial court has properly established subject matter and personal jurisdiction over an alleged juvenile offender, additional evidence of the juvenile's age is not essential to a finding of delinquency, unless one of the elements of the adult crime alleged requires specific proof of age." In re Burton S., 136 Ohio App. 3d 386, 392, 736 N.E.2d 928 (6th Dist. Ottawa County 1999).

[Section 2:6]

[1]For a discussion of the juvenile court's jurisdiction over an unborn fetus in neglect proceedings, see § 9:7, Neglect—Subsistence, education & medical care. See also Katz and Giannelli, Baldwin's Ohio Practice, Criminal Law (2d ed.) § 91:6 (infancy defense).

[2]Some Ohio juvenile courts have adopted a policy that children under a certain age (usually seven or 10) will not be charged officially with a delinquent or unruly act. If such children need court intervention, the court may proceed unofficially pursuant to Juv. R. 9; if the child's misbehavior is due to a lack of parental supervision, the child may be alleged to be neglected under RC 2151.03.

[3]In re Washington, 75 Ohio St. 3d 390, 1996-Ohio-186, 662 N.E.2d 346 (1996). See In Matter of Bowers, 1998 WL 46360 (Ohio Ct. App. 2d Dist. Greene County 1998).

[4]In re M.D., 38 Ohio St. 3d 149, 527 N.E.2d 286 (1988). See also In re Smith, 80 Ohio App. 3d 502, 609 N.E.2d 1281 (1st Dist. Hamilton County 1992).

While this court did mention this common-law rule in a more recent case, *In re M.D. . . .*, the issue of the rule's viability was not before the court in that case and it was mentioned only *in dicta*. Furthermore, the facts in that case are distinguishable from the present forced sexual conduct, as the children in *In re M.D.* were merely "playing doctor" when a twelve-year-old girl directed two five-year-olds to perform a sexual act. Thus, *In re M.D.* is not binding on this court as to the issue of whether such a presumption exists.[5]

Courts in some jurisdictions that do not have a statutory minimum age have held that since a delinquency complaint is based on the commission of a criminal offense, the common-law presumptions concerning criminal capacity should apply, making infancy a proper defense in a delinquency proceeding.[6] Thus, the common-law presumptions of criminal capacity based on age have been extended beyond criminal cases into juvenile proceedings. Other courts, however, have refused to recognize infancy as a relevant factor in juvenile proceedings.[7] These courts argue that since juvenile proceedings are civil rather than criminal and are designed to protect and rehabilitate children rather than to punish them, the traditional concept of incapacity is irrelevant.[8]

§ 2:7   Detention of "children" over the age of 18 years

A 2003 statutory amendment modifies the definition of "child."[1] Under this new definition, while a child continues to be someone subject to the court's jurisdiction until age 21, the detention options for a child once the child reaches age 18 expand beyond those places previously authorized by the Revised Code for the detention of children.[2] A "child" over age 18 years may be confined in adult facilities pursuant to RC 2152.26(F)(2).

Cross References

§ 2:2, Ch 22

Research References

Giannelli and Snyder, Baldwin's Ohio Practice, Evidence (2d ed.) § 301.3

Carlin, Baldwin's Ohio Practice, Merrick-Rippner Probate Law (6th ed.), Ch 105

---

[5]In re Washington, 75 Ohio St. 3d 390, 1996-Ohio-186, 662 N.E.2d 346 (1996).

[6]E.g., In re Gladys R., 1 Cal. 3d 855, 83 Cal. Rptr. 671, 464 P.2d 127 (1970); Com. v. Durham, 255 Pa. Super. 539, 389 A.2d 108 (1978).

[7]E.g., State v. D.H., 340 So. 2d 1163 (Fla. 1976); K. M. S. v. State, 129 Ga. App. 683, 200 S.E.2d 916 (1973).

[8]For a discussion of the effect that the child's attaining 21 years of age has on the continuing jurisdiction of the court, see Continuing Jurisdiction Ch 33.

[Section 2:7]

[1]Am. Sub. H.B. 400, eff. April 3, 2003.

[2]RC 2152.02(C)(6).

Chapter 3

Subject Matter Jurisdiction

> **KeyCite®:** Cases and other legal materials listed in KeyCite Scope can be researched through West's KeyCite service on Westlaw®. Use KeyCite to check citations for form, parallel references, prior and later history, and comprehensive citator information, including citations to other decisions and secondary materials.

§ 3:1   Subject matter jurisdiction—Introduction
§ 3:2   Exclusive original jurisdiction
§ 3:3   Concurrent jurisdiction

§ 3:1   Subject matter jurisdiction—Introduction

This chapter discusses the general requirements for subject matter jurisdiction. Subsequent chapters examine juvenile court jurisdiction for delinquency, juvenile traffic offenses, unruliness, neglect, abuse, and dependency.

§ 3:2   Exclusive original jurisdiction

Under the jurisdictional statute, RC 2151.23(A)(1), the juvenile court has exclusive original jurisdiction concerning any child, who on or about the date specified in the complaint, is alleged to be a juvenile traffic offender or a delinquent, unruly, abused, neglected, or dependent child.[1] Because this jurisdiction is both exclusive and original, all complaints regarding these children must be initially filed and processed in the appropriate juvenile court. Only after the juvenile court has assumed jurisdiction may any other type of court obtain jurisdiction (e.g., court of appeals in appellate cases,[2] or the general division of the court of common pleas in cases involving alleged delinquents transferred for criminal prosecution[3]).

Once a juvenile court assumes jurisdiction over a child, no other court of this state (with the possible exception of another juvenile court[4]) may assume jurisdiction over that child until the juvenile court's jurisdiction is terminated.[5] For instance, if a child is adjudged dependent by a juvenile court and is committed to the temporary custody of a county department of job and family services, and the parents thereafter are granted a divorce by a

---

[Section 3:2]

[1]See In re Lippitt, No. 38421 (8th Dist. Ct. App., Cuyahoga, 3-9-78), holding that RC 2151.23 is not definitional only, and that the juvenile court has exclusive, original jurisdiction over civil neglect cases. See also Reynolds v. Goll, 80 Ohio App. 3d 494, 609 N.E.2d 1276 (9th Dist. Lorain County 1992); In re Doe Children, 93 Ohio App. 3d 134, 637 N.E.2d 977 (6th Dist. Lucas County 1994).

[2]See Appeals and Habeas Corpus Ch 34.

[3]See Transfer of Jurisdiction Ch 22.

[4]See RC 2151.271; § 17:4, Transfer of venue.

[5]Children's Home of Marion County v. Fetter, 90 Ohio St. 110, 106 N.E. 761 (1914); In re Small, 114 Ohio App. 248, 19 Ohio Op. 2d 128, 181 N.E.2d 503 (2d Dist. Darke County 1960); Hartshorne v. Hartshorne, 89 Ohio L. Abs. 243, 185 N.E.2d 329 (Ct. App. 7th Dist. Columbiana County 1959); O'Donnell v. Franklin County Children Services, Starr Commonwealth Corporation, 1981 WL 3734 (Ohio Ct. App. 10th Dist. Franklin County 1981); State ex rel. Thompson v. Murray, 1984 WL 3422 (Ohio Ct. App. 12th Dist. Madison County 1984); Tingley v.

domestic relations court, that court is without authority to make any orders concerning the child's custody. In this situation the domestic relations court is authorized to certify its jurisdiction over custody and child support matters to the juvenile court if it finds that custody to either parent is not in the child's best interest,[6] or if the juvenile court consents.[7] Absent the best interest determination or juvenile court consent, the domestic relations court has no authority to certify its jurisdiction and would simply abstain from entering any child custody or support order.[8]

When a case is certified to a juvenile court, or when a juvenile court otherwise obtains jurisdiction over and enters orders regarding the custody and support of children, that court retains continuing and exclusive jurisdiction over such matters, and its attempted transfer of jurisdiction to a domestic relations court is a nullity.[9]

RC 2151.23 is broad enough to permit a juvenile court to decide a custody matter certified after denial of a divorce, provided that the certifying court is one of competent jurisdiction under RC 3105.21(B).[10] However, if the case has not been duly certified by a court of competent jurisdiction, the juvenile court does not obtain subject matter jurisdiction over the matter.[11]

§ 3:3   Concurrent jurisdiction

Although the assumption of jurisdiction over a child by a juvenile court precludes another court from assuming jurisdiction over such child, the reverse is not true. Several cases have held that if a domestic relations court grants custody of a child to a parent by virtue of a divorce decree, a juvenile court may subsequently assume jurisdiction over the child if he is alleged to be delinquent, unruly, neglected, dependent, abused, or a juvenile traffic offender.[1]

However, in *In re Poling*,[2] the Ohio Supreme Court viewed this issue in a slightly different light. In *Poling*, the parents were divorced with custody being granted to the mother by the domestic relations court. Subsequently, a neglect and dependency action with respect to the children was initiated in the juvenile court. The children were adjudged dependent and committed to the temporary custody of the children services board. Several months later, the custody of the children services board was terminated, and legal custody was awarded to the father. The Supreme Court held that, pursuant to RC 2151.23(A), the juvenile court has jurisdiction to determine the custody of a

---

Williams County Department of Human Services, 1993 WL 313710 (Ohio Ct. App. 6th Dist. Williams County 1993).

[6]RC 3109.04(A), RC 2151.23(D).

[7]RC 3109.06, RC 2151.23(D); In re Whaley, 86 Ohio App. 3d 304, 620 N.E.2d 954 (4th Dist. Athens County 1993); Lindon v. Lindon, 1989 WL 155730 (Ohio Ct. App. 5th Dist. Tuscarawas County 1989).

[8]See State ex rel. Easterday v. Zieba, 58 Ohio St. 3d 251, 569 N.E.2d 1028 (1991).

[9]Hardesty v. Hardesty, 16 Ohio App. 3d 56, 474 N.E.2d 368 (10th Dist. Franklin County 1984); Handelsman v. Handelsman, 108 Ohio App. 30, 9 Ohio Op. 2d 101, 160 N.E.2d 543 (7th Dist. Columbiana County 1958).

[10]State ex rel. Easterday v. Zieba, 58 Ohio St. 3d 251, 569 N.E.2d 1028 (1991).

[11]In re Whaley, 86 Ohio App. 3d 304, 620 N.E.2d 954 (4th Dist. Athens County 1993); Matter of Dych, 1990 WL 79028 (Ohio Ct. App. 5th Dist. Guernsey County 1990).

[Section 3:3]

[1]In re Greaser, 1995 WL 767983 (Ohio Ct. App. 5th Dist. Stark County 1995); James v. Child Welfare Bd., 9 Ohio App. 2d 299, 38 Ohio Op. 2d 347, 224 N.E.2d 358 (9th Dist. Summit County 1967); McFadden v. Kendall, 81 Ohio App. 107, 36 Ohio Op. 414, 77 N.E.2d 625 (3d Dist. Auglaize County 1946); In re L., 12 Ohio Misc. 251, 41 Ohio Op. 2d 341, 231 N.E.2d 253 (Juv. Ct. 1967); In re Jones, 33 Ohio Op. 331, 46 Ohio L. Abs. 132, 68 N.E.2d 97 (Juv. Ct. 1946); Matter of Likens, 1986 WL 11910 (Ohio Ct. App. 2d Dist. Greene County 1986); Matter of Schulte, 1993 WL 195853 (Ohio Ct. App. 6th Dist. Lucas County 1993).

[2]In re Poling, 64 Ohio St. 3d 211, 1992-Ohio-144, 594 N.E.2d 589 (1992).

child alleged to be abused, neglected, or dependent, but only if that child is not the ward of another court of this state.[3] However, in upholding the jurisdiction of the juvenile court to grant custody to the father, the Supreme Court determined that when a court in a divorce case grants custody of a child, the child does not become a "ward" of that court, even though the court retains jurisdiction to modify custody and support.[4] The Supreme Court further held that when a juvenile court seeks to exercise its concurrent jurisdiction where there is an existing custody decree from a domestic relations court, the juvenile court must do so in compliance with RC 2151.23(F)(1), which requires the court to consider the dictates of RC 3109.04.[5]

If a juvenile court obtains prior jurisdiction over a child, but does not issue orders concerning the child's custody, it does not retain continuing jurisdiction over that subject. Under such circumstances, a domestic relations court which grants a divorce has jurisdiction to issue custody orders with respect to that child.[6] Similarly, if a juvenile court terminates a previous custody order, and a probate court then assumes jurisdiction through the appointment of a guardian for the child, the juvenile court is without jurisdiction to grant custody of the child to another person until the guardianship has been terminated.[7] It has been held that a juvenile court does not have jurisdiction to determine a matter involving a child who is a ward of probate court due to the establishment of a guardianship.[8]

An appellate court has held that concurrent jurisdiction does not preclude a probate court from acquiring jurisdiction over adoption proceedings even though the juvenile court has jurisdiction over the child.[9] The rationale is that the rule of concurrent jurisdiction is based on sameness of claims or causes of action, and an adoption case, over which probate court has exclusive jurisdiction, is very different from an abuse, neglect, or dependency case, over which juvenile court has exclusive jurisdiction.[10] However, another appellate court decision, *In re Moran*,[11] apparently confused this distinction, holding that once a petition for adoption is filed, all matters concerning the adoption are strictly within the powers of the probate court, and the juvenile court has no authority to issue orders to the children services board or guardian ad litem once the matter is within the jurisdiction of the probate court.

---

[3]The Supreme Court cited RC 2151.23(A)(2) for the "ward of another court of this state" language. However, there is no such language in RC 2151.23(A)(1), which is the provision under which the juvenile court exercised its jurisdiction over the children alleged to be neglected and dependent. Even though the Supreme Court acknowledged that RC 2151.23(A)(1) and (A)(2) are independent of each other, it apparently considered them to be interdependent with respect to the juvenile court's custody jurisdiction.

[4]In considering the meaning of the term "ward," the Supreme Court did not cite Juv. R. 2(22) (now QQ), which defines "ward of court" as "a child over whom the court assumes continuing jurisdiction."

[5]In re Poling, 64 Ohio St. 3d 211, 1992-Ohio-144, 594 N.E.2d 589 (1992); Matter of Cheesman, 1993 WL 437666 (Ohio Ct. App. 12th Dist. Butler County 1993); In re Kennedy, 94 Ohio App. 3d 414, 640 N.E.2d 1176 (3d Dist. Marion County 1994); Kovalak v. Kovalak, 1998 WL 456506 (Ohio Ct. App. 8th Dist. Cuyahoga County 1998). See § 27:18, "Catch-all" provision.

[6]Huxley v. Huxley, 1984 WL 6176 (Ohio Ct. App. 9th Dist. Wayne County 1984). See also State ex rel. Clermont Cty. Dept. of Human Serv. v. Walsson, 108 Ohio App. 3d 125, 670 N.E.2d 287 (12th Dist. Clermont County 1995).

[7]In re Miller, 33 Ohio App. 3d 224, 515 N.E.2d 635 (8th Dist. Cuyahoga County 1986).

[8]Lake Cty. Dept. of Human Serv. v. Adams, 82 Ohio App. 3d 494, 612 N.E.2d 766 (11th Dist. Lake County 1992). This decision would apparently not be affected by the Supreme Court's determination of the meaning of the term "ward" in In re Poling, 64 Ohio St. 3d 211, 1992-Ohio-144, 594 N.E.2d 589 (1992). In *Poling*, the Supreme Court indicated that a "ward" is commonly associated with a guardianship.

[9]State ex rel. Hitchcock v. Cuyahoga Cty. Court of Common Pleas, Probate Div., 97 Ohio App. 3d 600, 647 N.E.2d 208 (8th Dist. Cuyahoga County 1994).

[10]State ex rel. Hitchcock v. Cuyahoga Cty. Court of Common Pleas, Probate Div., 97 Ohio App. 3d 600, 647 N.E.2d 208 (8th Dist. Cuyahoga County 1994).

[11]In re Moran, 1994 WL 123683 (Ohio Ct. App. 1st Dist. Hamilton County 1994).

The *Moran* decision seems to ignore both the body of law which governs the juvenile court's continuing jurisdiction over custody orders,[12] as well as the statute[13] requiring a guardian ad litem for a child to serve until a final decree of adoption has been issued.[14] Subsequent to *Moran*, the Eighth District Court of Appeals twice ruled that reliance on *Moran* for the proposition that the jurisdiction of the juvenile court ends when the jurisdiction of the probate court is invoked for adoption is unpersuasive.[15]

The probate court has no jurisdiction to determine the custody of a minor child once it terminates the guardianship of that minor. Once the guardianship is terminated, the juvenile court then has exclusive jurisdiction to determine the custody of the child under RC 2151.23(A)(2).[16] Similarly, where a divorce action has abated as a result of the death of the father, the domestic relations court is divested of jurisdiction, and the juvenile court has jurisdiction to determine the children's custody.[17] When a probate court vacates a final decree of adoption due to defective service, a prior temporary custody order made by a juvenile court remains in full force and effect.[18]

Transfer. Both statutory[19] and case law[20] provide that the juvenile court possesses exclusive original jurisdiction over the adjudication of delinquency offenses committed by children. However, in *State v. Tillman*,[21] it was held that the juvenile and general divisions of the court of common pleas possess concurrent jurisdiction over a child accused of a crime, and the rule vesting jurisdiction over the person of a child in the juvenile division does not divest the general division of jurisdiction over the subject matter of the alleged criminal offense. The dissent in *Tillman* argued that exclusive jurisdiction rests with the juvenile court, pointing out that the majority's reliance on *State ex rel. Leis v. Black*[22] and *State v. Klingenberger*[23] was misplaced because the former failed to consider RC 2151.26(E), and the latter was decided prior to the enactment of the statute.[24] This issue was finally put to rest by the Ohio Supreme Court in *State v. Wilson*,[25] in which the *Tillman* decision was overruled. The Court held that absent a proper bindover pursuant to RC 2151.26, the juvenile court has exclusive subject matter jurisdiction over any case concerning an alleged delinquent child, and further held that such jurisdiction cannot be waived.

If a case is transferred from a juvenile court to a criminal court under RC 2151.26, the juvenile court no longer has jurisdiction. Under such circum-

---

[12]See Continuing Jurisdiction Ch 33.

[13]RC 2151.281(G)(4).

[14]See Matter of Adoption of Nowowiejski, 1990 WL 187377 (Ohio Ct. App. 6th Dist. Lucas County 1990). See also § 23:6, Guardian ad litem.

[15]State ex rel. Cuyahoga Cty. Dept. of Children & Family Serv. v. Ferreri, 96 Ohio App. 3d 660, 645 N.E.2d 837 (8th Dist. Cuyahoga County 1994); State ex rel. Burich v. Ferreri, No. 69218 (8th Dist. Ct. App., Cuyahoga, 9-1-95).

[16]In re Guardianship of Harrison, 60 Ohio App. 3d 19, 572 N.E.2d 855 (1st Dist. Hamilton County 1989).

[17]In re Eng, 1992 WL 348184 (Ohio Ct. App. 2d Dist. Montgomery County 1992).

[18]In re Knipper, 39 Ohio App. 3d 35, 528 N.E.2d 1319 (1st Dist. Hamilton County 1987).

[19]RC 2151.23(A)(1), RC 2152.03, RC 2152.12(H).

[20]State v. Neguse, 71 Ohio App. 3d 596, 594 N.E.2d 1116 (10th Dist. Franklin County 1991); State v. Taylor, 26 Ohio App. 3d 69, 498 N.E.2d 211 (3d Dist. Auglaize County 1985); State v. Kimbler, No. 77AP-127 (10th Dist. Ct. App., Franklin, 9-20-77).

[21]State v. Tillman, 66 Ohio App. 3d 464, 585 N.E.2d 550 (9th Dist. Lorain County 1990).

[22]State ex rel. Leis v. Black, 45 Ohio App. 2d 191, 74 Ohio Op. 2d 270, 341 N.E.2d 853 (1st Dist. Hamilton County 1975).

[23]State v. Klingenberger, 113 Ohio St. 418, 3 Ohio L. Abs. 675, 149 N.E. 395 (1925).

[24]1969 H.B. 320.

[25]State v. Wilson, 73 Ohio St. 3d 40, 1995-Ohio-217, 652 N.E.2d 196 (1995). See also State ex rel. Harris v. Anderson, 76 Ohio St. 3d 193, 1996-Ohio-412, 667 N.E.2d 1 (1996); State v. Golphin, 78 Ohio St. 3d 1441, 676 N.E.2d 1187 (1997).

stances the criminal court has jurisdiction in the same manner as if the case had been originally commenced in that court.[26]

Moreover, it is possible for an individual to be treated both as a child subject to juvenile court jurisdiction for a parole violation based on a delinquent act committed before age 18, and as an adult subject to adult court jurisdiction for a separate offense committed after attaining age 18.[27]

Cross References
Ch 22, Ch 34
Research References
Giannelli and Snyder, Baldwin's Ohio Practice, Evidence (2d ed.) §§ 101.6, 101.8
Carlin, Baldwin's Ohio Practice, Merrick-Rippner Probate Law (6th ed.), Chs 105, 108

[26]RC 2151.23(H).

[27]In re Gillespie, 150 Ohio App. 3d 502, 507, 2002-Ohio-7025, 782 N.E.2d 140 (10th Dist. Franklin County 2002) ("[P]ursuant to Ohio's statutory scheme, if a person . . . is adjudicated delinquent prior to the age of 18, that person remains a child in the eyes of the juvenile court until the age of 21. And the juvenile court retains exclusive original jurisdiction over that child's progress through the juvenile system as the result of that adjudication. . . . [T]he juvenile court's jurisdiction did not reach appellant when he was indicted as an adult on charges alleging criminal activity at age 19. Rather, the common pleas court exercised jurisdiction over those charges. Appellant's parole violation constituted an entirely separate, but no less legitimate, matter."); In re Kelly, 1999 WL 132862 (Ohio Ct. App. 10th Dist. Franklin County 1999).

Chapter 4

Delinquent Child Jurisdiction

> **KeyCite®:** Cases and other legal materials listed in KeyCite Scope can be researched through West's KeyCite service on Westlaw®. Use KeyCite to check citations for form, parallel references, prior and later history, and comprehensive citator information, including citations to other decisions and secondary materials.

§ 4:1   Delinquent child jurisdiction—Introduction
§ 4:2   Delinquent child defined
§ 4:3   Federal penal law
§ 4:4   Ohio penal law
§ 4:5   Truancy
§ 4:6   Court order violations
§ 4:7   Transfer to adult criminal court
§ 4:8   Serious Youthful Offender (SYO)

§ 4:1   Delinquent child jurisdiction—Introduction

This chapter discusses juvenile court jurisdiction for delinquency cases. Subsequent chapters examine juvenile court jurisdiction for juvenile traffic offenses, unruliness, neglect, abuse, and dependency cases. Other related chapters include the adjudicatory hearing (Ch 23), transfer to adult courts (Ch 22), and delinquency dispositions (Ch 27).

Effective on January 1, 2002, the delinquency provisions, along with the juvenile traffic offender sections were transferred to new RC Chapter 2152.[1] This changed the applicable purposes and principles. In addition, a new category—Serious Youthful Offender—was recognized, along with blended (juvenile/adult) sentences.

Under the new delinquency and traffic offender chapter, the overriding purposes of the law are (1) protecting the public interest and safety, (2) holding offenders accountable, (3) restoring victims, (4) rehabilitating offenders, and (5) providing for the care, protection, and mental and physical development of children.[2] These purposes are to be achieved through a system of graduated sanctions and services. In contrast, prior law delineated the purposes as (1) providing for the care, protection, and mental and physical development of children, and (2) protecting the public interest by "removing the consequences of criminal behavior and the taint of criminality" from delinquent children and substituting a program of supervision, care, and rehabilitation. These purposes were to be achieved in a family environment, separating the child from parents only when necessary for the child's welfare or public safety.[3]

There are three alternatives for felony delinquency cases: (1) transfer or bindover to adult criminal court, (2) traditional juvenile dispositions, and (3) blended sentences for Serious Youthful Offenders.

[Section 4:1]
[1]S.B. 179.

[2]RC 2152.01(A).

[3]RC 2151.01. With the deletion of the quoted phrase, these purposes remain for abused, neglected, dependent, and unruly children. RC 2151.01(A).

S.B. 179 ELIGIBILITY TABLE

Prepared by the Ohio Criminal Sentencing Commission April, 2001.[4]

OFFENSE LEVEL	DT Eligible		Not DT Eligible	
AGES→	17 & 16	15 & 14	13 & 12	11 & 10
Aggravated Murder/Murder	MT	MT*/MSYO	DSYO	DSYO
Attempted Agg. Murder/Murder	MT	MT*/MSYO	DSYO	DSYO
F-1 Violent + Other Enhanced	MT**/MSYO	DSYO	DSYO	DSYO
F-1 Not Violent Enhanced	DSYO	DSYO	DSYO	TJ
F-1 Not Enhanced	DSYO	DSYO	TJ	TJ
F-2 Enhanced	MT**/DSYO	DSYO	DSYO	TJ
F-2 Not Enhanced	MT**/DSYO	DSYO	TJ	TJ
F-3 Enhanced	DSYO	DSYO	TJ	TJ
F-3 Not Enhanced	DSYO	TJ	TJ	TJ
F-4 Enhanced or F-5 Enhanced	DSYO	TJ	TJ	TJ
F-4 or F-5 Enhanced	TJ	TJ	TJ	TJ

*MT with prior DYS commitment for a Category 1 or 2 offense. Otherwise MSYO.

**If Category 2 (other than kidnapping), MT with prior DYS commitment for a Category 1 or 2 offense &/or used, displayed, or indicated a firearm in the act. Otherwise MSYO (F-1s) or DSYO (F-2s).

Key [§ 2152.11(J)]:

MT: Mandatory Transfer (must be bound over to adult court).

DT: Discretionary Transfer (may be bound over to adult court).

MSYO: Mandatory Serious Youthful Offender (''blended'') sentence.

DSYO: Discretionary Serious Youthful Offender sentence.

TJ: Traditional Juvenile dispositions (no MT or SYO).

Enhanced: One or more of the relevant enhancing factors is present (offense of violence, gun use, etc., or certain prior DYS terms). Relevant enhancements vary by offense and age.

Violent: Offense of violence as defined in § 2901.01(A)(9).

§ 4:2 Delinquent child defined

RC 2152.02(F) defines a delinquent child as any child who violates (1) a law of this state, (2) a law of the United States, (3) an ordinance of a political subdivision of this state,[1] which would be a crime if committed by an adult (except for traffic offenses), or (4) RC 2923.211(A).[2] In addition, the definition of delinquency includes a child who is a repeat habitual truant or chronic

---

[4]S.B. 179 Ohio Judicial College Course Materials (April 2001) prepared by David Diroll, Ohio Sentencing Commission.

[Section 4:2]

[1]See In re DeGeronimo, No. 40089 (8th Dist. Ct. App., Cuyahoga, 6-28-79), holding that violation of the rules of the Metropolitan Park Board is a delinquent act, since that board is a "political subdivision."

[2]RC 2923.211(A) prohibits a person under age 18 from purchasing or attempting to purchase a firearm.

truant, or who violates a lawful order of the juvenile court.[3]

Traffic offenses, however, are treated differently.[4]

§ 4:3 Federal penal law

A child who violates a federal law may be processed in either a federal district court or a state juvenile court. There is a preference for the state juvenile court. In order to prosecute a child in a federal court, the Attorney General or a United States Attorney must certify that the appropriate juvenile court does not have or refuses to assume jurisdiction, or does not have adequate programs and services to meet the child's needs.[1]

§ 4:4 Ohio penal law

A child who commits an act which would be a crime if committed by an adult (except for traffic offenses) falls within delinquency jurisdiction.[1]

Exceptions. By their terms, some crimes apply only to adults, and they are not considered delinquent acts if committed by children. For instance, the crimes of "Unlawful sexual conduct with a minor"[2] and "Importuning,"[3] which require the actor to be 18 years of age or older, are not delinquent acts if committed by a person under the age of 18.[4]

A child who commits a crime which specifies only that the victim must be a child may be charged as a delinquent. For example, the crimes of "Disseminating material harmful to juveniles,"[5] "Pandering obscenity involving a minor,"[6] "Pandering sexually oriented matter involving a minor,"[7] "Deception to obtain matter harmful to juveniles,"[8] "Contributing to delinquency of a child,"[9] "Endangering children,"[10] and "Interference with custody,"[11] which all require that the object of the offense be a person under 18 years of age, are delinquent acts if committed by a child since the subject of these offenses

---

[3]See In re Burgess, 13 Ohio App. 3d 374, 469 N.E.2d 967 (12th Dist. Preble County 1984), holding that a delinquent child is a child whose conduct would constitute a violation of any criminal statute, even a statute different from the one included in the delinquency complaint. See also In re Crowe, 1987 WL 7053 (Ohio Ct. App. 2d Dist. Montgomery County 1987).

[4]See Juvenile Traffic Offender Jurisdiction Ch 7.

[Section 4:3]
[1]18 U.S.C.A. §§ 5032 et seq.

[Section 4:4]
[1]E.g., State v. Lee, 1983 WL 5753 (Ohio Ct. App. 8th Dist. Cuyahoga County 1983) (possession of fireworks and marijuana); In the Matter of Pollard, 1981 WL 4690 (Ohio Ct. App. 8th Dist. Cuyahoga County 1981) (arson); State v. Majoros, No. 42062 (8th Dist. Ct. App., Cuyahoga, 11-13-80) (riot, disorderly conduct); In re White, No. 40971 (8th Dist. Ct. App., Cuyahoga, 7-31-80) (failure to report a crime, complicity to murder).

[2]RC 2907.04.

[3]RC 2907.07(C).

[4]However, it is arguable that a child may be unruly for committing these offenses. See RC 2151.022; In re J. P., 32 Ohio Misc. 5, 61 Ohio Op. 2d 24, 287 N.E.2d 926 (C.P. 1972).

[5]RC 2907.31.

[6]RC 2907.321.

[7]RC 2907.322. See In re Dalton, 115 Ohio App. 3d 794, 686 N.E.2d 345 (7th Dist. Belmont County 1996).

[8]RC 2907.33(A).

[9]RC 2919.24. State v. Bare, 153 Ohio App. 3d 193, 2003-Ohio-3062, 792 N.E.2d 732 (2d Dist. Champaign County 2003).

[10]RC 2919.22. This often involves the situation where a teen-age babysitter administers unwarranted disciplinary measures to a child.

[11]RC 2919.23(A)(1).

may be any "person."[12]

Drug and alcohol offenses. A substantial percentage of delinquency complaints involve drug and alcohol offenses. Courts have held that possession of liquor[13] or hallucinogens[14] by a child is an act of delinquency. Since the purchase of liquor is a crime if committed by an adult between the ages of 18 and 21,[15] and the purchase of beer is a crime if committed by an 18-year-old,[16] either would constitute a delinquent act if committed by a child. However, it could be argued that possession of less than 100 grams of marijuana, which is a minor misdemeanor if committed by an adult,[17] would not be a delinquent act if committed by a child. The strength of this argument rests on the interpretation given to RC 2925.11(D), which provides that "[a]rrest or conviction [of an adult] for a minor misdemeanor violation of this section does not constitute a criminal record." Attorneys representing alleged delinquents charged with possession of marijuana have asserted that since conviction of the offense does not lead to a "criminal record" for an adult, the offense is not a "crime" as used in the definition of a delinquent child.[18] The better position, however, is that possession of marijuana is a crime for an adult since it is included within Title 29 ("Crimes—Procedure") and is listed under the statute which classifies offenses.[19] Although the conviction of an adult for possession of marijuana does not constitute a criminal record, possession is still a crime for an adult and thus a delinquent act for a child.[20]

Second offender enhancements. Because the dispositional alternatives available to the juvenile court depend, in part, on whether the delinquent child has committed a felony or misdemeanor (according to adult standards),[21] there is added significance accorded those crimes which are elevated from misdemeanors to felonies based on an adult's prior conviction for a similar offense. For instance, based on the version of RC 2913.02 in effect prior to July 1996, if an adult had been convicted of a misdemeanor theft offense and had subsequently been convicted of a second theft offense, the second conviction constituted a felony regardless of the value of the property stolen.[22] In 1984, the Ohio Supreme Court in *In re Russell*,[23] held that a prior adjudication of delinquency predicated on a theft offense constituted a prior conviction of theft under RC 2913.02. Thus, a subsequent theft offense adjudication would amount to a delinquent-felony, permitting the juvenile court to commit the child to the legal custody of the Department of Youth Services.[24] The

---

[12]See In re Lomeli, 106 Ohio App. 3d 242, 665 N.E.2d 765 (3d Dist. Putnam County 1995); Matter of Popovich, 1993 WL 19619 (Ohio Ct. App. 7th Dist. Belmont County 1993).

[13]State v. Butler, 11 Supp. 18, 38 Ohio Law Abs. 211 (Juv., Tuscarawas 1943).

[14]In re Baker, 18 Ohio App. 2d 276, 47 Ohio Op. 2d 411, 248 N.E.2d 620 (4th Dist. Hocking County 1969).

[15]RC 4301.63.

[16]RC 4301.63.

[17]RC 2925.11(C)(3).

[18]RC 2151.02. However, the child may be charged as an unruly child. See RC 2151.022; Unruly Child Jurisdiction Ch 8.

[19]RC 2901.02(A) and (G) include minor misdemeanors.

[20]See State v. Lee, 1983 WL 5753 (Ohio Ct. App. 8th Dist. Cuyahoga County 1983), wherein a delinquency adjudication for possession of marijuana was upheld, although the issue of whether it constituted a delinquent act was not raised.

[21]For instance, under RC 2152.16(A), only a delinquency adjudication for commission of a felony may lead to a commitment to the Ohio Department of Youth Services. See also RC 2152.10 and RC 2152.12, concerning the transfer of a child to criminal court for trial as an adult if the child is charged with a delinquent-felony offense. See § 27:3, Department of Youth Services.

[22]RC 2913.02(B).

[23]In re Russell, 12 Ohio St. 3d 304, 466 N.E.2d 553 (1984). See also In re Reynolds, 1996 WL 379343 (Ohio Ct. App. 12th Dist. Madison County 1996).

[24]See § 27:3, Department of Youth Services.

amendment of RC 2913.02(B),[25] removing the felony enhancement based on a prior theft conviction, may render moot the specific holding of *Russell*,[26] but the principle established by the Supreme Court was significant. Subsequent to the decision, the General Assembly enacted RC 2151.355(D)(2) in recognition of the Supreme Court holding.[27] This statute provided that the juvenile court shall consider a previous delinquency adjudication as a conviction in determining the degree of offense for a current delinquent act, for purposes of entering an order of disposition.[28]

RC 2901.08 provides that delinquency adjudications are considered convictions for enhancement purposes.

Proof of prior adjudication. Where a child is charged as a delinquent-felon based on a prior adjudication, the prior adjudication becomes an element of the present offense and must be proved by the state beyond a reasonable doubt. This cannot be established by the court's merely taking judicial notice of the juvenile's prior adjudication,[29] but may be accomplished by producing a certified copy of the prior adjudication of delinquency and sufficient evidence to identify the child as the offender named in the prior order.[30]

§ 4:5 Truancy

In 2000,[1] some types of truancy were included in delinquency jurisdiction.

Repeat habitual truancy. A delinquent child includes "[a]ny child who is an habitual truant and who previously has been adjudicated an unruly child for being an habitual truant."[2] An "habitual truant" is a type of unruly child. A second habitual truancy adjudication escalates to delinquency. Habitual truancy is discussed in § 8:4, on unruly jurisdiction.

Chronic truancy. A new category—"chronic truant"—was created in 2000.[3] A "chronic truant" is defined as any child of compulsory school age[4] who is absent without legitimate excuse from the public school the child is supposed to attend for (1) seven or more consecutive school days,[5] (2) 10 or more school days in one school month,[6] or (3) 15 or more school days in a school year."[7]

§ 4:6 Court order violations

A child may be found delinquent not only for violating a criminal statute

---

[25]1995 S.B. 2, eff. 7-1-96.

[26]In re Russell, 12 Ohio St. 3d 304, 466 N.E.2d 553 (1984).

[27]1995 H.B. 1, eff. 1-1-96. See also Section 3(A) of 1995 H.B. 1, in which the General Assembly declares that its purpose in enacting RC 2151.355(D)(2) "is to recognize the holding of the Supreme Court in In re Russell, 12 Ohio St. 3d 304, 466 N.E.2d 553 (1984)."

[28]RC 2151.355(D)(2), language now found at RC 2152.17(C).

[29]In re Carlos O., 96 Ohio App. 3d 252, 644 N.E.2d 1084 (6th Dist. Wood County 1994).

[30]In re Hayes, 29 Ohio App. 3d 162, 504 N.E.2d 491 (10th Dist. Franklin County 1986); In re Williams, 31 Ohio App. 3d 241, 510 N.E.2d 832 (10th Dist. Franklin County 1986); Matter of Horton, 1985 WL 4585 (Ohio Ct. App. 10th Dist. Franklin County 1985).

[Section 4:5]

[1]S.B. 181.

[2]RC 2152.02(F)(4).

[3]RC 2152.02(F)(5) (any child who is a chronic truant).

[4]See RC 2151.011(B)(25) (" 'Of Compulsory School Age' has the same meaning as in Section 3321.01 of the revised code.").

[5]See RC 2151.011(B)(46) (" 'School Day' means the school day established by the state board of education pursuant to Section 3313.48 of the revised code.").

[6]See RC 2151.011(B)(47) (" 'School Month' and 'School Year' have the same meanings as in Section 3313.62 of the revised code.").

[7]RC 2152.02(D).

or ordinance, but also for violating a lawful juvenile court order.[1] Thus, if an unruly child (RC 2151.022) is placed on probation and violates the conditions of the probation order, a delinquency complaint may be filed.

This provision has stirred considerable controversy since it "transforms" an unruly child into a delinquent one even though the child may not have violated a criminal statute.[2] This was significant when the treatment and dispositional alternatives available for children in Ohio depended in large part on whether such children were delinquent or unruly.[3] However, since 1981, the distinction between a delinquent-felon and a delinquent-misdemeanant has had far more legal and practical significance than the difference between a delinquent child and an unruly child. For instance, only a delinquent-felon may be committed to the legal custody of the Ohio Department of Youth Services,[4] and only a child charged with a delinquent-felony may be transferred to a criminal court for prosecution as an adult.[5] The dispositions permitted for a delinquent-misdemeanant and an unruly child are quite similar.[6]

§ 4:7 Transfer to adult criminal court

There are three alternatives for felony delinquency cases: (1) transfer or bindover to adult criminal court, (2) traditional juvenile dispositions, and (3) blended sentences for Serious Youthful Offenders. Most, but not all, transfers are discretionary. Transfer of jurisdiction is discussed in Ch 22.

§ 4:8 Serious Youthful Offender (SYO)

S.B. 179 recognizes a new category of delinquency—Serious Youthful Offender (SYO), along with blended (juvenile/adult) sentences. This subject is discussed in Ch 5.

Cross References
Ch 8, § 19:7, § 22:6, § 27:3, § 33:9
Research References
Carlin, Baldwin's Ohio Practice, Merrick-Rippner Probate Law (6th ed.), Ch 106

[Section 4:6]
[1]RC 2152.02(F)(4).

[2]Despite this objection, the statute has been held constitutional against attacks of vagueness and overbreadth. See In re Boyer, No. 34724 (8th Dist. Ct. App., Cuyahoga, 12-31-75).

[3]See RC 2151.354 and RC 2151.355 prior to amendment by 1981 H.B. 440, eff. 11-23-81.

[4]RC 2152.16. See § 27:3, Department of Youth Services.

[5]RC 2152.10. See § 22:6, Probable cause requirement.

[6]RC 2152.19 and RC 2151.354, respectively.

Chapter 5

Serious Youthful Offenders

> **KeyCite®:** Cases and other legal materials listed in KeyCite Scope can be researched through West's KeyCite service on Westlaw®. Use KeyCite to check citations for form, parallel references, prior and later history, and comprehensive citator information, including citations to other decisions and secondary materials.

§ 5:1   Introduction
§ 5:2   Blended sentences
§ 5:3   SYO charging; preliminary hearing
§ 5:4   SYO venue
§ 5:5   SYO enhancements
§ 5:6   SYO adjudicatory hearing
§ 5:7   Mandatory SYO dispositions
§ 5:8   Discretionary SYO dispositions
§ 5:9   Procedural rights
§ 5:10   Invoking adult sentences
§ 5:11   Invoking adult sentence hearing
§ 5:12   Subsequent procedures
§ 5:13   SYO appeals

§ 5:1   Introduction

S.B. 179 recognized a new category of delinquency: Serious Youthful Offender (SYO), along with blended sentences.[1] Only SYOs are eligible for blended sentences, which contain both a juvenile disposition and an adult criminal sentence. The adult sentence is stayed while the juvenile term is served; the adult portion can then be invoked only for specified rule violations after the juvenile turns 14 years of age and after a hearing, as discussed below.

SYO classification depends on age, felony level, and enhancement factors. An SYO disposition may be discretionary or mandatory. Because of the possibility of an adult sentence, greater procedural safeguards—such as grand jury indictment and jury trials—are required in this context.

Ordinarily, juvenile cases may not be tried in the same courtrooms as adult criminal cases.[2] The statute, however, provides that a separate courtroom is not required for juveniles in SYO cases.[3] SYO cases must be heard by a judge; magistrates may not hear any portion of the case.[4]

§ 5:2   Blended sentences

"The theory underpinning [blended sentences] is that the juvenile system—even with its ability to bind over some of the worst offenders to the criminal court—needs greater flexibility in dealing with other serious juvenile

---

[Section 5:1]
[1]Effective Jan. 1, 2002.
[2]RC 2151.24(A).
[3]RC 2151.24(B).
[4]Juv. R. 40(C)(1). See also, § 24:3, Order of reference.

offenders. Bindover is not the best option for all serious offenders. The criminal court might be too lenient on some offenders, who are younger and appear less hardened than adult felons. It might be too harsh on others, who could benefit from the greater rehabilitative opportunities in the juvenile system."[1] The SYO category provides the court with more options. "The solution lies in a flexible sentencing structure involving both juvenile and adult sanctions. 'Blended sentencing' lets the court tailor a sentence using the treatment flexibility of the juvenile system and the more punitive sanctions of the criminal system. A blended sentence gives the court time to learn if the child simply needs guidance under the juvenile system and the tools to deal with a juvenile who poses an ongoing threat."[2]

The Sentencing Commission identified five different approaches to blended sentencing—some located in criminal court, some in juvenile court. In criminal court blending, the adult court controls the case from trial to sentencing and is authorized to impose juvenile sanctions. In one approach, "criminal-exclusive," the criminal court decides whether to impose *either* a juvenile disposition or an adult sentence on the juvenile.[3] In another approach, "criminal-inclusive," the criminal court must give *both* a juvenile disposition and an adult sentence. The adult sentence is stayed upon successful completion of the juvenile disposition. The adult sentence is imposed only for certain violations or designated serious disruptions to the juvenile's rehabilitative efforts.[4]

The other approaches involve the juvenile court. Under these approaches, the juvenile court controls the case and is authorized to impose adult criminal sanctions. Under a "juvenile-exclusive" approach, the juvenile court must impose *either* a juvenile disposition or an adult sentence.[5] The fourth approach, "juvenile-inclusive," requires the juvenile court to impose *both* a juvenile disposition and an adult sentence. The adult sentence is suspended pending successful completion of the juvenile term and is invoked only if the juvenile violates set conditions or institutional rules in such a way as to impede rehabilitation.[6] This is the approach adopted in Ohio. In the fifth approach—"juvenile-contiguous"—a juvenile sentence is imposed that may extend beyond the typical jurisdictional age limit of juvenile dispositions.[7]

§ 5:3   SYO charging; preliminary hearing

A blended sentence may be imposed only if the prosecutor obtains (1) an indictment, (2) an information,[1] or (3) a complaint that includes a request for an SYO sentence.[2]

Notice. In addition, the prosecutor may provide written notice of an intent to seek a blended sentence.[3] The notice must be filed within 20 days of the complaint or the date the juvenile court decides not to transfer a case to

---

[Section 5:2]

[1]Ohio Criminal Sentencing Commission, A Plan for Juvenile Sentencing in Ohio (Fall 1999).

[2]Ohio Criminal Sentencing Commission, A Plan for Juvenile Sentencing in Ohio (Fall 1999).

[3]California, Colorado, Florida, Idaho, Michigan, and Virginia use some form of the criminal-exclusive blend.

[4]Arkansas and Missouri use this approach.

[5]New Mexico employs this approach.

[6]Connecticut, Minnesota, and Montana use some form of the juvenile-inclusive blend.

[7]This approach was also part of the Sentencing Commission's recommendation but was not enacted.

[Section 5:3]

[1]RC 2152.13(A)(2). See also Juv. R. 29(F) (recognizing indictment and information procedure).

[2]RC 2152.13(A)(3).

[3]RC 2152.13(B).

adult court.[4] Juvenile Rule 22(E) provides that the filing of an SYO motion constitutes notice of intent to pursue SYO dispositions.[5]

The 20-day period may be extended by the court for good cause. The court must serve a copy of the notice on and advise the juvenile of the prosecutor's intent to pursue an SYO sentence.[6] Juvenile Rule 29, which governs the adjudicatory hearing, provides that the filing of a notice of intent or a "statement of interest" in pursuing an SYO sentence constitutes good cause for continuing the adjudicatory hearing and extending detention or shelter care.[7]

Preliminary hearing. A preliminary hearing is mandated, unless waived, if a complaint or the notice procedure is used. At the hearing, the court must determine whether there is probable cause that the juvenile committed the act charged and is age-eligible for an SYO sentence.[8] SYO proceedings must be conducted by juvenile judges, not magistrates.[9]

Despite this scheme, the Ohio constitutional requirement of a grand jury indictment would seem applicable to all such cases, unless it is waived.[10] Indeed, a different SYO section provides for the right to grand jury indictment.[11]

§ 5:4 SYO venue

Juvenile court jurisdiction usually entails dual venue, both in the county in which the act occurred or the county of residence.[1] SYO cases are treated differently. Like adult criminal cases,[2] venue lies only in the county in which the alleged act occurred.[3]

§ 5:5 SYO enhancements

SYO classification depends on age, felony level, and enhancement factors. An act may be "enhanced" in three ways.

Crimes of violence. First, an act is enhanced if it involves an offense of violence.[1] The Criminal Code defines the term "offense of violence"[2] to include such crimes as (1) aggravated murder,[3] murder,[4] voluntary manslaughter,[5] involuntary manslaughter,[6] felonious assault,[7] aggravated assault,[8] simple

---

[4]RC 2152.13(B)(1) and RC 2152.13(B)(2).

[5]See also Juv. R. 22(D)(5) (SYO motions).

[6]RC 2152.13(B).

[7]See Staff Note (2001) ("[B]ecause the rule contemplates a hearing within ten days, but the [SYO] statute grants a twenty day time period for making the charging decision, the amended rule also provides a mechanism by which a prosecuting attorney can preserve the twenty day time period by filing a 'statement of interest in pursuing a serious youthful offender sentence.' ").

[8]RC 2152.13(C).

[9]Juv. R. 40(C)(1).

[10]See Katz and Giannelli, Baldwin's Ohio Practice, Criminal Law (2d ed.), Ch 40 (indictments and information).

[11]RC 2152.13(D)(1).

[Section 5:4]

[1]See Venue Ch 17.

[2]See Katz and Giannelli, Baldwin's Ohio Practice, Criminal Law (2d ed.), Ch 56 (venue).

[3]RC 2151.271.

[Section 5:5]

[1]RC 2152.11(A)(1).

[2]RC 2901.01(A)(9).

[3]RC 2903.01. See also Katz and Giannelli, Baldwin's Ohio Practice, Criminal Law (2d ed.), Ch 95 (homicide).

[4]RC 2903.02.

[5]RC 2903.03.

[6]RC 2903.04.

assault,[9] aggravated menacing,[10] stalking-menacing,[11] simple menacing,[12] kidnapping,[13] abduction,[14] extortion,[15] rape,[16] sexual battery,[17] gross sexual imposition,[18] (former) felonious sexual penetration, aggravated arson,[19] arson,[20] aggravated robbery,[21] robbery,[22] aggravated burglary,[23] some burglaries,[24] inciting to violence,[25] aggravated riot,[26] riot,[27] inducing panic,[28] permitting child abuse,[29] child endangerment,[30] domestic violence,[31] intimidation,[32] intimidation of a victim or witness,[33] escape,[34] discharging a firearm into a home or school;[35] (2) conspiracy[36] or complicity,[37] or attempt[38] to commit any of the above crimes; (3) a current or former law or ordinance anywhere in the United States substantially equivalent to these offenses; and (4) a crime that is committed purposely or knowingly and involves physical harm to a person.

Guns. Second, an act is enhanced if it involves a firearm—i.e., the offender used, displayed, brandished, indicated possession of, or actually possessed a firearm.[39]

Prior DYS admission. Third, an act is enhanced if the juvenile had previously been *admitted* to a DYS facility for aggravated murder, murder, an

---

[7]RC 2903.11. See also Katz and Giannelli, Baldwin's Ohio Practice, Criminal Law (2d ed.), Ch 97 (assault and menacing).

[8]RC 2903.12.

[9]RC 2903.13.

[10]RC 2903.21.

[11]RC 2903.211.

[12]RC 2903.22.

[13]RC 2905.01. See also Katz and Giannelli, Baldwin's Ohio Practice, Criminal Law (2d ed.), Ch 98 (kidnapping).

[14]RC 2905.02.

[15]RC 2905.11.

[16]RC 2907.02. See also Katz and Giannelli, Baldwin's Ohio Practice, Criminal Law (2d ed.), Ch 99 (rape and related offenses).

[17]RC 2907.03.

[18]RC 2907.05.

[19]RC 2909.02. See also Katz and Giannelli, Baldwin's Ohio Practice, Criminal Law (2d ed.), Ch 103 (arson).

[20]RC 2909.03.

[21]RC 2911.01. See also Katz and Giannelli, Baldwin's Ohio Practice, Criminal Law (2d ed.), Ch 102 (robbery and extortion).

[22]RC 2911.02.

[23]RC 2911.11. See also Katz and Giannelli, Baldwin's Ohio Practice, Criminal Law (2d ed.), Ch 104 (burglary).

[24]RC 2911.12.

[25]RC 2917.01.

[26]RC 2917.02. See also Katz and Giannelli, Baldwin's Ohio Practice, Criminal Law (2d ed.), Ch 108 (offenses against public peace).

[27]RC 2917.03.

[28]RC 2917.31.

[29]RC 2903.15.

[30]RC 2919.22. See also Katz and Giannelli, Baldwin's Ohio Practice, Criminal Law (2d ed.), Ch 109 (offenses against family).

[31]RC 2919.25.

[32]RC 2921.03. See also Katz and Giannelli, Baldwin's Ohio Practice, Criminal Law (2d ed.), Ch 110 (offenses against justice).

[33]RC 2921.04.

[34]RC 2921.34.

[35]RC 2923.161.

[36]RC 2923.01.

[37]RC 2923.03.

[38]RC 2923.02.

[39]RC 2152.11(A)(2). See also RC 2152.02(M) (defining firearm as in RC 2923.11).

F-1, F-2, or F-3 offense of violence.[40] Commitment to a DYS facility is insufficient; actual admission is required. The facility may be a DYS contract facility or a comparable facility anywhere in the United States.[41]

§ 5:6 SYO adjudicatory hearing

The adjudicatory hearing in SYO cases differs from typical delinquency hearings[1] in several significant respects.[2]

Jury trial. The SYO statute recognizes the right to a jury trial in juvenile court.[3] Prior to the enactment of this provision, the right to trial by jury did not apply in delinquency proceedings.[4] The right to jury trial in criminal cases is grounded in the Sixth Amendment, the Ohio Constitution, and the Criminal Rules.[5]

Public trial. The SYO statute also recognizes the right to a public trial.[6] Prior to the enactment of this provision, this right did not apply in delinquency proceedings, although the juvenile court had discretion to open the proceeding.[7] Moreover, freedom of the press issues placed a number of constraints on the judge's authority to close juvenile proceedings.[8]

Trial judge. SYO proceedings must be conducted by juvenile judges, not magistrates—with or without a jury.[9]

SYO proceedings cease once the trier of fact determines that the child is not a serious youthful offender; they also end if the juvenile court decides not to impose a discretionary SYO disposition.[10]

§ 5:7 Mandatory SYO dispositions

If not transferred to adult court, a juvenile is subject to a mandatory blended sentence for (1) aggravated murder,[1] murder,[2] or an attempt[3] to commit either at the age of 14 or 15[4] or (2) an F-1 act at the age of 16 or 17 if an offense of violence and either the gun enhancement or prior DYS enhancement applies.[5] Juveniles from 10 to 13 years are not subject to MSYO.

For an MSYO sentence, the juvenile court must (1) impose an adult sentence under Chapter 2929 as if the juvenile were an adult (except for death and life without parole, which are not authorized), (2) impose one or

---

[40]RC 2152.11(A)(3).

[41]RC 2152.02(B).

[Section 5:6]

[1]See Adjudicatory Hearing Ch 23.

[2]See also § 5:9, Procedural rights.

[3]RC 2152.13(D)(1). See also Juv. R. 27(A)(3). The same statute also provides the right to a transcript.

[4]See § 23:10, Jury trials.

[5]See Katz and Giannelli, Baldwin's Ohio Practice, Criminal Law (2d ed.), Ch 62 (trial by jury).

[6]RC 2152.13(D)(1). See also Juv. R. 27(A)(1).

[7]See § 23:11, Public trials; gag orders. See generally Katz and Giannelli, Baldwin's Ohio Practice, Criminal Law (2d ed.) § 68:3 (right to public trial).

[8]See Katz and Giannelli, Baldwin's Ohio Practice, Criminal Law (2d ed.), Ch 66 (fair trial and free press).

[9]Juv. R. 40(C)(1).

[10]Juv. R. 2(LL) (defining SYO proceedings).

[Section 5:7]

[1]RC 2903.01.

[2]RC 2903.02.

[3]RC 2923.02.

[4]RC 2152.11(B)(1), RC 2152.11(C)(1).

[5]RC 2152.11(D)(1).

more traditional juvenile dispositions,[6] and (3) stay the adult sentence pending the successful completion of the juvenile dispositions.[7] In this context, the blended sentence is mandatory, but neither a DYS term nor the invoking of the adult portion of the sentence is mandatory.

§ 5:8 Discretionary SYO dispositions

A juvenile is subject to a discretionary blended sentence for:

(1) aggravated murder,[1] murder,[2] or an attempt[3] to commit either at the age of 10 to 13,[4]

(2) a F-1 act at age 16 or 17 not falling within MSYO,[5]

(3) a F-1 act at age 14 or 15,[6]

(4) a F-1 act at age 12 or 13 if any of the three enhancements applies,[7]

(5) a F-1 act at age 10 or 11 if an offense of violence and either the gun or prior DYS enhancement applies,[8]

(6) a F-2 act at age 14 to 17,[9]

(7) a F-2 act at age 12 or 13 if any of the three enhancements apply,[10]

(8) a F-3 act at age 16 or 17,[11]

(9) a F-3 act at age 14 or 15 if any of the three enhancements applies,[12] or

(10) a F-4 or F-5 act at age 16 or 17 if any of the three enhancements apply.[13]

For a DSYO sentence, the juvenile court has several options. First, the court may impose an adult sentence under Chapter 2929 as if the juvenile were an adult (except for death and life without parole, which are not authorized) under certain circumstances. The must court find, on the record, that there is not a reasonable expectation that the overriding purposes set forth in RC 2152.01 will be met.[14] In making this determination, the court must consider (1) the nature and circumstances of the violation, (2) the juvenile's history, and (3) the length of time, level of security, and types of juvenile programming and resources available. If this finding is not made, the court must impose as the sole disposition, one or more of the traditional juvenile dispositions under RC 2152.16, RC 2152.17 (if applicable), RC 2152.19, or RC 2152.20.[15]

Second, if the required findings are made, the court may impose one or

---

[6]See RC 2152.16, RC 2152.19.

[7]RC 2152.13(E)(1).

[Section 5:8]

[1]RC 2903.01.

[2]RC 2903.02.

[3]RC 2925.02.

[4]RC 2152.11(B)(2), RC 2152.11(C)(2).

[5]RC 2152.11(D)(2)(a).

[6]RC 2152.11(D)(2)(b)

[7]RC 2152.11(D)(2)(c).

[8]RC 2152.11(D)(2)(d).

[9]RC 2152.11(E)(1).

[10]RC 2152.11(E)(2).

[11]RC 2152.11(F)(1).

[12]RC 2152.11(F)(2).

[13]RC 2152.11(G)(1).

[14]RC 2152.13(D)(2)(a)(i).

[15]RC 2152.13(D)(2)(b).

more traditional juvenile dispositions.[16]

Finally, the court must stay the adult sentence pending the successful completion of the juvenile dispositions.[17]

§ 5:9 Procedural rights

Because the adult portion of a blended sentence is unquestionably a criminal sanction, the rights attendant to criminal trials are applicable.

Grand jury indictment.[1] This right includes a grand jury determination of probable cause that the child (1) committed the act charged and (2) is age eligible for a SYO dispositional sentence. The grand jury may be impaneled by the general division of the court of common pleas or the juvenile court. The right to grand jury indictment is found in the Ohio Constitution and Criminal Rule 7. The federal right to grand jury indictment has never been applied to the states.[2] Thus, although there are other ways to initiate SYO procedures—information, SYO complaint, and SYO notice—the juvenile nevertheless has a right to a grand jury determination, unless this right is waived.

Once the child is charged by indictment or information or the juvenile court finds the child eligible for SYO dispositions at the preliminary hearing,[3] other rights are triggered.

Speedy trial.[4] The Chapter 31 time limits[5] commence on the date on which the indictment, information, original SYO complaint, or SYO notice is filed, depending on the method used to initiate the SYO procedures. Prior to the enactment of this provision, the constitutional right to a speedy trial, but not the statutory right, applied in juvenile delinquency proceedings.[6]

Bail.[7] A detained juvenile awaiting adjudication upon an indictment or information has the same right to bail as an adult charged with the same offense. The right to bail did not exist until this legislation was enacted, although pre-adjudication release of the juvenile was preferred.[8] The right to bail is based upon the Eighth Amendment, the Ohio Constitution, and the Criminal Rules.[9]

Counsel.[10] The SYO statute provides that the right to counsel cannot be waived. This provision would seem to conflict with the right to self-representation, which is recognized in adult trials.[11] The right to counsel has been a hallmark of juvenile court proceedings since the *Gault* decision.[12]

---

[16]RC 2152.13(D)(2)(a)(ii). These dispositions are found in RC 2152.16, RC 2152.17 (if applicable), RC 2152.19, or RC 2152.20.

[17]RC 2152.13(D)(2)(a)(iii).

[Section 5:9]

[1]RC 2152.13(C)(1).

[2]See Katz and Giannelli, Baldwin's Ohio Practice, Criminal Law (2d ed.), Ch 40 (indictments and information).

[3]See § 5:3, SYO charging; preliminary hearing.

[4]RC 2152.13(C)(1).

[5]See Katz and Giannelli, Baldwin's Ohio Practice, Criminal Law (2d ed.), Ch 60 (statutory right to speedy trial).

[6]See also § 23:29, Speedy trial.

[7]RC 2152.13(C)(2).

[8]See § 19:9, Bail.

[9]See Katz and Giannelli, Baldwin's Ohio Practice, Criminal Law (2d ed.), Ch 37 (bail and preventive detention).

[10]RC 2152.13(C)(2).

[11]See Katz and Giannelli, Baldwin's Ohio Practice, Criminal Law (2d ed.) § 75:15 (self-representation).

[12]See § 23:3, Right to counsel.

Mental competency procedure.[13] The SYO statute recognizes the right to raise the issue of mental competency. Although the prior Ohio procedures did not explicitly provide for juvenile competency hearings, it was assumed that this right was part of the juvenile system because it is a fundamental due process right.[14]

Criminal Code and Rules.[15] The SYO statute specifies that all the provisions of Title 29 and the Criminal Rules apply, with the exception of RC 2152.14 proceedings, which govern the invocation of the adult portion of a blended sentence.[16]

Other rights. RC 2151.13(D)(2) provides that the SYO juvenile is to be "afforded all the rights afforded a person who is prosecuted for committing a crime." This is a catch-all provision, apparently intended to encompass rights that have not been explicitly enumerated in this section. One would expect that such a provision would spawn litigation for several years as the courts and legislature deal with unexpected issues.

§ 5:10 Invoking adult sentences

The adult part of a blended sentence may be invoked while the juvenile is in DYS custody or while the juvenile is in the community. Once invoked, a hearing may be required.[1]

From DYS. A juvenile serving a blended sentence who is at least 14 years of age and is either in or has escaped from DYS custody is subject to invocation of the adult sentence.[2] The DYS Director may request that the prosecutor from the committing county file a motion in the committing court to invoke the adult part of the sentence.

The motion must state that there is reasonable cause to believe that the juvenile has engaged in conduct that either (1) violates institutional rules that could be charged as a felony or a violent M-1 if committed by an adult, or (2) creates a substantial risk to the safety or security of the institution, community, or victim.[3] At least one incident of misconduct must have occurred after the juvenile reached age 14.

From the community. A juvenile serving a blended sentence in the community[4] who is at least 14 years old is subject to invocation of the adult sentence.[5] The DYS Director, the juvenile sentencing court, or the supervising probation department may request that the prosecutor from the committing county file a motion in the committing court to invoke the adult part of the sentence. The prosecutor also has authority to file the motion sua sponte.

The motion must state that there is reasonable cause to believe that the juvenile has engaged in conduct that either (1) violates the conditions of supervision and could be charged as a felony or a violent M-1 if committed by an adult, or (2) creates a substantial risk to the safety or security of the community or the victim. At least one incident of misconduct must have occurred after the child reached age 14.[6]

---

[13]RC 2152.13(C)(2).

[14]See § 23:7, Mental competency; Katz and Giannelli, Baldwin's Ohio Practice, Criminal Law (2d ed.), Ch 54 (competency to stand trial).

[15]RC 2152.13(C)(2).

[16]See § 5:10, Invoking adult sentences.

[Section 5:10]

[1]See § 5:11, Invoking adult sentence hearing.

[2]RC 2152.14(A)(1).

[3]RC 2152.14(A)(2).

[4]E.g., community control or parole.

[5]RC 2152.14(B).

[6]RC 2152.14(A)(2).

Prosecution refusal. If the prosecutor declines to file the motion within a reasonable time, the DYS or the probation department may file the motion. If the prosecutor declines to file the motion at the court's request within a reasonable time, the court may hear its own motion.[7]

§ 5:11 Invoking adult sentence hearing

After the motion to invoke the SYO adult sentence is filed, the juvenile court has the option to decline to consider the motion. If the court decides to consider the motion, it must hold a hearing.[1]

Rights. At the hearing, the juvenile is entitled (1) to be present, (2) to receive notice of the grounds for invoking the adult term, (3) to counsel, which cannot be waived, (4) to be advised of the procedures and protections in the Juvenile Rules, (5) to an open hearing, and (6) to present evidence, including evidence of mental illness or retardation.[2]

Findings. To invoke the adult part of the blended sentence, the court must find, by clear and convincing evidence, that the juvenile (1) is serving the juvenile part of an SYO sentence, (2) is at least 14 years old, (3) has been admitted to a DYS facility or has criminal charges pending, (4) has committed the acts charged, and (5) has demonstrated by this conduct that rehabilitation during the remaining period of juvenile jurisdiction is unlikely.[3]

§ 5:12 Subsequent procedures

The court may modify the adult sentence to any lesser prison term that could be imposed for the offense and/or to community control sanctions that the offender was eligible to receive at sentencing.[1]

If the court invokes the adult sentence, the juvenile disposition terminates and the DYS must transfer the person to the Department of Rehabilitation and Correction or place the person under another sanction imposed as part of the sentence.[2] Once invoked, the offender is not subject to juvenile court jurisdiction in future cases.

Credit. The court must specify in its order the number of days that the juvenile was detained during the juvenile part of the sentence. Any prison term must be reduced by this time period plus any days held awaiting transfer to the DRC.[3]

Sentencing cap. The total prison term cannot exceed the maximum available for an adult convicted of the same offenses, including the time credited.[4]

Prison release. Community control imposed as a condition of judicial release from prison is supervised by the adult probation system. Similarly, the Adult Parole Authority supervises any post-release control imposed after release from prison.[5]

---

[7]RC 2152.14(C).

[Section 5:11]
　[1]RC 2152.14(D).
　[2]RC 2152.14(D).
　[3]RC 2152.14(E)(1).

[Section 5:12]
　[1]RC 2152.14(E)(2).
　[2]RC 2152.14(F).
　[3]RC 2152.14(F).
　[4]RC 2152.14(F).
　[5]RC 2152.14(F).

§ 5:13 SYO appeals

The SYO statute[1] recognizes the juvenile's right to appeal the adult part of a blended sentence.[2] The appellate court must consider the appeal "as if the adult portion were not stayed."

[Section 5:13]

[1]RC 2152.13(D)(3).

[2]See RC 2953.08(A)(1), RC 2953.08(A)(3), RC 2953.08(A)(4), RC 2953.08(A)(5), RC 2953.08(A)(6) ("S.B. 2 appeals" (1996)); Katz and Giannelli, Baldwin's Ohio Practice, Criminal Law (2d ed.), Ch 80 (appeals).

Chapter 6

Sex Offender Law

> **KeyCite®:** Cases and other legal materials listed in KeyCite Scope can be researched through West's KeyCite service on Westlaw®. Use KeyCite to check citations for form, parallel references, prior and later history, and comprehensive citator information, including citations to other decisions and secondary materials.

§ 6:1   Introduction
§ 6:2   "Sexually oriented offender" defined
§ 6:3   Registration-exempt sexually oriented offenses
§ 6:4   "Habitual sex offender" defined
§ 6:5   "Sexual predator" defined
§ 6:6   "Child-victim oriented offender" defined
§ 6:7   "Habitual child-victim offender" defined
§ 6:8   "Child-victim predator" defined
§ 6:9   Juvenile offender registrant—Repeat offender classification
§ 6:10   Juvenile offender registrant—Mandatory classification
§ 6:11   Juvenile offender registrant—Discretionary classification
§ 6:12   Dispositional completion hearing
§ 6:13   Petitions for reclassification or declassification
§ 6:14   Registration requirements
§ 6:15   Notification requirements
§ 6:16   Internet dissemination
§ 6:17   Residence limitation

§ 6:1 Introduction

RC 2950.09, the sex offender registration and notification law, is the state's version of "Megan's Law." The first Megan's Law[1] was enacted in 1994 in New Jersey in response to the rape and murder of seven-year old Megan Kanka. Since then, all fifty states have enacted similar laws.[2] Also, Congress in 1994 enacted the Jacob Wetterling Crimes Against Children and Sexually Violent Offender Registration Act,[3] which in part requires states to enact similar laws in order to obtain federal funding.[4] Ohio case law interpreting this law as applied to adults is discussed in a companion text.[5]

RC 2152.191 makes certain provisions of RC Chapter 2950 applicable to children adjudicated delinquent for committing a "sexually oriented offense" or a child-victim oriented offense if fourteen or older at the time of the offense. In the case of juveniles, the registration and notification requirements continue for the statutorily mandated time period and do not lapse when the child reaches age 18 or 21.

[Section 6:1]

[1]N.J. Stat. Ann. 2C:7-1 et seq.

[2]State v. Cook, 83 Ohio St. 3d 404, 405–06, 1998-Ohio-291, 700 N.E.2d 570 (1998).

[3]42 U.S.C.A. 14071.

[4]While Ohio has had a sexual offender registration law since 1963, RC 2950.09 became effective on January 1, 1997 as the Ohio version of the federal sexual offender registration law.

[5]See Katz and Giannelli, Baldwin's Ohio Practice, Criminal Law (2d ed.) § 121:6.

The 1996 revision of Megan's law includes three classifications for offenders: (1) sexually oriented offender, (2) habitual sex offender, and (3) sexual predator. The registration and notification requirements differ for each of these categories. For example, sexual predators must register every 90 days for life, whereas habitual sex offenders must register annually for 20 years. Although these terms are also used in juvenile cases, they are defined somewhat differently in this context. In addition, the Juvenile Code employs the term "juvenile offender registrant" (JOR) to effectuate Megan's Law.[6]

In 2003, chapter 2950 was amended.[7] First, several new offender categories were created: (1) child-victim oriented offender, (2) habitual child-victim offender, and (3) child-victim predator. These categories reclassify crimes against children that are not committed with a sexual motivation. Automatic reclassification provisions were included for persons previously classified as sex offenders under the old law.[8] Second, new registration classifications were enacted: (1) presumptive registration-exempt sexually oriented offenses and (2) registration-exempt sexually oriented offenses. These provisions exempt certain first-time delinquent offenders from the registration requirements. Third, several crimes were added to the sex offender categories. Fourth, new registration and notification requirements became effective. Fifth, an offender residence limitation was established; a person convicted of a sexually oriented offense or child-victim oriented offense may not reside within 1,000 feet of a school. However, this provision does not apply to juveniles. Sixth, Internet databases, one for the public and one for law enforcement, were authorized. Seventh, penalties for noncompliance were increased.

§ 6:2   "Sexually oriented offender" defined

As applied to a person under 18 years of age,[1] a sexually oriented offender includes a child who commits any of the following offenses:

(1) rape,[2] sexual battery,[3] gross sexual imposition,[4] or importuning,[5] regardless of the victim's age;

(2) kidnapping for the purpose of engaging in sexual activity,[6] sexual imposition,[7] voyeurism,[8] compelling prostitution,[9] or certain types of child endangerment,[10] if the victim was under 18 years of age;

---

[6]RC 2950.01(J) defines a "juvenile sex offender registrant" as a child adjudicated delinquent for a sexually oriented offense, who was fourteen years or older at the time of the offense, and where a juvenile judge issues an order under RC 2152.82 through RC 2152.85 classifying the offender as a juvenile sex offender registrant and specifies a duty to register under RC 2950.04.

[7]The amendments were based on recommendations of the Governor's Sex Offender Registration and Notification Task Force generally conforming the law to federal guidelines.

[8]RC 2950.091.

[Section 6:2]

[1]RC 2907.01(D)(2). Adults are governed by RC 2950.01(D)(1). If the juvenile is transferred to adult court for prosecution, the adult provisions apply. RC 2950.01(D)(2)(i).

[2]RC 2907.02.

[3]RC 2907.03.

[4]RC 2907.05.

[5]RC 2907.07.

[6]RC 2905.01(A)(4).

[7]RC 2907.06.

[8]RC 2907.08.

[9]RC 2907.21 (if the person who is compelled, induced, procured, encouraged, solicited, requested, or facilitated to engage in, paid or agreed to be paid for, or allowed to engage in the sexual activity is under 18 years).

[10]RC 2919.22(B)(5) (sexually oriented matter or nudity-oriented matter).

(3) certain kidnappings,[11] menacing by stalking,[12] or (former) child steal-ing,[13] when the victim was under 18 years and the offense was com-mitted with sexual motivation;

(4) sexually violent offenses[14] of the first, second, third, or fourth degree felony;

(5) aggravated murder,[15] murder,[16] felonious assault,[17] kidnapping,[18] abduction,[19] or involuntary manslaughter[20] that is committed with sexual motivation;

(6) certain types of pandering obscenity involving a minor,[21] pandering sexually oriented matter involving a minor,[22] or illegal use of a minor in nudity-oriented material or performances,[23] if the juvenile is four years or more older than the minor victim;

(7) sexual imposition[24] and voyeurism[25] when the victim is 18 years or older; and menacing by stalking[26] when the victim is 18 years or older and the offense is committed with sexual motivation;

(8) violations of (a) former Ohio laws, (b) existing or former municipal ordinances or laws of another state or the United States, including military law, (c) Indian tribal law, or (d) the laws of another country, substantially equivalent to the above offenses if a first, second, third or fourth degree felony; or

(9) attempts, conspiracies, or complicity in connection with the above offenses.

In *State v. Cook*,[27] the Ohio Supreme Court observed that a "sexually oriented offender is one who has committed a 'sexually oriented offense' as that term is defined in R.C. 2950.01(D) but who does not fit the description of either an habitual sex offender or sexual predator." This classification arises automatically by law (not by determination of the trial judge), when the de-fendant is convicted of a sexually oriented offense that does not fall under the other classifications.[28]

As noted in the next section, certain offenses are registration exempt. A ju-venile judge may remove this classification at the dispositional completion

---

[11]RC 2905.01(A)(1), (2), (3) and (5).

[12]RC 2903.211.

[13]Former RC 2905.04.

[14]RC 2971.01(G) (includes a violent sex offense or a designated homicide, assault of kidnap-ping offense for which the offender also was convicted of a sexual motivation specification); RC 2971.01(L) (violent sex offenses are (1) rape (RC 2907.02); (2) sexual battery (RC 2907.03); (3) fe-lonious sexual penetration (RC 2907.12); (4) gross sexual imposition on a victim less than thirteen years old (RC 2907.05(A)(4)); (5) substantially equivalent former Ohio laws, (6) existing or former substantially equivalent laws of another state of the United States, and (7) felony at-tempts or complicity of the above offenses).

[15]RC 2903.01.

[16]RC 2903.02.

[17]RC 2903.11.

[18]RC 2905.01.

[19]RC 2905.02.

[20]RC 2903.04(A) (causing death while committing or attempting to commit a felony).

[21]RC 2907.321(A)(1) or RC 2907.321(A)(3).

[22]RC 2907.322(A)(1) or RC 2907.322(A)(3).

[23]RC 2907.323(A)(1) or RC 2907.323(A)(2).

[24]RC 2907.06.

[25]RC 2907.08.

[26]RC 2903.211.

[27]State v. Cook, 83 Ohio St. 3d 404, 1998-Ohio-291, 700 N.E.2d 570 (1998).

[28]State v. Moyers, 137 Ohio App. 3d 130, 133, 2000-Ohio-1669, 738 N.E.2d 90 (3d Dist. Seneca County 2000).

hearing[29] or upon petition of the juvenile.[30] Registration and notification requirements are discussed in later sections of this chapter.

§ 6:3   Registration-exempt sexually oriented offenses

A limited number of first-time offenses are presumptively excluded from the registration requirement—unless a court orders registration.[1] A prior adjudication of a sexually oriented or child-victim oriented offense disqualifies a child from this category.

Offenses subject to presumptive exemption include:

(1) sexual imposition[2] and voyeurism,[3] if the victim was 18 years or older.

(2) menacing by stalking[4] if victim was 18 years or older and committed with sexual motivation.

(3) violations of (a) former Ohio law, (b) existing or former municipal ordinances or laws of another state or the United States, or (c) Indian tribal law, substantially equivalent to a sexually oriented offense listed in RC 2950.01(D)(1).

(4) attempts, conspiracies, or complicity in connection with the above offenses.

Procedure. The judge decides pursuant to the criteria in RC 2950.02 and 2950.021 whether the child will not be exempt.[5]

§ 6:4   "Habitual sex offender" defined

As applied to juveniles, classification as an habitual sex offender requires satisfaction of two conditions: First, the child must be adjudicated a delinquent for a "sexually oriented offense" that is not registration-exempt committed when 14 years or older and classified as a "juvenile offender registrant."[1] Second, the child must have previously been convicted or adjudicated a delinquent for committing a sexually or child-victim oriented offense—regardless of when the offense was committed or age at the time.[2] The previous offense does not encompass multiple charges in the same case.[3] In effect, a habitual sex offender is a repeat offender.

A juvenile judge may remove this classification at the dispositional completion hearing[4] or upon petition of the juvenile.[5] Registration and notification requirements are discussed in later sections of this chapter.

---

[29]See § 6:12, Dispositional completion hearing.

[30]See § 6:13, Petitions for reclassification or declassification.

[Section 6:3]

[1]RC 2950.01(P).

[2]RC 2907.06.

[3]RC 2907.08.

[4]RC 2903.322.

[5]RC 2950.01(Q).

[Section 6:4]

[1]RC 2950.01(B)(1). Age is determined at the time of the offense and the registrant classification is for that adjudication (not a prior adjudication).

[2]RC 2950.01(B)(2).

[3]State v. West, 134 Ohio App. 3d 45, 730 N.E.2d 388 (1st Dist. Hamilton County 1999) (classification as habitual sexual offender cannot be based on multiple counts of battery in the same case; state must offer proof of other previous offenses.).

[4]See § 6:12, Dispositional completion hearing

[5]See § 6:13, Petitions for reclassification or declassification.

§ 6:5 "Sexual predator" defined

As applied to juveniles,[1] a "sexual predator" is defined as a person adjudicated as a delinquent for a sexually oriented offense that is not registration-exempt when 14 years or older and was classified as a "juvenile offender registrant" as a result of that adjudication and is likely to engage in sexually oriented offenses in the future.[2]

The juvenile's classification as a sexual predator arises in different ways for in-state and out-of-state juveniles. For an in-state juvenile, the classification occurs when a judge determines that the child is a sexual predator under RC 2950.09 or RC 2152.82 through RC 2152.85.[3] For an out-of-state juvenile, the classification occurs if (1) a delinquent of a sexually oriented offense that is not registration-exempt (regardless of date) is required to register under the out-of-state law as a sex offender until death and to verify his address at least quarterly and (2) resides in Ohio for more than five days unless a court determines that the child is not a sexual predator pursuant to RC 2950.09(F).[4]

A juvenile judge may remove this classification at the dispositional completion hearing[5] or upon petition of the juvenile.[6] Registration and notification requirements are discussed in later sections of this chapter.

§ 6:6 "Child-victim oriented offender" defined

Created by the 2003 amendment, this category reclassifies crimes against children that are not committed with a sexual motivation. As applied to a person under 18 years of age,[1] a "child-victim oriented offense" includes the following if the victim was under 18 years and was not the child of the offender:

(1) kidnapping except for the purpose of engaging in sexual activity;[2]

(2) (former) child stealing;[3]

(3) violations of (a) former Ohio law, (b) existing or former municipal ordinances or laws of another state or the United States, including military law, (c) Indian tribal law, or (d) the laws of another country that are substantially equivalent to the above offenses if a first, second, third or fourth degree felony; or

(4) attempts, conspiracies, or complicity in connection with the above

---

[Section 6:5]

[1]For adults, the predator classification may result from several methods: First, it attaches *automatically* if the defendant is convicted of a sexually violent offense as well as a sexually violent predator specification as alleged in the indictment or information. RC 2950.09(A). Second, a sentencing court may hold a *hearing* under RC 2950.09(B)to determine classification as a sexual predator or habitual sex offender for a defendant convicted of a sexually oriented offense. Third, a court may hold a hearing for an offender imprisoned for a sexually oriented offense offender. RC 2950.09(A) to RC 2950.09(C). See also RC 2950.01(G)(1), RC 2950.01(G)(2), or RC 2950.01(G)(4) (defining adjudication as a sexual predator).

[2]RC 2950.01(E)(2) (defining sexual predator). Age is determined at the time of the offense and the registrant classification is for that adjudication (not a prior adjudication). See also RC 2950.01(G) (defining "adjudication as a sexual predator").

[3]RC 2950.01(G)(3).

[4]RC 2950.01(G)(5) (in another state, or in a federal, military, or an Indian tribal court).

[5]See infra, § 6:12, Dispositional completion hearing

[6]See infra, § 6:13, Petitions for reclassification or declassification.

[Section 6:6]

[1]RC 2950.01(S)(1)(b). If the juvenile is transferred to adult court for prosecution, the adult provisions apply. RC 2950.01(S)(1)(b)(iv).

[2]RC 2905.01(A)(1), (2), (3) and (5). Kidnapping for the purpose of engaging in sexual activity is a sexually oriented offense. See § 6:2, "Sexually oriented offender" defined.

[3]Former RC 2905.04.

offenses.

This classification does not include any enumerated offense that is a sexually violent offense; such offenses are "sexually oriented offenses."[4] Automatic reclassification provisions apply for persons previously classified for the above offenses as sexually oriented offenses.[5]

A juvenile judge may remove this classification at the dispositional completion hearing[6] or upon petition of the juvenile.[7] Registration and notification requirements are discussed in later sections of this chapter.

§ 6:7 "Habitual child-victim offender" defined

As applied to juveniles, classification as a "habitual child-victim offender"[1] requires satisfaction of two conditions. First, the child must be adjudicated a delinquent for a child-victim oriented offense when 14 years or older and classified as a juvenile offender registrant based on that adjudication. Second, the child must have previously been convicted or adjudicated delinquent for committing a child-victim oriented offense—regardless of when the offense was committed or age at the time.

A juvenile judge may remove this classification at the dispositional completion hearing[2] or upon petition of the juvenile.[3] Registration and notification requirements are discussed in later sections of this chapter.

§ 6:8 "Child-victim predator" defined

As applied to juveniles, classification as a "child-victim predator"[1] is defined as a child who has been adjudicated delinquent for a child-victim oriented offense when 14 years or older and classified a juvenile offender registrant based on that adjudication and is likely to engage in child-victim oriented offenses in the future.

A juvenile judge may remove this classification at the dispositional completion hearing[2] or upon petition of the juvenile.[3] Registration and notification requirements are discussed in later sections of this chapter.

§ 6:9 Juvenile offender registrant—Repeat offender classification

In some cases, juvenile offender registrant (JOR) classification is mandatory. There are two types of mandatory classifications; repeat offenders are examined in this section, while the other mandatory procedure is considered in the next section.

Under RC 2152.82, the juvenile court is required to issue (as part of the dispositional order) a JOR classification order and specify that the child must comply with the registration, change of address, and address verification provisions if the child (1) is adjudicated a delinquent for a sexually oriented offense not registration-exempt or a child-victim offense; (2) was over 14 years

---

[4]RC 2950.01(S)(2).

[5]RC 2950.091.

[6]See § 6:12, Dispositional completion hearing

[7]See § 6:13, Petitions for reclassification or declassification.

[Section 6:7]

[1]RC 2950.01(T).

[2]See § 6:12, Dispositional completion hearing

[3]See § 6:13, Petitions for reclassification or declassification.

[Section 6:8]

[1]RC 2950.01(U)(2).

[2]See § 6:12, Dispositional completion hearing

[3]See § 6:13, Petitions for reclassification or declassification.

of age; and (3) had previously been convicted or adjudicated a delinquent for committing any sexually oriented or child-victim oriented offense, regardless of when committed or age at the time.[1]

Hearing. Prior to issuing a JOR classification order, the judge must hold a hearing[2] to determine if the offense is registration-exempt or the child is classifiable as a sexual or child-victim predator[3] or a habitual sex or child-victim offender.[4]

Orders. A JOR classification order must include the following: (1) a statement that the child is or is not a sexual or child-victim predator or habitual sex or child-victim offender with any related information, including any notification requirement necessary under RC 2950.09 or RC 2950.091; (2) a statement that upon completion of the disposition, a hearing will be held to determine whether the order is subject to modification or termination pursuant to RC 2152.84 or RC 2152.85; and (3) a statement specifying that the order was issued pursuant to RC 2152.82. In addition, a copy of the order must be provided to the child and legal guardian as part of the notice requirements under RC 2950.03.[5] No order is issued if the offense is registration-exempt.[6]

The order remains in effect for the period of time specified in RC 2950.07, subject to modification or termination under RC 2152.84 or RC 2152.85. The child's attainment of age 18 or 21 does not affect or terminate the order.[7]

§ 6:10 Juvenile offender registrant—Mandatory classification

In some cases, juvenile offender registrant (JOR) classification is mandatory. There are two types of mandatory classifications; repeat offenders are examined in the preceding section, while the other mandatory procedure is considered here.

Under RC 2152.83(A), the classification order may be issued at the time of the dispositional order or at the time a child is released from the secure facility. The juvenile court must issue a classification order and specify that the child must comply with the registration, change of address, and address verification provisions if (1) the child is adjudicated a delinquent for a sexually oriented offense that is not registration-exempt or a child-victim oriented offense; (2) the child was 16 years of age or older; and (3) classification is not required under RC 2152.82 as a repeat offender.[1]

Hearing. Prior to issuing a JOR order, the juvenile judge must hold a hearing to determine whether the offense is registration-exempt, and the child is classifiable as a sexual or child-victim predator or a habitual sex or child-victim offender.[2]

Orders. A JOR classification order must include the following: (1) a statement that the child is a sexual or child-victim predator or habitual sex or child-victim offender with any related information, including any notification

---

[Section 6:9]
[1]RC 2152.82(A). The offense must be committed on or after January 1, 2002. Age is determined at the time of that offense.
[2]RC 2152.82(B).
[3]As established by RC 2950.09(B).
[4]As established by RC 2950.09(C).
[5]RC 2152.82(B)(3).
[6]RC 2152.82(D).
[7]RC 2152.82(C).

[Section 6:10]
[1]See § 6:9, Juvenile offender registrant—Repeat offender classification.
[2]RC 2152.83(A)(2).

requirement necessary under RC 2950.09(B) or RC 2950.091,[3] (2) a statement that upon completion of the disposition, a hearing will be held to determine whether the order is subject to modification or termination pursuant to RC 2152.84 or RC 2152.85; and (3) a statement specifying that the order was issued pursuant to RC 2152.83. In addition, a copy of order must be provided to the child and legal guardian as part of the notice requirements under RC 2950.03.[4] No order is issued if the offense is registration-exempt.[5]

The order remains in effect for the period of time specified in RC 2950.07, subject to modification or termination under RC 2152.84. The child's attainment of age 18 or 21 does not affect or terminate the order.[6]

§ 6:11 Juvenile offender registrant—Discretionary classification

RC 2152.83(B) authorizes, but does not require, the juvenile judge to classify a child as a juvenile offender registrant. The JOR classification order may be issued at the time of the dispositional order or at the time a child is released from the secure facility. A classification order and registration notice under RC 2950.04may be issued if (1) the child is adjudicated a delinquent for a sexually oriented offense that is not registration-exempt or a child-victim oriented offense; (2) the child was 14 or 15 years of age; and (3) JOR classification is not required under RC 2152.82 as a repeat offender.[1]

Review hearing. A hearing to review the effectiveness of the disposition and of any treatment for a child placed in a secure setting is required.[2] The hearing may be conducted sua sponte or on the recommendation of a DYS officer or employee, probation officer, court employee, prosecutor, or law enforcement officer. At the conclusion of the hearing, the judge may (1) decline to issue an order or (2) issue a JOR classification order as a juvenile offender registrant.

Relevant factors. In making the above determinations, the court must consider all relevant factors including:

(1) the nature of the oriented offense;

(2) whether the child has shown genuine remorse or compunction;

(3) the public interest and safety;

(4) the factors in RC 2950.09(B)(3) or RC 2950.091;

(5) the factors in RC 2929.12(B) and (C) as applied to the child, offense, and victim; and

(6) the results of treatment and any follow-up professional assessment of the child.

Procedures. For sexual or child-victim predator classifications, the court must comply with the procedures of RC 2950.09(B) and RC 2950.091(B) respectively, and apply the "clear and convincing" evidence standard.[3] For a habitual sex or child-victim offender classification, the court must comply with the procedures of RC 2950.09(E) and RC 2950.091(E) respectively. The court may also impose community notification requirements on a habitual sex or child-victim offender.

---

[3]RC 2152.83(A)(2)

[4]RC 2152.83(D).

[5]RC 2152.83(G).

[6]RC 2152.83(F).

[Section 6:11]

[1]See § 6:9, Juvenile offender registrant—Repeat offender classification.

[2]RC 2152.83(B)(2).

[3]RC 2152.83(C).

The judge must provide a copy of the order to the child and legal guardian.[4]

The order remains in effect for the period of time specified in RC 2950.07, subject to modification or termination under RC 2152.84. The child's attainment of age 18 or 21 does not affect or terminate the order.[5]

§ 6:12 Dispositional completion hearing

Under RC 2152.84, the court must conduct a hearing at the completion of disposition to review the effectiveness of the disposition and of any treatment provided. The court must determine the risks that the child might re-offend and whether the prior classifications as a juvenile offender registrant, habitual sex offender, or sexual predator should be continued, modified or terminated.

Relevant factors. In making the above determinations, the court must consider the factors specified in RC 2152.83(E), including:

(1) the nature of the offense;

(2) whether the child has shown genuine remorse or compunction;

(3) the public interest and safety;

(4) the factors in RC 2950.09(B)(3) or RC 2950.091;

(5) the factors in RC 2929.12(B) and RC 2929.12(C) as applied to the child, offense, and victim; and

(6) the results of treatment and any follow-up professional assessment of the child.

At the completion of the hearing, the court is required to make one of several determinations: (1) continue the prior classification, including any predator or habitual offender determinations; (2) reclassify the child; or (3) terminate the classification.

§ 6:13 Petitions for reclassification or declassification

A juvenile offender registrant may petition the judge (or the judge's successor) to be reclassified or declassified[1] upon the expiration of one of the following time periods:

(1) the initial petition may be filed no earlier than three years after a mandatory hearing conducted under RC 2152.84;

(2) a second petition may be filed no earlier than three years after an order has been entered deciding the initial petition; or

(3) additional petitions may be filed no earlier than five years after an order has been entered deciding the second petition or the most recent petition filed.[2]

In making this determination, the judge may review the prior classification or determination and consider all relevant factors and information, including the factors in RC 2152.83(E).[3]

§ 6:14 Registration requirements

A juvenile adjudicated a delinquent for a nonexempt sexually oriented of-

---

[4]RC 2152.83(D).

[5]RC 2152.83(F).

[Section 6:13]

[1]RC 2152.85(A).

[2]RC 2152.85(B).

[3]RC 2152.85(C).

fense[1] or child-victim oriented offense[2] and classified a juvenile offender registrant must personally register with the sheriff within five days of entering the county where the juvenile resides or is temporarily domiciled. This requirement does not apply while the child is in a secure facility. The five-day period applies when the juvenile is released from a secure facility. There are also registration requirements when a child enters a county for school or employment.[3] Out-of-state offenders are also subject to the registration requirement for certain offenses.[4]

Offenders are required to provide a current address, current employment address, license plate number, and any other information required by the Bureau of Criminal Identification and Investigation.[5] The offender's photograph and fingerprints are taken at this time.

Address changes. Changes in resident, school, or employment addresses must be reported in writing to the sheriffs in both the old and new county.[6]

Verification. Under RC 2950.06 and RC 2950.07, this information must be updated periodically, depending on the classification.

(1) Sexually and child-victim oriented offenders must verify their addresses every year for ten years.

(2) Habitual offenders must reregister annually for twenty years.

(3) Predators must reregister every ninety days for life, unless the court issues a ruling that the offender is no longer classified as a predator.

Failure to comply with these requirements is a crime.[7]

§ 6:15   Notification requirements

Community. The community notification requirement applies to all predators and to habitual offenders if a court determines that they are subject to these provisions.[1] Under RC 2950.11(A), the sheriff notifies: (1) the offender's neighbors within a thousand feet in all directions, including apartment houses; (2) the director of the public children services agency within that county; (3) the superintendent of the school district or head of any nonpublic chartered schools; (4) directors of preschool programs and specified child day-care programs in the area; (5) the president of specified higher education institutions and the director of the state university law enforcement agency or campus police department that serves the institution; and (6) the chief of police.

Victim. The victim of a sexually oriented offender may request notification.[2]

§ 6:16   Internet dissemination

Two types of databases are authorized: public and law enforcement.[1] These databases operate differently for adults and juveniles.

[Section 6:14]
    [1]RC 2950.04(A)(2).
    [2]RC 2950.041(A)(2).
    [3]RC 2950.04(A)(3).
    [4]RC 2950.04(A)(3).
    [5]RC 2950.04(C); RC 2950.041(C).
    [6]RC 2950.05 (20 days before move).
    [7]RC 2950.99.

[Section 6:15]
    [1]The community notification provision applies no matter when the offense was committed.
    [2]RC 2950.10.

[Section 6:16]
    [1]The website is http://www.ag.state.oh.us.

For adult offenders, the public database must include at least the name, all registration addresses, and the nature of the offenses.[2] It must be searchable by name, county, zip code, and school district. The law enforcement database, which is available only to representatives of sheriffs and chiefs, includes additional information—motor vehicle license number, victim preference, last release data, and fingerprints.

Internet dissemination of juveniles registrants is prohibited,[3] except if the act that is the basis of the registration is aggravated murder,[4] murder,[5] kidnapping to gratify sexual needs and desires,[6] rape,[7] or attempts to commit these offenses.

§ 6:17   Residence limitation

An adult who has been convicted of a nonexempt sexually oriented offense or a child-victim oriented offense may not reside or occupy a residence within 1,000 feet of a school.[1] This limitation does not apply to juveniles.

---

[2]RC 2950.13.
[3]RC 2950.081(B); 2950.11(B).
[4]RC 2903.01.
[5]RC 2903.02.
[6]RC 2905.01.
[7]RC 2907.02.

[Section 6:17]
[1]RC 2950.031.

Chapter 7

Juvenile Traffic Offender Jurisdiction

> **KeyCite®:** Cases and other legal materials listed in KeyCite Scope can be researched through West's KeyCite service on Westlaw®. Use KeyCite to check citations for form, parallel references, prior and later history, and comprehensive citator information, including citations to other decisions and secondary materials.

§ 7:1   Juvenile traffic offender jurisdiction—Introduction
§ 7:2   Traffic offenders
§ 7:3   Juvenile traffic violations bureau
§ 7:4   Delinquency compared

§ 7:1   Juvenile traffic offender jurisdiction—Introduction

This chapter discusses juvenile court jurisdiction for juvenile traffic offense cases. Other chapters examine juvenile court jurisdiction for delinquency, unruliness, neglect, abuse, and dependency cases. Additional related chapters include the adjudicatory hearing (Chapter 23) and traffic offense dispositions (Chapter 28).

Effective on January 1, 2002, the Juvenile Traffic Offender sections (along with the delinquency sections) were transferred to new RC Chapter 2152.[1]

§ 7:2   Traffic offenders

RC 2152.02(N) defines a juvenile traffic offender as any child who violates any traffic law, ordinance, or regulation (with the exception of parking violations) of this state, the United States, or any political subdivision of this state.[1] This class of children comprises the largest single category of children coming before the juvenile court.

§ 7:3   Juvenile traffic violations bureau

In 2001, the General Assembly proposed a statutory amendment to permit the juvenile division of common pleas courts to establish violations bureaus for juvenile cases.[1] Such bureaus had been used in adult traffic cases for years to permit traffic offenders to admit to traffic violations and pay fines and court costs without having to appear in court. New Traffic Rule 13.1 provides that a juvenile traffic violations bureau may be established by local rule of court. The procedures set forth in Traffic Rule 13 apply in juvenile cases.

All juvenile traffic offenses may be disposed of by a violations bureau except

---

[Section 7:1]
  [1]S.B. 179.

[Section 7:2]
  [1]E.g., In re Farinacci, No. 37973 (8th Dist. Ct. App., Cuyahoga, 11-30-78) (speeding); In re Bernstein, Nos. 33531, 33532 (8th Dist. Ct. App., Cuyahoga, 1-2-75) (driving while under the influence; reckless operation).

[Section 7:3]
  [1]S.B. 179.

(1) certain specified offenses,[2] (2) a second or subsequent moving violation, or (3) an offense that involves an accident.[3]

§ 7:4 Delinquency compared

Determining whether a child who commits an offense involving the operation of a motor vehicle should be charged as a delinquent child or a juvenile traffic offender has caused some difficulty—especially where a death has resulted from the child's improper driving. The child may be responsible for an aggravated vehicular homicide or a vehicular homicide.[1]

In making this determination, one must consider the nature of the offense involved. If the offense is included in Title 29 ("Crimes—Procedure"), then the child should be charged as a delinquent. If the offense falls under Title 45 ("Motor Vehicles"), the child would fit within the more narrowly defined class of juvenile traffic offender.[2] Thus, the child accused of vehicular homicide, which is a "crime," must be prosecuted as a delinquent, not as a juvenile traffic offender.[3]

Since vehicular homicide does not depend upon the violation of a traffic offense, it would appear that a child who violates a traffic regulation and, in the process, causes the death of another could be charged as both a juvenile traffic offender (for the traffic offense) and a delinquent child (for the criminal offense). However, a court of appeals has held that the traffic offenses of driving while intoxicated and reckless operation are lesser included offenses of aggravated vehicular homicide, so that prosecution for both constitutes double jeopardy.[4]

Cross References
§ 4:2, Ch 28
Research References
Carlin, Baldwin's Ohio Practice, Merrick-Rippner Probate Law (6th ed.), Ch 106

---

[2]Traffic Rule 13.1 references Traffic Rule 13(B)(1) (indictable offenses); (B)(2) (DUI); (B)(3) (leaving the scene of an accident); (B)(4) (driving under suspension or revocation); (B)(5) (driving without a license except if expired for six months or less); (B)(7) (failure to stop for a school bus); (B)(8) (willfully eluding or fleeing a police officer); and (B)(9) (drag racing).

[3]Traf. R. 13.1(B).

[Section 7:4]
[1]RC 2903.06. See also Katz and Giannelli, Baldwin's Ohio Practice, Criminal Law (2d ed.), Ch 95 (homicide).

[2]In re Elliott, 87 Ohio App. 3d 816, 623 N.E.2d 217 (12th Dist. Fayette County 1993).

[3]In re Elliott, 87 Ohio App. 3d 816, 623 N.E.2d 217 (12th Dist. Fayette County 1993); In re Fox, 60 Ohio Misc. 31, 14 Ohio Op. 3d 80, 395 N.E.2d 918 (C.P. 1979). Contra State v. Gaida, No. 30423 (8th Dist. Ct. App., Cuyahoga, 3-2-72), holding that it is permissible, but not mandatory, to charge such child as a delinquent. *Gaida* was decided prior to the 1975 amendments to the Criminal Code, when vehicular homicide was termed "Homicide by Vehicle in the Second Degree" under RC Ch. 4511 ("Traffic Laws—Operation of Motor Vehicles"). See also In re Kuchinsky, No. 41944 (8th Dist. Ct. App., Cuyahoga, 10-23-80), in which a delinquency finding for aggravated vehicular homicide was reversed on other grounds (no proof that act was proximate cause of death).

[4]State v. Crowell, No. 42457 (8th Dist. Ct. App., Cuyahoga, 3-19-81). See, however, State v. Konicek, 16 Ohio App. 3d 17, 474 N.E.2d 363 (8th Dist. Cuyahoga County 1984), which distinguished *Crowell* in holding that if all the elements of the greater offense have not occurred when the state concludes prosecution for an included offense, prosecution for the greater offense is not thereby barred. See also State v. Long, 7 Ohio App. 3d 248, 455 N.E.2d 534 (10th Dist. Franklin County 1983).

Chapter 8

Unruly Child Jurisdiction

> **KeyCite®:** Cases and other legal materials listed in KeyCite Scope can be researched through West's KeyCite service on Westlaw®. Use KeyCite to check citations for form, parallel references, prior and later history, and comprehensive citator information, including citations to other decisions and secondary materials.

§ 8:1   Unruly child jurisdiction—Introduction
§ 8:2   Unruly child defined
§ 8:3   Unruly—Wayward or habitually disobedient
§ 8:4   Unruly—Truancy
§ 8:5   Unruly—Endangering conduct
§ 8:6   Unruly—Status offenses
§ 8:7   Unruly—Miscellaneous conduct

§ 8:1   Unruly child jurisdiction—Introduction

This chapter discusses juvenile court jurisdiction for unruly child cases. Other chapters examine juvenile court jurisdiction for delinquency, juvenile traffic offense, neglect, abuse, and dependency cases. Additional related chapters include the adjudicatory hearing (Ch 23) and unruly child dispositions (Ch 29).

In 2000, the truancy provision, division (B), was amended.[1] The phrase "habitual" truant was changed to "persistently truant" from home or school. The amendment was required because a new provision for "habitual" truants was created.[2]

Effective in 2002, the categories of unruly conduct were reduced to four.[3] Several categories were repealed: (1) truancy from home,[4] (2) attempt to marry without permission,[5] (3) disreputable places and people,[6] and (4) illegal occupations and immoral situations.[7]

§ 8:2   Unruly child defined

The term "unruly" in Ohio covers "status" offenses—conduct such as habit-

---

[Section 8:1]

[1]S.B. 181.

[2]RC 2151.022(B).

[3]S.B. 179.

[4]RC 2151.022(B). Runaways now fall under RC 2151.022(A) (wayward or habitually disobedient).

[5]RC 2151.022(E). These cases may come within RC 2151.022(A) (wayward or habitually disobedient), delinquency if the juvenile falsified his or her age, or emancipation (out of state marriages).

[6]RC 2151.022(F).

[7]RC 2151.022(G). Illegal prostitution can be charged as delinquency.

ual disobedience and truancy that do not apply to adults. RC 2151.022[1] defines an unruly child as

(A) Any child who does not submit to the reasonable control of the child's parents, teachers, guardian, or custodian, by reason of being wayward or habitually disobedient;[2]

(B) Any child who is an habitual truant from school and who previously has not been adjudicated an unruly child for being an habitual truant;

(C) Any child who behaves in a manner as to injure or endanger his or her health or morals or the health or morals of others;

(D) Any child who violates a law, other than RC 2923.211(A) or RC 2151.87, that is applicable only to a child.

The IJA-ABA Standards recommend that a child's unruly behavior that does not violate the criminal law should not constitute a ground for asserting juvenile court jurisdiction over the child and that voluntary social services should be substituted for coercive court intervention.[3]

§ 8:3 Unruly—Wayward or habitually disobedient

In order to prove a violation of RC 2151.022(A), the child must engage in a pattern of misconduct; one isolated instance of misconduct will not support a charge under this section.[1]

The 2002 amendment (S.B. 179) substituted the word "submit" for the phrase "subject the child's self." In addition, runaways are now governed by this provision because "truancy from home" was deleted from the truancy provision.

§ 8:4 Unruly—Truancy

In 2000, the truancy provision, division (B), was amended by H.B. 4. The phrase "habitual" truant was changed to "persistently truant" from home. The amended language was required because a new provision for "habitual" truants from school was created.[1] Later, S.B. 179 eliminated persistant truancy from home as unruly conduct,[2] leaving only "habitual truant from school" in the definition of unruly.

Habitual truancy. In 2000[3] a new category of unruliness was created: habitual truancy. An "habitual truant" is defined as any child of compulsory school age[4] who is absent without legitimate excuse from the public school

---

[Section 8:2]

[1]See In re Burgess, No. 3053 (9th Dist. Ct. App., Lorain, 11-5-80), and Matter of Popovich, 1993 WL 19619 (Ohio Ct. App. 7th Dist. Belmont County 1993), holding that the unruly statute is not unconstitutionally vague.

[2]See Rulison, 1981 WL 4326 (Ohio Ct. App. 11th Dist. Lake County 1981), holding that the term "wayward" as used in this section is not unconstitutionally vague.

[3]IJA-ABA Standards Relating to Noncriminal Misbehavior 23 (1980). See also Winick, Kress, Costello, "Wayward and Noncompliant" People With Mental Disabilities, 9 Psychol. Pub. Pol'y & L. 233 (2003).

[Section 8:3]

[1]In the Matter of Quillen, 1981 WL 5841 (Ohio Ct. App. 6th Dist. Huron County 1981).

[Section 8:4]

[1]RC 2151.022(C) (now RC 2151.022(B)).

[2]Runaways now fall under RC 2151.022(A) (wayward or habitually disobedient).

[3]S.B. 181.

[4]See RC 2151.011(B)(25) (" 'Of Compulsory School Age' has the same meaning as in Section 3321.01 of the revised code.").

the child is supposed to attend for five or more consecutive school days,[5] seven or more school days in one school month,[6] or 12 or more school days in a school year.[7]

Legitimate Excuse. A legitimate excuse for absence from public school includes situations in which the child (1) has enrolled and is attending another public or nonpublic school; (2) is excused from attendance at school for any of the reasons specified in RC 3321.04, or (3) has received an age and schooling certificate in accordance with RC 3331.01.[8] This is not an exclusive list of excuses.[9]

Delinquency. Truancy can also be the basis for delinquency jurisdiction. A delinquent child includes any child who is an habitual truant and who previously has been adjudicated an unruly child for being an habitual truant.[10] In addition, the 2000 statutory amendments included a new delinquency category—"chronic truant."[11] A "chronic truant" is defined as "any child of compulsory school age who is absent without legitimate excuse for absence from the public school the child is supposed to attend for seven or more consecutive school days, ten or more school days in one school month, or fifteen or more school days in a school year."[12] This provision is discussed in Chapter 4, along with other categories of delinquency.

§ 8:5 Unruly—Endangering conduct

A child who behaves in a manner that injures or endangers that child's or another person's health or morals may be adjudged unruly.[1] The 2002 amendment (S.B. 179) substituted the phrase "behaves in a manner" for the phrase "deports himself or herself." This provision, which may be the most all-encompassing provision of the statute, is sometimes used when there is insufficient evidence to file a delinquency complaint, but when there is nevertheless some justification for assuming jurisdiction over the child. For example, a court of appeals held that a child is unruly who engages in a single act of sexual intercourse with an adult, as it is inherently injurious to the morals of the child or others.[2] However, another court of appeals held that an isolated act of consensual sexual intercourse between two children did not establish the status of being unruly.[3]

Moreover, mere presence at a party where others were consuming alcohol does not constitute an unruly act because it does not indicate moral depravity, nor does it indicate any conduct which endangers the health of the child or others.[4]

§ 8:6 Unruly—Status offenses

This category covers any offense that is applicable only to children—other

---

[5]See RC 2151.011(B)(46) (" 'School Day' means the school day established by the state board of education pursuant to Section 3313.48 of the revised code.").

[6]See RC 2151.011(B)(47) (" 'School Month' and 'School Year' have the same meanings as in Section 3313.62 of the revised code.").

[7]RC 2151.011(B)(17) (defining "habitual truant").

[8]RC 2151.011(B)(20).

[9]See RC 2151.011(B)(20) ("but is not limited to").

[10]RC 2152.02(F)(4).

[11]RC 2152.02(F)(5).

[12]RC 2152.02(D).

[Section 8:5]

[1]RC 2151.022(D) superseded by RC 2151.022(C).

[2]State v. Lukens, 66 Ohio App. 3d 794, 586 N.E.2d 1099 (10th Dist. Franklin County 1990).

[3]Matter of Preston, 1993 WL 35682 (Ohio Ct. App. 5th Dist. Richland County 1993).

[4]State v. Aller, 82 Ohio App. 3d 9, 610 N.E.2d 1170 (6th Dist. Lucas County 1992).

than RC 2923.211(A), which governs the underage purchase of a firearm or handgun,[1] and RC 2151.87, which covers cigarette and tobacco products.

Included in this category are instances in which a child, for the purpose of obtaining material or gaining admission which is harmful to juveniles, either falsely represents or provides false identification concerning his age or marital status.[2]

Curfews. The most typical laws applicable only to children are curfew ordinances, most of which apply to all persons under the age of 18. Although the provisions of curfew ordinances vary among municipalities, the following features are common: graduated hours of restriction based on age, greater freedom during summer months and on weekends, applicability to all public places, and penalties for parents who permit their children to remain out beyond the curfew. Most of these ordinances also incorporate certain exceptions, such as for children accompanied by a parent or responsible adult, children engaged in lawful employment, and children returning home from a school- or church-sponsored event.[3]

Although curfew ordinances in other jurisdictions have been attacked on constitutional grounds as being vague[4] and violative of the First Amendment rights of assembly, association, and movement,[5] three Ohio courts of appeals have upheld the constitutionality of curfew ordinances. In *Eastlake v. Ruggiero*[6] the court held that a curfew ordinance which restricted children at nighttime was constitutionally valid, since it did not exceed the bounds of reasonableness. In upholding Eastlake's curfew ordinance, the court relied on the general notion that such laws are justified as police regulations necessary to control the activities of minors and to promote the welfare of the community. However, the court reversed the conviction of a parent who "allowed" the child to violate the curfew ordinance, holding that the proof must establish the parent's "actual or constructive knowledge" of the child's violation. In *In re Osman*,[7] the court upheld the constitutionality of the Ravenna curfew ordinance for similar reasons. Although the Ravenna ordinance did not define the term "legitimate business," the court determined that the ordinance used the least restrictive means of accomplishing its goals by including specific exceptions. In *In re Carpenter*,[8] the Franklin County Court of Appeals upheld the validity of a daytime curfew ordinance which prohibited children from being on the public streets when their attendance was required in school. As in *Ruggiero*, the court cautioned that the ordinance must not be unreasonable, arbitrary, or capricious and must bear a real and

---

[Section 8:6]

[1]This conduct constitutes a delinquent act. RC 2152.02(F)(3).

[2]RC 2907.33(B). Section (C) of this statute provides that any juvenile who violates section (B) "shall be adjudged an unruly child." This mandatory unruly adjudication is contrary to Juv. R. 29(F)(2)(d).

[3]The Cleveland curfew ordinance (Section 605.14) is typical. Children of the age of 12 or under may not be on the streets, sidewalks, parks, or other public places from darkness to dawn. For children aged 13 to 16, the curfew is 11 p.m. to 5 a.m. The curfew for 17-year-olds is midnight to 5 a.m. It is not a violation of curfew if the child is accompanied by a parent or guardian, or some other responsible person who is 21 or older, or a member of his family who is 18 or older. A parent who permits his child to violate the curfew ordinance is guilty of a minor misdemeanor.

[4]See Qutb v. Strauss, 11 F.3d 488 (5th Cir. 1993). E.g., Hayes v. Municipal Court of Oklahoma City, 1971 OK CR 274, 487 P.2d 974 (Okla. Crim. App. 1971); City of Seattle v. Pullman, 82 Wash. 2d 794, 514 P.2d 1059 (1973); In Interest of Doe, 54 Haw. 647, 513 P.2d 1385 (1973).

[5]Johnson v. City of Opelousas, 488 F. Supp. 433 (W.D. La. 1980); People v. Chambers, 66 Ill. 2d 36, 4 Ill. Dec. 308, 360 N.E.2d 55 (1976).

[6]City of Eastlake v. Ruggiero, 7 Ohio App. 2d 212, 36 Ohio Op. 2d 345, 220 N.E.2d 126 (7th Dist. Lake County 1966).

[7]In re Osman, 109 Ohio App. 3d 731, 672 N.E.2d 1114 (11th Dist. Portage County 1996).

[8]In re Carpenter, 31 Ohio App. 2d 184, 60 Ohio Op. 2d 287, 287 N.E.2d 399 (10th Dist. Franklin County 1972).

substantial relationship to the general public welfare.

§ 8:7 Unruly—Miscellaneous conduct

Several categories of unruly child were repealed in 2002: (1) truancy from home,[1] (2) attempt to marry without permission,[2] (3) disreputable places and people,[3] and (4) illegal occupations and immoral situations.[4]

Cross References
§ 4:5, Ch 29
Research References
Carlin, Baldwin's Ohio Practice, Merrick-Rippner Probate Law (6th ed.), Ch 106

[Section 8:7]

[1]Former RC 2151.022(B). Runaways now fall under RC 2151.022(A) (wayward or habitually disobedient).

[2]Former RC 2151.022(E). This provision had rarely been used; it covered the situation where a child frequents bars or associates with gangs. These cases may come within RC 2151.022(A) (wayward or habitually disobedient), delinquency if the juvenile falsified his or her age, or emancipations (out of state marriages).

[3]Former RC 2151.022(F). This section covered cases where a child is employed in violation of the child labor laws, RC Ch. 4109, or is without an age and schooling certificate where one is required. RC Ch. 3331. This may include situations in which the child is employed in an occupation which has been found to be hazardous or detrimental to the health and well-being of a child. There are also restrictions on the hours of employment, such as a provision prohibiting children from working more than three hours per day on school days. RC 4109.07.

[4]Former RC 2151.022(G). Illegal prostitution can be charged as delinquency.

Chapter 9

Neglected & Abused Child Jurisdiction

> **KeyCite®:** Cases and other legal materials listed in KeyCite Scope can be researched through West's KeyCite service on Westlaw®. Use KeyCite to check citations for form, parallel references, prior and later history, and comprehensive citator information, including citations to other decisions and secondary materials.

§ 9:1   Neglected & abused child jurisdiction—Introduction
§ 9:2   Parental rights
§ 9:3   Time of neglect
§ 9:4   Neglected child defined
§ 9:5   Neglect—Abandonment
§ 9:6   Neglect—Inadequate care due to parental fault
§ 9:7   Neglect—Subsistence, education & medical care
§ 9:8   Neglect—Special care for child's mental condition
§ 9:9   Neglect—Illegal placement
§ 9:10   Neglect—Physical or mental injury due to omissions
§ 9:11   Neglect—Out-of-home care neglect
§ 9:12   Abused child defined
§ 9:13   Abused child—Sexual victim
§ 9:14   Abused child—Child endangerment
§ 9:15   Abused child—Physical or mental injury exhibited
§ 9:16   Abused child—Physical or mental injury due to parents
§ 9:17   Abused child—Out-of-home abuse

§ 9:1   Neglected & abused child jurisdiction—Introduction

This chapter discusses juvenile court jurisdiction for neglect and abuse cases. Dependency cases are treated separately in Ch 10. Other chapters examine juvenile court jurisdiction for delinquency, juvenile traffic offense, and unruliness cases. Additional related chapters include the adjudicatory hearing (Ch 23) and neglect, abuse, and dependency dispositions (Ch 30).

§ 9:2   Parental rights

The United States Supreme Court's initial juvenile court cases dealt with delinquency proceedings, and when the Court granted due process rights in these cases, it carefully limited its holdings to delinquency cases. In the 1980s, however, the Court addressed due process issues in nondelinquency cases. For example, in *Lassiter v. Department of Social Services*,[1] the Court examined the applicability of due process rights in neglect cases. *Lassiter*, however, involved only one type of neglect proceeding—that involving the permanent termination of parental rights. Finding a parent's interest in such a proceeding to be "a commanding one,"[2] the Court held that due process

---

[Section 9:2]

[1]Lassiter v. Department of Social Services of Durham County, N. C., 452 U.S. 18, 101 S. Ct. 2153, 68 L. Ed. 2d 640 (1981).

[2]Lassiter v. Department of Social Services of Durham County, N. C., 452 U.S. 18, 27, 101 S. Ct. 2153, 68 L. Ed. 2d 640 (1981). See § 23:3, Right to counsel.

may require the appointment of counsel for indigent parents. The *Lassiter* holding requires assessing the right to counsel on a case-by-case basis.

Santosky v. Kramer[3] also involved proceedings to terminate parental custodial rights permanently. The issue before the Court was whether the "preponderance of evidence" standard, the burden of proof applied in civil cases, satisfied due process requirements in termination proceedings. The Court held that it did not: "In parental rights termination proceedings, the private interest affected is commanding; the risk of error from using a preponderance standard is substantial; and the countervailing governmental interest favoring that standard is comparatively slight."[4] Accordingly, the Court held that due process required "clear and convincing" proof in termination proceedings.

In *M.L.B. v. S.L.J.*,[5] the Court reviewed a state statute that required an indigent in a proceeding to terminate parental rights to pay an advance record fee of about $2,352 as a condition for an appeal. The Court ruled that the fee violated the Equal Protection and Due Process Clauses of the Fourteenth Amendment. The Court noted that it had "repeatedly noticed what sets parental status termination decrees apart from mine run civil actions, even from other domestic relations matters such as divorce, paternity, and child custody . . .. To recapitulate, termination decrees 'wor[k] a unique kind of deprivation.' . . . In contrast to matters modifiable at the parties' will or based on changed circumstances, termination adjudications involve the awesome authority of the State 'to destroy permanently all legal recognition of the parental relationship.' . . . We are therefore satisfied that the label 'civil' should not entice us to leave undisturbed the Mississippi courts' disposition of this case."[6]

Although parents have a fundamental, constitutionally protected right to raise their children,[7] this right may be forfeited under certain circumstances defined in the neglect,[8] dependency,[9] and abuse[10] statutes.

§ 9:3   Time of neglect

One issue which seems to be governed by statute[1] but which has divided the Ohio courts concerns when the neglect or dependency must exist in order for juvenile court jurisdiction to attach. RC 2151.23(A)(1) provides that the neglect or dependency must exist "on or about the date specified in the complaint." Several cases decided prior to this 1969 statutory amendment held that the dependency or neglect must exist at the time of the hearing.[2] Since 1969, the cases have split on this jurisdictional matter. Several cases

---

[3]Santosky v. Kramer, 455 U.S. 745, 102 S. Ct. 1388, 71 L. Ed. 2d 599 (1982).

[4]Santosky v. Kramer, 455 U.S. 745, 758, 102 S. Ct. 1388, 71 L. Ed. 2d 599 (1982). See § 23:13, Burden of proof. For a discussion of reasonable efforts to place child with parents, see § 25:14, Reasonable efforts determination.

[5]M.L.B. v. S.L.J., 519 U.S. 102, 117 S. Ct. 555, 136 L. Ed. 2d 473 (1996).

[6]M.L.B. v. S.L.J., 519 U.S. 102, 117 S. Ct. 555, 569–70, 136 L. Ed. 2d 473 (1996).

[7]E.g., State ex rel. Heller v. Miller, 61 Ohio St. 2d 6, 15 Ohio Op. 3d 3, 399 N.E.2d 66 (1980); In re Cunningham, 59 Ohio St. 2d 100, 13 Ohio Op. 3d 78, 391 N.E.2d 1034 (1979); Hughes v. Scaffide, 58 Ohio St. 2d 88, 12 Ohio Op. 3d 92, 388 N.E.2d 1233 (1979); In re Perales, 52 Ohio St. 2d 89, 6 Ohio Op. 3d 293, 369 N.E.2d 1047 (1977).

[8]RC 2151.03.

[9]RC 2151.04.

[10]RC 2151.031.

[Section 9:3]

[1]RC 2151.23(A)(1).

[2]In re Kronjaeger, 166 Ohio St. 172, 1 Ohio Op. 2d 459, 140 N.E.2d 773 (1957); In re Darst, 117 Ohio App. 374, 24 Ohio Op. 2d 144, 192 N.E.2d 287 (10th Dist. Franklin County 1963); In re Minton, 112 Ohio App. 361, 16 Ohio Op. 2d 283, 176 N.E.2d 252 (2d Dist. Darke County 1960); In re Burkhart, 15 Ohio Misc. 170, 44 Ohio Op. 2d 329, 239 N.E.2d 772 (Juv. Ct. 1968); In re

have held that the neglect or dependency must be established as of the date specified in the complaint.[3] These cases hold that RC 2151.23(A)(1) implicitly overruled the cases decided prior to the 1969 statutory amendment.[4] According to these cases, if the date of the hearing were to control, it would be possible for the parents to avoid juvenile court jurisdiction by temporarily correcting the neglectful conditions before the hearing date.[5] Other cases, however, have continued to follow the pre-1969 cases by requiring that evidence of neglect or dependency exist at the time of the adjudicatory hearing.[6] These cases hold that the 1969 statutory amendment[7] merely confers jurisdiction on the juvenile court, but that other statutes[8] require the court to find that the child "is" presently (at the time of the hearing) neglected or dependent in order to proceed to adjudication and disposition. According to these cases, it is necessary to establish neglect or dependency both as of the time specified in the complaint and the time of the hearing.[9]

Permanent custody. Where permanent custody is at issue, statutory and case law provide definitive standards for making these "timing" decisions.[10]

§ 9:4 Neglected child defined

RC 2151.03(A) defines a neglected child as any child

(1) Who is abandoned by the child's parents, guardian, or custodian;

(2) Who lacks adequate parental care because of the faults or habits of the child's parents, guardian, or custodian;

(3) Whose parents, guardian, or custodian neglects the child or refuses to provide proper or necessary subsistence, education, medical or surgical care or treatment, or other care necessary for the child's health, morals, or well-being;

(4) Whose parents, guardian, or custodian neglects the child or refuses to provide the special care made necessary by the child's mental condition;

(5) Whose parents, legal guardian, or custodian have placed or attempted to place the child in violation of sections 5103.16 and 5103.17 of the Revised Code.

(6) Who, because of the omission of the child's parents, guardian, or custodian, suffers physical or mental injury that harms or threatens to harm the child's health or welfare;

(7) Who is subjected to out-of-home care child neglect.

All these categories are discussed in subsequent sections.

Turner, 12 Ohio Misc. 171, 41 Ohio Op. 2d 264, 231 N.E.2d 502 (C.P. 1967); In re H------, 24 Ohio Op. 2d 334, 92 Ohio L. Abs. 436, 192 N.E.2d 683 (Juv. Ct. 1963).

[3]In re Sims, 13 Ohio App. 3d 37, 468 N.E.2d 111 (12th Dist. Preble County 1983); In re Siniard, No. C-78-063 (6th Dist. Ct. App., Lucas, 2-9-79); In re Feldman, No. 34223 (8th Dist. Ct. App., Cuyahoga, 12-23-75); In re Kidd, No. 34295 (8th Dist. Ct. App., Cuyahoga, 11-26-75); In re Linger, No. CA-2556 (5th Dist. Ct. App., Licking, 7-12-79); In re Baby Girl S., 32 Ohio Misc. 217, 61 Ohio Op. 2d 439, 290 N.E.2d 925 (C.P. 1972); Hood v. Hood, 1991 WL 123045 (Ohio Ct. App. 9th Dist. Summit County 1991); In re Hay, 1995 WL 324046 (Ohio Ct. App. 4th Dist. Lawrence County 1995).

[4]See § 30:8, Permanent custody—Defined.

[5]E.g., In re Bennett, No. CA 78-35 (5th Dist. Ct. App., Muskingum, 4-25-79).

[6]In Matter of Parker, 1981 WL 6774 (Ohio Ct. App. 3d Dist. Van Wert County 1981); In re Solarz, No. 42275 (8th Dist. Ct. App., Cuyahoga, 11-6-80); In re Guthrie, No. CA 6383 (2d Dist. Ct. App., Montgomery, 2-22-80); In re Justice, 59 Ohio App. 2d 78, 13 Ohio Op. 3d 139, 392 N.E.2d 897 (1st Dist. Clinton County 1978); Matter of Poth, 1982 WL 9371 (Ohio Ct. App. 6th Dist. Huron County 1982); In re Bishop, 36 Ohio App. 3d 123, 521 N.E.2d 838 (5th Dist. Ashland County 1987); Young v. Young, 1987 WL 5501 (Ohio Ct. App. 12th Dist. Clermont County 1987); Matter of Whiteman, 2 A.D.D. 386 (Ohio Ct. App. 6th Dist. Williams County 1993); Matter of Kasler, 1991 WL 100360 (Ohio Ct. App. 4th Dist. Athens County 1991); Mary Beth v. Howard, 1995 WL 601110 (Ohio Ct. App. 8th Dist. Cuyahoga County 1995).

[7]RC 2151.23(A)(1).

[8]RC 2151.03, RC 2151.04, RC 2151.35, RC 2151.353.

[9]E.g., In re Kidd, No. 34295 (8th Dist. Ct. App., Cuyahoga, 11-26-75).

[10]See § 30:8, Permanent custody—Defined.

§ 9:5   Neglect—Abandonment

The abandonment of a child consists of a willful leaving of the child by his parent, with the intention of causing a permanent separation.[1] The parent relinquishes his right to custody either by express agreement or unfavorable circumstances, making parental custody clearly detrimental to the welfare of the child.[2] Thus, the act of placing a child in a children's home[3] or with a relative[4] will not alone support a finding of neglect. Nor will a mother's placement of her illegitimate child for adoption and her subsequent withdrawal of consent to adoption constitute neglect since it does not demonstrate rejection of the child.[5] However, abandonment was established where the father did not provide financial support for the child, had no communication or other contact with the child for the three-year period immediately preceding the filing of the complaint, and was unsure of his child's birthday.[6]

According to RC 2151.011(C),[7] a child is presumed abandoned when the child's parents have failed to visit or maintain contact with the child for more than 90 days, regardless of whether they have resumed contact after the 90-day period.

§ 9:6   Neglect—Inadequate care due to parental fault

The majority of neglect complaints are processed under RC 2151.03(A)(2), which requires findings that (1) the child lacks adequate parental care, and (2) this lack of care is the fault of the parents, guardian, or custodian.

Prior to the 1996 amendment to RC 2151.03(A)(2),[1] the statute used the term "proper parental care," which is defined in RC 2151.05. The statutory amendment changed the standard to "adequate parental care," which is defined in RC 2151.011(B)(16). The RC 2151.05 definition of "proper parental care" is significantly broader and more inclusive than the RC 2151.011(B)(1) definition of "adequate parental care."

Lack of parental supervision. In *In re Zeiser*,[2] the court of appeals interpreted the phrase "adequate parental care," which is defined in RC 2151.011(B)(1), in part, as the provision of "adequate food, clothing, and shelter to ensure the child's health and physical safety." In this case two sons, ages eight and six, were found to have been left at home alone on a regular basis. The court construed the term "shelter" to include a lack of parental supervision: "We agree that parental supervision *per se* is not expressly mentioned in the definition of adequate parental care. . . . [W]e conclude that a reasonable interpretation of the intent of the statute would include the scenario by which small children are left alone with no adult supervision.

[Section 9:5]

[1]In re Kronjaeger, 166 Ohio St. 172, 1 Ohio Op. 2d 459, 140 N.E.2d 773 (1957); In re Masters, 165 Ohio St. 503, 60 Ohio Op. 474, 137 N.E.2d 752 (1956); Matter of Ferrell, 1990 WL 42275 (Ohio Ct. App. 4th Dist. Gallia County 1990).

[2]In re Perales, 52 Ohio St. 2d 89, 6 Ohio Op. 3d 293, 369 N.E.2d 1047 (1977); Gallagher v. Gallagher, 115 Ohio App. 453, 21 Ohio Op. 2d 74, 185 N.E.2d 571 (3d Dist. Henry County 1962).

[3]Gallagher v. Gallagher, 115 Ohio App. 453, 21 Ohio Op. 2d 74, 185 N.E.2d 571 (3d Dist. Henry County 1962); Dickerson, 1982 WL 3447 (Ohio Ct. App. 4th Dist. Lawrence County 1982).

[4]In re Reese, 4 Ohio App. 3d 59, 446 N.E.2d 482 (10th Dist. Franklin County 1982). But see Hughes v. Scaffide, 58 Ohio St. 2d 88, 12 Ohio Op. 3d 92, 388 N.E.2d 1233 (1979), a habeas corpus proceeding (RC 2151.23(A)(3)) in which the Ohio Supreme Court held that a parent forfeited his paramount right to custody by leaving the child with grandparents for nine years.

[5]In re O---, 28 Ohio Op. 2d 165, 95 Ohio L. Abs. 101, 199 N.E.2d 765 (Juv. Ct. 1964).

[6]Matter of Ferrell, 1990 WL 42275 (Ohio Ct. App. 4th Dist. Gallia County 1990).

[7]As enacted by 1998 H.B. 484, eff. 3-18-99.

[Section 9:6]

[1]1996 H.B. 274, eff. 8-8-96.

[2]In re Zeiser, 133 Ohio App. 3d 338, 340, 728 N.E.2d 10 (11th Dist. Lake County 1999).

The concept of 'shelter' would encompass such a situation. That circumstance certainly could constitute a danger to their physical health and safety and put them at undue risk."[3] The court went on to identify three factors that were relevant in this context. First, the age of the child. Second, the pattern, regularity, and length of the incidents of no supervision. Third, "the likelihood that the lack of supervision would continue because of the inability or unwillingness of appellant to acknowledge the implicit and immediate danger of such a situation."[4] The court concluded that "it constitutes neglect *per se* to allow a six-year-old child to be left alone for two entire days per week *on a regular basis* and to be regularly left at other times under the supervision of his eight-year-old sibling."[5]

Immoral lifestyle. Lack of "proper parental care" has often been equated by the courts with an allegedly immoral lifestyle.[6] For example, where the parents frequently engaged in adulterous behavior, were selfish and childish, and regularly told their children terrible things about each other, the children were found to be neglected.[7]

Faults or bad habits by themselves, however, do not constitute neglect. It must also be shown that as a result the child lacks proper care.[8] In the absence of evidence showing a detrimental impact upon the children, the mere fact that a mother is living with her boyfriend in the family home will not justify a finding that the children are neglected.[9] Nor will a mother's interracial marriage in itself establish a lack of proper parental care; there must be a finding of unfitness.[10] Furthermore, the fact that a parent is an alcoholic does not necessarily mean that his children are neglected. A causal link must be shown between the fault of the parent (i.e., alcoholism) and the neglected condition of the child.[11]

Temporary placement. Courts have considered the issue of whether temporary placement of a child with relatives constitutes neglect under RC 2151.03(A)(2).[12] Because such temporary placements do not constitute "abandonment" under RC 2151.03(A)(1)[13] nor "illegal placements" under RC 2151.03(A)(5),[14] it has been argued that they are evidence that the child lacks "proper parental care" because of parental "faults and habits."

It has been held that the fact that a child is temporarily living with relatives, by agreement with the mother during a period in which she is unable

---

[3]In re Zeiser, 133 Ohio App. 3d 338, 340, 728 N.E.2d 10 (11th Dist. Lake County 1999). The court also wrote: "We do not believe that the only type of situation that would justify immediate state intervention is one in which the parent decides to leave children alone in a house with an undue danger or dangerous condition, such as a gun . . .. [W]e believe that, regardless of maturity or intelligence, the ages alone of unsupervised children could constitute some clear and convincing evidence that showed that children of that age who were *regularly left alone for extended periods of time,* separately or together, were put at undue risk to their health and safety." In re Zeiser, 133 Ohio App. 3d 338, 347, 728 N.E.2d 10 (11th Dist. Lake County 1999).

[4]In re Zeiser, 133 Ohio App. 3d 338, 347, 728 N.E.2d 10 (11th Dist. Lake County 1999).

[5]In re Zeiser, 133 Ohio App. 3d 338, 348, 728 N.E.2d 10 (11th Dist. Lake County 1999).

[6]See In re Hayes, 62 Ohio App. 289, 16 Ohio Op. 10, 30 Ohio L. Abs. 568, 23 N.E.2d 956 (2d Dist. Franklin County 1939); In re Burrell, 58 Ohio St. 2d 37, 12 Ohio Op. 3d 43, 388 N.E.2d 738 (1979).

[7]In re Douglas, 11 Ohio Op. 2d 340, 82 Ohio L. Abs. 170, 164 N.E.2d 475 (Juv. Ct. 1959).

[8]The cases that follow relate to the former statutory language of "proper parental care."

[9]In re Burrell, 58 Ohio St. 2d 37, 12 Ohio Op. 3d 43, 388 N.E.2d 738 (1979).

[10]In re H., 37 Ohio Misc. 123, 66 Ohio Op. 2d 178, 66 Ohio Op. 2d 368, 305 N.E.2d 815 (C.P. 1973). See also Palmore v. Sidoti, 466 U.S. 429, 104 S. Ct. 1879, 80 L. Ed. 2d 421 (1984), holding that a divorce court judgment divesting a natural mother of custody of her infant child because of the mother's remarriage to a man of different race violates the Equal Protection Clause of the Fourteenth Amendment.

[11]In re Sims, 13 Ohio App. 3d 37, 468 N.E.2d 111 (12th Dist. Preble County 1983).

[12]E.g., In re Reese, 4 Ohio App. 3d 59, 446 N.E.2d 482 (10th Dist. Franklin County 1982).

[13]See § 9:5, Neglect—Abandonment.

[14]See § 9:9, Neglect—Illegal placement.

to care for the child, does not constitute neglect if the child is receiving proper care from the custodian.[15] In such situations, the state has no interest in assuming guardianship since the obligations of care, custody, and support are being met. However, the Ohio Supreme Court upheld an adjudication of neglect where the custody arrangement with the relative was initiated by a children services board caseworker, rather than pursuant to a voluntary agreement initiated by the child's parent.[16] The Supreme Court determined that if the trial court believed that the child's lack of proper care prior to the time the relative assumed responsibility for the child was due to circumstances within the parent's control, then a finding of fault, which was the basis of the neglect adjudication, would not be inappropriate.[17]

Confinement of parent. The neglect issue also arises when a child's parent is confined to a mental hospital or prison.[18] The Ohio Supreme Court has held that a mother's confinement in a mental hospital, during which time she had no funds to support her children and was unaware of their whereabouts, did not constitute neglect. Mental illness, which was the reason for the confinement, is involuntary and not willful or blameworthy.[19] Even where the conduct underlying the confinement is voluntary, such as the commission of a crime, neglect cannot be established without additional evidence showing a willful disregard of parental duty or indifference toward the child.[20] Such evidence must relate to the parent's character, morals, faults, or habits, rather than his inability to care for the child as a result of the confinement.[21]

§ 9:7 Neglect—Subsistence, education & medical care

The provisions of RC 2151.03(A)(3)[1] are similar to those of RC 2151.03(A)(2), except that RC 2151.03(A)(3) is more specific. It applies to distinct categories of neglect: a parent's failure or refusal to provide the child with proper subsistence, education, medical or surgical care, or anything else that may be necessary for his health or well-being.

Subsistence neglect. Evidence that shows only that a child is weak and sick, without any sign of physical neglect, will not establish that the parents have failed or refused to provide proper subsistence.[2]

Educational neglect. A child is not "educationally" neglected when he is excluded from public school because he has not been vaccinated, where the

---

[15]In re Reese, 4 Ohio App. 3d 59, 446 N.E.2d 482 (10th Dist. Franklin County 1982).

[16]In re Riddle, 79 Ohio St. 3d 259, 1997-Ohio-391, 680 N.E.2d 1227 (1997).

[17]In re Riddle, 79 Ohio St. 3d 259, 1997-Ohio-391, 680 N.E.2d 1227 (1997). The Supreme Court also determined that the terms "guardian" and "custodian" in RC 2151.03(A)(2) should not be limited to the definitions of those terms in RC 2151.011(B)(16) and RC 2151.011(B)(11), respectively, but rather could apply to any non-parent providing care for a child.

[18]In an adoption proceeding, the Ohio Supreme Court has held that the mere fact of a parent's incarceration does not constitute a willful failure to support a child. In re Schoeppner's Adoption, 46 Ohio St. 2d 21, 75 Ohio Op. 2d 12, 345 N.E.2d 608 (1976).

[19]In re Masters, 165 Ohio St. 503, 60 Ohio Op. 474, 137 N.E.2d 752 (1956). See also In re Pieper Children, 74 Ohio App. 3d 714, 600 N.E.2d 317 (12th Dist. Preble County 1991). However, under proper circumstances, the parent's mental illness may be grounds for a dependency action pursuant to RC 2151.04(B). See § 10:4, Dependency—Inadequate care due to parents' mental or physical condition.

[20]In re Thomas, Nos. 39494, 39495 (8th Dist. Ct. App., Cuyahoga, 7-19-79).

[21]In re Thomas, Nos. 39494, 39495 (8th Dist. Ct. App., Cuyahoga, 7-19-79).

[Section 9:7]

[1]This section has been held constitutional against vagueness attacks. See In re Lippitt, No. 38421 (8th Dist. Ct. App., Cuyahoga, 3-9-78); In re Artler, No. 34723 (8th Dist. Ct. App., Cuyahoga, 7-15-76).

[2]In re MacPherson, No. 34106 (8th Dist. Ct. App., Cuyahoga, 4-3-75). See also State v. Earich, 19 Ohio Op. 2d 39, 86 Ohio L. Abs. 90, 176 N.E.2d 191 (Juv. Ct. 1961), holding that a father's failure to ask for relief, thus permitting the child to go without proper subsistence, constituted criminal nonsupport.

evidence shows that his parent has attempted to enroll him into a proper public school and has not prevented the vaccination.[3]

Many cases of "educational" neglect[4] involve situations in which parents refuse to send their child to a certified school,[5] instead choosing to educate the child by themselves, through a correspondence school, or by enrolling the child in a noncertified private school.[6] An educational neglect adjudication was reversed where the evidence showed that the parents had unsuccessfully made several requests to their local school district superintendent for information on the requirements of home instruction, since these actions showed that the parents had not willfully refused to perform their parental duties.[7]

Ohio law recognizes a home education exception to its compulsory school attendance laws.[8] However, the right to home educate a child is not absolute, and is subject to reasonable government regulations designed to ensure that minimum educational standards prescribed by the state are met.[9] Where parents have failed to follow the procedures prescribed by law for asserting their rights to educate their children at home, they cannot legitimately claim an infringement of those rights.[10]

The parents' refusal to send their child to a certified school is often based on religious grounds. The United States Supreme Court, in *Wisconsin v. Yoder*,[11] has specifically exempted Amish children from attending public schools beyond the eighth grade, ruling that the Wisconsin state compulsory education law infringed upon their First Amendment rights. However, parents may not merely assert religious grounds as justification for not providing their children with an adequate education and properly qualified teachers.[12] In a case involving children who were taught at home, an Ohio court of appeals in *In re Lippitt*[13] held that in order to successfully assert religious grounds as justification for failing to send their children to school, parents must demonstrate how such an education would undermine their religious values and establish that they belong to an accepted religious group which offers a well-structured alternative.

In a similar "educational" neglect case, *In re Miller*,[14] a juvenile court dismissed a neglect complaint involving children who attended school in the basement of a home. The case was distinguishable both from *Yoder*, because the parents' objections to the public school's social and moral environment were not based on religious grounds, and from *Lippitt*, because the children's teacher was certified to teach elementary school subjects. In holding that violation of compulsory school laws does not necessarily constitute neglect, the court found that the children were receiving an adequate education and

---

[3]State v. Dunham, 154 Ohio St. 63, 42 Ohio Op. 133, 93 N.E.2d 286 (1950).

[4]Where the failure to attend school is the fault of the child rather than the parent, the child may be charged as an unruly child under RC 2151.022(B). See § 8:3, Unruly—Wayward or habitually disobedient.

[5]RC Ch. 3321.

[6]RC Ch. 3332.

[7]In the Matter of Nicholson, 1983 WL 3291 (Ohio Ct. App. 4th Dist. Hocking County 1983). See also State v. Schmidt, 29 Ohio St. 3d 32, 505 N.E.2d 627, 38 Ed. Law Rep. 1137 (1987) (Requirement of RC 3321.04(A)(2) that application be made to the local superintendent of schools for approval of a home education program is constitutional.).

[8]RC 3321.04(A)(2).

[9]State v. Schmidt, 29 Ohio St. 3d 32, 505 N.E.2d 627, 38 Ed. Law Rep. 1137 (1987); In Matter of Carroll, 1996 WL 535302 (Ohio Ct. App. 2d Dist. Greene County 1996).

[10]In Matter of Carroll, 1996 WL 535302 (Ohio Ct. App. 2d Dist. Greene County 1996).

[11]Wisconsin v. Yoder, 406 U.S. 205, 92 S. Ct. 1526, 32 L. Ed. 2d 15 (1972).

[12]In re Lippitt, No. 38421 (8th Dist. Ct. App., Cuyahoga, 3-9-78).

[13]In re Lippitt, No. 38421 (8th Dist. Ct. App., Cuyahoga, 3-9-78).

[14]In re Miller, Nos. 77-11-171 to 77-11-174 (Juv., Carroll 1978).

were thus not "educationally" neglected.[15] If the legislature had intended to equate nonattendance with neglect, it would have specifically so provided.[16]

Medical neglect. A child may be adjudged "medically" neglected when the evidence demonstrates that the child has suffered bruises on the face and buttocks that appear to have been inflicted by severe slaps.[17] Similarly, a mother's failure to provide medical care for her children who have been abused by their father constitutes neglect.[18] However, in reversing a juvenile court's adjudication that a child was neglected based on the "failure to thrive" syndrome, a court of appeals held that neglect was not established where the record overwhelmingly indicated that the mother had regularly sought proper medical treatment (i.e., eight times in a five-month period) for her child.[19]

As in the "educational" neglect cases, religion may be a factor in "medical" neglect cases. RC 2151.03(B) exempts from criminal liability a parent, guardian, or custodian of a child when, solely in the practice of his religious beliefs, he fails to provide adequate medical or surgical care or treatment for the child. However, the statute does not limit or abrogate any person's responsibility under RC 2151.421[20] to report known or suspected child abuse or neglect, or a threat of abuse or neglect; nor does it preclude the exercise of the authority of the state, any political subdivision, or any court to ensure that medical or surgical care or treatment is provided to a child when his health requires that he be provided with medical or surgical care or treatment.[21] When a child is in need of medical or surgical care or treatment, a complaint may be filed to secure a temporary court order allowing the treatment over the parents' or child's objections, and may include an order granting emergency temporary custody of the child to a county department of job and family services.[22] In *In re Clark*,[23] involving a badly burned child in critical need of blood transfusions, the court held that the child's right to live

---

[15]For a similar decision from another jurisdiction, see In re Interest of Rice, 204 Neb. 732, 285 N.W.2d 223 (1979).

[16]Instead of proceeding under the neglect statute, many of these nonattendance cases are processed as criminal prosecutions against the parents for failing to send their children to school (RC 3321.38). In fact, the *Yoder* case involved a criminal prosecution of parents under Wisconsin's compulsory attendance laws. Although many of the same legal principles apply, in one sense these cases are easier to prove since it is not necessary to establish that the children are neglected based on the quality of the alternative education. However, the Ohio Supreme Court has twice reversed the convictions of defendants whose children were attending nonchartered religious schools which did not comply with all of the minimum standards established by the State Board of Education. The court focused on the scope of the minimum standards, holding that they were so comprehensive as to abrogate the defendants' fundamental right of religious freedom. State ex rel. Nagle v. Olin, 64 Ohio St. 2d 341, 18 Ohio Op. 3d 503, 415 N.E.2d 279 (1980); State v. Whisner, 47 Ohio St. 2d 181, 1 Ohio Op. 3d 105, 351 N.E.2d 750 (1976).

[17]In re Artler, No. 34723 (8th Dist. Ct. App., Cuyahoga, 7-15-76).

[18]In re Sullivan, Nos. 79 AP-893, 79 AP-894 (10th Dist. Ct. App., Franklin, 12-16-80).

[19]In the Matter of Kuhn, 1982 WL 3392 (Ohio Ct. App. 4th Dist. Pickaway County 1982).

[20]See § 14:16, Abuse, neglect, & dependency investigations.

[21]RC 2151.03(B) was enacted in 1989 (1989 H.B. 257, eff. 8-3-89). The prior version of the statute exempted from the purview of the civil child neglect statute religious sects which provided spiritual treatment in lieu of medical treatment. The current RC 2151.03(B) has removed the civil child neglect exemption, but has included an exemption from criminal liability.

[22]RC 2151.33; Juv. R. 13(A). Where an unemancipated child has been removed from the custody of his parents and placed in the temporary custody of a county department of job and family services, the department may properly consent to surgical treatment for the child without consulting with the parents. Kilgallion v. Children's Hosp. Medical Center, 1987 WL 9742 (Ohio Ct. App. 1st Dist. Hamilton County 1987). The attorney general has ruled that where a child has been permanently committed to a child welfare board by order of the juvenile court, the board may properly consent to medical and surgical treatment for the child; but where the commitment is temporary, the juvenile court retains jurisdiction over the child and may consent to the treatment (OAG 51-689). See also Freedman, Consent to Medical Treatment for Minors Under Care of Children Services Board, 10 Capital L. Rev. 309 (1980). Under certain circumstances, the child may have the authority to consent to necessary treatment even without

took precedence over the parents' religious beliefs and granted the emergency order.[24]

A more difficult issue arises when a pregnant woman objects to medical or surgical treatment designed to save the life of her unborn fetus. Although at least one trial court has authorized emergency treatment under such circumstances,[25] the only reported appellate case viewed the issue differently. *Cox v. Franklin County Court of Common Pleas*[26] involved an original action requesting a writ of prohibition ordering the juvenile court to cease the exercise of jurisdiction over the mother in a neglect and dependency action. The neglect complaint alleged in part that the mother, who was an adult, was approximately seven months pregnant and a known drug user who had used cocaine and opiates throughout her pregnancy. She also had allegedly refused prenatal care for the child. The state had requested the court to find the mother in contempt of court for failure to obey and comply with former court orders to get prenatal care, a physical examination, and abstain from the use of illegal drugs. The court of appeals determined that it would not decide whether a fetus is a "child" or whether the juvenile court has jurisdiction over a fetus. The sole issue was whether the juvenile court had been conferred jurisdiction to compel a pregnant woman to take action for the alleged benefit of her unborn child. In granting the writ of prohibition, the court held that the jurisdictional statute[27] gave no such authority to juvenile courts.

However, there is authority from other jurisdictions upholding the right of the juvenile court to intercede in some circumstances on behalf of the unborn child.[28] Furthermore, in *In re Ruiz*, an Ohio trial court, after examining the developing body of law from other jurisdictions, held that "a child does have a right to begin life with a sound mind and body, and . . . a viable fetus is a child under the existing child abuse statute, and harm to it may be considered abuse under R.C. 2151.031."[29] Unlike the circumstances in *Cox*, the child who was the subject of the *Ruiz* case had been born prior to the commencement of the action, but the allegations of abuse in *Ruiz* were based on the prenatal heroin use of the mother. Similarly, an appellate court has held that a mother's use of cocaine during pregnancy constituted prenatal fault,

---

parental permission or court order. See Lacey v. Laird, 166 Ohio St. 12, 1 Ohio Op. 2d 158, 139 N.E.2d 25 (1956). See also Zaremski, Blood Transfusions and Elective Surgery: A Custodial Function of an Ohio Juvenile Court, 23 Clev. St. L. Rev. 231 (1974). The county welfare department was renamed the "county department of human services" by the amendment of RC 329.01 (1984 H.B. 401, eff. 7-20-84). The department was renamed "job and family services" (1999 H.B. 471, eff. 7-1-00).

[23]In re Clark, 21 Ohio Op. 2d 86, 90 Ohio L. Abs. 21, 185 N.E.2d 128 (C.P. 1962).

[24]The United States Supreme Court has often ruled that a state may legitimately regulate religious practices for the protection of society. E.g., Prince v. Massachusetts, 321 U.S. 158, 64 S. Ct. 438, 88 L. Ed. 645 (1944); Cantwell v. State of Connecticut, 310 U.S. 296, 60 S. Ct. 900, 84 L. Ed. 1213, 128 A.L.R. 1352 (1940). For cases from other jurisdictions upholding the right of the state to place limits on the parents' right to free exercise of religion in similar situations, see Jehovah's Witnesses in State of Wash. v. King County Hospital Unit No. 1 (Harborview), 278 F. Supp. 488 (W.D. Wash. 1967); Matter of Jensen, 54 Or. App. 1, 633 P.2d 1302 (1981); State v. Perricone, 37 N.J. 463, 181 A.2d 751 (1962); People ex rel. Wallace v. Labrenz, 411 Ill. 618, 104 N.E.2d 769, 30 A.L.R.2d 1132 (1952).

[25]E.g., In re Unborn Child Copeland, No. 7910111 (Juv., Cuyahoga, 6-9-79).

[26]Cox v. Court of Common Pleas of Franklin County, Div. of Domestic Relations, Juvenile Branch, 42 Ohio App. 3d 171, 537 N.E.2d 721 (10th Dist. Franklin County 1988).

[27]RC 2151.23.

[28]People v. Estergard, 169 Colo. 445, 457 P.2d 698 (1969) held that pending adjudication regarding the paternity of an unborn child, the juvenile court may issue such temporary orders for protection, support, or medical treatment as the child's best interest requires. See also Raleigh Fitkin-Paul Morgan Memorial Hospital and Ann May Memorial Foundation in Town of Neptune v. Anderson, 42 N.J. 421, 201 A.2d 537 (1964); Jehovah's Witnesses in State of Wash. v. King County Hospital Unit No. 1 (Harborview), 278 F. Supp. 488 (W.D. Wash. 1967).

[29]In re Ruiz, 27 Ohio Misc. 2d 31, 35, 500 N.E.2d 935 (C.P. 1986).

permitting an adjudication of neglect following the child's birth.[30] *In re Baby Boy Blackshear*, although an abuse case, may also be relevant.[31]

§ 9:8   Neglect—Special care for child's mental condition

Few cases are brought under RC 2151.03(A)(4). They might include instances in which parents fail or refuse to seek available care for a mentally retarded child. Because more often than not these parents are simply unable to find or afford necessary treatment,[1] but would be willing to accept such care if it were provided, these children more properly fit under the dependency statute.[2]

§ 9:9   Neglect—Illegal placement

The very specific provisions of RC 2151.03(A)(5) apply to cases where, pursuant to an agreement transferring parental rights or duties, a child is placed in the temporary or permanent custody of any person, association, or institution not certified by the department of job and family services without the consent of the department or the court.[1]

In many respects, complaints filed under this section may resemble "abandonment" complaints brought under RC 2151.03(A)(1),[2] although illegal placements may involve some temporary custody arrangements, whereas "abandonment" connotes a permanent forfeiture of parental rights.[3]

The temporary commitment of a child to a day-care center, nursery, or babysitter does not involve transfer of legal custody and thus would not constitute an illegal placement.[4] In addition, since RC 5103.16 exempts from its purview placements into the care of persons related by blood or marriage, this section would not cover cases where a child is being raised by a grandparent or other relative.

A child may be adjudged neglected under this section where he is placed for adoption, unless the placement is approved by the probate court or is made by a department or organization duly authorized to place children.[5]

A neglect adjudication may also result when a person, organization, hospital, or association which is not approved and certified knowingly

---

[30]In re Crawford, 1999 WL 100377 (Ohio Ct. App. 5th Dist. Stark County 1999).

[31]In re Baby Boy Blackshear, 90 Ohio St. 3d 197, 2000-Ohio-173, 736 N.E.2d 462 (2000). See § 9:16, Abused child—Physical or mental injury due to parents.

[Section 9:8]

[1]See In re Siniard, No. C-78-063 (6th Dist. Ct. App., Lucas, 2-9-79), in which the court held that where there was no evidence of the mother's inability to provide for her child's physical needs and where the child was enrolled in a school appropriate for his handicap, the child was not dependent. See also In re Duffy, 591 S.E.2d 598 (N.C. Ct. App. 2004).

[2]RC 2151.04(C). See § 10:5, Dependency—Detrimental condition or environment.

[Section 9:9]

[1]RC 5103.16 also provides that temporary placement with a person related by blood or marriage or in a legally licensed boarding home is legal. See In re Duncan, 62 Ohio L. Abs. 173, 107 N.E.2d 256 (Ct. App. 2d Dist. Preble County 1951), holding that a placement in violation of RC 5103.16 does not necessarily constitute dependency. This case was decided under a statute (GC 1352-13, recodified in 1953 as RC 5103.16 and amended in 1969) in which "illegal placements" were included within the definition of dependency. See also In re Whitmer, No. 28098 (8th Dist. Ct. App., Cuyahoga, 6-2-67); In re O---, 28 Ohio Op. 2d 165, 95 Ohio L. Abs. 101, 199 N.E.2d 765 (Juv. Ct. 1964).

[2]E.g., In re Kronjaeger, 166 Ohio St. 172, 1 Ohio Op. 2d 459, 140 N.E.2d 773 (1957).

[3]See § 9:5, Neglect—Abandonment.

[4]1952 OAG 159.

[5]RC 5103.16. See In re Harshey, 40 Ohio App. 2d 157, 69 Ohio Op. 2d 165, 318 N.E.2d 544, 83 A.L.R.3d 815 (8th Dist. Cuyahoga County 1974).

becomes a party to the separation of a child from its parents or guardians.[6] Where blood relatives of an unwed mother take temporary legal possession of her child whom she thereafter abandons, the relatives are not knowing parties to the separation of the child from its parent within the meaning of this section.[7]

§ 9:10 Neglect—Physical or mental injury due to omissions

RC 2151.03(A)(6), one of the two most recent additions to the child neglect statute,[1] covers a child who, because of parental omissions, suffers physical or mental injury that harms or threatens to harm the child's health or welfare. In cases decided prior to the enactment of this provision, situations in which a child was injured due to parental omissions were prosecuted under the child abuse statute, RC 2151.031.[2]

A parent's act of leaving children unattended with a loaded, unsecured gun is sufficient to support findings of both dependency and neglect.[3]

Mental injury. The most significant addition to Ohio law brought about by this statutory enactment is the inclusion of the concept of "mental" injury. The term "mental injury" is defined as "any behavioral, cognitive, emotional, or mental disorder in a child caused by an act or omission that is described in section 2919.22 of the Revised Code and is committed by the parent or other person responsible for the child's care."[4]

§ 9:11 Neglect—Out-of-home care neglect

RC 2151.03(A)(7), also enacted in 1989,[1] governs situations in which a child is subjected to out-of-home care child neglect. The term "out-of-home care child neglect," defined in RC 2151.011(B)(26), covers several omissions and commissions by a person responsible for the care of a child in out-of-home care. These include failure to provide reasonable supervision and failure to develop processes to ensure the proper administration of medication and the provision of care and subsistence for the child.[2]

Apparently, this provision was enacted to protect the growing numbers of children who spend significant amounts of time being cared for in day care centers and by other out-of-home providers. Although there is certainly a strong public policy to impose criminal sanctions against such providers who neglect the child's care, it is not readily apparent why this provision was added to the civil child neglect statute. The concept of civil neglect connotes the lack of proper care for a child due to the fault of a parent, guardian, or custodian,[3] and may result in the imposition of an array of dispositional options to protect the child, including the potential for parents to lose custody

---

[6]RC 5103.17.

[7]In re Tilton, 161 Ohio St. 571, 53 Ohio Op. 427, 120 N.E.2d 445 (1954).

[Section 9:10]

[1]1989 H.B. 257, eff. 8-3-89. A similar provision, which includes parental "acts" rather than "omissions," was added to the child abuse statute through the same legislation (RC 2151.031(D)). See § 9:12, Abused child defined.

[2]E.g., Matter of Weeks, 1991 WL 12147 (Ohio Ct. App. 12th Dist. Clermont County 1991).

[3]In re Leftwich, 1997 WL 202247 (Ohio Ct. App. 10th Dist. Franklin County 1997); In re Skeen, 71 Ohio St. 3d 1411, 641 N.E.2d 1110 (1994).

[4]RC 2151.011(B)(19).

[Section 9:11]

[1]1989 H.B. 257, eff. 8-3-89. A similar provision covering out-of-home care child abuse was added to the child abuse statute through the same legislation (RC 2151.031(E)). See § 9:12, Abused child defined.

[2]RC 2151.011(B)(25).

[3]See § 10:2, Dependent child defined.

of their child.[4] Unless the parents, guardian, or custodian[5] are somehow at fault for their selection of an out-of-home care provider, there seems to be no justification or rationale for invoking the civil jurisdiction of the juvenile court when out-of-home care neglect occurs.[6]

§ 9:12   Abused child defined

RC 2151.031 defines an abused child as any child who

(A) Is the victim of "sexual activity" as defined under Chapter 2907 of the Revised Code, where such activity would constitute an offense under that chapter, except that the court need not find that any person has been convicted of the offense in order to find that the child is an abused child;

(B) Is endangered as defined in section 2919.22 of the Revised Code, except that the court need not find that any person has been convicted under that section in order to find that the child is an abused child;

(C) Exhibits evidence of any physical or mental injury or death, inflicted other than by accidental means, or an injury or death which is at variance with the history given of it. Except as provided in division (D) of this section, a child exhibiting evidence of corporal punishment or other physical disciplinary measure by a parent, guardian, custodian, person having custody or control, or person in loco parentis of a child is not an abused child under this division if the measure is not prohibited under section 2919.22 of the Revised Code.

(D) Because of the acts of his parents, guardian, or custodian, suffers physical or mental injury that harms or threatens the child's health or welfare.

(E) Is subjected to out-of-home care child abuse.

Prior to the enactment of RC 2151.031, cases concerning children who had been physically or sexually abused were considered under the dependency[1] or neglect[2] statutes.

Parental fault. Divisions (A) to (C) of the abuse statute do not require that the abuser be a parent, guardian, or custodian, nor do they require parental fault. All that is necessary is that the child be a victim, regardless of who is responsible for the abuse.[3] However, some courts have held that if the parent has provided care and supervision, the child will not be considered abused if, despite those efforts, someone else abuses him.[4] Thus, a child was not an abused child where the evidence revealed that the child was abused by the mother's boyfriend, who had previously cared for the child properly and from whom the mother had no reason to expect such conduct.[5]

§ 9:13   Abused child—Sexual victim

Under RC 2151.031(A), an abused child includes a child who is the victim

---

[4]See § 30:2, General principles for abuse, neglect and dependency dispositions.

[5]The definitions of "guardian" (RC 2151.011(B)(16)) and "custodian" (RC 2151.011(B)(11)) would not ordinarily cover out-of-home care providers.

[6]An allegation of neglect committed by someone other than a parent, guardian, or custodian would be covered by the reporting statute, RC 2151.421. See § 14:16, Abuse, neglect, & dependency investigations.

[Section 9:12]

[1]RC 2151.04. E.g., In re Holcomb, No. 39694 (8th Dist. Ct. App., Cuyahoga, 10-4-79).

[2]RC 2151.03.

[3]In re Pitts, 38 Ohio App. 3d 1, 5, 525 N.E.2d 814 (5th Dist. Knox County 1987) ("The statute makes no reference to parental fault. All that is necessary is that the child be a victim, regardless of who is responsible for the abuse. The focus is upon harm to the child, not upon parental or custodial blame-worthiness."). See also Matter of Marshall, 1987 WL 19029 (Ohio Ct. App. 3d Dist. Putnam County 1987); Matter of Leu, 1993 WL 134004 (Ohio Ct. App. 6th Dist. Wood County 1993); In re Barger, 1996 WL 647631 (Ohio Ct. App. 2d Dist. Montgomery County 1996); In Matter of Dodson, 1996 WL 98730 (Ohio Ct. App. 3d Dist. Shelby County 1996).

[4]Under some circumstances, the child may be dependent or neglected. For discussion of dependency and neglect, see § 9:2, Parental rights; § 9:4, Neglected child defined.

[5]In re Collier, No. 8AP-825 (10th Dist. Ct. App., Franklin, 6-4-81). See also Dillon, 1981 WL 4218 (Ohio Ct. App. 9th Dist. Wayne County 1981).

of "sexual activity"[1] where such activity would be an offense under RC Chapter 2907. This includes crimes such as rape, sexual battery, sexual imposition, and gross sexual imposition.[2]

Like Divisions (B) and (C) of the abuse statute, this provision does not require that the abuser be a parent, guardian, or custodian, nor does it require parental fault. All that is necessary is that the child be a victim, regardless of who is responsible for the abuse.[3]

In a sense, the abuse statute is more narrowly drawn than either the neglect or dependency statutes. In order to establish neglect or dependency, it is not necessary that a specific person caused the neglect or dependency. A finding of abuse under RC 2151.031(A) (victim of sexual activity) or RC 2151.031(B) (endangered child) does not require a criminal conviction, but does require that there be sufficient evidence that a criminal offense has occurred.

§ 9:14 Abused child—Child endangerment

Under RC 2151.031(B), an abused child includes a child who is endangered.[1] Like Divisions (A) and (C) of the abuse statute, this provision does not require that the abuser be a parent, guardian, or custodian, nor does it require parental fault. All that is necessary is that the child be a victim, regardless of who is responsible for the abuse.[2]

A finding that a child is abused may be predicated solely on the prenatal conduct of the mother. Thus, a child who is born addicted to heroin because of the mother's regular use of heroin during pregnancy is an abused child, since it is from the point of viability that the state has an interest in the child's care, protection, and development.[3] *In re Baby Boy Blackshear* may also be relevant.[4]

§ 9:15 Abused child—Physical or mental injury exhibited

Like Divisions (A) and (B) of the abuse statute, RC 2151.031(C) does not require that the abuser be a parent, guardian, or custodian, nor does it require parental fault. All that is necessary is that the child be a victim, regardless of who is responsible for the abuse.[1]

[Section 9:13]

[1]RC 2907.01(C) defines "sexual activity" as including "sexual conduct" (which is defined in RC 2907.01(A) as vaginal, anal and oral intercourse) and "sexual contact" (which is defined in RC 2907.01(B) as touching erogenous zone of another).

[2]See Katz and Giannelli, Baldwin's Ohio Practice, Criminal Law (2d ed.), Ch 99 (rape and related offenses).

[3]See In re Pitts, 38 Ohio App. 3d 1, 5, 525 N.E.2d 814 (5th Dist. Knox County 1987) ("The statute makes no reference to parental fault. All that is necessary is that the child be a victim, regardless of who is responsible for the abuse. The focus is upon harm to the child, not upon parental or custodial blame-worthiness.").

[Section 9:14]

[1]RC 2919.22 defines endangerment. See Katz and Giannelli, Baldwin's Ohio Practice, Criminal Law (2d ed.) § 109:11 (child endangerment).

[2]See In re Pitts, 38 Ohio App. 3d 1, 5, 525 N.E.2d 814 (5th Dist. Knox County 1987) ("The statute makes no reference to parental fault. All that is necessary is that the child be a victim, regardless of who is responsible for the abuse. The focus is upon harm to the child, not upon parental or custodial blame-worthiness.").

[3]In re Ruiz, 27 Ohio Misc. 2d 31, 500 N.E.2d 935 (C.P. 1986). See also Roe v. Wade, 410 U.S. 113, 93 S. Ct. 705, 35 L. Ed. 2d 147 (1973) for discussion of the issue of viability of a fetus.

[4]See § 9:16, Abused child—Physical or mental injury due to parents.

[Section 9:15]

[1]See In re Pitts, 38 Ohio App. 3d 1, 5, 525 N.E.2d 814 (5th Dist. Knox County 1987) ("The statute makes no reference to parental fault. All that is necessary is that the child be a victim,

This provision covers situations where the child's injury[2] is nonaccidental or where it is at variance with the explanation given for it, except that corporal punishment or physical discipline administered by a parent or person in loco parentis does not constitute abuse if it is not prohibited by the "endangering children" statute, RC 2919.22.

In interpreting RC 2151.031(C), a court of appeals in *Watts v. Cuyahoga County Welfare Department*[3] held that a four-year-old child was abused where the record demonstrated that the mother punished him by whipping him with an electric appliance cord, causing internal injury and external bruises and lacerations. According to the mother, the reason for the whipping, which was not an isolated incident, was that the child had "badmouthed" his relatives. Such punishment was "excessive under the circumstances" and caused "serious physical harm" to the child.[4]

However, another court of appeals held that a mother's admission of punishing her thirteen-year-old daughter by beating her with a belt was not per se abusive.[5] The trial court must consider the totality of circumstances,[6] for example, the child's age, physical condition, emotional maturity, intelligence level, ability to understand and correct the offending behavior, response to noncorporal punishment, and the behavior being punished.[7] Similarly, in a criminal prosecution for "endangering children," an appellate court held that the defendant's son's bruised left eyelid, bruises, welts, and lacerations caused by belt whipping on his buttocks and lower legs, and his swollen hand, did not cause the son serious physical harm or threaten substantial risk of physical harm so as to sustain the defendant's conviction.[8] The injuries did not result in hospitalization, substantial risk of death, permanent incapacity, disfigurement, or substantial pain or suffering, but rather were the result of the imposition of corporal punishment by the father who determined that his son's conduct in school warranted strong physical disciplinary action.[9] Another court held that a mere finding that a parent's corporal punishment of his child was unwarranted and excessive is insufficient to establish abuse unless the punishment creates a substantial risk of serious physical harm, as required by RC 2919.22(B)(3).[10]

An adjudication of abuse under RC 2151.031(C) was upheld where the mother would not or could not protect her child.[11] She knew her husband was violent and that he had an uncontrollable temper. She admitted he disciplined the child in ways she did not approve, and that he had hit and

---

regardless of who is responsible for the abuse. The focus is upon harm to the child, not upon parental or custodial blame-worthiness.").

[2]The statute also includes situations where the child has died as a result of the abuse. Because abuse is a civil proceeding concerned with the issue of the child's custody, rather than a criminal proceeding against the abuser, it is not readily apparent why the legislature included this category. The reason may be that an adjudication of abuse based on the death of one child may be evidence of the dependency of the child's siblings under RC 2151.04(D).

[3]Watts v. Cuyahoga County Welfare Dep't, No. 40584 (8th Dist. Ct. App., Cuyahoga, 6-12-80).

[4]See also Matter of Wilson Children, 1995 WL 156326 (Ohio Ct. App. 5th Dist. Stark County 1995); In re Schuerman, 74 Ohio App. 3d 528, 599 N.E.2d 728 (3d Dist. Paulding County 1991); Matter of Rogers, 1989 WL 98423 (Ohio Ct. App. 3d Dist. Putnam County 1989).

[5]Matter of Bretz, 1990 WL 210753 (Ohio Ct. App. 5th Dist. Holmes County 1990).

[6]Clark v. Clark, 114 Ohio App. 3d 558, 683 N.E.2d 800 (12th Dist. Butler County 1996).

[7]Matter of Jandrew, 1997 WL 802848 (Ohio Ct. App. 4th Dist. Washington County 1997); Matter of Bretz, 1990 WL 210753 (Ohio Ct. App. 5th Dist. Holmes County 1990).

[8]State v. Ivey, 98 Ohio App. 3d 249, 648 N.E.2d 519 (8th Dist. Cuyahoga County 1994).

[9]State v. Ivey, 98 Ohio App. 3d 249, 648 N.E.2d 519 (8th Dist. Cuyahoga County 1994).

[10]Clark v. Clark, 114 Ohio App. 3d 558, 683 N.E.2d 800 (12th Dist. Butler County 1996).

[11]Matter of Weeks, 1991 WL 12147 (Ohio Ct. App. 12th Dist. Clermont County 1991). Under an amendment to the neglect statute occurring subsequent to this decision, a parent's omission which leads to the child's injury would now constitute neglect under RC 2151.03(A)(6). See § 9:10, Neglect—Physical or mental injury due to omissions.

shaken the child, yet she did nothing to stop him. Finally, she continued to live with her husband, even after their criminal convictions, and to deceive the authorities as to the cause of the child's injuries.[12]

Mental injury. RC 2151.031(C) does not define the term "mental injury," nor does it specifically require parental fault as the cause for the mental injury. However, the term "mental injury" is defined in the definitional statute as "any behavioral, cognitive, emotional or mental disorder in a child caused by an act or omission that is described in section 2919.22 of the Revised Code and is committed by the parent or other person responsible for the child's care."[13]

§ 9:16 Abused child—Physical or mental injury due to parents

RC 2151.031(D) is the only provision which specifically requires a finding of fault on the part of the parent, guardian, or custodian in order to establish abuse. Prior to its enactment, cases coming within the purview of this provision were initiated under the neglect statute.[1]

In *In re Baby Boy Blackshear*,[2] the Ohio Supreme Court held that "[w]hen a newborn child's toxicology screen yields a positive result for an illegal drug due to prenatal maternal drug abuse, the newborn is, for purposes of R.C. 2151.031(D), per se an abused child." The mother had argued that because the definition of child did not include a fetus, there was no abuse. The Court reframed the issue and focused on the child's condition after birth: "It is clear, and there can be no doubt, that an alleged abused child, once born, falls under the jurisdiction of the appropriate juvenile court. R.C. 2151.23. It is clear that a child has legal and constitutional rights and that juvenile courts were created, in part, to protect those rights and to empower the state to provide for the care and protection of Ohio's children. It is clear that there can be no more sacred or precious right of a newborn infant than the right to life and to begin that life, where medically possible, healthy, and uninjured."[3]

§ 9:17 Abused child—Out-of-home abuse

RC 2151.031(E) covers situations in which a child is subjected to out-of-home care child abuse. The term "out-of-home care child abuse," defined in RC 2151.011(B)(24), includes various abusive actions committed by a person responsible for the care of a child in out-of-home care.[1]

Cross References
§ 1:4, § 10:4, § 10:5, § 14:16, § 30:2, § 30:10, § 30:11
Research References
Giannelli and Snyder, Baldwin's Ohio Practice, Evidence (2d ed.) §§ 501.8, 601.6, 803.8
Carlin, Baldwin's Ohio Practice, Merrick-Rippner Probate Law (6th ed.), Chs 98, 106

---

[12]Matter of Weeks, 1991 WL 12147 (Ohio Ct. App. 12th Dist. Clermont County 1991).
[13]RC 2151.011(B)(19).

[Section 9:16]
[1]RC 2151.03.
[2]In re Baby Boy Blackshear, 90 Ohio St. 3d 197, 2000-Ohio-173, 736 N.E.2d 462 (2000) (syllabus).
[3]In re Baby Boy Blackshear, 90 Ohio St. 3d 197, 200, 2000-Ohio-173, 736 N.E.2d 462 (2000).

[Section 9:17]
[1]For a discussion of a similar provision in the child neglect statute, RC 2151.03(A)(7), see § 9:11, Neglect—Out-of-home care neglect.

Chapter 10

Dependent Child Jurisdiction

> **KeyCite®:** Cases and other legal materials listed in KeyCite Scope can be researched through West's KeyCite service on Westlaw®. Use KeyCite to check citations for form, parallel references, prior and later history, and comprehensive citator information, including citations to other decisions and secondary materials.

§ 10:1 Dependent child jurisdiction—Introduction
§ 10:2 Dependent child defined
§ 10:3 Dependency—Homeless, destitute or without adequate care
§ 10:4 Dependency—Inadequate care due to parents' mental or physical condition
§ 10:5 Dependency—Detrimental condition or environment
§ 10:6 Dependency—Danger of abuse of neglect

§ 10:1 Dependent child jurisdiction—Introduction

This chapter discusses juvenile court jurisdiction for dependency cases. Neglect and abuse cases are treated separately in Chapter 8. Other chapters examine juvenile court jurisdiction for delinquency, juvenile traffic offense, and unruly cases. Additional related chapters include the adjudicatory hearing (Chapter 22) and neglect, abuse, and dependency dispositions (Chapter 29).

§ 10:2 Dependent child defined

A dependent child as defined in RC 2151.04 includes any child

(A) Who is homeless or destitute or without adequate parental care[1] through no fault of the child's parents, guardian, or custodian;

(B) Who lacks adequate parental care by reason of the mental or physical condition of the child's parents, guardian, or custodian;

(C) Whose condition or environment is such as to warrant the state, in the interests of the child, in assuming the child's guardianship;[2]

(D) To whom both of the following apply:

(1) The child is residing in a household in which a parent, guardian, custodian, or other member of the household committed an act that was the basis for an adjudication that a sibling of the child or any other child who resides in the household is an abused, neglected, or dependent child.

(2) Because of the circumstances surrounding the abuse, neglect, or dependency of the sibling or other child and the other conditions in the household of the child, the child is in danger of being abused or neglected by that parent, guardian, custodian, or member of the household.

Although it is possible for a child to be both neglected and dependent,[3]

[Section 10:2]

[1]The term "adequate parental care" is defined in RC 2151.011(B)(1).

[2]RC 2151.04(B) was held constitutional in In re Boyer, No. 34724 (8th Dist. Ct. App., Cuyahoga, 12-31-75). RC 2151.04(C) has also been found to be constitutional. See Johnson, 1982 WL 8498 (Ohio Ct. App. 1st Dist. Hamilton County 1982); In re Forille, No. L-81-164 (6th Dist. Ct. App., Lucas, 2-12-82).

[3]State v. Griffin, 93 Ohio App. 299, 51 Ohio Op. 47, 63 Ohio L. Abs. 122, 106 N.E.2d 668 (2d Dist. Champaign County 1952); In re Douglas, 11 Ohio Op. 2d 340, 82 Ohio L. Abs. 170, 164

there is a clear distinction between the two terms.[4] Whereas a neglected child lacks proper care because of the fault of a parent, guardian, or custodian,[5] the dependency case focuses instead on the condition or environment of the child.[6]

Despite this difference in focus, parental fault is sometimes present in dependency cases and many of the issues raised in neglect cases may be important in dependency proceedings since both involve a lack of proper care.[7]

§ 10:3 Dependency—Homeless, destitute or without adequate care

As the neglect cases demonstrate, as long as the child is receiving appropriate care, he will generally not be found to be neglected. The same principle holds true in dependency cases. Thus, dependency is not established where the facts show only that the child is illegitimate;[1] the child's parents are divorced;[2] the parents are illegally married;[3] the father has been incarcerated in the state penitentiary;[4] the mother is a minor and a ward of the welfare department;[5] or the unmarried mother is openly living with her boyfriend.[6] Although in any one of these instances it may be in the best interest of the child to live with someone other than his parent(s), a finding of dependency requires more.[7] The dependency statute must be read in pari materia with the purpose statute, RC 2151.01 of the Juvenile Code, and with

---

N.E.2d 475 (Juv. Ct. 1959); In re Owens, 1995 WL 617630 (Ohio Ct. App. 5th Dist. Stark County 1995).

[4]For dispositional purposes there is no difference (RC 2151.353).

[5]In re Riddle, 79 Ohio St. 3d 259, 1997-Ohio-391, 680 N.E.2d 1227 (1997); In re Kronjaeger, 166 Ohio St. 172, 1 Ohio Op. 2d 459, 140 N.E.2d 773 (1957); In re East, 32 Ohio Misc. 65, 61 Ohio Op. 2d 38, 61 Ohio Op. 2d 108, 288 N.E.2d 343 (C.P. 1972); In the Matter of Kuhn, 1982 WL 3392 (Ohio Ct. App. 4th Dist. Pickaway County 1982); Matter of Whiteman, 2 A.D.D. 386 (Ohio Ct. App. 6th Dist. Williams County 1993); In re Pieper Children, 74 Ohio App. 3d 714, 600 N.E.2d 317 (12th Dist. Preble County 1991).

[6]In re Riddle, 79 Ohio St. 3d 259, 1997-Ohio-391, 680 N.E.2d 1227 (1997); In re Bibb, 70 Ohio App. 2d 117, 24 Ohio Op. 3d 159, 435 N.E.2d 96 (1st Dist. Hamilton County 1980); In re Darst, 117 Ohio App. 374, 24 Ohio Op. 2d 144, 192 N.E.2d 287 (10th Dist. Franklin County 1963); In re East, 32 Ohio Misc. 65, 61 Ohio Op. 2d 38, 61 Ohio Op. 2d 108, 288 N.E.2d 343 (C.P. 1972); In re Thomas, Nos. 39494, 39495 (8th Dist. Ct. App., Cuyahoga, 7-19-79); In re Bishop, 36 Ohio App. 3d 123, 521 N.E.2d 838 (5th Dist. Ashland County 1987); In re Burchfield, 51 Ohio App. 3d 148, 555 N.E.2d 325 (4th Dist. Athens County 1988); Matter of Duncan, 1993 WL 257269 (Ohio Ct. App. 12th Dist. Preble County 1993); Matter of Whiteman, 2 A.D.D. 386 (Ohio Ct. App. 6th Dist. Williams County 1993); Matter of Kasler, 1991 WL 100360 (Ohio Ct. App. 4th Dist. Athens County 1991); In re Tikyra A., 103 Ohio App. 3d 452, 659 N.E.2d 867 (6th Dist. Huron County 1995); In Matter of Price, 1997 WL 126833 (Ohio Ct. App. 3d Dist. Marion County 1997).

[7]Although dependency complaints often refer to more than one section of RC 2151.04, each section will be considered separately for purposes of illustration.

[Section 10:3]

[1]In re Gutman, 22 Ohio App. 2d 125, 51 Ohio Op. 2d 252, 259 N.E.2d 128 (1st Dist. Hamilton County 1969) (complaint filed pursuant to RC 2151.04(C)); Smith v. Privette & State, 13 Ohio L. Abs. 291, 1932 WL 1836 (Ct. App. 2d Dist. Franklin County 1932). See also In re Hobson, 44 Ohio L. Abs. 85, 44 Ohio L. Abs. 86, 62 N.E.2d 510 (Ct. App. 2d Dist. [sic] Franklin County 1945).

[2]Sonnenberg v. State, 40 Ohio App. 475, 10 Ohio L. Abs. 271, 178 N.E. 855 (2d Dist. Franklin County 1931).

[3]In re Solarz, No. 42275 (8th Dist. Ct. App., Cuyahoga, 11-6-80).

[4]In the Matter Of: Wiseman, 1981 WL 6404 (Ohio Ct. App. 5th Dist. Licking County 1981); In re Konneker, 30 Ohio App. 502, 7 Ohio L. Abs. 137, 165 N.E. 850 (9th Dist. Summit County 1929).

[5]In re Williams, No. 37370 (8th Dist. Ct. App., Cuyahoga, 4-27-78).

[6]In re Burrell, 58 Ohio St. 2d 37, 12 Ohio Op. 3d 43, 388 N.E.2d 738 (1979).

[7]In re Burkhart, 15 Ohio Misc. 170, 44 Ohio Op. 2d 329, 239 N.E.2d 772 (Juv. Ct. 1968); In re H------, 24 Ohio Op. 2d 334, 92 Ohio L. Abs. 436, 192 N.E.2d 683 (Juv. Ct. 1963); Ludy v. Ludy, 84 Ohio App. 195, 39 Ohio Op. 241, 53 Ohio L. Abs. 47, 82 N.E.2d 775 (2d Dist. Franklin

caselaw, both of which give parents the paramount right to custody unless there is a substantial threat of harm to the child's physical or mental health.[8]

Neglect cases compared. Many cases processed under RC 2151.04(A) resemble neglect cases in that parental fault is established. Courts have found dependency where the evidence showed that the mother's home was filthy and chaotic;[9] that the mother was an alcoholic who ignored her child's needs in favor of her abusive husband;[10] and that the father was irresponsible and a drug user.[11] In *In re Feldman*,[12] in which the record showed that the children had an irregular school attendance pattern, that the eight-year-old girl frequently slept in the same bed with her father, that the father had encouraged her and her 10-year-old brother to keep late hours, that the children were exposed to sexually suggestive materials and were told the details of the rape-murder of their cousin, and that the children frequently administered nonprescription drugs to their father, the children were found to be dependent.

It appears that many dependency cases would more properly fit within the "neglect" statute. As with neglect cases, many dependency cases focus on the lifestyles of the parents. Thus, marital discord,[13] a mother's sexual promiscuity,[14] and adultery[15] have been cited as factors in establishing dependency.

Lack of child-rearing skills. Dependency cases often rely on youthfulness, immaturity, and lack of child-rearing skills on the part of the parents to establish a lack of proper care.[16] Children have been adjudged dependent in cases in which the job and family services department attempted to provide training and counseling to the mother, who greeted these attempts with hostility, indifference, or a lack of motivation, and learned little if anything about raising a child.[17] A child may also be adjudged dependent when his mother is a high school student, desirous of completing school, unemployed, and living in a home with domestic problems.[18] A nine-month-old child with a 17-year-old mother was found to be dependent where the evidence showed that the child had severe burns on the buttocks, back, and hand, had suffered numerous injuries to her eyes and mouth, was underweight, and where the father was insensitive to the child's critical needs.[19]

Financial status. Financial instability on the part of the parents in combination with other factors often may be sufficient to establish dependency. Thus, where a child's 16-year-old mother wished to surrender temporary custody to a children's services agency, and the child's 18-year-old father sought custody for himself, the fact that he was almost destitute and was receiving only minimal wages as a probationary employee was considered

---

County 1948); In re Hayes, 62 Ohio App. 289, 16 Ohio Op. 10, 30 Ohio L. Abs. 568, 23 N.E.2d 956 (2d Dist. Franklin County 1939).

[8]In re Zerick, 57 Ohio Op. 331, 74 Ohio L. Abs. 525, 129 N.E.2d 661 (Juv. Ct. 1955).

[9]In the Matter Hawkins, 1981 WL 6687 (Ohio Ct. App. 3d Dist. Marion County 1981) (child also found neglected).

[10]In re Sullivan, Nos. 79 AP-893, 79 AP-894 (10th Dist. Ct. App., Franklin, 12-16-80).

[11]In re Hyrb, No. 36910 (8th Dist. Ct. App., Cuyahoga, 12-1-77).

[12]In re Feldman, No. 34223 (8th Dist. Ct. App., Cuyahoga, 12-23-75).

[13]In Matter of Parker, 1981 WL 6774 (Ohio Ct. App. 3d Dist. Van Wert County 1981).

[14]In re Bowman, No. 79AP-798 (10th Dist. Ct. App., Franklin, 6-26-80); In re East, 32 Ohio Misc. 65, 61 Ohio Op. 2d 38, 61 Ohio Op. 2d 108, 288 N.E.2d 343 (C.P. 1972).

[15]In re Turner, 12 Ohio Misc. 171, 41 Ohio Op. 2d 264, 231 N.E.2d 502 (C.P. 1967).

[16]Such cases are processed under RC 2151.04(C). See § 10:5, Dependency—Detrimental condition or environment.

[17]E.g., In re Bowman, No. 79AP-798 (10th Dist. Ct. App., Franklin, 6-26-80); In re Philpott, No. 41186 (8th Dist. Ct. App., Cuyahoga, 6-5-80); In re Heightland, No. 989 (4th Dist. Ct. App., Athens, 2-18-80); In re Feiler, No. C-780549 (1st Dist. Ct. App., Hamilton, 10-17-79).

[18]In re Trizzino, No. 40982 (8th Dist. Ct. App., Cuyahoga, 1-31-80).

[19]In re Holcomb, No. 39694 (8th Dist. Ct. App., Cuyahoga, 10-4-79) (Complaint based also on RC 2151.04(A). It appears that the child would also be neglected and abused.).

relevant by the court finding the child dependent.[20]

Illegitimacy. Although illegitimacy alone is insufficient to establish dependency, where a mother has four illegitimate children who are supported by public funds, the children may be dependent.[21] However, the dependency statute does not require that the source of support for the child in question be the parents' own income. As long as the parents are able to provide proper care, even if that entails obtaining financial assistance from the child's paternal grandfather, the child is not dependent.[22]

Homeless. The fact that a child is being cared for by relatives is immaterial to the determination of dependency, as long as the relatives are meeting the obligations of care, support, and custody which are owed to a child by his parents.[23] Under such circumstances the child is not "homeless," as defined by RC 2151.04(A), even if the child's parents are deceased[24] or otherwise unable to provide suitable care. In approving the rationale of these cases, the Ohio Supreme Court observed, "Given that fault (parental or otherwise) is not an issue in a R.C. 2151.04(A) dependency inquiry, so that the focus is exclusively on the child's situation, a child who is receiving proper care pursuant to an arrangement initiated by the parent with a caregiver is not a dependent child under R.C. 2151.04(A)."[25] However, where the mother was unable to care for her child and the grandparents were elderly and had not cared for any children in 22 years, the child was dependent despite the grandparents' willingness to care for her.[26] The mere allegation that a relative may be willing and able to care for a child, with no evidence of ability, is insufficient in challenging a dependency complaint.[27] Furthermore, where a child is being cared for by a nonparent pursuant to a court order, rather than at the parent's request, the parent's lack of interest in assuming responsibility for the child is a factor in determining dependency.[28]

§ 10:4 Dependency—Inadequate care due to parents' mental or physical condition

Mental condition. A substantial number of dependency complaints are filed under RC 2151.04(B) based on the mental condition of the child's parent(s). In such cases it must be proven that, as a result of the parent's condition, the child lacks proper care. Mental condition by itself, however, is

---

[20]In re McCarthy, No. 38243 (8th Dist. Ct. App., Cuyahoga, 4-20-78). See also Grubbs, 1982 WL 5285 (Ohio Ct. App. 8th Dist. Cuyahoga County 1982), in which the trial court's dismissal of a dependency complaint filed under RC 2151.04(C) was reversed in part because of the father's past failure to support the child.

[21]In re Dake, 87 Ohio L. Abs. 483, 180 N.E.2d 646 (Juv. Ct. 1961). See also In re McCall, No. 42420 (8th Dist. Ct. App., Cuyahoga, 3-5-81).

[22]In re Solarz, No. 42275 (8th Dist. Ct. App., Cuyahoga, 11-6-80).

[23]In re Darst, 117 Ohio App. 374, 24 Ohio Op. 2d 144, 192 N.E.2d 287 (10th Dist. Franklin County 1963); In the Matter Of: Crisp, 1981 WL 2983 (Ohio Ct. App. 10th Dist. Franklin County 1981); In Matter Of: Escue, 1981 WL 5930 (Ohio Ct. App. 4th Dist. Lawrence County 1981); In re Tikyra A., 103 Ohio App. 3d 452, 659 N.E.2d 867 (6th Dist. Huron County 1995); In re Collins, 1995 WL 688792 (Ohio Ct. App. 9th Dist. Summit County 1995).

[24]Dillon, 1981 WL 2676 (Ohio Ct. App. 4th Dist. Lawrence County 1981).

[25]In re Riddle, 79 Ohio St. 3d 259, 1997-Ohio-391, 680 N.E.2d 1227 (1997).

[26]In re Howell, No. 79-CA-16 (5th Dist. Ct. App., Coshocton, 1-31-80).

[27]In re McCarthy, No. 38243 (8th Dist. Ct. App., Cuyahoga, 4-20-78); Grubbs, 1982 WL 5285 (Ohio Ct. App. 8th Dist. Cuyahoga County 1982).

[28]In re Lee, No. CA-2856 (5th Dist. Ct. App., Licking, 11-1-82); Matter of Poth, 1982 WL 9371 (Ohio Ct. App. 6th Dist. Huron County 1982). See also In re Riddle, 79 Ohio St. 3d 259, 1997-Ohio-391, 680 N.E.2d 1227 (1997).

insufficient to establish dependency.[1]

In *In re McCall*,[2] where a mother had been an in-patient at a mental health center, had no relatives able to care for her child, and was still not stable enough to assume parental responsibility after her release, the child was found to be dependent.[3] In *In re Feke*[4] a court of appeals upheld a dependency adjudication where the father had been hospitalized several times with psychological problems and did not have a realistic view of the world, where the mother and both grandmothers were unable to provide a stable environment for the child, and where the child was vehement in his desire to continue to reside in a foster home.[5] In a third case, *In re Hadsell*,[6] a mother's history of mental illness and unwillingness to seek counseling and the father's past criminal record and current drug usage supported a finding that their children were dependent. Moreover, a child was correctly determined to be dependent where the mother's mental illness, her repeated hospitalizations on account of such illness, and her persistent refusal to follow prescribed drug therapy interfered with her ability to provide proper care and support for the child.[7]

In contrast, a finding of dependency was reversed in *In re Bibb*,[8] where the record showed that the mother had been frequently hospitalized for depression but had always made proper arrangements for the care of her children at these times.

Physical condition. Although the "mental condition of parents" provision of RC 2151.04(B) is often used to establish dependency, courts are more reluctant to base a finding of dependency on the "physical condition" of parents. Thus, where a mother who had multiple sclerosis had done an excellent job of raising her child, the court's anticipation of future problems could not justify a dependency adjudication.[9] However, evidence that a mother was a diabetic and had had numerous hypoglycemic reactions, that her child would have to take care of her, and that his grades had suffered was held sufficient to establish dependency.[10]

§ 10:5 Dependency—Detrimental condition or environment

Finding a child dependent under RC 2151.04(C) depends on whether the child is receiving proper care and support.[1] Therefore, the determination must be based on the child's condition, not on the parents' deficiencies.[2]

Newborns. Where it is believed that a newborn infant may be dependent,

---

[Section 10:4]

[1]In re H------, 24 Ohio Op. 2d 334, 92 Ohio L. Abs. 436, 192 N.E.2d 683 (Juv. Ct. 1963); Matter of Kasler, 1991 WL 100360 (Ohio Ct. App. 4th Dist. Athens County 1991).

[2]In re McCall, No. 42420 (8th Dist. Ct. App., Cuyahoga, 3-5-81).

[3]See also In re Kemp, No. 41320 (8th Dist. Ct. App., Cuyahoga, 6-26-80); In re Philpott, No. 41186 (8th Dist. Ct. App., Cuyahoga, 6-5-80).

[4]In re Feke, No. 42242 (8th Dist. Ct. App., Cuyahoga, 3-12-81).

[5]See also In re Justice, 59 Ohio App. 2d 78, 13 Ohio Op. 3d 139, 392 N.E.2d 897 (1st Dist. Clinton County 1978), which recognized that the potential harm to a child which might result from his separation from his foster parents is a factor supporting a dependency adjudication.

[6]In re Hadsell, No. 41004 (8th Dist. Ct. App., Cuyahoga, 6-19-80).

[7]In re Brown, 60 Ohio App. 3d 136, 573 N.E.2d 1217 (1st Dist. Hamilton County 1989).

[8]In re Bibb, 70 Ohio App. 2d 117, 24 Ohio Op. 3d 159, 435 N.E.2d 96 (1st Dist. Hamilton County 1980).

[9]Matter of Livingston, 1981 WL 2722 (Ohio Ct. App. 2d Dist. Clark County 1981).

[10]In re Ward, 75 Ohio App. 3d 377, 599 N.E.2d 431 (3d Dist. Defiance County 1992).

[Section 10:5]

[1]In re Brodbeck, 97 Ohio App. 3d 652, 647 N.E.2d 240 (3d Dist. Mercer County 1994).

[2]In re Brodbeck, 97 Ohio App. 3d 652, 647 N.E.2d 240 (3d Dist. Mercer County 1994).

a complaint is usually filed under RC 2151.04(C).[3] Even though the mother may never have had physical custody of the child, the determination of dependency under this section is based on what the child's "condition or environment" would be if the child were returned to the mother.[4] As one court has stated, "A juvenile court should not be forced to experiment with the health and safety of a newborn baby where the state can show, by clear and convincing evidence, that placing the child in such an environment would be threatening to the health and safety of the child."[5] Often these cases involve the child of an unmarried female[6] who is financially and emotionally unable to care for the child and who may have made plans for the baby's adoption but then changed her mind.[7]

In some cases, the objectionable nature of the "condition or environment" may be based in part on the fact that the mother herself is a ward of a county job and family services department.[8] However, this fact alone will not conclusively establish dependency if the mother is able to provide proper care for the child.[9]

Financial status. A mother's poverty by itself does not support a finding of dependency.[10] Such a finding must be based on the living conditions, such as evidence indicating that a large pool of sewage was located underneath her trailer, trash was piled up around the trailer, unprotected wiring was hanging at a level easily accessible to her child, and that the parents disregarded offers of assistance and recommendations to improve the conditions.[11]

Examples. Other circumstances which have led to a finding of dependency include an unmarried mother's adjudication for the commission of a delinquent-felony leading to her institutionalization, where the child's father is married and the mother's family is unstable;[12] a mother's cocaine addiction and inability to care for her child, her act of voluntarily surrendering custody to her mother, and the maternal grandmother's inability or unwillingness to

---

[3]This provision has been held to be not unconstitutionally vague. In re Barzak, 24 Ohio App. 3d 180, 493 N.E.2d 1011 (11th Dist. Trumbull County 1985).

[4]In re Campbell, 13 Ohio App. 3d 34, 468 N.E.2d 93 (12th Dist. Butler County 1983); Matter of Luke, 1984 WL 2667 (Ohio Ct. App. 5th Dist. Coshocton County 1984); In the Matter of Price, 1981 WL 4645 (Ohio Ct. App. 8th Dist. Cuyahoga County 1981); In re East, 32 Ohio Misc. 65, 61 Ohio Op. 2d 38, 61 Ohio Op. 2d 108, 288 N.E.2d 343 (C.P. 1972); In re Turner, 12 Ohio Misc. 171, 41 Ohio Op. 2d 264, 231 N.E.2d 502 (C.P. 1967); Bryant, 1982 WL 6001 (Ohio Ct. App. 12th Dist. Butler County 1982); In re Bishop, 36 Ohio App. 3d 123, 521 N.E.2d 838 (5th Dist. Ashland County 1987); Matter of Likens, 1986 WL 11910 (Ohio Ct. App. 2d Dist. Greene County 1986); In re Ruiz, 27 Ohio Misc. 2d 31, 500 N.E.2d 935 (C.P. 1986); In re Massengill, 76 Ohio App. 3d 220, 601 N.E.2d 206 (6th Dist. Lucas County 1991); In re Justice, 59 Ohio App. 2d 78, 13 Ohio Op. 3d 139, 392 N.E.2d 897 (1st Dist. Clinton County 1978); Matter of Kasler, 1991 WL 100360 (Ohio Ct. App. 4th Dist. Athens County 1991); Matter of Patterson, 1990 WL 41693 (Ohio Ct. App. 5th Dist. Coshocton County 1990); In re Pieper Children, 85 Ohio App. 3d 318, 619 N.E.2d 1059 (12th Dist. Preble County 1993); Mary Beth v. Howard, 1995 WL 601110 (Ohio Ct. App. 8th Dist. Cuyahoga County 1995).

[5]In re Collins, 1995 WL 688792 (Ohio Ct. App. 9th Dist. Summit County 1995).

[6]However, illegitimacy of the child, in itself, will not support a dependency adjudication. In re Gutman, 22 Ohio App. 2d 125, 51 Ohio Op. 2d 252, 259 N.E.2d 128 (1st Dist. Hamilton County 1969).

[7]E.g., In re Ware, No. 40983 (8th Dist. Ct. App., Cuyahoga, 7-17-80); In re Baby Girl S., 32 Ohio Misc. 217, 61 Ohio Op. 2d 439, 290 N.E.2d 925 (C.P. 1972).

[8]In re Williams, No. 37370 (8th Dist. Ct. App., Cuyahoga, 4-27-78) (adjudication also based on RC 2151.04(A)); In re Turner, 12 Ohio Misc. 171, 41 Ohio Op. 2d 264, 231 N.E.2d 502 (C.P. 1967).

[9]In re Williams, No. 37370 (8th Dist. Ct. App., Cuyahoga, 4-27-78).

[10]In re Brodbeck, 97 Ohio App. 3d 652, 647 N.E.2d 240 (3d Dist. Mercer County 1994).

[11]In re Brodbeck, 97 Ohio App. 3d 652, 647 N.E.2d 240 (3d Dist. Mercer County 1994).

[12]In re Turner, 12 Ohio Misc. 171, 41 Ohio Op. 2d 264, 231 N.E.2d 502 (C.P. 1967).

care for the child;[13] an unmarried father's involvement in criminal conduct and past failure to support or visit the child, where the mother is not interested in custody;[14] the refusal of parents, for religious reasons, to allow further medical treatment of their child suffering from a life-threatening illness;[15] a juvenile's refusal to accept necessary medical treatment for gonorrhea on the basis of his religious beliefs;[16] and a father's method of administering corporal punishment and the evidence of prior injury to the child.[17]

Evidence which shows that returning a child to his natural parent would be detrimental to him establishes dependency under RC 2151.04(C) even though the parent is capable of giving proper care and support to other children.[18] For example, harm that would result from removing a child from a foster home is a factor which would support a finding of dependency.[19]

An appellate court reversed a trial court's adjudication of dependency where the facts showed that the child lived with his father and his father's girlfriend in a residence found to be dirty and in disarray; where the child was exposed to nude photographs of his father's girlfriend, with whom he did not get along; and where the child feared his father, who had dressed in women's clothes.[20] The evidence was insufficient to sustain a finding of dependency since there was no evidence of any ill effects on the child, other than his unhappiness.

Another appellate court found that although mother admitted smoking marijuana, without evidence that her use negatively affects her care or supervision of the children, there is not clear and convincing evidence of dependency.[21]

§10:6 Dependency—Danger of abuse of neglect

The most recently enacted category of dependency includes circumstances in which a child resides in a household in which a parent, guardian, custodian, or other household member committed an act that was the basis for an abuse, neglect, or dependency adjudication involving a sibling of the child or any other child residing in the household, and in which the circumstances surrounding such abuse, neglect, or dependency and the other conditions in the household indicate that the child is in danger of being abused or neglected.[1] Prior to this enactment, these types of cases were initiated under the "condition or environment" provisions of the dependency statute.[2]

RC 2151.04(D) requires that an adjudication of abuse, neglect, or dependency of the sibling or other child is a condition precedent to the filing

---

[13]In re Massengill, 76 Ohio App. 3d 220, 601 N.E.2d 206 (6th Dist. Lucas County 1991).

[14]In re McCarthy, No. 38243 (8th Dist. Ct. App., Cuyahoga, 4-20-78). See also In re Infant Female Luallen, 27 Ohio App. 3d 29, 499 N.E.2d 358 (1st Dist. Hamilton County 1985).

[15]In re Willmann, 24 Ohio App. 3d 191, 493 N.E.2d 1380 (1st Dist. Hamilton County 1986). See In Matter of Stewart, 1996 WL 703406 (Ohio Ct. App. 11th Dist. Portage County 1996).

[16]In re J.J., 64 Ohio App. 3d 806, 582 N.E.2d 1138 (12th Dist. Butler County 1990).

[17]Matter of Jandrew, 1997 WL 802848 (Ohio Ct. App. 4th Dist. Washington County 1997).

[18]In re Justice, 59 Ohio App. 2d 78, 13 Ohio Op. 3d 139, 392 N.E.2d 897 (1st Dist. Clinton County 1978); Matter of Patterson, 1990 WL 41693 (Ohio Ct. App. 5th Dist. Coshocton County 1990).

[19]In re Justice, 59 Ohio App. 2d 78, 13 Ohio Op. 3d 139, 392 N.E.2d 897 (1st Dist. Clinton County 1978); Matter of Patterson, 1990 WL 41693 (Ohio Ct. App. 5th Dist. Coshocton County 1990).

[20]Matter of Sweat, 1987 WL 13054 (Ohio Ct. App. 12th Dist. Warren County 1987).

[21]In re RS, 2003-Ohio-1594, 2003 WL 1689595 (Ohio Ct. App. 9th Dist. Summit County 2003).

[Section 10:6]
[1]RC 2151.04(D), enacted by 1988 S.B. 89, eff. 1-1-89, amended by 1996 H.B. 274, eff. 8-8-96. See In re Overbay, 1997 WL 89160 (Ohio Ct. App. 12th Dist. Butler County 1997).

[2]RC 2151.04(C).

of a dependency complaint concerning the child.[3]

The test to be applied in RC 2151.04(D) proceedings "is not one of finding instances of past abuse of the allegedly dependent child, but one of the danger of prospective punishment of that child rising to the level of abuse to be drawn from the circumstances surrounding the prior abuse of another child in that environment."[4] In addition, a finding of dependency was supported where the abusive and neglectful parent would be residing in the home with the children he had previously abused and neglected, thereby placing these children in danger of being abused and neglected again.[5]

Cross References
§§ 9:3 to 9:11, § 14:16
Research References
Carlin, Baldwin's Ohio Practice, Merrick-Rippner Probate Law (6th ed.), Ch 106

---

[3]See In Matter of Surfer, 1998 WL 231012 (Ohio Ct. App. 10th Dist. Franklin County 1998); In re Darling, 2003-Ohio-7184, 2003 WL 23094930 (Ohio Ct. App. 9th Dist. Wayne County 2003).

[4]In re Schuerman, 74 Ohio App. 3d 528, 534, 599 N.E.2d 728 (3d Dist. Paulding County 1991). Another appellate court, in dicta, surmised that the abuse of a sibling may establish a rebuttable presumption that the subject child is dependent. In re Stevens, 1993 WL 265130 (Ohio Ct. App. 2d Dist. Montgomery County 1993); In re Rivas, 2002-Ohio-3747, 2002 WL 1626663 (Ohio Ct. App. 9th Dist. Lorain County 2002).

[5]In re Pieper Children, 85 Ohio App. 3d 318, 619 N.E.2d 1059 (12th Dist. Preble County 1993).

Chapter 11
Temporary & Permanent Custody Agreements

> **KeyCite®:** Cases and other legal materials listed in KeyCite Scope can be researched through West's KeyCite service on Westlaw®. Use KeyCite to check citations for form, parallel references, prior and later history, and comprehensive citator information, including citations to other decisions and secondary materials.

§ 11:1   Temporary & permanent custody agreements—Introduction
§ 11:2   Jurisdiction for custody agreements
§ 11:3   Temporary custody agreements
§ 11:4   Extension of temporary custody agreements
§ 11:5   Permanent custody agreements
§ 11:6   Parental revocation of permanent surrender

§ 11:1   Temporary & permanent custody agreements—Introduction

This chapter discusses juvenile court jurisdiction over agreements for temporary and permanent custody that are initiated by public or private agencies.

§ 11:2   Jurisdiction for custody agreements

In addition to the juvenile courts' authority to commit neglected, dependent, abused,[1] delinquent,[2] and unruly[3] children to the custody of a public children services agency or private child-placing agency, such courts have jurisdiction to hear and determine requests for the extension of temporary custody agreements and requests for court approval of permanent custody agreements.[4]

§ 11:3   Temporary custody agreements

The parents, guardian, or custodian of a child may enter into an agreement with such public or private agency for placement of the child in the temporary custody of the agency for up to 30 days without court approval; and up to 60 days without court approval if the agreement is executed solely for the purpose of obtaining the adoption of a child who is less than six months of age.[1]

§ 11:4   Extension of temporary custody agreements

The agency may request the juvenile court of the county in which the child

---

[Section 11:2]
   [1]RC 2151.353(A). See Abused, Neglected, or Dependent Child Dispositions Ch 30.

   [2]RC 2151.355(A). See Delinquent Child Dispositions Ch 27.

   [3]RC 2151.354(A). See Unruly Child Dispositions Ch 29.

   [4]RC 2151.23(A)(8). See also Juv. R. 2(C) (defining temporary custody agreement); Juv. R. 2(AA) (defining permanent surrender).

[Section 11:3]
   [1]RC 5103.15(A)(1); Juv. R. 38(A)(1).

has a residence or legal settlement[1] to extend the agreement for up to two 30-day periods.[2] When it files the request for an extension, the agency must file an original case plan or an updated version of the case plan.[3] The juvenile court may grant the requested extension if it finds that such action would be in the child's best interest. At the expiration of the period of extension, the agency must either return the child to his parents, guardian, or custodian, or file a complaint requesting temporary or permanent custody of the child.[4]

§ 11:5 Permanent custody agreements

In addition, the parents, guardian, or custodian of a child may enter into an agreement with such public or private agency surrendering the permanent custody of the child to the agency. All such agreements require juvenile court approval, except that an agreement with a private child-placing agency does not require court approval if the agreement is executed solely for the purpose of obtaining an adoption of a child who is less than six months of age on the date the agreement is executed.[1] When a request for approval of a permanent surrender agreement is filed, the juvenile court must determine whether the agreement is in the child's best interest and may approve the agreement if it is.[2]

§ 11:6 Parental revocation of permanent surrender

A proceeding to procure the consent of the juvenile court is not an adversary proceeding. The juvenile court's function in consenting to a voluntary surrender is to insure that the surrender is made by the parent voluntarily, with full knowledge of the legal import of the relinquishment of parental rights and to insure that the child welfare agency does not enter into improvident contracts.[1]

If a public agency subjects a single, minor mother unrepresented by counsel to undue influence that results in her signing a permanent surrender agreement, the consent is invalid and the mother retains custody.[2]

An agreement by a parent with the county board or job and family services department for permanent surrender of a child prior to consent of the juvenile court is not only revocable by the parent prior to consent of the juvenile court, but such parental revocation operates to dissolve the offer to sur-

---

[Section 11:4]

[1]Although the term "legal settlement" is not defined in the juvenile law, the term has been used in other areas of the law as the equivalent of "residence." See 1943 OAG 473.

[2]RC 5103.15(A)(2); Juv. R. 38(A)(1). If the agreement was made to obtain the adoption of a child under the age of six months, only one 30-day extension is permitted. RC 5103.15(A)(3); Juv. R. 38(A)(2).

[3]RC 5103.15(A)(2); Juv. R. 38(A)(2). See RC 2151.412; Dispositional Case Plans Ch 26.

[4]RC 5103.15(A)(2), RC 5103.15(A)(3); Juv. R. 38(A)(2). Presumably, pending hearing on the complaint, the child must be returned to his parent, guardian, or custodian unless the agency is granted temporary custody pending hearing. See § 30:4, Dispositional alternatives for abuse, neglect, or dependency.

[Section 11:5]

[1]RC 5103.15(B)(1); Juv. R. 38(B)(1), (2).

[2]RC 5103.15(B)(2); Juv. R. 38(B)(1). See § 33:11, Child custody agency commitment—Juvenile court dispositional review, for discussion of annual review requirements.

[Section 11:6]

[1]In re Plumley, 2004-Ohio-1161, 2004 WL 458310 (Ohio Ct. App. 11th Dist. Portage County 2004); In re Dunn, 102 Ohio App. 3d 217, 656 N.E.2d 1341 (3d Dist. Marion County 1995); In re Miller, 61 Ohio St. 2d 184, 15 Ohio Op. 3d 211, 399 N.E.2d 1262 (1980); In re K., 31 Ohio Misc. 218, 60 Ohio Op. 2d 134, 60 Ohio Op. 2d 388, 282 N.E.2d 370 (Juv. Ct. 1969).

[2]Marich v. Knox County Dept. of Human Services/Children Services Unit, 45 Ohio St. 3d 163, 543 N.E.2d 776 (1989).

render, and the public agency's continued retention of the child and refusal to return the child to the parent is illegal and gives rise to an action in habeas corpus.[3]

Cross References
Ch 27, Ch 29, Ch 30, § 33:11

[3]Angle v. Children's Services Division, Holmes County Welfare Dept., 63 Ohio St. 2d 227, 17 Ohio Op. 3d 140, 407 N.E.2d 524 (1980).

Chapter 12

Parental Notification of Abortion

> **KeyCite®:** Cases and other legal materials listed in KeyCite Scope can be researched through West's KeyCite service on Westlaw®. Use KeyCite to check citations for form, parallel references, prior and later history, and comprehensive citator information, including citations to other decisions and secondary materials.

§ 12:1   Parental notification of abortion—Introduction
§ 12:2   Jurisdictional requirements
§ 12:3   Complaint
§ 12:4   Attorney & guardian ad litem
§ 12:5   Venue
§ 12:6   Summons
§ 12:7   Scheduling the hearing
§ 12:8   Hearing
§ 12:9   Case law
§ 12:10 Appeals

§ 12:1   Parental notification of abortion—Introduction

This chapter discusses the jurisdiction of the juvenile court to hear complaints filed by pregnant, unmarried, unemancipated minor females who wish to have an abortion without parental notification. All procedural requirements, including the filing of appeals, are considered in this chapter.

§ 12:2   Jurisdictional requirements

RC 2151.85[1] provides the juvenile court with jurisdiction over certain issues dealing with abortion.[2] A pregnant, unmarried, unemancipated[3] minor female desiring an abortion without parental notification may file a complaint in juvenile court requesting authorization for her to consent to the abortion without such notification. The judge may grant the authorization if

---

[Section 12:2]

[1]The statute was found unconstitutional on several grounds in Akron Center for Reproductive Health v. Rosen, 633 F. Supp. 1123 (N.D. Ohio 1986); Akron Center for Reproductive Health v. Slaby, 854 F.2d 852 (6th Cir. 1988). However, the United States Supreme Court reversed the lower court decisions, upholding the constitutionality of the statute in Ohio v. Akron Center for Reproductive Health, 497 U.S. 502, 110 S. Ct. 2972, 111 L. Ed. 2d 405 (1990). See also Lambert v. Wicklund, 520 U.S. 292, 117 S. Ct. 1169, 137 L. Ed. 2d 464 (1997).

For comparison to other states, see generally, Planned Parenthood of Northern New England v. Heed, 296 F. Supp. 2d 59, 2003 DNH 222 (D.N.H. 2003); In re B.S., 205 Ariz. 611, 74 P.3d 285 (Ct. App. Div. 1 2003); In the Matter of Anonymous, 2003 WL 23325701 (Ala. Ct. Civil App.). See also Dick, Constitutional Law: Reaffirming Every Floridian's Broad and Fundamental Right of Privacy, 56 Fla. L. Rev. 447 (2004); Hubbard, *In Re T.W.*: Are the Privacy Rights of Florida's Female Pregnant Minors Limitless?, 4 Fla. Coastal L.J. 237 (2003); Kramer, Minors Have Rights, Too: The Supreme Court of New Jersey Protects the Fundamental Right of All Women to Chose an Abortion in *Planned Parenthood v. Farmer*, 11 Widener J. Pub. L. 515 (2002).

[2]The general juvenile court jurisdictional statute, RC 2151.23, contains no reference to the court's jurisdiction over the RC 2151.85 abortion issues.

[3]The term "unemancipated" is defined in RC 2151.85(I). Otherwise, Ohio does not statutorily recognize the emancipation of minors.

there is a finding that the child is sufficiently mature and well enough informed to make the decision on her own, or that she is a victim of parental abuse, or that notification is not in her best interests.[4] Alternatively, the requisite notification may be given to a specified adult brother or sister, stepparent, or grandparent if the minor female and specified relatives file affidavits in the juvenile court stating that the minor female is in fear of parental abuse, and that this fear is based on a pattern of abuse.[5]

§ 12:3 Complaint

A minor female's complaint for abortion must be made under oath and must include (1) a statement that the complainant is pregnant, unmarried, under 18 years of age, and unemancipated; (2) a statement that she wishes to have an abortion without the notification of her parents, guardian, or custodian; (3) an allegation of either or both of the following: (a) that she is sufficiently mature and well informed to intelligently decide whether to have an abortion without the notification of her parents, guardian, or custodian; (b) that one or both of her parents, her guardian, or custodian was engaged in a pattern of physical, sexual, or emotional abuse against her or that the notification otherwise is not in her best interests; and (4) a statement as to whether the complainant has retained an attorney and, if so, the name, address, and telephone number of her attorney.[1]

Rule 23(A) of the Rules of Superintendence for the Courts of Ohio provides that all actions pursuant to RC 2151.85 shall be commenced by filing a complaint on a form issued by the clerk of the Supreme Court of Ohio.[2] A certified copy of the second page, with the case number noted on it, shall be given to the complainant after she signs it. The original second page shall be removed from the file jacket and filed under seal in a safe or other secure place where access is limited to essential court personnel.[3]

Minors seeking to file an action under RC 2151.85 must be given prompt assistance by the clerk in a private, confidential setting. Assistance shall include performing the notary services necessary to file the complaint. The complaint shall be filed promptly upon the request of the minor, without cost to the minor.[4]

§ 12:4 Attorney & guardian ad litem

Upon the filing of the complaint, the court must appoint an attorney to represent the minor female, at no cost to her, if she is not already represented by an attorney.[1] In addition, the court must appoint a guardian ad litem to protect the interests of the minor female, without expense to her. The court may appoint the same person to serve as both the attorney and the guardian ad litem.[2]

---

[4]RC 2151.85(C). See also RC 2919.121(C), a criminal statute governing unlawful abortions, which in some respects conflicts with RC 2151.85 concerning a minor's right to consent to an abortion. See also Storrow and Martinez, "Special Weight" for Best-Interests Minors in the New Era of Parental Autonomy, 2003 Wis. L. Rev. 789.

[5]RC 2919.12(B)(1)(b); see Sup. R. 24.

[Section 12:3]

[1]RC 2151.85(A).

[2]See also RC 2151.85(G).

[3]Sup. R. 23(A).

[4]Sup. R. 23(A).

[Section 12:4]

[1]RC 2151.85(B)(2); Sup. R. 23(B).

[2]RC 2151.85(B)(2); Sup. R. 23(C); In re Jane Doe 01-01, 141 Ohio App. 3d 20, 26, 749 N.E.2d 807 (8th Dist. Cuyahoga County 2001) (McMonagle, J., dissenting).

§ 12:5 Venue

In proceedings in which a pregnant, unmarried, unemancipated female under the age of 18 is requesting an order authorizing her to consent to an abortion without parental notification,[1] the venue provisions are much more liberal than in other juvenile court proceedings. In such cases venue lies in the county in which the minor female has a residence or legal settlement, in any county that borders, to any extent, the county in which she has a residence or legal settlement, or in the county in which the hospital, clinic, or other facility in which the abortion would be performed or induced is located.[2]

§ 12:6 Summons

Unlike all other juvenile court proceedings, in proceedings in which a pregnant, unmarried, unemancipated female under the age of 18 is requesting an order authorizing her to consent to an abortion without parental notification,[1] the court must not notify the child's parents, guardian, or custodian that she is pregnant or that she wants to have an abortion.[2]

The Juvenile Rules do not apply "[i]n proceedings under section 2151.85 of the Revised Code to the extent that there is a conflict between these rules and section 2151.85 of the Revised Code."[3] As a result, the notice provisions of RC 2151.85(D) would apply to RC 2151.85 proceedings, and notice must not be provided to the child's parents.

§ 12:7 Scheduling the hearing

The court must conduct a hearing promptly after the filing of the complaint, if possible within 24 hours,[1] but not later than the fifth business day after the day that the complaint is filed.[2] The court must accommodate school hours if at all possible.[3]

If the hearing is not held by the fifth day, such failure shall be considered to be a constructive court order authorizing the minor female to consent to the abortion without parental notification, and the constructive order may be relied upon to the same extent as if the court actually had issued an order.[4]

§ 12:8 Hearing

The hearing on a minor female's complaint for authorization to consent to an abortion without parental notification must be conducted by a judge; no

---

[Section 12:5]
  [1]RC 2151.85.
  [2]RC 2151.85(A).

[Section 12:6]
  [1]RC 2151.85.
  [2]RC 2151.85(A), RC 2151.85(D); Sup. R. 23(H).
  [3]Juv. R. 1(C)(6).

[Section 12:7]
  [1]Sup. R. 23(D).
  [2]RC 2151.85(B)(1); Sup. R. 23(D).
  [3]Sup. R. 23(D).

  [4]RC 2151.85(B)(1). See also In re Jane Doe, 135 Ohio App. 3d 719, 719–20, 735 N.E.2d 504 (4th Dist. Scioto County 1999) ("On December 7, 1999, verification was filed in the trial court that no hearing was held. See, Sup.R. 23(I). The verification provides that the trial court did not hold a hearing to consider the complaint within five days of the date appellant filed her complaint. . . . Thus, pursuant to the statute's clear language, appellant and any other person may rely on the constructive order to the same extent as if the court had actually issued an order permitting the parental notification bypass procedure.").

portion of it may be referred to a magistrate.[1] The court must keep a record of all testimony and other oral proceedings in the action.[2]

Each hearing must be conducted in a manner that will preserve the anonymity of the complainant.[3] Not even the child's parents, guardian, or custodian may be notified of the hearing.[4] The hearings are to be closed to the public, and all persons except the complainant's witnesses, attorney, and guardian ad litem, and essential court personnel, must be excluded.[5] The complaint and all other papers and records that pertain to the action must be kept confidential and are not public records under RC 149.43.[6] Moreover, the complainant's name shall not appear on the record.[7]

The Ohio Supreme Court has held that "the public is entitled to secure from the records pertaining to each case filed under RC 2505.073:[8] (1) the docket number, (2) the name of the judge, and (3) the decision, including, if appropriate, a properly redacted opinion."[9] Presumably, the rationale of this decision would also apply to the same records maintained by a juvenile court under RC 2151.85.

If the complaint contains only the allegation concerning maturity,[10] and if the court finds that maturity has been proven by clear and convincing evidence, the court shall issue an order authorizing the minor female to consent to the abortion without parental notification. The court is required to dismiss the complaint if it does not make the finding.[11]

If the complaint contains only the allegation concerning parental abuse or best interest,[12] and if the court finds by clear and convincing evidence that there is a pattern of parental abuse or that parental notification otherwise is not in the best interest of the complainant, the court must issue the order of authorization. The failure of the court to make either finding requires dismissal of the complaint.[13]

If the complaint contains allegations concerning both maturity and either parental abuse or best interest, or if the complaint includes all three allegations, the court is required to rule on the issue of maturity first. Only if the court finds against the minor female on the issue of maturity shall it determine the other allegations of the complaint.[14] The court must dismiss the complaint if it determines that the minor female has not established any of the requisite allegations by clear and convincing evidence.[15]

Judgment must be entered on the complaint immediately after the hearing has concluded.[16] If the complaint is dismissed, the court must notify the

---

[Section 12:8]

[1]RC 2151.85(B)(1); Sup. R. 23(D).

[2]RC 2151.85(B)(1).

[3]RC 2151.85(F); Sup. R. 23(A), Sup. R. 23(D), Sup. R. 23(H). See also RC 2505.073(B).

[4]RC 2151.85(D) . See § 12:6, Summons.

[5]Sup. R. 23(D).

[6]RC 2151.85(F); Sup. R. 23(A), Sup. R. 23(H). See also RC 2505.073(B).

[7]Sup. R. 23(D).

[8]This statute provides the mechanism to appeal the dismissal of a complaint filed under RC 2151.85.

[9]State ex rel. The Cincinnati Post v. Second Dist. Court of Appeals, 65 Ohio St. 3d 378, 604 N.E.2d 153 (1992).

[10]RC 2151.85(A)(4)(a).

[11]RC 2151.85(C)(1); see Sup. R. 23(D), Sup. R. 23(E).

[12]RC 2151.85(A)(4)(b).

[13]RC 2151.85(C)(2); Sup. R. 23(D), Sup. R. 23(E).

[14]RC 2151.85(C)(3)(a); Sup. R. 23(D), Sup. R. 23(E).

[15]RC 2151.85(C)(3)(b); Sup. R. 23(E).

[16]RC 2151.85(B)(1); Sup. R. 23(E).

complainant of her right to appear pursuant to RC 2505.073,[17] and provide her with a copy of the notice of appeal.[18]

§12:9 Case law

The Ohio Supreme Court has determined that a reviewing court is to use an abuse of discretion standard of review in considering an appeal of the dismissal of a complaint by an unemancipated minor seeking to have an abortion without parental notification.[1] The Court upheld the decision of a juvenile court dismissing the child's complaint on the basis that the child was not sufficiently mature to make the judgment on her own, and that there was not sufficient evidence of a pattern of physical, sexual, or emotional abuse of the child by her parents.[2]

The evidence considered by the juvenile court on the issue of whether the child was sufficiently mature and well enough informed consisted of the following: she was a high school senior who planned to attend college; she had a prior abortion less than a year earlier; each pregnancy was the result of intercourse with a different man; and she had discontinued a program of birth control. With respect to the allegations that parental notification would not be in her best interest, or that her father was engaged in a pattern of physical and emotional abuse against her, the testimony indicated that her father threatened not to support her if she ever got pregnant, and that he had struck her on two occasions—once for coming home late and once for getting bad grades on her report card.[3] An appellate court affirmed a juvenile court's dismissal of a minor's complaint seeking abortion without parental notification where the testimony established that she was 17 years old, a high school senior with a 3.8 grade point average, and had worked as a secretary for approximately 20 hours per week, using a portion of her earnings to purchase school books.[4]

Following the reasoning in *In re Jane Doe 1*,[5] a court of appeals found no abuse of discretion in a juvenile court's dismissal of a child's complaint despite the fact that the child was 16 years, nine months old; she was a high school sophomore in good standing, getting grades of C and better; she wanted to go to college, but recognized that she could not do so and take care of a baby; her lapse in using birth control was a somewhat involuntary consequence of her having left her foster home without her pills, as a result of abuse she received in her foster home; and she had a poor relationship with her natural parents and stepfather.[6] Another appellate court has determined that the pregnancy of a minor female, by itself, does not evidence a lack of maturity sufficient to deny her complaint.[7]

The Franklin County Court of Appeals has on several occasions reversed decisions of a juvenile court dismissing a child's complaint and refusing her permission to terminate her pregnancy without parental notification. In the

---

[17]RC 2151.85(E); Sup. R. 23(E).

[18]Sup. R. 23(E).

[Section 12:9]

[1]In re Jane Doe 1, 57 Ohio St. 3d 135, 566 N.E.2d 1181 (1991).

[2]In re Jane Doe 1, 57 Ohio St. 3d 135, 566 N.E.2d 1181 (1991). The majority rejected the child's suggestion that the Court adopt a six-factor test for juvenile courts to weigh as factors that are indicative of a minor's maturity or competence to give informed consent.

[3]Because parents are not notified of these hearings, there is typically no opposing testimony presented. See § 12:6, Summons.

[4]In Matter of Jane Doe, 1990 WL 640269 (Ohio Ct. App. 8th Dist. Cuyahoga County 1990).

[5]In re Jane Doe 1, 57 Ohio St. 3d 135, 566 N.E.2d 1181 (1991).

[6]In re Doe, 1991 WL 96269 (Ohio Ct. App. 2d Dist. Montgomery County 1991).

[7]Complaint of Doe, 1998 WL 400769 (Ohio Ct. App. 10th Dist. Franklin County 1998).

first case,[8] the court of appeals held that the juvenile court's failure to find the existence of at least one of the prerequisites was an abuse of discretion in that the child had clearly demonstrated both that she was sufficiently mature and well enough informed to intelligently decide whether to have an abortion and that notification of her parents was not in her best interest. At the hearing, it was determined that the child was 17½ years old; had maintained a B grade average in school; had made plans for her future by enlisting in the military; had hoped, through her military service, to develop funds and benefits in order to attend college; had received counseling about the options other than abortion and the risks attendant to an abortion; and would be ordered out of her house without financial and emotional support if her mother found out that she was pregnant.

In the second case,[9] the court of appeals held that it was an abuse of discretion on the part of the trial court not to find clear and convincing evidence that the child was sufficiently mature and well enough informed to intelligently decide whether to have an abortion without parental notification. The court determined that the child had demonstrated sufficient maturity in that she was a high school senior and nearly 18 years old; had worked 13 hours each week and maintained a 3.6 grade point average; was involved in several extracurricular activities; would be attending college in the fall; and had an aunt in whom she could confide and a steady boyfriend who supported her decision, but did not wish to tell her mother of her pregnancy because she believed her mother would lose trust in her if she did so.

The third case[10] dealt with a situation in which a minor female made only the allegation that she was sufficiently mature and well enough informed to decide whether to have the abortion without parental notification.[11] The court of appeals determined that the trial court was authorized to find that the statutory criteria for the abortion based on the minor's maturity were not met, but further held that the trial court should have considered the other statutory criteria[12] for abortion without parental notification based on parental abuse. In this case the minor female was only a matter of days from her eighteenth birthday, and graphically described to the court a history of parental physical abuse and threats of further physical abuse. However, in a dissenting opinion, it was pointed out that RC 2151.85(C)(1) requires that if the complainant makes only one statutory allegation, and if the court does not make the appropriate finding with respect to that allegation, the complaint must be dismissed.[13]

The Cuyahoga County Court of Appeals reversed a juvenile court's dismissal of a child's complaint based on lack of maturity, where the evidence showed that she was a high school senior; three months short of age 18; planned to go to college; had average grades and had taken honors courses; worked part-time during the school year and full-time during the summer; lived with her mother, who suffered from pulmonary hypertension and a bad lung; had a good relationship with her mother; and had received counseling.[14]

---

[8]In re Complaint of Jane Doe, 83 Ohio App. 3d 904, 615 N.E.2d 1142 (10th Dist. Franklin County 1992).

[9]In re Complaint of Jane Doe, 83 Ohio App. 3d 98, 613 N.E.2d 1112 (10th Dist. Franklin County 1993). See also In re Petition of Doe, 2003-Ohio-6509, 2003 WL 22871690 (Ohio Ct. App. 10th Dist. Franklin County 2003).

[10]In re Complaint of Jane Doe, 96 Ohio App. 3d 435, 645 N.E.2d 134 (10th Dist. Franklin County 1994).

[11]RC 2151.85(A)(4)(a).

[12]RC 2151.85(A)(4)(b).

[13]In re Complaint of Jane Doe, 96 Ohio App. 3d 435, 645 N.E.2d 134 (10th Dist. Franklin County 1994).

[14]In re Jane Doe 93-1, No. 66355 (8th Dist. Ct. App., Cuyahoga, 11-1-93). See also In re Jane Doe 01-01, 141 Ohio App. 3d 20, 749 N.E.2d 807 (8th Dist. Cuyahoga County 2001) (No abuse of

In contrast to the fact situation in *Jane Doe 1*,[15] the facts indicated that her pregnancy was the result of a one-time mistake, and not a complete abandonment of a birth control program. The court also held that in order to establish that a child is well enough informed, it is only required that she understand the abortion procedure and consequences, and not that she describe them with complete technical accuracy.[16]

In another case, the Athens County Court of Appeals reversed a juvenile court's finding of lack of maturity, where the appellant was 17½ years of age; a high school senior; a first pregnancy; did not intend to become pregnant; regularly used birth control devices; hoped to attend college; was financially incapable of supporting a child; and feared her tenuous relationship with her parents would be destroyed.[17]

§ 12:10 Appeals

If a juvenile court dismisses a minor female's complaint for authorization to consent to an abortion without parental notification,[1] it must immediately notify her of her right to appeal under RC 2505.073.[2] If she files an appeal, the clerk of the juvenile court must immediately notify the court of appeals.[3] Within four days after the notice of appeal is filed, the juvenile court must deliver the notice of appeal and the record, except page two of the complaint which identifies the minor female,[4] to the court of appeals.[5]

If possible, the juvenile court must prepare a written transcript. If this cannot be prepared timely and the testimony is on audiotape, the tape may be forwarded to the court of appeals in lieu of a written transcript.[6]

The appellant must file her brief within four days after the appeal is

---

discretion in dismissal of a complaint by a minor seeking a judicial bypass to the parental consent statute where: the appellant was a 17 year old senior, an honor student with plans to attend college and law school, employed 20 hours per week, maintained her finances and savings from employment, and where a representative of the Juvenile Court Diagnostic Clinic testified that the minor was mature, had given much thought to the situation, and understood the procedure and consequences. The juvenile and appellate court gave great weight to the facts that the minor contacted the abortion clinic as soon as she found out she was pregnant, to them evincing that she had not thought through the consequences of her pregnancy, and that she indicated that she planned to go on birth control pills despite her statement that she intended to refrain from sexual activity, evincing poor credibility.).

[15]In re Jane Doe 1, 57 Ohio St. 3d 135, 566 N.E.2d 1181 (1991).

[16]In re Jane Doe 93-1, No. 66355 (8th Dist. Ct. App., Cuyahoga, 11-1-93).

[17]In re Complaint of Jane Doe, 134 Ohio App. 3d 569, 731 N.E.2d 751 (4th Dist. Athens County 1999). The court felt compelled to comment: "[W]e wish to emphasize that the issue before the court is an issue involving statutory interpretation and the application of the statute to the facts in this particular case. The issue of whether the termination of a pregnancy is lawful has been decided by the United States Supreme Court. Thus, under present law a person has a constitutional right to terminate a pregnancy. Arguments concerning the propriety of abortion in general are beyond the scope of this opinion and do not influence our decision. [Furthermore,] we emphasize that in a proceeding of this nature, the trial court's role and this court's role is to focus upon the factors prescribed by the Ohio General Assembly. It is not a court's function to question the wisdom of a legislative enactment." In re Complaint of Jane Doe, 134 Ohio App. 3d 569, 577, 731 N.E.2d 751 (4th Dist. Athens County 1999).

[Section 12:10]

[1]RC 2151.85. RC 2151.85(G) provides that the clerk of the supreme court shall prescribe the notice of appeal form.

[2]RC 2151.85(E).

[3]Sup. R. 23(F)(1); Sup. R. 25(B)(1).

[4]See Sup. R. 23(A).

[5]RC 2505.073; Sup. R. 23(F)(1), Sup. R. 25(B)(1). See Sup. R. 25(B)(4) for formula for counting days.

[6]Sup. R. 23(F)(2). The rule also provides that the juvenile court must ensure that the court of appeals has the necessary equipment to listen to the tape. See also Sup. R. 25(B)(2).

docketed.[7] Unless waived, the oral argument must be held within five days after docketing.[8] Judgment must be entered immediately after conclusion of oral argument or, if oral argument is waived, within five days after the appeal is docketed.[9] If the court of appeals fails to enter judgment by the fifth day, it will be considered a constructive order authorizing the child to give consent without parental notification.[10] Moreover, if the child files her notice of appeal on the same day as the dismissal of her complaint, the entire court process, from the juvenile court hearing through the appeal and decision, must be completed in 16 calendar days from the time the complaint was filed.[11]

The same stringent confidentiality requirements that apply to parental notification of abortion proceedings in juvenile court also apply in the court of appeals. All proceedings must be conducted in a manner that will preserve the anonymity of the appellant.[12] Oral arguments must be closed to the public and exclude all persons except the appellant, her attorney, her guardian ad litem, and essential court personnel.[13] Virtually all papers and records that pertain to an appeal shall be kept confidential and are not public records under RC 149.43.[14] The only exception is that the public may have access to the docket number, the name of the judge, the judgment entry and, if appropriate, a properly redacted opinion.[15] Any information in an opinion which would directly or indirectly identify the appellant must be removed.[16] After an opinion is written and before it is made available for public release, the appellant must be notified and given the option to appear and argue at a hearing if she believes the opinion may disclose her identity.[17]

A federal court has held that institutional abortion providers lack standing to challenge the constitutionality of Ohio's parental notification of abortion system, in that their complaint was that certain state judges were making wrong decisions under a constitutional statute.[18]

Cross References
§ 23:29
Research References
Katz and Giannelli, Baldwin's Ohio Practice, Criminal Law (2d ed.) § 7:14
Carlin, Baldwin's Ohio Practice, Merrick-Rippner Probate Law (6th ed.), Ch 107

---

[7]Sup. R. 25(B)(3).

[8]Sup. R. 25(B)(3).

[9]Sup. R. 25(D); RC 2505.073(A).

[10]RC 2505.073(A). See also Sup. R. 25(G).

[11]Sup. R. 23(G), Sup. R. 25(A).

[12]Sup. R. 25(C).

[13]Sup. R. 25(B)(3).

[14]Sup. R. 25(C).

[15]Sup. R. 25(E). See State ex rel. The Cincinnati Post v. Second Dist. Court of Appeals, 65 Ohio St. 3d 378, 604 N.E.2d 153 (1992).

[16]Sup. R. 25(E).

[17]Sup. R. 25(F).

[18]Cleveland Surgi-Center, Inc. v. Jones, 2 F.3d 686 (6th Cir. 1993).

Chapter 13

Removal Actions

> **KeyCite®:** Cases and other legal materials listed in KeyCite Scope can be researched through West's KeyCite service on Westlaw®. Use KeyCite to check citations for form, parallel references, prior and later history, and comprehensive citator information, including citations to other decisions and secondary materials.

§ 13:1   Removal actions—Introduction
§ 13:2   Jurisdictional requirements
§ 13:3   Venue
§ 13:4   Summons and notice
§ 13:5   Hearing
§ 13:6   Case law

§ 13:1   Removal actions—Introduction

This chapter discusses the jurisdiction of the juvenile court to hear complaints filed by school district superintendents to remove out-of-county children from in-county foster homes, where the child is alleged to be causing a significant and unreasonable disruption to the educational process. All substantive and procedural requirements are considered in this chapter.

§ 13:2   Jurisdictional requirements

RC 2151.55[1] governed certain issues involving the placement of children in foster homes outside of their home county. RC 2151.55(B) provided that prior to placing a child in an out-of-county foster home, the private or government entity responsible for the placement had to communicate directly with the intended foster caregiver, the juvenile court of the county in which the foster home is located, and the school district's board of education. The purpose of the communication was to provide relevant information concerning the reasons for the child's placement, if that information could be disclosed under federal and state law.

The superintendent of the school district in which the child resides in a foster home was authorized to file a complaint requesting that the child be removed from the county because the child was causing a significant and unreasonable disruption to the educational process in the school the child is attending.[2]

Division (A) of RC 2151.55 provided as follows:

> This section shall have no effect on and after the date the Supreme Court adopts, pursuant to its authority under Section 5 of Article IV, Ohio Constitution, rules governing procedure in the juvenile courts of the state that address the placement of a child in a foster home in a county other than the county in which the child resided at the time of being removed from home.

[Section 13:2]

[1]RC 2151.55 and RC 2151.23(A)(13), the jurisdictional statute, became effective on June 30, 1997 (1997 H.B. 215). As explained within, it appears that RC 2151.55 was automatically repealed on July 1, 1998. Therefore, the material in this chapter is not applicable unless the General Assembly enacts corrective legislation.

[2]RC 2151.55(C).

There appears to be a major jurisdictional problem with this provision. The Modern Courts Amendment to the Ohio Constitution[3] empowers the Supreme Court to promulgate procedural, but not substantive, rules. The rules may not "abridge, enlarge, or modify any substantive right."[4] By eliminating the jurisdictional basis for removal actions from the statute with the enactment of the rules, it is arguable that the jurisdiction of juvenile courts to hear these actions has been revoked. Although RC 2151.23(A)(13), which is not affected by the adoption of the rules, continues to provide that juvenile courts have jurisdiction "[c]oncerning an action commenced under section 2151.55 of the Revised Code," this provision appears to be rendered moot by the specific statement in RC 2151.55(A) that the enactment of the rules causes the statute to have no further effect.

Nonetheless, pursuant to RC 2151.55(A) the Supreme Court amended the following Juvenile Rules:[5]

- Rule 2(GG): Defines "removal action" as a "statutory action filed by the superintendent of a school district for the removal of a child in an out-of-county foster home placement."
- Rule 4(B)(7): Requires the appointment of a guardian ad litem for the child in removal actions.[6]
- Rule 10(A): Establishes venue for removal actions in the county where the foster home is located.
- Rule 11(B): Exempts removal actions from the mandatory transfer provisions where other proceedings are pending in the juvenile court of the child's resident county.
- Rule 15(B)(8): Requires the summons issued to the parties to include the specific disposition sought in a removal action.
- Rule 29(A): Requires the hearing of a removal action to be scheduled in accordance with Juvenile Rule 39(B).
- Rule 29(E)(4): Establishes a clear and convincing evidence standard in removal action adjudicatory hearings.

In addition, the Supreme Court enacted Juvenile Rule 39 to govern the out-of-county removal hearings.[7]

§ 13:3 Venue

In a removal action, the complaint must be filed in the county where the foster home is located.[1] This requirement clarifies the venue requirement where the boundaries of the school district extend beyond a single county.

Even if a proceeding involving the child is pending in the juvenile court of the county of the child's residence, removal actions shall not be transferred to that juvenile court.[2]

§ 13:4 Summons and notice

When the complaint is filed, the court in which the complaint is filed must

---

[3]Article IV, Section 5(B). See § 1:8, Rules of Juvenile Procedure.

[4]Article IV, Section 5(B).

[5]The amendments took effect on July 1, 1998.

[6]According to the Staff Note, the court may appoint the guardian ad litem initially appointed by the court that entered the original dispositional order, with the consent of that guardian ad litem, or may appoint a new guardian ad litem.

[7]See § 13:4, Summons and notice, and § 13:5, Hearing, for discussion of Juv. R. 39.

[Section 13:3]
[1]Juv. R. 10(A).
[2]Juv. R. 11(B).

contact the court that issued the original dispositional order to obtain information necessary for service of summons and issuance of notice.[1] The summons, which shall issue pursuant to Juvenile Rules 15 and 16,[2] must include a statement of the specific disposition sought.[3]

In addition to the issuance of summons, notice of the removal hearing must be sent by first class mail to the following, not otherwise summoned, at least five days prior to the hearing: the court issuing the dispositional order; the child's guardian ad litem; the child's legal counsel; the placing entity; the custodial entity; the complainant; the guardian ad litem and counsel presently representing the child in the court that issued the original dispositional order; and any other persons the court determines to be appropriate.[4] Persons or entities receiving a notice rather than a summons are not required to appear for the hearing, but should be aware that the hearing will be conducted.

§ 13:5 Hearing

The court shall hold the removal hearing as soon as possible, but not later than thirty days after service of summons is obtained.[1]

RC 2151.55(D) established the finding that the court was required to make.[2] According to the statute, the sole purpose of the hearing was to determine whether the child was causing a significant and unreasonable disruption to the educational process. A finding against the child mandated the court to order the entity that placed the child in the foster home to return the child from the county, whereas a finding for the child required dismissal of the complaint. An order removing the child from the county had to be sent to the juvenile court that journalized a case plan or issued any other order requiring the child's placement in the out-of-county foster home, whereupon that juvenile court was required to enter the notice on its journal and either change the case plan or issue a new dispositional order consistent with the removal order.[3]

According to Juvenile Rule 29(E)(4), complaints for removal actions must be established by clear and convincing evidence. Because the appropriate findings that a court must make are a matter of substantive law, Juvenile Rule 39(B) does not include any reference to these findings. The rule simply requires the court to send written notice of any removal order to the juvenile court that issued the original dispositional order.

§ 13:6 Case law

The only case interpreting RC 2151.55, decided before the amendment of the Juvenile Rules, found the statute unconstitutional.[1] Initially, the court found that the term "significant and unreasonable disruption to the

---

[Section 13:4]

[1]Juv. R. 39(A).

[2]Juv. R. 39(A).

[3]Juv. R. 15(B)(8).

[4]Juv. R. 39(A).

[Section 13:5]

[1]Juv. R. 29(A), Juv. R. 39(B). RC 2151.355(D), which is evidently of no further effect (see RC 2151.55(A)), predicates the scheduling of the hearing on the filing of the complaint rather than on service of summons.

[2]Due to the provisions of RC 2151.55(A), it appears that none of the statute is any longer in effect.

[3]RC 2151.55(E). Based on RC 2151.55(A), this statute is apparently no longer in effect.

[Section 13:6]

[1]In re T.B., No. K97-1055 (5th Dist. Ct. App., Licking, 1-26-98).

educational process"[2] was not unconstitutionally vague, and that the statute did not deprive a child of due process. Instead, the court found that the statute violated the equal protection clauses of both the United States and Ohio Constitutions because it requires the banishment of a child from the county, even though the child had not been found to be a criminal or a delinquent. Further, banishment may be contrary to the child's welfare and best interests, without regard to public safety. Moreover, the fact that juvenile courts must make decisions in removal actions based solely on the geographical boundaries of a county established an arbitrary classification with no legitimate state interest.[3]

---

[2]RC 2151.55(D).

[3]In re T.B., No. K97-1055 (5th Dist. Ct. App., Licking, 1-26-98).

Chapter 14

Investigations

> **KeyCite®:** Cases and other legal materials listed in KeyCite Scope can be researched through West's KeyCite service on Westlaw®. Use KeyCite to check citations for form, parallel references, prior and later history, and comprehensive citator information, including citations to other decisions and secondary materials.

§ 14:1   Investigations—Introduction
§ 14:2   Exclusionary rule
§ 14:3   Custody, arrests & stops
§ 14:4   Search & seizure
§ 14:5   Consent searches
§ 14:6   School searches
§ 14:7   Probation searches
§ 14:8   DNA databases
§ 14:9   Confessions—Due process
§ 14:10   Confessions—*Miranda*
§ 14:11   Confessions—Right to counsel
§ 14:12   Identification procedures—Self-incrimination
§ 14:13   Identification procedures—Right to counsel
§ 14:14   Identification procedures—Due process
§ 14:15   Fingerprints & photographs
§ 14:16   Abuse, neglect & dependency investigations
§ 14:17   Child abuse reporting statute

§ 14:1   Investigations—Introduction

A number of police investigative techniques implicate constitutional guarantees. For example, arrests and searches involve the Fourth Amendment's proscription against unreasonable searches and seizures; interrogation practices involve the Fifth Amendment privilege against compulsory self-incrimination, the right to counsel, and due process; and identification procedures, such as lineups, involve the right to counsel and due process. Generally, the courts have applied these constitutional rights to juvenile delinquency cases.[1]

Abuse and neglect investigations may also implicate constitutional issues. These issues are discussed in § 14:16. In addition, RC 2151.421 governs the reporting and investigation of child abuse and neglect, a subject examined in § 14:17.

Cross References
§ 14:16
Research References
Katz, Ohio Arrest, Search and Seizure, Ch 3

[Section 14:1]
[1]See IJA-ABA Standards Relating to Police Handling of Juvenile Problems 54–76 (1980); Rights of Juveniles: The Juvenile Justice System (2d ed.), Ch 3.

§ 14:2 Exclusionary rule

Evidence obtained in violation of constitutional guarantees is subject to exclusion at a criminal trial.[1] The United States Supreme Court, however, has recognized a "good faith" exception to the exclusionary rule where the police search pursuant to a warrant.[2]

Another aspect of the exclusionary rule relates to standing. Only a person whose constitutional rights have been violated has standing to invoke the exclusionary rule.[3]

Moreover, the exclusionary rule applies not only to primary evidence obtained as a direct result of unconstitutional conduct but also to evidence later discovered and found to be derivative of that conduct ("fruit of the poisonous tree").[4] There are several exceptions to the derivative evidence rule. Such evidence will not be excluded if the prosecution can establish that (1) there was an independent source for obtaining the evidence;[5] (2) the evidence would have been "inevitably discovered";[6] or (3) intervening events have sufficiently attenuated the taint of the original illegality.[7]

In Ohio, Juvenile Rule 22(D)(3) governs suppression motions.[8] In *State v. Whisenant*,[9] the court of appeals ruled that the juvenile judge is not required to rule on motions to suppress at the transfer hearing. The court wrote that "because the bindover proceeding is not adjudicative (the juvenile's guilt or innocence is not at issue), statutory and constitutional questions concerning the admissibility of evidence are premature and need not be addressed. Fundamental fairness and due process are not violated by the juvenile court's failure to rule on or to suppress evidence obtained in alleged violation of *Miranda* in this type of proceeding."[10] The court did acknowledge, however, that courts in other jurisdictions were split on this issue.

Juvenile Rule 22(F) provides for an appeal by the state under certain

---

[Section 14:2]

[1]See generally Katz and Giannelli, Baldwin's Ohio Practice, Criminal Law (2d ed.), Ch 29; Hall, Search and Seizure (3d ed.), Ch 1. See also Matter of Diane P., 110 A.D.2d 354, 494 N.Y. S.2d 881 (2d Dep't 1985) (exclusionary rule applicable in child protective proceedings).

[2]See U.S. v. Leon, 468 U.S. 897, 104 S. Ct. 3405, 82 L. Ed. 2d 677 (1984); Massachusetts v. Sheppard, 468 U.S. 981, 990, 104 S. Ct. 3424, 82 L. Ed. 2d 737 (1984) ("[T]he exclusionary rule should not be applied when the officer conducting the search acted in objectively reasonable reliance on a warrant issued by a detached and neutral magistrate that subsequently is determined to be invalid."). See generally Katz and Giannelli, Baldwin's Ohio Practice, Criminal Law (2d ed.), Ch 30.

[3]Rakas v. Illinois, 439 U.S. 128, 99 S. Ct. 421, 58 L. Ed. 2d 387 (1978); Rawlings v. Kentucky, 448 U.S. 98, 100 S. Ct. 2556, 65 L. Ed. 2d 633 (1980); Alderman v. U.S., 394 U.S. 165, 174, 89 S. Ct. 961, 22 L. Ed. 2d 176 (1969) ("Fourth Amendment rights are personal rights which . . . may not be vicariously asserted."). See generally Katz and Giannelli, Baldwin's Ohio Practice, Criminal Law (2d ed.), Ch 33.

[4]Nardone v. U.S., 308 U.S. 338, 341, 60 S. Ct. 266, 84 L. Ed. 307 (1939). See generally Katz and Giannelli, Baldwin's Ohio Practice, Criminal Law (2d ed.), Ch 32.

[5]See Murray v. U.S., 487 U.S. 533, 108 S. Ct. 2529, 101 L. Ed. 2d 472 (1988); Segura v. U.S., 468 U.S. 796, 104 S. Ct. 3380, 82 L. Ed. 2d 599 (1984).

[6]See Nix v. Williams, 467 U.S. 431, 104 S. Ct. 2501, 81 L. Ed. 2d 377 (1984).

[7]See Rawlings v. Kentucky, 448 U.S. 98, 100 S. Ct. 2556, 65 L. Ed. 2d 633 (1980); Brown v. Illinois, 422 U.S. 590, 95 S. Ct. 2254, 45 L. Ed. 2d 416 (1975). See generally Hall, Search and Seizure (3d ed.) § 11.4(a).

[8]See In re Baker, 18 Ohio App. 2d 276, 47 Ohio Op. 2d 411, 248 N.E.2d 620 (4th Dist. Hocking County 1969) (Failure to file a motion to suppress waives objections to the admissibility of evidence.). In re Clemens, 2002-Ohio-3370, 2002 WL 1401663 (Ohio Ct. App. 11th Dist. Lake County 2002).

[9]State v. Whisenant, 127 Ohio App. 3d 75, 711 N.E.2d 1016 (11th Dist. Portage County 1998).

[10]State v. Whisenant, 127 Ohio App. 3d 75, 85, 711 N.E.2d 1016 (11th Dist. Portage County 1998).

conditions if a motion to suppress evidence is granted in delinquency cases.[11] In *In re Mojica*,[12] the trial court did not hold a separate hearing for a motion to suppress based on Fourth Amendment grounds. Instead, at the judge's request both sides agreed to proceed with the trial and the defense would object when the evidence was offered. When the issue was raised at trial, the judge dismissed the case and granted the motion. The court of appeals wrote:

> We believe the state made a critical error by agreeing to go forward with the trial and not requesting a separate hearing on the motion to suppress. If the court would have strictly adhered to Crim.R. 12 and Juv.R. 22 and held a hearing on the motion to suppress, double jeopardy would not have been an issue since no factual finding of innocence would have been reached.

> Nevertheless, the trial court held a trial and after considering all the evidence determined that the case should be dismissed and the motion to suppress granted. Therefore, the fact finder reached a finding of innocence and double jeopardy attached at that point.[13]

§ 14:3 Custody, arrests & stops

RC 2151.31 and Juvenile Rule 6 set forth the conditions under which a child may be taken into custody.[1] These include:

(1) Pursuant to a court order under RC Chapter 2151[2] or RC 2930.05(B);[3]

(2) Pursuant to the law of arrest;[4]

(3) By a law enforcement officer or duly authorized officer of the court under specified conditions (see below); and

(4) By the judge or designated magistrate, ex parte, pending the outcome of an adjudication or dispositional hearing in an abuse, neglect, or dependency proceeding when it appears that the best interest and welfare of the child require immediate issuance of a shelter

---

[11]See In re Mojica, 107 Ohio App. 3d 461, 464, 669 N.E.2d 35 (8th Dist. Cuyahoga County 1995) ("[P]ursuant to R.C. 2945.67 and Juv.R. 22(F) the state may take an appeal from the granting of a motion to suppress as a matter of right. Therefore, the trial court did not have authority to grant a final verdict by dismissing the charges . . . and we retain jurisdiction to hear this appeal."); In re Hester, 1 Ohio App. 3d 24, 437 N.E.2d 1218 (10th Dist. Franklin County 1981). For a discussion of prosecution's right to appeal, see § 34:8, State appeals.

[12]In re Mojica, 107 Ohio App. 3d 461, 669 N.E.2d 35 (8th Dist. Cuyahoga County 1995).

[13]In re Mojica, 107 Ohio App. 3d 461, 466, 669 N.E.2d 35 (8th Dist. Cuyahoga County 1995).

[Section 14:3]

[1]RC 2151.31(B)(1) provides, "The taking of a child into custody is not and shall not be deemed an arrest except for the purpose of determining its validity under the constitution of this state or of the United States." In In re L---, 25 Ohio Op. 2d 369, 92 Ohio L. Abs. 475, 478, 194 N.E.2d 797 (Juv. Ct. 1963), the court held that the law of arrest does not apply in juvenile proceedings because they are "neither criminal nor penal in . . . nature." This view has been rejected by the post-*Gault* cases (Application of Gault, 387 U.S. 1, 87 S. Ct. 1428, 18 L. Ed. 2d 527 (1967)).

See also RC 2151.28(D) (service of summons and taking into custody). See generally IJA-ABA Standards Relating to Police Handling of Juvenile Problems 62–65 (1980); Rights of Juveniles: The Juvenile Justice System (2d ed.) §§ 3.1–3.5.

[2]See Juv. R. 15(D) ("If it appears that the summons will be ineffectual or the welfare of the child requires that the child be brought forthwith to the court, a warrant may be issued against the child.").

[3]This statute, a victim's rights provision, permits a prosecutor (upon a victim's affidavit) to file a motion for reconsideration of a juvenile's terms of release, including detention, where an act of violence has been threatened or committed against the victim, the victim's family, or the victim's representative. This provision also covers persons acting pursuant to a juvenile's direction.

[4]See In re Howard, 31 Ohio App. 3d 1, 508 N.E.2d 190 (1st Dist. Hamilton County 1987) (warrantless arrest of juvenile on probable cause).

care order.[5]

The conditions under which a law enforcement or court-authorized officer may take a child into custody [(3) above] include:

(a) When there are reasonable grounds to believe that the child is suffering from some illness or injury and is not receiving proper care, and the child's removal is necessary to prevent immediate or threatened physical or emotional harm;

(b) When there are reasonable grounds to believe that the child is in immediate danger from the child's surroundings and the child's removal is necessary to prevent immediate or threatened physical or emotional harm;[6]

(c) When there are reasonable grounds to believe that a parent, guardian, custodian, or other household member has abused or neglected another child in the same household, and the child is in danger of immediate or threatened physical or emotional harm;

(d) When there are reasonable grounds to believe that the child has run away from the child's parents, guardian, or other custodian;

(e) When there are reasonable grounds to believe that the conduct, conditions, or surroundings of the child are endangering the health, welfare, or safety of the child;

(f) When a complaint has been filed[7] or the child has been indicted or charged by information as a serious youthful offender (SYO).[8]

(g) When, during the pendency of court proceedings, there are reasonable grounds to believe that the child may abscond or be removed from the jurisdiction of the court or will not be brought to court;

(h) When there are reasonable grounds to believe the child committed a delinquent act and taking the child into custody is necessary to protect the public interest and safety;[9]

RC 2151.31(D) and Juvenile Rule 6(A)(3)(g) specify the conditions under which a juvenile court judge or a designated magistrate may issue an ex parte telephone order authorizing a child to be taken into emergency custody. RC 2151.31 and Juvenile Rule 6(B) require that a probable cause hearing be held before the end of the next business day, but not later than 72 hours if an ex parte emergency order is issued.[10]

Once in custody, the child must (with reasonable speed) be either (1) released to a parent, guardian, or other custodian, or (2) brought to the juvenile court or a court-designated place of detention or shelter care.[11]

Victim. Under RC 2930.05, a victim is entitled to notice of the detention of an alleged juvenile offender.

Law of arrest. In Ohio, the "law of arrest" is governed by statutory and constitutional provisions. An arrest is a seizure of the person within the meaning of the Fourth Amendment,[12] and thus must be based on probable

---

[5]See In re Jones, 114 Ohio App. 319, 19 Ohio Op. 2d 286, 182 N.E.2d 631 (3d Dist. Allen County 1961).

[6]See State v. Hunt, 2 Ariz. App. 6, 406 P.2d 208 (1965) (5-year-old child in danger).

[7]See RC 2151.27, RC 2152.021.

[8]See RC 2152.13. See also Serious Youthful Offenders Ch 5.

[9]RC 2151.31(A)(6)(d).

[10]See County of Riverside v. McLaughlin, 500 U.S. 44, 111 S. Ct. 1661, 114 L. Ed. 2d 49 (1991) (probable cause hearings in adult criminal cases are generally required within 48 hours of a warrantless arrest).

[11]Juv. R. 7(B). For a discussion of pretrial detention, see Detention or Shelter Care Ch 19.

[12]Kaupp v. Texas, 538 U.S. 626, 123 S. Ct. 1843, 155 L. Ed. 2d 814 (2003) (because arrest lacked probable cause, subsequent confession suppressed. "A 17-year-old boy was awakened in

cause;[13] that is, there must be reasonable grounds to believe that a crime has been committed and that the arrestee committed it.[14] According to the United States Supreme Court, an arrest warrant is not constitutionally required if a suspect is arrested in a public place.[15] Although an invalid arrest does not preclude subsequent prosecution,[16] it may nevertheless result in the exclusion of evidence that was the product of that arrest.[17]

RC 2935.04 provides that *any person*, upon reasonable cause, may arrest a felony suspect without a warrant. Misdemeanors are treated differently. Under RC 2935.03, only certain law enforcement officers may arrest without a warrant for (1) misdemeanors committed in their presence, or (2) specified drug, theft, and violence offenses not committed in their presence. In *State v. Jones*,[18] the Ohio Supreme Court held that "absent one or more of the exceptions specified in R.C. 2935.26, a full custodial arrest for a minor misdemeanor offense violates . . . Section 14, Article I of the Ohio Constitution, and evidence obtained incident to such an arrest is subject to suppression in accordance with the exclusionary rule."

Criminal Rule 4 governs the issuance and execution of arrest warrants.[19]

Stop & frisk. In addition to an arrest, the police may "stop and frisk" a suspect based upon reasonable suspicion that criminal activity is afoot.[20] Although an objective standard, "reasonable suspicion" is a lesser standard of proof than probable cause. However, the detention of a person pursuant to a stop is far less intrusive than an arrest; a stop is a temporary detention at the scene.[21] The courts have applied the stop and frisk doctrine to juveniles.[22]

---

his bedroom at three in the morning by at least three police officers, one of whom stated 'we need to go and talk.' He was taken out in handcuffs, without shoes, dressed only in his underwear in January, placed in a patrol car, driven to the scene of a crime and then to the sheriff's offices, where he was taken into an interrogation room and questioned.").

[13]Maryland v. Pringle, 124 S. Ct. 795, 800-01, 157 L. Ed. 2d 769 (U.S. 2003) ("The probable-cause standard is incapable of precise definition or quantification into percentages because it deals with probabilities and depends on the totality of the circumstances."; "Upon questioning, the three men [in the car] failed to offer any information with respect to the ownership of the cocaine or the money. ... We think it an entirely reasonable inference from these facts that any or all three of the occupants had knowledge of, and exercised dominion and control over, the cocaine. Thus a reasonable officer could conclude that there was probable cause to believe Pringle committed the crime of possession of cocaine, either solely or jointly."); Atwater v. City of Lago Vista, 532 U.S. 318, 354, 121 S. Ct. 1536, 149 L. Ed. 2d 549 (2001) (stating that "[i]f an officer has probable cause to believe that an individual has committed even a very minor criminal offense in his presence, he may, without violating the Fourth Amendment, arrest the offender.").

[14]E.g., In Interest of Tucker, 20 Ill. App. 3d 377, 314 N.E.2d 276 (1st Dist. 1974); Minor Boy v. State, 91 Nev. 456, 537 P.2d 477 (1975). See generally Katz and Giannelli, Baldwin's Ohio Practice, Criminal Law (2d ed.), Ch 6.

[15]U.S. v. Watson, 423 U.S. 411, 96 S. Ct. 820, 46 L. Ed. 2d 598 (1976).

[16]Gerstein v. Pugh, 420 U.S. 103, 95 S. Ct. 854, 43 L. Ed. 2d 54, 19 Fed. R. Serv. 2d 1499 (1975); In re Jackson, 46 Mich. App. 764, 208 N.W.2d 526 (1973).

[17]E.g., In re S., 36 A.D.2d 642, 319 N.Y.S.2d 752 (2d Dep't 1971).

[18]State v. Jones, 88 Ohio St. 3d 430, 440, 2000-Ohio-374, 727 N.E.2d 886 (2000), aff'd on state constitutional grounds, State v. Brown, 99 Ohio St. 3d 323, 2003-Ohio-3931, 792 N.E.2d 175 (2003).

[19]See Katz and Giannelli, Baldwin's Ohio Practice, Criminal Law (2d ed.), Ch 7.

[20]Terry v. Ohio, 392 U.S. 1, 88 S. Ct. 1868, 20 L. Ed. 2d 889 (1968). See Hall, Search and Seizure (3d ed.), Ch 9; Katz and Giannelli, Baldwin's Ohio Practice, Criminal Law (2d ed.), Ch 18.

[21]See Dunaway v. New York, 442 U.S. 200, 99 S. Ct. 2248, 60 L. Ed. 2d 824 (1979).

[22]E.g., In re Smalley, 62 Ohio App. 3d 435, 575 N.E.2d 1198 (8th Dist. Cuyahoga County 1989); In re Agosto, 85 Ohio App. 3d 188, 619 N.E.2d 475 (8th Dist. Cuyahoga County 1993) (gun suppressed due to invalid investigative stop); In re James D., 43 Cal. 3d 903, 239 Cal. Rptr. 663, 741 P.2d 161, 41 Ed. Law Rep. 722 (1987); In re Tony C., 21 Cal. 3d 888, 148 Cal. Rptr. 366, 582 P.2d 957 (1978); In the Matter of Thomas, 1983 WL 4689 (Ohio Ct. App. 8th Dist. Cuyahoga County 1983); In re Harvey, 222 Pa. Super. 222, 295 A.2d 93 (1972).

Cross References
Ch 19
Research References
Katz and Giannelli, Baldwin's Ohio Practice, Criminal Law (2d ed.), Chs 29, 30
Katz, Ohio Arrest, Search and Seizure, Chs 4 to 15

§ 14:4   Search & seizure

The Fourth Amendment reads:

> The right of the people to be secure in their persons, houses, papers, and effects, against unreasonable searches and seizures, shall not be violated, and no warrants shall issue, but upon probable cause, supported by oath or affirmation, and particularly describing the place to be searched, and the persons or things to be seized.

The Ohio Constitution contains a comparable provision.[1] The United States Supreme Court has applied the Fourth Amendment to juvenile cases.[2] The Ohio Supreme Court has also noted that "it is well-settled that a juvenile is as entitled as an adult to the constitutional protections of the Fourth Amendment."[3]

The threshold question when analyzing search and seizure issues is whether the Fourth Amendment applies. If the amendment is applicable, a search warrant and probable cause are usually required. There are, however, several well-recognized exceptions to the warrant requirement.

Applicability of the Fourth Amendment. The Fourth Amendment applies only to governmental searches. Searches by private citizens are not prohibited by the amendment.[4] However, if the police significantly expand upon a private search, it may evolve into a governmental search.[5] School officials are not private citizens in this context.[6]

Moreover, the Fourth Amendment applies only to certain governmental activities, that is, those activities that intrude upon a citizen's justifiable expectations of privacy.[7] Searches of homes, offices, cars, and containers are covered by the Fourth Amendment, as is the use of electronic eavesdropping and wiretapping,[8] and thermal-imaging devices aimed at a private home.[9] Police use of informants,[10] beepers,[11] aerial surveillance,[12] sniffing-dogs,[13] or pen registers[14] is not protected by the amendment. Searches of jail cells,[15]

See also Matter of Ronald B., 61 A.D.2d 204, 401 N.Y.S.2d 544 (2d Dep't 1978) (applying stop and frisk doctrine to school officials).

[Section 14:4]

[1]O. Const. art. I § 14.

[2]New Jersey v. T.L.O., 469 U.S. 325, 105 S. Ct. 733, 83 L. Ed. 2d 720, 21 Ed. Law Rep. 1122 (1985). See generally Rights of Juveniles: The Juvenile Justice System (2d ed.) § 3.6.

[3]In re Order Requiring Fingerprinting of a Juvenile, 42 Ohio St. 3d 124, 126, 537 N.E.2d 1286 (1989). See also State v. Davis, 56 Ohio St. 2d 51, 10 Ohio Op. 3d 87, 381 N.E.2d 641 (1978) ("Fourth Amendment applies to minors in the same manner as adults."); In re Morris, 29 Ohio Misc. 71, 72, 58 Ohio Op. 2d 126, 278 N.E.2d 701 (C.P. 1971) (Fourth Amendment applies to juveniles.).

[4]Burdeau v. McDowell, 256 U.S. 465, 41 S. Ct. 574, 65 L. Ed. 1048, 13 A.L.R. 1159 (1921); State v. Morris, 42 Ohio St. 2d 307, 71 Ohio Op. 2d 294, 329 N.E.2d 85 (1975). See generally Katz and Giannelli, Baldwin's Ohio Practice, Criminal Law (2d ed.), Ch 3.

[5]See U.S. v. Jacobsen, 466 U.S. 109, 104 S. Ct. 1652, 80 L. Ed. 2d 85 (1984); Walter v. U.S., 447 U.S. 649, 100 S. Ct. 2395, 65 L. Ed. 2d 410 (1980).

[6]See Text § 14:6, School searches.

[7]Katz v. U.S., 389 U.S. 347, 88 S. Ct. 507, 19 L. Ed. 2d 576 (1967). See Katz and Giannelli, Baldwin's Ohio Practice, Criminal Law (2d ed.), Ch 4; Hall, Search and Seizure (3d ed.), Ch 2.

[8]Katz v. U.S., 389 U.S. 347, 88 S. Ct. 507, 19 L. Ed. 2d 576 (1967).

[9]Kyllo v. U.S., 533 U.S. 27, 31, 121 S. Ct. 2038, 150 L. Ed. 2d 94 (2001).

[10]U.S. v. White, 401 U.S. 745, 91 S. Ct. 1122, 28 L. Ed. 2d 453 (1971).

open fields,[16] trash,[17] and bank records[18] also fall outside Fourth Amendment protection.[19]

Warrant & probable cause requirements. Searches must be based on probable cause and conducted pursuant to a search warrant unless a recognized exception to these requirements applies.[20] A search warrant must be issued by a neutral and detached magistrate[21] and describe with particularity the place to be searched and the items to be seized.[22]

Probable cause to search requires substantial evidence that the items sought are connected with a crime and that those items are located at the place to be searched. The United States Supreme Court has written, "In dealing with probable cause, however, as the very name implies, we deal with probabilities. These are not technical; they are the factual and practical considerations of everyday life on which reasonable and prudent men, not legal technicians, act."[23] Probable cause may be based on hearsay.[24] In order to determine whether information supplied by an informant satisfies the probable cause requirement, the totality of circumstances must be considered, including the informant's credibility, the basis for his knowledge, and the reliability of his information.[25]

Exceptions. There are a number of recognized exceptions to the warrant

---

[11]U.S. v. Knotts, 460 U.S. 276, 103 S. Ct. 1081, 75 L. Ed. 2d 55 (1983). But see U.S. v. Karo, 468 U.S. 705, 104 S. Ct. 3296, 82 L. Ed. 2d 530 (1984) (Monitoring beeper in a house is protected by the Fourth Amendment.).

[12]Florida v. Riley, 488 U.S. 445, 109 S. Ct. 693, 102 L. Ed. 2d 835 (1989); California v. Ciraolo, 476 U.S. 207, 106 S. Ct. 1809, 90 L. Ed. 2d 210 (1986).

[13]U.S. v. Place, 462 U.S. 696, 103 S. Ct. 2637, 77 L. Ed. 2d 110 (1983) (Use of a trained canine to detect drugs in luggage is not a search.).

[14]Smith v. Maryland, 442 U.S. 735, 99 S. Ct. 2577, 61 L. Ed. 2d 220 (1979).

[15]Hudson v. Palmer, 468 U.S. 517, 104 S. Ct. 3194, 82 L. Ed. 2d 393 (1984).

[16]U.S. v. Dunn, 480 U.S. 294, 107 S. Ct. 1134, 94 L. Ed. 2d 326 (1987); Oliver v. U.S., 466 U.S. 170, 104 S. Ct. 1735, 80 L. Ed. 2d 214 (1984); Hester v. U.S., 265 U.S. 57, 44 S. Ct. 445, 68 L. Ed. 898 (1924).

[17]California v. Greenwood, 486 U.S. 35, 108 S. Ct. 1625, 100 L. Ed. 2d 30 (1988).

[18]U.S. v. Miller, 425 U.S. 435, 96 S. Ct. 1619, 48 L. Ed. 2d 71 (1976) (Financial Privacy Act of 1978, 12 U.S.C.A. § 3401 to 12 U.S.C.A. § 3421, limits the holding in *Miller*.), superseded by statute as stated in McDonough v. Widnall, 891 F. Supp. 1439 (D. Colo. 1995).

[19]See also U.S. v. Dionisio, 410 U.S. 1, 93 S. Ct. 764, 35 L. Ed. 2d 67 (1973) (A person does not have reasonable expectation of privacy in the sound of his voice.); U.S. v. Mara, 410 U.S. 19, 93 S. Ct. 774, 35 L. Ed. 2d 99 (1973) (A person does not have a reasonable expectation of privacy in his handwriting.).

[20]Katz and Giannelli, Baldwin's Ohio Practice, Criminal Law (2d ed.), Ch 5. Probable cause is not required if a search is based on a validly obtained consent. Reasonable suspicion, not probable cause, is required for a stop and frisk.

[21]See Shadwick v. City of Tampa, 407 U.S. 345, 92 S. Ct. 2119, 32 L. Ed. 2d 783 (1972); Coolidge v. New Hampshire, 403 U.S. 443, 91 S. Ct. 2022, 29 L. Ed. 2d 564 (1971). See also Katz and Giannelli, Baldwin's Ohio Practice, Criminal Law (2d ed.) § 9:3.

[22]Maryland v. Garrison, 480 U.S. 79, 107 S. Ct. 1013, 94 L. Ed. 2d 72 (1987). See Groh v. Ramirez, 124 S. Ct. 1284, 157 L. Ed. 2d 1068 (U.S. 2004) ("This warrant did not simply omit a few items from a list of many to be seized, or misdescribe a few of several items. Nor did it make what fairly could be characterized as a mere technical mistake or typographical error. Rather, in the space set aside for a description of the items to be seized, the warrant stated that the items consisted of a 'single dwelling residence . . . blue in color.' In other words, the warrant did not describe the items to be seized at all."); Steele v. U.S., 267 U.S. 498, 45 S. Ct. 414, 69 L. Ed. 757 (1925) (place to be searched); Andresen v. Maryland, 427 U.S. 463, 96 S. Ct. 2737, 49 L. Ed. 2d 627 (1976) (items to be seized).

[23]Brinegar v. U.S., 338 U.S. 160, 175, 69 S. Ct. 1302, 93 L. Ed. 1879 (1949). See also Maryland v. Pringle, 124 S. Ct. 795, 800, 157 L. Ed. 2d 769 (U.S. 2003) ("The probable-cause standard is incapable of precise definition or quantification into percentages because it deals with probabilities and depends on the totality of the circumstances."); Katz and Giannelli, Baldwin's Ohio Practice, Criminal Law (2d ed.) § 5:6.

[24]Draper v. U.S., 358 U.S. 307, 79 S. Ct. 329, 3 L. Ed. 2d 327 (1959).

[25]Illinois v. Gates, 462 U.S. 213, 103 S. Ct. 2317, 76 L. Ed. 2d 527 (1983). See also Massachusetts v. Upton, 466 U.S. 727, 104 S. Ct. 2085, 80 L. Ed. 2d 721 (1984).

requirement. First, a warrant is not required for a search incident to arrest.[26] At the time of arrest, the police may search the arrestee[27] and the area within his immediate control.[28] A special rule applies when the police arrest an occupant of an automobile; in such a case the police may also search the passenger compartment of the automobile.[29] In addition, the police may inventory the property of an arrestee at the stationhouse if he or she is to be incarcerated.[30]

Second, the United States Supreme Court has recognized a broad exception for warrantless automobile searches. Automobiles stopped on the highway may be searched at the time of the stop or at the stationhouse if the police have probable cause to believe criminal evidence is in the automobile.[31] This search generally may extend to containers located in the automobile.[32] Validly seized automobiles may also be inventoried, under certain conditions, by the police at the place of impoundment.[33]

Third, the police may enter a house without a warrant if they are in hot pursuit of a suspect.[34] In the absence of exigent circumstances, however, an arrest warrant is required before the police may enter the home of a person subject to arrest.[35] A search warrant is required when the police enter the house of a third party to effect an arrest.[36]

Fourth, the police may seize an item without a warrant if it is in plain view, that is, when the police come across incriminating evidence during a lawful search.[37]

Fifth, consent searches, which are discussed in the next section, have long been recognized as an exception.

§ 14:5   Consent searches

Another exception to the warrant requirement is recognized for consent searches. Unlike other exceptions, a search based upon consent also does not

---

[26]See Katz and Giannelli, Baldwin's Ohio Practice, Criminal Law (2d ed.), Ch 12.

[27]U.S. v. Robinson, 414 U.S. 218, 94 S. Ct. 467, 38 L. Ed. 2d 427 (1973); Gustafson v. Florida, 414 U.S. 260, 94 S. Ct. 488, 38 L. Ed. 2d 456 (1973).

[28]Chimel v. California, 395 U.S. 752, 89 S. Ct. 2034, 23 L. Ed. 2d 685 (1969). For a juvenile case applying this rule, see In re Marsh, 40 Ill. 2d 53, 237 N.E.2d 529 (1968).

[29]New York v. Belton, 453 U.S. 454, 101 S. Ct. 2860, 69 L. Ed. 2d 768 (1981).

[30]Illinois v. Lafayette, 462 U.S. 640, 103 S. Ct. 2605, 77 L. Ed. 2d 65 (1983).

[31]Florida v. Meyers, 466 U.S. 380, 104 S. Ct. 1852, 80 L. Ed. 2d 381 (1984); Chambers v. Maroney, 399 U.S. 42, 90 S. Ct. 1975, 26 L. Ed. 2d 419 (1970). See also Katz and Giannelli, Baldwin's Ohio Practice, Criminal Law (2d ed.), Ch 12; Hall, Search and Seizure (3d ed.) § 7.2.

For a juvenile case on this issue, see In Interest of J. R. M., 487 S.W.2d 502 (Mo. 1972).

[32]California v. Acevedo, 500 U.S. 565, 111 S. Ct. 1982, 114 L. Ed. 2d 619 (1991); U.S. v. Ross, 456 U.S. 798, 102 S. Ct. 2157, 72 L. Ed. 2d 572 (1982).

[33]Florida v. Wells, 495 U.S. 1, 110 S. Ct. 1632, 109 L. Ed. 2d 1 (1990); Colorado v. Bertine, 479 U.S. 367, 107 S. Ct. 738, 93 L. Ed. 2d 739 (1987); South Dakota v. Opperman, 428 U.S. 364, 96 S. Ct. 3092, 49 L. Ed. 2d 1000 (1976).

[34]U.S. v. Santana, 427 U.S. 38, 96 S. Ct. 2406, 49 L. Ed. 2d 300 (1976); Warden, Md. Penitentiary v. Hayden, 387 U.S. 294, 87 S. Ct. 1642, 18 L. Ed. 2d 782 (1967).

[35]Payton v. New York, 445 U.S. 573, 100 S. Ct. 1371, 63 L. Ed. 2d 639 (1980). See also Minnesota v. Olson, 495 U.S. 91, 110 S. Ct. 1684, 109 L. Ed. 2d 85 (1990); Welsh v. Wisconsin, 466 U.S. 740, 104 S. Ct. 2091, 80 L. Ed. 2d 732 (1984) (Entry of a home to arrest for a nonjailable traffic offense does not constitute exigent circumstances.). See generally Katz and Giannelli, Baldwin's Ohio Practice, Criminal Law (2d ed.), Ch 11.

For a juvenile case on this issue, see Kwok T. v. Mauriello (In Matter of Kwok T.), 43 N.Y.2d 213, 401 N.Y.S.2d 52, 371 N.E.2d 814 (1977).

[36]Steagald v. U.S., 451 U.S. 204, 101 S. Ct. 1642, 68 L. Ed. 2d 38 (1981).

[37]Horton v. California, 496 U.S. 128, 110 S. Ct. 2301, 110 L. Ed. 2d 112 (1990); Arizona v. Hicks, 480 U.S. 321, 107 S. Ct. 1149, 94 L. Ed. 2d 347 (1987); Texas v. Brown, 460 U.S. 730, 103 S. Ct. 1535, 75 L. Ed. 2d 502 (1983); Coolidge v. New Hampshire, 403 U.S. 443, 91 S. Ct. 2022, 29 L. Ed. 2d 564 (1971). See generally Katz and Giannelli, Baldwin's Ohio Practice, Criminal Law (2d ed.), Ch 16.

require probable cause. A valid consent depends on three factors: (1) whether the consent was voluntary; (2) the scope of the consent; and (3) whether it was obtained from a person who may validly give consent.

Voluntariness. The voluntariness of a consent is determined by considering the "totality of all the circumstances," including factors such as the schooling and intelligence of the person consenting and the conduct of the police in obtaining consent.[1] Failure of the police to advise a person of the right to refuse to give consent is not determinative; it is merely one factor to be considered in assessing whether the consent is voluntary.[2] Nevertheless, neither mere submission to a claim by the police that they have authority to search[3] nor consent obtained by trickery is a voluntary consent.[4]

Scope of consent. The person giving consent can limit the scope of the consent.[5]

Third-party consent. Under certain circumstances, a third party may give consent. According to the United States Supreme Court, if the police reasonably believe that a third party has authority to consent ("apparent authority"), the consent is valid.[6] Generally, the courts have held that the consent of a parent to the search of a child's room is valid.[7] As one court has stated:

> In his capacity as the head of the household, a father has the responsibility and authority for the discipline, training and control of his children. In the exercise of his parental authority a father has full access to the room set aside for his son for purposes of fulfilling his right and duty to control his son's social behavior and to obtain obedience. . . . Permitting an officer to search a bedroom in order to determine if his son is using or trafficking in narcotics [is] a reasonable and necessary extension of a father's authority and control over his children's moral training, health and personal hygiene.[8]

In *State v. Reynolds*,[9] the Ohio Supreme Court ruled that "[p]arents may consent to a search of premises owned by them. Reynolds, Sr. owned the house that was searched and there was no agreement between him and Reynolds concerning the privacy of Reynolds's bedroom. Reynolds had not been paying rent, which would have given him a claim that he had a proprietary interest in his bedroom."

Parental consent, however, is not always valid. For example, one court has held that a father's consent to the search of a 17-year-old's toolbox was in-

---

[Section 14:5]

[1]Schneckloth v. Bustamonte, 412 U.S. 218, 227, 93 S. Ct. 2041, 36 L. Ed. 2d 854 (1973).

[2]Schneckloth v. Bustamonte, 412 U.S. 218, 227, 93 S. Ct. 2041, 36 L. Ed. 2d 854 (1973). See generally Katz and Giannelli, Baldwin's Ohio Practice, Criminal Law (2d ed.), Ch 21.

For a juvenile case in which the issue of consent is raised, see In re Ronny, 40 Misc. 2d 194, 242 N.Y.S.2d 844 (Fam. Ct. 1963). See also State v. Davis, 56 Ohio St. 2d 51, 10 Ohio Op. 3d 87, 381 N.E.2d 641 (1978) (A minor may consent and thereby waive his Fourth Amendment rights.).

[3]Bumper v. North Carolina, 391 U.S. 543, 88 S. Ct. 1788, 20 L. Ed. 2d 797 (1968); In re Brent, No. 35400 (8th Dist. Ct. App., Cuyahoga, 2-17-77).

[4]In re Robert T., 8 Cal. App. 3d 990, 88 Cal. Rptr. 37 (1st Dist. 1970).

[5]See Florida v. Jimeno, 500 U.S. 248, 251, 111 S. Ct. 1801, 114 L. Ed. 2d 297 (1991) ("The Fourth Amendment is satisfied when, under the circumstances, it is objectively reasonable for the officer to believe that the scope of the suspect's consent permitted him to open a particular container within the car.").

[6]Illinois v. Rodriguez, 497 U.S. 177, 110 S. Ct. 2793, 111 L. Ed. 2d 148 (1990). See generally Katz and Giannelli, Baldwin's Ohio Practice, Criminal Law (2d ed.) § 21:9.

[7]E.g., U.S. v. Wright, 564 F.2d 785, 2 Fed. R. Evid. Serv. 189, 48 A.L.R. Fed. 119 (8th Cir. 1977); U.S. v. Whitfield, 747 F. Supp. 807 (D.D.C. 1990); State v. Carder, 9 Ohio St. 2d 1, 38 Ohio Op. 2d 1, 222 N.E.2d 620 (1966); State of Ohio v. Bortree, 1982 WL 6755 (Ohio Ct. App. 3d Dist. Logan County 1982). See generally Katz and Giannelli, Baldwin's Ohio Practice, Criminal Law (2d ed.) § 21:11; Comment, "Who's Been Searching in My Room?" Parental Waiver of Children's Fourth Amendment Rights, 17 U.C.D. L. Rev. 359 (1983).

[8]Vandenberg v. Superior Court, 8 Cal. App. 3d 1048, 87 Cal. Rptr. 876 (2d Dist. 1970).

[9]State v. Reynolds, 80 Ohio St. 3d 670, 675, 1998-Ohio-171, 687 N.E.2d 1358 (1998).

valid where the son was present and objected: "The father claimed no interest in the box or its contents. He acknowledged that the son was owner, and the son did not consent to the search. Because those facts were known to the police there was no justification . . . for their relying on the father's consent to conduct the search."[10]

§ 14:6 School searches

The constitutionality of school searches raises a number of Fourth Amendment issues.[1] The United States Supreme Court resolved some of these issues in *New Jersey v. T.L.O.*[2] In that case, a student was taken to the vice-principal's office for smoking in the lavatory. A search of her purse revealed cigarettes as well as marijuana. This discovery led to the initiation of delinquency proceedings, at which the constitutionality of the search was challenged.

On review, the Supreme Court upheld the search. Initially, the Court declared the Fourth Amendment applicable to school searches. A number of courts had previously held that school officials were private citizens, acting in loco parentis, and thus not subject to the Fourth Amendment.[3] In response, the Court wrote:

> Such reasoning is in tension with contemporary reality and the teachings of this Court. . . . Today's public school officials do not merely exercise authority voluntarily conferred on them by individual parents; rather they act in furtherance of publicly mandated educational and disciplinary policies. . . . In carrying out searches and other disciplinary functions pursuant to such policies, school officials act as representatives of the State, not merely as surrogates for the parents, and they cannot claim the parents' immunity from the strictures of the Fourth Amendment.[4]

Next, the Court focused on the requirements of the Fourth Amendment in the school setting. In this context, the student's legitimate expectations of privacy are balanced against the school's legitimate need to maintain an environment in which learning can take place. The Court found that the warrant requirement imposed too high a burden on the proper functioning of school officials. Similarly, the Court believed that probable cause was too demanding an evidentiary standard in this setting. Instead, the Court held:

> [T]he legality of a search of a student should depend simply on the reasonableness, under all the circumstances, of the search. Determining reasonableness of any search involves a twofold inquiry: first, one must consider "whether the

---

[10]In re Scott K., 24 Cal. 3d 395, 405, 155 Cal. Rptr. 671, 595 P.2d 105 (1979). See also Reeves v. Warden, Md. Penitentiary, 346 F.2d 915 (4th Cir. 1965); People v. Flowers, 23 Mich. App. 523, 179 N.W.2d 56 (1970).

[Section 14:6]

[1]See generally Katz and Giannelli, Baldwin's Ohio Practice, Criminal Law (2d ed.) §§ 20:7 to 20:9; IJA-ABA Standards Relating to Schools and Education 150–59 (1982); Rights of Juveniles: The Juvenile Justice System (2d ed.) § 3.7; Hall, Search and Seizure (3d ed.) § 10.11; Parkey, Fourth Amendment Protections in the Elementary and Secondary School Settings, 38 Mercer L. Rev. 1417 (1987); Note, Student Fourth Amendment Rights: Defining the Scope of the T.L.O. School-Search Exception, 66 N.Y.U. L. Rev. 1077 (1991); Note, School Searches Under the Fourth Amendment: *New Jersey v. T.L.O.*, 72 Cornell L. Rev. 368 (1987); Admissibility, in criminal case, of evidence obtained by search conducted by school official or teacher, 49 A.L.R. 3d 978.

[2]New Jersey v. T.L.O., 469 U.S. 325, 105 S. Ct. 733, 83 L. Ed. 2d 720, 21 Ed. Law Rep. 1122 (1985).

[3]E.g., In re Donaldson, 269 Cal. App. 2d 509, 75 Cal. Rptr. 220 (3d Dist. 1969); People v. Stewart, 63 Misc. 2d 601, 313 N.Y.S.2d 253 (City Crim. Ct. 1970); Com. v. Dingfelt, 227 Pa. Super. 380, 323 A.2d 145 (1974); Mercer v. State, 450 S.W.2d 715 (Tex. Civ. App. Austin 1970).

See also State v. Wingerd, 40 Ohio App. 2d 236, 69 Ohio Op. 2d 217, 318 N.E.2d 866 (4th Dist. Athens County 1974) (College officials who searched a dormitory room are private citizens.).

[4]New Jersey v. T.L.O., 469 U.S. 325, 336, 105 S. Ct. 733, 83 L. Ed. 2d 720, 21 Ed. Law Rep. 1122 (1985).

. . . action was justified at its inception" . . .; second, one must determine whether the search as actually conducted "was reasonably related in scope to the circumstances which justified the interference in the first place" . . . . Under ordinary circumstances, a search of a student by a teacher or other school official will be "justified at its inception" when there are reasonable grounds for suspecting that the search will turn up evidence that the student has violated or is violating either the law or the rules of the school. Such a search will be permissible in its scope when the measures adopted are reasonably related to the objectives of the search and not excessively intrusive in light of the age and sex of the student and the nature of the infraction.[5]

The Court's decision in *T.L.O.* clarified two issues: (1) Fourth Amendment protections extend to the schoolhouse, and (2) reasonable suspicion (not probable cause) is the controlling standard in determining the constitutionality of these searches. A number of other issues, however, were left unresolved. First, the Court pointed out that its decision was limited to searches by school officials; the decision did not control searches conducted by school officials in conjunction with or at the behest of the police.[6] Second, the case involved the search of a purse, and the Court refused to say whether its rationale extended to searches of lockers, desks, or other school property used for storage by students.[7] For example, some lower courts have held that school officials may validly consent to a search of student lockers.[8] Finally, the Court refused to decide whether the exclusionary rule applied to school searches.[9]

The Ohio court of appeals in *In re Adam*[10] ruled that a locker search pursuant to RC 3313.20(B)(1)(a) is constitutional because that provision requires "reasonable suspicion." In contrast, the court believed that RC 3313.20(B)(1)(b) was unconstitutional because it sanctioned random searches without reasonable suspicion. In *In re Dengg*,[11] the court of appeals upheld the search of a car in a school parking lot under the automobile exception to the warrant requirement. In reaching this result, the court first held that a dog sniff of the automobile was not a "search" and once the dog alerted, the police had probable cause to search the vehicle.

Drug testing. In *Vernonia School District 47J v. Acton*,[12] the United States Supreme Court upheld random urinalysis drug testing for public high school students who participated in athletic programs. Based on *T.L.O.* and

---

[5]New Jersey v. T.L.O., 469 U.S. 325, 341–42, 105 S. Ct. 733, 83 L. Ed. 2d 720, 21 Ed. Law Rep. 1122 (1985).

[6]New Jersey v. T.L.O., 469 U.S. 325, 341 n.7, 105 S. Ct. 733, 83 L. Ed. 2d 720, 21 Ed. Law Rep. 1122 (1985). See also Cason v. Cook, 810 F.2d 188, 37 Ed. Law Rep. 473 (8th Cir. 1987) (Limited role of police liaison officer did not change nature of school search.).

[7]New Jersey v. T.L.O., 469 U.S. 325, 337 n.5, 105 S. Ct. 733, 83 L. Ed. 2d 720, 21 Ed. Law Rep. 1122 (1985). See also In Interest of Isiah B., 176 Wis. 2d 639, 500 N.W.2d 637, 83 Ed. Law Rep. 419 (1993) (Random locker searches by school officials do not violate Fourth Amendment.); State v. Joseph T., 175 W. Va. 598, 336 S.E.2d 728, 28 Ed. Law Rep. 1169 (1985) (Reasonable suspicion standard applied to locker search.).

[8]E.g., State v. Stein, 203 Kan. 638, 456 P.2d 1 (1969); People v. Overton, 20 N.Y.2d 360, 283 N.Y.S.2d 22, 229 N.E.2d 596 (1967) (Vice-principal could validly consent to search of student lockers.).

[9]New Jersey v. T.L.O., 469 U.S. 325, 333 n.3, 105 S. Ct. 733, 83 L. Ed. 2d 720, 21 Ed. Law Rep. 1122 (1985). See also State v. Young, 234 Ga. 488, 216 S.E.2d 586 (1975) (The exclusionary rule does not apply to searches conducted by public school officials.).

[10]In re Adam, 120 Ohio App. 3d 364, 697 N.E.2d 1100, 127 Ed. Law Rep. 1029 (11th Dist. Lake County 1997).

[11]In re Dengg, 132 Ohio App. 3d 360, 366, 724 N.E.2d 1255 (11th Dist. Portage County 1999) ("[T]he police officers were invited by school officials to conduct a search for illicit contraband at SHS, a public high school, and were deployed to the school's parking lots as part of that exercise. The police officers had probable cause to search the automobile driven by appellee to school because a police canine alerted its handler to the presence of drugs when it sniffed the exterior of appellee's vehicle.").

[12]Vernonia School Dist. 47J v. Acton, 515 U.S. 646, 115 S. Ct. 2386, 132 L. Ed. 2d 564, 101 Ed. Law Rep. 37 (1995).

prior cases upholding drug testing in other contexts,[13] the Court found the drug testing scheme at issue reasonable. "Fourth Amendment rights, no less than First and Fourteenth Amendment rights, are different in public schools than elsewhere; the 'reasonableness' inquiry cannot disregard the schools' custodial and tutelary responsibility for children."[14] In *Board of Education v. Earls*,[15] the Court expanded the holding of *Vernonia* to permit drug testing of all students participating in competitive extracurricular activities. The policy was "a reasonable means of furthering the School District's important interest in preventing and deterring drug use among its school children."

§ 14:7 Probation searches

RC 2152.19(F) authorizes a warrantless search by probation officers of a delinquent child on probation if there are reasonable grounds to believe that the child is not abiding by the law or conditions of probation.[1] This type of search also extends to the delinquent's residence, motor vehicle, and property. Both the child and parents, guardians, or custodians must be given written notice of this authority to search.

Cross References
§ 14:16
Research References
Katz, Ohio Arrest, Search and Seizure §§ 8:5 to 8:7
Katz and Giannelli, Baldwin's Ohio Practice, Criminal Law (2d ed.), Chs 9, 11

§ 14:8 DNA databases

RC 2152.74 specifies the circumstances under which delinquent juveniles are subject to DNA specimen collection. Every jurisdiction has enacted statutes that require blood samples for persons convicted of crimes, or a specific category of crime, such as felonies, violent crimes or sex offenders. Such provisions have challenged on Fourth Amendment grounds. In *State v. Olivas*,[1] the Washington Supreme Court rejected a search and seizure challenge to DNA identification sex offender law. According to the Court, this provision constituted a valid regulatory search. The Fourth Circuit reached the same result but under a different Fourth Amendment analysis—the diminished privacy rights of convicted persons.[2] The Ninth Circuit upheld an Oregon statute that required all persons convicted of murder or a sex offense to provide blood samples for a DNA data bank.[3] The court wrote:

Taking into account all of the factors discussed above—the reduced expecta-

---

[13]See National Treasury Employees Union v. Von Raab, 489 U.S. 656, 109 S. Ct. 1384, 103 L. Ed. 2d 685 (1989); Skinner v. Railway Labor Executives' Ass'n, 489 U.S. 602, 109 S. Ct. 1402, 103 L. Ed. 2d 639 (1989).

[14]Vernonia School Dist. 47J v. Acton, 515 U.S. 646, 115 S. Ct. 2386, 2392, 132 L. Ed. 2d 564, 101 Ed. Law Rep. 37 (1995). See also Buchter, Scriven & Sheeran, Ohio School Law, Ch. 47 (2003–04 rev. ed.) (Search and Seizure).

[15]Board of Education v. Earls, 536 U.S. 822, 838, 122 S. Ct. 2559, 153 L. Ed. 2d 735 (2002) (activities covered included the Academic Team, Future Farmers of America, Future Homemakers of America, band, choir, pom-pom, cheerleading, and athletics).

[Section 14:7]
[1]See generally Katz and Giannelli, Baldwin's Ohio Practice, Criminal Law (2d ed.) § 20:13.

[Section 14:8]
[1]State v. Olivas, 122 Wash. 2d 73, 856 P.2d 1076 (1993).

[2]Jones v. Murray, 962 F.2d 302 (4th Cir. 1992). See also Sanders v. Coman, 864 F. Supp. 496, 499–501 (E.D. N.C. 1994) (forcible drawing of blood for DNA databank violates neither the Fourth, Eighth, nor Fourteenth Amendments).

[3]Rise v. State of Or., 59 F.3d 1556 (9th Cir. 1995). See also Boling v. Romer, 101 F.3d 1336, 1340 (10th Cir. 1996) ("[W]hile obtaining and analyzing DNA or saliva of an inmate convicted of a sex offense is a search and seizure implicating Fourth Amendment concerns, it is a reasonable

tions of privacy held by persons convicted of one of the felonies to which [the statute] applies, the blood extractions' relatively minimal intrusion into these persons' privacy interests, the public's incontestable interest in preventing recidivism and identifying and prosecuting murderers and sexual offenders, and the likelihood that a DNA data bank will advance this interest—we conclude that [the statute] is reasonable and therefore constitutional under the Fourth Amendment.[4]

The court also noted that the statute left prison officials no discretion to choose which person must submit and also prohibited the use of this information for illegitimate purposes. Most later cases have also upheld DNA database searches.[5] Comparable juvenile statutes have also survived attack.[6]

The Ohio court of appeals upheld the DNA database statute in *In re Nicholson*.[7] The court found the statute to be reasonable within the meaning of the Fourth Amendment for several reasons. First, the statute required more than probable cause; it required a delinquency adjudication based upon the "beyond a reasonable doubt" standard or a constitutionally safeguarded admission by the juvenile. Second, the intrusion (blood sample) was minimal. Third, an inmate or probationer has diminished constitutional rights. Finally, the state's interest was significant: "[T]he state's legitimate interest in creating a DNA identification data bank not only deters a juvenile from committing future sex offenses, but also aids the police in the investigation of past and future crimes. These are legitimate state interests which outweigh the minimally intrusive drawing of blood."[8]

§ 14:9 Confessions—Due process

The admissibility of a confession may be challenged on several distinct constitutional grounds.[1] First, a confession may be involuntary and thus violate due process. Confessions obtained by means of physical or psychological coercion are examples of involuntary confessions. Second, a confession may be obtained in violation of the Fifth Amendment's privilege against com-

---

search and seizure. This is so in light of an inmate's diminished privacy rights; the minimal intrusion of saliva and blood tests; and the legitimate government interest in the investigation and prosecution of unsolved and future criminal acts by the use of DNA in a manner not significantly different from the use of fingerprints.") (also rejecting Fifth Amendment, due process, equal protection, and cruel and unusual punishment claims).

[4]Rise v. State of Or., 59 F.3d 1556, 1562 (9th Cir. 1995). See generally Krent, Of Diaries and Data Banks: Use Restrictions Under the Fourth Amendment, 74 Tex. L. Rev. 49 (1995); Note, Criminal DNA Data Banks: Revolution For Law Enforcement of Threat to Individual Privacy? 22 Am. J. Crim. L. 461 (1995).

[5]U.S. v. Kimler, 335 F.3d 1132, 1146, 61 Fed. R. Evid. Serv. 1024 (10th Cir. 2003), cert. denied, 124 S. Ct. 945, 157 L. Ed. 2d 759 (U.S. 2003) ("The DNA Act, while implicating the Fourth Amendment, is a reasonable search and seizure under the special needs exception to the Fourth Amendment's warrant requirement because the desire to build a DNA database goes beyond the ordinary law enforcement need."); U.S. v. Sczubelek, 255 F. Supp. 2d 315 (D. Del. 2003) ("Weighing the special need for DNA testing against defendant's diminished expectation of privacy and the minor intrusiveness of a blood test, the court finds the DNA Act testing requirements reasonable."); U.S. v. Reynard, 220 F. Supp. 2d 1142 (S.D. Cal. 2002); State v. Martinez, 276 Kan. 527, 78 P.3d 769, 775 (2003).

[6]Matter of Appeal in Maricopa County Juvenile Action Numbers JV-512600 and JV-512797, 187 Ariz. 419, 930 P.2d 496 (Ct. App. Div. 1 1996) (juvenile sex offenders).

[7]In re Nicholson, 132 Ohio App. 3d 303, 724 N.E.2d 1217 (8th Dist. Cuyahoga County 1999).

[8]In re Nicholson, 132 Ohio App. 3d 303, 309, 724 N.E.2d 1217 (8th Dist. Cuyahoga County 1999).

[Section 14:9]
[1]See In the Matter of Hawkins, 1983 WL 4091 (Ohio Ct. App. 9th Dist. Lorain County 1983) (Juv. R. 7(A), which requires a person taking a child into custody to bring the child to court, to deliver the child to a place of detention, or to release the child to his parents, does not prohibit the police from questioning a child taken into custody.).

pelled self-incrimination as defined in *Miranda v. Arizona.*[2] Third, a confession may be obtained in violation of the Sixth Amendment right to counsel.[3] Finally, a confession that is the product of an illegal search or seizure under the Fourth Amendment may be excludable as "fruit of the poisonous tree."[4] This section examines the due process issue.

Prior to *Miranda*, the United States Supreme Court examined the admissibility of confessions under the Due Process Clause.[5] In deciding these cases, the Court employed a "voluntariness test." Although the *Miranda* decision has overshadowed the voluntariness test, that test remains valid and important in a number of contexts. Accordingly, a statement may be involuntary and therefore inadmissible, even if the *Miranda* requirements are satisfied.[6] Moreover, an involuntary statement cannot be used to impeach a defendant, whereas a statement obtained in violation of *Miranda* may be used for impeachment.[7]

The Court summarized the voluntariness test as follows:

> The ultimate test . . . [is] voluntariness. Is the confession the product of an essentially free and unconstrained choice by its maker? If it is, if he has willed to confess, it may be used against him. If it is not, if his will has been overborne and his capacity for self-determination critically impaired, the use of his confession offends due process.[8]

The voluntariness test is based on the totality of circumstances and includes such factors as the defendant's age, education, intelligence, and mental condition. Other factors focus on police conduct. For example, failure to warn of rights, incommunicado detention, lengthy periods of questioning, use of relays in the interrogation, physical abuse, lack of food or sleep, deceptions, improper advice and promises are all relevant to a voluntariness determination.[9] However, the police must somehow be involved in the coercion.[10]

Two of the Court's voluntariness cases involved juveniles. These juveniles, however, were prosecuted in criminal, not juvenile, court. In *Haley v. Ohio*,[11] a 15-year-old male confessed to murder after several hours of questioning. The Court commented:

> What transpired would make us pause for careful inquiry if a mature man were involved. And when, as here, a mere child—an easy victim of the law—is before us, special care in scrutinizing the record must be used. Age 15 is a tender and difficult age for a boy of any race. He cannot be judged by the more exacting standards of maturity. That which would leave a man cold and

---

[2]Miranda v. Arizona, 384 U.S. 436, 86 S. Ct. 1602, 16 L. Ed. 2d 694, 10 A.L.R.3d 974 (1966). See § 14:10, Confessions—*Miranda*.

[3]See § 14:11, Confessions—Right to counsel.

[4]See Taylor v. Alabama, 457 U.S. 687, 102 S. Ct. 2664, 73 L. Ed. 2d 314 (1982); Dunaway v. New York, 442 U.S. 200, 99 S. Ct. 2248, 60 L. Ed. 2d 824 (1979); Brown v. Illinois, 422 U.S. 590, 95 S. Ct. 2254, 45 L. Ed. 2d 416 (1975). See also In re Appeal No. 245 (75) from Circuit Court for Kent County, 29 Md. App. 131, 349 A.2d 434 (1975) (applying fruit of poisonous tree doctrine to a juvenile case).

[5]See generally Katz and Giannelli, Baldwin's Ohio Practice, Criminal Law (2d ed.), Ch 23.

[6]See Arizona v. Fulminante, 499 U.S. 279, 111 S. Ct. 1246, 113 L. Ed. 2d 302 (1991); Miller v. Fenton, 474 U.S. 104, 106 S. Ct. 445, 88 L. Ed. 2d 405 (1985); State v. Kassow, 28 Ohio St. 2d 141, 57 Ohio Op. 2d 390, 277 N.E.2d 435 (1971).

[7]Compare Mincey v. Arizona, 437 U.S. 385, 98 S. Ct. 2408, 57 L. Ed. 2d 290 (1978) with Harris v. New York, 401 U.S. 222, 91 S. Ct. 643, 28 L. Ed. 2d 1 (1971).

[8]Culombe v. Connecticut, 367 U.S. 568, 602, 81 S. Ct. 1860, 6 L. Ed. 2d 1037 (1961).

[9]See generally 3 Wigmore, Evidence 352 n.11 (Chadbourn rev. 1970); Note, Developments in the Law—Confessions, 79 Harv. L. Rev. 935 (1966).

[10]Colorado v. Connelly, 479 U.S. 157, 165, 107 S. Ct. 515, 93 L. Ed. 2d 473 (1986) ("The most outrageous behavior by a private party seeking to secure evidence against a defendant does not make that evidence inadmissible under the Due Process Clause.").

[11]Haley v. State of Ohio, 332 U.S. 596, 68 S. Ct. 302, 92 L. Ed. 224 (1948).

unimpressed can overawe and overwhelm a lad in his early teens. This is the period of great instability which the crisis of adolescence produces. A 15-year-old lad, questioned through the dead of night by relays of police, is a ready victim of the inquisition.[12]

In *Gallegos v. Colorado*,[13] the Court, in holding a confession involuntary, again stressed the differences between juveniles and adults:

> He cannot be compared with an adult in full possession of his senses and knowledgeable of the consequences of his admissions. He would have no way of knowing what the consequences of his confession were without advice as to his rights—from someone concerned with securing him those rights—and without the aid of more mature judgment as to the steps he should take in the predicament in which he found himself. A lawyer or an adult relative or friend could have given the petitioner the protection which his own immaturity could not.[14]

Courts have applied the voluntariness test to juvenile cases: "Use of an involuntary confession in a juvenile court proceeding offends fundamental fairness because of the likelihood of its untrustworthiness."[15] In *State v. Evans*,[16] the Ohio court of appeals held that statements made as part of a residential treatment program were involuntary. The court commented:

> Evans received no instructions about his constitutional rights. Evans also did not have a parent or an interested adult present during the questioning. In fact, those adults who were expected to work with Evans for his benefit and sought to establish a trusting relationship with him were the very adults who ultimately divulged what he had told them. There is no doubt that Evans was isolated from any adult whose main priority was protecting Evans's interests.
>
> . . .
>
> What is remarkable about the court-ordered interrogation to which Evans was subjected is not its intensity or relative harshness, but rather its grinding duration and inevitability. Evans was warned when he arrived at Hillcrest that he must divulge incriminating information. It was not a question of whether Hillcrest would get the information; it was only a question of when Evans would succumb, as had all those who had preceded him. Hillcrest counselors institutionally and effectively employed both inducements and threats to insure that Evans would eventually give them what they wanted and thereby incriminate himself. While we find no fault with Hillcrest's procedures for purposes of therapy, our inquiry is far different when considering information obtained as a result.

§ 14:10 Confessions—*Miranda*

In *Miranda v. Arizona*,[1] the United States Supreme Court held that custodial interrogation constituted compulsion within the meaning of the Fifth Amendment privilege against compelled self-incrimination. To protect the privilege in this context, the Court required the reading of the now familiar *Miranda* warnings. Prior to any questioning, suspects must be warned

[12]Haley v. State of Ohio, 332 U.S. 596, 599, 68 S. Ct. 302, 92 L. Ed. 224 (1948).

[13]Gallegos v. Colorado, 370 U.S. 49, 82 S. Ct. 1209, 8 L. Ed. 2d 325, 87 A.L.R.2d 614 (1962).

[14]Gallegos v. Colorado, 370 U.S. 49, 54, 82 S. Ct. 1209, 8 L. Ed. 2d 325, 87 A.L.R.2d 614 (1962). See also State v. Bell, 48 Ohio St. 2d 270, 277, 2 Ohio Op. 3d 427, 358 N.E.2d 556 (1976); State v. Stewart, 176 Ohio St. 156, 27 Ohio Op. 2d 42, 198 N.E.2d 439 (1964).

[15]In re State in Interest of Carlo, 48 N.J. 224, 236, 225 A.2d 110 (1966). See also U.S. v. Ramsey, 367 F. Supp. 1307 (W.D. Mo. 1973); In re Garth D., 55 Cal. App. 3d 986, 127 Cal. Rptr. 881 (4th Dist. 1976); Matter of Dunlop, 1984 WL 14171 (Ohio Ct. App. 8th Dist. Cuyahoga County 1984); In re White, No. 40971 (8th Dist. Ct. App., Cuyahoga, 7-31-80). See generally Voluntariness and admissibility of minor's confession, 87 A.L.R. 2d 624.

[16]State v. Evans, 144 Ohio App. 3d 539, 563, 760 N.E.2d 909 (1st Dist. Hamilton County 2001).

[Section 14:10]
[1]Miranda v. Arizona, 384 U.S. 436, 86 S. Ct. 1602, 16 L. Ed. 2d 694, 10 A.L.R.3d 974 (1966). See also Dickerson v. U.S., 530 U.S. 428, 120 S. Ct. 2326, 147 L. Ed. 2d 405 (2000) (2003) (reaffirming *Miranda*).

that (1) they have the right to remain silent; (2) anything said can be used against them in a court of law; (3) they have the right to the presence of an attorney; and (4) if they cannot afford an attorney, one will be appointed prior to any questioning if they so desire.[2] The verbatim recital of the words of the *Miranda* opinion is not required, so long as the warnings fully convey the rights required by *Miranda*.[3] Although the warnings are required in misdemeanor as well as felony cases,[4] the Supreme Court has recognized a "public safety" exception where the warnings are not required.[5]

Custodial interrogation. The *Miranda* rights are triggered by "custodial interrogation."[6] If either custody or interrogation is absent, the warnings are not required. In *Miranda* the Court defined custodial interrogation as follows: "By custodial interrogation, we mean questioning initiated by law enforcement officers after a person has been taken into custody or otherwise deprived of his freedom of action in any significant way."[7] In a later case, the Court equated "custody" with "arrest." According to the Court, "[T]he ultimate inquiry is simply whether there is a 'formal arrest or restraint on freedom of movement' of the degree associated with a formal arrest."[8] Thus, even if the defendant is the focus of the police investigation, the warnings are not required unless he is in custody.[9] Moreover, questioning a suspect at the stationhouse does not necessarily mean that he is in custody.[10]

Even if the defendant is in custody, *Miranda* applies only when he is subjected to "interrogation." Volunteered statements are not subject to *Miranda*.[11] According to the Supreme Court, "the Miranda safeguards come into play whenever a person in custody is subjected to either express questioning or its functional equivalent."[12] The latter phrase includes "any words or actions on the part of the police (other than those normally attendant to arrest and custody) that the police should know are reasonably likely to elicit an incriminating response from the suspect."[13]

Waiver. After receiving *Miranda* warnings, a suspect may waive Fifth Amendment rights and make a statement.[14] The Court in *Miranda* indicated that the prosecution had a heavy burden in establishing a waiver; the failure to request counsel does not constitute a waiver, and a waiver will not be

---

[2]Miranda v. Arizona, 384 U.S. 436, 86 S. Ct. 1602, 16 L. Ed. 2d 694, 10 A.L.R.3d 974 (1966). See Katz and Giannelli, Baldwin's Ohio Practice, Criminal Law (2d ed.), Ch 24.

[3]Duckworth v. Eagan, 492 U.S. 195, 109 S. Ct. 2875, 106 L. Ed. 2d 166 (1989); California v. Prysock, 453 U.S. 355, 101 S. Ct. 2806, 69 L. Ed. 2d 696 (1981). See also State v. Harris, 48 Ohio St. 2d 351, 2 Ohio Op. 3d 472, 359 N.E.2d 67 (1976).

[4]Pennsylvania v. Bruder, 488 U.S. 9, 109 S. Ct. 205, 102 L. Ed. 2d 172 (1988); Berkemer v. McCarty, 468 U.S. 420, 104 S. Ct. 3138, 82 L. Ed. 2d 317 (1984). See also State v. Buchholz, 11 Ohio St. 3d 24, 462 N.E.2d 1222 (1984).

[5]New York v. Quarles, 467 U.S. 649, 104 S. Ct. 2626, 81 L. Ed. 2d 550 (1984).

[6]See generally Katz and Giannelli, Baldwin's Ohio Practice, Criminal Law (2d ed.), Ch 24.

[7]Miranda v. Arizona, 384 U.S. 436, 444, 86 S. Ct. 1602, 16 L. Ed. 2d 694, 10 A.L.R.3d 974 (1966).

[8]California v. Beheler, 463 U.S. 1121, 1125, 103 S. Ct. 3517, 77 L. Ed. 2d 1275 (1983). See also Berkemer v. McCarty, 468 U.S. 420, 104 S. Ct. 3138, 82 L. Ed. 2d 317 (1984); Minnesota v. Murphy, 465 U.S. 420, 430–31, 104 S. Ct. 1136, 79 L. Ed. 2d 409 (1984).

[9]Beckwith v. U.S., 425 U.S. 341, 96 S. Ct. 1612, 48 L. Ed. 2d 1 (1976). See also State v. Lipker, 16 Ohio App. 2d 21, 45 Ohio Op. 2d 34, 241 N.E.2d 171 (4th Dist. Lawrence County 1968).

[10]Oregon v. Mathiason, 429 U.S. 492, 97 S. Ct. 711, 50 L. Ed. 2d 714 (1977).

[11]State v. Perry, 14 Ohio St. 2d 256, 43 Ohio Op. 2d 434, 237 N.E.2d 891 (1968).

[12]Rhode Island v. Innis, 446 U.S. 291, 300–01, 100 S. Ct. 1682, 64 L. Ed. 2d 297 (1980).

[13]Rhode Island v. Innis, 446 U.S. 291, 301, 100 S. Ct. 1682, 64 L. Ed. 2d 297 (1980). See also Arizona v. Mauro, 481 U.S. 520, 107 S. Ct. 1931, 95 L. Ed. 2d 458 (1987).

[14]See generally Katz and Giannelli, Baldwin's Ohio Practice, Criminal Law (2d ed.), Ch 26.

presumed simply from the suspect's silence.[15] If no evidence is introduced at a suppression hearing to establish a knowing and intelligent waiver, the defendant's statements are inadmissible.[16]

In *North Carolina v. Butler*,[17] the Supreme Court considered the validity of a waiver where the defendant agreed to talk but refused to sign a waiver of rights form. The Court upheld the waiver, commenting:

> An express written or oral statement of waiver of the right to remain silent or of the right to counsel is usually strong proof of the validity of that waiver, but it is not inevitably either necessary or sufficient to establish waiver. The question is not one of form, but rather whether the defendant in fact knowingly and voluntarily waived the rights delineated in the *Miranda* case. . . . [M]ere silence is not enough. That does not mean that the defendant's silence, coupled with an understanding of his rights and a course of conduct indicating waiver, may never support a conclusion that the defendant has waived his rights. The courts must presume that a defendant did not waive his rights; the prosecution's burden is great; but in at least some cases waiver can be clearly inferred from the actions and words of the person interrogated.[18]

The Court has found a valid waiver where the defendant was not informed of all the crimes he was suspected of committing,[19] where the defendant was not informed that a lawyer had been retained for him,[20] and where a defendant refused to make a written statement but agreed to discuss a crime.[21]

Once a defendant invokes the right to remain silent or requests an attorney after receiving *Miranda* warnings, questioning must cease. The conditions under which interrogation may resume depend on which right the defendant has invoked. If the suspect indicates a desire to remain silent, but does not request counsel, questioning may resume if the police "scrupulously honor" the initial decision to remain silent. In *Michigan v. Mosley*,[22] the Court upheld the admission of a statement made during a second interrogation. Both interrogations were preceded by *Miranda* warnings; the defendant invoked the right to remain silent after the first interrogation. The Court emphasized several factors that demonstrated that the defendant's right to remain silent had been scrupulously honored: the second interrogation involved a different crime, was conducted by a different police officer, and occurred after a significant lapse of time. A different rule applies if the defendant requests counsel after receiving warnings. In such a case the prosecution must establish that the defendant (1) initiated the further communication with the police, and (2) validly waived the right to counsel.[23]

Impeachment. Impeachment is an attempt to diminish a witness's credibility or worthiness of belief. Statements obtained in violation of *Miranda* may nevertheless be used to impeach a defendant who testifies at trial.[24] If, however, the statement is involuntary (coerced), it is not admissible, even for

---

[15]Miranda v. Arizona, 384 U.S. 436, 86 S. Ct. 1602, 16 L. Ed. 2d 694, 10 A.L.R.3d 974 (1966).

[16]Tague v. Louisiana, 444 U.S. 469, 100 S. Ct. 652, 62 L. Ed. 2d 622 (1980).

[17]North Carolina v. Butler, 441 U.S. 369, 99 S. Ct. 1755, 60 L. Ed. 2d 286 (1979).

[18]North Carolina v. Butler, 441 U.S. 369, 373, 99 S. Ct. 1755, 60 L. Ed. 2d 286 (1979). See also State v. Scott, 61 Ohio St. 2d 155, 15 Ohio Op. 3d 182, 400 N.E.2d 375 (1980).

[19]Colorado v. Spring, 479 U.S. 564, 107 S. Ct. 851, 93 L. Ed. 2d 954 (1987).

[20]Moran v. Burbine, 475 U.S. 412, 106 S. Ct. 1135, 89 L. Ed. 2d 410 (1986).

[21]Connecticut v. Barrett, 479 U.S. 523, 107 S. Ct. 828, 93 L. Ed. 2d 920 (1987).

[22]Michigan v. Mosley, 423 U.S. 96, 96 S. Ct. 321, 46 L. Ed. 2d 313 (1975).

[23]Oregon v. Bradshaw, 462 U.S. 1039, 103 S. Ct. 2830, 77 L. Ed. 2d 405 (1983). See also Minnick v. Mississippi, 498 U.S. 146, 111 S. Ct. 486, 112 L. Ed. 2d 489 (1990); Arizona v. Roberson, 486 U.S. 675, 108 S. Ct. 2093, 100 L. Ed. 2d 704 (1988); Edwards v. Arizona, 451 U.S. 477, 101 S. Ct. 1880, 68 L. Ed. 2d 378 (1981); Wyrick v. Fields, 459 U.S. 42, 103 S. Ct. 394, 74 L. Ed. 2d 214 (1982).

[24]Oregon v. Hass, 420 U.S. 714, 95 S. Ct. 1215, 43 L. Ed. 2d 570 (1975); Harris v. New York, 401 U.S. 222, 91 S. Ct. 643, 28 L. Ed. 2d 1 (1971). See generally Katz and Giannelli, Baldwin's Ohio Practice, Criminal Law (2d ed.), Ch 31.

impeachment.[25]

Under some circumstances, a defendant's silence also may be used to impeach trial testimony. In *Doyle v. Ohio*,[26] the United States Supreme Court held that due process is violated when a defendant is impeached by his silence following *Miranda* warnings:

> [W]hile it is true that the *Miranda* warnings contain no express assurance that silence will carry no penalty, such assurance is implicit to any person who receives the warnings. In such circumstances, it would be fundamentally unfair and a deprivation of due process to allow the arrested person's silence to be used to impeach an explanation subsequently offered at trial.[27]

Doyle applies only when a suspect remains silent after receiving *Miranda* warnings. If the suspect makes a statement, he is subject to impeachment.[28] Moreover, silence prior to arrest[29] or prior to the reading of *Miranda* warnings[30] is admissible for impeachment.

Juvenile cases. The lower courts have applied the *Miranda* requirements to juvenile court proceedings.[31] Interestingly, in *Fare v. Michael C.*,[32] its only case involving the application of *Miranda* to juvenile proceedings, the United States Supreme Court suggested that this issue remains undecided:

> [T]his Court has not yet held that *Miranda* applies with full force to exclude evidence obtained in violation of its proscriptions from consideration in juvenile proceedings, which for certain purposes have been distinguished from formal criminal prosecutions. . . . We do not decide that issue today. In view of our disposition of this case, we assume without deciding that the *Miranda* principles were fully applicable to the present proceedings.[33]

The Court went on to hold that a juvenile's request to speak with his probation officer, after receiving *Miranda* warnings, is not a per se invocation of the right to remain silent.

Courts have held that statements made by juveniles are not subject to *Miranda* in the absence of custodial interrogation.[34] In *Yarborough v. Alvarado*,[35] the Supreme Court stated that the test to determine whether a person is in

---

[25]Mincey v. Arizona, 437 U.S. 385, 98 S. Ct. 2408, 57 L. Ed. 2d 290 (1978).

[26]Doyle v. Ohio, 426 U.S. 610, 96 S. Ct. 2240, 49 L. Ed. 2d 91 (1976).

[27]Doyle v. Ohio, 426 U.S. 610, 618, 96 S. Ct. 2240, 49 L. Ed. 2d 91 (1976). See also State v. Williams, 64 Ohio App. 2d 271, 276, 18 Ohio Op. 3d 262, 413 N.E.2d 1212 (8th Dist. Cuyahoga County 1979) ("An indirect comment on the accused's silence can be as devastating as a direct comment on his failure to speak."); State v. Eiding, 57 Ohio App. 2d 111, 11 Ohio Op. 3d 113, 385 N.E.2d 1332 (8th Dist. Cuyahoga County 1978).

[28]Anderson v. Charles, 447 U.S. 404, 100 S. Ct. 2180, 65 L. Ed. 2d 222 (1980). See also State v. Osborne, 50 Ohio St. 2d 211, 216, 4 Ohio Op. 3d 406, 364 N.E.2d 216 (1977) ("If a defendant voluntarily offers information to police, his toying with the authorities by allegedly telling only part of his story is certainly not protected by Miranda or Doyle."); State v. Jones, 53 Ohio App. 2d 308, 7 Ohio Op. 3d 391, 373 N.E.2d 1272 (9th Dist. Summit County 1977).

[29]Jenkins v. Anderson, 447 U.S. 231, 100 S. Ct. 2124, 65 L. Ed. 2d 86 (1980). See also State v. Sims, 3 Ohio App. 3d 321, 445 N.E.2d 235 (8th Dist. Cuyahoga County 1981).

[30]Fletcher v. Weir, 455 U.S. 603, 102 S. Ct. 1309, 71 L. Ed. 2d 490 (1982).

[31]E.g., In re R. A. H., 314 A.2d 133 (D.C. 1974); In re Creek, 243 A.2d 49 (D.C. 1968); In re M., 70 Cal. 2d 444, 75 Cal. Rptr. 1, 450 P.2d 296 (1969); State v. Whatley, 320 So. 2d 123 (La. 1975); State v. Loyd, 297 Minn. 442, 212 N.W.2d 671 (1973); In re L., 29 A.D.2d 182, 287 N.Y. S.2d 218 (2d Dep't 1968); Matter of Robert O., 109 Misc. 2d 238, 439 N.Y.S.2d 994 (Fam. Ct. 1981); Leach v. State, 428 S.W.2d 817 (Tex. Civ. App. Houston 14th Dist. 1968). See generally Holtz, *Miranda* in a Juvenile Setting: A Child's Right to Silence, 78 J. Crim. L. 534 (1987).

[32]Fare v. Michael C., 442 U.S. 707, 99 S. Ct. 2560, 61 L. Ed. 2d 197 (1979).

[33]Fare v. Michael C., 442 U.S. 707, 717 n.4, 99 S. Ct. 2560, 61 L. Ed. 2d 197 (1979).

[34]E.g., In re Haubeil, 2002-Ohio-4095, 2002 WL 1823001 (Ohio Ct. App. 4th Dist. Ross County 2002); State v. Evans, 144 Ohio App. 3d 539, 551-52, 760 N.E.2d 909 (1st Dist. Hamilton County 2001) ("*Miranda* warnings need only be given during custodial interrogation. . . . There is little doubt that Evans was in custody. . . . As the court-ordered guest of a court-operated residential treatment center, Evans properly understood his freedom to have been curtailed to a degree greater even than that associated with an arrest. He could not go home, leave the grounds without permission, or move freely throughout the facility."); State v. Whisenant, 127 Ohio App.

"custody" under *Miranda* is an objective test and thus a juvenile's age and experience is not relevant in this context: "Our Court has not stated that a suspect's age or experience is relevant to the *Miranda* custody analysis. . . ." Because the case arose during habeas proceedings, the legal issue was whether a state court's decision that the juvenile was not in custody was a reasonable one based on prior Supreme Court decisions. But the Court went beyond this narrow habeas issue, writing:

> [R]eliance on Alvarado's prior history with law enforcement was improper not only under the deferential standard of 28 U.S.C. § 2254(d)(1), but also as a *de novo* matter. In most cases, police officers will not know a suspect's interrogation history. Even if they do, the relationship between a suspect's past experiences and the likelihood a reasonable person with that experience would feel free to leave often will be speculative. True, suspects with prior law enforcement experience may understand police procedures and reasonably feel free to leave unless told otherwise. On the other hand, they may view past as prologue and expect another in a string of arrests. We do not ask police officers to consider these contingent psychological factors when deciding when suspects should be advised of their *Miranda* rights. The inquiry turns too much on the suspect's subjective state of mind and not enough on the "objective circumstances of the interrogation."[36]

Justice O'Connor, who voted with the majority in a 5-4 decision, added a concurrence:

> There may be cases in which a suspect's age will be relevant to the *Miranda* "custody" inquiry. In this case, however, Alvarado was almost 18 years old at the time of his interview. It is difficult to expect police to recognize that a suspect is a juvenile when he is so close to the age of majority. Even when police do know a suspect's age, it may be difficult for them to ascertain what bearing it has on the likelihood that the suspect would feel free to leave. That is especially true here; 17 1/2-year-olds vary widely in their reactions to police questioning, and many can be expected to behave as adults. Given these difficulties, I agree that the state court's decision in this case cannot be called an

---

3d 75, 87, 711 N.E.2d 1016 (11th Dist. Portage County 1998) (The sheriff "told appellant he was not under arrest and was free to leave at any time. Under these circumstances, a reasonable person would not have felt that he was not at liberty to terminate the discussion and leave. . . . Thus, Miranda warnings were not necessary when appellant made his first incriminating statement."); State v. Hopfer, 112 Ohio App. 3d 521, 546, 679 N.E.2d 321 (2d Dist. Montgomery County 1996) ("[A] reasonable person in Hopfer's [17-year-old suspect] position would have believed that she could have left the presence of the sheriff's deputies. The sheriff's deputies arrived at the Hopfer residence at 10:30 p.m., which was not an unreasonable hour considering the seriousness of the alleged crime [homicide]. They were invited inside by Mrs. Hopfer after announcing the purpose of their visit and were never asked to leave afterwards. When they spoke with Hopfer, her mother was either by her side or in the adjoining room, fully aware that her daughter was being questioned. Neither Hopfer nor her mother ever expressed a desire not to cooperate with the sheriff's deputies. The sheriff's deputies did not search the house. . . . Most important, the sheriff's deputies never expressed any intention to arrest Hopfer, and left the Hopfers' residence without doing so."); In re Travis, 110 Ohio App. 3d 684, 688, 675 N.E.2d 36 (10th Dist. Franklin County 1996) ("Nothing in the record indicates that appellant was threatened by the police or that he was under arrest at this time. The fact that appellant was subsequently placed in the police cruiser until his mother arrived on the scene does not change the nature of the initial [prior] questioning."); Matter of McCoy, 1993 WL 534660 (Ohio Ct. App. 12th Dist. Fayette County 1993) ("Neither appellant or Reed were formally arrested, nor was there evidence in the record that freedom of movement was restrained to a degree associated with arrest."); In re Smalley, 62 Ohio App. 3d 435, 443–44, 575 N.E.2d 1198 (8th Dist. Cuyahoga County 1989) ("We hold that Smalley was not in custody, within the meaning of *Miranda*, at any time before police discovered her true identity."); Matter of Norlin, 1990 WL 209855 (Ohio Ct. App. 8th Dist. Cuyahoga County 1990) (no "custody" where juvenile's pastor accompanies him to police station). See also In re Paul T., 15 Cal. App. 3d 886, 93 Cal. Rptr. 510 (1st Dist. 1971) (volunteered statement); In re Appeal No. 245 (75) from Circuit Court for Kent County, 29 Md. App. 131, 349 A.2d 434 (1975) (custody); Matter of Gage, 49 Or. App. 599, 624 P.2d 1076 (1980) (no custody); Matter of Killitz, 59 Or. App. 720, 651 P.2d 1382 (1982) (Juvenile questioned by police in principal's office was in custody.).

[35]Yarborough v. Alvarado, 124 S. Ct. 2140 (U.S. 2004).

[36]Yarborough v. Alvarado, 124 S. Ct. 2140 (U.S. 2004).

unreasonable application of federal law simply because it failed explicitly to mention Alvarado's age.[37]

The dissent argued that age could be incorporated into an objective standard: "Common sense, and an understanding of the law's basic purpose in this area, are enough to make clear that Alvarado's age—an objective, widely shared characteristic about which the police plainly knew—is also relevant to the inquiry."[38]

Statements made to persons other than police officers are also not covered by *Miranda*.[39] In *State v. Evans*,[40] the court of appeals held that staff members of a residential treatment center were not law enforcement officers for the purposes of *Miranda*. Moreover, statements obtained in violation of *Miranda* are admissible for impeachment.[41]

Waiver. The test for determining whether a juvenile has waived *Miranda* rights has divided the courts. Generally, courts have followed one of two approaches. One approach requires the presence of an interested adult—an attorney or a parent—before a child may validly waive *Miranda* rights.[42] This approach is supported by several studies. One study concluded, "[Y]ounger juveniles as a class do not understand the nature and significance of their *Miranda* rights to remain silent and to counsel. Consequently, their waivers of these rights cannot be considered intelligently, knowingly, and voluntarily made."[43]

Juvenile Rule 3 provides, in part, that no right of a child may be waived without permission of the juvenile court. The Ohio courts, however, have held that this provision does not apply to a child's waiver of *Miranda* rights.[44]

The second approach requires a consideration of the "totality of the circumstances" in determining the validity of a waiver, the same standard that ap-

---

[37]Yarborough v. Alvarado, 124 S. Ct. 2140 (U.S. 2004).

[38]Yarborough v. Alvarado, 124 S. Ct. 2140 (U.S. 2004). The dissent also commented: "What reasonable person in the circumstances—brought to a police station by his parents at police request, put in a small interrogation room, questioned for a solid two hours, and confronted with claims that there is strong evidence that he participated in a serious crime, could have thought to himself, 'Well, anytime I want to leave I can just get up and walk out'? If the person harbored any doubts, would he still think he might be free to leave once he recalls that the police officer has just refused to let his parents remain with him during questioning? Would he still think that he, rather than the officer, controls the situation?" Yarborough v. Alvarado, 124 S. Ct. 2140 (U.S. 2004).

[39]State v. Bolan, 27 Ohio St. 2d 15, 56 Ohio Op. 2d 8, 271 N.E.2d 839 (1971) (store security officer). See also In re Deborah C., 30 Cal. 3d 125, 177 Cal. Rptr. 852, 635 P.2d 446 (1981); R. W. v. State, 135 Ga. App. 668, 218 S.E.2d 674 (1975); In re Simmons, 24 N.C. App. 28, 210 S.E.2d 84 (1974).

[40]State v. Evans, 144 Ohio App. 3d 539, 553, 760 N.E.2d 909 (1st Dist. Hamilton County 2001) ("According to R.C. 2901.01(A)(11)(b), the definition of 'law enforcement official' includes an employee of the state 'upon whom, by statute, a duty to conserve the peace or to impose all or certain laws is imposed and the authority to arrest violators is conferred.' Since Evans has not directed us to any statutory provision vesting the staff at Hillcrest with such authority (and we can find none), we can only conclude that staff members were not law enforcement officials under the Revised Code and were consequently not law enforcement officials for the purposes of *Miranda* warnings. We therefore join other Ohio courts that have similarly held that those tangentially associated with the criminal justice system, but without the requisite statutory authority, are not law enforcement officials for the purposes of *Miranda*.").

[41]In re Larson's Welfare, 254 N.W.2d 388 (Minn. 1977); Matter of Michael P., 50 A.D.2d 598, 375 N.Y.S.2d 153 (2d Dep't 1975); In re Noble's Welfare, 15 Wash. App. 51, 547 P.2d 880 (Div. 1 1976).

[42]See Rights of Juveniles: The Juvenile Justice System (2d ed.) § 3.13; IJA-ABA Standards Relating to Police Handling of Juvenile Problems 69–73 (1980).

[43]Grisso, Juveniles' Capacities to Waive Miranda Rights: An Empirical Analysis, 68 Calif. L. Rev. 1134, 1166 (1980). See also Grisso, Juveniles' Waiver of Rights (1981); Ferguson & Douglas, A Study of Juvenile Waiver, 7 San Diego L. Rev. 39 (1970).

[44]In re Barber, 1993 WL 285902 (Ohio Ct. App. 11th Dist. Lake County 1993); In the Matter of Hawkins, 1983 WL 4091 (Ohio Ct. App. 9th Dist. Lorain County 1983); State of Ohio v. Hull, 1981 WL 5992 (Ohio Ct. App. 4th Dist. Athens County 1981).

plies in adult cases. The United States Supreme Court adopted this approach in *Fare v. Michael C.*[45] According to the Court, the totality of the circumstances requires an inquiry that would include "the juvenile's age, experience, education, background, and intelligence, and . . . whether he has the capacity to understand the warnings given him, the nature of his Fifth Amendment rights, and the consequences of waiving those rights."

The Ohio Supreme Court also has adopted the "totality of the circumstances" test. It has held that *Miranda* does not require that "the parents of a minor shall be read his constitutional rights along with their child."[46] In applying the totality of the circumstances test, however, the Court has recognized the special problems associated with juvenile waivers: "When a minor is sought to be interrogated, the question of whether he intelligently and voluntarily waives his rights cannot always be decided by the same criteria applied to mature adults."[47] The court went on to hold that the relevant factors in determining the validity of a waiver are the child's "age, emotional stability, physical condition, and mental capacity."[48]

The Court reaffirmed the "totality of the circumstances" approach in *In re Watson:*[49]

In construing whether a juvenile defendant's confession has been involuntarily

---

[45]Fare v. Michael C., 442 U.S. 707, 725, 99 S. Ct. 2560, 61 L. Ed. 2d 197 (1979).

[46]State v. Bell, 48 Ohio St. 2d 270, 276–77, 2 Ohio Op. 3d 427, 358 N.E.2d 556 (1976). See also In re Goins, 137 Ohio App. 3d 158, 165, 738 N.E.2d 385 (12th Dist. Clinton County 1999) ("We have previously found that a juvenile defendant has no right to have his mother present at any stage of the interrogation process."); State v. Holt, 132 Ohio App. 3d 601, 606, 725 N.E.2d 1155 (1st Dist. Hamilton County 1997) ("[W]hen an individual is in custody for an unrelated matter, any form of police questioning about another crime is interrogation and requires the recitation of the *Miranda* warnings—regardless of whether the individual is a suspect or a witness."); State v. Whisenant, 127 Ohio App. 3d 75, 86, 711 N.E.2d 1016 (11th Dist. Portage County 1998) ("It is . . . axiomatic that a juvenile may waive his Fifth Amendment rights with or without parental consent so long as the totality of the circumstances of the waiver, including the age of the juvenile, shows that the waiver is knowingly, intelligently, and voluntarily made.").

[47]State v. Bell, 48 Ohio St. 2d 270, 277, 2 Ohio Op. 3d 427, 358 N.E.2d 556 (1976).

[48]State v. Bell, 48 Ohio St. 2d 270, 277, 2 Ohio Op. 3d 427, 358 N.E.2d 556 (1976). See also In re Smalley, 62 Ohio App. 3d 435, 445, 575 N.E.2d 1198 (8th Dist. Cuyahoga County 1989) ("Waivers by minors must be scrutinized closely since the validity of the waiver is affected by the factors of age, emotional stability and mental capacity."); Toler, 1983 WL 4356 (Ohio Ct. App. 12th Dist. Preble County 1983); In the Matter of Hawkins, 1983 WL 4091 (Ohio Ct. App. 9th Dist. Lorain County 1983).

In West v. U.S., 399 F.2d 467, 469 (5th Cir. 1968), the court set forth the following factors for consideration in the waiver issue:

(1) the age of the accused; (2) education of the accused; (3) knowledge of the accused as to both the substance of the charge, if any has been filed, and the nature of his rights to consult with an attorney and remain silent; (4) whether the accused is held incommunicado or allowed to consult with relatives, friends or an attorney; (5) whether the accused was interrogated before or after formal charges had been filed; (6) methods used in interrogation; (7) length of interrogations; (8) whether vel non the accused refused to voluntarily give statements on prior occasions; and (9) whether the accused has repudiated an extra judicial statement at a later date.

[49]In re Watson, 47 Ohio St. 3d 86, 89–90, 548 N.E.2d 210 (1989). See also In re Goins, 137 Ohio App. 3d 158, 163, 738 N.E.2d 385 (12th Dist. Clinton County 1999) ("Appellee does not assert at any point in the proceedings that he was mistreated, deprived, or involuntarily induced into waiving his *Miranda* rights. [T]here was no evidence of any overt actions by Lester which were intended to intimidate appellee, no evidence of the existence of any physical deprivation or inducement, and the length, intensity and frequency of the interrogation were reasonable. Although appellee was eleven and three-quarters years old with no prior criminal experience at the time of his *Miranda* waiver, there is nothing in the record to suggest that he was of insufficient intelligence based upon his age or that he is mentally impaired and was unable to understand the nature of the waiver. Appellee stated that he could read and write. Appellee's testimony indicates that he is capable of understanding the meaning of 'silent,' and that he understood his constitutional rights."); State v. Mardis, 134 Ohio App. 3d 6, 24, 729 N.E.2d 1272 (10th Dist. Franklin County 1999) ("Appellant appeared to be in command of his faculties. He indicated that he was not under the influence of alcohol or drugs. He had completed the ninth grade and was currently in the tenth. He stated that he averaged 'Bs' and 'Cs' in school. The videotape fails to demonstrate that he was subjected to deprivation, mistreatment or harsh

induced, courts should consider the . . . totality of the circumstances, including the age, mentality, and prior criminal experience of the accused; the length, intensity and frequency of interrogation; the existence of physical deprivation or mistreatment; and the existence of threat or inducement. Given the above standard, the trial court can properly determine whether the juvenile appreciated his rights and voluntarily waived them in the absence of an interested adult or parent.

In one case, the juvenile court ruled that a special education student required greater protection in waiving *Miranda* rights. In this situation, the "officers of the interrogating agency must see that a person qualified, such as a special education teacher, an appropriate counsellor, or other capable specialist, is present during the interrogation to assure that the child to be interrogated is able to communicate accurately, understandably, truthfully, and free of any pressure or intimidation, whether intended or not."[50]

§ 14:11 Confessions—Right to counsel

A statement obtained in violation of a criminal defendant's right to counsel is inadmissible.[1] In *Brewer v. Williams,*[2] the United States Supreme Court wrote, "[O]nce adversary proceedings have commenced against an individual, he has a right to legal representation when the government interrogates him."[3] The right to counsel is a distinct ground for challenging the admissibility of a confession. Thus, even if the *Miranda* requirements are satisfied or are inapplicable, a violation of the Sixth Amendment requires suppression.

The right to counsel differs from *Miranda* in several respects. First, *Miranda* is triggered by "custodial interrogation." In contrast, the right to counsel is triggered by the initiation of adversary judicial proceedings, such as a formal charge, preliminary hearing, indictment, information, or

---

conditions, nor was he threatened or promised anything. Neither the length (approximately one hour) nor the intensity of the interrogation was unreasonable."); In re Howard, 119 Ohio App. 3d 33, 44, 694 N.E.2d 488 (12th Dist. Butler County 1997) ("Appellant had no right to have his mother present at any stage of the interrogation process, the interrogation process was not unreasonably lengthy or intense, the confession was clarified, not rewritten, and appellant voluntarily, and with his mother's approval, submitted to the [Computer Voice Stress Analyzer]."); State v. Hopfer, 112 Ohio App. 3d 521, 548, 679 N.E.2d 321 (2d Dist. Montgomery County 1996) (Juvenile "was an above-average high school student, in good health, and only three months shy of her eighteenth birthday. She was questioned in the familiar surroundings of her own home with her mother either by her side or within earshot. . . . Mrs. Hopfer contends that one sheriff's deputy made an explicit promise—Hopfer would get probation if she cooperated by writing a statement—and an explicit threat—Hopfer would get 'no mercy' unless she added an incriminating sentence to her written statement. While such promises and threats are improper, both of these allegations were denied by the three sheriff's deputies in their testimony."); In re Travis, 110 Ohio App. 3d 684, 689, 675 N.E.2d 36 (10th Dist. Franklin County 1996) ("There is no evidence to suggest that appellant was mentally or physically incapable or incompetent to make a written statement, and his mother was present during this time. Furthermore, as the court found, the limited length and intensity of the investigation, the lack of any inducements or threats, appellant's age and his willingness to cooperate are all factors which indicate that appellant's written statements were voluntary and were made with full knowledge of his rights."); State v. Bobo, 65 Ohio App. 3d 685, 689–90, 585 N.E.2d 429 (8th Dist. Cuyahoga County 1989) ("Though the greatest care must be taken to assure a juvenile's admissions are voluntary, parental presence is not constitutionally mandated. . . . [S]uch presence is only one factor in the totality of the circumstances surrounding the statements.").

[50]In re J.W., 85 Ohio Misc. 2d 1, 3, 682 N.E.2d 1109 (C.P. 1997).

[Section 14:11]

[1]See generally Katz and Giannelli, Baldwin's Ohio Practice, Criminal Law (2d ed.), Ch 27.

[2]Brewer v. Williams, 430 U.S. 387, 97 S. Ct. 1232, 51 L. Ed. 2d 424 (1977).

[3]Brewer v. Williams, 430 U.S. 387, 401, 97 S. Ct. 1232, 51 L. Ed. 2d 424 (1977). See also Estelle v. Smith, 451 U.S. 454, 101 S. Ct. 1866, 68 L. Ed. 2d 359 (1981); U.S. v. Henry, 447 U.S. 264, 100 S. Ct. 2183, 65 L. Ed. 2d 115 (1980); Massiah v. U.S., 377 U.S. 201, 84 S. Ct. 1199, 12 L. Ed. 2d 246 (1964).

arraignment.[4] A suspect who is not in custody but who is involved in adversary judicial proceedings is entitled to counsel but not *Miranda* warnings.[5] However, when a suspect is in custody and subjected to interrogation before adversary judicial proceedings have begun, the *Miranda* rule applies rather than the right to counsel.

Second, *Miranda* applies only when there is police interrogation—"words or actions . . . that the police should know are reasonably likely to elicit an incriminating response from the suspect."[6] The right to counsel is violated when the police "deliberately elicit" information from the defendant after the initiation of formal proceedings. Although interrogation would satisfy the "deliberately elicit" test, that test is not restricted to interrogation.[7] "By intentionally creating a situation likely to induce . . . incriminating statements,"[8] the government violates the right to counsel. Thus, even when a suspect is unaware that the person to whom he is speaking is a police officer, or an informant, the right to counsel may be violated,[9] but not *Miranda*.[10] However, passive listening by itself does not constitute deliberate elicitation.[11]

Waiver. The right to counsel may be waived, but the test for a valid waiver is stringent. The prosecution must establish an intentional relinquishment of a known right.[12] The United States Supreme Court has held that the waiver of *Miranda* rights also waives the right to counsel.[13]

Cross References
§ 1:4
Research References
Katz, Ohio Arrest, Search and Seizure, Ch 24
Carlin, Baldwin's Ohio Practice, Merrick-Rippner Probate Law (6th ed.), Ch 107

§ 14:12 Identification procedures—Self-incrimination

Along with confessions and searches, identification procedures play an important role in police investigations of crime. The use of these procedures raises a number of legal issues.

---

[4]Brewer v. Williams, 430 U.S. 387, 97 S. Ct. 1232, 51 L. Ed. 2d 424 (1977). See also People v. Fleming, 134 Ill. App. 3d 562, 89 Ill. Dec. 478, 480 N.E.2d 1221 (1st Dist. 1985) (Right to counsel attached when delinquency petition was filed and arrest warrant issued.); Edwards v. Arizona, 451 U.S. 477, 480 n.7, 101 S. Ct. 1880, 68 L. Ed. 2d 378 (1981).

[5]Massiah v. U.S., 377 U.S. 201, 84 S. Ct. 1199, 12 L. Ed. 2d 246 (1964).

[6]Rhode Island v. Innis, 446 U.S. 291, 301, 100 S. Ct. 1682, 64 L. Ed. 2d 297 (1980).

[7]Fellers v. U.S., 124 S. Ct. 1019, 1023, 157 L. Ed. 2d 1016 (U.S. 2004) ("The Court of Appeals erred in holding that the absence of an 'interrogation' foreclosed petitioner's claim that the jailhouse statements should have been suppressed as fruits of the statements taken from petitioner at his home. First, there is no question that the officers in this case 'deliberately elicited' information from petitioner. Indeed, the officers, upon arriving at petitioner's house, informed him that their purpose in coming was to discuss his involvement in the distribution of methamphetamine and his association with certain charged co-conspirators."); Rhode Island v. Innis, 446 U.S. 291, 300 n.4, 100 S. Ct. 1682, 64 L. Ed. 2d 297 (1980) ("The definitions of 'interrogation' under the Fifth and Sixth Amendments, if indeed the term 'interrogation' is even apt in the Sixth Amendment context, are not necessarily interchangeable, since the policies underlying the two constitutional protections are quite distinct."). See also U.S. v. Henry, 447 U.S. 264, 100 S. Ct. 2183, 65 L. Ed. 2d 115 (1980).

[8]U.S. v. Henry, 447 U.S. 264, 274, 100 S. Ct. 2183, 65 L. Ed. 2d 115 (1980).

[9]Maine v. Moulton, 474 U.S. 159, 106 S. Ct. 477, 88 L. Ed. 2d 481 (1985); U.S. v. Henry, 447 U.S. 264, 100 S. Ct. 2183, 65 L. Ed. 2d 115 (1980); Massiah v. U.S., 377 U.S. 201, 84 S. Ct. 1199, 12 L. Ed. 2d 246 (1964).

[10]Illinois v. Perkins, 496 U.S. 292, 110 S. Ct. 2394, 110 L. Ed. 2d 243 (1990).

[11]Kuhlmann v. Wilson, 477 U.S. 436, 106 S. Ct. 2616, 91 L. Ed. 2d 364 (1986).

[12]Brewer v. Williams, 430 U.S. 387, 404, 97 S. Ct. 1232, 51 L. Ed. 2d 424 (1977); State v. Cowans, 10 Ohio St. 2d 96, 39 Ohio Op. 2d 97, 227 N.E.2d 201 (1967). See also Michigan v. Jackson, 475 U.S. 625, 106 S. Ct. 1404, 89 L. Ed. 2d 631 (1986).

[13]Patterson v. Illinois, 487 U.S. 285, 108 S. Ct. 2389, 101 L. Ed. 2d 261 (1988).

The United States Supreme Court has limited the Fifth Amendment privilege against compelled self-incrimination[1] to "testimonial or communicative" evidence; the privilege does not prohibit the compelled production of "real or physical" evidence.[2] Accordingly, requiring a suspect to be photographed,[3] appear in a lineup,[4] speak for identification,[5] or provide blood specimens,[6] handwriting exemplars,[7] or fingerprints[8] does not violate the privilege.

§ 14:13 Identification procedures—Right to counsel

Because of the innumerable ways that identification procedures can erroneously affect eyewitness identifications[1] and the difficulty of reconstructing these procedures at trial, the United States Supreme Court in *United States v. Wade*[2] held that a lineup is a "critical stage" of the criminal process, thereby entitling the defendant to the assistance of counsel under the Sixth Amendment.[3] The presence of counsel, according to the Court, assures that a criminal defendant can effectively challenge a subsequent in-court identification based on a suggestive pretrial identification.[4] In *Kirby v. Illinois*,[5] however, the Court restricted the right to counsel, holding that it attaches only "at or after the initiation of adversary judicial criminal proceedings—whether by way of formal charge, preliminary hearing, indictment, information, or arraignment."[6] Thus, an arrest by itself does not trigger the right to counsel. The Court also has held that the right to counsel does not apply to photographic displays, even after the commencement of adversary proceedings.[7]

Waiver. If the right to counsel applies at an identification procedure, it

---

[Section 14:12]

[1]U.S. Const. amend. 5 ("No person . . . shall be compelled in any criminal case to be a witness against himself."). The privilege against compelled self-incrimination applies to state trials. Malloy v. Hogan, 378 U.S. 1, 84 S. Ct. 1489, 12 L. Ed. 2d 653 (1964). The Ohio Constitution also guarantees the privilege against self-incrimination (O. Const. art. I § 10).

[2]Schmerber v. California, 384 U.S. 757, 764, 86 S. Ct. 1826, 16 L. Ed. 2d 908 (1966). See Katz and Giannelli, Baldwin's Ohio Practice, Criminal Law (2d ed.) § 70:6.

[3]Schmerber v. California, 384 U.S. 757, 764, 86 S. Ct. 1826, 16 L. Ed. 2d 908 (1966).

[4]U.S. v. Wade, 388 U.S. 218, 87 S. Ct. 1926, 18 L. Ed. 2d 1149 (1967).

[5]U.S. v. Dionisio, 410 U.S. 1, 93 S. Ct. 764, 35 L. Ed. 2d 67 (1973).

[6]Schmerber v. California, 384 U.S. 757, 86 S. Ct. 1826, 16 L. Ed. 2d 908 (1966).

[7]U.S. v. Euge, 444 U.S. 707, 100 S. Ct. 874, 63 L. Ed. 2d 141 (1980); U.S. v. Mara, 410 U.S. 19, 93 S. Ct. 774, 35 L. Ed. 2d 99 (1973); Gilbert v. California, 388 U.S. 263, 87 S. Ct. 1951, 18 L. Ed. 2d 1178 (1967); State v. Ostrowski, 30 Ohio St. 2d 34, 59 Ohio Op. 2d 62, 282 N.E.2d 359 (1972).

[8]See Schmerber v. California, 384 U.S. 757, 86 S. Ct. 1826, 16 L. Ed. 2d 908 (1966).

[Section 14:13]

[1]See generally Katz and Giannelli, Baldwin's Ohio Practice, Criminal Law (2d ed.), Ch 28.

[2]U.S. v. Wade, 388 U.S. 218, 87 S. Ct. 1926, 18 L. Ed. 2d 1149 (1967).

[3]U.S. Const. amend. 6 ("In all criminal prosecutions, the accused shall enjoy the right . . . to have the assistance of counsel for his defence."). The right to counsel applies in state trials. Gideon v. Wainwright, 372 U.S. 335, 83 S. Ct. 792, 9 L. Ed. 2d 799, 93 A.L.R.2d 733 (1963). The Ohio Constitution also guarantees the right to counsel (O. Const. art. I § 10).

[4]U.S. v. Wade, 388 U.S. 218, 87 S. Ct. 1926, 18 L. Ed. 2d 1149 (1967). See also Gilbert v. California, 388 U.S. 263, 87 S. Ct. 1951, 18 L. Ed. 2d 1178 (1967).

[5]Kirby v. Illinois, 406 U.S. 682, 92 S. Ct. 1877, 32 L. Ed. 2d 411 (1972).

[6]Kirby v. Illinois, 406 U.S. 682, 689, 92 S. Ct. 1877, 32 L. Ed. 2d 411 (1972). See also Moore v. Illinois, 434 U.S. 220, 98 S. Ct. 458, 54 L. Ed. 2d 424 (1977) (Right to counsel attaches at preliminary hearing.); Edwards v. Arizona, 451 U.S. 477, 480 n.7, 101 S. Ct. 1880, 68 L. Ed. 2d 378 (1981) (indicating this issue is controlled by state law); State v. Stricklen, 63 Ohio St. 2d 47, 17 Ohio Op. 3d 29, 406 N.E.2d 1110 (1980); State v. Sheardon, 31 Ohio St. 2d 20, 60 Ohio Op. 2d 11, 285 N.E.2d 335 (1972); State v. Kiraly, 56 Ohio App. 2d 37, 10 Ohio Op. 3d 53, 381 N.E.2d 649 (8th Dist. Cuyahoga County 1977) (Setting bond triggers the right to counsel.); State v. Strodes, 42 Ohio App. 2d 8, 71 Ohio Op. 2d 49, 325 N.E.2d 899 (2d Dist. Clark County 1974).

[7]U.S. v. Ash, 413 U.S. 300, 93 S. Ct. 2568, 37 L. Ed. 2d 619 (1973).

may be waived. A stringent test determines whether there has been a valid waiver of the right to counsel. The prosecution must establish "an intentional relinquishment or abandonment of a known right or privilege"[8] and the "courts indulge in every reasonable presumption against waiver."[9]

Independent source rule. Testimony concerning a lineup identification at which the defendant has been denied the right to counsel is inadmissible.[10] Nevertheless, a subsequent *in-court* identification may be admissible if the prosecution can establish by clear and convincing evidence that the in-court identification was based upon an independent source.[11] A number of factors are considered when determining whether the in-court identification is derived from an independent source: the witness's prior opportunity to observe the criminal act, the existence of any discrepancy between a prelineup description and the defendant's actual description, an identification of another person, the identification by photograph of the defendant prior to the lineup, the failure to identify the defendant on a prior occasion, and the lapse of time between the crime and the lineup identification.[12]

Juvenile cases. Courts have applied the right-to-counsel requirement to juvenile cases.[13] The precise point at which the right attaches, however, is uncertain. One court has questioned whether juvenile court proceedings are adversarial judicial criminal proceedings under *Kirby*.[14]

§ 14:14   Identification procedures—Due process

Pretrial identification procedures are also subject to scrutiny under the Due Process Clause.[1] Due process rights are more comprehensive than the right to counsel. For example, due process applies to photographic displays[2] and to lineups conducted prior to the time the right to counsel attaches.[3] In *Stovall v. Denno*,[4] the United States Supreme Court held that due process requires the exclusion of a pretrial identification where the procedure used is "unnecessarily suggestive and conducive to irreparable mistaken identification."[5] The focus of this test is the reliability of the *procedure* used in the identification. If the procedure is both suggestive and unnecessary, the identification is inadmissible.

---

[8]Johnson v. Zerbst, 304 U.S. 458, 464, 58 S. Ct. 1019, 82 L. Ed. 1461, 146 A.L.R. 357 (1938).

[9]Brewer v. Williams, 430 U.S. 387, 404, 97 S. Ct. 1232, 51 L. Ed. 2d 424 (1977). See also State v. Hurt, 30 Ohio St. 2d 86, 59 Ohio Op. 2d 106, 282 N.E.2d 578 (1972) (waiver of counsel not found).

[10]Gilbert v. California, 388 U.S. 263, 87 S. Ct. 1951, 18 L. Ed. 2d 1178 (1967).

[11]U.S. v. Wade, 388 U.S. 218, 87 S. Ct. 1926, 18 L. Ed. 2d 1149 (1967).

[12]U.S. v. Wade, 388 U.S. 218, 87 S. Ct. 1926, 18 L. Ed. 2d 1149 (1967). See also State v. Lathan, 30 Ohio St. 2d 92, 59 Ohio Op. 2d 109, 282 N.E.2d 574 (1972) (no clear and convincing evidence of independent source); State v. Hurt, 30 Ohio St. 2d 86, 59 Ohio Op. 2d 106, 282 N.E.2d 578 (1972); State v. Kiraly, 56 Ohio App. 2d 37, 10 Ohio Op. 3d 53, 381 N.E.2d 649 (8th Dist. Cuyahoga County 1977).

[13]In re Carl T., 1 Cal. App. 3d 344, 81 Cal. Rptr. 655 (2d Dist. 1969); In Interest of Stoutzenberger, 235 Pa. Super. 500, 344 A.2d 668 (1975); In re Daniel T., 446 A.2d 1042 (R.I. 1982); In re Holley, 107 R.I. 615, 268 A.2d 723 (1970).

See also In re McKelvin, 258 A.2d 452 (D.C. 1969); In re Spencer, 288 Minn. 119, 121 n.1, 179 N.W.2d 95 (1970); Matter of Carlos B., 86 Misc. 2d 160, 382 N.Y.S.2d 655 (City Fam. Ct. 1976); IJA-ABA Standards Relating to Police Handling of Juvenile Problems 73–76 (1980).

[14]See Jackson v. State, 17 Md. App. 167, 300 A.2d 430 (1973).

[Section 14:14]

[1]See generally Katz and Giannelli, Baldwin's Ohio Practice, Criminal Law (2d ed.), Ch 28.

[2]See Simmons v. U.S., 390 U.S. 377, 88 S. Ct. 967, 19 L. Ed. 2d 1247 (1968). See also State v. Kaiser, 56 Ohio St. 2d 27, 10 Ohio Op. 3d 74, 381 N.E.2d 632 (1978); State v. Moody, 55 Ohio St. 2d 64, 9 Ohio Op. 3d 71, 377 N.E.2d 1008 (1978).

[3]Kirby v. Illinois, 406 U.S. 682, 92 S. Ct. 1877, 32 L. Ed. 2d 411 (1972).

[4]Stovall v. Denno, 388 U.S. 293, 87 S. Ct. 1967, 18 L. Ed. 2d 1199 (1967).

[5]Stovall v. Denno, 388 U.S. 293, 302, 87 S. Ct. 1967, 18 L. Ed. 2d 1199 (1967).

In a subsequent case, *Neil v. Biggers*,[6] the Court altered the due process test. The new test—whether a substantial likelihood of misidentification has occurred during the identification process—focuses on the reliability of the actual identification rather than on the reliability of the identification procedure itself. In applying this test, courts must consider the "totality of the circumstances," including the opportunity of the witness to view the criminal at the time of the crime, the witness's degree of attention, the accuracy of the witness's prior description of the criminal, the level of certainty demonstrated by the witness at the confrontation, and the length of time between the crime and the confrontation.[7]

The *Biggers* test was further refined in *Manson v. Brathwaite*.[8] After citing the factors listed in *Biggers*, the Court commented that these factors must be weighed against the "corrupting effect of the suggestive identification itself."[9] Thus, it appears that the present due process test combines both the *Biggers* and *Stovall* tests.[10]

Courts have applied the due process tests to identifications in juvenile cases.[11]

§ 14:15 Fingerprints & photographs

RC 2151.313 governs the fingerprinting and photographing of children. This statute generally prohibits fingerprinting or photographing of children without the consent of the juvenile court. There are, however, some exceptions involving conduct that would be a felony if committed by an adult. The statute also specifies the conditions under which fingerprints and photographs may be retained,[1] used, or released.[2]

Although a violation of the statute constitutes a misdemeanor,[3] exclusion of evidence is not a remedy.[4] According to the Ohio Supreme Court, the purpose of the statute is not to determine the admissibility of the evidence "but rather to conform to the theory that juvenile proceedings are not criminal in nature."[5]

In *In re Order Requiring Fingerprinting of a Juvenile*,[6] the statute was attacked on Fourth Amendment grounds. The juvenile court had ordered the fingerprinting of a juvenile who was neither in custody nor under arrest. The Ohio Supreme Court recognized that taking the juvenile into custody to obtain fingerprints "is clearly within the scope of the Fourth Amendment." The Court ruled that such an order is permissible if the juvenile court finds that (1) there is an articulable and specific basis in fact for suspecting crimi-

---

[6]Neil v. Biggers, 409 U.S. 188, 93 S. Ct. 375, 34 L. Ed. 2d 401 (1972).

[7]Neil v. Biggers, 409 U.S. 188, 93 S. Ct. 375, 34 L. Ed. 2d 401 (1972).

[8]Manson v. Brathwaite, 432 U.S. 98, 97 S. Ct. 2243, 53 L. Ed. 2d 140 (1977).

[9]Manson v. Brathwaite, 432 U.S. 98, 114, 97 S. Ct. 2243, 53 L. Ed. 2d 140 (1977).

[10]See dissenting opinion of Justice Marshall in *Manson*. See also State v. Madison, 64 Ohio St. 2d 322, 18 Ohio Op. 3d 491, 415 N.E.2d 272 (1980); State v. Moody, 55 Ohio St. 2d 64, 9 Ohio Op. 3d 71, 377 N.E.2d 1008 (1978).

[11]In re Carl T., 1 Cal. App. 3d 344, 81 Cal. Rptr. 655 (2d Dist. 1969); Matter of Mark J., 96 Misc. 2d 733, 412 N.Y.S.2d 549 (Fam. Ct. 1979); In re Howard, 31 Ohio App. 3d 1, 508 N.E.2d 190 (1st Dist. Hamilton County 1987); In the Matter Finley, 1984 WL 6377 (Ohio Ct. App. 8th Dist. Cuyahoga County 1984); In re Daniel T., 446 A.2d 1042 (R.I. 1982). See also IJA-ABA Standards Relating to Police Handling of Juvenile Problems 73–76 (1980).

[Section 14:15]

[1]RC 2151.313(A).

[2]RC 2151.313(B).

[3]RC 2151.99(B).

[4]State v. Davis, 56 Ohio St. 2d 51, 10 Ohio Op. 3d 87, 381 N.E.2d 641 (1978).

[5]State v. Carder, 9 Ohio St. 2d 1, 38 Ohio Op. 2d 1, 222 N.E.2d 620 (1966).

[6]In re Order Requiring Fingerprinting of a Juvenile, 42 Ohio St. 3d 124, 126, 537 N.E.2d 1286 (1989).

nal activity; (2) the intrusion is justified by substantial law enforcement interests; and (3) the intrusion is limited in scope, purpose and duration.

Research References
Katz, Ohio Arrest, Search and Seizure, Ch 23
Carlin, Baldwin's Ohio Practice, Merrick-Rippner Probate Law (6th ed.), Ch 107

§ 14:16   Abuse, neglect & dependency investigations

An investigation by welfare personnel to determine whether a child is abused, neglected, or dependent may raise Fourth Amendment and Fifth Amendment issues.

In addition, RC 2151.421 governs the reporting and investigation of child abuse and neglect; the statute is discussed in § 14:17.

Fourth Amendment. In *Wyman v. James*,[1] the United States Supreme Court considered whether the Fourth Amendment prohibition against unreasonable searches and seizures applied to a warrantless home visit by a caseworker. The visit was required as a condition for receipt of welfare assistance under the Aid to Families with Dependent Children program. James offered to answer all reasonable and relevant questions about her need for assistance but refused the home visit.

The Supreme Court rejected James's Fourth Amendment challenge. The Court first suggested that the Fourth Amendment was inapplicable because the home visit was not a "search." The Court wrote that the case was "not concerned here with any search . . . in the Fourth Amendment meaning of that term."[2] Commentators have severely criticized this aspect of the opinion: "[T]he Court is unquestionably incorrect in its assertion that a home visit is not a search."[3]

The Court also ruled that if the visit was a search, it was a reasonable search. According to the Court, the government had a legitimate interest in ensuring that dependent children received the aid and that tax money was properly spent. In addition, the means used were reasonable. Advanced written notice was required before the visit, and forcible entries were prohibited. Moreover, there were no alternative methods to a home visit that would produce the necessary information. Finally, the visit was conducted by a caseworker and not the police.

In *Ferguson v. City of Charleston*,[4] the Supreme Court considered the use of a mother's urine test to determine whether she had taken cocaine. Motivated by an apparent increase in cocaine use by patients receiving prenatal care, the Medical University of South Carolina [MUSC] instituted a policy to identify pregnant patients suspected of drug abuse and began conducting urine tests of obstetric patients pursuant to that policy. Ten patients who were arrested after testing positive for cocaine sued the City of Charleston, law enforcement officials who developed and enforced the policy, and representatives of MUSC alleging, inter alia, violation of the Fourth Amendment. The Court held that: (1) the urine tests conducted by MUSC were "searches" within the meaning of the Fourth Amendment, and (2) absent consent, the testing and subsequent reporting of positive test results to the police constituted unreasonable searches. The Court found that "[b]ecause the hospital seeks to justify its authority to conduct drug tests and

---

[Section 14:16]

[1]Wyman v. James, 400 U.S. 309, 91 S. Ct. 381, 27 L. Ed. 2d 408 (1971).

[2]Wyman v. James, 400 U.S. 309, 317, 91 S. Ct. 381, 27 L. Ed. 2d 408 (1971).

[3]LaFave, Search and Seizure: A Treatise on the Fourth Amendment (3d ed.) p 459 § 10.3.

[4]Ferguson v. City of Charleston, 532 U.S. 67, 121 S. Ct. 1281, 149 L. Ed. 2d 205 (2001). See also Smith, The Special Needs Doctrine After *Ferguson v. City of Charleston*, 32 U. Balt. L. Rev. 265 (2003).

to turn the results over to law enforcement agents without the knowledge or consent of the patients, this case differs from the four previous cases in which we have considered whether comparable drug tests 'fit within the closely guarded category of constitutionally permissible suspicionless searches.' "[5]

Fifth Amendment. *Baltimore City Department of Social Services v. Bouknight*[6] involved a Fifth Amendment challenge to a juvenile court order requiring the production of Bouknight's abused son. The son had previously been adjudicated a child in need of assistance and returned to Bouknight under the supervision of the Baltimore City Department of Social Services (BCDSS). The juvenile court subsequently granted the BCDSS's petition for the child's removal from Bouknight's custody. When the child could not be located, the BCDSS feared he might be dead or injured. The juvenile court held her in civil contempt for failure to produce the child as ordered. Bouknight argued that the contempt order violated the privilege against self-incrimination.

The United States Supreme Court rejected this argument. The Fifth Amendment covers only compelled *testimonial* or *communicative* evidence, and, typically, the act of producing evidence, in itself, is not testimonial. Moreover, "a person may not claim the Amendment's protections based upon the incrimination that may result from the contents or nature of the thing demanded."[7] Bouknight asserted that the "act of producing" her son was an implicit communication of her control over him and might aid the state in prosecuting her. The Court acknowledged this argument but ruled that this situation was analogous to the "required records" exception to the Fifth Amendment. This exception applies when "a person assumes control over items that are the legitimate object of the government's noncriminal regulatory powers."[8] Bouknight had accepted the care of her son subject to the custodial order's conditions, one of which was to cooperate with the BCDSS. She "submitted to the routine operation of the regulatory system and agreed to hold [her son] in a manner consonant with the State's regulatory interests and subject to inspection by BCDSS."[9] Because the state's interest in the child's well-being was unrelated to criminal law enforcement, the privilege did not apply.

Any person, including parents, may claim the Fifth Amendment privilege at an abuse, neglect, or dependency hearing. It is not the forum in which the privilege is asserted that is determinative, but whether the person could be subjected to future criminal prosecution.[10]

§ 14:17   Child abuse reporting statute

RC 2151.421(B) provides that any person who knows or suspects that a child is abused or neglected *may* report this information to a children services board, county job and family services department, or municipal or

---

[5]Ferguson v. City of Charleston, 532 U.S. 67, 77, 121 S. Ct. 1281, 149 L. Ed. 2d 205 (2001).

[6]Baltimore City Dept. of Social Services v. Bouknight, 493 U.S. 549, 110 S. Ct. 900, 107 L. Ed. 2d 992, 29 Fed. R. Evid. Serv. 273 (1990).

[7]Baltimore City Dept. of Social Services v. Bouknight, 493 U.S. 549, 555, 110 S. Ct. 900, 107 L. Ed. 2d 992, 29 Fed. R. Evid. Serv. 273 (1990).

[8]Baltimore City Dept. of Social Services v. Bouknight, 493 U.S. 549, 558, 110 S. Ct. 900, 107 L. Ed. 2d 992, 29 Fed. R. Evid. Serv. 273 (1990).

In Wilson v. U.S., 221 U.S. 361, 382, 31 S. Ct. 538, 55 L. Ed. 771 (1911), the Court wrote:

[W]here, by virtue of their character and the rules of law applicable to them, the books and papers are held subject to examination by the demanding authority, the custodian has no privilege to refuse production although their contents tend to criminate him. In assuming their custody he has accepted the incident obligation to permit inspection.

[9]Baltimore City Dept. of Social Services v. Bouknight, 493 U.S. 549, 559, 110 S. Ct. 900, 107 L. Ed. 2d 992, 29 Fed. R. Evid. Serv. 273 (1990).

[10]See § 23:27, Self-incrimination.

county peace officer. In contrast, division (A) *requires* certain "professionals," who, because of their line of work, are likely to come in contact with children, to report abuse or neglect. This category includes attorneys, physicians and other health care professionals, psychologists, speech pathologists, coroners, day care workers, school officials and teachers, social workers, clergy members, and others. Peace officers are required to transmit reports they receive to the children services board or county job and family services department.[1]

The statute also (1) provides criminal penalties for failure to make a required report, (2) specifies an exception to the attorney-client and physician-patient privileges, and (3) recognizes civil and criminal immunity for those who make reports.

Investigation. Upon receipt of a report, the children services agency must investigate the allegations within 24 hours and determine whether a complaint should be filed or other action taken to protect the child.[2] "When [Children Services Board (CSB)] receives a report that a child is suspected of being abused or neglected, CSB has a duty under the statute to begin an investigation within twenty-four hours. The mandate is to take affirmative action on behalf of a specifically identified individual. This individual is a minor whom the General Assembly has determined to be a proper recipient of the specialized care and protection that only the state through its political subdivisions is able to provide in many instances."[3] The investigation must be conducted in cooperation with law enforcement agencies. The children services agency is also required to report each case to a central registry and submit a written report to the law enforcement agency.

Immunity. The immunity provision, RC 2151.421(G), was amended in the early 1990s to shield only those who in good faith make a discretionary (as opposed to a mandatory) report. Immunity also extends to persons who are required to file mandatory abuse reports, even if the report is filed in bad faith.[4]

The Supreme Court has held that RC 2151.421(G) extends immunity to caseworkers and public children services agencies that investigate and participate in judicial proceedings after receiving a report of abuse and neglect: "[W]e conclude that [the statute] confers immunity upon those who, as a result of a report of a known or suspected incident of child abuse and/or ne-

---

[Section 14:17]

[1]RC 2151.421(D); Doe v. Roman, 2002-Ohio-6671, 2002 WL 31732468 (Ohio Ct. App. 5th Dist. Tuscarawas County 2002).

[2]RC 2151.421(F). With limited exceptions, abuse reports are confidential. RC 2151.421(H); State ex rel. Strothers v. Wertheim, 80 Ohio St. 3d 155, 157, 1997-Ohio-349, 684 N.E.2d 1239 (1997) (holding that records prepared by the Ombudsman Office in investigating complaints of child abuse and neglect are not covered by this provision).

[3]Brodie v. Summit County Children Services Bd., 51 Ohio St. 3d 112, 119, 554 N.E.2d 1301 (1990). See also Neuenschwander v. Wayne Cty. Children Serv. Bd., 92 Ohio App. 3d 767, 771, 637 N.E.2d 102 (9th Dist. Wayne County 1994) ("R.C. 2151.421 imposes a duty owed to a minor child who has allegedly been abused or neglected. It does not impose a duty to that child's grandparents or to any other member of the public who files a charge with a children services board.").

[4]Walters v. The Enrichment Ctr. of Wishing Well, Inc., 133 Ohio App. 3d 66, 73, 726 N.E.2d 1058 (8th Dist. Cuyahoga County 1999) ("In mandating that those persons listed in R.C. 2151.421(A) report known or suspected physical or mental abuse or neglect, it is clear that the societal benefits of preventing child abuse outweigh the individual harm which might arise from the filing of an occasional false report. The grant of immunity found in R.C. 2151.421(G)(1) for those persons reporting under the mandatory provisions of 2151.421(A) similarly promotes the public policy goal of protecting children from physical and mental abuse by ensuring that those persons who are required by law to report such abuse are not deterred from this duty by the daunting prospect of expensive and time-consuming litigation.").

glect, participate in a judicial proceeding."[5] The Court, however, has ruled that this immunity provision does not protect a caseworker and children services agency that fail to investigate and report findings as mandated by the statute.[6]

In *Surdel v. MetroHealth Med. Ctr.*,[7] the court of appeals rejected an argument that immunity extends only to the initial reporter, not a subsequent reporter: "So far as we can see, anyone who participates in a mandatory report under R.C. 2151.421(A) or who participates in good faith in a permissive report under R.C. 2151.421(B) is immune under R.C. 2151.421(G) (1) (a). It is immaterial whether the information provided is considered the initial report or merely corroborative of an earlier report." Similarly, the court rejected the notion that the immunity extends only if the reporter's suspicions are "reasonable." The court wrote: "The statute describes the kinds of indicators on which the reporter may rely. The qualifying language clarifies that the duty to report does not require absolute proof but rather is triggered when the condition reasonably indicates abuse or neglect. The statute's focus is on the condition, not the reporter. And to the extent Surdel contends that R.C. 2151.421(G) (1) (a) does not confer immunity where the report results from the reporter's alleged unreasonable misdiagnosis, we rejected the same argument."[8]

---

[5]Gersper v. Ashtabula County Children Services Bd., 59 Ohio St. 3d 127, 130, 570 N.E.2d 1120 (1991).

[6]Brodie v. Summit County Children Services Bd., 51 Ohio St. 3d 112, 554 N.E.2d 1301 (1990) ("Division (G) of R.C. 2151.421 does not confer immunity upon those who fail to carry out the mandate of the statute" (syl. 4)).

[7]Surdel v. MetroHealth Med. Ctr., 135 Ohio App. 3d 141, 148, 733 N.E.2d 281 (8th Dist. Cuyahoga County 1999).

[8]Surdel v. MetroHealth Med. Ctr., 135 Ohio App. 3d 141, 150, 733 N.E.2d 281 (8th Dist. Cuyahoga County 1999) (citing Criswell v. Brentwood Hosp., 49 Ohio App. 3d 163, 551 N.E.2d 1315 (8th Dist. Cuyahoga County 1989)).

Chapter 15

Intake, Diversion, & Mediation

> **KeyCite®:** Cases and other legal materials listed in KeyCite Scope can be researched through West's KeyCite service on Westlaw®. Use KeyCite to check citations for form, parallel references, prior and later history, and comprehensive citator information, including citations to other decisions and secondary materials.

§ 15:1   Intake, diversion, & mediation—Introduction
§ 15:2   Intake
§ 15:3   Diversion, youth services grant
§ 15:4   Mediation
§ 15:5   Arbitration
§ 15:6   Family & Children First Council—Dispute resolution process

§ 15:1   Intake, diversion, & mediation—Introduction

This chapter discusses the process by which decisions are made in handling cases which are referred to the juvenile court, including the utilization of alternative methods in lieu of official case processing. Additional related chapters include the complaint (Ch 16) and the summons (Ch 18).

§ 15:2   Intake

The intake process commences juvenile court proceedings. At intake, the intake officer decides whether the matter should be handled through official court action or diverted to a community services program. Juvenile Rule 9(A) provides that "[i]n all appropriate cases formal court action should be avoided and other community resources utilized to ameliorate situations brought to the attention of the court."[1]

Factual basis for complaint. In making this decision, the intake officer first determines whether the facts of the case justify the filing of a complaint and, if so, how to process the case. The facts are presented to the intake worker either directly from the complainant or through written reports supplied by the police, the job and family services department, or some other agency.[2] If the facts are legally insufficient to establish grounds for a complaint, the complainant may be referred to an appropriate alternative.[3]

Options. However, even if the facts justify the filing of a complaint, the

---

[Section 15:2]

[1]See In re M.D., 38 Ohio St. 3d 149, 527 N.E.2d 286 (1988), holding that the filing of delinquency charges based on allegations of complicity to rape against a child under the age of 13 is contrary to RC Ch. 2151 and Juv. R. 9(A) and constitutes a denial of due process of law. See also In re Smith, 80 Ohio App. 3d 502, 609 N.E.2d 1281 (1st Dist. Hamilton County 1992); In re Corcoran, 68 Ohio App. 3d 213, 587 N.E.2d 957 (11th Dist. Geauga County 1990); In re Carter, 1996 WL 103778 (Ohio Ct. App. 12th Dist. Butler County 1996); In re Frederick, 63 Ohio Misc. 2d 229, 622 N.E.2d 762 (C.P. 1993).

[2]Discovery of these reports is governed by Juv. R. 24. See § 21:2, Scope of discovery—Rule 24.

[3]For instance, if the facts are insufficient to file a delinquency complaint, the alleged victim might be referred to an attorney to explore the possibility of filing a civil action. A parent wishing to file a complaint against his child might be referred to a social service agency if the child's behavior does not fit within the definition of an unruly child.

intake worker has several options in handling the matter. These include (1) filing an official complaint;[4] (2) holding an informal mediation conference with the child, his parents, and the victim; or (3) diverting the matter to available community resources. This decision is based on such factors as the seriousness of the offense or behavior (in delinquency, unruly, and juvenile traffic offender cases), the living conditions of the child (in neglect, dependency, and abuse cases), the parties' prior involvement with the court or another agency, the child's age and attitude, and the family dynamics affecting the child.

These evidentiary and social history matters may be "informally screened prior to the filing of a complaint to determine whether the filing of a complaint is in the best interest of the child and the public."[5] In informal court proceedings, no written pleadings are filed, nor is the case docketed or recorded; but memoranda are maintained in the court's files.[6]

If the decision is made at the intake stage to handle the matter informally, the issue arises as to whether the complainant has an absolute right to demand that a complaint be accepted. RC 2151.27, RC 2152.021, and Juvenile Rule 10 provide that "any person having knowledge" that a child is delinquent, unruly, neglected, dependent, or abused or a juvenile traffic offender, "may file a sworn complaint with respect to that child." However, these provisions must be read in conjunction with Juvenile Rule 9(A), which provides that the court has discretion to avoid formal court action "in all appropriate cases." Although the complainant may not compel the filing of a complaint, he may appeal the intake decision to the prosecuting attorney's office or the juvenile judge. As the official who is responsible for maintaining court records[7] and managing the court staff,[8] the judge has the final authority regarding intake decisions, where those decisions are made by court staff.

Right to counsel. An issue which has not been ruled on by the Ohio appellate courts is whether the parties[9] have a right to counsel at the intake stage. Courts in other jurisdictions have generally denied such a right on the ground that the United States Supreme Court cases, including the constitutional rights of juveniles, have been limited to the adjudicatory stage of the proceedings.[10]

In Ohio, the right to counsel may attach at some point in the intake process. Juvenile Rule 4(A) provides that the right to counsel "shall arise when a person becomes a party to a juvenile court proceeding." Juvenile Rule 2(G) defines a "court proceeding" as "all action taken by a court from the earlier of (1) the time a complaint is filed and (2) the time a person first appears before an officer of a juvenile court until the court relinquishes jurisdiction over such child." Thus, if a child attends an informal intake mediation conference conducted by the juvenile court, he is entitled to legal representation.

---

[4]See Juv. R. 10; § 16:2, Standing to file complaint.

[5]Juv. R. 9(B).

[6]In re Douglas, 11 Ohio Op. 2d 340, 82 Ohio L. Abs. 170, 164 N.E.2d 475 (Juv. Ct. 1959). See also RC 2151.18, RC 2151.35.

[7]RC 2151.18. In all counties except those in which the domestic relations division of the common pleas court exercises juvenile jurisdiction, the juvenile judge serves also as the clerk of the juvenile court (RC 2151.12). In Cuyahoga County, the administrative juvenile judge is the clerk of court (RC 2153.08).

[8]RC 2151.13, RC 2153.08, RC 2153.09 (relating to Cuyahoga County Juvenile Court).

[9]Juv. R. 2(Y) defines a party as "a child who is the subject of a juvenile court proceeding, the child's spouse, if any, the child's parent or parents, or if the parent of a child is a child, the parent of that parent, in appropriate cases, the child's custodian, guardian, or guardian ad litem, the state, and any other person specifically designated by the court."

[10]E.g., In re S, 73 Misc. 2d 187, 341 N.Y.S.2d 11 (Fam. Ct. 1973); In re H., 71 Misc. 2d 1042, 337 N.Y.S.2d 118 (Fam. Ct. 1972).

Cross References
Ch 16, Ch 18, Ch 35
Research References
Carlin, Baldwin's Ohio Practice, Merrick-Rippner Probate Law (6th ed.), Ch 107

§ 15:3   Diversion, youth services grant

In furtherance of the general purpose clauses of the juvenile court statutes and rules[1] and the specific provision of Juvenile Rule 9(A), an increasingly popular alternative at intake is to divert the matter to appropriate "community resources."[2] These include diversion programs operated by the court or an outside agency whose primary purpose is to provide counseling or other treatment to children and their families. Because formal diversion programs are a relatively recent development, there is virtually no case law in Ohio concerning the due process rights of those referred to such programs.

A typical diversion program,[3] however, will establish the following guidelines:

(1) A child who is referred to a diversion program may choose instead to have the matter handled officially by the court;

(2) The child is not required to admit the alleged behavior in order to be eligible for diversion;[4]

(3) The child has a right to consult an attorney, retained or appointed, before agreeing to participate in diversion;[5]

(4) Any statements made by the child during participation in a diversion program or during negotiations leading to such participation are inadmissible as evidence in any subsequent judicial proceeding relative to the original charge.

In addition to these due process guidelines, diversion programs may also include the following provisions:

(1) Diversion should only be used as an alternative to court action. Therefore, diversion is inappropriate if there is insufficient evidence to file a complaint or if the matter is not serious enough to justify court action;

(2) Although the wishes of the complainant should be considered, the decision to divert should be based primarily on the child's best interest;[6]

(3) Because a primary purpose of diversion is to prevent official court involvement with the child,[7] diversion is inappropriate if the child already has an official record with the court; and

(4) If the child voluntarily enters a diversion program and thereafter

---

[Section 15:3]

[1]RC 2151.01; Juv. R. 1(B).

[2]According to the 2003 Annual Report of the Cuyahoga County Juvenile Court, 2,022 cases were referred to some type of diversion program.

[3]E.g., the diversion guidelines of the Cuyahoga County Juvenile Court, which were based in part on a similar program in Hamilton County, Ohio.

[4]It has been argued that admission should be a condition to eligibility for diversion because admitting one's misbehavior is essential to rehabilitation. On the other hand, a confession made to obtain the benefits of diversion could be deemed a "compelled" confession which may violate the child's Fifth Amendment privilege against self incrimination.

[5]For a discussion of the right to counsel at the intake stage, see § 15:2, Intake.

[6]This is authorized by Juv. R. 9(A) and (B).

[7]There is some research indicating that children who become wards of the court and are labeled delinquent have a high probability of recidivism. E.g., Faust, Delinquency Labeling, Its Consequences and Implications, 19 Crime and Delinquency 41 (1973).

violates the conditions of his participation, the court may choose to take formal action relative to the original charge.[8]

To further advance the general goal of avoiding official court action whenever possible, juvenile courts may participate with public or private county agencies in delinquency prevention and control programs.[9] The juvenile judge may assign employees to work with such programs and may accept and administer gifts, grants, bequests, and devises made to the court for delinquency prevention.[10]

In addition to diversion and prevention programs, there are a variety of other community resources which the juvenile court may use as alternatives to official court action. RC 5139.34 permits appropriation of funds to the Department of Youth Services. The funds are then channeled to counties as subsidies to establish prevention, early intervention, diversion, treatment and rehabilitation programs for alleged or adjudicated unruly or delinquent children or those at risk of becoming unruly or delinquent.[11] Because the purpose of these subsidies is to provide community-based programs for children in need, certain conditions have been placed on the receipt of subsidy money: (1) services provided in a facility or in out-of-home placement unless minimum standards adopted by the Department have been satisfied;[12] (2) the subsidy may not be used for foster care facilities which have not been certified, licensed, or properly approved;[13] (3) only certain percentages of the subsidy grant may be used for capital improvements;[14] and (4) the receipt of funds is contingent on the Department's approval of the juvenile court's grant agreement and application for funding.[15] Each county receives a minimum of $50,000 per fiscal year.[16] Any remaining portion of the Department's grant appropriation is distributed to larger counties on a per capita basis.[17]

Although the IJA-ABA Standards encourage intake screening and other nonjudicial methods of handling children, they warn against potential misuse of such methods. Because of the virtually unlimited discretion given intake workers, there is the possibility that cases that should be handled officially may be diverted or that cases that do not necessitate any court intervention will be processed through informal intake channels.[18]

Cross References
§ 1:5, §§ 14:9 to 14:11, § 15:2, § 20:2, § 23:3
Research References
Carlin, Baldwin's Ohio Practice, Merrick-Rippner Probate Law (6th ed.), Ch 104

§ 15:4 Mediation

The Supreme Court of Ohio began to explore mediation programs in the late 1980's as a means of improving the provision of legal services to Ohio

---

[8]Since the speedy trial provisions of RC 2945.71 do not apply to children's cases, the court is permitted to wait a reasonable time before commencing official proceedings. See § 23:29, Speedy trial.

[9]RC 2151.11.

[10]RC 2151.11.

[11]RC 5139.34(A), RC 5139.43(C)(2)(a).

[12]RC 5139.34(A).

[13]RC 5139.34(A).

[14]RC 5139.34(A).

[15]RC 5139.43(C)(3)(a).

[16]RC 5139.34(B)(1).

[17]RC 5139.34(B)(2).

[18]IJA-ABA Standards Relating to the Juvenile Probation Function 2–3 (1980).

citizens.[1] Following the recommendation of its Committee on Dispute Resolution, the Court established an Office of Dispute Resolution. That office recommended continuation of an existing program, known as the Circuit Rider Project, which helped local courts establish volunteer mediation programs. The Court then provided two year start up grants to courts of common pleas, with the goal of having mediation programs in every county, staffed by court employees, by 2005.[2]

Mediation is defined as "a range of practices designed to help parties in conflict. [T]he term is used to describe a process in which an impartial person helps those parties to communicate and to make voluntary informed choices in an effort to resolve their dispute."[3] A mediator does not define the goal, but provides ideas for resolution, and helps the parties set agendas which can build momentum to reach their goal.[4]

Mediation is different from other forms of dispute resolution such as arbitration because the mediator is neutral and has no decision making authority. Mediation focuses on the common ground between the parties, rather than their differences.

The recognized benefits of mediation include:

Empowerment. People participate in resolving their own problems and designing their own solutions. They maintain control over their situation.

Education. People learn to communicate more effectively and resolve issues.

Efficiency. Issues can be addressed soon after the dispute arises and before people become entrenched in their positions.

Affordability. Services are often provided at minimal or no cost.

Problem-solving. Dispute resolution processes focus on interests and needs rather than positions. The parties are encouraged to explore and address the underlying issues of the conflict.

Preservation of relationships. Dispute resolution and conflict management processes provide people with an opportunity to better understand each other and work together cooperatively.[5]

Ohio's juvenile rules require juvenile courts to use diversion methods which are an appropriate means of "ameliorating situations brought to the attention of the court."[6] Such methods would keep children out of the formal court process, and keep them from acquiring court records.

Juvenile courts are a perfect forum for implementing mediation. The benefits of mediation precisely address many of the issues presented in a juvenile court case. For example, if the mediation occurs soon after the family presents with its issues, the issues can be addressed swiftly, rather than be left to fester while the court works to get the complaint drafted, processed, and set for a court date, sometimes in several months. Only after the court resolves the complaint would the family begin to receive services. Mediation, on the other hand, works directly with the family to resolve its issues and secure agreements from each of the parties on services to be obtained and

---

[Section 15:4]

[1]Dispute Resolution—Court Connected Mediation Program Research in Ohio, http://www.sconet.state.oh.us/dispute_resolution/research.

[2]Dispute Resolution—Court Connected Mediation Program Research in Ohio, http://www.sconet.state.oh.us/dispute_resolution/research.

[3]Center for Dispute Settlement, et al., National Standards for Court Connected Mediation Programs, at iv.

[4]Center for Dispute Settlement, et al., National Standards for Court Connected Mediation Programs, at 9.4.

[5]The Ohio Commission on Dispute Resolution and Conflict Management, et al., Ohio Directory of Dispute Resolution and Conflict Management, at 1; see also Schepard, Bozzomo, Efficiency, Therapeutic Justice, Mediation and Evaluation: Reflections on a Survey of Unified Family Courts, 37 Fam. L. Q. 333 (2003).

[6]Juv. R. 9(A).

participated in. Further, the parties have the opportunity to raise and resolve the underlying issues as the agreements are being reached. All of this would occur in far less time that it would take the court to process an official complaint and get it in front of a jurist.

The Process. Juvenile courts throughout the state have identified areas of jurisdiction for which they will provide mediation services, including delinquency,[7] unruly and truancy,[8] dependency/neglect/abuse,[9] and private custody[10] cases. Parties can access the mediation before charges are filed with the court or after charges are filed, depending on the particular county's program.[11] Parties, and their attorneys, should check the local rules of court to determine the specific requirements of their jurisdiction.[12]

The Mediator. The mediator is a neutral or impartial third party, with no prior relationships to any of the individuals involved in the dispute.[13] Mediators have different styles; some are reticent about offering solutions, others may be active in offering ideas and suggestions. All will facilitate the meetings and keep the discussions moving towards a positive resolution. Mediators explain the process, including issues of voluntariness, cost, confidentiality, and enforceability. Mediators are bound by rules of ethics[14] and the Supreme Court of Ohio has issued standards for court employed mediators.[15]

The Participants. The parties in a mediation must come to the table in good faith, to work towards a resolution of their differences.[16] Parties with time constraints, or cultural or language barriers must raise them with the mediator. Parties who know of a history of violence or intimidation by another of the parties should raise it as well with the mediator.[17] Parties must have the capacity to reach agreements; a party unable to comprehend or negotiate on his/her own behalf may not be an appropriate participant in mediation.

Confidentiality. The social policy of promoting dispute resolution provides for confidentiality of the mediation proceedings.[18] No record (either written or audio) is made. Information shared in negotiations is privileged and cannot

---

[7]RC 2152.19(C). See Mika, The Practice and Prospect of Victim Offender Programs, 46 SMU L. Rev. 2191 (1993). See also Text § 27:20, Victim Mediation.

[8]Hurst, Planning Interventions for Unruly and Truant Youth, Children, Families and the Courts, Ohio Bulletin (2003).

[9]Shaw and Phear, Case Status Conferences for Child Protection and Placement Proceedings in the State of Connecticut, 29 Family and Conciliation Courts Review 270 (1991). See also State Justice Institute, et al., Abuse, Dependency, Neglect Case Facilitation/Mediation Workshop (1996).

[10]See, e.g., Stark County Court of Common Pleas, Family Court Division, Loc. R. 21.

[11]The Ohio Commission on Dispute Resolution and Conflict Management, et al., Ohio Directory of Dispute Resolution and Conflict Management.

[12]See, e.g., Stark County Court of Common Pleas, Family Court Division, Loc. R. 21; Summit County Court of Common Pleas, Juvenile Division, Loc. R. 21.

[13]The Ohio Commission on Dispute Resolution and Conflict Management, et al., Ohio Directory of Dispute Resolution and Conflict Management, at 5.

[14]Center for Dispute Settlement, et al., National Standards for Court Connected Mediation Programs, at 8.1.

[15]Sup. R. 16.

[16]The Ohio Commission on Dispute Resolution and Conflict Management, et al., Ohio Directory of Dispute Resolution and Conflict Management, at 6.

[17]CDR Associates for The Supreme Court of Ohio, Domestic Abuse Issues: Training for Mediators and Other Professionals (April 2003); Brigner, Family Violence Prevention Center at the Ohio Office of Criminal Justice Services, The Ohio Domestic Violence Benchbook, 2nd Edition, at 10.

[18]Center for Dispute Settlement, et al., National Standards for Court Connected Mediation Programs, at 9.1.

be used against one party or the other in courtroom proceedings.[19] Absent a waiver by both parties, the mediator cannot testify in court and is prevented from revealing information obtained in the mediation.[20]

There are two exceptions to the confidentiality of the proceedings. When a mediator knows that a felony has been or is being committed, the mediator must report that information to law enforcement.[21] In addition, when the mediator knows or has reasonable suspicion that a child is being neglected or abused, the mediator must report that information to law enforcement or to child welfare officials.[22] Of course, the mediator may release basic information such as where and when the parties meet.[23]

Enforceability. The agreement reached by the parties is enforceable in court. The agreement itself should set out the consequences for failure to comply with the terms reached, including charges filed or contempt proceedings.[24]

Types of Cases. Ohio's juvenile courts have developed mediation programs to address delinquency, unruly and truancy, abuse/dependency/neglect, and private custody cases.[25]

§ 15:5 Arbitration

Arbitration is another permissible method of alternative dispute resolution for use in juvenile court, if requested by all parties.[1] Arbitration in juvenile cases would primarily be used in the valuation of real and personal property.[2]

§ 15:6 Family & Children First Council—Dispute resolution process

RC 2151.23(A)(12) provides juvenile courts with exclusive, original jurisdiction concerning an action commenced under RC 121.38. Pursuant to RC 121.38, an agency that is represented on a county family and children first

---

[19]See Evid. R. 408; RC 2317.02. See also Center for Dispute Settlement, et al., National Standards for Court Connected Mediation Programs, at 12.1.

[20]Fowler, et al., Planning Mediation Programs: A Deskbook for Common Pleas Judges, at 9 20 (2000).

[21]RC 2921.22(A).

[22]RC 2151.421.

[23]Fowler, et al., Planning Mediation Programs: A Deskbook for Common Pleas Judges, at 9 14 (2000).

[24]Center for Dispute Settlement, et al., National Standards for Court Connected Mediation Programs, at 15 1.

[25]For a listing of mediation programs available in Ohio, see The Ohio Commission on Dispute Resolution and Conflict Management, et al., Ohio Directory of Dispute Resolution and Conflict Management. See also Daicoff, The Comprehensive Law Movement, 19 Touro L. Rev. 825 (2004); Bakker, Repairing the Breach and Reconciling the Discordant: Mediation in the Criminal Justice System, 72 N.C. L. Rev. 1479 (1994); Mika, The Practice and Prospect of Victim Offender Programs, 46 SMU L. Rev. 2191 (1993).

[Section 15:5]

[1]Sup. R. 15(B)(1).

The Rules of Superintendence for Courts of Ohio provide for arbitration in juvenile court cases. Rule 15(B) provides:

(B) Arbitration in Juvenile and Domestic Relations Cases.

(1) The judge or judges of a division of a court of common pleas having domestic relations or juvenile jurisdiction may, at the request of all parties, refer a case or a designated issue to arbitration.

(2) The parties shall propose an arbitrator to the court and identify all issues to be resolved by the arbitrator. The arbitrator shall consent to serve and shall have no interest in the determination of the case or relationship with the parties or their counsel that would interfere with the impartial consideration of the case. An arbitrator selected pursuant to this section is not required to be an attorney.

(3) The request for arbitration submitted by the parties shall provide for the manner of payment of the arbitrator.

(4) The arbitrator shall file a report and award pursuant to division (A)(2)(c) of this rule.

(5) Any party may appeal the report and award pursuant to division (A)(2)(d) of this rule.

[2]Sup. R. 15 Commentary.

council or local intersystem cluster[1] that disagrees with the council or cluster's decision concerning the services or funding for services that a child is to receive from council or cluster agencies may initiate a dispute resolution process. Not later than seven days after a determination has been issued pursuant to a dispute resolution process, the agency may file a motion (if the child has been alleged or adjudicated abused, neglected, dependent, unruly, delinquent, or a juvenile traffic offender),[2] or a complaint objecting to the determination (if the child is not presently within the court's jurisdiction).[3] Venue lies in the county in which the child's case is pending, or the county served by the council or cluster.[4]

No later than 90 days after the motion or complaint is filed, the court must conduct a hearing, and must issue written notice to each pertinent agency by first class mail at least five days before the hearing date.[5] At the conclusion of the hearing, the court shall issue an order directing one or more of the council or cluster agencies to provide services or funding for services to the child. An agency so ordered shall be a party to any juvenile court proceeding concerning the child.[6]

[Section 15:6]
[1]See RC 121.37.
[2]RC 121.38(B)(1).
[3]RC 121.38(B)(2).
[4]RC 121.38.
[5]RC 121.38(B)(2).
[6]RC 121.38(B)(2).

Chapter 16

Complaint

KeyCite®: Cases and other legal materials listed in KeyCite Scope can be researched through West's KeyCite service on Westlaw®. Use KeyCite to check citations for form, parallel references, prior and later history, and comprehensive citator information, including citations to other decisions and secondary materials.

§ 16:1   Complaint—Introduction
§ 16:2   Standing to file complaint
§ 16:3   Basis for complaint
§ 16:4   Time requirements—Custody; detention
§ 16:5   Parental identification
§ 16:6   Oath requirement
§ 16:7   Content of complaint; designating type of case
§ 16:8   Delinquency complaints
§ 16:9   Traffic offender complaints
§ 16:10   Unruly complaints
§ 16:11   Neglect & abuse complaints
§ 16:12   Dependency complaints
§ 16:13   Custody proceedings—Required information
§ 16:14   Permanent & temporary custody complaints; planned permanent living arrangements
§ 16:15   Certification or transfer from another court
§ 16:16   Amendment of complaints
§ 16:17   Objections to complaints

§ 16:1   Complaint—Introduction

This chapter discusses the requirements for the complaint, which is the document that initiates the juvenile court proceedings. Ch 18 considers summonses.

S.B. 179 and RC 2152.021 governs complaints in delinquency and traffic offender cases. RC 2151.27 deals only with unruly, abused, neglected, or dependent children. Serious Youthful Offender (SYO) cases may be initiated by indictment, information, complaint, or notice.[1]

Truancy. Juvenile Rule 10(A) was amended in 2001 to provide that delinquent or unruly complaints concerning chronic and habitual truants, including the parents, may be filed in the county in which the child is supposed to attend public school.[2]

The instrument that sets forth the allegations that form the basis for juvenile court jurisdiction is the complaint.[3] Unless a complaint is filed, the juvenile court has no jurisdiction to proceed with an adjudicatory or dispositional

---

[Section 16:1]
[1]See Serious Youthful Offenders Ch 5.
[2]This amendment was adopted to conform the rule to RC 2151.27(A)(2), which codified S.B. 181.
[3]Juv. R. 2(F).

hearing.[4] The requirements of a complaint are covered both by rule[5] and by statute.[6]

§ 16:2 Standing to file complaint

The question of standing to bring a complaint is a procedural matter governed by the Rules of Juvenile Procedure, which control over an inconsistent statute purporting to govern procedural matters.[1]

A complaint may be filed by "any person having knowledge"[2] that a child is within the court's jurisdiction. The term "person" is defined as "an individual, association, corporation, or partnership and the state or any of its political subdivisions, departments, or agencies."[3] Although this definition seems to permit any individual to file any type of complaint, there are some restrictions. For instance, a uniform traffic ticket must be used as the complaint in juvenile traffic offense proceedings.[4] Since such tickets may only be issued by law enforcement officers,[5] other persons would not be permitted to file complaints relative to juvenile traffic offenders.

§ 16:3 Basis for complaint

The complaint may be based upon "information and belief,"[1] and the filing of the complaint is a discretionary decision based on a consideration of available evidence.[2] In interpreting the "information and belief" standard in criminal proceedings, Ohio courts have held that it is not necessary that a complainant or affiant have personal knowledge of the facts constituting the elements of the offense or have observed the commission of the offense.[3] It is sufficient if such person has reasonable grounds to believe that the accused has committed the offense.[4] The complainant or affiant may rely upon the testimony and investigation of others to establish matters not within his personal knowledge.[5]

§ 16:4 Time requirements—Custody; detention

Custody. If an alleged abused, neglected, or dependent child is taken into custody pursuant to RC 2151.31(D) or is taken into custody pursuant to RC

---

[4]Howser v. Ashtabula County Children's Services Board, 1983 WL 6096 (Ohio Ct. App. 11th Dist. Ashtabula County 1983).

[5]Juv. R. 10.

[6]RC 2151.27.

[Section 16:2]

[1]In re Brofford, 83 Ohio App. 3d 869, 615 N.E.2d 1120 (10th Dist. Franklin County 1992); State ex rel. Lamier v. Lamier, 105 Ohio App. 3d 797, 664 N.E.2d 1384 (8th Dist. Cuyahoga County 1995).

[2]RC 2151.27; Juv. R. 10(A).

[3]Juv. R. 2(BB).

[4]Juv. R. 10(C); Traf. R. 3(A).

[5]Traf. R. 3(C), Traf. R. 3(E).

[Section 16:3]

[1]RC 2151.27(A); Juv. R. 10(B).

[2]Rich v. Erie Cty. Dept. of Human Resources, 106 Ohio App. 3d 88, 665 N.E.2d 278 (6th Dist. Erie County 1995).

[3]Sopko v. Maxwell, 3 Ohio St. 2d 123, 32 Ohio Op. 2d 99, 209 N.E.2d 201 (1965); State v. Villagomez, 44 Ohio App. 2d 209, 73 Ohio Op. 2d 215, 337 N.E.2d 167 (3d Dist. Defiance County 1974); State v. Biedenharn, 19 Ohio App. 2d 204, 48 Ohio Op. 2d 338, 250 N.E.2d 778 (1st Dist. Hamilton County 1969).

[4]Sopko v. Maxwell, 3 Ohio St. 2d 123, 32 Ohio Op. 2d 99, 209 N.E.2d 201 (1965).

[5]State v. Villagomez, 44 Ohio App. 2d 209, 73 Ohio Op. 2d 215, 337 N.E.2d 167 (3d Dist. Defiance County 1974). In some counties, the police departments of large municipalities assign to one officer the duty of signing all juvenile court complaints filed by the department.

2151.31(A) without the filing of a complaint, the complaint must be filed with respect to the child before the end of the next day after the day on which the child was taken into custody.[1]

Detention. With respect to any other child held in a place of detention or shelter care, the complaint must be filed not later than seventy-two hours after he is placed in detention or shelter care.[2]

§16:5 Parental identification

The complaint must contain the name and address of the child's parent, guardian, or custodian or, if such name and address is unknown, it must so state.[1] Where a permanent custody order has been entered against the child's parents,[2] it is unnecessary to include their names or addresses in any subsequent complaint because they would no longer be parties to the action.[3] In such cases the name and address of the child's guardian[4] or custodian[5] should be included. Where temporary custody of the child has been granted to one parent or to someone other than the parents,[6] Juvenile Rule 10(B) requires that the names and addresses of both parents as well as that of the custodian be listed in the complaint.

The rationale for requiring the inclusion of the parents' names and addresses is that the parents are parties to any juvenile court proceeding regarding their child,[7] unless their rights have been permanently divested. As parties they are entitled to certain due process safeguards, such as the rights to counsel[8] and notice.[9]

If the name or whereabouts of the child's parent, guardian, or custodian is unknown, the court is required to serve summons on that person by publication.[10]

§16:6 Oath requirement

Except for traffic cases, the complaint must be made under oath.[1] By entry in its journal, the juvenile court may authorize any deputy clerk to administer

---

[Section 16:4]

[1]RC 2151.27.

[2]RC 2151.314.

[Section 16:5]

[1]Juv. R. 10(B)(2).

[2]RC 2151.353(A)(4). See §§ 30:8 to 30:12, Permanent custody; Motions for Permanent Custody Ch 31.

[3]RC 2151.35(D), RC 2151.414(F).

[4]Juv. R. 2(N) defines a "guardian" as "a person, association, or corporation that is granted authority by a probate court pursuant to Chapter 2111 of the Revised Code to exercise parental rights over a child to the extent provided in the court's order and subject to the residual parental rights of the child's parents."

[5]Juv. R. 2(H) defines a "custodian" as "a person who has legal custody of a child or a public children services agency or private child placing agency that has permanent, temporary, or legal custody of a child."

[6]RC 2151.353(A). See § 25:14, Reasonable efforts determination; Dispositional Case Plans Ch 26.

[7]Juv. R. 2(Y) also provides that "in appropriate cases" the child's guardian or custodian may also be a party.

[8]See § 23:3, Right to counsel; § 23:6, Guardian ad litem.

[9]See Summons Ch 18.

[10]See § 18:4, Summons—Methods of service.

[Section 16:6]

[1]RC 2151.27(A); Juv. R. 10(B)(3). RC 3.20 provides that whenever an oath is required, an affirmation in lieu thereof may be taken by a person having conscientious scruples against taking an oath. An affirmation has the same effect as an oath.

oaths when necessary in the discharge of his duties.[2]

Although it is apparent from Juvenile Rule 10(B)(3) and RC 2151.27 that all complaints in non-traffic cases must be made under oath, this requirement has been relaxed in two unreported decisions. In one case, the complainant signed the complaint, but failed to do so under oath. The court held that the complainant had substantially complied with the rule and statute since at all times she realized the effect of signing the complaint and she corroborated at the adjudicatory hearing, under oath, the facts outlined in the complaint.[3] In the other case, the complaint was not even signed. However, the court determined that since the complainant appeared in court at the time the complaint was filed and testified under oath about the allegations in the complaint, the purpose and spirit of the rule had been served.[4]

Traffic cases. Despite the general rule requiring a sworn complaint, the complaint in juvenile traffic offenses need not be made under oath. Juvenile Rule 10(C) requires that a uniform traffic ticket be used as the complaint in juvenile traffic offense proceedings.[5] Traffic Rule 3(E) requires only that such tickets be "signed" by the law enforcement officer, not sworn to.[6]

§ 16:7 Content of complaint; designating type of case

The complaint must allege that the child is delinquent,[1] unruly, abused, neglected, dependent, or a juvenile traffic offender[2] and must state in ordinary and concise language the essential facts which bring the case within the court's jurisdiction.[3] Each type of complaint is discussed in the following sections.

Type of case. The rule requiring that the complaint specify the type of case involved has generally been followed by the Ohio courts. Thus, a neglect finding based on a dependency complaint,[4] a dependency finding based on a neglect[5] or unruly[6] complaint, and a juvenile traffic offender finding based on a delinquency complaint[7] have been held invalid. Since dependency, neglect, delinquency, and unruliness involve different conditions, the parent must be

---

[2]RC 2151.13.

[3]Matter of Lewandowski, 1986 WL 9211 (Ohio Ct. App. 7th Dist. Columbiana County 1986).

[4]Matter of Bridges, 1986 WL 7109 (Ohio Ct. App. 6th Dist. Lucas County 1986).

[5]See § 16:9, Traffic offender complaints.

[6]Prior to the 1975 amendment to Juv. R. 10, traffic tickets had to be made under oath. See In re Bernstein, Nos. 33531, 33532 (8th Dist. Ct. App., Cuyahoga, 1-2-75).

[Section 16:7]

[1]See RC 2925.42 for complaint requirements where a delinquency complaint alleges a felony drug abuse offense, and criminal forfeiture of property is sought.

[2]RC 2151.27(A); RC 2152.021(A). For the requirements of permanent custody complaints, see § 16:14, Permanent & temporary custody complaints; planned permanent living arrangements.

[3]Application of Gault, 387 U.S. 1, 87 S. Ct. 1428, 18 L. Ed. 2d 527 (1967); Juv. R. 10(B)(1). RC 2151.27(A) provides that the complaint must "allege the particular facts upon which the allegation . . . is based." These provisions overruled early court decisions which held that a complaint was valid if it merely used the words delinquent, dependent, or neglected, without alleging specific facts. See In re Duncan, 62 Ohio L. Abs. 173, 107 N.E.2d 256 (Ct. App. 2d Dist. Preble County 1951); In re Anteau, 67 Ohio App. 117, 21 Ohio Op. 129, 36 N.E.2d 47 (6th Dist. Lucas County 1941); In re Hayes, 62 Ohio App. 289, 16 Ohio Op. 10, 30 Ohio L. Abs. 568, 23 N.E.2d 956 (2d Dist. Franklin County 1939); Smith v. Privette & State, 13 Ohio L. Abs. 291, 1932 WL 1836 (Ct. App. 2d Dist. Franklin County 1932); In re Decker, 28 Ohio N.P. (n.s.) 433, 1930 WL 2382 (Juv. Ct. 1930).

[4]In re Thomas, Nos. 39494, 39495 (8th Dist. Ct. App., Cuyahoga, 7-19-79).

[5]Matter of Flynn, 1983 WL 3457 (Ohio Ct. App. 10th Dist. Franklin County 1983); In re Reed, No. CA 1325 (5th Dist. Ct. App., Tuscarawas, 7-24-79).

[6]In re Osborn, No. CA 1744 (5th Dist. Ct. App., Richland, 1-16-79).

[7]In re Elliott, 87 Ohio App. 3d 816, 623 N.E.2d 217 (12th Dist. Fayette County 1993).

provided sufficient notice of the category relied upon.[8] On the other hand, an Ohio court of appeals substituted a finding of dependency for a finding of neglect in a permanent custody case, although dependency had not been alleged in the complaint.[9]

An appellate court has held that a trial court's dismissal of a neglect complaint which erroneously contained a numerical reference to the dependency statute, instead of providing the complainant with an opportunity to cure the defect, was not a valid exercise of the court's discretion.[10]

§ 16:8   Delinquency complaints

The complaint must specify the type of case—i.e., delinquency.[1] The complaint must also state in ordinary and concise language the essential facts which bring the case within the court's jurisdiction.[2]

Numerical statute designation. In delinquency and juvenile traffic offense cases, the complaint must also contain the numerical designation of the statute or ordinance alleged to have been violated.[3] This requirement refers to the statute or ordinance which defines the particular offense and not to the general statutes which define a delinquent child[4] or a juvenile traffic offender.[5] However, a court of appeals has held that a delinquency complaint which inadvertently omitted some of the statutory language was not invalid.[6] In *State v. Burgun*,[7] a case interpreting a similar provision in Criminal Rule 3, the court held that inclusion of the numerical designation of the applicable criminal statute in a complaint does not cure failure to charge all of the essential elements of the crime.

The correction of mistaken section numbers is within the sound discretion of the trial court.[8]

Essential facts requirements. A delinquency complaint for disorderly conduct which alleges that the child is delinquent, which recites the statutory language of the criminal statute violated, and which describes the alleged conduct with particular facts relative to the time, place, and circumstances of the conduct is valid.[9] While all the facts relied upon to sustain the complaint need not be recited, the material elements of the offense must be stated.[10]

Moreover, a delinquency complaint does not need to be read as strictly as a

---

[8]In re Thomas, Nos. 39494, 39495 (8th Dist. Ct. App., Cuyahoga, 7-19-79).

[9]In re Sullivan, Nos. 79 AP-893, 79 AP-894 (10th Dist. Ct. App., Franklin, 12-16-80).

[10]In re Fetters, 110 Ohio App. 3d 483, 674 N.E.2d 766 (12th Dist. Preble County 1996).

[Section 16:8]

[1]RC 2152.021(A)(1).

[2]Juv. R. 10(B)(1). See also RC 2152.021(A)(1) ("the complaint shall allege the particular facts upon which the allegation . . . is based").

[3]Juv. R. 10(B)(1). In re Fetters, 110 Ohio App. 3d 483, 674 N.E.2d 766 (12th Dist. Preble County 1996); Matter of Vanek, 1995 WL 787429 (Ohio Ct. App. 11th Dist. Ashtabula County 1995).

[4]RC 2152.02(F).

[5]RC 2152.02(N).

[6]Matter of Pribanic, 1991 WL 3813 (Ohio Ct. App. 6th Dist. Erie County 1991).

[7]State v. Burgun, 49 Ohio App. 2d 112, 3 Ohio Op. 3d 177, 359 N.E.2d 1018 (8th Dist. Cuyahoga County 1976).

[8]State v. Hill, No. 76AP-504 (10th Dist. Ct. App., Franklin, 12-28-76).

[9]In Re: Davis, 1982 WL 2959 (Ohio Ct. App. 5th Dist. Tuscarawas County 1982) (complaint valid even though the only specific facts mentioned related to the date and county, with no facts given relative to the exact time, location, or victim); Corona, 1981 WL 4502 (Ohio Ct. App. 8th Dist. Cuyahoga County 1981) (complaint included particular facts relative to exact time and location and included the victims' names).

[10]State v. Burgun, 49 Ohio App. 2d 112, 3 Ohio Op. 3d 177, 359 N.E.2d 1018 (8th Dist. Cuyahoga County 1976).

criminal indictment.[11] Thus, even though a delinquency complaint designates a particular statute or statutes as being violated by a child, a juvenile court may find, on the basis of the facts alleged and proved, that the child is a delinquent child for the violation of an additional statute.[12]

Similarly, a delinquency complaint is sufficient under Juvenile Rule 10(B) to state a charge of complicity when it alleges that the juvenile "knowingly" aided another to commit robbery[13] in violation of RC 2923.03.[14] In *In re Howard*,[15] the court held that a delinquency complaint is sufficient even if it fails to specify exactly what theft offense was committed or attempted, and fails to specify the degree or degrees of culpability applicable to that theft offense.

Prior offenses. It is now provided by statute[16] that a prior delinquency adjudication shall be treated as a prior conviction in determining the degree of offense for a current delinquent act. The statute requires the court to determine the prior adjudication after adjudication on the current complaint, and prior to making any disposition involving a commitment to the Department of Youth Services. Neither RC 2152.021 nor Juvenile Rule 10 indicate whether the complaint for the current delinquent act must allege the prior delinquency adjudication as an additional element of the offense. RC 2945.75, which governs this same issue in the context of criminal cases, requires inclusion of "the degree of the offense which the accused is alleged to have committed, or . . . such additional element or elements" which elevate the offense to a more serious degree.

Firearms specification. The delinquent child dispositional statute provides that if a child is committed to the Department of Youth Services and the court determines that the child, if an adult, would be guilty of a firearm specification, the court may impose an additional term of commitment.[17] Again, neither RC 2152.021 nor Juvenile Rule 10 indicate whether the complaint must contain allegations regarding the firearm specification. Additional prison time on a firearm specification may not be imposed on an adult criminal defendant unless the indictment includes the specification.[18] However, in the juvenile context, an appellate court has held that the firearm specification need not be set forth in a delinquency complaint in order to impose the additional term of commitment.[19] In reaching its decision, the court relied on the catch-all provision in the dispositional statute,[20] and on the case law holding that delinquency complaints are not to be read as strictly as criminal indictments.[21]

Truancy. Juvenile Rule 10(A) was amended in 2001 to provide that delinquent or unruly complaints concerning chronic and habitual truants, including the parents, may be filed in the county in which the child is supposed to

---

[11]In re Burgess, 13 Ohio App. 3d 374, 469 N.E.2d 967 (12th Dist. Preble County 1984); In Matter of Rhodes, 1997 WL 143942 (Ohio Ct. App. 10th Dist. Franklin County 1997); In re Good, 118 Ohio App. 3d 371, 692 N.E.2d 1072 (12th Dist. Butler County 1997).

[12]In re Burgess, 13 Ohio App. 3d 374, 469 N.E.2d 967 (12th Dist. Preble County 1984). The court cautioned that its holding might differ if the complaint were intentionally abbreviated and the testimony at the adjudicatory hearing bore no relationship to the facts alleged in the complaint. See also In re Rough, 1989 WL 11513 (Ohio Ct. App. 12th Dist. Butler County 1989).

[13]RC 2911.01.

[14]In re Howard, 31 Ohio App. 3d 1, 508 N.E.2d 190 (1st Dist. Hamilton County 1987). See also Matter of Swackhammer, 1986 WL 13411 (Ohio Ct. App. 4th Dist. Ross County 1986).

[15]In re Howard, 31 Ohio App. 3d 1, 508 N.E.2d 190 (1st Dist. Hamilton County 1987).

[16]RC 2152.16(C).

[17]See § 27:3, Department of Youth Services commitment.

[18]State v. Loines, 20 Ohio App. 3d 69, 484 N.E.2d 727 (8th Dist. Cuyahoga County 1984).

[19]Matter of Laquatra, 1998 WL 23841 (Ohio Ct. App. 8th Dist. Cuyahoga County 1998).

[20]RC 2152.19(A)(8). See § 27:18, "Catch-all" provision.

[21]In re Burgess, 13 Ohio App. 3d 374, 469 N.E.2d 967 (12th Dist. Preble County 1984).

attend public school.[22]

§ 16:9 Traffic offender complaints

The complaint must specify the type of case—i.e., traffic offender case.[1] The complaint must also state in ordinary and concise language the essential facts which bring the case within the court's jurisdiction.[2]

In juvenile traffic offense proceedings, a uniform traffic ticket is used as the complaint.[3] Since juvenile court traffic proceedings are subject to the Ohio Traffic Rules, those rules determine the requirements of a ticket.[4] Unlike other complaints filed in the juvenile court, a traffic ticket need not be sworn to;[5] it may be issued only by a law enforcement officer.[6]

A properly issued uniform traffic ticket provides information relative to the time, place, and nature of the alleged violation, a narrative description of the offense, a synopsis of the road, weather, and traffic conditions,[7] and the numerical designation of the statute or ordinance alleged to have been violated.[8] In this respect, the traffic ticket is like other complaints; it informs the parties of the essential facts.

A uniform traffic ticket for speeding which fails to charge that the speed stated thereon is unreasonable fails to state an offense.[9] However, where a traffic ordinance prohibits driving faster or slower than is reasonable or proper and provides that exceeding any speed limit is prima facie unlawful, a traffic ticket alleging that the offender has exceeded the posted speed limit in effect also alleges that the offender's speed was prima facie unreasonable.[10]

§ 16:10 Unruly complaints

The complaint must specify the type of case—i.e., unruly child[1] and state in ordinary and concise language the essential facts which bring the case within the court's jurisdiction.[2]

Truancy. Juvenile Rule 10(A) was amended in 2001 to provide that delinquent or unruly complaints concerning habitual truants, including the parents, may be filed in the county in which the child is supposed to attend public school.[3]

§ 16:11 Neglect & abuse complaints

The complaint must specify the type of case—i.e., abused or neglected

---

[22]This amendment was adopted to conform the rule to RC 2151.27(A)(2), which codified S.B. 181.

[Section 16:9]

[1]RC 2152.021(A)(1).

[2]Juv. R. 10(B)(1). See also RC 2152.021(A)(1) ("the complaint shall allege the particular facts upon which the allegation . . . . is based").

[3]Juv. R. 10(C).

[4]Traf. R. 1(A), Traf. R. 2.

[5]Traf. R. 3(E).

[6]Traf. R. 3(C), Traf. R. 3(E).

[7]See Traffic Rules, Appendix of Forms.

[8]Juv. R. 10(B)(1).

[9]City of Medina v. Coles, 1987 WL 14424 (Ohio Ct. App. 9th Dist. Medina County 1987).

[10]In re Farinacci, No. 37973 (8th Dist. Ct. App., Cuyahoga, 11-30-78).

[Section 16:10]

[1]RC 2151.27(A)(1).

[2]Juv. R. 10(B)(1). See also RC 2151.27(A)(1) ("the complaint shall allege the particular facts upon which the allegation . . . . is based").

[3]This amendment was adopted to conform the rule to RC 2151.27(A)(2), which codified S.B. 181.

child.[1] It must also state in ordinary and concise language the essential facts which bring the case within the court's jurisdiction.[2] Complaints in custody proceedings are discussed in later sections.

An abuse complaint which did not specifically set forth the dates on which the abusive acts occurred has been held to satisfy the requirement of definiteness.[3]

§ 16:12 Dependency complaints

The complaint must specify the type of case—i.e., dependency.[1] The complaint must also state in ordinary and concise language the essential facts which bring the case within the court's jurisdiction.[2]

Essential facts requirement. A dependency complaint which recited only that the children "appear to be dependent in that their condition or environment is such as to warrant the state, in the interests of the children, in assuming their guardianship" was held to be defective.[3] Such a complaint merely reiterates the wording of the dependency statute (RC 2151.04(C)), without stating the particular facts supporting the complaint.[4] However, in another case in which the complaint merely repeated the wording of RC 2151.04(C), a court of appeals held that any insufficiency of the initial complaint was cured by the adjudicatory hearing, at which the parties had the opportunity to present evidence and establish facts on the issue of dependency.[5]

Dependency complaints which allege some details have generally been upheld against challenges of lack of specificity and definiteness. For example, a complaint which recited the wording of the dependency statute was upheld because it included the following supporting allegations: the parents' unstable living situation, their inability to provide for the child's support or medical care, the putative father's denial of paternity, the mother's lack of education and employment, and the mother's residence in a home fraught with

---

[Section 16:11]

[1]RC 2151.27(A)(1).

[2]Juv. R. 10(B)(1). See also RC 2151.27(A)(1) ("the complaint shall allege the particular facts upon which the allegation . . . is based"). The issue of whether a complaint contains "essential facts" arises more often in dependency and neglect proceedings than in delinquency proceedings. In dependency and neglect cases the "facts" are more generalized and the necessary elements are more nebulous than in delinquency cases, which involve a violation of a specific statute or ordinance.

[3]Matter of Gall, 1986 WL 7100 (Ohio Ct. App. 3d Dist. Paulding County 1986).

[Section 16:12]

[1]RC 2151.27(A)(1).

[2]Juv. R. 10(B)(1). See also RC 2151.27(A)(1) ("the complaint shall allege the particular facts upon which the allegation . . . is based"). The issue of whether a complaint contains "essential facts" arises more often in dependency and neglect proceedings than in delinquency proceedings. In dependency and neglect cases the "facts" are more generalized and the necessary elements are more nebulous than in delinquency cases, which involve a violation of a specific statute or ordinance.

[3]In re Hunt, 46 Ohio St. 2d 378, 75 Ohio Op. 2d 450, 348 N.E.2d 727 (1976). See also Baker, 1982 WL 6832 (Ohio Ct. App. 3d Dist. Hardin County 1982).

[4]In re Hunt, 46 Ohio St. 2d 378, 75 Ohio Op. 2d 450, 348 N.E.2d 727 (1976). For similar decisions holding that "boilerplate" complaints which merely recite the wording of the statute are defective, see Baker, 1982 WL 6832 (Ohio Ct. App. 3d Dist. Hardin County 1982); Matter of Willis, 1981 WL 6749 (Ohio Ct. App. 3d Dist. Henry County 1981); In Matter of Parker, 1981 WL 6774 (Ohio Ct. App. 3d Dist. Van Wert County 1981); In re Reed, No. CA 1325 (5th Dist. Ct. App., Tuscarawas, 7-24-79); In re Neff, No. 1-78-9 (3d Dist. Ct. App., Allen, 6-14-78); In Re: Spears, 1984 WL 5682 (Ohio Ct. App. 4th Dist. Athens County 1984).

[5]In re Rutherford, 1991 WL 65113 (Ohio Ct. App. 9th Dist. Summit County 1991). See In re Lester v. Lester, 1993 WL 392122 (Ohio Ct. App. 9th Dist. Summit County 1993); In re Dukes, 81 Ohio App. 3d 145, 610 N.E.2d 513 (9th Dist. Summit County 1991). In *Hunt*, a writ of habeas corpus had been filed for prior to the adjudicatory hearing.

domestic difficulties.[6] Complaints alleging even fewer details have met the requirement of definiteness. A mere allegation of "excessive punishment" has been held sufficient.[7]

Some courts have liberally interpreted the "necessary language" requirements of Juvenile Rule 10(B)(1). It has been held that the rule is not intended to force a complainant to state in the complaint every fact surrounding each incident described.[8] Thus, in proving its case in a neglect and dependency proceeding, the state is not limited to those facts which are specifically listed in the complaint.[9]

§ 16:13 Custody proceedings—Required information

RC 3109.27(A) requires every party in a custody proceeding to give information in his first pleading as to the child's present and past addresses and custodians and as to any custody proceedings concerning the child pending in other jurisdictions. This section is made applicable to juvenile court custody proceedings, including neglect and dependency cases, by RC 2151.23(F) and RC 3109.21(C) but does not apply to delinquency cases.[1]

The Ohio Supreme Court held that this mandatory jurisdictional requirement applies to a parent bringing an action, but does not apply to a public agency that initiates such an action.[2]

Subsequently, the statutes[3] were amended to specify that a public children services agency, acting pursuant to a complaint filed under RC 2151.27, is not subject to the requirements of RC 3109.27.[4]

§ 16:14 Permanent & temporary custody complaints; planned permanent living arrangements

In a case in which a child is alleged to be abused, neglected, or dependent, if the complainant desires permanent custody of the child, temporary custody of the child (whether as the preferred or an alternative disposition), or the placement of the child in a planned permanent living arrangement, the complaint must contain a prayer specifically requesting permanent custody, temporary custody, or the placement of the child in the planned arrangement.[1] If such a prayer is not included in the complaint, such a

---

[6]In re Trizzino, No. 40982 (8th Dist. Ct. App., Cuyahoga, 1-31-80).

[7]In re Brown, No. 3-CA-79 (5th Dist. Ct. App., Fairfield, 7-20-79).

[8]In re Sims, 13 Ohio App. 3d 37, 468 N.E.2d 111 (12th Dist. Preble County 1983); In re Pieper Children, 74 Ohio App. 3d 714, 600 N.E.2d 317 (12th Dist. Preble County 1991); In Matter of Rivera, 1996 WL 476448 (Ohio Ct. App. 8th Dist. Cuyahoga County 1996).

[9]In re Sims, 13 Ohio App. 3d 37, 468 N.E.2d 111 (12th Dist. Preble County 1983); In re Pieper Children, 74 Ohio App. 3d 714, 600 N.E.2d 317 (12th Dist. Preble County 1991).

[Section 16:13]

[1]In Matter of Trent, 1988 WL 36361 (Ohio Ct. App. 4th Dist. Ross County 1988).

[2]In re Palmer, 12 Ohio St. 3d 194, 465 N.E.2d 1312 (1984). See also Pasqualone v. Pasqualone, 63 Ohio St. 2d 96, 17 Ohio Op. 3d 58, 406 N.E.2d 1121 (1980); Cook v. Court of Common Pleas of Marion County, 28 Ohio App. 3d 82, 502 N.E.2d 245 (3d Dist. Marion County 1986); Matter of Infant Boy Reed, 1990 WL 187177 (Ohio Ct. App. 7th Dist. Columbiana County 1990); In Re Coe, 1983 WL 5648 (Ohio Ct. App. 5th Dist. Stark County 1983). But see In re Miller, No. 96AP09075 (5th Dist. Ct. App., Tuscarawas, 5-23-97) (unreported), which distinguished Palmer in holding that the doctrine of estoppel was inapplicable based on the specific facts of the case.

[3]RC 2151.27(G), RC 3109.27(D).

[4]1996 H.B. 274, eff. 8-8-96.

[Section 16:14]

[1]RC 2151.27(C). See also Juv. R. 10(D) to Juv. R. 10(F). Although the statutory provision requires this statement only in complaints which allege abuse, dependency, or neglect, the rule applies to any complaint. This includes delinquency and unruly cases since it is legally possible

dispositional order may not be made.[2] However, some courts have determined that the RC 2151.353(B) notice requirements do not apply under all circumstances. It has been held that the statutory requirement that the complaint state the requested dispositional order applies only to an initial dispositional hearing.[3] The court has discretion under RC 2151.415(A) at post-dispositional hearings to impose any of the dispositional options contained in that section according to the child's best interest.[4] Moreover, in a case in which a job and family services department appealed an order granting it long-term foster care after the agency's complaint had requested permanent custody, the court of appeals held that the fact that the agency did not request long-term foster care did not limit the juvenile court's discretion to make such a dispositional order.[5] In affirming the juvenile court, the court of appeals relied on the use of the discretionary word "may" in the dispositional statute[6] and on the rule[7] which permits juvenile courts to amend the pleadings. Another court of appeals held the same based on its finding that a trial court, pursuant to RC 2151.353(A), is vested with the inherent right to provide for a less restrictive dispositional option than was requested in the complaint.[8]

In *Smith*[9] and *Sullivan*,[10] post-dispositional motions had been filed requesting new dispositional orders, and in *Cremeans*[11] the original complaint had included a request for a specific dispositional order. In all three cases the courts of appeals upheld the juvenile courts' determinations to impose dispositional orders authorized by RC 2151.415(A) or RC 2151.353(A), although such orders were different from the orders requested in the motions or complaint. On the other hand, where a juvenile court conducts a dispositional review hearing pursuant to RC 2151.417(C),[12] and no written motions for a different dispositional option have been filed pursuant to RC 2151.353(A)(3) or RC 2151.415(A)(3) by any of the parties, it is a violation of the parent's procedural due process rights to grant an oral motion to award legal custody to a relative, which terminates the parent's reunification efforts with her child.[13]

As with other complaints, abuse, neglect, and dependency complaints must allege the particular facts on which the allegations of the complaint are

---

for permanent custody, temporary custody, or a planned permanent living arrangements to be ordered in such cases (RC 2151.354(A), RC 2151.355(A)(1)).

[2]RC 2151.353(B); Matter of Farace, 1997 WL 802819 (Ohio Ct. App. 4th Dist. Scioto County 1997); Matter of Brittany and Marcus B., 1996 WL 11135 (Ohio Ct. App. 6th Dist. Wood County 1996); In Matter of Buzzard, 1995 WL 739890 (Ohio Ct. App. 10th Dist. Franklin County 1995); Matter of McDaniel, 1993 WL 33308 (Ohio Ct. App. 4th Dist. Adams County 1993); In re Shackelford, 1990 WL 68954 (Ohio Ct. App. 2d Dist. Montgomery County 1990). See § 18:3, Summons—Contents and form.

[3]Matter of Smith Children, 1990 WL 70926 (Ohio Ct. App. 12th Dist. Warren County 1990); Matter of Sullivan, 1992 WL 42813 (Ohio Ct. App. 3d Dist. Seneca County 1992).

[4]Matter of Smith Children, 1990 WL 70926 (Ohio Ct. App. 12th Dist. Warren County 1990); Matter of Sullivan, 1992 WL 42813 (Ohio Ct. App. 3d Dist. Seneca County 1992).

[5]Matter of Cremeans, 1992 WL 47278 (Ohio Ct. App. 8th Dist. Cuyahoga County 1992); Matter of Duncan/Walker Children, 109 Ohio App. 3d 841, 673 N.E.2d 217 (5th Dist. Stark County 1996). The disposition of "long-term foster care" was replaced by "planned permanent living arrangement" by 1998 H.B. 484, eff. 3-18-99.

[6]RC 2151.353(A).

[7]Juv. R. 22(A).

[8]Matter of Stoffer, 1995 WL 347906 (Ohio Ct. App. 5th Dist. Stark County 1995); In Matter of Crenshaw, 1997 WL 219118 (Ohio Ct. App. 5th Dist. Stark County 1997).

[9]Matter of Smith Children, 1990 WL 70926 (Ohio Ct. App. 12th Dist. Warren County 1990).

[10]Matter of Sullivan, 1992 WL 42813 (Ohio Ct. App. 3d Dist. Seneca County 1992).

[11]Matter of Cremeans, 1992 WL 47278 (Ohio Ct. App. 8th Dist. Cuyahoga County 1992).

[12]See § 33:11, Child custody agency commitment—Juvenile court dispositional review.

[13]Matter of Fleming, 1993 WL 277186 (Ohio Ct. App. 8th Dist. Cuyahoga County 1993).

based.[14] The standard of definiteness which applies to complaints also applies to motions for permanent custody.[15]

Essential facts requirement. An adjudication of neglect or dependency for the purpose of obtaining permanent custody of a child will not be valid unless there has been a complaint filed containing a prayer requesting permanent custody which sufficiently apprises the parents of the grounds upon which the permanent custody order is to be based.[16] A motion for permanent custody based on a previous dependency adjudication which contains merely an allegation that "it would appear to be in the best interests of said minors that they be placed for adoption" is not sufficiently specific.[17] A "best interest" statement alone does not present the essential facts. A court does not have discretion to grant custody of a child to a third party solely on the ground that the best interest of the child will be promoted thereby.[18]

On the other hand, courts have upheld motions and complaints for permanent custody containing varying degrees of detail. A motion for permanent custody was held to be sufficiently definite when it alleged that the mother had failed to formulate any child-care plans in order to reunite her family, that she was living with but had not married the child's alleged father, and that she had visited her child only twice during the nine-month period that the child was in the temporary custody of the movant.[19] A permanent custody motion which was accompanied by an affidavit detailing the parents' marital troubles, the child's physical abuse, and the father's failure to protect the child was also held to be sufficiently specific.[20] A complaint seeking permanent custody was upheld where it alleged that the children lacked adequate supervision, that the mother was unable to maintain a proper home for the children and had often expressed her inability to care for them, and that she had recently attempted suicide and been admitted to a hospital psychiatric unit for alcohol and drug dependence.[21]

A neglect complaint for permanent custody was held sufficient even though it alleged facts pertaining to a previous temporary custody order that had since been terminated. Although a permanent custody hearing must be based on events occurring since the most recent grant of temporary custody, in this case the mother's continuing uncooperativeness and lack of effort to meet the

---

[14]RC 2151.27(A); Juv. R. 10(B)(1).

[15]In re Fassinger, 43 Ohio App. 2d 89, 72 Ohio Op. 2d 292, 334 N.E.2d 5 (8th Dist. Cuyahoga County 1974); In the Matter Of: Strowbridge, 1982 WL 3565 (Ohio Ct. App. 4th Dist. Lawrence County 1982); In Matter Of: Escue, 1981 WL 5930 (Ohio Ct. App. 4th Dist. Lawrence County 1981); Coulter, 1981 WL 9749 (Ohio Ct. App. 1st Dist. Hamilton County 1981); In re Holcomb, No. 39694 (8th Dist. Ct. App., Cuyahoga, 10-4-79); In re Neff, No. 1-78-9 (3d Dist. Ct. App., Allen, 6-14-78). But see Matter of Crose, 1982 WL 3824 (Ohio Ct. App. 2d Dist. Darke County 1982), holding that RC 2151.27 and Juv. R. 10(B) concern the sufficiency of complaints, whereas RC 2151.413 governs motions. See also In re Covin, 8 Ohio App. 3d 139, 456 N.E.2d 520 (1st Dist. Hamilton County 1982); In re Hadsell, No. 41004 (8th Dist. Ct. App., Cuyahoga, 6-19-80); In re Massie, No. 477 (4th Dist. Ct. App., Jackson, 3-30-84).

[16]In re Fassinger, 43 Ohio App. 2d 89, 72 Ohio Op. 2d 292, 334 N.E.2d 5 (8th Dist. Cuyahoga County 1974); In the Matter Of: Strowbridge, 1982 WL 3565 (Ohio Ct. App. 4th Dist. Lawrence County 1982); In the Matter Of: Lewis, 1982 WL 3527 (Ohio Ct. App. 4th Dist. Lawrence County 1982); Hutchison, 1982 WL 3455 (Ohio Ct. App. 4th Dist. Lawrence County 1982); In the Matter of Banks Griggs v. Griggs Banks Jones, 1981 WL 5593 (Ohio Ct. App. 6th Dist. Lucas County 1981); In Matter Of: Escue, 1981 WL 5930 (Ohio Ct. App. 4th Dist. Lawrence County 1981); In Matter of Evener, 1981 WL 6031 (Ohio Ct. App. 4th Dist. Athens County 1981); In re Osborn, No. CA 1744 (5th Dist. Ct. App., Richland, 1-16-79); Matter of Cox, 1986 WL 7900 (Ohio Ct. App. 4th Dist. Highland County 1986).

[17]In re Fassinger, 42 Ohio St. 2d 505, 71 Ohio Op. 2d 503, 330 N.E.2d 431 (1975).

[18]In re Fassinger, 42 Ohio St. 2d 505, 71 Ohio Op. 2d 503, 330 N.E.2d 431 (1975); Ludy v. Ludy, 84 Ohio App. 195, 39 Ohio Op. 241, 53 Ohio L. Abs. 47, 82 N.E.2d 775 (2d Dist. Franklin County 1948).

[19]In re Kemp, No. 41320 (8th Dist. Ct. App., Cuyahoga, 6-26-80).

[20]In re Holcomb, No. 39694 (8th Dist. Ct. App., Cuyahoga, 10-4-79).

[21]In re Pethel, No. 79CA25 (4th Dist. Ct. App., Washington, 11-9-81).

child's financial and medical needs met this test.[22]

Finally, a dependency complaint seeking permanent custody was held to state sufficiently particular facts where it cited only the parents' inability to provide a nurturing physical and emotional environment for the child.[23]

§ 16:15 Certification or transfer from another court

When a case concerning a child is transferred or certified from another court, the certification from the transferring court is considered the complaint.[1] "Transferred" cases are those in which a juvenile court of one county turns its jurisdiction of a matter over to a juvenile court of another county pursuant to Juvenile Rule 11.[2] "Certified" cases are typically those in which a juvenile court obtains jurisdiction from a domestic relations court pursuant to RC 2151.23(D)[3] or a probate court pursuant to RC 2151.23(E).[4]

Although a certification from domestic relations court constitutes a complaint, there is a split of authority as to whether a certification to a juvenile court that is not supplemented[5] by another type of complaint gives the juvenile court the jurisdiction to treat the child as a dependent or neglected child. In *Birch v. Birch*[6] the juvenile court had adopted the findings of fact and conclusions of law of the domestic relations court following certification. The juvenile court found the children to be dependent although apparently no dependency complaint had been filed. In affirming the juvenile court's order granting temporary custody to the human (job and family) services department, the Ohio Supreme Court, in dictum, rejected the argument that the juvenile court could not adopt the domestic relations court's findings of fact and conclusions of law without holding a new hearing. Similarly, in *Hartshorne v. Hartshorne*,[7] a court of appeals held that the certification of a divorce action that shows that the children are being neglected amounts to the filing of a neglect complaint under RC 2151.27. The court reasoned that since "any person having knowledge" may file a complaint and the purpose of filing a complaint with the juvenile court is to bring the matter to the court's attention, the certification itself constituted a neglect complaint.

On the other hand, the statutes[8] specify that any disposition made by a juvenile court after a case is certified to it must be made in accordance with RC 3109.04, the general custody statute, and several appellate court decisions have recognized this principle. Courts have held that the juvenile court is not permitted to use the more diverse dispositional alternatives available in other types of children's cases[9] unless the certification is supplemented by a

---

[22]In the Matter Bell, 1981 WL 6690 (Ohio Ct. App. 3d Dist. Shelby County 1981).

[23]In Re: Michelee Blankenship v. Collmar, 1981 WL 3920 (Ohio Ct. App. 9th Dist. Summit County 1981).

[Section 16:15]

[1]Juv. R. 10(A).

[2]See § 17:4, Transfer of venue.

[3]See RC 3109.04, RC 3109.06. A domestic relations court may not certify proceedings to a juvenile court under RC 3109.04 unless it finds after a full hearing that custody to either parent is not in the child's best interest. See Haslam v. Haslam, 1981 WL 4801 (Ohio Ct. App. 7th Dist. Monroe County 1981).

[4]See RC 2111.46, RC 3107.14.

[5]Juv. R. 10(A) provides that the juvenile court may order the certification supplemented upon its own motion or that of a party.

[6]Birch v. Birch, 11 Ohio St. 3d 85, 463 N.E.2d 1254 (1984).

[7]Hartshorne v. Hartshorne, 89 Ohio L. Abs. 243, 185 N.E.2d 329 (Ct. App. 7th Dist. Columbiana County 1959).

[8]RC 3109.06. See also RC 2151.23(F)(1).

[9]RC 3109.04(A) permits the court to grant custody to either parent, or to both parents jointly, or to a relative, but does not authorize the more wide-ranging dispositions of RC

complaint alleging dependency, neglect, abuse, delinquency, or unruliness.[10] Moreover, a certification from a domestic relations court which is supplemented by a motion alleging parental unsuitability is not sufficient to constitute a complaint of dependency or neglect.[11] In order for there to be a valid complaint, there must be an allegation that the child is dependent or neglected,[12] as well as a definite statement of the particular, essential facts which the parents will have to defend against.[13]

The authority of a juvenile court to dispose of a case certified from a probate court following the dismissal of an adoption petition (RC 3107.14(D)) is not as clearly defined as it is with a domestic relations court certification. Since probate court certifications result from the dismissal of an action, there would appear to be nothing to certify to the juvenile court. The Ohio Supreme Court has held in *State ex rel. Clark v. Allaman*[14] that such a certification, in itself, does not constitute a dependency or neglect complaint, nor even a complaint concerning the child's custody.[15] The court reasoned that there was no language in the statute[16] to indicate that the certification was to be considered a complaint. The only purpose of the certification statute was to provide a method for the juvenile court to conduct an investigation of the custody arrangements and, if warranted, to invoke the juvenile court's jurisdiction by having the appropriate complaint filed.[17] However, both *Allaman* and *In re Robert O.*[18] were decided prior to the promulgation of Juvenile Rule 10(A), which provides, in part, that "the certification from the transferring court shall be deemed to be the complaint." In view of the rule and the principles established by cases concerning domestic relations court certifications,[19] it appears that a certification from a probate court following the dismissal of an adoption petition constitutes a complaint for custody, with RC

2151.353, which permits a temporary or permanent commitment to a public child services agency or private child placing agency. Additionally, RC 2151.23(F) provides that the juvenile court shall follow the Uniform Child Custody Jurisdiction Law (RC 3109.21 to RC 3109.36) in exercising its jurisdiction in child custody matters. See also RC 2151.353 (disposition of abused, neglected, or dependent child); RC 2151.354 (disposition of unruly child); RC 2151.355 (disposition of delinquent child).

[10]In re Snider, 14 Ohio App. 3d 353, 471 N.E.2d 516 (3d Dist. Defiance County 1984); In re Height, 47 Ohio App. 2d 203, 1 Ohio Op. 3d 279, 353 N.E.2d 887 (3d Dist. Van Wert County 1975). See also In re Carter, No. 78-16 (6th Dist. Ct. App., Wood, 1-26-79); Union County Child Welfare Bd. v. Parker, 7 Ohio App. 2d 79, 36 Ohio Op. 2d 162, 218 N.E.2d 757 (3d Dist. Union County 1964); Thrasher v. Thrasher, 3 Ohio App. 3d 210, 444 N.E.2d 431 (9th Dist. Summit County 1981); In re Pryor, 86 Ohio App. 3d 327, 620 N.E.2d 973 (4th Dist. Athens County 1993); Gamble v. Dotson, 1991 WL 57229 (Ohio Ct. App. 9th Dist. Lorain County 1991); Matter of Knisley, 1998 WL 372703 (Ohio Ct. App. 4th Dist. Ross County 1998).

[11]Union County Child Welfare Bd. v. Parker, 7 Ohio App. 2d 79, 36 Ohio Op. 2d 162, 218 N.E.2d 757 (3d Dist. Union County 1964).

[12]RC 2151.27(A).

[13]RC 2151.27(A); Juv. R. 10(B)(1). Union County Child Welfare Bd. v. Parker, 7 Ohio App. 2d 79, 36 Ohio Op. 2d 162, 218 N.E.2d 757 (3d Dist. Union County 1964).

[14]State ex rel. Clark v. Allaman, 154 Ohio St. 296, 43 Ohio Op. 190, 95 N.E.2d 753 (1950).

[15]This interpretation finds support in a later case, In re O---, 28 Ohio Op. 2d 165, 95 Ohio L. Abs. 101, 199 N.E.2d 765 (Juv. Ct. 1964), which held that the certification in itself does not give the juvenile court jurisdiction to determine the custody of an illegitimate child. However, neither *Allaman* nor *Robert O.* mentioned an earlier court of appeals decision, State ex rel. Sparto v. Williams, 86 Ohio App. 377, 41 Ohio Op. 474, 55 Ohio L. Abs. 341, 86 N.E.2d 501 (2d Dist. Darke County 1949), in which it was held that such a certification did confer jurisdiction upon the juvenile court to determine the custody of the child. It should be noted that in *Sparto* the certification was supplemented by a neglect complaint, although the court indicated that this was not the basis for its decision.

[16]GC 10512-21, now RC 3107.14(D).

[17]State ex rel. Clark v. Allaman, 154 Ohio St. 296, 43 Ohio Op. 190, 95 N.E.2d 753 (1950).

[18]In re O---, 28 Ohio Op. 2d 165, 95 Ohio L. Abs. 101, 199 N.E.2d 765 (Juv. Ct. 1964).

[19]Thrasher v. Thrasher, 3 Ohio App. 3d 210, 444 N.E.2d 431 (9th Dist. Summit County 1981); In re Height, 47 Ohio App. 2d 203, 1 Ohio Op. 3d 279, 353 N.E.2d 887 (3d Dist. Van Wert County 1975).

3109.04 controlling the disposition. RC 3109.04 applies not only to divorce actions, but also to any custody determination in a juvenile court,[20] other than one involving a neglected, dependent,[21] delinquent, or unruly child.[22] If the custody alternatives available to a juvenile court in a case certified from probate court are limited to those in RC 3109.04, any child care agency seeking custody should supplement the certification with a dependency or neglect complaint.[23]

§ 16:16 Amendment of complaints

Any pleading, including a complaint,[1] may be amended at any time prior to the adjudicatory hearing, and may be amended after commencement of the adjudicatory hearing upon agreement of the parties, or if the interests of justice require, upon court order.[2] Where requested, a court order shall grant a party reasonable time in which to respond to an amendment.[3]

Delinquency complaints. Similar to Criminal Rule 7(D), Juvenile Rule 22(B) now specifically prohibits amending a delinquency complaint, unless agreed by the parties, if the proposed amendment would change the name or identity of the specific violation so that it would be considered a change of the crime charged if committed by an adult.

---

[20]But see In re Custody of Carpenter, 41 Ohio App. 3d 182, 534 N.E.2d 1216 (2d Dist. Greene County 1987), holding that RC 3109.04(B) has no application where a parent is seeking to extinguish an award of temporary custody to a nonparent and regain custody of the child.

[21]See In re Poling, 64 Ohio St. 3d 211, 1992-Ohio-144, 594 N.E.2d 589 (1992), in which the Ohio Supreme Court held that when a juvenile court seeks to exercise its jurisdiction over a dependent child where there is an existing custody decree from a domestic relations court, and jurisdiction has not been certified, the juvenile court must apply RC 3109.04. See also In re Cloud, 1997 WL 264264 (Ohio Ct. App. 12th Dist. Butler County 1997).

[22]In re Height, 47 Ohio App. 2d 203, 1 Ohio Op. 3d 279, 353 N.E.2d 887 (3d Dist. Van Wert County 1975). RC 2151.23(F) was amended in 1984 (1983 H.B. 93, eff. 3-19-84) to provide that the juvenile court shall exercise its jurisdiction in child custody matters in accordance with RC 3109.04. RC 3109.04(A) includes two significant legal principles. First, it limits the juvenile court's choices in granting custody to either a parent, both parents jointly, or another relative. Second, it adopts a "best interest" test for determining who shall receive custody. According to Boyer v. Boyer, 46 Ohio St. 2d 83, 75 Ohio Op. 2d 156, 346 N.E.2d 286 (1976), an Ohio Supreme Court case decided prior to the statutory amendment, the best interest standard applies to custody disputes between parents and a relative of the child. However, one year later in In re Perales, 52 Ohio St. 2d 89, 6 Ohio Op. 3d 293, 369 N.E.2d 1047 (1977), the Ohio Supreme Court appeared to meld the best interest test with a parental unsuitability test. Perales involved a custody dispute between a parent and the child's caretaker, who was neither a parent nor a relative. The court held that the nonparent could be awarded custody pursuant to an RC 2151.23(A)(2) action but only if the trial court made a finding of "parental unsuitability," a higher standard than the "best interest" test of RC 3109.04. In juvenile court custody disputes between parents, the "best interest" standard would apply. In re Byrd, 66 Ohio St. 2d 334, 20 Ohio Op. 3d 309, 421 N.E.2d 1284 (1981). See also Thrasher v. Thrasher, 3 Ohio App. 3d 210, 444 N.E.2d 431 (9th Dist. Summit County 1981), a juvenile court custody case originating from a domestic relations court certification. The court criticized Perales for apparently modifying the construction of RC 3109.04 from a "best interest" test to an "unsuitability" test and felt compelled to hold that the "unsuitability" test adopted by Perales must also apply to RC 3109.04 custody actions between a parent and a relative.

[23]Based on In re Perales, 52 Ohio St. 2d 89, 6 Ohio Op. 3d 293, 369 N.E.2d 1047 (1977), it appears that the certification could also be supplemented by an application to determine custody under RC 2151.23(A)(2). If a nonparent (including a job and family services department or children services board) filed such an application, Perales would require a finding of parental unsuitability before custody could be awarded to the nonparent. This is a higher standard than is required in dependency cases and would not permit an award of permanent custody. See §§ 30:8 to 29:12, Permanent custody; Motions for Permanent Custody Ch 31.

[Section 16:16]

[1]A complaint is included under the definition of pleadings (Juv. R. 22(A)).

[2]Juv. R. 22(B). In Matter of Barr, 1996 WL 608465 (Ohio Ct. App. 5th Dist. Stark County 1996).

[3]Juv. R. 22(B).

A complaint may be amended to reflect a lesser-included offense.[4] Criminal complaints and indictments are presumed to provide sufficient notice for a conviction of a lesser included offense, an offense of an inferior degree, or an attempt.[5]

Case law has also addressed the issue of whether a juvenile court may amend the specific nature of the complaint. It has been held that a juvenile court may not sua sponte amend a delinquency complaint to a juvenile traffic offender complaint,[6] or a delinquency complaint to an unruly complaint,[7] after the adjudicatory hearing. However, an appellate court has held that if the same facts formed the basis for both the original delinquency complaint and the amended unruly complaint, and the child was given the opportunity to prepare and present a defense on the allegations, it was not error for the juvenile court to amend the complaint.[8]

Relying on Criminal Rule 7(D), an appellate court has held that allegations of venue and the date of a charge may be amended at any time because such amendments do not alter the nature of the charged offense.[9]

In adult criminal proceedings, it has been held that a court is without authority to amend an affidavit without a new verification by the affiant.[10] However, the Ohio Supreme Court has held that where counsel has agreed to the amendment and has not objected to the lack of reverification, any objection thereto is waived.[11]

Neglect complaint. Although a juvenile court may not amend a neglect complaint by adding a child who was not included in the original complaint,

---

[4]In re Pennington, 150 Ohio App. 3d 205, 2002-Ohio-6381, 779 N.E.2d 1093 (2d Dist. Montgomery County 2002) ("A juvenile court has the discretion to amend a complaint . . . [T]he Supreme Court Rules Advisory Committee in its comments on the rule stated that such an amendment would be prohibited unless the amendment conforms to the evidence presented and also amounts to a lesser included offense of the crime charged."; holding disorderly conduct is a lesser included offense of gross sexual imposition with a minor under 13 years). In a case decided prior to this 1994 amendment to Juvenile Rule 22(B), In re Pollard, 1981 WL 4690 (Ohio Ct. App. 8th Dist. Cuyahoga County 1981) a delinquency complaint was amended from aggravated arson to arson was improper because it changed the identity of the complaint. See also State v. Kunkleman, No. L-79-156 (6th Dist. Ct. App., Lucas, 4-25-80); In re Burgess, 13 Ohio App. 3d 374, 469 N.E.2d 967 (12th Dist. Preble County 1984). The court of appeals in that case did not rule on whether a delinquency complaint could be amended to change the crime's name or identity but instead relied on Criminal Rule 31(C) to hold that it was not error to adjudge the child delinquent for arson, since arson is a lesser included offense of aggravated arson. See also In re L.D., 63 Ohio Misc. 2d 303, 626 N.E.2d 709 (C.P. 1993). In another case decided before the 1994 amendment, it was held that in the interest of justice, pursuant to Juvenile Rule 22, a delinquency complaint for aggravated burglary could be amended at the conclusion of the adjudicatory hearing to criminal trespass and petty theft, which conformed to the evidence at the hearing. In re L.D., 63 Ohio Misc. 2d 303, 626 N.E.2d 709 (C.P. 1993).

[5]See Katz and Giannelli, Baldwin's Ohio Practice, Criminal Law (2d ed.) §§ 35:5 and 40:7.

[6]In re Elliott, 87 Ohio App. 3d 816, 623 N.E.2d 217 (12th Dist. Fayette County 1993). In State v. Gaida, No. 30423 (8th Dist. Ct. App., Cuyahoga, 3-2-72), a pre-Juvenile Rules case, it was held that amending a complaint to charge a child with being a delinquent instead of a juvenile traffic offender, without objection by counsel, was not prejudicial error.

[7]State v. Aller, 82 Ohio App. 3d 9, 610 N.E.2d 1170 (6th Dist. Lucas County 1992). But see In re Frederick, 63 Ohio Misc. 2d 229, 622 N.E.2d 762 (C.P. 1993).

[8]In re Felton, 124 Ohio App. 3d 500, 706 N.E.2d 809 (3d Dist. Auglaize County 1997).

[9]In re Beeman, 1996 WL 494877 (Ohio Ct. App. 11th Dist. Lake County 1996). See also In re Smith, 142 Ohio App. 3d 16, 23–24, 753 N.E.2d 930 (8th Dist. Cuyahoga County 2001) (The court's decision to amend the complaint at the beginning of the adjudication hearing, by including the age of the defendant and the dates of the offenses that had been left out of the original compliant, did not prejudice the defendant because it did not change the name or identity of the offenses.).

[10]State v. Jackson, 90 Ohio L. Abs. 577, 190 N.E.2d 38 (Ct. App. 10th Dist. Franklin County 1960); City of Ironton v. Bundy, 98 Ohio App. 416, 57 Ohio Op. 451, 129 N.E.2d 831 (4th Dist. Lawrence County 1954); Diebler v. State, 43 Ohio App. 350, 13 Ohio L. Abs. 20, 183 N.E. 84 (5th Dist. Richland County 1932).

[11]State v. Chrisman, 9 Ohio St. 2d 27, 38 Ohio Op. 2d 16, 222 N.E.2d 649 (1966).

after the adjudicatory hearing and without agreement of the parties,[12] a dependency complaint may be amended to one of custody after all the evidence has been submitted.[13]

§ 16:17   Objections to complaints

In Ohio nonjurisdictional issues that have been neither brought to the attention of nor passed on by a lower court will generally not be ruled upon by appellate courts.[1] Whether the failure to include the particular facts in a complaint constitutes a jurisdictional defect, which may be raised at any time, is an issue that Ohio courts have not agreed upon.

Juvenile Rule 22(D) provides:

> Any defense, objection or request which is capable of determination without hearing on the allegations of the complaint may be raised before the adjudicatory hearing by motion. The following must be heard before the adjudicatory hearing, though not necessarily on a separate date: . . .
>
> (2) Defenses or objections based on defects in the complaint (other than failure to show jurisdiction in the court or to charge an offense which objections shall be noticed by the court at any time during the pendency of the proceeding).[2]

Furthermore, Juvenile Rule 22(E) provides that "[a]ll prehearing motions shall be filed by the earlier of (1) seven days prior to hearing, or (2) ten days after the appearance of counsel. The court in the interest of justice may extend the time for making prehearing motions."

In interpreting Juvenile Rule 22(D), the Ohio Supreme Court has held that objections to defects in a complaint must be raised in the juvenile court by an answer, a motion to dismiss, or a request for other relief.[3] The Eighth District Court of Appeals reached the same result with respect to an alleged failure of a delinquency complaint to set forth an offense.[4] It has also been held that the failure to include the particular facts in a permanent custody complaint is not a jurisdictional defect and may be waived if not timely objected to before the adjudicatory hearing pursuant to Juvenile Rule 22(D).[5]

On the other hand, several cases have held that the absence of specific facts in a complaint requesting permanent custody is a jurisdictional matter and may be raised for the first time in the appellate court. These courts reason that RC 2151.23(A)(1), which confers jurisdiction regarding neglected or dependent children, RC 2151.27, which sets forth complaint requirements, and RC 2151.03 and RC 2151.04, which define a neglected and dependent child, respectively, must be read in pari materia, and thus, the jurisdiction of the juvenile court is invoked only when a proper complaint is filed in accor-

---

[12]In re James, No. 30608 (8th Dist. Ct. App., Cuyahoga, 2-3-72).

[13]Matter of Likens, 1986 WL 11910 (Ohio Ct. App. 2d Dist. Greene County 1986). See also In the Matter Of: Dolibor, 1981 WL 5953 (Ohio Ct. App. 4th Dist. Ross County 1981).

[Section 16:17]

[1]In re Adoption of McDermitt, 63 Ohio St. 2d 301, 17 Ohio Op. 3d 195, 408 N.E.2d 680 (1980); State v. Williams, 51 Ohio St. 2d 112, 5 Ohio Op. 3d 98, 364 N.E.2d 1364 (1977); In re Lee, No. CA-2856 (5th Dist. Ct. App., Licking, 11-1-82).

[2]It is a well settled rule in criminal law that jurisdictional challenges may be raised at any time or by collateral attack (In re Lockhart, 157 Ohio St. 192, 47 Ohio Op. 129, 105 N.E.2d 35 (1952)). It is questionable whether the phrase "during the pendency of the proceeding" changes this rule for juvenile court proceedings.

[3]In re Hunt, 46 Ohio St. 2d 378, 75 Ohio Op. 2d 450, 348 N.E.2d 727 (1976). See also Matter of Bridges, 1986 WL 7109 (Ohio Ct. App. 6th Dist. Lucas County 1986); In Matter of Rhodes, 1997 WL 143942 (Ohio Ct. App. 10th Dist. Franklin County 1997).

[4]Corona, 1981 WL 4502 (Ohio Ct. App. 8th Dist. Cuyahoga County 1981).

[5]Matter of Crose, 1982 WL 3824 (Ohio Ct. App. 2d Dist. Darke County 1982); In the Matter Of: Daniels, 1981 WL 3907 (Ohio Ct. App. 9th Dist. Summit County 1981).

dance with these statutes.[6]

Cross References
§ 17:3, Ch 18, § 23:6, Ch 35, Ch 36
Research References
Giannelli and Snyder, Baldwin's Ohio Practice, Evidence (2d ed.) § 501.8
Katz and Giannelli, Baldwin's Ohio Practice, Criminal Law (2d ed.), Ch 35
Carlin, Baldwin's Ohio Practice, Merrick-Rippner Probate Law (6th ed.), Chs 105, 107, 108

---

[6]Hutchison, 1982 WL 3455 (Ohio Ct. App. 4th Dist. Lawrence County 1982); Bryant, 1982 WL 6001 (Ohio Ct. App. 12th Dist. Butler County 1982); In re Moore, No. CA291 (12th Dist. Ct. App., Preble, 5-20-81). See also Baker, 1982 WL 6832 (Ohio Ct. App. 3d Dist. Hardin County 1982); In Matter of Bundy, 1981 WL 6034 (Ohio Ct. App. 4th Dist. Lawrence County 1981); In re Nance, No. 1452 (4th Dist. Ct. App., Lawrence, 10-16-80); Union County Child Welfare Bd. v. Parker, 7 Ohio App. 2d 79, 36 Ohio Op. 2d 162, 218 N.E.2d 757 (3d Dist. Union County 1964); State ex rel. Clark v. Allaman, 154 Ohio St. 296, 43 Ohio Op. 190, 95 N.E.2d 753 (1950).

Chapter 17

Venue

KeyCite®: Cases and other legal materials listed in KeyCite Scope can be researched through West's KeyCite service on Westlaw®. Use KeyCite to check citations for form, parallel references, prior and later history, and comprehensive citator information, including citations to other decisions and secondary materials.

---

§ 17:1   Venue—Introduction
§ 17:2   Proper venue
§ 17:3   Proof of venue
§ 17:4   Transfer of venue

§ 17:1   Venue—Introduction

This chapter discusses the factors for determining which county or counties may conduct hearings relative to children's cases.

§ 17:2   Proper venue

Except for serious youth offender[1] and truancy cases,[2] complaints in children's cases may be filed either in the county where the child has a residence or legal settlement[3] or in the county where the traffic offense, delinquency, unruliness, neglect, dependency, or abuse occurred.[4] Thus, venue does not depend on having personal jurisdiction over the parents when the alleged conduct takes place outside of their county of residence.[5] In the absence of the mandatory provisions of Juvenile Rule 11(B), where transfer is required if other proceedings involving the child are pending in the juvenile court of the resident county, the juvenile court has discretion in determining venue.[6]

When a complaint is filed in the county of the parent's residence, the court retains jurisdiction even if the summons is not served until after the parent

---

[Section 17:2]

[1]Like adult criminal cases, venue lies only in the county in which the alleged act occurred. RC 2151.271. See § 5:4, SYO venue.

[2]Juvenile Rule 10(A) was amended in 2001 to provide that delinquent or unruly complaints concerning chronic and habitual truancy, including the parents, may be filed in the county in which the child is supposed to attend public school. This amendment was adopted to conform the rule to RC 2151.27(A)(2), which codified S.B. 181.

[3]Pursuant to RC 2151.06, "[A] child has the same residence or legal settlement as his parents, legal guardian of his person, or his custodian who stands in the relation of loco parentis." A child who is a ward of a job and family services department or children services board is a resident of the county in which the department or board is located. See In re Smith, 64 Ohio App. 3d 773, 582 N.E.2d 1117 (6th Dist. Lucas County 1990).

[4]RC 2151.27(A); RC 2152.021(A)(1); Juv. R. 10(A). State ex rel. Burchett v. Juvenile Court for Scioto County, 28 Ohio Op. 2d 116, 92 Ohio L. Abs. 357, 194 N.E.2d 912 (Ct. App. 4th Dist. Scioto County 1962); Matter of Bowen, 1987 WL 13696 (Ohio Ct. App. 6th Dist. Wood County 1987).

[5]Matter of Poth, 1982 WL 9371 (Ohio Ct. App. 6th Dist. Huron County 1982); In re MacPherson, No. 34106 (8th Dist. Ct. App., Cuyahoga, 4-3-75); In re Belk, 97 Ohio App. 114, 55 Ohio Op. 330, 123 N.E.2d 757 (3d Dist. Crawford County 1954).

[6]Ackerman v. Lucas County Children Services Bd., 49 Ohio App. 3d 14, 550 N.E.2d 549 (6th Dist. Lucas County 1989).

has moved to another county.[7] Similarly, it has been held that where the alleged incidents of neglect occurred while the parents and children resided in one county, and the majority of witnesses resided in that county, that county's juvenile court properly acquired venue even though the parents and children moved to another county before the complaint was filed.[8] However, when a child is moved from his resident county to another county and a complaint is immediately filed in the nonresident county, that county does not have venue if neither the child nor his parents reside there and none of the facts underlying the complaint occurred there.[9]

§ 17:3   Proof of venue

It has been held that, in a delinquency case, the prosecutor's failure to elicit specific testimony regarding venue was not prejudicial error where it was apparent beyond a reasonable doubt that the child was brought before the proper court.[1]

§ 17:4   Transfer of venue

A juvenile court acquiring jurisdiction over a child may, on its own motion or the motion of a party,[1] transfer the proceedings to the county of the child's residence[2] either after the filing of the complaint or after the adjudicatory or dispositional hearing.[3]

The determination of proper venue pursuant to the statute and rule is solely within the discretion of the juvenile court, and the transfer of venue may be ordered on the court's own motion without a hearing.[4] However, a juvenile court may not impose a fine and then transfer the matter to another jurisdiction for further dispositional proceedings. Once a final dispositional order is made, nothing remains to transfer to the other court.[5]

Where other proceedings involving the child are pending in the juvenile court of the county of his residence, transfer to that court is mandatory.[6] When a case against a child is pending in a foreign county, that case must be transferred to the child's home county if at any time prior to the disposition of that case, other proceedings against the child are pending in the home

---

[7]In re Goshorn, 82 Ohio L. Abs. 599, 167 N.E.2d 148 (Juv. Ct. 1959).

[8]In re Meyer, 98 Ohio App. 3d 189, 648 N.E.2d 52 (3d Dist. Defiance County 1994).

[9]State ex rel. Burchett v. Juvenile Court for Scioto County, 28 Ohio Op. 2d 116, 92 Ohio L. Abs. 357, 194 N.E.2d 912 (Ct. App. 4th Dist. Scioto County 1962).

[Section 17:3]

[1]In re Nickerson, No. 58639 (8th Dist. Ct. App., Cuyahoga, 6-4-90); In re Heater, 1997 WL 117136 (Ohio Ct. App. 5th Dist. Stark County 1997).

[Section 17:4]

[1]"Party" is defined in Juv. R. 2(Y).

[2]See RC 2151.06 for provisions regarding a child's residence.

[3]RC 2151.271; Juv. R. 11(A).

[4]In re Meyer, 98 Ohio App. 3d 189, 648 N.E.2d 52 (3d Dist. Defiance County 1994); Brakora v. Haudenschield, 1995 WL 695089 (Ohio Ct. App. 3d Dist. Hardin County 1995).

[5]In re Sekulich, 65 Ohio St. 2d 13, 19 Ohio Op. 3d 192, 417 N.E.2d 1014 (1981). However, it is common practice in Ohio to transfer probation supervision where the residence of the child changes after he is placed on probation. Since this does not involve a second dispositional order, it is proper. See also RC 2151.56 for provisions regarding the cooperative supervision of delinquent juveniles on probation or parole under the Interstate Compact.

[6]RC 2151.271; Juv. R. 11(B); In re Don B., 2003-Ohio-1400, 2003 WL 1448059 (Ohio Ct. App. 6th Dist. Huron County 2003). Removal actions are exempt from the mandatory transfer provisions. See § 13:3, Venue.

county.[7] In all other cases the decision to transfer is discretionary with the court in which the complaint is originally filed.[8] If either the transferring court or the receiving court[9] finds that the interests of justice and the convenience of the parties so require, the adjudicatory hearing will be held in the county where the complaint was filed.[10] After the adjudicatory hearing, the proceedings may be transferred to the county of the child's residence for disposition and must be transferred if there are proceedings involving the child pending in the resident county.[11] Transfer may also be made if the residence of the child changes.[12]

A juvenile court order transferring a dependency case to another county for dispositional hearing, for the reason that the parents resided in the transferee county, was held to be error because the children were in the custody of the job and family service department of the county where the original action was commenced, which was therefore the children's county of residence.[13] However, the appellate court further held that the erroneous decisions ordering and accepting transfer of venue did not automatically divest the transferee court of jurisdiction over the children.

Certified copies of all legal and social records pertaining to the proceeding must accompany any transfer.[14]

When a complaint concerning an alleged delinquent child is filed in the county of his residence, and that court transfers the proceedings to the common pleas court for criminal prosecution, the child is entitled to be tried in the county where the offense occurred.[15]

Research References

Carlin, Baldwin's Ohio Practice, Merrick-Rippner Probate Law (6th ed.), Chs 105, 107

---

[7]In re Frenz, 2003-Ohio-3653, 2003 WL 21545125 (Ohio Ct. App. 5th Dist. Tuscarawas County 2003), appeal not allowed, 99 Ohio St. 3d 1547, 2003-Ohio-4671, 795 N.E.2d 684 (2003); State v. Payne, 1982 WL 3487 (Ohio Ct. App. 4th Dist. Pickaway County 1982).

[8]RC 2151.271; Juv. R. 11(A). Squires v. Squires, 12 Ohio App. 3d 138, 468 N.E.2d 73 (12th Dist. Preble County 1983). When a child is on probation in his county of residence, it is reasonable for proceedings initiated in another county to be transferred to his resident county, at least for dispositional purposes. Whether or not transfer is mandatory depends on whether probation is considered a "pending proceeding." One interpretation is that probation is a final dispositional order and, therefore, not a "pending proceeding." On the other hand, because the court of the resident county maintains continuing jurisdiction over a child who is on probation, transfer to that court may be mandatory.

[9]Juv. R. 11(C) grants to either court the authority to make this determination, whereas RC 2151.271 grants it only to the court of the resident county, as the receiving court.

[10]The practice in Ohio is to conduct the adjudicatory hearing in the county in which the witnesses reside, even though a witness is generally not a "party" (Juv. R. 2(X)), and someone who is a "party" (i.e., the child) may be inconvenienced thereby. In re Meyer, 98 Ohio App. 3d 189, 648 N.E.2d 52 (3d Dist. Defiance County 1994).

[11]Juv. R. 11(B), Juv. R. 11(C). Such transfer is permitted only if the allegations of the complaint were admitted or proved at the adjudicatory hearing. See Juv. R. 29(F).

[12]Juv. R. 11(A).

[13]In re Smith, 64 Ohio App. 3d 773, 582 N.E.2d 1117 (6th Dist. Lucas County 1990); In Matter of Cantrell, 1996 WL 363816 (Ohio Ct. App. 5th Dist. Licking County 1996). See RC 2151.06 for definition of "residence."

[14]RC 2151.271; Juv. R. 11(D).

[15]In re Davis, 22 Ohio Op. 2d 108, 87 Ohio L. Abs. 222, 179 N.E.2d 198 (Juv. Ct. 1961).

Chapter 18

Summons

KeyCite®: Cases and other legal materials listed in KeyCite Scope can be researched through West's KeyCite service on Westlaw®. Use KeyCite to check citations for form, parallel references, prior and later history, and comprehensive citator information, including citations to other decisions and secondary materials.

§ 18:1   Summons—Introduction
§ 18:2   Issuance of summons: Proper parties
§ 18:3   Summons: Contents and form
§ 18:4   Summons: Methods of service
§ 18:5   Waiver of summons requirements

§ 18:1   Summons—Introduction

This chapter discusses the factors for determining who are appropriate parties to juvenile court proceedings, as well as the requirements for the issuance of notice to the parties. Additional related chapters include intake (Ch 15) and the complaint (Ch 16).

§ 18:2   Issuance of summons: Proper parties

The United States Supreme Court held in *In re Gault*[1] that timely notice must be given to the child and parents sufficiently in advance of scheduled court proceedings to afford a reasonable opportunity to prepare.[2] Ohio law provides that after a complaint has been filed, the court must promptly issue summons to the child, the parents, guardian, custodian, and any other persons who appear to be proper or necessary parties, requiring them to appear before the court at the time fixed to answer the allegations of the complaint.[3]

The term "party" applies to the child, the child's spouse, if any, the child's parent or parents, or if the parent is a child, the parent of such parent, and, where appropriate, the child's custodian, guardian, or guardian ad litem, the state, and any other person specifically designated by the court.[4]

Child. Although the child who is the subject of the complaint is a necessary party,[5] a child alleged to be abused, neglected, or dependent shall not be summoned unless the court so directs,[6] and such child may be excused from attending the hearings.[7] A summons issued for a child under 14 years of age

---

[Section 18:2]

[1]Application of Gault, 387 U.S. 1, 87 S. Ct. 1428, 18 L. Ed. 2d 527 (1967).

[2]See also In re Hoodlet, 72 Ohio App. 3d 115, 593 N.E.2d 478 (4th Dist. Athens County 1991).

[3]RC 2151.28(C), RC 2151.35(C); Juv. R. 15(A). The statutes and rule also provide that a copy of the complaint must accompany the summons. For discussion of complaints, see Complaint Ch 16.

[4]Juv. R. 2(Y), Juv. R. 4(E).

[5]Juv. R. 2(Y).

[6]RC 2151.28(C); Juv. R. 15(A).

[7]RC 2151.35(A); Juv. R. 27.

alleged to be delinquent, unruly, or a juvenile traffic offender shall be made by serving either the child's parents, guardian, or custodian.[8] Based on the language of Juv. R. 16(A), Civ. R. 4.2(2) would not apply to service of summons on a person under the age of 16, but might apply to service of process for pleadings other than the summons.

Parents. The Ohio Supreme Court has held that unless the parents of a child are given actual or constructive notice of the proceedings, the jurisdiction of the court does not attach, and any order or judgment rendered in such proceedings is void[9] and open to collateral attack.[10]

There are conflicting opinions as to the scope of this notice requirement. It has been held that where a mother did not receive notice of the original hearings in which her child was adjudicated dependent and committed to the temporary custody of a children services board, the jurisdiction of the juvenile court did not attach.[11] Thus, it was reversible error to terminate her parental rights following a hearing on a motion for permanent custody conducted two years later, even though the mother received notice of the permanent custody hearing.[12] However, in a case in which a child's father did not receive notice of the child's delinquency hearing in which temporary custody was granted, but did receive notice of a subsequent permanent custody motion filed in the same case, a court of appeals held that the original failure of service was not void but merely voidable; the defect creating that voidability was cured when he was given full notice and opportunity to be heard in the permanent custody proceeding.[13]

If the person who has physical custody of the child or with whom the child resides is other than the parent or guardian, then the parents or guardian shall also be summoned.[14]

If a court issues an order committing a child to the permanent custody of an appropriate agency, the parents of that child cease to be parties to that action.[15]

Noncustodial parent. A noncustodial father is a party in juvenile court

---

[8]Juv. R. 15(A); RC 2151.28(C).

[9]In re Corey, 145 Ohio St. 413, 31 Ohio Op. 35, 61 N.E.2d 892 (1945); Rarey v. Schmidt, 115 Ohio St. 518, 5 Ohio L. Abs. 12, 154 N.E. 914 (1926), which implicitly overruled Bleier v. Crouse, 13 Ohio App. 69, 1920 WL 515 (1st Dist. Hamilton County 1920), which had held that notice to the parent was not a condition precedent to the juvenile court's acquiring jurisdiction over a dependent child; In re Starkey, 150 Ohio App. 3d 612, 620, 2002-Ohio-6892, 782 N.E.2d 665 (7th Dist. Mahoning County 2002) ("The Supreme Court has long held that an order of permanent custody is void for want of jurisdiction if a party was not properly served with notice of the complaint. Until at least constructive notice is given to the parents, the jurisdiction of the juvenile court does not attach, making any judgment of permanent custody void. Based on these jurisdictional holdings, courts held that one parent has standing on appeal to challenge the permanent custody order as void for failing to serve the other parent.") (citations omitted); In re Stackhouse, 1991 WL 37940 (Ohio Ct. App. 4th Dist. Athens County 1991); Matter of McCurdy, 1993 WL 544430 (Ohio Ct. App. 5th Dist. Morrow County 1993); In re Ramsey Children, 1993 WL 500464 (Ohio Ct. App. 5th Dist. Stark County 1993); In re Mullenax, 108 Ohio App. 3d 271, 670 N.E.2d 551 (9th Dist. Lorain County 1996); In re Sitgraves, No. 71862 (8th Dist. Ct. App., Cuyahoga, 11-26-97); Matter of Williams, 1997 WL 317534 (Ohio Ct. App. 10th Dist. Franklin County 1997).

[10]Lewis v. Reed, 117 Ohio St. 152, 5 Ohio L. Abs. 420, 157 N.E. 897 (1927); In Matter Of: Tovar, 1984 WL 5678 (Ohio Ct. App. 4th Dist. Lawrence County 1984); In Matter of Dingess, 1997 WL 282191 (Ohio Ct. App. 4th Dist. Scioto County 1997).

[11]In re Brown, 98 Ohio App. 3d 337, 648 N.E.2d 576 (3d Dist. Marion County 1994).

[12]In re Brown, 98 Ohio App. 3d 337, 648 N.E.2d 576 (3d Dist. Marion County 1994).

[13]Brown v. Miami County Children's Service Bd., 1991 WL 47530 (Ohio Ct. App. 2d Dist. Miami County 1991). See also Matter of Jennifer L., 1998 WL 230808 (Ohio Ct. App. 6th Dist. Lucas County 1998).

[14]RC 2151.28(C); Juv. R. 15(A). It is not necessary to serve the parents if they have been permanently divested of the child's custody. See § 16:5, Parental identification; §§ 30:8 to 30:12, Permanent custody; Motions for Permanent Custody Ch 31.

[15]RC 2151.35(D), RC 2151.414(F).

cases[16] even if he is divorced from the mother or his whereabouts are unknown.[17] Under some circumstances, the father of an illegitimate child may be entitled to notice. In an Illinois dependency case, *Stanley v. Illinois*,[18] in which it was undisputed that the putative father was in fact the biological father, that he had lived with his two children all their lives, and that he had supported and reared them, the United States Supreme Court held that the father was a "parent" within the meaning of the Illinois dependency statute and, thus, was entitled to the same due process accorded to other parents.[19] The Ohio courts have varied considerably in determining the circumstances under which a biological father must be served. It has been held that if a social welfare agency discovers, through a paternity suit or otherwise, and prior to a grant of permanent custody, that a previously unidentified individual is the biological parent of the children, that parent is a party to the permanent custody proceedings.[20] Another court has gone even further, holding that even an apparently unconcerned or unknown putative father is entitled to the minimal protection of service by publication in a dependency proceeding.[21] Because such service is central to the court's subject matter jurisdiction, the child's mother may assert the failure of service upon the father.[22]

On the other hand, in a permanent custody case in which the mother appealed the judgment arguing that the juvenile court lacked jurisdiction because proper service had not been made on the biological father, the court held that the mother lacked standing to object to a purported defect in service upon another party.[23] In this case, the court found that there had been no involvement from the biological father, he had never made an appearance in the case, and he had not appealed the juvenile court order.[24]

Where the complainant is also the child's guardian (e.g., children services board), the mother's assertion that lack of service on the guardian deprived the court of personal and subject matter jurisdiction is unfounded.[25] Moreover, the jurisdiction of the juvenile court was proper in a proceeding to terminate parental rights despite the failure to serve the child's mother. The mother had voluntarily executed a permanent surrender of the child to a private agency and had actual notice of the proceeding via service on her husband, the legal father.[26]

Incarcerated parents. Special problems in terms of service and appearance for hearing result when a parent is incarcerated. In a case in which

---

[16]In Koogle, 1983 WL 2461 (Ohio Ct. App. 2d Dist. Greene County 1983); In re Rule, 1 Ohio App. 2d 57, 30 Ohio Op. 2d 76, 203 N.E.2d 501 (3d Dist. Crawford County 1963).

[17]For requirements for service by publication, see § 18:4, Summons—Methods of service.

[18]Stanley v. Illinois, 405 U.S. 645, 92 S. Ct. 1208, 31 L. Ed. 2d 551 (1972).

[19]See also Quilloin v. Walcott, 434 U.S. 246, 98 S. Ct. 549, 54 L. Ed. 2d 511 (1978), holding that where a putative father had provided virtually no care or support to an illegitimate child, a Georgia statute requiring only the mother's consent to adoption of the child did not deny the father due process or equal protection.

[20]Garabrandt v. Lucas County Children Services Bd., 47 Ohio App. 3d 119, 547 N.E.2d 997 (6th Dist. Lucas County 1988). See also In re Meacham, 1990 WL 200335 (Ohio Ct. App. 5th Dist. Stark County 1990).

[21]In re Ware, No. 40983 (8th Dist. Ct. App., Cuyahoga, 7-17-80).

[22]Where the identity of the father is unknown, the court would be required to try to serve the father through a "John Doe" publication, usually a futile attempt.

[23]Matter of Sours, 1988 WL 81057 (Ohio Ct. App. 3d Dist. Hancock County 1988). See also Matter of Reigle, 1993 WL 451203 (Ohio Ct. App. 3d Dist. Hancock County 1993); In Matter of Matis, 1995 WL 314683 (Ohio Ct. App. 9th Dist. Summit County 1995).

[24]See also In re Shackelford, 1990 WL 68954 (Ohio Ct. App. 2d Dist. Montgomery County 1990); In Matter of Ciara B., 1998 WL 355869 (Ohio Ct. App. 6th Dist. Lucas County 1998).

[25]In the Matter Bell, 1981 WL 6690 (Ohio Ct. App. 3d Dist. Shelby County 1981).

[26]In re Infant Female Luallen, 27 Ohio App. 3d 29, 499 N.E.2d 358 (1st Dist. Hamilton County 1985).

legal custody of four dependent and neglected children was given to their maternal great aunt, a court of appeals relied on RC 2317.06(B) in ruling that a juvenile court has discretion to determine whether an imprisoned father should be conveyed to appear for a hearing.[27] In this case, the father had not been present for the hearing, but had been served with summons and represented at the hearing by an attorney, who stated that it was in the father's best interest to agree to the legal custody motion, particularly because the order would not permanently divest him of his parental rights.

In another case concerning an imprisoned father who was summoned but not permitted to attend the hearing, the court adopted the *Mancino v. Lakewood*[28] and *Mathews v. Eldridge*[29] test in determining that the constitutional right to be present at a parental rights termination hearing is not absolute.[30] This test mandates consideration of three distinct factors: (1) the private interest that will be affected by the official action; (2) the risk of an erroneous deprivation of such interest through the procedures used, and the probable value, if any, of additional or substitute procedural safeguards; and (3) the government's interest, including the function involved and the fiscal and administrative burdens that the additional or substitute procedural requirements would entail.[31] Based on these factors, several courts have held that where a parent fails to take any steps to present testimony by an alternative method, such as a deposition, the parent's due process rights are not violated by the court's refusal to allow the parent to personally appear for the hearing.[32]

An incarcerated father's presence at the hearing may not be required where he was incarcerated for sexually abusing his children, was represented by counsel at the termination hearing, and was permitted to present his testimony by deposition.[33] However, not permitting an incarcerated father to be present for the hearing or to present his testimony by some other means constitutes reversible error.[34]

Moreover, where an incarcerated parent attempted to ascertain the correct hearing date by calling a public defender, who was given the wrong date by a court official, the juvenile court was required to vacate its findings made at the hearing since the parent took all steps available to her.[35]

Foster caregivers. It is provided by statute that foster caregivers, relatives with custody, and prospective adoptive parents are entitled to receive notice of most hearings concerning children in their care, and to present evidence at the hearings.[36] However, the notice and opportunity to present evi-

---

[27]Matter of Holewinski, 1993 WL 155636 (Ohio Ct. App. 6th Dist. Lucas County 1993). See also State ex rel. Vanderlaan v. Pollex, 96 Ohio App. 3d 235, 644 N.E.2d 1073 (6th Dist. Wood County 1994).

[28]Mancino v. City of Lakewood, 36 Ohio App. 3d 219, 523 N.E.2d 332 (8th Dist. Cuyahoga County 1987).

[29]Mathews v. Eldridge, 424 U.S. 319, 96 S. Ct. 893, 47 L. Ed. 2d 18 (1976).

[30]Matter of Vandale, 1993 WL 235599 (Ohio Ct. App. 4th Dist. Washington County 1993). See also In re Smith, 1995 WL 89455 (Ohio Ct. App. 9th Dist. Summit County 1995); In re Seymore, 1999 WL 247775 (Ohio Ct. App. 9th Dist. Lorain County 1999).

[31]Mathews v. Eldridge, 424 U.S. 319, 334, 96 S. Ct. 893, 47 L. Ed. 2d 18 (1976).

[32]In re Harding, 1995 WL 28993 (Ohio Ct. App. 9th Dist. Summit County 1995); In Matter of Yearian, 1996 WL 589264 (Ohio Ct. App. 11th Dist. Portage County 1996); Matter of Enochs, 1997 WL 117207 (Ohio Ct. App. 5th Dist. Stark County 1997); In re Sprague, 113 Ohio App. 3d 274, 680 N.E.2d 1041 (12th Dist. Butler County 1996); In re Fitzgerald, 1998 WL 46767 (Ohio Ct. App. 9th Dist. Summit County 1998).

[33]See Matter of Vandale, 1993 WL 235599 (Ohio Ct. App. 4th Dist. Washington County 1993); Matter of Elliott, 1993 WL 268846 (Ohio Ct. App. 4th Dist. Lawrence County 1993).

[34]Matter of Elliott, 1993 WL 268846 (Ohio Ct. App. 4th Dist. Lawrence County 1993).

[35]In re Maydock, 1997 WL 117081 (Ohio Ct. App. 5th Dist. Stark County 1997).

[36]RC 2151.424(A), RC 2151.424(B).

dence do not make them parties in the action or proceeding.[37] While Juvenile Rule 2(Y) allows a trial court to exercise discretion in determining whether to designate a person an additional party,[38] it does not mandate including a foster parent or any other persons not already specifically designated by the rule.[39] However, in a case decided prior to the enactment of RC 2151.424,[40] it was held that a trial court does not abuse its discretion in allowing foster parents to participate in hearings where their participation assists in fully developing the facts so that a more informed judgment can be made.[41]

In *In re Zhang*,[42] the court of appeals ruled: "While a foster parent is not automatically entitled to party status, the court has wide discretion to name parties to a juvenile court action, and this discretion includes naming foster parents as parties."

Relatives. Although the court's consideration of a relative for appointment as a temporary custodian does not make that relative a party to the proceedings,[43] under certain circumstances relatives may be considered parties if the court sends them notices and allows them to participate in the proceedings.[44]

Grandparents. A child's grandparents are necessary parties only if (1) they are the child's guardian or custodian;[45] (2) the parent (their child) is under age 18;[46] or (3) the grandparents have obtained through statute, court order, or other means a legal right to custody or visitation with the child.[47] Where the grandparents' claimed right to visitation is based on an order of temporary custody allowing the grandparents visitation rights, or is based on the placement of the children in their home by an agency having only temporary custody, the grandparents lack sufficient visitation rights to make their joinder as parties mandatory in dependency proceedings.[48] It has been held in a delinquency case that where the record shows that a child's grandmother stated to police that she has legal custody of the child, the juve-

---

[37]RC 2151.424(C). See Matter of Palmer, 1983 WL 6408 (Ohio Ct. App. 5th Dist. Stark County 1983).

[38]In re Hitchcock, 120 Ohio App. 3d 88, 696 N.E.2d 1090 (8th Dist. Cuyahoga County 1996); Matter of Byerly, 1998 WL 684178 (Ohio Ct. App. 11th Dist. Portage County 1998).

[39]In re Franklin, 88 Ohio App. 3d 277, 623 N.E.2d 720 (3d Dist. Marion County 1993); In Matter of Rundio, 1993 WL 379512 (Ohio Ct. App. 4th Dist. Pickaway County 1993); Matter of Rose, 1992 WL 110289 (Ohio Ct. App. 8th Dist. Cuyahoga County 1992); Matter of Jacquawn J., 1997 WL 458038 (Ohio Ct. App. 6th Dist. Sandusky County 1997).

[40]1998 H.B. 484, eff. 3-18-99.

[41]In Re: Spears, 1984 WL 5682 (Ohio Ct. App. 4th Dist. Athens County 1984); In re Parsons, 1996 WL 285370 (Ohio Ct. App. 9th Dist. Lorain County 1996).

[42]In re Zhang, 135 Ohio App. 3d 350, 354, 734 N.E.2d 379 (8th Dist. Cuyahoga County 1999) ("The best that can be said in this case is that the child welfare system failed miserably to protect the best interests of the child. The foster mother's understandable bond with the child placed her in the position of being an advocate for the child when those who had that responsibility failed to execute that responsibility.").

[43]RC 2151.28(B)(1), RC 2151.314(B)(2); In Matter of Voshel, 1995 WL 256186 (Ohio Ct. App. 9th Dist. Wayne County 1995).

[44]In Matter of Nelson, 1996 WL 200618 (Ohio Ct. App. 11th Dist. Geauga County 1996).

[45]RC 2151.424(A); Juv. R. 2(Y); In re D.H., 2003-Ohio-6478, 2003 WL 22861922 (Ohio Ct. App. 8th Dist. Cuyahoga County 2003); In re Bowman, 101 Ohio App. 3d 599, 656 N.E.2d 355 (9th Dist. Summit County 1995).

[46]Juv. R. 2(Y). In custody proceedings governed by RC 3109.04, a grandparent may become a party if custody to neither parent is in the child's best interest.

[47]In re Schmidt, 25 Ohio St. 3d 331, 496 N.E.2d 952 (1986). See also In Re Miller, 1984 WL 7022 (Ohio Ct. App. 1st Dist. Hamilton County 1984); In re Johnson, 1987 WL 16145 (Ohio Ct. App. 5th Dist. Licking County 1987); In re Thomas, 1993 WL 141597 (Ohio Ct. App. 9th Dist. Summit County 1993); Matter of McGinty, 1992 WL 67580 (Ohio Ct. App. 8th Dist. Cuyahoga County 1992); Matter of Thompson, 1990 WL 34242 (Ohio Ct. App. 4th Dist. Jackson County 1990).

[48]In re Goff, 2003-Ohio-6768, 2003 WL 22952808 (Ohio Ct. App. 11th Dist. Portage County 2003); In re Massengill, 76 Ohio App. 3d 220, 601 N.E.2d 206 (6th Dist. Lucas County 1991).

nile court does not err in finding that the grandmother is the child's custodian.[49]

Agency. The determination of who is a party requires special consideration when a child is committed to the custody of a children services agency. In a case in which two children were adjudicated unruly and committed to the temporary custody of a children services agency after the dispositional hearing, it was held that the agency was not a party to the adjudicatory or dispositional proceedings and thus had no standing to appeal the proceedings.[50] In a subsequent case decided by the same court of appeals, the court determined that where the children services agency was granted temporary custody before rather than after the dispositional hearing, the agency became a party to the action and was thus entitled to appear at the dispositional hearing.[51] When a public children services agency is an appropriate party, it must appear as a party through counsel.[52]

Prosecutor. When requested by the judge, or when a child denies the allegations of a complaint, the prosecuting attorney must assist the court by presenting the evidence in support of the allegations of the complaint.[53] In such a case, the prosecuting attorney, as a representative of the state, is also a party.[54]

School districts. RC 2151.27(F) requires juvenile courts to provide written notice to school districts where a delinquency complaint is filed against a child who is at least 16 years of age, and the offense is either a specified weapons or drug offense committed on school property or at a school sanctioned event; or a specified homicide, assault, or sex offense committed on school property or at a school sanctioned event, with a board of education employee as the victim.

Others. It has been held that a juvenile court's allowing a state witness's mother, a nonparty witness, to communicate extensively with the judge outside of the presence of the alleged delinquent raised questions about the appearance of unfairness of the proceedings and warranted vacation of the delinquency adjudication.[55] Even though the trial court apparently treated her as a "party," the judge did not comply with Juv. R. 2(Y) by "specifically designating" her a party, and did not require her to comply with the customary formalities required of a "party."[56]

§ 18:3 Summons: Contents and form

Juvenile Rule 15(B) sets forth the requirements for the content of summons. All must contain (1) the name of the person with whom the child is residing, or, if the name is unknown, any name or description by which the person can be identified with reasonable certainty; (2) a summary statement of the complaint; (3) a statement that any party is entitled to be represented by an attorney and that upon request the court will appoint an attorney for an indigent party entitled to appointed counsel under Juvenile Rule 4(A);[1] (4) an order to the person to appear at a stated time and place with a warning

---

[49]State v. Parks, 51 Ohio App. 3d 194, 555 N.E.2d 671 (2d Dist. Montgomery County 1988).

[50]In re Blakey, 65 Ohio App. 3d 341, 583 N.E.2d 1343 (10th Dist. Franklin County 1989).

[51]In re Lawson, 98 Ohio App. 3d 456, 648 N.E.2d 889 (10th Dist. Franklin County 1994).

[52]In re Lawson, 98 Ohio App. 3d 456, 648 N.E.2d 889 (10th Dist. Franklin County 1994).

[53]RC 2151.40; Juv. R. 29(E)(1). The rule permits the court to appoint another attorney in lieu of the prosecuting attorney.

[54]Juv. R. 2(Y).

[55]In re Ross, 107 Ohio App. 3d 35, 667 N.E.2d 1012 (10th Dist. Franklin County 1995).

[56]In re Ross, 107 Ohio App. 3d 35, 40, 667 N.E.2d 1012 (10th Dist. Franklin County 1995).

[Section 18:3]
[1]Pursuant to RC 2151.28(F)(1), the court may designate a public defender to represent an indigent party. In In re Trizzino, No. 40982 (8th Dist. Ct. App., Cuyahoga, 1-31-80), the follow-

that the person may lose valuable rights or be subject to court sanction for failure to appear.[2] and (5) contain the name and telephone number of the court employee designated by the court to arrange for the prompt appointment of counsel for indigent persons.[3]

A copy of the complaint must accompany the summons.[4]

There are additional requirements in certain types of cases. These requirements are discussed below.

Delinquency & traffic cases. In juvenile traffic offense and delinquency proceedings, summons must contain the numerical designation of the applicable statute or ordinance.[5]

Truancy cases. Juvenile Rule 15(B) was amended in 2001. In delinquent or unruly summons concerning chronic and habitual truancy, the summons must contain a statement that the parent or responsible adult must bring the child to a truancy hearing or be subject to court sanction, including contempt. This amendment was adopted to conform the rule to RC 2151.28(E)(2), which codified S.B. 181. "Adding this language to the summons alerts responsible adults to the need to ensure not only his or her own appearance, but that of the child as well."[6]

Case plans. In abuse, neglect, or dependency cases where no hearing has been conducted pursuant to RC 2151.314(A) or a parent, guardian, or custodian of the child does not attend the hearing, the summons must also contain a statement advising that a case plan may be prepared for the child, the general requirements of case plans, and the possible consequences of failure to comply with a journalized case plan.[7]

Loss of custody. If the complaint contains a prayer for permanent custody, temporary custody, or a planned permanent living arrangement in a case involving an alleged abused, neglected, or dependent child, the summons served on the parents must contain (1) an explanation that the granting of permanent custody permanently divests the parents of their parental rights and privileges; (2) an explanation that an adjudication of abuse, neglect, or dependency may result in an order of temporary custody that will cause the removal of the child from their legal custody until the court terminates temporary custody or orders permanent custody; or (3) an explanation that an order for a planned permanent living arrangement will

---

ing language, together with the phone number of the public defender's office, was held to sufficiently apprise the parents of their right to counsel:

> You and/or your child have the right to be represented by a lawyer at all stages of the proceedings or the rights to a lawyer may be waived. If you wish to be represented by a lawyer but are financially unable to employ one, you have a right to have a lawyer provided for you.

[2]A similar provision is contained in RC 2151.28(J). The juvenile court has the same power in contempt as do the courts of common pleas (RC 2151.21). See also RC 2705.01 to RC 2705.10; State ex rel. Turner v. Albin, 118 Ohio St. 527, 6 Ohio L. Abs. 341, 161 N.E. 792 (1928).

[3]RC 2151.28(C), RC 2151.314(D), RC 2151.414(A); Juv. R. 15(B)(9).

[4]Juv. R. 15(A). See also In re Smith, 142 Ohio App. 3d 16, 23, 753 N.E.2d 930 (8th Dist. Cuyahoga County 2001) ("We do not understand this argument to suggest that the juvenile had no notice of the charges against her. Her presence at the adjudicatory hearing necessarily implied that she had some notice of the complaint. Moreover, we see no reason to find that her failure to see the complaint until immediately before entering her admission somehow affected her admission. Absent some form of prejudice stemming from her failure to see the complaint at the time of the adjudicatory hearing, we cannot find error.").

[5]Juv. R. 15(B)(2).

[6]Staff Note (2001).

[7]RC 2151.28(F)(2). In re Moore, 153 Ohio App. 3d 641, 2003-Ohio-4250, at ¶ 15, 795 N.E.2d 149 (3d Dist. Hardin County 2003) ("[W]hile the trial court may have erred by not initially informing [Father] of the fact that permanent custody to DJFS was one possible consequence of failing to comply with the case plan, all of the subsequent information provided to him eliminated any prejudice that the initial error may have caused. Furthermore, even if [he] had fully complied with the case plan, this fact alone did not guarantee that permanent custody to DJFS would be denied.").

cause the removal of the child from the legal custody of the parents if the appropriate conditions are found to exist.[8] If the requisite explanation is not included in the summons, the corresponding dispositional order may not be made.[9] These requirements apply not only to original complaints, but also to motions for permanent custody.[10] Moreover, it is the responsibility of the court, not one of the parties, to issue the requisite notice.[11]

A court has no jurisdiction to award permanent custody when the summons contains only a cursory, confusing notice in fine print regarding the effects of permanent custody.[12] However, in a temporary custody proceeding, the parents were held to have received adequate notice even though the summons did not contain the required explanation.[13] The court determined that both parents had notice of the possibility that their son could be removed from their legal custody because (1) the language of the complaint itself gave that notice;[14] (2) both parties were individually represented by counsel; and (3) neither party objected to the court's exercise of jurisdiction at any time during or after the hearing until a complaint for permanent custody was filed.[15]

It has been held that the failure of a summons to explain adequately the effects of permanent custody is not a jurisdictional matter, but rather a matter of due process.[16]

The summons may also be endorsed with an order directing the parents, guardian, or other person with whom the child is residing to appear personally with the child.[17]

§ 18:4   Summons: Methods of service

Juvenile Rule 16(A) provides that except as otherwise provided in the juvenile rules, service of summons shall be governed by Civil Rules 4(A), (C), and (D), 4.1, 4.2, 4.3, 4.5, and 4.6.[1] Where service is made by certified mail pursuant to Civil Rule 4.1(1), the hearing may not be held before seven days after the date of mailing.[2]

---

[8]RC 2151.28(D); Juv. R. 15(B).

[9]RC 2151.353(B); In re Fassinger, 43 Ohio App. 2d 89, 72 Ohio Op. 2d 292, 334 N.E.2d 5 (8th Dist. Cuyahoga County 1974). See also In re Snider, 14 Ohio App. 3d 353, 471 N.E.2d 516 (3d Dist. Defiance County 1984); Reynolds v. Ross County Children's Services Agency, 5 Ohio St. 3d 27, 448 N.E.2d 816 (1983); Hutchison, 1982 WL 3455 (Ohio Ct. App. 4th Dist. Lawrence County 1982); Bryant, 1982 WL 6001 (Ohio Ct. App. 12th Dist. Butler County 1982); In the Matter of Banks Griggs v. Griggs Banks Jones, 1981 WL 5593 (Ohio Ct. App. 6th Dist. Lucas County 1981); In re Trizzino, No. 40982 (8th Dist. Ct. App., Cuyahoga, 1-31-80); In re Reed, No. CA 1325 (5th Dist. Ct. App., Tuscarawas, 7-24-79). See § 16:11, Neglect & abuse complaints.

[10]RC 2151.414(A).

[11]In re Shaeffer Children, 85 Ohio App. 3d 683, 621 N.E.2d 426 (3d Dist. Van Wert County 1993).

[12]In re Osborn, No. CA 1744 (5th Dist. Ct. App., Richland, 1-16-79) held that a summons containing the following language in fine print at the bottom was defective: "NOTICE: If the complaint contains a prayer for permanent custody in a neglect or dependency case, the parents are hereby advised that the granting of such custody permanently divests the parents of their parental rights and privileges."

[13]Matter of Cox, 1986 WL 7900 (Ohio Ct. App. 4th Dist. Highland County 1986).

[14]See § 16:11, Neglect & abuse complaints.

[15]See In re Shaeffer Children, 85 Ohio App. 3d 683, 621 N.E.2d 426 (3d Dist. Van Wert County 1993).

[16]In Re King, 1981 WL 4228 (Ohio Ct. App. 9th Dist. Summit County 1981).

[17]RC 2151.28(E); Juv. R. 15(C).

[Section 18:4]

[1]For provisions governing service of subpoenas, see RC 2151.28(J); Juv. R. 17.

[2]Juv. R. 16(A); RC 2151.29. The 1994 amendment to Juv. R. 16(A) reduced the requisite waiting period from 21 to seven days, thus eliminating the potential conflict with Juv. R. 29(A),

Personal service[3] or residence service[4] may be made in lieu of service by certified mail. Residence service may be perfected by leaving the process at the usual place of residence of the person to be served with a person of suitable age and discretion residing therein.[5]

When service of summons is made by certified mail, personal service, or residence service, there must be a signed certification attesting to the type of service.[6]

Service by publication. When a party's residence is unknown and cannot be ascertained with reasonable diligence,[7] service must be made by publication.[8] However, service by publication upon a non-custodial parent is not required in delinquency cases or unruly cases when the person alleged to have legal custody of the child has been served with summons; but the court may not enter any order or judgment against any person who has not been served with process or served by publication unless that person appears.[9]

Service by publication is a method of last resort and the requirements, as specified in Juvenile Rule 16(A) are mandatory and are strictly enforced.[10]

Methods. There are three alternatives for accomplishing service by publication: by newspaper publication, by posting and mail, or by a combination of these methods. Each court determines, by local rule, which method or methods to use.[11]

Affidavit. Before service by publication may be made, an affidavit must be filed with the court averring that service cannot be made because the residence of the party is unknown and cannot with reasonable diligence be ascertained. The affidavit must also include the last known address of the party to be served.[12] Service by publication without the filing of such an affidavit does not constitute proper service.[13]

Reasonable efforts. Once there is a challenge to a party's exercise of reasonable diligence, that party must support his claim that he used reasonable

---

which requires a hearing within 10 days of the filing of the complaint when the child is in detention or shelter care.

[3]Civ. R. 4.1(2) provides that in the event of failure to serve personally the party within 28 days, the clerk shall so notify the attorney or party who requested the service. This, too, would be in conflict with the 10-day rule of Juv. R. 29(A), which applies when the child is in detention or shelter care.

[4]Civ. R. 4.1(3). The rule includes the same 28-day provision discussed in the preceding footnote.

[5]Civ. R. 4.1(3). The rule includes the same 28-day provision discussed in the preceding footnote. See OAG 70-130 concerning the duty of the sheriff to serve summonses, notices, and subpoenas.

[6]Civ. R. 4.1. In re Osborn, No. CA 1744 (5th Dist. Ct. App., Richland, 1-16-79).

[7]"Reasonable diligence" has been defined as a "fair, proper, and due degree of care and activity, measured with reference to the particular circumstances; such diligence, care, or attention as might be expected from a (person) of ordinary prudence and activity," and requires the use of "common and readily available sources." Sizemore v. Smith, 6 Ohio St. 3d 330, 453 N.E.2d 632 (1983); Matter of Montasser, 1992 WL 348236 (Ohio Ct. App. 6th Dist. Lucas County 1992).

[8]Juv. R. 16(A).

[9]Juv. R. 16(A).

[10]In re Wilson, 21 Ohio App. 3d 36, 486 N.E.2d 152 (6th Dist. Huron County 1984).

[11]Juv. R. 16(A).

[12]Juv. R. 16(A).

[13]In re Osborn, No. CA 1744 (5th Dist. Ct. App., Richland, 1-16-79). See also Matter of Fraser, 1992 WL 238498 (Ohio Ct. App. 5th Dist. Stark County 1992); Matter of Bowman, 1992 WL 238457 (Ohio Ct. App. 5th Dist. Stark County 1992); In re Sitgraves, No. 71862 (8th Dist. Ct. App., Cuyahoga, 11-26-97). Both Juv. R. 16(A) and these decisions overruled In re Veselich, 22 Ohio App. 528, 5 Ohio L. Abs. 277, 154 N.E. 55 (8th Dist. Cuyahoga County 1926), which had held that service by publication on absent parents under former GC 1647 (now RC 2151.27) and former GC 1648 (now RC 2151.28) was sufficient even though an affidavit had not been filed (*Osborn* was based on an interpretation of Civ. R. 4.4, which is similar to Juv. R. 16(A), but which does not apply to children's cases).

diligence to locate the party served by publication.[14] However, compliance with Juvenile Rule 16(A) gives rise to a rebuttable presumption that reasonable efforts have been made.[15]

Content. Along with other information about the case, the publication must contain a summary statement of the object of the complaint[16] and, in permanent custody cases, a full explanation of the effect of permanent custody.[17]

Time requirements. The date of the hearing stated in the publication must not be less than seven days after the date of publication.[18]

Newspaper. If service by publication is made by newspaper publication, it shall be made in a newspaper of general circulation in the county in which the complaint is filed;[19] if no such newspaper exists, publication may be made in a newspaper of an adjoining county.[20] If service is by newspaper publication, the publisher or his agent must file with the court an affidavit showing the fact of publication together with a copy of the notice of publication.

Posting and mail. The newest option for publication is by posting and mail,[21] which is accomplished by posting the notice in a conspicuous place in the courthouse in which the juvenile court is located, and in additional public places in the county as designated by local rule. The number of additional places is either two, or the number of state representative districts that are contained in the county, whichever is greater. The notice shall be posted for seven consecutive days. In addition, the summons and accompanying pleadings must be sent by ordinary mail, address correction requested, to the party's last know address. If, within the seven-day period, the clerk is notified of a corrected or forwarding address for the party, the summons and pleadings must be mailed to that address.[22]

Service of publication by posting and mail must be noted on the docket by the clerk, including the locations and dates of the posting.[23]

§ 18:5   Waiver of summons requirements

A party other than the child may waive service of summons by written stipulation.[1]

Voluntary appearance. The Ohio Supreme Court has twice considered

---

[14]In re Miller, 33 Ohio App. 3d 224, 515 N.E.2d 635 (8th Dist. Cuyahoga County 1986). See also In re Wilson, 21 Ohio App. 3d 36, 486 N.E.2d 152 (6th Dist. Huron County 1984); Matter of Montasser, 1992 WL 348236 (Ohio Ct. App. 6th Dist. Lucas County 1992); In re Cowling, 72 Ohio App. 3d 499, 595 N.E.2d 470 (9th Dist. Summit County 1991); In re Shackelford, 1990 WL 68954 (Ohio Ct. App. 2d Dist. Montgomery County 1990); In re Mullenax, 108 Ohio App. 3d 271, 670 N.E.2d 551 (9th Dist. Lorain County 1996); In re Fitzgerald, 1998 WL 46767 (Ohio Ct. App. 9th Dist. Summit County 1998).

[15]In re Owen, 1990 WL 187084 (Ohio Ct. App. 5th Dist. Stark County 1990).

[16]Juv. R. 16(A).

[17]In re Brown, No. 3-CA-79 (5th Dist. Ct. App., Fairfield, 7-20-79).

[18]Juv. R. 16(A). See RC 2151.29. The July 1, 1998, amendment of the rule, reducing the waiting time from 14 to seven days, eliminates the conflict that previously existed with respect to a child in detention or shelter care. In such instances, Juv. R. 29(A) requires a hearing within 10 days of the filing of the complaint. See § 19:7, Time requirements.

[19]See In re Starkey, 150 Ohio App. 3d 612, 622, 2002-Ohio-6892, 782 N.E.2d 665 (7th Dist. Mahoning County 2002) ("[S]ervice by publication was not deficient merely because it was accomplished through the Daily Legal News.").

[20]Juv. R. 16(A).

[21]This addition to Juv. R. 16(A), which is modeled on Civil Rule 4.4(A)(2), took effect on July 1, 1998.

[22]Juv. R. 16(A).

[23]Juv. R. 16(A).

[Section 18:5]

[1]RC 2151.28(H). Civ. R. 4(D) is applicable to children's cases pursuant to Juv. R. 16(A).

the issue of waiver under a prior version of the statute (RC 2151.28), which required service of summons "unless the parties voluntarily appear." In *Ex parte Province*[2] the Court initially held that where a parent voluntarily appeared with counsel and participated in a dependency hearing regarding her child, she was deemed to have waived her right to prior notice of the hearing.[3] In *In re Frinzl*,[4] a later decision in which the mother participated in a permanent custody proceeding, but was not served with summons until the time of the hearing and was not represented by counsel, the Court held that the service was not made sufficiently in advance of the hearing.[5] Thus, the voluntary appearance of a party does not in itself constitute a waiver of service. However, a voluntary appearance may result in a waiver if the party consents and the court permits.[6]

It has also been held that a mother's purported waiver of summons in a permanent custody case is ineffective unless the waiver contains a full explanation of the effects of a permanent custody order.[7]

Although RC 2151.28(H) does not permit the child to waive service of summons, such waiver may arguably be valid under Juvenile Rule 3, which provides, "Other rights (other than counsel at bindover) of a child may be waived *with the permission of the court*" (emphasis added).[8]

Cross References
Ch 16, § 19:7, § 32:2
Research References
Katz and Giannelli, Baldwin's Ohio Practice, Criminal Law (2d ed.) § 7:15
Carlin, Baldwin's Ohio Practice, Merrick-Rippner Probate Law (6th ed.), Ch 107

---

[2]Ex parte Province, 127 Ohio St. 333, 188 N.E. 550 (1933).

[3]See also Mobley v. Allaman, 89 Ohio L. Abs. 473, 184 N.E.2d 707 (Prob. Ct. 1961); Matter of Garcia, 1993 WL 390100 (Ohio Ct. App. 6th Dist. Wood County 1993); In re Shaeffer Children, 85 Ohio App. 3d 683, 621 N.E.2d 426 (3d Dist. Van Wert County 1993).

[4]In re Frinzl, 152 Ohio St. 164, 39 Ohio Op. 456, 87 N.E.2d 583 (1949).

[5]See also Union County Child Welfare Bd. v. Parker, 7 Ohio App. 2d 79, 36 Ohio Op. 2d 162, 218 N.E.2d 757 (3d Dist. Union County 1964).

[6]Juv. R. 3; In re Smith, 64 Ohio App. 3d 773, 582 N.E.2d 1117 (6th Dist. Lucas County 1990); Lorain County Children Services v. Murray, 1996 WL 15843 (Ohio Ct. App. 9th Dist. Lorain County 1996).

[7]In re Brown, No. 3-CA-79 (5th Dist. Ct. App., Fairfield, 7-20-79).

[8]Prior to the 1994 amendment to Juv. R. 3, the rule stated, "No other right of a child may be waived without the permission of the court." The intent of the amended language is not clear.

Chapter 19

Detention or Shelter Care

> **KeyCite®:** Cases and other legal materials listed in KeyCite Scope can be researched through West's KeyCite service on Westlaw®. Use KeyCite to check citations for form, parallel references, prior and later history, and comprehensive citator information, including citations to other decisions and secondary materials.

§ 19:1   Detention or shelter care—Introduction
§ 19:2   Place of detention
§ 19:3   Admissions officer
§ 19:4   Detention hearing: Notice
§ 19:5   Detention hearing
§ 19:6   Standard for detention
§ 19:7   Time requirements
§ 19:8   Motions for release
§ 19:9   Bail
§ 19:10   Rights while detained
§ 19:11   Detention facilities
§ 19:12   Closure of hearing

§ 19:1 Detention or shelter care—Introduction

This chapter discusses the procedural and substantive requirements which govern the juvenile court's authority to place children in detention and shelter care facilities prior to the execution of a final court order.

Portions of Am. Sub. H.B. 400 became effective April 3, 2003. RC 2152.26(F)(2) permits children adjudicated delinquent to be placed in county, multi-county, or municipal jails or workhouses or other places where adults may be held. Further, children alleged to be delinquent who are not arrested or apprehended for a delinquent act before they turn 18 years of age, may be placed in county, multi-county or municipal jails or workhouses.[1] In addition, children adjudicated delinquent who turn 18 years of age before disposition may also be placed in county, multi-county or municipal jails or workhouses. Children alleged to be delinquent who are placed in county, multi-county or municipal jails or workhouses under this statute have the same rights to bail as an adult charged with the same offense who is confined in a jail, pending trial.[2]

Juvenile Rule 7 was amended in 2001 to reflect changes brought about by S.B. 179. The changes concern delinquency, including the new category, Serious Youthful Offender (SYO).[3] The phrase "or to protect the person or property of others" was added to Rule 7(A)(1)(b) to recognize the underling rationales of new RC Chapter 2152. The phrase "confinement is authorized by statute" was added as Rule 7(A)(5) for the same reason. RC 2152.04 permits the detention of a juvenile alleged or adjudicated to be delinquent for

---

[Section 19:1]
[1]RC 2152.26(F)(3).
[2]RC 2152.26(F)(3)(b).
[3]See Serious Youthful Offenders Ch 5.

90 days, during which time social history and other records may be gathered. RC 2151.31(C)(2) authorizes detention prior to implementation of a final disposition order for (1) an alleged delinquent child if authorized by RC 2152.04, or (2) an alleged SYO.[4]

§ 19:2   Place of detention

Pursuant to Am. Sub. H.B. 400 and S.B. 179, RC 2152.26 governs the place of detention for delinquents and juvenile traffic offenders.[1] RC 2151.312 now deals only with unruly, abused, neglected, or dependent children.

Truants. RC 2152.26(B) provides that a child alleged to be or adjudicated a delinquent child may be held in a detention home or center for delinquent children that is under the direction or supervision of the court or other public authority or private agency approved by the court. This provision, however, does not apply to a chronic truant, unless the child violated a lawful court order made pursuant to RC 2151.354(C)(1)(e). Similarly, it does not apply to a repeat habitual truant, unless the child violated a lawful court order made pursuant to RC 2151.354(C)(1)(e).

Further, a child adjudged delinquent who turns 18 years old prior to disposition (which arguably could include an habitual truant previously adjudicated an habitual truant), may be detained in a county, multi-county, or municipal jail or workhouse or other place where an adult convicted of crime, under arrest, or charged with a crime is held.[2]

When a child is taken into custody,[3] there are several restrictions regarding detention. The child may be released to his parents, guardian, or other custodian, or brought to the court or to a place of detention or shelter care designated by the court.[4]

Adult facilities. Before taking any of these actions, a person taking a child into custody may under certain circumstances hold the child in an adult facility.[5] A child who is taken into custody for an alleged delinquent felony offense may be held for up to six hours for processing purposes in a county, multicounty, or municipal jail or workhouse, or other place where an adult convicted of, under arrest for, or charged with a crime is held.[6] A child taken into custody for an alleged delinquent misdemeanor, unruly, or juvenile traffic offense may be held in the same types of facilities for processing purposes for up to three hours.[7]

Under all of the above circumstances, the child must be visually supervised by jail or workhouse personnel at all times, must remain beyond the range of

---

[4]See RC 2152.13 (SYO statute).

[Section 19:2]

[1]RC 2152.26(B) and RC 2152.26(F)(2).

[2]RC 2152.26(F)(3)(a).

[3]For discussion of when an alleged delinquent or unruly child may be arrested, see § 14:3, Custody, arrests, and stops. For discussion of when an alleged neglected, dependent, or abused child may be taken into custody, see Temporary Orders Pending Hearing Ch 20.

[4]RC 2151.311(A); Juv. R. 7(B)(1). See State v. Spencer, 1995 WL 363961 (Ohio Ct. App. 8th Dist. Cuyahoga County 1995). See RC 2151.011(B)(12) and Juv. R. 2(K) for definition of "detention." See also IJA-ABA Standards Relating to Interim Status: The Release, Control, and Detention of Accused Juvenile Offenders Between Arrest and Disposition 50 (1980).

[5]Am. Sub. H.B. 400 did not address RC 2151.311(C) which concerns the detention of children in adult facilities. The statute and the new legislation seem to be in conflict. One possible resolution might be that RC 2151.311(C) does not apply to the courts but rather to law enforcement officers. Consequently, law enforcement officers would be restricted in the time which they may detain children in facilities where adults may be detained. Once the court becomes involved, however, these restrictions do not apply. This, however, is mere speculation.

[6]RC 2151.311(C)(1)(a)(i). See also Juv. R. 7(H); State v. Johnson, 1996 WL 355288 (Ohio Ct. App. 8th Dist. Cuyahoga County 1996).

[7]RC 2151.311(C)(1)(b)(i).

touch of all adult detainees, and may not be handcuffed or otherwise physically secured to a stationary object during the detention.[8]

Am. Sub. H.B. 400 provides that an adjudicated delinquent or juvenile traffic offender may be held in facilities which include a county, multi-county, or municipal jail or workhouse, or a place where an adult convicted of a crime, under arrest or charged with a crime is held.[9]

Further, a person alleged to be a delinquent child may be held in places which include county, multi-county, or municipal jail or workhouse, if the child allegedly committed an offense which would be a felony if committed by an adult, and either the person reaches eighteen years of age before arrest or apprehension for that act, or the person is arrested or apprehended for the act before age eighteen, but passes age eighteen before the court orders disposition.[10] Such a child, held in an adult facility, has the same rights to bail as an adult charged with same offense who is confined in a jail pending trial.[11]

The only other instances in which a child may be held in any of the above adult facilities is if he has been transferred to an adult court for criminal prosecution,[12] or has been transferred from a department of youth services facility to a correctional medical center established by the department of rehabilitation and correction pursuant to RC 5139.06(C)(2) and RC 5120.162.[13]

Detention facilities. RC 2151.311(A)(2) provides that a child taken into custody may be brought to the court or delivered to a place of detention or shelter care[14] designated by the court.[15] Because of restrictions imposed by RC 2151.312, placement in a detention facility is generally limited to delinquent children.[16]

A child alleged to be or adjudicated a neglected, abused, or dependent child may not be held in an adult facility, a secure correctional facility,[17] or a detention home.[18] In addition, an alleged or adjudicated unruly child or juvenile traffic offender may not, with some exceptions, be held in any of the above facilities.[19] An unruly child or juvenile traffic offender may be held in a detention home for no more than 24 hours, or for an unspecified longer period if awaiting return to his or her home jurisdiction under the Interstate Compact on Juveniles (RC 2151.56 to RC 2151.61).[20] A juvenile traffic offender may also be held, under certain circumstances, in a detention center

---

[8]RC 2151.311(C)(1)(a)(ii), (iii), (iv); RC 2151.311(C)(1)(b)(ii), (iii), (iv). See also RC 341.11.

[9]RC 2152.26(F)(2).

[10]RC 2152.26(F)(3)(a).

[11]RC 2152.26(F)(3)(b).

[12]RC 2151.311(C)(2), RC 2151.312(D), RC 2151.312(F); In re Raypole, 2003-Ohio-1066, 2003 WL 928976 (Ohio Ct. App. 12th Dist. Fayette County 2003).

[13]RC 2151.312(B). See also Cox v. Turley, 506 F.2d 1347 (6th Cir. 1974), which held that keeping a juvenile in a jail with adult inmates violates due process.

[14]"Detention" is defined in RC 2151.011(B)(12) and Juv. R. 2(J). "Shelter" care is defined in RC 2151.011(B)(44) and Juv. R. 2(JJ). The primary distinction is that detention involves care in a physically restricted facility, whereas shelter care is nonrestrictive. See also RC 2152.26.

[15]See also Juv. R. 7(B)(2).

[16]RC 2151.312(B). But see RC 2152.26(B). In re Hennessey, 146 Ohio App. 3d 743, 746, 2001-Ohio-2267, 768 N.E.2d 663 (3d Dist. Mercer County 2001) ("R.C. 2151.312(D) like R.C. 2151.355(A)(25) does not permit the housing of delinquent children in any adult facility.").

[17]See RC 2151.011(B)(42) for definition of "secure correctional facility."

[18]RC 2151.312(C)(1), RC 2151.312(C)(2), RC 2151.312(D).

[19]RC 2151.312(C); RC 2152.21(A)(5); RC 2152.26(B); RC 2152.26(F).

[20]RC 2151.312(C)(2). RC 2151.312(C)(3) provides that an unruly child who is taken into custody on a Saturday, Sunday, or legal holiday may be held in a detention home until the next succeeding day. The statute does not address this extension with respect to a juvenile traffic offender. See Interstate Agreements Ch 36.

for up to five days in a post-dispositional status.[21]

Foster homes. There are other options in lieu of placing a child in an adult facility or detention facility. Three separate statutes govern the placement of children in foster homes and other similar facilities. RC 2151.312(A) provides that an alleged or adjudicated delinquent child, unruly child, or juvenile traffic offender may be held in a certified family foster home, in a home approved by the court, in a facility operated by a certified child welfare agency, or in any other suitable place designated by the court, which may include house arrest pending further hearing.[22]

RC 2151.331 addresses the same placement issues, but in a different manner. This statute allows an alleged or adjudicated abused, neglected, dependent, or unruly child or juvenile traffic offender to be detained in a certified family foster home for up to 60 days or until final disposition of the case, whichever occurs first. In addition, the statute[23] allows the court to arrange with a public children services agency or private child placing agency to receive, or with a private noncustodial agency for temporary care of, a child within the court's jurisdiction. Finally, this statute[24] allows the court to assign an alleged or adjudicated unruly child to an alternative diversion program for up to 60 days after a complaint is filed or until final disposition, whichever comes first.

The third statute, RC 2151.34, apparently limits the applicability of RC 2151.312(A) by providing that an alleged or adjudicated delinquent child may be held in a certified family foster home or other home approved by the court only for a period not exceeding 60 days or until final disposition, whichever comes first.

§ 19:3 Admissions officer

A person delivering a child to a shelter or detention facility (1) must give the admissions officer a signed report stating the reasons for taking the child into custody and for not releasing him and (2) must assist the admissions officer, if necessary, in notifying the child's parent.[1]

Based on this report and any further investigation as is feasible, the admissions officer must make an initial decision to release or hold the child.[2] The child must be released prior to implementation of a final disposition order except: (1) when detention or shelter care is required to protect the child from immediate or threatened physical or emotional harm; (2) when the child may abscond or be removed from the court's jurisdiction; (3) when the child has no parent or other person able to provide supervision and care and return the child to the court when required; or (4) when an order for the child's detention or shelter care has been made by the court.[3]

If the child is admitted to detention or shelter care, the admissions officer must (1) prepare a report containing the time of and reasons for admission;[4] (2) advise the child of his right to telephone parents and counsel, both immediately and at reasonable times thereafter;[5] (3) advise the child of the

---

[21]RC 2152.21(A)(5); RC 2152.21(A)(6). See § 28:6, Commitment to juvenile facility.

[22]State ex rel. Frazer v. Administrator/Director, Juvenile Court Detention Home, 107 Ohio App. 3d 245, 668 N.E.2d 546 (8th Dist. Cuyahoga County 1995).

[23]RC 2151.331.

[24]RC 2151.331.

[Section 19:3]
[1]Juv. R. 7(C).
[2]Juv. R. 7(D).
[3]RC 2151.31(C); Juv. R. 7(A).
[4]Juv. R. 7(E)(1).
[5]Juv. R. 7(E)(2).

time, place, and purpose of the detention (or shelter care) hearing;[6] and (4) use reasonable diligence to contact the child's parent, guardian, or custodian and advise him of the place of and reasons for detention; the time allowed for visitation; the time, place, and purpose of the detention hearing; and the right to counsel and to appointed counsel if indigent.[7]

§19:4 Detention hearing: Notice

Oral or written notice of the hearing must be given to the child and, if they can be found, to his parents, guardian, or custodian.[1] In abuse, neglect, or dependency cases, the notice must inform them that a case plan may be prepared for the child, the general requirements of case plans, and the possible consequences of failure to comply with a journalized case plan.[2]

Prior to the hearing, the parties must be informed of (1) their right to counsel, (2) their right to appointed counsel or a public defender if they are indigent,[3] and (3) the name and telephone number of a court employee who can be contacted during the normal business hours of the court to arrange for the prompt appointment of counsel for any party who is indigent.[4] They must also be advised of the child's right to remain silent with respect to any allegation of delinquency, unruliness, or juvenile traffic offense.[5]

Lack of notice. If a parent, guardian, or custodian did not receive notice of the initial detention hearing and did not appear or waive appearance at the hearing, upon a filing of an affidavit stating these facts, the court must rehear the matter promptly.[6] The Ohio Supreme Court has held that a parent alleging lack of notice of a shelter care hearing concerning his child must move the juvenile court for a rehearing pursuant to Juvenile Rule 7(G) before seeking a writ of habeas corpus.[7]

§19:5 Detention hearing

Juvenile Rule 2(L) defines a "detention hearing" as "a hearing to determine whether a child shall be held in detention or shelter care prior to or pending execution of a final dispositional order."[1]

The detention hearing is informal.[2] Any reports filed by the person delivering the child and by the admissions officer, as well as other evidence, may be considered without regard to formal rules of evidence.[3]

Although Juvenile Rule 7(F)(1) requires a juvenile court to conduct a shelter care hearing where a child has been involuntarily removed from his or her home following an allegation of neglect, dependency, or abuse,[4] a shelter care hearing is not required where an order transferring legal custody

---

[6]Juv. R. 7(E)(2).

[7]Juv. R. 7(E)(3).

[Section 19:4]

[1]RC 2151.314(A); Juv. R. 7(F)(1).

[2]RC 2151.314(A).

[3]RC 2151.314(A); Juv. R. 7(F)(2).

[4]RC 2151.314(A).

[5]RC 2151.314(A); Juv. R. 7(F)(2). The statute applies this right only to "any allegation of delinquency."

[6]RC 2151.314(A); Juv. R. 7(G).

[7]Linger v. Weiss, 57 Ohio St. 2d 97, 11 Ohio Op. 3d 281, 386 N.E.2d 1354 (1979).

[Section 19:5]

[1]For discussion of the 72-hour and other time limits concerning detained children, see §19:7, Time requirements.

[2]RC 2151.314(A).

[3]Juv. R. 7(F)(3).

[4]In re Pachin, 50 Ohio App. 3d 44, 552 N.E.2d 655 (2d Dist. Montgomery County 1988).

of a child to a children services board is considered a modification of a prior dispositional order.

§ 19:6   Standard for detention

Juvenile Rule 7 was amended in 2001 to reflect changes brought about by S.B. 179 (effective January 1, 2002). The changes concern delinquency, including the new category, Serious Youthful Offender (SYO).[1] The phrase "or to protect the person or property of others" was added to Rule 7(A)(1)(b) to recognize the underling rationales of new RC Chapter 2152. The phrase "confinement is authorized by statute" was added as Rule 7(A)(5) for the same reason. RC 2152.04 permits the detention of a juvenile alleged or adjudicated to be delinquent for 90 days,[2] during which time social history and other records may be gathered. RC 2151.31(C)(2) authorizes detention prior to implementation of a final disposition order for (1) an alleged delinquent child if authorized by RC 2152.04, or (2) an alleged SYO.[3]

In deciding whether to detain or release the child, the court[4] must apply the same standards used when the child is initially taken into custody[5] or brought to a detention or shelter care facility.[6] Thus, the child must be released unless (1) detention or care is required to protect the child from immediate or threatened physical or emotional harm;[7] (2) the child may abscond or be removed from the court's jurisdiction; (3) the child has no parent, guardian, or other person able to provide supervision and care and return the child to the court when required; or (4) an order for placement of the child in detention or shelter care has been made by the court.[8]

Also, RC 2151.314(B) provides that when the court conducts a detention or shelter care hearing, the court must:

(1) determine whether an alleged abused, neglected, or dependent child should remain in or be placed in shelter care;

(2) determine whether there are any relatives of the child who are willing to be temporary custodians of the child.[9] If any appropriate relatives are found, the court must appoint one of them as the child's temporary custodian instead of using shelter care placement. If the court determines that the appointment of a relative as custodian would not be appropriate, it must issue a written opinion setting forth its reasons and give a copy to all parties;

[Section 19:6]

[1]See Serious Youthful Offenders Ch 5.

[2]Note that this is detention, not commitment pursuant to RC 2152.19(A)(3), as amended by Am. Sub. H.B. 400, eff. January 1, 2004. That section permits the court to impose a 90-day commitment to a detention or district detention facility.

[3]See RC 2152.13 (SYO statute).

[4]In some counties, detention hearings are conducted by magistrates or other court personnel, rather than by judges.

[5]RC 2151.28(G), RC 2151.31(A); Juv. R. 6.

[6]Juv. R. 7(A), Juv. R. 7(F)(3).

[7]See Matter of Rozic, 1994 WL 393709 (Ohio Ct. App. 8th Dist. Cuyahoga County 1994).

[8]RC 2151.31(C); Juv. R. 7(A). The standards relative to the detention of children, as well as the elements of a detention hearing, have been considered by several federal courts. For example, although Ohio law does not specifically require a probable cause finding at the detention hearing, federal courts in other states whose detention laws are similar to Ohio's have imposed this additional procedural requirement in hearings for alleged delinquent and unruly children. E.g., R.W.T. v. Dalton, 712 F.2d 1225 (8th Cir. 1983); Moss v. Weaver, 383 F. Supp. 130 (S.D. Fla. 1974).

[9]See Juv. R. 7(F)(3). See Matter of Cory Y., 1995 WL 612929 (Ohio Ct. App. 6th Dist. Lucas County 1995).

(3) comply with the "reasonable efforts" provision, RC 2151.419.[10]

Juvenile Rule 27(B)(1) requires the court, in a proceeding where it orders detention, to determine whether the person who filed the complaint and removed the child from home has or will be given custody and has made reasonable efforts to:

(1) prevent the removal of the child from home;

(2) eliminate the continued removal of the child from home; or

(3) make it possible for the child to return home.

Preventive detention. The United States Supreme Court in *Schall v. Martin*[11] upheld the validity of a New York statute permitting the preventive detention of alleged delinquents when there is a "serious risk" that such children may commit a crime before their adjudicatory hearing. In holding that the statute was not invalid under the Due Process Clause of the Fourteenth Amendment, the Court reasoned that preventive detention serves the legitimate state objective of protecting the child and society from the hazards of pretrial crime and the procedural safeguards afforded by the statute provide sufficient protection against erroneous detention.[12]

§19:7 Time requirements

Both detention and shelter care facilities are intended to provide only temporary care pending adjudication or disposition, or execution of a court order.[1] The law places specific limits on the length of time that a child may be held before certain steps must be taken.

Seventy-two hour rule. Any child admitted to such a facility must be provided a hearing within 72 hours after admission, or on the next court day, whichever is earlier, to determine whether detention or shelter care is required.[2] This time limitation may not be extended by the court.[3] A complaint must also be filed within 72 hours of the child's admission.[4]

Regardless of when the detention hearing is held or what the outcome, an alleged or adjudicated unruly child or juvenile traffic offender may generally not be held for more than 24 hours in a detention home.[5]

Ten-day rule. If a decision is made at the detention or shelter care hearing to hold the child, the adjudicatory hearing must be held within 10 days after the complaint is filed.[6] Only upon a showing of good cause may the

---

[10]See also §25:14, Reasonable efforts determination.

[11]Schall v. Martin, 467 U.S. 253, 104 S. Ct. 2403, 81 L. Ed. 2d 207 (1984).

[12]See Katz and Giannelli, Baldwin's Ohio Practice, Criminal Law (2d ed.), Ch 37 (bail and preventive detention).

[Section 19:7]

[1]RC 2151.011(B)(12); Juv. R. 2(K), Juv. R. 2(MM).

[2]RC 2151.314(A); Juv. R. 7(F)(1). The statute does not include the "next court day" provision. For discussion of the detention hearing, see §19:5, Detention hearing.

[3]Juv. R. 18(B). See also Juv. R. 18(A), which indicates that if the 72-hour period *ends* on a Saturday, Sunday, or legal holiday, the detention or shelter care hearing may be extended to the next court day; but an *intermediate* Saturday, Sunday, or legal holiday shall be included in the 72-hour computation.

[4]RC 2151.314(A). Because the nature of the complaint bears on the question of detention, it should be filed prior to the hearing.

[5]RC 2151.312(C)(2), RC 2151.312(C)(3). See 42 U.S.C.A. §5601(A)(12); §19:2, Place of detention.

[6]Juv. R. 29(A). See also RC 2151.28(A)(1). Because RC 2151.314(A) allows up to 72 hours for filing the complaint, the adjudicatory hearing may, in some cases, be held 13 days after the child's admission to the facility.

adjudicatory hearing be continued and detention or shelter care extended.[7]

The Ohio Supreme Court held in *Linger v. Weiss*[8] that a juvenile court does not lose jurisdiction by failing to adhere to the 10-day time limit set forth in Juvenile Rule 29(A).[9] The Court reasoned that since the jurisdiction of the juvenile courts is statutory (RC 2151.23) and the juvenile rules govern procedural matters, the rules could not be construed to affect the juvenile court's jurisdiction. In support of its holding, the Court cited Juvenile Rule 44, which specifically provides that "[t]hese rules shall not be construed to extend or limit the jurisdiction of the juvenile court."

Whereas the *Linger* decision concerned a child in shelter care, an earlier court of appeals decision, *In re Therklidsen*,[10] ruled similarly regarding a child in detention.[11] In that case, the court held that a procedural rule (Juvenile Rule 29(A)) could not confer the right to a discharge for an alleged delinquent if the court failed to comply with the 10-day rule. There must be specific statutory authority for such a right. In contrast, another court of appeals in *State v. Newton*[12] has held that both the 72-hour (Juvenile Rule 7(F)(1)) and 10-day (Juvenile Rule 29(A)) time limits are mandatory rather than directory, so that a child in detention who is not provided a timely detention hearing or adjudicatory hearing is entitled to have the complaint dismissed.[13]

A child who is voluntarily placed in the custody of a children services bureau pending a hearing is in shelter care, but voluntary shelter care placement is not subject to the time limits for detention contained in Juvenile Rules 7 and 29(A).[14]

Ninety-day rule. RC 2151.34, which limits length of detention,[15] provides that a child who is alleged to be or adjudicated a delinquent child may be confined in a place of juvenile detention for a period not to exceed 90 days, during which time a social history and other pertinent studies and material may be prepared to assist the court in its disposition of the case. Although the prohibition in RC 2151.34 against the detention of alleged delinquents beyond 90 days is mandatory,[16] the Eighth District Court of Appeals has twice held that the 90-day limit does not apply if Juvenile Rule 30 bindover

---

[7]Juv. R. 29(A), Juv. R. 18(B); In re Miller, 2002-Ohio-3360, 2002 WL 1400544 (Ohio Ct. App. 11th Dist. Ashtabula County 2002).

[8]Linger v. Weiss, 57 Ohio St. 2d 97, 11 Ohio Op. 3d 281, 386 N.E.2d 1354 (1979).

[9]See also In re Carlos O., 96 Ohio App. 3d 252, 644 N.E.2d 1084 (6th Dist. Wood County 1994); In the Matter of Price, 1981 WL 4645 (Ohio Ct. App. 8th Dist. Cuyahoga County 1981).

[10]In re Therklidsen, 54 Ohio App. 2d 195, 8 Ohio Op. 3d 335, 376 N.E.2d 970 (10th Dist. Franklin County 1977).

[11]See also City of Seven Hills v. Gossick, 1984 WL 3582 (Ohio Ct. App. 8th Dist. Cuyahoga County 1984).

[12]State v. Newton, 1983 WL 6836 (Ohio Ct. App. 6th Dist. Fulton County 1983) (making no reference to either *Linger* or *Therklidsen*).

[13]The court initially held that the dismissal was without prejudice. However, in denying the child's application to reconsider the remedy and dismiss the complaint with prejudice, the court decided that "the facts of the case . . . render it unnecessary to decide that question at this time."

[14]In re Siniard, No. C-78-063 (6th Dist. Ct. App., Lucas, 2-9-79). See also RC 5153.16(A)(2), which authorizes a children services board or job and family services department to enter into voluntary agreements with parents with respect to the custody, care, or placement of their children.

[15]The statute makes no specific reference to shelter care, but it is reasonable to assume that it applies to shelter care as well.

[16]Matter Of: Hester, 1981 WL 3170 (Ohio Ct. App. 10th Dist. Franklin County 1981). Presumably, the 90-day limit would also apply to adjudicated delinquents awaiting the implementation of a final dispositional order.

proceedings are pending against the child.[17] In both cases, the appellate court cited Juvenile Rule 29(A) as justification for continuing detention prior to the holding of an adjudicatory hearing, which hearing may not be conducted until the completion of the bindover proceeding.[18]

§ 19:8 Motions for release

Any party, including the public children services agency and the child's guardian ad litem, may file a motion with the court requesting that the child be released from detention or shelter care.[1] The motion must state the reasons why the child should be released and must recite any changes in the situation of the child or the child's parents, guardian, or custodian since the initial hearing. On filing of the motion, the court must hold another shelter care hearing[2] within 72 hours.[3]

§ 19:9 Bail

Since a child who is alleged to be delinquent or unruly is not charged with a crime, the child is not entitled to bail under Section 9, Article I of the Ohio Constitution.[1] The restrictions on detention and the protection afforded to detained children by the statutes and rules[2] are considered to be an adequate substitute for bail.[3] Nevertheless, a juvenile court may grant bail in its discretion.

SYO cases, however, are different; there is a right to bail.[4]

Children alleged to be delinquent who are held in adult facilities pursuant to RC 2152.26(F)(3)(a) have the same rights to bail as an adult charged with the same offense who is confined in jail pending trial.[5]

§ 19:10 Rights while detained

A child admitted to a detention or shelter care facility has a right to telephone his parents and counsel both immediately and at reasonable times thereafter.[1] The child may be visited at reasonable visiting hours by his parents, adult family members, pastor, and teachers and at any time by his

---

[17]Rivera v. Morris, 1992 WL 877341 (Ohio Ct. App. 8th Dist. 1992); Ezell v. Manual, 1990 WL 746729 (Ohio Ct. App. 8th Dist. Cuyahoga County 1990). In both cases the court denied petitions for writs of habeas corpus.

[18]See § 22:21, Retention of jurisdiction.

[Section 19:8]

[1]RC 2151.314(C); Juv. R. 7(G).

[2]RC 2151.314(C); Juv. R. 7(G).

[3]Juv. R. 7(G).

[Section 19:9]

[1]In re Gillespie, 150 Ohio App. 3d 502, 509, 2002-Ohio-7025, 782 N.E.2d 140 (10th Dist. Franklin County 2002) ("[I]t is also widely held that 'a juvenile has no absolute constitutional right to bail.'") (quoting Kelly). State ex rel. Peaks v. Allaman, 51 Ohio Op. 321, 66 Ohio L. Abs. 403, 115 N.E.2d 849 (Ct. App. 2d Dist. Montgomery County 1952); In re Kelly, 1999 WL 132862 (Ohio Ct. App. 10th Dist. Franklin County 1999). For discussion of the right to bail pending appeal, see § 34:7, Appeal bond. For discussion of the right to bail subsequent to a transfer for criminal prosecution, see § 22:22, Transfer of jurisdiction.

[2]RC 2151.31 to RC 2151.314; Juv. R. 7.

[3]See Fulwood v. Stone, 394 F.2d 939 (D.C. Cir. 1967). Although the United States Supreme Court has not ruled specifically on this issue, there is dicta in both Application of Gault, 387 U.S. 1, 87 S. Ct. 1428, 18 L. Ed. 2d 527 (1967), and Kent v. U.S., 383 U.S. 541, 86 S. Ct. 1045, 16 L. Ed. 2d 84 (1966), which states that children have no right to bail.

[4]RC 2152.13(D)(2). See § 5:9, Procedural rights.

[5]RC 2152.26(F)(3)(b).

[Section 19:10]

[1]Juv. R. 7(E)(2), Juv. R. 7(J).

attorney.[2]

§ 19:11   Detention facilities

During the school year, when possible, school-age children must be provided with an educational program comparable to what they would receive in public schools, with competent, trained staff.[1]

In order to control health problems, the supervisor of a shelter or detention facility may provide for a physical examination of a child placed therein.[2]

Cross References
§ 14:3, Ch 20, Ch 35
Research References
Giannelli and Snyder, Baldwin's Ohio Practice, Evidence (2d ed.) § 101.10
Carlin, Baldwin's Ohio Practice, Merrick-Rippner Probate Law (6th ed.), Chs 104, 107

§ 19:12   Closure of hearing

In *State ex rel. Dispatch Co. v. Louden*,[1] the juvenile court closed the detention hearing. The Ohio Supreme Court reversed, finding that the judge abused his discretion by barring the press without any motion for closure, a hearing on the issue, or the required findings. The Court commented: "[The judge] did not hear evidence and argument on the issue of closing the detention hearing and did not make the requisite findings before adjudicating the issue in an informal, off-the-record procedure. In addition, no party to the delinquency proceeding sought closure of the detention hearing. In the absence of the foregoing, [the judge's] closure of the detention hearing was unjustified and constituted 'little more than [his] personal predilections.' "[2]

Juvenile Rule 27 was amended in 2001 in order to set forth a standard for determining closure in juvenile hearings. With the exception of SYO hearings (which are open to the public),[3] the court may exclude the general public from a hearing but may not exclude persons with a direct interest in the case or persons who demonstrate, at a hearing, a countervailing right to be present.[4]

---

[2]Juv. R. 7(E)(3)(b), Juv. R. 7(J); RC 2151.352.

[Section 19:11]

[1]RC 2152.42(C). The child's school district, as determined by the court, must pay the cost of educating the child based on the per capita cost of the educational facility within the detention home. See RC 2151.357.

[2]Juv. R. 7(I). However, medical treatment is authorized only upon court order. Juv. R. 13.

[Section 19:12]

[1]State ex rel. Dispatch Printing Co. v. Louden, 91 Ohio St. 3d 61, 2001-Ohio-268, 741 N.E.2d 517 (2001).

[2]State ex rel. Dispatch Printing Co. v. Louden, 91 Ohio St. 3d 61, 65, 2001-Ohio-268, 741 N.E.2d 517 (2001) (citations omitted). See also § 23:11, Public trials; gag orders.

[3]RC 2152.13(D)(1).

[4]See also Staff Note (2001) ("The rule seeks to conform to the Supreme Court's ruling in State ex rel. Plain Dealer Publishing Co. v. Geauga Cty. Court of Common Pleas, Juv. Div., 90 Ohio St. 3d 79, 2000-Ohio-35, 734 N.E.2d 1214 (2000).").

Chapter 20

Temporary Orders Pending Hearing

> **KeyCite®:** Cases and other legal materials listed in KeyCite Scope can be researched through West's KeyCite service on Westlaw®. Use KeyCite to check citations for form, parallel references, prior and later history, and comprehensive citator information, including citations to other decisions and secondary materials.

§ 20:1   Temporary orders pending hearing—Introduction
§ 20:2   Temporary care orders
§ 20:3   Emergency medical orders
§ 20:4   Required hearings
§ 20:5   Notice of hearing
§ 20:6   Time requirements

§ 20:1   Temporary orders pending hearing—Introduction

This chapter discusses the authority of the juvenile court to enter temporary pre-hearing orders with respect to a child under the court's jurisdiction, as well as orders controlling the conduct of other persons in order to protect a child.

§ 20:2   Temporary care orders

Before a hearing is held on a complaint, the juvenile court is authorized to make such temporary orders as may be necessary, both with respect to the care and custody of a child who is the subject of the complaint and the conduct of others toward that child.[1] For example, an emergency custody order was upheld where the evidence showed that the children were dirty, undernourished, and infected.[2]

RC 2151.33 and Juvenile Rule 13(B) provide that a juvenile court, prior to the final disposition of an abuse, neglect, or dependency case, and on the court's own motion or the oral or written motion of a party,[3] may issue any of the following temporary orders to protect the best interests of the child:

   (1) An order granting temporary child custody to a particular party;[4]
   (2) An order to take the child into custody pending the outcome of the adjudicatory and dispositional hearing;[5]
   (3) An order granting, limiting, or eliminating visitation rights;
   (4) An order requiring a party to vacate a residence that will be lawfully occupied by the child;

[Section 20:2]

[1]RC 2151.33(A); Juv. R. 13(A), Juv. R. 13(B). Notwithstanding these provisions, a county job and family services department or child services board is mandated to provide emergency care for any child it considers to be in need of such care, without agreement of the parents or commitment of the child (RC 5153.16(A)(7)). See also RC 2151.421(E).

[2]In re Douglas, 11 Ohio Op. 2d 340, 82 Ohio L. Abs. 170, 164 N.E.2d 475 (Juv. Ct. 1959).

[3]See RC 2151.33(C) for the notice requirements of the motion.

[4]See In re Bowman, 101 Ohio App. 3d 599, 656 N.E.2d 355 (9th Dist. Summit County 1995).

[5]A court issuing this type of order must comply with RC 2151.419. See § 25:14, Reasonable efforts determination.

(5) An order requiring a party to attend an appropriate counseling program that is reasonably available to that party; or

(6) Any other order that restrains or otherwise controls the conduct of any party that would not be in the child's best interest.[6]

Neither RC 2151.33 nor Juvenile Rule 13 requires the court to first find a parent unfit before placing an alleged dependent child in the temporary custody of someone other than a parent, since the determination of parental fitness is to be made at the adjudicatory hearing.[7]

Pending the outcome of the adjudicatory and dispositional hearings, the court may not issue an order granting temporary custody of a child to a public children services agency or private child-placing agency unless the court determines and specifically states in the order that the continued residence of the child in his current home will be contrary to his best interest and welfare.[8]

Moreover, any agency that receives temporary custody of a child pursuant to RC 2151.33 is required to maintain in the child's case record written documentation that it has placed the child, to the extent that it is consistent with the best interest, welfare, and special needs of the child, in the most family-like setting available and in close proximity to the home of the parents, custodian, or guardian of the child.[9]

A temporary custody order issued by a juvenile court pursuant to Juvenile Rule 13 or Juvenile Rule 29 is not a dispositional order under Juvenile Rule 34. Thus, it neither constitutes a final appealable order nor makes a dispositional hearing conducted thereafter a nullity.[10]

§ 20:3 Emergency medical orders

The court's authority to make temporary orders extends to emergency medical and surgical treatment for a child upon the certification of one or more reputable practicing physicians.[1] Although such treatment must appear to be "immediately necessary" for the child,[2] it has been held that the emergency need not be absolute; it is enough that the emergency might arise at any minute.[3]

§ 20:4 Required hearings

If a judge or magistrate issues an ex parte emergency order for taking an

---

[6]RC 2151.33(B); Juv. R. 13(B)(2); In re F.M., 2002-Ohio-3900, 2002 WL 1767396 (Ohio Ct. App. 8th Dist. Cuyahoga County 2002).

[7]Mary Beth v. Howard, 1995 WL 601110 (Ohio Ct. App. 8th Dist. Cuyahoga County 1995).

[8]RC 2151.33(E). See also 42 U.S.C.A. § 672.

[9]RC 2151.33(F). See also 42 U.S.C.A. § 675.

[10]Wayne, 1981 WL 3652 (Ohio Ct. App. 10th Dist. Franklin County 1981); Morrison v. Morrison, 45 Ohio App. 2d 299, 74 Ohio Op. 2d 441, 344 N.E.2d 144 (9th Dist. Summit County 1973).

[Section 20:3]
[1]RC 2151.33(A); Juv. R. 13(C). 1951 OAG 689. For a discussion of the court's right to authorize medical or surgical care for a child, despite religious objections of the parents, see § 9:7, Neglect—Subsistence, education & medical care.

[2]RC 2151.33(A); Juv. R. 13(C). 1951 OAG 689. For a discussion of the court's right to authorize medical or surgical care for a child, despite religious objections of the parents, see § 9:7, Neglect—Subsistence, education & medical care.

[3]In re Clark, 21 Ohio Op. 2d 86, 90 Ohio L. Abs. 21, 185 N.E.2d 128 (C.P. 1962). RC 2151.33(A) further provides that the court may order the parents, guardian, or custodian, if financially able, to reimburse the court for expenses involved in providing such treatment and enforce such order through contempt. If the child is a nonresident of the county and the expense cannot be recovered from the parent, guardian, or custodian, the board of county commissioners of the county in which the child has a legal settlement must reimburse the court for the reasonable cost of such treatment.

alleged abused, neglected, or dependent child into custody,[1] the court must conduct a hearing to determine whether probable cause for the order exists. If the court determines that probable cause does not exist, the child must be released to the custody of the child's parents, guardian, or custodian.[2]

If the court determines that probable cause does exist, the court must (1) ensure that a complaint is or has been filed, (2) make a reasonable efforts determination,[3] and (3) conduct a shelter care hearing.[4] Furthermore, if the court determines that there is probable cause that the child is abused, the court may: (1) on motion, issue reasonable protective orders concerning interviewing or deposing the child; (2) order the child's testimony be videotaped for preservation for possible use in any other proceedings in the case; or (3) set any additional conditions with respect to the child or the case that are in the child's best interest.[5]

§ 20:5   Notice of hearing

Wherever possible, the court must provide notice and an opportunity for a hearing prior to issuing the temporary or emergency order.[1] If the record does not reflect circumstances justifying an ex parte proceeding, the court may not issue a temporary custody order without providing notice and an opportunity for a hearing to the child's parents.[2]

If, however, it appears to the court that the interest and welfare of the child require immediate action, the court may proceed summarily without notice.[3] After issuing an ex parte order, the court must then give notice of the action it has taken to the parties and any other affected person and must provide them an opportunity for a hearing concerning the continuing effects of the order.[4]

§ 20:6   Time requirements

If the order was made ex parte in an abuse, neglect, or dependency proceeding, a hearing to review the order must be conducted within 72 hours hours after issuance or before the end of the next business day, whichever occurs first.[1]

If the court does not grant an ex parte order pursuant to the motion, the court must hold a shelter care hearing on the motion within 10 days after the motion is filed.[2] It has been held that if an ex parte emergency custody order is not requested or obtained, the time requirements of RC 2151.31(D) and (E) do not apply; instead, the child must be brought before the court

---

[Section 20:4]

[1]RC 2151.31(D) authorizes magistrates to grant by telephone an ex parte emergency order authorizing the taking of a child into custody. This is in conflict with Juv. R. 40 and RC 2151.16, which provide that magistrates may make only findings and recommendations, not court orders. Chill, Burden of Proof Begone: the Pernicious Effect of Emergency Removal in Child Protective Proceedings, 41 Fam. Ct. Rev. 457 (2003).

[2]RC 2151.31(E); Juv. R. 6(B). See Abused, Neglected, or Dependent Child Dispositions Ch 30.

[3]RC 2151.419. See also § 25:14, Reasonable efforts determination.

[4]RC 2151.31(E).

[5]RC 2151.31(F); Juv. R. 13(F).

[Section 20:5]

[1]RC 2151.33(D); Juv. R. 13(E).

[2]Williams v. Williams, 44 Ohio St. 2d 28, 73 Ohio Op. 2d 121, 336 N.E.2d 426 (1975).

[3]Juv. R. 13(D); RC 2151.33(D).

[4]Juv. R. 13(E); RC 2151.33(D).

[Section 20:6]

[1]RC 2151.33(D); Juv. R. 13(B)(3). These provisions also contain the notice requirements for the hearing.

[2]RC 2151.33(D); Juv. R. 13(B)(5).

with all reasonable speed under RC 2151.31(A)(2).[3]

The Ohio Supreme Court held in *Linger v. Weiss*[4] that where almost three years elapses between the time of an emergency shelter care order under Juvenile Rule 13 and the adjudicatory hearing, the juvenile court does not lose jurisdiction over the matter of the alleged neglected child for failing to adhere to the time limits mandated by Juvenile Rule 29(A).[5] However, this case was decided prior to the amendments of RC 2151.28(A)(2) and (B)(3),[6] which establish strict time frames for conducting the adjudicatory and dispositional hearings. The failure of a court to hold a dispositional hearing for an abused, neglected, or dependent child within 90 days after the date on which the complaint was filed requires that the complaint be dismissed without prejudice.[7]

Cross References
§ 9:6, § 30:2
Research References
Carlin, Baldwin's Ohio Practice, Merrick-Rippner Probate Law (6th ed.), Ch 107

---

[3]Portzer v. Cuyahoga County Dept. of Human Services, 1995 WL 350096 (Ohio Ct. App. 8th Dist. Cuyahoga County 1995).

[4]Linger v. Weiss, 57 Ohio St. 2d 97, 11 Ohio Op. 3d 281, 386 N.E.2d 1354 (1979).

[5]In this case, the juvenile court did not conduct the adjudicatory hearing until after a complaint for a writ of habeas corpus had been filed in the court of appeals. (In a footnote, the Supreme Court mentioned that the juvenile court had found the child to be neglected.) This case was appealed to the Licking County Court of Appeals on the basis that the adjudicatory hearing was not timely held. The court of appeals rejected that argument on the ground that the Supreme Court's footnote impliedly looked with favor upon the adjudication. See In re Linger, No. CA-2556 (5th Dist. Ct. App., Licking, 7-12-79). See also In re Caldwell, No. 420 (7th Dist. Ct. App., Carroll, 12-13-79), where the court of appeals held that a three-year delay in conducting an adjudicatory hearing, following an order granting emergency custody to a county human (job and family) services department, did not constitute prejudicial error and did not deprive the court of jurisdiction over an alleged dependent child.

[6]1988 S.B. 89, eff. 1-1-89.

[7]RC 2151.35(B)(1). See § 30:4, Dispositional alternatives for abuse, neglect or dependency.

Chapter 21

Discovery

> **KeyCite®:** Cases and other legal materials listed in KeyCite Scope can be researched through West's KeyCite service on Westlaw®. Use KeyCite to check citations for form, parallel references, prior and later history, and comprehensive citator information, including citations to other decisions and secondary materials.

§ 21:1   Discovery—Introduction
§ 21:2   Scope of discovery—Rule 24
§ 21:3   Discovery procedure—Rule 24
§ 21:4   Depositions
§ 21:5   Subpoenas
§ 21:6   Social history report
§ 21:7   Court records
§ 21:8   Victim impact statement

§ 21:1   Discovery—Introduction

This chapter discusses the parameters of a party's right to secure information from adverse parties as well as from the court and other parties. The discovery issues in bindover cases are discussed in the chapter on transfer.[1]

§ 21:2   Scope of discovery—Rule 24

Juvenile Rule 24 provides the means by which a party may discover material, to the extent that it is not privileged, which is in the possession of an adverse party. This includes the right to inspect, copy, or photograph (1) the names and addresses of each witness;[1] (2) copies of any written statements made by any party or witness;[2] (3) transcriptions, recordings, and summaries of any oral statements of any party or witness, except the work product of counsel;[3] (4) scientific and other reports, photographs, and physical evidence which a party intends to introduce at a hearing; and (5) except in delinquency and unruly proceedings, other evidence favorable to the requesting party and relevant to the subject matter involved in the action. In delinquency and unruly proceedings, the prosecuting attorney must disclose to the respondent's counsel all evidence, known or that may become known to the prosecuting attorney, favorable to the respondent and material either to guilt or punishment.[4]

A juvenile court is vested with broad discretion when considering matters

---

[Section 21:1]
 [1]See § 22:15, Access to reports & discovery.

[Section 21:2]
 [1]Juv. R. 24(A).

 [2]Juv. R. 24(A)(2). This rule is broader than Crim. R. 16, which does not permit discovery of witnesses' statements.

 [3]Juv. R. 24(A)(3).

 [4]Juv. R. 24(A)(1) to Juv. R. 24(A)(6). The terms "guilt" and "punishment" are taken from Crim. R. 16(B)(1)(f), and ordinarily are not used in delinquency and unruly proceedings.

relating to discovery.[5] Its decisions are reviewed by an appellate court under an abuse of discretion standard.[6]

A party does not bear a burden to produce documents which that party does not possess.[7] Thus, a county prosecutor is not responsible for producing documents in the possession of a department of job and family services, even though both are governmental agencies that sometimes work in concert.[8] As one court noted, "The rule does not require the responding party to gather all relevant evidence from other sources and hand it over to the requesting party; it imposes no onus on the prosecutor's office to conduct an investigation in appellant's behalf or make his case for him."[9]

Police reports. Ohio law is not clear on the issue of whether Juvenile Rule 24 permits discovery of police reports in delinquency proceedings. In *In re Hunter*,[10] an appellate court held that it is not an abuse of discretion for a juvenile court to deny the child an opportunity to view police reports. However, in another case the same court held that Juvenile Rule 24(A) unequivocally entitles the child's counsel to the production of the oral statement of a witness, where four requests and two court orders for the production of the statement had been ignored by the prosecutor.[11] Moreover, the court determined that there is no requirement that the statement be signed by the witness nor that it be taken verbatim.[12]

This issue is also governed by statutory law. RC 2151.352 provides that any report concerning a child who is taken into custody, which is used in any hearing and is pertinent thereto, must for good cause shown be made available to any attorney representing the child or parents, on written request prior to the hearing.[13]

Caseworker's file. In neglect, dependency, and abuse proceedings initiated by a county job and family services department, several Ohio courts have determined that a parent's attorney has a right to inspect or copy a caseworker's file, despite claims of work product and privilege.[14] RC 5153.17 provides, "Such records shall be confidential, but shall be open to inspection by the (children services) agency, the director of the county department of human services, and by any other persons, upon the written permission of

---

[5]In re Johnson, 61 Ohio App. 3d 544, 573 N.E.2d 184 (8th Dist. Cuyahoga County 1989).

[6]State v. Metz, 1997 WL 305220 (Ohio Ct. App. 4th Dist. Washington County 1997); State v. Crumedy, 1997 WL 37790 (Ohio Ct. App. 8th Dist. Cuyahoga County 1997).

[7]Matter of Bolser, 1996 WL 761216 (Ohio Ct. App. 11th Dist. Geauga County 1996).

[8]Matter of Bolser, 1996 WL 761216 (Ohio Ct. App. 11th Dist. Geauga County 1996). But see RC 305.14, which provides that the prosecuting attorney is the statutory counsel for county agencies.

[9]In re Henderson, 1997 WL 752633, at *3 (Ohio Ct. App. 11th Dist. Lake County 1997).

[10]In Re: Hunter, 1984 WL 5445 (Ohio Ct. App. 8th Dist. Cuyahoga County 1984).

[11]In re Johnson, 61 Ohio App. 3d 544, 573 N.E.2d 184 (8th Dist. Cuyahoga County 1989). See also State v. Workman, 14 Ohio App. 3d 385, 471 N.E.2d 853 (8th Dist. Cuyahoga County 1984) (holding that under Crim. R. 16(B) an oral statement given to the police by a witness is not discoverable in criminal cases).

[12]In re Johnson, 61 Ohio App. 3d 544, 573 N.E.2d 184 (8th Dist. Cuyahoga County 1989).

[13]See also RC 2151.14(D), which permits access to a variety of records in connection with the disposition of a child found to be delinquent, unruly, or a juvenile traffic offender. See § 25:6, Conduct of hearing.

[14]In re Barger, 1996 WL 647631 (Ohio Ct. App. 2d Dist. Montgomery County 1996); In re Trumbull County Children Services Bd., 32 Ohio Misc. 2d 11, 513 N.E.2d 360 (C.P. 1986); In re Barzak, 24 Ohio App. 3d 180, 493 N.E.2d 1011 (11th Dist. Trumbull County 1985); Matter of Evans, 1987 WL 26739 (Ohio Ct. App. 2d Dist. Miami County 1987); Matter of Strickland, 1987 WL 13057 (Ohio Ct. App. 12th Dist. Warren County 1987). These cases were decided prior to the 1994 amendment to Juv. R. 24(A), which permits discovery of material to the extent that it is not privileged.

the executive secretary."[15] The Ohio Attorney General has ruled[16] that pursuant to RC 5153.17, the executive secretary may grant written permission for access for good cause, which may be shown to exist where the best interests of the child require the release of the information or where denial of due process to one accused of child abuse or neglect would result from a refusal to grant access.[17]

Child abuse investigations. Records of child abuse and neglect investigations under RC 2151.421(H)(1) and RC 5153.17 are not "public records" within the meaning of RC 149.43.[18] In comparing RC 2151.421(H)(1) and RC 5153.17, an appellate court has noted that the former statute only references the "reports" which are made under RC 2151.421(A) and (B), and that "reports" is limited in scope and does not encompass any report made by anyone regarding the subject child.[19] On the other hand, RC 5153.17 is broader, so that it should be possible "to temper the sweeping authority of the latter statute with the specifics of the former and sort the file contents accordingly."[20] In this respect, appellate courts have held that the party requesting discovery of these confidential files is entitled to an in camera review by the trial court, with the final decision regarding discovery falling within the sound discretion of the court.[21]

It has been held that a social worker may not be compelled to reveal the name of the person who reported an instance of child abuse since such information is confidential under RC 2151.421.[22] Moreover, foster parents were properly denied the right to inspect a child abuse investigation report where they could not establish that their right to a fair trial was at stake.[23]

§ 21:3 Discovery procedure—Rule 24

Discovery requests. In order to obtain discovery, a party must serve a written request upon the opposing party.[1] If the opposing party is represented by an attorney, the request must be served upon the attorney, unless service is ordered by the court upon the party.[2] Requests for discovery must also be filed with the court simultaneously with or immediately after service.[3]

Continuing duty to disclose. Unlike Criminal Rule 16, Juvenile Rule 24 contains no requirement that disclosures be updated. Therefore, a party seeking current information must either repeat the request or move for an

---

[15]See also RC 2151.141, which governs access to certain records where an abuse, neglect, or dependency complaint has been filed, and the person requesting access is investigating the case, has custody of the child, is preparing a social history, or is providing services for the child.

[16]OAG 91-003, 1991 WL 576919.

[17]OAG 91-003, 1991 WL 576919.

[18]OAG 91-003, 1991 WL 576919.

[19]Sharpe v. Sharpe, 85 Ohio App. 3d 638, 620 N.E.2d 916 (11th Dist. Lake County 1993).

[20]Sharpe v. Sharpe, 85 Ohio App. 3d 638, 644, 620 N.E.2d 916 (11th Dist. Lake County 1993).

[21]In re Barzak, 24 Ohio App. 3d 180, 493 N.E.2d 1011 (11th Dist. Trumbull County 1985); In re Henderson, 1997 WL 752633 (Ohio Ct. App. 11th Dist. Lake County 1997).

[22]In re Hicks, No. H-78-7 (6th Dist. Ct. App., Huron, 11-17-78). See also Pennsylvania v. Ritchie, 480 U.S. 39, 107 S. Ct. 989, 94 L. Ed. 2d 40, 22 Fed. R. Evid. Serv. 1 (1987), holding that although a defendant has a due process right to access to child protection agency records in a criminal child abuse case, the court may first review these records in camera and remove information not relevant to the defense, including the identity of the reporter.

[23]State ex rel. Renfro v. Cuyahoga County Dept. of Human Services, 54 Ohio St. 3d 25, 560 N.E.2d 230 (1990).

[Section 21:3]

[1]Juv. R. 24(A).

[2]Juv. R. 20(A), Juv. R. 20(B). The method of service is governed by Civ. R. 5(B).

[3]Juv. R. 20(C).

order compelling discovery pursuant to Juvenile Rule 24(B).[4]

Discovery motions. If the request is refused or the material is not promptly produced, application may be made to the court for a discovery order, by means of a motion certifying that a request has been made and refused.[5] The court has several options in ruling on the motion. It may order the party to furnish the requested information and may make such discovery reciprocal for all parties, including the party requesting discovery.[6]

The court may also deny or limit discovery upon a showing that discovery would jeopardize the safety of a party, witness, or confidential informant, result in perjured evidence, endanger the existence of physical evidence, violate a privileged communication, or impede the criminal prosecution of a child as an adult in bindover proceedings or of an adult charged with an offense arising from the same transaction or occurrence.[7] Based upon this rule, a trial court has held that in a preliminary hearing in bindover proceedings, the state is not required to provide as full discovery as that required for delinquency adjudicatory hearings.[8] This principle is particularly applicable where the requested material, such as witness statements, would be subject to disclosure under Juvenile Rule 24 but not under Criminal Rule 16.[9]

Time requirement. Motions for discovery must be heard before the adjudicatory hearing, though not necessarily on a separate date.[10] They must be filed with the court seven days prior to hearing or 10 days after the appearance of counsel, whichever is earlier. The court, however, may extend the time in the interest of justice.[11] The failure to file a motion for discovery estops a party from thereafter raising the issue on appeal.[12]

Sanctions. If a party fails to comply with a court order for discovery, the court may grant a continuance, prohibit the party from introducing the material in evidence, or make other appropriate orders.[13] However, it is necessary that the party seeking discovery request the proper order from the court in order to obtain such remedies.[14] Where discovery is not provided until immediately before the adjudicatory hearing and the party who requested it agrees to proceed with the hearing after reviewing the material, that party may not claim on appeal that he was denied discovery.[15] Similarly, based on the broad discretion of a juvenile court to fashion an appropriate response to a party's failure to comply with a discovery order, it has been held that where the requested test results were provided at the adjudicatory hearing and the child's counsel was afforded a full opportunity to cross-examine the state's witnesses with respect to the results, it was neither an abuse of discretion nor a deprivation of the child's due process rights for the court to

---

[4]In re Gilbert, 1987 WL 17709 (Ohio Ct. App. 12th Dist. Butler County 1987).

[5]Juv. R. 24(B). Presumably, the same procedure applies if the request is simply not acted upon, though not technically refused. Juv. R. 24(A) requires the requested information to be produced "forthwith."

[6]Juv. R. 24(B). Presumably, the "work product" exception of Juv. R. 24(A)(3) applies to reciprocal discovery.

[7]Juv. R. 24(B). Presumably, the "work product" exception of Juv. R. 24(A)(3) applies to reciprocal discovery.

[8]In re Doss, 65 Ohio Misc. 2d 8, 640 N.E.2d 618 (C.P. 1994).

[9]State v. Metz, 1997 WL 305220 (Ohio Ct. App. 4th Dist. Washington County 1997).

[10]Juv. R. 22(D)(4).

[11]Juv. R. 22(E).

[12]State v. Lee, 1983 WL 5753 (Ohio Ct. App. 8th Dist. Cuyahoga County 1983). Although this was a juvenile delinquency case, the decision was based on Crim. R. 16(B), the adult criminal court counterpart to Juv. R. 24(B).

[13]Juv. R. 24(C).

[14]In re Hester, 3 Ohio App. 3d 458, 446 N.E.2d 202 (10th Dist. Franklin County 1982). See also In re Bernstein, Nos. 33531, 33532 (8th Dist. Ct. App., Cuyahoga, 1-2-75); In re Johnson, 61 Ohio App. 3d 544, 573 N.E.2d 184 (8th Dist. Cuyahoga County 1989).

[15]In re Wyrock, No. 41827 (8th Dist. Ct. App., Cuyahoga, 10-23-80).

refuse to order a new trial.[16]

It has been held that discovery violations in delinquency proceedings may be interpreted on analysis of Criminal Rule 16.[17] Thus, where the prosecution fails to comply with discovery and the record does not demonstrate (1) that the failure was willful, (2) that foreknowledge of the material would have benefited the accused in preparation of a defense, or (3) that the accused was prejudiced by admission of the material, it is not an abuse of discretion for the court to permit such evidence to be admitted.[18]

§ 21:4 Depositions

An additional device for obtaining discovery is the deposition. Authority to take the deposition of a party or other person may be granted by the court upon good cause shown and upon such conditions as the court may fix.[1] A juvenile court has discretion "to allow or disallow depositions and to control the manner and terms under which depositions are taken."[2]

Child victims. In any proceeding in which a child is charged with certain delinquent sex offenses, and the alleged victim was a child under age 11 when the complaint was filed, the testimony of the child victim may be taken by deposition.[3] If such a deposition is taken, the alleged delinquent has the right to attend the deposition, to be represented by counsel, and to cross-examine the child victim. If the deposition of a child victim is admitted as evidence in the delinquency proceeding, the child victim shall not be required to testify in person at the proceeding.[4] Under certain circumstances, the deposition of the child victim may be videotaped.[5]

In child abuse proceedings, the court may order that the testimony of the alleged abused child be taken by deposition in the presence of a judge or magistrate. On the motion of a party, or in its own discretion, the court may order that the deposition be videotaped. All or part of the deposition is admissible in evidence where all of the following apply:

    (1) It is filed with the clerk;

    (2) Counsel for all parties had an opportunity and similar motive to develop the testimony by examination; and

    (3) The judge or magistrate determines there is reasonable cause to believe that if the child were to testify at the hearing, the child would experience emotional trauma.[6]

§ 21:5 Subpoenas

The issuance of a subpoena may be used to gain discovery of certain documents or tangible things.[1] However, the law provides protection for persons subject to a subpoena to avoid imposing an undue burden or expense, or to

---

[16]Matter of Schroder, 1988 WL 100632 (Ohio Ct. App. 12th Dist. Brown County 1988).

[17]State v. Lee, 1983 WL 5753 (Ohio Ct. App. 8th Dist. Cuyahoga County 1983).

[18]In re Washington, 1996 WL 631105 (Ohio Ct. App. 8th Dist. Cuyahoga County 1996).

[Section 21:4]

[1]Juv. R. 25.

[2]In re Vaughn, 1990 WL 116936, at *6 (Ohio Ct. App. 12th Dist. Butler County 1990).

[3]RC 2151.3511(A)(1); In re Burchfield, 51 Ohio App. 3d 148, 555 N.E.2d 325 (4th Dist. Athens County 1988).

[4]RC 2151.3511(A)(1); In re Burchfield, 51 Ohio App. 3d 148, 555 N.E.2d 325 (4th Dist. Athens County 1988).

[5]RC 2151.3511(A)(2).

[6]RC 2151.35(G); Juv. R. 27(B)(3).

[Section 21:5]

[1]Juv. R. 17.

prevent divulging privileged or otherwise protected matter.[2]

For instance, a juvenile court was held to have properly quashed subpoenas received only six days before the individuals were to testify without prior notice of the hearing date, where the individuals would have had to reschedule numerous professional business appointments, and where the party issuing the subpoenas had failed to demonstrate a substantial need for the witnesses' testimony and had not offered the witnesses any compensation for their time.[3]

§ 21:6 Social history report

In addition to providing for the discovery of material in the possession of another party (Juvenile Rule 24), the law permits parties to inspect social history information in the possession of the court.[1] As a general rule, a social history of the child and the child's family may not be ordered or utilized by the court until there has been an admission or adjudication that the child is neglected, dependent, abused, delinquent, unruly, or a juvenile traffic offender.[2]

However, a social history or physical or mental examination may be ordered or utilized at any time after a complaint is filed, under any of the following limited circumstances: (1) upon the request of the party concerning whom it is to be made; (2) where transfer of the child for criminal prosecution[3] is in issue; (3) where the history is necessary to clarify a material allegation of a neglect, dependency, or abuse complaint; (4) where a party's legal responsibility for his acts or his competence to participate in the proceedings is an issue; (5) where a physical or mental examination is required to determine the need for emergency medical care under Juvenile Rule 13;[4] or (6) where the supervisor of a shelter or detention facility authorizes the physical examination of a child placed therein pursuant to Juvenile Rule 7(I).[5]

The right to inspect a social history or physical or mental examination report arises at a reasonable time before any hearing at which it is to be utilized.[6] However, this right is more limited and subject to greater restriction than the discovery rights provided by Juvenile Rule 24. While Juvenile Rule 24 permits discovery by all parties and allows inspection, copying, or photographing, Juvenile Rule 32 limits discovery to inspection, and then only by counsel.[7]

Upon a showing of good cause, the court may deny or limit the scope of inspection to specified portions of the history or report and may order that all

---

[2]Juv. R. 17(D), Juv. R. 17(G).

[3]In Matter of N.B., 1996 WL 174546 (Ohio Ct. App. 12th Dist. Butler County 1996).

[Section 21:6]

[1]Juv. R. 32. See also RC 2151.14, RC 2151.141, RC 2151.352.

[2]Juv. R. 32(B). For a discussion of the use of a social history for dispositional purposes, see § 25:6, Conduct of hearing. For a discussion of the use of a social history at the adjudicatory hearing, see § 23:16, Evidence—Hearsay.

[3]RC 2152.12(C); RC 2151.04; Juv. R. 30. See § 22:15, Access to reports & discovery.

[4]See Temporary Orders Pending Hearing Ch 20.

[5]Juv. R. 32(A). In a permanent custody case, In re Green, 18 Ohio App. 3d 43, 480 N.E.2d 492 (2d Dist. Montgomery County 1984), it was held that a juvenile court's consideration of a psychological evaluation of a mother did not violate her right as an indigent parent under the Due Process and Equal Protection Clauses, where the evaluation was requested by the mother pursuant to Juvenile Rule 32(A) and was understood to be for the purpose of assisting the juvenile court and not solely for the mother's defense.

[6]Juv. R. 32(C). See also § 35:2, Confidentiality requirement.

[7]In re Lawson, 98 Ohio App. 3d 456, 648 N.E.2d 889 (10th Dist. Franklin County 1994).

or part of its contents not be disclosed to specified persons.[8] If the court denies or limits inspection, the reasons constituting "good cause" must be stated to counsel.[9]

§21:7 Court records

The Attorney General has ruled that under RC 1347.08 a juvenile court must permit a juvenile or a duly authorized attorney who represents the juvenile to inspect court records pertaining to the juvenile unless the records are exempt under (1) RC 1347.04(A)(1)(e) (investigatory material compiled for law enforcement purposes), (2) RC 1347.08(C) (certain medical, psychiatric, or psychological information), or (3) RC 1347.08(E)(2) (confidential law enforcement investigatory records or trial preparation records).[1]

§21:8 Victim impact statement

Although a victim impact statement is confidential and is not a public record, the court may furnish copies of the statement to an adjudicated delinquent child or the child's counsel and the prosecuting attorney. The copies of the statement must be returned to the court immediately following an order of disposition.[1]

Cross References
§ 22:15, § 23:16
Research References
Giannelli and Snyder, Baldwin's Ohio Practice, Evidence (2d ed.) §§ 501.4, 501.9, 501.12
Katz and Giannelli, Baldwin's Ohio Practice, Criminal Law (2d ed.), Ch 34
Carlin, Baldwin's Ohio Practice, Merrick-Rippner Probate Law (6th ed.), Ch 107

[8]Juv. R. 32(C). The constitutionality of these restrictions was considered in J.P. v. DeSanti, No. C78-697 (N.D. Ohio, 12-18-78). Although a United States court of appeals ultimately reversed the decision, partly on the basis that the district court should have abstained from deciding those claims, J. P. v. DeSanti, 653 F.2d 1080 (6th Cir. 1981), the following language from the district court's opinion and order is worth noting:

Insofar as Rule 32(C) . . . authorizes the Juvenile Court to limit or deny access by a juvenile, his parents or guardian, or his legal counsel to any social history or family record concerning such juvenile prepared pursuant to Rule 32 prior to the juvenile's adjudicatory hearing, Rule 32(C) is inconsistent with the requirements of the Fifth, Sixth, and Fourteenth Amendments to the United States Constitution and the pronouncements of the Supreme Court in *Kent v. United States* and *In re Gault*, . . . and is to that extent hereby declared to be unconstitutional. Accordingly, any (such) social history or family record . . . shall be made available by the (court) to the juvenile concerned, his parents or guardian, and his legal counsel for inspection and copying upon written request not less than three days prior to the hearing.

[9]Juv. R. 32(C).

[Section 21:7]
[1]OAG 84-077. See RC 2152.19(D)(3) for provisions on discovery of victim impact statements.

[Section 21:8]
[1]RC 2152.19(D)(3).

Chapter 22

Transfer of Jurisdiction

> **KeyCite®:** Cases and other legal materials listed in KeyCite Scope can be researched through West's KeyCite service on Westlaw®. Use KeyCite to check citations for form, parallel references, prior and later history, and comprehensive citator information, including citations to other decisions and secondary materials.

§ 22:1   Transfer of jurisdiction—Introduction
§ 22:2   Rationale for transfer
§ 22:3   Constitutional issues
§ 22:4   Improper transfer—Lack of jurisdiction
§ 22:5   Transfer age requirement
§ 22:6   Probable cause requirement
§ 22:7   Mandatory transfer
§ 22:8   Discretionary transfer
§ 22:9   Amenability hearing procedures
§ 22:10   Mental examination
§ 22:11   Right to counsel
§ 22:12   Notice
§ 22:13   Rules of evidence
§ 22:14   Self-incrimination
§ 22:15   Access to reports & discovery
§ 22:16   Right to present evidence
§ 22:17   Statement of reasons
§ 22:18   Right to a transcript
§ 22:19   Public hearing—Victims—Gag orders
§ 22:20   Impartial judge
§ 22:21   Retention of jurisdiction
§ 22:22   Transfer of jurisdiction
§ 22:23   Appeals
§ 22:24   Double jeopardy
§ 22:25   Bail
§ 22:26   Motions to suppress

§ 22:1   Transfer of jurisdiction—Introduction

Transfer of jurisdiction refers to the process by which a juvenile court relinquishes jurisdiction and transfers a juvenile case to the criminal courts for prosecution. This process, variously described as waiver, certification, or bindover,[1] has been a unique part of the juvenile court system since the establishment of the first juvenile court in 1899.[2] As one court has observed: "There is no proceeding for adults comparable directly to the juvenile juris-

---

[Section 22:1]

[1]See State v. Whisenant, 127 Ohio App. 3d 75, 83, 711 N.E.2d 1016 (11th Dist. Portage County 1998) ("The juvenile court has original and exclusive jurisdiction over matters relating to allegedly delinquent children. . . . The juvenile court's determination to relinquish jurisdiction to the general division is what is meant by the term 'bindover.' "). See also RC 2152.02(AA)(defining transfer).

[2]Illinois Juvenile Court Act of 1899. 1899 Ill. Laws 131.

diction waiver hearing."[3]

Although virtually all jurisdictions permit transfer, the criteria and procedures for transfer vary from state to state.[4] Due process principles, however, apply to transfer hearings, and the double jeopardy clause precludes the transfer of jurisdiction after a child has been adjudicated delinquent.[5]

In Ohio, transfer proceedings are governed by RC 2152.10, RC 2152.12, and Juvenile Rule 30.[6] Transfer is permitted only for children of specified ages and for certain types of offenses. In addition, the court must find that there is probable cause to believe that the child has committed the offense. There are two types of transfer: mandatory and discretionary. Where transfer is discretionary, the court must also decide whether the child is amenable to treatment in the juvenile system.

The 1997 amendment to Juvenile Rule 30deleted several provisions in order to limit the rule to procedural issues. The rule no longer specifies an age requirement for transfer. Nor does the amended rule specify factors for consideration when determining transfer.

The 2002 amendment, S.B. 179, by codifying many of the Sentencing Commission's recommendations,[7] changed the law of juvenile transfer in certain respects. It moved the statutory section from RC 2151.26 to RC 2152.10 and RC 2152.12.

§ 22:2 Rationale for transfer

The purpose of transfer proceedings "is the assessment of the probability of rehabilitating the child within the juvenile justice system."[1] The concept of transfer entails a recognition that the juvenile court system should not be

---

[3]Kemplen v. State of Md., 428 F.2d 169, 173 (4th Cir. 1970).

[4]See IJA-ABA Standards Relating to Transfer Between Courts (1980); Rights of Juveniles: The Juvenile Justice System (2d ed.), Ch 4.

[5]See § 22:24, Double jeopardy.

[6]Until 1996, there was no direct conflict between the statute and the rule, although each had provisions not found in the other. The Ohio Supreme Court had indicated that the statute and rule should be construed together. See State v. Wilson, 73 Ohio St. 3d 40, 43, 1995-Ohio-217, 652 N.E.2d 196 (1995) ("R.C. 2151.26 and Juv.R. 30 provide a narrow exception to the general rule that juvenile courts have exclusive subject matter jurisdiction over any case involving a child."); State v. Watson, 47 Ohio St. 3d 93, 547 N.E.2d 1181 (1989) (referring to "Juv.R. 30, and its statutory counterpart, R.C. 2151.26"); State v. Douglas, 20 Ohio St. 3d 34, 485 N.E.2d 711 (1985) ("R.C. 2151.26 and Juv.R. 30 set forth the procedure to be followed by a juvenile court in a bind-over situation."); State v. Adams, 69 Ohio St. 2d 120, 123, 23 Ohio Op. 3d 164, 431 N.E.2d 326 (1982) ("R.C. 2151.26 and Juv.R. 30 provide the procedural mechanism by which a juvenile offender may be 'bound over' to the adult court."). The 1996 statutory amendments reduced the transfer age from 15 to 14 years and expanded the circumstances under which mandatory transfer applied. The juvenile court in In re Baker, No. 96JU-01-0268 (C.P., Franklin, 3-4-96), ruled that the amended statute and Juvenile Rule 30 did not conflict because the rule applied only to discretionary transfer. Moreover, the court found that the amended statute involved a substantive, rather than a procedural, issue under Section 5(B), Article IV, of the Ohio Constitution and thereby pre-empted the rule. See also State v. Agee, 86 Ohio St. 3d 1489, 716 N.E.2d 721 (1999); In re Langston, 119 Ohio App. 3d 1, 4, 694 N.E.2d 468 (5th Dist. Stark County 1997) ("Because the term 'may' denotes a discretionary provision, Juv.R. 30 affects only discretionary bindovers and not those mandated by R.C. 2151.26(B)."). The juvenile court in In re Snyder, No. 96-0098-DEF (C.P., Wayne, 2-26-96), reached the same result, albeit with a somewhat different rationale. The court found that the amended statute served to limit the jurisdiction of juvenile courts and therefore is a substantive provision, citing Juvenile Rule 44, which states that "[t]hese rules shall not be construed to extend or limit the jurisdiction of the juvenile court."

[7]Ohio Criminal Sentencing Commission, A Plan for Juvenile Sentencing in Ohio (Fall 1999). A number of the Commission's transfer proposals were not enacted. These include reducing the number of mandatory bindovers, creating a new category (presumed bindovers), making F-5s ineligible for transfer, and redefining Category One and Two offenses.

[Section 22:2]

[1]State v. Douglas, 20 Ohio St. 3d 34, 485 N.E.2d 711 (1985). Accord State v. Adams, 69 Ohio St. 2d 120, 123, 23 Ohio Op. 3d 164, 431 N.E.2d 326 (1982).

available to all children:

> Some acts are so offensive to the community that the arbitrary line drawn at eighteen cannot acceptably be used to protect the alleged wrongdoer. The serious offender should not be permitted to escape the criminal justice system simply because he or she is a day or a year short of eighteen. As age eighteen approaches, credible argument can be made that the juvenile court's always inadequate resources should not be devoted to those youthful wrongdoers whose offenses are so serious or who appear to be so incorrigible as to be unworthy of or beyond help.[2]

An Ohio court stated it this way:

> The purpose of [transfer] is to protect the public in those cases where rehabilitation appears unlikely and circumstances indicate that if the charge is ultimately established society would be better served by the criminal process by reason of the greater security which may be achieved or the deterring effect which that process is thought to accomplish.[3]

This view of transfer proceedings is not universally accepted. One commentary notes:

> Others argue that the existence of this loophole [transfer] in the juvenile system indicates a half-hearted commitment to treatment and a continued allegiance to retribution on the part of society, an allegiance that is particularly distasteful because it applies to the very persons whom the separate juvenile court system was designed to protect.[4]

In recent years, many jurisdictions have expanded the categories of juveniles who may be prosecuted in the criminal courts. "Since 1992, all but 10 jurisdictions have greatly eased the ability of the state to try juveniles as adults."[5] Ohio has followed this trend.[6]

§ 22:3 Constitutional issues

Constitutional considerations affect transfer procedures. In *Kent v. United States*,[1] the United States Supreme Court considered a challenge to transfer proceedings conducted pursuant to the D.C. Code.[2] Kent was taken into custody for rape. As a 16-year-old, he was subject to juvenile court jurisdiction. The juvenile court, however, transferred his case for trial as an adult. The transfer was accomplished without a hearing or written reasons. In addition, the court failed to provide Kent's attorney with access to Kent's

---

[2]IJA-ABA Standards Relating to Transfer Between Courts 3 (1980).

[3]In re Mack, 22 Ohio App. 2d 201, 203, 51 Ohio Op. 2d 400, 260 N.E.2d 619 (1st Dist. Hamilton County 1970).

[4]Piersma, Ganousis, Volenik, Swanger, & Connell, Law and Tactics in Juvenile Cases 274 (3d ed. 1977).

For articles and text on transfer, see Champion & Mays, Transferring Juveniles to Criminal Courts (1991); Dawson, An Empirical Study of Kent Style Juvenile Transfers to Criminal Court, 23 St. Mary's L. J. 975 (1992); Fagan & Deschenes, Determinants of Judicial Waiver Decisions for Violent Juvenile Offenders, 81 J. Crim. L. & Criminology 314 (1990); Feld, The Juvenile Court Meets the Principle of the Offense: Legislative Changes in Juvenile Waiver Statutes, 78 J. Crim. L. 471 (1987).

[5]See Shepard, Jr., Challenging Change: Legal Attacks on Juvenile Transfer Reform, Criminal Justice 55 (Fall 1997) ("[T]here has been a significant trend in the past decade to ease the traditional restrictions on trying juveniles in adult courts. Indeed, most states have acted affirmatively in recent years to try more youths as adults either by lowering the maximum age of juvenile court jurisdiction, dropping the minimum age for discretionary or mandatory transfer to criminal courts, broadening the range of offenses dictating placement in the adult system, and giving prosecutors broader discretion to file juvenile cases directly in the adult criminal court.").

[6]See § 22:7, Mandatory transfer.

[Section 22:3]

[1]Kent v. U.S., 383 U.S. 541, 86 S. Ct. 1045, 16 L. Ed. 2d 84 (1966).

[2]See generally Paulsen, *Kent v. United States*: The Constitutional Context of Juvenile Cases, 1966 Supreme Court Rev. 167.

social service file.

On review, the Supreme Court ruled the transfer proceedings invalid. According to the Court, transfer is a "critically important"[3] stage of the juvenile court process and "there is no place in our system of law for reaching a result of such tremendous consequences without ceremony—without hearing, without effective assistance of counsel, without a statement of reasons."[4]

Whether the Court intended to rest its decision in *Kent* on statutory or constitutional grounds is not entirely clear. At one point in the opinion, Justice Fortas wrote, "The Juvenile Court Act and the decisions of the United States Court of Appeals for the District of Columbia Circuit provide an adequate basis for decision of this case, and we go no further."[5] Moreover, the dissenting justices believed the case involved only a statutory issue.[6] Nevertheless, other parts of the Fortas opinion indicate a constitutional basis. One passage reads, "We believe that this result is required by the statute read in the context of constitutional principles relating to due process and the assistance of counsel."[7] In another passage the Court wrote that a transfer hearing "must measure up to the essentials of due process and fair treatment."[8] Significantly, the Court quoted this passage in *In re Gault*[9] and then wrote, "We reiterate this view . . . as a requirement which is part of the Due Process Clause of the Fourteenth Amendment of our Constitution."[10]

Although there are some exceptions,[11] most courts, including the Ohio courts, view *Kent* as establishing constitutional standards.[12] For example, the Third Circuit has stated, "[I]t is our view that *Kent*, particularly in light of the Supreme Court's subsequent opinion in *In re Gault* . . . sets forth certain principles of constitutional dimension."[13]

Courts have addressed a number of different due process challenges. They have ruled that due process does not require a transfer hearing; states are free to adopt mandatory transfer provisions or entrust the decision to prosecutorial discretion.[14] Recent challenges to the constitutionality of mandatory transfer statutes have been largely unsuccessful. "A review of state and federal decisions reveals that statutes providing, under stated cir-

---

[3]Kent v. U.S., 383 U.S. 541, 556, 86 S. Ct. 1045, 16 L. Ed. 2d 84 (1966).

[4]Kent v. U.S., 383 U.S. 541, 554, 86 S. Ct. 1045, 16 L. Ed. 2d 84 (1966).

[5]Kent v. U.S., 383 U.S. 541, 556, 86 S. Ct. 1045, 16 L. Ed. 2d 84 (1966).

[6]Kent v. U.S., 383 U.S. 541, 568, 86 S. Ct. 1045, 16 L. Ed. 2d 84 (1966) (dissenting opinion) ("This case involves the construction of a statute applicable only to the District of Columbia.").

[7]Kent v. U.S., 383 U.S. 541, 557, 86 S. Ct. 1045, 16 L. Ed. 2d 84 (1966).

[8]Kent v. U.S., 383 U.S. 541, 562, 86 S. Ct. 1045, 16 L. Ed. 2d 84 (1966).

[9]Application of Gault, 387 U.S. 1, 87 S. Ct. 1428, 18 L. Ed. 2d 527 (1967).

[10]Application of Gault, 387 U.S. 1, 30–31, 87 S. Ct. 1428, 18 L. Ed. 2d 527 (1967).

[11]E.g., State v. Steinhauer, 216 So. 2d 214 (Fla. 1968); In re Bullard, 22 N.C. App. 245, 206 S.E.2d 305 (1974); Cradle v. Peyton, 208 Va. 243, 156 S.E.2d 874 (1967).

[12]See State v. Adams, 69 Ohio St. 2d 120, 23 Ohio Op. 3d 164, 431 N.E.2d 326 (1982); State v. Payne, 118 Ohio App. 3d 699, 703, 693 N.E.2d 1159 (3d Dist. Seneca County 1997) ("A juvenile has due process rights and a right to fair treatment in the bindover process from juvenile court to criminal court.") (citing *Kent*); State v. Taylor, 26 Ohio App. 3d 69, 498 N.E.2d 211 (3d Dist. Auglaize County 1985); State v. Riggins, 68 Ohio App. 2d 1, 22 Ohio Op. 3d 1, 426 N.E.2d 504 (8th Dist. Cuyahoga County 1980); In re Mack, 22 Ohio App. 2d 201, 51 Ohio Op. 2d 400, 260 N.E.2d 619 (1st Dist. Hamilton County 1970).

[13]U. S. ex rel. Turner v. Rundle, 438 F.2d 839, 841–42 (3d Cir. 1971). Accord Oviedo v. Jago, 809 F.2d 326 (6th Cir. 1987); Geboy v. Gray, 471 F.2d 575 (7th Cir. 1973); Powell v. Hocker, 453 F.2d 652 (9th Cir. 1971); Kemplen v. State of Md., 428 F.2d 169 (4th Cir. 1970); Inge v. Slayton, 395 F. Supp. 560 (E.D. Va. 1975); Com. v. Wayne W., 414 Mass. 218, 606 N.E.2d 1323, 1326 (1993).

[14]See Woodard v. Wainwright, 556 F.2d 781 (5th Cir. 1977); Russell v. Parratt, 543 F.2d 1214 (8th Cir. 1976); Cox v. U. S., 473 F.2d 334 (4th Cir. 1973); U.S. v. Quinones, 516 F.2d 1309 (1st Cir. 1975); U.S. v. Bland, 472 F.2d 1329 (D.C. Cir. 1972); Vega v. Bell, 47 N.Y.2d 543, 419 N.Y. S.2d 454, 393 N.E.2d 450 (1979); People v. P.H., 145 Ill. 2d 209, 164 Ill. Dec. 137, 582 N.E.2d 700 (1991).

cumstances, for mandatory adult adjudication of offenders of otherwise juvenile age, routinely have been upheld against due process challenges based on *Kent*."[15]

The *Kent* decision addressed only the procedural aspects of transfer. The United States Supreme Court has yet to consider the constitutionality of the standards used in transfer proceedings. In *Breed v. Jones*,[16] the Court commented that it "has never attempted to prescribe criteria for, or the nature and quantum of evidence that must support, a decision to transfer a juvenile for trial in adult court."

Constitutional challenges to transfer statutes based on grounds other than due process have also been made. For example, attacks on vagueness grounds generally have been rejected.[17] Courts have also rejected challenges based upon separation-of-powers arguments.[18] In addition, most equal protection attacks have also failed.[19] There are, however, several exceptions.[20]

Cross References
§ 1:4, § 22:12
Research References
Carlin, Baldwin's Ohio Practice, Merrick-Rippner Probate Law (6th ed.), Ch 107

§ 22:4 Improper transfer—Lack of jurisdiction

Juvenile courts have exclusive jurisdiction over persons under the age of 18 who are charged with criminal conduct.[1] Only a child properly transferred may be prosecuted in the criminal courts. A criminal prosecution based on the mistaken belief that a defendant was 18 years of age or older at the time of the offense is a "nullity."[2]

Improper transfer. In *State v. Wilson*,[3] the Ohio Supreme Court addressed this issue. Wilson had been convicted and sentenced for theft in 1983. Twelve years later, Wilson sought to overturn his conviction on the

---

[15]State v. Angel C., 245 Conn. 93, 110, 715 A.2d 652, 662 (1998) (automatic transfer of person age 14 who is charged with certain enumerated offenses does not violate due process) (listing cases).

[16]Breed v. Jones, 421 U.S. 519, 537, 95 S. Ct. 1779, 44 L. Ed. 2d 346 (1975).

[17]See State v. Brown, 1987 WL 18253 (Ohio Ct. App. 8th Dist. Cuyahoga County 1987). See also Speck v. Auger, 558 F.2d 394 (8th Cir. 1977) (construing the Iowa statute); Donald L. v. Superior Court, 7 Cal. 3d 592, 102 Cal. Rptr. 850, 498 P.2d 1098 (1972); Davis v. State, 297 So. 2d 289 (Fla. 1974); State v. Gibbs, 94 Idaho 908, 500 P.2d 209 (1972); State v. Smagula, 117 N.H. 663, 377 A.2d 608 (1977); In re Bullard, 22 N.C. App. 245, 206 S.E.2d 305 (1974).

But see State in Interest of Hunter, 387 So. 2d 1086 (La. 1980). See also People v. Fields, 388 Mich. 66, 199 N.W.2d 217 (1972).

[18]See People v. J.S., 103 Ill. 2d 395, 83 Ill. Dec. 156, 469 N.E.2d 1090 (1984); State v. Behl, 547 N.W.2d 382 (Minn. Ct. App. 1996); Matter of Wood, 236 Mont. 118, 768 P.2d 1370 (1989); Jones v. State, 1982 OK CR 196, 654 P.2d 1080 (Okla. Crim. App. 1982); Hansen v. State, 904 P.2d 811 (Wyo. 1995).

[19]See Woodard v. Wainwright, 556 F.2d 781 (5th Cir. 1977); U.S. v. Bland, 472 F.2d 1329 (D.C. Cir. 1972); People v. Thorpe, 641 P.2d 935 (Colo. 1982); Bishop v. State, 265 Ga. 821, 462 S.E.2d 716 (1995); State v. Berard, 121 R.I. 551, 401 A.2d 448 (1979); Hansen v. State, 904 P.2d 811 (Wyo. 1995); Jahnke v. State, 692 P.2d 911 (Wyo. 1984).

[20]See Lamb v. Brown, 456 F.2d 18 (10th Cir. 1972) (providing juvenile treatment for females under 18 years of age but only males under 16 violates equal protection guarantee); Hughes v. State, 653 A.2d 241 (Del. 1994) (striking down the elimination of "reverse amenability process"); State v. Mohi, 901 P.2d 991 (Utah 1995) (statute giving prosecutors unguided discretion violates state constitution's "uniform operation of laws" provision).

[Section 22:4]
[1]RC 2151.23(A)(1), RC 2152.02(C) (defining the term "child"); § 2:3, Child subject to adult prosecution; § 2:4, Mistaken or concealed age. See also RC 2152.03 (transfer of cases from other courts to the juvenile court).

[2]RC 2152.12(H).

[3]State v. Wilson, 73 Ohio St. 3d 40, 1995-Ohio-217, 652 N.E.2d 196 (1995).

ground that he was only 17 years of age at the time of the offense.[4] The Court ruled that in the absence of a valid transfer, the juvenile court and not the criminal court had jurisdiction. Since the criminal court lacked subject matter jurisdiction, Wilson's conviction was "void *ab initio*."[5] The Court also held that the "exclusive subject matter jurisdiction of the juvenile court cannot be waived" and a "party's failure to challenge a court's subject matter jurisdiction cannot be used, in effect, to bestow jurisdiction on a court where there is none."[6]

In *Gaskins v. Shiplevy*,[7] the Ohio Supreme Court reaffirmed *Wilson* and also recognized the availability of habeas corpus as a means of challenging an improper transfer ruling. "[A]ppellant's amended petition stated a potentially good cause of action in habeas corpus, alleging, as it did, that the court of common pleas lacked jurisdiction over appellant."[8] Gaskins had alleged that he had not been represented by counsel when he was transferred for burglary in 1983 in violation of then-Juvenile Rule 3. He also alleged that a mental and physical examination was not conducted as required by then-RC 2151.26. The Ohio Supreme Court remanded the case for determinations on these issues.[9]

Later cases reaffirmed this position.[10]

Delayed apprehension. If a person who would otherwise have come

---

[4]Wilson, who was represented by counsel, never raised the age issue at his 1983 criminal trial. He was arrested, indicted, and pled guilty as an adult.

[5]State v. Wilson, 73 Ohio St. 3d 40, 44, 1995-Ohio-217, 652 N.E.2d 196 (1995). "Absent a proper bindover procedure, the juvenile court has the exclusive subject matter jurisdiction over any case concerning a child who is alleged to be a delinquent." State v. Wilson, 73 Ohio St. 3d 40, syl., para. 1, 1995-Ohio-217, 652 N.E.2d 196 (1995).

[6]State v. Wilson, 73 Ohio St. 3d 40, 46, 1995-Ohio-217, 652 N.E.2d 196 (1995). See also State v. Golphin, 1996 WL 673975 (Ohio Ct. App. 8th Dist. Cuyahoga County 1996) (Failure to conduct required physical examination deprives criminal court of jurisdiction.); State v. Taylor, 26 Ohio App. 3d 69, 498 N.E.2d 211 (3d Dist. Auglaize County 1985) (Failure to comply with notice requirements deprives criminal court of jurisdiction.); State v. Riggins, 68 Ohio App. 2d 1, 4, 22 Ohio Op. 3d 1, 426 N.E.2d 504 (8th Dist. Cuyahoga County 1980) ("Failure to comply with the provisions of R.C. 2151.26 . . . deprives the Court of Common Pleas of jurisdiction over a juvenile defendant.").

[7]Gaskins v. Shiplevy, 74 Ohio St. 3d 149, 151, 1995-Ohio-262, 656 N.E.2d 1282 (1995).

[8]Gaskins v. Shiplevy, 74 Ohio St. 3d 149, 151, 1995-Ohio-262, 656 N.E.2d 1282 (1995). See also State ex rel. Harris v. Anderson, 76 Ohio St. 3d 193, 196, 1996-Ohio-412, 667 N.E.2d 1 (1996) ("Harris alleged, with sufficient particularity to withstand dismissal, that he was a minor at the time of the commission of the offenses. There is no requirement that he provide supporting documentation of his age in his petition in order to satisfy the particularity requirement.").

[9]On remand, the state filed a return including a juvenile court journal entry. "The journal entry directly controverted Gaskins's statements in his motion to amend the petition that the bindover was improper. For example, the juvenile court entry states that Gaskins was represented by counsel at the bindover proceeding and that Gaskins knowingly and voluntarily waived his right to a mental and physical examination. The juvenile court entry establishes full compliance with the bindover procedure required by the applicable version of R.C. 2151.26." Gaskins v. Shiplevy, 76 Ohio St. 3d 380, 382, 1996-Ohio-387, 667 N.E.2d 1194 (1996) (habeas hearing not required).

[10]See Johnson v. Timmerman-Cooper, 93 Ohio St. 3d 614, 617, 2001-Ohio-1803, 757 N.E.2d 1153 (2001) ("Based on *Hanning* and the plain language of R.C. 2151.26(B)(4)(b), Johnson's sentencing court patently and unambiguously lacked jurisdiction to convict and sentence her on the charged offenses when she had not been lawfully transferred to that court. The resulting conviction and sentence are void, and the availability of alternative remedies do not prevent issuance of the writ."); State v. Golphin, 81 Ohio St. 3d 543, 546–47, 1998-Ohio-336, 692 N.E.2d 608 (1998) (no evidence in record of then-required physical examination; "[T]he amendments to the controlling statute and rule were made subsequent to the proceedings at issue, and may not be applied retroactively."); State ex rel. Harris v. Anderson, 76 Ohio St. 3d 193, 195, 1996-Ohio-412, 667 N.E.2d 1 (1996) ("Absent a proper bindover procedure pursuant to R.C. 2151.26, the jurisdiction of a juvenile court is exclusive and cannot be waived. A habeas corpus petition which alleges that the court lacked jurisdiction over the petitioner due to an improper bindover states a potentially good cause of action in habeas corpus. The petition requires the allowance of the writ and an order mandating the respondent to make a return in order that the court may determine whether the bindover was improper.") (citation omitted). See also State ex rel. Fryer-

under juvenile court jurisdiction for a delinquent act is not apprehended until after age 21, that person is treated as an adult and tried in criminal court.[11]

Acceptance of pleas. One court has held that transfer to the general division is mandatory. The juvenile court is obligated to determine whether there was probable cause to believe the child committed the alleged offense and, if so, to transfer the case as it has no jurisdiction to accept a plea.[12]

§22:5 Transfer age requirement

A child 14 years or older is subject to transfer to the criminal courts for trial.[1] Children under 14 years are not subject to transfer.[2] The child's age at that time of the offense, rather than the time of the transfer hearing, controls.[3]

In *In re C.*,[4] the alleged delinquent was not charged until after he was 21 years of age. The rape was alleged to have been committed when he was 14 years. At that time the age requirement for transfer was 15. A motion for bindover was dismissed because he was not 15 years at the time of the alleged conduct.[5] The court also ruled that it lacked jurisdiction over the "child" at the present time and therefore could not adjudicate the case.[6] Other cases,

---

son v. Tate, 84 Ohio St. 3d 481, 485, 1999-Ohio-465, 705 N.E.2d 353 (1999) ("The key deficiency in appellant's position is that in actuality he is not challenging the bindover; he is instead challenging the validity of subsequent events that took place after a technically correct bindover occurred. . . . Once appellant was properly bound over, the common pleas court had jurisdiction to proceed. It was only at the time of the proceedings in the common pleas court that possible error occurred, in that appellant had been bound over on charges involving Robinson and was prosecuted on the charges involving Jones. This consideration does not affect the essential validity of the bindover.") (habeas not available, other remedies available).

[11]RC 2152.12(J); RC 2152.02(C)(3). See also State v. Walls, 96 Ohio St. 3d 437, 442, 2002-Ohio-5059, 775 N.E.2d 829 (2002) ("Focusing on the date of Walls's offense, we conclude that the General Assembly intended that the 1997 amendments to R.C. Chapter 2151 apply retrospectively. The 1997 version of R.C. 2151.011(B)(6)(c) changed the definition of 'child' to *exclude* '[a]ny person who, while under eighteen years of age, commits an act that would be a felony if committed by an adult and who is not taken into custody or apprehended for that act until after that person attains twenty-one years of age.' Also effective in 1997, the General Assembly added R.C. 2151.23(I), which declared the juvenile court's lack of jurisdiction over a person 21 years of age who is apprehended for an offense committed prior to the person's 18th birthday. . . . These changes to the statutory scheme effectively removed anyone over 21 years of age from juvenile-court jurisdiction, regardless of the date on which the person allegedly committed the offense. In other words, the statutory amendments made the age of the *offender upon apprehension* the touchstone of determining juvenile-court jurisdiction without regard to whether the alleged offense occurred prior to the amendments' effective date. From these circumstances, we find an express legislative intent that the juvenile statutes apply retroactively.").

[12]In re Graham, 147 Ohio App. 3d 452, 459, 2002-Ohio-2407, 770 N.E.2d 1123 (7th Dist. Mahoning County 2002) ("The complaint against Jeremiah alleged that he was delinquent for committing aggravated robbery with a firearm specification. Aggravated robbery is a category two offense. . . . The complaint stated that Jeremiah was sixteen years of age when he committed the act. It also alleged that Jeremiah had a firearm on or about his person or under his control at the time. Given these facts, the juvenile court was obligated to determine whether there was probable cause to believe that Jeremiah committed the aggravated robbery and, if so, to transfer the case to the general division of the common pleas court. It appears that the juvenile court was without subject matter jurisdiction to accept Jeremiah's admission to the charges against him. Had the state amended the charges against Jeremiah so that he was no longer charged with a category two offense with a firearm specification, then the juvenile court would have had jurisdiction to accept Jeremiah's admission.").

[Section 22:5]

[1]RC 2152.10(A), RC 2152.12(B) (former RC 2151.26(B)).

[2]The 1995 statutory amendment reduced the transfer age from 15 years to 14 years. As amended in 1997, Juv. R. 30 deleted any reference to an age requirement.

[3]See Age Jurisdiction Ch 2.

[4]In re C., 61 Ohio Misc. 2d 610, 580 N.E.2d 1182 (C.P. 1991).

[5]In re C., 61 Ohio Misc. 2d 610, 612, 580 N.E.2d 1182 (C.P. 1991).

[6]In re C., 61 Ohio Misc. 2d 610, 614, 580 N.E.2d 1182 (C.P. 1991).

however, have reached the opposite conclusion.[7] Persons who are 21 years or older at the time of apprehension are no longer subject to juvenile court jurisdiction.[8]

§ 22:6   Probable cause requirement

Before a child may be transferred, the court must find that there is probable cause to believe that the child has committed the act charged.[1] There must be probable cause that (1) an offense has been committed, and (2) the child is the person who has committed that offense.[2] In *In re B.S.*,[3] the juvenile court ruled that the prosecution had established probable cause for aggravated burglary but not that the juvenile had employed a firearm to facilitate its commission. In the court's view, a mere allegation is insufficient; probable cause is required.

Once probable cause is determined,[4] the court proceeds differently depending on whether mandatory or discretionary transfer is sought, as discussed in the next sections.

§ 22:7   Mandatory transfer

In 2002, RC 2152.10 and RC 2152.12 superseded RC 2151.26. These statutes recognize two types of transfer: mandatory and discretionary. The latter is discussed in the next section. If one or more complaints allege both mandatory and discretionary transfer offenses, the mandatory offenses are considered first.[1]

RC 2152.10[2] specifies four circumstances in which transfer is mandatory:

(1) **Prior transfer and conviction**. The child has previously been

---

[7]See Matter of McCourt, 1993 WL 327677 (Ohio Ct. App. 7th Dist. Belmont County 1993); In re J.B., 71 Ohio Misc. 2d 63, 654 N.E.2d 216 (C.P. 1995).

[8]See Text § 22:4, Improper transfer—Lack of jurisdiction.

[Section 22:6]
[1]RC 2152.12(B)(2) (former RC 2151.26(A)); Juv. R. 30(A).

[2]In State v. Doyle, 1991 WL 286149, at *20 (Ohio Ct. App. 3d Dist. Allen County 1991), the court wrote:

Appellant also argues that there was no showing of probable cause pursuant to Juv.R. 30(A). . . . [T]he court need only find probable cause, not guilt beyond a reasonable doubt. Therefore, although Appellant may have raised doubts at the probable cause hearing as to whether Appellant was the perpetrator of the crime, a review of the hearing on the motion to transfer record indicates that there was probable cause sufficient to meet the parameters of Juv.R. 30(A).

See generally IJA-ABA Standards Relating to Transfer Between Courts 37–38 (1980); Davis, The Efficacy of a Probable Cause Requirement in Juvenile Proceedings, 59 N.C. L. Rev. 723 (1981).

[3]In re B.S., 103 Ohio Misc. 2d 34, 37, 725 N.E.2d 362 (C.P. 1998) ("Although a portion of the handgun was clearly visible as the juvenile fled, no evidence whatsoever suggested that B.S. displayed, brandished, indicated possession of, or used the firearm to facilitate the offense.").

[4]State v. Whisenant, 127 Ohio App. 3d 75, 83, 711 N.E.2d 1016 (11th Dist. Portage County 1998) ("At the first hearing, the court must determine whether there is probable cause to believe that the juvenile, aged fifteen to eighteen, committed the felonious act. . . . If the court finds probable cause, a second hearing will be held.").

[Section 22:7]
[1]RC 2152.12(F).

[2]Former RC 2151.26(B). The 1996 statutory amendment expanded significantly the number of cases subject to transfer to the criminal courts. This was accomplished by reducing the transfer age from 15 to 14 years and expanding the circumstances in which mandatory transfer applies. Under the prior statute, a child who had previously been adjudicated delinquent of aggravated murder or murder and was alleged to have again committed either of those crimes was subject to mandatory transfer upon a finding of probable cause.

transferred and convicted of a felony in criminal court.[3]

(2) **Out-of-state domiciliary**. The child is domiciled in another state and under the laws of that state would have been subject to criminal prosecution without a transfer hearing for the charged act.[4]

(3) **Category one offense**.[5] The child is charged with a category one offense and *either* (a) was 16 or 17 at the time of the act charged,[6] *or* (b) was 14 or 15 at the time of the act and had previously been adjudicated a category one or category two delinquent and committed to the Department of Youth Services as a result. Category one offenses include:[7] aggravated murder,[8] murder,[9] and an attempt[10] to commit either of those crimes.

(4) **Category two offense**.[11] The child is charged with a category two offense other than kidnapping, was 16 or 17 at the time of the act charged, and *either* (a) had previously been adjudicated a category one or two delinquent and committed to DYS as a result, *or* (b) is alleged to have had a firearm at the time of the act charged under specified conditions.[12] Category two offenses are:[13] voluntary manslaughter,[14] kidnapping,[15] rape,[16] aggravated arson,[17] aggravated robbery,[18] and aggravated burglary.[19] In addition, involuntary man-

---

[3]The statute specifies that the child either was convicted or pled guilty in the criminal case. RC 2152.12(A)(2)(a), RC 2152.10(A)(3)(former RC 2151.26(B)(1)) ("once an adult, always an adult" rule).

[4]RC 2152.12(A)(2)(b), RC 2152.10(A)(3)(former RC 2151.26(B)(2)). The new law limits this category to felonies. See also State v. Simpson, 148 Ohio App. 3d 221, 224-25, 2002-Ohio-3077, 772 N.E.2d 707 (5th Dist. Licking County 2002) (The statute "clearly was intended to prevent out-of-state minors from coming into Ohio and committing offenses which would subject them to punishment as an adult in their state of domicile but, in Ohio, are under the jurisdiction of the juvenile court."; domicile at the time of the offense, not domicile at the time of bindover hearing, controls).

[5]RC 2152.10(A)(1), RC 2152.12(A)(1)(a)(former RC 2151.26(B)(3)). See also RC 2152.02(BB)(defining category one offense).

[6]RC 2152.02(A) (former RC 2151.26(A)(4)) ("Act charged" is defined as "the act that is identified in a complaint, indictment, or information alleging that a child is a delinquent child.").

[7]RC 2152.02(BB) (former RC 2151.26(A)(1)).

[8]RC 2903.01.

[9]RC 2903.02.

[10]RC 2923.02.

[11]RC 2152.10(A)(2) and RC 2152.12(A)(1)(a) (former RC 2151.26(B)(4)). See also RC 2152.02(CC)(defining category two offense).

[12]RC 2152.02(M) (former RC 2151.26(A)(1)(c)) provides that the term "firearm" has the same meaning as in RC 2923.11. Also, the firearm must have been on or about the child's person or under the child's control at the time of the charged act, and the child must have displayed, brandished, indicated possession, or used the firearm to facilitate the commission of the act. See State v. Davis, 1997 WL 605193, at *3 (Ohio Ct. App. 2d Dist. Clark County 1997) ("[A]lthough the state's evidence at trial established that Dixon actually displayed and brandished the firearm, Davis also had control over the weapon as indicated by his statement to Reed, 'Give me your money, or I'll have my boy shoot you.' . . . This statement was sufficient evidence of Davis' control over the firearm to satisfy R.C. 2151.26(B)(4)(b). Furthermore, Davis aided and abetted Dixon, who possessed the firearm, in robbing Rudy."), appeal dismissed by 81 Ohio St.3d 1428, 689 N.E.2d 49 (1998); In re B.S., 103 Ohio Misc. 2d 34, 725 N.E.2d 362 (C.P. 1998) ("Although a portion of the handgun was clearly visible as the juvenile fled, no evidence whatsoever suggested that B.S. displayed, brandished, indicated possession, or used the firearm to facilitate the offense.").

[13]RC 2152.02(CC) (former RC 2151.26(A)(2)).

[14]RC 2903.03.

[15]RC 2905.01.

[16]RC 2907.02.

[17]RC 2909.02.

[18]RC 2911.01. See In re Graham, 147 Ohio App. 3d 452, 459, 2002-Ohio-2407, 770 N.E.2d 1123 (7th Dist. Mahoning County 2002).

[19]RC 2911.11.

slaughter is a category two offense if classified as a felony of the first degree (felony-manslaughter but not misdemeanor-manslaughter).[20]

In *State v. Hanning*,[21] the Ohio Supreme Court ruled that mandatory bindover does not apply unless the juvenile personally used the firearm as specified in the statute. The "bindover statute itself does not provide that a child can be bound over based on the fact that a firearm was used by an accomplice."[22] In other words, the complicity statute cannot be employed as a basis for transfer. *Hanning* is also noteworthy because it reflects the Court's view of transfer: "In most instances involving delinquency, juveniles can be effectively tried and handled in the juvenile justice system. However, in some extraordinary cases, involving older or violent offenders, the General Assembly enacted R.C. 2151.26 [now R.C. 2152.10] to provide special measures for transferring these juveniles to adult court."[23] The Court went on to describe mandatory bindover as a "narrow exception,"[24] noting that the legislature could have included complicity liability in the statute. Although an accomplice is treated the same as a principal under Ohio law, children are different: "But children are easily influenced and persuaded by adults. To require bindover for a child based on an adult accomplice's decision to use a firearm through application of the complicity statute runs contrary not only to the doctrine of *parens patriae*, upon which the General Assembly built the juvenile criminal justice system, but to common sense."[25]

Hearing. RC 2152.12(A)[26] requires a hearing for mandatory transfer. At this hearing, the court determines (1) whether the child was 14 years or older at the time of the act charged, (2) the existence of probable cause, and (3) the applicability of any of the four conditions specified for mandatory transfer.

Constitutionality. Cases discussing the constitutionality of mandatory bindover are found in § 22:3.

§ 22:8   Discretionary transfer

The Juvenile Code recognizes two types of transfers: mandatory and discretionary. If one or more complaints allege both mandatory and discretionary transfer offenses, the mandatory offenses are considered first.[1] Juvenile Rule 30 establishes a two-step hearing procedure for *discretionary* transfers.

Preliminary hearing. A preliminary hearing is first held to determine whether there is probable cause to believe the child has committed a felony.[2] Discretionary transfer is permitted only if the complaint alleges that the child has committed an act that would constitute a felony if committed by an adult.[3] The child, the prosecutor, or the court may move for a preliminary

---

[20]RC 2903.04. Felonious sexual penetration, RC 2907.12, was also a category two offense, but it has been repealed.

[21]State v. Hanning, 89 Ohio St. 3d 86, 2000-Ohio-436, 728 N.E.2d 1059 (2000) (Hanning had a plastic BB gun while the accomplice had a 9 mm).

[22]State v. Hanning, 89 Ohio St. 3d 86, 91, 2000-Ohio-436, 728 N.E.2d 1059 (2000).

[23]State v. Hanning, 89 Ohio St. 3d 86, 89–90, 2000-Ohio-436, 728 N.E.2d 1059 (2000).

[24]State v. Hanning, 89 Ohio St. 3d 86, 91, 2000-Ohio-436, 728 N.E.2d 1059 (2000).

[25]State v. Hanning, 89 Ohio St. 3d 86, 93, 2000-Ohio-436, 728 N.E.2d 1059 (2000).

[26]Former RC 2151.26(B). See also Juv. R. 30(B).

[Section 22:8]

[1]RC 2152.12(F).

[2]Juv. R. 30(A).

[3]RC 2152.10(B), RC 2152.12(B) (former RC 2151.26(C)(1)). There are no common-law crimes in Ohio—only statutory crimes. RC 2901.03(A). An offense specifically classified as a felony in the Revised Code is a felony regardless of the penalty that may be imposed. RC 2901.02(D).

hearing.[4]

Amenability hearing. If the court finds probable cause, the proceedings are continued until a full investigation is completed, at which time a second hearing is held to determine whether jurisdiction should be transferred to the criminal courts.[5] The focus of the second hearing is the amenability of the child to rehabilitation in the juvenile court system: "The purpose behind [the prior transfer statute] and Juv.R. 30 is the assessment of the probability of rehabilitating the child within the juvenile justice system."[6] A social history may be prepared and used for this purpose.[7] The procedural aspects of the amenability hearing are discussed in § 22:9.

Before a child may be transferred, the court must find that there are reasonable grounds to believe that (1) the child is not amenable to care or rehabilitation in the juvenile system, and (2) the safety of the community may require subjecting the child to adult sanctions.[8]

S.B. 179, adopted in 2002, provided a balancing test for determining discretionary bindover, along with the overriding principles under RC 2152.01. This test specified factors both "for" and "against" transfer.[9]

Factors favoring transfer. The court must consider the following factors (and other relevant factors) in favor of bindover:[10]

(1) The victim suffered physical, psychological, or serious economic harm;[11]

(2) The victim's physical or mental harm was exacerbated by the victim's physical or mental vulnerability or age;[12]

Similarly, an offense classified as a misdemeanor is a misdemeanor regardless of the penalty that may be imposed. RC 2901.02(D). Any offense not specifically classified is a felony if imprisonment for more than one year may be imposed as a penalty. RC 2901.02(E). Transfer of a felony charge does not relinquish juvenile court jurisdiction over misdemeanors committed by the child. State ex rel. Duganitz v. Court, 23 Ohio Op. 3d 572 (Ct. App. 8th Dist. Cuyahoga County 1981).

[4]Although a child may move for a hearing, "[t]here is no provision in the rule or in the Revised Code that a child can cause the juvenile court to surrender its jurisdiction." State v. Smith, 29 Ohio App. 3d 194, 196–97, 504 N.E.2d 1121 (8th Dist. Cuyahoga County 1985). Recognizing a child's right to move for transfer raises an issue of waiver because the child is giving up the right to treatment in the juvenile system. See U.S. v. Williams, 459 F.2d 903 (2d Cir. 1972) (Child should be advised of his right to be proceeded against as a child and of all the consequences of waiving that right.).

[5]Juv. R. 30(C).

[6]State v. Douglas, 20 Ohio St. 3d 34, 485 N.E.2d 711 (1985). Accord State v. Adams, 69 Ohio St. 2d 120, 23 Ohio Op. 3d 164, 431 N.E.2d 326 (1982).

[7]Juv. R. 32(A)(2).

[8]RC 2152.12(B)(3) (former RC 2151.26(C)(1)).

[9]The court must state "on the record" which factors were applicable and weighed. RC 2152.12(B)(3) (former RC 2151.26(F) (requiring only a statement of the reasons for transfer). Prior to the 1997 amendment, Juvenile Rule 30(F) required the court to consider six factors in determining whether a child was amenable to treatment:

(1) Age and mental-physical condition;

(2) Prior juvenile record;

(3) Previous efforts to treat or rehabilitate;

(4) Family environment;

(5) School record; and

(6) The specific facts of the offense that are relevant to physical or mental condition.

These factors were deleted from the rule because they were considered to be substantive, rather than procedural, in nature and thus beyond the Supreme Court's rulemaking authority.

[10]RC 2152.12(D).

[11]This is broader than merely looking to "physical harm" as in former law.

[12]This factor is no longer tied solely to the victims' younger or older ages or "permanent and total" disability.

(3) The juvenile's relationship with the victim facilitated the act;[13]

(4) The juvenile committed the act for hire or as part of a gang or other organized criminal activity;[14]

(5) The juvenile displayed, brandished, indicated, or used a firearm;[15]

(6) At the time of the act, the juvenile was awaiting adjudication or disposition for delinquency, was under a community sanction, or was on parole for a prior delinquency;[16]

(7) The results of previous juvenile sanctions and programs show rehabilitation will not occur in the juvenile system;[17]

(8) The juvenile is emotionally, physically, or psychologically mature enough for transfer;[18]

(9) There is not sufficient time for rehabilitation in the juvenile system.[19]

Factors against transfer. The court must consider these, and any other relevant factors, against bindover.[20]

(1) The victim induced or facilitated the act charged;[21]

(2) The juvenile acted under provocation;[22]

(3) The juvenile was not the principal offender or, at the time of the act, was under the negative influence or coercion of another;[23]

(4) The juvenile did not cause physical harm to person or property, or have reasonable cause to believe such harm would occur;[24]

(5) The juvenile was not previously found delinquent;[25]

(6) The juvenile is not emotionally, physically, or psychologically mature enough for transfer;[26]

---

[13]This is a new provision.

[14]This is a new provision.

[15]Same as former law. RC 2923.12 excepted.

[16]This is a new provision.

[17]This is broader than former law, which only required review of conduct in prior DYS terms, but prior cases mention this factor. See State v. Hanning, 89 Ohio St. 3d 86, 2000-Ohio-436, 728 N.E.2d 1059 (2000) ("The juvenile court must look at Hanning's unique characteristics and actions, including whether he has a history indicating a failure to be rehabilitated."); State v. Carter, 27 Ohio St. 2d 135, 56 Ohio Op. 2d 75, 272 N.E.2d 119 (1971) (prior commitment to correctional school); State v. Douglas, 20 Ohio St. 3d 34, 485 N.E.2d 711 (1985) ("lengthy prior juvenile record"); State v. Whisenant, 127 Ohio App. 3d 75, 91, 711 N.E.2d 1016 (11th Dist. Portage County 1998) ("evidence of appellant's juvenile record (several previous adjudications of delinquency)"); State v. Parks, 51 Ohio App. 3d 194, 555 N.E.2d 671 (2d Dist. Montgomery County 1988) (prior sentence to juvenile facility at Riverview Center and prior stay at Columbus juvenile facility marked by fights and poor attitude).

[18]This is a new provision.

[19]This is a new provision, but prior cases mention this factor. See State v. Watson, 47 Ohio St. 3d 93, 547 N.E.2d 1181 (1989) ("Because of a juvenile's age, there may not be sufficient time remaining for rehabilitation to take place before the twenty-first birthday, even though the juvenile is otherwise amenable to rehabilitation."); State v. Hopfer, 112 Ohio App. 3d 521, 534, 679 N.E.2d 321 (2d Dist. Montgomery County 1996) ("Hopfer's age at the time of the hearing, only three months short of eighteen, weighed against retaining jurisdiction.").

[20]RC 2152.12(E).

[21]This is a new provision.

[22]This is a new provision.

[23]This is a new provision.

[24]This is broader than only looking to "physical harm" as in former law.

[25]This is a new provision, but prior cases mention this factor. See State v. Watson, 47 Ohio St. 3d 93, 547 N.E.2d 1181 (1989) ("[N]o record of trouble with the juvenile authorities."); State v. Hopfer, 112 Ohio App. 3d 521, 536, 679 N.E.2d 321 (2d Dist. Montgomery County 1996) ("lack of criminal history").

[26]This is a new provision.

(7) The juvenile is mentally ill or mentally retarded;[27]

(8) There is sufficient time to rehabilitate in the juvenile system and the level of security available reasonably assures public safety.[28]

Some of the Ohio Supreme Court's decisions interpreting prior amenability criteria may still be relevant. In *State v. Carmichael*,[29] the Court recognized that the juvenile court "should have considerable latitude within which to determine whether it should retain jurisdiction."[30] In *State v. Watson*,[31] the Court stated that "[t]here is no requirement that each, or any, of the five factors [determining transfer] be resolved against the juvenile so long as the totality of the evidence supports a finding that the juvenile is not amenable to treatment."[32] Again, the Court noted that "the juvenile court enjoys wide latitude to retain or relinquish jurisdiction, and the ultimate decision lies within its sound discretion."[33] Other Ohio courts had commented that a juvenile court "is not bound by the experts' opinions in making its determination whether the defendant is amenable to rehabilitation."[34]

Cross References
§ 1:4, Ch 2, § 22:12, § 23:29

§ 22:9   Amenability hearing procedures

In Ohio, RC 2152.10, RC 2152.12,[1] and Juvenile Rule 30 govern the transfer hearing and investigation. In *Kent v. United States*,[2] the United States Supreme Court held that "an opportunity for a hearing which may be informal, must be given the child prior to entry of a waiver order." In explaining the hearing requirement, the Court wrote, "We do not mean by this to indicate that the hearing to be held must conform with all of the requirements of a criminal trial or even of the usual administrative hearing; but we do hold that the hearing must measure up to the essentials of due process and fair treatment."[3]

RC 2152.12(C) requires the court to order an investigation, including a

---

[27]This is a new provision, but prior cases mention this factor. See State v. Watson, 47 Ohio St. 3d 93, 547 N.E.2d 1181 (1989) ("[N]o evidence of any psychiatric disorder."); State v. Hopfer, 112 Ohio App. 3d 521, 534, 679 N.E.2d 321 (2d Dist. Montgomery County 1996) ("Based upon these interviews and discussions with Hopfer's parents, [the expert] concluded that Hopfer was suffering from a psychiatric disorder at the time she committed the alleged crimes and that the disorder was treatable.").

[28]This is a new provision.

[29]State v. Carmichael, 35 Ohio St. 2d 1, 64 Ohio Op. 2d 1, 298 N.E.2d 568 (1973).

[30]State v. Carmichael, 35 Ohio St. 2d 1, 1 syl. 1, 64 Ohio Op. 2d 1, 298 N.E.2d 568 (1973).

[31]State v. Watson, 47 Ohio St. 3d 93, 547 N.E.2d 1181 (1989).

[32]State v. Watson, 47 Ohio St. 3d 93, 547 N.E.2d 1181 (1989). The Court added:

Rule 30 calls for a broad assessment of individual circumstances. Mechanical application of a rigidly defined test would not serve the purpose of the public or the juvenile. Further, reduction of the bindover decision to a formula would constrain desirable judicial discretion. We agree with appellant that Rule 30(E) requires consideration of all the listed factors, but we discern nothing in the rule, or in the policy it serves, which prohibits consideration of other relevant factors.

State v. Watson, 47 Ohio St. 3d 93, 95–96, 547 N.E.2d 1181 (1989).

[33]State v. Watson, 47 Ohio St. 3d 93, 547 N.E.2d 1181 (1989).

[34]State v. Houston, 70 Ohio App. 3d 152, 590 N.E.2d 839 (6th Dist. Lucas County 1990), citing State v. Dickens, 1987 WL 17928 (Ohio Ct. App. 9th Dist. Summit County 1987). Accord State v. Lopez, 112 Ohio App. 3d 659, 679 N.E.2d 1155 (9th Dist. Lorain County 1996) ("Nor is the juvenile court bound by expert opinions in determining whether the child is amenable to rehabilitation."); State v. Tilley, 1993 WL 385318 (Ohio Ct. App. 5th Dist. Stark County 1993) (defendant bound over even though clinical psychologist recommended against transfer).

[Section 22:9]
[1]Former RC 2151.26.

[2]Kent v. U.S., 383 U.S. 541, 561, 86 S. Ct. 1045, 16 L. Ed. 2d 84 (1966).

[3]Kent v. U.S., 383 U.S. 541, 562, 86 S. Ct. 1045, 16 L. Ed. 2d 84 (1966).

mental examination,[4] before considering transfer. Similarly, Juvenile Rule 30(C) requires the court to continue the proceedings until a "full" investigation is completed, at which time an amenability hearing must be held.

Waiver. Under prior law, whether the investigation and hearing could be waived was unclear.[5] The statute and rule explicitly recognize the right to waive the mental examination. This, along with the mandatory language, suggest that waiver of the investigation or hearing is not permitted. However, Juvenile Rule 3 provides that, except for the right to counsel at transfer hearings, the "rights of a child may be waived with the permission of the court."

Standard of proof. RC 2152.12(B)(3) provides that the court shall consider whether the factors in favor of transfer "outweigh" the factors against transfer. This appears to adopt the preponderance-of-evidence standard ("more probable than not"). In other jurisdictions, the standard of proof on the issue of nonamenability varies. Some jurisdictions require "substantial evidence," while others require a "preponderance of evidence." Still others have adopted a "clear and convincing evidence" standard,[6] a standard also found in the IJA-ABA Standards.[7]

§ 22:10   Mental examination

RC 2512.12(C) and Juvenile Rule 30(C) provide for a mental examination by a public or private agency or other qualified person prior to a discretionary transfer decision. At one time, the "investigation" requirement also included a physical examination, but this requirement was deleted by the 1996 statutory amendments.[1]

Waiver. The mental examination may be waived by the child, and refusal to submit to the examination constitutes a waiver.[2]

In *State ex rel. Doe v. Tracy*,[3] the court ordered a mental examination. After this examination, the prosecution moved for a second mental examination by a psychologist of the state's choosing. The juvenile attempted to waive this examination, but the court refused. When the juvenile, on advice of counsel, refused to answer questions at the second examination, the court

---

[4]See Text § 22:10, Mental examination.

[5]In *State v. Newton*, 1983 WL 6836 (Ohio Ct. App. 6th Dist. Fulton County 1983), the court of appeals held that the investigation and hearing cannot be waived. Once probable cause is found at the preliminary hearing,

a *full investigation is required* and a hearing *must* be held on the matter to determine whether the court should transfer jurisdiction to the trial court. At least one purpose of this hearing is to create a record in which the factual basis of the transfer order might be shown. Therefore, we conclude that the Juvenile Court erred in accepting a "waiver" of these procedures, which are mandatory and cannot be waived.

In contrast, the court in *State v. Soke*, 1993 WL 266951 (Ohio Ct. App. 8th Dist. Cuyahoga County 1993), upheld such a waiver. The court wrote:

Defendant also maintains that there is no authority contained within R.C. Chapter 2151, or Juv.R. 30 which permits a defendant to waive bind over proceedings. We agree that there is no specific authority for waiver of a bind over hearing, but we note that there is likewise no prohibition for waiver of the hearing.

Defendant also maintains that pursuant to the pronouncements of the United States Supreme Court in *Kent v. United States* (1966), . . . a hearing on the issue of the bind over is a critical phase and is mandatory. Critical phases, however, may be knowingly, competently and intelligently waived.

[6]See Rights of Juveniles: The Juvenile Justice System (2d ed.) §§ 4–17; In re Winship, 397 U.S. 358, 90 S. Ct. 1068, 25 L. Ed. 2d 368 (1970), which held that the proper standard of proof in delinquency cases is proof beyond a reasonable doubt, was expressly limited to the adjudicatory hearing. See also State v. Carmichael, 35 Ohio St. 2d 1, 64 Ohio Op. 2d 1, 298 N.E.2d 568 (1973).

[7]IJA-ABA Standards Relating to Transfer Between Courts 39 (1980).

[Section 22:10]
[1]The 1997 rule amendment also eliminated the physical examination requirement.

[2]RC 2152.12(C) (Waiver must be "competently and intelligently made."); Juv. R. 30(F).

[3]State ex rel. Doe v. Tracy, 51 Ohio App. 3d 198, 555 N.E.2d 674 (12th Dist. Warren County 1988).

cited him for contempt. The appellate court upheld the juvenile's right to waive the examination:

> [The statute] makes it equally clear that the decision to submit to or waive the examination rests ultimately with the child. The only requirement is that any waiver must be competently and intelligently made. . . . Accordingly, where the child competently and intelligently waives the mental and physical examination, the court must complete its investigation without it. Any attempt on the part of the court to secure such an examination over a valid waiver would be unreasonable and would constitute an abuse of discretion.[4]

Constitutional issues. In *State ex rel. a Juvenile v. Hoose,*[5] the juvenile asserted his Fifth Amendment right with respect to a court ordered mental examination by the court psychiatrist. Citing *Ake v. Oklahoma,*[6] the juvenile also moved for the appointment of a private professional to evaluate the juvenile at the state's expense. In *Ake* the United States Supreme Court ruled that a criminal defendant had a due process right to a defense expert under some circumstances. The court of appeals ruled that *Ake* did not apply to transfer hearings because these hearings do not determine guilt or innocence, nor is liberty at stake.[7]

The court also rejected the juvenile's arguments regarding the right to effective assistance of counsel and the Fifth Amendment privilege against self-incrimination:

> In essence, the argument raised by counsel for petitioner is that he faces a dilemma in advising his client on whether to submit to a mental examination by a court psychologist because of the potential use of any incriminating statements made by him during such examination.
>
> Contrary to petitioner's concern here, it is our view that any incriminating matter which might be obtained during the mental examination with the court psychologist pertaining to the relinquishment proceeding is expressly precluded from being used for anything other than the waiver determination itself. Juv.R. 32(B).
>
> Consequently, if the juvenile court decides to retain its jurisdiction, the relevant juvenile rule prevents the use of any statements made by petitioner during the course of the ensuing hearing there in determining the status of the charge or charges there. This provision in our judgment also bars the use of such statements if the juvenile is treated as an adult offender in the general division of the common pleas court.[8]

§ 22:11   Right to counsel

RC 2151.352 provides for the right to counsel at all juvenile court hearings.[1]

---

[4]State ex rel. Doe v. Tracy, 51 Ohio App. 3d 198, 201, 555 N.E.2d 674 (12th Dist. Warren County 1988).

[5]State ex rel. A Juvenile v. Hoose, 43 Ohio App. 3d 109, 539 N.E.2d 704 (11th Dist. Lake County 1988).

[6]Ake v. Oklahoma, 470 U.S. 68, 105 S. Ct. 1087, 84 L. Ed. 2d 53 (1985).

[7]State ex rel. A Juvenile v. Hoose, 43 Ohio App. 3d 109, 111, 539 N.E.2d 704 (11th Dist. Lake County 1988), citing State v. R.G.D., 108 N.J. 1, 18, 527 A.2d 834 (1987); see also State v. Whisenant, 127 Ohio App. 3d 75, 89–90, 711 N.E.2d 1016 (11th Dist. Portage County 1998) ("[W]e reaffirm our conclusion in Hoose that a juvenile is not entitled to a court-appointed independent psychologist to assist him in determining whether to submit to or waive a Juv.R. 30 mental examination.").

[8]State ex rel. A Juvenile v. Hoose, 43 Ohio App. 3d 109, 112, 539 N.E.2d 704 (11th Dist. Lake County 1988). See also State v. McDonald, 1990 WL 78593, at *14 (Ohio Ct. App. 2d Dist. Montgomery County 1990); Com. v. Wayne W., 414 Mass. 218, 606 N.E.2d 1323, 1329 (1993) (compelled psychiatric examination violates the 5th Amendment; however, juvenile waives this right if he voluntarily choses to offer expert psychiatric evidence).

[Section 22:11]

[1]See also Juv. R. 4(A).

The right to counsel at transfer hearings is also constitutionally required.[2] In *Kent* the United States Supreme Court stated that "counsel must be afforded to the child in waiver proceedings"[3] and that "there is no place in our system of law for reaching a result of such tremendous consequences . . . without effective assistance of counsel."[4]

RC 2151.352 also provides that in the case of indigency, the child has the right to appointed counsel.[5] This right is also constitutionally required.[6] In criminal trials the Sixth Amendment right to counsel includes the right to appointed counsel for indigent defendants,[7] and in *In re Gault*,[8] the Court held that the appointment of counsel is required in a delinquency adjudication if the child is "unable to afford to employ counsel."

Waiver. Usually, the right to counsel may be waived. The standard for waiver is an "intentional relinquishment or abandonment" of a fully known right.[9] In Ohio, however, the right to counsel at a transfer hearing may not be waived. Juvenile Rule 3 provides that a child's "right to be represented by counsel at a hearing conducted pursuant to Juv.R. 30 may not be waived."

Effective assistance. The right to counsel includes the right to effective assistance of counsel. This is the rule regarding the Sixth Amendment right to counsel,[10] and the United States Supreme Court's references to "effective assistance" of counsel in *Kent*[11] indicate that the same rule applies to the due process right of counsel in transfer proceedings.[12]

Role. The function of counsel at a transfer hearing is to challenge the evidence offered by the prosecution[13] and to adduce evidence that the child is amenable to treatment in the juvenile system. As one court has commented, "The child's advocate should search for a plan, or perhaps a range of plans, which may persuade the court that the welfare of the child and the safety of the community can be served without waiver."[14]

---

[2]See Geboy v. Gray, 471 F.2d 575 (7th Cir. 1973); Kemplen v. State of Md., 428 F.2d 169 (4th Cir. 1970); Inge v. Slayton, 395 F. Supp. 560 (E.D. Va. 1975); James v. Cox, 323 F. Supp. 15 (E.D. Va. 1971); Steinhauer v. State, 206 So. 2d 25 (Fla. Dist. Ct. App. 3d Dist. 1967).

[3]Kent v. U.S., 383 U.S. 541, 562, 86 S. Ct. 1045, 16 L. Ed. 2d 84 (1966). See also Application of Gault, 387 U.S. 1, 36, 87 S. Ct. 1428, 18 L. Ed. 2d 527 (1967).

[4]Kent v. U.S., 383 U.S. 541, 554, 86 S. Ct. 1045, 16 L. Ed. 2d 84 (1966).

[5]Juv. R. 2(R) defines "indigent person."

[6]Kemplen v. State of Md., 428 F.2d 169 (4th Cir. 1970).

[7]See Gideon v. Wainwright, 372 U.S. 335, 83 S. Ct. 792, 9 L. Ed. 2d 799, 93 A.L.R.2d 733 (1963); Argersinger v. Hamlin, 407 U.S. 25, 92 S. Ct. 2006, 32 L. Ed. 2d 530 (1972); Scott v. Illinois, 440 U.S. 367, 99 S. Ct. 1158, 59 L. Ed. 2d 383 (1979).

[8]Application of Gault, 387 U.S. 1, 42, 87 S. Ct. 1428, 18 L. Ed. 2d 527 (1967).

[9]Application of Gault, 387 U.S. 1, 42, 87 S. Ct. 1428, 18 L. Ed. 2d 527 (1967), quoting Johnson v. Zerbst, 304 U.S. 458, 464, 58 S. Ct. 1019, 82 L. Ed. 1461, 146 A.L.R. 357 (1938).

[10]See Strickland v. Washington, 466 U.S. 668, 104 S. Ct. 2052, 80 L. Ed. 2d 674 (1984) (Sixth Amendment requires reasonably effective assistance of counsel.).

[11]Kent v. U.S., 383 U.S. 541, 558, 86 S. Ct. 1045, 16 L. Ed. 2d 84 (1966).

[12]See Geboy v. Gray, 471 F.2d 575 (7th Cir. 1973) (noting counsel showed a "notable lack of zeal" in attempting to find alternatives to transfer).

[13]See Kent v. U.S., 383 U.S. 541, 563, 86 S. Ct. 1045, 16 L. Ed. 2d 84 (1966) ("[I]f the staff's submissions include materials which are susceptible to challenge or impeachment, it is precisely the role of counsel to 'denigrate' such matter.").

[14]Haziel v. U. S., 404 F.2d 1275, 1279 (D.C. Cir. 1968). For a discussion of counsel's role at the transfer hearing, see IJA-ABA Standards Relating to Counsel for Private Parties 161–68 (1980); Feld, Juvenile Court Legislative Reform and the Serious Young Offender: Dismantling the "Rehabilitative Ideal," 65 Minn. L. Rev. 167 (1981).

§ 22:12 Notice

RC 2152.12(G)[1] requires the court to give written notice of the time, place, and purpose of the transfer hearing to the child's parents, guardian or other custodian, and the child's counsel at least three days prior to the hearing. Juvenile Rule 30(D) is similar but also includes notice to the state and provides for an on-the-record waiver of the written notice requirement.

Adequate notice is an essential aspect of due process.[2] Notice must be given sufficiently in advance of the hearing to permit adequate preparation.[3] It also must be sufficiently specific to appraise the parties of the nature of the charges[4] and the purpose of the hearing.[5] Finally, the proper parties must receive notice.[6]

In *State v. Taylor*,[7] the court of appeals ruled that the "notice of hearing requirements . . . are mandatory requirements, which cannot be waived by the juvenile by failing to object to non-compliance." The presence of the defendant's sister at the hearing did not satisfy this requirement because she was not the legal custodian. The court also held that the notice requirement was jurisdictional: "[T]he juvenile court, failing to comply with the notice of hearing provisions of R.C. 2151.26 [now R.C. 2152.12], was without jurisdiction to bind the defendant over to the criminal, or general, division of the common pleas court and the latter was without jurisdiction to proceed on an indictment against him."[8]

In *State v. Parks*,[9] the court of appeals distinguished *Taylor*. At the probable cause hearing a detective testified that the defendant's grandmother had told him that she was the legal custodian and guardian. Although the detective never asked for documentation, the court ruled that the "record thus supports that notice was properly made upon the defendant's legal custodian as required by law."

§ 22:13 Rules of evidence

In many jurisdictions the rules of evidence are relaxed in transfer hearings

---

[Section 22:12]

[1]Former RC 2151.26(D).

[2]See U.S. v. James Daniel Good Real Property, 510 U.S. 43, 114 S. Ct. 492, 501, 126 L. Ed. 2d 490 (1993) ("The right to prior notice and a hearing is central to the Constitution's command of due process."); Wolff v. McDonnell, 418 U.S. 539, 94 S. Ct. 2963, 41 L. Ed. 2d 935 (1974) (prison disciplinary hearings); Morrissey v. Brewer, 408 U.S. 471, 92 S. Ct. 2593, 33 L. Ed. 2d 484 (1972) (parole revocation hearings); Cole v. State of Ark., 333 U.S. 196, 68 S. Ct. 514, 92 L. Ed. 644 (1948) (criminal cases); In re Oliver, 333 U.S. 257, 68 S. Ct. 499, 92 L. Ed. 682 (1948) (criminal cases).

[3]See Geboy v. Gray, 471 F.2d 575 (7th Cir. 1973); Kemplen v. State of Md., 428 F.2d 169 (4th Cir. 1970); Miller v. Quatsoe, 332 F. Supp. 1269 (E.D. Wis. 1971). See also Application of Gault, 387 U.S. 1, 33, 87 S. Ct. 1428, 18 L. Ed. 2d 527 (1967) ("Notice, to comply with due process requirements, must be given sufficiently in advance of scheduled court proceedings so that reasonable opportunity to prepare will be afforded.").

[4]See U. S. ex rel. Turner v. Rundle, 438 F.2d 839 (3d Cir. 1971). See also Application of Gault, 387 U.S. 1, 33, 87 S. Ct. 1428, 18 L. Ed. 2d 527 (1967) ("Notice, to comply with due process requirements, . . . must 'set forth the alleged misconduct with particularity.' ").

[5]See James v. Cox, 323 F. Supp. 15 (E.D. Va. 1971); State v. Gibbs, 94 Idaho 908, 500 P.2d 209 (1972).

[6]See Miller v. Quatsoe, 332 F. Supp. 1269 (E.D. Wis. 1971); Crandell v. State, 1975 OK CR 127, 539 P.2d 398 (Okla. Crim. App. 1975).

[7]State v. Taylor, 26 Ohio App. 3d 69, 71, 498 N.E.2d 211 (3d Dist. Auglaize County 1985).

[8]State v. Taylor, 26 Ohio App. 3d 69, 72, 498 N.E.2d 211 (3d Dist. Auglaize County 1985).

[9]State v. Parks, 51 Ohio App. 3d 194, 196, 555 N.E.2d 671 (2d Dist. Montgomery County 1988).

because these hearings are considered dispositional in nature.[1] At least as a general rule, however, in Ohio the Rules of Evidence apply in transfer hearings

Evidence Rule 101 provides that the Rules of Evidence "govern proceedings in the courts of this state."[2] Accordingly, the Rules of Evidence apply in transfer hearings. There is, however, an important exception. Evidence Rule 101(C)(6) exempts from the Rules of Evidence proceedings in which other rules prescribed by the Ohio Supreme Court govern evidentiary matters. Thus, where the Rules of Evidence are in conflict with any other rule prescribed by the Ohio Supreme Court, the "other rule" prevails. For example, Juvenile Rule 32(A)(2) expressly permits the use of a social history in transfer proceedings, although much of the material contained in a social history would be inadmissible under the Rules of Evidence. Juvenile Rule 2 defines the social history as "the personal and family history of a child or any other party to a juvenile proceeding and may include the prior record of the person with the juvenile court or any other court."

Prior to the adoption of the Rules of Evidence, the Ohio Supreme Court in *State v. Carmichael*[3] had upheld the use of a social history at a transfer hearing, despite its hearsay character.[4] In that case, however, the Court also indicated that the psychiatrists and psychologists whose opinions appeared in the social history could have been called as witnesses: "[T]hey were never called, nor was any effort made to call them by defense counsel, even though counsel had access to those documents for more than two months prior to the hearing."[5]

The issue of whether the right of confrontation applies at a transfer hearing was raised in *State v. Riggins*.[6] In that case, the defendant contended that he was denied due process because he was deprived of the opportunity to confront the witnesses against him, i.e., the confession of a codefendant was read into evidence by a police officer. The court of appeals overruled this objection because the defendant failed to provide a transcript to support his allegations.[7] Under Evidence Rule 801, the confession of a codefendant is inadmissible hearsay.

Expert testimony concerning the juvenile's psychological condition and

---

[Section 22:13]

[1]See Rights of Juveniles: The Juvenile Justice System (2d ed.) §§ 4–17. But see In re Anonymous, Juvenile Court No. 6358-4, 14 Ariz. App. 466, 484 P.2d 235 (Div. 2 1971) (Only competent evidence is admissible.); In Interest of Harris, 218 Kan. 625, 544 P.2d 1403 (1976) (Transfer may not be based on inadmissible hearsay.); People v. Hana, 443 Mich. 202, 504 N.W.2d 166 (1993) (relaxed evidentiary standards apply only to dispositional phase of transfer hearing).

[2]See generally Giannelli and Snyder, Baldwin's Ohio Practice, Evidence (2d ed.) § 101.1.

[3]State v. Carmichael, 35 Ohio St. 2d 1, 64 Ohio Op. 2d 1, 298 N.E.2d 568 (1973).

[4]See also State v. Riggins, 68 Ohio App. 2d 1, 7, 22 Ohio Op. 3d 1, 426 N.E.2d 504 (8th Dist. Cuyahoga County 1980) ("The Ohio Supreme Court has held that hearsay evidence is admissible at a relinquishment proceeding in Juvenile Court in the form of psychiatric reports from the Ohio Youth Commission Juvenile Diagnostic Center."); State v. Cole, 1983 WL 4463 (Ohio Ct. App. 12th Dist. Butler County 1983).

[5]State v. Carmichael, 35 Ohio St. 2d 1, 3–4, 64 Ohio Op. 2d 1, 298 N.E.2d 568 (1973).

[6]State v. Riggins, 68 Ohio App. 2d 1, 22 Ohio Op. 3d 1, 426 N.E.2d 504 (8th Dist. Cuyahoga County 1980).

[7]State v. Riggins, 68 Ohio App. 2d 1, 22 Ohio Op. 3d 1, 426 N.E.2d 504 (8th Dist. Cuyahoga County 1980). See also People ex rel. Guggenheim v. Mucci, 77 Misc. 2d 41, 352 N.Y.S.2d 561 (Sup 1974) (Due process requires that probable cause determination be based on nonhearsay evidence.).

For a discussion of the right of confrontation at the adjudicatory hearing, see § 23:22, Right of confrontation.

potential for treatment is admissible.[8]

§22:14 Self-incrimination

The privilege against self-incrimination applies in transfer hearings.[1] In *In re Gault*,[2] the United States Supreme Court held the privilege applicable to adjudicatory hearings, and in other cases the Court has stated that the privilege is applicable in any proceeding "civil or criminal, formal or informal, where the answers might incriminate [a person] in future criminal proceedings."[3] The Court has also held that a criminal defendant's exercise of the right to remain silent may not be commented upon or used against the defendant in a criminal trial.[4]

By testifying at a transfer hearing, the child waives the privilege against self-incrimination. Whether the child's statement may be later used at a criminal trial or at an adjudicatory hearing is unclear. If the statements may be used against the child at a later time, the child is placed in an untenable position. The child either must give up the privilege or give up the right to be heard at the transfer hearing. The United States Supreme Court considered an analogous situation in *Simmons v. United States*,[5] which involved a similar choice facing criminal defendants in suppression hearings:

> Thus, in this case [the defendant] was obliged either to give up what he believed, with advice of counsel, to be a valid Fourth Amendment claim or, in legal effect, to waive his Fifth Amendment privilege against self-incrimination. In these circumstances, we find it intolerable that one constitutional right should have to be surrendered in order to assert another. We therefore hold that when a defendant testifies in support of a motion to suppress evidence on Fourth Amendment grounds, his testimony may not thereafter be admitted against him at trial on the issue of guilt unless he makes no objection.

Several courts in other jurisdictions have applied this reasoning to transfer hearings: "[C]andid testimony by the juvenile at the fitness hearing should be encouraged to aid in the determination of where best to try the minor; fairness to the minor requires that this testimony not be given at the expense of the privilege against self-incrimination."[6] Accordingly, statements made at a transfer hearing have been held inadmissible at subsequent criminal trials[7] and adjudicatory hearings.[8] This rule of exclusion does not, however,

---

[8]E.g., State v. Watson, 47 Ohio St. 3d 93, 547 N.E.2d 1181 (1989) ("At the hearing, the court clinic psychiatrist . . . testified that appellant showed 'no evidence of any psychiatric disorder.' "); State v. Parks, 51 Ohio App. 3d 194, 555 N.E.2d 671 (2d Dist. Montgomery County 1988) ("The social worker . . . testified it would be doubtful that the appellant would be amenable to rehabilitation in a juvenile institution."); State v. McDonald, 1990 WL 78593 (Ohio Ct. App. 2d Dist. Montgomery County 1990) (Chief psychologist indicated that "psychological tests 'suggested' that appellant was intensely hostile and destructive, and had a 'sadistic potential.' ").

[Section 22:14]

[1]R. E. M. v. State, 532 S.W.2d 645 (Tex. Civ. App. San Antonio 1975). See also IJA-ABA Standards Relating to Transfer Between Courts 50 (1980).

[2]Application of Gault, 387 U.S. 1, 87 S. Ct. 1428, 18 L. Ed. 2d 527 (1967).

[3]Lefkowitz v. Turley, 414 U.S. 70, 77, 94 S. Ct. 316, 38 L. Ed. 2d 274 (1973).

[4]Griffin v. California, 380 U.S. 609, 85 S. Ct. 1229, 14 L. Ed. 2d 106 (1965). See also U.S. v. Robinson, 485 U.S. 25, 108 S. Ct. 864, 99 L. Ed. 2d 23 (1988) (not a Fifth Amendment violation to comment on an accused's silence in response to defense counsel's tactics); In re Jackson, 21 Ohio St. 2d 215, 50 Ohio Op. 2d 447, 257 N.E.2d 74 (1970) (no *Griffin* violation found).

[5]Simmons v. U.S., 390 U.S. 377, 394, 88 S. Ct. 967, 19 L. Ed. 2d 1247 (1968).

[6]Sheila O. v. Superior Court, 125 Cal. App. 3d 812, 178 Cal. Rptr. 418 (1st Dist. 1981).

[7]Ramona R. v. Superior Court, 37 Cal. 3d 802, 210 Cal. Rptr. 204, 693 P.2d 789 (1985); Bryan v. Superior Court, 7 Cal. 3d 575, 102 Cal. Rptr. 831, 498 P.2d 1079 (1972); Com. v. Ransom, 446 Pa. 457, 288 A.2d 762 (1972).

[8]Ramona R. v. Superior Court, 37 Cal. 3d 802, 210 Cal. Rptr. 204, 693 P.2d 789 (1985); Sheila O. v. Superior Court, 125 Cal. App. 3d 812, 178 Cal. Rptr. 418 (1st Dist. 1981) (except for impeachment). See also IJA-ABA Standards Relating to Transfer Between Courts 50–51 (1980).

extend to the impeachment use of such statements.[9]

In *State ex rel. a Juvenile v. Hoose*,[10] an Ohio court of appeals addressed this issue in the context of the mental examination:

> In essence, the argument raised by counsel for petitioner is that he faces a dilemma in advising his client on whether to submit to a mental examination by a court psychologist because of the potential use of any incriminating statements made by him during such examination.
>
> Contrary to petitioner's concern here, it is our view that any incriminating matter which might be obtained during the mental examination with the court psychologist pertaining to the relinquishment proceeding is expressly precluded from being used for anything other than the waiver determination itself. Juv.R. 32(B).
>
> Consequently, if the juvenile court decides to retain its jurisdiction, the relevant juvenile rule prevents the use of any statements made by petitioner during the course of the ensuing hearing there in determining the status of the charge or charges there. This provision in our judgment also bars the use of such statements if the juvenile is treated as an adult offender in the general division of the common pleas court.

Whether this rationale also applies to the juvenile's statements at the hearing is unclear.

§ 22:15   Access to reports & discovery

Juvenile Rule 32(C) authorizes counsel to inspect a social history or report of a mental or physical examination a reasonable time prior to the transfer hearing. The United States Supreme Court in *Kent* held that counsel had a right of access to social service records. The Court left no doubt that the right of inspection was intended to permit counsel to challenge the accuracy of these reports:

> [I]f the staff's submissions include materials which are susceptible to challenge or impeachment, it is precisely the role of counsel to "denigrate" such matter. There is no irrebuttable presumption of accuracy attached to staff reports. If a decision on waiver is "critically important" it is equally of "critical importance" that the material submitted to the judge . . . be subjected . . . to examination, criticism and refutation. While the Juvenile Court judge may, of course, receive *ex parte* analyses and recommendations from his staff, he may not, for the purposes of a decision on waiver, receive and rely upon secret information, whether emanating from his staff or otherwise.[1]

Juvenile Rule 32(C) grants the court authority to deny or limit inspection for good cause. The court may also order that the contents of the report be withheld from specified persons. The court, however, must state reasons for its action.

Under RC 2151.352, any report used in a juvenile court hearing must be made available to the child's counsel prior to the hearing, upon a written request and a showing of good cause. This provision also applies to counsel for a parent, guardian, or custodian.

Discovery. Juvenile Rule 24 governs discovery. In *In re Doss*,[2] the juvenile court commented that in a preliminary (probable cause) hearing the "state need not provide as full a discovery as that required for an adjudica-

---

[9]People v. Macias, 16 Cal. 4th 739, 753, 66 Cal. Rptr. 2d 659, 941 P.2d 838 (1997) ("[N]othing in the state Constitution or our judicial decisions protects juveniles from impeachment if their voluntary trial testimony is inconsistent with the substantively immunized statements they make to their probation officers before their fitness hearings.").

[10]State ex rel. A Juvenile v. Hoose, 43 Ohio App. 3d 109, 112, 539 N.E.2d 704 (11th Dist. Lake County 1988).

[Section 22:15]

[1]Kent v. U.S., 383 U.S. 541, 563, 86 S. Ct. 1045, 16 L. Ed. 2d 84 (1966).

[2]In re Doss, 65 Ohio Misc. 2d 8, 10, 640 N.E.2d 618 (C.P. 1994). See also Discovery Ch 21.

tory hearing conducted under Juv.R. 29." The court did not, however, rely on this conclusion in deciding the discovery issue. Instead, the court based its decision on Juvenile Rule 24(B), which recognizes the court's authority to limit discovery if it would impede a criminal prosecution of an adult or a transferred juvenile. In the case, five individuals were charged with murder, two of whom were adults. In addition to Doss, two other juveniles were charged; one was under the transfer age and the other was awaiting transfer proceedings. The court ordered discovery of the names, addresses, and statements of only those witnesses that the prosecution intended to call at the preliminary hearing, as well as photographs, physical evidence, and reports that the prosecution intended to introduce at the hearing. If probable cause was established at the preliminary hearing, the prosecution was required to produce all material required by Criminal Rule 16.[3]

In re A.M.[4] held that Juvenile Rule 22(D)(4) specified that discovery under Rule 24 takes place before the adjudicatory hearing and, since a probable cause transfer hearing is not an adjudicatory hearing, discovery was not required. The prosecution had argued that discovery in a mandatory bindover hearing would provide the juvenile with more discovery than would be available under Criminal Rule 16 if the juvenile were transferred. Citing *Kent's* due process analysis, the court of appeals disagreed. The court wrote:

> The juvenile plainly has a legitimate interest in discovering the evidence that the prosecutor will offer to establish probable cause mandating transfer. We see no reason why the juvenile, in preparing for the only proceeding that will determine whether he will be tried as a juvenile or as an adult, should be denied the opportunity to discover the evidence the state will present to establish probable cause. While the discovery provided in anticipation of the mandatory bindover hearing under R.C. 2151.26(B) need not go beyond the limited issues that will be decided at the hearing, we find no support for the prosecutor's contention that the juvenile is not entitled to any discovery for that hearing.

The court noted, however, that the prosecution could request restrictions on discovery under Rule 24(B): "Upon a proper showing, Juv. R. 24(B) authorizes the juvenile court to limit discovery."[5] Finally, the juvenile court's decision "will not be disturbed on appeal absent an abuse of discretion."[6]

§ 22:16 Right to present evidence

Although the Juvenile Rules do not specifically recognize a child's right to present evidence at a transfer hearing, there seems little question that this right exists.[1] The right to counsel, the right to notice,[2] and the right of access to the social history all imply a right to present evidence. In a different context, the United States Supreme Court has commented, "Ordinarily, the right to present evidence is basic to a fair hearing."[3]

The Ohio Supreme Court has implicitly recognized this right. In one case the Court commented on a defense counsel's failure to make any effort to call

---

[3]The court reserved decision on whether additional discovery would be ordered if probable cause was not found or the child was found amenable to juvenile court jurisdiction.

[4]In re A.M., 139 Ohio App. 3d 303, 309, 743 N.E.2d 937 (8th Dist. Cuyahoga County 2000). The court of appeals overruled In re Hunter, 99 Ohio Misc. 2d 107, 111, 716 N.E.2d 802 (C.P. 1999).

[5]In re A.M., 139 Ohio App. 3d 303, 310, 743 N.E.2d 937 (8th Dist. Cuyahoga County 2000).

[6]In re A.M., 139 Ohio App. 3d 303, 310, 743 N.E.2d 937 (8th Dist. Cuyahoga County 2000).

[Section 22:16]

[1]See Summers v. State, 248 Ind. 551, 230 N.E.2d 320 (1967); In re Brown, 183 N.W.2d 731 (Iowa 1971); In re Doe, 86 N.M. 37, 519 P.2d 133 (Ct. App. 1974).

[2]See Wolff v. McDonnell, 418 U.S. 539, 564, 94 S. Ct. 2963, 41 L. Ed. 2d 935 (1974) (Prison disciplinary hearings: "Part of the function of notice is to give the charged party a chance to marshal the facts in his defense.").

[3]Wolff v. McDonnell, 418 U.S. 539, 566, 94 S. Ct. 2963, 41 L. Ed. 2d 935 (1974).

witnesses at a transfer hearing.[4]

§ 22:17 Statement of reasons

Juvenile Rule 30(G) requires the juvenile court to state reasons if it decides to transfer the child. RC 2152.12(I) adopts this requirement, and another provision requires the court to state on the record which of the factors "for" or "against" transfer are applicable and how they were weighed.[1]

The United States Supreme Court in *Kent* also required a statement of the reasons:

> Meaningful review requires that the reviewing court should review. It should not be remitted to assumptions. It must have before it a statement of the reasons motivating the waiver including, of course, a statement of the relevant facts. It may not "assume" that there are adequate reasons, nor may it merely assume that "full investigation" has been made. Accordingly, we hold that it is incumbent upon the Juvenile Court to accompany its waiver order with a statement of the reasons or considerations therefor. We do not read the statute as requiring that this statement must be formal or that it should necessarily include conventional findings of fact. But the statement should be sufficient to demonstrate that the statutory requirement of "full investigation" has been met; and that the question has received the careful consideration of the Juvenile Court; and it must set forth the basis for the order with sufficient specificity to permit meaningful review.[2]

In *State v. Oviedo*,[3] the court of appeals held that Juvenile Rule 30(G) is satisfied if the transfer order demonstrates that the "full investigation" requirement has been met and the issue has received the full attention of the court. In contrast, the court in *State v. Newton*[4] required more:

> Mere recitation of the conclusory language set forth in Juv.R. 30(C)(1) and (2) is *not* sufficient. Conclusions are not reasons, as contemplated by Juv.R. 30(G). The "reasonable grounds" for the court's belief that a juvenile is not amenable to rehabilitation and that the community's safety may require his legal restraint must be spelled out with reasonable specificity. Stated differently, Juv.R. 30(G) necessitates findings of fact from which to determine the prerequisites in Juv.R. 30(C)(1) and (2) and upon which to base the transfer order.[5]

In a later case, *State v. Douglas*,[6] the Ohio Supreme Court commented:

> Neither R.C. 2151.26 [R.C. 2152.12] nor Juv.R. 30 requires the juvenile court to make written findings as to the five factors listed in [then] Juv.R. 30(E). The rule simply requires the court to *consider* these factors in making its determination on the amenability issue. Although the better practice would be to address each factor, as long as sufficient, credible evidence pertaining to each factor exists in the record before the court, the bind-over order should not be reversed in the absence of an abuse of discretion.

The Court also stated that Juvenile Rule 30(H) "does not require written

---

[4]See State v. Carmichael, 35 Ohio St. 2d 1, 64 Ohio Op. 2d 1, 298 N.E.2d 568 (1973). See also State v. Yoss, 10 Ohio App. 2d 47, 39 Ohio Op. 2d 81, 225 N.E.2d 275 (7th Dist. Carroll County 1967) (*Kent* requires the juvenile court to consider additional evidence offered by a child in a transfer hearing.).

[Section 22:17]
[1]RC 2152.12(B)(3) ("The record shall indicate the specific factors that were applicable and that the court weighed.").

[2]Kent v. U.S., 383 U.S. 541, 561, 86 S. Ct. 1045, 16 L. Ed. 2d 84 (1966).

[3]State v. Oviedo, 5 Ohio App. 3d 168, 450 N.E.2d 700 (6th Dist. Wood County 1982).

[4]State v. Newton, 1983 WL 6836 (Ohio Ct. App. 6th Dist. Fulton County 1983).

[5]State v. Newton, 1983 WL 6836, at *7 (Ohio Ct. App. 6th Dist. Fulton County 1983) (emphasis by the court). See also State v. Reuss, 1981 WL 5748 (Ohio Ct. App. 6th Dist. Wood County 1981) (Bare recitation of factors in Juv. R. 30(E) is insufficient.).

[6]State v. Douglas, 20 Ohio St. 3d 34, 36, 485 N.E.2d 711 (1985).

findings on each of the five factors listed in [then] Juv.R. 30(E)."[7] "In a foot-note, the Court [in *Douglas*] noted that the juvenile court sufficiently stated is reasons for appellee's transfer as required by Juv.R. 30(G) although the juvenile court's journal entry relinquishing jurisdiction was couched in the conclusory language of R.C. 2151.26 [R.C. 2152.12]."[8]

Courts in other jurisdictions have insisted on specific reasons for transfer.[9]

§ 22:18 Right to a transcript

Juvenile Rule 37(A) governs the right to a recording of juvenile court hearings upon request. The 1996 amendment to Juvenile Rule 37, which made recording of adjudicatory and dispositional hearings mandatory, apparently does not apply to transfer hearings. A request to record transfer hearings should be made in every case. Moreover, one Ohio court, citing due process and equal protection grounds, has held that an indigent child has a right to a transcript in transfer proceedings.[1]

The importance of a transcript is illustrated by *State v. Riggins*,[2] in which the appellate court overruled an alleged error at a transfer hearing because the "appellant has failed to provide this court with a transcript of the hearing before the Juvenile Court at which this evidence was presented."[3]

§ 22:19 Public hearing—Victims—Gag orders

Juvenile Rule 27(A) was amended in 2001 to provide a standard for determining closure in juvenile hearings. SYO hearings are open to the

---

[7]State v. Douglas, 20 Ohio St. 3d 34, 36 n.2, 485 N.E.2d 711 (1985). The juvenile court in In re Snitzky, 73 Ohio Misc. 2d 52, 54, 657 N.E.2d 1379 (C.P. 1995), criticized the prior transfer procedure:

> Unfortunately, Ohio law regarding the transfer of juvenile offenders to the general division for prosecution as an adult is confused and contradictory. The proper weight which should be given to the degree of violence of the offense, versus the youth's prospects for rehabilitation, is unclear, with the rule, statute, and case law offering contradictory directives.
>
> In order to make the necessary public discourse possible, a court must honestly state the reasons for its decision, rather than camouflaging its rationale in the nonsensical intricacies of the statute, rule, and precedents. When a court choses [sic] to camouflage the reasons for a particular decision, it short-circuits the democratic process. In order for this process to function effectively, a juvenile court must honestly and openly articulate the rationale behind its decision whether or not to transfer a youth. Additionally, in order to meet constitutionally mandated due process requirements, a reviewing court must be able to meaningfully review such a decision.
>
> One effect of the lack of direction offered by the statute, rule, and precedents is transfer decisions which are subjected to only a cursory review, as any conclusion can be read to fit within the broad applicable law. In effect, the discretion of the juvenile court is largely unfettered. Beyond the obvious due process concerns, decisions made in such a vacuum contribute little to the evolution of juvenile justice because they hinder the ongoing dialogue between the courts and the legislature, which is an absolute necessity in crafting solutions to the ever-increasing problem of gang- and drug-related violent crimes.

[8]State v. McDonald, 1990 WL 78593, at *9 (Ohio Ct. App. 2d Dist. Montgomery County 1990).

[9]See Summers v. State, 248 Ind. 551, 230 N.E.2d 320 (1967); Risner v. Com., 508 S.W.2d 775 (Ky. 1974); Matter of Heising, 29 Or. App. 903, 565 P.2d 1105 (1977); Knott v. Langlois, 102 R.I. 517, 231 A.2d 767 (1967). See also IJA-ABA Standards Relating to Transfer Between Courts 33–34 (1980).

[Section 22:18]

[1]State v. Ross, 23 Ohio App. 2d 215, 52 Ohio Op. 2d 311, 262 N.E.2d 427 (2d Dist. Greene County 1970). See also State v. Harris, 1981 WL 3505 (Ohio Ct. App. 10th Dist. Franklin County 1981) (No due process violation for failure to provide a transcript where defendant did not attempt to use procedure provided in App. R. 9(C) for a statement of the evidence or proceedings when no transcript is available.).

[2]State v. Riggins, 68 Ohio App. 2d 1, 22 Ohio Op. 3d 1, 426 N.E.2d 504 (8th Dist. Cuyahoga County 1980).

[3]State v. Riggins, 68 Ohio App. 2d 1, 22 Ohio Op. 3d 1, 8, 426 N.E.2d 504 (8th Dist. Cuyahoga County 1980). See also Bailey & Rothblatt, Handling Juvenile Delinquency Cases 183 (1982) ("Insist that the proceedings be transcribed.").

public.[1] In all other hearings, the court may exclude the general public but may not exclude persons with a direct interest in the case or persons who demonstrate, at a hearing, a countervailing right to be present.[2] RC 2151.35(A) is comparable.

Victims. RC 2930.09[3] recognizes the right of a victim[4] to be present whenever an alleged juvenile offender is present during any on-the-record stage of the case, unless the court determines that exclusion of the victim is necessary to protect the juvenile's right to a fair delinquency hearing. At the victim's request, the victim has the right to be accompanied by an individual to provide support to the victim, unless the court determines that exclusion of that individual is necessary to protect the juvenile's right to a fair delinquency hearing.

Closure. In *State ex rel. Fyffe v. Pierce,*[5] the Ohio Supreme Court refused to issue a writ of prohibition to close a transfer hearing. The Court pointed out that both the rule and the statute make closure discretionary: "The word 'may' is clearly not mandatory; therefore, the court was not required to close the hearing, but could exercise its discretion."[6] Moreover, the Court found an adequate remedy at law. According to the Court, "If tried as adults, they can move for change of venue to alleviate any unfairness that pretrial publicity may cause. If change of venue is denied, and relators are subsequently convicted, they can appeal."[7]

In *In re T.R.,*[8] the Supreme Court once again addressed the closure issue, albeit in a dependency case. The Court first recognized that the public has a qualified constitutional right of access to court proceedings. However, "the open courts provision of the Ohio Constitution [Art. I, sec. 16] creates no greater right of public access to court proceedings than that accorded by the [free speech and free press clauses of federal and state constitutions]."[9] In light of the need for confidentiality in dependency cases, the Court concluded that "there is no qualified right of public access to juvenile court proceedings to determine if a child is abused, neglected, or dependent, or to determine custody of a minor child."[10] These proceedings are "neither presumptively open nor presumptively closed to the press and public."[11]

The Court then examined the competing interests involved—the public's interest in judicial proceedings and the child's interest in confidentiality. "While the public's interest in access is important and deserving of protection, the state also has a compelling interest in the protection of children."[12] A trial court may close such a proceeding "if, after hearing evidence and argument on the issue, it finds that: (1) there exists a reasonable and substantial basis for believing that public access could harm the child or endanger the fairness of the proceeding, and (2) the potential for harm

---

[1]See Text Ch 5.

[2]See also Staff Note (2001) ("The rule seeks to conform to the Supreme Court's ruling in State ex rel. Plain Dealer Publishing Co. v. Geauga Cty. Court of Common Pleas, Juv. Div., 90 Ohio St. 3d 79, 2000-Ohio-35, 734 N.E.2d 1214 (2000).").

[3]This statute was enacted pursuant to the Victims' Rights provision of the Ohio Constitution. O. Const. art. I § 10a.

[4]RC 2930.02provides a procedure for the designation of a victim's representative, who is authorized to exercise the victim's rights under RC Ch. 2930.

[5]State ex rel. Fyffe v. Pierce, 40 Ohio St. 3d 8, 531 N.E.2d 673 (1988).

[6]State ex rel. Fyffe v. Pierce, 40 Ohio St. 3d 8, 9, 531 N.E.2d 673 (1988).

[7]State ex rel. Fyffe v. Pierce, 40 Ohio St. 3d 8, 9, 531 N.E.2d 673 (1988).

[8]In re T.R., 52 Ohio St. 3d 6, 556 N.E.2d 439 (1990).

[9]In re T.R., 52 Ohio St. 3d 6, 14, 556 N.E.2d 439 (1990).

[10]In re T.R., 52 Ohio St. 3d 6, 17, 556 N.E.2d 439 (1990).

[11]In re T.R., 52 Ohio St. 3d 6, 18, 556 N.E.2d 439 (1990).

[12]In re T.R., 52 Ohio St. 3d 6, 18, 556 N.E.2d 439 (1990).

outweighs the benefits of public access."[13] The Court went on to hold that the juvenile court had not abused its discretion in closing the proceedings and issuing a gag order on the litigants and attorneys in the case, although the order had to be modified because it was overbroad.

The Ohio Supreme Court applied *T.R.* to transfer hearings in *State ex rel. Plain Dealer Publishing Co. v. Geauga County Court of Common Pleas.*[14] The Court noted that it had observed in *T.R.* that the need for confidentiality was less compelling in delinquency cases than in cases involving an abused, neglected, or dependent child because the "delinquent child is at least partially responsible for the case being in court." Moreover, the Court, for the first time, held explicitly that

> the burden is borne by the party seeking closure to the proceeding because in the absence of evidence and findings supporting those factors, the juvenile court cannot close the proceedings. In other words, if there is no evidence that there exists a reasonable and substantial basis for believing that public access could harm the child or endanger the fairness of the adjudication, that the potential for harm outweighs the benefits of public access, and that there are no reasonable alternatives to closure, a closure order is not justified. Consequently, the risk of non-persuasion is on the party seeking closure.[15]

The Court found that the harms cited by the trial court were "little more than the personal predilections of the judge that are not susceptible of judicial notice and, if accepted as appropriate, would arguably justify the closure of all juvenile delinquency proceedings."[16]

After *T.R.* was decided but before *Plain Dealer* was handed down, juvenile courts had addressed the issue. One juvenile court concluded that "the holding in *T.R.*, which provides that certain juvenile court hearings are neither presumptively open nor presumptively closed, should be applied to both the preliminary and amenability hearings in Juv.R. 30 proceedings."[17] Another court had ruled that "[p]ublic access ought to remain open to those portions of the bindover proceedings which directly relate to the nature of the crime alleged to have been committed. Therefore, the public will have access to the probable cause hearing."[18] The amenability hearing was treated differently. "Certain portions of any amenability hearing ought to be closed, because some portions of such hearings often involve information about a child's

---

[13]In re T.R., 52 Ohio St. 3d 6, 18–19, 556 N.E.2d 439 (1990).

[14]State ex rel. Plain Dealer Publishing Co. v. Geauga Cty. Court of Common Pleas, Juv. Div., 90 Ohio St. 3d 79, 83, 2000-Ohio-35, 734 N.E.2d 1214 (2000). The Court noted the historic rationale for juvenile courts: "Juvenile court proceedings have historically been closed to the public, and public access to these proceedings does not necessarily play a significant positive role in the juvenile court process. . . . These traditional interests of confidentiality and rehabilitation prevent the public from having a qualified constitutional right of access to juvenile delinquency proceedings." The Court went on to conclude: "Juvenile delinquency proceedings should not be presumed closed because many legitimate interests favor public access to these proceedings." State ex rel. Plain Dealer Publishing Co. v. Geauga Cty. Court of Common Pleas, Juv. Div., 90 Ohio St. 3d 79, 84, 2000-Ohio-35, 734 N.E.2d 1214 (2000).

[15]State ex rel. Plain Dealer Publishing Co. v. Geauga Cty. Court of Common Pleas, Juv. Div., 90 Ohio St. 3d 79, 85–86, 2000-Ohio-35, 734 N.E.2d 1214 (2000).

[16]State ex rel. Plain Dealer Publishing Co. v. Geauga Cty. Court of Common Pleas, Juv. Div., 90 Ohio St. 3d 79, 87, 2000-Ohio-35, 734 N.E.2d 1214 (2000). The Court also wrote: "These factors—the public interest in the juvenile proceedings, J.H.'s near-adult age at the time of the alleged offenses, the minimal likelihood that the probable cause hearing will disclose confidential information of the sort specified in T.R., the gravity of the charged offenses, and the fact that J.H. will be subject to mandatory bindover to adult court if probable cause is found—outweigh J.H.'s attorney's bare assertion that permitting access would not be in J.H.'s best interest." State ex rel. Plain Dealer Publishing Co. v. Geauga Cty. Court of Common Pleas, Juv. Div., 90 Ohio St. 3d 79, 88, 2000-Ohio-35, 734 N.E.2d 1214 (2000).

[17]In re D.R., 63 Ohio Misc. 2d 273, 279, 624 N.E.2d 1120 (C.P. 1993).

[18]In re N.H., 63 Ohio Misc. 2d 285, 297, 626 N.E.2d 697 (C.P. 1992).

psychological, social and family histories."[19]

Gag orders. In *State ex rel. News Herald v. Ottawa County Court of Common Pleas, Juvenile Division*,[20] the juvenile court ruled the transfer hearing open to the public but then issued a "gag order" prohibiting the media from reporting the case until a transfer order was entered. The Ohio Supreme Court granted a writ of prohibition to dissolve the gag order. The Court commented: "The order of the trial court . . . is a classic order of prior restraint. The order prohibited publication of information legally obtained by relators [newspapers]."[21]

Cross References
§ 1:4, § 23:11, § 23:22, § 34:9, § 35:2

§ 22:20   Impartial judge

In *In re Disqualification of Ruben*,[1] the prosecutor filed an affidavit of disqualification of the juvenile court judge on the grounds that the judge held a predisposition against the transfer of certain juveniles for prosecution as adults—an expressed reluctance to transfer unless the juvenile had previously been committed to the custody of the Department of Youth Services. The prosecutor alleged that this reluctance imposed a higher standard than required by law for transfer. The Chief Justice ruled against disqualification, pointing out that the juvenile judge had "granted motions to transfer an alleged juvenile delinquent for prosecution as an adult in more than one-half of the cases in which the motions were considered, including cases in which the juvenile had no prior commitment to the custody of the Department of Youth Services."[2]

In *State v. Payne*,[3] the defendant argued that a comment by the juvenile judge during the preliminary transfer hearing that the defendant had committed the offense beyond a reasonable doubt demonstrated the judge's lack of impartiality in the subsequent amenability proceeding. The court of appeals rejected this argument, finding the judge's personal opinion on this issue irrelevant. The court commented: "The juvenile court judge may believe that the juvenile committed the offense, but that the juvenile is completely amenable to rehabilitation."[4]

§ 22:21   Retention of jurisdiction

If the juvenile court decides to retain jurisdiction, it must schedule a hearing on the merits.[1] One court has stated that a juvenile judge is not disqualified from presiding at an adjudicatory hearing because of the judge's involvement in a prior transfer hearing.[2] In contrast, the IJA-ABA Standards

---

[19]In re N.H., 63 Ohio Misc. 2d 285, 298, 626 N.E.2d 697 (C.P. 1992).

[20]State ex rel. News Herald v. Ottawa Cty. Court of Common Pleas, Juv. Div., 77 Ohio St. 3d 40, 1996-Ohio-354, 671 N.E.2d 5 (1996).

[21]State ex rel. News Herald v. Ottawa Cty. Court of Common Pleas, Juv. Div., 77 Ohio St. 3d 40, 45, 1996-Ohio-354, 671 N.E.2d 5 (1996).

[Section 22:20]
[1]In re Disqualification of Ruben, 77 Ohio St. 3d 1232, 674 N.E.2d 348 (1995).

[2]In re Disqualification of Ruben, 77 Ohio St. 3d 1232, 674 N.E.2d 348 (1995).

[3]State v. Payne, 118 Ohio App. 3d 699, 703, 693 N.E.2d 1159 (3d Dist. Seneca County 1997) ("The issue of whether a juvenile court judge denied a juvenile a fair and impartial amenability hearing appears to be a case of first impression in this state.").

[4]State v. Payne, 118 Ohio App. 3d 699, 704, 693 N.E.2d 1159 (3d Dist. Seneca County 1997).

[Section 22:21]
[1]Juv. R. 30(E).

[2]In re Terry H., 1 O.B.R. 377 (C.P., Cuyahoga 1982). See also § 23:28, Impartial judge.

recognize a child's right to disqualify the transfer hearing judge from participating in subsequent proceedings: "No matter how fair the waiver judge may be in subsequent proceedings, an impression of unfairness will exist."[3]

§ 22:22 Transfer of jurisdiction

The criminal court to which jurisdiction has been transferred may not "review the factual findings of the juvenile court on the issue of amenability."[1]

Bail. If the juvenile court decides to transfer jurisdiction, it will set the terms and conditions for release of the child in accordance with Criminal Rule 46.[2] If the child is in detention, the child may be transferred to the appropriate officer or detention facility in accordance with the law governing the detention of adults,[3] provided certain conditions are satisfied.

Abatement of jurisdiction. RC 2152.12(I)[4] provides that "transfer abates the jurisdiction of the juvenile court with respect to the delinquent *acts alleged in the complaint*, and upon the transfer, all further proceedings pertaining to *the act charged* shall be discontinued in the juvenile court, and the case then shall be within the jurisdiction of the court to which it is transferred." This provision, added in 1996,[5] supersedes *State v. Adams*,[6] in which the Ohio Supreme Court had held that once a child is properly transferred, the child is considered bound over for *all* felonies, even if the other felonies have not been subject to transfer proceedings.

Once the person is transferred, that person is no longer a "child" in the transferred case.[7] Moreover, once the juvenile court has transferred the case, it lacks subject matter jurisdiction in the case and may not consider a motion for relief from judgment under Civil Rule 60(B).[8]

Criminal trial. Once the child is transferred, the child is subject to punishment as an adult—with the exception of the death penalty, which cannot be imposed on a person who was not 18 years at the time of the offense.[9] A grand jury may indict for any offense appropriate under the facts; the grand jury is not limited to the charges filed in juvenile court.[10] Moreover, a criminal defendant's statutory right to a speedy trial does not commence

---

[3]IJA-ABA Standards Relating to Transfer Between Courts 49 (1980). See also Donald L. v. Superior Court, 7 Cal. 3d 592, 598, 102 Cal. Rptr. 850, 498 P.2d 1098 (1972) ("[I]f the referee or judge who hears the issue of fitness decides that the minor should be retained in the juvenile court, he may not thereafter properly preside at a contested hearing on the issue of jurisdiction.").

[Section 22:22]

[1]State v. Whiteside, 6 Ohio App. 3d 30, 36, 452 N.E.2d 332 (3d Dist. Allen County 1982).

[2]Juv. R. 30(H). For a discussion of Crim. R. 46, see Katz and Giannelli, Baldwin's Ohio Practice, Criminal Law (2d ed.). See also RC 2152.12(I).

[3]RC 2151.312(C). The child must be confined in a room totally separated by sight and sound from adult detainees.

[4]Former RC 2151.26(F).

[5]1995 H.B. 1.

[6]State v. Adams, 69 Ohio St. 2d 120, 23 Ohio Op. 3d 164, 431 N.E.2d 326 (1982).

[7]RC 2152.02(C)(4).

[8]In re Williams, 111 Ohio App. 3d 120, 125, 675 N.E.2d 1254 (10th Dist. Franklin County 1996).

[9]See RC 2929.023.

[10]State v. Adams, 69 Ohio St. 2d 120, 126–27, 23 Ohio Op. 3d 164, 431 N.E.2d 326 (1982) (A grand jury does not exceed its authority by returning indictments on charges that were not originally filed in juvenile court.); State v. Klingenberger, 113 Ohio St. 418, 3 Ohio L. Abs. 675, 149 N.E. 395 (1925). See also State v. Whisenant, 127 Ohio App. 3d 75, 81, 711 N.E.2d 1016 (11th Dist. Portage County 1998) ("[T]he grand jury was within its power to indict appellant for counts that were not alleged in the juvenile proceedings.").

until the juvenile court relinquishes jurisdiction.[11] In addition, a defendant is entitled to good time credit for the time spent in juvenile custody.[12] By pleading guilty in criminal court, a defendant does not waive the right to contest the validity of the transfer decision.[13] If the case goes to trial, the prosecution is usually prohibited from commenting on the transfer decision: "Generally, the state is not permitted to refer to previous trials or hearings of the same cause of action for the same defendant."[14]

Future cases. A transferred person who is convicted is no longer a "child" in any future case.[15]

Cross References
§ 23:12

§ 22:23 Appeals

In Ohio, a juvenile court order transferring jurisdiction to the criminal courts is not a final appealable order.[1] Thus, a transfer order may be challenged on appeal only after trial and conviction in the criminal courts. Similarly, a writ of prohibition may not be used to challenge a transfer order.[2] Although a number of jurisdictions permit appeals of transfer orders, the Ohio rule appears to be the majority rule.[3] The Ohio Supreme Court has reasoned:

> To permit interlocutory review of such an order would obviously delay the prosecution of any proceeding in either the juvenile or the criminal division, with the result that the prospect of a just disposition would be jeopardized. In either proceeding the primary issue is the ascertainment of the innocence or guilt of the person charged. To permit interlocutory review would subordinate that primary issue and defer its consideration while the question of the punishment appropriate for a suspect whose guilt has not yet been ascertained is be-

[11]State v. Bickerstaff, 10 Ohio St. 3d 62, 461 N.E.2d 892 (1984); State ex rel. Williams v. Court of Common Pleas of Lucas County, 42 Ohio St. 2d 433, 71 Ohio Op. 2d 410, 329 N.E.2d 680 (1975); State v. Steele, 8 Ohio App. 3d 137, 456 N.E.2d 513 (10th Dist. Franklin County 1982); State v. Trapp, 52 Ohio App. 2d 189, 6 Ohio Op. 3d 175, 368 N.E.2d 1278 (1st Dist. Hamilton County 1977); State v. Young, 44 Ohio App. 2d 387, 73 Ohio Op. 2d 462, 339 N.E.2d 668 (10th Dist. Franklin County 1975).

[12]State v. Young, 44 Ohio App. 2d 387, 73 Ohio Op. 2d 462, 339 N.E.2d 668 (10th Dist. Franklin County 1975).

[13]State v. Riggins, 68 Ohio App. 2d 1, 22 Ohio Op. 3d 1, 426 N.E.2d 504 (8th Dist. Cuyahoga County 1980).

[14]State v. Hopfer, 112 Ohio App. 3d 521, 540, 679 N.E.2d 321 (2d Dist. Montgomery County 1996) ("In light of the innocuous nature of these comments, along with the procedural nature of the amenability hearing itself, we conclude that the prosecutor's references to the amenability hearing were not improper and did not prejudice Hopfer's right to a fair trial.").

[15]RC 2152.02(C)(5); former RC 2151.011(B)(5)(e). Some language in the former law was deleted as unnecessary.

[Section 22:23]

[1]In re Becker, 39 Ohio St. 2d 84, 68 Ohio Op. 2d 50, 314 N.E.2d 158 (1974). Accord State ex rel. Torres v. Simmons, 68 Ohio St. 2d 118, 22 Ohio Op. 3d 340, 428 N.E.2d 862 (1981); State v. Houston, 70 Ohio App. 3d 152, 590 N.E.2d 839 (6th Dist. Lucas County 1990); State v. Whiteside, 6 Ohio App. 3d 30, 452 N.E.2d 332 (3d Dist. Allen County 1982). See generally Comment, Juvenile Court and Direct Appeal from Waiver of Jurisdiction in Ohio, 8 Akron L. Rev. 499 (1975). For a further discussion of appeals, see Appeals and Habeas Corpus Ch 34.

[2]State ex rel. Torres v. Simmons, 68 Ohio St. 2d 118, 22 Ohio Op. 3d 340, 428 N.E.2d 862 (1981). See also In re Writ of Habeas Corpus for Baker, 116 Ohio App. 3d 580, 586, 688 N.E.2d 1068 (10th Dist. Franklin County 1996) ("Like the petitioner in Torres, petitioner here is challenging the bindover as ineffective to vest jurisdiction in the general division and is doing so prior to any conviction. Under such circumstances, neither prohibition nor habeas corpus will lie."; challenge to constitutionality of mandatory transfer statute after bindover but before the criminal trial).

[3]See IJA-ABA Standards Relating to Transfer Between Courts 53 (1980).

ing litigated in reviewing courts. We are unwilling to sanction such a procedure.[4]

There is, however, a serious disadvantage to this rule. The time consumed during the prosecution of the case in criminal court and during the appellate process may place the defendant beyond the age jurisdiction of the juvenile court. In this event, an appellate court that finds error in a transfer proceeding must either free the improperly transferred individual, because neither juvenile nor criminal court has jurisdiction, or reconstruct the transfer process to determine whether a hearing free from error would have resulted in transfer.[5]

The *Kent* case illustrates this problem. By the time the United States Supreme Court reversed Morris Kent's conviction, he was over 21 years of age and thus no longer subject to juvenile court jurisdiction. The Court remanded the case to the district court for a de novo consideration of the transfer issue, i.e., a reconstructed waiver hearing.[6] The difficulty with this procedure is that the reconstructed hearing must "attempt to imagine" the child as he was at the time of the original transfer hearing.[7]

Cross References

Ch 34

§ 22:24 Double jeopardy

In *Breed v. Jones*,[1] the United States Supreme Court reviewed a California procedure that permitted transfer *after* a child had been found delinquent in an adjudicatory hearing. The Court held that this procedure violated the Double Jeopardy Clause:[2]

> We believe it is simply too late in the day to conclude . . . that a juvenile is not put in jeopardy at a proceeding whose object is to determine whether he has committed acts that violate a criminal law and whose potential consequences include both the stigma inherent in such a determination and the deprivation of liberty for many years.[3]

In a footnote, however, the Court distinguished the California process from a transfer procedure requiring only a finding of probable cause:

> We note that nothing decided today forecloses States from requiring, as a prerequisite to the transfer of a juvenile, substantial evidence that he committed the offense charged, so long as the showing required is not made in an adjudicatory proceeding. . . . The instant case is not one in which the judicial determi-

---

[4]In re Becker, 39 Ohio St. 2d 84, 68 Ohio Op. 2d 50, 314 N.E.2d 158 (1974), quoting People v. Jiles, 43 Ill. 2d 145, 150, 251 N.E.2d 529 (1969). See also State v. Brown, 1990 WL 94223, at *4 (Ohio Ct. App. 9th Dist. Lorain County 1990) (The Ohio procedure on transfer appeals does not violate the due clauses of the U.S. and Ohio Constitutions.).

[5]IJA-ABA Standards Relating to Transfer Between Courts 53 (1980).

[6]Kent v. U.S., 383 U.S. 541, 86 S. Ct. 1045, 16 L. Ed. 2d 84 (1966). On appeal after remand, the D.C. Circuit held that Kent had been improperly transferred. See Kent v. U. S., 401 F.2d 408 (D.C. Cir. 1968). For other cases requiring a reconstructed waiver hearing, see U. S. ex rel. Turner v. Rundle, 438 F.2d 839 (3d Cir. 1971); Kemplen v. State of Md., 428 F.2d 169 (4th Cir. 1970).

[7]IJA-ABA Standards Relating to Transfer Between Courts 53 (1980).

[Section 22:24]

[1]Breed v. Jones, 421 U.S. 519, 95 S. Ct. 1779, 44 L. Ed. 2d 346 (1975).

[2]U.S. Const. amend. 5 ("[N]or shall any person be subject for the same offence to be twice put in jeopardy of life or limb."). For a further discussion of double jeopardy, see § 23:31, Double jeopardy.

[3]Breed v. Jones, 421 U.S. 519, 529, 95 S. Ct. 1779, 44 L. Ed. 2d 346 (1975).

nation was simply a finding of, e.g., probable cause. Rather, it was an adjudication that respondent had violated a criminal statute.[4]

In *Sims v. Engle*,[5] the Sixth Circuit held that the Ohio procedure operative at that time suffered from the same deficiencies that marked the California procedure in *Breed*. Under that procedure, a juvenile court was required to make a delinquency finding prior to transfer.[6] According to the Sixth Circuit, this procedure violated the double jeopardy guarantee:

> Once the Juvenile Court, possessing the jurisdiction and power to enter final orders levying a wide range of possible sanctions, began a hearing, not limited in scope by statute to a preliminary hearing or probable cause hearing, jeopardy attached and appellant possessed the constitutional right to have the Juvenile Court, as the original trier of fact, determine his fate.[7]

The statute that the Sixth Circuit found constitutionally defective in *Sims* was subsequently amended. Unlike the former procedure, the present transfer procedure requires only a finding of probable cause and not a determination of delinquency. The Sixth Circuit has upheld the constitutionality of this procedure: "We reject the contention that the introduction of evidence of probable cause to believe appellant committed the alleged offense without more, transformed the hearing into an adjudicatory proceeding."[8]

In *State v. Reddick*,[9] the referee accepted the juvenile's admission before the prosecutor decided to seek a transfer. The court of appeals ruled that jeopardy had attached and thus the subsequent transfer was improper. The court wrote: "There is no question that an adjudicatory hearing began and the referee took all of the evidence he was required to take, given Drayton Reddick's admission to the allegations of the complaint."[10]

In *In re K.W.*,[11] a 17-year-old juvenile was alleged to have committed aggravated robbery. At the transfer hearing, the court found that the juvenile was amenable to treatment in the juvenile justice system. The juvenile was released but failed to appear for the adjudicatory hearing. Having turned 18 during the pendency of the proceedings, K.W. was later arrested for carrying a concealed weapon. He then escaped from detention and was subsequently rearrested for receiving stolen property and carrying a concealed weapon. The prosecution moved for reconsideration of the initial amenability finding. The juvenile court ruled that double jeopardy had not attached and ordered the case transferred. "[U]ntil the juvenile court either begins to hear evidence in an adjudicatory hearing or divest itself of jurisdiction by transferring the child for prosecution as an adult, the determination of the child's amenability is subject to reconsideration upon motion filed by a party." The court pointed out that there had been neither a delinquency adjudication nor an adjudicatory hearing. No final orders had been entered. The court's ruling

---

[4]Breed v. Jones, 421 U.S. 519, 538 n.18, 95 S. Ct. 1779, 44 L. Ed. 2d 346 (1975).

[5]Sims v. Engle, 619 F.2d 598 (6th Cir. 1980). Accord State v. Turner, No. 39951 (8th Dist. Ct. App., Cuyahoga, 5-3-79).

[6]See State v. Carter, 27 Ohio St. 2d 135, 56 Ohio Op. 2d 75, 272 N.E.2d 119 (1971); In re Jackson, 21 Ohio St. 2d 215, 50 Ohio Op. 2d 447, 257 N.E.2d 74 (1970).

[7]Sims v. Engle, 619 F.2d 598, 605 (6th Cir. 1980). See also Johnson v. Perini, 644 F.2d 573 (6th Cir. 1981) (*Sims* does not apply if the record plainly establishes that the transfer hearing was limited to a probable cause determination.).

In DuBose v. Court of Common Pleas of Trumbull County, 64 Ohio St. 2d 169, 18 Ohio Op. 3d 385, 413 N.E.2d 1205 (1980), the court held that the refusal to grant a motion to dismiss on double jeopardy grounds is appealable and thus not subject to a writ of prohibition. The double jeopardy grounds asserted were based on *Breed*.

[8]Keener v. Taylor, 640 F.2d 839, 841–42, 22 Ohio Op. 3d 248 (6th Cir. 1981). Accord State v. Salmon, 1981 WL 4980 (Ohio Ct. App. 8th Dist. Cuyahoga County 1981); In re Doss, 65 Ohio Misc. 2d 8, 10, 640 N.E.2d 618 (C.P. 1994).

[9]State v. Reddick, 113 Ohio App. 3d 788, 682 N.E.2d 38 (9th Dist. Lorain County 1996).

[10]State v. Reddick, 113 Ohio App. 3d 788, 793, 682 N.E.2d 38 (9th Dist. Lorain County 1996).

[11]In re K.W., 73 Ohio Misc. 2d 20, 23, 657 N.E.2d 611 (C.P. 1995).

is consistent with the rule in adult cases, which specifies that jeopardy does not attach in a bench trial until the first witness is sworn.[12]

A different double jeopardy issue arose in *State v. Penrod*.[13] Four complaints were filed against the juvenile. Based on the juvenile's statement at the adjudicatory hearing, the referee found him delinquent on two of the complaints. The referee proceeded to disposition, and his recommendations were accepted by the court without objection. Within a week, the prosecution filed additional complaints and a motion to transfer. In response, the juvenile moved to dismiss charges that had been part of the prior adjudication, citing the double jeopardy clause. The juvenile court granted the motion. The prosecution argued that jeopardy does not attach when a complaint against a juvenile is dismissed following an adjudicatory hearing. The appellate court disagreed because the referee proceeded to the adjudicatory hearing: "The juvenile's liberty was placed at risk on all four complaints when the court proceeded to determine issues. At that point, the juvenile court was no longer a mere advisor of rights, but a trier of fact. The adjudicatory hearing did not adjourn but continued to adjudication and disposition."[14]

In *State v. Payne*,[15] the court of appeals held that a "statement by a judge that the state met its burden of proving probable cause and, in addition, demonstrated the offender's guilt beyond a reasonable doubt in the preliminary hearing does not transform the evidentiary hearing to an adjudicatory hearing or trial. Appellant was not adjudged delinquent during the preliminary hearing, he was not subjected to any sanctions, nor was he otherwise punished in any way as a result of the judge's statement. The judge's statement was merely extraneous."

Cross References
§ 23:31

§ 22:25 Bail

In *In re K.G.*,[1] the juvenile judge ruled, as a matter of first impression, that the court had discretion to release a person on bail in a transfer case. While neither the United States nor the Ohio Supreme Court had recognized the right to bail in transfer cases, nothing in Ohio law prohibited it. The legislature, in the court's view, has remained silent. "This court notes that K.G.'s petition for a commensurate increase in constitutional protections, i.e., bail, is consistent with the state's request to deprive K.G. of the rights attendant to juvenile proceedings, thereby exposing him to treatment as an adult."[2] In addition, the Ohio Constitution's bail clause extends to "all persons."

§ 22:26 Motions to suppress

In *State v. Whisenant*,[1] the court of appeals ruled that the juvenile judge is not required to rule on motions to suppress at transfer hearings. The court wrote that "because the bindover proceeding is not adjudicative (the juvenile's

---

[12]See Katz and Giannelli, Baldwin's Ohio Practice, Criminal Law (2d ed.) § 74:2 (attachment of jeopardy).

[13]State v. Penrod, 62 Ohio App. 3d 720, 577 N.E.2d 424 (9th Dist. Summit County 1989).

[14]State v. Penrod, 62 Ohio App. 3d 720, 724, 577 N.E.2d 424 (9th Dist. Summit County 1989).

[15]State v. Payne, 118 Ohio App. 3d 699, 705, 693 N.E.2d 1159 (3d Dist. Seneca County 1997).

[Section 22:25]

[1]In re K.G., 89 Ohio Misc. 2d 16, 693 N.E.2d 1186 (C.P. 1997).

[2]In re K.G., 89 Ohio Misc. 2d 16, 20, 693 N.E.2d 1186 (C.P. 1997).

[Section 22:26]

[1]State v. Whisenant, 127 Ohio App. 3d 75, 85, 711 N.E.2d 1016 (11th Dist. Portage County 1998).

guilt or innocence is not at issue), statutory and constitutional questions concerning the admissibility of evidence are premature and need not be addressed. Fundamental fairness and due process are not violated by the juvenile court's failure to rule on or to suppress evidence obtained in alleged violation of *Miranda* in this type of proceeding."[2] The court did acknowledge, however, that the courts in other jurisdictions were split on this issue.

___

[2]State v. Whisenant, 127 Ohio App. 3d 75, 85, 711 N.E.2d 1016 (11th Dist. Portage County 1998).

Chapter 23

Adjudicatory Hearings

> **KeyCite®:** Cases and other legal materials listed in KeyCite Scope can be researched through West's KeyCite service on Westlaw®. Use KeyCite to check citations for form, parallel references, prior and later history, and comprehensive citator information, including citations to other decisions and secondary materials.

§ 23:1   Adjudicatory hearings—Introduction
§ 23:2   Constitutional issues
§ 23:3   Right to counsel
§ 23:4   Waiver of right to counsel
§ 23:5   Ineffective assistance of counsel
§ 23:6   Guardian ad litem
§ 23:7   Mental competency
§ 23:8   Pleas
§ 23:9   Uncontested cases
§ 23:10   Jury trials
§ 23:11   Public trials; gag orders
§ 23:12   Right to be present
§ 23:13   Burden of proof
§ 23:14   Rules of evidence
§ 23:15   Evidence—Privileges
§ 23:16   Evidence—Hearsay
§ 23:17   Evidence—Separation of witnesses
§ 23:18   Evidence—Competency of witnesses
§ 23:19   Evidence—Experts
§ 23:20   Evidence—Impeachment
§ 23:21   Evidence—Corroboration rules
§ 23:22   Right of confrontation
§ 23:23   Confrontation—Face-to-face confrontation
§ 23:24   Confrontation—Cross-examination
§ 23:25   Confrontation—Hearsay
§ 23:26   Confrontation—Waiver
§ 23:27   Self-incrimination
§ 23:28   Impartial judge
§ 23:29   Speedy trial
§ 23:30   Right to a transcript
§ 23:31   Double jeopardy
§ 23:32   Juvenile & adult cases—Truancy

§ 23:1 Adjudicatory hearings—Introduction

The adjudicatory hearing is the fact-determining stage in juvenile cases.[1] It is analogous to the trial in a criminal or civil case. The party with the

---

[Section 23:1]

[1]Juv. R. 2(B) defines adjudicatory hearing as a "hearing to determine whether a child is a juvenile traffic offender, delinquent, unruly, abused, neglected, or dependent or is otherwise within the jurisdiction of the court or whether temporary legal custody should be converted to permanent custody."

burden of persuasion is required at this stage to introduce sufficient evidence to sustain its burden of persuasion on the issues before the court—for example, establishing that the child is delinquent, neglected, or dependent. The opposing party, of course, has the right to challenge this evidence through cross-examination and the introduction of its own evidence.

The adjudicatory hearing should be distinguished from the dispositional hearing, which is governed by Juvenile Rule 34.[2] Only after there has been an adjudication may the court consider matters relating to disposition.[3] For example, the Supreme Court has written:

> The law commands that the proceedings be bifurcated into separate adjudicatory and dispositional hearings because the issues raised and the procedures used at each hearing differ. The issue at the adjudicatory stage of a dependency case is whether petitioner has proven, by clear and convincing evidence, that the child is in fact dependent. The issue at the dispositional stage involves a determination of what is in the child's best interests. There must be strict adherence to the Rules of Evidence at the adjudicatory stage. Yet, "any evidence that is material and relevant, including hearsay, opinion and documentary evidence," is admissible at the dispositional stage. Juv.R. 34(B)(2).[4]

In Ohio, RC 2151.35 and Juvenile Rule 29 generally govern procedures in adjudicatory hearings. These procedures must comply with due process requirements.

§ 23:2   Constitutional issues

In *In re Gault*[1] the United States Supreme Court for the first time held that due process safeguards applied to juvenile adjudicatory hearings. Specifically, the Court held that the right to notice, right to counsel, right of confrontation, and the privilege against compelled self-incrimination applied in delinquency hearings. In subsequent cases, the Court held that the constitutional standard of proof in criminal cases (proof beyond a reasonable doubt)[2] and the Double Jeopardy Clause[3] also applied to delinquency cases. The Court, however, refused to extend the right to jury trial to juvenile

---

[2]For a discussion of the dispositional hearing, see Dispositional Hearings Ch 25.

[3]Juv. R. 34(A) expressly recognizes the distinction between the adjudicatory and dispositional hearings. It refers to a "separate dispositional hearing." Similarly, Juv. R. 29 also recognizes the distinction. Juv. R. 29(F)(2) grants the court several options if the allegations in the complaint are either admitted or proved: Among other actions, the court may (a) enter an adjudication and proceed to disposition, or (b) enter an adjudication and continue the matter for disposition for not more than six months.

[4]In re Baby Girl Baxter, 17 Ohio St. 3d 229, 479 N.E.2d 257 (1985). See also In re Cunningham, 59 Ohio St. 2d 100, 13 Ohio Op. 3d 78, 391 N.E.2d 1034 (1979) (emphasizing the differences between the adjudicatory and dispositional stages); In re Brofford, 83 Ohio App. 3d 869, 873, 615 N.E.2d 1120 (10th Dist. Franklin County 1992) (permanent custody hearings are adjudicatory hearings and, therefore, inadmissible hearsay should have been excluded); In re Pitts, 38 Ohio App. 3d 1, 4, 525 N.E.2d 814 (5th Dist. Knox County 1987) ("[T]he trial court erred in considering dispositional matters and issues at the adjudication phase."); Elmer v. Lucas County Children Services Bd., 36 Ohio App. 3d 241, 246, 523 N.E.2d 540 (6th Dist. Lucas County 1987) ("If a hearing is held which is to cover both the adjudicatory and dispositional phases of the proceeding, the court must bifurcate the proceedings into two distinct phases in order to accommodate the different standards of proof.").

For a discussion of this issue, see § 25:3, Bifurcated hearings.

[Section 23:2]

[1]Application of Gault, 387 U.S. 1, 87 S. Ct. 1428, 18 L. Ed. 2d 527 (1967). For a further discussion of *Gault*, see § 1:4, Due process revolution.

[2]In re Winship, 397 U.S. 358, 90 S. Ct. 1068, 25 L. Ed. 2d 368 (1970). See § 23:13, Burden of proof.

[3]Illinois v. Vitale, 447 U.S. 410, 100 S. Ct. 2260, 65 L. Ed. 2d 228 (1980); Swisher v. Brady, 438 U.S. 204, 98 S. Ct. 2699, 57 L. Ed. 2d 705, 25 Fed. R. Serv. 2d 1463 (1978); Breed v. Jones, 421 U.S. 519, 95 S. Ct. 1779, 44 L. Ed. 2d 346 (1975). See § 23:31, Double jeopardy.

cases.[4]

In addition, the United States Supreme Court has considered the due process rights applicable to neglect cases in which the permanent termination of parental rights is at issue. It has held that an indigent parent has the right to appointed counsel under some circumstances[5] and that the state must introduce "clear and convincing" proof before parental rights may be terminated.[6]

Which due process rights the Court would extend to other types of juvenile cases is uncertain. Some lower courts have found the *Gault* rationale applicable to nondelinquency cases. For example, one court has commented, "While an adjudication of unruliness . . . is not based upon a finding that the accused committed a crime, we believe it still carries a significant degree of stigmatization, which, when taken together with the possible loss of liberty, mandates application of constitutional safeguards."[7]

Cross References

§ 1:4, § 23:6, § 23:10, § 23:13, § 23:29, Ch 25

Research References

Carlin, Baldwin's Ohio Practice, Merrick-Rippner Probate Law (6th ed.), Ch 107

§ 23:3 Right to counsel

Juvenile Rule 4(A) and RC 2151.352 govern the right to counsel in juvenile court proceedings.

U.S. Constitution. The Ohio provisions go beyond federal constitutional requirements.[1] Although the Supreme Court in *Gault* recognized that a child and his parents had the right to appointed counsel if they could not afford counsel,[2] the *Gault* decision applied only to delinquency cases. In *Lassiter v. Department of Social Services*,[3] the Court held that in some cases due process requires the appointment of counsel for indigent parents where the perma-

---

[4]McKeiver v. Pennsylvania, 403 U.S. 528, 91 S. Ct. 1976, 29 L. Ed. 2d 647 (1971). See § 23:10, Jury trials.

[5]Lassiter v. Department of Social Services of Durham County, N. C., 452 U.S. 18, 101 S. Ct. 2153, 68 L. Ed. 2d 640 (1981). See § 23:3, Right to counsel; § 23:6, Guardian ad litem.

[6]Santosky v. Kramer, 455 U.S. 745, 102 S. Ct. 1388, 71 L. Ed. 2d 599 (1982). See § 23:13, Burden of proof. See also M.L.B. v. S.L.J., 519 U.S. 102, 117 S. Ct. 555, 136 L. Ed. 2d 473 (1996) (equal protection and due process violation to require an indigent to pay a fee as a condition for an appeal in a parental rights termination case).

[7]Smith v. Grossmann, 6 O.B.R. 83, 88 (S.D. Ohio 1982).

[Section 23:3]

[1]See State ex rel. Asberry v. Payne, 82 Ohio St. 3d 44, 46, 1998-Ohio-596, 693 N.E.2d 794 (1998) ("Ohio, through R.C. 2151.352, provides a statutory right to appointed counsel that goes beyond constitutional requirements."). See also In re Williams, 101 Ohio St. 3d 398, 402, 2004-Ohio-1500, 805 N.E.2d 1110 (2004) (citing *Asberry*); In re Moore, 153 Ohio App. 3d 641, 648, 2003-Ohio-4250, 795 N.E.2d 149 (3d Dist. Hardin County 2003) ("This court has previously held that '[t]his statutory right to appointment of counsel expands beyond the federal and state constitutional requirements to afford the right to counsel at juvenile proceedings in general'.") (citation omitted); In re Kriak, 30 Ohio App. 3d 83, 506 N.E.2d 556 (9th Dist. Medina County 1986) (Indigent juvenile traffic offender's statutory, but not constitutional, right to counsel was violated.); Sabrina J. v. Robbin C., 2002-Ohio-2691, 2002 WL 1303148 (Ohio Ct. App. 6th Dist. Lucas County 2002) (Parent and child entitled to counsel in custody proceedings.).

[2]Application of Gault, 387 U.S. 1, 87 S. Ct. 1428, 18 L. Ed. 2d 527 (1967). See also McKeiver v. Pennsylvania, 403 U.S. 528, 532, 91 S. Ct. 1976, 29 L. Ed. 2d 647 (1971) (Due process requires "right to counsel, retained or appointed."); In re Agler, 19 Ohio St. 2d 70, 48 Ohio Op. 2d 85, 249 N.E.2d 808 (1969) (Constitutional fairness requires provision for counsel at state expense.).

[3]Lassiter v. Department of Social Services of Durham County, N. C., 452 U.S. 18, 101 S. Ct. 2153, 68 L. Ed. 2d 640 (1981).

nent termination of parental rights is at issue.[4] According to the Court, whether counsel's appointment is constitutionally required must be decided on a case-by-case basis. The Court has yet to decide whether the right to counsel is required in other contexts, such as in status offense (unruly) cases.[5]

Notice. Several provisions require that the parties be informed of the right to counsel.[6] Juvenile Rule 15(B)(3) and RC 2151.28(F) require the summons to include a statement informing the parties of the right to counsel. Similarly, Juvenile Rule 29(B)(3) requires the juvenile court judge to inform unrepresented parties of the right to counsel at the commencement of the adjudicatory hearing.

In *Gault* the United States Supreme Court commented on the importance of counsel:

> The juvenile needs the assistance of counsel to cope with problems of law, to make skilled inquiry into the facts, to insist upon regularity of the proceedings, and to ascertain whether he has a defense and to prepare and submit it. The child "requires the guiding hand of counsel at every step in the proceedings against him."[7]

A 1989 study, however, concluded:

> In the two decades since *Gault*, the promise of counsel remains unrealized. Although there is a scarcity of data in many states, including Minnesota, less than fifty percent of juveniles adjudicated delinquent receive the assistance of counsel to which they are constitutionally entitled. Although national statistics are not available, surveys of representation by counsel in several jurisdictions suggest that "there is reason to think that lawyers still appear much less often than might have been expected." The most comprehensive study to date reports that in half of the six states surveyed, only 37.5%, 47.7%, and 52.7% of the juveniles were represented.[8]

A more recent study has concluded that not much has changed, at least in Ohio:

> The findings and recommendations of the study . . . are compelling and indicative of a system plagued with poor policies and practices, lack of funding, and perhaps most important, lack of any real leadership to effect positive reforms on behalf of poor children and youth in our courts. . . . [Approximately] half of the youth waived counsel at the detention hearing stage, and nearly as many waive the right to counsel in non-detained cases . . . . [I]n all but two of the twelve jurisdictions reviewed . . . waiver of counsel was a common and

---

[4]In State ex rel. Heller v. Miller, 61 Ohio St. 2d 6, 15 Ohio Op. 3d 3, 399 N.E.2d 66 (1980), the Ohio Supreme Court held that both the United States and Ohio Constitutions guarantee the right to counsel on appeal to indigent parents in proceedings to permanently terminate parental rights. In In re Miller, 12 Ohio St. 3d 40, 465 N.E.2d 397 (1984), the Court held that there is no constitutional right to counsel in temporary custody proceedings.

[5]Compare In re Walker, 282 N.C. 28, 191 S.E.2d 702 (1972) (no constitutional right to counsel in status offense proceedings) with State ex rel. Wilson v. Bambrick, 156 W. Va. 703, 195 S.E.2d 721 (1973) (*Gault* requires right to counsel for juvenile arrested as a runaway.).

[6]In re Williams, 2004-Ohio-678, at ¶ 13, 2004 WL 285560 (Ohio Ct. App. 10th Dist. Franklin County) (Mother was repeatedly "informed of her right to counsel and the procedures necessary to obtain appointed counsel, but she failed to avail herself of such rights. Thus, [mother] was not denied the right to counsel afforded by Juv.R. 4. . . ."); In re Doyle, 122 Ohio App. 3d 767, 772, 702 N.E.2d 970 (2d Dist. 1997) ("Further, R.C. 2151.352 requires that a juvenile be made aware of her right to be provided with counsel if she is an indigent person. The record does not provide any indication that the trial court (or the referee) ever inquired about Doyle's financial status.").

[7]Application of Gault, 387 U.S. 1, 36, 87 S. Ct. 1428, 18 L. Ed. 2d 527 (1967). As the Ohio Supreme Court recognized in In re Agler, 19 Ohio St. 2d 70, 48 Ohio Op. 2d 85, 249 N.E.2d 808 (1969), *Gault* overruled prior Ohio cases that had held the right to counsel inapplicable to adjudicatory delinquency proceedings. E.g., Cope v. Campbell, 175 Ohio St. 475, 26 Ohio Op. 2d 88, 196 N.E.2d 457 (1964). See generally Katz and Giannelli, Baldwin's Ohio Practice, Criminal Law (2d ed.), Ch 75.

[8]Feld, The Right to Counsel in Juvenile Court: An Empirical Study of When Lawyers Appear and the Difference They Make, 79 J. Crim. L. & Criminology 1185, 1188–89 (1989).

pervasive practice, with as many as 80% of youth proceeding through the system without the benefit of counsel. These findings were true in urban, small urban and rural counties alike.[9]

Withdrawal by counsel. The right to counsel may be violated by an improper withdrawal: "To allow counsel to withdraw from representation on the day of the dispositional hearing, in his client's absence, without prior motion or notice to his client, without a demonstration to the court that the client had rendered it unreasonably difficult for the attorney to represent him, and without appointing new counsel and/or continuing the hearing, and to require the client to proceed immediately without representation, was both erroneous and prejudicial."[10]

In *In re Zhang*,[11] the court of appeals upheld a juvenile court decision that let counsel withdraw from the case. The court found no abuse of discretion: "Chen abducted her child from the child's foster parents' home in violation of existing court orders and voluntarily absconded from the court's jurisdiction and has chosen not to contact either her counsel or the court; Chen's counsel advised the court that she did not know what her client wanted her to do and therefore could not zealously represent her client; and the Juvenile Court Rules authorized Chen's guardian ad litem, also an attorney, to serve as her counsel." In addition, the juvenile court was not required to continue the case: "A court need not grant a continuance for purposes of securing new counsel where the request plausibly can be viewed as simply a delaying tactic or as otherwise unreasonable. Time was of the essence in conducting the hearing for termination of the mother's parental rights. The experts agreed that the child had primarily bonded to the foster mother, and the longer she remained captive in China, the more likely it would be that the child would suffer emotional harm from the separation."[12]

Indigency. Juvenile Rule 4(A) provides: "Every party shall have the right to be represented by counsel and every child, parent, custodian, or other person in loco parentis the right to appointed counsel if indigent." This provision addresses two issues: the right to retained counsel and the right to appointed counsel in cases of indigency.[13] Similarly, Juvenile Rule 29(B)(4) requires the court at an adjudicatory hearing to appoint counsel for "any unrepresented party under Juv. R. 4(A)." Rule 2 defines an indigent person

[9]American Bar Association et al., Justice Cut Short: An Assessment of Access to Counsel and Quality of Representation in Delinquency Proceedings in Ohio, March, 2003, at I and 25.

[10]In re M.L.R., 150 Ohio App. 3d 39, 44, 2002-Ohio-5958, 779 N.E.2d 772 (8th Dist. Cuyahoga County 2002) ("An attorney may ethically withdraw when his or her client '[b]y other conduct renders it unreasonably difficult for the lawyer to carry out his employment effectively.' DR 2-110(C)(1)(d). Before the court can decide whether alleged uncooperativeness has made it unreasonably difficult for an attorney to represent the client effectively, it must ascertain the source of the uncooperativeness."). See also In re Alyssa C., 153 Ohio App. 3d 10, 2003-Ohio-2673, 790 N.E.2d 803 (6th Dist. Lucas County 2003) ("[N]o counsel was ever appointed to represent appellant father. Appellant mother's counsel appeared at the dispositional hearing and advised the court that she had not contacted him for more than six months. Because of this lack of communication, counsel sought and was granted leave to withdraw. . . . In any event, it is clear that both appellants were denied their statutory right to representation at the dispositional hearing. To proceed without representation for a party in such a circumstance is plainly erroneous.").

[11]In re Zhang, 135 Ohio App. 3d 350, 354, 734 N.E.2d 379 (8th Dist. Cuyahoga County 1999).

[12]In re Zhang, 135 Ohio App. 3d 350, 355, 734 N.E.2d 379 (8th Dist. Cuyahoga County 1999). See also In re T.C., 140 Ohio App. 3d 409, 417–418, 2000-Ohio-1769, 747 N.E.2d 881 (3d Dist. Allen County 2000); In re Hayes, 2002-Ohio-2446, 2002 WL 819216 (Ohio Ct. App. 5th Dist. Tuscarawas County 2002); but see, In re B.P., 2002-Ohio-6318, 2002 WL 31619047 (Ohio Ct. App. 8th Dist. Cuyahoga County 2002).

[13]See generally IJA-ABA Standards Relating to Counsel for Private Parties (1980); Right of juvenile court defendant to be represented during court proceedings by parent, 11 A.L.R. 4th 719; Right of indigent parent to appointed counsel in proceeding for involuntary termination of parental rights, 80 A.L.R. 3d 1141; Right to and appointment of counsel in juvenile court proceedings, 60 A.L.R. 2d 691.

as "a person who, at the time need is determined, is unable by reason of lack of property or income to provide for full payment of legal counsel and all other necessary expenses of representation."

RC 2151.352 also addresses this right.[14] It differs from Juvenile Rule 4(A) because it requires the appointment of counsel pursuant to RC Chapter 120, which governs representation by public defenders.[15]

The right to retained counsel has not caused problems. The right to appointed counsel, however, has proved controversial. Several cases had held that former Juvenile Rule 4(A) was more expansive than RC 2151.352. According to these cases, the statute is limited "to status cases involving delinquency, unruliness, juvenile traffic offenders, dependency, abuse, and neglect. Juv. R. 4(A) . . . applies to those cases outside the scope of R.C. 2151.352. "[16] In particular, the rule was held to require court-appointed counsel in visitation hearings.[17]

In January 1994, the Supreme Court proposed an amendment to Juvenile Rule 4(A) that would have overruled these cases.[18] The accompanying Staff Note (Jan. 1994) cited two situations in which the proposed rule would not

---

The right to appointed counsel does not require the appointment of a particular attorney to represent an indigent party. See State ex rel. Butler v. Demis, 66 Ohio St. 2d 123, 132–33, 20 Ohio Op. 3d 121, 420 N.E.2d 116 (1981) ("Pursuant to . . . inherent power, a trial judge may decide not to appoint a particular attorney to represent an indigent party in a proceeding before the court."). See also Matter of Church, 1983 WL 3182 (Ohio Ct. App. 4th Dist. Lawrence County 1983) (Refusal to appoint counsel of party's choice without stating reasons was an abuse of discretion.).

[14]See In Matter of Rushing, 1981 WL 6066 (Ohio Ct. App. 4th Dist. Lawrence County 1981) (RC 2151.352 imposes a mandatory duty upon the trial court to ascertain whether a party is indigent.).

[15]Pursuant to RC 2151.352, a child, parent, custodian, or other person in loco parentis, if indigent, is entitled to be represented in all juvenile proceedings by a public defender in accordance with the comprehensive system set forth in RC Ch. 120, regardless of whether the outcome of the proceeding could result in a loss of liberty (OAG 84-023, 1984 WL 196617).

[16]Fortney v. Hines, 1990 WL 173358 (Ohio Ct. App. 5th Dist. Tuscarawas County 1990); Custody of Stover, 1993 WL 385313 (Ohio Ct. App. 5th Dist. Guernsey County 1993). Other courts have interpreted the statute more expansively. E.g., Lowry v. Lowry, 48 Ohio App. 3d 184, 188–89, 549 N.E.2d 176 (4th Dist. Ross County 1988) (custody proceedings); In re Kriak, 30 Ohio App. 3d 83, 506 N.E.2d 556 (9th Dist. Medina County 1986) (statute applies to all juvenile proceedings).

[17]See McKinney v. McClure, 102 Ohio App. 3d 165, 167, 656 N.E.2d 1310 (12th Dist. Butler County 1995) ("Juv. R. 4(A) and R.C. 2151.352 guarantee the right to appointed counsel for all indigent parties in juvenile court proceedings. . . . The right to appointed counsel applies to all matters properly brought before the juvenile court, including custody and visitation issues."); Holley v. Higgins, 86 Ohio App. 3d 240, 620 N.E.2d 251 (10th Dist. Franklin County 1993) (indigent grandparent seeking visitation rights entitled to court-appointed counsel in custody suit).

[18]See 67 Ohio Bar lxxi (Feb. 14, 1994). The amendment was not adopted in this form. Under this proposal, counsel was required to be provided to:

(1) An alleged delinquent child;

(2) An alleged juvenile traffic offender under certain circumstances;

(3) An alleged unruly child;

(4) A party who (a) faces the state as an adversary, or (b) faces a party for whom representation has been provided by the state in actions establishing a parent-child relationship (RC 3111) or actions involving the establishment or modification of child support (excluding, however, parentage proceedings involving visitation or custody);

(5) A parent in parental rights termination proceedings;

(6) An adult charged with other than a minor misdemeanor in juvenile court;

(7) A child or adult charged with contempt of court;

(8) Any party in abuse, neglect, or dependency cases when the state is a party;

(9) A child in RC 2151.85 actions (abortion hearing for a minor);

(10) A child in probation revocation proceedings;

(11) A person when necessary for a fair hearing; and

(12) A person when required by the United States or Ohio Constitution or by statute.

extend the right to appointed counsel: (1) "custody, visitation, and modification of child support" actions[19] and (2) so-called "private" child abuse, neglect or dependency actions.[20] This proposed amendment to Juvenile Rule 4(A) was vigorously attacked as limiting the right to appointed counsel for the poor. As a result, the Supreme Court withdrew the proposal and substituted a different amendment. This substituted amendment retained the language of prior Juvenile Rule 4(A) but added a final sentence, which reads: "This rule shall not be construed to provide a right to appointed counsel in cases in which that right is not otherwise provided for by constitution or statute." The revised Staff Note (July 1994) states that this sentence was added "to clarify that Juv. R. 4 does not create a right to court-appointed counsel, and that the right to appointed counsel arises from other sources of law."[21] Accordingly, the issue is left to the courts to decide whether "other sources of law" extend the right to appointed counsel to all juvenile court proceedings.

In *State ex rel. Asberry v. Payne*,[22] the Ohio Supreme Court ruled that RC 2151.352 requires the appointment of counsel in custody actions brought by private persons in juvenile court. The Court held that the reference to RC Chapter 120 in the statute "does not limit the circumstances in which a person is entitled to appointed counsel under R.C. 2151.352; it instead incorporates statutory procedures to provide appointed counsel."[23] The Court also held that the 1994 amendment to Juvenile Rule 4(A) did not affect the statute: "Asberry's right to appointed counsel emanates from R.C. 2151.352, and the amendment to Juv.R. 4(A) does not abrogate that right."[24]

In *In re Williams*,[25] the Ohio Supreme Court held that the statute providing for the right to counsel should be read in light of Juvenile Rule 2, which

---

[19]Typically, custody actions in juvenile court involve an action between unmarried parents, or an action of a relative or neighbor against the parent.

[20]Private parties may bring abuse, neglect, or dependency actions without state involvement. See also State ex rel. Cody v. Toner, 8 Ohio St. 3d 22, 24, 456 N.E.2d 813 (1983) ("[T]he denial of court-appointed counsel for an indigent paternity defendant who faces the state as an adversary, when the complainant-mother and her child are recipients of public assistance, violates the due process guarantees of the Ohio and United States Constitutions."); Douglas v. Boykin, 121 Ohio App. 3d 140, 143, 699 N.E.2d 123 (12th Dist. Butler County 1997) ("An indigent paternity defendant has a constitutional right to appointed counsel when the state is a plaintiff in a paternity action.") (citing *Cody*); Sabrina J. v. Robbin C., 2002-Ohio-2691, 2002 WL 1303148 (Ohio Ct. App. 6th Dist. Lucas County 2002) (Parent and child are entitled to counsel in custody proceedings.).

[21]A 1995 amendment changed the title of Juv. R. 4 and of division (A) from "right to counsel" to "assistance of counsel."

[22]State ex rel. Asberry v. Payne, 82 Ohio St. 3d 44, 1998-Ohio-596, 693 N.E.2d 794 (1998).

[23]State ex rel. Asberry v. Payne, 82 Ohio St. 3d 44, 47, 1998-Ohio-596, 693 N.E.2d 794 (1998). See also State ex rel. Butler v. Demis, 66 Ohio St. 2d 123, 126–27, 20 Ohio Op. 3d 121, 420 N.E.2d 116 (1981) (right to appointed counsel under RC 2151.352 is not limited to the proceedings specified in RC 120.16(A)).

[24]State ex rel. Asberry v. Payne, 82 Ohio St. 3d 44, 48, 1998-Ohio-596, 693 N.E.2d 794 (1998). See also In re Janie M., 131 Ohio App. 3d 637, 639, 723 N.E.2d 191 (6th Dist. Lucas County 1999) (change of custody proceeding; "Under the plain language of R.C. 2151.352, indigent children are entitled to appointed counsel in all juvenile court proceedings.").

[25]In re Williams, 101 Ohio St. 3d 398, 2004-Ohio-1500, 805 N.E.2d 1110 (2004) (syl.). See also Smiles, A Child's Due Process Right to Legal Counsel in Abuse and Neglect Dependency Proceedings, 37 Fam. L.Q. 485 (2003). In *In re Stacey S.*, 136 Ohio App. 3d 503, 513 n.3, 1999-Ohio-989, 737 N.E.2d 92 (6th Dist. Lucas County 1999), the court of appeals stated, "Appellee's argument that the specific reference to the appointment of counsel for an alleged abused child in the rule restricts the right to only alleged abused children is unavailing. The rules and the case law clearly define who is to be afforded counsel and when the right attaches." The court rejected the argument that Rule 4 required appointment of counsel for a child only in an "abuse case, not a neglect or dependency case." According to the court, the "right to counsel attaches as soon as a complaint is filed, . . . or the child is taken into custody pursuant to Juv.R. 6. . . . Consequently, the six children who were the subject of this action had a right to counsel which attached in January 1996, when the children were removed from the home and one should have been appointed for them at their first court appearance. The record reflects that no counsel for the children was ever appointed."

defined a child as a party: "Pursuant to R.C. 2151.352, as clarified by Juv.R. 4(A) and Juv.R. 2(Y), a child who is the subject of a juvenile court proceeding to terminate parental rights is a party to that proceeding and, therefore, is entitled to independent counsel in certain circumstances."

The Attorney General has adopted the view that under RC 2151.352 and Juvenile Rule 4(A) a juvenile traffic offender is entitled to public defender appointment in all cases regardless of whether the outcome could result in a loss of liberty.[26]

Guardian ad litem. The appointment of a guardian ad litem who happens to be an attorney does not necessarily satisfy the right to counsel.[27]

§ 23:4   Waiver of right to counsel

Typically, the right to counsel may be waived.[1] However, the SYO statute[2] provides that the right to counsel cannot be waived.[3] This provision would seem to conflict with the right to self-representation, which is recognized in adult trials.

As indicated in *Gault*, the standard for waiving the right to counsel is stringent; there must be an " 'intentional relinquishment or abandonment' of a fully known right."[4]

RC 2151.352 and Juvenile Rule 29(B)(3) require the court to inform the parties of their right to counsel at the beginning of an adjudicatory hearing and to determine whether they intend to waive this right.[5]

In discussing a court's responsibility in determining whether a waiver of the right to counsel in criminal cases is valid, the United States Supreme Court has written:

> To discharge this duty properly in light of the strong presumption against

---

[26]OAG 97-040, 1997 WL 561203.

[27]In re Amos, 154 Ohio App. 3d 434, 436, 2003-Ohio-5014, 797 N.E.2d 568 (3d Dist. Crawford County 2003) ("The trial court appointed the guardian ad litem but did not appoint separate counsel. Indigent children are entitled to appointed counsel in all juvenile court proceedings. Although the guardian ad litem was an attorney, the trial court should not presume dual appointment, absent express dual appointment, as the roles of guardian ad litem and attorney are different. Thus, the trial court erred by neither appointing counsel to represent the indigent child nor by obtaining a waiver of counsel from the guardian ad litem.") (citations omitted). See infra, § 23:6, Guardian ad litem.

[Section 23:4]

[1]See Faretta v. California, 422 U.S. 806, 95 S. Ct. 2525, 45 L. Ed. 2d 562 (1975) (Defendant has a right to represent himself.). See generally Katz and Giannelli, Baldwin's Ohio Practice, Criminal Law (2d ed.) § 75:14.

See also In re Bolden, 37 Ohio App. 2d 7, 14, 66 Ohio Op. 2d 26, 306 N.E.2d 166 (3d Dist. Allen County 1973):

The law does not require continuances to be granted and trials postponed indefinitely until counsel is obtained. The record reveals that the parties were given a reasonable opportunity to obtain same and we find no error of the trial court in not granting a continuance and in proceeding with the trial under these circumstances.

[2]See Serious Youthful Offenders Ch 5.

[3]RC 2152.13(C)(2).

[4]Application of Gault, 387 U.S. 1, 42, 87 S. Ct. 1428, 18 L. Ed. 2d 527 (1967). See also Juv. R. 3 (waiver of rights).

[5]In re Hinko, 84 Ohio App. 3d 89, 95, 616 N.E.2d 515 (8th Dist. Cuyahoga County 1992) (error to proceed without advising parties of right to counsel). Pursuant to RC 2151.352, a child, parents, custodian, or other person in loco parentis, if indigent, is entitled to be represented in all juvenile proceedings by a public defender in accordance with the comprehensive system set forth in RC Ch. 120, regardless of whether the outcome of the proceeding could result in a loss of liberty (OAG 84-023, 1984 WL 196617). In In re Ramsey Children, 102 Ohio App. 3d 168, 656 N.E.2d 1311 (5th Dist. Stark County 1995), the court of appeals ruled that the mother in an abuse case, in which long-term foster care was granted, had not been denied her statutory right to counsel. She had been served by certified mail with a copy of the complaint but did not contact the public defender's office for representation.

waiver of the constitutional right to counsel, a judge must investigate as long and as thoroughly as the circumstances of the case before him demand. The fact that an accused may tell him that he is informed of his right to counsel and desires to waive this right does not automatically end the judge's responsibility. To be valid such waiver must be made with an apprehension of the nature of the charges, the statutory offenses included within them, the range of allowable punishments thereunder, possible defenses to the charges and circumstances in mitigation thereof, and all other facts essential to a broad understanding of the whole matter. A judge can make certain that an accused's professed waiver of counsel is understandingly and wisely made only from a penetrating and comprehensive examination of all the circumstances under which such a plea is tendered.[6]

The Ohio courts have applied this standard in juvenile cases.[7] The court of appeals in *In re Johnson*[8] stated the standard as follows:

When a defendant waives his or her right to counsel, the court must make sufficient inquiry to determine whether the defendant has done so knowingly, intelligently and voluntarily. The court's inquiry must encompass the totality of the circumstances before the court can be satisfied that the waiver was given knowingly, intelligently and voluntarily. In applying the totality-of-the circumstances test to juveniles, courts must give close scrutiny to factors such as a juvenile's age, emotional stability, mental capacity, and prior criminal experience.

At the initial hearing, the referee asked Johnson, "Do you want a lawyer?" Johnson replied, "No." The referee then told Johnson to sign the waiver form. "This was the extent of the inquiry, and clearly failed to take into account all

---

[6]Von Moltke v. Gillies, 332 U.S. 708, 723–24, 68 S. Ct. 316, 92 L. Ed. 309 (1948).

[7]In re Smith, 142 Ohio App. 3d 16, 22, 753 N.E.2d 930 (8th Dist. Cuyahoga County 2001) ("The court must personally address the child to determine whether the admission is knowing and voluntary. Here, the court told the juvenile that she was entitled to counsel and that the state would appoint counsel if she could not afford it. This colloquy was insufficient, under the circumstances, to establish a knowing waiver of the right to counsel.") (citations omitted); In re Doyle, 122 Ohio App. 3d 767, 771, 702 N.E.2d 970 (2d Dist. 1997) ("[T]he record demonstrates that the magistrate did not adequately inform Doyle of her right to counsel. The magistrate discussed Doyle's right to counsel only in terms of representation if she were to elect to proceed to trial. The magistrate's explanation of the right to counsel was confusing, if not misleading, and could have led Doyle to believe that she was not entitled to counsel while deciding whether to admit or to deny the complaint. . . . Therefore, despite the fact that Doyle did sign a waiver of rights form, we conclude that the record does not show that Doyle knowingly and intelligently waived her right to counsel."); In re Miller, 119 Ohio App. 3d 52, 56, 694 N.E.2d 500 (2d Dist. Clark County 1997) ("[T]he court must make a sufficient inquiry which encompasses the totality of the circumstances, giving close scrutiny to factors such as the juvenile's age, emotional stability, mental capacity, and prior criminal experience. . . . No specific mention was made of the right to appointment of counsel, however. . . . [T]here was no specific colloquy between the court and Wayne in which the court inquired whether Wayne wished to waive his right to counsel. Rather, the court simply gave Wayne and his mother a 'statement of rights and waiver form' to review and sign."); In In re East, 105 Ohio App. 3d 221, 223, 663 N.E.2d 983 (8th Dist. Cuyahoga County 1995), the court wrote: "[C]ase law regarding an adult's waiver of counsel provides guidance." The court went on to state: "[T]he referee's report/journal entry affirmatively states that '[t]he referee explained legal rights' . . .. Although the appellant's mother signed a waiver of counsel form, this does not constitute a waiver of appellant's right to counsel as no case in Ohio 'has held that a parent can waive the constitutional right of a minor in a Juvenile Court or criminal case.' " In re East, 105 Ohio App. 3d 221, 224–25, 663 N.E.2d 983 (8th Dist. Cuyahoga County 1995) (citing In re Collins, 20 Ohio App. 2d 319, 322, 49 Ohio Op. 2d 448, 253 N.E.2d 824 (8th Dist. Cuyahoga County 1969)). See also In re Montgomery, 117 Ohio App. 3d 696, 700, 691 N.E.2d 349 (8th Dist. Cuyahoga County 1997) ("Case law concerning an adult's waiver of counsel can be utilized to determine whether a juvenile has entered a valid waiver of the constitutional right to counsel. . . . The court must fully and clearly explain to defendant his right to counsel, and the defendant must then affirmatively waive that right on record."); In re Nation, 61 Ohio App. 3d 763, 767, 573 N.E.2d 1155 (3d Dist. Shelby County 1989) (waiver invalid where record showed delinquent "uncertain" as to whether she should waive the right to counsel); Matter of Wilson, 1981 WL 6717 (Ohio Ct. App. 3d Dist. Paulding County 1981) (Waiver of counsel will not be presumed from a silent record.).

[8]In re Johnson, 106 Ohio App. 3d 38, 41, 665 N.E.2d 247 (1st Dist. Hamilton County 1995) (citations omitted).

of the circumstances necessary to determine whether Johnson waived his right to counsel, knowingly, intelligently, and voluntarily. Within the totality-of-circumstances test, the court was required to take special care given Johnson's age (13). Instead, the referee did not even explain to Johnson his rights."[9] Reliance on a waiver form does not satisfy the constitutional test for waiver.[10]

There is a presumption against waiver[11] and

> [s]pecial caution must be taken when dealing with juveniles in the justice system because children do not have the life experience that would assist them in making the best decisions to safeguard their personal and constitutional rights. . . . Where juveniles are not represented, the court has a duty to advise them of the right to counsel and the right to have counsel appointed for those who are indigent. The opportunity for independent representation of a minor is important, as parents do not always represent the child's best interests and are sometimes adverse thereto.[12]

In *Godinez v. Moran*,[13] the United States Supreme Court ruled that the mental competency required to plead guilty and to waive counsel was the same as that required to stand trial; the issue is whether the accused "has the capacity to understand the proceedings and to assist counsel."[14] The Court rejected the view that a "heightened" standard of competence applied to these decisions. Although the mental competence standard is the same, the issues are not. A waiver of counsel "must also be intelligent and voluntary before it can be accepted."[15] Similarly, a valid guilty plea requires the trial court to determine that the waiver of "constitutional rights is knowing and voluntary."[16]

Some jurisdictions have taken the position that a child cannot waive the

---

[9] In re Johnson, 106 Ohio App. 3d 38, 41, 665 N.E.2d 247 (1st Dist. Hamilton County 1995). See also In re Franklin, 1997 WL 624844, at *1 (Ohio Ct. App. 2d Dist. Clark County 1997) ("In effect, the inability of the trial court to provide a transcript to the appellant was tantamount to denying him his right to appeal. And when the record is silent, such as it is here, the burden rests upon the State to show compliance with Juv.R. 29(D) and to demonstrate a valid waiver of the appellant's right to representation."); In re Ward, 1997 WL 321492, at *2 (Ohio Ct. App. 8th Dist. Cuyahoga County 1997) ("A journal entry indicating that the juvenile waived his right to counsel was not adequate to demonstrate that the trial court explained the statutory right to counsel and informed him that counsel would be appointed if he were indigent."); In re Kimble, 114 Ohio App. 3d 136, 140–41, 682 N.E.2d 1066 (3d Dist. Crawford County 1996) ("[T]here is no indication from the record that the trial court ever made a determination concerning defendant's indigency or that the court advised defendant that he had the right to appointed counsel based on his indigency. Moreover, aside from the aforementioned dialogue in which the court asked, 'Since you are here without an attorney am I to assume that you wish to proceed without an attorney?' and defendant responded 'yes,' there is no evidence in the record that the trial court made a sufficient inquiry to determine whether defendant's purported waiver of counsel was made knowingly and voluntarily.").

[10] In re Royal, 132 Ohio App. 3d 496, 504–05, 725 N.E.2d 685 (7th Dist. Mahoning County 1999) ("[T]he waiver form is merely a boilerplate document listing some of the rights of the child, including the right to counsel and the right to appointed counsel if indigent. . . . The form does not indicate that any meaningful dialogue occurred between appellant and the magistrate. . . . A waiver form is not a valid substitute for the court's duty to personally address the juvenile.").

[11] Douglas v. Boykin, 121 Ohio App. 3d 140, 143, 699 N.E.2d 123 (12th Dist. Butler County 1997) ("Courts are to indulge every reasonable presumption against the waiver of a fundamental constitutional right, including the right to be represented by counsel. Therefore, a waiver may not be presumed from a silent record. Rather, the waiver must affirmatively appear in the record.") (citations omitted).

[12] In re Rogers, 124 Ohio App. 3d 392, 395, 706 N.E.2d 390 (9th Dist. Summit County 1997) (citations omitted).

[13] Godinez v. Moran, 509 U.S. 389, 113 S. Ct. 2680, 125 L. Ed. 2d 321 (1993).

[14] Godinez v. Moran, 509 U.S. 389, 113 S. Ct. 2680, 2688, 125 L. Ed. 2d 321 (1993).

[15] Godinez v. Moran, 509 U.S. 389, 113 S. Ct. 2680, 2688, 125 L. Ed. 2d 321 (1993); In re Bays, 2003-Ohio-1256, 2003 WL 1193787 (Ohio Ct. App. 2d Dist. Greene County 2003); In re Husk, 2002-Ohio-4000, 2002 WL 1803698 (Ohio Ct. App. 4th Dist. Washington County 2002).

[16] Godinez v. Moran, 509 U.S. 389, 113 S. Ct. 2680, 2687, 125 L. Ed. 2d 321 (1993).

right to counsel without the advice of counsel,[17] and the IJA-ABA Standards do not permit the right to counsel to be waived.[18] In contrast, Juvenile Rule 3 provides that, except for the right to counsel at transfer hearings, the rights of a child may be waived with permission of the court.

One court has held that it was inappropriate to expect a child to hire an attorney, that being a task to be performed by an adult.[19] Failure by the parents to do so, and the child's inadequate attempts to hire an attorney did not constitute waiver of counsel.

Research References
Carlin, Baldwin's Ohio Practice, Merrick-Rippner Probate Law (6th ed.), Ch 107

§ 23:5 Ineffective assistance of counsel

The right to counsel includes the right to the effective assistance of counsel.[1] Whether a criminal defendant has been denied this right is judged by a "reasonably effective assistance" standard. In *Strickland v. Washington*,[2] the United States Supreme Court wrote: "When a convicted defendant complains of the ineffectiveness of counsel's assistance, the defendant must show that counsel's representation fell below an objective standard of reasonableness."[3] The second part of the *Strickland* test requires the defendant to "show that the deficient performance prejudiced the defense."[4] The *Strickland* standard applies in delinquency cases.[5] It may also apply in all cases in which there is a right to appointed counsel.[6] For example, "the two-part test for ineffective assistance of counsel used in criminal cases, announced in *Strickland v. Washington* . . ., is equally applicable in actions by the state to force the permanent, involuntary termination of parental rights."[7]

---

[17]State ex rel. J. M. v. Taylor, 166 W. Va. 511, 276 S.E.2d 199, 25 A.L.R.4th 1063 (1981).

[18]IJA-ABA Standards Relating to Adjudication 14 (1980).

[19]In re Johnston, 142 Ohio App. 3d 314, 319, 755 N.E.2d 457 (11th Dist. Ashtabula County 2001).

[Section 23:5]

[1]McMann v. Richardson, 397 U.S. 759, 771 n.14, 90 S. Ct. 1441, 25 L. Ed. 2d 763 (1970) ("It has long been recognized that the right to counsel is the right to the effective assistance of counsel."). See generally Katz and Giannelli, Baldwin's Ohio Practice, Criminal Law (2d ed.), Ch 76; LaFave & Israel, Criminal Procedure Ch. 11 (1984); Whitebread & Slobogin, Criminal Procedure Ch. 31 (3d ed. 1992).

[2]Strickland v. Washington, 466 U.S. 668, 104 S. Ct. 2052, 80 L. Ed. 2d 674 (1984).

[3]Strickland v. Washington, 466 U.S. 668, 687–88, 104 S. Ct. 2052, 80 L. Ed. 2d 674 (1984).

[4]Strickland v. Washington, 466 U.S. 668, 687, 104 S. Ct. 2052, 80 L. Ed. 2d 674 (1984).

[5]In re Terrance P., 129 Ohio App. 3d 418, 426, 717 N.E.2d 1160 (6th Dist. Lucas County 1998) (citing *Strickland*, court found ineffectiveness in proffering an "admission"; "In the present case, it is clear that appellant's trial counsel was not acting as his counsel in the proceedings below."); Pendleton v. State, 1990 WL 104964 (Ohio Ct. App. 8th Dist. Cuyahoga County 1990); In re Hannah, 106 Ohio App. 3d 766, 667 N.E.2d 76 (8th Dist. Cuyahoga County 1995) ("The failure to request a recording device for a verbatim transcript is not *per se* ineffective assistance of counsel even when the juvenile's liberty is at issue.").

[6]In re Wise, 96 Ohio App. 3d 619, 629, 645 N.E.2d 812 (9th Dist. Wayne County 1994) ("A strong presumption exists that licensed attorneys are competent and that the challenged action is the product of a sound trial strategy.") (termination of parental rights).

[7]In re Moore, 153 Ohio App. 3d 641, 652, 2003-Ohio-4250, 795 N.E.2d 149 (3d Dist. Hardin County 2003) (*Strickland* test "'has been utilized to give effect to R.C. 2151.352 and Juv.R. 4(A).'") (citation omitted); Jones v. Lucas County Children Services Bd., 46 Ohio App. 3d 85, 86, 546 N.E.2d 471 (6th Dist. Lucas County 1988) (finding counsel's performance not deficient). Accord In re Baby Girl Doe, 149 Ohio App. 3d 717, 741, 2002-Ohio-4470, 778 N.E.2d 1053 (6th Dist. Lucas County 2002) ("A trial counsel's choice of tactics must be given deference. A litigant bears the burden of proving that his trial counsel was ineffective. An appellate court need not address both components of the *Strickland* analysis if one component fails." (citations omitted)); In re Wingo, 143 Ohio App. 3d 652, 668, 2001-Ohio-2477, 758 N.E.2d 780 (4th Dist. Ross County 2001) ("[J]udicial scrutiny of counsel's performance must be highly deferential. Tactical or stra-

One type of ineffective assistance involves conflicts of interest.[8] RC 2151.352 provides that if the interests of two or more parties conflict, separate counsel shall be provided for each party.[9] Similarly, Juvenile Rule 4(A) requires the appointment of counsel to represent the child in abuse cases. Moreover, as discussed in the next section, conflicts may arise because an attorney is functioning in dual roles—as counsel and as guardian ad litem.

§ 23:6   Guardian ad litem

RC 2151.281 and Juvenile Rule 4(B) provide for the appointment of a guardian ad litem[1] to protect the interests of a child when:

(1) The child has no parent, guardian, or legal custodian;

(2) The interests of the child and the parents may conflict;

(3) The parent is under 18 years of age or appears to be mentally incompetent;

(4) The court believes the parent is incapable of representing the best interests of the child;

(5) A proceeding involves allegations of abuse or neglect, voluntary surrender of permanent custody, or termination of parental rights;

(6) There is an agreement for voluntary surrender of temporary custody under RC 5103.15 and thereafter a request for an extension is made;

(7) The child is subject to a removal action;[2] or

---

tegic trial decisions, even if ultimately unsuccessful, do not generally constitute ineffective assistance of counsel."); In re T.C., 140 Ohio App. 3d 409, 408, 2000-Ohio-1769, 747 N.E.2d 881 (3d Dist. Allen County 2000); In re Glenn, 139 Ohio App. 3d 105, 114, 742 N.E.2d 1210 (8th Dist. Cuyahoga County 2000) ("The two-part standard set forth in *Strickland v. Washington* . . . for proving ineffective assistance of counsel in criminal cases also applies in cases where the state attempts to gain involuntary and permanent termination of parental rights."); In re Heston, 129 Ohio App. 3d 825, 827, 719 N.E.2d 93 (1st Dist. Hamilton County 1998) ("The right to counsel, guaranteed in these proceedings by R.C. 2151.352 and Juv.R. 4, includes the right to the effective assistance of counsel. Where the proceeding contemplates the loss of parents' 'essential' and 'basic' civil rights to raise their children, the test for ineffective assistance of counsel used in criminal cases is equally applicable to actions seeking to force the permanent, involuntary termination of parental custody.") (citations omitted); Matter of Cobb, 1996 WL 65840, at *7 (Ohio Ct. App. 8th Dist. Cuyahoga County 1996) ("The [*Strickland*] test [is] applicable to permanent custody proceedings . . . ."); In re Travis Children, 80 Ohio App. 3d 620, 625, 609 N.E.2d 1356 (5th Dist. Stark County 1992) ("[F]ailure to object to so fundamental a matter as jurisdiction must be considered ineffective."); In re Curley/Brown Children, 1993 WL 473832 (Ohio Ct. App. 9th Dist. Summit County 1993); Matter of Kuzel, 1993 WL 93331 (Ohio Ct. App. 3d Dist. Allen County 1993). See also Williams County Department of Social Services v. Gilman, 1982 WL 6438 (Ohio Ct. App. 6th Dist. Williams County 1982) (RC 2151.352 and RC 2151.353(B) entitle party to effective assistance of counsel in neglect cases.).

[8]See Cuyler v. Sullivan, 446 U.S. 335, 100 S. Ct. 1708, 64 L. Ed. 2d 333 (1980) (multiple representation); Holloway v. Arkansas, 435 U.S. 475, 98 S. Ct. 1173, 55 L. Ed. 2d 426 (1978).

See also Appeal of A Juvenile, 61 Ohio App. 2d 235, 15 Ohio Op. 3d 400, 401 N.E.2d 937 (11th Dist. Lake County 1978) (Juvenile court cannot deny representation by an attorney on the grounds that the attorney is an assistant law director of an adjoining county.).

[9]In re Brodbeck, 97 Ohio App. 3d 652, 657, 647 N.E.2d 240 (3d Dist. Mercer County 1994) (finding no conflict of interest because there was no evidence in record that the parents intended to separate at that time).

[Section 23:6]

[1]See In re Barzak, 24 Ohio App. 3d 180, 493 N.E.2d 1011 (11th Dist. Trumbull County 1985) (Appointment of a guardian ad litem is not required in dependency proceedings.); In re Height, 47 Ohio App. 2d 203, 1 Ohio Op. 3d 279, 353 N.E.2d 887 (3d Dist. Van Wert County 1975) (Appointment of guardian ad litem is procedural, not jurisdictional.); Matter of Church, 1983 WL 3182 (Ohio Ct. App. 4th Dist. Lawrence County 1983) (Appointment of guardian ad litem is mandatory.); In the Matter Of: Strowbridge, 1982 WL 3565 (Ohio Ct. App. 4th Dist. Lawrence County 1982); In Matter of Myer, 1981 WL 6316 (Ohio Ct. App. 5th Dist. Delaware County 1981).

[2]A 1998 amendment to Juvenile Rule 4(B) provided for the appointment of a guardian ad litem in removal actions, as defined in present Juvenile Rule 2(GG) and governed by Rule 39.

(8) It is necessary to meet the requirements of a fair hearing.

RC 2151.281(C) provides for the appointment of a guardian ad litem for a parent in delinquency, unruly, abuse, neglect, or dependency cases if the parent appears to be mentally incompetent[3] or is under 18 years of age.

RC 2151.281(G) specifies the point in time at which the guardian ad litem's appointment terminates.[4]

Role of guardian ad litem. Juvenile Rule 2(N) defines guardian ad litem as a "person appointed to protect the interests of a party in a juvenile court proceeding."[5] According to one court, the guardian ad litem for the child should be a person "who can serve uninhibited by any ties or loyalties with either the mother of [the child] or the proposed adoptive parents."[6] Another court has stated that the "role of a guardian *ad litem* is to investigate the ward's situation and then to ask the court to do what the guardian feels is the ward's best interest . . .. This does not necessarily require an exact knowledge of the applicable law or an ability to submit the guardian's recommendation with great legal precision."[7] In permanent custody proceedings, RC 2151.414(C) requires the guardian ad litem to submit a written report to the court prior to or at the time of the hearing.[8] The guardian ad litem is also authorized to bring a civil action against any person required to report child

---

"At the discretion of the court, the court may appoint the guardian *ad litem* initially appointed for the child by the court that entered the original dispositional placement order, with the consent of that guardian *ad litem*. Alternatively, the court may appoint a new guardian *ad litem*." Staff Note (1998). See Removal Actions Ch 13.

[3]In re K.P., 2004-Ohio-1448, 2004 WL 583867 (Ohio Ct. App. 8th Dist. Cuyahoga County) (The mother did not need a guardian ad litem appointed for her, did not appear mentally incompetent at any stage of the proceedings, and did not request appointment of a guardian ad litem.); In re Anderson, No. 02CA38 (4th Dist. Athens County 2002).

[4]In re Moran, 1994 WL 123683, at *5–6 (Ohio Ct. App. 1st Dist. Hamilton County 1994):

[T]he award of permanent custody to CSS [Catholic Social Services] does not terminate the association of the guardian ad litem at that point in the proceedings because CSS is not a person within the meaning of R.C. 2151.281(G)(3). However, when CSS places the child in a home, and a person is given legal custody of the child, the services of the guardian ad litem are extinguished. However, if matters involving the care of a child arise during that period, the juvenile court continues to have jurisdiction . . . if the jurisdiction of the probate court has yet to be invoked by the filing of a petition for adoption, as the child cannot be left in a jurisdictional vacuum between the two courts . . . . The provision of R.C. 2151.281(G)(4) states that the presence of the guardian ad litem in the case will cease when a final decree of adoption is issued with respect to the child. Until that time, if no person has legal custody of the child, and a petition for adoption has not been filed activating the jurisdiction of the probate court, the guardian ad litem shall continue to serve and may meet with the child and report to the juvenile court on the child's behalf.

See also Matter of Adoption of Nowowiejski, 1990 WL 187377 (Ohio Ct. App. 6th Dist. Lucas County 1990) ("In construing Civ. R. 24 and R.C. 2151.281 in pari materia, we hold that a guardian ad litem, appointed for a child during a permanent custody action, can intervene as a matter of right in a subsequent adoption proceeding.").

[5]See In re Etter, 134 Ohio App. 3d 484, 731 N.E.2d 694 (1st Dist. Hamilton County 1998) ("The purpose of a guardian ad litem is to secure for the juvenile or incompetent person a proper defense or an adequate protection of his or her rights. It is the guardian ad litem's duty to protect the best interests of the incompetent. A guardian ad litem is considered an officer of the court, and must be distinguished from a general guardian who has the general care and control of the person. While a guardian ad litem has a protective role to play in any waiver of his or her ward's rights, that role does not preempt application of Juv.R. 29(D). Neither Young's attorney nor her guardian ad litem had the authority to make the decision for her to enter an admission. That decision belonged to Young uniquely. Particularly in light of Young's diminished mental capacity, it was incumbent upon the magistrate, notwithstanding the statement from Young's guardian ad litem, to comply with the mandate of Juv.R. 29(D) to personally address Young.") (citations omitted).

[6]In re Christopher, 54 Ohio App. 2d 137, 144, 8 Ohio Op. 3d 271, 376 N.E.2d 603 (5th Dist. Morrow County 1977). Accord In re Height, 47 Ohio App. 2d 203, 206, 1 Ohio Op. 3d 279, 353 N.E.2d 887 (3d Dist. Van Wert County 1975) (guardian ad litem has no duty to protect parental interests).

[7]In re Pryor, 86 Ohio App. 3d 327, 620 N.E.2d 973 (4th Dist. Athens County 1993).

[8]Matter of Eplin, 1995 WL 495451 (Ohio Ct. App. 5th Dist. Stark County 1995) (judgment reversed because the "record is devoid of any written guardian ad litem report," a mandatory requirement); In re Shaeffer Children, 85 Ohio App. 3d 683, 693, 621 N.E.2d 426 (3d Dist. Van Wert County 1993) (reading report into the record in open court at the close of the evidence, but

abuse or neglect if that person fails to file the report and injury or harm to the child results.[9] The guardian ad litem may not be the attorney responsible for presenting evidence alleging that the child is abused or neglected. The guardian ad litem may file the complaint, "However, after the complaint is filed, the guardian ad litem is required to step aside. Thereafter, the duty falls on the children services agency to investigate the situation and, if necessary, prosecute the complaint."[10]

In *In re Doe*,[11] the court severely criticized the guardian ad litem's performance:

> [T]he guardian *ad litem* did in fact submit his report late . . . . Additionally, and much more to his discredit, the record shows that the "investigation" consisted of no more than reading through the [Board's] case file prior to writing his report. The only "independent" aspect consisted of some brief conversations with the parents in the courthouse halls after hearings. The record also indicates that the guardian's written report contains no new information or insight into the case.

> [T]he court feels compelled to address the unacceptable manner in which the guardian of these three small children neglected his responsibilities. The guardian's contribution in the form of work and work product was essentially nonexistent. Due to his inaction, the trial court did not receive the benefit of any of the contributions and insight a guardian *ad litem* could and should give. . . . This type of deficient performance should not have been overlooked or tolerated by the trial court and should not be in the future.[12]

Parent-child conflicts. RC 2151.281(B)(1) requires the mandatory appointment of a guardian ad litem in cases of alleged abuse or neglect. Another provision, RC 2151.281(A)(2), requires appointment in delinquency and unruly cases if there is a conflict between the parent (legal guardian or custodian) and the child.[13]

---

prior to closing arguments, satisfies this requirement); In re Salsgiver, 2003-Ohio-1206, 2003 WL 1193784 (Ohio Ct. App. 8th Dist. Cuyahoga County 2003) (Were parties given sufficient notice of the guardian ad litem's position to rebut assertions contained in the report?).

[9]RC 2151.281(B)(2).

[10]In re Kheirkhah, 2004-Ohio-521, at ¶ 17, 2004 WL 231495 (Ohio Ct. App. 11th Dist. Lake County).

[11]Matter of Doe, 1993 WL 355692 (Ohio Ct. App. 6th Dist. Lucas County 1993).

[12]Matter of Doe, 1993 WL 355692, at *21–23 (Ohio Ct. App. 6th Dist. Lucas County 1993). See also Matter of Doe, 1993 WL 541121, at *6 (Ohio Ct. App. 6th Dist. Lucas County 1993) ("Once again, we would note that the guardian *ad litem* in this case, whether through ignorance or willful neglect, was somewhat remiss in fulfilling his responsibilities to the children he represented. Home visits, parent conferences, and independent visitations with all the children, wherever they may be in placement, are certainly threshold duties of a diligent guardian *ad litem*. The performance of the guardian *ad litem* should be monitored by the court to insure that the children's best interest are, in fact, being represented.").

[13]In re Spradlin, 140 Ohio App. 3d 402, 407, 2000-Ohio-2003, 747 N.E.2d 877 (4th Dist. Highland County 2000) (When juvenile's grandfather, who had custody, informed the court about a recent unruly report he had filed against the juvenile for the purpose of ascertaining the status of the claim, rather than for the best interest of the child, the court was required at a minimum to inquire further into the necessity of a guardian ad litem due to the strong possibility of a conflict of interest. Failure to do so was reversible error.); In re Miller, 119 Ohio App. 3d 52, 55, 694 N.E.2d 500 (2d Dist. Clark County 1997) ("[T]he only person who appeared on Wayne Miller's behalf at the adjudicatory proceeding was his mother, Mrs. Miller, who is also the mother of the nine-year-old girl Wayne was alleged to have raped. . . . [T]he conflict between Wayne's interest and that of his mother is obvious."). In In re Sappington, 123 Ohio App. 3d 448, 704 N.E.2d 339 (2d Dist. Montgomery County 1997), the court of appeals ruled that the juvenile court had abused its discretion by not appointing a guardian ad litem where the record indicated a strong possibility of conflicting interests between the juvenile and his father, who represented him at the adjudicatory and dispositional hearing of delinquency proceedings. The court wrote: "We are persuaded, from our review of [the Ohio] cases, that the different lines of authority can be reconciled. We agree with those authorities that have found that Juv.R. 4(B) does not require an actual conflict of interest to trigger the need for a guardian ad litem. The plain language of the rule mandates that the possibility that interests 'may conflict' will suffice. Nevertheless, the juvenile court is in the best position to weigh the relevant facts in determining

In *In re Johnson*,[14] a delinquency case, the referee appointed the grandmother guardian ad litem of a 13-year-old child charged with theft. There was no indication that she understood her role; her only action at the initial hearing was to sign a waiver-of-counsel form. At the adjudicatory hearing, during the cross-examination of a police officer, she accused Johnson of lying to her. Later, she advised the court that confinement was the best solution for him. The court of appeals reversed, commenting:

> It seems clear that [the grandmother] did not protect Johnson's interest as required by R.C. 2151.281(A) because she damaged Johnson's credibility and recommended a stiff penalty.

> By failing to appoint a guardian *ad litem* capable of assisting the court in ensuring that the child's statutory rights are protected, the court failed to discharge its duty under R.C. 2151.281(D).

> We find this assignment of error is well taken, especially in light of the fact that Johnson had no representation by counsel.

The problem in delinquency cases is determining what is meant by a conflict of interest. In *In re Howard*,[15] the court of appeals refused to adopt a bright-line rule requiring the appointment of a guardian ad litem whenever a parent speaks against the child's penal interest, i.e., recommending commitment to DYS. Such a position, however, requires an inquiry into the possibility of a conflict.[16] The court observed: "Howard's mother spoke in some detail about why she believed that Howard would be better off in the DYS. Parents are not compelled to advocate what the child wants if they believe such a result would not be in the child's best interest. There was nothing in this record to suggest that Howard's mother was acting other than in Howard's best interest. The fact that her position was in her son's best interest was validated by the testimony of the representative from Hillcrest School."[17]

Attorney-guardian ad litem conflicts. RC 2151.281(H) and Juvenile

---

whether a potential conflict of interest exists between the parent and child. . . . We believe, therefore, that an abuse of discretion standard should apply." In re Sappington, 123 Ohio App. 3d 448, 454, 704 N.E.2d 339 (2d Dist. Montgomery County 1997) (internal citations omitted).

Compare In re Adoption of Howell, 77 Ohio App. 3d 80, 92, 601 N.E.2d 92 (4th Dist. Lawrence County 1991) (guardian ad litem required under Juv. R. 4(B)(2) where child's and parent's interests "could conflict"); In re Christopher, 54 Ohio App. 2d 137, 143, 8 Ohio Op. 3d 271, 376 N.E.2d 603 (5th Dist. Morrow County 1977) (reversing lower court where court of appeals concluded that interests "may" conflict), with In re Nation, 61 Ohio App. 3d 763, 767, 573 N.E.2d 1155 (3d Dist. Shelby County 1989) (abuse of discretion).

[14]In re Johnson, 106 Ohio App. 3d 38, 43, 665 N.E.2d 247 (1st Dist. Hamilton County 1995).

[15]In re Howard, 119 Ohio App. 3d 201, 206, 695 N.E.2d 1 (1st Dist. Hamilton County 1997) ("It is also the basic responsibility of a parent, the natural guardian, to look out for the best interest of the child. In theory, then, the parent and guardian *ad litem* have the same responsibility. That is not always the reality, however. A parent may clearly have her own agenda, or be advocating her own best interest, which may or may not also be the child's."). See also Stuckey, Guardians Ad Litem as Surrogate Parents: Implications for Role Definition and Confidentiality, 64 Fordham L. Rev. 1785 (1996).

[16]In re Howard, 119 Ohio App. 3d 201, 207, 695 N.E.2d 1 (1st Dist. Hamilton County 1997) ("We do not believe that either the statute or the rule requires that every time a parent and child disagree, a guardian *ad litem* must be appointed. Nor will we write a bright-line rule that any time a parent speaks against a child's penal interest, it is not in the child's best interest. Nevertheless, we caution the court and counsel that in a delinquency case, when a parent does speak against a child's penal interest, a colorable claim of a conflict is at least raised, requiring thorough inquiry."). See also In re Smith, 142 Ohio App. 3d 16, 20, 753 N.E.2d 930 (8th Dist. Cuyahoga County 2001) ("The fact that a parent or custodian acting in what they believe to be the child's best interests conflicts with the child's best legal interests is not sufficient to warrant the appointment of a guardian ad litem."); In re K.J.F., 2004-Ohio-263, 2004 WL 102847 (Ohio Ct. App. 2d Dist. Clark County) (Child appealed rape adjudication where victim was his sister and mother indicated to court she could not make choices in child's best interests. The trial court did not appoint a guardian ad litem to represent the child's best interests, and the court of appeals found that to be reversible error.).

[17]In re Howard, 119 Ohio App. 3d 201, 207, 695 N.E.2d 1 (1st Dist. Hamilton County 1997).

Rule 4(C) provide that a guardian ad litem who is an Ohio attorney may also serve as counsel, provided no conflict between these roles exists.[18] In *In re Duncan/Walker Children*,[19] the court of appeals held that an explicit dual appointment was required. The court wrote: "The issue presented is, When an attorney is appointed as guardian ad litem for a juvenile, does the attorney automatically become the attorney for the ward? We think not. The attorney may serve as attorney for the ward and guardian only when there is no conflict of interest, and who better to determine that issue but the court? Therefore, we find that for an attorney to act as guardian ad litem and attorney for the ward, there must be a dual appointment, and a finding that no conflict exists."[20]

In *In re Baby Girl Baxter*,[21] the Ohio Supreme Court recognized that these two roles are not always compatible:

> The duty of a lawyer to his client and the duty of a guardian ad litem to his ward are not always identical and, in fact, may conflict. The role of guardian ad litem is to investigate the ward's situation and then to ask the court to do what the guardian feels is in the child's best interest. The role of the attorney is to zealously represent his client within the bounds of the law. . . .

---

[18]See In re Stacey S., 136 Ohio App. 3d 503, 513–14, 1999-Ohio-989, 737 N.E.2d 92 (6th Dist. Lucas County 1999) ("The rule specifically permits an attorney to act as both guardian ad litem and attorney to the ward, but recognizes the inherent danger of conflict in these roles. A lawyer for the child has an ethical duty to zealously represent his client within the bounds of the law. The attorney is the spokesperson for the ward's wishes. The role of the guardian ad litem is to investigate the ward's situation and then ask the court to do that which the guardian ad litem believes is in the ward's best interests. It is held that for an attorney to act in both capacities, the court must first make a '* * * dual appointment and a finding that no conflict exists.' In this case, the court appointed a lay guardian ad litem and an attorney for the guardian, but never an attorney for the children."); In re Zhang, 135 Ohio App. 3d 350, 357, 734 N.E.2d 379 (8th Dist. Cuyahoga County 1999) ("Examination of the record in this case reveals the interests of the guardian ad litem for Sue Chen aligned with those of the role of her counsel, and hence representation by the guardian ad litem does not present any conflict of interest problem in this case. Because Sue Chen's guardian ad litem participated in the juvenile court proceedings on behalf of Chen and no conflict existed between her role as guardian ad litem and as counsel, Sue Chen had counsel during the juvenile court proceedings."). But see In re Curry, 2004-Ohio-750, at ¶ 46, 2004 WL 307476 (Ohio Ct. App. 4th Dist. Washington County) ("Appellant has not established that the [non-attorney] guardian ad litem's questioning of witnesses seriously affected the basic fairness, integrity, or public reputation of the judicial process. Consequently, based on the foregoing reasons, we disagree with appellant that the guardian ad litem's questioning of witnesses constituted plain error and mandates a reversal of the trial court's judgment.").

[19]Matter of Duncan/Walker Children, 109 Ohio App. 3d 841, 673 N.E.2d 217 (5th Dist. Stark County 1996).

[20]Matter of Duncan/Walker Children, 109 Ohio App. 3d 841, 844–45, 673 N.E.2d 217 (5th Dist. Stark County 1996). The court went on to note: "Since we find that the guardian ad litem was not counsel for the ward, the guardian ad litem had no authority to file findings of fact and conclusions of law, and the court should not have ordered the guardian to do so. . . . [T]he findings of fact submitted by the guardian ad litem are based upon the investigative report that was not submitted under oath. Therefore, the report is pure hearsay. The guardian ad litem did not testify and was not subjected to direct or cross-examination, and therefore the report cannot be considered evidence." Matter of Duncan/Walker Children, 109 Ohio App. 3d 841, 845, 673 N.E.2d 217 (5th Dist. Stark County 1996).

[21]In re Baby Girl Baxter, 17 Ohio St. 3d 229, 479 N.E.2d 257 (1985). See also In re Howard, 119 Ohio App. 3d 201, 206, 695 N.E.2d 1 (1st Dist. Hamilton County 1997) ("If the juvenile has a lawyer, the role of the lawyer is to represent his or her client zealously within the bounds of the law. The job of a guardian *ad litem* is to investigate the minor's situation, and ask the court to do what the guardian *ad litem* believes is in the minor's best interest. A lawyer can take on both responsibilities, but as noted in *Baxter*, the duties of a lawyer and the duties of a guardian *ad litem* may conflict. In that circumstance, one lawyer cannot perform both functions. Generally, it is counsel who must bring potential conflicts to the attention of the court, but where counsel fails to perceive a conflict, or fails to bring it to the court's attention, the court may be obliged to act *sua sponte*.").

If the attorney feels there is a conflict between his role as attorney and his role as guardian, he should petition the court for an order allowing him to withdraw as guardian. The court should not hesitate to grant such request.[22]

A new guardian ad litem should be appointed if either the court or the attorney finds there is a conflict.[23]

In *In re Smith*,[24] the trial court terminated a mother's parental rights. At the close of the hearing, the guardian ad litem referred to the "rather difficult position" he was in being both guardian ad litem and counsel for the mother. The appellees attempted to distinguish *In re Baby Girl Baxter* on the ground that no direct conflict had been shown in this case. The court of appeals rejected such a requirement:

> To accept appellees' position would be to require showing the commission of an act or acts by the guardian/counsel indicative of conflict. This would place an intolerable burden on the appellant in instances where a conflict manifests itself not in the commission of an act antithetical to the client's interest, but by the omission of an act or acts which might prove favorable to the client's wishes. We decline to require an appellant to, in effect, prove a negative.

Research References

Carlin, Baldwin's Ohio Practice, Merrick-Rippner Probate Law (6th ed.), Ch 107

§ 23:7 Mental competency

Mental competency refers to a criminal defendant's mental condition at the time of trial and should be distinguished from insanity, which refers to the defendant's mental condition at the time of the crime. The United States Supreme Court has held that "the failure to observe procedures adequate to protect a defendant's right not to be tried or convicted while incompetent to

---

[22]In re Baby Girl Baxter, 17 Ohio St. 3d 229, 479 N.E.2d 257 (1985). See also RC 2151.281(H).

[23]RC 2151.281(H) and Juv. R. 4(C)(2). In re Williams, 101 Ohio St. 3d 398, 2004-Ohio-1500, 805 N.E.2d 1110 (2004) ("[A] child who is the subject of a juvenile court proceeding to terminate parental rights is a party to that proceeding and, therefore, is entitled to independent counsel in certain circumstances."); In Re Ridenour, 2004-Ohio-1958, at ¶ 47, 2004 WL 834579 (Ohio Ct. App. 11th Dist. Lake County) ("[I]t was error for the juvenile court to rely on the testimony of [the child's] caseworker as evidence of his wishes regarding his custody. The statute clearly provides that the court is to consider '[t]he wishes of the child, *as expressed directly by the child or through the child's guardian ad litem*.'"). See also In re Emery, 2003-Ohio-2206, at ¶ 21, 2004 WL 2003811 (Ohio Ct. App. 4th Dist. Lawrence County) ("In summary, we find that [mother] is entitled to assert her children's right to counsel and did not waive that right."); In re Johnson, 2003-Ohio-3278, at ¶ 12, 2004 WL 21446385 (Ohio Ct. App. 7th Dist. Columbiana County) (It was an abuse of discretion for the trial court to fail to hear evidence on mother's motion for appointment of guardian ad litem for the children.); In re Janie M., 131 Ohio App. 3d 637, 723 N.E.2d 191 (6th Dist. Lucas County 1999) (change of custody proceeding; "The roles of guardian *ad litem* and attorney are different. Therefore, absent an express dual appointment, courts should not presume a dual appointment when the appointed guardian *ad litem* is also an attorney. . . . At the time of the initial hearing, the magistrate was aware that Tyler's wishes were clearly different from those of the guardian. Therefore, we conclude that the court erred in not appointing counsel to represent Tyler.") (citations omitted). In In Matter of Spaulding, 1993 WL 115934, at *11 (Ohio Ct. App. 6th Dist. Lucas County 1993), the court noted that the statute requires the guardian/counsel to give up the guardian duties in the event of a conflict. "The problem with this rule is evident in the present circumstances where the same attorney is appointed as guardian *ad litem* and counsel for three children and only one of the three children objects to the guardian's recommendation." In re Emery, 2003-Ohio-2206, 2003 WL 2003811, at *13 (Ohio Ct. App. 4th Dist. Lawrence County 2003) ("We conclude the court's hearing on [mother's] motion was deficient because the court did not consider the proper factors in determining whether a conflict existed between the children's desires and the GAL's position.") In re Micheal Legg, 2002-Ohio-4582, 2002 WL 2027290 (Ohio Ct. App. 8th Dist. Cuyahoga County 2002).

[24]In re Smith, 77 Ohio App. 3d 1, 13–14, 601 N.E.2d 45 (6th Dist. Ottawa County 1991).

stand trial deprives him of his due process right to a fair trial."[1] The test for competency is whether the defendant "has sufficient present ability to consult with his lawyer with a reasonable degree of rational understanding—and whether he has a rational as well as factual understanding of the proceedings against him."[2]

In Ohio, RC 2945.37 governs the competency issue.[3] Under this statute, a defendant is presumed competent to stand trial unless it is proved by a preponderance of the evidence that the defendant is incapable of understanding the nature and objective of the proceedings or of presently assisting in the defense. This statute, however, applies only to a "criminal action."

There is no comparable provision for juvenile cases. Nevertheless, Juvenile Rule 32(A)(4) does provide that the court may order a mental examination where a party's "competence to participate in the proceedings is an issue." In addition, the SYO statute recognizes the right to raise the issue of mental competency.[4] More importantly, due process requires that an alleged delinquent be competent to stand trial. The court of appeals in *In re McWhorter*[5] wrote:

> [T]here is no statutory basis in Ohio for a juvenile to plead that he or she is incompetent to stand for adjudication as a delinquent. Nevertheless, certain constitutional requirements associated with an adult criminal trial are equally applicable to adjudicative juvenile proceedings. . . . The conviction of an accused not legally competent to stand trial is a violation of due process.

After a court-ordered competency evaluation, a psychologist concluded that the child was competent to stand for adjudication in juvenile court. At the competency hearing, the psychologist indicated that the child might not be competent to stand trial as an adult—citing a simpler vocabulary. The juvenile judge also mentioned that practical differences existed in the two different courts. The court of appeals held: "We do not believe that the trial court adopted an erroneous standard for establishing competency in juvenile proceedings. Instead, the trial court simply recognized that there are practical differences between juvenile delinquency proceedings and adult criminal prosecutions. The court could consider these differences in determining whether a defendant is capable of understanding the nature and objective of the particular proceeding and assisting in his or her defense."[6]

In *In re Williams*,[7] the court of appeals held that a juvenile with an IQ of 40 was incompetent to stand trial. Although there is no statutory standard

---

[Section 23:7]

[1]Drope v. Missouri, 420 U.S. 162, 172, 95 S. Ct. 896, 43 L. Ed. 2d 103 (1975). See also Cooper v. Oklahoma, 517 U.S. 348, 116 S. Ct. 1373, 134 L. Ed. 2d 498 (1996); Medina v. California, 505 U.S. 437, 453, 112 S. Ct. 2572, 120 L. Ed. 2d 353 (1992); Pate v. Robinson, 383 U.S. 375, 86 S. Ct. 836, 15 L. Ed. 2d 815 (1966); State v. Chapin, 67 Ohio St. 2d 437, 21 Ohio Op. 3d 273, 424 N.E.2d 317 (1981).

[2]Dusky v. U.S., 362 U.S. 402, 402, 80 S. Ct. 788, 4 L. Ed. 2d 824 (1960). See also Godinez v. Moran, 509 U.S. 389, 113 S. Ct. 2680, 2688, 125 L. Ed. 2d 321 (1993) (The issue is whether the accused "has the capacity to understand the proceedings and to assist counsel.").

[3]Katz and Giannelli, Baldwin's Ohio Practice, Criminal Law (2d ed.), Ch 54.

[4]RC 2152.13(C)(2).

[5]In re McWhorter, 1994 WL 673098, at *2 (Ohio Ct. App. 12th Dist. Butler County 1994). See also In re Bailey, 150 Ohio App. 3d 664, 667, 2002-Ohio-6792, 782 N.E.2d 1177 (2d Dist. Montgomery County 2002) ("Although Bailey is not a criminal defendant, the right not to be tried or convicted while incompetent is as fundamental in juvenile proceedings as it is in criminal trials of adults. . . . [T]he standard enunciated in R.C. 2945.37(G) governs the competency evaluations of juveniles so long as it is applied in light of juvenile rather than adult norms." (citations omitted)).

[6]In re McWhorter, 1994 WL 673098, at *3 (Ohio Ct. App. 12th Dist. Butler County 1994).

[7]In re Williams, 116 Ohio App. 3d 237, 241, 687 N.E.2d 507 (2d Dist. Montgomery County 1997) ("Although Nicholas is not a criminal defendant, this court has held that 'the right not to be tried while incompetent' is as fundamental in juvenile proceedings as it is in criminal trials of adults.").

specified for juvenile cases, the court ruled that "the standard enunciated in R.C. 2945.37(A) governs competency evaluations of juveniles, so long as it is applied in light of juvenile rather than adult norms."[8]

Courts in other jurisdictions that have considered the issue have applied the competency requirements to juvenile proceedings. As one court has noted, "Since the right not to be tried while incompetent is a due process-fundamental fairness right . . . it should . . . be applicable to juvenile proceedings, unless some essential end of the juvenile justice system will be thwarted by its application."[9]

Cross References

§ 1:4

Research References

Katz and Giannelli, Baldwin's Ohio Practice, Criminal Law (2d ed.), Ch 54

§ 23:8 Pleas

Juvenile Rule 29(C) requires the parties to admit or deny the allegations in the complaint. Failure or refusal to admit the allegations constitutes a denial. Juvenile Rule 29(D) governs the procedures applicable if a party enters an admission. These uncontested cases are discussed in the next

---

[8]In re Williams, 116 Ohio App. 3d 237, 242, 687 N.E.2d 507 (2d Dist. Montgomery County 1997). See also In re Stone, 2003-Ohio-3071, 2003 WL 21373156 (Ohio Ct. App. 12th Dist. Clinton County 2003), appeal not allowed, 100 Ohio St. 3d 1432, 2003-Ohio-5396, 797 N.E.2d 512 (2003); In re Adams, 2003-Ohio-4112, at ¶ 33, 2004 WL 21783682 (Ohio Ct. App 7th Dist. Mahoning County) (A low IQ is not, in and of itself, enough to find a defendant incompetent. "Therefore, a defendant being mentally retarded does not per se raise 'sufficient indicia of incompetence' to require a trial court to sua sponte raise competency and order a hearing."); In re Bailey, 150 Ohio App. 3d 664, 668, 2002-Ohio-6792, 782 N.E.2d 1177 (2d Dist. Montgomery County 2002) ("There is authority to support a juvenile court's finding that while a child may be incompetent to stand trial in adult court, he or she may nevertheless be competent to enter an admission and stand for adjudication in juvenile court, because of the differences in the complexities in adult criminal proceedings versus juvenile proceedings. A juvenile court can properly consider those differences in determining whether a child is competent to enter an admission per R.C. 2945.37(G), because that statutory standard must be assessed in light of juvenile, rather than adult, norms.") (citations omitted); In re York, 142 Ohio App. 3d 524, 536, 756 N.E.2d 191 (8th Dist. Cuyahoga County 2001) ("R.C. 2945.37(A) governs competency evaluations of juveniles, as well as adults, so long as it is applied in light of juvenile rather than adult norms.") ; In re Grimes, 147 Ohio App. 3d 192, 422–423, 2002-Ohio-1547, 769 N.E.2d 420 (7th Dist. Monroe County 2002) ("This court has previously acknowledged that the right not to be tried while incompetent applies to juvenile proceedings just as it does in criminal trial of adults."); In Matter of Lloyd, 1997 WL 115886, at *2 (Ohio Ct. App. 5th Dist. Richland County 1997) ("The right not to be tried while incompetent is applicable to the juvenile system just as in the adult system."); In Re: Johnson, 1983 WL 2516 (Ohio Ct. App. 2d Dist. Montgomery County 1983) ("[T]he right not to be tried while incompetent is as fundamental and essential in the juvenile system as it is in adult criminal trials." (citation omitted); In re D.G., 91 Ohio Misc. 2d 226, 229, 698 N.E.2d 533 (C.P. 1998) ("[T]he Due Process Clauses . . . require a juvenile court to observe procedures sufficient to safeguard the child's right not to be adjudicated while incompetent to stand trial. The court further finds well taken the juvenile's request for application of the adult competency statute to juvenile proceedings, provided the court assesses the juvenile by juvenile norms rather than adult.).

[9]State In Interest of Causey, 363 So. 2d 472, 476 (La. 1978). See also State ex rel. Dandoy v. Superior Court In and For Pima County, 127 Ariz. 184, 619 P.2d 12 (1980); Matter of W.A.F., 573 A.2d 1264, 1267 (D.C. 1990); Tate v. State, 864 So. 2d 44 (Fla. Dist. Ct. App. 4th Dist. 2003); Matter of S. W. T.'s Welfare, 277 N.W.2d 507 (Minn. 1979); In re Jeffrey C., 81 Misc. 2d 651, 366 N.Y.S.2d 826 (Fam. Ct. 1975); In re N.S., 2004 WL 254215 (Tex. App. Waco 2004). See generally Grisso, Juvenile Competency to Stand Trial: Questions in an Era of Punitive Reform, 12 Criminal Justice 4 (Fall 1997).

See also In re Atwell, Nos. 40667, 40719 (8th Dist. Ct. App., Cuyahoga, 1-17-80) (Mental competency of child considered.).

section.[1] If the party denies the allegations or the court does not accept an admission, the case is tried.

No-contest plea. In contrast to Criminal Rule 11, for a long time Juvenile Rule 29 did not recognize a plea of "no contest."[2] In a criminal case, a plea of no contest does not waive a defendant's right to challenge a pretrial ruling on a motion to suppress evidence. Criminal Rule 12(H) provides that a "plea of no contest does not preclude a defendant from asserting upon appeal that the trial court prejudicially erred in ruling on a pretrial motion, including a pretrial motion to suppress evidence." There is no comparable provision in juvenile cases. Instead, Juvenile Rule 29(D)(2) provides that an admission waives a party's right to challenge the evidence against him or her. In 2001, the option to plead no contest was added to Juvenile Rule 29(C); the court must consent to the entry of this plea.

Insanity plea. In *In re Chambers*,[3] the court of appeals held that the affirmative defense of insanity could not be raised in juvenile court, noting that "no provision for an insanity plea exists in Juv.R. 29 such as exists in Crim.R. 11."

Cross References
§ 23:9
Research References
Katz and Giannelli, Baldwin's Ohio Practice, Criminal Law (2d ed.) § 42.2

§ 23:9 Uncontested cases

Before a juvenile court may accept an admission,[1] it must personally address the party[2] to determine whether the admission is voluntarily and intel-

---

[Section 23:8]

[1]See § 23:9, Uncontested cases. See generally Katz and Giannelli, Baldwin's Ohio Practice, Criminal Law (2d ed.), Ch 45.

[2]See In re Green, 4 Ohio App. 3d 196, 447 N.E.2d 129 (10th Dist. Franklin County 1982); Juniper, 1982 WL 4229 (Ohio Ct. App. 10th Dist. Franklin County 1982); Langrehr, 1981 WL 4294 (Ohio Ct. App. 11th Dist. Trumbull County 1981).

Since the Traffic Rules apply in juvenile traffic offender cases, a child may plead "no contest" in such a case. Traf. R. 10(A). See also In the Matter Of: Kahan, 1982 WL 6596 (Ohio Ct. App. 6th Dist. Lucas County 1982) (Failure to inform child that no contest plea could result in revocation of driving privileges invalidated the plea.).

[3]Matter of Chambers, 116 Ohio App. 3d 312, 314, 688 N.E.2d 25 (3d Dist. Logan County 1996).

[Section 23:9]

[1]An admission must demonstrate that the child is in fact delinquent, neglected, or dependent. See In re Hobson, 44 Ohio L. Abs. 85, 44 Ohio L. Abs. 86, 62 N.E.2d 510 (Ct. App. 2d Dist. [sic] Franklin County 1945) (Mere fact that mother desires to place her baby for adoption is not enough to constitute dependency.). See also In re Sims, 13 Ohio App. 3d 37, 468 N.E.2d 111 (12th Dist. Preble County 1983) (An admission does not bar a parent from participating in an adjudicatory hearing on neglect.). RC 2151.35(H)(1), which became effective in 1996 as H.B. 1, uses the terms "guilty" and "no contest" pleas. These pleas are not permitted under Juv. R. 29. The statute also erroneously cites RC 2151.26; the correct cite should be RC 2151.355. The statute reads: "Before accepting from an alleged delinquent child a plea of guilty or no contest to the commission of an act that is a category one or category two offense, the court shall inform the child of the possible length of commitment to the legal custody of the Department of Youth Services to which the child could be subject under section 21.51.26 [RC 2151.355]."

[2]See In re Beechler, 115 Ohio App. 3d 567, 571–72, 685 N.E.2d 1257 (4th Dist. Ross County 1996) ("This rule places an affirmative duty upon the juvenile court. Prior to accepting an admission, the juvenile court must *personally* address the actual party before the court and determine that that party, and not merely the attorney, understands the nature of the allegations and the consequences of entering the admission. Furthermore, the test for the accused delinquent's understanding of the charges is subjective, rather than objective, in that it is not sufficient that a hypothetical reasonable party would understand. The person actually before the court must do so. . . . Strict adherence to the procedures imposed by these rules is not constitutionally mandated; however, courts have interpreted them as requiring substantial compliance with

ligently made, i.e., with an understanding of the nature of the allegations[3] and the consequences of the admission.[4] A possible loss of liberty is a consequence that a juvenile must understand.[5] In contrast, providing a DNA sample is not.[6]

their provisions. . . . The failure of a lower court to substantially comply with the requirements of Juv.R. 29 constitutes prejudicial error." (emphasis added); see also In re Montgomery, 117 Ohio App. 3d 696, 700, 691 N.E.2d 349 (8th Dist. Cuyahoga County 1997) ("[A] trial court violates Juv.R. 29 when it accepts a juvenile's admission of delinquency when the trial court did not address the juvenile personally to determine if appellant understood the consequences of his admission and the rights waived."). But see In re Adams, 2003-Ohio-4112, 2003 WL 21783682 (Ohio Ct. App. 7th Dist. Mahoning County).

[3]See In re Morgan, 2003-Ohio-2543, 2003 WL 21135298 (Ohio Ct. App. 12th Dist. Butler County); In re Fulk, 132 Ohio App. 3d 470, 472, 1999-Ohio-840, 725 N.E.2d 357 (3d Dist. Crawford County 1999) ("[T]he trial court did not apprise appellant of the nature of the charge against her, nor did the court inform her of the possible consequences of an admission."); In re Terrance P., 129 Ohio App. 3d 418, 425, 717 N.E.2d 1160 (6th Dist. Lucas County 1998) ("[T]he court's subsequent questioning of appellant revealed that appellant did not understand and in fact contested the knowledge element of the crime of receiving stolen property."); In re Doyle, 122 Ohio App. 3d 767, 773, 702 N.E.2d 970 (2d Dist. 1997) ("[T]he magistrate merely read the complaint into the record, and . . . he did not make any effort to ascertain whether Doyle understood it. . . . The lack of any further explanation of the nature of the charge is exacerbated by its nature; we doubt whether the elements of complicity to receive stolen property would be known and understood by most adults, let alone by a juvenile."); In re Brooks, 112 Ohio App. 3d 54, 57, 677 N.E.2d 1229 (9th Dist. Summit County 1996) ("In this case, the trial court, in accepting the appellant's admission, established only that the appellant was making his plea voluntarily. No inquiry was made of the appellant as to whether he understood the nature of the charges before him or the consequences of his plea, as required by Juv.R. 29(D)(1). Indeed, the appellant's obvious confusion at his first dispositional hearing highlights his complete lack of understanding as to the consequences of his admission. Further, no personal inquiry was made by the court of the appellant as to any of the elements set forth in Juv.R. 29(D)(2).").

[4]See In re J.J., 2004-Ohio-1429, 2004 WL 574135 (Ohio Ct. App. 9th Dist. Summit County); In re Graham, 147 Ohio App. 3d 452, 456-57, 2002-Ohio-2407, 770 N.E.2d 1123 (7th Dist. Mahoning County 2002) ("Although the court asked Jeremiah if he understood the nature of the charges and whether he understood the consequences of the admission, it never personally advised Jeremiah of these charges and consequences. In order to have demonstrated substantial compliance with the mandates of Juv.R. 29(D), the court should have *explained* to Jeremiah the nature of charges against him and the potential penalties he faced."); In re Kimble, 114 Ohio App. 3d 136, 141, 682 N.E.2d 1066 (3d Dist. Crawford County 1996) ("[T]he record indicates that the trial court failed to advise defendant of the purpose of the hearing, the possible penalties for the alleged truancy violation, the ramifications of an admission to the charge, as well as defendant's right to remain silent, offer evidence, cross-examine witnesses and have a record made of the proceedings as mandated by Juv.R. 29(B) and (D).").

[5]See In re Holcomb, 147 Ohio App. 3d 31, 2002-Ohio-2042, 768 N.E.2d 722 (8th Dist. Cuyahoga County 2002) (no substantial compliance where court failed to inform juvenile of term of possible commitment); In re Doyle, 122 Ohio App. 3d 767, 773, 702 N.E.2d 970 (2d Dist. 1997) ("[P]erhaps most significantly, we find that the magistrate failed to apprise Doyle of the consequences of her admission. . . . [H]e made no mention of the possible length of any commitment."); In Matter of Keck, 1997 WL 473097, at *4 (Ohio Ct. App. 8th Dist. Cuyahoga County 1997) ("While the term 'consequences,' as used in this rule, has received minimal attention by the courts of this state, . . . commitment to ODYS for [a] period of several years is a significant enough consequence to warrant mention by the trial court."); In re Hendrickson, 114 Ohio App. 3d 290, 293, 683 N.E.2d 76 (2d Dist. Greene County 1996) ("In particular, we find troubling the judge's failure to provide Hendrickson with any information concerning the possible sentence the court could impose. . . . Neither party cites, nor can this court locate, any cases construing the term 'consequences' as used in Juv.R. 29(D). In our view, however, the potential for commitment to the Ohio Department of Youth Services for a period of one to six years is a significant consequence that the judge should have mentioned to Hendrickson. Indeed, in the eyes of a fifteen-year old who is unrepresented by counsel, the possibility of a lengthy commitment well may be the most important consequence imaginable.").

[6]In In re Nicholson, 132 Ohio App. 3d 303, 307–08, 724 N.E.2d 1217 (8th Dist. Cuyahoga County 1999), the court of appeals ruled that a juvenile need not be informed of the requirement of a mandatory sample for the DNA databank statute. First, the court ruled that a failure to withdraw the plea or vacate the adjudication waived the issue for appeal. Second, the court held that this requirement was not a "consequence" within the meaning of Juvenile Rule 29(D)(1). It was a collateral consequence because it did not have an immediate and direct effect upon the range of punishment.

The court must also ensure that the party understands that an admission waives the right to challenge the witnesses and evidence against the party,[7] the right to remain silent,[8] and the right to introduce evidence[9] at the hearing.[10] In *In re Jenkins*,[11] the court of appeals commented:

> Juv. R. 29(D) has been held to be analogous to Crim. R. 11(C)(2), which provides that the trial judge in an adult criminal proceeding must personally address the defendant before accepting a plea of guilty . . .. Although the trial judge addressed the elements contained in Juv. R. 29(D). There was no discussion by the trial court to determine whether appellant understood that by entering his admission he was waiving his rights to challenge the witnesses and evidence against him, to remain silent, and to introduce evidence at the adjudicatory hearing, as required under subsection (D)(2). Therefore, there was no compliance, substantial or otherwise, with the requirement of Juv. R. 29(D)(2).[12]

---

[7]In re Morgan, 2003-Ohio-2543, 2003 WL 21135298 (Ohio Ct. App. 12th Dist. Butler County); In re Hendrickson, 114 Ohio App. 3d 290, 293, 683 N.E.2d 76 (2d Dist. Greene County 1996) ("[T]he judge informed Hendrickson that his admission would result in a waiver of his right to a trial. We are unpersuaded, however, that a fifteen-year-old child necessarily would infer that a trial encompasses the right to challenge the witnesses and evidence against him.").

[8]See In re Onion, 128 Ohio App. 3d 498, 503, 715 N.E.2d 604 (11th Dist. Ashtabula County 1998) (In rejecting the applicability of the substantial-compliance test for constitutional rights, the court wrote that "when . . . a trial court fails to inform a defendant of one of his or her *critical constitutional rights*, including the privilege against self-incrimination, that failure is *per se* prejudicial.").

[9]In re Hairston, 1996 WL 465249, at *2 (Ohio Ct. App. 10th Dist. Franklin County 1996) ("The magistrate specifically advised appellant that there would be 'no trial, no right to remain silent, no right to question witnesses, no appeal.' The only item specifically enumerated in Juv.R. 29(D)(2), which was not directly covered by the magistrate, was appellant's ability to introduce his own evidence at the adjudicatory hearing. As a factual matter, the magistrate did not strictly comply with Juv.R. 29; however, this court finds that, under the circumstances, the magistrate substantially complied with the rule."); State v. Miller, No. 33127 (8th Dist. Ct. App., Cuyahoga, 1-23-75) (Juv. R. 29(D) violated where record failed to show that child understood the consequences of his admission to delinquency charges or his right to introduce evidence in his own behalf).

[10]Juv. R. 29(D). See also In re West, 128 Ohio App. 3d 356, 360, 714 N.E.2d 988 (8th Dist. Cuyahoga County 1998) ("More alarming is the fact that there is no discussion regarding the rights that appellant would be waiving by entering an admission and only a cursory attempt at inquiring of appellant's right to counsel."); In re Montgomery, 117 Ohio App. 3d 696, 700, 691 N.E.2d 349 (8th Dist. Cuyahoga County 1997) ("[A] trial court violates Juv.R. 29 when it accepts a juvenile's admission of delinquency when the trial court did not address the juvenile personally to determine if appellant understood the consequences of his admission and the rights waived."); In re Brooks, 112 Ohio App. 3d 54, 57, 677 N.E.2d 1229 (9th Dist. Summit County 1996) ("In this case, the trial court, in accepting the appellant's admission, established only that the appellant was making his plea voluntarily. No inquiry was made of the appellant as to whether he understood the nature of the charges before him or the consequences of his plea, as required by Juv.R. 29(D)(1). Indeed, the appellant's obvious confusion at his first dispositional hearing highlights his complete lack of understanding as to the consequences of his admission. Further, no personal inquiry was made by the court of the appellant as to any of the elements set forth in Juv.R. 29(D)(2)."); In re Flynn, 101 Ohio App. 3d 778, 782–83, 656 N.E.2d 737 (8th Dist. Cuyahoga County 1995) ("[T]he lower court did not adequately explain to the appellant the right he was waiving by choosing to enter an admission. . . . Appellant's counsel did acknowledge on the record that he had explained to appellant his rights. However, this is insufficient to demonstrate a knowing and voluntary waiver, as the court itself must address the appellant. . . . [A]lthough the appellant also signed a form in which he waived his rights, this does not constitute a substitute for the court's duty to address the appellant."); In re McKenzie, 102 Ohio App. 3d 275, 277, 656 N.E.2d 1377 (8th Dist. Cuyahoga County 1995) ("Juv.R. 29 requires the judge to address the youth personally and conduct an on-the-record exchange to determine whether the admission is knowing and voluntary. . . . Review of an admission pursuant to Juv.R. 29(D) is similar to review of a guilty plea pursuant to Crim.R. 11(C)(2) . . .. A valid waiver cannot be presumed from a silent record.").

[11]In re Jenkins, 101 Ohio App. 3d 177, 655 N.E.2d 238 (12th Dist. Butler County 1995).

[12]In re Jenkins, 101 Ohio App. 3d 177, 179–80, 655 N.E.2d 238 (12th Dist. Butler County 1995). See also In re Beechler, 115 Ohio App. 3d 567, 571, 685 N.E.2d 1257 (4th Dist. Ross County 1996) ("An admission in a juvenile proceeding pursuant to Juv.R. 29(D) is analogous to a guilty plea made by an adult pursuant to Crim.R. 11(C)."); In re Hendrickson, 114 Ohio App. 3d 290, 292, 683 N.E.2d 76 (2d Dist. Greene County 1996) ("This state's courts have construed

Another court of appeals has adopted a different view. In *In re Harris*,[13] the court concluded that the referee had substantially complied with the requirements of Juvenile Rule 29(D)(1) but not Juvenile Rule 29(D)(2). Nevertheless, the court ruled that Harris's due process rights had not been violated. The court observed:

> The juvenile contends that the accepting of an "admission of responsibility" is so analogous to accepting a guilty plea in [a] felony case that the requirements of Crim.R. 11(C)(2) should apply. We disagree. This [Criminal] rule was drafted, at least in part, in order to satisfy constitutional requirements set forth in several criminal cases in the United States Supreme Court. Juv.R. 29(D)(2) appears to have been drafted in order to satisfy due process and fairness requirements of juveniles in juvenile court proceedings. *In re Gault* . . . Unlike adults a child has a "right not to liberty but to custody." . . .
>
> The differences between adult criminal proceedings and juvenile delinquency proceedings were succinctly pointed out in *Kent* . . .
>
> Ohio courts have also held that "[t]he procedure for pleas in juvenile court in relation to a delinquency complaint differs substantially from the pleas provided by Crim.R. 11 in adult criminal proceedings."

In any event, the courts have emphasized that "[s]pecial caution must be taken when dealing with juveniles in the justice system because children do not have the life experience that would assist them in making the best decisions to safeguard their personal and constitutional rights. When accepting an admission, the court must personally address the party and determine that the admission is voluntary and made with an understanding of the nature of the charges and potential consequences."[14] Moreover, the signing of a rights-waiver form by itself is not sufficient, nor are group sessions.[15] Finally, a journal entry without a transcript is also insufficient.[16]

The Ohio Supreme Court compared Juvenile Rule 29 and Criminal Rule 11

Juv.R. 29(D) as being 'similar to' or 'analogous to' Crim.R. 11(C)(2)."); In re Brooks, 112 Ohio App. 3d 54, 57, 677 N.E.2d 1229 (9th Dist. Summit County 1996) ("An admission in a delinquency case is similar to a guilty plea entered by an adult in a criminal case in that it involves a waiver of the juvenile's right to challenge the allegations of the complaint and to confront witnesses. . . . Juv.R. 29(D) is analogous to Crim.R. 11(C)(2) in that, before accepting an admission of guilt, the trial court must personally address the juvenile on the record with respect to the areas of inquiry set forth in the rule."); In re William H., 105 Ohio App. 3d 761, 766, 664 N.E.2d 1361 (6th Dist. Lucas County 1995) ("trial court did substantially comply with the requirements of Juv. R. 29 when it accepted appellant's admission"); In re Christopher R., 101 Ohio App. 3d 245, 247–48, 655 N.E.2d 280 (6th Dist. Lucas County 1995) ("Ohio courts have held that in a delinquency case, an admission is similar to a guilty plea made by an adult pursuant to Crim. R. 11(C) . . .. [T]he trial court failed to substantially comply with the requirements of Juv. R. 29(D).").

[13]In re Harris, 104 Ohio App. 3d 324, 327, 662 N.E.2d 34 (2d Dist. Montgomery County 1995) (citing In re Green, 4 Ohio App. 3d 196, 198, 447 N.E.2d 129 (10th Dist. Franklin County 1982)).

[14]In re Rogers, 124 Ohio App. 3d 392, 395, 706 N.E.2d 390 (9th Dist. Summit County 1997) ("The magistrate did not conduct any type of meaningful colloquy with Fawn, either to ensure her complete understanding of her right to counsel or to ensure that she understood the consequences of her plea. Most of the remarks were addressed to Fawn's mother, who was the person who had filed the unruly-child complaint. Most references to Fawn were in the third person, and the magistrate addressed her directly concerning her rights only briefly, almost as an afterthought. This court has recently held that the record must reflect that a juvenile is clearly made aware of his or her rights and understands any waiver of them.") (citations omitted).

[15]In re Miller, 119 Ohio App. 3d 52, 57, 694 N.E.2d 500 (2d Dist. Clark County 1997) (collective colloquy in lieu of an individual colloquy was not sufficient; nor was waiver of rights form) ("The purpose of Juv.R. 29(D) is to ensure that minors are afforded their due process right to fundamentally fair treatment in juvenile court proceedings. . . . This procedure is somewhat analogous to the plea procedure mandated in adult felony criminal cases by Crim.R. 11(C)(2)."). But see In re Holcomb, 147 Ohio App. 3d 31, 2002-Ohio-2042, 768 N.E.2d 722 (8th Dist. Cuyahoga County 2002) (Fact that juvenile court intermingled acceptance of juvenile's plea with that of his brother did not mean court failed to personally address juvenile, where the court individually addressed each brother after each major component of its colloquy).

[16]In re Amos, 154 Ohio App. 3d 434, 436-37, 2003-Ohio-5014, 797 N.E.2d 568 (3d Dist. Crawford County 2003) ("Without a transcript to review, there is no way to review the admissions and to ensure that the trial court complied with the rule. The journal entry alone does not

in *In re Kirby*.[17] In that case, the juvenile attempted to proffer an *Alford* plea, which involves entering a guilty plea in a criminal case while at the same time maintaining innocence.[18] Although the Court recognized that "[p]rocedural and systemic differences . . . exist between the juvenile courts and the adult criminal courts," the decision turned on a provision found in Juvenile Rule 29 but not in Criminal Rule 11:

> While Crim.R. 11 and Juv.R. 29 are similar, they are not identical. Significantly, Juv.R. 29 has a provision not found in Crim.R. 11: a juvenile's "failure or refusal to admit the allegations *shall be deemed a denial*." (Emphasis added.) Juv.R. 29(C). In the case of a denial, the juvenile court is required to follow the procedure set forth in division (E) of Juv.R. 29, which provides that the juvenile court considers the evidence and determines the issues. Juv.R. 29(E)(3) and (4).[19]

The Court went on to conclude that *Alford* pleas were not permitted under the Juvenile Rules: "Thus, Juv.R. 29(C) mandates the procedure for the juvenile court to follow when a juvenile offender fails or refuses to admit to allegations: the court must treat that failure or refusal as a denial. Therefore, acceptance of an *Alford* plea by a juvenile court is inconsistent with the objectives, procedures, and rules of the juvenile court system."[20]

The procedure for accepting admissions, at least in *delinquency* cases,[21] should be based on the constitutional requirements applicable in criminal trials. In *McCarthy v. United States*,[22] the United States Supreme Court wrote:

> A defendant who enters such a plea [of guilty] simultaneously waives several constitutional rights, including his privilege against compulsory self-incrimination, his right to trial by jury, and his right to confront his accusers. For this waiver to be valid under the Due Process Clause, it must be "an intentional relinquishment or abandonment of a known right or privilege." . . . Consequently, if a defendant's guilty plea is not equally voluntary and knowing, it has been obtained in violation of due process and is therefore void. Moreover, because a guilty plea is an admission of all the elements of a formal criminal charge, it cannot be truly voluntary unless the defendant possesses an understanding of the law in relation to the facts.[23]

Courts in other jurisdictions have applied the constitutional standards relat-

---

provide sufficient support for this court to review whether the rule was followed. When the record as a whole is silent, the state bears the burden of proving that the admissions were properly made. . . . The state has presented no brief, so fails to meet its burden.").

[17]In re Kirby, 101 Ohio St. 3d 312, 2004-Ohio-970, 804 N.E.2d 476 (2004).

[18]North Carolina v. Alford, 400 U.S. 25, 91 S. Ct. 160, 27 L. Ed. 2d 162 (1970). The Ohio Supreme Court first found that the U.S. Supreme Court's decision did not require the acceptance of *Alford* pleas; instead, the Court held only that such pleas were not unconstitutional.

[19]In re Kirby, 101 Ohio St. 3d 312, 316-17, 2004-Ohio-970, 804 N.E.2d 476 (2004).

[20]In re Kirby, 101 Ohio St. 3d 312, 317, 2004-Ohio-970, 804 N.E.2d 476 (2004).

[21]See In re Clark, 141 Ohio App. 3d 55, 59, 2001-Ohio-4126, 749 N.E.2d 833 (8th Dist. Cuyahoga County 2001) ("The determination of whether a party's admission complies with Juv.R. 29 is similar to that used in determining whether a criminal defendant's guilty plea complies with Crim.R. 11" (citations omitted); "The issue is not whether the judge strictly complied with rote, but whether the parties adequately understood their rights and the effect of their admissions."); In the Matter of Banks Griggs v. Griggs Banks Jones, 1981 WL 5593 (Ohio Ct. App. 6th Dist. Lucas County 1981) (Pleading requirements for criminal cases also apply to admissions regarding dependency.); In re Theodore F., 47 A.D.2d 945, 367 N.Y.S.2d 103 (2d Dep't 1975) (applying pleading rules to status offender cases).

[22]McCarthy v. U.S., 394 U.S. 459, 89 S. Ct. 1166, 22 L. Ed. 2d 418 (1969).

[23]McCarthy v. U.S., 394 U.S. 459, 466, 89 S. Ct. 1166, 22 L. Ed. 2d 418 (1969). See also Henderson v. Morgan, 426 U.S. 637, 96 S. Ct. 2253, 49 L. Ed. 2d 108 (1976); Boykin v. Alabama, 395 U.S. 238, 89 S. Ct. 1709, 23 L. Ed. 2d 274 (1969). See generally Katz and Giannelli, Baldwin's Ohio Practice, Criminal Law (2d ed.), Ch 43; LaFave & Israel, Criminal Procedure Ch. 20 (1984); Whitebread & Slobogin, Criminal Procedure Ch. 6 (3d ed. 1992).

ing to guilty pleas in criminal trials to delinquency cases.[24]

Mental competence. In *Godinez v. Moran*,[25] the United States Supreme Court ruled that the mental competency required to plead guilty and to waive counsel was the same as that required to stand trial; the issue is whether the accused "has the capacity to understand the proceedings and to assist counsel."[26] The Court rejected the view that a "heightened" standard of competence applied to these decisions. Although the mental competence standard is the same, the issues are not. A waiver of counsel "must also be intelligent and voluntary before it can be accepted."[27] Similarly, a valid guilty plea requires the trial court to determine that the waiver of "constitutional rights is knowing and voluntary."[28]

Counsel waiver. If a party also wishes to waive the right to counsel, the court must ensure that this waiver is intelligently and voluntarily made.[29] In *In re Nation*,[30] the court ruled that the juvenile's admissions to delinquency charges were invalid because the transcript showed "her uncertainty as to whether she should waive counsel."[31] In addition, the court may hear testimony, review documents, and make further inquiry in connection with the plea.

Plea bargains. If a juvenile enters an admission pursuant to a "plea bargain," due process requires the prosecution to honor its part of the bargain.[32] One juvenile court has held that "the federal and state due process guarantees bar the refiling of a charge in a juvenile delinquency proceeding which has been dismissed pursuant to a plea agreement."[33]

Non-delinquency cases. The requirements of Juvenile Rule 29(D), however, are not limited to delinquency cases. For example, in a dependency case a court has written:

---

[24]E.g., In re Mary B., 20 Cal. App. 3d 816, 98 Cal. Rptr. 178 (3d Dist. 1971); G. M. K. v. State, 312 So. 2d 538 (Fla. Dist. Ct. App. 2d Dist. 1975); In re Appeal No. 544 September Term, 1974 from Circuit Court for Cecil County Sitting as a Juvenile Court, 25 Md. App. 26, 332 A.2d 680 (1975); Matter of Chavis, 31 N.C. App. 579, 230 S.E.2d 198 (1976); State ex rel. Juvenile Dept. of Coos County and Children's Services Div. v. Clements, 95 Or. App. 640, 770 P.2d 937 (1989); State ex rel. Juvenile Dept. of Coos County v. Welch, 12 Or. App. 400, 501 P.2d 991 (1972); State ex rel. J. M. v. Taylor, 166 W. Va. 511, 276 S.E.2d 199, 25 A.L.R.4th 1063 (1981).

[25]Godinez v. Moran, 509 U.S. 389, 113 S. Ct. 2680, 125 L. Ed. 2d 321 (1993). See § 23:7, Mental competency.

[26]Godinez v. Moran, 509 U.S. 389, 113 S. Ct. 2680, 2688, 125 L. Ed. 2d 321 (1993).

[27]Godinez v. Moran, 509 U.S. 389, 113 S. Ct. 2680, 2688, 125 L. Ed. 2d 321 (1993).

[28]Godinez v. Moran, 509 U.S. 389, 113 S. Ct. 2680, 2687, 125 L. Ed. 2d 321 (1993).

[29]In Iowa v. Tovar, 124 S. Ct. 1379, 1383, 158 L. Ed. 2d 209 (U.S. 2004), the U.S. Supreme Court held that when accepting a guilty plea from a defendant who has waived counsel, the trial court is not required to advise the defendant that waiving the assistance of counsel entails the risk that a viable defense will be overlooked or that by waiving counsel he will lose the opportunity to obtain an independent opinion on whether, under the facts and applicable law, it is wise to plead guilty. Instead, "[t]he constitutional requirement is satisfied when the trial court informs the accused of the nature of the charges against him, of his right to be counseled regarding his plea, and of the range of allowable punishments attendant upon the entry of a guilty plea."

[30]In re Nation, 61 Ohio App. 3d 763, 573 N.E.2d 1155 (3d Dist. Shelby County 1989). See § 23:4, Waiver of right to counsel.

[31]In re Nation, 61 Ohio App. 3d 763, 766, 573 N.E.2d 1155 (3d Dist. Shelby County 1989). See also In re Doyle, 122 Ohio App. 3d 767, 771, 702 N.E.2d 970 (2d Dist. 1997) ("[T]he record demonstrates that the magistrate did not adequately inform Doyle of her right to counsel. The magistrate discussed Doyle's right to counsel only in terms of representation if she were to elect to proceed to trial. The magistrate's explanation of the right to counsel was confusing, if not misleading, and could have led Doyle to believe that she was not entitled to counsel while deciding whether to admit or to deny the complaint. . . . Therefore, despite the fact that Doyle did sign a waiver of rights form, we conclude that the record does not show that Doyle knowingly and intelligently waived her right to counsel.").

[32]See Santobello v. New York, 404 U.S. 257, 92 S. Ct. 495, 30 L. Ed. 2d 427 (1971). See generally Katz and Giannelli, Baldwin's Ohio Practice, Criminal Law (2d ed.), Ch 44.

[33]In re Leonhardt, 62 Ohio Misc. 2d 783, 791, 610 N.E.2d 1238 (C.P. 1993).

The record before us is devoid of any showing that these provisions were complied with. In a case where parental rights are permanently terminated, it is of utmost importance that the parties fully understand their rights and that any waiver is made with full knowledge of those rights and the consequences which will follow.[34]

Research References

Katz and Giannelli, Baldwin's Ohio Practice, Criminal Law (2d ed.) §§ 43.12, 43.13, 43.17

§ 23:10 Jury trials

With the exception of SYO cases,[1] Juvenile Rule 27(A) and RC 2151.35(A) require the juvenile court to "hear and determine all cases of children without a jury."

The Ohio cases have repeatedly held that juveniles do not have a right to trial by jury.[2] The same rule applies to abuse, neglect, and dependency cases; in addition, the "failure to provide a jury trial does not render the procedures used fundamentally unfair or inaccurate."[3]

The Sixth Amendment guarantees the right to trial by jury in adult criminal cases.[4] The United States Supreme Court has held this right to be fundamental and therefore applicable to state criminal trials.[5] In *McKeiver v. Pennsylvania*,[6] however, the Court held that trial by jury is not a constitutional requirement in juvenile cases. The Court reasoned that mandating jury trials would "remake the juvenile proceeding into a fully adversary process and . . . put an effective end to what has been the idealistic prospect of

---

[34]Elmer v. Lucas County Children Services Bd., 36 Ohio App. 3d 241, 245, 523 N.E.2d 540 (6th Dist. Lucas County 1987). Accord In re Etter, 134 Ohio App. 3d 484, 489, 731 N.E.2d 694 (1st Dist. Hamilton County 1998) ("While the rule is normally thought of in the context of delinquency hearings, reviewing courts have recognized that faithful adherence to Juv.R. 29(D) is of 'utmost importance' in dependency cases that threaten the permanent loss of parental rights. . . . Juv.R. 29(D) is, therefore, no less applicable in the adjudicatory phase of a dependency proceeding than it is in a delinquency hearing."); In re Smith, 77 Ohio App. 3d 1, 16, 601 N.E.2d 45 (6th Dist. Ottawa County 1991) ("A termination of parental rights is the family law equivalent of the death penalty in a criminal case. The parties to such an action must be afforded every procedural and substantive protection the law allows. In the case at bar, appellants were denied the procedural safeguards of Juv.R. 29(D). Appellants' admissions to the neglect and dependency of their children are, therefore, invalid."); In re N.D., 2002-Ohio-3791, 2002 WL 1728880 (Ohio Ct. App. 8th Dist. Cuyahoga County 2002); In re White Children, 2002-Ohio-5949, 2002 WL 31426250 (Ohio Ct. App. 5th Dist. Stark County 2002); In re Aldridge, 2002-Ohio-5988, 2002 WL 31439807 (Ohio Ct. App. 4th Dist. Ross County). See also Stanley v. Illinois, 405 U.S. 645, 651, 92 S. Ct. 1208, 31 L. Ed. 2d 551 (1972) ("The rights to conceive and to raise one's children have been deemed 'essential, . . . basic civil rights of man,' . . . and 'rights far more precious . . . than property rights.' ") (citations omitted).

[Section 23:10]

[1]RC 2152.13(C)(1) ("open and speedy trial by jury in juvenile court"). See Serious Youthful Offenders Ch 5.

[2]See State v. Ostrowski, 30 Ohio St. 2d 34, 59 Ohio Op. 2d 62, 282 N.E.2d 359 (1972); In re Agler, 19 Ohio St. 2d 70, 48 Ohio Op. 2d 85, 249 N.E.2d 808 (1969); Cope v. Campbell, 175 Ohio St. 475, 26 Ohio Op. 2d 88, 196 N.E.2d 457 (1964); In re Darnell, 173 Ohio St. 335, 19 Ohio Op. 2d 269, 182 N.E.2d 321 (1962); Prescott v. State, 19 Ohio St. 184, 1869 WL 42 (1869); In re Tsesmilles, 24 Ohio App. 2d 153, 53 Ohio Op. 2d 363, 265 N.E.2d 308 (7th Dist. Columbiana County 1970); In re Benn, 18 Ohio App. 2d 97, 47 Ohio Op. 2d 170, 247 N.E.2d 335 (8th Dist. Cuyahoga County 1969). See also Ex parte Januszewski, 196 F. 123 (C.C.S.D. Ohio 1911).

[3]In re Adkins Children, 1990 WL 95043, at *7 (Ohio Ct. App. 12th Dist. Butler County 1990).

[4]U.S. Const. amend. 6 ("In all criminal prosecutions, the accused shall enjoy the right to a speedy and public trial, by an impartial jury."). The Ohio Constitution also guarantees the right to jury trial (O. Const. art. I § 5). See generally Katz and Giannelli, Baldwin's Ohio Practice, Criminal Law (2d ed.), Ch 62.

[5]Duncan v. State of La., 391 U.S. 145, 88 S. Ct. 1444, 20 L. Ed. 2d 491 (1968).

[6]McKeiver v. Pennsylvania, 403 U.S. 528, 91 S. Ct. 1976, 29 L. Ed. 2d 647 (1971).

an intimate, informal protective proceeding."[7]

In *McKeiver* the Court also commented, "If, in its wisdom, any State feels the jury trial is desirable in all cases, or in certain kinds, there appears to be no impediment to its installing a system embracing that feature."[8] A majority of jurisdictions in this country do not provide for jury trials in juvenile cases.[9] Nevertheless, a number of jurisdictions recognize such a right by statute,[10] and one jurisdiction recognizes it as a matter of state constitutional law.[11]

The IJA-ABA Standards also provide for the right to jury trial upon request. Under these Standards, the jury would consist of six persons. The right to a jury trial on demand is supported by the following reasons:

> The importance of the availability of jury trials in juvenile cases goes beyond neutralizing the biased juvenile court judge. A jury trial gives enhanced visibility to the adjudicative process. A jury trial requires the trial court judge to articulate his or her views of the applicable law in the case through jury instructions, thereby facilitating appellate court review of the legal issues involved. Without the focus on legal issues that such an exercise entails, the danger is great that the applicable law may be misperceived or misapplied and that the error will go uncorrected on appeal. In addition, many significant evidentiary protections in the adjudicative process are based on the assumption that preliminary rulings on admissibility will be made by the trial judge and that a jury will receive the evidence only if it has been ruled admissible. When a jury is not present, the evidentiary questions tend to become blurred and appellate review of evidentiary questions is made extremely difficult by the universal presumption that the trial judge disregarded inadmissible evidence and relied only upon competent evidence in arriving at his or her decision.[12]

Cross References
§ 1:4

§ 23:11 Public trials; gag orders

With the exception of SYO cases,[1] Juvenile Rule 27(A) and RC 2151.35(A) permit the exclusion of the general public from juvenile court hearings; only persons with a direct interest in the case may attend. RC 2151.352 expressly recognizes a parent's or guardian's right to attend all hearings.[2]

Exclusion of the public from juvenile proceedings is designed to protect the child. As Chief Justice Rehnquist has written:

> It is a hallmark of our juvenile justice system in the United States that virtually from its inception at the end of the last century its proceedings have been conducted outside of the public's full gaze and the youths brought before our juvenile courts have been shielded from publicity. . . . This insistence on

---

[7]McKeiver v. Pennsylvania, 403 U.S. 528, 545, 91 S. Ct. 1976, 29 L. Ed. 2d 647 (1971).

[8]McKeiver v. Pennsylvania, 403 U.S. 528, 547, 91 S. Ct. 1976, 29 L. Ed. 2d 647 (1971).

[9]E.g., People in Interest of T.M., 742 P.2d 905 (Colo. 1987); State ex rel. Juvenile Dept. of Klamath County v. Reynolds, 317 Or. 560, 857 P.2d 842, 850 (1993) (no right to jury trial under state constitution); State v. Schaaf, 109 Wash. 2d 1, 743 P.2d 240 (1987).

[10]See Rights of Juveniles: The Juvenile Justice System (2d ed.) § 5.3. See also Right to jury trial in juvenile court delinquency proceedings, 100 A.L.R. 2d 1241.

[11]RLR v. State, 487 P.2d 27 (Alaska 1971).

[12]IJA-ABA Standards Relating to Adjudication 53 (1980).

[Section 23:11]

[1]There is a right to a public trial in SYO cases. RC 2152.13(C)(1) ("open and speedy trial by jury in juvenile court"). See Serious Youthful Offenders Ch 5.

[2]See State v. Ostrowski, 30 Ohio St. 2d 34, 59 Ohio Op. 2d 62, 282 N.E.2d 359 (1972) (Exclusion of parents until they have testified does not violate RC 2151.352.). But see § 23:17, Evidence—Separation of witnesses.

confidentiality is born of a tender concern for the welfare of the child, to hide his youthful errors and "bury them in the graveyard of the forgotten past."[3]

Sixth Amendment. In contrast, the Sixth Amendment guarantees the right to a public trial in adult criminal trials.[4] Justice Brennan focused on a child's right to a public trial in *McKeiver v. Pennsylvania*,[5] in which the Supreme Court held that the right to jury trial did not apply to juvenile cases. *McKeiver* involved the consolidation of several cases for the purpose of appeal. Justice Brennan concurred in the Court's decision in the Pennsylvania cases, but dissented in the North Carolina cases. In his view, the difference between the two jurisdictions was that Pennsylvania provided the right to a public trial, a right which provided "similar protection" to the right to jury trial:

> The availability of trial by jury allows an accused to protect himself against possible oppression by what is in essence an appeal to the community conscience, as embodied in the jury that hears his case. To some extent, however, a similar protection may be obtained when an accused may in essence appeal to the community at large, by focusing public attention upon the facts of his trial, exposing improper judicial behavior to public view, and obtaining, if necessary, executive redress through the medium of public indignation.[6]

For similar reasons, the Alaska Supreme Court has recognized a child's right to public trial as a matter of state constitutional law.[7] The IJA-ABA Standards also provide for the right to public trial in juvenile cases.[8]

First Amendment. In addition to a criminal defendant's Sixth Amendment right to a public trial, the United States Supreme Court has recognized a First Amendment right of access on the part of the public and press to attend adult criminal trials. In *Richmond Newspapers, Inc. v. Virginia*,[9] the Court wrote, "We hold that the right to attend criminal trials is implicit in the guarantees of the First Amendment; without the freedom to attend such trials . . . important aspects of freedom of speech and 'of the press could be eviscerated.' "[10]

Courts in other jurisdictions have split over the applicability of the right of

---

[3]Smith v. Daily Mail Pub. Co., 443 U.S. 97, 107, 99 S. Ct. 2667, 61 L. Ed. 2d 399 (1979) (concurring opinion).

[4]U.S. Const. amend. 6 ("In all criminal prosecutions, the accused shall enjoy the right to a speedy and public trial."). The right to a public trial applies to state trials. In re Oliver, 333 U.S. 257, 68 S. Ct. 499, 92 L. Ed. 682 (1948). See also Gannett Co., Inc. v. DePasquale, 443 U.S. 368, 99 S. Ct. 2898, 61 L. Ed. 2d 608 (1979) (Right to public trial may be waived by the accused.); Waller v. Georgia, 467 U.S. 39, 104 S. Ct. 2210, 81 L. Ed. 2d 31 (1984) (Right to a public trial extends to suppression hearings.).

The Ohio Constitution also guarantees the right to a public trial (O. Const. art. I § 10). See generally Katz and Giannelli, Baldwin's Ohio Practice, Criminal Law (2d ed.), Ch 66.

[5]McKeiver v. Pennsylvania, 403 U.S. 528, 91 S. Ct. 1976, 29 L. Ed. 2d 647 (1971).

[6]McKeiver v. Pennsylvania, 403 U.S. 528, 554–55, 91 S. Ct. 1976, 29 L. Ed. 2d 647 (1971).

[7]RLR v. State, 487 P.2d 27 (Alaska 1971). But see In re Jesse McM., 105 Cal. App. 3d 187, 164 Cal. Rptr. 199 (1st Dist. 1980) (no constitutional right to a public trial in juvenile cases). See also Matter of L., 24 Or. App. 257, 546 P.2d 153 (1976) (statutory right to public trial on request).

[8]IJA-ABA Standards Relating to Adjudication 70 (1980). Open hearings in juvenile cases have been proposed in Ohio. See Willey, The Proposed Ohio Juvenile Code of 1977–1978, 39 Ohio St. L. J. 273 (1978).

[9]Richmond Newspapers, Inc. v. Virginia, 448 U.S. 555, 100 S. Ct. 2814, 65 L. Ed. 2d 973 (1980).

[10]Richmond Newspapers, Inc. v. Virginia, 448 U.S. 555, 580, 100 S. Ct. 2814, 65 L. Ed. 2d 973 (1980). See also Press-Enterprise Co. v. Superior Court of California for Riverside County, 478 U.S. 1, 106 S. Ct. 2735, 92 L. Ed. 2d 1 (1986) (Right of access applies to preliminary hearing.); Press-Enterprise Co. v. Superior Court of California, Riverside County, 464 U.S. 501, 104 S. Ct. 819, 78 L. Ed. 2d 629 (1984) (Right of access applies to voir dire examinations of jurors.); Globe Newspaper Co. v. Superior Court for Norfolk County, 457 U.S. 596, 102 S. Ct. 2613, 73 L. Ed. 2d 248 (1982) (Mandatory closure of trial during testimony of sex offense victim unconstitutional.).

access in juvenile proceedings.[11]

Ohio cases. The Ohio Supreme Court has decided several cases involving the closure of juvenile proceedings. In *State ex rel. Fyffe v. Pierce*,[12] the Court held that Juvenile Rule 27 and RC 2151.35 make closure discretionary: "The word 'may' is clearly not mandatory; therefore, the court was not required to close the hearing, but could exercise its discretion."[13]

In *In re T.R.*,[14] the Supreme Court again addressed the closure issue, albeit in a dependency case. The Court first recognized that the public has a constitutional qualified right of access to court proceedings. However, "the open courts provision of the Ohio Constitution [Art. I, sec. 16] creates no greater right of public access to court proceedings than that accorded by the [free speech and free press clauses of federal and state constitutions]."[15] In light of the need for confidentiality in dependency cases, the Court concluded that "there is no qualified right of public access to juvenile court proceedings to determine if a child is abused, neglected, or dependent, or to determine custody of a minor child."[16] These proceedings are "neither presumptively open nor presumptively closed to the press and public."[17]

The Court then examined the competing interests involved, the public's interest in judicial proceedings and the child's interest in confidentiality. "While the public's interest in access is important and deserving of protection, the state also has a compelling interest in the protection of children."[18] A trial court may close such a proceeding "if, after hearing evidence and argument on the issue, it finds that: (1) there exists a reasonable and substantial basis for believing that public access could harm the child or endanger the fairness of the proceeding, and (2) the potential for harm outweighs the benefits of public access."[19]

The Court went on to hold that the juvenile court had not abused its discretion in closing the proceedings and issuing a gag order on the litigants and attorneys in the case, although the order had to be modified because it was overbroad.

Whether this analysis also applies to delinquency cases is unclear. At one point the Court commented:

> The need for confidentiality is even more compelling in the case of a child who is abused, neglected, or dependent. The delinquent child is at least partially responsible for the case being in court; an abused, neglected, or dependent child is wholly innocent of wrongdoing. While the public arguably has an interest in delinquency proceedings which is analogous to its interest in criminal proceedings, . . . (public has qualified right of access because "the public is a party to all criminal proceedings"), this interest is not present in abuse, neglect, and dependency proceedings.[20]

The Supreme Court once again addressed this issue in *State ex rel.*

---

[11]E.g., State ex rel. Oregonian Pub. Co. v. Deiz, 289 Or. 277, 613 P.2d 23 (1980) (State constitution guarantees public and press right of access to juvenile proceedings.); In re Jones, 46 Ill. 2d 506, 263 N.E.2d 863 (1970) (statutory right of news media to attend juvenile proceedings); In re J. S., 140 Vt. 458, 438 A.2d 1125 (1981) (right of access does not apply).

See also Note, The Public Right of Access to Juvenile Delinquency Hearings, 81 Mich. L. Rev. 1540 (1983); Note, The Right of Access and Juvenile Delinquency Hearings: The Future of Confidentiality, 16 Ind. L. Rev. 911 (1983).

[12]State ex rel. Fyffe v. Pierce, 40 Ohio St. 3d 8, 531 N.E.2d 673 (1988).

[13]State ex rel. Fyffe v. Pierce, 40 Ohio St. 3d 8, 531 N.E.2d 673 (1988).

[14]In re T.R., 52 Ohio St. 3d 6, 556 N.E.2d 439 (1990).

[15]In re T.R., 52 Ohio St. 3d 6, 14, 556 N.E.2d 439 (1990).

[16]In re T.R., 52 Ohio St. 3d 6, 17, 556 N.E.2d 439 (1990).

[17]In re T.R., 52 Ohio St. 3d 6, 18, 556 N.E.2d 439 (1990).

[18]In re T.R., 52 Ohio St. 3d 6, 18, 556 N.E.2d 439 (1990).

[19]In re T.R., 52 Ohio St. 3d 6, 18–19, 556 N.E.2d 439 (1990).

[20]In re T.R., 52 Ohio St. 3d 6, 16, 556 N.E.2d 439 (1990).

Dispatch Printing Co. v. Lias,[21] which involved the closure of a custody proceeding. The Court reaffirmed *T.R.*: "We reaffirm that any restriction shielding court proceedings from public scrutiny should be narrowly tailored to serve the competing interests of protecting the welfare of the child or children and of not unduly burdening the public's right of access."[22] The weighing of these interests has to be determined on a "case-by-case basis." The Court also observed that "the doors to the courtroom 'may be closed to the general public only on a rare occasion after a determination that in *no* other way can justice be served.' "[23]

The Court outlined the procedure for determining closure issues. Unless a motion for closure is summarily denied, the trial court must conduct an evidentiary hearing ("closure hearing"). If a party asserts the closure hearing itself should be closed, the court shall use an *in camera* inspection proceeding to decide this issue. The party seeking closure must provide the court

> for its *in camera* inspection, a written or recorded summary of any testimony sought to be excluded from the public domain. Such summary must contain sufficient information for the juvenile court to make an informed decision, pursuant to the standards set forth in *T.R.*, as to whether any or all of the testimony sought to be excluded from public disclosure should be excluded.[24]

Counsel for the parties, the press, and the public (if any) have a right to participate in the *in camera* inspection, including the right to review the summary of testimony. At the conclusion of the inspection, counsel must be given the opportunity to object to the court's findings. Upon objection, the findings become "a final order subject to appeal as affecting a substantial right in a special proceeding."[25] Testimony subject to objection shall be sealed and preserved as part of the record for possible appellate review. The court proceedings may continue until there is an appeal. In addition, all persons participating in the *in camera* inspection are subject to contempt for disseminating any information excluded from public disclosure until a competent authority determines the information may be released to the public.

In *State ex rel. Scripps Howard Broadcasting Co. v. Cuyahoga County Court of Common Pleas, Juvenile Division,*[26] the juvenile court held an attorney for and the director of Children and Family Services in contempt for failing to timely produce subpoenaed records in a permanent custody proceeding. A television station videotaped and then televised the contempt hearing. Scripps Howard Broadcasting Company, the owner of a different TV station, sought to obtain a transcript of the hearing. When the court refused this request, the news company instituted a mandamus action. The Supreme Court held that the "right of access includes both the live proceedings and the transcripts which document those proceedings."[27] Because the contempt proceeding itself had been open to the public and there was no risk that the child would be harmed by public access to the contempt proceeding transcript,

---

[21]State ex rel. Dispatch Printing Co. v. Lias, 68 Ohio St. 3d 497, 1994-Ohio-335, 628 N.E.2d 1368 (1994).

[22]State ex rel. Dispatch Printing Co. v. Lias, 68 Ohio St. 3d 497, 503, 1994-Ohio-335, 628 N.E.2d 1368 (1994).

[23]State ex rel. Dispatch Printing Co. v. Lias, 68 Ohio St. 3d 497, 503–504, 1994-Ohio-335, 628 N.E.2d 1368 (1994), quoting Lexington Herald Leader Co., Inc. v. Tackett, 601 S.W.2d 905, 906 (Ky. 1980) (emphasis by Ohio Supreme Court).

[24]State ex rel. Dispatch Printing Co. v. Lias, 68 Ohio St. 3d 497, 503, 1994-Ohio-335, 628 N.E.2d 1368 (1994).

[25]State ex rel. Dispatch Printing Co. v. Lias, 68 Ohio St. 3d 497, 503, 1994-Ohio-335, 628 N.E.2d 1368 (1994).

[26]State ex rel. Scripps Howard Broadcasting Co. v. Cuyahoga Cty. Court of Common Pleas, Juv. Div., 73 Ohio St. 3d 19, 652 N.E.2d 179 (1995).

[27]State ex rel. Scripps Howard Broadcasting Co. v. Cuyahoga Cty. Court of Common Pleas, Juv. Div., 73 Ohio St. 3d 19, 21, 652 N.E.2d 179 (1995).

the Court ruled that denial of the transcript was not justified: "Therefore, when Juv. R. 37(B) is construed consistently with the constitutional right of public access, the juvenile court cannot withhold the requested transcript from relator."[28]

In *In re Joanne M.*,[29] the County Children's Service Board moved for closure of proceedings in an abuse, neglect, and dependency case. The motion was summarily denied, and the Board appealed. The court of appeals ruled that the juvenile court had abused its discretion.

> Here, we have severe physical injury to a young child. The nature of that injury and the information provided by her two sisters give rise to an inference that evidence may be offered, which if made public, will be psychologically damaging to all three children. Further, this is a case in which the media has already expressed an interest. Finally, none of the parties to the case under consideration objected to a closure hearing.
>
> Moreover, the juvenile court apparently relied on an incorrect presumption in reaching its decision. Nothing in *Lias* suggests that the holding in *In re T.R.* was modified or overruled. Therefore, in determining whether to summarily deny a motion for closure without a hearing, any presumption in favor of a public proceeding in an abuse, neglect, dependency and/or custody proceeding is erroneous.

Juvenile Rule 27 was amended in 2001 in order to set forth a standard for determining closure in juvenile hearings. SYO hearings are open to the public. In all other hearings, the court may exclude the general public but may not exclude persons with a direct interest in the case or persons who demonstrate, at a hearing, a countervailing right to be present.[30]

Gag orders. In *State ex rel. News Herald v. Ottawa County Court of Common Pleas, Juvenile Division*,[31] the juvenile court ruled that the transfer hearing would be open to the public but then issued a "gag order" prohibiting the media from reporting the case until a transfer order was entered. The Ohio Supreme Court granted a writ of prohibition to dissolve the gag order. The Court commented: "The order of the trial court . . . is a classic order of prior restraint. The order prohibited publication of information legally obtained by relators [newspapers]."[32]

Cross References
§ 1:4, § 22:19

§ 23:12 Right to be present

The parties to a juvenile court proceeding have a right to attend and participate in the adjudicatory hearing. In an adult criminal prosecution, this right is part of the right of confrontation. The United States Supreme Court has observed: "One of the most basic of the rights guaranteed by the Confrontation Clause is the accused's right to be present in the courtroom at every stage of his trial."[1] An alleged delinquent's right to attend the adjudicatory hearing is discussed in § 23:23.

---

[28]State ex rel. Scripps Howard Broadcasting Co. v. Cuyahoga Cty. Court of Common Pleas, Juv. Div., 73 Ohio St. 3d 19, 22, 652 N.E.2d 179 (1995) (citations omitted).

[29]In re Joanne M., 103 Ohio App. 3d 447, 451, 659 N.E.2d 864 (6th Dist. Lucas County 1995).

[30]See also Staff Note (2001) ("The rule seeks to conform to the Supreme Court's ruling in State ex rel. Plain Dealer Publishing Co. v. Geauga Cty. Court of Common Pleas, Juv. Div., 90 Ohio St. 3d 79, 2000-Ohio-35, 734 N.E.2d 1214 (2000).").

[31]State ex rel. News Herald v. Ottawa Cty. Court of Common Pleas, Juv. Div., 77 Ohio St. 3d 40, 1996-Ohio-354, 671 N.E.2d 5 (1996).

[32]State ex rel. News Herald v. Ottawa Cty. Court of Common Pleas, Juv. Div., 77 Ohio St. 3d 40, 45, 1996-Ohio-354, 671 N.E.2d 5 (1996).

[Section 23:12]
[1]Illinois v. Allen, 397 U.S. 337, 338, 90 S. Ct. 1057, 25 L. Ed. 2d 353 (1970).

The right to be present at other types of juvenile court proceedings is guaranteed as a matter of due process. "Due process of law implies, in its most comprehensive sense, the right of the person affected thereby to be present before the tribunal which pronounces judgment upon a question of life, liberty or property."[2] This right is separate from and in addition to the right to notice.[3]

Parents. A number of Ohio courts have addressed the applicability of this right at proceedings to terminate parental rights. *In re Elliott*[4] recognized a parent's right to be present at a hearing concerning termination of parental rights, but the court of appeals qualified the right because the parent was in prison. The court ruled:

> Permitting Philip Elliott to be present would be the optimal arrangement. However, allowing some other means of presenting his testimony would clearly serve the state's goal and the children's interest, and it would not impose any undue fiscal or administrative burden upon the state. The trial court did not err in overruling Philip Elliott's motion to be present at the hearing. However, due process required that Philip Elliott be afforded some other means of presenting his testimony, *e.g.*, by deposition.[5]

The court of appeals reaffirmed *Elliott* in a later case, again recognizing that a parent had a due process right to attend termination of parental rights hearings. This right, however, is not absolute. The court found no error because the incarcerated parent was represented by counsel at the hearing and was permitted to present his testimony by deposition.[6]

Another court of appeals has ruled that a parent's right to be present at a permanent custody hearing may be waived: "Where counsel for the parent was present at the hearing and actually cross-examined witnesses, neither counsel nor the parent objected to the parent's absence, and the parent cannot show prejudice from her absence, her right to attend the hearing is effectively waived."[7]

Victims. RC 2930.09[8] recognizes the right of a victim[9] to be present whenever an alleged juvenile offender is present during any on the record stage of the case, unless the court determines that exclusion of the victim is necessary to protect the juvenile's right to a fair delinquency hearing. At the victim's request, the victim has the right to be accompanied by an individual to provide support to the victim, unless the court determines that exclusion of the individual is necessary to protect the juvenile's right to a fair delinquency hearing.

§ 23:13 Burden of proof

Juvenile Rule 29(E)(4) and RC 2151.35(A) require proof "beyond a reason-

---

[2]Lowry v. Lowry, 48 Ohio App. 3d 184, 190, 549 N.E.2d 176 (4th Dist. Ross County 1988).

[3]Notice is discussed in Summons Ch 18.

[4]Matter of Elliott, 1993 WL 268846 (Ohio Ct. App. 4th Dist. Lawrence County 1993).

[5]Matter of Elliott, 1993 WL 268846, at *10 (Ohio Ct. App. 4th Dist. Lawrence County 1993).

[6]Matter of Vandale, 1993 WL 235599 (Ohio Ct. App. 4th Dist. Washington County 1993). See also State ex rel. Vanderlaan v. Pollex, 96 Ohio App. 3d 235, 644 N.E.2d 1073 (6th Dist. Wood County 1994).

[7]In re Curley/Brown Children, 1993 WL 473832, at *3 (Ohio Ct. App. 9th Dist. Summit County 1993).

[8]This statute was enacted pursuant to the Victims' Rights provision of the Ohio Constitution. O. Const. art. I § 10a.

[9]RC 2930.02 provides a procedure for the designation of a victim's representative, who is authorized to exercise the victim's rights under RC Ch. 2930.

able doubt" in delinquency, unruly,[1] and juvenile traffic offender cases. These same provisions require a less demanding standard of proof—"clear and convincing" evidence—in abuse, neglect, and dependency cases.[2] A "preponderance of evidence" standard (more probable than not) applies in all other cases. In addition, RC 2151.414(E) requires the "clear and convincing evidence" standard in permanent custody proceedings,[3] and RC 2151.415(C)(1) requires clear and convincing evidence in long-term foster care placements.[4] A 1998 amendment to Juvenile Rule 29(E) requires the "clear and convincing evidence" standard in removal actions as defined in Rule 2(GG) and governed by Rule 39.

The Ohio definition of proof "beyond a reasonable doubt" is found in RC 2901.05(D):

"Reasonable doubt" is present when the jurors, after they have carefully considered and compared all the evidence, cannot say they are firmly convinced of the truth of the charge. It is a doubt based on reason and common sense. Reasonable doubt is not mere possible doubt, because everything relating to human affairs or depending on moral evidence is open to some possible or imaginary doubt. "Proof beyond a reasonable doubt" is proof of such character that an ordinary person would be willing to rely and act upon it in the most important of his own affairs.[5]

The Ohio Supreme Court has defined "clear and convincing evidence" as

that measure or degree of proof which is more than a mere "preponderance of the evidence," but not to the extent of such certainty as is required "beyond a reasonable doubt" in criminal cases, and which will produce in the mind of the trier of facts a firm belief or conviction as to the facts sought to be established.[6]

The Ohio courts have applied this standard on numerous occasions.[7] The

---

[Section 23:13]

[1]See In re Osman, 109 Ohio App. 3d 731, 736, 672 N.E.2d 1114 (11th Dist. Portage County 1996) (police officer's testimony that he "believed" that the juvenile was the person that he had stopped for a curfew violation satisfied burden of proof for unruliness).

[2]The Ohio Supreme Court has ruled that the Ohio Constitution does not require the "beyond-a-reasonable-doubt" standard in proceedings involving the termination of parental rights. In re Schmidt, 25 Ohio St. 3d 331, 496 N.E.2d 952 (1986); In re Tikyra A., 103 Ohio App. 3d 452, 454, 659 N.E.2d 867 (6th Dist. Huron County 1995) ("In the instant case for whatever reason, appellee chose to charge only under R.C. 2151.04(A). The curiosity here is that while appellee may have proved that the children were neglected (generally considered to be the more serious allegation), it failed to prove any of the elements which define dependency. These children were not homeless, destitute, without proper care or without support. It is undisputed that their needs for shelter, food and other necessaries were satisfied.").

[3]See In re William S., 75 Ohio St. 3d 95, 101, 1996-Ohio-182, 661 N.E.2d 738 (1996) ("[P]ermanent custody may not be granted unless the trial court finds clear and convincing evidence.").

[4]See In re Bacorn, 116 Ohio App. 3d 489, 494, 688 N.E.2d 575 (11th Dist. Portage County 1996).

[5]See generally Katz and Giannelli, Baldwin's Ohio Practice, Criminal Law (2d ed.), Ch 86.

[6]State v. Schiebel, 55 Ohio St. 3d 71, 74, 564 N.E.2d 54 (1990).

[7]E.g., In re Knotts, 109 Ohio App. 3d 267, 271, 671 N.E.2d 1357 (3d Dist. Mercer County 1996) (Because a court can only take judicial notice of its own proceedings in the same case, there was no evidence of abuse or dependency.); In re Makuch, 101 Ohio App. 3d 45, 47, 654 N.E.2d 1331 (9th Dist. Lorain County 1995) (Dependency proved by clear and convincing evidence in termination of parental rights hearing.); In re Brodbeck, 97 Ohio App. 3d 652, 657, 659–60, 647 N.E.2d 240 (3d Dist. Mercer County 1994) (Dependency proved by clear and convincing evidence in termination of parental rights hearing.); In re Doe Children, 93 Ohio App. 3d 134, 144, 637 N.E.2d 977 (6th Dist. Lucas County 1994) ("[T]here was clear and convincing evidence . . . that the four Doe children could not be placed with either of their parents within a reasonable time."); In re Pieper Children, 85 Ohio App. 3d 318, 619 N.E.2d 1059 (12th Dist. Preble County 1993) (Dependency proved by clear and convincing evidence.); In re McCrary, 75 Ohio App. 3d 601, 600 N.E.2d 347 (12th Dist. Madison County 1991) (Clear and convincing evidence that child's best interest was to award permanent custody.); In re Wall, 60 Ohio App. 3d 6, 572 N.E.2d 248 (9th Dist. Wayne County 1989) (Neglect not proved by clear and convincing evidence.); In re Bishop, 36 Ohio App. 3d 123, 521 N.E.2d 838 (5th Dist. Ashland County 1987) (Dependency established by clear and convincing evidence.); In re Green, 18 Ohio App. 3d 43,

courts have also indicated that a certain amount of deference should be accorded the juvenile court in this context.[8]

In some instances, the Ohio provisions codify due process requirements; in other instances they go beyond constitutional standards. In *In re Winship*,[9] the United States Supreme Court held that the Due Process Clause protects "against conviction except upon proof beyond a reasonable doubt of every fact necessary to constitute the crime . . . charged."[10] This standard, according to the Court, protects against erroneous convictions and assures community respect and confidence in the criminal process; it applies to delinquency proceedings as well as to criminal trials.

In *Santosky v. Kramer*,[11] the Supreme Court considered the standard of proof in neglect proceedings involving the permanent termination of parental rights. According to the Court, the "preponderance of evidence" standard, the typical standard applied in civil litigation, did not satisfy due process: "In parental rights termination proceedings, the private interest affected is commanding; the risk of error from using a preponderance standard is substantial; and the countervailing governmental interest favoring that standard is comparatively slight."[12] The Court went on to require a more demanding standard of proof—clear and convincing evidence—in these cases.

Winship and *Santosky* are the United States Supreme Court's only juvenile court standard of proof cases. In *Winship* the Court pointed out that it was not deciding the required standard of proof for status offense (unruly) cases,[13] and courts in other jurisdictions are divided over the proper standard in these cases.[14]

Affirmative defenses. *Winship* speaks only to the prosecution's burden of persuasion with respect to the elements of the charged offense. It does not expressly deal with the burden of persuasion for affirmative defenses.[15] In criminal trials, RC 2901.05 provides that the "burden of going forward with

---

480 N.E.2d 492 (2d Dist. Montgomery County 1984) (Dependency established by clear and convincing evidence.); In re Bibb, 70 Ohio App. 2d 117, 24 Ohio Op. 3d 159, 435 N.E.2d 96 (1st Dist. Hamilton County 1980) (Dependency not proved by clear and convincing evidence.); In re Fassinger, 43 Ohio App. 2d 89, 72 Ohio Op. 2d 292, 334 N.E.2d 5 (8th Dist. Cuyahoga County 1974) (Present neglect or dependency not established by clear and convincing evidence.).

[8]See In re Meyer, 98 Ohio App. 3d 189, 195, 648 N.E.2d 52 (3d Dist. Defiance County 1994) ("Once the clear and convincing standard has been met to the satisfaction of the trial court, a reviewing court 'must examine the record and determine if the trier of fact had sufficient evidence before it to satisfy this burden of proof.' ") (quoting In re Adoption of Holcomb, 18 Ohio St. 3d 361, 481 N.E.2d 613 (1985); In re Awkal, 95 Ohio App. 3d 309, 316, 642 N.E.2d 424 (8th Dist. Cuyahoga County 1994) ("The discretion which the juvenile court enjoys in determining whether an order of permanent custody is in the best interest of a child should be accorded the utmost respect, given the nature of the proceeding and the impact the court's determination will have on the lives of the parties concerned. Moreover, the knowledge the juvenile court gains at the adjudicatory hearing through viewing the witnesses and observing their demeanor, gestures and voice inflections and using these observations in weighing the credibility of the proffered testimony cannot be conveyed to a reviewing court by a printed record."). But see In re M.W., 2004-Ohio-438, 2004 WL 199962 (Ohio Ct. App. 9th Dist. Lorain County).

[9]In re Winship, 397 U.S. 358, 90 S. Ct. 1068, 25 L. Ed. 2d 368 (1970). In V. v. City of New York, 407 U.S. 203, 92 S. Ct. 1951, 32 L. Ed. 2d 659 (1972), the Court held *Winship* retroactive.

[10]In re Winship, 397 U.S. 358, 364, 90 S. Ct. 1068, 25 L. Ed. 2d 368 (1970). *Winship* overruled prior Ohio cases on this issue. E.g., In re Agler, 19 Ohio St. 2d 70, 48 Ohio Op. 2d 85, 249 N.E.2d 808 (1969) (clear and convincing evidence standard); State v. Shardell, 107 Ohio App. 338, 8 Ohio Op. 2d 262, 79 Ohio L. Abs. 534, 153 N.E.2d 510 (8th Dist. Cuyahoga County 1958) (preponderance of evidence standard).

[11]Santosky v. Kramer, 455 U.S. 745, 102 S. Ct. 1388, 71 L. Ed. 2d 599 (1982).

[12]Santosky v. Kramer, 455 U.S. 745, 758, 102 S. Ct. 1388, 71 L. Ed. 2d 599 (1982).

[13]In re Winship, 397 U.S. 358, 359 n.1, 90 S. Ct. 1068, 25 L. Ed. 2d 368 (1970).

[14]Compare In re D., 36 A.D.2d 970, 321 N.Y.S.2d 510 (2d Dep't 1971) (proof beyond a reasonable doubt) with In Interest of Potter, 237 N.W.2d 461 (Iowa 1976) (clear and convincing evidence).

[15]See Martin v. Ohio, 480 U.S. 228, 107 S. Ct. 1098, 94 L. Ed. 2d 267 (1987) (Allocating burden of proving self-defense to defendant does not violate due process.); Patterson v. New

the evidence of an affirmative defense, and the burden of proof, by a preponderance of the evidence, for an affirmative defense, is upon the accused."[16]

Burden of production. In delinquency cases, the burden of production (burden of going forward with evidence) is the same as in criminal prosecutions, which is governed by Criminal Rule 29 and due process.[17]

Cross References
§ 1:4

§ 23:14   Rules of evidence

The Ohio Rules of Evidence apply at the adjudicatory hearing.[1] Evidence Rule 101 provides that the Rules "govern proceedings in the courts of this state." None of the exceptions specified in Evidence Rule 101(C) apply to the adjudicatory hearing. Even prior to the adoption of the Rules of Evidence, the Ohio Supreme Court indicated that evidentiary rules applied in adjudicatory hearings: "We are in complete agreement that at the adjudicatory stage the use of clearly incompetent evidence to prove a youth's involvement is not justifiable."[2] In particular, inadmissible hearsay evidence was prohibited.[3]

Although the Rules of Evidence do not distinguish between the applicability of the Rules in jury and bench trials, there nevertheless is a difference.

York, 432 U.S. 197, 97 S. Ct. 2319, 53 L. Ed. 2d 281 (1977) (Allocating burden of proving extreme emotional disturbance to homicide defendant does not violate due process.); Mullaney v. Wilbur, 421 U.S. 684, 95 S. Ct. 1881, 44 L. Ed. 2d 508 (1975) (Allocating burden of proving heat of passion to homicide defendant violates due process.).

[16]See generally Katz and Giannelli, Baldwin's Ohio Practice, Criminal Law (2d ed.) § 86.7.

[17]See In re McCoy, 138 Ohio App. 3d 774, 742 N.E.2d 247 (2d Dist. Greene County 2000) (inducing panic) ("A sufficiency of the evidence argument challenges whether the State has presented adequate evidence on each element of the offense to allow the case to go to the jury or sustain the verdict as a matter of law. . . . An appellate court's function when reviewing the sufficiency of the evidence to support a criminal conviction is to examine the evidence admitted at trial to determine whether such evidence, if believed, would convince the average mind of the defendant's guilt beyond a reasonable doubt. The relevant inquiry is whether, after viewing the evidence in a light most favorable to the prosecution, any rational trier of fact could have found the essential elements of the crime proven beyond a reasonable doubt."); State v. Matha, 107 Ohio App. 3d 756, 759, 669 N.E.2d 504 (9th Dist. Lorain County 1995); Katz and Giannelli, Baldwin's Ohio Practice, Criminal Law (2d ed.) § 86:6.

[Section 23:14]
[1]In re Baby Girl Baxter, 17 Ohio St. 3d 229, 479 N.E.2d 257 (1985) ("There must be strict adherence to the Rules of Evidence at the adjudicatory stage."); In Matter of Neighbors, 1993 WL 564218 (Ohio Ct. App. 5th Dist. Richland County 1993) ("The focus in the adjudicatory phase is on the ability of the parents to provide adequate care to the child, while the focus of the dispositional phase becomes the best interest of the child. The reason for this is that in the adjudicatory phase, the rules of evidence must be strictly adhered to, but in the dispositional hearing, all relevant evidence is admitted, including hearsay, opinion, and documentary evidence . . . . It appears on this record that the trial court skipped the adjudicatory hearing, and went directly to the dispositional hearing."). See generally Giannelli and Snyder, Baldwin's Ohio Practice, Evidence (2d ed.) § 101.1. See also Applicability of rules of evidence in juvenile delinquency proceedings, 43 A.L.R. 2d 1128.

[2]State v. Carmichael, 35 Ohio St. 2d 1, 7, 64 Ohio Op. 2d 1, 298 N.E.2d 568 (1973). See also In re Michael, 119 Ohio App. 3d 112, 121, 694 N.E.2d 538 (2d Dist. Montgomery County 1997) (challenging rape shield law as violating right of confrontation and compulsory process) ("[E]vidence that Christopher [age 8] had been sexually abused in the past was essential to Bryan's [age 14] defense, particularly where, as here, Christopher had been sexually abused in the identical manner which he claims to have been abused by Bryan. . . . Introduction of such evidence, however, would also serve the more important purpose of affording Bryan the opportunity to establish an alternative explanation for Christopher's sexual knowledge.").

[3]See In re Agler, 19 Ohio St. 2d 70, 48 Ohio Op. 2d 85, 249 N.E.2d 808 (1969); In re Tsesmilles, 24 Ohio App. 2d 153, 53 Ohio Op. 2d 363, 265 N.E.2d 308 (7th Dist. Columbiana County 1970); State v. Shardell, 107 Ohio App. 338, 8 Ohio Op. 2d 262, 79 Ohio L. Abs. 534, 153 N.E.2d 510 (8th Dist. Cuyahoga County 1958).

Many of the exclusionary Rules of Evidence are designed to insulate juries from evidence that is thought to be too unreliable or too inflammatory. Since trial judges are presumed capable of properly evaluating such evidence, exclusionary rules are treated differently in bench trials, at least to the extent that appellate courts will less readily find error in a bench trial than in a jury trial.[4] For example, one court of appeals has written, "It is presumed that the Juvenile Court Judge would reject any incompetent and prejudicial evidence and only consider the competent and relevant evidence. A reviewing court may not presume that the trial court deliberately committed error."[5]

Evidence obtained in violation of a child's constitutional rights may be inadmissible at the adjudicatory hearing. Juvenile Rule 22(D)(3) governs motions to suppress evidence.[6]

"[E]videntiary rulings and the overall conduct of a trial are within the discretion of the trial court."[7]

§ 23:15 Evidence—Privileges

The law of privilege,[1] including the constitutional privilege against compelled self-incrimination,[2] applies in adjudicatory hearings.[3] The physician-patient[4] and psychologist-client[5] privileges, however, do not apply to physical and mental examinations that are ordered by the court.[6] Moreover, a special exemption from the coverage of a privilege often applies in abuse or neglect cases.[7]

In *In re Wieland*,[8] the Ohio Supreme Court refused to carve out an exception to physician and patient, psychologist and client, and counselor-social worker and client privileges for statements made by a parent in the course of treatment ordered as part of a reunification plan in an action for dependency and neglect. The Court wrote: " 'The purpose of the [physician-patient privilege] statute is to create an atmosphere of confidentiality, encouraging the patient to be completely candid and open with his or her physician, thereby

---

[4]See In re Watson, 47 Ohio St. 3d 86, 91, 548 N.E.2d 210 (1989) ("[T]he trial court can be presumed to apply the law correctly."); State v. Eubank, 60 Ohio St. 2d 183, 14 Ohio Op. 3d 416, 398 N.E.2d 567 (1979) ("[A] judge is presumed to consider only the relevant, material and competent evidence in arriving at a judgment, unless the contrary affirmatively appears from the record."); State v. White, 15 Ohio St. 2d 146, 44 Ohio Op. 2d 132, 239 N.E.2d 65 (1968).

[5]In re Baker, 18 Ohio App. 2d 276, 283, 47 Ohio Op. 2d 411, 248 N.E.2d 620 (4th Dist. Hocking County 1969).

[6]See Investigations Ch 14.

[7]In re S., 102 Ohio App. 3d 338, 343, 657 N.E.2d 307 (6th Dist. Lucas County 1995).

[Section 23:15]
[1]See Evid. R. 501. See also RC 2317.02 (attorney-client, physician-patient, clergyman-penitent, husband-wife, counselor-client, and social worker-client privilege), RC 4732.19 (psychologist-client privilege), RC 2739.04 (broadcasters' confidential source privilege), RC 2739.12 (reporters' confidential source privilege). See Giannelli and Snyder, Baldwin's Ohio Practice, Evidence (2d ed.) § 501.1. See also Bennett, Secret Reflections: Some Thoughts about Secrets and Court Processes in Child Protection Matters, 45 Ariz. L. Rev. 713 (2003) (discussing secrets in a family, in therapy, in adoption, with lawyers, with parents, and the role each can play in the child protective case).

[2]See § 23:27, Self-incrimination.

[3]E.g., In re Decker, 20 Ohio App. 3d 203, 485 N.E.2d 751 (3d Dist. Van Wert County 1984) (applying psychiatrist-patient privileges in dependency and neglect proceeding).

[4]RC 2317.02(B).

[5]RC 4732.19.

[6]See In re Smith, 7 Ohio App. 3d 75, 454 N.E.2d 171 (2d Dist. Greene County 1982); In re Winstead, 67 Ohio App. 2d 111, 21 Ohio Op. 3d 422, 425 N.E.2d 943 (9th Dist. Summit County 1980).

[7]RC 2151.421. See In re Aristotle R., 2004-Ohio-217, 2004 WL 88588 (Ohio Ct. App. 6th Dist. Sandusky County).

[8]In re Wieland, 89 Ohio St. 3d 535, 538–39, 2000-Ohio-233, 733 N.E.2d 1127 (2000) (citations omitted).

enabling more complete treatment.' Otherwise, the fear of disclosure 'could seriously impede the patient's chances for a recovery.' The same purpose, of course, underlies each of the testimonial privilege statutes. The same concerns are prevalent where a parent is required, under the terms of a reunification plan, to utilize medical, psychological, or other social and rehabilitative services in an effort to remedy the problems that initially caused the child to be placed outside the home so that the child can return home."

While some courts have recognized a parent-child privilege,[9] the majority have not.[10] Although welfare records are confidential,[11] they are not protected by an absolute privilege.[12]

In delinquency cases, the counselor privilege may apply to statements made during therapy.[13] In addition, there is a federal statute pertaining to the confidentiality of patient records in federally assisted substance-abuse programs.[14]

§ 23:16 Evidence—Hearsay

The hearsay rule applies in adjudicatory hearings.[1] The right of confronta-

---

[9]See In re Agosto, 553 F. Supp. 1298, 12 Fed. R. Evid. Serv. 639 (D. Nev. 1983); Application of A and M, 61 A.D.2d 426, 403 N.Y.S.2d 375, 6 A.L.R.4th 532 (4th Dep't 1978); People v. Fitzgerald, 101 Misc. 2d 712, 422 N.Y.S.2d 309 (County Ct. 1979). See also Idaho Code § 9-203(7) (1988 supp.).

See generally Testimonial privilege for confidential communications between relatives other than husband and wife—state cases, 6 A.L.R. 4th 544; Kandoian, The Parent-Child Privilege and the Parent-Child Crime: Observations on *State v. DeLong* and *In re Agosto*, 36 Me. L. Rev. 59 (1984); Stanton, Child-Parent Privilege for Confidential Communications: An Examination and Proposal, 16 Fam. L. Quar. 1 (1982); Watts, The Parent-Child Privileges: Hardly a New or Revolutionary Concept, 28 Wm. & Mary L. Rev. 583 (1987); Note, Parent-Child Loyalty and Testimonial Privilege, 100 Harv. L. Rev. 910 (1987).

[10]See In the Matter of Hawkins, 1983 WL 4091 (Ohio Ct. App. 9th Dist. Lorain County 1983) (There is no parent-child privilege in Ohio.); Grand Jury Proceedings of John Doe v. U.S., 842 F.2d 244, 25 Fed. R. Evid. Serv. 1081 (10th Cir. 1988); Port v. Heard, 764 F.2d 423 (5th Cir. 1985); U.S. v. Ismail, 756 F.2d 1253, 17 Fed. R. Evid. Serv. 1450 (6th Cir. 1985); In re Terry W., 59 Cal. App. 3d 745, 130 Cal. Rptr. 913 (2d Dist. 1976); State v. DeLong, 456 A.2d 877 (Me. 1983); Three Juveniles v. Com., 390 Mass. 357, 455 N.E.2d 1203 (1983).

[11]RC 5153.17.

[12]In re Barzak, 24 Ohio App. 3d 180, 493 N.E.2d 1011 (11th Dist. Trumbull County 1985).

[13]RC 2317.02(G)(1); RC Ch. 4757.

[14]42 U.S.C.A. § 290dd-2.

[Section 23:16]

[1]Evid. R. 801 to Evid. R. 807. See In re Mack, 148 Ohio App. 3d 626, 629-30, 2002-Ohio-4161, 774 N.E.2d 1243 (3d Dist. Crawford County 2002) ("[T]he Rules of Evidence applied during the permanent custody hearing. The Rules of Evidence prohibit the use of hearsay . . . . The report of the psychological evaluation contained the opinion of Dr. Don McIntire, the psychologist who examined the appellant, yet he did not testify at the permanent custody hearing. The report was offered in evidence to aid in proving that the appellant was not a suitable caretaker for the children, and, as such, constituted inadmissible hearsay."); In re Washington, 143 Ohio App. 3d 576, 582, 758 N.E.2d 724 (8th Dist. Cuyahoga County 2001) ("The Rules of Evidence applied during the permanent custody hearing and, as such, the report of the psychological evaluation of the parents constituted inadmissible hearsay. The trial court erred, therefore, in allowing its admission into evidence."). Hearsay is a written or oral statement made by a declarant out of court and offered for the truth of the assertions contained in the statement. See generally Giannelli and Snyder, Baldwin's Ohio Practice, Evidence (2d ed.) § 801.1.

See also In re Carter, 123 Ohio App. 3d 532, 539, 541, 704 N.E.2d 625 (4th Dist. Pickaway County 1997) ("A record showing that subpoenas were issued unsuccessfully, without sworn testimony, is insufficient to demonstrate the unavailability of the witness [under Evid. R. 804(A)]."; "In this case, the consequences of Folley's statements weigh heavily against the statements' trustworthiness. . . . Folley's statements do not substitute herself for Carter. In fact, it is likely that Folley believed that she could exculpate herself somewhat, if not entirely, by identifying Carter as a drug dealer and the owner of the cocaine in her purse. Thus, the trustworthiness inherent in a traditional statement-against-interest scenario is absent in this case."); In re

tion is often implicated when hearsay evidence is introduced.[2]

Admissions of the parties are admissible under Evidence Rule 801(D)(2). In addition, Evidence Rules 803 and 804 recognize twenty-seven exceptions to the hearsay rule. One of the most important exceptions in juvenile cases is Evidence Rule 803(8), which governs the admissibility of public records. Police, welfare,[3] and school records[4] are often admissible under this exception. Typically, these records are also self-authenticating[5] and certified copies may be admitted.[6] Hospital and medical records are admissible as business records under Evidence Rule 803(6).[7] These documents, however, often raise double hearsay issues.[8]

Physical and sexual abuse cases present special problems. Statements made by children in these cases have sometimes been admitted as excited utterances, Evid. R. 803(2),[9] or as statements made for the purpose of medical

---

Barzak, 24 Ohio App. 3d 180, 493 N.E.2d 1011 (11th Dist. Trumbull County 1985) (hearsay inadmissible in dependency cases); In re Vickers Children, 14 Ohio App. 3d 201, 470 N.E.2d 438 (12th Dist. Butler County 1983) (hearsay inadmissible in neglect cases); In re Sims, 13 Ohio App. 3d 37, 468 N.E.2d 111 (12th Dist. Preble County 1983) (hearsay inadmissible in neglect cases); Matter of Crose, 1982 WL 3824 (Ohio Ct. App. 2d Dist. Darke County 1982) (Hearsay evidence is inadmissible in adjudicatory hearings unless it falls within a recognized exception.); In re Legg, 68 Ohio Misc. 2d 1, 3–4, 646 N.E.2d 266 (C.P. 1993) ("[I]f the evidence is offered by the state to show the effect [the victim's] statement had on her mother or the police officer instead of for the truth of the matter asserted, it may not be hearsay, but it is inadmissible because it is irrelevant.").

[2]See § 23:25, Confrontation—Hearsay.

[3]In re Dukes, 81 Ohio App. 3d 145, 152, 610 N.E.2d 513 (9th Dist. Summit County 1991) (caseworker report admitted as a business record); In re Lucas, 29 Ohio App. 3d 165, 173, 504 N.E.2d 472 (3d Dist. Putnam County 1985) (caseworker's case notes admitted as public record).

[4]See Admissibility of school records under hearsay exceptions, 57 A.L.R. 4th 1111.

[5]Evid. R. 902. See Matter of Knipp, 1983 WL 3161 (Ohio Ct. App. 4th Dist. Scioto County 1983) (Georgia state reports that have not been certified as authentic are inadmissible.).

[6]Evid. R. 1005 (admissibility of certified copies of public records).

[7]See In re Heston, 129 Ohio App. 3d 825, 827, 719 N.E.2d 93 (1st Dist. Hamilton County 1998) ("admission of the children's hospital records, as exceptions to the hearsay rule pursuant to Evid.R. 803(4) and 803(6)"); In re Smart, 21 Ohio App. 3d 31, 34, 486 N.E.2d 147 (10th Dist. Franklin County 1984). See also In re Robert S., 98 Ohio App. 3d 84, 94, 647 N.E.2d 869 (6th Dist. Huron County 1994) ("[T]he court admitted the records [in a dependency hearing] under the business records exception to the hearsay rule. Evid. R. 803(6). In our view, however, the records were admissible because they were not introduced to prove the truth of the matter asserted . . . .. The records in question were not admitted to prove that Robert had severe emotional and behavioral problems. Rather, they were admitted to establish that information about Robert was known to [the Department] prior to the adoption but was kept from appellees.").

[8]See Evid. R. 805; Matter of Workman, 1993 WL 222843 (Ohio Ct. App. 5th Dist. Tuscarawas County 1993) (double hearsay in social worker's record not admitted).

[9]In State v. Taylor, 66 Ohio St. 3d 295, 612 N.E.2d 316 (1993), the Court wrote:

In the cases of statements made by children who say they were sexually assaulted, we have upheld the admission of those statements even when made after a substantial lapse of time, but in those cases we have done so because we recognize that children are likely to remain in a state of nervous excitement longer than would an adult. . . .

This trend of liberalizing the requirements for an excited utterance when applied to young children who are the victims of sexual assault is also based on the recognition of their limited reflective powers. Inability to fully reflect makes it likely that the statements are trustworthy.

See also State v. Boston, 46 Ohio St. 3d 108, 545 N.E.2d 1220 (1989); State v. Wallace, 37 Ohio St. 3d 87, 524 N.E.2d 466 (1988), superseded by statute on other grounds as stated in State v. Uhler, 80 Ohio App. 3d 113, 608 N.E.2d 1091 (9th Dist. Wayne County 1992); State v. Duncan, 53 Ohio St. 2d 215, 7 Ohio Op. 3d 380, 373 N.E.2d 1234 (1978); In re Michael, 119 Ohio App. 3d 112, 130, 131, 694 N.E.2d 538 (2d Dist. Montgomery County 1997) (Two weeks after the alleged abuse, "five-year-old Myra started crying and became very upset while watching a soap opera in which the actors were kissing. She pointed to the television and stated that Bryan had done the same things to her.") ("[T]he record does not demonstrate, either directly or inferentially, that Lovely asked Myra leading questions regarding the alleged sexual abuse that destroyed the spontaneity or unreflectiveness of Myra's responses."); State v. Wagner, 30 Ohio App. 3d 261, 508 N.E.2d 164 (8th Dist. Cuyahoga County 1986); State v. Fowler, 27 Ohio App. 3d 149, 500 N.E.2d 390 (8th Dist. Cuyahoga County 1985); In re Legg, 68 Ohio Misc. 2d 1, 4, 646 N.E.2d 266 (C.P. 1993) (child victim's statement made weeks after startling event is

treatment or diagnoses, Evid. R. 803(4).[10]

A statute, RC 2151.35(F), recognizing a residual or open-ended hearsay exception in abuse, neglect, and dependency cases was struck down as inconsistent with the Rules of Evidence by the Ohio Supreme Court.[11] The Court, however, also promulgated Evidence Rule 807, which is similar.[12]

Depositions, including videotape depositions, may be admissible in abuse cases[13] and in delinquency cases when specified sex offenses are alleged for victims under 11 years of age.[14] The Ohio Supreme Court has upheld the use of a videotape deposition in a criminal prosecution for child abuse.[15]

A specific rule governs the use of social histories, which often contain hearsay evidence. Juvenile Rule 32(B) provides that a social history may not be used until after an admission or adjudication.

§ 23:17 Evidence—Separation of witnesses

Juvenile Rule 29(E)(2) provides for the separation or exclusion of witnesses upon request. Evidence Rule 615 contains a comparable provision. Evidence Rule 615, however, recognizes exceptions for (1) a party who is a natural person, (2) an officer or employee of a party which is not a natural person, and (3) a person whose presence is shown by a party to be essential to the presentation of his cause.[1]

Since parents are "parties" to juvenile cases under Juvenile Rule 2(Y), Ev-

---

inadmissible). In re Rossantelli Children, 2002-Ohio-2525, 2002 WL 999301 (Ohio Ct. App. 5th Dist. Delaware County 2002).

[10]In re Corry M., 134 Ohio App. 3d 274, 281–83, 730 N.E.2d 1047 (11th Dist. Lake County 1999) ("[W]hile most hearsay declarations offered into admission under Evid.R. 803(4) will involve situations where a patient seeks diagnosis or treatment of a physical or psychological condition from a medical doctor, the rule does not require that such a declaration necessarily be made to a physician. Indeed, a statement may fit within the scope of this hearsay exception if it is directed to other physical and mental health professions including nurses, psychologists, and therapists. . . . In the present case, the state offered absolutely no evidence from which this court can discern the child's motivation for participating in the interview with Ms. Pomeroy. The child was never told the purpose of her visit with the social worker and Ms. Pomeroy herself testified that she was only conducting an intake interview to investigate allegations of abuse. . . . Furthermore, while the white lab coats and medical instruments traditionally seen at a doctor's office might signal in a child's mind the seriousness of the situation and the necessity to tell the truth, . . . there is no indication that a typically dressed social worker carrying an anatomically correct doll would evoke a similar reaction in the eyes of a child."). The application of this exception in child sexual abuse prosecutions has proved troublesome. Compare State v. Dever, 64 Ohio St. 3d 401, 1992-Ohio-41, 596 N.E.2d 436 (1992), with State v. Boston, 46 Ohio St. 3d 108, 545 N.E.2d 1220 (1989). See also State v. Storch, 66 Ohio St. 3d 280, 1993-Ohio-38, 612 N.E.2d 305 (1993) (modifying *Dever*); In re Rossantelli Children, 2002-Ohio-2525, 2002 WL 999301 (Ohio Ct. App. 5th Dist. Delaware County 2002).

[11]In re Coy, 67 Ohio St. 3d 215, 1993-Ohio-202, 616 N.E.2d 1105 (1993) (RC 2151.35(F) is inconsistent with the Rules of Evidence and is therefore unconstitutional under Art. IV, § 5(B) of the Ohio Constitution).

[12]See also In re Coy, 67 Ohio St. 3d 215, 1993-Ohio-202, 616 N.E.2d 1105 (1993) (Evid. R. 807 should be used in abuse cases); State v. Storch, 66 Ohio St. 3d 280, 1993-Ohio-38, 612 N.E.2d 305 (1993) (Evid. R. 807 accords with the right of confrontation.); In re Corry M., 134 Ohio App. 3d 274, 284, 730 N.E.2d 1047 (11th Dist. Lake County 1999) ("In this case, the trial court determined that the child's hearsay statements to Ms. Pomeroy did not provide particularized guarantees of trustworthiness based on the social worker's admissions that the alleged victim may not have been truthful as well as concerns that the child may have been coached into making false allegations against appellee. These concerns are adequately borne out in the record on appeal and we cannot hold that the trial court abused its discretion under these circumstances.").

[13]RC 2151.35(G).

[14]RC 2151.3511.

[15]State v. Self, 56 Ohio St. 3d 73, 564 N.E.2d 446 (1990).

[Section 23:17]

[1]Lowry v. Lowry, 48 Ohio App. 3d 184, 549 N.E.2d 176 (4th Dist. Ross County 1988) (applying Evid. R. 615 in custody proceeding); In re Morris, 2002-Ohio-5881, 2002 WL 31414557 (Ohio Ct. App. 12th Dist. Butler County 2002); see also, RC 2152.81.

idence Rule 615 would appear to supersede a prior Ohio case that upheld the exclusion of parents who were also witnesses.[2] One court, however, has held that the juvenile court retains discretion to exclude parents at a delinquency hearing.[3]

Victims. RC 2930.09[4] recognizes the right of a victim[5] to be present whenever an alleged juvenile offender is present during any on the record stage of the case, unless the court determines that exclusion of the victim is necessary to protect the juvenile's right to a fair delinquency hearing. At the victim's request, the victim has the right to be accompanied by an individual to provide support to the victim, unless the court determines that exclusion of the individual is necessary to protect the juvenile's right to a fair delinquency hearing.

If the victim, the victim's designee, or the individual accompanying the victim are witnesses, there may be a conflict with Juvenile Rule 29(E)(2), which specifies that the court shall order the separation of witnesses, upon request of any party. Whether the statute or the rule controls depends on whether the statute is considered "substantive" or "procedural." If procedural, the statute would ordinarily be unconstitutional. In this situation, however, the issue is more complex because the Ohio Constitution has been amended to include a Victims' Rights provision.[6] The victims' rights provision may supersede the constitutional provision dealing with the Supreme Court's rulemaking authority.

§ 23:18   Evidence—Competency of witnesses

Evidence Rule 601(A) governs the competency of a child witness. Under this rule, children under the age of 10 who do not appear capable of "receiving just impressions of the facts and transactions respecting which they are examined, or of relating them truly" are incompetent.[1]

Ten years. A child 10 years of age is considered prima facie competent,[2] even if the child was younger than 10 at the time of the events about which the child will testify.[3] According to the Ohio Supreme Court in *State v. Clark*,[4] "[t]he rule addresses competency as of the time of trial, not as of the time at which the incident in question occurred." When a child is over 10 years of age at the time of the trial, "[a] trial judge, in the exercise of his or her discretion, may choose to conduct a voir-dire examination of the child witness

---

[2]State v. Ostrowski, 30 Ohio St. 2d 34, 59 Ohio Op. 2d 62, 282 N.E.2d 359 (1972).

[3]In re Vaughn, 1990 WL 116936 (Ohio Ct. App. 12th Dist. Butler County 1990).

[4]This statute was enacted pursuant to the Victims' Rights provision of the Ohio Constitution. O. Const. art. I § 10a.

[5]RC 2930.02 provides a procedure for the designation of a victim's representative, who is authorized to exercise the victim's rights under RC Ch. 2930.

[6]O. Const. art. I § 10a. This provision specifically authorizes the General Assembly to enact laws giving victims "access" to the criminal justice process.

[Section 23:18]

[1]State v. Workman, 14 Ohio App. 3d 385, 471 N.E.2d 853 (8th Dist. Cuyahoga County 1984); State v. Lee, 9 Ohio App. 3d 282, 459 N.E.2d 910 (9th Dist. Summit County 1983); Philpot v. Williams, 8 Ohio App. 3d 241, 456 N.E.2d 1315 (1st Dist. Hamilton County 1983); State v. Lewis, 4 Ohio App. 3d 275, 448 N.E.2d 487 (3d Dist. Union County 1982); In re Black, No. 40247 (8th Dist. Ct. App., Cuyahoga, 1-25-80). See generally Giannelli and Snyder, Baldwin's Ohio Practice, Evidence (2d ed.) § 501.1.

[2]See State v. Carey, 107 Ohio App. 149, 8 Ohio Op. 2d 49, 157 N.E.2d 381 (2d Dist. Miami County 1958).

[3]State v. Clark, 71 Ohio St. 3d 466, 471, 1994-Ohio-43, 644 N.E.2d 331 (1994).

[4]State v. Clark, 71 Ohio St. 3d 466, 470–71, 1994-Ohio-43, 644 N.E.2d 331 (1994) (This conclusion followed from "the plain meaning of Evid. R. 601(A).").

if the judge has reason to question the child's competency."[5]

Under 10 years. A child witness under 10 years of age "is not presumed incompetent, but rather, the proponent of the witness's testimony bears the burden of proving that the witness" is competent.[6] In such cases, the trial judge must conduct a voir dire examination to determine the witness's competence.[7]

Determining the competency of a child witness is a decision that is entrusted to the discretion of the court.[8] The Supreme Court has stated:

> Such determination of competency is within the sound discretion of the trial judge. The trial judge has the opportunity to observe the child's appearance, his or her manner of responding to the questions, general demeanor and any indicia of ability to relate the facts accurately and truthfully. Thus, the responsibility of the trial judge is to determine through questioning whether the child of tender years is capable of receiving just impressions of facts and events and to accurately relate them.[9]

The parties are entitled to introduce evidence, including expert testimony, on this issue.

The Ohio Supreme Court stated in *State v. Said*[10] that "[c]ompetency under Evid.R. 601(A) contemplates several characteristics" which "can be broken down into three elements":

> First, the individual must have the ability to receive accurate impressions of fact. Second, the individual must be able to accurately recollect those impressions. Third, the individual must be able to relate those impressions truthfully.

The Court noted, in *State v. Frazier*,[11] that in making the competency decision

> the trial court must take into consideration (1) the child's ability to receive accurate impressions of fact or to observe acts about which he or she will testify, (2) the child's ability to recollect those impressions or observations, (3) the child's ability to communicate what was observed, (4) the child's understanding of truth and falsity and (5) the child's appreciation of his or her responsibility to be truthful.[12]

The trial judge need not, however, make explicit findings as to the *Frazier* factors. The Court in *Schulte v. Schulte*[13] stated that a requirement of express findings "would unduly burden our trial courts with unnecessary formality." The trial court's obligation is "merely . . . to consider the *Frazier* factors

---

[5]State v. Clark, 71 Ohio St. 3d 466, 471, 1994-Ohio-43, 644 N.E.2d 331 (1994). See also State v. Moreland, 50 Ohio St. 3d 58, 61, 552 N.E.2d 894 (1990).

[6]State v. Clark, 71 Ohio St. 3d 466, 469, 1994-Ohio-43, 644 N.E.2d 331 (1994).

[7]State v. Said, 71 Ohio St. 3d 473, 476, 1994-Ohio-402, 644 N.E.2d 337 (1994). The Court in *Said* characterized the competency hearing as "an indispensable tool" in child witness cases:

A court cannot determine the competency of a child through consideration of the child's out-of-court statements standing alone. . . . [T]he essential questions of competency can be answered only through an in-person hearing: "The child's appearance, fear or composure, general demeanor and manner of answering, and any indication of coaching or instruction as to answers to be given are as significant as the words used in answering during the examination, to determine competency . . ..

Such important and necessary observations cannot be made unless the child appears personally before the court.

State v. Said, 71 Ohio St. 3d 473, 476, 1994-Ohio-402, 644 N.E.2d 337 (1994) (quoting State v. Wilson, 156 Ohio St. 525, 532, 46 Ohio Op. 437, 103 N.E.2d 552, 30 A.L.R.2d 763 (1952)).

[8]State v. Holt, 17 Ohio St. 2d 81, 46 Ohio Op. 2d 408, 246 N.E.2d 365 (1969).

[9]State v. Frazier, 61 Ohio St. 3d 247, 251, 574 N.E.2d 483 (1991).

[10]State v. Said, 71 Ohio St. 3d 473, 1994-Ohio-402, 644 N.E.2d 337 (1994).

[11]State v. Frazier, 61 Ohio St. 3d 247, 251, 574 N.E.2d 483 (1991).

[12]State v. Frazier, 61 Ohio St. 3d 247, 251, 574 N.E.2d 483 (1991).

[13]Schulte v. Schulte, 71 Ohio St. 3d 41, 43, 1994-Ohio-459, 641 N.E.2d 719 (1994).

while making the competency determination."[14]

Procedure. RC 2317.01 and Juvenile Rule 27(B)(2) provide that in an abuse, neglect, or dependency case an examination of a child to determine competency shall be conducted in an office or room other than a courtroom. In addition, only those persons considered necessary by the court for the conduct of the examination or the well-being of the child may be present. The prosecutor, guardian ad litem, or attorney for any party may submit questions for use by the court in determining competency. This provision would permit the exclusion of parties and perhaps counsel.

In *Kentucky v. Stincer*,[15] the United States Supreme Court ruled that the exclusion of a criminal defendant from a hearing to determine the competency of a child witness did not violate the right of confrontation. The defendant's attorney, however, was present and participated in the hearing. One Ohio court of appeals has written: "Even if, as here, no prejudice to the defendant results, the appearance of the judge and a witness [a child] closeting themselves without a representative of the defendant is one which raises the specter of impropriety. It should be avoided."[16]

§ 23:19 Evidence—Experts

Expert testimony is admissible if (1) it relates to matters beyond the knowledge or experience possessed by lay persons or dispels a misconception among lay persons, and (2) the witness is qualified by knowledge, skill, experience, training, or education to express an opinion on that matter.[1] An expert may base an opinion on personal observation or on evidence admitted at the hearing.[2] The latter situation typically involves the use of a hypothetical question. If it will assist the court, an expert may express an opinion on the ultimate issues in the case.[3]

Testimony by psychologists, caseworkers, and counselors is often admitted in dependency and neglect cases.[4] Medical testimony concerning the "battered child syndrome" is admissible in physical abuse cases.[5] A number of

---

[14]Schulte v. Schulte, 71 Ohio St. 3d 41, 43, 1994-Ohio-459, 641 N.E.2d 719 (1994). See State v. Kittle, 2003-Ohio-3097, 2003 WL 21385035 (Ohio Ct. App. 6th Dist. Lucas County 2003), appeal allowed, judgment rev'd, 100 Ohio St. 3d 247, 2003-Ohio-5759, 797 N.E.2d 1283 (2003).

[15]Kentucky v. Stincer, 482 U.S. 730, 107 S. Ct. 2658, 96 L. Ed. 2d 631, 22 Fed. R. Evid. Serv. 1164 (1987).

[16]State v. McMillan, 62 Ohio App. 3d 565, 568, 577 N.E.2d 91 (9th Dist. Lorain County 1989).

[Section 23:19]

[1]Evid. R. 702. See In re Baby Girl Doe, 149 Ohio App. 3d 717, 735, 2002-Ohio-4470, 778 N.E.2d 1053 (6th Dist. Lucas County 2002) ("The decision that a witness is or is not qualified to testify as an expert is a matter within the sound discretion of the trial court, and a court's ruling thereon will not be reversed unless there is a clear showing of an abuse of this discretion."). See generally Giannelli and Snyder, Baldwin's Ohio Practice, Evidence (2d ed.) § 702.1.

[2]Evid. R. 703.

[3]Evid. R. 704.

[4]E.g., In re Awkal, 95 Ohio App. 3d 309, 318, 642 N.E.2d 424 (8th Dist. Cuyahoga County 1994) ("In reaching its conclusion, the court specifically noted the expert testimony of [the] psychologist."); In re Webb, 64 Ohio App. 3d 280, 581 N.E.2d 570 (1st Dist. Hamilton County 1989) (physician's clinical impression that children had been sexually abused admitted); In re Brown, 60 Ohio App. 3d 136, 139, 573 N.E.2d 1217 (1st Dist. Hamilton County 1989) (social worker's testimony about mother's "past parenting history and her ability to comply with prior reunification plans regarding her other children" admitted); In re Green, 18 Ohio App. 3d 43, 480 N.E.2d 492 (2d Dist. Montgomery County 1984).

[5]E.g., U.S. v. Bowers, 660 F.2d 527, 529, 9 Fed. R. Evid. Serv. 387 (5th Cir. 1981); State v. Durfee, 322 N.W.2d 778, 783-84 (Minn. 1982); State v. Holland, 346 N.W.2d 302, 307–08 (S.D. 1984). See also Giannelli & Imwinkelried, Scientific Evidence 72–73 (2d ed. 1993); Admissibility of expert medical testimony on battered child syndrome, 98 A.L.R. 3d 306.

other syndromes have been raised — e.g., sudden infant death syndrome,[6] shaken baby syndrome,[7] parent alienation syndrome,[8] and reactive attachment disorder.[9]

The admissibility of expert testimony concerning the "child sexual abuse accommodation syndrome"[10] has been controversial. In *State v. Boston*,[11] the Supreme Court ruled that an "expert may not testify as to the expert's opinion of the veracity of the statements of a child declarant."[12]

In *In re Bennett*,[13] the court of appeals upheld the identification of marijuana by an experienced police officer.

In *In re Burton S.*,[14] the parties stipulated to the admission of polygraph test results and the magistrate admitted the results. The magistrate, however, later decided to give those results no weight based only upon the admissibility requirements of *Souel*. According to the court of appeals, "this was a clear abuse of discretion. Once the test results were admitted, the magistrate was then bound to consider them."

In *Ake v. Oklahoma*,[15] the United States Supreme Court recognized that an indigent criminal defendant has a due process right to expert assistance in some cases. Several Ohio courts have extended *Ake* to permanent custody proceedings.[16] For example, in *In re Brown*,[17] the court of appeals wrote:

> [The] due process clause of the United States Constitution and the due course

---

[6]See Wilson v. State, 370 Md. 191, 803 A.2d 1034, 1044 (2002) (use of product rule in calculating statistics as applied to multiple sudden infant deaths not generally accepted; "Stated another way, there is not general agreement in the medical community that multiple SIDS deaths in a single family are genetically unrelated.").

[7]See People v. Cauley, 32 P.3d 602, 605 (Colo. Ct. App. 2001); State v. McClary, 207 Conn. 233, 541 A.2d 96 (1988); State v. Compton, 304 N.J. Super. 477, 701 A.2d 468 (App. Div. 1997) (collecting cases); State v. Lopez, 306 S.C. 362, 412 S.E.2d 390 (1991).

[8]See Bruch, Parental Alienation Syndrome and Parental Alienation: Getting It Wrong in Child Custody Cases, 35 FAM. L.Q. 527 (2001) (criticizing underlying research).

[9]In re Priser, 2004-Ohio-1315, 2004 WL 541124 (Ohio Ct. App. 2d Dist. Montgomery County).

[10]See Giannelli & Imwinkelried, Scientific Evidence § 9-5 (3d ed. 1999).

[11]State v. Boston, 46 Ohio St. 3d 108, 545 N.E.2d 1220 (1989).

[12]State v. Boston, 46 Ohio St. 3d 108, 545 N.E.2d 1220 (1989) (syllabus). In a later case, the Court wrote:

> *Boston* stands for the proposition that expert testimony cannot be used to show that a child is telling the *truth* or that the child accurately testified. We came to this conclusion because the trier of fact, and not the expert, is burdened with assessing the credibility and veracity of witnesses.

State v. Moreland, 50 Ohio St. 3d 58, 62, 552 N.E.2d 894 (1990).

[13]In re Bennett, 134 Ohio App. 3d 699, 700, 731 N.E.2d 1226 (12th Dist. Brown County 1999) ("[I]t is well-established that expert testimony from experienced police officers is properly admitted. The Supreme Court of Ohio stated in that case that because 'marijuana, not being an extract or preparation difficult or impossible to characterize without chemical analysis, but consisting of the dried leaves, stems, and seeds of a plant which anyone reasonably familiar therewith should be able to identify by appearance, it is not error to permit officers who have had experience in searching for and obtaining marijuana to testify that a certain substance is marijuana; and other police officers have also been held qualified to testify.' ") (citing State v. Maupin, 42 Ohio St. 2d 473, 479–80, 71 Ohio Op. 2d 485, 330 N.E.2d 708 (1975)).

[14]In re Burton S., 136 Ohio App. 3d 386, 392, 736 N.E.2d 928 (6th Dist. Ottawa County 1999).

[15]Ake v. Oklahoma, 470 U.S. 68, 105 S. Ct. 1087, 84 L. Ed. 2d 53 (1985).

[16]E.g., In re Stanley, 1993 WL 512502 (Ohio Ct. App. 10th Dist. Franklin County 1993) ("Where the juvenile court grants the state's request for a psychological examination of an indigent parent to be performed by an examiner selected and paid by the state [FCCS], the parent is entitled to an expert of his or her own. Funds to employ her own psychologist should have been awarded appellant in order to afford her a meaningful opportunity to rebut the allegations of FCCS's expert. We agree with the court in *In re Angelo Brown* . . .. Our holding is limited, however, to situations where the court orders an indigent parent to undergo an evaluation by an examiner selected and paid by the non-parent party seeking to destroy parental rights. In essence, the playing field must be level."); In re Egbert Children, 99 Ohio App. 3d 492, 495, 651 N.E.2d 38 (12th Dist. Butler County 1994) (quoting *In re Brown*) ("There is no evidence that the $300 in fees awarded by the juvenile court in this case was inadequate . . . to retain a competent psychiatrist to assist in the preparation of her defense."); In re Shaeffer Children, 85 Ohio App. 3d 683, 621 N.E.2d 426 (3d Dist. Van Wert County 1993).

of law provision under the Ohio Constitution require the appointment of a psychiatrist to assist an indigent parent in permanent custody proceedings in which the parent's mental condition is at issue.

§ 23:20   Evidence—Impeachment

Evidence Rule 609 governs impeachment by prior conviction. Evidence Rule 609(D) provides, "Evidence of juvenile adjudications is not admissible except as provided by statute enacted by the General Assembly." RC 2151.358(H) is the applicable statute. When the Rules of Evidence were adopted in 1980, the statute read:

> The disposition of a child under the judgment rendered or any evidence given in court is not admissible as evidence against the child in any other case or proceeding in any other court, except that the judgment rendered and the disposition of the child may be considered by any court only as to the matter of sentence or to the granting of probation.

In *In re Johnson*,[1] the court of appeals held that Evidence Rule 609(D) and the statute precluded the impeachment of an alleged delinquent with a prior adjudication of delinquency. The same court, however, had reached the opposite result in prior cases.[2]

In *State v. Shedrick*,[3] the Supreme Court held that evidence introduced at a prior juvenile adjudication could not be used as "other acts" evidence, Evid. R. 404(B), in a criminal trial. RC 2151.358(H) was subsequently amended to change this result. It now prohibits the use of a juvenile judgment only if offered "to impeach the credibility of the child in any action or proceeding. Otherwise, . . . the judgment rendered or any evidence given in court is admissible as evidence for or against the child in any action or proceeding in any court in accordance with the Rules of Evidence."

The use of juvenile court records in other proceedings is discussed in a later chapter.[4]

§ 23:21   Evidence—Corroboration rules

The Ohio courts have applied "corroboration" rules in criminal cases. For example, a confession is inadmissible unless there is some independent evidence of the corpus delicti.[1] This rule applies to juvenile cases.[2] In addition, by statute a criminal defendant may not be convicted of conspiracy based solely on the testimony of a co-conspirator, unsupported by other evidence.[3] At one time a similar rule applied to accomplice testimony and complicity

---

[17]In re Brown, 1986 WL 13385 (Ohio Ct. App. 1st Dist. Hamilton County 1986).

[Section 23:20]

[1]In re Johnson, 61 Ohio App. 3d 544, 549, 573 N.E.2d 184 (8th Dist. Cuyahoga County 1989).

[2]In re Wyrock, No. 41827 (8th Dist. Ct. App., Cuyahoga, 10-23-80); State v. Eppinger, No. 30798 (8th Dist. Ct. App., Cuyahoga, 12-9-71) (RC 2151.358's use of the phrase "any other court" clearly excludes the juvenile court from the restrictions contained in the statute.). See generally Herbert & Sinclair, Adversary Juvenile Delinquency Proceedings: Impeachment of Juvenile Defendants by the Use of Previous Adjudications of Delinquency, 8 Akron L. Rev. 443 (1975).

See also In re Hayes, 29 Ohio App. 3d 162, 504 N.E.2d 491 (10th Dist. Franklin County 1986) (Evidence of prior adjudication is admissible as prior conviction to enhance degree of theft offense.).

[3]State v. Shedrick, 61 Ohio St. 3d 331, 574 N.E.2d 1065 (1991).

[4]See § 33:3, Other proceedings.

[Section 23:21]

[1]See State v. Black, 54 Ohio St. 2d 304, 8 Ohio Op. 3d 296, 376 N.E.2d 948 (1978); State v. Edwards, 49 Ohio St. 2d 31, 3 Ohio Op. 3d 18, 358 N.E.2d 1051 (1976); State v. King, 10 Ohio App. 3d 161, 460 N.E.2d 1383 (1st Dist. Hamilton County 1983); State v. Ralston, 67 Ohio App. 2d 81, 21 Ohio Op. 3d 403, 425 N.E.2d 916 (1st Dist. Clermont County 1979). See generally McCormick on Evidence (4th ed.) § 145; LaFave and Scott, Handbook on Criminal Law (2d ed.) § 18.

prosecutions, but the statute[4] has since been amended.[5]

Cross References
Ch 14, § 23:13, § 23:22, § 23:27

§ 23:22 Right of confrontation

The right of confrontation was one of the due process rights expressly applied to adjudicatory hearings in *Gault*: "We now hold that . . . a determination of delinquency and an order of commitment to a state institution cannot be sustained in the absence of sworn testimony subjected to the opportunity for cross-examination in accordance with our law and constitutional requirements."[1] Although the *Gault* decision was limited to delinquency cases, there seems little question that due process requires the right of confrontation in most juvenile cases.[2]

Most of the United States Supreme Court's cases in this area have focused on the Sixth Amendment Confrontation Clause.[3] There are several aspects to the right of confrontation, which are discussed in the following sections.

§ 23:23 Confrontation—Face-to-face confrontation

At the very least, the right of confrontation guarantees an accused the right to be present during trial, a subject that is discussed in section 20.12. "One of the most basic of the rights guaranteed by the Confrontation Clause is the accused's right to be present in the courtroom at every stage of his trial."[1] This right is implicitly recognized in Juvenile Rule 27[2] and RC 2151.35.[3]

The right to be present at the proceedings, however, can be waived by a defendant's obstructive conduct[4] or his voluntary absence after the hearing

---

[2]See Toler, 1983 WL 4356 (Ohio Ct. App. 12th Dist. Preble County 1983); In the Interest of Way, 319 So. 2d 651 (Miss. 1975); In re State In Interest of W. J., 116 N.J. Super. 462, 282 A.2d 770 (App. Div. 1971).

[3]RC 2923.01(H).

[4]RC 2923.03(D).

[5]See State v. Mullins, 34 Ohio App. 3d 192, 517 N.E.2d 945 (5th Dist. Fairfield County 1986) (Amendment applies prospectively.).

[Section 23:22]

[1]Application of Gault, 387 U.S. 1, 57, 87 S. Ct. 1428, 18 L. Ed. 2d 527 (1967).

[2]The right of confrontation as a due process requirement applies in a variety of contexts. See Goldberg v. Kelly, 397 U.S. 254, 90 S. Ct. 1011, 25 L. Ed. 2d 287 (1970) (Right of confrontation applies in welfare termination hearings.); Morrissey v. Brewer, 408 U.S. 471, 92 S. Ct. 2593, 33 L. Ed. 2d 484 (1972) (Conditional right of confrontation applies in parole revocation hearings.).

[3]U.S. Const. amend. 6 ("In all criminal prosecutions, the accused shall enjoy the right . . . to be confronted with the witnesses against him."). The right of confrontation applies to state trials. Pointer v. Texas, 380 U.S. 400, 85 S. Ct. 1065, 13 L. Ed. 2d 923 (1965).

The Ohio Constitution also guarantees the right of confrontation (O. Const. art. I § 10).

[Section 23:23]

[1]Illinois v. Allen, 397 U.S. 337, 338, 90 S. Ct. 1057, 25 L. Ed. 2d 353 (1970). See also In re Oliver, 333 U.S. 257, 68 S. Ct. 499, 92 L. Ed. 682 (1948); Lewis v. U.S., 146 U.S. 370, 13 S. Ct. 136, 36 L. Ed. 1011 (1892); Katz and Giannelli, Baldwin's Ohio Practice, Criminal Law (2d ed.), Ch 69.

The right to be present has been applied to juvenile cases. See RLR v. State, 487 P.2d 27 (Alaska 1971).

[2]Juv. R. 27(A) provides, "The court may excuse the attendance of the child at the hearing in neglect, dependency, or abuse cases."

[3]RC 2151.35(A) is identical to Juv. R. 27 in this respect ("The court may excuse the attendance of the child at the hearing in cases involving abused, neglected, or dependent children.").

[4]Illinois v. Allen, 397 U.S. 337, 90 S. Ct. 1057, 25 L. Ed. 2d 353 (1970). See also § 23:26, Confrontation—Waiver.

has commenced.[5]

The right to be present includes the right to "face-to-face" confrontation. In *Coy v. Iowa*,[6] the United States Supreme Court found a Sixth Amendment violation where a screen was used to separate the accused and the alleged child sexual abuse victims during their testimony. However, an important concurring opinion, citing statutes which permit the use of closed-circuit television, indicated that the right to face-to-face confrontation is not absolute; the state interest in protecting the child could outweigh the defendant's right if case-specific findings of necessity are made by the trial court.[7] Two years later, in *Maryland v. Craig*,[8] the Court rejected a confrontation challenge to a procedure permitting a child witness to testify outside the courtroom via closed circuit television. Here, the trial court had made a fact-specific inquiry to determine whether the child would be traumatized by testifying in the presence of the accused.

The Ohio statute, RC 2151.3511, on testifying via closed-circuit television applies when specified sex offenses are charged and the alleged victim is under 11 years of age when the complaint is filed. The court of appeals in *In re Howard*[9] addressed the constitutionality of the statute. The court noted that the closed circuit television procedure is permissible if the state proves necessity on a case-by-case basis after a hearing and the entry of findings. A psychologist testified about the effect of trauma on a child compelled to testify in front of the alleged abuser. In this case, the court found that the trial court's failure to enter findings was harmless error. The court also held that a child who witnesses the sexual abuse of another child can be considered a "victim" under the statute "where there is sufficient evidence for the trial court to determine that a child witness would be unable to testify in the defendant's presence due to fear and the substantial likelihood of emotional trauma."[10]

§ 23:24   Confrontation—Cross-examination

The right of confrontation includes the right of cross-examination. For example, in *Davis v. Alaska*,[1] an accused was prohibited from cross-examining a prosecution witness concerning the witness's status as a juvenile probationer. This curtailment of cross-examination was based on a state statute designed to protect the confidentiality of juvenile adjudications. On review, the United States Supreme Court reversed: "The State's policy interest in protecting the confidentiality of a juvenile offender's record cannot require yielding of so vital a constitutional right as the effective cross-

---

[5]Taylor v. U.S., 414 U.S. 17, 94 S. Ct. 194, 38 L. Ed. 2d 174 (1973). See also In re Jason R., 77 Ohio Misc. 2d 37, 41, 666 N.E.2d 666 (C.P. 1995) ("The *Taylor* decision is most analogous to the case before this court. As reflected by the trial record, Jason attended the prior proceedings against him, including the adjudicatory hearing. By virtue of his mother's testimony at the dispositional hearing, Jason had notice and knowledge of the scheduled dispositional hearing, yet chose not to attend. Thus, by the *Taylor* rationale, Jason waived his right to be present at the dispositional hearing through his voluntary absence.").

[6]Coy v. Iowa, 487 U.S. 1012, 108 S. Ct. 2798, 101 L. Ed. 2d 857, 25 Fed. R. Evid. Serv. 865 (1988).

[7]Coy v. Iowa, 487 U.S. 1012, 2803, 108 S. Ct. 2798, 101 L. Ed. 2d 857, 25 Fed. R. Evid. Serv. 865 (1988) (Justice O'Connor). See also State v. Eastham, 39 Ohio St. 3d 307, 530 N.E.2d 409 (1988) (Use of video violated right of confrontation where no particularized findings of necessity established.).

[8]Maryland v. Craig, 497 U.S. 836, 110 S. Ct. 3157, 111 L. Ed. 2d 666, 30 Fed. R. Evid. Serv. 1 (1990).

[9]In re Howard, 119 Ohio App. 3d 33, 38, 694 N.E.2d 488 (12th Dist. Butler County 1997).

[10]In re Howard, 119 Ohio App. 3d 33, 40, 694 N.E.2d 488 (12th Dist. Butler County 1997).

[Section 23:24]
[1]Davis v. Alaska, 415 U.S. 308, 94 S. Ct. 1105, 39 L. Ed. 2d 347 (1974). See also Katz and Giannelli, Baldwin's Ohio Practice, Criminal Law (2d ed.), Ch 69.

examination for bias of an adverse witness."[2]

Juvenile Rule 29(B)(5) implicitly recognizes the right of cross-examination. It provides that a party who waives the right to counsel, must be informed of certain rights, including the right "to cross-examine witness."[3]

Whether interviewing the child in camara violates the due process right of confrontation in an abuse, neglect, or dependency hearing has not been definitely decided in Ohio.[4] Some courts have indicated that this decision falls within the trial court's discretion.[5] Other courts have demonstrated more concern. "We most certainly do not encourage all in-camera interviews to be conducted in the same manner as in the case now before us. In addition to obtaining a list of questions from counsel, the better procedure, in our view, would have been to permit counsel for all interested parties to attend the interview. Had Krista become emotional or frightened, counsel could have been asked to leave. After the interview, counsel could have also been permitted to ask a list of follow-up questions."[6]

§ 23:25 Confrontation—Hearsay

The Confrontation Clause also places some limitations on the use of hearsay evidence. The United States Supreme Court has addressed this issue on several occasions. Because a hearsay declarant is, in effect, a "witness," a literal application of the Confrontation Clause would preclude the prosecution from introducing any hearsay statement, notwithstanding the applicability of a recognized hearsay exception. The Supreme Court, however, has rejected this interpretation: "[I]f thus applied, the Clause would abrogate virtually every hearsay exception, a result long rejected as unintended and too extreme."[1]

The Confrontation Clause could also be interpreted as requiring only the right to cross-examine in-court witnesses and not out-of-court declarants. Under this interpretation, the admissibility of statements falling within any recognized hearsay exception would not violate the confrontation guarantee. But the Court has also rejected this view: "It seems apparent that the Sixth Amendment's Confrontation Clause and the evidentiary hearsay rule stem from the same roots. But this Court has never equated the two, and we decline to do so now."[2]

Instead, the Court has adopted a middle ground, but one that has changed

---

[2]Davis v. Alaska, 415 U.S. 308, 320, 94 S. Ct. 1105, 39 L. Ed. 2d 347 (1974). See also Smith v. State of Illinois, 390 U.S. 129, 88 S. Ct. 748, 19 L. Ed. 2d 956 (1968).

[3]See Matter of Eplin, 1995 WL 495451 (Ohio Ct. App. 5th Dist. Stark County 1995) ("The language of Juv.R. 29(B)(5) is mandatory.").

[4]Juv. R. 27(A) and RC 2151.35(A) provide that the court may excuse the attendance of the child at the hearing in neglect, dependency, or abuse cases; it does not say that the child may be excused from cross-examination if the child is a witness. Juv. R. 27(B) governs procedures for determining the competency of witnesses. Juv. R. 27(C) and RC 2151.35(G) provide for the use of depositions in such cases.

[5]In re S., 102 Ohio App. 3d 338, 343, 657 N.E.2d 307 (6th Dist. Lucas County 1995) ("[T]he trial court gave extensive consideration as to whether to allow the children to be called as witnesses. The court even requested proposed questions for an *in camera* examination. In the end, however, the court made the determination that calling the children was not in their best interests. We cannot say that such a carefully contemplated determination exhibited the type of attitude which characterizes an abuse of discretion.").

[6]In re House, 1992 WL 35038 (Ohio Ct. App. 12th Dist. Butler County 1992). The court recognized that the Sixth Amendment right of confrontation did not apply, but also acknowledged that due process might provide a basis for requiring a right to cross-examine in this context.

[Section 23:25]
[1]Ohio v. Roberts, 448 U.S. 56, 63, 100 S. Ct. 2531, 65 L. Ed. 2d 597, 7 Fed. R. Evid. Serv. 1 (1980).

[2]Dutton v. Evans, 400 U.S. 74, 86, 91 S. Ct. 210, 27 L. Ed. 2d 213 (1970). See also Crawford v. Washington, 124 S. Ct. 1354, 1364, 158 L. Ed. 2d 177, 63 Fed. R. Evid. Serv. 1077 (U.S. 2004) ("[W]e once again reject the view that the Confrontation Clause applies of its own force only to

over time. The Court jettisoned nearly 25 years of confrontation jurisprudence in *Crawford v. Washington*[3] by overruling *Ohio v. Roberts*.[4] *Roberts* had established reliability as a critical component in the confrontation analysis of hearsay statements. *Crawford* rejected reliability as a relevant factor. Instead, the Court focused on cross-examination as the determinative factor when hearsay statements have a "testimonial" component.

In *Crawford*, the Court wrote: "The *Roberts* test allows a jury to hear evidence, untested by the adversary process, based on a mere judicial determination of reliability. It thus replaces the constitutionally prescribed method of assessing reliability [cross-examination] with a wholly foreign one. In this respect, it is very different from exceptions to the Confrontation Clause that make no claim to be a surrogate means of assessing reliability."[5] In addition, the Court found that the *Roberts'* "framework is so unpredictable that it fails to provide meaningful protection from even core confrontation violations. Reliability is an amorphous, if not entirely subjective, concept. There are countless factors bearing on whether a statement is reliable; the nine-factor balancing test applied by the Court of Appeals below is representative."[6]

In the Court's view, history established two things. "First, the principal evil at which the Confrontation Clause was directed was the civil-law mode of criminal procedure, and particularly its use of *ex parte* examinations as evidence against the accused."[7] Thus, out-of-court "testimonial" statements were the root concern of the Framers, rather than off-hand remarks.[8]

The second inference that can be drawn from history, according to the Court, was "that the Framers would not have allowed admission of testimonial statements of a witness who did not appear at trial unless he was unavailable to testify, and the defendant had had a prior opportunity for cross-examination."[9]

The critical and sometimes difficult task will be defining what is "testimonial" in this context. Although, the Court wrote that it left "for another day any effort to spell out a comprehensive definition of 'testimonial'," it added that "[w]hatever else the term covers, it applies at a minimum to prior testimony at a preliminary hearing, before a grand jury, or at a former trial; and to police interrogations. These are the modern practices with closest kinship to the abuses at which the Confrontation Clause was directed."[10]

---

in-court testimony . . . ."); California v. Green, 399 U.S. 149, 90 S. Ct. 1930, 26 L. Ed. 2d 489 (1970).

[3]Crawford v. Washington, 124 S. Ct. 1354, 158 L. Ed. 2d 177, 63 Fed. R. Evid. Serv. 1077 (U.S. 2004). The defendant was charged with assault and attempted murder. To rebut his claim of self-defense, the prosecution offered a statement made by his wife during a stationhouse interrogation.

[4]Ohio v. Roberts, 448 U.S. 56, 100 S. Ct. 2531, 65 L. Ed. 2d 597, 7 Fed. R. Evid. Serv. 1 (1980).

[5]Crawford v. Washington, 124 S. Ct. 1354, 1370, 158 L. Ed. 2d 177, 63 Fed. R. Evid. Serv. 1077 (U.S. 2004).

[6]Crawford v. Washington, 124 S. Ct. 1354, 1371, 158 L. Ed. 2d 177, 63 Fed. R. Evid. Serv. 1077 (U.S. 2004).

[7]Crawford v. Washington, 124 S. Ct. 1354, 1363, 158 L. Ed. 2d 177, 63 Fed. R. Evid. Serv. 1077 (U.S. 2004).

[8]Crawford v. Washington, 124 S. Ct. 1354, 1364, 158 L. Ed. 2d 177, 63 Fed. R. Evid. Serv. 1077 (U.S. 2004) ("An accuser who makes a formal statement to government officers bears testimony in a sense that a person who makes a casual remark to an acquaintance does not.").

[9]Crawford v. Washington, 124 S. Ct. 1354, 1364, 158 L. Ed. 2d 177, 63 Fed. R. Evid. Serv. 1077 (U.S. 2004).

[10]Crawford v. Washington, 124 S. Ct. 1354, 1374, 158 L. Ed. 2d 177, 63 Fed. R. Evid. Serv. 1077 (U.S. 2004). In another passage, the Court noted:

Various formulations of this core class of "testimonial" statements exist: "*ex parte* in-court testimony or its functional equivalent—that is, material such as affidavits, custodial examinations, prior testimony that the defendant was unable to cross-examine, or similar pretrial statements that declarants would reasonably expect to be used prosecutorially,"; "extrajudicial statements . . . contained in formalized testimonial

Moreover, "[s]tatements taken by police officers in the course of interrogations are also testimonial under even a narrow standard."[11]

The Court noted that the results (if not the rationale) of most of its past cases were consistent with this new approach. Prior testimony, such as that given at a preliminary hearing, was inadmissible in the absence of cross-examination. In addition, accomplice statements provided to the police have been excluded.

Two footnotes raise further questions. One involved the dying declaration exception. "Although many dying declarations may not be testimonial, there is authority for admitting even those that clearly are. We need not decide in this case whether the Sixth Amendment incorporates an exception for testimonial dying declarations. If this exception must be accepted on historical grounds, it is *sui generis*."[12] The second is the excited utterance exception: "It is questionable whether testimonial statements would ever have been admissible on that ground in 1791; to the extent the hearsay exception for spontaneous declarations existed at all, it required that the statements be made 'immediat[ely] upon the hurt received, and before [the declarant] had time to devise or contrive any thing for her own advantage.' *Thompson v. Trevanion*, Skin. 402, 90 Eng. Rep. 179 (K.B.1694)."[13]

Another issue concerns the treatment of "nontestimonial" statements. Are they subject to some type of reliability test under the Confrontation Clause or do they fall outside the Clause—i.e., left to evidence law governing hearsay? The Court offered only one comment regarding such statements: "Where nontestimonial hearsay is at issue, it is wholly consistent with the Framers' design to afford the States flexibility in their development of hearsay law—as does *Roberts*, and as would an approach that exempted such statements from Confrontation Clause scrutiny altogether."[14]

In sum, the new confrontation framework consists of two distinctions. The first involves situations where there is in-court examination of a declarant (i.e., the witness and the declarant are the same person). This satisfies the Confrontation Clause. In other words, *California v. Green*[15] remains intact.[16] The second distinction is between "testimonial" and "nontestimonial" statements. The former requires the opportunity to cross-examine at the time the statement was made.[17]

---

materials, such as affidavits, depositions, prior testimony, or confessions,"; "statements that were made under circumstances which would lead an objective witness reasonably to believe that the statement would be available for use at a later trial." These formulations all share a common nucleus and then define the Clause's coverage at various levels of abstraction around it. Regardless of the precise articulation, some statements qualify under any definition—for example, *ex parte* testimony at a preliminary hearing.
Crawford v. Washington, 124 S. Ct. 1354, 1364, 158 L. Ed. 2d 177, 63 Fed. R. Evid. Serv. 1077 (U.S. 2004). The Court cited A. Amar, The Constitution and Criminal Procedure 125-31 (1997), and Friedman, Confrontation: The Search for Basic Principles, 86 Geo. L.J. 1011 (1998), as advocates of this position.

[11]Crawford v. Washington, 124 S. Ct. 1354, 1364, 158 L. Ed. 2d 177, 63 Fed. R. Evid. Serv. 1077 (U.S. 2004).

[12]Crawford v. Washington, 124 S. Ct. 1354, 1367 n. 6, 158 L. Ed. 2d 177, 63 Fed. R. Evid. Serv. 1077 (U.S. 2004) (citations omitted).

[13]Crawford v. Washington, 124 S. Ct. 1354, 1368 n. 8, 158 L. Ed. 2d 177, 63 Fed. R. Evid. Serv. 1077 (U.S. 2004) (citations omitted).

[14]Crawford v. Washington, 124 S. Ct. 1354, 1364, 158 L. Ed. 2d 177, 63 Fed. R. Evid. Serv. 1077 (U.S. 2004).

[15]California v. Green, 399 U.S. 149, 90 S. Ct. 1930, 26 L. Ed. 2d 489 (1970).

[16]Crawford v. Washington, 124 S. Ct. 1354, 1369 n. 9, 158 L. Ed. 2d 177, 63 Fed. R. Evid. Serv. 1077 (U.S. 2004).

[17]See State v. Cutlip, 2004-Ohio-2120, 2004 WL 895980 (Ohio Ct. App. 9th Dist. Medina County 2004) (reversing conviction because of admission of statements of two alleged accomplices, who were unavailable, made during police interrogation).

In *State v. Storch*,[18] the Ohio Supreme Court stated that the admission of a statement pursuant to a firmly rooted hearsay exception may nevertheless violate the state constitution. According to the Court, the current interpretation of the Sixth Amendment by the United States Supreme Court "provides less protection for the accused than the protection provided by the Sixth Amendment as traditionally construed and by the express words of Section 10, Article I of the Ohio Constitution."[19]

> We construe the right to confrontation contained in Section 10, Article I to require live testimony where reasonably possible. However, circumstances may exist where the evidence clearly indicates that a child may suffer significant emotional harm by being forced to testify in the actual presence of a person he or she is accusing of abuse. In such circumstances, the child may be considered unavailable for purposes of the Rules of Evidence and the out-of-court statements admitted without doing violence to Section 10 Article I, assuming Evid.R. 807 is otherwise satisfied.[20]

The Court also commented: "Evid.R. 807 accords with the Sixth Amendment right to confrontation and of the confrontation rights in Section 10, Article I of the Ohio Constitution."[21]

§ 23:26   Confrontation—Waiver

The right of confrontation may be waived. In some cases the United States Supreme Court has applied a stringent waiver standard, requiring "an intentional relinquishment or abandonment of a known right or privilege."[1] In other cases the Court has found a waiver by conduct.[2] In *In re Gantt*,[3] a juvenile court considered a witness's transfer hearing testimony during the adjudicatory hearing, even though the witness did not testify at that hearing. On review, the appellate court held that the child had waived his right of confrontation by failing to object to the use of the transfer hearing testimony.[4]

§ 23:27   Self-incrimination

In *Gault* the United States Supreme Court held the Fifth Amendment privilege against compelled self-incrimination[1] applicable in adjudicatory delinquency proceedings, despite the state's argument that such proceedings were "civil" in nature. According to the Court, proceedings "which may lead to commitment to a state institution, must be regarded as 'criminal' for purposes of the privilege against self-incrimination. To hold otherwise would be to disregard substance because of the feeble enticement of the 'civil' label-

---

[18]State v. Storch, 66 Ohio St. 3d 280, 1993-Ohio-38, 612 N.E.2d 305 (1993).

[19]State v. Storch, 66 Ohio St. 3d 280, 291, 1993-Ohio-38, 612 N.E.2d 305 (1993).

[20]State v. Storch, 66 Ohio St. 3d 280, 293, 1993-Ohio-38, 612 N.E.2d 305 (1993).

[21]State v. Storch, 66 Ohio St. 3d 280, 289, 1993-Ohio-38, 612 N.E.2d 305 (1993).

[Section 23:26]

[1]Brookhart v. Janis, 384 U.S. 1, 4, 86 S. Ct. 1245, 16 L. Ed. 2d 314 (1966).

[2]Taylor v. U.S., 414 U.S. 17, 94 S. Ct. 194, 38 L. Ed. 2d 174 (1973); Illinois v. Allen, 397 U.S. 337, 90 S. Ct. 1057, 25 L. Ed. 2d 353 (1970). See § 23:23, Confrontation—Face-to-face confrontation.

[3]Matter of Gantt, 61 Ohio App. 2d 44, 15 Ohio Op. 3d 67, 398 N.E.2d 800 (6th Dist. Wood County 1978).

[4]Matter of Gantt, 61 Ohio App. 2d 44, 48, 15 Ohio Op. 3d 67, 398 N.E.2d 800 (6th Dist. Wood County 1978).

[Section 23:27]

[1]U.S. Const. amend. 5 ("No person . . . shall be compelled in any criminal case to be a witness against himself."). The privilege applies in state trials. Malloy v. Hogan, 378 U.S. 1, 84 S. Ct. 1489, 12 L. Ed. 2d 653 (1964). See generally Katz and Giannelli, Baldwin's Ohio Practice, Criminal Law (2d ed.), Ch 70; LaFave, et.al., Criminal Procedure (3d ed.), Ch 15.

The Ohio Constitution also guarantees the right against self-incrimination (O. Const. art. I § 10).

of-convenience which has been attached to juvenile proceedings."[2] The Court also has held that the privilege prohibits a court from considering a criminal defendant's failure to testify as evidence of guilt.[3] This rule applies in juvenile cases.[4]

Waiver. The privilege against self-incrimination may be waived. A child waives the privilege by taking the stand and testifying in his own defense. In *Gault* the Court commented:

> We appreciate that special problems may arise with respect to waiver of the privilege by or on behalf of children, and that there may well be some differences in technique—but not in principle—depending upon the age of the child and the presence and competence of parents. The participation of counsel will, of course, assist the police, Juvenile Courts and appellate tribunals in administering the privilege. If counsel was not present for some permissible reason when an admission was obtained, the greatest care must be taken to assure that the admission was voluntary, in the sense not only that it was not coerced or suggested, but also that it was not the product of ignorance of rights or of adolescent fantasy, fright or despair.[5]

In *In re Johnson*,[6] the juvenile, without counsel, stipulated to a prior theft offense. The court of appeals ruled that the juvenile's Fifth Amendment rights had been violated: "Johnson cannot be considered to have waived his rights without a voluntary, knowing and intelligent waiver."

Advisement of right. Juvenile Rule 29(B)(5) requires the court to inform parties who have waived the right to counsel of the right to remain silent.[7] In *In re Collins*,[8] the court of appeals stated that the explanation of the privilege "must include the facts that there is an unqualified right to remain silent, that a statement made may be used against him, and that his refusal to testify will not be held against him."[9] The court also ruled that only the child could waive the privilege: "No case . . . has held that a parent could waive the constitutional right of a minor in a Juvenile Court or criminal case."[10]

In *In re Johnson*,[11] the court of appeals noted that the "referees and the judge failed under each element of Juv.R.29(B) at each hearing. . . . The court must comply with Juv.R. 29(B). This rule protects juveniles from the type of violations of right that occurred in this case."

---

[2]Application of Gault, 387 U.S. 1, 49–50, 87 S. Ct. 1428, 18 L. Ed. 2d 527 (1967). As the Ohio Supreme Court acknowledged in In re Agler, 19 Ohio St. 2d 70, 48 Ohio Op. 2d 85, 249 N.E.2d 808 (1969), *Gault* overruled prior Ohio cases which had held the privilege inapplicable in juvenile cases. See State v. Shardell, 107 Ohio App. 338, 8 Ohio Op. 2d 262, 79 Ohio L. Abs. 534, 153 N.E.2d 510 (8th Dist. Cuyahoga County 1958).

[3]Griffin v. California, 380 U.S. 609, 85 S. Ct. 1229, 14 L. Ed. 2d 106 (1965). But see U.S. v. Robinson, 485 U.S. 25, 108 S. Ct. 864, 99 L. Ed. 2d 23 (1988) (not a Fifth Amendment violation to comment on an accused's silence in response to defense counsel's tactics).

[4]See In re Collins, 20 Ohio App. 2d 319, 49 Ohio Op. 2d 448, 253 N.E.2d 824 (8th Dist. Cuyahoga County 1969); In re State in Interest of D.A.M., 132 N.J. Super. 192, 333 A.2d 270 (App. Div. 1975).

[5]Application of Gault, 387 U.S. 1, 55, 87 S. Ct. 1428, 18 L. Ed. 2d 527 (1967).

[6]In re Johnson, 106 Ohio App. 3d 38, 45, 665 N.E.2d 247 (1st Dist. Hamilton County 1995).

[7]Matter of Eplin, 1995 WL 495451 (Ohio Ct. App. 5th Dist. Stark County 1995) ("The language of Juv.R. 29(B)(5) is mandatory.").

[8]In re Collins, 20 Ohio App. 2d 319, 49 Ohio Op. 2d 448, 253 N.E.2d 824 (8th Dist. Cuyahoga County 1969).

[9]In re Collins, 20 Ohio App. 2d 319, 322, 49 Ohio Op. 2d 448, 253 N.E.2d 824 (8th Dist. Cuyahoga County 1969).

[10]In re Collins, 20 Ohio App. 2d 319, 322, 49 Ohio Op. 2d 448, 253 N.E.2d 824 (8th Dist. Cuyahoga County 1969).

[11]In re Johnson, 106 Ohio App. 3d 38, 45, 665 N.E.2d 247 (1st Dist. Hamilton County 1995).

Statements made during treatment. In *State v. Evans*,[12] the court of appeals ruled that statements made at a residential treatment center for juveniles were properly suppressed as violative of the Fifth Amendment. "By procuring two incriminating statements as a condition of court-ordered therapy and under threat of substantial penalty, Hillcrest placed Evans in the 'classic penalty' situation. His privilege against self-incrimination therefore became self-executing, and the resulting confessions could not be used against him in a criminal trial."[13]

The United States Supreme Court subsequently addressed the same issue but in a different context. In *McKune v Lile*,[14] the Court upheld a prison sex offender treatment program that required inmates to reveal their entire sexual history or lose privileges and be transferred to a more secure facility. A divided Court ruled that the program did not involve "compulsion" in the Fifth Amendment sense. The Court had previously recognized that lawful conviction and incarceration necessarily placed limitations on the exercise of a defendant's privilege against self-incrimination. The plurality wrote: "A prison clinical rehabilitation program, which is acknowledged to bear a rational relation to a legitimate penological objective, does not violate the privilege against self-incrimination if the adverse consequences an inmate faces for not participating are related to the program objectives and do not constitute atypical and significant hardships in relation to the ordinary incidents of prison life." Justice O'Connor stated that this standard was too narrow but nevertheless concurred in the judgment because she did "not believe that the alterations in respondent's prison conditions as a result of his failure to participate in the Sexual Abuse Treatment Program (SATP) were so great as to constitute compulsion for the purposes of the Fifth Amendment privilege against self-incrimination."[15]

Abuse, neglect, and dependency cases. The United States Supreme Court has held that the privilege is applicable in any proceeding "civil or criminal, formal or informal, where the answers might incriminate [a person] in future criminal proceedings."[16] This rule applies to abuse, neglect, and dependency hearings if a future criminal prosecution is possible.[17]

In *In re Amanda W.*,[18] the court of appeals held that the privilege was violated because the father was required to admit he had sexually abused his daughter in order to obtain the group counseling required under his case plan. Moreover, any statement about the father's abuse of his child could subject her mother to prosecution for child endangerment. In addition, failure to comply with the case plan could result in the loss of permanent custody. The court wrote that "this is the type of compelling sanction that forces an individual to admit to offenses in violation of his right not to incriminate himself. Accordingly, the privilege was self-executing. Therefore, in order to avoid a Fifth Amendment infringement, the state was required to offer [the parents] protection from the use of any compelled statements and

---

[12]State v. Evans, 144 Ohio App. 3d 539, 556, 760 N.E.2d 909 (1st Dist. Hamilton County 2001).

[13]State v. Evans, 144 Ohio App. 3d 539, 558, 760 N.E.2d 909 (1st Dist. Hamilton County 2001) ("Evans was unconstitutionally forced to choose between a substantial penalty and self-incrimination.").

[14]McKune v. Lile, 536 U.S. 24, 122 S. Ct. 2017, 153 L. Ed.2d 47 (2002).

[15]McKune v. Lile, 536 U.S. 24, 48-49, 122 S. Ct. 2017, 153 L. Ed.2d 47 (2002).

[16]Lefkowitz v. Turley, 414 U.S. 70, 77, 94 S. Ct. 316, 38 L. Ed. 2d 274 (1973).

[17]In re Billman, 92 Ohio App. 3d 279, 634 N.E.2d 1050 (8th Dist. Cuyahoga County 1993).

[18]In re Amanda W., 124 Ohio App. 3d 136, 140, 705 N.E.2d 724 (6th Dist. Lucas County 1997) ("The type of proceeding does not determine the availability of the privilege; rather, it turns upon whether the statement or admission is or may be inculpatory. . . . Furthermore, the privilege is self-executing, that is, it does not have to be expressly raised [in some circumstances]. Thus, if the state, expressly or by implication, imposes a penalty for the exercise of the privilege, the failure to assert the privilege is excused.").

any evidence derived from those answers in a subsequent criminal case against either one or both of them."[19]

Cross References

§ 1:4

Research References

Carlin, Baldwin's Ohio Practice, Merrick-Rippner Probate Law (6th ed.), Ch 107

§ 23:28 Impartial judge

Due process guarantees the right to an impartial judge. According to the United States Supreme Court, "A fair trial in a fair tribunal is a basic requirement of due process. Fairness of course requires an absence of actual bias in the trial of cases. But our system of law has always endeavored to prevent even the probability of unfairness."[1]

An issue of impartiality may arise when the same judge who decides the issue of transfer subsequently presides at an adjudicatory hearing. Evidence admissible at a transfer hearing may not be admissible at the adjudicatory hearing. For example, a social history may be considered at the transfer hearing but not at the adjudicatory hearing.[2] Accordingly, some juvenile court statutes preclude, over the objection of the child, the same judge from presiding at both the transfer and adjudicatory hearing.[3] Moreover, the California Supreme Court has written:

> [I]f the referee or judge who hears the issue of fitness [transfer] decides that the minor should be retained in the juvenile court, he may not thereafter properly preside at a contested hearing on the issue of jurisdiction. Basic principles of fairness underlying the Juvenile Court Law require that the minor be protected against premature resolution of the jurisdictional issue on the basis of incompetent background material adduced on the issue of amenability to juvenile court treatment.[4]

The IJA-ABA Standards also adopt this position.[5]

Nevertheless, one Ohio court has stated that a juvenile judge is not disqualified from presiding at an adjudicatory hearing by reason of the judge's involvement in a prior transfer hearing.[6] Judges are often exposed to inadmissible evidence, such as evidence excluded as a result of a motion to suppress,

---

[19]In re Amanda W., 124 Ohio App. 3d 136, 141, 705 N.E.2d 724 (6th Dist. Lucas County 1997). See also In re Stacey S., 136 Ohio App. 3d 503, 511, 1999-Ohio-989, 737 N.E.2d 92 (6th Dist. Lucas County 1999) ("We have held that a case plan which requires a parent to complete a course of treatment, admission to which requires him to admit that he is a sexual offender, is a violation of his right against self-incrimination protected by the Fifth Amendment of the Constitution of the United States and Article I, Section 10 of the Ohio Constitution. Here, however, the record reflects that appellant father did not complete the anger management and sexual abuse groups to which he was assigned because he either refused to attend or behaved so inappropriately that he was rejected. Accordingly, appellants' second assignment of error is not well-taken.") (citing In re Amanda W.); In re Knight, 135 Ohio App. 3d 172, 175, 733 N.E.2d 303 (8th Dist. Cuyahoga County 1999) (mother tested positive for cocaine; "When an allegation of neglect is made, a showing of fault on the part of the parents must be found. Appellant raised below the possibility of being charged with child endangering because of her testimony. Under Billman, this is sufficient to invoke a parent's Fifth Amendment privilege against self-incrimination.").

[Section 23:28]

[1]In re Murchison, 349 U.S. 133, 136, 75 S. Ct. 623, 99 L. Ed. 942 (1955).

[2]See Juv. R. 32.

[3]E.g., Tenn. Code Ann. § 37-1-134(f) (1984); Wyo. Stat. § 14-6-237(f) (1977) .

[4]Donald L. v. Superior Court, 7 Cal. 3d 592, 598, 102 Cal. Rptr. 850, 498 P.2d 1098 (1972).

[5]IJA-ABA Standards Relating to Transfer Between Courts 49 (1980) ("No matter how fair the waiver judge may be in subsequent proceedings, an impression of unfairness will exist.").

[6]In re Terry H., 1 O.B.R. 377 (C.P., Cuyahoga 1982).

and they are presumed capable of disregarding such evidence.[7] "A judge need not recuse himself on the basis that he acquired knowledge of the facts during a prior proceeding. What a judge learns in his judicial capacity, whether from pretrial proceedings, co-defendant pleas, or evidence presented in a prior case, is properly considered as judicial observations and creates no personal bias requiring recusal."[8] Moreover, refusal to accept a plea bargain is not evidence of trial court bias.[9]

In *In re Simons*,[10] the court of appeals ruled that ex parte communications between an Ohio and a Kentucky judge on procedural issues did not violate due process or violate the Code of Judicial Conduct. The court concluded that "communications regarding the status of other pending cases are essential to the fulfillment of the purposes of the [Uniform Child Custody Jurisdiction Act]. . . . [W]here there is no evidence that the trial judges exchanged evidence or conducted communications regarding the substantive issues of the pending cases, we cannot say there is a violation of any party's due process rights."[11]

§ 23:29 Speedy trial

RC 2151.28(A) requires the adjudicatory hearing to be scheduled no later than 72 hours after the complaint is filed[1] and to hold an adjudicatory hearing within 30 days in abuse, neglect, and dependency cases.[2] Juvenile Rule 29(A) provides that the adjudicatory hearing for a child in detention or shelter care must be held within 10 days of the filing of the complaint. The hearing, however, may be continued upon a showing of good cause.

Remedy. Juvenile Rule 29(A) does not specify a remedy for a violation of the 10-day rule. In *In re Therklidsen*,[3] a court of appeals held that dismissal was not an appropriate remedy. "In the absence of a specific statutory provision for a discharge constituting a bar to further prosecution, a provision requiring a trial within a certain period of time does not entitle the defendant to discharge."[4] In contrast, a different court in *State v. Newton*[5] held that Juvenile Rule 29(A)'s time limits were mandatory and that the proper

---

[7]See In re A., 65 Misc. 2d 1034, 319 N.Y.S.2d 691 (Fam. Ct. 1971) (The customary ground for disqualification of a judge is personal bias and not prior judicial exposure to the issues or parties.).

[8]In re Daniel E., 122 Ohio App. 3d 139, 140–41, 701 N.E.2d 408 (6th Dist. Sandusky County 1997) (juvenile judge presided over co-defendant's trial) (citing State v. D'Ambrosio, 67 Ohio St. 3d 185, 188, 1993-Ohio-170, 616 N.E.2d 909 (1993)).

[9]In re Daniel E., 122 Ohio App. 3d 139, 141, 701 N.E.2d 408 (6th Dist. Sandusky County 1997) ("[I]t is well settled that the decision of whether to accept a plea bargain rests within the sound discretion of the trial court.").

[10]In re Simons, 118 Ohio App. 3d 622, 693 N.E.2d 1111 (2d Dist. Montgomery County 1997).

[11]In re Simons, 118 Ohio App. 3d 622, 632, 693 N.E.2d 1111 (2d Dist. Montgomery County 1997). See also In re Disqualification of Floyd, 101 Ohio St. 3d 1215, 2003-Ohio-7354, 803 N.E.2d 816 (2003) (ex parte communication); In re Myers, 2004-Ohio-539, at ¶ 8, 2004 WL 231796 (Ohio Ct. App. 3d Dist. Seneca County) ("[A] trial court is permitted to question witnesses called by a party as long as the questions are relevant and the questioning is done impartially.").

[Section 23:29]
[1]1996 H.B. 274, eff. 8-8-96.

[2]Under certain circumstances, extensions are permitted. See also RC 2151.28(A)(1) (adjudicatory hearings in delinquency, unruly, and juvenile traffic offense cases shall be held in accordance with Juvenile Rules).

[3]In re Therklidsen, 54 Ohio App. 2d 195, 8 Ohio Op. 3d 335, 376 N.E.2d 970 (10th Dist. Franklin County 1977).

[4]In re Therklidsen, 54 Ohio App. 2d 195, 199, 8 Ohio Op. 3d 335, 376 N.E.2d 970 (10th Dist. Franklin County 1977).

[5]State v. Newton, 1983 WL 6836 (Ohio Ct. App. 6th Dist. Fulton County 1983).

remedy was dismissal without prejudice.[6] The court of appeals reaffirmed *Newton* in *In re Carlos O.*,[7] noting that the "time limitation set forth in Juv. R. 29(A) is a mandatory procedural requirement to which the juvenile court must strictly adhere."[8]

The 1994 amendment to Rule 29(A) provides that the failure to meet the time limits does not provide the "basis for contesting the jurisdiction of the court or the validity of any order of the court."[9]

Speedy trial statute. RC 2945.71(C) provides a statutory right to a speedy trial in criminal prosecutions.[10] That section, however, applies only to a "person against whom a charge of felony is pending." Based on this language, the Ohio Supreme Court has ruled the statute inapplicable to juveniles cases. According to the Court, the statute applies "only if and when the Juvenile Court relinquishes jurisdiction over the case and transfers it to the appropriate 'adult' court."[11]

The statute also does not apply to juvenile traffic offender cases.[12]

SYO cases. The speedy trial statute does apply to serious youthful offender cases.[13]

Constitutional right. In adult cases the Sixth Amendment guarantees the right to a speedy trial in criminal prosecutions.[14] The United States Supreme Court has held that four factors are relevant in determining whether this right has been violated: (1) the length of the delay, (2) the reason for the delay, (3) whether and when the defendant asserted the right to a speedy trial, and (4) whether the defendant has suffered actual prejudice from the delay.[15] The sole remedy for a denial of the constitutional right to a speedy trial is dismissal.[16]

Courts in other jurisdictions have held that the constitutional right to a

---

[6]See § 19:7, Time restrictions.

[7]In re Carlos O., 96 Ohio App. 3d 252, 254, 644 N.E.2d 1084 (6th Dist. Wood County 1994) (dismissing one delinquency complaint with prejudice).

[8]In re Carlos O., 96 Ohio App. 3d 252, 254, 644 N.E.2d 1084 (6th Dist. Wood County 1994).

[9]In Linger v. Weiss, 57 Ohio St. 2d 97, 11 Ohio Op. 3d 281, 386 N.E.2d 1354 (1979), the Ohio Supreme Court held that a juvenile court does not lose jurisdiction by failing to adhere to the time limits of Juv. R. 29(A).

[10]See generally Katz and Giannelli, Baldwin's Ohio Practice, Criminal Law (2d ed.), Ch 60.

[11]State ex rel. Williams v. Court of Common Pleas of Lucas County, 42 Ohio St. 2d 433, 435, 71 Ohio Op. 2d 410, 329 N.E.2d 680 (1975). Accord State v. Bickerstaff, 10 Ohio St. 3d 62, 461 N.E.2d 892 (1984); In re Corcoran, 68 Ohio App. 3d 213, 218, 587 N.E.2d 957 (11th Dist. Geauga County 1990); State v. Reed, 54 Ohio App. 2d 193, 194, 8 Ohio Op. 3d 333, 376 N.E.2d 609 (5th Dist. Coshocton County 1977) ("[T]he statutory speedy trial provisions for adults in Ohio do not apply to juveniles."); In re T.L.K., 2 Ohio Op.3d 324 (C.P., Ross 1976) (Juv. R. 29 controls over statute.). In re Milgrim, 2001 WL 112123 (Ohio Ct. App. 8th Dist. Cuyahoga County 2001).

Other courts have also held that the statute is triggered only after juvenile court jurisdiction has been transferred to the criminal courts. State v. Steele, 8 Ohio App. 3d 137, 456 N.E.2d 513 (10th Dist. Franklin County 1982); State v. Trapp, 52 Ohio App. 2d 189, 6 Ohio Op. 3d 175, 368 N.E.2d 1278 (1st Dist. Hamilton County 1977); State v. Young, 44 Ohio App. 2d 387, 73 Ohio Op. 2d 462, 339 N.E.2d 668 (10th Dist. Franklin County 1975).

See also State v. Robinson, 1983 WL 5630 (Ohio Ct. App. 8th Dist. Cuyahoga County 1983) (Right to speedy trial commences on date court makes pronouncement of transfer and not date the entry is journalized.).

[12]In re Washburn, 70 Ohio App. 3d 178, 181, 590 N.E.2d 855 (3d Dist. Wyandot County 1990).

[13]RC 2152.13(C)(1) ("open and speedy trial by jury in juvenile court"). See Serious Youthful Offenders Ch 5.

[14]U.S. Const. amend. 6 ("In all criminal prosecutions, the accused shall enjoy the right to a speedy and public trial."). The right to a speedy trial applies to state trials. Klopfer v. State of N. C., 386 U.S. 213, 87 S. Ct. 988, 18 L. Ed. 2d 1 (1967). See generally Katz and Giannelli, Baldwin's Ohio Practice, Criminal Law (2d ed.), Ch 59.

The Ohio Constitution also guarantees the right to a speedy trial (O. Const. art. I § 10).

[15]Barker v. Wingo, 407 U.S. 514, 92 S. Ct. 2182, 33 L. Ed. 2d 101 (1972). Accord Doggett v. U.S., 505 U.S. 647, 112 S. Ct. 2686, 120 L. Ed. 2d 520 (1992).

[16]Strunk v. U.S., 412 U.S. 434, 93 S. Ct. 2260, 37 L. Ed. 2d 56 (1973).

speedy trial applies to delinquency cases.[17] Although the Ohio Supreme Court has not yet addressed this issue,[18] one Ohio court has commented, "With respect to the constitutional right to a speedy trial, the rationale and progeny of *In re Gault* . . . suggests there is no distinction between adults and juveniles."[19]

Abuse, neglect, & dependency. RC 2151.28(A)(2) and Juvenile Rule 29(A) require an adjudicatory hearing to be held within 30 days of the filing of a complaint in abuse, neglect, and dependency cases. The hearing may be continued for 10 days to allow a party to obtain counsel or for 30 days to allow for service on all parties and any necessary evaluation. In either event, the hearing must be held within sixty days of the filing of the complaint. An inordinate delay in this context could give rise to a due process violation.[20]

Cross References
§ 19:7

§ 23:30   Right to a transcript

Juvenile Rule 37(A), as amended in 1996, requires a record of (1) adjudicatory and dispositional proceedings in abuse, neglect, dependency, unruly and delinquency cases; (2) permanent custody cases; and (3) proceedings before magistrates.[1] In all other proceedings, a record shall be made upon the motion of the court or the request of a party.[2] The term proceeding "includes the

---

[17]See R.D.S.M. v. Intake Officer, 565 P.2d 855 (Alaska 1977); In Interest of C. T. F., 316 N.W.2d 865 (Iowa 1982); State in Interest of H. M. T., 159 N.J. Super. 104, 387 A.2d 368 (App. Div. 1978); State v. Henry, 78 N.M. 573, 434 P.2d 692 (1967); In re Benjamin L., 92 N.Y.2d 660, 685 N.Y.S.2d 400, 404, 708 N.E.2d 156, 160 (1999) ("These same [speedy trial] concerns are even more compelling in the juvenile context. Minimizing the time between arrest and disposition in juvenile delinquency cases may be especially desirable because of the nature of adolescence. Indeed, a delay in the proceedings may undermine a court's ability to act in its adjudicative and rehabilitative capacities. . . . In light of the need for swift and certain adjudication at all phases of a delinquency proceeding, we conclude that the speedy trial protections afforded under the Due Process Clause are not for criminal proceedings alone and are not at odds with the goals of juvenile proceedings.") (citations omitted); Matter of Anthony P., 104 Misc. 2d 1024, 430 N.Y. S.2d 479 (Fam. Ct. 1980); Piland v. Clark County Juvenile Court Services, 85 Nev. 489, 457 P.2d 523 (1969). See also Butts, Speedy Trial in the Juvenile Court, 23 Am. J. Crim. L. 515 (1996).

[18]State ex rel. Williams v. Court of Common Pleas of Lucas County, 42 Ohio St. 2d 433, 435 n.4, 71 Ohio Op. 2d 410, 329 N.E.2d 680 (1975).

[19]State v. Reed, 54 Ohio App. 2d 193, 194, 8 Ohio Op. 3d 333, 376 N.E.2d 609 (5th Dist. Coshocton County 1977). See also In re Hester, 3 Ohio App. 3d 458, 446 N.E.2d 202 (10th Dist. Franklin County 1982).

[20]Cf. In re Omosun Children, 106 Ohio App. 3d 813, 818, 667 N.E.2d 431 (11th Dist. Trumbull County 1995) ("[T]wenty-eight months of limbo in a juvenile dispositional hearing is, in our opinion, a per se due process violation, barring extraordinary circumstances.").

[Section 23:30]

[1]In re Amos, 154 Ohio App. 3d 434, 436, 2003-Ohio-5014, 797 N.E.2d 568 (3d Dist. Crawford County 2003) ("Amos claims that the trial court erred by not making a record of the hearings. . . . The failure to make these records prevents the preparation of a transcript for appellate review. . . . Since the trial court did not make records of any of the adjudicatory or dispositional hearings at issue, the trial court abused its discretion."); In re Collins, 127 Ohio App. 3d 278, 280, 712 N.E.2d 798 (8th Dist. Cuyahoga County 1998) ("[S]ince no record was made, it is clear that the trial court failed to comply with the mandates of Juv.R. 37(A). . . . This matter is reversed.").

[2]Juv. R. 37(A) also provides that the recording "shall be taken in shorthand, stenotype, or by any other adequate mechanical, electronic, or video recording device." It is within the trial court's discretion to determine which method of recording shall be used. In re Glenn, No. 35352 (8th Dist. Ct. App., Cuyahoga, 1-20-77). However, if an electronic recording device malfunctions, the party's right to a transcript may be infringed. In re Roberts, No. 34232 (8th Dist. Ct. App., Cuyahoga, 11-13-75).

receiving of any admission or denial, as well as evidentiary hearings."[3] RC 2151.35 contains a comparable, but not identical, provision.[4] It requires recordings in permanent custody proceedings (RC 2151.414 and RC 2151.353). In addition, RC 2152.13(C)(1) requires a transcript in SYO cases. Juvenile Rule 29(B)(5) requires the court to inform parties who are not represented by counsel that they have the right, upon request, to a record of all proceedings at public expense if indigent.

Although the right to a transcript was raised in *Gault*, the Supreme Court declined to rule on this issue.[5] In a concurring and dissenting opinion, Justice Harlan expressed the view that a "written record, or its equivalent, adequate to permit effective review on appeal or in collateral proceedings" should be required as a matter of due process.[6]

In criminal cases, the United States Supreme Court has held, on equal protection and due process grounds, that an indigent is entitled to a free transcript if the state provides the right to appeal.[7] In *State ex rel. Heller v. Miller*,[8] the Ohio Supreme Court extended the right to a transcript to indigent parents in proceedings to permanently terminate parental rights.

In *State ex rel. Howard v. Ferreri*,[9] the juvenile court refused to file-stamp transcripts of permanent custody hearings and make them available at state expense to Howard or his attorney. Noting that the right to a transcript under *Heller* requires a showing of indigency[10] and the filing of an appeal,[11] the Ohio Supreme Court issued a writ of mandamus because (1) Howard had a clear legal right to a copy of the complete transcript, (2) the juvenile court had a clear legal duty to provide the transcript, and (3) Howard lacked an adequate remedy at law.[12]

Similarly, an Ohio court of appeals, citing due process and equal protection grounds, has held that an indigent child has a right to a transcript in transfer

---

See also In re Menich, No. 42727 (8th Dist. Ct. App., Cuyahoga, 3-26-81) (Local rules conditioning right to a transcript upon prepayment of costs are not inconsistent with Juv. R. 37 where they permit avoidance of costs by filing a poverty affidavit.).

See also § 34:9, Right to transcript.

[3]Staff Note (1996). Under the pre-1996 rule, the juvenile court was required to make a transcript only upon request. In re Wright, 88 Ohio App. 3d 539, 624 N.E.2d 347 (2d Dist. Montgomery County 1993). According to one court, this requirement did not violate due process or equal protection. In re Hannah, 106 Ohio App. 3d 766, 667 N.E.2d 76 (8th Dist. Cuyahoga County 1995).

[4]See In re Wyrock, No. 41305 (8th Dist. Ct. App., Cuyahoga, 6-5-80) (Juv. R. 37(A) supersedes RC 2151.35.).

[5]Application of Gault, 387 U.S. 1, 87 S. Ct. 1428, 18 L. Ed. 2d 527 (1967).

[6]Application of Gault, 387 U.S. 1, 72, 87 S. Ct. 1428, 18 L. Ed. 2d 527 (1967).

[7]Griffin v. Illinois, 351 U.S. 12, 76 S. Ct. 585, 100 L. Ed. 891, 55 A.L.R.2d 1055 (1956). See also Mayer v. City of Chicago, 404 U.S. 189, 92 S. Ct. 410, 30 L. Ed. 2d 372 (1971) (right to transcript in cases where a fine is imposed). See generally Katz and Giannelli, Baldwin's Ohio Practice, Criminal Law (2d ed.) § 80:6.

[8]State ex rel. Heller v. Miller, 61 Ohio St. 2d 6, 15 Ohio Op. 3d 3, 399 N.E.2d 66 (1980) (right to transcript based on United States and Ohio Constitutions' Due Process and Equal Protection Clauses). See also In re Hitchcock, 81 Ohio St. 3d 1222, 2000-Ohio-436, 689 N.E.2d 43 (1998).

[9]State ex rel. Howard v. Ferreri, 70 Ohio St. 3d 587, 1994-Ohio-234, 639 N.E.2d 1189 (1994).

[10]"The right to a free transcript pursuant to *Heller* hinges on the parent's indigency status; thus, a request for a transcript at state expense may be properly denied where the juvenile court finds that the party has adequate financial means to obtain the transcript." State ex rel. Howard v. Ferreri, 70 Ohio St. 3d 587, 590, 1994-Ohio-234, 639 N.E.2d 1189 (1994).

[11]State ex rel. Howard v. Ferreri, 70 Ohio St. 3d 587, 592, 1994-Ohio-234, 639 N.E.2d 1189 (1994) (finding no right to a transcript in one of the two cases because an appeal had not been filed).

[12]"[S]ince the right to a transcript under *Heller* applies only to state-initiated permanent custody cases, an indigent, noncustodial parent is not entitled to a transcript where temporary custody is given to the other parent." State ex rel. Howard v. Ferreri, 70 Ohio St. 3d 587, 591, 1994-Ohio-234, 639 N.E.2d 1189 (1994).

proceedings.[13] Courts in other jurisdictions have also ruled that juveniles have a constitutional right to a transcript.[14]

Cross References
§ 34:9
Research References
Carlin, Baldwin's Ohio Practice, Merrick-Rippner Probate Law (6th ed.), Ch 107

§ 23:31 Double jeopardy

The Fifth Amendment protects a criminal defendant from being put in jeopardy twice for the same offense.[1] The Double Jeopardy Clause consists of three separate guarantees: "It protects against a second prosecution for the same offense after acquittal. It protects against a second prosecution for the same offense after conviction. And it protects against multiple punishments for the same offense."[2]

In *Breed v. Jones*,[3] the United States Supreme Court held the Double Jeopardy Clause applicable to delinquency proceedings:[4]

> We believe it is simply too late in the day to conclude . . . that a juvenile is not put in jeopardy at a proceeding whose object is to determine whether he has committed acts that violate a criminal law and whose potential consequences include both the stigma inherent in such a determination and the deprivation of liberty for many years.[5]

According to the Court, jeopardy attached "when the Juvenile Court, as the trier of the facts, began to hear evidence."[6] *Breed* involved double jeopardy issues relating to transfer proceedings.[7]

The Court also addressed double jeopardy issues in *Swisher v. Brady*,[8] which involved the use of a master. The issue was whether the state's filing of exceptions to a master's proposals required the child to stand trial a second time, i.e., before the juvenile court judge. The Court held that the Maryland procedure involved in *Swisher* did not violate the Double Jeopardy Clause. The Court, however, emphasized several factors regarding the Maryland pro-

---

[13]State v. Ross, 23 Ohio App. 2d 215, 52 Ohio Op. 2d 311, 262 N.E.2d 427 (2d Dist. Greene County 1970).

[14]E.g., In re State in Interest of Aaron, 266 So. 2d 726 (La. Ct. App. 3d Cir. 1972). See generally Comment, Appellate Review for Juveniles: A "Right" to a Transcript, 4 Colum. Hum. Rts. L. Rev. 485 (1972); Comment, The Right of an Indigent Juvenile in Ohio to a Transcript at State Expense, 5 Akron L. Rev. 117 (1972).

[Section 23:31]

[1]U.S. Const. amend. 5 ("[N]or shall any person be subject for the same offence to be twice put in jeopardy of life or limb."). The Supreme Court has held that the Double Jeopardy Clause applies to state trials. Benton v. Maryland, 395 U.S. 784, 89 S. Ct. 2056, 23 L. Ed. 2d 707 (1969). See generally Katz and Giannelli, Baldwin's Ohio Practice, Criminal Law (2d ed.), Ch 72.

The Ohio Constitution also prohibits double jeopardy (O. Const. art. I § 10).

[2]North Carolina v. Pearce, 395 U.S. 711, 717, 89 S. Ct. 2072, 23 L. Ed. 2d 656 (1969).

[3]Breed v. Jones, 421 U.S. 519, 95 S. Ct. 1779, 44 L. Ed. 2d 346 (1975).

[4]See generally Applicability of double jeopardy to juvenile court proceedings, 5 A.L.R. 4th 234.

[5]Breed v. Jones, 421 U.S. 519, 529, 95 S. Ct. 1779, 44 L. Ed. 2d 346 (1975). *Breed* overruled several Ohio cases that had held the Double Jeopardy Clause inapplicable to juvenile cases on the grounds that these cases were civil and not criminal. See In re Mack, 22 Ohio App. 2d 201, 51 Ohio Op. 2d 400, 260 N.E.2d 619 (1st Dist. Hamilton County 1970); In re Whittington, 17 Ohio App. 2d 164, 46 Ohio Op. 2d 237, 245 N.E.2d 364 (5th Dist. Fairfield County 1969).

[6]Breed v. Jones, 421 U.S. 519, 531, 95 S. Ct. 1779, 44 L. Ed. 2d 346 (1975). See also Serfass v. U.S., 420 U.S. 377, 95 S. Ct. 1055, 43 L. Ed. 2d 265 (1975) (In a bench trial jeopardy attaches when the first witness is sworn.).

[7]For a discussion of this issue, see § 22:24, Double jeopardy.

[8]Swisher v. Brady, 438 U.S. 204, 98 S. Ct. 2699, 57 L. Ed. 2d 705, 25 Fed. R. Serv. 2d 1463 (1978).

cedure that were critical to its decision. First, under that procedure the prosecution is not given a "second crack" at winning its case in the proceeding before the juvenile judge: "The State presents its evidence once before the master. The record is then closed, and additional evidence can be received by the Juvenile Court judge only with the consent of the minor."[9] Second, the master's recommendations are not binding; only the juvenile court judge is authorized to enter a judgment.[10]

An issue raised by the dissent in *Swisher*, but not decided by the Court, focused on whether the Maryland procedure violated due process because the juvenile judge, who was the ultimate factfinder, did not personally conduct the trial. The Arizona Supreme Court has held that such a procedure violates due process.[11]

In *Illinois v. Vitale*,[12] a child was first prosecuted and convicted in criminal court for failure to reduce speed to avoid an accident. A petition was subsequently filed in juvenile court alleging involuntary manslaughter by reckless operation of a motor vehicle. Both the criminal prosecution and the juvenile petition were based on the same incident. The United States Supreme Court held that the test for determining whether two offenses are the same offense for purposes of the Double Jeopardy Clause is the same in criminal and juvenile cases. "The applicable rule is that where the same act or transaction constitutes a violation of two distinct statutory provisions, the test to be applied to determine whether there are two offenses or only one, is whether each provision requires proof of a fact which the other does not."[13] The Court, however, was uncertain whether a careless failure to slow is always a necessary element of manslaughter by automobile under state law and thus remanded the case to the state supreme court.

In *In re Gilbert*,[14] an Ohio appellate court held that the Double Jeopardy Clause precluded the prosecution from appealing a verdict in favor of a child after an adjudicatory hearing.[15] Such a postverdict appeal should be distinguished from a pretrial appeal. For example, Juvenile Rule 22(F) provides for the right of appeal by the prosecution where the juvenile court grants a motion to suppress evidence. This rule does not violate the double jeopardy provision because jeopardy has not yet attached[16] and such a ruling is not an acquittal.[17]

In *In re Williams*,[18] a juvenile was charged with felony theft based on prior adjudications for petit theft. The referee sua sponte declared a mistrial because of her own intervention in the examination of a witness concerning the prior adjudications. The appellate court ruled that the Double Jeopardy

[9]Swisher v. Brady, 438 U.S. 204, 216, 98 S. Ct. 2699, 57 L. Ed. 2d 705, 25 Fed. R. Serv. 2d 1463 (1978).

[10]Swisher v. Brady, 438 U.S. 204, 216, 98 S. Ct. 2699, 57 L. Ed. 2d 705, 25 Fed. R. Serv. 2d 1463 (1978). See also Magistrates Ch 24.

[11]Matter of Pima County, Juvenile Action, No. 63212-2, 129 Ariz. 371, 631 P.2d 526 (1981) (en banc) (Juvenile judge reversed referee's finding that evidence did not establish offense beyond a reasonable doubt.).

[12]Illinois v. Vitale, 447 U.S. 410, 100 S. Ct. 2260, 65 L. Ed. 2d 228 (1980).

[13]Brown v. Ohio, 432 U.S. 161, 166, 97 S. Ct. 2221, 53 L. Ed. 2d 187 (1977).

[14]In re Gilbert, 45 Ohio App. 2d 308, 74 Ohio Op. 2d 480, 345 N.E.2d 79 (9th Dist. Summit County 1974).

[15]See also In re Lee, 145 Ohio App. 3d 167, 169, 762 N.E.2d 396 (8th Dist. Cuyahoga County 2001) ("The court reached a final verdict in this case, and the state is statutorily precluded from appealing that verdict."; In re Hampton, 24 Ohio App. 2d 69, 53 Ohio Op. 2d 192, 263 N.E.2d 910 (8th Dist. Cuyahoga County 1970) (A juvenile court's overruling of a plea in bar on double jeopardy grounds is not a final appealable order.).

[16]Breed v. Jones, 421 U.S. 519, 531, 95 S. Ct. 1779, 44 L. Ed. 2d 346 (1975).

[17]See U.S. v. Scott, 437 U.S. 82, 98 S. Ct. 2187, 57 L. Ed. 2d 65 (1978).

For a discussion of the state's right to appeal, see § 34:8, State appeals.

[18]In re Williams, 31 Ohio App. 3d 241, 510 N.E.2d 832 (10th Dist. Franklin County 1986).

Clause precluded a retrial for felony theft but not for petit theft.

In *In re Phommarath*,[19] the referee recommended dismissal based on insufficient evidence. The trial court entered judgment, noting that it had carefully and independently reviewed the referee's report. Upon the prosecution's motion, which argued that the state had proved the offense beyond a reasonable doubt, the trial court reversed itself. The court of appeals found a double jeopardy violation. In its view, the "judgment entry adopting the referee's report was an adjudication of the factual and legal issues, effective and binding when approved and entered as a matter of record by the court pursuant to Juv.R. 40(D)(5). . . . [T]o permit the court to then vacate its judgment and enter an adjudication of delinquency violates principles of double jeopardy."

The court reserved judgment on whether Juvenile Rule 40(D)(7) is unconstitutional on its face. The "rule does not mandate the court to enter a judgment, interim or otherwise, before the period for objections expires. There is no constitutional impediment to the court's power to modify its decisions, provided such a modification does not subject an individual to double jeopardy. . . . Our decision is limited to the facts."[20] To support these comments, the court cited a New York case, *In re Lionel F.*,[21] which held that a juvenile court could entertain reargument and reverse its earlier ruling of dismissal while the proceeding was still pending and before the evidence was closed.

A different double jeopardy issue arose in *State v. Penrod*.[22] Four complaints were filed against the juvenile. Based on the juvenile's statement at the adjudicatory hearing, the referee found him delinquent on two of the complaints. The referee proceeded to disposition, and his recommendations were accepted by the court without objection. Within a week, the prosecution filed additional complaints and a motion to transfer. In response, the juvenile moved to dismiss charges that had been part of the prior adjudication, citing the Double Jeopardy Clause. The juvenile court granted the motion. The prosecution argued that jeopardy does not attach when a complaint against a juvenile is dismissed following an adjudicatory hearing. The appellate court disagreed because the referee proceeded to the adjudicatory hearing: "The juvenile's liberty was placed at risk on all four complaints when the court proceeded to determine issues. At that point, the juvenile court was no longer a mere advisor of rights, but a trier of fact. The adjudicatory hearing did not adjourn but continued to adjudication and disposition."[23]

Whether the Double Jeopardy Clause applies to nondelinquency cases remains uncertain. One court, however, has held that the double jeopardy guarantee bars delinquency proceedings based on conduct that was earlier

---

[19]Matter of Phommarath, 1995 WL 681213, at *10 (Ohio Ct. App. 10th Dist. Franklin County 1995). The court also wrote:

> [T]he court, which had the power to adjudicate appellant a delinquent minor and impose punishment, entered a judgment in favor of the accused. We are persuaded that, permitting the trial court to revisit and re-adjudicate the issues after it had independently reviewed the evidence and conclusions of the referee and entered judgment provided the prosecution the forbidden "second crack." Therefore, the trial court's adjudication of delinquency following its initial finding that the state had failed to prove beyond a doubt that appellant was guilty of carrying a concealed weapon violated appellant's rights under the Double Jeopardy Clause.

Matter of Phommarath, 1995 WL 681213, at *12 (Ohio Ct. App. 10th Dist. Franklin County 1995).

[20]Matter of Phommarath, 1995 WL 681213, at *13 (Ohio Ct. App. 10th Dist. Franklin County 1995). See also In re Carter, 123 Ohio App. 3d 532, 542, 704 N.E.2d 625 (4th Dist. Pickaway County 1997) ("the sufficiency-of-the evidence issue affects Carter's constitutional protection against double jeopardy"; evidence not sufficient to show constructive possession of cocaine).

[21]Matter of Lionel F., 76 N.Y.2d 747, 559 N.Y.S.2d 228, 558 N.E.2d 30 (1990).

[22]State v. Penrod, 62 Ohio App. 3d 720, 577 N.E.2d 424 (9th Dist. Summit County 1989).

[23]State v. Penrod, 62 Ohio App. 3d 720, 724, 577 N.E.2d 424 (9th Dist. Summit County 1989).

the subject of a "status" offender proceeding.[24]

Cross References
§ 1:4, § 22:24, § 23:30, § 34:8

§ 23:32 Juvenile & adult cases—Truancy

As a general rule, cases involving juveniles are heard "separately and apart" from the trials of cases against adults.[1] There is, however, an exception for habitual or chronic truancy cases. In these cases, the children's and parents' responsibilities are determined jointly.[2]

[24]In Interest of R. L. K., 67 Ill. App. 3d 451, 23 Ill. Dec. 737, 384 N.E.2d 531 (4th Dist. 1978). See also Garrison v. Jennings, 1974 OK CR 216, 529 P.2d 536 (Okla. Crim. App. 1974) (Jeopardy attached in status offender hearing based on criminal conduct.).

[Section 23:32]

[1]RC 2151.35(A)(1) .

[2]RC 2151.35(A)(1). See also Juv. R. 27(A)(2). See also McMullen, "You Can't Make Me!": How Expectations of Parental Control Over Adolescents Influence the Law, 35 Loy. U. Chi. L.J. 603 (2004).

Chapter 24

Magistrates

> **KeyCite®:** Cases and other legal materials listed in KeyCite Scope can be researched through West's KeyCite service on Westlaw®. Use KeyCite to check citations for form, parallel references, prior and later history, and comprehensive citator information, including citations to other decisions and secondary materials.

§ 24:1   Magistrates—Introduction
§ 24:2   Qualifications
§ 24:3   Order of reference
§ 24:4   Pretrial orders
§ 24:5   Hearings
§ 24:6   Recording of proceedings
§ 24:7   Magistrate's decision
§ 24:8   Objections
§ 24:9   Court action

§ 24:1   Magistrates—Introduction

Magistrates play an important role in the juvenile court system. In 1995, Juvenile Rule 40 was significantly amended, including the substitution of the term "magistrate" for "referee."[1] RC 2151.16 continues to use the term "referee."[2] The rule, however, also provides that "magistrates shall continue to be authorized to enter orders when authority to enter orders is specifically conveyed by statute or rule to magistrates or referees."[3]

§ 24:2   Qualifications

The rule and statute set forth several qualifications as well as limitations on the appointment of magistrates. After July 1995, magistrates must be attorneys admitted to practice in Ohio.[1] A magistrate appointed under Juvenile Rule 40 may also serve as a magistrate under Criminal Rule 19.

A person who has contemporaneous responsibility for working with or supervising children subject to juvenile court dispositional orders may not be

---

[Section 24:1]

[1]Juv. R. 40 is similar but not identical to Civ. R. 53, which governs the appointment and powers of magistrates in civil cases. See generally Klein, Darling and Terez, Baldwin's Ohio Practice, Civil Practice. See also Traf. R. 14 (magistrates in traffic cases).

[2]RC 2151.16 provides that referees shall have the usual powers of masters in chancery cases. In State v. Eddington, 52 Ohio App. 2d 312, 6 Ohio Op. 3d 317, 369 N.E.2d 1054 (3d Dist. Marion County 1976), the court held that neither of these provisions authorizes the appointment of a referee to hear a case involving an adult charged with child abuse, even though such a case is subject to juvenile court jurisdiction.

[3]Juv. R. 40(C)(3)(d). See also Staff Note (1995) ("If otherwise applicable, this rule is intended to apply to 'referees' as that term continues to exist in rule and statute."). The term magistrate is used in this text even when referring to the statute.

[Section 24:2]

[1]See Staff Note (1995) (Rule "permits those who are not attorneys and are presently serving as referees (prior to July 1, 1995) to continue to serve as magistrates.").

appointed a magistrate.[2] Where possible, a female "referee" must be appointed for the trial of females.[3]

§ 24:3 Order of reference

Juvenile Rule 40(C)(1) specifies the types of duties a magistrate may be assigned. These include: (1) pretrial or post-judgment motions or proceedings, (2) the trial of any case, except those requiring a jury, and (3) jury trials upon the unanimous written consent of the parties.[1] SYO proceedings[2] must be conducted by juvenile judges, not magistrates—with or without a jury.[3]

Generally, the magistrate's order or decision has the same effect whether the parties have consented or not.[4]

The order of reference may be for a specific case, a specific proceeding, or categories of motions, cases, or proceedings. The order may also specify the magistrate's powers, direct the magistrate to report only upon particular issues, perform particular acts, or receive and report evidence only. In addition, the order may fix the time and place for commencing and adjourning hearings and for the filing of the magistrate's decision or order. It may also authorize the magistrates to hear and recommend dispositions on official cases assigned to them.[5]

§ 24:4 Pretrial orders

Unless limited by the order of reference, Juvenile Rule 40(C)(3)(a) authorizes the magistrate to enter orders without court approval concerning: (1) pretrial proceedings under Civil Rule 16; (2) discovery proceedings under Civil Rules 26 to 37 and Juvenile Rules 24 to 25;[1] (3) appointment of counsel or guardian ad litem under Juvenile Rules 4 and 29(B)(4);[2] (4) taking children into custody under Juvenile Rule 6;[3] (5) detention hearings under Juvenile Rule 7;[4] (6) temporary orders under Juvenile Rule 13; (7) extension of temporary orders under Juvenile Rule 14; (8) summons and warrants under Juvenile Rule 15; (9) preliminary conferences under Juvenile Rule 21; (10) continuances under Juvenile Rule 23; (11) disposition orders under Juvenile Rule 27(B)(3);[5] (12) orders for social histories and physical and mental examinations under Juvenile Rule 32; and (13) other orders necessary to

---

[2]Juv. R. 40(A).

[3]RC 2151.16.

[Section 24:3]

[1]See Staff Note (1995) (Specific language was added, "consistent with the Court's ruling in Hartt v. Munobe (1993), 67 Ohio St.3d 3, that permits magistrates to conduct jury trials and, in order to obviate the consent issue in *Munobe*, requires that consent of the parties must be in writing.").

[2]See Serious Youthful Offenders Ch 5.

[3]Juv. R. 40(C)(1). Section 3 of Am. Sub. H.B. 393 states as follows: "The General Assembly hereby encourages the Supreme Court to amend the Juvenile Rules to do . . . the following: (A) make clear that while a Magistrate may not try or sentence a case involving an alleged or adjudicated SYO, a Magistrate may handle ministerial duties in that type of case, including arraignment and setting bail . . . ."

[4]Juv. R. 40(C)(1)(a)(iii) recognizes an exception for jury trial cases. See also Staff Note (1995) (Language added to make clear that with the exception for jury trials, "the consent of the parties to the order of reference is not required.").

[5]State ex rel. Nalls v. Russo, 96 Ohio St.3d 410, 2002-Ohio-4907, 775 N.E.2d 522 (2002).

[Section 24:4]

[1]See Discovery Ch 21.

[2]See § 23:3, Right to counsel; § 23:6, Guardian ad litem.

[3]See § 14:3, Custody, arrests, and stops.

[4]See § 19:5, Detention hearing.

[5]See Dispositional Hearings Ch 25.

regulate the proceedings.

All orders must be written, signed by the magistrate, identified as a magistrate's order, filed with the clerk, and served on all parties or their attorneys.[6]

Any person may appeal a pretrial order to the juvenile court by filing a "motion to set aside" within 10 days after the order is entered.[7] The motion must state the party's objections with particularity. The rule also provides for contempt in the magistrate's presence.[8]

§ 24:5 Hearings

Generally, a hearing before a magistrate is conducted in the same manner as a hearing before a juvenile court judge. Unless otherwise provided in the order of reference, the magistrate may (1) issue subpoenas for the attendance of witnesses and the production of documents; (2) rule on the admissibility of evidence;[1] (3) place witnesses under oath and examine them; and (4) call parties and examine them under oath.[2]

In contempt cases, the magistrate may issue an attachment for the alleged contemnor if necessary to obtain the contemnor's presence for a contempt hearing. The magistrate may also set bail for the contemnor in accordance with Criminal Rule 46.

The jurist is permitted to ask questions of witnesses called by one of the parties, as long as the questions are relevant and the questioning is done impartially.[3]

§ 24:6 Recording of proceedings

Juvenile Rule 40(D) requires all proceedings before magistrates to be recorded.

§ 24:7 Magistrate's decision

The magistrate is required to promptly hold proceedings necessary for decision of the referred matter. The magistrate's decision must be filed with the clerk, who is required to serve copies on the parties or their attorneys.[1] The magistrate is required to make findings of fact and conclusions of law only if (1) requested by a party under Civil Rule 52, (2) required by law, or (3)

---

[6]Juv. R. 40(C)(3)(e).

[7]Juv. R. 40(C)(3)(b).

[8]Juv. R. 40(C)(3)(c).

[Section 24:5]

[1]See In re Zindle, 107 Ohio App. 3d 342, 349, 668 N.E.2d 969 (9th Dist. Summit County 1995) ("A referee has discretion in the admission and exclusion of evidence, and his or her evidentiary decisions will not be reversed on appeal absent a clear abuse of discretion which materially prejudiced the objecting party.").

[2]Juv. R. 40(C)(2).

[3]In re Myers, 2004-Ohio-539, at ¶ 8, 2004 WL 231796 (Ohio Ct. App. 3d Dist. Seneca County 2004).

[Section 24:7]

[1]Prior to the 1995 amendment, "referees" issued reports; they did not render decisions. A body of case law developed on this subject. See In re Weimer, 19 Ohio App. 3d 130, 483 N.E.2d 173 (8th Dist. Cuyahoga County 1984) (Failure to provide juvenile with supplemental report is error.); Nolte v. Nolte, 60 Ohio App. 2d 227, 14 Ohio Op. 3d 215, 396 N.E.2d 807 (8th Dist. Cuyahoga County 1978) (Referee's report must contain a statement of facts forming the basis for the referee's recommendation.); In re Hobson, 44 Ohio L. Abs. 85, 44 Ohio L. Abs. 86, 62 N.E.2d 510, 512 (Ct. App. 2d Dist. [sic] Franklin County 1945) (The "findings and recommendations by the referee are required by statute to be in writing.").

required by the order of reference.[2] The magistrates findings and conclusions must "indicate conspicuously" that a party must make a timely and specific objection to the court's adoption of any findings and conclusions — or waive the issue on appeal.

§ 24:8 Objections

A party may file objections to the magistrate's decision within 14 days of filing—regardless of whether the court has adopted the decision.[1] If objections are filed, other parties may file their own objections within 10 days of the filing of the first objections.[2]

Objections must be specific, stating the grounds with particularity.[3] If the parties stipulate to the facts in writing, only errors of law may be the subject of objection.[4] An objection to a finding of fact must be supported with a transcript of all the evidence relevant to the objection. If a transcript is unavailable, an affidavit of the evidence is acceptable. Failure to object to the court's adoption of any finding of fact or conclusion of law waives the parties right to appeal on the issue.[5]

§ 24:9 Court action

The magistrate's decision becomes effective when adopted by and journalized by the juvenile court.[1] In a delinquency case, the journal entry triggers

---

[2]Juv. R. 40(E)(1) and Juv. R. 40(E)(2). If the Civ. R. 52 request is made after the magistrate's decision is filed, an amended decision including the findings and conclusions is required.

[Section 24:8]

[1]In In re Ross, 107 Ohio App. 3d 35, 667 N.E.2d 1012 (10th Dist. Franklin County 1995), the mother of an assault victim filed objections to the referee's report. The court of appeals found this procedure and the ensuing ex parte hearing improper. The court wrote:

> Quite simply, Anderson's status in this case was no more than that of mother of a state's witness; since Anderson was never properly made a party nor required to adhere to the formalities required of a party [e.g., failure to serve the delinquent], we view her "objections" as a nullity of no legal significance.
>
> In reviewing the improperly filed objections and conducting an ex parte hearing thereon, the judge allowed a nonparty witness to communicate extensively out of the presence of one of the parties, namely, the accused delinquent minor. This procedure raises significant questions regarding the appearance of unfairness of the proceedings.
>
> Given the judge's ultimate resolution of the objections filed on behalf of the state, there arguably exists an appearance that one party (the state) gained an unfair advantage over the opposing party (appellant) through an ex parte communication involving the decisionmaker regarding the substantive merits of the matter in controversy.

In re Ross, 107 Ohio App. 3d 35, 40–41, 667 N.E.2d 1012 (10th Dist. Franklin County 1995).

[2]Juv. R. 40(E)(3)(a). If a delayed request under Civ. R. 52 is made, the time period commences when the magistrate files the findings of fact and conclusions of law in the magistrate's amended decision.

[3]Juv. R. 40(E)(3)(b).

[4]Juv. R. 40(E)(3)(c).

[5]Juv. R. 40(E)(3)(d); In re Clemens, 2002-Ohio-3370, 2002 WL 1401663 (Ohio Ct. App. 11th Dist. Geauga County 2002); In re K.M., 2003-Ohio-5781, at ¶ 4, 2003 WL 22439756 (Ohio Ct. App. 9th Dist. Summit County 2003) (Mother "failed to file any objections to the magistrate's decisions. Because [she] failed to preserve any of these challenges to the findings of fact or conclusions of law of the magistrate, she is precluded from raising them on appeal . . . ."); In re Harper, 2003-Ohio-6666, 2003 WL 22927248 (Ohio Ct. App. 2d Dist. Montgomery County 2003) (The appellant failed to file objections with the trial court, and so has waived all but plain error.).

[Section 24:9]

[1]Juv. R. 40(E)(4)(a). Prior to the 1995 amendment, "referees" issued reports; they did not render decisions. The referee's report was not binding until approved and entered as a matter of record by the juvenile court judge. See In re Zakov, 107 Ohio App. 3d 716, 717, 669 N.E.2d 344 (11th Dist. Geauga County 1995) ("'[T]he adoption or rejection of the referee's report is not the matter which has been submitted to the court, rather the report is merely an additional resource at the court's disposal in determining the issues before it. This determination must sufficiently address those issues so that the parties may know of their rights and obligations by referring only to that document known as the judgment entry.'"); In re Fusik, No. 41569 (8th Dist. Ct.

double jeopardy protection.[2]

A journal entry signed by both the assigned judge and the magistrate who presided over the proceedings is not a "combination entry."[3] One court of appeals has ruled that such an entry is not in compliance with Juv. R. 40. "[T]he trial court must journalize a judgment that unequivocally orders the relief provided to the parties and cannot merely adopt or affirm the magistrate's decision."[4]

In the absence of written objections, the court may adopt the decision unless there is an error of law or other defect.[5]

If objections are filed, the court may adopt, reject, or modify the magistrate's decision, hear additional evidence, recommit the issue to the magistrate with instructions, or hear the matter itself.[6] A 1998 amendment requires the court to rule on objections.[7] In delinquency, unruly, or juvenile traffic offender cases, the court may hear additional evidence or hear the matter itself only with the consent of the child.[8] The court may refuse to consider additional evidence if the objecting party cannot demonstrate that this evidence could not have been produced with reasonable diligence for the magistrate's consideration.[9]

The court may adopt a magistrate's decision and enter judgment without

---

App., Cuyahoga, 6-12-80) (Juvenile court referee has no authority to enter a judgment.). One court had stated that "[r]eferees serve only in an advisory capacity and have no authority to render final judgments." In re Moorehead, 75 Ohio App. 3d 711, 720, 600 N.E.2d 778 (2d Dist. Montgomery County 1991). Another commented, "Although reports of referees may frequently be adopted by the trial court, the rule does not contemplate that the trial court rubber-stamp all reports by referees." In re Bradford, 30 Ohio App. 3d 87, 88, 506 N.E.2d 925 (10th Dist. Franklin County 1986).

The juvenile judge "has the responsibility to critically review and verify to its own satisfaction the correctness of the report." Sharpe v. Sharpe, 85 Ohio App. 3d 638, 643, 620 N.E.2d 916 (11th Dist. Lake County 1993). One opinion comments:

[B]ecause the report and judgment entry were entered at the same time, the trial judge could not possibly have made an independent analysis of the report. He merely "rubber stamped" it, a practice which has been severely condemned. . . . The trial court erred in failing to independently analyze the referee's report. We cannot condone such a practice.

Matter of Smith Children, 1990 WL 70926, at *6 (Ohio Ct. App. 12th Dist. Warren County 1990).

[2]See Matter of Phommarath, 1995 WL 681213 (Ohio Ct. App. 10th Dist. Franklin County 1995); § 23:31, Double jeopardy.

[3]In re D.N., 2004-Ohio-1106, 2004 WL 439965 (Ohio Ct. App. 8th Dist. Cuyahoga County 2004).

[4]In re D.N., 2004-Ohio-1106, at ¶ 15, 2004 WL 439965 (Ohio Ct. App. 8th Dist. Cuyahoga County 2004).

[5]In re Adams, 2003-Ohio-4112, at ¶ 5, 2003 WL 21783682 (Ohio Ct. App. 7th Dist. Mahoning County 2003) (In dicta, the Court commented "The mere adoption of a magistrate's decision without entering a judgment defining the rights and obligations of the parties is not a final order." The Court went on to resolve the case on the merits.)

[6]Juv. R. 40(E)(4)(b). See also In re Zindle, 107 Ohio App. 3d 342, 346, 668 N.E.2d 969 (9th Dist. Summit County 1995) ("Juv.R. 40(D)(2) and 40(D)(6) do not require that the trial court hold a hearing when objections and an affidavit about evidence have been filed. Further consideration is required, but a hearing is within the discretion of the court. We are not persuaded that the trial court did not consider appellant's objections and affidavit about evidence.").

[7]See Staff Note (1998) ("The amendment was made because some trial judges apparently had avoided ruling upon objections to magistrates' reports since the previous rule appeared to require only 'consideration' of the objections.").

[8]See Staff Note (1995) (The rule contains a "new provision that limits the court's power to hear additional evidence or hear the matter itself in certain situations thereby eliminating the double jeopardy issues raised in Swisher v. Brady, 438 U.S. 204, 98 S. Ct. 2699, 57 L. Ed. 2d 705, 25 Fed. R. Serv. 2d 1463 (1978)."). See also § 23:31, Double jeopardy.

[9]The former rule also did not require a hearing. In re Stall, 36 Ohio St. 2d 139, 65 Ohio Op. 2d 338, 304 N.E.2d 596 (1973); In re Swain, 68 Ohio App. 3d 737, 741, 589 N.E.2d 483 (11th Dist. Portage County 1991) ("[T]he appellant did not request an oral hearing and Juv.R. 40 does not mandate one.").

waiting for timely objections.[10] The filing of timely written objections, however, operates as an automatic stay of execution until the court disposes of the objections.

The court may also enter an interim order without waiting for objections "where immediate relief is justified."[11] The filing of objections does not stay an interim order. The order, however, may not extend for more than 28 days, unless for good cause shown the court extends the order for an additional 28 days.

Research References

Carlin, Baldwin's Ohio Practice, Merrick-Rippner Probate Law (6th ed.), Ch 107

---

[10]Juv. R. 40(E)(4)(c) .

[11]Juv. R. 40(E)(4)(c).

Chapter 25

Dispositional Hearings

> **KeyCite®:** Cases and other legal materials listed in KeyCite Scope can be researched through West's KeyCite service on Westlaw®. Use KeyCite to check citations for form, parallel references, prior and later history, and comprehensive citator information, including citations to other decisions and secondary materials.

§ 25:1   Dispositional hearings—Introduction
§ 25:2   Bifurcated hearings
§ 25:3   Judge or magistrate
§ 25:4   Time requirements
§ 25:5   Right to attend dispositional hearing
§ 25:6   Conduct of hearing
§ 25:7   Advisement of rights
§ 25:8   Burden of proof
§ 25:9   Evidence
§ 25:10   Social history & medical examinations
§ 25:11   Victim participation
§ 25:12   Transcripts
§ 25:13   Judgment & records
§ 25:14   Reasonable efforts determination—Abuse, neglect & dependency

§ 25:1   Dispositional hearings—Introduction

This chapter discusses the procedural issues that relate to juvenile court dispositional hearings. Dispositional case plans are examined in Ch 26. The requirements attending the different types of juvenile court dispositions are explored in subsequent chapters: delinquency (Ch 27), juvenile traffic offenses (Ch 28), unruliness (Ch 29), and neglect, abuse, and dependency (Ch 30).

§ 25:2   Bifurcated hearings

If the child is found to be within the jurisdiction of the court at the adjudicatory hearing, a dispositional hearing is subsequently held to determine what action should be taken concerning the child.[1]

Ohio law mandates that adjudication and disposition take place at bifurcated hearings.[2] Consideration of dispositional interests, including a de-

---

[Section 25:2]

[1]Juv. R. 2(M); RC 2151.35(B)(1). See In Matter of Davis, 1995 WL 723155 (Ohio Ct. App. 3d Dist. Marion County 1995).

[2]Juv. R. 29(E)(4), Juv. R. 34; In re Baby Girl Baxter, 17 Ohio St. 3d 229, 479 N.E.2d 257 (1985); In re Cunningham, 59 Ohio St. 2d 100, 13 Ohio Op. 3d 78, 391 N.E.2d 1034 (1979); In re Pieper Children, 74 Ohio App. 3d 714, 600 N.E.2d 317 (12th Dist. Preble County 1991); In re Vickers Children, 14 Ohio App. 3d 201, 470 N.E.2d 438 (12th Dist. Butler County 1983); Matter of Whiteman, 2 A.D.D. 386 (Ohio Ct. App. 6th Dist. Williams County 1993); Matter of Hodgkin, 1990 WL 235496 (Ohio Ct. App. 12th Dist. Preble County 1990); Matter of Parish, 1990 WL 68912 (Ohio Ct. App. 6th Dist. Lucas County 1990). But see Matter of Lannom, 1997 WL 761323 (Ohio Ct. App. 2d Dist. Clark County 1997), holding that any error resulting from combining the adjudicatory and dispositional hearings is waived if the parties fail to object to the procedure. See § 25:5, Right to attend dispositional hearing; § 30:8 to § 30:12, Permanent custody.

termination of the child's best interests, may not enter into the adjudicatory phase of the proceedings.[3] Those matters become a proper focus only when the emphasis has shifted to a consideration of the statutorily permissible alternatives. A finding of dependency, neglect, or abuse, which is at some point journalized, must precede the disposition of the case because there are different substantive inquiries to be undertaken in each phase with concomitant differences in evidence and standards of review.[4]

Although a bifurcated hearing process is required where permanent custody is sought at the initial disposition,[5] hearings on motions for permanent custody are considered dispositional hearings and need not be bifurcated.[6]

Furthermore, where the juvenile court hears some evidence on disposition during the adjudicatory phase but understands the distinction between the two stages, the court does not commit reversible error.[7] This is particularly so where the issues of dependency (adjudication) and custody (disposition) are so interrelated as to make it impossible to conduct a dependency hearing devoid of all dispositional aspects.[8]

Waiver. Although prejudice need not be shown in order to justify reversal where the hearings are not bifurcated,[9] it has been held that such error is waived if there is no objection to the combined hearings.[10]

§ 25:3 Judge or magistrate

The judge or magistrate who presided at the adjudicatory hearing must, if possible, preside at the dispositional hearing.[1] However, the failure of the parent to object to the dispositional hearing being conducted by a different

---

[3]In re Cunningham, 59 Ohio St. 2d 100, 13 Ohio Op. 3d 78, 391 N.E.2d 1034 (1979); In re Pitts, 38 Ohio App. 3d 1, 525 N.E.2d 814 (5th Dist. Knox County 1987); Matter of Whiteman, 2 A.D.D. 386 (Ohio Ct. App. 6th Dist. Williams County 1993); In re Knotts, 109 Ohio App. 3d 267, 671 N.E.2d 1357 (3d Dist. Mercer County 1996).

[4]Johnson, 1982 WL 8498 (Ohio Ct. App. 1st Dist. Hamilton County 1982); Bryant, 1982 WL 6001 (Ohio Ct. App. 12th Dist. Butler County 1982); In re Black, No. C-800021 (1st Dist. Ct. App., Hamilton, 1-28-81). See also In re Moore, No. CA291 (12th Dist. Ct. App., Preble, 5-20-81); In re Bowman, No. 79AP-798 (10th Dist. Ct. App., Franklin, 6-26-80); In re Brown, No. 3-CA-79 (5th Dist. Ct. App., Fairfield, 7-20-79); In re Darst, 117 Ohio App. 374, 24 Ohio Op. 2d 144, 192 N.E.2d 287 (10th Dist. Franklin County 1963); In re Baby Girl Baxter, 17 Ohio St. 3d 229, 479 N.E.2d 257 (1985); In re Pitts, 38 Ohio App. 3d 1, 525 N.E.2d 814 (5th Dist. Knox County 1987); In re Smart, 21 Ohio App. 3d 31, 486 N.E.2d 147 (10th Dist. Franklin County 1984); Moore v. Moore, 1991 WL 13905 (Ohio Ct. App. 4th Dist. Gallia County 1991); In Matter of Neighbors, 1993 WL 564218 (Ohio Ct. App. 5th Dist. Richland County 1993).

[5]In re Baby Girl Baxter, 17 Ohio St. 3d 229, 479 N.E.2d 257 (1985); In re Cunningham, 59 Ohio St. 2d 100, 13 Ohio Op. 3d 78, 391 N.E.2d 1034 (1979); In re Brofford, 83 Ohio App. 3d 869, 615 N.E.2d 1120 (10th Dist. Franklin County 1992). See also RC 2151.353(A)(4).

[6]Juv. R. 34(I). See § 31:4, Nature of proceedings.

[7]In re Bibb, 70 Ohio App. 2d 117, 24 Ohio Op. 3d 159, 435 N.E.2d 96 (1st Dist. Hamilton County 1980); In re Feiler, No. C-780549 (1st Dist. Ct. App., Hamilton, 10-17-79). See also In the Matter Of: Skaggs, 1981 WL 5904 (Ohio Ct. App. 4th Dist. Scioto County 1981).

[8]In re Kemp, No. 41320 (8th Dist. Ct. App., Cuyahoga, 6-26-80); In re Feldman, No. 34223 (8th Dist. Ct. App., Cuyahoga, 12-23-75).

[9]In re Vickers Children, 14 Ohio App. 3d 201, 470 N.E.2d 438 (12th Dist. Butler County 1983); In Matter of Parker, 1981 WL 6774 (Ohio Ct. App. 3d Dist. Van Wert County 1981). But see In re Feldman, No. 34223 (8th Dist. Ct. App., Cuyahoga, 12-23-75), and Matter of Parish, 1990 WL 68912 (Ohio Ct. App. 6th Dist. Lucas County 1990), which determined that prejudice must be shown.

[10]In re Guthrie, No. CA 6383 (2d Dist. Ct. App., Montgomery, 2-22-80); In re Feldman, No. 34223 (8th Dist. Ct. App., Cuyahoga, 12-23-75).

[Section 25:3]

[1]Juv. R. 34(B)(1); RC 2151.35(B)(2)(a).

judge constitutes waiver of any error resulting therefrom.[2] Moreover, where it is not possible for a magistrate to preside over both hearings, and the parties are not prejudiced by having different individuals preside over the adjudicatory and dispositional hearings, no error exists.[3]

§ 25:4 Time requirements

Abuse, neglect, & dependency cases. In abuse, neglect, and dependency proceedings, the date for the dispositional hearing must be scheduled by the court at the conclusion of the adjudicatory hearing.[1] The dispositional hearing may be held immediately after the adjudicatory hearing if all parties were served prior to the adjudicatory hearing with all necessary documents.[2]

Thirty-day rule. The dispositional hearing may not be held more than 30 days after the adjudicatory hearing is held.[3] It has been held that any error in setting the dispositional hearing beyond 30 days after the adjudicatory hearing, without objection, does not constitute a due process violation.[4] On the request of any party, the court may continue the dispositional hearing to enable a party to obtain or consult counsel.[5]

Ninety-day rule. However, the dispositional hearing in neglect, abuse, and dependency cases must be held within 90 days after the complaint was filed, and if the court fails to meet this time limit, it is required to dismiss the complaint without prejudice.[6] In interpreting this requirement, a trial court has held that it is mandatory to *conclude* both the adjudicatory and dispositional hearings no later than 90 days after the filing of the complaint.[7] However, the appellate courts do not agree, some courts holding that *commencement* of the dispositional hearing within 90 days is sufficient.[8] One court justified this interpretation by arguing that "any other conclusion would have been contrary to legislative intent to expedite hearings in child-

---

[2]In re Shampine, 1991 WL 232156 (Ohio Ct. App. 8th Dist. Cuyahoga County 1991); Hood v. Hood, 1991 WL 123045 (Ohio Ct. App. 9th Dist. Summit County 1991).

[3]In re Johnson, 106 Ohio App. 3d 38, 665 N.E.2d 247 (1st Dist. Hamilton County 1995).

[Section 25:4]
[1]RC 2151.28(B)(3).

[2]RC 2151.35(B)(1). Matter of Hart, 1998 WL 183863 (Ohio Ct. App. 8th Dist. Cuyahoga County 1998). Prior to the 1996 amendment to the statute (1996 H.B. 274, eff. 8-8-96), the statute required, under certain circumstances, a one-day delay between the adjudicatory and dispositional hearings. In 1994, Juv. R. 34(A) was amended to conform with the statute. Now that the statute has been amended, the statute and rule are in conflict. See § 1:8, Rules of Juvenile Procedure.

[3]RC 2151.35(B)(1); Juv. R. 34(A).

[4]In re Rodgers, 1990 WL 187334 (Ohio Ct. App. 6th Dist. Lucas County 1990). See Matter of Cass, 1995 WL 631650 (Ohio Ct. App. 12th Dist. Preble County 1995); In Matter of Velentine, 1995 WL 498958 (Ohio Ct. App. 5th Dist. Coshocton County 1995); In Matter of Taeovonni, 1995 WL 495564 (Ohio Ct. App. 5th Dist. Tuscarawas County 1995); Matter of Grimm, 1993 WL 544362 (Ohio Ct. App. 5th Dist. Tuscarawas County 1993).

[5]In re Rodgers, 1990 WL 187334 (Ohio Ct. App. 6th Dist. Lucas County 1990). See also RC 2151.28(B)(3); Juv. R. 34(A).

[6]RC 2151.35(B)(1); Juv. R. 34(A); In re Olah, 142 Ohio App. 3d 176, 177, 754 N.E.2d 1271 (9th Dist. Lorain County 2000) ("The language employed by the General Assembly indicates that the matter *shall* be dismissed if the dispositional hearing is held outside the juvenile court's ninety-day window. Moreover, juvenile matters demand prompt administration. This court concludes, therefore, that the statute requires a juvenile court to dismiss without prejudice, on its own motion, when it cannot hold a timely dispositional hearing, *i.e.*, within ninety days of the filing of a complaint."); In re Rodgers, 1990 WL 187334 (Ohio Ct. App. 6th Dist. Lucas County 1990). See also RC 2151.28(B)(3); Matter of Grimm, 1993 WL 544362 (Ohio Ct. App. 5th Dist. Tuscarawas County 1993); Matter of Chapman, 1998 WL 258418 (Ohio Ct. App. 11th Dist. Ashtabula County 1998).

[7]In re Gandarilla, No. 89JU-05-3985 (Juv., Franklin, 11-15-89).

[8]Matter of Dixon, 1992 WL 277966 (Ohio Ct. App. 6th Dist. Erie County 1992); In re Brown, 96 Ohio App. 3d 306, 644 N.E.2d 1117 (2d Dist. Montgomery County 1994); In re Gibson, 1994 WL 520842 (Ohio Ct. App. 8th Dist. Cuyahoga County 1994); In Matter of Davis, 1996 WL

custody cases, frustrated judicial process, and arguably amounted to withdrawal of due process rights of parties, particularly those of the child."[9]

Waiver. Other appellate courts have held that the 90-day requirement
may, under certain circumstances, be waived. Thus, a parent waives by
implication her right to have an abuse complaint dismissed upon grounds
that the dispositional hearing was not held within 90 days after the filing of
the complaint where she did not move for dismissal at a time when it was
within her right to do so, but instead moved for a continuance, and then on
the next hearing date moved for dismissal when it became obvious that another continuance would not be granted.[10] Other appellate courts have held
that absent express statutory language divesting the juvenile court of jurisdiction when it fails to adhere to the time limits of RC 2151.28 and RC
2151.35, the jurisdictional grant to the juvenile court is not defeated by the
lapse of time or the failure to meet the time requirements.[11] Thus, a writ of
prohibition would not lie where a third dependency action is filed after the
court had failed to comply with the 90-day requirement in two previous
dependency actions.[12]

It has also been held that Civil Rule 41(A)(1), governing voluntary dismiss-
als in civil cases, is not applicable to a juvenile court custody proceeding
which is voluntarily dismissed due to the impending 90-day statutory
deadline.[13] Thus, a second notice of dismissal of a neglect, dependency, or
abuse complaint does not operate as an adjudication on the merits.[14]

Delinquency, unruly, & traffic cases. In all other cases (e.g., delinquency, unruly, and traffic cases), this hearing may be conducted either immediately after the adjudicatory hearing or at a later date,[15] and the 90-day
requirement does not apply.[16] If the dispositional hearing is held immediately
after the adjudicatory hearing, a party may request that the hearing be
continued for a reasonable time to obtain or consult counsel.[17] Where a party
does not request a continuance, the court may proceed immediately to
disposition.[18] Moreover, where a county children services board is a party,
the request for a continuance must be made through counsel, and not by a

---

752861 (Ohio Ct. App. 5th Dist. Stark County 1996); In re White, 1999 WL 43321 (Ohio Ct. App.
8th Dist. Cuyahoga County 1999).

[9]In re Brown, 96 Ohio App. 3d 306, 644 N.E.2d 1117 (2d Dist. Montgomery County 1994).

[10]In re Kutzli, 71 Ohio App. 3d 843, 595 N.E.2d 1026 (3d Dist. Paulding County 1991). See
also Hood v. Hood, 1991 WL 123045 (Ohio Ct. App. 9th Dist. Summit County 1991); In Matter of
Keller, 1994 WL 695338 (Ohio Ct. App. 8th Dist. Cuyahoga County 1994); In Matter of N.B.,
1996 WL 174546 (Ohio Ct. App. 12th Dist. Butler County 1996); Matter of Cass, 1995 WL
631650 (Ohio Ct. App. 12th Dist. Preble County 1995); Matter of George, 1995 WL 399137 (Ohio
Ct. App. 12th Dist. Brown County 1995); In Matter of Price, 1997 WL 126833 (Ohio Ct. App. 3d
Dist. Marion County 1997); In Matter of N.B., 1996 WL 174546 (Ohio Ct. App. 12th Dist. Butler
County 1996); In Matter of Bailey D., 1998 WL 196287 (Ohio Ct. App. 6th Dist. Lucas County
1998); In re Jessica M. B., 2004-Ohio-1040, 2004 WL 413307 (Ohio Ct. App. 6th Dist. Ottawa
County 2004).

[11]State ex rel. Howard v. Ferreri, No. 66559 (8th Dist. Ct. App., Cuyahoga, 2-10-94); In Matter of Keller, 1994 WL 695338 (Ohio Ct. App. 8th Dist. Cuyahoga County 1994); In Matter of
Bailey D., 1998 WL 196287 (Ohio Ct. App. 6th Dist. Lucas County 1998).

[12]State ex rel. Howard v. Ferreri, No. 66559 (8th Dist. Ct. App., Cuyahoga, 2-10-94); In Matter of Keller, 1994 WL 695338 (Ohio Ct. App. 8th Dist. Cuyahoga County 1994). See In re Scott,
1995 WL 476200 (Ohio Ct. App. 12th Dist. Butler County 1995).

[13]In Matter of Pritt, 1996 WL 132250 (Ohio Ct. App. 5th Dist. Stark County 1996).

[14]In Matter of Jones, 1996 WL 724757 (Ohio Ct. App. 9th Dist. Lorain County 1996).

[15]RC 2151.35(A); Juv. R. 34(A). See Juv. R. 29(F)(2)(a) to Juv. R. 29(F)(2)(d).

[16]Juv. R. 34(A).

[17]Juv. R. 34(A).

[18]In re Howell, No. 79-CA-16 (5th Dist. Ct. App., Coshocton, 1-31-80); In re Bolden, 37 Ohio
App. 2d 7, 66 Ohio Op. 2d 26, 306 N.E.2d 166 (3d Dist. Allen County 1973); In Matter of
Johnson, 1995 WL 229118 (Ohio Ct. App. 8th Dist. Cuyahoga County 1995).

nonattorney caseworker.[19]

Rescheduling. If the juvenile court decides to schedule the dispositional hearing at a later date, such hearing must be conducted within six months of the adjudicatory hearing.[20] However, the Ohio Supreme Court has held in *Linger v. Weiss*[21] that the juvenile court does not lose jurisdiction by failing to adhere to the time limits set forth in Juvenile Rule 34(A). The court in *Linger* reasoned that since the Ohio Rules of Juvenile Procedure may not extend or limit the jurisdiction of the juvenile court,[22] a procedural violation has no effect on jurisdictional issues, which are governed by statutory law. Because almost three years had elapsed since the adjudicatory hearing and no dispositional hearing had ever been scheduled,[23] the court relied on Juvenile Rule 34, rather than Juvenile Rule 29(F)(2)(b), in reaching its decision. The same outcome would have resulted if the dispositional hearing had been held in conformity with Juvenile Rule 34(A) but after the six-month limit of Juvenile Rule 29(F)(2)(b) .[24] Where an untimely delay occurs between the adjudicatory and dispositional hearings, a party's only recourse is to file a complaint for a writ of procedendo[25] or mandamus,[26] rather than filing an appeal[27] or a writ of habeas corpus.[28]

Cross References
§ 19:7, § 25:5, § 30:10 to § 30:12, § 33:4

§ 25:5 Right to attend dispositional hearing

In neglect, dependency, and abuse cases the child's attendance may be excused,[1] but it appears that the child's presence is required in delinquency, unruly, and juvenile traffic offender dispositional hearings.[2]

Waiver. A trial court has held that a juvenile waived his right to be present at a delinquency dispositional hearing by blatantly disregarding it after receiving adequate notice.[3]

Victims. RC 2930.09[4] recognizes the right of a victim[5] to be present whenever an alleged juvenile offender is present during any on the record stage of the case, unless the court determines that exclusion of the victim is necessary to protect the juvenile's right to a fair delinquency hearing. At the

---

[19]In re Lawson, 98 Ohio App. 3d 456, 648 N.E.2d 889 (10th Dist. Franklin County 1994).

[20]Juv. R. 29(F)(2)(b).

[21]Linger v. Weiss, 57 Ohio St. 2d 97, 11 Ohio Op. 3d 281, 386 N.E.2d 1354 (1979).

[22]Juv. R. 44.

[23]There was some question as to whether an adjudicatory hearing had even been held. For discussion of this issue, see § 23:29, Time restrictions.

[24]In re Fusik, No. 41569 (8th Dist. Ct. App., Cuyahoga, 6-12-80).

[25]See footnote 5 of the Supreme Court's decision in Linger v. Weiss, 57 Ohio St. 2d 97, 11 Ohio Op. 3d 281, 386 N.E.2d 1354 (1979).

[26]In re Fusik, No. 41569 (8th Dist. Ct. App., Cuyahoga, 6-12-80); Matter of Chapman, 1998 WL 258418 (Ohio Ct. App. 11th Dist. Ashtabula County 1998).

[27]In re Fusik, No. 41569 (8th Dist. Ct. App., Cuyahoga, 6-12-80).

[28]Linger v. Weiss, 57 Ohio St. 2d 97, 11 Ohio Op. 3d 281, 386 N.E.2d 1354 (1979).

[Section 25:5]
[1]Juv. R. 27(A).

[2]See Matter of James J., 1995 WL 283884 (Ohio Ct. App. 6th Dist. Huron County 1995); In re R.W., 2003-Ohio-401, 2003 WL 194771 (Ohio Ct. App. 8th Dist. Cuyahoga County 2003) (A juvenile has the right to be present at a hearing whenever his sentence is changed from the one stated at disposition.).

[3]In re Jason R., 77 Ohio Misc. 2d 37, 666 N.E.2d 666 (C.P. 1995).

[4]This statute was enacted pursuant to the Victims' Rights provision of the Ohio Constitution. O. Const. art. I § 10a.

[5]RC 2930.02 provides a procedure for the designation of a victim's representative, who is authorized to exercise the victim's rights under RC Ch. 2930.

victim's request, the victim has the right to be accompanied by an individual to provide support to the victim, unless the court determines that exclusion of the individual is necessary to protect the juvenile's right to a fair delinquency hearing.

Public & press. The general public may be excluded.[6]

§ 25:6 Conduct of hearing

The dispositional hearing in children's cases shares certain aspects with the adjudicatory hearing. For example, the court may conduct a dispositional hearing in an informal manner and may adjourn the hearing from time to time.[1]

§ 25:7 Advisement of rights

Commencement of hearing. Some appellate courts have determined that at the commencement of the dispositional hearing the court is not required to reiterate the relevant rights enumerated in Juvenile Rule 29(B) which apply to the adjudicatory hearing.[1] However, other courts of appeals have held that RC 2151.352 mandates the juvenile court to advise the parties of their right to counsel at the dispositional hearing.[2]

Conclusion of hearing. At the conclusion of the hearing, the court must advise the child of his right to record expungement (in delinquency, unruly, and juvenile traffic offender cases) and, where any part of the proceeding was contested, the court must advise the parties of their right to appeal.[3] However, failure of the court to advise the child of his or her right to expungement[4] or appeal[5] does not constitute reversible error where no prejudice is shown.

§ 25:8 Burden of proof

The standard of proof at the adjudicatory hearing is proof beyond a reasonable doubt or clear and convincing evidence.[1] The standard of proof at the dispositional portion of the proceedings for permanent custody[2] and planned permanent living arrangement is clear and convincing evidence.[3] The Revised Code and the Juvenile Rules are silent as to the standard of proof in other

---

[6]In re T.R., 52 Ohio St. 3d 6, 556 N.E.2d 439 (1990); In re D.R., 63 Ohio Misc. 2d 273, 624 N.E.2d 1120 (C.P. 1993); In re N.H., 63 Ohio Misc. 2d 285, 626 N.E.2d 697 (C.P. 1992). See § 23:11, Public trials; gag orders.

[Section 25:6]
[1]Juv. R. 27(A).

[Section 25:7]
[1]In Matter of Copeland, 1995 WL 453422 (Ohio Ct. App. 11th Dist. Ashtabula County 1995); In re Burton, 1997 WL 473099 (Ohio Ct. App. 8th Dist. Cuyahoga County 1997).

[2]In re Johnson, 106 Ohio App. 3d 38, 665 N.E.2d 247 (1st Dist. Hamilton County 1995); In re Fambro, 1997 WL 165427 (Ohio Ct. App. 2d Dist. Clark County 1997).

[3]Juv. R. 34(J).

[4]In re Haas, 45 Ohio App. 2d 187, 74 Ohio Op. 2d 231, 341 N.E.2d 638 (5th Dist. Stark County 1975). See In re Hairston, 1996 WL 465249 (Ohio Ct. App. 10th Dist. Franklin County 1996), in which the court of appeals affirmed the juvenile court but remanded the matter to the juvenile court to bring the child back to the court to properly advise him of his right to expungement.

[5]In Matter of Hendricks, 1996 WL 202856 (Ohio Ct. App. 11th Dist. Ashtabula County 1996); Matter of Holtgreven, 1995 WL 368841 (Ohio Ct. App. 3d Dist. Hancock County 1995); In re Hairston, 1996 WL 465249 (Ohio Ct. App. 10th Dist. Franklin County 1996).

[Section 25:8]
[1]Juv. R. 29(E)(4); RC 2151.35(A).
[2]RC 2151.353(A)(4).
[3]RC 2151.353(A)(5).

cases.[4]

§ 25:9 Evidence

Applicability of Ohio Rules of Evidence. Although the Ohio Rules of Evidence apply to juvenile court proceedings,[1] their applicability at the dispositional stage is somewhat limited. Evidence Rule 101(C)(6) provides that the evidence rules are inapplicable in "proceedings in which other rules prescribed by the supreme court govern matters relating to evidence." Both the rules[2] and the statutes[3] governing the procedure for the dispositional hearing in children's cases permit the court to admit any evidence that is material and relevant, including, but not limited to, hearsay, opinion, and documentary evidence.[4] Thus, these types of evidence are properly admitted at dispositional hearings without the restrictions imposed by Evidence Rule 802 and Articles VII and IX of the Rules of Evidence.

However, the Rules of Evidence do apply in hearings on motions for permanent custody, even though such hearings are considered dispositional in nature.[5] Moreover, an appellate court has held that although Juvenile Rule 34(I) refers to "motions" and not to "complaints," in light of the gravity of permanent custody proceedings, the Rules of Evidence apply to any permanent custody dispositional hearing.[6]

Oath requirement. It has been held that the evidence which is admissible in dispositional hearings must be in the form of sworn testimony, despite the informal nature of such hearings.[7]

Hearsay. The nature of hearsay evidence that is admissible includes the report of a guardian ad litem,[8] the contents of a social history or report of a mental or physical examination ordered under Juvenile Rule 32,[9] testimony regarding a child's drug problem which allegedly contributed to the child's parole violation,[10] allegations of sexual conduct between parents and their children,[11] and evidence as to whether a parent had obtained an evaluation for detoxification as required by a comprehensive reunification plan (case

---

[4]In re Willmann, 24 Ohio App. 3d 191, 493 N.E.2d 1380 (1st Dist. Hamilton County 1986) cites both RC 2151.353(A) and Juv. R. 29(E)(4) for the proposition that the standard of proof at disposition is preponderance of the evidence. However, Juv. R. 29(E) discusses standards of proof in adjudicatory hearings only. Juv. R. 29(F) which discusses dispositional proceedings is silent as to the standard of proof.

[Section 25:9]

[1]Evid. R. 101(A). See § 23:14, Rules of evidence.

[2]Juv. R. 34(B)(2).

[3]RC 2151.35(B)(2).

[4]See In Matter of Kennedy, 1995 WL 495816 (Ohio Ct. App. 5th Dist. Guernsey County 1995); Matter of Lamar L., 1995 WL 112903 (Ohio Ct. App. 6th Dist. Lucas County 1995).

[5]Juv. R. 34(B)(2), Juv. R. 34(I); In re Mack, 148 Ohio App. 3d 626, 629-30, 2002-Ohio-4161, 774 N.E.2d 1243 (3d Dist. Crawford County 2002) ("[T]he Rules of Evidence applied during the permanent custody hearing. The Rules of Evidence prohibit the use of hearsay . . . . The report of the psychological evaluation contained the opinion of Dr. Don McIntire, the psychologist who examined the appellant, yet he did not testify at the permanent custody hearing. The report was offered in evidence to aid in proving that the appellant was not a suitable caretaker for the children, and, as such, constituted inadmissible hearsay."); Matter of Antonio M., 1997 WL 525092 (Ohio Ct. App. 6th Dist. Lucas County 1997).

[6]In Matter of Davon B., 1997 WL 243574 (Ohio Ct. App. 6th Dist. Lucas County 1997).

[7]In re Ramsey Children, 102 Ohio App. 3d 168, 656 N.E.2d 1311 (5th Dist. Stark County 1995); Matter of Deehan, 1995 WL 560870 (Ohio Ct. App. 10th Dist. Franklin County 1995); Matter of Fleming, 1993 WL 277186 (Ohio Ct. App. 8th Dist. Cuyahoga County 1993).

[8]Matter of Hogan, 1990 WL 178092 (Ohio Ct. App. 6th Dist. Lucas County 1990).

[9]Matter of Crose, 1982 WL 3824 (Ohio Ct. App. 2d Dist. Darke County 1982); Matter of Gilbert, 1990 WL 25084 (Ohio Ct. App. 3d Dist. Marion County 1990); In re Lovejoy, 1998 WL 114400 (Ohio Ct. App. 9th Dist. Lorain County 1998).

[10]Matter of Holewinski, 1993 WL 155636 (Ohio Ct. App. 6th Dist. Lucas County 1993).

[11]In re Smith, 77 Ohio App. 3d 1, 601 N.E.2d 45 (6th Dist. Ottawa County 1991).

plan).[12] However, the admissibility of hearsay evidence at a dispositional hearing is not absolute. It is within the discretion of the court to determine whether to admit hearsay, and the evidentiary rules of competency and relevancy (Evidence Rules 601, 602, 401, 402, and 104) remain in force.[13]

Cross-examination. Evidence Rule 611(B), governing cross-examination of witnesses, is superseded by RC 2151.35(B)(2)(c) and Juvenile Rule 34(B)(3), which prohibit the cross-examination of medical examiners and investigators who prepare a social history, except on consent of all the parties or the court.[14]

Rebuttal evidence. In *In re Sadiku*,[15] the court of appeals found a due process violation where the appellant was precluded from offering evidence to rebut the guardian ad litem's statement. The court of appeals noted that RC 2151.35(B)(2)(c) permits a party to dispute "any information contained in the social history or other reports that may be used by the court in determining disposition."[16]

§ 25:10   Social history & medical examinations

Inspection. If a social history is prepared or a mental or physical examination is conducted prior to the dispositional hearing, counsel is entitled to inspect the contents of the history or report a reasonable time before the hearing.[1] For good cause shown, the court may deny inspection or may limit its scope to specified portions of the history or report and may order that its contents not be disclosed to specified persons. The court must state its reasons for denial or limitation of inspection or disclosure to counsel.[2] It has been held that the ordering of a psychological assessment and evaluation prior to commitment is within the sound discretion of the juvenile court.[3]

Rebuttal. Any party may offer evidence supplementing, explaining, or disputing the information contained in the social history or other reports utilized by the court at disposition.[4] However, it has been held that an addendum to a psychological report offered by a probation officer was admis-

---

[12]Matter of Stertzbach, 1990 WL 52454 (Ohio Ct. App. 5th Dist. Stark County 1990).

[13]RC 2151.35(B)(2)(b); Juv. R. 34(B)(2); Matter of Seymour, 1993 WL 49263 (Ohio Ct. App. 4th Dist. Hocking County 1993); In Matter of Spaulding, 1993 WL 115934 (Ohio Ct. App. 6th Dist. Lucas County 1993); In re Stanley, 1993 WL 512502 (Ohio Ct. App. 10th Dist. Franklin County 1993).

[14]See also In re Guthrie, No. CA 6383 (2d Dist. Ct. App., Montgomery, 2-22-80), holding that where the adjudicatory and dispositional hearings were combined, a parent had a right to call as a witness a psychologist who had prepared a report.

[15]In re Sadiku, 139 Ohio App. 3d 263, 268, 743 N.E.2d 507 (9th Dist. Summit County 2000) ("[I]n light of the most serious nature of these proceedings, this court finds that the trial court abused its discretion and violated due process in denying appellant the opportunity to rebut the statements of the guardian ad litem.").

[16]In re Sadiku, 139 Ohio App. 3d 263, 268, 743 N.E.2d 507 (9th Dist. Summit County 2000) ("The record before this court discloses that appellant requested the opportunity to present rebuttal testimony specifically as to the statements of the guardian ad litem regarding the conditions of the house and living situation as well as the statements demeaning Ms. Cook's own efforts to go back to school. Significantly, these matters were not contained in the guardian ad litem's written report and were not previously addressed by Ms. Cook in her earlier testimony. Therefore, they are properly subject to rebuttal.").

[Section 25:10]

[1]Juv. R. 32(C); Matter of Crose, 1982 WL 3824 (Ohio Ct. App. 2d Dist. Darke County 1982). See § 21:6, Social history report.

[2]Juv. R. 32(C).

[3]In re Nunn, 1995 WL 768544 (Ohio Ct. App. 5th Dist. Morgan County 1995).

[4]Juv. R. 34(B)(3). See also In re Sadiku, 139 Ohio App. 3d 263, 268, 743 N.E.2d 507 (9th Dist. Summit County 2000) (due process violation where the appellant was precluded from offering rebuttal evidence to guardian ad litem's statement; the trial court did not consider the statement "evidence" but court of appeals disagreed, noting that RC 2151.35(B)(2)(c) permits a party to dispute "any information contained in the social history or other reports that may be used by

sible at a delinquency dispositional hearing, even though the children services board with temporary custody of the delinquent child was not provided an opportunity to obtain an expert to assist the board in interpreting and rebutting the report.[5] The court reasoned that the addendum did not change the psychologist's initial recommendation, and thus its admission was not erroneous, an abuse of discretion, or prejudicial.[6]

§25:11 Victim participation

Victim impact statement. If a child is adjudicated a delinquent for a felony or offense of violence, the court is required to order, prior to disposition, preparation of a victim impact statement.[1] The court is also required to consider the statement in making its disposition.[2]

Victim statement. Before disposition is imposed in a delinquency case, the victim may make a statement.[3] Written statements may be given to the juvenile or counsel. The court may redact any information contained in a written statement that is not relevant to and will not be considered in the disposition. The statement is confidential and not a public record. The court is required to consider the statement along with other factors in making the disposition.[4] The court, however, may not rely on new material facts unless it continues the dispositional hearing or takes other appropriate action to allow the juvenile an adequate opportunity to respond to the new material.

§25:12 Transcripts

Juvenile Rule 37 requires a record in dispositional proceedings in abuse, neglect, dependent, unruly, and delinquent cases and permanent custody cases.[1]

Statutory requirements are comparable; a record of all testimony and other oral proceedings is required in all cases where permanent custody of the child may be granted at the original dispositional hearing (RC 2151.353(A)(4)) or pursuant to a motion for permanent custody (RC 2151.414), and in any other proceedings a record must be made upon request.[2] The denial of a request for a court reporter is not prejudicial error, since alternative methods of reporting trial proceedings, including a full narrative statement based on Appellate Rule 9(C), are permissible if they place before the appellate court an equivalent report of the events at trial.[3]

§25:13 Judgment & records

Seven-day rule. RC 2151.35(B)(3) and Juvenile Rule 34(C) provide that within seven days of the conclusion of the dispositional hearing, the court

---

the court in determining disposition"); In re Simon, No. CA1011 (2d Dist. Ct. App., Darke, 10-15-80).

[5]In re Lawson, 98 Ohio App. 3d 456, 648 N.E.2d 889 (10th Dist. Franklin County 1994).

[6]In re Lawson, 98 Ohio App. 3d 456, 648 N.E.2d 889 (10th Dist. Franklin County 1994).

[Section 25:11]
[1]RC 2152.19(D).
[2]RC 2152.19(D).
[3]RC 2930.14(A).
[4]RC 2930.14(B).

[Section 25:12]
[1]Juv. R. 37(A); In re Solis, 124 Ohio App. 3d 547, 706 N.E.2d 839 (8th Dist. Cuyahoga County 1997); In re Collins, 127 Ohio App. 3d 278, 712 N.E.2d 798 (8th Dist. Cuyahoga County 1998).

[2]RC 2151.35(A). See also RC 2301.20.

[3]In re Holcomb, No. 39694 (8th Dist. Ct. App., Cuyahoga, 10-4-79), citing Draper v. State of Wash., 372 U.S. 487, 83 S. Ct. 774, 9 L. Ed. 2d 899 (1963).

must enter an appropriate judgment. In interpreting this constraint, the Ohio Supreme Court has held that the seven-day time limit in abuse, neglect, and dependency cases is directory, not mandatory, and failure to comply with it will not deprive a court of jurisdiction.[1] If a court violates the seven-day time limit, the appropriate remedy is the filing of a petition for a writ of procedendo with the court of appeals requesting a directive to the trial court to comply immediately with the requirement.[2] The failure to seek a writ of procedendo precludes the party from challenging the delay in the issuance of the judgment.[3]

Copies. Juvenile Rule 34(C) also requires the court to provide a copy of the judgment to any party requesting it. However, it appears that a copy of the judgment must be served on all parties whether or not a request is made. RC 2151.35(B)(3), which applies to abuse, neglect, and dependency proceedings, requires a copy of the judgment to be served on all parties. Moreover, the Ohio Supreme Court has held that within three days of the entry of any final appealable judgment or order, the clerk of courts must serve a notice of the entry on every party who is not in default for failure to appear.[4] Since a dispositional order is a final appealable order,[5] this case would supersede Juvenile Rule 34(C).

Records. In connection with the disposition of a delinquent child, unruly child, or juvenile traffic offender, the court may order various public and private agencies to provide copies of specified records with respect to the child to the child, the child's attorney or guardian, the child's parent, and other specified individuals or entities who are providing services to the child.[6] A similar provision applies in abuse, neglect, and dependency proceedings.[7]

Cross References
§ 1:4, Ch 23, § 34:4
Research References
Giannelli and Snyder, Baldwin's Ohio Practice, Evidence (2d ed.) §§ 101.10, 611.4, 701.1, 702.7, 802.6, 901.1

Carlin, Baldwin's Ohio Practice, Merrick-Rippner Probate Law (6th ed.), Ch 107

§ 25:14 Reasonable efforts determination—Abuse, neglect & dependency

As a general rule, at any hearing held pursuant to RC 2151.28 (complaint filed), RC 2151.31 (taken into custody), RC 2151.314 (detention or shelter care), RC 2151.33 (temporary orders), or RC 2151.353 (disposition) in which the court removes a child from the child's home or continues the removal, the court must determine whether the agency that filed the complaint, removed the child, has custody of the child, or will be given custody of the child has

---

[Section 25:13]

[1]In re Davis, 84 Ohio St. 3d 520, 1999-Ohio-419, 705 N.E.2d 1219 (1999). This case resolved a conflict among the appellate courts on this issue. See, for example, In re Omosun Children, 106 Ohio App. 3d 813, 667 N.E.2d 431 (11th Dist. Trumbull County 1995), and In re Fleming, 76 Ohio App. 3d 30, 600 N.E.2d 1112 (6th Dist. Lucas County 1991).

[2]In re Davis, 84 Ohio St. 3d 520, 1999-Ohio-419, 705 N.E.2d 1219 (1999). See also In re Fleming, 76 Ohio App. 3d 30, 600 N.E.2d 1112 (6th Dist. Lucas County 1991); In re Galloway, 77 Ohio App. 3d 61, 601 N.E.2d 83 (6th Dist. Lucas County 1991); Matter of Moses, 1992 WL 32117 (Ohio Ct. App. 6th Dist. Lucas County 1992); Matter of Doe, 1993 WL 541121 (Ohio Ct. App. 6th Dist. Lucas County 1993).

[3]In re Davis, 84 Ohio St. 3d 520, 1999-Ohio-419, 705 N.E.2d 1219 (1999). See § 31:3, Time requirements for permanent custody motions.

[4]Atkinson v. Grumman Ohio Corp., 37 Ohio St. 3d 80, 523 N.E.2d 851 (1988).

[5]See § 34:4, Final order requirement.

[6]RC 2151.14(D), RC 2152.18(C).

[7]RC 2151.141.

made reasonable efforts to (1) prevent the removal, (2) eliminate the continued removal, or (3) make it possible for the child to return safely home. The agency has the burden of proving that it has made reasonable efforts. In determining whether reasonable efforts have been made, the child's health and safety are paramount.[1]

A 1999 amendment provides that the court is not precluded from finding that reasonable efforts had been made where an emergency removal is based on an unsafe home and the agency did not have prior contact with the child.

Exceptions. The court must make a determination that the agency is not required to make reasonable efforts if:

(1) The parent from whom the child was removed has been convicted of:
   (a) RC 2903.01 (aggravated murder), RC 2903.02 (murder), or RC 2903.03 (voluntary manslaughter) or an existing or former law of this state, any other state, or the United States that is substantially equivalent to one of those offenses, where the victim was the sibling of the child or another child who lived in the parent's household at the time of the offense;[2] or a conspiracy or attempt to commit, or complicity in committing, any such offense.[3]
   (b) RC 2903.11 (felonious assault), RC 2903.12 (aggravated assault), RC 2903.13 (assault), or RC 2919.22(B)(2) (child endangerment), or an existing or former law of this state, any other state, or the United States that is substantially equivalent to one of those offenses, where the victim is the child, a sibling of the child, or another child who lived in the parent's household at the time of the offense.[4]
   (c) RC 2907.02 (rape), RC 2907.03 (sexual battery), RC 2907.04 (corruption of a minor), RC 2907.05 (gross sexual imposition), or RC 2907.06 (sexual imposition), or an existing or former law of this state, any other state, or the United States that is substantially equivalent to one of those offenses, where the victim is the child, a sibling of the child, or another child who lived in the parent's household at the time of the offense;[5] or a conspiracy or attempt to commit, or complicity in committing, any such offense.[6]
(2) The parent has repeatedly withheld medical treatment or food from the child when the parent has the means to provide the treatment or food. If the parent has withheld medical treatment in order to treat the physical or medical illness or defect of the child by spiritual means through prayer in accordance with the tenets of a recognized religious body, a reasonable efforts determination is required.[7]
(3) The parent has placed the child at substantial risk of harm two or

---

[Section 25:14]

[1]RC 2151.419(A)(1); In re Kutzli, 71 Ohio App. 3d 843, 595 N.E.2d 1026 (3d Dist. Paulding County 1991); In re Leveck, 2003-Ohio-1269, 2003 WL 1205082 (Ohio Ct. App. 3d Dist. Hancock County 2003) (what constitutes "reasonable" and "diligent"); In re Nelson, 2004-Ohio-268, 2004 WL 103021 (Ohio Ct. App. 2d Dist. Montgomery County 2004). See 42 U.S.C.A. § 672. See also Juv. R. 27(B)(1), which includes the reasonable efforts determination as a requirement in any proceeding where the court orders detention. See also Glennon, Walking with Them: Advocating for Parents with Mental Illnesses in the Child Welfare System, 12 Temp. Pol. & Civ. Rts. L. Rev. 273 (2003).

[2]RC 2151.419(A)(2)(a)(i).

[3]RC 2151.419(A)(2)(a)(v).

[4]RC 2151.419(A)(2)(a)(ii), RC 2151.419(A)(2)(a)(iii).

[5]RC 2151.419(A)(2)(a)(iv).

[6]RC 2151.419(A)(2)(a)(v).

[7]RC 2151.419(A)(2)(b). See § 9:6, Neglect—Inadequate care due to parental fault.

more times due to alcohol or drug abuse and has rejected treatment two or more times or has refused to participate in further treatment two or more times after a case plan pursuant to RC 2151.412 requiring treatment was journalized as part of a dispositional order issued with respect to the child, or an order was issued by any other court requiring treatment of the parent.[8]

(4) The parent has abandoned the child.[9]

(5) The parent has had parental rights involuntarily terminated pursuant to RC 2151.353, RC 2151.414, or RC 2151.415 with respect to a sibling of the child.[10]

The court is permitted to issue an order returning the child home even if the conditions described in RC 2151.419(A)(2)(a) to (e) are present.[11] Under such circumstances the court must issue written findings of fact setting forth the reasons supporting its decision.[12]

Applicability. Although this requirement is intended to apply mainly to abuse, neglect, or dependency proceedings where such public and private agencies are involved, by the wording of the statute its applicability is extended to other cases under certain circumstances. Thus, the requirement applies in any proceeding (e.g., abuse, neglect, dependency, delinquency, and unruly cases) where the removal order is made at an adjudicatory hearing.[13] However, if the removal order is made at a dispositional hearing, the reasonable efforts determination is required only if the dispositional hearing was held following an adjudication of abuse, neglect, or dependency.[14]

Moreover, the reasonable efforts determination is not necessary where a custody order is made pursuant to RC 3109.04 following the certification of the case from the domestic relations court to the juvenile court.[15] Nor was the determination required when a mother placed her child with a certified child-placing agency, where the mother represented the identity of the father, who then sought custody.[16]

Although the reasonable efforts determination is required where an initial dispositional order of permanent custody is made,[17] appellate courts interpreting a prior version of RC 2151.413 held that the statute did not expressly invoke the reasonable efforts requirement where a motion for permanent custody had been filed.[18] However, the current version of the statute generally requires a reasonable efforts determination under such circumstances.[19]

It has been held that where a juvenile court modifies a prior custody order pursuant to RC 2151.417 and returns custody of the child to the child's

---

[8]RC 2151.419(A)(2)(c).

[9]RC 2151.419(A)(2)(d). See RC 2151.011(C).

[10]RC 2151.419(A)(2)(e).

[11]RC 2151.419(A)(3).

[12]RC 2151.419(B)(2).

[13]RC 2151.419(A)(1). See RC 2151.28(B); Matter of Hogan, 1990 WL 178092 (Ohio Ct. App. 6th Dist. Lucas County 1990); Ch 23, Adjudicatory Hearings.

[14]RC 2151.419(A)(1). See RC 2151.353(H); § 30:4, Dispositional alternatives for abuse, neglect or dependency.

[15]Gamble v. Dotson, 1991 WL 57229 (Ohio Ct. App. 9th Dist. Lorain County 1991).

[16]Mary Beth v. Howard, 1995 WL 601110 (Ohio Ct. App. 8th Dist. Cuyahoga County 1995).

[17]RC 2151.419(A)(1); Matter of Hogan, 1990 WL 178092 (Ohio Ct. App. 6th Dist. Lucas County 1990).

[18]In re Stevens, 1993 WL 265130 (Ohio Ct. App. 2d Dist. Montgomery County 1993); Matter of Rowe, 1998 WL 65460 (Ohio Ct. App. 4th Dist. Scioto County 1998); Matter of Cramer, 1998 WL 430544 (Ohio Ct. App. 5th Dist. Licking County 1998); Matter of Knisley, 1998 WL 372703 (Ohio Ct. App. 4th Dist. Ross County 1998).

[19]RC 2151.413(D)(3)(b).

mother, the reasonable efforts finding is not required.[20]

Written findings. If a court is required to make a determination that the agency is or is not required to make reasonable efforts, it must issue written findings of fact setting forth its reasons. If the court determines that the agency is required to make reasonable efforts, it shall include a brief description of the relevant services provided by the agency to the child's family and why those services did not prevent the child's removal from home or enable the child to return safely home.[21]

In interpreting a prior version of RC 2151.419,[22] courts of appeals have reversed trial court judgments where the trial court failed to include in the record any indication that it made the required reasonable efforts determination or any written findings of fact detailing the services provided by the agency to the family and why the services did not prevent the children's removal.[23] Other appellate court decisions construing the prior statute have indicated that although it is advisable for a juvenile court to make express factual findings and conclusions with respect to the reasonable efforts determination,[24] failure to do so is not reversible error as long as the record reflects that diligent efforts have been made to prevent the child's removal.[25] However, in another appellate decision interpreting the same statute, it was held that it was not reversible error for a trial court to fail to make the written findings of fact where the mother, who in effect admitted noncooperation with the agency, was not prejudiced by the failure.[26] Similarly, a trial court's failure to make the determination was held not to be error where the child had no home from which the removal could have been prevented; the mother had viciously abused the child and the father had "not one redeeming factor in his character."[27]

---

[20]Matter of Mull, 1997 WL 155412 (Ohio Ct. App. 3d Dist. Seneca County 1997).

[21]RC 2151.419(B)(1).

[22]The statute was amended by 1998 H.B. 484, eff. 3-18-99.

[23]Matter of Hogan, 1990 WL 178092 (Ohio Ct. App. 6th Dist. Lucas County 1990). See RC 2151.419(B); Matter of Duncan/Walker Children, 1995 WL 434114 (Ohio Ct. App. 5th Dist. Stark County 1995); In Matter of Lawson/Reid Children, 1997 WL 189379 (Ohio Ct. App. 2d Dist. Clark County 1997); In re Conley/Wilt Children, 1998 WL 72266 (Ohio Ct. App. 2d Dist. Clark County 1998).

[24]See Matter of Moses, 1992 WL 32117 (Ohio Ct. App. 6th Dist. Lucas County 1992).

[25]In re Pieper Children, 85 Ohio App. 3d 318, 619 N.E.2d 1059 (12th Dist. Preble County 1993); Matter of Hulsey, 1995 WL 544019 (Ohio Ct. App. 4th Dist. Adams County 1995); In Matter of Hainline, 1995 WL 9402 (Ohio Ct. App. 3d Dist. Van Wert County 1995); Matter of Cass, 1995 WL 631650 (Ohio Ct. App. 12th Dist. Preble County 1995); Matter of Flanagan, 1998 WL 195866 (Ohio Ct. App. 3d Dist. Seneca County 1998).

[26]Matter of Gentry, 1990 WL 12115 (Ohio Ct. App. 5th Dist. Licking County 1990).

[27]Matter of Jones, 1991 WL 273988, at *3 (Ohio Ct. App. 7th Dist. Mahoning County 1991).

Chapter 26

Dispositional Case Plans

> **KeyCite®:** Cases and other legal materials listed in KeyCite Scope can be researched through West's KeyCite service on Westlaw®. Use KeyCite to check citations for form, parallel references, prior and later history, and comprehensive citator information, including citations to other decisions and secondary materials.

§ 26:1 Dispositional case plans—Introduction
§ 26:2 Requirements
§ 26:3 Time requirements for case plans
§ 26:4 Court approval; journalization
§ 26:5 Case plan amendments
§ 26:6 Goals & priorities
§ 26:7 Due process

§ 26:1 Dispositional case plans—Introduction

This chapter discusses the requirements under which case plans must be prepared for children under the jurisdiction of the juvenile court. The dispositional options available for neglected, abused, and dependent children are examined in Ch 30. Motions for permanent custody are considered in Ch 31.

§ 26:2 Requirements

An agency must prepare and maintain a case plan for any child to whom the agency is providing services if: (1) the agency filed a complaint alleging that the child is abused, neglected, or dependent; (2) the agency has temporary or permanent custody of the child; (3) the child is living at home subject to an order for protective supervision; or (4) the child is in a planned permanent living arrangement.[1]

RC 2151.412(A) does not require a case plan if no public children services agency or private child placing agency is providing services to the child.[2] However, some courts have determined that case plans should be prepared for children placed with relatives, who are not otherwise served by an agency.[3]

[Section 26:2]

[1]RC 2151.412(A); 42 U.S.C.A. § 671. See RC 2151.412(A) and RC 5103.153 for case plan requirements where a private child placing agency is providing services to a child who is the subject of a permanent surrender agreement. The Director of Job and Family Services is required to adopt rules concerning the content and format of case plans and procedures for developing, implementing, and changing case plans. RC 2151.412(A)(1), RC 2151.412(A)(2); In re Stevens, 1993 WL 265130 (Ohio Ct. App. 2d Dist. Montgomery County 1993); Matter of Fulton, 1992 WL 238898 (Ohio Ct. App. 4th Dist. Athens County 1992); Matter of Ferrell, 1990 WL 42275 (Ohio Ct. App. 4th Dist. Gallia County 1990).

[2]See Matter of Johnson, 1995 WL 146064 (Ohio Ct. App. 4th Dist. Ross County 1995); Matter of Mathe, 1985 WL 4436 (Ohio Ct. App. 11th Dist. Ashtabula County 1985); In re Timberlake, 2003-Ohio-1183, 2003 WL 1094078 (Ohio Ct. App. 10th Dist. Franklin County 2003).

[3]In re Patterson, 16 Ohio App. 3d 214, 475 N.E.2d 160 (12th Dist. Madison County 1984); Matter of Cummings, 1989 WL 104753 (Ohio Ct. App. 5th Dist. Guernsey County 1989); Matter of Likens, 1986 WL 11910 (Ohio Ct. App. 2d Dist. Greene County 1986).

§ 26:3   Time requirements for case plans

The case plan must be filed with the court prior to the child's adjudicatory hearing, but no later than 30 days after the complaint was filed or the child was first placed into shelter care, whichever is earlier.[1] If insufficient information is available prior to the hearing to complete the plan, the agency must complete the plan by 30 days after the adjudicatory hearing or the date of the dispositional hearing, whichever is earlier.[2]

It has been held that allowing the case plan to be filed on the second day of a hearing was harmless error since the parties were not prejudiced.[3]

§ 26:4   Court approval; journalization

In preparing the case plan, the agency must attempt to obtain an agreement among all parties regarding its content.[1] If this is accomplished, and the court approves it, the court must journalize the case plan as part of its dispositional order.[2]

If, on the other hand, agreement cannot be reached, or the court does not approve the case plan, the court must decide its contents at the dispositional hearing based on the child's best interest.[3] The journalized case plan will then bind all parties.[4] Any party who fails to comply with the terms of the journalized case plan may be held in contempt.[5]

§ 26:5   Case plan amendments

If a party wishes to propose changes to a substantive part of a case plan, the party must file the proposed change with the court and provide written notice to all parties before the end of the day after the day of filing. Although the term "substantive part" is not defined by the statute, the statute includes the child's placement and the visitation rights of any party as examples of such parts.[1]

Request for hearing. Any party may object to and request a hearing on the proposed change within seven days from the date the notice is sent.[2] If a timely request is made for a hearing, the hearing must be held within 30 days after the request is received by the court, with notice to the parties. Unless emergency circumstances exist, the agency may not implement the proposed change unless it is approved by the court.[3]

No request. If a timely request for a hearing is not made, the court may approve the proposed change without a hearing. If this is done, the court

---

[Section 26:3]

[1]RC 2151.412(C); Juv. R. 34(F).

[2]RC 2151.412(C); Juv. R. 34(F).

[3]In Matter of Ackert, 1996 WL 72617 (Ohio Ct. App. 5th Dist. Holmes County 1996).

[Section 26:4]

[1]RC 2151.412(D); In re Stevens, 1993 WL 265130 (Ohio Ct. App. 2d Dist. Montgomery County 1993); In Matter of Wilson Children, 1996 WL 363434 (Ohio Ct. App. 5th Dist. Stark County 1996).

[2]RC 2151.412(D). See RC 2151.353(D); Juv. R. 34(F); In re Moloney, 24 Ohio St. 3d 22, 492 N.E.2d 805 (1986); In re Beasley, 1993 WL 468401 (Ohio Ct. App. 9th Dist. Summit County 1993); In re Thomas, No. 15813 (9th Dist. Ct. App., Summit, 3-10-93).

[3]RC 2151.412(D); Juv. R. 34(F).

[4]RC 2151.412(E)(1). See § 31:8, Implementation of case plan.

[5]RC 2151.412(E)(1).

[Section 26:5]

[1]See In re Smith, 1995 WL 348431 (Ohio Ct. App. 12th Dist. Butler County 1995), which equated "substantive part" with "significant changes" in the plan.

[2]RC 2151.412(E)(2).

[3]RC 2151.412(E)(2)(a).

must journalize the case plan with the change within 14 days after the change is filed.[4] If the court does not approve the proposed change, a hearing must be held within 30 days after the 14-day period expires, with notice to all parties. However, the agency may implement the proposed change not earlier than 15 days after it is submitted to the court if the court neither approves and journalizes the proposed change nor conducts a hearing.[5]

Emergency circumstances. If emergency circumstances exist and an immediate change in the case plan is needed to prevent harm to the child, the agency may implement the change without prior agreement or court approval.[6] Before the end of the next day after the change is made, the agency must notify all parties and the court. Before the end of the third day, the agency must file a statement of the change with the court, with notice to the parties.

Within 10 days from the date the notice is sent, any party may object to and request a hearing on the change.[7] If a timely request for a hearing is made, the court must schedule a hearing within the same time frames that apply to other proposed changes in the case plan.[8] If it does not receive a timely request for a hearing, the court may approve the change without a hearing, or schedule a hearing according to the above time frames.[9]

§ 26:6 Goals & priorities

All case plans for children in temporary custody must have the following general goals: (1) consistent with the best interest and special needs of the child, to achieve a safe out-of-home placement in the least restrictive, most family-like setting available and in close proximity to the home from which the child was removed or the home in which the child will be permanently placed; and (2) to eliminate with all due speed the need for the out-of-home placement so the child can safely return home.[1]

If the child is or has been the victim of abuse or neglect or witnessed, in the child's household, abuse or neglect of a sibling, parent, or other household member, the case plan for a child in temporary custody must also include a requirement that the child's parents, guardian, or custodian participate in mandatory counseling and any supportive services included in the case plan.[2]

RC 2151.412(F)(2) provides that the Director of Job and Family Services must adopt rules setting forth the general goals of case plans for children in protective supervision, planned permanent living arrangements, or permanent custody. However, another statute, RC 2151.415(C)(2)(b), provides that the case plan for a child in planned permanent living arrangements shall be designed to assist the child in finding a permanent home outside of the parents' home. Moreover, it has been held that the goal of long-term foster care is not reunification with the child's parents.[3]

Cases interpreting both the former version of RC 2151.412, which required comprehensive reunification plans rather than case plans, and the current version of the statute have upheld court-approved plans denying visitation

---

[4]RC 2151.412(E)(2)(b).

[5]RC 2151.412(E)(2)(b).

[6]RC 2151.412(E)(3).

[7]RC 2151.412(E)(3).

[8]RC 2151.412(E)(3)(a). See RC 2151.417.

[9]RC 2151.412(E)(3)(b).

[Section 26:6]

[1]RC 2151.412(F)(1). See Matter of Brown Chilren, 1995 WL 347821 (Ohio Ct. App. 5th Dist. Stark County 1995).

[2]RC 2151.412(H).

[3]Matter of Brown Chilren, 1995 WL 347821 (Ohio Ct. App. 5th Dist. Stark County 1995); In re Lee, 1996 WL 665058 (Ohio Ct. App. 4th Dist. Athens County 1996).

between the parents and child in exceptional cases.[4] It is not unreasonable for a plan to condition reunification with the child on the parent's abstention from alcohol.[5] However, a case plan that requires a parent to admit that he sexually abused his child in order to be reunited with that child violates the parent's right against compulsory self-incrimination as guaranteed by the Fifth Amendment.[6]

The agency developing the case plan, as well as the court reviewing it, must consider the child's health and safety as the paramount concern and be guided by the following general priorities.[7] A child who is residing with or can be placed with his parents within a reasonable time should remain in their legal custody, even if an order of protective supervision is required.[8] If return to the parents is not feasible, the child should be placed in the legal custody of a suitable member of the child's extended family or, if none exists, a suitable nonrelative.[9] If the above options cannot be implemented, the child should be placed in the temporary custody of an appropriate agency.[10] As a last resort, the child should be committed to the permanent custody of an agency if the agency has a reasonable expectation of placing the child for adoption.[11] The placement of a child for adoption or foster care may not be delayed or denied solely on the basis of the race, color, or national origin of the child or the adoptive or foster family.[12]

A case plan may include, as a supplement, a plan for locating a permanent family placement for the child, but the agency need not attempt to obtain agreement among all the parties to the supplement, nor must the court review or approve the supplement.[13]

It has been held that the statutory language listing the general priorities of case plans is precatory rather than mandatory; it does not require the court or the agency to act in any specific manner but merely suggests certain criteria in developing case plan goals.[14] Thus, RC 2151.412(G) does not require a juvenile court to follow the priorities enumerated in the statute in

---

[4]In re Jones, 29 Ohio App. 3d 176, 504 N.E.2d 719 (8th Dist. Cuyahoga County 1985); In re Erica, 65 Ohio Misc. 2d 17, 640 N.E.2d 623 (C.P. 1994).

[5]Johnson v. Trumbull County Children Services Bd., 1990 WL 162587 (Ohio Ct. App. 11th Dist. Trumbull County 1990).

[6]In re Amanda W., 124 Ohio App. 3d 136, 705 N.E.2d 724 (6th Dist. Lucas County 1997). See § 23:27, Self-incrimination.

[7]RC 2151.412(G).

[8]RC 2151.412(G)(1).

[9]RC 2151.412(G)(2), RC 2151.412(G)(3).

[10]RC 2151.412(G)(4).

[11]RC 2151.412(G)(5). The statute does not include long-term foster care among any of the priorities.

[12]RC 2151.412(G)(6).

[13]RC 2151.412(I), citing RC 2151.412(D).

[14]In re Hiatt, 86 Ohio App. 3d 716, 621 N.E.2d 1222 (4th Dist. Adams County 1993); In Matter of Butler, 1996 WL 132238 (Ohio Ct. App. 5th Dist. Stark County 1996); In re Cundiff, 1995 WL 768599 (Ohio Ct. App. 5th Dist. Stark County 1995); In Matter of Seven A. Children, 1995 WL 557329 (Ohio Ct. App. 6th Dist. Fulton County 1995); In re Dye, 1995 WL 231214 (Ohio Ct. App. 9th Dist. Summit County 1995); Matter of Clark, 1995 WL 153010 (Ohio Ct. App. 7th Dist. Harrison County 1995); In re Balazy, 1993 WL 164790 (Ohio Ct. App. 9th Dist. Lorain County 1993); Matter of Cremeans, 1992 WL 47278 (Ohio Ct. App. 8th Dist. Cuyahoga County 1992); Matter of Dixon, 1991 WL 325657 (Ohio Ct. App. 6th Dist. Lucas County 1991); Matter of Leverett, 1998 WL 141192 (Ohio Ct. App. 8th Dist. Cuyahoga County 1998). But see Matter of Taylor, 1990 WL 193601, at *7 (Ohio Ct. App. 4th Dist. Scioto County 1990), in which the court stated, "There is a presumption in favor of placement with a relative under the current statutory scheme, much as there has always been in the statutes, case law, and traditional ethos of Americans. But this factor must be balanced with other factors." Accord Matter of Taceia R., 1996 WL 71003 (Ohio Ct. App. 6th Dist. Lucas County 1996). In re Gordon, 2002-Ohio-4959, 2002 WL 31107543 (Ohio Ct. App. 11th Dist. Trumbull County 2002) (An agency is not required to set forth an exact plan of adoption until permanent custody is granted.).

making a permanent custody decision.[15]

An appellate court has held that although a juvenile court may order a public children services agency to provide certain services to a dependent child, the court must first permit the agency to present evidence that it could not provide such services.[16]

§ 26:7 Due process

A federal district court held that the Due Process Clause of the United States Constitution does not require states to carry out a reunification plan before making a final adjudication of abuse or dependency.[1] The court further held that although federal law[2] provides that the amount of federal tax money granted to states for child welfare programs will be reduced unless the state has a "replacement preventive service program," the statute is a mere funding provision and creates no federal "right" to such a reunification program.

A court of appeals held that a case plan designed to secure an alternative permanent living arrangement for a child does not deprive the father of due process of law by failing to include him in the case plan, inasmuch as RC 2151.412 sanctions alternative living arrangements.[3]

Cross References
§ 1:4, Ch 30

---

[15]In re Hiatt, 86 Ohio App. 3d 716, 621 N.E.2d 1222 (4th Dist. Adams County 1993); Matter of Gilbert, 1996 WL 435426 (Ohio Ct. App. 12th Dist. Butler County 1996).

[16]Matter of Richard Carl S., 1998 WL 667044 (Ohio Ct. App. 6th Dist. Sandusky County 1998).

[Section 26:7]
[1]Lesher v. Lavrich, 632 F. Supp. 77 (N.D. Ohio 1984); Garabrandt v. Lucas County Children Services Bd., 47 Ohio App. 3d 119, 547 N.E.2d 997 (6th Dist. Lucas County 1988).

[2]42 U.S.C.A. § 627(b)(3).

[3]Mary Beth v. Howard, 1995 WL 601110 (Ohio Ct. App. 8th Dist. Cuyahoga County 1995).

Chapter 27

Delinquent Child Dispositions

KeyCite®: Cases and other legal materials listed in KeyCite Scope can be researched through West's KeyCite service on Westlaw®. Use KeyCite to check citations for form, parallel references, prior and later history, and comprehensive citator information, including citations to other decisions and secondary materials.

§ 27:1   Delinquent child dispositions—Introduction
§ 27:2   Dispositional alternatives
§ 27:3   Department of Youth Services commitment
§ 27:4   DYS release
§ 27:5   Child protective services
§ 27:6   County or private facility commitment
§ 27:7   Community control sanctions
§ 27:8   Probation
§ 27:9   Drug & alcohol dispositions
§ 27:10   House arrest & electronic monitoring
§ 27:11   Driving privileges
§ 27:12   Fines
§ 27:13   Restitution
§ 27:14   Forfeiture
§ 27:15   Costs & reimbursements
§ 27:16   Truancy dispositions
§ 27:17   Court custody
§ 27:18   "Catch-all" provision
§ 27:19   Plural dispositions
§ 27:20   Victim-mediation

§ 27:1   Delinquent child dispositions—Introduction

This chapter discusses dispositions in delinquent child cases. The procedural issues that relate to juvenile court dispositional hearings are examined in Chapter 24. The substantive requirements attending other types of juvenile court jurisdiction are explored in subsequent chapters: juvenile traffic offenses (Chapter 27), unruliness (Chapter 28), and neglect, abuse, and dependency (Chapter 29).

SYO sentencing is discussed in Chapter 5 and sex offender registration in Chapter 6.

General principles. In 2002, the juvenile disposition provisions were transferred to RC 2152.16 to RC 2152.20, which reorganized RC 2151.355. The underpinning philosophy for delinquency and traffic offender cases was distinguished from that of abuse, neglect, dependence, and unruly cases.[1]

§ 27:2   Dispositional alternatives

RC 2152.19(A) provides that if a child is adjudged delinquent, the court

---

[Section 27:1]
[1]See § 4:1, Delinquent child jurisdiction—Introduction.

may make any of several dispositional orders. Although the disposition of cases is substantive in nature and is thus governed by statute, Juvenile Rule 29(F)(2)(d) permits dismissal of the complaint where it is in the best interests of the child and the community, even if the allegations of the complaint are admitted or proven.

Moving away from probation, S.B. 179 designates a number of community control sanctions, including basic probation and intensive probation.[1] In addition, the court may impose a host of other sanctions, such as day reporting, community service, school and work requirements, curfew, monitored time, house arrest and electronic monitoring.[2] In addition, two drug dispositions are recognized: drug monitoring and drug assessment and treatment.[3] Various driver's license dispositions are also authorized.[4]

Financial sanctions include fines,[5] restitution,[6] forfeiture,[7] costs and reimbursements.[8] There are also special truancy dispositions.[9] Finally, the court can make dispositions relating to child protective services.[10] county and private facility dispositions,[11] and court custody.[12] These dispositions are discussed in the following sections.

Commitment to the Department of Youth Services is the most drastic disposition.[13] SYO commitments are discussed in Chapter 5.

§ 27:3   Department of Youth Services commitment

If a child has been adjudicated a delinquent child for the commission of a felony, he or she may be committed to the legal custody of the Department of Youth Services for institutionalization.[1]

Unlike commitments to county, district, or private agencies authorized by RC 2151.355(A)(1) and (3), a commitment to the state-operated Department of Youth Services may only be ordered for a delinquent-felon.[2] In addition, a commitment to the department is accompanied by a minimum period of institutionalization,[3] whereas commitment to other agencies is usually for an open-ended period of time. When the court commits a child to the department, the department determines to which facility the child will be sent. The court may not designate a specific institution but instead must specify that the child is to be institutionalized or that the institutionalization is to be in a

---

[Section 27:2]

[1]See § 27:8, Probation.

[2]See § 27:10, House arrest & electronic monitoring.

[3]See § 27:9, Drug & alcohol dispositions.

[4]See § 27:11, Driving privileges.

[5]See § 27:12, Fines.

[6]See § 27:13, Restitution.

[7]See § 27:14, Forfeiture.

[8]See § 27:15, Costs & reimbursements.

[9]See § 27:16, Truancy dispositions.

[10]See § 27:5, Child protective services.

[11]See § 27:6, County or private facility commitment.

[12]See § 27:17, Court custody.

[13]See § 27:3, Department of Youth Services commitment.

[Section 27:3]

[1]RC 2152.16. In re Joseph S., 1996 WL 185160 (Ohio Ct. App. 6th Dist. Lucas County 1996).

[2]Because the degree of offense is paramount in determining whether and for how long a child may remain in the custody of the Department of Youth Services, plea-bargaining occurs frequently in the juvenile justice system.

[3]For provisions regarding the department's procedures and requirements prior to releasing a child, see § 33:9, Department of Youth Services.

secure facility.[4]

Similarly, a juvenile court may not order the department to place a parole violator at a specific institution or at a private out-of-state school.[5] Commitments to the Department of Youth Services may not exceed the child's attainment of age 21.[6]

It has been held that RC 2151.355 does not require the court to exhaust all other options before imposing a commitment to the Department of Youth Services; the court may order institutionalization without first attempting other forms of rehabilitation.[7] Absent a request from the child, a juvenile court is not required to order psychological testing or a social history prior to imposing the commitment.[8] Moreover, when placing a delinquent child on probation, the court need not first impose and suspend a commitment to the Department in order to subsequently order a commitment after the child violates probation.[9]

Relevant factors. Prior to 2002, the following factors had to be considered in favor of imposing an order committing a child to a facility for delinquent children, including the Department of Youth Services, but should not have controlled the court's decision:

(1) A victim was age five or younger, regardless of whether the child knew the age of the victim;

(2) A victim sustained physical harm during the commission of or otherwise as a result of the offense; and

(3) A victim was age 65 or older or permanently and totally disabled at the time of the offense, regardless of whether the child knew the age of the victim, and the delinquent act was an offense of violence.[10]

S.B. 179 eliminated the above approach and focused on the broader goals of new RC 2152.01, which includes protection of the public and restoring the victim. Consequently, a victim's vulnerability and loss are relevant factors.[11]

The Ohio Supreme Court has determined that the length of commitment should be based on the delinquent act as well as the child's overall conduct and behavior, the child's history, the remorse shown by the child, and other relevant societal factors.[12]

Minimum age. The minimum age is at least 12 years old at the time of the commitment. S.B. 179 reduces the minimum age to 10 at the time of the charged act, but only 10- and 11-year-olds adjudicated delinquent for aggravated murder, murder, a violent F-1 or F-2, or arson are eligible.[13]

---

[4]RC 2152.18(A), RC 5139.05(A).

[5]In re Sanders, 72 Ohio App. 3d 655, 595 N.E.2d 974 (8th Dist. Cuyahoga County 1991). See § 33:9, Department of Youth Services.

[6]RC 2152.16, RC 2151.38, RC 5139.05(A). For a discussion of the termination of juvenile court jurisdiction, see § 33:4, Abuse, neglect, and dependency proceedings.

[7]In Matter of Copeland, 1995 WL 453422 (Ohio Ct. App. 11th Dist. Ashtabula County 1995); Matter of Jasmine V., 1997 WL 440921 (Ohio Ct. App. 6th Dist. Williams County 1997).

[8]Matter of Joey O., 1997 WL 785621 (Ohio Ct. App. 6th Dist. Lucas County 1997).

[9]In Matter of Kelly, 1995 WL 656944 (Ohio Ct. App. 10th Dist. Franklin County 1995); In re Barnhouse, 1996 WL 39650 (Ohio Ct. App. 10th Dist. Franklin County 1996); In re Peggy L., 1995 WL 803443 (Ohio Ct. App. 6th Dist. Lucas County 1995).

[10]RC 2151.355(E)(1), now repealed. See RC 2151.355(A)(3) to RC 2151.355(A)(6), now repealed. According to the Legislative Service Commission analysis of 1995 H.B. 1, eff. 1-1-96, "A juvenile court is required to consider a combination of the offense of violence factor any of the victim factors in favor of ordering the commitment of the delinquent child."

[11]RC 2152.16.

[12]In re Caldwell, 76 Ohio St. 3d 156, 1996-Ohio-410, 666 N.E.2d 1367 (1996). See also In re Houston, 1998 WL 827608 (Ohio Ct. App. 8th Dist. Cuyahoga County 1998).

[13]RC 5139.05(A). The offender must be housed separately from older juveniles until age 12. RC 5139.05(A)(4). See also Executive Order 20001-01T.

Maximum term. A DYS term cannot extend beyond age 21.[14]

Terms. S.B. 179, as finally enacted, did not change the ranges of DYS terms, whether these terms are imposed as a traditional juvenile (TJ) or as the juvenile portion of a blended (SYO) sentence. The period of the commitment is dependent on the seriousness of the offense, as follows:

Murders. Aggravated murder (RC 2903.01) or murder (RC 2903.02) until age 21.[15]

Attempted murders. Minimum period of six to seven years and maximum period not to exceed age 21, for attempted aggravated murder (RC 2923.01) or attempted murder (RC 2923.02).[16]

Certain category two offenses. Minimum period of one to three years and maximum period not to exceed age 21, for the following offenses: (1) voluntary manslaughter (RC 2903.03); (2) involuntary manslaughter, where the death was the proximate result of the commission of a felony (RC 2903.04(A)); (3) kidnapping (RC 2905.01); (4) aggravated arson (RC 2909.02); (5) aggravated robbery (RC 2911.01); and (6) rape (RC 2907.02) "other than division (A)(1)(b) [victim under age 13] of that section when the sexual conduct or insertion involved was consensual and when the victim of the violation of division (A)(1)(b) of that section was older than the delinquent child, was the same age as the delinquent child, or was less than three years younger than the delinquent child."[17]

Other F-1 and F-2 offenses. Minimum period of one year and maximum period not to exceed age 21 for any other felony of the first or second degree.[18]

F-3, F-4 and F-5 offenses. Minimum period of six months and maximum period not to exceed age 21, for a felony of the third, fourth, or fifth degree, or for violating RC 2923.211 (underage purchase of firearm or handgun).[19]

In this context, "minimum" does not mean a mandatory minimum term. Rather, it refers to the time the juvenile court retains control over the disposition—the term during which the court has authority to release the juvenile.[20]

Specifications. The above terms may be augmented by gun or gang specifications provided that they are charged and proved. Many, but not all, of these specifications specify mandatory terms.

There is a five-year maximum for multiple specifications.[21] No commitment may extend beyond age 21.[22]

Gun specification. There are several different types of gun specifications. They apply to an accomplice.[23]

If the underlying offense involves *possession* of a firearm,[24] other than the offense of carrying a concealed weapon (RC 2923.12), the child may receive

---

[14]RC 2152.17(D).

[15]RC 2152.16(A)(1)(a). Lack of a minimum term means that commitment to age 21 is the only option. RC 5139.05(A)(2).

[16]RC 2152.16(A)(1)(b), RC 5139.05(A)(1).

[17]RC 2152.16(A)(1)(c). See RC 5139.05(A)(1). In re C.M., 2004-Ohio-1927, 2004 WL 829937 (Ohio Ct. App. 12th Dist. Butler County 2004).

[18]RC 2152.16(A)(1)(d), RC 5139.05(A)(1). In re R.W.J., 155 Ohio App. 3d 52, 2003-Ohio-5407, 798 N.E.2d 1206 (2d Dist. Clark County 2003).

[19]RC 2152.16(A)(1)(e), RC 5139.05(A)(1). Under S.B. 179 the status offense of purchasing or attempting to purchase a firearm while under 18 years of age is classified as an F-4 delinquent act.

[20]See § 27:4, DYS release.

[21]RC 2152.17(D).

[22]RC 2152.17(D).

[23]RC 2152.17(B) ("to the same extent" as adult accomplices).

[24]See RC 2941.141.

an additional term of commitment of one year, but only if the court determines that a DYS term is warranted.[25] Although this term is served consecutive and prior to the underlying DYS term,[26] this is true only if the court elects to impose a DYS term for the underlying offense and elects to add specification time.[27]

If the underlying offense involves using, indicating, brandishing, or displaying a firearm,[28] the child must receive an additional term of commitment of one year to three years and be committed to DYS for the underlying delinquent act.[29]

If the underlying offense involves an automatic, muffled, or silenced weapon,[30] the child must receive an additional term of commitment of one year to five years and be committed to DYS for the underlying delinquent act.[31]

If the underlying offense involves a drive-by shooting,[32] the child must receive an additional term of commitment of one year to five years.[33]

If the complaint includes a specification that the child discharged a firearm at a peace officer or corrections officer while committing the underlying offense, the child shall be committed to DYS on the underlying offense and receive an additional definite period of not less than one and not more than five years.[34]

These additional terms must be served consecutively and prior to the child's regular term of commitment, provided that the total of all periods of commitment may not exceed age 21.[35] It has been held that this additional term of commitment may be imposed even if the complaint did not include the firearm specification.[36]

Gang specification. If the underlying offense is aggravated murder, murder, or a violent F-1, F-2, or F-3 act while participating in gang activity,[37] the child must receive an additional term of commitment of one year to three years.[38]

Under pre-S.B. 179 law, if the child was committed to the Department of Youth Services pursuant to RC 2151.355(A)(5) or (6) for committing a category one or category two offense,[39] and if the court determined that if the child were guilty of a specification concerning an offense of violence while participating in criminal gang activity,[40] the court was required to commit the child for a period of not less than one year or more than three years, provided the total period of commitment did not exceed age 21.[41]

Consecutive terms. If a child is committed to the Department of Youth

---

[25]RC 2152.17(A)(1).

[26]See RC 2152.17(D).

[27]The new S.B. 179 language is intended to clarify whether specification time is mandatory or optional.

[28]See RC 2941.145.

[29]RC 2152.17(A)(2), RC 5139.05(A)(3).

[30]See RC 2941.144.

[31]RC 2152.17(A)(3).

[32]See RC 2941.146.

[33]RC 2152.17(A)(3).

[34]RC 2941.1412(A) and RC 2152.17.

[35]RC 2152.17(D), RC 5139.05(A)(3).

[36]Matter of Laquatra, 1998 WL 23841 (Ohio Ct. App. 8th Dist. Cuyahoga County 1998). See § 16:8, Delinquency complaints.

[37]See RC 2941.142.

[38]RC 2152.17(C); former RC 2151.355(A)(7) (not as broad).

[39]See RC 2151.26(A).

[40]See RC 2941.142.

[41]RC 2151.355(A)(7)(b).

Services for two or more felonies, the court may order consecutive commitments.[42] If the child received an additional term due to a firearms or gang specification, any consecutive terms shall be served immediately following the expiration of the additional firearms specification term, but the child may not be committed for a period that exceeds age 21.[43]

Appellate courts have indicated that a juvenile court is specifically mandated by RC 2921.34 to impose a consecutive commitment order on a juvenile found delinquent of escape.[44] The court in *In re Woodson*[45] relied on RC 2921.34(C)(3), which provides, "Sentence of confinement imposed for escape shall be served consecutively to any other sentence of confinement imposed on such offender." Although the term "commitment" rather than "sentence" is used in the context of the juvenile law,[46] the courts determined that the mandatory provision applies to juveniles because the remainder of the statute[47] specifically refers to alleged or adjudicated delinquents.

Repeat violent offenders. If a delinquent child is committed to the DYS for aggravated murder, murder, rape, felonious sexual penetration,[48] involuntary manslaughter, a F-1 or F-2 act resulting in death or physical harm, complicity in or an attempt to commit any of the above offenses, or any substantially equivalent offense, the adjudication is considered a conviction for purposes of determining whether the child is a repeat violent offender as defined in RC 2929.01.[49]

Credit. A delinquent child committed to the Department of Youth Services pursuant to RC Chapter 2152 is entitled to credit for the total number of days held in detention prior to the transfer of physical custody of the child to the department.[50] A child committed to the department, who has been confined as an adult in an adult jail, must also be granted credit for time served while awaiting his juvenile court dispositional hearing.[51] However, based on a strict interpretation of the statute,[52] one court has held that a child detained pending commitment for a parole violation offense is not entitled to credit for time held in detention where the parole violation offense does not constitute a felony.[53] Moreover, in an adult criminal case, it was held that a defendant is not entitled to credit for the time he spent under electronic home monitoring pending trial.[54] Time in a rehabilitation center while on probation does not meet the definition of detention and is not

---

[42]RC 2152.17(E), RC 5139.05(A)(4).

[43]RC 2152.17(E).

[44]Matter of Bremmer, 1993 WL 95556 (Ohio Ct. App. 8th Dist. Cuyahoga County 1993); In re Woodson, 98 Ohio App. 3d 678, 649 N.E.2d 320 (10th Dist. Franklin County 1994). See § 4:6, Court order violations, and § 27:3, Department of Youth Services commitment.

[45]In re Woodson, 98 Ohio App. 3d 678, 649 N.E.2d 320 (10th Dist. Franklin County 1994).

[46]See RC 2151.355(A).

[47]RC 2921.34.

[48]Former RC 2907.12.

[49]RC 2152.17(F).

[50]RC 2152.18(B). In re Hughley, 1998 WL 57380 (Ohio Ct. App. 1st Dist. Hamilton County 1998); In re Roux, 1998 WL 551990 (Ohio Ct. App. 7th Dist. Noble County 1998). This statute overrules In re Vaughn, 1990 WL 116936 (Ohio Ct. App. 12th Dist. Butler County 1990). See State v. James, 106 Ohio App. 3d 686, 666 N.E.2d 1185 (9th Dist. Summit County 1995), holding that a defendant in adult court who was convicted subsequent to a bindover is entitled to receive credit for the time that he was held in a juvenile detention facility awaiting the bindover proceedings. In re Caplinger, 2002-Ohio-3087, 2002 WL 1343653 (Ohio Ct. App. 5th Dist. Muskingham County 2002); In re Mills, 2002-Ohio-2503, 2002 WL 925270 (Ohio Ct. App. 5th Dist. Ashland County 2002); In re Ringo, 2002-Ohio-1218, 2002 WL 418968 (Ohio Ct. App. 3d Dist. Crawford County 2002).

[51]In re Smith, 32 Ohio App. 3d 82, 513 N.E.2d 1387 (12th Dist. Butler County 1986).

[52]RC 2151.355(F)(6).

[53]Matter of Fee, 1993 WL 541133 (Ohio Ct. App. 6th Dist. Erie County 1993); In re Mills, 2002-Ohio-2503, 2002 WL 925270 (Ohio Ct. App. 5th Dist. Ashland County 2002).

[54]State v. Faulkner, 102 Ohio App. 3d 602, 657 N.E.2d 602 (3d Dist. Marion County 1995).

counted as time served.[55]

Court responsibilities. When a juvenile court commits a child to the Department of Youth Services, it must provide notification and documentation to DYS, the school district, and the victim.

First, the court must provide the department with the child's medical records, reports of any court-ordered mental examinations, the section(s) of the Revised Code violated and the degree of the violation, the warrant to convey the child, a copy of the journal entry containing the commitment order, a copy of the arrest record pertaining to the subject delinquent act, a copy of any victim impact statement pertaining to that act, and any other information concerning the child that the department reasonably requests. The court must also complete the form for the standard disposition investigation report, and provide the completed form to the department.[56] The department may refuse to accept physical custody of the child until all of the above documents have been provided.[57]

Second, within 20 working days the court must provide the department with a certified copy of the child's birth certificate or social security number, or, if the court made all reasonable efforts to obtain the information but was unsuccessful, with documentation of the efforts made to obtain the information.[58] A copy of the journal entry ordering the commitment must be sent to the child's school, which, upon receiving the entry, must provide the department with the child's school transcript.[59]

Third, the court must also notify the juvenile's school district of the commitment within 14 days.[60] For specified persons 14 and older, the school district must be provided certain information under S.B. 181 within 10 days.[61]

Fourth, the court must notify the victim of any right to recover damages from the juvenile's parents or reparations from the state.[62]

DYS release. Upon releasing the child, the department must provide within 14 days the court and the school with an updated copy of the child's school transcript and must provide the court with a summary of the child's institutional record. The department must also furnish the court with a copy of any portion of the child's institutional record that the court specifically requests, within five working days of the request.[63]

Expenses. The Department of Youth Services is eligible to receive educational tuition pursuant to RC 3313.64(I) and RC 3313.64(C)(2) for a child committed to an institution operated by the department.[64] Under RC 5139.01(A)(3), the department is responsible for payment of medical bills incurred by a child in the department's custody.[65]

§ 27:4 DYS release

A DYS disposition is a temporary order. A committed juvenile may be

---

[55]In re Henderson, 2002-Ohio-2575, 2002 WL 1160073 (Ohio Ct. App. 12th Dist. Butler County 2002).

[56]RC 2152.18(C)(1). See RC 5139.04.

[57]RC 2152.18(C)(1).

[58]RC 2152.18(C)(2).

[59]RC 2152.18(D)(3).

[60]RC 2152.18(D)(3).

[61]RC 2152.18(D)(1) & RC 2152.18(D)(2).

[62]RC 2152.18(E).

[63]RC 2152.18(D)(4).

[64]OAG 88-23.

[65]Northern Columbiana County Community Hosp. Ass'n v. Department of Youth Services, 38 Ohio St. 3d 102, 526 N.E.2d 802 (1988).

released from DYS commitment in several ways.[1]

First, the juvenile court may release the juvenile. This method of release is discussed below.

Second, DYS may release the juvenile. Once the minimum period (court control) has expired, the DYS has authority to release the offender.[2]

Third, the juvenile may be transferred to DRC if the adult part of a blended SYO sentence is invoked.[3]

Finally, the juvenile may reach the age of 21 or secure a medical release.[4] These two methods are rare.

Court control. The court retains jurisdiction over the juvenile committed to DYS for the "minimum" period. Generally, this permits the court to release the juvenile. Moreover, during this time DYS cannot release the child or move the child to a nonsecure environment without the court's permission.[5]

There are two types of judicial release: (1) judicial release to court supervision (formerly called "judicial release") and (2) judicial release to DYS supervision (formerly "early release"). This classification depends on committed time served. Judicial release to court supervision is limited to the first 90 days for F-3, F-4 or F-5 conduct[6] and 180 days for F-1 and F-2 conduct.[7] For murder or aggravated murder, the time period is the first half for juveniles committed to age 21 with no minimum.[8]

Judicial release to court supervision. A request for release may be filed by the offender, the offender's parents, or DYS.[9] In response to a request or on its own motion, the court may (1) approve the request by journal entry, (2) schedule a hearing within 30 days,[10] or (3) deny the request by journal entry without a hearing.[11] The court may hold the hearing without the child or order DYS to deliver the child. The court may also require a DYS report on the juvenile's progress and recommendations for release conditions.[12]

If the court rejects an offender or parental request, one later request may be made but not earlier than 30 days after the first request was filed. Denial of a request does not preclude a later application for judicial release to DYS supervision.

If release is granted the local probation department provides supervision. The court's staff must prepare a plan that may specify release conditions recommended by DYS.

Judicial release to DYS supervision. As noted above, this type of release is limited to the latter part of the "minimum" commitment.[13] The procedures and options are similar to the judicial release to court supervision. The supervision is provided by DYS. If the court rejects an offender or parental request, only one request every 90 days is permitted.[14]

[Section 27:4]

[1]See § 33:9, Department of Youth Services.

[2]RC 2152.16(B) & RC 5139.05(B).

[3]See Serious Youth Offenders Ch 5.

[4]RC 5139.54.

[5]RC 2152.16(A)(2).

[6]RC 2152.22(B)(1)(a). Former law used the terms "first half" and "second half."

[7]RC 2152.22(B)(1)(b).

[8]RC 2152.22(B)(1)(c). S.B. 179 is silent as to attempted murders.

[9]RC 2152.22(B)(1) to RC 2152.22(B)(3).

[10]Former law was 20 days.

[11]RC 2152.22(B)(2).

[12]RC 2152.22(B)(3).

[13]RC 2152.22(C)(1) to RC 2152.22(C)(3).

[14]RC 2152.22(C)(2).

If a hearing is held, DYS must provide a post-release treatment plan.[15] If release is granted, the actual date of release is contingent on DYS finding suitable placement. DYS must discuss the release plan and conditions with the juvenile court and the parents before the release.[16] It must also file regular progress reports to the committing court for those on judicial release to DYS supervision.[17]

Violations. If serious violations of release conditions are found after a hearing, the court of the placement county may return the juvenile to DYS or make another disposition.[18]

DYS parole. The committing juvenile court retains jurisdiction over violations by juveniles released on DYS parole pursuant to RC 5139.51 and RC 5139.52.[19]

§ 27:5   Child protective services

In a delinquency disposition, a court may make "[a]ny order that is authorized by section 2151.353 of the Revised Code."[1] Pursuant to this dispositional alternative, the court may utilize any disposition allowable for an abused, neglected, or dependent child. This would include commitment of the child to the temporary custody[2] and permanent custody of an authorized agency as long as all required findings have been made.[3] However, it is unclear whether the stringent procedural and substantive safeguards applicable to the commitment of abused, neglected, and dependent children apply to a delinquent child. For instance, RC 2151.353(B) provides that no permanent or temporary custody order may be made unless both the summons and complaint served on the parents contain an explanation of their rights and of the possible consequences of the order. The language of this provision seems to limit its applicability to abuse, neglect, and dependency proceedings. On the other hand, it is arguable that whenever a court treats a delinquent child as an abused, neglected, or dependent child pursuant to RC 2151.355(A)(1), the statutory requirements imposed in the latter proceedings apply. For instance, it is clear that a case plan must be prepared and maintained for a delinquent child who is in the temporary or permanent custody of an appropriate agency.[4]

Before a juvenile court issues an order of disposition under RC 2151.355(A)(1) committing a delinquent child to the custody of a public children services agency, it must provide the agency with notice of the intended order pursuant to the Juvenile Rules.[5]

§ 27:6   County or private facility commitment

Another alternative is to commit the delinquent child to the temporary custody of any school, camp, institution, or other facility for delinquent children operated by the county, by a district, or by a private agency within or

---

[15]RC 2152.22(C)(3).
[16]RC 2152.22(E).
[17]RC 2152.22(F).
[18]RC 2152.22(D).
[19]RC 2152.22(G).

[Section 27:5]
[1]RC 2152.19(A)(1).
[2]See RC 5103.10.
[3]RC 2151.353(A)(4).
[4]RC 2151.412(A)(2).
[5]RC 2151.3510.

outside the state.[1] A juvenile court is authorized to order placement of a delinquent child, who is in the temporary custody of a children services board, into a residential treatment facility.[2]

Prior to April 3, 2003 and the implementation of Am. Sub. H.B. 400, a final order of disposition for a delinquent child could not include confinement to a juvenile detention center. Since that date, a child could be committed to a detention facility or district detention facility operated under RC 2152.41 for a period of up to 90 days.[3] However, a district detention home approved for such purpose by the Department of Youth Services may receive children committed to its temporary custody under this statute and may provide the care, treatment, and training required.[4]

When a county or district operates a school, camp, or other facility for delinquent children pursuant to RC 2151.65, the juvenile court must determine which children are to be admitted to the facility, the duration of their commitment, and the date of release or transfer.[5]

Residual parental rights, privileges, and responsibilities, including the duty of support, remain with the parents upon the commitment of their child to a county-operated facility for delinquent children.[6]

§ 27:7 Community control sanctions

Under S.B. 179, the court may place a delinquent juvenile on "community control" under any sanctions, services, and conditions the court prescribes.[1] Moving away from probation, the new law designates a number of community control sanctions, including basic probation and intensive probation. In addition, the court may impose a host of other sanctions, such as day reporting, community service, school and work requirements, curfew, monitored time, house arrest, and electronic monitoring. In addition, two drug dispositions are recognized: drug monitoring and drug assessment and treatment. Moreover, various driver's license dispositions are authorized. Some of these dispositions are discussed in the following sections. Other are discussed below.

Community control includes:

Day reporting.[2] In day reporting, the child is required each day to report to and leave an approved reporting location at specified times in order to participate in work, education or training, treatment, and other approved programs.

Community service.[3] The court may impose a period of community service of up to (1) 500 hours for a felony or M-1, (2) 200 hours for an M-2, M-3, or M-4, and (3) 30 hours for minor misdemeanor.

[Section 27:6]

[1]RC 2152.19(A)(2).

[2]In re Lawson, 98 Ohio App. 3d 456, 648 N.E.2d 889 (10th Dist. Franklin County 1994).

[3]RC 2152.19(A)(3). Note that the legislature did not include language in RC 2152.41(A) authorizing post-dispositional use of confinement in a detention facility. See § 27:18, "Catch-all" provision. But see, In re Hennessey, 146 Ohio App. 3d 743, 2001-Ohio-2267, 768 N.E.2d 663 (3d Dist. Mercer County 2001).

[4]RC 2151.34. See Matter of Hale, 1986 WL 4925 (Ohio Ct. App. 6th Dist. Wood County 1986); RC 5139.281.

[5]RC 2151.65.

[6]In re Hinko, 84 Ohio App. 3d 89, 616 N.E.2d 515 (8th Dist. Cuyahoga County 1992).

[Section 27:7]

[1]RC 2152.19(A)(4).

[2]RC 2152.19(A)(3)(c).

[3]RC 2152.19(A)(3)(d).

School and work.[4] The court may require the child to obtain (1) a high school diploma, (2) a high school equivalence certificate, (3) vocation training, or (4) employment.

Curfew.[5] The court may impose a curfew involving daytime or evening hours.[6]

Monitored time.[7] Monitored time imposes only the obligation to obey the law during the specified time period.[8]

Abide by law.[9] The court must require any juvenile on community control to abide by the law during the period of community control. This is in addition to any other sanction.

§ 27:8 Probation

The law designates a number of community control sanctions, including basic probation and intensive probation. Basic probation requires the offender to maintain contact with a person appointed by the court to supervise the child in accordance with the sanctions imposed.[1] In contrast, intensive probation supervision requires the offender to maintain *frequent* contact with a person appointed by the court to supervise the child while the child is seeking or maintaining employment and participating in training, education, and treatment programs in accordance with the sanctions imposed.[2]

Probation is a frequently used disposition for a delinquent child.[3] Prior to the enactment of S.B. 179, "probation" was defined as a legal status created by court order following an adjudication that a child is delinquent, unruly, or a juvenile traffic offender, whereby the child is permitted to remain in his parent's, guardian's, or custodian's home subject to supervision or under the supervision of any agency designated by the court. The child could be returned to the court for violation of probation at any time during the probationary period.[4] In all cases in which a child is placed on probation, such child must be provided a written statement of the conditions of probation and must be instructed regarding them.[5] Probation conditions which prohibited a child from going to a specified place of business, from associating with a specified individual, and from dressing as a female were held to be unreasonable, arbitrary, and capricious and an abuse of discretion.[6]

Term. The length of time for which a child is to remain on probation may be fixed at the dispositional hearing or at a later date and may extend until

---

[4]RC 2152.19(A)(3)(e).

[5]RC 2152.19(A)(3)(h).

[6]See also RC 2929.02(H) ("a requirement that an offender during a specified period of time be at a designated place."

[7]RC 2152.19(A)(3)(i).

[8]RC 2152.02(U) (monitored time is defined in RC 2929.01(Z) ("a period of time during which an offender continues to be under the control of the sentencing court or parole board, subject to no conditions other than leading a law abiding life").

[9]RC 2152.19(A)(3). Streamlines former RC 2151.355(A)(2), which included the phrase "gun laws."

[Section 27:8]

[1]RC 2152.19(A)(3)(a); RC 2151.355(A)(17).

[2]RC 2152.19(A)(3)(b).

[3]RC 2152.19(A)(3). See Matter of McCourt, 1993 WL 327677 (Ohio Ct. App. 7th Dist. Belmont County 1993).

[4]RC 2151.011(B)(34), repealed by S.B. 179.

[5]RC 2151.14, repealed by S.B. 179; Juv. R. 34(C). All children placed on probation by the Cuyahoga County Juvenile Court are subject to certain standard conditions such as attending school, obeying parents, and maintaining appointments with the probation officer.

[6]In re Miller, 82 Ohio App. 3d 81, 611 N.E.2d 451 (6th Dist. Lucas County 1992).

the time the child reaches age 21.[7] The court order placing the child on probation continues until it expires by its own terms or is revoked or terminated by court order. Thus, the authority of a probation officer to supervise a child on probation does not include the authority to terminate court-ordered probation.[8] The termination of a probation order by the court deprives the court of its continuing jurisdiction, preventing the court from revoking the suspension of a permanent commitment to the Department of Youth Services even though the child had been released from official probation.[9]

Conditions. RC 2152.19(B) mandates that if a child is placed on probation after having been found delinquent, the court must require the child as a condition of probation to abide by the law, including complying with the provisions of RC Chapter 2923 relating to the possession, sale, furnishing, transfer, disposition, purchase, acquisition, carrying, conveying, or use of, or other conduct involving a firearm or dangerous ordnance, as defined in RC 2923.11.

Restitution. If a child is adjudged delinquent for the offenses of vandalism (RC 2909.05), criminal damaging or endangering (RC 2909.06), or criminal mischief (RC 2909.07), and if restitution is appropriate under the circumstances of the case, the court must require the child to make restitution for the property damage as a condition of probation.[10] Restitution may also be made a condition of probation for any child adjudged delinquent for violation of any other Revised Code section. In such cases, restitution is limited to the amount of any property damage and the value of any property that was the subject of a theft offense.[11] A restitution order may also be appropriate as an independent disposition apart from probation.[12]

Restitution may take many forms, including a cash reimbursement (paid in a lump sum or in installments), the performance of repair work (to restore any damaged property to its original condition), the performance of a reasonable amount of labor for the victim (approximately equal to the value of the property that was damaged or stolen), the performance of community service or community work, or any combination of these forms.[13]

Probation department. The court's probation department, under the direction of the juvenile judge and the chief probation officer, must keep informed concerning the conduct and condition of each person under its supervision and must report thereon to the judge as he directs.[14] Each probation officer is required to use all suitable methods to aid persons on probation and to bring about improvement in their conduct and condition. The department must maintain full records of its work, which records are considered

---

[7]In re DeGeronimo, No. 40089 (8th Dist. Ct. App., Cuyahoga, 6-28-79); In re Weber, 61 Ohio App. 3d 636, 573 N.E.2d 730 (8th Dist. Cuyahoga County 1989). See also § 33:4, Abuse, neglect, and dependency proceedings.

[8]In re Burton, 1997 WL 473099 (Ohio Ct. App. 8th Dist. Cuyahoga County 1997).

[9]In re Cross, 96 Ohio St. 3d 328, 2002-Ohio-4183, 774 N.E.2d 258 (2002) ("A juvenile court does not have the jurisdiction to reimpose a suspended commitment to a Department of Youth Services facility after a juvenile has been released from probation.") (syllabus). See § 33:7, Suspended commitments.

[10]RC 2152.20. Victims of delinquent acts may also be entitled to compensation from the Reparations Rotary Fund established pursuant to RC 2743.70. See § 27:13, Restitution.

[11]RC 2152.20(A)(3).

[12]RC 2152.20(A)(3). See § 27:13, Restitution.

[13]RC 2152.20(A)(3). Many juvenile courts have established programs which are funded by a state subsidy (RC 5139.34) and which provide delinquents with temporary, part-time jobs in the community. Typically, the majority of the money earned by the child is given directly to the victim, with the child receiving a minimal wage.

[14]RC 2151.14(A).

confidential and not available to the public.[15]

Foster care. A juvenile court may transfer to any foster facility certified by the Department of Job and Family Services any child between the ages of 12 and 18, other than a psychotic or mentally retarded child, who has been found delinquent for violating any law or ordinance and placed on probation.[16]

§ 27:9 Drug & alcohol dispositions

There are two drug dispositions as part of community control sanctions. First, the court may impose a period of drug or alcohol monitoring.[1] Second, the court may require (1) alcohol or drug assessment or counseling, or (2) a period in an alcohol or drug treatment program with a level of security as determined by the court.[2]

If a child is adjudged delinquent for any drug abuse offense[3] or disorderly conduct while intoxicated,[4] the court, in addition to imposing any discretionary order of disposition, is required to both (1) order the child to participate in a drug abuse or alcohol abuse counseling program and (2) suspend or revoke the child's temporary instruction permit or probationary operator's license until the child attains the age of 18 years or attends, at the court's discretion, and satisfactorily completes a drug abuse or alcohol abuse education, intervention, or treatment program specified by the court.[5] During the time that the child is attending the program, the court must retain the child's permit or license and return it to the child after he satisfactorily completes the program.[6]

Within 10 days after the adjudication, the court must notify the Bureau of Motor Vehicles of the adjudicatory order.[7] If the child satisfactorily completes a drivers' intervention program, the program operator must promptly notify the court,[8] whereupon the court must immediately notify the Bureau of Motor Vehicles.[9]

§ 27:10 House arrest & electronic monitoring

As part of community control sanctions, the court may impose house arrest, electronic monitoring, or both.

S.B. 179 permits house arrest with or without electronic monitoring.[1] (Prior law tied house "detention" to electronic monitoring.[2]) In addition, the court may impose electronic monitoring, with or without house arrest, that

---

[15]RC 2151.14(A). For further discussion of the confidentiality of juvenile court records, see § 35:2, Confidentiality requirement; § 35:3, Non-juvenile court proceedings.

[16]RC 5139.39.

[Section 27:9]

[1]RC 2152.19(A)(3)(f).

[2]RC 2152.19(A)(3)(g).

[3]"Drug abuse offense" is defined in RC 2925.01.

[4]RC 2917.11(B).

[5]RC 2152.19(B)(2). See also RC 4507.162. If the child does not yet own a temporary instruction permit or probationary operator's license, he may not be issued one until he satisfactorily completes the program (RC 4507.08).

[6]RC 2152.19(B)(2). For discussion of the period of time for which the license may be suspended, see § 28:2, Suspension or revocation.

[7]RC 4507.021(D)(2)(a). Although this order is mandated by the dispositional statute (RC 2151.355(B)), it is made at the adjudicatory hearing, which may be held well before the dispositional hearing (see Juv. R. 34(A)).

[8]RC 3793.10.

[9]RC 4507.021(D)(2)(b).

[Section 27:10]

[1]RC 2152.19(A)(4)(j).

[2]RC 2151.355(A)(13).

does not exceed the maximum prison term available to an adult for the same offense.[3] Several changes in electronic monitoring were made. First, electronic monitoring can continue until the juvenile reaches age 21[4] Second, the definition of electronic monitoring broadened to include any technology that can adequately track and determine the location of a subject, approved by Department of Rehabilitation and Corrections. It includes, but is not limited to, satellite surveillance, voice tracking, and retinal scanning.[5] Third, juveniles can be subject to electronic monitoring at school and in workplaces in addition to house arrest.[6]

If the child's adjudication of delinquency is based on a criminal offense that would qualify an adult as an eligible offender,[7] the court may impose a period of electronically monitored house detention in accordance with RC 2151.355(J) that does not exceed the maximum sentence of imprisonment that could be imposed upon an adult who commits the same act,[8] and does not extend beyond the child's eighteenth birthday.[9] A period of electronically monitored house detention may be imposed in addition to or in lieu of any other dispositional order.[10]

If a court imposes a period of electronically monitored house detention upon a child, the child is required to enter into a written contract with the court agreeing to comply with all court-imposed restrictions and requirements, and agreeing to pay any fee imposed by the court for the costs of the monitoring.[11] The child must also agree to waive the right to receive credit for any time served on electronically monitored house detention toward the period of any other dispositional order imposed upon him for the act for which electronically monitored house detention was imposed if he violates any of the restrictions or requirements of electronically monitored house detention.[12]

§ 27:11 Driving privileges

The court may suspend the juvenile's driver's license, probationary driver's license, or temporary instruction. In addition, the court may suspend the registration of all motor vehicles registered in the child's name.[1] The suspension or revocation may remain in effect until the child's twenty-first birthday.[2]

If a child is found delinquent (1) for a weapons violation committed on school property,[3] (2) for a drug offense, or (3) for some disorderly conduct while intoxicated, the court, in addition to any other order of disposition, must revoke the child's temporary instruction permit and deny the child the issuance of another temporary permit, or must suspend any other driver's

---

[3]RC 2152.19(A)(4)(k). Former RC 2151.355(A)(10) repealed.

[4]RC 2152.19(A)(3)(k).

[5]RC 2152.02(K) (citing RC 2929.23).

[6]RC 2152.19(A)(4)(k).

[7]See RC 2929.23(A)(3).

[8]RC 2151.355(A)(10). See also RC 2151.355(A)(12).

[9]RC 2151.355(J)(2).

[10]RC 2151.355(J)(2).

[11]RC 2152.19(A)(4)(k). See RC 2929.23(E).

[12]RC 2152.19(A)(4)(k).

[Section 27:11]

[1]RC 2152.19(A)(4)(l). For discussion of this alternative, see Juvenile Traffic Offender Dispositions Ch 28.

[2]In re Mason, 1997 WL 803083 (Ohio Ct. App. 9th Dist. Summit County 1997). The child is ineligible for issuance of a license or permit during the period of suspension. After the suspension ends, the child must pay any applicable reinstatement fee and comply with all requirements governing license reinstatement.

[3]RC 2923.122.

license of the child, or deny the child the issuance of any other driver's license.[4]

§ 27:12 Fines

The juvenile court may impose maximum fines according to a graduated schedule:

(1) Minor misdemeanor or unclassified misdemeanor: $50;

(2) Fourth degree misdemeanor: $100;

(3) Third degree misdemeanor: $150;

(4) Second degree misdemeanor: $200;

(5) First degree misdemeanor: $250;

(6) Fifth degree felony or unclassified felony: $300;

(7) Fourth degree felony: $400;

(8) Third degree felony: $750;

(9) Second degree felony: $1,000;

(10) First degree felony: $1,500; and

(11) Aggravated murder or murder: $2,000.[1]

The imposition of a fine and costs often accompanies other dispositions and may include an order directing the child to perform work assignments to earn money to pay the fine and costs.[2] However, since the assessment of a fine and costs constitutes a final order, once it is ordered the court may not also transfer the case to the juvenile court of the child's resident county for further disposition.[3]

A juvenile court may not commit a child who has been adjudged delinquent to a county jail or juvenile detention home upon the failure, refusal, or inability of the child to pay a fine and/or court costs.[4]

§ 27:13 Restitution

The child may be ordered to make restitution for all or part of the property damage caused by his delinquent act and for all or part of the value of the property that was the subject of his delinquent theft offense.[1] Citing RC 2151.355(A)(10),[2] an appellate court has held that a juvenile court may order restitution for the victim's medical expenses even though RC 2151.355(A)(8) provided for restitution involving theft and property damage only.[3]

Restitution may be ordered independently of any other order.[4]

---

[4]RC 2152.19(B)(1) & RC 2152.19(B)(2).

[Section 27:12]

[1]RC 2152.20(A)(1).

[2]See RC 2152.20(A)(3). See also § 27:8, Probation; § 27:13, Restitution.

[3]In re Sekulich, 65 Ohio St. 2d 13, 19 Ohio Op. 3d 192, 417 N.E.2d 1014 (1981).

[4]In re Rinehart, 10 Ohio App. 3d 318, 462 N.E.2d 448 (4th Dist. Ross County 1983).

[Section 27:13]

[1]RC 2152.20(A)(3).

[2]Now RC 2152.20(A)(3).

[3]In re Lambert, 63 Ohio App. 3d 121, 577 N.E.2d 1184 (4th Dist. Lawrence County 1989); In re Joshua S., 1996 WL 256596 (Ohio Ct. App. 6th Dist. Erie County 1996). See § 27:18, "Catch-all" provision.

[4]The variety of forms of restitution is discussed in § 27:8, Probation. See In re Jacobs, 148 Ohio App. 3d 173, 2002-Ohio-2844, 772 N.E.2d 671 (3d Dist. Seneca County 2002) ("[W]e note the appellant's assertion that if the 'catch-all' provision of R.C. 2151.355(A) is utilized, the juvenile court is confined to imposing a disposition prescribed by another statute within the Juvenile Code. The appellant contends that no such disposition is authorized by the Juvenile Code. This argument is without merit. The statute neither says such a disposition is so restricted, nor do

It is error for a juvenile court to order restitution without holding an evidentiary hearing on the existence of damages and the proper amount of restitution.[5] However, there is no denial of due process or equal protection when the court equally divides damages among three juveniles, who, by their joint and concerted efforts and actions, seriously damaged another's property.[6]

A juvenile court does not have jurisdiction to order a parent to make restitution for the destructive acts of his or her children, since recovery from the parent may only be gained through a civil suit under RC 3109.09, RC 3109.10,[7] or RC 2307.70. Nor may a juvenile court award compensation to foster parents for the damaging acts of a county.[8]

S.B. 179 authorized restitution in an amount based on the victim's economic loss.[9] The court determines the amount based on a figure recommended by the victim, the victim's survivor, the delinquent, a presentence investigation report, estimates or receipts for repairing or replacing property, or any other information. If there is a dispute, a hearing is required.

Restitution may be paid directly to the victim in open court, or through the probation department or court clerk. Any restitution is credited against losses recovered by the victim in a civil action. A surcharge of up to 5% of the restitution amount may be imposed to defray collection and processing costs.

A motion to modify, based on a substantial change in the offender's ability to pay, may be filed by the juvenile or the victim (through the prosecutor).

§ 27:14 Forfeiture

If a child is found delinquent for violating RC 2923.32,[1] in addition to any other order of disposition, the court must enter an order of criminal forfeiture against the child.[2]

If a child is found delinquent for violation of a felony drug abuse offense,[3] the child loses any right to the possession of, and forfeits to the state any right, title, and interest he may have in property derived from or used in the crime,[4] provided that (1) the complaint specifies the nature of the right, title, or interest of the child in the property that is potentially subject to forfeiture, or a description of the child's property that is potentially subject to forfeiture, to the extent that the child's right, title, or interest in the property or the

---

we find that such a restriction is in place. Even if such a proviso did exist, R.C. 2151.356(A)(5) allowed a juvenile court to require a juvenile traffic offender to 'make restitution for all damages caused by the child's traffic violation or any part of the damages.' Ordering the appellant to make restitution for the cost of Faber's funeral expenses clearly falls within the former R.C. 2151.356.").

[5]In re Hall, 65 Ohio App. 3d 88, 582 N.E.2d 1055 (10th Dist. Franklin County 1989); In re Holmes, 70 Ohio App. 2d 75, 24 Ohio Op. 3d 93, 434 N.E.2d 747 (1st Dist. Hamilton County 1980); In re Alonzo B., 1999 WL 63649 (Ohio Ct. App. 6th Dist. Erie County 1999); In re Hatfield, 2003-Ohio-5404, 2003 WL 22318010 (Ohio Ct. App. 4th Dist. Lawrence County 2003).

[6]Daudt v. Daudt, 1987 WL 13715 (Ohio Ct. App. 12th Dist. Butler County 1987).

[7]In re Watkins, No. 42409 (8th Dist. Ct. App., Cuyahoga, 1-22-81); In re Daudt, 1986 WL 9630 (Ohio Ct. App. 12th Dist. Butler County 1986); In re Joshua S., 1996 WL 256596 (Ohio Ct. App. 6th Dist. Erie County 1996).

[8]Tingley v. Williams County Department of Human Services, 1993 WL 313710 (Ohio Ct. App. 6th Dist. Williams County 1993). See also Tingley v. Williams Cty. Dept. of Human Serv., 100 Ohio App. 3d 385, 654 N.E.2d 148 (6th Dist. Williams County 1995).

[9]RC 2152.20(A)(3). Former law required restitution, "if appropriate under the circumstances," for vandalism, criminal damaging, and criminal mischief. RC 2151.355(A)(2). It also permitted restitution in other cases. RC 2151.355(A)(9).

[Section 27:14]
[1]RC 2923.32 governs the offense of "engaging in a pattern of corrupt activity."
[2]RC 2152.20(B)(1). See RC 2923.32(B) to RC 2923.32(F).
[3]"Felony drug abuse offense" is defined in RC 2925.01. See RC 2152.20(B)(2).
[4]RC 2152.20(B)(2), RC 2925.42(A). See RC 2925.41 to RC 2925.45.

property is known at the time of the filing of the complaint;[5] or (2) the property in question was not reasonably foreseen to be subject to forfeiture at the time of the filing of the complaint, the prosecuting attorney gave prompt notice to the child when the property was discovered to be subject to forfeiture, and the child is found delinquent for the offense.[6]

Proceedings for forfeiture of property are governed by RC 2925.42(B) (criminal forfeiture) and RC 2925.43(E) (civil forfeiture). Forfeiture proceedings under RC 2923.44 to RC 2923.47 apply to children who are or could be adjudicated delinquent for criminal gang activity under RC 2923.42.[7] Ohio law also permits the court to order forfeiture for seizures of other types of contraband.[8] Forfeiture of contraband constitutes a separate disposition in addition to any other disposition utilized by the court for the underlying delinquency offense.[9] Ten percent of the proceeds of property forfeited by a juvenile court must be applied to one or more certified alcohol and drug addiction programs.[10]

§ 27:15 Costs & reimbursements

A delinquent may be required to pay court costs.[1] In addition, reimbursements for other expenses are authorized, such as the cost of implementing community control sanctions, including a supervision fee.[2] The costs of confinement in a DYS institution or residential facility, including a per diem for room and board, medical and dental costs, and cost of repairing property damaged by the delinquent while confined may be assessed against the juvenile.[3]

§ 27:16 Truancy dispositions

In 2000[1] some types of truancy were included in delinquency jurisdiction: (1) repeat habitual truancy and (2) chronic truancy.[2] S.B. 179 transfered these provisions to the new chapter.

The court may require a delinquent child "not to be" absent without legitimate excuse for (1) five or more consecutive days, (2) seven or more school days in one school month, or (3) 12 or more school days in a school year.[3]

A chronic truant or a repeat habitual truant may be required to participate in a truancy prevention mediation program.[4] In addition, the court may impose any other sanction with certain limitations. The child may not be placed in a child facility,[5] unless child violated a lawful court order.[6] However,

---

[5]RC 2925.42(B)(1)(a).

[6]RC 2925.42(B)(1)(b). See RC 2152.20(B).

[7]RC 2152.20(B)(3).

[8]RC 2933.43. In re Harman, 63 Ohio Misc. 2d 529, 635 N.E.2d 96 (C.P. 1994).

[9]RC 2152.19(A), RC 2152.20(B). See State v. Casalicchio, 58 Ohio St. 3d 178, 569 N.E.2d 916 (1991).

[10]RC 2923.35(D)(1)(a). See RC 2925.44, RC 2933.41(E), RC 2933.43, RC 2933.44.

[Section 27:15]

[1]RC 2152.20(A)(2). In re Graham, 2002-Ohio-6615, 2002 WL 31718885 (Ohio Ct. App. 7th Dist. Mahoning County 2002) (No court costs should be assessed against a juvenile when a delinquency case is dismissed.).

[2]RC 2152.20(A)(4)(a).

[3]RC 2152.20(A)(4)(b).

[Section 27:16]

[1]S.B. 181.

[2]See § 4:5, Truancy.

[3]RC 2152.19(A)(5).

[4]RC 2152.19(A)(6)(a)(i).

[5]See § 27:6, County or private facility commitment.

the child may be placed in a detention facility or district facility for up to 90 days.[7]

Parental control. If the court determines that the parent, guardian, or custodian failed to send the child to school,[8] it may require that person to participate (1) in a truancy prevention mediation program, or (2) in any community service program, preferably one that requires involvement the child's school.[9]

§ 27:17 Court custody

An additional statutory option for the disposition of a delinquent child permits the court to commit the child to the custody of the court itself.[1] This allows juvenile courts to seek reimbursement under Title IV-E of the Social Security Act for foster care maintenance costs incurred by the courts for children under their jurisdiction.[2]

§ 27:18 "Catch-all" provision

The delinquency dispositional statute also includes a catch-all provision,[1] permitting the court to make any further disposition that it finds proper. Prior to a 1990 amendment to the statute,[2] the authority of the juvenile court to impose an adult sentence on a delinquent who had reached the age of 18 or 21 pending final disposition was an issue which had resulted in inconsistent decisions from the appellate courts.[3] But, pursuant to RC 2152.26(F)(2), as amended by Am. Sub. H.B. 400 and effective April 3, 2003, an adjudicated child may be held under a court-ordered disposition in a county, multi-county, or municipal jail or workhouse or other place where an adult, convicted of a crime, under arrest, or charged with crime may be held.[4]

Pursuant to the catch-all provision, a court may order a school district to establish a detailed educational program for a delinquent child who is hand-

---

[6]RC 2152.19(A)(6)(a)(ii).

[7]RC 2152.19(A)(3), effective January 1, 2004.

[8]As required by RC 3321.38.

[9]RC 2152.19(A)(6)(b).

[Section 27:17]
[1]RC 2152.19(A)(4).

[2]See 42 U.S.C.A. § 672; RC 5101.141.

[Section 27:18]
[1]RC 2152.19(A)(7) (former RC 2151.355(A)(25)). This division was amended by 1998 H.B. 526, eff. 9-1-98. The division was renumbered by 1998 H.B. 2, eff.1-1-99, but did not include the language of the prior amendment. Harmonization pursuant to RC 1.52 is possible.

[2]1989 H.B. 166, eff. 2-14-90.

[3]See Corona, 1981 WL 4502 (Ohio Ct. App. 8th Dist. Cuyahoga County 1981), and In re Cox, 36 Ohio App. 2d 65, 65 Ohio Op. 2d 51, 301 N.E.2d 907 (7th Dist. Mahoning County 1973), holding that imprisonment in an adult facility was permissible. See In re Lambert, 63 Ohio App. 3d 121, 577 N.E.2d 1184 (4th Dist. Lawrence County 1989); State v. Grady, 3 Ohio App. 3d 174, 176, 444 N.E.2d 51 (8th Dist. Cuyahoga County 1981); and In re Day, No. 669 (11th Dist. Ct. App., Geauga, 8-23-76), holding that imprisonment in an adult facility was not within the jurisdiction of the juvenile court.

[4]In re Hennessey, 146 Ohio App. 3d 743, 746, 2001-Ohio-2267, 768 N.E.2d 663 (3d Dist. Mercer County 2001) ("While R.C. 2151.355 and 2151.312 provide a juvenile court with wide latitude in sentencing a delinquent child by allowing the court to make 'any further disposition that the court finds proper,' or to order a commitment to '[a]ny other suitable place designated by the court,' these options do not include placement in an adult county jail because the plain language of R.C. 2151.355(A)(25) and 2151.312(D) prohibits the court from ordering a delinquent child to serve any time in the county jail even though he is chronologically an adult."). But see In Matter of McKinley, 1998 WL 355874 (Ohio Ct. App. 7th Dist. Belmont County 1998), affirming a juvenile court order "sentencing" a child to county jail where the child had reached age 18 prior to his juvenile court "trial."

icapped,[5] may order a child's parents to participate in counseling,[6] and may order a delinquent child to make restitution to a victim for medical bills resulting from assault.[7] Although the provision has resulted in innovative dispositions designed to meet the specific rehabilitative needs of the child, it has also resulted in several controversial dispositions. The broad discretionary power provided by the statute is limited by those statutory provisions governing the juvenile court's jurisdiction.[8] It has also been held that the "choice of places to which a court can send a juvenile offender is essentially a legislative rather than a judicial prerogative. . . . In short, the court's authority to make 'any further disposition' has been ruled to be confined to a choice of dispositions provided for in other statutes of the Juvenile Code."[9] The disposition of a child may include, by legislative decree, confinement for up to 90 days for disposition[10] but not for failure to pay a fine or costs.[11] In addition, neither this provision nor any other statute permits the juvenile court to order a parent to pay for the destructive acts of his or her child.[12] Although RC 2152.17(E) permits a juvenile court to order a child to serve consecutive commitments to the Department of Youth Services, the court may not designate a specific department institution for the child.[13]

It has been held that the catch-all provision[14] authorizes a juvenile court to impose an additional term of commitment to the Department of Youth Services for a delinquency offense involving a firearm specification, even if the specification was never averred to in the complaint.[15] Furthermore, the provision, along with the jurisdictional statute (RC 2151.23), gives juvenile courts jurisdiction to hear and decide forfeiture proceedings involving delinquent children.[16]

§ 27:19 Plural dispositions

Under certain circumstances the court may choose to impose more than one disposition for a child adjudged delinquent, such as restitution and commitment to the Department of Youth Services,[1] and electronic monitoring and any other dispositional order.[2] However, the court's authority to order

---

[5]Matter of Bremmer, 1993 WL 95556 (Ohio Ct. App. 8th Dist. Cuyahoga County 1993).

[6]In re Joshua S., 1996 WL 256596 (Ohio Ct. App. 6th Dist. Erie County 1996); Matter of Joey O., 1997 WL 785621 (Ohio Ct. App. 6th Dist. Lucas County 1997).

[7]In re Lambert, 63 Ohio App. 3d 121, 577 N.E.2d 1184 (4th Dist. Lawrence County 1989).

[8]In re Hoodlet, 72 Ohio App. 3d 115, 593 N.E.2d 478 (4th Dist. Athens County 1991); In Matter of Kelly, 1995 WL 656944 (Ohio Ct. App. 10th Dist. Franklin County 1995).

[9]State v. Grady, 3 Ohio App. 3d 174, 444 N.E.2d 51 (8th Dist. Cuyahoga County 1981). See In re Sanders, 72 Ohio App. 3d 655, 595 N.E.2d 974 (8th Dist. Cuyahoga County 1991).

[10]RC 2152.19(A)(3), effective January 1, 2004.

[11]In re Hennessey, 146 Ohio App. 3d 743, 746, 2001-Ohio-2267, 768 N.E.2d 663 (3d Dist. Mercer County 2001); In re Rinehart, 10 Ohio App. 3d 318, 462 N.E.2d 448 (4th Dist. Ross County 1983); In re Bolden, 37 Ohio App. 2d 7, 66 Ohio Op. 2d 26, 306 N.E.2d 166 (3d Dist. Allen County 1973); OAG 70-143. See § 27:6, County or private facility commitment.

[12]In re Watkins, No. 42409 (8th Dist. Ct. App., Cuyahoga, 1-22-81).

[13]See § 33:9, Department of Youth Services. See also RC 2152.18(A).

[14]RC 2152.19(A).

[15]Matter of Laquatra, 1998 WL 23841 (Ohio Ct. App. 8th Dist. Cuyahoga County 1998). See § 27:3, Department of Youth Services commitment.

[16]In re Harman, 63 Ohio Misc. 2d 529, 635 N.E.2d 96 (C.P. 1994); State v. Corrado, 1993 WL 76234 (Ohio Ct. App. 11th Dist. Lake County 1993). Criminal statutes which govern forfeiture include RC 2923.32(B)(3), RC 2925.42, RC 2925.43, RC 2933.42, and RC 2933.43. See § 27:2, Dispositional alternatives.

[Section 27:19]

[1]Matter of Wood, 1986 WL 4947 (Ohio Ct. App. 3d Dist. Marion County 1986).

[2]RC 2152.19.

more than one disposition is not unlimited. In *In re Bolden*,[3] in which a child was adjudged delinquent on three separate assault complaints, the juvenile court judge committed the child to the custody of the Ohio Youth Commission (now Ohio Department of Youth Services) for diagnostic study[4] on one complaint, placed him in the physical care and custody of his parents on the second complaint, and placed him on probation with the court's probation department on the third complaint.[5] On appeal, it was held that plural delinquency findings constitute a finding of a single legal status and permit either one disposition common to all the complaints and findings of delinquency or separate dispositions for each finding based on a single complaint, which findings must be consistent with and not mutually exclusive of each other. Because it was impossible to simultaneously place the child on probation, return him to his parents, and place him in the custody of the Ohio Youth Commission (now Department of Youth Services), the dispositions imposed by the juvenile court were inconsistent. Other courts have held that a juvenile court may simultaneously place a delinquent child on probation on one complaint, while committing the child to a residential treatment facility on a second complaint.[6]

It has also been held that where a juvenile court issues only one finding of delinquency, even though based on three separate delinquency complaints, it is without authority to enter additional dispositions on the other two underlying offenses by ordering separate court costs on each.[7] The court also held that RC 2941.25(A), which provides that adults indicted for allied offenses may be convicted of only one, does not apply to delinquents because children are not charged with crimes.[8]

In *State ex rel. Duganitz v. Court of Common Pleas*,[9] involving a child who was charged with several delinquency complaints, some of which were classified as felonies and some misdemeanors, the juvenile court judge transferred the felony complaints to the adult court for criminal prosecution[10] and retained jurisdiction over the disposition of the misdemeanor complaints. This action was approved by a court of appeals because there is no provision for transferring to adult court the trial of juveniles for misdemeanors.

A juvenile court may not impose a fine and court costs on a delinquent child and also transfer the matter to the juvenile court of the child's resident county for further disposition.[11] Since the imposition of a fine pursuant to RC 2151.355 is a final dispositional order, nothing remains for transfer to the other juvenile court.

§ 27:20 Victim-mediation

With the assent of the victim, the juvenile court may require the child to participate in a reconciliation or mediation program that includes a meeting in which the child and the victim discuss the criminal act, discuss restitu-

---

[3]In re Bolden, 37 Ohio App. 2d 7, 66 Ohio Op. 2d 26, 306 N.E.2d 166 (3d Dist. Allen County 1973).

[4]RC 2152.19 no longer permits a temporary commitment for diagnostic study.

[5]See also Matter of Hill, 1993 WL 291068 (Ohio Ct. App. 3d Dist. Union County 1993).

[6]State v. Matha, 107 Ohio App. 3d 756, 669 N.E.2d 504 (9th Dist. Lorain County 1995); In re Taylor, 1995 WL 134754 (Ohio Ct. App. 9th Dist. Lorain County 1995).

[7]Matter of Lugo, 1991 WL 106085 (Ohio Ct. App. 6th Dist. Wood County 1991).

[8]Matter of Lugo, 1991 WL 106085 (Ohio Ct. App. 6th Dist. Wood County 1991). See also In Matter Of: Skeens, 1982 WL 3994 (Ohio Ct. App. 10th Dist. Franklin County 1982); In re Durham, 1998 WL 635107 (Ohio Ct. App. 10th Dist. Franklin County 1998).

[9]State, ex rel. Duganitz v. Court of Common Pleas of Cuyahoga County, 69 Ohio St. 2d 270, 23 Ohio Op. 3d 267, 432 N.E.2d 163 (1982).

[10]See RC 2151.26. See also Juv. R. 30. Transfer to the adult court is technically not a disposition, since it is a pre-adjudicatory order.

[11]In re Sekulich, 65 Ohio St. 2d 13, 19 Ohio Op. 3d 192, 417 N.E.2d 1014 (1981).

tion, and consider other sanctions for the criminal act.[1]

Cross References
§ 4:4, Ch 28, Ch 33, Ch 35
Research References
Katz and Giannelli, Baldwin's Ohio Practice, Criminal Law (2d ed.) § 78:1
Carlin, Baldwin's Ohio Practice, Merrick-Rippner Probate Law (6th ed.), Ch 107

[Section 27:20]
[1]RC 2152.19(C).

Chapter 28

Juvenile Traffic Offender Dispositions

> **KeyCite®:** Cases and other legal materials listed in KeyCite Scope can be researched through West's KeyCite service on Westlaw®. Use KeyCite to check citations for form, parallel references, prior and later history, and comprehensive citator information, including citations to other decisions and secondary materials.

§ 28:1   Juvenile traffic offender dispositions—Introduction
§ 28:2   Suspension or revocation
§ 28:3   Financial sanctions
§ 28:4   Community control and probation
§ 28:5   Restitution
§ 28:6   Commitment to juvenile facility
§ 28:7   Seat belt law violations
§ 28:8   Revocation of probationary operator's license
§ 28:9   Occupational driving privileges
§ 28:10   Imposition of adult penalties
§ 28:11   Parental orders

§ 28:1 Juvenile traffic offender dispositions—Introduction

This chapter discusses dispositions in juvenile traffic offenses cases. Traffic offender jurisdiction is considered in Ch 7.

The procedural issues that relate to juvenile court dispositional hearings are examined in Ch 25. The requirements attending other types of juvenile court jurisdiction are explored in separate chapters: delinquency (Ch 27), unruliness (Ch 29), and neglect, abuse, and dependency (Ch 30).

In 2002, the juvenile traffic offender sections (along with the delinquency sections) were transferred to new RC Chapter 2152.[1]

§ 28:2 Suspension or revocation

If a child is adjudicated a juvenile traffic offender, the juvenile court may suspend the child's probationary driver's license or the registration of any motor vehicles registered in the name of the child for such period as the court prescribes.[1]

In some juvenile courts, the child's driver's license is restricted for a period of time, permitting the child to drive for limited, specified purposes. The record of any revocation or suspension must be sent to the registrar of the Bureau of Motor Vehicles pursuant to RC 4507.15.

Although it is settled that a juvenile court does not have the authority to permanently revoke a child's driver's license,[2] the maximum period for which a juvenile court may suspend or revoke a license was not clear. In 2002, RC

[Section 28:1]
[1]S.B. 179.

[Section 28:2]
[1]RC 2152.21(A)(2).

[2]In re Finlaw, 69 Ohio App. 3d 474, 590 N.E.2d 1340 (2d Dist. Greene County 1990); In re Weber, 61 Ohio App. 3d 636, 573 N.E.2d 730 (8th Dist. Cuyahoga County 1989).

2151.356 was transferred to RC 2152.21(A)(2), and the language "for the period that the court prescribes" was replaced with language stating that the suspension is not to exceed two years. Moreover, the statutory language concerning revocation was repealed because it is covered by suspensions. In addition, the "registration of vehicle" language is deleted because it is virtually meaningless.

DUI cases. If a child is adjudicated a juvenile traffic offender for driving while intoxicated under RC 4511.19(A), the court is required to suspend or revoke the child's temporary instruction permit or probationary driver's license until the child's eighteenth birthday or until the child attends, at the court's discretion, and satisfactorily completes a drug abuse or alcohol abuse education, intervention, or treatment program specified by the court.[3] If the child does not yet own a temporary instruction permit or probationary operator's license, the child may not be issued one until he or she satisfactorily completes the program (RC 4507.08). It appears that the period of suspension or revocation may extend beyond age 18, until the child completes the program.[4] During the time that the child is attending the program, the court must retain the child's permit or license and return it to the child after he satisfactorily completes the program.[5]

If a child is adjudicated a juvenile traffic offender for driving while intoxicated under RC 4511.19(B),[6] the court must suspend the child's temporary instruction permit or probationary driver's license for the shorter period of 60 days or until the child attains the age of 18 years.[7]

The maximum period of license suspension for a child adjudicated a juvenile traffic offender under RC 4511.19(B), age 18, is potentially shorter than for a child adjudicated for a less serious traffic offense. Moreover, it appears that if the child is age 18 at the time of the hearing, his or her permit or license may not be suspended for any period of time.

Within 10 days after the adjudication, the court must notify the Bureau of Motor Vehicles of the adjudicatory order.[8] If the child satisfactorily completes a drivers' intervention program, the program operator must promptly notify the court,[9] whereupon the court must immediately notify the Bureau of Motor Vehicles.[10]

A license suspension imposed for violation of RC 4511.19(B) may not extend beyond the child's eighteenth birthday.

§ 28:3   Financial sanctions

If a child is found to be a juvenile traffic offender, the court may impose costs and a maximum fine according to the following graduated schedule:

(1) Minor misdemeanor or unclassified misdemeanor: $50;

---

[3]RC 2152.21(B) (replacing "time prescribed by the court" with at least three months but not more than two years) (former RC 2151.356(B)). See also RC 4507.162.

[4]Under a previous version of RC 2151.356(B), the period of license suspension ended when the child reached age 18. See State v. Rice, 1990 WL 97687 (Ohio Ct. App. 6th Dist. Lucas County 1990).

[5]RC 2152.21(B).

[6]RC 4511.19(B) requires a lesser concentration of alcohol than RC 4511.19(A).

[7]RC 2152.21(B) (replacing "60 days to two years" with "at least three months but not more than two years") (former RC 2151.356(B)). In re Eric W., 113 Ohio App. 3d 367, 680 N.E.2d 1275 (6th Dist. Erie County 1996); State v. Rice, 1990 WL 97687 (Ohio Ct. App. 6th Dist. Lucas County 1990).

[8]RC 4507.021(D)(2)(a). Although this order is mandated by the dispositional statute (RC 2151.356(B)), it is made at the adjudicatory hearing, which may be held well before the dispositional hearing (see Juv. R. 34(A)).

[9]RC 3793.10.

[10]RC 4507.021(D)(2)(b).

    (2) Fourth degree misdemeanor: $75;

    (3) Third degree misdemeanor: $125;

    (4) Second degree misdemeanor: $175;

    (5) First degree misdemeanor: $225;

    (6) Fifth degree felony or unclassified felony: $300;

    (7) Fourth degree felony: $400;

    (8) Third degree felony: $750;

    (9) Second degree felony: $1,000;

    (10) First degree felony: $1,450.[1]

§ 28:4 Community control and probation

If a child is adjudicated a juvenile traffic offender, the court may place the child on probation, now known as community control sanctions.[1]

It is arguable that if a child is placed on probation for the traffic offense, with the condition of a license revocation, the revocation may extend until the child reaches age 21, which is also the maximum age for institutionalization.[2] Moreover, in an unreported decision, the Fifth District Court of Appeals held that RC 2151.356 does not limit the court's authority to make orders that extend beyond the child's eighteenth birthday, reasoning that there is no statute which expressly provides that a probationary license expires at age 18.[3]

§ 28:5 Restitution

The court may also require the child to make restitution for all damages caused by his traffic violation or any part of the damages.[1] An appellate court has held that a juvenile court may order a juvenile traffic offender to make restitution to a victim's family for funeral, medical, and out-of-pocket expenses, but must first hold an evidentiary hearing to determine the precise amount and extent of the expenses.[2]

§ 28:6 Commitment to juvenile facility

Under certain circumstances, a juvenile traffic offender may be committed

---

[Section 28:3]
    [1]RC 2152.20, RC 2152.21(A)(1).

[Section 28:4]
    [1]RC 2152.21(A)(3) and RC 2151.21(A)(6). For a discussion of probation as it applies to the disposition of a delinquent child, see § 27:8, Probation.

    [2]In re Weber, 61 Ohio App. 3d 636, 573 N.E.2d 730 (8th Dist. Cuyahoga County 1989). See § 33:5, Other proceedings.

    [3]Matter of Tobin, 1995 WL 495305 (Ohio Ct. App. 5th Dist. Licking County 1995).

[Section 28:5]
    [1]RC 2152.21(A)(4) (deleting phrase "or any part of the damages" unnecessary) (former RC 2151.356(A)(5)). For a discussion of restitution as it applies to the disposition of a delinquent child, see § 27:13, Restitution.

    [2]In Matter of Brown, 1998 WL 430028 (Ohio Ct. App. 5th Dist. Richland County 1998). See also In re Jacobs, 148 Ohio App. 3d 173, 176, 2002-Ohio-2844, 772 N.E.2d 671 (3d Dist. Seneca County 2002) ("[W]e note the appellant's assertion that if the 'catch-all' provision of R.C. 2151.355(A) is utilized, the juvenile court is confined to imposing a disposition prescribed by another statute within the Juvenile Code. The appellant contends that no such disposition is authorized by the Juvenile Code. This argument is without merit. The statute neither says such a disposition is so restricted, nor do we find that such a restriction is in place. Even if such a proviso did exist, R.C. 2151.356(A)(5) allowed a juvenile court to require a juvenile traffic offender to 'make restitution for all damages caused by the child's traffic violation or any part of the damages.' Ordering the appellant to make restitution for the cost of Faber's funeral expenses clearly falls within the former R.C. 2151.356." (citations omitted)).

to a detention home or an institution. A child adjudicated a juvenile traffic offender for driving while intoxicated[1] may be committed for not longer than five days to the temporary custody of a detention home or district detention home, or to any school, camp, institution, or other facility for juvenile traffic offenders.[2] If the child is committed to the temporary custody of a detention home[3] or district detention home, he must be kept separate and apart from alleged delinquent children.[4] If the child is committed to the temporary custody of a detention home, district detention home, school, camp, institution, or facility, the length of commitment shall not be reduced as a credit for any time held in detention or shelter care prior to disposition.[5]

Except as provided in division (A)(5) of RC 2152.21, an initial dispositional order for a juvenile traffic offender may not include commitment to an institution or agency. However, if after making a disposition under RC 2152.21(A)(1) to (A)(5) , the court finds upon further hearing that the child has failed to comply with the orders of the court and that the child's operation of a motor vehicle constitutes a danger to the child and others, the court may make any disposition authorized for delinquent children under RC 2152.19(A)(1), (A)(4), (A)(5), and (A)(8),[6] with some exceptions. The child may not be committed to or placed in a secure correctional facility[7] unless authorized by RC 2152.21(A)(5), and commitment to or placement in a detention home may not exceed 24 hours. Alternately, the child may be charged as a delinquent child under RC 2152.02(F)(2) for violating a court order.

§ 28:7 Seat belt law violations

Specific dispositional alternatives are provided for children who violate the seat belt law.[1] If a child is found to be a juvenile traffic offender for operating an automobile without wearing a seat belt,[2] the child must be fined $25.[3] Although RC 2152.21(C) provides that the court must impose the appropriate fine set forth in RC 4513.99 for a child who operates an automobile in which a front seat passenger is not wearing a seat belt,[4] RC 4513.99 contains no fine or other penalty for such violation.[5] If a child 16 years of age or older is found to be a juvenile traffic offender for occupying a front seat without wearing a seat belt,[6] the child must be fined $15.[7] However, if the child is under

---

[Section 28:6]

[1]This applies to violations of RC 4511.19 as well as a substantially comparable municipal ordinance. For required dispositional orders on a child adjudged for driving while intoxicated, see § 29:2, Unruly—Dispositional alternatives.

[2]RC 2152.21(A)(5).

[3]RC 2152.21(A)(5)(i) is the only statute that allows a child to be committed to the *temporary custody* of a detention home. Under RC 2151.011(B)(9), the detention home would have legal custody of the child. All other statutes relating to a child's containment in a detention home (e.g., RC 2151.312(A)(3)) refer to the child being "held," rather than committed to temporary custody. RC 2152.21(A)(5)(i) is also the only dispositional statute which specifically permits the use of a detention home as a dispositional option. See § 27:17, Court custody.

[4]RC 2152.41(B).

[5]RC 2152.21(A)(5)(b).

[6]RC 2152.21(A)(6).

[7]See RC 2151.011(B)(48) for definition of "secure correctional facility."

[Section 28:7]

[1]RC 2152.21(C), RC 4513.263.

[2]RC 4513.263(B)(1).

[3]RC 2152.21(C), RC 4513.99(F).

[4]RC 4513.263(B)(2).

[5]An earlier version of RC 4513.99(G) required the imposition of a $10 fine on the driver for each such passenger, up to a maximum of $30. Its omission from the current statute is apparently a legislative oversight.

[6]RC 4513.263(B)(3).

16 he or she may not be fined, but may be placed on probation.[8]

§ 28:8 Revocation of probationary operator's license

In addition to the juvenile court's authority to revoke a child's driver's license, the Bureau of Motor Vehicles must revoke for a period of one year the probationary operator's license issued to a child between the ages of 16 and 18 years if the child has, before reaching his or her eighteenth birthday, been convicted of, pleaded guilty to, or adjudicated in juvenile court of committing three separate moving violations in a two-year period.[1] These violations must come within the purview of RC 2903.06, RC 2903.07, RC 2903.08, RC 2921.331, RC 4511.12, RC 4511.13, RC 4511.15, RC 4511.191, RC 4511.192, RC 4511.20, RC 4511.201, RC 4511.202, RC 4511.21, RC 4511.22, RC 4511.23, RC 4511.25 to RC 4511.48, RC 4511.57 to RC 4511.65, RC 4511.75, RC 4549.02, RC 4549.021, RC 4549.03, or RC 2903.04(D), or of any municipal ordinance relating to the offenses covered in these statutes.[2] The mandatory revocation also applies to one violation of RC 4511.19 or a substantially similar municipal ordinance.[3]

RC 4507.162 differs from the general rule governing the disposition of children's cases in that the adjudication on the third violation must occur prior to the child's eighteenth birthday in order for mandatory revocation to apply.[4] The general rule in other cases is that a child who violates a law shall be deemed a child irrespective of age at the time the complaint is filed or the hearing is had thereon, and any permissible disposition may be made even if the child reaches age 18 prior to adjudication.[5]

§ 28:9 Occupational driving privileges

If a child is adjudicated on a third violation of RC 4511.12, RC 4511.13, RC 4511.15, RC 4511.20 to RC 4511.23, RC 4511.25, RC 4511.26 to RC 4511.48, RC 4511.57 to RC 4511.65, or RC 4511.75, or any similar municipal ordinance within a two-year period, the court may grant the child occupational driving privileges if the court finds that the child will reach age 18 before the end of the mandatory suspension period, and further finds reasonable cause to believe that such suspension, if continued beyond the child's eighteenth birthday, will seriously affect his or her ability to continue in employment.[1] If granted, the occupational driving privileges take effect on the child's eighteenth birthday, and during the period following that birthday for which the suspension would otherwise be imposed.[2] If a person who has been granted

---

[7]RC 4513.99(G).

[8]RC 2152.21(C). It is not clear from the statute whether the child's age should be determined as of the date of the issuance of the ticket, or the date of the hearing.

[Section 28:8]

[1]RC 4507.162(A). The terms "convicted" and "pleaded guilty" are not ordinarily used in children's cases. See Juv. R. 29.

[2]RC 4507.162(A)(1).

[3]RC 4507.162(A)(2).

[4]The attorney general has ruled that the probationary operator's license of a person who commits a third moving traffic violation before his or her eighteenth birthday, but who neither is convicted of nor pleads guilty to the violation until after his or her eighteenth birthday, may not be suspended under RC 4507.162 (OAG 79-092). However, the juvenile court may still suspend his or her license pursuant to RC 2151.356(A)(2).

[5]RC 2151.011(B)(6)(a). See § 2:2, Age jurisdiction.

[Section 28:9]

[1]RC 4507.162(C).

[2]RC 4507.162(C).

occupational driving privileges violates any conditions imposed by the court,[3] or commits a subsequent violation of the Revised Code sections contained in RC 4507.162(A), the court must revoke the occupational driving privileges, and the registrar must suspend the person's license for a period of one year.[4]

§ 28:10 Imposition of adult penalties

Generally, the penalty provisions applicable to an adult traffic offender may not be imposed on a juvenile traffic offender unless expressly permitted by the dispositional statute, RC 2152.21.[1] Thus, except as provided in RC 2152.21(A)(5), a final dispositional order for a juvenile traffic offender may not include commitment to a county jail[2] or confinement in a juvenile detention home,[3] even if the child has committed a traffic offense which, if committed by an adult, would require incarceration.[4] Thus, the minimum three-day imprisonment required by RC 4511.99 for an adult convicted of driving while intoxicated pursuant to RC 4511.19 does not apply to a juvenile traffic offender, since it is not specifically provided for in RC 2152.21.[5]

On the other hand, if permitted by the dispositional statute, the court may impose a stricter dispositional order on a juvenile traffic offender than could be imposed on an adult convicted of the same traffic violation.[6] Because the special Code provisions relating to juveniles supersede the more general provisions governing the operation of motor vehicles,[7] a child's driver's license may be suspended for a speeding violation under RC 2152.21(A)(2), whereas an adult's license could not be suspended for the same offense.

Moreover, a juvenile traffic offender is subject to some of the same penalties which are imposed on an adult traffic offender by the Bureau of Motor Vehicles. For instance, the accumulation of points for moving violations applies equally to juvenile and adult traffic offenders.[8] In addition, a juvenile traffic offender is subject to the provisions of RC 4509.01 to RC 4509.78, the Ohio Financial Responsibility Act.[9]

§ 28:11 Parental orders

As of January 1, 2002, the juvenile court may issue orders to control parental conduct when a child is adjudicated a juvenile traffic offender.[1] Moreover, the parent can be required to post bond to ensure compliance with

---

[3]See RC 4507.02.

[4]RC 4507.162(D).

[Section 28:10]

[1]See State v. Rice, 1990 WL 97687 (Ohio Ct. App. 6th Dist. Lucas County 1990).

[2]RC 2152.26(C)(1)(a). OAG 70-143.

[3]RC 2152.21(A)(5); OAG 63-553.

[4]In Re: Martin, 1981 WL 6463 (Ohio Ct. App. 5th Dist. Ashland County 1981).

[5]In Re: Martin, 1981 WL 6463 (Ohio Ct. App. 5th Dist. Ashland County 1981).

[6]In re Farinacci, No. 37973 (8th Dist. Ct. App., Cuyahoga, 11-30-78).

[7]In re Farinacci, No. 37973 (8th Dist. Ct. App., Cuyahoga, 11-30-78).

[8]RC 4507.021. Gebell ♥. Dollison, 57 Ohio App. 2d 198, 9 Ohio Op. 3d 23, 11 Ohio Op. 3d 187, 386 N.E.2d 845 (1st Dist. Clermont County 1978), held that RC 2151.358 does not prohibit the use of records pertaining to traffic violations, kept pursuant to RC 4507.40 (now RC 4507.021), in a driver's license revocation hearing conducted after the accused has attained majority.

[9]RC 2152.21(D), RC 4509.011. Matter of Chapa, 1996 WL 156743 (Ohio Ct. App. 3d Dist. Hancock County 1996). The 1977 amendment to RC 2151.356 and the enactment of RC 4509.011 overrule Lapp v. Ohio Bureau of Motor Vehicles, No. 1128 (5th Dist. Ct. App., Muskingum, 9-25-75), which held that RC 4509.31 did not apply to juvenile traffic offenders since, at that time, they were not specifically included within its purview.

[Section 28:11]

[1]RC 2152.61(A).

these judicial orders.[2] In addition, parents are subject to contempt proceedings for failure to comply with these orders.[3]

Cross References
Ch 2, § 7:2, § 27:4, § 27:8, § 28:3, § 33:5
Research References
Carlin, Baldwin's Ohio Practice, Merrick-Rippner Probate Law (6th ed.), Ch 107

---

[2]RC 2152.61(B).
[3]RC 2152.61(C).

Chapter 29

Unruly Child Dispositions

> **KeyCite®:** Cases and other legal materials listed in KeyCite Scope can be researched through West's KeyCite service on Westlaw®. Use KeyCite to check citations for form, parallel references, prior and later history, and comprehensive citator information, including citations to other decisions and secondary materials.

§ 29:1   Unruly child dispositions—Introduction
§ 29:2   Unruly—Dispositional alternatives
§ 29:3   Unruly—Delinquency dispositions
§ 29:4   Unruly—Drug & alcohol cases
§ 29:5   Unruly—Truancy cases

§ 29:1   Unruly child dispositions—Introduction

This chapter discusses dispositions in unruly child cases. The procedural issues that relate to juvenile court dispositional hearings are examined in Chapter 24. The dispositional alternatives attending other types of juvenile court jurisdiction are explored in separate chapters: delinquency (Chapter 26), juvenile traffic offenses (Chapter 27), and neglect, abuse, and dependency (Chapter 29).

RC 2151.354 governs dispositions for unruly children. Some dispositions for unruly children are mandatory, while most are discretionary. S.B. 179 (effective January 1, 2002) amended the definition of child in RC 2152.011(B)(5) to clarify that the juvenile court has jurisdiction over any person adjudicated unruly until that person reaches the age of 21.

§ 29:2   Unruly—Dispositional alternatives

If the child is adjudged unruly, the juvenile court may impose a number of discretionary dispositions. First, the court may impose any of the dispositions authorized for neglected, dependent, and abused children under RC 2151.353.[1]

Second, the court may impose any community control sanction permitted under RC 2152.19(A)(3) for delinquents.[2] Prior to 2002, the statute permitted only the placement of the child on probation under such conditions as the court prescribes. The same rules governing probation for delinquent children apply to unruly children.[3]

Third, the court may suspend or revoke the child's driving privileges or the

---

[Section 29:2]

[1] RC 2151.354(A)(1) cites to RC 2151.353. See In re Kessler, 90 Ohio App. 3d 231, 628 N.E.2d 153 (6th Dist. Huron County 1993); In re Kidd, 2002-Ohio-7264, 2002 WL 31886759 (Ohio Ct. App. 11th Dist. Lake County 2002); § 30:4, Dispositional alternatives for abuse, neglect or dependency. For a discussion of whether the procedural requirements applicable to the disposition of neglected, dependent, and abused children would apply to the disposition of delinquent (and unruly) children, see § 27:3, Department of Youth Services commitment.

[2] RC 2151.354(A)(2). See § 27:7, Community control sanctions.

[3] See § 27:8, Probation.

registration of motor vehicles issued to the child.[4]

Fourth, the court may commit the child to the temporary or permanent custody of the court.[5]

Fifth, the court may impose delinquency dispositions under specified conditions, as discussed in the next section.

Sixth, the court may impose a period of community service not to exceed 175 hours.[6]

In addition, there are mandatory sanctions in certain drug and alcohol cases,[7] and special provisions for truancy cases.[8]

§ 29:3 Unruly—Delinquency dispositions

If, after making its disposition, the court finds, upon further hearing, that the child is not amenable to treatment or rehabilitation under such disposition, it may make a disposition authorized for a delinquent child under RC 2152.19(A)(1), (4), (5), or (8), except that the child may not be committed to or placed in a secure correctional facility, and commitment to or placement in a detention home may generally not exceed 24 hours unless authorized by RC 2151.312 or RC 2151.56 to RC 2151.61.[1]

This further finding may result from the filing of a motion to review the original order, notice of which must be served in the same manner provided for service of process.[2] A complaint for violation of probation[3] or a delinquency complaint for violation of a court order[4] may also trigger this reexamination of the original disposition. However, an unruly child may not be committed to or placed in a detention home for five days without the further hearing to determine whether the child was amenable to treatment or rehabilitation, even if the original "sentence" was suspended.[5]

§ 29:4 Unruly—Drug & alcohol cases

If a child is adjudged unruly for any drug abuse offense[1] or for disorderly conduct while intoxicated,[2] the court, in addition to any discretionary order of disposition, is required to both (1) order the child to participate in a drug abuse or alcohol abuse counseling program; and (2) suspend or revoke the child's temporary instruction permit or probationary operator's license until the child's eighteenth birthday or the child attends, at the court's discretion, and satisfactorily completes a drug abuse or alcohol abuse education,

---

[4]RC 2151.354(A)(3) (including driver's license, probationary driver's license, or temporary instruction permit). The same rules governing a disposition relative to a juvenile traffic offender apply to unruly children. See Juvenile Traffic Offender Dispositions Ch 28.

[5]RC 2151.354(A)(4).

[6]RC 2151.354(A)(2) (effective July 2, 2002).

[7]See § 29:4, Unruly: Drug & alcohol cases.

[8]See § 29:5, Unruly: Truancy cases.

[Section 29:3]

[1]RC 2151.354(A). The use of the catch-all provision of division (A)(12) of RC 2151.355 (now RC 2152.19(A)(8)) was apparently not permitted prior to 2001.

[2]Juv. R. 35(A).

[3]See Juv. R. 35(B). See also § 33:6, Revocation of probation.

[4]RC 2152.02(F)(2). See § 4:2, Delinquent child defined.

[5]In re Osman, 109 Ohio App. 3d 731, 672 N.E.2d 1114 (11th Dist. Portage County 1996). However, it is unclear whether the legislature intended to authorize the courts to commit children, originally found to be unruly, then delinquent by reason of a violation of court order, to a detention facility for 90 days under RC 2152.19(A)(3).

[Section 29:4]

[1]"Drug abuse offense" is defined in RC 2925.01.

[2]RC 2917.11(B). It is not clear why either of these offenses is included in the dispositional statute for unruly children since both are delinquency offenses.

intervention, or treatment program specified by the court.[3] During the time that the child is attending the program, the court must retain the child's permit or license and return it to the child after he satisfactorily completes the program.[4]

Within 10 days after the adjudication, the court must notify the Bureau of Motor Vehicles of the adjudicatory order.[5] If the child satisfactorily completes a drivers' intervention program, the program operator must promptly notify the court,[6] whereupon the court must immediately notify the Bureau of Motor Vehicles.[7]

§ 29:5   Unruly—Truancy cases

In addition to or in lieu of other dispositions, under RC 2151.354(C)(1) an habitual truant may be required to (1) attend an alternative school if one has been established under RC 3313.533,[1] (2) participate in any academic program or community service program; (3) participate in a drug abuse or alcohol abuse counseling program; or (4) receive appropriate medical or psychological treatment or counseling. Moreover, the court may make any other order that the court finds proper to address the child's habitual truancy, including ordering the child to not be absent without legitimate excuse from public school for five or more consecutive days, seven or more school days in one school month, or 12 or more school days in a school year and including ordering the child to participate in a truancy prevention mediation program.[2]

Cross References
§ 4:4, § 27:4, § 30:2, § 33:6
Research References
Carlin, Baldwin's Ohio Practice, Merrick-Rippner Probate Law (6th ed.), Ch 107

---

[3]RC 2151.354(B). See also RC 4507.162. If the child does not yet own a temporary instruction permit or probationary operator's license, the child may not be issued one until he or she satisfactorily completes the program (RC 4507.08).

[4]RC 2151.354(B)(2). For discussion of the period of time for which the license may be suspended, see § 28:2, Suspension or revocation.

[5]RC 4507.021(D)(2)(a) . Although this order is mandated by the dispositional statute (RC 2151.354(B)), it is not made at the adjudicatory hearing, which may be held well before the dispositional hearing (see Juv. R. 34(A)).

[6]RC 3793.10.

[7]RC 4507.021(D)(2)(b).

[Section 29:5]
[1]In this situation, the court orders the board of education of the child's school district or the governing board of the educational service center in the child's school district to require the child to attend the alternative school if the child is entitled to attend that school.

[2]RC 2151.354(C)(2) specifies the court's control over parents, guardians, or other person having care of the child who has failed to cause the child's attendance at school in violation of RC 3321.38.

Chapter 30

Abused, Neglected, or Dependent Child Dispositions

> **KeyCite®:** Cases and other legal materials listed in KeyCite Scope can be researched through West's KeyCite service on Westlaw®. Use KeyCite to check citations for form, parallel references, prior and later history, and comprehensive citator information, including citations to other decisions and secondary materials.

§ 30:1   Abused, neglected, or dependent child dispositions—Introduction
§ 30:2   General principles for abuse, neglect and dependency dispositions
§ 30:3   Costs of dispositions
§ 30:4   Dispositional alternatives for abuse, neglect or dependency
§ 30:5   Protective supervision
§ 30:6   Temporary custody
§ 30:7   Legal custody
§ 30:8   Permanent custody—Defined
§ 30:9   Permanent custody—Requirements
§ 30:10   Permanent custody—Parental placement within reasonable time
§ 30:11   Permanent custody—"Best interest" factors
§ 30:12   Permanent custody—Procedural issues
§ 30:13   Planned permanent living arrangement
§ 30:14   Jurisdiction over parents

§ 30:1 Abused, neglected, or dependent child dispositions— Introduction

This chapter discusses dispositions in neglect, abuse, and dependency cases. The procedural issues that relate to juvenile court dispositional hearings are examined in Ch 25. The dispositional alternatives attending other types of juvenile court jurisdiction are explored in separate chapters: delinquency (Ch 27), juvenile traffic offenses (Ch 28), and unruliness (Ch 29). The process required upon the filing of a motion for permanent custody is discussed in Ch 31.

§ 30:2 General principles for abuse, neglect and dependency dispositions

The primary consideration in the disposition of all children's cases is the best interests and welfare of the child.[1] The court must focus its disposition on providing for the care, protection, and mental and physical development of the child.[2]

Whenever possible, the child should be cared for in a family environment,

---

[Section 30:2]

[1]In re Pryor, 86 Ohio App. 3d 327, 620 N.E.2d 973 (4th Dist. Athens County 1993); In Matter of Rundio, 1993 WL 379512 (Ohio Ct. App. 4th Dist. Pickaway County 1993); In re Overbay, 1997 WL 89160 (Ohio Ct. App. 12th Dist. Butler County 1997). For a discussion of this issue in the context of permanent custody cases, see § 25:5, Right to attend dispositional hearing; § 30:8 to § 30:12, Permanent custody.

[2]RC 2151.01(A), RC 2151.01(B).

separated from parents only when necessary for the child's welfare or in the interests of public safety.[3] Parents have a natural, paramount right to raise their children, the loss of which must be safeguarded by due process protections.[4]

Religious faith. If the child is placed in the guardianship or custody of someone other than a parent, the court must, when practicable, select a person, institution, or agency of the same religious faith as the child's parents; in case of a difference in the religious faith of the parents, the selection may be based on the religious faith of the child or, if this is not ascertainable, on that of either parent.[5] Where the parent has stated an indifference to the religious upbringing of the child, the county welfare department (now county job and family services department) which has obtained custody of the child is not required to place the child with persons of the parent's religion.[6]

County or district facility. If a county or district establishes a school, camp, or other facility for the training, treatment, and rehabilitation of children adjudged to be delinquent, dependent, neglected, abused, unruly, or juvenile traffic offenders, the juvenile court is responsible for determining which children shall be admitted to the facility, the period of commitment, and removal and transfer from the facility.[7]

§ 30:3 Costs of dispositions

Educational. Whenever the court makes an order that removes a child from his or her home or that vests legal or permanent custody of the child with a parent or governmental agency, the court must determine the school district responsible for bearing the cost of the child's education,[1] unless the child is not of school age or enrolled in any educational program.[2]

If a child is placed in a detention home[3] or a juvenile facility established under RC 2151.65, or if he has been committed to the custody of the Department of Youth Services, his school district as determined by the court must pay the cost of the child's education.[4] This requirement applies to any child,

---

[3]RC 2151.01(A); In Matter Of: Escue, 1981 WL 5930 (Ohio Ct. App. 4th Dist. Lawrence County 1981); In re Wright, 1996 WL 397143 (Ohio Ct. App. 9th Dist. Lorain County 1996).

[4]State ex rel. Heller v. Miller, 61 Ohio St. 2d 6, 15 Ohio Op. 3d 3, 399 N.E.2d 66 (1980); In re Cunningham, 59 Ohio St. 2d 100, 13 Ohio Op. 3d 78, 391 N.E.2d 1034 (1979); In re Perales, 52 Ohio St. 2d 89, 6 Ohio Op. 3d 293, 369 N.E.2d 1047 (1977); In re Gutman, 22 Ohio App. 2d 125, 51 Ohio Op. 2d 252, 259 N.E.2d 128 (1st Dist. Hamilton County 1969); In re Shaeffer Children, 85 Ohio App. 3d 683, 621 N.E.2d 426 (3d Dist. Van Wert County 1993); In re Awkal, 95 Ohio App. 3d 309, 642 N.E.2d 424 (8th Dist. Cuyahoga County 1994); In re Mahley, 2004-Ohio-1772, 2004 WL 740003 (Ohio Ct. App. 5th Dist. Guernsey County 2004).

[5]RC 2151.32.

[6]In re Doe, 167 N.E.2d 396 (Ohio Juv. Ct. 1956).

[7]RC 2151.65.

[Section 30:3]

[1]RC 2151.357, RC 2151.35(B)(3); Juv. R. 34(C). RC 3313.64 prescribes the manner in which this determination is to be made. See Board of Educ. v. Day, 30 Ohio Misc. 2d 25, 506 N.E.2d 1239, 39 Ed. Law Rep. 271 (C.P. 1986). OAG 89-92 discussed the responsibility of a children services board to assure payment to a receiving state when a child in its custody is placed with a relative in the other state. OAG 94-070, 1994 WL 577271, discussed the factors to be used in determining the appropriate school district for a child who is in the temporary custody of a children services board.

[2]Matter of Hogan, 1990 WL 178092 (Ohio Ct. App. 6th Dist. Lucas County 1990).

[3]Placement in a detention home may not be used as a final disposition. See § 27:18, "Catch-all" provision.

[4]RC 2151.357; Christman v. Washington Court House [School Dist.], 30 Ohio App. 3d 228, 507 N.E.2d 384, 39 Ed. Law Rep. 283 (12th Dist. Fayette County 1986); OAG 88-23.

including children with special needs.[5] If the child is placed in a private institution, school, residential treatment center, or other private facility, the state must pay the court a subsidy, not to exceed $2,500 per year, to help defray the expense of educating the child.[6]

Parental support. Whenever a child has been committed the court shall order the parent, guardian, or person charged with the child's support to pay for the care, support, maintenance, and education of the child.[7] Juv. R. 34(C) makes an order of parental support permissible rather than mandatory. The court is required, prior to final disposition, to order the parents, guardian, or person charged with the child's support to pay support for the child,[8] and to continue to maintain or obtain health insurance coverage for the child.[9]

Any expenses ordered by the court for the care, support, maintenance, education, orthopedic, medical or surgical treatment, or special care of a child, except that part paid by the state or federal government or by the parent or other person charged with support, shall be paid from the county treasury.[10]

§ 30:4 Dispositional alternatives for abuse, neglect or dependency

If a child is adjudicated abused, neglected, or dependent, the court may issue any order described in RC 2151.33.[1] Because the juvenile court's subject matter jurisdiction is limited to that which the General Assembly has specifically conferred upon it, the court may not make a disposition other than the alternatives included in the statutes.[2]

The juvenile court is not limited to only one dispositional alternative, and thus may issue both a legal custody and protective supervision order with respect to the same child.[3] Additionally, the court may issue dissimilar dispositional orders with respect to siblings.[4]

Even if the allegations of a complaint are proven at the adjudicatory hearing, a juvenile court may still dismiss the complaint.[5]

Alternatives. RC 2151.353(A)[6] and Juvenile Rule 34(D)[7] authorize the court to make any of the following dispositional orders:

---

[5]Matter of Fetters, 1998 WL 102997 (Ohio Ct. App. 12th Dist. Preble County 1998).

[6]RC 2151.357. The statute contains a formula for determining the specific amount of the subsidy.

[7]RC 2151.35(B)(3), RC 2151.36.

[8]RC 2151.33(B)(2)(a). See RC 3113.21 to RC 3113.219.

[9]RC 2151.33(B)(2)(b). See RC 3113.217.

[10]RC 2151.36; In re Hoodlet, 72 Ohio App. 3d 115, 593 N.E.2d 478 (4th Dist. Athens County 1991); OAG 89-6.

[Section 30:4]

[1]RC 2151.35(B)(4). See § 9:4, Neglected child defined; § 9:12, Abused child defined; § 10:2, Dependent child defined.

[2]In re Gibson, 61 Ohio St. 3d 168, 573 N.E.2d 1074 (1991).

[3]In re Pryor, 86 Ohio App. 3d 327, 620 N.E.2d 973 (4th Dist. Athens County 1993); Matter of Coffey, 1991 WL 57153 (Ohio Ct. App. 5th Dist. Tuscarawas County 1991).

[4]In re Pryor, 86 Ohio App. 3d 327, 620 N.E.2d 973 (4th Dist. Athens County 1993).

[5]In Matter of Dodson, 1996 WL 98730 (Ohio Ct. App. 3d Dist. Shelby County 1996).

[6]The statute, in a previous but similar version, was held not unconstitutionally vague or broad. In re Williams, 7 Ohio App. 3d 324, 455 N.E.2d 1027 (1st Dist. Hamilton County 1982). The current version of the statute was held to comport with due process and equal protection requirements. Matter of Whiteman, 2 A.D.D. 386 (Ohio Ct. App. 6th Dist. Williams County 1993). Because the amendments to the statute did not change the substantive requirements, the new version is effective as to all proceedings pending at the time of its effective date (1-1-89). Matter of Butcher, 1991 WL 62145 (Ohio Ct. App. 4th Dist. Athens County 1991).

[7]Juv. R. 34(D).

(1) Place the child in protective supervision;[8]

(2) Commit the child to the temporary custody of a public children services agency, a private child placing agency, either parent, a relative
residing within or without the state, a probation officer for placement in a certified family foster, or in any other home approved by
the court;[9]

(3) Award legal custody of the child to either parent or to any other
person;[10]

(4) Commit the child to the permanent custody of an agency;[11] or

(5) Place the child in a planned permanent living arrangement.[12]

Removal of persons from home. In addition to making orders concerning the custodial status of the child, the court may order the removal from
the child's home of the person responsible for the neglect, abuse, or
dependency, and may order any person not to have contact with the child or
the child's siblings.[13] Prior to issuance of these orders, the court must provide
the person with notice and a copy of the motion or application, the grounds
for the motion or application, an opportunity for a hearing, and an opportunity to be represented by counsel at the hearing.[14]

Medical treatment. The court has the authority to order a dependent
child "to submit to medical treatment for contagious and potentially life-
threatening disease even though such would violate the juvenile's religious
beliefs."[15]

Case plans. Although the court reviewing a case plan must be guided by
certain priorities, RC 2151.353 does not mandate that the dispositional options be applied in any particular order; the appropriate decision is within
the court's discretion.[16] In exercising this discretion, the court must consider
the totality of the circumstances.[17] If the disposition being considered by the
court would modify any existing custody decree, the court must also consider
the factors set forth in RC 3109.04.[18]

§ 30:5 Protective supervision

Protective supervision is an order of disposition in which the court permits
a child to remain in the custody of the child's parents, guardian, or custodian
and stay at home, subject to any conditions and limitations upon the child,
parents, guardian, custodian, or any other person that the court prescribes,
including supervision as directed by the court for the protection of the child.[1]
These conditions and limitations include, but are not limited to, any of the
following:

---

[8]RC 2151.353(A)(1); Juv. R. 34(D)(1). See § 30:5, Protective supervision.

[9]RC 2151.353(A)(2); Juv. R. 34(D)(2). See § 30:6, Temporary custody.

[10]RC 2151.353(A)(3); Juv. R. 34(D)(3). See § 30:7, Legal custody.

[11]RC 2151.353(A)(4); Juv. R. 34(D)(4). See § 30:8, Permanent custody—Defined.

[12]RC 2151.353(A)(5). See § 30:13, Planned permanent living arrangement. But see Juv. R.
34(D)(5), which refers to the former disposition of long-term foster care.

[13]RC 2151.353(A)(6).

[14]RC 2151.353(I).

[15]In re J.J., 64 Ohio App. 3d 806, 811, 582 N.E.2d 1138 (12th Dist. Butler County 1990).

[16]In Matter of Crenshaw, 1997 WL 219118 (Ohio Ct. App. 5th Dist. Stark County 1997). See
§ 26:6, Goals and priorities.

[17]In re Pryor, 86 Ohio App. 3d 327, 620 N.E.2d 973 (4th Dist. Athens County 1993).

[18]In re Poling, 64 Ohio St. 3d 211, 1992-Ohio-144, 594 N.E.2d 589 (1992); In re Cloud, 1997
WL 264264 (Ohio Ct. App. 12th Dist. Butler County 1997); In Matter of Black, 1997 WL 567924
(Ohio Ct. App. 3d Dist. Defiance County 1997). See § 3:3, Concurrent jurisdiction.

[Section 30:5]
[1]RC 2151.011(B)(35).

(1) The court may order a party, effective within 48 hours after the issuance of the order, to vacate the child's home indefinitely or for a
specified period of time;

(2) The court may order a party to prevent any particular person from
having contact with the child; or

(3) The court may issue an order restraining or otherwise controlling
the conduct of any person whose conduct would not be in the child's
best interest.[2]

An order of protective supervision is an appropriate disposition in an
abuse case where the perpetrator of the abuse is unknown.[3]

Time requirements. No later than one year after the date on which the
complaint was filed or the child was first placed in shelter care, whichever is
earlier, a party may file a written request for a six-month extension or
termination of the order, with notice to the other parties before the end of
the day after the day of filing. If no party requests extension or termination,
the court must notify the parties that the court will extend or terminate the
order without a hearing, unless a party requests a hearing within seven days
from the date the notice is sent.[4]

If a timely request for a hearing is made, the court must conduct a hearing
within 30 days, with notice to the parties. The decision to extend or terminate
the order must be based on a determination of the child's best interest.[5] If a
timely request is not made, the court may extend the order for six months or
terminate it without a hearing, and journalize the order within 14 days.
Alternatively, the court may conduct a hearing within 30 days after the
expiration of the 14-day period, and determine, based on the child's best
interest, whether to extend or terminate the order.[6]

If the order is extended, a party may, prior to the termination of the extension, file a request for an additional six-month extension or for termination of
the order.[7] The procedure for ruling on the request is the same as that which
applies to initial requests for extension or termination. If the additional six-
month extension is granted, the court must terminate the order for protective supervision at the end of the extension.[8]

§ 30:6 Temporary custody

The juvenile court may commit the child to the temporary custody of a
public children services agency,[1] a private child placing agency,[2] either parent, a relative residing within or without the state, or a probation officer for

---

[2]RC 2151.353(C); Juv. R. 34(E).

[3]In Matter of Dodson, 1996 WL 98730 (Ohio Ct. App. 3d Dist. Shelby County 1996).

[4]RC 2151.353(G)(1).

[5]RC 2151.353(G)(1)(a).

[6]RC 2151.353(G)(1)(b).

[7]RC 2151.353(G)(2).

[8]RC 2151.353(G)(3). See In re Carroll, 124 Ohio App. 3d 51, 705 N.E.2d 402 (2d Dist. Greene
County 1997); In re Dunham/Lewers Children, 1995 WL 434172 (Ohio Ct. App. 5th Dist. Stark
County 1995).

[Section 30:6]

[1]A juvenile court does not have the authority to order a mental health board to take custody
of a dependent child. In re Shott, 75 Ohio App. 3d 270, 599 N.E.2d 363 (12th Dist. Warren
County 1991). See Jurisdiction Over Parents and Others Ch 32.

[2]Hereinafter, the terms "public children services agency" and "private child placing agency"
will be referred to as "agency." See RC 2151.011(A)(3) and Juv. R. 2(FF) and (EE) for definitions
of these terms.

placement in a certified family foster home[3] or in any other home approved by the court;[4]

Defined. Temporary custody is defined as legal custody of a child who is removed from his home, which custody may be terminated at any time by the court in its discretion or, if the legal custody is granted in an agreement for temporary custody, by the person who executed the agreement.[5] An appellate court has upheld the authority of a juvenile court, per RC 2151.359, to place conditions on a temporary custody award to a children services board.[6]

Termination date. Any temporary custody order must terminate one year after the earlier of the date on which the complaint was filed or the date on which the child was first placed into shelter care.[7]

It has been held that when a job and family services department previously was given protective supervision over a child, the one-year limitation on a subsequent temporary custody order began running on the date of the department's request for temporary custody, rather than on the date the complaint was originally filed.[8] The court chose to read the statute in light of all the provisions of RC 2151.353 in lieu of a strict interpretation, and further concluded that it was the legislative intent to interpret the word "complaint" in RC 2151.353(F) to include "filing a motion."[9]

Extension of termination date. Under certain circumstances, the one-year termination date may be extended.[10] Except in cases in which a motion for permanent custody is required to be made under RC 2151.413(D)(1),[11] not later than 30 days prior to either the scheduled termination date or the scheduled dispositional review hearing date[12] the agency is required to file a motion with the court requesting any of the following dispositional orders:

  (1) An order that the child be returned to the child's home and the custody of the child's parents, guardian, or custodian without any restrictions;

  (2) An order for protective supervision;

---

[3]A foster home is a family home in which a child is received apart from his parents for care, supervision, or training (RC 2151.011(B)(15)). A certified family foster home is a foster home operated by persons holding a permit issued under RC 5103.03 (RC 2151.011(B)(5)). Any foster home is considered to be a residential use of property for purposes of municipal, county, and township zoning and is a permitted use in all zoning districts in which residential uses are permitted (RC 2151.418).

[4]RC 2151.353(A)(2); Juv. R. 34(D)(2). See § 30:6, Temporary custody. See In re Phillips, 1998 WL 177556 (Ohio Ct. App. 2d Dist. Montgomery County 1998). For discussion of agreements for temporary custody, see § 11:3, Temporary custody agreements.

[5]RC 2151.011(B)(46) and Juv. R. 2(OO). See RC 2151.011(B)(15) and RC 2151.011(B)(5) for definitions of foster home and certified foster home, respectively.

[6]In re Pead, No. 79AP-906 (10th Dist. Ct. App., Franklin, 6-10-80).

[7]RC 2151.353(F); Juv. R. 14(A). In re Travis Children, 80 Ohio App. 3d 620, 609 N.E.2d 1356 (5th Dist. Stark County 1992). Headnote number 1 of *Travis* provides, "Juvenile Court loses jurisdiction over custodial matters concerning children in temporary custody on the 'sunset date,' one year *after the temporary custody order is issued*, if there are no extensions granted" (emphasis added). The text of the opinion, however, correctly places the sunset date one year after the filing of the complaint or the placement of the child into shelter care. Pursuant to Rule 2(F) of the Supreme Court Rules for the Reporting of Opinions, the text of the opinion is the controlling statement of law.

[8]In re Ward, 75 Ohio App. 3d 377, 599 N.E.2d 431 (3d Dist. Defiance County 1992). See also In Matter of Keller, 1994 WL 695338 (Ohio Ct. App. 8th Dist. Cuyahoga County 1994).

[9]In re Ward, 75 Ohio App. 3d 377, 382, 599 N.E.2d 431 (3d Dist. Defiance County 1992). See also McNeal v. Miami County Childrens Services Bd., 1991 WL 19395 (Ohio Ct. App. 2d Dist. Miami County 1991).

[10]RC 2151.415(D).

[11]See § 31:2, Filing of motion.

[12]See RC 2151.415, RC 2151.35(B)(3), RC 2151.42; Temporary and Permanent Custody Agreements Ch 12.

(3) An order that the child be placed in the legal custody[13] of a relative or other interested individual;

(4) An order permanently terminating the parental rights of the child's parents;

(5) An order that the child be placed in long-term foster care; or

(6) An order for the extension of temporary custody.[14]

The Ohio Supreme Court has held that the passing of the statutory time period established by RC 2151.353(F) ("sunset date") does not divest juvenile courts of jurisdiction to enter dispositional orders when the problems that led to the original temporary custody order remain unsolved.[15] The court determined that temporary custody is terminated upon the passing of the sunset date when no motion is filed under RC 2151.415(A), but that the *jurisdiction* of the juvenile court is not affected. The court reasoned that other statutes[16] indicate a legislative intent that juvenile courts have continuing jurisdiction in that a child's welfare should always be subject to court review. The court cautioned, however, that the duty to file a motion 30 days prior to the sunset date is still required, and the failure to file is not harmless error.[17] Moreover, the court held that where the original problems have been resolved or sufficiently mitigated, a juvenile court may not make a further dispositional order based on the original complaint. Finally, the court ruled that when a new complaint is filed based on past facts discovered subsequent to the original complaint, the new complaint establishes its own sunset date.

The Supreme Court decision in *In re Young Children*[18] resolved a split of authority among the appellate courts concerning the effect of the passing of the sunset date on the juvenile court's jurisdiction.[19] One appellate court has held that where the court itself extends a temporary custody order on its own motion pursuant to RC 2151.417(B), the agency's failure to file a motion to extend temporary custody not later than 30 days before the scheduled termination date is of no consequence.[20]

Upon the filing of the motion, the temporary custody order continues in ef-

---

[13]See RC 2151.011(B)(17) and Juv. R. 2(V) for definition of legal custody.

[14]RC 2151.415(A); Juv. R. 14(A). See Matter of Fleming, 1993 WL 277186 (Ohio Ct. App. 8th Dist. Cuyahoga County 1993).

[15]In re Young Children, 76 Ohio St. 3d 632, 1996-Ohio-45, 669 N.E.2d 1140 (1996). See also Holloway v. Clermont County Dept. of Human Services, 80 Ohio St. 3d 128, 1997-Ohio-131, 684 N.E.2d 1217 (1997); In Matter of Lewis, 1997 WL 217573 (Ohio Ct. App. 4th Dist. Athens County 1997); In Matter of Knotts, 1997 WL 38084 (Ohio Ct. App. 3d Dist. Mercer County 1997); In Matter of Greer, 1996 WL 753162 (Ohio Ct. App. 5th Dist. Guernsey County 1996); Matter of Hare, 1998 WL 118039 (Ohio Ct. App. 4th Dist. Scioto County 1998).

[16]RC 2151.01(A), RC 2151.353(E)(1).

[17]In making this statement, the court cited Endsley v. Endsley, 89 Ohio App. 3d 306, 624 N.E.2d 270 (9th Dist. Wayne County 1993). However, the court in *Endsley* held that the 30-day filing requirement is directory and that the "failure to file . . . constituted [no] more than harmless error." Endsley v. Endsley, 89 Ohio App. 3d 306, 308, 624 N.E.2d 270 (9th Dist. Wayne County 1993).

[18]In re Young Children, 76 Ohio St. 3d 632, 1996-Ohio-45, 669 N.E.2d 1140 (1996).

[19]In the decision in *Young*, the Supreme Court reversed the holdings in four cases decided by the Fifth District Court of Appeals: Matter of Young Children, 1995 WL 434274 (Ohio Ct. App. 5th Dist. Stark County 1995); In Matter of Bunting Children, 1995 WL 507604 (Ohio Ct. App. 5th Dist. Stark County 1995); Matter of Brock Children, 1995 WL 495414 (Ohio Ct. App. 5th Dist. Stark County 1995); Matter of Farrar, 1995 WL 495471 (Ohio Ct. App. 5th Dist. Guernsey County 1995). Following its decision in *Young*, the Supreme Court reversed additional decisions of the Fifth District: In re Graybill/Rowe Children, 77 Ohio St. 3d 373, 1997-Ohio-267, 674 N.E.2d 676 (1997); In re Kleich Children, 77 Ohio St. 3d 373, 1997-Ohio-266, 674 N.E.2d 676 (1997); In re Norris Children, 77 Ohio St. 3d 374, 1997-Ohio-30, 674 N.E.2d 677 (1997); In re Turner, 77 Ohio St. 3d 375, 674 N.E.2d 677 (1997).

[20]Matter of Harris, 1995 WL 472917 (Ohio Ct. App. 8th Dist. Cuyahoga County 1995).

fect until the court issues a new dispositional order.[21] The court must conduct the dispositional hearing on the date set at the initial dispositional hearing.[22] After the dispositional hearing that follows the agency's motion, or at a date after such dispositional hearing that is not later than one year after the earlier of the date on which the complaint was filed or the date on which the child was first placed into shelter care, the court must issue a dispositional order from among those listed in RC 2151.415(A), in accordance with the child's best interest.[23] However, all orders for permanent custody must be in accordance with the statutes governing permanent custody.[24] Moreover, in issuing a dispositional order under RC 2151.415(B), the court must comply with RC 2151.42.[25]

If the agency requests an extension of temporary custody for up to six months, it must include in its motion an explanation of the progress on the child's case plan[26] and its expectations of reunifying the child with its family, or placing the child in a permanent placement, within the extension period.[27] Failure to include the explanation of progress made under the case plan and expectations for reunification in a motion to extend temporary custody is not prejudicial to parents where they were given notice of hearing and were afforded an opportunity to appear.[28] The court may extend the temporary custody order for up to six months if, after hearing, it determines by clear and convincing evidence that (1) the extension is in the child's best interest, (2) there has been significant progress on the child's case plan, and (3) there is reasonable cause to believe that the child will be reunified with one of his parents or otherwise permanently placed within the period of extension.[29]

Prior to the end of an extension granted by the court, the agency must file a motion with the court requesting one of the dispositional orders set forth in RC 2151.415(A)(1) to (5), or requesting an additional six-month extension of the temporary custody order.[30] If the agency requests one of the orders set forth in RC 2151.415(A)(1) to (5), or does not file any motion, the court must conduct a hearing[31] and issue an appropriate order of disposition.[32] The court has discretion to impose any of the dispositional alternatives contained in RC 2151.415(A) after considering the evidence and the child's best interest,[33] and may order a different dispositional option than the one requested by the agency.[34] If the agency requests an additional six-month extension of temporary custody, the court may, after hearing, grant the additional extension if it makes the same findings required for the original six-month extension.[35]

Prior to the end of the second extension of a temporary custody order, the agency must file the same type of motion that it filed with respect to the first

---

[21]RC 2151.353(F). In Matter of Kirksey Children, 1996 WL 74086 (Ohio Ct. App. 5th Dist. Stark County 1996).

[22]RC 2151.415(B). See RC 2151.35(B)(3); Juv. R. 14(B).

[23]RC 2151.415(B).

[24]RC 2151.415(B). See RC 2151.413, RC 2151.414; § 11:5, Permanent custody agreements.

[25]See § 33:4, Abuse, neglect, and dependency proceedings.

[26]See Dispositional Case Plans Ch 26.

[27]RC 2151.415(D)(1); Juv. R. 14(B). See RC 2151.42.

[28]Endsley v. Endsley, 89 Ohio App. 3d 306, 624 N.E.2d 270 (9th Dist. Wayne County 1993).

[29]Endsley v. Endsley, 89 Ohio App. 3d 306, 624 N.E.2d 270 (9th Dist. Wayne County 1993). If the court extends temporary custody, upon request it must issue findings of fact.

[30]RC 2151.415(D)(2); Juv. R. 14(B). See RC 2151.42.

[31]See RC 2151.415(B).

[32]RC 2151.415(D)(2); Juv. R. 14(B).

[33]Matter of Smith Children, 1990 WL 70926 (Ohio Ct. App. 12th Dist. Warren County 1990).

[34]Matter of McDaniel, 1993 WL 33308 (Ohio Ct. App. 4th Dist. Adams County 1993); In Matter of Crenshaw, 1997 WL 219118 (Ohio Ct. App. 5th Dist. Stark County 1997).

[35]RC 2151.415(D)(2); Juv. R. 14(B).

extension. The court, after hearing, must then issue the appropriate dispositional order.[36] No further extension of temporary custody may be ordered by the court.[37]

§ 30:7 Legal custody

Legal custody is defined as a legal status which vests in the custodian (1) the physical care and control of the child and to determine where and with whom the child shall live, and (2) the right and duty to protect, train, and discipline the child and to provide the child with food, shelter, education, and medical care, all subject to any residual parental rights, privileges, and responsibilities.[1]

Any person wishing legal custody of a child must, prior to the dispositional hearing, file a motion requesting legal custody of the child.[2] It is clear that the requirement of filing a motion prior to the dispositional hearing applies to relatives of the child.[3] However, while the Fourth District has held that this requirement also applies to the child's parents themselves,[4] the Twelfth District has determined that, based on a parent's inherent right to custody, a parent is not required to file a pre-dispositional motion for legal custody of his or her child.[5]

Although a juvenile court's custody determination must be in accordance with the general custody statute (RC 3109.04) if an existing custody decree is being modified,[6] a disposition of legal custody to a parent does not change the nature of a dependency action to a custody modification proceeding.[7]

Residual parental rights. Residual parental rights, privileges, and responsibilities are those remaining with the natural parent after the transfer of legal custody of the child. These include but are not limited to the privilege of reasonable visitation, consent to adoption, the privilege to determine the child's religious affiliation, and the responsibility for support.[8]

Termination date. The jurisdiction of the juvenile court terminates one

---

[36]RC 2151.415(D)(3).

[37]RC 2151.415(D)(4). In In re Travis Children, 80 Ohio App. 3d 620, 624, 609 N.E.2d 1356 (5th Dist. Stark County 1992), the court held that there is "a total of two years that these children may remain in the temporary custody of the department." Actually, the period is less than two years because under RC 2151.353(F), the time is measured beginning at the earlier of the filing of the complaint or placement of the child into shelter care. But see In re N.B., 2003-Ohio-3656, 2003 WL 21545142 (Ohio Ct. App. 8th Dist. Cuyahoga County 2003), appeal not allowed, 100 Ohio St. 3d 1425, 2003-Ohio-5232, 797 N.E.2d 93 (2003).

[Section 30:7]

[1]RC 2151.011(B)(17); Juv. R. 2(V). See In re Orwell, 1993 WL 531958 (Ohio Ct. App. 2d Dist. Montgomery County 1993).

[2]RC 2151.353(A)(3). Matter of Fleming, 1993 WL 277186 (Ohio Ct. App. 8th Dist. Cuyahoga County 1993).

[3]Matter of Leverett, 1998 WL 141192 (Ohio Ct. App. 8th Dist. Cuyahoga County 1998). But see, In re Allen, 2002-Ohio-5555, 2002 WL 31312392 (Ohio Ct. App. 5th Dist. Delaware County 2002).

[4]Matter of Farace, 1997 WL 802819 (Ohio Ct. App. 4th Dist. Scioto County 1997). See also Matter of Barcelo, 1998 WL 553165 (Ohio Ct. App. 11th Dist. Geauga County 1998).

[5]In re Motter, 1998 WL 314362 (Ohio Ct. App. 12th Dist. Butler County 1998).

[6]In re Poling, 64 Ohio St. 3d 211, 1992-Ohio-144, 594 N.E.2d 589 (1992); In Matter of Black, 1997 WL 567924 (Ohio Ct. App. 3d Dist. Defiance County 1997). See § 3:3, Concurrent jurisdiction.

[7]In re D.R., 153 Ohio App. 3d 156, 2003-Ohio-2852, 792 N.E.2d 203 (9th Dist. Summit County 2003) (The trial court should have used a best interest standard, rather than requiring grandmother to prove the mother unfit.); In re C.F., 2003-Ohio-3260, 2003 WL 21434769 (Ohio Ct. App. 8th Dist. Cuyahoga County 2003); In re Pryor, 86 Ohio App. 3d 327, 620 N.E.2d 973 (4th Dist. Athens County 1993).

[8]RC 2151.011(B)(41); Juv. R. 2(II). See In re Hitchcock, 120 Ohio App. 3d 88, 696 N.E.2d 1090 (8th Dist. Cuyahoga County 1996); Matter of Coffey, 1998 WL 24341 (Ohio Ct. App. 12th Dist. Madison County 1998).

year after the date of the award of legal custody, or the date of the latest further action after the award, if the legal custodian either resides in a county of this state other than the county in which the court is located, or moves to a different county prior to the one-year period. The court in the county in which the legal custodian resides shall then have jurisdiction.[9]

§ 30:8 Permanent custody—Defined

The most drastic dispositional alternative available to the juvenile court is to commit an abused, neglected, or dependent child to the permanent custody of a public children services agency or private child placing agency.[1]

Permanent custody is a legal status which vests the agency with all parental rights, duties, and obligations, including the right to consent to adoption, and divests the natural parents or adoptive parents of any and all parental rights, privileges, and obligations, including all residual rights and obligations.[2]

Because the purpose clause (RC 2151.01(A)) of the Juvenile Code expresses a preference that children be cared for in a family environment with their parents, permanent custody should be used only as a last resort. Judicial reluctance to grant permanent custody recognizes the importance of maintaining the family structure and protecting the rights of parents, as well as protecting the child's right to the companionship of the child's siblings.[3] One court has stated that "where there is a true parent-child relationship and true love exchanged between the parent and child, permanent commitment is out of the question, even though the mother is unable to provide a proper home for her children."[4]

A juvenile court may not condition an award of permanent custody to a children services board upon the children remaining in the home of their aunt and uncle,[5] or upon the children's placement in a specific adoptive home.[6]

Methods of obtaining permanent custody. Ohio law provides two means by which an authorized agency may obtain permanent custody.[7] The agency may either request permanent custody as part of the initial abuse,

---

[9]RC 2151.353(J).

[Section 30:8]

[1]RC 2151.353(A)(4). See Stanley v. Illinois, 405 U.S. 645, 651, 92 S. Ct. 1208, 31 L. Ed. 2d 551 (1972) (parent's right to raise his or her children is an "essential" and "basic civil right"); In re Perales, 52 Ohio St. 2d 89, 6 Ohio Op. 3d 293, 369 N.E.2d 1047 (1977) (parent's right to custody of child is "paramount."); In re Campbell, 138 Ohio App. 3d 786, 790, 742 N.E.2d 663 (10th Dist. Franklin County 2000) ("Termination of the rights of a birth parent is an alternative of last resort, but is sanctioned when necessary for the welfare of the child."); In re Smith, 77 Ohio App. 3d 1, 16, 601 N.E.2d 45 (6th Dist. Ottawa County 1991) ("A termination of (parental) rights is the family law equivalent of the death penalty in a criminal case. The parties to such an action must be afforded every procedural and substantive protection the law allows.").

[2]RC 2151.011(B)(26); Juv. R. 2(Z). See RC 3107.06. When a permanent custody complaint is filed prior to a mother's attempt to petition the probate court for the children's adoption, the mother may not contest the custody determination by interposing her residual adoptive rights. In re Palmer, 12 Ohio St. 3d 194, 465 N.E.2d 1312 (1984).

[3]In re M., 65 Ohio Misc. 7, 18 Ohio Op. 3d 283, 19 Ohio Op. 3d 112, 416 N.E.2d 669 (C.P. 1979).

[4]In re Gibson, No. 78AP-856 (10th Dist. Ct. App., Franklin, 7-19-79).

[5]In the Matter of Lenard, 1984 WL 4275 (Ohio Ct. App. 4th Dist. Athens County 1984).

[6]In re Morris, 1991 WL 96271 (Ohio Ct. App. 2d Dist. Montgomery County 1991).

[7]An award of permanent custody should not be confused with a permanent surrender action governed by RC 5103.15. Permanent surrender results from a voluntary agreement between a parent and an appropriate agency and does not require a finding that the child is neglected, dependent, or abused. Furthermore, where such an agreement is with a county department of job and family services, it is revocable by the parent prior to the consent of the juvenile court. See In re Williams, 7 Ohio App. 3d 324, 455 N.E.2d 1027 (1st Dist. Hamilton County 1982). For discussion of permanent surrenders, see Temporary & Permanent Custody Agreements Ch 12.

neglect, or dependency proceeding,[8] or it may first obtain temporary custody or a planned permanent living arrangement and thereafter file a motion for permanent custody.[9]

The court may grant permanent custody as the initial dispositional order if it determines in accordance with RC 2151.414(E) that the child cannot be placed with one of his parents within a reasonable time or should not be placed with either parent, and determines in accordance with RC 2151.414(D) that the permanent commitment is in the child's best interest.[10] Both of these determinations focus on the child, not on the parents.[11] Permanent custody should be granted as the initial disposition only in extreme situations where reunification is not possible.[12] However, neither the case law nor statutory law requires a finding that reunification would be "futile" before a court may grant permanent custody.[13]

Where neglect has been proven with respect to the acts of one parent, but the evidence is insufficient to establish a finding of neglect on behalf of the other parent, the court may not terminate the parental rights of the parent innocent of wrongdoing.[14]

§ 30:9   Permanent custody—Requirements

Under RC 2151.414(B), a juvenile court may grant permanent custody only if the court first determines, by clear and convincing evidence, that one of the following conditions apply: (1) the child is abandoned, (2) the child is orphaned and no relatives are able to take permanent custody, (3) the child has been in temporary custody of one or more public or private agencies for 12 or more months of a consecutive 22-month period,[1] or (4) the child cannot be placed with either parent within a reasonable time or should not be placed with the parents.[2] In addition, the court must then determine that it is in the child's best interest to grant permanent custody.[3]

§ 30:10   Permanent custody—Parental placement within reasonable time

The court must consider all relevant evidence before determining that the

---

[8]RC 2151.353(A)(4); In re Massengill, 76 Ohio App. 3d 220, 601 N.E.2d 206 (6th Dist. Lucas County 1991); In Matter of Cooperman, 1995 WL 23162 (Ohio Ct. App. 8th Dist. Cuyahoga County 1995); Matter of Woods, 1993 WL 19546 (Ohio Ct. App. 8th Dist. Cuyahoga County 1993).

[9]For discussion of this procedure, see Motions for Permanent Custody Ch 31.

[10]RC 2151.353(A)(4); In re Cunningham, 59 Ohio St. 2d 100, 13 Ohio Op. 3d 78, 391 N.E.2d 1034 (1979); In re Pachin, 50 Ohio App. 3d 44, 552 N.E.2d 655 (2d Dist. Montgomery County 1988); Matter of Price, 1993 WL 76957 (Ohio Ct. App. 2d Dist. Greene County 1993); In re Brown, 98 Ohio App. 3d 337, 648 N.E.2d 576 (3d Dist. Marion County 1994).

[11]In re Awkal, 95 Ohio App. 3d 309, 642 N.E.2d 424 (8th Dist. Cuyahoga County 1994).

[12]In re Smart, 21 Ohio App. 3d 31, 486 N.E.2d 147 (10th Dist. Franklin County 1984); In re Pachin, 50 Ohio App. 3d 44, 552 N.E.2d 655 (2d Dist. Montgomery County 1988); In Matter of Cooperman, 1995 WL 23162 (Ohio Ct. App. 8th Dist. Cuyahoga County 1995).

[13]In Matter of Shawn W., 1996 WL 549223 (Ohio Ct. App. 6th Dist. Lucas County 1996).

[14]In re Pieper Children, 74 Ohio App. 3d 714, 600 N.E.2d 317 (12th Dist. Preble County 1991). See In re Belden/Haywood Children, 1995 WL 347924 (Ohio Ct. App. 5th Dist. Stark County 1995).

[Section 30:9]

[1]In re C.W., 2004-Ohio-1987, at ¶ 17, 2004 WL 840124 (Ohio Ct. App. 9th Dist. Summit County 2004), motion to certify allowed, 102 Ohio St. 3d 1481, 2004-Ohio-3069 (2004) (The first prong of the permanent custody test may not be satisfied by RC 2151.414(B)(1)(d) when the agency filed a motion for permanent custody before the child had been in temporary custody for 12 months.)

[2]See § 30:10, Permanent custody—Parental placement within reasonable time.

[3]In re Muldrew, 2004-Ohio-2044, 2004 WL 870427 (Ohio Ct. App. 2d Dist. Montgomery County 2004). See § 30:11, Permanent custody—"Best interests" factors.

child cannot be placed with either parent within a reasonable time or that the child should not be placed with the parents.[1] Such a finding *must* be made if the court finds, by clear and convincing evidence,[2] that any of the following circumstances, or other relevant circumstances, exist with respect to each of the child's parents:

(1) **Parental failure in six-month period.** Following the placement of the child outside the child's home and notwithstanding reasonable case planning and diligent efforts by the agency to assist the parents to remedy the problems that initially caused the outside placement, the parent has failed continuously and repeatedly for a period of six months or more to substantially remedy the conditions that caused the outside placement.

In making this determination, the court must consider parental utilization of medical, psychiatric, psychological, and other social and rehabilitative services and material resources made available to the parents for the purpose of changing parental conduct to allow them to resume and maintain parental duties.[3]

[Section 30:10]

[1]RC 2151.414(E). This statute was amended by both 1996 H.B. 419, eff. 9-18-96, and 1996 H.B. 274, eff. 8-8-96. Because the amendments do not appear to be substantively irreconcilable, the above analysis attempts to harmonize the amendments to give effect to each of them.

[2]RC 2151.414(E); In re Weaver, 79 Ohio App. 3d 59, 606 N.E.2d 1011 (12th Dist. Butler County 1992); Matter of Gilbert, 1990 WL 25084 (Ohio Ct. App. 3d Dist. Marion County 1990); In the Matter Of: Foos, 1985 WL 7370 (Ohio Ct. App. 3d Dist. Marion County 1985); In re Egbert Children, 99 Ohio App. 3d 492, 651 N.E.2d 38 (12th Dist. Butler County 1994); In re Meyer, 98 Ohio App. 3d 189, 648 N.E.2d 52 (3d Dist. Defiance County 1994); In re Brodbeck, 97 Ohio App. 3d 652, 647 N.E.2d 240 (3d Dist. Mercer County 1994); In re Doe Children, 93 Ohio App. 3d 134, 637 N.E.2d 977 (6th Dist. Lucas County 1994); Matter of Queen, 1993 WL 285943 (Ohio Ct. App. 4th Dist. Pickaway County 1993); Matter of Harding, 1993 WL 7914 (Ohio Ct. App. 8th Dist. Cuyahoga County 1993); In re Shanequa H., 109 Ohio App. 3d 142, 671 N.E.2d 1113 (6th Dist. Lucas County 1996).

[3]RC 2151.414(E)(1). See In re Glenn, 139 Ohio App. 3d 105, 113, 742 N.E.2d 1210 (8th Dist. Cuyahoga County 2000) ("The evidence demonstrated that Glenn and Young maintained a continuing and abusive relationship. Although the violence was not directed at the children, they could be expected to be emotionally and psychologically damaged as a result of the parents' actions. Further, the evidence showed a pattern of behavior suggesting Glenn planned to continue her relationship with Young upon his release from jail. Additionally, the evidence demonstrated Glenn failed to address the issues of violence in a timely manner by allowing approximately one and a half years to pass before choosing to participate in a course. The evidence demonstrated Young exhibited a pattern of violence toward women. The record showed Young was currently incarcerated and has a history of repeated incarcerations."); In re Campbell, 138 Ohio App. 3d 786, 793, 742 N.E.2d 663 (10th Dist. Franklin County 2000) ("[M]agistrate found appellant failed to substantially remedy the conditions causing Sabastian to be placed in foster care in 1996. . . . Non-compliance with a case plan is grounds for termination of parental rights."); In re Rodgers, 138 Ohio App. 3d 510, 520, 741 N.E.2d 901 (12th Dist. Preble County 2000) ("Appellant failed to fully comply with the case plan. One of the most important goals of the case plan was to assess and address drug dependency by appellant and Bruce Rodgers. Both parents were ordered to submit to random drug testing, and visitation with Oza was conditioned upon taking these tests. Appellant failed to comply with the drug testing requirements."); In re Stacey S., 136 Ohio App. 3d 503, 520–21, 1999-Ohio-989, 737 N.E.2d 92 (6th Dist. Lucas County 1999) ("[A]ppellant father's bizarre behavior is well-documented and it is undoubtedly one of, if not the, principal reason the children were removed from the home. There was ample evidence at the dispositional hearing that this behavior continues and this evidence, along with appellant father's refusal to avail himself of the services offered by appellee, in our view, could be found to establish by clear and convincing evidence that appellant father failed to remedy a condition which caused the children to be removed from the home. With respect to appellant mother, she was and is unable to restrain appellant father's behavior. Therefore, the trial court could have found that she, too, had failed to remedy a problem that caused removal of the children."); Drushal v. Drushal, 1983 WL 4058 (Ohio Ct. App. 9th Dist. Summit County 1983); Orwell v. Orwell, 1990 WL 157170 (Ohio Ct. App. 2d Dist. Montgomery County 1990); In re Stanley, 1993 WL 512502 (Ohio Ct. App. 10th Dist. Franklin County 1993); Matter of Queen, 1993 WL 285943 (Ohio Ct. App. 4th Dist. Pickaway County 1993); Matter of Reynolds, 1993 WL 220253 (Ohio Ct. App. 12th Dist. Butler County 1993); Matter of Lewis, 1992 WL 150202 (Ohio Ct. App. 7th Dist. Mahoning County 1992); In re M. W., 2004-Ohio-438, 2004 WL 199962 (Ohio Ct. App. 9th Dist. Lorain County 2004). See also Text § 30:10 at footnote 12.

If an agency seeks to argue that a parent did not rectify the causes for removal of the child, the agency must give the parent a case plan and an opportunity to correct the situation.[4]

It has been held that the factors set forth in RC 2151.414(E)(1) refer to conditions existing at the time of the child's removal, even if those conditions were remedied after the child was removed.[5]

(2) **Chronic illnesses, physical disability or chemical dependency.** Chronic mental or emotional illness, mental retardation, physical disability, or chemical dependency of the parent that is so severe that it makes the parent unable to provide an adequate permanent home for the child at the present time and, as anticipated, within one year after the permanent custody hearing is held.[6] Although a mere finding that a mother is an alcoholic is insufficient to satisfy this requirement,[7] evidence that a mother had not stopped drinking, was intoxicated at least once during visitation with her children, and had been arrested twice following the case plan for disorderly conduct while intoxicated was deemed sufficient to meet the statutory requirement.[8]

If a parent's severe and chronic mental illness is being controlled by medication, therapy, and treatment, and does not make the parent unable to provide an adequate permanent home for the child at the present time and in the foreseeable future, a juvenile court order terminating parental rights is improper.[9]

(3) **Parental abuse or neglect after original complaint.** The parent committed any abuse as described in RC 2151.031, caused the child to suffer any neglect as described in RC 2151.03, or allowed the child to suffer any neglect as described in RC 2151.03 between the date that the original complaint alleging abuse or neglect was filed and the date of the filing of the motion[10] for permanent custody.[11]

(4) **Lack of parental commitment.** The parent has demonstrated a lack of commitment toward the child by failing to regularly support, visit, or communicate with the child when able to do so, or by other actions showing an unwillingness to provide an adequate permanent home for the child.[12]

---

[4]In re Mark H., 1999 WL 253163 (Ohio Ct. App. 6th Dist. Lucas County 1999).

[5]In Matter of Shawn W., 1996 WL 549223 (Ohio Ct. App. 6th Dist. Lucas County 1996); Matter of Linda M., 1998 WL 200161 (Ohio Ct. App. 6th Dist. Lucas County 1998).

[6]RC 2151.414(E)(2). See In re Ison, 47 Ohio App. 3d 103, 547 N.E.2d 420 (9th Dist. Wayne County 1989). The statute has been held not unconstitutional when applied to retarded parents. Matter of Mayle, 1991 WL 100527 (Ohio Ct. App. 5th Dist. Stark County 1991); Matter of Cannon, 1990 WL 237462 (Ohio Ct. App. 5th Dist. Stark County 1990); Matter of Norton, 1990 WL 187073 (Ohio Ct. App. 5th Dist. Stark County 1990); In re Egbert Children, 99 Ohio App. 3d 492, 651 N.E.2d 38 (12th Dist. Butler County 1994).

[7]Matter of Dixon, 1992 WL 277966 (Ohio Ct. App. 6th Dist. Erie County 1992).

[8]Matter of Queen, 1993 WL 285943 (Ohio Ct. App. 4th Dist. Pickaway County 1993).

[9]In re Arvin, 1990 WL 37783 (Ohio Ct. App. 1st Dist. Hamilton County 1990).

[10]It is presumed that this applies to original complaints requesting permanent custody, as well as motions for permanent custody. See RC 2151.415(A).

[11]RC 2151.414(E)(3). See In the Matter Of: Wellinger, 1983 WL 2645 (Ohio Ct. App. 8th Dist. Cuyahoga County 1983); In the Matter Of: Lucas, 1982 WL 3444 (Ohio Ct. App. 4th Dist. Lawrence County 1982).

[12]RC 2151.414(E)(4). See In re Baby Girl Doe, 149 Ohio App. 3d 717, 739, 2002-Ohio-4470, 778 N.E.2d 1053 (6th Dist. Lucas County 2002) ("Natalie and her parents' failure ever to visit the baby or inquire about the baby and their request that the baby not be brought to a meeting speak volumes about the level of their commitment to the baby, as does Kevin's selection of an optional swim-team training over visiting and caring for the baby. Additionally, both Natalie and Kevin sought consent for a third-party adoption."); In re McCrary, 75 Ohio App. 3d 601, 600 N.E.2d 347 (12th Dist. Madison County 1991); In re Stevens, 1993 WL 265130 (Ohio Ct. App. 2d Dist. Montgomery County 1993); In re Crager, 2003-Ohio-5548, 2003 WL 22386961 (Ohio Ct.

The Supreme Court has determined that the term "unwillingness," as used in the statute, is not synonymous with "inability."[13]

(5) **Incarceration for crime against child or sibling.** The parent is incarcerated for an offense committed against the child or a sibling of the child.[14]

(6) **Conviction: child or sibling victim.** The parent has been convicted of one of a variety of criminal offenses[15] and the child or the child's sibling was a victim of the offense; or the parent has been convicted of an offense under RC 2903.04 where the child's sibling was the victim, and the parent poses an ongoing danger to the child or a sibling.[16] It has been held that even if the conviction occurred prior to the birth of the child who is the subject of the permanent custody proceeding, the conviction is relevant in determining the parent's fitness since the statute does not draw any distinction based on when the crime was committed.[17]

(7) **Conviction: child or sibling victim.** The parent has been convicted of:

(a) RC 2903.01 (aggravated murder), RC 2903.02 (murder), or RC 2903.03 (voluntary manslaughter) or an existing or former law of this state, any other state, or the United States that is substantially equivalent to one of those offenses, where the victim was the sibling of the child or another child who lived in the parent's household at the time of the offense;[18] or a conspiracy or attempt to commit, or complicity in committing, any such offense;[19]

(b) RC 2903.11 (felonious assault), RC 2903.12 (aggravated assault), RC 2903.13 (assault), or RC 2919.22(B)(2) (child endangerment), or an existing or former law of this state, any other state, or the United States that is substantially equivalent to one of those offenses, where the victim is the child, a sibling of the child, or another child who lived in the parent's household at the time of the offense;[20]

(c) RC 2907.02 (rape), RC 2907.03 (sexual battery), RC 2907.04 (corruption of a minor), RC 2907.05 (gross sexual imposition), or RC 2907.06 (sexual imposition), or an existing or former law of this state, any other state, or the United States that is substantially equivalent to one of those offenses, where the victim is the child, a sibling of the child, or another child who lived in the parent's household at the time of the offense;[21] or a conspiracy or attempt to commit, or complicity in committing, any such offense.[22]

(8) **Withholding medical treatment or food.** The parent has repeatedly withheld medical treatment or food from the child when the parent

---

App. 4th Dist. Lawrence County 2003) (Were parents financially unable to support their children?).

[13]In re William S., 75 Ohio St. 3d 95, 1996-Ohio-182, 661 N.E.2d 738 (1996). See In re Shawnta J., 1998 WL 161101 (Ohio Ct. App. 6th Dist. Lucas County 1998).

[14]RC 2151.414(E)(5). See In the Matter Of: Espy, 1982 WL 2490 (Ohio Ct. App. 8th Dist. Cuyahoga County 1982).

[15]These include RC 2919.22(A), RC 2919.22(C), RC 2903.16, RC 2903.21, RC 2903.34, RC 2905.01, RC 2905.02, RC 2905.03, RC 2905.04, RC 2905.05, RC 2907.07, RC 2907.08, RC 2907.09, RC 2907.12, RC 2907.21, RC 2907.22, RC 2907.23, RC 2907.25, RC 2907.31, RC 2907.32, RC 2907.321, RC 2907.322, RC 2907.323, RC 2911.01, RC 2911.02, RC 2911.11, RC 2911.12, RC 2919.12, RC 2919.24, RC 2919.25, RC 2923.12, RC 2923.161, RC 2925.02, and RC 3716.11.

[16]RC 2151.414(E)(6).

[17]In Matter of Marrs, 1998 WL 896669 (Ohio Ct. App. 2d Dist. Clark County 1998).

[18]RC 2151.414(E)(7)(a).

[19]RC 2151.414(E)(7)(e).

[20]RC 2151.414(E)(7)(b), RC 2151.414(E)(7)(c).

[21]RC 2151.414(E)(7)(d).

[22]RC 2151.414(E)(7)(e).

has the means to provide the treatment or food. In the case of medical treatment, the parent withheld it for a purpose other than to treat the physical or medical illness or defect of the child by spiritual means through prayer in accordance with the tenets of a recognized religious body.[23]

(9) **Alcohol and drug abuse.** The parent has placed the child at substantial risk of harm two or more times due to alcohol or drug abuse and has rejected treatment two or more times or has refused to participate in further treatment two or more times after a case plan pursuant to RC 2151.412 requiring treatment was journalized as part of a dispositional order issued with respect to the child, or an order was issued by any other court requiring treatment of the parent.[24]

(10) **Abandonment.** The parent has abandoned the child.[25]

(11) **Termination of rights with respect to sibling.** The parent has had parental rights involuntarily terminated pursuant to RC 2151.353, RC 2151.414, or RC 2151.415 with respect to a sibling of the child.[26]

(12) **Incarceration for 18 months.** The parent is incarcerated at the time of the filing of the motion for permanent custody or the dispositional hearing and will not be available to care for the child for at least 18 months.[27] Because the statute phrases the dates as alternatives, if a parent is unavailable because of imprisonment either 18 months from the initial filing or 18 months from the date of the dispositional hearing, the parent is not fit for placement within a reasonable time.[28] The mere possibility of parole or early release within a time less than the 18-month term is not sufficient to overcome the clear and convincing evidence that a sentence of imprisonment provides.[29] A prison sentence for longer than 18 months is sufficient to prove that the parent will be incarcerated for that time, and the burden is on the parent to produce evidence that the prison sentence will terminate within a lesser time.[30]

(13) **Repeated incarceration.** The parent is repeatedly incarcerated and the repeated incarceration prevents the parent from providing care for the child.[31] This factor does not require that the parent be incarcerated at the time of the hearing; the court must examine the series of incarcerations, their effect on the children, and whether the parent's criminality shows an inclination to continue violating the law in the future.[32]

(14) **Unwilling to provide basic necessities.** The parent for any reason is unwilling to provide food, clothing, shelter, and other basic necessi-

---

[23]RC 2151.414(E)(8). See § 9:7, Neglect—Subsistence, education & medical care.

[24]RC 2151.414(E)(9).

[25]RC 2151.414(E)(10). See RC 2151.011(C).

[26]RC 2151.414(E)(11). In re Richardson, 2004-Ohio-2170, at ¶ 20, 2004 WL 911316 (Ohio Ct. App. 5th Dist. Guernsey County 2004) (Parents "had each had their parental rights with respect to [child's] siblings previously terminated. Therefore, the statute exempts CSB from the reasonable effort requirement of R.C. 2151.419.").

[27]RC 2151.414(E)(12). See In re Hederson, 30 Ohio App. 3d 187, 507 N.E.2d 418 (9th Dist. Summit County 1986); Matter of Davis, 1984 WL 5666 (Ohio Ct. App. 4th Dist. Hocking County 1984); In re T.K., 2003-Ohio-2634, 2003 WL 21185949 (Ohio Ct. App. 9th Dist. Wayne County 2003) (Father had been incarcerated throughout child's lifetime and would continue to be incarcerated for at least another eighteen months following the permanent custody hearing.).

[28]In Matter of Marrs, 1998 WL 896669 (Ohio Ct. App. 2d Dist. Clark County 1998).

[29]In re Hederson, 30 Ohio App. 3d 187, 507 N.E.2d 418 (9th Dist. Summit County 1986); In re Hiatt, 86 Ohio App. 3d 716, 621 N.E.2d 1222 (4th Dist. Adams County 1993); In re V. S., 2003-Ohio-5612, 2003 WL 22399705 (Ohio Ct. App. 9th Dist. Lorain County 2003); Matter of Uehlein v. Fuller, 1993 WL 129333 (Ohio Ct. App. 9th Dist. Lorain County 1993); Matter of Cook, 1990 WL 157225 (Ohio Ct. App. 2d Dist. Clark County 1990); Lorain County Children Services v. Simmons, 1990 WL 121102 (Ohio Ct. App. 9th Dist. Lorain County 1990).

[30]Matter of Uehlein v. Fuller, 1993 WL 129333 (Ohio Ct. App. 9th Dist. Lorain County 1993).

[31]RC 2151.414(E)(13).

[32]In Matter of Hendricks, 1996 WL 202856 (Ohio Ct. App. 11th Dist. Ashtabula County 1996).

ties for the child or to prevent the child from suffering physical, emotional, or sexual abuse or physical, emotional, or mental neglect.[33] Permanent custody may be granted when a mother is unable to protect her children from a foreseeable abusive situation, even if she herself is not the abuser.[34]

(15) **Likely recurrence of abuse or neglect.** The parent has abused or neglected the child, and the seriousness, nature, or likelihood of recurrence of abuse or neglect makes the child's placement with the child's parent a threat to the child's safety.[35]

(16) **Other factors.** Any other factor the court considers relevant.[36]

Even before the 1996 amendments to RC 2151.414(E),[37] several appellate decisions had held that only one of the eight statutory conditions needs to exist to support a finding that a child cannot be placed within a reasonable time with either parent.[38] Moreover, no one statutory factor should be given more weight than any other, nor must the court specifically cite the statute or use the exact language of the statute, as long as all factors relevant to a determination of the child's best interests are considered by the court.[39] The focus is on the specific needs of the child and whether a parent can meet those needs.[40] Even where it cannot be proven that a parent is unfit under one of the designated factors, permanent custody may be granted if the court finds that the children services agency has met its burden to prove the parent to be unsuitable given the child's specific needs.[41]

§ 30:11 Permanent custody—"Best interest" factors

In determining the best interest of a child at a permanent custody hearing,

---

[33]RC 2151.414(E)(14). See In re Mark H., 1999 WL 253163 (Ohio Ct. App. 6th Dist. Lucas County 1999).

[34]In re Szabat, No. 94-P-0049 (11th Dist. Ct. App., Portage, 9-1-95); Matter of Ranker, 1996 WL 761159 (Ohio Ct. App. 11th Dist. Portage County 1996).

[35]RC 2151.414(E)(15). See In re Baby Girl Doe, 149 Ohio App. 3d 717, 739, 2002-Ohio-4470, 778 N.E.2d 1053 (6th Dist. Lucas County 2002) ("R.C. 2151.414(E)(15) also provides that a finding that a child cannot or should not be reunified with the parents is to be made if the trial court determines that the seriousness or nature of the abuse or neglect makes placement with the parents a threat to the child's safety. In regard to Natalie, given where and in what condition the baby was found, this court cannot find that the trial court erred in its reliance upon R.C. 2151.414(E)(15).").

[36]RC 2151.414(E)(16), overruling In re William S., 75 Ohio St. 3d 95, 1996-Ohio-182, 661 N.E.2d 738 (1996). See Matter of Keltner, 1995 WL 22722 (Ohio Ct. App. 12th Dist. Butler County 1995); Matter of Kasler, 1991 WL 100360 (Ohio Ct. App. 4th Dist. Athens County 1991); In Matter of Cooperman, 1995 WL 23162 (Ohio Ct. App. 8th Dist. Cuyahoga County 1995); In re Hodge/Burchett Children, 1995 WL 470540 (Ohio Ct. App. 12th Dist. Butler County 1995); Matter of Shahan, 1997 WL 374517 (Ohio Ct. App. 4th Dist. Hocking County 1997).

[37]1996 H.B. 419, eff. 9-18-96, and 1996 H.B. 274, eff. 8-8-96.

[38]In re Weaver, 79 Ohio App. 3d 59, 606 N.E.2d 1011 (12th Dist. Butler County 1992); Matter of Whiteman, 2 A.D.D. 386 (Ohio Ct. App. 6th Dist. Williams County 1993); Matter of Runyon, 1993 WL 79291 (Ohio Ct. App. 4th Dist. Highland County 1993); Matter of McDaniel, 1993 WL 33308 (Ohio Ct. App. 4th Dist. Adams County 1993); Matter of Stapleton, 1991 WL 110217 (Ohio Ct. App. 4th Dist. Scioto County 1991); Matter of Butcher, 1991 WL 62145 (Ohio Ct. App. 4th Dist. Athens County 1991); Matter of Dillen, 1990 WL 42303 (Ohio Ct. App. 4th Dist. Hocking County 1990); In re Brown, 98 Ohio App. 3d 337, 648 N.E.2d 576 (3d Dist. Marion County 1994); Matter of Queen, 1993 WL 285943 (Ohio Ct. App. 4th Dist. Pickaway County 1993); In Matter of Hendricks, 1996 WL 202856 (Ohio Ct. App. 11th Dist. Ashtabula County 1996); Matter of Coles, 1994 WL 237974 (Ohio Ct. App. 11th Dist. Trumbull County 1994); In Matter of Robinson, 1997 WL 599156 (Ohio Ct. App. 4th Dist. Scioto County 1997).

[39]Matter of Jennings, 1993 WL 99444 (Ohio Ct. App. 3d Dist. Allen County 1993); Matter of Catherine M., 1995 WL 326354 (Ohio Ct. App. 6th Dist. Lucas County 1995); In Matter of Mills, 1996 WL 132286 (Ohio Ct. App. 5th Dist. Licking County 1996).

[40]Hoff v. Hoff, 1993 WL 280455 (Ohio Ct. App. 9th Dist. Wayne County 1993).

[41]In re Higby, 81 Ohio App. 3d 466, 611 N.E.2d 403 (9th Dist. Wayne County 1992); In re Stevens, 1993 WL 265130 (Ohio Ct. App. 2d Dist. Montgomery County 1993); In re Pickett, 1993 WL 386259 (Ohio Ct. App. 12th Dist. Butler County 1993); In Matter of Matis, 1995 WL 314683 (Ohio Ct. App. 9th Dist. Summit County 1995).

the court must consider all relevant factors,[1] including but not limited to the following:

(1) **Interaction of child.** The interaction and interrelationship of the child with parents, siblings, relatives, foster parents, and out-of-home providers, and any other person who may significantly affect the child.[2]

(2) **Child's wishes.** The wishes of the child, as expressed directly by the child or through the child's guardian ad litem, with due regard for the maturity of the child.[3]

(3) **Custodial history.** The custodial history of the child, including whether the child has been in the temporary custody of one or more agencies for 12 or more months of a consecutive 22-month period ending on or after March 18, 1999.[4] An appellate court has held that this provision mandates only that the court consider a child's custodial history and not the reasons why the child was first placed with the agency.[5] However, another court of appeals overturned a permanent custody order in part because the record was silent as to the conditions which caused the child to be initially placed outside the home.[6]

[Section 30:11]

[1]RC 2151.414(D). See In re Hensley, 1993 WL 119959 (Ohio Ct. App. 12th Dist. Butler County 1993); Matter of Addison, 1996 WL 732440 (Ohio Ct. App. 8th Dist. Cuyahoga County 1996); In re J.O., 2004-Ohio-2121, 2004 WL 894571 (Ohio Ct. App. 9th Dist. Wayne County 2004); In re M.B., 2004-Ohio-597, 2004 WL 239924 (Ohio Ct. App. 9th Dist. Summit County 2004).

[2]RC 2151.414(D)(1). See In re Patterson, 134 Ohio App. 3d 119, 124, 730 N.E.2d 439 (9th Dist. Summit County 1999) ("Eric has Downs syndrome. At the time of the trial, Eric was four years old. He was described as a very loveable, active child. Although there was testimony that Eric had a bond with his mother, there was also overwhelming testimony that Eric bonded easily with everyone. He was described as being able to adjust to different situations with no problems. Eric has bonded with his current foster family and has made significant progress in his therapy."). Several cases decided prior to the 1989 amendment to the statute (1988 S.B. 89, eff. 1-1-89) held that where the child has become a stranger to the parent and has become psychologically and emotionally attached to foster parents, termination of parental rights may be justified. Matter of Luke, 1984 WL 2667 (Ohio Ct. App. 5th Dist. Coshocton County 1984); In the Matter Of: Wellinger, 1983 WL 2645 (Ohio Ct. App. 8th Dist. Cuyahoga County 1983); In the Matter Of: Espy, 1982 WL 2490 (Ohio Ct. App. 8th Dist. Cuyahoga County 1982); Matter Of: Wayne, 1981 WL 3452 (Ohio Ct. App. 10th Dist. Franklin County 1981); In re Justice, 59 Ohio App. 2d 78, 13 Ohio Op. 3d 139, 392 N.E.2d 897 (1st Dist. Clinton County 1978); In re Christopher, 54 Ohio App. 2d 137, 8 Ohio Op. 3d 271, 376 N.E.2d 603 (5th Dist. Morrow County 1977); Matter of Clark, 1995 WL 153010 (Ohio Ct. App. 7th Dist. Harrison County 1995); In re R. K., 2004-Ohio-439, 2004 WL 200002 (Ohio Ct. App. 9th Dist. Lorain County 2004).

[3]RC 2151.414(D)(2). See In re Patterson, 134 Ohio App. 3d 119, 124, 730 N.E.2d 439 (9th Dist. Summit County 1999) ("Eric was not sufficiently mature to express his desires, however, his guardian ad litem recommended that he be placed with CSB."); In re Fotiou Children, 1991 WL 3213 (Ohio Ct. App. 12th Dist. Madison County 1991); Matter of Gordon, 1990 WL 138358 (Ohio Ct. App. 12th Dist. Madison County 1990); In re Staten, 1998 WL 735949 (Ohio Ct. App. 2d Dist. Montgomery County 1998); In Matter of Reid, 1998 WL 409115 (Ohio Ct. App. 3d Dist. Paulding County 1998).

[4]RC 2151.414(D)(3). Temporary custody includes custody of one or more public children services agencies or private child placing agencies. Custody commences on the date the child is adjudicated pursuant to RC 2151.28 or 60 days after removal from the home, whichever is earlier. See also In re Patterson, 134 Ohio App. 3d 119, 124, 730 N.E.2d 439 (9th Dist. Summit County 1999) ("Eric had been out of his mother's custody for over twelve months. Testimony indicated that he had made significant progress in his therapy while in foster care because he was getting his therapy on a consistent basis."); In Re P. C., 2004-Ohio-1230, 2004 WL 509368 (Ohio Ct. App. 9th Dist. Summit County 2004); In re Joiner, 2004-Ohio-1158, 2004 WL 473260 (Ohio Ct. App. 11th Dist. Ashtabula County 2004), appeal not allowed, 102 Ohio St. 3d 1425, 2004-Ohio-2003, 807 N.E.2d 368 (2004).

[5]Matter of Bacorn, 1996 WL 762005 (Ohio Ct. App. 11th Dist. Portage County 1996).

[6]Matter of Mesko, 1997 WL 205279 (Ohio Ct. App. 7th Dist. Belmont County 1997).

(4) **Child's need for permanent placement.** The child's need for a legally secure permanent placement and whether that type of placement can be achieved without a grant of permanent custody to the agency.[7]

(5) **Other factors.** Whether any of the factors in RC 2151.414(E)(7) to (12) apply in relation to the parents and child.[8]

In making these determinations, the court may not consider the effect that the granting of permanent custody would have on any parent of the child.[9]

The court is not required to find that each and every statutory condition exist before making a best interest determination; the decision may be based solely on the existence of one of the conditions.[10] No one statutory factor should be given more weight than another, as long as all factors relevant to the child's best interests are considered,[11] including factors not enumerated in the statute.[12] Moreover, the court is not required to use the exact language of the statute in making its determination.[13]

A court does not abuse its discretion by not granting permanent custody even when it finds every statutory factor in the state's favor, because RC 2151.414(B) provides only that the court *may* grant permanent custody when it makes a best interest determination.[14]

The time frame to keep in mind in deciding permanent custody cases is whatever is in the child's best interests.[15]

Parental unfitness. Long before its codification, the "best interest" stan-

---

[7]RC 2151.414(D)(4). See In re Campbell, 138 Ohio App. 3d 786, 791–92, 742 N.E.2d 663 (10th Dist. Franklin County 2000) ("Appellant was unable to provide a stable environment, as she had failed to obtain stable housing or employment. Her lack of commitment to her case plan and to reunifying with Sabastian, as well as her inability to meet his needs for a secure environment through employment and housing stability, indicate divestiture of custody is the only means to advance a secure placement for Sabastian."); In re Patterson, 134 Ohio App. 3d 119, 124, 730 N.E.2d 439 (9th Dist. Summit County 1999) ("Eric has special health and educational needs. He requires ongoing and consistent physical, occupational and speech therapies. The juvenile court found that Eric needed a legally secure permanent placement and that that placement could not be achieved without a grant of permanent custody to CSB."); In re Lindsay, 1991 WL 131494 (Ohio Ct. App. 9th Dist. Summit County 1991); In re Johnson, 1991 WL 123047 (Ohio Ct. App. 9th Dist. Lorain County 1991); Matter of Tackett, 1990 WL 34369 (Ohio Ct. App. 4th Dist. Adams County 1990); In re Hall, 65 Ohio App. 3d 88, 582 N.E.2d 1055 (10th Dist. Franklin County 1989); In re Mourey, 2003-Ohio-1870, 2003 WL 1869911 (Ohio Ct. App. 4th Dist. Athens County 2003).

[8]RC 2151.414(D)(5). See § 30:9, Permanent custody—Requirements.

[9]RC 2151.414(C). See Matter of McDaniel, 1993 WL 33308 (Ohio Ct. App. 4th Dist. Adams County 1993); Matter of Clark, 1995 WL 153010 (Ohio Ct. App. 7th Dist. Harrison County 1995); Matter of Hurlow, 1998 WL 655414 (Ohio Ct. App. 4th Dist. Gallia County 1998).

[10]Matter of Butcher, 1991 WL 62145 (Ohio Ct. App. 4th Dist. Athens County 1991); In re Shaeffer Children, 85 Ohio App. 3d 683, 621 N.E.2d 426 (3d Dist. Van Wert County 1993).

[11]Matter of Winegardner, 1995 WL 657113 (Ohio Ct. App. 3d Dist. Hardin County 1995); In Matter of Heyman, 1996 WL 465238 (Ohio Ct. App. 10th Dist. Franklin County 1996); Matter of Hommes, 1996 WL 760920 (Ohio Ct. App. 11th Dist. Ashtabula County 1996); Matter of Alexander, 1997 WL 799517 (Ohio Ct. App. 11th Dist. Trumbull County 1997); In re J. H., 2003-Ohio-5611, 2003 WL 22399693 (Ohio Ct. App. 9th Dist. Summit County 2003) (The court reviewed all of the factors relevant to the child's best interests.) However, see In re Robinson, 2004-Ohio-376, 2004 WL 177720 (Ohio Ct. App. 5th Dist. Stark County 2004) (Failure to conduct a best interests hearing or to hear evidence on best interests before awarding permanent custody was reversible error.).

[12]Matter of Brittany and Marcus B., 1996 WL 11135 (Ohio Ct. App. 6th Dist. Wood County 1996).

[13]In Matter of Mills, 1996 WL 132286 (Ohio Ct. App. 5th Dist. Licking County 1996).

[14]Matter of Seymour, 1993 WL 49263 (Ohio Ct. App. 4th Dist. Hocking County 1993); Matter of Catherine M., 1995 WL 326354 (Ohio Ct. App. 6th Dist. Lucas County 1995).

[15]In re Cornell, 2003-Ohio-5007, at ¶ 28, 2003 WL 22171435 (Ohio Ct. App. 11th Dist. Portage County 2003) ([Mother,] "in general, argues that although she has failed to accomplish the objectives of her case plan, she is currently *attempting* to do so. [She] maintains if she were given more time, she would satisfy her case plan and have a better chance of reuniting with [the child.] . . . . [H]owever, a permanent custody hearing must be grounded upon the child's best interests.").

dard was recognized as the primary consideration in permanent custody cases.[16] However, there appears to be considerable overlap between the "best interests" test and a "parental fitness" standard. The Ohio Supreme Court held in *In re Perales*[17] that in a custody dispute between a parent and a nonparent under RC 2151.23(A)(2), the welfare of the child is the first consideration, but suitable parents have a paramount right to custody.[18] In effect, the court defined "suitability" in terms of the best interests of the child[19] when it stated that a parent is unsuitable if "a preponderance of the evidence indicates abandonment, contractual relinquishment of custody, total inability to provide care or support, or that the parent is otherwise unsuitable—that is, that an award of custody would be detrimental to the child."[20] A specific "parental unsuitability" finding is not required in a permanent custody proceeding concerning a child who has been adjudicated neglected, dependent, or abused because an award of permanent custody constitutes an implicit finding that the parents are unsuitable.[21] On the other hand, a custody decision made under RC 2151.23(A)(2) does not require a preliminary finding that the child is neglected, dependent, or abused[22] and is based on a lesser standard of proof—preponderance of the evidence[23] rather than clear and convincing evidence.[24]

In comparing the concepts of "parental unfitness" and "the best interests of the child" as they apply to the disposition of dependency cases, the Ohio

---

[16]E.g., In re Cunningham, 59 Ohio St. 2d 100, 13 Ohio Op. 3d 78, 391 N.E.2d 1034 (1979); In re Young, 58 Ohio St. 2d 90, 12 Ohio Op. 3d 93, 388 N.E.2d 1235 (1979); In re Tilton, 161 Ohio St. 571, 53 Ohio Op. 427, 120 N.E.2d 445 (1954); Children's Home of Marion County v. Fetter, 90 Ohio St. 110, 106 N.E. 761 (1914); Clark v. Bayer, 32 Ohio St. 299, 1877 WL 120 (1877); Gishwiler v. Dodez, 4 Ohio St. 615, 1855 WL 28 (1855); In the Matter Of: Espy, 1982 WL 2490 (Ohio Ct. App. 8th Dist. Cuyahoga County 1982); Matter of Poth, 1982 WL 9371 (Ohio Ct. App. 6th Dist. Huron County 1982); In the Matter of Banks Griggs v. Griggs Banks Jones, 1981 WL 5593 (Ohio Ct. App. 6th Dist. Lucas County 1981); In re Bowman, No. 79AP-798 (10th Dist. Ct. App., Franklin, 6-26-80); In re Hadsell, No. 41004 (8th Dist. Ct. App., Cuyahoga, 6-19-80); In re Collier, No. 39343 (8th Dist. Ct. App., Cuyahoga, 12-13-79); In re Holcomb, No. 39694 (8th Dist. Ct. App., Cuyahoga, 10-4-79); In re Christopher, 54 Ohio App. 2d 137, 8 Ohio Op. 3d 271, 376 N.E.2d 603 (5th Dist. Morrow County 1977).

[17]In re Perales, 52 Ohio St. 2d 89, 6 Ohio Op. 3d 293, 369 N.E.2d 1047 (1977).

[18]In a more recent case, the court held that the best interests standard applies to a custody case between the parents of an illegitimate child. In re Byrd, 66 Ohio St. 2d 334, 20 Ohio Op. 3d 309, 421 N.E.2d 1284 (1981). This case also held that an *alleged* natural father, who has participated in the nurturing process of his illegitimate child, has standing to seek custody pursuant to RC 2151.23(A)(2). This decision was apparently overruled by the 1982 revision of RC 3111.13(C) which now states, *"After entry of the judgment or order* (establishing the existence of the parent-child relationship), the father may petition for custody of the child or for visitation rights in a proceeding separate from any action to establish paternity" (emphasis added). The statute was amended again in 1998 (1997 H.B. 352, eff. 1-1-98), but the amendment did not change the substance of the statute. But see Madison v. Jameson, 1997 WL 416319 (Ohio Ct. App. 9th Dist. Summit County 1997), holding that the principle of law set forth in *Byrd* is still applicable.

[19]For this interpretation of *Perales*, see Thrasher v. Thrasher, 3 Ohio App. 3d 210, 444 N.E.2d 431 (9th Dist. Summit County 1981).

[20]In re Perales, 52 Ohio St. 2d 89, 6 Ohio Op. 3d 293, 369 N.E.2d 1047 (1977). This standard also applies in habeas corpus proceedings involving child custody. Reynolds v. Ross County Children's Services Agency, 5 Ohio St. 3d 27, 448 N.E.2d 816 (1983); In re Hua, 62 Ohio St. 2d 227, 16 Ohio Op. 3d 270, 405 N.E.2d 255 (1980); Reynolds v. Goll, 75 Ohio St. 3d 121, 1996-Ohio-153, 661 N.E.2d 1008 (1996).

[21]In re Stillman, 155 Ohio App. 3d 333, 2003-Ohio-6228, 801 N.E.2d 475 (11th Dist. Ashtabula County 2003), appeal not allowed, 101 Ohio St. 3d 1425, 2004-Ohio-123, 802 N.E.2d 155 (2004); Matter of Gordon, 1996 WL 434122 (Ohio Ct. App. 4th Dist. Gallia County 1996); In re Richard, Laqueeda, Shennell & Dominique, 1994 WL 702071 (Ohio Ct. App. 2d Dist. Montgomery County 1994); Hoff v. Hoff, 1993 WL 280455 (Ohio Ct. App. 9th Dist. Wayne County 1993).

[22]In re Torok, 161 Ohio St. 585, 53 Ohio Op. 433, 120 N.E.2d 307 (1954).

[23]Juv. R. 29(E)(4).

[24]Juv. R. 29(E)(4); RC 2151.35, RC 2151.414(B).

Supreme Court in *In re Cunningham*[25] noted a subtle relationship between the two criteria. While elements of parental unfitness figure strongly in the best interests test, elements of the child's best interests weigh in any consideration of whether a parent is fit to have custody of his or her child. The court emphasized, however, that the two concepts have different meanings. The fundamental inquiry at the dispositional hearing is what the child's best interests are and not whether the parents of a dependent child are fit or unfit.[26] Because parental unfitness is not a mandatory prerequisite to an award of permanent custody in this type of case, a fit parent is not automatically entitled to custody if the specific needs of the child require termination of parental rights.[27]

A court is not required to grant custody to a blood relative of the child,[28] nor to a specific family requested by the mother, as long as it acts in the child's best interests.[29]

§ 30:12   Permanent custody—Procedural issues

Guardian ad litem report. A written report of the child's guardian ad litem must be submitted to the court prior to or at the time of the permanent custody hearing, but it need not be submitted under oath.[1] However, the report is hearsay and cannot be considered evidence where it is not submitted under oath, and the guardian ad litem does not testify and is not subjected to direct or cross-examination.[2] It has been held that the filing of the report is mandatory, and the absence of the written report from the record constitutes reversible error.[3]

It is not improper for the guardian ad litem to submit the report just prior to the end of the hearing before the closing arguments.[4] Moreover, the report may be submitted at the time of the hearing regardless of whether notice had been provided to the other parties.[5] Even submission of the report a full week after the hearing was held to be harmless error where the parties were

---

[25]In re Cunningham, 59 Ohio St. 2d 100, 13 Ohio Op. 3d 78, 391 N.E.2d 1034 (1979).

[26]See In re Awkal, 95 Ohio App. 3d 309, 642 N.E.2d 424 (8th Dist. Cuyahoga County 1994).

[27]In re Cunningham, 59 Ohio St. 2d 100, 13 Ohio Op. 3d 78, 391 N.E.2d 1034 (1979).

[28]Montgomery County Children Services Board v. Kiszka, 1983 WL 2483 (Ohio Ct. App. 2d Dist. Montgomery County 1983); Coulter, 1981 WL 9749 (Ohio Ct. App. 1st Dist. Hamilton County 1981); In re Baby Girl S., 32 Ohio Misc. 217, 61 Ohio Op. 2d 439, 290 N.E.2d 925 (C.P. 1972); In Matter of Seven A. Children, 1995 WL 557329 (Ohio Ct. App. 6th Dist. Fulton County 1995); In re Dye, 1995 WL 231214 (Ohio Ct. App. 9th Dist. Summit County 1995); In re Leonard, 1997 WL 208137 (Ohio Ct. App. 12th Dist. Butler County 1997); Matter of Gilbert, 1996 WL 435426 (Ohio Ct. App. 12th Dist. Butler County 1996); Matter of Mastin, Nat'l Disability Law Rep. 1 Disability Law Rep.", 1997 WL 795809 (Ohio Ct. App. 9th Dist. Lorain County 1997); In re Leonard, 1997 WL 208137 (Ohio Ct. App. 12th Dist. Butler County 1997); Matter of Gary M., 1998 WL 336904 (Ohio Ct. App. 6th Dist. Lucas County 1998); In re C.F., 2003-Ohio-3260, 2003 WL 21434769 (Ohio Ct. App. 8th Dist. Cuyahoga County 2003).

[29]In re Baumgartner, 50 Ohio App. 2d 37, 4 Ohio Op. 3d 22, 361 N.E.2d 501 (10th Dist. Franklin County 1976).

[Section 30:12]

[1]RC 2151.414(C). See Juv. R. 4(B). See also § 23:6, Guardian ad litem.

[2]Matter of Duncan/Walker Children, 109 Ohio App. 3d 841, 673 N.E.2d 217 (5th Dist. Stark County 1996). See In Matter of Nelson, 1999 WL 4273 (Ohio Ct. App. 5th Dist. Stark County 1998), holding that cross-examination of the guardian ad litem is prohibited by the statute.

[3]In Matter of Webb, 1995 WL 499007 (Ohio Ct. App. 5th Dist. Stark County 1995); Matter of Eplin, 1995 WL 495451 (Ohio Ct. App. 5th Dist. Stark County 1995).

[4]In re Shaeffer Children, 85 Ohio App. 3d 683, 621 N.E.2d 426 (3d Dist. Van Wert County 1993). See Matter of McCutchen, 1991 WL 34881 (Ohio Ct. App. 5th Dist. Knox County 1991).

[5]In re Watts, 1995 WL 592249 (Ohio Ct. App. 9th Dist. Summit County 1995); In re Huber, 1995 WL 765940 (Ohio Ct. App. 2d Dist. Montgomery County 1995); In re Holloway, 1997 WL 102016 (Ohio Ct. App. 2d Dist. Montgomery County 1997).

not prejudiced.[6] The court may also continue the hearing to allow the guardian ad litem to submit the report.[7] Moreover, a juvenile court does not abuse
its discretion in granting permanent custody where the guardian ad litem
failed to issue a written report and no objection was offered at the hearing;[8]
or where the report was given orally at the hearing rather than in writing;[9]
or where the guardian ad litem participated in the hearing and the court
permitted a post-hearing written report with the option to counsel to request
cross-examination of the guardian ad litem.[10]

There is nothing in the statute or rules which requires a juvenile court to
follow the recommendation of the guardian ad litem.[11]

The guardian ad litem may be cross-examined by the parties on the content
of the report and the basis for custody recommendations when the report of
the guardian ad litem will be a factor in the trial court's decision.[12]

Findings and conclusions of law. If the court grants permanent custody,
the court, on the request of any party, must file a written opinion setting
forth its findings of fact and conclusions of law in relation to the proceeding.[13]
It has been held that since the statute requires the juvenile court to make
these findings only if requested by a party, the court is under no duty to
make the findings if no request is made.[14] Moreover, the trial court's failure
to make findings of fact and conclusions of law following a grant of permanent custody of a child to an agency does not constitute prejudicial error
where the parties agree generally to the facts of the case.[15] Further, the
determinations to be made by the court in a permanent custody hearing need
not be listed in the court's judgment entry,[16] and may be made in a separate
judgment entry incorporating the findings and the statutory requirements.[17]
These determinations would be appropriately included within the court's
findings of fact and conclusions of law, if they were requested by any of the
parties.[18]

If a guardian ad litem is not also acting as counsel to his or her ward, the
guardian ad litem has no authority to file findings of fact and conclusions of

---

[6]In Matter of Ackert, 1996 WL 72617 (Ohio Ct. App. 5th Dist. Holmes County 1996).

[7]Matter of Hogan, 1990 WL 178092 (Ohio Ct. App. 6th Dist. Lucas County 1990).

[8]Cordell v. Cordell, 1992 WL 67629 (Ohio Ct. App. 8th Dist. Cuyahoga County 1992); Shiflett
v. Korp, 1990 WL 139741 (Ohio Ct. App. 8th Dist. Cuyahoga County 1990); Matter of Tackett,
1990 WL 34369 (Ohio Ct. App. 4th Dist. Adams County 1990).

[9]Matter of Searcy, 1992 WL 62189 (Ohio Ct. App. 8th Dist. Cuyahoga County 1992).

[10]Matter of Taylor, 1995 WL 497614 (Ohio Ct. App. 5th Dist. Coshocton County 1995).

[11]Matter of Gilbert, 1990 WL 25084 (Ohio Ct. App. 3d Dist. Marion County 1990).

[12]In re Hoffman, 97 Ohio St. 3d 92, 2002-Ohio-5368, 776 N.E.2d 485 (2002). See also, In re
Spillman, 2003-Ohio-713, 2003 WL 352477 (Ohio Ct. App. 12th Dist. Clinton County 2003); In re
Salsgiver, 2003-Ohio-1203, 2003 WL 1193789 (Ohio Ct. App. 11th Dist. Geauga County 2003).

[13]RC 2151.353(A)(4). See Matter of Gilbert, 1990 WL 25084 (Ohio Ct. App. 3d Dist. Marion
County 1990); In re Hiatt, 86 Ohio App. 3d 716, 621 N.E.2d 1222 (4th Dist. Adams County
1993); In re Fotiou Children, 1991 WL 3213 (Ohio Ct. App. 12th Dist. Madison County 1991); In
re McCune/Warnken Children, 2004-Ohio-293, 2004 WL 113483 (Ohio Ct. App. 5th Dist. Stark
County 2004).

[14]In re Carl, 1995 WL 363820 (Ohio Ct. App. 8th Dist. Cuyahoga County 1995); In Matter of
Brandon M., 1998 WL 196288 (Ohio Ct. App. 6th Dist. Lucas County 1998); Matter of Jennifer
L., 1998 WL 230808 (Ohio Ct. App. 6th Dist. Lucas County 1998); Matter of Eppinger, 1994 WL
55786 (Ohio Ct. App. 8th Dist. Cuyahoga County 1994).

[15]In the Matter Of: Hollins, 1983 WL 5102 (Ohio Ct. App. 5th Dist. Guernsey County 1983).

[16]In re Covin, 8 Ohio App. 3d 139, 456 N.E.2d 520 (1st Dist. Hamilton County 1982); In Matter of Brandon M., 1998 WL 196288 (Ohio Ct. App. 6th Dist. Lucas County 1998).

[17]In Matter of Hoeflick, 1995 WL 495829 (Ohio Ct. App. 5th Dist. Licking County 1995).

[18]In re Covin, 8 Ohio App. 3d 139, 456 N.E.2d 520 (1st Dist. Hamilton County 1982); In re
Holcomb, No. 39694 (8th Dist. Ct. App., Cuyahoga, 10-4-79).

law, and the court may not order the guardian ad litem to do so.[19]

Judgment entry. Although the judgment entry supporting a court's decision to grant permanent custody need not contain specific words to establish the statutory findings,[20] there must be some facts set forth on the record showing that the court found clear and convincing evidence to support its findings.[21] A cursory judgment which simply stated that, "while each individual act of the parents . . . might not warrant a granting of permanent custody . . ., the totality of the acts, and the pattern of the parent(s') behavior over the three-year period . . . more than satisfied the court that permanent custody requirements have been met," violated the parents' constitutional rights with respect to the custody of their children.[22]

In preparing findings of fact, the judge is not required to state the negative of each rejected contention as well as the affirmative of those found to be correct; nor must the judge make findings on a particular issue if other issues are decisive of the case.[23]

§ 30:13   Planned permanent living arrangement

A planned permanent living arrangement is a dispositional order pursuant to which both of the following apply:

(1) Legal custody[1] of a child is given to an agency without the termination of parental rights; and

(2) The agency is permitted to make an appropriate placement of the child and to enter into a written agreement with a foster care provider or with any other person or agency with whom the child is placed.[2]

Requirements. In order for a child to be placed in a planned permanent living arrangement, the agency must request that the court make such an order, and the court must find, by clear and convincing evidence, that a planned permanent living arrangement is in the child's best interest and that one of the following exists:

(1) The child, because of physical, mental, or psychological problems or needs, is unable to function in a family-like setting and must remain in residential or institutional care;

(2) The parents of the child have significant physical, mental, or psychological problems and are unable to care for the child because of those problems, adoption is not in the best interest of the child, and the child retains a significant and positive relationship with a parent or relative;

---

[19]Matter of Duncan/Walker Children, 109 Ohio App. 3d 841, 673 N.E.2d 217 (5th Dist. Stark County 1996).

[20]Matter of Hart, 1993 WL 69694 (Ohio Ct. App. 3d Dist. Marion County 1993); In Matter of Buzzard, 1995 WL 739890 (Ohio Ct. App. 10th Dist. Franklin County 1995); In Matter of Lawson/Reid Children, 1997 WL 189379 (Ohio Ct. App. 2d Dist. Clark County 1997); Matter of Bacorn, 1996 WL 762005 (Ohio Ct. App. 11th Dist. Portage County 1996); In Matter of Christopher B., 1997 WL 379631 (Ohio Ct. App. 6th Dist. Lucas County 1997). But see, In re Belanger, 2002-Ohio-4956, 2002 WL 31107545 (Ohio Ct. App. 11th Dist. Ashtabula County 2002).

[21]In re Brown, 98 Ohio App. 3d 337, 648 N.E.2d 576 (3d Dist. Marion County 1994); In re Omosun Children, 106 Ohio App. 3d 813, 667 N.E.2d 431 (11th Dist. Trumbull County 1995); Matter of Hommes, 1996 WL 760920 (Ohio Ct. App. 11th Dist. Ashtabula County 1996); Matter of Mesko, 1997 WL 205279 (Ohio Ct. App. 7th Dist. Belmont County 1997); In re Sellers, 1998 WL 654119 (Ohio Ct. App. 1st Dist. Hamilton County 1998).

[22]In re Brown, 98 Ohio App. 3d 337, 648 N.E.2d 576 (3d Dist. Marion County 1994).

[23]In Matter of Burrows, 17 A.D.D. 379 (Ohio Ct. App. 4th Dist. Athens County 1996).

[Section 30:13]
[1]The term "legal custody" is defined in RC 2151.011(B)(17) and Juv. R. 2(V).

[2]RC 2151.011(B)(27). This dispositional option replaced the former option of long-term foster care by the 1999 amendment to RC 2151.353. See 1998 H.B. 484, eff. 3-18-99; Juv. R. 2(DD) and Juv. R. 34(D)(5).

(3) The child is age 16 or older, has been counseled on the permanent placement options available to him, is unwilling to accept or unable to adopt to a permanent placement, and is in an agency program preparing him for independent living.[3]

Prior to the 1999 amendment to RC 2151.353(A)(5) and RC 2151.415(C)(1)(c),[4] the disposition of "planned permanent living arrangement" was known as "long-term foster care." Although the label for this disposition has changed, the conditions under which the disposition could be ordered have generally remained the same. Therefore, the case law governing the former disposition of long-term foster care would, for the most part, apply to the current disposition of planned permanent living arrangement.

Appellate courts have held that as long as the statutory factors are present, the fact that the agency did not request long-term foster care did not thereby limit the discretion of the court to issue such an order.[5] However, other courts have held that a court could not place a child in long-term foster care unless the complaint or motion requested such placement.[6] It has also been held that only a private child services agency, and not a parent, could request long-term foster care.[7]

As with long-term foster care, a planned permanent living arrangement may also be used as a further dispositional alternative after a prior temporary custody order has expired.[8] In such cases, the agency must present to the court evidence indicating why a planned permanent living arrangement is appropriate for the child, including, but not limited to, evidence that the agency has tried or considered all other possible dispositions for the child.[9] Before the court may place the child in a planned permanent living arrangement, it must make the same findings when a planned permanent living arrangement is requested as an original order of disposition.[10] If the court then makes the planned permanent living arrangement order, it must

---

[3]RC 2151.353(A)(5). See RC 2151.415(C)(2). See also RC 2151.55 for special provisions governing the placement of a child in a foster home in a county other than the county in which the child resided at the time of being removed from home. In re D.B., 2003-Ohio-3521, 2003 WL 21511310 (Ohio Ct. App. 8th Dist. Cuyahoga County 2003).

[4]1998 H.B. 484, eff. 3-18-99.

[5]In re Tanker, 142 Ohio App. 3d 159, 164, 754 N.E.2d 813 (8th Dist. Cuyahoga County 2001); Matter of Cremeans, 1992 WL 47278 (Ohio Ct. App. 8th Dist. Cuyahoga County 1992); In Matter of Crenshaw, 1997 WL 219118 (Ohio Ct. App. 5th Dist. Stark County 1997); In Matter of Buchanan, 1997 WL 451472 (Ohio Ct. App. 2d Dist. Clark County 1997); In re C.R., 2004-Ohio-131, 2004 WL 63623 (Ohio Ct. App. 8th Dist. Cuyahoga County 2004).

[6]Matter of McDaniel, 1993 WL 33308 (Ohio Ct. App. 4th Dist. Adams County 1993); Matter of Smith Children, 1990 WL 70926 (Ohio Ct. App. 12th Dist. Warren County 1990); In re Shackelford, 1990 WL 68954 (Ohio Ct. App. 2d Dist. Montgomery County 1990); In re Brodbeck, 97 Ohio App. 3d 652, 647 N.E.2d 240 (3d Dist. Mercer County 1994).

[7]In Matter of Stamper, 1997 WL 722784 (Ohio Ct. App. 3d Dist. Union County 1997).

[8]See RC 2151.415(A)(5); § 30:6, Temporary custody.

[9]RC 2151.415(C)(1). See In re Muldrew, 2002-Ohio-7288, 2002 WL 31888158 (Ohio Ct. App. 2d Dist. Montgomery County 2002).

[10]RC 2151.415(C)(1). See RC 2151.353(A)(5). See also In re Tanker, 142 Ohio App. 3d 159, 164, 754 N.E.2d 813 (8th Dist. Cuyahoga County 2001) ("The court recognized that all four children had been together in foster care. There seemed to be no disagreement that permanent custody leading to adoption would break up the children, and there also seemed to be no disagreement that one of the children was likely to be adopted. The children each had special needs, all of which were being met by the foster parents. In short, as the guardian ad litem noted, the foster home provided the children with a stable home environment and support for their physical and emotional needs. The court knew that the foster parents who provided this stable environment for the children were unwilling to adopt the children. The foster parents are in their sixties and candidly said that the adoption subsidy was less than the foster care subsidy, so adoption would not make financial sense. Certainly, the prospects for anyone else adopting one child, much less all four, remained remote. So the court rationally decided that continuing foster care under these circumstances was preferable to the inevitability of breaking up the family. The court also heard testimony that the parents were not a lost cause.").

issue a finding of fact setting forth its reasons.[11] Thereafter, the agency may make any appropriate placement for the child and must develop a case plan that is designed to assist the child in finding a permanent home outside of the home of the parents.[12] Moreover, the agency may not remove the child from the residential placement in which the child is originally placed without court approval except under emergency circumstances.[13]

In interpreting the former disposition, it has been held that long-term foster care under RC 2151.415(C)(1)(c) applied only to children who were age 16 or older at the time they expressed their opinions regarding long-term foster care and when they received the mandated counseling.[14]

§ 30:14   Jurisdiction over parents

Under certain circumstances, the court is mandated to make specific dispositional orders in cases where a child has been adjudicated neglected, abused, or dependent. If the court issues an original dispositional order of temporary custody or protective supervision and the alcohol or other drug addiction of a parent or other caregiver was the basis for the adjudication of neglect, abuse, or dependency, the court must issue an order requiring the parent or caregiver to submit to an assessment and, if needed, treatment from a certified alcohol and drug addiction program.[1]

The parent or caregiver may be ordered to submit to alcohol or other drug testing during and/or after the treatment.[2] Any order for alcohol or other drug testing shall require one test per month for 12 consecutive months.[3] The certified program that conducts the tests is required to send the test results, along with treatment recommendations, to the court and to the public children services agency providing services to the family.[4]

---

[11]RC 2151.415(C)(2)(a). RC 2151.415(C)(2) still refers to the disposition of long-term foster care rather than planned permanent living arrangement, apparently due to a legislative oversight. In re C.R., 2004-Ohio-131, 2004 WL 63623 (Ohio Ct. App. 8th Dist. Cuyahoga County 2004).

[12]RC 2151.415(C)(2)(b).

[13]RC 2151.415(G). Apparently this requirement applies only if a planned permanent living arrangement follows a prior temporary custody order, and not if a planned permanent living arrangement is the original dispositional order.

[14]In re Bacorn, 116 Ohio App. 3d 489, 688 N.E.2d 575 (11th Dist. Portage County 1996).

[Section 30:14]
[1]RC 2151.3514(B). RC 2151.3514(A)(1) provides that "alcohol and drug addiction program" has the same meaning as in RC 3793.01.

[2]RC 2151.3514(B).

[3]RC 2151.3514(C).

[4]RC 2151.3514(D).

Chapter 31

Motions for Permanent Custody

KeyCite®: Cases and other legal materials listed in KeyCite Scope can be researched through West's KeyCite service on Westlaw®. Use KeyCite to check citations for form, parallel references, prior and later history, and comprehensive citator information, including citations to other decisions and secondary materials.

§ 31:1   Motions for permanent custody—Introduction
§ 31:2   Filing of motion
§ 31:3   Time requirements for permanent custody motions
§ 31:4   Hearings on permanent custody motions
§ 31:5   Evidence
§ 31:6   Findings
§ 31:7   Foster parents as "psychological parents"
§ 31:8   Implementation of case plan
§ 31:9   Effect on parental rights

§ 31:1   Motions for permanent custody—Introduction

This chapter discusses the procedures for obtaining permanent custody through the filing of a motion subsequent to an original order of temporary custody or long-term foster care. Original orders of permanent custody upon an adjudication of neglect, abuse, or dependency are discussed in Ch 30.

In addition to ordering permanent custody at the dispositional hearing on the original complaint of abuse, neglect, or dependency,[1] permanent custody may be ordered on a motion (1) where a child who is not abandoned or orphaned has been committed to the temporary custody of an agency,[2] and (2) where a child has been placed in a planned permanent living arrangement.[3] Where a child in temporary custody is orphaned, the motion may be filed whenever the agency can show that no relative of the child is able to take legal custody of the child.[4]

§ 31:2   Filing of motion

As a general rule, if a child has been in temporary custody for 12 or more

---

[Section 31:1]
[1]RC 2151.353(A)(4).

[2]RC 2151.413(A).

[3]RC 2151.413(C).

[4]RC 2151.413(B). The references to abandoned and orphaned children are vestiges of earlier versions of the statute, when the timing for the filing of a motion for permanent custody was, in part, dependent on whether the child was abandoned or orphaned. Those time constraints have been removed from the current version of the statute. Moreover, it is not clear from divisions (A) and (B) of RC 2151.413 whether a motion for permanent custody may be filed with respect to a child who is abandoned, although division (D) of the statute would apparently apply to abandoned children.

months of a consecutive 22-month period,[1] the agency with custody must file a motion for permanent custody in the court that issued the current order for temporary custody.[2] In addition, if a court makes a determination under RC 2151.419(A)(2),[3] the agency required to develop the permanency plan for the child pursuant to RC 2151.417(K)[4] must file a motion for permanent custody.[5]

Exceptions. There are exceptions to these general requirements. A motion for permanent custody shall not be filed by the agency if: (1) the agency documents in the case plan or permanency plan a compelling reason that permanent custody is not in the best interest of the child; (2) if reasonable efforts to return the child home are required under RC 2151.419, the agency has not provided the services required by the case plan to the child or the child's parents to ensure the child's safe return home; (3) the agency has already been granted permanent custody; (4) the child has been returned home pursuant to a court order issued under RC 2151.419(A)(3).[6]

In addition to the provisions of RC 2151.413, RC 2151.415(F) permits the court to conduct a hearing on its own motion—or on the motion of the agency, the person with legal custody of the child, the child's guardian ad litem, or any other party—to determine whether a dispositional order should be modified or terminated. This apparently allows for the filing of a motion for permanent custody by any party. In rendering a decision under this statute, the court must comply with RC 2151.42.[7]

Case plans. Any agency that files a motion for permanent custody must include in the case plan of the child a specific plan of the agency's actions to seek an adoptive family for the child and to prepare the child for adoption.[8] Since the statute does not specify when such plan must be filed, it has been held that the adoption plan need not be filed until permanent custody has been granted, making adoption a viable option.[9] The court reasoned that because a substantive change to a case plan may be made only by agreement of all parties or after a hearing,[10] to require the agency to go through the amendment process to add the adoptive case plan before parental rights are terminated would "undermine the agency's efforts to help parents deal with their problems and work toward reunifying the family."[11]

A public children services agency, acting pursuant to a complaint or action filed under RC 2151.27, is not subject to RC 3109.27, which requires the filing of a child custody affidavit.[12]

If a juvenile court has determined pursuant to RC 2151.419(A)(2) that the agency is not required to make reasonable efforts,[13] the agency files a motion for permanent custody under RC 2151.413(D)(2) and no dispositional hearing has been held, the court may hear the motion in the dispositional hearing required by RC 2151.35(B). If the court grants permanent custody pursuant

---

[Section 31:2]

[1]Temporary custody includes custody of one or more public children services agencies or private child placing agencies. Custody commences on the date the child is adjudicated pursuant to RC 2151.28 or 60 days after removal from the home, whichever is earlier.

[2]RC 2151.413(D)(1).

[3]See § 25:14, Reasonable efforts determination.

[4]See § 33:11, Child custody agency commitment—Juvenile court dispositional review.

[5]RC 2151.413(D)(2). See also RC 2151.414(A)(2) and § 31:3, Time requirements for permanent custody motions.

[6]RC 2151.413(D).

[7]RC 2151.415(F). See § 33:4, Abuse, neglect, and dependency proceedings.

[8]RC 2151.413(E).

[9]Matter of McCutchen, 1991 WL 34881 (Ohio Ct. App. 5th Dist. Knox County 1991).

[10]RC 2151.412(E)(2), RC 2151.412(E)(3).

[11]Matter of McCutchen, 1991 WL 34881, at *9 (Ohio Ct. App. 5th Dist. Knox County 1991).

[12]RC 2151.27(G), RC 3109.27(D). In re Palmer, 12 Ohio St. 3d 194, 465 N.E.2d 1312 (1984).

[13]See § 25:14, Reasonable efforts determination.

to RC 2151.353,[14] the court shall immediately dismiss the motion for permanent custody filed under RC 2151.413(D)(2).[15]

§ 31:3　Time requirements for permanent custody motions

The hearing on the motion for permanent custody must be held no later than 120 days after the motion is filed, except that the court may continue the hearing for a reasonable period of time for good cause.[1] The motion must be disposed of, and the order journalized, no later than 200 days after the motion is filed. However, the failure of the court to comply with the time periods does not affect the court's authority to issue orders and does not provide a basis for attacking the court's jurisdiction or the validity of the court's orders.[2]

§ 31:4　Hearings on permanent custody motions

Cases interpreting both the prior version[1] and the amended version of RC 2151.414[2] have held that hearings on motions for permanent custody need not be bifurcated where an adjudication of neglect, dependency, or abuse and a temporary custody order had previously been made.[3] In such proceedings, the only dispositional option available is to grant or deny the motion for permanent custody.[4] However, it has been held that if the court denies the motion, it may proceed pursuant to RC 2151.415 and make any disposition listed in the statute.[5]

Juvenile Rule 34(I), which was adopted in 1994, provides that hearings to determine whether temporary orders should be modified to permanent custody orders shall be considered dispositional hearings and need not be bifurcated. Prior to its 1998 amendment, Juvenile Rule 2(B) provided that a hearing on a motion to determine "whether temporary legal custody should be converted to permanent custody" was adjudicatory in nature. That phrase has now been removed from Juvenile Rule 2(B), thus eliminating the disparity between the two rules.

Notice. Parties must receive adequate notice, defined as notice which reasonably conveys information about the time and location of the permanent

---

[14]See § 30:9, Permanent custody—Requirements.

[15]RC 2151.414(A)(2).

[Section 31:3]

[1]RC 2151.414(A)(2).

[2]RC 2151.414(A)(2); Matter of Hare, 1998 WL 118039 (Ohio Ct. App. 4th Dist. Scioto County 1998); Matter of Goodwin, 1998 WL 517688 (Ohio Ct. App. 5th Dist. Licking County 1998).

[Section 31:4]

[1]In re Foust, 57 Ohio App. 3d 149, 567 N.E.2d 1042 (3d Dist. Crawford County 1989); In re Jones, 29 Ohio App. 3d 176, 504 N.E.2d 719 (8th Dist. Cuyahoga County 1985); Matter of Collins, 1990 WL 36309 (Ohio Ct. App. 11th Dist. Lake County 1990); Matter of Hughes, 1990 WL 7970 (Ohio Ct. App. 3d Dist. Logan County 1990); Matter of Grimes, 1988 WL 80498 (Ohio Ct. App. 3d Dist. Logan County 1988); In re Owens, 1986 WL 14515 (Ohio Ct. App. 8th Dist. Cuyahoga County 1986); In Matter of Hattery, 1986 WL 9657 (Ohio Ct. App. 3d Dist. Marion County 1986).

[2]1988 S.B. 89, eff. 1-1-89; 1996 H.B. 419, eff. 9-18-96; 1996 H.B. 274, eff. 8-8-96.

[3]In re Brofford, 83 Ohio App. 3d 869, 615 N.E.2d 1120 (10th Dist. Franklin County 1992); In re Hopkins, 78 Ohio App. 3d 92, 603 N.E.2d 1138 (4th Dist. Hocking County 1992); Poole v. Cuyahoga County Dept. of Human Services, 1993 WL 35586 (Ohio Ct. App. 8th Dist. Cuyahoga County 1993); Matter of Taylor, 1995 WL 497614 (Ohio Ct. App. 5th Dist. Coshocton County 1995). See In re Michael D., 1995 WL 584516 (Ohio Ct. App. 4th Dist. Jackson County 1995).

[4]Matter of McDaniel, 1993 WL 33308 (Ohio Ct. App. 4th Dist. Adams County 1993); Matter of Lyons, 1987 WL 15482 (Ohio Ct. App. 4th Dist. Ross County 1987).

[5]Matter of McDaniel, 1993 WL 33308 (Ohio Ct. App. 4th Dist. Adams County 1993); Matter of Lyons, 1987 WL 15482 (Ohio Ct. App. 4th Dist. Ross County 1987); In re Brofford, 83 Ohio App. 3d 869, 615 N.E.2d 1120 (10th Dist. Franklin County 1992).

custody hearing. Failure to so notify is a violation of due process rights.[6]

§ 31:5 Evidence

Although several pre-1994 cases held that such hearings were adjudicatory,[1] both Juvenile Rule 34(I) and pre-1994 case law[2] state that the Rules of Evidence apply to hearings on motions for permanent custody.[3]

Although hearsay evidence is not admissible,[4] the right to confront and to cross-examine adverse witnesses does not apply.[5]

A juvenile court may not take judicial notice of a previous adjudication and journal entry to establish abuse and dependency of children in a subsequent case, where the journal entry was the result of another proceeding which had different case numbers and separate dockets.[6] Thus, where the journal entry of the prior adjudication was not admitted as part of the record, the juvenile court erred by concluding that the children were abused or dependent.[7]

A court may consider any admissible evidence relevant to disposition upon a motion for permanent custody.[8]

A case interpreting the former version of RC 2151.414 held that it is reversible error to limit the evidence to factual matters occurring before the filing of the motion for permanent custody, and to refuse to consider evidence relating to the adequacy of parental care based on facts occurring after the filing of the motion.[9]

Experts. It has been held that where an indigent parent's mental or emotional health is the predominant, determinative issue in a permanent custody hearing, the parent's timely request for the assistance of a court-appointed psychiatric expert must be granted pursuant to the Fourteenth Amendment of the United States Constitution.[10]

§ 31:6 Findings

The court may grant permanent custody to the agency if the court

---

[6]In re Babbs, 2004-Ohio-583, 2004 WL 249608 (Ohio Ct. App. 10th Dist. Franklin County 2004).

[Section 31:5]

[1]In re Hopkins, 78 Ohio App. 3d 92, 603 N.E.2d 1138 (4th Dist. Hocking County 1992); Matter of Workman, 1993 WL 222843 (Ohio Ct. App. 5th Dist. Tuscarawas County 1993); Davis v. Smith, 1993 WL 277536 (Ohio Ct. App. 9th Dist. Summit County 1993).

[2]In re Brofford, 83 Ohio App. 3d 869, 615 N.E.2d 1120 (10th Dist. Franklin County 1992); Matter of Greene, 1992 WL 341385 (Ohio Ct. App. 10th Dist. Franklin County 1992).

[3]But see Matter of Duncan/Walker Children, 109 Ohio App. 3d 841, 673 N.E.2d 217 (5th Dist. Stark County 1996). In this case, which was decided after the 1994 amendment to Juv. R. 34(I), the court did not cite either Juv. R. 2(B) or Juv. R. 34(I) in its holding that a permanent commitment hearing under RC 2151.414 is adjudicatory in nature. See also In Matter of Ritter, 1996 WL 635798 (Ohio Ct. App. 11th Dist. Trumbull County 1996), in which the court recognized the prior conflict between Juv. R. 2(B) and Juv. R. 34(I), but determined that the conflict had no bearing on the outcome of the case.

[4]Matter of Taylor, 1995 WL 497614 (Ohio Ct. App. 5th Dist. Coshocton County 1995).

[5]In re Starkey, 1996 WL 148656 (Ohio Ct. App. 9th Dist. Summit County 1996).

[6]In re Knotts, 109 Ohio App. 3d 267, 671 N.E.2d 1357 (3d Dist. Mercer County 1996).

[7]In re Knotts, 109 Ohio App. 3d 267, 671 N.E.2d 1357 (3d Dist. Mercer County 1996).

[8]Matter of McCutchen, 1991 WL 34881 (Ohio Ct. App. 5th Dist. Knox County 1991).

[9]In re Foust, 57 Ohio App. 3d 149, 567 N.E.2d 1042 (3d Dist. Crawford County 1989).

[10]In re Shaeffer Children, 85 Ohio App. 3d 683, 621 N.E.2d 426 (3d Dist. Van Wert County 1993); In re Brown, 1986 WL 13385 (Ohio Ct. App. 1st Dist. Hamilton County 1986); In re Hess, 2003-Ohio-1429, 2003 WL 1465190 (Ohio Ct. App. 7th Dist. Jefferson County 2003); In re B.G., 2003-Ohio-3256, 2003 WL 21434172 (Ohio Ct. App. 8th Dist. Cuyahoga County 2003), appeal not allowed, 99 Ohio St. 3d 1547, 2003-Ohio-4671, 795 N.E.2d 684 (2003); In re J.D., 2004-Ohio-358, 2004 WL 170338 (Ohio Ct. App. 8th Dist. Cuyahoga County 2004); In re Elliott, 2004-Ohio-388, 2004 WL 187413 (Ohio Ct. App. 7th Dist. Jefferson County 2004).

determines at the hearing, by clear and convincing evidence,[1] that it is in the best interest of the child to grant permanent custody and that any of the following apply: (1) the child is not abandoned or orphaned or has not been in the temporary custody of one or more agencies for 12 or more months of a consecutive 22-month period ending on or after March 18, 1999, and the child cannot be placed with either of the child's parents within a reasonable time or should not be placed with his or her parents;[2] (2) the child is abandoned;[3] (3) the child is orphaned and there are no relatives able to take permanent custody;[4] (4) the child has been in the temporary custody of one or more agencies for 12 or more months of a consecutive 22-month period ending on or after March 18, 1999.[5] If the motion for permanent custody is made pursuant to RC 2151.413(D)(2)[6] where the court has made a determination that the agency is not required to make reasonable efforts,[7] the court is required to grant permanent custody if the court determines that the child cannot be placed with one of the child's parents within a reasonable time or should not be placed with either parent, and that permanent custody is in the child's best interest.[8]

In making the above determinations, the court is to consider the same factors that it considers when permanent custody is requested at the original dispositional hearing following an adjudication of abuse, neglect, or dependency.[9] However, the adjudication that the child is abused, neglected, or dependent and any dispositional order issued pursuant to the adjudication shall not be readjudicated at the permanent custody hearing or affected by a denial of the motion for permanent custody.[10]

In a multi-child permanent custody proceeding, the court must make an

---

[Section 31:6]

[1]RC 2151.414(B)(1). Santosky v. Kramer, 455 U.S. 745, 102 S. Ct. 1388, 71 L. Ed. 2d 599 (1982); In re Schmidt, 25 Ohio St. 3d 331, 496 N.E.2d 952 (1986); In re Brodbeck, 97 Ohio App. 3d 652, 647 N.E.2d 240 (3d Dist. Mercer County 1994).

[2]RC 2151.414(B)(1)(a). In re Awkal, 95 Ohio App. 3d 309, 642 N.E.2d 424 (8th Dist. Cuyahoga County 1994); In re Makuch, 101 Ohio App. 3d 45, 654 N.E.2d 1331 (9th Dist. Lorain County 1995). Temporary custody includes custody of one or more public children services agencies or private child placing agencies. Custody commences on the date the child is adjudicated pursuant to RC 2151.28 or 60 days after removal from the home, whichever is earlier.

[3]RC 2151.414(B)(1)(b). See RC 2151.011(C). Where the record reveals that the agency holding temporary custody has been unable to maintain contact with the mother because of her frequent changes in address and that the mother has expressed no interest in regaining custody of her children on the infrequent occasions when she has contacted the agency, the mother's conduct constitutes abandonment. Fields, 1982 WL 6650 (Ohio Ct. App. 6th Dist. Williams County 1982).

[4]RC 2151.414(B)(1)(c). See Matter of Long, 1993 WL 329975 (Ohio Ct. App. 12th Dist. Brown County 1993); Matter of Snook, 1992 WL 98879 (Ohio Ct. App. 3d Dist. Seneca County 1992). It has been held that this provision pertains only to a situation where the child is found to be an orphan. If the child is not orphaned, Ohio law does not give blood relatives any superior right to custody, particularly where they would not be able to provide adequate parental care for the child's special needs. Montgomery County Children Services Board v. Kiszka, 1983 WL 2483 (Ohio Ct. App. 2d Dist. Montgomery County 1983).

[5]RC 2151.414(B)(1)(d). Temporary custody includes custody of one or more public children services agencies or private child placing agencies. Custody commences on the date the child is adjudicated pursuant to RC 2151.28 or 60 days after removal from the home, whichever is earlier.

[6]See § 31:2, Filing of motion.

[7]See RC 2151.419(A)(2) and § 25:14, Reasonable efforts determination.

[8]RC 2151.414(B)(2).

[9]RC 2151.414(C) to RC 2151.414(E). See Hoff v. Hoff, 1993 WL 280455 (Ohio Ct. App. 9th Dist. Wayne County 1993); In re Higby, 81 Ohio App. 3d 466, 611 N.E.2d 403 (9th Dist. Wayne County 1992); Matter of Kasler, 1991 WL 100360 (Ohio Ct. App. 4th Dist. Athens County 1991); In re Belanger, 2002-Ohio-4956, 2002 WL 31107545 (Ohio Ct. App. 11th Dist. Ashtabula County 2002) (Failure to fully discuss these factors renders the court's decision facially defective and warrants reversal of the decision.). See § 30:11, Permanent custody—"Best interest" factors.

[10]See Matter of Barnett, 1990 WL 85131 (Ohio Ct. App. 6th Dist. Sandusky County 1990); Matter of Collins, 1990 WL 36309 (Ohio Ct. App. 11th Dist. Lake County 1990). See also Matter

independent determination of the relevant statutory criteria and evidence for each child.[11] However, how a parent mistreats one child in the household may be relevant to the permanent custody determination of another child who is not mistreated in the same manner.[12]

The hearing officer must fully and specifically discuss all five factors enumerated in RC 2151.414(D). Failure to do so constitutes reversible error.[13]

§ 31:7   Foster parents as "psychological parents"

Where permanent custody is requested several years after an initial temporary custody order, the passage of time and the resultant psychological and emotional development of the child become especially important in determining the child's best interests. Thus, in *In re Christopher*,[1] where the evidence indicated that between the time of the temporary and permanent custody hearings the mother had married, sought counseling, and now demonstrated normal maternal concern for her child, the court properly granted permanent custody on the basis that the separation of the parent and child had resulted in the child becoming a stranger to the parent.[2] In such situations, where there is no strong relationship between the parent and child, the difficult challenge that the resumption of parenthood would demand is a significant factor.[3]

In addition, the fact that a child in the temporary custody of a job and family services department has become psychologically and emotionally dependent on his foster parents and has been fully integrated into their family may justify a best interests decision to terminate parental rights.[4] Even where a bond exists between the children and their mother,[5] or where a placement with relatives may be possible,[6] an order of permanent custody may be proper.

However, the mere existence of an exemplary foster home is insufficient,

---

of Jeroncic, 1991 WL 127255 (Ohio Ct. App. 8th Dist. Cuyahoga County 1991), which criticized the statute for not requiring that all efforts be made to unify a family; In re Hartney, 1996 WL 137432 (Ohio Ct. App. 9th Dist. Summit County 1996).

[11]In re Hiatt, 86 Ohio App. 3d 716, 621 N.E.2d 1222 (4th Dist. Adams County 1993).

[12]In re Hiatt, 86 Ohio App. 3d 716, 621 N.E.2d 1222 (4th Dist. Adams County 1993).

[13]In re Smith, 2003-Ohio-800, 2003 WL 470198 (Ohio Ct. App. 11th Dist. Ashtabula County 2003).

[Section 31:7]

[1]In re Christopher, 54 Ohio App. 2d 137, 8 Ohio Op. 3d 271, 376 N.E.2d 603 (5th Dist. Morrow County 1977).

[2]See also Goldstein, Freud, and Solnit, Beyond the Best Interests of the Child (1973), for a discussion of the importance of psychological factors in making child-placement decisions; Mnookin, The Guardianship of Phillip B.: Jay Spears' Achievement, 40 Stan. L. Rev. 841 (1988).

[3]In re Philpott, No. 41186 (8th Dist. Ct. App., Cuyahoga, 6-5-80); In re Christopher, 54 Ohio App. 2d 137, 8 Ohio Op. 3d 271, 376 N.E.2d 603 (5th Dist. Morrow County 1977). See also The Matter of Ferguson, 1983 WL 2929 (Ohio Ct. App. 8th Dist. Cuyahoga County 1983).

[4]Matter of Luke, 1984 WL 2667 (Ohio Ct. App. 5th Dist. Coshocton County 1984); In the Matter Of: Wellinger, 1983 WL 2645 (Ohio Ct. App. 8th Dist. Cuyahoga County 1983); In the Matter Of: Espy, 1982 WL 2490 (Ohio Ct. App. 8th Dist. Cuyahoga County 1982); Wayne, 1981 WL 3652 (Ohio Ct. App. 10th Dist. Franklin County 1981); In re Justice, 59 Ohio App. 2d 78, 13 Ohio Op. 3d 139, 392 N.E.2d 897 (1st Dist. Clinton County 1978); In re Webb, 64 Ohio App. 3d 280, 581 N.E.2d 570 (1st Dist. Hamilton County 1989); In re Stanley, 1993 WL 512502 (Ohio Ct. App. 10th Dist. Franklin County 1993).

[5]In re Hensley, 1993 WL 119959 (Ohio Ct. App. 12th Dist. Butler County 1993).

[6]Matter of Moore, 1993 WL 172263 (Ohio Ct. App. 6th Dist. Lucas County 1993); Matter of Dowell, 1992 WL 200887 (Ohio Ct. App. 6th Dist. Lucas County 1992); Matter of Dixon, 1991 WL 325657 (Ohio Ct. App. 6th Dist. Lucas County 1991); In Matter of Crenshaw, 1997 WL 219118 (Ohio Ct. App. 5th Dist. Stark County 1997); In Matter of Knotts, 1997 WL 38084 (Ohio Ct. App. 3d Dist. Mercer County 1997).

by itself, to justify a permanent custody order.[7] Moreover, where a parent has continuous visitation and an ongoing relationship with his children in foster care, the likelihood that the foster parents will become "psychological parents" is negligible.[8] It is up to the agency holding temporary custody to make a conscientious effort to rehabilitate and reunite the family by attempting to maintain contact and communication between parent and child.[9] Thus, difficulties in transportation, where, for instance, the foster home is 60 miles from the mother's home, do not justify the agency's denial of regular and frequent visits between a parent and child.[10]

Appellate courts have held that the Americans with Disabilities Act (ADA), with its "reasonable accommodation" requirements, applies in cases involving the termination of parental rights.[11]

§ 31:8 Implementation of case plan

Amendments to the permanent custody statute[1] apparently have resolved questions raised by a prior version of the statute. It is now specifically provided that the juvenile court may not deny an agency's motion for permanent custody solely because the agency failed to implement any particular aspect of the child's case plan.[2] Prior to the enactment of this provision, the cases seemed at odds with the statute. The statute had required the court to decide whether the agency had made a good faith effort to implement reunification plans. Although proof of such good faith effort was a factor to be considered, the *statute* did not specifically require the submission of the reunification plans as a condition precedent to granting the motion for permanent custody. However, the *court decisions* were unclear regarding whether a plan had to be submitted before a permanent custody order.[3]

Despite the amendment to RC 2151.414(C) providing that permanent custody may be granted even if the agency failed to implement any particular aspect of the case plan, and the amendment to RC 2151.414(A) removing the requirement that the court determine that the agency has made a good faith effort to implement a plan to reunify the parents and child, there exists a disparity in the case law. Citing the general purpose statute's requirement that a child should be separated from its parents "only when necessary for his welfare or in the interests of public safety,"[4] it has been held that an agency's complete failure to implement any case plan, as opposed merely to a "particular aspect" of a case plan, requires the denial of a motion for perma-

---

[7]In re Stevens, 1993 WL 265130 (Ohio Ct. App. 2d Dist. Montgomery County 1993).

[8]In re M., 65 Ohio Misc. 7, 18 Ohio Op. 3d 283, 19 Ohio Op. 3d 112, 416 N.E.2d 669 (C.P. 1979).

[9]See RC 2151.412. See also In the Matter Of: Skaggs, 1981 WL 5904 (Ohio Ct. App. 4th Dist. Scioto County 1981); In re Stanley, 1993 WL 512502 (Ohio Ct. App. 10th Dist. Franklin County 1993). See § 31:8, Implementation of case plan.

[10]In the Matter Of: Skaggs, 1981 WL 5904 (Ohio Ct. App. 4th Dist. Scioto County 1981). See Orwell v. Orwell, 1990 WL 157170 (Ohio Ct. App. 2d Dist. Montgomery County 1990).

[11]Matter of Whiteman, 2 A.D.D. 386 (Ohio Ct. App. 6th Dist. Williams County 1993); In Matter of Burrows, 17 A.D.D. 379 (Ohio Ct. App. 4th Dist. Athens County 1996); Matter of Mastin, Nat'l Disability Law Rep. 1 Disability Law Rep.", 1997 WL 795809 (Ohio Ct. App. 9th Dist. Lorain County 1997).

[Section 31:8]

[1]RC 2151.414, amended by 1988 S.B. 89, eff. 1-1-89.

[2]RC 2151.414(C). See Matter of Workman, 1993 WL 33316 (Ohio Ct. App. 4th Dist. Jackson County 1993); Dispositional Case Plans Ch 26.

[3]See, e.g., In the Matter Of: Stewart, 1985 WL 7212 (Ohio Ct. App. 5th Dist. Licking County 1985); In Re Miller, 1984 WL 7022 (Ohio Ct. App. 1st Dist. Hamilton County 1984); In the Matter of Wurtzel, 1984 WL 4268 (Ohio Ct. App. 4th Dist. Pickaway County 1984).

[4]RC 2151.01(C).

nent custody.[5] Similarly, in spite of the change in RC 2151.414(A), appellate courts have held that due process implies the same good faith effort at reunification on the part of the agency.[6]

Other courts, while not specifically addressing the meaning of the amended statute, have determined that the agency must still make a good faith effort to reunify the parents and child.[7] These courts have defined "good faith effort" as "an honest, purposeful effort, free of malice and the design to defraud or to seek an unconscionable advantage," and "lack of good faith effort" as "importing dishonest purpose, conscious wrongdoing or breach of known duty based on some ulterior motive, or ill will in nature of fraud."[8] Thus, a case plan which tends to preordain the result of permanent custody, by providing for only brief, sporadic, supervised visitations between the parent and child at the agency's facility, does not satisfy the good faith requirement.[9]

Also, a case plan that requires a parent to admit that he sexually abused his child in order to be reunited with that child does not meet the good faith requirement because it violates the parent's privilege against self-incrimination.[10]

Other courts, while implying that a good faith effort at reunification is still required, have recognized that there is no need to implement a reunification plan when such an attempt would be futile.[11] It has also been held that a reunification plan is not required when permanent custody is sought as the original disposition under RC 2151.353(A)(4).[12]

Other courts have determined that the amendments to RC 2151.414(A) and (C) have eliminated the need for juvenile courts to make a "good faith ef-

---

[5]Matter of Ferrell, 1990 WL 42275 (Ohio Ct. App. 4th Dist. Gallia County 1990).

[6]Matter of Baldridge, 1991 WL 96335 (Ohio Ct. App. 10th Dist. Franklin County 1991); In re Silvia, 1993 WL 464606 (Ohio Ct. App. 10th Dist. Franklin County 1993); In re Brown, 98 Ohio App. 3d 337, 648 N.E.2d 576 (3d Dist. Marion County 1994); In re Forrest, 1996 WL 434180 (Ohio Ct. App. 10th Dist. Franklin County 1996); Matter of Hurlow, 1997 WL 701328 (Ohio Ct. App. 4th Dist. Gallia County 1997); Matter of Rowe, 1998 WL 65460 (Ohio Ct. App. 4th Dist. Scioto County 1998).

[7]See In re Weaver, 79 Ohio App. 3d 59, 606 N.E.2d 1011 (12th Dist. Butler County 1992); Matter of Price, 1993 WL 76957 (Ohio Ct. App. 2d Dist. Greene County 1993); Matter of Hart, 1993 WL 69694 (Ohio Ct. App. 3d Dist. Marion County 1993); In re Fotiou Children, 1991 WL 3213 (Ohio Ct. App. 12th Dist. Madison County 1991); In Matter of Lawson/Reid Children, 1997 WL 189379 (Ohio Ct. App. 2d Dist. Clark County 1997); In re Mark H., 1999 WL 253163 (Ohio Ct. App. 6th Dist. Lucas County 1999).

[8]See In re Weaver, 79 Ohio App. 3d 59, 606 N.E.2d 1011 (12th Dist. Butler County 1992); Matter of Price, 1993 WL 76957 (Ohio Ct. App. 2d Dist. Greene County 1993); Matter of Hart, 1993 WL 69694 (Ohio Ct. App. 3d Dist. Marion County 1993); In re Fotiou Children, 1991 WL 3213 (Ohio Ct. App. 12th Dist. Madison County 1991).

[9]Matter of Baldridge, 1991 WL 96335 (Ohio Ct. App. 10th Dist. Franklin County 1991). See also Matter of Jeroncic, 1991 WL 127255 (Ohio Ct. App. 8th Dist. Cuyahoga County 1991).

[10]In re Amanda W., 124 Ohio App. 3d 136, 705 N.E.2d 724 (6th Dist. Lucas County 1997). See also § 23:27, Self-incrimination.

[11]See In Matter of Greenwalt, 1993 WL 116111 (Ohio Ct. App. 5th Dist. Tuscarawas County 1993); Matter of Ferrell, 1990 WL 42275 (Ohio Ct. App. 4th Dist. Gallia County 1990). These cases relied on Elmer v. Lucas County Children Services Bd., 36 Ohio App. 3d 241, 523 N.E.2d 540 (6th Dist. Lucas County 1987), which was decided prior to the 1989 amendment of RC 2151.414. In re Baby Boy Puckett, 1996 WL 174607 (Ohio Ct. App. 12th Dist. Butler County 1996); In Matter of Crosten, 1996 WL 130937 (Ohio Ct. App. 4th Dist. Athens County 1996); In re Noe, 1997 WL 411594 (Ohio Ct. App. 12th Dist. Butler County 1997); Matter of Efaw, 1998 WL 224905 (Ohio Ct. App. 4th Dist. Athens County 1998).

[12]In re Baby Girl Baxter, 17 Ohio St. 3d 229, 479 N.E.2d 257 (1985); In Matter of Greenwalt, 1993 WL 116111 (Ohio Ct. App. 5th Dist. Tuscarawas County 1993); Matter of Stantz, 1991 WL 249431 (Ohio Ct. App. 5th Dist. Stark County 1991); Matter of Cannon, 1990 WL 237462 (Ohio Ct. App. 5th Dist. Stark County 1990); Matter of Parks, 1990 WL 121866 (Ohio Ct. App. 6th Dist. Lucas County 1990). See § 30:9, Permanent custody—Requirements.

fort" finding prior to awarding permanent custody to an agency.[13] According to these cases, only if the trial court relies on RC 2151.414(E)(1) as the basis for determining "whether a child cannot be placed with either of his parents within a reasonable time or should not be placed with his parents"[14] is the court required to find that the agency engaged in "reasonable case planning" and made "diligent efforts" to assist the parents.[15]

The Seventh District Court of Appeals has indicated that the "good faith effort" requirement contained in the former version of RC 2151.414(A) has been replaced by the "reasonable effort" standard set forth in RC 2151.419(A).[16] However, other appellate courts have held that by the very language of the statute, RC 2151.419(A) is not applicable to proceedings on motions for permanent custody.[17]

Although there is some disparity in the case law as to the agency's responsibility with respect to the case plan, it is clear that if the parents have failed to comply with the requirements of the case plan despite the agency's efforts to assist them, permanent custody is appropriate.[18] This outcome applies even where the case plan has imposed difficult conditions for reunification on the parents, such as abstention from alcohol[19] or requiring the parent to return to Ohio for supervised visits with the child.[20]

Moreover, permanent custody is not an abuse of discretion where a parent has historically failed to comply with a case plan for several years, and then makes a last-minute effort for a period of a few weeks.[21] It has been held that even where the mother has complied with the goals in the case plan, her parental rights may be terminated for a reason not in the case plan.[22] As one court stated, "The issue is not whether the parent has substantially complied

---

[13]See Matter of McDaniel, 1993 WL 33308 (Ohio Ct. App. 4th Dist. Adams County 1993); Matter of Wadsworth, 1991 WL 147748 (Ohio Ct. App. 5th Dist. Tuscarawas County 1991); Matter of Butcher, 1991 WL 62145 (Ohio Ct. App. 4th Dist. Athens County 1991); In Matter of McKenzie, 1995 WL 608285 (Ohio Ct. App. 9th Dist. Wayne County 1995); In re Moore, 1995 WL 338489 (Ohio Ct. App. 9th Dist. Summit County 1995); Matter of Brittany and Marcus B., 1996 WL 11135 (Ohio Ct. App. 6th Dist. Wood County 1996); In re Watkins v. Harris, 1995 WL 513118 (Ohio Ct. App. 9th Dist. Summit County 1995); Matter of Brewer, 1996 WL 65939 (Ohio Ct. App. 7th Dist. Belmont County 1996); In re Everhart, 1996 WL 724774 (Ohio Ct. App. 9th Dist. Summit County 1996).

[14]See § 30:12, Permanent custody—Procedural issues.

[15]Matter of McDaniel, 1993 WL 33308 (Ohio Ct. App. 4th Dist. Adams County 1993); Matter of Wadsworth, 1991 WL 147748 (Ohio Ct. App. 5th Dist. Tuscarawas County 1991); In Matter of Gipson, 1997 WL 665741 (Ohio Ct. App. 3d Dist. Hardin County 1997). In Matter of Butcher, 1991 WL 62145, at *11 (Ohio Ct. App. 4th Dist. Athens County 1991), the court initially held that the "good faith effort" requirement finding was no longer required, but also held that "the agency still has to prove that the children cannot or should not be placed with the parents. The agency still cannot meet that burden of proof without clear and convincing evidence that reunification was tried but failed."

[16]Matter of Brewer, 1996 WL 65939 (Ohio Ct. App. 7th Dist. Belmont County 1996); Matter of Tirado, 1998 WL 30097 (Ohio Ct. App. 7th Dist. Mahoning County 1998); Matter of Honeycutt, 1998 WL 124518 (Ohio Ct. App. 7th Dist. Belmont County 1998).

[17]In re Stevens, 1993 WL 265130 (Ohio Ct. App. 2d Dist. Montgomery County 1993); Matter of Rowe, 1998 WL 65460 (Ohio Ct. App. 4th Dist. Scioto County 1998).

[18]In re Brofford, 83 Ohio App. 3d 869, 615 N.E.2d 1120 (10th Dist. Franklin County 1992); In re Weaver, 79 Ohio App. 3d 59, 606 N.E.2d 1011 (12th Dist. Butler County 1992); In re Brown, 60 Ohio App. 3d 136, 573 N.E.2d 1217 (1st Dist. Hamilton County 1989); In re Spurlock Children, 1992 WL 12778 (Ohio Ct. App. 12th Dist. Butler County 1992); McKeown v. McKeown, 1991 WL 149718 (Ohio Ct. App. 9th Dist. Summit County 1991); In re Meyer, 98 Ohio App. 3d 189, 648 N.E.2d 52 (3d Dist. Defiance County 1994).

[19]Johnson v. Trumbull County Children Services Bd., 1990 WL 162587 (Ohio Ct. App. 11th Dist. Trumbull County 1990).

[20]Matter of Price, 1993 WL 76957 (Ohio Ct. App. 2d Dist. Greene County 1993).

[21]In re Swisher, 1997 WL 164311 (Ohio Ct. App. 9th Dist. Summit County 1997); In re Mills, 1997 WL 576384 (Ohio Ct. App. 9th Dist. Summit County 1997).

[22]Matter of McCutchen, 1991 WL 34881 (Ohio Ct. App. 5th Dist. Knox County 1991). See In re Stanley, 1993 WL 512502 (Ohio Ct. App. 10th Dist. Franklin County 1993); In re Dettweiler,

with the case plan, but whether the parent has substantially remedied the conditions that caused the child's removal."[23]

§ 31:9 Effect on parental rights

Once the court issues an order granting permanent custody pursuant to the filing of a motion for permanent custody, the child's biological parents cease to be parties to the action except for purposes of appeal.[1] In such instances, the parents have no standing to challenge the permanent custody order through the filing of a motion for a new trial.[2] Moreover, relatives of parents whose parental rights are terminated have no standing to assert visitation rights,[3] or shared parenting agreements.[4]

A juvenile court order vacating permanent custody and giving legal custody of children to foster parents results in the restoration of the parents' residual rights to the children.[5]

It has been held that a juvenile court has jurisdiction to terminate parental rights pursuant to RC 2151.415(F) and RC 2151.415(A)(4),[6] upon the motion of individuals who have been awarded legal custody of a dependent child.[7] When such a termination of rights is ordered, it would directly affect only the legal status of the child's parents, not the legal status of the child, thus permitting the legal custodians to initiate a separate proceeding for the adoption of the child in the probate court.[8]

Cross References
Ch 9, Ch 10, Ch 11, Ch 26

1993 WL 471405 (Ohio Ct. App. 5th Dist. Stark County 1993); Matter of VanGundy, 1998 WL 181644 (Ohio Ct. App. 4th Dist. Ross County 1998).

[23]In Matter of McKenzie, 1995 WL 608285, at *4 (Ohio Ct. App. 9th Dist. Wayne County 1995). See In Matter of Marshall, 1996 WL 648742 (Ohio Ct. App. 11th Dist. Geauga County 1996); In Matter of Stewart, 1996 WL 703406 (Ohio Ct. App. 11th Dist. Portage County 1996).

[Section 31:9]
[1]RC 2151.414(F). Presumably, this would also apply where permanent custody is granted at the original dispositional hearing pursuant to RC 2151.353(A)(4).

[2]Matter of Adkins Children, 1992 WL 56768 (Ohio Ct. App. 12th Dist. Butler County 1992); Matter of Butkus, 1997 WL 401527 (Ohio Ct. App. 12th Dist. Warren County 1997).

[3]Farley v. Farley, 85 Ohio App. 3d 113, 619 N.E.2d 427 (5th Dist. Licking County 1992); In Matter of Nelson, 1996 WL 200618 (Ohio Ct. App. 11th Dist. Geauga County 1996).

[4]Matter of Deanna B., 1995 WL 112895 (Ohio Ct. App. 6th Dist. Lucas County 1995); Matter of Jasper, 1998 WL 729234 (Ohio Ct. App. 12th Dist. Warren County 1998).

[5]In re Hitchcock, 120 Ohio App. 3d 88, 696 N.E.2d 1090 (8th Dist. Cuyahoga County 1996).

[6]See § 33:4, Abuse, neglect, and dependency proceedings.

[7]In re Bennett, 1995 WL 675968 (Ohio Ct. App. 1st Dist. Hamilton County 1995).

[8]In re Bennett, 1995 WL 675968 (Ohio Ct. App. 1st Dist. Hamilton County 1995).

Chapter 32

Jurisdiction Over Parents and Others

> **KeyCite®:** Cases and other legal materials listed in KeyCite Scope can be researched through West's KeyCite service on Westlaw®. Use KeyCite to check citations for form, parallel references, prior and later history, and comprehensive citator information, including citations to other decisions and secondary materials.

§ 32:1   Jurisdiction over parents and others—Introduction
§ 32:2   Jurisdiction over parents and others
§ 32:3   Responsibilities to victims and others

§ 32:1   Jurisdiction over parents and others—Introduction

This chapter discusses the extent of juvenile court jurisdiction over the parents of children who are under the court's jurisdiction, as well as its jurisdiction over victims and others.

§ 32:2   Jurisdiction over parents and others

The juvenile court's jurisdiction over the disposition of children's cases may, in some instances, extend beyond the child himself. Under certain circumstances the court may impose orders on the child's parents.[1]

However, the juvenile court's authority over parents is not unlimited. The court does not have jurisdiction to order a parent to pay for the destructive acts of his child.[2] Nor does the court have jurisdiction to regulate the conduct of a pregnant adult for the purpose of protecting her unborn child's health.[3]

Medical costs. Based on the legal duty of parents to support their children, it has been held that the court may order the parents, if able to do so, to reimburse the court for the expense involved in providing emergency medical or surgical treatment to a child.[4] A juvenile court is not required to determine a mother's ability to pay before ordering her to pay her dependent child's costs of medical treatment; the issue of her ability to pay should be

---

[Section 32:2]

[1]For authority of court to impose restrictions on a parent following an order of protective supervision, see RC 2151.353(C) and § 30:5, Protective supervision. See also McMullen, You Can't Make Me!: How Expectations of Parental Control Over Adolescents Influence the Law, 35 Loy. U. Chi. L.J. 603 (2004).

[2]In re Watkins, No. 42409 (8th Dist. Ct. App., Cuyahoga, 1-22-81); In re Daudt, 1986 WL 9630 (Ohio Ct. App. 12th Dist. Butler County 1986); In re Joshua S., 1996 WL 256596 (Ohio Ct. App. 6th Dist. Erie County 1996).

[3]Cox v. Court of Common Pleas of Franklin County, Div. of Domestic Relations, Juvenile Branch, 42 Ohio App. 3d 171, 537 N.E.2d 721 (10th Dist. Franklin County 1988). See § 9:7, Neglect—Subsistence, education & medical care.

[4]RC 2151.33(A). See In re J.J., 64 Ohio App. 3d 806, 582 N.E.2d 1138 (12th Dist. Butler County 1990); Children's Hospital of Akron v. Johnson, 68 Ohio App. 2d 17, 22 Ohio Op. 3d 11, 426 N.E.2d 515 (9th Dist. Summit County 1980); St. Thomas Medical Center v. Morgan, 1984 WL 5207 (Ohio Ct. App. 9th Dist. Summit County 1984). See RC 2151.36, amended by 1996 H.B. 274, eff. 8-8-96, which apparently requires the court to order the parents to pay the expenses for medical or surgical treatment for the child.

addressed at the time that the charges are actually assessed.[5]

Legal costs. The court may also order the parents to pay the costs for the services of appointed counsel and guardians ad litem.[6] However, parents may not be ordered to pay a bill prepared by a public defender's office for their son's representation in delinquency proceedings where the court failed to address the parents, inform them of their status as parties, or advise them of their right to counsel prior to the dispositional hearing.[7]

Support order. When a child has been committed pursuant to RC Chapter 2151 or RC Chapter 2152, the court shall issue an order pursuant to RC 3113.21 to 3113.219 that the parent, guardian, or person charged with the child's support pay for the care, support, maintenance, and education of the child and for expenses involved in providing orthopedic, medical, or surgical treatment for, or special care of, the child.[8] Further, the court must enter a judgment for the amount due and enforce the judgment by execution.[9]

An order requiring the parents to provide support for their delinquent child under RC 2151.36 may extend until the child reaches age 21, based on the definition of "child" contained in RC 2151.011(B)(6).[10] In a case decided prior to the 1996 amendment to RC 2151.36,[11] which now mandates the court to enter the support order, it was held that an order requiring a parent to pay the cost of his or her child's placement without first examining the parent's income was prejudicial error.[12] Other appellate courts have held that the calculations of the parent's child support duty must be done in accordance with RC 3113.215.[13]

In addition to the mandatory child support provisions of RC 2151.36, RC 2151.33(B)(2) provides that prior to final disposition in an abuse, neglect, or dependency case, the court must issue both a child support order and an order requiring the parents, guardian or person charged with the child's support to maintain or obtain health insurance coverage for the child.

Handicapped child. The statute[14] defining "handicapped child" for purposes of determining a child's eligibility for special education cannot serve as the basis for a juvenile court's exercise of jurisdiction to order a father to maintain medical coverage for his 18-year-old unruly, diabetic daughter until she is 21.[15] However, because diabetes is a "physical handicap," the juvenile court does have jurisdiction to order the father to carry his daughter on his insurance until she turns 21 pursuant to the statute[16] governing the continuing jurisdiction of the juvenile court.[17]

Probation bond. In any case where a delinquent child is placed on probation, if the court finds that the parents or the custodial parent has failed to

---

[5]In re J.J., 64 Ohio App. 3d 806, 582 N.E.2d 1138 (12th Dist. Butler County 1990).

[6]Juv. R. 4(G). See In Re: Vaughn, 1987 WL 18479 (Ohio Ct. App. 8th Dist. Cuyahoga County 1987).

[7]In re Hinko, 84 Ohio App. 3d 89, 616 N.E.2d 515 (8th Dist. Cuyahoga County 1992).

[8]RC 2151.36; Juv. R. 34(C); OAG 62-2938. Where permanent custody is awarded, the parents are divested of all legal obligations towards the child, including the duty of support. See RC 2151.011(B)(26), RC 2151.35(B)(3).

[9]RC 2151.36. The statute also contains provisions governing situations where the child resides in a foreign state or country.

[10]In re Hinko, 84 Ohio App. 3d 89, 616 N.E.2d 515 (8th Dist. Cuyahoga County 1992).

[11]1996 H.B. 274, eff. 8-8-96.

[12]In Koogle, 1983 WL 2461 (Ohio Ct. App. 2d Dist. Greene County 1983).

[13]In re Krechting, 108 Ohio App. 3d 435, 670 N.E.2d 1081 (12th Dist. Clermont County 1996); In Matter of King, 1996 WL 368236 (Ohio Ct. App. 3d Dist. Auglaize County 1996); Matter of Mundy, 1998 WL 60502 (Ohio Ct. App. 12th Dist. Preble County 1998).

[14]RC 3323.01(A).

[15]In re Kessler, 90 Ohio App. 3d 231, 628 N.E.2d 153 (6th Dist. Huron County 1993).

[16]RC 2151.353(E)(1).

[17]In re Kessler, 90 Ohio App. 3d 231, 628 N.E.2d 153 (6th Dist. Huron County 1993).

exercise reasonable parental control and that such failure is the proximate cause of the child's delinquent act, the court may require the parent to post a recognizance bond in an amount not over $500, conditioned upon the faithful discharge of the parent's duties under the probation order.[18] Under certain circumstances, this bond may be forfeited if the child commits a second delinquent act or violates the conditions of probation, where the parent's failure to exercise his or her duties is the proximate cause thereof. The proceeds from the forfeited recognizance are applied toward payment of any damages caused by the child or are paid into the county treasury. The court's authority under this section is in addition to that contained in other provisions relating to failure or neglect to exercise proper parental control.[19]

Probation searches. If a delinquent child is placed on probation, the court shall provide written notice to the child's parents, guardian, or custodian, informing them that authorized probation officers may conduct searches as described in RC 2152.19(F) during the period of probation if they have reasonable grounds to believe that the child is not abiding by the law or otherwise is not complying with the conditions of probation.[20] The notice must state that the search might extend to a motor vehicle, other personal property, or a place of residence or other real property in which the parent, guardian, or custodian has a right, title, or interest and that the child is expressly or impliedly permitted to use, occupy, or possess.[21]

Restraining order. Additionally, the court may grant a restraining order controlling the conduct of a parent, guardian, custodian, or any other party, if it is necessary to control any conduct or relationship which may be harmful to the child and may tend to defeat the execution of a dispositional order. Due notice, the grounds for the application, and an opportunity to be heard must be given to the person against whom the order is directed.[22] In a case in which a father's parental rights had been terminated due to his sexual abuse and neglect of his children, an order that the mother not allow any contact or communication between the father and children was upheld as necessary to prevent further harm to the children.[23] However, the court's order limiting contact between the mother and father was held to be overly broad because it was not necessary to serve the best interests of the children and it imposed an undue restriction upon the exercise of fundamental marital rights.[24]

Counseling. Pursuant to the catch-all provision in the delinquency dispositional statute,[25] the court may order the parents of a child who has been found delinquent to participate in counseling.[26]

Drug testing. Where a parent has admitted to past use of marijuana and has indicated his intention to continue using it, and where his child has been adjudged delinquent for a drug offense and placed on probation in the custody of his parents, the court may order the custodial parent to submit to a urine

---

[18]RC 2152.61(B). See RC 2152.61(C).

[19]RC 2152.61(A).

[20]RC 2152.19(F).

[21]RC 2152.19(F).

[22]RC 2151.359 and RC 2152.61(A); Juv. R. 34(H). Included under the definition of party in Juv. R. 2(Y) is "any other person specifically designated by the court." By such action, the court would be authorized to order virtually anyone not to associate with the child and would be able to enforce such an order through its contempt powers (RC 2151.21 and RC 2152.61(C)).

[23]In re Pieper Children, 85 Ohio App. 3d 318, 619 N.E.2d 1059 (12th Dist. Preble County 1993).

[24]In re Pieper Children, 85 Ohio App. 3d 318, 619 N.E.2d 1059 (12th Dist. Preble County 1993).

[25]RC 2152.19(A)(7). See § 27:2, Dispositional alternatives.

[26]In re Joshua S., 1996 WL 256596 (Ohio Ct. App. 6th Dist. Erie County 1996); Matter of Joey O., 1997 WL 785621 (Ohio Ct. App. 6th Dist. Lucas County 1997).

analysis test to check for use of marijuana.[27]

Public agencies. Under certain circumstances, the court may exercise jurisdiction over certain public agencies who have responsibility for providing services to children.[28] Thus, a juvenile court may lawfully order a school district to establish a detailed educational program for a handicapped delinquent child.[29] In a case decided prior to the amendment to RC 2151.23(A)(4),[30] it was held that a juvenile court may order the Ohio Department of Mental Retardation and Developmental Disabilities to serve as the guardian of a mentally retarded child without the agency's consent.[31] However, the juvenile court's jurisdiction over public agencies is limited by the juvenile court jurisdictional statute, RC 2151.23.[32] The court may not order the state or local Department of Mental Health to pay the cost of care for a child placed in a private psychiatric hospital,[33] even with a finding that the child is a mentally ill child subject to hospitalization pursuant to RC 2151.23(A)(4).[34] Absent judicial commitment procedures under RC 2151.23(A)(4), a juvenile court may not order a county mental health agency to take custody of a dependent child.[35] Appellate courts have also determined that a juvenile court is without jurisdiction to order the Ohio Department of Mental Retardation and Developmental Disabilities to provide supervised day care services for a dependent child,[36] or to order the Ohio Department of Youth Services to pay for the private placement of a child in the Department's custody,[37] or to order a county to provide compensation to foster parents for the damaging acts of the county.[38]

§ 32:3   Responsibilities to victims and others

In recognition of the juvenile court's responsibility to protect the welfare of the community,[1] the court is authorized, and in some cases required, to consider the interests of the victim in delinquency cases. In any case in which a child is found delinquent for a felony and the child caused, attempted to cause, threatened to cause, or created the risk of physical harm to the victim, the court must order the preparation of a victim impact statement, and must consider the statement in determining the order of disposition for

---

[27]Matter of Dague, 1987 WL 19093 (Ohio Ct. App. 5th Dist. Delaware County 1987).

[28]See RC 121.38.

[29]State ex rel. Nace v. Johnston, 1984 WL 3476 (Ohio Ct. App. 4th Dist. Hocking County 1984).

[30]1993 S.B. 21, eff. 10-30-93, eliminated from the jurisdiction of the juvenile court cases of mentally retarded children subject to institutionalization.

[31]In re Brown, 43 Ohio App. 3d 212, 540 N.E.2d 317 (1st Dist. Hamilton County 1988).

[32]In re Hoodlet, 72 Ohio App. 3d 115, 593 N.E.2d 478 (4th Dist. Athens County 1991).

[33]In re Hoodlet, 72 Ohio App. 3d 115, 593 N.E.2d 478 (4th Dist. Athens County 1991); In re Hamil, 69 Ohio St. 2d 97, 23 Ohio Op. 3d 151, 431 N.E.2d 317 (1982); In re Lozano, 66 Ohio App. 3d 583, 585 N.E.2d 889 (8th Dist. Cuyahoga County 1990); In re Beckett, 1992 WL 29233 (Ohio Ct. App. 12th Dist. Butler County 1992).

[34]1993 S.B. 21, eff. 10-30-93, which amended RC 2151.23(A)(4) to eliminate jurisdiction over mentally retarded children subject to institutionalization, did not affect the juvenile court's jurisdiction over mentally ill children subject to hospitalization.

[35]In re Shott, 75 Ohio App. 3d 270, 599 N.E.2d 363 (12th Dist. Warren County 1991).

[36]In re Parker, 7 Ohio App. 3d 38, 453 N.E.2d 1285 (6th Dist. Lucas County 1982).

[37]In re Sanders, 72 Ohio App. 3d 655, 595 N.E.2d 974 (8th Dist. Cuyahoga County 1991).

[38]Tingley v. Williams County Department of Human Services, 1993 WL 313710 (Ohio Ct. App. 6th Dist. Williams County 1993). See also Tingley v. Williams Cty. Dept. of Human Serv., 100 Ohio App. 3d 385, 654 N.E.2d 148 (6th Dist. Williams County 1995).

[Section 32:3]

[1]Juv. R. 1(B)(3), Juv. R. 30(C)(2).

the child.[2] The court may also order the child to make restitution to the victim of the delinquent act.[3] The victim's status may also be a relevant factor in determining whether to relinquish jurisdiction of an alleged delinquent for the purpose of criminal prosecution.[4] and also in determining the appropriate order of disposition for a child adjudicated delinquent.[5]

The court is also required, under certain circumstances, to issue various types of notices to victims. When a complaint has been filed alleging that a child is delinquent for having committed certain sex offenses,[6] and the arresting authority, the court, or a probation officer discovers that the child or a person whom the child caused to engage in sexual activity has a communicable disease, the arresting authority, court, or probation officer must immediately notify the victim of the delinquent act of the nature of the disease.[7] If a child age 16 or older is alleged to have committed certain delinquent acts on or involving school district property, within 10 days after the filing of the complaint, and again within 10 days after the adjudication, the court must provide the superintendent of the school district with written notice of the complaint[8] and the adjudication,[9] respectively. Moreover, at any hearing at which a child is adjudicated delinquent, or as soon as possible thereafter, the court must notify all victims that they may be entitled to a recovery under RC 3109.09 (compensatory damages from child's parents for acts of theft or vandalism), RC 3109.10 (compensatory damages from child's parents for willful and malicious assaults committed by the child), and RC 2743.51 to RC 2743.72 (award of reparations).[10]

It is also provided by statute that an agency may not place a child found delinquent for certain offenses in a foster home until specific written information concerning the child is given to the foster caregivers.[11]

Cross References
§ 27:8, § 33:9
Research References
Carlin, Baldwin's Ohio Practice, Merrick-Rippner Probate Law (6th ed.), Ch 107

---

[2]See RC 2152.19(D) for required contents of the victim impact statement and for confidentiality requirements of the statement.

[3]See RC 2152.20(A)(3). See also § 27:13, Restitution.

[4]See RC 2152.12(D). See Transfer of Jurisdiction Ch 22.

[5]See RC 2152.19(D)(1). See § 33:9, Department of Youth Services.

[6]These offenses include violations of RC 2907.02 to RC 2907.06, or RC 2907.12.

[7]RC 2151.14(C).

[8]RC 2152.021(C).

[9]RC 2152.18(D).

[10]RC 2152.18(E).

[11]RC 2152.72.

Chapter 33

Continuing Jurisdiction

KeyCite®: Cases and other legal materials listed in KeyCite Scope can be researched through West's KeyCite service on Westlaw®. Use KeyCite to check citations for form, parallel references, prior and later history, and comprehensive citator information, including citations to other decisions and secondary materials.

§ 33:1   Continuing jurisdiction—Introduction
§ 33:2   Motions
§ 33:3   Detention
§ 33:4   Abuse, neglect, and dependency proceedings
§ 33:5   Other proceedings
§ 33:6   Revocation of probation
§ 33:7   Suspended commitments
§ 33:8   Contempt
§ 33:9   Department of Youth Services
§ 33:10   Child custody agency commitment—Semiannual administrative review
§ 33:11   Child custody agency commitment—Juvenile court dispositional review

§ 33:1   Continuing jurisdiction—Introduction

This chapter discusses the authority of juvenile courts to exercise jurisdiction subsequent to a final order of disposition in children's cases.

§ 33:2   Motions

The continuing jurisdiction of the juvenile court is invoked by motion filed in the original proceeding, notice of which must be served in the manner provided for the service of process.[1] Juvenile courts lack continuing jurisdiction to modify prior orders when the requirements for service of motions to modify have not been satisfied.[2] Despite the language of Juvenile Rule 35(A), the label placed on the initiating document is unimportant. Thus, the court's continuing jurisdiction may be invoked by the filing of a new complaint rather than a motion, as long as the parties are given notice and an opportunity to be heard.[3]

The time period provided for certain acts and proceedings is not affected or limited by the expiration of a term of court which in no way affects the authority of a juvenile court.[4]

The grounds for modification and vacation of judgments contained in Civil Rule 60 appear to apply to juvenile court judgments. These grounds include fraud or misrepresentation, lack of jurisdiction, and any other reason justify-

---

[Section 33:2]

[1]Juv. R. 35(A).

[2]In re Miller, 33 Ohio App. 3d 224, 515 N.E.2d 635 (8th Dist. Cuyahoga County 1986); In Matter of Thomas, 1995 WL 363895 (Ohio Ct. App. 8th Dist. Cuyahoga County 1995).

[3]Matter of Luke, 1984 WL 2667 (Ohio Ct. App. 5th Dist. Coshocton County 1984).

[4]Juv. R. 18(C). For special provisions relating to the Cuyahoga County Juvenile Court, see RC 2153.15. The term of any juvenile court is one calendar year (RC 2151.22).

ing relief from the judgment.[5]

A motion invoking the court's continuing jurisdiction, like any other motion, must state with particularity the grounds upon which it is made and must set forth the relief or order sought. It must also be supported by a brief and may be supported by an affidavit. To expedite its business, unless otherwise provided by statute or rule, the court may provide by rule or order for the submission and determination of motions without oral hearing upon brief written statements of reasons in support and opposition.[6]

§ 33:3 Detention

During the pendency of proceedings pursuant to a motion invoking the court's continuing jurisdiction, a child may be placed in detention in accordance with the provisions of Juvenile Rule 7.[1]

§ 33:4 Abuse, neglect, and dependency proceedings

Special provisions apply regarding the extent of the juvenile court's jurisdiction in cases in which legal custody has been awarded to a legal custodian who resides or moves out of the county in which the court is located. The court's jurisdiction terminates one year after the date of the legal custody award, or the date of the latest further action involving the award, if the legal custodian either resides in another county in Ohio, or moves to another county within one year after the date of the award or the latest further action.[1] In such cases the court in the resident county of the legal custodian shall have jurisdiction.[2]

Once the court issues an original dispositional order[3] or a further dispositional order following the expiration of a temporary custody order in abuse, neglect, and dependency proceedings,[4] the court's jurisdiction over the child continues until age 18 for a child who is not mentally retarded, developmentally disabled, or physically impaired;[5] age 21 for a child who is mentally retarded, developmentally disabled, or physically impaired; or until the child is adopted.[6] Thus, a juvenile court retains jurisdiction to order a father to maintain medical coverage for his unruly daughter with diabetes until she is 21.[7] Moreover, the court may make a journal entry retaining jurisdiction over a child and continuing any order of disposition for a specified period of time to enable the child to graduate from high school or vocational

---

[5]Civ. R. 60(B). E.g., In re Frinzl, 152 Ohio St. 164, 39 Ohio Op. 456, 87 N.E.2d 583 (1949).

[6]Juv. R. 19.

[Section 33:3]
[1]Juv. R. 35(C).

[Section 33:4]
[1]RC 2151.353(J).

[2]RC 2151.353(J).

[3]See RC 2151.353(A); § 30:2, General principles for abuse, neglect and dependency dispositions.

[4]See RC 2151.415(B).

[5]See RC 2151.011(B)(21) and RC 5123.01(K) for definition of "mentally retarded person." See RC 2151.011(B)(13) and RC 5123.01(N) for definition of "developmental disability." See RC 2151.011(B)(30) for definition of "physically impaired."

[6]RC 2151.353(E)(1), RC 2151.415(E). See In Matter of Kost, 1994 WL 24374 (Ohio Ct. App. 10th Dist. Franklin County 1994); In re Doe Children, 93 Ohio App. 3d 134, 637 N.E.2d 977 (6th Dist. Lucas County 1994); Matter of Harris, 1995 WL 472917 (Ohio Ct. App. 8th Dist. Cuyahoga County 1995); State ex rel. Burich v. Ferreri, No. 69218 (8th Dist. Ct. App., Cuyahoga, 9-1-95); In re Hitchcock, 120 Ohio App. 3d 88, 696 N.E.2d 1090 (8th Dist. Cuyahoga County 1996).

[7]In re Kessler, 90 Ohio App. 3d 231, 235, 628 N.E.2d 153 (6th Dist. Huron County 1993).

school.[8]

However, notwithstanding the jurisdictional provisions of RC 2151.353(E)(1), juvenile court proceedings do not divest the probate court of jurisdiction over adoptions.[9]

A juvenile court does not lose its authority to protect children merely because it has entered an order returning custody of children adjudged neglected to their parents.[10]

On the motion of any party to modify or terminate a dispositional order, or on the court's own motion, the court is required to conduct a further dispositional hearing and may modify or terminate a dispositional order in accordance with the child's best interest.[11] Although it is not clear from the statutes, appellate courts have held that the parent bears the burden to show by clear and convincing evidence that the modification returning the child to the parent's custody is in the child's best interest.[12] Moreover, a dispositional order granting legal custody is intended to be permanent in nature, and shall not be modified or terminated unless the court finds, based on facts that have arisen since the order was issued or were unknown to the court at that time, that a change of circumstances of the child or legal custodian has occurred and that modification or termination is in the child's best interest.[13]

It is provided by statute[14] that if a child has been placed in a foster home or is in the custody of a relative, other than a parent, notice of the hearing must be provided to the foster caregiver or relative. If the agency has permanent custody of the child and has filed a petition to adopt the child, the prospective adoptive parent must be given notice.[15] At the hearing, the foster caregiver, relative, or prospective adoptive parent may present evidence,[16] but is not considered a party to the action.[17]

§ 33:5   Other proceedings

RC 2151.38(A) provides that when a child is committed to the legal custody of the Department of Youth Services,[1] the juvenile court's jurisdiction with respect to the child terminates, with certain exceptions.[2]

RC 2151.38(A) further provides that, subject to other provisions of law that

---

[8]RC 2151.353(E)(1), RC 2151.415(E). See In Matter of Kost, 1994 WL 24374 (Ohio Ct. App. 10th Dist. Franklin County 1994).

[9]State ex rel. Hitchcock v. Cuyahoga Cty. Court of Common Pleas, Probate Div., 97 Ohio App. 3d 600, 647 N.E.2d 208 (8th Dist. Cuyahoga County 1994). See Subject Matter Jurisdictions Ch 3.

[10]In Matter of Spaulding, 1993 WL 115934 (Ohio Ct. App. 6th Dist. Lucas County 1993).

[11]RC 2151.353(E)(2), RC 2151.415(F), RC 2151.417(B), RC 2151.42(A); Juv. R. 14(C), Juv. R. 34(G), Juv. R. 36(A).

[12]In re Patterson, 16 Ohio App. 3d 214, 475 N.E.2d 160 (12th Dist. Madison County 1984); In re Sopher, 1986 WL 2354 (Ohio Ct. App. 8th Dist. Cuyahoga County 1986); In re Christopher, 54 Ohio App. 2d 137, 8 Ohio Op. 3d 271, 376 N.E.2d 603 (5th Dist. Morrow County 1977).

[13]RC 2151.42(B).

[14]RC 2151.424(A).

[15]RC 2151.424(B).

[16]RC 2151.424(A), RC 2151.424(B).

[17]RC 2151.424(C). Cases decided prior to the 1999 enactment of RC 2151.424 held that the legal custodian was a party to the action and had standing to file a motion requesting modification of the dispositional order and a termination of parental rights. See In re Bowman, 101 Ohio App. 3d 599, 656 N.E.2d 355 (9th Dist. Summit County 1995); In re Bennett, 1995 WL 675968 (Ohio Ct. App. 1st Dist. Hamilton County 1995).

[Section 33:5]

[1]See § 27:3, Department of Youth Services commitment.

[2]See § 33:9, Department of Youth Services.

specify a different duration for a commitment,[3] "all other dispositional orders made by the court shall be temporary and shall continue for a period that is designated by the court in its order, until terminated or modified by the court or until the child attains 21 years of age."[4] For example, it has been held that a juvenile court may place a delinquent child on probation until he reaches the age of 21 years,[5] and suspend a delinquent child's driver's license until her twenty-first birthday.[6]

According to one juvenile court, when a child adjudicated delinquent becomes 21 years old during the pendency of appeals from the adjudication, all jurisdiction of the juvenile court terminates and that court has no authority to vacate its previous order of commitment.[7] This issue was discussed by the United States Supreme Court in *Kent v. United States*[8] in relation to a Washington D.C. statute which, like the former Ohio statute,[9] provides that the juvenile court may no longer exercise jurisdiction over a child who reaches 21 years of age during the period that his appeal is pending final determination.[10] In *Kent* the Supreme Court overturned a juvenile court order transferring jurisdiction over a child from the juvenile court to the district court for prosecution as an adult. Because the child had passed the age of 21 by the time of the Supreme Court's decision, the Court concluded that the juvenile court had lost jurisdiction over the child. Thus, the case was remanded to the district court for a hearing de novo on the issue of waiver.

In *Kent* the juvenile court's waiver order had been effectuated prior to the child's attaining 21 years of age. There is some disagreement among the Ohio courts concerning the termination of juvenile court jurisdiction when the juvenile court is unable to assume jurisdiction or enforce its orders until after the child attains the age of 21.[11]

§ 33:6 Revocation of probation

The juvenile court may not revoke a child's probation except after a hearing at which the child is present[1] and is apprised of the grounds for the proposed revocation. All parties to a probation revocation proceeding have a right to retain counsel, or to have counsel appointed if indigent.[2] It is reversible error if the child does not knowingly and intelligently waive the right to counsel,[3] or if the child is denied proper notice of the hearing[4] or the grounds

---

[3]See, for example, RC 2151.38(B), RC 2151.38(C), RC 2151.353, and RC 2151.411 to RC 2151.421.

[4]RC 2151.38(A).

[5]In re DeGeronimo, No. 40089 (8th Dist. Ct. App., Cuyahoga, 6-28-79); see In re J.B., 71 Ohio Misc. 2d 63, 654 N.E.2d 216 (C.P. 1995). For discussion of the maximum period for which a child's driver's license may be revoked or suspended, see § 28:3, Financial sanctions.

[6]In re Mason, 1997 WL 803083 (Ohio Ct. App. 9th Dist. Summit County 1997).

[7]In re J. F., 17 Ohio Misc. 40, 46 Ohio Op. 2d 49, 242 N.E.2d 604 (Juv. Ct. 1968).

[8]Kent v. U.S., 383 U.S. 541, 86 S. Ct. 1045, 16 L. Ed. 2d 84 (1966).

[9]RC 2151.38.

[10]RC 2151.38. For further discussion, see § 22:23, Appeals.

[11]See § 2:2, Age jurisdiction, for discussion of this issue and other issues involving age jurisdiction.

[Section 33:6]

[1]In re Nowak, 133 Ohio App. 3d 396, 398, 728 N.E.2d 411 (11th Dist. Geauga County 1999) ("Thus, when [the juvenile] allegedly failed to comply with the terms of his probation, the proper action would have been a probation violation proceeding rather than a contempt-of-court hearing. The distinction is important because appellant could not have been found in violation of his probation unless he was present at the hearing.").

[2]Juv. R. 35(B).

[3]Matter of Fries, 1997 WL 428649 (Ohio Ct. App. 8th Dist. Cuyahoga County 1997). See In re Burton, 1997 WL 473099 (Ohio Ct. App. 8th Dist. Cuyahoga County 1997), in which the court held that where the child expressly waived counsel at the beginning of the provocation revoca-

for revocation.[5] However, probation violation hearings do not fall within the Juvenile Rule 2(B) definition of an adjudicatory hearing, and are thus not governed by Juvenile Rule 29[6] nor by the formal procedures used in adult probation revocation cases.[7] As such, at a probation violation hearing the juvenile court is not required to inform the juvenile of the consequences of his or her plea and the right to present evidence.[8]

Probation may not be revoked unless it is found that the child has violated a condition of probation of which he or she was notified pursuant to Juvenile Rule 34(C).[9] The standard of proof required to establish the violation is not provided by statute or rule. However, in a proceeding charging an unruly child as a delinquent for violation of the conditions of probation,[10] proof beyond a reasonable doubt would be required.[11]

It has been held that a child may be committed to the Department of Youth Services after violating the terms of probation even though the initial dispositional order does not include an underlying suspended order of commitment, despite claims of double jeopardy[12] and res judicata.[13]

Although there is no provision specifying the dispositional alternatives available to the court for a child in violation of probation, it appears that any disposition authorized at the time of the original dispositional hearing would be permitted.[14]

§33:7 Suspended commitments

It has been held that the due process requirements which attach to probation revocation proceedings pursuant to Juvenile Rule 35(B) do not apply to proceedings in which a suspended commitment to the Department of Youth Services is lifted, thereby resulting in the child's commitment.[1]

Where a court suspends an order committing a child to the Department of Youth Services and places him or her on probation, the commitment order

---

tion hearing, the juvenile court is not required to advise him again of his right to counsel where the hearing had been continued to a subsequent date.

[4]Matter of Caruso, 1991 WL 82985 (Ohio Ct. App. 6th Dist. Lucas County 1991). But see Matter of Cottrill, 1998 WL 377675 (Ohio Ct. App. 4th Dist. Ross County 1998), holding that the failure to timely object to due process violations during a probation revocation proceeding waives any error.

[5]In re Royal, 132 Ohio App. 3d 496, 725 N.E.2d 685 (7th Dist. Mahoning County 1999).

[6]In re Griffin, 1996 WL 547921 (Ohio Ct. App. 3d Dist. Union County 1996); In re Bennett, 1997 WL 321149 (Ohio Ct. App. 8th Dist. Cuyahoga County 1997).

[7]Matter of Hall, 1991 WL 44356 (Ohio Ct. App. 12th Dist. Preble County 1991).

[8]In re Motley, 110 Ohio App. 3d 641, 674 N.E.2d 1268 (9th Dist. Summit County 1996).

[9]Juv. R. 35(B). See In re Reynolds, 1996 WL 379343 (Ohio Ct. App. 12th Dist. Madison County 1996); In re Guy, 1997 WL 133527 (Ohio Ct. App. 12th Dist. Butler County 1997); In re Edwards, 117 Ohio App. 3d 108, 690 N.E.2d 22 (8th Dist. Cuyahoga County 1996); In re Royal, 132 Ohio App. 3d 496, 725 N.E.2d 685 (7th Dist. Mahoning County 1999).

[10]See RC 2151.02(B).

[11]RC 2151.35; Juv. R. 29(E)(4). But see In re Boyer, No. 34724 (8th Dist. Ct. App., Cuyahoga, 12-31-75), in which the court stated, "Violation [of probation] is not a separate crime in Ohio (cf. Ohio Revised Code 2951.09) if committed by an adult. However, even if it were criminal in an adult requiring proof beyond a reasonable doubt, such proof was obviously present in this case."

[12]In re Barnhouse, 1996 WL 39650 (Ohio Ct. App. 10th Dist. Franklin County 1996); In Matter of Kelly, 1995 WL 656944 (Ohio Ct. App. 10th Dist. Franklin County 1995); In re Herring, 1996 WL 385611 (Ohio Ct. App. 9th Dist. Summit County 1996); In re Guy, 1997 WL 133527 (Ohio Ct. App. 12th Dist. Butler County 1997).

[13]In re Peggy L., 1995 WL 803443 (Ohio Ct. App. 6th Dist. Lucas County 1995).

[14]In re Guy, 1997 WL 133527 (Ohio Ct. App. 12th Dist. Butler County 1997). For an adult defendant who has violated probation, the court may impose any sentence which might originally have been imposed (RC 2951.09).

[Section 33:7]
[1]Matter of Anthony M., 1995 WL 96786 (Ohio Ct. App. 6th Dist. Lucas County 1995).

may not be reimposed if the child violates the conditions of the suspended commitment order and the period of probation has expired.[2]

§ 33:8   Contempt

The juvenile court, as a division of the courts of common pleas, has the inherent power to punish for contempt.[1] Anyone who is summoned or subpoenaed to appear for a hearing and who fails to do so may be punished for contempt of court.[2] This sanction also applies to a parent who fails to obey a summons ordering him or her to bring a child to the hearing.[3] However, parents may not be held in contempt if the evidence indicates that they do not know the child's whereabouts.[4]

A party who fails to comply with the terms of a journalized case plan may be held in contempt.[5] However, based on the principle that a written and journalized court order must form the basis for the alleged acts of contempt, it has been held that an order of protective supervision, without further specification, does not by itself compel a parent to obey an agent of a department of job and family services under risk of contempt of court.[6]

Contempt is also an available option where the parent, guardian, or custodian of an adjudicated delinquent child has failed to obey an order to exercise appropriate and necessary control and authority over the child to ensure the child's compliance with the terms and conditions of probation.[7]

No officer or employee of the Department of Youth Services may be prosecuted for contempt for refusing to accept physical custody of a delinquent child who is committed to the legal custody of the department if the juvenile court fails to provide the documents specified in RC 2152.18(C)(1) at the time the court transfers physical custody of the child to the department.[8]

Contempt is sometimes used to compel a party or witness to answer questions addressed to him. Where the mother of a child who is the subject of a dependency action fails to answer deposition questions[9] after being granted immunity under RC 2945.44, she may be held in contempt. The juvenile court has authority to grant immunity even though no criminal case is pending against the grantee.[10] However, the result is different where immunity has not been granted. For example, a juvenile witness (who was charged with being a delinquent and was under indictment for manslaughter) is not guilty of contempt for refusing to testify in the criminal trial of a defendant charged with selling liquor to a minor in answer to questions about whether he had purchased liquor from the defendant or had seen him sell liquor to

---

[2]In re Cross, 96 Ohio St. 3d 328, 2002-Ohio-4183, 774 N.E.2d 258 (2002) ("A juvenile court does not have the jurisdiction to reimpose a suspended commitment to a Department of Youth Services facility after a juvenile has been released from probation.") (syllabus).

[Section 33:8]

[1]RC 2151.21. See RC 2705.01 to RC 2705.10. State ex rel. Turner v. Albin, 118 Ohio St. 527, 6 Ohio L. Abs. 341, 161 N.E. 792 (1928).

[2]RC 2151.28(J). See also Juv. R. 15(B)(4), relative to failure to appear in response to a summons, and Juv. R. 17(F), which provides that the contempt power may be applied against any person who fails to obey a subpoena "without adequate excuse."

[3]See Juv. R. 15(C).

[4]State v. Hershberger, 83 Ohio L. Abs. 62, 168 N.E.2d 13 (Ct. App. 9th Dist. Wayne County 1959).

[5]RC 2151.412(E)(1).

[6]In Matter of Webster Children, 1996 WL 132234 (Ohio Ct. App. 5th Dist. Stark County 1996).

[7]RC 2151.411(C)(1).

[8]RC 2152.18(C)(1).

[9]See Juv. R. 25.

[10]In re Poth, 2 Ohio App. 3d 361, 442 N.E.2d 105 (6th Dist. Huron County 1981).

minors.[11]

Contempt penalties may also be used to prevent persons present and participating at an *in camera* inspection from disseminating any information determined by the juvenile court to be excluded from public disclosure.[12]

The traditional due process requirements of notice and hearing, which are applicable to contempt proceedings, must be adhered to in a juvenile court action brought against a child for failure to pay court costs ordered by the court.[13] However, another court has held that a contempt proceeding is not the proper method by which to collect court costs because an order to pay court costs is essentially a judgment on a contractual debt, which is governed by the methods provided for the collection of civil judgments.[14] Moreover, contempt may not be used to deal with a probation violation.[15]

§ 33:9 Department of Youth Services

As a general rule, two legal consequences result from a juvenile court's commitment of a child to the legal custody of the Department of Youth Services: (1) the court's jurisdiction over the child terminates,[1] and (2) the department assumes legal custody[2] of the child until the child attains 21 years of age.[3] However, subsequent to the commitment the juvenile court retains jurisdiction over certain decisions concerning judicial release,[4] early release,[5] and supervised release[6] of the child.[7]

---

[11]In re Newton, 12 Ohio App. 2d 191, 41 Ohio Op. 2d 290, 231 N.E.2d 880 (1st Dist. Hamilton County 1967).

[12]State ex rel. Dispatch Printing Co. v. Lias, 68 Ohio St. 3d 497, 1994-Ohio-335, 628 N.E.2d 1368 (1994).

[13]In re Rinehart, 10 Ohio App. 3d 318, 462 N.E.2d 448 (4th Dist. Ross County 1983).

[14]In re Buffington, 89 Ohio App. 3d 814, 627 N.E.2d 1013 (6th Dist. Huron County 1993).

[15]In re Nowak, 133 Ohio App. 3d 396, 398, 728 N.E.2d 411 (11th Dist. Geauga County 1999) ("Thus, when [the juvenile] allegedly failed to comply with the terms of his probation, the proper action would have been a probation violation proceeding rather than a contempt-of-court hearing. The distinction is important because appellant could not have been found in violation of his probation unless he was present at the hearing.").

[Section 33:9]
[1]RC 2151.38(A), RC 5139.05(B). See State v. McCallister, 1987 WL 27857 (Ohio Ct. App. 5th Dist. Stark County 1987).

[2]RC 2152.16(A) uses the term "legal custody" rather than "permanent custody" when referring to the status of the department relative to a child committed to it. "Legal custody," as defined in RC 2151.011(B)(19) and Juv. R. 2(V), creates a different status than "permanent custody," defined in RC 2151.011(B)(30) and Juv. R. 2(Z). However, RC 5139.05(B), which governs the Department of Youth Services, provides that an order committing a child to the department shall state that the commitment is permanent. RC Ch. 5139 also includes definitions of the terms "legal custody" (RC 5139.01(A)(3)) and "permanent commitment" (RC 5139.01(A)(2)), which differ from the meaning of those terms as used in RC Ch. 2151 and the Juvenile Rules. These definitions clearly establish the custodial responsibilities of the department with respect to a child committed to it.

[3]RC 5139.05(B). See also In re Cox, 36 Ohio App. 2d 65, 65 Ohio Op. 2d 51, 301 N.E.2d 907 (7th Dist. Mahoning County 1973).

[4]See RC 5139.01(A)(25).

[5]See RC 5139.01(A)(26). See In re Howard, 150 Ohio App. 3d 1, 3, 2002-Ohio-6004, 778 N.E.2d 1106 (7th Dist. Mahoning County 2002) ("[U]nder the former version of the applicable statute, a juvenile is eligible for early release after serving half of the prescribed minimum term of commitment. That former version of the statute contains no exceptions for terms of commitment a juvenile is serving for a firearm specification. Therefore, the trial court did not abuse its discretion in granting this juvenile early release from commitment.").

[6]See RC 5139.01(A)(21); RC 5139.51, RC 5139.52.

[7]RC 5139.05(B).

§ 33:10 Child custody agency commitment—Semiannual administrative review

Both federal[1] and state[2] laws require periodic reviews of cases of children who are in the custody of public children services agencies and private child-placing agencies.

An agency that is required to prepare a case plan[3] for a child must complete a semiannual administrative review of the case plan no later than six months after the earlier of the date on which the complaint was filed or the date on which the child was first placed in shelter care, and no later than every six months thereafter.[4] If the court issues an order pursuant to the filing of a motion for permanent custody[5] or pursuant to a motion to extend or modify temporary custody,[6] the agency's administrative review must be conducted no later than six months after the court order, and every six months thereafter.[7]

The requirement that agencies must conduct semiannual review may sometimes be satisfied by court review hearings. For instance, the agency's administrative review may be replaced by a hearing held pursuant to the agency's motion to extend or modify a temporary custody order,[8] or it can be replaced by a court hearing to review the child's placement or custody arrangement.[9] If a court hearing is used instead of the agency's semiannual review, the court must do all of the following:

(1) Determine the continued necessity for and the appropriateness of the child's placement;

(2) Determine the extent of compliance with the child's case plan;

(3) Determine the extent of progress that has been made toward alleviating or mitigating the causes necessitating the child's placement in foster care;

(4) Project likely date by which the child may be returned to the child's home or placed for adoption or legal guardianship; and

(5) Approve the permanency plan for the child consistent with RC 2151.417.[10]

Administrative reviews which are conducted by the agency rather than the court are to be conducted by a review panel of at least three persons, including but not limited to the child's caseworker and another person not responsible for the child's case management or service delivery.[11] It has been held that the phrase "including but not limited to" as used in the statute creates neither a clear legal right enforceable in mandamus for anyone, other than the specified individuals, to attend the reviews, nor a clear legal duty to allow anyone, upon the invitation of the parent, to attend the reviews.[12] The review must include a meeting by the panel with the child's parents, guard-

---

[Section 33:10]

[1] 42 U.S.C.A. § 675.

[2] RC 2151.416, RC 2151.417.

[3] See RC 2151.412.

[4] RC 2151.416(A); Juv. R. 36(C).

[5] RC 2151.414.

[6] RC 2151.415.

[7] RC 2151.416(A).

[8] See RC 2151.415.

[9] See RC 2151.416(A), RC 2151.417.

[10] RC 2151.415(H), RC 2151.417(J).

[11] RC 2151.416(B).

[12] State ex rel. Strothers v. Colon, 1999 WL 125847 (Ohio Ct. App. 8th Dist. Cuyahoga County 1999).

ian, custodian, guardian ad litem, and foster care provider, unless any of these persons cannot be located or declines to participate.[13] The review must result in a written summary which includes all of the following:

(1) A conclusion regarding the safety and appropriateness of the child's foster care placement;

(2) The extent of the compliance with the case plan of all parties;

(3) The extent of progress that has been made toward alleviating the circumstances that required the agency to assume temporary custody of the child;

(4) An estimated date by which the child may be returned to and safely maintained in the child's home or placed for adoption or legal custody;

(5) An updated case plan that includes any changes that the agency is proposing in the case plan;

(6) The agency's recommendation as to which agency or person should be given custodial rights over the child for the six-month period after the administrative review; and

(7) The names of all persons who participated in the administrative review.[14]

If it is determined at the administrative review that changes in the case plan are needed, the agency and the court must follow the same procedures that apply to any other changes in case plans.[15] Regardless of whether changes in the case plan are needed, the agency must submit its written summary of the administrative review to the court no later than seven days after the completion of the administrative review.[16] If the court determines that the custody or care arrangement is not in the child's best interest, it may terminate the agency's custody and place the child in the custody of another public or private organization, society, association, agency, or individual certified pursuant to RC 5103.02 and RC 5103.03.[17]

§ 33:11 Child custody agency commitment—Juvenile court dispositional review

In addition to the agency's semiannual administrative review, provision is made for the juvenile court to conduct its own custody review proceedings.

Any dispositional order made in abuse, neglect, or dependency proceedings[1] may be reviewed by the court at any time[2] and must be reviewed one year after the earlier of the date on which the complaint was filed or the date on which the child was first placed into shelter care.[3] Such orders must be reviewed by the court annually thereafter until the child is adopted or returned to the child's parents, or until the court terminates the child's

---

[13]RC 2151.416(C). See Matter of Brittany and Marcus B., 1996 WL 11135 (Ohio Ct. App. 6th Dist. Wood County 1996).

[14]RC 2151.416(D).

[15]See RC 2151.416(E), RC 2151.412(E)(2), RC 2151.412(E)(3), RC 2151.417(D); Juv. R. 36(C). See § 26:5, Case plan amendments.

[16]RC 2151.416(G); Juv. R. 36(C).

[17]Juv. R. 36(C); RC 2151.416(G).

[Section 33:11]

[1]See RC 2151.353, RC 2151.414, RC 2151.415.

[2]RC 2151.417(A); Juv. R. 36(A).

[3]RC 2151.417(C); Juv. R. 36(A). The dispositional hearing held pursuant to RC 2151.415 shall take the place of the first review hearing.

placement or custody arrangement.[4]

If a court determines pursuant to RC 2151.419[5] that the agency is not required to make reasonable efforts concerning the child's removal from and return to home, and the court does not return the child home, the court must conduct a review hearing to approve the child's permanency plan, and may make changes to the child's case plan and placement or custody arrangement. The court may hold the hearing immediately following the determination under RC 2151.419 and must hold it no later than 30 days after making that determination.[6]

Whenever the court is required to approve a permanency plan under RC 2151.417 or RC 2151.415, the agency is required to develop a permanency plan for the child and file the plan with the court prior to the review hearing.[7] The permanency plan must specify whether and, if applicable, when the child will be safely returned home or placed for adoption or legal custody, or why a planned permanent living arrangement is otherwise in the child's best interest.[8]

The court may appoint a magistrate or a citizens review board to conduct the review hearings, subject to the review and approval of the court.[9]

The court must give notice of the review hearings to every interested party and must give them an opportunity to testify and present other evidence at the hearing.[10] The court may even require a party to testify or present other evidence when necessary to a proper determination of the issues.[11] The scope of the court's review includes the following:

(1) The child's placement or custody arrangement;

(2) The child's case plan;

(3) The agency's actions in implementing the case plan;

(4) The child's permanency plan, if a permanency plan has been approved;

(5) The actions taken by the child's custodian;

(6) The need for a change in the child's custodian or caseworker;

(7) The need for any specific action to be taken with respect to the child; and

(8) Any other aspects of the child's placement or custody arrangement.[12]

After the review hearing, the court may require any party to take any reasonable action that the court determines is necessary and in the best interest of the child, or it may require that a party discontinue any action that is not in the child's best interest.[13] After the review hearing, the court must determine whether the conclusions of any administrative review conducted

---

[4]RC 2151.417(C). The court must schedule the first annual review hearing when it holds the original dispositional hearing, and all subsequent review hearings must be scheduled at the time of the prior review hearing. Juv. R. 36(A). See also Juv. R. 38(B)(2), which requires the annual reviews for a child who is the subject of permanent custody. See § 11:5, Permanent custody agreements.

[5]See § 25:14, Reasonable efforts determination.

[6]RC 2151.417(E).

[7]RC 2151.417(K)(1).

[8]RC 2151.417(K)(2). If the permanency plan was developed as a result of a determination made under RC 2151.419(A)(2), it may not include any provision requiring the child to be returned home.

[9]RC 2151.417(H).

[10]RC 2151.417(A), RC 2151.417(F). See Matter of Deehan, 1995 WL 560870 (Ohio Ct. App. 10th Dist. Franklin County 1995).

[11]RC 2151.417(F).

[12]RC 2151.417(A), RC 2151.417(F).

[13]RC 2151.417(A).

by the agency are supported by a preponderance of the evidence, and approve or modify the case plan based on that evidence.[14] If the hearing was held under RC 2151.417(C) or (E),[15] the court must also approve a permanency plan for the child that specifies whether and, if applicable, when the child will be safely returned home or placed for adoption, legal custody, or in a planned permanent living arrangement.[16] If the child is in temporary custody, the court must determine the child's custody status, and in so doing must comply with RC 2151.42.[17] If the child is in permanent custody, the court must determine what actions need to be taken to facilitate the child's adoption, including any necessary transfer of permanent custody.[18] The court must also journalize the terms of the child's updated case plan[19] and send a copy of its determination to all the parties.[20]

An order of disposition issued under RC 2151.417 granting legal custody of a child to a person is intended to be permanent in nature, and may not be modified or terminated unless the court finds a change of circumstances of the child or legal custodian and that modification or termination is in the child's best interest.[21]

Cross References
§ 11:5, Ch 22, § 27:5, Ch 30
Research References
Giannelli and Snyder, Baldwin's Ohio Practice, Evidence (2d ed.) §§ 101.7, 101.8
Katz and Giannelli, Baldwin's Ohio Practice, Criminal Law (2d ed.) § 81:4
Carlin, Baldwin's Ohio Practice, Merrick-Rippner Probate Law (6th ed.), Chs 105, 107

---

[14]RC 2151.417(G)(1); Juv. R. 36(C)(1).

[15]RC 2151.417(C) governs reviews of dispositional orders issued pursuant to RC 2151.353, RC 2151.414, or RC 2151.415. RC 2151.417(E) governs reviews conducted pursuant to RC 2151.419.

[16]RC 2151.417(G)(2). If the permanency plan was approved after a hearing under RC 2151.417(E), it shall not include any provision requiring the child to be returned home.

[17]RC 2151.417(G)(3); Juv. R. 36(C)(2). See § 33:4, Abuse, neglect, and dependency proceedings.

[18]RC 2151.417(G)(4); Juv. R. 36(C)(3).

[19]RC 2151.417(G)(5); Juv. R. 36(C)(4).

[20]RC 2151.417(I).

[21]RC 2151.42(B). But see, In re Timberlake, 2003-Ohio-1183, 2003 WL 1094078 (Ohio Ct. App. 10th Dist. Franklin County 2003).

Chapter 34

Appeals and Habeas Corpus

> **KeyCite®:** Cases and other legal materials listed in KeyCite Scope can be researched through West's KeyCite service on Westlaw®. Use KeyCite to check citations for form, parallel references, prior and later history, and comprehensive citator information, including citations to other decisions and secondary materials.

§ 34:1   Appeals and habeas corpus—Introduction
§ 34:2   Types of cases
§ 34:3   Standing
§ 34:4   Final order requirement
§ 34:5   Notice of appeal
§ 34:6   Stay of proceedings
§ 34:7   Appeal bond
§ 34:8   State appeals
§ 34:9   Right to transcript
§ 34:10   Right to counsel
§ 34:11   Effect on further juvenile court proceedings
§ 34:12   Habeas corpus

§ 34:1 Appeals and habeas corpus—Introduction

This chapter discusses the procedural and substantive law governing the appeal of children's cases to the appellate courts. The chapter also examines the applicability of the extraordinary writ of habeas corpus with respect to the decisions of the juvenile court.

§ 34:2 Types of cases

RC 2501.02 provides that the courts of appeals have jurisdiction over judgments or final orders of courts of record inferior to the court of appeals, "including the finding, order, or judgment of a juvenile court that a child is delinquent, neglected, abused, or dependent, for prejudicial error committed by such lower court."[1] Although juvenile traffic offender proceedings are not specifically included within the statute, the Ohio Supreme Court has held in *In re Hartman*[2] that the statute gives the court of appeals jurisdiction over such proceedings.[3] The court ruled that the classification of juvenile court judgments specifically enumerated following the term "including" in RC 2501.02(A) is not an exhaustive listing, but merely contains examples of appealable juvenile court judgments.

In *Hartman*, the Supreme Court interpreted the term "including" as a word of expansion rather than one of limitation. However, in a prior decision,

---

[Section 34:2]

[1]RC 2153.17, which applies exclusively to the Cuyahoga County Juvenile Court, provides that the sections of the Revised Code regulating the manner and grounds of appeal from any judgment, order, or decree rendered by the common pleas court in the exercise of juvenile jurisdiction shall apply to the juvenile court.

[2]In re Hartman, 2 Ohio St. 3d 154, 443 N.E.2d 516 (1983).

[3]The meaning of "final orders" is discussed in § 34:4, Final order requirement.

In re Becker,[4] the court stated that absent a finding that a child is delinquent, neglected, or dependent, no appeal is available from the juvenile court.[5] In *Becker*, the court specifically held that a juvenile court order transferring a child to the common pleas court for criminal prosecution is not a final appealable order since no finding of delinquency is made in such a case.[6]

If one follows the rationale of *Hartman*, it appears that a final order adjudicating a child unruly is appealable even though the category of unruly cases is not specifically included in RC 2501.02. The rule[7] that authorizes the stay pending appeal of final orders in unruly cases implicitly recognizes the right of appeal in such cases.[8]

§ 34:3 Standing

It appears that any party,[1] with the exception of the prosecuting attorney in delinquency cases,[2] may appeal the final order of a juvenile court. Thus, an appeal may be filed by a mother or father who has been denied custody, even if someone else is the child's legal guardian.[3] Where a grandmother was permitted to testify at a child neglect dispositional hearing and the court considered her request to have the children placed with her, she was held to have standing to appeal a permanent custody order even though she was not specifically made a party to the neglect proceedings.[4] Similarly, foster parents who unsuccessfully attempted to intervene as parties in a permanent custody proceeding were held to have a right of direct appeal because of their present interest in the case and resulting prejudice from the juvenile court's judgment.[5] However, a child's stepfather, who is not a party unless so designated by the court, does not have standing to appeal a permanent

---

[4]In re Becker, 39 Ohio St. 2d 84, 68 Ohio Op. 2d 50, 314 N.E.2d 158 (1974).

[5]*Becker* was decided prior to the 1975 amendment to RC 2501.02(A), which added abuse cases to the listing.

[6]Accord In re Morales, No. 33919 (8th Dist. Ct. App., Cuyahoga, 4-24-75). See also § 22:23, Appeals.

[7]App. R. 7.

[8]However, there is some support for the argument that unruly cases are not subject to appeal. According to the dissenting opinions in *Hartman*, the *Becker* decision established the rule that the list of appealable orders contained in RC 2501.02 is complete and exclusive. Moreover, one of the dissenting justices argued that there were no constitutional problems inherent in limiting appellate jurisdiction to those juvenile court cases specifically listed in the statute. O. Const. art. IV § 3(B)(2) provides that the "courts of appeals shall have jurisdiction *as may be provided by law* to review and affirm, modify, or reverse judgments or final orders of the courts of record inferior to the court of appeals" (emphasis in dissenting opinion of Justice Krupansky, Hartman, 2 Ohio St.3d at 158). Although the juvenile court is a court of record pursuant to RC 2151.07, inferior to the court of appeals, the dissent proposed that "as provided by law," only the juvenile proceedings specifically enumerated in RC 2501.02(A) are appealable to the court of appeals. Justice Krupansky further argued that "the majority's analysis conveniently ignores the fact that only *one* category [i.e., juvenile traffic offender] of a mere five possible categories is missing from the 'partial' list in RC 2151.02(A)" (emphasis in original). However, a sixth category, that of the unruly child, is also excluded from the list.

[Section 34:3]

[1]The term "party" is defined in Juv. R. 2(Y).

[2]See § 34:8, State appeals.

[3]In re Rule, 1 Ohio App. 2d 57, 30 Ohio Op. 2d 76, 203 N.E.2d 501 (3d Dist. Crawford County 1963); In re Neff, No. 1-78-9 (3d Dist. Ct. App., Allen, 6-14-78). But see Matter of Soboslay, 1986 WL 12865 (Ohio Ct. App. 8th Dist. Cuyahoga County 1986) (court stated in a footnote that it seriously doubted that the child's mother had standing to raise issues on the appeal of her son's delinquency adjudication, but decided to hear the case since the state had not challenged her standing); In re Phillips, 2003-Ohio-5107, at ¶ 6, 2003 WL 22227364 (Ohio Ct. App. 12th Dist. Butler County 2003) (Putative fathers may have standing in a permanent custody proceeding.).

[4]In re Travis Children, 80 Ohio App. 3d 620, 609 N.E.2d 1356 (5th Dist. Stark County 1992); In Matter of Nelson, 1996 WL 200618 (Ohio Ct. App. 11th Dist. Geauga County 1996).

[5]In Matter of Rundio, 1993 WL 379512 (Ohio Ct. App. 4th Dist. Pickaway County 1993).

custody order.[6] Moreover, a children services board to which unruly children were committed was held not to have been a party to the proceedings in which the children were determined to be unruly, and thus could not appeal from the unruly adjudication.[7]

The appealing party may complain of error committed against a nonappealing party when error is prejudicial to the appellant's rights.[8]

§ 34:4 Final order requirement

The jurisdiction of the court of appeals over final orders[1] of lower courts includes the finding, order, or judgment of a juvenile court that a child is delinquent, neglected, abused, or dependent.[2] In interpreting this rule, the courts generally have held that a finding of delinquency must be accompanied by an order of disposition to be subject to appeal.[3] Juvenile Rule 34, which governs the procedural aspects of the dispositional hearing, must be followed scrupulously before an appeal may be pursued;[4] absent a disposition, the child has not been prejudiced.[5]

How final the disposition must be in order to permit appeal is an issue often raised. Clearly, an order which finds children neglected and commits them to the permanent custody of a welfare board is a final appealable order.[6] Moreover, an order dismissing a neglect complaint and allocating court costs constitutes a final appealable order.[7] However, another court has held that a juvenile court order denying a children services agency's motion for permanent custody, and continuing an order for the child's temporary custody with the agency complete an investigation of a potential custodian, is not a final appealable order.[8] The court reasoned that the order did not affect a substantial right.

It is not necessary that the dispositional order be final in all respects in order to permit appeal. The Ohio Supreme Court has determined that "the question of whether an order is final and appealable turns on the effect which the order has on the pending action rather than the name attached to it, or its general nature."[9] Thus, an adjudication that a child is neglected or dependent followed by a disposition awarding temporary custody to a public children services agency pursuant to RC 2151.353(A)(2) constitutes a final

---

[6]In re Neff, No. 1-78-9 (3d Dist. Ct. App., Allen, 6-14-78).

[7]In re Blakey, 65 Ohio App. 3d 341, 583 N.E.2d 1343 (10th Dist. Franklin County 1989).

[8]In re Smith, 77 Ohio App. 3d 1, 601 N.E.2d 45 (6th Dist. Ottawa County 1991); In re Hitchcock, 120 Ohio App. 3d 88, 696 N.E.2d 1090 (8th Dist. Cuyahoga County 1996); Matter of Giffin, 1997 WL 691473 (Ohio Ct. App. 4th Dist. Athens County 1997); Matter of Cook, 1998 WL 719524 (Ohio Ct. App. 3d Dist. Hancock County 1998); In Matter of Ciara B., 1998 WL 355869 (Ohio Ct. App. 6th Dist. Lucas County 1998).

[Section 34:4]

[1]See RC 2505.02 for definition of "final orders."

[2]RC 2501.02. See § 34:2, Types of cases.

[3]E.g., In re Sekulich, 65 Ohio St. 2d 13, 19 Ohio Op. 3d 192, 417 N.E.2d 1014 (1981); In Matter of Short, 1981 WL 6049 (Ohio Ct. App. 4th Dist. Lawrence County 1981); In re Shaeffer Children, 85 Ohio App. 3d 683, 621 N.E.2d 426 (3d Dist. Van Wert County 1993).

[4]State v. Wylie, 1983 WL 5631 (Ohio Ct. App. 8th Dist. Cuyahoga County 1983).

[5]State v. Wylie, 1983 WL 5631 (Ohio Ct. App. 8th Dist. Cuyahoga County 1983).

[6]In re Masters, 165 Ohio St. 503, 60 Ohio Op. 474, 137 N.E.2d 752 (1956); Matter of Hurlow, 1997 WL 701328 (Ohio Ct. App. 4th Dist. Gallia County 1997).

[7]In re Fetters, 110 Ohio App. 3d 483, 674 N.E.2d 766 (12th Dist. Preble County 1996).

[8]In re Wilkinson, 1996 WL 132196 (Ohio Ct. App. 2d Dist. Montgomery County 1996); In re D.H., 2003-Ohio-6478, 2003 WL 22861922 (Ohio Ct. App. 8th Dist. Cuyahoga County 2003).

[9]In re Murray, 52 Ohio St. 3d 155, 556 N.E.2d 1169 (1990).

appealable order.[10] Even though the temporary custody order is subject to further review,[11] it could continue for an indefinite period of time, thereby depriving the parents of a means to regain custody.[12] For the same reasons, a later modification or continuation of a temporary custody order is also a final appealable order.[13] Similarly, the Ohio Supreme Court has rejected the argument that a finding of delinquency unaccompanied by a "final dispositional order" is not a final appealable order.[14] The imposition of a penalty pursuant to RC 2151.355 is a dispositional order and, as such, is a final appealable order.[15] Moreover, a juvenile court's finding of closure or nonclosure of a proceeding is a final order subject to appeal as affecting a substantial right in a special proceeding.[16]

It has also been held that a juvenile court order changing temporary custody of children adjudged neglected and dependent from one county children services board to another county children services board, following a transfer of jurisdiction to that county's juvenile court, is a final appealable order, even though a final dispositional hearing is pending.[17] However, until the receiving court accepts or rejects the transfer of the case, the orders of the transferring court granting temporary custody and transferring the case are temporary interlocutory orders, not final appealable orders.[18]

When a court refused to order the return to Ohio of children placed outside of Ohio by the court while a second motion for permanent custody was heard, the court of appeals held that "the order to return the children to this jurisdiction in order to determine the best interests of the children pending a hearing on appellant's successive motion for permanent custody is not a final appealable order under R.C.2505.02."[19]

With respect to the issue of mootness, a court of appeals has held that the appeal of an adjudication of neglect and dependency was moot because the judgment appealed from granted the appellant legal custody of the children and terminated the involvement of the Children Services Board.[20]

Where a domestic relations court, as part of a final determination of a divorce action, finds it not in the best interest of the child to award custody to either parent and certifies the issue of custody to juvenile court pursuant to RC 3109.04, the certification order is appealable as part of the divorce

---

[10]In re Murray, 52 Ohio St. 3d 155, 556 N.E.2d 1169 (1990); Matter of Price, 1994 WL 245663 (Ohio Ct. App. 8th Dist. Cuyahoga County 1994); In Matter of Caputo, 1998 WL 170205 (Ohio Ct. App. 12th Dist. Butler County 1998).

[11]See RC 2151.412, RC 2151.417.

[12]In re Murray, 52 Ohio St. 3d 155, 556 N.E.2d 1169 (1990).

[13]Motill, 1981 WL 4586 (Ohio Ct. App. 8th Dist. Cuyahoga County 1981); In re Rule, 1 Ohio App. 2d 57, 30 Ohio Op. 2d 76, 203 N.E.2d 501 (3d Dist. Crawford County 1963); In re Siniard, No. C-78-063 (6th Dist. Ct. App., Lucas, 2-9-79); In re Patterson, 16 Ohio App. 3d 214, 475 N.E.2d 160 (12th Dist. Madison County 1984); Matter of Myers, 1986 WL 3917 (Ohio Ct. App. 5th Dist. Delaware County 1986).

[14]In re Sekulich, 65 Ohio St. 2d 13, 19 Ohio Op. 3d 192, 417 N.E.2d 1014 (1981). *Sekulich* involved an adjudication of delinquency and an order of disposition requiring the child to pay a fine and court costs, followed by an order that the matter be certified to another juvenile court. Because the court held that the juvenile court was not authorized to certify the matter to another court, a final dispositional order was made.

[15]In re Sekulich, 65 Ohio St. 2d 13, 19 Ohio Op. 3d 192, 417 N.E.2d 1014 (1981).

[16]State ex rel. Dispatch Printing Co. v. Lias, 68 Ohio St. 3d 497, 1994-Ohio-335, 628 N.E.2d 1368 (1994).

[17]In re Smith, 61 Ohio App. 3d 788, 573 N.E.2d 1170 (6th Dist. Lucas County 1989).

[18]In re Devlin, 78 Ohio App. 3d 543, 605 N.E.2d 467 (10th Dist. Franklin County 1992).

[19]In re N.B., 2004-Ohio-859, at ¶ 2, 2004 WL 350947 (Ohio Ct. App. 8th Dist. Cuyahoga County 2004).

[20]Matter of Duncan, 1993 WL 257269 (Ohio Ct. App. 12th Dist. Preble County 1993).

judgment and constitutes a final appealable order.[21]

On the other hand, where the court order neither fully determines the action nor presents a judgment, it is not a final appealable order as defined by RC 2505.02.[22] Thus, a juvenile court's granting of overnight visitation rights to a child's mother as part of a proposed reunification plan is not a final appealable order.[23] A juvenile court order which overrules the child's objections to the magistrate's report but defers the issue of restitution for a later time, without specifying the amount of restitution or the method of payment, is a continuing order and thus not a final appealable order.[24] Likewise, a finding of delinquency accompanied only by a commitment to the temporary custody of the Department of Youth Services for the purpose of diagnostic study and report is not a final order subject to appeal, as it is merely a procedural incident.[25] For similar reasons, a juvenile court order transferring a child to the common pleas court for criminal prosecution,[26] a predispositional temporary custody order made pursuant to Juvenile Rule 13 or Juvenile Rule 29(F)(2)(b), and an ex parte temporary restraining order[27] are not final appealable orders.[28] Similarly, a juvenile court order overruling a plea in bar in a delinquency proceeding is not a final appealable order and cannot be the vehicle which brings the issue of double jeopardy to the appellate court.[29]

It has been held that the dismissal without prejudice of a dependency case for failure to conduct the dispositional hearing within 90 days[30] is not a final determination of the parties' rights, and thus does not constitute a final appealable order because refiling or amending of the complaint is possible.[31]

A juvenile court temporary custody order which is not accompanied by findings of fact[32] is not a final appealable order because it deprives the appellate court of the means to conduct a meaningful appellate review.[33]

In interpreting former Civil Rule 53, the Ohio Supreme Court held in

---

[21]Robinson v. Robinson, 19 Ohio App. 3d 323, 484 N.E.2d 710 (10th Dist. Franklin County 1984).

[22]See Matter of Kinstle, 1998 WL 148075 (Ohio Ct. App. 3d Dist. Logan County 1998).

[23]In re Boehmke, 44 Ohio App. 3d 125, 541 N.E.2d 630 (8th Dist. Cuyahoga County 1988).

[24]In re Holmes, 70 Ohio App. 2d 75, 24 Ohio Op. 3d 93, 434 N.E.2d 747 (1st Dist. Hamilton County 1980). See In re Zakov, 107 Ohio App. 3d 716, 669 N.E.2d 344 (11th Dist. Geauga County 1995); In re Alonzo B., 1999 WL 63649 (Ohio Ct. App. 6th Dist. Erie County 1999); In Matter of Brown, 1998 WL 430028 (Ohio Ct. App. 5th Dist. Richland County 1998).

[25]In re Bolden, 37 Ohio App. 2d 7, 66 Ohio Op. 2d 26, 306 N.E.2d 166 (3d Dist. Allen County 1973); In re Whittington, 17 Ohio App. 2d 164, 46 Ohio Op. 2d 237, 245 N.E.2d 364 (5th Dist. Fairfield County 1969). A temporary commitment to the Department of Youth Services is no longer permitted by RC 2151.355.

[26]In re Becker, 39 Ohio St. 2d 84, 68 Ohio Op. 2d 50, 314 N.E.2d 158 (1974); In re Williams, 111 Ohio App. 3d 120, 675 N.E.2d 1254 (10th Dist. Franklin County 1996); In re Morales, No. 33919 (8th Dist. Ct. App., Cuyahoga, 4-24-75). But see In re Langston, 119 Ohio App. 3d 1, 694 N.E.2d 468 (5th Dist. Stark County 1997). See also § 22:23, Appeals.

[27]Cavanaugh v. Sealey, 1997 WL 25521 (Ohio Ct. App. 8th Dist. Cuyahoga County 1997).

[28]Howard v. Catholic Social Serv. of Cuyahoga Cty., Inc., 70 Ohio St. 3d 141, 1994-Ohio-219, 637 N.E.2d 890 (1994); Morrison v. Morrison, 45 Ohio App. 2d 299, 74 Ohio Op. 2d 441, 344 N.E.2d 144 (9th Dist. Summit County 1973) (This case involved an application to determine custody filed under RC 2151.23(A)(2).). See Matter of Johnson, 1995 WL 21690 (Ohio Ct. App. 9th Dist. Lorain County 1995).

[29]In re Hampton, 24 Ohio App. 2d 69, 53 Ohio Op. 2d 192, 263 N.E.2d 910 (8th Dist. Cuyahoga County 1970). See Matter of Szymczak, 1998 WL 414924 (Ohio Ct. App. 8th Dist. Cuyahoga County 1998).

[30]See RC 2151.35(B)(1).

[31]Matter of Mary Beth v. Timothy H., 1995 WL 250236 (Ohio Ct. App. 8th Dist. Cuyahoga County 1995).

[32]See RC 2151.353(H) and RC 2151.419(B).

[33]In Matter of Hill, 1997 WL 473098 (Ohio Ct. App. 8th Dist. Cuyahoga County 1997).

Normandy Place Associates v. Beyer[34] that the filing of an objection to a magistrate's report is not a prerequisite for appellate review of a finding or recommendation made by a magistrate and adopted by a trial court. However, Juvenile Rule 40(E)(3)(b) provides, "A party shall not assign as error on appeal the court's adoption of any finding of fact or conclusion of law unless the party has objected to that finding or conclusion under this rule."[35] Some courts have apparently ignored Juvenile Rule 40, holding that, based on Civil Rule 53 and *Normandy Place*, the filing of an objection is not a prerequisite to appeal.[36] Other courts have recognized that Juvenile Rule 40 is the applicable rule, which requires the filing of written objections in order to assert the issues on appeal.[37]

A juvenile court journal entry in which the court simply adopted the findings and recommendations of the magistrate was held not to be a final appealable order because the entry merely incorporated the magistrate's recommendations.[38]

A judgment entry which is not signed by the juvenile court judge, but which merely contains the judge's rubber stamp signature, is not a final appealable order.[39]

§ 34:5   Notice of appeal

To initiate an appeal, a notice of appeal must be filed in the juvenile court within 30 days of the date of entry of the judgment or order subject to appeal.[1] The running of the time for filing a notice of appeal is suspended where a timely motion is filed in the juvenile court for judgment under Civil Rule 50(B) or for a new trial under Civil Rule 59.[2] However, neither a motion for rehearing nor a motion for reconsideration stays the time within which an appeal may be taken.[3]

In *In re Anderson*,[4] the Supreme Court held that both the Civil Rules of Procedure and the Appellate Rules are applicable to the filing of a civil notice of appeal in an appeal from a juvenile court. The Court further ruled that the records did not show that appellant was served with notice of judgment; therefore, the time for filing an appeal had not run, and the appellant had filed a timely appeal under both Civil Rule 58(B) and Appellate Rule 4(A).

When an appellant makes a post-judgment request of the trial court seek-

---

[34]Normandy Place Associates v. Beyer, 2 Ohio St. 3d 102, 443 N.E.2d 161 (1982). Accord In re Marriage of Sisinger, 5 Ohio App. 3d 28, 448 N.E.2d 842 (10th Dist. Franklin County 1982); Zacek v. Zacek, 11 Ohio App. 3d 91, 463 N.E.2d 391 (10th Dist. Franklin County 1983).

[35]This provision was originally promulgated in 1985 and was contained in Juv. R. 40(D)(6) until the 1995 amendment to the rule moved it to Juv. R. 40(E)(3)(b).

[36]In re Flynn, 101 Ohio App. 3d 778, 656 N.E.2d 737 (8th Dist. Cuyahoga County 1995); Matter of Smith Children, 1990 WL 70926 (Ohio Ct. App. 12th Dist. Warren County 1990).

[37]Matter of Williams, 1995 WL 380063 (Ohio Ct. App. 3d Dist. Allen County 1995); Matter of Green, 1990 WL 190134 (Ohio Ct. App. 10th Dist. Franklin County 1990); Matter of Shuman, 1997 WL 33298 (Ohio Ct. App. 9th Dist. Lorain County 1997).

[38]In re Zakov, 107 Ohio App. 3d 716, 669 N.E.2d 344 (11th Dist. Geauga County 1995).

[39]In re Mitchell, 93 Ohio App. 3d 153, 637 N.E.2d 989 (8th Dist. Cuyahoga County 1994); Matter of Carolyn Wheat, 1996 WL 695664 (Ohio Ct. App. 8th Dist. Cuyahoga County 1996).

[Section 34:5]

[1]App. R. 4(A). See Matter of Domineck, 1990 WL 170674 (Ohio Ct. App. 12th Dist. Butler County 1990); In re Shaeffer Children, 85 Ohio App. 3d 683, 621 N.E.2d 426 (3d Dist. Van Wert County 1993); In Matter of Caputo, 1998 WL 170205 (Ohio Ct. App. 12th Dist. Butler County 1998); In Matter of Christopher B., 1997 WL 379631 (Ohio Ct. App. 6th Dist. Lucas County 1997).

[2]In re Shaeffer Children, 85 Ohio App. 3d 683, 621 N.E.2d 426 (3d Dist. Van Wert County 1993). The juvenile rules do not apply to procedures upon appeal. See Juv. R. 1(C)(1).

[3]Motill, 1981 WL 4586 (Ohio Ct. App. 8th Dist. Cuyahoga County 1981).

[4]In re Anderson, 92 Ohio St. 3d 63, 66–67, 2001-Ohio-131, 748 N.E.2d 67 (2001) (A juvenile court proceeding is a civil action).

ing findings of fact and conclusions of law on motions upon which the court did not make any factual determinations, the request is a nullity, and does not toll the time for filing a notice of appeal.[5]

§ 34:6 Stay of proceedings

Unless a juvenile court order is stayed pending the determination of an appeal, it remains in full force and effect. In the absence of a stay, the juvenile court may enforce its judgment by issuing a *nunc pro tunc* order where such action does not interfere with the power of the appellate court to review the judgment under appeal.[1] In order to secure a stay of the execution of a court order, the party seeking the stay must apply to the juvenile court which made the order.[2] If application to the juvenile court is not practicable, or if the juvenile court has by journal entry denied an application, a motion to stay may be made to the court of appeals or a judge thereof.[3] No order, judgment, or decree of a juvenile court that concerns a dependent, neglected, unruly, abused, or delinquent child may be stayed upon appeal unless suitable provision is made for the maintenance, care, and custody of such child pending the appeal.[4] Furthermore, appeals concerning such children shall have precedence over all other cases in the court to which the appeal is taken.[5]

It has been held that the filing of a notice of appeal deprives the juvenile court of jurisdiction to dispose of a motion for reconsideration filed in the juvenile court in the same case.[6]

In delinquency cases in which the state appeals the granting of a motion to suppress evidence, it is specifically provided that a child in detention or shelter care may be released pending the appeal.[7]

§ 34:7 Appeal bond

Although bond is not required as a condition of granting a stay, the court of appeals may condition a stay upon the filing of a bond or other appropriate security in the trial court.[1] The procedure for determining the amount and approval of a supersedeas bond pending appeal is the same as that for applying for a stay. The original application is made in the juvenile court, but a motion for such relief may be filed in the appellate court if it shows that application to the juvenile court is not practicable or has been denied.[2] Since there is no constitutional provision guaranteeing the right to an appeal bond, a juvenile court does not err in refusing to grant bail pending appeal to a de-

---

[5]In re Wells, 2004-Ohio-1572, at ¶ 19, 2004 WL 1152844 (Ohio Ct. App. 7th Dist. Belmont County 2004).

[Section 34:6]
[1]In re Kessler, 90 Ohio App. 3d 231, 628 N.E.2d 153 (6th Dist. Huron County 1993).

[2]App. R. 7(A).

[3]App. R. 7(A).

[4]App. R. 7(C). Although the rule does not include abuse or juvenile traffic offender proceedings, it appears that these cases would be subject to their provisions since a final order in such cases is appealable. See § 34:2, Types of cases.

[5]App. R. 7(C). See also RC 3109.04(E) and RC 3109.06, which provide that appeals taken from custody decisions must be given calendar priority and handled expeditiously by the court of appeals.

[6]In Matter of Jane Doe, 1990 WL 640269 (Ohio Ct. App. 8th Dist. Cuyahoga County 1990).

[7]Juv. R. 22(F).

[Section 34:7]
[1]App. R. 7(B).

[2]App. R. 7(A).

linquent child who has been committed to an institution.[3]

The IJA-ABA Standards recommend that once an appeal is filed, the child should be released, with or without conditions, unless the court orders otherwise. The Standards suggest that only children needing secure incarceration should be detained pending appeal and then only if certain conditions exist.[4]

§ 34:8 State appeals

As a general rule, the state may not appeal the final order of a juvenile court dismissing a delinquency complaint for failure to prove the allegations of the complaint beyond a reasonable doubt. An appeal by the state under such circumstances is barred by the constitutional protection against double jeopardy, since a court proceeding which may result in incarceration places a person, adult or juvenile, in jeopardy.[1]

However, certain decisions in delinquency cases may be appealed by the state. As with other appeals in juvenile court cases,[2] an appeal by the state following the granting of a motion to suppress takes precedence over all other appeals.[3] For example, the state may appeal the grant of a motion to dismiss a complaint and, by leave of the court to which the appeal is taken, any other decision of the juvenile court in a delinquency case except the final verdict.[4] The state may also appeal the juvenile court's granting of a motion to suppress evidence if, in addition to filing a notice of appeal, the prosecuting attorney certifies that (1) the appeal is not taken for the purpose of delay, and (2) the granting of the motion has rendered the state's case so weak that any reasonable possibility of proving the complaint's allegations has been destroyed.[5] In such cases, the notice of appeal and the certification by the prosecutor must be filed with the clerk of the juvenile court within seven days after the date of the entry of the order granting the motion to suppress.[6] Where the state has timely filed a notice of appeal, but has failed to make a proper certification as required by Juvenile Rule 22(F), a court of appeals may allow amendment of the timely filed notice of appeal and certification.[7]

In a criminal case, *State v. Felty*,[8] it was held that where a trial court sustains a portion of the defendant's motion to suppress and the state fails to appeal that ruling pursuant to Criminal Rule 12(J) (the equivalent of Juvenile Rule 22(F)) and Appellate Rule 4(B), the state is precluded from contesting that portion of the suppression ruling in the defendant's appeal of his conviction based upon evidence which was not suppressed.

An appellate court has held that an appeal by the state from an order denying mandatory bindover became a final appealable order following the

---

[3]State v. Fullmer, 76 Ohio App. 335, 32 Ohio Op. 53, 43 Ohio L. Abs. 193, 62 N.E.2d 268 (2d Dist. Montgomery County 1945).

[4]IJA-ABA Standards Relating to Appeals and Collateral Review 41 (1980).

[Section 34:8]

[1]In re Gilbert, 45 Ohio App. 2d 308, 74 Ohio Op. 2d 480, 345 N.E.2d 79 (9th Dist. Summit County 1974). See § 23:31, Double jeopardy.

[2]App. R. 7(C).

[3]Juv. R. 22(F).

[4]RC 2945.67(A). See In re Mojica, 107 Ohio App. 3d 461, 669 N.E.2d 35 (8th Dist. Cuyahoga County 1995).

[5]Juv. R. 22(F). See also RC 2945.67(A).

[6]Juv. R. 22(F); App. R. 4(B).

[7]In re Hester, 1 Ohio App. 3d 24, 437 N.E.2d 1218 (10th Dist. Franklin County 1981).

[8]State v. Felty, 2 Ohio App. 3d 62, 440 N.E.2d 803 (1st Dist. Hamilton County 1981).

amenability hearing where the child was bound over by the juvenile court.[9]

§ 34:9 Right to transcript

In *In re Gault*[1] the United States Supreme Court chose not to rule on the question of whether a child has a right to a transcript on appeal. However, in *Gault* the Court commented that the failure to prepare a transcript imposes a burden upon the reviewing process.

Ohio law provides that in all juvenile court hearings a complete record of all testimony and other oral proceedings must be made upon the request of a party or upon the court's own motion.[2] When a hearing is conducted on a motion for permanent custody pursuant to RC 2151.414, or on a complaint requesting a permanent custody order under RC 2151.353(A)(4), a record is mandatory.[3] No public use may be made of any juvenile court record or transcript except in the course of an appeal or as authorized by the court.[4]

When a transcript of proceedings is requested pursuant to Appellate Rule 9, it is the responsibility of the juvenile court to prepare it.[5] It has been held that a presumption of regularity attached to juvenile court proceedings where the child provided a copy of videotapes of the proceedings and where the child provided on appeal only those transcribed portions of the proceedings that were favorable to his claim that the adjudication of delinquency had been against the manifest weight of the evidence, rather than a transcript of all testimony relevant to his claim.[6] In actions instituted by the state to permanently terminate parental rights, the United States and Ohio Constitutions' guarantees of due process and equal protection require the juvenile court to provide indigent parents with a transcript at public expense for appeals as of right.[7] However, a party's right to a free transcript on appeal turns on that party's status as an indigent, and a motion for a free transcript may be denied where the juvenile court finds that the party has adequate financial means to obtain the transcript.[8] Moreover, since the right to a transcript applies only in a state-instituted permanent custody case, an indigent, noncustodial parent is not entitled to a transcript where temporary custody is given to the other parent.[9]

§ 34:10 Right to counsel

An indigent parent in a state-instituted action to permanently terminate parental rights is also entitled to appointed counsel on appeal, although the responsibility for affording this right rests with the court of appeals rather

---

[9]In re Langston, 119 Ohio App. 3d 1, 694 N.E.2d 468 (5th Dist. Stark County 1997). But see In re Becker, 39 Ohio St. 2d 84, 68 Ohio Op. 2d 50, 314 N.E.2d 158 (1974), holding that a bindover order is not a final appealable order. See also § 22:23, Appeals.

[Section 34:9]

[1]Application of Gault, 387 U.S. 1, 87 S. Ct. 1428, 18 L. Ed. 2d 527 (1967).

[2]RC 2151.35(A); Juv. R. 37(A). State v. Eppinger, No. 30798 (8th Dist. Ct. App., Cuyahoga, 12-9-71).

[3]RC 2151.35(A).

[4]Juv. R. 37(B); State ex rel. Scripps Howard Broadcasting Co. v. Cuyahoga Cty. Court of Common Pleas, Juv. Div., 73 Ohio St. 3d 19, 652 N.E.2d 179 (1995).

[5]State ex rel. Heller v. Miller, 61 Ohio St. 2d 6, 15 Ohio Op. 3d 3, 399 N.E.2d 66 (1980). See also In re Lippitt, No. 38421 (8th Dist. Ct. App., Cuyahoga, 3-9-78); In re Brown, 60 Ohio App. 3d 136, 573 N.E.2d 1217 (1st Dist. Hamilton County 1989); In re Edgerson, 144 Ohio App.3d 113, 2001-Ohio-4237, 759 N.E.2d 806 (8th Dist. Cuyahoga County 2001).

[6]In re Corcoran, 68 Ohio App. 3d 213, 587 N.E.2d 957 (11th Dist. Geauga County 1990).

[7]M.L.B. v. S.L.J., 519 U.S. 102, 117 S. Ct. 555, 136 L. Ed. 2d 473 (1996); State ex rel. Heller v. Miller, 61 Ohio St. 2d 6, 15 Ohio Op. 3d 3, 399 N.E.2d 66 (1980).

[8]State ex rel. Henry v. Grossmann, 5 Ohio St. 3d 235, 450 N.E.2d 1156 (1983).

[9]State ex rel. Howard v. Ferreri, 70 Ohio St. 3d 587, 1994-Ohio-234, 639 N.E.2d 1189 (1994); In re Alexander, No. H-82-23 (6th Dist. Ct. App., Huron, 12-28-82).

than with the juvenile court.[1] The procedures set forth in *Anders v. California*[2] are applicable to appeals involving the termination of parental rights when appointed counsel cannot find any merit in his client's appeal and wishes to withdraw.[3]

In any delinquency proceeding in which a prosecuting attorney appeals a juvenile court decision granting a motion to dismiss a complaint or a motion to suppress evidence,[4] the juvenile court must appoint counsel in accordance with RC Chapter 120 to represent any indigent person who is not represented by counsel and who has not waived the right to counsel.[5]

§ 34:11 Effect on further juvenile court proceedings

When a case has been appealed, the juvenile court retains all jurisdiction not inconsistent with the appellate court's jurisdiction to reverse, modify, or affirm the judgment.[1] However, an appeal divests the juvenile court of jurisdiction to consider a Civil Rule 60(B) motion for relief from judgment, unless the appellate court confers such jurisdiction through an order remanding the matter for consideration of the motion.[2] Moreover, a juvenile court does not have the authority to consider whether the appellant has validly invoked the jurisdiction of the appellate court.[3]

If the court of appeals finds that the juvenile court did not commit prejudicial error, it must affirm the ruling of the juvenile court.[4] Following an unsuccessful appeal from the sustaining of a motion to suppress, the state is not barred from continuing its prosecution as long as its Juvenile Rule 22(F) certification, that the suppressed evidence was of such a nature that the prosecution could not be successful without it, was made in good faith.[5] If the certification was not made in good faith, the time consumed in the appeal process, from the grant of the motion, must be charged to the state as undue delay in determining whether the child's constitutional right to a speedy trial

---

[Section 34:10]

[1]State ex rel. Heller v. Miller, 61 Ohio St. 2d 6, 15 Ohio Op. 3d 3, 399 N.E.2d 66 (1980). This holding was not affected by the later decision of the United States Supreme Court in Lassiter v. Department of Social Services of Durham County, N. C., 452 U.S. 18, 101 S. Ct. 2153, 68 L. Ed. 2d 640 (1981), which held that the Due Process Clause of the Fourteenth Amendment does not require appointment of counsel in every parental status termination proceeding. This decision, which was based on narrow factual grounds, dealt with the right to appointed counsel for the juvenile court proceedings and not for purposes of appeal.

[2]Anders v. State of Cal., 386 U.S. 738, 87 S. Ct. 1396, 18 L. Ed. 2d 493 (1967). *Anders* specifies three requirements that the defense attorney must perform: (1) advise the court that the appeal is frivolous and request permission to withdraw, (2) submit a brief referring to anything in the record that might arguably support the appeal, and (3) furnish the client with a copy of the brief and afford the client time to raise any points the client chooses. See generally Katz and Giannelli, Baldwin's Ohio Practice, Criminal Law (2d ed.) § 75:11 (discussing *Anders* briefs).

[3]Morris v. Lucas County Children Services Bd., 49 Ohio App. 3d 86, 550 N.E.2d 980 (6th Dist. Lucas County 1989). See also In re Booker, 133 Ohio App. 3d 387, 391, 728 N.E.2d 405 (1st Dist. Hamilton County 1999) (*Anders* violated; brief did not refer to any matters that arguably support the appeal, nor did it show that Booker was provided with a copy or that counsel discussed the brief with Booker).

[4]See § 34:8, State appeals.

[5]RC 2945.67(B).

[Section 34:11]

[1]Howard v. Catholic Social Serv. of Cuyahoga Cty., Inc., 70 Ohio St. 3d 141, 1994-Ohio-219, 637 N.E.2d 890 (1994).

[2]Howard v. Catholic Social Serv. of Cuyahoga Cty., Inc., 70 Ohio St. 3d 141, 1994-Ohio-219, 637 N.E.2d 890 (1994); In re Phillips, 2003-Ohio-5107, 2003 WL 22227364 (Ohio Ct. App. 12th Dist. Butler County 2003) (once the child is adopted, the juvenile court loses jurisdiction to hear the alleged father's Civil Rule 60(B) motion.).

[3]In re Terrance P., 124 Ohio App. 3d 487, 706 N.E.2d 801 (6th Dist. Lucas County 1997).

[4]App. R. 12(B).

[5]In re Hester, 3 Ohio App. 3d 458, 446 N.E.2d 202 (10th Dist. Franklin County 1982).

has been violated.[6]

If the court of appeals determines that the juvenile court committed prejudicial error and the appellant is entitled to final judgment, the court must reverse the juvenile court order and either enter the appropriate judgment or remand the matter to the juvenile court with instructions to enter an appropriate order.[7] If prejudicial error is found, the court of appeals may also modify the judgment or final order of the juvenile court if appropriate.[8] In *In re Ewing*,[9] in which a juvenile court adjudged a child delinquent for aggravated burglary and grand theft, a court of appeals modified the judgment by finding the child delinquent for criminal trespass only and remanded the case for a new dispositional hearing. This modification was based on the failure of the evidence to establish a nexus between the child and the alleged stolen property. Similarly, a juvenile court order adjudging a child delinquent for theft and disorderly conduct was modified by a court of appeals to a judgment of delinquency based solely on the theft offense, because the disorderly conduct charge was not proven.[10]

If the court of appeals finds (1) that the juvenile court order is against the manifest weight of the evidence, (2) that there is no other prejudicial error, and (3) that the appellee is not entitled to judgment, it must reverse the juvenile court order and either render the appropriate order or remand the case to the juvenile court for further proceedings.[11] Where the testimony presented to a juvenile court in a neglect proceeding indicated that the child was weak and sick but showed no sign of physical neglect, the court of appeals in *In re MacPherson*[12] reversed the neglect adjudication and entered judgment for the appellant-parents. On the other hand, in *In re Grubbs*,[13] where a juvenile court found a child not dependent, the court of appeals reversed the judgment, found the child dependent, and remanded the matter to the juvenile court for further proceedings based on the fact that the evidence established dependency.

When a court of appeals remands the matter of disposition to the juvenile court, there is no specified number of days within which the hearing is to be held. Thus, the juvenile court's delay in conducting the hearing is not a denial of the parents' due process rights, particularly where the parents have failed to object to the time lapse.[14]

In *In re Solarz*,[15] in which a court of appeals reversed for insufficient evidence a juvenile court's dependency adjudication, the court of appeals refused to enter final judgment for the parents. Because the parents had separated during the pendency of the appeal, the cause was remanded to the juvenile court for a determination of the child's custody pursuant to RC 2151.23(A)(2) (to determine the custody of a child not a ward of another court of this state) and RC 2151.23(E) (to determine the case of any child certified to the court by any court of competent jurisdiction). The court of appeals further ordered that if the juvenile court found that neither parent was capable of assuming legal custody of the child, new dependency proceedings should be instituted. It has been held that an appellate court's reversal of a juvenile court's per-

---

[6]In re Hester, 3 Ohio App. 3d 458, 446 N.E.2d 202 (10th Dist. Franklin County 1982).

[7]App. R. 12(B).

[8]App. R. 12(B).

[9]In the Matter of Ewing, 1983 WL 4671 (Ohio Ct. App. 8th Dist. Cuyahoga County 1983).

[10]In re Brown, No. 34450 (8th Dist. Ct. App., Cuyahoga, 1-8-76).

[11]App. R. 12(C). Matter of Hurlow, 1997 WL 701328 (Ohio Ct. App. 4th Dist. Gallia County 1997).

[12]In re MacPherson, No. 34106 (8th Dist. Ct. App., Cuyahoga, 4-3-75).

[13]Grubbs, 1982 WL 5285 (Ohio Ct. App. 8th Dist. Cuyahoga County 1982).

[14]Wayne, 1981 WL 3652 (Ohio Ct. App. 10th Dist. Franklin County 1981).

[15]In re Solarz, No. 42275 (8th Dist. Ct. App., Cuyahoga, 11-6-80).

manent custody order leaves a prior temporary custody order in effect.[16]

§ 34:12   Habeas corpus

Because habeas corpus is an extraordinary remedy,[1] it may not be used either as a substitute for appeal or where an adequate remedy at law exists.[2] Habeas corpus relief is the exception rather than the general rule in child custody actions.[3] The Ohio Supreme Court has held that in order to prevail on habeas corpus in a child custody case, the petitioner must establish that the child is being unlawfully detained, and the petitioner has the superior legal right to custody of the child.[4]

Accordingly, when a child has been committed to an institution by the juvenile court in proceedings regular in all particulars, a writ of habeas corpus may not issue from another court on the ground that the child is unlawfully restrained.[5] Similarly, a parent alleging that he failed to receive notice of a hearing concerning the prehearing shelter care of his child must request a rehearing in the juvenile court pursuant to Juvenile Rule 7(G) before seeking habeas corpus relief.[6] Despite the fact that Juvenile Rule 7(G) relates to predispositional detention and shelter care orders, it has been cited as an adequate remedy at law, justifying the denial of a writ of habeas corpus where children were found dependent and committed to the temporary custody of a county job and family services department.[7] It has also been held that habeas corpus is not an appropriate remedy to challenge a defective dependency

---

[16]In Matter of Parker, 1981 WL 6774 (Ohio Ct. App. 3d Dist. Van Wert County 1981); In re Neff, No. 1-78-9 (3d Dist. Ct. App., Allen, 6-14-78).

[Section 34:12]

[1]This section covers the use of habeas corpus as an alternative to appeal of juvenile court decisions. It does not include habeas corpus as an original action in juvenile court pursuant to RC 2151.23(A)(3). In re Bailey, 98 Ohio St. 3d 309, 310, 2003-Ohio-859, 784 N.E.2d 109 (2003) ("In order to withstand dismissal, the Baileys were required to allege with particularity the extraordinary circumstances entitling them to the requested extraordinary relief in habeas corpus. 'Unsupported conclusions contained in a habeas corpus petition are not considered admitted and are insufficient to withstand dismissal.' The Baileys' petition contained unsupported conclusions, e.g., that they had been denied due process and that they had no adequate alternative remedy at law available, rather than specific facts supporting their claim for the writ.") (citations omitted).

[2]In re Bailey, 98 Ohio St. 3d 309, 311, 2003-Ohio-859, 784 N.E.2d 109 (2003) ("[T]he Baileys' attack on the constitutionality of certain legislation is better suited to an action in a common pleas court than in an extraordinary writ action filed here."); Rammage v. Saros, 97 Ohio St. 3d 430, 431, 2002-Ohio-6669, 780 N.E.2d 278 (2002) ("She has or had adequate legal remedies in the ordinary course of law to raise her claims. . . . This principle applies equally to child custody actions, where habeas corpus relief is the exception rather than the general rule."); Luchene v. Wagner, 12 Ohio St. 3d 37, 465 N.E.2d 395 (1984); In re Piazza, 7 Ohio St. 2d 102, 36 Ohio Op. 2d 84, 218 N.E.2d 459 (1966). See also State ex rel. Spitler v. Seiber, 16 Ohio St. 2d 117, 45 Ohio Op. 2d 463, 243 N.E.2d 65 (1968); In re Butt, 20 Ohio Misc. 2d 15, 486 N.E.2d 255 (C.P. 1984); McNeal v. Miami Cty. Children's Services Bd., 64 Ohio St. 3d 208, 594 N.E.2d 587 (1992); State ex rel. Frazer v. Administrator/Director, Juvenile Court Detention Home, 107 Ohio App. 3d 245, 668 N.E.2d 546 (8th Dist. Cuyahoga County 1995); State ex rel. Fryerson v. Tate, 84 Ohio St. 3d 481, 1999-Ohio-465, 705 N.E.2d 353 (1999).

[3]Holloway v. Clermont County Dept. of Human Services, 80 Ohio St. 3d 128, 1997-Ohio-131, 684 N.E.2d 1217 (1997); Barnebey v. Zschach, 71 Ohio St. 3d 588, 646 N.E.2d 162 (1995); Howard v. Catholic Social Serv. of Cuyahoga Cty., Inc., 70 Ohio St. 3d 141, 1994-Ohio-219, 637 N.E.2d 890 (1994).

[4]In re Bailey, 98 Ohio St. 3d 309, 310, 2003-Ohio-859, 784 N.E.2d 109 (2003); State ex rel. Bruggeman v. Auglaize Cty. Court of Common Pleas, 87 Ohio St. 3d 257, 1999-Ohio-52, 719 N.E.2d 543 (1999) ("[I]n order to prevail on a petition for a writ of habeas corpus in a child custody case, the petitioner must establish that (1) the child is being unlawfully detained, and (2) the petitioner has the superior legal right to custody of the child."); Holloway v. Clermont County Dept. of Human Services, 80 Ohio St. 3d 128, 1997-Ohio-131, 684 N.E.2d 1217 (1997); Pegan v. Crawmer, 76 Ohio St. 3d 97, 1996-Ohio-419, 666 N.E.2d 1091 (1996).

[5]Children's Home of Marion County v. Fetter, 90 Ohio St. 110, 106 N.E. 761 (1914).

[6]Linger v. Weiss, 57 Ohio St. 2d 97, 11 Ohio Op. 3d 281, 386 N.E.2d 1354 (1979).

[7]Pettry v. McGinty, 60 Ohio St. 2d 92, 14 Ohio Op. 3d 331, 397 N.E.2d 1190 (1979).

complaint where a motion to dismiss pursuant to Juvenile Rule 22(D)(2) could have been filed.[8]

However, habeas corpus actions have been allowed to proceed in child custody actions where appeal was not speedy enough, such as where the permanent surrender of an infant is at issue,[9] or where parents are being denied contact with their children on the authority of an emergency shelter care order.[10]

Moreover, where an imprisoned father was not served with a summons for temporary and permanent custody hearings in a dependency case, the order of permanent custody and a subsequent order of adoption were determined to be void in a habeas corpus proceeding.[11] Without proper service of process on the parents, a final dispositional order is void, since the court has no jurisdiction to make such order.[12] It has also been held that habeas is the proper remedy to enforce the due process right of indigent parents to appointed counsel.[13]

The Ohio Supreme Court has ruled that where a juvenile court journal entry stated that "all writs heretofore issued herein have been duly served according to law and that all persons interested are now before the Court," such recital should be taken as true when attacked by a writ of habeas corpus.[14] However, in another habeas corpus proceeding, a father who was imprisoned at the time of a permanent custody hearing regarding his children was permitted to demonstrate that he had not been served with a summons, even though a fill-in-blank form journal entry indicated that all interested parties had been served.[15]

The Eighth District Court of Appeals has held that habeas corpus does not lie to challenge the detention of a child held beyond ninety days, in contravention of RC 2151.34, where a Juvenile Rule 30 bindover proceeding was pending against the child. The court relied on Juvenile Rule 29(A) which authorizes continuing detention prior to the adjudicatory hearing.[16]

The United States Supreme Court has held that the federal habeas corpus statute[17] does not confer jurisdiction on federal courts to consider collateral challenges to a state court judgment which involuntarily terminates parental rights.[18]

---

[8]In re Hunt, 46 Ohio St. 2d 378, 75 Ohio Op. 2d 450, 348 N.E.2d 727 (1976).

[9]Marich v. Knox County Dept. of Human Services/Children Services Unit, 45 Ohio St. 3d 163, 543 N.E.2d 776 (1989).

[10]Matter of Smith, 1991 WL 325699 (Ohio Ct. App. 6th Dist. Ottawa County 1991).

[11]Reynolds v. Ross County Children's Services Agency, 1981 WL 6057 (Ohio Ct. App. 4th Dist. Ross County 1981) (After service was made on the father and a further hearing was conducted, the court of appeals determined that the father was not a suitable custodian of his children and denied the writ.).

[12]In re Frinzl, 152 Ohio St. 164, 39 Ohio Op. 456, 87 N.E.2d 583 (1949); In re Corey, 145 Ohio St. 413, 31 Ohio Op. 35, 61 N.E.2d 892 (1945); Lewis v. Reed, 117 Ohio St. 152, 5 Ohio L. Abs. 420, 157 N.E. 897 (1927); Rarey v. Schmidt, 115 Ohio St. 518, 5 Ohio L. Abs. 12, 154 N.E. 914 (1926).

[13]Sink v. Auglaize County Welfare Dep't, No. 2-80-15 (3d Dist. Ct. App., Auglaize, 4-15-80).

[14]Linger v. Weiss, 57 Ohio St. 2d 97, 11 Ohio Op. 3d 281, 386 N.E.2d 1354 (1979). This ruling was included in a footnote to the decision and was based on the fact that the parent had a right to attack the decision by a direct proceeding under Juv. R. 7(G). Accord In re Bibb, 70 Ohio App. 2d 117, 24 Ohio Op. 3d 159, 435 N.E.2d 96 (1st Dist. Hamilton County 1980).

[15]Reynolds v. Ross County Children's Services Agency, 1981 WL 6057 (Ohio Ct. App. 4th Dist. Ross County 1981).

[16]Rivera v. Morris, 1992 WL 877341 (Ohio Ct. App. 8th Dist. 1992); Ezell v. Manual, 1990 WL 746729 (Ohio Ct. App. 8th Dist. Cuyahoga County 1990). See also State ex rel. Driscoll v. Hunter, 1998 WL 102477 (Ohio Ct. App. 8th Dist. Cuyahoga County 1998).

[17]28 U.S.C.A. § 2254.

[18]Lehman v. Lycoming County Children's Services Agency, 458 U.S. 502, 102 S. Ct. 3231, 73 L. Ed. 2d 928 (1982).

Chapter 35

Juvenile Court Records

> **KeyCite®:** Cases and other legal materials listed in KeyCite Scope can be researched through West's KeyCite service on Westlaw®. Use KeyCite to check citations for form, parallel references, prior and later history, and comprehensive citator information, including citations to other decisions and secondary materials.

§ 35:1   Juvenile court records—Introduction
§ 35:2   Confidentiality requirement
§ 35:3   Non-juvenile court proceedings
§ 35:4   Expungement and sealing

§ 35:1   Juvenile court records—Introduction

This chapter discusses miscellaneous aspects of the law governing juvenile court records, including their use in proceedings in courts other than juvenile courts. An additional related chapter examines the discovery of various records (Ch 21).

§ 35:2   Confidentiality requirement

Both legal and social history information is included in juvenile court records.[1] Legal records, including an appearance docket, a journal, and court transcripts, must be maintained for all official cases.[2] The parents of any child affected, if living, or the nearest of kin, if the parents are deceased, may inspect these records, either in person or by counsel. The Ohio Supreme Court has held that mandamus is the appropriate remedy when a juvenile court refuses to provide access to these records to a person who has a clear legal right to access.[3]

Social history records contain the personal and family history of a child or any other party to a juvenile proceeding and may include the prior record of the person with the juvenile court or any other court.[4] Counsel may inspect the social history a reasonable time before any hearing at which it is utilized, although the court may deny inspection for good cause, limit its scope, or order that the contents of the history not be disclosed to specified persons.[5]

As with juvenile court proceedings involving children,[6] the concept of confidentiality applies to juvenile court records involving children. As a general rule, no public use may be made of any juvenile court record except in

---

[Section 35:2]

  [1]See Sup. R. 26.03(H) for the retention schedule for case files maintained by juvenile courts.

  [2]RC 2151.18(A). See also RC 2151.35(A)(2) and RC 2152.71. The statute requires that a separate docket be kept for traffic offenses. See also RC 2151.40.

  [3]State ex rel. Howard v. Ferreri, 70 Ohio St. 3d 587, 1994-Ohio-234, 639 N.E.2d 1189 (1994).

  [4]Juv. R. 2(NN).

  [5]Juv. R. 32(C). See also RC 2151.352, which permits counsel access to additional records. See § 21:2, Scope of discovery—Rule 24.

  [6]RC 2151.35; Juv. R. 27.

the course of an appeal or as authorized by court order.[7] The purpose of this rule is to keep confidential juvenile court records involving children, since their welfare is a primary consideration.[8] However, the extent of confidentiality of such records is subject to the provisions of the Public Record Act.[9] RC 149.43(A)(1) generally defines a "public record" as "any record that is kept by any public office," but exempts "records the release of which is prohibited by state or federal law." Specific provisions in Ohio law ensure the confidentiality of various nonpublic juvenile court records, including the reports and records of the probation department;[10] court-ordered mental and physical examinations of children;[11] child abuse, neglect, and dependency investigative records;[12] victim impact statements;[13] confidential law enforcement investigatory records;[14] records relating to parental notification of abortion proceedings;[15] fingerprints or photographs of a child arrested or taken into custody;[16] and sealed or expunged juvenile adjudications or arrests.[17]

Federal courts have held that the Constitution does not encompass a general right to nondisclosure of private information.[18] Thus, the postadjudication release of social histories of children by employees of a juvenile court[19] and the act of publishing the name of an alleged delinquent in a newspaper[20] do not violate any constitutional right to privacy.

The Attorney General is permitted to obtain all juvenile court records relative to a delinquent child in order to comply with RC 2743.51 et seq., the Victims' Reparation Act.[21]

§ 35:3 Non-juvenile court proceedings

The confidentiality issue often arises when there is an attempt to introduce juvenile court records into evidence in other proceedings, and has led to controversial court decisions and resultant statutory amendments. The relevant statute, RC 2151.358(H), provides that a juvenile court judgment does not impose any of the civil disabilities ordinarily imposed by conviction of a crime, nor shall it operate to disqualify a child in any future civil service examination, appointment, or application. A former version of the statute also provided that neither the disposition of the child nor the evidence given in

---

[7]Juv. R. 37(B). See Matter of Etchell, 1987 WL 10613 (Ohio Ct. App. 8th Dist. Cuyahoga County 1987), holding that it is not error for a juvenile court to deny a request for a transcript made prior to the filing of the notice of appeal.

[8]State ex rel. Scripps Howard Broadcasting Co. v. Cuyahoga Cty. Court of Common Pleas, Juv. Div., 73 Ohio St. 3d 19, 652 N.E.2d 179 (1995).

[9]RC 149.43 et seq. See also RC 1347.08.

[10]RC 2151.14. This provision applies only to the records of the juvenile court probation department and not to those of a state institution to which the child has been committed. State v. Sherow, 101 Ohio App. 169, 1 Ohio Op. 2d 100, 138 N.E.2d 444 (4th Dist. Gallia County 1956). The records of the Department of Youth Services are confidential, accessible only to department employees, except upon consent of the department or order of the court. See RC 5139.05(D). See also RC 149.43(A)(1)(b), RC 149.43(A)(1)(l)

[11]Juv. R. 32(B); OAG 90-101, 1990 WL 547011.

[12]RC 5153.17, RC 2151.421(H)(1); OAG 91-003, 1991 WL 576919; State ex rel. Renfro v. Cuyahoga County Dept. of Human Services, 54 Ohio St. 3d 25, 560 N.E.2d 230 (1990); In re Fuhrman, No. 91-0206 (1st Dist. Ct. App., Hamilton, 11-22-91).

[13]RC 2152.19(D)(3).

[14]RC 2151.141(B)(2)(b); OAG 90-101, 1990 WL 547011.

[15]RC 2151.85(F), RC 149.43(A)(1)(c). See § 12:8, Hearing.

[16]RC 2151.313; OAG 90-101, 1990 WL 547011.

[17]RC 2151.358; OAG 90-101, 1990 WL 547011. See § 35:4, Expungement and sealing.

[18]J. P. v. DeSanti, 653 F.2d 1080 (6th Cir. 1981).

[19]J. P. v. DeSanti, 653 F.2d 1080 (6th Cir. 1981).

[20]Murphy v. Plain Dealer Pub. Co., 19 Media L. Rep. (BNA) 1556, 1991 WL 337361 (N.D. Ohio 1991).

[21]In re Flemming, No. 83-5591-09 (Ct. of Claims 1983).

the juvenile court was admissible against the child in any proceeding in another court, except for purposes of sentencing and the granting of probation.[1] Case law interpreting the former statute held that neither a delinquency judgment nor evidence of the acts which formed the basis of the delinquency adjudication was admissible against the child in either a civil action[2] or a criminal proceeding[3] in another court. It was also held that because the former statutory prohibition against the introduction of a juvenile record applied only to "any other case or proceeding in any other court,"[4] confessions used in a juvenile court hearing, after which the child was transferred to the general division for criminal prosecution, were admissible in the criminal court proceedings, since those proceedings were part of the same case.[5]

However, the validity of these decisions was significantly impacted by two Ohio Supreme Court decisions and subsequent statutory amendments. In *State v. Shedrick* (*Shedrick I*),[6] the Supreme Court broadly interpreted former RC 2151.358(H) as barring testimony, documents, or exhibits presented against a child in a delinquency proceeding from being used against him in any other case or proceeding, including a subsequent criminal prosecution. The Court further held that where a witness had testified in a juvenile court proceeding, the statute prohibited that witness from giving essentially the same testimony in any other case or proceeding.[7] Because this strict prohibition would also prevent the introduction of testimony given in a delinquency proceeding from being used in a criminal prosecution subsequent to bindover, or in a subsequent civil action, originating from the same conduct that formed the basis of the delinquency prosecution, the Supreme Court granted a motion for rehearing. In *State v. Shedrick* (*Shedrick II*),[8] the Court vacated and clarified its opinion in *Shedrick I* by holding that the prohibition against the use of juvenile court testimony applied only in any subsequent *criminal* proceeding. However, subsequent to *Shedrick I* but prior to *Shedrick II*, the General Assembly amended RC 2151.358(H).[9] Under this amendment, the juvenile court disposition and evidence were deemed not admissible in any other action in any other court except for purposes of sentence or probation, and in any bindover hearing, in any criminal prosecution of the child subsequent to bindover, and in any civil action arising out of the conduct of the child that was the subject of the juvenile court proceeding. Then, subsequent to *Shedrick II*, the General Assembly again amended RC 2151.358(H).[10] Pursuant to this amendment, the juvenile court disposition and evidence are "not admissible to impeach the credibility of the child in any action or proceeding."[11] However, the disposition or evidence is admissible "as evidence for or against the child in any action or proceeding in any court in accordance with the Rules of Evidence and also may be considered

---

[Section 35:3]

[1]See State v. Blogna, 60 Ohio App. 3d 141, 573 N.E.2d 1223 (5th Dist. Stark County 1990).

[2]Beatty v. Riegel, 115 Ohio App. 448, 21 Ohio Op. 2d 71, 185 N.E.2d 555 (2d Dist. Montgomery County 1961). See also Allstate Ins. Co. v. Cook, 324 F.2d 752, 26 Ohio Op. 2d 192 (6th Cir. 1963), holding that the improper admission of such records was not prejudicial error where there was other testimony in the record sufficient to sustain the findings of fact.

[3]State v. Hall, 57 Ohio App. 3d 144, 567 N.E.2d 305 (8th Dist. Cuyahoga County 1989).

[4]RC 2151.358(H), amended by 1991 H.B. 27 and 1992 H.B. 154.

[5]State v. Lowder, 79 Ohio App. 237, 34 Ohio Op. 568, 72 N.E.2d 785 (5th Dist. Stark County 1946).

[6]State v. Shedrick, 59 Ohio St. 3d 146, 572 N.E.2d 59 (1991).

[7]State v. Shedrick, 59 Ohio St. 3d 146, 572 N.E.2d 59 (1991).

[8]State v. Shedrick, 61 Ohio St. 3d 331, 574 N.E.2d 1065 (1991).

[9]1991 H.B. 27, eff. 10-10-91. *Shedrick I* was decided on May 8, 1991; H.B. 27 was passed on June 26, 1991; and *Shedrick II* was decided on August 7, 1991.

[10]1992 H.B. 154, eff. 7-31-92.

[11]RC 2151.358(H).

by any court as to the matter of sentence or to the granting of probation."[12]

The above statutory amendment has resulted in some confusion. For instance, the meaning of the phrase "in accordance with the Rules of Evidence," as used in RC 2151.358(H), is not clear. Evidence Rule 609(D) provides, "Evidence of juvenile adjudications[13] is not admissible except as provided by statute enacted by the General Assembly."[14] Thus, the statute refers to the Rules of Evidence for authority, and the Rules of Evidence refer to the statute for authority. A possible way to reconcile the statute and rule is to consider that the statute controls the types of juvenile court records that are admissible, while the Rules control the procedure for introduction of these records.[15] Under this interpretation, the prohibition in Evidence Rule 609(D) would be of no further effect because RC 2151.358(H) generally permits the use of juvenile court records in any proceeding and for any purpose, except for impeachment.

Both before and after the amendments to RC 2151.358(H), Ohio courts have ruled that a witness's prior juvenile record may not be used to impeach the witness's general credibility.[16] However, the United States Supreme Court has ruled that a defendant's right to confront witnesses and to present probative evidence for his or her defense includes the right to cross-examine a witness about the witness's juvenile record in order to show bias.[17] The specific bias in *Davis v. Alaska* was the witness's vulnerable status as a probationer and his possible concern that he might be a suspect in the crime under investigation. In *State v. Cox*,[18] the juvenile record of a state witness was admissible to demonstrate the deteriorating relationship between the witness and her mother, for whose murder the defendant was being tried.[19]

In order to determine whether a witness's juvenile court records are relevant[20] in a criminal prosecution to determine the potential bias of the wit-

---

[12]RC 2151.358(H).

[13]The statute, RC 2151.358(H), uses the phrase "disposition of a child under the judgment rendered or any evidence given in court," whereas Evid. R. 609(D) uses the phrase "evidence of juvenile adjudications." It is not clear whether the statute and rule are referring to the same types of evidence.

[14]Prior to the current version of RC 2151.358(H), the general rule of Evid. R. 609(D) applied if a juvenile adjudication was sought to be introduced at a proceeding not involving sentencing or the granting of probation. See State v. Robinson, 98 Ohio App. 3d 560, 649 N.E.2d 18 (8th Dist. Cuyahoga County 1994); In re Johnson, 61 Ohio App. 3d 544, 573 N.E.2d 184 (8th Dist. Cuyahoga County 1989).

[15]See Evid. R. 102.

[16]State v. White, 6 Ohio App. 3d 1, 451 N.E.2d 533 (8th Dist. Cuyahoga County 1982); State v. Mann, 1982 WL 5770 (Ohio Ct. App. 11th Dist. Ashtabula County 1982); State v. Williams, 16 Ohio App. 3d 484, 477 N.E.2d 221 (1st Dist. Hamilton County 1984); State v. Marks, 1987 WL 6763 (Ohio Ct. App. 4th Dist. Athens County 1987); State v. Newton, 1991 WL 3214 (Ohio Ct. App. 12th Dist. Warren County 1991); State v. Robinson, 98 Ohio App. 3d 560, 649 N.E.2d 18 (8th Dist. Cuyahoga County 1994); State v. Fred Podeyn, 1996 WL 20873 (Ohio Ct. App. 6th Dist. Huron County 1996); State v. Cole, 1995 WL 753956 (Ohio Ct. App. 8th Dist. Cuyahoga County 1995); State v. Neiderhelman, 1995 WL 550030 (Ohio Ct. App. 12th Dist. Clermont County 1995); State v. Bayless, 1995 WL 328029 (Ohio Ct. App. 3d Dist. Crawford County 1995); State v. Gilroy, 1995 WL 243440 (Ohio Ct. App. 3d Dist. Auglaize County 1995); State v. Willman, 77 Ohio App. 3d 344, 602 N.E.2d 323 (1st Dist. Hamilton County 1991); State v. Reyes-Cairo, 1997 WL 256670 (Ohio Ct. App. 6th Dist. Lucas County 1997); State v. Pratt, 1997 WL 666788 (Ohio Ct. App. 9th Dist. Summit County 1997); State v. Hawkins, 1998 WL 134321 (Ohio Ct. App. 10th Dist. Franklin County 1998); State v. Fox, 1998 WL 525577 (Ohio Ct. App. 5th Dist. Stark County 1998).

[17]Davis v. Alaska, 415 U.S. 308, 94 S. Ct. 1105, 39 L. Ed. 2d 347 (1974).

[18]State v. Cox, 42 Ohio St. 2d 200, 71 Ohio Op. 2d 186, 327 N.E.2d 639 (1975).

[19]See also State v. McGuire, 1987 WL 31129 (Ohio Ct. App. 11th Dist. Lake County 1987).

[20]Since Evid. R. 402 provides that evidence which is not relevant is not admissible, RC 2151.358(H) would not permit the introduction of this evidence unless it is relevant.

ness, the trial court should conduct an in camera review of the records.[21] A trial court's refusal to release the records after an in camera review will be upheld if the defendant is unable to demonstrate a specific need for the records.[22] Even where an in camera review was not conducted, any potential error in limiting cross-examination of the child witness was held to be harmless where additional evidence corroborated the child's account of the crime, and the defendant was allowed some opportunity to cross-examine the child as to the issue of bias.[23] In the same case it was held that the county children's services' records of a child victim and her school records were not admissible in a prosecution for contributing to the unruliness of that child because the records were not relevant to the child's credibility as it related to her testimony regarding the incident in question.[24]

A federal court has held that where a juvenile confederate of a defendant is called as a prosecution witness, and testimony has already established that the juvenile is in the custody of the Department of Youth Services for his part in the burglary with which the defendant is charged, the jury has sufficient information to appraise the witness's motives and possible bias, and the defendant has no right under the Sixth Amendment to inquire into earlier findings of the juvenile delinquency.[25]

Although juvenile adjudications may not be introduced for the purpose of general impeachment, other valid uses may allow the introduction of such evidence.[26] Thus, where a defendant charged with offenses of violence introduces on direct examination evidence of his peaceful character, the prosecution may cross-examine the defendant concerning his juvenile adjudication and his gang faction's activities.[27] Two cases decided prior to the amendments to RC 2151.358(H) and prior to the effective date of the Ohio Rules of Evidence[28] held that if the defendant does not put his character in issue, it is prejudicial error to permit cross-examination of him as to the disposition of a juvenile adjudication.[29] A court of appeals has held that a mere reference to a criminal defendant's juvenile record is not prejudicial if, pursuant to Criminal Rule 52(A), it does not affect substantial rights.[30]

Confidential child abuse and neglect investigatory reports made under the mandatory reporting statute[31] are admissible in a criminal proceeding in accordance with the Rules of Evidence, and are subject to discovery in accordance with the Rules of Criminal Procedure.[32]

The amendments to RC 2151.358(H) and the enactment of Evidence Rule 609(D) make it clear that the legal principles applicable to the admissibility

---

[21]State v. Hawkins, 66 Ohio St. 3d 339, 612 N.E.2d 1227 (1993); State v. Lukens, 66 Ohio App. 3d 794, 586 N.E.2d 1099 (10th Dist. Franklin County 1990).

[22]State v. Hawkins, 66 Ohio St. 3d 339, 612 N.E.2d 1227 (1993).

[23]State v. Lukens, 66 Ohio App. 3d 794, 586 N.E.2d 1099 (10th Dist. Franklin County 1990).

[24]State v. Lukens, 66 Ohio App. 3d 794, 586 N.E.2d 1099 (10th Dist. Franklin County 1990).

[25]Mann v. Gray, 622 F. Supp. 1225 (N.D. Ohio 1985).

[26]See State v. Robinson, 98 Ohio App. 3d 560, 649 N.E.2d 18 (8th Dist. Cuyahoga County 1994), citing RC 2151.358(H) and Evid. R. 609(D).

[27]State v. Robinson, 98 Ohio App. 3d 560, 649 N.E.2d 18 (8th Dist. Cuyahoga County 1994). See also State v. Marinski, 139 Ohio St. 559, 23 Ohio Op. 50, 41 N.E.2d 387 (1942); State v. Hale, 21 Ohio App. 2d 207, 50 Ohio Op. 2d 340, 256 N.E.2d 239 (10th Dist. Franklin County 1969); State v. Koballa, 2003-Ohio-3535, 2003 WL 21513041 (Ohio Ct. App. 8th Dist. Cuyahoga County 2003).

[28]July 1, 1980.

[29]Malone v. State, 130 Ohio St. 443, 5 Ohio Op. 59, 200 N.E. 473 (1936); Workman v. Cardwell, 338 F. Supp. 893, 31 Ohio Misc. 99, 60 Ohio Op. 2d 187, 60 Ohio Op. 2d 250 (N.D. Ohio 1972); State v. Koballa, 2003-Ohio-3535, 2003 WL 21513041 (Ohio Ct. App. 8th Dist. Cuyahoga County 2003).

[30]State v. Brewster, 1 Ohio Op.3d 372 (App., Franklin 1976).

[31]RC 2151.421.

[32]RC 2151.421(H)(1).

of juvenile court records apply equally in criminal prosecutions as well as juvenile court adjudicatory hearings.[33]

If a person is alleged to have committed an offense, and if that person previously has been adjudicated a delinquent child or a juvenile traffic offender for violating a law or ordinance, the adjudication is considered a conviction for purposes of determining the appropriate offense to charge, and if the person pleads guilty to or is convicted of the offense, the appropriate sentence to be imposed.[34]

§ 35:4   Expungement and sealing

One of the primary purposes of RC Chapter 2151 is to remove "the consequences of criminal behavior and the taint of criminality from children committing delinquent acts."[1] To this end, Ohio law has provided a means for expunging or sealing the juvenile court and arrest records of children who are adjudged delinquent, unruly, or juvenile traffic offenders, as well as the records of those who have such complaints dismissed.[2] As a result, once a record is expunged or sealed, the proceedings in the case are treated as if they never occurred. The expungement/sealing process is not available, apparently, to children whose delinquency, unruly, or juvenile traffic offender complaint is withdrawn prior to adjudication.[3] Moreover, since the juvenile court's expungement authority arises only after a child comes within its jurisdiction, the statute does not provide for the expungement of arrest records concerning a child who is arrested but has no complaint filed against him or her.[4]

Once the court issues an order pursuant to RC 2151.358, the juvenile court records are either expunged or sealed. Expungement is available only if the juvenile court proceedings do not result in an adjudication that the child is delinquent, unruly,[5] or a juvenile traffic offender. Where the child has been adjudicated delinquent, unruly, or a juvenile traffic offender, the records may be sealed but may not be destroyed.[6] Sealed records are removed from the

---

[33]For earlier cases on this issue, see In re Johnson, 61 Ohio App. 3d 544, 573 N.E.2d 184 (8th Dist. Cuyahoga County 1989); In re Wyrock, No. 41827 (8th Dist. Ct. App., Cuyahoga, 10-23-80); State v. Eppinger, No. 30798 (8th Dist. Ct. App., Cuyahoga, 12-9-71).

[34]RC 2901.08. See In re Hayes, 29 Ohio App. 3d 162, 504 N.E.2d 491 (10th Dist. Franklin County 1986); State v. Blogna, 60 Ohio App. 3d 141, 573 N.E.2d 1223 (5th Dist. Stark County 1990); State v. Kelly, 154 Ohio App. 3d 285, 2003-Ohio-4783, 797 N.E.2d 104 (9th Dist. Medina County 2003), appeal not allowed, 101 Ohio St. 3d 1421, 2004-Ohio-123, 802 N.E.2d 153 (2004) (Appellant challenged the use of his juvenile DUI record, claiming his admission was uncounselled. "Appellant did not testify that he was not informed of his right to counsel; he only testified that he did not remember whether he was informed. This is insufficient.").

[Section 35:4]
[1]RC 2151.01(B).

[2]RC 2151.358(C), RC 2151.358(F). In considering the expungement process for adults, governed by RC 2953.31, an appellate court held that a trial court does not have discretion to grant judicial (i.e., extrastatutory) expungement relief to adults convicted of an offense. State v. Weber, 19 Ohio App. 3d 214, 484 N.E.2d 207 (1st Dist. Hamilton County 1984).

[3]According to a letter from the Ohio Legislative Service Commission (February 24, 1981), the term "dismissed" as used in RC 2151.358(F) has a very limited meaning. The letter states, in part:

    If a juvenile is arrested, charged with being a delinquent or unruly child, and the court drops the case, or otherwise does not bring the case to a conclusion, without formally dismissing the charges against the juvenile . . . the juvenile cannot have his arrest record expunged under division (F) of section 2151.358.

    Such a case could not be expunged under section (C) either, since there has been no adjudication.

[4]A letter from the Ohio Legislative Service Commission (February 24, 1981) stated that "if a juvenile is arrested and then released without being formally charged in a case, the juvenile cannot have his arrest record expunged under division (F) of section 2151.358."

[5]RC 2151.358(F).

[6]RC 2151.358(C) to RC 2151.358(E).

main file of similar records and are secured in a separate file that contains only sealed records and is accessible only to the juvenile court.[7]

The juvenile court's authority to seal a record arises two years after the termination of any court order or two years after the unconditional discharge of a person from the Department of Youth Services or other institution or facility.[8] The juvenile court is not authorized to seal a record prior to the expiration of this two-year period.[9] Once the person has been discharged, the department, institution, or facility must notify the court, and the court must note the date of discharge on a separate record of such discharges.[10] After the prescribed two-year period, the court must order the record of an adjudicated unruly child sealed.[11] If the person was adjudicated a delinquent child, or a juvenile traffic offender,[12] the court must either order the record sealed or send the person notice of his right to have the record sealed. If notice is sent, it must be sent by certified mail, return receipt requested, to the person's last known address within 90 days after the expiration of the two-year period. The notice must state that the person may apply to the court for an order to seal his record, explain what sealing a record means, and explain the possible consequences of not having the record sealed.[13]

In those cases in which a child timely files an application for an order to seal his or her record, the court must hold a hearing within 60 days after the application is received. Notice of the hearing must be given to the prosecuting attorney and to any other public office or agency known to have a record of the prior adjudication. If the court finds that the rehabilitation of the person has been attained to a satisfactory degree, it may order the record sealed.[14] It has been held that where an applicant for record sealing repeatedly violated the terms of his parole and was sporadically incarcerated for a 10-year period after his original delinquency adjudication, it was not an abuse of discretion when the juvenile court found that he was not "satisfactorily" rehabilitated, thus denying his request for sealing.[15]

The two-year period does not apply to those cases in which the child has been adjudicated not delinquent, unruly, or a juvenile traffic offender or has had the charges against him dismissed.[16] In such cases the child may at any time apply to the court for expungement of his record. The court must notify the prosecuting attorney of any hearing on the application. In delinquency

---

[7]RC 2151.358(A).

[8]RC 2151.358(C).

[9]In re Manuel, 1997 WL 761311 (Ohio Ct. App. 2d Dist. Montgomery County 1997); In re Dulaney, 1998 WL 310746 (Ohio Ct. App. 2d Dist. Montgomery County 1998).

[10]RC 2151.358(B).

[11]RC 2151.358(C)(1).

[12]The statute authorizing the expungement or sealing of juvenile court records, RC 2151.358, was amended in 1995 (1995 H.B. 1, eff. 1-1-96) to add juvenile traffic offender proceedings to the category of cases eligible for expungement or sealing. Section 3(C) of the act amending the statute provides that the amendments apply to persons who were adjudicated or charged with being juvenile traffic offenders prior to January 1, 1996, regardless of their age on that date. A person who was adjudicated or charged with being a juvenile traffic offender prior to January 1, 1996, may file an application pursuant to RC 2151.358(D) or (F) for sealing or expungement, after which the juvenile court must conduct a hearing. Section 3(C) further states that the juvenile court is not required to send notice under RC 2151.358(C)(1)(b) to a person who was adjudicated a juvenile traffic offender prior to January 1, 1996, if on January 1, 1996, more than 90 days has expired after the expiration of the two-year period described in RC 2151.358(C)(1).

[13]RC 2151.358(C)(2).

[14]RC 2151.358(D). In making this finding, the court may rely on the type of information gathered by a probation officer and included in a social history pursuant to Juv. R. 32.

[15]State v. Lowe, 1995 WL 470543 (Ohio Ct. App. 12th Dist. Fayette County 1995).

[16]RC 2151.358(F). This section states that "[a]ny person who has been *arrested* and charged . . . and who is adjudicated *not guilty* of the charges" may apply for expungement (emphasis added). Many delinquent and unruly children and juvenile traffic offenders are never arrested, and the term "not guilty" is not used in children's cases.

and juvenile traffic offender cases, the court may initiate the expungement proceedings on its own motion. The court must initiate such proceedings in unruly cases if an application for expungement is not filed. If the court determines that the charges were dismissed or the person was adjudicated "not guilty," the court must order the records expunged.[17]

Both expungement and sealing have several beneficial effects for the child. Once the record is expunged or sealed, the proceedings in the case are deemed never to have occurred.[18] With regard to sealed records, all index references to the case and to the person must be deleted, and the person and the court may properly reply to inquiries that no record exists. Sealed records may be inspected with court permission, but only upon application by the person who is the subject of the sealed records and only by the persons that are named in the application.[19] With regard to expunged records, in addition to deleting all index references, the court must also destroy or delete all records of the case, including any pictures and fingerprints taken of the person at arrest.[20] After the expungement order has been issued, the court must, and the person may properly, reply that no record of the case exists.[21]

The expungement/sealing process affects the record-keeping of other governmental bodies in addition to the juvenile court. When a juvenile court record is expunged, the court must order the appropriate persons and governmental agencies to destroy, erase, or delete all index references to the case and all references to the arrest that are maintained by the state or any political subdivision. However, an arrest record may be retained if it is maintained only for purposes of compiling statistical data and does not contain any reference to the person. In addition, if the applicant for an expungement order does not waive in writing his or her right to bring a civil action based on the arrest to which the expungement order relates, the court must order that a copy of all records of the case, except fingerprints held by the court or a law enforcement agency, be delivered to it. These records are to be sealed with other sealed records and are to be destroyed (1) after the statute of limitations expires for any civil action based on the arrest; (2) after any pending litigation based on the arrest is terminated; or (3) after the applicant files a written waiver of his or her right to bring the civil action.[22]

The court must send notice of the order to expunge or seal to any public office or agency that it has reason to believe may have a record of the expunged or sealed record.[23] Whereas the disposition of an expunged record depends on whether the waiver of civil action is signed, a sealed record must be destroyed by all persons and governmental bodies except the juvenile court.[24] RC 2151.358(G) provides that, except for boards of education that maintain records of an individual who has been permanently excluded under RC 3301.121 and RC 3313.662, an order to seal or expunge applies to all public offices and agencies, regardless of whether they receive notice of the expungement/sealing hearing or a copy of the order to expunge or seal. Despite this language, the statute further indicates that the person whose rec-

---

[17]RC 2151.358(F).

[18]RC 2151.358(E), RC 2151.358(F).

[19]RC 2151.358(E). Despite this provision, section (H) of the statute permits the introduction of juvenile court records in other proceedings under certain circumstances. Presumably, section (H) would not apply to an expunged or sealed record. See RC 2151.358(I), and § 35:3, Non-juvenile court proceedings.

[20]RC 2151.358(F). See also RC 2151.313(B)(4), which applies to fingerprints and photographs subject to both an expungement and sealing order.

[21]RC 2151.358(F).

[22]RC 2151.358(F). But see Carrion, Rethinking Expungement of Juvenile Records in Massachusetts: the Case of *Commonwealth v. Gavin G.*, 38 New Eng. L. Rev. 331 (2004).

[23]RC 2151.358(G).

[24]RC 2151.358(A).

ord has been expunged or sealed may make a written request of the office or agency to have the record destroyed. Upon receipt of the request and a copy of the order, the office or agency must destroy its record of the adjudication or arrest, with the exception of certain statistical data.[25]

A board of education that maintains a record of an individual who has been permanently excluded under RC 3301.121 and RC 3313.662 may maintain records of the individual's delinquency adjudication that formed the basis for the exclusion, regardless of a court order to seal the record. Moreover, an order to seal does not revoke the adjudication order of the superintendent to exclude the individual.[26]

In any application for employment, license, or other right or privilege, any appearance as a witness, or any other inquiry, a person may not be questioned with respect to any arrest for which the records were expunged.[27] If such an inquiry is made, the person may respond as if the expunged arrest had not occurred, and the person may not be subjected to any adverse action because of the arrest or the response.[28] However, the Ohio Supreme Court has held that all information requested by any authorized committee, board, or the Supreme Court, reviewing the character and fitness of an applicant seeking to be admitted to the practice of law in Ohio, shall be fully, honestly, and completely provided by the applicant, including expunged or sealed juvenile court records.[29]

RC 2151.358(J) also establishes the offense of divulging confidential information, a misdemeanor of the fourth degree, for certain governmental officers or employees who release information concerning expunged or sealed records.[30]

Cross References

Ch 21, §§ 23:14 to 22:21, § 23:28

Research References

Giannelli and Snyder, Baldwin's Ohio Practice, Evidence (2d ed.) §§ 609.8, 609.9

Katz and Giannelli, Baldwin's Ohio Practice, Criminal Law (2d ed.) § 47:7

Carlin, Baldwin's Ohio Practice, Merrick-Rippner Probate Law (6th ed.), Ch 107

---

[25]Boards of education maintaining records governed by RC 2151.358(K) are not subject to this requirement.

[26]RC 2151.358(K).

[27]RC 2151.358(I). It is not clear why this prohibition does not also apply to sealed records.

[28]RC 2151.358(I). There have been instances in which children whose records were expunged and who enlisted in the armed services were subject to court martial proceedings for not revealing the expunged record. The armed services' argument was that Ohio law did not bind them. See also, Nelson v. State, 120 Wash. App. 470, 85 P.3d 912 (Div. 1 2003) (Where child's juvenile records are expunged, Washington's statutes do "not make it unlawful for the child to carry a firearm so long as he has no convictions other than those expunged.")

[29]Application of Watson, 31 Ohio St. 3d 220, 509 N.E.2d 1240 (1987).

[30]Pursuant to RC 2151.23(A)(5), the juvenile court has exclusive original jurisdiction over such criminal prosecutions.

Chapter 36

Interstate Agreements

> **KeyCite®:** Cases and other legal materials listed in KeyCite Scope can be researched through West's KeyCite service on Westlaw®. Use KeyCite to check citations for form, parallel references, prior and later history, and comprehensive citator information, including citations to other decisions and secondary materials.

§ 36:1 Interstate agreements—Introduction
§ 36:2 Interstate Compact on Juveniles
§ 36:3 Extradition

§ 36:1 Interstate agreements—Introduction

This chapter discusses the authority of juvenile courts in Ohio to enter into arrangements with officials in another state with respect to children who are residing or domiciled in the other state.

§ 36:2 Interstate Compact on Juveniles

Ohio law authorizes the governor to enter into compacts with other states with respect to (1) the return of runaways to their home state; (2) the return of juvenile absconders and escapees to the state from which they have absconded or escaped; (3) the out-of-state placement and supervision of delinquent juveniles;[1] and (4) additional cooperative measures for the care and protection of juveniles and the public.[2]

Upon the receipt of a requisition demanding the return of a runaway juvenile, the court or executive authority to whom the requisition is addressed must issue an order to any peace officer or other appropriate person directing that the juvenile be taken into custody and detained. Before the juvenile may be returned, he must be taken before a judge of a court in the state in which he is found. If the judge finds that the requisition is in order, the juvenile must be delivered to the officer appointed by the demanding court to receive him.[3]

A juvenile who has run away from another state may be taken into custody without a requisition and brought before the appropriate court. After a hearing, that court must determine whether sufficient cause exists to hold the juvenile, for his own protection and welfare, for up to 90 days until such other state issues a proper requisition. Any criminal or delinquency proceedings pending or anticipated in the state in which the child is found take precedence over the requisition.[4]

Provision is also made for the return of delinquent juveniles who have absconded from probation or parole supervision or who have escaped from

---

[Section 36:2]

[1]RC 2151.39, RC 2151.56, RC 5103.20.

[2]RC 2151.56.

[3]RC 2151.56, Article IV. The term "juvenile" means any person who is a minor under the law of the state of residence of the parent, guardian, person, or agency entitled to the legal custody of the minor.

[4]RC 2151.56, Article V.

institutional custody. The procedures involved in such cases are the same as those for runaways.[5]

Any runaway or delinquent juvenile who has absconded or escaped may consent to his immediate return. The consent must be in writing and signed by the juvenile and his counsel or guardian ad litem, if any. Before the consent may be executed or subscribed, the court must advise the juvenile of his rights under the compact.[6]

Under certain circumstances, a delinquent juvenile placed on probation or parole may be permitted to reside in another state. If the sending state thereafter determines it to be necessary, the juvenile may thereafter be returned to the sending state.[7]

The states that take part in the interstate compact subscribe to the policy that, to the extent possible, no juvenile shall be placed or detained in any prison, jail, or lockup, and shall not be detained or transported in association with criminal, vicious, or dissolute persons.[8]

For the purposes of RC 2151.56, a person over the age of 21 may qualify as a "delinquent juvenile," provided that (1) the person has been adjudged delinquent by the sending state, and (2) at the time the provisions of RC 2151.56 are invoked, the person is subject to the jurisdiction of the court in the sending state that made the adjudication or is subject to the jurisdiction or supervision of an agency or institution pursuant to an order of such court.[9]

The payment of any transportation costs involved in the return of runaways, absconders, or escapees is the responsibility of the state to which they are returned.[10] The cost of transporting probationers or parolees to or from the receiving state is the sending state's responsibility.[11] Any participating state or subdivision thereof may assert any right against any person, agency, or other entity in regard to costs for which that state or subdivision is responsible.[12]

§ 36:3   Extradition

The remedies and procedures provided by the interstate compact are in addition to and not in place of other rights, remedies, and procedures.[1] Although the Interstate Compact on Juveniles includes a provision dealing with the transfer of a juvenile to another state when a juvenile commits a crime in a state other than his home state,[2] extradition appears to be another remedy available for the return of alleged or adjudicated delinquents who have escaped or absconded to another state.[3] The attorney general has ruled that when an alleged delinquent flees to another state prior to a final determination of his or her case, the alleged delinquent may be returned to

---

[5]RC 2151.56, Article V.

[6]RC 2151.56, Article VI.

[7]RC 2151.56, Article VII.

[8]RC 2151.56, Article IX.

[9]OAG 88-50; OAG 89-107, 1989 WL 455446.

[10]RC 2151.56, Articles IV and V.

[11]RC 2151.56, Article VII.

[12]RC 2151.56, Article VIII; OAG 89-107, 1989 WL 455446.

[Section 36:3]

[1]RC 2151.56, Article II.

[2]RC 2151.61.

[3]See RC 2963.20. Extradition might be used in cases where the state to which the child has fled is not a party to the Interstate Compact on Juveniles but is a party to the Uniform Extradition Act. See Extradition of juveniles, 73 A.L.R. 3d 700 (discussion of laws of other states).

Ohio pursuant to the Uniform Extradition Act.[4] Upon the child's return, he or she is to be taken before the juvenile court. If the child is taken before any other court, that court must transfer the case to the juvenile court and discontinue all further proceedings with respect to the child.[5]

On the other hand, the Uniform Extradition Act does not apply if the juvenile court has exercised jurisdiction to the extent of ordering a final disposition committing the child to a state institution.[6] Thus, if the child escapes from that institution and flees to another state, the Interstate Compact on Juveniles would be the appropriate remedy to secure his return.[7]

It has been held that RC Chapter 2151 does not confer authority or jurisdiction on a juvenile court to apprehend a child and return him or her to another state without a hearing as to whether the return is in the child's best interests.[8]

The expense of transporting children by police or other officers acting upon a juvenile court order is to be paid from the county treasury.[9] In addition, the expense of returning fugitives who have violated RC Chapter 2151 is to be paid from the county general expense fund.[10] This applies to children as well as adults.[11]

Cross References
Ch 2, Ch 3, Ch 4, Ch 7, Ch 8, Ch 9, Ch 10, Ch 11.
Research References
Giannelli and Snyder, Baldwin's Ohio Practice, Evidence (2d ed.) § 101.7
Carlin, Baldwin's Ohio Practice, Merrick-Rippner Probate Law (6th ed.), Ch 107

---

[4]RC 2963.01 et seq. See also 1945 OAG 509. This opinion was issued prior to Ohio's adoption of the Interstate Compact on Juveniles on June 18, 1957.

[5]1945 OAG 509.

[6]1946 OAG 770.

[7]RC 2151.56, Article V.

[8]In re Messner, 19 Ohio App. 2d 33, 48 Ohio Op. 2d 31, 249 N.E.2d 532 (6th Dist. Huron County 1969).

[9]RC 2151.54.

[10]RC 2151.45.

[11]1945 OAG 509.

OHIO REVISED CODE
(Selected Provisions)

CHAPTER 2151

JUVENILE COURTS—GENERAL PROVISIONS

Publisher's Note: Until 1968, when the Modern Courts Amendment to the Ohio Constitution was adopted, Ohio court procedure was governed entirely by statute and case law. The Modern Courts Amendment required the Supreme Court of Ohio, subject to the approval of the General Assembly, to "prescribe rules governing practice and procedure in all courts of the state." Rules of practice and procedure are the Civil, Criminal, Appellate, and Juvenile Rules, Rules of the Court of Claims, and the Ohio Rules of Evidence. Pursuant to Ohio Constitution Article IV, Section 5(B), such rules "shall not abridge, enlarge, or modify any substantive right," and " [a]ll laws in conflict with such rules shall be of no further force or effect." Provisions of Chapter 2151 should be read with this in mind.

CONSTRUCTION; DEFINITIONS

Section

2151.01	Construction; purpose
2151.011	Definitions
2151.022	"Unruly child" defined
2151.03	"Neglected child" defined
2151.031	"Abused child" defined
2151.04	"Dependent child" defined
2151.05	Child without proper parental care
2151.06	Residence or legal settlement

ADMINISTRATION, OFFICIALS, AND JURISDICTION

2151.07	Creation and powers of juvenile court; assignment of judge
2151.08	Juvenile court in Hamilton county
2151.09	Separate building and site may be purchased or leased
2151.10	Appropriation for expenses of the court and maintenance of children; hearing; action in court of appeals; limitation of contempt power
2151.12	Clerk; judge as clerk; bond
2151.13	Employees; compensation; bond
2151.14	Duties and powers of probation department; records; command assistance; notice to victim of accused sex offender's communicable disease; order to provide copies of records
2151.141	Requests for copies of records
2151.142	Confidentiality of residential addresses; exceptions
2151.15	Powers and duties vested in county department of probation
2151.151	Juvenile court may contract for services to children on probation
2151.152	Agreement to reimburse juvenile court for foster care maintenance costs and associated administrative and training costs
2151.16	Referees; powers and duties

Section

2151.17	Rules governing practice and procedure
2151.18	Records of cases; annual report
2151.19	Summons; expense
2151.20	Seal of court; dimensions
2151.21	Jurisdiction in contempt
2151.211	Employee's attendance at proceeding; employer may not penalize
2151.22	Terms of court; sessions
2151.23	Jurisdiction of juvenile court; orders for child support
2151.231	Action for child support order
2151.232	Action for child support order before acknowledgment becomes final
2151.24	Separate room for hearings

PRACTICE AND PROCEDURE

2151.27	Complaint
2151.271	Transfer to juvenile court of another county
2151.28	Summons
2151.281	Guardian ad litem
2151.29	Service of summons
2151.30	Issuance of warrant
2151.31	Apprehension, custody, and detention
2151.311	Procedure upon apprehension
2151.312	Place of detention
2151.313	Fingerprinting or photographing child in an investigation
2151.314	Detention hearing
2151.32	Selection of custodian
2151.33	Temporary care; emergency medical treatment; reimbursement
2151.331	Detention in certified foster home; arrangement for temporary care; alternative diversion programs

HEARING AND DISPOSITION

2151.35	Hearing procedure; findings; record
2151.352	Right to counsel

Section

2151.353 Disposition of abused, neglected, or dependent child

2151.354 Disposition of unruly child; driver's license suspension; habitual truants

2151.355 Repealed

2151.355 Disposition where child adjudicated delinquent (second version)

2151.357 Cost of education

2151.358 Under what conditions records are to be sealed or expunged; procedures; effects; offense of divulging confidential information

2151.359 Control of conduct of parent, guardian, or custodian; contempt

2151.3510 Notice of intended dispositional order

2151.3514 Orders requiring alcohol and drug addiction assessment, treatment, and testing of parents or caregivers

2151.3515 Definitions

2151.3516 Persons authorized to take possession of deserted child

2151.3517 Duties of persons taking possession of deserted child

2151.3518 Duties of public children services agencies

2151.3519 Emergency hearings; adjudications

2151.3520 Temporary custody orders

2151.3521 Deserted child treated as neglected child

2151.3522 Case plans, investigations, administrative reviews, and services

2151.3523 Immunity from criminal liability; exceptions

2151.3524 Anonymity of parent; exceptions

2151.3525 Completion of medical information forms by parents

2151.3526 Refusal of parents to accept written materials

2151.3527 Coercion prohibited

2151.3528 DNA testing of parents

2151.3529 Medical information forms; written materials

2151.3530 Distribution of forms and materials by job and family services department

2151.36 Support of child

2151.361 Payment for care, support, maintenance, and education of child

2151.37 Institution receiving children required to make report

2151.38 Temporary nature of dispositional orders

2151.39 Placement of children from other states

2151.40 Cooperation with court

GENERAL PROVISIONS

2151.412 Case plans

2151.413 Motion for permanent custody

2151.414 Procedures upon motion

2151.415 Motions for dispositional orders; procedure

Section

2151.416 Administrative review of case plans

2151.417 Review by court issuing dispositional orders

2151.419 Hearings on efforts of agencies to prevent removal of children from homes

2151.42 Modification or termination of dispositional order

2151.421 Persons required to report injury or neglect; procedures on receipt of report

2151.422 Investigations concerning children in domestic violence or homeless shelters; services; custody; confidentiality of information

2151.424 Notice of dispositional hearings

ADULT CASES

2151.43 Charges against adults; defendant bound over to grand jury

2151.44 Complaint after hearing

2151.49 Suspension of sentence

2151.50 Forfeiture of bond

2151.52 Appeals on questions of law

2151.53 Physical and mental examinations; records of examination; expenses

FEES AND COSTS

2151.54 Fees and costs; waiver

2151.541 Additional fees for computer services

PLACEMENT OF CHILDREN IN FOSTER HOMES OUTSIDE COUNTIES OF RESIDENCE

2151.55 Persons entitled to oral communication of intended placement

2151.551 Requirements of oral communication of intended placement

2151.552 Time for provision of written information

2151.553 School district procedures for receiving information

2151.554 Provision of written information to juvenile court

INTERSTATE COMPACT ON JUVENILES

2151.56 Interstate compact on juveniles

2151.57 Compact administrator; powers and duties

2151.58 Supplementary agreements

2151.59 Discharge of financial obligations

2151.60 Enforcement by agencies of state and subdivisions

2151.61 Additional article

FACILITIES FOR TRAINING, TREATMENT, AND REHABILITATION OF JUVENILES

2151.65 Facilities for treatment of juveniles; joint boards; admission

2151.651 Application for financial assistance for acquisition or construction of facilities

2151.653 Program of education; teachers

Section

2151.654　Agreements for admission of children from counties not maintaining facilities

2151.655　County taxing authority may submit securities issue to electors for support of schools, detention homes, forestry camps, or other facilities

2151.66　Annual tax assessments

2151.67　Receipt and use of gifts, grants, devises, bequests and public moneys

2151.68　Board of trustees

2151.69　Board meetings; compensation

2151.70　Appointment of superintendent; bond; compensation; duties

2151.71　Operation of facilities

2151.72　Selection of site for district facility

2151.73　Apportionment of trustees; executive committee

2151.74　Removal of trustee

2151.75　Interim duties of trustees; trustees fund; reports

2151.76　Authority for choice, construction, and furnishing of district facility

2151.77　Capital and current expenses of district

2151.78　Withdrawal of county from district; continuity of district tax levy

2151.79　Designation of fiscal officer of district; duties of county auditors

2151.80　Expenses of members of boards of county commissioners

INDEPENDENT LIVING SERVICES

2151.81　Definitions

2151.82　Independent living services

2151.83　Joint agreement for provision of independent living services

2151.84　Model agreements

MISCELLANEOUS PROVISIONS

2151.85　Minor female's complaint for abortion; hearing; appeal

2151.86　Criminal records check; disqualification from employment

2151.87　Prohibitions relating to cigarettes or tobacco products

PENALTIES

2151.99　Penalties

Uncodified Law

2000 S 179, § 10, eff. 4–9–01, reads:

The General Assembly hereby states its intention to do the following in the remainder of the 123rd General Assembly and in the 124th General Assembly:

(A) Address the issue of competency in juvenile proceedings and its various aspects;

(B) Review and continue to support the RECLAIM Ohio program and the alternative schools program;

(C) Review and address the anticipated costs of implementing this act.

1997 H 215, § 163, eff. 6–30–97, reads:

The General Assembly hereby requests that the Supreme Court adopt, pursuant to its authority under Ohio Constitution, Article IV, Section 5, rules governing procedure in juvenile courts of the state that address the placement of children in foster homes in a county other than the county in which the child resided at the time of the removal.

Comparative Laws

Ariz.—A.R.S.　§ 8-201 et seq.
Minn.—M.S.A.　§ 260.011 et seq.
N.D.—NDCC 27–20–01 et seq.
Va.—Code 1950, § 16.1–226 et seq.
Wyo.—Wyo.Stat.Ann., § 14–6–201.

Cross References

Adoption, search of putative father registry prior to adoption, exemptions, 3107.064

Affidavit of disqualification for prejudice filed against judge, powers pending resolution, 2701.03

Birth parent or sibling's request for assistance in finding adoptee's name by adoption, requirements, 3107.49

Common pleas courts; probate and other divisions; jurisdiction, O Const Art IV §4

County children services boards, powers and duties, 5153.16

County public children services agencies, emergency assistance and funding, 5153.165

Courts of record, premature judgment deemed clerical error, 2701.18

Curfew for persons under eighteen, 307.71

Cuyahoga county juvenile court, jurisdiction and powers, 2153.16

Deception to obtain matter harmful to juveniles, 2907.33

Department of youth services, powers and duties, 5139.04

Factors to consider in felony sentencing, 2929.12

Guardianship of mentally retarded minors, 5123.93

Job and family services department, payments for services to children, 5101.14

Humane societies, protection of children, 1717.14

Judges of the division of domestic relations, certain counties; juvenile court powers, 2301.03

Judicial power vested in courts, O Const Art IV §1

Juvenile court jurisdiction over juvenile capital facilities, 307.021

Minor employees, conditions on employment, 4109.08

Parent convicted of killing other parent, termination of custody order deemed new complaint for institutional custody, 3109.46

Rules of criminal procedure; scope, applicability, construction, exceptions, Crim R 1

Rules of juvenile procedure, Juv R 1 to 48

School pupils, withdrawal, habitual absence, suspension, or expulsion from school, notice to juvenile court judge, 3321.13

Townships, curfews for minors, violators, 505.89

Transfer of child to foster care facility, 5139.39

Transfer of children to correctional medical center, 5139.06

Trial, magistrate courts, applicability to juveniles, 2938.02

Visitation rights, juvenile court powers not limited, 3109.051, 3109.11, 3109.12

When consent not required for adoption, 3107.07

Youth commission, powers with respect to children, 5139.05

Ohio Administrative Code References

Authority to assume and retain custody of a child, OAC 5101:2–42–04

Library References

Inclusion or exclusion of the day of birth in computing one's age. 5 ALR2d 1143

Marriage as affecting jurisdiction of juvenile court over delinquent or dependent. 14 ALR2d 336

Homicide by juvenile as within jurisdiction of a juvenile court. 48 ALR2d 663

CONSTRUCTION; DEFINITIONS

2151.01   Construction; purpose

The sections in Chapter 2151. of the Revised Code, with the exception of those sections providing for the criminal prosecution of adults, shall be liberally interpreted and construed so as to effectuate the following purposes:

(A) To provide for the care, protection, and mental and physical development of children subject to Chapter 2151. of the Revised Code, whenever possible, in a family environment, separating the child from the child's parents only when necessary for the child's welfare or in the interests of public safety;

(B) To provide judicial procedures through which Chapters 2151. and 2152. of the Revised Code are executed and enforced, and in which the parties are assured of a fair hearing, and their constitutional and other legal rights are recognized and enforced.

(2000 S 179, § 3, eff. 1–1–02; 1969 H 320, eff. 11–19–69)

Historical and Statutory Notes

Ed. Note: Former 2151.01 repealed by 1969 H 320, eff. 11–19–69; 1953 H 1; GC 1639–1; see now 2151.011 for provisions analogous to former 2151.01.

Pre–1953 H 1 Amendments: 121 v 557

Amendment Note: 2000 S 179, § 3, eff. 1–1–02, rewrote this section, which prior thereto read:

"The sections in Chapter 2151. of the Revised Code, with the exception of those sections providing for the criminal prosecution of adults, shall be liberally interpreted and construed so as to effectuate the following purposes:

"(A) To provide for the care, protection, and mental and physical development of children subject to Chapter 2151. of the Revised Code;

"(B) To protect the public interest in removing the consequences of criminal behavior and the taint of criminality from children committing delinquent acts and to substitute therefor a program of supervision, care, and rehabilitation;

"(C) To achieve the foregoing purposes, whenever possible, in a family environment, separating the child from its parents only when necessary for his welfare or in the interests of public safety;

"(D) To provide judicial procedures through which Chapter 2151. of the Revised Code is executed and enforced, and in which the parties are assured of a fair hearing, and their constitutional and other legal rights are recognized and enforced."

Cross References

Applicability and construction, Juv R 1

Authority of grandparent to execute caretaker authorization certificate, 3109.65.

Grandparents, form and content of power of attorney, 3109.53

Hearing, notice, de novo review, 3109.77

Intake, Juv R 9

Judges of the court of domestic relations, juvenile court responsibility, 2301.03

Judges of the divisions of domestic relations, 2301.03

Power of attorney, conditions determining execution of power by one or both parents, 3109.56

Power of attorney, notice to nonresidential parent and guardian, 3109.55.

Waiver of rights, Juv R 3

Library References

Infants ⬥12, 132.

Westlaw Topic No. 211.

C.J.S. Infants §§ 5, 6, 10, 32, 41, 43, 44, 95.

OJur 3d: 22, Courts and Judges § 18; 48, Family Law § 1531, 1636

Katz & Giannelli, Baldwin's Ohio Practice, Criminal Law § 119.2 (1996).

Carlin, Baldwin's Ohio Practice, Merrick–Rippner Probate Law § 104.3, 106.4, 107.1, 107.73, 107.84, 107.116, 108.10, 108.12, 108.26 (2003).

2151.011   Definitions

(A) As used in the Revised Code:

(1) "Juvenile court" means whichever of the following is applicable that has jurisdiction under this chapter and Chapter 2152. of the Revised Code:

(a) The division of the court of common pleas specified in section 2101.022 or 2301.03 of the Revised Code as having jurisdiction under this chapter and Chapter 2152. of the Revised Code or as being the juvenile division or the juvenile division combined with one or more other divisions;

(b) The juvenile court of Cuyahoga county or Hamilton county that is separately and independently created by section 2151.08 or Chapter 2153. of the Revised Code and that has jurisdiction under this chapter and Chapter 2152. of the Revised Code;

(c) If division (A)(1)(a) or (b) of this section does not apply, the probate division of the court of common pleas.

(2) "Juvenile judge" means a judge of a court having jurisdiction under this chapter.

(3) "Private child placing agency" means any association, as defined in section 5103.02 of the Revised Code, that is certified under section 5103.03 of the Revised Code to accept temporary, permanent, or legal custody of children and place the children for either foster care or adoption.

(4) "Private noncustodial agency" means any person, organization, association, or society certified by the department of job and family services that does not accept temporary or permanent legal custody of children, that is privately operated in this state, and that does one or more of the following:

(a) Receives and cares for children for two or more consecutive weeks;

(b) Participates in the placement of children in certified foster homes;

(c) Provides adoption services in conjunction with a public children services agency or private child placing agency.

(B) As used in this chapter:

(1) "Adequate parental care" means the provision by a child's parent or parents, guardian, or custodian of adequate food, clothing, and shelter to ensure the child's health and physical safety and the provision by a child's parent or parents of specialized services warranted by the child's physical or mental needs.

(2) "Adult" means an individual who is eighteen years of age or older.

(3) "Agreement for temporary custody" means a voluntary agreement authorized by section 5103.15 of the Revised Code that transfers the temporary custody of a child to a public children services agency or a private child placing agency.

(4) "Certified foster home" means a foster home, as defined in section 5103.02 of the Revised Code, certified under section 5103. 03 of the Revised Code.

(5) "Child" means a person who is under eighteen years of age, except that the juvenile court has jurisdiction over any person who is adjudicated an unruly child prior to attaining eighteen years of age until the person attains twenty-one years of age, and, for purposes of that jurisdiction related to that adjudication, a person who is so adjudicated an unruly child shall be deemed a "child" until the person attains twenty-one years of age.

(6) "Child day camp," "child day-care," "child day-care center," "part-time child day-care center," "type A family day-care home," "certified type B family day-care home," "type B home," "administrator of a child day-care center," "administrator of a type A family day-care home," "in-home aide," and "authorized provider" have the same meanings as in section 5104.01 of the Revised Code.

(7) "Child day-care provider" means an individual who is a child-care staff member or administrator of a child day-care center, a type A family day-care home, or a type B family day-care home, or an in-home aide or an individual who is licensed, is regulated, is approved, operates under the direction of, or otherwise is certified by the department of job and family services, department of mental retardation and developmental disabilities, or the early childhood programs of the department of education.

(8) "Chronic truant" has the same meaning as in section 2152.02 of the Revised Code.

(9) "Commit" means to vest custody as ordered by the court.

(10) "Counseling" includes both of the following:

(a) General counseling services performed by a public children services agency or shelter for victims of domestic violence to assist a child, a child's parents, and a child's siblings in alleviating identified problems that may cause or have caused the child to be an abused, neglected, or dependent child.

(b) Psychiatric or psychological therapeutic counseling services provided to correct or alleviate any mental or emotional illness or disorder and performed by a licensed psychiatrist, licensed psychologist, or a person licensed under Chapter 4757. of the Revised Code to engage in social work or professional counseling.

(11) "Custodian" means a person who has legal custody of a child or a public children services agency or private child placing agency that has permanent, temporary, or legal custody of a child.

(12) "Delinquent child" has the same meaning as in section 2152.02 of the Revised Code.

(13) "Detention" means the temporary care of children pending court adjudication or disposition, or execution of a court order, in a public or private facility designed to physically restrict the movement and activities of children.

(14) "Developmental disability" has the same meaning as in section 5123. 01 of the Revised Code.

(15) "Foster caregiver" has the same meaning as in section 5103.02 of the Revised Code.

(16) "Guardian" means a person, association, or corporation that is granted authority by a probate court pursuant to Chapter 2111. of the Revised Code to exercise parental rights over a child to the extent provided in the court's order and subject to the residual parental rights of the child's parents.

(17) "Habitual truant" means any child of compulsory school age who is absent without legitimate excuse for absence from the public school the child is supposed to attend for five or more consecutive school days, seven or more school days in one school month, or twelve or more school days in a school year.

(18) "Juvenile traffic offender" has the same meaning as in section 2152.02 of the Revised Code.

(19) "Legal custody" means a legal status that vests in the custodian the right to have physical care and control of the child and to determine where and with whom the child shall live, and the right and duty to protect, train, and discipline the child and to provide the child with food, shelter, education, and medical care, all subject to any residual parental rights, privileges, and responsibilities. An individual granted legal custody shall exercise the rights and responsibilities personally unless otherwise authorized by any section of the Revised Code or by the court.

(20) A "legitimate excuse for absence from the public school the child is supposed to attend" includes, but is not limited to, any of the following:

(a) The fact that the child in question has enrolled in and is attending another public or nonpublic school in this or another state;

(b) The fact that the child in question is excused from attendance at school for any of the reasons specified in section 3321.04 of the Revised Code;

(c) The fact that the child in question has received an age and schooling certificate in accordance with section 3331.01 of the Revised Code.

(21) "Mental illness" and "mentally ill person subject to hospitalization by court order" have the same meanings as in section 5122.01 of the Revised Code.

(22) "Mental injury" means any behavioral, cognitive, emotional, or mental disorder in a child caused by an act or omission that is described in section 2919.22 of the Revised Code and is committed by the parent or other person responsible for the child's care.

(23) "Mentally retarded person" has the same meaning as in section 5123. 01 of the Revised Code.

(24) "Nonsecure care, supervision, or training" means care, supervision, or training of a child in a facility that does not confine or prevent movement of the child within the facility or from the facility.

(25) "Of compulsory school age" has the same meaning as in section 3321. 01 of the Revised Code.

(26) "Organization" means any institution, public, semipublic, or private, and any private association, society, or agency located or operating in the state, incorporated or unincorporated, having among its functions the furnishing of protective services or care for children, or the placement of children in certified foster homes or elsewhere.

(27) "Out-of-home care" means detention facilities, shelter facilities, certified foster homes, placement in a prospective adoptive home prior to the issuance of a final decree of adoption, organizations, certified organizations, child day-care centers, type A family day-care homes, child day-care provided by type B family day-care home providers and by in-home aides, group home providers, group homes, institutions, state institutions, residential facilities, residential care facilities, residential camps, day camps, public schools, chartered nonpublic schools, educational service centers, hospitals, and medical clinics that are responsible for the care, physical custody, or control of children.

(28) "Out-of-home care child abuse" means any of the following when committed by a person responsible for the care of a child in out-of-home care:

(a) Engaging in sexual activity with a child in the person's care;

(b) Denial to a child, as a means of punishment, of proper or necessary subsistence, education, medical care, or other care necessary for a child's health;

(c) Use of restraint procedures on a child that cause injury or pain;

(d) Administration of prescription drugs or psychotropic medication to the child without the written approval and ongoing supervision of a licensed physician;

(e) Commission of any act, other than by accidental means, that results in any injury to or death of the child in out-of-home care or commission of any act by accidental means that results in an injury to or death of a child in out-of-home care and that is at variance with the history given of the injury or death.

(29) "Out-of-home care child neglect" means any of the following when committed by a person responsible for the care of a child in out-of-home care:

(a) Failure to provide reasonable supervision according to the standards of care appropriate to the age, mental and physical condition, or other special needs of the child;

(b) Failure to provide reasonable supervision according to the standards of care appropriate to the age, mental and physical condition, or other special needs of the child, that results in sexual or physical abuse of the child by any person;

(c) Failure to develop a process for all of the following:

(i) Administration of prescription drugs or psychotropic drugs for the child;

(ii) Assuring that the instructions of the licensed physician who prescribed a drug for the child are followed;

(iii) Reporting to the licensed physician who prescribed the drug all unfavorable or dangerous side effects from the use of the drug.

(d) Failure to provide proper or necessary subsistence, education, medical care, or other individualized care necessary for the health or well-being of the child;

(e) Confinement of the child to a locked room without monitoring by staff;

(f) Failure to provide ongoing security for all prescription and nonprescription medication;

(g) Isolation of a child for a period of time when there is substantial risk that the isolation, if continued, will impair or retard the mental health or physical well-being of the child.

(30) "Permanent custody" means a legal status that vests in a public children services agency or a private child placing agency, all parental rights, duties, and obligations, including the right to consent to adoption, and divests the natural parents or adoptive parents of all parental rights, privileges, and obligations, including all residual rights and obligations.

(31) "Permanent surrender" means the act of the parents or, if a child has only one parent, of the parent of a child, by a voluntary agreement authorized by section 5103.15 of the Revised Code, to transfer the permanent custody of the child to a public children services agency or a private child placing agency.

(32) "Person responsible for a child's care in out-of-home care" means any of the following:

(a) Any foster caregiver, in-home aide, or provider;

(b) Any administrator, employee, or agent of any of the following: a public or private detention facility; shelter facility; organization; certified organization; child day-care center; type A family day-care home; certified type B family day-care home; group home; institution; state institution; residential facility; residential care facility; residential camp; day camp; school district; community school; chartered nonpublic school; educational service center; hospital; or medical clinic;

(c) Any person who supervises or coaches children as part of an extracurricular activity sponsored by a school district, public school, or chartered nonpublic school;

(d) Any other person who performs a similar function with respect to, or has a similar relationship to, children.

(33) "Physically impaired" means having one or more of the following conditions that substantially limit one or more of an individual's major life activities, including self-care, receptive and expressive language, learning, mobility, and self-direction:

(a) A substantial impairment of vision, speech, or hearing;

(b) A congenital orthopedic impairment;

(c) An orthopedic impairment caused by disease, rheumatic fever or any other similar chronic or acute health problem, or amputation or another similar cause.

(34) "Placement for adoption" means the arrangement by a public children services agency or a private child placing agency with a person for the care and adoption by that person of a child of whom the agency has permanent custody.

(35) "Placement in foster care" means the arrangement by a public children services agency or a private child placing agency for the out-of-home care of a child of whom the agency has temporary custody or permanent custody.

(36) "Planned permanent living arrangement" means an order of a juvenile court pursuant to which both of the following apply:

(a) The court gives legal custody of a child to a public children services agency or a private child placing agency without the termination of parental rights.

(b) The order permits the agency to make an appropriate placement of the child and to enter into a written agreement with a foster care provider or with another person or agency with whom the child is placed.

(37) "Practice of social work" and "practice of professional counseling" have the same meanings as in section 4757.01 of the Revised Code.

(38) "Sanction, service, or condition" means a sanction, service, or condition created by court order following an adjudication that a child is an unruly child that is described in division (A)(4) of section 2152.19 of the Revised Code.

(39) "Protective supervision" means an order of disposition pursuant to which the court permits an abused, neglected, dependent, or unruly child to remain in the custody of the child's parents, guardian, or custodian and stay in the child's home, subject to any conditions and limitations upon the child, the child's parents, guardian, or custodian, or any other person that the court prescribes, including supervision as directed by the court for the protection of the child.

(40) "Psychiatrist" has the same meaning as in section 5122.01 of the Revised Code.

(41) "Psychologist" has the same meaning as in section 4732.01 of the Revised Code.

(42) "Residential camp" means a program in which the care, physical custody, or control of children is accepted overnight for recreational or recreational and educational purposes.

(43) "Residential care facility" means an institution, residence, or facility that is licensed by the department of mental health under section 5119.22 of the Revised Code and that provides care for a child.

(44) "Residential facility" means a home or facility that is licensed by the department of mental retardation and developmental disabilities under section 5123.19 of the Revised Code and in which a child with a developmental disability resides.

(45) "Residual parental rights, privileges, and responsibilities" means those rights, privileges, and responsibilities remaining with the natural parent after the transfer of legal custody of the child, including, but not necessarily limited to, the privilege of reasonable visitation, consent to adoption, the privilege to determine the child's religious affiliation, and the responsibility for support.

(46) "School day" means the school day established by the state board of education pursuant to section 3313.48 of the Revised Code.

(47) "School month" and "school year" have the same meanings as in section 3313.62 of the Revised Code.

(48) "Secure correctional facility" means a facility under the direction of the department of youth services that is designed to physically restrict the movement and activities of children and used for the placement of children after adjudication and disposition.

(49) "Sexual activity" has the same meaning as in section 2907.01 of the Revised Code.

(50) "Shelter" means the temporary care of children in physically unrestricted facilities pending court adjudication or disposition.

(51) "Shelter for victims of domestic violence" has the same meaning as in section 3113.33 of the Revised Code.

(52) "Temporary custody" means legal custody of a child who is removed from the child's home, which custody may be terminated at any time at the discretion of the court or, if the legal custody is granted in an agreement for temporary custody, by the person who executed the agreement.

(C) For the purposes of this chapter, a child shall be presumed abandoned when the parents of the child have failed to visit or maintain contact with the child for more than ninety days, regardless of whether the parents resume contact with the child after that period of ninety days.

(2004 H 106, eff. 9–16–04; 2002 H 400, eff. 4–3–03; 2000 S 179, § 3, eff. 1–1–02; 2000 H 332, eff. 1–1–01; 2000 H 448, eff. 10–5–00; 2000 S 181, eff. 9–4–00; 1999 H 470, eff. 7–1–00; 1998 H 484, eff. 3–18–99; 1998 S 212, eff. 9–30–98; 1997 H 408, eff. 10–1–97; 1996 S 223, eff. 3–18–97; 1996 H 124, eff. 3–31–97; 1996 H 265, eff. 3–3–97; 1996 H 274, § 4, eff. 8–8–96; 1996 H 274, § 1, eff. 8–8–96; 1995 S 2, eff. 7–1–96; 1995 H 1, eff. 1–1–96; 1994 H 715, eff. 7–22–94; 1993 S 21, eff. 10–29–93; 1993 H 152, eff. 7–1–93; 1992 H 356; 1991 H 155; 1990 H 38; 1989 H 257; 1988 H 403)

Uncodified Law

1996 H 445, § 3: See Uncodified Law under 2151.14.

1995 H 1, § 3, eff. 1–1–96, reads in part: (B) The General Assembly hereby declares that its purpose in enacting the language in division (B) of section 2151.011 and divisions (B) and (C) of section 2151.26 of the Revised Code that exists on and after the effective date of this act is to overrule the holding in **State v. Adams** (1982), 69 Ohio St. 2d 120, regarding the effect of binding a child over for trial as an adult.

Historical and Statutory Notes

Ed. Note: Former 2151.011 repealed by 1988 H 403, eff. 1–1–89; 1988 S 89, H 399; 1986 H 428; 1983 S 210; 1981 H 440; 1980 H 695; 1969 H 320.

Ed. Note: Former 2151.011 contained provisions analogous to former 2151.01 repealed by 1969 H 320, eff. 11–19–69.

Amendment Note: 2004 H 106 inserted "public schools, chartered nonpublic schools, educational service centers," in division (B)(27); "school district; community school; chartered nonpublic school; educational service center;" in division (B)(32)(a); "Any person who supervises or coaches children as part of an extracurricular activity sponsored by a school district, public school, or chartered nonpublic school;" in division (B)(32)(c); and redesignated former (B)(32)(c) as new division (B)(32)(d).

Amendment Note: 2002 H 400 substituted "(4)" for "(3)" in division (B)(38).

Amendment Note: 2000 S 179, § 3, eff. 1–1–02, rewrote this section. See *Baldwin's Ohio Legislative Service Annotated*, 2000, page 11/L-3601, or the OH-LEGIS or OH-LEGIS-OLD database on WESTLAW, for prior version of this section.

Amendment Note: 2000 H 332 substituted "under" for "pursuant to" in division (A)(3) and "certified" for "family" in division (A)(4)(b); deleted former division (B)(4), (B)(14), (B)15) and (B)(27); redesignated former divisions (B)(5) to (B)(46) as new divisions (B)(4) to (B)(43); deleted "family" before "foster" twice and substituted "as defined in

section 5103.02 of the Revised Code, certified" for "operated by persons holding a certificate in force, issued" in new division (B)(4); substituted "(5)" for "(6)" throughout new division (B)(5); deleted "foster homes" after "shelter facilities" in former division (B)(23); and added new division (B)(29). Prior to deletion former divisions (B)(4), (B)(14), (B)(15) and (B)(27) read:

"(4)'Babysitting care' means care provided for a child while the parents, guardian, or legal custodian of the child are temporarily away.

"(14)'Family foster home' means a private residence in which children are received apart from their parents, guardian, or legal custodian by an individual for hire, gain, or reward for nonsecure care, supervision, or training twenty four hours a day. 'Family foster home' does not include babysitting care provided for a child in the home of a person other then the home of the parents, guardian, or legal custodian of the child.

"(15)'Foster home' means a family home in which any child is received apart from the child's parents for care, supervision, or training

"(27)'Planned permanent living arrangement' means an order of a juvenile court pursuant to which both of the following apply:

"(a)The court gives legal custody of a child to a public children services agency or a private child placing agency without the termination of parental rights.

"(b)The order permits the agency to make an appropriate placement of the child and to enter into a written agreement with a foster care provider or with another person or agency with whom the child is placed."

Amendment Note: 2000 H 448 substituted "certified" for "family" in division (A)(4)(b); deleted former divisions (B)(4), (B)(14), (B)(27); redesignated former divisions (B)(5) to (B)(46) as new divisions (B)(4) to (B)(44); rewrote former division (B)(5); substituted "(5)" for "(6)" throughout new division (B)(5); rewrote former division (B)(15); inserted "certified" in new division (20); deleted "foster homes" in new division (B)(21); substituted "caregiver" for "parent" in new division (B)(26); and added new division (B)(30). Prior to deletion or amendment, division (B)(4), (B)(5), (B)(14), (B)(15) and (B)(27) read:

"(4) 'Babysitting care' means care provided for a child while the parents, guardian, or legal custodian of the child are temporarily away.

"(5) 'Certified family foster home' means a family foster home operated by persons holding a certificate in force, issued under section 5103.03 of the Revised Code.

"(14) 'Family foster home' means a private residence in which children are received apart from their parents, guardian, or legal custodian by an individual for hire, gain, or reward for nonsecure care, supervision, or training twenty-four hours a day. 'Family foster home' does not include babysitting care provided for a child in the home of a person other than the home of the parents, guardian, or legal custodian of the child.

"(15) 'Foster home' means a family home in which any child is received apart from the child's parents for care, supervision, or training.

"(27) 'Planned permanent living arrangement' means an order of a juvenile court pursuant to which both of the following apply:

"(a) The court gives legal custody of a child to a public children services agency or a private child placing agency without the termination of parental rights.

"(b) The order permits the agency to make an appropriate placement of the child and to enter into a written agreement with a foster care provider or with another person or agency with whom the child is placed."

Amendment Note: 2000 S 181 added new division (B)(9); redesignated former divisions (B)(9) through (B)(16) as new divisions (B)(10) through (B)(17); added new division (B)(18); redesignated former divisions (B)(17) and (B)(18) as new divisions (B)(19) and (B)(20); added new division (B)(20); redesignated former divisions (B)(18) through (B)(21) as new divisions (B)(21) through (B)(24); added new division (B)(25); redesignated former divisions (B)(22) through (B)(41) as new divisions (B)(26) through (B)(45); added new divisions (B)(46) and (B)(47); and redesignated former divisions (B)(42) through (B)(46) as new divisions (B)(48) through (B)(52).

Amendment Note: 1999 H 470 substituted "section 5103.03" for "sections 5103.03 to 5103.05" in division (A)(3); and substituted "job and family" for "human" in division (A)(4).

Amendment Note: 1998 S 212 substituted "mentally" for "mental" in division (B)(19); substituted "in foster care" for "for adoption" in division (B)(32); and rewrote division (B)(38), which prior to amendment read:

"(38) 'Residential camp' means a public or private facility that engages or accepts the care, physical custody, or control of children during summer months and that is licensed, regulated, approved, operated under the direction of, or otherwise certified by the department of health for the American camping association."

Amendment Note: 1998 H 484 deleted former division (B)(18); redesignated former division (B)(19) through (B)(27) as new divisions (B)(18) through (B)(26); and added new division (B)(27). Prior to deletion, former division (B)(18) read:

"(18) 'Long–term foster care' means an order of a juvenile court pursuant to which both of the following apply:

"(a) Legal custody of a child is given to a public children services agency or a private child placing agency without the termination of parental rights.

"(b) The agency is permitted to make an appropriate placement of the child and to enter into a written long-term foster care agreement with a foster care provider or with another person or agency with whom the child is placed."

Amendment Note: 1997 H 408 rewrote this section; see *Baldwin's Ohio Legislative Service Annotated,* 1997, p 7/L–764, or the OH–LEGIS or OH–LEGIS–OLD database on WESTLAW, for text of previous version.

Amendment Note: 1996 S 223 rewrote division (B)(29); deleted former divisions (B)(33) and (B)(34); redesignated former divisions (B)(35) through (B)(52) as divisions (B)(33) through (B)(50); substituted "Practice of social work" for "Social work" in division (B)(33); and made other nonsubstantive changes. Prior to amendment, division (B)(29), and former divisions (B)(33) and (B)(34), read, respectively:

"(29) 'Therapeutic counseling' means psychiatric or psychological services performed by a licensed psychiatrist or psychologist, a licensed or certified social worker, or licensed professional counselor to correct or alleviate any mental or emotional handicap or disorder of a person."

"(33) 'Social worker' means any person who is licensed or certified under Chapter 4757. of the Revised Code to engage in social work.

"(34) 'Licensed professional counselor' means any person who is licensed under Chapter 4757. of the Revised Code to engage in the practice of professional counseling."

Amendment Note: 1996 H 124 rewrote division (B)(1), which prior thereto read:

"(1)(a) 'Child' means a person who is under eighteen years of age, except that any person who violates a federal or state law or municipal ordinance prior to attaining eighteen years of age shall be deemed a "child" irrespective of that person's age at the time the complaint is filed or the hearing on the complaint is held and except that any person whose case is transferred for criminal prosecution pursuant to division (B) or (C) of section 2151.26 of the Revised Code and subsequently is convicted in that case shall after the transfer be deemed not to be a child in any of the following cases:

"(i) The transferred case;

"(ii) A case in which the person is alleged to have committed prior to the transfer an act that would be an offense if committed by an adult;

"(iii) A case in which the person is alleged to have committed subsequent to the transfer an act that would be an offense if committed by an adult.

"(b) Divisions (B)(1)(a)(ii) and (iii) of this section apply to a case regardless of whether the prior or subsequent act that is alleged in the case and that would be an offense if committed by an adult allegedly was committed in the same county in which the case was transferred or in another county and regardless of whether the complaint in the case involved was filed in the same county in which the case was transferred or in another county. Division (B)(1)(a)(ii) of this section applies to a case only when the prior act alleged in the case has not been disposed of by a juvenile court or trial court."

Amendment Note: 1996 H 265 rewrote division (B)(3); and added division (B)(55). Prior to amendment, division (B)(3) read:

"(3) 'Detention' means the temporary care of children in restricted facilities pending court adjudication or disposition."

Amendment Note: 1996 H 274, § 1, eff. 8–8–96, inserted "family" before "foster home operated by" in division (B)(6); substituted "illness" for "handicap" in division (B)(29); substituted "children" for "no more than five children, or in which all the children in a sibling group," in division (B)(48); added divisions (B)(53), (B)(54), and (C); and made changes to reflect gender neutral language.

Amendment Note: 1996 H 274, § 4, eff. 8–8–96, harmonized the versions of this section as amended by 1995 S 2, § 1, eff. 7–1–96, and 1996 H 274, § 1, eff. 8–8–96; and deleted division (C), which prior thereto read:

"(C) This is an interim section effective until July 1, 1996."

Amendment Note: 1995 S 2 deleted ", an aggravated felony of the first or second degree," from and inserted ", or third" in division (B)(1); and made changes to reflect gender neutral language.

Amendment Note: 1995 H 1 rewrote division (B)(1); and made changes to reflect gender neutral language and other nonsubstantive changes. Prior to amendment, division (B)(1) read:

"(1) "Child" means a person who is under the age of eighteen years, except that any person who violates a federal or state law or municipal ordinance prior to attaining eighteen years of age shall be deemed a "child" irrespective of his age at the time the complaint is filed or the hearing on the complaint is held and except that any person whose case is transferred for criminal prosecution pursuant to section 2151.26 of the Revised Code and is subsequently convicted in that case shall after the transfer be deemed not to be a child in any case in which he is alleged to have committed an act that if committed by an adult would constitute murder or aggravated murder, an aggravated felony of the first or second degree, or a felony of the first or second degree."

Amendment Note: 1993 H 152 inserted "family", changed "permit" to "certificate", and changed a reference to sections 5103.03 to 5103.05 to a reference to section 5103.03, in division (B)(6); deleted former division (B)(7); redesignated former divisions (B)(8) through (50) as divisions (B)(7) through (49), respectively; deleted "approved foster care," prior to "placement" in division (B)(41); and added divisions (B)(50) through (B)(54). Prior to amendment, division (B)(7) read:

"(7) 'Approved foster care' means facilities approved by the department of youth services under section 5139.37 of the Revised Code.";

Amendment Note: 1993 S 21 deleted "and 'mentally retarded person subject to institutionalization by court order' have" from division (B)(20); substituted "5123.01" for "5123.19" in division (B)(44); removed former divisions (B)(46) and (47), which duplicated divisions (B)(21) and (20), respectively; and redesignated former divisions (B)(48) through (50) as divisions (B)(46) through (48), respectively.

Amendment Note: 1994 H 715 corrected the designations of divisions (B)(45) through (B)(52); and rewrote division (B)(50), which previously read:

"(52) 'Private noncustodial agency' means any person, organization, association, or society certified by the department of human services that does not accept temporary or permanent legal custody of children, that is privately operated in the state, that receives and cares for children for two or more consecutive weeks, and that participates in the placement of children in family foster homes or provides adoption services in conjunction with a public children services agency or private child placing agency."

Cross References

Additional definitions applicable to juvenile courts, Juv R 2

Body piercing and tattooing, custodian defined, 3730.01

Disability assistance, annual report of number of children requiring services from children services agency due to denial of, 5115.012

Foster parent or relative wanting to adopt child, permanent custody defined, 5103.161

Job and family services department, agreements to make payments to encourage adoptive placement of children with agencies, permanent custody defined, 5103.12

Infant hearing-impairment screening, custodian defined, 3701.503

Judges of the court of domestic relations, juvenile court responsibility, 2301.03

Juvenile court jurisdiction over juvenile capital facilities, 307.021

Obstructing justice, adult and child defined, 2921.32

Permanent exclusion of pupils, out-of-home care defined, 3313.662

Permanent exclusion of pupils, out-of-home care and legal custody defined, 3301.121, 3313.662

Power of attorney, certain pending actions prohibiting creation, 3109.58.

Procedure under Criminal Rules, exceptions, Crim R 1

Sex offender registration, notification of public children services agency, 2950.11

Social administration division, private child placing agency, private noncustodial agency, public children services agency, and treatment foster home defined, 5103.02

Voyeurism, babysitting care defined, 2907.08

Ohio Administrative Code References

Department of public welfare, social services, eligibility of child for subsidized adoption, OAC 5101:2–44–05

Library References

Infants ⟲12, 131.

Westlaw Topic No. 211.

C.J.S. Infants §§ 5, 6, 10, 31 to 54, 95.

OJur 3d: 22, Courts and Judges § 3, 18, 69; 28, Criminal Law § 2012; 48, Family Law § 1490, 1500 to 1503, 1535, 1561, 1566, 1734

Am Jur 2d: 47, Juvenile Courts and Delinquent and Dependent Children § 26, 27

Inclusion or exclusion of the day of birth in computing one's age. 5 ALR2d 1143

Age of child at time of alleged offense or delinquency, or at time of legal proceedings, as criterion of jurisdiction of juvenile court. 89 ALR2d 506

Baldwin's Ohio Legislative Service, 1988 Laws of Ohio, S 89—LSC Analysis, p 5–571

Gotherman & Babbit, Ohio Municipal Law, Text 27.05.

Adrine & Ruden, Ohio Domestic Violence Law (2002 Ed.), Text 12.11.

Carlin, Baldwin's Ohio Practice, Merrick–Rippner Probate Law § 104.11, 105.8, 105.9, 105.10, 106.1, 106.8, 106.11, 106.14, 106.17, 107.70, 107.74, 107.76, 107.77, 107.78, 107.79, 107.80, 107.82, 107.84, 107.108, 108.1 (2003).

2151.022 "Unruly child" defined

As used in this chapter, "unruly child" includes any of the following:

(A) Any child who does not submit to the reasonable control of the child's parents, teachers, guardian, or custodian, by reason of being wayward or habitually disobedient;

(B) Any child who is an habitual truant from school and who previously has not been adjudicated an unruly child for being an habitual truant;

(C) Any child who behaves in a manner as to injure or endanger the child's own health or morals or the health or morals of others;

(D) Any child who violates a law, other than division (A) of section 2923.211 or section 2151.87 of the Revised Code, that is applicable only to a child.

(2000 S 179, § 3, eff. 1–1–02; 2000 S 218, eff. 3–15–01; 2000 S 181, eff. 9–4–00; 1995 H 4, eff. 11–9–95; 1969 H 320, eff. 11–19–69)

Uncodified Law

1995 H 4, § 3, eff. 11–9–95, reads: Sections 2151.02, 2151.022, 2151.355, 2151.411, 2913.02, 2913.51, 2913.71, 2921.13, 2923.21, 2947.061, 2951.02, 2967.01, and 2967.15 of the Revised Code, as amended by this act, and sections 2923.211 and 2967.131 of the Revised Code, as enacted by this act, apply to any offense, delinquent act, or unruly act committed on or after the effective date of this act. Sections 2151.02, 2151.022, 2151.355, 2151.411, 2913.02, 2913.51, 2913.71, 2921.13, 2923.21, 2947.061, 2951.02, 2967.01, and 2967.15 of the Revised Code, as they existed immediately prior to the effective date of this act, apply to any offense, delinquent act, or unruly act committed before the effective date of this act.

Historical and Statutory Notes

Ed. Note: A special endorsement by the Legislative Service Commission states, "Comparison of these amendments [2000 S 179, § 3, eff. 1–1–02 and 2000 S 218, eff. 3–15–01] in pursuance of section 1.52 of the Revised Code discloses that they are not irreconcilable so that they are required by that section to be harmonized to give effect to each amendment." In recognition of this rule of construction, changes made by 2000 S 179, § 3, eff. 1–1–02 and 2000 S 218, eff. 3–15–01, have been incorporated in the above amendment. See *Baldwin's Ohio Legislative Service Annotated*, 2000, pages 11/L–3606 and 11/L–2881, or the OH–LEGIS or OH–LEGIS–OLD database on WESTLAW, for original versions of these Acts.

Amendment Note: 2000 S 179, § 3, eff. 1–1–02, rewrote this section, which prior thereto read:

"As used in this chapter, 'unruly child' includes any of the following:

"(A) Any child who does not subject the child's self to the reasonable control of the child's parents, teachers, guardian, or custodian, by reason of being wayward or habitually disobedient;

"(B) Any child who is persistently truant from home;

"(C) Any child who is an habitual truant from school and who previously has not been adjudicated an unruly child for being an habitual truant;

"(D) Any child who so deports the child's self as to injure or endanger the child's own health or morals or the health or morals of others;

"(E) Any child who attempts to enter the marriage relation in any state without the consent of the child's parents, custodian, or legal guardian or other legal authority;

"(F) Any child who is found in a disreputable place, visits or patronizes a place prohibited by law, or associates with vagrant, vicious, criminal, notorious, or immoral persons;

"(G) Any child who engages in an occupation prohibited by law or is in a situation dangerous to life or limb or injurious to the child's own health or morals or the health or morals of others;

"(H) Any child who violates a law, other than division (A) of section 2923.211 of the Revised Code, that is applicable only to a child."

Amendment Note: 2000 S 218 inserted "or section 2151.87" in division (H).

Amendment Note: 2000 S 181 substituted "persistently" for "an habitual", and deleted "or school" from the end of, division (B); added new division (C); redesignated former divisions (C) through (G) as new divisions (D) through (H); and made changes to reflect gender neutral language.

Amendment Note: 1995 H 4 substituted "this chapter" for "sections 2151.01 to 2151.54, inclusive, of the Revised Code" and "of the following:" for "child" in the first paragraph; substituted "Any child who" for "Who" in divisions (A) through (F); added "the health or morals of" to divisions (C) and (F); rewrote division (G), which formerly read "Who has violated a law applicable only to a child."; and made changes to reflect gender neutral language and other nonsubstantive changes throughout.

Cross References

Contributing to unruliness or delinquency, 2919.24
Right to counsel, guardian ad litem, Juv R 4
Standards of operation and construction for facilities for rehabilitation of delinquent juveniles, 5139.27
Waiver of rights, Juv R 3
Youth services department, unruly child defined, 5139.01

Library References

Infants ☞153.
Westlaw Topic No. 211.
C.J.S. Infants §§ 31 to 67.
OJur 3d: 26, Criminal Law § 859, 861; 29, Criminal Law § 3152, 3154; 48, Family Law § 1489, 1735
Marriage as affecting jurisdiction of juvenile court over delinquent or dependent. 14 ALR2d 336
Truancy as indicative of delinquency or incorrigibility, justifying commitment of infant or juvenile. 5 ALR4th 1211
Katz & Giannelli, Baldwin's Ohio Practice, Criminal Law § 109.13 (1996).
Carlin, Baldwin's Ohio Practice, Merrick–Rippner Probate Law § 106.8, 107.25, 107.137, 108.2 (2003).

2151.03   "Neglected child" defined

(A) As used in this chapter, "neglected child" includes any child:

(1) Who is abandoned by the child's parents, guardian, or custodian;

(2) Who lacks adequate parental care because of the faults or habits of the child's parents, guardian, or custodian;

(3) Whose parents, guardian, or custodian neglects the child or refuses to provide proper or necessary subsistence, education, medical or surgical care or treatment, or other care necessary for the child's health, morals, or well being;

(4) Whose parents, guardian, or custodian neglects the child or refuses to provide the special care made necessary by the child's mental condition;

(5) Whose parents, legal guardian, or custodian have placed or attempted to place the child in violation of sections 5103.16 and 5103.17 of the Revised Code;

(6) Who, because of the omission of the child's parents, guardian, or custodian, suffers physical or mental injury that

harms or threatens to harm the child's health or welfare;

(7) Who is subjected to out-of-home care child neglect.

(B) Nothing in this chapter shall be construed as subjecting a parent, guardian, or custodian of a child to criminal liability when, solely in the practice of religious beliefs, the parent, guardian, or custodian fails to provide adequate medical or surgical care or treatment for the child. This division does not abrogate or limit any person's responsibility under section 2151.421 of the Revised Code to report known or suspected child abuse, known or suspected child neglect, and children who are known to face or are suspected of facing a threat of suffering abuse or neglect and does not preclude any exercise of the authority of the state, any political subdivision, or any court to ensure that medical or surgical care or treatment is provided to a child when the child's health requires the provision of medical or surgical care or treatment.

(1996 H 274, eff. 8–8–96; 1989 H 257, eff. 8–3–89; 1969 H 320; 1953 H 1; GC 1639–3)

Historical and Statutory Notes
Pre–1953 H 1 Amendments: 117 v 520

Amendment Note: 1996 H 274 substituted "adequate" for "proper" in division (A)(2); and made changes to reflect gender neutral language and other nonsubstantive changes.

Cross References
Duty of husband to support family, wife to assist, duration of duty to support, 3103.03
False report of child abuse or neglect, 2921.14
Nonsupport of dependents, 2919.21
Right to counsel, guardian ad litem, Juv R 4
Shared parenting, neglected child defined, 3109.04
Taking into custody, Juv R 6
Uniform child custody jurisdiction, neglected child defined, 3109.27
Visitation rights, effect of finding child neglected, 3109.051
Waiver of rights, Juv R 3

Library References
Infants ☞156.
Westlaw Topic No. 211.
C.J.S. Infants §§ 31 to 62.
OJur 3d: 27, Criminal Law § 1073; 47, Family Law § 1079, 1138; 48, Family Law § 1490, 1568, 1664, 1665, 1735
Am Jur 2d: 47, Juvenile Courts and Delinquent and Dependent Children § 24, 25
Inclusion or exclusion of the day of birth in computing one's age. 5 ALR2d 1143
Marriage as affecting jurisdiction of juvenile court over delinquent or dependent. 14 ALR2d 336
Parent's involuntary confinement, or failure to care for child as result thereof, as evincing neglect, unfitness, or the like in dependency or divestiture proceeding. 79 ALR3d 417

Adrine & Ruden, Ohio Domestic Violence Law (2002 Ed.), Text 8.5.
Carlin, Baldwin's Ohio Practice, Merrick–Rippner Probate Law § 98.15, 98.23, 105.7, 106.11, 106.17, 107.138, 108.16 (2003).

2151.031   "Abused child" defined

As used in this chapter, an "abused child" includes any child who:

(A) Is the victim of "sexual activity" as defined under Chapter 2907. of the Revised Code, where such activity would constitute an offense under that chapter, except that the court need not find that any person has been convicted of the offense in order to find that the child is an abused child;

(B) Is endangered as defined in section 2919.22 of the Revised Code, except that the court need not find that any person has been convicted under that section in order to find that the child is an abused child;

(C) Exhibits evidence of any physical or mental injury or death, inflicted other than by accidental means, or an injury or death which is at variance with the history given of it. Except as provided in division (D) of this section, a child exhibiting evidence of corporal punishment or other physical disciplinary measure by a parent, guardian, custodian, person having custody or control, or person in loco parentis of a child is not an abused child under this division if the measure is not prohibited under section 2919.22 of the Revised Code.

(D) Because of the acts of his parents, guardian, or custodian, suffers physical or mental injury that harms or threatens to harm the child's health or welfare.

(E) Is subjected to out-of-home care child abuse.

(1989 H 257, eff. 8–3–89; 1988 S 89; 1975 H 85)

Cross References
Domestic violence, defined, 3113.31
Endangering children (child abuse), 2919.22
Failure to report a felony, including child abuse, 2921.22
False report of child abuse or neglect, 2921.14
Prevention of child abuse and child neglect, 3109.13 to 3109.18
Requirement to report child abuse, 2151.421
Sexual activity, defined, 2907.01
Shared parenting, abused child defined, 3109.04
Uniform child custody jurisdiction, abused child defined, 3109.27
Visitation rights, effect of finding child abused, 3109.051

Library References

Infants ☞156.

Westlaw Topic No. 211.

C.J.S. Infants §§ 31 to 62.

OJur 3d: 47, Family Law § 1079, 1138, 1175; 48, Family Law § 1492, 1664, 1679, 1735

Sexual child abuser's civil liability to child's parent. 54 ALR4th 93

Baldwin's Ohio Legislative Service, 1988 Laws of Ohio, S 89—LSC Analysis, p 5–571

Adrine & Ruden, Ohio Domestic Violence Law (2002 Ed.), Text 8.5, 11.11.

Carlin, Baldwin's Ohio Practice, Merrick–Rippner Probate Law § 106.17, 107.138 (2003).

2151.04 "Dependent child" defined

As used in this chapter, "dependent child" means any child:

(A) Who is homeless or destitute or without adequate parental care, through no fault of the child's parents, guardian, or custodian;

(B) Who lacks adequate parental care by reason of the mental or physical condition of the child's parents, guardian, or custodian;

(C) Whose condition or environment is such as to warrant the state, in the interests of the child, in assuming the child's guardianship;

(D) To whom both of the following apply:

(1) The child is residing in a household in which a parent, guardian, custodian, or other member of the household committed an act that was the basis for an adjudication that a sibling of the child or any other child who resides in the household is an abused, neglected, or dependent child.

(2) Because of the circumstances surrounding the abuse, neglect, or dependency of the sibling or other child and the other conditions in the household of the child, the child is in danger of being abused or neglected by that parent, guardian, custodian, or member of the household.

(1996 H 274, eff. 8–8–96; 1988 S 89, eff. 1–1–89; 1969 H 320; 129 v 1778; 1953 H 1; GC 1639–4)

Historical and Statutory Notes

Pre–1953 H 1 Amendments: 117 v 520, § 1

Amendment Note: 1996 H 274 rewrote the section, which prior thereto read:

"As used in this chapter, "dependent child" includes any child:

"(A) Who is homeless or destitute or without proper care or support, through no fault of his parents, guardian, or custodian;

"(B) Who lacks proper care or support by reason of the mental or physical condition of his parents, guardian, or custodian;

"(C) Whose condition or environment is such as to warrant the state, in the interests of the child, in assuming his guardianship;

"(D) To whom both of the following apply:

"(1) He is residing in a household in which a parent, guardian, custodian, or other member of the household has abused or neglected a sibling of the child;

"(2) Because of the circumstances surrounding the abuse or neglect of the sibling and the other conditions in the household of the child, the child is in danger of being abused or neglected by that parent, guardian, custodian, or member of the household."

Cross References

Nonsupport of dependents, 2919.21

School attendance, juvenile court proceedings, 3321.22

Taking into custody, Juv R 6

Library References

Infants ☞154.1.

Westlaw Topic No. 211.

OJur 3d: 27, Criminal Law § 1073; 48, Family Law § 1494, 1495, 1497, 1677, 1735, 1746

Am Jur 2d: 47, Juvenile Courts and Delinquent and Dependent Children § 24, 25

Jurisdiction to award custody of child having legal domicile in another state. 4 ALR2d 7

Baldwin's Ohio Legislative Service, 1988 Laws of Ohio, S 89—LSC Analysis, p 5–571

Carlin, Baldwin's Ohio Practice, Merrick–Rippner Probate Law § 101.28, 105.7, 106.14, 106.17, 107.74, 107.138, 108.2 (2003).

2151.05 Child without proper parental care

Under sections 2151.01 to 2151.54 of the Revised Code, a child whose home is filthy and unsanitary; whose parents, stepparents, guardian, or custodian permit him to become dependent, neglected, abused, or delinquent; whose parents, stepparents, guardian, or custodian, when able, refuse or neglect to provide him with necessary care, support, medical attention, and educational facilities; or whose parents, stepparents, guardian, or custodian fail to subject such child to necessary discipline is without proper parental care or guardianship.

(1975 H 85, eff. 11–28–75; 1953 H 1; GC 1639–5)

Historical and Statutory Notes

Pre–1953 H 1 Amendments: 117 v 520, § 1

Cross References

Taking into custody, Juv R 6

Library References

Infants ☞154.1.

Westlaw Topic No. 211.

OJur 3d: 48, Family Law § 1493

Parent's mental deficiency as factor in termination of parental rights. 1 ALR5th 469

Parent's use of drugs as factor in award of custody of children, visitation rights, or termination of parental rights. 20 ALR5th 534

Carlin, Baldwin's Ohio Practice, Merrick–Rippner Probate Law § 106.11, 106.14, 108.1 (2003).

2151.06   Residence or legal settlement

Under sections 2151.01 to 2151.54, inclusive, of the Revised Code, a child has the same residence or legal settlement as his parents, legal guardian of his person, or his custodian who stands in the relation of loco parentis.

(1953 H 1, eff. 10–1–53; GC 1639–6)

Historical and Statutory Notes

Pre–1953 H 1 Amendments: 121 v 557; 117 v 520

Library References

Domicile ⟜1.

Westlaw Topic No. 135.

C.J.S. Domicile § 1 et seq.

OJur 3d: 36, Domicil § 10; 48, Family Law § 1585

ADMINISTRATION, OFFICIALS, AND JURISDICTION

2151.07   Creation and powers of juvenile court; assignment of judge

The juvenile court is a court of record within the court of common pleas. The juvenile court has and shall exercise the powers and jurisdiction conferred in Chapters 2151. and 2152. of the Revised Code.

Whenever the juvenile judge of the juvenile court is sick, is absent from the county, or is unable to attend court, or the volume of cases pending in court necessitates it, upon the request of the administrative juvenile judge, the presiding judge of the court of common pleas pursuant to division (DD) of section 2301.03 of the Revised Code shall assign a judge of any division of the court of common pleas of the county to act in the juvenile judge's place or in conjunction with the juvenile judge. If no judge of the court of common pleas is available for that purpose, the chief justice of the supreme court shall assign a judge of the court of common pleas, a juvenile judge, or a probate judge from a different county to act in the place of that juvenile judge or in conjunction with that juvenile judge. The assigned judge shall receive the compensation and expenses for so serving that is provided by law for judges assigned to hold court in courts of common pleas.

(2003 H 86, eff. 11–13–03; 2003 H 26, eff. 8–8–03; 2001 H 11, § 3, eff. 1–1–02; 2000 S 179, § 3, eff. 1–1–02; 1972 H 574, eff. 6–29–72; 1969 H 320; 127 v 847; 1953 H 1; GC 1639–7)

Historical and Statutory Notes

Ed. Note: Guidelines for Assignment of Judges were announced by the Chief Justice of the Ohio Supreme Court on 5–24–88, and revised 2–25–94 and 3–25–94, but not adopted as rules pursuant to O Const Art IV, §5. For the full text, see 37 OS(3d) xxxix, 61 OBar A–2 (6–13–88), and 69 OS(3d) xcix, 67 OBar xiii (4–18–94).

Pre–1953 H 1 Amendments: 122 v S 50

Amendment Note: 2003 H 86 substituted "(DD)" for "(CC)" in the second paragraph.

Amendment Note: 2003 H 26 substituted "(CC)" for "(BB)" in the second paragraph of the section.

Amendment Note: 2001 H 11, § 3 substituted "(BB)" for "(AA)".

Amendment Note: 2000 S 179, § 3, eff. 1–1–02, rewrote this section, which prior thereto read:

"The juvenile court is a court of record and within the division of domestic relations or probate of the court of common pleas, except that the juvenile courts of Cuyahoga county and Hamilton county shall be separate divisions of the court of common pleas. The juvenile court has and shall exercise the powers and jurisdiction conferred in sections 2151.01 to 2151.99 of the Revised Code.

"Whenever the juvenile judge of the juvenile court is absent from the county, or is unable to attend court, or the volume of cases pending in court necessitates it, upon the request of said judge, the presiding judge of the court of common pleas shall assign a judge of the court of common pleas of the county to act in his place or in conjunction with him. If no such judge is available for said purpose, the chief justice of the supreme court shall assign a judge of the court of common pleas, a juvenile judge, or a probate judge from some other county to act in the place of such judge or in conjunction with him, who shall receive such compensation and expenses for his services as is provided by law for judges assigned to hold court in courts of common pleas."

Cross References

Compensation and expenses of judges holding court outside county of residence, 141.07

Cuyahoga county juvenile court administrative judge shall be clerk of court, may appoint deputies and clerks, bonds, 2153.08

Library References

Courts ⟜175.

Judges ⟜29.

Westlaw Topic Nos. 106, 227.

C.J.S. Judges §§ 69, 70.

OJur 3d: 22, Courts and Judges § 14, 18, 71, 104, 105, 265; 48, Family Law § 1534

Am Jur 2d: 47, Juvenile Courts and Delinquent and Dependent Children § 2 to 6

Carlin, Baldwin's Ohio Practice, Merrick–Rippner Probate Law § 104.11, 104.20 (2003).

2151.08 Juvenile court in Hamilton county

In Hamilton county, the powers and jurisdiction of the juvenile court as conferred by Chapters 2151. and 2152. of the Revised Code shall be exercised by the judge of the court of common pleas whose term begins on January 1, 1957, and that judge's successors and by the judge of the court of common pleas whose term begins on February 14, 1967, and that judge's successors as provided by section 2301.03 of the Revised Code. This conferral of powers and jurisdiction on the specified judges shall be deemed a creation of a separately and independently created and established juvenile court in Hamilton county, Ohio. The specified judges shall serve in each and every position where the statutes permit or require a juvenile judge to serve.

(2000 S 179, § 3, eff. 1–1–02; 131 v H 165, eff. 11–16–65; 127 v 84)

Historical and Statutory Notes

Ed. Note: Former 2151.08 repealed by 126 v 778, eff. 10–11–55; 1953 H 1; GC 1639–8.

Pre–1953 H 1 Amendments: 117 v S 20, § 1

Amendment Note: 2000 S 179, § 3, eff. 1–1–02, added the reference to Chapter 2152; and made changes to reflect gender neutral language and other nonsubstantive changes.

Library References

Judges ☞23.

Westlaw Topic No. 227.

C.J.S. Judges §§ 53 to 62.

OJur 3d: 22, Courts and Judges § 69

Carlin, Baldwin's Ohio Practice, Merrick–Rippner Probate Law § 104.11 (2003).

2151.09 Separate building and site may be purchased or leased

Upon the advice and recommendation of the juvenile judge, the board of county commissioners may provide by purchase, lease, or otherwise a separate building and site to be known as "the juvenile court" at a convenient location within the county which shall be appropriately constructed, arranged, furnished, and maintained for the convenient and efficient transaction of the business of the court and all parts thereof and its employees, including adequate facilities to be used as laboratories, dispensaries, or clinics for the use of scientific specialists connected with the court.

(1953 H 1, eff. 10–1–53; GC 1639–15)

Historical and Statutory Notes

Pre–1953 H 1 Amendments: 117 v 520, § 1

Library References

Courts ☞72 to 74.

Westlaw Topic No. 106.

C.J.S. Courts §§ 7, 121.

OJur 3d: 22, Courts and Judges § 172; 48, Family Law § 1536

2151.10 Appropriation for expenses of the court and maintenance of children; hearing; action in court of appeals; limitation of contempt power

The juvenile judge shall annually submit a written request for an appropriation to the board of county commissioners that shall set forth estimated administrative expenses of the juvenile court that the judge considers reasonably necessary for the operation of the court, including reasonably necessary expenses of the judge and such officers and employees as the judge may designate in attending conferences at which juvenile or welfare problems are discussed, and such sum each year as will provide for the maintenance and operation of the detention facility, the care, maintenance, education, and support of neglected, abused, dependent, and delinquent children, other than children eligible to participate in the Ohio works first program established under Chapter 5107. of the Revised Code, and for necessary orthopedic, surgical, and medical treatment, and special care as may be ordered by the court for any neglected, abused, dependent, or delinquent children. The board shall conduct a public hearing with respect to the written request submitted by the judge and shall appropriate such sum of money each year as it determines, after conducting the public hearing and considering the written request of the judge, is reasonably necessary to meet all the administrative expenses of the court. All disbursements from such appropriations shall be upon specifically itemized vouchers, certified to by the judge.

If the judge considers the appropriation made by the board pursuant to this section insufficient to meet all the administrative expenses of the court, the judge shall commence an action under Chapter 2731. of the Revised Code in the court of appeals for the judicial district for a determination of the duty of the board of county commissioners to appropriate the amount of money in dispute. The court of appeals shall give priority to the action filed by the juvenile judge over all cases pending on its docket. The burden shall be on the juvenile judge to prove that the appropriation requested is reasonably necessary to meet all administrative expenses of the court. If, prior to the filing of an action under Chapter 2731. of the Revised Code or during the pendency of the action, the judge exercises the judge's contempt power in order to obtain the sum of money in dispute, the judge shall not order the imprisonment of any member of the board of county commissioners notwithstanding sections 2705.02 to 2705.06 of the Revised Code.

(2000 S 179, § 3, eff. 1–1–02; 1997 H 408, eff. 10–1–97; 1979 S 63, eff. 7–26–79; 1975 H 85; 1953 H 1; GC 1639–57)

Historical and Statutory Notes

Pre–1953 H 1 Amendments: 121 v 557; 119 v 731; 117 v 520

Amendment Note: 2000 S 179, § 3, eff. 1–1–02, substituted "facility" for "home" in the first paragraph.

Amendment Note: 1997 H 408 substituted "eligible to participate in the Ohio works first program established under Chapter 5107." for "entitled to aid under sections 5107.01 to 5107.16" in the first paragraph; and made changes to reflect gender neutral language.

Cross References

Board of county commissioners, appropriation for court of common pleas; juvenile court excepted, 307.01
Judicial and court fund, tax levy, 5707.02

Library References

Contempt ⊕36.
Counties ⊕138.
Westlaw Topic Nos. 93, 104.
C.J.S. Contempt § 53 et seq.
C.J.S. Counties §§ 177, 177, 178.
OJur 3d: 48, Family Law § 1542, 1725
Carlin, Baldwin's Ohio Practice, Merrick–Rippner Probate Law § 104.13 (2003).

2151.12 Clerk; judge as clerk; bond

(A) Except as otherwise provided in this division, whenever a court of common pleas, division of domestic relations, exercises the powers and jurisdictions conferred in Chapters 2151. and 2152. of the Revised Code, the judge or judges of that division or, if applicable, the judge of that division who specifically is designated by section 2301.03 of the Revised Code as being responsible for administering sections 2151.13, 2151.16, 2151.17, 2151.18, and 2152.71 of the Revised Code shall be the clerk of the court for all records filed with the court pursuant to Chapter 2151. or 2152. of the Revised Code or pursuant to any other section of the Revised Code that requires documents to be filed with a juvenile judge or a juvenile court. If, in a division of domestic relations of a court of common pleas that exercises the powers and jurisdiction conferred in Chapters 2151. and 2152. of the Revised Code, the judge of the division, both judges in a two-judge division, or a majority of the judges in a division with three or more judges and the clerk of the court of common pleas agree in an agreement that is signed by the agreeing judge or judges and the clerk and entered into formally in the journal of the court, the clerk of courts of common pleas shall keep the records filed with the court pursuant to Chapter 2151. or 2152. of the Revised Code or pursuant to any other section of the Revised Code that requires documents to be filed with a juvenile judge or a juvenile court.

Whenever the juvenile judge, or a majority of the juvenile judges of a multi-judge juvenile division, of a court of common pleas, juvenile division, and the clerk of the court of common pleas agree in an agreement that is signed by the judge and the clerk and entered formally in the journal of the court, the clerks of courts of common pleas shall keep the records of those courts. In all other cases, the juvenile judge shall be the clerk of the judge's own court.

(B) In counties in which the juvenile judge is clerk of the judge's own court, before entering upon the duties of office as the clerk, the judge shall execute and file with the county treasurer a bond in a sum to be determined by the board of county commissioners, with sufficient surety to be approved by the board, conditioned for the faithful performance of duties as clerk. The bond shall be given for the benefit of the county, the state, or any person who may suffer loss by reason of a default in any of the conditions of the bond.

(2000 S 179, § 3, eff. 1–1–02; 1996 H 423, eff. 10–31–96; 1977 S 336, eff. 3–3–78; 1953 H 1; GC 1639–17)

Historical and Statutory Notes

Pre–1953 H 1 Amendments: 117 v 520, § 1

Amendment Note: 2000 S 179, § 3, eff. 1–1–02, added references to Chapter 2152 throughout; inserted "and 2152.71" in the first paragraph; and made other nonsubstantive changes.

Amendment Note: 1996 H 423 rewrote this section, which prior thereto read:

"Whenever the courts of common pleas, division of domestic relations, exercise the powers and jurisdictions conferred in sections 2151.01 to 2151.54 of the Revised Code, or whenever the juvenile judge, or a majority of the juvenile judges of a multi-judge juvenile division, of a court of common pleas, juvenile division and the clerk of the court of common pleas agree in an agreement that is signed by the judge and the clerk and entered formally in the journal of the court, the clerks of courts of common pleas shall keep the records of such courts. In all other cases, the juvenile judge shall be the clerk of his own court.

"In counties in which the juvenile judge is clerk of his own court, before entering upon the duties of his office as such clerk, he shall execute and file with the county treasurer a bond in a sum to be determined by the board of county commissioners, with sufficient surety to be approved by the board, conditioned for the faithful performance of his duties as clerk. The bond shall be given for the benefit of the county, the state, or any person who may suffer loss by reason of a default in any of the conditions of the bond."

Cross References

Registry of custody documents, duty of clerk of courts, 3109.33

Library References

OJur 3d: 22, Courts and Judges § 38, 188; 48, Family Law § 1540
Katz & Giannelli, Baldwin's Ohio Practice, Criminal Law § 119.2 (1996).
Carlin, Baldwin's Ohio Practice, Merrick–Rippner Probate Law § 104.14, 104.21 (2003).

2151.13 Employees; compensation; bond

The juvenile judge may appoint such bailiffs, probation officers, and other employees as are necessary and may designate their titles and fix their duties, compensation, and expense allowances. The juvenile court may by entry on its journal authorize any deputy clerk to administer oaths when necessary in the discharge of his duties. Such employees shall serve during the pleasure of the judge.

The compensation and expenses of all employees and the salary and expenses of the judge shall be paid in semimonthly installments by the county treasurer from the money appropriated for the operation of the court, upon the warrant of the county auditor, certified to by the judge.

The judge may require any employee to give bond in the sum of not less than one thousand dollars, conditioned for the honest and faithful performance of his duties. The sureties on such bonds shall be approved in the manner provided by section 2151.12 of the Revised Code. The judge shall not be personally liable for the default, misfeasance, or nonfeasance of any employee from whom a bond has been required.

(1953 H 1, eff. 10–1–53; GC 1639–18)

Historical and Statutory Notes

Pre–1953 H 1 Amendments: 121 v 557; 117 v 520

Cross References

Judges of the court of domestic relations, juvenile court responsibility, 2301.03
Peace officer training, 109.73 et seq.

Library References

Courts ☞55 to 58.
Westlaw Topic No. 106.
C.J.S. Courts §§ 107 to 110.
OJur 3d: 22, Courts and Judges § 112, 188, 199; 48, Family Law § 1540
Gotherman & Babbit, Ohio Municipal Law, Text 33.11.
Carlin, Baldwin's Ohio Practice, Merrick–Rippner Probate Law § 104.16, 104.22, 104.23, 104.24, 104.25, 107.41, 107.43, 107.47, 107.102 (2003).

2151.14 Duties and powers of probation department; records; command assistance; notice to victim of accused sex offender's communicable disease; order to provide copies of records

(A) The chief probation officer, under the direction of the juvenile judge, shall have charge of the work of the probation department. The department shall make any investigations that the judge directs, keep a written record of the investigations, and submit the record to the judge or deal with them as the judge directs. The department shall furnish to any person placed on community control a statement of the conditions of community control and shall instruct the person regarding them. The department shall keep informed concerning the conduct and condition of each person under its supervision and shall report on their conduct and condition to the judge as the judge directs. Each probation officer shall use all suitable methods to aid persons on community control and to bring about improvement in their conduct and condition. The department shall keep full records of its work, keep accurate and complete accounts of money collected from persons under its supervision, give receipts for the money, and make reports on the money as the judge directs.

(B) Except as provided in this division or in division (C) or (D) of this section, the reports and records of the department shall be considered confidential information and shall not be made public. If an officer is preparing pursuant to section 2947.06 or 2951.03 of the Revised Code or Criminal Rule 32.2 a presentence investigation report pertaining to a person, the department shall make available to the officer, for use in preparing the report, any reports and records it possesses regarding any adjudications of that person as a delinquent child or regarding the dispositions made relative to those adjudications. A probation officer may serve the process of the court within or without the county, make arrests without warrant upon reasonable information or upon view of the violation of this chapter or Chapter 2152. of the Revised Code, detain the person arrested pending the issuance of a warrant, and perform any other duties, incident to the office, that the judge directs. All sheriffs, deputy sheriffs, constables, marshals, deputy marshals, chiefs of police, municipal corporation and township police officers, and other peace officers shall render assistance to probation officers in the performance of their duties when requested to do so by any probation officer.

(C) When a complaint has been filed alleging that a child is delinquent by reason of having committed an act that would constitute a violation of section 2907.02, 2907.03, 2907.05, or 2907.06 of the Revised Code if committed by an adult and the arresting authority, a court, or a probation officer discovers that the child or a person whom the child caused to engage in sexual activity, as defined in section 2907.01 of the Revised Code, has a communicable disease, the arresting authority, court, or probation officer immediately shall notify the victim of the delinquent act of the nature of the disease.

(D)(1) In accordance with division (D)(2) of this section, subject to the limitation specified in division (D)(4) of this section, and in connection with a disposition pursuant to section 2151.354 of the Revised Code when a child has been found to be an unruly child, a disposition pursuant to sections 2152.19 and 2152.20 of the Revised Code when a child has been found to be a delinquent child, or a disposition pursuant to sections 2152.20 and 2152.21 of the Revised Code when a child has been found to be a juvenile traffic offender, the court may issue an order requiring boards of education, governing bodies of chartered nonpublic schools, public children services agencies, private child placing agencies, probation departments, law enforcement agencies, and prosecuting attorneys that have records related to the child in question to provide copies of one or more specified records, or specified information in one or more specified records, that the individual or entity has with respect to the child to any of the following individuals or entities that request the records in accordance with division (D)(3)(a) of this section:

(a) The child;

(b) The attorney or guardian ad litem of the child;

(c) A parent, guardian, or custodian of the child;

(d) A prosecuting attorney;

(e) A board of education of a public school district;

(f) A probation department of a juvenile court;

(g) A public children services agency or private child placing agency that has custody of the child, is providing services to the child or the child's family, or is preparing a social history or performing any other function for the juvenile court;

(h) The department of youth services when the department has custody of the child or is performing any services for the child that are required by the juvenile court or by statute;

(i) The individual in control of a juvenile detention or rehabilitation facility to which the child has been committed;

(j) An employee of the juvenile court that found the child to be an unruly child, a delinquent child, or a juvenile traffic offender;

(k) Any other entity that has custody of the child or is providing treatment, rehabilitation, or other services for the child pursuant to a court order, statutory requirement, or other arrangement.

(2) Any individual or entity listed in divisions (D)(1)(a) to (k) of this section may file a motion with the court that requests the court to issue an order as described in division (D)(1) of this section. If such a motion is filed, the court shall conduct a hearing on it. If at the hearing the movant demonstrates a need for one or more specified records, or for information in one or more specified records, related to the child in question and additionally demonstrates the relevance of the information sought to be obtained from those records, and if the court determines that the limitation specified in division (D)(4) of this section does not preclude the provision of a specified record or specified information to the movant, then the court may issue an order to

a designated individual or entity to provide the movant with copies of one or more specified records or with specified information contained in one or more specified records.

(3)(a) Any individual or entity that is authorized by an order issued pursuant to division (D)(1) of this section to obtain copies of one or more specified records, or specified information, related to a particular child may file a written request for copies of the records or for the information with any individual or entity required by the order to provide copies of the records or the information. The request shall be in writing, describe the type of records or the information requested, explain the need for the records or the information, and be accompanied by a copy of the order.

(b) If an individual or entity that is required by an order issued pursuant to division (D)(1) of this section to provide one or more specified records, or specified information, related to a child receives a written request for the records or information in accordance with division (D)(3)(a) of this section, the individual or entity immediately shall comply with the request to the extent it is able to do so, unless the individual or entity determines that it is unable to comply with the request because it is prohibited by law from doing so, or unless the requesting individual or entity does not have authority to obtain the requested records or information. If the individual or entity determines that it is unable to comply with the request, it shall file a motion with the court that issued the order requesting the court to determine the extent to which it is required to comply with the request for records or information. Upon the filing of the motion, the court immediately shall hold a hearing on the motion, determine the extent to which the movant is required to comply with the request for records or information, and issue findings of fact and conclusions of law in support of its determination. The determination of the court shall be final. If the court determines that the movant is required to comply with the request for records or information, it shall identify the specific records or information that must be supplied to the individual or entity that requested the records or information.

(c) If an individual or entity is required to provide copies of one or more specified records pursuant to division (D)

of this section, the individual or entity may charge a fee for the copies that does not exceed the cost of supplying them.

(4) Division (D) of this section does not require, authorize, or permit the dissemination of any records or any information contained in any records if the dissemination of the records or information generally is prohibited by any provision of the Revised Code and a specific provision of the Revised Code does not specifically authorize or permit the dissemination of the records or information pursuant to division (D) of this section.

(2002 H 247, eff. 5–30–02; 2000 S 179, § 3, eff. 1–1–02; 2000 H 442, eff. 10–17–00; 1996 H 445, eff. 9–3–96; 1990 S 258, eff. 8–22–90; 1986 H 468; 1953 H 1; GC 1639–19)

Uncodified Law

1996 H 445, § 3, eff. 9–3–96, reads:

(A) When a complaint is filed alleging that a child is a delinquent child for committing felonious sexual penetration in violation of former section 2907.12 of the Revised Code and the arresting authority, a court, or a probation officer discovers that the child or a person whom the child caused to engage in sexual activity has a communicable disease, the arresting authority, court, or probation officer shall notify the victim of the delinquent act of the nature of the disease in accordance with division (C) of section 2151.14 of the Revised Code.

As used in division (A) of Section 3 of this act:

(1) "Child" has the same meaning as in section 2151.011 of the Revised Code.

(2) "Delinquent child" has the same meaning as in section 2151.02 of the Revised Code.

(3) "Sexual activity" has the same meaning as in section 2907.01 of the Revised Code.

(B) If a child is adjudicated a delinquent child for violating any provision of former section 2907.12 of the Revised Code other than division (A)(1)(b) of that section when the insertion involved was consensual and when the victim of the violation of division (A)(1)(b) of that section was older than the delinquent child, was the same age as the delinquent child, or was less that three years younger than the delinquent child, the juvenile court with jurisdiction over the child may commit the child to the legal custody of the department of youth services pursuant to division (A)(5)(a) of section 2151.355 of the Revised Code, as amended by this act, and all provisions of the Revised Code that apply to a disposition otherwise imposed pursuant to division (A)(5)(a) of section 2151.355 of the Revised Code, as amended by this act, apply to a disposition imposed in accordance with division (B) of Section 3 of this act.

As used in division (B) of Section 3 of this act:

(1) "Child" and "legal custody" have the same meanings as in section 2151.011 of the Revised Code.

(2) "Delinquent child" has the same meaning as in section 2151.02 of the Revised Code.

(C) Section 2151.3511 of the Revised Code, as amended by this act, applies to a proceeding in juvenile court involving a complaint in which a child is charged with committing an act that if committed by an adult would be felonious sexual penetration in violation of former section 2907.12 of the Revised Code and in which an alleged victim of the act was a child who was under eleven years of age when the complaint was filed.

As used in division (C) of Section 3 of this act, "child" has the same meaning as in section 2151.011 of the Revised Code.

(D) Division (E) of section 2743.62 of the Revised Code applies to a claim for an award of reparations arising out of the commission of felonious sexual penetration in violation of former section 2907.12 of the Revised Code.

(E) Section 2907.11 of the Revised Code, as amended by this act, applies to a prosecution for felonious sexual penetration committed in violation of former section 2907.12 of the Revised Code.

(F) Division (A) of section 2907.28 and sections 2907.29 and 2907.30 of the Revised Code, as amended by this act, apply to a victim of felonious sexual penetration committed in violation of former section 2907.12 of the Revised Code.

(G) Sections 2907.41 and 2945.49 of the Revised Code, as amended by this act, apply to a trial or other proceeding involving a charge of felonious sexual penetration in violation of former section 2907.12 of the Revised Code in which an alleged victim of the offense was a child who was under eleven years of age when the complaint, indictment, or information was filed relative to the trial or other proceeding.

(H) Divisions (B) and (C) of section 2937.11 of the Revised Code, as amended by this act, apply to a case involving an alleged commission of the offense of felonious sexual penetration in violation of former section 2907.12 of the Revised Code.

(I) Notwithstanding section 2967.13 of the Revised Code, as amended by this act, a prisoner serving a term of imprisonment for life for committing the offense of felonious sexual penetration in violation of former section 2907.12 of the Revised Code becomes eligible for parole after serving a term of ten full years' imprisonment.

(J) Notwithstanding section 2967.18 of the Revised Code, as amended by this act, no reduction of sentence pursuant to division (B)(1) of section 2967.18 of the Revised Code shall be given to a person who is serving a term of imprisonment for the commission of felonious sexual penetration in violation of former section 2907.12 of the Revised Code.

Historical and Statutory Notes

Pre–1953 H 1 Amendments: 117 v 520, § 1

Amendment Note: 2002 H 247 inserted "this division or in" before "division (C)" in the first sentence of division (B); added the second sentence of division (B); and substituted "2152.20" for "2156.20" in division (D)(1).

Amendment Note: 2000 S 179, § 3, eff. 1–1–02, substituted "community control" for "probation" three times in division (A); inserted "or Chapter 2152. of the Revised Code" in division (B); and substituted "sections 2152.19 and 2152.20" for "section 2151.355" and "sections 2152.20 and 2152.21" for "section 2151.356" in the introductory paragraph in division (D)(1).

Amendment Note: 2000 H 442 deleted "2907.04," after "2907.03" in division (C).

Amendment Note: 1996 H 445 removed a reference to section 2907.12 from division (C); and made changes to reflect gender neutral language and other nonsubstantive changes.

Cross References

Bureau of aftercare services, contract with county agency, 5139.18
Dispositional hearing, Juv R 34
Limits on public access to records concerning pupils, 3319.321
Personal information systems, applicability of chapter, 1347.04
Presentence investigation reports, mandatory consideration of certain information, 2951.03
Process: service, Juv R 16
Social history, physical and mental examinations, custody investigation, Juv R 32
Subpoena, Juv R 17

Library References

Courts ⚖55.
Infants ⚖17, 131, 133.
Westlaw Topic Nos. 106, 211.
C.J.S. Courts §§ 107 to 109.
C.J.S. Infants §§ 8, 9, 31 to 57, 69 to 85.
OJur 3d: 48, Family Law § 1541, 1568, 1658, 1680
Baldwin's Ohio Legislative Service, 1990 Laws of Ohio, S 258—LSC Analysis, p 5–954
Carlin, Baldwin's Ohio Practice, Merrick–Rippner Probate Law § 107.61, 107.84, 107.114 (2003).

2151.141   Requests for copies of records

(A) If a complaint filed with respect to a child pursuant to section 2151.27 of the Revised Code alleges that a child is an abused, neglected, or dependent child, any individual or entity that is listed in divisions (D)(1)(a) to (k) of section 2151.14 of the Revised Code and that is investigating whether the child is an abused, neglected, or dependent child, has custody of the child, is preparing a social history for the child, or is providing any services for the child may request any board of education, governing body of a chartered nonpublic school, public children services agency, private child placing agency, probation department, law enforcement agency, or prosecuting attorney that has any records related to the child to provide the individual or entity with a copy of the records. The request shall be in writing, describe the type of records requested, explain the need for the records, be accompanied by a copy of the complaint, and describe the relationship of the requesting individual or entity to the child. The individual or entity shall provide a copy of the request to the child in question, the attorney or guardian ad litem of the child, and the parent, guardian, or custodian of the child.

(B)(1) Any board of education, governing body of a chartered nonpublic school, public children services agency, private child placing agency, probation department, law enforcement agency, or prosecuting attorney that has any records related to a child who is the subject of a complaint as described in division (A) of this section and that receives a request for a copy of the records pursuant to division (A) of this section shall comply with the request, unless the individual or entity determines that it is unable to do so because it is prohibited by law from complying with the request, the request does not comply with division (A) of this section, or a complaint as described in division (A) of this section has not been filed with respect to the child who is the subject of the requested records. If the individual or entity determines that it is unable to comply with the request, it shall file a motion with the court in which the complaint as described in division (A) of this section was filed or was alleged to have been filed requesting the court to determine the extent to which it is required to comply with the request for records. Upon the filing of the motion, the court immediately shall hold a hearing on the motion, determine the extent to which the movant is required to comply with the request for records, and issue findings of fact and conclusions of law in support of its determination. The determination of the court shall be final. If the court determines that the movant is required to comply with the request for records, it shall identify the specific records that must be supplied to the individual or entity that requested them.

(2) In addition to or in lieu of the motion described in division (B)(1) of this section, a law enforcement agency or prosecuting attorney that receives a request for a copy of records pursuant to division (A) of this section may file a motion for a protective order as described in this division with the court in which the complaint as described in division (A) of this section was filed or alleged to have been filed. Upon the filing of a motion of that nature, the court shall conduct a hearing on the motion. If at the hearing the law enforcement agency or prosecuting attorney demonstrates that any of the following applies and if, after considering the purposes for which the records were requested pursuant to division (A) of this section, the best interest of the child, and any demonstrated need to prevent specific information in the records from being disclosed, the court determines that the issuance of a protective order is necessary, then the court shall issue a protective order that appropriately limits the disclosure of one or more specified records or specified information in one or more specified records:

(a) The records or information in the records relate to a case in which the child is alleged to be a delinquent child or a case in which a child is transferred for trial as an adult pursuant to section 2152.12 of the Revised Code and Juvenile Rule 30, and the adjudication hearing in the case, the trial in the case, or other disposition of the case has not been concluded.

(b) The records in question, or the records containing the information in question, are confidential law enforcement investigatory records, as defined in section 149.43 of the Revised Code.

(c) The records or information in the records relate to a case in which the child is or was alleged to be a delinquent child or to a case in which a child is or was transferred for trial as an adult pursuant to section 2152.12 of the Revised Code and Juvenile Rule 30; another case is pending against any child or any adult in which the child is alleged to be a delinquent child, the child is so transferred for trial as an adult, or the adult is alleged to be a criminal offender; the allegations in the case to which the records or information relate and the allegations in the other case are based on the same act or transaction, are based on two or more connected transactions or constitute parts of a common scheme or plan, or are part of a course of criminal conduct; and the adjudication hearing in, trial in, or other disposition of the other case has not been concluded.

(C) If an individual or entity is required to provide copies of records pursuant to this section, the individual or entity may charge a fee for the copies that does not exceed the cost of supplying them.

(D) This section does not require, authorize, or permit the dissemination of any records or any information contained in any records if the dissemination of the records or information generally is prohibited by section 2151.142 or another section of the Revised Code and a waiver as described in division (B)(1) of section 2151.142 of the Revised Code or a specific provision of the Revised Code does not specifically authorize or permit the dissemination of the records or information pursuant to this section.

(2000 S 179, § 3, eff. 1–1–02; 2000 H 412, eff. 4–10–01; 1990 S 258, eff. 8–22–90)

Historical and Statutory Notes

Ed. Note: A special endorsement by the Legislative Service Commission states, "Comparison of these amendments [2000 S 179, § 3, eff. 1–1–02 and 2000 H 412, eff. 4–10–01] in pursuance of section 1.52 of the Revised Code discloses that they are not irreconcilable so that they are required by that section to be harmonized to give effect to each amendment." In recognition of this rule of construction, changes made by 2000 S 179, § 3, eff. 1–1–02 and 2000 H 412, eff. 4–10–01, have been incorporated in the above amendment. See *Baldwin's Ohio Legislative Service Annotated*, 2000, pages 11/L–3610 and 11/L–3174, or the OH–LEGIS or OH–LEGIS–OLD database on WESTLAW, for original versions of these Acts.

Amendment Note: 2000 S 179, § 3, eff. 1–1–02, substituted "transferred" for "bound over" and "2152.12" for "2151.26" throughout divisions (B)(2)(a) and (B)(2)(c).

Amendment Note: 2000 H 412 inserted "of that nature" in division (B)(2); deleted "shall not be construed to require, authorize, or permit, and," before "does not require, authorize, or permit", substituted "section 2151.142 or another section" for "any provision," and inserted "waiver as described in division (B)(1) of section 2151.142 of the Revised Code or a" in division (D); and made other nonsubstantive changes.

Cross References

Limits on public access to records concerning pupils, 3319.321
Personal information systems, applicability of chapter, 1347.04

Ohio Administrative Code References

Family and children services information system (FACSIS) reporting requirements, OAC 5101:2–33–05

Library References

Baldwin's Ohio Legislative Service, 1990 Laws of Ohio, S 258—LSC Analysis, p 5–954

2151.142 Confidentiality of residential addresses; exceptions

(A) As used in this section, "public record" and "journalist" have the same meanings as in section 149.43 of the Revised Code.

(B) Both of the following apply to the residential address of each officer or employee of a public children services agency or a private child placing agency who performs official responsibilities or duties described in section 2151.14, 2151.141, 2151.33, 2151.353, 2151.412, 2151.413, 2151.414, 2151.415, 2151.416, 2151.417, or 2151.421 or another section of the Revised Code and to the residential address of persons related to that officer or employee by consanguinity or affinity:

(1) Other officers and employees of a public children services agency, private child placing agency, juvenile court, or law enforcement agency shall consider those residential addresses to be confidential information. The officer or employee of the public children services agency or private child placing agency may waive the confidentiality of those residential addresses by giving express permission for their disclosure to other officers or employees of a public children services agency, private child placing agency, juvenile court, or law enforcement agency.

(2) To the extent that those residential addresses are contained in public records kept by a public children services agency, private child placing agency, juvenile court, or law enforcement agency, they shall not be considered to be information that is subject to inspection or copying as part of a public record under section 149.43 of the Revised Code.

(C) Except as provided in division (D) of this section, in the absence of a waiver as described in division (B)(1) of this section, no officer or employee of a public children services agency, private child placing agency, juvenile court, or law enforcement agency shall disclose the residential address of an officer or employee of a public children services agency or private child placing agency, or the residential address of a person related to that officer or employee by consanguinity or affinity, that is confidential information under division (B)(1) of this section to any person, when the disclosing officer or employee knows that the person is or may be a subject of an investigation, interview, examination, criminal case, other case, or other matter with which the officer or employee to whom the residential address relates currently is or has been associated.

(D) If, on or after the effective date of this section, a journalist requests a public children services agency, private child placing agency, juvenile court, or law enforcement agency to disclose a residential address that is confidential information under division (B)(1) of this section, the agency or juvenile court shall disclose to the journalist the residential address if all of the following apply:

(1) The request is in writing, is signed by the journalist, includes the journalist's

name and title, and includes the name and address of the journalist's employer.

(2) The request states that disclosure of the residential address would be in the public interest.

(3) The request adequately identifies the person whose residential address is requested.

(4) The public children services agency, private child placing agency, juvenile court, or law enforcement agency receiving the request is one of the following:

(a) The agency or juvenile court with which the official in question serves or with which the employee in question is employed;

(b) The agency or juvenile court that has custody of the records of the agency with which the official in question serves or with which the employee in question is employed.

(2000 H 412, eff. 4–10–01)

2151.15 Powers and duties vested in county department of probation

When a county department of probation has been established in the county and the juvenile judge does not establish a probation department within the juvenile court as provided in section 2151.14 of the Revised Code, all powers and duties of the probation department provided for in sections 2151.01 to 2151.54, inclusive, of the Revised Code, shall vest in and be imposed upon such county department of probation.

In counties in which a county department of probation has been or is hereafter established the judge may transfer to such department all or any part of the powers and duties of his own probation department; provided that all juvenile cases shall be handled within a county department of probation exclusively by an officer or division separate and distinct from the officers or division handling adult cases.

(1953 H 1, eff. 10–1–53; GC 1639–20)

Historical and Statutory Notes
Pre-1953 H 1 Amendments: 121 v 557; 117 v 520

Cross References
Advertising for children for adoption or foster homes forbidden, 5103.17
Bureau of aftercare services, contract with county agency, 5139.18

Library References
Infants ⚖225.

Westlaw Topic No. 211.
C.J.S. Infants §§ 57, 69 to 85.
OJur 3d: 48, Family Law § 1541

2151.151 Juvenile court may contract for services to children on probation

(A) The juvenile judge may contract with any agency, association, or organization, which may be of a public or private, or profit or nonprofit nature, or with any individual for the provision of supervisory or other services to children placed on probation who are under the custody and supervision of the juvenile court.

(B) The juvenile judges of two or more adjoining or neighboring counties may join together for purposes of contracting with any agency, association, or organization, which may be of a public or private, or profit or nonprofit nature, or with any individual for the provision of supervisory or other services to children placed on probation who are under the custody and supervision of the juvenile court of any of the counties that joins [sic.] together.

(1981 H 440, eff. 11–23–81)

Ohio Administrative Code References
Community corrections facilities—fiscal rules and procedures, OAC Ch 5139–63
Community juvenile corrections facilities program—rules and procedures, OAC Ch 5139–61

Library References
Infants ⚖225.
Westlaw Topic No. 211.
C.J.S. Infants §§ 57, 69 to 85.
OJur 3d: 48, Family Law § 1537
Carlin, Baldwin's Ohio Practice, Merrick–Rippner Probate Law § 104.19 (2003).

2151.152 Agreement to reimburse juvenile court for foster care maintenance costs and associated administrative and training costs

The juvenile judge may enter into an agreement with the department of job and family services pursuant to section 5101.11 of the Revised Code for the purpose of reimbursing the court for foster care maintenance costs and associated administrative and training costs incurred on behalf of a child eligible for payments under Title IV–E of the "Social Security Act," 94 Stat. 501, 42 U.S.C.A. 670 (1980) and who is in the temporary or permanent custody of the court or subject to a disposition issued under division (A)(5) of section 2151.354 or division (A)(7) (a)(ii) or (A)(8) of section 2152.19 of the Revised Code. The agreement shall govern the responsibilities and duties the court shall perform in providing services to the child.

(2002 H 400, eff. 4–3–03; 2001 H 57, eff. 2–19–02; 1999 H 471, eff. 7–1–00; 1996 H 274, eff. 8–8–96)

Historical and Statutory Notes

Amendment Note: 2002 H 400 substituted "(7)" for "(6)" and "(8)" for "(7)".

Amendment Note: 2001 H 57 rewrote this section, which prior thereto read:

"The juvenile judge may enter into an agreement with the department of job and family services pursuant to section 5101.11 of the Revised Code for the purpose of reimbursing the court for foster care maintenance costs and administrative and training costs incurred on behalf of a child eligible for payments under Title IV–E of the 'Social Security Act,' 94 Stat. 501, 42 U.S.C.A. 670 (1980). The agreement shall govern the responsibilities and duties the court shall perform in providing services to the child."

Amendment Note: 1999 H 471 substituted "job and family" for "human".

Library References

Baldwin's Ohio Legislative Service, 1996 H 274—LSC Analysis, p 5/L–697

2151.16 Referees; powers and duties

The juvenile judge may appoint and fix the compensation of referees who shall have the usual power of masters in chancery cases, provided, in all such cases submitted to them by the juvenile court, they shall hear the testimony of witnesses and certify to the judge their findings upon the case submitted to them, together with their recommendation as to the judgment or order to be made in the case in question. The court, after notice to the parties in the case of the presentation of such findings and recommendation, may make the order recommended by the referee, or any other order in the judgment of the court required by the findings of the referee, or may hear additional testimony, or may set aside said findings and hear the case anew. In appointing a referee for the trial of females, a female referee shall be appointed where possible.

(1953 H 1, eff. 10–1–53; GC 1639–21)

Historical and Statutory Notes

Pre–1953 H 1 Amendments: 117 v 520, § 1

Cross References

Advertising for children for adoption or foster homes forbidden, 5103.17

Judges of the court of domestic relations, juvenile court responsibility, 2301.03
Referees, Juv R 40

Library References

Infants ☞206.
Westlaw Topic No. 211.
C.J.S. Infants §§ 63, 68.
OJur 3d: 48, Family Law § 1645, 1647, 1650, 1651
Carlin, Baldwin's Ohio Practice, Merrick–Rippner Probate Law § 107.49, 107.119, 107.179 (2003).

2151.17 Rules governing practice and procedure

Except as otherwise provided by rules promulgated by the supreme court, the juvenile court may prescribe rules regulating the docketing and hearing of causes, motions, and demurrers, and such other matters as are necessary for the orderly conduct of its business and the prevention of delay, and for the government of its officers and employees, including their conduct, duties, hours, expenses, leaves of absence, and vacations.

(1969 H 320, eff. 11–19–69; 1953 H 1; GC 1639–11)

Historical and Statutory Notes

Pre–1953 H 1 Amendments: 121 v 557; 117 v 520

Cross References

Judges of the court of domestic relations, juvenile court responsibility, 2301.03
Procedure not otherwise specified, Juv R 45
Rules of civil procedure; scope, applicability, construction, exceptions, Civ R 1

Library References

Courts ☞55, 81.
Infants ☞191.
Westlaw Topic Nos. 106, 211.
C.J.S. Courts §§ 107 to 109, 129.
C.J.S. Infants §§ 42, 53, 54.
OJur 3d: 48, Family Law § 1538, 1540
Carlin, Baldwin's Ohio Practice, Merrick–Rippner Probate Law § 107.50 (2003).

2151.18 Records of cases; annual report

(A) The juvenile court shall maintain records of all official cases brought before it, including, but not limited to, an appearance docket, a journal, and records of the type required by division (A)(2) of section 2151.35 of the Revised Code. The parents, guardian, or other custodian of any child affected, if living, or the nearest of kin of the child, if the parents would be entitled to inspect the records but are deceased, may inspect these records, either in person or by counsel, during the hours in which the court is open.

(B) Not later than June of each year, the court shall prepare an annual report covering the preceding calendar year showing the number and kinds of cases that have come before it, the disposition of the cases, and any other data pertaining to the work of the court that the juvenile judge directs. The court shall file copies of the report with the board of county commissioners. With the approval of the board, the court may print or cause to be printed copies of the report for distribution to persons and agencies interested in the court or community program for dependent, neglected, abused, or delinquent children and juvenile traffic offenders. The court shall include the number of copies ordered printed and the estimated cost of each printed copy on each copy of the report printed for distribution.

(2002 H 393, eff. 7–5–02; 2000 S 179, § 3, eff. 1–1–02)

Historical and Statutory Notes

Ed. Note: Former 2151.18 amended and recodified as 2152.71 by 2000 S 179, § 3, eff. 1–1–02; 2000 S 181, eff. 9–4–00; 1999 H 3, eff. 11–22–99; 1998 H 2, eff. 1–1–99; 1996 H 124, eff. 3–31–97; 1995 H 1, eff. 1–1–96; 1993 H 152, eff. 7–1–93; 1990 S 268; 1984 S 5; 1981 H 440; 1979 H 394; 1975 H 85; 127 v 547; 1953 H 1; GC 1639–13.

Pre–1953 H 1 Amendments: 123 v 367; 121 v 557; 117 v 520

Amendment Note: 2002 H 393 added the last sentence to division (A).

Library References

Carlin, Baldwin's Ohio Practice, Merrick–Rippner Probate Law § 106.1, 107.1, 107.86, 107.114, 107.115 (2003).

2151.19 Summons; expense

The summons, warrants, citations, subpoenas, and other writs of the juvenile court may issue to a probation officer of any such court or to the sheriff of any county or any marshal, constable, or police officer, and the provisions of law relating to the subpoenaing of witnesses in other cases shall apply in so far as they are applicable.

When a summons, warrant, citation, subpoena, or other writ is issued to any such officer, other than a probation officer, the expense in serving the same shall be paid by the county, township, or municipal corporation in the manner prescribed for the payment of sheriffs, deputies, assistants, and other employees.

(1953 H 1, eff. 10–1–53; GC 1639–52, 1639–53)

Historical and Statutory Notes

Pre–1953 H 1 Amendments: 117 v 520, § 1

Cross References

Process, issuance, form, Juv R 15
Right to compulsory process to obtain witnesses, O Const Art I §10

Library References

Counties ⊕138.
Infants ⊕207.
Municipal Corporations ⊕262.
Westlaw Topic Nos. 104, 211, 268.
C.J.S. Counties §§ 175, 177, 178.
C.J.S. Infants §§ 51, 52, 62 to 67.
C.J.S. Municipal Corporations § 1030.
OJur 3d: 48, Family Law § 1605, 1618, 1719

2151.20 Seal of court; dimensions

Juvenile courts within the probate court shall have a seal which shall consist of the coat of arms of the state within a circle one and one-fourth inches in diameter and shall be surrounded by the words "juvenile court _____ county."

The seal of other courts exercising the powers and jurisdiction conferred in sections 2151.01 to 2151.54, inclusive, of the Revised Code, shall be attached to all writs and processes.

(132 v H 164, eff. 12–15–67; 1953 H 1; GC 1639–9)

Historical and Statutory Notes

Pre–1953 H 1 Amendments: 117 v 520, § 1

Library References

OJur 3d: 48, Family Law § 1537

2151.21 Jurisdiction in contempt

The juvenile court has the same jurisdiction in contempt as courts of common pleas.

(1953 H 1, eff. 10–1–53; GC 1639–10)

Historical and Statutory Notes

Pre–1953 H 1 Amendments: 117 v 520, § 1

Cross References

Contempt of court, Ch 2705

Library References

Contempt ⊕44.
Westlaw Topic No. 93.
C.J.S. Contempt § 64.
OJur 3d: 48, Family Law § 1545

Am Jur 2d: 47, Juvenile Courts and Delinquent and Dependent Children § 5

Court's power to punish for contempt a child within the age group subject to jurisdiction of juvenile court. 77 ALR2d 1004

Interference with enforcement of judgment in criminal or juvenile delinquent case as contempt. 8 ALR3d 657

Carlin, Baldwin's Ohio Practice, Merrick–Rippner Probate Law § 107.127 (2003).

2151.211 Employee's attendance at proceeding; employer may not penalize

No employer shall discharge or terminate from employment, threaten to discharge or terminate from employment, or otherwise punish or penalize any employee because of time lost from regular employment as a result of the employee's attendance at any proceeding pursuant to a subpoena under this chapter or Chapter 2152. of the Revised Code. This section generally does not require and shall not be construed to require an employer to pay an employee for time lost as a result of attendance at any proceeding under either chapter. However, if an employee is subpoenaed to appear at a proceeding under either chapter and the proceeding pertains to an offense against the employer or an offense involving the employee during the course of the employee's employment, the employer shall not decrease or withhold the employee's pay for any time lost as a result of compliance with the subpoena. Any employer who knowingly violates this section is in contempt of court.

(2000 S 179, § 3, eff. 1–1–02; 1984 S 172, eff. 9–26–84)

Historical and Statutory Notes

Amendment Note: 2000 S 179, § 3, eff. 1–1–02, substituted "under this chapter or Chapter 2152. of the Revised Code" for "in a delinquency case" in the first sentence; substituted "under either chapter" for "in a delinquency case" in the second and third sentences; and made changes to reflect gender neutral language.

Cross References

Victim's rights pamphlet, publication and distribution, 109.42

Library References

Master and Servant ⬥30(6.10).

Westlaw Topic No. 255.

C.J.S. Master and Servant § 42.

OJur 3d: 48, Family Law § 1618

Carlin, Baldwin's Ohio Practice, Merrick–Rippner Probate Law § 107.127 (2003).

2151.22 Terms of court; sessions

The term of any juvenile or domestic relations court, whether a division of the court of common pleas or an independent court, is one calendar year. All actions and other business pending at the expiration of any term of court is automatically continued without further order. The judge may adjourn court or continue any case whenever, in his opinion, such continuance is warranted.

Sessions of the court may be held at such places throughout the county as the judge shall from time to time determine.

(1976 H 390, eff. 8–6–76; 1953 H 1; GC 1639–12)

Historical and Statutory Notes

Pre–1953 H 1 Amendments: 117 v 520, § 1

Library References

Courts ⬥75.

Westlaw Topic No. 106.

C.J.S. Courts § 120.

OJur 3d: 48, Family Law § 1536

Carlin, Baldwin's Ohio Practice, Merrick–Rippner Probate Law § 104.12, 107.89 (2003).

2151.23 Jurisdiction of juvenile court; orders for child support

(A) The juvenile court has exclusive original jurisdiction under the Revised Code as follows:

(1) Concerning any child who on or about the date specified in the complaint, indictment, or information is alleged to have violated section 2151.87 of the Revised Code or an order issued under that section or to be a juvenile traffic offender or a delinquent, unruly, abused, neglected, or dependent child and, based on and in relation to the allegation pertaining to the child, concerning the parent, guardian, or other person having care of a child who is alleged to be an unruly or delinquent child for being an habitual or chronic truant;

(2) Subject to divisions (G) and (V) of section 2301.03 of the Revised Code, to determine the custody of any child not a ward of another court of this state;

(3) To hear and determine any application for a writ of habeas corpus involving the custody of a child;

(4) To exercise the powers and jurisdiction given the probate division of the court of common pleas in Chapter 5122. of the Revised Code, if the court has probable cause to believe that a child

otherwise within the jurisdiction of the court is a mentally ill person subject to hospitalization by court order, as defined in section 5122.01 of the Revised Code;

(5) To hear and determine all criminal cases charging adults with the violation of any section of this chapter;

(6) To hear and determine all criminal cases in which an adult is charged with a violation of division (C) of section 2919.21, division (B)(1) of section 2919.22, section 2919.222, division (B) of section 2919.23, or section 2919.24 of the Revised Code, provided the charge is not included in an indictment that also charges the alleged adult offender with the commission of a felony arising out of the same actions that are the basis of the alleged violation of division (C) of section 2919.21, division (B)(1) of section 2919.22, section 2919.222, division (B) of section 2919.23, or section 2919.24 of the Revised Code;

(7) Under the interstate compact on juveniles in section 2151.56 of the Revised Code;

(8) Concerning any child who is to be taken into custody pursuant to section 2151.31 of the Revised Code, upon being notified of the intent to take the child into custody and the reasons for taking the child into custody;

(9) To hear and determine requests for the extension of temporary custody agreements, and requests for court approval of permanent custody agreements, that are filed pursuant to section 5103.15 of the Revised Code;

(10) To hear and determine applications for consent to marry pursuant to section 3101.04 of the Revised Code;

(11) Subject to divisions (G) and (V) of section 2301.03 of the Revised Code, to hear and determine a request for an order for the support of any child if the request is not ancillary to an action for divorce, dissolution of marriage, annulment, or legal separation, a criminal or civil action involving an allegation of domestic violence, or an action for support brought under Chapter 3115. of the Revised Code;

(12) Concerning an action commenced under section 121.38 of the Revised Code;

(13) To hear and determine violations of section 3321.38 of the Revised Code;

(14) To exercise jurisdiction and authority over the parent, guardian, or oth-er person having care of a child alleged to be a delinquent child, unruly child, or juvenile traffic offender, based on and in relation to the allegation pertaining to the child;

(15) To conduct the hearings, and to make the determinations, adjudications, and orders authorized or required under sections 2152.82 to 2152.85 and Chapter 2950. of the Revised Code regarding a child who has been adjudicated a delinquent child and to refer the duties conferred upon the juvenile court judge under sections 2152.82 to 2152.85 and Chapter 2950. of the Revised Code to magistrates appointed by the juvenile court judge in accordance with Juvenile Rule 40.

(B) Except as provided in divisions (G) and (I) of section 2301.03 of the Revised Code, the juvenile court has original jurisdiction under the Revised Code:

(1) To hear and determine all cases of misdemeanors charging adults with any act or omission with respect to any child, which act or omission is a violation of any state law or any municipal ordinance;

(2) To determine the paternity of any child alleged to have been born out of wedlock pursuant to sections 3111.01 to 3111.18 of the Revised Code;

(3) Under the uniform interstate family support act in Chapter 3115. of the Revised Code;

(4) To hear and determine an application for an order for the support of any child, if the child is not a ward of another court of this state;

(5) To hear and determine an action commenced under section 3111.28 of the Revised Code;

(6) To hear and determine a motion filed under section 3119.961 of the Revised Code.

(C) The juvenile court, except as to juvenile courts that are a separate division of the court of common pleas or a separate and independent juvenile court, has jurisdiction to hear, determine, and make a record of any action for divorce or legal separation that involves the custody or care of children and that is filed in the court of common pleas and certified by the court of common pleas with all the papers filed in the action to the juvenile court for trial, provided that no certification of that nature shall be made to any juvenile court unless the consent of the juvenile judge first is obtained. After a certification of that nature is made and consent is obtained, the juvenile court shall proceed as if the action originally had been begun in that court, except as to awards for spousal support or support due and unpaid at the time of certification, over which the juvenile court has no jurisdiction.

(D) The juvenile court, except as provided in divisions (G) and (I) of section 2301.03 of the Revised Code, has jurisdiction to hear and determine all matters as to custody and support of children duly certified by the court of common pleas to the juvenile court after a divorce decree has been granted, including jurisdiction to modify the judgment and decree of the court of common pleas as the same relate to the custody and support of children.

(E) The juvenile court, except as provided in divisions (G) and (I) of section 2301.03 of the Revised Code, has jurisdiction to hear and determine the case of any child certified to the court by any court of competent jurisdiction if the child comes within the jurisdiction of the juvenile court as defined by this section.

(F)(1) The juvenile court shall exercise its jurisdiction in child custody matters in accordance with sections 3109.04, 3109.21 to 3109.36, and 5103.20 to 5103.28 of the Revised Code.

(2) The juvenile court shall exercise its jurisdiction in child support matters in accordance with section 3109.05 of the Revised Code.

(G) Any juvenile court that makes or modifies an order for child support shall comply with Chapters 3119., 3121., 3123., and 3125. of the Revised Code. If any person required to pay child support under an order made by a juvenile court on or after April 15, 1985, or modified on or after December 1, 1986, is found in contempt of court for failure to make support payments under the order, the court that makes the finding, in addition to any other penalty or remedy imposed, shall assess all court costs arising out of the contempt proceeding against the person and require the person to pay any reasonable attorney's fees of any adverse party, as determined by the court, that arose in relation to the act of contempt.

(H) If a child who is charged with an act that would be an offense if committed by an adult was fourteen years of age or older and under eighteen years of age at the time of the alleged act and if the case is transferred for criminal prosecution pursuant to section 2152.12 of the Revised Code, the juvenile court does not have jurisdiction to hear or determine the case subsequent to the transfer. The court to which the case is transferred for criminal prosecution pursuant to that section has jurisdiction subsequent to the transfer to hear and determine the case in the same manner as if the case originally had been commenced in that court, including, but not limited to, jurisdiction to accept a plea of guilty or another plea authorized by Criminal Rule 11 or another section of the Revised Code and jurisdiction to accept a verdict and to enter a judgment of conviction pursuant to the Rules of Criminal Procedure against the child for the commission of the offense that was the basis of the transfer of the case for criminal prosecution, whether the conviction is for the same degree or a lesser degree of the offense charged, for the commission of a lesser-included offense, or for the commission of another offense that is different from the offense charged.

(I) If a person under eighteen years of age allegedly commits an act that would be a felony if committed by an adult and if the person is not taken into custody or apprehended for that act until after the person attains twenty-one years of age, the juvenile court does not have jurisdiction to hear or determine any portion of the case charging the person with committing that act. In those circumstances, divisions (A) and (B) of section 2152.12 of the Revised Code do not apply regarding the act, and the case charging the person with committing the act shall be a criminal prosecution commenced and heard in the appropriate court having jurisdiction of the offense as if the person had been eighteen years of age or older when the person committed the act. All proceedings pertaining to the act shall be within the jurisdiction of the court having jurisdiction of the offense, and that court has all the authority and duties in the case that it has in other criminal cases in that court.

(2004 H 38, eff. 6–17–04; 2001 S 3, eff. 1–1–02; 2000 S 179, § 3, eff. 1–1–02; 2000 S 180, eff. 3–22–01; 2000 S 218, eff. 3–15–01; 2000 H 583, eff. 6–14–00; 2000 S 181, eff. 9–4–00; 1997 H 352, eff. 1–1–98; 1997 H 215, eff. 6–30–97; 1996 H 124, eff. 3–31–97; 1996 H 377, eff. 10–17–96; 1996 S 269, eff. 7–1–96; 1996 H 274, eff. 8–8–96; 1995 H 1, eff. 1–1–96; 1993 H 173, eff. 12–31–93; 1993 S 21; 1992 S 10; 1990 S 3, H 514, S 258, H 591; 1988 S 89; 1986 H 428, H 509, H 476; 1984 H 614; 1983 H 93; 1982 H 515; 1981 H 1; 1977 S 135; 1976 H 244; 1975 H 85; 1970 H 931; 1969 H 320)

Historical and Statutory Notes

Ed. Note: Former 2151.23 repealed by 1969 H 320, eff. 11–19–69; 130 v S 187; 127 v 547; 1953 H 1; GC 1639–16.

Ed. Note: Former RC 2151.23(G)(2) related to the duration of child support orders beyond the child's eighteenth birthday. See now RC 3119.86 for provisions analogous to former RC 2151.23(G)(2).

Pre–1953 H 1 Amendments: 121 v 557; 117 v 520

Amendment Note: 2001 S 3 added new division (A)(15).

Amendment Note: 2000 S 179 inserted ", indictment, or information" in division (A)(1); substituted "2152.12" for "2151.26" in division (H); substituted "divisions (A) and (B) of section 2152.12" for "divisions (B) and (C) of section 2151.26" in division (I); and made corrective internal numbering changes and other nonsubstantive changes.

Amendment Note: 2000 S 180 redesignated divisions (A)(14) and (A)(15) as (A)(13) and (A)(14); substituted "3111.18" for "3111.19" in division (B)(2) and "3111.28" for "5101.34" in division (B)(5); inserted new division (B)(6); rewrote division (G); and made other nonsubstantive amendments. Prior to amendment division (G) read:

"(G)(1) Each order for child support made or modified by a juvenile court shall include as part of the order a general provision, as described in division (A)(1) of section 3113.21 of the Revised Code, requiring the withholding or deduction of income or assets of the obligor under the order as described in division (D) of section 3113.21 of the Revised Code, or another type of appropriate requirement as described in division (D)(3), (D)(4), or (H) of that section, to ensure that withholding or deduction from the income or assets of the obligor is available from the commencement of the support order for collection of the support and of any arrearages that occur; a statement requiring all parties to the order to notify the child support enforcement agency in writing of their current mailing address, current residence address, current residence telephone number, and current driver's license number, and any changes to that information; and a notice that the requirement to notify the child support enforcement agency of all changes to that information continues until further notice from the court. Any juvenile court that makes or modifies an order for child support shall comply with sections 3113.21 to 3113.219 of the Revised Code. If any person required to pay child support under an order made by a juvenile court on or after April 15, 1985, or modified on or after December 1, 1986, is found in contempt of court for failure to make support payments under the order, the court that makes the finding, in addition to any other penalty or remedy imposed, shall assess all court costs arising out of the contempt proceeding against the person and require the person to pay any reasonable attorney's fees of any adverse party, as determined by the court, that arose in relation to the act of contempt.

"(2) Notwithstanding section 3109.01 of the Revised Code, if a juvenile court issues a child support order under this chapter, the order shall remain in effect beyond the child's eighteenth birthday as long as the child continuously attends on a full-time basis any recognized and accredited high school or the order provides that the duty of support of the child continues beyond the child's eighteenth birthday. Except in cases in which the order provides that the duty of support continues for any period after the child reaches nineteen years of age the order shall not remain in effect after the child reaches nineteen years of age. Any parent ordered to pay support under a child support order issued under this chapter shall continue to pay support under the order, including during seasonal vacation periods, until the order terminates."

Amendment Note: 2000 S 218 inserted "have violated section 2151.87 of the Revised Code or an order issued under that section or to" in division (A)(1); and made corrective internal numbering changes.

Amendment Note: 2000 H 583 deleted former division (A)(13); inserted "except as provided in division (I) of section 2301.03 of the Revised Code," in divisions (B), (D), and (E); and made other nonsubstantive changes. Prior to deletion, former division (A)(13) read:

"(13) Concerning an action commenced under section 2151.55 of the Revised Code."

Amendment Note: 2000 S 181 inserted "and, based on and in relation to the allegation pertaining to the child, concerning the parent, guardian, or other person having care of a child who is alleged to be an unruly or delinquent child for being an habitual or chronic truant" in division (A)(1); inserted "section 2919.222," twice in division (A)(6); and added divisions (A)(14) and (A)(15).

Amendment Note: 1997 H 352 substituted "uniform interstate family support act" for "uniform reciprocal enforcement of support act" in division (B)(3); added division (B)(5); deleted "on or after December 31, 1993," before "shall include", substituted "income" for "wages" twice and "(D)(3), (D)(4)" for "(D)(6), (D)(7)", inserted "current residence telephone number, current driver's license number," and deleted "on or after April 12, 1990," before "shall comply", in division (G)(1); inserted "or the order provides that the duty of support of the child continues beyond the child's eighteenth birthday" and added the second sentence in division (G)(2); and made other nonsubstantive changes.

Amendment Note: 1997 H 215 added division (A)(13).

Amendment Note: 1996 H 124 removed the designation of division (H)(1); deleted former division (H)(2); and added division (I). Prior to deletion, former division (H)(2) read:

"(2) The department of rehabilitation and correction shall house an inmate who is fourteen years of age or older and under eighteen years of age in a housing unit in a state correctional institution separate from inmates who are eighteen years of age or older, if the inmate who is under eighteen years of age observes the rules and regulations of the institution and does not otherwise create a security risk by being housed separately. When an inmate attains eighteen years of age, the department may house the inmate with the adult population of the state correctional institution. If the department receives too few inmates who are under eighteen years of age to fill a housing unit in the state correctional institution separate from inmates who are eighteen years or older, the department also may assign to the housing unit inmates who are eighteen years of age or older and under twenty-one years of age."

Amendment Note: 1996 H 377 inserted "as follows" in the introductory paragraph of division (A); inserted "Subject to division (V) of section 2301.03 of the Revised Code," in divisions (A)(2) and (A)(11); and made other nonsubstantive changes.

Amendment Note: 1996 S 269 changed statutory references from section 2919.21(B) to 2919.21(C) throughout in division (A)(6).

Amendment Note: 1996 H 274 added division (A)(12).

Amendment Note: 1995 H 1 added division (H); and made other nonsubstantive changes.

Amendment Note: 1993 S 21 removed a reference to Chapter 5123 in, and deleted "or a mentally retarded person subject to institutionalization by court order, as defined in section 5123.01 of the Revised Code" from the end of, division (A)(4).

Amendment Note: 1993 H 173 rewrote division (G)(1) before the first semi-colon, which previously read:

"(G)(1) Each order for child support made or modified by a juvenile court on or after December 1, 1986, shall be accompanied by one or more orders described in division (D) or (H) of section 3113.21 of the Revised Code, whichever is appropriate under the requirements of that section".

Cross References

Custody of minor children, 3109.03, 3109.04
Duty of parents to support children of unemancipated minor children, 3109.19
Failure to send child to school, 3321.38
Interfering with action to issue or modify support order, 2919.231
Marriage, method of consent, 3101.02
Minor female's complaint for abortion, juvenile court to hear, 2151.85
Nonsupport of dependents, 2919.21
Paternity proceedings, jurisdiction of courts, 3111.06
Placing of children, 5103.16
Rules of procedure do not affect jurisdiction, Juv R 44
Scope of rules, Juv R 1
Uniform child custody jurisdiction law, 3109.21 to 3109.37
Uniform Interstate Family Support Act, venue of actions, 3115.56

Ohio Administrative Code References

Child support enforcement agency's responsibility in custody situations, OAC 5101:1–29–01
Child support, procedural matters, OAC 5101:1–30–501

Library References

Courts ☞175.
Infants ☞196.
Parent and Child ☞3.3(2).
Westlaw Topic Nos. 106, 211, 285.
C.J.S. Infants §§ 42, 53, 54.
C.J.S. Parent and Child § 74.
OJur 3d: 46, Family Law § 570, 571; 47, Family Law § 1058, 1188, 1198, 1201, 1222, 1300, 1301, 1306, 1308; 48, Family Law § 1484, 1495, 1544 to 1547, 1549, 1550 to 1555, 1557, 1558, 1590, 1624, 1662, 1735 to 1737, 1739; 53, Habeas Corpus and Post Conviction Remedies § 40
Am Jur 2d: 47, Juvenile Courts and Delinquent and Dependent Children § 16 to 21
Homicide by juvenile as within jurisdiction of a juvenile court. 48 ALR2d 663
Long-arm statutes: obtaining jurisdiction over nonresident parent in filiation or support proceeding. 76 ALR3d 708
Authority of court to order juvenile delinquent incarcerated in adult penal institution. 95 ALR3d 568
Baldwin's Ohio Legislative Service, 1988 Laws of Ohio, S 89—LSC Analysis, p 5–571; 1990 Laws of Ohio, S 258—LSC Analysis, p 5–954, H 591—LSC Analysis, p 5–576
Gotherman & Babbit, Ohio Municipal Law, Text 27.05.

Sowald & Morganstern, Baldwin's Ohio Practice, Domestic Relations Law § 3.8, 3.12, 19.1, 22.4.2 (1997).
Adrine & Ruden, Ohio Domestic Violence Law (2002 Ed.), Text 12.11, 14.5.
Carlin, Baldwin's Ohio Practice, Merrick–Rippner Probate Law § 3.5, 19.2, 19.6, 62.59, 101.22, 105.1, 105.2, 105.3, 105.4, 105.5, 105.6, 105.7, 105.8, 105.10, 105.11, 105.13, 106.19, 107.2, 107.67, 107.88, 107.117, 107.118, 107.121, 107.133, 107.134, 107.139, 107.140, 107.141, 107.177, 108.1, 108.3, 108.13, 108.14, 108.15, 108.16, 108.17, 108.20, 108.23, 108.26, 108.31, 108.34, 108.38, 108.41 (2003).

2151.231 Action for child support order

The parent, guardian, or custodian of a child, the person with whom a child resides, or the child support enforcement agency of the county in which the child, parent, guardian, or custodian of the child resides may bring an action in a juvenile court or other court with jurisdiction under section 2101.022 or 2301.03 of the Revised Code under this section requesting the court to issue an order requiring a parent of the child to pay an amount for the support of the child without regard to the marital status of the child's parents. No action may be brought under this section against a person presumed to be the parent of a child based on an acknowledgment of paternity that has not yet become final under former section 3111.211 or 5101.314 or section 2151.232, 3111.25, or 3111.821 of the Revised Code.

The parties to an action under this section may raise the issue of the existence or nonexistence of a parent-child relationship, unless a final and enforceable determination of the issue has been made with respect to the parties pursuant to Chapter 3111. of the Revised Code or an acknowledgment of paternity signed by the child's parents has become final pursuant to former section 3111.211 or 5101.314 or section 2151.232, 3111.25, or 3111.821 of the Revised Code. If a complaint is filed under this section and an issue concerning the existence or nonexistence of a parent-child relationship is raised, the court shall treat the action as an action pursuant to sections 3111.01 to 3111.18 of the Revised Code. An order issued in an action under this section does not preclude a party to the action from bringing a subsequent action pursuant to sections 3111.01 to 3111.18 of the Revised Code if the issue concerning the existence or nonexistence of the parent-child relationship was not determined with respect to the party pursuant to a proceeding under this section, a proceeding under Chapter 3111. of the Revised Code, or an acknowledgment of paternity that has become final under former section 3111.211 or 5101.314 or section 2151.232, 3111.25, or 3111.821 of the Revised Code. An order issued pursuant to this section shall remain effective until an order is issued pursuant to sections 3111.01 to 3111.18 of the Revised Code that a parent-child relationship does not exist between the alleged father of the child and the child or until the occurrence of an event described in section 3119.88 of the Revised Code that would require the order to terminate.

The court, in accordance with sections 3119.29 to 3119.56 of the Revised Code, shall include in each support order made under this section the requirement that one or both of the parents provide for the health care needs of the child to the satisfaction of the court.

(2002 H 657, eff. 12–13–02; 2000 S 180, eff. 3–22–01; 1997 H 352, eff. 1–1–98; 1996 H 710, § 7, eff. 6–11–96; 1995 H 167, eff. 6–11–96; 1992 S 10, eff. 7–15–92)

Uncodified Law

1996 H 710, § 15, eff. 6–11–96, reads, in part:

(A) The amendments to sections 2151.231, 2301.34, 2301.35, 2301.351, 2301.358, 2705.02, 3111.20, 3111.21, 3111.22, 3111.23, 3111.241, 3111.242, 3111.27, 3111.28, 3111.99, 3113.21, 3113.214, 3113.215, 3113.99, 4723.07, and 4723.09 of the Revised Code by Sub. H.B. 167 of the 121st General Assembly take effect, and their existing interim versions are correspondingly repealed, on the date this act takes effect and not on November 15, 1996 [.]

Historical and Statutory Notes

Ed. Note: The effective date of the amendment of this section by 1995 H 167 was changed from 11–15–96 to 6–11–96 by 1996 H 710, § 7, eff. 6–11–96.

Amendment Note: 2002 H 657 substituted "3119.29" for "3119.30" and "3119.56" for "3119.58" in the last paragraph of the section.

Amendment Note: 2000 S 180 rewrote this section, which prior thereto read:

"The parent, guardian, or custodian of a child, the person with whom a child resides, or the child support enforcement agency of the county in which the child, parent, guardian, or custodian of the child resides may bring an action in a juvenile court under this section requesting the court to issue an order requiring a parent of the child to pay an amount for the support of the child without regard to the marital status of the child's parents.

"The parties to an action under this section may raise the issue of the existence or nonexistence of a parent-child relationship, unless a final and enforceable determination of the issue has been made with respect to the parties pursuant to Chapter 3111. of the Revised Code or an acknowledgment of paternity signed by the child's parents has become final pursu-

ant to section 2151.232, 3111.211, or 5101.314 of the Revised Code. If a complaint is filed under this section and an issue concerning the existence or nonexistence of a parent-child relationship is raised, the court shall treat the action as an action pursuant to sections 3111.01 to 3111.19 of the Revised Code. An order issued in an action under this section does not preclude a party to the action from bringing a subsequent action pursuant to sections 3111.01 to 3111.19 of the Revised Code if the issue concerning the existence or nonexistence of the parent-child relationship was not determined with respect to the party pursuant to a proceeding under this section, a proceeding under Chapter 3111. of the Revised Code, or an acknowledgment of paternity that has become final under section 2151.232, 3111.211, or 5101.314 of the Revised Code. An order issued pursuant to this section shall remain effective until an order is issued pursuant to sections 3111.01 to 3111.19 of the Revised Code that a parent-child relationship does not exist between the alleged father of the child and the child or until the occurrence of an event described in division (G)(4)(a) of section 3113.21 of the Revised Code that would require the order to terminate.

"The court, in accordance with section 3113.217 of the Revised Code, shall include in each support order made under this section the requirement that one or both of the parents provide for the health care needs of the child to the satisfaction of the court."

Amendment Note: 1997 H 352 inserted "or an acknowledgment of paternity signed by the child's parents has become final pursuant to section 2151.232, 3111.211, or 5101.314 of the Revised Code" and "pursuant to a proceeding under this section, a proceeding under Chapter 3111. of the Revised Code, or an acknowledgment of paternity that has become final under section 2151.232, 3111.211, or 5101.314 of the Revised Code" in the second paragraph; and added the third paragraph.

Amendment Note: 1995 H 167 inserted ", the person with whom a child resides, or the child support enforcement agency of the county in which the child, parent, guardian, or custodian of the child resides" in the first paragraph; and added the second paragraph.

Cross References

Child support orders, penalties, child support order defined, 3113.99

Interfering with action to issue or modify support order, 2919.231

Nonsupport of dependents, court costs and attorney fees, 2919.21

Parental duty of support, 3111.20

Review of administrative child support orders, 3111.27

Support orders, withholding or deduction requirements and notices, 3113.21

Library References

OJur 3d: 47, Family Law § 1027, 1046, 1222

Sowald & Morganstern, Baldwin's Ohio Practice, Domestic Relations Law § 3.2, 3.4, 3.8, 19.1, 22.13 (1997).

Carlin, Baldwin's Ohio Practice, Merrick–Rippner Probate Law § 19.2, 19.6, 19.10, 107.134, 108.1, 108.13, 108.20, 108.33, 108.34 (2003).

2151.232 Action for child support order before acknowledgment becomes final

If an acknowledgment has been filed and entered into the birth registry pursuant to section 3111.24 of the Revised Code but has not yet become final, either parent who signed the acknowledgment may bring an action in the juvenile court or other court with jurisdiction under section 2101.022 or 2301.03 of the Revised Code under this section requesting that the court issue an order requiring a parent of the child to pay an amount for the support of the child in accordance with Chapters 3119., 3121., 3123., and 3125. of the Revised Code.

The parties to an action under this section may raise the issue of the existence or nonexistence of a parent-child relationship. If an action is commenced pursuant to this section and the issue of the existence or nonexistence of a parent-child relationship is raised, the court shall treat the action as an action commenced pursuant to sections 3111.01 to 3111.18 of the Revised Code. If the issue is raised, the court shall promptly notify the office of child support in the department of job and family services that it is conducting proceedings in compliance with sections 3111.01 to 3111.18 of the Revised Code. On receipt of the notice by the office, the acknowledgment of paternity signed by the parties and filed pursuant to section 3111.23 of the Revised Code shall be considered rescinded.

If the parties do not raise the issue of the existence or nonexistence of a parent-child relationship in the action and an order is issued pursuant to this section prior to the date the acknowledgment filed and entered on the birth registry becomes final, the acknowledgment shall be considered final as of the date of the issuance of the order. An order issued pursuant to this section shall not affect an acknowledgment that becomes final pursuant to section 3111.25 of the Revised Code prior to the issuance of the order.

(2000 S 180, eff. 3–22–01; 1999 H 471, eff. 7–1–00; 1997 H 352, eff. 1–1–98)

Historical and Statutory Notes

Amendment Note: 2000 S 180 rewrote this section, which prior thereto read:

"If an acknowledgment has been filed and entered into the birth registry pursuant to section 5101.314 of the Revised Code but has not yet become final, either parent who signed the acknowledgment may bring an action in the juvenile court under this section requesting that the court issue an order requiring a parent of the child to pay an amount for the support of the child in accordance with sections 3113.21 to 3113.219 of the Revised Code.

"The parties to an action under this section may raise the issue of the existence or nonexistence of a

parent-child relationship. If an action is commenced pursuant to this section and the issue of the existence or nonexistence of a parent-child relationship is raised, the court shall treat the action as an action commenced pursuant to sections 3111.01 to 3111.19 of the Revised Code. If the issue is raised, the court shall promptly notify the division of child support in the department of job and family services that it is conducting proceedings in compliance with sections 3111.01 to 3111.19 of the Revised Code. On receipt of the notice by the division, the acknowledgment of paternity signed by the parties and filed pursuant to section 5101.314 of the Revised Code shall be considered rescinded.

"If the parties do not raise the issue of the existence or nonexistence of a parent-child relationship in the action and an order is issued pursuant to this section prior to the date the acknowledgment filed and entered on the birth registry under section 5101.314 of the Revised Code becomes final, the acknowledgment shall be considered final as of the date of the issuance of the order. An order issued pursuant to this section shall not affect an acknowledgment that becomes final pursuant to section 5101.314 of the Revised Code prior to the issuance of the order."

Amendment Note: 1999 H 471 substituted "job and family" for "human" in the second paragraph.

Cross References

Adoption, consents required, 3107.06
Adoption, exception to requirement of search of putative father registry, 3107.064
Child support orders, penalties, child support order defined, 3113.99
Duty of parents to support children of unemancipated minor children, complaints regarding, 3109.19
Filing of birth certificate upon acknowledgement of paternity, 3705.09
Interfering with action to issue or modify support order, 2919.231
Nonsupport of dependents, court costs and attorney fees, 2919.21
Parental duty of support, raising issue of existence of parent-child relationship, 3111.20
Parental duty of support, when arising, 3103.031
Presumptions regarding father-child relationship, 3111.03
Visitation rights of grandparents and other relatives, complaints for, 3109.12

Library References

OJur 3d: 47, Family Law § 892, 908.1, 965, 1008, 1027, 1038, 1039, 1198, 1201, 1222, 1300, 1301, 1308
Validity and construction of putative father's promise to support or provide for illegitimate child. 20 ALR3d 500
Sowald & Morganstern, Baldwin's Ohio Practice, Domestic Relations Law § 19.1, 19.2 (1997).
Carlin, Baldwin's Ohio Practice, Merrick–Rippner Probate Law § 19.1, 19.2, 19.4, 19.6, 19.7, 19.10, 98.30, 98.31, 98.32, 98.34, 98.38, 98.49, 108.13, 108.20, 108.22, 108.24, 108.26, 108.31, 108.34 (2003).

2151.24 Separate room for hearings

(A) Except as provided in division (B) of this section, the board of county commissioners shall provide a special room not used for the trial of criminal or adult cases, when available, for the hearing of the cases of dependent, neglected, abused, and delinquent children.

(B) Division (A) of this section does not apply to the case of an alleged delinquent child when the case is one in which the prosecuting attorney seeks a serious youthful offender disposition under section 2152.13 of the Revised Code.

(2000 S 179, § 3, eff. 1–1–02; 1975 H 85, eff. 11–28–75; 1953 H 1; GC 1639–14)

Historical and Statutory Notes

Pre–1953 H 1 Amendments: 117 v 520, § 1

Amendment Note: 2000 S 179 designated division (A) and inserted "Except as provided in division (B) of this section," therein; and added division (B).

Library References

Infants ⚬74.

Westlaw Topic No. 211.

C.J.S. Infants §§ 221, 226.

OJur 3d: 48, Family Law § 1536

Carlin, Baldwin's Ohio Practice, Merrick–Rippner Probate Law § 107.52 (2003).

PRACTICE AND PROCEDURE

2151.27 Complaint

(A)(1) Subject to division (A)(2) of this section, any person having knowledge of a child who appears to have violated section 2151.87 of the Revised Code or to be a juvenile traffic offender or to be an unruly, abused, neglected, or dependent child may file a sworn complaint with respect to that child in the juvenile court of the county in which the child has a residence or legal settlement or in which the violation, unruliness, abuse, neglect, or dependency allegedly occurred. If an alleged abused, neglected, or dependent child is taken into custody pursuant to division (D) of section 2151.31 of the Revised Code or is taken into custody pursuant to division (A) of section 2151.31 of the Revised Code without the filing of a complaint and placed into shelter care pursuant to division (C) of that section, a sworn complaint shall be filed with respect to the child before the end of the next day after the day on which the child was taken into custody. The sworn complaint may be upon information and belief, and, in addition to the allegation that the child committed the violation or is an unruly, abused, neglected, or dependent child, the complaint shall allege the particular facts upon which the allegation that the child committed the violation or is an unruly, abused, neglected, or dependent child is based.

(2) Any person having knowledge of a child who appears to be an unruly child for being an habitual truant may file a sworn complaint with respect to that child and the parent, guardian, or other person having care of the child in the juvenile court of the county in which the child has a residence or legal settlement or in which the child is supposed to attend public school. The sworn complaint may be upon information and belief and shall contain the following allegations:

(a) That the child is an unruly child for being an habitual truant and, in addition, the particular facts upon which that allegation is based;

(b) That the parent, guardian, or other person having care of the child has failed to cause the child's attendance at school in violation of section 3321.38 of the Revised Code and, in addition, the particular facts upon which that allegation is based.

(B) If a child, before arriving at the age of eighteen years, allegedly commits an act for which the child may be adjudicated an unruly child and if the specific complaint alleging the act is not filed or a hearing on that specific complaint is not held until after the child arrives at the age of eighteen years, the court has jurisdiction to hear and dispose of the complaint as if the complaint were filed and the hearing held before the child arrived at the age of eighteen years.

(C) If the complainant in a case in which a child is alleged to be an abused, neglected, or dependent child desires permanent custody of the child or children, temporary custody of the child or children, whether as the preferred or an alternative disposition, or the placement of the child in a planned permanent living arrangement, the complaint shall contain a prayer specifically requesting permanent custody, temporary custody, or the placement of the child in a planned permanent living arrangement.

(D) Any person with standing under applicable law may file a complaint for the determination of any other matter over which the juvenile court is given jurisdiction by section 2151.23 of the Revised Code. The complaint shall be filed in the county in which the child who is the subject of the complaint is found or was last known to be found.

(E) A public children services agency, acting pursuant to a complaint or an action on a complaint filed under this section, is not subject to the requirements of section 3109.27 of the Revised Code.

(F) Upon the filing of a complaint alleging that a child is an unruly child, the court may hold the complaint in abeyance pending the child's successful completion of actions that constitute a method to divert the child from the juvenile court system. The method may be adopted by a county pursuant to divisions (D) and (E) of section 121.37 of the Revised Code or it may be another method that the court considers satisfactory. If the child completes the actions to the court's satisfaction, the court may dismiss the complaint. If the child fails to complete the actions to the court's satisfaction, the court may consider the complaint.

(2001 H 57, eff. 2–19–02; 2000 S 179, § 3, eff. 1–1–02; 2000 S 218, eff. 3–15–01; 2000 S 181, eff. 9–4–00; 1998 H 484, eff. 3–18–99; 1996 H 445, eff. 9–3–96; 1996 H 274, § 4, eff. 8–8–96; 1996 H 274, § 1, eff. 8–8–96; 1995 S 2, eff. 7–1–96; 1992 H 154, eff. 7–31–92; 1988 S 89; 1984 S 5; 1975 H 85; 1969 H 320)

Historical and Statutory Notes

Ed. Note: Former 2151.27 repealed by 1969 H 320, eff. 11–19–69; 127 v 547; 1953 H 1; GC 1639–23.

Pre–1953 H 1 Amendments: 121 v 557; 117 v 520

Amendment Note: 2001 H 57 added new division (F).

Amendment Note: 2000 S 179 rewrote this section, which prior thereto read:

"(A) (1) Subject to division (A)(2) of this section, any person having knowledge of a child who appears to be a juvenile traffic offender or to be a delinquent, unruly, abused, neglected, or dependent child may file a sworn complaint with respect to that child in the juvenile court of the county in which the child has a residence or legal settlement or in which the traffic offense, delinquency, unruliness, abuse, neglect, or dependency allegedly occurred. If an alleged abused, neglected, or dependent child is taken into custody pursuant to division (D) of section 2151.31 of the Revised Code or is taken into custody pursuant to division (A) of section 2151.31 of the Revised Code without the filing of a complaint and placed into shelter care pursuant to division (C) of that section, a sworn complaint shall be filed with respect to the child before the end of the next day after the day on which the child was taken into custody. The sworn complaint may be upon information and belief, and, in addition to the allegation that the child is a delinquent, unruly, abused, neglected, or dependent child or a juvenile traffic offender, the complaint shall allege the particular facts upon which the allegation that the child is a delinquent, unruly, abused, neglected, or dependent child or a juvenile traffic offender is based.

"(2) Any person having knowledge of a child who appears to be an unruly or delinquent child for being an habitual or chronic truant may file a sworn complaint with respect to that child and the parent, guardian, or other person having care of the child in the juvenile court of the county in which the child has a residence or legal settlement or in which the child is supposed to attend public school. The sworn complaint may be upon information and belief and shall contain the following allegations:

"(a) That the child is an unruly child for being an habitual truant or the child is a delinquent child for being a chronic truant or an habitual truant who previously has been adjudicated an unruly child for being an habitual truant and, in addition, the particular facts upon which that allegation is based;

"(b) That the parent, guardian, or other person having care of the child has failed to cause the child's attendance at school in violation of section 3321.38 of the Revised Code and, in addition, the particular facts upon which that allegation is based.

"(B) If a child, before arriving at the age of eighteen years, allegedly commits an act for which the child may be adjudicated a delinquent child, an unruly child, or a juvenile traffic offender and if the specific complaint alleging the act is not filed or a hearing on that specific complaint is not held until after the child arrives at the age of eighteen years, the court has jurisdiction to hear and dispose of the complaint as if the complaint were filed and the hearing held before the child arrived at the age of eighteen years.

"(C) If the complainant in a case in which a child is alleged to be an abused, neglected, or dependent child desires permanent custody of the child or children, temporary custody of the child or children, whether as the preferred or an alternative disposition, or the placement of the child in a planned permanent living arrangement, the complaint shall contain a prayer specifically requesting permanent custody, temporary custody, or the placement of the child in a planned permanent living arrangement.

"(D) For purposes of the record to be maintained by the clerk under division (B) of section 2151.18 of the Revised Code, when a complaint is filed that alleges that a child is a delinquent child, the court shall determine if the victim of the alleged delinquent act was sixty-five years of age or older or permanently and totally disabled at the time of the alleged commission of the act.

"(E) Any person with standing under applicable law may file a complaint for the determination of any other matter over which the juvenile court is given jurisdiction by section 2151.23 of the Revised Code. The complaint shall be filed in the county in which the child who is the subject of the complaint is found or was last known to be found.

"(F) Within ten days after the filing of a complaint, the court shall give written notice of the filing of the complaint and of the substance of the complaint to the superintendent of a city, local, exempted village, or joint vocational school district if the complaint alleges that a child committed an act that would be a criminal offense if committed by an adult, that the child was sixteen years of age or older at the time of the commission of the alleged act, and that the alleged act is any of the following:

"(1) A violation of section 2923.122 of the Revised Code that relates to property owned or controlled by, or to an activity held under the auspices of, the board of education of that school district;

"(2) A violation of section 2923.12 of the Revised Code, of a substantially similar municipal ordinance, or of section 2925.03 of the Revised Code that was committed on property owned or controlled by, or at an activity held under the auspices of, the board of education of that school district;

"(3) A violation of section 2925.11 of the Revised Code that was committed on property owned or controlled by, or at an activity held under the auspices of, the board of education of that school district, other than a violation of that section that would be a minor drug possession offense, as defined in section 2925.01 of the Revised Code, if committed by an adult;

"(4) A violation of section 2903.01, 2903.02, 2903.03, 2903.04, 2903.11, 2903.12, 2907.02, or 2907.05 of the Revised Code, or a violation of former section 2907.12 of the Revised Code, that was committed on property owned or controlled by, or at an activity held under the auspices of, the board of education of that school district, if the victim at the time of the commission of the alleged act was an employee of the board of education of that school district.

"(5) Complicity in any violation described in division (F)(1), (2), (3), or (4) of this section that was alleged to have been committed in the manner described in division (F)(1), (2), (3), or (4) of this section, regardless of whether the act of complicity was committed on property owned or controlled by, or at an activity held under the auspices of, the board of education of that school district.

"(G) A public children services agency, acting pursuant to a complaint or an action on a complaint filed under this section, is not subject to the requirements of section 3109.27 of the Revised Code."

Amendment Note: 2000 S 218 inserted "have violated section 2151.87 of the Revised Code or to", "violation," and "committed the violation or" twice, in division (A)(1).

Amendment Note: 2000 S 181 designated division (A)(1) and inserted "Subject to division (A)(2) of this section," therein; and added division (A)(2).

Amendment Note: 1998 H 484 substituted "a planned permanent living arrangement" for "long-term foster care" twice in division (C).

Amendment Note: 1996 H 445 changed a reference to section 2907.12 to the reference to former section 2907.12 in division (F)(4); and made other nonsubstantive changes.

Amendment Note: 1996 H 274, § 4, eff. 8–8–96, harmonized the versions of this section as amended by 1995 S 2, § 1, eff. 7–1–96, and 1996 H 274, § 1, eff. 8–8–96; and deleted division (H), which prior thereto read:

"(H) This is an interim section effective until July 1, 1996."

Amendment Note: 1996 H 274, § 1, eff. 8–8–96, deleted "business" after "next" in division (A); added divisions (G) and (H); and made changes to reflect gender neutral language.

Amendment Note: 1995 S 2 substituted "adjudicated" for "adjudged" in division (B); deleted "division (A)(1), (4), (5), (6), (7), (9), or (10) of" before "section 2925.03" in division (F)(2); added division (F)(3); redesignated former divisions (F)(3) and (F)(4) as divisions (F)(4) and (F)(5); inserted "or (4)" twice in division (F)(5); and made changes to reflect gender neutral language and other nonsubstantive changes.

Cross References

Complaint, Juv R 10
Extension of expulsion of pupils, 3313.66
Minor, diversion program, 4301.69

Parent convicted of killing other parent, termination of custody order deemed new complaint for institutional custody, 3109.46
Placing of child in institution, agency filing complaint and case plan, 5103.15
Power of attorney or caretaker authorization affidavit, hearing, notice, de novo review, 3109.77

Ohio Administrative Code References

Obtaining permanent custody: termination of parental rights, OAC 5101:2–42–95

Library References

Infants ☞152, 197.
Westlaw Topic No. 211.
C.J.S. Infants §§ 31 to 91.
OJur 3d: 48, Family Law § 1486, 1550, 1556, 1586, 1590, 1593, 1595, 1601, 1684, 1699
Age of child at time of alleged offense or delinquency, or at time of legal proceedings, as criterion of jurisdiction of juvenile court. 89 ALR2d 506
Baldwin's Ohio Legislative Service, 1988 Laws of Ohio, S 89—LSC Analysis, p 5–571
Katz & Giannelli, Baldwin's Ohio Practice, Criminal Law § 35.11 (1996).
Carlin, Baldwin's Ohio Practice, Merrick–Rippner Probate Law § 104.5, 105.8, 105.13, 107.2, 107.3, 107.4, 107.5, 107.7, 107.8, 107.50, 107.84, 107.136, 107.137, 107.138, 108.16 (2003).

2151.271 Transfer to juvenile court of another county

Except in a case in which the child is alleged to be a serious youthful offender under section 2152.13 of the Revised Code, if the child resides in a county of the state and the proceeding is commenced in a juvenile court of another county, that court, on its own motion or a motion of a party, may transfer the proceeding to the county of the child's residence upon the filing of the complaint or after the adjudicatory, or dispositional hearing, for such further proceeding as required. The court of the child's residence shall then proceed as if the original complaint had been filed in that court. Transfer may also be made if the residence of the child changes. The proceeding shall be so transferred if other proceedings involving the child are pending in the juvenile court of the county of the child's residence.

Whenever a case is transferred to the county of the child's residence and it appears to the court of that county that the interests of justice and the convenience of the parties requires that the adjudicatory hearing be had in the county in which the complaint was filed, the court may return the proceeding to the county in which the complaint was filed for the purpose of the adjudicatory hearing. The court may thereafter proceed as to the transfer to the county of the child's legal residence as provided in this section.

Certified copies of all legal and social records pertaining to the case shall accompany the transfer.

(2000 S 179, § 3, eff. 1–1–02; 1969 H 320, eff. 11–19–69)

Historical and Statutory Notes

Amendment Note: 2000 S 179, § 3, eff. 1–1–02, inserted "Except in a case in which the child is alleged to be a serious youthful offender under section 2152.13 of the Revised Code," in the first paragraph; and made changes to reflect gender neutral language and other nonsubstantive changes.

Cross References

Complaint, Juv R 10
Transfer to another county, Juv R 11

Library References

Infants ☞196.
Westlaw Topic No. 211.
C.J.S. Infants §§ 42, 53, 54.
OJur 3d: 46, Family Law § 453; 48, Family Law § 1587, 1588
Carlin, Baldwin's Ohio Practice, Merrick–Rippner Probate Law § 107.7 (2003).

2151.28   Summons

(A) No later than seventy-two hours after the complaint is filed, the court shall fix a time for an adjudicatory hearing. The court shall conduct the adjudicatory hearing within one of the following periods of time:

(1) Subject to division (C) of section 2152.13 of the Revised Code and division (A)(3) of this section, if the complaint alleged that the child violated section 2151.87 of the Revised Code or is a delinquent or unruly child or a juvenile traffic offender, the adjudicatory hearing shall be held and may be continued in accordance with the Juvenile Rules.

(2) If the complaint alleged that the child is an abused, neglected, or dependent child, the adjudicatory hearing shall be held no later than thirty days after the complaint is filed, except that, for good cause shown, the court may continue the adjudicatory hearing for either of the following periods of time:

(a) For ten days beyond the thirty-day deadline to allow any party to obtain counsel;

(b) For a reasonable period of time beyond the thirty-day deadline to obtain service on all parties or any necessary evaluation, except that the adjudicatory hearing shall not be held later than sixty days after the date on which the complaint was filed.

(3) If the child who is the subject of the complaint is in detention and is charged with violating a section of the Revised Code that may be violated by an adult, the hearing shall be held not later than fifteen days after the filing of the complaint. Upon a showing of good cause, the adjudicatory hearing may be continued and detention extended.

(B) At an adjudicatory hearing held pursuant to division (A)(2) of this section, the court, in addition to determining whether the child is an abused, neglected, or dependent child, shall determine whether the child should remain or be placed in shelter care until the dispositional hearing. When the court makes the shelter care determination, all of the following apply:

(1) The court shall determine whether there are any relatives of the child who are willing to be temporary custodians of the child. If any relative is willing to be a temporary custodian, the child otherwise would remain or be placed in shelter care, and the appointment is appropriate, the court shall appoint the relative as temporary custodian of the child, unless the court appoints another relative as custodian. If it determines that the appointment of a relative as custodian would not be appropriate, it shall issue a written opinion setting forth the reasons for its determination and give a copy of the opinion to all parties and the guardian ad litem of the child.

The court's consideration of a relative for appointment as a temporary custodian does not make that relative a party to the proceedings.

(2) The court shall comply with section 2151.419 of the Revised Code.

(3) The court shall schedule the date for the dispositional hearing to be held pursuant to section 2151.35 of the Revised Code. The parents of the child have a right to be represented by counsel; however, in no case shall the dispositional hearing be held later than ninety days after the date on which the complaint was filed.

(C)(1) The court shall direct the issuance of a summons directed to the child except as provided by this section, the parents, guardian, custodian, or other person with whom the child may be, and any other persons that appear to the court to be proper or necessary parties to the proceedings, requiring them to appear before the court at the time fixed to answer the allegations of the complaint. The summons shall contain the name and telephone number of the court employee designated by the court pursuant to section 2151.314 of the Revised Code to arrange for the prompt appointment of counsel for indigent persons. A child alleged to be an abused, neglected, or dependent child shall not be summoned unless the court so directs. A summons issued for a child who is under fourteen years of age and who is alleged to be a delinquent child, unruly child, or a juvenile traffic offender shall be served on the parent, guardian, or custodian of the child in the child's behalf.

If the person who has physical custody of the child, or with whom the child resides, is other than the parent or guardian, then the parents and guardian also shall be summoned. A copy of the complaint shall accompany the summons.

(2) In lieu of appearing before the court at the time fixed in the summons and prior to the date fixed for appearance in the summons, a child who is alleged to have violated section 2151.87 of the Revised Code and that child's parent, guardian, or custodian may sign a waiver of appearance before the clerk of the juvenile court and pay a fine of one hundred dollars. If the child and that child's parent, guardian, or custodian do not waive the court appearance, the court shall proceed with the adjudicatory hearing as provided in this section.

(D) If the complaint contains a prayer for permanent custody, temporary custody, whether as the preferred or an alternative disposition, or a planned permanent living arrangement in a case involving an alleged abused, neglected, or dependent child, the summons served on the parents shall contain as is appropriate an explanation that the granting of permanent custody permanently divests the parents of their parental rights and privileges, an explanation that an adjudication that the child is an abused, neglected, or dependent child may result in an order of temporary custody that will cause the removal of the child from their legal custody until the court terminates the order of temporary custody or permanently divests the parents of their parental rights, or an explanation that the issuance of an order for a planned permanent living arrangement will cause the

removal of the child from the legal custody of the parents if any of the conditions listed in divisions (A)(5)(a) to (c) of section 2151.353 of the Revised Code are found to exist.

(E)(1) Except as otherwise provided in division (E)(2) of this section, the court may endorse upon the summons an order directing the parents, guardian, or other person with whom the child may be to appear personally at the hearing and directing the person having the physical custody or control of the child to bring the child to the hearing.

(2) In cases in which the complaint alleges that a child is an unruly or delinquent child for being an habitual or chronic truant and that the parent, guardian, or other person having care of the child has failed to cause the child's attendance at school, the court shall endorse upon the summons an order directing the parent, guardian, or other person having care of the child to appear personally at the hearing and directing the person having the physical custody or control of the child to bring the child to the hearing.

(F)(1) The summons shall contain a statement advising that any party is entitled to counsel in the proceedings and that the court will appoint counsel or designate a county public defender or joint county public defender to provide legal representation if the party is indigent.

(2) In cases in which the complaint alleges a child to be an abused, neglected, or dependent child and no hearing has been conducted pursuant to division (A) of section 2151.314 of the Revised Code with respect to the child or a parent, guardian, or custodian of the child does not attend the hearing, the summons also shall contain a statement advising that a case plan may be prepared for the child, the general requirements usually contained in case plans, and the possible consequences of failure to comply with a journalized case plan.

(G) If it appears from an affidavit filed or from sworn testimony before the court that the conduct, condition, or surroundings of the child are endangering the child's health or welfare or those of others, that the child may abscond or be removed from the jurisdiction of the court, or that the child will not be brought to the court, notwithstanding the service of the summons, the court may endorse upon the summons an order that a law enforcement officer serve the summons and take the child into immediate custody and bring the child forthwith to the court.

(H) A party, other than the child, may waive service of summons by written stipulation.

(I) Before any temporary commitment is made permanent, the court shall fix a time for hearing in accordance with section 2151.414 of the Revised Code and shall cause notice by summons to be served upon the parent or guardian of the child and the guardian ad litem of the child, or published, as provided in section 2151.29 of the Revised Code. The summons shall contain an explanation that the granting of permanent custody permanently divests the parents of their parental rights and privileges.

(J) Any person whose presence is considered necessary and who is not summoned may be subpoenaed to appear and testify at the hearing. Anyone summoned or subpoenaed to appear who fails to do so may be punished, as in other cases in the court of common pleas, for contempt of court. Persons subpoenaed shall be paid the same witness fees as are allowed in the court of common pleas.

(K) The failure of the court to hold an adjudicatory hearing within any time period set forth in division (A)(2) of this section does not affect the ability of the court to issue any order under this chapter and does not provide any basis for attacking the jurisdiction of the court or the validity of any order of the court.

(L) If the court, at an adjudicatory hearing held pursuant to division (A) of this section upon a complaint alleging that a child is an abused, neglected, dependent, delinquent, or unruly child or a juvenile traffic offender, determines that the child is a dependent child, the court shall incorporate that determination into written findings of fact and conclusions of law and enter those findings of fact and conclusions of law in the record of the case. The court shall include in those findings of fact and conclusions of law specific findings as to the existence of any danger to the child and any underlying family problems that are the basis for the court's determination that the child is a dependent child.

(2002 H 393, eff. 7–5–02; 2002 H 180, eff. 5–16–02; 2000 S 179, § 3, eff. 1–1–02; 2000 S 218, eff. 3–15–01; 2000 S 181, eff. 9–4–00; 1998 H 484, eff. 3–18–99; 1996 H 274, eff. 8–8–96; 1996 H 419, eff. 9–18–96; 1988 S 89, eff. 1–1–89; 1975 H 164, H 85; 1969 H 320)

Uncodified Law

2002 H 180, § 3, eff. 5–16–02, reads, in part:

The General Assembly hereby requests the Supreme Court to promptly modify Rule 29 of the Rules of Juvenile Procedure pursuant to its authority under the Ohio Constitution to make that rule consistent with the amendments of this act to section 2151.28 of the Revised Code.

Historical and Statutory Notes

Ed. Note: Former 2151.28 repealed by 1969 H 320, eff. 11–19–69; 1953 H 1; GC 1639–24.

Pre–1953 H 1 Amendments: 121 v 557; 117 v 520

Amendment Note: 2002 H 393 substituted "(C)" for "(D)" in division (A)(1).

Amendment Note: 2002 H 180 inserted "and division (A)(3) of this section" after "Revised Code" in division (A)(1); and added new division (A)(3).

Amendment Note: 2000 S 179, § 3, eff. 1–1–02, inserted "Subject to division (D) of section 2152.13 of the Revised Code," in division (A)(1).

Amendment Note: 2000 S 218 inserted "violated section 2151.87 of the Revised Code or" in division (A)(1); designated division (C)(1); and added division (C)(2).

Amendment Note: 2000 S 181 designated division (E)(1) and inserted "Except as otherwise provided in division (E)(2) of this section," therein; and added division (E)(2).

Amendment Note: 1998 H 484 substituted "comply with" for "make the determination and issue the written finding of facts required by" in division (B)(2); substituted "a planned permanent living arrangement" for "long-term foster care" twice in division (D); and made other nonsubstantive changes.

Amendment Note: 1996 H 274 substituted "No later than seventy-two hours after the complaint is filed" for "After the complaint has been filed" in the first paragraph in division (A); designated division (F)(1); and added division (F)(2).

Amendment Note: 1996 H 419 added division (L) and made changes to reflect gender neutral language throughout.

Cross References

Adjudicatory hearing, Juv R 29
Definitions, Juv R 2
Learnfare program, requirements for participation, 5107.281
Process, issuance, form, Juv R 15
Process, service, Juv R 16
Right to counsel, O Const Art I §10
Subpoena, Juv R 17
Taking into custody, Juv R 6

Library References

Infants ⬤198, 204.
Westlaw Topic No. 211.
C.J.S. Infants §§ 51 to 67.
OJur 3d: 48, Family Law § 1545, 1556, 1568, 1609 to 1614, 1620, 1654, 1660, 1665, 1677, 1678, 1719
Am Jur 2d: 47, Juvenile Courts and Delinquent and Dependent Children § 43
Right to and appointment of counsel in juvenile court proceedings. 60 ALR2d 691
Necessity of service of process upon infant itself in juvenile delinquency and dependency proceedings. 90 ALR2d 293
Right of juvenile court defendant to be represented during court proceedings by parent. 11 ALR4th 719

Validity and efficacy of minor's waiver of right to counsel—modern cases. 25 ALR4th 1072

Court appointment of attorney to represent without compensation indigent in civil action. 52 ALR4th 1063

Baldwin's Ohio Legislative Service, 1988 Laws of Ohio, S 89—LSC Analysis, p 5–571

Klein & Darling, Baldwin's Ohio Practice, Civil Practice § 52–4 (1997).

Katz & Giannelli, Baldwin's Ohio Practice, Criminal Law § 61.10 (1996).

Giannelli & Snyder, Baldwin's Ohio Practice, Evidence § 804.8 (2d ed. 2001).

Carlin, Baldwin's Ohio Practice, Merrick–Rippner Probate Law § 107.9, 107.10, 107.26, 107.43, 107.56, 107.72, 107.74, 107.127, 107.161, 107.162, 107.163, 107.164 (2003).

2151.281   Guardian ad litem

(A) The court shall appoint a guardian ad litem to protect the interest of a child in any proceeding concerning an alleged or adjudicated delinquent child or unruly child when either of the following applies:

(1) The child has no parent, guardian, or legal custodian.

(2) The court finds that there is a conflict of interest between the child and the child's parent, guardian, or legal custodian.

(B)(1) The court shall appoint a guardian ad litem to protect the interest of a child in any proceeding concerning an alleged abused or neglected child and in any proceeding held pursuant to section 2151.414 of the Revised Code. The guardian ad litem so appointed shall not be the attorney responsible for presenting the evidence alleging that the child is an abused or neglected child and shall not be an employee of any party in the proceeding.

(2) The guardian ad litem appointed for an alleged or adjudicated abused or neglected child may bring a civil action against any person, who is required by division (A)(1) of section 2151.421 of the Revised Code to file a report of known or suspected child abuse or child neglect, if that person knows or suspects that the child for whom the guardian ad litem is appointed is the subject of child abuse or child neglect and does not file the required report and if the child suffers any injury or harm as a result of the known or suspected child abuse or child neglect or suffers additional injury or harm after the failure to file the report.

(C) In any proceeding concerning an alleged or adjudicated delinquent, unruly, abused, neglected, or dependent child in which the parent appears to be mentally incompetent or is under eighteen years of age, the court shall appoint a guardian ad litem to protect the interest of that parent.

(D) The court shall require the guardian ad litem to faithfully discharge the guardian ad litem's duties and, upon the guardian ad litem's failure to faithfully discharge the guardian ad litem's duties, shall discharge the guardian ad litem and appoint another guardian ad litem. The court may fix the compensation for the service of the guardian ad litem, which compensation shall be paid from the treasury of the county.

(E) A parent who is eighteen years of age or older and not mentally incompetent shall be deemed sui juris for the purpose of any proceeding relative to a child of the parent who is alleged or adjudicated to be an abused, neglected, or dependent child.

(F) In any case in which a parent of a child alleged or adjudicated to be an abused, neglected, or dependent child is under eighteen years of age, the parents of that parent shall be summoned to appear at any hearing respecting the child, who is alleged or adjudicated to be an abused, neglected, or dependent child.

(G) In any case involving an alleged or adjudicated abused or neglected child or an agreement for the voluntary surrender of temporary or permanent custody of a child that is made in accordance with section 5103.15 of the Revised Code, the court shall appoint the guardian ad litem in each case as soon as possible after the complaint is filed, the request for an extension of the temporary custody agreement is filed with the court, or the request for court approval of the permanent custody agreement is filed. In any case involving an alleged dependent child in which the parent of the child appears to be mentally incompetent or is under eighteen years of age, there is a conflict of interest between the child and the child's parents, guardian, or custodian, or the court believes that the parent of the child is not capable of representing the best interest of the child, the court shall appoint a guardian ad litem for the child. The guardian ad litem or the guardian ad litem's replacement shall continue to serve until any of the following occur:

(1) The complaint is dismissed or the request for an extension of a temporary custody agreement or for court approval

of the permanent custody agreement is withdrawn or denied;

(2) All dispositional orders relative to the child have terminated;

(3) The legal custody of the child is granted to a relative of the child, or to another person;

(4) The child is placed in an adoptive home or, at the court's discretion, a final decree of adoption is issued with respect to the child;

(5) The child reaches the age of eighteen if the child is not mentally retarded, developmentally disabled, or physically impaired or the child reaches the age of twenty-one if the child is mentally retarded, developmentally disabled, or physically impaired;

(6) The guardian ad litem resigns or is removed by the court and a replacement is appointed by the court.

If a guardian ad litem ceases to serve a child pursuant to division (G)(4) of this section and the petition for adoption with respect to the child is denied or withdrawn prior to the issuance of a final decree of adoption or prior to the date an interlocutory order of adoption becomes final, the juvenile court shall reappoint a guardian ad litem for that child. The public children services agency or private child placing agency with permanent custody of the child shall notify the juvenile court if the petition for adoption is denied or withdrawn.

(H) If the guardian ad litem for an alleged or adjudicated abused, neglected, or dependent child is an attorney admitted to the practice of law in this state, the guardian ad litem also may serve as counsel to the ward. If a person is serving as guardian ad litem and counsel for a child and either that person or the court finds that a conflict may exist between the person's roles as guardian ad litem and as counsel, the court shall relieve the person of duties as guardian ad litem and appoint someone else as guardian ad litem for the child. If the court appoints a person who is not an attorney admitted to the practice of law in this state to be a guardian ad litem, the court also may appoint an attorney admitted to the practice of law in this state to serve as counsel for the guardian ad litem.

(I) The guardian ad litem for an alleged or adjudicated abused, neglected, or dependent child shall perform whatever functions are necessary to protect the best interest of the child, including, but not limited to, investigation, mediation, monitoring court proceedings, and monitoring the services provided the child by the public children services agency or private child placing agency that has temporary or permanent custody of the child, and shall file any motions and other court papers that are in the best interest of the child.

The guardian ad litem shall be given notice of all hearings, administrative reviews, and other proceedings in the same manner as notice is given to parties to the action.

(J)(1) When the court appoints a guardian ad litem pursuant to this section, it shall appoint a qualified volunteer whenever one is available and the appointment is appropriate.

(2) Upon request, the department of job and family services shall provide for the training of volunteer guardians ad litem.

(1999 H 471, eff. 7–1–00; 1996 H 274, eff. 8–8–96; 1996 H 419, eff. 9–18–96; 1988 S 89, eff. 1–1–89; 1986 H 529; 1984 S 321; 1980 H 695; 1975 H 85; 1969 H 320)

Uncodified Law

1996 H 274, § 12, eff. 8–8–96, reads: Section 2151.281 of the Revised Code as amended by this act shall take effect the earliest time permitted by law, but division (G)(4) and the last unnumbered paragraph of division (G) of the section as amended or added by Am. Sub. H.B. 419 of the 121st General Assembly shall not be applied until the later of the earliest time permitted by law or September 18, 1996.

Historical and Statutory Notes

Amendment Note: 1999 H 471 substituted "job and family" for "human" in division (J)(2).

Amendment Note: 1996 H 274 inserted "either of the following applies" in the first paragraph in division (A); inserted "any injury or harm as a result of the known or suspected child abuse or child neglect or suffers" in division (B)(2); substituted "retarded, developmentally disabled, or physically impaired" for "or physically handicapped" twice in division (G)(5); deleted "guardian," after "mediation," in the first paragraph in division (I); deleted former division (K); and made other nonsubstantive changes. Prior to amendment, former division (K) read:

"(K) A guardian ad litem appointed pursuant to this section on or after the effective date of this amendment may be compensated an amount not exceeding four hundred dollars for the appointment."

Amendment Note: 1996 H 419 substituted "The child is placed in an adoptive home or, at the court's discretion, a" for "A" at the beginning of division (G)(4); added the second and third sentences to division (G)(6); added division (K); and made changes to reflect gender neutral language throughout.

Cross References

Competency of child as witness, submission of questions to determine, 2317.01
Persons required to report injury or neglect, 2151.421
Right to counsel, guardian ad litem, Juv R 4
Waiver of rights, Juv R 3

Library References

Infants ☞205.
Westlaw Topic No. 211.
C.J.S. Infants §§ 51 to 67.
OJur 3d: 5A, Alternative Dispute Resolution § 201; 48, Family Law § 1609, 1629 to 1631, 1722
Am Jur 2d: 47, Juvenile Courts and Delinquent and Dependent Children § 29, 30
Allowance of fees for guardian ad litem appointed for infant defendant, as costs. 30 ALR2d 1148
Baldwin's Ohio Legislative Service, 1988 Laws of Ohio, S 89—LSC Analysis, p 5–571
Sowald & Morganstern, Baldwin's Ohio Practice, Domestic Relations Law § 15.60.1 (1997).
Carlin, Baldwin's Ohio Practice, Merrick–Rippner Probate Law § 107.45, 107.46, 108.13, 108.31 (2003).

2151.29   Service of summons

Service of summons, notices, and subpoenas, prescribed by section 2151.28 of the Revised Code, shall be made by delivering a copy to the person summoned, notified, or subpoenaed, or by leaving a copy at the person's usual place of residence. If the juvenile judge is satisfied that such service is impracticable, the juvenile judge may order service by registered or certified mail. If the person to be served is without the state but the person can be found or the person's address is known, or the person's whereabouts or address can with reasonable diligence be ascertained, service of the summons may be made by delivering a copy to the person personally or mailing a copy to the person by registered or certified mail.

Whenever it appears by affidavit that after reasonable effort the person to be served with summons cannot be found or the person's post-office address ascertained, whether the person is within or without a state, the clerk shall publish such summons once in a newspaper of general circulation throughout the county. The summons shall state the substance and the time and place of the hearing, which shall be held at least one week later than the date of the publication. A copy of the summons and the complaint, indictment, or information shall be sent by registered or certified mail to the last known address of the person summoned unless it is shown by affidavit that a reasonable effort has been made, without success, to obtain such address.

A copy of the advertisement, the summons, and the complaint, indictment, or information, accompanied by the certificate of the clerk that such publication has been made and that the summons and the complaint, indictment, or information have been mailed as required by this section, is sufficient evidence of publication and mailing. When a period of one week from the time of publication has elapsed, the juvenile court shall have full jurisdiction to deal with such child as provided by sections 2151.01 to 2151.99 of the Revised Code.

(2000 S 179, § 3, eff. 1–1–02; 1969 H 320, eff. 11–19–69)

Historical and Statutory Notes

Ed. Note: Former 2151.29 repealed by 1969 H 320, eff. 11–19–69; 1953 H 1; GC 1639–25.

Pre–1953 H 1 Amendments: 121 v 557; 117 v 520

Amendment Note: 2000 S 179, § 3, eff. 1–1–02, inserted ", indictment, or information" throughout the section; and made changes to reflect gender neutral language and other nonsubstantive changes.

Cross References

Process, service, Juv R 16
Subpoena, Juv R 17

Library References

Infants ☞198.
Westlaw Topic No. 211.
C.J.S. Infants § 56.
OJur 3d: 48, Family Law § 1612; 76, Process § 58
Am Jur 2d: 47, Juvenile Courts and Delinquent and Dependent Children § 43
Necessity of service of process upon infant itself in juvenile delinquency and dependency proceedings. 90 ALR2d 293
Katz & Giannelli, Baldwin's Ohio Practice, Criminal Law § 61.10 (1996).
Giannelli & Snyder, Baldwin's Ohio Practice, Evidence § 804.8 (2d ed. 2001).
Carlin, Baldwin's Ohio Practice, Merrick–Rippner Probate Law § 107.165, 107.166 (2003).

2151.30   Issuance of warrant

In any case when it is made to appear to the juvenile judge that the service of a citation under section 2151.29 of the Revised Code will be ineffectual or the welfare of the child requires that he be brought forthwith into the custody of the juvenile court, a warrant may be issued against the parent, custodian, or guardian, or against the child himself.

(1953 H 1, eff. 10–1–53; GC 1639–26)

Historical and Statutory Notes

Pre–1953 H 1 Amendments: 117 v 520, § 1

Cross References

Process, issuance, form, Juv R 15
Process, service, Juv R 16

Library References

Infants ☞192.
Westlaw Topic No. 211.
C.J.S. Infants §§ 42, 53 to 55.
OJur 3d: 48, Family Law § 1615
Carlin, Baldwin's Ohio Practice, Merrick–Rippner
 Probate Law § 107.167 (2003).

2151.31 Apprehension, custody, and detention

(A) A child may be taken into custody in any of the following ways:

(1) Pursuant to an order of the court under this chapter or pursuant to an order of the court upon a motion filed pursuant to division (B) of section 2930.05 of the Revised Code;

(2) Pursuant to the laws of arrest;

(3) By a law enforcement officer or duly authorized officer of the court when any of the following conditions are present:

(a) There are reasonable grounds to believe that the child is suffering from illness or injury and is not receiving proper care, as described in section 2151.03 of the Revised Code, and the child's removal is necessary to prevent immediate or threatened physical or emotional harm;

(b) There are reasonable grounds to believe that the child is in immediate danger from the child's surroundings and that the child's removal is necessary to prevent immediate or threatened physical or emotional harm;

(c) There are reasonable grounds to believe that a parent, guardian, custodian, or other household member of the child's household has abused or neglected another child in the household and to believe that the child is in danger of immediate or threatened physical or emotional harm from that person.

(4) By an enforcement official, as defined in section 4109.01 of the Revised Code, under the circumstances set forth in section 4109.08 of the Revised Code;

(5) By a law enforcement officer or duly authorized officer of the court when there are reasonable grounds to believe that the child has run away from the child's parents, guardian, or other custodian;

(6) By a law enforcement officer or duly authorized officer of the court when any of the following apply:

(a) There are reasonable grounds to believe that the conduct, conditions, or surroundings of the child are endangering the health, welfare, or safety of the child.

(b) A complaint has been filed with respect to the child under section 2151.27 or 2152.021 of the Revised Code or the child has been indicted under division (A) of section 2152.13 of the Revised Code or charged by information as described in that section and there are reasonable grounds to believe that the child may abscond or be removed from the jurisdiction of the court.

(c) The child is required to appear in court and there are reasonable grounds to believe that the child will not be brought before the court when required.

(d) There are reasonable grounds to believe that the child committed a delinquent act and that taking the child into custody is necessary to protect the public interest and safety.

(B)(1) The taking of a child into custody is not and shall not be deemed an arrest except for the purpose of determining its validity under the constitution of this state or of the United States.

(2) Except as provided in division (C) of section 2151.311 of the Revised Code, a child taken into custody shall not be held in any state correctional institution, county, multicounty, or municipal jail or workhouse, or any other place where any adult convicted of crime, under arrest, or charged with crime is held.

(C)(1) Except as provided in division (C)(2) of this section, a child taken into custody shall not be confined in a place of juvenile detention or placed in shelter care prior to the implementation of the court's final order of disposition, unless detention or shelter care is required to protect the child from immediate or threatened physical or emotional harm, because the child is a danger or threat to one or more other persons and is charged with violating a section of the Revised Code that may be violated by an adult, because the child may abscond or be removed from the jurisdiction of the court, because the child has no parents, guardian, or custodian or other person able to provide supervision and care for the child and return the child to the court when required, or because an order for placement of the child in detention or shelter care has been made by the court pursuant to this chapter.

(2) A child alleged to be a delinquent child who is taken into custody may be confined in a place of juvenile detention prior to the implementation of the court's final order of disposition if the confinement is authorized under section 2152.04 of the Revised Code or if the child is alleged to be a serious youthful offender under section 2152.13 of the Revised Code and is not released on bond.

(D) Upon receipt of notice from a person that the person intends to take an alleged abused, neglected, or dependent child into custody pursuant to division (A)(3) of this section, a juvenile judge or a designated referee may grant by telephone an ex parte emergency order authorizing the taking of the child into custody if there is probable cause to believe that any of the conditions set forth in divisions (A)(3)(a) to (c) of this section are present. The judge or referee shall journalize any ex parte emergency order issued pursuant to this division. If an order is issued pursuant to this division and the child is taken into custody pursuant to the order, a sworn complaint shall be filed with respect to the child before the end of the next business day after the day on which the child is taken into custody and a hearing shall be held pursuant to division (E) of this section and the Juvenile Rules. A juvenile judge or referee shall not grant an emergency order by telephone pursuant to this division until after the judge or referee determines that reasonable efforts have been made to notify the parents, guardian, or custodian of the child that the child may be placed into shelter care and of the reasons for placing the child into shelter care, except that, if the requirement for notification would jeopardize the physical or emotional safety of the child or result in the child being removed from the court's jurisdiction, the judge or referee may issue the order for taking the child into custody and placing the child into shelter care prior to giving notice to the parents, guardian, or custodian of the child.

(E) If a judge or referee pursuant to division (D) of this section issues an ex parte emergency order for taking a child into custody, the court shall hold a hearing to determine whether there is probable cause for the emergency order. The hearing shall be held before the end of the next business day after the day on which the emergency order is issued, except that it shall not be held later than seventy-two hours after the emergency order is issued.

If the court determines at the hearing that there is not probable cause for the issuance of the emergency order issued pursuant to division (D) of this section, it shall order the child released to the custody of the child's parents, guardian, or custodian. If the court determines at the hearing that there is probable cause for the issuance of the emergency order issued pursuant to division (D) of this section, the court shall do all of the following:

(1) Ensure that a complaint is filed or has been filed;

(2) Comply with section 2151.419 of the Revised Code;

(3) Hold a hearing pursuant to section 2151.314 of the Revised Code to determine if the child should remain in shelter care.

(F) If the court determines at the hearing held pursuant to division (E) of this section that there is probable cause to believe that the child is an abused child, as defined in division (A) of section 2151.031 of the Revised Code, the court may do any of the following:

(1) Upon the motion of any party, the guardian ad litem, the prosecuting attorney, or an employee of the public children services agency, or its own motion, issue reasonable protective orders with respect to the interviewing or deposition of the child;

(2) Order that the child's testimony be videotaped for preservation of the testimony for possible use in any other proceedings in the case;

(3) Set any additional conditions with respect to the child or the case involving the child that are in the best interest of the child.

(G) This section is not intended, and shall not be construed, to prevent any person from taking a child into custody, if taking the child into custody is necessary in an emergency to prevent the physical injury, emotional harm, or neglect of the child.

(2002 H 180, eff. 5–16–02; 2000 S 179, § 3, eff. 1–1–02; 1999 H 3, eff. 11–22–99; 1999 H 176, eff. 10–29–99; 1998 H 484, eff. 3–18–99; 1997 H 408, eff. 10–1–97; 1994 H 571, eff. 10–6–94; 1989 H 166, eff. 2–14–90; 1988 S 89; 1978 H 883; 1969 H 320)

Uncodified Law

2002 H 180, § 3, eff. 5–16–02, reads, in part:

The General Assembly further requests the Supreme Court to promptly modify Rule 7 of the Rules of Juvenile Procedure pursuant to its authority under the Ohio Constitution to make that rule consistent with the amendments of this act to section 2151.31 of the Revised Code.

Historical and Statutory Notes

Ed. Note: Former 2151.31 repealed by 1969 H 320, eff. 11–19–69; 1953 H 1; GC 1639–27.

Pre–1953 H 1 Amendments: 121 v 557; 117 v 520

Amendment Note: 2002 H 180 inserted "because the child is a danger or threat to one or more other persons and is charged with violating a section of the Revised Code that may be violated by an adult" in division (C)(1).

Amendment Note: 2000 S 179, § 3, eff. 1–1–02, inserted "or 2152.021" and "or the child has been indicted under division (A) of section 2152.13 of the Revised Code or charged by information as described in that section" in division (A)(6)(b); added division (A)(6)(d); designated division (C)(1) and inserted "Except as provided in division (C)(2) of this section," therein; and added division (C)(2).

Amendment Note: 1999 H 3 inserted "or pursuant to an order of the court upon a motion filed pursuant to division (B) of section 2930.05 of the Revised Code" in division (A)(1).

Amendment Note: 1999 H 176 added new division (E)(2); redesignated former division (E)(2) as division (E)(3); and made other nonsubstantive changes.

Amendment Note: 1998 H 484 deleted former division (E)(3); and made other nonsubstantive changes. Prior to deletion, former division (E)(3) read:

"(3) At the hearing held pursuant to section 2151.314 of the Revised Code, make the determination and issue the written finding of facts required by section 2151.419 of the Revised Code."

Amendment Note: 1997 H 408 substituted "public children services agency" for "children services board or the county department of human services exercising the children services function" in division (F)(1); and made changes to reflect gender neutral language.

Amendment Note: 1994 H 571 substituted "correctional" for "penal or reformatory" in division (B)(2).

Cross References

Caretaker authorization affidavit not permitted when certain proceedings are pending, 3109.68
Detention and shelter care, Juv R 7
Delinquent children, information provided to foster caregivers regarding, 2152.72
Power of attorney, certain pending actions prohibiting creation, 3109.58
Taking into custody, Juv R 6
Youth services department, taking into custody child violating supervised release from, 5139.52

Administrative Code References

Emergency removal and placement of the Indian child, OAC 5101:2–42–57

Library References

Infants ⚭68.3, 192.
Westlaw Topic No. 211.
C.J.S. Infants §§ 42, 53 to 55.

OJur 3d: 48, Family Law § 1546, 1568 to 1570, 1590, 1654
Am Jur 2d: 47, Juvenile Courts and Delinquent and Dependent Children § 35
Baldwin's Ohio Legislative Service, 1988 Laws of Ohio, S 89—LSC Analysis, p 5–571
Klein & Darling, Baldwin's Ohio Practice, Civil Practice § 52–4 (1997).
Carlin, Baldwin's Ohio Practice, Merrick–Rippner Probate Law § 104.9, 105.1, 107.5, 107.13, 107.25, 107.26, 107.41, 107.49, 107.74, 107.152 (2003).

2151.311 Procedure upon apprehension

(A) A person taking a child into custody shall, with all reasonable speed and in accordance with division (C) of this section, either:

(1) Release the child to the child's parents, guardian, or other custodian, unless the child's detention or shelter care appears to be warranted or required as provided in section 2151.31 of the Revised Code;

(2) Bring the child to the court or deliver the child to a place of detention or shelter care designated by the court and promptly give notice thereof, together with a statement of the reason for taking the child into custody, to a parent, guardian, or other custodian and to the court.

(B) If a parent, guardian, or other custodian fails, when requested by the court, to bring the child before the court as provided by this section, the court may issue its warrant directing that the child be taken into custody and brought before the court.

(C)(1) Before taking any action required by division (A) of this section, a person taking a child into custody may hold the child for processing purposes in a county, multicounty, or municipal jail or workhouse, or other place where an adult convicted of crime, under arrest, or charged with crime is held for either of the following periods of time:

(a) For a period not to exceed six hours, if all of the following apply:

(i) The child is alleged to be a delinquent child for the commission of an act that would be a felony if committed by an adult;

(ii) The child remains beyond the range of touch of all adult detainees;

(iii) The child is visually supervised by jail or workhouse personnel at all times during the detention;

(iv) The child is not handcuffed or otherwise physically secured to a stationary object during the detention.

(b) For a period not to exceed three hours, if all of the following apply:

(i) The child is alleged to be a delinquent child for the commission of an act that would be a misdemeanor if committed by an adult, is alleged to be a delinquent child for being a chronic truant or an habitual truant who previously has been adjudicated an unruly child for being an habitual truant, or is alleged to be an unruly child or a juvenile traffic offender;

(ii) The child remains beyond the range of touch of all adult detainees;

(iii) The child is visually supervised by jail or workhouse personnel at all times during the detention;

(iv) The child is not handcuffed or otherwise physically secured to a stationary object during the detention.

(2) If a child has been transferred to an adult court for prosecution for the alleged commission of a criminal offense, subsequent to the transfer, the child may be held as described in division (F) of section 2152.26 or division (B) of section 5120.16 of the Revised Code.

(D) As used in division (C)(1) of this section, "processing purposes" means all of the following:

(1) Fingerprinting, photographing, or fingerprinting and photographing the child in a secure area of the facility;

(2) Interrogating the child, contacting the child's parent or guardian, arranging for placement of the child, or arranging for transfer or transferring the child, while holding the child in a nonsecure area of the facility.

(2000 S 179, § 3, eff. 1–1–02; 2000 S 181, eff. 9–4–00; 1996 H 124, eff. 3–31–97; 1996 H 480, eff. 10–16–96; 1994 H 571, eff. 10–6–94; 1989 H 166, eff. 2–14–90; 1972 S 445; 1970 H 931; 1969 H 320)

Historical and Statutory Notes

Amendment Note: 2000 S 179, § 3, eff. 1–1–02, substituted "2152.26" for "2151.312" in division (C)(2).

Amendment Note: 2000 S 181 inserted ", is alleged to be a delinquent child for being a chronic truant or an habitual truant who previously has been adjudicated an unruly child for being an habitual truant," in division (C)(1)(b)(i); and substituted "(F)" for "(C)" in division (C)(2).

Amendment Note: 1996 H 124 rewrote division (C)(2), which prior thereto read:

"(2) If a child has been transferred to an adult court for prosecution for the alleged commission of a criminal offense, subsequent to the transfer, the child may be held as described in division (C) of section 2151.312 of the Revised Code or, if that division does not apply, may be held in a state correctional institution or other place where an adult convicted of crime, under arrest, or charged with crime is held."

Amendment Note: 1996 H 480 rewrote the section, which prior thereto read:

"(A) A person taking a child into custody shall, with all reasonable speed and in accordance with division (C) of this section, either:

"(1) Release the child to his parents, guardian, or other custodian, unless his detention or shelter care appears to be warranted or required as provided in section 2151.31 of the Revised Code;

"(2) Bring the child to the court or deliver him to a place of detention or shelter care designated by the court and promptly give notice thereof, together with a statement of the reason for taking the child into custody, to a parent, guardian, or other custodian and to the court.

"(B) If a parent, guardian, or other custodian fails, when requested by the court, to bring the child before the court as provided by this section, the court may issue its warrant directing that the child be taken into custody and brought before the court.

"(C)(1) Before taking any action required by division (A) of this section, a person taking a child into custody may hold the child for processing purposes in a county, multicounty, or municipal jail or workhouse, or other place where an adult convicted of crime, under arrest, or charged with crime is held for either of the following periods of time:

"(a) For a period not to exceed six hours, if all of the following apply:

"(i) The child is alleged to be a delinquent child for the commission of an act that would be a felony if committed by an adult;

"(ii) The detention is in a room totally separate and removed by both sight and sound from all adult detainees;

"(iii) The child is supervised at all times during the detention.

"(b) For a period not to exceed three hours, if all of the following apply:

"(i) The child is alleged to be a delinquent child for the commission of an act that would be a misdemeanor if committed by an adult or is alleged to be an unruly child or a juvenile traffic offender;

"(ii) The detention is in a room totally separate and removed by both sight and sound from all adult detainees;

"(iii) The child is supervised at all times during the detention.

"(2) If a child has been transferred to an adult court for prosecution for the alleged commission of a criminal offense, the child is convicted of a criminal offense, and sentence is imposed upon the child subsequent to the conviction, the child, during the period of time that he is subject to that sentence and for any action related to that sentence, may be held in a state correctional institution or other place where an adult convicted of crime, under arrest, or charged with crime is held."

Amendment Note: 1994 H 571 substituted "correctional" for "penal institution, reformatory" in division (C)(2).

Cross References

Confinement of minors in county, multicounty, or municipal jails, 341.11

Detention and shelter care, release to parents, procedure, Juv R 7

Library References

Infants ☞68.3, 192.

Westlaw Topic No. 211.

C.J.S. Infants §§ 42, 53 to 55.

OJur 3d: 48, Family Law § 1570, 1574; 73, Penal and Correctional Institutions § 94

Am Jur 2d: 47, Juvenile Courts and Delinquent and Dependent Children § 35

Carlin, Baldwin's Ohio Practice, Merrick–Rippner Probate Law § 107.25, 107.27, 107.29, 107.152, 107.169 (2003).

2151.312   Place of detention

(A) A child alleged to be or adjudicated an unruly child may be held only in the following places:

(1) A certified family foster home or a home approved by the court;

(2) A facility operated by a certified child welfare agency;

(3) Any other suitable place designated by the court.

(B)(1) Except as provided under division (C)(1) of section 2151.311 of the Revised Code, a child alleged to be or adjudicated a neglected child, an abused child, a dependent child, or an unruly child may not be held in any of the following facilities:

(a) A state correctional institution, county, multicounty, or municipal jail or workhouse, or other place in which an adult convicted of a crime, under arrest, or charged with a crime is held;

(b) A secure correctional facility.

(2) Except as provided under sections 2151.26 to 2151.61 of the Revised Code and division (B)(3) of this section, a child alleged to be or adjudicated an unruly child may not be held for more than twenty-four hours in a detention facility. A child alleged to be or adjudicated a neglected child, an abused child, or a dependent child shall not be held in a detention facility.

(3) A child who is alleged to be or adjudicated an unruly child and who is taken into custody on a Saturday, Sunday, or legal holiday, as listed in section 1.14 of the Revised Code, may be held in a detention facility until the next succeeding day that is not a Saturday, Sunday, or legal holiday.

(2000 S 179, § 3, eff. 1–1–02)

Historical and Statutory Notes

Ed. Note: Former 2151.312 amended and recodified as 2152.26 by 2000 S 179, § 3, eff. 1–1–02; 2000 H 332, eff. 1–1–01; 2000 H 448, eff. 10–5–00; 2000 S 181, eff. 9–4–00; 1997 H 1, eff. 7–1–98; 1996 H 124, eff. 3–31–97; 1996 H 265, eff. 3–3–97; 1994 H 571, eff. 10–6–94; 1993 H 152, eff. 7–1–93; 1992 S 331; 1989 H 166; 1981 H 440; 1975 H 85; 1969 H 320.

Library References

Carlin, Baldwin's Ohio Practice, Merrick–Rippner Probate Law § 107.27, 107.28, 107.29, 107.108 (2003).

2151.313   Fingerprinting or photographing child in an investigation

(A)(1) Except as provided in division (A)(2) of this section and in sections 109.57, 109.60, and 109.61 of the Revised Code, no child shall be fingerprinted or photographed in the investigation of any violation of law without the consent of the juvenile judge.

(2) Subject to division (A)(3) of this section, a law enforcement officer may fingerprint and photograph a child without the consent of the juvenile judge when the child is arrested or otherwise taken into custody for the commission of an act that would be an offense, other than a traffic offense or a minor misdemeanor, if committed by an adult, and there is probable cause to believe that the child may have been involved in the commission of the act. A law enforcement officer who takes fingerprints or photographs of a child under division (A)(2) of this section immediately shall inform the juvenile court that the fingerprints or photographs were taken and shall provide the court with the identity of the child, the number of fingerprints and photographs taken, and the name and address of each person who has custody and control of the fingerprints or photographs or copies of the fingerprints or photographs.

(3) This section does not apply to a child to whom either of the following applies:

(a) The child has been arrested or otherwise taken into custody for committing, or has been adjudicated a delinquent child for committing, an act that would be a felony if committed by an adult or has been convicted of or pleaded guilty to committing a felony.

(b) There is probable cause to believe that the child may have committed an act that would be a felony if committed by an adult.

(B)(1) Subject to divisions (B)(4), (5), and (6) of this section, all fingerprints and photographs of a child obtained or taken under division (A)(1) or (2) of this section, and any records of the arrest or custody of the child that was the basis for the taking of the fingerprints or photographs, initially may be retained only until the expiration of thirty days after the date taken, except that the court may limit the initial retention of fingerprints and photographs of a child obtained under division (A)(1) of this section to a shorter period of time and except that, if the child is adjudicated a delinquent child for the commission of an act described in division (B)(3) of this section or is convicted of or pleads guilty to a criminal offense for the commission of an act described in division (B)(3) of this section, the fingerprints and photographs, and the records of the arrest or custody of the child that was the basis for the taking of the fingerprints and photographs, shall be retained in accordance with division (B)(3) of this section. During the initial period of retention, the fingerprints and photographs of a child, copies of the fingerprints and photographs, and records of the arrest or custody of the child shall be used or released only in accordance with division (C) of this section. At the expiration of the initial period for which fingerprints and photographs of a child, copies of fingerprints and photographs of a child, and records of the arrest or custody of a child may be retained under this division, if no complaint, indictment, or information is pending against the child in relation to the act for which the fingerprints and photographs originally were obtained or taken and if the child has neither been adjudicated a delinquent child for the commission of that act nor been convicted of or pleaded guilty to a criminal offense based on that act subsequent to a transfer of the child's case for criminal prosecution pursuant to section 2152.12 of the Revised Code, the fingerprints and photographs of the child, all copies of the fingerprints and photographs, and all records of the arrest or custody of the child that was the basis of the taking of the fingerprints and photographs shall be removed from the file and delivered to the juvenile court.

(2) If, at the expiration of the initial period of retention set forth in division (B)(1) of this section, a complaint, indictment, or information is pending against the child in relation to the act for which the fingerprints and photographs originally were obtained or the child either has been adjudicated a delinquent child for the commission of an act other than an act described in division (B)(3) of this section or has been convicted of or pleaded guilty to a criminal offense for the commission of an act other than an act described in division (B)(3) of this section subsequent to transfer of the child's case, the fingerprints and photographs of the child, copies of the fingerprints and photographs, and the records of the arrest or custody of the child that was the basis of the taking of the fingerprints and photographs may further be retained, subject to division (B)(4) of this section, until the earlier of the expiration of two years after the date on which the fingerprints or photographs were taken or the child attains eighteen years of age, except that, if the child is adjudicated a delinquent child for the commission of an act described in division (B)(3) of this section or is convicted of or pleads guilty to a criminal offense for the commission of an act described in division (B)(3) of this section, the fingerprints and photographs, and the records of the arrest or custody of the child that was the basis for the taking of the fingerprints and photographs, shall be retained in accordance with division (B)(3) of this section.

Except as otherwise provided in division (B)(3) of this section, during this additional period of retention, the fingerprints and photographs of a child, copies of the fingerprints and photographs of a child, and records of the arrest or custody of a child shall be used or released only in accordance with division (C) of this section. At the expiration of the additional period, if no complaint, indictment, or information is pending against the child in relation to the act for which the fingerprints originally were obtained or taken or in relation to another act for which the fingerprints were used as authorized by division (C) of this section and that would be a felony if committed by an adult, the fingerprints of the child, all copies of the fingerprints, and all records of the arrest or custody of the child that was the basis of the taking of the fingerprints shall be removed from the file and delivered to the juvenile court, and, if no complaint, indictment, or information is pending against the child concerning the act for which the photographs originally were obtained or taken or concerning an act that would be a felony if committed by an adult, the photographs and all copies of the photographs, and, if no fingerprints were taken at the time the photographs were taken, all records of the arrest or custody that was the basis of the taking of the photographs shall be removed from the file and delivered to the juvenile court. In either case, if, at the expiration of the applicable additional period, such a complaint, indictment, or information is pending against the child, the photographs and copies of the photographs of the child, or the fingerprints and copies of the fingerprints of the child, whichever is applicable, and the records of the arrest or custody of the child may be retained, subject to division (B)(4) of this section, until final disposition of the complaint, indictment, or information, and, upon final disposition of the complaint, indictment, or information, they shall be removed from the file and delivered to the juvenile court, except that, if the child is adjudicated a delinquent child for the commission of an act described in division (B)(3) of this section or is convicted of or pleads guilty to a criminal offense for the commission of an act described in division (B)(3) of this section, the fingerprints and photographs, and the records of the arrest or custody of the child that was the basis for the taking of the fingerprints and photographs, shall be retained in accordance with division (B)(3) of this section.

(3) If a child is adjudicated a delinquent child for violating section 2923.42 of the Revised Code or for committing an act that would be a misdemeanor offense of violence if committed by an adult, or is convicted of or pleads guilty to a violation of section 2923.42 of the Revised Code, a misdemeanor offense of violence, or a violation of an existing or former municipal ordinance or law of this state, another state, or the United States that is substantially equivalent to section 2923.42 of the Revised Code or any misdemeanor offense of violence, both of the following apply:

(a) Originals and copies of fingerprints and photographs of the child obtained or taken under division (A)(1) of this section, and any records of the arrest or custody that was the basis for the taking of the fingerprints or photographs, may be retained for the period of time speci-

fied by the juvenile judge in that judge's grant of consent for the taking of the fingerprints or photographs. Upon the expiration of the specified period, all originals and copies of the fingerprints, photographs, and records shall be delivered to the juvenile court or otherwise disposed of in accordance with any instructions specified by the juvenile judge in that judge's grant of consent. During the period of retention of the photographs and records, all originals and copies of them shall be retained in a file separate and apart from all photographs taken of adults. During the period of retention of the fingerprints, all originals and copies of them may be maintained in the files of fingerprints taken of adults. If the juvenile judge who grants consent for the taking of fingerprints and photographs under division (A)(1) of this section does not specify a period of retention in that judge's grant of consent, originals and copies of the fingerprints, photographs, and records may be retained in accordance with this section as if the fingerprints and photographs had been taken under division (A)(2) of this section.

(b) Originals and copies of fingerprints and photographs taken under division (A)(2) of this section, and any records of the arrest or custody that was the basis for the taking of the fingerprints or photographs, may be retained for the period of time and in the manner specified in division (B)(3)(b) of this section. Prior to the child's attainment of eighteen years of age, all originals and copies of the photographs and records shall be retained and shall be kept in a file separate and apart from all photographs taken of adults. During the period of retention of the fingerprints, all originals and copies of them may be maintained in the files of fingerprints taken of adults. Upon the child's attainment of eighteen years of age, all originals and copies of the fingerprints, photographs, and records shall be disposed of as follows:

(i) If the juvenile judge issues or previously has issued an order that specifies a manner of disposition of the originals and copies of the fingerprints, photographs, and records, they shall be delivered to the juvenile court or otherwise disposed of in accordance with the order.

(ii) If the juvenile judge does not issue and has not previously issued an order that specifies a manner of disposition of the originals and copies of the fingerprints not maintained in adult files, photographs, and records, the law enforcement agency, in its discretion, either shall remove all originals and copies of them from the file in which they had been maintained and transfer them to the files that are used for the retention of fingerprints and photographs taken of adults who are arrested for, otherwise taken into custody for, or under investigation for the commission of a criminal offense or shall remove them from the file in which they had been maintained and deliver them to the juvenile court. If the originals and copies of any fingerprints of a child who attains eighteen years of age are maintained in the files of fingerprints taken of adults or if pursuant to division (B)(3)(b)(ii) of this section the agency transfers the originals and copies of any fingerprints not maintained in adult files, photographs, or records to the files that are used for the retention of fingerprints and photographs taken of adults who are arrested for, otherwise taken into custody for, or under investigation for the commission of a criminal offense, the originals and copies of the fingerprints, photographs, and records may be maintained, used, and released after they are maintained in the adult files or after the transfer as if the fingerprints and photographs had been taken of, and as if the records pertained to, an adult who was arrested for, otherwise taken into custody for, or under investigation for the commission of a criminal offense.

(4) If a sealing or expungement order issued under section 2151.358 of the Revised Code requires the sealing or destruction of any fingerprints or photographs of a child obtained or taken under division (A)(1) or (2) of this section or of the records of an arrest or custody of a child that was the basis of the taking of the fingerprints or photographs prior to the expiration of any period for which they otherwise could be retained under division (B)(1), (2), or (3) of this section, the fingerprints, photographs, and arrest or custody records that are subject to the order and all copies of the fingerprints, photographs, and arrest or custody records shall be sealed or destroyed in accordance with the order.

(5) All fingerprints of a child, photographs of a child, records of an arrest or custody of a child, and copies delivered to a juvenile court in accordance with division (B)(1), (2), or (3) of this section shall be destroyed by the court, provided that, if a complaint is filed against the child in relation to any act to which the records pertain, the court shall maintain all records of an arrest or custody of a child so delivered for at least three years after the final disposition of the case or after the case becomes inactive.

(6)(a) All photographs of a child and records of an arrest or custody of a child retained pursuant to division (B) of this section and not delivered to a juvenile court shall be kept in a file separate and apart from fingerprints, photographs, and records of an arrest or custody of an adult. All fingerprints of a child retained pursuant to division (B) of this section and not delivered to a juvenile court may be maintained in the files of fingerprints taken of adults.

(b) If a child who is the subject of photographs or fingerprints is adjudicated a delinquent child for the commission of an act that would be an offense, other than a traffic offense or a minor misdemeanor, if committed by an adult or is convicted of or pleads guilty to a criminal offense, other than a traffic offense or a minor misdemeanor, all fingerprints not maintained in the files of fingerprints taken of adults and all photographs of the child, and all records of the arrest or custody of the child that is the basis of the taking of the fingerprints or photographs, that are retained pursuant to division (B) of this section and not delivered to a juvenile court shall be kept in a file separate and apart from fingerprints, photographs, and arrest and custody records of children who have not been adjudicated a delinquent child for the commission of an act that would be an offense, other than a traffic offense or a minor misdemeanor, if committed by an adult and have not been convicted of or pleaded guilty to a criminal offense other than a traffic offense or a minor misdemeanor.

(C) Until they are delivered to the juvenile court or sealed, transferred in accordance with division (B)(3)(b) of this section, or destroyed pursuant to a sealing or expungement order, the originals and copies of fingerprints and photographs of a child that are obtained or taken pursuant to division (A)(1) or (2) of this section, and the records of the arrest or custody of the child that was the basis of the taking of the fingerprints or photographs, shall be used or released only as follows:

(1) During the initial thirty-day period of retention, originals and copies of fingerprints and photographs of a child, and records of the arrest or custody of a child, shall be used, prior to the filing of a complaint or information against or the obtaining of an indictment of the child in relation to the act for which the fingerprints and photographs were originally obtained or taken, only for the investigation of that act and shall be released, prior to the filing of the complaint, only to a court that would have jurisdiction of the child's case under this chapter. Subsequent to the filing of a complaint or information or the obtaining of an indictment, originals and copies of fingerprints and photographs of a child, and records of the arrest or custody of a child, shall be used or released during the initial thirty-day period of retention only as provided in division (C)(2)(a), (b), or (c) of this section.

(2) Originals and copies of fingerprints and photographs of a child, and records of the arrest or custody of a child, that are retained beyond the initial thirty-day period of retention subsequent to the filing of a complaint or information or the obtaining of an indictment, a delinquent child adjudication, or a conviction of or guilty plea to a criminal offense shall be used or released only as follows:

(a) Originals and copies of photographs of a child, and, if no fingerprints were taken at the time the photographs were taken, records of the arrest or custody of the child that was the basis of the taking of the photographs, may be used only as follows:

(i) They may be used for the investigation of the act for which they originally were obtained or taken; if the child who is the subject of the photographs is a suspect in the investigation, for the investigation of any act that would be an offense if committed by an adult; and for arresting or bringing the child into custody.

(ii) If the child who is the subject of the photographs is adjudicated a delinquent child for the commission of an act that would be a felony if committed by an adult or is convicted of or pleads guilty to a criminal offense that is a felony as a result of the arrest or custody that was the basis of the taking of the photographs, a law enforcement officer may use the photographs for a photo line-up conducted as part of the investigation of any act that would be a felony if committed by an adult, whether or not the child who is the subject of the photographs is a suspect in the investigation.

(b) Originals and copies of fingerprints of a child, and records of the arrest or custody of the child that was the basis of the taking of the fingerprints, may be used only for the investigation of the act for which they originally were obtained or taken; if a child is a suspect in the investigation, for the investigation of another act that would be an offense if committed by an adult; and for arresting or bringing the child into custody.

(c) Originals and copies of fingerprints, photographs, and records of the arrest or custody that was the basis of the taking of the fingerprints or photographs shall be released only to the following:

(i) Law enforcement officers of this state or a political subdivision of this state, upon notification to the juvenile court of the name and address of the law enforcement officer or agency to whom or to which they will be released;

(ii) A court that has jurisdiction of the child's case under Chapters 2151. and 2152. of the Revised Code or subsequent to a transfer of the child's case for criminal prosecution pursuant to section 2152.12 of the Revised Code.

(D) No person shall knowingly do any of the following:

(1) Fingerprint or photograph a child in the investigation of any violation of law other than as provided in division (A)(1) or (2) of this section or in sections 109.57, 109.60, and 109.61 of the Revised Code;

(2) Retain fingerprints or photographs of a child obtained or taken under division (A)(1) or (2) of this section, copies of fingerprints or photographs of that nature, or records of the arrest or custody that was the basis of the taking of fingerprints or photographs of that nature other than in accordance with division (B) of this section;

(3) Use or release fingerprints or photographs of a child obtained or taken under division (A)(1) or (2) of this section, copies of fingerprints or photographs of that nature, or records of the arrest or custody that was the basis of the taking of fingerprints or photographs of

that nature other than in accordance with division (B) or (C) of this section.

(2000 S 179, § 3, eff. 1–1–02; 2000 S 181, eff. 9–4–00; 1998 H 2, eff. 1–1–99; 1996 H 124, eff. 3–31–97; 1996 H 445, eff. 9–3–96; 1995 H 1, eff. 1–1–96; 1992 H 198, eff. 10–6–92; 1984 H 258; 1977 H 315; 1973 S 1; 1969 H 320)

Historical and Statutory Notes

Amendment Note: 2000 S 179, § 3, eff. 1–1–02, added references to indictments and informations throughout the section; substituted "2152.12" for "2151.26" in divisions (B)(1) and (C)(2)(c)(ii); and added the reference to Chapter 2152 in division (C)(2)(c)(ii).

Amendment Note: 2000 S 181 inserted ", provided that, if a complaint is filed against the child in relation to any act to which the records pertain, the court shall maintain all records of an arrest or custody of a child so delivered for at least three years after the final disposition of the case or after the case becomes inactive" in division (B)(5); and made other nonsubstantive changes.

Amendment Note: 1998 H 2 substituted "an offense, other than a traffic offense or a minor misdemeanor," for "a felony" in division (A)(2); rewrote divisions (A)(3) and (B)(3); substituted "an offense, other than a traffic offense or a minor misdemeanor," for "a felony" and "other than a traffic offense or a minor misdemeanor" for "that is a felony" twice each in division (B)(6)(b); deleted "No later than ninety days after a law enforcement officer uses the photographs in a photo line up, the officer shall return them to the file from which the officer obtained them." from the end of division (C)(2)(a)(ii); and made other nonsubstantive changes. Prior to amendment, divisions (A)(3) and (B)(3) read:

"(3) This section does not apply to a child who is fourteen years of age or older and under eighteen years of age and to whom either of the following applies:

"(a) The child has been arrested or otherwise taken into custody for committing, has been adjudicated a delinquent child for committing, or has been convicted of or pleaded guilty to committing a designated delinquent act or juvenile offense, as defined in section 109.57 of the Revised Code.

"(b) There is probable cause to believe that the child may have committed a designated delinquent act or juvenile offense, as defined in section 109.57 of the Revised Code."

"(3) If a child is adjudicated a delinquent child for the commission of an act in violation of, or is convicted of or pleads guilty to a criminal offense for the commission of an act that is a violation of, section 2903.01, 2903.02, 2903.03, 2903.04, 2903.11, 2903.12, 2903.13, 2903.21, 2903.22, 2905.01, 2905.02, 2905.11, 2907.02, 2907.03, 2907.05, 2909.02, 2909.03, 2911.01, 2911.02, 2911.11, 2911.12, 2911.13, 2921.34, or 2921.35 of the Revised Code, section 2913.02 of the Revised Code involving the theft of a motor vehicle, former section 2907.12 of the Revised Code, or an existing or former municipal ordinance or law of this state, another state, or the United States that is substantially equivalent to any of those sections, both of the following apply [.]"

Amendment Note: 1996 H 124 rewrote division (A)(3), which prior thereto read:

"(3) This section does not apply to a child who is fourteen years of age or older and under eighteen years of age and who has been arrested or otherwise taken into custody for committing an act that is a category one offense or a category two offense, as defined in section 2151.26 of the Revised Code, has been adjudicated a delinquent child for committing an act that is a category one offense or a category two offense, has been convicted of or pleaded guilty to a category one offense or a category two offense, or is a child with respect to whom there is probable cause to believe that the child may have committed an act that is a category one offense or a category two offense."

Amendment Note: 1996 H 445 changed a reference to section 2907.12 to the reference to former section 2907.12 in the first paragraph in division (B)(3).

Amendment Note: 1995 H 1 inserted "and in sections 109.57, 109.60, and 109.61 of the Revised Code" in division (A)(1); added "Subject to division (A)(3) of this section," at the beginning of division (A)(2); added division (A)(3); inserted "or in sections 109.57, 109.60, and 109.61 of the Revised Code" in division (D)(1); and made changes to reflect gender neutral language and other nonsubstantive changes.

Cross References

Penalty: 2151.99
Duties of the superintendent of the bureau of criminal investigation, 109.57

Library References

Infants ☞68.3, 133, 192.
Westlaw Topic No. 211.
C.J.S. Infants §§ 42, 53 to 57, 69 to 85.
OJur 3d: 29, Criminal Law § 2961; 48, Family Law § 1572, 1573, 1737, 1749
Expungement of juvenile court records. 71 ALR3d 753
Carlin, Baldwin's Ohio Practice, Merrick–Rippner Probate Law § 107.21, 107.22, 107.23, 107.24, 107.154, 107.155, 108.1 (2003).

2151.314   Detention hearing

(A) When a child is brought before the court or delivered to a place of detention or shelter care designated by the court, the intake or other authorized officer of the court shall immediately make an investigation and shall release the child unless it appears that the child's detention or shelter care is warranted or required under section 2151.31 of the Revised Code.

If the child is not so released, a complaint under section 2151.27 or 2152.021 or an information under section 2152.13 of the Revised Code shall be filed or an indictment under division (B) of section 2152.13 of the Revised Code shall be sought and an informal detention or shelter care hearing held promptly, not later than seventy-two hours after the child is placed in detention or shelter care, to determine whether detention or shelter care is required. Reasonable oral or written notice of the time, place, and purpose of the detention or shelter care hearing shall be given to the child and, if they can be found, to the child's parents, guardian, or custodian. In cases in which the complaint alleges a child to be an abused, neglected, or dependent child, the notice given the parents, guardian, or custodian shall inform them that a case plan may be prepared for the child, the general requirements usually contained in case plans, and the possible consequences of the failure to comply with a journalized case plan.

Prior to the hearing, the court shall inform the parties of their right to counsel and to appointed counsel or to the services of the county public defender or joint county public defender, if they are indigent, of the child's right to remain silent with respect to any allegation of delinquency, and of the name and telephone number of a court employee who can be contacted during the normal business hours of the court to arrange for the prompt appointment of counsel for any party who is indigent. Unless it appears from the hearing that the child's detention or shelter care is required under the provisions of section 2151.31 of the Revised Code, the court shall order the child's release as provided by section 2151.311 of the Revised Code. If a parent, guardian, or custodian has not been so notified and did not appear or waive appearance at the hearing, upon the filing of an affidavit stating these facts, the court shall rehear the matter without unnecessary delay.

(B) When the court conducts a hearing pursuant to division (A) of this section, all of the following apply:

(1) The court shall determine whether an alleged abused, neglected, or dependent child should remain or be placed in shelter care;

(2) The court shall determine whether there are any relatives of the child who are willing to be temporary custodians of the child. If any relative is willing to be a temporary custodian, the child would otherwise be placed or retained in shelter care, and the appointment is appropriate, the court shall appoint the relative as temporary custodian of the child, unless the court appoints another relative as temporary custodian. If it determines that the appointment of a relative as custodian would not be appropriate, it shall issue a written opinion setting forth the reasons for its determination and give a copy of the opinion to all parties and to the guardian ad litem of the child.

The court's consideration of a relative for appointment as a temporary custodian does not make that relative a party to the proceedings.

(3) The court shall comply with section 2151.419 of the Revised Code.

(C) If a child is in shelter care following the filing of a complaint pursuant to section 2151.27 or 2152.021 of the Revised Code, the filing of an information, or the obtaining of an indictment or following a hearing held pursuant to division (A) of this section, any party, including the public children services agency, and the guardian ad litem of the child may file a motion with the court requesting that the child be released from shelter care. The motion shall state the reasons why the child should be released from shelter care and, if a hearing has been held pursuant to division (A) of this section, any changes in the situation of the child or the parents, guardian, or custodian of the child that have occurred since that hearing and that justify the release of the child from shelter care. Upon the filing of the motion, the court shall hold a hearing in the same manner as under division (A) of this section.

(D) Each juvenile court shall designate at least one court employee to assist persons who are indigent in obtaining appointed counsel. The court shall include in each notice given pursuant to division (A) or (C) of this section and in each summons served upon a party pursuant to this chapter, the name and telephone number at which each designated employee can be contacted during the normal business hours of the court to arrange for prompt appointment of counsel for indigent persons.

(2002 H 393, eff. 7–5–02; 2000 S 179, § 3, eff. 1–1–02; 1999 H 176, eff. 10–29–99; 1998 H 484, eff. 3–18–99; 1996 H 274, eff. 8–8–96; 1988 S 89, eff. 1–1–89; 1975 H 164; 1969 H 320)

Historical and Statutory Notes

Amendment Note: 2002 H 393 substituted "(B)" for "(C)" in the second paragraph of division (A).

Amendment Note: 2000 S 179, § 3, eff. 1–1–02, inserted "or 2152.021 or an information under section 2152.13" and "or an indictment under division (C) of section 2152.13 of the Revised Code shall be sought" in the first paragraph in division (A); inserted "or 2152.021" and ", the filing of an information, or the obtaining of an indictment" in division (C); and inserted "at least" and substituted "each" for "the" in division (D).

Amendment Note: 1999 H 176 added division (B)(3); and made other nonsubstantive changes.

Amendment Note: 1998 H 484 deleted former division (B)(3); and made other nonsubstantive changes. Prior to deletion, former division (B)(3) read:

"(3) The court shall make the determination and issue the written finding of facts required by section 2151.419 of the Revised Code."

Amendment Note: 1996 H 274 added the third sentence in the second paragraph in division (A); inserted ", including the public children services agency," in division (C); and made changes to reflect gender neutral language.

Cross References

Caretaker authorization affidavit not permitted when certain proceedings are pending, 3109.68
Detention and shelter care, release to parents, hearing, Juv R 7
Power of attorney, certain pending actions prohibiting creation, 3109.58.
Temporary disposition, Juv R 13

Library References

Infants ⟨⟩203.
Westlaw Topic No. 211.
C.J.S. Infants §§ 51 to 67.
OJur 3d: 48, Family Law § 1574, 1576 to 1579, 1601, 1609, 1626, 1654
Am Jur 2d: 47, Juvenile Courts and Delinquent and Dependent Children § 44
Applicability of rules of evidence in juvenile delinquency proceeding. 43 ALR2d 1128
Right to and appointment of counsel in juvenile court proceedings. 60 ALR2d 691
Right to jury trial in juvenile court delinquency proceedings. 100 ALR2d 1241
Right of bail in proceedings in juvenile courts. 53 ALR3d 848
Baldwin's Ohio Legislative Service, 1988 Laws of Ohio, S 89—LSC Analysis, p 5–571
Klein & Darling, Baldwin's Ohio Practice, Civil Practice § 52–4 (1997).
Carlin, Baldwin's Ohio Practice, Merrick–Rippner Probate Law § 107.5, 107.9, 107.30, 107.42, 107.74, 107.172 (2003).

2151.32 Selection of custodian

In placing a child under any guardianship or custody other than that of its parent, the juvenile court shall, when practicable, select a person or an institution or agency governed by persons of like religious faith as that of the parents of such child, or in case of a difference in the religious faith of the parents, then of the religious faith of the child, or if the religious faith of the child is not ascertained, then of either of the parents.

(1953 H 1, eff. 10–1–53; GC 1639–33)

Historical and Statutory Notes
Pre–1953 H 1 Amendments: 117 v 520, § 1

Library References
Infants ⟨⟩226.
Westlaw Topic No. 211.
C.J.S. Infants §§ 57, 70 to 84.

OJur 3d: 48, Family Law § 1686; 53, Guardian and Ward § 30
Consideration and weight of religious affiliations in appointment or removal of guardian for minor child. 22 ALR2d 696
Carlin, Baldwin's Ohio Practice, Merrick–Rippner Probate Law § 107.73 (2003).

2151.33 Temporary care; emergency medical treatment; reimbursement

(A) Pending hearing of a complaint filed under section 2151.27 of the Revised Code or a motion filed or made under division (B) of this section and the service of citations, the juvenile court may make any temporary disposition of any child that it considers necessary to protect the best interest of the child and that can be made pursuant to division (B) of this section. Upon the certificate of one or more reputable practicing physicians, the court may summarily provide for emergency medical and surgical treatment that appears to be immediately necessary to preserve the health and well-being of any child concerning whom a complaint or an application for care has been filed, pending the service of a citation upon the child's parents, guardian, or custodian. The court may order the parents, guardian, or custodian, if the court finds the parents, guardian, or custodian able to do so, to reimburse the court for the expense involved in providing the emergency medical or surgical treatment. Any person who disobeys the order for reimbursement may be adjudged in contempt of court and punished accordingly.

If the emergency medical or surgical treatment is furnished to a child who is found at the hearing to be a nonresident of the county in which the court is located and if the expense of the medical or surgical treatment cannot be recovered from the parents, legal guardian, or custodian of the child, the board of county commissioners of the county in which the child has a legal settlement shall reimburse the court for the reasonable cost of the emergency medical or surgical treatment out of its general fund.

(B)(1) After a complaint, petition, writ, or other document initiating a case dealing with an alleged or adjudicated abused, neglected, or dependent child is filed and upon the filing or making of a motion pursuant to division (C) of this section, the court, prior to the final disposition of the case, may issue any of the following temporary orders to protect the best interest of the child:

(a) An order granting temporary custody of the child to a particular party;

(b) An order for the taking of the child into custody pursuant to section 2151.31 of the Revised Code pending the outcome of the adjudicatory and dispositional hearings;

(c) An order granting, limiting, or eliminating parenting time or visitation rights with respect to the child;

(d) An order requiring a party to vacate a residence that will be lawfully occupied by the child;

(e) An order requiring a party to attend an appropriate counseling program that is reasonably available to that party;

(f) Any other order that restrains or otherwise controls the conduct of any party which conduct would not be in the best interest of the child.

(2) Prior to the final disposition of a case subject to division (B)(1) of this section, the court shall do both of the following:

(a) Issue an order pursuant to Chapters 3119. to 3125. of the Revised Code requiring the parents, guardian, or person charged with the child's support to pay support for the child.

(b) Issue an order requiring the parents, guardian, or person charged with the child's support to continue to maintain any health insurance coverage for the child that existed at the time of the filing of the complaint, petition, writ, or other document, or to obtain health insurance coverage in accordance with sections 3119.29 to 3119.56 of the Revised Code.

(C)(1) A court may issue an order pursuant to division (B) of this section upon its own motion or if a party files a written motion or makes an oral motion requesting the issuance of the order and stating the reasons for it. Any notice sent by the court as a result of a motion pursuant to this division shall contain a notice that any party to a juvenile proceeding has the right to be represented by counsel and to have appointed counsel if the person is indigent.

(2) If a child is taken into custody pursuant to section 2151.31 of the Revised Code and placed in shelter care, the public children services agency or private child placing agency with which the child is placed in shelter care shall file or make a motion as described in division (C)(1) of this section before the end of the next day immediately after the date on which the child was taken into custody and, at a minimum, shall request an order for temporary custody under division (B)(1)(a) of this section.

(3) A court that issues an order pursuant to division (B)(1)(b) of this section shall comply with section 2151.419 of the Revised Code.

(D) The court may grant an ex parte order upon its own motion or a motion filed or made pursuant to division (C) of this section requesting such an order if it appears to the court that the best interest and the welfare of the child require that the court issue the order immediately. The court, if acting on its own motion, or the person requesting the granting of an ex parte order, to the extent possible, shall give notice of its intent or of the request to the parents, guardian, or custodian of the child who is the subject of the request. If the court issues an ex parte order, the court shall hold a hearing to review the order within seventy-two hours after it is issued or before the end of the next day after the day on which it is issued, whichever occurs first. The court shall give written notice of the hearing to all parties to the action and shall appoint a guardian ad litem for the child prior to the hearing.

The written notice shall be given by all means that are reasonably likely to result in the party receiving actual notice and shall include all of the following:

(1) The date, time, and location of the hearing;

(2) The issues to be addressed at the hearing;

(3) A statement that every party to the hearing has a right to counsel and to court-appointed counsel, if the party is indigent;

(4) The name, telephone number, and address of the person requesting the order;

(5) A copy of the order, except when it is not possible to obtain it because of the exigent circumstances in the case.

If the court does not grant an ex parte order pursuant to a motion filed or made pursuant to division (C) of this section or its own motion, the court shall hold a shelter care hearing on the motion within ten days after the motion is filed. The court shall give notice of the hearing to all affected parties in the same manner as set forth in the Juvenile Rules.

(E) The court, pending the outcome of the adjudicatory and dispositional hearings, shall not issue an order granting temporary custody of a child to a public children services agency or private child placing agency pursuant to this section, unless the court determines and specifically states in the order that the continued residence of the child in the child's current home will be contrary to the child's best interest and welfare and the court complies with section 2151.419 of the Revised Code.

(F) Each public children services agency and private child placing agency that receives temporary custody of a child pursuant to this section shall maintain in the child's case record written documentation that it has placed the child, to the extent that it is consistent with the best interest, welfare, and special needs of the child, in the most family-like setting available and in close proximity to the home of the parents, custodian, or guardian of the child.

(G) For good cause shown, any court order that is issued pursuant to this section may be reviewed by the court at any time upon motion of any party to the action or upon the motion of the court.

(2002 H 657, eff. 12–13–02; 2000 S 180, eff. 3–22–01; 1999 H 176, eff. 10–29–99; 1998 H 484, eff. 3–18–99; 1997 H 352, eff. 1–1–98; 1996 H 274, eff. 8–8–96; 1988 S 89, eff. 1–1–89; 1953 H 1; GC 1639–28)

Historical and Statutory Notes

Pre–1953 H 1 Amendments: 121 v 557; 119 v 731; 117 v 520

Amendment Note: 2002 H 657 substituted "3119.29" for "3119.30" and "3119.56" for "3119.58" in division (B)(2)(b).

Amendment Note: 2000 S 180 substituted "Chapters 3119. to 3125." for "sections 3113.21 to 3113.219" in division (B)(2)(a) and "sections 3119.30 to 3119.58" for "section 3113.217" in division (B)(2)(b).

Amendment Note: 1999 H 176 added division (B)(3); and inserted "and the court complies with section 2151.419 of the Revised Code" in division (E).

Amendment Note: 1998 H 484 deleted former division (C)(3); deleted "and makes the determination and issues the written finding of facts required by section 2151.419 of the Revised Code" from the end of division (E); and made other nonsubstantive changes. Prior to deletion, former division (C)(3) read:

"(3) Any court that issues an order pursuant to division (B)(1)(b) of this section shall make the determination and issue the written finding of facts required by section 2151.419 of the Revised Code."

Amendment Note: 1997 H 352 substituted "in accordance with" for "pursuant to" in division (B)(2)(b).

Amendment Note: 1996 H 274 rewrote divisions (B) and (C) and the first paragraph in division (D); inserted "or its own motion" in the final paragraph in division (D); and made changes to reflect gender neutral language. Prior to amendment, divisions (B) and (C) and the first paragraph in division (D) read:

"(B) After a complaint, petition, writ, or other document initiating a case dealing with an alleged or adjudicated abused, neglected, or dependent child is filed and upon the filing or making of a motion pursuant to division (C) of this section, the court, prior to the final disposition of the case, may issue any of the following temporary orders to protect the best interest of the child:

"(1) An order granting temporary custody of the child to a particular party;

"(2) An order for the taking of the child into custody pursuant to section 2151.31 of the Revised Code pending the outcome of the adjudicatory and dispositional hearings;

"(3) An order granting, limiting, or eliminating visitation rights with respect to the child;

"(4) An order for the payment of child support for the child and the continued maintenance of any medical, surgical, or hospital policies of insurance for the child that existed at the time of the filing of the complaint, petition, writ, or other document;

"(5) An order requiring a party to vacate a residence that will be lawfully occupied by the child;

"(6) An order requiring a party to attend an appropriate counseling program that is reasonably available to that party;

"(7) Any other order that restrains or otherwise controls the conduct of any party which conduct would not be in the best interest of the child.

"(C)(1) A court may issue an order pursuant to division (B) of this section only if a party files a written motion or makes an oral motion requesting the issuance of the order and stating the reasons for it. Any notice sent by the court as a result of the filing or making of a motion pursuant to this division shall contain a notice that any party to a juvenile proceeding has the right to be represented by counsel and to have counsel appointed for him if he is an indigent person.

"(2) If a child is taken into custody pursuant to section 2151.31 of the Revised Code and placed in shelter care, the public children services agency or private child placing agency with which the child is placed in shelter care shall file or make a motion as described in division (C)(1) of this section before the end of the next business day immediately after the date on which the child was taken into custody and, at a minimum, shall request an order for temporary custody under division (B)(1)(a) of this section.

"(3) Any court that issues an order pursuant to division (B)(2) of this section shall make the determination and issue the written finding of facts required by section 2151.419 of the Revised Code.

"(D) If a motion filed or made pursuant to division (C) of this section requests the issuance of an ex parte order, the court may grant an ex parte order if it appears to the court that the best interest and the welfare of the child require that the court issue the order immediately. The person requesting the granting of an ex parte order, to the extent possible, shall give notice of the request to the parents, guardian, or custodian of the child who is the subject of the request. If the court issues the requested ex parte order, the court shall hold a hearing to review the order within seventy-two hours after it is issued or before the end of the next business day after the day on which it is issued, whichever occurs first. The court shall give written notice of the hearing to all parties to the action and shall appoint a guardian ad litem for the child prior to the hearing."

Cross References

Caretaker authorization affidavit not permitted when certain proceedings are pending, 3109.68

Foster caregivers, information regarding delinquent children provided to, 2152.72

Interfering with action to issue or modify support order, 2919.231

Nonsupport of dependents, 2919.21

Power of attorney, certain pending actions prohibiting creation, 3109.58

Social history, physical and mental examinations, custody investigation, Juv R 32

Temporary disposition, emergency medical and surgical treatment, Juv R 13

Library References

Infants ⊕228.

Westlaw Topic No. 211.

C.J.S. Infants §§ 42, 53, 54, 57, 69 to 85.

OJur 3d: 47, Family Law § 1430; 48, Family Law § 1632 to 1634, 1654, 1724

Power of court or other public agency to order medical treatment over parental religious objections for child whose life is not immediately endangered. 52 ALR3d 1118

Power of court or other public agency to order medical treatment for child over parental objections not based on religious grounds. 97 ALR3d 421

Baldwin's Ohio Legislative Service, 1988 Laws of Ohio, S 89—LSC Analysis, p 5–571

Klein & Darling, Baldwin's Ohio Practice, Civil Practice § 52–4 (1997).

Carlin, Baldwin's Ohio Practice, Merrick–Rippner Probate Law § 107.41, 107.74, 107.76, 107.78, 107.152, 107.153 (2003).

2151.331 Detention in certified foster home; arrangement for temporary care; alternative diversion programs

A child alleged to be or adjudicated an abused, neglected, dependent, or unruly child or a juvenile traffic offender may be detained after a complaint is filed in a certified foster home for a period not exceeding sixty days or until the final disposition of the case, whichever comes first. The court also may arrange with a public children services agency or private child placing agency to receive, or with a private noncustodial agency for temporary care of, the child within the jurisdiction of the court. A child alleged to be or adjudicated an unruly child also may be assigned to an alternative diversion program established by the court for a period not exceeding sixty days after a complaint is filed or until final disposition of the case, whichever comes first.

If the court arranges for the board of a child temporarily detained in a certified foster home or arranges for the board of a child through a private child placing agency, the board of county commissioners shall pay a reasonable sum, which the court shall fix, for the board of the child. In order to have certified foster homes available for service, an agreed monthly subsidy may be paid in addition to a fixed rate per day for care of a child actually residing in the certified foster home.

(2000 H 332, eff. 1–1–01; 2000 H 448, eff. 10–5–00; 1996 H 265, eff. 3–3–97)

Historical and Statutory Notes

Ed. Note: The amendment of this section by 2000 H 332, eff. 1–1–01, and 2000 H 448, eff. 10–5–00, was identical. See *Baldwin's Ohio Legislative Service Annotated*, 2000, pages 6/L–2155 and 6/L–2219, or the OH–LEGIS or OH–LEGIS–OLD database on WESTLAW, for original versions of these Acts.

Amendment Note: 2000 H 332 deleted "family" before "foster home" throughout the section.

Amendment Note: 2000 H 448 deleted "family" after "certified" throughout the section.

HEARING AND DISPOSITION

2151.35 Hearing procedure; findings; record

(A)(1) Except as otherwise provided by division (A)(3) of this section or in section 2152.13 of the Revised Code, the juvenile court may conduct its hearings in an informal manner and may adjourn its hearings from time to time. The court may exclude the general public from its hearings in a particular case if the court holds a separate hearing to determine whether that exclusion is appropriate. If the court decides that exclusion of the general public is appropriate, the court still may admit to a particular hearing or all of the hearings relating to a particular case those persons who have a direct interest in the case and those who demonstrate that their need for access outweighs the interest in keeping the hearing closed.

Except cases involving children who are alleged to be unruly or delinquent children for being habitual or chronic truants and except as otherwise provided in section 2152.13 of the Revised Code, all cases involving children shall be heard separately and apart from the trial of cases against adults. The court may excuse the attendance of the child at the hearing in cases involving abused, neglected, or dependent children. The court shall hear and determine all cases of children without a jury, except cases involving serious youthful offenders under section 2152.13 of the Revised Code.

If a complaint alleges a child to be a delinquent child, unruly child, or juvenile traffic offender, the court shall require the parent, guardian, or custodian of the child to attend all proceedings of the court regarding the child. If a parent, guardian, or custodian fails to so attend, the court may find the parent, guardian, or custodian in contempt.

If the court finds from clear and convincing evidence that the child violated section 2151.87 of the Revised Code, the court shall proceed in accordance with divisions (F) and (G) of that section.

If the court at the adjudicatory hearing finds from clear and convincing evidence that the child is an abused, neglected, or dependent child, the court shall proceed, in accordance with division (B) of this section, to hold a dispositional hearing and hear the evidence as to the proper disposition to be made under section 2151.353 of the Revised Code. If the court at the adjudicatory hearing finds beyond a reasonable doubt that the child is a delinquent or unruly child or a juvenile traffic offender, the court shall proceed immediately, or at a postponed hearing, to hear the evidence as to the proper disposition to be made under section 2151.354 or Chapter 2152. of the Revised Code. If the court at the adjudicatory hearing finds beyond a reasonable doubt that the child is an unruly child for being an habitual truant, or that the child is an unruly child for being an habitual truant and that the parent, guardian, or other person having care of the child has failed to cause the child's attendance at school in violation of section 3321.38 of the Revised Code, the court shall proceed to hold a hearing to hear the evidence as to the proper disposition to be made in regard to the child under division (C)(1) of section 2151.354 of the Revised Code and the proper action to take in regard to the parent, guardian, or other person having care of the child under division (C)(2) of section 2151.354 of the Revised Code. If the court at the adjudicatory hearing finds beyond a reasonable doubt that the child is a delinquent child for being a chronic truant or for being an habitual truant who previously has been adjudicated an unruly child for being an habitual truant, or that the child is a delinquent child for either of those reasons and the parent, guardian, or other person having care of the child has failed

to cause the child's attendance at school in violation of section 3321.38 of the Revised Code, the court shall proceed to hold a hearing to hear the evidence as to the proper disposition to be made in regard to the child under division (A)(7) (a) of section 2152.19 of the Revised Code and the proper action to take in regard to the parent, guardian, or other person having care of the child under division (A)(7) (b) of section 2152.19 of the Revised Code.

If the court does not find the child to have violated section 2151.87 of the Revised Code or to be an abused, neglected, dependent, delinquent, or unruly child or a juvenile traffic offender, it shall order that the case be dismissed and that the child be discharged from any detention or restriction theretofore ordered.

(2) A record of all testimony and other oral proceedings in juvenile court shall be made in all proceedings that are held pursuant to section 2151.414 of the Revised Code or in which an order of disposition may be made pursuant to division (A)(4) of section 2151.353 of the Revised Code, and shall be made upon request in any other proceedings. The record shall be made as provided in section 2301.20 of the Revised Code.

(3) The authority of a juvenile court to exclude the general public from its hearings that is provided by division (A)(1) of this section does not limit or affect any right of a victim of a crime or delinquent act, or of a victim's representative, under Chapter 2930. of the Revised Code.

(B)(1) If the court at an adjudicatory hearing determines that a child is an abused, neglected, or dependent child, the court shall not issue a dispositional order until after the court holds a separate dispositional hearing. The court may hold the dispositional hearing for an adjudicated abused, neglected, or dependent child immediately after the adjudicatory hearing if all parties were served prior to the adjudicatory hearing with all documents required for the dispositional hearing. The dispositional hearing may not be held more than thirty days after the adjudicatory hearing is held. The court, upon the request of any party or the guardian ad litem of the child, may continue a dispositional hearing for a reasonable time not to exceed the time limits set forth in this division to enable a party to obtain or consult counsel. The dispositional hearing shall not be held more than ninety days after the date on which the complaint in the case was filed.

If the dispositional hearing is not held within the period of time required by this division, the court, on its own motion or the motion of any party or the guardian ad litem of the child, shall dismiss the complaint without prejudice.

(2) The dispositional hearing shall be conducted in accordance with all of the following:

(a) The judge or referee who presided at the adjudicatory hearing shall preside, if possible, at the dispositional hearing;

(b) The court may admit any evidence that is material and relevant, including, but not limited to, hearsay, opinion, and documentary evidence;

(c) Medical examiners and each investigator who prepared a social history shall not be cross-examined, except upon consent of the parties, for good cause shown, or as the court in its discretion may direct. Any party may offer evidence supplementing, explaining, or disputing any information contained in the social history or other reports that may be used by the court in determining disposition.

(3) After the conclusion of the dispositional hearing, the court shall enter an appropriate judgment within seven days and shall schedule the date for the hearing to be held pursuant to section 2151.415 of the Revised Code. The court may make any order of disposition that is set forth in section 2151.353 of the Revised Code. A copy of the judgment shall be given to each party and to the child's guardian ad litem. If the judgment is conditional, the order shall state the conditions of the judgment. If the child is not returned to the child's own home, the court shall determine which school district shall bear the cost of the child's education and shall comply with section 2151.36 of the Revised Code.

(4) As part of its dispositional order, the court may issue any order described in division (B) of section 2151.33 of the Revised Code.

(C) The court shall give all parties to the action and the child's guardian ad litem notice of the adjudicatory and dispositional hearings in accordance with the Juvenile Rules.

(D) If the court issues an order pursuant to division (A)(4) of section 2151.353 of the Revised Code committing a child to the permanent custody of a public children services agency or a private child placing agency, the parents of the child whose parental rights were terminated cease to be parties to the action upon the issuance of the order. This division is not intended to eliminate or restrict any right of the parents to appeal the permanent custody order issued pursuant to division (A)(4) of section 2151.353 of the Revised Code.

(E) Each juvenile court shall schedule its hearings in accordance with the time requirements of this chapter.

(F) In cases regarding abused, neglected, or dependent children, the court may admit any statement of a child that the court determines to be excluded by the hearsay rule if the proponent of the statement informs the adverse party of the proponent's intention to offer the statement and of the particulars of the statement, including the name of the declarant, sufficiently in advance of the hearing to provide the party with a fair opportunity to prepare to challenge, respond to, or defend against the statement, and the court determines all of the following:

(1) The statement has circumstantial guarantees of trustworthiness;

(2) The statement is offered as evidence of a material fact;

(3) The statement is more probative on the point for which it is offered than any other evidence that the proponent can procure through reasonable efforts;

(4) The general purposes of the evidence rules and the interests of justice will best be served by the admission of the statement into evidence.

(G) If a child is alleged to be an abused child, the court may order that the testimony of the child be taken by deposition. On motion of the prosecuting attorney, guardian ad litem, or any party, or in its own discretion, the court may order that the deposition be videotaped. Any deposition taken under this division shall be taken with a judge or referee present.

If a deposition taken under this division is intended to be offered as evidence at the hearing, it shall be filed with the court. Part or all of the deposition is admissible in evidence if counsel for all parties had an opportunity and similar motive at the time of the taking of the deposition to develop the testimony by direct, cross, or redirect examination and the judge determines that there is reasonable cause to believe that if the child were to testify in person at the hearing, the child would experience emotional trauma as a result of participating at the hearing.

(2002 H 400, eff. 4–3–03; 2000 S 179, § 3, eff. 1–1–02; 2000 S 179, § 1, eff. 4–9–01; 2000 S 218, eff. 3–15–01; 2000 S 181, eff. 9–4–00; 1996 H 124, eff. 3–31–97; 1996 H 274, eff. 8–8–96; 1995 H 1, eff. 1–1–96; 1988 S 89, eff. 1–1–89; 1980 H 695; 1975 H 85; 1969 H 320)

Historical and Statutory Notes

Ed. Note: Former 2151.35 repealed by 1969 H 320, eff. 11–19–69; 1969 S 49; 132 v S 278; 130 v H 299, H 879; 127 v 547; 125 v 324; 1953 H 1; GC 1639–30; see now 2151.352 for provisions analogous to former 2151.35.

Pre–1953 H 1 Amendments: 121 v 557; 119 v 731; 117 v 520

Amendment Note: 2002 H 400 substituted "(7)" for "(6)" twice in the last sentence of the fifth paragraph of division (A).

Amendment Note: 2000 S 179, § 3, eff. 1–1–02, rewrote division (A), which prior thereto read:

"(A)(1) The juvenile court may conduct its hearings in an informal manner and may adjourn its hearings from time to time. In the hearing of any case, the general public may be excluded and only those persons admitted who have a direct interest in the case.

"Except cases involving children who are alleged to be unruly or delinquent children for being habitual or chronic truants, all cases involving children shall be heard separately and apart from the trial of cases against adults. The court may excuse the attendance of the child at the hearing in cases involving abused, neglected, or dependent children. The court shall hear and determine all cases of children without a jury.

"If a complaint alleges a child to be a delinquent child, unruly child, or juvenile traffic offender, the court shall require the parent, guardian, or custodian of the child to attend all proceedings of the court regarding the child. If a parent, guardian, or custodian fails to so attend, the court may find the parent, guardian, or custodian in contempt.

"If the court at the adjudicatory hearing finds from clear and convincing evidence that the child is an abused, neglected, or dependent child, the court shall proceed, in accordance with division (B) of this section, to hold a dispositional hearing and hear the evidence as to the proper disposition to be made under section 2151.353 of the Revised Code. If the court at the adjudicatory hearing finds beyond a reasonable doubt that the child is a delinquent or unruly child or a juvenile traffic offender, the court shall proceed immediately, or at a postponed hearing, to hear the evidence as to the proper disposition to be made under sections 2151.352 to 2151.355 of the Revised Code. If the court at the adjudicatory hearing finds beyond a reasonable doubt that the child is an unruly child for being an habitual truant, or that the child is an unruly child for being an habitual truant and that the parent, guardian, or other person having care of the child has failed to cause the child's attendance at school in violation of section 3321.38 of the Revised Code, the court shall

proceed to hold a hearing to hear the evidence as to the proper disposition to be made in regard to the child under division (C)(1) of section 2151.354 of the Revised Code and the proper action to take in regard to the parent, guardian, or other person having care of the child under division (C)(2) of section 2151.354 of the Revised Code. If the court at the adjudicatory hearing finds beyond a reasonable doubt that the child is a delinquent child for being a chronic truant or for being an habitual truant who previously has been adjudicated an unruly child for being an habitual truant, or that the child is a delinquent child for either of those reasons and the parent, guardian, or other person having care of the child has failed to cause the child's attendance at school in violation of section 3321.38 of the Revised Code, the court shall proceed to hold a hearing to hear the evidence as to the proper disposition to be made in regard to the child under division (A)(24)(a) of section 2151.355 of the Revised Code and the proper action to take in regard to the parent, guardian, or other person having care of the child under division (A)(24)(b) of section 2151.355 of the Revised Code.

"If the court does not find the child to be an abused, neglected, dependent, delinquent, or unruly child or a juvenile traffic offender, it shall order that the complaint be dismissed and that the child be discharged from any detention or restriction theretofore ordered.

"(2) A record of all testimony and other oral proceedings in juvenile court shall be made in all proceedings that are held pursuant to section 2151.414 of the Revised Code or in which an order of disposition may be made pursuant to division (A)(4) of section 2151.353 of the Revised Code, and shall be made upon request in any other proceedings. The record shall be made as provided in section 2301.20 of the Revised Code."

Amendment Note: 2000 S 179, § 1, eff. 4–9–01, deleted ", except that section 2151.47 of the Revised Code shall apply in cases involving a complaint that jointly alleges that a child is an unruly or delinquent child for being an habitual or chronic truant and that a parent, guardian, or other person having care of the child failed to cause the child's attendance at school" from the end of the second paragraph in division (A)(1).

Amendment Note: 2000 S 218 added the fourth paragraph in division (A)(1); and inserted "have violated section 2151.87 of the Revised Code or to" in the sixth paragraph in division (A)(1).

Amendment Note: 2000 S 181 designated and rewrote division (A)(1); and designated division (A)(2). Prior to designation and amendment, division (A)(1) read:

"(A) The juvenile court may conduct its hearings in an informal manner and may adjourn its hearings from time to time. In the hearing of any case, the general public may be excluded and only those persons admitted who have a direct interest in the case.

"All cases involving children shall be heard separately and apart from the trial of cases against adults. The court may excuse the attendance of the child at the hearing in cases involving abused, neglected, or dependent children. The court shall hear and determine all cases of children without a jury.

"If the court at the adjudicatory hearing finds from clear and convincing evidence that the child is an abused, neglected, or dependent child, the court shall proceed, in accordance with division (B) of this section, to hold a dispositional hearing and hear the evidence as to the proper disposition to be made under section 2151.353 of the Revised Code. If the court at the adjudicatory hearing finds beyond a reasonable doubt that the child is a delinquent or unruly child or a juvenile traffic offender, the court shall proceed immediately, or at a postponed hearing, to hear the evidence as to the proper disposition to be made under sections 2151.352 to 2151.355 of the Revised Code. If the court does not find the child to be an abused, neglected, dependent, delinquent, or unruly child or a juvenile traffic offender, it shall order that the complaint be dismissed and that the child be discharged from any detention or restriction theretofore ordered."

Amendment Note: 1996 H 124 deleted former division (H), which read:

"(H)(1) Before accepting from an alleged delinquent child a plea of guilty or no contest to the commission of an act that is a category one or category two offense, the court shall inform the child of the possible length of commitment to the legal custody of the department of youth services to which the child could be subject under section 2151.26 of the Revised Code.

"(2) As used in division (H) of this section, 'category one offense' and 'category two offense' have the same meanings as in section 2151.26 of the Revised Code."

Amendment Note: 1996 H 274 rewrote the second sentence in the first paragraph in division (B)(1); added the third sentence in the first paragraph in division (B)(1); and substituted "shall comply with section 2151.36 of the Revised Code" for "may fix an amount of support to be paid by the responsible parent or to be paid from public funds" in division (B)(3). Prior to amendment, the second sentence in the first paragraph in division (B)(1) read:

"The dispositional hearing for an adjudicated abused, neglected, or dependent child shall be held at least one day but not more than thirty days after the adjudicatory hearing is held, except that the dispositional hearing may be held immediately after the adjudicatory hearing if all parties were served prior to the adjudicatory hearing with all documents required for the dispositional hearing and all parties consent to the dispositional hearing being held immediately after the adjudicatory hearing."

Amendment Note: 1995 H 1 added division (H); and made changes to reflect gender neutral language and other nonsubstantive changes.

Cross References

Adjudicatory hearing, Juv R 29
Child sex offense victims, deposition, 2152.81
Disposition of child committed to youth services department, 5139.06
Hearings, Juv R 27
Juvenile court proceedings for truancy, 3321.22
Recordings of proceedings, Juv R 37
Trial by jury, O Const Art I, § 5
Waiver of rights, Juv R 3

Library References

Infants ☞203, 210, 246.
Westlaw Topic No. 211.
C.J.S. Infants §§ 51 to 68, 86 to 91.
OJur 3d: 22, Courts and Judges § 18; 44, Evidence and Witnesses § 926; 48, Family Law § 1653, 1655 to 1657, 1670, 1672, 1674, 1677 to 1679, 1682, 1693
Am Jur 2d: 47, Juvenile Courts and Delinquent and Dependent Children § 48 to 62; 57A, Negligence § 94 to 99, 130 to 141, 233 to 256; 62, Premises Liability § 6 to 28, 37 to 41, 83, 133 to 135
Applicability of rules of evidence in juvenile delinquency proceeding. 43 ALR2d 1128

Propriety of exclusion of press or other media representatives from civil trial. 79 ALR3d 401
Right of juvenile court defendant to be represented during court proceedings by parent. 11 ALR4th 719
Baldwin's Ohio Legislative Service, 1988 Laws of Ohio, S 89—LSC Analysis, p 5–571
Katz & Giannelli, Baldwin's Ohio Practice, Criminal Law § 1.6 (1996).
Giannelli & Snyder, Baldwin's Ohio Practice, Evidence § 102.5, 402.5, 802.5, 807, 807.1, 807.3 (2d ed. 2001).
Carlin, Baldwin's Ohio Practice, Merrick–Rippner Probate Law § 104.1, 104.5, 105.7, 106.2, 106.7, 106.9, 106.12, 106.15, 106.18, 107.1, 107.9, 107.10, 107.40, 107.43, 107.47, 107.50, 107.52, 107.56, 107.57, 107.59, 107.60, 107.72, 107.76, 107.78, 107.115, 107.122, 107.173, 107.174, 107.175, 107.176 (2003).

2151.352   Right to counsel

A child, or the child's parents, custodian, or other person in loco parentis of such child is entitled to representation by legal counsel at all stages of the proceedings under this chapter or Chapter 2152. of the Revised Code and if, as an indigent person, any such person is unable to employ counsel, to have counsel provided for the person pursuant to Chapter 120. of the Revised Code. If a party appears without counsel, the court shall ascertain whether the party knows of the party's right to counsel and of the party's right to be provided with counsel if the party is an indigent person. The court may continue the case to enable a party to obtain counsel or to be represented by the county public defender or the joint county public defender and shall provide counsel upon request pursuant to Chapter 120. of the Revised Code. Counsel must be provided for a child not represented by the child's parent, guardian, or custodian. If the interests of two or more such parties conflict, separate counsel shall be provided for each of them.

Section 2935.14 of the Revised Code applies to any child taken into custody. The parents, custodian, or guardian of a child taken into custody, and any attorney at law representing them or the child, shall be entitled to visit the child at any reasonable time, be present at any hearing involving the child, and be given reasonable notice of the hearing.

Any report or part of a report concerning the child, which is used in the hearing and is pertinent to the hearing, shall for good cause shown be made available to any attorney at law representing the child and to any attorney at law representing the parents, custodian, or guardian of the child, upon written request prior to any hearing involving the child.

(2003 H 95, eff. 9–26–03; 2000 S 179, § 3, eff. 1–1–02; 1975 H 164, eff. 1–13–76; 1969 H 320)

Historical and Statutory Notes

Ed. Note: 2151.352 contains provisions analogous to former 2151.35 repealed by 1969 H 320, eff. 11–19–69.

Amendment Note: 2003 H 95 made nonsubstantive changes to the second and third paragraphs of the section.

Amendment Note: 2000 S 179, § 3, eff. 1–1–02, inserted "under this chapter or Chapter 2152. of the Revised Code" in the first paragraph; and made changes to reflect gender neutral language and other nonsubstantive changes.

Cross References

Adjudicatory hearing, court to state right to counsel, Juv R 29
Right to counsel, O Const Art I §10
Right to counsel, guardian ad litem, procedure, Juv R 4
Social history, physical and mental examinations, custody investigation, availability of reports to counsel, Juv R 32
Waiver of rights, Juv R 3

Library References

Infants ☞205.
Westlaw Topic No. 211.
C.J.S. Infants §§ 51 to 67.
OJur 3d: 48, Family Law § 1575, 1626 to 1628, 1638, 1655
Am Jur 2d: 47, Juvenile Courts and Delinquent and Dependent Children § 38, 39
Right to and appointment of counsel in juvenile court proceedings. 60 ALR2d 691
Right of indigent parent to appointed counsel in proceeding for involuntary termination of parental rights. 80 ALR3d 1141
Right of juvenile court defendant to be represented during court proceedings by parent. 11 ALR4th 719
Validity and efficacy of minor's waiver of right to counsel—modern cases. 25 ALR4th 1072
Sowald & Morganstern, Baldwin's Ohio Practice, Domestic Relations Law § 15.60, 15.60.1 (1997).
Carlin, Baldwin's Ohio Practice, Merrick–Rippner Probate Law § 104.5, 107.33, 107.36, 107.45, 107.55, 107.56, 108.13, 108.25, 108.31 (2003).

2151.353 Disposition of abused, neglected, or dependent child

(A) If a child is adjudicated an abused, neglected, or dependent child, the court may make any of the following orders of disposition:

(1) Place the child in protective supervision;

(2) Commit the child to the temporary custody of a public children services agency, a private child placing agency, either parent, a relative residing within or outside the state, or a probation officer for placement in a certified foster home or in any other home approved by the court;

(3) Award legal custody of the child to either parent or to any other person who, prior to the dispositional hearing, files a motion requesting legal custody of the child;

(4) Commit the child to the permanent custody of a public children services agency or private child placing agency, if the court determines in accordance with division (E) of section 2151.414 of the Revised Code that the child cannot be placed with one of the child's parents within a reasonable time or should not be placed with either parent and determines in accordance with division (D) of section 2151.414 of the Revised Code that the permanent commitment is in the best interest of the child. If the court grants permanent custody under this division, the court, upon the request of any party, shall file a written opinion setting forth its findings of fact and conclusions of law in relation to the proceeding.

(5) Place the child in a planned permanent living arrangement with a public children services agency or private child placing agency, if a public children services agency or private child placing agency requests the court to place the child in a planned permanent living arrangement and if the court finds, by clear and convincing evidence, that a planned permanent living arrangement is in the best interest of the child and that one of the following exists:

(a) The child, because of physical, mental, or psychological problems or needs, is unable to function in a family-like setting and must remain in residential or institutional care.

(b) The parents of the child have significant physical, mental, or psychological problems and are unable to care for the child because of those problems, adoption is not in the best interest of the child, as determined in accordance with division (D) of section 2151.414 of the Revised Code, and the child retains a significant and positive relationship with a parent or relative.

(c) The child is sixteen years of age or older, has been counseled on the permanent placement options available to the child, is unwilling to accept or unable to adapt to a permanent placement, and is in an agency program preparing the child for independent living.

(6) Order the removal from the child's home until further order of the court of the person who committed abuse as described in section 2151.031 of the Revised Code against the child, who caused or allowed the child to suffer neglect as described in section 2151.03 of the Revised Code, or who is the parent, guardian, or custodian of a child who is adjudicated a dependent child and order any person not to have contact with the child or the child's siblings.

(B) No order for permanent custody or temporary custody of a child or the placement of a child in a planned permanent living arrangement shall be made pursuant to this section unless the complaint alleging the abuse, neglect, or dependency contains a prayer requesting permanent custody, temporary custody, or the placement of the child in a planned permanent living arrangement as desired, the summons served on the parents of the child contains as is appropriate a full explanation that the granting of an order for permanent custody permanently divests them of their parental rights, a full explanation that an adjudication that the child is an abused, neglected, or dependent child may result in an order of temporary custody that will cause the removal of the child from their legal custody until the court terminates the order of temporary custody or permanently divests the parents of their parental rights, or a full explanation that the granting of an order for a planned permanent living arrangement will result in the removal of the child from their legal custody if any of the conditions listed in divisions (A)(5)(a) to (c) of this section are found to exist, and the summons served on the parents contains a full explanation of their right to be represented by counsel and to have counsel appointed pursuant to Chapter 120. of the Revised Code if they are indigent.

If after making disposition as authorized by division (A)(2) of this section, a motion is filed that requests permanent custody of the child, the court may grant permanent custody of the child to the movant in accordance with section 2151.414 of the Revised Code.

(C) If the court issues an order for protective supervision pursuant to division (A)(1) of this section, the court may place any reasonable restrictions upon the child, the child's parents, guardian, or custodian, or any other person, including, but not limited to, any of the following:

(1) Order a party, within forty-eight hours after the issuance of the order, to vacate the child's home indefinitely or for a specified period of time;

(2) Order a party, a parent of the child, or a physical custodian of the child to prevent any particular person from having contact with the child;

(3) Issue an order restraining or otherwise controlling the conduct of any person which conduct would not be in the best interest of the child.

(D) As part of its dispositional order, the court shall journalize a case plan for the child. The journalized case plan shall not be changed except as provided in section 2151.412 of the Revised Code.

(E)(1) The court shall retain jurisdiction over any child for whom the court issues an order of disposition pursuant to division (A) of this section or pursuant to section 2151.414 or 2151.415 of the Revised Code until the child attains the age of eighteen years if the child is not mentally retarded, developmentally disabled, or physically impaired, the child attains the age of twenty-one years if the child is mentally retarded, developmentally disabled, or physically impaired, or the child is adopted and a final decree of adoption is issued, except that the court may retain jurisdiction over the child and continue any order of disposition under division (A) of this section or under section 2151.414 or 2151.415 of the Revised Code for a specified period of time to enable the child to graduate from high school or vocational school. The court shall make an entry continuing its jurisdiction under this division in the journal.

(2) Any public children services agency, any private child placing agency, the department of job and family services, or any party, other than any parent whose parental rights with respect to the child have been terminated pursuant to an order issued under division (A)(4) of this section, by filing a motion with the court, may at any time request the court to modify or terminate any order of disposition issued pursuant to division (A) of this section or section 2151.414 or 2151.415 of the Revised Code. The court shall hold a hearing upon the motion as if the hearing were the original dispositional hearing and shall give all parties to the action and the guardian ad litem notice of the hearing pursuant to the

Juvenile Rules. If applicable, the court shall comply with section 2151.42 of the Revised Code.

(F) Any temporary custody order issued pursuant to division (A) of this section shall terminate one year after the earlier of the date on which the complaint in the case was filed or the child was first placed into shelter care, except that, upon the filing of a motion pursuant to section 2151.415 of the Revised Code, the temporary custody order shall continue and not terminate until the court issues a dispositional order under that section.

(G)(1) No later than one year after the earlier of the date the complaint in the case was filed or the child was first placed in shelter care, a party may ask the court to extend an order for protective supervision for six months or to terminate the order. A party requesting extension or termination of the order shall file a written request for the extension or termination with the court and give notice of the proposed extension or termination in writing before the end of the day after the day of filing it to all parties and the child's guardian ad litem. If a public children services agency or private child placing agency requests termination of the order, the agency shall file a written status report setting out the facts supporting termination of the order at the time it files the request with the court. If no party requests extension or termination of the order, the court shall notify the parties that the court will extend the order for six months or terminate it and that it may do so without a hearing unless one of the parties requests a hearing. All parties and the guardian ad litem shall have seven days from the date a notice is sent pursuant to this division to object to and request a hearing on the proposed extension or termination.

(a) If it receives a timely request for a hearing, the court shall schedule a hearing to be held no later than thirty days after the request is received by the court. The court shall give notice of the date, time, and location of the hearing to all parties and the guardian ad litem. At the hearing, the court shall determine whether extension or termination of the order is in the child's best interest. If termination is in the child's best interest, the court shall terminate the order. If extension is in the child's best interest, the

court shall extend the order for six months.

(b) If it does not receive a timely request for a hearing, the court may extend the order for six months or terminate it without a hearing and shall journalize the order of extension or termination not later than fourteen days after receiving the request for extension or termination or after the date the court notifies the parties that it will extend or terminate the order. If the court does not extend or terminate the order, it shall schedule a hearing to be held no later than thirty days after the expiration of the applicable fourteen-day time period and give notice of the date, time, and location of the hearing to all parties and the child's guardian ad litem. At the hearing, the court shall determine whether extension or termination of the order is in the child's best interest. If termination is in the child's best interest, the court shall terminate the order. If extension is in the child's best interest, the court shall issue an order extending the order for protective supervision six months.

(2) If the court grants an extension of the order for protective supervision pursuant to division (G)(1) of this section, a party may, prior to termination of the extension, file with the court a request for an additional extension of six months or for termination of the order. The court and the parties shall comply with division (G)(1) of this section with respect to extending or terminating the order.

(3) If a court grants an extension pursuant to division (G)(2) of this section, the court shall terminate the order for protective supervision at the end of the extension.

(H) The court shall not issue a dispositional order pursuant to division (A) of this section that removes a child from the child's home unless the court complies with section 2151.419 of the Revised Code and includes in the dispositional order the findings of fact required by that section.

(I) If a motion or application for an order described in division (A)(6) of this section is made, the court shall not issue the order unless, prior to the issuance of the order, it provides to the person all of the following:

(1) Notice and a copy of the motion or application;

(2) The grounds for the motion or application;

(3) An opportunity to present evidence and witnesses at a hearing regarding the motion or application;

(4) An opportunity to be represented by counsel at the hearing.

(J) The jurisdiction of the court shall terminate one year after the date of the award or, if the court takes any further action in the matter subsequent to the award, the date of the latest further action subsequent to the award, if the court awards legal custody of a child to either of the following:

(1) A legal custodian who, at the time of the award of legal custody, resides in a county of this state other than the county in which the court is located;

(2) A legal custodian who resides in the county in which the court is located at the time of the award of legal custody, but moves to a different county of this state prior to one year after the date of the award or, if the court takes any further action in the matter subsequent to the award, one year after the date of the latest further action subsequent to the award.

The court in the county in which the legal custodian resides then shall have jurisdiction in the matter.

(2000 H 332, eff. 1–1–01; 2000 H 448, eff. 10–5–00; 1999 H 471, eff. 7–1–00; 1998 H 484, eff. 3–18–99; 1996 H 265, eff. 3–3–97; 1996 H 274, eff. 8–8–96; 1996 H 419, eff. 9–18–96; 1993 H 152, eff. 7–1–93; 1988 S 89; 1986 H 428; 1981 H 440; 1980 H 695; 1975 H 85; 1969 H 320)

Historical and Statutory Notes

Ed. Note: The amendment of this section by 2000 H 332, eff. 1–1–01, and 2000 H 448, eff. 10–5–00, was identical. See *Baldwin's Ohio Legislative Service Annotated*, 2000, pages 6/L–2157 and 6/L–2220, or the OH–LEGIS or OH–LEGIS–OLD database on WESTLAW, for original versions of these Acts.

Amendment Note: 2000 H 332 deleted "family" before "foster home" in division (A)(2); and inserted "years" twice in division (E)(1).

Amendment Note: 2000 H 448 deleted "family" after "certified" in division (A)(2).

Amendment Note: 1999 H 471 substituted "job and family" for "human" in division (E)(2).

Amendment Note: 1998 H 484 substituted "a planned permanent living arrangement" for "long-term foster care" throughout division (A)(5) and (B); added the third sentence in division (E)(2); substituted "complies with" for "makes the determination required by" in division (H); and made other nonsubstantive changes.

Amendment Note: 1996 H 265 inserted "or in any other home approved by the court" in division (A)(2).

Amendment Note: 1996 H 274 added division (A)(6); substituted "retarded, developmentally disabled, or physically impaired" for "or physically handicapped" twice in division (E)(1); deleted former division (G); added divisions (G), (I), and (J); and made changes to reflect gender neutral language. Prior to amendment, former division (G) read:

"(G) Any order for protective supervision issued pursuant to division (A)(1) of this section shall terminate one year after the earlier of the date on which the complaint in the case was filed or the child was first placed into shelter care, unless the public children services agency or private child placing agency that prepared the child's case plan files a motion with the court requesting the extension for a period of up to six months of the original dispositional order or the extension of a previously granted extension for an additional period of up to six months. Upon the filing of the motion and the court's giving notice of the date, time, and location of the hearing to all parties and the guardian ad litem, the court shall hold a hearing on the motion. If the court determines at the hearing that the extension of the original dispositional order or of any previously granted extension is in the best interest of the child, the court shall issue an order extending the original dispositional order or previously granted extension for an additional period of up to six months.

"At any time after the court issues an order extending an original order for protective supervision issued under division (A)(1) of this section or a previously granted extension, the agency that filed the motion requesting the extension may request the court to terminate the dispositional order, and the court, upon receipt of the motion, shall terminate the dispositional order."

Amendment Note: 1996 H 419 made changes to reflect gender neutral language throughout, and made other nonsubstantive changes.

Amendment Note: 1993 H 152 inserted "family" in, and deleted "or approved foster care" from the end of division (A)(2); and inserted "family" in division (A)(5).

Cross References

Adjudicatory hearing, Juv R 29

Day-care facilities, certain persons not to be employed by, 5104.09

Dispositional hearing, procedure, Juv R 34

Lists of prospective adoptive children and parents, 5103.16

Services for children with special needs, 5153.163

Ohio Administrative Code References

Protective supervision by PCSAs and PCPAs, OAC 5101:2–39–30

Library References

Infants ⚲222, 226.

Westlaw Topic No. 211.

C.J.S. Infants §§ 57, 69 to 85.

OJur 3d: 48, Family Law § 1544, 1550, 1602, 1610, 1662, 1632, 1657, 1691, 1693, 1694, 1703, 1706, 1711

Am Jur 2d: 42, Infants § 56, 57; 47, Juvenile Courts and Delinquent and Dependent Children § 29 to 33

Physical abuse of child by parent as ground for termination of parent's right to child. 53 ALR3d 605

Sexual abuse of child by parent as ground for termination of parent's right to child. 58 ALR3d 1074

Liability of parent for support of child institutionalized by juvenile court. 59 ALR3d 636

Parent's involuntary confinement, or failure to care for child as result thereof, as evincing neglect, unfitness, or the like in dependency or divestiture proceeding. 79 ALR3d 417

Right of indigent parent to appointed counsel in proceeding for involuntary termination of parental rights. 80 ALR3d 1141

Validity of state statute providing for termination of parental rights. 22 ALR4th 774

Validity and application of statute allowing endangered child to be temporarily removed from parental custody. 38 ALR4th 756

Failure of state or local government entity to protect child abuse victim as violation of federal constitutional right. 79 ALR Fed 514

Baldwin's Ohio Legislative Service, 1996 H 274—LSC Analysis, p 5/L–697

Baldwin's Ohio Legislative Service, 1988 Laws of Ohio, S 89—LSC Analysis, p 5–571

Klein & Darling, Baldwin's Ohio Practice, Civil Practice § 24–12 (1997).

Sowald & Morganstern, Baldwin's Ohio Practice, Domestic Relations Law § 15.67 (1997).

Carlin, Baldwin's Ohio Practice, Merrick–Rippner Probate Law § 98.15, 98.20, 98.23, 98.41, 101.63, 105.7, 106.10, 107.4, 107.10, 107.72, 107.74, 107.75, 107.76, 107.77, 107.78, 107.79, 107.80, 107.81, 107.82, 107.83, 107.84, 107.90, 107.112, 107.118, 107.120, 107.161, 107.174, 107.175, 107.176, 108.13, 108.14 (2003).

2151.354 Disposition of unruly child; driver's license suspension; habitual truants

(A) If the child is adjudicated an unruly child, the court may:

(1) Make any of the dispositions authorized under section 2151.353 of the Revised Code;

(2) Place the child on community control under any sanctions, services, and conditions that the court prescribes, as described in division (A)(4) of section 2152.19 of the Revised Code, provided that, if the court imposes a period of community service upon the child, the period of community service shall not exceed one hundred seventy-five hours;

(3) Suspend the driver's license, probationary driver's license, or temporary instruction permit issued to the child for a period of time prescribed by the court and suspend the registration of all motor vehicles registered in the name of the child for a period of time prescribed by the court. A child whose license or permit is so suspended is ineligible for issuance of a license or permit during the period of suspension. At the end of the period of suspension, the child shall not be reissued a license or permit until the child has paid any applicable reinstatement fee and complied with all requirements governing license reinstatement.

(4) Commit the child to the temporary or permanent custody of the court;

(5) Make any further disposition the court finds proper that is consistent with sections 2151.312 and 2151.56 to 2151.61 of the Revised Code;

(6) If, after making a disposition under division (A)(1), (2), or (3) of this section, the court finds upon further hearing that the child is not amenable to treatment or rehabilitation under that disposition, make a disposition otherwise authorized under divisions (A)(1), (4), (5), and (8) of section 2152.19 of the Revised Code that is consistent with sections 2151.312 and 2151.56 to 2151.61 of the Revised Code.

(B) If a child is adjudicated an unruly child for committing any act that, if committed by an adult, would be a drug abuse offense, as defined in section 2925.01 of the Revised Code, or a violation of division (B) of section 2917.11 of the Revised Code, in addition to imposing, in its discretion, any other order of disposition authorized by this section, the court shall do both of the following:

(1) Require the child to participate in a drug abuse or alcohol abuse counseling program;

(2) Suspend the temporary instruction permit, probationary driver's license, or driver's license issued to the child for a period of time prescribed by the court. The court, in its discretion, may terminate the suspension if the child attends and satisfactorily completes a drug abuse or alcohol abuse education, intervention, or treatment program specified by the court. During the time the child is attending a program as described in this division, the court shall retain the child's temporary instruction permit, probationary driver's license, or driver's license, and the court shall return the permit or license if it terminates the suspension.

(C)(1) If a child is adjudicated an unruly child for being an habitual truant, in addition to or in lieu of imposing any other order of disposition authorized by this section, the court may do any of the following:

(a) Order the board of education of the child's school district or the governing board of the educational service center in the child's school district to require the child to attend an alternative school if an alternative school has been established pursuant to section 3313.533 of the Revised Code in the school district in which the child is entitled to attend school;

(b) Require the child to participate in any academic program or community service program;

(c) Require the child to participate in a drug abuse or alcohol abuse counseling program;

(d) Require that the child receive appropriate medical or psychological treatment or counseling;

(e) Make any other order that the court finds proper to address the child's habitual truancy, including an order requiring the child to not be absent without legitimate excuse from the public school the child is supposed to attend for five or more consecutive days, seven or more school days in one school month, or twelve or more school days in a school year and including an order requiring the child to participate in a truancy prevention mediation program.

(2) If a child is adjudicated an unruly child for being an habitual truant and the court determines that the parent, guardian, or other person having care of the child has failed to cause the child's attendance at school in violation of section 3321.38 of the Revised Code, in addition to any order of disposition authorized by this section, all of the following apply:

(a) The court may require the parent, guardian, or other person having care of the child to participate in any community service program, preferably a community service program that requires the involvement of the parent, guardian, or other person having care of the child in the school attended by the child.

(b) The court may require the parent, guardian, or other person having care of the child to participate in a truancy prevention mediation program.

(c) The court shall warn the parent, guardian, or other person having care of the child that any subsequent adjudication of the child as an unruly or delinquent child for being an habitual or chronic truant may result in a criminal charge against the parent, guardian, or other person having care of the child for a violation of division (C) of section 2919.21 or section 2919.24 of the Revised Code.

(2002 H 400, § 4, eff. 1–1–04; 2002 H 400, § 1, eff. 4–3–03; 2002 S 123, eff. 1–1–04; 2002 H 393, eff. 7–5–02; 2001 H 57, eff. 2–19–02; 2000 S 179, § 3, eff. 1–1–02; 2000 S 181, eff. 9–4–00; 1997 S 35, eff. 1–1–99; 1996 H 265, eff. 3–3–97; 1996 H 274, eff. 8–8–96; 1992 H 154, eff. 7–31–92; 1990 S 258, S 131; 1989 H 381, H 330, H 329; 1988 H 643; 1969 H 320)

Historical and Statutory Notes

Amendment Note: 2002 H 400 changed "(A)(3)" to "(A)(4)" in division (A)(2); and changed "(A)(1), (3), (4), and (7)" to "(A)(1), (4), (5), and (8)" in division (A)(6).

Amendment Note: 2002 S 123 rewrote divisions (A) and (B) of this section, which prior thereto read:

"(A) If the child is adjudicated an unruly child, the court may:

"(1) Make any of the dispositions authorized under section 2151.353 of the Revised Code;

"(2) Place the child on community control under any sanctions, services, and conditions that the court prescribes, as described in division (A)(3) of section 2152.19 of the Revised Code, provided that, if the court imposes a period of community service upon the child, the period of community service shall not exceed one hundred seventy-five hours;

"(3) Suspend or revoke the driver's license, probationary driver's license, or temporary instruction permit issued to the child and suspend or revoke the registration of all motor vehicles registered in the name of the child. A child whose license or permit is so suspended or revoked is ineligible for issuance of a license or permit during the period of suspension or revocation. At the end of the period of suspension or revocation, the child shall not be reissued a license or permit until the child has paid any applicable reinstatement fee and complied with all requirements governing license reinstatement.

"(4) Commit the child to the temporary or permanent custody of the court;

"(5) Make any further disposition the court finds proper that is consistent with sections 2151.312 and 2151.56 to 2151.61 of the Revised Code;

"(6) If, after making a disposition under division (A)(1), (2), or (3) of this section, the court finds upon further hearing that the child is not amenable to treatment or rehabilitation under that disposition, make a disposition otherwise authorized under divisions (A)(1), (3), (4), and (7) of section 2152.19 of the Revised Code that is consistent with sections

2151.312 and 2151.56 to 2151.61 of the Revised Code.

"(B) If a child is adjudicated an unruly child for committing any act that, if committed by an adult, would be a drug abuse offense, as defined in section 2925.01 of the Revised Code, or a violation of division (B) of section 2917.11 of the Revised Code, then, in addition to imposing, in its discretion, any other order of disposition authorized by this section, the court shall do both of the following:

"(1) Require the child to participate in a drug abuse or alcohol abuse counseling program;

"(2) Suspend or revoke the temporary instruction permit, probationary driver's license, or driver's license issued to the child for a period of time prescribed by the court or, at the discretion of the court, until the child attends and satisfactorily completes a drug abuse or alcohol abuse education, intervention, or treatment program specified by the court. During the time the child is attending the program, the court shall retain any temporary instruction permit, probationary driver's license, or driver's license issued to the child and shall return the permit or license when the child satisfactorily completes the program."

Amendment Note: 2002 H 393 inserted ", provided that, if the court imposes a period of community service upon the child, the period of community service shall not exceed one hundred seventy-five hours;" in division (A)(2).

Amendment Note: 2001 H 57 inserted new division (A)(5), redesignated former division (A)(5) as new division (A)(6); and rewrote new division (A)(6), which as former division (A)(5) read:

"If, after making a disposition under division (A)(1), (2), or (3) of this section, the court finds upon further hearing that the child is not amenable to treatment or rehabilitation under that disposition, make a disposition otherwise authorized under divisions (A)(1), (3), (4) and (7) of section 2152.19 of the Revised Code, except that the child may not be committed to or placed in a secure correctional facility, and commitment to or placement in a detention facility may not exceed twenty-four hours unless authorized by division (C)(3) of section 2151.312 or sections 2151.56 to 2151.61 of the Revised Code."

Amendment Note: 2000 S 179, § 3, eff. 1–1–02, substituted "community control" for "probation" and inserted "sanctions, services, and" and "as described in division (A) of section 2152.19 of the Revised Code" in division (A)(2); and substituted "divisions (A)(1), (3), (4), and (7) of section 2152.19" for "divisions (A)(1), (2), and (A)(8) to (12) of section 2151.355", "facility" for "home", and "division (B)(3)" for "division (C)(3)", in division (A)(5).

Amendment Note: 2000 S 181 substituted "(A)(8) to (12)" for "(A)(7) to (11)" in division (A)(5); and added division (C).

Amendment Note: 1997 S 35 inserted "probationary driver's license, or temporary instruction permit" and added the second and third sentences in division (A)(3); rewrote division (B)(2); and made other nonsubstantive changes. Prior to amendment, division (B)(2) read:

"(2) Suspend or revoke the temporary instruction permit or probationary operator's license issued to the child until the child attains the age of eighteen years or, at the discretion of the court, attends and satisfactorily completes a drug abuse or alcohol abuse education, intervention, or treatment program specified by the court. During the time the child is attending the program, the court shall retain any temporary instruction permit or probationary license issued to the child and shall return the permit or license when the child satisfactorily completes the program."

Amendment Note: 1996 H 265 substituted "(A)(1), (2), and (A)(7) to (11)" for "(A)(1) to (3) and (A)(6) to (10)" and inserted ", except that the child may not be committed to or placed in a secure correctional facility, and commitment to or placement in a detention home may not exceed twenty-four hours unless authorized by division (C)(3) of section 2151.312 or sections 2151.56 to 2151.61 of the Revised Code" in division (A)(5).

Amendment Note: 1996 H 274 added division (A)(4); and redesignated former division (A)(4) as division (A)(5).

Cross References

Adjudicatory hearing, Juv R 29

Deception to obtain matter harmful to juveniles, 2907.33

Dispositional hearing, procedure, Juv R 34

Foster caregivers, information regarding delinquent children provided to, 2152.72

Registrar of motor vehicles, revocation of probationary driver's license, 4507.162

Library References

Automobiles ⊂⇒144.

Infants ⊂⇒223.1.

Westlaw Topic Nos. 48A, 211.

C.J.S. Motor Vehicles § 164.1 et seq.

OJur 3d: 48, Family Law § 1688

Am Jur 2d: 42, Infants § 56, 57; 47, Juvenile Courts and Delinquent and Dependent Children § 29 to 33

Physical abuse of child by parent as ground for termination of parent's right to child. 53 ALR3d 605

Sexual abuse of child by parent as ground for termination of parent's right to child. 58 ALR3d 1074

Liability of parent for support of child institutionalized by juvenile court. 59 ALR3d 636

Parent's involuntary confinement, or failure to care for child as result thereof, as evincing neglect, unfitness, or the like in dependency or divestiture proceeding. 79 ALR3d 417

Right of indigent parent to appointed counsel in proceeding for involuntary termination of parental rights. 80 ALR3d 1141

Validity of state statute providing for termination of parental rights. 22 ALR4th 774

Validity and application of statute allowing endangered child to be temporarily removed from parental custody. 38 ALR4th 756

Failure of state or local government entity to protect child abuse victim as violation of federal constitutional right. 79 ALR Fed 514

Baldwin's Ohio Legislative Service, 1990 Laws of Ohio, S 258—LSC Analysis, p 5–954

Carlin, Baldwin's Ohio Practice, Merrick–Rippner Probate Law § 107.111, 107.112, 107.113 (2003).

2151.355 Orders of disposition for delinquent child; records; notice to victims; electronically monitored house detention; notice to school districts; searches authorized—Repealed (first version)

Note: See also following version, Publisher's Note, and Uncodified Law.

(2000 S 179, § 4, eff. 1–1–02; 2002 H 130, eff. 4–7–03; 2000 S 222, eff. 3–22–01; 2000 S 181, eff. 9–4–00; 1999 H 3, eff. 11–22–99; 1998 H 526, § 4, eff. 1–1–99; 1998 H 526, § 1, eff. 9–1–98; 1998 H 2, eff. 1–1–99; 1997 S 35, eff. 1–1–99; 1997 H 1, eff. 7–1–98; 1997 H 215, § 7, eff. 9–30–97; 1997 H 215, § 1, eff. 9–29–97; 1996 H 124, eff. 9–30–97; 1996 S 269, eff. 7–1–96; 1996 H 445, eff. 9–3–96; 1996 H 274, § 4, eff. 8–8–96; 1996 H 274, § 1, eff. 8–8–96; 1995 S 2, eff. 7–1–96; 1995 H 1, eff. 1–1–96; 1995 H 4, eff. 11–9–95; 1994 H 571, eff. 10–6–94; 1992 H 725, eff. 4–16–93; 1992 S 331, H 154; 1990 S 258, H 51, H 266, H 513, S 131; 1989 H 166, H 381, H 330, H 329; 1988 H 643; 1983 S 210; 1982 H 209; 1981 H 440; 1978 H 565, S 119; 1977 H 1; 1976 H 1196; 1974 H 1067; 1973 S 324; 1972 H 494; 1970 H 931; 1969 H 320)

Note: See also following version, Publisher's Note, and Uncodified Law.

2151.355 Disposition where child adjudicated delinquent (second version)

Note: See also preceding repeal, Publisher's Note, and Uncodified Law.

(A) If a child is adjudicated a delinquent child, the court may make any of the following orders of disposition:

(1) Any order that is authorized by section 2151.353 of the Revised Code;

(2) Place the child on probation under any conditions that the court prescribes. If the child is adjudicated a delinquent child for violating section 2909.05, 2909.06, or 2909.07 of the Revised Code and if restitution is appropriate under the circumstances of the case, the court shall require the child to make restitution for the property damage caused by the child's violation as a condition of the child's probation. If the child is adjudicated a delinquent child because the child violated any other section of the Revised Code, the court may require the child as a condition of the child's probation to make restitution for the property damage caused by the child's violation and for the value of the property that was the subject of the violation the child committed if it would be a theft offense, as defined in division (K) of section 2913.01 of the Revised Code, if committed by an adult. The restitution may be in the form of a cash reimbursement paid in a lump sum or in installments, the performance of repair work to restore any damaged property to its original condition, the performance of a reasonable amount of labor for the victim approximately equal to the value of the property damage caused by the child's violation or to the value of the property that is the subject of the violation if it would be a theft offense if committed by an adult, the performance of community service or community work, any other form of restitution devised by the court, or any combination of the previously described forms of restitution.

If the child is adjudicated a delinquent child for violating a law of this state or the United States, or an ordinance or regulation of a political subdivision of this state, that would be a crime if committed by an adult or for violating division (A) of section 2923.211 of the Revised Code, the court, in addition to all other required or permissive conditions of probation that the court imposes upon the delinquent child pursuant to division (A)(2) of this section, shall require the child as a condition of the child's probation to abide by the law during the period of probation, including, but not limited to, complying with the provisions of Chapter 2923. of the Revised Code relating to the possession, sale, furnishing, transfer, disposition, purchase, acquisition, carrying, conveying, or use of, or other conduct involving, a firearm or dangerous ordnance, as defined in section 2923.11 of the Revised Code.

(3) Commit the child to the temporary custody of any school, camp, institution, or other facility operated for the care of delinquent children by the county, by a district organized under section 2151.34 or 2151.65 of the Revised Code, or by a private agency or organization, within or without the state, that is authorized and qualified to provide the care, treatment, or placement required;

(4) If the child is adjudicated a delinquent child for committing an act that would be a felony of the third, fourth, or

fifth degree if committed by an adult or for violating division (A) of section 2923.211 of the Revised Code, commit the child to the legal custody of the department of youth services for institutionalization for an indefinite term consisting of a minimum period of six months and a maximum period not to exceed the child's attainment of twenty-one years of age;

(5)(a) If the child is adjudicated a delinquent child for violating section 2903.03, 2905.01, 2909.02, or 2911.01 or division (A) of section 2903.04 of the Revised Code or for violating any provision of section 2907.02 of the Revised Code other than division (A)(1)(b) of that section when the sexual conduct or insertion involved was consensual and when the victim of the violation of division (A)(1)(b) of that section was older than the delinquent child, was the same age as the delinquent child, or was less than three years younger than the delinquent child, commit the child to the legal custody of the department of youth services for institutionalization in a secure facility for an indefinite term consisting of a minimum period of one to three years, as prescribed by the court, and a maximum period not to exceed the child's attainment of twenty-one years of age;

(b) If the child is adjudicated a delinquent child for violating section 2923.02 of the Revised Code and if the violation involves an attempt to commit a violation of section 2903.01 or 2903.02 of the Revised Code, commit the child to the legal custody of the department of youth services for institutionalization in a secure facility for an indefinite term consisting of a minimum period of six to seven years, as prescribed by the court, and a maximum period not to exceed the child's attainment of twenty-one years of age;

(c) If the child is adjudicated a delinquent child for committing an act that is not described in division (A)(5)(a) or (b) of this section and that would be a felony of the first or second degree if committed by an adult, commit the child to the legal custody of the department of youth services for institutionalization in a secure facility for an indefinite term consisting of a minimum period of one year and a maximum period not to exceed the child's attainment of twenty-one years of age.

(6) If the child is adjudicated a delinquent child for committing a violation of section 2903.01 or 2903.02 of the Revised Code, commit the child to the legal custody of the department of youth services for institutionalization in a secure facility until the child's attainment of twenty-one years of age;

(7)(a) If the child is adjudicated a delinquent child for committing an act, other than a violation of section 2923.12 of the Revised Code, that would be a felony if committed by an adult and is committed to the legal custody of the department of youth services pursuant to division (A)(4), (5), or (6) of this section and if the court determines that the child, if the child was an adult, would be guilty of a specification of the type set forth in section 2941.141, 2941.144, 2941.145, 2941.146, or 2941.1412 of the Revised Code in relation to the act for which the child was adjudicated a delinquent child, commit the child to the legal custody of the department of youth services for institutionalization in a secure facility for the following period of time, subject to division (A)(7)(d) of this section:

(i) If the child would be guilty of a specification of the type set forth in section 2941.141 of the Revised Code, a period of one year;

(ii) If the child would be guilty of a specification of the type set forth in section 2941.144, 2941.145, 2941.146, or 2941.1412 of the Revised Code, a period of three years.

(b) If the child is adjudicated a delinquent child for committing a category one offense or a category two offense and is committed to the legal custody of the department of youth services pursuant to division (A)(5) or (6) of this section and if the court determines that the child, if the child was an adult, would be guilty of a specification of the type set forth in section 2941.142 of the Revised Code in relation to the act for which the child was adjudicated a delinquent child, the court shall commit the child to the legal custody of the department of youth services for institutionalization in a secure facility for a period of not less than one year or more than three years, subject to division (A)(7)(d) of this section.

(c) If the child is adjudicated a delinquent child for committing an act that would be an offense of violence that is a felony if committed by an adult and is committed to the legal custody of the department of youth services pursuant to division (A)(4), (5), or (6) of this section and if the court determines that the child, if the child was an adult, would be guilty of a specification of the type set forth in section 2941.1411 of the Revised Code in relation to the act for which the child was adjudicated a delinquent child, the court may commit the child to the custody of the department of youth services for institutionalization in a secure facility for two years, subject to division (A)(7)(d) of this section.

(d) A court that imposes a period of commitment under division (A)(7)(a) of this section is not precluded from imposing an additional period of commitment under division (A)(7)(b) or (c) of this section, a court that imposes a period of commitment under division (A)(7)(b) of this section is not precluded from imposing an additional period of commitment under division (A)(7)(a) or (c) of this section, and a court that imposes a period of commitment under division (A)(7)(c) of this section is not precluded from imposing an additional period of commitment under division (A)(7)(a) or (b) of this section. The court shall not commit a child to the legal custody of the department of youth services pursuant to division (A)(7)(a), (b), or (c) of this section for a period of time that exceeds three years. The period of commitment imposed pursuant to division (A)(7)(a), (b), or (c) of this section shall be in addition to, and shall be served consecutively with and prior to, a period of commitment ordered pursuant to division (A)(4), (5), or (6) of this section, provided that the total of all the periods of commitment shall not exceed the child's attainment of twenty-one years of age.

(8) Impose a fine and costs in accordance with the schedule set forth in section 2151.3512 of the Revised Code;

(9) Require the child to make restitution for all or part of the property damage caused by the child's delinquent act and for all or part of the value of the property that was the subject of any delinquent act the child committed that would be a theft offense, as defined in division (K) of section 2913.01 of the Revised Code, if committed by an adult. If the court determines that the victim of the child's delinquent act was sixty-five years of age or older or permanently and totally disabled at the time of the commission of the act, the court, regardless of whether or not the child knew the age of the victim, shall consider that fact in favor of imposing restitution, but that fact shall not control the

decision of the court. The restitution may be in the form of a cash reimbursement paid in a lump sum or in installments, the performance of repair work to restore any damaged property to its original condition, the performance of a reasonable amount of labor for the victim, the performance of community service or community work, any other form of restitution devised by the court, or any combination of the previously described forms of restitution.

(10) Subject to division (D) of this section, suspend or revoke the driver's license, probationary driver's license, or temporary instruction permit issued to the child or suspend or revoke the registration of all motor vehicles registered in the name of the child. A child whose license or permit is so suspended or revoked is ineligible for issuance of a license or permit during the period of suspension or revocation. At the end of the period of suspension or revocation, the child shall not be reissued a license or permit until the child has paid any applicable reinstatement fee and complied with all requirements governing license reinstatement.

(11) If the child is adjudicated a delinquent child for committing an act that, if committed by an adult, would be a criminal offense that would qualify the adult as an eligible offender pursuant to division (A)(3) of section 2929.23 of the Revised Code, impose a period of electronically monitored house detention in accordance with division (J) of this section that does not exceed the maximum sentence of imprisonment that could be imposed upon an adult who commits the same act;

(12) Impose a period of day reporting in which the child is required each day to report to and leave a center or other approved reporting location at specified times in order to participate in work, education or training, treatment, and other approved programs at the center or outside the center;

(13) Impose a period of electronically monitored house arrest in accordance with division (J) of this section;

(14) Impose a period of community service of up to five hundred hours;

(15) Impose a period in an alcohol or drug treatment program with a level of security for the child as determined necessary by the court;

(16) Impose a period of intensive supervision, in which the child is required to maintain frequent contact with a person appointed by the court to supervise the child while the child is seeking or maintaining employment and participating in training, education, and treatment programs as the order of disposition;

(17) Impose a period of basic supervision, in which the child is required to maintain contact with a person appointed to supervise the child in accordance with sanctions imposed by the court;

(18) Impose a period of drug and alcohol use monitoring;

(19) Impose a period in which the court orders the child to observe a curfew that may involve daytime or evening hours;

(20) Require the child to obtain a high school diploma, a certificate of high school equivalence, or employment;

(21) If the court obtains the assent of the victim of the criminal act committed by the child, require the child to participate in a reconciliation or mediation program that includes a meeting in which the child and the victim may discuss the criminal act, discuss restitution, and consider other sanctions for the criminal act;

(22) Commit the child to the temporary or permanent custody of the court;

(23) Require the child to not be absent without legitimate excuse from the public school the child is supposed to attend for five or more consecutive days, seven or more school days in one school month, or twelve or more school days in a school year;

(24)(a) If a child is adjudicated a delinquent child for being a chronic truant or an habitual truant who previously has been adjudicated an unruly child for being an habitual truant, do either or both of the following:

(i) Require the child to participate in a truancy prevention mediation program;

(ii) Make any order of disposition as authorized by this section, except that the court shall not commit the child to a facility described in division (A)(3) of this section unless the court determines that the child violated a lawful court order made pursuant to division (C)(1)(e) of section 2151.354 of the Revised Code or division (A)(23) of this section.

(b) If a child is adjudicated a delinquent child for being a chronic truant or

an habitual truant who previously has been adjudicated an unruly child for being an habitual truant and the court determines that the parent, guardian, or other person having care of the child has failed to cause the child's attendance at school in violation of section 3321.38 of the Revised Code, do either or both of the following:

(i) Require the parent, guardian, or other person having care of the child to participate in a truancy prevention mediation program;

(ii) Require the parent, guardian, or other person having care of the child to participate in any community service program, preferably a community service program that requires the involvement of the parent, guardian, or other person having care of the child in the school attended by the child.

(25) Make any further disposition that the court finds proper, except that the child shall not be placed in any state correctional institution, county, multicounty, or municipal jail or workhouse, or other place in which an adult convicted of a crime, under arrest, or charged with a crime is held.

(B)(1) If a child is adjudicated a delinquent child for violating section 2923.32 of the Revised Code, the court, in addition to any order of disposition it makes for the child under division (A) of this section, shall enter an order of criminal forfeiture against the child in accordance with divisions (B)(3), (4), (5), and (6) and (C) to (F) of section 2923.32 of the Revised Code.

(2) If a child is adjudicated a delinquent child for being a chronic truant or an habitual truant who previously has been adjudicated an unruly child for being an habitual truant and the court determines that the parent, guardian, or other person having care of the child has failed to cause the child's attendance at school in violation of section 3321.38 of the Revised Code, in addition to any order of disposition it makes under this section, the court shall warn the parent, guardian, or other person having care of the child that any subsequent adjudication of the child as an unruly or delinquent child for being an habitual or chronic truant may result in a criminal charge against the parent, guardian, or other person having care of the child for a violation of division (C) of section 2919.21 or section 2919.24 of the Revised Code.

(3) If a child is adjudicated a delinquent child for committing two or more acts that would be felonies if committed by an adult and if the court entering the delinquent child adjudication orders the commitment of the child, for two or more of those acts, to the legal custody of the department of youth services for institutionalization or institutionalization in a secure facility pursuant to division (A)(4), (5), or (6) of this section, the court may order that all of the periods of commitment imposed under those divisions for those acts be served consecutively in the legal custody of the department of youth services and, if applicable, be in addition to and commence immediately following the expiration of all periods of commitment that the court imposes pursuant to division (A)(7)(a), (b), or (c) of this section. A court shall not commit a delinquent child to the legal custody of the department of youth services under division (B)(2) of this section for a period that exceeds the child's attainment of twenty-one years of age.

(C) If a child is adjudicated a delinquent child for committing an act that, if committed by an adult, would be a drug abuse offense, as defined in section 2925.01 of the Revised Code, or for violating division (B) of section 2917.11 of the Revised Code, in addition to imposing in its discretion any other order of disposition authorized by this section, the court shall do both of the following:

(1) Require the child to participate in a drug abuse or alcohol abuse counseling program;

(2) Suspend or revoke the temporary instruction permit, probationary driver's license, or driver's license issued to the child for a period of time prescribed by the court or, at the discretion of the court, until the child attends and satisfactorily completes, a drug abuse or alcohol abuse education, intervention, or treatment program specified by the court. During the time the child is attending the program, the court shall retain any temporary instruction permit, probationary driver's license, or driver's license issued to the child, and the court shall return the permit or license when the child satisfactorily completes the program.

(D) If a child is adjudicated a delinquent child for violating section 2923.122 of the Revised Code, the court, in addition to any order of disposition it makes for the child under division (A), (B), or (C) of this section, shall revoke the temporary instruction permit and deny the child the issuance of another temporary instruction permit in accordance with division (F)(1)(b) of section 2923.122 of the Revised Code or shall suspend the probationary driver's license, restricted license, or nonresident operating privilege of the child or deny the child the issuance of a probationary driver's license, restricted license, or temporary instruction permit in accordance with division (F)(1)(a), (c), (d), or (e) of section 2923.122 of the Revised Code.

(E)(1) At the dispositional hearing and prior to making any disposition pursuant to division (A) of this section, the court shall determine whether a victim of the delinquent act committed by the child was five years of age or younger at the time the delinquent act was committed, whether a victim of the delinquent act sustained physical harm to the victim's person during the commission of or otherwise as a result of the delinquent act, whether a victim of the delinquent act was sixty-five years of age or older or permanently and totally disabled at the time the delinquent act was committed, and whether the delinquent act would have been an offense of violence if committed by an adult. If the victim was five years of age or younger at the time the delinquent act was committed, sustained physical harm to the victim's person during the commission of or otherwise as a result of the delinquent act, or was sixty-five years of age or older or permanently and totally disabled at the time the act was committed, regardless of whether the child knew the age of the victim, and if the act would have been an offense of violence if committed by an adult, the court shall consider those facts in favor of imposing commitment under division (A)(3), (4), (5), or (6) of this section, but those facts shall not control the court's decision.

(2) At the dispositional hearing and prior to making any disposition pursuant to division (A)(4), (5), or (6) of this section, the court shall determine whether the delinquent child previously has been adjudicated a delinquent child for a violation of a law or ordinance. If the delinquent child previously has been adjudicated a delinquent child for a violation of a law or ordinance, the court, for purposes of entering an order of disposition for the delinquent child under this section, shall consider the previous delinquent child adjudication as a conviction of a violation of the law or ordinance in

determining the degree of offense the current delinquent act would be had it been committed by an adult.

(F)(1) When a juvenile court commits a delinquent child to the custody of the department of youth services pursuant to this section, the court shall not designate the specific institution in which the department is to place the child but instead shall specify that the child is to be institutionalized or that the institutionalization is to be in a secure facility if that is required by division (A) of this section.

(2) When a juvenile court commits a delinquent child to the custody of the department of youth services, the court shall provide the department with the child's medical records, a copy of the report of any mental examination of the child ordered by the court, the section or sections of the Revised Code violated by the child and the degree of the violation, the warrant to convey the child to the department, a copy of the court's journal entry ordering the commitment of the child to the legal custody of the department, a copy of the arrest record pertaining to the act for which the child was adjudicated a delinquent child, a copy of any victim impact statement pertaining to the act, and any other information concerning the child that the department reasonably requests. The court also shall complete the form for the standard disposition investigation report that is developed and furnished by the department of youth services pursuant to section 5139.04 of the Revised Code and provide the department with the completed form. The department may refuse to accept physical custody of a delinquent child who is committed to the legal custody of the department until the court provides to the department the documents specified in division (F)(2) of this section. No officer or employee of the department who refuses to accept physical custody of a delinquent child who is committed to the legal custody of the department shall be subject to prosecution or contempt of court for the refusal if the court fails to provide the documents specified in division (F)(2) of this section at the time the court transfers the physical custody of the child to the department.

(3) Within twenty working days after the department of youth services receives physical custody of a delinquent child from a juvenile court, the court shall provide the department with a certified copy of the child's birth certificate or the child's social security number, or, if the court made all reasonable efforts to obtain the information but was unsuccessful, the court shall provide the department with documentation of the efforts it made to obtain the information.

(4) When a juvenile court commits a delinquent child to the custody of the department of youth services, the court shall give notice to the school attended by the child of the child's commitment by sending to that school a copy of the court's journal entry ordering the commitment. As soon as possible after receipt of the notice described in this division, the school shall provide the department with the child's school transcript. However, the department shall not refuse to accept a child committed to it, and a child committed to it shall not be held in a county or district detention home, because of a school's failure to provide the school transcript that it is required to provide under division (F)(4) of this section.

(5) The department of youth services shall provide the court and the school with an updated copy of the child's school transcript and shall provide the court with a summary of the institutional record of the child when it releases the child from institutional care. The department also shall provide the court with a copy of any portion of the child's institutional record that the court specifically requests within five working days of the request.

(6) When a juvenile court commits a delinquent child to the custody of the department of youth services pursuant to division (A)(4) or (5) of this section, the court shall state in the order of commitment the total number of days that the child has been held, as of the date of the issuance of the order, in detention in connection with the delinquent child complaint upon which the order of commitment is based. The department shall reduce the minimum period of institutionalization or minimum period of institutionalization in a secure facility specified in division (A)(4) or (5) of this section by both the total number of days that the child has been so held in detention as stated by the court in the order of commitment and the total number of any additional days that the child has been held in detention subsequent to the order of commitment but prior to the transfer of physical custody of the child to the department.

(G)(1) At any hearing at which a child is adjudicated a delinquent child or as soon as possible after the hearing, the court shall notify all victims of the delinquent act, who may be entitled to a recovery under any of the following sections, of the right of the victims to recover, pursuant to section 3109.09 of the Revised Code, compensatory damages from the child's parents; of the right of the victims to recover, pursuant to section 3109.10 of the Revised Code, compensatory damages from the child's parents for willful and malicious assaults committed by the child; and of the right of the victims to recover an award of reparations pursuant to sections 2743.51 to 2743.72 of the Revised Code.

(2) If a child is adjudicated a delinquent child for committing an act that, if committed by an adult, would be aggravated murder, murder, rape, felonious sexual penetration in violation of former section 2907.12 of the Revised Code, involuntary manslaughter, a felony of the first or second degree resulting in the death of or physical harm to a person, complicity in or an attempt to commit any of those offenses, or an offense under an existing or former law of this state that is or was substantially equivalent to any of those offenses and if the court in its order of disposition for that act commits the child to the custody of the department of youth services, the court may make a specific finding that the adjudication should be considered a conviction for purposes of a determination in the future, pursuant to Chapter 2929. of the Revised Code, as to whether the child is a repeat violent offender as defined in section 2929.01 of the Revised Code. If the court makes a specific finding as described in this division, it shall include the specific finding in its order of disposition and in the record in the case.

(H)(1) If a child is adjudicated a delinquent child for committing an act that would be a felony or offense of violence if committed by an adult, the court, prior to issuing an order of disposition under this section, shall order the preparation of a victim impact statement by the probation department of the county in which the victim of the act resides, by the court's own probation department, or by a victim assistance program that is operated by the state, a county, a municipal corporation, or another governmental entity. The court shall consider the victim impact statement in determining the order of disposition to issue for the child.

(2) Each victim impact statement shall identify the victim of the act for which the child was adjudicated a delinquent child, itemize any economic loss suffered by the victim as a result of the act, identify any physical injury suffered by the victim as a result of the act and the seriousness and permanence of the injury, identify any change in the victim's personal welfare or familial relationships as a result of the act and any psychological impact experienced by the victim or the victim's family as a result of the act, and contain any other information related to the impact of the act upon the victim that the court requires.

(3) A victim impact statement shall be kept confidential and is not a public record, as defined in section 149.43 of the Revised Code. However, the court may furnish copies of the statement to the department of youth services pursuant to division (F)(3) of this section or to both the adjudicated delinquent child or the adjudicated delinquent child's counsel and the prosecuting attorney. The copy of a victim impact statement furnished by the court to the department pursuant to division (F)(3) of this section shall be kept confidential and is not a public record, as defined in section 149.43 of the Revised Code. The copies of a victim impact statement that are made available to the adjudicated delinquent child or the adjudicated delinquent child's counsel and the prosecuting attorney pursuant to division (H)(3) of this section shall be returned to the court by the person to whom they were made available immediately following the imposition of an order of disposition for the child under this section.

(I)(1) Sections 2925.41 to 2925.45 of the Revised Code apply to children who are adjudicated or could be adjudicated by a juvenile court to be delinquent children for an act that, if committed by an adult, would be a felony drug abuse offense. Subject to division (B) of section 2925.42 and division (E) of section 2925.43 of the Revised Code, a delinquent child of that nature loses any right to the possession of, and forfeits to the state any right, title, and interest that the delinquent child may have in, property as defined in section 2925.41 and further described in section 2925.42 or 2925.43 of the Revised Code.

(2) Sections 2923.44 to 2923.47 of the Revised Code apply to children who are adjudicated or could be adjudicated by a juvenile court to be delinquent children for an act in violation of section 2923.42 of the Revised Code. Subject to division (B) of section 2923.44 and division (E) of section 2923.45 of the Revised Code, a delinquent child of that nature loses any right to the possession of, and forfeits to the state any right, title, and interest that the delinquent child may have in, property as defined in section 2923.41 of the Revised Code and further described in section 2923.44 or 2923.45 of the Revised Code.

(J)(1) A juvenile court, pursuant to division (A)(11) of this section, may impose a period of electronically monitored house detention upon a child who is adjudicated a delinquent child for committing an act that, if committed by an adult, would be a criminal offense that would qualify the adult as an eligible offender pursuant to division (A)(3) of section 2929.23 of the Revised Code. The court may impose a period of electronically monitored house detention in addition to or in lieu of any other dispositional order imposed upon the child, except that any period of electronically monitored house detention shall not extend beyond the child's eighteenth birthday. If a court imposes a period of electronically monitored house detention upon a child, it shall require the child to wear, otherwise have attached to the child's person, or otherwise be subject to monitoring by a certified electronic monitoring device or to participate in the operation of and monitoring by a certified electronic monitoring system; to remain in the child's home or other specified premises for the entire period of electronically monitored house detention except when the court permits the child to leave those premises to go to school or to other specified premises; to be monitored by a central system that monitors the certified electronic monitoring device that is attached to the child's person or that otherwise is being used to monitor the child and that can monitor and determine the child's location at any time or at a designated point in time or to be monitored by the certified electronic monitoring system; to report periodically to a person designated by the court; and, in return for receiving a dispositional order of electronically monitored house detention, to enter into a written contract with the court agreeing to comply with all restrictions and requirements imposed by the court, agreeing to pay any fee imposed by the court for the costs of the electronically monitored house detention imposed by the court pursuant to division (E) of section 2929.23 of the Revised Code, and agreeing to waive the right to receive credit for any time served on electronically monitored house detention toward the period of any other dispositional order imposed upon the child for the act for which the dispositional order of electronically monitored house detention was imposed if the child violates any of the restrictions or requirements of the dispositional order of electronically monitored house detention. The court also may impose other reasonable restrictions and requirements upon the child.

(2) If a child violates any of the restrictions or requirements imposed upon the child as part of the child's dispositional order of electronically monitored house detention, the child shall not receive credit for any time served on electronically monitored house detention toward any other dispositional order imposed upon the child for the act for which the dispositional order of electronically monitored house detention was imposed.

(K)(1) Within ten days after completion of the adjudication, the court shall give written notice of an adjudication that a child is a delinquent child to the superintendent of a city, local, exempted village, or joint vocational school district, and to the principal of the school the child attends, if the basis of the adjudication was the commission of an act that would be a criminal offense if committed by an adult, if the act was committed by the delinquent child when the child was fourteen years of age or older, and if the act is any of the following:

(a) An act that would be a felony or an offense of violence if committed by an adult, an act in the commission of which the child used or brandished a firearm, or an act that is a violation of section 2907.04, 2907.06, 2907.07, 2907.08, 2907.09, 2907.24, or 2907.241 of the Revised Code and that would be a misdemeanor if committed by an adult;

(b) A violation of section 2923.12 of the Revised Code or of a substantially similar municipal ordinance that would be a misdemeanor if committed by an adult and that was committed on property owned or controlled by, or at an activity held under the auspices of, the board of education of that school district;

(c) A violation of division (A) of section 2925.03 or 2925.11 of the Revised Code that would be a misdemeanor if committed by an adult, that was committed on property owned or controlled by, or at an activity held under the auspices of, the board of education of that school district, and that is not a minor drug possession offense;

(d) Complicity in any violation described in division (K)(1)(a) of this section, or complicity in any violation described in division (K)(1)(b) or (c) of this section that was alleged to have been committed in the manner described in division (K)(1)(b) or (c) of this section, and regardless of whether the act of complicity was committed on property owned or controlled by, or at an activity held under the auspices of, the board of education of that school district.

(2) The notice given pursuant to division (K)(1) of this section shall include the name of the child who was adjudicated to be a delinquent child, the child's age at the time the child committed the act that was the basis of the adjudication, and identification of the violation of the law or ordinance that was the basis of the adjudication.

(L) During the period of a delinquent child's probation granted under division (A)(2) of this section, authorized probation officers who are engaged within the scope of their supervisory duties or responsibilities may search, with or without a warrant, the person of the delinquent child, the place of residence of the delinquent child, and a motor vehicle, another item of tangible or intangible personal property, or other real property in which the delinquent child has a right, title, or interest or for which the delinquent child has the express or implied permission of a person with a right, title, or interest to use, occupy, or possess if the probation officers have reasonable grounds to believe that the delinquent child is not abiding by the law or otherwise is not complying with the conditions of the delinquent child's probation. The court that places a delinquent child on probation under division (A)(2) of this section shall provide the delinquent child with a written notice that informs the delinquent child that authorized probation officers who are engaged within the scope of their supervisory duties or responsibilities may conduct those types of searches during the period of probation if they have reasonable grounds to believe that the delinquent child is not abiding by the law or otherwise is not complying with the conditions of the delinquent child's probation. The court also shall provide the written notice described in division (C)(2)(b) of section 2151.411 of the Revised Code to each parent, guardian, or custodian of the delinquent child who is described in division (C)(2)(a) of that section.

(M) As used in this section:

(1) "Certified electronic monitoring device," "certified electronic monitoring system," "electronic monitoring device," and "electronic monitoring system" have the same meanings as in section 2929.23 of the Revised Code.

(2) "Electronically monitored house detention" means a period of confinement of a child in the child's home or in other premises specified by the court, during which period of confinement all of the following apply:

(a) The child wears, otherwise has attached to the child's person, or otherwise is subject to monitoring by a certified electronic monitoring device or is subject to monitoring by a certified electronic monitoring system.

(b) The child is required to remain in the child's home or other premises specified by the court for the specified period of confinement, except for periods of time during which the child is at school or at other premises as authorized by the court.

(c) The child is subject to monitoring by a central system that monitors the certified electronic monitoring device that is attached to the child's person or that otherwise is being used to monitor the child and that can monitor and determine the child's location at any time or at a designated point in time, or the child is required to participate in monitoring by a certified electronic monitoring system.

(d) The child is required by the court to report periodically to a person designated by the court.

(e) The child is subject to any other restrictions and requirements that may be imposed by the court.

(3) "Felony drug abuse offense" and "minor drug possession offense" have the same meanings as in section 2925.01 of the Revised Code.

(4) "Firearm" has the same meaning as in section 2923.11 of the Revised Code.

(5) "Sexually oriented offense" has the same meaning as in section 2950.01 of the Revised Code.

(6) "Theft offense" has the same meaning as in section 2913.01 of the Revised Code.

(2002 H 130, eff. 4–7–03; 2000 S 179, § 4, eff. 1–1–02; 2000 S 222, eff. 3–22–01; 2000 S 181, eff. 9–4–00; 1999 H 3, eff. 11–22–99; 1998 H 526, § 4, eff. 1–1–99; 1998 H 526, § 1, eff. 9–1–98; 1998 H 2, eff. 1–1–99; 1997 S 35, eff. 1–1–99; 1997 H 1, eff. 7–1–98; 1997 H 215, § 7, eff. 9–30–97; 1997 H 215, § 1, eff. 9–29–97; 1996 H 124, eff. 9–30–97; 1996 S 269, eff. 7–1–96; 1996 H 445, eff. 9–3–96; 1996 H 274, § 4, eff. 8–8–96; 1996 H 274, § 1, eff. 8–8–96; 1995 S 2, eff. 7–1–96; 1995 H 1, eff. 1–1–96; 1995 H 4, eff. 11–9–95; 1994 H 571, eff. 10–6–94; 1992 H 725, eff. 4–16–93; 1992 S 331, H 154; 1990 S 258, H 51, H 266, H 513, S 131; 1989 H 166, H 381, H 330, H 329; 1988 H 643; 1983 S 210; 1982 H 209; 1981 H 440; 1978 H 565, S 119; 1977 H 1; 1976 H 1196; 1974 H 1067; 1973 S 324; 1972 H 494; 1970 H 931; 1969 H 320)

Note: See also preceding repeal, Publisher's Note, and Uncodified Law.

Uncodified Law

2002 H 130, § 4, eff. 4–7–03, reads:

The amendment of section 2151.355 of the Revised Code is not intended to supersede the earlier repeal, with delayed effective date, of that section.

2001 S 3, § 5, eff. 10–26–01, reads:

Section 2152.19 of the Revised Code, as presented in this act, includes matter that was amended into former section 2151.355 of the Revised Code by Am. Sub. S.B. 181 of the 123rd General Assembly. Paragraphs of former section 2151.355 of the Revised Code containing S.B. 181 amendments were transferred to section 2152.19 of the Revised Code by Am. Sub. S.B. 179 of the 123rd General Assembly as part of its general revision of the juvenile sentencing laws. The General Assembly, applying the principle stated in division (B) of section 1.52 of the Revised Code that amendments are to be harmonized if reasonably capable of simultaneous operation, finds that the version of section 2152.19 of the Revised Code presented in this act is the resulting version of the section in effect prior to the effective date of the section as presented in this act.

1996 H 445, § 3: See Uncodified Law under 2151.14.

1995 H 1, § 3, eff. 1–1–96, reads in part: (A) The General Assembly hereby declares that its purpose in enacting the language of division (A)(2) of section 2151.18 and division (D)(2) of section 2151.355 of the Revised Code that exists on and after the effective

date of this act is to recognize the holding of the Supreme Court in *In re Russell* (1984), 12 Ohio St. 3d 304.

1995 H 4, § 3: See Uncodified Law under 2151.022.

1990 H 51, § 3, eff. 11–8–90, reads: This act does not apply to any criminal sentence or dispositional order imposed prior to the effective date of this act, which sentence or dispositional order requires an offender or delinquent child to serve a period of time restricted to his home or any other specified premises for specified periods of time and requires the offender or delinquent child to be monitored by some type of electronic monitoring device, unless the court that imposed the sentence or dispositional order modifies the sentence or dispositional order and specifically makes the provisions of this act applicable to the criminal sentence or dispositional order.

Historical and Statutory Notes

Publisher's Note: 2151.355 was repealed by 2000 S 179, § 4, eff. 1–1–02, and amended by 2002 H 130, eff. 4–7–03. The legal effect of these actions, pursuant to 2002 H 130, § 4, is in question. See *Baldwin's Ohio Legislative Service Annotated*, 2000, page 11/L–3793, and 2002, page 12/L–2943, or the OH–LEGIS or OH–LEGIS–OLD database on Westlaw, for original versions of these Acts.

Ed. Note: See now 2152.18, 2152.19 and 2152.20 for provisions analogous to former 2151.355, repealed by 2000 S 179, § 4, eff. 1–1–02.

Amendment Note: 2002 H 130 inserted ", or 2941.1412" in divisions (A)(7)(a) and (A)(7)(a)(ii); and made other nonsubstantive changes.

2151.357 Cost of education

In the manner prescribed by division (C)(2) of section 3313.64 of the Revised Code, the court, at the time of making any order that removes a child from the child's own home or that vests legal or permanent custody of the child in a person other than the child's parent or a government agency, shall determine the school district that is to bear the cost of educating the child. The court shall make the determination a part of the order that provides for the child's placement or commitment.

Whenever a child is placed in a detention facility established under section 2152.41 of the Revised Code or a juvenile facility established under section 2151.65 of the Revised Code, the child's school district as determined by the court shall pay the cost of educating the child based on the per capita cost of the educational facility within the detention home or juvenile facility.

Whenever a child is placed by the court in a private institution, school, or residential treatment center or any other private facility, the state shall pay to the court a subsidy to help defray the expense of educating the child in an amount equal to the product of the daily per capita educational cost of the private facility, as determined pursuant to this section, and the number of days the child resides at the private facility, provided that the subsidy shall not exceed twenty-five hundred dollars per year per child. The daily per capita educational cost of a private facility shall be determined by dividing the actual program cost of the private facility or twenty-five hundred dollars, whichever is less, by three hundred sixty-five days or by three hundred sixty-six days for years that include February twenty-ninth. The state shall pay seventy-five per cent of the total subsidy for each year quarterly to the court. The state may adjust the remaining twenty-five per cent of the total subsidy to be paid to the court for each year to an amount that is less than twenty-five per cent of the total subsidy for that year based upon the availability of funds appropriated to the department of education for the purpose of subsidizing courts that place a child in a private institution, school, or residential treatment center or any other private facility and shall pay that adjusted amount to the court at the end of the year.

(2000 S 179, § 3, eff. 1–1–02; 1995 H 117, eff. 6–30–95; 1981 S 140, eff. 7–1–81; 1970 S 518; 1969 H 320)

Historical and Statutory Notes

Amendment Note: 2000 S 179, § 3, eff. 1–1–02, substituted "facility" for "home" and "2152.42" for "2151.34" in the second paragraph.

Amendment Note: 1995 H 117 rewrote this section, which previously read:

"In the manner prescribed by division (C)(2) of section 3313.64 of the Revised Code, the court shall, at the time of making any order that removes a child from his own home or that vests legal or permanent custody of the child in a person or government agency other than his parent, determine the school district that is to bear the cost of educating the child. Such determination shall be made a part of the order that provides for the child's placement or commitment.

Whenever a child is placed in a detention home established under section 2151.34 of the Revised Code or a juvenile facility established under section 2151.65 of the Revised Code, his school district as determined by the court shall pay the cost of educating the child based on the per capita cost of the educational facility within such detention home or juvenile facility. Whenever a child is placed by the court in a private institution, school, residential treatment center, or other private facility, the state shall pay to the court a subsidy to help defray the expense of educating the child in an amount equal to the product of the daily per capita educational cost of such facility and the number of days the child resides at the facility, provided that such subsidy shall not exceed five hundred dollars per year. The subsidy shall be paid quarterly to the court."

Cross References

Boards of education, residency for attendance purposes, acceptance of certain tuition requirements, enforcement, 3313.64
Dispositional hearing, Juv R 34
Education of handicapped children, definitions, 3323.01
Permanent exclusion of pupils, cost of educating child, 3313.662
Permanent exclusion of pupils, duty to pay for cost of education not relieved, 3313.662

Library References

Infants ⟚222, 223.1.
Westlaw Topic No. 211.
C.J.S. Infants §§ 57, 69 to 85.
OJur 3d: 48, Family Law § 1718
Carlin, Baldwin's Ohio Practice, Merrick–Rippner Probate Law § 107.73, 107.174, 107.175, 107.176 (2003).

2151.358 Under what conditions records are to be sealed or expunged; procedures; effects; offense of divulging confidential information

(A) As used in this section, "seal a record" means to remove a record from the main file of similar records and to secure it in a separate file that contains only sealed records and that is accessible only to the juvenile court. A record that is sealed shall be destroyed by all persons and governmental bodies except the juvenile court.

(B) The department of youth services and any other institution or facility that unconditionally discharges a person who has been adjudicated a delinquent child, an unruly child, or a juvenile traffic offender shall immediately give notice of the discharge to the court that committed the person. The court shall note the date of discharge on a separate record of discharges of those natures.

(C)(1)(a) Two years after the termination of any order made by the court or two years after the unconditional discharge of a person from the department of youth services or another institution or facility to which the person may have been committed, the court that issued the order or committed the person shall do whichever of the following is applicable:

(i) If the person was adjudicated an unruly child, order the record of the person sealed;

(ii) If the person was adjudicated a delinquent child for committing an act other than a violation of section 2903.01, 2903.02, 2907.02, 2907.03, or 2907.05 of the Revised Code or was adjudicated a juvenile traffic offender, either order the record of the person sealed or send the person notice of the person's right to have that record sealed.

(b) Division (C)(1)(a) of this section does not apply regarding a person who was adjudicated a delinquent child for committing a violation of section 2903.01, 2903.02, 2907.02, 2907.03, or 2907.05 of the Revised Code.

(2) The court shall send the notice described in division (C)(1)(a)(ii) of this section within ninety days after the expiration of the two-year period described in division (C)(1)(a) of this section by certified mail, return receipt requested, to the person's last known address. The notice shall state that the person may apply to the court for an order to seal the person's record, explain what sealing a record means, and explain the possible consequences of not having the person's record sealed.

(D)(1) At any time after the two-year period described in division (C)(1)(a) of this section has elapsed, any person who has been adjudicated a delinquent child for committing an act other than a violation of section 2903.01, 2903.02, 2907.02, 2907.03, or 2907.05 of the Revised Code or who has been adjudicated a juvenile traffic offender may apply to the court for an order to seal the person's record. The court shall hold a hearing on each application within sixty days after the application is received. Notice of the hearing on the application shall be given to the prosecuting attorney and to any other public office or agency known to have a record of the prior adjudication. If the court finds that the rehabilitation of the person who was adjudicated a delinquent child or a juvenile traffic offender has been attained to a satisfactory degree, the court may order the record of the person sealed.

(2) Division (D)(1) of this section does not apply regarding a person who was adjudicated a delinquent child for committing a violation of section 2903.01, 2903.02, 2907.02, 2907.03, or 2907.05 of the Revised Code.

(3) If a child who was charged with violating division (E)(1) of section 4301.69 of the Revised Code successfully completes a diversion program under division (E)(2)(a) of section 4301.69 of the Revised Code with respect to that charge, the court shall order the person's record in that case sealed.

(E)(1) If the court orders the adjudication record or other record of a person sealed pursuant to division (C) or (D) of this section, the court, except as provided in division (K) of this section, shall order that the proceedings in the case in which the person was adjudicated a juvenile traffic offender, a delinquent child, or an unruly child, or in which the person was the subject of a complaint alleging the person to have violated division (E)(1) of section 4301.69 of the Revised Code, be deemed never to have occurred. Except as provided in division (G)(2) of this section, all index references to the case and the person shall be deleted, and the person and the court properly may reply that no record exists with respect to the person upon any inquiry in the matter.

(2) Inspection of records that have been ordered sealed under division (E)(1) of this section may be made only by the following persons or for the following purposes:

(a) If the records in question pertain to an act that would be an offense of violence that would be a felony if committed by an adult, by any law enforcement officer or any prosecutor, or the assistants of a law enforcement officer or prosecutor, for any valid law enforcement or prosecutorial purpose;

(b) Upon application by the person who is the subject of the sealed records, by the persons that are named in that application;

(c) If the records in question pertain to an alleged violation of division (E)(1) of section 4301.69 of the Revised Code, by any law enforcement officer or any prosecutor, or the assistants of a law enforcement officer or prosecutor, for the purpose of determining whether the person is eligible for diversion under division (E)(2) of section 4301.69 of the Revised Code.

(F) Any person who has been arrested and charged with being a delinquent child or a juvenile traffic offender and who is adjudicated not guilty of the charges in the case or has the charges in the case dismissed may apply to the court for an expungement of the record in the case. The application may be filed at any time after the person is adjudicated not guilty or the charges against the person are dismissed. The court shall give notice to the prosecuting attorney of any hearing on the application. The court may initiate the expungement proceedings on its own motion.

Any person who has been arrested and charged with being an unruly child and who is adjudicated not guilty of the charges in the case or has the charges in the case dismissed may apply to the court for an expungement of the record in the case. The court shall initiate the expungement proceedings on its own motion if an application for expungement is not filed.

If the court upon receipt of an application for expungement or upon its own motion determines that the charges against any person in any case were dismissed or that any person was adjudicated not guilty in any case, the court shall order that the records of the case be expunged and that the proceedings in the case be deemed never to have occurred. If the applicant for the expungement order, with the written consent of the applicant's parents or guardian if the applicant is a minor and with the written approval of the court, waives in writing the applicant's right to bring any civil action based on the arrest for which the expungement order is applied, the court shall order the appropriate persons and governmental agencies to delete all index references to the case; destroy or delete all court records of the case; destroy all copies of any pictures and fingerprints taken of the person pursuant to the expunged arrest; and destroy, erase, or delete any reference to the arrest that is maintained by the state or any political subdivision of the state, except a record of the arrest that is maintained for compiling statistical data and that does not contain any reference to the person.

If the applicant for an expungement order does not waive in writing the right to bring any civil action based on the arrest for which the expungement order is applied, the court, in addition to ordering the deletion, destruction, or erasure of all index references and court records of the case and of all references to the arrest that are maintained by the state or any political subdivision of the state, shall order that a copy of all records of the case, except fingerprints held by the court or a law enforcement agency, be delivered to the court. The court shall seal all of the records delivered to the court in a separate file in which only sealed records are maintained. The sealed records shall be kept by the court until the statute of limitations expires for any civil action based on the arrest, any pending litigation based on the arrest is terminated, or the applicant files a writ-

ten waiver of the right to bring a civil action based on the arrest. After the expiration of the statute of limitations, the termination of the pending litigation, or the filing of the waiver, the court shall destroy the sealed records.

After the expungement order has been issued, the court shall, and the person may properly, reply that no record of the case with respect to the person exists.

(G)(1) The court shall send notice of the order to expunge or seal to any public office or agency that the court has reason to believe may have a record of the expunged or sealed record. Except as provided in division (K) of this section, an order to seal or expunge under this section applies to every public office or agency that has a record of the prior adjudication or arrest, regardless of whether it receives notice of the hearing on the expungement or sealing of the record or a copy of the order to expunge or seal the record. Except as provided in division (K) of this section, upon the written request of a person whose record has been expunged and the presentation of a copy of the order to expunge, a public office or agency shall destroy its record of the prior adjudication or arrest, except a record of the adjudication or arrest that is maintained for compiling statistical data and that does not contain any reference to the person who is the subject of the order to expunge.

(2) The person, or the public office or agency, that maintains sealed records pertaining to an adjudication of a child as a delinquent child may maintain a manual or computerized index to the sealed records. The index shall contain only the name of, and alphanumeric identifiers that relate to, the persons who are the subject of the sealed records, the word "sealed," and the name of the person, or the public office or agency that has custody of the sealed records and shall not contain the name of the delinquent act committed. The person who has custody of the sealed records shall make the index available only for the purposes set forth in divisions (E)(2) and (H) of this section.

(H) The judgment rendered by the court under this chapter shall not impose any of the civil disabilities ordinarily imposed by conviction of a crime in that the child is not a criminal by reason of the adjudication and no child shall be charged with or convicted of a crime in any court except as provided by this chapter. The disposition of a child under the judgment rendered or any evidence given in court shall not operate to disqualify a child in any future civil service examination, appointment, or application. Evidence of a judgment rendered and the disposition of a child under the judgment is not admissible to impeach the credibility of the child in any action or proceeding. Otherwise, the disposition of a child under the judgment rendered or any evidence given in court is admissible as evidence for or against the child in any action or proceeding in any court in accordance with the Rules of Evidence and also may be considered by any court as to the matter of sentence or to the granting of probation, and a court may consider the judgment rendered and the disposition of a child under that judgment for purposes of determining whether the child, for a future criminal conviction or guilty plea, is a repeat violent offender, as defined in section 2929.01 of the Revised Code.

(I) In any application for employment, license, or other right or privilege, any appearance as a witness, or any other inquiry, a person may not be questioned with respect to any arrest for which the records were expunged. If an inquiry is made in violation of this division, the person may respond as if the expunged arrest did not occur, and the person shall not be subject to any adverse action because of the arrest or the response.

(J) An officer or employee of the state or any of its political subdivisions who knowingly releases, disseminates, or makes available for any purpose involving employment, bonding, licensing, or education to any person or to any department, agency, or other instrumentality of the state or of any of its political subdivisions any information or other data concerning any arrest, complaint, indictment, information, trial, hearing, adjudication, or correctional supervision, the records of which have been expunged or sealed pursuant to this section and the release, dissemination, or making available of which is not expressly permitted by this section, is guilty of divulging confidential information, a misdemeanor of the fourth degree.

(K) Notwithstanding any provision of this section that requires otherwise, a board of education of a city, local, exempted village, or joint vocational school district that maintains records of an individual who has been permanently excluded under sections 3301.121 and 3313.662 of the Revised Code is permitted to maintain records regarding an adjudication that the individual is a delinquent child that was used as the basis for the individual's permanent exclusion, regardless of a court order to seal the record. An order issued under this section to seal the record of an adjudication that an individual is a delinquent child does not revoke the adjudication order of the superintendent of public instruction to permanently exclude the individual who is the subject of the sealing order. An order issued under this section to seal the record of an adjudication that an individual is a delinquent child may be presented to a district superintendent as evidence to support the contention that the superintendent should recommend that the permanent exclusion of the individual who is the subject of the sealing order be revoked. Except as otherwise authorized by this division and sections 3301.121 and 3313.662 of the Revised Code, any school employee in possession of or having access to the sealed adjudication records of an individual that were the basis of a permanent exclusion of the individual is subject to division (J) of this section.

(2002 H 17, eff. 10–11–02; 2000 S 179, § 3, eff. 1–1–02; 2000 S 181, eff. 9–4–00; 1995 S 2, eff. 7–1–96; 1995 H 1, eff. 1–1–96; 1992 H 154, eff. 7–31–92; 1991 H 27; 1984 H 37; 1981 H 440; 1977 H 315; 1969 H 320)

Uncodified Law

1999 H 121, § 3, eff. 11–3–99, amended 1997 H 215, § 50.52.5, as amended by 1998 H 650, § 5, and by 1998 H 770, § 8, to read:

Each contract entered into between a sponsor and the governing authority of a community school shall specify the following:

(A) That the school shall be established as a nonprofit corporation established under Chapter 1702. of the Revised Code;

(B) The education program of the school, including the school's mission, the characteristics of the students the school is expected to attract, the ages and grades of students, and the focus of the curriculum;

(C) Performance standards and assessments by which the success of the school will be evaluated by the sponsor, which shall include the statewide proficiency tests;

(D) The admission standards of Subsection 8 of this section;

(E) Dismissal procedures;

(F) The ways by which the school will achieve racial and ethnic balance reflective of the community it serves;

(G) Requirements and procedures for financial audits by the Auditor of State. The contract shall require financial records of the school to be maintained in the same manner as are financial records of school districts, pursuant to rules of the Auditor of State, and the audits shall be conducted in accordance with section 117.10 of the Revised Code.

(H) Facilities to be used, their location, and their method of acquisition;

(I) Qualifications of teachers, including a requirement that the school's classroom teachers be certificated in accordance with sections 3319.22 to 3319.31 of the Revised Code, except that a community school may engage noncertificated persons to teach up to twelve hours per week pursuant to section 3319.301 of the Revised Code;

(J) That the school will comply with the following requirements:

(1) The school will provide learning opportunities to a minimum of twenty-five students for a minimum of nine hundred twenty hours per school year;

(2) The governing authority will purchase liability insurance, or otherwise provide for the potential liability of the school;

(3) The school will be nonsectarian in its programs, admission policies, employment practices, and all other operations, and will not be operated by a sectarian school or religious institution;

(4) The school will comply with sections 9.90, 9.91, 109.65, 121.22, 149.43, 2151.358, 2151.421, 2313.18, 3301.0710, 3301.0711, 3301.0714, 3313.33, 3313.50, 3313.643, 3313.66, 3313.661, 3313.662, 3313.67, 3313.672, 3313.673, 3313.69, 3313.71, 3313.716, 3313.80, 3313.96, 3319.321, 3319.39, 3321.01, 3327.10, 4111.17, and 4113.52 and Chapters 102., 117., 1347., 2744., 4112., 4123., 4141., and 4167. of the Revised Code as if it were a school district;

(5) The school will comply with sections 3313.61 and 3313.611 of the Revised Code, except that the requirement in those sections that a person must successfully complete the curriculum in any high school prior to receiving a high school diploma may be met by completing the curriculum adopted by the governing authority of the community school rather than the curriculum specified in Title XXXIII of the Revised Code or any rules of the State Board of Education;

(6) The school governing authority will submit an annual report of its activities and progress in meeting the goals and standards of division (C) of this subsection and its financial status to the sponsor, the parents of all students enrolled in the school, and the Legislative Office of Education Oversight. The financial statement shall be in such form as shall be prescribed by the Auditor of State.

(K) Arrangements for providing health and other benefits to employees;

(L) The length of the contract, which shall not exceed five years nor extend beyond June 30, 2003;

(M) The governing authority of the school, which shall be responsible for carrying out the provisions of the contract, and a description of the process by which the governing authority will be selected in the future;

(N) A financial plan detailing an estimated school budget for each year of the period of the contract and specifying the total estimated per pupil expenditure amount for each such year. The plan shall specify for each year the base formula amount that will be used for purposes of funding calculations under Subsection 10 of this section. This base formula amount for any year shall not exceed the formula amount defined in section 3317.02 of the Revised Code.

(O)(1) Requirements and procedures regarding the disposition of employees, equipment, materials, supplies, and facilities of the school in the event the contract is terminated or not renewed pursuant to this section;

(2) Provisions to ensure that, if for any reason a school must close prior to June 30, 2003, the school will be kept open for students to attend until the end of the school year in which it is determined that the school must close;

(3) Provisions establishing procedures for resolving disputes or differences of opinion between the sponsor and the governing authority of the community school.

(P) Whether or not the school is to be created by converting all or part of an existing public school and, if it is, specification of any duties or responsibilities of an employer that the board of education that operated the school before conversion is delegating to the governing authority of the community school with respect to all or any specified group of employees provided the delegation is not prohibited by a collective bargaining agreement applicable to such employees;

(Q) Any additional details concerning the management and administration of the school;

(R) If the proposed community school is a currently existing public school, alternative arrangements, approved by the board of education of the school district in which the school is located, for current public school students who choose not to attend the school and teachers who choose not to teach in the school after conversion;

(S) That the school shall be the custodian of all money received during the first full fiscal year of its operation and during subsequent years unless another custodian is designated in the contract to receive and maintain the first-year revenue.

1995 H 1, § 3, eff. 1–1–96, reads, in part: (C) The amendments made by this act to section 2151.358 of the Revised Code apply to persons who were adjudicated juvenile traffic offenders or charged with being juvenile traffic offenders prior to the effective date of this act, regardless of their age on that date. A person who was adjudicated a juvenile traffic offender or charged with being a juvenile traffic offender prior to the effective date of this act may file an application in accordance with division (D) or (F) of section 2151.358 of the Revised Code on or after the effective date of this act for the sealing of the record of the person's adjudication as a juvenile traffic offender or the expungement of the record of the case in which the person was adjudicated not guilty of being a juvenile traffic offender or the charges of being a juvenile traffic offender were dismissed, and the juvenile court involved shall proceed with a hearing on the application in accordance with division (D) or (F) of that section. A juvenile court is not required to send the notice described in division (C)(1)(b) of section 2151.358 of the Revised Code to a person who was adjudicated a juvenile traffic offender prior to the effective date of this act if, on the effective date of this act, more than ninety days has expired after the expiration of the two-year period described in division (C)(1) of section 2151.358 of the Revised Code.

Historical and Statutory Notes

Amendment Note: 2002 H 17 added new divisions (D)(3) and (E)(2)(c); inserted "or other record" after "adjudication record" and inserted "or in which the person was the subject of a complaint alleging the person to have violated division (E)(1) of section 4301.69 of the Revised Code" in division (E)(1).

Amendment Note: 2000 S 179, § 3, eff. 1–1–02, inserted "indictment, information," in division (J).

Amendment Note: 2000 S 181 designated new division (C)(1)(a); redesignated former divisions (C)(1)(a) and (C)(1)(b) as new divisions (C)(1)(a)(i) and (C)(1)(a)(ii); inserted "for committing an act other than a violation of section 2903.01, 2903.02, 2907.02, 2907.03, or 2907.05 of the Revised Code" in new division (C)(1)(a)(ii); added new division (C)(1)(b); substituted "(C)(1)(a)(ii)" for "(C)(1)(b)" in division (C)(2); designated division (D)(1) and inserted "(a)" and "for committing an act other than a violation of section 2903.01, 2903.02, 2907.02, 2907.03, or 2907.05 of the Revised Code" therein; added division (D)(2); rewrote division (E); designated division (G)(1) and deleted references to sealed records therefrom; added division (G)(2); inserted "and the release, dissemination, or making available of which is not expressly permitted by this section" in division (J); and made other nonsubstantive changes. Prior to amendment, division (E) read:

"(E) If the court orders the adjudication record of a person sealed pursuant to division (C) or (D) of this section, the court shall order that the proceedings in the case in which the person was adjudicated a juvenile traffic offender, a delinquent child, or an unruly child be deemed never to have occurred. All index references to the case and the person shall be deleted, and the person and the court properly may reply that no record exists with respect to the person upon any inquiry in the matter. Inspection of records that have been ordered sealed may be permitted by the court only upon application by the person who is the subject of the sealed records and only by the persons that are named in the that application."

Amendment Note: 1995 S 2 inserted ", and a court may consider the judgment rendered and the disposition of a child under that judgment for purposes of determining whether the child, for a future criminal conviction or guilty plea, is a repeat violent offender, as defined in section 2929.01 of the Revised Code" in division (H); and made changes to reflect gender neutral language and other nonsubstantive changes.

Amendment Note: 1995 H 1 added all references to juvenile traffic offenders throughout; designated division (C)(1); redesignated former divisions (C)(1) and (C)(2) as divisions (C)(1)(a) and (C)(1)(b); designated division (C)(2) and inserted "described in division (C)(1)(b) of this section", "described in division (C)(1) of this section", and ", return receipt requested," therein; inserted "described in division (C)(1) of this section" in division (D); substituted "employee" for "employer" in division (J); and made changes to reflect gender neutral language and other nonsubstantive changes.

Comparative Laws

Ariz.—A.R.S. § 8-247.
Conn.—C.G.S.A. § 46b-146.
Ga.—O.C.G.A. § 15-11-61.
Idaho—I.C. § 16-1816A.
Ind.—West's A.I.C. 31–6–8–2.
Mo.—V.A.M.S. § 211.321.
Tex.—V.T.C.A. Family Code § 51.16.
W.Va.—Code, 49–5–17.

Cross References

Advising child of right to expungement, Juv R 34
Community schools, required terms of contracts, 3314.03
Education management information system, collection and reporting of data, 3301.0714

Expungement in adult cases, 2953.31 to 2953.55
Foster caregivers, information regarding delinquent children provided to, 2152.72

Library References

Infants ☞133.
Westlaw Topic No. 211.
C.J.S. Infants §§ 57, 69 to 85.
OJur 3d: 48, Family Law § 1659, 1712, 1713
Am Jur 2d: 47, Juvenile Courts and Delinquent and Dependent Children § 59
Use of judgment in prior juvenile court proceeding to impeach credibility of witness. 63 ALR3d 1112
Giannelli & Snyder, Baldwin's Ohio Practice, Evidence § 404.25, 501.4, 609, 609.11, 609.12, 609.13 (2d ed. 2001).
Carlin, Baldwin's Ohio Practice, Merrick–Rippner Probate Law § 22.5, 106.4, 107.22, 107.51, 107.52, 107.114, 107.116, 107.158, 107.159 (2003).

2151.359 Control of conduct of parent, guardian, or custodian; contempt

(A)(1) In any proceeding in which a child has been adjudicated an unruly, abused, neglected, or dependent child, on the application of a party, or on the court's own motion, the court may make an order restraining or otherwise controlling the conduct of any parent, guardian, or other custodian in the relationship of that individual to the child if the court finds that an order of that type is necessary to do either of the following:

(a) Control any conduct or relationship that will be detrimental or harmful to the child.

(b) Control any conduct or relationship that will tend to defeat the execution of the order of disposition made or to be made.

(2) The court shall give due notice of the application or motion under division (A) of this section, the grounds for the application or motion, and an opportunity to be heard to the person against whom an order under this division is directed. The order may include a requirement that the child's parent, guardian, or other custodian enter into a recognizance with sufficient surety, conditioned upon the faithful discharge of any conditions or control required by the court.

(B) The authority to make an order under division (A) of this section and any order made under that authority is in addition to the authority to make an order pursuant to division (C)(2) of section 2151.354 or division (A)(7) (b) of section 2152.19 of the Revised Code and to any order made under either division.

(C) A person's failure to comply with any order made by the court under this section is contempt of court under Chapter 2705. of the Revised Code.

(2002 H 400, eff. 4–3–03; 2000 S 179, § 3, eff. 1–1–02; 2000 S 181, eff. 9–4–00; 1975 H 85, eff. 11–28–75; 1969 H 320)

Historical and Statutory Notes

Amendment Note: 2002 H 400 substituted "(7)" for "(6)" in division (B).

Amendment Note: 2000 S 179, § 3, eff. 1–1–02, rewrote this section, which prior thereto read:

"(A)(1) In any proceeding in which a child has been adjudicated a delinquent, unruly, abused, neglected, or dependent child, on the application of a party, or on the court's own motion, the court may make an order restraining or otherwise controlling the conduct of any parent, guardian, or other custodian in the relationship of that individual to the child if the court finds both of the following:

"(a) An order of that nature is necessary to control any conduct or relationship that will be detrimental or harmful to the child.

"(b) That conduct or relationship will tend to defeat the execution of the order of disposition made or to be made.

"(2) The court shall give due notice of the application or motion, the grounds for the application or motion, and an opportunity to be heard to the person against whom an order under this division is directed.

"(B) The authority to make an order under division (A) of this section and any order made under that authority is in addition to the authority to make an order pursuant to division (C)(2) of section 2151.354 or division (A)(24)(b) of section 2151.355 of the Revised Code and to any order made under either division."

Amendment Note: 2000 S 181 rewrote this section, which prior thereto read:

"In any proceeding wherein a child has been adjudged delinquent, unruly, abused, neglected, or dependent, on the application of a party, or the court's own motion, the court may make an order restraining or otherwise controlling the conduct of any parent, guardian, or other custodian in the relationship of such individual to the child if the court finds that such an order is necessary to:

"(A) Control any conduct or relationship that will be detrimental or harmful to the child;

"(B) Where such conduct or relationship will tend to defeat the execution of the order of disposition made or to be made.

"Due notice of the application or motion and the grounds therefor, and an opportunity to be heard shall be given to the person against whom such order is directed."

Cross References

Dispositional hearing, Juv R 34
Temporary disposition, Juv R 13

Library References

Infants ☞221.
Westlaw Topic No. 211.
C.J.S. Infants §§ 57, 69 to 85.
OJur 3d: 46, Family Law § 534; 48, Family Law § 1690

Carlin, Baldwin's Ohio Practice, Merrick–Rippner Probate Law § 64.17, 107.73, 107.113, 107.127 (2003).

2151.3510   Notice of intended dispositional order

Before a juvenile court issues an order of disposition pursuant to division (A)(1) of section 2151.354 or 2152.19 of the Revised Code committing an unruly or delinquent child to the custody of a public children services agency, it shall give the agency notice in the manner prescribed by the Juvenile Rules of the intended dispositional order.

(2000 S 179, § 3, eff. 1–1–02; 1996 H 274, eff. 8–8–96; 1991 H 298, eff. 7–26–91)

Historical and Statutory Notes

Amendment Note: 2000 S 179, § 3, eff. 1–1–02, substituted "2152.19" for "2151.355".

Amendment Note: 1996 H 274 deleted "temporary or permanent" before "custody".

Library References

Carlin, Baldwin's Ohio Practice, Merrick–Rippner Probate Law § 107.84 (2003).

2151.3514   Orders requiring alcohol and drug addiction assessment, treatment, and testing of parents or caregivers

(A) As used in this section:

(1) "Alcohol and drug addiction program" has the same meaning as in section 3793.01 of the Revised Code;

(2) "Chemical dependency" means either of the following:

(a) The chronic and habitual use of alcoholic beverages to the extent that the user no longer can control the use of alcohol or endangers the user's health, safety, or welfare or that of others;

(b) The use of a drug of abuse to the extent that the user becomes physically or psychologically dependent on the drug or endangers the user's health, safety, or welfare or that of others.

(3) "Drug of abuse" has the same meaning as in section 3719.011 of the Revised Code.

(4) "Medicaid" means the program established under Chapter 5111. of the Revised Code.

(B) If the juvenile court issues an order of temporary custody or protective supervision under division (A) of section 2151.353 of the Revised Code with respect to a child adjudicated to be an abused, neglected, or dependent child and the alcohol or other drug addiction of a parent or other caregiver of the child was the basis for the adjudication of abuse, neglect, or dependency, the court shall issue an order requiring the parent or other caregiver to submit to an assessment and, if needed, treatment from an alcohol and drug addiction program certified by the department of alcohol and drug addiction services. The court may order the parent or other caregiver to submit to alcohol or other drug testing during, after, or both during and after, the treatment. The court shall send any order issued pursuant to this division to the public children services agency that serves the county in which the court is located for use as described in section 340.15 of the Revised Code.

(C) Any order requiring alcohol or other drug testing that is issued pursuant to division (B) of this section shall require one alcohol or other drug test to be conducted each month during a period of twelve consecutive months beginning the month immediately following the month in which the order for alcohol or other drug testing is issued. Arrangements for administering the alcohol or other drug tests, as well as funding the costs of the tests, shall be locally determined in accordance with sections 340.033 and 340.15 of the Revised Code. If a parent or other caregiver required to submit to alcohol or other drug tests under this section is not a recipient of medicaid, the agency that refers the parent or caregiver for the tests may require the parent or caregiver to reimburse the agency for the cost of conducting the tests.

(D) The certified alcohol and drug addiction program that conducts any alcohol or other drug tests ordered in accordance with divisions (B) and (C) of this section shall send the results of the tests, along with the program's recommendations as to the benefits of continued treatment, to the court and to the public children services agency providing services to the involved family, according to federal regulations set forth in 42 C.F.R. Part 2, and division (B) of section 340.15 of the Revised Code. The court shall consider the results and the recommendations sent to it under this division in any adjudication or review by the court, according to section 2151.353, 2151.414, or 2151.419 of the Revised Code.

(1998 H 484, eff. 3–18–99)

Library References

OJur 3d: 55, Incompetent Persons § 150 to 154
Am Jur 2d: 24, Divorce and Separation § 99
Carlin, Baldwin's Ohio Practice, Merrick–Rippner Probate Law § 107.77, 107.78 (2003).

2151.3515 Definitions

As used in sections 2151.3515 to 2151.3530 of the Revised Code:

(A) "Deserted child" means a child whose parent has voluntarily delivered the child to an emergency medical service worker, peace officer, or hospital employee without expressing an intent to return for the child.

(B) "Emergency medical service organization," "emergency medical technician–basic," "emergency medical technician–intermediate," "first responder," and "paramedic" have the same meanings as in section 4765.01 of the Revised Code.

(C) "Emergency medical service worker" means a first responder, emergency medical technician-basic, emergency medical technician-intermediate, or paramedic.

(D) "Hospital" has the same meaning as in section 3727.01 of the Revised Code.

(E) "Hospital employee" means any of the following persons:

(1) A physician who has been granted privileges to practice at the hospital;

(2) A nurse, physician assistant, or nursing assistant employed by the hospital;

(3) An authorized person employed by the hospital who is acting under the direction of a physician described in division (E)(1) of this section.

(F) "Law enforcement agency" means an organization or entity made up of peace officers.

(G) "Nurse" means a person who is licensed under Chapter 4723. of the Revised Code to practice as a registered nurse or licensed practical nurse.

(H) "Nursing assistant" means a person designated by a hospital as a nurse aide or nursing assistant whose job is to aid nurses, physicians, and physician assistants in the performance of their duties.

(I) "Peace officer" means a sheriff, deputy sheriff, constable, police officer of a township or joint township police district, marshal, deputy marshal, municipal police officer, or a state highway patrol trooper.

(J) "Physician" and "physician assistant" have the same meanings as in section 4730.01 of the Revised Code.

(2000 H 660, eff. 4–9–01)

Library References
OJur 3d: 48, Family Law § 1576 to 1579

2151.3516 Persons authorized to take possession of deserted child

The following persons, while acting in an official capacity, shall take possession of a child who is seventy-two hours old or younger if that child's parent has voluntarily delivered the child to that person without the parent expressing an intent to return for the child:

(A) A peace officer on behalf of the law enforcement agency that employs the officer;

(B) A hospital employee on behalf of the hospital that has granted the person privilege to practice at the hospital or that employs the person;

(C) An emergency medical service worker on behalf of the emergency medical service organization that employs the worker or for which the worker provides services.

(2000 H 660, eff. 4–9–01)

Library References
OJur 3d: 48, Family Law § 1415, 1419, 1424

2151.3517 Duties of persons taking possession of deserted child

(A) On taking possession of a child pursuant to section 2151.3516 of the Revised Code, a law enforcement agency, hospital, or emergency medical service organization shall do all the following:

(1) Perform any act necessary to protect the child's health or safety;

(2) Notify the public children services agency of the county in which the agency, hospital, or organization is located that the child has been taken into possession;

(3) If possible, make available to the parent who delivered the child forms developed under section 2151.3529 of the Revised Code that are designed to gather medical information concerning the child and the child's parents;

(4) If possible, make available to the parent who delivered the child written materials developed under section 2151.3529 of the Revised Code that describe services available to assist parents and newborns;

(5) If the child has suffered a physical or mental wound, injury, disability, or condition of a nature that reasonably indicates abuse or neglect of the child, attempt to identify and pursue the person who delivered the child.

(B) An emergency medical service worker who takes possession of a child shall, in addition to any act performed under division (A)(1) of this section, perform any medical service the worker is authorized to perform that is necessary to protect the physical health or safety of the child.

(2000 H 660, eff. 4–9–01)

Library References
OJur 3d: 48, Family Law § 1415 et seq.

2151.3518 Duties of public children services agencies

On receipt of a notice given pursuant to section 2151.3517 of the Revised Code that an emergency medical service organization, a law enforcement agency, or hospital has taken possession of a child and in accordance with rules of the department of job and family services, a public children services agency shall do all of the following:

(A) Consider the child to be in need of public care and protective services;

(B) Accept and take emergency temporary custody of the child;

(C) Provide temporary emergency care for the child, without agreement or commitment;

(D) Make an investigation concerning the child;

(E) File a motion with the juvenile court of the county in which the agency is located requesting that the court grant temporary custody of the child to the agency or to a private child placing agency;

(F) Provide any care for the child that the public children services agency considers to be in the best interest of the child, including placing the child in shelter care;

(G) Provide any care and perform any duties that are required of public children services agencies under section 5153.16 of the Revised Code;

(H) Prepare and keep written records of the investigation of the child, of the care and treatment afforded the child, and any other records required by the department of job and family services.

(2000 H 660, eff. 4–9–01)

Ohio Administrative Code References

PCSA requirements for a deserted child investigation, OAC 5101:2–34–321

Library References

OJur 3d: 48, Family Law § 1441, 1443 to 1456

2151.3519 Emergency hearings; adjudications

When a public children services agency files a motion pursuant to division (E) of section 2151.3518 of the Revised Code, the juvenile court shall hold an emergency hearing as soon as possible to determine whether the child is a deserted child. The court is required to give notice to the parents of the child only if the court has knowledge of the names of the parents. If the court determines at the initial hearing or at any other hearing that a child is a deserted child, the court shall adjudicate the child a deserted child and enter its findings in the record of the case.

(2000 H 660, eff. 4–9–01)

Library References

OJur 3d: 48, Family Law § 1653 et seq.

2151.3520 Temporary custody orders

If a juvenile court adjudicates a child a deserted child, the court shall commit the child to the temporary custody of a public children services agency or a private child placing agency. The court shall consider the order committing the child to the temporary custody of the agency to be an order of disposition issued under division (A)(2) of section 2151.353 of the Revised Code with respect to a child adjudicated a neglected child.

(2000 H 660, eff. 4–9–01)

Library References

OJur 3d: 48, Family Law § 1653 et seq.

2151.3521 Deserted child treated as neglected child

A court that issues an order pursuant to section 2151.3520 of the Revised Code shall treat the child who is the subject of the order the same as a child adjudicated a neglected child when performing duties under Chapter 2151. of the Revised Code with respect to the child, except that there is a rebuttable presumption that it is not in the child's best interest to return the child to the natural parents.

(2000 H 660, eff. 4–9–01)

Library References

OJur 3d: 48, Family Law § 1526 et seq.

2151.3522 Case plans, investigations, administrative reviews, and services

A public children services agency or private child placing agency that receives temporary custody of a child adjudicated a deserted child shall prepare case plans, conduct investigations, conduct periodic administrative reviews of case plans, and provide services for the deserted child as if the child were adjudicated a neglected child and shall follow the same procedures under this chapter in performing those functions as if the deserted child was a neglected child.

(2000 H 660, eff. 4–9–01)

Library References

OJur 3d: 48, Family Law § 1526 et seq.

2151.3523 Immunity from criminal liability; exceptions

(A) A parent does not commit a criminal offense under the laws of this state and shall not be subject to criminal prosecution in this state for the act of voluntarily delivering a child under section 2151.3516 of the Revised Code.

(B) A person who delivers or attempts to deliver a child who has suffered any physical or mental wound, injury, disability, or condition of a nature that reasonably indicates abuse or neglect of the child is not immune from civil or criminal liability for abuse or neglect.

(C) A person or governmental entity that takes possession of a child pursuant to section 2151.3516 of the Revised Code or takes emergency temporary custody of and provides temporary emergency care for a child pursuant to section 2151.3518 of the Revised Code is immune from any civil liability that might otherwise be incurred or imposed as a result of these actions, unless the person or entity has acted in bad faith or with malicious purpose. The immunity provided by this division does not apply if the person or governmental entity has immunity from civil liability under section 9.86, 2744.02, or 2744.03 of the Revised Code for the action in question.

(D) A person or governmental entity that takes possession of a child pursuant to section 2151.3516 of the Revised Code or takes emergency temporary custody of and provides temporary emergency care for a child pursuant to section 2151.3518 of the Revised Code is immune from any criminal liability that might otherwise be incurred or imposed as a result of these actions, unless the person or entity has acted in bad faith or with malicious purpose.

(E) Divisions (C) and (D) of this section do not create a new cause of action or substantive legal right against a person or governmental entity, and do not affect any immunities from civil liability or defenses established by another section of the Revised Code or available at common law, to which a person or governmental entity may be entitled under circumstances not covered by this section.

(2000 H 660, eff. 4–9–01)
Library References
OJur 3d: 48, Family Law § 1526 et seq.

2151.3524 Anonymity of parent; exceptions

(A) A parent who voluntarily delivers a child under section 2151.3516 of the Revised Code has the absolute right to remain anonymous. The anonymity of a parent who voluntarily delivers a child does not affect any duty imposed under sections 2151.3516 or 2151.3517 of the Revised Code. A parent who voluntarily delivers a child may leave the place at which the parent delivers the child at any time after the delivery of the child.

(B) Notwithstanding division (A) of this section, a parent who delivers or attempts to deliver a child who has suffered any physical or mental wound, injury, disability, or condition of a nature that reasonably indicates abuse or neglect of the child does not have the right to remain anonymous and may be sub-

ject to arrest pursuant to Chapter 2935. of the Revised Code.

(2000 H 660, eff. 4–9–01)
Library References
OJur 3d: 48, Family Law § 1526 et seq.

2151.3525 Completion of medical information forms by parents

A parent who voluntarily delivers a child under section 2151.3516 of the Revised Code may complete all or any part of the medical information forms the parent receives under division (A)(3) of section 2151.3517 of the Revised Code. The parent may deliver the fully or partially completed forms at the same time as delivering the child or at a later time. The parent is not required to complete all or any part of the forms.

(2000 H 660, eff. 4–9–01)
Library References
OJur 3d: 48, Family Law § 1526 et seq.

2151.3526 Refusal of parents to accept written materials

A parent who voluntarily delivers a child under section 2151.3516 of the Revised Code may refuse to accept the materials made available under division (A)(4) of section 2151.3517 of the Revised Code.

(2000 H 660, eff. 4–9–01)
Library References
OJur 3d: 48, Family Law § 1526 et seq.

2151.3527 Coercion prohibited

(A) No person described in section 2151.3516 of the Revised Code shall do the following with respect to a parent who voluntarily delivers a child under that section:

(1) Coerce or otherwise try to force the parent into revealing the identity of the child's parents;

(2) Pursue or follow the parent after the parent leaves the place at which the child was delivered;

(3) Coerce or otherwise try to force the parent not to desert the child;

(4) Coerce or otherwise try to force the parent to complete all or any part of the medical information forms received under division (A)(3) of section 2151.3517 of the Revised Code;

(5) Coerce or otherwise try to force the parent to accept the materials made available under division (A)(4) of section 2151.3517 of the Revised Code.

(B) Divisions (A)(1) and (2) of this section do not apply to a person who delivers or attempts to deliver a child who has suffered any physical or mental wound, injury, disability, or condition of a nature that reasonably indicates abuse or neglect of the child.

(2000 H 660, eff. 4–9–01)

Library References

OJur 3d: 48, Family Law § 1526 et seq.

2151.3528 DNA testing of parents

If a child is adjudicated a deserted child and a person indicates to the court that the person is the parent of the child and that the person seeks to be reunited with the child, the court that adjudicated the child shall require the person, at the person's expense, to submit to a DNA test to verify that the person is a parent of the child.

(2000 H 660, eff. 4–9–01)

Library References

OJur 3d: 48, Family Law § 1526 et seq.

2151.3529 Medical information forms; written materials

(A) The director of job and family services shall promulgate forms designed to gather pertinent medical information concerning a deserted child and the child's parents. The forms shall clearly and unambiguously state on each page that the information requested is to facilitate medical care for the child, that the forms may be fully or partially completed or left blank, that completing the forms or parts of the forms is completely voluntary, and that no adverse legal consequence will result from failure to complete any part of the forms.

(B) The director shall promulgate written materials to be given to the parents of a child delivered pursuant to section 2151.3516 of the Revised Code. The materials shall describe services available to assist parents and newborns and shall include information directly relevant to situations that might cause parents to desert a child and information on the procedures for a person to follow in order to reunite with a child the person delivered under section 2151.3516 of the

Revised Code, including notice that the person will be required to submit to a DNA test, at that person's expense, to prove that the person is the parent of the child.

(C) If the department of job and family services determines that money in the putative father registry fund created under section 2101.16 of the Revised Code is more than is needed for its duties related to the putative father registry, the department may use surplus moneys in the fund for costs related to the development and publication of forms and materials promulgated pursuant to divisions (A) and (B) of this section.

(2003 H 95, eff. 6–26–03; 2000 H 660, eff. 4–9–01)

Historical and Statutory Notes

Amendment Note: 2003 H 95 added division (C).

Cross References

Probate court; fees; cost of investigations; advance deposit, 2101.16.

Library References

OJur 3d: 48, Family Law § 1526 et seq.

2151.3530 Distribution of forms and materials by job and family services department

(A) The director of job and family services shall distribute the medical information forms and written materials promulgated under section 2151.3529 of the Revised Code to entities permitted to receive a deserted child, to public children services agencies, and to other public or private agencies that, in the discretion of the director, are best able to disseminate the forms and materials to the persons who are most in need of the forms and materials.

(B) If the department of job and family services determines that money in the putative father registry fund created under section 2101.16 of the Revised Code is more than is needed to perform its duties related to the putative father registry, the department may use surplus moneys in the fund for costs related to the distribution of forms and materials pursuant to this section.

(2003 H 95, eff. 6–26–03; 2000 H 660, eff. 4–9–01)

Historical and Statutory Notes

Amendment Note: 2003 H 95 designated the language of the former section as Division (A); and added Division (B).

Cross References

Probate court; fees; cost of investigations; advance deposit, 2101.16.

Library References

OJur 3d: 48, Family Law § 1526 et seq.

2151.36   Support of child

Except as provided in section 2151.361 of the Revised Code, when a child has been committed as provided by this chapter or Chapter 2152. of the Revised Code, the juvenile court shall issue an order pursuant to Chapters 3119., 3121., 3123., and 3125. of the Revised Code requiring that the parent, guardian, or person charged with the child's support pay for the care, support, maintenance, and education of the child. The juvenile court shall order that the parents, guardian, or person pay for the expenses involved in providing orthopedic, medical, or surgical treatment for, or for special care of, the child, enter a judgment for the amount due, and enforce the judgment by execution as in the court of common pleas.

Any expenses incurred for the care, support, maintenance, education, orthopedic, medical, or surgical treatment, and special care of a child who has a legal settlement in another county shall be at the expense of the county of legal settlement if the consent of the juvenile judge of the county of legal settlement is first obtained. When the consent is obtained, the board of county commissioners of the county in which the child has a legal settlement shall reimburse the committing court for the expenses out of its general fund. If the department of job and family services considers it to be in the best interest of any delinquent, dependent, unruly, abused, or neglected child who has a legal settlement in a foreign state or country that the child be returned to the state or country of legal settlement, the juvenile court may commit the child to the department for the child's return to that state or country.

Any expenses ordered by the court for the care, support, maintenance, education, orthopedic, medical, or surgical treatment, or special care of a dependent, neglected, abused, unruly, or delinquent child or of a juvenile traffic offender under this chapter or Chapter 2152. of the Revised Code, except the part of the expense that may be paid by the state or federal government or paid by the parents, guardians, or person charged with the child's support pursuant to this section, shall be paid from the county treasury upon specifically itemized vouchers, certified to by the judge. The court shall not be responsible for any expenses resulting from the commitment of children to any home, public children services agency, private child placing agency, or other institution, association, or agency, unless the court authorized the expenses at the time of commitment.

(2001 S 27, § 3, eff. 3–15–02; 2001 S 27, § 1, eff. 3–15–02; 2000 S 179, § 3, eff. 1–1–02; 2000 S 180, eff. 3–22–01; 1999 H 471, eff. 7–1–00; 1996 H 274, eff. 8–8–96; 1988 S 89, eff. 1–1–89; 1986 H 428; 1975 H 85; 1969 S 49, H 320; 1953 H 1; GC 1639–34)

Historical and Statutory Notes

Pre–1953 H 1 Amendments: 121 v 557; 119 v 731; 117 v 520

Amendment Note: 2001 S 27, § 1 and 3 substituted "Except as provided in section 2151.361 of the Revised Code, when" for "When" at the beginning of the section; and deleted "sections" after "order pursuant to" in the first sentence.

Amendment Note: 2000 S 179, § 3, eff. 1–1–02, inserted "or Chapter 2152. of the Revised Code" in the first and third paragraphs.

Amendment Note: 2000 S 180 substituted "Chapters 3119., 3121., 3123., and 3125." for "3113.21 to 3113.219" in the first paragraph.

Amendment Note: 1999 H 471 substituted "job and family" for "human" in the second paragraph.

Amendment Note: 1996 H 274 rewrote the section, which prior thereto read:

"When a child has been committed as provided by this chapter, the juvenile court may make an examination regarding the income of the parents, guardian, or person charged with the child's support, and may then order that the parent, guardian, or person pay for the care, maintenance, and education of the child and for expenses involved in providing orthopedic, medical or surgical treatment for, or special care of, the child. The court may enter judgment for the money due and enforce the judgment by execution as in the court of common pleas.

"Any expenses incurred for the care, support, maintenance, education, medical or surgical treatment, special care of a child, who has a legal settlement in another county, shall be at the expense of the county of legal settlement, if the consent of the juvenile judge of the county of legal settlement is first obtained. When the consent is obtained, the board of county commissioners of the county in which the child has a legal settlement shall reimburse the committing court for the expense out of its general fund. If the department of human services considers it to be in the best interest of any delinquent, dependent, unruly, abused, or neglected child who has a legal settlement in a foreign state or country, that the child be returned to the state or country of legal settlement, the child may be committed to the department for the return.

"Any expense ordered by the court for the care, maintenance, and education of dependent, neglected, abused, unruly, or delinquent children, or for orthopedic, medical or surgical treatment, or special care of such children under this chapter, except the part of the expense as may be paid by the state or federal government, shall be paid from the county treasury upon specifically itemized vouchers, certified to by the judge. The court shall not be responsible for any expense resulting from the commitment of children to any home, public children services agency, private child placing agency, or other institution, association, or agency, unless such expense has been authorized by the court at the time of commitment.''

Cross References

Duty of husband to support family, wife to assist, 3103.03
Interfering with action to issue or modify support order, 2919.231

Library References

Infants ⊙228, 279.
Westlaw Topic No. 211.
C.J.S. Infants §§ 42 to 85.
OJur 3d: 47, Family Law § 1198, 1201, 1222, 1300, 1301, 1308; 48, Family Law § 1545, 1710, 1715 to 1717
Liability of parent for support of child institutionalized by juvenile court. 59 ALR3d 636
Baldwin's Ohio Legislative Service, 1988 Laws of Ohio, S 89—LSC Analysis, p 5–571
Carlin, Baldwin's Ohio Practice, Merrick–Rippner Probate Law § 106.19, 107.73, 107.76, 108.1, 108.34 (2003).

2151.361 Payment for care, support, maintenance, and education of child

(A) If the parents of a child enter into an agreement with a public children services agency or private child placing agency to place the child into the temporary custody of the agency or the child is committed as provided by this chapter, the juvenile court, at its discretion, may issue an order pursuant to Chapters 3119., 3121., 3123., and 3125. of the Revised Code requiring that the parents pay for the care, support, maintenance, and education of the child if the parents adopted the child.

(B) When determining whether to issue an order under division (A) of this section, the juvenile court shall consider all pertinent issues, including, but not limited to, all of the following:

(1) The ability of the parents to pay for the care, support, maintenance, and education of the child;

(2) The chances for reunification of the parents and child;

(3) Whether issuing the order will encourage the reunification of the parents and child or undermine that reunification;

(4) Whether the problem underlying the agreement to place the child into temporary custody existed prior to the parents' adoption of the child and whether the parents were informed of the problem prior to that adoption;

(5) Whether the problem underlying the agreement to place the child into temporary custody began after the parents' adoption of the child;

(6) Whether the parents have contributed to the child's problems;

(7) Whether the parents are part of the solution to the child's problems.

(2001 S 27, eff. 3–15–02)

Cross References

Interfering with action to issue or modify support order, 2919.231

2151.37 Institution receiving children required to make report

At any time the juvenile judge may require from an association receiving or desiring to receive children, such reports, information, and statements as he deems necessary. He may at any time require from an association or institution reports, information, or statements concerning any child committed to it by such judge under sections 2151.01 to 2151.54, inclusive, of the Revised Code.

(1953 H 1, eff. 10–1–53; GC 1639–36)

Historical and Statutory Notes
Pre–1953 H 1 Amendments: 117 v 520, § 1

Library References

Infants ⊙271.
Westlaw Topic No. 211.
C.J.S. Reformatories §§ 1 to 5.
OJur 3d: 48, Family Law § 1537

2151.38 Temporary nature of dispositional orders

Subject to sections 2151.353 and 2151.412 to 2151.421 of the Revised Code, and any other provision of law that specifies a different duration for a dispositional order, all dispositional orders made by the court under this chapter shall be temporary and shall continue for a period that is designated by the court in its order, until terminated or modified by the court or until the child attains twenty-one years of age.

(2002 H 393, eff. 7–5–02; 2000 S 179, § 3, eff. 1–1–02; 1999 H 3, eff. 11–22–99; 1998 H 526, eff. 9–1–98; 1997 H 1, eff. 7–1–98; 1996 H 124, eff. 3–31–97; 1995 H 1, eff. 1–1–96; 1994 H 314, eff. 9–29–94; 1994 H 715, eff. 7–22–94; 1993 H 152, eff. 7–1–93; 1992 S 241; 1988 S 89; 1986 H 428; 1983 H 291; 1981 H 440, H 1; 1980 H 695; 1969 H 320, S 49; 130 v H 299; 1953 H 1; GC 1639–35)

Historical and Statutory Notes

Pre–1953 H 1 Amendments: 121 v 557; 117 v 520

Amendment Note: 2002 H 393 rewrote the section which prior thereto read:

"(A) Subject to sections 2151.353 and 2151.412 to 2151.421 of the Revised Code, and any other provision of law that specifies a different duration for a dispositional order, all dispositional orders made by the court under this chapter shall be temporary and shall continue for a period that is designated by the court in its order, until terminated or modified by the court or until the child attains twenty-one years of age.

"The release authority of the department of youth services shall not release the child from institutional care or institutional care in a secure facility and as a result shall not discharge the child or order the child's release on supervised release prior to the expiration of the prescribed minimum period of institutionalization or institutionalization in a secure facility or prior to the child's attainment of twenty-one years of age, whichever is applicable under the order of commitment."

Amendment Note: 2000 S 179, § 3, eff. 1–1–02, rewrote this section. See *Baldwin's Ohio Legislative Service Annotated*, 2000, page 11/L–3635, or the OH–LEGIS or OH–LEGIS–OLD database on WESTLAW, for prior version of this section.

Amendment Note: 1999 H 3 rewrote divisions (B)(2) and (C)(2); and deleted "treatment" before "plan" in division (E)(4). Prior to amendment, divisions (B)(2) and (C)(2) read:

"(2) If a court schedules a hearing under division (B)(1) of this section to determine whether a child should be granted a judicial release, it may order the department to deliver the child to the court on the date set for the hearing and may order the department to present to the court a report on the child's progress in the institution to which the child was committed and recommendations for terms and conditions of supervision of the child by the court after release. The court may conduct the hearing without the child being present. The court shall determine at the hearing whether the child should be granted a judicial release from institutionalization or institutionalization in a secure facility. If the court approves the judicial release, the court shall order its staff to prepare a written treatment and rehabilitation plan for the child that may include any terms and conditions of the child's release that were recommended by the department and approved by the court. The committing court shall send the juvenile court of the county in which the child is placed a copy of the recommended plan and the terms and conditions set by the committing court. The court of the county in which the child is placed may adopt the recommended terms and conditions set by the committing court as an order of the court and may add any additional consistent terms and conditions it considers appropriate. If a child is granted a judicial release, the judicial release discharges the child from the custody of the department of youth services."

"(2) If a court schedules a hearing under division (C)(1) of this section to determine whether a child committed to the department should be granted an early release, it may order the department to deliver the child to the court on the date set for the hearing and shall order the department to present to the court at that time a treatment plan for the child's post-institutional care. The court may conduct the hearing without the child being present. The court shall determine at the hearing whether the child should be granted an early release from institutional-ization or institutionalization in a secure facility. If the court approves the early release, the department shall prepare a written treatment and rehabilitation plan for the child pursuant to division (E) of this section that shall include the terms and conditions of the child's release. It shall send the committing court and the juvenile court of the county in which the child is placed a copy of the plan and the terms and conditions that it fixed. The court of the county in which the child is placed may adopt the terms and conditions set by the department as an order of the court and may add any additional consistent terms and conditions it considers appropriate, provided that the court may not add any term or condition that decreases the level or degree of supervision specified by the department in its plan, that substantially increases the financial burden of supervision that will be experienced by the department, or that alters the placement specified by the department in its plan. If the court of the county in which the child is placed adds to the department's plan any additional terms and conditions, it shall enter those additional terms and conditions in its journal and shall send to the department a copy of the journal entry of the additional terms and conditions."

Amendment Note: 1998 H 526 deleted "the most serious act for" after "prescribed minimum term for" in divisions (B)(1) and (C)(1); added the seventh sentence in division (B)92); added division (C)(3); inserted ", and, if the child was released under division (C) of this section, divisions (A) to (E) of section 5139.52 of the Revised Code apply regarding the child", and deleted "specialized supervised release" before "revocation program" twice, in division (D); and made other nonsubstantive changes.

Amendment Note: 1997 H 1 rewrote this section; see *Baldwin's Ohio Legislative Service Annotated*, 1997, page 9/L–2444, or the OH–LEGIS or OH–LEGIS–OLD database on WESTLAW, for text of previous version.

Amendment Note: 1996 H 124 substituted "dispositional order" for "commitment" and "dispositional orders" for "commitments" in division (A); and made changes to reflect gender neutral language.

Amendment Note: 1995 H 1 added the third sentence in division (A); designated division (B)(1)(a) and inserted "in division (B)(1)(b) and (c) of this section and" twice and "or institutionalization in a secure facility" therein; added divisions (B)(1)(b) and (B)(1)(c); inserted "if it desires to release a child committed to it pursuant to division (A)(7) of that section from institutional care in a secure facility prior to the expiration of the period of commitment required to be imposed by that division and prior to the expiration of the prescribed minimum period of institutionalization or institutionalization in a secure facility under division (A)(4) or (5) of that section if either of those divisions applies or prior to the child's attainment of twenty-one years of age if division (A)(6) of that section applies, or if it desires to release a child committed to it under the circumstances described in division (B)(1)(c) of this section prior to the expiration of the prescribed minimum periods or prescribed periods of institutionalization or institutionalization in a secure facility described in that division" in division (B)(2)(a); substituted "as described in division (B)(1)(a), (b), or (c) of this section" for "whichever is applicable, prior to the expiration of the prescribed minimum period of institutionalization or prior to the child's attainment of the age of twenty-one years, whichever is applicable" in division (B)(2)(b); inserted "or prescribed period" in division (B)(2)(c); and made changes to reflect gender neutral language and other nonsubstantive changes.

Amendment Note: 1994 H 314 added ", or shall reject the request by journal entry without conducting a hearing" at the end of division (B)(2)(a).

Amendment Note: 1994 H 715 deleted a reference to section 5139.38 from division (A).

Amendment Note: 1993 H 152 added references to section 5139.38 throughout divisions (A), (B)(1), and (B)(2)(a); and added "or until the child successfully completes a specialized parole revocation program of a duration of not less than thirty days operated either by the department or by an entity with whom the department has contracted to provide a specialized parole revocation program" at the end of divisions (B) and (C).

Cross References

Commitment of child to department of youth services, 5139.05 to 5139.10
Commitment of child to youth services department, permanent assignment defined, 5139.05
Department of youth services as legal custodian, release and placement defined, 5139.01
Department of youth services, early releases in emergency overcrowding condition, 5139.20
Duties of the department of youth services to reduce and control delinquency, 5139.11
Interference with custody, 2919.23
Victims' rights pamphlet, contents, 109.42
Youth services department, placement of released children, applicability, 5139.18

Library References

Infants ⊕222, 226, 278.
Westlaw Topic No. 211.
C.J.S. Infants §§ 57, 69 to 85, 198 to 214.
OJur 3d: 48, Family Law § 1517, 1704, 1705
Am Jur 2d: 47, Juvenile Courts and Delinquent and Dependent Children § 32, 33
Baldwin's Ohio Legislative Service, 1988 Laws of Ohio, S 89—LSC Analysis, p 5–571
Carlin, Baldwin's Ohio Practice, Merrick–Rippner Probate Law § 105.10, 107.73, 107.89, 107.121, 107.184, 107.185 (2003).

2151.39 Placement of children from other states

No person, association or agency, public or private, of another state, incorporated or otherwise, shall place a child in a family home or with an agency or institution within the boundaries of this state, either for temporary or permanent care or custody or for adoption, unless such person or association has furnished the department of job and family services with a medical and social history of the child, pertinent information about the family, agency, association, or institution in this state with whom the sending party desires to place the child, and any other information or financial guaranty required by the department to determine whether the proposed placement will meet the needs of the child. The department may require the party desiring the placement to agree to promptly receive and remove from the state a child brought into the state whose placement has not proven satisfactorily responsive to the needs of the child at any time until the child is adopted, reaches majority, becomes self-supporting or is discharged with the concurrence of the department. All placements proposed to be made in this state by a party located in a state which is a party to the interstate compact on the placement of children shall be made according to the provisions of sections 5103.20 to 5103.28 of the Revised Code.

(1999 H 471, eff. 7–1–00; 1986 H 428, eff. 12–23–86; 1975 H 247; 126 v 1165; 1953 H 1; GC 1639–37)

Historical and Statutory Notes

Pre–1953 H 1 Amendments: 117 v 520, § 1

Amendment Note: 1999 H 471 substituted "job and family" for "human".

Cross References

Placing of children, 5103.16
Social administration division, enforcement by job and family services department, 5103.14

Ohio Administrative Code References

Agency and court interstate placement requirements, OAC 5101:2–42–21
Interstate placements of children into or from Ohio, foreign-born children, OAC 5101:2–42–20 to 5101:2–42–27

Library References

Infants ⊕229.
Westlaw Topic No. 211.
C.J.S. Infants §§ 57, 69 to 85.
OJur 3d: 48, Family Law § 1524
Carlin, Baldwin's Ohio Practice, Merrick–Rippner Probate Law § 98.6, 107.128 (2003).

2151.40 Cooperation with court

Every county, township, or municipal official or department, including the prosecuting attorney, shall render all assistance and co-operation within his jurisdictional power which may further the objects of sections 2151.01 to 2151.54 of the Revised Code. All institutions or agencies to which the juvenile court sends any child shall give to the court or to any officer appointed by it such information concerning such child as said court or officer requires. The court may seek the co-operation of all societies or organizations having for their object the protection or aid of children.

On the request of the judge, when the child is represented by an attorney, or when a trial is requested the prosecuting attorney shall assist the court in presenting the evidence at any hearing or proceeding concerning an alleged or adjudicated delinquent, unruly, abused, neglected, or dependent child or juvenile traffic offender.

(1975 H 85, eff. 11–28–75; 1969 H 320; 1953 H 1; GC 1639–55)

Historical and Statutory Notes
Pre–1953 H 1 Amendments: 117 v 520, § 1
Cross References
Adjudicatory hearing, Juv R 29
Library References
Infants ☞17.
Westlaw Topic No. 211.
C.J.S. Infants §§ 8, 9.
OJur 3d: 48, Family Law § 1567
Carlin, Baldwin's Ohio Practice, Merrick–Rippner Probate Law § 104.15, 107.48 (2003).

GENERAL PROVISIONS

2151.412 Case plans

(A) Each public children services agency and private child placing agency shall prepare and maintain a case plan for any child to whom the agency is providing services and to whom any of the following applies:

(1) The agency filed a complaint pursuant to section 2151.27 of the Revised Code alleging that the child is an abused, neglected, or dependent child;

(2) The agency has temporary or permanent custody of the child;

(3) The child is living at home subject to an order for protective supervision;

(4) The child is in a planned permanent living arrangement.

Except as provided by division (A)(2) of section 5103.153 of the Revised Code, a private child placing agency providing services to a child who is the subject of a voluntary permanent custody surrender agreement entered into under division (B)(2) of section 5103.15 of the Revised Code is not required to prepare and maintain a case plan for that child.

(B)(1) The director of job and family services shall adopt rules pursuant to Chapter 119. of the Revised Code setting forth the content and format of case plans required by division (A) of this section and establishing procedures for developing, implementing, and changing the case plans. The rules shall at a minimum comply with the requirements of Title IV–E of the "Social Security Act," 94 Stat. 501, 42 U.S.C. 671 (1980), as amended.

(2) The director of job and family services shall adopt rules pursuant to Chapter 119. of the Revised Code requiring public children services agencies and private child placing agencies to maintain case plans for children and their families who are receiving services in their homes from the agencies and for whom case plans are not required by division (A) of this section. The agencies shall maintain case plans as required by those rules; however, the case plans shall not be subject to any other provision of this section except as specifically required by the rules.

(C) Each public children services agency and private child placing agency that is required by division (A) of this section to maintain a case plan shall file the case plan with the court prior to the child's adjudicatory hearing but no later than thirty days after the earlier of the date on which the complaint in the case was filed or the child was first placed into shelter care. If the agency does not have sufficient information prior to the adjudicatory hearing to complete any part of the case plan, the agency shall specify in the case plan the additional information necessary to complete each part of the case plan and the steps that will be taken to obtain that information. All parts of the case plan shall be completed by the earlier of thirty days after the adjudicatory hearing or the date of the dispositional hearing for the child.

(D) Any agency that is required by division (A) of this section to prepare a case plan shall attempt to obtain an agreement among all parties, including, but not limited to, the parents, guardian, or custodian of the child and the guardian ad litem of the child regarding the content of the case plan. If all parties agree to the content of the case plan and the court approves it, the court shall journalize it as part of its dispositional order. If the agency cannot obtain an agreement upon the contents of the case plan or the court does not approve it, the parties shall present evidence on the contents of the case plan at the dispositional hearing. The court, based upon the evidence presented at the dispositional hearing and the best interest of the child, shall determine the contents of the case plan and journalize it as part of the dispositional order for the child.

(E)(1) All parties, including the parents, guardian, or custodian of the child, are bound by the terms of the journalized case plan. A party that fails to comply with the terms of the journalized case plan may be held in contempt of court.

(2) Any party may propose a change to a substantive part of the case plan, including, but not limited to, the child's placement and the visitation rights of any party. A party proposing a change to the case plan shall file the proposed change with the court and give notice of the proposed change in writing before the end of the day after the day of filing it to all parties and the child's guardian ad litem. All parties and the guardian ad litem shall have seven days from the date the notice is sent to object to and request a hearing on the proposed change.

(a) If it receives a timely request for a hearing, the court shall schedule a hearing pursuant to section 2151.417 of the Revised Code to be held no later than thirty days after the request is received by the court. The court shall give notice of the date, time, and location of the hearing to all parties and the guardian ad litem. The agency may implement the proposed change after the hearing, if the court approves it. The agency shall not implement the proposed change unless it is approved by the court.

(b) If it does not receive a timely request for a hearing, the court may approve the proposed change without a hearing. If the court approves the proposed change without a hearing, it shall journalize the case plan with the change not later than fourteen days after the change is filed with the court. If the court does not approve the proposed change to the case plan, it shall schedule a hearing to be held pursuant to section 2151.417 of the Revised Code no later than thirty days after the expiration of the fourteen-day time period and give notice of the date, time, and location of the hearing to all parties and the guardian ad litem of the child. If, despite the requirements of division (E)(2) of this section, the court neither approves and journalizes the proposed change nor conducts a hearing, the agency may implement the proposed change not earlier than fifteen days after it is submitted to the court.

(3) If an agency has reasonable cause to believe that a child is suffering from illness or injury and is not receiving proper care and that an appropriate change in the child's case plan is necessary to prevent immediate or threatened physical or emotional harm, to believe that a child is in immediate danger from the child's surroundings and that an immediate change in the child's case plan is necessary to prevent immediate or threatened physical or emotional harm to the child, or to believe that a parent, guardian, custodian, or other member of the child's household has abused or neglected the child and that the child is in danger of immediate or threatened physical or emotional harm from that person unless the agency makes an appropriate change in the child's case plan, it may implement the change without prior agreement or a court hearing and, before the end of the next day after the change is made, give all parties, the guardian ad litem of the child, and the court notice of the change. Before the end of the third day after implementing the change in the case plan, the agency shall file a statement of the change with the court and give notice of the filing accompanied by a copy of the statement to all parties and the guardian ad litem. All parties and the guardian ad litem shall have ten days from the date the notice is sent to object to and request a hearing on the change.

(a) If it receives a timely request for a hearing, the court shall schedule a hearing pursuant to section 2151.417 of the Revised Code to be held no later than thirty days after the request is received by the court. The court shall give notice of the date, time, and location of the hearing to all parties and the guardian ad litem. The agency shall continue to administer the case plan with the change after the hearing, if the court approves the change. If the court does not approve the change, the court shall make appropriate changes to the case plan and shall journalize the case plan.

(b) If it does not receive a timely request for a hearing, the court may approve the change without a hearing. If the court approves the change without a hearing, it shall journalize the case plan with the change within fourteen days after receipt of the change. If the court does not approve the change to the case plan, it shall schedule a hearing under section 2151.417 of the Revised Code to be held no later than thirty days after the expiration of the fourteen-day time period and give notice of the date, time, and location of the hearing to all parties and the guardian ad litem of the child.

(F)(1) All case plans for children in temporary custody shall have the following general goals:

(a) Consistent with the best interest and special needs of the child, to achieve a safe out-of-home placement in the least restrictive, most family-like setting available and in close proximity to the home from which the child was removed or the home in which the child will be permanently placed;

(b) To eliminate with all due speed the need for the out-of-home placement so that the child can safely return home.

(2) The director of job and family services shall adopt rules pursuant to Chapter 119. of the Revised Code setting forth the general goals of case plans for children subject to dispositional orders for protective supervision, a planned permanent living arrangement, or permanent custody.

(G) In the agency's development of a case plan and the court's review of the case plan, the child's health and safety shall be the paramount concern. The agency and the court shall be guided by the following general priorities:

(1) A child who is residing with or can be placed with the child's parents within a reasonable time should remain in their legal custody even if an order of protective supervision is required for a reasonable period of time;

(2) If both parents of the child have abandoned the child, have relinquished custody of the child, have become incapable of supporting or caring for the child even with reasonable assistance, or have a detrimental effect on the health, safety, and best interest of the child, the child should be placed in the legal custody of a suitable member of the child's extended family;

(3) If a child described in division (G)(2) of this section has no suitable member of the child's extended family to accept legal custody, the child should be placed in the legal custody of a suitable nonrelative who shall be made a party to the proceedings after being given legal custody of the child;

(4) If the child has no suitable member of the child's extended family to accept legal custody of the child and no suitable nonrelative is available to accept legal custody of the child and, if the child temporarily cannot or should not be placed with the child's parents, guardian, or custodian, the child should be placed in the temporary custody of a public children services agency or a private child placing agency;

(5) If the child cannot be placed with either of the child's parents within a rea-

sonable period of time or should not be placed with either, if no suitable member of the child's extended family or suitable nonrelative is available to accept legal custody of the child, and if the agency has a reasonable expectation of placing the child for adoption, the child should be committed to the permanent custody of the public children services agency or private child placing agency;

(6) If the child is to be placed for adoption or foster care, the placement shall not be delayed or denied on the basis of the child's or adoptive or foster family's race, color, or national origin.

(H) The case plan for a child in temporary custody shall include at a minimum the following requirements if the child is or has been the victim of abuse or neglect or if the child witnessed the commission in the child's household of abuse or neglect against a sibling of the child, a parent of the child, or any other person in the child's household:

(1) A requirement that the child's parents, guardian, or custodian participate in mandatory counseling;

(2) A requirement that the child's parents, guardian, or custodian participate in any supportive services that are required by or provided pursuant to the child's case plan.

(I) A case plan may include, as a supplement, a plan for locating a permanent family placement. The supplement shall not be considered part of the case plan for purposes of division (D) of this section.

(1999 H 471, eff. 7–1–00; 1998 H 484, eff. 3–18–99; 1996 H 274, eff. 8–8–96; 1996 H 419, eff. 9–18–96; 1988 H 403, eff. 1–1–89)

Uncodified Law

1988 S 89, § 4: See Uncodified Law under 2151.414.

Historical and Statutory Notes

Ed. Note: Former 2151.412 repealed by 1988 H 403, eff. 1–1–89; 1988 S 89. Prior 2151.412 repealed by 1988 S 89, eff. 1–1–89; 1988 H 399; 1986 H 428; 1980 H 695.

Amendment Note: 1999 H 471 substituted "director of job and family services" for "department of human services" in divisions (B)(1), (B)(2), and (F)(2).

Amendment Note: 1998 H 484 substituted "a planned permanent living arrangement" for "long-term foster care" in divisions (A)(4) and (F)(2); inserted "safe" in division (F)(1)(a); rewrote division (F)(1)(b); inserted "child's health and safety shall be the paramount concern. The" in the first paragraph in division (G); deleted "solely" after "denied" in division (G)(6); added division (I); and made other nonsubstantive changes. Prior to amendment, division (F)(1)(b) read:

"(b) To do either of the following:

"(i) With all due speed eliminate the need for the out-of-home placement so that the child can return home;

"(ii) If return to the child's home is not imminent and desirable, develop and implement an alternative permanent living arrangement for the child."

Amendment Note: 1996 H 274 rewrote division (E), which prior thereto read:

"(E)(1) All parties are bound by the terms of the journalized case plan.

"(2) No party shall change a substantive part of the case plan, including, but not limited to, the child's placement and the visitation rights of any party, unless the proposed change has been approved by all parties and the guardian ad litem. The proposed change shall be submitted to the court within seven days of approval. If the court approves the proposed change, it shall journalize the case plan with the change within fourteen days after receipt of the proposed change. The agency may implement the proposed change fourteen days after it is submitted to the court for approval, unless the court schedules a hearing under section 2151.417 of the Revised Code to consider the proposed change. If the court does not approve the proposed change to the case plan, it shall schedule a hearing under section 2151.417 of the Revised Code to be held no later than thirty days after the expiration of the fourteen-day time period and give notice of the date, time, and location of the hearing to all parties and the guardian ad litem of the child. The agency shall not implement any proposed change to a case plan pursuant to this division, unless the proposed change has been approved by the court or the court has failed to either approve and journalize the proposed change or schedule a hearing pursuant to section 2151.417 of the Revised Code on the proposed change within fourteen days after the proposed change was submitted to the court.

"(3) If an agency has reasonable cause to believe that a child is suffering from illness or injury and is not receiving proper care and that an appropriate change in the child's case plan is necessary to prevent immediate or threatened physical or emotional harm, to believe that a child is in immediate danger from the child's surroundings and that an immediate change in the child's case plan is necessary to prevent immediate or threatened physical or emotional harm to the child, or to believe that a parent, guardian, custodian, or other member of the child's household has abused or neglected the child and that the child is in danger of immediate or threatened physical or emotional harm from that person unless the agency makes an appropriate change in the child's case plan, it may implement the change without prior agreement or a court hearing and, before the end of the next business day after the change is made, give all parties, the guardian ad litem of the child, and the court notice of the change. If the agency, within seven days after implementing the change pursuant to this division, can obtain an agreement on the change to the case plan that is signed by all parties and the child's guardian ad litem, it shall immediately file the change with the court. If the court approves the change, it shall journalize the case plan with the change within fourteen days after receipt of the change. If the court does not approve the change to the case plan, it shall schedule a hearing under section 2151.417 of the Revised Code to be held no later than thirty days after the expiration of the fourteen-day time period

and give notice of the date, time, and location of the hearing to all parties and the guardian ad litem of the child. If the agency cannot obtain the approval of all parties and the child's guardian ad litem to a change to the case plan, it shall request the court to schedule a hearing under section 2151.417 of the Revised Code to consider the change. The court shall schedule the requested hearing to be held within fourteen days after the request and give notice of the date, time, and location of the hearing to all parties and the guardian ad litem of the child."

Amendment Note: 1996 H 419 added the second sentence to division (A)(4); added division (G)(6); made changes to reflect gender neutral language throughout; and made other nonsubstantive changes.

Cross References

Child day-care, protective day-care defined, 5104.01
Foster caregivers, information regarding delinquent children provided to, 2152.72
Ohio works first program, eligibility, 5107.10
Placing of child in institution, agency filing complaint and case plan, 5103.15
Review hearing of adoption agreement, case plan, 5103.153

Ohio Administrative Code References

Children services, definition of terms, OAC 5101:2–1–01
"Child's education and health information" form, OAC 5101:2–39–082
PCPA and PNA case plans and administrative case reviews for direct placements, OAC 5101:2–5–34
PCPA case plan for children in custody or under court-ordered protective supervision, OAC 5101:2–39–10
Public children services agency case plan, OAC 5101:2–39–07 to 5101:2–39–081, 5101:2–39–10
Removal of a child from his own home, OAC 5101:2–39–12 et seq.

Library References

Infants ☞17, 155 to 158, 222.
Westlaw Topic No. 211.
C.J.S. Infants §§ 8, 9, 31 to 85.
OJur 3d: 48, Family Law § 1426 to 1428, 1699, 1700, 1702; 78, Public Welfare § 49
Am Jur 2d: 47, Juvenile Courts and Delinquent and Dependent Children § 29, 30, 55
Baldwin's Ohio Legislative Service, 1996 H 274—LSC Analysis, p 5/L–697
Baldwin's Ohio Legislative Service, 1988 Laws of Ohio, S 89—LSC Analysis, p 5–571
Sowald & Morganstern, Baldwin's Ohio Practice, Domestic Relations Law § 37.12 (1997).
Carlin, Baldwin's Ohio Practice, Merrick–Rippner Probate Law § 98.8, 98.11, 98.17, 107.54, 107.75, 107.119, 107.175 (2003).

2151.413 Motion for permanent custody

(A) A public children services agency or private child placing agency that, pursuant to an order of disposition under division (A)(2) of section 2151.353 of the Revised Code or under any version of section 2151.353 of the Revised Code that existed prior to January 1, 1989, is granted temporary custody of a child who is not abandoned or orphaned may file a motion in the court that made the disposition of the child requesting permanent custody of the child.

(B) A public children services agency or private child placing agency that, pursuant to an order of disposition under division (A)(2) of section 2151.353 of the Revised Code or under any version of section 2151.353 of the Revised Code that existed prior to January 1, 1989, is granted temporary custody of a child who is orphaned may file a motion in the court that made the disposition of the child requesting permanent custody of the child whenever it can show that no relative of the child is able to take legal custody of the child.

(C) A public children services agency or private child placing agency that, pursuant to an order of disposition under division (A)(5) of section 2151.353 of the Revised Code, places a child in a planned permanent living arrangement may file a motion in the court that made the disposition of the child requesting permanent custody of the child.

(D)(1) Except as provided in division (D)(3) of this section, if a child has been in the temporary custody of one or more public children services agencies or private child placing agencies for twelve or more months of a consecutive twenty-two month period ending on or after March 18, 1999, the agency with custody shall file a motion requesting permanent custody of the child. The motion shall be filed in the court that issued the current order of temporary custody. For the purposes of this division, a child shall be considered to have entered the temporary custody of an agency on the earlier of the date the child is adjudicated pursuant to section 2151.28 of the Revised Code or the date that is sixty days after the removal of the child from home.

(2) Except as provided in division (D)(3) of this section, if a court makes a determination pursuant to division (A)(2) of section 2151.419 of the Revised Code, the public children services agency or private child placing agency required to develop the permanency plan for the child under division (K) of section 2151.417 of the Revised Code shall file a motion in the court that made the determination requesting permanent custody of the child.

(3) An agency shall not file a motion for permanent custody under division (D)(1) or (2) of this section if any of the following apply:

(a) The agency documents in the case plan or permanency plan a compelling reason that permanent custody is not in the best interest of the child.

(b) If reasonable efforts to return the child to the child's home are required under section 2151.419 of the Revised Code, the agency has not provided the services required by the case plan to the parents of the child or the child to ensure the safe return of the child to the child's home.

(c) The agency has been granted permanent custody of the child.

(d) The child has been returned home pursuant to court order in accordance with division (A)(3) of section 2151.419 of the Revised Code.

(E) Any agency that files a motion for permanent custody under this section shall include in the case plan of the child who is the subject of the motion, a specific plan of the agency's actions to seek an adoptive family for the child and to prepare the child for adoption.

(F) The department of job and family services may adopt rules pursuant to Chapter 119. of the Revised Code that set forth the time frames for case reviews and for filing a motion requesting permanent custody under division (D)(1) of this section.

(1999 H 471, eff. 7–1–00; 1999 H 176, eff. 10–29–99; 1998 H 484, eff. 3–18–99; 1996 H 419, eff. 9–18–96; 1988 S 89, eff. 1–1–89; 1980 H 695)

Historical and Statutory Notes

Amendment Note: 1999 H 471 substituted "job and family" for "human" in division (F).

Amendment Note: 1999 H 176 rewrote division (D)(1); and made other nonsubstantive changes. Prior to amendment, division (D)(1) read:

"(D)(1) Except as provided in division (D)(3) of this section, if a child has been in temporary custody for twelve or more months of a consecutive twenty-two month period ending on or after the effective date of this amendment pursuant to an order of disposition that was issued under division (A)(2) of section 2151.353 of the Revised Code or pursuant to an order that extends temporary custody and was issued prior to the effective date of this amendment under division (D) of section 2151.415 of the Revised Code, the public children services agency or private child placing agency with custody shall file a motion requesting permanent custody of the child. The motion shall be filed in the court that issued the order of disposition."

Amendment Note: 1998 H 484 rewrote this section, which prior thereto read:

"(A) A public children services agency or private child placing agency that, pursuant to an order of disposition under division (A)(2) of section 2151.353

of the Revised Code or under any version of section 2151.353 of the Revised Code that existed prior to January 1, 1989, is granted temporary custody of a child who is not abandoned or orphaned or of an abandoned child whose parents have been located may file a motion in the court that made the disposition of the child requesting permanent custody of the child.

"(B) A public children services agency or private child placing agency that, pursuant to an order of disposition under division (A)(2) of section 2151.353 of the Revised Code or under any version of section 2151.353 of the Revised Code that existed prior to January 1, 1989, is granted temporary custody of a child who is abandoned or orphaned may file a motion in the court that made the disposition of the child requesting permanent custody of the child, if the child is abandoned, whenever it can show the court that the parents cannot be located and, if the child is orphaned, whenever it can show that no relative of the child is able to take legal custody of the child.

"(C) A public children services agency or private child placing agency that, pursuant to an order of disposition under division (A)(5) of section 2151.353 of the Revised Code, places a child in long-term foster care may file a motion in the court that made the disposition of the child requesting permanent custody of the child.

"(D) Any agency that files a motion for permanent custody under this section shall include in the case plan of the child who is the subject of the motion, a specific plan of the agency's actions to seek an adoptive family for the child and to prepare the child for adoption."

Amendment Note: 1996 H 419 substituted "January 1, 1989" for "the effective date of this amendment" in divisions (A) and (B); deleted "if a period of at least six months has elapsed since the order of temporary custody was issued or the initial filing of the case plan with the court if the child is an abandoned child whose parents have been located" from the end of division (A); added division (C); and redesignated former division (C) as (D).

Ohio Administrative Code References

Extension of "Agreement for Temporary Custody of Child" (JFS 01645), OAC 5101:2–42–07
Obtaining permanent custody: termination of parental rights, OAC 5101:2–42–95

Library References

Infants ⬩155 to 158, 222.
Westlaw Topic No. 211.
C.J.S. Infants §§ 31 to 85.
OJur 3d: 48, Family Law § 1612, 1663
Baldwin's Ohio Legislative Service, 1988 Laws of Ohio, S 89—LSC Analysis, p 5–571
Carlin, Baldwin's Ohio Practice, Merrick–Rippner Probate Law § 107.78, 107.80, 107.83 (2003).

2151.414 Procedures upon motion

(A)(1) Upon the filing of a motion pursuant to section 2151.413 of the Revised Code for permanent custody of a child, the court shall schedule a hearing and give notice of the filing of the motion and of the hearing, in accordance with section 2151.29 of the Revised Code, to all parties to the action and to the child's guardian ad litem. The notice also shall

contain a full explanation that the granting of permanent custody permanently divests the parents of their parental rights, a full explanation of their right to be represented by counsel and to have counsel appointed pursuant to Chapter 120. of the Revised Code if they are indigent, and the name and telephone number of the court employee designated by the court pursuant to section 2151.314 of the Revised Code to arrange for the prompt appointment of counsel for indigent persons.

The court shall conduct a hearing in accordance with section 2151.35 of the Revised Code to determine if it is in the best interest of the child to permanently terminate parental rights and grant permanent custody to the agency that filed the motion. The adjudication that the child is an abused, neglected, or dependent child and any dispositional order that has been issued in the case under section 2151.353 of the Revised Code pursuant to the adjudication shall not be readjudicated at the hearing and shall not be affected by a denial of the motion for permanent custody.

(2) The court shall hold the hearing scheduled pursuant to division (A)(1) of this section not later than one hundred twenty days after the agency files the motion for permanent custody, except that, for good cause shown, the court may continue the hearing for a reasonable period of time beyond the one-hundred-twenty-day deadline. The court shall issue an order that grants, denies, or otherwise disposes of the motion for permanent custody, and journalize the order, not later than two hundred days after the agency files the motion.

If a motion is made under division (D)(2) of section 2151.413 of the Revised Code and no dispositional hearing has been held in the case, the court may hear the motion in the dispositional hearing required by division (B) of section 2151.35 of the Revised Code. If the court issues an order pursuant to section 2151.353 of the Revised Code granting permanent custody of the child to the agency, the court shall immediately dismiss the motion made under division (D)(2) of section 2151.413 of the Revised Code.

The failure of the court to comply with the time periods set forth in division (A)(2) of this section does not affect the authority of the court to issue any order under this chapter and does not provide any basis for attacking the jurisdiction of the court or the validity of any order of the court.

(B)(1) Except as provided in division (B)(2) of this section, the court may grant permanent custody of a child to a movant if the court determines at the hearing held pursuant to division (A) of this section, by clear and convincing evidence, that it is in the best interest of the child to grant permanent custody of the child to the agency that filed the motion for permanent custody and that any of the following apply:

(a) The child is not abandoned or orphaned or has not been in the temporary custody of one or more public children services agencies or private child placing agencies for twelve or more months of a consecutive twenty-two month period ending on or after March 18, 1999, and the child cannot be placed with either of the child's parents within a reasonable time or should not be placed with the child's parents.

(b) The child is abandoned.

(c) The child is orphaned, and there are no relatives of the child who are able to take permanent custody.

(d) The child has been in the temporary custody of one or more public children services agencies or private child placing agencies for twelve or more months of a consecutive twenty-two month period ending on or after March 18, 1999.

For the purposes of division (B)(1) of this section, a child shall be considered to have entered the temporary custody of an agency on the earlier of the date the child is adjudicated pursuant to section 2151.28 of the Revised Code or the date that is sixty days after the removal of the child from home.

(2) With respect to a motion made pursuant to division (D)(2) of section 2151.413 of the Revised Code, the court shall grant permanent custody of the child to the movant if the court determines in accordance with division (E) of this section that the child cannot be placed with one of the child's parents within a reasonable time or should not be placed with either parent and determines in accordance with division (D) of this section that permanent custody is in the child's best interest.

(C) In making the determinations required by this section or division (A)(4) of

section 2151.353 of the Revised Code, a court shall not consider the effect the granting of permanent custody to the agency would have upon any parent of the child. A written report of the guardian ad litem of the child shall be submitted to the court prior to or at the time of the hearing held pursuant to division (A) of this section or section 2151.35 of the Revised Code but shall not be submitted under oath.

If the court grants permanent custody of a child to a movant under this division, the court, upon the request of any party, shall file a written opinion setting forth its findings of fact and conclusions of law in relation to the proceeding. The court shall not deny an agency's motion for permanent custody solely because the agency failed to implement any particular aspect of the child's case plan.

(D) In determining the best interest of a child at a hearing held pursuant to division (A) of this section or for the purposes of division (A)(4) or (5) of section 2151.353 or division (C) of section 2151.415 of the Revised Code, the court shall consider all relevant factors, including, but not limited to, the following:

(1) The interaction and interrelationship of the child with the child's parents, siblings, relatives, foster caregivers and out-of-home providers, and any other person who may significantly affect the child;

(2) The wishes of the child, as expressed directly by the child or through the child's guardian ad litem, with due regard for the maturity of the child;

(3) The custodial history of the child, including whether the child has been in the temporary custody of one or more public children services agencies or private child placing agencies for twelve or more months of a consecutive twenty-two month period ending on or after March 18, 1999;

(4) The child's need for a legally secure permanent placement and whether that type of placement can be achieved without a grant of permanent custody to the agency;

(5) Whether any of the factors in divisions (E)(7) to (11) of this section apply in relation to the parents and child.

For the purposes of this division, a child shall be considered to have entered the temporary custody of an agency on the earlier of the date the child is adjudicated pursuant to section 2151.28 of the Revised Code or the date that is sixty days after the removal of the child from home.

(E) In determining at a hearing held pursuant to division (A) of this section or for the purposes of division (A)(4) of section 2151.353 of the Revised Code whether a child cannot be placed with either parent within a reasonable period of time or should not be placed with the parents, the court shall consider all relevant evidence. If the court determines, by clear and convincing evidence, at a hearing held pursuant to division (A) of this section or for the purposes of division (A)(4) of section 2151.353 of the Revised Code that one or more of the following exist as to each of the child's parents, the court shall enter a finding that the child cannot be placed with either parent within a reasonable time or should not be placed with either parent:

(1) Following the placement of the child outside the child's home and notwithstanding reasonable case planning and diligent efforts by the agency to assist the parents to remedy the problems that initially caused the child to be placed outside the home, the parent has failed continuously and repeatedly to substantially remedy the conditions causing the child to be placed outside the child's home. In determining whether the parents have substantially remedied those conditions, the court shall consider parental utilization of medical, psychiatric, psychological, and other social and rehabilitative services and material resources that were made available to the parents for the purpose of changing parental conduct to allow them to resume and maintain parental duties.

(2) Chronic mental illness, chronic emotional illness, mental retardation, physical disability, or chemical dependency of the parent that is so severe that it makes the parent unable to provide an adequate permanent home for the child at the present time and, as anticipated, within one year after the court holds the hearing pursuant to division (A) of this section or for the purposes of division (A)(4) of section 2151.353 of the Revised Code;

(3) The parent committed any abuse as described in section 2151.031 of the Revised Code against the child, caused the child to suffer any neglect as described in section 2151.03 of the Revised Code, or allowed the child to suffer any neglect as described in section 2151.03 of the Revised Code between the date that the original complaint alleging abuse or neglect was filed and the date of the filing of the motion for permanent custody;

(4) The parent has demonstrated a lack of commitment toward the child by failing to regularly support, visit, or communicate with the child when able to do so, or by other actions showing an unwillingness to provide an adequate permanent home for the child;

(5) The parent is incarcerated for an offense committed against the child or a sibling of the child;

(6) The parent has been convicted of or pleaded guilty to an offense under division (A) or (C) of section 2919.22 or under section 2903.16, 2903.21, 2903.34, 2905.01, 2905.02, 2905.03, 2905.04, 2905.05, 2907.07, 2907.08, 2907.09, 2907.12, 2907.21, 2907.22, 2907.23, 2907.25, 2907.31, 2907.32, 2907.321, 2907.322, 2907.323, 2911.01, 2911.02, 2911.11, 2911.12, 2919.12, 2919.24, 2919.25, 2923.12, 2923.13, 2923.161, 2925.02, or 3716.11 of the Revised Code and the child or a sibling of the child was a victim of the offense or the parent has been convicted of or pleaded guilty to an offense under section 2903.04 of the Revised Code, a sibling of the child was the victim of the offense, and the parent who committed the offense poses an ongoing danger to the child or a sibling of the child.

(7) The parent has been convicted of or pleaded guilty to one of the following:

(a) An offense under section 2903.01, 2903.02, or 2903.03 of the Revised Code or under an existing or former law of this state, any other state, or the United States that is substantially equivalent to an offense described in those sections and the victim of the offense was a sibling of the child or the victim was another child who lived in the parent's household at the time of the offense;

(b) An offense under section 2903.11, 2903.12, or 2903.13 of the Revised Code or under an existing or former law of this state, any other state, or the United States that is substantially equivalent to an offense described in those sections and the victim of the offense is the child, a sibling of the child, or another child who lived in the parent's household at the time of the offense;

(c) An offense under division (B)(2) of section 2919.22 of the Revised Code or under an existing or former law of this state, any other state, or the United States that is substantially equivalent to the offense described in that section and the child, a sibling of the child, or another child who lived in the parent's household at the time of the offense is the victim of the offense;

(d) An offense under section 2907.02, 2907.03, 2907.04, 2907.05, or 2907.06 of the Revised Code or under an existing or former law of this state, any other state, or the United States that is substantially equivalent to an offense described in those sections and the victim of the offense is the child, a sibling of the child, or another child who lived in the parent's household at the time of the offense;

(e) A conspiracy or attempt to commit, or complicity in committing, an offense described in division (E)(7)(a) or (d) of this section.

(8) The parent has repeatedly withheld medical treatment or food from the child when the parent has the means to provide the treatment or food, and, in the case of withheld medical treatment, the parent withheld it for a purpose other than to treat the physical or mental illness or defect of the child by spiritual means through prayer alone in accordance with the tenets of a recognized religious body.

(9) The parent has placed the child at substantial risk of harm two or more times due to alcohol or drug abuse and has rejected treatment two or more times or refused to participate in further treatment two or more times after a case plan issued pursuant to section 2151.412 of the Revised Code requiring treatment of the parent was journalized as part of a dispositional order issued with respect to the child or an order was issued by any other court requiring treatment of the parent.

(10) The parent has abandoned the child.

(11) The parent has had parental rights involuntarily terminated pursuant to this section or section 2151.353 or 2151.415 of the Revised Code with respect to a sibling of the child.

(12) The parent is incarcerated at the time of the filing of the motion for permanent custody or the dispositional hearing of the child and will not be available to care for the child for at least eighteen months after the filing of the motion for permanent custody or the dispositional hearing.

(13) The parent is repeatedly incarcerated, and the repeated incarceration prevents the parent from providing care for the child.

(14) The parent for any reason is unwilling to provide food, clothing, shelter, and other basic necessities for the child or to prevent the child from suffering physical, emotional, or sexual abuse or physical, emotional, or mental neglect.

(15) The parent has committed abuse as described in section 2151.031 of the Revised Code against the child or caused or allowed the child to suffer neglect as described in section 2151.03 of the Revised Code, and the court determines that the seriousness, nature, or likelihood of recurrence of the abuse or neglect makes the child's placement with the child's parent a threat to the child's safety.

(16) Any other factor the court considers relevant.

(F) The parents of a child for whom the court has issued an order granting permanent custody pursuant to this section, upon the issuance of the order, cease to be parties to the action. This division is not intended to eliminate or restrict any right of the parents to appeal the granting of permanent custody of their child to a movant pursuant to this section.

(2000 H 448, eff. 10–5–00; 1999 H 176, eff. 10–29–99; 1998 H 484, eff. 3–18–99; 1996 H 274, eff. 8–8–96; 1996 H 419, eff. 9–18–96; 1988 S 89, eff. 1–1–89; 1980 H 695)

Uncodified Law

1988 S 89, § 4, eff. 1–1–89, reads:

If a child is in the permanent custody of a public children services agency or private child placing agency on the effective date of this act, both of the following apply:

(A) The agency shall do both of the following:

(1) Prepare and file with the court a case plan for the child in accordance with section 2151.412 of the Revised Code, as enacted by this act, on or before July 1, 1989, and, after the case plan is prepared and filed with the court, comply with all provisions of section 2151.412 of the Revised Code, as enacted by this act.

(2) Conduct an administrative review of the child's case plan in accordance with section 2151.416 of the Revised Code, as renumbered and amended by this act, on or before the sixth month after the court conducts its first review hearing as required by division (B) of this section and continue to conduct administrative reviews of the child's case plan no

later than every six months in accordance with that section until the child attains the age of eighteen if the child is not mentally or physically handicapped, the child attains the age of twenty-one if the child is mentally or physically handicapped, the child is adopted and a final decree of adoption is issued, or the court otherwise terminates the custody arrangement.

(B) The court with jurisdiction over the child shall conduct its first review hearing in accordance with division (C) of section 2151.417 of the Revised Code to review the child's case plan after the case plan is filed pursuant to division (A)(1) of this section and on or before July 1, 1989, and shall continue to hold review hearings no later than every twelve months in accordance with division (C) of section 2151.417 of the Revised Code until the child attains the age of eighteen if the child is not mentally or physically handicapped, the child attains the age of twenty-one if the child is mentally or physically handicapped, the child is adopted and a final decree of adoption is issued, or the court otherwise terminates the custody arrangement.

Historical and Statutory Notes

Ed. Note: Per In re Vickers Children, 14 App(3d) 201, 14 OBR 228, 470 NE(2d) 438 (Butler 1983), 2151.414 is in conflict with Juvenile Rule 29 and 34.

Amendment Note: 2000 H 448 substituted "caregivers" for "parents" in division (D)(1); and inserted "this section or" and deleted "2151.414" after "2151.353" in division (E)(11).

Amendment Note: 1999 H 176 rewrote divisions (B)(1)(a), (B)(1)(d), and (D)(3); substituted "(11)" for "(12)" in division (D)(5); and added the final paragraph in division (D). Prior to amendment, divisions (B)(1)(a), (B)(1)(d), and (D)(3) read:

"(a) The child is not abandoned or orphaned or has not been in the temporary custody of a public children services agency or private child placing agency under one or more separate orders of disposition issued under section 2151.353 or 2151.415 of the Revised Code for twelve or more months of a consecutive twenty-two month period ending on or after the effective date of this amendment, and the child cannot be placed with either of the child's parents within a reasonable time or should not be placed with the child's parents."

"(d) The child has been in the temporary custody of a public children services agency or private child placing agency under one or more separate orders of disposition issued under section 2151.353 of the Revised Code for twelve or more months of a consecutive twenty-two month period ending on or after the effective date of this amendment."

"(3) The custodial history of the child, including whether the child has been in the temporary custody of a public children services agency or private child placing agency under one or more separate orders of disposition issued under section 2151.353 or 2151.415 of the Revised Code for twelve or more months of a consecutive twenty-two month period ending on or after the effective date of this amendment;"

Amendment Note: 1998 H 484 rewrote this section, which prior thereto read:

"(A)(1) Upon the filing of a motion pursuant to section 2151.413 of the Revised Code for permanent custody of a child by a public children services agency or private child placing agency that has temporary custody of the child or has placed the child in long-term foster care, the court shall schedule a hearing and give notice of the filing of the motion and of the hearing, in accordance with section

2151.29 of the Revised Code, to all parties to the action and to the child's guardian ad litem. The notice also shall contain a full explanation that the granting of permanent custody permanently divests the parents of their parental rights, a full explanation of their right to be represented by counsel and to have counsel appointed pursuant to Chapter 120. of the Revised Code if they are indigent, and the name and telephone number of the court employee designated by the court pursuant to section 2151.314 of the Revised Code to arrange for the prompt appointment of counsel for indigent persons.

"The court shall conduct a hearing in accordance with section 2151.35 of the Revised Code to determine if it is in the best interest of the child to permanently terminate parental rights and grant permanent custody to the agency that filed the motion. The adjudication that the child is an abused, neglected, or dependent child and the grant of temporary custody to the agency that filed the motion or placement into long-term foster care shall not be readjudicated at the hearing and shall not be affected by a denial of the motion for permanent custody.

"(2) The court shall hold the hearing scheduled pursuant to division (A)(1) of this section not later than one hundred twenty days after the agency files the motion for permanent custody, except that, for good cause shown, the court may continue the hearing for a reasonable period of time beyond the one-hundred-twenty-day deadline. The court shall issue an order that grants, denies, or otherwise disposes of the motion for permanent custody, and journalize the order, not later than two hundred days after the agency files the motion.

"The failure of the court to comply with the time periods set forth in division (A)(2) of this section does not affect the authority of the court to issue any order under this chapter and does not provide any basis for attacking the jurisdiction of the court or the validity of any order of the court.

"(B) The court may grant permanent custody of a child to a movant if the court determines at the hearing held pursuant to division (A) of this section, by clear and convincing evidence, that it is in the best interest of the child to grant permanent custody of the child to the agency that filed the motion for permanent custody and that any of the following apply:

"(1) The child is not abandoned or orphaned and the child cannot be placed with either of the child's parents within a reasonable time or should not be placed with the child's parents;

"(2) The child is abandoned and the parents cannot be located;

"(3) The child is orphaned and there are no relatives of the child who are able to take permanent custody.

"(C) In making the determinations required by this section or division (A)(4) of section 2151.353 of the Revised Code, a court shall not consider the effect the granting of permanent custody to the agency would have upon any parent of the child. A written report of the guardian ad litem of the child shall be submitted to the court prior to or at the time of the hearing held pursuant to division (A) of this section or section 2151.35 of the Revised Code but shall not be submitted under oath.

"If the court grants permanent custody of a child to a movant under this division, the court, upon the request of any party, shall file a written opinion setting forth its findings of fact and conclusions of law in relation to the proceeding. The court shall not deny an agency's motion for permanent custody solely because the agency failed to implement any particular aspect of the child's case plan.

"(D) In determining the best interest of a child at a hearing held pursuant to division (A) of this section or for the purposes of division (A)(4) or (5) of section 2151.353 or division (C) of section 2151.415 of the Revised Code, the court shall consider all relevant factors, including, but not limited to, the following:

"(1) The interaction and interrelationship of the child with the child's parents, siblings, relatives, foster parents and out-of-home providers, and any other person who may significantly affect the child;

"(2) The wishes of the child, as expressed directly by the child or through the child's guardian ad litem, with due regard for the maturity of the child;

"(3) The custodial history of the child;

"(4) The child's need for a legally secure permanent placement and whether that type of placement can be achieved without a grant of permanent custody to the agency.

"(E) In determining at a hearing held pursuant to division (A) of this section or for the purposes of division (A)(4) of section 2151.353 of the Revised Code whether a child cannot be placed with either parent within a reasonable period of time or should not be placed with the parents, the court shall consider all relevant evidence. If the court determines, by clear and convincing evidence, at a hearing held pursuant to division (A) of this section or for the purposes of division (A)(4) of section 2151.353 of the Revised Code that one or more of the following exist as to each of the child's parents, the court shall enter a finding that the child cannot be placed with either parent within a reasonable time or should not be placed with either parent:

"(1) Following the placement of the child outside the child's home and notwithstanding reasonable case planning and diligent efforts by the agency to assist the parents to remedy the problems that initially caused the child to be placed outside the home, the parent has failed continuously and repeatedly to substantially remedy the conditions causing the child to be placed outside the child's home. In determining whether the parents have substantially remedied those conditions, the court shall consider parental utilization of medical, psychiatric, psychological, and other social and rehabilitative services and material resources that were made available to the parents for the purpose of changing parental conduct to allow them to resume and maintain parental duties.

"(2) Chronic mental illness, chronic emotional illness, mental retardation, physical disability, or chemical dependency of the parent that is so severe that it makes the parent unable to provide an adequate permanent home for the child at the present time and, as anticipated, within one year after the court holds the hearing pursuant to division (A) of this section or for the purposes of division (A)(4) of section 2151.353 of the Revised Code;

"(3) The parent committed any abuse as described in section 2151.031 of the Revised Code against the child, caused the child to suffer any neglect as described in section 2151.03 of the Revised Code, or allowed the child to suffer any neglect as described in section 2151.03 of the Revised Code between the date that the original complaint alleging abuse or neglect was filed and the date of the filing of the motion for permanent custody;

"(4) The parent has demonstrated a lack of commitment toward the child by failing to regularly support, visit, or communicate with the child when able to do so, or by other actions showing an unwill-

ingness to provide an adequate permanent home for the child;

"(5) The parent is incarcerated for an offense committed against the child or a sibling of the child;

"(6) The parent violated section 2903.11, 2903.12, 2903.13, 2903.16, 2903.21, 2903.34, 2905.01, 2905.02, 2905.03, 2905.04, 2905.05, 2907.02, 2907.03, 2907.04, 2907.05, 2907.06, 2907.07, 2907.08, 2907.09, 2907.12, 2907.21, 2907.22, 2907.23, 2907.25, 2907.31, 2907.32, 2907.321, 2907.322, 2907.323, 2911.01, 2911.02, 2911.11, 2911.12, 2919.12, 2919.22, 2919.24, 2919.25, 2923.12, 2923.13, 2923.161, 2925.02, or 3716.11 of the Revised Code and the child or a sibling of the child was a victim of the violation or the parent violated section 2903.01, 2903.02, 2903.03, or 2903.04 of the Revised Code, a sibling of the child was the victim of the violation, and the parent who committed the violation poses an ongoing danger to the child or a sibling of the child.

"(7) The parent is incarcerated at the time of the filing of the motion for permanent custody or the dispositional hearing of the child and will not be available to care for the child for at least eighteen months after the filing of the motion for permanent custody or the dispositional hearing;

"(8) The parent is repeatedly incarcerated and the repeated incarceration prevents the parent from providing care for the child;

"(9) The parent for any reason is unwilling to provide food, clothing, shelter, and other basic necessities for the child or to prevent the child from suffering physical, emotional, or sexual abuse or physical, emotional, or mental neglect;

"(10) The parent has committed abuse as described in section 2151.031 of the Revised Code against the child or caused or allowed the child to suffer neglect as described in section 2151.03 of the Revised Code and the court determines that the seriousness, nature, or likelihood of recurrence of the abuse or neglect makes the child's placement with the child's parent a threat to the child's safety;

"(11) The parent committed abuse as described in section 2151.031 of the Revised Code against the child or caused or allowed the child to suffer neglect as described in section 2151.03 of the Revised Code and a sibling of the child previously has been permanently removed from the home of the child's parents because the parent abused or neglected the sibling.

"(12) Any other factor the court considers relevant.

"(F) The parents of a child for whom the court has issued an order granting permanent custody pursuant to this section, upon the issuance of the order, cease to be parties to the action. This division is not intended to eliminate or restrict any right of the parents to appeal the granting of permanent custody of their child to a movant pursuant to this section."

Amendment Note: 1996 H 274 rewrote the first paragraph in division (E); and added division (E)(12). Prior to amendment, the first paragraph in division (E) read:

"(E) In determining at a hearing held pursuant to division (A) of this section or for the purposes of division (A)(4) of section 2151.353 of the Revised Code whether a child cannot be placed with either of the child's parents within a reasonable period of time or should not be placed with the child's parents, the court shall make its findings based upon all relevant evidence, including evidence of the circumstances described in divisions (E)(1) to (11) of this section. If the court determines, by clear and convincing evidence, at a hearing held pursuant to division (A) of this section or for the purposes of division (A)(4) of section 2151.353 of the Revised Code, that the child cannot be placed with either of the child's parents within a reasonable time or should not be placed with the child's parents, the court shall enter a finding to that effect. Factors the court shall consider include the following and any other factor the court considers relevant:"

Amendment Note: 1996 H 419 rewrote this section, which previously read:

"(A) Upon the filing of a motion pursuant to section 2151.413 of the Revised Code for permanent custody of a child by a public children services agency or private child placing agency that has temporary custody of the child, the court shall schedule a hearing and give notice of the filing of the motion and of the hearing, in accordance with section 2151.29 of the Revised Code, to all parties to the action and to the child's guardian ad litem. The notice also shall contain a full explanation that the granting of permanent custody permanently divests the parents of their parental rights, a full explanation of their right to be represented by counsel and to have counsel appointed pursuant to Chapter 120. of the Revised Code if they are indigent, and the name and telephone number of the court employee designated by the court pursuant to section 2151.314 of the Revised Code to arrange for the prompt appointment of counsel for indigent persons. The court shall conduct a hearing in accordance with section 2151.35 of the Revised Code to determine if it is in the best interest of the child to permanently terminate parental rights and grant permanent custody to the agency that filed the motion. The adjudication that the child is an abused, neglected, or dependent child and the grant of temporary custody to the agency that filed the motion shall not be readjudicated at the hearing and shall not be affected by a denial of the motion for permanent custody.

"(B) The court may grant permanent custody of a child to a movant if the court determines at the hearing held pursuant to division (A) of this section, by clear and convincing evidence, that it is in the best interest of the child to grant permanent custody of the child to the agency that filed the motion for permanent custody and that any of the following apply:

"(1) The child is not abandoned or orphaned and the child cannot be placed with either of his parents within a reasonable time or should not be placed with his parents;

"(2) The child is abandoned and the parents cannot be located;

"(3) The child is orphaned and there are no relatives of the child who are able to take permanent custody.

"(C) In making the determinations required by this section or division (A)(4) of section 2151.353 of the Revised Code, a court shall not consider the effect the granting of permanent custody to the agency would have upon any parent of the child. A written report of the guardian ad litem of the child shall be submitted to the court prior to or at the time of the hearing held pursuant to division (A) of this section or section 2151.35 of the Revised Code but shall not be submitted under oath.

"If the court grants permanent custody of a child to a movant under this division, the court, upon the request of any party, shall file a written opinion setting forth its findings of fact and conclusions of law in relation to the proceeding. The court shall not deny an agency's motion for permanent custody solely because the agency failed to implement any particular aspect of the child's case plan.

"(D) In determining the best interest of a child at a hearing held pursuant to division (A) of this section or for the purposes of division (A)(4) of section 2151.353 of the Revised Code, the court shall consider all relevant factors, including, but not limited to, the following:

"(1) The reasonable probability of the child being adopted, whether an adoptive placement would positively benefit the child, and whether a grant of permanent custody would facilitate an adoption;

"(2) The interaction and interrelationship of the child with his parents, siblings, relatives, foster parents and out-of-home providers, and any other person who may significantly affect the child;

"(3) The wishes of the child, as expressed directly by the child or through his guardian ad litem, with due regard for the maturity of the child;

"(4) The custodial history of the child;

"(5) The child's need for a legally secure permanent placement and whether that type of placement can be achieved without a grant of permanent custody to the agency.

"(E) In determining at a hearing held pursuant to division (A) of this section or for the purposes of division (A)(4) of section 2151.353 of the Revised Code whether a child cannot be placed with either of his parents within a reasonable period of time or should not be placed with his parents, the court shall consider all relevant evidence. If the court determines, by clear and convincing evidence, at a hearing held pursuant to division (A) of this section or for the purposes of division (A)(4) of section 2151.353 of the Revised Code that one or more of the following exist as to each of the child's parents, the court shall enter a finding that the child cannot be placed with either of his parents within a reasonable time or should not be placed with his parents:

"(1) Following the placement of the child outside his home and notwithstanding reasonable case planning and diligent efforts by the agency to assist the parents to remedy the problems that initially caused the child to be placed outside the home, the parent has failed continuously and repeatedly for a period of six months or more to substantially remedy the conditions causing the child to be placed outside his home. In determining whether the parents have substantially remedied those conditions, the court shall consider parental utilization of medical, psychiatric, psychological, and other social and rehabilitative services and material resources that were made available to the parents for the purpose of changing parental conduct to allow them to resume and maintain parental duties.

"(2) The severe and chronic mental illness, severe and chronic emotional illness, severe mental retardation, severe physical disability, or chemical dependency of the parent makes the parent unable to provide an adequate permanent home for the child at the present time and in the forseeable future;

"(3) The parent committed any abuse as described in section 2151.031 of the Revised Code against the child, caused the child to suffer any neglect as described in section 2151.03 of the Revised Code, or allowed the child to suffer any neglect as described in section 2151.03 of the Revised Code between the date that the original complaint alleging abuse or neglect was filed and the date of the filing of the motion for permanent custody;

"(4) The parent has demonstrated a lack of commitment toward the child by failing to regularly support, visit, or communicate with the child when able to do so, or by other actions showing an unwillingness to provide an adequate permanent home for the child;

"(5) The parent is incarcerated for an offense committed against the child or a sibling of the child;

"(6) The parent is incarcerated at the time of the filing of the motion for permanent custody or the dispositional hearing of the child and will not be available to care for the child for at least eighteen months after the filing of the motion for permanent custody or the dispositional hearing;

"(7) The parent is repeatedly incarcerated and the repeated incarceration prevents the parent from providing care for the child;

"(8) The parent for any reason is unwilling to provide food, clothing, shelter, and other basic necessities for the child or to prevent the child from suffering physical, emotional, or sexual abuse or physical, emotional, or mental neglect.

"(F) The parents of a child for whom the court has issued an order granting permanent custody pursuant to this section, upon the issuance of the order, cease to be parties to the action. This division is not intended to eliminate or restrict any right of the parents to appeal the granting of permanent custody of their child to a movant pursuant to this section."

Cross References

Adjudicatory hearing, Juv R 29
Dispositional hearing, Juv R 34

Ohio Administrative Code References

Obtaining permanent custody: termination of parental rights, OAC 5101:2–42–95

Library References

Infants ⊕155 to 158, 178 to 181, 198, 203, 222, 226.
Westlaw Topic No. 211.
C.J.S. Infants §§ 31 to 85.
OJur 3d: 47, Family Law § 1107; 48, Family Law § 1612, 1629, 1657, 1663, 1664, 1694, 1711
Right of indigent parent to appointed counsel in proceeding for involuntary termination of parental rights. 80 ALR3d 1141
Baldwin's Ohio Legislative Service, 1988 Laws of Ohio, S 89—LSC Analysis, p 5–571
Carlin, Baldwin's Ohio Practice, Merrick–Rippner Probate Law § 107.10, 107.46, 107.60, 107.72, 107.78, 107.80, 107.81, 107.83, 107.119, 107.120, 107.175 (2003).

2151.415 Motions for dispositional orders; procedure

(A) Except for cases in which a motion for permanent custody described in division (D)(1) of section 2151.413 of the Revised Code is required to be made, a public children services agency or private child placing agency that has been given temporary custody of a child pursuant to section 2151.353 of the Revised Code, not later than thirty days prior to the earlier of the date for the termination of the custody order pursuant to division (F) of section 2151.353 of the Revised Code or the date set at the dispositional hearing for the hearing to be held pursuant to this section, shall file a motion with the court that issued the order of disposition requesting that any of the fol-

lowing orders of disposition of the child be issued by the court:

(1) An order that the child be returned home and the custody of the child's parents, guardian, or custodian without any restrictions;

(2) An order for protective supervision;

(3) An order that the child be placed in the legal custody of a relative or other interested individual;

(4) An order permanently terminating the parental rights of the child's parents;

(5) An order that the child be placed in a planned permanent living arrangement;

(6) In accordance with division (D) of this section, an order for the extension of temporary custody.

(B) Upon the filing of a motion pursuant to division (A) of this section, the court shall hold a dispositional hearing on the date set at the dispositional hearing held pursuant to section 2151.35 of the Revised Code, with notice to all parties to the action in accordance with the Juvenile Rules. After the dispositional hearing or at a date after the dispositional hearing that is not later than one year after the earlier of the date on which the complaint in the case was filed or the child was first placed into shelter care, the court, in accordance with the best interest of the child as supported by the evidence presented at the dispositional hearing, shall issue an order of disposition as set forth in division (A) of this section, except that all orders for permanent custody shall be made in accordance with sections 2151.413 and 2151.414 of the Revised Code. In issuing an order of disposition under this section, the court shall comply with section 2151.42 of the Revised Code.

(C)(1) If an agency pursuant to division (A) of this section requests the court to place a child into a planned permanent living arrangement, the agency shall present evidence to indicate why a planned permanent living arrangement is appropriate for the child, including, but not limited to, evidence that the agency has tried or considered all other possible dispositions for the child. A court shall not place a child in a planned permanent living arrangement, unless it finds, by clear and convincing evidence, that a planned permanent living arrangement is in the best interest of the child and that one of the following exists:

(a) The child, because of physical, mental, or psychological problems or needs, is unable to function in a family-like setting and must remain in residential or institutional care.

(b) The parents of the child have significant physical, mental, or psychological problems and are unable to care for the child because of those problems, adoption is not in the best interest of the child, as determined in accordance with division (D) of section 2151.414 of the Revised Code, and the child retains a significant and positive relationship with a parent or relative;

(c) The child is sixteen years of age or older, has been counseled on the permanent placement options available, is unwilling to accept or unable to adapt to a permanent placement, and is in an agency program preparing for independent living.

(2) If the court issues an order placing a child in a planned permanent living arrangement, both of the following apply:

(a) The court shall issue a finding of fact setting forth the reasons for its finding;

(b) The agency may make any appropriate placement for the child and shall develop a case plan for the child that is designed to assist the child in finding a permanent home outside of the home of the parents.

(D)(1) If an agency pursuant to division (A) of this section requests the court to grant an extension of temporary custody for a period of up to six months, the agency shall include in the motion an explanation of the progress on the case plan of the child and of its expectations of reunifying the child with the child's family, or placing the child in a permanent placement, within the extension period. The court shall schedule a hearing on the motion, give notice of its date, time, and location to all parties and the guardian ad litem of the child, and at the hearing consider the evidence presented by the parties and the guardian ad litem. The court may extend the temporary custody order of the child for a period of up to six months, if it determines at the hearing, by clear and convincing evidence, that the extension is in the best interest of the child, there has been significant progress on the case plan of the child, and there is reasonable cause to believe that the child will be reunified with one of the parents or otherwise per-manently placed within the period of extension. In determining whether to extend the temporary custody of the child pursuant to this division, the court shall comply with section 2151.42 of the Revised Code. If the court extends the temporary custody of the child pursuant to this division, upon request it shall issue findings of fact.

(2) Prior to the end of the extension granted pursuant to division (D)(1) of this section, the agency that received the extension shall file a motion with the court requesting the issuance of one of the orders of disposition set forth in divisions (A)(1) to (5) of this section or requesting the court to extend the temporary custody order of the child for an additional period of up to six months. If the agency requests the issuance of an order of disposition under divisions (A)(1) to (5) of this section or does not file any motion prior to the expiration of the extension period, the court shall conduct a hearing in accordance with division (B) of this section and issue an appropriate order of disposition. In issuing an order of disposition, the court shall comply with section 2151.42 of the Revised Code.

If the agency requests an additional extension of up to six months of the temporary custody order of the child, the court shall schedule and conduct a hearing in the manner set forth in division (D)(1) of this section. The court may extend the temporary custody order of the child for an additional period of up to six months if it determines at the hearing, by clear and convincing evidence, that the additional extension is in the best interest of the child, there has been substantial additional progress since the original extension of temporary custody in the case plan of the child, there has been substantial additional progress since the original extension of temporary custody toward reunifying the child with one of the parents or otherwise permanently placing the child, and there is reasonable cause to believe that the child will be reunified with one of the parents or otherwise placed in a permanent setting before the expiration of the additional extension period. In determining whether to grant an additional extension, the court shall comply with section 2151.42 of the Revised Code. If the court extends the temporary custody of the child for an additional period pursuant to this division, upon request it shall issue findings of fact.

(3) Prior to the end of the extension of a temporary custody order granted pursuant to division (D)(2) of this section, the agency that received the extension shall file a motion with the court requesting the issuance of one of the orders of disposition set forth in divisions (A)(1) to (5) of this section. Upon the filing of the motion by the agency or, if the agency does not file the motion prior to the expiration of the extension period, upon its own motion, the court, prior to the expiration of the extension period, shall conduct a hearing in accordance with division (B) of this section and issue an appropriate order of disposition. In issuing an order of disposition, the court shall comply with section 2151.42 of the Revised Code.

(4) No court shall grant an agency more than two extensions of temporary custody pursuant to division (D) of this section.

(E) After the issuance of an order pursuant to division (B) of this section, the court shall retain jurisdiction over the child until the child attains the age of eighteen if the child is not mentally retarded, developmentally disabled, or physically impaired, the child attains the age of twenty-one if the child is mentally retarded, developmentally disabled, or physically impaired, or the child is adopted and a final decree of adoption is issued, unless the court's jurisdiction over the child is extended pursuant to division (E) of section 2151.353 of the Revised Code.

(F) The court, on its own motion or the motion of the agency or person with legal custody of the child, the child's guardian ad litem, or any other party to the action, may conduct a hearing with notice to all parties to determine whether any order issued pursuant to this section should be modified or terminated or whether any other dispositional order set forth in divisions (A)(1) to (5) of this section should be issued. After the hearing and consideration of all the evidence presented, the court, in accordance with the best interest of the child, may modify or terminate any order issued pursuant to this section or issue any dispositional order set forth in divisions (A)(1) to (5) of this section. In rendering a decision under this division, the court shall comply with section 2151.42 of the Revised Code.

(G) If the court places a child in a planned permanent living arrangement with a public children services agency or a private child placing agency pursuant to this section, the agency with which the child is placed in a planned permanent living arrangement shall not remove the child from the residential placement in which the child is originally placed pursuant to the case plan for the child or in which the child is placed with court approval pursuant to this division, unless the court and the guardian ad litem are given notice of the intended removal and the court issues an order approving the removal or unless the removal is necessary to protect the child from physical or emotional harm and the agency gives the court notice of the removal and of the reasons why the removal is necessary to protect the child from physical or emotional harm immediately after the removal of the child from the prior setting.

(H) If the hearing held under this section takes the place of an administrative review that otherwise would have been held under section 2151.416 of the Revised Code, the court at the hearing held under this section shall do all of the following in addition to any other requirements of this section:

(1) Determine the continued necessity for and the appropriateness of the child's placement;

(2) Determine the extent of compliance with the child's case plan;

(3) Determine the extent of progress that has been made toward alleviating or mitigating the causes necessitating the child's placement in foster care;

(4) Project a likely date by which the child may be returned to the child's home or placed for adoption or legal guardianship;

(5) Approve the permanency plan for the child consistent with section 2151.417 of the Revised Code.

(1999 H 176, eff. 10–29–99; 1998 H 484, eff. 3–18–99; 1996 H 274, eff. 8–8–96; 1988 S 89, eff. 1–1–89)

Historical and Statutory Notes

Amendment Note: 1999 H 176 substituted "a planned permanent living arrangement" for "long-term foster care" in the first paragraph in division (C)(2).

Amendment Note: 1998 H 484 inserted "Except for cases in which a motion for permanent custody described in division (D)(1) of section 2151.413 of the Revised Code is required to be made," in the first paragraph in division (A); substituted "a planned permanent living arrangement" for "long-term foster care" throughout divisions (A)(5), (C)(1), and (G);

added the third sentence in division (B); added the fourth sentence in division (D)(1); added the third sentence in the first paragraph in division (D)(2); added the third sentence in the second paragraph in division (D)(2); added the third sentence in division (D)(3); added the third sentence in division (F); substituted "Approve the permanency plan for the child consistent with section 2151.417 of the Revised Code" for "Determine the future status of the child" in division (H)(5); and made changes to reflect gender neutral language and other nonsubstantive changes.

Amendment Note: 1996 H 274 substituted "retarded, developmentally disabled, or physically impaired" for "or physically handicapped" twice in division (E); and made changes to reflect gender neutral language.

Library References

Infants ☞221, 222, 226, 231.

Westlaw Topic No. 211.

C.J.S. Infants §§ 57, 69 to 85.

OJur 3d: 48, Family Law § 1602, 1632, 1679, 1681, 1701, 1706

Am Jur 2d: 47, Juvenile Courts and Delinquent and Dependent Children § 29, 30, 55

Baldwin's Ohio Legislative Service, 1988 Laws of Ohio, S 89—LSC Analysis, p 5–571

Carlin, Baldwin's Ohio Practice, Merrick–Rippner Probate Law § 107.78, 107.79, 107.82, 107.118, 107.119, 107.120 (2003).

2151.416 Administrative review of case plans

(A) Each agency that is required by section 2151.412 of the Revised Code to prepare a case plan for a child shall complete a semiannual administrative review of the case plan no later than six months after the earlier of the date on which the complaint in the case was filed or the child was first placed in shelter care. After the first administrative review, the agency shall complete semiannual administrative reviews no later than every six months. If the court issues an order pursuant to section 2151.414 or 2151.415 of the Revised Code, the agency shall complete an administrative review no later than six months after the court's order and continue to complete administrative reviews no later than every six months after the first review, except that the court hearing held pursuant to section 2151.417 of the Revised Code may take the place of any administrative review that would otherwise be held at the time of the court hearing. When conducting a review, the child's health and safety shall be the paramount concern.

(B) Each administrative review required by division (A) of this section shall be conducted by a review panel of at least three persons, including, but not limited to, both of the following:

(1) A caseworker with day-to-day responsibility for, or familiarity with, the management of the child's case plan;

(2) A person who is not responsible for the management of the child's case plan or for the delivery of services to the child or the parents, guardian, or custodian of the child.

(C) Each semiannual administrative review shall include, but not be limited to, a joint meeting by the review panel with the parents, guardian, or custodian of the child, the guardian ad litem of the child, and the child's foster care provider and shall include an opportunity for those persons to submit any written materials to be included in the case record of the child. If a parent, guardian, custodian, guardian ad litem, or foster care provider of the child cannot be located after reasonable efforts to do so or declines to participate in the administrative review after being contacted, the agency does not have to include them in the joint meeting.

(D) The agency shall prepare a written summary of the semiannual administrative review that shall include, but not be limited to, all of the following:

(1) A conclusion regarding the safety and appropriateness of the child's foster care placement;

(2) The extent of the compliance with the case plan of all parties;

(3) The extent of progress that has been made toward alleviating the circumstances that required the agency to assume temporary custody of the child;

(4) An estimated date by which the child may be returned to and safely maintained in the child's home or placed for adoption or legal custody;

(5) An updated case plan that includes any changes that the agency is proposing in the case plan;

(6) The recommendation of the agency as to which agency or person should be given custodial rights over the child for the six-month period after the administrative review;

(7) The names of all persons who participated in the administrative review.

(E) The agency shall file the summary with the court no later than seven days after the completion of the administrative review. If the agency proposes a change to the case plan as a result of the administrative review, the agency shall file the proposed change with the court at the time it files the summary. The agency shall give notice of the summary and proposed change in writing before the end of the next day after filing them to all parties and the child's guardian ad litem. All parties and the guardian ad litem shall have seven days after the date the notice is sent to object to and request a hearing on the proposed change.

(1) If the court receives a timely request for a hearing, the court shall schedule a hearing pursuant to section 2151.417 of the Revised Code to be held not later than thirty days after the court receives the request. The court shall give notice of the date, time, and location of the hearing to all parties and the guardian ad litem. The agency may implement the proposed change after the hearing, if the court approves it. The agency shall not implement the proposed change unless it is approved by the court.

(2) If the court does not receive a timely request for a hearing, the court may approve the proposed change without a hearing. If the court approves the proposed change without a hearing, it shall journalize the case plan with the change not later than fourteen days after the change is filed with the court. If the court does not approve the proposed change to the case plan, it shall schedule a review hearing to be held pursuant to section 2151.417 of the Revised Code no later than thirty days after the expiration of the fourteen-day time period and give notice of the date, time, and location of the hearing to all parties and the guardian ad litem of the child. If, despite the requirements of this division and division (D) of section 2151.417 of the Revised Code, the court neither approves and journalizes the proposed change nor conducts a hearing, the agency may implement the proposed change not earlier than fifteen days after it is submitted to the court.

(F) The director of job and family services may adopt rules pursuant to Chapter 119. of the Revised Code for procedures and standard forms for conducting administrative reviews pursuant to this section.

(G) The juvenile court that receives the written summary of the administrative review, upon determining, either from the written summary, case plan, or otherwise, that the custody or care arrangement is not in the best interest of the child, may terminate the custody of an agency and place the child in the custody of another institution or association certified by the department of job and family services under section 5103.03 of the Revised Code.

(H) The department of job and family services shall report annually to the public and to the general assembly on the results of the review of case plans of each agency and on the results of the summaries submitted to the department under section 3107.10 of the Revised Code. The annual report shall include any information that is required by the department, including, but not limited to, all of the following:

(1) A statistical analysis of the administrative reviews conducted pursuant to this section and section 2151.417 of the Revised Code;

(2) The number of children in temporary or permanent custody for whom an administrative review was conducted, the number of children whose custody status changed during the period, the number of children whose residential placement changed during the period, and the number of residential placement changes for each child during the period;

(3) An analysis of the utilization of public social services by agencies and parents or guardians, and the utilization of the adoption listing service of the department pursuant to section 5103.154 of the Revised Code;

(4) A compilation and analysis of data submitted to the department under section 3107.10 of the Revised Code.

(1999 H 471, eff. 7–1–00; 1998 H 484, eff. 3–18–99; 1996 H 274, eff. 8–8–96; 1996 H 419, eff. 9–18–96; 1988 S 89, eff. 1–1–89)

Uncodified Law

1988 S 89, § 4: See Uncodified Law under 2151.414.

Historical and Statutory Notes

Ed. Note: 2151.416 is former 5103.151 amended and recodified by 1988 S 89, eff. 1–1–89; 1986 H 428; 1980 H 695; 1978 H 832; 1976 H 156.

Amendment Note: 1999 H 471 substituted "director of job and family services" for "department of human services" in division (F); and substituted "job and family" for "human" in divisions (G) and (H).

Amendment Note: 1998 H 484 added the fourth sentence in division (A); inserted "safety and" in division (D)(1); and inserted "and safely maintained in" in division (D)(4).

Amendment Note: 1996 H 274 rewrote division (E), which prior thereto read:

"(E)(1) If the agency, the parents, guardian, or custodian of the child, and the guardian ad litem and the attorney of the child agree to the need for changes in the case plan of the child and the terms of the changes, the revised case plan shall be signed by all parties and the guardian ad litem of the child and filed with the court together with the written summary of the administrative review no later than seven days after the completion of the administrative review. If the court does not object to the revised case plan, it shall journalize the case plan, within fourteen days after it is filed with the court. The agency may implement the proposed changes fourteen days after they are submitted to the court for approval, unless the court schedules a hearing under section 2151.417 of the Revised Code to consider the proposed changes. If the court does not approve of the revised case plan, it shall schedule a review hearing to be held pursuant to section 2151.417 of the Revised Code no later than thirty days after the filing of the case plan and written summary and give notice of the date, time, and location of the hearing to all parties and the guardian ad litem of the child.

"(2) If the agency, the parents, guardian, or custodian of the child, and the guardian ad litem and the attorney of the child do not agree to the need for changes to the case plan and to all of the proposed changes, the agency shall file its written summary of the administrative review with the court no later than seven days after the completion of the administrative review and request the court to conduct a review hearing pursuant to section 2151.417 of the Revised Code. The court shall schedule the hearing to be held no later than thirty days after the written summary was filed with the court and shall give notice of the date, time, and location of the hearing to all parties and the guardian ad litem of the child."

Amendment Note: 1996 H 419 substituted "the child's" for "his" in division (D)(4); substituted "institution or association certified by the department of human services under section 5103.03 of the Revised Code." for "public or private organization, society, association, agency, or individual certified pursuant to sections 5103.02 and 5103.03 of the Revised Code." in division (G); and substituted "5103.154" for "5103.152" in division (H)(3).

Ohio Administrative Code References

Requirements of semiannual administrative review, OAC 5101:2–42–43

Library References

Infants ⊕17, 226, 230.1.
Westlaw Topic No. 211.
C.J.S. Infants §§ 8, 9, 57, 70 to 84.
OJur 3d: 48, Family Law § 1429, 1602, 1633, 1711
Am Jur 2d: 47, Juvenile Courts and Delinquent and Dependent Children § 33
Baldwin's Ohio Legislative Service, 1996 H 274—LSC Analysis, p 5/L–697
Baldwin's Ohio Legislative Service, 1988 Laws of Ohio, S 89—LSC Analysis, p 5–571
Carlin, Baldwin's Ohio Practice, Merrick–Rippner Probate Law § 98.16, 98.17, 98.18, 98.19, 107.119 (2003).

2151.417 Review by court issuing dispositional orders

(A) Any court that issues a dispositional order pursuant to section 2151.353, 2151.414, or 2151.415 of the Revised Code may review at any time the child's placement or custody arrangement, the case plan prepared for the child pursuant to section 2151.412 of the Revised Code, the actions of the public children services agency or private child placing agency in implementing that case plan, the child's permanency plan, if the child's permanency plan has been approved and any other aspects of the child's placement or custody arrangement. In conducting the review, the court shall determine the appropriateness of any agency actions, the safety and appropriateness of continuing the child's placement or custody arrangement, and whether any changes should be made with respect to the child's permanency plan or placement or custody arrangement or with respect to the actions of the agency under the child's placement or custody arrangement. Based upon the evidence presented at a hearing held after notice to all parties and the guardian ad litem of the child, the court may require the agency, the parents, guardian, or custodian of the child, and the physical custodians of the child to take any reasonable action that the court determines is necessary and in the best interest of the child or to discontinue any action that it determines is not in the best interest of the child.

(B) If a court issues a dispositional order pursuant to section 2151.353, 2151.414, or 2151.415 of the Revised Code, the court has continuing jurisdiction over the child as set forth in division (E)(1) of section 2151.353 of the Revised Code. The court may amend a dispositional order in accordance with division (E)(2) of section 2151.353 of the Revised Code at any time upon its own motion or upon the motion of any interested party. The court shall comply with section 2151.42 of the Revised Code in amending any dispositional order pursuant to this division.

(C) Any court that issues a dispositional order pursuant to section 2151.353, 2151.414, or 2151.415 of the Revised Code shall hold a review hearing one year after the earlier of the date on which the complaint in the case was filed or the child was first placed into shelter care to review the case plan prepared pursuant to section 2151.412 of the Revised Code and the child's placement or custody arrangement, to approve or review the permanency plan for the child, and to make changes to the case plan and placement or custody arrangement consistent with the permanency plan. The court shall schedule the review hearing at the time that it holds the dispositional hearing pursuant to section 2151.35 of the Revised Code.

The court shall hold a similar review hearing no later than every twelve months after the initial review hearing until the child is adopted, returned to the parents, or the court otherwise terminates the child's placement or custody arrangement, except that the dispositional hearing held pursuant to section 2151.415 of the Revised Code shall take the place of the first review hearing to be held under this section. The court shall schedule each subsequent review hearing at the conclusion of the review hearing immediately preceding the review hearing to be scheduled.

(D) If, within fourteen days after a written summary of an administrative review is filed with the court pursuant to section 2151.416 of the Revised Code, the court does not approve the proposed change to the case plan filed pursuant to division (E) of section 2151.416 of the Revised Code or a party or the guardian ad litem requests a review hearing pursuant to division (E) of that section, the court shall hold a review hearing in the same manner that it holds review hearings pursuant to division (C) of this section, except that if a review hearing is required by this division and if a hearing is to be held pursuant to division (C) of this section or section 2151.415 of the Revised Code, the hearing held pursuant to division (C) of this section or section 2151.415 of the Revised Code shall take the place of the review hearing required by this division.

(E) If a court determines pursuant to section 2151.419 of the Revised Code that a public children services agency or private child placing agency is not required to make reasonable efforts to prevent the removal of a child from the child's home, eliminate the continued removal of a child from the child's home, and return the child to the child's home, and the court does not return the child to the child's home pursuant to division (A)(3) of section 2151.419 of the Revised Code, the court shall hold a review hearing to approve the permanency plan for the child and, if appropriate, to make changes to the child's case plan and the child's placement or custody arrangement consistent with the permanency plan. The court may hold the hearing immediately following the determination under section 2151.419 of the Revised

Code and shall hold it no later than thirty days after making that determination.

(F) The court shall give notice of the review hearings held pursuant to this section to every interested party, including, but not limited to, the appropriate agency employees who are responsible for the child's care and planning, the child's parents, any person who had guardianship or legal custody of the child prior to the custody order, the child's guardian ad litem, and the child. The court shall summon every interested party to appear at the review hearing and give them an opportunity to testify and to present other evidence with respect to the child's custody arrangement, including, but not limited to, the following: the case plan for the child the *[sic]* permanency plan, if one exists; the actions taken by the child's custodian; the need for a change in the child's custodian or caseworker; and the need for any specific action to be taken with respect to the child. The court shall require any interested party to testify or present other evidence when necessary to a proper determination of the issues presented at the review hearing.

(G) After the review hearing, the court shall take the following actions based upon the evidence presented:

(1) If an administrative review has been conducted, determine whether the conclusions of the review are supported by a preponderance of the evidence and approve or modify the case plan based upon that evidence;

(2) If the hearing was held under division (C) or (E) of this section, approve a permanency plan for the child that specifies whether and, if applicable, when the child will be safely returned home or placed for adoption, for legal custody, or in a planned permanent living arrangement. a permanency plan approved after a hearing under division (E) of this section shall not include any provision requiring the child to be returned to the child's home.

(3) If the child is in temporary custody, do all of the following:

(a) Determine whether the child can and should be returned home with or without an order for protective supervision;

(b) If the child can and should be returned home with or without an order for protective supervision, terminate the order for temporary custody;

(c) If the child cannot or should not be returned home with an order for protective supervision, determine whether the agency currently with custody of the child should retain custody or whether another public children services agency, private child placing agency, or an individual should be given custody of the child.

The court shall comply with section 2151.42 of the Revised Code in taking any action under this division.

(4) If the child is in permanent custody, determine what actions are required by the custodial agency and of any other organizations or persons in order to facilitate an adoption of the child and make any appropriate orders with respect to the custody arrangement or conditions of the child, including, but not limited to, a transfer of permanent custody to another public children services agency or private child placing agency;

(5) Journalize the terms of the updated case plan for the child.

(H) The court may appoint a referee or a citizens review board to conduct the review hearings that the court is required by this section to conduct, subject to the review and approval by the court of any determinations made by the referee or citizens review board. If the court appoints a citizens review board to conduct the review hearings, the board shall consist of one member representing the general public and four members who are trained or experienced in the care or placement of children and have training or experience in the fields of medicine, psychology, social work, education, or any related field. Of the initial appointments to the board, two shall be for a term of one year, two shall be for a term of two years, and one shall be for a term of three years, with all the terms ending one year after the date on which the appointment was made. Thereafter, all terms of the board members shall be for three years and shall end on the same day of the same month of the year as did the term that they succeed. Any member appointed to fill a vacancy occurring prior to the expiration of the term for which the member's predecessor was appointed shall hold office for the remainder of the term.

(I) A copy of the court's determination following any review hearing held pursuant to this section shall be sent to the custodial agency, the guardian ad litem of the child who is the subject of the review hearing, and, if that child is not the subject of a permanent commitment hearing, the parents of the child.

(J) If the hearing held under this section takes the place of an administrative review that otherwise would have been held under section 2151.416 of the Revised Code, the court at the hearing held under this section shall do all of the following in addition to any other requirements of this section:

(1) Determine the continued necessity for and the safety and appropriateness of the child's placement;

(2) Determine the extent of compliance with the child's case plan;

(3) Determine the extent of progress that has been made toward alleviating or mitigating the causes necessitating the child's placement in foster care;

(4) Project a likely date by which the child may be safely returned home or placed for adoption or legal custody.

(K)(1) Whenever the court is required to approve a permanency plan under this section or section 2151.415 of the Revised Code, the public children services agency or private child placing agency that filed the complaint in the case, has custody of the child, or will be given custody of the child shall develop a permanency plan for the child. The agency must file the plan with the court prior to the hearing under this section or section 2151.415 of the Revised Code.

(2) The permanency plan developed by the agency must specify whether and, if applicable, when the child will be safely returned home or placed for adoption or legal custody. If the agency determines that there is a compelling reason why returning the child home or placing the child for adoption or legal custody is not in the best interest of the child, the plan shall provide that the child will be placed in a planned permanent living arrangement. A permanency plan developed as a result of a determination made under division (A)(2) of section 2151.419 of the Revised Code may not include any provision requiring the child to be returned home.

(1998 H 484, eff. 3–18–99; 1996 H 274, eff. 8–8–96; 1988 S 89, eff. 1–1–89)

Uncodified Law

1988 S 89, § 4: See Uncodified Law under 2151.414.

Historical and Statutory Notes

Amendment Note: 1998 H 484 rewrote this section, which prior thereto read:

"(A) Any court that issues a dispositional order pursuant to section 2151.353, 2151.414, or 2151.415 of the Revised Code may review at any time the child's placement or custody arrangement, the case plan prepared for the child pursuant to section 2151.412 of the Revised Code, the actions of the public children services agency or private child placing agency in implementing that case plan, and any other aspects of the child's placement or custody arrangement. In conducting the review, the court shall determine the appropriateness of any agency actions, the appropriateness of continuing the child's placement or custody arrangement, and whether any changes should be made with respect to the child's placement or custody arrangement or with respect to the actions of the agency under the child's placement or custody arrangement. Based upon the evidence presented at a hearing held after notice to all parties and the guardian ad litem of the child, the court may require the agency, the parents, guardian, or custodian of the child, and the physical custodians of the child to take any reasonable action that the court determines is necessary and in the best interest of the child or to discontinue any action that it determines is not in the best interest of the child.

"(B) If a court issues a dispositional order pursuant to section 2151.353, 2151.414, or 2151.415 of the Revised Code, the court has continuing jurisdiction over the child as set forth in division (E)(1) of section 2151.353 of the Revised Code. The court may amend a dispositional order in accordance with division (E)(2) of section 2151.353 of the Revised Code at any time upon its own motion or upon the motion of any interested party.

"(C) Any court that issues a dispositional order pursuant to section 2151.353, 2151.414, or 2151.415 of the Revised Code shall hold a review hearing one year after the earlier of the date on which the complaint in the case was filed or the child was first placed into shelter care to review the case plan prepared pursuant to section 2151.412 of the Revised Code and to review the child's placement or custody arrangement. The court shall schedule the review hearing at the time that it holds the dispositional hearing pursuant to section 2151.35 of the Revised Code.

"The court shall hold a similar review hearing no later than every twelve months after the initial review hearing until the child is adopted, returned to the parents, or the court otherwise terminates the child's placement or custody arrangement, except that the dispositional hearing held pursuant to section 2151.415 of the Revised Code shall take the place of the first review hearing to be held under this section. The court shall schedule each subsequent review hearing at the conclusion of the review hearing immediately preceding the review hearing to be scheduled.

"(D) If, within fourteen days after a written summary of an administrative review is filed with the court pursuant to section 2151.416 of the Revised Code, the court does not approve the proposed change to the case plan filed pursuant to division (E) of section 2151.416 of the Revised Code or a party or the guardian ad litem requests a review hearing pursuant to division (E) of that section, the court shall hold a review hearing in the same manner that it holds review hearings pursuant to division (C) of this section, except that if a review hearing is required by this division and if a hearing is to be held pursuant to division (C) of this section or section 2151.415 of the Revised Code, the hearing held pursuant to division (C) of this section or section 2151.415 of the Revised Code shall take the place of the review hearing required by this division.

"(E) The court shall give notice of the review hearings held pursuant to this section to every interested party, including, but not limited to, the appropriate agency employees who are responsible for the child's care and planning, the child's parents, any person who had guardianship or legal custody of the child prior to the custody order, the child's guardian ad litem, and the child. The court shall summon every interested party to appear at the review hearing and give them an opportunity to testify and to present other evidence with respect to the child's custody arrangement, including, but not limited to, the case plan for the child, the actions taken by the child's custodian, the need for a change in the child's custodian or caseworker, or the need for any specific action to be taken with respect to the child. The court shall require any interested party to testify or present other evidence when necessary to a proper determination of the issues presented at the review hearing.

"(F) After the review hearing, the court shall take the following actions based upon the evidence presented:

"(1) Determine whether the conclusions of the administrative review are supported by a preponderance of the evidence and approve or modify the case plan based upon that evidence;

"(2) If the child is in temporary custody, do all of the following:

"(a) Determine whether the child can and should be returned home with or without an order for protective supervision;

"(b) If the child can and should be returned home with or without an order for protective supervision, terminate the order for temporary custody;

"(c) If the child cannot or should not be returned home with an order for protective supervision, determine whether the agency currently with custody of the child should retain custody or whether another public children services agency, private child placing agency, or an individual should be given custody of the child.

"(3) If the child is in permanent custody, determine what actions are required by the custodial agency and of any other organizations or persons in order to facilitate an adoption of the child and make any appropriate orders with respect to the custody arrangement or conditions of the child, including, but not limited to, a transfer of permanent custody to another public children services agency or private child placing agency;

"(4) Journalize the terms of the updated case plan for the child.

"(G) The court may appoint a referee or a citizens review board to conduct the review hearings that the court is required by this section to conduct, subject to the review and approval by the court of any determinations made by the referee or citizens review board. If the court appoints a citizens review board to conduct the review hearings, the board shall consist of one member representing the general public and four members who are trained or experienced in the care or placement of children and have training or experience in the fields of medicine, psychology, social work, education, or any related field. Of the initial appointments to the board, two shall be for a term of one year, two shall be for a term of two years, and one shall be for a term of three years, with all the terms ending one year after the date on which the appointment was made. Thereafter, all terms of the board members shall be for three years and shall end on the same day of the same month of the year as did the term that they succeed. Any member appointed to fill a vacancy occurring prior to the expiration of the term for which the member's predecessor was appointed shall hold office for the remainder of the term.

"(H) A copy of the court's determination following any review hearing held pursuant to this section shall be sent to the custodial agency, the guardian ad litem of the child who is the subject of the review hearing, and, if that child is not the subject of a permanent commitment hearing, the parents of the child.

"(I) If the hearing held under this section takes the place of an administrative review that otherwise would have been held under section 2151.416 of the Revised Code, the court at the hearing held under this section shall do all of the following in addition to any other requirements of this section:

"(1) Determine the continued necessity for and the appropriateness of the child's placement;

"(2) Determine the extent of compliance with the child's case plan;

"(3) Determine the extent of progress that has been made toward alleviating or mitigating the causes necessitating the child's placement in foster care;

"(4) Project a likely date by which the child may be returned home or placed for adoption or legal guardianship;

"(5) Determine the future status of the child."

Amendment Note: 1996 H 274 substituted "proposed change to the case plan filed pursuant to division (E) of section 2151.416 of the Revised Code or a party or the guardian ad litem requests a review hearing pursuant to division (E) of that section" for "revised case plan filed pursuant to division (E)(1) of section 2151.416 of the Revised Code or the agency requests a review hearing pursuant to division (E)(2) of section 2151.416 of the Revised Code" in division (D); and made changes to reflect gender neutral language.

Cross References

Public children services agencies, powers and duties, 5153.16

Library References

Infants ⬦226, 230.1.

Westlaw Topic No. 211.

C.J.S. Infants §§ 57, 70 to 84.

OJur 3d: 48, Family Law § 1711

Am Jur 2d: 47, Juvenile Courts and Delinquent and Dependent Children § 57, 60, 62

Baldwin's Ohio Legislative Service, 1988 Laws of Ohio, S 89—LSC Analysis, p 5–571

Carlin, Baldwin's Ohio Practice, Merrick–Rippner Probate Law § 107.74, 107.118, 107.119, 107.120, 107.174, 107.175, 107.176 (2003).

2151.419 Hearings on efforts of agencies to prevent removal of children from homes

(A)(1) Except as provided in division (A)(2) of this section, at any hearing held pursuant to section 2151.28, division (E) of section 2151.31, or section 2151.314, 2151.33, or 2151.353 of the Revised Code at which the court removes a child from the child's home or continues the removal of a child from the child's home, the court shall determine whether the public children services agency or private child placing agency that filed the complaint in the case, removed the child from home, has custody of the child, or will be given custody of the child has made reasonable efforts to prevent the removal of the child from the child's home, to eliminate the continued removal of the child from the child's home, or to make it possible for the child to return safely home. The agency shall have the burden of proving that it has made those reasonable efforts. If the agency removed the child from home during an emergency in which the child could not safely remain at home and the agency did not have prior contact with the child, the court is not prohibited, solely because the agency did not make reasonable efforts during the emergency to prevent the removal of the child, from determining that the agency made those reasonable efforts. In determining whether reasonable efforts were made, the child's health and safety shall be paramount.

(2) If any of the following apply, the court shall make a determination that the agency is not required to make reasonable efforts to prevent the removal of the child from the child's home, eliminate the continued removal of the child from the child's home, and return the child to the child's home:

(a) The parent from whom the child was removed has been convicted of or pleaded guilty to one of the following:

(i) An offense under section 2903.01, 2903.02, or 2903.03 of the Revised Code or under an existing or former law of this state, any other state, or the United States that is substantially equivalent to an offense described in those sections and the victim of the offense was a sibling of the child or the victim was another child who lived in the parent's household at the time of the offense;

(ii) An offense under section 2903.11, 2903.12, or 2903.13 of the Revised Code or under an existing or former law of this state, any other state, or the United States that is substantially equivalent to an offense described in those sections and the victim of the offense is the child, a sibling of the child, or another child who lived in the parent's household at the time of the offense;

(iii) An offense under division (B)(2) of section 2919.22 of the Revised Code or under an existing or former law of this state, any other state, or the United States that is substantially equivalent to the offense described in that section and the child, a sibling of the child, or another child who lived in the parent's household at the time of the offense is the victim of the offense;

(iv) An offense under section 2907.02, 2907.03, 2907.04, 2907.05, or 2907.06 of the Revised Code or under an existing or former law of this state, any other state, or the United States that is substantially equivalent to an offense described in those sections and the victim of the offense is the child, a sibling of the child, or another child who lived in the parent's household at the time of the offense;

(v) A conspiracy or attempt to commit, or complicity in committing, an offense described in division (A)(2)(a)(i) or (iv) of this section.

(b) The parent from whom the child was removed has repeatedly withheld medical treatment or food from the child when the parent has the means to provide the treatment or food. If the parent has withheld medical treatment in order to treat the physical or mental illness or defect of the child by spiritual means through prayer alone, in accordance with the tenets of a recognized religious body, the court or agency shall comply with the requirements of division (A)(1) of this section.

(c) The parent from whom the child was removed has placed the child at substantial risk of harm two or more times due to alcohol or drug abuse and has rejected treatment two or more times or refused to participate in further treatment two or more times after a case plan issued pursuant to section 2151.412 of the Revised Code requiring treatment of the parent was journalized as part of a dispositional order issued with respect to the child or an order was issued by any other court requiring such treatment of the parent.

(d) The parent from whom the child was removed has abandoned the child.

(e) The parent from whom the child was removed has had parental rights involuntarily terminated pursuant to section 2151.353, 2151.414, or 2151.415 of the Revised Code with respect to a sibling of the child.

(3) At any hearing in which the court determines whether to return a child to the child's home, the court may issue an order that returns the child in situations in which the conditions described in divisions (A)(2)(a) to (e) of this section are present.

(B)(1) A court that is required to make a determination as described in division (A)(1) or (2) of this section shall issue written findings of fact setting forth the reasons supporting its determination. If the court makes a written determination under division (A)(1) of this section, it shall briefly describe in the findings of fact the relevant services provided by the agency to the family of the child and why those services did not prevent the removal of the child from the child's home or enable the child to return safely home.

(2) If a court issues an order that returns the child to the child's home in situations in which division (A)(2)(a), (b), (c), (d), or (e) of this section applies, the court shall issue written findings of fact setting forth the reasons supporting its determination.

(C) If the court makes a determination pursuant to division (A)(2) of this section, the court shall conduct a review hearing pursuant to section 2151.417 of the Revised Code to approve a permanency plan with respect to the child, unless the court issues an order returning the child home pursuant to division (A)(3) of this section. The hearing to approve the permanency plan may be held immediately following the court's determination pursuant to division (A)(2) of this section and shall be held no later than thirty days following that determination.

(1999 H 176, eff. 10–29–99; 1998 H 484, eff. 3–18–99; 1988 S 89, eff. 1–1–89)

Historical and Statutory Notes

Amendment Note: 1999 H 176 inserted ", division (E) of section 2151.31, or section 2151.314, 2151.33," and "removed the child from home," and added the third sentence in division (A)(1).

Amendment Note: 1998 H 484 rewrote this section, which prior thereto read:

"(A) At any hearing held pursuant to section 2151.28, division (E) of section 2151.31, or section 2151.314, 2151.33, or 2151.353 of the Revised Code at which the court removes a child from his home or continues the removal of a child from his home, the court shall determine whether the public children services agency or private child placing agency that filed the complaint in the case, removed the child from his home, has custody of the child, or will be given custody of the child has made reasonable efforts to prevent the removal of the child from his home, to eliminate the continued removal of the child from his home, or to make it possible for the child to return home. The agency shall have the burden of proving that it has made those reasonable efforts. If the agency removed the child from his home during an emergency in which the child could not safely remain at home and the agency did not have prior contact with the child, the court is not prohibited, solely because the agency did not make the reasonable efforts during the emergency to prevent the removal of the child, from determining that the agency made those reasonable efforts.

"(B) The court shall issue written finding of facts setting forth its determination under division (A) of this section. In its written finding of facts, the court shall briefly describe the relevant services provided by the agency to the family of the child and why those services did not prevent the removal of the child from his home or enable the child to return home."

Cross References

Public children services agencies, powers and duties, 5153.16

Ohio Administrative Code References

Reasonable efforts, OAC 5101:2–39–05

Library References

Infants ⊗17, 226, 230.1.
Westlaw Topic No. 211.
C.J.S. Infants §§ 8, 9, 57, 70 to 84.
OJur 3d: 48, Family Law § 1632, 1634, 1654, 1678, 1691
Baldwin's Ohio Legislative Service, 1988 Laws of Ohio, S 89—LSC Analysis, p 5–571
Klein & Darling, Baldwin's Ohio Practice, Civil Practice § 52–4 (1997).
Carlin, Baldwin's Ohio Practice, Merrick–Rippner Probate Law § 107.30, 107.41, 107.74, 107.78, 107.81, 107.83 (2003).

2151.42 Modification or termination of dispositional order

(A) At any hearing in which a court is asked to modify or terminate an order of disposition issued under section 2151.353, 2151.415, or 2151.417 of the Revised Code, the court, in determining whether to return the child to the child's parents, shall consider whether it is in the best interest of the child.

(B) An order of disposition issued under division (A)(3) of section 2151.353, division (A)(3) of section 2151.415, or section 2151.417 of the Revised Code granting legal custody of a child to a person is intended to be permanent in nature. A court shall not modify or terminate an order granting legal custody of a child unless it finds, based on facts that have arisen since the order was issued or that were unknown to the court at that time, that a change has occurred in the circumstances of the child or the person who was granted legal custody, and that modification or termination of the order is necessary to serve the best interest of the child.

(1999 H 176, eff. 10–29–99; 1998 H 484, eff. 3–18–99)

Historical and Statutory Notes

Ed. Note: Former 2151.42 repealed by 1972 H 511, eff. 1–1–74; 130 v H 83; 1953 H 1; GC 1639–46; see now 2919.21 and 2919.22 for provisions analogous to former 2151.42.

Pre–1953 H 1 Amendments: 121 v 557; 119 v 731; 117 v 520

Amendment Note: 1999 H 176 rewrote the section, which prior thereto read:

"(A) At any hearing in which a court is asked to modify or terminate an order of disposition issued under section 2151.353, 2151.415, or 2151.417 of the Revised Code, the court, in determining whether to return the child to the child's parents, shall consider whether it is in the best interest of the child. If the order of disposition that is the subject of a hearing under this section involves a previous award of legal custody under division (A)(3) of section 2151.353 of the Revised Code and is governed by division (E) of section 3109.04 of the Revised Code, the court shall comply with the requirements of division (E) of section 3109.04 of the Revised Code in its modification or termination of the order of disposition.

"(B) Additionally, an order of disposition issued under division (A)(3) of section 2151.353, division (A)(3) of section 2151.415, or section 2151.417 of the Revised Code granting legal custody of a child to a person is intended to be permanent in nature. A court shall not modify or terminate an order issued under either of those divisions or that section granting legal custody of a child to a person unless it finds, based on facts that have arisen since the order was issued or that were unknown to the court at that time, that a change has occurred in the circumstances of the child, the child's parents, or the person, and that modification or termination of the order is necessary to serve the best interest of the child."

Library References

OJur 3d: 46, Family Law § 711, 1602
Carlin, Baldwin's Ohio Practice, Merrick–Rippner Probate Law § 107.79 (2003).

2151.421 Persons required to report injury or neglect; procedures on receipt of report

(A)(1)(a) No person described in division (A)(1)(b) of this section who is acting in an official or professional capacity and knows or suspects that a child under eighteen years of age or a mentally retarded, developmentally disabled, or physically impaired child under twenty-one years of age has suffered or faces a threat of suffering any physical or mental wound, injury, disability, or condition of a nature that reasonably indicates abuse or neglect of the child, shall fail to immediately report that knowledge or suspicion to the entity or persons specified in this division. Except as provided in section 5120.173 of the Revised Code, the person making the report shall make it to the public children services agency or a municipal or county peace officer in the county in which the child resides or in which the abuse or neglect is occurring or has occurred. In the circumstances described in section 5120.173 of the Revised Code, the person making the report shall make it to the entity specified in that section.

(b) Division (A)(1)(a) of this section applies to any person who is an attorney; physician, including a hospital intern or resident; dentist; podiatrist; practitioner of a limited branch of medicine as specified in section 4731.15 of the Revised Code; registered nurse; licensed practical nurse; visiting nurse; other health care professional; licensed psychologist; licensed school psychologist; independent marriage and family therapist or marriage and family therapist; speech pathologist or audiologist; coroner; administrator or employee of a child day-care center; administrator or employee of a residential camp or child day camp; administrator or employee of a certified child care agency or other public or private children services agency; school teacher; school employee; school authority; person engaged in social work or the practice of professional counseling; agent of a county humane society; person rendering spiritual treatment through prayer in accordance with the tenets of a well-recognized religion; superintendent, board member, or employee of a county board of mental retardation; investigative agent contracted with by a county board of mental retardation; or employee of the department of mental retardation and developmental disabilities.

(2) An attorney or a physician is not required to make a report pursuant to division (A)(1) of this section concerning any communication the attorney or physician receives from a client or patient in an attorney-client or physician-patient relationship, if, in accordance with division (A) or (B) of section 2317.02 of the Revised Code, the attorney or physician could not testify with respect to that communication in a civil or criminal proceeding, except that the client or patient is deemed to have waived any testimonial privilege under division (A) or (B) of section 2317.02 of the Revised Code with respect to that communication and the attorney or physician shall make a report pursuant to division (A)(1) of this section with respect to that communication, if all of the following apply:

(a) The client or patient, at the time of the communication, is either a child under eighteen years of age or a mentally retarded, developmentally disabled, or physically impaired person under twenty-one years of age.

(b) The attorney or physician knows or suspects, as a result of the communication or any observations made during that communication, that the client or patient has suffered or faces a threat of suffering any physical or mental wound, injury, disability, or condition of a nature that reasonably indicates abuse or neglect of the client or patient.

(c) The attorney-client or physician-patient relationship does not arise out of the client's or patient's attempt to have an abortion without the notification of her parents, guardian, or custodian in accordance with section 2151.85 of the Revised Code.

(B) Anyone, who knows or suspects that a child under eighteen years of age or a mentally retarded, developmentally disabled, or physically impaired person under twenty-one years of age has suffered or faces a threat of suffering any physical or mental wound, injury, disability, or other condition of a nature that reasonably indicates abuse or neglect of the child may report or cause reports to be made of that knowledge or suspicion to the entity or persons specified in this division. Except as provided in section 5120.173 of the Revised Code, a person making a report or causing a report to be made under this division shall make it or cause it to be made to the public children services agency or to a municipal or county peace officer. In the circumstances described in section 5120.173 of the Revised Code, a person making a report or causing a report to be made under this division shall make it or cause it to be made to the entity specified in that section.

(C) Any report made pursuant to division (A) or (B) of this section shall be made forthwith either by telephone or in person and shall be followed by a written report, if requested by the receiving agency or officer. The written report shall contain:

(1) The names and addresses of the child and the child's parents or the person or persons having custody of the child, if known;

(2) The child's age and the nature and extent of the child's known or suspected injuries, abuse, or neglect or of the known or suspected threat of injury,

abuse, or neglect, including any evidence of previous injuries, abuse, or neglect;

(3) Any other information that might be helpful in establishing the cause of the known or suspected injury, abuse, or neglect or of the known or suspected threat of injury, abuse, or neglect.

Any person, who is required by division (A) of this section to report known or suspected child abuse or child neglect, may take or cause to be taken color photographs of areas of trauma visible on a child and, if medically indicated, cause to be performed radiological examinations of the child.

(D)(1) When a municipal or county peace officer receives a report concerning the possible abuse or neglect of a child or the possible threat of abuse or neglect of a child, upon receipt of the report, the municipal or county peace officer who receives the report shall refer the report to the appropriate public children services agency.

(2) When a public children services agency receives a report pursuant to this division or division (A) or (B) of this section, upon receipt of the report, the public children services agency shall comply with section 2151.422 of the Revised Code.

(E) No township, municipal, or county peace officer shall remove a child about whom a report is made pursuant to this section from the child's parents, stepparents, or guardian or any other persons having custody of the child without consultation with the public children services agency, unless, in the judgment of the officer, and, if the report was made by physician, the physician, immediate removal is considered essential to protect the child from further abuse or neglect. The agency that must be consulted shall be the agency conducting the investigation of the report as determined pursuant to section 2151.422 of the Revised Code.

(F)(1) Except as provided in section 2151.422 of the Revised Code, the public children services agency shall investigate, within twenty-four hours, each report of known or suspected child abuse or child neglect and of a known or suspected threat of child abuse or child neglect that is referred to it under this section to determine the circumstances surrounding the injuries, abuse, or neglect or the threat of injury, abuse, or neglect, the cause of the injuries, abuse, neglect, or threat, and the person or per-

sons responsible. The investigation shall be made in cooperation with the law enforcement agency and in accordance with the memorandum of understanding prepared under division (J) of this section. A failure to make the investigation in accordance with the memorandum is not grounds for, and shall not result in, the dismissal of any charges or complaint arising from the report or the suppression of any evidence obtained as a result of the report and does not give, and shall not be construed as giving, any rights or any grounds for appeal or post-conviction relief to any person. The public children services agency shall report each case to a central registry which the department of job and family services shall maintain in order to determine whether prior reports have been made in other counties concerning the child or other principals in the case. The public children services agency shall submit a report of its investigation, in writing, to the law enforcement agency.

(2) The public children services agency shall make any recommendations to the county prosecuting attorney or city director of law that it considers necessary to protect any children that are brought to its attention.

(G)(1)(a) Except as provided in division (H)(3) of this section, anyone or any hospital, institution, school, health department, or agency participating in the making of reports under division (A) of this section, anyone or any hospital, institution, school, health department, or agency participating in good faith in the making of reports under division (B) of this section, and anyone participating in good faith in a judicial proceeding resulting from the reports, shall be immune from any civil or criminal liability for injury, death, or loss to person or property that otherwise might be incurred or imposed as a result of the making of the reports or the participation in the judicial proceeding.

(b) Notwithstanding section 4731.22 of the Revised Code, the physician-patient privilege shall not be a ground for excluding evidence regarding a child's injuries, abuse, or neglect, or the cause of the injuries, abuse, or neglect in any judicial proceeding resulting from a report submitted pursuant to this section.

(2) In any civil or criminal action or proceeding in which it is alleged and proved that participation in the making of a report under this section was not in

good faith or participation in a judicial proceeding resulting from a report made under this section was not in good faith, the court shall award the prevailing party reasonable attorney's fees and costs and, if a civil action or proceeding is voluntarily dismissed, may award reasonable attorney's fees and costs to the party against whom the civil action or proceeding is brought.

(H)(1) Except as provided in divisions (H)(4) and (M) of this section, a report made under this section is confidential. The information provided in a report made pursuant to this section and the name of the person who made the report shall not be released for use, and shall not be used, as evidence in any civil action or proceeding brought against the person who made the report. In a criminal proceeding, the report is admissible in evidence in accordance with the Rules of Evidence and is subject to discovery in accordance with the Rules of Criminal Procedure.

(2) No person shall permit or encourage the unauthorized dissemination of the contents of any report made under this section.

(3) A person who knowingly makes or causes another person to make a false report under division (B) of this section that alleges that any person has committed an act or omission that resulted in a child being an abused child or a neglected child is guilty of a violation of section 2921.14 of the Revised Code.

(4) If a report is made pursuant to division (A) or (B) of this section and the child who is the subject of the report dies for any reason at any time after the report is made, but before the child attains eighteen years of age, the public children services agency or municipal or county peace officer to which the report was made or referred, on the request of the child fatality review board, shall submit a summary sheet of information providing a summary of the report to the review board of the county in which the deceased child resided at the time of death. On the request of the review board, the agency or peace officer may, at its discretion, make the report available to the review board.

(5) A public children services agency shall advise a person alleged to have inflicted abuse or neglect on a child who is the subject of a report made pursuant to this section in writing of the disposition of the investigation. The agency shall

not provide to the person any information that identifies the person who made the report, statements of witnesses, or police or other investigative reports.

(I) Any report that is required by this section, other than a report that is made to the state highway patrol as described in section 5120.173 of the Revised Code, shall result in protective services and emergency supportive services being made available by the public children services agency on behalf of the children about whom the report is made, in an effort to prevent further neglect or abuse, to enhance their welfare, and, whenever possible, to preserve the family unit intact. The agency required to provide the services shall be the agency conducting the investigation of the report pursuant to section 2151.422 of the Revised Code.

(J)(1) Each public children services agency shall prepare a memorandum of understanding that is signed by all of the following:

(a) If there is only one juvenile judge in the county, the juvenile judge of the county or the juvenile judge's representative;

(b) If there is more than one juvenile judge in the county, a juvenile judge or the juvenile judges' representative selected by the juvenile judges or, if they are unable to do so for any reason, the juvenile judge who is senior in point of service or the senior juvenile judge's representative;

(c) The county peace officer;

(d) All chief municipal peace officers within the county;

(e) Other law enforcement officers handling child abuse and neglect cases in the county;

(f) The prosecuting attorney of the county;

(g) If the public children services agency is not the county department of job and family services, the county department of job and family services;

(h) The county humane society.

(2) A memorandum of understanding shall set forth the normal operating procedure to be employed by all concerned officials in the execution of their respective responsibilities under this section and division (C) of section 2919.21, division (B)(1) of section 2919.22, division (B) of section 2919.23, and section 2919.24 of the Revised Code and shall

have as two of its primary goals the elimination of all unnecessary interviews of children who are the subject of reports made pursuant to division (A) or (B) of this section and, when feasible, providing for only one interview of a child who is the subject of any report made pursuant to division (A) or (B) of this section. A failure to follow the procedure set forth in the memorandum by the concerned officials is not grounds for, and shall not result in, the dismissal of any charges or complaint arising from any reported case of abuse or neglect or the suppression of any evidence obtained as a result of any reported child abuse or child neglect and does not give, and shall not be construed as giving, any rights or any grounds for appeal or post-conviction relief to any person.

(3) A memorandum of understanding shall include all of the following:

(a) The roles and responsibilities for handling emergency and nonemergency cases of abuse and neglect;

(b) Standards and procedures to be used in handling and coordinating investigations of reported cases of child abuse and reported cases of child neglect, methods to be used in interviewing the child who is the subject of the report and who allegedly was abused or neglected, and standards and procedures addressing the categories of persons who may interview the child who is the subject of the report and who allegedly was abused or neglected.

(K)(1) Except as provided in division (K)(4) of this section, a person who is required to make a report pursuant to division (A) of this section may make a reasonable number of requests of the public children services agency that receives or is referred the report to be provided with the following information:

(a) Whether the agency has initiated an investigation of the report;

(b) Whether the agency is continuing to investigate the report;

(c) Whether the agency is otherwise involved with the child who is the subject of the report;

(d) The general status of the health and safety of the child who is the subject of the report;

(e) Whether the report has resulted in the filing of a complaint in juvenile court or of criminal charges in another court.

(2) A person may request the information specified in division (K)(1) of this section only if, at the time the report is made, the person's name, address, and telephone number are provided to the person who receives the report.

When a municipal or county peace officer or employee of a public children services agency receives a report pursuant to division (A) or (B) of this section the recipient of the report shall inform the person of the right to request the information described in division (K)(1) of this section. The recipient of the report shall include in the initial child abuse or child neglect report that the person making the report was so informed and, if provided at the time of the making of the report, shall include the person's name, address, and telephone number in the report.

Each request is subject to verification of the identity of the person making the report. If that person's identity is verified, the agency shall provide the person with the information described in division (K)(1) of this section a reasonable number of times, except that the agency shall not disclose any confidential information regarding the child who is the subject of the report other than the information described in those divisions.

(3) A request made pursuant to division (K)(1) of this section is not a substitute for any report required to be made pursuant to division (A) of this section.

(4) If an agency other than the agency that received or was referred the report is conducting the investigation of the report pursuant to section 2151.422 of the Revised Code, the agency conducting the investigation shall comply with the requirements of division (K) of this section.

(L) The director of job and family services shall adopt rules in accordance with Chapter 119. of the Revised Code to implement this section. The department of job and family services may enter into a plan of cooperation with any other governmental entity to aid in ensuring that children are protected from abuse and neglect. The department shall make recommendations to the attorney general that the department determines are necessary to protect children from child abuse and child neglect.

(M)(1) As used in this division:

(a) "Out-of-home care" includes a nonchartered nonpublic school if the alleged child abuse or child neglect, or alleged threat of child abuse or child neglect, described in a report received by a public children services agency allegedly occurred in or involved the nonchartered nonpublic school and the alleged perpetrator named in the report holds a certificate, permit, or license issued by the state board of education under section 3301.071 or Chapter 3319. of the Revised Code.

(b) "Administrator, director, or other chief administrative officer" means the superintendent of the school district if the out-of-home care entity subject to a report made pursuant to this section is a school operated by the district.

(2) No later than the end of the day following the day on which a public children services agency receives a report of alleged child abuse or child neglect, or a report of an alleged threat of child abuse or child neglect, that allegedly occurred in or involved an out-of-home care entity, the agency shall provide written notice of the allegations contained in and the person named as the alleged perpetrator in the report to the administrator, director, or other chief administrative officer of the out-of-home care entity that is the subject of the report unless the administrator, director, or other chief administrative officer is named as an alleged perpetrator in the report. If the administrator, director, or other chief administrative officer of an out-of-home care entity is named as an alleged perpetrator in a report of alleged child abuse or child neglect, or a report of an alleged threat of child abuse or child neglect, that allegedly occurred in or involved the out-of-home care entity, the agency shall provide the written notice to the owner or governing board of the out-of-home care entity that is the subject of the report. The agency shall not provide witness statements or police or other investigative reports.

(3) No later than three days after the day on which a public children services agency that conducted the investigation as determined pursuant to section 2151.422 of the Revised Code makes a disposition of an investigation involving a report of alleged child abuse or child neglect, or a report of an alleged threat of child abuse or child neglect, that allegedly occurred in or involved an out-of-home care entity, the agency shall send written notice of the disposition of the investigation to the administrator, director, or other chief administrative offi-

cer and the owner or governing board of the out-of-home care entity. The agency shall not provide witness statements or police or other investigative reports.

(2004 H 106, eff. 9–16–04; 2004 S 178, eff. 1–30–04; 2002 S 221, eff. 4–9–03; 2002 H 374, eff. 4–7–03; 2002 H 510, eff. 3–31–03; 2000 H 448, eff. 10–5–00; 1999 H 471, eff. 7–1–00; 1998 H 606, eff. 3–9–99; 1998 S 212, eff. 9–30–98; 1997 H 408, eff. 10–1–97; 1997 H 215, eff. 6–30–97; 1996 S 223, eff. 3–18–97; 1996 S 269, eff. 7–1–96; 1996 H 274, eff. 8–8–96; 1992 H 154, eff. 7–31–92; 1990 S 3, H 44; 1989 H 257; 1986 H 529, H 528; 1985 H 349; 1984 S 321; 1977 H 219; 1975 H 85; 1969 H 338, S 49; 131 v H 218; 130 v H 765)

Uncodified Law

1999 H 121, § 3: See Uncodified Law under 2151.358

1990 S 3, § 6, eff. 4–11–91, reads: Each county shall amend its county plan of cooperation to comply with division (J) of section 2151.421 of the Revised Code, as amended by this act, when the plan is regularly scheduled to be revised. Prior to that time, the county does not have to amend its plan of cooperation; however, the appropriate officials of the county shall comply with division (J) of section 2151.421 of the Revised Code, as amended by this act, to the greatest extent possible.

Historical and Statutory Notes

Amendment Note: 2004 H 106 deleted ", and (N)" in division (H)(1); added divisions (M)(1), (M)(1)(a) and (M)(1)(b); and designated division (M)(2) and redesignated former division (N) as new division (M)(3).

Amendment Note: 2004 S 178 inserted "; superintendent, board member, or employee of a county board of mental retardation; investigative agent contracted with by a county board of mental retardation; or employee of the department of mental retardation and developmental disabilities" at the end of division (A)(1)(b).

Amendment Note: 2002 S 221 added "agent of a county humane society;" to division (A)(1)(b); and added division (J)(1)(h).

Amendment Note: 2002 H 374 inserted "independent marriage and family therapist or marriage and family therapist;" preceding "speech pathologist" in division (A)(1)(b).

Amendment Note: 2002 H 510 inserted "to the entity or persons specified in this division. Except as provided in section 5120.173 of the Revised Code, the person making the report shall make it" and "In the circumstances described in section 5120.173 of the Revised Code, the person making the report shall make it to the entity specified in that section." in division (A)(1)(a); inserted "to the entity or persons specified in this division. Except as provided in section 5120.173 of the Revised Code, a person making a report or causing a report to be made under this division shall make it or cause it to be made" and "In the circumstances described in section 5120.173 of the Revised Code, a person making a report or causing a report to be made under this division shall make it or cause it to be made to the entity specified in that section." to division (B); substituted "When a municipal or county peace officer receives" with "Upon the receipt of" and inserted "upon receipt of the report," in division (D)(1); substituted "When a public children services agency receives" for "On receipt of" and inserted "upon receipt of the report," in division (D)(2); and inserted ", other than a report that is made to the state highway patrol as described in section 5120.173 of the Revised Code," in division (I).

Amendment Note: 2000 H 448 added new division (H)(4); redesignated former division (H)(4) as new division (H)(5); and inserted "in writing" in new division (H)(5).

Amendment Note: 1999 H 471 substituted "department of job and family services" for "state department of human services" in division (F)(1); substituted "job and family" for "human" twice in division (J)(1)(g); substituted "director of job and family services" for "department of human services" and inserted "of job and family services" in division (L); and made other nonsubstantive changes.

Amendment Note: 1998 H 606 deleted "or surgery" after "limited branch of medicine" and substituted "specified" for "defined" in division (A)(1)(b); designated divisions (G)(1)(a) and (G)(1)(b); and made other nonsubstantive changes.

Amendment Note: 1998 S 212 deleted "listed" following "No person described" in division (A)(1)(a); inserted "administrator or employee of a residential camp or child day camp;" in division (A)(1)(b); deleted "public" following "attorney of the county;" in division (J)(1)(f); deleted "agency" following "of human services" in division (J)(1)(g); and made other nonsubstantive changes.

Amendment Note: 1997 H 408 rewrote division (A)(1); changed references to county human services departments and county children services boards to references to public children services agencies throughout; and made corrective changes and other nonsubstantive changes. Prior to amendment, division (A)(1) read:

"(A)(1) No attorney, physician, including a hospital intern or resident, dentist, podiatrist, practitioner of a limited branch of medicine or surgery as defined in section 4731.15 of the Revised Code, registered nurse, licensed practical nurse, visiting nurse, other health care professional, licensed psychologist, licensed school psychologist, speech pathologist or audiologist, coroner, administrator or employee of a child day care center, administrator or employee of a certified child care agency or other public or private children services agency, school teacher, school employee, school authority, person engaged in social work or the practice of professional counseling, or person rendering spiritual treatment through prayer in accordance with the tenets of a well recognized religion, who is acting in an official or professional capacity and knows or suspects that a child under eighteen years of age or a mentally retarded, developmentally disabled, or physically impaired child under twenty-one years of age has suffered or faces a threat of suffering any physical or mental wound, injury, disability, or condition of a nature that reasonably indicates abuse or neglect of the child, shall fail to immediately report that knowledge or suspicion to the children services board, the county department of human services exercising the children services function, or a municipal or county peace officer in the county in which the child resides or in which the abuse or neglect is occurring or has occurred."

Amendment Note: 1997 H 215 rewrote this section; see *Baldwin's Ohio Legislative Service Annotat-*

ed, 1997, page 8/L–1492, or the OH–LEGIS or OH–LEGIS–OLD database on WESTLAW, for text of previous version.

Amendment Note: 1996 S 223 substituted "person engaged in social work or the practice of professional counseling," for "social worker, licensed professional counselor," in division (A)(1); added the reference to township peace officers in division (E); rewrote division (K); and made changes to reflect gender neutral language and other nonsubstantive changes. Prior to amendment, division (K) read:

"(K)(1) When a municipal or county peace officer or an employee of a county department of human services or children services board receives a report pursuant to division (A) or (B) of this section, the person who receives the report, at the time he receives the report, shall inform the person making the report that, if the person making the report is required to make the report pursuant to division (A) of this section and if he provides his name, address, and telephone number at the time he makes the report, subject to verification of his identity, he may make a reasonable number of requests of the county department of human services or children services board that receives or is referred the report to provide him with the following information:

"(a) Whether the department or board has initiated an investigation of the report;

"(b) Whether the department or board is continuing to investigate the report;

"(c) Whether the department or board is otherwise involved with the child who is the subject of the report;

"(d) The general status of the health and safety of the child who is the subject of the report;

"(e) Whether the report has resulted in the filing of a complaint in juvenile court or of criminal charges in another court.

"(2) Any municipal or county peace officer or employee of a county department of human services or children services board who informs a person making a report pursuant to division (A) or (B) of this section of the person's right to request the information described in divisions (K)(1)(a) to (e) of this section shall include in the initial child abuse or child neglect report that the person making the report was so informed and, if provided at the time of the making of the report, shall include the person's name, address, and telephone number in the report.

"(3) Any person, who is required to make a report pursuant to division (A) of this section and who provides his name, address, and telephone number at the time he makes the report, may make a reasonable number of requests of the county department of human services or children services board that receives or is referred the report to provide him with the information described in divisions (K)(1)(a) to (e) of this section. Each request is subject to verification of the person's identity. A request made pursuant to division (K)(3) of this section is not a substitute for any report required to be made pursuant to division (A) of this section.

"(4) If the county department of human services or children services board receives or is referred a report pursuant to this section, if the person making the report is required to make the report pursuant to division (A) of this section, if that person provides his name, address, and telephone number at the time he makes the report, if that person requests the department or board to provide the information described in divisions (K)(1)(a) to (e) of this section, and if that person's identity is verified, the department or board shall provide the person with the information described in divisions (K)(1)(a) to (e) of this section a reasonable number of times, except that the department or board shall not disclose any confidential information regarding the child who is the subject of the report other than the information described in those divisions."

Amendment Note: 1996 S 269 changed a statutory reference from "division (B) of section 2919.21" to "division (C) of section 2919.21" in division (J); made changes to reflect gender neutral language; and made other nonsubstantive changes.

Amendment Note: 1996 H 274 substituted "mentally retarded, developmentally disabled, or physically impaired person" for "physically or mentally handicapped person" throughout; inserted "Except as provided in division (H)(4) of this section," in division (H)(1); added division (H)(4); added the second and third sentences in division (L); added divisions (M) and (N); and made changes to reflect gender neutral language.

Cross References

Penalty: 2151.99(A)

Abuse or neglect of minor inmate to be reported to state highway patrol, 5120.173

Anti-stalking protection orders, persons who may seek relief, 2903.214

Child abuse prevention, in-service training for school employees, 3319.073

Community schools, required terms of contracts, 3314.03

County children services boards, powers and duties, 5153.16

Evidence, privileged communications and acts, duty to report child abuse, 2317.02

Failure to report a felony or certain suspicious circumstances, 2921.22

Filing of power of attorney or affidavit with juvenile court, accompanying information, report to public children services agency, investigation, 3109.74

Memorandum of understanding to outline normal operating procedure, 5126.058

Mental retardation and developmental disabilities department, investigation of abuse or neglect by employees, 5123.51

Outpatient mental health services for minors, obligations of mental health professionals, 5122.04

Petition alleging domestic violence against minor children, 3113.31

Prevention of child abuse and child neglect, 3109.13 to 3109.18

Sealing of records, official records defined, 2953.51

Verification of power of attorney or affidavit, 3109.75

Ohio Administrative Code References

Child abuse and neglect, interstate and intrastate referral procedures, protective service alerts, locating the child, OAC 5101:2–35–62 et seq.

Children services, definition of terms, OAC 5101:2–1–01

Children's protective services, OAC Ch 5101:2–34, Ch 5101:2–36

Documentation of comprehensive health care for children in custody, OAC 5101:2–42–662

Documentation of comprehensive health care for children in placement, OAC 5101:2–42–66.2

Family and children services information system (FACSIS) reporting requirements, OAC 5101:2–33–05

Joint planning and sharing of information among the PCSA and CDJFS, OAC 5101:2–39–51

Major unusual incidents, OAC 5123:2–17–02

PCSA requirements for conducting out-of-home perpetrator investigations and alleged child victim assessments, OAC 5101:2–34–36

Procedures for intervening in cases involving alleged withholding of appropriate nutrition, hydration, medication, or medically indicated treatment from disabled infants with life-threatening conditions, OAC 5101:2–35–77

Protective service alerts, OAC 5101:2–35–67

Submittal of central registry reports on child abuse or neglect, OAC 5101:2–35–16

Supportive services, OAC Ch 5101:2–39

The child abuse and neglect memorandum of understanding, OAC 5101:2–34–71

Library References

Infants ⊜13.

Westlaw Topic No. 211.

C.J.S. Infants §§ 5, 92 to 98.

OJur 3d: 26, Criminal Law § 738; 27, Criminal Law § 1417; 35, Defamation and Privacy § 75; 46, Family Law § 315; 48, Family Law § 1474 to 1477, 1479, 1736, 1749

Civil liability of physician for failure to diagnose or report battered child syndrome. 97 ALR3d 338

Validity, construction, and application of statute limiting physician-patient privilege in judicial proceedings relating to child abuse or neglect. 44 ALR4th 649

Power of court or other public agency to order medical treatment over parental religious objections for child whose life is not immediately endangered. 21 ALR5th 248

Baldwin's Ohio Legislative Service, 1996 H 274— LSC Analysis, p 5/L–697

Giannelli & Snyder, Baldwin's Ohio Practice, Evidence § 501.4, 501.13, 501.21, 501.22, 501.27 (2d ed. 2001).

Gotherman & Babbit, Ohio Municipal Law, Text 32.03.

Adrine & Ruden, Ohio Domestic Violence Law (2002 Ed.), Text 8.5.

Carlin, Baldwin's Ohio Practice, Merrick–Rippner Probate Law § 5.12, 101.16, 107.34, 107.46, 107.52, 107.54, 107.114, 108.1, 108.15 (2003).

2151.422 Investigations concerning children in domestic violence or homeless shelters; services; custody; confidentiality of information

(A) As used in this section, "homeless shelter" means a facility that provides accommodations to homeless individuals.

(B) On receipt of a notice pursuant to division (A), (B), or (D) of section 2151.421 of the Revised Code, the public children services agency shall determine whether the child subject to the report is living in a shelter for victims of domestic violence or a homeless shelter and whether the child was brought to that shelter pursuant to an agreement with a shelter in another county. If the child is living in a shelter and was brought there from another county, the agency shall immediately notify the public children services agency of the county from which the child was brought of the report and all the information contained in the report. On receipt of the notice pursuant to this division, the agency of the county from which the child was brought shall conduct the investigation of the report required pursuant to section 2151.421 of the Revised Code and shall perform all duties required of the agency under this chapter with respect to the child who is the subject of the report. If the child is not living in a shelter or the child was not brought to the shelter from another county, the agency that received the report pursuant to division (A), (B), or (D) of section 2151.421 of the Revised Code shall conduct the investigation required pursuant to section 2151.421 of the Revised Code and shall perform all duties required of the agency under this chapter with respect to the child who is the subject of the report. The agency of the county in which the shelter is located in which the child is living and the agency of the county from which the child was brought may ask the shelter to provide information concerning the child's residence address and county of residence to the agency.

(C) If a child is living in a shelter for victims of domestic violence or a homeless shelter and the child was brought to that shelter pursuant to an agreement with a shelter in another county, the public children services agency of the county from which the child was brought shall provide services to or take custody of the child if services or custody are needed or required under this chapter or section 5153.16 of the Revised Code.

(D) When a homeless shelter provides accommodations to a person, the shelter, on admitting the person to the shelter, shall determine, if possible, the person's last known residential address and county of residence. The information concerning the address and county of residence is confidential and may only be released to a public children services agency pursuant to this section.

(1997 H 215, eff. 6–30–97)

Historical and Statutory Notes

Ed. Note: Former 2151.422 repealed by 1978 H 565, eff. 11–1–78; 132 v S 316.

Cross References

Public children services agencies, powers and duties, 5153.16
Release of last known residential address of domestic violence shelter resident, 3113.40

Library References

OJur 3d: 46, Family Law § 319, 1457, 1468

2151.424   Notice of dispositional hearings

(A) If a child has been placed in a certified foster home or is in the custody of a relative of the child, other than a parent of the child, a court, prior to conducting any hearing pursuant to division (E)(2) or (3) of section 2151.412 or section 2151.28, 2151.33, 2151.35, 2151.414, 2151.415, 2151.416, or 2151.417 of the Revised Code with respect to the child, shall notify the foster caregiver or relative of the date, time, and place of the hearing. At the hearing, the foster caregiver or relative may present evidence.

(B) If a public children services agency or private child placing agency has permanent custody of a child and a petition to adopt the child has been filed under Chapter 3107. of the Revised Code, the agency, prior to conducting a review under section 2151.416 of the Revised Code, or a court, prior to conducting a hearing under division (E)(2) or (3) of section 2151.412 or section 2151.416 or 2151.417 of the Revised Code, shall notify the prospective adoptive parent of the date, time, and place of the review or hearing. At the review or hearing, the prospective adoptive parent may present evidence.

(C) The notice and the opportunity to present evidence do not make the foster caregiver, relative, or prospective adoptive parent a party in the action or proceeding pursuant to which the review or hearing is conducted.

(2000 H 448, eff. 10–5–00; 1998 H 484, eff. 3–18–99)

Historical and Statutory Notes

Amendment Note: 2000 H 448 inserted "certified" in division (A).

Library References

OJur 3d: 46, Family Law § 711, 1602
Carlin, Baldwin's Ohio Practice, Merrick–Rippner Probate Law § 107.56 (2003).

ADULT CASES

2151.43   Charges against adults; defendant bound over to grand jury

In cases against an adult under sections 2151.01 to 2151.54 of the Revised Code, any person may file an affidavit with the clerk of the juvenile court setting forth briefly, in plain and ordinary language, the charges against the accused who shall be tried thereon. When the child is a recipient of aid pursuant to

Chapter 5107. or 5115. of the Revised Code, the county department of job and family services shall file charges against any person who fails to provide support to a child in violation of section 2919.21 of the Revised Code, unless the department files charges under section 3113.06 of the Revised Code, or unless charges of nonsupport are filed by a relative or guardian of the child, or unless action to enforce support is brought under Chapter 3115. of the Revised Code.

In such prosecution an indictment by the grand jury or information by the prosecuting attorney shall not be required. The clerk shall issue a warrant for the arrest of the accused, who, when arrested, shall be taken before the juvenile judge and tried according to such sections.

The affidavit may be amended at any time before or during the trial.

The judge may bind such adult over to the grand jury, where the act complained of constitutes a felony.

(1999 H 471, eff. 7–1–00; 1995 H 249, eff. 7–17–95; 1991 H 298, eff. 7–26–91; 1986 H 428; 1972 H 511; 1969 H 361; 132 v H 390; 127 v 847; 1953 H 1; GC 1639–39)

Historical and Statutory Notes

Pre–1953 H 1 Amendments: 119 v 731; 117 v 520, § 1

Amendment Note: 1999 H 471 substituted "job and family" for "human" in the first paragraph.

Amendment Note: 1995 H 249 removed a reference to Chapter 5113.

Cross References

Failure to pay maintenance cost, 3113.06

Library References

Courts ☞472.1.

Parent and Child ☞17.

Westlaw Topic Nos. 106, 285.

C.J.S. Courts §§ 186, 187.

C.J.S. Parent and Child § 165.

OJur 3d: 48, Family Law § 1738 to 1741; 78, Public Welfare § 120

Civil liability of physician for failure to diagnose or report battered child syndrome. 97 ALR3d 338

Validity, construction, and application of statute limiting physician-patient privilege in judicial proceedings relating to child abuse or neglect. 44 ALR4th 649

Carlin, Baldwin's Ohio Practice, Merrick–Rippner Probate Law § 107.170, 108.3, 108.4, 108.5, 108.6, 108.7 (2003).

2151.44   Complaint after hearing

If it appears at the hearing of a child that any person has abused or has aided, induced, caused, encouraged, or contributed to the dependency, neglect, or delinquency of a child or acted in a way tending to cause delinquency in such child, or that a person charged with the care, support, education, or maintenance of any child has failed to support or sufficiently contribute toward the support, education, and maintenance of such child, the juvenile judge may order a complaint filed against such person and proceed to hear and dispose of the case as provided in sections 2151.01 to 2151.54, inclusive, of the Revised Code.

On the request of the judge, the prosecuting attorney shall prosecute all adults charged with violating such sections.

(1953 H 1, eff. 10–1–53; GC 1639–40, 1639–42)

Historical and Statutory Notes

Pre–1953 H 1 Amendments: 117 v 520, § 1

Library References

Courts ☞472.1.

Infants ☞13.

Parent and Child ☞17.

Westlaw Topic Nos. 106, 211, 285.

C.J.S. Courts §§ 186, 187.

C.J.S. Infants §§ 5, 92 to 98.

C.J.S. Parent and Child § 165.

OJur 3d: 48, Family Law § 1739

Civil liability of physician for failure to diagnose or report battered child syndrome. 97 ALR3d 338

Validity, construction, and application of statute limiting physician-patient privilege in judicial proceedings relating to child abuse or neglect. 44 ALR4th 649

Carlin, Baldwin's Ohio Practice, Merrick–Rippner Probate Law § 106.10, 108.8 (2003).

2151.49   Suspension of sentence

In every case of conviction under sections 2151.01 to 2151.54 of the Revised Code, where imprisonment is imposed as part of the punishment, the juvenile judge may suspend sentence, before or during commitment, upon such condition as the juvenile judge imposes. In the case of conviction for nonsupport of a child who is receiving aid under Chapter 5107. or 5115. of the Revised Code, if the juvenile judge suspends sentence on condition that the person make payments for support, the payment shall be made to the county department of job and family services rather than to the child or custodian of the child.

The court, in accordance with sections 3119.29 to 3119.56 of the Revised Code, shall include in each support order made under this section the requirement that one or both of the parents provide for the health care needs of the child to the satisfaction of the court.

(2002 H 657, eff. 12–13–02; 2000 S 180, eff. 3–22–01; 1999 H 471, eff. 7–1–00; 1997 H 352, eff. 1–1–98; 1995 H 249, eff. 7–17–95; 1991 H 298, eff. 7–26–91; 1986 H 428; 132 v H 390; 1953 H 1; GC 1639–49)

Historical and Statutory Notes

Pre–1953 H 1 Amendments: 117 v 520, § 1

Amendment Note: 2002 H 657 substituted "3119.29" for "3119.30" and "3119.56" for "3119.58" in the last paragraph of the section.

Amendment Note: 2000 S 180 substituted "non-support" for "non support" in the first paragraph and "sections 3119.30 to 3119.58" for "section 3113.217" in the second paragraph.

Amendment Note: 1999 H 471 substituted "job and family" for "human" in the first paragraph.

Amendment Note: 1997 H 352 added the second paragraph; and made changes to reflect gender neutral language.

Amendment Note: 1995 H 249 removed a reference to Chapter 5113.

Cross References

Interfering with action to issue or modify support order, 2919.231
Modification of sentence, 2929.51
Presentence investigation, Crim R 32.2
Sentencing procedure, Crim R 32
Support of dependents, withholding personal earnings to pay support, bond, 3115.23

Library References

Criminal Law ☞982.1, 982.3, 982.5.
Westlaw Topic No. 110.
C.J.S. Criminal Law §§ 1550, 1552, 1556.
OJur 3d: 47, Family Law § 1198, 1201, 1222, 1241, 1300, 1301, 1308; 48, Family Law § 1750
Am Jur 2d: 21, Criminal Law § 557 to 566
Inherent power of court to suspend for indefinite period execution of sentence in whole or in part. 73 ALR3d 474
Carlin, Baldwin's Ohio Practice, Merrick–Rippner Probate Law § 108.1, 108.12, 108.48 (2003).

2151.50   Forfeiture of bond

When, as a condition of suspension of sentence under section 2151.49 of the Revised Code, bond is required and given, upon the failure of a person giving such bond to comply with the conditions thereof, such bond may be forfeited, the suspension terminated by the juvenile judge, the original sentence executed as though it had not been suspended, and the term of any sentence imposed in such case shall commence from the date of imprisonment of such person after such forfeiture and termination of suspension. Any part of such sentence which may have been served shall be deducted from any such period of imprisonment. When such bond is forfeited the judge may issue execution thereon without further proceedings.

(1953 H 1, eff. 10–1–53; GC 1639–50)

Historical and Statutory Notes

Pre–1953 H 1 Amendments: 117 v 520, § 1

Library References

OJur 3d: 48, Family Law § 1750
Carlin, Baldwin's Ohio Practice, Merrick–Rippner Probate Law § 108.4, 108.12 (2003).

2151.52   Appeals on questions of law

The sections of the Revised Code and rules relating to appeals on questions of law from the court of common pleas shall apply to prosecutions of adults under this chapter, and from such prosecutions an appeal on a question of law may be taken to the court of appeals of the county under laws or rules governing appeals in other criminal cases to such court of appeals.

(1986 H 412, eff. 3–17–87; 129 v 290; 1953 H 1; GC 1639–51)

Historical and Statutory Notes

Pre–1953 H 1 Amendments: 117 v 520, § 1

Cross References

Applicability of rules of appellate procedure, scope, App R 1

Library References

Criminal Law ☞1068 1/2.
Westlaw Topic No. 110.
C.J.S. Criminal Law § 1685.
OJur 3d: 48, Family Law § 1753
Whiteside, Ohio Appellate Practice (2003 Ed.), Text 1.23.
Carlin, Baldwin's Ohio Practice, Merrick–Rippner Probate Law § 108.40 (2003).

2151.53   Physical and mental examinations; records of examination; expenses

Any person coming within sections 2151.01 to 2151.54 of the Revised Code may be subjected to a physical examination by competent physicians, physician assistants, clinical nurse specialists, and certified nurse practitioners, and a mental examination by competent psychologists, psychiatrists, and clinical nurse specialists that practice the specialty of mental health or psychiatric mental health to be appointed by the juvenile court. Whenever any child is committed to any institution by virtue of such sections, a record of such examinations shall be sent with the commitment to such institution. The compensation of such physicians, physician assistants, clinical nurse specialists, certified nurse practitioners, psychologists, and psychiatrists and the expenses of such examinations shall be paid by the county treasurer upon specifically itemized vouchers, certified by the juvenile judge.

(2002 S 245, eff. 3–31–03; 1953 H 1, eff. 10–1–53; GC 1639–54)

Historical and Statutory Notes

Pre–1953 H 1 Amendments: 117 v 520, § 1

Amendment Note: 2002 S 245 rewrote this section, which prior thereto read:

"Any person coming within sections 2151.01 to 2151.54, inclusive, of the Revised Code, may be subjected to a physical and mental examination by competent physicians, psychologists, and psychiatrists to be appointed by the juvenile court. Whenever any child is committed to any institution by virtue of such sections, a record of such examinations shall be sent with the commitment to such institution. The compensation of such physicians, psychologists, and psychiatrists and the expenses of such examinations shall be paid by the county treasurer upon specifically itemized vouchers, certified by the juvenile judge.".

Cross References

Social history, physical or mental examination, custody investigation, procedure, Juv R 32

Library References

Infants ⚏208.

Westlaw Topic No. 211.

C.J.S. Infants §§ 51 to 85.

OJur 3d: 48, Family Law § 1636, 1723, 1743

FEES AND COSTS

2151.54 Fees and costs; waiver

The juvenile court shall tax and collect the same fees and costs as are allowed the clerk of the court of common pleas for similar services. No fees or costs shall be taxed in cases of delinquent, unruly, dependent, abused, or neglected children except as required by section 2743.70 or 2949.091 of the Revised Code or when specifically ordered by the court. The expense of transportation of children to places to which they have been committed, and the transportation of children to and from another state by police or other officers, acting upon order of the court, shall be paid from the county treasury upon specifically itemized vouchers certified to by the judge.

If a child is adjudicated to be a delinquent child or a juvenile traffic offender and the juvenile court specifically is required, by section 2743.70 or 2949.091 of the Revised Code or any other section of the Revised Code, to impose a specified sum of money as court costs in addition to any other court costs that the court is required or permitted by law to impose, the court shall not waive the payment of the specified additional court costs that the section of the Revised Code specifically requires the court to impose unless the court determines that the child is indigent and the court either waives the payment of all court costs or enters an order in its journal stating that no court costs are to be taxed in the case.

(1990 S 131, eff. 7–25–90; 1980 H 238; 1975 H 85; 1970 H 931; 1953 H 1; GC 1639–56)

Historical and Statutory Notes

Pre–1953 H 1 Amendments: 119 v 731; 117 v 520, § 1

Cross References

Common pleas court, fees and costs, Ch 2335

Library References

Infants ⚏212.

Westlaw Topic No. 211.

C.J.S. Infants §§ 57, 69 to 85.

OJur 3d: 48, Family Law § 1714, 1725, 1752

Baldwin's Ohio Legislative Service, 1990 Laws of Ohio, S 131—LSC Analysis, p 5–623

Carlin, Baldwin's Ohio Practice, Merrick–Rippner Probate Law § 107.111, 107.129, 108.10, 108.12 (2003).

2151.541 Additional fees for computer services

(A)(1) The juvenile judge may determine that, for the efficient operation of the juvenile court, additional funds are required to computerize the court, to make available computerized legal research services, or both. Upon making a determination that additional funds are required for either or both of those purposes, the judge shall do one of the following:

(a) If he is clerk of the court, charge one additional fee not to exceed three dollars on the filing of each cause of action or appeal under division (A), (Q), or (U) of section 2303.20 of the Revised Code;

(b) If the clerk of the court of common pleas serves as the clerk of the juvenile court pursuant to section 2151.12 of the Revised Code, authorize and direct the clerk to charge one additional fee not to exceed three dollars on the filing of each cause of action or appeal under division (A), (Q), or (U) of section 2303.20 of the Revised Code.

(2) All moneys collected under division (A)(1) of this section shall be paid to the

county treasurer. The treasurer shall place the moneys from the fees in a separate fund to be disbursed, upon an order of the juvenile judge, in an amount no greater than the actual cost to the court of procuring and maintaining computerization of the court, computerized legal research services, or both.

(3) If the court determines that the funds in the fund described in division (A)(2) of this section are more than sufficient to satisfy the purpose for which the additional fee described in division (A)(1) of this section was imposed, the court may declare a surplus in the fund and expend those surplus funds for other appropriate technological expenses of the court.

(B)(1) If the juvenile judge is the clerk of the juvenile court, he may determine that, for the efficient operation of his court, additional funds are required to computerize the clerk's office and, upon that determination, may charge an additional fee, not to exceed ten dollars, on the filing of each cause of action or appeal, on the filing, docketing, and endorsing of each certificate of judgment, or on the docketing and indexing of each aid in execution or petition to vacate, revive, or modify a judgment under divisions (A), (P), (Q), (T), and (U) of section 2303.20 of the Revised Code. Subject to division (B)(2) of this section, all moneys collected under this division shall be paid to the county treasurer to be disbursed, upon an order of the juvenile judge and subject to appropriation by the board of county commissioners, in an amount no greater than the actual cost to the juvenile court of procuring and maintaining computer systems for the clerk's office.

(2) If the juvenile judge makes the determination described in division (B)(1) of this section, the board of county commissioners may issue one or more general obligation bonds for the purpose of procuring and maintaining the computer systems for the office of the clerk of the juvenile court. In addition to the purposes stated in division (B)(1) of this section for which the moneys collected under that division may be expended, the moneys additionally may be expended to pay debt charges on and financing costs related to any general obligation bonds issued pursuant to this division as they become due. General obligation bonds issued pursuant to this division are Chapter 133. securities.

(1992 S 246, eff. 3–24–93; 1992 H 405)

Cross References

Net indebtedness of county, securities not considered in calculation of, 133.07

Library References

OJur 3d: 22, Courts and Judges § 69

PLACEMENT OF CHILDREN IN FOSTER HOMES OUTSIDE COUNTIES OF RESIDENCE

2151.55 Persons entitled to oral communication of intended placement

When a private or governmental entity intends to place a child in a certified foster home in a county other than the county in which the child resided at the time of being removed from home, a representative of the placing entity shall orally communicate the intended placement to the foster caregiver with whom the child is to be placed and, if the child will attend the schools of the district in which the certified foster home is located, a representative of the school district's board of education.

(2000 H 332, eff. 1–1–01; 2000 H 448, eff. 10–5–00; 1999 H 283, eff. 9–29–99)

Historical and Statutory Notes

Ed. Note: The amendment of this section by 2000 H 332, eff. 1–1–01, and 2000 H 448, eff. 10–5–00, was identical. See *Baldwin's Ohio Legislative Service Annotated*, 2000, pages 6/L–2160 and 6/L–2233, or the OH–LEGIS or OH–LEGIS–OLD database on WESTLAW, for original versions of these Acts.

Ed. Note: Former 2151.55 repealed by 1999 H 283, eff. 9–29–99; 1997 H 215, eff. 6–30–97.

Ed. Note: Prior 2151.55 repealed by 130 v H 299, eff. 10–7–63; 1953 H 1; GC 1639–59.

Pre–1953 H 1 Amendments: 117 v 520, § 1

Amendment Note: 2000 H 332 inserted "certified" twice throughout the section.

Amendment Note: 2000 H 448 inserted "certified" twice.

Library References

Carlin, Baldwin's Ohio Practice, Merrick–Rippner Probate Law § 105.1, 107.46 (2003).

2151.551 Requirements of oral communication of intended placement

During the oral communication described in section 2151.55 of the Revised Code, the representative of the placing entity shall do the following:

(A) Discuss safety and well-being concerns regarding the child and, if the child attends school, the students, teachers, and personnel of the school;

(B) Provide the following information:

(1) A brief description of the reasons the child was removed from home;

(2) Services the child is receiving;

(3) The name of the contact person for the placing entity that is directly responsible for monitoring the child's placement;

(4) The telephone number of the placing entity and, if the child is in the temporary, permanent, or legal custody of a private or government entity other than the placing entity, the telephone number of the entity with custody;

(5) The previous school district attended by the child;

(6) The last known address of the child's parents.

(1999 H 283, eff. 9–29–99)

Library References

OJur 3d: 46, Family Law § 1415 et seq.

2151.552 Time for provision of written information

No later than five days after a child described in section 2151.55 of the Revised Code is enrolled in school in the district described in that section, the placing entity shall provide in writing the information described in division (B) of section 2151.551 of the Revised Code to the school district and the child's foster caregiver.

(1999 H 283, eff. 9–29–99)

Library References

OJur 3d: 46, Family Law § 1415 et seq.

2151.553 School district procedures for receiving information

Each school district board of education shall implement a procedure for receiving the information described in section 2151.552 of the Revised Code.

(1999 H 283, eff. 9–29–99)

Library References

OJur 3d: 46, Family Law § 1415 et seq.

2151.554 Provision of written information to juvenile court

When a private or governmental entity places a child who has been adjudicated to be an unruly or delinquent child in a certified foster home in a county other than the county in which the child resided at the time of being removed from home, the placing entity shall provide the following information in writing to the juvenile court of the county in which the certified foster home is located:

(A) The information listed in divisions (B)(2) to (4) of section 2151.551 of the Revised Code;

(B) A brief description of the facts supporting the adjudication that the child is unruly or delinquent;

(C) The name and address of the foster caregiver;

(D) Safety and well-being concerns with respect to the child and community.

(2000 H 332, eff. 1–1–01; 2000 H 448, eff. 10–5–00; 1999 H 283, eff. 9–29–99)

Historical and Statutory Notes

Ed. Note: The amendment of this section by 2000 H 332, eff. 1–1–01, and 2000 H 448, eff. 10–5–00, was identical. See *Baldwin's Ohio Legislative Service Annotated*, 2000, pages 6/L–2160 and 6/L–2233, or the OH–LEGIS or OH–LEGIS–OLD database on WESTLAW, for original versions of these Acts.

Amendment Note: 2000 H 332 inserted "certified" twice in the introductory paragraph.

Amendment Note: 2000 H 448 inserted "certified" twice in the introductory paragraph.

Library References

OJur 3d: 46, Family Law § 1415 et seq.

INTERSTATE COMPACT ON JUVENILES

2151.56 Interstate compact on juveniles

The governor is hereby authorized to execute a compact on behalf of this state with any other state or states legally joining therein in the form substantially as follows:

THE INTERSTATE COMPACT ON JUVENILES

The contracting states solemnly agree:

Article I —Findings and Purposes

That juveniles who are not under proper supervision and control, or who have absconded, escaped or run away, are likely to endanger their own health, morals and welfare, and the health, morals and welfare of others. The cooperation of the states party to this compact is therefore necessary to provide for the welfare and protection of juveniles and of the public with respect to (1) cooperative supervision of delinquent juveniles on probation or parole; (2) the return, from one state to another, of delinquent juveniles who have escaped or absconded; (3) the return, from one state to another, of nondelinquent juveniles who have run away from home; and (4) additional measures for the protection of juveniles and of the public, which any two or more of the party states may find desirable to undertake cooperatively. In carrying out the provisions of this compact the party states shall be guided by the noncriminal, reformative and protective policies which guide their laws concerning delinquent, neglected or dependent juveniles generally. It shall be the policy of the states party to this compact to cooperate and observe their respective responsibilities for the prompt return and acceptance of juveniles and delinquent juveniles who become subject to the provisions of this compact. The provisions of this compact shall be reasonably and liberally construed to accomplish the foregoing purposes.

Article II —Existing Rights and Remedies

That all remedies and procedures provided by this compact shall be in addition to and not in substitution for other rights, remedies and procedures, and shall not be in derogation of parental rights and responsibilities.

Article III —Definitions

That, for the purposes of this compact, "delinquent juvenile" means any juvenile who has been adjudged delinquent and who, at the time the provisions of this compact are invoked, is still subject to the jurisdiction of the court that has made such adjudication or to the jurisdiction or supervision of an agency or institution pursuant to an order of such court; "probation or parole" means any kind of conditional release of juveniles authorized under the laws of the states party hereto; "court" means any court having jurisdiction over delinquent, neglected or dependent children; "state" means any state, territory or possessions of the United States, the District of Columbia, and the Commonwealth of Puerto Rico; and "residence" or any variant thereof means a place at which a home or regular place of abode is maintained.

Article IV —Return of Runaways

(a) That the parent, guardian, person or agency entitled to legal custody of a juvenile who has not been adjudged de-linquent but who has run away without the consent of such parent, guardian, person or agency may petition the appropriate court in the demanding state for the issuance of a requisition for his return. The petition shall state the name and age of the juvenile, the name of the petitioner and the basis of entitlement to the juvenile's custody, the circumstances of his running away, his location if known at the time application is made, and such other facts as may tend to show that the juvenile who has run away is endangering his own welfare or the welfare of others and is not an emancipated minor. The petition shall be verified by affidavit, shall be executed in duplicate, and shall be accompanied by two certified copies of the document or documents on which the petitioner's entitlement to the juvenile's custody is based, such as birth records, letters of guardianship, or custody decrees. Such further affidavits and other documents as may be deemed proper may be submitted with such petition. The judge of the court to which this application is made may hold a hearing thereon to determine whether for the purposes of this compact the petitioner is entitled to the legal custody of the juvenile, whether or not it appears that the juvenile has in fact run away without consent, whether or not he is an emancipated minor, and whether or not it is in the best interest of the juvenile to compel his return to the state. If the judge determines, either with or without a hearing, that the juvenile should be returned, he shall present to the appropriate court or to the executive authority of the state where the juvenile is alleged to be located a written requisition for the return of such juvenile. Such requisition shall set forth the name and age of the juvenile, the determination of the court that the juvenile has run away without the consent of a parent, guardian, person or agency entitled to his legal custody, and that it is in the best interest and for the protection of such juvenile that he be returned. In the event that a proceeding for the adjudication of the juvenile as a delinquent, neglected or dependent juvenile is pending in the court at the time when such juvenile runs away, the court may issue a requisition for the return of such juvenile upon its own motion, regardless of the consent of the parent, guardian, person or agency entitled to legal custody, reciting therein the nature and circumstances of the pending proceeding. The requisition shall in every case be executed in duplicate and shall be signed by the judge. One copy of the requisition shall be filed with the compact administrator of the demanding state, there to remain on file subject to the provisions of law governing records of such court. Upon the receipt of a requisition demanding the return of a juvenile who has run away, the court or the executive authority to whom the requisition is addressed shall issue an order to any peace officer or other appropriate person directing him to take into custody and detain such juvenile. Such detention order must substantially recite the facts necessary to the validity of its issuance hereunder. No juvenile detained upon such order shall be delivered over to the officer whom the court demanding him shall have appointed to receive him, unless he shall first be taken forthwith before a judge of a court in the state, who shall inform him of the demand made for his return, and who may appoint counsel or guardian ad litem for him. If the judge of such court shall find that the requisition is in order, he shall deliver such juvenile over to the officer whom the court demanding him shall have appointed to receive him. The judge, however, may fix a reasonable time to be allowed for the purpose of testing the legality of the proceeding.

Upon reasonable information that a person is a juvenile who has run away from another state party to this compact without the consent of a parent, guardian, person or agency entitled to his legal custody, such juvenile may be taken into custody without a requisition and brought forthwith before a judge of the appropriate court who may appoint counsel or guardian ad litem for such juvenile and who shall determine after a hearing whether sufficient cause exists to hold the person, subject to the order of the court, for his own protection and welfare, for such a time not exceeding ninety days as will enable his return to another state party to this compact pursuant to a requisition for his return from a court of that state. If, at the time when a state seeks the return of a juvenile who has run away, there is pending in the state wherein he is found any criminal charge, or any proceeding to have him adjudicated a delinquent juvenile for an act committed in such state, or if he is suspected of having committed within such state a criminal offense or an act of juvenile delinquency, he shall not be returned without the consent of such state until discharged from prosecution or other form of proceeding, imprisonment, detention or supervision for such offense or juvenile delinquency. The duly accredited officers of any state party to this compact, upon the establishment of their authority and the identity of the juvenile being returned, shall be permitted to transport such juvenile through any and all states party to this compact, without interference. Upon his return to the state from which he ran away, the juvenile shall be subject to such further proceedings as may be appropriate under the laws of that state.

(b) That the state to which a juvenile is returned under this Article shall be responsible for payment of the transportation costs of such return.

(c) That "juvenile" as used in this Article means any person who is a minor under the law of the state of residence of the parent, guardian, person or agency entitled to the legal custody of such minor.

Article V —Return of Escapees and Absconders

(a) That the appropriate person or authority from whose probation or parole supervision a delinquent juvenile has absconded or from whose institutional custody he has escaped shall present to the appropriate court or to the executive authority of the state where the delinquent juvenile is alleged to be located a written requisition for the return of such delinquent juvenile. Such requisition shall state the name and age of the delinquent juvenile, the particulars of his adjudication as a delinquent juvenile, the circumstances of the breach of the terms of his probation or parole or of his escape from an institution or agency vested with his legal custody or supervision, and the location of such delinquent juvenile, if known, at the time the requisition is made. The requisition shall be verified by affidavit, shall be executed in duplicate, and shall be accompanied by two certified copies of the judgment, formal adjudication, or order of commitment which subjects such delinquent juvenile to probation or parole or to the legal custody of the institution or agency concerned. Such further affidavits and other documents as may be deemed proper may be submitted with such requisition. One copy of the requisition shall be filed with the compact administrator of the demanding state, there to remain on file subject to the provisions of law governing records of the appropriate court. Upon the receipt of a requisition demanding the return of a delinquent juvenile who has absconded or escaped, the court or the executive authority to whom the requisition is addressed shall issue an order to any peace officer or other appropriate person directing him to take into custody and detain such delinquent juvenile. Such detention order must substantially recite the facts necessary to the validity of its issuance hereunder. No delinquent juvenile detained upon such order shall be delivered over to the officer whom the appropriate person or authority demanding him shall have appointed to receive him, unless he shall first be taken forthwith before a judge of an appropriate court in the state, who shall inform him of the demand made for his return and who may appoint counsel or guardian ad litem for him. If the judge of such court shall find that the requisition is in order, he shall deliver such delinquent juvenile over to the officer whom the appropriate person or authority demanding him shall have appointed to receive him. The judge, however, may fix a reasonable time to be allowed for the purpose of testing the legality of the proceeding.

Upon reasonable information that a person is a delinquent juvenile who has absconded while on probation or parole, or escaped from an institution or agency vested with his legal custody or supervision in any state party to this compact, such person may be taken into custody in any other state party to this compact without a requisition. But in such event, he must be taken forthwith before a judge of the appropriate court, who may appoint counsel or guardian ad litem for such person and who shall determine, after a hearing, whether sufficient cause exists to hold the person subject to the order of the court for such a time, not exceeding ninety days, as will enable his detention under a detention order issued on a requisition pursuant to this Article. If, at the time when a state seeks the return of a delinquent juvenile who has either absconded while on probation or parole or escaped from an institution or agency vested with his legal custody or supervision, there is pending in the state wherein he is detained any criminal charge or any proceeding to have him adjudicated a delinquent juvenile for an act committed in such state, or if he is suspected of having committed within such state a criminal offense or an act of

juvenile delinquency, he shall not be returned without the consent of such state until discharged from prosecution or other form of proceeding, imprisonment, detention or supervision for such offense or juvenile delinquency. The duly accredited officers of any state party to this compact, upon the establishment of their authority and the identity of the delinquent juvenile being returned, shall be permitted to transport such delinquent juvenile through any and all states party to this compact, without interference. Upon his return to the state from which he escaped or absconded, the delinquent juvenile shall be subject to such further proceedings as may be appropriate under the laws of that state.

(b) That the state to which a delinquent juvenile is returned under this Article shall be responsible for the payment of the transportation costs of such return.

Article VI —Voluntary
Return Procedure

That any delinquent juvenile who has absconded while on probation or parole, or escaped from an institution or agency vested with his legal custody or supervision in any state party to this compact, and any juvenile who has run away from any state party to this compact, who is taken into custody without a requisition in another state party to this compact under the provisions of Article IV (a) or of Article V (a), may consent to his immediate return to the state from which he absconded, escaped or ran away. Such consent shall be given by the juvenile or delinquent juvenile and his counsel or guardian ad litem if any, by executing or subscribing a writing, in the presence of a judge of the appropriate court, which states that the juvenile or delinquent juvenile and his counsel or guardian ad litem, if any, consent to his return to the demanding state. Before such consent shall be executed or subscribed, however, the judge, in the presence of counsel or guardian ad litem, if any, shall inform the juvenile or delinquent juvenile of his rights under this compact. When the consent has been duly executed, it shall be forwarded to and filed with the compact administrator of the state in which the court is located and the judge shall direct the officer having the juvenile or delinquent juvenile in custody to deliver him to the duly accredited officer or officers of the state demanding his return, and shall cause to be delivered to such officer or officers a copy of the consent. The court may, however, upon the request of the state to which the juvenile or delinquent juvenile is being returned, order him to return unaccompanied to such state and shall provide him with a copy of such court order; in such event a copy of the consent shall be forwarded to the compact administrator of the state to which said juvenile or delinquent juvenile is ordered to return.

Article VII —Cooperative Supervision of Probationers and Parolees

(a) That the duly constituted judicial and administrative authorities of a state party to this compact (herein called "sending state") may permit any delinquent juvenile within such state, placed on probation or parole, to reside in any other state party to this compact (herein called "receiving state") while on probation or parole, and the receiving state shall accept such delinquent juvenile, if the parent, guardian or person entitled to the legal custody of such delinquent juvenile is residing or undertakes to reside within the receiving state. Before granting such permission, opportunity shall be given to the receiving state to make such investigations as it deems necessary. The authorities of the sending state shall send to the authorities of the receiving state copies of pertinent court orders, social case studies and all other available information which may be of value to and assist the receiving state in supervising a probationer or parolee in this compact. A receiving state, in its discretion, may agree to accept supervision of a probationer or parolee in cases where the parent, guardian or person entitled to the legal custody of the delinquent juvenile is not a resident of the receiving state, and if so accepted the sending state may transfer supervision accordingly.

(b) That each receiving state will assume the duties of visitation and of supervision over any such delinquent juvenile and in the exercise of those duties will be governed by the same standards of visitation and supervision that prevail for its own delinquent juveniles released on probation or parole.

(c) That, after consultation between the appropriate authorities of the sending state and of the receiving state as to the desirability and necessity of returning such a delinquent juvenile, the duly accredited officers of a sending state may enter a receiving state and there appre-

hend and retake any such delinquent juvenile on probation or parole. For that purpose, no formalities will be required, other than establishing the authority of the officer and the identity of the delinquent juvenile to be retaken and returned. The decision of the sending state to retake a delinquent juvenile on probation or parole shall be conclusive upon and not reviewable within the receiving state, but if, at the time the sending state seeks to retake a delinquent juvenile on probation or parole, there is pending against him within the receiving state any criminal charge or any proceeding to have him adjudicated a delinquent juvenile for any act committed in such state, or if he is suspected of having committed within such state a criminal offense or an act of juvenile delinquency, he shall not be returned without the consent of the receiving state until discharged from prosecution or other form of proceeding, imprisonment, detention or supervision for such offense or juvenile delinquency. The duly accredited officers of the sending state shall be permitted to transport delinquent juveniles being so returned through any and all states party to this compact, without interference.

(d) That the sending state shall be responsible under this Article for paying the costs of transporting any delinquent juvenile to the receiving state or of returning any delinquent juvenile to the sending state.

Article VIII —Responsibility for Costs

(a) That the provisions of Articles IV(b), V(b) and VII(d) of this compact shall not be construed to alter or affect any internal relationship among the departments, agencies and officers of and in the government of a party state, or between a party state and its subdivisions, as to the payment of costs, or responsibilities therefor.

(b) That nothing in this compact shall be construed to prevent any party state or subdivision thereof from asserting any right against any person, agency or other entity in regard to costs for which such party state or subdivision thereof may be responsible pursuant to Articles IV(b), V(b) or VII(d) of this compact.

Article IX —Detention Practices

That, to every extent possible, it shall be the policy of states party to this compact that no juvenile or delinquent juvenile shall be placed or detained in any prison, jail or lockup nor be detained or transported in association with criminal, vicious or dissolute persons.

Article X —Supplementary Agreements

That the duly constituted administrative authorities of a state party to this compact may enter into supplementary agreements with any other state or states party hereto for the cooperative care, treatment and rehabilitation of delinquent juveniles whenever they shall find that such agreements will improve the facilities or programs available for such care, treatment and rehabilitation. Such care, treatment and rehabilitation may be provided in an institution located within any state entering into such supplementary agreement. Such supplementary agreements shall (1) provide the rates to be paid for the care, treatment and custody of such delinquent juveniles, taking into consideration the character of facilities, services and subsistence furnished; (2) provide that the delinquent juvenile shall be given a court hearing prior to his being sent to another state for care, treatment and custody; (3) provide that the state receiving such a delinquent juvenile in one of its institutions shall act solely as agent for the state sending such delinquent juvenile; (4) provide that the sending state shall at all times retain jurisdiction over delinquent juveniles sent to an institution in another state; (5) provide for reasonable inspection of such institutions by the sending state; (6) provide that the consent of the parent, guardian, person or agency entitled to the legal custody of said delinquent juvenile shall be secured prior to his being sent to another state; and (7) make provision for such other matters and details as shall be necessary to protect the rights and equities of such delinquent juveniles and of the cooperating states.

Article XI —Acceptance of Federal and Other Aid

That any state party to this compact may accept any and all donations, gifts and grants of money, equipment and services from the federal or any local government, or any agency thereof and from any person, firm or corporation, for any of the purposes and functions of this compact, and may receive and utilize the same subject to the terms, conditions and regulations governing such donations, gifts and grants.

Article XII —Compact Administrators

That the governor of each state party to this compact shall designate an officer who, acting jointly with like officers of other party states, shall promulgate rules and regulations to carry out more effectively the terms and provisions of this compact.

Article XIII —Execution of Compact

That this compact shall become operative immediately upon its execution by any state as between it and any other state or states so executing. When executed it shall have the full force and effect of law within such state, the form of execution to be in accordance with the laws of the executing state.

Article XIV —Renunciation

That this compact shall continue in force and remain binding upon each executing state until renounced by it. Renunciation of this compact shall be by the same authority which executed it, by sending six months' notice in writing of its intention to withdraw from the compact to the other states party hereto. The duties and obligations of a renouncing state under Article VII hereof shall continue as to parolees and probationers residing therein at the time of withdrawal until retaken or finally discharged. Supplementary agreements entered into under Article X hereof shall be subject to renunciation as provided by such supplementary agreements, and shall not be subject to the six months' renunciation notice of the present Article.

Article XV —Severability

That the provisions of this compact shall be severable and if any phrase, clause, sentence or provision of this compact is declared to be contrary to the constitution of any participating state or of the United States or the applicability thereof to any government, agency, person or circumstance is held invalid, the validity of the remainder of this compact and the applicability thereof to any government, agency, person or circumstance shall not be affected thereby. If this compact shall be held contrary to the constitution of any state participating therein, the compact shall remain in full force and effect as to the remaining states and in full force and effect as to the state affected as to all severable matters.

(1988 H 790, eff. 3–16–89; 127 v 530)

Comparative Laws

Ala.—Code 1975, § 44–2–1 to 44–2–7.
Alaska—AS 47.15.010 to 47.15.080.
Ariz.—A.R.S. § 8-361 to 8–367.
Ark.—A.C.A. § 9-29-101 to 9–29–108.
Cal.—West's Ann.Cal.Welf. & Inst.Code, § 1300.
Colo.—West's C.R.S.A. § 24–60–701 to 24–60–708.
Conn.—C.G.S.A. § 17-75 to 17–81.
D.C.—D.C. Code 1981, § 32–1101 to 32–1106.
Del.—31 Del.C. § 5203, 5221 to 5228.
Fla.—West's F.S.A. § 985.501 to 985.507.
Ga.—O.C.G.A. § 39-3-1 to 39–3–7.
Hawaii—HRS § 582–1 to 582–8.
Idaho—I.C. § 16-1901 to 16–1910.
Ill.—45 ILCS 10/0.01 to 10/7.
Ind.—West's A.I.C. 31–37–23–1 to 31–37–23–10.
Iowa—I.C.A. § 232.171, 232.172.
Kan.—K.S.A. 38-1001 to 38–1006.
Ky.—Baldwin's KRS 615.010, 615.020.
La.—LSA-C.C. arts. 1623 to 1657.
Mass.—M.G.L.A. c. 119 App., § 1–1 to 1–7.
Md.—Code 1957, art. 83C, § 3–102 to 3–109.
Me.—34-A M.R.S.A. § 9001 to 9016.
Mich.—M.C.L.A. § 3.701 to 3.706.
Minn.—M.S.A. § 260.51 to 260.57.
Miss.—Code 1972, § 43–25–1 to 43–25–17.
Mo.—V.A.M.S. § 210.570 to 210.600.
Mont.—MCA 41–6–101 to 41–6–106.
N.C.—G.S. § 7B-2800 to 7B–2827.
N.D.—NDCC 27–22–01 to 27–22–06.
Neb.—R.R.S.1943, § 43–1001 to 43–1009.
Nev.—N.R.S. 214.010 to 214.060.
N.H.—RSA 169–A:1 to 169–A:9.
N.J.—N.J.S.A. 9:23-1 to 9:23–4.
N.M.—NMSA 1978, § 32–3–1 to 32–3–8.
N.Y.—McKinney's Unconsol. Laws, § 1801 to 1806.
Okl.—10 Okl.St.Ann. § 531 to 537.
Ore.—ORS 417.010 to 417.080.
Pa.—62 P.S. § 731 et seq.
R.I.—Gen.Laws 1956, § 14–6–1 to 14–6–11.
S.C.—Code 1976, § 20–7–2080.
S.D.—SDCL 26–12–1 to 26–12–13.
Tenn.—T.C.A. § 37-4-101 to 37–4–106.
Tex.—V.T.C.A., Family Code § 60.001 to 60.009.
Utah—U.C.A.1953, 55–12–1 to 55–12–6.
Va.—Code 1950, § 16.1–323 to 16.1–330.
Vt.—33 V.S.A. § 5701 to 5703.
Wash.—West's RCWA 13.24.010 to 13.24.900.
Wis.—W.S.A. 48.991 to 48.997.
W.Va.—Code, 49–8–1 to 49–8–7.
Wyo.—Wyo.Stat.Ann., § 14–5–101.

Cross References

Jurisdiction of juvenile court under interstate compact, 2151.23
Procedure not otherwise specified, Juv R 45

Library References

Infants ⟐131.
States ⟐6.
Westlaw Topic Nos. 211, 360.
C.J.S. Infants §§ 31 to 54.
C.J.S. States §§ 31, 32, 143.
OJur 3d: 48, Family Law § 1523, 1524
Extradition of juveniles. 73 ALR3d 700
Carlin, Baldwin's Ohio Practice, Merrick–Rippner Probate Law § 105.1, 107.128, 107.129 (2003).

2151.57 Compact administrator; powers and duties

Pursuant to section 2151.56 of the Revised Code, the governor is hereby authorized and empowered, with the advice and consent of the senate, to designate an officer who shall be the compact administrator and who, acting jointly with like officers of other party states, shall promulgate rules and regulations to carry out more effectively the terms of the compact. Such compact administrator shall serve subject to the pleasure of the governor. The compact administrator is hereby authorized, empowered and directed to cooperate with all departments, agencies and officers of and in the government of this state and its subdivisions in facilitating the proper administration of the compact or of any supplementary agreement or agreements entered into by this state thereunder.

(127 v 530, eff. 9–17–57)

Library References

OJur 3d: 48, Family Law § 1524
Extradition of juveniles. 73 ALR3d 700
Carlin, Baldwin's Ohio Practice, Merrick–Rippner Probate Law § 107.128 (2003).

2151.58 Supplementary agreements

The compact administrator is hereby authorized and empowered to enter into supplementary agreements with appropriate officials of other states pursuant to the compact. In the event that such supplementary agreement shall require or contemplate the use of any institution or facility of this state or require or contemplate the provision of any service by this state, said supplementary agreement shall have no force or effect until approved by the head of the department or agency under whose jurisdiction the institution or facility is operated or whose department or agency will be charged with the rendering of such service.

(127 v 530, eff. 9–17–57)

Library References

OJur 3d: 48, Family Law § 1524
Extradition of juveniles. 73 ALR3d 700

2151.59 Discharge of financial obligations

The compact administrator, subject to the approval of the director of budget and management, may make or arrange for any payments necessary to discharge any financial obligations imposed upon this state by the compact or by any supplementary agreement entered into thereunder.

(1985 H 201, eff. 7–1–85; 127 v 530)

Library References

OJur 3d: 48, Family Law § 1524

Extradition of juveniles. 73 ALR3d 700

Carlin, Baldwin's Ohio Practice, Merrick–Rippner Probate Law § 107.128 (2003).

2151.60   Enforcement by agencies of state and subdivisions

The courts, departments, agencies and officers of this state and its subdivisions shall enforce this compact and shall do all things appropriate to the effectuation of its purposes and intent which may be within their respective jurisdictions.

(127 v 530, eff. 9–17–57)

Library References

OJur 3d: 48, Family Law § 1525

2151.61   Additional article

In addition to any procedure provided in Articles IV and VI of the compact for the return of any runaway juvenile, the particular states, the juvenile or his parents, the courts, or other legal custodian involved may agree upon and adopt any other plan or procedure legally authorized under the laws of this state and the other respective party states for the return of any such runaway juvenile.

Article XVI —Additional Article

The governor is hereby authorized and directed to execute, with any other state or states legally joining in the same, an amendment to the interstate compact on juveniles in substantially the following form:

"(a) That this Article shall provide additional remedies, and shall be binding only as among and between those party states which specifically execute the same.

(b) For the purposes of Article XVI(c), "child", as used herein, means any minor within the jurisdictional age limits of any court in the home state.

(c) When any child is brought before a court of a state of which such child is not a resident, and such state is willing to permit such child's return to the home state of such child, such home state, upon being so advised by the state in which such proceeding is pending, shall immediately institute proceedings to determine the residence and jurisdictional facts as to such child in such home state, and upon finding that such child is in fact a resident of said state and subject to the jurisdiction of the court thereof, shall within five days authorize the return of such child to the home state, and to the parent or custodial agency legally authorized to accept such custody in such home state, and at the expense of such home state, to be paid from such funds as such home state may procure, designate, or provide, prompt action being of the essence.

(d) All provisions and procedures of Articles V and VI of the interstate compact on juveniles shall be construed to apply to any juvenile charged with being a delinquent juvenile for the violation of any criminal law. Any juvenile charged with being a delinquent juvenile for violating any criminal law shall be returned to the requesting state upon a requisition to the state where the juvenile may be found. A petition in the case shall be filed in a court of competent jurisdiction in the requesting state where the violation of criminal law is alleged to have been committed. The petition may be filed regardless of whether the juvenile has left the state before or after the filing of the petition. The requisition described in Article V of the compact shall be forwarded by the judge of the county in which the petition has been filed."

(1992 H 154, eff. 7–31–92; 127 v 530)

Cross References

Judges of the division of domestic relations, 2301.03

Library References

OJur 3d: 48, Family Law § 1523

Carlin, Baldwin's Ohio Practice, Merrick–Rippner Probate Law § 107.128 (2003).

FACILITIES FOR TRAINING, TREATMENT, AND REHABILITATION OF JUVENILES

2151.65   Facilities for treatment of juveniles; joint boards; admission

Upon the advice and recommendation of the juvenile judge, the board of county commissioners may provide by purchase, lease, construction, or otherwise a school, forestry camp, or other facility or facilities where delinquent children, as defined in section 2152.02 of the Revised Code, dependent children, abused children, unruly children, as defined in section 2151.022 of the Revised Code, or neglected children or juvenile traffic offenders may be held for training, treatment, and rehabilitation. Upon the joint advice and recommendation of the juvenile judges of two or more adjoining or neighboring counties, the boards of county commissioners of such counties may form themselves into a joint board and proceed to organize a district for the establishment and support of a school, forestry camp, or other facility or facilities for the use of the juvenile courts of such counties, where delinquent, dependent, abused, unruly, or neglected children, or juvenile traffic offenders may be held for treatment, training, and rehabilitation, by using a site or buildings already established in one such county, or by providing for the purchase of a site and the erection of the necessary buildings thereon. Such county or district school, forestry camp, or other facility or facilities shall be maintained as provided in Chapters 2151. and 2152. of the Revised Code. Children who are adjudged to be delinquent, dependent, neglected, abused, unruly, or juvenile traffic offenders may be committed to and held in any such school, forestry camp, or other facility or facilities for training, treatment, and rehabilitation.

The juvenile court shall determine:

(A) The children to be admitted to any school, forestry camp, or other facility maintained under this section;

(B) The period such children shall be trained, treated, and rehabilitated at such facility;

(C) The removal and transfer of children from such facility.

(2000 S 179, § 3, eff. 1–1–02; 1980 S 168, eff. 10–2–80; 1975 H 85; 130 v H 879)

Historical and Statutory Notes

Amendment Note: 2000 S 179, § 3, eff. 1–1–02, substituted "2152.02" for "2151.02" and "Chapters 2151. and 2152." for "sections 2151.01 to 2151.80" in the first paragraph; and made other nonsubstantive changes.

Cross References

Acquisition, construction, or renovation of facilities, 307.021

Additional disposition orders for delinquent children; 2152.19

Adoption of rules for payment of assistance, 5139.29

Resolution relative to tax levy in excess of ten-mill limitation, 5705.19

Standards of construction prerequisite to financial assistance of facilities for rehabilitation of delinquent juveniles, 5139.27

Tax levy law, detention home district is "subdivision," 5705.01

Transfer of child committed to facility, 5139.30

Uniform bond law, fiscal officer, subdivision and taxing authority defined, definitions, 133.01

Withdrawal of county from district, continuity of district tax levy, 2151.78

Library References

OJur 3d: 48, Family Law § 1718; 73, Penal and Correctional Institutions § 53; 86, Taxation § 62

Carlin, Baldwin's Ohio Practice, Merrick–Rippner Probate Law § 104.18, 107.73, 107.84 (2003).

2151.651 Application for financial assistance for acquisition or construction of facilities

The board of county commissioners of a county which, either separately or as part of a district, is planning to establish a school, forestry camp, or other facility under section 2151.65 of the Revised Code, to be used exclusively for the rehabilitation of children between the ages of twelve to eighteen years, other than psychotic or mentally retarded children, who are designated delinquent children, as defined in section 2152.02 of the Revised Code, or unruly children, as defined in section 2151.022 of the Revised Code, by order of a juvenile court, may make application to the department of youth services, created under section 5139.01 of the Revised Code, for financial assistance in defraying the county's share of the cost of acquisition or construction of such school, camp, or other facility, as provided in section 5139.27 of the Revised Code. Such application shall be made on forms prescribed and furnished by the department.

(2000 S 179, § 3, eff. 1–1–02; 1981 H 440, eff. 11–23–81; 1980 S 168; 131 v H 943)

Historical and Statutory Notes

Amendment Note: 2000 S 179, § 3, eff. 1–1–02, substituted "2152.02" for "2151.01"; deleted "division (B) of" before "section 5139.01"; and made other nonsubstantive changes.

Cross References

Inspection of youth rehabilitation facilities, 5139.31

Standards of construction prerequisite to financial assistance of facilities for rehabilitation of delinquent juveniles, 5139.27

Library References

Infants ⬯271, 272, 273, 279.

Westlaw Topic No. 211.

C.J.S. Infants §§ 57, 69 to 85.

C.J.S. Reformatories §§ 1 to 19.

OJur 3d: 73, Penal and Correctional Institutions § 56

Carlin, Baldwin's Ohio Practice, Merrick–Rippner Probate Law § 104.18 (2003).

2151.653 Program of education; teachers

The board of county commissioners of a county or the board of trustees of a district maintaining a school, forestry camp, or other facility established under section 2151.65 of the Revised Code, shall provide a program of education for the youths admitted to such school, forestry camp, or other facility. Either of such boards and the board of education of any school district may enter into an agreement whereby such board of education provides teachers for such school, forestry camp, or other facility, or permits youths admitted to such school, forestry camp, or other facility to attend a school or schools within such school district, or both. Either of such boards may enter into an agreement with the appropriate authority of any university, college, or vocational institution to assist in providing a program of education for the youths admitted to such school, forestry camp, or other facility.

(131 v H 943, eff. 8–10–65)

2151.654 Agreements for admission of children from counties not maintaining facilities

The board of county commissioners of a county or the board of trustees of a district maintaining a school, forestry camp, or other facility established under section 2151.65 of the Revised Code, may enter into an agreement with the board of county commissioners of a county which does not maintain such a school, forestry camp, or other facility, to admit to such school, forestry camp, or other facility a child from the county not maintaining such a school, forestry camp, or other facility.

(131 v H 943, eff. 8–10–65)

2151.655 County taxing authority may submit securities issue to electors for support of schools, detention homes, forestry camps, or other facilities

(A) The taxing authority of a county may issue general obligation securities of the county under Chapter 133. of the Revised Code to pay such county's share, either separately or as a part of a district, of the cost of acquiring schools, detention facilities, forestry camps, or other facilities, or any combination thereof, un-

der section 2152.41 or 2151.65 of the Revised Code, or of acquiring sites for and constructing, enlarging, or otherwise improving such schools, detention facilities, forestry camps, other facilities, or combinations thereof.

(B) The taxing authority of a detention facility district, or a district organized under section 2151.65 of the Revised Code, or of a combined district organized under sections 2152.41 and 2151.65 of the Revised Code, may submit to the electors of the district the question of issuing general obligation bonds of the district to pay the cost of acquiring, constructing, enlarging, or otherwise improving sites, buildings, and facilities for any purposes for which the district was organized. The election on such question shall be submitted and held under section 133.18 of the Revised Code.

(2000 S 179, § 3, eff. 1–1–02; 1989 H 230, eff. 10–30–89)

Historical and Statutory Notes

Ed. Note: 2151.655 is former 133.151, amended and recodified by 1989 H 230, eff. 10–30–89; 1972 H 258; 1970 H 1135; 131 v H 943.

Amendment Note: 2000 S 179, § 3, eff. 1–1–02, substituted "facilities" for "homes" twice and "2152.41" for "2151.34" in division (A); and substituted "facility" for "home" and "2152.41" for "2151.34" in division (B).

Cross References

Uniform bond law, definitions, 133.01

Library References

Counties ☞149.

Infants ☞279.

Westlaw Topic Nos. 104, 211.

C.J.S. Counties §§ 185, 187.

C.J.S. Infants §§ 57, 69 to 85.

Baldwin's Ohio Legislative Service, 1989 Laws of Ohio, H 230—LSC Analysis, p 5–925

2151.66 Annual tax assessments

The joint boards of county commissioners of district schools, forestry camps, or other facility or facilities created under section 2151.65 of the Revised Code, shall make annual assessments of taxes sufficient to support and defray all necessary expenses of such school, forestry camp, or other facility or facilities.

(130 v H 879, eff. 10–14–63)

Library References

OJur 3d: 73, Penal and Correctional Institutions § 56

2151.67 Receipt and use of gifts, grants, devises, bequests and public moneys

The board of county commissioners of a county or the board of trustees of a district maintaining a school, forestry camp, or other facility established or to be established under section 2151.65 of the Revised Code may receive gifts, grants, devises, and bequests, either absolutely or in trust, and may receive any public moneys made available to it. Each of such boards shall use such gifts, grants, devises, bequests, and public moneys in whatever manner it determines is most likely to carry out the purposes for which such school, forestry camp, or other facility was or is to be established.

(132 v H 1, eff. 2–21–67; 131 v H 943)

Historical and Statutory Notes
Ed. Note: Former 2151.67 repealed by 131 v H 943, eff. 8–10–65; 130 v H 879.

Library References
OJur 3d: 73, Penal and Correctional Institutions § 56

2151.68 Board of trustees

Immediately upon the organization of the joint board of county commissioners as provided by section 2151.65 of the Revised Code, or so soon thereafter as practicable, such joint board of county commissioners shall appoint a board of not less than five trustees, which shall hold office and perform its duties until the first annual meeting after the choice of an established site and buildings, or after the selection and purchase of a building site, at which time such joint board of county commissioners shall appoint a board of not less than five trustees, one of whom shall hold office for a term of one year, one for the term of two years, one for the term of three years, half of the remaining number for the term of four years, and the remainder for the term of five years. Annually thereafter, the joint board of county commissioners shall appoint one or more trustees, each of whom shall hold office for the term of five years, to succeed any trustee whose term of office expires. A trustee may be appointed to succeed himself upon such board of trustees, and all appointments to such board of trustees shall be made from persons who are recommended and approved by the juvenile court judge or judges of the county of

which such person is a resident. The annual meeting of the board of trustees shall be held on the first Tuesday in May in each year.

(130 v H 879, eff. 10–14–63)

Ohio Administrative Code References
County department of job and family services responsibilities for certification, OAC 5101:2–14–61

Library References
OJur 3d: 73, Penal and Correctional Institutions § 54

2151.69 Board meetings; compensation

A majority of the trustees appointed under section 2151.68 of the Revised Code constitutes a quorum. Board meetings shall be held at least quarterly. The presiding juvenile court judge of each of the counties of the district organized pursuant to section 2151.65 of the Revised Code shall attend such meetings, or shall designate a member of his staff to do so. The members of the board shall receive no compensation for their services, except their actual traveling expenses, which, when properly certified, shall be allowed and paid by the treasurer.

(130 v H 879, eff. 10–14–63)

Library References
OJur 3d: 73, Penal and Correctional Institutions § 54

2151.70 Appointment of superintendent; bond; compensation; duties

The judge, in a county maintaining a school, forestry camp, or other facility or facilities created under section 2151.65 of the Revised Code, shall appoint the superintendent of any such facility. In the case of a district facility created under such section, the board of trustees shall appoint the superintendent. A superintendent, before entering upon his duties, shall give bond with sufficient surety to the judge or to the board, as the case may be, in such amount as may be fixed by the judge or the board, such bond being conditioned upon the full and faithful accounting of the funds and properties coming into his hands.

Compensation of the superintendent and other necessary employees of a school, forestry camp, or other facility or facilities shall be fixed by the judge in the case of a county facility, or by the board of trustees in the case of a district facility. Such compensation and other expenses of maintaining the facility shall be paid in the manner prescribed in section 2151.13 of the Revised Code in the case of a county facility, or in accordance with rules and regulations provided for in section 2151.77 of the Revised Code in the case of a district facility.

The superintendent of a facility shall appoint all employees of such facility. All such employees, except the superintendent, shall be in the classified civil service.

The superintendent of a school, forestry camp, or other facility shall have entire executive charge of such facility, under supervision of the judge, in the case of a county facility, or under supervision of the board of trustees, in the case of a district facility. The superintendent shall control, manage, and operate the facility, and shall have custody of its property, files, and records.

(130 v H 879, eff. 10–14–63)

Cross References

Classified civil service defined, 124.01
Official bond, 3.30 to 3.34

Library References

OJur 3d: 73, Penal and Correctional Institutions § 55

2151.71   Operation of facilities

District schools, forestry camps, or other facilities created under section 2151.65 of the Revised Code shall be established, operated, maintained, and managed in the same manner, so far as applicable, as county schools, forestry camps, or other facilities.

(130 v H 879, eff. 10–14–63)

Library References

OJur 3d: 73, Penal and Correctional Institutions § 53

2151.72   Selection of site for district facility

When the board of trustees appointed under section 2151.68 of the Revised Code does not choose an established institution in one of the counties of the district, it may select a suitable site for the erection of a district school, forestry camp, or other facility or facilities created under section 2151.65 of the Revised Code.

(130 v H 879, eff. 10–14–63)

Library References

OJur 3d: 73, Penal and Correctional Institutions § 54

2151.73   Apportionment of trustees; executive committee

Each county in the district, organized under section 2151.65 of the Revised Code, shall be entitled to one trustee, and in districts composed of but two counties, each county shall be entitled to not less than two trustees. In districts composed of more than four counties, the number of trustees shall be sufficiently increased so that there shall always be an uneven number of trustees constituting such board. The county in which a district school, forestry camp, or other facility created under section 2151.65 of the Revised Code is located shall have not less than two trustees, who, in the interim period between the regular meetings of the board of trustees, shall act as an executive committee in the discharge of all business pertaining to the school, forestry camp, or other facility.

(130 v H 879, eff. 10–14–63)

Library References

OJur 3d: 73, Penal and Correctional Institutions § 54

2151.74   Removal of trustee

The joint board of county commissioners organized under section 2151.65 of the Revised Code may remove any trustee appointed under section 2151.68 of the Revised Code, but no such removal shall be made on account of the religious or political convictions of such trustee. The trustee appointed to fill any vacancy shall hold his office for the unexpired term of his predecessor.

(130 v H 879, eff. 10–14–63)

Library References

OJur 3d: 73, Penal and Correctional Institutions § 54

2151.75   Interim duties of trustees; trustees fund; reports

In the interim, between the selection and purchase of a site, and the erection and occupancy of a district school, forestry camp, or other facility or facilities created under section 2151.65 of the Revised Code, the joint board of county commissioners provided by section 2151.65 of the Revised Code may delegate to a board of trustees appointed under section 2151.68 of the Revised Code, such powers and duties as, in its judgment, will be of general interest or aid to the institution. Such joint board of county commissioners may appropriate a trustees' fund, to be expended by the board of trustees in payment of such contracts, purchases, or other expenses necessary to the wants or requirements of the school, forestry camp, or other facility or facilities which are not otherwise provided for. The board of trustees shall make a complete settlement with the joint board of county commissioners once each six months, or quarterly if required, and shall make a full report of the condition of the school, forestry camp, or other facility or facilities and inmates, to the board of county commissioners, and to the juvenile court of each of the counties.

(130 v H 879, eff. 10–14–63)

Library References

OJur 3d: 73, Penal and Correctional Institutions § 54

2151.76 Authority for choice, construction, and furnishing of district facility

The choice of an established site and buildings, or the purchase of a site, stock, implements, and general farm equipment, should there be a farm, the erection of buildings, and the completion and furnishing of the district school, forestry camp, or other facility or facilities for occupancy, shall be in the hands of the joint board of county commissioners organized under section 2151.65 of the Revised Code. Such joint board of county commissioners may delegate all or a portion of these duties to the board of trustees provided for under section 2151.68 of the Revised Code, under such restrictions and regulations as the joint board of county commissioners imposes.

(130 v H 879, eff. 10–14–63)

Library References

OJur 3d: 73, Penal and Correctional Institutions § 54

2151.77 Capital and current expenses of district

When an established site and buildings are used for a district school, forestry camp, or other facility or facilities created under section 2151.65 of the Revised Code the joint board of county commissioners organized under section 2151.65 of the Revised Code shall cause the value of such site and buildings to be properly appraised. This appraisal value, or in case of the purchase of a site, the purchase price and the cost of all betterments and additions thereto, shall be paid by the counties comprising the district, in proportion to the taxable property of each county, as shown by its tax duplicate. The current expenses of maintaining the school, forestry camp, or other facility or facilities and the cost of ordinary repairs thereto shall be paid by each such county in accordance with one of the following methods as approved by the joint board of county commissioners:

(A) In proportion to the number of children from such county who are maintained in the school, forestry camp, or other facility or facilities during the year;

(B) By a levy submitted by the joint board of county commissioners under division (A) of section 5705.19 of the Revised Code and approved by the electors of the district;

(C) In proportion to the taxable property of each county, as shown by its tax duplicate;

(D) In any combination of the methods for payment described in division (A), (B), or (C) of this section.

The board of trustees shall, with the approval of the joint board of county commissioners, adopt rules for the management of funds used for the current expenses of maintaining the school, forestry camp, or other facility or facilities.

(1988 H 365, eff. 6–14–88; 1972 H 258; 130 v H 879)

Library References

Counties ☞131.
Infants ☞271.
Westlaw Topic Nos. 104, 211.
C.J.S. Counties § 172.
C.J.S. Reformatories §§ 1 to 5.
OJur 3d: 73, Penal and Correctional Institutions § 56

2151.78 Withdrawal of county from district; continuity of district tax levy

The board of county commissioners of any county within a school, forestry camp, or other facility or facilities district may, upon the recommendation of the juvenile court of such county, withdraw from such district and dispose of its interest in such school, forestry camp, or other facility or facilities selling or leasing its right, title, and interest in the site, buildings, furniture, and equipment to any counties in the district, at such price and upon such terms as are agreed upon among the boards of county commissioners of the counties concerned. Section 307.10 of the Revised Code does not apply to this section. The net proceeds of any such sale or lease shall be paid into the treasury of the withdrawing county.

Any county withdrawing from such district or from a combined district organized under sections 2152.41 and 2151.65 of the Revised Code shall continue to have levied against its tax duplicate any tax levied by the district during the period in which the county was a member of the district for current operating expenses, permanent improvements, or the retirement of bonded indebtedness. Such levy shall continue to be a levy against such duplicate of the county until such time that it expires or is renewed.

Members of the board of trustees of a district school, forestry camp, or other facility or facilities who are residents of a county withdrawing from such district are deemed to have resigned their positions upon the completion of the withdrawal procedure provided by this section. Vacancies then created shall be filled according to sections 2151.68 and 2151.74 of the Revised Code.

(2000 S 179, § 3, eff. 1–1–02; 1972 H 258, eff. 1–27–72; 130 v H 879)

Historical and Statutory Notes
Amendment Note: 2000 S 179, § 3, eff. 1–1–02, substituted "2152.41" for "2151.34" in the second paragraph; and made other nonsubstantive changes.

Library References
OJur 3d: 73, Penal and Correctional Institutions § 53

2151.79 Designation of fiscal officer of district; duties of county auditors

The county auditor of the county having the greatest population, or, with the unanimous concurrence of the county auditors of the counties composing a facilities district, the auditor of the county wherein the facility is located, shall be the fiscal officer of a district organized under section 2151.65 of the Revised Code or a combined district organized under sections 2152.41 and 2151.65 of the Revised Code. The county auditors of the several counties composing a school, forestry camp, or other facility or

facilities district, shall meet at the district school, forestry camp, or other facility or facilities not less than once in each six months, to review accounts and to transact such other duties in connection with the institution as pertain to the business of their office.

(2000 S 179, § 3, eff. 1–1–02; 1974 H 1033, eff. 10–2–74; 1972 H 258; 130 v H 879)

Historical and Statutory Notes
Amendment Note: 2000 S 179, § 3, eff. 1–1–02, substituted "2152.41" for "2151.34".

Library References
OJur 3d: 73, Penal and Correctional Institutions § 56

2151.80 Expenses of members of boards of county commissioners

Each member of the board of county commissioners who meets by appointment to consider the organization of a district school, forestry camp, or other facility or facilities shall, upon presentation of properly certified accounts, be paid his necessary expenses upon a warrant drawn by the county auditor of his county.

(130 v H 879, eff. 10–14–63)

INDEPENDENT LIVING SERVICES

2151.81 Definitions

As used in sections 2151.82 to 2151.84 of the Revised Code:

(A) "Independent living services" means services and other forms of support designed to aid children and young adults to successfully make the transition to independent adult living and to achieve emotional and economic self-sufficiency. "Independent living services" may include the following:

(1) Providing housing;

(2) Teaching decision-making skills;

(3) Teaching daily living skills such as securing and maintaining a residence, money management, utilization of community services and systems, personal health care, hygiene and safety, and time management;

(4) Assisting in obtaining education, training, and employment skills;

(5) Assisting in developing positive adult relationships and community supports.

(B) "Young adult" means a person eighteen years of age or older but under twenty-one years of age who was in the temporary or permanent custody of, or was provided care in a planned permanent living arrangement by, a public children services agency or private child placing agency on the date the person attained age eighteen.

(2002 H 38, eff. 11–1–02)

Cross References

Children services board, county; powers and duties, 5153.16
Medicaid plan amendment, 5111.0111
Workforce development plans, 6301.07

2151.82 Independent living services

A public children services agency or private child placing agency, that has temporary or permanent custody of, or is providing care in a planned permanent living arrangement to, a child who is sixteen or seventeen years of age, shall provide independent living services to the child. The services to be provided shall be determined based on an evaluation of the strengths and weaknesses of the child, completed or obtained by the agency. If housing is provided as part of the services, the child shall be placed in housing that is supervised or semi-supervised by an adult.

The services shall be included as part of the case plan established for the child pursuant to section 2151.412 of the Revised Code.

(2002 H 38, eff. 11–1–02)

Cross References

Children services board, county; powers and duties, 5153.16
Medicaid plan amendment, 5111.0111
Workforce development plans, 6301.07

Library References

Carlin, Baldwin's Ohio Practice, Merrick–Rippner Probate Law § 107.100 (2003).

2151.83 Joint agreement for provision of independent living services

(A) A public children services agency or private child placing agency, on the request of a young adult, shall enter into a jointly prepared written agreement with the young adult that obligates the agency to ensure that independent living services are provided to the young adult and sets forth the responsibilities of the young adult regarding the services. The agreement shall be developed based on the young adult's strengths, needs, and circumstances. The agreement shall be designed to promote the young adult's successful transition to independent adult living and emotional and economic self-sufficiency.

(B) If the young adult appears to be eligible for services from one or more of the following entities, the agency must contact the appropriate entity to determine eligibility:

(1) An entity, other than the agency, that is represented on a county family and children first council established pursuant to section 121.37 of the Revised Code. If the entity is a board of alcohol, drug addiction, and mental health services, an alcohol and drug addiction services board, or a community mental health board, the agency shall contact the provider of alcohol, drug addiction, or mental health services that has been designated by the board to determine the young adult's eligibility for services.

(2) The rehabilitation services commission;

(3) A metropolitan housing authority established pursuant to section 3735.27 of the Revised Code.

If an entity described in this division determines that the young adult qualifies for services from the entity, that entity, the young adult, and the agency to which the young adult made the request for independent living services shall enter into a written addendum to the jointly prepared agreement entered into under division (A) of this section. The addendum shall indicate how services under the agreement and addendum are to be coordinated and allocate the service responsibilities among the entities and agency that signed the addendum.

(2003 H 95, eff. 9–26–03; 2002 H 38, eff. 11–1–02)

Historical and Statutory Notes

Amendment Note: 2003 H 95 deleted "and the availability of funds provided pursuant to section 2151.84 of the Revised Code" from the end of the second sentence in Division (A).

Cross References

Children services board, county; powers and duties, 5153.16
Medicaid plan amendment, 5111.0111
Workforce development plans, 6301.07

Library References

Carlin, Baldwin's Ohio Practice, Merrick–Rippner Probate Law § 107.100 (2003).

2151.84 Model agreements

The department of job and family services shall establish model agreements that may be used by public children services agencies and private child placing agencies required to provide services under an agreement with a young adult pursuant to section 2151.83 of the Revised Code. The model agreements shall include provisions describing the specific independent living services to be provided, the duration of the services and the agreement, the duties and responsibilities of each party under the agreement, and grievance procedures regarding disputes that arise regarding the agreement or services provided under it.

(2003 H 95, eff. 9–26–03; 2002 H 38, eff. 11–1–02)

Historical and Statutory Notes

Amendment Note: 2003 H 95 deleted "to the extent funds are provided pursuant to this section" following "independent living services to be provided" in the first paragraph; and deleted the second paragraph, which prior thereto read:

"To facilitate the provision of independent living services, the department shall provide funds to meet the requirement of state matching funds needed to qualify for federal funds under the 'Foster Care Independence Act of 1999,' 113 Stat. 1822 (1999), 42 U.S.C. 677, as amended. The department shall seek controlling board approval of any fund transfers necessary to meet this requirement."

Cross References

Children services board, county; powers and duties, 5153.16
Medicaid plan amendment, 5111.0111
Workforce development plans, 6301.07

MISCELLANEOUS PROVISIONS

2151.85 Minor female's complaint for abortion; hearing; appeal

(A) A woman who is pregnant, unmarried, under eighteen years of age, and unemancipated and who wishes to have an abortion without the notification of her parents, guardian, or custodian may file a complaint in the juvenile court of the county in which she has a residence or legal settlement, in the juvenile court of any county that borders to any extent the county in which she has a residence or legal settlement, or in the juvenile court of the county in which the hospital, clinic, or other facility in which the abortion would be performed or induced is located, requesting the issuance of an order authorizing her to consent to the performance or inducement of an abortion without the notification of her parents, guardian, or custodian.

The complaint shall be made under oath and shall include all of the following:

(1) A statement that the complainant is pregnant;

(2) A statement that the complainant is unmarried, under eighteen years of age, and unemancipated;

(3) A statement that the complainant wishes to have an abortion without the notification of her parents, guardian, or custodian;

(4) An allegation of either or both of the following:

(a) That the complainant is sufficiently mature and well enough informed to intelligently decide whether to have an abortion without the notification of her parents, guardian, or custodian;

(b) That one or both of her parents, her guardian, or her custodian was engaged in a pattern of physical, sexual, or emotional abuse against her, or that the notification of her parents, guardian, or custodian otherwise is not in her best interest.

(5) A statement as to whether the complainant has retained an attorney and, if she has retained an attorney, the name, address, and telephone number of her attorney.

(B)(1) The court shall fix a time for a hearing on any complaint filed pursuant to division (A) of this section and shall keep a record of all testimony and other oral proceedings in the action. The court shall hear and determine the action and shall not refer any portion of it to a referee. The hearing shall be held at the earliest possible time, but not later than the fifth business day after the day that the complaint is filed. The court shall enter judgment on the complaint immediately after the hearing is concluded. If the hearing required by this division is not held by the fifth business day after the complaint is filed, the failure to hold the hearing shall be considered to be a constructive order of the court authorizing the complainant to consent to the performance or inducement of an abortion without the notification of her parent, guardian, or custodian, and the complainant and any other person may rely on the constructive order to the same extent as if the court actually had issued an order under this section authorizing the complainant to consent to the performance or inducement of an abortion without such notification.

(2) The court shall appoint a guardian ad litem to protect the interests of the complainant at the hearing that is held pursuant to this section. If the complainant has not retained an attorney, the court shall appoint an attorney to represent her. If the guardian ad litem is an attorney admitted to the practice of law in this state, the court also may appoint him to serve as the complainant's attorney.

(C)(1) If the complainant makes only the allegation set forth in division (A)(4)(a) of this section and if the court finds, by clear and convincing evidence, that the complainant is sufficiently mature and well enough informed to decide intelligently whether to have an abortion, the court shall issue an order authorizing the complainant to consent to the performance or inducement of an abortion without the notification of her parents, guardian, or custodian. If the court does not make the finding specified in this division, it shall dismiss the complaint.

(2) If the complainant makes only the allegation set forth in division (A)(4)(b) of this section and if the court finds, by clear and convincing evidence, that there is evidence of a pattern of physical, sexual, or emotional abuse of the complainant by one or both of her parents, her guardian, or her custodian, or that the notification of the parents, guardian, or custodian of the complainant otherwise is not in the best interest of the complainant, the court shall issue an order authorizing the complainant to consent to the performance or inducement of an abortion without the notification of her parents, guardian, or custodian. If the court does not make the finding specified in this division, it shall dismiss the complaint.

(3) If the complainant makes both of the allegations set forth in divisions (A)(4)(a) and (b) of this section, the court shall proceed as follows:

(a) The court first shall determine whether it can make the finding specified in division (C)(1) of this section and, if so, shall issue an order pursuant to that division. If the court issues such an order, it shall not proceed pursuant to division (C)(3)(b) of this section. If the court does not make the finding specified in division (C)(1) of this section, it shall proceed pursuant to division (C)(3)(b) of this section.

(b) If the court pursuant to division (C)(3)(a) of this section does not make the finding specified in division (C)(1) of this section, it shall proceed to determine whether it can make the finding specified in division (C)(2) of this section and, if so, shall issue an order pursuant to that division. If the court does not make the finding specified in division (C)(2) of this section, it shall dismiss the complaint.

(D) The court shall not notify the parents, guardian, or custodian of the complainant that she is pregnant or that she wants to have an abortion.

(E) If the court dismisses the complaint, it immediately shall notify the complainant that she has a right to appeal under section 2505.073 of the Revised Code.

(F) Each hearing under this section shall be conducted in a manner that will preserve the anonymity of the complainant. The complaint and all other papers and records that pertain to an action commenced under this section shall be kept confidential and are not public records under section 149.43 of the Revised Code.

(G) The clerk of the supreme court shall prescribe complaint and notice of appeal forms that shall be used by a complainant filing a complaint under this section and by an appellant filing an appeal under section 2505.073 of the Revised Code. The clerk of each juvenile court shall furnish blank copies of the forms, without charge, to any person who requests them.

(H) No filing fee shall be required of, and no court costs shall be assessed against, a complainant filing a complaint under this section or an appellant filing an appeal under section 2505.073 of the Revised Code.

(I) As used in this section, "unemancipated" means that a woman who is unmarried and under eighteen years of age has not entered the armed services of the United States, has not become employed and self-subsisting, or has not otherwise become independent from the care and control of her parent, guardian, or custodian.

(1985 H 319, eff. 3–24–86)

Cross References

Appeal from dismissal of minor female's complaint for abortion, 2505.073

Attempt to have abortion without parental notice not
    creating   patient-physician   relationship,
    2151.421

Library References

Abortion and Birth Control ⊸.50.

Westlaw Topic No. 4.

C.J.S. Abortion and Birth Control; Family Planning
    §§ 4 to 8.

OJur 3d: 26, Criminal Law § 807; 29, Criminal Law
    § 3097; 48, Family Law § 1481, 1482

Right of minor to have abortion performed without
    parental consent. 42 ALR3d 1406

Whiteside, Ohio Appellate Practice (2003 Ed.), Text
    3.27.

Gotherman & Babbit, Ohio Municipal Law, Text
    6.12.

Ohio Administrative Law Handbook and Agency Di-
    rectory, OAC Vol. 17, Text 8.14.

Carlin, Baldwin's Ohio Practice, Merrick–Rippner
    Probate Law § 106.21, 106.22, 106.32, 106.33,
    107.2, 107.7, 107.10, 107.43, 107.45, 107.46,
    107.49,   107.52,   107.59,   107.60,   107.62,
    107.72, 107.114, 107.124, 107.147, 107.187,
    107.188 (2003).

2151.86 Criminal records check; disqualification from employment

(A)(1) The appointing or hiring officer
of any entity that appoints or employs
any person responsible for a child's care
in out-of-home care shall request the superintendent of BCII to conduct a criminal records check with respect to any
person who is under final consideration
for appointment or employment as a person responsible for a child's care in out-
of-home care, except that section 3319.39
of the Revised Code shall apply instead of
this section if the out-of-home care entity
is a public school, educational service
center, or chartered nonpublic school.

(2) The administrative director of an
agency, or attorney, who arranges an
adoption for a prospective adoptive parent shall request the superintendent of
BCII to conduct a criminal records check
with respect to that prospective adoptive
parent and all persons eighteen years of
age or older who reside with the prospective adoptive parent.

(3) Before a recommending agency
submits a recommendation to the department of job and family services on
whether the department should issue a
certificate to a foster home under section
5103.03 of the Revised Code, the administrative director of the agency shall request that the superintendent of BCII
conduct a criminal records check with
respect to the prospective foster caregiver and all other persons eighteen years of
age or older who reside with the foster
caregiver.

(B) If a person subject to a criminal
records check does not present proof that
the person has been a resident of this
state for the five-year period immediately
prior to the date upon which the criminal
records check is requested or does not
provide evidence that within that five-
year period the superintendent of BCII
has requested information about the person from the federal bureau of investigation in a criminal records check, the appointing or hiring officer, administrative
director, or attorney shall request that
the superintendent of BCII obtain information from the federal bureau of investigation as a part of the criminal records
check. If the person subject to the criminal records check presents proof that the
person has been a resident of this state
for that five-year period, the officer, director, or attorney may request that the
superintendent of BCII include information from the federal bureau of investigation in the criminal records check.

An appointing or hiring officer, administrative director, or attorney required by
division (A) of this section to request a
criminal records check shall provide to
each person subject to a criminal records
check a copy of the form prescribed pursuant to division (C)(1) of section
109.572 of the Revised Code and a standard impression sheet to obtain fingerprint impressions prescribed pursuant to
division (C)(2) of section 109.572 of the
Revised Code, obtain the completed form
and impression sheet from the person,
and forward the completed form and impression sheet to the superintendent of
BCII at the time the criminal records
check is requested.

Any person subject to a criminal records check who receives pursuant to this
division a copy of the form prescribed
pursuant to division (C)(1) of section
109.572 of the Revised Code and a copy
of an impression sheet prescribed pursuant to division (C)(2) of that section and
who is requested to complete the form
and provide a set of fingerprint impressions shall complete the form or provide
all the information necessary to complete
the form and shall provide the impression sheet with the impressions of the
person's fingerprints. If a person subject
to a criminal records check, upon request, fails to provide the information
necessary to complete the form or fails to
provide impressions of the person's fingerprints, the appointing or hiring officer
shall not appoint or employ the person as
a person responsible for a child's care in

out-of-home care, a probate court may not issue a final decree of adoption or an interlocutory order of adoption making the person an adoptive parent, and the department of job and family services shall not issue a certificate authorizing the prospective foster caregiver to operate a foster home.

(C)(1) No appointing or hiring officer shall appoint or employ a person as a person responsible for a child's care in out-of-home care, the department of job and family services shall not issue a certificate under section 5103.03 of the Revised Code authorizing a prospective foster caregiver to operate a foster home, and no probate court shall issue a final decree of adoption or an interlocutory order of adoption making a person an adoptive parent if the person or, in the case of a prospective foster caregiver or prospective adoptive parent, any person eighteen years of age or older who resides with the prospective foster caregiver or prospective adoptive parent previously has been convicted of or pleaded guilty to any of the following, unless the person meets rehabilitation standards established in rules adopted under division (F) of this section:

(a) A violation of section 2903.01, 2903.02, 2903.03, 2903.04, 2903.11, 2903.12, 2903.13, 2903.16, 2903.21, 2903.34, 2905.01, 2905.02, 2905.05, 2907. 02, 2907.03, 2907.04, 2907.05, 2907.06, 2907.07, 2907.08, 2907.09, 2907.21, 2907.22, 2907.23, 2907.25, 2907.31, 2907.32, 2907.321, 2907.322, 2907.323, 2909.02, 2909.03, 2911.01, 2911.02, 2911.11, 2911.12, 2919.12, 2919.22, 2919.24, 2919.25, 2923. 12, 2923.13, 2923.161, 2925.02, 2925.03, 2925.04, 2925.05, 2925.06, or 3716.11 of the Revised Code, a violation of section 2905.04 of the Revised Code as it existed prior to July 1, 1996, a violation of section 2919.23 of the Revised Code that would have been a violation of section 2905.04 of the Revised Code as it existed prior to July 1, 1996, had the violation been committed prior to that date, a violation of section 2925.11 of the Revised Code that is not a minor drug possession offense, or felonious sexual penetration in violation of former section 2907.12 of the Revised Code;

(b) A violation of an existing or former law of this state, any other state, or the United States that is substantially equivalent to any of the offenses described in division (C)(1)(a) of this section.

(2) The appointing or hiring officer may appoint or employ a person as a person responsible for a child's care in out-of-home care conditionally until the criminal records check required by this section is completed and the officer receives the results of the criminal records check. If the results of the criminal records check indicate that, pursuant to division (C)(1) of this section, the person subject to the criminal records check does not qualify for appointment or employment, the officer shall release the person from appointment or employment.

(D) The appointing or hiring officer, administrative director, or attorney shall pay to the bureau of criminal identification and investigation the fee prescribed pursuant to division (C)(3) of section 109.572 of the Revised Code for each criminal records check conducted in accordance with that section upon a request pursuant to division (A) of this section. The officer, director, or attorney may charge the person subject to the criminal records check a fee for the costs the officer, director, or attorney incurs in obtaining the criminal records check. A fee charged under this division shall not exceed the amount of fees the officer, director, or attorney pays for the criminal records check. If a fee is charged under this division, the officer, director, or attorney shall notify the person who is the applicant at the time of the person's initial application for appointment or employment, an adoption to be arranged, or a certificate to operate a foster home of the amount of the fee and that, unless the fee is paid, the person who is the applicant will not be considered for appointment or employment or as an adoptive parent or foster caregiver.

(E) The report of any criminal records check conducted by the bureau of criminal identification and investigation in accordance with section 109.572 of the Revised Code and pursuant to a request made under division (A) of this section is not a public record for the purposes of section 149.43 of the Revised Code and shall not be made available to any person other than the person who is the subject of the criminal records check or the person's representative; the appointing or hiring officer, administrative director, or attorney requesting the criminal records check or the officer's, director's, or attorney's representative; the department of job and family services or a county department of job and family services; and any court, hearing officer, or other necessary individual involved in a case dealing with the denial of employment, a final decree of adoption or interlocutory order of adoption, or a foster home certificate.

(F) The director of job and family services shall adopt rules in accordance with Chapter 119. of the Revised Code to implement this section. The rules shall include rehabilitation standards a person who has been convicted of or pleaded guilty to an offense listed in division (C)(1) of this section must meet for an appointing or hiring officer to appoint or employ the person as a person responsible for a child's care in out-of-home care, a probate court to issue a final decree of adoption or interlocutory order of adoption making the person an adoptive parent, or the department to issue a certificate authorizing the prospective foster caregiver to operate a foster home.

(G) An appointing or hiring officer, administrative director, or attorney required by division (A) of this section to request a criminal records check shall inform each person who is the applicant, at the time of the person's initial application for appointment or employment, an adoption to be arranged, or a foster home certificate, that the person subject to the criminal records check is required to provide a set of impressions of the person's fingerprints and that a criminal records check is required to be conducted and satisfactorily completed in accordance with section 109.572 of the Revised Code.

(H) The department of job and family services may waive the requirement that a criminal records check based on fingerprints be conducted for an adult resident of a prospective adoptive or foster home or the home of a foster caregiver if the recommending agency documents to the department's satisfaction that the adult resident is physically unable to comply with the fingerprinting requirement and poses no danger to foster children or adoptive children who may be placed in the home. In such cases, the recommending or approving agency shall request that the bureau of criminal identification and investigation conduct a criminal records check using the person's name and social security number.

(I) As used in this section:

(1) "Children's hospital" means any of the following:

(a) A hospital registered under section 3701.07 of the Revised Code that provides general pediatric medical and surgical care, and in which at least seventy-five per cent of annual inpatient discharges for the preceding two calendar years were individuals less than eighteen years of age;

(b) A distinct portion of a hospital registered under section 3701.07 of the Revised Code that provides general pediatric medical and surgical care, has a total of at least one hundred fifty registered pediatric special care and pediatric acute care beds, and in which at least seventy-five per cent of annual inpatient discharges for the preceding two calendar years were individuals less than eighteen years of age;

(c) A distinct portion of a hospital, if the hospital is registered under section 3701.07 of the Revised Code as a children's hospital and the children's hospital meets all the requirements of division (I)(3)(a) of this section.

(2) "Criminal records check" has the same meaning as in section 109.572 of the Revised Code.

(3) "Minor drug possession offense" has the same meaning as in section 2925.01 of the Revised Code.

(4) "Person responsible for a child's care in out-of-home care" has the same meaning as in section 2151.011 of the Revised Code, except that it does not include a prospective employee of the department of youth services or a person responsible for a child's care in a hospital or medical clinic other than a children's hospital.

(5) "Person subject to a criminal records check" means the following:

(a) A person who is under final consideration for appointment or employment as a person responsible for a child's care in out-of-home care;

(b) A prospective adoptive parent;

(c) A prospective foster caregiver;

(d) A person eighteen years old or older who resides with a prospective foster caregiver or a prospective adoptive parent.

(6) "Recommending agency" means a public children services agency, private child placing agency, or private noncustodial agency to which the department of job and family services has delegated a

duty to inspect and approve foster homes.

(7) "Superintendent of BCII" means the superintendent of the bureau of criminal identification and investigation.

(2004, H 106, eff. 9–16–04; 2004 H 117, eff. 9–3–04; 2000 H 448, eff. 10–5–00; 1999 H 471, eff. 7–1–00; 1998 H 446, eff. 8–5–98; 1996 S 269, eff. 7–1–96; 1996 H 445, eff. 9–3–96; 1995 S 2, eff. 7–1–96; 1993 S 38, eff. 10–29–93)

Uncodified Law

1999 H 128, § 1 and 2, eff. 7–28–99, read:

Section 1. (A) There is hereby created the Employment Disqualification Study Committee consisting of eleven members. The Speaker of the House of Representatives shall appoint three members from the House of Representatives, no more than two of whom shall be from the same political party. The President of the Senate shall appoint three members from the Senate, no more than two of whom shall be from the same political party. The Attorney General shall appoint one member to represent the office of the Attorney General. The Superintendent of Public Instruction shall appoint one member to represent the Department of Education. The Director of Rehabilitation and Correction shall appoint one member to represent the Department of Rehabilitation and Correction. The Director of Human Services shall appoint one member to represent the Department of Human Services. The Supterintendent of Public Instruction shall appoint one member who shall be a teacher or a school administrator.

The initial appointments to the Employment Disqualification Study Committee shall be made within thirty days after this section's effective date. A vacancy on the committee shall be filled in the same manner as the original appointment. The Speaker of the House of Representatives shall appoint the chairperson of the committee. The members of the committee shall serve without compensation. The Department of Human Services shall provide facilities in which the committee shall meet, provide any clerical or other services required by the committee in performing its official duties, and be responsible for any administrative expenses incurred by the committee in performing its official duties.

(B) The Employment Disqualification Study Committee shall do all of the following:

(1) Hold its first meeting within fourteen days after the initial appointments to the committee described in division (A) of this section have been made;

(2) Review sections 173.41, 2151.86, 3301.32, 3301.541, 3319.31, 3319.311, 3319.39, 3701.881, 3712.09, 3721.121, 3722.151, 5104.012, 5104.013, 5126.28, 5126.281, and 5153.111 of the Revised Code and the offenses listed or described in those sections;

(3) Determine the impact of sections 173.41, 2151.86, 3301.32, 3301.541, 3319.31, 3319.311, 3319.39, 3701.881, 3712.09, 3721.121, 3722.151, 5104.012, 5104.013, 5126.28, 5126.281, and 5153.111 of the Revised Code on the ability of the Ohio Works First program to help the program's participants find self-sufficiency through employment;

(4) Seek any funds available under Title IV–A of the "Social Security Act," 49 Stat. 620 (1935), 42 U.S.C. 301, as amended, to assist the committee in fulfilling its duties;

(5) Develop recommendations regarding sections 173.41, 2151.86, 3301.32, 3301.541, 3319.31, 3319.311, 3319.39, 3701.881, 3712.09, 3721.121, 3722.151, 5104.012, 5104.013, 5126.28, 5126.281, and 5153.111 of the Revised Code and the offenses specified in those sections that shall include recommendations regarding all of the following:

(a) Whether a person who is convicted of or pleads guilty to committing more than one of the offenses specified in any of those sections should be permanently prevented or prevented for a specified period of time from obtaining the employment, contract, or licensing described in any of those sections or from being permitted to perform the duties described in any of those sections;

(b) Whether a person who has been convicted of or pleads guilty to committing only one of the offenses specified in any of those sections should be permanently prevented or prevented for a specified period of time from obtaining the employment, contract, or licensing described in any of those sections or from being permitted to perform the duties described in any of those sections;

(c) Whether a person who is convicted of or pleads guilty to committing one or more of the offenses specified in any of those sections can be sufficiently rehabilitated as to merit the person obtaining the employment, contract, or licensing described in any of those sections or being permitted to perform the duties described in any of those sections and, if the person can be sufficiently rehabilitated, what standard should be used to determine whether the person has been sufficiently rehabilitated;

(d) Which of the offenses described in any of those sections, if any, the conviction of or plea of guilty to which merit permanently preventing a person from obtaining the employment, contract, or licensing described in any of those sections or from being permitted to perform the duties described in any of those sections and which of those offenses, if any, the conviction of or plea of guilty to which merit preventing a person from obtaining the employment, contract, or licensing described in any of those sections or from being permitted to perform the duties described in any of those sections for a specified period of time;

(e) If the conviction of or plea of guilty to one of the offenses specified in any of those sections merits preventing a person from obtaining the employment, contract, or licensing described in any of those sections or from being permitted to perform the duties described in any of those sections for a specified period of time, what that period of time should be.

(6) Within six months after the effective date of this section, submit a report of its findings and recommendations to the Speaker and Minority Leader of the House of Representatives and the President and Minority Leader of the Senate.

(C) The Employment Disqualification Study Committee shall cease to exist six months after the effective date of this section.

(D) As used in this section:

(1) "License" has the same meaning as in section 3319.31 of the Revised Code.

(2) "Licensing" means the issuance of a license.

Section 2. This act shall expire six months after its effective date.

1993 S 38, § 3, eff. 10–29–93, reads: Sections 3301.54, 5104.09, and 5126.28 of the Revised Code, as amended by this act, and sections 109.572,

2151.86, 3301.32, 3301.541, 3319.39, 3701.881, 5104.012, 5104.013, and 5153.111 of the Revised Code, as enacted by this act, apply only to persons who apply for employment for a position on or after the effective date of this act.

Historical and Statutory Notes

Ed. Note: Comparison of these amendments [2004 H 106, eff. 9–16–04 and 2004 H 117, eff. 9–3–04] in pursuance of section 1.52 of the Revised Code discloses that they are not substantively irreconcilable so that they are required by that section to be harmonized to give effect to each amendment. In recognition of this rule of construction, changes made by 2004 H 106, eff. 9–16–04 and 2004 H 117, eff. 9–3–04, have been incorporated in the above amendment. See *Baldwin's Ohio Legislative Service Annotated*, 2004, pages 5/L–1034 and 5/L–733, or the OH-LEGIS or OH-LEGIS-OLD databases on Westlaw, for original versions of these Acts.

Amendment Note: 2004 H 106, eff. 9–16–04, inserted ", except that section 3319.39 of the Revised Code shall apply instead of this section if the out-of-home care entity is a public school, educational service center, or chartered nonpublic school" in division (A)(1).

Amendment Note: 2004 H 117 inserted "and all persons eighteen years of age or older who reside with the prospective adoptive parent" in division (A)(2); inserted ", the department of job and family services shall not issue a certificate under section 5103.03 of the Revised Code authorizing a prospective foster caregiver to operate a foster home," and "or, in the case of a prospective foster caregiver or prospective adoptive parent, any person eighteen years of age or older who resides with the prospective foster caregiver or prospective adoptive parent" in division (C)(1); inserted "2909.02, 2909.03" in division (C)(1)(a); deleted division (C)(2) through (C)(2)(b); deleted the paragraph designation in division (C)(3); deleted "or (2)" in division (F); added division (H); designated division (I); substituted "(I)" for "(H)" in newly division (I)(c); and inserted "or a prospective adoptive parent" in division (I)(5)(d). Prior to amendment, deleted division (C)(2) through (C)(2)(b) read:

"(2) The department of job and family services shall not issue a certificate under section 5103.03 of the Revised Code authorizing a prospective foster caregiver to operate a foster home if the department has been notified that the foster caregiver or any person eighteen years of age or older who resides with the foster caregiver has been convicted of or pleaded guilty to a violation of one of the following offenses, unless the foster caregiver or other person meets rehabilitation standards established in rules adopted under division (F) of this section:

"(a) Any offense listed in division (C)(1)(a) of this section or section 2909.02 or 2909.03 of the Revised Code;

"(b) An existing or former law of this state, any other state, or the United States that is substantially equivalent to any offense listed in division (C)(1)(a) of this section or section 2909.02 or 2909.03 of the Revised Code."

Amendment Note: 2000 H 448 rewrote this section, which prior thereto read:

"(A)(1) The appointing or hiring officer of any entity that employs any person responsible for a child's care in out-of-home care shall request the superintendent of the bureau of criminal identification and investigation to conduct a criminal records check with respect to any applicant who has applied to the entity for employment as a person responsible for a child's care in out-of-home care. The adminis-

trative director of any entity that designates a person as a prospective adoptive parent or as a prospective foster parent shall request the superintendent to conduct a criminal records check with respect to that person. If the applicant, prospective adoptive parent, or prospective foster parent does not present proof that the applicant or prospective adoptive or foster parent has been a resident of this state for the five-year period immediately prior to the date upon which the criminal records check is requested or does not provide evidence that within that five-year period the superintendent has requested information about the applicant or prospective adoptive or foster parent from the federal bureau of investigation in a criminal records check, the appointing or hiring officer or administrative director shall request that the superintendent obtain information from the federal bureau of investigation as a part of the criminal records check. If the applicant, prospective adoptive parent, or prospective foster parent presents proof that the applicant or prospective adoptive or foster parent has been a resident of this state for that five-year period, the appointing or hiring officer or administrator may request that the superintendent include information from the federal bureau of investigation in the criminal records check.

"(2) Any person required by division (A)(1) of this section to request a criminal records check shall provide to each applicant, prospective adoptive parent, or prospective foster parent a copy of the form prescribed pursuant to division (C)(1) of section 109.572 of the Revised Code and a standard impression sheet to obtain fingerprint impressions prescribed pursuant to division (C)(2) of section 109.572 of the Revised Code, obtain the completed form and impression sheet from each applicant, prospective adoptive parent, or prospective foster parent, and forward the completed form and impression sheet to the superintendent of the bureau of criminal identification and investigation at the time the person requests a criminal records check pursuant to division (A)(1) of this section.

"(3) Any applicant, prospective adoptive parent, or prospective foster parent who receives pursuant to division (A)(2) of this section a copy of the form prescribed pursuant to division (C)(1) of section 109.572 of the Revised Code and a copy of an impression sheet prescribed pursuant to division (C)(2) of that section and who is requested to complete the form and provide a set of fingerprint impressions shall complete the form or provide all the information necessary to complete the form and shall provide the impression sheet with the impressions of the applicant's or prospective adoptive or foster parent's fingerprints. If an applicant, prospective adoptive parent, or prospective foster parent, upon request, fails to provide the information necessary to complete the form or fails to provide impressions of the applicant's or prospective adoptive or foster parent's fingerprints, the entity shall not employ that applicant for any position for which a criminal records check is required by division (A)(1) of this section and shall not consider the prospective adoptive parent or prospective foster parent as an adoptive parent or foster parent.

"(B)(1) No entity shall employ a person as a person responsible for a child's care in out-of-home care or permit a person to become an adoptive parent or foster parent if the person previously has been convicted of or pleaded guilty to any of the following, unless the person meets rehabilitation standards established in rules adopted under division (E) of this section:

"(a) A violation of section 2903.01, 2903.02, 2903.03, 2903.04, 2903.11, 2903.12, 2903.13, 2903.16, 2903.21, 2903.34, 2905.01, 2905.02,

2905.05, 2907.02, 2907.03, 2907.04, 2907.05, 2907.06, 2907.07, 2907.08, 2907.09, 2907.21, 2907.22, 2907.23, 2907.25, 2907.31, 2907.32, 2907.321, 2907.322, 2907.323, 2911.01, 2911.02, 2911.11, 2911.12, 2919.12, 2919.22, 2919.24, 2919.25, 2923.12, 2923.13, 2923.161, 2925.02, 2925.03, 2925.04, 2925.05, 2925.06, or 3716.11 of the Revised Code, a violation of section 2905.04 of the Revised Code as it existed prior to July 1, 1996, a violation of section 2919.23 of the Revised Code that would have been a violation of section 2905.04 of the Revised Code as it existed prior to July 1, 1996, had the violation been committed prior to that date, a violation of section 2925.11 of the Revised Code that is not a minor drug possession offense, or felonious sexual penetration in violation of former section 2907.12 of the Revised Code;

"(b) A violation of an existing or former law of this state, any other state, or the United States that is substantially equivalent to any of the offenses described in division (B)(1)(a) of this section.

"(2) An out-of-home care entity may employ an applicant conditionally until the criminal records check required by this section is completed and the entity receives the results of the criminal records check. If the results of the criminal records check indicate that, pursuant to division (B)(1) of this section, the applicant does not qualify for employment, the entity shall release the applicant from employment.

"(C)(1) The out-of-home care entity shall pay to the bureau of criminal identification and investigation the fee prescribed pursuant to division (C)(3) of section 109.572 of the Revised Code for each criminal records check conducted in accordance with that section upon a request pursuant to division (A)(1) of this section.

"(2) An out-of-home care entity may charge an applicant, prospective adoptive parent, or prospective foster parent a fee for the costs it incurs in obtaining a criminal records check under this section. A fee charged under this division shall not exceed the amount of fees the entity pays under division (C)(1) of this section. If a fee is charged under this division, the entity shall notify the applicant, prospective adoptive parent, or prospective foster parent at the time of the person's initial application for employment or for becoming an adoptive parent or foster parent of the amount of the fee and that, unless the fee is paid, the entity will not consider the person for employment or as an adoptive parent or foster parent.

"(D) The report of any criminal records check conducted by the bureau of criminal identification and investigation in accordance with section 109.572 of the Revised Code and pursuant to a request made under division (A)(1) of this section is not a public record for the purposes of section 149.43 of the Revised Code and shall not be made available to any person other than the applicant, prospective adoptive parent, or prospective foster parent who is the subject of the criminal records check or the applicant's or prospective adoptive or foster parent's representative; the entity requesting the criminal records check or its representative; the department of job and family services or a county department of job and family services; and any court, hearing officer, or other necessary individual involved in a case dealing with the denial of employment to the applicant or the denial of consideration as an adoptive parent or foster parent.

"(E) The director of job and family services shall adopt rules pursuant to Chapter 119. of the Revised Code to implement this section. The rules shall include rehabilitation standards a person who has been convicted of or pleaded guilty to an offense listed in division (B)(1) of this section must meet for an entity to employ the person as a person responsible for a child's care in out-of-home care or permit the person to become an adoptive parent or foster parent.

"(F) Any person required by division (A)(1) of this section to request a criminal records check shall inform each person, at the time of the person's initial application for employment with an entity as a person responsible for a child's care in out-of-home care or the person's initial application for becoming an adoptive parent or foster parent, that the person is required to provide a set of impressions of the person's fingerprints and that a criminal records check is required to be conducted and satisfactorily completed in accordance with section 109.572 of the Revised Code if the person comes under final consideration for appointment or employment as a precondition to employment for that position or if the person is to be given final consideration as an adoptive parent or foster parent.

"(G) As used in this section:

"(1) 'Applicant' means a person who is under final consideration for appointment or employment as a person responsible for a child's care in out-of-home care.

"(2) 'Person responsible for a child's care in out-of-home care' has the same meaning as in section 2151.011 of the Revised Code, except that it does not include a prospective employee of the department of youth services or a person responsible for a child's care in a hospital or medical clinic other than a children's hospital.

"(3) 'Children's hospital' means any of the following:

"(a) A hospital registered under section 3701.07 of the Revised Code that provides general pediatric medical and surgical care, and in which at least seventy-five per cent of annual inpatient discharges for the preceding two calendar years were individuals less than eighteen years of age;

"(b) A distinct portion of a hospital registered under section 3701.07 of the Revised Code that provides general pediatric medical and surgical care, has a total of at least one hundred fifty registered pediatric special care and pediatric acute care beds, and in which at least seventy-five per cent of annual inpatient discharges for the preceding two calendar years were individuals less than eighteen years of age;

"(c) A distinct portion of a hospital, if the hospital is registered under section 3701.07 of the Revised Code as a children's hospital and the children's hospital meets all the requirements of division (G)(3)(a) of this section.

"(4) 'Criminal records check' has the same meaning as in section 109.572 of the Revised Code.

"(5) 'Minor drug possession offense' has the same meaning as in section 2925.01 of the Revised Code.''

Amendment Note: 1999 H 471 substituted "department of job and family services or a county department of job and family services" for "state department of human services or a county department of human services" in division (D); and substituted "director of job and family services" for "department of human services" in division (E).

Amendment Note: 1998 H 446 rewrote the first paragraph in division (B)(1) and division (E), which prior thereto read:

"(B)(1) Except as provided in rules adopted by the department of human services in accordance with division (E) of this section, no entity shall employ a person as a person responsible for a child's care in out-of-home care or permit a person to become an adoptive parent or foster parent if the person previously has been convicted of or pleaded guilty to any of the following:"

"(E) The department of human services shall adopt rules pursuant to Chapter 119. of the Revised Code to implement this section, including rules specifying circumstances under which an out-of-home care entity may hire a person who has been convicted of an offense listed in division (B)(1) of this section but who meets standards in regard to rehabilitation set by the department."

Amendment Note: 1996 S 269 deleted a statutory reference to section "2905.04," following "2905.02," and inserted "a violation of section 2905.04 of the Revised Code as it existed prior to July 1, 1996, a violation of section 2919.23 of the Revised Code that would have been a violation of section 2905.04 of the Revised Code as it existed prior to July 1, 1996, had the violation been committed prior to that date," in division (B)(1)(a).

Amendment Note: 1996 H 445 substituted "the entity shall not employ that applicant for any position for which a criminal records check is required by division (A)(1) of this section and shall not consider the prospective adoptive parent or prospective foster parent as an adoptive parent or foster parent" for "that applicant or prospective adoptive or foster parent shall not be employed for any position for which a criminal records check is required by division (A)(1) of this section or be considered as a prospective adoptive parent or prospective foster parent" in division (A)(3); removed a reference to section 2907.12 from, and inserted "or felonious sexual penetration in violation of former section 2907.12 of the Revised Code" in, division (B)(1)(a); and made other nonsubstantive changes.

Amendment Note: 1995 S 2 inserted "2925.04, 2925.05, 2925.06," and "or a violation of section 2925.11 of the Revised Code that is not a minor drug possession offense" in division (B)(1)(a); added division (G)(5); and made changes to reflect gender neutral language and other nonsubstantive changes.

Cross References

Adoption, issuance of final decree or interlocutory order, 3107.14
Application for adoption by foster caregiver seeking to adopt foster child, 3107.012
Requests for criminal records checks by criminal identification and investigation bureau, 109.57

Ohio Administrative Code References

Application for professional certification, OAC 5101:2–14–02
Criminal records check required for prospective employees and foster caregivers, OAC 5101:2–5–091
Definitions, criminal records check, OAC 5101:2–14–01
General requirements for initial application for child placement, OAC 5101:2–7–02
Limited certification, OAC 5101:2–14–55 et seq.
Offenses which disqualify persons from being a certified child care provider, an emergency caregiver or substitute caregiver, OAC 5101:2–14–11
Personnel, OAC 5139–35–05, 5139–37–05
Personnel and prohibited convictions for employment, OAC 5101:2–5–09
Restrictions concerning provision of adoption services, OAC 5101:2–48–10
Restrictions concerning provision of adoption services, OAC 5101:2–48–10

Library References

OJur 3d: 26, Criminal Law § 678
Adrine & Ruden, Ohio Domestic Violence Law (2002 Ed.), Text 7.12.
Carlin, Baldwin's Ohio Practice, Merrick–Rippner Probate Law § 98.12, 107.76 (2003).

2151.87 Prohibitions relating to cigarettes or tobacco products

(A) As used in this section:

(1) "Cigarette" and "tobacco product" have the same meanings as in section 2927.02 of the Revised Code.

(2) "Youth smoking education program" means a private or public agency program that is related to tobacco use, prevention, and cessation, that is carried out or funded by the tobacco use prevention and control foundation pursuant to section 183.07 of the Revised Code, that utilizes educational methods focusing on the negative health effects of smoking and using tobacco products, and that is not more than twelve hours in duration.

(B) No child shall do any of the following unless accompanied by a parent, spouse who is eighteen years of age or older, or legal guardian of the child:

(1) Use, consume, or possess cigarettes, other tobacco products, or papers used to roll cigarettes;

(2) Purchase or attempt to purchase cigarettes, other tobacco products, or papers used to roll cigarettes;

(3) Order, pay for, or share the cost of cigarettes, other tobacco products, or papers used to roll cigarettes;

(4) Except as provided in division (E) of this section, accept or receive cigarettes, other tobacco products, or papers used to roll cigarettes.

(C) No child shall knowingly furnish false information concerning that child's name, age, or other identification for the purpose of obtaining cigarettes, other tobacco products, or papers used to roll cigarettes.

(D) A juvenile court shall not adjudicate a child a delinquent or unruly child for a violation of division (B)(1), (2), (3), or (4) or (C) of this section.

(E)(1) It is not a violation of division (B)(4) of this section for a child to accept or receive cigarettes, other tobacco products, or papers used to roll cigarettes if the child is required to do so in the performance of the child's duties as an employee of that child's employer and the child's acceptance or receipt of cigarettes, other tobacco products, or papers used to roll cigarettes occurs exclusively within the scope of the child's employment.

(2) It is not a violation of division (B)(1), (2), (3), or (4) of this section if the child possesses, purchases or attempts to purchase, orders, pays for, shares the cost of, or accepts or receives cigarettes, other tobacco products, or papers used to roll cigarettes while participating in an inspection or compliance check conducted by a federal, state, local, or corporate entity at a location at which cigarettes, other tobacco products, or papers used to roll cigarettes are sold or distributed.

(3) It is not a violation of division (B)(1) or (4) of this section for a child to accept, receive, use, consume, or possess cigarettes, other tobacco products, or papers used to roll cigarettes while participating in a research protocol if all of the following apply:

(a) The parent, guardian, or legal custodian of the child has consented in writing to the child participating in the research protocol.

(b) An institutional human subjects protection review board, or an equivalent entity, has approved the research protocol.

(c) The child is participating in the research protocol at the facility or location specified in the research protocol.

(F) If a juvenile court finds that a child violated division (B)(1), (2), (3), or (4) or (C) of this section, the court may do either or both of the following:

(1) Require the child to attend a youth smoking education program or other smoking treatment program approved by the court, if one is available;

(2) Impose a fine of not more than one hundred dollars.

(G) If a child disobeys a juvenile court order issued pursuant to division (F) of this section, the court may do any or all of the following:

(1) Increase the fine imposed upon the child under division (F)(2) of this section;

(2) Require the child to perform not more than twenty hours of community service;

(3) Suspend for a period of thirty days the temporary instruction permit, probationary driver's license, or driver's license issued to the child.

(H) A child alleged or found to have violated division (B) or (C) of this section shall not be detained under any provision of this chapter or any other provision of the Revised Code.

(2002 H 393, eff. 7–5–02; 2000 S 218, eff. 3–15–01)

Historical and Statutory Notes

Amendment Note: 2002 H 393 added new division (E)(3).

Library References

OJur 3d: 48, Family Law § 1534 et seq.
Carlin, Baldwin's Ohio Practice, Merrick–Rippner Probate Law § 105.1, 106.1, 106.8, 106.25 (2003).

PENALTIES

2151.99   Penalties

(A) Whoever violates division (D)(2) or (3) of section 2151.313 or division (A)(1) or (H)(2) of section 2151.421 of the Revised Code is guilty of a misdemeanor of the fourth degree.

(B) Whoever violates division (D)(1) of section 2151.313 of the Revised Code is guilty of a minor misdemeanor.

(2000 S 179, § 3, eff. 1–1–02; 1998 H 173, eff. 7–29–98; 1989 H 257, eff. 8–3–89; 1986 H 529; 1985 H 349; 1984 H 258; 1972 H 511; 1969 H 320; 130 v H 765; 1953 H 1)

Historical and Statutory Notes

Amendment Note: 2000 S 179, § 3, eff. 1–1–02, deleted former division (C), which read:

"(C) Whoever violates division (C) of section 2151.62 of the Revised Code is guilty of a minor misdemeanor."

Amendment Note: 1998 H 173 added division (C).

Cross References

Imposing sentence for misdemeanor, 2929.22
Judges of the court of domestic relations, juvenile court responsibility, 2301.03
Penalties for misdemeanor, 2929.21

Library References

Infants ⟨key⟩20.

Westlaw Topic No. 211.

C.J.S.   Infants §§ 95 to 107.

OJur 3d: 48, Family Law § 1476, 1572, 1736, 1737, 1749

Gotherman & Babbit, Ohio Municipal Law, Text 32.03.

Carlin, Baldwin's Ohio Practice, Merrick–Rippner Probate Law § 107.24, 107.114, 108.1, 108.9 (2003).

CHAPTER 2152

JUVENILE COURTS—CRIMINAL PROVISIONS

GENERAL PROVISIONS

Section
2152.01 Purposes; applicability of law
2152.02 Definitions
2152.021 Complaint; indictment
2152.03 Transfer of cases to juvenile court
2152.04 Social histories of delinquent children

DISPOSITIONAL ORDERS

2152.10 Mandatory transfer; discretionary transfer
2152.11 More restrictive dispositions for commission of enhanced acts
2152.12 Transfer of cases from juvenile court
2152.13 Serious youthful offender dispositional sentence
2152.14 Invoking adult portion of sentence
2152.16 Commitment of delinquent children to custody of youth services department
2152.17 Felony specifications
2152.18 Place and duration of institutionalization; records; notice to schools and victims
2152.19 Additional disposition orders for delinquent children
2152.19 Additional disposition orders for delinquent children (later effective date)
2152.191 Application of certain sections of Revised Code to child adjudicated a delinquent child for committing sexually oriented offense
2152.20 Fines; costs; restitution; forfeitures
2152.201 Recovery of costs where offense constitutes act of terrorism
2152.21 Disposition of juvenile traffic offender
2152.22 Relinquishment of juvenile court control; judicial release

PLACE OF DETENTION

2152.26 Delinquent child or juvenile traffic offender to be held only in specified places

DETENTION FACILITIES

2152.41 Juvenile detention facility
2152.42 Superintendents of facilities
2152.43 Assistance in operation of facilities from department of youth services; tax assessment
2152.44 District detention facility trustees

ORDERS RESTRAINING PARENTS

2152.61 Orders restraining parents, guardians, or custodians

JURY TRIALS

2152.67 Jury trial; procedure

Section

MISCELLANEOUS PROVISIONS

2152.71 Records and reports; statistical summaries
2152.72 Information provided to foster caregivers or prospective adoptive parents regarding delinquent children; psychological examination
2152.73 Court participation in delinquency prevention activities
2152.74 DNA specimen collected from juvenile adjudged delinquent

SEX OFFENSES

2152.81 Deposition of child sex offense victim

JUVENILE OFFENDER REGISTRANTS

2152.811 Child adjudicated a child delinquent for committing a sexually oriented offense
2152.82 Juvenile offender registrant
2152.821 Testimony of mentally retarded or developmentally disabled victim
2152.83 Order classifying child as juvenile offender registrant; hearing to review effectiveness of disposition and treatment
2152.84 Hearings; orders
2152.85 Petitioning of judge by juvenile offender registrant
2152.851 Effect of redesignation of offense on existing order

PENALTIES

2152.99 Penalties

GENERAL PROVISIONS

Uncodified Law

2000 S 179, § 10, eff. 4–9–01, reads:

The General Assembly hereby states its intention to do the following in the remainder of the 123rd General Assembly and in the 124th General Assembly:

(A) Address the issue of competency in juvenile proceedings and its various aspects;

(B) Review and continue to support the RECLAIM Ohio program and the alternative schools program;

(C) Review and address the anticipated costs of implementing this act.

Cross References

Corrupt activity, engaging in pattern of, penalties not limited, 2923.32, 2923.34

2152.01 Purposes; applicability of law

(A) The overriding purposes for dispositions under this chapter are to provide for the care, protection, and mental and physical development of children subject to this chapter, protect the public interest and safety, hold the offender accountable for the offender's actions, restore the victim, and rehabilitate the offender. These purposes shall be achieved by a system of graduated sanctions and services.

(B) Dispositions under this chapter shall be reasonably calculated to achieve the overriding purposes set forth in this section, commensurate with and not demeaning to the seriousness of the delinquent child's or the juvenile traffic offender's conduct and its impact on the victim, and consistent with dispositions for similar acts committed by similar delinquent children and juvenile traffic offenders. The court shall not base the disposition on the race, ethnic background, gender, or religion of the delinquent child or juvenile traffic offender.

(C) To the extent they do not conflict with this chapter, the provisions of Chapter 2151. of the Revised Code apply to the proceedings under this chapter.

(2000 S 179, § 3, eff. 1–1–02)

Cross References

Judges of the divisions of domestic relations, 2301.03

Library References

OJur 3d: 48, Family Law § 1534 to 1565
Carlin, Baldwin's Ohio Practice, Merrick–Rippner
    Probate Law § 104.3, 106.4, 107.73, 107.84,
    107.85, 107.86, 107.87, 107.89, 107.102
    (2003).

2152.02 Definitions

As used in this chapter:

(A) "Act charged" means the act that is identified in a complaint, indictment, or information alleging that a child is a delinquent child.

(B) "Admitted to a department of youth services facility" includes admission to a facility operated, or contracted for, by the department and admission to a comparable facility outside this state by another state or the United States.

(C)(1) "Child" means a person who is under eighteen years of age, except as otherwise provided in divisions (C)(2) to (6) of this section.

(2) Subject to division (C)(3) of this section, any person who violates a federal or state law or a municipal ordinance prior to attaining eighteen years of age shall be deemed a "child" irrespective of that person's age at the time the complaint with respect to that violation is

filed or the hearing on the complaint is held.

(3) Any person who, while under eighteen years of age, commits an act that would be a felony if committed by an adult and who is not taken into custody or apprehended for that act until after the person attains twenty-one years of age is not a child in relation to that act.

(4) Any person whose case is transferred for criminal prosecution pursuant to section 2152.12 of the Revised Code shall be deemed after the transfer not to be a child in the transferred case.

(5) Any person whose case is transferred for criminal prosecution pursuant to section 2152.12 of the Revised Code and who subsequently is convicted of or pleads guilty to a felony in that case, and any person who is adjudicated a delinquent child for the commission of an act, who has a serious youthful offender dispositional sentence imposed for the act pursuant to section 2152.13 of the Revised Code, and whose adult portion of the dispositional sentence is invoked pursuant to section 2152.14 of the Revised Code, shall be deemed after the transfer or invocation not to be a child in any case in which a complaint is filed against the person.

(6) The juvenile court has jurisdiction over a person who is adjudicated a delinquent child or juvenile traffic offender prior to attaining eighteen years of age until the person attains twenty-one years of age, and, for purposes of that jurisdiction related to that adjudication, except as otherwise provided in this division, a person who is so adjudicated a delinquent child or juvenile traffic offender shall be deemed a "child" until the person attains twenty-one years of age. If a person is so adjudicated a delinquent child or juvenile traffic offender and the court makes a disposition of the person under this chapter, at any time after the person attains eighteen years of age, the places at which the person may be held under that disposition are not limited to places authorized under this chapter solely for confinement of children, and the person may be confined under that disposition, in accordance with division (F)(2) of section 2152.26 of the Revised Code, in places other than those authorized under this chapter solely for confinement of children.

(D) "Chronic truant" means any child of compulsory school age who is absent without legitimate excuse for absence from the public school the child is supposed to attend for seven or more consecutive school days, ten or more school days in one school month, or fifteen or more school days in a school year.

(E) "Community corrections facility," "public safety beds," "release authority," and "supervised release" have the same meanings as in section 5139.01 of the Revised Code.

(F) "Delinquent child" includes any of the following:

(1) Any child, except a juvenile traffic offender, who violates any law of this state or the United States, or any ordinance of a political subdivision of the state, that would be an offense if committed by an adult;

(2) Any child who violates any lawful order of the court made under this chapter or under Chapter 2151. of the Revised Code other than an order issued under section 2151.87 of the Revised Code;

(3) Any child who violates division (A) of section 2923.211 of the Revised Code;

(4) Any child who is a habitual truant and who previously has been adjudicated an unruly child for being a habitual truant;

(5) Any child who is a chronic truant.

(G) "Discretionary serious youthful offender" means a person who is eligible for a discretionary SYO and who is not transferred to adult court under a mandatory or discretionary transfer.

(H) "Discretionary SYO" means a case in which the juvenile court, in the juvenile court's discretion, may impose a serious youthful offender disposition under section 2152.13 of the Revised Code.

(I) "Discretionary transfer" means that the juvenile court has discretion to transfer a case for criminal prosecution under division (B) of section 2152.12 of the Revised Code.

(J) "Drug abuse offense," "felony drug abuse offense," and "minor drug possession offense" have the same meanings as in section 2925.01 of the Revised Code.

(K) "Electronic monitoring" and "electronic monitoring device" have the same meanings as in section 2929.01 of the Revised Code.

(L) "Economic loss" means any economic detriment suffered by a victim of a delinquent act or juvenile traffic offense as a direct and proximate result of the delinquent act or juvenile traffic offense and includes any loss of income due to lost time at work because of any injury caused to the victim and any property loss, medical cost, or funeral expense incurred as a result of the delinquent act or juvenile traffic offense. "Economic loss" does not include non-economic loss or any punitive or exemplary damages.

(M) "Firearm" has the same meaning as in section 2923.11 of the Revised Code.

(N) "Juvenile traffic offender" means any child who violates any traffic law, traffic ordinance, or traffic regulation of this state, the United States, or any political subdivision of this state, other than a resolution, ordinance, or regulation of a political subdivision of this state the violation of which is required to be handled by a parking violations bureau or a joint parking violations bureau pursuant to Chapter 4521. of the Revised Code.

(O) A "legitimate excuse for absence from the public school the child is supposed to attend" has the same meaning as in section 2151.011 of the Revised Code.

(P) "Mandatory serious youthful offender" means a person who is eligible for a mandatory SYO and who is not transferred to adult court under a mandatory or discretionary transfer.

(Q) "Mandatory SYO" means a case in which the juvenile court is required to impose a mandatory serious youthful offender disposition under section 2152.13 of the Revised Code.

(R) "Mandatory transfer" means that a case is required to be transferred for criminal prosecution under division (A) of section 2152.12 of the Revised Code.

(S) "Mental illness" has the same meaning as in section 5122.01 of the Revised Code.

(T) "Mentally retarded person" has the same meaning as in section 5123.01 of the Revised Code.

(U) "Monitored time" and "repeat violent offender" have the same meanings as in section 2929.01 of the Revised Code.

(V) "Of compulsory school age" has the same meaning as in section 3321.01 of the Revised Code.

(W) "Public record" has the same meaning as in section 149.43 of the Revised Code.

(X) "Serious youthful offender" means a person who is eligible for a mandatory SYO or discretionary SYO but who is not transferred to adult court under a mandatory or discretionary transfer.

(Y) "Sexually oriented offense," "habitual sex offender," "juvenile offender registrant," " sexual predator," "presumptive registration-exempt sexually oriented offense," "registration-exempt sexually oriented offense," "child-victim oriented offense," " habitual child-victim offender," and "child-victim predator" have the same meanings as in section 2950.01 of the Revised Code.

(Z) "Traditional juvenile" means a case that is not transferred to adult court under a mandatory or discretionary transfer, that is eligible for a disposition under sections 2152.16, 2152.17, 2152.19, and 2152.20 of the Revised Code, and that is not eligible for a disposition under section 2152.13 of the Revised Code.

(AA) "Transfer" means the transfer for criminal prosecution of a case involving the alleged commission by a child of an act that would be an offense if committed by an adult from the juvenile court to the appropriate court that has jurisdiction of the offense.

(BB) "Category one offense" means any of the following:

(1) A violation of section 2903.01 or 2903.02 of the Revised Code;

(2) A violation of section 2923.02 of the Revised Code involving an attempt to commit aggravated murder or murder.

(CC) "Category two offense" means any of the following:

(1) A violation of section 2903.03, 2905.01, 2907.02, 2909.02, 2911.01, or 2911.11 of the Revised Code;

(2) A violation of section 2903.04 of the Revised Code that is a felony of the first degree;

(3) A violation of section 2907.12 of the Revised Code as it existed prior to September 3, 1996.

(DD) "Non–economic loss" means nonpecuniary harm suffered by a victim of a delinquent act or juvenile traffic offense as a result of or related to the delinquent act or juvenile traffic offense, including, but not limited to, pain and suffering; loss of society, consortium, companionship, care, assistance, attention, protection, advice, guidance, counsel, instruction, training, or education; mental anguish; and any other intangible loss.

(2004 H 52, eff. 6–1–04; 2003 S 5, § 3, eff. 1–1–04; 2003 S 5, § 1, eff. 7–31–03; 2002 H 490, eff. 1–1–04; 2002 H 400, eff. 4–3–03; 2001 S 3, eff. 1–1–02; 2000 S 179, § 3, eff. 1–1–02)

Uncodified Law

2001 S 3, § 4, eff. 10–26–01, reads, in part:

Section 2152.02 of the Revised Code, as presented in this act, includes matter that was amended into former section 2151.02 of the Revised Code by S.B. 218 of the 123rd General Assembly. Paragraphs of former section 2151.02 of the Revised Code were transferred to section 2152.02 of the Revised Code by S.B. 179 of the 123rd General Assembly as part of its general revision of the juvenile sentencing laws. The General Assembly, applying the principle stated in division (B) of section 1.52 of the Revised Code that amendments are to be harmonized if reasonably capable of simultaneous operation, finds that the version of section 2152.02 of the Revised Code presented in this act is the resulting version of the section in effect prior to the date of the section as presented in this act.

Historical and Statutory Notes

Ed. Note: RC 2152.02 contains, in part, provisions analogous to former RC 2151.02 and 2151.021, repealed by 2000 S 179, eff. 1–1–02.

Amendment Note: 2004 H 52 inserted "or juvenile traffic offense" throughout division (L); inserted "direct and proximate" in the first sentence of division (L); added the last sentence of division (L); and added new division (DD).

Amendment Note: 2003 S 5, § 1 and 3, rewrote division (Y), which prior thereto read:

"(Y) 'Sexually oriented offense,' 'habitual sex offender,' 'juvenile sex offender registrant,' and 'sexual predator' have the same meanings as in section 2950.01 of the Revised Code."

Amendment Note: 2002 H 490 rewrote division (K), which prior thereto read:

"(K) "Electronic monitoring device," "certified electronic monitoring device," "electronically monitored house arrest," "electronic monitoring system," and "certified electronic monitoring system" have the same meanings as in section 2929.23 of the Revised Code."

Amendment Note: 2002 H 400 rewrote division (C)(6), which prior thereto read:

"(6) The juvenile court has jurisdiction over a person who is adjudicated a delinquent child or juvenile traffic offender prior to attaining eighteen years of age until the person attains twenty-one years of age, and, for purposes of that jurisdiction related to that adjudication, a person who is so adjudicated a delinquent child or juvenile traffic offender shall be deemed a 'child' until the person attains twenty-one years of age."

Amendment Note: 2001 S 3 rewrote division (Y) which prior thereto read:

"(Y) 'Sexually oriented offense' has the same meaning as in section 2950.01 of the Revised Code."

Library References

OJur 3d: 48, Family Law § 1534 to 1565

Katz & Giannelli, Baldwin's Ohio Practice, Criminal Law § 109.13 (1996).
Painter, Ohio Driving Under the Influence Law (2003 Ed.), Text 19.44.
Carlin, Baldwin's Ohio Practice, Merrick–Rippner Probate Law § 105.8, 106.1, 107.65, 107.136 (2003).

2152.021 Complaint; indictment

(A)(1) Subject to division (A)(2) of this section, any person having knowledge of a child who appears to be a juvenile traffic offender or to be a delinquent child may file a sworn complaint with respect to that child in the juvenile court of the county in which the child has a residence or legal settlement or in which the traffic offense or delinquent act allegedly occurred. The sworn complaint may be upon information and belief and, in addition to the allegation that the child is a delinquent child or a juvenile traffic offender, the complaint shall allege the particular facts upon which the allegation that the child is a delinquent child or a juvenile traffic offender is based.

If a child appears to be a delinquent child who is eligible for a serious youthful offender dispositional sentence under section 2152.11 of the Revised Code and if the prosecuting attorney desires to seek a serious youthful offender dispositional sentence under section 2152.13 of the Revised Code in regard to the child, the prosecuting attorney of the county in which the alleged delinquency occurs may initiate a case in the juvenile court of the county by presenting the case to a grand jury for indictment, by charging the child in a bill of information as a serious youthful offender pursuant to section 2152.13 of the Revised Code, by requesting a serious youthful offender dispositional sentence in the original complaint alleging that the child is a delinquent child, or by filing with the juvenile court a written notice of intent to seek a serious youthful offender dispositional sentence.

(2) Any person having knowledge of a child who appears to be a delinquent child for being an habitual or chronic truant may file a sworn complaint with respect to that child and the parent, guardian, or other person having care of the child in the juvenile court of the county in which the child has a residence or legal settlement or in which the child is supposed to attend public school. The sworn complaint may be upon information and belief and shall contain the following allegations:

(a) That the child is a delinquent child for being a chronic truant or an habitual truant who previously has been adjudicated an unruly child for being a habitual truant and, in addition, the particular facts upon which that allegation is based;

(b) That the parent, guardian, or other person having care of the child has failed to cause the child's attendance at school in violation of section 3321.38 of the Revised Code and, in addition, the particular facts upon which that allegation is based.

(B) Any person with standing under applicable law may file a complaint for the determination of any other matter over which the juvenile court is given jurisdiction by section 2151.23 of the Revised Code. The complaint shall be filed in the county in which the child who is the subject of the complaint is found or was last known to be found.

(C) Within ten days after the filing of a complaint or the issuance of an indictment, the court shall give written notice of the filing of the complaint or the issuance of an indictment and of the substance of the complaint or indictment to the superintendent of a city, local, exempted village, or joint vocational school district if the complaint or indictment alleges that a child committed an act that would be a criminal offense if committed by an adult, that the child was sixteen years of age or older at the time of the commission of the alleged act, and that the alleged act is any of the following:

(1) A violation of section 2923.122 of the Revised Code that relates to property owned or controlled by, or to an activity held under the auspices of, the board of education of that school district;

(2) A violation of section 2923.12 of the Revised Code, of a substantially similar municipal ordinance, or of section 2925.03 of the Revised Code that was committed on property owned or controlled by, or at an activity held under the auspices of, the board of education of that school district;

(3) A violation of section 2925.11 of the Revised Code that was committed on property owned or controlled by, or at an activity held under the auspices of, the board of education of that school district, other than a violation of that section that would be a minor drug possession offense if committed by an adult;

(4) A violation of section 2903.01, 2903.02, 2903.03, 2903.04, 2903.11,

2903.12, 2907.02, or 2907.05 of the Revised Code, or a violation of former section 2907.12 of the Revised Code, that was committed on property owned or controlled by, or at an activity held under the auspices of, the board of education of that school district, if the victim at the time of the commission of the alleged act was an employee of the board of education of that school district;

(5) Complicity in any violation described in division (C)(1), (2), (3), or (4) of this section that was alleged to have been committed in the manner described in division (C)(1), (2), (3), or (4) of this section, regardless of whether the act of complicity was committed on property owned or controlled by, or at an activity held under the auspices of, the board of education of that school district.

(D) A public children services agency, acting pursuant to a complaint or an action on a complaint filed under this section, is not subject to the requirements of section 3109.27 of the Revised Code.

(E) For purposes of the record to be maintained by the clerk under division (B) of section 2152.71 of the Revised Code, when a complaint is filed that alleges that a child is a delinquent child, the court shall determine if the victim of the alleged delinquent act was sixty-five years of age or older or permanently and totally disabled at the time of the alleged commission of the act.

(2000 S 179, § 3, eff. 1–1–02)

Library References

OJur 3d: 48, Family Law § 1534 to 1565
Carlin, Baldwin's Ohio Practice, Merrick–Rippner Probate Law § 104.5, 107.2, 107.3, 107.7, 107.8, 107.84, 107.136 (2003).

2152.03 Transfer of cases to juvenile court

When a child is arrested under any charge, complaint, affidavit, or indictment for a felony or a misdemeanor, proceedings regarding the child initially shall be in the juvenile court in accordance with this chapter. If the child is taken before a judge of a county court, a mayor, a judge of a municipal court, or a judge of a court of common pleas other than a juvenile court, the judge of the county court, mayor, judge of the municipal court, or judge of the court of common pleas shall transfer the case to the juvenile court, and, upon the transfer, the proceedings shall be in accordance with this chapter. Upon the transfer, all further proceedings under the charge, complaint, information, or indictment shall be discontinued in the court of the judge of the county court, mayor, municipal judge, or judge of the court of common pleas other than a juvenile court subject to section 2152.12 of the Revised Code. The case relating to the child then shall be within the exclusive jurisdiction of the juvenile court, subject to section 2152.12 of the Revised Code.

(2000 S 179, § 3, eff. 1–1–02)

Historical and Statutory Notes

Ed. Note: 2152.03 is former 2151.25, amended and recodified by 2000 S 179, § 3, eff. 1–1–02; 1995 H 1, eff. 1–1–96; 1975 H 205, eff. 1–1–76; 1969 H 320; 129 v 582; 1953 H 1; GC 1639–29.

Amendment Note: 2000 S 179, § 3, eff. 1–1–02, substituted "2152.12" for "2151.26" twice; and made other nonsubstantive changes.

Amendment Note: 1995 H 1 inserted "subject to section 2151.26 of the Revised Code" throughout, and made other nonsubstantive changes.

Cross References

Certification to juvenile court, 3109.06
Minor under sixteen not to be confined with adult prisoner, 341.11
Right to counsel, 2151.352

Library References

Infants ⬯68.6, 68.7.
Westlaw Topic No. 211.
C.J.S. Infants §§ 45 to 48, 203.
OJur 3d: 48, Family Law § 1534 to 1565
Am Jur 2d: 47, Juvenile Courts and Delinquent and Dependent Children § 16, 20
Homicide by juvenile as within jurisdiction of a juvenile court. 48 ALR2d 663
Carlin, Baldwin's Ohio Practice, Merrick–Rippner Probate Law § 105.9, 107.14 (2003).

2152.04 Social histories of delinquent children

A child who is alleged to be, or who is adjudicated, a delinquent child may be confined in a place of juvenile detention provided under section 2152.41 of the Revised Code for a period not to exceed ninety days, during which time a social history may be prepared to include court record, family history, personal history, school and attendance records, and any other pertinent studies and material that will be of assistance to the juvenile court in its disposition of the charges against that alleged or adjudicated delinquent child.

(2000 S 179, § 3, eff. 1–1–02)

Library References

OJur 3d: 48, Family Law § 1534 to 1565

Carlin, Baldwin's Ohio Practice, Merrick–Rippner Probate Law § 107.28 (2003).

DISPOSITIONAL ORDERS

2152.10 Mandatory transfer; discretionary transfer

(A) A child who is alleged to be a delinquent child is eligible for mandatory transfer and shall be transferred as provided in section 2152.12 of the Revised Code in any of the following circumstances:

(1) The child is charged with a category one offense and either of the following apply:

(a) The child was sixteen years of age or older at the time of the act charged.

(b) The child was fourteen or fifteen years of age at the time of the act charged and previously was adjudicated a delinquent child for committing an act that is a category one or category two offense and was committed to the legal custody of the department of youth services upon the basis of that adjudication.

(2) The child is charged with a category two offense, other than a violation of section 2905.01 of the Revised Code, the child was sixteen years of age or older at the time of the commission of the act charged, and either or both of the following apply:

(a) The child previously was adjudicated a delinquent child for committing an act that is a category one or a category two offense and was committed to the legal custody of the department of youth services on the basis of that adjudication.

(b) The child is alleged to have had a firearm on or about the child's person or under the child's control while committing the act charged and to have displayed the firearm, brandished the firearm, indicated possession of the firearm, or used the firearm to facilitate the commission of the act charged.

(3) Division (A)(2) of section 2152.12 of the Revised Code applies.

(B) Unless the child is subject to mandatory transfer, if a child is fourteen years of age or older at the time of the act charged and if the child is charged with an act that would be a felony if committed by an adult, the child is eligible for discretionary transfer to the appropriate court for criminal prosecution. In determining whether to transfer the child for criminal prosecution, the juvenile court shall follow the procedures in

section 2152.12 of the Revised Code. If the court does not transfer the child and if the court adjudicates the child to be a delinquent child for the act charged, the court shall issue an order of disposition in accordance with section 2152.11 of the Revised Code.

(2002 H 393, eff. 7–5–02; 2000 S 179, § 3, eff. 1–1–02)

Historical and Statutory Notes

Amendment Note: 2002 H 393 inserted "brandished the firearm," in division (A)(2)(b).

Library References

OJur 3d: 48, Family Law § 1679 to 1702

Katz & Giannelli, Baldwin's Ohio Practice, Criminal Law § 119.2 (1996).

Carlin, Baldwin's Ohio Practice, Merrick–Rippner Probate Law § 107.64, 107.65, 107.66, 107.69, 107.189 (2003).

2152.11 More restrictive dispositions for commission of enhanced acts

(A) A child who is adjudicated a delinquent child for committing an act that would be a felony if committed by an adult is eligible for a particular type of disposition under this section if the child was not transferred under section 2152.12 of the Revised Code. If the complaint, indictment, or information charging the act includes one or more of the following factors, the act is considered to be enhanced, and the child is eligible for a more restrictive disposition under this section;

(1) The act charged against the child would be an offense of violence if committed by an adult.

(2) During the commission of the act charged, the child used a firearm, displayed a firearm, brandished a firearm, or indicated that the child possessed a firearm and actually possessed a firearm.

(3) The child previously was admitted to a department of youth services facility for the commission of an act that would have been aggravated murder, murder, a felony of the first or second degree if committed by an adult, or an act that would have been a felony of the third degree and an offense of violence if committed by an adult.

(B) If a child is adjudicated a delinquent child for committing an act that would be aggravated murder or murder if committed by an adult, the child is eligible for whichever of the following is appropriate:

(1) Mandatory SYO, if the act allegedly was committed when the child was fourteen or fifteen years of age;

(2) Discretionary SYO, if the act was committed when the child was ten, eleven, twelve, or thirteen years of age;

(3) Traditional juvenile, if divisions (B)(1) and (2) of this section do not apply.

(C) If a child is adjudicated a delinquent child for committing an act that would be attempted aggravated murder or attempted murder if committed by an adult, the child is eligible for whichever of the following is appropriate:

(1) Mandatory SYO, if the act allegedly was committed when the child was fourteen or fifteen years of age;

(2) Discretionary SYO, if the act was committed when the child was ten, eleven, twelve, or thirteen years of age;

(3) Traditional juvenile, if divisions (C)(1) and (2) of this section do not apply.

(D) If a child is adjudicated a delinquent child for committing an act that would be a felony of the first degree if committed by an adult, the child is eligible for whichever of the following is appropriate:

(1) Mandatory SYO, if the act allegedly was committed when the child was sixteen or seventeen years of age, and the act is enhanced by the factors described in division (A)(1) and either division (A)(2) or (3) of this section;

(2) Discretionary SYO, if any of the following applies:

(a) The act was committed when the child was sixteen or seventeen years of age, and division (D)(1) of this section does not apply.

(b) The act was committed when the child was fourteen or fifteen years of age.

(c) The act was committed when the child was twelve or thirteen years of age, and the act is enhanced by any factor described in division (A)(1), (2), or (3) of this section.

(d) The act was committed when the child was ten or eleven years of age, and the act is enhanced by the factors described in division (A)(1) and either division (A)(2) or (3) of this section.

(3) Traditional juvenile, if divisions (D)(1) and (2) of this section do not apply.

(E) If a child is adjudicated a delinquent child for committing an act that would be a felony of the second degree if committed by an adult, the child is eligible for whichever of the following is appropriate:

(1) Discretionary SYO, if the act was committed when the child was fourteen, fifteen, sixteen, or seventeen years of age;

(2) Discretionary SYO, if the act was committed when the child was twelve or thirteen years of age, and the act is enhanced by any factor described in division (A)(1), (2), or (3) of this section;

(3) Traditional juvenile, if divisions (E)(1) and (2) of this section do not apply.

(F) If a child is adjudicated a delinquent child for committing an act that would be a felony of the third degree if committed by an adult, the child is eligible for whichever of the following is appropriate:

(1) Discretionary SYO, if the act was committed when the child was sixteen or seventeen years of age;

(2) Discretionary SYO, if the act was committed when the child was fourteen or fifteen years of age, and the act is enhanced by any factor described in division (A)(1), (2), or (3) of this section;

(3) Traditional juvenile, if divisions (F)(1) and (2) of this section do not apply.

(G) If a child is adjudicated a delinquent child for committing an act that would be a felony of the fourth or fifth degree if committed by an adult, the child is eligible for whichever of the following dispositions is appropriate:

(1) Discretionary SYO, if the act was committed when the child was sixteen or seventeen years of age, and the act is enhanced by any factor described in division (A)(1), (2), or (3) of this section;

(2) Traditional juvenile, if division (G)(1) of this section does not apply.

(H) The following table describes the dispositions that a juvenile court may impose on a delinquent child:

OFFENSE CATEGORY (Enhancement factors)	AGE 16 & 17	AGE 14 & 15	AGE 12 & 13	AGE 10 & 11
Murder/aggravated Murder	N/A	MSYO, TJ	DSYO, TJ	DSYO, TJ
Attempted Murder/Attempted Aggravated Murder	N/A	MSYO, TJ	DSYO, TJ	DSYO, TJ

OFFENSE CATEGORY (Enhancement factors)	AGE 16 & 17	AGE 14 & 15	AGE 12 & 13	AGE 10 & 11
F1 (enhanced by offense of violence factor and either disposition firearm factor or previous DYS admission factor)	MSYO,	DSYO, TJ	DSYO, TJ	DSYO, TJ
F1 (enhanced by any single or other combination of enhancement factors)	DSYO, TJ	DSYO, TJ	DSYO, TJ	TJ
F1 (not enhanced)	DSYO, TJ	DSYO, TJ	TJ	TJ
F2 (enhanced by any enhancement factor)	DSYO, TJ	DSYO, TJ	DSYO, TJ	TJ
F2 (not enhanced)	DSYO, TJ	DSYO, TJ	TJ	TJ
F3 (enhanced by any enhancement factor)	DSYO, TJ	DSYO, TJ	TJ	TJ
F3 (not enhanced)	DSYO, TJ	TJ	TJ	TJ
F4 (enhanced by any enhancement factor)	DSYO, TJ	TJ	TJ	TJ
F4 (not enhanced)	TJ	TJ	TJ	TJ
F5 (enhanced by any enhancement factor)	DSYO, TJ	TJ	TJ	TJ
F5 (not enhanced)	TJ	TJ	TJ	TJ

(I) The table in division (H) of this section is for illustrative purposes only. If the table conflicts with any provision of divisions (A) to (G) of this section, divisions (A) to (G) of this section shall control.

(J) Key for table in division (H) of this section:

(1) "Any enhancement factor" applies when the criteria described in division (A)(1), (2), or (3) of this section apply.

(2) The "disposition firearm factor" applies when the criteria described in division (A)(2) of this section apply.

(3) "DSYO" refers to discretionary serious youthful offender disposition.

(4) "F1" refers to an act that would be a felony of the first degree if committed by an adult.

(5) "F2" refers to an act that would be a felony of the second degree if committed by an adult.

(6) "F3" refers to an act that would be a felony of the third degree if committed by an adult.

(7) "F4" refers to an act that would be a felony of the fourth degree if committed by an adult.

(8) "F5" refers to an act that would be a felony of the fifth degree if committed by an adult.

(9) "MSYO" refers to mandatory serious youthful offender disposition.

(10) The "offense of violence factor" applies when the criteria described in division (A)(1) of this section apply.

(11) The "previous DYS admission factor" applies when the criteria described in division (A)(3) of this section apply.

(12) "TJ" refers to traditional juvenile.

(2000 S 179, § 3, eff. 1–1–02)

Library References

OJur 3d: 48, Family Law § 1679 to 1702
Carlin, Baldwin's Ohio Practice, Merrick–Rippner Probate Law § 107.102, 107.103 (2003).

2152.12   Transfer of cases from juvenile court

(A)(1)(a) After a complaint has been filed alleging that a child is a delinquent child for committing an act that would be aggravated murder, murder, attempted aggravated murder, or attempted murder if committed by an adult, the juvenile court at a hearing shall transfer the case if the child was sixteen or seventeen years of age at the time of the act charged and there is probable cause to believe that the child committed the act charged. The juvenile court also shall transfer the case at a hearing if the child was fourteen or fifteen years of age at the time of the act charged, if section 2152.10 of the Revised Code provides that the child is eligible for mandatory transfer, and if there is probable cause to believe that the child committed the act charged.

(b) After a complaint has been filed alleging that a child is a delinquent child by reason of committing a category two offense, the juvenile court at a hearing shall transfer the case if section 2152.10 of the Revised Code requires the mandatory transfer of the case and there is probable cause to believe that the child committed the act charged.

(2) The juvenile court also shall transfer a case in the circumstances described in division (C)(5) of section 2152.02 of the Revised Code or if either of the following applies:

(a) A complaint is filed against a child who is eligible for a discretionary transfer under section 2152.10 of the Revised Code and who previously was convicted of or pleaded guilty to a felony in a case that was transferred to a criminal court.

(b) A complaint is filed against a child who is domiciled in another state alleging that the child is a delinquent child for committing an act that would be a felony if committed by an adult, and, if the act charged had been committed in that other state, the child would be subject to criminal prosecution as an adult under the law of that other state without the need for a transfer of jurisdiction from a juvenile, family, or similar noncriminal court to a criminal court.

(B) Except as provided in division (A) of this section, after a complaint has been filed alleging that a child is a delinquent child for committing an act that would be a felony if committed by an adult, the juvenile court at a hearing may transfer the case if the court finds all of the following:

(1) The child was fourteen years of age or older at the time of the act charged.

(2) There is probable cause to believe that the child committed the act charged.

(3) The child is not amenable to care or rehabilitation within the juvenile system, and the safety of the community may require that the child be subject to adult sanctions. In making its decision under this division, the court shall consider whether the applicable factors under division (D) of this section indicating that the case should be transferred outweigh the applicable factors under division (E) of this section indicating that the case should not be transferred. The record shall indicate the specific factors that were applicable and that the court weighed.

(C) Before considering a transfer under division (B) of this section, the juvenile court shall order an investigation, including a mental examination of the child by a public or private agency or a person qualified to make the examination. The child may waive the examination required by this division if the court finds that the waiver is competently and intelligently made. Refusal to submit to a mental examination by the child constitutes a waiver of the examination.

(D) In considering whether to transfer a child under division (B) of this section, the juvenile court shall consider the following relevant factors, and any other relevant factors, in favor of a transfer under that division:

(1) The victim of the act charged suffered physical or psychological harm, or serious economic harm, as a result of the alleged act.

(2) The physical or psychological harm suffered by the victim due to the alleged act of the child was exacerbated because of the physical or psychological vulnerability or the age of the victim.

(3) The child's relationship with the victim facilitated the act charged.

(4) The child allegedly committed the act charged for hire or as a part of a gang or other organized criminal activity.

(5) The child had a firearm on or about the child's person or under the child's control at the time of the act charged, the act charged is not a violation of section 2923.12 of the Revised Code, and the child, during the commission of the act charged, allegedly used or displayed the firearm, brandished the firearm, or indicated that the child possessed a firearm.

(6) At the time of the act charged, the child was awaiting adjudication or disposition as a delinquent child, was under a community control sanction, or was on parole for a prior delinquent child adjudication or conviction.

(7) The results of any previous juvenile sanctions and programs indicate that rehabilitation of the child will not occur in the juvenile system.

(8) The child is emotionally, physically, or psychologically mature enough for the transfer.

(9) There is not sufficient time to rehabilitate the child within the juvenile system.

(E) In considering whether to transfer a child under division (B) of this section, the juvenile court shall consider the following relevant factors, and any other relevant factors, against a transfer under that division:

(1) The victim induced or facilitated the act charged.

(2) The child acted under provocation in allegedly committing the act charged.

(3) The child was not the principal actor in the act charged, or, at the time of the act charged, the child was under the

negative influence or coercion of another person.

(4) The child did not cause physical harm to any person or property, or have reasonable cause to believe that harm of that nature would occur, in allegedly committing the act charged.

(5) The child previously has not been adjudicated a delinquent child.

(6) The child is not emotionally, physically, or psychologically mature enough for the transfer.

(7) The child has a mental illness or is a mentally retarded person.

(8) There is sufficient time to rehabilitate the child within the juvenile system and the level of security available in the juvenile system provides a reasonable assurance of public safety.

(F) If one or more complaints are filed alleging that a child is a delinquent child for committing two or more acts that would be offenses if committed by an adult, if a motion is made alleging that division (A) of this section applies and requires that the case or cases involving one or more of the acts charged be transferred for, and if a motion also is made requesting that the case or cases involving one or more of the acts charged be transferred pursuant to division (B) of this section, the juvenile court, in deciding the motions, shall proceed in the following manner:

(1) Initially, the court shall decide the motion alleging that division (A) of this section applies and requires that the case or cases involving one or more of the acts charged be transferred.

(2) If the court determines that division (A) of this section applies and requires that the case or cases involving one or more of the acts charged be transferred, the court shall transfer the case or cases in accordance with the that division. After the transfer pursuant to division (A) of this section, the court shall decide, in accordance with division (B) of this section, whether to grant the motion requesting that the case or cases involving one or more of the acts charged be transferred pursuant to that division. Notwithstanding division (B) of this section, prior to transferring a case pursuant to division (A) of this section, the court is not required to consider any factor specified in division (D) or (E) of this section or to conduct an investigation under division (C) of this section.

(3) If the court determines that division (A) of this section does not require that the case or cases involving one or more of the acts charged be transferred, the court shall decide in accordance with division (B) of this section whether to grant the motion requesting that the case or cases involving one or more of the acts charged be transferred pursuant to that division.

(G) The court shall give notice in writing of the time, place, and purpose of any hearing held pursuant to division (A) or (B) of this section to the child's parents, guardian, or other custodian and to the child's counsel at least three days prior to the hearing.

(H) No person, either before or after reaching eighteen years of age, shall be prosecuted as an adult for an offense committed prior to becoming eighteen years of age, unless the person has been transferred as provided in division (A) or (B) of this section or unless division (J) of this section applies. Any prosecution that is had in a criminal court on the mistaken belief that the person who is the subject of the case was eighteen years of age or older at the time of the commission of the offense shall be deemed a nullity, and the person shall not be considered to have been in jeopardy on the offense.

(I) Upon the transfer of a case under division (A) or (B) of this section, the juvenile court shall state the reasons for the transfer on the record, and shall order the child to enter into a recognizance with good and sufficient surety for the child's appearance before the appropriate court for any disposition that the court is authorized to make for a similar act committed by an adult. The transfer abates the jurisdiction of the juvenile court with respect to the delinquent acts alleged in the complaint, and, upon the transfer, all further proceedings pertaining to the act charged shall be discontinued in the juvenile court, and the case then shall be within the jurisdiction of the court to which it is transferred as described in division (H) of section 2151.23 of the Revised Code.

(J) If a person under eighteen years of age allegedly commits an act that would be a felony if committed by an adult and if the person is not taken into custody or apprehended for that act until after the person attains twenty-one years of age, the juvenile court does not have jurisdiction to hear or determine any portion of the case charging the person with committing that act. In those circumstances, divisions (A) and (B) of this section do not apply regarding the act, and the case charging the person with committing the act shall be a criminal prosecution commenced and heard in the appropriate court having jurisdiction of the offense as if the person had been eighteen years of age or older when the person committed the act. All proceedings pertaining to the act shall be within the jurisdiction of the court having jurisdiction of the offense, and that court has all the authority and duties in the case as it has in other criminal cases in that court.

(2000 S 179, § 3, eff. 1–1–02)

Uncodified Law

1995 H 1, § 3: See Uncodified Law under 2151.011.

1991 H 27, § 3, eff. 10–10–91, reads: The provisions of section 2151.26 of the Revised Code, as amended by this act, apply only to offenses that are committed on or after the effective date of this act.

Historical and Statutory Notes

Ed. Note: 2152.12 is former 2151.26, amended and recodified by 2000 S 179, § 3, eff. 1–1–02; 1996 H 124, eff. 3–31–97; 1996 S 269, eff. 7–1–96; 1995 S 2, eff. 7–1–96; 1995 H 1, eff. 1–1–96; 1991 H 27, eff. 10–10–91; 1986 H 499; 1983 S 210; 1981 H 440; 1978 S 119; 1971 S 325; 1969 H 320.

Amendment Note: 2000 S 179, § 3, eff. 1–1–02, rewrote this section. See *Baldwin's Ohio Legislative Service Annotated*, 2000, page 11/L–3649, or the OH–LEGIS or OH–LEGIS–OLD database on WESTLAW, for prior version of this section.

Amendment Note: 1996 H 124 deleted a reference to former section 2907.12 from division (A)(2)(a); added division (A)(2)(c); inserted "and subject to division (C)(4) of this section" in the first paragraph in division (C)(1); inserted "Subject to division (C)(4) of this section," in the first paragraph in division (C)(2); added division (C)(4); inserted "or unless division (G) of this section applies" in division (E); added division (G); and made other nonsubstantive changes.

Amendment Note: 1996 S 269 substituted "a felony" for "an aggravated felony" in division (A)(2)(b); added division (a)(4); inserted "or the act charged" in the introductory paragraph of division (B); deleted "be alleged in the complaint" preceding "When determining" in division (C)(2); and made other nonsubstantive changes.

Amendment Note: 1995 S 2 deleted a reference to section 2901.01 from division (B)(1); deleted "would constitute an aggravated felony of the first or second degree or" from and inserted ", or third" in division (G); and made changes to reflect gender neutral language and other nonsubstantive changes.

Amendment Note: 1995 H 1 rewrote this section, which previously read:

"(A)(1) Except as provided in division (A)(2) of this section, after a complaint has been filed alleging that a child is a delinquent child for committing an act that would constitute a felony if committed by an adult, the court at a hearing may transfer the case for criminal prosecution to the appropriate court having

jurisdiction of the offense, after making the following determinations:

"(a) The child was fifteen years of age or older at the time of the conduct charged;

"(b) There is probable cause to believe that the child committed the act alleged;

"(c) After an investigation, including a mental and physical examination of the child made by a public or private agency or a person qualified to make the examination, and after consideration of all relevant information and factors, including any fact required to be considered by division (B)(2) of this section, that there are reasonable grounds to believe that:

"(i) He is not amenable to care or rehabilitation or further care or rehabilitation in any facility designed for the care, supervision, and rehabilitation of delinquent children;

"(ii) The safety of the community may require that he be placed under legal restraint, including, if necessary, for the period extending beyond his majority.

"(2) After a complaint has been filed alleging that a child is a delinquent child for committing an act that would constitute aggravated murder or murder if committed by an adult, the court at a hearing shall transfer the case for criminal prosecution to the appropriate court having jurisdiction of the offense, if the court determines at the hearing that both of the following apply:

"(a) There is probable cause to believe that the child committed the alleged act.

"(b) The child previously has been adjudicated a delinquent child for the commission of an act that would constitute aggravated murder or murder if committed by an adult.

"(B)(1) The court, when determining whether to transfer a case pursuant to division (A)(1) of this section, shall determine if the victim of the delinquent act was sixty-five years of age or older or permanently and totally disabled at the time of the commission of the act and whether the act alleged, if actually committed, would be an offense of violence, as defined in section 2901.01 of the Revised Code, if committed by an adult. Regardless of whether or not the child knew the age of the victim, if the court determines that the victim was sixty-five years of age or older or permanently and totally disabled, that fact shall be considered by the court in favor of transfer, but shall not control the decision of the court. Additionally, if the court determines that the act alleged, if actually committed, would be an offense of violence, as defined in section 2901.01 of the Revised Code, if committed by an adult, that fact shall be considered by the court in favor of transfer, but shall not control the decision of the court.

"(2)(a) As used in division (B)(2)(b) of this section, "foreign jurisdiction" means any state other than this state, any foreign country or nation, or any province, territory, or other political subdivision of any foreign country or nation.

"(b) The court, when determining whether to transfer a case pursuant to division (A)(1) of this section, shall determine whether the child is domiciled in this state or in a foreign jurisdiction and, if the child is domiciled in a foreign jurisdiction, whether the law of that foreign jurisdiction would subject him to criminal prosecution as an adult for the alleged act without the need for any transfer of jurisdiction from a juvenile, family, or similar noncriminal court to a criminal court if that act had been committed in that foreign jurisdiction. If the court determines that the child is domiciled in a foreign jurisdiction and that, if the alleged act had been committed in that foreign jurisdiction, the law of that foreign jurisdiction would subject him to criminal prosecution as an adult for that act without the need for any transfer of jurisdiction from a juvenile, family, or similar noncriminal court to a criminal court, the court shall consider that fact, along with all other relevant information and factors, in determining whether there are reasonable grounds to believe that the child is not amenable to care or rehabilitation or further care or rehabilitation, as described in division (A)(1)(c)(i) of this section, and whether there are reasonable grounds to believe that the safety of the community may require that the child be placed under legal restraint, as described in division (A)(1)(c)(ii) of this section.

"(C) The child may waive the examination required by division (A)(1)(c) of this section, if the court finds the waiver competently and intelligently made. Refusal to submit to a mental and physical examination by the child constitutes waiver of the examination.

"(D) Notice in writing of the time, place, and purpose of any hearing held pursuant to division (A) of this section shall be given to the child's parents, guardian, or other custodian and his counsel at least three days prior to the hearing.

"(E) No child, either before or after reaching eighteen years of age, shall be prosecuted as an adult for an offense committed prior to becoming eighteen, unless the child has been transferred as provided in this section. Any prosecution that is had in a criminal court on the mistaken belief that the child was eighteen years of age or older at the time of the commission of the offense shall be deemed a nullity, and the child shall not be considered to have been in jeopardy on the offense.

"(F) Upon such transfer, the juvenile court shall state the reasons for the transfer and order the child to enter into a recognizance with good and sufficient surety for his appearance before the appropriate court for any disposition that the court is authorized to make for a like act committed by an adult. The transfer abates the jurisdiction of the juvenile court with respect to the delinquent acts alleged in the complaint.

"(G) Any child whose case is transferred for criminal prosecution pursuant to this section and who subsequently is convicted in that case thereafter shall be prosecuted as an adult in the appropriate court for any future act that he is alleged to have committed that if committed by an adult would constitute the offense of murder or aggravated murder, or would constitute an aggravated felony of the first or second degree or a felony of the first or second degree."

Cross References

Imprisoned minors deemed emancipated for purpose of consent to medical treatment, 5120.172
Relinquishment of jurisdiction, procedure, Juv R 30
Sex offenders, definitions, 2950.01.
Social history, physical and mental examinations, custody investigation, Juv R 32
Youth services department, category one offense and category two offense defined, 5139.01

Library References

Infants ☞68.7.
Westlaw Topic No. 211.
C.J.S. Infants §§ 45 to 48, 203.
OJur 3d: 48, Family Law § 1561, 1562, 1564, 1565, 1580, 1679 to 1702
Am Jur 2d: 47, Juvenile Courts and Delinquent and Dependent Children § 19

Right of other person on trial for crime to invoke privilege as to communications by a juvenile delinquent to juvenile court. 2 ALR2d 652
Homicide by juvenile as within jurisdiction of a juvenile court. 48 ALR2d 663
Applicability of rules of evidence to juvenile transfer, waiver, or certification hearings. 37 ALR5th 703
Katz & Giannelli, Baldwin's Ohio Practice, Criminal Law § 119.2 (1996).
Carlin, Baldwin's Ohio Practice, Merrick–Rippner Probate Law § 107.64, 107.65, 107.66, 107.69, 107.102, 107.189 (2003).

2152.13 Serious youthful offender dispositional sentence

(A) A juvenile court may impose a serious youthful offender dispositional sentence on a child only if the prosecuting attorney of the county in which the delinquent act allegedly occurred initiates the process against the child in accordance with this division, and the child is an alleged delinquent child who is eligible for the dispositional sentence. The prosecuting attorney may initiate the process in any of the following ways:

(1) Obtaining an indictment of the child as a serious youthful offender;

(2) The child waives the right to indictment, charging the child in a bill of information as a serious youthful offender;

(3) Until an indictment or information is obtained, requesting a serious youthful offender dispositional sentence in the original complaint alleging that the child is a delinquent child;

(4) Until an indictment or information is obtained, if the original complaint does not request a serious youthful offender dispositional sentence, filing with the juvenile court a written notice of intent to seek a serious youthful offender dispositional sentence within twenty days after the later of the following, unless the time is extended by the juvenile court for good cause shown:

(a) The date of the child's first juvenile court hearing regarding the complaint;

(b) The date the juvenile court determines not to transfer the case under section 2152.12 of the Revised Code.

After a written notice is filed under division (A)(4) of this section, the juvenile court shall serve a copy of the notice on the child and advise the child of the prosecuting attorney's intent to seek a serious youthful offender dispositional sentence in the case.

(B) If an alleged delinquent child is not indicted or charged by information as described in division (A)(1) or (2) of this section and if a notice or complaint as described in division (A)(3) or (4) of this section indicates that the prosecuting attorney intends to pursue a serious youthful offender dispositional sentence in the case, the juvenile court shall hold a preliminary hearing to determine if there is probable cause that the child committed the act charged and is by age eligible for, or required to receive, a serious youthful offender dispositional sentence.

(C) (1) A child for whom a serious youthful offender dispositional sentence is sought has the right to a grand jury determination of probable cause that the child committed the act charged and that the child is eligible by age for a serious youthful offender dispositional sentence. The grand jury may be impaneled by the court of common pleas or the juvenile court.

Once a child is indicted, or charged by information or the juvenile court determines that the child is eligible for a serious youthful offender dispositional sentence, the child is entitled to an open and speedy trial by jury in juvenile court and to be provided with a transcript of the proceedings. The time within which the trial is to be held under Title XXIX of the Revised Code commences on whichever of the following dates is applicable:

(a) If the child is indicted or charged by information, on the date of the filing of the indictment or information.

(b) If the child is charged by an original complaint that requests a serious youthful offender dispositional sentence, on the date of the filing of the complaint.

(c) If the child is not charged by an original complaint that requests a serious youthful offender dispositional sentence, on the date that the prosecuting attorney files the written notice of intent to seek a serious youthful offender dispositional sentence.

(2) If the child is detained awaiting adjudication, upon indictment or being charged by information, the child has the same right to bail as an adult charged with the offense the alleged delinquent act would be if committed by an adult. Except as provided in division (D) of section 2152.14 of the Revised Code, all provisions of Title XXIX of the Revised Code and the Criminal Rules shall apply in the case and to the child. The juvenile court shall afford the child all rights afforded a person who is prosecuted for committing a crime including the right to counsel and the right to raise the issue of competency. The child may not waive the right to counsel.

(D) (1) If a child is adjudicated a delinquent child for committing an act under circumstances that require the juvenile court to impose upon the child a serious youthful offender dispositional sentence under section 2152.11 of the Revised Code, all of the following apply:

(a) The juvenile court shall impose upon the child a sentence available for the violation, as if the child were an adult, under Chapter 2929. of the Revised Code, except that the juvenile court shall not impose on the child a sentence of death or life imprisonment without parole.

(b) The juvenile court also shall impose upon the child one or more traditional juvenile dispositions under sections 2152.16, 2152.19, and 2152.20, and, if applicable, section 2152.17 of the Revised Code.

(c) The juvenile court shall stay the adult portion of the serious youthful offender dispositional sentence pending the successful completion of the traditional juvenile dispositions imposed.

(2)(a) If a child is adjudicated a delinquent child for committing an act under circumstances that allow, but do not require, the juvenile court to impose on the child a serious youthful offender dispositional sentence under section 2152.11 of the Revised Code, all of the following apply:

(i) If the juvenile court on the record makes a finding that, given the nature and circumstances of the violation and the history of the child, the length of time, level of security, and types of programming and resources available in the juvenile system alone are not adequate to provide the juvenile court with a reasonable expectation that the purposes set forth in section 2152.01 of the Revised Code will be met, the juvenile court may impose upon the child a sentence available for the violation, as if the child were an adult, under Chapter 2929. of the Revised Code, except that the juvenile court shall not impose on the child a sentence of death or life imprisonment without parole.

(ii) If a sentence is imposed under division (D) (2)(a)(i) of this section, the juvenile court also shall impose upon the child one or more traditional juvenile dispositions under sections 2152.16, 2152.19, and 2152.20 and, if applicable, section 2152.17 of the Revised Code.

(iii) The juvenile court shall stay the adult portion of the serious youthful offender dispositional sentence pending the successful completion of the traditional juvenile dispositions imposed.

(b) If the juvenile court does not find that a sentence should be imposed under division (D) (2)(a)(i) of this section, the juvenile court may impose one or more traditional juvenile dispositions under sections 2152.16, 2152.19, 2152.20, and, if applicable, section 2152.17 of the Revised Code.

(3) A child upon whom a serious youthful offender dispositional sentence is imposed under division (D) (1) or (2) of this section has a right to appeal under division (A)(1), (3), (4), (5), or (6) of section 2953.08 of the Revised Code the adult portion of the serious youthful offender dispositional sentence when any of those divisions apply. The child may appeal the adult portion, and the court shall consider the appeal as if the adult portion were not stayed.

(2002 H 393, eff. 7–5–02; 2000 S 179, § 3, eff. 1–1–02)

Uncodified Law

2000 S 179, § 8, eff. 4–9–01, reads:

The General Assembly hereby encourages the Supreme Court to take appropriate action to collect data from each juvenile court in this state on both the number of alleged delinquent children for whom a serious youthful offender dispositional sentence is sought pursuant to section 2152.13 of the Revised Code and the number of jury trials held in the juvenile courts annually as a result of serious youthful offender dispositional sentences being sought for alleged delinquent children, and to prepare and submit to the General Assembly a report containing the data so collected.

Historical and Statutory Notes

Amendment Note: 2002 H 393 rewrote this section which prior thereto read:

"(A) A juvenile court may impose a serious youthful offender dispositional sentence on a child only if the prosecuting attorney of the county in which the delinquent act allegedly occurred initiates the process against the child in accordance with this division or division (B) of this section, and the child is an alleged delinquent child who is eligible for the dispositional sentence. The prosecuting attorney may initiate the process in any of the following ways:

"(1) The child is indicted as a serious youthful offender or is charged in a bill of information as a serious youthful offender.

"(2) The original complaint alleging that the child is a delinquent child requests a serious youthful offender dispositional sentence.

"(B) Unless the original complaint includes a notice of intent to seek that type of sentence, the prose-

cuting attorney shall file with the juvenile court a written notice of intent to seek a serious youthful offender dispositional sentence within twenty days after the later of the following, unless the time is extended by the juvenile court for good cause shown:

"(1) The date of the child's first juvenile court hearing regarding the complaint;

"(2) The date the juvenile court determines not to transfer the case under section 2152.12 of the Revised Code.

"After a written notice is filed under this division, the juvenile court shall serve a copy of the notice on the child and advise the child of the prosecuting attorney's intent to seek a serious youthful offender dispositional sentence in the case.

"(C) If an alleged delinquent child is not indicted or charged by information as described in division (A) of this section and if a notice or complaint as described in division (A)(3) or (B) of this section indicates that the prosecuting attorney intends to pursue a serious youthful offender dispositional sentence in the case, the juvenile court shall hold a preliminary hearing to determine if there is probable cause that the child committed the act charged and is by age eligible for, or required to receive, a serious youthful offender dispositional sentence.

"(D)(1) A child for whom a serious youthful offender dispositional sentence is sought has the right to a grand jury determination of probable cause that the child committed the act charged and that the child is eligible by age for a serious youthful offender dispositional sentence. The grand jury may be impaneled by the court of common pleas or the juvenile court.

"Once a child is indicted, or charged by information or the juvenile court determines that the child is eligible for a serious youthful offender dispositional sentence, the child is entitled to an open and speedy trial by jury in juvenile court and to be provided with a transcript of the proceedings. The time within which the trial is to be held under Title XXIX of the Revised Code commences on whichever of the following dates is applicable:

"(a) If the child is indicted or charged by information, on the date of the filing of the indictment or information.

"(b) If the child is charged by an original complaint that requests a serious youthful offender dispositional sentence, on the date of the filing of the complaint.

"(c) If the child is not charged by an original complaint that requests a serious youthful offender dispositional sentence, on the date that the prosecuting attorney files the written notice of intent to seek a serious youthful offender dispositional sentence.

"(2) If the child is detained awaiting adjudication, upon indictment or being charged by information, the child has the same right to bail as an adult charged with the offense the alleged delinquent act would be if committed by an adult. Except as provided in division (D) of section 2152.14 of the Revised Code, all provisions of Title XXIX of the Revised Code and the Criminal Rules shall apply in the case and to the child. The juvenile court shall afford the child all rights afforded a person who is prosecuted for committing a crime including the right to counsel and the right to raise the issue of competency. The child may not waive the right to counsel.

"(E)(1) If a child is adjudicated a delinquent child for committing an act under circumstances that require the juvenile court to impose upon the child a serious youthful offender dispositional sentence under section 2152.11 of the Revised Code, all of the following apply:

"(a) The juvenile court shall impose upon the child a sentence available for the violation, as if the child were an adult, under Chapter 2929. of the Revised Code, except that the juvenile court shall not impose on the child a sentence of death or life imprisonment without parole.

"(b) The juvenile court also shall impose upon the child one or more traditional juvenile dispositions under sections 2152.16 and 2152.19 of the Revised Code.

"(c) The juvenile court shall stay the adult portion of the serious youthful offender dispositional sentence pending the successful completion of the traditional juvenile dispositions imposed.

"(2)(a) If a child is adjudicated a delinquent child for committing an act under circumstances that allow, but do not require, the juvenile court to impose on the child a serious youthful offender dispositional sentence under section 2152.11 of the Revised Code, all of the following apply:

"(i) If the juvenile court on the record makes a finding that, given the nature and circumstances of the violation and the history of the child, the length of time, level of security, and types of programming and resources available in the juvenile system alone are not adequate to provide the juvenile court with a reasonable expectation that the purposes set forth in section 2152.01 of the Revised Code will be met, the juvenile court may impose upon the child a sentence available for the violation, as if the child were an adult, under Chapter 2929. of the Revised Code, except that the juvenile court shall not impose on the child a sentence of death or life imprisonment without parole.

"(ii) If a sentence is imposed under division (E)(2)(a)(i) of this section, the juvenile court also shall impose upon the child one or more traditional juvenile dispositions under sections 2152.16, 2152.19, and 2152.20 and, if applicable, section 2152.17 of the Revised Code.

"(iii) The juvenile court shall stay the adult portion of the serious youthful offender dispositional sentence pending the successful completion of the traditional juvenile dispositions imposed.

"(b) If the juvenile court does not find that a sentence should be imposed under division (E)(2)(a)(i) of this section, the juvenile court may impose one or more traditional juvenile dispositions under sections 2152.16, 2152.19, and, if applicable, section 2152.17 of the Revised Code.

"(3) A child upon whom a serious youthful offender dispositional sentence is imposed under division (E)(1) or (2) of this section has a right to appeal under division (A)(1), (3), (4), (5), or (6) of section 2953.08 of the Revised Code the adult portion of the serious youthful offender dispositional sentence when any of those divisions apply. The child may appeal the adult portion, and the court shall consider the appeal as if the adult portion were not stayed."

Library References

OJur 3d: 48, Family Law § 1679 to 1702

Carlin, Baldwin's Ohio Practice, Merrick–Rippner Probate Law § 107.52, 107.65, 107.89, 107.102, 107.104, 107.168, 107.189 (2003).

2152.14 Invoking adult portion of sentence

(A)(1) The director of youth services may request the prosecuting attorney of the county in which is located the juvenile court that imposed a serious youthful offender dispositional sentence upon a person to file a motion with that juvenile court to invoke the adult portion of the dispositional sentence if all of the following apply to the person:

(a) The person is at least fourteen years of age.

(b) The person is in the institutional custody, or an escapee from the custody, of the department of youth services.

(c) The person is serving the juvenile portion of the serious youthful offender dispositional sentence.

(2) The motion shall state that there is reasonable cause to believe that either of the following misconduct has occurred and shall state that at least one incident of misconduct of that nature occurred after the person reached fourteen years of age:

(a) The person committed an act that is a violation of the rules of the institution and that could be charged as any felony or as a first degree misdemeanor offense of violence if committed by an adult.

(b) The person has engaged in conduct that creates a substantial risk to the safety or security of the institution, the community, or the victim.

(B) If a person is at least fourteen years of age, is serving the juvenile portion of a serious youthful offender dispositional sentence, and is on parole or aftercare from a department of youth services facility, or on community control, the director of youth services, the juvenile court that imposed the serious youthful offender dispositional sentence on the person, or the probation department supervising the person may request the prosecuting attorney of the county in which is located the juvenile court to file a motion with the juvenile court to invoke the adult portion of the dispositional sentence. The prosecuting attorney may file a motion to invoke the adult portion of the dispositional sentence even if no request is made. The motion shall state that there is reasonable cause to believe that either of the following occurred and shall state that at least one incident of misconduct of that nature occurred after the person reached fourteen years of age:

(1) The person committed an act that is a violation of the conditions of supervision and that could be charged as any felony or as a first degree misdemeanor offense of violence if committed by an adult.

(2) The person has engaged in conduct that creates a substantial risk to the safety or security of the community or of the victim.

(C) If the prosecuting attorney declines a request to file a motion that was made by the department of youth services or the supervising probation department under division (A) or (B) of this section or fails to act on a request made under either division by the department within a reasonable time, the department of youth services or the supervising probation department may file a motion of the type described in division (A) or (B) of this section with the juvenile court to invoke the adult portion of the serious youthful offender dispositional sentence. If the prosecuting attorney declines a request to file a motion that was made by the juvenile court under division (B) of this section or fails to act on a request from the court under that division within a reasonable time, the juvenile court may hold the hearing described in division (D) of this section on its own motion.

(D) Upon the filing of a motion described in division (A), (B), or (C) of this section, the juvenile court may hold a hearing to determine whether to invoke the adult portion of a person's serious juvenile offender dispositional sentence. The juvenile court shall not invoke the adult portion of the dispositional sentence without a hearing. At the hearing the person who is the subject of the serious youthful offender disposition has the right to be present, to receive notice of the grounds upon which the adult sentence portion is sought to be invoked, to be represented by counsel including counsel appointed under Juvenile Rule 4(A), to be advised on the procedures and protections set forth in the Juvenile Rules, and to present evidence on the person's own behalf, including evidence that the person has a mental illness or is a mentally retarded person. The person may not waive the right to counsel. The hearing shall be open to the public. If the person presents evidence that the person has a mental illness or is a mentally retarded person, the juvenile court

shall consider that evidence in determining whether to invoke the adult portion of the serious youthful offender dispositional sentence.

(E)(1) The juvenile court may invoke the adult portion of a person's serious youthful offender dispositional sentence if the juvenile court finds all of the following on the record by clear and convincing evidence:

(a) The person is serving the juvenile portion of a serious youthful offender dispositional sentence.

(b) The person is at least fourteen years of age and has been admitted to a department of youth services facility, or criminal charges are pending against the person.

(c) The person engaged in the conduct or acts charged under division (A), (B), or (C) of this section, and the person's conduct demonstrates that the person is unlikely to be rehabilitated during the remaining period of juvenile jurisdiction.

(2) The court may modify the adult sentence the court invokes to consist of any lesser prison term that could be imposed for the offense and, in addition to the prison term or in lieu of the prison term if the prison term was not mandatory, any community control sanction that the offender was eligible to receive at sentencing.

(F) If a juvenile court issues an order invoking the adult portion of a serious youthful offender dispositional sentence under division (E) of this section, the juvenile portion of the dispositional sentence shall terminate, and the department of youth services shall transfer the person to the department of rehabilitation and correction or place the person under another sanction imposed as part of the sentence. The juvenile court shall state in its order the total number of days that the person has been held in detention or in a facility operated by, or under contract with, the department of youth services under the juvenile portion of the dispositional sentence. The time the person must serve on a prison term imposed under the adult portion of the dispositional sentence shall be reduced by the total number of days specified in the order plus any additional days the person is held in a juvenile facility or in detention after the order is issued and before the person is transferred to the custody of the department of rehabilitation and correction. In no case shall the total prison term as calculated under this division exceed the maximum prison term available for an adult who is convicted of violating the same sections of the Revised Code.

Any community control imposed as part of the adult sentence or as a condition of a judicial release from prison shall be under the supervision of the entity that provides adult probation services in the county. Any post-release control imposed after the offender otherwise is released from prison shall be supervised by the adult parole authority.

(2002 H 393, eff. 7–5–02; 2000 S 179, § 3, eff. 1–1–02)

Historical and Statutory Notes

Amendment Note: 2002 H 393 inserted "and shall state that at least one incident of misconduct of that nature occurred after the person reached fourteen years of age:" at the end of division (B); and rewrote division (E) which prior thereto read:

"(E) The juvenile court may invoke the adult portion of a person's serious youthful offender dispositional sentence if the juvenile court finds all of the following on the record by clear and convincing evidence:

"(1) The person is serving the juvenile portion of a serious youthful offender dispositional sentence.

"(2) The person is at least fourteen years of age and has been admitted to a department of youth services facility, or criminal charges are pending against the person.

"(3) The person engaged in the conduct or acts charged under division (A), (B), or (C) of this section, and the person's conduct demonstrates that the person is unlikely to be rehabilitated during the remaining period of juvenile jurisdiction."

Library References

OJur 3d: 48, Family Law § 1679 to 1702
Carlin, Baldwin's Ohio Practice, Merrick–Rippner Probate Law § 107.65, 107.102, 107.104, 107.189 (2003).

2152.16 Commitment of delinquent children to custody of youth services department

(A)(1) If a child is adjudicated a delinquent child for committing an act that would be a felony if committed by an adult, the juvenile court may commit the child to the legal custody of the department of youth services for secure confinement as follows:

(a) For an act that would be aggravated murder or murder if committed by an adult, until the offender attains twenty-one years of age;

(b) For a violation of section 2923.02 of the Revised Code that involves an attempt to commit an act that would be aggravated murder or murder if commit-

ted by an adult, a minimum period of six to seven years as prescribed by the court and a maximum period not to exceed the child's attainment of twenty-one years of age;

(c) For a violation of section 2903.03, 2905.01, 2909.02, or 2911.01 or division (A) of section 2903.04 of the Revised Code or for a violation of any provision of section 2907.02 of the Revised Code other than division (A)(1)(b) of that section when the sexual conduct or insertion involved was consensual and when the victim of the violation of division (A)(1)(b) of that section was older than the delinquent child, was the same age as the delinquent child, or was less than three years younger than the delinquent child, for an indefinite term consisting of a minimum period of one to three years, as prescribed by the court, and a maximum period not to exceed the child's attainment of twenty-one years of age;

(d) If the child is adjudicated a delinquent child for committing an act that is not described in division (A)(1)(b) or (c) of this section and that would be a felony of the first or second degree if committed by an adult, for an indefinite term consisting of a minimum period of one year and a maximum period not to exceed the child's attainment of twenty-one years of age.

(e) For committing an act that would be a felony of the third, fourth, or fifth degree if committed by an adult or for a violation of division (A) of section 2923.211 of the Revised Code, for an indefinite term consisting of a minimum period of six months and a maximum period not to exceed the child's attainment of twenty-one years of age.

(2) In each case in which a court makes a disposition under this section, the court retains control over the commitment for the minimum period specified by the court in divisions (A)(1)(a) to (e) of this section. During the minimum period, the department of youth services shall not move the child to a nonsecure setting without the permission of the court that imposed the disposition.

(B) (1) Subject to division (B)(2) of this section, if a delinquent child is committed to the department of youth services under this section, the department may release the child at any time after the minimum period specified by the court in division (A)(1) of this section ends.

(2) A commitment under this section is subject to a supervised release or to a discharge of the child from the custody of the department for medical reasons pursuant to section 5139.54 of the Revised Code, but, during the minimum period specified by the court in division (A)(1) of this section, the department shall obtain court approval of a supervised release or discharge under that section.

(C) If a child is adjudicated a delinquent child, at the dispositional hearing and prior to making any disposition pursuant to this section, the court shall determine whether the delinquent child previously has been adjudicated a delinquent child for a violation of a law or ordinance. If the delinquent child previously has been adjudicated a delinquent child for a violation of a law or ordinance, the court, for purposes of entering an order of disposition of the delinquent child under this section, shall consider the previous delinquent child adjudication as a conviction of a violation of the law or ordinance in determining the degree of the offense the current act would be had it been committed by an adult. This division also shall apply in relation to the imposition of any financial sanction under section 2152.19 of the Revised Code.

(2002 H 393, eff. 7–5–02; 2000 S 179, § 3, eff. 1–1–02)

Historical and Statutory Notes

Amendment Note: 2002 H 393 inserted "minimum" before and deleted "of court control" after "period" in division (A)(2); and rewrote division (B) which prior thereto read:

"(B) If a delinquent child is committed to the department of youth services under this section, the department may release the child at any time after the period of court control imposed under division (A)(1) of this section ends."

Cross References

Order of commitment to department of youth services, 5139.05

Library References

OJur 3d: 48, Family Law § 1679 to 1702
Carlin, Baldwin's Ohio Practice, Merrick–Rippner Probate Law § 107.89, 107.102, 107.105 (2003).

2152.17 Felony specifications

(A) Subject to division (D) of this section, if a child is adjudicated a delinquent child for committing an act, other than a violation of section 2923.12 of the Revised Code, that would be a felony if committed by an adult and if the court determines that, if the child was an adult,

the child would be guilty of a specification of the type set forth in section 2941.141, 2941.144, 2941.145, 2941.146, 2941.1412, 2941.1413[1], or 2941.1414[2] of the Revised Code, in addition to any commitment or other disposition the court imposes for the underlying delinquent act, all of the following apply:

(1) If the court determines that the child would be guilty of a specification of the type set forth in section 2941.141 of the Revised Code, the court may commit the child to the department of youth services for the specification for a definite period of up to one year.

(2) If the court determines that the child would be guilty of a specification of the type set forth in section 2941.145 of the Revised Code or if the delinquent act is a violation of division (A)(1) or (2) of section 2903.06 of the Revised Code and the court determines that the child would be guilty of a specification of the type set forth in section 2941.1414[2] of the Revised Code, the court shall commit the child to the department of youth services for the specification for a definite period of not less than one and not more than three years, and the court also shall commit the child to the department for the underlying delinquent act under sections 2152.11 to 2152.16 of the Revised Code.

(3) If the court determines that the child would be guilty of a specification of the type set forth in section 2941.144, 2941.146, or 2941.1412 of the Revised Code or if the delinquent act is a violation of division (A)(1) or (2) of section 2903.06 of the Revised Code and the court determines that the child would be guilty of a specification of the type set forth in section 2941.1413[1] of the Revised Code, the court shall commit the child to the department of youth services for the specification for a definite period of not less than one and not more than five years, and the court also shall commit the child to the department for the underlying delinquent act under sections 2152.11 to 2152.16 of the Revised Code.

(B) Division (A) of this section also applies to a child who is an accomplice to the same extent the firearm specifications would apply to an adult accomplice in a criminal proceeding.

(C) If a child is adjudicated a delinquent child for committing an act that would be aggravated murder, murder, or a first, second, or third degree felony offense of violence if committed by an adult and if the court determines that, if the child was an adult, the child would be guilty of a specification of the type set forth in section 2941.142 of the Revised Code in relation to the act for which the child was adjudicated a delinquent child, the court shall commit the child for the specification to the legal custody of the department of youth services for institutionalization in a secure facility for a definite period of not less than one and not more than three years, subject to division (D)(2) of this section, and the court also shall commit the child to the department for the underlying delinquent act.

(D)(1) If the child is adjudicated a delinquent child for committing an act that would be an offense of violence that is a felony if committed by an adult and is committed to the legal custody of the department of youth services pursuant to division (A)(1) of section 2152.16 of the Revised Code and if the court determines that the child, if the child was an adult, would be guilty of a specification of the type set forth in section 2941.1411 of the Revised Code in relation to the act for which the child was adjudicated a delinquent child, the court may commit the child to the custody of the department of youth services for institutionalization in a secure facility for up to two years, subject to division (D)(2) of this section.

(2) A court that imposes a period of commitment under division (A) of this section is not precluded from imposing an additional period of commitment under division (C) or (D)(1) of this section, a court that imposes a period of commitment under division (C) of this section is not precluded from imposing an additional period of commitment under division (A) or (D)(1) of this section, and a court that imposes a period of commitment under division (D)(1) of this section is not precluded from imposing an additional period of commitment under division (A) or (C) of this section.

(E) The court shall not commit a child to the legal custody of the department of youth services for a specification pursuant to this section for a period that exceeds five years for any one delinquent act. Any commitment imposed pursuant to division (A), (B), (C), or (D)(1) of this section shall be in addition to, and shall be served consecutively with and prior to, a period of commitment ordered under this chapter for the underlying delinquent act, and each commitment imposed pursuant to division (A), (B), (C),

or (D)(1) of this section shall be in addition to, and shall be served consecutively with, any other period of commitment imposed under those divisions. If a commitment is imposed under division (A) or (B) of this section and a commitment also is imposed under division (C) of this section, the period imposed under division (A) or (B) of this section shall be served prior to the period imposed under division (C) of this section.

In each case in which a court makes a disposition under this section, the court retains control over the commitment for the entire period of the commitment.

The total of all the periods of commitment imposed for any specification under this section and for the underlying offense shall not exceed the child's attainment of twenty-one years of age.

(F) If a child is adjudicated a delinquent child for committing two or more acts that would be felonies if committed by an adult and if the court entering the delinquent child adjudication orders the commitment of the child for two or more of those acts to the legal custody of the department of youth services for institutionalization in a secure facility pursuant to section 2152.13 or 2152.16 of the Revised Code, the court may order that all of the periods of commitment imposed under those sections for those acts be served consecutively in the legal custody of the department of youth services, provided that those periods of commitment shall be in addition to and commence immediately following the expiration of a period of commitment that the court imposes pursuant to division (A), (B), (C), or (D)(1) of this section. A court shall not commit a delinquent child to the legal custody of the department of youth services under this division for a period that exceeds the child's attainment of twenty-one years of age.

(G) If a child is adjudicated a delinquent child for committing an act that if committed by an adult would be aggravated murder, murder, rape, felonious sexual penetration in violation of former section 2907.12 of the Revised Code, involuntary manslaughter, a felony of the first or second degree resulting in the death of or physical harm to a person, complicity in or an attempt to commit any of those offenses, or an offense under an existing or former law of this state that is or was substantially equivalent to any of those offenses and if the court in its order of disposition for that act commits the child to the custody of the department of youth services, the adjudication shall be considered a conviction for purposes of a future determination pursuant to Chapter 2929. of the Revised Code as to whether the child, as an adult, is a repeat violent offender.

(2004 H 52, eff. 6–1–04; 2002 H 130, § 3, eff. 1–1–02 [3]; 2002 H 393, eff. 7–5–02; 2000 S 179, § 3, eff. 1–1–02)

[1] RC 2941.1413 renumbered to 2941.1414 by the Legislative Service Commission.
[2] RC 2941.1414 renumbered to 2941.1415 by the Legislative Service Commission.
[3] O Const Art II, § 1c and 1d, and RC 1.471, state that codified sections of law are subject to the referendum unless providing for tax levies, state appropriations, or are emergency in nature. Since this Act is apparently not an exception, and 1–1–02 is within the ninety-day period, the effective date should probably be 4–7–03.

Uncodified Law

2002 H 130, § 5, eff. 4–7–03, reads, in part:

(B) Section 2152.17 of the Revised Code, as presented in this act, includes matter that was amended into former section 2151.355 of the Revised Code by Am. Sub. S.B. 222 of the 123rd General Assembly. Paragraphs of former section 2151.355 of the Revised Code containing Am. Sub. S.B. 222 amendments were transferred to section 2152.17 of the Revised Code by Am. Sub. S.B. 179 of the 123rd General Assembly as part of its general revision of the juvenile sentencing laws. The General Assembly, applying the principle stated in division (B) of section 1.52 of the Revised Code that amendments are to be harmonized if reasonably capable of simultaneous operation, finds that the version of section 2152.17 of the Revised Code presented in this act is the resulting version of the section in effect prior to the effective date of the section as presented in this act.

Historical and Statutory Notes

Amendment Note: 2004 H 52 inserted "2941.1413, or 2941.1414 in division (A); inserted "or if the delinquent act is a violation of division (A)(1) or (2) of section 2903.06 of the Revised Code and the court determines that the child would be guilty of a specification of the type set forth in section 2941.1414 of the Revised Code" in division (A)(2); inserted "or if the delinquent act is a violation of division (A)(1) or (2) of section 2903.06 of the Revised Code and the court determines that the child would be guilty of specification of the type set forth in section 2941.1413 of the Revised Code"; and made other nonsubstantive changes.

Amendment Note: 2002 H 130 inserted ", or 2941.1412" in divisions (A) and (A)(3); inserted "(2)" after "subject to division (D)" in division (C); rewrote the first two paragraphs of division (D); redesignated the last two paragraphs of former division (D) as new division (E) and inserted "or (D)(1)" twice; redesignated former division (E) as new division (F) and inserted "or (D)(1)"; redesignated former division (F) as new division (G); and made other nonsubstantive changes. Prior to amendment the first two paragraphs of division (D) read:

"(D) If the child is adjudicated a delinquent child for committing an act that would be an offense of violence that is a felony if committed by an adult and is committed to the legal custody of the department

of youth services pursuant to division (A)(4), (5), or (6) of this section and if the court determines that the child, if the child was an adult, would be guilty of a specification of the type set forth in section 2941.1411 of the Revised Code in relation to the act for which the child was adjudicated a delinquent child, the court may commit the child to the custody of the department of youth services for institutionalization in a secure facility for two years, subject to division (A)(7)(d) of this section.

"(d) A court that imposes a period of commitment under division (A)(7)(a) of this section is not precluded from imposing an additional period of commitment under division (A)(7)(b) or (c) of this section, a court that imposes a period of commitment under division (A)(7)(b) of this section is not precluded from imposing an additional period of commitment under division (A)(7)(a) or (c) of this section, and a court that imposes a period of commitment under division (A)(7)(c) of this section is not precluded from imposing an additional period of commitment under division (A)(7)(a) or (b) of this section."

Amendment Note: 2002 H 393 added "(2)" to division (C); and rewrote divisions (D) through (F), which prior thereto read:

"(D) If the child is adjudicated a delinquent child for committing an act that would be an offense of violence that is a felony if committed by an adult and is committed to the legal custody of the department of youth services pursuant to division (A)(4), (5), or (6) of this section and if the court determines that the child, if the child was an adult, would be guilty of a specification of the type set forth in section 2941.1411 of the Revised Code in relation to the act for which the child was adjudicated a delinquent child, the court may commit the child to the custody of the department of youth services for institutionalization in a secure facility for two years, subject to division (A)(7)(d) of this section.

"(d) A court that imposes a period of commitment under division (A)(7)(a) of this section is not precluded from imposing an additional period of commitment under division (A)(7)(b) or (c) of this section, a court that imposes a period of commitment under division (A)(7)(b) of this section is not precluded from imposing an additional period of commitment under division (A)(7)(a) or (c) of this section, and a court that imposes a period of commitment under division (A)(7)(c) of this section is not precluded from imposing an additional period of commitment under division (A)(7)(a) or (b) of this section.

"The court shall not commit a child to the legal custody of the department of youth services for a specification pursuant to this section for a period that exceeds five years for any one delinquent act. Any commitment imposed pursuant to division (A), (B), or (C) of this section shall be in addition to, and shall be served consecutively with and prior to, a period of commitment ordered under this chapter for the underlying delinquent act, and each commitment imposed pursuant to division (A), (B), or (C) of this section shall be in addition to, and shall be served consecutively with, any other period of commitment imposed under those divisions. If a commitment is imposed under division (A) or (B) of this section and a commitment also is imposed under division (C) of this section, the period imposed under division (A) or (B) of this section shall be served prior to the period imposed under division (C) of this section.

"The total of all the periods of commitment imposed for any specification under this section and for the underlying offense shall not exceed the child's attainment of twenty-one years of age.

"(E) If a child is adjudicated a delinquent child for committing two or more acts that would be felonies if committed by an adult and if the court entering the delinquent child adjudication orders the commitment of the child for two or more of those acts to the legal custody of the department of youth services for institutionalization in a secure facility pursuant to section 2152.13 or 2152.16 or the Revised Code, the court may order that all of the periods of commitment imposed under those sections for those acts be served consecutively in the legal custody of the department of youth services, provided that those periods of commitment shall be in addition to and commence immediately following the expiration of a period of commitment that the court imposes pursuant to division (A), (B), or (C) of this section. A court shall not commit a delinquent child to the legal custody of the department of youth services under this division for a period that exceeds the child's attainment of twenty-one years of age.

"(F) If a child is adjudicated a delinquent child for committing an act that if committed by an adult would be aggravated murder, murder, rape, felonious sexual penetration in violation of former section 2907.12 of the Revised Code, involuntary manslaughter, a felony of the first or second degree resulting in the death of or physical harm to a person, complicity in or an attempt to commit any of those offenses, or an offense under an existing or former law of this state that is or was substantially equivalent to any of those offenses and if the court in its order of disposition for that act commits the child to the custody of the department of youth services, the adjudication shall be considered a conviction for purposes of a future determination pursuant to Chapter 2929. of the Revised Code as to whether the child, as an adult, is a repeat violent offender."

Cross References

Specifications concerning drug or alcohol related vehicular homicide of peace officer in construction zone and prior convictions, 2941.1415

Library References

OJur 3d: 48, Family Law § 1679 to 1702
Carlin, Baldwin's Ohio Practice, Merrick–Rippner Probate Law § 107.89, 107.92, 107.102 (2003).

2152.18   Place and duration of institutionalization; records; notice to schools and victims

(A) When a juvenile court commits a delinquent child to the custody of the department of youth services pursuant to this chapter, the court shall not designate the specific institution in which the department is to place the child but instead shall specify that the child is to be institutionalized in a secure facility.

(B) When a juvenile court commits a delinquent child to the custody of the department of youth services pursuant to this chapter, the court shall state in the order of commitment the total number of days that the child has been held in detention in connection with the delinquent child complaint upon which the order of commitment is based. The department shall reduce the minimum period of institutionalization that was ordered by both the total number of days that the

child has been so held in detention as stated by the court in the order of commitment and the total number of any additional days that the child has been held in detention subsequent to the order of commitment but prior to the transfer of physical custody of the child to the department.

(C)(1) When a juvenile court commits a delinquent child to the custody of the department of youth services pursuant to this chapter, the court shall provide the department with the child's medical records, a copy of the report of any mental examination of the child ordered by the court, the Revised Code section or sections the child violated and the degree of each violation, the warrant to convey the child to the department, a copy of the court's journal entry ordering the commitment of the child to the legal custody of the department, a copy of the arrest record pertaining to the act for which the child was adjudicated a delinquent child, a copy of any victim impact statement pertaining to the act, and any other information concerning the child that the department reasonably requests. The court also shall complete the form for the standard predisposition investigation report that the department furnishes pursuant to section 5139.04 of the Revised Code and provide the department with the completed form.

The department may refuse to accept physical custody of a delinquent child who is committed to the legal custody of the department until the court provides to the department the documents specified in this division. No officer or employee of the department who refuses to accept physical custody of a delinquent child who is committed to the legal custody of the department shall be subject to prosecution or contempt of court for the refusal if the court fails to provide the documents specified in this division at the time the court transfers the physical custody of the child to the department.

(2) Within twenty working days after the department of youth services receives physical custody of a delinquent child from a juvenile court, the court shall provide the department with a certified copy of the child's birth certificate and the child's social security number or, if the court made all reasonable efforts to obtain the information but was unsuccessful, with documentation of the efforts it made to obtain the information.

(3) If an officer is preparing pursuant to section 2947.06 or 2951.03 of the Revised Code or Criminal Rule 32.2 a presentence investigation report pertaining to a person, the department shall make available to the officer, for use in preparing the report, any records or reports it possesses regarding that person that it received from a juvenile court pursuant to division (C)(1) of this section or that pertain to the treatment of that person after the person was committed to the custody of the department as a delinquent child.

(D)(1) Within ten days after an adjudication that a child is a delinquent child, the court shall give written notice of the adjudication to the superintendent of a city, local, exempted village, or joint vocational school district, and to the principal of the school the child attends, if the basis of the adjudication was the commission of an act that would be a criminal offense if committed by an adult, if the act was committed by the delinquent child when the child was fourteen years of age or older, and if the act is any of the following:

(a) An act that would be a felony or an offense of violence if committed by an adult, an act in the commission of which the child used or brandished a firearm, or an act that is a violation of section 2907.06, 2907.07, 2907.08, 2907.09, 2907.24, or 2907.241 of the Revised Code and that would be a misdemeanor if committed by an adult;

(b) A violation of section 2923.12 of the Revised Code or of a substantially similar municipal ordinance that would be a misdemeanor if committed by an adult and that was committed on property owned or controlled by, or at an activity held under the auspices of, the board of education of that school district;

(c) A violation of division (A) of section 2925.03 or 2925.11 of the Revised Code that would be a misdemeanor if committed by an adult, that was committed on property owned or controlled by, or at an activity held under the auspices of, the board of education of that school district, and that is not a minor drug possession offense;

(d) An act that would be a criminal offense if committed by an adult and that results in serious physical harm to persons or serious physical harm to property while the child is at school, on any other property owned or controlled by the board, or at an interscholastic competition, an extracurricular event, or any other school program or activity;

(e) Complicity in any violation described in division (D)(1)(a), (b), (c), or (d) of this section that was alleged to have been committed in the manner described in division (D)(1)(a), (b), (c), or (d) of this section, regardless of whether the act of complicity was committed on property owned or controlled by, or at an activity held under the auspices of, the board of education of that school district.

(2) The notice given pursuant to division (D)(1) of this section shall include the name of the child who was adjudicated to be a delinquent child, the child's age at the time the child committed the act that was the basis of the adjudication, and identification of the violation of the law or ordinance that was the basis of the adjudication.

(3) Within fourteen days after committing a delinquent child to the custody of the department of youth services, the court shall give notice to the school attended by the child of the child's commitment by sending to that school a copy of the court's journal entry ordering the commitment. As soon as possible after receipt of the notice described in this division, the school shall provide the department with the child's school transcript. However, the department shall not refuse to accept a child committed to it, and a child committed to it shall not be held in a county or district detention facility, because of a school's failure to provide the school transcript that it is required to provide under this division.

(4) Within fourteen days after discharging or releasing a child from an institution under its control, the department of youth services shall provide the court and the superintendent of the school district in which the child is entitled to attend school under section 3313.64 or 3313.65 of the Revised Code with the following:

(a) An updated copy of the child's school transcript;

(b) A report outlining the child's behavior in school while in the custody of the department;

(c) The child's current individualized education program, as defined in section 3323.01 of the Revised Code, if such a program has been developed for the child;

(d) A summary of the institutional record of the child's behavior.

The department also shall provide the court with a copy of any portion of the child's institutional record that the court specifically requests, within five working days of the request.

(E) At any hearing at which a child is adjudicated a delinquent child or as soon as possible after the hearing, the court shall notify all victims of the delinquent act who may be entitled to a recovery under any of the following sections of the right of the victims to recover, pursuant to section 3109.09 of the Revised Code, compensatory damages from the child's parents; of the right of the victims to recover, pursuant to section 3109.10 of the Revised Code, compensatory damages from the child's parents for willful and malicious assaults committed by the child; and of the right of the victims to recover an award of reparations pursuant to sections 2743.51 to 2743.72 of the Revised Code.

(2004 H 106, eff. 9–16–04; 2002 H 393, eff. 7–5–02; 2002 H 247, eff. 5–30–02; 2000 S 179, § 3, eff. 1–1–02)

Uncodified Law

2002 H 393, § 5, eff. 7–5–02, reads, in part:

(B) Section 2152.18 of the Revised Code, as presented in this act, includes matter that was amended into former section 2151.355 of the Revised Code by Am. Sub. S.B. 181 of the 123rd General Assembly. Paragraphs of former section 2151.355 of the Revised Code containing S.B. 181 amendments were transferred to section 2152.18 of the Revised Code by S.B. 179 of the 123rd General Assembly as part of its general revision of the juvenile sentencing laws. The General Assembly, applying the principle stated in division (B) of section 1.52 of the Revised Code that amendments are to be harmonized if reasonably capable of simultaneous operation, finds that the version of section 2152.18 of the Revised Code presented in this act is the resulting version of the section in effect prior to the effective date of the section as presented in this act.

2002 H 247, § 3, eff. 5–30–02, reads:

Section 2152.18 of the Revised Code, as presented in this act, includes matter that was amended into former section 2151.355 of the Revised Code by Am. Sub. S.B. 181 of the 123rd General Assembly. Paragraphs of former section 2151.355 of the Revised Code containing S.B. 181 amendments were transferred to section 2152.18 of the Revised Code by S.B. 179 of the 123rd General Assembly as part of its general revision of the juvenile sentencing laws. The General Assembly, applying the principle stated in division (B) of section 1.52 of the Revised Code that amendments are to be harmonized if reasonably capable of simultaneous operation, finds that the version of section 2152.18 of the Revised Code presented in this act is the resulting version of the section in effect prior to the effective date of the section as presented in this act.

Historical and Statutory Notes

Ed. Note: 2152.18, 2152.19 and 2152.20 contain provisions analogous to former 2151.355, repealed by 2000 S 179, § 4, eff. 1–1–02.

Amendment Note: 2004 H 106 Rewrote division (D)(4). Prior to amendment, division (D)(4) read, "Within fourteen days after releasing a child from an institution under its control, the department of youth services shall provide the court and the school with an updated copy of the child's school transcript and a summary of the institutional record of the child. The department also shall provide the court with a copy of any portion of the child's institutional record that the court specifically requests, within five working days of the request."

Amendment Note: 2002 H 393 deleted "2907.04" before "2907.06" in division (D)(1)(a); and substituted "(D)" for "(K)" in division (D)(2).

Amendment Note: 2002 H 247 added new division (C)(3); deleted "2907.04" before "2907.06" in division (D)(1)(a); and substituted "(D)" for "(K)" after "pursuant to division" in division (D)(2).

Cross References

Presentence investigation reports, mandatory consideration of certain information, 2951.03

Library References

OJur 3d: 48, Family Law § 1679 to 1702
Carlin, Baldwin's Ohio Practice, Merrick–Rippner Probate Law § 107.84, 107.105 (2003).

2152.19 Additional disposition orders for delinquent children

Note: See also following version of this section, eff. 9–23–04.

(A) If a child is adjudicated a delinquent child, the court may make any of the following orders of disposition, in addition to any other disposition authorized or required by this chapter:

(1) Any order that is authorized by section 2151.353 of the Revised Code for the care and protection of an abused, neglected, or dependent child;

(2) Commit the child to the temporary custody of any school, camp, institution, or other facility operated for the care of delinquent children by the county, by a district organized under section 2152.41 or 2151.65 of the Revised Code, or by a private agency or organization, within or without the state, that is authorized and qualified to provide the care, treatment, or placement required, including, but not limited to, a school, camp, or facility operated under section 2151.65 of the Revised Code;

(3) Place the child in a detention facility or district detention facility operated under section 2152.41 of the Revised Code, for up to ninety days;

(4) Place the child on community control under any sanctions, services, and

conditions that the court prescribes. As a condition of community control in every case and in addition to any other condition that it imposes upon the child, the court shall require the child to abide by the law during the period of community control. As referred to in this division, community control includes, but is not limited to, the following sanctions and conditions:

(a) A period of basic probation supervision in which the child is required to maintain contact with a person appointed to supervise the child in accordance with sanctions imposed by the court;

(b) A period of intensive probation supervision in which the child is required to maintain frequent contact with a person appointed by the court to supervise the child while the child is seeking or maintaining employment and participating in training, education, and treatment programs as the order of disposition;

(c) A period of day reporting in which the child is required each day to report to and leave a center or another approved reporting location at specified times in order to participate in work, education or training, treatment, and other approved programs at the center or outside the center;

(d) A period of community service of up to five hundred hours for an act that would be a felony or a misdemeanor of the first degree if committed by an adult, up to two hundred hours for an act that would be a misdemeanor of the second, third, or fourth degree if committed by an adult, or up to thirty hours for an act that would be a minor misdemeanor if committed by an adult;

(e) A requirement that the child obtain a high school diploma, a certificate of high school equivalence, vocational training, or employment;

(f) A period of drug and alcohol use monitoring;

(g) A requirement of alcohol or drug assessment or counseling, or a period in an alcohol or drug treatment program with a level of security for the child as determined necessary by the court;

(h) A period in which the court orders the child to observe a curfew that may involve daytime or evening hours;

(i) A requirement that the child serve monitored time;

(j) A period of house arrest without electronic monitoring;

(k) A period of electronic monitoring without house arrest or house arrest with electronic monitoring that does not exceed the maximum sentence of imprisonment that could be imposed upon an adult who commits the same act.

A period of house arrest with electronic monitoring imposed under this division shall not extend beyond the child's twenty-first birthday. If a court imposes a period of house arrest with electronic monitoring upon a child under this division, it shall require the child: to remain in the child's home or other specified premises for the entire period of house arrest with electronic monitoring except when the court permits the child to leave those premises to go to school or to other specified premises; to be monitored by a central system that can determine the child's location at designated times; to report periodically to a person designated by the court; and to enter into a written contract with the court agreeing to comply with all requirements imposed by the court, agreeing to pay any fee imposed by the court for the costs of the house arrest with electronic monitoring, and agreeing to waive the right to receive credit for any time served on house arrest with electronic monitoring toward the period of any other dispositional order imposed upon the child if the child violates any of the requirements of the dispositional order of house arrest with electronic monitoring. The court also may impose other reasonable requirements upon the child.

Unless ordered by the court, a child shall not receive credit for any time served on house arrest with electronic monitoring toward any other dispositional order imposed upon the child for the act for which was imposed the dispositional order of house arrest with electronic monitoring.

(*l*) A suspension of the driver's license, probationary driver's license, or temporary instruction permit issued to the child for a period of time prescribed by the court, or a suspension of the registration of all motor vehicles registered in the name of the child for a period of time prescribed by the court. A child whose license or permit is so suspended is ineligible for issuance of a license or permit during the period of suspension. At the end of the period of suspension, the child shall not be reissued a license or permit until the child has paid any applicable reinstatement fee and complied with all requirements governing license reinstatement.

(5) Commit the child to the custody of the court;

(6) Require the child to not be absent without legitimate excuse from the public school the child is supposed to attend for five or more consecutive days, seven or more school days in one school month, or twelve or more school days in a school year;

(7)(a) If a child is adjudicated a delinquent child for being a chronic truant or an habitual truant who previously has been adjudicated an unruly child for being a habitual truant, do either or both of the following:

(i) Require the child to participate in a truancy prevention mediation program;

(ii) Make any order of disposition as authorized by this section, except that the court shall not commit the child to a facility described in division (A)(2) or (3) of this section unless the court determines that the child violated a lawful court order made pursuant to division (C)(1)(e) of section 2151.354 of the Revised Code or division (A)(6) of this section.

(b) If a child is adjudicated a delinquent child for being a chronic truant or a habitual truant who previously has been adjudicated an unruly child for being a habitual truant and the court determines that the parent, guardian, or other person having care of the child has failed to cause the child's attendance at school in violation of section 3321.38 of the Revised Code, do either or both of the following:

(i) Require the parent, guardian, or other person having care of the child to participate in a truancy prevention mediation program;

(ii) Require the parent, guardian, or other person having care of the child to participate in any community service program, preferably a community service program that requires the involvement of the parent, guardian, or other person having care of the child in the school attended by the child.

(8) Make any further disposition that the court finds proper, except that the child shall not be placed in any of the following:

(a) A state correctional institution, a county, multicounty, or municipal jail or workhouse, or another place in which an adult convicted of a crime, under arrest, or charged with a crime is held;

(b) A community corrections facility, if the child would be covered by the definition of public safety beds for purposes of sections 5139.41 to 5139.43 of the Revised Code if the court exercised its authority to commit the child to the legal custody of the department of youth services for institutionalization or institutionalization in a secure facility pursuant to this chapter.

(B) If a child is adjudicated a delinquent child, in addition to any order of disposition made under division (A) of this section, the court, in the following situations and for the specified periods of time, shall suspend the child's temporary instruction permit, restricted license, probationary driver's license, or nonresident operating privilege, or suspend the child's ability to obtain such a permit:

(1) If the child is adjudicated a delinquent child for violating section 2923.122 of the Revised Code, impose a class four suspension of the child's license, permit, or privilege from the range specified in division (A)(4) of section 4510.02 of the Revised Code or deny the child the issuance of a license or permit in accordance with division (F)(1) of section 2923.122 of the Revised Code.

(2) If the child is adjudicated a delinquent child for committing an act that if committed by an adult would be a drug abuse offense or for violating division (B) of section 2917.11 of the Revised Code, suspend the child's license, permit, or privilege for a period of time prescribed by the court. The court, in its discretion, may terminate the suspension if the child attends and satisfactorily completes a drug abuse or alcohol abuse education, intervention, or treatment program specified by the court. During the time the child is attending a program described in this division, the court shall retain the child's temporary instruction permit, probationary driver's license, or driver's license, and the court shall return the permit or license if it terminates the suspension as described in this division.

(C) The court may establish a victim-offender mediation program in which victims and their offenders meet to discuss the offense and suggest possible restitution. If the court obtains the assent of the victim of the delinquent act committed by the child, the court may require the child to participate in the program.

(D)(1) If a child is adjudicated a delinquent child for committing an act that would be a felony if committed by an adult and if the child caused, attempted to cause, threatened to cause, or created a risk of physical harm to the victim of the act, the court, prior to issuing an order of disposition under this section, shall order the preparation of a victim impact statement by the probation department of the county in which the victim of the act resides, by the court's own probation department, or by a victim assistance program that is operated by the state, a county, a municipal corporation, or another governmental entity. The court shall consider the victim impact statement in determining the order of disposition to issue for the child.

(2) Each victim impact statement shall identify the victim of the act for which the child was adjudicated a delinquent child, itemize any economic loss suffered by the victim as a result of the act, identify any physical injury suffered by the victim as a result of the act and the seriousness and permanence of the injury, identify any change in the victim's personal welfare or familial relationships as a result of the act and any psychological impact experienced by the victim or the victim's family as a result of the act, and contain any other information related to the impact of the act upon the victim that the court requires.

(3) A victim impact statement shall be kept confidential and is not a public record. However, the court may furnish copies of the statement to the department of youth services if the delinquent child is committed to the department or to both the adjudicated delinquent child or the adjudicated delinquent child's counsel and the prosecuting attorney. The copy of a victim impact statement furnished by the court to the department pursuant to this section shall be kept confidential and is not a public record. If an officer is preparing pursuant to section 2947.06 or 2951.03 of the Revised Code or Criminal Rule 32.2 a presentence investigation report pertaining to a person, the court shall make available to the officer, for use in preparing the report, a copy of any victim impact statement regarding that person. The copies of a victim impact statement that are made available to the adjudicated delinquent child or the adjudicated delinquent child's counsel and the prosecuting attorney pursuant to this division shall be returned to the court by the person to whom they were made available immediately following the imposition of an order of disposition for the child under this chapter.

The copy of a victim impact statement that is made available pursuant to this division to an officer preparing a criminal presentence investigation report shall be returned to the court by the officer immediately following its use in preparing the report.

(4) The department of youth services shall work with local probation departments and victim assistance programs to develop a standard victim impact statement.

(E) If a child is adjudicated a delinquent child for being a chronic truant or an habitual truant who previously has been adjudicated an unruly child for being an habitual truant and the court determines that the parent, guardian, or other person having care of the child has failed to cause the child's attendance at school in violation of section 3321.38 of the Revised Code, in addition to any order of disposition it makes under this section, the court shall warn the parent, guardian, or other person having care of the child that any subsequent adjudication of the child as an unruly or delinquent child for being an habitual or chronic truant may result in a criminal charge against the parent, guardian, or other person having care of the child for a violation of division (C) of section 2919.21 or section 2919.24 of the Revised Code.

(F)(1) During the period of a delinquent child's community control granted under this section, authorized probation officers who are engaged within the scope of their supervisory duties or responsibilities may search, with or without a warrant, the person of the delinquent child, the place of residence of the delinquent child, and a motor vehicle, another item of tangible or intangible personal property, or other real property in which the delinquent child has a right, title, or interest or for which the delinquent child has the express or implied permission of a person with a right, title, or interest to use, occupy, or possess if the probation officers have reasonable grounds to believe that the delinquent child is not abiding by the law or otherwise is not complying with the conditions of the delinquent child's community control. The court that places a delinquent child on community control under this section shall provide the delinquent child with a written notice that informs the delinquent child that authorized probation officers who are engaged within the scope of their supervisory duties or responsibilities may conduct those types of searches during the period of community control if they have reasonable grounds to believe that the delinquent child is not abiding by the law or otherwise is not complying with the conditions of the delinquent child's community control. The court also shall provide the written notice described in division (E)(2) of this section to each parent, guardian, or custodian of the delinquent child who is described in that division.

(2) The court that places a child on community control under this section shall provide the child's parent, guardian, or other custodian with a written notice that informs them that authorized probation officers may conduct searches pursuant to division (E)(1) of this section. The notice shall specifically state that a permissible search might extend to a motor vehicle, another item of tangible or intangible personal property, or a place of residence or other real property in which a notified parent, guardian, or custodian has a right, title, or interest and that the parent, guardian, or custodian expressly or impliedly permits the child to use, occupy, or possess.

(G) If a juvenile court commits a delinquent child to the custody of any person, organization, or entity pursuant to this section and if the delinquent act for which the child is so committed is a sexually oriented offense that is not a registration-exempt sexually oriented offense or is a child-victim oriented offense, the court in the order of disposition shall do one of the following:

(1) Require that the child be provided treatment as described in division (A)(2) of section 5139.13 of the Revised Code;

(2) Inform the person, organization, or entity that it is the preferred course of action in this state that the child be provided treatment as described in division (A)(2) of section 5139.13 of the Revised Code and encourage the person, organization, or entity to provide that treatment.

(2003 S 5, § 3, eff. 1–1–04; 2003 S 5, § 1, eff. 7–31–03; 2003 H 95, § 3.13, eff. 1–1–04; 2003 H 95, § 1, eff. 9–26–03; 2002 H 490, eff. 1–1–04; 2002 H 400, § 4, eff. 1–1–04; 2002 H 400, § 1, eff. 4–3–03; 2002 S 123, eff. 1–1–04; 2002 H 393, eff. 7–5–02; 2002 H 247, eff. 5–30–02; 2001 S 3, eff. 1–1–02; 2000 S 179, § 3, eff. 1–1–02)

Note: See also following version of this section, eff. 9–23–04.

2152.19 Additional disposition orders for delinquent children (later effective date)

Note: See also preceding version of this section, in effect until 9–23–04.

(A) If a child is adjudicated a delinquent child, the court may make any of the following orders of disposition, in addition to any other disposition authorized or required by this chapter:

(1) Any order that is authorized by section 2151.353 of the Revised Code for the care and protection of an abused, neglected, or dependent child;

(2) Commit the child to the temporary custody of any school, camp, institution, or other facility operated for the care of delinquent children by the county, by a district organized under section 2152.41 or 2151.65 of the Revised Code, or by a private agency or organization, within or without the state, that is authorized and qualified to provide the care, treatment, or placement required, including, but not limited to, a school, camp, or facility operated under section 2151.65 of the Revised Code;

(3) Place the child in a detention facility or district detention facility operated under section 2152.41 of the Revised Code, for up to ninety days;

(4) Place the child on community control under any sanctions, services, and conditions that the court prescribes. As a condition of community control in every case and in addition to any other condition that it imposes upon the child, the court shall require the child to abide by the law during the period of community control. As referred to in this division, community control includes, but is not limited to, the following sanctions and conditions:

(a) A period of basic probation supervision in which the child is required to maintain contact with a person appointed to supervise the child in accordance with sanctions imposed by the court;

(b) A period of intensive probation supervision in which the child is required to maintain frequent contact with a person appointed by the court to supervise the child while the child is seeking or maintaining employment and participating in training, education, and treatment programs as the order of disposition;

(c) A period of day reporting in which the child is required each day to report to and leave a center or another approved reporting location at specified times in order to participate in work, education or training, treatment, and other approved programs at the center or outside the center;

(d) A period of community service of up to five hundred hours for an act that would be a felony or a misdemeanor of the first degree if committed by an adult, up to two hundred hours for an act that would be a misdemeanor of the second, third, or fourth degree if committed by an adult, or up to thirty hours for an act that would be a minor misdemeanor if committed by an adult;

(e) A requirement that the child obtain a high school diploma, a certificate of high school equivalence, vocational training, or employment;

(f) A period of drug and alcohol use monitoring;

(g) A requirement of alcohol or drug assessment or counseling, or a period in an alcohol or drug treatment program with a level of security for the child as determined necessary by the court;

(h) A period in which the court orders the child to observe a curfew that may involve daytime or evening hours;

(i) A requirement that the child serve monitored time;

(j) A period of house arrest without electronic monitoring or continuous alcohol monitoring;

(k) A period of electronic monitoring or continuous alcohol monitoring without house arrest, or house arrest with electronic monitoring or continuous alcohol monitoring or both electronic monitoring and continuous alcohol monitoring, that does not exceed the maximum sentence of imprisonment that could be imposed upon an adult who commits the same act.

A period of house arrest with electronic monitoring or continuous alcohol monitoring or both electronic monitoring and continuous alcohol monitoring, imposed under this division, shall not extend beyond the child's twenty-first birthday. If a court imposes a period of house arrest with electronic monitoring or continuous alcohol monitoring or both electronic monitoring and continuous alcohol monitoring, upon a child under this division, it shall require the child: to remain in the child's home or other specified premises for the entire period of house arrest with electronic monitoring or continuous alcohol monitoring or both except when the court permits the child to leave those premises to go to school or to other specified premises . Regarding electronic monitoring, the court also shall require the child to be monitored by a central system that can determine the child's location at designated times; to report periodically to a person designated by the court; and to enter into a written contract with the court agreeing to comply with all requirements imposed by the court, agreeing to pay any fee imposed by the court for the costs of the house arrest with electronic monitoring, and agreeing to waive the right to receive credit for any time served on house arrest with electronic monitoring toward the period of any other dispositional order imposed upon the child if the child violates any of the requirements of the dispositional order of house arrest with electronic monitoring. The court also may impose other reasonable requirements upon the child.

Unless ordered by the court, a child shall not receive credit for any time served on house arrest with electronic monitoring or continuous alcohol monitoring or both toward any other dispositional order imposed upon the child for the act for which was imposed the dispositional order of house arrest with electronic monitoring or continuous alcohol monitoring. As used in this division and division (A)(4)(*l*) of this section, "continuous alcohol monitoring" has the same meaning as in section 2929.01 of the Revised Code.

(*l*) A suspension of the driver's license, probationary driver's license, or temporary instruction permit issued to the child for a period of time prescribed by the court, or a suspension of the registration of all motor vehicles registered in the name of the child for a period of time prescribed by the court. A child whose license or permit is so suspended is ineligible for issuance of a license or permit during the period of suspension. At the end of the period of suspension, the child shall not be reissued a license or permit until the child has paid any applicable reinstatement fee and complied with all requirements governing license reinstatement.

(5) Commit the child to the custody of the court;

(6) Require the child to not be absent without legitimate excuse from the public

school the child is supposed to attend for five or more consecutive days, seven or more school days in one school month, or twelve or more school days in a school year;

(7)(a) If a child is adjudicated a delinquent child for being a chronic truant or a habitual truant who previously has been adjudicated an unruly child for being a habitual truant, do either or both of the following:

(i) Require the child to participate in a truancy prevention mediation program;

(ii) Make any order of disposition as authorized by this section, except that the court shall not commit the child to a facility described in division (A)(2) or (3) of this section unless the court determines that the child violated a lawful court order made pursuant to division (C)(1)(e) of section 2151.354 of the Revised Code or division (A)(6) of this section.

(b) If a child is adjudicated a delinquent child for being a chronic truant or a habitual truant who previously has been adjudicated an unruly child for being a habitual truant and the court determines that the parent, guardian, or other person having care of the child has failed to cause the child's attendance at school in violation of section 3321.38 of the Revised Code, do either or both of the following:

(i) Require the parent, guardian, or other person having care of the child to participate in a truancy prevention mediation program;

(ii) Require the parent, guardian, or other person having care of the child to participate in any community service program, preferably a community service program that requires the involvement of the parent, guardian, or other person having care of the child in the school attended by the child.

(8) Make any further disposition that the court finds proper, except that the child shall not be placed in any of the following:

(a) A state correctional institution, a county, multicounty, or municipal jail or workhouse, or another place in which an adult convicted of a crime, under arrest, or charged with a crime is held;

(b) A community corrections facility, if the child would be covered by the definition of public safety beds for purposes of sections 5139.41 to 5139.43 of the Re-

vised Code if the court exercised its authority to commit the child to the legal custody of the department of youth services for institutionalization or institutionalization in a secure facility pursuant to this chapter.

(B) If a child is adjudicated a delinquent child, in addition to any order of disposition made under division (A) of this section, the court, in the following situations and for the specified periods of time, shall suspend the child's temporary instruction permit, restricted license, probationary driver's license, or nonresident operating privilege, or suspend the child's ability to obtain such a permit:

(1) If the child is adjudicated a delinquent child for violating section 2923.122 of the Revised Code, impose a class four suspension of the child's license, permit, or privilege from the range specified in division (A)(4) of section 4510.02 of the Revised Code or deny the child the issuance of a license or permit in accordance with division (F)(1) of section 2923.122 of the Revised Code.

(2) If the child is adjudicated a delinquent child for committing an act that if committed by an adult would be a drug abuse offense or for violating division (B) of section 2917.11 of the Revised Code, suspend the child's license, permit, or privilege for a period of time prescribed by the court. The court, in its discretion, may terminate the suspension if the child attends and satisfactorily completes a drug abuse or alcohol abuse education, intervention, or treatment program specified by the court. During the time the child is attending a program described in this division, the court shall retain the child's temporary instruction permit, probationary driver's license, or driver's license, and the court shall return the permit or license if it terminates the suspension as described in this division.

(C) The court may establish a victim-offender mediation program in which victims and their offenders meet to discuss the offense and suggest possible restitution. If the court obtains the assent of the victim of the delinquent act committed by the child, the court may require the child to participate in the program.

(D)(1) If a child is adjudicated a delinquent child for committing an act that would be a felony if committed by an adult and if the child caused, attempted to cause, threatened to cause, or created a risk of physical harm to the victim of the act, the court, prior to issuing an order of disposition under this section, shall order the preparation of a victim impact statement by the probation department of the county in which the victim of the act resides, by the court's own probation department, or by a victim assistance program that is operated by the state, a county, a municipal corporation, or another governmental entity. The court shall consider the victim impact statement in determining the order of disposition to issue for the child.

(2) Each victim impact statement shall identify the victim of the act for which the child was adjudicated a delinquent child, itemize any economic loss suffered by the victim as a result of the act, identify any physical injury suffered by the victim as a result of the act and the seriousness and permanence of the injury, identify any change in the victim's personal welfare or familial relationships as a result of the act and any psychological impact experienced by the victim or the victim's family as a result of the act, and contain any other information related to the impact of the act upon the victim that the court requires.

(3) A victim impact statement shall be kept confidential and is not a public record. However, the court may furnish copies of the statement to the department of youth services if the delinquent child is committed to the department or to both the adjudicated delinquent child or the adjudicated delinquent child's counsel and the prosecuting attorney. The copy of a victim impact statement furnished by the court to the department pursuant to this section shall be kept confidential and is not a public record. If an officer is preparing pursuant to section 2947.06 or 2951.03 of the Revised Code or Criminal Rule 32.2 a presentence investigation report pertaining to a person, the court shall make available to the officer, for use in preparing the report, a copy of any victim impact statement regarding that person. The copies of a victim impact statement that are made available to the adjudicated delinquent child or the adjudicated delinquent child's counsel and the prosecuting attorney pursuant to this division shall be returned to the court by the person to whom they were made available immediately following the imposition of an order of disposition for the child under this chapter.

The copy of a victim impact statement that is made available pursuant to this division to an officer preparing a criminal presentence investigation report shall be returned to the court by the officer immediately following its use in preparing the report.

(4) The department of youth services shall work with local probation departments and victim assistance programs to develop a standard victim impact statement.

(E) If a child is adjudicated a delinquent child for being a chronic truant or a habitual truant who previously has been adjudicated an unruly child for being a habitual truant and the court determines that the parent, guardian, or other person having care of the child has failed to cause the child's attendance at school in violation of section 3321.38 of the Revised Code, in addition to any order of disposition it makes under this section, the court shall warn the parent, guardian, or other person having care of the child that any subsequent adjudication of the child as an unruly or delinquent child for being a habitual or chronic truant may result in a criminal charge against the parent, guardian, or other person having care of the child for a violation of division (C) of section 2919.21 or section 2919.24 of the Revised Code.

(F)(1) During the period of a delinquent child's community control granted under this section, authorized probation officers who are engaged within the scope of their supervisory duties or responsibilities may search, with or without a warrant, the person of the delinquent child, the place of residence of the delinquent child, and a motor vehicle, another item of tangible or intangible personal property, or other real property in which the delinquent child has a right, title, or interest or for which the delinquent child has the express or implied permission of a person with a right, title, or interest to use, occupy, or possess if the probation officers have reasonable grounds to believe that the delinquent child is not abiding by the law or otherwise is not complying with the conditions of the delinquent child's community control. The court that places a delinquent child on community control under this section shall provide the delinquent child with a written notice that informs the delinquent child that authorized probation officers who are engaged within the scope of their supervisory duties or responsibilities may conduct those types of searches during the period of community control if they have reasonable grounds to believe that the delinquent child is not abiding by the law or otherwise is not complying with the conditions of the delinquent child's community control. The court also shall provide the written notice described in division (E)(2) of this section to each parent, guardian, or custodian of the delinquent child who is described in that division.

(2) The court that places a child on community control under this section shall provide the child's parent, guardian, or other custodian with a written notice that informs them that authorized probation officers may conduct searches pursuant to division (E)(1) of this section. The notice shall specifically state that a permissible search might extend to a motor vehicle, another item of tangible or intangible personal property, or a place of residence or other real property in which a notified parent, guardian, or custodian has a right, title, or interest and that the parent, guardian, or custodian expressly or impliedly permits the child to use, occupy, or possess.

(G) If a juvenile court commits a delinquent child to the custody of any person, organization, or entity pursuant to this section and if the delinquent act for which the child is so committed is a sexually oriented offense that is not a registration-exempt sexually oriented offense or is a child-victim oriented offense, the court in the order of disposition shall do one of the following:

(1) Require that the child be provided treatment as described in division (A)(2) of section 5139.13 of the Revised Code;

(2) Inform the person, organization, or entity that it is the preferred course of action in this state that the child be provided treatment as described in division (A)(2) of section 5139.13 of the Revised Code and encourage the person, organization, or entity to provide that treatment.

(2004 H 163, eff. 9–23–04; 2003 S 5, § 3, eff. 1–1–04; 2003 S 5, § 1, eff. 7–31–03; 2003 H 95, § 3.13, eff. 1–1–04; 2003 H 95, § 1, eff. 9–26–03; 2002 H 490, eff. 1–1–04; 2002 H 400, § 4, eff. 1–1–04; 2002 H 400, § 1, eff. 4–3–03; 2002 S 123, eff. 1–1–04; 2002 H 393, eff. 7–5–02; 2002 H 247, eff. 5–30–02; 2001 S 3, eff. 1–1–02; 2000 S 179, § 3, eff. 1–1–02)

Note: See also preceding version of this section, in effect until 9–23–04.

Uncodified Law

2001 S 3, § 5, eff. 10–26–01, reads:

Section 2152.19 of the Revised Code, as presented in this act, includes matter that was amended into former section 2151.355 of the Revised Code by Am. Sub. S.B. 181 of the 123rd General Assembly. Paragraphs of former section 2151.355 of the Revised Code containing S.B. 181 amendments were transferred to section 2152.19 of the Revised Code by Am. Sub. S.B. 179 of the 123rd General Assembly as part of its general revision of the juvenile sentencing laws. The General Assembly, applying the principle stated in division (B) of section 1.52 of the Revised Code that amendments are to be harmonized if reasonably capable of simultaneous operation, finds that the version of section 2152.19 of the Revised Code presented in this act is the resulting version of the section in effect prior to the effective date of the section as presented in this act.

Historical and Statutory Notes

Amendment Note: 2004 H 163 inserted "or continuous alcohol monitoring", "or both electronic monitoring and continuous alcohol monitoring," and "or continuous alcohol monitoring or both" throughout subdivisions (A)(4)(j) and (k); inserted ". Regarding electronic monitoring, the court also shall require the child" preceding "to be monitored by a central system" in the second paragraph of subdivision (A)(4)(k); inserted the last sentence of subdivision (A)(4)(k); and made other nonsubstantive changes.

Ed. Note: A special endorsement by the Legislative Service Commission states, "Comparison of these amendments [2003 S 5, § 3, eff. 1–1–04, 2003 H 95, § 3.13, eff. 1–1–04, 2002 H 490, eff. 1–1–04, and 2002 H 400, § 4, eff. 1–1–04] in pursuance of section 1.52 of the Revised Code discloses that they are not irreconcilable so that they are required by that section to be harmonized to give effect to each amendment." In recognition of this rule of construction, changes made by 2003 S 5, § 3, eff. 1–1–04, 2003 H 95, § 3.13, eff. 1–1–04, 2002 H 490, eff. 1–1–04, and 2002 H 400, § 4, eff. 1–1–04, have been incorporated in the above amendment. See *Baldwin's Ohio Legislative Service Annotated*, 2003, pages 7/L–1994 and 6/L–1415, and 2002, pages 12/L–2669 and 12/L–2622, or the OH–LEGIS or OH–LEGIS–OLD database on Westlaw, for original versions of these Acts.

Ed. Note: 2152.18, 2152.19 and 2152.20 contain provisions analogous to former 2151.355, repealed by 2000 S 179, § 4, eff. 1–1–02.

Amendment Note: 2003 S 5 inserted "that is not a registration-exempt sexually oriented offense or is a child-victim oriented offense" in division (G).

Amendment Note: 2003 H 95, § 1 and 3, substituted "5139.43" for "5139.45" in Division (A)(8)(b).

Amendment Note: 2002 H 490 substituted "with electronic monitoring" for "electronically monitored" throughout the section; and deleted "to wear, otherwise have attached to the child's person, or otherwise be subject to monitoring by a certified electronic monitoring device or to participate in the operation of and monitoring by a certified electronic monitoring system;" after "the child:" in the first paragraph of division (A)(3)(k).

Amendment Note: 2002 H 400, § 1, added ", including, but not limited to, a school, camp, or facility operated under section 2151.65 of the Revised Code;" to division (A)(2); added new (A)(3); renumbered existing divisions (A)(3) through (A)(7) as (A)(4) through (A)(8); added "or (3)" to division

(A)(7)(a)(ii); and changed "(5)" to "(6)" in division (A)(7)(a)(ii).

Amendment Note: 2002 S 123 inserted "for a period of time prescribed by the court" twice in division (A)(3)(*l*); and rewrote division (B), which prior thereto read:

"(B) If a child is adjudicated a delinquent child, in addition to any order of disposition made under division (A) of this section, the court, in the following situations, shall suspend the child's temporary instruction permit, restricted license, probationary driver's license, or nonresident operating privilege, or suspend the child's ability to obtain such a permit:

"(1) The child is adjudicated a delinquent child for violating section 2923.122 of the Revised Code, with the suspension and denial being in accordance with division (E)(1)(a), (c), (d), or (e) of section 2923.122 of the Revised Code.

"(2) The child is adjudicated a delinquent child for committing an act that if committed by an adult would be a drug abuse offense or for violating division (B) of section 2917.11 of the Revised Code, with the suspension continuing until the child attends and satisfactorily completes a drug abuse or alcohol abuse education, intervention, or treatment program specified by the court. During the time the child is attending the program, the court shall retain any temporary instruction permit, probationary driver's license, or driver's license issued to the child, and the court shall return the permit or license when the child satisfactorily completes the program."

Amendment Note: 2002 H 393 rewrote division (G) which prior thereto read:

"(G) If a juvenile court commits a delinquent child to the custody of any person, organization, or entity pursuant to this section and if the delinquent act for which the child is so committed is a sexually oriented offense, the court in the order of disposition shall inform the person, organization, or entity that it is the preferred course of action in this state that the child be provided treatment as described in division (A)(2) of section 5139.13 of the Revised Code and shall encourage the person, organization, or entity to provide that treatment."

Amendment Note: 2002 H 247 made nonsubstantive changes and rewrote division (D)(3), which prior thereto read:

"(3) A victim impact statement shall be kept confidential and is not a public record. However, the court may furnish copies of the statement to the department of youth services if the delinquent child is committed to the department or to both the adjudicated delinquent child or the adjudicated delinquent child's counsel and the prosecuting attorney. The copy of a victim impact statement furnished by the court to the department pursuant to this section shall be kept confidential and is not a public record. The copies of a victim impact statement that are made available to the adjudicated delinquent child or the adjudicated delinquent child's counsel and the prosecuting attorney pursuant to this division shall be returned to the court by the person to whom they were made available immediately following the imposition of an order of disposition for the child under this chapter."

Amendment Note: 2001 S 3 added new division (G).

Cross References

Agreement to reimburse juvenile court for foster care maintenance costs and associated administrative and training costs, 2151.152

Presentence investigation reports, mandatory consideration of certain information, 2951.03

Library References

OJur 3d: 48, Family Law § 1679 to 1702
Carlin, Baldwin's Ohio Practice, Merrick–Rippner Probate Law § 107.61, 107.89, 107.90, 107.101, 107.102, 107.105, 107.113, 107.180 (2003).

2152.191 Application of certain sections of Revised Code to child adjudicated a delinquent child for committing sexually oriented offense

If a child is adjudicated a delinquent child for committing a sexually oriented offense that is not a registration-exempt sexually oriented offense or for committing a child-victim oriented offense, if the child is fourteen years of age or older at the time of committing the offense, and if the child committed the offense on or after January 1, 2002, both of the following apply:

(A) Sections 2152.82 to 2152.85 and Chapter 2950. of the Revised Code apply to the child and the adjudication.

(B) In addition to any order of disposition it makes of the child under this chapter, the court may make any determination, adjudication, or order authorized under sections 2152.82 to 2152.85 and Chapter 2950. of the Revised Code and shall make any determination, adjudication, or order required under those sections and that chapter.

(2003 S 5, eff. 7–31–03; 2001 S 3, eff. 1–1–02)

Historical and Statutory Notes

Amendment Note: 2003 S 5 inserted "that is not a registration-exempt sexually oriented offense or for committing a child-victim oriented offense" and substituted "January 1, 2002, both" for "the effective date of this section, all" in the first paragraph.

Library References

OJur 3d: 48, Family Law § 1679 to 1702

2152.20 Fines; costs; restitution; forfeitures

(A) If a child is adjudicated a delinquent child or a juvenile traffic offender, the court may order any of the following dispositions, in addition to any other disposition authorized or required by this chapter:

(1) Impose a fine in accordance with the following schedule:

(a) For an act that would be a minor misdemeanor or an unclassified misdemeanor if committed by an adult, a fine not to exceed fifty dollars;

(b) For an act that would be a misdemeanor of the fourth degree if committed by an adult, a fine not to exceed one hundred dollars;

(c) For an act that would be a misdemeanor of the third degree if committed by an adult, a fine not to exceed one hundred fifty dollars;

(d) For an act that would be a misdemeanor of the second degree if committed by an adult, a fine not to exceed two hundred dollars;

(e) For an act that would be a misdemeanor of the first degree if committed by an adult, a fine not to exceed two hundred fifty dollars;

(f) For an act that would be a felony of the fifth degree or an unclassified felony if committed by an adult, a fine not to exceed three hundred dollars;

(g) For an act that would be a felony of the fourth degree if committed by an adult, a fine not to exceed four hundred dollars;

(h) For an act that would be a felony of the third degree if committed by an adult, a fine not to exceed seven hundred fifty dollars;

(i) For an act that would be a felony of the second degree if committed by an adult, a fine not to exceed one thousand dollars;

(j) For an act that would be a felony of the first degree if committed by an adult, a fine not to exceed one thousand five hundred dollars;

(k) For an act that would be aggravated murder or murder if committed by an adult, a fine not to exceed two thousand dollars.

(2) Require the child to pay costs;

(3) Unless the child's delinquent act or juvenile traffic offense would be a minor misdemeanor if committed by an adult or could be disposed of by the juvenile traffic violations bureau serving the court under Traffic Rule 13.1 if the court has established a juvenile traffic violations bureau, require the child to make restitution to the victim of the child's delinquent act or juvenile traffic offense or, if the victim is deceased, to a survivor of the victim in an amount based upon the victim's economic loss caused by or related to the delinquent act or juvenile traffic offense. The court may not re-

quire a child to make restitution pursuant to this division if the child's delinquent act or juvenile traffic offense would be a minor misdemeanor if committed by an adult or could be disposed of by the juvenile traffic violations bureau serving the court under Traffic Rule 13.1 if the court has established a juvenile traffic violations bureau. If the court requires restitution under this division, the restitution shall be made directly to the victim in open court or to the probation department that serves the jurisdiction or the clerk of courts on behalf of the victim.

If the court requires restitution under this division, the restitution may be in the form of a cash reimbursement paid in a lump sum or in installments, the performance of repair work to restore any damaged property to its original condition, the performance of a reasonable amount of labor for the victim or survivor of the victim, the performance of community service work, any other form of restitution devised by the court, or any combination of the previously described forms of restitution.

If the court requires restitution under this division, the court may base the restitution order on an amount recommended by the victim or survivor of the victim, the delinquent child, the juvenile traffic offender, a presentence investigation report, estimates or receipts indicating the cost of repairing or replacing property, and any other information, provided that the amount the court orders as restitution shall not exceed the amount of the economic loss suffered by the victim as a direct and proximate result of the delinquent act or juvenile traffic offense. If the court decides to order restitution under this division and the amount of the restitution is disputed by the victim or survivor or by the delinquent child or juvenile traffic offender, the court shall hold a hearing on the restitution. If the court requires restitution under this division, the court shall determine, or order the determination of, the amount of restitution to be paid by the delinquent child or juvenile traffic offender. All restitution payments shall be credited against any recovery of economic loss in a civil action brought by or on behalf of the victim against the delinquent child or juvenile traffic offender or the delinquent child's or juvenile traffic offender's parent, guardian, or other custodian.

If the court requires restitution under this division, the court may order that the delinquent child or juvenile traffic offender pay a surcharge, in an amount not exceeding five per cent of the amount of restitution otherwise ordered under this division, to the entity responsible for collecting and processing the restitution payments.

The victim or the survivor of the victim may request that the prosecuting authority file a motion, or the delinquent child or juvenile traffic offender may file a motion, for modification of the payment terms of any restitution ordered under this division. If the court grants the motion, it may modify the payment terms as it determines appropriate.

(4) Require the child to reimburse any or all of the costs incurred for services or sanctions provided or imposed, including, but not limited to, the following:

(a) All or part of the costs of implementing any community control imposed as a disposition under section 2152.19 of the Revised Code, including a supervision fee;

(b) All or part of the costs of confinement in a residential facility described in section 2152.19 of the Revised Code or in a department of youth services institution, including, but not limited to, a per diem fee for room and board, the costs of medical and dental treatment provided, and the costs of repairing property the delinquent child damaged while so confined. The amount of reimbursement ordered for a child under this division shall not exceed the total amount of reimbursement the child is able to pay as determined at a hearing and shall not exceed the actual cost of the confinement. The court may collect any reimbursement ordered under this division. If the court does not order reimbursement under this division, confinement costs may be assessed pursuant to a repayment policy adopted under section 2929.37 of the Revised Code and division (D) of section 307.93, division (A) of section 341.19, division (C) of section 341.23 or 753.16, or division (B) of section 341.14, 753.02, 753.04, 2301.56, or 2947.19 of the Revised Code.

(B)(1) If a child is adjudicated a delinquent child for violating section 2923.32 of the Revised Code, the court shall enter an order of criminal forfeiture against the child in accordance with divisions (B)(3), (4), (5), and (6) and (C) to (F) of section 2923.32 of the Revised Code.

(2) Sections 2925.41 to 2925.45 of the Revised Code apply to children who are adjudicated or could be adjudicated by a juvenile court to be delinquent children for an act that, if committed by an adult, would be a felony drug abuse offense. Subject to division (B) of section 2925.42 and division (E) of section 2925.43 of the Revised Code, a delinquent child of that nature loses any right to the possession of, and forfeits to the state any right, title, and interest that the delinquent child may have in, property as defined in section 2925.41 of the Revised Code and further described in section 2925.42 or 2925.43 of the Revised Code.

(3) Sections 2923.44 to 2923.47 of the Revised Code apply to children who are adjudicated or could be adjudicated by a juvenile court to be delinquent children for an act in violation of section 2923.42 of the Revised Code. Subject to division (B) of section 2923.44 and division (E) of section 2923. 45 of the Revised Code, a delinquent child of that nature loses any right to the possession of, and forfeits to the state any right, title, and interest that the delinquent child may have in, property as defined in section 2923.41 of the Revised Code and further described in section 2923.44 or 2923. 45 of the Revised Code.

(C) The court may hold a hearing if necessary to determine whether a child is able to pay a sanction under this section.

(D) If a child who is adjudicated a delinquent child is indigent, the court shall consider imposing a term of community service under division (A) of section 2152.19 of the Revised Code in lieu of imposing a financial sanction under this section. If a child who is adjudicated a delinquent child is not indigent, the court may impose a term of community service under that division in lieu of, or in addition to, imposing a financial sanction under this section. The court may order community service for an act that if committed by an adult would be a minor misdemeanor.

If a child fails to pay a financial sanction imposed under this section, the court may impose a term of community service in lieu of the sanction.

(E) The clerk of the court, or another person authorized by law or by the court to collect a financial sanction imposed under this section, may do any of the following:

(1) Enter into contracts with one or more public agencies or private vendors for the collection of the amounts due under the financial sanction, which amounts may include interest from the date of imposition of the financial sanction;

(2) Permit payment of all, or any portion of, the financial sanction in installments, by credit or debit card, by another type of electronic transfer, or by any other reasonable method, within any period of time, and on any terms that the court considers just, except that the maximum time permitted for payment shall not exceed five years. The clerk may pay any fee associated with processing an electronic transfer out of public money and may charge the fee to the delinquent child.

(3) To defray administrative costs, charge a reasonable fee to a child who elects a payment plan rather than a lump sum payment of a financial sanction.

(2004 H 52, eff. 6–1–04; 2002 H 490, eff. 1–1–04; 2002 H 170, eff. 9–6–02; 2000 S 179, § 3, eff. 1–1–02)

Historical and Statutory Notes

Ed. Note: 2152.18, 2152.19 and 2152.20 contain provisions analogous to former 2151.355, repealed by 2000 S 179, § 4, eff. 1–1–02.

Amendment Note: 2004 H 52 rewrote division (A)(3), which prior thereto read:

"(3) Require the child to make restitution to the victim of the child's delinquent act or, if the victim is deceased, to a survivor of the victim in an amount based upon the victim's economic loss caused by or related to the delinquent act. Restitution required under this division shall be made directly to the victim in open court or to the probation department that serves the jurisdiction or the clerk of courts on behalf of the victim. The restitution may include reimbursement to third parties, other than the delinquent child's insurer, for amounts paid to the victim or to any survivor of the victim for economic loss resulting from the delinquent act. If reimbursement to a third party is required, the reimbursement shall be made to any governmental agency to repay any amounts the agency paid to the victim or any survivor of the victim before any reimbursement is made to any other person.

"Restitution required under this division may be in the form of a cash reimbursement paid in a lump sum or in installments, the performance of repair work to restore any damaged property to its original condition, the performance of a reasonable amount of labor for the victim or survivor of the victim, the performance of community service work, any other form of restitution devised by the court, or any combination of the previously described forms of restitution.

"The court may base the restitution order under this division on an amount recommended by the victim or survivor of the victim, the delinquent child, a presentence investigation report, estimates or receipts indicating the cost of repairing or replacing property, and any other information. If the amount of the restitution is disputed by the victim or survivor or by the delinquent child, the court shall hold a hearing on the restitution. The court shall determine, or order the determination of, the amount of restitution to be paid by the delinquent child. All restitution payments shall be credited against any recovery of economic loss in a civil action brought by or on behalf of the victim against the delinquent child or the delinquent child's parent, guardian, or other custodian.

"The court may order that the delinquent child pay a surcharge, in an amount not exceeding five per cent of the amount of restitution otherwise ordered under this division, to the entity responsible for collecting and processing the restitution payments.

"The victim or the survivor of the victim may request that the prosecuting authority file a motion, or the delinquent child may file a motion, for modification of the payment terms of any restitution ordered under this division. If the court grants the motion, it may modify the payment terms as it determines appropriate."

Amendment Note: 2002 H 490 rewrote the fifth paragraph of division (A)((3), which prior thereto read:

"The victim or the survivor of the victim may request that the prosecuting authority file a motion, or the delinquent child may file a motion, for modification of the payment terms of any restitution ordered under this division, based on a substantial change in the delinquent child's ability to pay."

Amendment Note: 2002 H 170 rewrote the last sentence of division (A)(4)(b), which prior thereto read:

"If the court does not order reimbursement under this division, confinement costs may be assessed pursuant to a repayment policy adopted under division (E) of section 307.93, division (A) of section 341.06, division (C) of section 341.23, or division (C) of section 753.02, 753.04, 2301.56, or 2947.19 of the Revised Code."

Library References

OJur 3d: 48, Family Law § 1679 to 1702
Painter, Ohio Driving Under the Influence Law (2003 Ed.), Text 19.45.
Carlin, Baldwin's Ohio Practice, Merrick–Rippner Probate Law § 107.91, 107.102, 107.130 (2003).

2152.201   Recovery of costs where offense constitutes act of terrorism

(A) In addition to any other dispositions authorized or required by this chapter, the juvenile court making disposition of a child adjudicated a delinquent child for committing a violation of section 2909.22, 2909.23, or 2909.24 of the Revised Code or a violation of section 2921.32 of the Revised Code when the offense or act committed by the person aided or to be aided as described in that section is an act of terrorism may order the child to pay to the state, municipal, or county law enforcement agencies that handled the investigation and prosecution all of the costs that the state, municipal corporation, or county reasonably incurred in the investigation and prosecution of the violation. The court shall hold a hearing to determine the amount of costs to be imposed under this section. The court may hold the hearing as part of the dispositional hearing for the child.

(B) If a child is adjudicated a delinquent child for committing a violation of section 2909.23 or 2909.24 of the Revised Code and if any political subdivision incurred any response costs as a result of, or in making any response to, the threat of the specified offense involved in the violation of section 2909.23 of the Revised Code or the actual specified offense involved in the violation of section 2909.24 of the Revised Code, in addition to any other dispositions authorized or required by this chapter, the juvenile court making disposition of the child for the violation may order the child to reimburse the involved political subdivision for the response costs it so incurred.

(C) As used in this section, "response costs" and "act of terrorism" have the same meanings as in section 2909.21 of the Revised Code.

(2002 S 184, eff. 5–15–02)

Library References
OJur 3d: 48, Family Law § 1679 to 1702

2152.21 Disposition of juvenile traffic offender

(A) Unless division (C) of this section applies, if a child is adjudicated a juvenile traffic offender, the court may make any of the following orders of disposition:

(1) Impose costs and one or more financial sanctions in accordance with section 2152.20 of the Revised Code;

(2) Suspend the child's driver's license, probationary driver's license, or temporary instruction permit for a definite period not exceeding two years or suspend the registration of all motor vehicles registered in the name of the child for a definite period not exceeding two years. A child whose license or permit is so suspended is ineligible for issuance of a license or permit during the period of suspension. At the end of the period of suspension, the child shall not be reissued a license or permit until the child has paid any applicable reinstatement fee and complied with all requirements governing license reinstatement.

(3) Place the child on community control;

(4) If the child is adjudicated a juvenile traffic offender for an act other than an act that would be a minor misdemeanor if committed by an adult and other than an act that could be disposed of by the juvenile traffic violations bureau serving the court under Traffic Rule 13.1 if the court has established a juvenile traffic violations bureau, require the child to make restitution pursuant to division (A)(3) of section 2152.20 of the Revised Code;

(5)(a) If the child is adjudicated a juvenile traffic offender for committing a violation of division (A) of section 4511.19 of the Revised Code or of a municipal ordinance that is substantially equivalent to that division, commit the child, for not longer than five days, to either of the following:

(i) The temporary custody of a detention facility or district detention facility established under section 2152.41 of the Revised Code;

(ii) The temporary custody of any school, camp, institution, or other facility for children operated in whole or in part for the care of juvenile traffic offenders of that nature by the county, by a district organized under section 2151.65 or 2152.41 of the Revised Code, or by a private agency or organization within the state that is authorized and qualified to provide the care, treatment, or placement required.

(b) If an order of disposition committing a child to the temporary custody of a home, school, camp, institution, or other facility of that nature is made under division (A)(5)(a) of this section, the length of the commitment shall not be reduced or diminished as a credit for any time that the child was held in a place of detention or shelter care, or otherwise was detained, prior to entry of the order of disposition.

(6) If, after making a disposition under divisions (A)(1) to (5) of this section, the court finds upon further hearing that the child has failed to comply with the orders of the court and the child's operation of a motor vehicle constitutes the child a danger to the child and to others, the court may make any disposition authorized by divisions (A)(1), (4), (5), and (8) of section 2152.19 of the Revised Code, except that the child may not be committed to or placed in a secure correctional facility unless authorized by division (A)(5) of this section, and commitment to or

placement in a detention facility may not exceed twenty-four hours.

(B) If a child is adjudicated a juvenile traffic offender for violating division (A) or (B) of section 4511.19 of the Revised Code, in addition to any order of disposition made under division (A) of this section, the court shall impose a class six suspension of the temporary instruction permit, probationary driver's license, or driver's license issued to the child from the range specified in division (A)(6) of section 4510.02 of the Revised Code. The court, in its discretion, may terminate the suspension if the child attends and satisfactorily completes a drug abuse or alcohol abuse education, intervention, or treatment program specified by the court. During the time the child is attending a program as described in this division, the court shall retain the child's temporary instruction permit, probationary driver's license, or driver's license issued, and the court shall return the permit or license if it terminates the suspension as described in this division.

(C) If a child is adjudicated a juvenile traffic offender for violating division (B)(1) of section 4513.263 of the Revised Code, the court shall impose the appropriate fine set forth in division (G) of that section. If a child is adjudicated a juvenile traffic offender for violating division (B)(3) of section 4513.263 of the Revised Code and if the child is sixteen years of age or older, the court shall impose the fine set forth in division (G)(2) of that section. If a child is adjudicated a juvenile traffic offender for violating division (B)(3) of section 4513.263 of the Revised Code and if the child is under sixteen years of age, the court shall not impose a fine but may place the child on probation or community control.

(D) A juvenile traffic offender is subject to sections 4509.01 to 4509.78 of the Revised Code.

(2004 H 52, eff. 6–1–04; 2002 H 400, § 4, eff. 1–1–04; 2002 H 400, § 1, eff. 4–3–03; 2002 S 123, eff. 1–1–04; 2000 S 179, § 3, eff. 1–1–02)

Historical and Statutory Notes

Ed. Note: 2152.21 is former 2151.356, amended and recodified by 2000 S 179, § 3, eff. 1–1–02; 2000 S 181, eff. 9–4–00; 1998 H 2, eff. 1–1–99; 1997 S 35, eff. 1–1–99; 1996 H 265, eff. 3–3–97; 1995 H 1, eff. 1–1–96; 1992 S 98, eff. 11–12–92; 1992 H 154, H 118; 1990 S 131; 1989 H 381, H 330, H 329; 1988 H 643; 1986 H 428, S 54; 1977 H 222, H 1; 1970 H 931; 1969 H 320.

Amendment Note: 2004 H 52 rewrote division (A)(4) and substituted "or 2152.41" for "2152.41 or" in division (A)(5)(a)(ii). Prior to amendment, division (A)(4) read:

"(4) Require the child to make restitution for all damages caused by the child's traffic violation;"

Amendment Note: 2002 H 400, § 1, rewrote "divisions (A)(1), (3), (4), and (7) of section 2152.19" as "divisions (A)(1), (4), (5), and (8) of section 2152.19" in division (A)(6).

Amendment Note: 2002 S 123 inserted "for a definite period not exceeding two years" in division (A)(2); made other nonsubstantive changes to the section; and rewrote division (B), which prior thereto read:

"(B) If a child is adjudicated a juvenile traffic offender for violating division (A) or (B) of section 4511.19 of the Revised Code, in addition to any order of disposition made under division (A) of this section, the court shall suspend the temporary instruction permit, probationary driver's license, or driver's license issued to the child for a definite period of at least three months but not more than two years or, at the discretion of the court, until the child attends and satisfactorily completes a drug abuse or alcohol abuse education, intervention, or treatment program specified by the court. During the time the child is attending the program, the court shall retain any temporary instruction permit, probationary driver's license, or driver's license issued to the child and shall return the permit or license when the child satisfactorily completes the program."

Amendment Note: 2000 S 179, § 3, eff. 1–1–02, rewrote this section, which prior thereto read:

"(A) Unless division (C) of this section applies, if a child is adjudicated a juvenile traffic offender, the court may make any of the following orders of disposition:

"(1) Impose a fine and costs in accordance with the schedule set forth in section 2151.3512 of the Revised Code;

"(2) Suspend the child's driver's license, probationary driver's license, or temporary instruction permit or the registration of all motor vehicles registered in the name of the child for the period that the court prescribes. A child whose license or permit is so suspended is ineligible for issuance of a license or permit during the period of suspension. At the end of the period of suspension, the child shall not be reissued a license or permit until the child has paid any applicable reinstatement fee and complied with all requirements governing license reinstatement.

"(3) Revoke the child's driver's license, probationary driver's license, or temporary instruction permit or the registration of all motor vehicles registered in the name of the child. A child whose license or permit is so revoked is ineligible for issuance of a license or permit during the period of revocation. At the end of the period of revocation, the child shall not be reissued a license or permit until the child has paid any applicable reinstatement fee and complied with all requirements governing license reinstatement.

"(4) Place the child on probation;

"(5) Require the child to make restitution for all damages caused by the child's traffic violation or any part of the damages;

"(6) If the child is adjudicated a juvenile traffic offender for committing a violation of division (A) of section 4511.19 of the Revised Code or of a municipal ordinance that is substantially comparable to that division, commit the child, for not longer than five days, to the temporary custody of a detention home or district detention home established under section 2151.34 of the Revised Code, or to the temporary custody of any school, camp, institution, or other facility for children operated in whole or in part for the care of juvenile traffic offenders of that nature by the county, by a district organized under section 2151.34 or 2151.65 of the Revised Code, or by a private agency or organization within the state that is authorized and qualified to provide the care, treatment, or placement required. If an order of disposition committing a child to the temporary custody of a home, school, camp, institution, or other facility of that nature is made under division (A)(6) of this section, the length of the commitment shall not be reduced or diminished as a credit for any time that the child was held in a place of detention or shelter care, or otherwise was detained, prior to entry of the order of disposition.

"(7) If, after making a disposition under divisions (A)(1) to (6) of this section, the court finds upon further hearing that the child has failed to comply with the orders of the court and the child's operation of a motor vehicle constitutes the child a danger to the child and to others, the court may make any disposition authorized by divisions (A)(1), (A)(2), (A)(10) to (11), and (A)(22) of section 2151.355 of the Revised Code, except that the child may not be committed to or placed in a secure correctional facility unless authorized by division (A)(6) of this section, and commitment to or placement in a detention home may not exceed twenty-four hours.

"(B) If a child is adjudicated a juvenile traffic offender for violating division (A) of section 4511.19 of the Revised Code, the court shall suspend or revoke the temporary instruction permit, probationary driver's license, or driver's license issued to the child for a period of time prescribed by the court or, at the discretion of the court, until the child attends and satisfactorily completes a drug abuse or alcohol abuse education, intervention, or treatment program specified by the court. During the time the child is attending the program, the court shall retain any temporary instruction permit, probationary driver's license, or driver's license issued to the child and shall return the permit or license when the child satisfactorily completes the program. If a child is adjudicated a juvenile traffic offender for violating division (B) of section 4511.19 of the Revised Code, the court shall suspend the temporary instruction permit, probationary driver's license, or driver's license issued to the child for a period of not less than sixty days nor more than two years.

"(C) If a child is adjudicated a juvenile traffic offender for violating division (B)(1) or (2) of section 4513.263 of the Revised Code, the court shall impose the appropriate fine set forth in section 4513.99 of the Revised Code. If a child is adjudicated a juvenile traffic offender for violating division (B)(3) of section 4513.263 of the Revised Code and if the child is sixteen years of age or older, the court shall impose the fine set forth in division (G) of section 4513.99 of the Revised Code. If a child is adjudicated a juvenile traffic offender for violating division (B)(3) of section 4513.263 of the Revised Code and if the child is under sixteen years of age, the court shall not impose a fine but may place the child on probation.

"(D) A juvenile traffic offender is subject to sections 4509.01 to 4509.78 of the Revised Code."

Amendment Note: 2000 S 181 substituted "(A)(10) to (11), and (A)(22)" for "(A)(7) to (A)(10), and (A)(21)" in division (A)(7).

Amendment Note: 1998 H 2 substituted "(A)(2), (A)(7) to (A)(10), and (A)(21)" for "(2), and (A)(7) to (11)" in division (A)(7).

Amendment Note: 1997 S 35 inserted "driver's license" and "or temporary instruction permit", substituted "driver's" for "operator's", and added the second and third sentences, in division (A)(2); inserted "driver's license" and "or temporary instruction permit", and added the second and third sentences, in division (A)(3); rewrote division (B); and made other nonsubstantive changes. Prior to amendment, division (B) read:

"(B) If a child is adjudicated a juvenile traffic offender for violating division (A) of section 4511.19 of the Revised Code, the court shall suspend or revoke the temporary instruction permit or probationary driver's license issued to the child until the child attains eighteen years of age or attends, at the discretion of the court, and satisfactorily completes a drug abuse or alcohol abuse education, intervention, or treatment program specified by the court. During the time the child is attending the program, the court shall retain any temporary instruction permit or probationary license issued to the child and shall return the permit or license when the child satisfactorily completes the program. If a child is adjudicated a juvenile traffic offender for violating division (B) of section 4511.19 of the Revised Code, the court shall suspend the temporary instruction permit or probationary driver's license issued to the child for the shorter period of sixty days or until the child attains eighteen years of age."

Amendment Note: 1996 H 265 substituted "the child's" for "his" in division (A)(5); and substituted "(A)(1), (2), and (A)(7) to (11)" for "(A)(1) to (3) and (A)(6) to (10)" and inserted ", except that the child may not be committed to or placed in a secure correctional facility unless authorized by division (A)(6) of this section, and commitment to or placement in a detention home may not exceed twenty-four hours" in division (A)(7).

Amendment Note: 1995 H 1 substituted "adjudicated" for "found to be" throughout; substituted "and costs in accordance with the schedule set forth in section 2151.3512 of the Revised Code" for "not to exceed fifty dollars and costs" in division (A)(1); substituted "violating" for "having committed any act that if committed by an adult would be a drug abuse offense, as defined in section 2925.01 of the Revised Code, a violation of division (B) of section 2917.11 of the Revised Code, or a violation of" in division (B); substituted "violating" for "having committed an act that if committed by an adult would be a violation of" throughout division (C); and made changes to reflect gender neutral language and other nonsubstantive changes.

Cross References

Adjudicatory hearing, procedure, Juv R 29
Dispositional hearing, procedure, Juv R 34

Library References

Infants ⟪⟫223.1.

Westlaw Topic No. 211.

OJur 3d: 7, Automobiles and Other Vehicles § 177; 28, Criminal Law § 2762; 48, Family Law § 1547, 1548, 1679 to 1702

Am Jur 2d: 47, Juvenile Courts and Delinquent and Dependent Children § 29

Baldwin's Ohio Legislative Service, 1990 Laws of Ohio, S 131—LSC Analysis, p 5–623

Painter, Ohio Driving Under the Influence Law (2003 Ed.), Text 19.44, 19.45.

Carlin, Baldwin's Ohio Practice, Merrick–Rippner Probate Law § 107.106, 107.107, 107.108, 107.109 (2003).

2152.22 Relinquishment of juvenile court control; judicial release

(A) When a child is committed to the legal custody of the department of youth services under this chapter, the juvenile court relinquishes control with respect to the child so committed, except as provided in divisions (B), (C), and (G) of this section or in sections 2152.82 to 2152.85 of the Revised Code. Subject to divisions (B) and (C) of this section, sections 2151.353 and 2151.412 to 2151.421 of the Revised Code, sections 2152.82 to 2152.85 of the Revised Code, and any other provision of law that specifies a different duration for a dispositional order, all other dispositional orders made by the court under this chapter shall be temporary and shall continue for a period that is designated by the court in its order, until terminated or modified by the court or until the child attains twenty-one years of age.

The department shall not release the child from a department facility and as a result shall not discharge the child or order the child's release on supervised release prior to the expiration of the minimum period specified by the court in division (A)(1) of section 2152.16 of the Revised Code and any term of commitment imposed under section 2152.17 of the Revised Code or prior to the child's attainment of twenty-one years of age, except upon the order of a court pursuant to division (B) or (C) of this section or in accordance with section 5139.54 of the Revised Code.

(B)(1) The court that commits a delinquent child to the department may grant judicial release of the child to court supervision under this division during the first half of the prescribed minimum term for which the child was committed to the department or, if the child was committed to the department until the child attains twenty-one years of age, during the first half of the prescribed period of commitment that begins on the first day of commitment and ends on the child's twenty-first birthday, provided any commitment imposed under division (A), (B), (C), or (D) of section 2152.17 of the Revised Code has ended.

(2) If the department of youth services desires to release a child during a period specified in division (B)(1) of this section, it shall request the court that committed the child to grant a judicial release of the child to court supervision. During whichever of those periods is applicable, the child or the parents of the child also may request that court to grant a judicial release of the child to court supervision. Upon receipt of a request for a judicial release to court supervision from the department, the child, or the child's parent, or upon its own motion, the court that committed the child shall do one of the following: approve the release by journal entry; schedule within thirty days after the request is received a time for a hearing on whether the child is to be released; or reject the request by journal entry without conducting a hearing.

If the court rejects an initial request for a release under this division by the child or the child's parent, the child or the child's parent may make one additional request for a judicial release to court supervision within the applicable period. The additional request may be made no earlier than thirty days after the filing of the prior request for a judicial release to court supervision. Upon the filing of a second request for a judicial release to court supervision, the court shall either approve or disapprove the release by journal entry or schedule within thirty days after the request is received a time for a hearing on whether the child is to be released.

(3) If a court schedules a hearing under division (B)(2) of this section, it may order the department to deliver the child to the court on the date set for the hearing and may order the department to present to the court a report on the child's progress in the institution to which the child was committed and recommendations for conditions of supervision of the child by the court after release. The court may conduct the hearing without the child being present. The court shall determine at the hearing whether the child should be granted a judicial release to court supervision.

If the court approves the release, it shall order its staff to prepare a written treatment and rehabilitation plan for the child that may include any conditions of the child's release that were recommended by the department and approved by the court. The committing court shall send the juvenile court of the county in which the child is placed a copy of the recommended plan. The court of the county in which the child is placed may adopt the recommended conditions set by the committing court as an order of the court and may add any additional consistent conditions it considers appropriate. If a child is granted a judicial release to court supervision, the release discharges the child from the custody of the department of youth services.

(C)(1) The court that commits a delinquent child to the department may grant judicial release of the child to department of youth services supervision under this division during the second half of the prescribed minimum term for which the child was committed to the department or, if the child was committed to the department until the child attains twenty-one years of age, during the second half of the prescribed period of commitment that begins on the first day of commitment and ends on the child's twenty-first birthday, provided any commitment imposed under division (A), (B), (C), or (D) of section 2152.17 of the Revised Code has ended.

(2) If the department of youth services desires to release a child during a period specified in division (C)(1) of this section, it shall request the court that committed the child to grant a judicial release to department of youth services supervision. During whichever of those periods is applicable, the child or the child's parent also may request the court that committed the child to grant a judicial release to department of youth services supervision. Upon receipt of a request for judicial release to department of youth services supervision, the child, or the child's parent, or upon its own motion at any time during that period, the court shall do one of the following: approve the release by journal entry; schedule a time within thirty days after receipt of the request for a hearing on whether the child is to be released; or reject the request by journal entry without conducting a hearing.

If the court rejects an initial request for release under this division by the child or the child's parent, the child or the child's parent may make one or more subsequent requests for a release within the applicable period, but may make no more than one request during each period of ninety days that the child is in a secure department facility after the filing of a prior request for early release. Upon the filing of a request for release under this division subsequent to an initial request, the court shall either approve or disapprove the release by journal entry or schedule a time within thirty days after receipt of the request for a

hearing on whether the child is to be released.

(3) If a court schedules a hearing under division (C)(2) of this section, it may order the department to deliver the child to the court on the date set for the hearing and shall order the department to present to the court at that time a treatment plan for the child's post-institutional care. The court may conduct the hearing without the child being present. The court shall determine at the hearing whether the child should be granted a judicial release to department of youth services supervision.

If the court approves the judicial release to department of youth services supervision, the department shall prepare a written treatment and rehabilitation plan for the child pursuant to division (E) of this section that shall include the conditions of the child's release. It shall send the committing court and the juvenile court of the county in which the child is placed a copy of the plan. The court of the county in which the child is placed may adopt the conditions set by the department as an order of the court and may add any additional consistent conditions it considers appropriate, provided that the court may not add any condition that decreases the level or degree of supervision specified by the department in its plan, that substantially increases the financial burden of supervision that will be experienced by the department, or that alters the placement specified by the department in its plan. If the court of the county in which the child is placed adds to the department's plan any additional conditions, it shall enter those additional conditions in its journal and shall send to the department a copy of the journal entry of the additional conditions.

If the court approves the judicial release to department of youth services supervision, the actual date on which the department shall release the child is contingent upon the department finding a suitable placement for the child. If the child is to be returned to the child's home, the department shall return the child on the date that the court schedules for the child's release or shall bear the expense of any additional time that the child remains in a department facility. If the child is unable to return to the child's home, the department shall exercise reasonable diligence in finding a suitable placement for the child, and the child shall remain in a department facility while the department finds the suitable placement.

(D) If a child is released under division (B) or (C) of this section and the court of the county in which the child is placed has reason to believe that the child's deportment is not in accordance with the conditions of the child's judicial release, the court of the county in which the child is placed shall schedule a time for a hearing to determine whether the child violated any of the post-release conditions, and, if the child was released under division (C) of this section, divisions (A) to (E) of section 5139.52 of the Revised Code apply regarding the child.

If that court determines at the hearing that the child violated any of the post-release conditions, the court, if it determines that the violation was a serious violation, may order the child to be returned to the department for institutionalization, consistent with the original order of commitment of the child, or in any case may make any other disposition of the child authorized by law that the court considers proper. If the court of the county in which the child is placed orders the child to be returned to a department of youth services institution, the time during which the child was held in a secure department facility prior to the child's judicial release shall be considered as time served in fulfilling the prescribed period of institutionalization that is applicable to the child under the child's original order of commitment. If the court orders the child returned to a department institution, the child shall remain in institutional care for a minimum of three months or until the child successfully completes a revocation program of a duration of not less than thirty days operated either by the department or by an entity with which the department has contracted to provide a revocation program.

(E) The department of youth services, prior to the release of a child pursuant to division (C) of this section, shall do all of the following:

(1) After reviewing the child's rehabilitative progress history and medical and educational records, prepare a written treatment and rehabilitation plan for the child that includes conditions of the release;

(2) Completely discuss the conditions of the plan prepared pursuant to division (E)(1) of this section and the possible penalties for violation of the plan with the child and the child's parents, guardian, or legal custodian;

(3) Have the plan prepared pursuant to division (E)(1) of this section signed by the child, the child's parents, legal guardian, or custodian, and any authority or person that is to supervise, control, and provide supportive assistance to the child at the time of the child's release pursuant to division (C) of this section;

(4) Prior to the child's release, file a copy of the treatment plan prepared pursuant to division (E)(1) of this section with the committing court and the juvenile court of the county in which the child is to be placed.

(F) The department of youth services shall file a written progress report with the committing court regarding each child released pursuant to division (C) of this section at least once every thirty days unless specifically directed otherwise by the court. The report shall indicate the treatment and rehabilitative progress of the child and the child's family, if applicable, and shall include any suggestions for altering the program, custody, living arrangements, or treatment. The department shall retain legal custody of a child so released until it discharges the child or until the custody is terminated as otherwise provided by law.

(G) When a child is committed to the legal custody of the department of youth services, the court retains jurisdiction to perform the functions specified in section 5139.51 of the Revised Code with respect to the granting of supervised release by the release authority and to perform the functions specified in section 5139.52 of the Revised Code with respect to violations of the conditions of supervised release granted by the release authority and to the revocation of supervised release granted by the release authority.

(2002 H 393, eff. 7–5–02; 2001 S 3, eff. 1–1–02; 2000 S 179, § 3, eff. 1–1–02)

Historical and Statutory Notes

Amendment Note: 2002 H 393 rewrote divisions (A), (B), and (C)(1) which prior thereto read:

"(A) When a child is committed to the legal custody of the department of youth services under this chapter, the juvenile court relinquishes control with respect to the child so committed, except as provided in divisions (B), (C), and (G) of this section or in sections 2152.82 to 2152.85 of the Revised Code. Subject to divisions (B) and (C) of this section, sections 2151.353 and 2151.412 to 2151.421 of the Revised Code, sections 2152.82 to 2152.85 of the Revised Code, and any other provision of law that specifies a different duration for a dispositional order, all other dispositional orders made by the court under this chapter shall be temporary and shall continue for a period that is designated by the court in its order, until terminated or modified by the court or until the child attains twenty-one years of age.

"The department shall not release the child from a department facility and as a result shall not discharge the child or order the child's release on supervised release prior to the expiration of the period of court control over the child or prior to the child's attainment of twenty-one years of age, except upon the order of a court pursuant to division (B) or (C) of this section or in accordance with section 5139.54 of the Revised Code.

"(B)(1) The court that commits a delinquent child to the department may grant judicial release of the child to court supervision under this division, during any of the following periods that are applicable, provided any commitment imposed under division (A), (B), or (C) of section 2152.17 of the Revised Code has ended:

"(a) If the child was given a disposition under section 2152.16 of the Revised Code for committing an act that would be a felony of the third, fourth, or fifth degree if committed by an adult, at any time during the first ninety days of the period of court control over the child;

"(b) If the child was given a disposition under section 2152.13 or 2152.16 of the Revised Code, or both of those sections, for committing an act that would be a felony of the first or second degree if committed by an adult, at any time during the first one hundred eighty days of the period of court control over the child;

"(c) If the child was committed to the department until the child attains twenty-one years of age for an act that would be aggravated murder or murder if committed by an adult, at any time during the first half of the prescribed period of that commitment of the child.

"(2) If the department of youth services desires to release a child during a period specified in division (B)(1) of this section, it shall request the court that committed the child to grant a judicial release of the child to court supervision. During whichever of those periods is applicable, the child or the parents of the child also may request that court to grant a judicial release of the child to court supervision. Upon receipt of a request for a judicial release to court supervision from the department, the child, or the child's parent, or upon its own motion, the court that committed the child shall do one of the following: approve the release by journal entry; schedule within thirty days after the request is received a time for a hearing on whether the child is to be released; or reject the request by journal entry without conducting a hearing.

"If the court rejects an initial request for a release under this division by the child or the child's parent, the child or the child's parent may make one additional request for a judicial release to court supervision within the applicable period. The additional request may be made no earlier than thirty days after the filing of the prior request for a judicial release to court supervision. Upon the filing of a second request for a judicial release to court supervision, the court shall either approve or disapprove the release by journal entry or schedule within thirty days after the request is received a time for a hearing on whether the child is to be released.

"(3) If a court schedules a hearing under division (B)(2) of this section, it may order the department to deliver the child to the court on the date set for the hearing and may order the department to present to the court a report on the child's progress in the institution to which the child was committed and recommendations for conditions of supervision of the child by the court after release. The court may conduct the hearing without the child being present. The court shall determine at the hearing whether the child should be granted a judicial release to court supervision.

"If the court approves the release, it shall order its staff to prepare a written treatment and rehabilitation plan for the child that may include any conditions of the child's release that were recommended by the department and approved by the court. The committing court shall send the juvenile court of the county in which the child is placed a copy of the recommended plan. The court of the county in which the child is placed may adopt the recommended conditions set by the committing court as an order of the court and may add any additional consistent conditions it considers appropriate. If a child is granted a judicial release to court supervision, the release discharges the child from the custody of the department of youth services.

"(C)(1) The court that commits a delinquent child to the department may grant judicial release of the child to department of youth services supervision under this division, during any of the following periods that are applicable, provided any commitment imposed under division (A), (B), or (C) of section 2152.17 of the Revised Code has ended:

"(a) If the child was given a disposition under section 2152.16 of the Revised Code for an act that would be a felony of the third, fourth, or fifth degree if committed by an adult, at any time during the period of court control over the child, provided that at least ninety days of that period have elapsed;

"(b) If the child was given a disposition under section 2152.13 or 2152.16 of the Revised Code, or both of those sections, for an act that would be a felony of the first or second degree if committed by an adult, at any time during the period of court control over the child, provided that at least one hundred eighty days of that period have elapsed;

"(c) If the child was committed to the department for an act that would be aggravated murder or murder if committed by an adult until the child attains twenty-one years of age, at any time during the second half of the prescribed period of that commitment of the child."

Amendment Note: 2001 S 3 inserted "or in sections 2152.82 to 2152.85 of the Revised Code" and "sections 2152.82 to 2152.85 of the Revised Code" in the first paragraph of division (A)

Library References

OJur 3d: 48, Family Law § 1679 to 1702
Carlin, Baldwin's Ohio Practice, Merrick–Rippner
    Probate Law § 107.89, 107.121, 107.146,
    107.184, 107.185 (2003).

PLACE OF DETENTION

2152.26 Delinquent child or juvenile traffic offender to be held only in specified places

(A) Except as provided in divisions (B) and (F) of this section, a child alleged to be or adjudicated a delinquent child or a juvenile traffic offender may be held only in the following places:

(1) A certified foster home or a home approved by the court;

(2) A facility operated by a certified child welfare agency;

(3) Any other suitable place designated by the court.

(B) In addition to the places listed in division (A) of this section, a child alleged to be or adjudicated a delinquent child may be held in a detention facility for delinquent children that is under the direction or supervision of the court or other public authority or of a private agency and approved by the court and a child adjudicated a delinquent child may be held in accordance with division (F)(2) of this section in a facility of a type specified in that division. Division (B) of this section does not apply to a child alleged to be or adjudicated a delinquent child for chronic truancy, unless the child violated a lawful court order made pursuant to division (A)(6) of section 2152.19 of the Revised Code. Division (B) of this section also does not apply to a child alleged to be or adjudicated a delinquent child for being an habitual truant who previously has been adjudicated an unruly child for being an habitual truant, unless the child violated a lawful court order made pursuant to division (C)(1)(e) of section 2151.354 of the Revised Code.

(C)(1) Except as provided under division (C)(1) of section 2151.311 of the Revised Code or division (A)(5) of section 2152.21 of the Revised Code, a child alleged to be or adjudicated a juvenile traffic offender may not be held in any of the following facilities:

(a) A state correctional institution, county, multicounty, or municipal jail or workhouse, or other place in which an adult convicted of crime, under arrest, or charged with a crime is held.

(b) A secure correctional facility.

(2) Except as provided under this section, sections 2151.56 to 2151.61, and divisions (A)(5) and (6) of section 2152.21 of the Revised Code, a child alleged to be or adjudicated a juvenile traffic offender may not be held for more than twenty-four hours in a detention facility.

(D) Except as provided in division (F) of this section or in division (C) of section 2151.311, in division (C)(2) of section 5139.06 and section 5120.162, or in division (B) of section 5120.16 of the Revised Code, a child who is alleged to be or is adjudicated a delinquent child may not be held in a state correctional institution, county, multicounty, or municipal jail or workhouse, or other place where an adult convicted of crime, under arrest, or charged with crime is held.

(E) Unless the detention is pursuant to division (F) of this section or division (C) of section 2151.311, division (C)(2) of section 5139.06 and section 5120.162, or division (B) of section 5120.16 of the Revised Code, the official in charge of the institution, jail, workhouse, or other facility shall inform the court immediately when a child, who is or appears to be under the age of eighteen years, is received at the facility, and shall deliver the child to the court upon request or transfer the child to a detention facility designated by the court.

(F)(1) If a case is transferred to another court for criminal prosecution pursuant to section 2152.12 of the Revised Code, the child may be transferred for detention pending the criminal prosecution in a jail or other facility in accordance with the law governing the detention of persons charged with crime. Any child so held shall be confined in a manner that keeps the child beyond the range of touch of all adult detainees. The child shall be supervised at all times during the detention.

(2) If a person is adjudicated a delinquent child or juvenile traffic offender and the court makes a disposition of the person under this chapter, at any time after the person attains eighteen years of age, the person may be held under that disposition in places other than those specified in division (A) of this section, including, but not limited to, a county, multicounty, or municipal jail or workhouse, or other place where an adult convicted of crime, under arrest, or charged with crime is held.

(3)(a) A person alleged to be a delinquent child may be held in places other than those specified in division (A) of this section, including, but not limited to, a county, multicounty, or municipal jail, if the delinquent act that the child allegedly committed would be a felony if committed by an adult, and if either of the following applies:

(i) The person attains eighteen years of age before the person is arrested or apprehended for that act.

(ii) The person is arrested or apprehended for that act before the person attains eighteen years of age, but the person attains eighteen years of age before the court orders a disposition in the case.

(b) If, pursuant to division (F)(3)(a) of this section, a person is held in a place other than a place specified in division (A) of this section, the person has the same rights to bail as an adult charged with the same offense who is confined in a jail pending trial.

(2002 H 400, eff. 4–3–03; 2000 S 179, § 3, eff. 1–1–02)

Historical and Statutory Notes

Ed. Note: 2152.26 is former 2151.312, amended and recodified by 2000 S 179, § 3, eff. 1–1–02; 2000 H 332, eff. 1–1–01; 2000 H 448, eff. 10–5–00; 2000 S 181, eff. 9–4–00; 1997 H 1, eff. 7–1–98; 1996 H 124, eff. 3–31–97; 1996 H 265, eff. 3–3–97; 1994 H 571, eff. 10–6–94; 1993 H 152, eff. 7–1–93; 1992 S 331; 1989 H 166; 1981 H 440; 1975 H 85; 1969 H 320.

Amendment Note: 2002 H 400 added "and a child adjudicated a delinquent child may be held in accordance with division (F)(2) of this section in a facility of a type specified in that division" to the first sentence of division (B); changed "(A)(5)" to "(A)(6)" in the second sentence of division (B); changed "division (A)(5)" to "divisions (A)(5) and (6)" in division (C)(2); and rewrote division (F), which prior thereto read:

"(F) If a case is transferred to another court for criminal prosecution pursuant to section 2152.12 of the Revised Code, the child may be transferred for detention pending the criminal prosecution in a jail or other facility in accordance with the law governing the detention of persons charged with crime. Any child so held shall be confined in a manner that keeps the child beyond the range of touch of all adult detainees. The child shall be supervised at all times during the detention."

Amendment Note: 2000 S 179, § 3, eff. 1–1–02, rewrote this section, which prior thereto read:

"(A) Except as provided in divisions (B) and (F) of this section, a child alleged to be or adjudicated a delinquent child, an unruly child, or a juvenile traffic offender may be held only in the following places:

"(1) A certified foster home or a home approved by the court;

"(2) A facility operated by a certified child welfare agency;

"(3) Any other suitable place designated by the court.

"(B) In addition to the places listed in division (A) of this section, a child alleged to be or adjudicated a delinquent child may be held in a detention home or center for delinquent children that is under the direction or supervision of the court or other public authority or of a private agency and approved by the court. Division (B) of this section does not apply to a child alleged to be or adjudicated a delinquent child for chronic truancy, unless the child violated a lawful court order made pursuant to division (A)(23) of section 2151.355 of the Revised Code. Division (B) of this section also does not apply to a child alleged to be or adjudicated a delinquent child for being an habitual truant who previously has been adjudicated an unruly child for being an habitual

truant, unless the child violated a lawful court order made pursuant to division (C)(1)(e) of section 2151.354 of the Revised Code.

"(C)(1) Except as provided under division (C)(1) of section 2151.311 of the Revised Code or division (A)(6) of section 2151.356 of the Revised Code, a child alleged to be or adjudicated a neglected child, an abused child, a dependent child, an unruly child, or a juvenile traffic offender may not be held in any of the following facilities:

"(a) A state correctional institution, county, multi-county, or municipal jail or workhouse, or other place in which an adult convicted of crime, under arrest, or charged with a crime is held;

"(b) A secure correctional facility.

"(2) Except as provided under sections 2151.56 to 2151.61 and division (A)(6) of section 2151.356 of the Revised Code and division (C)(3) of this section, a child alleged to be or adjudicated an unruly child or a juvenile traffic offender may not be held for more than twenty-four hours in a detention home. A child alleged to be or adjudicated a neglected child, an abused child, or a dependent child shall not be held in a detention home.

"(3) A child who is alleged to be or who is adjudicated an unruly child and who is taken into custody on a Saturday, Sunday, or legal holiday, as listed in section 1.14 of the Revised Code, may be held in a detention home until the next succeeding day that is not a Saturday, Sunday, or legal holiday.

"(D) Except as provided in division (F) of this section or in division (C) of section 2151.311, in division (C)(2) of section 5139.06 and section 5120.162, or in division (B) of section 5120.16 of the Revised Code, a child who is alleged to be or is adjudicated a delinquent child may not be held in a state correctional institution, county, multicounty, or municipal jail or workhouse, or other place where an adult convicted of crime, under arrest, or charged with crime is held.

"(E) Unless the detention is pursuant to division (F) of this section or division (C) of section 2151.311, division (C)(2) of section 5139.06 and section 5120.162, or division (B) of section 5120.16 of the Revised Code, the official in charge of the institution, jail, workhouse, or other facility shall inform the court immediately when a child, who is or appears to be under the age of eighteen years, is received at the facility, and shall deliver the child to the court upon request or transfer the child to a detention facility designated by the court.

"(F) If a case is transferred to another court for criminal prosecution pursuant to section 2151.26 of the Revised Code, the child may be transferred for detention pending the criminal prosecution in a jail or other facility in accordance with the law governing the detention of persons charged with crime. Any child so held shall be confined in a manner that keeps the child beyond the range of touch of all adult detainees. The child shall be supervised at all times during the detention."

Amendment Note: 2000 H 332 deleted "family" before "foster home" in division (A)(1).

Amendment Note: 2000 H 448 deleted "family" after "certified" in division (A)(1).

Amendment Note: 2000 S 181 added the second and third sentences in division (B).

Amendment Note: 1997 H 1 substituted "(F)" for "(C)" and "(C)(2)" for "(C)(3)" in divisions (D) and (E).

Amendment Note: 1996 H 124 added the references to sections 2151.312(C) and 5120.16(B) throughout division (B); substituted "a manner that keeps the child beyond the range of touch of" for "a room totally separate by both sight and sound from" in division (C); and made changes to reflect gender neutral language and other nonsubstantive changes.

Amendment Note: 1996 H 265 rewrote this section, which prior thereto read:

"(A) A child alleged to be a delinquent child, an unruly child, or a juvenile traffic offender may be held only in the following places:

"(1) A certified family foster home or a home approved by the court;

"(2) A facility operated by a certified child welfare agency;

"(3) A detention home or center for delinquent children which is under the direction or supervision of the court or other public authority or of a private agency and approved by the court;

"(4) Any other suitable place designated by the court.

"(B) Except as provided in division (C) of section 2151.311 or in division (C)(3) of section 5139.06 and section 5120.162 of the Revised Code, a child shall not be held in a state correctional institution, county, multicounty, or municipal jail or workhouse, or other place where an adult convicted of crime, under arrest, or charged with crime is held. Unless the detention is pursuant to division (C) of section 2151.311 or pursuant to division (C)(3) of section 5139.06 and section 5120.162 of the Revised Code, the official in charge of the institution, jail, workhouse, or other facility shall inform the court immediately when a child, who is or appears to be under the age of eighteen years, is received at the facility, and shall deliver him to the court upon request or transfer him to a detention facility designated by the court.

"(C) If a case is transferred to another court for criminal prosecution pursuant to section 2151.26 of the Revised Code, the child may be transferred for detention pending the criminal prosecution in a jail or other facility in accordance with the law governing the detention of persons charged with crime. Any child so held shall be confined in a room totally separate by both sight and sound from all adult detainees. The child shall be supervised at all times during the detention.

"(D) A child who is alleged to be a neglected, abused, or dependent child shall not be held in a state correctional institution, county, multicounty, or municipal jail, or other place where any adult convicted of crime, under arrest, or charged with crime is held. The alleged neglected, abused, or dependent child shall not be held in a detention home or a center for children who are alleged to be delinquent children."

Amendment Note: 1994 H 571 substituted "correctional" for "penal or reformatory" in divisions (B) and (D).

Amendment Note: 1993 H 152 inserted "family" in division (A)(1).

Cross References

Detention and shelter care, Juv R 7

Library References

Infants ⊕68.3, 192.

Westlaw Topic No. 211.

C.J.S. Infants §§ 42, 53 to 55.

OJur 3d: 48, Family Law § 1580 to 1583

Painter, Ohio Driving Under the Influence Law (2003 Ed.), Text 19.44.

Carlin, Baldwin's Ohio Practice, Merrick–Rippner Probate Law § 107.27, 107.28 (2003).

DETENTION FACILITIES

2152.41   Juvenile detention facility

(A) Upon the recommendation of the judge, the board of county commissioners shall provide, by purchase, lease, construction, or otherwise, a detention facility that shall be within a convenient distance of the juvenile court. The facility shall not be used for the confinement of adults charged with criminal offenses. The facility may be used to detain alleged delinquent children until final disposition for evaluation pursuant to section 2152.04 of the Revised Code, to confine children who are adjudicated delinquent children and placed in the facility pursuant to division (A)(3) of section 2152.19 of the Revised Code, and to confine children who are adjudicated juvenile traffic offenders and committed to the facility under division (A)(5) or (6) of section 2152.21 of the Revised Code.

(B) Upon the joint recommendation of the juvenile judges of two or more neighboring counties, the boards of county commissioners of the counties shall form themselves into a joint board and proceed to organize a district for the establishment and support of a detention facility for the use of the juvenile courts of those counties, in which alleged delinquent children may be detained as provided in division (A) of this section, by using a site or buildings already established in one of the counties or by providing for the purchase of a site and the erection of the necessary buildings on the site.

A child who is adjudicated to be a juvenile traffic offender for having committed a violation of division (A) of section 4511.19 of the Revised Code or of a municipal ordinance that is substantially comparable to that division may be confined in a detention facility or district detention facility pursuant to division (A)(5) of section 2152.21 of the Revised Code, provided the child is kept separate and apart from alleged delinquent children.

Except as otherwise provided by law, district detention facilities shall be established, operated, maintained, and managed in the same manner so far as applicable as county detention facilities.

Members of the board of county commissioners who meet by appointment to consider the organization of a district detention home, upon presentation of properly certified accounts, shall be paid their necessary expenses upon a warrant drawn by the county auditor of their county.

The county auditor of the county having the greatest population or, with the unanimous concurrence of the county auditors of the counties composing a district, the auditor of the county in which the detention facility is located shall be the fiscal officer of a detention facility district. The county auditors of the several counties composing a detention facility district shall meet at the district detention facility, not less than once in six months, to review accounts and to transact any other duties in connection with the institution that pertain to the business of their office.

(C) In any county in which there is no detention facility or that is not served by a district detention facility, the juvenile court may enter into a contract, subject to the approval of the board of county commissioners, with another juvenile court, another county's detention facility, or a joint county detention facility. Alternately, the board of county commissioners shall provide funds for the boarding of children, who would be eligible for detention under division (A) of this section, temporarily in private homes or in certified foster homes approved by the court for a period not exceeding sixty days or until final disposition of their cases, whichever comes first. The court also may arrange with any public children services agency or private child placing agency to receive, or private noncustodial agency for temporary care of, children within the jurisdiction of the court.

If the court arranges for the board of children temporarily detained in certified foster homes or through any private child placing agency, the county shall pay a reasonable sum to be fixed by the court for the board of those children. In order to have certified foster homes available for service, an agreed monthly subsidy may be paid and a fixed rate per day for care of children actually residing in the certified foster home.

(D) The board of county commissioners of any county within a detention facility district, upon the recommendation of the juvenile court of that county, may withdraw from the district and sell or lease its right, title, and interest in the site, buildings, furniture, and equipment of the facility to any counties in the district, at any price and upon any such terms that are agreed upon among the boards of county commissioners of the counties concerned. Section 307.10 of the Revised Code does not apply to this division. The net proceeds of any sale or lease under this division shall be paid into the treasury of the withdrawing county.

The members of the board of trustees of a district detention facility who are residents of a county withdrawing from the district are deemed to have resigned their positions upon the completion of the withdrawal procedure provided by this division. The vacancies then created shall be filled as provided in this section.

(E) The children to be admitted for care in a county or district detention facility established under this section, the period during which they shall be cared for in the facility, and the removal and transfer of children from the facility shall be determined by the juvenile court that ordered the child's detention.

(2002 H 400, eff. 4–3–03; 2000 S 179, § 3, eff. 1–1–02)

Historical and Statutory Notes

Ed. Note: 2152.41 is former 2151.34, amended and recodified by 2000 S 179, § 3, eff. 1–1–02; 2000 H 332, eff. 1–1–01; 2000 H 448, eff. 10–5–00; 1996 H 265, eff. 3–3–97; 1993 H 152, eff. 7–1–93; 1990 H 837, S 131; 1989 H 166; 1988 S 89; 1986 H 428; 1981 H 440; 1976 H 1196; 1975 H 85; 1970 H 931; 1969 H 320, S 49; 128 v 1211; 1953 H 1; GC 1639–22.

Pre–1953 H 1 Amendments: 121 v 557; 117 v 520

Amendment Note: 2002 H 400 rewrote division (A), which prior thereto read:

"(A) Upon the recommendation of the judge, the board of county commissioners shall provide, by purchase, lease, construction, or otherwise, a detention facility that shall be within a convenient distance of the juvenile court. The facility shall not be used for the confinement of adults charged with criminal offenses. The facility may be used to detain alleged delinquent children until final disposition for evaluation pursuant to section 2152.04 of the Revised Code and for children adjudicated juvenile traffic offenders under division (A)(5) or (6) of section 2152.21 of the Revised Code."

Amendment Note: 2000 S 179, § 3, eff. 1–1–02, rewrote this section, which prior thereto read:

"A child who is alleged to be or adjudicated a delinquent child may be confined in a place of juvenile detention for a period not to exceed ninety days, during which time a social history may be prepared to include court record, family history, personal history, school and attendance records, and any other pertinent studies and material that will be of assistance to the juvenile court in its disposition of the charges against that juvenile offender.

"Upon the advice and recommendation of the judge, the board of county commissioners shall provide, by purchase, lease, construction, or otherwise, a place to be known as a detention home that shall be within a convenient distance of the juvenile court and shall not be used for the confinement of adults charged with criminal offenses and in which delinquent children may be detained until final disposition. Upon the joint advice and recommendation of the juvenile judges of two or more adjoining or neighboring counties, the boards of county commissioners of the counties shall form themselves into a joint board and proceed to organize a district for the establishment and support of a detention home for the use of the juvenile courts of those counties, in which delinquent children may be detained until final disposition, by using a site or buildings already established in one of the counties or by providing for the purchase of a site and the erection of the necessary buildings on the site.

"A child who is adjudicated to be a juvenile traffic offender for having committed a violation of division (A) of section 4511.19 of the Revised Code or of a municipal ordinance that is substantially comparable to that division may be confined in a detention home or district detention home pursuant to division (A)(6) of section 2151.356 of the Revised Code, provided the child is kept separate and apart from alleged delinquent children.

"The county or district detention home shall be maintained as provided in sections 2151.01 to 2151.54 of the Revised Code. In any county in which there is no detention home or that is not served by a district detention home, the board of county commissioners shall provide funds for the boarding of such children temporarily in private homes. Children who are alleged to be or have been adjudicated delinquent children may be detained after a complaint is filed in the detention home until final disposition of their cases or in certified foster homes or in any other home approved by the court, if any are available, for a period not exceeding sixty days or until final disposition of their cases, whichever comes first. The court also may arrange with any public children services agency or private child placing agency to receive, or private noncustodial agency for temporary care of, the children within the jurisdiction of the court. A district detention home approved for such purpose by the department of youth services under section 5139.281 of the Revised Code may receive children committed to its temporary custody under section 2151.355 of the Revised Code and provide the care, treatment, and training required.

"If a detention home is established as an agency of the court or a district detention home is established by the courts of several counties as provided in this section, it shall be furnished and carried on, as far as possible, as a family home in charge of a superintendent or matron in a nonpunitive neutral atmosphere. The judge, or the directing board of a district detention home, may appoint a superintendent, a matron, and other necessary employees for the home and fix their salaries. During the school year, when possible, a comparable educational program with competent and trained staff shall be provided for those children of school age. A sufficient number of trained recreational personnel shall be included among the staff to assure wholesome and profitable leisure-time activities. Medical and mental health services shall be made available to ensure the courts all possible treatment facilities shall be given to those children placed under their care. In the case of a county detention home, the salaries shall be paid in the same manner as is provided by section 2151.13 of the Revised Code for other employees of the court, and the necessary expenses incurred in maintaining the detention home shall be paid by the county. In the case of a district detention home, the salaries and the necessary expenses incurred in maintaining the district detention home shall be paid as provided in sections 2151.341 to 2151.3415 of the Revised Code.

"If the court arranges for the board of children temporarily detained in certified foster homes or arranges for the board of those children through any private child placing agency, a reasonable sum to be fixed by the court for the board of those children shall be paid by the county. In order to have certified foster homes available for service, an agreed monthly subsidy may be paid and a fixed rate per day for care of children actually residing in the certified foster home."

Amendment Note: 2000 H 332 deleted "family" before "foster home in the fourth paragraph; substituted "certified" for "family" throughout the last paragraph; and made other nonsubstantive changes.

Amendment Note: 2000 H 448 deleted "family" after "certified" in the third sentence in the third paragraph; substituted "certified" for "family" three times in the last paragraph; and made other nonsubstantive changes.

Amendment Note: 1996 H 265 inserted "or adjudicated" in the first sentence in the first paragraph; removed references to unruly, dependent, neglected, and abused children and juvenile traffic offenders throughout this section; and rewrote the fourth paragraph, which prior thereto read:

"The county or district detention home shall be maintained as provided in sections 2151.01 to 2151.54 of the Revised Code. In any county in which there is no detention home or that is not served by a district detention home, the board of county commissioners shall provide funds for the boarding of such children temporarily in private homes. Children who are alleged to be or have been adjudicated delinquent, unruly, dependent, neglected, or abused children or juvenile traffic offenders, after a complaint is filed, may be detained in the detention home or in certified family foster homes until final disposition of their case. The court may arrange for the boarding of such children in certified family foster homes or in uncertified family foster homes for a period not exceeding sixty days, subject to the supervision of the court, or may arrange with any children services agency, or private child placing agency to receive, or private noncustodial agency for temporary care children within the jurisdiction of the court. A district detention home approve for such purpose by the department of youth services under section 5139.281 of the Revised Code may receive children committed to its temporary custody under section 2151.355 of the Revised Code and provide the care, treatment, and training required."

Amendment Note: 1993 H 152 changed "foster home" to "family foster home" throughout; and deleted "may enter into a contract with a public children services agency," before "private child placing agency" in the final paragraph.

Cross References

Actions against political subdivisions, negligence or omission in performing governmental or proprietary functions, Ch 2744
Adoption of rules for payment of assistance, 5139.29
Conditions of financial assistance for construction or acquisition of detention home, 5139.271
Detention and shelter care, Juv R 7
Division of social administration, examination of institutions, 5103.03
Resolution relative to tax levy in excess of ten-mill limitation, 5705.19
Tax levy law, detention home districts, 5705.01
Uniform bond law, fiscal officer, subdivision and taxing authority defined, definitions, 133.01

Withdrawal of county from district, continuity of
    district tax levy, 2151.78

Library References

Infants ⊕192, 223.1, 271.

Westlaw Topic No. 211.

C.J.S. Infants §§ 42, 53 to 55.

C.J.S. Reformatories §§ 1 to 5.

OJur 3d: 48, Family Law § 1504 to 1508, 1540, 1580
    to 1583

Am Jur 2d: 60, Penal and Correctional Institutions
    § 41 et seq.

Baldwin's Ohio Legislative Service, 1988 Laws of
    Ohio, S 89—LSC Analysis, p 5–571; 1990
    Laws of Ohio, S 131—LSC Analysis, p 5–623

Painter, Ohio Driving Under the Influence Law (2003
    Ed.), Text 19.45.

Carlin, Baldwin's Ohio Practice, Merrick–Rippner
    Probate Law § 104.13, 104.17, 107.88,
    107.108 (2003).

2152.42 Superintendents of facilities

(A) Any detention facility established under section 2152.41 of the Revised Code shall be under the direction of a superintendent. The superintendent shall be appointed by, and under the direction of, the judge or judges or, for a district facility, the board of trustees of the facility. The superintendent serves at the pleasure of the juvenile court or, in a district detention facility, at the pleasure of the board of trustees.

Before commencing work as superintendent, the person appointed shall obtain a bond, with sufficient surety, conditioned upon the full and faithful accounting of the funds and properties under the superintendent's control.

The superintendent, under the supervision and subject to the rules and regulations of the board, shall control, manage, operate, and have general charge of the facility and shall have the custody of its property, files, and records.

(B) For a county facility, the superintendent shall appoint all employees of the facility, who shall be in the unclassified civil service. The salaries shall be paid as provided by section 2151.13 of the Revised Code for other employees of the court, and the necessary expenses incurred in maintaining the facility shall be paid by the county.

For a district facility, the superintendent shall appoint other employees of the facility and fix their compensation, subject to approval of the board of trustees. Employees of a district facility, except for the superintendent, shall be in the classified civil service.

(C) During the school year, when possible, a comparable educational program with competent and trained staff shall be provided for children of school age who are in the facility. A sufficient number of trained recreational personnel shall be included among the staff. Medical and mental health services shall be made available.

(2000 S 179, § 3, eff. 1–1–02)

Library References

OJur 3d: 48, Family Law § 1504 to 1508, 1580 to
    1583

Carlin, Baldwin's Ohio Practice, Merrick–Rippner
    Probate Law § 104.17 (2003).

2152.43 Assistance in operation of facilities from department of youth services; tax assessment

(A) A board of county commissioners that provides a detention facility and the board of trustees of a district detention facility may apply to the department of youth services under section 5139.281 of the Revised Code for assistance in defraying the cost of operating and maintaining the facility. The application shall be made on forms prescribed and furnished by the department.

The board of county commissioners of each county that participates in a district detention facility may apply to the department of youth services for assistance in defraying the county's share of the cost of acquisition or construction of the facility, as provided in section 5139.271 of the Revised Code. Application shall be made in accordance with rules adopted by the department. No county shall be reimbursed for expenses incurred in the acquisition or construction of a district detention facility that serves a district having a population of less than one hundred thousand.

(B)(1) The joint boards of county commissioners of district detention facilities shall defray all necessary expenses of the facility not paid from funds made available under section 5139.281 of the Revised Code, through annual assessments of taxes, through gifts, or through other means.

If any county withdraws from a district under division (D) of section 2152.41 of the Revised Code, it shall continue to have levied against its tax duplicate any tax levied by the district during the period in which the county was a member of the district for current operating expenses, permanent improvements, or the retirement of bonded indebtedness. The levy shall continue to be a levy against the tax duplicate of the county until the time that it expires or is renewed.

(2) The current expenses of maintaining the facility not paid from funds made available under section 5139.281 of the Revised Code or division (C) of this section, and the cost of ordinary repairs to the facility, shall be paid by each county in accordance with one of the following methods as approved by the joint board of county commissioners:

(a) In proportion to the number of children from that county who are maintained in the facility during the year;

(b) By a levy submitted by the joint board of county commissioners under division (A) of section 5705.19 of the Revised Code and approved by the electors of the district;

(c) In proportion to the taxable property of each county, as shown by its tax duplicate;

(d) In any combination of the methods for payment described in division (B)(2)(a), (b), or (c) of this section.

(C) When any person donates or bequeaths any real or personal property to a county or district detention facility, the juvenile court or the trustees of the facility may accept and use the gift, consistent with the best interest of the institution and the conditions of the gift.

(2000 S 179, § 3, eff. 1–1–02)

Historical and Statutory Notes

Ed. Note: 2152.43 is former 2151.341, amended and recodified by 2000 S 179, § 3, eff. 1–1–02; 1981 H 440, eff. 11–23–81; 1977 S 221; 1976 H 1196; 128 v 1211.

Amendment Note: 2000 S 179, § 3, eff. 1–1–02, rewrote this section, which prior thereto read:

"A board of county commissioners that provides a detention home and the board of trustees of a district detention home may make application to the department of youth services under section 5139.281 of the Revised Code for financial assistance in defraying the cost of operating and maintaining the home. Such application shall be made on forms prescribed and furnished by the department. The joint boards of county commissioners of district detention homes shall make annual assessments of taxes sufficient to support and defray all necessary expenses of such home not paid from funds made available under section 5139.281 of the Revised Code."

Cross References

Inspection of facilities by youth commission, 5139.31

Library References

Counties ☞138.
Infants ☞279.
Westlaw Topic Nos. 104, 211.

C.J.S. Counties §§ 175, 177, 178.
C.J.S. Infants §§ 57, 69 to 85.
OJur 3d: 48, Family Law § 1504 to 1508, 1510, 1580 to 1583

2152.44 District detention facility trustees

(A) As soon as practical after the organization of the joint board of county commissioners as provided by section 2152.41 of the Revised Code, the joint board shall appoint a board of not less than five trustees. The board shall hold office until the first annual meeting after the choice of an established site and buildings, or after the selection and purchase of a building site. At that time, the joint board of county commissioners shall appoint a board of not less than five trustees, one of whom shall hold office for a term of one year, one for a term of two years, one for a term of three years, half of the remaining number for a term of four years, and the remainder for a term of five years. Annually thereafter, the joint board of county commissioners shall appoint one or more trustees, each of whom shall hold office for a term of five years, to succeed the trustee or trustees whose term of office expires. A trustee may be appointed to successive terms. Any person appointed as a trustee shall be recommended and approved by the juvenile court judge or judges of the county of which the person resides.

At least one trustee shall reside in each county in the district. In districts composed of two counties, each county shall be entitled to not less than two trustees. In districts composed of more than four counties, the number of trustees shall be sufficiently increased, provided that there shall always be an uneven number of trustees on the board. The county in which a district detention facility is located shall have not less than two trustees, who, in the interim period between the regular meetings of the trustees, shall act as an executive committee in the discharge of all business pertaining to the facility.

The joint board of county commissioners may remove any trustee for good cause. The trustee appointed to fill any vacancy shall hold the office for the unexpired term of the predecessor trustee.

(B) The annual meeting of the board of trustees shall be held on the first Tuesday in May in each year.

A majority of the board constitutes a quorum. Other board meetings shall be held at least quarterly. The juvenile court judge of each county of the district, or the judge's designee, shall attend the meetings. The members of the board shall receive no compensation for their services, except their actual and necessary expenses. The treasurer shall pay the member's traveling expenses when properly certified.

(C) When the board of trustees does not choose an established institution in one of the counties of the district, it may select a suitable site for the erection of a district detention facility. The site must be easily accessible, conducive to health, economy in purchasing or in building, and the general interest of the facility and its residents, and be as near as practicable to the geographical center of the district.

In the interim between the selection and purchase of a site, and the erection and occupancy of the district detention facility, the joint board of county commissioners provided under section 2151.41 of the Revised Code may delegate to the board of trustees any powers and duties that, in its judgment, will be of general interest or aid to the institution. The joint board of county commissioners may appropriate a trustees' fund, to be expended by the trustees for contracts, purchases, or other necessary expenses of the facility. The trustees shall make a complete settlement with the joint board of county commissioners once each six months, or quarterly if required, and shall make to the board of county commissioners and to the juvenile court of each of the counties a full report of the condition of the facility and residents.

(D) The choice of an established site and buildings, or the purchase of a site, stock, implements, and general farm equipment, should there be a farm, the erection of buildings, and the completion and furnishing of the district detention facility for occupancy, shall be in the hands of the joint board of county commissioners organized under section 2152.41 of the Revised Code. The joint board of county commissioners may delegate all or a portion of these duties to the board of trustees, under any restrictions that the joint board of county commissioners imposes.

When an established site and buildings are used for a district detention facility,

the joint board of county commissioners shall cause the value of that site and those buildings to be properly appraised. This appraisal value, or in case of the purchase of a site, the purchase price and the cost of all improvements thereto, shall be paid by the counties comprising the district, in proportion to the taxable property of each county, as shown by its tax duplicate.

(E) Once a district is established, the trustees shall operate, maintain, and manage the facility as provided in sections 2152.41 to 2152.43 of the Revised Code.

(2000 S 179, § 3, eff. 1–1–02)

Historical and Statutory Notes

Ed. Note: 2152.44 is former 2151.343, amended and recodified by 2000 S 179, § 3, eff. 1–1–02; 128 v 1211, eff. 11–2–59.

Amendment Note: 2000 S 179, § 3, eff. 1–1–02, rewrote this section, which prior thereto read:

"Immediately upon the organization of the joint board of county commissioners as provided by section 2151.34 of the Revised Code, or so soon thereafter as practicable, such joint board of county commissioners shall appoint a board of not less than five trustees, which shall hold office and perform its duties until the first annual meeting after the choice of an established site and buildings, or after the selection and purchase of a building site, at which time such joint board of county commissioners shall appoint a board of not less than five trustees, one of whom shall hold office for a term of one year, one for the term of two years, one for the term of three years, half of the remaining number for the term of four years, and the remainder for the term of five years. Annually thereafter, the joint board of county commissioners shall appoint one or more trustees, each of whom shall hold office for the term of five years, to succeed the trustee or trustees whose term of office shall expire. A trustee may be appointed to succeed himself upon such board of trustees, and all appointments to such board of trustees shall be made from persons who are recommended and approved by the juvenile court judge or judges of the county of which such person is resident. The annual meeting of the board of trustees shall be held on the first Tuesday in May in each year."

Library References

Infants ⚮273.

Westlaw Topic No. 211.

C.J.S. Reformatories §§ 6 to 8.

OJur 3d: 48, Family Law § 1504 to 1508, 1512, 1580 to 1583

ORDERS RESTRAINING PARENTS

2152.61 Orders restraining parents, guardians, or custodians

(A) In any proceeding in which a child has been adjudicated a delinquent child or a juvenile traffic offender, on the application of a party or the court's own motion, the court may make an order restraining or otherwise controlling the conduct of any parent, guardian, or other custodian in the relationship of the individual to the child if the court finds that an order of that type necessary to do either of the following:

(1) Control any conduct or relationship that will be detrimental or harmful to the child;

(2) Control any conduct or relationship that will tend to defeat the execution of the order of disposition made or to be made.

(B) Due notice of the application or motion and the grounds for the application or motion under division (A) of this section, and an opportunity to be heard, shall be given to the person against whom the order under that division is directed. The order may include a requirement that the child's parent, guardian, or other custodian enter into a recognizance with sufficient surety, conditioned upon the faithful discharge of any conditions or control required by the court.

(C) A person's failure to comply with any order made by the court under this section is contempt of court under Chapter 2705. of the Revised Code.

(2000 S 179, § 3, eff. 1–1–02)

Library References

OJur 3d: 48, Family Law § 1690
Carlin, Baldwin's Ohio Practice, Merrick–Rippner Probate Law § 107.113, 107.127 (2003).

JURY TRIALS

2152.67   Jury trial; procedure

Any adult who is arrested or charged under any provision in this chapter and who is charged with a crime may demand a trial by jury, or the juvenile judge upon the judge's own motion may call a jury. A demand for a jury trial shall be made in writing in not less than three days before the date set for trial, or within three days after counsel has been retained, whichever is later. Sections 2945.17 and 2945.23 to 2945.36 of the Revised Code, relating to the drawing and impaneling of jurors in criminal cases in the court of common pleas, other than in capital cases, shall apply to a jury trial under this section. The compensation of jurors and costs of the clerk and sheriff shall be taxed and paid in the same manner as in criminal cases in the court of common pleas.

(2000 S 179, § 3, eff. 1–1–02)

Historical and Statutory Notes

Ed. Note: 2152.67 is former 2151.47, recodified by 2000 S 179, § 3; 2000 S 181, eff. 9–4–00; 1969 H 1, eff. 3–18–69; 132 v S 55; 1953 H 1; GC 1639–44.

Amendment Note: 2000 S 181 rewrote this section, which prior thereto read:

"Any adult arrested under section 2151.01 to 2151.54, inclusive, of the Revised Code, may demand a trial by jury, or the juvenile judge upon his own motion may call a jury. A demand for a jury trial must be made in writing in not less than three days before the date set for trial, or within three days after counsel has been retained, whichever is later. Sections 2945.17 and 2945.22 to 2945.36, inclusive, of the Revised Code, relating to the drawing and impaneling of jurors in criminal cases in the court of common pleas, other than in capital cases, shall apply to such jury trial. The compensation of jurors and costs of the clerk and sheriff shall be taxed and paid as in criminal cases in the court of common pleas."

Cross References

Jury trial, Crim R 23

Library References

Jury ⟲19.5.
Westlaw Topic No. 230.
C.J.S. Juries § 68.
OJur 3d: 48, Family Law § 1656, 1738, 1744, 1752
Am Jur 2d: 47, Jury § 7 et seq.
Right of accused, in state criminal trial, to insist, over prosecutor's or court's objection, on trial by court without jury. 37 ALR4th 304

MISCELLANEOUS PROVISIONS

2152.71   Records and reports; statistical summaries

(A)(1) The juvenile court shall maintain records of all official cases brought before it, including, but not limited to, an appearance docket, a journal, and, in cases pertaining to an alleged delinquent child, arrest and custody records, complaints, journal entries, and hearing summaries. The court shall maintain a separate docket for traffic cases and shall record all traffic cases on the separate docket instead of on the general appearance docket. The parents, guardian, or other custodian of any child affected, if they are living, or the nearest of kin of the child, if the parents are deceased, may inspect these records, either in person or by counsel, during the hours in which the court is open. Division (A)(1) of this section does not require the release or authorize the inspection of arrest or incident reports, law enforcement investigatory reports or records, or witness statements.

(2) The juvenile court shall send to the superintendent of the bureau of criminal identification and investigation, pursuant to section 109.57 of the Revised Code, a weekly report containing a summary of

each case that has come before it and that involves the disposition of a child who is a delinquent child for committing an act that would be a felony or an offense of violence if committed by an adult.

(B) The clerk of the court shall maintain a statistical record that includes all of the following:

(1) The number of complaints that are filed with, or indictments or information made to, the court that allege that a child is a delinquent child, in relation to which the court determines under division (D) of section 2151.27 of the Revised Code that the victim of the alleged delinquent act was sixty-five years of age or older or permanently and totally disabled at the time of the alleged commission of the act;

(2) The number of complaints, indictments, or information described in division (B)(1) of this section that result in the child being adjudicated a delinquent child;

(3) The number of complaints, indictments, or information described in division (B)(2) of this section in which the act upon which the delinquent child adjudication is based caused property damage or would be a theft offense, as defined in division (K) of section 2913.01 of the Revised Code, if committed by an adult;

(4) The number of complaints, indictments, or information described in division (B)(3) of this section that result in the delinquent child being required as an order of disposition made under division (A) of section 2152.20 of the Revised Code to make restitution for all or part of the property damage caused by the child's delinquent act or for all or part of the value of the property that was the subject of the delinquent act that would be a theft offense if committed by an adult;

(5) The number of complaints, indictments, or information described in division (B)(2) of this section in which the act upon which the delinquent child adjudication is based would have been an offense of violence if committed by an adult;

(6) The number of complaints, indictments, or information described in division (B)(5) of this section that result in the delinquent child being committed as an order of disposition made under section 2152.16, divisions (A) and (B) of

section 2152.17, or division (A)(2) of section 2152.19 of the Revised Code to any facility for delinquent children operated by the county, a district, or a private agency or organization or to the department of youth services;

(7) The number of complaints, indictments, or information described in division (B)(1) of this section that result in the case being transferred for criminal prosecution to an appropriate court having jurisdiction of the offense under section 2152.12 of the Revised Code.

(C) The clerk of the court shall compile an annual summary covering the preceding calendar year showing all of the information for that year contained in the statistical record maintained under division (B) of this section. The statistical record and the annual summary shall be public records open for inspection. Neither the statistical record nor the annual summary shall include the identity of any party to a case.

(D) Not later than June of each year, the court shall prepare an annual report covering the preceding calendar year showing the number and kinds of cases that have come before it, the disposition of the cases, and any other data pertaining to the work of the court that the juvenile judge directs. The court shall file copies of the report with the board of county commissioners. With the approval of the board, the court may print or cause to be printed copies of the report for distribution to persons and agencies interested in the court or community program for dependent, neglected, abused, or delinquent children and juvenile traffic offenders. The court shall include the number of copies ordered printed and the estimated cost of each printed copy on each copy of the report printed for distribution.

(E) If an officer is preparing pursuant to section 2947.06 or 2951.03 of the Revised Code or Criminal Rule 32.2 a presentence investigation report pertaining to a person, the court shall make available to the officer, for use in preparing the report, any records it possesses regarding any adjudications of that person as a delinquent child or regarding the dispositions made relative to those adjudications. The records to be made available pursuant to this division include, but are not limited to, any social history or report of a mental or physical examination regarding the person that was prepared pursuant to Juvenile Rule 32.

(2002 H 393, eff. 7–5–02; 2002 H 247, eff. 5–30–02; 2000 S 179, § 3, eff. 1–1–02)

Historical and Statutory Notes

Ed. Note: A special endorsement by the Legislative Service Commission states, "Comparison of these amendments [2002 H 393, eff. 7–5–02 and 2002 H 247, eff. 5–30–02] in pursuance of section 1.52 of the Revised Code discloses that they are not irreconcilable so that they are required by that section to be harmonized to give effect to each amendment." In recognition of this rule of construction, changes made by 2002 H 393, eff. 7–5–02, and 2002 H 247, eff. 5–30–02, have been incorporated in the above amendment. See *Baldwin's Ohio Legislative Service Annotated*, 2002 pages 3/L–553 and 2/L–121, or the OH–LEGIS or OH–LEGIS–OLD database on WESTLAW, for original versions of these Acts.

Ed. Note: 2152.71 is former 2151.18, amended and recodified by 2000 S 179, § 3, eff. 1–1–02; 2000 S 181, eff. 9–4–00; 1999 H 3, eff. 11–22–99; 1998 H 2, eff. 1–1–99; 1996 H 124, eff. 3–31–97; 1995 H 1, eff. 1–1–96; 1993 H 152, eff. 7–1–93; 1990 S 268; 1984 S 5; 1981 H 440; 1979 H 394; 1975 H 85; 127 v 547; 1953 H 1; GC 1639–13.

Amendment Note: 2002 H 393 inserted the last two sentences in division (A)(1); and substituted "2152.19" for "2159.19" in division (B)(6).

Amendment Note: 2002 H 247 substituted "2152.19" for "2159.19" in division (B)(6); and added new division (E).

Amendment Note: 2000 S 179, § 3, eff. 1–1–02, rewrote division (A)(1); added references to indictments and informations throughout the section; substituted "section 2152.16, divisions (A) and (B) of section 2152.17, or division (A)(2) of section 2152.19" for "division (A)(3), (4), (5), (6), or (7) of section 2151.355" in division (B)(6); and substituted "2152.12" for '2151.26" in division (B)(8). Prior to amendment, division (A)(1) read:

"(A)(1) The juvenile court shall maintain records of all official cases brought before it, including, but not limited to, an appearance docket, a journal, a cashbook, records of the type required by division (A)(2) of section 2151.35 of the Revised Code, and, in cases pertaining to an alleged delinquent child, arrest and custody records, complaints, journal entries, and hearing summaries. The court shall maintain a separate docket for traffic cases and shall record all traffic cases on the separate docket instead of on the general appearance docket. The parents of any child affected, if they are living, or the nearest of kin of the child, if the parents are deceased, may inspect these records, either in person or by counsel during the hours in which the court is open."

Amendment Note: 2000 S 181 inserted ", but not limited to," and ", records of the type required by division (A)(2) of section 2151.35 of the Revised Code, and, in cases pertaining to an alleged delinquent child, arrest and custody records, complaints, journal entries, and hearing summaries" in division (A)(1); substituted "(A)(9)" for "(A)(8)(b)" in division (B)(4); and made other nonsubstantive changes.

Amendment Note: 1999 H 3 substituted "the disposition of a child who" for "an adjudication of a child" in division (A)(2).

Amendment Note: 1998 H 2 rewrote division (A)(2); and made other changes to reflect gender neutral language. Prior to amendment, division (A)(2) read:

"(2) The juvenile court shall send to the superintendent of the bureau of criminal identification and investigation, pursuant to section 109.57 of the Revised Code, a weekly report containing a summary of each case that has come before it and that involves an adjudication that a child is a delinquent child for committing a designated delinquent act or juvenile offense, as defined in section 109.57 of the Revised Code."

Amendment Note: 1996 H 124 substituted "a designated delinquent act or juvenile offense, as defined in section 109.57" for "an act that is a category one offense or a category two offense, as defined in section 2151.26" in division (A)(2).

Amendment Note: 1995 H 1 designated division (A)(1); added division (A)(2); rewrote division (B)(7); and made other nonsubstantive changes. Prior to amendment, division (B)(7) read:

"(7) The number of complaints described in division (B)(1) of this section that result in the case being transferred for criminal prosecution to an appropriate court having jurisdiction of the offense, under division (A) of section 2151.26 of the Revised Code, or that involve an act of a child that is required to be prosecuted in an appropriate court having jurisdiction of the offense, under division (G) of that section."

Amendment Note: 1993 H 152 substituted "cases" for "offenses" in division (A); designated division (C); inserted "statistical" before "record" in division (C); deleted former division (C); and deleted "or that the department of youth services requests" following "juvenile judge directs" and "department and with the" prior to "board of county commissioners" in division (D). Prior to amendment, division (C) read:

"(C) The juvenile court shall submit quarterly to the department of youth services, on forms provided by the department, the number of juveniles who were adjudicated delinquent children during the immediately preceding month for the commission of an act that would be a felony if committed by an adult, the number of those delinquent children who were committed to the department, and any other data regarding all official cases of the court that the department reasonably requests. The department shall publish this data on a statewide basis in statistical form at least annually. The department shall not publish the identity of any party to a case."

Cross References

Judges of the court of domestic relations, juvenile court responsibility, 2301.03
Presentence investigation reports, mandatory consideration of certain information, 2951.03

Library References

Infants ⚖133.

Westlaw Topic No. 211.

C.J.S. Infants §§ 57, 69 to 85.

OJur 3d: 1, Actions § 82; 22, Courts and Judges § 205, 207; 48, Family Law § 1534 to 1539, 1566 et seq.

Carlin, Baldwin's Ohio Practice, Merrick–Rippner Probate Law § 106.1, 107.1, 107.86, 107.114, 107.115 (2003).

2152.72 Information provided to foster caregivers or prospective adoptive parents regarding delinquent children; psychological examination

(A) This section applies only to a child who is or previously has been adjudicated a delinquent child for an act to which any of the following applies:

(1) The act is a violation of section 2903.01, 2903.02, 2903.03, 2903.04, 2903.11, 2903.12, 2903.13, 2907.02, 2907.03, or 2907.05 of the Revised Code.

(2) The act is a violation of section 2923.01 of the Revised Code and involved an attempt to commit aggravated murder or murder.

(3) The act would be a felony if committed by an adult, and the court determined that the child, if an adult, would be guilty of a specification found in section 2941.141, 2941.144, or 2941.145 of the Revised Code or in another section of the Revised Code that relates to the possession or use of a firearm during the commission of the act for which the child was adjudicated a delinquent child.

(4) The act would be an offense of violence that is a felony if committed by an adult, and the court determined that the child, if an adult, would be guilty of a specification found in section 2941.1411 of the Revised Code or in another section of the Revised Code that relates to the wearing or carrying of body armor during the commission of the act for which the child was adjudicated a delinquent child.

(B)(1) Except as provided in division (E) of this section, a public children services agency, private child placing agency, private noncustodial agency, or court, the department of youth services, or another private or government entity shall not place a child in a certified foster home or for adoption until it provides the foster caregivers or prospective adoptive parents with all of the following:

(a) A written report describing the child's social history;

(b) A written report describing all the acts committed by the child the entity knows of that resulted in the child being adjudicated a delinquent child and the disposition made by the court, unless the records pertaining to the acts have been sealed pursuant to section 2151.358 of the Revised Code;

(c) A written report describing any other violent act committed by the child of which the entity is aware;

(d) The substantial and material conclusions and recommendations of any psychiatric or psychological examination conducted on the child or, if no psychological or psychiatric examination of the child is available, the substantial and material conclusions and recommendations of an examination to detect mental and emotional disorders conducted in compliance with the requirements of Chapter 4757. of the Revised Code by an independent social worker, social worker, professional clinical counselor, or professional counselor licensed under that chapter. The entity shall not provide any part of a psychological, psychiatric, or mental and emotional disorder examination to the foster caregivers or prospective adoptive parents other than the substantial and material conclusions.

(2) Notwithstanding section 2151.358 of the Revised Code, if records of an adjudication that a child is a delinquent child have been sealed pursuant to that section and an entity knows the records have been sealed, the entity shall provide the foster caregivers or prospective adoptive parents a written statement that the records of a prior adjudication have been sealed.

(C)(1) The entity that places the child in a certified foster home or for adoption shall conduct a psychological examination of the child unless either of the following applies:

(a) An entity is not required to conduct the examination if an examination was conducted no more than one year prior to the child's placement, and division (C)(1)(b) of this section does not apply.

(b) An entity is not required to conduct the examination if a foster caregiver seeks to adopt the foster caregiver's foster child, and an examination was conducted no more than two years prior to the date the foster caregiver seeks to adopt the child.

(2) No later than sixty days after placing the child, the entity shall provide the foster caregiver or prospective adoptive parents a written report detailing the substantial and material conclusions and · recommendations of the examination conducted pursuant to this division.

(D)(1) Except as provided in divisions (D)(2) and (3) of this section, the expenses of conducting the examinations and preparing the reports and assessment required by division (B) or (C) of this section shall be paid by the entity that places the child in the certified foster home or for adoption.

(2) When a juvenile court grants temporary or permanent custody of a child pursuant to any section of the Revised

Code, including section 2151.33, 2151.353, 2151.354, or 2152.19 of the Revised Code, to a public children services agency or private child placing agency, the court shall provide the agency the information described in division (B) of this section, pay the expenses of preparing that information, and, if a new examination is required to be conducted, pay the expenses of conducting the examination described in division (C) of this section. On receipt of the information described in division (B) of this section, the agency shall provide to the court written acknowledgment that the agency received the information. The court shall keep the acknowledgment and provide a copy to the agency. On the motion of the agency, the court may terminate the order granting temporary or permanent custody of the child to that agency, if the court does not provide the information described in division (B) of this section.

(3) If one of the following entities is placing a child in a certified foster home or for adoption with the assistance of or by contracting with a public children services agency, private child placing agency, or a private noncustodial agency, the entity shall provide the agency with the information described in division (B) of this section, pay the expenses of preparing that information, and, if a new examination is required to be conducted, pay the expenses of conducting the examination described in division (C) of this section:

(a) The department of youth services if the placement is pursuant to any section of the Revised Code including section 2152.22, 5139.06, 5139.07, 5139.38, or 5139.39 of the Revised Code;

(b) A juvenile court with temporary or permanent custody of a child pursuant to section 2151.354 or 2152.19 of the Revised Code;

(c) A public children services agency or private child placing agency with temporary or permanent custody of the child.

The agency receiving the information described in division (B) of this section shall provide the entity described in division (D)(3)(a) to (c) of this section that sent the information written acknowledgment that the agency received the information and provided it to the foster caregivers or prospective adoptive parents. The entity shall keep the acknowledgment and provide a copy to the agency.

An entity that places a child in a certified foster home or for adoption with the assistance of or by contracting with an agency remains responsible to provide the information described in division (B) of this section to the foster caregivers or prospective adoptive parents unless the entity receives written acknowledgment that the agency provided the information.

(E) If a child is placed in a certified foster home as a result of an emergency removal of the child from home pursuant to division (D) of section 2151.31 of the Revised Code, an emergency change in the child's case plan pursuant to division (E)(3) of section 2151.412 of the Revised Code, or an emergency placement by the department of youth services pursuant to this chapter or Chapter 5139. of the Revised Code, the entity that places the child in the certified foster home shall provide the information described in division (B) of this section no later than ninety-six hours after the child is placed in the certified foster home.

(F) On receipt of the information described in divisions (B) and (C) of this section, the foster caregiver or prospective adoptive parents shall provide to the entity that places the child in the foster caregiver's or prospective adoptive parents' home a written acknowledgment that the foster caregiver or prospective adoptive parents received the information. The entity shall keep the acknowledgment and provide a copy to the foster caregiver or prospective adoptive parents.

(G) No person employed by an entity subject to this section and made responsible by that entity for the child's placement in a certified foster home or for adoption shall fail to provide the foster caregivers or prospective adoptive parents with the information required by divisions (B) and (C) of this section.

(H) It is not a violation of any duty of confidentiality provided for in the Revised Code or a code of professional responsibility for a person or government entity to provide the substantial and material conclusions and recommendations of a psychiatric or psychological examination, or an examination to detect mental and emotional disorders, in accordance with division (B)(1)(d) or (C) of this section.

(I) As used in this section:

(1) "Body armor" has the same meaning as in section 2941.1411 of the Revised Code.

(2) "Firearm" has the same meaning as in section 2923.11 of the Revised Code.

(2001 S 27, eff. 3–15–02; 2000 S 179, § 3, eff. 1–1–02)

Uncodified Law

2001 S 27, § 7, eff. 3–15–02, reads:

The amendment of section 2151.62 of the Revised Code is not intended to supersede its amendment and renumbering by Am. Sub. S.B. 179 of the 123rd General Assembly. Paragraphs of section 2151.62 of the Revised Code that are amended by this act were moved to section 2152.72 of the Revised Code by Am. Sub. S.B. 179, effective January 1, 2002, as part of its revision of the juvenile sentencing laws. Therefore, section 2152.72 of the Revised Code is amended by this act to continue, on and after January 1, 2002, the amendments this act is making to section 2151.62 of the Revised Code; section 2151.62 of the Revised Code as amended by this act is superseded on January 1, 2002, by the section as it results from its amendment and renumbering by Am. Sub. S.B. 179; and section 2152.72 of the Revised Code as amended by this act takes effect on January 1, 2002 [1]

[1] O Const Art II, § 1c and 1d, and RC 1.471 state that codified sections of law are subject to the referendum unless providing for tax levies, state appropriations, or are emergency in nature. Since this Act is apparently not an exception, and January 1, 2002, is within the ninety-day period, the Secretary of State has assigned an effective date of March 15, 2002.

Historical and Statutory Notes

Ed. Note: 2152.72 is former 2151.62, amended and recodified by 2000 S 179, § 3, eff. 1–1–02; 2000 S 222, eff. 3–22–01; 2000 H 332, eff. 1–1–01; 2000 H 448, eff. 10–5–00; 1998 H 173, eff. 7–29–98.

Amendment Note: 2001 S 27 inserted "or for adoption" and "or prospective adoptive parents" throughout the section; rewrote division (C); and made other nonsubstantive changes throughout the section. Prior to amendment, division (C) read:

"(C) The entity that places the child in a certified foster home shall conduct a psychological examination of the child, except that the entity is not required to conduct the examination if such an examination was conducted no more than one year prior to the child's placement. No later than sixty days after placing the child, the entity shall provide the foster caregiver a written report detailing the substantial and material conclusions and recommendations of the examination conducted pursuant to this division."

Amendment Note: 2000 S 179, § 3, eff. 1–1–02, substituted "2152.19" for "2151.355' in divisions (D)(2) and (D)(3)(b); substituted "2152,22" for "2151.38" in division (D)(3)(a); and made other nonsubstantive changes.

Amendment Note: 2000 S 222 deleted ", as defined in section 2923.11 of the Revised Code," after "firearm" in division (A)(3); and added divisions (A)(4) and (I).

Amendment Note: 2000 H 332 inserted "certified" throughout the section.

Amendment Note: 2000 H 448 inserted "certified" before "foster home" throughout the section.

Cross References

Content of preplacement training program, 5103.039

Administrative Code References

Adoptive placement procedures, OAC 5101:2–48–16

Library References

OJur 3d: 48, Family Law § 1534 to 1539, 1566 et seq., 1695 et seq.

Carlin, Baldwin's Ohio Practice, Merrick–Rippner Probate Law § 107.84 (2003).

2152.73 Court participation in delinquency prevention activities

A juvenile court may participate with other public or private agencies of the county served by the court in programs that have as their objective the prevention and control of juvenile delinquency. The juvenile judge may assign employees of the court, as part of their regular duties, to work with organizations concerned with combatting conditions known to contribute to delinquency, providing adult sponsors for children who have been found to be delinquent children, and developing wholesome youth programs.

The juvenile judge may accept and administer on behalf of the court gifts, grants, bequests, and devises made to the court for the purpose of preventing delinquency.

(2000 S 179, § 3, eff. 1–1–02)

Historical and Statutory Notes

Ed. Note: 2152.73 is former 2151.11, amended and recodified by 2000 S 179, § 3, eff. 1–1–02; 131 v H 449, eff. 11–11–65.

Amendment Note: 2000 S 179, § 3, eff. 1–1–02, made nonsubstantive changes.

Cross References

Intake, Juv R 9

Library References

Courts ⬤55.

Judges ⬤24.

Westlaw Topic Nos. 106, 227.

C.J.S. Courts §§ 107 to 109.

C.J.S. Judges §§ 35, 53 to 65.

OJur 3d: 48, Family Law § 1534 to 1539, 1566 et seq.

Carlin, Baldwin's Ohio Practice, Merrick–Rippner Probate Law § 104.19 (2003).

2152.74 DNA specimen collected from juvenile adjudged delinquent

(A) As used in this section, "DNA analysis" and "DNA specimen" have the same meanings as in section 109.573 of the Revised Code.

(B)(1) A child who is adjudicated a delinquent child for committing an act listed in division (D) of this section and who is committed to the custody of the department of youth services, placed in a detention facility or district detention facility pursuant to division (A)(3) of section 2152.19 of the Revised Code, or placed in a school, camp, institution, or other facility for delinquent children described in division (A)(2) of section 2152.19 of the Revised Code shall submit to a DNA specimen collection procedure administered by the director of youth services if committed to the department or by the chief administrative officer of the detention facility, district detention facility, school, camp, institution, or other facility for delinquent children to which the child was committed or in which the child was placed. If the court commits the child to the department of youth services, the director of youth services shall cause the DNA specimen to be collected from the child during the intake process at an institution operated by or under the control of the department. If the court commits the child to or places the child in a detention facility, district detention facility, school, camp, institution, or other facility for delinquent children, the chief administrative officer of the detention facility, district detention facility, school, camp, institution, or facility to which the child is committed or in which the child is placed shall cause the DNA specimen to be collected from the child during the intake process for the detention facility, district detention facility, school, camp, institution, or facility. In accordance with division (C) of this section, the director or the chief administrative officer shall cause the DNA specimen to be forwarded to the bureau of criminal identification and investigation no later than fifteen days after the date of the collection of the DNA specimen. The DNA specimen shall be collected from the child in accordance with division (C) of this section.

(2) If a child is adjudicated a delinquent child for committing an act listed in division (D) of this section, is committed to or placed in the department of youth services, a detention facility or district detention facility, or a school, camp, institution, or other facility for delinquent children, and does not submit to a DNA specimen collection procedure pursuant to division (B)(1) of this section, prior to the child's release from the custody of the department of youth services,

from the custody of the detention facility or district detention facility, or from the custody of the school, camp, institution, or facility, the child shall submit to, and the director of youth services or the chief administrator of the detention facility, district detention facility, school, camp, institution, or facility to which the child is committed or in which the child was placed shall administer, a DNA specimen collection procedure at the institution operated by or under the control of the department of youth services or at the detention facility, district detention facility, school, camp, institution, or facility to which the child is committed or in which the child was placed. In accordance with division (C) of this section, the director or the chief administrative officer shall cause the DNA specimen to be forwarded to the bureau of criminal identification and investigation no later than fifteen days after the date of the collection of the DNA specimen. The DNA specimen shall be collected in accordance with division (C) of this section.

(C) If the DNA specimen is collected by withdrawing blood from the child or a similarly invasive procedure, a physician, registered nurse, licensed practical nurse, duly licensed clinical laboratory technician, or other qualified medical practitioner shall collect in a medically approved manner the DNA specimen required to be collected pursuant to division (B) of this section. If the DNA specimen is collected by swabbing for buccal cells or a similarly noninvasive procedure, this section does not require that the DNA specimen be collected by a qualified medical practitioner of that nature. No later than fifteen days after the date of the collection of the DNA specimen, the director of youth services or the chief administrative officer of the detention facility, district detention facility, school, camp, institution, or other facility for delinquent children to which the child is committed or in which the child was placed shall cause the DNA specimen to be forwarded to the bureau of criminal identification and investigation in accordance with procedures established by the superintendent of the bureau under division (H) of section 109.573 of the Revised Code. The bureau shall provide the specimen vials, mailing tubes, labels, postage, and instruction needed for the collection and forwarding of the DNA specimen to the bureau.

(D) The director of youth services and the chief administrative officer of a detention facility, district detention facility, school, camp, institution, or other facility for delinquent children shall cause a DNA specimen to be collected in accordance with divisions (B) and (C) of this section from each child in its custody who is adjudicated a delinquent child for committing any of the following acts:

(1) A violation of section 2903.01, 2903.02, 2903.11, 2905.01, 2907.02, 2907.03, 2907.05, 2911.01, 2911.02, 2911.11, or 2911.12 of the Revised Code;

(2) A violation of section 2907.12 of the Revised Code as it existed prior to September 3, 1996;

(3) An attempt to commit a violation of section 2903.01, 2903.02, 2907.02, 2907.03, or 2907.05 of the Revised Code or to commit a violation of section 2907.12 of the Revised Code as it existed prior to September 3, 1996;

(4) A violation of any law that arose out of the same facts and circumstances and same act as did a charge against the child of a violation of section 2903.01, 2903.02, 2905.01, 2907.02, 2907.03, 2907.05, or 2911.11 of the Revised Code that previously was dismissed or amended or as did a charge against the child of a violation of section 2907.12 of the Revised Code as it existed prior to September 3, 1996, that previously was dismissed or amended;

(5) A violation of section 2905.02 or 2919.23 of the Revised Code that would have been a violation of section 2905.04 of the Revised Code as it existed prior to July 1, 1996, had the violation been committed prior to that date;

(6) A felony violation of any law that arose out of the same facts and circumstances and same act as did a charge against the child of a violation of section 2903.11, 2911.01, 2911.02, or 2911.12 of the Revised Code that previously was dismissed or amended;

(7) A violation of section 2923.01 of the Revised Code involving a conspiracy to commit a violation of section 2903.01, 2903.02, 2905.01, 2911.01, 2911.02, 2911.11, or 2911.12 of the Revised Code;

(8) A violation of section 2923.03 of the Revised Code involving complicity in committing a violation of section 2903.01, 2903.02, 2903.11, 2905.01, 2907.02, 2907.03, 2907.04, 2907.05, 2911.01, 2911.02, 2911.11, or 2911.12 of the Revised Code or a violation of section 2907.12 of the Revised Code as it existed prior to September 3, 1996.

(E) The director of youth services and the chief administrative officer of a detention facility, district detention facility, school, camp, institution, or other facility for delinquent children is not required to comply with this section in relation to the following acts until the superintendent of the bureau of criminal identification and investigation gives agencies in the juvenile justice system, as defined in section 181.51 of the Revised Code, in the state official notification that the state DNA laboratory is prepared to accept DNA specimens of that nature:

(1) A violation of section 2903.11, 2911.01, 2911.02, or 2911.12 of the Revised Code;

(2) An attempt to commit a violation of section 2903.01 or 2903.02 of the Revised Code;

(3) A felony violation of any law that arose out of the same facts and circumstances and same act as did a charge against the child of a violation of section 2903.11, 2911.01, 2911.02, or 2911.12 of the Revised Code that previously was dismissed or amended;

(4) A violation of section 2923.01 of the Revised Code involving a conspiracy to commit a violation of section 2903.01, 2903.02, 2905.01, 2911.01, 2911.02, 2911.11, or 2911.12 of the Revised Code;

(5) A violation of section 2923.03 of the Revised Code involving complicity in committing a violation of section 2903.01, 2903.02, 2903.11, 2905.01, 2907.02, 2907.03, 2907.04, 2907.05, 2911.01, 2911.02, 2911.11, or 2911.12 of the Revised Code or a violation of section 2907.12 of the Revised Code as it existed prior to September 3, 1996.

(2002 H 400, eff. 4–3–03; 2002 H 427, eff. 8–29–02; 2000 S 179, § 3, eff. 1–1–02)

Historical and Statutory Notes

Ed. Note: 2152.74 is former 2151.315, amended and recodified by 2000 S 179, § 3, eff. 1–1–02; 2000 H 442, eff. 10–17–00; 1998 H 526, eff. 9–1–98; 1996 H 124, eff. 3–31–97; 1996 S 269, eff. 7–1–96; 1995 H 5, eff. 8–30–95.

Amendment Note: 2002 H 400 added "detention facility, district detention facility," in divisions (C), (D) and (E); added "or in which the child was placed" to the third sentence of division (C); and rewrote division (B), which prior thereto read:

"(B)(1) A child who is adjudicated a delinquent child for committing an act listed in division (D) of this section and who is committed to the custody of the department of youth services or to a school, camp, institution, or other facility for delinquent children described in division (A)(2) of section 2152.19 of the Revised Code shall submit to a DNA specimen collection procedure administered by the director of youth services if committed to the department or by the chief administrative officer of the school, camp, institution, or other facility for delinquent children to which the child was committed. If the court commits the child to the department of youth services, the director of youth services shall cause the DNA specimen to be collected from the child during the intake process at an institution operated by or under the control of the department. If the court commits the child to a school, camp, institution, or other facility for delinquent children, the chief administrative officer of the school, camp, institution, or facility to which the child is committed shall cause the DNA specimen to be collected from the child during the intake process for the school, camp, institution, or facility. In accordance with division (C) of this section, the director or the chief administrative officer shall cause the DNA specimen to be forwarded to the bureau of criminal identification and investigation no later than fifteen days after the date of the collection of the DNA specimen. The DNA specimen shall be collected from the child in accordance with division (C) of this section.

"(2) If a child is adjudicated a delinquent child for committing an act listed in division (D) of this section, is committed to the department of youth services or to a school, camp, institution, or other facility for delinquent children, and does not submit to a DNA specimen collection procedure pursuant to division (B)(1) of this section, prior to the child's release from the custody of the department of youth services or from the custody of the school, camp, institution, or facility, the child shall submit to, and the director of youth services or the chief administrator of the school, camp, institution, or facility to which the child is committed shall administer, a DNA specimen collection procedure at the institution operated by or under the control of the department of youth services or at the school, camp, institution, or facility to which the child is committed. In accordance with division (C) of this section, the director or the chief administrative officer shall cause the DNA specimen to be forwarded to the bureau of criminal identification and investigation no later than fifteen days after the date of the collection of the DNA specimen. The DNA specimen shall be collected in accordance with division (C) of this section.".

Amendment Note: 2002 H 427 rewrote divisions (C), (D) and (E), which prior thereto read:

"(C) A physician, registered nurse, licensed practical nurse, duly licensed clinical laboratory technician, or other qualified medical practitioner shall collect in a medically approved manner the DNA specimen required to be collected pursuant to division (B) of this section. No later than fifteen days after the date of the collection of the DNA specimen, the director of youth services or the chief administrative officer of the school, camp, institution, or other facility for delinquent children to which the child is committed shall cause the DNA specimen to be forwarded to the bureau of criminal identification and investigation in accordance with procedures established by the superintendent of the bureau under division (H) of section 109.573 of the Revised Code. The bureau shall provide the specimen vials, mailing tubes, labels, postage, and instruction needed for the collection and forwarding of the DNA specimen to the bureau.

"(D) The director of youth services and the chief administrative officer of a school, camp, institution, or other facility for delinquent children shall cause a

DNA specimen to be collected in accordance with divisions (B) and (C) of this section from each child in its custody who is adjudicated a delinquent child for committing any of the following acts:

"(1) A violation of section 2903.01, 2903.02, 2905.01, 2907.02, 2907.03, 2907.05, or 2911.11 of the Revised Code;

"(2) A violation of section 2907.12 of the Revised Code as it existed prior to September 3, 1996;

"(3) An attempt to commit a violation of section 2907.02, 2907.03, or 2907.05 of the Revised Code or to commit a violation of section 2907.12 of the Revised Code as it existed prior to September 3, 1996;

"(4) A violation of any law that arose out of the same facts and circumstances and same act as did a charge against the child of a violation of section 2903.01, 2903.02, 2905.01, 2907.02, 2907.03, 2907.05, or 2911.11 of the Revised Code that previously was dismissed or amended or as did a charge against the child of a violation of section 2907.12 of the Revised Code as it existed prior to September 3, 1996, that previously was dismissed or amended;

"(5) A violation of section 2905.02 or 2919.23 of the Revised Code that would have been a violation of section 2905.04 of the Revised Code as it existed prior to July 1, 1996, had the violation been committed prior to that date.

"(E) The director of youth services and the chief administrative officer of a school, camp, institution, or other facility for delinquent children is not required to comply with this section until the superintendent of the bureau of criminal identification and investigation gives agencies in the juvenile justice system, as defined in section 181.51 of the Revised Code, in the state official notification that the state DNA laboratory is prepared to accept DNA specimens."

Amendment Note: 2000 S 179, § 3, eff. 1–1–02, substituted "division (2) of section 2152.19" for "division (3) of section 2151.355" in division (B)(1).

Amendment Note: 2000 H 442 deleted "2907.04," after "2907.03" in divisions (D)(1), (D)(3), and (D)(4).

Amendment Note: 1998 H 526 added references to sections 2903.01, 2903.02, 2905.01, and 2911.11 and inserted "or amended" twice in division (D)(4).

Amendment Note: 1996 H 124 rewrote division (D), which prior thereto read:

"(D) The director of youth services and the chief administrative officer of a school, camp, institution, or other facility for delinquent children shall cause a DNA specimen to be collected in accordance with divisions (B) and (C) of this section from each child in its custody who is adjudicated a delinquent child for committing any of the following acts:

"(1) A violation of section 2903.01, 2903.02, 2905.01, 2907.02, 2907.03, 2907.04, 2907.05, 2907.12, or 2911.11 of the Revised Code;

"(2) An attempt to commit a violation of section 2907.02, 2907.03, 2907.04, 2907.05, or 2907.12 of the Revised Code;

"(3) A violation of any law that arose out of the same facts and circumstances and same act as did a charge against the child of a violation of section 2907.02, 2907.03, 2907.04, 2907.05, or 2907.12 of the Revised Code that previously was dismissed;

"(4) A violation of section 2905.02 or 2919.23 of the Revised Code that would have been a violation of section 2905.04 of the Revised Code as it existed prior to July 1, 1996, had the violation been committed prior to that date."

Amendment Note: 1996 S 269 deleted "that if committed by an adult would be an offense" following "an act" in divisions (B)(1) and (B)(2); substituted "is adjudicated" for "was adjudicated", "is committed" for "was committed", and "does not submit" for "did not submit" in division (B)(2); substituted "any of the following acts" for "an act that if committed by an adult would be one of the following offenses" in the introductory paragraph of division (D); added division (D)(4); and made other nonsubstantive changes.

Cross References

Reparations fund, DNA specimens, administration and analysis costs, 2743.191

Library References

OJur 3d: 48, Family Law § 1534 to 1539, 1566 et seq.
Am Jur 2d: 37A, Freedom Of Information Act § 127; 62, Privacy § 101, 103, 117
Baldwin's Ohio Legislative Service, 1995 H 5—LSC Analysis, p 5/L–336

SEX OFFENSES

2152.81   Deposition of child sex offense victim

(A)(1) As used in this section, "victim" includes any of the following persons:

(a) A person who was a victim of a violation identified in division (A)(2) of this section or an act that would be an offense of violence if committed by an adult;

(b) A person against whom was directed any conduct that constitutes, or that is an element of, a violation identified in division (A)(2) of this section or an act that would be an offense of violence if committed by an adult.

(2) In any proceeding in juvenile court involving a complaint, indictment, or information in which a child is charged with a violation of section 2905.03, 2905.05, 2907.02, 2907.03, 2907.05, 2907.06, 2907.07, 2907.09, 2907.21, 2907.23, 2907.24, 2907.31, 2907.32, 2907.321, 2907.322, 2907.323, or 2919.22 of the Revised Code or an act that would be an offense of violence if committed by an adult and in which an alleged victim of the violation or act was a child who was less than thirteen years of age when the complaint or information was filed or the indictment was returned, the juvenile judge, upon motion of an attorney for the prosecution, shall order that the testimony of the child victim be taken by deposition. The prosecution also may request that the deposition be videotaped in accordance with division (A)(3) of this section. The judge shall notify the child victim whose deposition is to be taken, the prosecution, and the attorney for the child who is charged

with the violation or act of the date, time, and place for taking the deposition. The notice shall identify the child victim who is to be examined and shall indicate whether a request that the deposition be videotaped has been made. The child who is charged with the violation or act shall have the right to attend the deposition and the right to be represented by counsel. Depositions shall be taken in the manner provided in civil cases, except that the judge in the proceeding shall preside at the taking of the deposition and shall rule at that time on any objections of the prosecution or the attorney for the child charged with the violation or act. The prosecution and the attorney for the child charged with the violation or act shall have the right, as at an adjudication hearing, to full examination and cross-examination of the child victim whose deposition is to be taken. If a deposition taken under this division is intended to be offered as evidence in the proceeding, it shall be filed in the juvenile court in which the action is pending and is admissible in the manner described in division (B) of this section. If a deposition of a child victim taken under this division is admitted as evidence at the proceeding under division (B) of this section, the child victim shall not be required to testify in person at the proceeding. However, at any time before the conclusion of the proceeding, the attorney for the child charged with the violation or act may file a motion with the judge requesting that another deposition of the child victim be taken because new evidence material to the defense of the child charged has been discovered that the attorney for the child charged could not with reasonable diligence have discovered prior to the taking of the admitted deposition. Any motion requesting another deposition shall be accompanied by supporting affidavits. Upon the filing of the motion and affidavits, the court may order that additional testimony of the child victim relative to the new evidence be taken by another deposition. If the court orders the taking of another deposition under this provision, the deposition shall be taken in accordance with this division; if the admitted deposition was a videotaped deposition taken in accordance with division (A)(3) of this section, the new deposition also shall be videotaped in accordance with that division, and, in other cases, the new deposition may be videotaped in accordance with that division.

(3) If the prosecution requests that a deposition to be taken under division (A)(2) of this section be videotaped, the juvenile judge shall order that the deposition be videotaped in accordance with this division. If a juvenile judge issues an order to video tape the deposition, the judge shall exclude from the room in which the deposition is to be taken every person except the child victim giving the testimony, the judge, one or more interpreters if needed, the attorneys for the prosecution and the child who is charged with the violation or act, any person needed to operate the equipment to be used, one person chosen by the child victim giving the deposition, and any person whose presence the judge determines would contribute to the welfare and well-being of the child victim giving the deposition. The person chosen by the child victim shall not be a witness in the proceeding and, both before and during the deposition, shall not discuss the testimony of the child victim with any other witness in the proceeding. To the extent feasible, any person operating the recording equipment shall be restricted to a room adjacent to the room in which the deposition is being taken, or to a location in the room in which the deposition is being taken that is behind a screen or mirror so that the person operating the recording equipment can see and hear, but cannot be seen or heard by, the child victim giving the deposition during the deposition. The child who is charged with the violation or act shall be permitted to observe and hear the testimony of the child victim giving the deposition on a monitor, shall be provided with an electronic means of immediate communication with the attorney of the child who is charged with the violation or act during the testimony, and shall be restricted to a location from which the child who is charged with the violation or act cannot be seen or heard by the child victim giving the deposition, except on a monitor provided for that purpose. The child victim giving the deposition shall be provided with a monitor on which the child victim can observe, while giving testimony, the child who is charged with the violation or act. The judge, at the judge's discretion, may preside at the deposition by electronic means from outside the room in which the deposition is to be taken; if the judge presides by electronic means, the judge shall be provided with monitors on which the judge can see each person in the room in which the deposition is to be taken and with an electronic means of communication with each person in that room, and each person in the room shall be provided with a monitor on which that person can see the judge and with an electronic means of communication with the judge. A deposition that is videotaped under this division shall be taken and filed in the manner described in division (A)(2) of this section and is admissible in the manner described in this division and division (B) of this section, and, if a deposition that is videotaped under this division is admitted as evidence at the proceeding, the child victim shall not be required to testify in person at the proceeding. No deposition videotaped under this division shall be admitted as evidence at any proceeding unless division (B) of this section is satisfied relative to the deposition and all of the following apply relative to the recording:

(a) The recording is both aural and visual and is recorded on film or videotape, or by other electronic means.

(b) The recording is authenticated under the Rules of Evidence and the Rules of Criminal Procedure as a fair and accurate representation of what occurred, and the recording is not altered other than at the direction and under the supervision of the judge in the proceeding.

(c) Each voice on the recording that is material to the testimony on the recording or the making of the recording, as determined by the judge, is identified.

(d) Both the prosecution and the child who is charged with the violation or act are afforded an opportunity to view the recording before it is shown in the proceeding.

(B)(1) At any proceeding in relation to which a deposition was taken under division (A) of this section, the deposition or a part of it is admissible in evidence upon motion of the prosecution if the testimony in the deposition or the part to be admitted is not excluded by the hearsay rule and if the deposition or the part to be admitted otherwise is admissible under the Rules of Evidence. For purposes of this division, testimony is not excluded by the hearsay rule if the testimony is not hearsay under Evidence Rule 801; if the testimony is within an exception to the hearsay rule set forth in Evidence Rule 803; if the child victim who gave the testimony is unavailable as a witness, as defined in Evidence Rule 804, and the testimony is admissible under that rule; or if both of the following apply:

(a) The child who is charged with the violation or act had an opportunity and similar motive at the time of the taking of the deposition to develop the testimony by direct, cross, or redirect examination.

(b) The judge determines that there is reasonable cause to believe that, if the child victim who gave the testimony in the deposition were to testify in person at the proceeding, the child victim would experience serious emotional trauma as a result of the child victim's participation at the proceeding.

(2) Objections to receiving in evidence a deposition or a part of it under division (B) of this section shall be made as provided in civil actions.

(3) The provisions of divisions (A) and (B) of this section are in addition to any other provisions of the Revised Code, the Rules of Juvenile Procedure, the Rules of Criminal Procedure, or the Rules of Evidence that pertain to the taking or admission of depositions in a juvenile court proceeding and do not limit the admissibility under any of those other provisions of any deposition taken under division (A) of this section or otherwise taken.

(C) In any proceeding in juvenile court involving a complaint, indictment, or information in which a child is charged with a violation listed in division (A)(2) of this section or an act that would be an offense of violence if committed by an adult and in which an alleged victim of the violation or offense was a child who was less than thirteen years of age when the complaint or information was filed or indictment was returned, the prosecution may file a motion with the juvenile judge requesting the judge to order the testimony of the child victim to be taken in a room other than the room in which the proceeding is being conducted and be televised, by closed circuit equipment, into the room in which the proceeding is being conducted to be viewed by the child who is charged with the violation or act and any other persons who are not permitted in the room in which the testimony is to be taken but who would have been present during the testimony of the child victim had it been given in the room in which the proceeding is being conducted. Except for good cause shown, the prosecution shall file a motion under this division at least seven days before the date of the proceeding. The juvenile judge may issue the order

upon the motion of the prosecution filed under this division, if the judge determines that the child victim is unavailable to testify in the room in which the proceeding is being conducted in the physical presence of the child charged with the violation or act, due to one or more of the reasons set forth in division (E) of this section. If a juvenile judge issues an order of that nature, the judge shall exclude from the room in which the testimony is to be taken every person except a person described in division (A)(3) of this section. The judge, at the judge's discretion, may preside during the giving of the testimony by electronic means from outside the room in which it is being given, subject to the limitations set forth in division (A)(3) of this section. To the extent feasible, any person operating the televising equipment shall be hidden from the sight and hearing of the child victim giving the testimony, in a manner similar to that described in division (A)(3) of this section. The child who is charged with the violation or act shall be permitted to observe and hear the testimony of the child victim giving the testimony on a monitor, shall be provided with an electronic means of immediate communication with the attorney of the child who is charged with the violation or act during the testimony, and shall be restricted to a location from which the child who is charged with the violation or act cannot be seen or heard by the child victim giving the testimony, except on a monitor provided for that purpose. The child victim giving the testimony shall be provided with a monitor on which the child victim can observe, while giving testimony, the child who is charged with the violation or act.

(D) In any proceeding in juvenile court involving a complaint, indictment, or information in which a child is charged with a violation listed in division (A)(2) of this section or an act that would be an offense of violence if committed by an adult and in which an alleged victim of the violation or offense was a child who was less than thirteen years of age when the complaint or information was filed or the indictment was returned, the prosecution may file a motion with the juvenile judge requesting the judge to order the testimony of the child victim to be taken outside of the room in which the proceeding is being conducted and be recorded for showing in the room in which the proceeding is being conducted before the judge, the child who is charged with the violation or act, and any other persons who would have been present during the testimony of the child victim had it been given in the room in which the proceeding is being conducted. Except for good cause shown, the prosecution shall file a motion under this division at least seven days before the date of the proceeding. The juvenile judge may issue the order upon the motion of the prosecution filed under this division, if the judge determines that the child victim is unavailable to testify in the room in which the proceeding is being conducted in the physical presence of the child charged with the violation or act, due to one or more of the reasons set forth in division (E) of this section. If a juvenile judge issues an order of that nature, the judge shall exclude from the room in which the testimony is to be taken every person except a person described in division (A)(3) of this section. To the extent feasible, any person operating the recording equipment shall be hidden from the sight and hearing of the child victim giving the testimony, in a manner similar to that described in division (A)(3) of this section. The child who is charged with the violation or act shall be permitted to observe and hear the testimony of the child victim giving the testimony on a monitor, shall be provided with an electronic means of immediate communication with the attorney of the child who is charged with the violation or act during the testimony, and shall be restricted to a location from which the child who is charged with the violation or act cannot be seen or heard by the child victim giving the testimony, except on a monitor provided for that purpose. The child victim giving the testimony shall be provided with a monitor on which the child victim can observe, while giving testimony, the child who is charged with the violation or act. No order for the taking of testimony by recording shall be issued under this division unless the provisions set forth in divisions (A)(3)(a), (b), (c), and (d) of this section apply to the recording of the testimony.

(E) For purposes of divisions (C) and (D) of this section, a juvenile judge may order the testimony of a child victim to be taken outside of the room in which a proceeding is being conducted if the judge determines that the child victim is unavailable to testify in the room in the physical presence of the child charged with the violation or act due to one or more of the following circumstances:

(1) The persistent refusal of the child victim to testify despite judicial requests to do so;

(2) The inability of the child victim to communicate about the alleged violation or offense because of extreme fear, failure of memory, or another similar reason;

(3) The substantial likelihood that the child victim will suffer serious emotional trauma from so testifying.

(F)(1) If a juvenile judge issues an order pursuant to division (C) or (D) of this section that requires the testimony of a child victim in a juvenile court proceeding to be taken outside of the room in which the proceeding is being conducted, the order shall specifically identify the child victim to whose testimony it applies, the order applies only during the testimony of the specified child victim, and the child victim giving the testimony shall not be required to testify at the proceeding other than in accordance with the order. The authority of a judge to close the taking of a deposition under division (A)(3) of this section or a proceeding under division (C) or (D) of this section is in addition to the authority of a judge to close a hearing pursuant to section 2151.35 of the Revised Code.

(2) A juvenile judge who makes any determination regarding the admissibility of a deposition under divisions (A) and (B) of this section, the videotaping of a deposition under division (A)(3) of this section, or the taking of testimony outside of the room in which a proceeding is being conducted under division (C) or (D) of this section, shall enter the determination and findings on the record in the proceeding.

(2000 S 179, § 3, eff. 1–1–02)

Historical and Statutory Notes

Ed. Note: 2152.81 is former 2151.3511, amended and recodified by 2000 S 179, § 3, eff. 1–1–02; 2000 H 442, eff. 10–17–00; 1997 S 53, eff. 10–14–97; 1996 H 445, eff. 9–3–96; 1986 H 108, eff. 10–14–86.

Amendment Note: 2000 S 179, § 3, eff. 1–1–02, added references to indictments and informations throughout the section.

Amendment Note: 2000 H 442 deleted "2907.04," after "2907.03" in division (A)(2).

Amendment Note: 1997 S 53 added division (A)(1); redesignated former division (A)(2) as division (A)(3); designated division (A)(2); inserted references to Revised Code sections 2905.03, 2905.05, 2907.07, 2907.09, 2907.23 and 2907.24 in division (A)(2); substituted references to division (A)(2) with references to division (A)(3) throughout; substituted "less than thirteen" for "under eleven" in divisions (A)(2), (C) and (D); inserted "or an act that would be an offense of violence if committed by an adult" in divisions (A)(2), (C) and (D); and made changes to reflect gender neutral language and other nonsubstantive changes.

Amendment Note: 1996 H 445 removed a reference to section 2907.12 from the first sentence in division (A)(1); and made changes to reflect gender neutral language and other nonsubstantive changes.

Cross References

Bureau of criminal identification and investigation, recording and televising equipment for child sex offense victims, 109.54

Library References

Infants ⚖201, 207.

Westlaw Topic No. 211.

C.J.S. Infants §§ 42, 51 to 67.

OJur 3d: 48, Family Law § 1534, 1537, 1538, 1641

Am Jur 2d: 21A, Criminal Law § 960; 47, Juvenile Courts and Delinquent and Dependent Children § 49, 52

Carlin, Baldwin's Ohio Practice, Merrick–Rippner Probate Law § 107.35 (2003).

JUVENILE OFFENDER REGISTRANTS

2152.811   Child adjudicated a child delinquent for committing a sexually oriented offense

If a court adjudicates a child a delinquent child for committing a presumptive registration-exempt sexually oriented offense, the court may determine pursuant to section 2950.021 of the Revised Code, prior to making an order of disposition for the child, that the child potentially should be subjected to classification as a juvenile offender registrant under sections 2152.82, 2152.83, 2152.84, or 2152.85 of the Revised Code and to registration under section 2950.04 of the Revised Code and all other duties and responsibilities generally imposed under Chapter 2950. of the Revised Code upon persons who are adjudicated delinquent children for committing a sexually oriented offense other than a presumptive registration-exempt sexually oriented offense. If the court so determines, divisions (B)(1) and (3) of section 2950.021 of the Revised Code apply, and the court shall proceed as described in those divisions.

(2003 S 5, eff. 7–31–03)

2152.82   Juvenile offender registrant

(A) The court that adjudicates a child a delinquent child shall issue as part of the dispositional order an order that classifies the child a juvenile offender regis-

trant and specifies that the child has a duty to comply with sections 2950.04, 2950.041, 2950.05, and 2950.06 of the Revised Code if all of the following apply:

(1) The act for which the child is adjudicated a delinquent child is a sexually oriented offense that is not a registration-exempt sexually oriented offense or is a child-victim oriented offense that the child committed on or after January 1, 2002.

(2) The child was fourteen, fifteen, sixteen, or seventeen years of age at the time of committing the offense.

(3) The court has determined that the child previously was convicted of, pleaded guilty to, or was adjudicated a delinquent child for committing any sexually oriented offense or child-victim oriented offense, regardless of when the prior offense was committed and regardless of the child's age at the time of committing the offense.

(B) An order required under division (A) of this section shall be issued at the time the judge makes the orders of disposition for the delinquent child. Prior to issuing the order required by division (A) of this section, the judge shall conduct the hearing and make the determinations required by division (B) of section 2950.09 of the Revised Code regarding a sexually oriented offense that is not a registration-exempt sexually oriented offense or division (B) of section 2950.091 of the Revised Code regarding a child-victim oriented offense to determine if the child is to be classified a sexual predator or a child-victim predator, shall make the determinations required by division (E) of section 2950.09 of the Revised Code regarding a sexually oriented offense that is not a registration-exempt sexually oriented offense or division (E) of section 2950.091 of the Revised Code regarding a child-victim oriented offense to determine if the child is to be classified a habitual sex offender or a habitual child-victim offender, and shall otherwise comply with those divisions. When a judge issues an order under division (A) of this section, all of the following apply:

(1) The judge shall include in the order any determination that the delinquent child is, or is not, a sexual predator or child-victim predator or is, or is not, a habitual sex offender or habitual child-victim offender that the judge makes pursuant to division (B) or (E) of section 2950.09 or 2950.091 of the Revised Code and any related information required or

authorized under the division under which the determination is made, including, but not limited to, any requirement imposed by the court subjecting a child who is a habitual sex offender or habitual child-victim offender to community notification provisions as described in division (E) of section 2950.09 or 2950.091 of the Revised Code.

(2) The judge shall include in the order a statement that, upon completion of the disposition of the delinquent child that was made for the sexually oriented offense or child-victim oriented offense upon which the order is based, a hearing will be conducted, and the order and any determinations included in the order are subject to modification or termination pursuant to sections 2152.84 and 2152.85 of the Revised Code.

(3) The judge shall provide to the delinquent child and to the delinquent child's parent, guardian, or custodian the notice required under divisions (A) and (B) of section 2950.03 of the Revised Code and shall provide as part of that notice a copy of the order.

(4) The judge shall include the order in the delinquent child's dispositional order and shall specify in the dispositional order that the order issued under division (A) of this section was made pursuant to this section.

(C) An order issued under division (A) of this section and any determinations included in the order shall remain in effect for the period of time specified in section 2950.07 of the Revised Code, subject to a modification or termination of the order under section 2152.84 or 2152.85 of the Revised Code, and section 2152.851 of the Revised Code applies regarding the order and the determinations. If an order is issued under division (A) of this section, the child's attainment of eighteen or twenty-one years of age does not affect or terminate the order, and the order remains in effect for the period of time described in this division.

(D) A court that adjudicates a child a delinquent child for a sexually oriented offense that is a registration-exempt sexually oriented offense shall not issue based on that adjudication an order under this section that classifies the child a juvenile offender registrant and specifies that the child has a duty to comply with

sections 2950.04, 2950.041, 2950.05, and 2950.06 of the Revised Code.

(2003 S 5, eff. 7–31–03; 2002 H 393, eff. 7–5–02; 2001 S 3, eff. 1–1–02)

Historical and Statutory Notes

Amendment Note: 2003 S 5 substituted "comply with sections" for "register under section" and inserted ", 2950.041, 2950.05, and 2950.06" before "of the Revised Code" in the first paragraph; inserted "that is not a registration-exempt sexually oriented offense or is a child-victim oriented offense" to division (1); inserted "or child-victim oriented offense" to division (3); inserted "regarding a sexually oriented offense that is not a registration-exempt sexually oriented offense or division (B) of section 2950.091 of the Revised Code regarding a child-victim oriented offense" before "to determine if the child" and inserted "or a child-victim predator" before "shall make the determinations", deleted "that" after "by division (E) of", inserted "2950.09 of the Revised Code regarding a sexually oriented offense that is not a registration-exempt sexually oriented offense or division (E) of section 2950.091 of the Revised Code regarding a child-victim oriented offense" before "to determine if the child is to be classified as a habitual sex offender", inserted "or a habitual child-victim offender" before ", and shall otherwise comply", inserted ", or is not," before "sexual predator", inserted "or child-victim predator" before "or is", inserted ",or is not," before "a habitual sex offender", inserted "or habitual child-victim offender" before "that the judge makes", inserted "or 2950.091" before "of the Revised Code", inserted "or habitual child-victim offender" before "to community notification", deleted "that" after "division (E) of", and inserted "2950.09.09 or 2950.091 of the Revised Code" to division (B)(1); inserted "or child-victim oriented offense" before "upon which the order is based" in division (B)(2); deleted "a copy of the order" before "to the delinquent", deleted ", as part of" before "the notice", substituted "required" for "provided" before "under divisions (A) and (B)" and inserted "and shall provide as part of that notice a copy of the order" to division (B)(3); inserted ", and section 2152.851 of the Revised Code applies regarding the order and the determinations" to the end of the first sentence in division (C); and added new division (D).

Amendment Note: 2002 H 393 rewrote divisions (A) and (B) which prior thereto read:

"(A) If a child is adjudicated a delinquent child for committing on or after the effective date of this section a sexually oriented offense, the juvenile court judge who adjudicates the child a delinquent child shall issue an order that classifies the child a juvenile sex offender registrant and specifies that the child has a duty to register under section 2950.04 of the Revised Code if the delinquent child was fourteen, fifteen, sixteen, or seventeen years of age at the time of committing the offense, and the delinquent child previously was adjudicated a delinquent child for committing any sexually oriented offense, regardless of when the prior offense was committed and regardless of the delinquent child's age at the time of committing the offense.

"(B) An order required under division (A) of this section shall be issued at the time the judge makes the orders of disposition for the delinquent child. Prior to issuing the order, the judge shall conduct the hearing and make the determinations required by, and otherwise comply with, divisions (B) and (E) of section 2950.09 of the Revised Code. When a judge issues an order under division (A) of this section, all of the following apply:"

Cross References

Adjudication of offender as sexual predator or as habitual sex offender; exclusion of registration-exempt sexually oriented offense, 2950.09.
Child-victim oriented offenses; duty of registration of offender or delinquent child, 2950.041.
Determination of offender as child-victim predator; hearing, 2950.091.
Determination of requirement to register as sex offender with sheriff, 2950.021.
Manner of registering as sex offenders, 2950.04.
Notice of duty to register as sex offender and related requirements, 2950.03.
Sex offenders, definitions, 2950.01.

Library References

OJur 3d: 48, Family Law § 1534, 1537, 1538
Carlin, Baldwin's Ohio Practice, Merrick–Rippner Probate Law § 107.89, 107.93, 107.94, 107.95, 107.96, 107.97, 107.100 (2003).

2152.821 Testimony of mentally retarded or developmentally disabled victim

(A) As used in this section:

(1) "Mentally retarded person" and "developmentally disabled person" have the same meanings as in section 5123.01 of the Revised Code.

(2) "Mentally retarded or developmentally disabled victim" includes any of the following persons:

(a) A mentally retarded person or developmentally disabled person who was a victim of a violation identified in division (B)(1) of this section or an act that would be an offense of violence if committed by an adult;

(b) A mentally retarded person or developmentally disabled person against whom was directed any conduct that constitutes, or that is an element of, a violation identified in division (B)(1) of this section or an act that would be an offense of violence if committed by an adult.

(B)(1) In any proceeding in juvenile court involving a complaint, indictment, or information in which a child is charged with a violation of section 2903.16, 2903.34, 2903.341, 2907.02, 2907.03, 2907.05, 2907.21, 2907. 23, 2907.24, 2907.32, 2907.321, 2907.322, or 2907.323 of the Revised Code or an act that would be an offense of violence if committed by an adult and in which an alleged victim of the violation or act was a mentally retarded person or developmentally disabled person, the juvenile judge, upon motion of the prosecution, shall order that the testimony of the men-tally retarded or developmentally disabled victim be taken by deposition. The prosecution also may request that the deposition be videotaped in accordance with division (B)(2) of this section. The judge shall notify the mentally retarded or developmentally disabled victim whose deposition is to be taken, the prosecution, and the attorney for the child who is charged with the violation or act of the date, time, and place for taking the deposition. The notice shall identify the mentally retarded or developmentally disabled victim who is to be examined and shall indicate whether a request that the deposition be videotaped has been made. The child who is charged with the violation or act shall have the right to attend the deposition and the right to be represented by counsel. Depositions shall be taken in the manner provided in civil cases, except that the judge in the proceeding shall preside at the taking of the deposition and shall rule at that time on any objections of the prosecution or the attorney for the child charged with the violation or act. The prosecution and the attorney for the child charged with the violation or act shall have the right, as at an adjudication hearing, to full examination and cross-examination of the mentally retarded or developmentally disabled victim whose deposition is to be taken.

If a deposition taken under this division is intended to be offered as evidence in the proceeding, it shall be filed in the juvenile court in which the action is pending and is admissible in the manner described in division (C) of this section. If a deposition of a mentally retarded or developmentally disabled victim taken under this division is admitted as evidence at the proceeding under division (C) of this section, the mentally retarded or developmentally disabled victim shall not be required to testify in person at the proceeding.

At any time before the conclusion of the proceeding, the attorney for the child charged with the violation or act may file a motion with the judge requesting that another deposition of the mentally retarded or developmentally disabled victim be taken because new evidence material to the defense of the child charged has been discovered that the attorney for the child charged could not with reasonable diligence have discovered prior to the taking of the admitted deposition. Any motion requesting another deposition shall be accompanied by supporting affidavits. Upon the filing of the motion and affidavits, the court may order that additional testimony of the mentally retarded or developmentally disabled victim relative to the new evidence be taken by another deposition. If the court orders the taking of another deposition under this provision, the deposition shall be taken in accordance with this division. If the admitted deposition was a videotaped deposition taken in accordance with division (B)(2) of this section, the new deposition also shall be videotaped in accordance with that division. In other cases, the new deposition may be videotaped in accordance with that division.

(2) If the prosecution requests that a deposition to be taken under division (B)(1) of this section be videotaped, the juvenile judge shall order that the deposition be videotaped in accordance with this division. If a juvenile judge issues an order to video tape the deposition, the judge shall exclude from the room in which the deposition is to be taken every person except the mentally retarded or developmentally disabled victim giving the testimony, the judge, one or more interpreters if needed, the attorneys for the prosecution and the child who is charged with the violation or act, any person needed to operate the equipment to be used, one person chosen by the mentally retarded or developmentally disabled victim giving the deposition, and any person whose presence the judge determines would contribute to the welfare and well-being of the mentally retarded or developmentally disabled victim giving the deposition. The person chosen by the mentally retarded or developmentally disabled victim shall not be a witness in the proceeding and, both before and during the deposition, shall not discuss the testimony of the victim with any other witness in the proceeding. To the extent feasible, any person operating the recording equipment shall be restricted to a room adjacent to the room in which the deposition is being taken, or to a location in the room in which the deposition is being taken that is behind a screen or mirror so that the person operating the recording equipment can see and hear, but cannot be seen or heard by, the mentally retarded or developmentally disabled victim giving the deposition during the deposition.

The child who is charged with the violation or act shall be permitted to observe and hear the testimony of the mentally retarded or developmentally disabled victim giving the deposition on a monitor, shall be provided with an electronic means of immediate communication with the attorney of the child who is charged with the violation or act during the testimony, and shall be restricted to a location from which the child who is charged with the violation or act cannot be seen or heard by the mentally retarded or developmentally disabled victim giving the deposition, except on a monitor provided for that purpose. The mentally retarded or developmentally disabled victim giving the deposition shall be provided with a monitor on which the mentally retarded or developmentally disabled victim can observe, while giving testimony, the child who is charged with the violation or act. The judge, at the judge's discretion, may preside at the deposition by electronic means from outside the room in which the deposition is to be taken; if the judge presides by electronic means, the judge shall be provided with monitors on which the judge can see each person in the room in which the deposition is to be taken and with an electronic means of communication with each person in that room, and each person in the room shall be provided with a monitor on which that person can see the judge and with an electronic means of communication with the judge. A deposition that is videotaped under this division shall be taken and filed in the manner described in division (B)(1) of this section and is admissible in the manner described in this division and division (C) of this section. If a deposition that is videotaped under this division is admitted as evidence at the proceeding, the mentally retarded or developmentally disabled victim shall not be required to testify in person at the proceeding. No deposition videotaped under this division shall be admitted as evidence at any proceeding unless division (C) of this section is satisfied relative to the deposition and all of the following apply relative to the recording:

(a) The recording is both aural and visual and is recorded on film or videotape, or by other electronic means.

(b) The recording is authenticated under the Rules of Evidence and the Rules of Criminal Procedure as a fair and accurate representation of what occurred, and the recording is not altered other than at the direction and under the supervision of the judge in the proceeding.

(c) Each voice on the recording that is material to the testimony on the recording or the making of the recording, as determined by the judge, is identified.

(d) Both the prosecution and the child who is charged with the violation or act are afforded an opportunity to view the recording before it is shown in the proceeding.

(C)(1) At any proceeding in relation to which a deposition was taken under division (B) of this section, the deposition or a part of it is admissible in evidence upon motion of the prosecution if the testimony in the deposition or the part to be admitted is not excluded by the hearsay rule and if the deposition or the part to be admitted otherwise is admissible under the Rules of Evidence. For purposes of this division, testimony is not excluded by the hearsay rule if the testimony is not hearsay under Evidence Rule 801; the testimony is within an exception to the hearsay rule set forth in Evidence Rule 803; the mentally retarded or developmentally disabled victim who gave the testimony is unavailable as a witness, as defined in Evidence Rule 804, and the testimony is admissible under that rule; or both of the following apply:

(a) The child who is charged with the violation or act had an opportunity and similar motive at the time of the taking of the deposition to develop the testimony by direct, cross, or redirect examination.

(b) The judge determines that there is reasonable cause to believe that, if the mentally retarded or developmentally disabled victim who gave the testimony in the deposition were to testify in person at the proceeding, the mentally retarded or developmentally disabled victim would experience serious emotional trauma as a result of the mentally retarded or developmentally disabled victim's participation at the proceeding.

(2) Objections to receiving in evidence a deposition or a part of it under division (C) of this section shall be made as provided in civil actions.

(3) The provisions of divisions (B) and (C) of this section are in addition to any other provisions of the Revised Code, the Rules of Juvenile Procedure, the Rules of Criminal Procedure, or the Rules of Evidence that pertain to the taking or admission of depositions in a juvenile court proceeding and do not limit the admissibility under any of those other provisions of any deposition taken under division (B) of this section or otherwise taken.

(D) In any proceeding in juvenile court involving a complaint, indictment, or information in which a child is charged with a violation listed in division (B)(1) of this section or an act that would be an offense of violence if committed by an adult and in which an alleged victim of the violation or offense was a mentally retarded or developmentally disabled person, the prosecution may file a motion with the juvenile judge requesting the judge to order the testimony of the mentally retarded or developmentally disabled victim to be taken in a room other than the room in which the proceeding is being conducted and be televised, by closed circuit equipment, into the room in which the proceeding is being conducted to be viewed by the child who is charged with the violation or act and any other persons who are not permitted in the room in which the testimony is to be taken but who would have been present during the testimony of the mentally retarded or developmentally disabled victim had it been given in the room in which the proceeding is being conducted. Except for good cause shown, the prosecution shall file a motion under this division at least seven days before the date of the proceeding. The juvenile judge may issue the order upon the motion of the prosecution filed under this division, if the judge determines that the mentally retarded or developmentally disabled victim is unavailable to testify in the room in which the proceeding is being conducted in the physical presence of the child charged with the violation or act for one or more of the reasons set forth in division (F) of this section. If a juvenile judge issues an order of that nature, the judge shall exclude from the room in which the testimony is to be taken every person except a person described in division (B)(2) of this section. The judge, at the judge's discretion, may preside during the giving of the testimony by electronic means from outside the room in which it is being given, subject to the limitations set forth in division (B)(2) of this section. To the extent feasible, any person operating the televising equipment shall be hidden from the sight and hearing of the mentally retarded or developmentally disabled victim giving the testimony, in a manner similar to that described in division (B)(2) of this section. The child who is charged with the violation or act shall be permitted to observe and hear the testimony of the mentally retarded or developmentally disabled victim giving the testimony on a monitor, shall be provided with an electronic means of immediate communication with the attorney of the child who is charged with the violation or act during the testimony, and shall be restricted to a location from which the child who is charged with the violation or act cannot be seen or heard by the mentally retarded or developmentally disabled victim giving the testimony, except on a monitor provided for that purpose. The mentally retarded or developmentally disabled victim giving the testimony shall be provided with a monitor on which the mentally retarded or developmentally disabled victim can observe, while giving testimony, the child who is charged with the violation or act.

(E) In any proceeding in juvenile court involving a complaint, indictment, or information in which a child is charged with a violation listed in division (B)(1) of this section or an act that would be an offense of violence if committed by an adult and in which an alleged victim of the violation or offense was a mentally retarded or developmentally disabled person, the prosecution may file a motion with the juvenile judge requesting the judge to order the testimony of the mentally retarded or developmentally disabled victim to be taken outside of the room in which the proceeding is being conducted and be recorded for showing in the room in which the proceeding is being conducted before the judge, the child who is charged with the violation or act, and any other persons who would have been present during the testimony of the mentally retarded or developmentally disabled victim had it been given in the room in which the proceeding is being conducted. Except for good cause shown, the prosecution shall file a motion under this division at least seven days before the date of the proceeding. The juvenile judge may issue the order upon the motion of the prosecution filed under this division, if the judge determines that the mentally retarded or developmentally disabled victim is unavailable to testify in the room in which the proceeding is being conducted in the physical presence of the child charged with the violation or act, due to one or more of the reasons set forth in division (F) of this section. If a juvenile judge issues an order of that nature, the judge

shall exclude from the room in which the testimony is to be taken every person except a person described in division (B)(2) of this section. To the extent feasible, any person operating the recording equipment shall be hidden from the sight and hearing of the mentally retarded or developmentally disabled victim giving the testimony, in a manner similar to that described in division (B)(2) of this section. The child who is charged with the violation or act shall be permitted to observe and hear the testimony of the mentally retarded or developmentally disabled victim giving the testimony on a monitor, shall be provided with an electronic means of immediate communication with the attorney of the child who is charged with the violation or act during the testimony, and shall be restricted to a location from which the child who is charged with the violation or act cannot be seen or heard by the mentally retarded or developmentally disabled victim giving the testimony, except on a monitor provided for that purpose. The mentally retarded or developmentally disabled victim giving the testimony shall be provided with a monitor on which the mentally retarded or developmentally disabled victim can observe, while giving testimony, the child who is charged with the violation or act. No order for the taking of testimony by recording shall be issued under this division unless the provisions set forth in divisions (B)(2)(a), (b), (c), and (d) of this section apply to the recording of the testimony.

(F) For purposes of divisions (D) and (E) of this section, a juvenile judge may order the testimony of a mentally retarded or developmentally disabled victim to be taken outside of the room in which a proceeding is being conducted if the judge determines that the mentally retarded or developmentally disabled victim is unavailable to testify in the room in the physical presence of the child charged with the violation or act due to one or more of the following circumstances:

(1) The persistent refusal of the mentally retarded or developmentally disabled victim to testify despite judicial requests to do so;

(2) The inability of the mentally retarded or developmentally disabled victim to communicate about the alleged violation or offense because of extreme fear, failure of memory, or another similar reason;

(3) The substantial likelihood that the mentally retarded or developmentally disabled victim will suffer serious emotional trauma from so testifying.

(G)(1) If a juvenile judge issues an order pursuant to division (D) or (E) of this section that requires the testimony of a mentally retarded or developmentally disabled victim in a juvenile court proceeding to be taken outside of the room in which the proceeding is being conducted, the order shall specifically identify the mentally retarded or developmentally disabled victim to whose testimony it applies, the order applies only during the testimony of the specified mentally retarded or developmentally disabled victim, and the mentally retarded or developmentally disabled victim giving the testimony shall not be required to testify at the proceeding other than in accordance with the order. The authority of a judge to close the taking of a deposition under division (B)(2) of this section or a proceeding under division (D) or (E) of this section is in addition to the authority of a judge to close a hearing pursuant to section 2151.35 of the Revised Code.

(2) A juvenile judge who makes any determination regarding the admissibility of a deposition under divisions (B) and (C) of this section, the videotaping of a deposition under division (B)(2) of this section, or the taking of testimony outside of the room in which a proceeding is being conducted under division (D) or (E) of this section shall enter the determination and findings on the record in the proceeding.

(2004 S 178, eff. 1–30–04)

2152.83 Order classifying child as juvenile offender registrant; hearing to review effectiveness of disposition and treatment

(A)(1) The court that adjudicates a child a delinquent child shall issue as part of the dispositional order or, if the court commits the child for the delinquent act to the custody of a secure facility, shall issue at the time of the child's release from the secure facility, an order that classifies the child a juvenile offender registrant and specifies that the child has a duty to comply with sections 2950.04, 2950.041, 2950.05, and 2950.06 of the Revised Code if all of the following apply:

(a) The act for which the child is or was adjudicated a delinquent child is a sexually oriented offense that is not a registration-exempt sexually oriented offense or is a child-victim oriented offense that the child committed on or after January 1, 2002.

(b) The child was sixteen or seventeen years of age at the time of committing the offense.

(c) The court was not required to classify the child a juvenile offender registrant under section 2152.82 of the Revised Code.

(2) Prior to issuing the order required by division (A)(2) of this section, the judge shall conduct the hearing and make the determinations required by division (B) of section 2950.09 of the Revised Code regarding a sexually oriented offense that is not a registration-exempt sexually oriented offense or division (B) of section 2950.091 of the Revised Code regarding a child-victim oriented offense to determine if the child is to be classified a sexual predator or a child-victim predator, shall make the determinations required by division (E) of section 2950.09 of the Revised Code regarding a sexually oriented offense that is not a registration-exempt sexually oriented offense or division (E) of section 2950.091 of the Revised Code regarding a child-victim oriented offense to determine if the child is to be classified a habitual sex offender or a habitual child-victim offender, and shall otherwise comply with those divisions. When a judge issues an order under division (A)(1) of this section, the judge shall include in the order all of the determinations and information identified in division (B)(1) of section 2152.82 of the Revised Code that are relevant.

(B)(1) The court that adjudicates a child a delinquent child, on the judge's own motion, may conduct at the time of disposition of the child or, if the court commits the child for the delinquent act to the custody of a secure facility, may conduct at the time of the child's release from the secure facility, a hearing for the purposes described in division (B)(2) of this section if all of the following apply:

(a) The act for which the child is adjudicated a delinquent child is a sexually oriented offense that is not a registration-exempt sexually oriented offense or is a child-victim oriented offense that the child committed on or after January 1, 2002.

(b) The child was fourteen or fifteen years of age at the time of committing the offense.

(c) The court was not required to classify the child a juvenile offender registrant under section 2152.82 of the Revised Code.

(2) A judge shall conduct a hearing under division (B)(1) of this section to review the effectiveness of the disposition made of the child and of any treatment provided for the child placed in a secure setting and to determine whether the child should be classified a juvenile offender registrant. The judge may conduct the hearing on the judge's own initiative or based upon a recommendation of an officer or employee of the department of youth services, a probation officer, an employee of the court, or a prosecutor or law enforcement officer. If the judge conducts the hearing, upon completion of the hearing, the judge, in the judge's discretion and after consideration of the factors listed in division (E) of this section, shall do either of the following:

(a) Decline to issue an order that classifies the child a juvenile offender registrant and specifies that the child has a duty to comply with sections 2950.04, 2950.041, 2950.05, and 2950.06 of the Revised Code;

(b) Issue an order that classifies the child a juvenile offender registrant and specifies that the child has a duty to comply with sections 2950.04, 2950.041, 2950.05, and 2950.06 of the Revised Code and, if the judge conducts a hearing as described in division (C) of this section to determine whether the child is a sexual predator or child-victim predator or a habitual sex offender or habitual child-victim offender, include in the order a statement that the judge has determined that the child is, or is not, a sexual predator , child-victim predator, habitual sex offender, or habitual child-victim offender, whichever is applicable.

(C) A judge may issue an order under division (B) of this section that contains a determination that a delinquent child is a sexual predator or child-victim predator only if the judge, in accordance with the procedures specified in division (B) of section 2950.09 of the Revised Code regarding sexual predators or division (B) of section 2950.091 of the Revised Code regarding child-victim predators, determines at the hearing by clear and convincing evidence that the child is a sexual predator or a child-victim predator. A

judge may issue an order under division (B) of this section that contains a determination that a delinquent child is a habitual sex offender or a habitual child-victim offender only if the judge at the hearing determines as described in division (E) of section 2950.09 of the Revised Code regarding habitual sex offenders or division (E) of section 2950.091 of the Revised Code regarding habitual child-victim offenders that the child is a habitual sex offender or a habitual child-victim offender. If the judge issues an order under division (B) of this section that contains a determination that a delinquent child is a habitual sex offender or a habitual child-victim offender, the judge may impose a requirement subjecting the child to community notification provisions as described in division (E) of section 2950.09 or 2950.091 of the Revised Code, whichever is applicable. If the court conducts a hearing as described in this division to determine whether the child is a sexual predator or child-victim predator or a habitual sex offender or habitual child-victim offender, the judge shall comply with division (B) or (E) of section 2950.09 or 2950.091 of the Revised Code, whichever is applicable, in all regards.

(D) If a judge issues an order under division (A) or (B) of this section, the judge shall provide to the delinquent child and to the delinquent child's parent, guardian, or custodian a copy of the order and a notice containing the information described in divisions (A) and (B) of section 2950.03 of the Revised Code. The judge shall provide the notice at the time of the issuance of the order and shall comply with divisions (B) and (C) of that section regarding that notice and the provision of it.

The judge also shall include in the order a statement that, upon completion of the disposition of the delinquent child that was made for the sexually oriented offense or child-victim oriented offense upon which the order is based, a hearing will be conducted and the order is subject to modification or termination pursuant to section 2152.84 of the Revised Code.

(E) In making a decision under division (B) of this section as to whether a delinquent child should be classified a juvenile offender registrant and, if so, whether the child also is a sexual predator or child-victim predator or a habitual sex offender or habitual child-victim offender, a judge shall consider all relevant factors, including, but not limited to, all of the following:

(1) The nature of the sexually oriented offense that is not a registration-exempt sexually oriented offense or the child-victim oriented offense committed by the child;

(2) Whether the child has shown any genuine remorse or compunction for the offense;

(3) The public interest and safety;

(4) The factors set forth in division (B)(3) of section 2950.09 or 2950.091 of the Revised Code, whichever is applicable;

(5) The factors set forth in divisions (B) and (C) of section 2929.12 of the Revised Code as those factors apply regarding the delinquent child, the offense, and the victim;

(6) The results of any treatment provided to the child and of any follow-up professional assessment of the child.

(F) An order issued under division (A) or (B) of this section and any determinations included in the order shall remain in effect for the period of time specified in section 2950.07 of the Revised Code, subject to a modification or termination of the order under section 2152.84 of the Revised Code, and section 2152.851 of the Revised Code applies regarding the order and the determinations. The child's attainment of eighteen or twenty-one years of age does not affect or terminate the order, and the order remains in effect for the period of time described in this division.

(G) A court that adjudicates a child a delinquent child for a sexually oriented offense that is a registration-exempt sexually oriented offense shall not issue based on that adjudication an order under this section that classifies the child a juvenile offender registrant and specifies that the child has a duty to comply with sections 2950.04, 2950.041, 2950.05, and 2950.06 of the Revised Code.

(H) As used in the section, "secure facility" has the same meaning as in section 2950.01 of the Revised Code.

(2003 S 5, eff. 7–31–03; 2002 H 393, eff. 7–5–02; 2001 S 3, eff. 1–1–02)

Historical and Statutory Notes

Amendment Note: 2003 S 5 rewrote the section, which prior thereto read:

"(A)(1) The court that adjudicates a child a delinquent child shall issue as part of the dispositional order or, if the court commits the child for the delinquent act to the custody of a secure facility, shall issue at the time of the child's release from the secure facility, an order that classifies the child a juvenile sex offender registrant and specifies that the child has a duty to register under section 2950.04 of the Revised Code if all of the following apply:

"(a) The act for which the child is or was adjudicated a delinquent child is a sexually oriented offense that the child committed on or after January 1, 2002.

"(b) The child was sixteen or seventeen years of age at the time of committing the offense.

"(c) The court was not required to classify the child a juvenile sex offender registrant under section 2152.82 of the Revised Code.

"(2) Prior to issuing the order required by division (A)(2) of this section, the judge shall conduct the hearing and make the determinations required by division (B) of section 2950.09 of the Revised Code to determine if the child is to be classified as a sexual predator, shall make the determinations required by division (E) of that section to determine if the child is to be classified as a habitual sex offender, and shall otherwise comply with those divisions. When a judge issues an order under division (A)(1) of this section, the judge shall include in the order all of the determinations and information identified in division (B)(1) of section 2152. 82 of the Revised Code that are relevant.

"(B)(1) The court that adjudicates a child a delinquent child, on the judge's own motion, may conduct at the time of disposition of the child or, if the court commits the child for the delinquent act to the custody of a secure facility, may conduct at the time of the child's release from the secure facility, a hearing for the purposes described in division (B)(2) of this section if all of the following apply:

"(a) The act for which the child is adjudicated a delinquent child is a sexually oriented offense that the child committed on or after January 1, 2002.

"(b) The child was fourteen or fifteen years of age at the time of committing the offense.

"(c) The court was not required to classify the child a juvenile sex offender registrant under section 2152.82 of the Revised Code.

"(2) A judge shall conduct a hearing under division (B)(1) of this section to review the effectiveness of the disposition made of the child and of any treatment provided for the child placed in a secure setting and to determine whether the child should be classified a juvenile sex offender registrant. The judge may conduct the hearing on the judge's own initiative or based upon a recommendation of an officer or employee of the department of youth services, a probation officer, an employee of the court, or a prosecutor or law enforcement officer. If the judge conducts the hearing, upon completion of the hearing, the judge, in the judge's discretion and after consideration of the factors listed in division (E) of this section, shall do either of the following:

"(a) Decline to issue an order that classifies the child a juvenile sex offender registrant and specifies that the child has a duty to register under section 2950.04 of the Revised Code;

"(b) Issue an order that classifies the child a juvenile sex offender registrant and specifies that the child has a duty to register under section 2950.04 of the Revised Code and, if the judge determines as described in division (C) of this section that the child is a sexual predator or a habitual sex offender, include in the order a statement that the judge has determined that the child is a sexual predator or a habitual sex offender, whichever is applicable.

"(C) A judge may issue an order under division (B) of this section that contains a determination that a delinquent child is a sexual predator only if the judge, in accordance with the procedures specified in division (B) of section 2950.09 of the Revised Code, determines at the hearing by clear and convincing evidence that the child is a sexual predator. A judge may issue an order under division (B) of this section that contains a determination that a delinquent child is a habitual sex offender only if the judge at the hearing determines as described in division (E) of section 2950.09 of the Revised Code that the child is a habitual sex offender. If the judge issues an order under division (B) of this section that contains a determination that a delinquent child is a habitual sex offender, the judge may impose a requirement subjecting the child to community notification provisions as described in division (E) of section 2950.09 of the Revised Code.

"(D) If a judge issues an order under division (A) or (B) of this section, the judge shall provide to the delinquent child and to the delinquent child's parent, guardian, or custodian a copy of the order and a notice containing the information described in divisions (A) and (B) of section 2950.03 of the Revised Code. The judge shall provide the notice at the time of the issuance of the order, shall provide the notice as described in division (B)(1)(c) of that section, and shall comply with divisions (B)(1), (B)(2), and (C) of that section regarding that notice.

"The judge also shall include in the order a statement that, upon completion of the disposition of the delinquent child that was made for the sexually oriented offense upon which the order is based, a hearing will be conducted and the order is subject to modification or termination pursuant to section 2152.84 of the Revised Code.

"(E) In making a decision under division (B) of this section as to whether a delinquent child should be classified a juvenile sex offender registrant and, if so, whether the child also is a sexual predator or a habitual sex offender, a judge shall consider all relevant factors, including, but not limited to, all of the following:

"(1) The nature of the sexually oriented offense committed by the child;

"(2) Whether the child has shown any genuine remorse or compunction for the offense;

"(3) The public interest and safety;

"(4) The factors set forth in division (B)(3) of section 2950.09 of the Revised Code;

"(5) The factors set forth in divisions (B) and (C) of section 2929.12 of the Revised Code as those factors apply regarding the delinquent child, the offense, and the victim;

"(6) The results of any treatment provided to the child and of any follow-up professional assessment of the child.

"(F) An order issued under division (A) or (B) of this section shall remain in effect for the period of time specified in section 2950.07 of the Revised Code, subject to a modification or termination of the order under section 2152.84 of the Revised Code. The child's attainment of eighteen or twenty-one years of age does not affect or terminate the order, and the order remains in effect for the period of time described in this division.

"(G) As used in the section, 'secure facility' has the same meaning as in section 2950.01 of the Revised Code."

Amendment Note: 2002 H 393 rewrote divisions (A), (B), and (C) which prior thereto read:

"(A) If a child is adjudicated a delinquent child for committing on or after the effective date of this section a sexually oriented offense, if the child was sixteen or seventeen years of age at the time of committing the offense, and if the juvenile court judge was not required to classify the child a juvenile sex offender registrant under section 2152.82 of the Revised Code, upon the child's discharge or release from a secure facility or at the time of disposition if the judge does not commit the child to the custody of a secure facility, the juvenile court judge who adjudicated the child a delinquent child, or that judge's successor in office, shall issue an order that classifies the child a juvenile sex offender registrant and specifies that the child has a duty to register under section 2950.04 of the Revised Code. Prior to issuing the order, the judge shall conduct the hearing and make the determinations required by, and otherwise comply with, divisions (B) and (E) of section 2950.09 of the Revised Code. When a judge issues an order under division (A) of this section, the judge shall include in the order any determination that the delinquent child is a sexual predator or is a habitual sex offender that the judge makes pursuant to division (B) or (E) of section 2950.09 of the Revised Code and any related information required or authorized under the division under which the determination is made, including, but not limited to, any requirement imposed by the court subjecting a child who is a habitual sex offender to community notification provisions as described in division (E) of that section.

"(B) If a child is adjudicated a delinquent child for committing on or after the effective date of this section a sexually oriented offense, if the delinquent child was fourteen or fifteen years of age at the time of committing the offense, and if the juvenile court judge was not required to classify the child a juvenile sex offender registrant under section 2152.82 of the Revised Code, upon the child's discharge or release from a secure facility or at the time of disposition if the judge does not commit the child to the custody of a secure facility, the juvenile court judge who adjudicated the child a delinquent child, or that judge's successor in office, may, on the judge's own motion, conduct a hearing to review the effectiveness of the disposition and of any treatment provided for a child placed in a secure setting and to determine whether the child should be classified a juvenile sex offender registrant. The judge may conduct the hearing on the judge's own initiative or based upon a recommendation of an officer or employee of the department of youth services, a probation officer, an employee of the court, or a prosecutor or law enforcement officer. If the judge conducts the hearing, upon completion of the hearing, the judge, in the judge's discretion and after consideration of the factors listed in division (E) of this section, shall do either of the following:

"(1) Decline to issue an order that classifies the child a juvenile sex offender registrant and specifies that the child has a duty to register under section 2950.04 of the Revised Code;

"(2) Issue an order that classifies the child a juvenile sex offender registrant and specifies that the child has a duty to register under section 2950.04 of the Revised Code and, if the judge determines as described in division (C) of this section that the child is a sexual predator or a habitual sex offender, include in the order a statement that the judge has determined that the child is a sexual predator or a habitual sex offender, whichever is applicable.

"(C) A judge may issue an order under division (B) of this section that contains a determination that a delinquent child is a sexual predator only if the judge, in accordance with the procedures specified in division (B) of section 2950.09 of the Revised Code, determines at the hearing by clear and convincing evidence that the child is a sexual predator. A judge may issue an order under division (B) of this section that contains a determination that a delinquent child is a habitual sex offender only if the judge determines at the hearing as described in division (E) of section 2950.09 of the Revised Code that the child is a habitual sex offender. If the judge issues an order under division (B) of this section that contains a determination that a delinquent child is a habitual sex offender, the judge may impose a requirement subjecting the child to community notification provisions as described in division (E) of section 2950.09 of the Revised Code.''

Cross References

Adjudication of offender as sexual predator or as habitual sex offender; exclusion of registration-exempt sexually oriented offense, 2950.09.
Child-victim oriented offenses; duty of registration of offender or delinquent child, 2950.041.
Community notification of sex offender registration, 2950.11
Determination of offender as child-victim predator; hearing, 2950.091.
Determination of requirement to register as sex offender with sheriff, 2950.021.
Manner of registering as sex offenders, 2950.04.
Notice of duty to register as sex offender and related requirements, 2950.03.
Sex offenders, definitions, 2950.01.

Library References

OJur 3d: 48, Family Law § 1534, 1537, 1538
Carlin, Baldwin's Ohio Practice, Merrick–Rippner Probate Law § 107.93, 107.94, 107.95, 107.96, 107.97, 107.100 (2003).

2152.84 Hearings; orders

(A)(1) When a juvenile court judge issues an order under section 2152.82 or division (A) or (B) of section 2152.83 of the Revised Code that classifies a delinquent child a juvenile offender registrant and specifies that the child has a duty to comply with sections 2950.04, 2950.041, 2950.05, and 2950.06 of the Revised Code, upon completion of the disposition of that child made for the sexually oriented offense that is not a registration-exempt sexually oriented offense or the child-victim oriented offense on which the juvenile offender registrant order was based, the judge or the judge's successor in office shall conduct a hearing to review the effectiveness of the disposition and of any treatment provided for the child, to determine the risks that the child might re-offend, and to determine whether the prior classification of the child as a juvenile offender registrant and, if applicable, as a sexual predator or child-victim predator or as a habitual sex offender or habitual child-victim offender should be continued, modified, or terminated as provided under division (A)(2) of this section.

(2) Upon completion of a hearing under division (A)(1) of this section, the judge, in the judge's discretion and after consideration of the factors listed in division (E) of section 2152.83 of the Revised Code, shall do one of the following, as applicable:

(a) Enter an order that continues the classification of the delinquent child made in the prior order issued under section 2152.82 or division (A) or (B) of section 2152.83 of the Revised Code, and any sexual predator, child-victim predator, habitual sex offender, or habitual child-victim offender determination included in the order;

(b) If the prior order was issued under section 2152.82 or division (A) of section 2152.83 of the Revised Code and includes a determination by the judge that the delinquent child is a sexual predator or child-victim predator, enter, as applicable, an order that contains a determination that the child no longer is a sexual predator, the reason or reasons for that determination, and either a determination that the child is a habitual sex offender or a determination that the child remains a juvenile offender registrant but is not a sexual predator or habitual sex offender, or an order that contains a determination that the child no longer is a child-victim predator, the reason or reasons for that determination, and either a determination that the child is a habitual child-victim offender or a determination that the child remains a juvenile offender registrant but is not a child-victim predator or habitual child-victim offender;

(c) If the prior order was issued under section 2152.82 or division (A) of section 2152.83 of the Revised Code and does not include a sexual predator or child-victim predator determination as described in division (A)(2)(b) of this section but includes a determination by the judge that the delinquent child is a habitual sex offender or a habitual child-victim offender, enter, as applicable, an order that contains a determination that the child no longer is a habitual sex offender and a determination that the child remains a juvenile sex offender registrant but is not a habitual offender, or an order that contains a determination that the child no longer is a habitual child-victim offender and a determination that the child remains a juvenile offender registrant but is not a habitual child-victim offender;

(d) If the prior order was issued under division (B) of section 2152.83 of the Revised Code and includes a determination by the judge that the delinquent child is a sexual predator or child-victim predator, enter, as applicable, an order that contains a determination that the child no longer is a sexual predator, the reason or reasons for that determination, and either a determination that the child is a habitual sex offender, a determination that the child remains a juvenile offender registrant but is not a sexual predator or habitual sex offender, or a determination that the child no longer is a juvenile offender registrant and no longer has a duty to comply with sections 2950.04, 2950.05, and 2950.06 of the Revised Code, or an order that contains a determination that the child no longer is a child-victim predator, the reason or reasons for that determination, and either a determination that the child is a habitual child-victim offender, a determination that the child remains a juvenile offender registrant but is not a child-victim predator or habitual child-victim offender, or a determination that the child no longer is a juvenile offender registrant and no longer has a duty to comply with sections 2950.041, 2950.05, and 2950.06 of the Revised Code;

(e) If the prior order was issued under division (B) of section 2152.83 of the Revised Code and does not include a sexual predator or child-victim predator determination as described in division (A)(2)(d) of this section but includes a determination by the judge that the delinquent child is a habitual sex offender or habitual child-victim offender, enter, as applicable, an order that contains a determination that the child no longer is a habitual sex offender and either a determination that the child remains a juvenile offender registrant but is not a sexual predator or habitual sex offender or a determination that the child no longer is a juvenile offender registrant and no longer has a duty to comply with sections 2950.04, 2950.05, and 2950.06 of the Revised Code, or an order that contains a determination that the child no longer is a habitual child-victim offender and either a determination that the child remains a juvenile offender registrant but is not a child-victim predator or habitual child-victim offender or a determination that the child no longer is a juvenile offender registrant and no longer has a duty to comply with sections 2950.041,

2950.05, and 2950.06 of the Revised Code;

(f) If the prior order was issued under division (B) of section 2152.83 of the Revised Code and does not include a sexual predator or child-victim predator determination or a habitual sex offender or habitual child-victim offender determination as described in divisions (A)(2)(d) and (e) of this section, enter, as applicable, an order that contains a determination that the delinquent child no longer is a juvenile offender registrant and no longer has a duty to comply with sections 2950.04, 2950.05, and 2950.06 of the Revised Code, or an order that contains a determination that the delinquent child no longer is a juvenile offender registrant and no longer has a duty to comply with sections 2950.041, 2950.05, and 2950.06 of the Revised Code.

(B) If a judge issues an order under division (A)(2)(a) of this section that continues the prior classification of the delinquent child as a juvenile offender registrant and any sexual predator or habitual sex offender determination included in the order, or that continues the prior classification of the delinquent child as a juvenile offender registrant and any child-victim predator or habitual child-victim offender determination included in the order, the prior classification and the prior determination, if applicable, shall remain in effect.

A judge may issue an order under division (A)(2) of this section that contains a determination that a child no longer is a sexual predator or no longer is a child-victim predator only if the judge, in accordance with the procedures specified in division (D)(1) of section 2950.09 of the Revised Code regarding a sexual predator, determines at the hearing by clear and convincing evidence that the delinquent child is unlikely to commit a sexually oriented offense in the future, or the judge, in accordance with the procedures specified in division (D)(1) of section 2950.091 of the Revised Code regarding a child-victim predator, determines at the hearing by clear and convincing evidence that the delinquent child is unlikely to commit a child-victim oriented offense in the future. If the judge issues an order of that type, the judge shall provide the notifications described in division (D)(1) of section 2950.09 or 2950.091 of the Revised Code, whichever is applicable, and the recipient of the notification shall comply with the provisions of that division.

If a judge issues an order under division (A)(2) of this section that otherwise reclassifies the delinquent child, the judge shall provide a copy of the order to the bureau of criminal identification and investigation, and the bureau, upon receipt of the copy of the order, promptly shall notify the sheriff with whom the child most recently registered under section 2950.04 or 2950.041 of the Revised Code of the reclassification.

(C) If a judge issues an order under any provision of division (A)(2) of this section, the judge shall provide to the delinquent child and to the delinquent child's parent, guardian, or custodian a copy of the order and a notice containing the information described in divisions (A) and (B) of section 2950.03 of the Revised Code. The judge shall provide the notice at the time of the issuance of the order and shall comply with divisions (B) and (C) of that section regarding that notice and the provision of it.

(D) In making a decision under division (A) of this section, a judge shall consider all relevant factors, including, but not limited to, the factors listed in division (E) of section 2152.83 of the Revised Code.

(E) An order issued under division (A)(2) of this section and any determinations included in the order shall remain in effect for the period of time specified in section 2950.07 of the Revised Code, subject to a modification or termination of the order under section 2152.85 of the Revised Code, and section 2152.851 of the Revised Code applies regarding the order and the determinations. If an order is issued under division (A)(2) of this section, the child's attainment of eighteen or twenty-one years of age does not affect or terminate the order, and the order remains in effect for the period of time described in this division.

(2003 S 5, eff. 7–31–03; 2002 H 393, eff. 7–5–02; 2001 S 3, eff. 1–1–02)

Historical and Statutory Notes

Amendment Note: 2003 S 5 rewrote the section, which prior thereto read:

"(A)(1) When a juvenile court judge issues an order under section 2152.82 or division (A) or (B) of section 2152.83 of the Revised Code that classifies a delinquent child a juvenile sex offender registrant and specifies that the child has a duty to register under section 2950.04 of the Revised Code, upon completion of the disposition of that child made for the sexually oriented offense on which the juvenile

sex offender registrant order was based, the judge or the judge's successor in office shall conduct a hearing to review the effectiveness of the disposition and of any treatment provided for the child, to determine the risks that the child might re-offend, and to determine whether the prior classification of the child as a juvenile sex offender registrant and, if applicable, as a sexual predator or habitual sex offender should be continued, modified, or terminated as provided under division (A)(2) of this section.

"(2) Upon completion of a hearing under division (A)(1) of this section, the judge, in the judge's discretion and after consideration of the factors listed in division (E) of section 2152.83 of the Revised Code, shall do one of the following, as applicable:

"(a) Enter an order that continues the classification of the delinquent child made in the prior order issued under section 2152.82 or division (A) or (B) of section 2152.83 of the Revised Code, and any sexual predator or habitual sex offender determination included in the order;

"(b) If the prior order was issued under section 2152.82 or division (A) of section 2152.83 of the Revised Code and includes a determination by the judge that the delinquent child is a sexual predator, enter an order that contains a determination that the delinquent child no longer is a sexual predator and that also contains either a determination that the delinquent child is a habitual sex offender or a determination that the delinquent child remains a juvenile sex offender registrant but is not a sexual predator or habitual sex offender;

"(c) If the prior order was issued under section 2152.82 or division (A) of section 2152.83 of the Revised Code and does not include a sexual predator determination as described in division (A)(2)(b) of this section but includes a determination by the judge that the delinquent child is a habitual sex offender, enter an order that contains a determination that the delinquent child no longer is a habitual sex offender and that also contains a determination that the delinquent child remains a juvenile sex offender registrant but is not a habitual sex offender;

"(d) If the prior order was issued under division (B) of section 2152.83 of the Revised Code and includes a determination by the judge that the delinquent child is a sexual predator, enter an order that contains a determination that the delinquent child no longer is a sexual predator and that also contains a determination that the delinquent child is a habitual sex offender, a determination that the delinquent child remains a juvenile sex offender registrant but is not a sexual predator or habitual sex offender, or a determination that specifies that the delinquent child no longer is a juvenile sex offender registrant and no longer has a duty to register under section 2950.04 of the Revised Code;

"(e) If the prior order was issued under division (B) of section 2152.83 of the Revised Code and does not include a sexual predator determination as described in division (A)(2)(d) of this section but includes a determination by the judge that the delinquent child is a habitual sex offender, enter an order that contains a determination that the child no longer is a habitual sex offender and that also contains either a determination that the child remains a juvenile sex offender registrant but is not a sexual predator or habitual sex offender or a determination that specifies that the child no longer is a juvenile sex offender registrant and no longer has a duty to register under section 2950.04 of the Revised Code;

"(f) If the prior order was issued under division (B) of section 2152.83 of the Revised Code and does not include a sexual predator determination or a habitual sex offender determination as described in divisions (A)(2)(d) and (e) of this section, enter an order that contains a determination that the delinquent child no longer is a juvenile sex offender registrant and no longer has a duty to register under section 2950.04 of the Revised Code.

"(B) If a judge issues an order under division (A)(2)(a) of this section that continues the prior classification of the delinquent child as a juvenile sex offender registrant and any sexual predator or habitual sex offender determination included in the order, the prior classification and the prior determination, if applicable, shall remain in effect.

"A judge may issue an order under division (A)(2) of this section that contains a determination that a child no longer is a sexual predator only if the judge, in accordance with the procedures specified in division (D)(1) of section 2950.09 of the Revised Code, determines at the hearing by clear and convincing evidence that the delinquent child is unlikely to commit a sexually oriented offense in the future. If the judge issues an order of that type, the judge shall provide the notifications described in division (D)(1) of section 2950.09 of the Revised Code, and the recipient of the notification shall comply with the provisions of that division.

"If a judge issues an order under division (A)(2) of this section that otherwise reclassifies the delinquent child, the judge shall provide a copy of the order to the bureau of criminal identification and investigation, and the bureau, upon receipt of the copy of the order, promptly shall notify the sheriff with whom the child most recently registered under section 2950.04 of the Revised Code of the reclassification.

"(C) If a judge issues an order under any provision of division (A)(2) of this section, the judge shall provide to the delinquent child and to the delinquent child's parent, guardian, or custodian a copy of the order and a notice containing the information described in divisions (A) and (B) of section 2950.03 of the Revised Code. The judge shall provide the notice at the time of the issuance of the order, shall provide the notice as described in division (B)(1)(c) of that section, and shall comply with divisions (B)(1), (B)(2), and (C) of that section regarding that notice.

"(D) In making a decision under division (A) of this section, a judge shall consider all relevant factors, including, but not limited to, the factors listed in division (E) of section 2152.83 of the Revised Code.

"(E) An order issued under division (A)(2) of this section and any determinations included in the order shall remain in effect for the period of time specified in section 2950.07 of the Revised Code, subject to a modification or termination of the order under section 2152.85 of the Revised Code. If an order is issued under division (A)(2) of this section, the child's attainment of eighteen or twenty-one years of age does not affect or terminate the order, and the order remains in effect for the period of time described in this division."

Amendment Note: 2002 H 393 rewrote this section which prior thereto read:

"(A)(1) When a juvenile court judge issues an order under section 2152.82 or division (A) or (B) of section 2152.83 of the Revised Code that classifies a delinquent child a juvenile sex offender registrant and specifies that the child has a duty to register under section 2950.04 of the Revised Code, upon completion of the disposition of that delinquent child that the judge made for the sexually oriented offense on which the juvenile sex offender registrant order was based, the judge or the judge's successor in office shall conduct a hearing to do all of the following:

"(a) Review the effectiveness of the disposition and of any treatment provided for the child;

"(b) If the order also contains a determination that the delinquent child is a sexual predator or habitual sex offender that the court made pursuant to division (B) or (E) of section 2950.09 of the Revised Code, determine whether the classification of the child as a sexual predator, habitual sex offender, or juvenile sex offender registrant should be continued or modified or, regarding an order issued under division (B) of section 2152.83 of the Revised Code, terminated;

"(c) If the order was issued under division (B) of section 2152.83 of the Revised Code and does not contain a sexual predator determination that the court makes as described in division (A)(1)(b) of this section, determine whether the classification of the child as a juvenile sex offender registrant should be continued, modified, or terminated.

"(2) Upon completion of a hearing under division (A)(1) of this section, the judge, in the judge's discretion and after consideration of the factors listed in division (E) of this section, shall do one of the following, as applicable:

"(a) Enter an order that continues the classification of the delinquent child made in the order issued under section 2152.82 or division (A) or (B) of section 2152.83 of the Revised Code, and any sexual predator or habitual sex offender determination included in the order;

"(b) If the order was issued under section 2152.82 or division (A) of section 2152.83 of the Revised Code and includes a determination by the judge that the delinquent child is a sexual predator, enter an order that contains a determination that the delinquent child no longer is a sexual predator and that also contains either a determination that the delinquent child is a habitual sex offender or a determination that the delinquent child remains a juvenile sex offender registrant but is not a sexual predator or habitual sex offender;

"(c) If the order was issued under section 2152.82 or division (A) of section 2152.83 of the Revised Code and does not include a sexual predator determination as described in division (A)(2)(b) of this section but includes a determination by the judge that the delinquent child is a habitual sex offender, enter an order that contains a determination that the delinquent child no longer is a habitual sex offender and that also contains a determination that the delinquent child remains a juvenile sex offender registrant but is not a habitual sex offender;

"(d) If the order was issued under division (B) of section 2152.83 of the Revised Code and includes a determination by the judge that the delinquent child is a sexual predator, enter an order that contains a determination that the delinquent child no longer is a sexual predator and that also contains a determination that the delinquent child is a habitual sex offender, a determination that the delinquent child remains a juvenile sex offender registrant but is not a sexual predator or habitual sex offender, or a determination that specifies that the delinquent child no longer is a juvenile sex offender registrant and no longer has a duty to register under section 2950.04 of the Revised Code;

"(e) If the order was issued under division (B) of section 2152.83 of the Revised Code and does not include a sexual predator determination as described in division (A)(2)(d) of this section but includes a determination by the judge that the delinquent child is a habitual sex offender, enter an order that contains a determination that the child no longer is a habitual sex offender and that also contains either a determination that the child remains a juvenile sex offender registrant but is not a sexual predator or habitual sex offender or a determination that specifies that the child no longer is a juvenile sex offender registrant and no longer has a duty to register under section 2950.04 of the Revised Code;

"(f) If the order was issued under division (B) of section 2152.83 of the Revised Code and the order does not include a sexual predator determination or a habitual sex offender determination as described in divisions (A)(2)(d) and (e) of this section, enter an order that contains a determination that the delinquent child no longer is a juvenile sex offender registrant and no longer has a duty to register under section 2950.04 of the Revised Code.

"(B) If a judge issues an order under division (A)(2)(a) of this section that continues the prior classification of the delinquent child as a juvenile sex offender registrant and any sexual predator or habitual sex offender determination included in the order, the prior classification and the prior determination, if applicable, shall remain in effect.

"A judge may issue an order under division (A)(2) of this section that contains a determination that a child no longer is a sexual predator only if the judge, in accordance with the procedures specified in division (D)(1) of section 2950.09 of the Revised Code, determines at the hearing by clear and convincing evidence that the delinquent child is unlikely to commit a sexually oriented offense in the future. If the judge issues an order of that type, the judge shall provide the notifications described in division (D)(1) of section 2950.09 of the Revised Code, and the recipient of the notification shall comply with the provisions of that division.

"(C) If a judge issues an order under any provision of division (A)(2) of this section, the judge shall provide to the delinquent child and to the delinquent child's parent, guardian, or custodian a copy of the order and a notice containing the information described in divisions (A) and (B) of section 2950.03 of the Revised Code. The judge shall provide the notice at the time of the issuance of the order, shall provide the notice as described in division (B)(1)(c) of that section, and shall comply with divisions (B)(1), (B)(2), and (C) of that section regarding that notice.

"(D) In making a decision under division (A) of this section, a judge shall consider all relevant factors, including, but not limited to, the factors listed in division (E) of section 2152.83 of the Revised Code.

"(E) An order issued under division (A)(2) of this section and any determinations included in the order shall remain in effect for the period of time specified in section 2950.07 of the Revised Code, subject to a modification or termination of the order under section 2152.85 of the Revised Code. If an order is issued under division (A)(2) of this section, the child's attainment of eighteen or twenty-one years of age does not affect or terminate the order, and the order remains in effect for the period of time described in this division."

Cross References

Adjudication of offender as sexual predator or as habitual sex offender; exclusion of registration-exempt sexually oriented offense, 2950.09.
Child-victim oriented offenses; duty of registration of offender or delinquent child, 2950.041.
Community notification of sex offender registration, 2950.11.
Determination of offender as child-victim predator; hearing, 2950.091.
Determination of requirement to register as sex offender with sheriff, 2950.021.
Manner of registering as sex offenders, 2950.04.

Notice of duty to register as sex offender and related requirements, 2950.03.
Sex offenders, definitions, 2950.01.
Verification of current address of residence, school, or place of employment, 2950.06.

Ohio Administrative Code References
Completion and transmittal of forms, OAC 109:5–2–02

Library References
OJur 3d: 48, Family Law § 1534, 1537, 1538
Carlin, Baldwin's Ohio Practice, Merrick–Rippner Probate Law § 107.93, 107.94, 107.95, 107.96, 107.97, 107.100 (2003).

2152.85 Petitioning of judge by juvenile offender registrant

(A) Upon the expiration of the applicable period of time specified in division (B)(1) or (2) of this section, a delinquent child who has been classified pursuant to this section or section 2152.82 or 2152.83 of the Revised Code a juvenile offender registrant may petition the judge who made the classification, or that judge's successor in office, to do one of the following:

(1) If the order containing the juvenile offender registrant classification also includes a determination by the juvenile court judge that the delinquent child is a sexual predator or child-victim predator in the manner described in section 2152.82 or 2152.83 of the Revised Code and that determination remains in effect, to enter, as applicable, an order that contains a determination that the child no longer is a sexual predator, the reason or reasons for that determination, and either a determination that the child is a habitual sex offender or a determination that the child remains a juvenile offender registrant but is not a sexual predator or habitual sex offender, or an order that contains a determination that the child no longer is a child-victim predator, the reason or reasons for that determination, and either a determination that the child is a habitual child-victim offender or a determination that the child remains a juvenile offender registrant but is not a child-victim predator or habitual child-victim offender;

(2) If the order containing the juvenile offender registrant classification under section 2152.82 or 2152.83 of the Revised Code or under division (C)(2) of this section pursuant to a petition filed under division (A) of this section does not include a sexual predator or child-victim predator determination as described in division (A)(1) of this section but includes a determination by the juvenile court

judge that the delinquent child is a habitual sex offender or a habitual child-victim offender in the manner described in section 2152.82 or 2152.83 of the Revised Code, or in this section, and that determination remains in effect, to enter, as applicable, an order that contains a determination that the child no longer is a habitual sex offender and either a determination that the child remains a juvenile offender registrant or a determination that the child no longer is a juvenile offender registrant and no longer has a duty to comply with sections 2950.04, 2950.05, and 2950.06 of the Revised Code, or an order that contains a determination that the child no longer is a habitual child-victim offender and either a determination that the child remains a juvenile offender registrant or a determination that the child no longer is a juvenile offender registrant and no longer has a duty to comply with sections 2950.041, 2950.05, and 2950.06 of the Revised Code;

(3) If the order containing the juvenile offender registrant classification under section 2152.82 or 2152.83 of the Revised Code or under division (C)(2) of this section pursuant to a petition filed under division (A) of this section does not include a sexual predator or child-victim predator determination or a habitual sex offender or habitual child-victim offender determination as described in division (A)(1) or (2) of this section, to enter, as applicable, an order that contains a determination that the child no longer is a juvenile offender registrant and no longer has a duty to comply with sections 2950.04, 2950.05, and 2950.06 of the Revised Code, or an order that contains a determination that the child no longer is a juvenile offender registrant and no longer has a duty to comply with sections 2950.041, 2950.05, and 2950.06 of the Revised Code.

(B) A delinquent child who has been adjudicated a delinquent child for committing on or after January 1, 2002, a sexually oriented offense that is not a registration-exempt sexually oriented offense and who has been classified a juvenile offender registrant relative to that offense or who has been adjudicated a delinquent child for committing on or after that date a child-victim oriented offense and who has been classified a juvenile offender registrant relative to that offense may file a petition under division (A) of this section requesting reclassification or declassification as de-

scribed in that division after the expiration of one of the following periods of time:

(1) The delinquent child initially may file a petition not earlier than three years after the entry of the juvenile court judge's order after the mandatory hearing conducted under section 2152.84 of the Revised Code.

(2) After the delinquent child's initial filing of a petition under division (B)(1) of this section, the child may file a second petition not earlier than three years after the judge has entered an order deciding the petition under division (B)(1) of this section.

(3) After the delinquent child's filing of a petition under division (B)(2) of this section, thereafter, the delinquent child may file a petition under this division upon the expiration of five years after the judge has entered an order deciding the petition under division (B)(2) of this section or the most recent petition the delinquent child has filed under this division.

(C) Upon the filing of a petition under divisions (A) and (B) of this section, the judge may review the prior classification or determination in question and, upon consideration of all relevant factors and information, including, but not limited to the factors listed in division (E) of section 2152.83 of the Revised Code, the judge, in the judge's discretion, shall do one of the following:

(1) Enter an order denying the petition;

(2) Issue an order that reclassifies or declassifies the delinquent child, in the requested manner specified in division (A)(1), (2), or (3) of this section.

(D) If a judge issues an order under division (C) of this section that denies a petition, the prior classification of the delinquent child as a juvenile offender registrant, and the prior determination that the child is a sexual predator, child-victim predator, habitual sex offender, or habitual child-victim offender, if applicable, shall remain in effect.

A judge may issue an order under division (C) of this section that contains a determination that a child no longer is a sexual predator or no longer is a child-victim predator only if the judge conducts a hearing and, in accordance with the procedures specified in division (D)(1) of section 2950.09 of the Revised Code regarding a sexual predator, determines at the hearing by clear and convincing evidence that the delinquent child is unlikely to commit a sexually oriented offense in the future, or, in accordance with the procedures specified in division (D)(1) of section 2950.091 of the Revised Code regarding a child-victim predator, determines at the hearing by clear and convincing evidence that the delinquent child is unlikely to commit a child-victim oriented offense in the future. If the judge issues an order of that type, the judge shall provide the notifications described in division (D)(1) of section 2950.09 or 2950.091 of the Revised Code, whichever is applicable, and the recipient of the notification shall comply with the provisions of that division.

A judge may issue an order under division (C) of this section that contains a determination that a delinquent child is a habitual sex offender or a habitual child-victim offender only if the judge conducts a hearing and determines at the hearing as described in division (E) of section 2950.09 of the Revised Code regarding habitual sex offenders or division (E) of section 2950.091 of the Revised Code regarding habitual child-victim offenders that the child is a habitual sex offender or a habitual child-victim offender. If the judge issues an order that contains a determination that a delinquent child is a habitual sex offender or a habitual child-victim offender, the judge may impose a requirement subjecting the child to community notification provisions as described in that division.

(E) If a judge issues an order under division (C) of this section, the judge shall provide to the delinquent child and to the delinquent child's parent, guardian, or custodian a copy of the order and a notice containing the information described in divisions (A) and (B) of section 2950.03 of the Revised Code. The judge shall provide the notice at the time of the issuance of the order and shall comply with divisions (B) and (C) of that section regarding that notice and the provision of it.

(F) An order issued under division (C) of this section shall remain in effect for the period of time specified in section 2950.07 of the Revised Code, subject to a further modification or a termination of the order under this section, and section 2152.851 of the Revised Code applies regarding the order and the determinations. If an order is issued under division (C) of this section, the child's at-

tainment of eighteen or twenty-one years of age does not affect or terminate the order, and the order remains in effect for the period of time described in this division.

(2003 S 5, eff. 7–31–03; 2001 S 3, eff. 1–1–02)

Historical and Statutory Notes

Amendment Note: 2003 S 5 rewrote the section, which prior thereto read:

"(A) Upon the expiration of the applicable period of time specified in division (B)(1) or (2) of this section, a delinquent child who has been classified pursuant to this section or section 2152.82 or 2152.83 of the Revised Code a juvenile sex offender registrant may petition the judge who made the classification, or that judge's successor in office, to do one of the following:

"(1) If the order containing the juvenile sex offender registrant classification also includes a determination by the juvenile court judge that the delinquent child is a sexual predator relative to the sexually oriented offense in the manner described in section 2152.82 or 2152.83 of the Revised Code and that determination remains in effect, to enter an order that contains a determination that the child no longer is a sexual predator and that also contains either a determination that the child is a habitual sex offender or a determination that the child remains a juvenile sex offender registrant but is not a sexual predator or habitual sex offender;

"(2) If the order containing the juvenile sex offender registrant classification under section 2152.82 or 2152.83 of the Revised Code or under division (C)(2) of this section pursuant to a petition filed under division (A) of this section does not include a sexual predator determination as described in division (A)(1) of this section but includes a determination by the juvenile court judge that the delinquent child is a habitual sex offender relative to the sexually oriented offense in the manner described in section 2152.82 or 2152.83 of the Revised Code, or in this section, and that determination remains in effect, to enter an order that contains a determination that the child no longer is a habitual sex offender and that also contains either a determination that the child remains a juvenile sex offender registrant or a determination that the child no longer is a juvenile sex offender registrant and no longer has a duty to register under section 2950.04 of the Revised Code;

"(3) If the order containing the juvenile sex offender registrant classification under section 2152.82 or 2152.83 of the Revised Code or under division (C)(2) of this section pursuant to a petition filed under division (A) of this section does not include a sexual predator or habitual sex offender determination as described in division (A)(1) or (2) of this section, to enter an order that contains a determination that the child no longer is a juvenile sex offender registrant and no longer has a duty to register under section 2950.04 of the Revised Code.

"(B) A delinquent child who has been adjudicated a delinquent child for committing on or after the effective date of this section a sexually oriented offense and who has been classified a juvenile sex offender registrant relative to that sexually oriented offense may file a petition under division (A) of this section requesting reclassification or declassification as described in that division after the expiration of one of the following periods of time:

"(1) The delinquent child initially may file a petition not earlier than three years after the entry of the juvenile court judge's order after the mandatory hearing conducted under section 2152.84 of the Revised Code.

"(2) After the delinquent child's initial filing of a petition under division (B)(1) of this section, the child may file a second petition not earlier than three years after the judge has entered an order deciding the petition under division (B)(1) of this section.

"(3) After the delinquent child's filing of a petition under division (B)(2) of this section, thereafter, the delinquent child may file a petition under this division upon the expiration of five years after the judge has entered an order deciding the petition under division (B)(2) of this section or the most recent petition the delinquent child has filed under this division.

"(C) Upon the filing of a petition under divisions (A) and (B) of this section, the judge may review the prior classification or determination in question and, upon consideration of all relevant factors and information, including, but not limited to the factors listed in division (E) of section 2152.83 of the Revised Code, the judge, in the judge's discretion, shall do one of the following:

"(1) Enter an order denying the petition;

"(2) Issue an order that reclassifies or declassifies the delinquent child, in the requested manner specified in division (A)(1), (2), or (3) of this section.

"(D) If a judge issues an order under division (C) of this section that denies a petition, the prior classification of the delinquent child as a juvenile sex offender registrant, and the prior determination that the child is a sexual predator or habitual sex offender, if applicable, shall remain in effect.

"A judge may issue an order under division (C) of this section that contains a determination that a child no longer is a sexual predator only if the judge conducts a hearing and, in accordance with the procedures specified in division (D)(1) of section 2950.09 of the Revised Code, determines at the hearing by clear and convincing evidence that the delinquent child is unlikely to commit a sexually oriented offense in the future. If the judge issues an order of that type, the judge shall provide the notifications described in division (D)(1) of section 2950.09 of the Revised Code, and the recipient of the notification shall comply with the provisions of that division.

"A judge may issue an order under division (C) of this section that contains a determination that a delinquent child is a habitual sex offender only if the judge conducts a hearing and determines at the hearing as described in division (E) of section 2950.09 of the Revised Code that the child is a habitual sex offender. If the judge issues an order that contains a determination that a delinquent child is a habitual sex offender , the judge may impose a requirement subjecting the child to community notification provisions as described in that division.

"(E) If a judge issues an order under division (C) of this section, the judge shall provide to the delinquent child and to the delinquent child's parent, guardian, or custodian a copy of the order and a notice containing the information described in divisions (A) and (B) of section 2950.03 of the Revised Code. The judge shall provide the notice at the time of the issuance of the order, shall provide the notice as described in division (B)(1)(c) of section 2950.03 of the Revised Code, and shall comply with divisions (B)(1), (B)(2), and (C) of that section regarding that notice.

"(F) An order issued under division (C) of this section shall remain in effect for the period of time specified in section 2950.07 of the Revised Code, subject to a further modification or a termination of the order under this section. If an order is issued under division (C) of this section, the child's attainment of eighteen or twenty-one years of age does not affect or terminate the order, and the order remains in effect for the period of time described in this division."

Cross References

Adjudication of offender as sexual predator or as habitual sex offender; exclusion of registration-exempt sexually oriented offense, 2950.09.
Child-victim oriented offenses; duty of registration of offender or delinquent child, 2950.041.
Community notification of sex offender registration, 2950.11
Determination of offender as child-victim predator; hearing, 2950.091.
Determination of requirement to register as sex offender with sheriff, 2950.021.
Manner of registering as sex offenders, 2950.04.
Notice of duty to register as sex offender and related requirements, 2950.03.
Sex offenders, definitions, 2950.01.
Verification of current address of residence, school, or place of employment, 2950.06.

Ohio Administrative Code References

Completion and transmittal of forms, OAC 109:5–2–02

Library References

OJur 3d: 48, Family Law § 1534, 1537, 1538
Carlin, Baldwin's Ohio Practice, Merrick–Rippner Probate Law § 107.89, 107.93, 107.94, 107.95, 107.96, 107.97, 107.100 (2003).

2152.851 Effect of redesignation of offense on existing order

(A) If, prior to the effective date of this section, a judge issues an order under section 2152.82, 2152.83, 2152.84, or 2152.85 of the Revised Code that classifies a delinquent child a juvenile offender registrant and if, on and after the effective date of this section, the sexually oriented offense upon which the order was based no longer is considered a sexually oriented offense but instead is a child-victim oriented offense, notwithstanding the redesignation of the offense, the order shall remain in effect for the period described in the section under which it was issued, the order shall be considered for all purposes to be an order that classifies the child a juvenile offender registrant, division (A)(2)(b) of section 2950.041 of the Revised Code applies regarding the child, and the duty to register imposed pursuant to that division shall be considered, for purposes of section 2950.07 of the Revised Code and for all other purposes, to be a continuation of the duty imposed upon the child prior to the effective date of this section under the order issued under section 2152.82,

2152.83, 2152.84, or 2152.85 and Chapter 2950. of the Revised Code.

(B) If an order of the type described in division (A) of this section included a classification or determination that the delinquent child was a sexual predator or habitual sex offender, notwithstanding the redesignation of the offense upon which the determination was based, all of the following apply:

(1) Divisions (A)(1) and (2) or (E)(1) and (2) of section 2950.091 of the Revised Code apply regarding the child and the judge's order made prior to the effective date of this section shall be considered for all purposes to be an order that classifies the child as described in those divisions;

(2) The child's classification or determination under divisions (A)(1) and (2) or (E)(1) and (2) of section 2950.091 of the Revised Code shall be considered, for purposes of section 2950.07 of the Revised Code and for all other purposes, to be a continuation of classification or determination made prior to the effective date of this section;

(3) The child's duties under Chapter 2950. of the Revised Code relative to that classification or determination shall be considered for all purposes to be a continuation of the duties related to that classification or determination as they existed prior to the effective date of this section.

(2003 S 5, eff. 7–31–03)

PENALTIES

2152.99 **Penalties**

Whoever violates division (G) of section 2152.72 of the Revised Code is guilty of a minor misdemeanor.

(2000 S 179, § 3, eff. 1–1–02)

Library References

OJur 3d: 48, Family Law § 1534, 1537, 1538

RULES OF JUVENILE PROCEDURE

Publisher's Note: These Rules are published as they appear in the *Ohio Official Reports*.

Publisher's Note: Until 1968, when the Modern Courts Amendment to the Ohio Constitution was adopted, Ohio court procedure was governed entirely by statute and case law. The Modern Courts Amendment required the Supreme Court of Ohio, subject to the approval of the General Assembly, to "prescribe rules governing practice and procedure in all courts of the state." Rules of practice and procedure are the Civil, Criminal, Appellate, and Juvenile Rules, Rules of the Court of Claims, and the Ohio Rules of Evidence. Pursuant to Ohio Constitution Article IV, Section 5(B), such rules "shall not abridge, enlarge, or modify any substantive right," and " [a]ll laws in conflict with such rules shall be of no further force or effect."

Publisher's Note: The Supreme Court Rules Advisory Committee prepared Staff Notes for each of the substantive rule amendments. The Staff Note follows the applicable rule. Although the Supreme Court used the Staff Notes as background for its deliberations, the Staff Notes are not adopted by the Court and are not a part of the rule. Where they interpret the law, describe present conditions, or predict future practices, the Staff Notes represent the views of the Rules Advisory Committee and not necessarily the views of the Supreme Court. Each staff note should be read in light of the language of the rule at the time of its adoption or amendment.

Rule
1 Scope of rules: applicability; construction; exceptions
2 Definitions
3 Waiver of rights
4 Assistance of counsel; guardian ad litem
5 [Reserved]
6 Taking into custody
7 Detention and shelter care
8 Filing by electronic means
9 Intake
10 Complaint
11 Transfer to another county
12 [Reserved]
13 Temporary disposition; temporary orders; emergency medical and surgical treatment
14 Termination, extension or modification of temporary custody orders
15 Process: issuance, form
16 Process: service
17 Subpoena
18 Time
19 Motions
20 Service and filing of papers when required subsequent to filing of complaint
21 Preliminary conferences
22 Pleadings and motions; defenses and objections
23 Continuance
24 Discovery
25 Depositions
26 [Reserved]
27 Hearings: general
28 [Reserved]
29 Adjudicatory hearing
30 Relinquishment of jurisdiction for purposes of criminal prosecution
31 [Reserved]
32 Social history; physical examination; mental examination; investigation involving the allocation of parental rights and responsibilities for the care of children
33 [Reserved]

Rule
34 Dispositional hearing
35 Proceedings after judgment
36 Dispositional review
37 Recording of proceedings
38 Voluntary surrender of custody
39 Out of county removal hearings
40 Magistrates
41 [Reserved]
42 Consent to marry
43 Reference to Ohio Revised Code
44 Jurisdiction unaffected
45 Rules by juvenile courts; procedure not otherwise specified
46 Forms
47 Effective date
48 Title

Cross References

Cuyahoga county juvenile court, jurisdiction, 2153.16

Humane societies, protection of children, 1717.14

Judges of the court of domestic relations, juvenile court responsibility, 2301.03

Trial, magistrate courts, applicability of chapter, 2938.02

Youth commission, commitment of children, assignment to juvenile diagnostic center, 5139.05

Law Review and Journal Commentaries

An Answer to the Challenge of Kent, Daniels W. McLean. 53 A B A J 456 (May 1967).

Evidence in Cuyahoga County Juvenile Court, Elaine J. Columbro. 10 Clev–Marshall L Rev 524 (September 1961).

In re Gault, Juvenile Courts and Lawyers, Norman Lefstein. 53 A B A J 811 (September 1967).

The Juvenile Court—A Court of Law, Walter G. Whitlatch. 18 W Reserve U L Rev 1239 (May 1967).

The Juvenile Court: Effective Justice or Benevolent Despotism?, Bertram Polow. 53 A B A J 31 (January 1967).

Juvenile Court: "Neglected Child" of the Judiciary, Hon. Albert A. Woldman. 37 Clev B J 257 (September 1966).

Juvenile Court: Time for Change, Charles Auerbach. 37 Clev B J 179 (June 1966).

The Kent Case and the Juvenile Court: A Challenge to Lawyers, Robert Gardner. 52 A B A J 923 (October 1966).

A legal look at Juvenile Court, Paul W. Alexander. 27 Clev B J 171 (August 1956).

Rights of Children: The Legal Vacuum, Lois G. Forer. 55 A B A J 1151 (December 1969).

Role of the Attorney in Juvenile Court, Julian Greenspun. 18 Clev St L Rev 599 (September 1969).

Rules of the Juvenile Court of Cuyahoga County. Vol 33 Cuyahoga County B Ass'n Bull, No. 8.

A synopsis of Ohio Juvenile Court Law, Hon. Don J. Young, Jr. 31 U Cin L Rev 131 (Spring 1962).

A Way Out of Juvenile Delinquency, Roman C. Pucinski. 54 A B A J 33 (January 1968).

Juv R 1   Scope of rules: applicability; construction; exceptions

(A) Applicability

These rules prescribe the procedure to be followed in all juvenile courts of this state in all proceedings coming within the jurisdiction of such courts, with the exceptions stated in subdivision (C).

(B) Construction

These rules shall be liberally interpreted and construed so as to effectuate the following purposes:

(1) to effect the just determination of every juvenile court proceeding by ensuring the parties a fair hearing and the recognition and enforcement of their constitutional and other legal rights;

(2) to secure simplicity and uniformity in procedure, fairness in administration, and the elimination of unjustifiable expense and delay;

(3) to provide for the care, protection, and mental and physical development of children subject to the jurisdiction of the juvenile court, and to protect the welfare of the community; and

(4) to protect the public interest by treating children as persons in need of supervision, care and rehabilitation.

(C) Exceptions

These rules shall not apply to procedure (1) Upon appeal to review any judgment, order, or ruling; (2) Upon the trial of criminal actions; (3) Upon the trial of actions for divorce, annulment, legal separation, and related proceedings; (4) In proceedings to determine parent-child relationships, provided, however that appointment of counsel shall be in accordance with Rule 4(A) of the Rules of Juvenile Procedure; (5) In the commitment of the mentally ill and mentally retarded; (6) In proceedings under sec-

tion 2151.85 of the Revised Code to the extent that there is a conflict between these rules and section 2151.85 of the Revised Code.

When any statute provides for procedure by general or specific reference to the statutes governing procedure in juvenile court actions, procedure shall be in accordance with these rules.

(Adopted eff. 7–1–72; amended eff. 7–1–91, 7–1–94, 7–1–95)

Historical and Statutory Notes

Amendment Note: The 7–1–95 amendment deleted "(4)" after "Rule 4(A)" in the first paragraph in division (C).

Amendment Note: The 7–1–94 amendment consolidated the first paragraph of division (C) and divisions (C)(1) through (C)(6) into a single paragraph; and inserted ", and related proceedings" and substituted "parent-child relationships, provided, however that appointment of counsel shall be in accordance with Rule 4(A)(4) of the Rules of Juvenile Procedure" for "the paternity of any child born out of wedlock" in the first paragraph of division (C).

Commentary

Staff Notes
1995:

Rule 1(C) Exceptions

The amendment effective July 1, 1994 contained an error that is corrected by this revision. The 1994 amendment erroneously referred to division (A)(4) of Rule 4, when no division (A)(4) exists.

1994:

Rule 1(C) Exceptions

Juv. R. 1(C)(4) now reflects current terminology used in Revised Code Sections 3111.01 through 3111.19 regarding the establishment of the parent and child relationship. Additionally, the division clarifies that Juv. R. 4(A)(4), regarding appointment of counsel for certain parties, now applies in actions to establish the parent and child relationship.

Cross References

Powers and duties of supreme court, administrative director, rules, O Const Art IV §5
Rules of Criminal Procedure, application to juvenile proceedings limited, Crim R 1

Library References

Infants ⚖68.1, 68.2, 132, 191.
Westlaw Topic No. 211.
C.J.S. Infants §§ 32, 41 to 54, 95, 198, 199.
Giannelli & Snyder, Baldwin's Ohio Practice, Evidence § 101, 102.3 (2d ed. 2001).
Carlin, Baldwin's Ohio Practice, Merrick–Rippner Probate Law § 104.3, 106.4, 106.21, 107.1, 107.50, 107.84, 108.4 (2003).

Law Review and Journal Commentaries

Juvenile Delinquency, Hon. Richard L. Davis. (Ed. note: Observations from twenty-two years on the bench concerning the decline of family values as delinquency's cause.) 14 Ohio N U L Rev 195 (1987).

Notes of Decisions

Authority of judges   6

Constitutional issues 1
Exceptions 2
Jurisdiction 5
Liberal construction 4
Rules, applicability 3

---

1. Constitutional issues

Traditional interests of confidentiality and rehabilitation prevent the public from having a qualified constitutional right of access to juvenile delinquency proceedings. State ex rel. Plain Dealer Publishing Co. v. Geauga Cty. Court of Common Pleas, Juv. Div. (Ohio 2000) 90 Ohio St.3d 79, 734 N.E.2d 1214, 2000 –Ohio- 35.

News media did not have qualified constitutional right of access to delinquency proceedings involving juvenile charged in connection with murder and robbery, including proceedings on motion to transfer case to adult court. State ex rel. Plain Dealer Publishing Co. v. Geauga Cty. Court of Common Pleas, Juv. Div. (Ohio 2000) 90 Ohio St.3d 79, 734 N.E.2d 1214, 2000 –Ohio- 35.

When, in an adjudicatory hearing held pursuant to Juv R 29, the only evidence of guilt utilized by the court is testimony presented at the preliminary hearing, where the accused exercised adequate rights of cross-examination, he is denied no constitutional right. Matter of Gantt (Wood 1978) 61 Ohio App.2d 44, 398 N.E.2d 800, 15 O.O.3d 67.

2. Exceptions

Although a parentage action brought by a natural mother takes place in a juvenile division of the common pleas court, the civil rules apply rather than the juvenile rules; thus, a motion for judgment on the pleadings under Civ R 12(C) is permissible in a parentage action. Nelson v. Pleasant (Lawrence 1991) 73 Ohio App.3d 479, 597 N.E.2d 1137.

3. Rules, applicability

Juvenile was not entitled to acquittal in delinquency proceedings pursuant to rule of criminal procedure, because rules of criminal procedure did not apply to juvenile proceeding. In re Barchet (Ohio App. 3 Dist., Hancock, 10-09-2002) No. 5-02-27, No. 5-02-30, No. 5-02-28, No. 5-02-31, No. 5-02-29, No. 5-02-32, 2002-Ohio-5420, 2002 WL 31255290, Unreported. Infants ☞ 195

A hearing on a complaint for permanent custody must be bifurcated according to Juv R 29 and 34 into separate adjudicatory and dispositional hearings, notwithstanding the contrary provisions of RC 2151.414, since Juv R 1(A) provides that all proceedings in a juvenile court are governed by the Rules of Juvenile Procedure. In re Vickers Children (Butler 1983) 14 Ohio App.3d 201, 470 N.E.2d 438, 14 O.B.R. 228.

4. Liberal construction

The juvenile statutes are designed primarily for the protection of dependent children and reformation of delinquent children and must be given a liberal construction. (Annotation from former RC 2151.05.) In re Decker (Ohio Juv. 1930) 28 Ohio N.P.(N.S.) 433.

5. Jurisdiction

The juvenile and general divisions of a court of common pleas possess concurrent jurisdiction over a juvenile accused of a crime, and the juvenile division has not been divested of personal jurisdiction over one whose disposition is returned to it after the accused initially waived his right to be judged in that tribunal. State ex rel. Leis v. Black (Hamilton 1975) 45 Ohio App.2d 191, 341 N.E.2d 853, 74 O.O.2d 270.

6. Authority of judges

Mother's claim on appeal that trial court erred in determining child support when it failed to complete a child support computation worksheet was not waived by her failure to provide juvenile court with a transcript of the proceedings before magistrate which set father's child support obligation; issue was purely legal, the resolution of which did not require a review of the hearing transcript. Estes v. Smith (Ohio App. 12 Dist., Butler, 10-07-2002) No. CA2001-09-206, 2002-Ohio-5448, 2002 WL 31255745, Unreported. Child Support ☞ 542

A juvenile judge has no authority to commit the trial of a criminal charge against an adult to a referee, and any proceedings so committed are null and void. State v. Eddington (Marion 1976) 52 Ohio App.2d 312, 369 N.E.2d 1054, 6 O.O.3d 317. Criminal Law ☞ 254.1

Juv R 2   Definitions

As used in these rules:

(A) "Abused child" has the same meaning as in section 2151.031 of the Revised Code.

(B) "Adjudicatory hearing" means a hearing to determine whether a child is a juvenile traffic offender, delinquent, unruly, abused, neglected, or dependent or otherwise within the jurisdiction of the court.

(C) "Agreement for temporary custody" means a voluntary agreement that is authorized by section 5103.15 of the Revised Code and transfers the temporary custody of a child to a public children services agency or a private child placing agency.

(D) "Child" has the same meaning as in sections 2151.011 and 2152.02 of the Revised Code.

(E) "Chronic truant" has the same meaning as in section 2151.011 of the Revised Code.

(F) "Complaint" means the legal document that sets forth the allegations that form the basis for juvenile court jurisdiction.

(G) "Court proceeding" means all action taken by a court from the earlier of (1) the time a complaint is filed and (2) the time a person first appears before an officer of a juvenile court until the court relinquishes jurisdiction over such child.

(H) "Custodian" means a person who has legal custody of a child or a public children's services agency or private child-placing agency that has permanent, temporary, or legal custody of a child.

(I) "Delinquent child" has the same meaning as in section 2152.02 of the Revised Code.

(J) "Dependent child" has the same meaning as in section 2151.04 of the Revised Code.

(K) "Detention" means the temporary care of children in restricted facilities pending court adjudication or disposition.

(L) "Detention hearing" means a hearing to determine whether a child shall be held in detention or shelter care prior to or pending execution of a final dispositional order.

(M) "Dispositional hearing" means a hearing to determine what action shall be taken concerning a child who is within the jurisdiction of the court.

(N) "Guardian" means a person, association, or corporation that is granted authority by a probate court pursuant to Chapter 2111 of the Revised Code to exercise parental rights over a child to the extent provided in the court's order and subject to the residual parental rights of the child's parents.

(O) "Guardian ad litem" means a person appointed to protect the interests of a party in a juvenile court proceeding.

(P) "Habitual truant" has the same meaning as in section 2151.011 of the Revised Code.

(Q) "Hearing" means any portion of a juvenile court proceeding before the court, whether summary in nature or by examination of witnesses.

(R) "Indigent person" means a person who, at the time need is determined, is unable by reason of lack of property or income to provide for full payment of legal counsel and all other necessary expenses of representation.

(S) "Juvenile court" means a division of the court of common pleas, or a juvenile court separately and independently created, that has jurisdiction under Chapters 2151 and 2152 of the Revised Code.

(T) "Juvenile judge" means a judge of a court having jurisdiction under Chapters 2151 and 2152 of the Revised Code.

(U) "Juvenile traffic offender" has the same meaning as in section 2151.021 of the Revised Code.

(V) "Legal custody" means a legal status that vests in the custodian the right to have physical care and control of the child and to determine where and with whom the child shall live, and the right and duty to protect, train, and discipline the child and provide the child with food, shelter, education, and medical care, all subject to any residual parental rights, privileges, and responsibilities. An individual granted legal custody shall exercise the rights and responsibilities personally unless otherwise authorized by any section of the Revised Code or by the court.

(W) "Mental examination" means an examination by a psychiatrist or psychologist.

(X) "Neglected child" has the same meaning as in section 2151.03 of the Revised Code.

(Y) "Party" means a child who is the subject of a juvenile court proceeding, the child's spouse, if any, the child's parent or parents, or if the parent of a child is a child, the parent of that parent, in appropriate cases, the child's custodian, guardian, or guardian ad litem, the state, and any other person specifically designated by the court.

(Z) "Permanent custody" means a legal status that vests in a public children's services agency or a private child-placing agency, all parental rights, duties, and obligations, including the right to consent to adoption, and divests the natural parents or adoptive parents of any and all parental rights, privileges, and obligations, including all residual rights and obligations.

(AA) "Permanent surrender" means the act of the parents or, if a child has only one parent, of the parent of a child, by a voluntary agreement authorized by section 5103.15 of the Revised Code, to transfer the permanent custody of the child to a public children's services agency or a private child-placing agency.

(BB) "Person" includes an individual, association, corporation, or partnership and the state or any of its political subdivisions, departments, or agencies.

(CC) "Physical examination" means an examination by a physician.

(DD) "Planned permanent living arrangement" means an order of a juvenile court pursuant to which both of the following apply:

(1) The court gives legal custody of a child to a public children's services agen-

cy or a private child-placing agency without the termination of parental rights;

(2) The order permits the agency to make an appropriate placement of the child and to enter into a written planned permanent living arrangement agreement with a foster care provider or with another person or agency with whom the child is placed.

(EE) "Private child-placing agency" means any association, as defined in section 5103.02 of the Revised Code that is certified pursuant to sections 5103.03 to 5103.05 of the Revised Code to accept temporary, permanent, or legal custody of children and place the children for either foster care or adoption.

(FF) "Public children's services agency" means a children's services board or a county department of human services that has assumed the administration of the children's services function prescribed by Chapter 5153 of the Revised Code.

(GG) "Removal action" means a statutory action filed by the superintendent of a school district for the removal of a child in an out-of-county foster home placement.

(HH) "Residence or legal settlement" means a location as defined by section 2151.06 of the Revised Code.

(II) "Residual parental rights, privileges, and responsibilities" means those rights, privileges, and responsibilities remaining with the natural parent after the transfer of legal custody of the child, including but not limited to the privilege of reasonable visitation, consent to adoption, the privilege to determine the child's religious affiliation, and the responsibility for support.

(JJ) "Rule of court" means a rule promulgated by the Supreme Court or a rule concerning local practice adopted by another court that is not inconsistent with the rules promulgated by the Supreme Court and that is filed with the Supreme Court.

(KK) "Serious youthful offender" means a child eligible for sentencing as described in sections 2152.11 and 2152.13 of the Revised Code.

(LL) "Serious youthful offender proceedings" means proceedings after a probable cause determination that a child is eligible for sentencing as described in sections 2152.11 and 2152.13 of the Revised Code. Serious youthful offender proceedings cease to be serious youthful offender proceedings once a child has been determined by the trier of fact not to be a serious youthful offender or the juvenile judge has determined not to impose a serious youthful offender disposition on a child eligible for discretionary serious youthful offender sentencing.

(MM) "Shelter care" means the temporary care of children in physically unrestricted facilities, pending court adjudication or disposition.

(NN) "Social history" means the personal and family history of a child or any other party to a juvenile proceeding and may include the prior record of the person with the juvenile court or any other court.

(OO) "Temporary custody" means legal custody of a child who is removed from the child's home, which custody may be terminated at any time at the discretion of the court or, if the legal custody is granted in an agreement for temporary custody, by the person or persons who executed the agreement.

(PP) "Unruly child" has the same meaning as in section 2151.022 of the Revised Code.

(QQ) "Ward of court" means a child over whom the court assumes continuing jurisdiction.

(Adopted eff. 7–1–72; amended eff. 7–1–94, 7–1–98, 7–1–01, 7–1–02)

Historical and Statutory Notes

Amendment Note: The 7–1–02 amendment deleted former divisions (W), (W)(1) and (W)(2), relating to "Long term foster care" and redesignated former divisions (X) through (DD) as new divisions (W) through (CC), respectively; added new divisions (DD), (DD)(1) and (DD)(2).

Amendment Note: The 7–1–01 amendment substituted "2151.011 and 2152.02" for "2151.011(B)(1)" in division (D); created new divisions (E) and (P); made nonsubstantive changes to new divisions (F), (H), (W), (AA), (BB), (EE) and (FF); redesignated former divisions (E) through (N) as new divisions (F) through (O), respectively; redesignated former divisions (O) through (HH) as new divisions (Q) through (JJ); created new divisions (KK) and (LL); redesignated former divisions (II) through (MM) as new divisions (MM) through (QQ); substituted "2152.02" for "2151.02" in new division (I); and added "and 2152" after "2151" in new divisions (S) and (T).

Amendment Note: The 7–1–98 amendment deleted "or whether temporary legal custody should be converted to permanent custody" from the end of division (B); rewrote new division (D); added new division (EE); and redesignated former divisions (EE) through (LL) as new divisions (FF) through (MM). Prior to amendment, division (D) read:

"(D) 'Child' means a person who is under the age of eighteen years except as it relates to transfer of jurisdiction pursuant to Juv. R. 30 for purposes of criminal prosecution. A child who violates a federal or state law or municipal ordinance prior to attaining eighteen years of age shall be considered a child irrespective of age at the time the complaint is filed or hearing is had."

Amendment Note: The 7–1–94 amendment added divisions (A), (C), (H), (I), (S), (T), (U), (W), (Y), (Z), (CC), (DD), (EE), (FF), (JJ), and (KK); redesignated former divisions (1) through (22) as divisions (B), (D), (E), (F), (G), (J), (K), (L), (M), (N), (O), (P), (Q), (R), (V), (X), (AA), (BB), (GG), (HH), (II), and (LL), respectively; inserted "abused," in division (B); inserted "except as it relates to transfer of jurisdiction pursuant to Juv. R. 30 for purposes of criminal prosecution" in division (D); substituted "legal custody of a child or a public children services agency or private child placing agency that has permanent, temporary, or legal custody of a child" for "been granted custody of a child by a court" in division (G); deleted ", or execution of a court order" from the end of division (J); substituted "person, association, or corporation that is granted authority by a probate court pursuant to Chapter 2111. of the Revised Code to exercise parental rights over a child to the extent provided in the court's order and subject to the residual parental rights of the child's parents" for "court appointed guardian of the person of a child" in division (M); and deleted ", or execution of a court order" from the end of division (HH).

Commentary

Staff Notes

2002:

Juvenile Rule 2 Definitions

The July 1, 2002, amendments substituted the language of "planned permanent living arrangement" for the former language of "long term foster care," to conform to the new legislative designation for these child-placing arrangements. Former division (W), "Long term foster care," was deleted, a new division (DD), "Planned permanent living arrangement," was added, and other divisions were relettered accordingly.

The amendments to Juv. R. 2 conform to section 2151.011 of the Revised Code. Juvenile Rules 10, 15, and 34 also were amended effective July 1, 2002 to reflect this change in terminology.

2001:

Rule 2 Definitions

Several definitions in Rule 2 were amended to correct the language: Rules 2(F), (H), (W), (AA), (BB), (EE), and (FF).

Rule 2(D) was amended to reflect that the definition of "child" in the Revised Code had been placed into two new sections, i.e., R. C. 2151.011 and 2152.02.

Rules 2(E) and (P) were added to reflect the new categories of chronic truant [defined in Revised Code section 2151.011(B)(9)] and habitual truant [defined in Revised Code section 2151.011(B)(18)], added by Sub. Sen. Bill 181, which became effective September 4, 2000. Other rules that were amended to reflect changes necessitated by the chronic and habitual truancy bill are Rule 10(A), Rule 15(B), Rule 27(A), Rule 29(F), and Rule 37.

Rules 2(I), (S) and (T) were amended to reflect the reorganization of the Revised Code made by Sub. Sen. Bill 179, effective January 1, 2002. The reorganization moved delinquency into a new chapter, Chapter 2152 of the Revised Code, thus necessitating

that "juvenile court" and "juvenile judge" be redefined to include those having jurisdiction under Chapter 2152 as well as under Chapter 2151, and that "delinquent child" be amended to reflect it is now defined in section 2152.02.

Rule 2(KK) was added to reflect the new category of "serious youthful offender" created by Sub. Sen. Bill 179. Although the Revised Code does not define serious youthful offender specifically, sections 2152.11 and 2152.13 describe in detail the predicate offenses and other predicates to treatment as a serious youthful offender, as well as the types of dispositional sentencing available for each. Other rules that were amended to reflect changes necessitated by the serious youthful offender bill are Rule 7(A), Rule 22(D) and (E), Rule 27(A), and Rule 29(A), (C) and (F).

Rule 2(LL) defines "serious youthful offender proceedings." The new category of serious youthful offender created by Sub. Sen. Bill 179 contemplates imposition of an adult sentence in addition to a juvenile disposition upon conviction. Therefore, serious youthful offenders have statutory and constitutional rights commensurate with those of adults. Some proceedings in juvenile court needed to be altered to ensure adult substantive and procedural protections where appropriate. The amendment makes clear that juvenile protections and confidentiality apply both before a probable cause determination that a child may be subject to serious youthful offender disposition, and after a determination that the child shall not be given a serious youthful offender disposition.

1998:

Rule 2 Definitions

Rule 2(B) Adjudicatory hearing

Included under the prior definition of "adjudicatory hearing" in Juv. R. 2(B) were proceedings in which "temporary legal custody should be converted to permanent custody." This provision, which had been included in Juv. R. 2 since its adoption in 1972, appeared to conflict with the 1994 enactment of Juv. R. 34(I), which provides, "Hearings to determine whether temporary orders regarding custody should be modified to orders for permanent custody shall be considered dispositional hearings and need not be bifurcated. The Rules of Evidence shall apply in hearings on motions for permanent custody." Similarly, section 2151.414(A) of the Revised Code provides, "The adjudication that the child is an abused, neglected, or dependent child and the grant of temporary custody to the agency that filed the motion or placement into long-term foster care shall not be readjudicated at the hearing and shall not be affected by a denial of the motion for permanent custody."

The case law on this issue is in conflict. Several pre–1994 cases have held that hearings on motions for permanent custody are adjudicatory in nature. See *In re Hopkins* (1992), 78 Ohio App. 3d 92; *In re Workman* (June 14, 1993), Tuscarawas App. No. 92 AP080055, unreported; *In re Davis* (July 21, 1993), Summit App. No. 16051, unreported. The most recent reported decision, *In re Duncan/Walker Children*, (1996), 109 Ohio App. 3d 841, held that a permanent custody hearing under R.C. 2151.414 is adjudicatory, and did not make reference to either Juv. R. 2(B) or Juv. R. 34(I).

By deleting the final phrase of Juv. R. 2(B) with this amendment, Juv. R. 34(I) becomes the sole authority on this issue with the Rules of Juvenile Procedure.

Rule 2(D) Child

The definition of "child" contained in Juv. R. 2(D) has been amended to conform to the definition of the term found in sections 2151.011(B)(1)(a) of the Revised Code, as amended by legislation (1996 H 124, eff. 3–31–97, and 1996 H 265, eff. 3–3–97). Because the definition of the term "child" appears to be a matter of substantive law since it deals with a jurisdiction issue, the amended definition of the term simply makes reference to the statutory definition.

Rule 2(EE) Removal action

The definition of the term "removal action" added as Juv. R. 2(EE) refers to the cause of action first created by section 2151.55 of the Revised Code (1996 H 215, eff. 9–29–97). This new cause of action applies exclusively to a child in out-of-county foster home placement who is alleged to be causing a significant and unreasonable disruption to the educational process in the school the child is attending.

The addition of division (EE) required the relettering of previous divisions (EE) through (LL) to divisions (FF) through (MM).

1994:

Rule 2 Definitions

Definitions in Juv. R. 2 have been amended or added to reflect definitions found in Revised Code 2151.011, as amended by legislation (Am. Sub. S.B. 89 of the 117th General Assembly and Am. Sub. S.B. 3 of the 118th General Assembly). Amended language exists for the following terms: adjudicatory hearing; child; custodian; guardian; shelter care.

New terms defined in accordance with new statutes are: agreement for temporary custody; delinquent child; dependent child; juvenile traffic offender; legal custody; long term foster care; neglected child; permanent custody; permanent surrender; private child placing agency; public children services agency; residence or legal settlement; residual parental rights, privileges and responsibilities; temporary custody; unruly child.

All other changes in the definitions are to assure gender neutral language.

Library References

Infants ⟊68.1, 131.

Westlaw Topic No. 211.

C.J.S. Infants §§ 31 to 54, 198, 199.

OJur 3d: 22, Courts and Judges § 69; 28, Criminal Law § 1970

Klein & Darling, Baldwin's Ohio Practice, Civil Practice § 24–12 (1997).

Katz & Giannelli, Baldwin's Ohio Practice, Criminal Law § 1.6, 1.9, 35.11 (1996).

Carlin, Baldwin's Ohio Practice, Merrick–Rippner Probate Law § 105.8, 105.10, 107.9, 107.48, 107.51, 107.78, 107.79, 107.110, 107.114 (2003).

Notes of Decisions

Compatibility of offices 5
Delinquent child 3
Evidence 4
Final orders 2
Hearings 7
Jurisdiction 6

Parties 1

---

1. Parties

Grandparents were not prejudiced by denial of motion to intervene in dependency proceedings involving grandson; grandparents were not parties to juvenile proceeding under juvenile rule governing such proceedings, and there was no showing that grandparents had legally protectable interest in custody or visitation or that they acted in loco parentis with respect to child. In re Goff (Ohio App. 11 Dist., Portage, 12-12-2003) No. 2001-P-0144, 2003-Ohio-6768, 2003 WL 22952808, Unreported. Infants ⟊ 200

Paternal grandparents of allegedly dependent child, who was born to underage mother who allegedly was artificially inseminated by step-father, were not entitled to intervene regarding motion for permanent custody of child that was filed by county department of job and family services, since grandparents were not parties for purposes of juvenile proceedings, grandparents did not state how their presence was necessary condition to court's determination of child's best interests, grandparents did not have right to custody or visitation, and trial court's determination that intervention in this case was against public policy was neither arbitrary nor unreasonable. In re Goff (Ohio App. 11 Dist., Portage, 11-14-2003) No. 2003-P-0068, 2003-Ohio-6087, 2003 WL 22697969, Unreported. Infants ⟊ 200

Putative father had standing to file a motion to set aside judgment, in termination of parental rights case; father was named in the proceedings, he was served with pleading, and he was represented by counsel during the proceedings. In re Phillips (Ohio App. 12 Dist., Butler, 09-29-2003) No. CA2003-03-062, 2003-Ohio-5107, 2003 WL 22227364, Unreported. Infants ⟊ 230.1

Dismissal of paternal grandmother's appeal was warranted, based on failure to demonstrate a final appealable order, of the trial court's denial of her motion to intervene in dependency proceeding; trial court permitted grandmother to have visitation with child and ordered county department of job and family services to investigate grandmother for possible relative placement. In re Cunningham (Ohio App. 5 Dist., Stark, 08-11-2003) No. 2003CA00161, 2003-Ohio-4271, 2003 WL 21919874, Unreported. Infants ⟊ 247

Failing to appoint counsel to represent children in termination of parental rights proceeding involving allegations of child abuse was harmless error, where allegations of abuse were dismissed by agreement of parties and court attempted to determine each child's wishes by conducting in camera interview. In re Joshua B. (Ohio App. 6 Dist., Sandusky, 06-13-2003) No. S-02-018, No. S-02-021, No. S-02-019, No. S-02-020, 2003-Ohio-3096, 2003 WL 21384883, Unreported. Infants ⟊ 253

Juvenile has a right to counsel in a proceeding to terminate parental rights, based on the juvenile's status as a party to the proceeding; courts should make a determination, on a case-by-case basis, whether the child actually needs independent counsel, taking into account the maturity of the child and the possibility of the child's guardian ad litem being appointed to represent the child. In re Williams (Ohio, 04-14-2004) 101 Ohio St.3d 398, 805 N.E.2d 1110, 2004-Ohio-1500. Infants ⟊ 205

Any error was harmless as to trial court's failure to name child as party to paternity and child support action and its failure to appoint counsel for child, where child's interest did not appear to conflict with mother's interests. Still v. Hayman (Ohio App. 7 Dist., 07-30-2003) 153 Ohio App.3d 487, 794 N.E.2d 751, 2003-Ohio-4113. Children Out-of-wedlock ⟨≈⟩ 72.1

A child's grandparents are necessary parties to a permanent custody proceeding only if they have obtained through statute, court order, or other means a legal right to custody or visitation with the child. In re Schmidt (Ohio 1986) 25 Ohio St.3d 331, 496 N.E.2d 952, 25 O.B.R. 386.

Permitting foster mother to become a party to action to terminate mother's parental rights was not an abuse of discretion; mother cared more for her own selfish interests than those of her child, repeatedly telling her doctors that she only took her psychotropic medication to get her child back and that, once reunified, she would discontinue her medication because she did not believe she suffered from any mental illness; mother showed an inability to perform rudimentary parenting skills; county continued to advocate reunification, despite mother's discouraging lack of progress; and mother refused to fight for the child after child had been abducted to China. In re Zhang (Ohio App. 8 Dist. 1999) 135 Ohio App.3d 350, 734 N.E.2d 379, dismissed, appeal not allowed 87 Ohio St.3d 1417, 717 N.E.2d 1105, reconsideration stricken 87 Ohio St.3d 1437, 719 N.E.2d 2. Infants ⟨≈⟩ 200

Juvenile court has wide discretion in affording any individual party status in proceeding for custody. In re Hitchcock (Ohio App. 8 Dist., 11-21-1996) 120 Ohio App.3d 88, 696 N.E.2d 1090, stay granted 77 Ohio St.3d 1462, 672 N.E.2d 1119, stay denied 77 Ohio St.3d 1502, 673 N.E.2d 921, motion to vacate stay denied 77 Ohio St.3d 1521, 674 N.E.2d 373, appeal allowed 78 Ohio St.3d 1455, 677 N.E.2d 815, appeal dismissed as improvidently allowed 81 Ohio St.3d 1222, 689 N.E.2d 43, 1998-Ohio-653, stay denied 81 Ohio St.3d 1469, 690 N.E.2d 1288, stay denied 81 Ohio St.3d 1476, 691 N.E.2d 294. Child Custody ⟨≈⟩ 409

Juvenile court did not abuse its discretion by permitting couple legally ineligible to adopt children to remain as parties to post-dispositional custody proceeding while court examined merits of couple's motion for legal custody; motion presented additional disposition option, which court was required to consider as part of its obligation to consider best interests of children. In re Hitchcock (Ohio App. 8 Dist., 11-21-1996) 120 Ohio App.3d 88, 696 N.E.2d 1090, stay granted 77 Ohio St.3d 1462, 672 N.E.2d 1119, stay denied 77 Ohio St.3d 1502, 673 N.E.2d 921, motion to vacate stay denied 77 Ohio St.3d 1521, 674 N.E.2d 373, appeal allowed 78 Ohio St.3d 1455, 677 N.E.2d 815, appeal dismissed as improvidently allowed 81 Ohio St.3d 1222, 689 N.E.2d 43, 1998-Ohio-653, stay denied 81 Ohio St.3d 1469, 690 N.E.2d 1288, stay denied 81 Ohio St.3d 1476, 691 N.E.2d 294. Infants ⟨≈⟩ 230.1

Trial court's allowing state witness' mother, a nonparty witness, to communicate extensively out of presence of one of the parties, namely, accused delinquent minor, about referee's findings and recommendations raised questions regarding appearance of unfairness of proceedings and warranted vacation of adjudication of delinquency based upon attempted felonious assault finding and remand for hearing and ruling on objections to initial referee's report and recommendations. In re Ross (Franklin 1995) 107 Ohio App.3d 35, 667 N.E.2d 1012. Infants ⟨≈⟩ 207; Infants ⟨≈⟩ 254

County child support enforcement agency (CSEA) had standing, as collecting agent of Department of Human Services (DHS), to bring action in juvenile court to determine child support and to make deter-

mination of reimbursement for amount of support already provided by DHS to children of mothers receiving public assistance who had assigned their rights to child support to DHS; even if statute authorizing only parent, guardian, or custodian of child to bring action in juvenile court requesting child support order did not authorize state to bring such action, Juvenile Rules of Procedure giving state or its agencies standing to file complaint to order child support payments controlled over statute. State ex rel. Lamier v. Lamier (Cuyahoga 1995) 105 Ohio App.3d 797, 664 N.E.2d 1384.

Question of standing, i.e., of who is proper party to bring complaint, is procedural matter governed by Rules of Juvenile Procedure; these rules control over inconsistent statute purporting to govern procedural matters. State ex rel. Lamier v. Lamier (Cuyahoga 1995) 105 Ohio App.3d 797, 664 N.E.2d 1384.

Indigent father was entitled to have counsel appointed to represent him on custody and visitation issues in child support action under statute and juvenile court rule; both rule and statute guarantee right to appointed counsel for all indigent parties in juvenile court proceedings, father, being natural father and parent of children, was a party to juvenile court proceeding under juvenile court rules, and father was indigent as defined in rules. McKinney v. McClure (Butler 1995) 102 Ohio App.3d 165, 656 N.E.2d 1310. Children Out-of-wedlock ⟨≈⟩ 20.4

While statute regarding dispositional review hearings does not list a child's legal custodian at the time review hearing is ordered as an "interested party" entitled to notice of the review hearing, the list is not exhaustive. In re Bowman (Summit 1995) 101 Ohio App.3d 599, 656 N.E.2d 355. Infants ⟨≈⟩ 230.1

Grandmother became an "interested party," entitled to notice of dispositional hearing, when court awarded her legal custody of dependent child. In re Bowman (Summit 1995) 101 Ohio App.3d 599, 656 N.E.2d 355. Infants ⟨≈⟩ 230.1

Although individual party may represent himself, such right of self-representation does not extend to parties who are not natural persons. In re Lawson (Ohio App. 10 Dist., 11-08-1994) 98 Ohio App.3d 456, 648 N.E.2d 889. Attorney And Client ⟨≈⟩ 62

Foster parents were not entitled to party status, in proceedings by county childrens services board that had temporary custody of child to accept permanent voluntary surrender of natural mother's rights for purposes of adoption, by virtue of juvenile court rule defining party by virtue of rule's reference to "any other party specifically designated by court"; rule merely afforded procedural device permitting trial court to include individuals not specifically otherwise designated party but whose presence was necessary to fully litigate issue presented in action, and such action was within trial court's sound discretion. In re Franklin (Marion 1993) 88 Ohio App.3d 277, 623 N.E.2d 720. Infants ⟨≈⟩ 200

In a delinquency proceeding, a trial court does not err in ordering that the regional consortium for children be made a party following the final disposition hearing where (1) a representative for the consortium was given notice and appeared as a witness for the state, (2) the court asked whether the consortium was represented by counsel at the beginning of the second dispositional hearing, and (3) the consortium representative was given the opportunity to question other witnesses. In re Hoodlet (Athens 1991) 72 Ohio App.3d 115, 593 N.E.2d 478. Infants ⟨≈⟩ 253

A county children services agency may not appeal an order of a juvenile court finding two minors to be unruly because of habitual truancy and committing them to the agency's custody, as the agency is not a party to the litigation under Juv R 2(16). In re Blakey (Franklin 1989) 65 Ohio App.3d 341, 583 N.E.2d 1343.

A father is a party to proceedings in a juvenile court in which his children are found to be neglected and in which temporary custody is given to the mother; he is also a party to a subsequent proceeding in the same court modifying such temporary custody order and is entitled to appear in an appeal from such order and move to dismiss such appeal. In re Rule (Crawford 1963) 1 Ohio App.2d 57, 203 N.E.2d 501, 30 O.O.2d 76.

The father of a juvenile adjudged delinquent is a party as defined in Juv R 2(16) and is subject to orders of the court. In re Dague, No. 87–CA–12 (5th Dist Ct App, Delaware, 10–22–87).

Foster parents who had cared for a child for over two years are not parties in interest in a dependency case because they have no property or liberty rights which would require a juvenile court to permit their intervention. In re Palmer, No. CA–6026 (5th Dist Ct App, Stark, 4–12–83).

2. Final orders

A temporary order of a juvenile court changing custody under Juv R 13 or 29 is not a dispositional order under Juv R 34, and hence is not a final appealable order. Morrison v. Morrison (Summit 1973) 45 Ohio App.2d 299, 344 N.E.2d 144, 74 O.O.2d 441.

3. Delinquent child

A juvenile who has been placed in a residential treatment center by order of a juvenile court and who leaves such premises without permission may properly be adjudicated delinquent, as the act of leaving the center without permission constitutes escape. In re Wells, No. CA–8287, CA–8347, and CA–8307 (5th Dist Ct App, Stark, 3–18–91).

4. Evidence

In an adjudicatory hearing to convert temporary custody of a minor to permanent custody pursuant to Juv R 2(1), the trial court erred in admitting into evidence reports of a child welfare agency where no foundation was laid to admit such report as a business records exception or public records exception to hearsay. In re Knipp, No. 1388 (4th Dist Ct App, Scioto, 3–28–83).

5. Compatibility of offices

The office of probate and juvenile judge is incompatible with the office of county court judge. (Annotation from former RC 2151.011.) 1957 OAG 880.

6. Jurisdiction

Rule requiring the state to respond to discovery requests in juvenile matters applies to "mandatory bindover" or waiver of jurisdiction proceedings wherein the court determines whether probable cause exists to transfer the matter for prosecution of the juvenile as an adult. In re A.M. (Ohio Com.Pl. 1998) 92 Ohio Misc.2d 4, 699 N.E.2d 574, affirmed 139 Ohio App.3d 303, 743 N.E.2d 937, appeal not allowed 91 Ohio St.3d 1431, 741 N.E.2d 895. Infants ⟲ 68.7(3)

Under authority of this act, juvenile court has exclusive jurisdiction of all persons under eighteen charged with arson or other burnings as contained in GC 12433 (RC 2907.02) and GC 12436 (RC 2907.07). (Annotation from former RC 2151.25.) 1939 OAG 726.

7. Hearings

Error cannot be predicated on the juvenile court's holding a dispositional hearing immediately following an adjudicatory hearing and its failure to continue the dispositional hearing for a reasonable time to enable the party to obtain or consult counsel, as prescribed by Juv R 34(A), unless it affirmatively appears in the record that the affected nonindigent party has requested such continuance. In re Bolden (Allen 1973) 37 Ohio App.2d 7, 306 N.E.2d 166, 66 O.O.2d 26.

Probable cause hearing in a "mandatory bindover" or waiver of jurisdiction proceeding is both an "adjudicatory hearing" and a "hearing" as those terms are used in the rules governing juvenile matters. In re A.M. (Ohio Com.Pl. 1998) 92 Ohio Misc.2d 4, 699 N.E.2d 574, affirmed 139 Ohio App.3d 303, 743 N.E.2d 937, appeal not allowed 91 Ohio St.3d 1431, 741 N.E.2d 895. Infants ⟲ 68.7(3)

Juv R 3   Waiver of rights

A child's right to be represented by counsel at a hearing conducted pursuant to Juv. R. 30 may not be waived. Other rights of a child may be waived with the permission of the court.

(Adopted eff. 7–1–72; amended eff. 7–1–94)

Historical and Statutory Notes

Amendment Note: The 7–1–94 amendment rewrote this rule, which previously read:

"A child's right to be represented by counsel at a hearing to determine whether the juvenile court shall relinquish its jurisdiction for purposes of criminal prosecution may not be waived. No other right of a child may be waived without the permission of the court."

Commentary

Staff Notes

1994:

Rule 3 Waiver of Rights

Prior to this revision, some courts had interpreted Juv. R. 3 to permit a juvenile to waive the right to counsel at the probable cause hearing phase of the bindover process. Juv. R. 3 now makes specific reference to bindover proceedings delineated in Juv. R. 30 to remind the court and practitioners that a juvenile cannot waive counsel at any stage of the bindover procedure.

Cross References

Relinquishment of jurisdiction for purpose of criminal prosecution, Juv R 30

Library References

Infants ⟲68.7(3), 191.

Westlaw Topic No. 211.

C.J.S. Infants §§ 42 to 54.

Am Jur 2d: 47, Juvenile Courts and Delinquent and Dependent Children § 39

Validity and efficacy of minor's waiver of right to counsel—modern cases. 25 ALR4th 1072

Carlin, Baldwin's Ohio Practice, Merrick–Rippner Probate Law § 104.5, 107.14, 107.45, 107.67 (2003).

Law Review and Journal Commentaries

Do Juveniles Facing Civil Commitment Have a Right to Counsel? A Therapeutic Jurisprudence Brief. Bruce J. Winick and Ginger Lerner-Wren, 71 U Cin L Rev 115 (Fall 2002).

Notes of Decisions

Confessions, admissibility 2
Constitutional issues 1
Miranda warnings 3

_____

1. Constitutional issues

Application of 180-day time period in which to file motion for postconviction relief to juvenile did not amount to a waiver of his right to file a motion for post-conviction relief in violation of rule requiring permission of court for waiver of rights; since juvenile had no constitutional right to post-conviction relief, and the legislature provided a time limitation for filing petitions for post-conviction relief, trial court did not violate rule by dismissing his motion as untimely filed. In re Snyder (Ohio App. 4 Dist., Highland, 06-26-2002) No. 01CA11, 2002-Ohio-6137, 2002 WL 31520119, Unreported. Infants ⬤ 230.1

Juvenile court's limited inquiry at dispositional hearing and 14–year–old juvenile's limited responses, including court's asking whether juvenile recalled the rights explained to him at adjudicatory hearing and juvenile's response, "Um-hum," were insufficient to establish valid admission or valid waiver of right to counsel under the federal and state due process clauses. In re Royal (Ohio App. 7 Dist., 03-01-1999) 132 Ohio App.3d 496, 725 N.E.2d 685. Constitutional Law ⬤ 43(1); Infants ⬤ 199; Infants ⬤ 205

Trial court accepted 13–year–old juvenile's waiver of counsel without proper assurances that waiver was knowing, intelligent and voluntary; referee gave basic explanation to juvenile on his right to counsel at initial hearing and adjudicatory hearing, and asked juvenile to sign waiver form, but failed to inquire into any circumstances that would demonstrate that juvenile knowingly, intelligently, and voluntarily waived his right to counsel, and trial judge did not address subject of right to counsel at dispositional hearing. In re Johnson (Ohio App. 1 Dist., 08-23-1995) 106 Ohio App.3d 38, 665 N.E.2d 247. Infants ⬤ 205

Where a juvenile has received the following essentials of due process and fair treatment: (1) written notice of the specific charge or factual allegations, given to the juvenile and his parents or guardian sufficiently in advance of the hearing to permit preparation; (2) notification to the juvenile and his parents of the juvenile's right to be represented by counsel retained by them, or, if they are unable to afford counsel, that counsel will be appointed to represent the juvenile; (3) application of the constitutional privileges against self-incrimination; and (4), absent a valid confession, a determination of delinquency and an order of commitment based only on sworn testimony subjected to the opportunity for cross-examination in accordance with constitutional requirements, such juvenile has not been deprived of due process under either the Constitution of the United States or the Constitution of the State of Ohio. (Annotation from former RC 2151.35.) In re Baker (Hocking 1969) 18 Ohio App.2d 276, 248 N.E.2d 620, 47 O.O.2d 411.

A trial court does not fulfill its duty to ascertain whether a juvenile knows of his right to be provided with counsel if he is indigent simply by asking the juvenile if he has received a copy of the statement of rights and whether he has any questions about those rights where (1) the statement of rights is two pages in length, (2) single-spaced, and (3) the right of counsel if indigent is not stated until near the top of the second page; under such circumstances, the juvenile even with a parent present, is likely to sign a form he has not fully read or does not fully understand while at the same time telling a judge otherwise. In re Shane, No. 1523, 2001 WL 62550 (2d Dist Ct App, Darke, 1–26–01).

Federal and state due process rights extend to juvenile court proceedings, so that a plea agreement may not be broken by refiling charges. In re Leonhardt (Ohio Com.Pl. 1993) 62 Ohio Misc.2d 783, 610 N.E.2d 1238.

A juvenile taken into custody as a delinquent has certain rights guaranteed by the Due Process Clause of the United States Constitution in delinquency proceedings by the state which include the following: (1) notice of the charge, (2) right to counsel, (3) right to confrontation and cross-examination, and (4) privilege against self incrimination. Application of Gault (U.S.Ariz. 1967) 87 S.Ct. 1428, 387 U.S. 1, 18 L.Ed.2d 527, 40 O.O.2d 378.

2. Confessions, admissibility

Juvenile's waiver of rights and statement to police implicating himself, made at correctional facility, were voluntary; juvenile was 15-years-old at time of incident, he could read, understand and write English, he was not handcuffed or under any other physical restraint, nor was he subject to any apparent coercion at time of questioning, and he was aware that he had right to remain silent and right to have attorney present. In re Hill (Ohio App. 10 Dist., Franklin, 11-20-2003) No. 03AP-82, 2003-Ohio-6185, 2003 WL 22725297, Unreported. Infants ⬤ 174

Neither juvenile's waiver of counsel nor his admission to charges against him were made in a knowing manner, for purposes of delinquency proceedings, where juvenile was never informed of nature of charges against him, trial court made no mention of possible defenses or mitigating circumstances that related to juvenile's situation, and juvenile was not informed that if he admitted to the charges he would be losing certain rights associated with trial. In re Styer (Ohio App. 3 Dist., Union, 11-19-2002) No. 14-02-12, 2002-Ohio-6273, 2002 WL 31555992, Unreported. Infants ⬤ 205

A voluntary confession to the perpetration of murder obtained from a sixteen and three-fourths year old high school junior, which confession was made before indictment and while the accused was detained for investigation, is admissible in evidence (1) where the accused had been allowed to consult with an attorney prior to being questioned; (2) where the accused first was advised that he did not have to talk; (3) where the accused, when told that his parents and another attorney were there and waiting to see him, stated that he did not want to see them; and (4) where there is no showing that the confession was obtained by inquisitorial processes. (Annotation from former RC 2151.31.) State v. Carder (Fairfield 1965) 3 Ohio App.2d 381, 210 N.E.2d 714, 32 O.O.2d 524, affirmed 9 Ohio St.2d 1, 222 N.E.2d 620, 38 O.O.2d 1.

A voluntary confession to the perpetration of murder, obtained from a seventeen-year-old high school senior, which confession was made before indictment on said charge and while the accused was under arrest for a misdemeanor, is admissible in evidence where (1) the accused was first advised that "he would not be compelled to give a statement... if he wanted to give a statement it would be by his own free will and that statement would be used for or against him in court;" (2) the accused was further advised that "he could secure the services of an attorney;" and (3) there is no showing that the confession was obtained by inquisitorial processes, without the procedural safeguards of due process, and by such compulsion that the confession is irreconcilable with the possession of mental freedom. (Annotation from former RC 2151.31.) State v. Stewart (Summit 1963) 120 Ohio App. 199, 201 N.E.2d 793, 29 O.O.2d 4, affirmed 176 Ohio St. 156, 198 N.E.2d 439, 27 O.O.2d 42, certiorari denied 85 S.Ct. 443, 379 U.S. 947, 13 L.Ed.2d 544.

3. Miranda warnings

Juvenile court erred in delinquency proceeding by allowing prosecutor to prove elements of state's case by questioning juvenile, an unrepresented minor held in custody, without informing him of his *Miranda* rights against self-incrimination, where juvenile was asked to stipulate to prior theft offense needed for disposition chosen. In re Johnson (Ohio App. 1 Dist., 08-23-1995) 106 Ohio App.3d 38, 665 N.E.2d 247. Infants ☞ 199; Infants ☞ 207

Unrepresented juvenile who did not receive *Miranda* warning could not be bound to stipulation that he had committed prior offense. In re Johnson (Ohio App. 1 Dist., 08-23-1995) 106 Ohio App.3d 38, 665 N.E.2d 247. Infants ☞ 199

Where a fourteen-year-old minor, without counsel, made a statement to police implicating herself in setting a fire which killed her father, and the court psychologist testified that such minor was of average intelligence, the minor's statement is properly admitted into evidence where the minor had waived her Miranda rights and during the course of such statement the minor answered intelligently, coherently, and gave no indication of undue influence. In re Hawkins, No. 3430 (9th Dist Ct App, Lorain, 5–11–83).

Juv R 4 Assistance of counsel; guardian ad litem

(A) Assistance of counsel

Every party shall have the right to be represented by counsel and every child, parent, custodian, or other person in loco parentis the right to appointed counsel if indigent. These rights shall arise when a person becomes a party to a juvenile court proceeding. When the complaint alleges that a child is an abused child, the court must appoint an attorney to represent the interests of the child. This rule shall not be construed to provide for a right to appointed counsel in cases in which that right is not otherwise provided for by constitution or statute.

(B) Guardian ad litem; when appointed

The court shall appoint a guardian *ad litem* to protect the interests of a child or incompetent adult in a juvenile court proceeding when:

(1) The child has no parents, guardian, or legal custodian;

(2) The interests of the child and the interests of the parent may conflict;

(3) The parent is under eighteen years of age or appears to be mentally incompetent;

(4) The court believes that the parent of the child is not capable of representing the best interest of the child.

(5) Any proceeding involves allegations of abuse or neglect, voluntary surrender of permanent custody, or termination of parental rights as soon as possible after the commencement of such proceeding.

(6) There is an agreement for the voluntary surrender of temporary custody that is made in accordance with section 5103.15 of the Revised Code, and thereafter there is a request for extension of the voluntary agreement.

(7) The proceeding is a removal action.

(8) Appointment is otherwise necessary to meet the requirements of a fair hearing.

(C) Guardian ad litem as counsel

(1) When the guardian ad litem is an attorney admitted to practice in this state, the guardian may also serve as counsel to the ward providing no conflict between the roles exist.

(2) If a person is serving as guardian ad litem and as attorney for a ward and either that person or the court finds a conflict between the responsibilities of the role of attorney and that of guardian ad litem, the court shall appoint another person as guardian ad litem for the ward.

(3) If a court appoints a person who is not an attorney admitted to practice in this state to be a guardian ad litem, the court may appoint an attorney admitted to pracice [sic.] in this state to serve as attorney for the guardian ad litem.

(D) Appearance of attorneys

An attorney shall enter appearance by filing a written notice with the court or by appearing personally at a court hearing and informing the court of said representation.

(E) Notice to guardian ad litem

The guardian ad litem shall be given notice of all proceedings in the same manner as notice is given to other parties to the action.

(F) Withdrawal of counsel or guardian ad litem

An attorney or guardian ad litem may withdraw only with the consent of the court upon good cause shown.

(G) Costs

The court may fix compensation for the services of appointed counsel and guardians ad litem, tax the same as part of the costs and assess them against the child, the child's parents, custodian, or other person in loco parentis of such child.

(Adopted eff. 7–1–72; amended eff. 7–1–76, 7–1–94, 7–1–95, 7–1–98)

Historical and Statutory Notes

Amendment Note: The 7–1–98 amendment added new division (B)(7); and redesignated former division (B)(7) as new division (B)(8).

Amendment Note: The 7–1–95 amendment rewrote the titles of this rule and of division (A), which previously read:

"Rule 4. Appointment of Counsel; Guardian Ad Litem

"(A) Right to counsel; when arises."

Amendment Note: The 7–1–94 amendment added the final sentence of division (A); added divisions (B)(4) through (B)(6); redesignated former division (B)(4) as division (B)(7); rewrote division (C); added division (E); redesignated former divisions (E) and (F) as divisions (F) and (G); and made changes to reflect gender-neutral language. Prior to amendment, division (C) read:

"(C) Guardian ad litem as counsel

When the guardian ad litem is an attorney admitted to practice in this state, he may also serve as counsel to his ward."

Commentary

Staff Notes

1998:

Rule 4(B) Guardian ad litem; when appointed

The 1998 amendment added division (B)(7), requiring the appointment of a guardian *ad litem* for removal actions, as defined in Juv. R. 2(EE), also added in the amendments effective July 1, 1998. At the discretion of the court, the court may appoint the guardian *ad litem* initially appointed for the child by the court that entered the original dispositional placement order, with the consent of that guardian *ad litem.* Alternatively, the court may appoint a new guardian *ad litem.*

The addition of a new division (B)(7) required the renumbering of the former division to what is now division (B)(8).

1995:

Rule 4. Assistance of Counsel; Guardian Ad Litem

The 1995 amendment changed the title of this rule and of division (A) to more accurately reflect the substance of the rule. There were no changes to the text of the rule.

1994:

Rule 4 Right to Counsel; Guardian Ad Litem

Masculine references throughout Juv. R. 4 have been replaced by gender neutral language.

Rule 4(A) Right to counsel; when arises

The 1994 amendment added a new sentence to the end of division (A) to clarify that Juv. R. 4 does not create a right to court-appointed counsel, and that the right to appointed counsel arises from other sources of law.

Rule 4(B) Guardian ad litem; when appointed

Juv. R. 4(B) governs the appointment of a guardian ad litem (GAL). New sections specify the appointment of a GAL as required by section 2151.281 of the Revised Code.

Rule 4(C) Guardian ad litem as counsel

Juv. R. 4(C) requires the appointment of a new GAL when an attorney serving as GAL is also the child's attorney and a conflict of interest exists. (Revised Code 2151.281(H)).

Rule 4(E) Notice to guardian ad litem

Juv. R. 4(E) specifies notice requirements to GALs pursuant to section 2151.281(I) of the Revised Code.

Cross References

Child, parents and custodian, right to legal counsel, 2151.352
Guardian ad litem to be appointed in proceeding concerning delinquent or unruly child, 2151.281
Paternity proceedings, representation of child's interests, 3111.07

Library References

Infants ⬥68.4, 68.7(3), 205.
Westlaw Topic No. 211.
C.J.S. Infants §§ 46 to 52, 62 to 67, 201, 202.
OJur 3d: 48, Family Law § 1647, 1667
Am Jur 2d: 47, Juvenile Courts and Delinquent and Dependent Children § 22, 38, 58
Right to and appointment of counsel in juvenile court proceeding. 60 ALR2d 691
Right of indigent parent to appointed counsel in proceeding for involuntary termination of parental rights. 80 ALR3d 1141
Ineffective assistance of counsel: right of attorney to withdraw, as appointed defense counsel, due to self-avowed incompetence. 16 ALR5th 118
Carlin, Baldwin's Ohio Practice, Merrick–Rippner Probate Law § 104.5, 104.10, 107.45, 107.46, 107.104, 107.164 (2003).

Law Review and Journal Commentaries

The Criminal Defense Lawyer in the Juvenile Justice System, David A. Harris. 26 U Tol L Rev 751 (Summer 1995).

Do Juveniles Facing Civil Commitment Have a Right to Counsel? A Therapeutic Jurisprudence Brief. Bruce J. Winick and Ginger Lerner-Wren, 71 U Cin L Rev 115 (Fall 2002).

Lassiter v. Department of Social Services: The Due Process Right to Appointed Counsel Left Hanging Uneasily in the Mathews v. Eldrodge Balance, Jane E. Jackson. 8 N Ky L Rev 513 (1981).

Legal Representation Of A Fetus: The Mother And Child Disunion, Comment. 18 Cap U L Rev 591 (Winter 1989).

Manipulated by *Miranda*: A Critical Analysis of Bright Lines and Voluntary Confessions Under *Unit-*

ed States v. Dickerson, Casenote. 68 U Cin L Rev 555 (Winter 2000).

The Right to Remain Silent: The Use of Pre–Arrest Silence in *United States v. Oplinger*, 150 F.3d 1061 (5th Cir. 1998), Casenote. 68 U Cin L Rev 505 (Winter 2000).

Notes of Decisions

Cause of action 10
Constitutional issues 1
Damages 8
Effective assistance of counsel 4
Equitable actions 2
Fees and costs 5
Guardian ad litem 9
Jurisdiction 11
Persons represented 6
Right to counsel 7
Waiver of counsel 3

---

1. Constitutional issues

There is no constitutional right to appointment of counsel for indigent parents in a hearing on a complaint by a county social services department for temporary custody of allegedly neglected children. (Annotation from former RC 2151.352.) In re Miller (Ohio 1984) 12 Ohio St.3d 40, 465 N.E.2d 397, 12 O.B.R. 35.

Juvenile court magistrate's judgment entry, indicating only a finding that "subject child, after first being advised of all procedural and constitutional rights, including the right to counsel and a continuance herein, asserts said rights and ADMITS the allegations as they appear in the complaint," did not establish under the federal and state due process clauses a valid waiver of counsel or that the admission was voluntarily, knowingly, and intelligently made. In re Royal (Ohio App. 7 Dist., 03-01-1999) 132 Ohio App.3d 496, 725 N.E.2d 685. Constitutional Law ☞ 43(1); Infants ☞ 199; Infants ☞ 205

There is no material difference with respect to constitutional right to counsel between adult and juvenile proceedings. In re East (Cuyahoga 1995) 105 Ohio App.3d 221, 663 N.E.2d 983, dismissed, appeal not allowed 74 Ohio St.3d 1482, 657 N.E.2d 1375. Infants ☞ 205

Where a juvenile has received the following essentials of due process and fair treatment: (1) written notice of the specific charge or factual allegations, given to the juvenile and his parents or guardian sufficiently in advance of the hearing to permit preparation; (2) notification to the juvenile and his parents of the juvenile's right to be represented by counsel retained by them, or, if they are unable to afford counsel, that counsel will be appointed to represent the juvenile; (3) application of the constitutional privileges against self-incrimination; and (4), absent a valid confession, a determination of delinquency and an order of commitment based only on sworn testimony subjected to the opportunity for cross-examination in accordance with constitutional requirements, such juvenile has not been deprived of due process under either the Constitution of the United States or the Constitution of the State of Ohio. (Annotation from former RC 2151.35.) In re Baker (Hocking 1969) 18 Ohio App.2d 276, 248 N.E.2d 620, 47 O.O.2d 411.

In a complaint against a juvenile for gross sexual imposition it is not necessary for the juvenile to be given Miranda rights during a noncustodial interview that takes place in the juvenile's home at the kitchen table. State v Gray, No. 00CA007695, 2001 WL 251345 (9th Dist Ct App, Lorain, 3–14–01).

Appointment of the guardian ad litem for the children as counsel for child did not violate child's constitutional right to counsel, in termination of parental rights proceeding; there was no conflict of interest between counsel's roles as guardian ad litem and as attorney for child since the children both expressed a desire to remain with their foster mother. In re Legg, Nos. 80542+, 2002-Ohio-4582, 2002 WL 2027290 (8th Dist Ct App, 9-05-02).

The trial court has the discretion to decide, in the interests of due process, whether there should be an appointment of counsel for the indigent in every parental status termination hearing, and the failure to appoint counsel does not presumptively deny the parent of constitutional rights where the presence of counsel could not have made a determinative difference. Lassiter v. Department of Social Services of Durham County, N. C. (U.S.N.C. 1981) 101 S.Ct. 2153, 452 U.S. 18, 68 L.Ed.2d 640, rehearing denied 102 S.Ct. 889, 453 U.S. 927, 69 L.Ed.2d 1023.

A juvenile taken into custody as a delinquent has certain rights guaranteed by the Due Process Clause of the United States Constitution in delinquency proceedings by the state which include the following: (1) notice of the charge, (2) right to counsel, (3) right to confrontation and cross-examination, and (4) privilege against self incrimination. Application of Gault (U.S.Ariz. 1967) 87 S.Ct. 1428, 387 U.S. 1, 18 L.Ed.2d 527, 40 O.O.2d 378.

2. Equitable actions

Indigent parent was entitled to writ of mandamus commanding juvenile court judge to appoint counsel for her in child custody action commenced by her; parent had a clear legal right to relief prayed for, judge was under clear legal duty to appoint counsel for mother, and mother had no plain and adequate remedy in the ordinary course of law. State ex rel. Lunsford v. Buck (Meigs 1993) 88 Ohio App.3d 425, 623 N.E.2d 1356.

3. Waiver of counsel

Mother's failure to cooperate with appointed counsel and court constituted waiver of her right to counsel in termination of parental rights proceeding; mother did not appear at disposition hearing in spite of receiving notice, counsel made continued attempts to contact mother without success, caseworker had not had recent contact with mother, other evidence showed that mother was disinterested in welfare of child since birth, and court permitted counsel to withdraw. In re Savanah M. (Ohio App. 6 Dist., Lucas, 10-31-2003) No. L-03-1112, 2003-Ohio-5855, 2003 WL 22462478, Unreported. Infants ☞ 205

Neither juvenile's waiver of counsel nor his admission to charges against him were made in a knowing manner, for purposes of delinquency proceedings, where juvenile was never informed of nature of charges against him, trial court made no mention of possible defenses or mitigating circumstances that related to juvenile's situation, and juvenile was not informed that if he admitted to the charges he would be losing certain rights associated with trial. In re Styer (Ohio App. 3 Dist., Union, 11-19-2002) No. 14-02-12, 2002-Ohio-6273, 2002 WL 31555992, Unreported. Infants ☞ 205

Juvenile's waiver of right to counsel at probation violation hearing was not voluntary, knowing, and intelligent, where trial court did not engage juvenile in meaningful discussion to determine whether juvenile understood rights she was waiving. In re Vaughters (Ohio App. 8 Dist., Cuyahoga, 10-24-2002)

No. 80650, 2002-Ohio-5843, 2002 WL 31401623, Unreported. Infants ⇔ 205

Trial court abused its discretion in failing to either appoint counsel to represent indigent child in delinquency proceedings or to obtain a waiver of counsel from guardian ad litem, even though guardian had counsel; court could not presume dual appointment absent express dual appointment. In re Amos (Ohio App. 3 Dist., 09-22-2003) 154 Ohio App.3d 434, 797 N.E.2d 568, 2003-Ohio-5014. Infants ⇔ 205

To be effective, a waiver of a juvenile's right to counsel must be voluntary, knowing and intelligent. In re Johnston (Ohio App. 11 Dist., 04-30-2001) 142 Ohio App.3d 314, 755 N.E.2d 457. Infants ⇔ 205

Juvenile court's limited inquiry at dispositional hearing and 14–year–old juvenile's limited responses, including court's asking whether juvenile recalled the rights explained to him at adjudicatory hearing and juvenile's response, "Um-hum," were insufficient to establish valid admission or valid waiver of right to counsel under the federal and state due process clauses. In re Royal (Ohio App. 7 Dist., 03-01-1999) 132 Ohio App.3d 496, 725 N.E.2d 685. Constitutional Law ⇔ 43(1); Infants ⇔ 199; Infants ⇔ 205

Presence of 14–year–old juvenile's mother at the adjudicatory hearing did not provide dispositive proof that the juvenile waived his rights and gave his admission voluntarily, knowingly, and intelligently. In re Royal (Ohio App. 7 Dist., 03-01-1999) 132 Ohio App.3d 496, 725 N.E.2d 685. Infants ⇔ 199; Infants ⇔ 205

Since juvenile was advised of his right to counsel and waived it when he entered his admission to robbery charge, it was not necessary for court to again advise juvenile of his right at disposition hearing. In re East (Cuyahoga 1995) 105 Ohio App.3d 221, 663 N.E.2d 983, dismissed, appeal not allowed 74 Ohio St.3d 1482, 657 N.E.2d 1375. Infants ⇔ 203

Fact that juvenile's mother signed waiver of counsel form did not amount to waiver of juvenile's right to counsel, but fact that mother was present when waiver took place indicated that waiver was voluntary and knowing. In re East (Cuyahoga 1995) 105 Ohio App.3d 221, 663 N.E.2d 983, dismissed, appeal not allowed 74 Ohio St.3d 1482, 657 N.E.2d 1375. Infants ⇔ 205

Referee's report/journal entry and supplemental report, stating that juvenile was advised of his right to counsel and he chose to waive this right, were adequate to show juvenile's waiver of his right to counsel, absent request for transcript of admission hearing. In re East (Cuyahoga 1995) 105 Ohio App.3d 221, 663 N.E.2d 983, dismissed, appeal not allowed 74 Ohio St.3d 1482, 657 N.E.2d 1375. Infants ⇔ 246

An alleged delinquent's response of "don't think so" in response to the juvenile court judge's questions as to whether she desired the representation of counsel is insufficient to support the court's finding that the right to counsel was waived. In re Nation (Shelby 1989) 61 Ohio App.3d 763, 573 N.E.2d 1155.

Colloquy prior to juvenile's admission of delinquency allegations, in which trial court informed juvenile that she had the right to an attorney and that one would be appointed for her if she could not afford one, asked whether juvenile wished to have an attorney, and was told "no" by juvenile, was not sufficient to establish a knowing, voluntary, and intelligent waiver of juvenile's right to counsel. In re K.J. (Ohio App. 8 Dist., Cuyahoga, 05-23-2002) No. 79612, No. 79940, 2002-Ohio-2615, 2002 WL 1041818, Unreported.

A trial court does not fulfill its duty to ascertain whether a juvenile knows of his right to be provided with counsel if he is indigent simply by asking the juvenile if he has received a copy of the statement of rights and whether he has any questions about those rights where (1) the statement of rights is two pages in length, (2) single-spaced, and (3) the right of counsel if indigent is not stated until near the top of the second page; under such circumstances, the juvenile even with a parent present, is likely to sign a form he has not fully read or does not fully understand while at the same time telling a judge otherwise. In re Shane, No. 1523, 2001 WL 62550 (2d Dist Ct App, Darke, 1–26–01).

A juvenile does not knowingly and intelligently waive her right to counsel (1) in absence of any examination by the court regarding such right in deciding whether to admit or deny the complaint, (2) where the complaint states that the juvenile is a delinquent child by reason of committing an act that would constitute complicity to receiving stolen property if she were an adult, and (3) where the magistrate fails to ascertain whether the juvenile understands the charge against her or the possible length of any commitment in the custody of the Department of Youth Services. In re Doyle (App. 2 Dist., 10-03-1997) 122 Ohio App.3d 767, 702 N.E.2d 970.

4. Effective assistance of counsel

Counsel's failure to object when guardian ad litem for the children questioned witnesses during termination of parental rights hearing did not constitute ineffective assistance; mother failed to overcome the strong presumption that counsel's failure to object was reasonable trial strategy, and mother failed to establish that counsel's failure to object to the questioning by guardian ad litem prejudiced mother or affected the outcome of trial. In re Curry (Ohio App. 4 Dist., Washington, 02-11-2004) No. 03CA51, 2004-Ohio-750, 2004 WL 307476, Unreported. Infants ⇔ 205

Father's counsel at termination of parental rights hearing was not ineffective for failing to ask questions on cross examination or present witnesses; failing to question witnesses on cross examination and choosing not to present witnesses fell within realm of trial strategy, and father failed to demonstrate how counsel's alleged deficient performance affected outcome of proceedings. In re Riley (Ohio App. 4 Dist., Washington, 07-25-2003) No. 03CA19, 2003-Ohio-4109, 2003 WL 21783373, Unreported. Infants ⇔ 205

Trial court's error in failing to either make express dual appointment of guardian ad litem to serve as dependent child's guardian and attorney, or to make separate appointments for child's guardian ad litem and child's attorney at outset of child dependency proceeding did not prejudice child; child's attorney and guardian ad litem entered her appearance at probable cause and dependency hearings, and no conflict existed, given that child asked to be placed in Planned Permanent Living Arrangement (PPLA), and attorney/guardian ad litem's recommendation as guardian was that court place child in PPLA. In re Beasley (Ohio App. 4 Dist., Scioto, 05-28-2003) No. 03CA2874, 2003-Ohio-2857, 2003 WL 21278912, Unreported. Infants ⇔ 253

Father failed to establish that he was prejudiced by his trial counsel's alleged failure to be more involved in the parental rights termination hearing, counsel's representation of mother and father and the same time, and counsel's failure to arrange for father's presence at the hearing; none of counsel's alleged deficiencies affected the outcome at trial. In re

Joseph P. (Ohio App. 6 Dist., Lucas, 05-02-2003) No. L-02-1385, 2003-Ohio-2217, 2003 WL 2007268, Unreported. Infants ⬡ 205

Juvenile did not validly waive her right to counsel in delinquency proceeding; while juvenile court orally informed juvenile that she had a right to an attorney at date in which juvenile was not admit or deny guilt to delinquency charge, trial court made no mention of the counsel issue at adjudication hearing and merely asked whether juvenile was ready to proceed, and juvenile court never inquired whether juvenile was waiving her right to counsel. In re Bays (Ohio App. 2 Dist., Greene, 03-14-2003) No. 2002-CA-52, No. 2002-CA-56, 2003-Ohio-1256, 2003 WL 1193787, Unreported. Infants ⬡ 205

For purposes of ineffective assistance claim, minor mother and her parents did not make necessary showing that mother was prejudiced, in dependency proceeding that culminated in judgment terminating mother's parental rights to infant child, by failure of mother's counsel to appear at a pretrial hearing, where counsel made unsuccessful request for continuance of pretrial hearing, and all information shared at hearing was to be shared with mother's counsel. In re Baby Girl Doe (Ohio App., 08-30-2002) 149 Ohio App.3d 717, 778 N.E.2d 1053, 2002-Ohio-4470, appeal not allowed 97 Ohio St.3d 1425, 777 N.E.2d 278, 2002-Ohio-5820. Infants ⬡ 205

Where the proceeding contemplates the loss of parents' essential and basic civil rights to raise their children, the test for ineffective assistance of counsel used in criminal cases is equally applicable to actions seeking to force the permanent, involuntary termination of parental custody. In re Baby Girl Doe (Ohio App. 6 Dist., 08-30-2002) 149 Ohio App.3d 717, 778 N.E.2d 1053, 2002-Ohio-4470, appeal not allowed 97 Ohio St.3d 1425, 777 N.E.2d 278, 2002-Ohio-5820. Infants ⬡ 205

Even assuming that testimony of protective services supervisor for county children's services agency, that child's maternal grandmother told on-call social worker and supervisor that she was upset that she could not have custody of child and that "she was just going to 'go' over and just take him," was inadmissible hearsay, any deficient performance of father's counsel in failing to object at the shelter care hearing was not prejudicial; court was not bound by formal rules of evidence at the hearing, and there was abundant evidence establishing that father's relatives were no longer able to care for child and that child should be placed in foster care. In re Wingo (Ohio App. 4 Dist., 06-01-2001) 143 Ohio App.3d 652, 758 N.E.2d 780, 2001-Ohio-2477. Infants ⬡ 173.1; Infants ⬡ 253

Even assuming father's counsel provided deficient performance by failing to object that testimony of protective services supervisor for county children's services agency involved events and statements outside her personal knowledge, father was not prejudiced at hearing on agency's motion to terminate parental rights; much of the information was also testified to by other witnesses who had firsthand knowledge of events. In re Wingo (Ohio App. 4 Dist., 06-01-2001) 143 Ohio App.3d 652, 758 N.E.2d 780, 2001-Ohio-2477. Infants ⬡ 205; Infants ⬡ 253

Assuming that father's counsel provided deficient performance by failing to submit written argument to court regarding whether child was dependent child and by failing to appear at the hearing extending temporary custody, father was not prejudiced; at that juncture of the case, county children's services agency was attempting to reunify child with mother and place him with a relative until such goal could be accomplished, father had expressed no desire to

gain custody of child, and child's relatives were either not interested in custody or were considered improper placements by agency. In re Wingo (Ohio App. 4 Dist., 06-01-2001) 143 Ohio App.3d 652, 758 N.E.2d 780, 2001-Ohio-2477. Infants ⬡ 205; Infants ⬡ 253

Where proceeding contemplates loss of parents' essential and basic civil rights to raise their children, test for ineffective assistance of counsel used in criminal cases is equally applicable to actions seeking to force permanent, involuntary termination of parental custody. In re Heston (Ohio App. 1 Dist., 09-18-1998) 129 Ohio App.3d 825, 719 N.E.2d 93. Infants ⬡ 205

Statutory right to counsel in child protection proceedings includes right to effective assistance of counsel. In re Heston (Ohio App. 1 Dist., 09-18-1998) 129 Ohio App.3d 825, 719 N.E.2d 93. Infants ⬡ 205

The two-part test for ineffective assistance of counsel used in criminal cases, announced in Strickland v Washington, 466 US 668, 104 SCt 2052, 80 LEd(2d) 674 (1984), is equally applicable in actions by the state to force the permanent, involuntary termination of parental rights. Jones v. Lucas County Children Services Bd. (Lucas 1988) 46 Ohio App.3d 85, 546 N.E.2d 471. Infants ⬡ 205

5. Fees and costs

Trial court's approval of request of guardian ad litem for fees and equal division of fees between former husband and former wife in proceeding on former husband's motion for temporary custody of his and former wife's children did not constitute abuse of discretion; approval implicitly rejected husband's claim that guardian did not act in ward's best interest, notwithstanding husband's claims that guardian was biased against him. Beatley v. Beatley (Ohio App. 5 Dist., Delaware, 08-15-2003) No. 03CAF02010, 2003-Ohio-4375, 2003 WL 21962540, Unreported. Infants ⬡ 83

Court did not err in ruling on motion of guardian ad litem for fees in proceeding on former husband's motion for temporary custody of his and former wife's children, without holding evidentiary hearing on issue; record reflected parties were given opportunity to be heard on fee issue, former husband filed memorandum in opposition to fee request, parties were almost continuously in front of court on variety of issues, and the same judge had been involved with case since its inception. Beatley v. Beatley (Ohio App. 5 Dist., Delaware, 08-15-2003) No. 03CAF02010, 2003-Ohio-4375, 2003 WL 21962540, Unreported. Infants ⬡ 83

Parents should not have been ordered to pay bill prepared by Public Defender's Office for representation of their son in delinquency proceedings, where, at no time prior to dispositional hearing did court address parents, inform them of their status as parties to action, or advise them of their right to counsel. In re Hinko (Cuyahoga 1992) 84 Ohio App.3d 89, 616 N.E.2d 515. Infants ⬡ 205

In an action brought against a parent and his child for damages caused by a fire in a rental unit, where the court finds the child alone liable for such damages in that the child was responsible for starting the fire, the fees and expenses of a court-appointed guardian ad litem are properly charged to the indigent minor child and not to his parent, as part of the court costs. Nationwide Mut. Ins. Co. v. Wymer (Franklin 1986) 33 Ohio App.3d 318, 515 N.E.2d 987.

Pursuant to Juv R 4(F), the juvenile court is authorized to order a child's parents to pay the costs for the services of appointed counsel and guardians ad litem. In re Vaughn, No. 53462 (8th Dist Ct App, Cuyahoga, 10–15–87).

6. Persons represented

Juvenile court was not authorized to proceed with custody hearing and grant permanent and legal custody of children, where father, who had been represented by counsel during much of custody proceedings, was not represented by counsel at custody hearing, and juvenile court had not consented to withdrawal of father's attorney. In re B.P. (Ohio App. 8 Dist., Cuyahoga, 11-21-2002) No. 80659, 2002-Ohio-6318, 2002 WL 31619047, Unreported. Child Custody ⟐ 500

Parents are denied proper representation when the attorney for their children acts as both guardian ad litem and attorney in an action wherein custody is challenged by a county agency. In re Smith (Ottawa 1991) 77 Ohio App.3d 1, 601 N.E.2d 45.

Pursuant to RC 2151.352, a child, his parents, custodian, or other persons in loco parentis, if indigent, is entitled to be represented in all juvenile proceedings by a public defender in accordance with the comprehensive system set forth in RC Ch 120, regardless of whether the outcome of the proceeding could result in a loss of liberty. (Annotation from former RC 2151.352.) OAG 84–023, approved and followed by OAG 97–040.

7. Right to counsel

Child's lack of attorney did not require reversal of order granting temporary custody of child to father and grandmother; order was interlocutory order subject to later modification, record reflected that mother, although informed of child's right to counsel, failed to request counsel, and record reflected that child was subsequently represented by counsel on appeal. In re S.M. (Ohio App. 8 Dist., Cuyahoga, 03-18-2004) No. 81566, 2004-Ohio-1243, 2004 WL 527925, Unreported. Child Custody ⟐ 923(5)

Mother was not denied her right to counsel, in child dependency proceeding; trial court complied with the juvenile court rules when the notice of the permanent custody hearing informed mother of her right to counsel and explained how mother could request the appointment of counsel, and mother failed to pursue counsel. In re Williams (Ohio App. 10 Dist., Franklin, 02-12-2004) No. 03AP-1007, 2004-Ohio-678, 2004 WL 285560, Unreported. Infants ⟐ 205

Fact that incarcerated father did not face jail time was not a proper basis for denying him appointed counsel in child support arrearage proceedings. Jones v. Bowens (Ohio App. 11 Dist., Ashtabula, 09-30-2003) No. 2002-A-0034, 2003-Ohio-5224, 2003 WL 22235372, Unreported. Child Support ⟐ 491

Incarcerated father had not been formally adjudicated indigent, for purposes of child support arrearage proceedings, and thus his right to appointed counsel had not been triggered. Jones v. Bowens (Ohio App. 11 Dist., Ashtabula, 09-30-2003) No. 2002-A-0034, 2003-Ohio-5224, 2003 WL 22235372, Unreported. Child Support ⟐ 491

When a guardian ad litem who is also appointed as the juvenile's attorney in a proceeding for the termination of parental rights recommends a disposition that conflicts with the juvenile's wishes, the juvenile court must appoint independent counsel to represent the child. In re Williams (Ohio, 04-14-2004) 101 Ohio St.3d 398, 805 N.E.2d 1110, 2004-Ohio-1500. Infants ⟐ 205

Guardian ad litem can, in some situations, serve a dual role, in a proceeding for the termination of parental rights, as both the guardian ad litem and the juvenile's attorney, and thereby fulfill the juvenile's right to counsel, provided there has been an express dual appointment by the juvenile court. In re Williams (Ohio, 04-14-2004) 101 Ohio St.3d 398, 805 N.E.2d 1110, 2004-Ohio-1500. Infants ⟐ 205

Child who was subject of juvenile court proceeding to terminate parental rights was party to that proceeding, and entitled to independent counsel; abrogating In re Alfrey, Clark App. No. 01CA0083, 2003-Ohio-608, 2003 WL 262587. In re Williams (Ohio, 04-14-2004) 101 Ohio St.3d 398, 805 N.E.2d 1110, 2004-Ohio-1500. Infants ⟐ 205

County child support enforcement agency (CSEA) lacked standing to appeal trial court's failure to appoint counsel for indigent mother in paternity and child support action, because agency was not prejudiced by any error; agency's ability to assert its claim that laches did not bar establishment of paternity or bar issuance of child support order was not affected, because agency could have subpoenaed mother to testify and because agency presented, without mother's testimony, her explanation for delay in revealing father's identity. Still v. Hayman (Ohio App. 7 Dist., 07-30-2003) 153 Ohio App.3d 487, 794 N.E.2d 751, 2003-Ohio-4113. Children Out-of-wedlock ⟐ 73

Indigent mother was entitled to have the trial court appoint counsel for her in paternity and child support action, even if funding in the account for payment of court-appointed counsel was lacking. Still v. Hayman (Ohio App. 7 Dist., 07-30-2003) 153 Ohio App.3d 487, 794 N.E.2d 751, 2003-Ohio-4113. Children Out-of-wedlock ⟐ 57

RC 120.33(B) does not impose a clear legal duty upon a judge to appoint as counsel of record the attorney personally selected by an indigent party. State ex rel. Butler v. Demis (Ohio 1981) 66 Ohio St.2d 123, 420 N.E.2d 116, 20 O.O.3d 121.

The trial court's failure to consider child's desire to reside with mother prejudiced mother, in permanent custody proceeding, and warranted remand for a new hearing; child had a right to be represented by counsel at the hearing, counsel for child had a duty to advocate for child's position, and mother was entitled to cross-examine the supplemental evidence concerning child's wishes. In re Williams (Ohio App. 11 Dist., Geauga, 07-03-2003) No. 2003-G-2498, No. 2003-G-2499, 2003-Ohio-3550, 2003 WL 21517986, Unreported. Infants ⟐ 254

Failing to appoint counsel to represent children in termination of parental rights proceeding involving allegations of child abuse was harmless error, where allegations of abuse were dismissed by agreement of parties and court attempted to determine each child's wishes by conducting in camera interview. In re Joshua B. (Ohio App. 6 Dist., Sandusky, 06-13-2003) No. S-02-018, No. S-02-021, No. S-02-019, No. S-02-020, 2003-Ohio-3096, 2003 WL 21384883, Unreported. Infants ⟐ 253

Mother of dependent children did not waive right to assert children's right to counsel in termination of parental rights proceeding, where mother filed motion raising issue of counsel one week after guardian ad litem (GAL) interviewed children and they indicated desire to reunify. In re Emery (Ohio App. 4 Dist., Lawrence, 04-25-2003) No. 02CA40, 2003-Ohio-2206, 2003 WL 2003811, Unreported. Infants ⟐ 200

Mother of dependent children was entitled to assert children's right to counsel in termination of parental rights proceeding, where both mother and children desired reunification. In re Emery (Ohio App. 4 Dist., Lawrence, 04-25-2003) No. 02CA40,

2003-Ohio-2206, 2003 WL 2003811, Unreported. Infants ⚬ 200

Dependent children were not represented by counsel in termination of parental rights proceeding; although individual appointed as guardian ad litem (GAL) was licensed attorney, there was nothing to indicate that court made dual appointment so that individual could also serve as children's attorney. In re Emery (Ohio App. 4 Dist., Lawrence, 04-25-2003) No. 02CA40, 2003-Ohio-2206, 2003 WL 2003811, Unreported. Infants ⚬ 205

Indigent dependent children were parties to termination of parental rights proceeding who had right to appointed counsel upon being name in complaints. In re Emery (Ohio App. 4 Dist., Lawrence, 04-25-2003) No. 02CA40, 2003-Ohio-2206, 2003 WL 2003811, Unreported. Infants ⚬ 205

Trial court's failure to inquire as to appointment of counsel for mother in father's proceeding to modify shared parenting plan was harmless error, where, at trial, mother admitted that she made too much money to be considered indigent, and thus, mother would not have been entitled to appointment of counsel. In re Lemon (Ohio App. 5 Dist., Stark, 11-12-2002) No. 2002 CA 00098, 2002-Ohio-6263, 2002 WL 31546216, Unreported. Child Custody ⚬ 923(4)

County child support enforcement agency (CSEA) lacked standing to appeal trial court's failure to appoint counsel for indigent mother in paternity and child support action, because agency was not prejudiced by any error; agency's ability to assert its claim that laches did not bar establishment of paternity or bar issuance of child support order was not affected, because agency could have subpoenaed mother to testify and because agency presented, without mother's testimony, her explanation for delay in revealing father's identity. Still v. Hayman (Ohio App. 7 Dist., 07-30-2003) 153 Ohio App.3d 487, 794 N.E.2d 751, 2003-Ohio-4113. Children Out-of-wedlock ⚬ 73

Indigent mother was entitled to have the trial court appoint counsel for her in paternity and child support action, even if funding in the account for payment of court-appointed counsel was lacking. Still v. Hayman (Ohio App. 7 Dist., 07-30-2003) 153 Ohio App.3d 487, 794 N.E.2d 751, 2003-Ohio-4113. Children Out-of-wedlock ⚬ 57

Parents were denied their statutory right to counsel in termination of parental rights proceedings, where father was never represented, mother's counsel withdrew at dispositional hearing for lack of contact with mother, and hearing continued ex parte. In re Alyssa C. (Ohio App. 6 Dist., 05-23-2003) 153 Ohio App.3d 10, 790 N.E.2d 803, 2003-Ohio-2673. Infants ⚬ 205

In order to sustain commitment of a juvenile offender to a state institution in a delinquency proceeding, where such commitment will deprive the child of his liberty, the alleged delinquent must have been afforded representation by counsel, appointed at state expense in case of indigency. (Annotation from former RC 2151.35.) In re Agler (Ohio 1969) 19 Ohio St.2d 70, 249 N.E.2d 808, 48 O.O.2d 85. Infants ⚬ 205

An adjudication proceeding cannot go forward unless the juvenile is represented by counsel or there has been a valid waiver of the right to counsel. In re Johnston (Ohio App. 11 Dist., 04-30-2001) 142 Ohio App.3d 314, 755 N.E.2d 457. Infants ⚬ 205

Juvenile was entitled to representation by counsel in adjudication for vandalism and criminal trespass, where juvenile did not waive his right to counsel, and conviction on charges could result in juvenile having his liberty curtailed. In re Johnston (Ohio App. 11 Dist., 04-30-2001) 142 Ohio App.3d 314, 755 N.E.2d 457. Infants ⚬ 205

Custodian's statement to court that she advised juvenile to admit to the charges if true or deny them if false did not urge juvenile to admit to something she did not do, nor did it recommend to the court any suggested disposition of the matter, and thus custodian did not act contrary to juvenile's best legal interests. In re Smith (Ohio App. 8 Dist., 03-26-2001) 142 Ohio App.3d 16, 753 N.E.2d 930. Infants ⚬ 205

Children who were subject of action to terminate parental rights had right to appointed counsel that attached when they were removed from the home. In re Stacey S. (Ohio App. 6 Dist., 12-30-1999) 136 Ohio App.3d 503, 737 N.E.2d 92, 1999-Ohio-989. Infants ⚬ 205

Complaint to terminate parental rights claiming that children were neglected and dependent, which included facts showing that both physical and sexual abuse were believed to be at issue, was sufficient to allege that children were 'abused,'' such that children had right to appointed counsel. In re Stacey S. (Ohio App. 6 Dist., 12-30-1999) 136 Ohio App.3d 503, 737 N.E.2d 92, 1999-Ohio-989. Infants ⚬ 197; Infants ⚬ 205

Appointment of guardian ad litem and attorney for the guardian ad litem was not sufficient to satisfy children's right to counsel in action to terminate parental rights. In re Stacey S. (Ohio App. 6 Dist., 12-30-1999) 136 Ohio App.3d 503, 737 N.E.2d 92, 1999-Ohio-989. Infants ⚬ 205

Appointment of attorney for guardian ad litem as the substitute guardian ad litem in parental rights termination proceeding did not satisfy children's right to counsel, even though attorney claimed she performed as counsel to children, where court failed to make finding that there was no conflict between the attorney's dual roles as guardian ad litem and attorney for children and suggestions were raised during dispositional hearing that a conflict did exist. In re Stacey S. (Ohio App. 6 Dist., 12-30-1999) 136 Ohio App.3d 503, 737 N.E.2d 92, 1999-Ohio-989. Infants ⚬ 205

Child is entitled to counsel at all stages of juvenile proceedings. In re Solis (Ohio App. 8 Dist., 12-22-1997) 124 Ohio App.3d 547, 706 N.E.2d 839. Infants ⚬ 205

Juvenile adjudicated delinquent and provisionally placed in foster care was entitled to counsel at dispositional hearing, as provisional placement was not equivalent of probation and dispositional hearing was not equivalent of probation revocation hearing. In re Solis (Ohio App. 8 Dist., 12-22-1997) 124 Ohio App.3d 547, 706 N.E.2d 839. Infants ⚬ 205

Trial court failed to adequately advise juvenile of her right to counsel, where court did not conduct any meaningful colloquy with juvenile, made most of its remarks to juvenile's mother, who had filed unruly child complaint, and addressed child directly only briefly, almost as an afterthought. In re Rogers (Ohio App. 9 Dist., 12-10-1997) 124 Ohio App.3d 392, 706 N.E.2d 390. Infants ⚬ 205

Magistrate who presided over arraignment in juvenile proceeding failed to adequately inform juvenile of her right to counsel; magistrate discussed right to counsel only in terms of representation if she were to proceed to trial, and gave explanation of right to counsel that was confusing, if not misleading, and could have led juvenile to believe that she was not entitled to counsel while deciding whether to admit or deny complaint. In re Doyle (App. 2 Dist., 10-03-1997) 122 Ohio App.3d 767, 702 N.E.2d 970. Infants ⚬ 205

Prior to juvenile's admission to habitual truancy charge, trial court failed to adequately advise juvenile of his constitutional rights and of consequences of his admission and also failed to sufficiently ascertain whether juvenile's purported waiver of counsel was made knowingly and voluntarily; there was no indication in record that trial court ever made determination concerning juvenile's indigency or advised juvenile that he had right to appointed counsel based on his indigency; trial court had merely asked juvenile whether it could be assumed that juvenile wished to proceed without attorney since juvenile was there without attorney, and trial court had not advised juvenile of purpose of hearing, possible penalties for alleged truancy violation, ramifications of admission to charge or of juvenile's rights to remain silent, offer evidence, cross-examine witnesses and have record made of proceedings. In re Kimble (Ohio App. 3 Dist., 09-25-1996) 114 Ohio App.3d 136, 682 N.E.2d 1066. Infants ☞ 199; Infants ☞ 205

Indigent father was entitled to have counsel appointed to represent him on custody and visitation issues in child support action under statute and juvenile court rule; both rule and statute guarantee right to appointed counsel for all indigent parties in juvenile court proceedings, father, being natural father and parent of children, was a party to juvenile court proceeding under juvenile court rules, and father was indigent as defined in rules. McKinney v. McClure (Butler 1995) 102 Ohio App.3d 165, 656 N.E.2d 1310. Children Out-of-wedlock ☞ 20.4

Right to appointed counsel for indigent parties applies to all matters properly brought before juvenile court, including custody and visitation issues. McKinney v. McClure (Butler 1995) 102 Ohio App.3d 165, 656 N.E.2d 1310. Child Custody ☞ 500

Juvenile rule and statute guarantee right to counsel for all indigent parties in juvenile proceedings. Holley v. Higgins (Franklin 1993) 86 Ohio App.3d 240, 620 N.E.2d 251. Infants ☞ 205

Indigent parties to juvenile court proceedings have a right to counsel under RC 2151.312 and Juv R 4(A). Lowry v. Lowry (Ross 1988) 48 Ohio App.3d 184, 549 N.E.2d 176.

The guarantee of the right to be represented by counsel set forth in Juv R 4(A) does not, as to a nonindigent party, require that trial be continued indefinitely until counsel can be obtained, but merely requires, if it does not appear that counsel could not be obtained through the exercise of reasonable diligence and a willingness to enter into reasonable contractual arrangements for counsel's services, that a reasonable opportunity be given to the party before trial to employ such counsel. In re Bolden (Allen 1973) 37 Ohio App.2d 7, 306 N.E.2d 166, 66 O.O.2d 26.

Trial court was not required to unilaterally appoint counsel for dependent child regarding action by county child services to modify disposition of child from temporary custody to permanent custody and to terminate father's parental rights, where no allegation of abuse was set forth in complaint. In re Graham (Ohio App. 4 Dist., Athens, 08-02-2002) No. 01CA57, 2002-Ohio-4411, 2002 WL 1978881, Unreported.

Juvenile court commits reversible error when it violates a parent's statutory right to be represented by counsel at a dispositional hearing to modify temporary custody of her son to long term foster care by failing to advise the parent of her right to counsel and her right to appointed counsel if she is indigent. In re Lander, No. CA99-05-096, 2000 WL 819775 (12th Dist Ct App, Butler, 6-26-00).

A child dependency proceeding invokes a parent's right to counsel under Juv R 4(A), and a court abuses its discretion in revoking the pro hac vice status of a parent's attorney without a hearing where there are only bald accusations that the attorney is engaging in egregious misconduct. In re N.B. & S.B, Nos. CA93-09-183+, 1994 WL 394972 (12th Dist Ct App, Butler, 8-1-94).

Stepmother's and her allegedly abused stepson's interests were aligned and any error prejudicial to stepson was prejudicial to stepmother, and thus, stepmother had standing to raise as assignment of error whether stepson's right to be represented by counsel was violated, even though stepson did not appeal from judgment ordering protective supervision. (Per O'Neill, P.J., with one judge concurring in judgment only.) In re Calvin, Anthony, Alyshia (Ohio App. 11 Dist., Geauga, 11-22-2002) No. 2001-G-2379, 2002-Ohio-6468, 2002 WL 31663562, Unreported, stay granted 98 Ohio St.3d 1459, 783 N.E.2d 518, 2003-Ohio-644, appeal not allowed 98 Ohio St.3d 1513, 786 N.E.2d 63, 2003-Ohio-1572. Infants ☞ 242

Allegedly abused child was entitled to have counsel appointed to represent his interests in dependency proceedings. (Per O'Neill, P.J., with one judge concurring in judgment only.) In re Calvin, Anthony, Alyshia (Ohio App. 11 Dist., Geauga, 11-22-2002) No. 2001-G-2379, 2002-Ohio-6468, 2002 WL 31663562, Unreported, stay granted 98 Ohio St.3d 1459, 783 N.E.2d 518, 2003-Ohio-644, appeal not allowed 98 Ohio St.3d 1513, 786 N.E.2d 63, 2003-Ohio-1572. Infants ☞ 205

An indigent child is entitled pursuant to RC 2151.352 and Juv R 4(A) to be represented by the county public defender in all juvenile court proceedings pertaining to a complaint alleging the child to be a juvenile traffic offender, regardless of whether the outcome of the proceeding could result in a loss of liberty, except when the right to counsel is waived or the juvenile court pursuant to RC 120.16(E) appoints counsel other than the county public defender or allows an indigent child to select his own personal counsel to represent him. OAG 97–040.

8. Damages

Since the decision to appoint or refuse to appoint an attorney to represent indigent juvenile litigants rests entirely in the discretion of the juvenile court judge, it follows that neither the court administrator, county board of commissioners, nor the county juvenile court can be held liable for any damages suffered by the attorney when his name is removed by the juvenile court judge from the court-appointment list. Eichenberger v. Petree (Franklin 1992) 76 Ohio App.3d 779, 603 N.E.2d 366, motion overruled 64 Ohio St.3d 1409, 592 N.E.2d 846. Counties ☞ 59; Courts ☞ 55; Judges ☞ 36

9. Guardian ad litem

The trial court's failure to appoint a guardian ad litem for juvenile when a conflict of interest existed between juvenile and his parents constituted reversible error; the victim of juvenile's crime was his half-sister, juvenile's stepfather informed the court at juvenile's arraignment that they did not want juvenile to return to their home, juvenile's mother informed the court that she did not feel that she could make choices that were in juvenile's best interest, and juvenile was not represented by counsel at his probation revocation hearing. In re K.J.F. (Ohio App. 2 Dist., Clark, 01-23-2004) No. 2003 CA 41, 2004-Ohio-263, 2004 WL 102847, Unreported. Infants ☞ 253

Mother waived her appellate argument that the trial court erred when it failed to permit counsel for mother to examine the guardian ad litem with respect to the contents of his report submitted after the hearing, in child dependency proceeding, where mother failed to object to the manner in which guardian ad litem performed his duties, she did not object when the guardian ad litem failed to submit his report at the hearing, and she failed to object when the trial judge expressed an intention to receive and consider the guardian ad litem's report after the hearing. In re La.B. (Ohio App. 8 Dist., Cuyahoga, 12-18-2003) No. 81981, 2003-Ohio-6852, 2003 WL 22966171, Unreported. Infants ☞ 243

Magistrate's failure to appoint guardian ad litem in delinquency proceeding, despite fact that minor's mother requested treatment for minor, while minor desired commitment to Department of Youth Services, was not plain error; transcript of proceeding revealed no anger or tension between minor and mother, which may have necessitated appointment of guardian ad litem. In re Harper (Ohio App. 2 Dist., Montgomery, 12-12-2003) No. 19948, 2003-Ohio-6666, 2003 WL 22927248, Unreported. Infants ☞ 243

Trial court acted within its discretion in denying mother's motion for a separate guardian ad litem without a hearing, in proceedings in which mother sought to suspend father's visitation based on alleged sexual abuse, even though original guardian allegedly spent only an hour with family, where guardian ad litem's report revealed reasons for her recommendations and did not reveal bias, and mother did not show any other basis for appointment of separate guardian. Edwards v. Livingstone (Ohio App. 11 Dist., Ashtabula, 08-01-2003) No. 2001-A-0082, No. 2002-A-0060, 2003-Ohio-4099, 2003 WL 21782596, Unreported. Infants ☞ 80(1)

Trial court should have either made express dual appointment of guardian ad litem to serve as dependent child's guardian and attorney, or should have made separate appointments for child's guardian ad litem and child's attorney at outset of child dependency proceeding. In re Beasley (Ohio App. 4 Dist., Scioto, 05-28-2003) No. 03CA2874, 2003-Ohio-2857, 2003 WL 21278912, Unreported. Infants ☞ 205

Trial court was required to appoint a guardian ad litem for children in termination of parental rights case, whereas the court was not likewise required to appoint counsel to represent them. In re Alfrey (Ohio App. 2 Dist., Clark, 02-07-2003) No. 01CA0083, 2003-Ohio-608, 2003 WL 262587, Unreported. Infants ☞ 205

Although an attorney may represent an indigent mother who is also incompetent as her counsel and as guardian ad litem, if he feels there is a conflict between the two roles of representing his client's wishes and asking the court to do what is in the best interests of his ward, he should withdraw so that the client/ward have proper representation at the hearing. In re Baby Girl Baxter (Ohio 1985) 17 Ohio St.3d 229, 479 N.E.2d 257, 17 O.B.R. 469.

Failure to appoint guardian at litem for juvenile or at least inquire further into whether guardian ad litem was necessary was reversible error in delinquency proceedings after juvenile's grandfather, his legal guardian, informed court that he had recently filed unruly charge against juvenile, thereby suggesting strong possibility of conflict of interest, particularly where grandfather apparently acted for purpose of ascertaining status of this additional charge rather than out of concern for juvenile's best interests, as evidenced by his refusal to explain circumstances surrounding charge. In re Spradlin (Ohio App. 4

Dist. 2000) 140 Ohio App.3d 402, 747 N.E.2d 877, 2000 -Ohio- 2003. Infants ☞ 253

Permitting mother's counsel to withdraw from proceedings to terminate mother's parental rights was neither error nor an abuse of discretion; mother abducted child from foster parents' home in violation of existing court orders and voluntarily absconded from the court's jurisdiction to China, choosing not to contact either her counsel or the court, counsel advised the court that she did not know what her client wanted her to do and therefore could not zealously represent her client, and the Juvenile Court Rules authorized mother's guardian ad litem, also an attorney, to serve as her counsel. In re Zhang (Ohio App. 8 Dist. 1999) 135 Ohio App.3d 350, 734 N.E.2d 379, dismissed, appeal not allowed 87 Ohio St.3d 1417, 717 N.E.2d 1105, reconsideration stricken 87 Ohio St.3d 1437, 719 N.E.2d 2. Infants ☞ 205

Strong possibility of conflict of interest between juvenile involved in delinquency adjudication proceeding and his father, who represented him in such proceeding, mandated appointment of guardian ad litem for juvenile; juvenile's parents had previously brought him before juvenile court on domestic violence charge, and father attempted to persuade juvenile court to act in manner which may have been against juvenile's interests and persuaded juvenile not to exercise his statutory right to attorney. In re Sappington (Ohio App. 2 Dist. 1997) 123 Ohio App.3d 448, 704 N.E.2d 339. Infants ☞ 205

Failure of court to appoint guardian ad litem for juvenile, when such appointment is required under applicable rule or statute, constitutes reversible error. In re Sappington (Ohio App. 2 Dist. 1997) 123 Ohio App.3d 448, 704 N.E.2d 339. Infants ☞ 205; Infants ☞ 253

Appellate court should find reversible error in juvenile court's failure to appoint guardian ad litem for juvenile involved in proceedings before it when record from below reveals strong enough possibility of conflict of interest between parent and child to show that juvenile court abused its discretion by not so finding. In re Sappington (Ohio App. 2 Dist. 1997) 123 Ohio App.3d 448, 704 N.E.2d 339. Infants ☞ 205; Infants ☞ 253

Lawyer may, in proper circumstances, take on duties of both counsel for juvenile subjected to delinquency proceeding and juvenile's guardian ad litem; however, as lawyer's role is to represent client zealously within boundaries of law, and guardian's role is to investigate juvenile's situation and ask court to do what is in juvenile's best interest, duties of counsel and guardian may conflict to extent rendering lawyer incapable of performing both functions. In re Howard (Ohio App. 1 Dist., 04-16-1997) 119 Ohio App.3d 201, 695 N.E.2d 1. Infants ☞ 205

In action to terminate parental rights, guardian ad litem's report was hearsay and could not be considered evidence, where report was not submitted under oath and guardian did not testify and was not subjected to direct or cross-examination. Matter of Duncan/Walker Children (Stark 1996) 109 Ohio App.3d 841, 673 N.E.2d 217. Infants ☞ 174

Since guardian ad litem was not counsel for ward in action to terminate parental rights, guardian had no authority to file findings of fact and conclusions of law, and court should not have ordered guardian to do so. Matter of Duncan/Walker Children (Stark 1996) 109 Ohio App.3d 841, 673 N.E.2d 217. Infants ☞ 210

For attorney to act as guardian ad litem and attorney for ward, there must be dual appointment, and finding that no conflict exists. Matter of Duncan/Walker Children (Stark 1996) 109 Ohio App.3d

841, 673 N.E.2d 217. Attorney And Client ⇔ 21.5(1); Infants ⇔ 81

Guardian ad litem has absolute immunity from actions arising out of performance of duties mandated by guardian's role as advocate for child in judicial proceedings. Penn v. McMonagle (Huron 1990) 60 Ohio App.3d 149, 573 N.E.2d 1234, motion overruled 58 Ohio St.3d 704, 569 N.E.2d 512. Infants ⇔ 85

Where an infant child has been in the custody of prospective adoptive parents as a result of a permanent order of custody in a dependency action and that permanent order is subsequently vacated and the parent moves to terminate temporary custody, it appears that the interests of the child and parent may conflict and a guardian ad litem must be appointed for the child pursuant to Juv R 4(B) prior to the hearing on the mother's motion to terminate custody. In re Christopher (Morrow 1977) 54 Ohio App.2d 137, 376 N.E.2d 603, 8 O.O.3d 271. Infants ⇔ 78(1)

The guardian ad litem appointed for a child in a dependency action where the interest of the child and the parent may conflict must have no ties or loyalties to anyone with an adversary interest in the outcome such as a natural parent or the prospective adoptive parents. In re Christopher (Morrow 1977) 54 Ohio App.2d 137, 376 N.E.2d 603, 8 O.O.3d 271. Infants ⇔ 81

Appointment of guardian ad litem (GAL) did not constitute an appointment to act as child's attorney in proceeding which sought custody of child; there was no evidence of a dual appointment, such as mention on judgment entry that GAL was also acting as child's attorney or inclusion of an attorney number on documents bearing signature of GAL. Sabrina J. v Robbin C, No. L-00-1374, 2002-Ohio-2691, 2002 WL 1303148 (6th Dist Ct App, Lucas, 5-31-02).

The trial court errs in failing to inform the parent of her rights to remain silent, to cross-examine witnesses, and to offer evidence at the adjudicatory hearing and in granting permanent custody when no guardian ad litem's report is filed with the court. Matter of Eplin (Ohio App. 5 Dist., Stark, 06-29-1995) No. 94 CA 0311, 1995 WL 495451, Unreported.

10. Cause of action

Contempt judgment could not be entered for failure to pay court costs imposed in proceeding in which juvenile was found to be unruly child. In re Buffington (Huron 1993) 89 Ohio App.3d 814, 627 N.E.2d 1013, motion overruled 68 Ohio St.3d 1429, 624 N.E.2d 1066. Contempt ⇔ 20

In an attorney's action against a juvenile court administrative judge brought after the attorney's name is removed from the list of attorneys appointed to represent indigent clients appearing before the court, the attorney's allegation that the removal of his name prevented him from practicing law in the juvenile court is merely a conclusion about the consequences of the removal which need not be accepted as true for purposes of a motion to dismiss; the attorney failed to allege facts that the judge attempted to control the practice of law in juvenile court, and the removal of the attorney's name did not prevent him from representing indigent clients pro bono or from representing other clients. Eichenberger v. Petree (Franklin 1992) 76 Ohio App.3d 779, 603 N.E.2d 366, motion overruled 64 Ohio St.3d 1409, 592 N.E.2d 846. Pretrial Procedure ⇔ 652

Before withdrawing as appointed counsel in an appeal from a termination of parental rights on the ground that counsel finds the case wholly frivolous, the attorney should so advise the court, request permission to withdraw, and submit with the request a brief referring to anything in the record that might arguably support the appeal; a copy of the brief should be given the appellant and time allowed him to raise any points he chooses, after which the court will fully examine the proceedings to decide whether the case is wholly frivolous. Morris v. Lucas County Children Services Bd. (Lucas 1989) 49 Ohio App.3d 86, 550 N.E.2d 980.

11. Jurisdiction

Where a court, having acquired jurisdiction over a child by virtue of a divorce action between the child's parents, certifies the matter of the child's custody to a juvenile court, the consent of the juvenile court having been first obtained, the juvenile court has exclusive jurisdiction over the child's custody by virtue of RC 3109.06 and 2151.23(D) and a finding of unfitness of the parents or that there is no suitable relative to have custody is not a necessary prerequisite to such certification, and while such certification shall be deemed to be the complaint in the juvenile court, it does not constitute a complaint in the juvenile court that such child is dependent or neglected and those dispositions provided for under RC 2151.353, 2151.354, and 2151.355 are not applicable to the disposition of such a child, disposition thereof being subject to and controlled by RC 3109.04. In re Height (Van Wert 1975) 47 Ohio App.2d 203, 353 N.E.2d 887, 1 O.O.3d 279. Courts ⇔ 472.1

Juv R 5 [Reserved]

Juv R 6 Taking into custody

(A) A child may be taken into custody:

(1) pursuant to an order of the court;

(2) pursuant to the law of arrest;

(3) by a law enforcement officer or duly authorized officer of the court when any of the following conditions exist:

(a) There are reasonable grounds to believe that the child is suffering from illness or injury and is not receiving proper care, and the child's removal is necessary to prevent immediate or threatened physical or emotional harm;

(b) There are reasonable grounds to believe that the child is in immediate danger from the child's surroundings and that the child's removal is necessary to prevent immediate or threatened physical or emotional harm;

(c) There are reasonable grounds to believe that a parent, guardian, custodian, or other household member of the child has abused or neglected another child in the household, and that the child is in danger of immediate or threatened physical or emotional harm;

(d) There are reasonable grounds to believe that the child has run away from the child's parents, guardian, or other custodian;

(e) There are reasonable grounds to believe that the conduct, conditions, or surroundings of the child are endangering the health, welfare, or safety of the child;

(f) During the pendency of court proceedings, there are reasonable grounds to believe that the child may abscond or be removed from the jurisdiction of the court or will not be brought to the court;

(g) A juvenile judge or designated magistrate has found that there is probable cause to believe any of the conditions set forth in division (A)(3)(a), (b), or (c) of this rule are present, has found that reasonable efforts have been made to notify the child's parents, guardian ad litem or custodian that the child may be placed into shelter care, except where notification would jeopardize the physical or emotional safety of the child or result in the child's removal from the court's jurisdiction, and has ordered ex parte, by telephone or otherwise, the taking of the child into custody.

(4) By the judge or designated magistrate ex parte pending the outcome of the adjudicatory and dispositional hearing in an abuse, neglect, or dependency proceeding, where it appears to the court that the best interest and welfare of the child require the immediate issuance of a shelter care order.

(B) Probable cause hearing

When a child is taken into custody pursuant to an ex parte emergency order pursuant to division (A)(3)(g) or (A)(4) of this rule, a probable cause hearing shall be held before the end of the next business day after the day on which the order is issued but not later than seventy-two hours after the issuance of the emergency order.

(Adopted eff. 7–1–72; amended eff. 7–1–94, 7–1–96)

Historical and Statutory Notes

Amendment Note: The 7–1–96 amendment substituted "magistrate" for "referee" in divisions (A)(3)(g) and (A)(4).

Amendment Note: The 7–1–94 amendment rewrote this rule, which previously read:

"A child may be taken into custody: (1) pursuant to an order of the court, (2) pursuant to the law of arrest, (3) by a law enforcement officer or duly authorized officer of the court when there are reasonable grounds to believe that the child is suffering from illness or injury and is not receiving proper care, or is in immediate danger from his surroundings, and that his removal is necessary, (4) by a law enforcement officer or duly authorized officer of the court when there are reasonable grounds to believe

that the child has run away from his parents, guardian, or other custodian, and (5) where, during the pendency of court proceedings, it appears to the court that the conduct, condition or surroundings of the child are endangering the health, welfare, person or property of himself or others, or that he may abscond or be removed from the jurisdiction of the court or will not be brought to the court."

Commentary

Staff Notes

1996:

The amendment changed the rule's reference from "referee" to "magistrate" in divisions (A)(3)(G) [sic.] and (A)(4) in order to harmonize the rule with the language adopted in the 1995 amendments to Juv. R. 40. The amendment is technical only and no substantive change is intended.

1994:

Rule 6 Taking Into Custody

The 1994 amendment modified Juv. R. 6 to comply with section 2151.31 of the Revised Code, which requires particular conditions to exist to permit a law enforcement officer or a duly authorized officer of the court to take a child into emergency custody. Juv. R. 6(A)(3)(g) specifies when such taking into custody may be authorized by an ex parte telephone order pursuant to section 2151.31(D) of the Revised Code. Juv. R. 6(B) delineates time deadlines for a probable cause hearing to be held after the issuance of an emergency order.

Cross References

Custody of child by public agency, 2151.38
Disposition of abused, neglected, or dependent child, 2151.353
Disposition of unruly child, 2151.354

Ohio Administrative Code References

Authority to assume and retain custody of a child, OAC 5101:2–42–04

Library References

Infants ⚖68.3, 192.
Westlaw Topic No. 211.
C.J.S. Infants §§ 42, 53 to 55.
Am Jur 2d: 47, Juvenile Courts and Delinquent and Dependent Children § 35, 44 to 48
Validity and application of statute allowing endangered child to be temporarily removed from parental custody. 38 ALR4th 756
Carlin, Baldwin's Ohio Practice, Merrick–Rippner Probate Law § 107.25, 107.152 (2003).

Law Review and Journal Commentaries

The Plight of the Interstate Child in American Courts, Leona Mary Hudak. 9 Akron L Rev 257 (Fall 1975).

Notes of Decisions

Confessions, admissibility 2
Hearings 1
Release from custody 3
Taking minor into custody 4
Waiver of Miranda rights 5

---

1. Hearings

RC 2151.28 and 2151.31 do not require a hearing as a condition precedent to the taking of a child into custody, pursuant to order of a juvenile court, during pendency of an action in such court. (Annotation from former RC 2151.31.) In re Jones (Allen 1961) 114 Ohio App. 319, 182 N.E.2d 631, 19 O.O.2d 286.

2. Confessions, admissibility

Three minors, suspected of murder, were apprehended; prior to their being taken before any court and before any charges were filed against them, signed confessions were obtained from each of them; they were then taken before juvenile court which conducted investigation, and nature of crime being apparent, cases were referred to common pleas court where accused were indicted, tried and convicted; in each instance confession obtained was used against one making it, in both juvenile court and court of common pleas; confessions were admissible in evidence, even though accused were not taken immediately before juvenile court as directed by this section; fact that confessions were used in juvenile court did not render them inadmissible in court of common pleas under GC 1639–30 (RC 2151.35) because there was but one case or proceeding. (Annotation from former RC 2151.31.) State v. Lowder (Stark 1946) 79 Ohio App. 237, 72 N.E.2d 785, 34 O.O. 568, appeal dismissed 147 Ohio St. 340, 70 N.E.2d 905, 34 O.O. 249, certiorari granted 67 S.Ct. 1728, 331 U.S. 803, 91 L.Ed. 1826, reversed 68 S.Ct. 302, 332 U.S. 596, 92 L.Ed. 224, 36 O.O. 530, appeal dismissed 147 Ohio St. 530, 72 N.E.2d 102, 34 O.O. 423, appeal dismissed 147 Ohio St. 531, 72 N.E.2d 81, 34 O.O. 423, appeal dismissed 151 Ohio St. 80, 84 N.E.2d 217, 38 O.O. 531, certiorari denied 69 S.Ct. 1501, 337 U.S. 945, 93 L.Ed. 1748.

3. Release from custody

A minor detained on delinquency charges is not charged with an offense and hence is not entitled to release on bail. (Annotation from former RC 2151.31.) State ex rel. Peaks v. Allaman (Montgomery 1952) 115 N.E.2d 849, 66 Ohio Law Abs. 403, 51 O.O. 321.

4. Taking minor into custody

The warrantless arrest of a juvenile is on probable cause when the arresting officer has sufficient information, from the victim's description of the group responsible for a robbery and from a subsequent radio report concerning a disturbance created by a similar group in the same general area, to warrant a reasonable belief that a felony has been committed and that the arrestee is one of the perpetrators. In re Howard (Hamilton 1987) 31 Ohio App.3d 1, 508 N.E.2d 190, 31 O.B.R. 14.

Under RC 2151.14 and 2151.31 it is the manifest duty of enforcement officers to cooperate with and assist the juvenile authorities in the performance of their duties when such officers are specifically requested to do so by the juvenile authorities; and such officers may avoid liability in an action for false imprisonment by showing that they were justified in the detention or restraint of the juvenile made under the specific direction and order of the juvenile authorities. (Annotation from former RC 2151.31.) Garland v. Dustman (Portage 1969) 19 Ohio App.2d 292, 251 N.E.2d 153, 48 O.O.2d 408. False Imprisonment ⟐ 11; Infants ⟐ 192

Under Ohio law, unless matters of public safety are involved, a child alleged to be abused, neglected, or dependent may be removed from his home by court order only upon a judicial determination that continuation in the home would be contrary to the child's best interest. OAG 87–105.

5. Waiver of Miranda rights

Where police apprehended a fourteen-year-old minor for questioning following a fire, police may properly question such minor at the police station before

delivering her to a place of detention or bringing her to court. In re Hawkins, No. 3430 (9th Dist Ct App, Lorain, 5–11–83).

Where a fourteen-year-old minor, without counsel, made a statement to police implicating herself in setting a fire which killed her father, and the court psychologist testified that such minor was of average intelligence, the minor's statement is properly admitted into evidence where the minor had waived her Miranda rights and during the course of such statement the minor answered intelligently, coherently, and gave no indication of undue influence. In re Hawkins, No. 3430 (9th Dist Ct App, Lorain, 5–11–83).

Juv R 7   Detention and shelter care

(A) Detention: standards

A child taken into custody shall not be placed in detention or shelter care prior to final disposition unless any of the following apply:

(1) Detention or shelter care is required:

(a) to protect the child from immediate or threatened physical or emotional harm; or

(b) to protect the person or property of others from immediate or threatened physical or emotional harm.

(2) The child may abscond or be removed from the jurisdiction of the court;

(3) The child has no parent, guardian, custodian or other person able to provide supervision and care for the child and return the child to the court when required;

(4) An order for placement of the child in detention or shelter care has been made by the court;

(5) Confinement is authorized by statute.

(B) Priorities in placement prior to hearing

A person taking a child into custody shall, with all reasonable speed, do either of the following:

(1) Release the child to a parent, guardian, or other custodian;

(2) Where detention or shelter care appears to be required under the standards of division (A) of this rule, bring the child to the court or deliver the child to a place of detention or shelter care designated by the court.

(C) Initial procedure upon detention

Any person who delivers a child to a shelter or detention facility shall give the admissions officer at the facility a signed report stating why the child was taken into custody and why the child was not released to a parent, guardian or custodian, and shall assist the admissions officer, if necessary, in notifying the parent pursuant to division (E)(3) of this rule.

(D) Admission

The admissions officer in a shelter or detention facility, upon receipt of a child, shall review the report submitted pursuant to division (C) of this rule, make such further investigation as is feasible and do either of the following:

(1) Release the child to the care of a parent, guardian or custodian;

(2) Where detention or shelter care is required under the standards of division (A) of this rule, admit the child to the facility or place the child in some appropriate facility.

(E) Procedure after admission

When a child has been admitted to detention or shelter care the admissions officer shall do all of the following:

(1) Prepare a report stating the time the child was brought to the facility and the reasons the child was admitted;

(2) Advise the child of the right to telephone parents and counsel immediately and at reasonable times thereafter and the time, place, and purpose of the detention hearing;

(3) Use reasonable diligence to contact the child's parent, guardian, or custodian and advise that person of all of the following:

(a) The place of and reasons for detention;

(b) The time the child may be visited;

(c) The time, place, and purpose of the detention hearing;

(d) The right to counsel and appointed counsel in the case of indigency.

(F) Detention hearing

(1) Hearing: time; notice. When a child has been admitted to detention or shelter care, a detention hearing shall be held promptly, not later than seventy-two hours after the child is placed in detention or shelter care or the next court day, whichever is earlier, to determine whether detention or shelter care is required. Reasonable oral or written notice of the time, place, and purpose of the detention hearing shall be given to the child and the parents, guardian, or other custodi-

an, if that person or those persons can be found.

(2) Hearing: advisement of rights. Prior to the hearing, the court shall inform the parties of the right to counsel and to appointed counsel if indigent and the child's right to remain silent with respect to any allegation of a juvenile traffic offense, delinquency, or unruliness.

(3) Hearing procedure. The court may consider any evidence, including the reports filed by the person who brought the child to the facility and the admissions officer, without regard to formal rules of evidence. Unless it appears from the hearing that the child's detention or shelter care is required under division (A) of this rule, the court shall order the child's release to a parent, guardian, or custodian. Whenever abuse, neglect, or dependency is alleged, the court shall determine whether there are any appropriate relatives of the child who are willing to be temporary custodians and, if so, appoint an appropriate relative as the temporary custodian of the child. The court shall make a reasonable efforts determination in accordance with Juv. R. 27(B)(1).

(G) Rehearing

If a parent, guardian, or custodian did not receive notice of the initial hearing and did not appear or waive appearance at the hearing, the court shall rehear the matter promptly. After a child is placed in shelter care or detention care, any party and the guardian ad litem of the child may file a motion with the court requesting that the child be released from detention or shelter care. Upon the filing of the motion, the court shall hold a hearing within seventy-two hours.

(H) Separation from adults

No child shall be placed in or committed to any prison, jail, lockup, or any other place where the child can come in contact or communication with any adult convicted of crime, under arrest, or charged with crime.

(I) Physical examination

The supervisor of a shelter or detention facility may provide for a physical examination of a child placed in the shelter or facility.

(J) Telephone and visitation rights

A child may telephone the child's parents and attorney immediately after being admitted to a shelter or detention facility and at reasonable times thereafter.

The child may be visited at reasonable visiting hours by the child's parents and adult members of the family, the child's pastor, and the child's teachers. The child may be visited by the child's attorney at any time.

(Adopted eff. 7–1–72; amended eff. 7–1–94, 7–1–01)

Uncodified Law

2002 H 180, § 3, eff. 5–16–02, reads, in part:

The General Assembly further requests the Supreme Court to promptly modify Rule 7 of the Rules of Juvenile Procedure pursuant to its authority under the Ohio Constitution to make that rule consistent with the amendments of this act to section 2151.31 of the Revised Code.

Historical and Statutory Notes

Amendment Note: The 7–1–01 amendment redesignated former division (1) as divisions (1) and (1)(a); and added new division (1)(b) and new division (5).

Amendment Note: The 7–1–94 amendment designated divisions (A)(1) through (A)(3); inserted "shelter" and substituted "child from immediate or threatened physical or emotional harm" for "person and property of others or those of the child" in division (A)(1); added division (A)(4); added the final two sentences in division (F)(3); deleted "Any decision relating to detention or shelter care may be reviewed at any time upon motion of any party." from the beginning of, and added the final two sentences in, division (G); deleted the second and third paragraphs in division (H); substituted "Physical" for "Medical" in the title of division (I); and made changes to reflect gender-neutral language. Prior to amendment, the second and third paragraphs in division (H) read:

"A child may be detained in jail or other facility for detention of adults only if the child is alleged to be delinquent, there is no detention center for delinquent children under the supervision of the court or other agency approved by the court, and the detention is in a room separate and removed from those for adults. The court may order that a child over the age of fifteen years who is alleged to be delinquent be detained in a jail in a room separate and removed from adults if public safety or protection of the child or others reasonably requires such detention.

"A child alleged to be neglected or dependent shall not be detained in jail or other facility intended or used for detention of adults charged with criminal offenses or of children alleged to be delinquent unless upon order of the court."

Commentary

Staff Notes

2001:

Rule 7(A) Detention: standards

Rule 7(A) was amended to add two rationales for placing a child in detention or shelter care: one, that the child is endangering the person or property of others [(A)(1)(b)] and two, that a statutory provision authorizes confinement [(A)(5)]. Rule 7(A)(1)(b) conforms to Sub. Sen. Bill 179 (January 1, 2002 effective date), Revised Code section 2151.31(A)(6)(b) and (d). Rule 7(A)(5) ensures that statutory provisions, i.e., Revised Code sections 2152.04 and 2151.31 (C)(2),

that contemplate placing a child in detention are recognized as valid rationales by the Juvenile Rules.

1994:

Rule 7 Detention and Shelter Care

Am. Sub. S.B. 89, effective January 1, 1989, changed the parameters under which a child could be detained. The law removed the authority to detain a child to protect the person and property of others or to protect the property of the child, so such language in Juv. R. 7(A)(1) has been deleted. Juv. R. 7(A)(1) does define the right to place a child in shelter care because of immediate or threatened physical or emotional harm pursuant to Revised Code 2151.31.

Juv. R. 7(F)(3) requires the court to determine the issues of the opportunity for suitable placement with relatives and of reasonable efforts made by agencies to prevent removal or to return the child home, in accordance with Revised Code 2151.314(B)(2) and 2151.419. "Reasonable efforts" are further defined by amended Juv. R. 27(B)(1).

Juv. R. 7(G) has been modified to include the seventy-two hour shelter care hearing requirement imposed by Revised Code 2151.31(E).

The title for Juv. R. 7(I) was changed from "Medical Examination" to "Physical Examination" to conform it to the definition specified in Juv. R. 2.

Cross References

Detention or shelter care hearing, 2151.314

Ohio Administrative Code References

Operational procedures for detention centers to conform to Ohio Rules of Juvenile Procedure, OAC 5139–7–04

Standards for administration of detention center; confinement to be in accordance with Juv R 7, OAC 5139–37–03

Standards for admission to detention center, OAC 5139–37–17

Library References

Infants ⚖68.3, 192, 208.

Westlaw Topic No. 211.

C.J.S. Infants §§ 42, 51 to 85.

Am Jur 2d: 47, Juvenile Courts and Delinquent and Dependent Children § 35, 44 to 54

Validity and application of statute allowing endangered child to be temporarily removed from parental custody. 38 ALR4th 756

Giannelli & Snyder, Baldwin's Ohio Practice, Evidence § 101.13, 101, 101.16 (2d ed. 2001).

Carlin, Baldwin's Ohio Practice, Merrick–Rippner Probate Law § 104.9, 107.25, 107.26, 107.27, 107.28, 107.29, 107.30, 107.36, 107.117, 107.121, 107.125, 107.152, 107.172 (2003).

Notes of Decisions

Constitutional issues   2
Employees' status   5
Fees and costs   6
Habeas corpus   1
Release from custody   3
Taking minor into custody   4

---

1. Habeas corpus

Habeas corpus will not lie at the request of the father of children found to be dependent and placed in the temporary care and custody of the county welfare department. Pettry v. McGinty (Ohio 1979) 60 Ohio St.2d 92, 397 N.E.2d 1190, 14 O.O.3d 331.

A parent, alleging that he failed to receive notice of a hearing concerning the shelter care of his child, must move the juvenile court for a rehearing, pursuant to Juv R 7(G), before seeking a writ of habeas corpus. Linger v. Weiss (Ohio 1979) 57 Ohio St.2d 97, 386 N.E.2d 1354, 11 O.O.3d 281, certiorari denied 100 S.Ct. 128, 444 U.S. 862, 62 L.Ed.2d 83. Habeas Corpus ⬥ 280

Habeas corpus relief was not available from decision of the juvenile court awarding temporary custody of father's children to county, which had alleged that one child was neglected; juvenile court had jurisdiction to make the award of temporary custody under applicable statutes, appeal provided an adequate remedy, and alleged errors actually attacked findings of the court. Rothacker v McCafferty, No. 81427, 2002-Ohio-4927, 2002 WL 31087671 (8th Dist Ct App, 9-19-02).

2. Constitutional issues

The due process clause of US Const Am 14 is not violated where a state statute provides for (1) the pretrial detention of a juvenile delinquent where there is a finding, following notice and a hearing, and a statement of reasons and facts, that there is a "serious risk" that the child might commit a crime before return date; and (2) a more formal hearing within a maximum of seventeen days where detention is ordered. (Ed. note: New York law construed in light of federal constitution.) Schall v. Martin (U.S.N.Y. 1984) 104 S.Ct. 2403, 467 U.S. 253, 81 L.Ed.2d 207.

Under the present Juvenile Code and Rules, a juvenile court cannot change a "temporary" commitment to the Ohio youth commission to an "permanent" commitment without hearing; further, the commitment of an unruly child, not declared "delinquent", is a violation of due process and any hearing held on the above matters requires the presence of the youth involved. OAG 72–071.

3. Release from custody

A minor detained on delinquency charges is not charged with an offense and hence is not entitled to release on bail. (Annotation from former RC 2151.27.) State ex rel. Peaks v. Allaman (Montgomery 1952) 115 N.E.2d 849, 66 Ohio Law Abs. 403, 51 O.O. 321.

RC 2151.311(A)(1), 2151.314(A), and Juv R 7(B) do not authorize the release of a child to the peace officer who took the child into custody. OAG 96–061.

4. Taking minor into custody

Where an allegedly neglected, dependent, or abused child is committed to the temporary, emergency custody of a children services board after a shelter care hearing under Juv R 7, the court need not order a reunification plan where it has not finally adjudged and disposed of the matter under RC 2151.353. In re Moloney (Ohio 1986) 24 Ohio St.3d 22, 492 N.E.2d 805, 24 O.B.R. 18.

Even assuming that testimony of protective services supervisor for county children's services agency, that child's maternal grandmother told on-call social worker and supervisor that she was upset that she could not have custody of child and that "she was just going to 'go' over and just take him," was inadmissible hearsay, any deficient performance of father's counsel in failing to object at the shelter care hearing was not prejudicial; court was not bound by formal rules of evidence at the hearing, and there was abundant evidence establishing that father's relatives were no longer able to care for child and that child should be placed in foster care. In re Wingo (Ohio App. 4 Dist., 06-01-2001) 143 Ohio App.3d 652, 758 N.E.2d 780, 2001-Ohio-2477. Infants ⬥ 173.1; Infants ⬥ 253

If a peace officer determines that the detention or shelter care of a child appears to be required as provided in RC 2151.31(C) and Juv R 7(A), the peace officer is required by RC 2151.311(A) and Juv R 7(B) to bring the child to the court or deliver the child to a place of detention or shelter care designated by the court. A peace officer who determines that the detention or shelter care of a child appears to be required may contact the juvenile court by telephone to determine the place of detention or shelter care to which to deliver the child. OAG 96–061.

Under Ohio law, unless matters of public safety are involved, a child alleged to be abused, neglected, or dependent may be removed from his home by court order only upon a judicial determination that continuation in the home would be contrary to the child's best interest. OAG 87–105.

The placement or detention of delinquent, dependent, neglected children, or juvenile traffic offenders, is upon final disposition of the juvenile court and does not include placement in a detention home provided under RC 2151.34. (Annotation from former RC 2151.35.) 1963 OAG 553.

5. Employees' status

Employees of a five-county joint juvenile detention center who are responsible for the supervision, education, and care of detained juveniles are not "officers of the [juvenile] courts" within the meaning of that term in RC 4117.01 where they have no independent authority to decide the disposition of juveniles but merely make recommendations; nor are these workers employees "of the courts" where the relations between the courts and the center are characterized by the following circumstances: (1) the juvenile court judges recommend and approve a list of potential trustees; (2) county commissioners then choose the trustees; (3) these trustees make all decisions about running the center, although the judges may give advice and recommend actions; (4) the trustees hire a superintendent, who in turn hires the other employees; (5) center employees are in the classified civil service; (6) the hours, duties, and schedules of employees are set by the trustees and superintendent; (7) employees often make daily reports to judges about admissions to and incidents at the center, and the superintendent reports to the courts each month; the relations between the courts and the center mandated by Juv R 7 are not enough standing alone to make center employees "court employees"; the employees are instead employees of a "public" or "special" district and are therefore covered by RC Ch 4117. Five–County Joint Juvenile Detention Center v SERB, 1989 SERB 4–81 (10th Dist Ct App, Franklin, 7–18–89), vacated by 57 OS(3d) 4 (1991).

6. Fees and costs

A judge of a juvenile court may not commit a child who has been found to be a delinquent child, or a juvenile traffic offender, to the county jail upon the failure, refusal, or inability of such child to pay a fine and court costs. (Annotation from former RC 2151.23.) OAG 70–143.

Juv R 8   Filing by electronic means

A court may provide, by local rules adopted pursuant to the Rules of Superintendence, for the filing of documents by electronic means. If the court adopts such local rules, they shall include all of the following:

(A) Any signature on electronically transmitted documents shall be considered that of the attorney or party it purports to be for all purposes. If it is established that the documents were transmitted without authority, the court shall order the filing stricken.

(B) A provision shall specify the days and hours during which electronically transmitted documents will be received by the court, and a provision shall specify when documents received electronically will be considered to have been filed.

(C) Any document filed electronically that requires a filing fee may be rejected by the clerk of court unless the filer has complied with the mechanism established by the court for the payment of filing fees.

(Adopted eff. 7–1–94, amended eff. 7–1–96, 7–1–01)

Historical and Statutory Notes

Amendment Note: The 7–1–01 amendment completely rewrote the section to bring it into conformity with the electronic filing procedures in place throughout the procedural rules of Ohio. See *Baldwin's Ohio Legislative Service Annotated*, 2001, page 6/R–64, or the OH–LEGIS or OH–LEGIS–OLD database on Westlaw, for prior version of this rule.

Amendment Note: The 7–1–96 amendment substituted "or magistrate, or both" for "and/or referee" and "this" for "such" in division (A)(2).

Commentary

Staff Notes

2001:

Rule 8 Filing by Electronic Means

The amendments to this rule were part of a group of amendments that were submitted by the Ohio Courts Digital Signatures Task Force to establish minimum standards for the use of information systems, electronic signatures, and electronic filing. The substantive amendment to this rule was the addition of the first sentence of the rule and of divisions (B) and (C). The title of the rule was changed from "Filing by Facsimile Transmission." Comparable amendments were made to Civil Rule 5, Civil Rule 73 (for probate courts), Criminal Rule 12, and Appellate Rule 13.

As part of this electronic filing and signature project, the following rules were amended effective July 1, 2001: Civil Rules 5, 11, and 73; Criminal Rule 12; Juvenile Rule 8; and Appellate Rules 13 and 18. In addition, Rule 26 of the Rules of Superintendence for Courts of Ohio was amended and Rule of Superintendence 27 was added to complement the rules of procedure. Superintendence Rule 27 establishes a process by which minimum standards for information technology are promulgated, and requires that courts submit any local rule involving the use of information technology to a technology standards committee designated by the Supreme Court for approval.

1996:

The amendment changed the rule's reference from "referee" to "magistrate" in division (A)(2) in order to harmonize the rule with the language adopted in the 1995 amendments to Juv. R. 40. The amendment is technical only and no substantive change is intended.

1994:

Rule 8 Filing by Facsimile Transmission

Juv. R. 8 is an attempt to facilitate juvenile court filings by electronic means. Concerns about the reliability of facsimile transmission are addressed in several divisions. The rule sets forth the form and procedural requirements necessary for proper facsimile transmission in an effort to minimize unauthorized filings. Division 8(B) also requires the court to meet certain standards in paper and equipment in order to assure that the electronic filings will be able to be read and handled by court personnel.

Juv R 9   Intake

(A) Court action to be avoided

In all appropriate cases formal court action should be avoided and other community resources utilized to ameliorate situations brought to the attention of the court.

(B) Screening; referral

Information that a child is within the court's jurisdiction may be informally screened prior to the filing of a complaint to determine whether the filing of a complaint is in the best interest of the child and the public.

(Adopted eff. 7–1–72)

Cross References

Scope of rules, applicability, construction, exceptions, Juv R 1

Library References

Infants ⚖191.

Westlaw Topic No. 211.

C.J.S. Infants §§ 42, 53, 54.

Am Jur 2d: 47, Juvenile Courts and Delinquent and Dependent Children § 40

Carlin, Baldwin's Ohio Practice, Merrick–Rippner Probate Law § 107.1 (2003).

Notes of Decisions

Constitutional issues   1
Formal court action   4
Juvenile considered "suspect"   2
Review of complaint   3

---

1. Constitutional issues

The prosecution of a twelve-year-old girl as a delinquent based on a charge of complicity to commit rape violates RC Ch 2151, Juv R 9(A), local court intake policy, public policy, and due process of law where such prosecution arises from an incident of three children "playing doctor," with the adjudicated delinquent directing a five-year-old boy to drop his pants and place his penis in a five-year-old girl's mouth in order to take her temperature, because no offense was actually committed and the failure to raise the issue of the constitutionality of applying the rape statute to children under the age of thirteen does not preclude consideration of the constitutional challenge on appeal. In re M.D. (Ohio 1988) 38 Ohio St.3d 149, 527 N.E.2d 286.

2. Juvenile considered "suspect"

For purposes of the confidential law enforcement investigatory records exception under RC 149.43(A), a juvenile may be considered a "suspect" when no charge, arrest, complaint, or referral to the juvenile court pursuant to Juv R 9 has been made. 1990 OAG 101.

For purposes of the confidential law enforcement investigatory records exception under RC 149.43(A), a juvenile ceases to be a "suspect" upon arrest, being charged, the filing of a complaint, or a referral to the juvenile court pursuant to Juv R 9. 1990 OAG 101.

A decision, at a particular point in time, not to charge, arrest, file a complaint with, or refer a juvenile to the juvenile court pursuant to Juv R 9 does not require disclosure or terminate the juvenile's status as a "suspect," pursuant to RC 149.43(A). 1990 OAG 101.

3. Review of complaint

The juvenile court is entitled to review the appropriateness of filing a complaint against a ten-year old boy for rape and to dismiss the complaint because it would not further the policies of the state. In re Smith (Hamilton 1992) 80 Ohio App.3d 502, 609 N.E.2d 1281, dismissed, jurisdictional motion overruled 65 Ohio St.3d 1441, 600 N.E.2d 683.

4. Formal court action

Formal court action is permissible in appropriate juvenile cases and it is within the discretion of the juvenile court to proceed in such a manner. In re Corcoran (Geauga 1990) 68 Ohio App.3d 213, 587 N.E.2d 957, dismissed 56 Ohio St.3d 702, 564 N.E.2d 703.

Complete lack of any record of adjudicatory and dispositional hearings before the magistrate required reversal of juvenile's delinquency adjudication; missing record concerned waiver of counsel and admission to complaint, and lack of record prevented finding that magistrate complied with juvenile procedure rule requiring courts to make every effort to avoid the use of formal court proceedings in cases involving children. In re L.B. (Ohio App. 8 Dist., Cuyahoga, 07-25-2002) No. 79370, No. 79942, 2002-Ohio-3767, 2002 WL 1729905, Unreported.

Juv R 10   Complaint

(A) Filing

Any person having knowledge of a child who appears to be a juvenile traffic offender, delinquent, unruly, neglected, dependent, or abused may file a complaint with respect to the child in the juvenile court of the county in which the child has a residence or legal settlement, or in which the traffic offense, delinquency, unruliness, neglect, dependency, or abuse occurred.

Persons filing complaints that a child appears to be an unruly or delinquent child for being an habitual or chronic truant and the parent, guardian, or other person having care of the child has failed to cause the child to attend school may also file the complaint in the county in which the child is supposed to attend public school.

Any person may file a complaint to have determined the custody of a child not a ward of another court of this state, and any person entitled to the custody of a child and unlawfully deprived of such custody may file a complaint requesting a writ of habeas corpus. Complaints concerning custody shall be filed in the county where the child is found or was last known to be.

Any person with standing may file a complaint for the determination of any other matter over which the juvenile court is given jurisdiction by the Revised Code. The complaint shall be filed in the county in which the child who is the subject of the complaint is found or was last known to be. In a removal action, the complaint shall be filed in the county where the foster home is located.

When a case concerning a child is transferred or certified from another court, the certification from the transferring court shall be considered the complaint. The juvenile court may order the certification supplemented upon its own motion or that of a party.

(B) Complaint: general form

The complaint, which may be upon information and belief, shall satisfy all of the following requirements:

(1) State in ordinary and concise language the essential facts that bring the proceeding within the jurisdiction of the court, and in juvenile traffic offense and delinquency proceedings, shall contain the numerical designation of the statute or ordinance alleged to have been violated;

(2) Contain the name and address of the parent, guardian, or custodian of the child or state that the name or address is unknown;

(3) Be made under oath.

(C) Complaint: juvenile traffic offense

A Uniform Traffic Ticket shall be used as a complaint in juvenile traffic offense proceedings.

(D) Complaint: permanent custody

A complaint seeking permanent custody of a child shall state that permanent custody is sought.

(E) Complaint: temporary custody

A complaint seeking temporary custody of a child shall state that temporary custody is sought.

(F) Complaint: planned permanent living arrangement

A complaint seeking the placement of a child into a planned permanent living arrangement shall state that placement into a planned permanent living arrangement is sought.

(G) Complaint: habeas corpus

Where a complaint for a writ of habeas corpus involving the custody of a child is based on the existence of a lawful court order, a certified copy of the order shall be attached to the complaint.

(Adopted eff. 7–1–72; amended eff. 7–1–75, 7–1–76, 7–1–94, 7–1–98, 7–1–01, 7–1–02)

Historical and Statutory Notes

Amendment Note: The 7–1–02 amendment substituted "a planned permanent living arrangement" for "long term foster care" throughout division (F).

Amendment Note: The 7–1–01 amendment added the second paragraph in division (A).

Amendment Note: The 7–1–98 amendment deleted "section 2151.23 of" before "the Revised Code" and added the third sentence in the third paragraph in division (A).

Amendment Note: The 7–1–94 amendment added the third paragraph in division (A) and divisions (E) and (F); and redesignated former division (E) as division (G).

Commentary

Staff Notes

2002:

Juvenile Rule 10(F) Complaint: planned permanent living arrangement

The July 1, 2002, amendment to Juv. R. 10(F) substituted the language of "planned permanent living arrangement" for the former language of "long term foster care," to conform to the new legislative designation for these child-placing arrangements.

The amendment to Juv. R. 10(F) conforms to sections 2151.27(C) and 2151.353(B) of the Revised Code. Juvenile Rules 2, 15, and 34 also were amended effective July 1, 2002 to reflect this change in terminology.

2001:

Rule 10(A) Filing

Rule 10(A) was amended to conform to the Sub. Sen. Bill 181 (effective September 4, 2000) changes that provide in R. C. section 2151.27(A)(2) that chronic and habitual truancy complaints against both children and adults responsible for them may also be properly venued in the county in which the child is supposed to be attending public school.

1998:

Rule 10(A) Filing

The 1998 amendment revised the third paragraph of Juv. R. 10(A) by adding a reference to removal actions, which are defined in Juv. R. 2(EE), also added by the 1998 amendments. The provision that the complaint in removal actions must be filed in the county where the foster home is located clarifies the venue requirement where the boundaries of the school district extend beyond single county.

The 1998 amendment also deleted from the third paragraph a reference to section 2151.23 of Revised Code.

1994:

Rule 10 Complaint

Division (A) of Juv. R. 10 now includes a residual category of persons who may file a complaint in juvenile court. Juv. R. 10(E) and 10(F) have been modified to require that complainants specifically plead whether or not temporary custody or long term foster care is sought. All changes are pursuant to section 2151.27 of the Revised Code, as amended by S.B. 89.

Cross References

Adjudicatory hearing, Juv R 29
Complaint, Crim R 3
Complaint may be filed regarding a delinquent, unruly, abused, or neglected child in juvenile court, 2151.27
Warrant or summons, Crim R 7

Library References

Habeas Corpus ⌐670(10), 671.
Infants ⌐197, 200.
Westlaw Topic Nos. 197, 211.
C.J.S. Habeas Corpus §§ 167 to 169.
C.J.S. Infants §§ 42, 53 to 55.
Am Jur 2d: 47, Juvenile Courts and Delinquent and Dependent Children § 40 to 42
Katz & Giannelli, Baldwin's Ohio Practice, Criminal Law § 35.11 (1996).
Carlin, Baldwin's Ohio Practice, Merrick–Rippner Probate Law § 104.5, 107.2, 107.3, 107.4, 107.7, 107.136, 107.137, 107.138 (2003).

Notes of Decisions

Constitutional issues 7
Evidence 6
Habeas corpus 4
Jurisdiction 3
Permanent custody 5
Procedural issues 2
Sufficiency of complaint 1

---

1. Sufficiency of complaint

Child dependency complaint filed by the county department of children and family services was sufficient to put father on notice of the issues and did not deprive father of due process; complaint alleged that child was born while mother tested positive for drugs, mother's drug problem prevented her from caring for child, mother had other children that were not in her custody, mother failed to comply with her agency caseplan, father failed to provide care or support for child, and complaint sought an award of permanent custody to county department of children and family services. In re I.M. (Ohio App. 8 Dist., Cuyahoga, 12-24-2003) No. 82669, No. 82695, 2003-Ohio-7069, 2003 WL 23010024, Unreported. Infants ⌐197

Parents' complaint alleging that child suffered neglect while in foster care should not have been dismissed even though complaint incorrectly cited dependency statute, rather than child neglect statute, where complaint demonstrated good faith effort to comply with rules, and adequately notified opposing party of the claim; thus, dismissal of complaint would be reversed and cause remanded to allow parents opportunity to cure the defect. In re Fetters (Preble 1996) 110 Ohio App.3d 483, 674 N.E.2d 766, on reconsideration. Infants ⚭ 17

A complaint to terminate parental custody in juvenile court is sufficient if the allegations therein notify the opposing party of the nature of the claim against her even if no specific facts or dates are mentioned. In re Pieper Children (Preble 1991) 74 Ohio App.3d 714, 600 N.E.2d 317, dismissed, jurisdictional motion overruled 66 Ohio St.3d 1410, 607 N.E.2d 9.

An allegation in a motion filed in juvenile court seeking to have that court "determine and award the future care and custody" of a child, that "neither parent is a suitable person to have the care and custody of said child," does not constitute a charge that such child is "neglected" or "dependent" and is not sufficiently definite to constitute the "complaint" necessitated by RC 2151.27. (Annotation from former RC 2151.03.) Union County Child Welfare Bd. v. Parker (Union 1964) 7 Ohio App.2d 79, 218 N.E.2d 757, 36 O.O.2d 162. Infants ⚭ 197

The recitation in the complaint of the numerical designations alone is insufficient to inform a defendant of the crime alleged even where the referee defines the statute enumerated in the complaint at the arraignment. In re Coen, No. 94-AP-090060, 1995 WL 495384 (5th Dist Ct App, Tuscarawas, 6-14-95).

2. Procedural issues

RC 3109.27(A), which requires every party in a custody proceeding to give information in his first pleading as to the child's present and past addresses and custodians and as to any custody proceedings concerning the child pending in other jurisdictions, does not apply to a public agency that initiates a dependency complaint. In re Palmer (Ohio 1984) 12 Ohio St.3d 194, 465 N.E.2d 1312, 12 O.B.R. 259, certiorari denied 105 S.Ct. 918, 469 U.S. 1162, 83 L.Ed.2d 930.

Under RC 2151.353, the filing of a complaint containing a prayer requesting permanent custody of minor children, sufficiently apprising the parents of the grounds upon which the order is to be based, and the service of summons upon the parents, explaining that the granting of such an order permanently divests them of their parental rights, are prerequisite to a valid adjudication that a child is neglected or dependent for the purpose of obtaining an order for permanent custody divesting parental rights. In re Fassinger (Ohio 1975) 42 Ohio St.2d 505, 330 N.E.2d 431, 71 O.O.2d 503.

County child support enforcement agency (CSEA) had standing, as collecting agent of Department of Human Services (DHS), to bring action in juvenile court to determine child support and to make determination of reimbursement for amount of support already provided by DHS to children of mothers receiving public assistance who had assigned their rights to child support to DHS; even if statute authorizing only parent, guardian, or custodian of child to bring action in juvenile court requesting child support order did not authorize state to bring such action, Juvenile Rules of Procedure giving state or its agencies standing to file complaint to order child support payments controlled over statute. State ex rel. Lamier v. Lamier (Cuyahoga 1995) 105 Ohio App.3d 797, 664 N.E.2d 1384.

Rules of Juvenile Procedure authorizing state or its agencies to file complaint in juvenile court to order child support payments was not inconsistent with statute authorizing only parent, guardian, or custodian of child to bring action in juvenile court requesting child support order, where statute, although specifying that parent, guardian, or custodian could bring support action, neither expressly authorized nor excluded state from bringing such action. State ex rel. Lamier v. Lamier (Cuyahoga 1995) 105 Ohio App.3d 797, 664 N.E.2d 1384.

Question of standing, i.e., of who is proper party to bring complaint, is procedural matter governed by Rules of Juvenile Procedure; these rules control over inconsistent statute purporting to govern procedural matters. State ex rel. Lamier v. Lamier (Cuyahoga 1995) 105 Ohio App.3d 797, 664 N.E.2d 1384.

Where public children services agency did not have requisite grant of temporary custody, instead of filing postdispositional motion for permanent custody, agency should have sought grant of temporary custody by asking court to modify its disposition terminating agency's grant of temporary custody or by filing a new complaint based on more recent allegations of abuse or on dependency theory. In re Miller (Montgomery 1995) 101 Ohio App.3d 199, 655 N.E.2d 252. Infants ⚭ 230.1

In accordance with Juv R 10(A), anyone who knows that a child is abused, neglected, or dependent may bring a complaint to the juvenile court. In re Dukes (Summit 1991) 81 Ohio App.3d 145, 610 N.E.2d 513, motion overruled 63 Ohio St.3d 1411, 585 N.E.2d 835.

A complaint filed with the juvenile court in a child abuse case must be made under oath and contain the facts of the abuse or neglect, sections of the Ohio Revised Code that have been violated, names and addresses of the parents, and a prayer for custody which must specifically indicate permanent custody, temporary custody, or long-term foster care. In re Dukes (Summit 1991) 81 Ohio App.3d 145, 610 N.E.2d 513, motion overruled 63 Ohio St.3d 1411, 585 N.E.2d 835.

A complaint which contains all the essential elements and facts but is not signed by the complainant under oath is defective, and the person who makes the complaint under oath must be the same person who signs the complaint. In re Dukes (Summit 1991) 81 Ohio App.3d 145, 610 N.E.2d 513, motion overruled 63 Ohio St.3d 1411, 585 N.E.2d 835.

A party must object to a defect in a complaint of child abuse by a prehearing motion before the adjudicatory hearing, within the time requirements of Juv R 22(E). In re Dukes (Summit 1991) 81 Ohio App.3d 145, 610 N.E.2d 513, motion overruled 63 Ohio St.3d 1411, 585 N.E.2d 835.

The juvenile court is entitled to review the appropriateness of filing a complaint against a ten-year old boy for rape and to dismiss the complaint because it would not further the policies of the state. In re Smith (Hamilton 1992) 80 Ohio App.3d 502, 609 N.E.2d 1281, dismissed, jurisdictional motion overruled 65 Ohio St.3d 1441, 600 N.E.2d 683.

A delinquency complaint which alleges that a juvenile "knowingly" aided another to commit robbery is sufficient to state a charge of complicity under Juv R 10(B). In re Howard (Hamilton 1987) 31 Ohio App.3d 1, 508 N.E.2d 190, 31 O.B.R. 14.

A properly served summons containing the "full explanation" required by RC 2151.353(B) must be accompanied by a copy of the complaint, amended or not, if the complaint seeks, temporarily or permanently, to divest a parent of his parental rights. In re Wilson (Huron 1984) 21 Ohio App.3d 36, 486 N.E.2d 152, 21 O.B.R. 38.

When a case concerning a child is transferred or certified from another court, such certification does not constitute a complaint in the juvenile court that such a child is neglected, dependent, or abused, and those dispositions provided for under RC 2151.353 pertaining to neglected, dependent, or abused children, including an award of permanent custody to a county welfare department which has assumed the administration of child welfare, are not applicable to such a child, disposition thereof being subject to and controlled by RC 3109.04. In re Snider (Defiance 1984) 14 Ohio App.3d 353, 471 N.E.2d 516, 14 O.B.R. 420. Infants ⊕ 197; Infants ⊕ 222

Even though a delinquency complaint designates a particular statute or statutes as being violated by a child, a juvenile court may find, on the basis of the facts alleged and proved, that the child is a delinquent child for the violation of an additional statute. In re Burgess (Preble 1984) 13 Ohio App.3d 374, 469 N.E.2d 967, 13 O.B.R. 456. Infants ⊕ 210

In a juvenile proceeding where a complaining witness designates two statutes she claims were violated, the court is free to find that the facts prove the violation of an additional statute and may find the accused to be a delinquent child. In re Burgess (Preble 1984) 13 Ohio App.3d 374, 469 N.E.2d 967, 13 O.B.R. 456. Infants ⊕ 210

Juv R 10(B) is not meant to force a complainant to state every fact surrounding every incident described in the complaint, and therefore, in proving its case in a neglect and dependency proceeding, the state need not limit its proof to the habits and faults of the custodial parent that are actually listed in the complaint. In re Sims (Preble 1983) 13 Ohio App.3d 37, 468 N.E.2d 111, 13 O.B.R. 40.

While the certification shall be deemed to be the complaint in the juvenile court, such certification does not constitute a complaint in the juvenile court that such child is dependent or neglected and those dispositions provided for under RC 2151.353, 2151.354, and 2151.355 pertaining to unruly, delinquent, dependent, or neglected children are not applicable to the disposition of such a child, disposition thereof being subject to and controlled by RC 3109.04. In re Height (Van Wert 1975) 47 Ohio App.2d 203, 353 N.E.2d 887, 1 O.O.3d 279. Courts ⊕ 488(1); Infants ⊕ 197

Proceedings, wherein the juvenile court determines in response to such motion that such child is a neglected and dependent child and orders such child placed in the temporary custody of the county welfare board, are void ab initio for want of a complaint filed as prescribed by RC 2151.27, and such proceedings cannot be the foundation for a determination of dependency or neglect necessary to support an order awarding custody of such child. (Annotation from former RC 2151.27.) Union County Child Welfare Bd. v. Parker (Union 1964) 7 Ohio App.2d 79, 218 N.E.2d 757, 36 O.O.2d 162. Infants ⊕ 197

Where an affidavit is filed in support of a motion for a new trial, alleging that the child was a neglected child within the meaning of this section, on which charges a hearing was had, the juvenile court has jurisdiction in such matter and may grant a motion for new trial. (Annotation from former RC 2151.27.) State ex rel. Sparto v. Williams (Darke 1949) 86 Ohio App. 377, 86 N.E.2d 501, 55 Ohio Law Abs. 341, 41 O.O. 474.

In complaint under this section, that a child of separated parents is dependent, a judgment of common pleas court that the child is dependent awarding its custody to its father "until further order of the court," is a final order from which appeal to the court of appeals may be taken. (Annotation from former RC 2151.27.) In re Anteau (Lucas 1941) 67 Ohio App. 117, 36 N.E.2d 47, 21 O.O. 129.

Any person has standing to bring an action for child custody under RC 2151.23; such a person need not be a parent, need not have established paternity and need not have legitimized the child. Harris v Hopper, No. L–81–187 (6th Dist Ct App, Lucas, 1–15–82).

There is a distinction between a "putative" father and a father who has been adjudicated as such by his own admission, in that a father adjudicated as such by his own admission has legal standing to seek custody of his illegitimate child against the world, including the mother. In re Wright (Ohio Com.Pl. 1977) 52 Ohio Misc. 4, 367 N.E.2d 931, 6 O.O.3d 31.

A certification by a common pleas court of its record to the juvenile court constitutes a filing of a complaint within the meaning of RC 2151.27. (Annotation from former RC 2151.27.) Hartshorne v. Hartshorne (Columbiana 1959) 185 N.E.2d 329, 89 Ohio Law Abs. 243.

3. Jurisdiction

A complaint under Juv R 10 and RC 2151.27 alleging that a child is dependent must state the essential facts which bring the proceeding within the jurisdiction of the court. In re Hunt (Ohio 1976) 46 Ohio St.2d 378, 348 N.E.2d 727, 75 O.O.2d 450. Infants ⊕ 197

Where a court, having acquired jurisdiction over a child by virtue of a divorce action between the child's parents, certifies the matter of the child's custody to a juvenile court, the consent of the juvenile court having been first obtained, the juvenile court has exclusive jurisdiction over the child's custody by virtue of RC 3109.06 and 2151.23(D) and a finding of unfitness of the parents or that there is no suitable relative to have custody is not a necessary prerequisite to such certification, and while such certification shall be deemed to be the complaint in the juvenile court, it does not constitute a complaint in the juvenile court that such child is dependent or neglected and those dispositions provided for under RC 2151.353, 2151.354, and 2151.355 are not applicable to the disposition of such a child, disposition thereof being subject to and controlled by RC 3109.04. In re Height (Van Wert 1975) 47 Ohio App.2d 203, 353 N.E.2d 887, 1 O.O.3d 279. Courts ⊕ 472.1

An Ohio juvenile court, in a dependency proceeding pursuant to RC 2151.27 et seq., has no jurisdiction to interfere with a mother's legal custody of her children, in the absence of proof and a finding of unfitness of such parent, merely for the purpose of releasing such children to the officers of the court of a foreign state, and the court need not give full faith and credit to a Michigan decree where that decree was obtained by the husband in an ex parte custody determination, subsequent to a divorce decree, in which the Michigan court had no personal jurisdiction over the nonresident wife. (Annotation from former RC 2151.27.) In re Messner (Huron 1969) 19 Ohio App.2d 33, 249 N.E.2d 532, 48 O.O.2d 31.

Where a neglected child proceeding is instituted in the juvenile court by a parent of such child, and a divorce action is later instituted by such parent, the juvenile court has exclusive original jurisdiction to determine whether the child is neglected, the power to determine his custody and the authority to place the child with a relative. (Annotation from former

RC 2151.27.) In re Small (Darke 1960) 114 Ohio App. 248, 181 N.E.2d 503, 19 O.O.2d 128.

The juvenile court of the county in which acts constituting neglect or dependency of a minor child occur has jurisdiction over complaints concerning such child whether or not the parent or minor child was a nonresident of such county. (Annotation from former RC 2151.27.) In re Belk (Crawford 1954) 97 Ohio App. 114, 123 N.E.2d 757, 55 O.O. 330. Infants ⬥ 196

The juvenile court is given original jurisdiction in a proper proceeding to determine the right of custody of any child where such child is not a ward of another court, and it is not necessary in the exercise of such jurisdiction that the juvenile court first determine that such child is a dependent, neglected or delinquent child. (Annotation from former RC 2151.27.) In re Lorok (Cuyahoga 1952) 93 Ohio App. 251, 114 N.E.2d 65, 51 O.O. 10. Child Custody ⬥ 920

Juvenile court has no jurisdiction to adjudicate a child as a dependent child until after filing of a complaint charging such dependency and notice given to the parent or parents. (Annotation from former RC 2151.27.) State ex rel. Clark v. Allaman (Montgomery 1950) 87 Ohio App. 101, 90 N.E.2d 394, 57 Ohio Law Abs. 17, 42 O.O. 330, affirmed 154 Ohio St. 296, 95 N.E.2d 753, 43 O.O. 190.

In an action to remove a child from her mother's custody, the mere allegation that such child is dependent, where the complaint fails to state the essential facts upon which the allegation of dependency is based and which allegations bring the proceeding within the jurisdiction of the court, such complaint is insufficient to confer jurisdiction upon the trial court. In re Baker, No. 6-81-12 (3d Dist Ct App, Hardin, 7-14-82).

The juvenile court has the authority to hear and determine the case of a "neglected child" notwithstanding the fact that the child is at the time within the continuing jurisdiction of the common pleas court by virtue of a divorce decree. (Annotation from former RC 2151.27.) In re L. (Ohio Juv. 1967) 12 Ohio Misc. 251, 231 N.E.2d 253, 41 O.O.2d 341. Courts ⬥ 475(15)

In order for a juvenile court to have jurisdiction to declare a child to be dependent, it must be shown that either the residence of the child is in the county or that the acts constituting neglect or dependency occurred in the county. (Annotation from former RC 2151.27.) State ex rel. Burchett v. Juvenile Court for Scioto County (Scioto 1962) 194 N.E.2d 912, 92 Ohio Law Abs. 357, 28 O.O.2d 116.

Where a juvenile court in the jurisdiction in which an offender resides waives jurisdiction so that the offender will be tried by a common pleas court, such defendant is entitled to a trial in the county where the offense occurred. (Annotation from former RC 2151.27.) In re Davis (Ohio Juv. 1961) 179 N.E.2d 198, 87 Ohio Law Abs. 222, 22 O.O.2d 108.

Where an affidavit was filed charging that children were neglected and dependent and the mother unfit, and such children were taken into custody by the county welfare department at a time when the mother and children were residents of the county, the juvenile court had jurisdiction of such proceedings even though citation was not served on the mother until after her removal to another county. (Annotation from former RC 2151.27.) In re Goshorn (Ohio Juv. 1959) 167 N.E.2d 148, 82 Ohio Law Abs. 599.

4. Habeas corpus

Habeas corpus relief is the exception rather than the general rule in child custody actions. Barnebey v. Zschach (Ohio 1995) 71 Ohio St.3d 588, 646 N.E.2d 162. Habeas Corpus ⬥ 532(1)

Habeas corpus will not lie where a child has been adjudicated a neglected and dependent child and committed by a juvenile court. (Annotation from former RC 2151.23.) Byington v. Byington (Ohio 1964) 175 Ohio St. 513, 196 N.E.2d 588, 26 O.O.2d 176.

Habeas corpus in a court of competent jurisdiction as prescribed in RC Ch 2725 is the proper proceeding to raise the question of rightful custody of minor children, where it is alleged that the restraint is illegal, or where a parent or other person claims that he or she has been unlawfully deprived of custody of a minor child; and, as part of such proceedings, the best interests and welfare of the child is a primary question and determining factor, and all other matters must yield accordingly, including the comity existing between states. (Annotation from former RC 2151.23.) In re Messner (Huron 1969) 19 Ohio App.2d 33, 249 N.E.2d 532, 48 O.O.2d 31.

An application for a writ of habeas corpus will be denied where a complaint is duly filed in the county of legal residence, pursuant to RC 2151.27, charging a child with being a dependent or neglected child, notwithstanding the court of common pleas of another county in this state, as a result of a divorce action there heard, gave custody of the child to the mother who subsequently moved with the child to the county where the affidavit of dependency and neglect was filed. (Annotation from former RC 2151.27.) James v. Child Welfare Bd. (Summit 1967) 9 Ohio App.2d 299, 224 N.E.2d 358, 38 O.O.2d 347.

Where, in an action in habeas corpus instituted by the natural mother to gain custody of her minor child, the respondents, who have the child in their custody, are unable to show a valid judgment or order of the court that has jurisdiction to issue such order, it is error for the trial court to determine on the principle "what is for the best interests of the child" that the custody of such child should remain in the respondents and to deny custody to the natural mother. (Annotation from former RC 2151.23.) In re McTaggart (Cuyahoga 1965) 2 Ohio App.2d 214, 207 N.E.2d 562, 31 O.O.2d 336, on rehearing 4 Ohio App.2d 359, 212 N.E.2d 663, 33 O.O.2d 447.

An award of custody of a child in a divorce action is conclusive only as to the parties to such action, and the remedy of habeas corpus is available to obtain such child where a party other than the parties to the divorce action is involved; and it is not necessary to apply to the court which originally awarded custody of such child. (Annotation from former RC 3109.04.) In re Howland (Highland 1961) 115 Ohio App. 186, 184 N.E.2d 228, 20 O.O.2d 277.

Where a juvenile court assumes jurisdiction in a habeas corpus proceeding relating to the rights of a parent to custody of his children, it may exercise such further powers as are necessary to the complete resolution of the entire issue, including retention of continuing jurisdiction to make further orders, although the petition for writ of habeas corpus is denied. (Annotation from former RC 2151.23.) Baker v. Rose (Ohio Com.Pl. 1970) 28 Ohio Misc. 200, 270 N.E.2d 678, 57 O.O.2d 57, 57 O.O.2d 351.

Where a juvenile court has acquired jurisdiction over the question of custody of a child, the court of common pleas may not thereafter inquire into such custody in a habeas corpus proceeding. (Annotation from former RC 2151.23.) In re Ruth (Ohio Com.Pl. 1961) 176 N.E.2d 187, 88 Ohio Law Abs. 1, 16 O.O.2d 408.

On the evidence in a habeas corpus action the court will permit two boys to remain with their father rather than being given to their mother or separated. (Annotation from former RC 3109.04.) Trout v. Trout (Ohio Com.Pl. 1956) 136 N.E.2d 474, 73 Ohio Law Abs. 91, appeal dismissed 167 Ohio St. 476, 149 N.E.2d 728, 5 O.O.2d 156.

5. Permanent custody

Mother was required to state with particularity in her habeas corpus petition the extraordinary circumstances which entitled her to a writ of habeas corpus; mother's petition which alleged that she was entitled to custody of the children and that the trial court lacked jurisdiction to deprive mother of custody was insufficient to support her petition. Holloway v. Clermont Cty. Dept. of Human Serv. (Ohio 2001) 92 Ohio St.3d 553, 751 N.E.2d 1055, 2001 –Ohio- 1282.

Res judicata barred mother from filing successive habeas corpus petitions to obtain custody of her children, where mother failed to allege any facts or circumstances which arose after she filed her second habeas corpus petition, and the allegations and attachments to mother's third habeas corpus petition restated the claims of her previous habeas corpus actions. Holloway v. Clermont Cty. Dept. of Human Serv. (Ohio 2001) 92 Ohio St.3d 553, 751 N.E.2d 1055, 2001 –Ohio- 1282.

A proceeding, instituted in the juvenile court under RC 2151.27 may not be used by the complainant either to force an adoption or as a substitute for an adoption proceeding. (Annotation from former RC 2151.27.) In re Minton (Darke 1960) 112 Ohio App. 361, 176 N.E.2d 252, 16 O.O.2d 283. Infants ☞ 131

Court not bound to deliver a child to a parent upon the claim of mere legal right but should in the exercise of sound discretion and after careful consideration of the facts award custody to one other than the parent. (Annotation from former RC 2151.23.) Ex parte Justice (Ohio Com.Pl. 1956) 135 N.E.2d 285, 72 Ohio Law Abs. 323. Child Custody ☞ 22; Child Custody ☞ 76

6. Evidence

In a proceeding in the juvenile court, instituted by the filing of a complaint under RC 2151.27, a finding by the court that a child is "neglected," in that it "lacked proper parental care because of the faults and habits of his parents" and "dependent " in that its "condition and environment... is such as to warrant the court... in assuming his guardianship" must be based on evidence with respect to whether the child was receiving proper parental care in a proper environment in its home at the time of the hearing. (Annotation from former RC 2151.04.) In re Minton (Darke 1960) 112 Ohio App. 361, 176 N.E.2d 252, 16 O.O.2d 283. Infants ☞ 156

7. Constitutional issues

While it was uncertain whether typed complaint which included firearm specification was ever prepared in juvenile delinquency case, record would have led reasonable person to believe that juvenile had prior notice of his alleged misconduct, and thus, there was no violation of juvenile's due process rights in finding that he violated statute prohibiting possession of firearm while committing felony. In re Good (Ohio App. 12 Dist., 02-24-1997) 118 Ohio App.3d 371, 692 N.E.2d 1072, appeal not allowed 79 Ohio St.3d 1418, 680 N.E.2d 156. Constitutional Law ☞ 255(4); Infants ☞ 198

Due process requires that before being found delinquent, juvenile must be given written notice of alleged misconduct. In re Good (Ohio App. 12 Dist., 02-24-1997) 118 Ohio App.3d 371, 692 N.E.2d 1072, dismissed, appeal not allowed 79 Ohio St.3d 1418, 680 N.E.2d 156. Constitutional Law ☞ 255(4)

Juv R 11 Transfer to another county

(A) Residence in another county; transfer optional

If the child resides in a county of this state and the proceeding is commenced in a court of another county, that court, on its own motion or a motion of a party, may transfer the proceeding to the county of the child's residence upon the filing of the complaint or after the adjudicatory or dispositional hearing for such further proceeding as required. The court of the child's residence shall then proceed as if the original complaint had been filed in that court. Transfer may also be made if the residence of the child changes.

(B) Proceedings in another county; transfer required

The proceedings, other than a removal action, shall be so transferred if other proceedings involving the child are pending in the juvenile court of the county of the child's residence.

(C) Adjudicatory hearing in county where complaint filed

Where either the transferring or receiving court finds that the interests of justice and the convenience of the parties so require, the adjudicatory hearing shall be held in the county wherein the complaint was filed. Thereafter the proceeding may be transferred to the county of the child's residence for disposition.

(D) Transfer of records

Certified copies of all legal and social records pertaining to the proceeding shall accompany the transfer.

(Adopted eff. 7–1–72; amended eff. 7–1–94, 7–1–98)

Historical and Statutory Notes

Amendment Note: The 7–1–98 amendment inserted ", other than a removal action," in division (B).

Amendment Note: The 7–1–94 amendment substituted "the child's" for "his" in division (B).

Commentary

Staff Notes

1998:

Rule 11(B) Proceedings in another county; transfer required

An exception to the mandatory transfer provisions of Juv. R. 11(B) was added by this amendment to cover removal actions, which are defined in Juv. R. 2(EE), also added by the 1998 amendments. Mandatory transfer of the action to the county of the child's residence would be inconsistent with the purpose of a removal action.

1994:

Rule 11 Transfer to Another County

The 1994 amendments were made to reflect gender neutral language.

Cross References

Transfer to juvenile court of another county, 2151.271

Library References

Infants ⊕196.

Westlaw Topic No. 211.

C.J.S. Courts §§ 249 et seq.

C.J.S. Infants §§ 42, 53, 54.

Carlin, Baldwin's Ohio Practice, Merrick–Rippner Probate Law § 107.7, 108.13 (2003).

Notes of Decisions

County of residence   2
Transfer after adjudication   3
Venue   1

---

1. Venue

Pursuant to Juv R 11(A), a case may be transferred only to a court in the county of the child's residence; transfer to a court in the county of the parents' residence is improper. In re Smith (Lucas 1989) 61 Ohio App.3d 788, 573 N.E.2d 1170, reconsideration denied.

Proper venue for child custody dispute was a matter within discretion of trial court where no other proceedings were pending in juvenile court of county of child's legal residence. Ackerman v. Lucas County Children Services Bd. (Lucas 1989) 49 Ohio App.3d 14, 550 N.E.2d 549. Infants ⊕ 196

2. County of residence

Transfer of abused child case to county where child legally resided and matters were pending was mandatory despite court's failure to complete an adjudicatory hearing; child's parents resided in other county, and that county's children and family services agency held emergency temporary custody of the child pursuant to an order of the juvenile court. In re Don B. (Ohio App. 6 Dist., Huron, 03-21-2003) No. H-02-033, 2003-Ohio-1400, 2003 WL 1448059, Unreported. Venue ⊕ 45

Although parents and children had moved to Paulding County before complaint in neglect and dependency was filed, Defiance County common pleas court did not abuse its discretion in denying parents' motion to dismiss case, noting that alleged incidents of neglect occurred while children resided in Defiance County and that majority of witnesses resided in Defiance County. In re Meyer (Defiance 1994) 98 Ohio App.3d 189, 648 N.E.2d 52, corrected. Infants ⊕ 196

Transfer of a permanent custody hearing from the county where the children have been found to be neglected and dependent and are the subjects of a temporary custody order to the county in which the children's parents currently reside is improper as the residency of the children, not the parents, controls jurisdiction. In re Smith (Lucas 1990) 64 Ohio App.3d 773, 582 N.E.2d 1117.

Forum county was proper venue in child custody dispute as both custodian in loco parentis and natural father of child were residents of that county, even though child's mother resided in another county. Ackerman v. Lucas County Children Services Bd. (Lucas 1989) 49 Ohio App.3d 14, 550 N.E.2d 549. Infants ⊕ 196

Venue in a custody proceeding in the juvenile division of common pleas court is governed by Juv R 11, which provides for an optional transfer of venue where the child resides in one county and the custody proceeding is brought in another county. Squires v. Squires (Preble 1983) 12 Ohio App.3d 138, 468 N.E.2d 73, 12 O.B.R. 460.

Proceedings declaring a child neglected by the juvenile court of another county do not prevent a child from thereafter becoming a school resident in a county to which he moves with his family. (Annotation from former RC 2151.27.) In re Larichchiuta (Preble 1968) 16 Ohio App.2d 164, 243 N.E.2d 111, 45 O.O.2d 456.

The juvenile court of the county in which acts constituting neglect or dependency of a minor child occur has jurisdiction over complaints concerning such child whether or not the parent or minor child was a nonresident of such county. (Annotation from former RC 2151.23.) In re Belk (Crawford 1954) 97 Ohio App. 114, 123 N.E.2d 757, 55 O.O. 330. Infants ⊕ 196

Where a case is pending against a juvenile in a foreign county, such case must be transferred to the juvenile's home county, if, at any time prior to dispositional order, proceedings against the juvenile are pending in his home county. Furthermore, such mandatory transfer may not be avoided by the foreign county through the use of a bindover proceeding. State v Payne, No. 81–CA–22 (4th Dist Ct App, Pickaway, 7–28–82).

A juvenile court has jurisdiction to declare any child dependent which is found within the county under facts and circumstances constituting dependency and the legal residence of the child or its parents, or those standing in loco parentis does not determine the jurisdiction of the court; the county in which such court assumes jurisdiction and declares such child to be dependent will be responsible for the support of such child. (Annotation from former RC 2151.23.) (See also 1929 OAG 755.) 1935 OAG 4172.

3. Transfer after adjudication

A juvenile court may not impose a fine and then transfer the case to another jurisdiction for further dispositional proceedings; once a final dispositional order is made, nothing remains to transfer to the other court. In re Sekulich (Ohio 1981) 65 Ohio St.2d 13, 417 N.E.2d 1014, 19 O.O.3d 192.

A juvenile court's erroneous transfer of a custodial proceeding subsequent to a dependency and neglect adjudication, but before a dispositional hearing, does not render subsequent collateral decisions by the receiving court null and void. In re Smith (Lucas 1990) 64 Ohio App.3d 773, 582 N.E.2d 1117.

Juv R 12   [Reserved]

Juv R 13 Temporary disposition; temporary orders; emergency medical and surgical treatment

(A) Temporary disposition

Pending hearing on a complaint, the court may make such temporary orders concerning the custody or care of a child who is the subject of the complaint as the child's interest and welfare may require.

(B) Temporary orders

(1) Pending hearing on a complaint, the judge or magistrate may issue temporary orders with respect to the relations and conduct of other persons toward a child who is the subject of the complaint as the child's interest and welfare may require.

(2) Upon the filing of an abuse, neglect, or dependency complaint, any party may by motion request that the court issue any of the following temporary orders to protect the best interest of the child:

(a) An order granting temporary custody of the child to a particular party;

(b) An order for the taking of the child into custody pending the outcome of the adjudicatory and dispositional hearings;

(c) An order granting, limiting, or eliminating visitation rights with respect to the child;

(d) An order for the payment of child support and continued maintenance of any medical, surgical, or hospital policies of insurance for the child that existed at the time of the filing of the complaint, petition, writ, or other document;

(e) An order requiring a party to vacate a residence that will be lawfully occupied by the child;

(f) An order requiring a party to attend an appropriate counseling program that is reasonably available to that party;

(g) Any other order that restrains or otherwise controls the conduct of any party which conduct would not be in the best interest of the child.

(3) The orders permitted by division (B)(2) of this rule may be granted ex parte if it appears that the best interest and welfare of the child require immediate issuance. If the court issues the requested ex parte order, the court shall hold a hearing to review the order within seventy-two hours after it is issued or before the end of the next court day after the day on which it is issued, whichever occurs first. The court shall appoint a guardian ad litem for the child prior to the hearing. The court shall give written notice of the hearing by means reasonably likely to result in the party's receiving actual notice and include all of the following:

(a) The date, time, and location of the hearing;

(b) The issues to be addressed at the hearing;

(c) A statement that every party to the hearing has a right to counsel and to court appointed counsel, if the party is indigent;

(d) The name, telephone number, and address of the person requesting the order;

(e) A copy of the order, except when it is not possible to obtain it because of the exigent circumstances in the case.

(4) The court may review any order under this rule at any time upon motion of any party for good cause shown or upon the motion of the court.

(5) If the court does not grant an ex parte order, the court shall hold a shelter care hearing on the motion within ten days after the motion is filed.

(C) Emergency medical and surgical treatment

Upon the certification of one or more reputable practicing physicians, the court may order such emergency medical and surgical treatment as appears to be immediately necessary for any child concerning whom a complaint has been filed.

(D) Ex parte proceedings

In addition to the ex parte proceeding described in division (B) of this rule, the court may proceed summarily and without notice under division (A), (B), or (C) of this rule, where it appears to the court that the interest and welfare of the child require that action be taken immediately.

(E) Hearing; notice

In addition to the procedures specified in division (B) of this rule and wherever possible, the court shall provide an opportunity for hearing before proceeding under division (D) of this rule. Where the court has proceeded without notice under division (D) of this rule, it shall give notice of the action it has taken to the parties and any other affected person and provide them an opportunity for a hearing concerning the continuing effects of the action.

(F) Probable cause finding

Upon the finding of probable cause at a shelter care hearing that a child is an abused child, the court may do any of the following:

(1) Upon motion by the court or of any party, issue reasonable protective orders with respect to the interviewing or deposition of the child;

(2) Order that the child's testimony be videotaped for preservation of the testimony for possible use in any other proceedings in the case;

(3) Set any additional conditions with respect to the child or the case involving the child that are in the best interest of the child.

(G) Payment

The court may order the parent, guardian, or custodian, if able, to pay for any emergency medical or surgical treatment provided pursuant to division (C) of this rule. The order of payment may be enforced by judgment, upon which execution may issue, and a failure to pay as ordered may be punished as contempt of court.

(Adopted eff. 7–1–72; amended eff. 7–1–94, 7–1–96)

Historical and Statutory Notes

Amendment Note: The 7–1–96 amendment substituted "magistrate" for "referee" in division (B)(1).

Amendment Note: The 7–1–94 amendment rewrote divisions (B), (D), and (E); added division (F); and redesignated former division (F) as division (G). Prior to amendment, divisions (B), (D), and (E) read:

"(B) Temporary orders. Pending hearing on a complaint, the court may issue such temporary orders with respect to the relations and conduct of other persons toward a child who is the subject of the complaint as the child's interest and welfare may require.

"(D) Ex parte proceedings. Where it appears to the court that the interest and welfare of the child require that action be taken immediately, the court may proceed summarily and without notice under subdivision (A), (B) or (C).

"(E) Hearing; notice. Wherever possible, the court shall provide an opportunity for hearing before proceeding under subdivision (A), (B) or (C) and shall give notice of the time and place of the hearing to the parties and any other person who may be affected by the proposed action. Where the court has proceeded without notice under subdivision (D), it shall give notice of the action it has taken to the parties and any other affected person and provide them an opportunity for a hearing concerning the continuing effects of such action."

Commentary

Staff Notes

1996:

The amendment changed the rule's reference from "referee" to "magistrate" in division (B)(1) in order to harmonize the rule with the language adopted in the 1995 amendments to Juv. R. 40. The amend-

ment is technical only and no substantive change is intended.

1994:

Rule 13 Temporary Disposition; Temporary Orders; Emergency Medical and Surgical Treatment

S.B. 89 amended section 2151.33 of the Revised Code to clarify the court's previously existing authority to issue emergency orders for children and Juv. R. 13 has been revised to reflect those amendments. Division (B) sets forth the type of temporary orders a court is authorized to make in an abuse, neglect or dependency case, as well as the procedure to be followed for notice and hearings when orders are made ex parte.

Division (D) clarifies that other kinds of ex parte hearings other than those specified in division (B) are still permitted, and division (E) emphasizes notice and hearing requirements where possible with hearings under division (D).

In accordance with section 2151.33(B) of the Revised Code, division (F)(1), (2), and (3) list the actions the court may take after finding, at a shelter care hearing, probable cause to believe that a child is an abused child.

Library References

Infants ⊜68.3, 192, 228.

Westlaw Topic No. 211.

C.J.S. Infants §§ 42, 53 to 57, 69 to 85.

Am Jur 2d: 47, Juvenile Court and Delinquent and Dependent Children § 29 to 33, 35, 36

Validity and application of statute allowing endangered child to be temporarily removed from parental custody. 38 ALR4th 756

Adrine & Ruden, Ohio Domestic Violence Law (2002 Ed.), Text 11.11.

Carlin, Baldwin's Ohio Practice, Merrick–Rippner Probate Law § 107.36, 107.41, 107.122, 107.152, 107.153 (2003).

Law Review and Journal Commentaries

Consent to Medical Treatment for Minors Under Care of Children Services Board, Stephen D. Freedman. 10 Cap U L Rev 309 (Winter 1980).

Emergency Custody in Domestic Relations Court: A Proposed Procedural and Substantive Litmus Test, Hon. V. Michael Brigner. 49 Dayton B Briefs 19 (December 1999).

Rethinking The Relationship Between Juvenile Courts And Treatment Agencies—An Administrative Law Approach, Leslie J. Harris. 28 J Fam L 217 (1990).

Notes of Decisions

Constitutional issues 1
Emergency medical treatment 2
Final orders 3
Orders from other states 6
Removal of minor from home 5
Temporary custody 4

---

1. Constitutional issues

Due process is not denied to the parent of a severely abused child by a court holding a temporary custody hearing ex parte under Juv R 13 without appointing a guardian ad litem under RC 2151.281. Parker v. Children Services Bd. of Trumbull County (Trumbull 1984) 21 Ohio App.3d 115, 487 N.E.2d 341, 21 O.B.R. 123.

Under the present Juvenile Code and Rules, a juvenile court cannot change a "temporary" commitment to the Ohio youth commission to an "permanent" commitment without hearing; further, the commitment of an unruly child, not declared "delinquent", is a violation of due process and any hearing held on the above matters requires the presence of the youth involved. OAG 72–071.

2. Emergency medical treatment

Where an unemancipated child has been removed from the custody of his parents and placed in the temporary custody of a county department of human services, the department may properly consent to surgical treatment for the child without consulting with the parents. Kilgallion v Children's Hospital Medical Center, Nos. C–850644 and C–860342 (1st Dist Ct App, Hamilton, 4–15–87).

Juvenile court properly authorized hospital to administer blood transfusions to child over religious objections of parents. (Annotation from former RC 2151.33.) In re Clark (Ohio Com.Pl. 1962) 185 N.E.2d 128, 90 Ohio Law Abs. 21, 21 O.O.2d 86.

When a complaint or application for care concerning a child has been filed with the juvenile court, such court may, pending service of a citation on the child's parents, guardian or custodian, order the provision of emergency medical or surgical treatment. (Annotation from former RC 2151.33.) 1951 OAG 898.

Where a child has been permanently committed to a child welfare board by order of the juvenile court, such board may properly consent to medical and surgical treatment of such child; where a child has been temporarily so committed, the child remains a ward of juvenile court, and such court may properly consent to medical and surgical treatment of such child. (Annotation from former RC 2151.35.) 1951 OAG 898.

3. Final orders

A temporary order of a juvenile court changing custody under Juv R 13 or 29 is not a dispositional order under Juv R 34, and hence is not a final appealable order. Morrison v. Morrison (Summit 1973) 45 Ohio App.2d 299, 344 N.E.2d 144, 74 O.O.2d 441.

It is reversible error for a trial court to grant permanent custody of the parties' minor child to the father solely because the mother was incarcerated for child stealing at the time of the hearing and without first determining the best interest of the child. Dunn v Martin, No. 15208, 1996 WL 430867 (2d Dist Ct App, Montgomery, 8–2–96).

4. Temporary custody

Court of Appeals was without jurisdiction to address mother's claim that trial court erred in awarding temporary custody of mother's child to child's father and grandmother because there was no motion pending and no finding of suitability was determined; order awarded temporary custody "until further order," and was thus not final, appealable order. In re S.M. (Ohio App. 8 Dist., Cuyahoga, 03-18-2004) No. 81566, 2004-Ohio-1243, 2004 WL 527925, Unreported. Child Custody ⟳ 902

A comprehensive reunification plan need be prepared only when a child is committed to the temporary custody of the department of public welfare under RC 2151.353(A)(2) or 2151.353(A)(3); this is the plain meaning of RC 2151.412(C), which does not, it follows, require preparation of a plan when a temporary custody order is based on Juv R 13(A) and

13(D). In re Koballa, Nos. 48417 and 48480 (8th Dist Ct App, Cuyahoga, 1–24–85).

5. Removal of minor from home

Under Ohio law, unless matters of public safety are involved, a child alleged to be abused, neglected, or dependent may be removed from his home by court order only upon a judicial determination that continuation in the home would be contrary to the child's best interest. OAG 87–105.

6. Orders from other states

Where a court of another state has awarded custody of a minor child pursuant to a valid in personam order, and there is no evidence of a subsequent change in circumstances affecting the best interests of the child, the courts of this state will give full faith and credit to that order. Williams v. Williams (Ohio 1975) 44 Ohio St.2d 28, 336 N.E.2d 426, 73 O.O.2d 121.

Juv R 14 Termination, extension or modification of temporary custody orders

(A) Termination

Any temporary custody order issued shall terminate one year after the earlier of the date on which the complaint in the case was filed or the child was first placed into shelter care. A temporary custody order shall extend beyond a year and until the court issues another dispositional order, where any public or private agency with temporary custody, not later than thirty days prior to the earlier of the date for the termination of the custody order or the date set at the dispositional hearing for the hearing to be held pursuant to division (A) of section 2151.415 of the Revised Code, files a motion requesting that any of the following orders of disposition be issued:

(1) An order that the child be returned home with custody to the child's parents, guardian, or custodian without any restrictions;

(2) An order for protective supervision;

(3) An order that the child be placed in the legal custody of a relative or other interested individual;

(4) An order terminating parental rights;

(5) An order for long term foster care;

(6) An order for the extension of temporary custody.

(B) Extension

Upon the filing of an agency's motion for the extension of temporary custody, the court shall schedule a hearing and give notice to all parties in accordance with these rules. The agency shall include in the motion an explanation of the progress on the case plan and of its expectations of reunifying the child with the child's family, or placing the child in a permanent placement, within the extension period. The court may extend the temporary custody order for a period of up to six months. Prior to the end of the extension period, the agency may request one additional extension of up to six months. The court shall grant either extension upon finding that it is in the best interest of the child, that there has been significant progress on the case plan, and that there is reasonable cause to believe that the child will be reunited with one of the child's parents or otherwise permanently placed within the period of extension. Prior to the end of either extension, the agency that received the extension shall file a motion and the court shall issue one of the orders of disposition set forth in division (A) of this rule. Upon the agency's motion or upon its own motion, the court shall conduct a hearing and issue an appropriate order of disposition.

(C) Modification

The court, upon its own motion or that of any party, shall conduct a hearing with notice to all parties to determine whether any order issued should be modified or terminated, or whether any other dispositional order set forth in division (A) should be issued. The court shall so modify or terminate any order in accordance with the best interest of the child.

(Adopted eff. 7–1–94)

Commentary

Staff Notes

1994:

Rule 14 Termination, Extension or Modification of Temporary Orders

S.B. 89 required new time periods to be established for the termination of abuse, neglect, and dependency cases; for the timing of possible final orders to terminate a case; and for the conditions, procedures, and limitations for seeking an extension. Juv. R. 14, previously reserved, has been written in accordance with the requirements of Revised Code 2151.353 and 2151.415.

Juv R 15   Process: issuance, form

(A) Summons: issuance

After the complaint has been filed, the court shall cause the issuance of a summons directed to the child, the parents, guardian, custodian, and any other persons who appear to the court to be proper or necessary parties. The summons shall require the parties to appear before the court at the time fixed to answer the allegations of the complaint. A child alleged to be abused, neglected, or dependent shall not be summoned unless the court so directs.

A summons issued for a child under fourteen years of age alleged to be delinquent, unruly, or a juvenile traffic offender shall be made by serving either the child's parents, guardian, custodian, or other person with whom the child lives or resides. If the person who has physical custody of the child or with whom the child resides is other than the parent or guardian, then the parents and guardian also shall be summoned. A copy of the complaint shall accompany the summons.

(B) Summons: form

The summons shall contain:

(1) The name of the party or person with whom the child may be or, if unknown, any name or description by which the party or person can be identified with reasonable certainty.

(2) A summary statement of the complaint and in juvenile traffic offense and delinquency proceedings the numerical designation of the applicable statute or ordinance.

(3) A statement that any party is entitled to be represented by an attorney and that upon request the court will appoint an attorney for an indigent party entitled to appointed counsel under Juv. R. 4(A).

(4) An order to the party or person to appear at a stated time and place with a warning that the party or person may lose valuable rights or be subject to court sanction if the party or person fails to appear at the time and place stated in the summons.

(5) An order to the parent, guardian, or other person having care of a child alleged to be an unruly or delinquent child for being an habitual or chronic truant, to appear personally at the hearing and all proceedings, and an order directing the person having the physical custody or control of the child to bring the child to the hearing, with a warning that if the child fails to appear, the parent, guardian, or other person having care of the child may be subject to court sanction, including a finding of contempt.

(6) A statement that if a child is adjudicated abused, neglected, or dependent and the complaint seeks an order of per-

manent custody, an order of permanent custody would cause the parents, guardian, or legal custodian to be divested permanently of all parental rights and privileges.

(7) A statement that if a child is adjudicated abused, neglected, or dependent and the complaint seeks an order of temporary custody, an order of temporary custody will cause the removal of the child from the legal custody of the parents, guardian, or other custodian until the court terminates the order of temporary custody or permanently divests the parents of their parental rights.

(8) A statement that if the child is adjudicated abused, neglected, or dependent and the complaint seeks an order for a planned permanent living arrangement, an order for a planned permanent living arrangement will cause the removal of the child from the legal custody of the parent, guardian, or other custodian.

(9) A statement, in a removal action, of the specific disposition sought.

(10) The name and telephone number of the court employee designated by the court to arrange for the prompt appointment of counsel for indigent persons.

(C) Summons: endorsement

The court may endorse upon the summons an order directed to the parents, guardian, or other person with whom the child may be, to appear personally and bring the child to the hearing.

(D) Warrant: issuance

If it appears that the summons will be ineffectual or the welfare of the child requires that the child be brought forthwith to the court, a warrant may be issued against the child. A copy of the complaint shall accompany the warrant.

(E) Warrant: form

The warrant shall contain the name of the child or, if that is unknown, any name or description by which the child can be identified with reasonable certainty. It shall contain a summary statement of the complaint and in juvenile traffic offense and delinquency proceedings the numerical designation of the applicable statute or ordinance. A copy of the complaint shall be attached to the warrant. The warrant shall command that the child be taken into custody and be

brought before the court that issued the warrant without unnecessary delay.

(Adopted eff. 7–1–72; amended eff. 7–1–94, 7–1–98, 7–1–01, 7–1–02)

Historical and Statutory Notes

Amendment Note: The 7–1–02 amendment substituted "a planned permanent living arrangement" for "long term foster care" throughout division (B)(8).

Amendment Note: The 7–1–01 amendment added new division (B)(5) and redesignated former divisions (B)(5) through (B)(9) as new divisions (B)(6) through (B)(10).

Amendment Note: The 7–1–98 amendment deleted "or other person with whom the child may be living" before "and any other person" in division (A).

Amendment Note: The 7–1–94 amendment rewrote divisions (A) and (B)(5); added divisions (B)(6) through (B)(8); substituted "parents, guardian, or other" for "party or" in division (C); and made changes to reflect gender-neutral language. Prior to amendment, divisions (A) and (B)(5) read:

"(A) Summons: issuance. After the complaint has been filed, the clerk shall promptly issue summons to the parties and to any person with whom the child may be, requiring the parties or person to appear before the court at the time fixed for hearing. A copy of the complaint shall accompany the summons.

"(5) If a complaint requests permanent custody a statement that the parent, guardian or other custodian may be permanently divested of all parental rights."

Commentary

Staff Notes

2002:

Juvenile Rule 15(B) Summons: form

The July 1, 2002, amendment to Juv. R. 15(B)(8) substituted the language of "planned permanent living arrangement" for the former language of "long term foster care," to conform to the new legislative designation for these child-placing arrangements.

The amendment to Juv. R. 15(B)(8) conforms to sections 2151.28(D) and 2151.353(B) of the Revised Code. Juvenile Rules 2, 10, and 34 also were amended effective July 1, 2002 to reflect this change in terminology.

2001:

Rule 15(B) Summons: form

Rule 15(B) was amended to add new division (5), which deals with orders to be placed on a summons to parents or other responsible adults when a child or adult is summoned to court pursuant to a complaint of chronic or habitual truancy. The new section tracks the language of Revised Code section 2151.28 (E)(2), as amended by Sub. Sen. Bill 181 (effective September 4, 2000), and makes clear that the parent or responsible adult must bring the child to truancy hearings or be subject to court sanction, including a finding of contempt. Adding this language to the summons alerts responsible adults to the need to ensure not only his or her own appearance, but that of the child as well. Prior divisions (B)(5) through (B)(9) were renumbered (B)(6) through (B)(10) to reflect this interpolation.

1998:

Rule 15 Process: Issuance, Form

The 1998 amendment to the first paragraph of Juv. R. 15(A) was intended to clarify the requirement that summons must be issued to the child and to all of the following persons: the parents, guardian, custodian, and any other persons who appear to the court to be proper or necessary parties. Under the prior version of the rule, the use of the word "or" made it unclear whether summons was required to be issued to all of the listed persons. The 1998 amendment also deleted the phrase "other person with whom the child may be living," because this person would be covered by the remaining list of designated persons.

Pursuant to section 2151.55 of the Revised Code, which first created removal actions, the written notice issued to the school superintendent and to the entity that placed the child in the foster home must include an explanation of the purpose of the removal hearing. In furtherance of this notification objective, the 1998 addition of Juv. R. 15(B)(8) requires that those persons receiving a summons for the removal hearing also be notified of the purpose of the hearing and possible disposition.

1994:

Rule 15 Process: Issuance, Form

Pursuant to Revised Code 2151.28 (S.B. 89), Juv. R. 15 now sets forth the form of the summons issued in juvenile court. The revised statute requires the summons in an abuse, neglect, or dependency case to state precisely the potential consequences of an unfavorable adjudication, including permanent loss of parental rights. Therefore, those requirements are listed in divisions (B)(5), (6), (7), and (8).

Cross References

Issuance of warrant against parent, custodian, guardian, or child, 2151.30

Summons on juvenile complaint, 2151.28

Warrant or summons, Crim R 4

Library References

Infants ⊃198.

Westlaw Topic No. 211.

C.J.S. Infants § 56.

Am Jur 2d: 47, Juvenile Courts and Delinquent and Dependent Children § 43

Necessity of service of process upon infant itself in juvenile delinquency and dependency proceedings. 90 ALR2d 293

Failure to give adequate notice to juvenile's parents as ground for reversal of determination of juvenile delinquency under Federal Juvenile Delinquency Act (18 USC secs. 5031–5042). 30 ALR Fed 745

Carlin, Baldwin's Ohio Practice, Merrick–Rippner Probate Law § 106.21, 107.10, 107.11, 107.13, 107.127, 107.161, 107.167 (2003).

Notes of Decisions

Constitutional issues   2

Hearings   8

Jurisdiction   3

Notice   4

Orders from other states   1

Parties   9

Right to counsel   5

Summons   7

Warrants   6

---

1. Orders from other states

Where a court of another state has awarded custody of a minor child pursuant to a valid in personam order, and there is no evidence of a subsequent change in circumstances affecting the best interests of the child, the courts of this state will give full faith and credit to that order. Williams v. Williams (Ohio 1975) 44 Ohio St.2d 28, 336 N.E.2d 426, 73 O.O.2d 121.

2. Constitutional issues

Due process entitles a party to reasonable notice of the setting of a trial date. Lowry v. Lowry (Ross 1988) 48 Ohio App.3d 184, 549 N.E.2d 176.

The notice provisions of RC 2151.85(D) violate the rulemaking authority of the Supreme Court, in O Const Art IV §5(B), as Juv R 15(A) requires that parents of a juvenile be notified of any proceedings involving the child; therefore, RC 2151.85 is unconstitutional. Further CP Sup R 76(H), promulgated in furtherance of RC 2151.85, conflicts with Juv R 15(A), and in such situations, the juvenile rule controls. In re Doe (Ohio Com.Pl. 1990) 57 Ohio Misc.2d 20, 565 N.E.2d 891.

3. Jurisdiction

In case of arrest of a minor, upon a warrant issued by a juvenile court, arising out of a complaint charging such minor with delinquency, the juvenile court has jurisdiction of the proceedings even though a citation has not been issued to the parents, guardian or other person having custody and control of such child. (Annotation from former RC 2151.28.) State ex rel. Heth v. Moloney (Ohio 1933) 126 Ohio St. 526, 186 N.E. 362.

Juvenile court has no jurisdiction to adjudicate a child as dependent until after filing of a complaint charging such dependency and notice given to the parent or parents. (Annotation from former RC 2151.28.) State ex rel. Clark v. Allaman (Montgomery 1950) 87 Ohio App. 101, 90 N.E.2d 394, 57 Ohio Law Abs. 17, 42 O.O. 330, affirmed 154 Ohio St. 296, 95 N.E.2d 753, 43 O.O. 190.

A juvenile court does not have jurisdiction to make commitments of children under former GC 1653 (Repealed) unless service, either actual or constructive, is first had on the father of such child or on the person having the custody of such child. (Annotation from former RC 2151.36.) 1929 OAG 281.

4. Notice

Under this section, the parents of a minor child or children are entitled to notice, actual or constructive, in a proceeding instituted in the juvenile court upon a complaint of dependency of such children; without such notice jurisdiction of the court does not attach and a judgment of commitment in proceeding is void. (Annotation from former RC 2151.28.) In re Corey (Ohio 1945) 145 Ohio St. 413, 61 N.E.2d 892, 31 O.O. 35. Infants ⊃ 198

Failure to serve a parent with a summons in a permanent custody action does not require dismissal of the action where the parent has actual notice of the action and has been served with a complaint. In re Webb (Hamilton 1989) 64 Ohio App.3d 280, 581 N.E.2d 570, dismissed, jurisdictional motion overruled 48 Ohio St.3d 704, 549 N.E.2d 1191.

Regular legal notice by service of process on the parent is an indispensable prerequisite to jurisdiction of juvenile court to make commitment of a minor child in delinquency cases. (Annotation from former RC 2151.28.) Ex parte Flickinger (Ohio Com.Pl. 1940) 5 Ohio Supp. 252, 33 Ohio Law Abs. 8, 20 O.O. 224.

5. Right to counsel

Juvenile rule and statute guarantee right to counsel for all indigent parties in juvenile proceedings. Holley v. Higgins (Franklin 1993) 86 Ohio App.3d 240, 620 N.E.2d 251. Infants ⬤ 205

6. Warrants

Under this section, a juvenile court may either issue a citation, requiring a minor charged with being dependent, neglected or delinquent and its parents or guardian or other person to appear, or the judge may in the first instance issue a warrant for the arrest of such minor. (Annotation from former RC 2151.28.) State ex rel. Heth v. Moloney (Ohio 1933) 126 Ohio St. 526, 186 N.E. 362.

7. Summons

A properly served summons containing the "full explanation" required by RC 2151.353(B) must be accompanied by a copy of the complaint, amended or not, if the complaint seeks, temporarily or permanently, to divest a parent of his parental rights. In re Wilson (Huron 1984) 21 Ohio App.3d 36, 486 N.E.2d 152, 21 O.B.R. 38.

The sheriff is required to serve summons, notices, and subpoenas which are directed to him by the juvenile court, and whether the juvenile court requests the summons, notices or subpoenas to be served personally or to be delivered by registered or certified mail, the sheriff's office is legally required to serve them in accordance with such directions of the juvenile court; and if the person to be served is out of the state and his address is known, service of summons may be made by the sheriff by delivering a copy to him personally or mailing a copy to him by registered or certified mail. (Annotation from former RC 2151.19.) OAG 70–130.

8. Hearings

RC 2151.28 and 2151.31 do not require a hearing as a condition precedent to the taking of a child into custody, pursuant to order of a juvenile court, during pendency of an action in such court. (Annotation from former RC 2151.28.) In re Jones (Allen 1961) 114 Ohio App. 319, 182 N.E.2d 631, 19 O.O.2d 286.

9. Parties

A father is a party to proceedings in a juvenile court in which his children are found to be neglected and in which temporary custody is given to the mother; and he is also a party to a subsequent proceeding in the same court modifying such temporary custody order and is entitled to appear in an appeal from such order and to move to dismiss such appeal. (Annotation from former RC 2151.28.) In re Rule (Crawford 1963) 1 Ohio App.2d 57, 203 N.E.2d 501, 30 O.O.2d 76.

Juv R 16 Process: service

(A) Summons: service, return

Except as otherwise provided in these rules, summons shall be served as provided in Civil Rules 4(A), (C) and (D), 4.1, 4.2, 4.3, 4.5 and 4.6. The summons shall direct the party served to appear at a stated time and place. Where service is by certified mail, the time shall not be less than seven days after the date of mailing.

Except as otherwise provided in this rule, when the residence of a party is unknown and cannot be ascertained with reasonable diligence, service shall be made by publication. Service by publication upon a non-custodial parent is not required in delinquent child or unruly child cases when the person alleged to have legal custody of the child has been served with summons pursuant to this rule, but the court may not enter any order or judgment against any person who has not been served with process or served by publication unless that person appears. Before service by publication can be made, an affidavit of a party or party's counsel shall be filed with the court. The affidavit shall aver that service of summons cannot be made because the residence of the person is unknown to the affiant and cannot be ascertained with reasonable diligence and shall set forth the last known address of the party to be served.

Service by publication shall be made by newspaper publication, by posting and mail, or by a combination of these methods. The court, by local rule, shall determine which method or methods of publication shall be used. If service by publication is made by newspaper publication, upon the filing of the affidavit, the clerk shall serve notice by publication in a newspaper of general circulation in the county in which the complaint is filed. If no newspaper is published in that county, then publication shall be in a newspaper published in an adjoining county. The publication shall contain the name and address of the court, the case number, the name of the first party on each side, and the name and last known address, if any, of the person or persons whose residence is unknown. The publication shall also contain a summary statement of the object of the complaint and shall notify the person to be served that the person is required to appear at the time and place stated. The time stated shall not be less than seven days after the date of publication. The publication shall be published once and service shall be complete on the date of publication.

After the publication, the publisher or the publisher's agent shall file with the court an affidavit showing the fact of publication together with a copy of the notice of publication. The affidavit and copy of the notice shall constitute proof of service.

If service by publication is made by posting and mail, upon the filing of the affidavit, the clerk shall cause service of notice to be made by posting in a conspicuous place in the courthouse in which the division of the common pleas court exercising jurisdiction over the complaint is located and in additional public places in the county that have been designated by local rule for the posting of notices pursuant to this rule. The number of additional public places to be designated shall be either two places or the number of state representative districts that are contained wholly or partly in the county in which the courthouse is located, whichever is greater. The notice shall contain the same information required to be contained in a newspaper publication. The notice shall be posted in the required locations for seven consecutive days. The clerk also shall cause the summons and accompanying pleadings to be mailed by ordinary mail, address correction requested, to the last known address of the party to be served. The clerk shall obtain a certificate of mailing from the United States Postal Service. If the clerk is notified of a corrected or forwarding address of the party to be served within the seven day period that notice is posted pursuant to this rule, the clerk shall cause the summons and accompanying pleadings to be mailed to the corrected or forwarding address. The clerk shall note the name, address, and date of each mailing in the docket.

After the seven days of posting, the clerk shall note on the docket where and when notice was posted. Service shall be complete upon the entry of posting.

(B) Warrant: execution; return

(1) By whom. The warrant shall be executed by any officer authorized by law.

(2) Territorial limits. The warrant may be executed at any place within this state.

(3) Manner. The warrant shall be executed by taking the party against whom it is issued into custody. The officer is not required to have possession of the warrant at the time it is executed, but in such case the officer shall inform the party of the complaint made and the fact that the warrant has been issued. A copy of the warrant shall be given to the person named in the warrant as soon as possible.

(4) Return. The officer executing a warrant shall make return thereof to the issuing court. Unexecuted warrants shall upon request of the issuing court be returned to that court.

A warrant returned unexecuted and not cancelled or a copy thereof may, while the complaint is pending, be delivered by the court to an authorized officer for execution.

An officer executing a warrant shall take the person named therein without unnecessary delay before the court which issued the warrant.

(Adopted eff. 7–1–72; amended eff. 7–1–94, 7–1–98)

Historical and Statutory Notes

Amendment Note: The 7–1–98 amendment inserted "and shall set forth the last known address of the party to be served" at the end of the first paragraph in division (A); added the first two sentences, inserted "If service by publication is made by newspaper publication," and substituted "seven" for "fourteen" in the second paragraph in division (A); added the fourth and fifth paragraphs in division (A); and made other nonsubstantive changes.

Amendment Note: The 7–1–94 amendment rewrote the first two paragraphs in division (A); and made changes to reflect gender-neutral language. Prior to amendment, the first two paragraphs in division (A) read:

"(A) Summons: service, return. Summons shall be served as provided in Civil Rules 4(A), (C) and (D), 4.1, 4.2, 4.3, 4.5 and 4.6. The summons shall direct the party served to appear at a stated time and place; where service is by certified mail such time shall not be less than twenty-one days after the date of mailing.

"When the residence of a party is unknown, and cannot with reasonable diligence be ascertained, service shall be made by publication. Before service by publication can be made, an affidavit of a party or his counsel must be filed with the court. The affidavit shall aver that service of summons cannot be made because the residence of the defendant is unknown to the affiant and cannot with reasonable diligence be ascertained."

Commentary

Staff Notes

1998:

Rule 16(A) Summons: service, return

The amendments to division (A) address the issue of service by publication where the residence of a party is unknown. Prior to the amendment, the rule only provided for publication in a newspaper of general circulation. This amendment changed the nature of service by publication in juvenile court cases.

Under this amendment, which is modeled partly on Civ. R. 4.4(A)(2), service by publication in all cases governed by the Juvenile Rules would be accomplished either by the traditional method of newspaper publication, by posting and mail, or by a combination of these methods. The court, by local rule, determines which method of service to select.

Civ. R. 4.4(A)(2) mandates posting and mail publication in divorce, annulment, or legal separation actions where the plaintiff is proceeding *in forma pauperis*. Because most juvenile court cases are initiated by a complaint being filed by a parent (e.g., custody and unruly cases) or by an agency of the state (e.g., delinquency and unruly complaints filed by police departments and boards of education; neglect, dependency, and abuse complaints filed by children's services boards), the rationale which apparently supports Civ. R. 4.4(A)(2) would equally apply to juvenile court cases. Moreover, since the type of case and the status of the complainant should have no bearing on the method of service, the posting and mail form of publication should be permitted in all cases governed by the Juvenile Rules.

Another amendment relates to time frames. The prior rule provided that the publication had to occur not less than fourteen days prior to the scheduled hearing date. The amendment reduced the publication time frame to seven days. This amendment was based on several reasons. First, a 1994 amendment to Juv. R. 16(A) reduced the requisite waiting period for service by certified mail from twenty-one to seven days. Thus, the change to seven days for publication is consistent with the 1994 amendment. Second, Juv. R. 29(A) requires an adjudicatory hearing within ten days of the filing of a complaint when a child is in detention or shelter care. Although this hearing may be continued upon a showing of good cause, the amendment to Juv. R. 16(A) eliminated the potential conflict between the two rules. Third, Juv. R. 29(A) requires an adjudicatory hearing within thirty days after the filing of a complaint in all cases of abuse, neglect, or dependency. Although this hearing may be continued for a reasonable time beyond thirty days to obtain service on all parties, under no circumstances may the hearing be held later than sixty days after the complaint is filed. The condensed time frame for perfecting service by publication would facilitate conducting the hearing within the mandated time periods. Finally, section 2151.29 of the Revised Code, which has been in effect since 1969 (and which conflicts with both the prior and new versions of Juv. R. 16(A)), provides for a one week time frame for service by publication.

1994:

Rule 16 Process: Service

Juv. R. 29(A) requires that, when a child is in detention or shelter care, an adjudicatory hearing be set no later than ten days after the filing of the complaint. Certified mail service must, therefore, be completed prior to the ten day period. Juv. R. 16(A) now requires that a hearing shall be held not less than seven days after the date of mailing.

Service by publication permits fourteen days notice prior to the date of the hearing; however, new language has been added to Juv. R. 16(A) to eliminate the necessity of serving a non-custodial parent whose address is unknown, so long as the person with legal custody has been served with summons. Further safeguards have been added to the rule in that the court may not enter an order against any person who has not been served with process or served by publication unless that person appears.

Cross References

Issuance of warrant against parent, custodian, guardian, or child, 2151.30
Process: summons, Civ R 4 et seq.
Service of summons on juvenile complaint, 2151.29
Style of process, 7.01
Summons; expense, 2151.19
Summons on juvenile complaint, 2151.28
Warrant or summons, Crim R 4

Library References

Infants ⟜198.
Westlaw Topic No. 211.
C.J.S. Infants § 56.
Am Jur 2d: 47, Juvenile Courts and Delinquent and Dependent Children § 43
Necessity of service of process upon infant itself in juvenile delinquency and dependency proceedings. 90 ALR2d 293
Failure to give adequate notice to juvenile's parents as ground for reversal of determination of juvenile delinquency under Federal Juvenile Delinquency Act (18 USC secs. 5031–5042). 30 ALR Fed 745
Klein & Darling, Baldwin's Ohio Practice, Civil Practice § 4.1–6 (1997).
Carlin, Baldwin's Ohio Practice, Merrick–Rippner Probate Law § 107.11, 107.12, 107.13, 107.50, 107.166, 107.167 (2003).

Notes of Decisions

Jurisdiction 3
Notice 2
Orders from other states 1
Service 4

---

1. Orders from other states

Where a court of another state has awarded custody of a minor child pursuant to a valid in personam order, and there is no evidence of a subsequent change in circumstances affecting the best interests of the child, the courts of this state will give full faith and credit to that order. Williams v. Williams (Ohio 1975) 44 Ohio St.2d 28, 336 N.E.2d 426, 73 O.O.2d 121.

2. Notice

Minor mother's legal guardian received sufficient notice of temporary custody hearing to provide court with jurisdiction in matter, even though mother claimed no notice was provided, where notice was endorsed and left at guardian's residence. In re D.H. (Ohio App. 8 Dist., Cuyahoga, 12-04-2003) No. 82533, 2003-Ohio-6478, 2003 WL 22861922, Unreported. Infants ⟜ 198

Mother received proper notice of motion filed by county department of children and family services seeking permanent custody of dependent child; record indicated that mother was personally served with notice some six months after filing of motion to modify temporary custody and seven months prior to the hearing for permanent custody. In re R.K. (Ohio App. 8 Dist., Cuyahoga, 11-26-2003) No. 82374, 2003-Ohio-6333, 2003 WL 22804937, Unreported. Infants ⟜ 198

Where only notice given mother of hearing to change child's temporary commitment to a permanent one was served on mother within an hour before such hearing, and she had no opportunity to either prepare for such hearing or to engage counsel to represent her, such notice is insufficient in law, and an order for permanent custody made at such hearing is void for want of jurisdiction of court in making it, even though mother was present at hearing; attack made upon it by an application for a writ of habeas corpus is proper even though judgment appears to be regular and valid upon its face. (Annotation from former RC 2151.29.) In re Frinzl (Ohio 1949) 152 Ohio St. 164, 87 N.E.2d 583, 39 O.O. 456.

The matters required to be shown under former GC 1648 (GC 1639–24; RC 2151.28) as a prerequisite to notice by publication of proceedings as to dependency of minor children were jurisdictional. In such case an attack upon a judgment for fraud in its procurement is direct, and is permitted, notwithstanding that the judgment questioned may appear on its face regular and valid. (Annotation from former RC 2151.29.) Lewis v. Reed (Ohio 1927) 117 Ohio St. 152, 157 N.E. 897, 5 Ohio Law Abs. 420, 25 Ohio Law Rep. 386.

Under GC 1648 (GC 1639–24; RC 2151.28), the mother of an illegitimate child is entitled to notice, actual or constructive, of proceedings upon a complaint of dependency instituted in the juvenile court in reference to such child; and until notice of such proceedings has been given to the mother, the jurisdiction of the juvenile court does not attach and a judgment of permanent commitment rendered in such dependency proceeding is void. (Annotation from former RC 2151.29.) Lewis v. Reed (Ohio 1927) 117 Ohio St. 152, 157 N.E. 897, 5 Ohio Law Abs. 420, 25 Ohio Law Rep. 386.

A published notice under Juv R 16 that lacks the last known address is defective as notice by publication; the requirements of Juv R 16 are mandatory and are to be strictly construed. In re Holloway, No. CA95-09-064, 1996 WL 227481 (12th Dist Ct App, Clermont, 5-6-96).

Where a complaint for dependency is filed, an unknown father must be served by publication; even an apparently unconcerned putative father is entitled to notice by publication, and the mother's statement that she does not know who the father is does not justify dispensing with the notice. In re Ware, No. 79–03243 (8th Dist Ct App, Cuyahoga, 7–17–80).

The Common Pleas Court had jurisdiction to grant permanent custody of mother's two children to the county job and family services agency, even though notice to mother of the dispositional hearing was returned undeliverable; mother appeared with counsel at an earlier shelter-care hearing, at the shelter-care hearing the trial court noted the date of the adjudicatory hearing, counsel for mother appeared at the dispositional hearing, and neither mother or her counsel objected to the notice provided to mother. In re Billingsley (Ohio App. 3 Dist., Putnam, 01-28-2003) No. 12-02-07, No. 12-02-08, 2003-Ohio-344, 2003 WL 178661, Unreported. Infants ☞ 198

Father waived on appeal in termination of parental rights proceeding issue of whether trial court lacked jurisdiction to enter order awarding permanent custody of children to county department of children and family services, based on his allegation that court did not provide proper notice to mother of proceedings, as he failed to raise issue in trial court. (Per O'Donnell, J., with two judges concurring in judgment only). In re Harlston (Ohio App. 8 Dist., Cuyahoga, 01-23-2003) No. 80672, 2003-Ohio-282, 2003 WL 152939, Unreported. Infants ☞ 243

Mother's absence at termination of parental rights hearing did not prejudice father's rights; not only was there no evidence that mother would have been awarded custody of children, but mother was in agreement with permanent custody of children being awarded to county department of children and family services. (Per O'Donnell, J., with two judges concurring in judgment only). In re Harlston (Ohio App. 8 Dist., Cuyahoga, 01-23-2003) No. 80672, 2003-Ohio-282, 2003 WL 152939, Unreported. Infants ☞ 253

Daily legal newspaper that was designated as official law journal of county was "newspaper of general circulation" by special exemption of statutes defining publications that qualify as newspapers of general circulation, and thus, publication of notice of complaint and summons in official law journal to fathers of dependent children was sufficient for juvenile court to assert jurisdiction over fathers for hearing on state's motion for permanent custody. In re Starkey (Ohio App. 7 Dist., 12-11-2002) 150 Ohio App.3d 612, 782 N.E.2d 665, 2002-Ohio-6892. Infants ☞ 198; Process ☞ 105

3. Jurisdiction

Juvenile court is without jurisdiction to make permanent a temporary commitment of child unless notice of time and place of hearing is served on parent or guardian either by delivering a copy to the person to be notified, by leaving a copy at his usual place of residence, by service by registered mail, or by publication, as provided by this section; such notice must be served sufficiently in advance of hearing to allow reasonable time to obtain counsel and prepare for participation in such hearing. (Annotation from former RC 2151.29.) In re Frinzl (Ohio 1949) 152 Ohio St. 164, 87 N.E.2d 583, 39 O.O. 456. Infants ☞ 198

4. Service

Trial court did not have jurisdiction to award permanent custody of child to Department of Children and Family Services, even though mother had notice of preliminary hearing, where service was not attempted on mother in regards to trial. In re D.H. (Ohio App. 8 Dist., Cuyahoga, 12-04-2003) No. 82533, 2003-Ohio-6478, 2003 WL 22861922, Unreported. Infants ☞ 198

Service by publication, in child protection proceedings, was not rendered defective when affidavit incorrectly listed affiant, where affidavit contained a statement by the notary certifying that content was sworn to and it was subscribed in her presence. In re D.H. (Ohio App. 8 Dist., Cuyahoga, 12-04-2003) No. 82533, 2003-Ohio-6478, 2003 WL 22861922, Unreported. Infants ☞ 198

Trial court lacked personal jurisdiction over father to enter child support order against him, due to defective service of process of motion to set support; docket sheet showed that father was served with motion to set child support by ordinary mail only, rather than by certified mail, or express mail, as required by rule, so continuing jurisdiction of juvenile court was not invoked, and, due to failure to provide notice, any subsequent order based on void order was nullity. In re Brandon P. (Ohio App. 6 Dist., Lucas, 04-11-2003) No. L-02-1230, 2003-Ohio-1861, 2003 WL 1861564, Unreported. Child Support ☞ 180

An order of a juvenile court declaring a minor child to be a dependent child and awarding its custody to a stranger, obtained without service upon the parent, the guardian, or a person having the custody of such child by operation of law or awarded by a judicial order, judgment, or decree, confers upon such stranger no power to consent to the adoption of such child by any one. (Annotation from former RC 2151.29.) Rarey v. Schmidt (Ohio 1926) 115 Ohio St. 518, 154 N.E. 914, 5 Ohio Law Abs. 12, 25 Ohio Law Rep. 134.

Where a minor child has neither legal guardian nor custodian, other than a parent, and the residence of the parent is known, service, actual or constructive, must be had upon such parent before a juvenile court has jurisdiction to declare such child a dependent child. (Annotation from former RC 2151.29.) Rarey v. Schmidt (Ohio 1926) 115 Ohio St. 518, 154 N.E. 914, 5 Ohio Law Abs. 12, 25 Ohio Law Rep. 134.

Alleged father waived appellate review of sufficiency of service of process, through publication, for initial hearing regarding temporary custody of dependent, neglected, and abused child, where summons and complaint for permanent custody proceeding was properly served on alleged father once he was found in prison, alleged father was afforded an appointed attorney at hearing on permanent custody, and, at best, attorney referred only in passing, at hearing on permanent custody, to insufficiency of service of process for initial hearing on temporary custody. In re T.C. (Ohio App. 3 Dist., 12-13-2000) 140 Ohio App.3d 409, 747 N.E.2d 881, 2000-Ohio-1769. Infants ⇐ 243

Jurisdiction of juvenile court does not attach until notice of proceedings has been provided to parties; if parties do not receive notice of proceedings, judgment of court is void. In re Mullenax (Lorain 1996) 108 Ohio App.3d 271, 670 N.E.2d 551. Infants ⇐ 198; Infants ⇐ 223.1

Social services organization which filed application for permanent custody of child demonstrated reasonable diligence in attempting to ascertain residence of child's biological father, and therefore service on child's biological father by publication was permissible, though child's putative father contended that child's mother lied about her inability to identify him and that someone on hospital staff would have identified him as child's father if inquiry had been made, where child's guardian ad litem testified that child's mother could not identify father or anyone else she had had sex with at time surrounding conception, caseworker for social services organization testified that child's mother and grandmother could not identify child's biological father, and putative father produced no evidence that inquiry of hospital staff would have had possibility of success. In re Mullenax (Lorain 1996) 108 Ohio App.3d 271, 670 N.E.2d 551. Child Custody ⇐ 409

Service by publication is proper in a case in which a county children's services board files a motion for permanent custody of a mother's children where the board adequately establishes that it exercised reasonable diligence in attempting to locate the mother; the mother's history of sporadic contact coupled with her inability to obtain stable housing, ten addresses within one year, or provide the board with an address to send notices made it extremely impractical, if not impossible, to serve the mother in any other manner than by publication. In re Cowling (Summit 1991) 72 Ohio App.3d 499, 595 N.E.2d 470. Infants ⇐ 198

Service by publication pursuant to Juv R 16(A) is defective when the notice fails to include the last known address of the party to be served and where only minimal efforts are made discover the whereabouts of the party to be served. In re Miller (Cuyahoga 1986) 33 Ohio App.3d 224, 515 N.E.2d 635.

Where a challenge to a party's claim that reasonable diligence was exercised to locate a party served by publication under Juv R 16(A) is raised, the party claiming use of reasonable diligence must support such a claim. In re Miller (Cuyahoga 1986) 33 Ohio App.3d 224, 515 N.E.2d 635.

Service of summons by publication is defective if the published notice fails to include a last known address, when such an address is known, and fails to include a summary statement of the object of the complaint. In re Wilson (Huron 1984) 21 Ohio App.3d 36, 486 N.E.2d 152, 21 O.B.R. 38. Infants ⇐ 198

Service of a complaint alleging that children are dependent and neglected and notice of hearing by regular mail the day before the hearing and receipt of same the day after the hearing deprives the defending parent of sufficient notice and due process under the law; the report of the referee and judgment of the juvenile court are rendered a nullity,

despite the fact that such service complies with the letter of the procedural rules. In re Marshall, No. C–830874 (1st Dist Ct App, Hamilton, 8–15–84).

The sheriff is required to serve summons, notices, and subpoenas which are directed to him by the juvenile court, and whether the juvenile court requests the summons, notices or subpoenas to be served personally or to be delivered by registered or certified mail, the sheriff's office is legally required to serve them in accordance with such directions of the juvenile court; and if the person to be served is out of the state and his address is known, service of summons may be made by the sheriff by delivering a copy to him personally or mailing a copy to him by registered or certified mail. (Annotation from former RC 2151.29.) OAG 70–130.

Preparing an envelope for certified mailing and then placing it into an "Express Mail" envelope is not the equivalent of actually sending the document by certified mail, but will instead be treated as an ordinary mailing, where the sender did not pay for certified mail delivery, did not have the post office affix a post mark to the envelope or a "domestic return receipt," and did not use the inner envelope in the mailing. It is unfortunate that the party was encouraged by the post office to use a form of delivery that resulted in the untimely filing. Little Tykes Co v Summit County Bd of Revision, BTA 96–T–1156, 1997 WL 39919 (1–24–97).

Juv R 17   Subpoena

(A) Form; issuance

(1) Every subpoena shall do all of the following:

(a) State the name of the court from which it is issued, the title of the action, and the case number;

(b) Command each person to whom it is directed, at a time and place specified in the subpoena, to do one or more of the following:

(i) Attend and give testimony at a trial, hearing, proceeding, or deposition;

(ii) Produce documents or tangible things at a trial, hearing, proceeding, or deposition;

(iii) Produce and permit inspection and copying of any designated documents that are in the possession, custody, or control of the person;

(iv) Produce and permit inspection and copying, testing, or sampling of any tangible things that are in the possession, custody, or control of the person.

(c) Set forth the text of divisions (D) and (E) of this rule.

A command to produce and permit inspection may be joined with a command to attend and give testimony, or may be issued separately.

(2) The clerk shall issue a subpoena, signed but otherwise in blank, to a party requesting it, who shall complete it be-

fore service. An attorney who has filed an appearance on behalf of a party in an action also may sign and issue a subpoena on behalf of the court in which the action is pending.

(3) If the issuing attorney modifies the subpoena in any way, the issuing attorney shall give prompt notice of the modifications to all other parties.

(B) Parties unable to pay

The court shall order at any time that a subpoena be issued for service on a named witness upon an ex parte application of a party and upon a satisfactory showing that the presence of the witness is necessary and that the party is financially unable to pay the witness fees required by division (C) of this rule. If the court orders the subpoena to be issued, the costs incurred by the process and the fees of the witness so subpoenaed shall be paid in the same manner that similar costs and fees are paid in case of a witness subpoenaed in behalf of the state in a criminal prosecution.

(C) Service

A subpoena may be served by a sheriff, bailiff, coroner, clerk of court, constable, probation officer, or a deputy of any, by an attorney or the attorney's agent, or by any person designated by order of the court who is not a party and is not less than eighteen years of age. Service of a subpoena upon a person named in the subpoena shall be made by delivering a copy of the subpoena to the person, by reading it to him or her in person, or by leaving it at the person's usual place of residence, and by tendering to the person upon demand the fees for one day's attendance and the mileage allowed by law. The person serving the subpoena shall file a return of the subpoena with the clerk. If the witness being subpoenaed resides outside the county in which the court is located, the fees for one day's attendance and mileage shall be tendered without demand. The return may be forwarded through the postal service or otherwise.

(D) Protection of persons subject to subpoenas

(1) A party or an attorney responsible for the issuance and service of a subpoena shall take reasonable steps to avoid imposing undue burden or expense on a person subject to that subpoena.

(2) (a) A person commanded to produce under division (A)(1)(b)(ii), (iii), or (iv) of this rule is not required to appear in person at the place of production or inspection unless commanded to attend and give testimony at a trial, hearing, proceeding, or deposition.

(b) Subject to division (E)(2) of this rule, a person commanded to produce under division (A)(1)(b)(ii), (iii), or (iv) of this rule may serve upon the party or attorney designated in the subpoena written objections to production. The objections must be served within fourteen days after service of the subpoena or before the time specified for compliance if that time is less than fourteen days after service. If objection is made, the party serving the subpoena shall not be entitled to production except pursuant to an order of the court that issued the subpoena. If objection has been made, the party serving the subpoena, upon notice to the person commanded to produce, may move at any time for an order to compel the production. An order to compel production shall protect any person who is not a party or an officer of a party from significant expense resulting from the production commanded.

(3) On timely motion, the court from which the subpoena was issued shall quash or modify the subpoena, or order appearance or production only under specified conditions, if the subpoena does any of the following:

(a) Fails to allow reasonable time to comply;

(b) Requires disclosure of privileged or otherwise protected matter and no exception or waiver applies;

(c) Requires disclosure of a fact known or opinion held by an expert not retained or specially employed by any party in anticipation of litigation or preparation for trial if the fact or opinion does not describe specific events or occurrences in dispute and results from study by that expert that was not made at the request of any party;

(d) Subjects a person to undue burden.

(4) Before filing a motion pursuant to division (D)(3)(d) of this rule, a person resisting discovery under this rule shall attempt to resolve any claim of undue burden through discussions with the issuing attorney. A motion filed pursuant to division (D)(3)(d) of this rule shall be supported by an affidavit of the subpoenaed person or a certificate of that per-

son's attorney of the efforts made to resolve any claim of undue burden.

(5) If a motion is made under division (D)(3)(c) or (D)(3)(d) of this rule, the court shall quash or modify the subpoena unless the party in whose behalf the subpoena is issued shows a substantial need for the testimony or material that cannot be otherwise met without undue hardship and assures that the person to whom the subpoena is addressed will be reasonably compensated.

(E) Duties in responding to subpoena

(1) A person responding to a subpoena to produce documents shall, at the person's option, produce the documents as they are kept in the usual course of business or organized and labeled to correspond with the categories in the subpoena. A person producing documents pursuant to a subpoena for them shall permit their inspection and copying by all parties present at the time and place set in the subpoena for inspection and copying.

(2) When information subject to a subpoena is withheld on a claim that it is privileged or subject to protection as trial preparation materials, the claim shall be made expressly and shall be supported by a description of the nature of the documents, communications, or things not produced that is sufficient to enable the demanding party to contest the claim.

(F) Sanctions

Failure by any person without adequate excuse to obey a subpoena served upon that person may be a contempt of the court from which the subpoena issued. A subpoenaed person or that person's attorney who frivolously resists discovery under this rule may be required by the court to pay the reasonable expenses, including reasonable attorney's fees, of the party seeking the discovery. The court from which a subpoena was issued may impose upon a party or attorney in breach of the duty imposed by division (D)(1) of this rule an appropriate sanction, that may include, but is not limited to, lost earnings and reasonable attorney's fees.

(G) Privileges

Nothing in this rule shall be construed to authorize a party to obtain information protected by any privilege recognized by law or to authorize any person to disclose such information.

(H) Time

Nothing in this rule shall be construed to expand any other time limits imposed by rule or statute. All issues concerning subpoenas shall be resolved prior to the time otherwise set for hearing or trial.

(Adopted eff. 7–1–72; amended eff. 7–1–94)

Historical and Statutory Notes

Amendment Note: The 7–1–94 amendment rewrote division (A); substituted "(C)" for "(D)" in division (B); deleted former division (C); redesignated former division (D) as division (C); deleted former divisions (E) and (F); added divisions (D) and (E); redesignated former division (G) as division (F) and rewrote this division; added divisions (G) and (H); and made changes to reflect gender-neutral language. Prior to amendment, divisions (A), (C), (E), (F), and (G) read:

"(A) For attendance of witnesses; form; issuance. Every subpoena issued by the clerk shall be under the seal of the court, shall state the name of the court and the title of the action, and shall command each person to whom it is directed to attend and give testimony at a time and place therein specified. The clerk shall issue a subpoena, or a subpoena for the production of documentary evidence, signed and sealed but otherwise in blank, to a party requesting it, who shall fill it in and file a copy thereof with the clerk before service.

"(C) For production of documentary evidence. A subpoena may also command the person to whom it is directed to produce the books, papers, documents or other objects designated therein; but the court upon motion made promptly and in any event at or before the time specified in the subpoena for compliance therewith may quash or modify the subpoena if compliance would be unreasonable or oppressive. The court may direct that the books, papers, documents or other objects designated in the subpoena be produced before the court at a time prior to the hearing or prior to the time they are offered in evidence and may upon their production permit them or portions thereof to be inspected by the parties or their attorneys.

"(E) Subpoena for taking depositions; place of examination. When the attendance of a witness before an official authorized to take depositions is required, the subpoena shall be issued by such person and shall command the person to whom it is directed to attend and give testimony at a time and place specified therein. The subpoena may command the person to whom it is directed to produce designated books, papers, documents or tangible objects which constitute or contain evidence relating to any of the matters within the scope of the examination permitted by Rule 25.

"A person whose deposition is to be taken may be required to attend an examination in the county wherein he resides or is employed or transacts his business in person, or at such other convenient place as is fixed by an order of court.

"(F) Subpoena for a hearing. At the request of any party subpoenas for attendance at a hearing shall be issued by the clerk of the court in which the hearing is held. A subpoena requiring the attendance of a witness at a hearing may be served at any place within this state.

"(G) Contempt. Failure by any person without adequate excuse to obey a subpoena served upon him may be deemed a contempt of the court or officer issuing the subpoena.''

Commentary

Staff Notes

1994:

Rule 17 Subpoena

Juv. R. 17 has been revised to control the issuance and enforcement of subpoenas. Because of the special nature of juvenile proceedings, Juv. R. 17 must be read in conjunction with Juv. R. 24 and 25. Juv. R. 25 provides that the court may grant authority to take a deposition only upon good cause shown. Juv. R. 24 governs the scope of discovery, which is subject to the assertion of privilege.

Cross References

Subpoena, Civ R 45; Crim R 17

Library References

Infants ⚖201, 207.

Witnesses ⚖16, 21.

Westlaw Topic Nos. 211, 410.

C.J.S. Infants §§ 42, 51 to 67.

C.J.S. Witnesses §§ 25, 27.

Am Jur 2d: 47, Juvenile Courts and Delinquent and Dependent Children § 44, 49

Giannelli & Snyder, Baldwin's Ohio Practice, Evidence § 804.8, 1004.4 (2d ed. 2001).

Carlin, Baldwin's Ohio Practice, Merrick–Rippner Probate Law § 107.127, 107.162, 107.163 (2003).

Law Review and Journal Commentaries

White Collar Crime: Second Annual Survey of Law; Subpoena, Dona A. Nutini and Patricia J. Pannell. 19 Am Crim L Rev 173 (1981).

Notes of Decisions

Court costs   2
Service   1

------

1. Service

Court's refusal to grant juvenile's request for a continuance in aggravated burglary case, on grounds that subpoenas that defense counsel had filed with the clerk's office had not been served, did not violate juvenile's right to compel production of witnesses, where defense counsel did not explain why the witnesses were material, did not give any indication what the testimony would have been, and did not request continuance until shortly before trial was to begin. State v. K.W. (Ohio App. 8 Dist., Cuyahoga, 01-30-2003) No. 80951, 2003-Ohio-425, 2003 WL 194857, Unreported. Infants ⚖ 204

The sheriff is required to serve summons, notices, and subpoenas which are directed to him by the juvenile court, and whether the juvenile court requests the summons, notices or subpoenas to be served personally or to be delivered by registered or certified mail, the sheriff's office is legally required to serve them in accordance with such directions of the juvenile court; and if the person to be served is out of the state and his address is known, service of summons may be made by the sheriff by delivering a copy to him personally or mailing a copy to him by registered or certified mail. (Annotation from former RC 2151.19.) OAG 70–130.

2. Court costs

Trial court did not abuse its discretion by denying juvenile defendant's motion for appointment of an expert at State's expense in delinquency proceeding in order to rebut juvenile victim's statements to police of alleged sexual abuse; State presented no evidence as to what was said or displayed during victim's interviews, and thus, it was not relevant or reasonably necessary that an expert witness be appointed. In re Bright (Ohio App. 11 Dist., Trumbull, 05-23-2003) No. 2001-T-0095, No. 2001-T-0097, 2003-Ohio-2835, 2003 WL 21267810, Unreported. Infants ⚖ 212

In juvenile court cases in which the Ohio rules of juvenile procedure apply, Ohio Juv R 17(B) grants a juvenile court the authority to tax as costs and collect from a party the fees of the county sheriff in serving subpoenas issued by the court and the fees of witnesses subpoenaed by the court. However, pursuant to RC 2151.54, such fees may not be taxed as costs and collected by a juvenile court in cases of delinquent, unruly, dependent, abused, or neglected children except when specifically ordered by the court. OAG 98–021.

Juv R 18   Time

(A) Time: computation

In computing any period of time prescribed or allowed by these rules, by the local rules of any court, by order of court, or by any applicable statute, the date of the act or event from which the designated period of time begins to run shall not be included. The last day of the period so computed shall be included, unless it is a Saturday, a Sunday, or a legal holiday, in which event the period runs until the end of the next day that is not a Saturday, a Sunday or a legal holiday. Such extension of time includes, but is not limited to, probable cause, shelter care, and detention hearings.

Except in the case of probable cause, shelter care, and detention hearings when the period of time prescribed or allowed is less than seven days, intermediate Saturdays, Sundays, and legal holidays shall be excluded in computation.

(B) Time: enlargement

When an act is required or allowed to be performed at or within a specified time, the court for cause shown may at any time in its discretion (1) with or without motion or notice, order the period enlarged if application therefor is made before expiration of the period originally prescribed or of that period as extended by a previous order, or (2) upon motion permit the act to be done after expiration of the specified period if the failure to act on time was the result of excusable neglect or would result in injustice to a party, but the court may not extend the time for taking any action under Rule 7(F)(1), Rule 22(F), Rule

29(A) and Rule 29(F)(2)(b), except to the extent and under the conditions stated in them.

(C) Time: unaffected by expiration of term

The period of time provided for the doing of any act or the taking of any proceeding is not affected or limited by the expiration of a term of court. The expiration of a term of court in no way affects the power of a court to do any act in a juvenile proceeding.

(D) Time: for motions; affidavits

A written motion, other than one which may be heard ex parte, and notice of the hearing thereof, shall be served not later than seven days before the time specified for the hearing unless a different period is fixed by rule or order of the court. For cause shown such an order may be made on ex parte application. When a motion is supported by affidavit, the affidavit shall be served with the motion, and opposing affidavits may be served not less than one day before the hearing unless the court permits them to be served at a later time.

(E) Time: additional time after service by mail

Whenever a party has the right or is required to do an act within a prescribed period after the service of a notice or other paper upon the person and the notice or other paper is served upon the person by mail, three days shall be added to the prescribed period. This division does not apply to service of summons.

(Adopted eff. 7–1–72; amended eff. 7–1–94)

Historical and Statutory Notes

Amendment Note: The 7–1–94 amendment redesignated division (A) into two paragraphs; added the final sentence in the first paragraph of division (A); added "Except in the case of probable cause, shelter care, and detention hearings" at the beginning of the second paragraph of division (A); and made changes to reflect gender-neutral language.

Commentary

Staff Notes

1994:

Rule 18 Time

Juv. R. 18(A) now clarifies that the computation of time allowed or prescribed by rules or statutes for probable cause, shelter care, and detention hearings shall not exclude intermediate Saturdays, Sundays, and legal holidays.

Cross References

Computation of time, 1.45

Standard time, official legal proceedings to be governed by, 1.04
Time, Civ R 6; Crim R 45

Library References

Infants ⟐152, 193, 204.

Westlaw Topic No. 211.

C.J.S. Infants §§ 31 to 91.

Carlin, Baldwin's Ohio Practice, Merrick–Rippner Probate Law § 107.10, 107.30, 107.42, 107.50, 107.117 (2003).

Notes of Decisions

Constitutional issues 4
Discretion of court 2
Enlargement of time to file 3
Excusable neglect 1

---

1. Excusable neglect

Attorney ignorance as to the filing deadlines provided under juvenile court rules was insufficient to constitute excusable neglect under juvenile rule governing motion for extension of time to file. In re Malone (Ohio App. 10 Dist., Franklin, 12-30-2003) No. 03AP-489, 2003-Ohio-7156, 2003 WL 23024377, Unreported. Infants ⟐ 204

To determine whether a defendant's conduct constitutes "excusable neglect," for purposes of juvenile rule governing motion for extension of time to file, all of the surrounding facts and circumstances must be considered, and courts must be mindful of the admonition that cases should be decided on their merits where possible, rather than procedural grounds. In re Malone (Ohio App. 10 Dist., Franklin, 12-30-2003) No. 03AP-489, 2003-Ohio-7156, 2003 WL 23024377, Unreported. Infants ⟐ 204

Juvenile procedure rules, rather than civil procedure rules, governed motion for extension of time to file objections to magistrate's decision in juvenile dependency proceedings. In re Malone (Ohio App. 10 Dist., Franklin, 12-30-2003) No. 03AP-489, 2003-Ohio-7156, 2003 WL 23024377, Unreported. Infants ⟐ 204

2. Discretion of court

Court's determination under juvenile rule governing motion for extension of time to file rests within the sound discretion of the trial court and will not be disturbed on appeal absent a showing of an abuse of discretion. In re Malone (Ohio App. 10 Dist., Franklin, 12-30-2003) No. 03AP-489, 2003-Ohio-7156, 2003 WL 23024377, Unreported. Infants ⟐ 204

3. Enlargement of time to file

Juvenile court's failure to grant enlargement of time to mother to file objections to magistrate's decision in dependency proceedings did not result in an injustice to mother within meaning of juvenile rule governing enlargement of time to file; mother had a full and fair opportunity to litigate the matters before the magistrate, and failure to file resulted from attorney's ignorance as to filing deadlines. In re Malone (Ohio App. 10 Dist., Franklin, 12-30-2003) No. 03AP-489, 2003-Ohio-7156, 2003 WL 23024377, Unreported. Infants ⟐ 204

4. Constitutional issues

Mother failed to show prejudice resulting from attorney's failure to file timely objections to magistrate's decision in juvenile dependency proceedings, and thus such failure would not constitute ineffective assistance of counsel, where objections would have been without merit. In re Malone (Ohio App. 10

Dist., Franklin, 12-30-2003) No. 03AP-489, 2003-Ohio-7156, 2003 WL 23024377, Unreported. Infants ⟐ 205

Juv R 19   Motions

An application to the court for an order shall be by motion. A motion other than one made during trial or hearing shall be in writing unless the court permits it to be made orally. It shall state with particularity the grounds upon which it is made and shall set forth the relief or order sought. It shall be supported by a memorandum containing citations of authority and may be supported by an affidavit.

To expedite its business, unless otherwise provided by statute or rule, the court may make provision by rule or order for the submission and determination of motions without oral hearing upon brief written statements of reasons in support and opposition.

(Adopted eff. 7–1–72; amended eff. 7–1–94)

Historical and Statutory Notes

Amendment Note: The 7–1–94 amendment inserted "unless otherwise provided by statute or rule," in the second paragraph.

Commentary

Staff Notes

1994:

Rule 19 Motions

Revised Code 2151.353, as amended by S.B. 89, mandates that an oral hearing be held, with notice to all parties and the guardian ad litem, on any motion to extend an original order for protective supervision. The language "unless otherwise provided by statute or law" is designed to prohibit the court from deciding, without an oral hearing, a motion for extension of protective supervision.

Cross References

Continuing jurisdiction to be invoked by motion, Juv R 35

Pleadings and motions, Civ R 7

Library References

Infants ⟐191.

Westlaw Topic No. 211.

C.J.S. Infants §§ 42, 53, 54.

Am Jur 2d: 56, Motions, Rules, and Orders § 1 et seq.

Carlin, Baldwin's Ohio Practice, Merrick–Rippner Probate Law § 107.42, 107.50, 107.77 (2003).

Notes of Decisions

Constitutional issues   1
Procedural issues   2

---

1. Constitutional issues

Rules governing filing and service of motions in juvenile court are designed to safeguard due process rights of all litigants by creating orderly procedure to ensure adequate notice to all interested parties. In re Robert S. (Ohio App. 6 Dist., 12-09-1994) 98 Ohio App.3d 84, 647 N.E.2d 869. Infants ⟐ 132; Infants ⟐ 198

Huron County Department of Human Services (HCDHS) substantially complied with notice requirements of juvenile rule in filing motion seeking to require Cuyahoga County Department of Children and Family Services CCDCFS to contribute to support of adopted child; trial court erred in submission of postjudgment entry and supporting affidavits with recommendations for financial responsibility CCDCFS should bear for reimbursing HCDHS for past and future treatment of adopted child, HCDHS filed its motion to determine support obligations, and although HCDHS did not file supporting affidavits or memorandum, CCDCFS did not object. In re Robert S. (Ohio App. 6 Dist., 12-09-1994) 98 Ohio App.3d 84, 647 N.E.2d 869. Social Security And Public Welfare ⟐ 194.30

2. Procedural issues

Trial court denial of mother's motion to dismiss father's motion to modify visitation based on father's failure to include citations of authority within his motion was not an abuse of discretion; mother's motion was untimely since it was orally made at the hearing on father's motion to modify visitation, and father's motion provided adequate notice for mother to respond and defend herself. In re Lane (Ohio App. 4 Dist., Washington, 06-25-2003) No. 02CA61, 2003-Ohio-3755, 2003 WL 21652176, Unreported. Child Custody ⟐ 609

Juv R 20   Service and filing of papers when required subsequent to filing of complaint

(A) Service: when required

Written notices, requests for discovery, designation of record on appeal and written motions, other than those which are heard ex parte, and similar papers shall be served upon each of the parties.

(B) Service: how made

Whenever under these rules or by an order of the court service is required or permitted to be made upon a party represented by an attorney, the service shall be made upon the attorney unless service is ordered by the court upon the party. Service upon the attorney or upon the party shall be made in the manner provided in Civ. R. 5(B).

(C) Filing

All papers required to be served upon a party shall be filed simultaneously with or immediately after service. Papers filed with the court shall not be considered until proof of service is endorsed thereon or separately filed. The proof of service shall state the date and the manner of service and shall be signed and filed in the manner provided in Civil Rule 5(D).

(Adopted eff. 7–1–72; amended eff. 7–1–94)

Historical and Statutory Notes

Amendment Note: The 7–1–94 amendment added "when required subsequent to filing of complaint" to the title of the rule; and made changes to reflect gender-neutral language.

Commentary

Staff Notes

1994:

Rule 20 Service and Filing of Papers When Required Subsequent to Filing of Complaint

The words "when required subsequent to filing of complaint" have been added to the title of Juv. R. 20 to distinguish it from the requirements of initial service of process described under Juv. R. 16. Otherwise, the only changes to the rule are to render it gender neutral.

Cross References

Expense of service of process, 2151.19
Probation officer may serve process, 2151.14
Service and filing of papers, Crim R 49
Service and filing of pleadings and other papers subsequent to the original complaint, Civ R 5
Service of summons, 2151.29
Style of process, 7.01

Library References

Infants ⊜198, 201, 244.1.
Westlaw Topic No. 211.
C.J.S. Infants §§ 42, 53, 54, 56, 86 to 91.
Necessity of service of process upon infant itself in juvenile delinquency and dependency proceedings. 90 ALR2d 293
Carlin, Baldwin's Ohio Practice, Merrick–Rippner Probate Law § 107.50 (2003).

Juv R 21   Preliminary conferences

At any time after the filing of a complaint, the court upon motion of any party or upon its own motion may order one or more conferences to consider such matters as will promote a fair and expeditious proceeding.

(Adopted eff. 7–1–72)

Cross References

Indictment and information, Crim R 7

Library References

Infants ⊜191.
Westlaw Topic No. 211.
C.J.S. Infants §§ 42, 53, 54.

Juv R 22   Pleadings and motions; defenses and objections

(A) Pleadings and motions

Pleadings in juvenile proceedings shall be the complaint and the answer, if any, filed by a party. A party may move to dismiss the complaint or for other appropriate relief.

(B) Amendment of pleadings

Any pleading may be amended at any time prior to the adjudicatory hearing. After the commencement of the adjudicatory hearing, a pleading may be amended upon agreement of the parties or, if the interests of justice require, upon order of the court. A complaint charging an act of delinquency may not be amended unless agreed by the parties, if the proposed amendment would change the name or identity of the specific violation of law so that it would be considered a change of the crime charged if committed by an adult. Where requested, a court order shall grant a party reasonable time in which to respond to an amendment.

(C) Answer

No answer shall be necessary. A party may file an answer to the complaint, which, if filed, shall contain specific and concise admissions or denials of each material allegation of the complaint.

(D) Prehearing motions

Any defense, objection or request which is capable of determination without hearing on the allegations of the complaint may be raised before the adjudicatory hearing by motion. The following must be heard before the adjudicatory hearing, though not necessarily on a separate date:

(1) Defenses or objections based on defects in the institution of the proceeding;

(2) Defenses or objections based on defects in the complaint (other than failure to show jurisdiction in the court or to charge an offense which objections shall be noticed by the court at any time during the pendency of the proceeding);

(3) Motions to suppress evidence on the ground that it was illegally obtained;

(4) Motions for discovery;

(5) Motions to determine whether the child is eligible to receive a sentence as a serious youthful offender.

(E) Motion time

Except for motions filed under division (D)(5) of this rule, all prehearing motions shall be filed by the earlier of:

(1) seven days prior to the hearing, or

(2) ten days after the appearance of counsel.

Rule 22(D)(5) motions shall be filed by the later of:

(1) twenty days after the date of the child's initial appearance in juvenile court; or

(2) twenty days after denial of a motion to transfer.

The filing of the Rule 22(D)(5) motion shall constitute notice of intent to pursue a serious youthful offender disposition.

The court in the interest of justice may extend the time for making prehearing motions.

The court for good cause shown may permit a motion to suppress evidence under division (D)(3) of this rule to be made at the time the evidence is offered.

(F) State's right to appeal upon granting a motion to suppress

In delinquency proceedings the state may take an appeal as of right from the granting of a motion to suppress evidence if, in addition to filing a notice of appeal, the prosecuting attorney certifies that (1) the appeal is not taken for the purpose of delay and (2) the granting of the motion has rendered proof available to the state so weak in its entirety that any reasonable possibility of proving the complaint's allegations has been destroyed.

Such appeal shall not be allowed unless the notice of appeal and the certification by the prosecuting attorney are filed with the clerk of the juvenile court within seven days after the date of the entry of the judgment or order granting the motion. Any appeal which may be taken under this rule shall be diligently prosecuted.

A child in detention or shelter care may be released pending this appeal when the state files the notice of appeal and certification.

This appeal shall take precedence over all other appeals.

(Adopted eff. 7–1–72; amended eff. 7–1–77, 7–1–94, 7–1–01)

Historical and Statutory Notes

Amendment Note: The 7-1-01 amendment added new division (D)(5); and rewrote division (E), which prior thereto read:

"All prehearing motions shall be filed by the earlier of (1) seven days prior to hearing, or (2) ten days after the appearance of counsel. The court in the interest of justice may extend the time for making prehearing motions.

The court for good cause shown may permit a motion to suppress evidence under subsection (D)(3) to be made at the time such evidence is offered."

Amendment Note: The 7-1-94 amendment added the third sentence in division (B).

Commentary

Staff Notes

2001:

Rule 22(D) Prehearing motions

Rule 22 (D) was amended to add a fifth category of prehearing motions, the motion of the prosecuting attorney to have the court hold a probable cause hearing to determine whether or not a child is eligible under Revised Code sections 2152.11 or 2152.13 to receive a sentence as a serious youthful offender. These motions provide a timely opportunity for the needed probable cause determination of eligibility for treatment as a serious youthful offender, in circumstances in which the prosecuting attorney does not have sufficient time to seek a grand jury determination of such eligibility.

Rule 22(E) Motion time

Rule 22(E) was amended to conform to Sub. Sen. Bill 179 (effective date January 1, 2002) by reflecting that motions for determination of eligibility for treatment as a serious youthful offender are subject to a different time frame than other prehearing motions. It is important for the prosecuting attorney to have sufficient time to investigate before making the significant charging decision to pursue serious youthful offender sentencing. Revised Code section 2152.13(B) provides that the prosecuting attorney has twenty days after a child's initial appearance within which to file a notice of intent to pursue a serious youthful offender dispositional sentence. Juvenile rule time frames applicable in all other cases would truncate this statutory latitude. For instance, Juvenile Rule 29(A) contemplates that ordinarily the adjudicatory hearing of a child held in detention must occur within ten days. Since these are the most serious cases, it is not unlikely that the child will be in detention. Thus, the ordinary time frames of Rule 22(E) would require the motion to be filed well before the statutory period of twenty days has elapsed. Amended Rule 22(E) also clarifies that the prosecuting attorney has the statutory twenty-day time period for filing a notice of intent to pursue serious youthful offender dispositional sentencing after a transfer is denied.

Finally, Rule 22(E) as amended specifically provides that a Rule 22(D)(5) motion shall serve as the statutory "notice of intent" to pursue serious youthful offender dispositional sentencing. This serves to create a recognized procedural mechanism for the notice and to clarify that a motion is indeed the required notice. It also clarifies that the motion starts the speedy trial time clock running [see also Revised Code section 2152.13(D)(1)].

Other changes to Rule 22(E) were in form only, and were not intended to be substantive.

1994:

Rule 22 Pleadings and Motions; Defenses and Objections

The revision to Juv. R. 22(B) prohibits the amendment of a pleading after the commencement or termination of the adjudicatory hearing unless the amendment conforms to the evidence presented and also amounts to a lesser included offense of the crime charged. Because juveniles can be bound over as adults and become subject to the jurisdiction of the criminal division of the common pleas courts, it is important that Juv. R. 22(B) conform with Crim. R. 7(D), which similarly prohibits any amendment which would result in a change in the identity of the crime charged.

Cross References

Amended and supplemental pleadings, Civ R 15
General rules of pleading, Civ R 8
Indictment and information, Crim R 7
Pleadings and motions before trial: defenses and objections, Crim R 12
Pleadings and motions, Civ R 7

Library References

Infants ⊷197, 242.
Westlaw Topic No. 211.
C.J.S. Infants §§ 55, 86 to 91.
Am Jur 2d: 47, Juvenile Courts and Delinquent and Dependent Children § 40 to 43
Whiteside, Ohio Appellate Practice (2003 Ed.), Text 3.6.
Carlin, Baldwin's Ohio Practice, Merrick–Rippner Probate Law § 106.3, 107.6, 107.20, 107.42, 107.122 (2003).

Law Review and Journal Commentaries

Access to "Confidential" Welfare Records in the Course of Child Protection Proceedings, Richard Steven Levine. 14 J Fam L 535 (1975–76).

The Fourth Amendment Exclusionary Rule: The Desirability of a Good Faith Exception, Donald L. Willits. 32 Case W Res L Rev 443 (1982).

Notes of Decisions

Appeals 8
Complaints 1
Constitutional issues 4
Jurisdiction 5
Miranda warnings 7
Prosecutions 6
Service, notice 3
Time limitations 2

---

1. Complaints

A complaint under Juv R 10 and RC 2151.27 alleging that a child is dependent must state the essential facts which bring the proceeding within the jurisdiction of the court. In re Hunt (Ohio 1976) 46 Ohio St.2d 378, 348 N.E.2d 727, 75 O.O.2d 450. Infants ⊷ 197

After adjudicatory hearing in juvenile delinquency proceeding, trial court could not amend original complaint charging acts constituting third-degree attempted felonious assault if committed by adult, so that juvenile could be found delinquent based on acts constituting second-degree felonious assault by means of deadly weapon; amended offense was not lesser included offense of originally charged offense, amendment made significant difference in juvenile's potential confinement if juvenile violated probation, and addition of "deadly weapon" element surprised juvenile. In re Reed (Ohio App. 8 Dist., 01-17-2002) 147 Ohio App.3d 182, 769 N.E.2d 412, 2002-Ohio-43. Infants ⊷ 197

Amended charge of acts constituting second-degree felonious assault by means of deadly weapon if committed by adult was not lesser included offense of original charge of third-degree attempted felonious assault, for purposes of amending the complaint after adjudicatory hearing in juvenile delinquency proceeding; second–degree felony adjudication carried

longer minimum term of confinement for juvenile than third-degree felony adjudication, attempted felonious assault could be committed without felonious assault by means of deadly weapon also being committed, and attempted felonious assault did not contain deadly weapon element. In re Reed (Ohio App. 8 Dist., 01-17-2002) 147 Ohio App.3d 182, 769 N.E.2d 412, 2002-Ohio-43. Infants ⊷ 197

Court's decision to amend indictment to state juvenile's age and date of offenses did not prejudice the juvenile because it did not change the name or identity of the offenses. In re Smith (Ohio App. 8 Dist., 03-26-2001) 142 Ohio App.3d 16, 753 N.E.2d 930. Infants ⊷ 197

Referral for juvenile adjudication of parochial school student disciplined by school for sexual harassment and sexual violence did not amount to malicious civil prosecution, despite resolution of juvenile court complaint in student's favor, absent any allegation that student's person or body was seized. Iwenofu v. St. Luke School (Ohio App. 8 Dist., 02-16-1999) 132 Ohio App.3d 119, 724 N.E.2d 511, appeal not allowed 86 Ohio St.3d 1407, 711 N.E.2d 234. Malicious Prosecution ⊷ 11

Juvenile court properly amended complaint in delinquency adjudication proceeding to charge juvenile with unruliness as lesser included offense of charged conduct, which would, if committed by adult, have constituted third-degree misdemeanor sexual imposition; record of proceeding demonstrated that central issue of proceeding was whether juvenile grabbed a girl's breast, and amended complaint was based on same facts as original charge. In re Felton (Ohio App. 3 Dist. 1997) 124 Ohio App.3d 500, 706 N.E.2d 809, dismissed, appeal not allowed 81 Ohio St.3d 1497, 691 N.E.2d 1058. Infants ⊷ 197

A party must object to a defect in a complaint of child abuse by a prehearing motion before the adjudicatory hearing, within the time requirements of Juv R 22(E). In re Dukes (Summit 1991) 81 Ohio App.3d 145, 610 N.E.2d 513, motion overruled 63 Ohio St.3d 1411, 585 N.E.2d 835.

Juvenile court abused its discretion in modifying delinquency adjudication for robbery to misdemeanor theft after disposition, where rule cited by juvenile for amendment of pleading did not authorize the court to amend the complaint after the juvenile's adjudication and disposition, and no other rule authorized juvenile court to modify the adjudication. In re Harris, No. 2001-P-0117, 2002-Ohio-3848, 2002 WL 1752261 (4th Dist Ct App, Lawrence, 7-26-02).

A juvenile court may amend a complaint, after all the evidence has been submitted, from one of dependency to one of custody. In re Likens, No. 85 CA 80 (2d Dist Ct App, Greene, 10–24–86).

The juvenile court errs in permitting the county department of children and family services to orally amend its complaint for temporary custody to one which seeks permanent custody on the day of trial since the department has only been granted emergency temporary custody, and the court should proceed on the motion for temporary custody and provide the parents with an opportunity to prepare for a permanent custody hearing. In re Vandivner, Nos. 77963+, 2001 WL 175542 (8th Dist Ct App, Cuyahoga, 2–22–01).

Trial court was authorized to amend murder charge at juvenile's dispositional hearing to murder by committing felonious assault to conform to the evidence, where amendment did not change the name or identity of the offense. In re B.M. (Ohio App. 8 Dist., Cuyahoga, 02-27-2003) No. 80909, 2003-Ohio-870, 2003 WL 548359, Unreported. Infants ⊷ 197

Juvenile waived error claim to trial court's amendment of complaint from murder to murder by committing felonious assault, where he failed to object to amendment at dispositional hearing. In re B.M. (Ohio App. 8 Dist., Cuyahoga, 02-27-2003) No. 80909, 2003-Ohio-870, 2003 WL 548359, Unreported. Infants ☞ 243

2. Time limitations

Any error arising from failure of magistrate to hold hearing on juvenile's motion to suppress prior to adjudicatory hearing did not prejudice juvenile, in delinquency proceeding, especially in light of fact that motion was technically not properly before the court, given its untimeliness. In re Hill (Ohio App. 10 Dist., Franklin, 11-20-2003) No. 03AP-82, 2003-Ohio-6185, 2003 WL 22725297, Unreported. Infants ☞ 253

The time requirement for filing a prehearing motion in juvenile court is seven days prior to the hearing or ten days after the appearance of counsel, whichever is earlier. In re Dukes (Summit 1991) 81 Ohio App.3d 145, 610 N.E.2d 513, motion overruled 63 Ohio St.3d 1411, 585 N.E.2d 835. Infants ☞ 203

The time requirement for filing a prehearing motion in juvenile court is not met when counsel makes his first appearance several months before the adjudicatory hearing where an objection is made to a defective complaint; thus, the objection is not timely. In re Dukes (Summit 1991) 81 Ohio App.3d 145, 610 N.E.2d 513, motion overruled 63 Ohio St.3d 1411, 585 N.E.2d 835.

3. Service, notice

Juvenile had sufficient notice of the complaint, although she first saw complaint at time of adjudicatory hearing, as her presence at hearing necessarily implied she had some notice of complaint. In re Smith (Ohio App. 8 Dist., 03-26-2001) 142 Ohio App.3d 16, 753 N.E.2d 930. Infants ☞ 198

Mother was provided with adequate notice of hearing to place her two minor children in permanent custody of Department of Human Services (DHS), despite her claim that DHS's motion for permanent custody failed to meet statutory notice requirements, in view of fact that statutory notice must be provided by court, not DHS, that notice given to mother by trial court contained all information required by statute, that mother waived any objection to inadequacies of notice when she elected to appear and participate with counsel, and that she did not raise issue of adequacy of notice at trial level. In re Shaeffer Children (Van Wert 1993) 85 Ohio App.3d 683, 621 N.E.2d 426, dismissed, jurisdictional motion overruled 67 Ohio St.3d 1451, 619 N.E.2d 419. Infants ☞ 198

Service of a complaint alleging that children are dependent and neglected and notice of hearing by regular mail the day before the hearing and receipt of same the day after the hearing deprives the defending parent of sufficient notice and due process under the law; the report of the referee and judgment of the juvenile court are rendered a nullity, despite the fact that such service complies with the letter of the procedural rules. In re Marshall, No. C-830874 (1st Dist Ct App, Hamilton, 8-15-84).

The Common Pleas Court had jurisdiction to grant permanent custody of mother's two children to the county job and family services agency, even though notice to mother of the dispositional hearing was returned undeliverable; mother appeared with counsel at an earlier shelter-care hearing, at the shelter-care hearing the trial court noted the date of the adjudicatory hearing, counsel for mother appeared at the dispositional hearing, and neither mother or her counsel objected to the notice provided to mother. In re Billingsley (Ohio App. 3 Dist., Putnam, 01-28-2003) No. 12-02-07, No. 12-02-08, 2003-Ohio-344, 2003 WL 178661, Unreported. Infants ☞ 198

Father waived on appeal in termination of parental rights proceeding issue of whether trial court lacked jurisdiction to enter order awarding permanent custody of children to county department of children and family services, based on his allegation that court did not provide proper notice to mother of proceedings, as he failed to raise issue in trial court. (Per O'Donnell, J., with two judges concurring in judgment only). In re Harlston (Ohio App. 8 Dist., Cuyahoga, 01-23-2003) No. 80672, 2003-Ohio-282, 2003 WL 152939, Unreported. Infants ☞ 243

Mother's absence at termination of parental rights hearing did not prejudice father's rights; not only was there no evidence that mother would have been awarded custody of children, but mother was in agreement with permanent custody of children being awarded to county department of children and family services. (Per O'Donnell, J., with two judges concurring in judgment only). In re Harlston (Ohio App. 8 Dist., Cuyahoga, 01-23-2003) No. 80672, 2003-Ohio-282, 2003 WL 152939, Unreported. Infants ☞ 253

4. Constitutional issues

Minor's speedy trial rights were not violated by the fact that delinquency complaint was filed 17 months after the last act alleged in the complaint; minor was not in custody between the time police were contacted to conduct investigation and when the complaint was filed. In re N.K. (Ohio App. 8 Dist., Cuyahoga, 12-24-2003) No. 82332, 2003-Ohio-7059, 2003 WL 23009113, Unreported. Infants ☞ 204

Notice to mother of adjudicatory hearing in dependency proceeding satisfied due process, where county children services agency filed amended complaint upon learning identities of child's birth parents, amended complaint that was served on mother included notices of pretrial hearing the next day and of adjudicatory hearing nine days later, mother's counsel filed entry of appearance five days before service on mother of amended complaint, mother did not object to any defects in complaint prior to adjudicatory hearing, and she did not challenge adequacy of notice at trial level. In re Baby Girl Doe (Ohio App. 6 Dist., 08-30-2002) 149 Ohio App.3d 717, 778 N.E.2d 1053, 2002-Ohio-4470, appeal not allowed 97 Ohio St.3d 1425, 777 N.E.2d 278, 2002-Ohio-5820. Constitutional Law ☞ 274(5); Infants ☞ 198

An appeal by the state from a finding of not guilty, on a charge of "delinquency by reason of murder," by the juvenile division of the court of common pleas is barred by the constitutional protection against former jeopardy. In re Gilbert (Summit 1974) 45 Ohio App.2d 308, 345 N.E.2d 79, 74 O.O.2d 480.

The matter of unlawful search and seizure under US Const Am 4 applies to juveniles. (Annotation from former RC 2151.01.) In re Morris (Ohio Com. Pl. 1971) 29 Ohio Misc. 71, 278 N.E.2d 701, 58 O.O.2d 126.

The federal courts will abstain from interfering in state proceedings where juveniles seek an injunction against the use of social histories in pre-adjudication instances, although they may hear an issue involving the constitutionality of post-adjudicatory dissemination of the social histories where state law is not clear and the proper factual issues were not decided; the dissemination of social histories compiled by probation officers during juvenile proceedings do not violate a constitutional right to privacy. J. P. v. DeSanti (C.A.6 (Ohio) 1981) 653 F.2d 1080.

5. Jurisdiction

In a juvenile proceeding an objection, raised after trial and submission, based on a failure of the testimony to establish the age of the accused juvenile, relates to jurisdiction over the person and not to jurisdiction in the court, and is waived under Juv R 22(D)(2). In re Fudge (Clark 1977) 59 Ohio App.2d 129, 392 N.E.2d 1262, 13 O.O.3d 176.

The failure to include the particular facts in a permanent custody complaint is not a jurisdictional defect and may be waived if not timely objected to before the adjudicatory hearing pursuant to Juv R 22(D). In re Crose, No. 1055 (2d Dist Ct App, Darke, 10–18–82).

Juvenile waived all but plain error in trial court's alleged failure to establish jurisdiction over him in delinquency proceeding, where juvenile did not raise that objection below. In re Ball (Ohio App. 3 Dist., Allen, 01-30-2003) No. 1-02-72, 2003-Ohio-395, 2003 WL 193519, Unreported. Infants ⟜ 243

Trial court established proper jurisdiction in juvenile delinquency proceeding by eliciting testimony by subject of proceeding, at preliminary hearing, that he was 16 years old and by making a finding in judgment entry of commitment that subject of proceeding was born on a particular date and was therefore a juvenile. In re Ball (Ohio App. 3 Dist., Allen, 01-30-2003) No. 1-02-72, 2003-Ohio-395, 2003 WL 193519, Unreported. Infants ⟜ 196

6. Prosecutions

Magistrate's decision to hold suppression hearing simultaneously with adjudicatory hearing was not abuse of discretion, in delinquency proceeding; same or similar testimony was necessary for motion to suppress as well as adjudication, when magistrate considered motion, juvenile had full opportunity to have any concerns about confession and waiver addressed by the court, and magistrate ruled on motion prior to adjudication. In re Hill (Ohio App. 10 Dist., Franklin, 11-20-2003) No. 03AP-82, 2003-Ohio-6185, 2003 WL 22725297, Unreported. Infants ⟜ 203

Even though a complaining witness may designate a particular statute or statutes as being violated by a child, a juvenile court is free to find, on the basis of the facts alleged and proved, a violation of an additional statute and that the accused is a delinquent child. In re Burgess (Preble 1984) 13 Ohio App.3d 374, 469 N.E.2d 967, 13 O.B.R. 456. Infants ⟜ 210

The state is not barred from prosecution following an unsuccessful appeal from the sustaining of a motion to suppress so long as the state's certification upon appeal pursuant to Juv R 22(F) or Crim R 12(J), that the evidence suppressed was of such nature that the prosecution could not be successful without it, was made in good faith; if such certification were not made in good faith, the time consumed in determining the appeal from the motion to suppress must be charged to the state as undue delay in prosecution of the accused with respect to a determination of whether there has been a violation of the accused's right to a speedy trial. In re Hester (Franklin 1982) 3 Ohio App.3d 458, 446 N.E.2d 202, 3 O.B.R. 539. Criminal Law ⟜ 577.12(1)

Complaint charging 13–year–old juvenile with aggravated burglary for entering unlocked door of friend's home and, after no one answered, taking pack of cigarettes from top of refrigerator would be amended, in interest of justice, to charge criminal trespass and petty theft; there was no evidence that intent to steal was formed prior to entry, and relative potential for harm to persons was minimal as result of juvenile's conduct. In re L.D. (Ohio Com.Pl., 11-

09-1993) 63 Ohio Misc.2d 303, 626 N.E.2d 709. Infants ⟜ 197

7. Miranda warnings

Where a juvenile is asked to take a polygraph examination as a potential witness to a murder but is not charged, arrested, photographed, fingerprinted or considered a suspect, such juvenile is not in custody and Miranda has no application. In re Johnson, No. 7998 (2d Dist Ct App, Montgomery, 10–25–83).

8. Appeals

Father waived his appellate argument that the complaint for permanent custody failed to set forth allegations in compliance with statute, in child dependency proceeding, where father failed to object to the sufficiency of the complaint until ten months after he was first served with the summons and complaint. In re I.M. (Ohio App. 8 Dist., Cuyahoga, 12-24-2003) No. 82669, No. 82695, 2003-Ohio-7069, 2003 WL 23010024, Unreported. Infants ⟜ 243

Juvenile's appeal of trial court's amendment of complaint after adjudicatory hearing in delinquency proceeding, to increase the level of the charged offense, was not "moot," though minimum confinement period for which juvenile could be sentenced had expired, where trial court had not stated a time limit for probation and trial court retained jurisdiction over the juvenile until he reached age of 21. In re Reed (Ohio App. 8 Dist., 01-17-2002) 147 Ohio App.3d 182, 769 N.E.2d 412, 2002-Ohio-43. Infants ⟜ 247

Trial court did not have authority to grant final verdict by dismissing charges in juvenile delinquency proceeding so as to defeat state's right to appeal granting of juveniles' motion to suppress evidence granted during trial; state could appeal from granting of motion to suppress as matter of right. In re Mojica (Ohio App. 8 Dist., 11-20-1995) 107 Ohio App.3d 461, 669 N.E.2d 35. Infants ⟜ 202; Infants ⟜ 242

Where the state has timely filed a notice of appeal from the granting of a motion to suppress, but has failed to make a proper certification as required by Juv R 22(F), a court of appeals may, pursuant to App R 3(E), allow the amendment of the timely filed notice of appeal and certification so that there may be full compliance with Juv R 22(F). In re Hester (Franklin 1981) 1 Ohio App.3d 24, 437 N.E.2d 1218, 1 O.B.R. 85.

Juvenile's appeal of delinquency adjudication and disposition was timely pursuant to rule of appellate procedure requiring filing of notice of appeal within thirty days of service of the notice of judgment and its entry, although notice of appeal was filed more than a year after disposition order was approved and journalized, and juvenile allegedly had actual notice of adjudication and disposition, where there was no evidence that juvenile court served or attempted to serve any of judge's or magistrate's journal entries on juvenile, or, on any other party. In re L.B. (Ohio App. 8 Dist., Cuyahoga, 07-25-2002) No. 79370, No. 79942, 2002-Ohio-3767, 2002 WL 1729905, Unreported.

Juv R 23 Continuance

Continuances shall be granted only when imperative to secure fair treatment for the parties.

(Adopted eff. 7–1–72)

Cross References

Actions pending at end of term automatically continued, 2151.22

Library References

Infants ☞204.

Westlaw Topic No. 211.

C.J.S. Infants §§ 51, 52, 62 to 67.

Notes of Decisions

Hearings 3
Right to counsel 2
Time limitations 1

_____

1. Time limitations

Father was not entitled to reversal of trial court judgment terminating parental rights and granting permanent custody to county children services board based on time delay in case due to numerous continuances and extensions; services board was not responsible for all continuances, continuances were based on unavailability of key witnesses, father did not object to all continuances, and father did not file objection to the trial court from the magistrate's grant of continuances. In re Hess (Ohio App. 7 Dist., Jefferson, 03-21-2003) No. 02 JE 37, 2003-Ohio-1429, 2003 WL 1465190, Unreported. Infants ☞ 253

The ten-day period of limitations in Juv R 29(A) is procedural only and such rule confers no substantive right upon an accused to have his case dismissed if he is not tried within the designated time. In re Therklidsen (Franklin 1977) 54 Ohio App.2d 195, 376 N.E.2d 970, 8 O.O.3d 335.

Juvenile's request to call an additional witness at a later time in delinquency proceeding did not constitute a formal request for a continuance. In re Neff (Ohio App. 5 Dist., Tuscarawas, 02-04-2003) No. 2002AP080063, 2003-Ohio-569, 2003 WL 255739, Unreported. Infants ☞ 204

Juvenile court was warranted in denying juvenile's motion for a continuance to call an additional witness at a later time in the delinquency proceeding, where juvenile did not subpoena witness until three days before trial, and entire trial was completed except for State's calling of the rape victim as a rebuttal witness when juvenile requested the continuance. In re Neff (Ohio App. 5 Dist., Tuscarawas, 02-04-2003) No. 2002AP080063, 2003-Ohio-569, 2003 WL 255739, Unreported. Infants ☞ 204

Court's refusal to grant juvenile's request for a continuance in aggravated burglary case, on grounds that subpoenas that defense counsel had filed with the clerk's office had not been served, did not violate juvenile's right to compel production of witnesses, where defense counsel did not explain why the witnesses were material, did not give any indication what the testimony would have been, and did not request continuance until shortly before trial was to begin. State v. K.W. (Ohio App. 8 Dist., Cuyahoga, 01-30-2003) No. 80951, 2003-Ohio-425, 2003 WL 194857, Unreported. Infants ☞ 204

Five and a half month delay between the finding of delinquency and the disposition did not divest the court of jurisdiction; juvenile rule provided that after adjudication a court may continue a matter for disposition for not more than six months, and juvenile did not object to the continuances entered by the court. In re Homan (Ohio App. 5 Dist., Tuscarawas, 01-27-2003) No. 2002AP080067, 2003-Ohio-352, 2003 WL 183811, Unreported. Infants ☞ 223.1

Extending permanent custody proceedings so that county could present newly discovered evidence was consistent with juvenile code's purpose to provide for the care, protection, and mental and physical development of children, where evidence exposed fact that father had lied to county when he told county that he had no other children, when, in fact, he had another son who resided with him, allegedly had been victim of sexual abuse perpetrated by father and father's brother, and was also a perpetrator of sexual abuse. In re Sullivan (Ohio App. 12 Dist., Butler, 01-21-2003) No. CA2002-03-061, 2003-Ohio-195, 2003 WL 138665, Unreported. Infants ☞ 207

2. Right to counsel

Trial court was not required to continue dispositional hearing arising from minor's adjudication as delinquent to allow county children services board to have counsel present, as nonattorney caseworker could not properly request continuance on behalf of board. In re Lawson (Ohio App. 10 Dist., 11-08-1994) 98 Ohio App.3d 456, 648 N.E.2d 889. Infants ☞ 204

The guarantee of the right to be represented by counsel set forth in Juv R 4(A) does not, as to a nonindigent party, require that trial be continued indefinitely until counsel can be obtained, but merely requires, if it does not appear that counsel could not be obtained through the exercise of reasonable diligence and a willingness to enter into reasonable contractual arrangements for counsel's services, that a reasonable opportunity be given to the party before trial to employ such counsel. In re Bolden (Allen 1973) 37 Ohio App.2d 7, 306 N.E.2d 166, 66 O.O.2d 26.

3. Hearings

Trial court was not required to continue dispositional hearing arising from minor's adjudication as delinquent at request of county children services board which sought to have expert prepare second psychological report; request for continuance was not properly made because board did not appear as party through counsel at hearing, and minor's need for treatment outweighed need for additional report. In re Lawson (Ohio App. 10 Dist., 11-08-1994) 98 Ohio App.3d 456, 648 N.E.2d 889. Infants ☞ 204

Where the juvenile court (1) has gone through the process of hearing pursuant to RC 2151.417, (2) has reviewed placement of the child with his mother, and (3) has satisfied itself as to such placement, it is not an abuse of discretion for the court to deny a motion for continuance brought by the child's former custodian. In re Mull, No. 13–96–38, 1997 WL 155412 (3d Dist Ct App, Seneca, 3–24–97).

When a party does not request a continuance of a dispositional hearing which is to be held immediately after an adjudicatory hearing, the court may proceed immediately to disposition. In re Howell, No. 79–CA–16 (5th Dist Ct App, Coshocton, 1–31–80).

Juv R 24   Discovery

(A) Request for discovery

Upon written request, each party of whom discovery is requested shall, to the extent not privileged, produce promptly for inspection, copying, or photographing the following information, documents, and material in that party's custody, control, or possession:

(1) The names and last known addresses of each witness to the occurrence that forms the basis of the charge or defense;

(2) Copies of any written statements made by any party or witness;

(3) Transcriptions, recordings, and summaries of any oral statements of any party or witness, except the work product of counsel;

(4) Any scientific or other reports that a party intends to introduce at the hearing or that pertain to physical evidence that a party intends to introduce;

(5) Photographs and any physical evidence which a party intends to introduce at the hearing;

(6) Except in delinquency and unruly child proceedings, other evidence favorable to the requesting party and relevant to the subject matter involved in the pending action. In delinquency and unruly child proceedings, the prosecuting attorney shall disclose to respondent's counsel all evidence, known or that may become known to the prosecuting attorney, favorable to the respondent and material either to guilt or punishment.

(B) Order granting discovery: limitations; sanctions

If a request for discovery is refused, application may be made to the court for a written order granting the discovery. Motions for discovery shall certify that a request for discovery has been made and refused. An order granting discovery may make such discovery reciprocal for all parties to the proceeding, including the party requesting discovery. Notwithstanding the provisions of subdivision (A), the court may deny, in whole or part, or otherwise limit or set conditions on the discovery authorized by such subdivision, upon its own motion, or upon a showing by a party upon whom a request for discovery is made that granting discovery may jeopardize the safety of a party, witness, or confidential informant, result in the production of perjured testimony or evidence, endanger the existence of physical evidence, violate a privileged communication, or impede the criminal prosecution of a minor as an adult or of an adult charged with an offense arising from the same transaction or occurrence.

(C) Failure to comply

If at any time during the course of the proceedings it is brought to the attention of the court that a person has failed to comply with an order issued pursuant to this rule, the court may grant a continuance, prohibit the person from introducing in evidence the material not disclosed, or enter such other order as it deems just under the circumstances.

(Adopted eff. 7–1–72; amended eff. 7–1–94)

Historical and Statutory Notes

Amendment Note: The 7–1–94 amendment substituted "promptly" for "forthwith", inserted ", to the extent not privileged," and made changes to reflect gender-neutral language in the first paragraph of division (A); and added division (A)(6).

Commentary

Staff Notes

1994:

Rule 24 Discovery

Juv. R. 24 governs the scope of discovery. It adds a new category under Juv. R. 24(A)(6) permitting the requesting party to discover relevant evidence which is favorable to the requesting party, except that in delinquency and unruly child proceedings, the requirement imposed upon prosecuting attorneys is to disclose only such favorable evidence which is material to guilt or punishment of the respondent. All categories of discovery are subject to the assertion of a privilege.

Cross References

Discovery and inspection, Crim R 16
General provisions governing discovery, Civ R 26
Production of documents and things for inspection, copying, testing and entry upon land for inspection and other purposes, Civ R 34

Library References

Infants ☞201.
Westlaw Topic No. 211.
C.J.S. Infants §§ 42, 53, 54.
Am Jur 2d: 23, Depositions and Discovery § 400 to 467
Carlin, Baldwin's Ohio Practice, Merrick–Rippner Probate Law § 107.32, 107.33, 107.67, 107.156, 107.157 (2003).

Notes of Decisions

Access to records 4
Appeals 8
Failure to comply 5
Final orders 1
Limitations on discovery 2
Orders compelling discovery 7
Subpoenas 3
Witness' statement 6

---

1. Final orders

Under the discovery provisions of the Civil Rules, the court has a discretionary power, not a ministerial duty; an interlocutory order, overruling a motion to compel answers to interrogatories involving opinions, contentions, and legal conclusions, is not a final appealable order. State ex rel. Daggett v. Gessaman (Ohio 1973) 34 Ohio St.2d 55, 295 N.E.2d 659, 63 O.O.2d 88.

2. Limitations on discovery

A prosecutor is under a duty, imposed by the due process clauses of the state and federal constitutions and by the rule governing discovery in juvenile proceedings, to disclose to a juvenile respondent all evidence in the state's possession favorable to the juvenile respondent and material either to guilt or punishment that is known at the time of a mandatory bindover hearing and that may become known to the prosecuting attorney after the bindover. State v. Iacona (Ohio 2001) 93 Ohio St.3d 83, 752 N.E.2d 937, 2001 –Ohio- 1292, on remand. Constitutional Law ⊕ 255(4); Infants ⊕ 68.7(3)

The juvenile court is authorized, upon a proper showing, to limit discovery. In re A.M. (Ohio App. 8 Dist., 09-05-2000) 139 Ohio App.3d 303, 743 N.E.2d 937, appeal not allowed 91 Ohio St.3d 1431, 741 N.E.2d 895. Infants ⊕ 201

Juv R 24 does not permit discovery of police reports in delinquency cases. In re Hunter, No. 46019 (8th Dist Ct App, Cuyahoga, 4–5–84).

A social worker may not be compelled to reveal the name of the person who reported an instance of child abuse since such information is confidential under RC 2151.421. In re Hicks, No. H–78–7 (6th Dist Ct App, Huron, 11–17–78).

Justification existed for limiting juvenile's discovery on motion to transfer juvenile delinquency proceedings to criminal court for trial as adult, where five individuals had been formally charged with offenses arising from same transaction which formed basis of complaint filed against juvenile, two of whom were adults and two of whom had transfer proceedings pending, and granting full discovery might impede criminal prosecution of adult codefendants and potential criminal prosecution of child and his alleged codelinquent. In re Doss (Ohio Com.Pl., 05-11-1994) 65 Ohio Misc.2d 8, 640 N.E.2d 618. Infants ⊕ 68.7(1)

Although rule is generally move expansive than statute governing discovery in juvenile delinquency proceedings, nature of proceedings for which discovery is sought is relevant in determining extent to which discovery will be granted under rule. In re Doss (Ohio Com.Pl., 05-11-1994) 65 Ohio Misc.2d 8, 640 N.E.2d 618. Infants ⊕ 201

Order limiting scope of mother's discovery with respect to guardian ad litem did not deprive mother of right to prepare for trial, in proceedings to place mother's children in permanent custody of county children's services board; mother's discovery requests were overly broad and went beyond scope of allowable discovery, mother did not bring any discrepancies in guardian ad litem's information to court's attention, and mother never called guardian ad litem to testify at hearing. In re Adams (Ohio App. 2 Dist., Miami, 02-07-2003) No. 2002 CA 45, 2003-Ohio-618, 2003 WL 264357, Unreported. Infants ⊕ 201

3. Subpoenas

Where the parents of an alleged dependent child have filed a praecipe for a subpoena duces tecum of a children services board (the party filing the complaint) seeking to obtain or view the agency's records, it is error for the court to sustain a motion to quash the subpoena on the basis that the records are privileged and confidential; the court should allow counsel for the parents reasonable access to the files in order to use the parts which are relevant to the issues being presented to the court. In re Barzak (Trumbull 1985) 24 Ohio App.3d 180, 493 N.E.2d 1011, 24 O.B.R. 270.

4. Access to records

RC Ch 1347 and Ch 5153 do not conflict, and these chapters impose upon the keeper of the files of the county children services board an obligation to provide reasonable access to them for inspection by an involved party. In re Trumbull County Children Services Bd. (Ohio Com.Pl. 1986) 32 Ohio Misc.2d 11, 513 N.E.2d 360.

5. Failure to comply

At mandatory bindover proceedings involving juvenile who allegedly murdered her newborn child, state committed *Brady* violation by not providing child's blood culture laboratory report, which indicated the presence of a potentially deadly bacterium, to the defense in time for use at the hearing. State v. Iacona (Ohio 2001) 93 Ohio St.3d 83, 752 N.E.2d 937, 2001 –Ohio- 1292, on remand. Infants ⊕ 68.7(3)

At mandatory bindover proceedings involving juvenile who allegedly murdered her newborn child, reversible error did not occur through state's committing *Brady* violation by not providing child's blood culture laboratory report, which indicated the presence of a potentially deadly bacterium, to the defense in time for use at the hearing, as trial court would have found probable cause even if juvenile possessed report. State v. Iacona (Ohio 2001) 93 Ohio St.3d 83, 752 N.E.2d 937, 2001 –Ohio- 1292, on remand. Infants ⊕ 68.8

In prosecution of defendant for involuntary manslaughter of her newborn child, state did not conceal significance of child's blood culture laboratory report, which indicated the presence of a potentially deadly bacterium, that it provided during pretrial discovery, even though faxed copy of report was unclear and hand-delivered copy was less-than-perfect. State v. Iacona (Ohio 2001) 93 Ohio St.3d 83, 752 N.E.2d 937, 2001 –Ohio- 1292, on remand. Criminal Law ⊕ 700(3)

Where a party fails to comply with a court order for discovery, the party seeking discovery must request the proper remedial order from the court in order to obtain such remedies. In re Hester (Franklin 1982) 3 Ohio App.3d 458, 446 N.E.2d 202, 3 O.B.R. 539.

In termination of parental rights case, juvenile court properly refused father's motion in limine to exclude testimony from clinical psychologist and case worker because state failed to respond to father's request for documents, as father never filed a motion to compel discovery, but instead waited until the day of the permanent custody hearing, which was nearly two weeks after the filing of his document request, to raise the issue with the court for the first time. In re Funk, Nos. 2002-P-0035+, 2002-Ohio-4958, 2002 WL 31107531 (11th Dist Ct App, 9-20-02).

Where discovery is not provided until immediately before the adjudicatory hearing and the party who requested it agrees to proceed with the hearing after reviewing the material, the party may not claim on appeal that he was denied discovery. In re Wyrock, Nos. 41827, 41828, and 41904 (8th Dist Ct App, Cuyahoga, 10–23–80).

6. Witness' statement

Under juvenile procedure rule and upon timely request, juvenile charged with rape was entitled to production of complaining witness' narrative to police on date of alleged offense, even though narrative was not signed by witness and was not taken verbatim. In re Johnson (Cuyahoga 1989) 61 Ohio App.3d 544, 573 N.E.2d 184. Infants ⊕ 201

There is nothing in Juv R 24 mandating the witness' signature on a narrative, nor does that rule specify that the statement must be taken verbatim. In re Johnson, No. 55204 (8th Dist Ct App, Cuyahoga, 3–23–89).

7. Orders compelling discovery

Juvenile was entitled to discovery prior to hearing to determine whether juvenile would be tried in adult court, even though discovery available under juvenile rule was more expansive than that which was available to adult, as hearing was critically important, and juvenile had legitimate interest in discovering evidence that prosecutor would offer to establish probable cause mandating transfer. In re A.M. (Ohio App. 8 Dist., 09-05-2000) 139 Ohio App.3d 303, 743 N.E.2d 937, appeal not allowed 91 Ohio St.3d 1431, 741 N.E.2d 895. Infants ☞ 68.7(3)

Because Juv R 24 contains no requirement that disclosures be updated, a party seeking current information must either repeat the discovery request or move for an order compelling discovery pursuant to Juv R 24(B). In re Gilbert, No. CA 86–10–144 (12th Dist Ct App, Butler, 9–28–87).

Rule requiring the state to respond to discovery requests in juvenile matters applies to "mandatory bindover" or waiver of jurisdiction proceedings wherein the court determines whether probable cause exists to transfer the matter for prosecution of the juvenile as an adult. In re A.M. (Ohio Com.Pl. 1998) 92 Ohio Misc.2d 4, 699 N.E.2d 574, affirmed 139 Ohio App.3d 303, 743 N.E.2d 937, appeal not allowed 91 Ohio St.3d 1431, 741 N.E.2d 895. Infants ☞ 68.7(3)

8. Appeals

The failure to file a motion for discovery estops a party from thereafter raising the issue on appeal. State v Lee, No. 44902 (8th Dist Ct App, Cuyahoga, 2–10–83).

Juv R 25 Depositions

The court upon good cause shown may grant authority to take the deposition of a party or other person upon such terms and conditions and in such manner as the court may fix.

(Adopted eff. 7–1–72)

Cross References

Deposition, Crim R 15

Perpetuation of testimony, depositions before action or pending appeal, Civ R 27

Library References

Infants ☞201.

Westlaw Topic No. 211.

C.J.S. Infants §§ 42, 53, 54.

Am Jur 2d: 23, Depositions and Discovery § 400 to 467

Giannelli & Snyder, Baldwin's Ohio Practice, Evidence § 804.8, 804.10 (2d ed. 2001).

Carlin, Baldwin's Ohio Practice, Merrick–Rippner Probate Law § 107.35 (2003).

Notes of Decisions

Contempt of court   1

Procedures   2

_____

1. Contempt of court

Where the mother of a child who is the subject of a dependency action fails to answer deposition questions after being granted immunity under RC 2945.44, she may be held in contempt of court. In re Poth (Huron 1981) 2 Ohio App.3d 361, 442 N.E.2d 105, 2 O.B.R. 417.

2. Procedures

The trial court has discretion to allow or disallow depositions and to control the manner and terms under which depositions are taken. In re Vaughn, No. CA89–11–162 (12th Dist Ct App, Butler, 8–13–90).

Admission of deposition of psychologist was not an abuse of discretion, in child dependency proceeding; psychologist qualified as a medical expert, the rules of civil procedure provided that the deposition of a medical expert was admissible as if the expert were present and testifying, defense counsel was present during psychologist's deposition and had an opportunity to cross-examine him, and defendant was not precluded from calling the psychologist to testify at the hearing. In re Mraz (Ohio App. 12 Dist., Brown, 12-30-2002) No. CA2002-05-011, No. CA2002-07-014, 2002-Ohio-7278, 2002 WL 31883343, Unreported. Infants ☞ 173.1

Juv R 26 [Reserved]

Juv R 27 Hearings: general

(A) General provisions

Unless otherwise stated in this rule, the juvenile court may conduct its hearings in an informal manner and may adjourn its hearings from time to time.

The court may excuse the attendance of the child at the hearing in neglect, dependency, or abuse cases.

(1) Public access to hearings. In serious youthful offender proceedings, hearings shall be open to the public. In all other proceedings, the court may exclude the general public from any hearing, but may not exclude either of the following:

(a) persons with a direct interest in the case;

(b) persons who demonstrate, at a hearing, a countervailing right to be present.

(2) Separation of juvenile and adult cases. Cases involving children shall be heard separate and apart from the trial of cases against adults, except for cases involving chronic or habitual truancy.

(3) Jury trials. The court shall hear and determine all cases of children without a jury, except for the adjudication of a serious youthful offender complaint, indictment, or information in which trial by jury has not been waived.

Unless otherwise stated in this rule, the juvenile court may conduct its hearings in an informal manner and may adjourn its hearings from time to time.

The court may excuse the attendance of the child at the hearing in neglect, dependency, or abuse cases.

(B) Special provisions for abuse, neglect, and dependency proceedings

(1) In any proceeding involving abuse, neglect, or dependency at which the court removes a child from the child's home or continues the removal of a child from the child's home, or in a proceeding where the court orders detention, the court shall determine whether the person who filed the complaint in the case and removed the child from the child's home has custody of the child or will be given custody and has made reasonable efforts to do any of the following:

(a) Prevent the removal of the child from the child's home;

(b) Eliminate the continued removal of the child from the child's home;

(c) Make it possible for the child to return home.

(2) In a proceeding involving abuse, neglect, or dependency, the examination made by the court to determine whether a child is a competent witness shall comply with all of the following:

(a) Occur in an area other than a courtroom or hearing room;

(b) Be conducted in the presence of only those individuals considered necessary by the court for the conduct of the examination or the well being of the child;

(c) Be recorded in accordance with Juv. R. 37 or Juv. R. 40. The court may allow the prosecutor, guardian ad litem, or attorney for any party to submit questions for use by the court in determining whether the child is a competent witness.

(3) In a proceeding where a child is alleged to be an abused child, the court may order that the testimony of the child be taken by deposition in the presence of a judge or a magistrate. On motion of the prosecuting attorney, guardian ad litem, or a party, or in its own discretion, the court may order that the deposition be videotaped. All or part of the deposition is admissible in evidence where all of the following apply:

(a) It is filed with the clerk;

(b) Counsel for all parties had an opportunity and similar motive at the time of the taking of the deposition to develop the testimony by direct, cross, or redirect examination;

(c) The judge or magistrate determines there is reasonable cause to believe that if the child were to testify in person at the hearing, the child would experience emotional trauma as a result of the child's participation at the hearing.

(Adopted eff. 7–1–72; amended eff. 7–1–76, 7–1–94, 7–1–96, 7–1–01)

Historical and Statutory Notes

Amendment Note: The 7–1–01 amendment rewrote division (A), which prior thereto read:

"The juvenile court may conduct its hearings in an informal manner and may adjourn its hearings from time to time. In the hearing of any case the general public may be excluded and only persons admitted who have a direct interest in the case.

"All cases involving children shall be heard separate and apart from the trial of cases against adults. The court may excuse the attendance of the child at the hearing in neglect, dependency or abuse cases. The court shall hear and determine all cases of children without a jury."; the amendment further inserted "for abuse, neglect, and dependency proceedings" to the caption of division (B).

Amendment Note: The 7–1–96 amendment substituted "magistrate" for "referee" throughout division (B)(3).

Amendment Note: The 7–1–94 amendment designated division (A) and added division (B).

Commentary

Staff Notes

2001:

Rule 27(A) General provisions

Rule 27(A) was completely rewritten and reorganized to conform to changes necessitated by Sub. Sen. Bill 179 (serious youthful offenders) (effective date January 1, 2002), and Sub. Sen. Bill 181 (chronic and habitual truants) (effective date September 4, 2000).

Rule 27(A) as amended deals separately with the informality of hearings [division (A)], public access to hearings [division (A)(1)], separation of juvenile and adult cases [division (A)(2)], and jury trials [division (A)(3)].

Division (A)(1) clarifies that in serious youthful offender proceedings, adult rules about public access shall apply, and thus a qualified presumption of public access is appropriate. The rule seeks to conform to the Supreme Court's ruling in *State ex rel. New World Communications of Ohio, Inc. v. Geauga County Court of Common Pleas, Juvenile Division* (2000), 90 Ohio St. 3d 79, 734 N.E.2d 1214. In juvenile proceedings, there is no qualified right of public access, and no presumption that the proceedings be either open or closed. The amended rule recognizes that the policies of confidentiality and rehabilitation important in juvenile proceedings may justify closure to those without a direct interest after a hearing. In that hearing, the party seeking closure bears the burden of proof, but Rule 27(A)(1)(b) clarifies that closure is justified unless there is a "comparable competing interest" for public access, which the rule describes as a countervailing right. The amendment also conforms to Revised Code section 2151.35 (A) as amended by Sub. Sen. Bill 179.

Rule 27(A)(2) conforms to Revised Code section 2151.35 (A)(1), which provides that in cases in which both a child and an adult are charged for chronic or habitual truancy, the cases need not be heard separately, while preserving separate proceedings in all other cases.

Rule 27(A)(3) conforms to Revised Code section 2152.13(D) providing for a jury determination in cases seeking a serious youthful offender dispositional sentence, while preserving nonjury proceedings in all other cases.

Rule 27(B) Special Provisions for Abuse, Neglect, and Dependency Proceedings

Rule 27(B) was not amended, but was recaptioned to clarify that its provisions apply to abuse, neglect and dependency proceedings.

1996:

The amendment changed the rule's reference from "referee" to "magistrate" in division (B)(3) and (B)(3)(c) in order to harmonize the rule with the language adopted in the 1995 amendments to Juv. R. 40. The amendment is technical only and no substantive change is intended.

1994:

Rule 27 Hearings: General

S.B. 89 set forth several additional criteria to be observed in the course of hearings in juvenile court. The revisions to Juv. R. 27 reflect the general policy of that legislation to protect children and to assure that all reasonable measures have been taken to keep children with their original families.

Juv. R. 27(B)(1) specifies the "reasonable efforts" determination necessary to assure that, as much as possible, children can remain with their families or return to them without undue trauma. Revised Code 2151.419.

Juv. R. 27(B)(1) [1] sets forth the requirements of the court's determination as to whether a child is a competent witness. Revised Code 2317.01.

Juv. R. 27(B)(3) details a procedure to permit a child's testimony to be taken by deposition in the presence of a judge or a referee. Revised Code 2151.35(G).

Cross References

Charges against adults, 2151.43
Hearing on abortion without parental consent, 2151.85
Hearing procedures; findings, record, 2151.35
Release of child from youth services department institution, 2151.38

Library References

Infants ⟨⟩68.7(3), 203, 204.
Westlaw Topic No. 211.
C.J.S. Infants §§ 46 to 67.
OJur 3d: 22, Courts and Judges § 18
Am Jur 2d: 47, Juvenile Courts and Delinquent and Dependent Children § 44 to 48
Propriety of exclusion of press or other media representatives from civil trial. 79 ALR3d 401
Carlin, Baldwin's Ohio Practice, Merrick–Rippner Probate Law § 104.5, 107.47, 107.50, 107.52, 107.56 (2003).

[1] So in original; should this read "Juv. R.

Law Review and Journal Commentaries

Confidentiality of Juvenile Court Proceedings, William A. Kurtz. 1 Prob L J Ohio 115 (May/June 1991).

The Effect of the Double Jeopardy Clause on Juvenile Proceedings, James G. Carr. 6 U Tol L Rev 1 (Fall 1974).

In re T.R.: Not In Front of the Children, Bill Dickhaut. I Ky Children's Rts J 10 (July 1991).

Interviewing Child Victims/Witnesses, Mary A. Lentz. 9 Baldwin's Ohio Sch L J 25 (July/August 1997).

Interviewing the child witness: Do's and don't's, how's and why's, Nancy E. Walker and Matthew Nguyen. 29 Creighton L Rev 1587 (1996).

Notes of Decisions

Constitutional issues 2
Discretion of court 4
Equitable actions 1
Public access 3

---

1. Equitable actions

It is within the discretion of a juvenile court judge to determine whether or not to close from the general public a hearing on the transfer of jurisdiction from the juvenile division to the court of common pleas, and thus a writ of prohibition to prevent the judge from conducting an open hearing will not lie. State ex rel. Fyffe v. Pierce (Ohio 1988) 40 Ohio St.3d 8, 531 N.E.2d 673.

2. Constitutional issues

At closure hearing in juvenile proceeding, court may entertain summaries of testimony by witnesses who may subsequently testify at permanent commitment hearing, resolution of closure issues may be predicated upon those summaries, and the rules of evidence are necessarily relaxed to allow the presentation of the information in summary form. State ex rel. Dispatch Printing Co. v. Lias (Ohio 1994) 68 Ohio St.3d 497, 628 N.E.2d 1368.

Juvenile court did not violate double jeopardy principles when, after defendant began serving sentence, it issued amended sentencing entry and nunc pro tunc entry which corrected its original sentencing entry, which erroneously indicated that defendant's sentence had been suspended, to reflect juvenile court's actual decision at sentencing hearing that sentence was not suspended. State v. Parsons (Ohio App. 12 Dist. 1997) 122 Ohio App.3d 284, 701 N.E.2d 732. Double Jeopardy ⟨⟩ 33

Due process clause of Fourteenth Amendment applies when child is charged with misconduct for which he may be incarcerated in institution, so child is entitled to notice of charges, counsel, confrontation and cross-examination, and privilege against self-incrimination. In re Jason R. (Ohio Com.Pl. 1995) 77 Ohio Misc.2d 37, 666 N.E.2d 666. Constitutional Law ⟨⟩ 255(4)

Proceeding with dispositional hearing in juvenile's absence did not violate due process; juvenile effectively waived his right to be present, as he had notice of hearing but blatantly disregarded it. In re Jason R. (Ohio Com.Pl. 1995) 77 Ohio Misc.2d 37, 666 N.E.2d 666. Constitutional Law ⟨⟩ 255(4); Infants ⟨⟩ 203

Right to be present at every stage of trial, as encompassed by right of confrontation, applies to 27(B)(2)"?

both adult criminal trials and juvenile proceedings. In re Jason R. (Ohio Com.Pl. 1995) 77 Ohio Misc.2d 37, 666 N.E.2d 666. Criminal Law ☞ 662.70; Infants ☞ 203; Infants ☞ 207

Although juvenile's right to be present at dispositional hearing was implied by rule stating that court may excuse attendance of child at hearing in neglect, dependency, or abuse cases, and rule requiring court at conclusion of dispositional hearing to advise child of child's right to record expungement and right to appeal, juvenile nonetheless waived his right to be present at dispositional hearing by blatantly disregarding it after receiving adequate notice. In re Jason R. (Ohio Com.Pl. 1995) 77 Ohio Misc.2d 37, 666 N.E.2d 666. Infants ☞ 203

Proceeding with dispositional hearing in juvenile's absence did not violate his right of allocution, as he waived his right to be present by blatantly disregarding hearing after receiving adequate notice, thus waiving his right to address court passing judgment upon him. In re Jason R. (Ohio Com.Pl. 1995) 77 Ohio Misc.2d 37, 666 N.E.2d 666. Infants ☞ 203

Under the present Juvenile Code and Rules, a juvenile court cannot change a "temporary" commitment to the Ohio youth commission to an "permanent" commitment without hearing; further, the commitment of an unruly child, not declared "delinquent", is a violation of due process and any hearing held on the above matters requires the presence of the youth involved. OAG 72–071.

3. Public access

Closure of delinquency proceedings for 17–year–old charged with aggravated murder, aggravated attempted murder, and aggravated robbery was abuse of discretion; public interest in proceedings outweighed bare assertion by juvenile's attorney that permitting access would not be in juvenile's best interest, in view of juvenile's near-adult age at time of alleged offenses, minimal likelihood that probable cause hearing would disclose confidential information, gravity of offenses, and fact that juvenile would be subject to mandatory bindover to adult court if probable cause hearing was found. State ex rel. Plain Dealer Publishing Co. v. Geauga Cty. Court of Common Pleas, Juv. Div. (Ohio 2000) 90 Ohio St.3d 79, 734 N.E.2d 1214, 2000 –Ohio- 35.

Decision to close juvenile proceedings to general public will be upheld unless juvenile court abused its discretion. State ex rel. Plain Dealer Publishing Co. v. Geauga Cty. Court of Common Pleas, Juv. Div. (Ohio 2000) 90 Ohio St.3d 79, 734 N.E.2d 1214, 2000 –Ohio- 35.

Party seeking closure of juvenile proceedings bears burden of proof on relevant factors. State ex rel. Plain Dealer Publishing Co. v. Geauga Cty. Court of Common Pleas, Juv. Div. (Ohio 2000) 90 Ohio St.3d 79, 734 N.E.2d 1214, 2000 –Ohio- 35.

Since juvenile proceedings to determine if child is abused, neglected, or dependent or to determine custody of minor child are neither presumptively open nor presumptively closed to public, juvenile court may restrict public access to those proceedings if it finds, after hearing evidence and argument on issue, that there exists reasonable and substantial basis for believing that public access could harm child or endanger fairness of adjudication, and that potential for harm outweighs benefits of public access. State ex rel. Scripps Howard Broadcasting Co. v. Cuyahoga Cty. Court of Common Pleas, Juv. Div. (Ohio, 07-13-1995) 73 Ohio St.3d 19, 652 N.E.2d 179.

Those persons present and participating at in camera inspection held to determine whether closure hearing in juvenile proceeding should be closed are prohibited, under penalty of contempt, from disseminating any information determined by the juvenile court to be excluded from public disclosure, unless and until it is determined by competent authority that the information may be released to the public. State ex rel. Dispatch Printing Co. v. Lias (Ohio 1994) 68 Ohio St.3d 497, 628 N.E.2d 1368.

Proceedings in juvenile court to determine if a child is abused, neglected, or dependent, or to determine custody of a minor child, are neither presumptively open nor presumptively closed to the public; the juvenile court may restrict public access to these proceedings pursuant to Juv R 27 and RC 2151.35 if the court finds, after hearing evidence and argument on the issue, that (1) there exists a reasonable and substantial basis for believing that public access could harm the child or endanger the fairness of the adjudication, and (2) the potential for harm outweighs the benefits of public access. In re T.R. (Ohio 1990) 52 Ohio St.3d 6, 556 N.E.2d 439, certiorari denied 111 S.Ct. 386, 498 U.S. 958, 112 L.Ed.2d 396. Infants ☞ 172; Infants ☞ 203

Alleged falsity of news broadcast in suggesting that juvenile had prior record for rape and kidnapping did not require closing probable cause and amenability hearings in juvenile delinquency case, even though the broadcast would likely endanger fairness of trial as adult; state's agents and judge knew difference between facts of prior case and scenario presented in broadcast, and there was no reason to believe that any more harm would result from permitting public access to further proceedings. In re N.H. (Ohio Com.Pl. 1992) 63 Ohio Misc.2d 285, 626 N.E.2d 697. Infants ☞ 203

Public had First Amendment right of access to probable cause hearing in juvenile delinquency case and to parts of amenability hearing involving prior juvenile record, but public had no right of access to portions of amenability hearing involving information about child's psychological, social, and family histories. In re N.H. (Ohio Com.Pl. 1992) 63 Ohio Misc.2d 285, 626 N.E.2d 697. Constitutional Law ☞ 90.1(3); Infants ☞ 203

Juvenile court proceedings in delinquency cases are not presumed to be opened or closed; rather, in each case juvenile court must weigh competing interests for and against public access. In re N.H. (Ohio Com.Pl. 1992) 63 Ohio Misc.2d 285, 626 N.E.2d 697. Infants ☞ 203

4. Discretion of court

"Evidence," for purposes of statute providing that juvenile court at dispositional hearing may admit any evidence that is material and relevant, contemplates sworn testimony, despite informal nature of such hearing. In re Ramsey Children (Stark 1995) 102 Ohio App.3d 168, 656 N.E.2d 1311. Infants ☞ 173.1

Juvenile failed to show that he was prejudiced by juvenile court's refusal to conduct informal proceedings, rather than formal court proceedings, on charges of criminal mischief. In re Corcoran (Geauga 1990) 68 Ohio App.3d 213, 587 N.E.2d 957, dismissed 56 Ohio St.3d 702, 564 N.E.2d 703. Infants ☞ 253

Juv R 28   [Reserved]

Juv R 29   Adjudicatory hearing

(A) Scheduling the hearing

The date for the adjudicatory hearing shall be set when the complaint is filed or as soon thereafter as is practicable. If the child is the subject of a complaint alleging a violation of a section of the Revised Code that may be violated by an adult and that does not request a serious youthful offender sentence, and if the child is in detention or shelter care, the hearing shall be held not later than fifteen days after the filing of the complaint. Upon a showing of good cause, the adjudicatory hearing may be continued and detention or shelter care extended.

The prosecuting attorney's filing of either a notice of intent to pursue or a statement of an interest in pursuing a serious youthful offender sentence shall constitute good cause for continuing the adjudicatory hearing date and extending detention or shelter care.

The hearing of a removal action shall be scheduled in accordance with Juv. R. 39(B).

If the complaint alleges abuse, neglect, or dependency, the hearing shall be held no later than thirty days after the complaint is filed. For good cause shown, the adjudicatory hearing may extend beyond thirty days either for an additional ten days to allow any party to obtain counsel or for a reasonable time beyond thirty days to obtain service on all parties or complete any necessary evaluations. However, the adjudicatory hearing shall be held no later than sixty days after the complaint is filed.

The failure of the court to hold an adjudicatory hearing within any time period set forth in this rule does not affect the ability of the court to issue any order otherwise provided for in statute or rule and does not provide any basis for contesting the jurisdiction of the court or the validity of any order of the court.

(B) Advisement and findings at the commencement of the hearing

At the beginning of the hearing, the court shall do all of the following:

(1) Ascertain whether notice requirements have been complied with and, if not, whether the affected parties waive compliance;

(2) Inform the parties of the substance of the complaint, the purpose of the hearing, and possible consequences of the hearing, including the possibility that the cause may be transferred to the appropriate adult court under Juv. R. 30 where the complaint alleges that a child fourteen years of age or over is delinquent by conduct that would constitute a felony if committed by an adult;

(3) Inform unrepresented parties of their right to counsel and determine if those parties are waiving their right to counsel;

(4) Appoint counsel for any unrepresented party under Juv. R. 4(A) who does not waive the right to counsel;

(5) Inform any unrepresented party who waives the right to counsel of the right: to obtain counsel at any stage of the proceedings, to remain silent, to offer evidence, to cross-examine witnesses, and, upon request, to have a record of all proceedings made, at public expense if indigent.

(C) Entry of admission or denial

The court shall request each party against whom allegations are being made in the complaint to admit or deny the allegations. A failure or refusal to admit the allegations shall be deemed a denial, except in cases where the court consents to entry of a plea of no contest.

(D) Initial procedure upon entry of an admission

The court may refuse to accept an admission and shall not accept an admission without addressing the party personally and determining both of the following:

(1) The party is making the admission voluntarily with understanding of the nature of the allegations and the consequences of the admission;

(2) The party understands that by entering an admission the party is waiving the right to challenge the witnesses and evidence against the party, to remain silent, and to introduce evidence at the adjudicatory hearing.

The court may hear testimony, review documents, or make further inquiry, as it considers appropriate, or it may proceed directly to the action required by division (F) of this rule.

(E) Initial procedure upon entry of a denial

If a party denies the allegations the court shall:

(1) Direct the prosecuting attorney or another attorney-at-law to assist the court by presenting evidence in support of the allegations of a complaint;

(2) Order the separation of witnesses, upon request of any party;

(3) Take all testimony under oath or affirmation in either question-answer or narrative form; and

(4) Determine the issues by proof beyond a reasonable doubt in juvenile traffic offense, delinquency, and unruly proceedings; by clear and convincing evidence in dependency, neglect, and abuse cases, and in a removal action; and by a preponderance of the evidence in all other cases.

(F) Procedure upon determination of the issues

Upon the determination of the issues, the court shall do one of the following:

(1) If the allegations of the complaint, indictment, or information were not proven, dismiss the complaint;

(2) If the allegations of the complaint, indictment, or information are admitted or proven, do any one of the following, unless precluded by statute:

(a) Enter an adjudication and proceed forthwith to disposition;

(b) Enter an adjudication and continue the matter for disposition for not more than six months and may make appropriate temporary orders;

(c) Postpone entry of adjudication for not more than six months;

(d) Dismiss the complaint if dismissal is in the best interest of the child and the community.

(3) Upon request make written findings of fact and conclusions of law pursuant to Civ. R. 52.

(4) Ascertain whether the child should remain or be placed in shelter care until the dispositional hearing in an abuse, neglect, or dependency proceeding. In making a shelter care determination, the court shall make written finding of facts with respect to reasonable efforts in accordance with the provisions in Juv. R. 27(B)(1) and to relative placement in accordance with Juv. R. 7(F)(3).

(Adopted eff. 7–1–72; amended eff. 7–1–76, 7–1–94, 7–1–98, 7–1–01, 7–1–04)

Uncodified Law

2002 H 180, § 3, eff. 5–16–02, reads, in part:

The General Assembly hereby requests the Supreme Court to promptly modify Rule 29 of the Rules of Juvenile Procedure pursuant to its authority under the Ohio Constitution to make that rule consistent with the amendments of this act to section 2151.28 of the Revised Code.

2000 S 179, § 6, eff. 4–9–01, reads:

The General Assembly hereby encourages the Supreme Court to amend the Juvenile Rules to be consistent with the changes in the Juvenile Laws pertaining to delinquent children, particularly the laws relating to serious youthful offender dispositional sentences.

The General Assembly hereby encourages the Supreme Court to amend Rule 29(C) to permit "no contest" pleas in juvenile traffic offender and nontraffic cases with the consent of the juvenile court in a manner similar to Criminal Rule 11. Children paying fines to juvenile traffic violations bureaus should be required to admit guilt, with parental knowledge.

The General Assembly hereby encourages the Supreme Court to amend the Rules for the Government of the Judiciary of Ohio or other appropriate rules, or to take other appropriate action, to encourage cooperation between divisions of the courts of common pleas to better implement this act, including, but not limited to, the provisions of this act authorizing, in specified circumstances, jury trials in juvenile courts.

Historical and Statutory Notes

Amendment Note: The 7–1–04 amendment rewrote the second sentence of the first paragraph of division (A) which previously read, "If the child who is the subject of a complaint that does not request a serious youthful offender sentence is in detention or shelter care, the hearing shall be held not later than ten days after the filing of the complaint."; substituted "fourteen" for "fifteen" in division (B)(2); and made other nonsubstantive changes.

Amendment Note: The 7–1–01 amendment inserted "that does not request a serious youthful offender sentence" between "complaint" and "is in detention" in the second sentence of the first paragraph of division (A); added the second paragraph of division (A); inserted the phrase "except in cases where the court consents to entry of a plea of no contest" at the end of division (C); substituted "proven" for "proved" throughout division (F); and substituted "complaint, indictment, or information" for "complaint" in divisions (F)(1) and (F)(2).

Amendment Note: The 7–1–98 amendment added the second paragraph in division (A); substituted "abuse cases, and in a removal action;" for "child abuse proceedings," in division (E)(4); substituted "entry" for "judgment" in division (F)(2)(c); and made other nonsubstantive changes.

Amendment Note: The 7–1–94 amendment added the second and third paragraphs in division (A), and division (F)(4); and made changes to reflect gender-neutral language.

Commentary

Staff Notes

2004:

(A) Scheduling the hearing

Division (A) was amended to conform the language of the rule to R.C. 2151. 28, as amended effective May 16, 2002.

(B) Advisement and findings at the commencement of the hearing

Division (C) was amended to conform the language of the rule to R.C. 2151. 10 and 2151.12, which allow the transfer of juveniles age fourteen and over to adult court for trial.

2001:

Rule 29(A) Scheduling the hearing

Rule 29(A) was amended to conform to Revised Code section 2152.13(B), which provides that the prosecuting attorney has twenty days after a child's initial appearance in juvenile court within which to file a notice of intent to pursue a serious youthful offender dispositional sentence. The rule preserves the ten-day time period within which to hold an adjudicatory hearing for all other cases in which the child is in detention or shelter care. However, because the rule contemplates a hearing within ten days, but the statute grants a twenty-day time period for making the charging decision, the amended rule also provides a mechanism by which a prosecuting attorney can preserve the twenty-day time period by filing a "statement of interest in pursuing a serious youthful offender sentence." The amended rule states that either the notice of intent (i.e., a Rule 22(D)(5) motion) or a statement of interest shall be good cause for extending both the date for an adjudicatory hearing and detention or shelter care. If the prosecuting attorney does not file a notice of intent to pursue a serious youthful offender sentence before the twenty-day time period lapses, the ordinary juvenile time frames again become operative. If the prosecuting attorney does not obtain an indictment or information, or the court denies the Rule 22(D)(5) motion, the ordinary juvenile time frames will again become operative. If the child is determined to be eligible for a serious youthful offender sentence, the ordinary juvenile time frames do not apply. Instead, adult time frames, i.e., speedy trial provisions, become operative [Revised Code section 2152.13(D)(1)].

Rule 29(C) Entry of admission or denial

Rule 29(C) was amended in response to Section 3 of Sub. Sen. Bill 179 (effective January 1, 2002), in which the General Assembly encouraged the Supreme Court to amend Rule 29(C) to permit "no contest" pleas with the consent of the court, similar to the provisions in Criminal Rule 11.

Rule 29(F) Procedure upon determination of the issues

Rule 29(F) was amended in response to both the chronic and habitual truancy act and the serious youthful offender act. Divisions (F)(1) and (2) include recognition that a serious youthful offender case will proceed by indictment or information. Division (F)(2) also recognizes that certain dispositions within the power of the juvenile court may be precluded by statute for certain types of cases. The amendment removes any perception of conflict between statutorily authorized dispositions and those authorized in the rule. Specifically, the division conforms to Revised Code section 2152.13(E), which controls the dispositions in serious youthful offender cases. The division also recognizes that chronic or habitual truant dispositions are heavily regulated by statute.

1998:

Rule 29 Adjudicatory hearing

The 1998 amendment to Juv. R. 29(A) makes reference to Juv. R. 39(B), which governs service of process and the scheduling of hearings in removal actions.

The 1998 amendment to Juv. R. 29(E)(4) establishes a clear and convincing standard in removal

actions for determining whether the child is causing a significant and unreasonable disruption to the educational process. This standard recognizes the significant consequences that will result if the allegations of the complaint are established.

1994:

Rule 29 Adjudicatory Hearing

The 1994 amendment revised Juv. R. 29(A) to require specific time deadlines for holding the adjudicatory hearing in abuse, neglect, and dependency cases. Specifically in abuse, neglect, and dependency cases, an adjudicatory hearing is to be conducted no later than thirty days after the complaint is filed, with the possibility of a ten day extension for obtaining counsel, and a reasonable time extension to perfect service of process. In any event, the time for the adjudicatory hearing is not to exceed ninety days from the filing of a complaint. Revised Code 2151.28 (amended by S.B. 89).

Masculine references have been replaced by gender neutral language.

Cross References

Arraignment, Crim R 10

Hearing procedure; findings, record, 2151.35

Pleas, rights upon plea, Crim R 11

Library References

Infants ⟲199, 203.

Westlaw Topic No. 211.

C.J.S. Infants §§ 42 to 67.

Am Jur 2d: 47, Juvenile Courts and Delinquent and Dependent Children § 44 to 57

Applicability of rules of evidence in juvenile court proceeding. 43 ALR2d 1128

Giannelli & Snyder, Baldwin's Ohio Practice, Evidence § 615.1, 615.3 (2d ed. 2001).

Carlin, Baldwin's Ohio Practice, Merrick–Rippner Probate Law § 104.1, 104.15, 106.2, 106.5, 106.7, 106.9, 106.12, 106.15, 106.18, 107.12, 107.20, 107.41, 107.43, 107.48, 107.50, 107.51, 107.53, 107.55, 107.56, 107.57, 107.59, 107.60, 107.68, 107.72, 107.79, 107.84, 107.122, 107.173, 108.14 (2003).

Law Review and Journal Commentaries

The Criminal Defense Lawyer in the Juvenile Justice System, David A. Harris. 26 U Tol L Rev 751 (Summer 1995).

Discrimination Perfected to a Science: The Evolution of the Supreme Court's War on Drugs, Note. 30 U Tol L Rev 677 (Summer 1999).

Juvenile Delinquency Proceedings in Ohio: Due Process and the Hearsay Dilemma, Comment. 24 Clev St L Rev 356 (Spring 1975).

Juvenile Delinquent and Unruly Proceedings in Ohio: Unconstitutional Adjudications, Note. 24 Clev St L Rev 602 (1975).

Notes of Decisions

Admissions 4

Bifurcated hearings 5

Consequences of hearing 13

Constitutional issues 3

Delinquency not crime 10

Double jeopardy 8

Evidence and standards 6

Final orders 9

Insanity defense 14

Judge's duty to inform
    In general   15
    Right to counsel   2
Jurisdiction   1
No contest pleas   12
Notice   16
Preservation of error for review   17
Time limitations   7
Waiver of counsel   11

---

1. Jurisdiction

Trial court was without jurisdiction to accept juvenile's admission to aggravated robbery offense and adjudicate him as delinquent, where notice regarding juvenile delinquency proceedings was not given to juvenile's parents. In re Brunner (Ohio App. 4 Dist., Scioto, 03-10-2003) No. 02CA2865, 2003-Ohio-2590, 2003 WL 21152500, Unreported. Infants ☞ 198

The juvenile court has exclusive original jurisdiction, pursuant to RC 2151.23(A), concerning any child who is alleged in a proper complaint to be neglected, and the court does not lose jurisdiction by failing to adhere to the time limits set forth in Juv R 29(A) and 34(A). Linger v. Weiss (Ohio 1979) 57 Ohio St.2d 97, 386 N.E.2d 1354, 11 O.O.3d 281, certiorari denied 100 S.Ct. 128, 444 U.S. 862, 62 L.Ed.2d 83.

2. —Right to counsel, judge's duty to inform

The trial court was not required to inform mother of her right to counsel at hearing to modify custody of child, in child dependency proceeding; Juvenile Rules required the trial court to inform parents of their right to counsel at the adjudicatory hearing, trial court informed mother of her right to counsel at the adjudicatory hearing, and there was no Juvenile Rule regarding counsel for modification of custody hearings. In re Williams (Ohio App. 10 Dist., Franklin, 02-12-2004) No. 03AP-1007, 2004-Ohio-678, 2004 WL 285560, Unreported. Infants ☞ 230.1

Mother in dependency proceedings was not prejudiced by juvenile court's alleged failure to inform parties of the substance of complaint, the purpose of hearing, the possible consequences of hearing prior to adjudicatory hearing, and the right to appeal after the dispositional hearing; mother contested the matter, was represented by counsel at trial, a full hearing was held on the merits, and mother appealed the juvenile court's judgment. In re Malone (Ohio App. 10 Dist., Franklin, 12-30-2003) No. 03AP-489, 2003-Ohio-7156, 2003 WL 23024377, Unreported. Infants ☞ 203

An indigent parent is entitled to a transcript and counsel on appeal from a judgment permanently terminating his parental rights. State ex rel. Heller v. Miller (Ohio 1980) 61 Ohio St.2d 6, 399 N.E.2d 66, 15 O.O.3d 3.

Juvenile court did not abuse its discretion by denying juvenile a continuance, and forcing him to go to trial on rape and attempted rape charges without the presence of his retained lawyer, where length of delay requested was open-ended in a case that had been on docket for almost a year and a half, court had granted other continuances, State would have been forced to subpoena its witnesses again, two of whom were minors who would have had to miss school, assigned visiting judge would have had to travel again from another county, juvenile contributed to need for request, having had at least a month to inform counsel of date of his final adjudicatory hearing, and case had been delayed due to fact that juvenile had changed lawyers four times between his first and last adjudicatory hearings. In re Daniel K.

(Ohio App. 6 Dist., Ottawa, 03-14-2003) No. OT-02-025T-02-023, 2003-Ohio-1409, 2003 WL 1465043, Unreported. Infants ☞ 204

Failure to advise juvenile, who was adjudicated delinquent by reason of rape and attempted rape, of his adjudicatory hearing rights until ultimate stage of his final hearing was reversible error. In re Daniel K. (Ohio App. 6 Dist., Ottawa, 03-14-2003) No. OT-02-025T-02-023, 2003-Ohio-1409, 2003 WL 1465043, Unreported. Infants ☞ 203; Infants ☞ 253

Juvenile court failed to substantially comply with rule requiring court to personally question juvenile defendant concerning voluntariness of admission and advise him of the rights he was waiving by entering admission; although court did question juvenile defendant as to the voluntariness of his admission, court failed to advise juvenile defendant that he was waiving his right to challenge witnesses and evidence against him, the right to remain silent, and the right to introduce evidence. In re Graham (Ohio App. 7 Dist., 05-17-2002) 147 Ohio App.3d 452, 770 N.E.2d 1123, 2002-Ohio-2407. Infants ☞ 174

An adjudication proceeding cannot go forward unless the juvenile is represented by counsel or there has been a valid waiver of the right to counsel. In re Johnston (Ohio App. 11 Dist., 04-30-2001) 142 Ohio App.3d 314, 755 N.E.2d 457. Infants ☞ 205

Juvenile was entitled to representation by counsel in adjudication for vandalism and criminal trespass, where juvenile did not waive his right to counsel, and conviction on charges could result in juvenile having his liberty curtailed. In re Johnston (Ohio App. 11 Dist., 04-30-2001) 142 Ohio App.3d 314, 755 N.E.2d 457. Infants ☞ 205

Child is entitled to counsel at all stages of juvenile proceedings. In re Solis (Ohio App. 8 Dist., 12-22-1997) 124 Ohio App.3d 547, 706 N.E.2d 839. Infants ☞ 205

Juvenile adjudicated delinquent and provisionally placed in foster care was entitled to counsel at dispositional hearing, as provisional placement was not equivalent of probation and dispositional hearing was not equivalent of probation revocation hearing. In re Solis (Ohio App. 8 Dist., 12-22-1997) 124 Ohio App.3d 547, 706 N.E.2d 839. Infants ☞ 205

Magistrate who presided over arraignment in juvenile proceeding failed to adequately inform juvenile of her right to counsel; magistrate discussed right to counsel only in terms of representation if she were to proceed to trial, and gave explanation of right to counsel that was confusing, if not misleading, and could have led juvenile to believe that she was not entitled to counsel while deciding whether to admit or deny complaint. In re Doyle (App. 2 Dist., 10-03-1997) 122 Ohio App.3d 767, 702 N.E.2d 970. Infants ☞ 205

Juvenile court failed to ascertain that juvenile understood charge against her, or possible consequences of admitting it, and thus failed to substantially comply with rule requiring it to make determination that admission by juvenile is being made voluntarily before accepting any admission; record was devoid of any indication that magistrate had determined whether juvenile had understanding of nature of allegations, and while juvenile was told that admission could result in her being placed in custody, no mention was made of possible length of any commitment. In re Doyle (App. 2 Dist., 10-03-1997) 122 Ohio App.3d 767, 702 N.E.2d 970. Infants ☞ 199

Juvenile court failed to make sufficient inquiry, in delinquency proceeding, to determine whether juvenile's waiver of his right to counsel was knowing, intelligent and voluntary, though court addressed group of juveniles collectively as to their right to counsel, where court did not specifically mention in its group address the right to appointment of counsel, court only inquired of juvenile personally as to whether he heard and understood what court said earlier, and court simply gave juvenile and his mother "statement of rights and waiver form" to review and sign. In re Miller (Ohio App. 2 Dist., 04-04-1997) 119 Ohio App.3d 52, 694 N.E.2d 500. Infants ⟜ 205

County children services board was "party" to action in which minor was adjudicated delinquent when board was granted temporary custody of minor and board was thus entitled to appear at dispositional hearing through counsel. In re Lawson (Ohio App. 10 Dist., 11-08-1994) 98 Ohio App.3d 456, 648 N.E.2d 889. Infants ⟜ 200; Infants ⟜ 205

Juvenile rule and statute guarantee right to counsel for all indigent parties in juvenile proceedings. Holley v. Higgins (Franklin 1993) 86 Ohio App.3d 240, 620 N.E.2d 251. Infants ⟜ 205

The guarantee of the right to be represented by counsel set forth in Juv R 4(A) does not, as to a nonindigent party, require that trial be continued indefinitely until counsel can be obtained, but merely requires, if it does not appear that counsel could not be obtained through the exercise of reasonable diligence and a willingness to enter into reasonable contractual arrangements for counsel's services, that a reasonable opportunity be given to the party before trial to employ such counsel. In re Bolden (Allen 1973) 37 Ohio App.2d 7, 306 N.E.2d 166, 66 O.O.2d 26.

A trial court's failure to make a record of an adjudicatory hearing in a stolen car delinquency case in accordance with the mandates of Juv R 37(A) and Juv R 40(D)(2) prevents a finding that an affirmative waiver of the constitutional right to counsel took place, and the trial court magistrate's journal entry, which is the only record of the adjudicatory hearing in question, fails to even minimally satisfy the requirements of Juv R 29 since the magistrate did not check the box indicating whether the juvenile admitted or denied the allegations of the complaint and whether counsel was waived; although the informal detention hearing journal entry sets forth that an express waiver of counsel took place, the journal entry is not adequate evidence of a knowing, voluntary and intelligent waiver of counsel. In re Ward (Ohio App. 8 Dist., Cuyahoga, 06-12-1997) No. 71245, 1997 WL 321492, Unreported.

Juvenile court's failure to advise mother of her rights in dependency proceeding precluded it from accepting mother's plea of true to allegation that she repeatedly struck stepchild, where court did not inform mother of her right to counsel, to remain silent, to cross-examine witnesses, or to offer evidence, court did not inform her that she could request to have a record of the proceedings made at public expense if she were indigent, and court did not ascertain that mother understood consequences of making an admission. (Per O'Neill, P.J., with one judge concurring in judgment only.) In re Calvin, Anthony, Alyshia (Ohio App. 11 Dist., Geauga, 11-22-2002) No. 2001-G-2379, 2002-Ohio-6468, 2002 WL 31663562, Unreported, stay granted 98 Ohio St.3d 1459, 783 N.E.2d 518, 2003-Ohio-644, appeal not allowed 98 Ohio St.3d 1513, 786 N.E.2d 63, 2003-Ohio-1572. Infants ⟜ 199

3. Constitutional issues

Trial court complied with juvenile procedure rule mandates when accepting mother's admissions at adjudication phase of procedure terminating her custody of her children, and thus did not violate mother's due process rights; record indicated mother acknowledged and fully comprehended that by admitting to allegations of abuse in amended complaint, she was waiving her right to challenge witnesses and evidence on that issue, waiving her right to remain silent, and waiving her right to introduce evidence on that issue, trial court read allegations of abuse to mother and asked her if she understood what each allegation and subsequent admission meant, and if mother stated that she did not understand, the trial court explained until mother stated that she understood. In re K.P. (Ohio App. 8 Dist., Cuyahoga, 03-25-2004) No. 82709, 2004-Ohio-1448, 2004 WL 583867, Unreported. Constitutional Law ⟜ 274(5)

Trial counsel's alleged failure to raise issue of juvenile's lack of competence did not establish ineffective assistance in delinquency proceeding in which juvenile admitted that he was guilty of rape, where court was made aware that juvenile was diagnosed as having bipolar disorder and attention deficit hyperactive disorder, record did not indicate and juvenile did not demonstrate that these disorders affected juvenile's understanding of issues involved in case, juvenile was properly informed of consequences of admission of guilt, and juvenile failed to show how he was prejudiced by counsel's actions. In re J. J. (Ohio App. 9 Dist., Summit, 03-24-2004) No. 21386, 2004-Ohio-1429, 2004 WL 574135, Unreported. Infants ⟜ 205

Minor's counsel in delinquency proceeding was not insufficient for failing to raise issue of negligent investigation into charges against minor in a motion to dismiss, where counsel raised the issue at trial by arguing that the investigation harmed the credibility of all of the State's evidence. In re N.K. (Ohio App. 8 Dist., Cuyahoga, 12-24-2003) No. 82332, 2003-Ohio-7059, 2003 WL 23009113, Unreported. Infants ⟜ 205

There was no evidence in the record that testimony from social worker would have aided minor during his delinquency proceeding, and thus, minor's counsel was not insufficient in failing to call social worker as a witness. In re N.K. (Ohio App. 8 Dist., Cuyahoga, 12-24-2003) No. 82332, 2003-Ohio-7059, 2003 WL 23009113, Unreported. Infants ⟜ 205

Mother waived her appellate argument that the trial court committed reversible error when it failed to comply with the Juvenile Procedural rule pertaining to the adjudicatory hearing, during adjudicatory hearing in child dependency proceeding, where mother failed to file a timely notice of appeal regarding any errors that occurred at the adjudicatory hearing. In re C.H. (Ohio App. 8 Dist., Cuyahoga, 12-18-2003) No. 82258, No. 82852, 2003-Ohio-6854, 2003 WL 22966248, Unreported. Infants ⟜ 244.1

Juvenile was not informed that by entering guilty plea to assault he would be waiving other constitutional rights, and thus his guilty plea was not voluntarily and intelligently made, where juvenile was only informed that if he entered plea he would not have the right to a trial. In re Adams (Ohio App. 7 Dist., Mahoning, 07-29-2003) No. 01 CA 237, No. 01 CA 238, No. 02 CA 120, 2003-Ohio-4112, 2003 WL 21783682, Unreported. Infants ⟜ 199

Juvenile understood constitutional rights he would be waiving by entering admission to charge of burglary, for purposes of determining whether his guilty plea was voluntarily and intelligently made, where court asked juvenile if he understood that he had right to trial, that he could make prosecutor prove case against him, that he could cross-examine and confront witnesses, and that he was giving up those rights by pleading, and juvenile said yes; trial court was not required to make additional inquiries following juvenile's affirmative responses. In re Adams (Ohio App. 7 Dist., Mahoning, 07-29-2003) No. 01 CA 237, No. 01 CA 238, No. 02 CA 120, 2003-Ohio-4112, 2003 WL 21783682, Unreported. Infants ⊸ 199

Assuming that mother's counsel was derelict in failing to timely move for appointment of new counsel due to conflict of interest and in failing to follow up on motion, mother did not show prejudice, and thus, mother could not establish ineffective assistance of counsel in proceeding for permanent custody of dependent children; Montgomery County Children Services (MCCS) proved its case by clear and convincing evidence and nothing in record suggested any viable objections. In re Lakes (Ohio App. 2 Dist., 08-02-2002) 149 Ohio App.3d 128, 776 N.E.2d 510, 2002-Ohio-3917. Infants ⊸ 205

If the defendant, in seeking appointment of new counsel, alleges facts which, if true, would require relief, the trial court must inquire into the defendant's complaint and make the inquiry part of the record; the inquiry may be brief and minimal, but it must be made if the allegations are sufficiently specific. In re Lakes (Ohio App. 2 Dist., 08-02-2002) 149 Ohio App.3d 128, 776 N.E.2d 510, 2002-Ohio-3917. Criminal Law ⊸ 641.10(2)

Sixteen-year-old suspect was not in "custody" when he made videotaped confession at police station, as element for requiring *Miranda* warnings before interrogation, where suspect and his father voluntarily accompanied detective to the police station and suspect was not placed under arrest. State v. Noggle (Ohio App. 3 Dist., 09-18-2000) 140 Ohio App.3d 733, 749 N.E.2d 309, 2000-Ohio-1927, appeal allowed 91 Ohio St.3d 1431, 741 N.E.2d 894, appeal dismissed as improvidently granted 91 Ohio St.3d 1280, 747 N.E.2d 827, 2001-Ohio-117. Criminal Law ⊸ 412.2(2); Infants ⊸ 174

Police, by telling 16–year–old suspect that suspect's father was his "legal advisor," did not mislead suspect into believing his right to counsel had been satisfied before he made videotaped confession; rather, police merely told suspect his father could act as his legal counsel if he desired. State v. Noggle (Ohio App. 3 Dist., 09-18-2000) 140 Ohio App.3d 733, 749 N.E.2d 309, 2000-Ohio-1927, appeal allowed 91 Ohio St.3d 1431, 741 N.E.2d 894, appeal dismissed as improvidently granted 91 Ohio St.3d 1280, 747 N.E.2d 827, 2001-Ohio-117. Infants ⊸ 174

Following juvenile's acquittal in delinquency proceeding, Court of Appeals exercised its discretion to review state's challenge to trial court's evidentiary ruling that identification of controlled substance had to be done in laboratory by a chemist, though principles of double jeopardy barred retrial, as issue was capable of repetition yet evading review. In re Bennett (Ohio App. 12 Dist., 09-20-1999) 134 Ohio App.3d 699, 731 N.E.2d 1226. Infants ⊸ 248.1

Guardian ad litem appointed for mother during dependency proceeding by reason of mother's diminished mental capacity lacked authority to consent to waiver of mother's fundamental constitutional rights, and guardian's indication that there was no objection to finding of dependency based upon complaint did not satisfy or lessen magistrate's obligation to ascertain that mother's waiver of her rights was knowing, intelligent and voluntary. In re Etter (Ohio App. 1 Dist., 06-12-1998) 134 Ohio App.3d 484, 731 N.E.2d 694. Infants ⊸ 205

Juvenile was deprived of constitutionally adequate representation on his appeal from his permanent commitment to Department of Youth Services following delinquency adjudication for domestic violence, where his appointed counsel filed *Anders* brief, setting forth conclusion that there was no infirmity in

juvenile's adjudication for drug trafficking, but made no request to withdraw, did not refer to matters of record that might arguably support appeal, and failed to indicate that counsel consulted with, sought advice of, or notified juvenile regarding conclusion that appeal was frivolous. In re Booker (Ohio App. 1 Dist., 03-05-1999) 133 Ohio App.3d 387, 728 N.E.2d 405. Infants ⊸ 241

Dispositional hearing transcript's reference to juvenile court telling juvenile he had been advised of his right to trial at adjudicatory hearing at which his admission was accepted did not substantially comply with mandates of Juvenile Rule 29(D), requiring court to address juvenile personally and determine that admission was being made voluntarily and with understanding of juvenile's rights; it could not be presumed that 14–year–old juvenile would infer that trial encompassed the right to challenge witnesses and evidence against him. In re Royal (Ohio App. 7 Dist., 03-01-1999) 132 Ohio App.3d 496, 725 N.E.2d 685.

Juvenile court magistrate's judgment entry, indicating only a finding that "subject child, after first being advised of all procedural and constitutional rights, including the right to counsel and a continuance herein, asserts said rights and ADMITS the allegations as they appear in the complaint," did not establish under the federal and state due process clauses a valid waiver of counsel or that the admission was voluntarily, knowingly, and intelligently made. In re Royal (Ohio App. 7 Dist., 03-01-1999) 132 Ohio App.3d 496, 725 N.E.2d 685. Constitutional Law ⊸ 43(1); Infants ⊸ 199; Infants ⊸ 205

Juvenile court's limited inquiry at dispositional hearing and 14–year–old juvenile's limited responses, including court's asking whether juvenile recalled the rights explained to him at adjudicatory hearing and juvenile's response, "Um-hum," were insufficient to establish valid admission or valid waiver of right to counsel under the federal and state due process clauses. In re Royal (Ohio App. 7 Dist., 03-01-1999) 132 Ohio App.3d 496, 725 N.E.2d 685. Constitutional Law ⊸ 43(1); Infants ⊸ 199; Infants ⊸ 205

Minor's admission to offense of disorderly conduct was not entered knowingly, voluntarily, and intelligently, as necessary to comport with due process, where trial court did not apprise minor of the nature of charge against her, inform her of possible consequences of her admission, or advise her of rights she would waive by entering admission. In re Fulk (Ohio App. 3 Dist., 08-06-1999) 132 Ohio App.3d 470, 725 N.E.2d 357, 1999-Ohio-840. Constitutional Law ⊸ 255(4); Infants ⊸ 174

Required collection of blood sample for DNA identification purposes from juveniles who are adjudicated delinquent on certain charges does not constitute an unreasonable search and seizure under the Fourth Amendment; reasonable doubt standard for proof of delinquency imposes substantially greater burden than the probable cause standard required for a search warrant, and the minimal intrusion of taking a blood sample is outweighed by state's legitimate interest in recording the identity of a person who is lawfully incarcerated, committed to a secure care facility, or on probation. In re Nicholson (Ohio App. 8 Dist., 02-16-1999) 132 Ohio App.3d 303, 724 N.E.2d 1217, dismissed, appeal not allowed 86 Ohio St.3d 1403, 711 N.E.2d 231. Infants ⊸ 201; Searches And Seizures ⊸ 78

Counsel's examination of his juvenile client during admission colloquy in delinquency proceeding, in apparent attempt to establish juvenile's knowledge that car he had been driving at time of his arrest had been stolen, fell below objective standard of reasonableness, and amounted to ineffective assistance, where juvenile had just contested knowledge element of crime of receiving stolen property. In re Terrance P. (Ohio App. 6 Dist., 08-14-1998) 129 Ohio App.3d 418, 717 N.E.2d 1160. Infants ☞ 205

Juvenile who enters an admission of true to a delinquency count must be informed that he is waiving his right to remain silent at the adjudicatory hearing, in the same manner as an adult criminal defendant who enters guilty plea. In re Onion (Ohio App. 11 Dist., 06-22-1998) 128 Ohio App.3d 498, 715 N.E.2d 604. Infants ☞ 199

Failure of trial court to address juvenile personally to determine whether he understood that he was waiving the privilege against self-incrimination, before accepting juvenile's admission of true on rape count, was reversible error. In re Onion (Ohio App. 11 Dist., 06-22-1998) 128 Ohio App.3d 498, 715 N.E.2d 604. Infants ☞ 199; Infants ☞ 253

Even if juvenile adjudicated delinquent was improperly denied counsel at dispositional hearing, such denial did not mandate or permit reversal of underlying adjudication, where juvenile's counsel was present at adjudication hearing. In re Solis (Ohio App. 8 Dist., 12-22-1997) 124 Ohio App.3d 547, 706 N.E.2d 839. Infants ☞ 254

Trial court did not make determination that juvenile's admission to having received stolen vehicle was knowing, voluntary, and intelligent, as required by due process clause, prior to accepting admission and adjudicating juvenile delinquent; court did not conduct meaningful colloquy with juvenile to ensure that she understood consequences of plea, most of court's references to juvenile were in the third person, and court addressed juvenile directly concerning her rights only briefly, almost as an afterthought. In re Rogers (Ohio App. 9 Dist., 12-10-1997) 124 Ohio App.3d 392, 706 N.E.2d 390. Constitutional Law ☞ 255(4); Infants ☞ 199

Trial court failed to adequately advise juvenile of her right to counsel, where court did not conduct any meaningful colloquy with juvenile, made most of its remarks to juvenile's mother, who had filed unruly child complaint, and addressed child directly only briefly, almost as an afterthought. In re Rogers (Ohio App. 9 Dist., 12-10-1997) 124 Ohio App.3d 392, 706 N.E.2d 390. Infants ☞ 205

Purpose of rule governing initial procedure upon juvenile's entry of admission to charge is to ensure that minors are afforded their due process right to fundamentally fair treatment in juvenile court proceedings. In re Miller (Ohio App. 2 Dist., 04-04-1997) 119 Ohio App.3d 52, 694 N.E.2d 500. Constitutional Law ☞ 255(4)

Juvenile court erroneously adopted referee's report and proposed journal entry indicating that juvenile knowingly and voluntarily waived counsel and entered admission where there was no indication that referee addressed juvenile personally and determined that he understood nature of allegations and consequences of his admission, that juvenile knowingly and intelligently entered admission, or that he understood nature and ramifications of adjudicatory proceedings before he waived counsel and entered admission; referee's report and proposed journal entry consisted of one page with boilerplate language and check-off boxes to indicate proceedings. In re Montgomery (Ohio App. 8 Dist., 01-21-1997) 117 Ohio App.3d 696, 691 N.E.2d 349, dismissed, appeal not allowed 78 Ohio St.3d 1490, 678 N.E.2d 1228. Infants ☞ 206

Trial court violated juvenile's constitutional rights to due process by accepting juvenile's admission to

charge of rape without complying with statutory requirement that court personally address juvenile and determine whether juvenile understood nature of allegations made in complaint or consequences of entering admission to such allegations. In re Beechler (Ohio App. 4 Dist., 07-25-1996) 115 Ohio App.3d 567, 685 N.E.2d 1257. Constitutional Law ☞ 255(4); Infants ☞ 199

General statement that juvenile was waiving right to trial was insufficient to inform 15–year–old that, by entering admission, he was waiving his right to challenge adverse evidence and witnesses. In re Hendrickson (Ohio App. 2 Dist., 09-27-1996) 114 Ohio App.3d 290, 683 N.E.2d 76. Infants ☞ 199

Prior to juvenile's admission to habitual truancy charge, trial court failed to adequately advise juvenile of his constitutional rights and of consequences of his admission and also failed to sufficiently ascertain whether juvenile's purported waiver of counsel was made knowingly and voluntarily; there was no indication in record that trial court ever made determination concerning juvenile's indigency or advised juvenile that he had right to appointed counsel based on his indigency; trial court had merely asked juvenile whether it could be assumed that juvenile wished to proceed without attorney since juvenile was there without attorney, and trial court had not advised juvenile of purpose of hearing, possible penalties for alleged truancy violation, ramifications of admission to charge or of juvenile's rights to remain silent, offer evidence, cross-examine witnesses and have record made of proceedings. In re Kimble (Ohio App. 3 Dist., 09-25-1996) 114 Ohio App.3d 136, 682 N.E.2d 1066. Infants ☞ 199; Infants ☞ 205

Rights dialogue in juvenile proceeding is mandatory, and failure to advise juvenile of constitutionally afforded protections constitutes reversible error. In re Kimble (Ohio App. 3 Dist., 09-25-1996) 114 Ohio App.3d 136, 682 N.E.2d 1066. Infants ☞ 199; Infants ☞ 253

Minor who entered plea of admission to delinquency by reason of rape was denied due process where, although trial court accepting plea established that minor made plea voluntarily, trial court did not substantially comply with rule requiring that court inquire as to whether minor understood nature of charges, consequences of plea, and that minor was waiving certain rights. In re Brooks (Ohio App. 9 Dist., 06-26-1996) 112 Ohio App.3d 54, 677 N.E.2d 1229. Constitutional Law ☞ 255(4); Infants ☞ 199

Juvenile court did not comply with rule setting forth duties to ensure that juveniles are afforded minimum protection under the Constitution; referee failed to ascertain whether notice requirements were met, failed to disclose either purpose of hearing or possible penalties, failed to determine whether juvenile waived his right to counsel voluntarily and failed to inform juvenile of his rights. In re Johnson (Ohio App. 1 Dist., 08-23-1995) 106 Ohio App.3d 38, 665 N.E.2d 247. Infants ☞ 198; Infants ☞ 199; Infants ☞ 205

Representations by juvenile defendant's attorney that defendant understood rights waived and consequences of his plea are not sufficient to demonstrate knowing and voluntary waiver. In re McKenzie (Ohio App. 8 Dist., 03-30-1995) 102 Ohio App.3d 275, 656 N.E.2d 1377. Infants ☞ 199

Acknowledgement on the record by juvenile's counsel that counsel had explained juvenile's rights to juvenile is insufficient to demonstrate knowing and voluntary waiver by juvenile, as the court itself must address juvenile. In re Flynn (Ohio App. 8 Dist., 05-25-1995) 101 Ohio App.3d 778, 656 N.E.2d 737. Infants ☞ 199

Juvenile's signing of waiver of rights form does not constitute substitute for the court's duty to address the juvenile. In re Flynn (Ohio App. 8 Dist., 05-25-1995) 101 Ohio App.3d 778, 656 N.E.2d 737. Infants ⟐ 199

At hearing to accept juvenile's admission to charges of resisting arrest and unauthorized use of motor vehicle, juvenile court violated rule governing acceptance of juvenile admissions and denied juvenile due process, where juvenile court failed to determine whether juvenile was making admission voluntarily and failed to determine whether juvenile understood that by entering admission, he was waiving his right to challenge witnesses and evidence against him, his right to remain silent, and his right to introduce evidence. In re Christopher R. (Ohio App. 6 Dist., 06-16-1995) 101 Ohio App.3d 245, 655 N.E.2d 280. Constitutional Law ⟐ 255(4); Infants ⟐ 199

There are no constitutional violations in an adjudicatory hearing held pursuant to Juv R 29 when the court uses evidence of guilt that was presented at the preliminary hearing where the accused was afforded cross-examination of witnesses. Matter of Gantt (Wood 1978) 61 Ohio App.2d 44, 398 N.E.2d 800, 15 O.O.3d 67.

An alleged delinquent child should be specifically advised by the court concerning his right not to testify in his own behalf, that any statement made by him may be used against him, and that a refusal to testify may not be held against him. In re Collins (Cuyahoga 1969) 20 Ohio App.2d 319, 253 N.E.2d 824, 49 O.O.2d 448. Infants ⟐ 191

Where a juvenile has received the following essentials of due process and fair treatment: (1) written notice of the specific charge or factual allegations given to the juvenile and his parents or guardian sufficiently in advance of the hearing to permit preparation; (2) notification to the juvenile and his parents of the juvenile's right to be represented by counsel retained by them, or, if they are unable to afford counsel, that counsel will be appointed to represent the juvenile; (3) application of the constitutional privileges against self-incrimination; and (4), absent a valid confession, a determination of delinquency and an order of commitment based only on sworn testimony subjected to the opportunity for cross-examination in accordance with constitutional requirements, such juvenile has not been deprived of due process under either the Constitution of the United States or the Constitution of the State of Ohio. (Annotation from former RC 2151.35.) In re Baker (Hocking 1969) 18 Ohio App.2d 276, 248 N.E.2d 620, 47 O.O.2d 411.

Juvenile defendant waived any right to confront the witnesses against him when he entered an admission to raping his six year old half sister. In re Panko (Ohio App. 12 Dist., Brown, 05-13-2002) No. CA2001-05-008, 2002-Ohio-2306, 2002 WL 975135, Unreported.

Juvenile defendant, who admitted raping six year old half sister, waived his right to challenge on appeal evidentiary issues, including a motion to suppress. In re Panko (Ohio App. 12 Dist., Brown, 05-13-2002) No. CA2001-05-008, 2002-Ohio-2306, 2002 WL 975135, Unreported.

The trial court errs in failing to inform the parent of her rights to remain silent, to cross-examine witnesses, and to offer evidence at the adjudicatory hearing and in granting permanent custody when no guardian ad litem's report is filed with the court. Matter of Eplin (Ohio App. 5 Dist., Stark, 06-29-1995) No. 94 CA 0311, 1995 WL 495451, Unreported.

A juvenile court errs when it revokes a juvenile's probation status without affording the right to counsel at the dispositional hearing and by failing to provide the opportunity to secure counsel for the probation revocation hearing where (1) the juvenile pleads true at the adjudication hearing and is not informed of right to counsel, (2) there is no inquiry into the desire for counsel, and (3) there is no indication of a waiver of right to counsel. In re Sproule, Nos. 00CA007575 and 00CA007580, 2001 WL 39594 (9th Dist Ct App, Lorain, 1–17–01).

Juvenile who was adjudicated delinquent by reason of rape lacked standing to challenge constitutionality of juvenile sex offender registration and notification law on basis that law deprived juveniles of a jury trial for sexual offender designations, where the law was not applied to juvenile in case. In re Nooks (Ohio App. 2 Dist., Montgomery, 10-25-2002) No. 19374, 2002-Ohio-5824, 2002 WL 31398607, Unreported. Constitutional Law ⟐ 42.1(1)

Juvenile court's continued exercise of jurisdiction over juvenile regarding his parole violation in delinquency matter, when the parole violation was committed by juvenile when he was 19, was not an act of discrimination treating juvenile differently from other adults, but, rather, an act recognizing juvenile's ongoing status as a juvenile; pursuant to statute, juvenile court retained jurisdiction over the juvenile, who was adjudicated delinquent prior to age of 18, until he turned 21. In re Gillespie (Ohio App. 10 Dist., 12-19-2002) 150 Ohio App.3d 502, 782 N.E.2d 140, 2002-Ohio-7025, appeal not allowed 98 Ohio St.3d 1513, 786 N.E.2d 63, 2003-Ohio-1572. Infants ⟐ 281

Juvenile court's continued exercise of jurisdiction over juvenile in delinquency matter, after juvenile committed parole violation when he was 19 years old, did not arbitrarily or capriciously deny juvenile's right to bail in violation of due process, although common pleas court had released juvenile on bail on the adult charges underlying parole violation while juvenile court revoked juvenile's parole and returned him to custody; common pleas court's exercise of power over juvenile with respect to adult charges did not eviscerate juvenile court's coexisting power to hold juvenile pursuant to his parole violation, and juvenile had no absolute constitutional right to bail as a juvenile. In re Gillespie (Ohio App. 10 Dist., 12-19-2002) 150 Ohio App.3d 502, 782 N.E.2d 140, 2002-Ohio-7025, appeal not allowed 98 Ohio St.3d 1513, 786 N.E.2d 63, 2003-Ohio-1572. Constitutional Law ⟐ 255(4); Infants ⟐ 281

In delinquency matter, a juvenile is not entitled to indictment by grand jury, to a public trial, or to trial by jury. In re Gillespie (Ohio App. 10 Dist., 12-19-2002) 150 Ohio App.3d 502, 782 N.E.2d 140, 2002-Ohio-7025, appeal not allowed 98 Ohio St.3d 1513, 786 N.E.2d 63, 2003-Ohio-1572. Infants ⟐ 197; Infants ⟐ 203; Jury ⟐ 19.5

A juvenile has no absolute constitutional right to bail in a delinquency case. In re Gillespie (Ohio App. 10 Dist., 12-19-2002) 150 Ohio App.3d 502, 782 N.E.2d 140, 2002-Ohio-7025, appeal not allowed 98 Ohio St.3d 1513, 786 N.E.2d 63, 2003-Ohio-1572. Infants ⟐ 134

The exclusion on Fourth Amendment grounds of the contents of a fourteen-year-old schoolgirl's purse from delinquency proceedings is erroneous where a teacher discovered the pupil smoking in violation of school rules inasmuch as (1) the teacher's report supported a suspicion on the part of the principal that the pupil had violated school rules; (2) the principal's suspicion gave him reason to suspect the pupil had cigarettes in her purse, her denials notwithstanding, and a search of the purse for cigarettes was, therefore, proper; (3) the discovery in plain view of rolling papers on removal of the cigarette pack gave the principal reason to suspect the presence of marijuana; and (4) reasonable suspicion of the presence of marijuana justified a thorough search which turned up marijuana, letters implicating the pupil in dope dealing, and other evidence of drug-related activities. (Annotation from US Const Am 4.) New Jersey v. T.L.O. (U.S.N.J. 1985) 105 S.Ct. 733, 469 U.S. 325, 83 L.Ed.2d 720.

Juveniles who are charged with felony crimes are not entitled to a jury trial because the applicable due process standard for juvenile proceedings is fundamental fairness, and a jury, is not necessary for adequate factfinding. McKeiver v. Pennsylvania (U.S.Pa. 1971) 91 S.Ct. 1976, 403 U.S. 528, 29 L.Ed.2d 647.

A juvenile taken into custody as a delinquent has certain rights guaranteed by the Due Process Clause of the United States Constitution in delinquency proceedings by the state which include the following: (1) notice of the charge, (2) right to counsel, (3) right to confrontation and cross-examination, and (4) privilege against self incrimination. Application of Gault (U.S.Ariz. 1967) 87 S.Ct. 1428, 387 U.S. 1, 18 L.Ed.2d 527, 40 O.O.2d 378.

Under the present Juvenile Code and Rules, a juvenile court cannot change a "temporary" commitment to the Ohio youth commission to an "permanent" commitment without hearing; further, the commitment of an unruly child, not declared "delinquent", is a violation of due process and any hearing held on the above matters requires the presence of the youth involved. OAG 72–071.

4. Admissions

Trial court substantially complied with requirements of rule related to acceptance of admission of guilt in juvenile delinquency proceeding, where court questioned juvenile concerning his awareness of charge against him, possible penalties stemming from admission, and rights he would be waiving by entering admission, and there was nothing to support contention that juvenile did not understand implications of entering guilty plea. In re J. J. (Ohio App. 9 Dist., Summit, 03-24-2004) No. 21386, 2004-Ohio-1429, 2004 WL 574135, Unreported. Infants ⟳ 199

Trial court order granting children services temporary custody of mother's two children was not an abuse of discretion; mother was a heavy prescription drug user, she had been arrested four times in the past three years, she missed several counseling appointments and was terminated from services, and she refused to comply with the case management plan. In re Barnosky (Ohio App. 4 Dist., Athens, 03-09-2004) No. 03CA32, 2004-Ohio-1127, 2004 WL 444527, Unreported. Infants ⟳ 154.1

Magistrate's acceptance of minor's admission to charge in delinquency complaint was not plain error; minor was represented by counsel when she entered her admission, no guardian ad litem was required, and minor agreed with magistrate's statements concerning minor's understanding of circumstances of her offense, consequences of an admission, and the voluntariness of her acceptance of responsibility without any apparent hesitation, confusion, or misgivings. In re Harper (Ohio App. 2 Dist., Montgomery, 12-12-2003) No. 19948, 2003-Ohio-6666, 2003 WL 22927248, Unreported. Infants ⟳ 243

Evidence supported trial court finding that juvenile's admission to gross sexual imposition and rape was knowing, intelligent, and voluntary; juvenile's responses to magistrate during plea colloquy were appropriate, and there was no evidence that juvenile's admission was other than knowing and volun-

tary. In re J.W. (Ohio App. 2 Dist., Montgomery, 09-26-2003) No. 19869, 2003-Ohio-5096, 2003 WL 22220345, Unreported. Infants ⟳ 199

Juvenile gained understanding of factual circumstances surrounding charges of burglary from juvenile's counsel, despite trial court's failure to explain elements of burglary, for purposes of determining whether his guilty plea was voluntarily and intelligently made, where counsel stated he had gone through the factual bases with juvenile, and juvenile stated he understood what his lawyer stated regarding the charges. In re Adams (Ohio App. 7 Dist., Mahoning, 07-29-2003) No. 01 CA 237, No. 01 CA 238, No. 02 CA 120, 2003-Ohio-4112, 2003 WL 21783682, Unreported. Infants ⟳ 199

Trial court adequately determined that juvenile entered admission voluntarily and with an understanding of the nature of the allegations against him and the consequences of the admission; juvenile heard from prosecutor all the charges for which the hearing was called, as well as the purpose of the proceedings, prosecutor then gave an extensive recitation of all the specifics of each offense before juvenile admitted them, and trial court verified that juvenile understood rights he was giving up, that his thinking was clear, and that he had no questions about the proceeding. State v. D.M. (Ohio App. 8 Dist., Cuyahoga, 06-19-2003) No. 81641, 2003-Ohio-3228, 2003 WL 21419595, Unreported. Infants ⟳ 199

Because hearing regarding motion to modify temporary custody to permanent custody was a dispositional hearing, rather than an adjudicatory hearing, juvenile court rule setting forth procedures to be followed by trial court upon filing of a complaint and its resolution by admission did not apply. In re L.D. (Ohio App. 8 Dist., Cuyahoga, 05-15-2003) No. 81397, 2003-Ohio-2471, 2003 WL 21101101, Unreported. Infants ⟳ 230.1

Complaint and summons in juvenile delinquency proceeding did not have to provide notice of potential disposition that juvenile could be placed in foster care; juvenile rule only required that trial court advise juvenile, prior to accepting an admission to complaint, of nature of allegations and consequences of admission, including possible dispositions. In re Hutzel (Ohio App. 5 Dist., Tuscarawas, 04-29-2003) No. 2002AP110087, 2003-Ohio-2288, 2003 WL 21025820, Unreported. Infants ⟳ 198

Prior to accepting juvenile's admission to offense of gross sexual imposition, trial court failed to determine whether juvenile fully understood consequences of his admission, thus mandating reversal of delinquency adjudication, even though trial court asked juvenile if he understood that he would have been subject to a six-month minimum term of commitment and juvenile replied affirmatively, where court failed to inform him of any maximum potential term of commitment available, juvenile was not entering admission to avoid prosecution as an adult, he was only 16 at time of hearing, and proceeding was conducted in an abrupt manner. In re A.H. (Ohio App. 8 Dist., Cuyahoga, 04-17-2003) No. 81214, 2003-Ohio-1953, 2003 WL 1900952, Unreported. Infants ⟳ 253

Revocation of juvenile's probation on two counts of raping his younger sister, following hearing at which juvenile moved unsuccessfully to withdraw his admission to those offenses based on allegations that his parents had coerced him into making admission, was not abuse of discretion; juvenile had repeatedly been brought back into court and warned that he would be sent to Department of Youth Services if his improper behavior did not cease, and he did not present adequate evidence to support allegations of coercion by parents. In re McElfresh (Ohio App. 7 Dist., Belmont, 03-07-2003) No. 02 BA 12, 2003-Ohio-1079, 2003 WL 932342, Unreported. Infants ⊛ 225

Denial of juvenile's motion to withdraw admission to two counts of raping his younger sister, brought on basis of allegation that juvenile's parents coerced him into making admission, was not abuse of discretion in view of insufficient supporting evidence; while juvenile testified that his parents were engaging in sexual activity with him and his siblings and that they advised him to enter an admission, he did not testify that they coerced into following that advice by engaging in sexual activity or any other means. In re McElfresh (Ohio App. 7 Dist., Belmont, 03-07-2003) No. 02 BA 12, 2003-Ohio-1079, 2003 WL 932342, Unreported. Infants ⊛ 199

Juvenile court failed to substantially comply with rule governing acceptance of admissions during neglected child proceedings, where it failed to question father in order to determine whether his admission was voluntary or inform him that by admitting to the neglect charge the court could terminate his parental rights. In re Aldridge (Ohio App. 4 Dist., Ross, 10-30-2002) No. 02CA2661, 2002-Ohio-5988, 2002 WL 31439807, Unreported. Infants ⊛ 199

Biological mother's surrender of parental rights over four of her children was voluntary, despite fact that she made it in return for dismissal of permanent custody motion as to one of her five children; trial court engaged in discussion with her concerning this promise, and mother indicated that she desired to surrender permanent custody as to other four children in exchange for this promise. In re White Children (Ohio App. 5 Dist., Stark, 10-28-2002) No. 2002CA00216, 2002-Ohio-5949, 2002 WL 31426250, Unreported. Infants ⊛ 157

Court complied with rule requiring it to address biological mother personally and to conduct discussion to determine whether her admission was entered knowingly and voluntarily prior to accepting stipulation regarding permanent custody of four of her children by county agency; record reflected court advised mother of options available to her, explained procedure, explained meaning of permanent custody, and mother acknowledged that she understood. In re White Children (Ohio App. 5 Dist., Stark, 10-28-2002) No. 2002CA00216, 2002-Ohio-5949, 2002 WL 31426250, Unreported. Infants ⊛ 199

Juvenile procedural rule's mandate that a juvenile's failure or refusal to admit allegations shall be deemed a denial barred trial court from accepting juvenile's *Alford* plea, in delinquency proceeding in which it was alleged that juvenile had committed two counts of rape of a child under 13, as juvenile made no admission of culpability, which had to be deemed a denial. In re Kirby (Ohio, 03-17-2004) 101 Ohio St.3d 312, 804 N.E.2d 476, 2004-Ohio-970. Infants ⊛ 199

Waiver by minor mother's counsel of mother's appearance at adjudication hearing in child dependency proceeding did not involve an "admission" by mother and thus did not implicate juvenile procedure rule that prohibits a court from accepting an admission from a juvenile unless it addresses the party personally. In re Baby Girl Doe (Ohio App. 6 Dist., 08-30-2002) 149 Ohio App.3d 717, 778 N.E.2d 1053, 2002-Ohio-4470, appeal not allowed 97 Ohio St.3d 1425, 777 N.E.2d 278, 2002-Ohio-5820. Infants ⊛ 199

The best method for the trial court to comply with rule requiring court to personally question juvenile concerning voluntariness of admission and knowing waiver of rights is to use the language of the rule itself, carefully tailored to the child's level of understanding, stopping after each right and asking whether the child understands the right and knows that he is waiving it by entering an admission. In re Graham (Ohio App. 7 Dist., 05-17-2002) 147 Ohio App.3d 452, 770 N.E.2d 1123, 2002-Ohio-2407. Infants ⊛ 174

Juvenile court's attempt, at dispositional hearing, to remedy its failure at adjudication hearing to advise juvenile defendant of the rights he was waiving by entering admission, was inadequate; court was required to advise juvenile defendant of his rights before accepting his admission, not after. In re Graham (Ohio App. 7 Dist., 05-17-2002) 147 Ohio App.3d 452, 770 N.E.2d 1123, 2002-Ohio-2407. Infants ⊛ 174

To satisfy requirements of rule governing acceptance of juvenile admissions, court must address juvenile personally and conduct an on-the-record discussion to determine whether admission is being entered knowingly and voluntarily. In re Holcomb (Ohio App. 8 Dist., 02-04-2002) 147 Ohio App.3d 31, 768 N.E.2d 722, 2002-Ohio-2042. Infants ⊛ 174

Although strict compliance with rule governing acceptance of juvenile admissions is not required, courts must substantially comply with procedures specified therein. In re Holcomb (Ohio App. 8 Dist., 02-04-2002) 147 Ohio App.3d 31, 768 N.E.2d 722, 2002-Ohio-2042. Infants ⊛ 174

Fact that juvenile court intermingled acceptance of juvenile's plea with that of his brother did not mean that court failed to personally address juvenile, as required by rule governing acceptance of juvenile admissions, where court individually addressed each brother after each major component of its colloquy. In re Holcomb (Ohio App. 8 Dist., 02-04-2002) 147 Ohio App.3d 31, 768 N.E.2d 722, 2002-Ohio-2042. Infants ⊛ 174

Juvenile court properly determined whether juvenile made his admissions voluntarily by inquiring as to whether he was under influence of any alcohol or drugs that would cloud his judgment and whether anybody made any promises or threats to force either him to make admissions. In re Holcomb (Ohio App. 8 Dist., 02-04-2002) 147 Ohio App.3d 31, 768 N.E.2d 722, 2002-Ohio-2042. Infants ⊛ 174

Trial court properly made determination as to whether juvenile, who made an admission, understood charges against him, where state had read charges into record and provided detailed summary of evidence against juvenile. In re Holcomb (Ohio App. 8 Dist., 02-04-2002) 147 Ohio App.3d 31, 768 N.E.2d 722, 2002-Ohio-2042. Infants ⊛ 174

Juvenile court failed to substantially comply with rule governing acceptance of juvenile admissions, where it failed to inform juvenile of term of his possible commitment. In re Holcomb (Ohio App. 8 Dist., 02-04-2002) 147 Ohio App.3d 31, 768 N.E.2d 722, 2002-Ohio-2042. Infants ⊛ 174

The determination of whether a party's admission at a juvenile adjudicatory hearing complies with the governing juvenile rule is similar to that used in determining whether a criminal defendant's guilty plea complies with the governing criminal rule. In re Clark (Ohio App. 8 Dist., 01-29-2001) 141 Ohio App.3d 55, 749 N.E.2d 833, 2001-Ohio-4126. Infants ⊛ 174

Family court judge conducting proceedings on county Department of Child and Family Services' (DCFS) petition for permanent custody of mother's three children substantially complied with rule governing admissions at juvenile adjudicatory hearings; judge explained mother's rights at initial hearing, she was represented by lawyer throughout proceedings, when judge personally addressed mother at hearing at which she admitted allegations of amended complaint he asked her specifically, inter alia, whether she had discussed case with her attorney and whether she understood that her admission would result in finding of neglect, and mother indicated her understanding of these consequences in presence of attorney. In re Clark (Ohio App. 8 Dist., 01-29-2001) 141 Ohio App.3d 55, 749 N.E.2d 833, 2001-Ohio-4126. Infants ⟜ 174

Magistrate's questions to counsel for parties to dependency proceeding, asking whether modification of one word in complaint was acceptable, and then whether there was any objection to her making adjudication of dependency based upon stipulation to complaint as amended, did not satisfy her obligation to determine whether mother was making knowing, intelligent and voluntary admission to facts; magistrate never addressed mother personally, and made no real inquiry into whether mother understood nature of charges in complaint, consequences of making admission to facts, or rights she would be waiving as consequence of admission. In re Etter (Ohio App. 1 Dist., 06-12-1998) 134 Ohio App.3d 484, 731 N.E.2d 694. Infants ⟜ 199

Magistrate's failure, in dependency proceeding, to satisfy her obligation to determine whether mother was making knowing, intelligent and voluntary admission to facts in complaint was plain error, and mother's failure to object thereto did not waive appellate review of magistrate's failure to comply with applicable rule. In re Etter (Ohio App. 1 Dist., 06-12-1998) 134 Ohio App.3d 484, 731 N.E.2d 694. Infants ⟜ 243

Presence of 14–year–old juvenile's mother at the adjudicatory hearing did not provide dispositive proof that the juvenile waived his rights and gave his admission voluntarily, knowingly, and intelligently. In re Royal (Ohio App. 7 Dist., 03-01-1999) 132 Ohio App.3d 496, 725 N.E.2d 685. Infants ⟜ 199; Infants ⟜ 205

A waiver form is not a valid substitute for the court's duty to personally address the juvenile and determine that the admission is being made voluntarily and with an understanding of the juvenile's rights. In re Royal (Ohio App. 7 Dist., 03-01-1999) 132 Ohio App.3d 496, 725 N.E.2d 685. Infants ⟜ 199

Judgment entry of disposition, which merely stated that "upon inquiry, the 'Juvenile' Court finds said plea was entered voluntarily and intelligently and the Court accepts the same and affirms the decision submitted by the Magistrate," did not substantially comply with mandates of Juvenile Rule 29(D), requiring court to address juvenile personally and determine that admission was being made voluntarily and with understanding of juvenile's rights. In re Royal (Ohio App. 7 Dist., 03-01-1999) 132 Ohio App.3d 496, 725 N.E.2d 685. Infants ⟜ 199

Court would not presume regularity of adjudicatory hearing at which 14–year–old juvenile's admission was accepted, where juvenile was unrepresented by counsel at the hearing and nothing in the record indicated that juvenile court complied with the juvenile rules by informing juvenile of his rights if he waived counsel, including the right to request a transcript of any of the proceedings. In re Royal (Ohio App. 7 Dist., 03-01-1999) 132 Ohio App.3d 496, 725 N.E.2d 685. Infants ⟜ 250

If the juvenile court fails to substantially comply with Juvenile Rule 29(D), requiring the court to address the juvenile personally and determine that the admission is being made voluntarily and with an understanding of the juvenile's rights, the adjudica-

tion must be reversed so that the juvenile may plead anew. In re Royal (Ohio App. 7 Dist., 03-01-1999) 132 Ohio App.3d 496, 725 N.E.2d 685.

Requirement that juvenile who admitted delinquency on charge of gross sexual imposition provide a DNA sample was not a "consequence" of the admission of which trial court was obligated to inform him prior to accepting the admission; requirement was remedial and did not have a direct and immediate effect upon the range of juvenile's punishment. In re Nicholson (Ohio App. 8 Dist., 02-16-1999) 132 Ohio App.3d 303, 724 N.E.2d 1217, dismissed, appeal not allowed 86 Ohio St.3d 1403, 711 N.E.2d 231. Infants ⟜ 199

Whether State Department of Youth Services could properly require that juvenile provide blood sample for DNA identification, after failing to inform him of that requirement when he admitted his delinquency on charge of gross sexual imposition, was waived in proceeding to enjoin department from taking blood sample, where juvenile failed to seek a withdrawal of his admission. In re Nicholson (Ohio App. 8 Dist., 02-16-1999) 132 Ohio App.3d 303, 724 N.E.2d 1217, dismissed, appeal not allowed 86 Ohio St.3d 1403, 711 N.E.2d 231. Infants ⟜ 243

For purposes of determining voluntariness, juvenile's admission in delinquency proceeding is analogous to guilty plea made by adult in criminal proceeding and constitutes waiver of rights to challenge allegations in complaint. In re Terrance P. (Ohio App. 6 Dist., 08-14-1998) 129 Ohio App.3d 418, 717 N.E.2d 1160. Infants ⟜ 199

Court's initial questioning of juvenile concerning his understanding of charges against him in delinquency proceeding prior to explaining such charges was attempt to ascertain whether juvenile understood charges, rather than acceptance of his admissions to those charges, despite fact that juvenile's responses to questions were phrased as admissions, and juvenile's responses therefore did not amount to unknowing or involuntary waiver of his right to challenge allegations in complaint. In re Terrance P. (Ohio App. 6 Dist., 08-14-1998) 129 Ohio App.3d 418, 717 N.E.2d 1160. Infants ⟜ 199

Juvenile's challenge to knowledge element of crime of receiving stolen property with which he was charged in delinquency complaint invalidated his subsequent admission thereto; juvenile stated, in response to questioning by court, that he did not know car he had been driving at time of his arrest was stolen because insurance papers were in glove compartment. In re Terrance P. (Ohio App. 6 Dist., 08-14-1998) 129 Ohio App.3d 418, 717 N.E.2d 1160. Infants ⟜ 199

To comply with juvenile rule governing acceptance of admission by youth, court must address the youth personally and conduct an on-the-record discussion to determine whether the admission is being entered knowingly and voluntarily. In re West (Ohio App. 8 Dist., 06-15-1998) 128 Ohio App.3d 356, 714 N.E.2d 988. Infants ⟜ 199

Trial court improperly accepted juvenile's admission to burglary, even though court personally addressed juvenile, where there was only minimal discussion of charged offense and possible penalties, a cursory discussion of juvenile's right to counsel, and no discussion regarding the rights juvenile was waiving by entering admission. In re West (Ohio App. 8 Dist., 06-15-1998) 128 Ohio App.3d 356, 714 N.E.2d 988. Infants ⟜ 199

Absent a showing of prejudice, appellate court will not disturb admission by youth on appeal if trial court substantially complied with juvenile rule governing acceptance of admissions; test for prejudice is whether admission would otherwise have been made. In re West (Ohio App. 8 Dist., 06-15-1998) 128 Ohio App.3d 356, 714 N.E.2d 988. Infants ⟋ 253

Failure of juvenile court to substantially comply with rule requiring it to make determination that admission is being made voluntarily before accepting any admission has prejudicial effect necessitating reversal of adjudication, so that juvenile may plead anew. In re Doyle (App. 2 Dist., 10-03-1997) 122 Ohio App.3d 767, 702 N.E.2d 970. Infants ⟋ 205; Infants ⟋ 253

Juvenile court failed, during delinquency proceeding, to substantially comply with required procedures for accepting juvenile's admission to rape charge, where court only addressed group of juveniles regarding what rights they would be giving up if they entered admission to charge, no such colloquy was repeated when court addressed juvenile personally, and court merely asked whether juvenile had heard and understood what court previously said, asked both juvenile and his mother if juvenile understood his rights and knew what he was doing and provided juvenile and mother with "statement of rights and waiver form" which, while informing juvenile of his rights, did not specifically state that juvenile would waive those rights by entering admission. In re Miller (Ohio App. 2 Dist., 04-04-1997) 119 Ohio App.3d 52, 694 N.E.2d 500. Infants ⟋ 199

Best method for juvenile court to satisfy its obligations, in delinquency proceeding, under rule setting forth initial procedure upon entry of admission to charge is to use language contained in the rule, though carefully tailored to child's level of understanding, stopping after each right and asking whether child understands right and knows that he is waiving it by entering admission; absent that form of colloquy, substantial compliance with rule must be clearly demonstrated. In re Miller (Ohio App. 2 Dist., 04-04-1997) 119 Ohio App.3d 52, 694 N.E.2d 500. Infants ⟋ 199

Failure of juvenile court in delinquency proceeding to comply, at least substantially, with requirements of rule setting forth initial procedure upon entry of admission to charge constitutes reversible error. In re Miller (Ohio App. 2 Dist., 04-04-1997) 119 Ohio App.3d 52, 694 N.E.2d 500. Infants ⟋ 199; Infants ⟋ 253

Trial court violates rule governing adjudicatory hearings in delinquency proceedings if it accepts juvenile's admission of delinquency when trial court did not address juvenile personally to determine if he understood consequences of his admission and rights waived. In re Montgomery (Ohio App. 8 Dist., 01-21-1997) 117 Ohio App.3d 696, 691 N.E.2d 349, dismissed, appeal not allowed 78 Ohio St.3d 1490, 678 N.E.2d 1228. Infants ⟋ 199

Prior to accepting juvenile's admission to delinquency complaint, juvenile court must personally address actual juvenile before court and determine that juvenile, and not merely attorney, understands nature of allegations and consequences of entering admission, and test for accused delinquent's understanding of charges is subjective, such that juvenile must actually understand. In re Beechler (Ohio App. 4 Dist., 07-25-1996) 115 Ohio App.3d 567, 685 N.E.2d 1257. Infants ⟋ 199

Juvenile court's failure to substantially comply with statutory requirements for accepting juvenile's admission constitutes prejudicial error that requires reversal of adjudication in order to permit party to plead anew. In re Beechler (Ohio App. 4 Dist., 07-25-1996) 115 Ohio App.3d 567, 685 N.E.2d 1257. Infants ⟋ 199; Infants ⟋ 253

Lack of substantial compliance with requirements for accepting juvenile's admission requires reversal of delinquency adjudication and opportunity for juvenile to plead anew. In re Hendrickson (Ohio App. 2 Dist., 09-27-1996) 114 Ohio App.3d 290, 683 N.E.2d 76. Infants ⟋ 199; Infants ⟋ 253

Juvenile court was required, under rule requiring court to inform juvenile of "consequences" of admission, to tell juvenile that he faced potential commitment of up to six years in legal custody of Department of Youth Services. In re Hendrickson (Ohio App. 2 Dist., 09-27-1996) 114 Ohio App.3d 290, 683 N.E.2d 76. Infants ⟋ 199

Admission in delinquency case involves waiver of juvenile's right to challenge allegations of complaint and to confront witnesses. In re Brooks (Ohio App. 9 Dist., 06-26-1996) 112 Ohio App.3d 54, 677 N.E.2d 1229. Infants ⟋ 199

Before accepting admission of guilt to charge of delinquency, trial court must personally address juvenile on record with respect to areas of inquiry set forth in rule and may accept juvenile's admission only upon court's substantial compliance with rule; in absence of such compliance, adjudication must be reversed and juvenile permitted to plead again. In re Brooks (Ohio App. 9 Dist., 06-26-1996) 112 Ohio App.3d 54, 677 N.E.2d 1229. Infants ⟋ 199; Infants ⟋ 253

Trial court is required to substantially comply with juvenile rule setting forth procedure for acceptance of admission of criminal conduct, and strict scrutiny is not required. In re William H. (Ohio App. 6 Dist., 08-18-1995) 105 Ohio App.3d 761, 664 N.E.2d 1361. Infants ⟋ 199

Referee in juvenile delinquency proceeding erred when he failed to comply with juvenile rule stating that court shall not accept admission without determining if party understands that, by entering admission, party is waiving the right to challenge witnesses and evidence, to remain silent, and to introduce evidence at adjudicatory hearing, but this error was neither prejudicial nor plain since juvenile was given due process in these proceedings. In re Harris (Ohio App. 2 Dist., 05-05-1995) 104 Ohio App.3d 324, 662 N.E.2d 34. Constitutional Law ⟋ 255(4); Infants ⟋ 199; Infants ⟋ 253

Juvenile rule stating that court, in juvenile delinquency proceedings, shall not accept admission without determining that party understands that, by entering admission, party is waiving the right to challenge witnesses and evidence and to remain silent was drafted in order to satisfy due process and fairness requirements for juveniles in juvenile court proceedings. In re Harris (Ohio App. 2 Dist., 05-05-1995) 104 Ohio App.3d 324, 662 N.E.2d 34. Constitutional Law ⟋ 255(4); Infants ⟋ 199

Referee in juvenile delinquency hearing substantially complied with juvenile rule stating that court shall not accept admission without determining if party is making admission voluntarily with understanding of nature of the allegations and consequences of the admission; immediately after plea negotiation took place, referee asked juvenile "By admitting to these you are in fact stating you are responsible for these charges. Do you understand that?" and juvenile replied "yes" and later in the proceedings, juvenile's attorney stated that juvenile was "aware of the results of the plea." In re Harris (Ohio App. 2 Dist., 05-05-1995) 104 Ohio App.3d 324, 662 N.E.2d 34. Infants ⟋ 199

Trial court improperly accepted youth's admission to amended complaint alleging attempted receipt of stolen property without addressing him personally to ascertain whether he understood consequences of admission or rights he was waiving. In re McKenzie (Ohio App. 8 Dist., 03-30-1995) 102 Ohio App.3d 275, 656 N.E.2d 1377. Infants ⟂ 199

Prosecutor must affirmatively demonstrate that judge addressed youth personally and conducted on-the-record exchange to determine whether admission was knowing and voluntary. In re McKenzie (Ohio App. 8 Dist., 03-30-1995) 102 Ohio App.3d 275, 656 N.E.2d 1377. Infants ⟂ 199

As in criminal case in which defendant offers plea of guilty, juvenile court must make careful inquiry before accepting admission in juvenile case. In re Flynn (Ohio App. 8 Dist., 05-25-1995) 101 Ohio App.3d 778, 656 N.E.2d 737. Infants ⟂ 199

While admission in juvenile case is not deemed to be guilty plea under rules governing pleas in criminal cases, it is a waiver of the right to challenge the allegations raised in the complaint. In re Flynn (Ohio App. 8 Dist., 05-25-1995) 101 Ohio App.3d 778, 656 N.E.2d 737. Infants ⟂ 199

Court of Appeals' review of juvenile adjudication hearing is similar to its review of entry of guilty plea in criminal case. In re Flynn (Ohio App. 8 Dist., 05-25-1995) 101 Ohio App.3d 778, 656 N.E.2d 737. Infants ⟂ 248.1

Juvenile court's acceptance of juvenile's admission did not comply with rule governing entry of admissions at adjudicatory hearings where juvenile's counsel acknowledged on the record that he had explained to juvenile his rights, court asked juvenile if he understood that he was waiving his right to trial, court did not specifically ask juvenile about waiver of his rights to challenge witnesses and evidence, to remain silent, and to introduce evidence, and juvenile was only 14 years old and it was doubtful he understood that waiver of trial would encompass those other rights, even though juvenile signed waiver of rights form and clearly understood the charges against him. In re Flynn (Ohio App. 8 Dist., 05-25-1995) 101 Ohio App.3d 778, 656 N.E.2d 737. Infants ⟂ 199

Juvenile's failure to file objection to referee's recommendation did not prevent Court of Appeals from reviewing the voluntariness of juvenile's plea. In re Flynn (Ohio App. 8 Dist., 05-25-1995) 101 Ohio App.3d 778, 656 N.E.2d 737. Infants ⟂ 243

Trial court did not substantially comply with rule setting forth required colloquy with juvenile before acceptance of admission, necessitating reversal of delinquency adjudication, where there was no discussion by trial court to determine whether juvenile understood by entering his admission he was waiving his rights to challenge witnesses and evidence against him, to remain silent, and to introduce evidence at adjudicatory hearing. In re Jenkins (Ohio App. 12 Dist., 02-13-1995) 101 Ohio App.3d 177, 655 N.E.2d 238. Infants ⟂ 199

In a juvenile proceeding the trial court asks each party whether he admits or denies each allegation in the complaint to determine how the court will proceed, as the admission or denial of the allegations determines whether the court proceeds in accordance with Juv R 29(D) or 29(E). In re Dukes (Summit 1991) 81 Ohio App.3d 145, 610 N.E.2d 513, motion overruled 63 Ohio St.3d 1411, 585 N.E.2d 835.

While the trial court does not strictly follow the Juvenile Rules for an admission or denial to the allegations in the complaint, there is no prejudice against the parents where their behavior before the court indicates they will deny the allegations and the court proceeds in accordance with Juv R 29(E). In re Dukes (Summit 1991) 81 Ohio App.3d 145, 610

N.E.2d 513, motion overruled 63 Ohio St.3d 1411, 585 N.E.2d 835.

A parent's admission of neglect of the children in an action to terminate custody is invalid when the record shows that the parents were not personally addressed by the court, the court did not advise them of their rights, and there was no evidence their acts were voluntary. In re Smith (Ottawa 1991) 77 Ohio App.3d 1, 601 N.E.2d 45.

In a delinquency case, a juvenile's plea is an admission or denial of the facts contained in the complaint; an admission is not a guilty plea but a waiver of rights to challenge the allegations; a juvenile is not a delinquent child until so adjudicated; a denial is an assertion of the juvenile's right to challenge the allegations; if the allegations of the complaint are not proved, the complaint must be dismissed. State v. Penrod (Summit 1989) 62 Ohio App.3d 720, 577 N.E.2d 424, motion overruled 44 Ohio St.3d 715, 542 N.E.2d 1112.

Where a complaint alleges that a child is neglected or dependent within the meaning of RC 2151.03(B) and 2151.04(A), 2151.04(B), and 2151.04(C), the child's mother is not prohibited by Juv R 29(D)(2) from taking part in the adjudicatory hearing by the fact that she entered a plea of "admitted" to the allegations in the complaint. In re Sims (Preble 1983) 13 Ohio App.3d 37, 468 N.E.2d 111, 13 O.B.R. 40.

Juv R 29(C) provides that a failure or refusal to admit the allegations of the complaint shall be deemed a denial. In re Green (Franklin 1982) 4 Ohio App.3d 196, 447 N.E.2d 129, 4 O.B.R. 300.

Prosecutor's threat to file charges against complaining witness, if she were to testify to facts contrary to her signed affidavit, did not render involuntary juvenile's admission to charge that he was delinquent because he took a minivan without consent; during adjudicatory hearing, juvenile denied that anyone made threats or promises or otherwise forced him into admitting charge, juvenile, his father, and his guardian ad litem signed waiver that included a statement that no promises, threats, or inducements had been made to secure waiver, and prosecutor's statement was not related in any way to juvenile's admission. In re Hudnall (Ohio App. 4 Dist., Lawrence, 09-27-2002) No. 02CA21, 2002-Ohio-5364, 2002 WL 31230578, Unreported.

Trial court substantially complied with admissions rule, in accepting mother's admission that her two children were dependent, although court did not advise her of her right to remain silent and to introduce evidence at adjudicatory hearing; court held discussion with mother on the record, and determined that she entered admission knowingly and voluntarily. In re N.D. (Ohio App. 8 Dist., Cuyahoga, 07-25-2002) No. 80559, 2002-Ohio-3791, 2002 WL 1728880, Unreported.

At the time of a juvenile's "admit" plea where there is no record made of the proceeding there is no record for the judge to review in determining whether the juvenile's motion to withdraw his plea and vacate his sentence should be granted; as a result, a conviction for operating a motor vehicle under the influence of alcohol after underage consumption is vacated with instructions to conduct a new adjudicatory hearing which is properly recorded. In re L.D. (Ohio App. 8 Dist., Cuyahoga, 12-13-2001) No. 78750, 2001 WL 1612114, Unreported.

Juvenile court's failure to apprise a fourteen-year-old of the potential penalty which he faces in making an admission to the charge of burglary fails to comply with the requirements of Juv R 29(D). In re

Gilbert (Ohio App. 7 Dist., Jefferson, 03-29-1999) No. 96-JE-34, 1999 WL 182526, Unreported.

A juvenile does not knowingly and intelligently waive her right to counsel (1) in absence of any examination by the court regarding such right in deciding whether to admit or deny the complaint, (2) where the complaint states that the juvenile is a delinquent child by reason of committing an act that would constitute complicity to receiving stolen property if she were an adult, and (3) where the magistrate fails to ascertain whether the juvenile understands the charge against her or the possible length of any commitment in the custody of the Department of Youth Services. In re Doyle (App. 2 Dist., 10-03-1997) 122 Ohio App.3d 767, 702 N.E.2d 970.

A homeowner's liability insurer has no duty to defend or indemnify its insured pursuant to the exclusion provision for expected or intentional injuries where the insured's son is adjudicated delinquent as a result of throwing a broken pool cue at another juvenile from a distance of fifteen feet with the intention of hurting him. Horace Mann Companies v. Harris (Ohio App. 12 Dist., Madison, 08-11-1997) No. CA96-11-051, 1997 WL 451371, Unreported.

Trial court adequately determined that juvenile entered plea voluntarily and with an understanding of the nature of the allegations against him and the consequences; the court advised juvenile that he was giving up his right to trial, his right to have the State prove he committed the offense beyond a reasonable doubt, his right to present his own defense, and his right to an appeal, and juvenile and his parents stated that they understood those rights. In re Homan (Ohio App. 5 Dist., Tuscarawas, 01-27-2003) No. 2002AP080067, 2003-Ohio-352, 2003 WL 183811, Unreported. Infants ☞ 199

Juvenile court in dependency proceeding abused its discretion by denying mother's motion to withdraw her plea of true without conducting a hearing to determine whether there was a reasonable and legitimate basis for withdrawal. (Per O'Neill, P.J., with one judge concurring in judgment only.) In re Calvin, Anthony, Alyshia (Ohio App. 11 Dist., Geauga, 11-22-2002) No. 2001-G-2379, 2002-Ohio-6468, 2002 WL 31663562, Unreported, stay granted 98 Ohio St.3d 1459, 783 N.E.2d 518, 2003-Ohio-644, appeal not allowed 98 Ohio St.3d 1513, 786 N.E.2d 63, 2003-Ohio-1572. Infants ☞ 199

5. Bifurcated hearings

Mother was entitled to adjudicatory hearing on her complaint alleging that father abused child and seeking order to protect child; trial court was not permitted to dismiss complaint without first conducting adjudicatory hearing. In re Robinson (Ohio App. 5 Dist., Perry, 11-02-2002) No. 02CA7, 2002-Ohio-6020, 2002 WL 31458237, Unreported. Breach Of The Peace ☞ 20

In proceedings where parental rights are subject to termination, it is reversible error not to provide separate adjudicatory and dispositional hearings as required by RC 2151.35, Juv R 29(F)(2)(a), and 34. In re Baby Girl Baxter (Ohio 1985) 17 Ohio St.3d 229, 479 N.E.2d 257, 17 O.B.R. 469.

A bifurcated hearing on a permanent custody complaint is required due to the evidentiary and waiver requirements of Juv R 29 and due to the different standards of proof applicable to the adjudicatory and dispositional stages, and where the record does not reflect separate stages, a remand for further proceedings on the matter is proper. Elmer v. Lucas County Children Services Bd. (Lucas 1987) 36 Ohio App.3d 241, 523 N.E.2d 540.

In an action where the county files a motion for permanent custody of a child, the child's mother files a motion for permanent custody, and the court grants the county's motion at the close of the evidence, there is no requirement to bifurcate the permanent custody hearing into separate adjudicatory and dispositional stages since there is no dispositional option as either the mother's rights are terminated, or the motion is denied. In re Jones (Cuyahoga 1985) 29 Ohio App.3d 176, 504 N.E.2d 719, 29 O.B.R. 206.

A hearing on a complaint for permanent custody must be bifurcated according to Juv R 29 and 34 into separate adjudicatory and dispositional hearings, notwithstanding the contrary provisions of RC 2151.414, since Juv R 1(A) provides that all proceedings in a juvenile court are governed by the Rules of Juvenile Procedure. In re Vickers Children (Butler 1983) 14 Ohio App.3d 201, 470 N.E.2d 438, 14 O.B.R. 228.

6. Evidence and standards

Finding that juvenile was delinquent due to his commission of attempted burglary was not against manifest weight of evidence; juvenile's confession, and eyewitness testimony that juvenile attempted to break into residence, weighed heavily against juvenile's own testimony, and testimony of other juveniles, and, even without juvenile's confession, eyewitness testimony was competent, credible evidence of juvenile's guilt. In re Bays (Ohio App. 12 Dist., Warren, 03-01-2004) No. CA2003-02-026, 2004-Ohio-915, 2004 WL 369039, Unreported. Infants ☞ 176

Admission of juvenile's confession in evidence at delinquency hearing, before state had established corpus delicti of crime, was not error; state presented strong evidence of guilt independent of juvenile's confession, and testimony of witness that she saw juvenile attempting to break into residence came immediately after testimony of deputy sheriff who testified that juvenile had confessed to offense. In re Bays (Ohio App. 12 Dist., Warren, 03-01-2004) No. CA2003-02-026, 2004-Ohio-915, 2004 WL 369039, Unreported. Infants ☞ 174

Trial court adjudication of delinquency based on juvenile's commission of robbery was not against the manifest weight of the evidence; juvenile admitted that she hit and kicked the victim, victim's daughter testified that she saw juvenile kick and punch the victim, and victim testified that juvenile took her cigarette case, cigarettes, house keys, driver's license, and four dollars. In re J.G. (Ohio App. 2 Dist., Montgomery, 02-20-2004) No. 20074, 2004-Ohio-774, 2004 WL 316443, Unreported. Infants ☞ 176

Minor who engaged in non-forcible sexual contact with a five-year-old girl was delinquent, even though girl consented to the conduct, where minor was nine or ten at the time of the offense, minor was presumably of greater physical and intellectual development, and evidence indicated that minor used manipulative threats to obtain compliance from other victim. In re N.K. (Ohio App. 8 Dist., Cuyahoga, 12-24-2003) No. 82332, 2003-Ohio-7059, 2003 WL 23009113, Unreported. Infants ☞ 153

Evidence was sufficient to support trial court's finding that minor had forced sexual conduct with five-year-old girl so as to adjudicate minor delinquent; victim testified that minor threatened her by telling her he would tell her friends not to play with her if she did not perform oral sex, and that minor pushed her head down to gain compliance. In re N.K. (Ohio App. 8 Dist., Cuyahoga, 12-24-2003) No. 82332, 2003-Ohio-7059, 2003 WL 23009113, Unreported. Infants ☞ 176

Trial court finding that child was a dependent child was not against the sufficiency of the evidence; mother had a history of being unable to provide for her children and for being unable to provide adequate housing, mother was unemployed, psychological testing of mother indicated a lack of efficacy and a lack of independence, and, at the hearing on mother's objections to dependency finding, the court found out that mother had moved out of the state and had not been in contact with child or inquired about child's welfare. In re Barker (Ohio App. 5 Dist., Stark, 11-24-2003) No. 03-CA-279, 2003-Ohio-6406, 2003 WL 22843907, Unreported. Infants ☞ 158

Trial court finding of juvenile delinquency was not against the manifest weight of the evidence; police officers testified that, after they activated their lights and attempted to box in vehicle juvenile was driving, he drove vehicle at police officer, he rammed police vehicle, and he only stopped his vehicle after he was involved in another collision. In re B.B. (Ohio App. 8 Dist., Cuyahoga, 11-06-2003) No. 81948, 2003-Ohio-5920, 2003 WL 22510518, Unreported. Infants ☞ 153

Evidence was sufficient to support juvenile's adjudication of delinquency based on the commission of felonious assault, and thus denial of juvenile's motion for judgment of acquittal was proper; defendant admitted that he punched the victim in the face, and the victim sustained a broken jaw as a result of the punch. In re D.P. (Ohio App. 8 Dist., Cuyahoga, 10-30-2003) No. 82151, 2003-Ohio-5821, 2003 WL 22456992, Unreported. Infants ☞ 209

There was competent credible evidence to show that child suffered from acute pain of lasting duration, to support finding that child was abused; doctor testified that multiple bruises found on child's body were from one to five days old, were not in typical locations of common toddler bruises, and were in the outline of a hand. In re K.B. (Ohio App. 9 Dist., Summit, 07-16-2003) No. 21365, 2003-Ohio-3784, 2003 WL 21658319, Unreported. Infants ☞ 179

Trial court's error in admitting hearsay testimony from officer in delinquency proceeding for assault offense, in which officer testified about what victim and witness told him about assault, did not result in prejudice to juvenile; trial judge made specific, detailed findings of fact, which focused less on the genesis of the assault, and more on the extent of juvenile's involvement once other individual and the victim fell to the ground. In re J.P. (Ohio App. 8 Dist., Cuyahoga, 07-03-2003) No. 81486, 2003-Ohio-3522, 2003 WL 21511316, Unreported. Infants ☞ 253

Juvenile's placement of his hand in victim's pants would be sufficient to support delinquency adjudication for attempted rape if he commented, after victim removed his hand, that victim had "let other guys finger" her. In re Hardie (Ohio App. 4 Dist., Washington, 03-14-2003) No. 02CA55, 2003-Ohio-1388, 2003 WL 1423403, Unreported. Infants ☞ 153

Delinquency adjudication for violating condition of parole for attempted gross sexual imposition that prohibited unsupervised contact with any individuals under age of 18 years was not against manifest weight of evidence, where social worker who had given juvenile permission to go to store with his 17-year-old girlfriend but had not given permission for contact with any other minors observed juvenile at store with girlfriend and with two persons under age of three. In re Raypole (Ohio App. 12 Dist., Fayette, 03-10-2003) No. CA2002-01-001, No. CA2002-01-002, 2003-Ohio-1066, 2003 WL 928976, Unreported. Infants ☞ 225

Evidence that juvenile was at store with his 17-year-old girlfriend and with two persons under age of three supported a finding beyond a reasonable doubt that juvenile violated rule of parole on delinquency adjudication for attempted gross sexual imposition that prohibited any unsupervised contact with any individuals under age of 18 years; while social worker had given juvenile permission to go to store with girlfriend, juvenile had not sought permission to have contact with the other minors. In re Raypole (Ohio App. 12 Dist., Fayette, 03-10-2003) No. CA2002-01-001, No. CA2002-01-002, 2003-Ohio-1066, 2003 WL 928976, Unreported. Infants ☞ 225

Offense of breaking and entering does not require specific proof of age, and thus state did not have to prove juvenile's age for court to have found that juvenile committed offense and to have adjudicated juvenile a delinquent. In re Tressler (Ohio App. 3 Dist., Paulding, 11-19-2002) No. 11-02-06, 2002-Ohio-6276, 2002 WL 31555996, Unreported. Infants ☞ 153

Evidence existed that gas station was unoccupied, as required to support finding of juvenile delinquency based on offense of breaking and entering; evidence indicated that break-ins occurred after hours, owner's wife operated store by herself, and owner was with wife when wife closed store at night. In re Tressler (Ohio App. 3 Dist., Paulding, 11-19-2002) No. 11-02-06, 2002-Ohio-6276, 2002 WL 31555996, Unreported. Infants ☞ 176

Adjudication of juvenile as delinquent for his involvement in burglary was not against the manifest weight of the evidence; although main evidence against defendant was testimony of co-defendant who testified as part of plea bargain, co-defendant's testimony was not inherently unreliable as a result of plea bargain, and his testimony about telephone call made to ensure that burglary victim was home was corroborated by telephone records. In re Barchet (Ohio App. 3 Dist., Hancock, 10-09-2002) No. 5-02-27, No. 5-02-30, No. 5-02-28, No. 5-02-31, No. 5-02-29, No. 5-02-32, 2002-Ohio-5420, 2002 WL 31255290, Unreported. Infants ☞ 176

A juvenile court's determination of parental unsuitability for custody of minor children must be supported by a preponderance of the evidence. Reynolds v. Ross County Children's Services Agency (Ohio 1983) 5 Ohio St.3d 27, 448 N.E.2d 816, 5 O.B.R. 87.

In a neglect case, the juvenile court may proceed to find neglect at the adjudication stage upon the admission of the parent charged; no other evidence is required, even when the standard is clear and convincing evidence. In re Lakes (Ohio App. 2 Dist., 08-02-2002) 149 Ohio App.3d 128, 776 N.E.2d 510, 2002-Ohio-3917. Infants ☞ 179

Uncontroverted evidence that juvenile and his sister, with whom juvenile resided, engaged in physical altercation over the issue of whether juvenile would be leaving the house, and that juvenile's sister sustained physical injuries as consequence of this encounter, was sufficient to support juvenile's adjudication as delinquent on basis of his commission of acts which, if committed by adult, would have constituted offense of domestic violence. In re Booker (Ohio App. 1 Dist., 03-05-1999) 133 Ohio App.3d 387, 728 N.E.2d 405. Infants ☞ 176

Parochial school student disciplined by school officials for sexual harassment could also be referred for adjudication as delinquent for acts of sexual violence, consistent with student handbook, as disciplinary options available to school under sexual harassment and sexual violence provisions of handbook were not mutually exclusive and student's admissions and complaints of other students gave school reason to believe student had committed acts of sexual violence, triggering mandatory reporting requirement. Iwenofu v. St. Luke School (Ohio App. 8 Dist., 02-16-1999) 132 Ohio App.3d 119, 724 N.E.2d 511, appeal not allowed 86 Ohio St.3d 1407, 711 N.E.2d 234. Schools ☞ 8

Trial court's erroneous admission, in delinquency adjudication proceeding, of hearsay statement of juvenile's adult codefendant, was prejudicial to juvenile and required reversal of adjudication, where evidence remaining after exclusion of hearsay statement was not overwhelming evidence of juvenile's guilt and reasonable probability existed that exclusion of statement from adjudication proceeding would have affected result. In re Carter (Ohio App. 4 Dist., 11-06-1997) 123 Ohio App.3d 532, 704 N.E.2d 625. Infants ☞ 174; Infants ☞ 253

Evidence that juvenile passenger in car stopped by police used alias upon being questioned, which was sole admissible evidence of guilt presented in delinquency adjudication proceeding, was insufficient to convince reasonable trier of fact, beyond reasonable doubt, that juvenile knowingly exercised dominion and control over cocaine found in purse of adult passenger, as required to support juvenile's adjudication as delinquent by reason of acts which would, if committed by adult, constituted felony drug abuse; only evidence that juvenile exerted actual control over purse at any time was improperly admitted hearsay. In re Carter (Ohio App. 4 Dist., 11-06-1997) 123 Ohio App.3d 532, 704 N.E.2d 625. Infants ☞ 176

Credible evidence that juvenile was part of group of boys who attacked victim and shouted threats at him in attempt to steal money from him was sufficient to support adjudication of delinquency based upon finding that juvenile had committed what would be crime of robbery were he an adult. In re Howard (Ohio App. 1 Dist., 04-16-1997) 119 Ohio App.3d 201, 695 N.E.2d 1. Infants ☞ 176

Adjudication of juvenile delinquency must be supported by proof beyond a reasonable doubt. In re Howard (Ohio App. 1 Dist., 04-16-1997) 119 Ohio App.3d 201, 695 N.E.2d 1. Infants ☞ 176

Evidence that juvenile deliberately wrapped shirt around neck of her newborn son and tightened it supported adjudication of delinquency based upon commission of felony of murder. Matter of Chambers (Ohio App. 3 Dist., 12-13-1996) 116 Ohio App.3d 312, 688 N.E.2d 25, dismissed, appeal not allowed 78 Ohio St.3d 1464, 678 N.E.2d 221. Infants ☞ 156

Issue of juvenile's sanity was properly reviewed at disposition hearing following her adjudication as delinquent for murder of her newborn son. Matter of Chambers (Ohio App. 3 Dist., 12-13-1996) 116 Ohio App.3d 312, 688 N.E.2d 25, dismissed, appeal not allowed 78 Ohio St.3d 1464, 678 N.E.2d 221. Infants ☞ 203

"Clear and convincing evidence of dependency" is evidence by which trial court could form firm belief or conviction that essential statutory elements for dependency have been established. In re Tikyra A. (Ohio App. 6 Dist., 05-12-1995) 103 Ohio App.3d 452, 659 N.E.2d 867. Infants ☞ 177

Because clear and convincing evidence standard must be met before permanent custody of children is granted to county and parental rights terminated, permanent custody hearing should be adjudicatory and not dispositional hearing; hearsay will not be admissible in adjudicatory proceedings unless exception is applicable. In re Brofford (Franklin 1992) 83 Ohio App.3d 869, 615 N.E.2d 1120. Infants ☞ 173.1; Infants ☞ 203

Although a finding of dependency may be made only upon the presentation of clear and convincing

evidence, if the parties agree to waive such a hearing and stipulate to certain facts, then Juv R 29(D) must be fully complied with and the facts set forth in the record must sufficiently support a finding of dependency. Elmer v. Lucas County Children Services Bd. (Lucas 1987) 36 Ohio App.3d 241, 523 N.E.2d 540.

Although Juv R 29 provides for juvenile proceedings to be conducted in an informal manner, hearsay evidence that is otherwise inadmissible will not be admitted at the adjudicatory stage of a neglect and dependency proceeding since the importance of parental interests requires an accurate finding of the facts underlying a complaint which alleges neglect or dependency and requires substantial compliance with the Ohio Rules of Evidence. In re Sims (Preble 1983) 13 Ohio App.3d 37, 468 N.E.2d 111, 13 O.B.R. 40. Infants ☞ 173.1

Proof of possession, use, or control by a juvenile of a hallucinogen is sufficient evidence upon which a juvenile court can find such juvenile a delinquent under RC Ch 2151. (Annotation from former RC 2151.35.) In re Baker (Hocking 1969) 18 Ohio App.2d 276, 248 N.E.2d 620, 47 O.O.2d 411.

In preliminary hearing on motion to transfer juvenile proceedings to criminal court, state need not provide as full discovery as that required for adjudicatory hearing in juvenile proceedings. In re Doss (Ohio Com.Pl., 05-11-1994) 65 Ohio Misc.2d 8, 640 N.E.2d 618. Infants ☞ 68.7(1)

Evidence was sufficient to support adjudication of delinquency by reason of murder by committing felonious assault; juvenile made admissions to detectives, several members of his family, and infant's mother that he beat his infant son when the infant did not stop crying, and medical evidence showed that infant's death was a homicide and resulted from head and abdominal injuries inflicted within 24 hours prior to death. In re B.M. (Ohio App. 8 Dist., Cuyahoga, 02-27-2003) No. 80909, 2003-Ohio-870, 2003 WL 548359, Unreported. Infants ☞ 176

Testimony by juvenile's companion at time of charged incident, who had previously entered admission in his own juvenile proceeding to his involvement in robbery, that he and juvenile approached victim as victim was playing basketball, asked him for his money and then slammed him to ground and kicked him when he resisted, removed victim's cash and pocket knife from victim's person, and fled the scene was sufficient to support delinquency adjudication for complicity to robbery. In re Ball (Ohio App. 3 Dist., Allen, 01-30-2003) No. 1-02-72, 2003-Ohio-395, 2003 WL 193519, Unreported. Infants ☞ 176

Testimony against juvenile by his companion at time of charged incident was not so self-serving as to affect his credibility in delinquency proceeding involving charge of complicity to robbery, where companion had already entered an admission to involvement in robbery in his own delinquency proceeding complaint and was already in the custody of Department of Youth Services, and companion testified that he was not offered promises regarding his testimony and insisted that he made the decision to testify on his own. In re Ball (Ohio App. 3 Dist., Allen, 01-30-2003) No. 1-02-72, 2003-Ohio-395, 2003 WL 193519, Unreported. Infants ☞ 176

Adjudication of delinquency for complicity to robbery was not against manifest weight of evidence; while two of juvenile's witnesses testified that juvenile's companion was victim's sole assailant, one of those witnesses admitted previously identifying juvenile to police as one of the assailants, victim and juvenile's companion presented similar versions of charged incident that both implicated juvenile, and investigating officer testified that victim immediately identified his assailants by name and positively identified juvenile and companion from photo line-up. In re Ball (Ohio App. 3 Dist., Allen, 01-30-2003) No. 1-02-72, 2003-Ohio-395, 2003 WL 193519, Unreported. Infants ⟜ 176

7. Time limitations

Adjudicatory hearing held more than two weeks after complaint was filed against juvenile required dismissal of complaint with prejudice. In re Carlos O. (Ohio App. 6 Dist., 07-29-1994) 96 Ohio App.3d 252, 644 N.E.2d 1084. Infants ⟜ 204

Adjudicatory hearing that was held on December 14, 1993 and December 21, 1993 for complaint that was filed on December 13, 1993 was timely. In re Carlos O. (Ohio App. 6 Dist., 07-29-1994) 96 Ohio App.3d 252, 644 N.E.2d 1084. Infants ⟜ 204

The speedy trial provisions of RC 2945.71(C) do not apply to delinquency proceedings. In re Corcoran (Geauga 1990) 68 Ohio App.3d 213, 587 N.E.2d 957, dismissed 56 Ohio St.3d 702, 564 N.E.2d 703. Infants ⟜ 204

The ten-day period of limitations in Juv R 29(A) is procedural only and such rule confers no substantive right upon an accused to have his case dismissed if he is not tried within the designated time. In re Therklidsen (Franklin 1977) 54 Ohio App.2d 195, 376 N.E.2d 970, 8 O.O.3d 335.

Five and a half month delay between the finding of delinquency and the disposition did not divest the court of jurisdiction; juvenile rule provided that after adjudication a court may continue a matter for disposition for not more than six months, and juvenile did not object to the continuances entered by the court. In re Homan (Ohio App. 5 Dist., Tuscarawas, 01-27-2003) No. 2002AP080067, 2003-Ohio-352, 2003 WL 183811, Unreported. Infants ⟜ 223.1

8. Double jeopardy

Proceedings conducted in a juvenile court for the purpose of determining whether or not to bind over a juvenile defendant to be tried as an adult do not constitute an adjudicatory hearing in the sense that the evidence is put to the trier of fact or that jeopardy attaches. In re A.M. (Ohio App. 8 Dist., 09-05-2000) 139 Ohio App.3d 303, 743 N.E.2d 937, appeal not allowed 91 Ohio St.3d 1431, 741 N.E.2d 895. Infants ⟜ 68.7(3)

Jeopardy attached when juvenile's adjudicatory hearing began, for purposes of double jeopardy challenge to amendment of charge from unauthorized use of motor vehicle to robbery and transfer for prosecution as adult; because state failed to make transfer decision prior to adjudicatory hearing, juvenile's liberty was placed at risk when court proceeded with adjudicatory hearing. State v. Reddick (Ohio App. 9 Dist., 09-04-1996) 113 Ohio App.3d 788, 682 N.E.2d 38. Double Jeopardy ⟜ 62

Once a juvenile who has had complaints filed against him elects to proceed with an adjudicatory hearing, jeopardy attaches as to all the complaints so as to prevent the state from prosecuting him as an adult for acts underlying the complaints; the fact that the juvenile did not admit to all the allegations contained in the complaints and that no additional evidence was presented, does not prevent the attaching of jeopardy. State v. Penrod (Summit 1989) 62 Ohio App.3d 720, 577 N.E.2d 424, motion overruled 44 Ohio St.3d 715, 542 N.E.2d 1112.

Ohio juvenile adjudication of felonious assault and adult conviction of aggravated robbery did not violate double jeopardy clause; felonious assault contained element of knowledge in causing physical harm, and aggravated robbery contained element of theft. Robertson v. Morgan (C.A.6 (Ohio), 09-14-2000) 227 F.3d 589, rehearing denied. Double Jeopardy ⟜ 33

9. Final orders

Delinquency adjudication without disposition is not final appealable order. In re Solis (Ohio App. 8 Dist., 12-22-1997) 124 Ohio App.3d 547, 706 N.E.2d 839. Infants ⟜ 242

Order changing temporary custody of children, who had been adjudged neglected and dependent, pending final dispositional hearing was a "final, appealable order." In re Smith (Lucas 1989) 61 Ohio App.3d 788, 573 N.E.2d 1170, reconsideration denied. Infants ⟜ 242

A temporary order of a juvenile court changing custody under Juv R 13 or 29 is not a dispositional order under Juv R 34, and hence is not a final appealable order. Morrison v. Morrison (Summit 1973) 45 Ohio App.2d 299, 344 N.E.2d 144, 74 O.O.2d 441.

The finding of a juvenile court in an adjudicatory hearing is a final appealable order. In re Becker, No. 3301 (11th Dist Ct App, Trumbull, 3–9–84).

10. Delinquency not crime

Being found a juvenile delinquent is different from being found guilty of crime. In re Good (Ohio App. 12 Dist., 02-24-1997) 118 Ohio App.3d 371, 692 N.E.2d 1072, dismissed, appeal not allowed 79 Ohio St.3d 1418, 680 N.E.2d 156. Infants ⟜ 153

Juvenile court is neither criminal nor penal in nature, but is administrative police regulation of corrective nature. In re Good (Ohio App. 12 Dist., 02-24-1997) 118 Ohio App.3d 371, 692 N.E.2d 1072, dismissed, appeal not allowed 79 Ohio St.3d 1418, 680 N.E.2d 156. Infants ⟜ 194.1

Complaint in juvenile court alleging delinquency does not need to be read as strictly as criminal indictment. In re Good (Ohio App. 12 Dist., 02-24-1997) 118 Ohio App.3d 371, 692 N.E.2d 1072, dismissed, appeal not allowed 79 Ohio St.3d 1418, 680 N.E.2d 156. Infants ⟜ 197

As an adjudication of delinquency does not constitute a conviction for commission of a crime, RC 2941.25(A) does not apply to juvenile delinquency adjudications. In re Lugo, No. WD–90–38 (6th Dist Ct App, Wood, 6–14–91).

11. Waiver of counsel

Juvenile court's colloquy with 13-year-old juvenile, in which the court simply asked if juvenile had any questions and asked whether juvenile wanted to be represented by a lawyer in the juvenile delinquency proceeding, did not establish that juvenile knowingly waived his right to counsel before admitting to committing acts constituting burglary. In A.C. (Ohio App. 8 Dist., Cuyahoga, 10-16-2003) No. 82289, 2003-Ohio-5496, 2003 WL 22351114, Unreported. Infants ⟜ 199

Juvenile did not validly waive her right to counsel in delinquency proceeding; while juvenile court orally informed juvenile that she had a right to an attorney at date in which juvenile was not admit or deny guilt to delinquency charge, trial court made no mention of the counsel issue at adjudication hearing and merely asked whether juvenile was ready to proceed, and juvenile court never inquired whether juvenile was waiving her right to counsel. In re Bays (Ohio App. 2 Dist., Greene, 03-14-2003) No. 2002-CA-52, No. 2002-CA-56, 2003-Ohio-1256, 2003 WL 1193787, Unreported. Infants ⟜ 205

To be effective, a waiver of a juvenile's right to counsel must be voluntary, knowing and intelligent. In re Johnston (Ohio App. 11 Dist., 04-30-2001) 142 Ohio App.3d 314, 755 N.E.2d 457. Infants ⬲ 205

Court's colloquy did not establish that juvenile fully understood nature of right that she was waiving when she entered admission, where court told juvenile, "you have the right to an attorney. If you cannot afford one, one will be appointed for you. Do you wish to have an attorney?" and when the juvenile replied, "No," the court said "the juvenile waives her right to an attorney." In re Smith (Ohio App. 8 Dist., 03-26-2001) 142 Ohio App.3d 16, 753 N.E.2d 930. Infants ⬲ 205

Sixteen-year-old suspect waived his right against self-incrimination and right to counsel knowingly, intelligently, and voluntarily before he made videotaped confession at police station, despite suspect's age and diminished IQ, where police made a thorough effort on three separate occasions to warn suspect of his *Miranda* rights and to obtain from him an acknowledgement that he understood and waived those rights. State v. Noggle (Ohio App. 3 Dist., 09-18-2000) 140 Ohio App.3d 733, 749 N.E.2d 309, 2000-Ohio-1927, appeal allowed 91 Ohio St.3d 1431, 741 N.E.2d 894, appeal dismissed as improvidently granted 91 Ohio St.3d 1280, 747 N.E.2d 827, 2001-Ohio-117. Criminal Law ⬲ 412.2(5); Infants ⬲ 174

At adjudicatory delinquency hearing, referee must personally address juvenile and ensure validity of waiver of right to counsel before accepting admission to charges. In re Montgomery (Ohio App. 8 Dist., 01-21-1997) 117 Ohio App.3d 696, 691 N.E.2d 349, dismissed, appeal not allowed 78 Ohio St.3d 1490, 678 N.E.2d 1228. Infants ⬲ 199

Journal entry indicating that juvenile waived his right to counsel in delinquency proceeding was not adequate to show that court explained juvenile's statutory right to counsel and informed him that counsel would be appointed if he was indigent. In re Montgomery (Ohio App. 8 Dist., 01-21-1997) 117 Ohio App.3d 696, 691 N.E.2d 349, dismissed, appeal not allowed 78 Ohio St.3d 1490, 678 N.E.2d 1228. Infants ⬲ 199

Trial court accepted 13-year-old juvenile's waiver of counsel without proper assurances that waiver was knowing, intelligent and voluntary; referee gave basic explanation to juvenile on his right to counsel at initial hearing and adjudicatory hearing, and asked juvenile to sign waiver form, but failed to inquire into any circumstances that would demonstrate that juvenile knowingly, intelligently, and voluntarily waived his right to counsel, and trial judge did not address subject of right to counsel at dispositional hearing. In re Johnson (Ohio App. 1 Dist., 08-23-1995) 106 Ohio App.3d 38, 665 N.E.2d 247. Infants ⬲ 205

In applying totality-of-the-circumstances test to waiver of counsel by juveniles, courts must give close scrutiny to factors such as juvenile's age, emotional stability, mental capacity, and prior criminal experience. In re Johnson (Ohio App. 1 Dist., 08-23-1995) 106 Ohio App.3d 38, 665 N.E.2d 247. Infants ⬲ 205

Valid waiver by juvenile may not be presumed from silent record. In re McKenzie (Ohio App. 8 Dist., 03-30-1995) 102 Ohio App.3d 275, 656 N.E.2d 1377. Infants ⬲ 250

Magistrate did not commit plain error in accepting juvenile's waiver of counsel before obtaining his admission to preparing crack cocaine for sale; magistrate informed juvenile of his right to counsel and made sufficient inquiry, employing informal language and encompassing the totality of the circumstances present, to determine whether juvenile knowingly, intelligently, and voluntarily waived his right to counsel, and juvenile and his mother additionally signed a waiver-of-counsel-and-rights form which the magistrate journalized in the court record. In re Sweeten (Ohio App. 1 Dist., Hamilton, 05-24-2002) No. C-010314, 2002-Ohio-2552, 2002 WL 1040229, Unreported.

Waiver of counsel will not be presumed from a silent record. In re Wilson, No. 11-80-28 (3d Dist Ct App, Paulding, 11-12-81).

12. No contest pleas

The trial court's refusal to accept juvenile's *Alford*-type plea was not an abuse of discretion, in juvenile delinquency proceeding; juvenile failed to admit the allegations in the complaint or a factual basis supporting the offense. In re Kirby (Ohio App. 12 Dist., Clinton, 12-16-2002) No. CA2002-03-015, 2002-Ohio-6881, 2002 WL 31798390, Unreported. Infants ⬲ 199

Where a juvenile entered a no contest plea to a delinquency complaint apparently on the basis that she would be able to appeal the juvenile court's ruling on the pretrial motion to suppress, as would be true in an adult criminal case, the court erroneously disposed of the case on such a plea. In re Green (Franklin 1982) 4 Ohio App.3d 196, 447 N.E.2d 129, 4 O.B.R. 300. Infants ⬲ 199

The no contest plea in a juvenile proceeding is not the unequivocal admission of the allegations of the complaint contemplated by Juv R 29(D), and it must be construed as a denial and the prosecuting attorney must prove the issues of delinquency beyond a reasonable doubt. In re Green (Franklin 1982) 4 Ohio App.3d 196, 447 N.E.2d 129, 4 O.B.R. 300. Infants ⬲ 176; Infants ⬲ 199

There is no statement in Crim R 11 that a no contest plea results in a waiver of a defendant's right to challenge evidence against him as is specifically provided for by Juv R 29(D)(2) in relation to an admission of allegations of the complaint. In re Green (Franklin 1982) 4 Ohio App.3d 196, 447 N.E.2d 129, 4 O.B.R. 300.

13. Consequences of hearing

Trial court's disposition of juvenile adjudicated delinquent for murder of her newborn son, suspending her commitment pending successful completion of probation and adherence to recommendations of mental health professionals, was necessary and appropriate. Matter of Chambers (Ohio App. 3 Dist., 12-13-1996) 116 Ohio App.3d 312, 688 N.E.2d 25, dismissed, appeal not allowed 78 Ohio St.3d 1464, 678 N.E.2d 221. Infants ⬲ 225

Juvenile was properly put on notice of a potential commitment to Department of Youth Services (DYS) for probation violation, even though at first adjudicatory hearing, court did not impose a suspended commitment to DYS; juvenile court informed juvenile during adjudicatory hearing that probation violation could have resulted in commitment to DYS. In re Rumph (Ohio App. 9 Dist., Summit, 09-04-2002) No. 20886, 2002-Ohio-4525, 2002 WL 2009212, Unreported.

In a juvenile traffic offender proceeding, failure to inform the child that a no contest plea could result in revocation of his driving privileges invalidated such plea. In re Kahan, No. L-82-170 (6th Dist Ct App, Lucas, 10-22-82).

14. Insanity defense

In juvenile proceedings, juvenile may not assert affirmative defense of insanity, although issue of sanity is factor to be considered during trial court's determination of delinquency; plea of not guilty by reason of insanity is feature of criminal cases, and child should not be dealt with on basis of criminal laws for felony out of which delinquency charge sprang. Matter of Chambers (Ohio App. 3 Dist., 12-13-1996) 116 Ohio App.3d 312, 688 N.E.2d 25, dismissed, appeal not allowed 78 Ohio St.3d 1464, 678 N.E.2d 221. Infants ☞ 199

15. Judge's duty to inform—In general

Trial court substantially complied with rule governing adjudicatory hearings, which required court to give juvenile certain advisements at beginning of juvenile's adjudicatory hearing, in delinquency proceeding; juvenile received detailed advisements required by rule at initial hearing, and, although court did not repeat advisements at adjudicatory hearing, both sides acknowledged that rape counts were being tried, full adversarial trial was conducted, and juvenile had opportunity to present and confront witnesses. In re Pyles (Ohio App. 2 Dist., Montgomery, 10-11-2002) No. 19354, 2002-Ohio-5539, 2002 WL 31317249, Unreported. Infants ☞ 203

16. Notice

Statutory notice requirements of juvenile delinquency proceeding were met by providing juvenile's guardian with notice, instead of juvenile's father, where juvenile was in permanent county custody and had a guardian who was not his father. State v. D.M. (Ohio App. 8 Dist., Cuyahoga, 06-19-2003) No. 81641, 2003-Ohio-3228, 2003 WL 21419595, Unreported. Infants ☞ 198

17. Preservation of error for review

Juvenile failed to preserve for appellate review in juvenile delinquency case his claims that trial court failed to comply with requirements of rule governing admissions, where juvenile failed at any time before appeal to withdraw pleas admitting parole violation and failure to comply with order or signal of police officer. In re M.F. (Ohio App. 8 Dist., Cuyahoga, 09-11-2003) No. 82018, 2003-Ohio-4807, 2003 WL 22100124, Unreported. Infants ☞ 243

Juv R 30 Relinquishment of jurisdiction for purposes of criminal prosecution

(A) Preliminary hearing

In any proceeding where the court considers the transfer of a case for criminal prosecution, the court shall hold a preliminary hearing to determine if there is probable cause to believe that the child committed the act alleged and that the act would be an offense if committed by an adult. The hearing may be upon motion of the court, the prosecuting attorney, or the child.

(B) Mandatory transfer

In any proceeding in which transfer of a case for criminal prosecution is required by statute upon a finding of probable cause, the order of transfer shall be entered upon a finding of probable cause.

(C) Discretionary transfer

In any proceeding in which transfer of a case for criminal prosecution is permitted, but not required, by statute, and in which probable cause is found at the preliminary hearing, the court shall continue the proceeding for full investigation. The investigation shall include a mental examination of the child by a public or private agency or by a person qualified to make the examination. When the investigation is completed, an amenability hearing shall be held to determine whether to transfer jurisdiction. The criteria for transfer shall be as provided by statute.

(D) Notice

Notice in writing of the time, place, and purpose of any hearing held pursuant to this rule shall be given to the state, the child's parents, guardian, or other custodian and the child's counsel at least three days prior to the hearing, unless written notice has been waived on the record.

(E) Retention of jurisdiction

If the court retains jurisdiction, it shall set the proceedings for hearing on the merits.

(F) Waiver of mental examination

The child may waive the mental examination required under division (C) of this rule. Refusal by the child to submit to a mental examination or any part of the examination shall constitute a waiver of the examination.

(G) Order of transfer

The order of transfer shall state the reasons for transfer.

(H) Release of child

With respect to the transferred case, the juvenile court shall set the terms and conditions for release of the child in accordance with Crim. R. 46.

(Adopted eff. 7–1–72; amended eff. 7–1–76, 7–1–94, 7–1–97)

Historical and Statutory Notes

Amendment Note: The 7–1–97 amendment substituted "considers the transfer of a case for criminal prosecution" for "may transfer a child fifteen or more years of age for prosecution as an adult" and "act would be an offense" for "act alleged would be a felony" in division (A); added division (B); redesignated former divisions (B), (C), (G), (H), and (I) as divisions (C), (D), (F), (G), and (H), respectively; deleted former divisions (D) and (F); substituted "Discretionary transfer. In any proceeding in which transfer of a case for criminal prosecution is permitted, but not required, by statute, and in which probable cause is found at the preliminary hearing, the court shall continue the proceeding for full investigation." for "Investigation. If the court finds probable cause it shall continue the proceedings for full investigation." and "an amenability hearing" for "a hearing" in division (C); added the last sentence in division (C); deleted "division (A) or (B) of" following "hearing held pursuant to" in division (D); deleted "and physical" in the caption and following "waive the mental" in division (F); substituted "(C)" for "(B)" in division (F); rewrote division (H); and made other nonsubstantive changes. Prior to deletion and amendment, former divisions (D), (F), and (H) read:

"(D) Prerequisites to transfer. The proceedings may be transferred if the court finds there are reasonable grounds to believe both of the following:

"(1) The child is not amenable to care or rehabilitation in any facility designed for the care, supervision, and rehabilitation of delinquent children;

"(2) The safety of the community may require that the child be placed under legal restraint for a period extending beyond the child's majority.

"(F) Determination of amenability to rehabilitation. In determining whether the child is amenable to the treatment or rehabilitative processes available to the juvenile court, the court shall consider the following relevant circumstances:

"(1) The child's age and mental and physical condition;

"(2) The child's prior juvenile record;

"(3) Efforts previously made to treat or rehabilitate the child;

"(4) The child's family environment;

"(5) The child's school record;

"(6) The specific facts relating to the offense for which probable cause was found, to the extent relevant to the child's physical or mental condition.

"(I) Release of transferred child. The juvenile court shall set terms and conditions for the release of the transferred child in accordance with Criminal Rule 46. The transfer abates the jurisdiction of the juvenile court with respect to the delinquent acts alleged in the complaint."

Amendment Note: The 7-1-94 amendment deleted "the Ohio Youth Commission" before "a public or private agency" in, and deleted "Written notice of the time, place and nature of the hearing shall be given to the parties at least three days prior to the hearing." from the end of, division (B); added division (C); redesignated former divisions (C) through (H) as divisions (D) through (I), respectively; inserted "the following relevant circumstances" in the first paragraph of division (F); substituted "condition" for "health" in division (F)(1); inserted "child's" in division (F)(5); added division (F)(6); added the final sentence in division (I); and made changes to reflect gender-neutral language.

Commentary

Staff Notes

1997:

With the passage of 1995 H1, effective January 1, 1996, major conflicts resulted between the statute governing bindover proceedings (Revised Code 2151.26) and the provisions of Juv.R. 30. The 1997 amendment to Juv.R. 30 eliminates these conflicts by removing from the rule all provisions governing substantive law, thus confining the rule to procedural matters. A significant amendment to Juv.R. 30(A) is the deletion of any reference to a minimum age at which a juvenile could be subject to bindover, since age jurisdiction is more appropriately covered by statute.

Revisions to Juv.R. 30(B) and (C) recognize the statutory distinctions between mandatory and discretionary bindover. Once probable cause has been established for mandatory bindover under Juv.R. 30(B), the only procedural step remaining is to enter the order of transfer. All references to the investigation contained in the former version of Juv.R. 30(B) have been removed from the current version. Similarly, Juv.R. 30(C) provides that the transfer of jurisdiction with respect to discretionary bindover shall be governed by statute.

The notice requirements of Juv.R. 30(D) (formerly Juv.R. 30(C)) have been changed to clarify that the three-day notice is required before any hearing held under Juv.R. 30. This language is consistent with similar language contained in Revised Code 2151.26(D).

In conformity with the decision to remove substantive law language from the rule, the amenability factors included in the former version of Juv.R. 30(F) have been deleted in their entirety, and the jurisdictional language in the former Juv.R. 30(I) has been eliminated from the new version of Juv.R. 30(H).

H. B. 1 also deleted the requirement for a physical examination of the juvenile as part of the background investigation in connection with a discretionary bindover. Accordingly, the requirement was deleted from divisions (C) and (F) of this rule (formerly divisions (B) and (G)).

1994:

Rule 30 Relinquishment of Jurisdiction for Purposes of Criminal Prosecution

Juv. R. 30 deals with bindover proceedings to determine whether or not to transfer a juvenile to the adult criminal justice system. The revision to Juv. R. 30(C) clarifies that written notice of the time, place, and purpose of any hearing under this rule be given in writing at least three days prior to the hearing to the state, the child's parents, guardian or other custodian, and the child's counsel, as required by Revised Code 2151.26(D), unless notice is waived on the record.

Revisions to Juv. R. 30(F) present an additional criterion for the court to consider in determining if the juvenile is amenable to rehabilitation. Juvenile courts may now consider the specific facts relating to the offense for which probable cause was found, to the extent relevant to the child's mental or physical condition, along with the other criteria specified in Juv. R. 30. While there is a danger that taking note of the facts surrounding a particularly heinous crime could prejudice a court's deliberations on the rehabilitation question, the Supreme Court of Ohio approved a court's ability to consider the totality of the circumstances which have brought the juvenile before the court in *State v. Watson* (1989), 47 Ohio St. 3d 93.

Library References

Infants ⬅68.7(1) to 68.7(5).

Westlaw Topic No. 211.

C.J.S. Infants §§ 45 to 48, 203.

OJur 3d: 28, Criminal Law § 2013 to 2014

Am Jur 2d: 47, Juvenile Courts and Delinquent and Dependent Children § 19, 20

Katz & Giannelli, Baldwin's Ohio Practice, Criminal Law § 1.9 (1996).

Carlin, Baldwin's Ohio Practice, Merrick–Rippner Probate Law § 104.5, 105.9, 106.4, 107.33, 107.36, 107.45, 107.50, 107.52, 107.63, 107.66, 107.67, 107.69, 107.70, 107.186 (2003).

Law Review and Journal Commentaries

A Brief History of Ohio Gang Trends—Changes in Legislation as a Result of Gangs and Successful Prevention Methods, Linda M. Schmidt. 10 Baldwin's Ohio Sch L J 69 (November/December 1998).

The Effect of the Double Jeopardy Clause on Juvenile Proceedings, James G. Carr. 6 U Tol L Rev 1 (Fall 1974).

Judge's Column, Hon. William W. Weaver. (Ed. note: Judge Weaver of the Lake County Juvenile Court highlights the effects of 1995 H 1 on juvenile law and procedure and provides flow charts to explain the new procedures.) 19 Lake Legal Views 1 (January 1996).

Rights of passage: Analysis of waiver of juvenile court jurisdiction. 64 Fordham L Rev 2425 (1995).

Symposium: They Grow Up So Fast: When Juveniles Commit Adult Crimes, Hon. W. Don Reader, et al. 29 Akron L Rev 473 (Spring 1996).

Notes of Decisions

Adjudicatory hearing   13
Amenability to rehabilitation   5
Constitutional issues   9
County of transfer   11
Criminal charges and indictments   4
Final orders   1
Habeas corpus   15
Improper transfer   10
Investigation   8
Judge   12
Notice   6
Prerequisites to transfer   2
Sentences   14
Time limitations   3
Waiver of examination   7

---

1. Final orders

An order by a juvenile court pursuant to RC 2151.26 transferring a child to the court of common pleas for criminal prosecution is not a final appealable order. In re Becker (Ohio 1974) 39 Ohio St.2d 84, 314 N.E.2d 158, 68 O.O.2d 50. Infants ☞ 68.8

In cases involving challenges to certification of juveniles to adult courts, counsel is required to include specific language in the text of the praecipe to the clerk of courts requesting all pertinent documents from both the juvenile division and the general division of the court of common pleas to establish that the case is a final appealable order. State v. Houston (Lucas 1990) 70 Ohio App.3d 152, 590 N.E.2d 839. Infants ☞ 68.8

2. Prerequisites to transfer

Juvenile, who attempted to challenge his confinement at a juvenile detention center with a pending order to transfer him to the Division of Youth Services, was not entitled to a writ of mandamus to compel his release from the juvenile detention facility; juvenile had adequate remedies at law through an appeal and a motion for contempt to raise the issue of whether juvenile court judge, on remand, had violated a Court of Appeals mandate. State ex rel. Borden v. Hendon (Ohio 2002) 96 Ohio St.3d 64, 771 N.E.2d 247, 2002 –Ohio- 3525.

Legislative elimination of requirement that allegedly delinquent child be given physical examination before juvenile court relinquishes jurisdiction could not be applied retroactively. State v. Golphin (Ohio 1998) 81 Ohio St.3d 543, 692 N.E.2d 608, 1998 – Ohio- 336. Infants ☞ 68.2

Under former versions of statute and rule governing bind-over procedures, juvenile court failed to properly relinquish jurisdiction over allegedly delinquent child where no physical examination was performed; thus, prosecution of child in common pleas court was void ab initio. State v. Golphin (Ohio 1998) 81 Ohio St.3d 543, 692 N.E.2d 608, 1998 – Ohio- 336. Infants ☞ 68.7(1)

Former rulings of a juvenile court judge demonstrating that the motion to transfer a youth for prosecution as an adult was granted in more than one-half of the cases in which the motion was considered are contrary to a claim that former rulings demonstrate a predisposition to deny such motions and therefore the rulings do not provide grounds for disqualification. In re Disqualification of Ruben (Ohio 1995) 77 Ohio St.3d 1232, 674 N.E.2d 348.

In deciding whether to relinquish jurisdiction over a child, a juvenile court may consider the seriousness of the alleged offense when determining pursuant to Juv R 30(C)(1) if the juvenile is "not amenable to care or rehabilitation" in the juvenile justice system. State v. Watson (Ohio 1989) 47 Ohio St.3d 93, 547 N.E.2d 1181. Infants ☞ 68.7(2)

Where the record before a juvenile court contains sufficient credible evidence pertaining to each factor listed in Juv R 30(E), the court's determination to transfer the case for trial of the juvenile as an adult will be upheld, absent an abuse of discretion, even without any written statement of the court on those factors. State v. Douglas (Ohio 1985) 20 Ohio St.3d 34, 485 N.E.2d 711, 20 O.B.R. 282.

To bind juvenile over as an adult, it is not necessary that court resolve each of pertinent rule's factors against juvenile. State v. Lopez (Lorain 1996) 112 Ohio App.3d 659, 679 N.E.2d 1155. Infants ☞ 68.7(2)

Juvenile court enjoys wide latitude in determining whether to relinquish jurisdiction of juvenile, and its ultimate decision will not be reversed absent abuse of discretion. State v. Lopez (Lorain 1996) 112 Ohio App.3d 659, 679 N.E.2d 1155. Infants ☞ 68.7(2); Infants ☞ 68.8

Juvenile court is not bound by expert opinions in determining whether juvenile is amenable to rehabilitation and should thus not be bound over as an adult. State v. Lopez (Lorain 1996) 112 Ohio App.3d 659, 679 N.E.2d 1155. Infants ☞ 68.7(3)

In deciding whether to relinquish its jurisdiction and permit state to prosecute child as adult, juvenile court enjoys wide latitude of discretion. State v. Hopfer (Ohio App. 2 Dist., 07-12-1996) 112 Ohio App.3d 521, 679 N.E.2d 321, dismissed, appeal not allowed 77 Ohio St.3d 1488, 673 N.E.2d 146, reconsideration denied 77 Ohio St.3d 1550, 674 N.E.2d 1187. Infants ☞ 68.7(2)

In reviewing juvenile court's decision to permit state to prosecute child as adult, test is not whether appellate court would have reached same result upon evidence before juvenile court; test is whether juvenile court abused discretion confided in it. State v. Hopfer (Ohio App. 2 Dist., 07-12-1996) 112 Ohio App.3d 521, 679 N.E.2d 321, dismissed, appeal not allowed 77 Ohio St.3d 1488, 673 N.E.2d 146, reconsideration denied 77 Ohio St.3d 1550, 674 N.E.2d 1187. Infants ☞ 68.8

In deciding whether juvenile court abused its discretion in permitting state to prosecute child as adult, appellate court had to determine whether juvenile court's decision was "unreasonable" (that is, without any reasonable basis), arbitrary, or unconscionable. State v. Hopfer (Ohio App. 2 Dist., 07-12-1996) 112 Ohio App.3d 521, 679 N.E.2d 321, dismissed, appeal not allowed 77 Ohio St.3d 1488, 673 N.E.2d 146, reconsideration denied 77 Ohio St.3d 1550, 674 N.E.2d 1187. Infants ⇐ 68.8

Any evidence that reasonably supports juvenile court's decision to relinquish jurisdiction over child and permit state to prosecute child as adult will suffice to sustain that court's judgment. State v. Hopfer (Ohio App. 2 Dist., 07-12-1996) 112 Ohio App.3d 521, 679 N.E.2d 321, dismissed, appeal not allowed 77 Ohio St.3d 1488, 673 N.E.2d 146, reconsideration denied 77 Ohio St.3d 1550, 674 N.E.2d 1187. Infants ⇐ 68.8

A juvenile court may consider the nature and seriousness of an alleged crime when deciding if the defendant, who struck the murder victim on the back of the head with a bat, should be tried as an adult. State v. Campbell (Hamilton 1991) 74 Ohio App.3d 352, 598 N.E.2d 1244, dismissed, jurisdictional motion overruled 62 Ohio St.3d 1431, 578 N.E.2d 823.

Possession of a loaded firearm while engaged in drug trafficking by a sixteen-year-old constitutes sufficient evidence that the juvenile poses a danger to the safety of the community to warrant his transfer to the general division of the court of common pleas. State v. Houston (Lucas 1990) 70 Ohio App.3d 152, 590 N.E.2d 839.

A juvenile faced with a bind-over attempt in juvenile court is not entitled to the appointment of a private psychiatric examiner, at the state's expense, instead of a court psychologist for purposes of determining whether juvenile court jurisdiction should be waived. State ex rel. A Juvenile v. Hoose (Lake 1988) 43 Ohio App.3d 109, 539 N.E.2d 704, cause dismissed 39 Ohio St.3d 713, 534 N.E.2d 94.

A minor does not have the right to be tried as an adult and there is no provision for bind-over upon motion of a minor. State v. Smith (Cuyahoga 1985) 29 Ohio App.3d 194, 504 N.E.2d 1121, 29 O.B.R. 237.

When there is sufficient evidence to show that a juvenile charged with murder is unresponsive to juvenile care or rehabilitation, the juvenile court has met its duty to find reasonable grounds for the relinquishment of jurisdiction to the county trial court, and the probable cause requirement of Juv R 30 is fulfilled. State v. Whiteside (Allen 1982) 6 Ohio App.3d 30, 452 N.E.2d 332, 6 O.B.R. 140.

Juvenile's case fell under statute governing requirements for a juvenile's transfer to adult court for criminal prosecution, thus meeting first requirement for case's mandatory transfer to adult court, where juvenile was charged with four category two offenses, was sixteen years old at the time of offenses, and complaint specifically alleged that juvenile had a firearm on his person and displayed such during the acts charged. State v. Fender (Ohio App. 9 Dist., Lorain, 06-26-2002) No. 01CA007934, 2002-Ohio-3184, 2002 WL 1371090, Unreported.

Evidence supported juvenile court's finding of probable cause that juvenile committed acts alleged in complaint, that is, two counts of aggravated robbery, two counts of kidnapping, and two counts of theft, and a gun specification on five of the six charges, as alleged in complaint, and thus, second requirement for mandatory transfer of case to adult court for criminal prosecution was met; juvenile knowingly and voluntarily waived probable cause

hearing on charges, he stipulated to probable cause for all six offenses, and he did not dispute gun charges. State v. Fender (Ohio App. 9 Dist., Lorain, 06-26-2002) No. 01CA007934, 2002-Ohio-3184, 2002 WL 1371090, Unreported.

Evidence that a juvenile was sixteen years and seven months old at the time of the murder and in seemingly satisfactory mental and physical health, his past adjudications as a delinquent, the juvenile's admission to selling drugs and using both drugs and alcohol, his association with friends with whom he had engaged in criminal behavior, and his expulsion from high school for setting fire to a trash can, supports a trial court decision to bind the juvenile over to be tried as an adult pursuant to Juv R 30(E) and RC 2151.26. State v Ruple, No. 15726, 1993 WL 290201 (9th Dist Ct App, Summit, 8-4-93).

Rule requiring the state to respond to discovery requests in juvenile matters applies to "mandatory bindover" or waiver of jurisdiction proceedings wherein the court determines whether probable cause exists to transfer the matter for prosecution of the juvenile as an adult. In re A.M. (Ohio Com.Pl. 1998) 92 Ohio Misc.2d 4, 699 N.E.2d 574, affirmed 139 Ohio App.3d 303, 743 N.E.2d 937, appeal not allowed 91 Ohio St.3d 1431, 741 N.E.2d 895. Infants ⇐ 68.7(3)

Juvenile who was almost 18 years old when he allegedly murdered 14-year-old girl after considering candidates for murder for approximately two months was not amenable to rehabilitation, and safety of community required that juvenile be placed under legal restrictions beyond age of majority despite fact that juvenile had no prior record, achieved above average grades in school, and worked steadily since junior high and, thus, jurisdiction of juvenile could be transferred for prosecution as adult. In re Snitzky (Ohio Com.Pl. 1995) 73 Ohio Misc.2d 52, 657 N.E.2d 1379. Infants ⇐ 68.7(2)

Justification existed for limiting juvenile's discovery on motion to transfer juvenile delinquency proceedings to criminal court for trial as adult, where five individuals had been formally charged with offenses arising from same transaction which formed basis of complaint filed against juvenile, two of whom were adults and two of whom had transfer proceedings pending, and granting full discovery might impede criminal prosecution of adult codefendants and potential criminal prosecution of child and his alleged codelinquent. In re Doss (Ohio Com.Pl., 05-11-1994) 65 Ohio Misc.2d 8, 640 N.E.2d 618. Infants ⇐ 68.7(1)

In preliminary hearing on motion to transfer juvenile proceedings to criminal court, state need not provide as full discovery as that required for adjudicatory hearing in juvenile proceedings. In re Doss (Ohio Com.Pl., 05-11-1994) 65 Ohio Misc.2d 8, 640 N.E.2d 618. Infants ⇐ 68.7(1)

3. Time limitations

If a juvenile is accused of committing a felony, the ninety-day period established by RC 2945.71(C)(2) and 2945.71(D) for commencing trial does not begin to run until the juvenile court relinquishes jurisdiction and transfers the accused to the "adult" court. State ex rel. Williams v. Court of Common Pleas of Lucas County (Ohio 1975) 42 Ohio St.2d 433, 329 N.E.2d 680, 71 O.O.2d 410.

4. Criminal charges and indictments

Juvenile court considered relevant factors before allowing juvenile to be bound over for adult prosecution for murder and robbery offenses; stipulation existed that victims sustained physical harm to their persons during the robbery and that juvenile used a firearm to commit the robbery, record further demonstrated that both victims were over the age of five and under the age of sixty-five at the time of the robbery, evidence established that neither victim was disabled and that juvenile had never been committed to rehabilitation prior to the offense, and juvenile court appropriately considered the seriousness of the offense, as evidence was presented that revealed juvenile's actions were premeditated and occurred in a deliberate manner. State v. Moorer (Ohio App. 11 Dist., Geauga, 10-24-2003) No. 2001-G-2353, No. 2001-G-2354, 2003-Ohio-5698, 2003 WL 22427822, Unreported. Infants ☞ 68.7(2)

Juvenile court did not abuse its discretion by ordering that juvenile defendant be bound over for adult prosecution for murder and robbery offenses; evidence at the amenability hearing established that defendant was manipulative and exploited the trust of those who cared for him, evidence indicated that even in the restricted setting of his foster home the criminal nature of juvenile's behavior was escalating, and psychological evaluation of court-appointed psychologist concluded that any behavioral improvements displayed by juvenile were superficial. State v. Moorer (Ohio App. 11 Dist., Geauga, 10-24-2003) No. 2001-G-2353, No. 2001-G-2354, 2003-Ohio-5698, 2003 WL 22427822, Unreported. Infants ☞ 68.7(2)

Trial court did not abuse its discretion in relinquishing its jurisdiction of juvenile's case and transferring juvenile for prosecution as adult; several witnesses testified that juvenile was threat to community and himself and that juvenile had engaged in violent behavior which had escalated, and none of the witnesses was able to state that juvenile would be amenable to rehabilitation in juvenile justice system or that there would be no need for legal restraint beyond age of 21. State v. Shreves (Ohio App. 6 Dist., Lucas, 06-06-2003) No. L-02-1075, 2003-Ohio-2911, 2003 WL 21299925, Unreported. Infants ☞ 68.7(3)

Once a juvenile is bound over in any county in Ohio pursuant to RC 2151.26 and Juv R 30, that juvenile is bound over for all felonies committed in other counties of this state, as well as for future felonies he may commit. State v. Adams (Ohio 1982) 69 Ohio St.2d 120, 431 N.E.2d 326, 23 O.O.3d 164. Infants ☞ 68.7(4)

When a minor is transferred from the juvenile court to the court of common pleas on a charge which would constitute a felony if committed by an adult, the grand jury is empowered to return any indictment under the facts submitted to it and is not confined to returning indictments only on charges originally filed in the juvenile court. State v. Adams (Ohio 1982) 69 Ohio St.2d 120, 431 N.E.2d 326, 23 O.O.3d 164.

If a juvenile offender meets defined criteria, the juvenile court may, or in specific cases shall, transfer the case to the general division of the common pleas court; in specified situations, transfer to the general division is mandatory, one such mandatory transfer situation is where the juvenile is alleged to have used a firearm in commission of certain crimes. In re Graham (Ohio App. 7 Dist., 05-17-2002) 147 Ohio App.3d 452, 770 N.E.2d 1123, 2002-Ohio-2407. Infants ☞ 68.7(1)

Statute requiring mandatory bindover to adult criminal court after a probable cause finding did not conflict with juvenile rule relating to bindover, as by its very language, juvenile rule was a discretionary provision and only affected discretionary bindovers, not those mandated by criminal statute. In Matter of Langston (Ohio App. 5 Dist. 1997) 119 Ohio App.3d 1, 694 N.E.2d 468. Infants ☞ 68.2

In determining whether juvenile could be bound over as an adult on charges of burglary and assault, juvenile court could consider testimony of arresting officer as to violent nature of crime. State v. Lopez (Lorain 1996) 112 Ohio App.3d 659, 679 N.E.2d 1155. Infants ☞ 68.7(3)

A juvenile court's bindover decision and conviction on two counts of murder are affirmed where at age fifteen defendant lures his girlfriend to a wooded area and drops a rock on her abdomen killing both her and the couple's unborn baby. State v. Steele (Ohio App. 10 Dist., Franklin, 06-28-2001) No. 00AP-499, 2001 WL 721806, Unreported, dismissed, appeal not allowed 93 Ohio St.3d 1459, 756 N.E.2d 1235.

The juvenile court was well within its discretion in determining that there were reasonable grounds to believe that a seventeen-year-old charged with aggravated murder was not amenable to rehabilitation in a juvenile treatment facility and in transferring jurisdiction to the general division after a full evidentiary hearing and careful examination of all the statutory factors showed that (1) the defendant was adjudicated delinquent in 1990 and 1991 for acts which if committed by an adult would be violent felonies, (2) rehabilitation after these offenses was not successful, (3) school officials were unsuccessful at disciplining him and his family was not cooperative in rectifying his disrespectful behavior, and (4) the murder victim was seventy-seven years old and was shot three times in the head at point-blank range while he was lying on the floor. State v Metz, No. 96CA03, 1997 WL 305220 (4th Dist Ct App, Washington, 6–4–97).

In a felonious assault committed in a beating of a gang initiation member, where the initiate member cannot positively state whether the defendant-juvenile attacked him, there is sufficient evidence to conclude that the defendant's presence, companionship and conduct indicates his complicity where (1) the defendant is a member of the Folks gang and is seen riding his bicycle alongside the group of four members who were performing the initiation, (2) a detective sees the defendant confer with the four youths shortly before the attack, and (3) another gang member names the defendant as a participant in the assault. In re Meredith (Ohio App. 8 Dist., Cuyahoga, 02-22-1996) No. 68938, 1996 WL 75696, Unreported, dismissed, appeal not allowed 76 Ohio St.3d 1434, 667 N.E.2d 985.

5. Amenability to rehabilitation

Evidence was sufficient to support court finding that there were reasonable grounds to believe juvenile was not amenable to rehabilitation in the juvenile court, and thus order binding juvenile over to the general division was proper; juvenile was 17 years old when the offenses occurred, juvenile was charged with aggravated murder, which was a category one offense and had a mandatory bindover, and juvenile was in sole possession of the murder weapon for awhile on the date of the crime, she participated in the robbery, and she drove the car when the murder weapon was discarded. State v. Holder (Ohio App. 11 Dist., Geauga, 12-20-2002) No. 2001-G-2345, No. 2001-G-2350, 2002-Ohio-7124, 2002 WL 31862684, Unreported, appeal not allowed 98 Ohio St.3d 1513, 786 N.E.2d 63, 2003-Ohio-1572, denial of post-conviction relief affirmed 2003-Ohio-5860, 2003 WL 22470862. Infants ☞ 68.7(3)

Evidence in a juvenile murder suspect's bindover proceeding, including the gruesome facts of the murder, supported the conclusion that the suspect was not amenable to rehabilitation in the juvenile court, even though prior attempts at such rehabilitation had been limited to probation. State v. Whisenant (Ohio App. 11 Dist., 03-30-1998) 127 Ohio App.3d 75, 711

N.E.2d 1016, dismissed, appeal not allowed 83 Ohio St.3d 1416, 698 N.E.2d 1005. Infants ☞ 68.7(3)

Juvenile court judge's personal opinion as to whether juvenile committed offenses alleged is not related to whether juvenile is amenable to rehabilitation, as will preclude transfer of juvenile to criminal court for prosecution as adult. State v. Payne (Ohio App. 3 Dist. 1997) 118 Ohio App.3d 699, 693 N.E.2d 1159. Infants ☞ 68.7(3)

Juvenile court need not find that any of the statutory circumstances for determining child's amenability to care or rehabilitation within juvenile penal system specifically weighs against child before it relinquishes jurisdiction over child and permits state to prosecute child as adult, as long as totality of evidence supports finding that child is not amenable to treatment. State v. Hopfer (Ohio App. 2 Dist., 07-12-1996) 112 Ohio App.3d 521, 679 N.E.2d 321, dismissed, appeal not allowed 77 Ohio St.3d 1488, 673 N.E.2d 146, reconsideration denied 77 Ohio St.3d 1550, 674 N.E.2d 1187. Infants ☞ 68.7(3)

Juvenile court did not abuse its discretion in relinquishing jurisdiction over 17–year–old child and permitting state to prosecute her as adult for murdering her newborn baby and grossly abusing its corpse, notwithstanding child's excellent academic record, lack of criminal history, clean disciplinary record, and previously stable family, where psychologist provided sufficient expert testimony about child's lack of remorse and skewed, self-focused value system to support conclusion that she would not be amenable to rehabilitation or treatment within juvenile penal system, child's age at time of hearing was only three months short of 18, and nature and severity of child's alleged act suggested callous indifference for human life which could pose threat to community even after she turned 21. State v. Hopfer (Ohio App. 2 Dist., 07-12-1996) 112 Ohio App.3d 521, 679 N.E.2d 321, dismissed, appeal not allowed 77 Ohio St.3d 1488, 673 N.E.2d 146, reconsideration denied 77 Ohio St.3d 1550, 674 N.E.2d 1187. Infants ☞ 68.7(3)

In assessing probability of rehabilitating child within juvenile justice system, juvenile court enjoys wide latitude to entertain or relinquish jurisdiction, and ultimate decision lies within its sound discretion. In re Williams (Franklin 1996) 111 Ohio App.3d 120, 675 N.E.2d 1254, dismissed, appeal not allowed 77 Ohio St.3d 1470, 673 N.E.2d 136. Infants ☞ 68.7(2)

A sixteen-year-old in good physical and mental health and possessing above average intelligence who makes a conscious decision to terminate employment in order to traffic in drugs which pays more than his $4.50/hour job and who has previously been adjudicated a delinquent in another state due to drug trafficking is properly determined to be unamenable to rehabilitation in juvenile facilities. State v. Houston (Lucas 1990) 70 Ohio App.3d 152, 590 N.E.2d 839.

A prior rape adjudication should not be admitted in a rape prosecution where neither sentencing nor probation is involved; cross–examination of the juvenile about the inadmissible prior conviction is not prejudicial, however, where the judge is aware of it from the amenability hearing on the prosecutor's motion to bind the boy over for trial as an adult, there is no jury trial before laypersons, and the judge says that he put the adjudication out of his mind. In re Johnson (Cuyahoga 1989) 61 Ohio App.3d 544, 573 N.E.2d 184.

When a juvenile court determines whether a juvenile is amenable to rehabilitation, all five factors of Juv R 30(E) must be considered, but the court is not required to resolve all five factors against the juvenile in order to justify his transfer for prosecution as an adult. State v. Oviedo (Wood 1982) 5 Ohio App.3d 168, 450 N.E.2d 700, 5 O.B.R. 351.

A sixteen-year-old delinquent child who purposely causes the death of her father in violation of RC 2903.02 and 2151.02 is not amenable to rehabilitation within the juvenile system despite the lack of a physical examination where testimony and evidence coupled with the nature and severity of the act suggest a callous indifference for human life that could pose a threat to the community even beyond the juvenile's twenty-first birthday. State v Berenyi, No. 11–97–01, 1997 WL 576357 (3d Dist Ct App, Paulding, 9–18–97).

A penalty enhancement accompanying a prosecution of a juvenile as an adult, rather than in a juvenile delinquency proceeding, is not a factor to be considered by a juvenile court pursuant to Juv R 30(E) when determining whether the juvenile is amenable to rehabilitation. State v Ingram, No. CA–15049 (9th Dist Ct App, Summit, 12–26–91).

The decision to relinquish juvenile court jurisdiction rests with the juvenile court; expert testimony as to the amenability of a defendant to rehabilitation in juvenile facilities is not binding on the court. State v Dickens, No. 12967 (9th Dist Ct App, Summit, 9–23–87).

A judge is only required to find reasonable grounds to believe the accused would be amenable to rehabilitation, not that the accused cannot be rehabilitated. State v Barnum, No. 81–C–60 (7th Dist Ct App, Columbiana, 6–22–82).

Until juvenile court either begins to hear evidence in an adjudicatory hearing, or divests itself of jurisdiction by transferring child for prosecution as an adult, determination of child's amenability to care and rehabilitation in juvenile justice system is subject to reconsideration upon motion filed by party. In re K.W. (Ohio Com.Pl. 1995) 73 Ohio Misc.2d 20, 657 N.E.2d 611. Infants ☞ 68.7(4)

6. Notice

Where a grandmother states to a juvenile court that she has legal custody of a minor in a "bindover" proceeding, the notice requirements of RC 2151.26 have been satisfied when the grandmother has been given proper notice. State v. Parks (Montgomery 1988) 51 Ohio App.3d 194, 555 N.E.2d 671.

7. Waiver of examination

Juvenile is not entitled to a court-appointed independent psychologist to assist him in determining whether to submit to or waive a mental examination in a bindover proceeding. State v. Whisenant (Ohio App. 11 Dist., 03-30-1998) 127 Ohio App.3d 75, 711 N.E.2d 1016, dismissed, appeal not allowed 83 Ohio St.3d 1416, 698 N.E.2d 1005. Infants ☞ 68.7(3)

According to RC 2151.26(C), the decision to submit to or waive the mental and physical examination authorized by RC 2151.26(A)(1)(c) rests ultimately with the child. The only requirement is that any waiver must be competently and intelligently made. State ex rel. Doe v. Tracy (Warren 1988) 51 Ohio App.3d 198, 555 N.E.2d 674, cause dismissed 39 Ohio St.3d 713, 534 N.E.2d 95.

8. Investigation

Pursuant to Juv R 30(G), an order of transfer is sufficient if it demonstrates that the statutory requirement of "full investigation" has been met and that the issue has received the full attention of the juvenile court. State v. Oviedo (Wood 1982) 5 Ohio App.3d 168, 450 N.E.2d 700, 5 O.B.R. 351. Infants ☞ 68.7(4)

9. Constitutional issues

Statute providing for transfer of certain juveniles to General Division for criminal prosecution as an adult did not violate juvenile's due process or equal protection rights, nor did it conflict with juvenile procedure rule governing relinquishment of jurisdiction for purposes of criminal prosecution. State v. Agee (Ohio App. 2 Dist. 1999) 133 Ohio App.3d 441, 728 N.E.2d 442, dismissed, appeal not allowed 86 Ohio St.3d 1489, 716 N.E.2d 721, denial of habeas corpus affirmed 92 Ohio St.3d 540, 751 N.E.2d 1043. Constitutional Law ⊜ 242.1(4); Constitutional Law ⊜ 255(4); Infants ⊜ 68.7(2)

Juvenile who was transferred to criminal court for prosecution as adult on assault charges received fair and impartial hearing, as required by due process clause, on his amenability for rehabilitation as juvenile, even though juvenile court judge had made statement during preliminary hearing that juvenile had, beyond a reasonable doubt, committed offense in question. State v. Payne (Ohio App. 3 Dist. 1997) 118 Ohio App.3d 699, 693 N.E.2d 1159. Constitutional Law ⊜ 255(4); Infants ⊜ 68.7(3)

Prosecutor's references to result of prior juvenile court hearing concerning defendant's amenability to treatment and rehabilitation within juvenile penal system were not improper and did not prejudice defendant's right to fair trial on charges of murdering her newborn baby and grossly abusing its corpse, where references were innocuous efforts to explain to potential jurors why state was prosecuting defendant as adult, to clarify one witness' comment that sheriff's deputy had called her before "first trial," and to establish chronological order of events in cross-examination of defendant, especially considering procedural nature of amenability hearings, which do not address merits of accusations against juvenile. State v. Hopfer (Ohio App. 2 Dist., 07-12-1996) 112 Ohio App.3d 521, 679 N.E.2d 321, dismissed, appeal not allowed 77 Ohio St.3d 1488, 673 N.E.2d 146, reconsideration denied 77 Ohio St.3d 1550, 674 N.E.2d 1187. Criminal Law ⊜ 713

Jeopardy attached as to all four delinquency complaints filed against juvenile, so that juvenile could no longer be prosecuted as adult for acts underlying complaints, once juvenile requested that adjudicatory hearing proceed; fact that juvenile did not admit to all of the allegations contained in complaints and that no additional evidence was presented did not prevent attaching of jeopardy. State v. Penrod (Summit 1989) 62 Ohio App.3d 720, 577 N.E.2d 424, motion overruled 44 Ohio St.3d 715, 542 N.E.2d 1112. Double Jeopardy ⊜ 33

When, in an adjudicatory hearing held pursuant to Juv R 29, the only evidence of guilt utilized by the court is testimony presented at the preliminary hearing, where the accused exercised adequate rights of cross-examination, he is denied no constitutional right. Matter of Gantt (Wood 1978) 61 Ohio App.2d 44, 398 N.E.2d 800, 15 O.O.3d 67.

Trial counsel did not render ineffective assistance by arranging plea agreement for juvenile, even though juvenile was committed to Department of Youth Services (DYS) for violating probation that resulted from plea agreement in which juvenile pled guilty to gross sexual imposition; plea agreement reduced juvenile's charge of first-degree felony rape to third-degree felony gross sexual imposition, counsel actively sought to obtain probation for juvenile rather than commitment to DYS when he negotiated plea bargain, and juvenile was aware when he pled guilty to gross sexual imposition that a possible disposition was that juvenile could have been sent to DYS. In re Staugler, No. 2001 CA 33, 2002–Ohio–2376, 2002 WL 1000602 (2d Dist Ct App, Miami, 5–17–02).

In a bindover proceeding a juvenile is denied effective assistance of counsel where his attorney fails to present any evidence in opposition to the prosecutor's bindover request and the record contains very little information concerning (1) the juvenile's prior offenses, (2) disposition of those offenses, (3) extent of the probation services offered, and (4) previous attempts to rehabilitate the juvenile. State v Lett, No. 95-CA-2094, 1996 WL 511732 (4th Dist Ct App, Ross, 9-11-96).

Statutes are presumed constitutional and the burden is on a defendant to demonstrate the contrary; therefore, where a defendant alleges, without analysis, that RC 2151.26 and Juv R 30(E) are unconstitutionally void for vagueness, because they fail to provide a workable standard to insure equal treatment among juvenile defendants, that burden is not met. State v Brown, No. 52757 (8th Dist Ct App, Cuyahoga, 10–8–87).

While juvenile's probable cause hearing must measure up to essentials of due process and fair treatment, hearing need not conform with all requirements of criminal trial, adjudicatory hearing, or administrative hearing, and juvenile need not be afforded all rights that he or she may have for trial. In re Hunter (Ohio Com.Pl. 1999) 99 Ohio Misc.2d 107, 716 N.E.2d 802. Constitutional Law ⊜ 255(4); Infants ⊜ 203

Denial of juvenile's motion to compel discovery at probable cause hearing is not prejudicial to juvenile's right to fair trial. In re Hunter (Ohio Com.Pl. 1999) 99 Ohio Misc.2d 107, 716 N.E.2d 802. Infants ⊜ 201

Juvenile court may, in its discretion, admit juvenile to bail in action wherein request for waiver of jurisdiction has been made seeking transfer of matter for prosecution as adult. Matter of K.G. (Ohio Com.Pl. 1997) 89 Ohio Misc.2d 16, 693 N.E.2d 1186. Infants ⊜ 68.3

Jeopardy does not attach to probable cause determination made at preliminary hearing on motion to transfer juvenile to criminal court for trial as adult. In re Doss (Ohio Com.Pl., 05-11-1994) 65 Ohio Misc.2d 8, 640 N.E.2d 618. Double Jeopardy ⊜ 33

There is a violation of the Double Jeopardy Clause of the US Constitution where a juvenile is subjected to a hearing at juvenile court where evidence is heard to determine if he committed acts that violated a criminal law, he is found unfit to be treated as a juvenile and then bound over to superior court for trial, because even though he was only subject to one punishment, he still faced the risk of two trials for the same offense. Breed v. Jones (U.S.Cal. 1975) 95 S.Ct. 1779, 421 U.S. 519, 44 L.Ed.2d 346, on remand 519 F.2d 1314.

Although a juvenile court has considerable latitude in determining whether it will retain or waive jurisdiction over a child, there must be sufficient procedural regularity to satisfy the requirements of due process, which include a full investigation, and where the judge fails to rule on various motions affecting the accused, fails to hold a hearing or confer with the accused, his parents, or counsel, and fails to recite any reasons for waiver of jurisdiction, the waiver order is invalid. Kent v. U. S. (U.S.Dist. Col. 1966) 86 S.Ct. 1045, 383 U.S. 541, 11 Ohio Misc. 53, 16 L.Ed.2d 84, 40 O.O.2d 270.

A decision of an Ohio juvenile court to transfer a fifteen-year-old to court because of deterrence and retribution rather than rehabilitation does not violate due process. Deel v. Jago (C.A.6 (Ohio) 1992) 967

F.2d 1079. Constitutional Law ⬥ 255(4); Infants ⬥ 68.7(2)

A juvenile who has been bound over to be tried as an adult for murder does not have his due process guarantees violated when the juvenile court considers the factors in Juv R 30(E) but does not formally receive the reports in evidence at the transfer hearing. Oviedo v. Jago (C.A.6 (Ohio) 1987) 809 F.2d 326.

Where the order of a juvenile court contained a finding only that there was probable cause to believe that the juvenile had committed an act which would be a felony if committed by an adult, the hearing in juvenile court was not an adjudicatory hearing and the subsequent trial of defendant as an adult in the court of common pleas did not subject him to double jeopardy. Johnson v. Perini (C.A.6 (Ohio) 1981) 644 F.2d 573. Double Jeopardy ⬥ 33

A juvenile court proceeding to determine whether petitioner should be treated as a juvenile or transferred to the court of common pleas to be tried as an adult on a murder charge was not an adjudicatory proceeding to which double jeopardy attached and hence did not preclude a subsequent trial of petitioner as an adult, notwithstanding that the state presented evidence of probable cause in proceeding to believe that petitioner had committed the alleged offense, where probable cause evidence was heard solely for juvenile court to decide which judicial treatment of petitioner would serve his interests and those of the community, not for juvenile court to decide petitioner's guilt. Keener v. Taylor (C.A.6 (Ohio) 1981) 640 F.2d 839, 22 O.O.3d 248. Double Jeopardy ⬥ 33

Where Ohio statute required full investigation of facts underlying charge of delinquency and finding of delinquency prior to bindover of juvenile for trial as an adult, once juvenile court, possessing jurisdiction and power to enter final orders levying a wide range of possible sanctions, began a hearing, not limited in scope by statute to preliminary or probable cause hearing, jeopardy attached, with the result that subsequent criminal prosecution for the same acts contravened his constitutional protection against double jeopardy. Sims v. Engle (C.A.6 (Ohio) 1980) 619 F.2d 598, certiorari denied 101 S.Ct. 1403, 450 U.S. 936, 67 L.Ed.2d 372. Double Jeopardy ⬥ 33

10. Improper transfer

Absent proper bindover procedure pursuant to statute, jurisdiction of juvenile court is exclusive and cannot be waived. State ex rel. Harris v. Anderson (Ohio, 07-31-1996) 76 Ohio St.3d 193, 667 N.E.2d 1, 1996-Ohio-412.

Juvenile court's failure to state with reasonable specificity the factual basis underlying its order to transfer a juvenile to common pleas court for prosecution as an adult renders the common pleas court without jurisdiction. State v Newton, No. F–82–17 (6th Dist Ct App, Fulton, 6–10–83).

11. County of transfer

Where a case is pending against a juvenile in a foreign county, such case must be transferred to the juvenile's home county, if, at any time prior to dispositional order, proceedings against the juvenile are pending in his home county. Furthermore, such mandatory transfer may not be avoided by the foreign county through the use of a bindover proceeding. State v Payne, No. 81–CA–22 (4th Dist Ct App, Pickaway, 7–28–82).

12. Judge

It would be apex juris and unreasonable to hold that every judge who presides over a preliminary hearing in a criminal or juvenile matter must thereafter disqualify himself because his impartiality might "reasonably" be questioned. In re Terry H, 1 OBR 377 (CP, Cuyahoga 1982).

13. Adjudicatory hearing

Closure of delinquency proceedings for 17–year–old charged with aggravated murder, aggravated attempted murder, and aggravated robbery was abuse of discretion; public interest in proceedings outweighed bare assertion by juvenile's attorney that permitting access would not be in juvenile's best interest, in view of juvenile's near-adult age at time of alleged offenses, minimal likelihood that probable cause hearing would disclose confidential information, gravity of offenses, and fact that juvenile would be subject to mandatory bindover to adult court if probable cause was found. State ex rel. Plain Dealer Publishing Co. v. Geauga Cty. Court of Common Pleas, Juv. Div. (Ohio 2000) 90 Ohio St.3d 79, 734 N.E.2d 1214.

Information which is normally considered confidential in juvenile court proceedings, such as a social history or mental examination, is not relevant to a juvenile court's probable cause determination at preliminary hearing. State ex rel. Plain Dealer Publishing Co. v. Geauga Cty. Court of Common Pleas, Juv. Div. (Ohio 2000) 90 Ohio St.3d 79, 734 N.E.2d 1214.

Informal proceedings conducted in a juvenile court in 1962 for the purpose of determining whether or not to bind over a juvenile defendant to be tried as an adult do not constitute an "adjudicatory hearing" as described in Breed v Jones, 421 US 519, 95 SCt 1779, 44 LEd(2d) 346 (1975). (But see Sims v Engle, 619 F(2d) 598 (6th Cir Ohio 1980).) State v. Sims (Cuyahoga 1977) 55 Ohio App.2d 285, 380 N.E.2d 1350, 9 O.O.3d 417. Double Jeopardy ⬥ 33

Preliminary hearing in delinquency adjudication proceeding to determine probable cause was not adjudicatory hearing for purposes of filing of discovery motions; juvenile's guilt or innocence was not at issue, and bindover to adult court was still possibility. In re Hunter (Ohio Com.Pl. 1999) 99 Ohio Misc.2d 107, 716 N.E.2d 802. Infants ⬥ 201

General rule that court may deny or limit discovery in delinquency adjudication proceeding upon showing that granting discovery may impede criminal prosecution of minor as adult or of an adult charged with offense arising from same transaction, while applicable when there is adjudicatory hearing pending on juvenile and that juvenile has co-delinquent who has pending bindover hearing and/or adult co-defendant who has trial pending, is not applicable to preliminary probable cause hearings. In re Hunter (Ohio Com.Pl. 1999) 99 Ohio Misc.2d 107, 716 N.E.2d 802. Infants ⬥ 201

Original determination, that child was amenable to care and rehabilitation in juvenile justice system, would be set aside prior to adjudicatory hearing and jurisdiction would be transferred to Common Pleas Court; child failed to appear for adjudicatory hearing and after turning age 18 was arrested as an adult for carrying concealed weapon, escaped from juvenile detention center one week after being placed there, and was rearrested for receiving stolen property and carrying concealed weapon. In re K.W. (Ohio Com.Pl. 1995) 73 Ohio Misc.2d 20, 657 N.E.2d 611. Infants ⬥ 68.7(4)

Preliminary and amenability hearings in proceedings to transfer child for prosecution as adult are neither presumptively open nor presumptively closed. In re D.R. (Ohio Com.Pl. 1993) 63 Ohio Misc.2d 273, 624 N.E.2d 1120. Infants ⊕ 68.7(3)

Preliminary hearing to determine whether 17–year–old juvenile should be transferred to be tried as adult for offenses of murder and felonious assault would be open to media and public; evidence did not indicate that there existed reasonable and substantial basis for believing that public access could harm child or endanger fairness of adjudication, or that potential for harm outweighed benefits of public access. In re D.R. (Ohio Com.Pl. 1993) 63 Ohio Misc.2d 273, 624 N.E.2d 1120. Infants ⊕ 68.7(3)

14. Sentences

Defendant was not entitled to $30 per day credit towards his fine since defendant was not confined pursuant to statute providing that, if fine is imposed as part of sentence and if court determines that offender is able to pay but refuses to do so, court may order offender confined until fine is paid; time that defendant served in juvenile detention facility was prior to sentencing and, thus, he was not ordered to serve this time in satisfaction of his fine and even at time of sentencing, there was no issue raised as to defendant's ability or willingness to pay the $1,000 fine. State v. James (Summit 1995) 106 Ohio App.3d 686, 666 N.E.2d 1185. Fines ⊕ 12

Trial court committed reversible error by failing to specify in defendant's record of conviction that he had served 179 days in juvenile detention facility or to order that defendant's sentence be reduced by the number of days he served in that facility. State v. James (Summit 1995) 106 Ohio App.3d 686, 666 N.E.2d 1185. Criminal Law ⊕ 1177

Since defendant was unable to leave juvenile detention facility of his own volition, he was "confined" within meaning of statute stating that jailor shall reduce sentence of prisoner by the total number of days prisoner was "confined" for any reason, and, thus, defendant should have received credit for the 179 days that he served in juvenile detention facility. State v. James (Summit 1995) 106 Ohio App.3d 686, 666 N.E.2d 1185. Sentencing And Punishment ⊕ 1157

Unless juvenile court exceeds statutory sentencing guidelines or abuses its discretion, Court of Appeals will not reverse decision of juvenile court. In re William H. (Ohio App. 6 Dist., 08-18-1995) 105 Ohio App.3d 761, 664 N.E.2d 1361. Infants ⊕ 251; Infants ⊕ 252

"Abuse of discretion" sufficient to overturn a sentencing decision by juvenile court, connotes more than an error of law of judgment; it implies that court's attitude is unreasonable, arbitrary or unconscionable. In re William H. (Ohio App. 6 Dist., 08-18-1995) 105 Ohio App.3d 761, 664 N.E.2d 1361. Infants ⊕ 251

An accused in a court of common pleas who has been bound over from a juvenile court is entitled to have his "jail time," service while under the jurisdiction of the latter, deducted from his sentence. State v. Young (Franklin 1975) 44 Ohio App.2d 387, 339 N.E.2d 668, 73 O.O.2d 462.

Trial court erred when it failed to credit days that juvenile was held in county juvenile detention center, and other facilities, toward the balance of his commitment to the Ohio Department of Youth Services after he violated probation. In re Keeran, No. 01CA69, 2002–Ohio–1580, 2002 WL 1653799 (5th Dist Ct App, Licking, 3–28–02).

15. Habeas corpus

Doctrine of res judicata barred inmate from filing third petition for writ of habeas corpus, in which he claimed that his conviction and sentence were void due to fact he was never given physical examination before juvenile court bound him over for trial as an adult, where inmate could have raised such claim in his two prior habeas corpus actions. State ex rel. Childs v. Lazaroff (Ohio 2001) 90 Ohio St.3d 519, 739 N.E.2d 802, 2001 –Ohio– 9.

Direct appeal of indictment and conviction provided defendant with adequate remedy for claim that he was improperly convicted of crimes for which he was never bound over from juvenile court, such that habeas relief was not available; petition challenged validity of subsequent indictment, conviction, and sentencing by common pleas court after a technically correct bindover on charges for which defendant was not prosecuted. State ex rel. Fryerson v. Tate (Ohio 1999) 84 Ohio St.3d 481, 705 N.E.2d 353, 1999 –Ohio– 465, reconsideration denied 85 Ohio St.3d 1448, 708 N.E.2d 212.

Habeas petition in which petitioner who alleged that conviction for which he was incarcerated occurred when he was 17 years old and that no bindover from juvenile court to adult court occurred stated potentially good cause of action in habeas corpus, even though petitioner may have possessed adequate remedy at law. State ex rel. Harris v. Anderson (Ohio, 07-31-1996) 76 Ohio St.3d 193, 667 N.E.2d 1, 1996-Ohio-412.

Habeas corpus petition which alleges that court lacked jurisdiction over petitioner due to improper bindover from juvenile court states potentially good cause of action in habeas corpus. State ex rel. Harris v. Anderson (Ohio, 07-31-1996) 76 Ohio St.3d 193, 667 N.E.2d 1, 1996-Ohio-412.

Contention by petitioner, who sought habeas corpus relief on basis that no proper bindover from juvenile court had occurred prior to his conviction, that he was 17 years old at time of commission of offenses was sufficient to meet particularity requirement to withstand dismissal, as petitioner was not required to provide supporting documentation of his age in petition in order to satisfy particularity requirement. State ex rel. Harris v. Anderson (Ohio, 07-31-1996) 76 Ohio St.3d 193, 667 N.E.2d 1, 1996-Ohio-412.

Juv R 31 [Reserved]

Juv R 32 Social history; physical examination; mental examination; investigation involving the allocation of parental rights and responsibilities for the care of children

(A) Social history and physical or mental examination: availability before adjudication

The court may order and utilize a social history or physical or mental examination at any time after the filing of a complaint under any of the following circumstances:

(1) Upon the request of the party concerning whom the history or examination is to be made;

(2) Where transfer of a child for adult prosecution is an issue in the proceeding;

(3) Where a material allegation of a neglect, dependency, or abused child complaint relates to matters that a history or examination may clarify;

(4) Where a party's legal responsibility for the party's acts or the party's competence to participate in the proceedings is an issue;

(5) Where a physical or mental examination is required to determine the need for emergency medical care under Juv. R. 13; or

(6) Where authorized under Juv. R. 7(I).

(B) Limitations on preparation and use

Until there has been an admission or adjudication that the child who is the subject of the proceedings is a juvenile traffic offender, delinquent, unruly, neglected, dependent, or abused, no social history, physical examination or mental examination shall be ordered except as authorized under subdivision (A) and any social history, physical examination or mental examination ordered pursuant to subdivision (A) shall be utilized only for the limited purposes therein specified. The person preparing a social history or making a physical or mental examination shall not testify about the history or examination or information received in its preparation in any juvenile traffic offender, delinquency, or unruly child adjudicatory hearing, except as may be required in a hearing to determine whether a child should be transferred to an adult court for criminal prosecution.

(C) Availability of social history or investigation report

A reasonable time before the dispositional hearing, or any other hearing at which a social history or physical or mental examination is to be utilized, counsel shall be permitted to inspect any social history or report of a mental or physical examination. The court may, for good cause shown, deny such inspection or limit its scope to specified portions of the history or report. The court may order that the contents of the history or report, in whole or part, not be disclosed to specified persons. If inspection or disclosure is denied or limited, the court shall state its reasons for such denial or limitation to counsel.

(D) Investigation: allocation of parental rights and responsibilities for the care of children; habeas corpus

On the filing of a complaint for the allocation of parental rights and responsibilities for the care of children or for a writ of habeas corpus to determine the allocation of parental rights and responsibilities for the care of a child, or on the filing of a motion for change in the allocation of parental rights and responsibilities for the care of children, the court may cause an investigation to be made as to the character, health, family relations, past conduct, present living conditions, earning ability, and financial worth of the parties to the action. The report of the investigation shall be confidential, but shall be made available to the parties or their counsel upon written request not less than three days before hearing. The court may tax as costs all or any part of the expenses of each investigation.

(Adopted eff. 7–1–72; amended eff. 7–1–73, 7–1–76, 7–1–91, 7–1–94)

Historical and Statutory Notes

Amendment Note: The 7–1–94 amendment made changes to reflect gender-neutral language.

Commentary

Staff Notes

1994:

Rule 32 Social History; Physical Examination; Mental Examination; Investigation Involving the Allocation of Parental Rights and Responsibilities for the Care of Children

Masculine references were replaced by gender neutral language and other nonsubstantive grammatical changes were made.

Cross References

Detention, and shelter care, Juv R 7
Divorce, annulment and alimony actions, Civ R 75
Relinquishment of jurisdiction for purposes of criminal prosecution, Juv R 30
Report concerning child in custody may be made available for good cause shown to attorney representing child, parents, or custodian, 2151.352
Temporary disposition, temporary orders, emergency medical and surgical treatment, Juv R 13

Library References

Habeas Corpus ⬤688.
Infants ⬤208.
Westlaw Topic Nos. 197, 211.
C.J.S. Habeas Corpus §§ 159, 207 to 220.
C.J.S. Infants §§ 51 to 85.
Carlin, Baldwin's Ohio Practice, Merrick–Rippner Probate Law § 107.36, 107.53, 107.66, 107.114 (2003).

Law Review and Journal Commentaries

In re T.R.: Not In Front of the Children, Bill Dickhaut. I Ky Children's Rts J 10 (July 1991).

Juvenile Delinquency Proceedings in Ohio: Due Process and the Hearsay Dilemma, Comment. 24 Clev St L Rev 356 (Spring 1975).

Notes of Decisions

Confidentiality 1
Constitutional issues 2
Mental evaluation 3
Social history 4

_____

1. Confidentiality

Pursuant to Juv R 32(B), 37(B) and RC 2151.14, juvenile court records, the records of social, mental, and physical examinations pursuant to court order, and records of the juvenile court probation department are not public records under RC 149.43. OAG 90–101.

Under RC 1347.08 a juvenile court must permit a juvenile or a duly authorized attorney who represents the juvenile to inspect court records pertaining to the juvenile unless the records are exempt under RC 1347.04(A)(1)(e) (investigatory material compiled for law enforcement purposes) RC 1347.08(C) (certain medical, psychiatric, or psychological information), or RC 1347.08(E)(2) (confidential law enforcement investigatory records or trial preparation records). OAG 84–077.

2. Constitutional issues

The federal courts will abstain from interfering in state proceedings where juveniles seek an injunction against the use of social histories in pre-adjudication instances, although they may hear an issue involving the constitutionality of post-adjudicatory dissemination of the social histories where state law is not clear and the proper factual issues were not decided; the dissemination of social histories compiled by probation officers during juvenile proceedings do not violate a constitutional right to privacy. J. P. v. DeSanti (C.A.6 (Ohio) 1981) 653 F.2d 1080.

In proceedings to terminate father's parental rights and grant permanent custody to county children services board, father was not entitled, as a matter of due process, to appointment of a child psychologist at state expense to rebut the psychological finding of unsuitability made by the State's expert who evaluated mother; father was not faced with an allegation of a mental illness which he needed to counter, father's mental condition was not at issue, and father was not ordered to undergo psychological or psychiatric treatment. In re Hess (Ohio App. 7 Dist., Jefferson, 03-21-2003) No. 02 JE 37, 2003-Ohio-1429, 2003 WL 1465190, Unreported. Infants ⚖ 212

3. Mental evaluation

Evidence supported trial court's determination that juvenile was competent to stand trial; although physician's conclusions as to juvenile's competency were mixed, she testified juvenile was not mentally ill and that he understood charge against him, and trial court properly evaluated juvenile's competency by juvenile norms, finding that juvenile's deficiencies in understanding nature of proceedings against him could be compensated for by special measures allowed by juvenile court. In re Stone (Ohio App. 12 Dist., Clinton, 06-16-2003) No. CA2002-09-035, 2003-Ohio-3071, 2003 WL 21373156, Unreported. Infants ⚖ 208

Trial court did not abuse its discretion in denying mother's request for independent psychiatric evaluation in proceedings to determine if her child was dependent child; trial court had wide latitude in determining the need for a psychiatric examination, and court had granted state's motion for psychological evaluation. In re Fazio (Ohio App. 5 Dist., Licking, 10-11-2002) No. 2002CA0057, 2002-Ohio-5554, 2002 WL 31312276, Unreported. Infants ⚖ 208

Juvenile should have been afforded a hearing to assess his competence to stand trial for gross sexual imposition, as competency evaluation raised sufficient indicia of incompetence; report noted that juvenile had limited communication abilities due to his deafness, and psychologist concluded that juvenile was incompetent to stand trial because he was not able to aid his defense. In re Grimes (Ohio App. 7 Dist. 2002) 147 Ohio App.3d 192, 769 N.E.2d 420, 2002 –Ohio- 1547. Infants ⚖ 203

Juvenile court committed plain error by not holding hearing to assess juvenile's competence to be tried for gross sexual imposition, where psychologist concluded in competency evaluation that juvenile was incompetent because his deafness rendered him incapable of aiding his defense. In re Grimes (Ohio App. 7 Dist. 2002) 147 Ohio App.3d 192, 769 N.E.2d 420, 2002 –Ohio- 1547. Infants ⚖ 248.1

Rule prohibiting state from using any incriminating evidence obtained during court-ordered mental examination of juvenile defendant in any proceeding other than juvenile amenability hearing does not apply to mental examinations by persons hired by juvenile defendant to bolster defendant's case. State v. Hopfer (Ohio App. 2 Dist., 07-12-1996) 112 Ohio App.3d 521, 679 N.E.2d 321, dismissed, appeal not allowed 77 Ohio St.3d 1488, 673 N.E.2d 146, reconsideration denied 77 Ohio St.3d 1550, 674 N.E.2d 1187. Criminal Law ⚖ 393(1)

Addendum to psychological report offered by probation officer was admissible at dispositional hearing, though county children's services board with temporary custody of minor was not given opportunity to respond to report, as court was permitted to have psychological report conducted after adjudication of minor as delinquent, and addendum did not change recommendation of psychologist. In re Lawson (Ohio App. 10 Dist., 11-08-1994) 98 Ohio App.3d 456, 648 N.E.2d 889. Infants ⚖ 208

A juvenile faced with a bind-over attempt in juvenile court is not entitled to the appointment of a private psychiatric examiner, at the state's expense, instead of a court psychologist for purposes of determining whether juvenile court jurisdiction should be waived. State ex rel. A Juvenile v. Hoose (Lake 1988) 43 Ohio App.3d 109, 539 N.E.2d 704, cause dismissed 39 Ohio St.3d 713, 534 N.E.2d 94.

Where a court orders a psychological evaluation on the request of an indigent party, pursuant to Juv R 32(A)(1), the court may admit the evaluation into evidence over the objection of the party. In re Green (Montgomery 1984) 18 Ohio App.3d 43, 480 N.E.2d 492, 18 O.B.R. 155.

4. Social history

Admission of testimony from psychologist, who testified about mother's prior social history, was not an abuse of discretion in child dependency proceeding; dependency complaint made allegations regarding mother's past difficulties with parenting and stable housing, expert's testimony clarified the past issues for the court, and psychologist was permitted to testify as to issues that mother deemed were "confidential" since psychologist performed a competency examination of mother pursuant to a referral from the court. In re Barker (Ohio App. 5 Dist., Stark, 11-24-2003) No. 03-CA-279, 2003-Ohio-6406, 2003 WL 22843907, Unreported. Infants ⚖ 173.1

In a hearing to determine whether a child is dependent, hearsay evidence contained in a social history report may not be used as evidence of the truth of the complaint, although, pursuant to Juv R 32(A)(3), the report may be used to clarify allegations of the complaint. In re Barzak (Trumbull 1985) 24 Ohio App.3d 180, 493 N.E.2d 1011, 24 O.B.R. 270.

Juv R 33   [Reserved]

Juv R 34   Dispositional hearing

(A) Scheduling the hearing

Where a child has been adjudicated as an abused, neglected, or dependent child, the court shall not issue a dispositional order until after it holds a separate dispositional hearing. The dispositional hearing for an adjudicated abused, neglected, or dependent child shall be held at least one day but not more than thirty days after the adjudicatory hearing is held. The dispositional hearing may be held immediately after the adjudicatory hearing if all parties were served prior to the adjudicatory hearing with all documents required for the dispositional hearing and all parties consent to the dispositional hearing being held immediately after the adjudicatory hearing. Upon the request of any party or the guardian ad litem of the child, the court may continue a dispositional hearing for a reasonable time not to exceed the time limit set forth in this division to enable a party to obtain or consult counsel. The dispositional hearing shall not be held more than ninety days after the date on which the complaint in the case was filed. If the dispositional hearing is not held within this ninety day period of time, the court, on its own motion or the motion of any party or the guardian ad litem of the child, shall dismiss the complaint without prejudice.

In all other juvenile proceedings, the dispositional hearing shall be held pursuant to Juv. R. 29(F)(2)(a) through (d) and the ninety day requirement shall not apply. Where the dispositional hearing is to be held immediately following the adjudicatory hearing, the court, upon the request of any party, shall continue the hearing for a reasonable time to enable the party to obtain or consult counsel.

(B) Hearing procedure

The hearing shall be conducted in the following manner:

(1) The judge or magistrate who presided at the adjudicatory hearing shall, if possible, preside;

(2) Except as provided in division (I) of this rule, the court may admit evidence that is material and relevant, including, but not limited to, hearsay, opinion, and documentary evidence;

(3) Medical examiners and each investigator who prepared a social history shall not be cross-examined, except upon consent of all parties, for good cause shown, or as the court in its discretion may direct. Any party may offer evidence supplementing, explaining, or disputing any information contained in the social history or other reports that may be used by the court in determining disposition.

(C) Judgment

After the conclusion of the hearing, the court shall enter an appropriate judgment within seven days. A copy of the judgment shall be given to any party requesting a copy. In all cases where a child is placed on probation, the child shall receive a written statement of the conditions of probation. If the judgment is conditional, the order shall state the conditions. If the child is not returned to the child's home, the court shall determine the school district that shall bear the cost of the child's education and may fix an amount of support to be paid by the responsible parent or from public funds.

(D) Dispositional Orders

Where a child is adjudicated an abused, neglected, or dependent child, the court may make any of the following orders of disposition:

(1) Place the child in protective supervision;

(2) Commit the child to the temporary custody of a public or private agency, either parent, a relative residing within or outside the state, or a probation officer for placement in a certified foster home or approved foster care;

(3) Award legal custody of the child to either parent or to any other person who, prior to the dispositional hearing, files a motion requesting legal custody;

(4) Commit the child to the permanent custody of a public or private agency, if the court determines that the child cannot be placed with one of the child's parents within a reasonable time or should not be placed with either parent and determines that the permanent commitment is in the best interest of the child;

(5) Place the child in a planned permanent living arrangement with a public or private agency if the agency requests the court for placement, if the court finds

that a planned permanent living arrangement is in the best interest of the child, and if the court finds that one of the following exists:

(a) The child because of physical, mental, or psychological problems or needs is unable to function in a family-like setting;

(b) The parents of the child have significant physical, mental or psychological problems and are unable to care for the child, adoption is not in the best interest of the child and the child retains a significant and positive relationship with a parent or relative;

(c) The child is sixteen years of age or older, has been counseled, is unwilling to accept or unable to adapt to a permanent placement and is in an agency program preparing the child for independent living.

(E) Protective supervision

If the court issues an order for protective supervision, the court may place any reasonable restrictions upon the child, the child's parents, guardian, or any other person including, but not limited to, any of the following:

(1) Ordering a party within forty-eight hours to vacate the child's home indefinitely or for a fixed period of time;

(2) Ordering a party, parent, or custodian to prevent any particular person from having contact with the child;

(3) Issuing a restraining order to control the conduct of any party.

(F) Case plan

As part of its dispositional order, the court shall journalize a case plan for the child. The agency required to maintain a case plan shall file the case plan with the court prior to the child's adjudicatory hearing but not later than thirty days after the earlier of the date on which the complaint in the case was filed or the child was first placed in shelter care. The plan shall specify what additional information, if any, is necessary to complete the plan and how the information will be obtained. All parts of the case plan shall be completed by the earlier of thirty days after the adjudicatory hearing or the date of the dispositional hearing for the child. If all parties agree to the content of the case plan and the court approves it, the court shall journalize the plan as part of its dispositional order. If no agreement is reached, the court,

based upon the evidence presented at the dispositional hearing and the best interest of the child, shall determine the contents of the case plan and journalize it as part of the dispositional order for the child.

(G) Modification of temporary order

The department of human services or any other public or private agency or any party, other than a parent whose parental rights have been terminated, may at any time file a motion requesting that the court modify or terminate any order of disposition. The court shall hold a hearing upon the motion as if the hearing were the original dispositional hearing and shall give all parties and the guardian ad litem notice of the hearing pursuant to these rules. The court, on its own motion and upon proper notice to all parties and any interested agency, may modify or terminate any order of disposition.

(H) Restraining orders

In any proceeding where a child is made a ward of the court, the court may grant a restraining order controlling the conduct of any party if the court finds that the order is necessary to control any conduct or relationship that may be detrimental or harmful to the child and tend to defeat the execution of a dispositional order.

(I) Bifurcation; Rules of Evidence

Hearings to determine whether temporary orders regarding custody should be modified to orders for permanent custody shall be considered dispositional hearings and need not be bifurcated. The Rules of Evidence shall apply in hearings on motions for permanent custody.

(J) Advisement of rights after hearing

At the conclusion of the hearing, the court shall advise the child of the child's right to record expungement and, where any part of the proceeding was contested, advise the parties of their right to appeal.

(Adopted eff. 7–1–72; amended eff. 7–1–94, 7–1–96, 7–1–02)

Historical and Statutory Notes

Amendment Note: The 7–1–02 amendment substituted "a planned permanent living arrangement" for "long term foster care" throughout division (D)(5).

Amendment Note: The 7–1–96 amendment substituted "magistrate" for "referee" in division (B)(1).

Amendment Note: The 7–1–94 amendment rewrote division (A); inserted "or referee" in division (B)(1); inserted "Except as provided in division (I) of this rule," and ", but not limited to," in division (B)(2); added divisions (D) through (G); redesignated former division (D) as division (H); added division (I); redesignated former division (E) as division (J); and made changed to reflect gender-neutral language. Prior to amendment, division (A) read:

"(A) Scheduling the hearing. The dispositional hearing may be held immediately following the adjudicatory hearing or at a later time fixed by the court. Where the dispositional hearing is to be held immediately following the adjudicatory hearing, the court, upon the request of a party shall continue the hearing for a reasonable time to enable the party to obtain or consult counsel."

Commentary

Staff Notes

2002:

Juvenile Rule 34(D) Dispositional orders

The July 1, 2002, amendment to Juv. R. 34(D)(5) substituted the language of "planned permanent living arrangement" for the former language of "long term foster care," to conform to the new legislative designation for these child-placing arrangements.

The amendment to Juv. R. 34(D)(5) conforms to section 2151.353(A)(5) of the Revised Code. Juvenile Rules 2, 10, and 15 also were amended effective July 1, 2002 to reflect this change in terminology.

1996:

The amendment changed the rule's reference from "referee" to "magistrate" in division (B)(1) in order to harmonize the rule with the language adopted in the 1995 amendments to Juv. R. 40. The amendment is technical only and no substantive change is intended.

1994:

Rule 34 Dispositional Hearing

Changes in Juv. R. 34 now bring the rule into conformity with Revised Code 2151.35 as amended by S.B. 89.

Juv. R. 34(A) delineates the ninety day deadline for dispositional hearings in abuse, neglect, and dependency cases and clarifies that the ninety day rule does not apply in unruly and delinquency cases. Revised Code 2151.35(B)(1)

Juv. R. 34(B)(1) specifies that the judge or referee who presided at the adjudicatory hearing shall, if possible, preside at the dispositional hearing. Revised Code 2151.35(B)(2)(a).

Juv. R. 34(D) restates the dispositional alternatives for an adjudicated abused, neglected, or dependent child as set forth in Revised Code 2151.353(A)(1), (2), (3), (4), and (5).

Juv. R. 34(F) sets forth the utilization of the case plan as part of the dispositional order and restates the provisions of Revised Code 2151.353(D) and 2151.412.

Juv. R. 34(G) restates Revised Code 2151.353(E) regarding the procedure for modifying a temporary order.

Juv. R. 34(I) is new and attempts to eliminate the need to bifurcate a motion for permanent custody into adjudicatory and dispositional hearings. A good explanation of the state of current case law in appellate courts in Ohio on the subject of bifurcation is

[1] Footnote 1: A motion to certify the record in *Lucas*, *supra*, to the Supreme Court of Ohio was

found in *In the Matter of Amy Lyons, Alleged Dependent Child*, No. 1411 (4th District Court of Appeals of Ohio, Ross County, decided August 11, 1987). A concurring opinion states:

"There is a conflict in Ohio law as to whether hearings for permanent custody under Revised Code 2151.414 must be bifurcated into separate adjudicatory and dispositional stages. Kurtz and Giannelli, Ohio Juvenile Law (1985), T 13.04(D)(5). The Third and Twelfth District Courts of Appeals have held that Juv. R. 29 and Juv. R. 34 control over R.C. 2151.414 to require a bifurcated hearing. *In re Vickers Children* (1983), 14 Ohio App. 3d 210; *In re Lucas* (1985), 29 Ohio App. 3d 165. [1] However, the Eighth District Court of Appeals has held that only one hearing which is purely adjudicatory is required and that, contrary to *Vickers*, *supra*, there is no conflict between R.C. 2151.414 and the applicable Juvenile Rules.

"By contrast, however, in the case at bar, there is no dispositional option. Either the motion is granted, in which case the mother's parental rights are terminated, or else the motion is denied. The single hearing prescribed by R.C. 2151.414 is purely adjudicatory. The foregoing analysis is consistent with Juv. R. 2(1), which states:

"'Adjudicatory hearing' means a hearing to determine whether a child is a juvenile traffic offender, delinquent, unruly, neglected, or dependent or otherwise within the jurisdiction of the court or whether temporary legal custody should be converted to permanent custody.

"Consequently, this court holds that the juvenile court did not err in failing to bifurcate the permanent custody hearing into separate adjudicatory and dispositional stages." *In re Jones* (1985), 29 Ohio App. 3d 176, 179.

"Although permanent custody is clearly a dispositional order, Juv. R. 2(1)'s definition of "adjudicatory hearing" appears sufficiently broad to require only one hearing or one "stage". See Kurtz and Giannelli, Ohio Juvenile Law (1985), T 13.04, p. 164 at fn. 155. When a permanent custody motion is filed pursuant to R.C. 2151.414, unlike an original disposition pursuant to R.C. 2151.353(A), there is no dispositional option in that the trial court, as the majority opinion notes, can only either terminate parental rights by granting the permanent custody motion or not terminate parental rights by overruling the permanent custody motion. *Jones*, *supra*; Juv. R. 2(1).

"Assuming, arguendo, that pursuant to *Vickers* and *Lucas*, *supra*, a bifurcated hearing was required herein, any error was waived by the failure of appellate to object to the lack of such bifurcation below. *Jones*, *supra* at p. 179; *Vickers*, *supra*. Accordingly, I concur in the judgment."

Because the cases cited seemed to interpret the need for bifurcation based upon the current Juvenile Rules, Juv. R. 34(I) now seeks to clarify that the need to bifurcate a permanent custody hearing is unnecessary.

Library References

Infants ⚖203, 204, 221, 223.1 to 225.

Westlaw Topic No. 211.

C.J.S. Infants §§ 51 to 85.

Am Jur 2d: 47, Juvenile Courts and Delinquent and Dependent Children § 44 to 62

overruled on May 21, 1986.

Whiteside, Ohio Appellate Practice (2003 Ed.), Text 2.5.

Giannelli & Snyder, Baldwin's Ohio Practice, Evidence § 101.16, 802.7 (2d ed. 2001).

Carlin, Baldwin's Ohio Practice, Merrick–Rippner Probate Law § 107.43, 107.50, 107.51, 107.72, 107.73, 107.75, 107.80, 107.84, 107.85, 107.106, 107.111, 107.113, 107.121, 107.122, 107.158, 107.159, 107.180 (2003).

Law Review and Journal Commentaries

Access to "Confidential" Welfare Records in the Course of Child Protection Proceedings, Richard Steven Levine. 14 J Fam L 535 (1975–76).

Juvenile Delinquency Proceedings in Ohio: Due Process and the Hearsay Dilemma, Comment. 24 Clev St L Rev 356 (Spring 1975).

Navigating Between Scylla and Charybdis: Ohio's Efforts to Protect Children Without Eviscerating the Rights of Criminal Defendants–Evidentiary Considerations and the Rebirth of Confrontation Clause Analysis in Child Abuse Cases, Myrna S. Raeder. 25 U Tol L Rev 43 (1994).

Rethinking The Relationship Between Juvenile Courts And Treatment Agencies—An Administrative Law Approach, Leslie J. Harris. 28 J Fam L 217 (1990).

Notes of Decisions

Bifurcated hearings 1
Case plan 12
Dispositional hearing
    Timing 11
Dispositional orders 6
Evidence 9
Fees and costs 5
Final orders 4
Judgment 3
Jurisdiction 2
Probation 7
Right to counsel 8
Rights of juvenile 10

1. Bifurcated hearings

Mother in dependency proceedings was not prejudiced by juvenile court's alleged failure to inform parties of the substance of complaint, the purpose of hearing, the possible consequences of hearing prior to adjudicatory hearing, and the right to appeal after the dispositional hearing; mother contested the matter, was represented by counsel at trial, a full hearing was held on the merits, and mother appealed the juvenile court's judgment. In re Malone (Ohio App. 10 Dist., Franklin, 12-30-2003) No. 03AP-489, 2003-Ohio-7156, 2003 WL 23024377, Unreported. Infants ⚮ 203

In proceedings where parental rights are subject to termination, it is reversible error not to provide separate adjudicatory and dispositional hearings as required by RC 2151.35, Juv R 29(F)(2)(a), and 34. In re Baby Girl Baxter (Ohio 1985) 17 Ohio St.3d 229, 479 N.E.2d 257, 17 O.B.R. 469.

In an action where the county files a motion for permanent custody of a child, the child's mother files a motion for permanent custody, and the court grants the county's motion at the close of the evidence, there is no requirement to bifurcate the permanent custody hearing into separate adjudicatory and dispositional stages since there is no dispositional option as either the mother's rights are terminated, or the motion is denied. In re Jones (Cuyahoga

1985) 29 Ohio App.3d 176, 504 N.E.2d 719, 29 O.B.R. 206.

A hearing on a complaint for permanent custody must be bifurcated according to Juv R 29 and 34 into separate adjudicatory and dispositional hearings, notwithstanding the contrary provisions of RC 2151.414, since Juv R 1(A) provides that all proceedings in a juvenile court are governed by the Rules of Juvenile Procedure. In re Vickers Children (Butler 1983) 14 Ohio App.3d 201, 470 N.E.2d 438, 14 O.B.R. 228.

2. Jurisdiction

The juvenile court has exclusive original jurisdiction, pursuant to RC 2151.23(A), concerning any child who is alleged in a proper complaint to be neglected, and the court does not lose jurisdiction by failing to adhere to the time limits set forth in Juv R 29(A) and 34(A). Linger v. Weiss (Ohio 1979) 57 Ohio St.2d 97, 386 N.E.2d 1354, 11 O.O.3d 281, certiorari denied 100 S.Ct. 128, 444 U.S. 862, 62 L.Ed.2d 83.

An Ohio juvenile court, in a dependency proceeding pursuant to RC 2151.27 et seq., has no jurisdiction to interfere with a mother's legal custody of her children, in the absence of proof and a finding of unfitness of such parent, merely for the purpose of releasing such children to the officers of the court of a foreign state, and the court need not give full faith and credit to a Michigan decree where that decree was obtained by the husband in an ex parte custody determination, subsequent to a divorce decree, in which the Michigan court had no personal jurisdiction over the nonresident wife. (Annotation from former RC 2151.35.) In re Messner (Huron 1969) 19 Ohio App.2d 33, 249 N.E.2d 532, 48 O.O.2d 31.

Where a defendant is a juvenile at the time he commits theft but is an adult at the time he receives the stolen property, the judgment of conviction for theft is vacated where no complaint for delinquency was ever brought against the defendant in juvenile court, there was no bindover from juvenile court to common pleas court, and the defendant was indicted, charged, and tried as an adult in common pleas court without subject matter jurisdiction for an offense committed while a juvenile. State v Wilson, No. C-930429, 1994 WL 176901 (1st Dist Ct App, Hamilton, 5-11-94), affirmed by 73 Ohio St.3d 40 (1995).

3. Judgment

During dispositional phase of dependency proceeding, lower court properly considered matters other than original violence allegations in the complaint. In re Pryor (Athens 1993) 86 Ohio App.3d 327, 620 N.E.2d 973. Infants ⚮ 197

While the seven-day requirement for filing a report is mandatory in a custody action, a trial court's failure to comply with the rule is not ground for reversal of its decision to terminate parental custody since the proper remedy would be for the complaining party to file a writ of procedendo compelling the court to finalize the decision. In re Galloway (Lucas 1991) 77 Ohio App.3d 61, 601 N.E.2d 83, motion overruled 62 Ohio St.3d 1503, 583 N.E.2d 974, denial of post-conviction relief affirmed.

The seven day time requirement of RC 2151.35(B)(3) and Juv R 34(C) is mandatory and must be applied as such and it may not be relaxed or eliminated. In re Fleming (Lucas 1991) 76 Ohio App.3d 30, 600 N.E.2d 1112.

The seven day rule of RC 2151.35(B)(3) and Juv R 34(C) can be applied consistently with Juv R 40(D), which (1) mandates the preparation and filing of findings of fact and recommendations by the referee; (2) provides an allowance of fourteen days from the filing of the referee's report for the filing of objections by the parties; and (3) provides for a hearing on the objections; when the dispositional hearing is conducted before a referee, the referee has seven days from the time the case becomes decisional in which to issue his findings of fact and recommendations and at the expiration of the fourteen day period for filing objections, if no objections are filed, the case is decisional and the trial court has seven days to issue its final judgment; however, if objections are filed pursuant to Juv R 40 and a hearing is held, the judge has seven days from the conclusion of the hearing to enter his final judgment. In re Fleming (Lucas 1991) 76 Ohio App.3d 30, 600 N.E.2d 1112.

In a proceeding to terminate a father's parental rights, a trial court's failure to comply with RC 2151.35(B)(3) and Juv R 34(C), which requires judgment to be entered within seven days of dispositional hearings, does not (1) result in a denial of the father's due process rights; (2) deprive the court of jurisdiction to enter a final determination; or (3) require reversal of the court's final judgment. In re Fleming (Lucas 1991) 76 Ohio App.3d 30, 600 N.E.2d 1112. Constitutional Law ⬤➡ 274(5); Infants ⬤➡ 221; Infants ⬤➡ 254

The proper remedy in cases where a trial court fails to meet the seven day requirement imposed by RC 2151.35(B)(3) and/or Juv R 34(C) is for counsel for the parents or county children services board to file, on expiration of the seven day time period, a petition for a writ of procedendo with the court of appeals requesting the court to direct the trial court to comply immediately with those requirements and proceed to final judgment. In re Fleming (Lucas 1991) 76 Ohio App.3d 30, 600 N.E.2d 1112. Courts ⬤➡ 207.1

When a child is placed in the permanent custody of the youth services department, the court shall determine the school district responsible for the costs of educating the child as provided by RC 2151.357; Juv R 34(C) is not inconsistent with RC 2151.357, and gives the court no discretion to determine such school district in any other manner. Christman v. Washington Court House (Fayette 1986) 30 Ohio App.3d 228, 507 N.E.2d 384, 30 O.B.R. 386.

Although RC 2151.35(B)(3) and Juv R 34(C) require that final judgment in the dispositional phase of an institutional child custody action be rendered within seven days of the dispositional hearing, failure to render judgment within seven days does not require reversal of the judgment ultimately rendered; procedendo is the proper remedy to compel a court to comply with the time limits. Galloway v Lucas County Children Services Bd, No. L–90–197 (6th Dist Ct App, Lucas, 9–6–91).

4. Final orders

Temporary custody orders entered pursuant to Juv R 34 are final, appealable orders when entered. Ackerman v. Lucas County Children Services Bd. (Lucas 1989) 49 Ohio App.3d 14, 550 N.E.2d 549.

A further dispositional order which continues an original order of temporary custody constitutes a final appealable order within the meaning of RC 2505.02. In re Patterson (Madison 1984) 16 Ohio App.3d 214, 475 N.E.2d 160, 16 O.B.R. 229. Infants ⬤➡ 242

A temporary order of a juvenile court changing custody under Juv R 13 or 29 is not a dispositional order under Juv R 34, and hence is not a final appealable order. Morrison v. Morrison (Summit 1973) 45 Ohio App.2d 299, 344 N.E.2d 144, 74 O.O.2d 441.

5. Fees and costs

A court that commits a child to the custody of the youth services department is required to determine which school district shall bear the cost of educating the child. OAG 88–023.

Where a juvenile court commits a child to a specialized school in another state, the court must itself pay expenses occasioned by the commitment and authorized by the court at the time of commitment, which expenses are paid out of funds appropriated to the court by the board of county commissioners under RC 2151.10; and the court may order the parents, guardian, or person charged with the child's support to reimburse the court for such payments. (Annotation from former RC 2151.35.) 1962 OAG 2938.

6. Dispositional orders

Juvenile court's failure in dependency proceedings to wait at least one day between the adjudicatory and dispositional hearings was not improper, where parties consented to hold dispositional hearing immediately after adjudicatory hearing. In re Malone (Ohio App. 10 Dist., Franklin, 12-30-2003) No. 03AP-489, 2003-Ohio-7156, 2003 WL 23024377, Unreported. Infants ⬤➡ 210

Trial court lacked authority to place children in a Planned Permanent Living Arrangement (PPLA) as an alternative to terminating father's parental rights; there was no evidence to suggest that father or county department of children and family services sought a PPLA, and there was no evidence presented to establish any of the other statutory requirements necessary for court to place children in a PPLA. (Per O'Donnell, J., with two judges concurring in judgment only). In re Harlston (Ohio App. 8 Dist., Cuyahoga, 01-23-2003) No. 80672, 2003-Ohio-282, 2003 WL 152939, Unreported. Infants ⬤➡ 222

A juvenile court may, upon finding that a child is neglected, dependent, or delinquent, commit the child to any person or institution meeting the requirements of RC 5103.02 and 5103.03, even though a county child welfare board exists and could provide care and support for the child; and the board of county commissioners has a duty to appropriate each year such sum as will provide the court with necessary funds for the care, maintenance, education, and support of neglected, dependent, and delinquent children. (Annotation from former RC 2151.10.) 1962 OAG 3489.

Juvenile court is empowered to commit a child to a foster home and to make such terms respecting such commitment as may be proper and suitable under the circumstances. (Annotation from former RC 2151.35.) 1941 OAG 3353.

7. Probation

The length of time for which a child is to remain on probation may be fixed at the dispositional hearing or at a later date and may extend until the time the child reaches age twenty-one. In re De Geronimo, No. 40089 (8th Dist Ct App, Cuyahoga, 6–28–79).

8. Right to counsel

The trial court was not required to inform mother of her right to counsel at hearing to modify custody of child, in child dependency proceeding; Juvenile Rules required the trial court to inform parents of their right to counsel at the adjudicatory hearing, trial court informed mother of her right to counsel at the adjudicatory hearing, and there was no Juvenile Rule regarding counsel for modification of custody hearings. In re Williams (Ohio App. 10 Dist., Franklin, 02-12-2004) No. 03AP-1007, 2004-Ohio-678, 2004 WL 285560, Unreported. Infants ⊕ 230.1

Trial court committed reversible error in allowing father's attorney to withdraw at outset of dispositional hearing regarding termination of father's rights to minor child, on basis of father's tardiness at hearing and alleged failure to cooperate with attorney beforehand, where statute provided that parents were entitled to representation by legal counsel at all stages of such proceedings, father's attorney did not make requisite good cause showing to withdraw, from ethical perspective, attorney could not withdraw from employment until attorney had taken reasonable steps to avoid foreseeable prejudice to rights of client, and father could not have been deemed to have waived right to counsel. In re M.L.R. (Ohio App. 8 Dist. 2002) 2002–Ohio–5958, 2002 WL 31429749.

Assuming that mother's counsel was derelict in failing to timely move for appointment of new counsel due to conflict of interest and in failing to follow up on motion, mother did not show prejudice, and thus, mother could not establish ineffective assistance of counsel in proceeding for permanent custody of dependent children; Montgomery County Children Services (MCCS) proved its case by clear and convincing evidence and nothing in record suggested any viable objections. In re Lakes (Ohio App. 2 Dist., 08-02-2002) 149 Ohio App.3d 128, 776 N.E.2d 510, 2002-Ohio-3917. Infants ⊕ 205

If the defendant, in seeking appointment of new counsel, alleges facts which, if true, would require relief, the trial court must inquire into the defendant's complaint and make the inquiry part of the record; the inquiry may be brief and minimal, but it must be made if the allegations are sufficiently specific. In re Lakes (Ohio App. 2 Dist., 08-02-2002) 149 Ohio App.3d 128, 776 N.E.2d 510, 2002-Ohio-3917. Criminal Law ⊕ 641.10(2)

Error cannot be predicated on the juvenile court's holding a dispositional hearing immediately following an adjudicatory hearing and its failure to continue the dispositional hearing for a reasonable time to enable the party to obtain or consult counsel, as prescribed by Juv R 34(A), unless it affirmatively appears in the record that the affected nonindigent party has requested such continuance. In re Bolden (Allen 1973) 37 Ohio App.2d 7, 306 N.E.2d 166, 66 O.O.2d 26.

The guarantee of the right to be represented by counsel set forth in Juv R 4(A) does not, as to a nonindigent party, require that trial be continued indefinitely until counsel can be obtained, but merely requires, if it does not appear that counsel could not be obtained through the exercise of reasonable diligence and a willingness to enter into reasonable contractual arrangements for counsel's services, that a reasonable opportunity be given to the party before trial to employ such counsel. In re Bolden (Allen 1973) 37 Ohio App.2d 7, 306 N.E.2d 166, 66 O.O.2d 26.

9. Evidence

Mother's ongoing criminal legal problems (some involving dishonesty), her failure to provide stable housing, and her failure to financially support her children constituted clear and convincing evidence that county agency should be awarded permanent custody of dependent child. In re Ashley E.D. (Ohio App. 6 Dist., Huron, 11-15-2002) No. H-02-025, 2002-Ohio-6238, 2002 WL 31529030, Unreported. Infants ⊕ 157

Any error in admitting father's testimony was harmless at motion for permanent custody of dependent child, as there was more than sufficient evidence absent father's testimony to support trial court's findings. In re Ashley E.D. (Ohio App. 6 Dist., Huron, 11-15-2002) No. H-02-025, 2002-Ohio-6238, 2002 WL 31529030, Unreported. Infants ⊕ 253

Lay opinions of social workers and dependent child's guardian ad litem were admissible on motion for permanent custody on issue of whether child's best interest was served by granting permanent custody to county department of jobs and family services. In re Ashley E.D. (Ohio App. 6 Dist., Huron, 11-15-2002) No. H-02-025, 2002-Ohio-6238, 2002 WL 31529030, Unreported. Infants ⊕ 173.1

Rules of Evidence applied at motion for permanent custody of dependent child. In re Ashley E.D. (Ohio App. 6 Dist., Huron, 11-15-2002) No. H-02-025, 2002-Ohio-6238, 2002 WL 31529030, Unreported. Infants ⊕ 173.1

At dispositional hearing in child dependency proceeding, trial court should have considered both grandmother's motion for legal custody of dependent child and mother's motion for return of custody based on best interest standard, without requiring grandmother to establish that mother was unsuitable before her motion would be considered. In re D.R. (Ohio App. 9 Dist., 06-04-2003) 153 Ohio App.3d 156, 792 N.E.2d 203, 2003-Ohio-2852. Infants ⊕ 231

At the dispositional stage of a neglect case, evidence other than the parent's admission is required to determine whether a particular placement is in the child's best interest. In re Lakes (Ohio App. 2 Dist., 08-02-2002) 149 Ohio App.3d 128, 776 N.E.2d 510, 2002-Ohio-3917. Infants ⊕ 179

In dispositional hearing related to permanent custody of neglected children, trial court was not required to engage in colloquy with mother similar to that required at adjudicatory hearing in determining whether mother knowingly, intelligently, and voluntarily relinquished custody of children. In re Lakes (Ohio App. 2 Dist., 08-02-2002) 149 Ohio App.3d 128, 776 N.E.2d 510, 2002-Ohio-3917. Infants ⊕ 203

Mother whose children were subjects of county's motion for permanent custody had statutory right to rebut guardian ad litem's unsworn testimony concerning suitability of placement with mother's sister and condition of her home, as these matters were not contained in guardian ad litem's written report and were not previously addressed by sister in her earlier testimony; thus, refusal to permit such rebuttal evidence violated due process. In re Sadiku (Ohio App. 9 Dist., 11-22-2000) 139 Ohio App.3d 263, 743 N.E.2d 507. Constitutional Law ⊕ 274(5); Infants ⊕ 207

The right of parents to raise their children is basic and essential, protected by due process of law. In re Sadiku (Ohio App. 9 Dist., 11-22-2000) 139 Ohio App.3d 263, 743 N.E.2d 507. Constitutional Law ⊕ 274(5)

Due process requires "fundamentally fair procedures" when a state attempts to terminate parental rights. In re Sadiku (Ohio App. 9 Dist., 11-22-2000) 139 Ohio App.3d 263, 743 N.E.2d 507. Constitutional Law ⊕ 274(5)

The proper scope of rebuttal testimony in a parental rights termination case lies within the sound discretion of the trial court. In re Sadiku (Ohio App. 9 Dist., 11-22-2000) 139 Ohio App.3d 263, 743 N.E.2d 507. Infants ⊕ 207

A trial court's decision regarding the scope of rebuttal testimony in a parental rights termination case will not be reversed unless the trial court's decision was unreasonable, arbitrary, or unconscionable. In re Sadiku (Ohio App. 9 Dist., 11-22-2000) 139 Ohio App.3d 263, 743 N.E.2d 507. Infants ☞ 252

"Evidence," for purposes of statute providing that juvenile court at dispositional hearing may admit any evidence that is material and relevant, contemplates sworn testimony, despite informal nature of such hearing. In re Ramsey Children (Stark 1995) 102 Ohio App.3d 168, 656 N.E.2d 1311. Infants ☞ 173.1

Testimony regarding a child's home environment and parental care is admissible in an action to terminate parental custody, even if it is hearsay, so long as it is material and relevant to the best interest of the child. In re Smith (Ottawa 1991) 77 Ohio App.3d 1, 601 N.E.2d 45.

10. Rights of juvenile

Twenty-eight months of limbo in juvenile dispositional hearing is a per se due process violation, barring extraordinary circumstances. In re Omosun Children (Trumbull 1995) 106 Ohio App.3d 813, 667 N.E.2d 431. Constitutional Law ☞ 274(5); Infants ☞ 204

Juvenile court did not err by conducting dispositional hearing with judge after referee conducted adjudicatory hearing, absent showing that juvenile was prejudiced or that it was possible for referee to preside over both hearings. In re Johnson (Ohio App. 1 Dist., 08-23-1995) 106 Ohio App.3d 38, 665 N.E.2d 247. Infants ☞ 253

Where no part of a proceeding conducted pursuant to Juv R 34(E) is contested, a juvenile court is not required to advise an accused of his right to appeal. In re Haas (Stark 1975) 45 Ohio App.2d 187, 341 N.E.2d 638, 74 O.O.2d 231.

Admission of reports of workers at juvenile rehabilitation center during dispositional hearing on revocation of juvenile's probation did not violate his right to due process, even though workers did not testify and were not subject to cross-examination, where program director of rehabilitation center and probation officer testified, and both were subject to cross-examination. In re Henderson (Ohio App. 12 Dist., Butler, 06–03–2002) No. CA2001–07–162, No. CA2001–09–228, 2002–Ohio–2575, 2002 WL 1160073, Unreported.

Procedural rule that requires a criminal defendant to be present at sentencing is applicable to a delinquency adjudication. In re Sweeten (Ohio App. 1 Dist., Hamilton, 05-24-2002) No. C-010314, 2002-Ohio-2552, 2002 WL 1040229, Unreported.

Due process clause of Fourteenth Amendment applies when child is charged with misconduct for which he may be incarcerated in institution, so child is entitled to notice of charges, counsel, confrontation and cross-examination, and privilege against self-incrimination. In re Jason R. (Ohio Com.Pl. 1995) 77 Ohio Misc.2d 37, 666 N.E.2d 666. Constitutional Law ☞ 255(4)

Proceeding with dispositional hearing in juvenile's absence did not violate due process; juvenile effectively waived his right to be present, as he had notice of hearing but blatantly disregarded it. In re Jason R. (Ohio Com.Pl. 1995) 77 Ohio Misc.2d 37, 666 N.E.2d 666. Constitutional Law ☞ 255(4); Infants ☞ 203

Right to be present at every stage of trial, as encompassed by right of confrontation, applies to both adult criminal trials and juvenile proceedings. In re Jason R. (Ohio Com.Pl. 1995) 77 Ohio Misc.2d 37, 666 N.E.2d 666. Criminal Law ☞ 662.70; Infants ☞ 203; Infants ☞ 207

Although juvenile's right to be present at dispositional hearing was implied by rule stating that court may excuse attendance of child at hearing in neglect, dependency, or abuse cases, and rule requiring court at conclusion of dispositional hearing to advise child of child's right to record expungement and right to appeal, juvenile nonetheless waived his right to be present at dispositional hearing by blatantly disregarding it after receiving adequate notice. In re Jason R. (Ohio Com.Pl. 1995) 77 Ohio Misc.2d 37, 666 N.E.2d 666. Infants ☞ 203

Proceeding with dispositional hearing in juvenile's absence did not violate his right of allocution, as he waived his right to be present by blatantly disregarding hearing after receiving adequate notice, thus waiving his right to address court passing judgment upon him. In re Jason R. (Ohio Com.Pl. 1995) 77 Ohio Misc.2d 37, 666 N.E.2d 666. Infants ☞ 203

Variance between one year sentence in judgment entry, and six-month sentence pronounced at hearing in delinquency proceeding, required vacation of sentence and remand for resentencing, where juvenile was not present when trial court imposed one year confinement stated in judgment entry. State v. R.W. (Ohio App. 8 Dist., Cuyahoga, 01-30-2003) No. 80631, 2003-Ohio-401, 2003 WL 194771, Unreported. Infants ☞ 254

11. —Timing, dispositional hearing

County children services' complaint for temporary custody of minor was statutorily required to be dismissed, where dispositional hearing was held some five months after date complaint was filed, rather than within mandated 90 days of filing. In re Olah (Ohio App. 9 Dist. 2000) 142 Ohio App.3d 176, 754 N.E.2d 1271, motion to certify allowed 90 Ohio St.3d 1491, 739 N.E.2d 816, appeal allowed 90 Ohio St.3d 1493, 739 N.E.2d 817, cause dismissed 93 Ohio St.3d 1404, 753 N.E.2d 208. Infants ☞ 204

12. Case plan

Mother in dependency proceedings failed to show she was prejudiced by failure of county children services to file case plan prior to adjudicatory hearing; there was no evidence to demonstrate lack of action on behalf of county children services, any lack of action on behalf of county children services was not the result of any error by magistrate or trial court, and trial counsel's failure to raise issue with regard to such failure may have been result of strategy to avoid further delays. In re Malone (Ohio App. 10 Dist., Franklin, 12-30-2003) No. 03AP-489, 2003-Ohio-7156, 2003 WL 23024377, Unreported. Infants ☞ 191

Juv R 35 Proceedings after judgment

(A) Continuing jurisdiction; invoked by motion

The continuing jurisdiction of the court shall be invoked by motion filed in the original proceeding, notice of which shall be served in the manner provided for the service of process.

(B) Revocation of probation

The court shall not revoke probation except after a hearing at which the child shall be present and apprised of the grounds on which revocation is proposed. The parties shall have the right to counsel and the right to appointed counsel where entitled pursuant to Juv. R. 4(A). Probation shall not be revoked except upon a finding that the child has violated a condition of probation of which the child had, pursuant to Juv. R. 34(C), been notified.

(C) Detention

During the pendency of proceedings under this rule, a child may be placed in detention in accordance with the provisions of Rule 7.

(Adopted eff. 7–1–72; amended eff. 7–1–94)

Historical and Statutory Notes

Amendment Note: The 7–1–94 amendment made changes to reflect gender-neutral language.

Commentary

Staff Notes

1994:

Rule 35 Proceedings After Judgment

Masculine references were replaced by gender neutral language and other grammar changes were made; no substantive change was intended.

Cross References

Divorce, annulment and alimony actions, Civ R 75
Sentence, Crim R 32

Library References

Infants ☞225, 230.1, 231.
Westlaw Topic No. 211.
C.J.S. Adoption of Persons §§ 10 to 12.
C.J.S. Infants §§ 57, 69 to 85.
Am Jur 2d: 47, Juvenile Courts and Delinquent Children § 60 to 62
Probation revocation: insanity as defense. 56 ALR4th 1178
Carlin, Baldwin's Ohio Practice, Merrick–Rippner Probate Law § 107.117, 107.121 (2003).

Notes of Decisions

Constitutional issues
   Due process 3
Court's duty to inform 2
Jurisdiction 1
Procedural issues 4

---

1. Jurisdiction

Trial court lacked personal jurisdiction over father to enter child support order against him, due to defective service of process of motion to set support; docket sheet showed that father was served with motion to set child support by ordinary mail only, rather than by certified mail, or express mail, as required by rule, so continuing jurisdiction of juvenile court was not invoked, and, due to failure to provide notice, any subsequent order based on void order was nullity. In re Brandon P. (Ohio App. 6 Dist., Lucas, 04-11-2003) No. L-02-1230, 2003-Ohio-1861, 2003 WL 1861564, Unreported. Child Support ☞180

Juvenile court's jurisdiction concerning any child who on or about date specified in complaint is al-

leged to be delinquent child is continuing and may be invoked at any time by motion before juvenile court. In re Bracewell (Ohio App. 1 Dist. 1998) 126 Ohio App.3d 133, 709 N.E.2d 938, dismissed, appeal not allowed 82 Ohio St.3d 1481, 696 N.E.2d 1087. Infants ☞ 230.1

Juvenile court's jurisdiction to reinstate order of commitment upon juvenile adjudicated delinquent by reason of acts which, if committed by adult, would have constituted third-degree felony of carrying concealed weapon, continued after juvenile was released from official probation; at dispositional hearing, order of commitment was stayed, and juvenile was informed that he would not have to appear before court again unless he got himself into some "more difficulty" or violated his probation. In re Bracewell (Ohio App. 1 Dist. 1998) 126 Ohio App.3d 133, 709 N.E.2d 938, dismissed, appeal not allowed 82 Ohio St.3d 1481, 696 N.E.2d 1087. Infants ☞ 230.1

The court's continuing jurisdiction may be invoked by the filing of a new complaint rather than a motion, as long as the parties are given notice and an opportunity to be heard. In re Luke, No. 83–CA–09 (5th Dist Ct App, Coshocton, 1–13–84).

2. Court's duty to inform

Revocation of juvenile's probation violated due process notice rights, where juvenile was unrepresented by counsel and neither Ohio transcript of dispositional hearing, docket, nor judgment entry of disposition mentioned a probation violation or informed juvenile of the condition of probation that he was alleged to have violated, and juvenile court made no finding that juvenile violated a probation condition. In re Royal (Ohio App. 7 Dist., 03-01-1999) 132 Ohio App.3d 496, 725 N.E.2d 685. Constitutional Law ☞ 255(4); Infants ☞ 225

Juvenile court must give the minor notice as to why a previously suspended commitment is ordered reinstated, if the court imposes a previously suspended commitment as a further disposition. In re Royal (Ohio App. 7 Dist., 03-01-1999) 132 Ohio App.3d 496, 725 N.E.2d 685. Infants ☞ 198

Court of Common Pleas did not "reopen" juvenile's case at probation department's request; although court placed entry in docket sheet about "reopening" case, no journal entry supported notation, and nothing in record showed that probation department had terminated probation. In re Edwards (Ohio App. 8 Dist. 1996) 117 Ohio App.3d 108, 690 N.E.2d 22. Infants ☞ 230.1

Court of Common Pleas never adequately determined that juvenile was probation violator after date on which it continued his probation; court in judgment entry neither identified condition allegedly violated, nor "found" juvenile had violated condition. In re Edwards (Ohio App. 8 Dist. 1996) 117 Ohio App.3d 108, 690 N.E.2d 22. Infants ☞ 230.1

At hearing for probation violation, juvenile court was not required to inform juvenile of consequences of his plea and right to present evidence during hearing. In re Motley (Summit 1996) 110 Ohio App.3d 641, 674 N.E.2d 1268. Infants ☞ 225

3. —Due process, constitutional issues

Juvenile had due process right to be present at hearing in order to show cause why he should not be held in contempt for his alleged failure to complete treatment program into which he was ordered in delinquency adjudication proceeding, as such proceeding should have been treated as probation revocation hearing at which juvenile had statutory right to be present. In re Nowak (Ohio App. 11 Dist.

1999) 133 Ohio App.3d 396, 728 N.E.2d 411. Constitutional Law ⊗ 273; Infants ⊗ 230.1

Admission of reports of workers at juvenile rehabilitation center during dispositional hearing on revocation of juvenile's probation did not violate his right to due process, even though workers did not testify and were not subject to cross-examination, where program director of rehabilitation center and probation officer testified, and both were subject to cross-examination. In re Henderson (Ohio App. 12 Dist., Butler, 06–03–2002), No. CA2001–07–162, No. CA2001–09–228, 2002–Ohio–2575, 2002 WL 1160073, Unreported.

Sentence entry informed juvenile of a suspended commitment to the Ohio Department of Youth Services, and thus there was no violation of due process and equal protection, and juvenile was not subjected to double jeopardy, when he was committed to the Ohio Department of Youth Services after he violated his probation. In re Keeran, No. 01CA69, 2002–Ohio–1580, 2002 WL 1653799 (5th Dist Ct App, Licking, 3–28–02).

4. Procedural issues

Revocation of juvenile's probation on two counts of raping his younger sister, following hearing at which juvenile moved unsuccessfully to withdraw his admission to those offenses based on allegations that his parents had coerced him into making admission, was not abuse of discretion; juvenile had repeatedly been brought back into court and warned that he would be sent to Department of Youth Services if his improper behavior did not cease, and he did not present adequate evidence to support allegations of coercion by parents. In re McElfresh (Ohio App. 7 Dist., Belmont, 03-07-2003) No. 02 BA 12, 2003-Ohio-1079, 2003 WL 932342, Unreported. Infants ⊗ 225

Court of Appeals could not address juvenile's challenges to actions taken and omissions made concerning original adjudication of delinquency, by reason of having committed burglary, and disposition, and juvenile's subsequent placement into custody of Department of Youth Services, where juvenile failed to file notices of appeal from juvenile court's orders; juvenile court's decision to suspend the commitment in order to permit juvenile to remain on probation did not affect its finality for purposes of appeal. In re R.M. (Ohio App. 8 Dist., Cuyahoga, 02-27-2003) No. 81085, 2003-Ohio-872, 2003 WL 549904, Unreported. Infants ⊗ 244.1

Trial court, in delinquency proceeding, had authority to initiate contempt proceedings against juvenile's mother based on a violation of order that required mother to attend parenting classes, even though a stay of execution of such order on was issued next day; stay of execution only dealt with juvenile's ninety-day sentence to juvenile detention center, and thus order to attend parenting classes was still in effect at all times. In re Cunningham (Ohio App. 7 Dist., Harrison, 10-18-2002) No. 02-537-CA, 2002-Ohio-5875, 2002 WL 31412256, Unreported. Contempt ⊗ 22

Juvenile court improperly proceeded against juvenile in contempt for his alleged failure to complete treatment program into which he was ordered in delinquency adjudication proceeding, as such alleged failure, if proved, would have amounted to probation violation; proper action would have been probation violation proceeding rather than contempt of court hearing. In re Nowak (Ohio App. 11 Dist. 1999) 133 Ohio App.3d 396, 728 N.E.2d 411. Infants ⊗ 230.1

Trial court could not revoke juvenile's probation without notifying juvenile of grounds on which revocation was proposed and without finding that juvenile had violated a condition of probation. In re Lett, No. 01 CA 222, 2002–Ohio–5023, 2002 WL 31115583 (7th Dist Ct App, 9–18–02).

Juv R 36   Dispositional review

(A) Court review

A court that issues a dispositional order in an abuse, neglect, or dependency case may review the child's placement or custody arrangement, the case plan, and the actions of the public or private agency implementing that plan at any time. A court that issues a dispositional order shall hold a review hearing one year after the earlier of the date on which the complaint in the case was filed or the child was first placed into shelter care. The court shall schedule the review hearing at the time that it holds the dispositional hearing. The court shall hold a similar review hearing no later than every twelve months after the initial review hearing until the child is adopted, returned to the child's parents, or the court otherwise terminates the child's placement or custody arrangement. A hearing pursuant to section 2151.415 of the Revised Code shall take the place of the first review hearing. The court shall schedule each subsequent review hearing at the conclusion of the review hearing immediately preceding the review hearing to be scheduled. Review hearings may be conducted by a judge or magistrate.

(B) Citizens' review board

The court may appoint a citizens' review board to conduct review hearings, subject to the review and approval by the court.

(C) Agency review

Each agency required to prepare a case plan for a child shall complete a semiannual administrative review of the case plan no later than six months after the earlier of the date on which the complaint in the case was filed or the child was first placed in shelter care. After the first administrative review, the agency shall complete semiannual administrative reviews no later than every six months. The agency shall prepare and file a written summary of the semiannual administrative review that shall include an updated case plan. If the agency, parents, guardian, or custodian of the child and guardian ad litem stipulate to the revised case plan, the plan shall be signed by all parties and filed with the written summary of the administrative review no later than seven days after the completion of the administrative review. If the court does not object to the revised case plan, it shall journalize the case plan within fourteen days after it is filed with the court. If the court does not approve of the revised case plan or if the agency, parties, guardian ad litem, and the attorney of the child do not agree to the need for changes to the case plan and to all of the proposed changes, the agency shall file its written summary and request a hearing. The court shall schedule a review hearing to be held no later than thirty days after the filing of the case plan or written summary or both, if required. The court shall give notice of the date, time, and location of the hearing to all interested parties and the guardian ad litem of the child. The court shall take one of the following actions:

(1) Approve or modify the case plan based upon the evidence presented;

(2) Return the child home with or without protective supervision and terminate temporary custody or determine which agency shall have custody;

(3) If the child is in permanent custody determine what actions would facilitate adoption;

(4) Journalize the terms of the updated case plan.

(Adopted eff. 7–1–94; amended eff. 7–1–96)

Historical and Statutory Notes

Amendment Note: The 7–1–96 amendment deleted "also" after "may" and substituted "judge or magistrate" for "referee" in the last sentence in division (A).

Commentary

Staff Notes

1996:

The amendment changed the rule's reference from "referee" to "magistrate" in division (A) in order to harmonize the rule with the language adopted in the 1995 amendments to Juv. R. 40. The amendment is technical only and no substantive change is intended.

1994:

Rule 36 Dispositional Review

Juv. R. 36 was previously reserved. The 1994 amendment was drafted to address requirements of dispositional review imposed by S.B. 89.

Revised Code 2151.353 and 2151.417(B) permit the court on its own motion or any public children's services agency or private child placing agency, the Department of Human Services, or any party at any time to move to modify or terminate any dispositional order on an abused, neglected, or dependent child.

Juv. R. 34 sets out the procedures for such a hearing to terminate or modify a dispositional order. Juv. R. 36(A) provides requirements for notice to all parties and the guardian ad litem.

Revised Code 2151.417(G) allows the appointment of a citizens' review board to review dispositional orders. Juv. R. 36(B) delineates that provision.

Juv. R. 36(C) delineates procedures for preparing case plans and conducting administrative reviews in accordance with Revised Code 2151.416(F).

Notes of Decisions

Court review 1

———

1. Court review

While statute requires juvenile court to review dispositional order if any party files motion requesting modification or termination of order, statute and rule additionally allow juvenile court to review child's placement or custody arrangement at any time. In re Bowman (Summit 1995) 101 Ohio App.3d 599, 656 N.E.2d 355. Infants ☞ 230.1

If a juvenile court, in making disposition of an unruly or delinquent child pursuant to RC 2151.354 or RC 2151.355, places the child into the temporary custody of the county department of human services in accordance with RC 2151.353, the juvenile court is required to hold periodic reviews pursuant to RC 2151.417 and Juv R 36(A). OAG 99–041.

Juv R 37 Recording of proceedings

(A) Record of proceedings

The juvenile court shall make a record of adjudicatory and dispositional proceedings in abuse, neglect, dependent, unruly, and delinquent cases; permanent custody cases; and proceedings before magistrates. In all other proceedings governed by these rules, a record shall be made upon request of a party or upon motion of the court. The record shall be taken in shorthand, stenotype, or by any other adequate mechanical, electronic, or video recording device.

(B) Restrictions on use of recording or transcript

No public use shall be made by any person, including a party, of any juvenile court record, including the recording or a transcript of any juvenile court hearing, except in the course of an appeal or as authorized by order of the court or by statute.

(Adopted eff. 7–1–72; amended eff. 7–1–96, 7–1–01)

Historical and Statutory Notes

Amendment Note: The 7–1–01 amendment inserted "or by statute" at the end of division (B).

Amendment Note: The 7–1–96 amendment rewrote this rule, which prior thereto read:

"(A) Recording of hearings.

"In all juvenile court hearings, upon request of a party, or upon the court's own motion, a complete record of all testimony, or other oral proceedings shall be taken in shorthand, stenotype or by any other adequate mechanical or electronic recording device.

"(B) Restrictions on use of recording or transcript.

"No public use shall be made by any person, including a party, of any juvenile court record, including the recording or a transcript thereof of any juvenile court hearing, except in the course of an appeal or as authorized by order of the court."

Commentary

Staff Notes

2001:

Rule 37(B) Restrictions on use of recording or transcript

Division (B) of this rule was amended to conform the rule with Revised Code section 2151.358 (E)(2), which provides for law enforcement personnel to have access to certain juvenile court records. The amendment was not intended to designate juvenile court records as public documents or to enlarge access to juvenile records beyond that specifically designated by a statute directed at juvenile court records.

1996:

Division (A) of this rule was modified to require the making of a record in adjudication and dispositional proceedings in abuse, neglect, dependent, unruly, and delinquent cases; in permanent custody cases; and in all proceedings before magistrates. It should be noted that the making of a record is mandatory in adjudicatory and dispositional proceedings. "Proceedings" includes the receiving of any admission or denial, as well as evidentiary hearings. The rule is consistent with section 2151.35(A) of the Revised Code requiring a record of permanent custody proceedings.

Division (B), which was not changed by the 1996 amendment, further provides that no public use shall be made of a transcript except upon appeal or upon authorization by the court.

The preparation of a transcript shall be at public expense if the party is indigent, in accordance with Juvenile Rule 29(B)(5).

Library References

Infants ☞133, 203, 246.
Westlaw Topic No. 211.
C.J.S. Infants §§ 51 to 91.
Am Jur 2d: 47, Juvenile Courts and Delinquent and Dependent Children § 56
Giannelli & Snyder, Baldwin's Ohio Practice, Evidence § 103.10 (2d ed. 2001).
Carlin, Baldwin's Ohio Practice, Merrick–Rippner Probate Law § 19.10, 19.12, 107.33, 107.60, 107.114 (2003).

Notes of Decisions

Lack of record, effect 6
Method of recording 3
Motion for transcript 1
Public records 4
Retention of record; time limitations 7
Right to counsel 5
Right to transcript 2

---

1. Motion for transcript

In absence of motion by mother for transcript of oral proceedings on her motion to reopen custody cases of her two children, and to recover legal custody of those children, no transcript was required; it was not matter determining permanent custody, but only motion to change legal custody. In re Wright (Montgomery 1993) 88 Ohio App.3d 539, 624 N.E.2d 347. Child Custody ☞ 907

2. Right to transcript

Television station was entitled to purchase copy of transcript of contempt proceeding against family services director and attorney arising out of child custody case; court did not make requisite findings before denying public access to transcript, proceeding itself was open to press, and there was no evidence that child could be harmed by access to transcript. State ex rel. Scripps Howard Broadcasting Co. v. Cuyahoga Cty. Court of Common Pleas, Juv. Div. (Ohio, 07-13-1995) 73 Ohio St.3d 19, 652 N.E.2d 179.

Juvenile court's order refusing to release transcript of contempt proceeding arising out of child custody case impinged on public's constitutional right of access and, as such, court was required to make findings that there existed reasonable and substantial basis for believing that public access could harm child or endanger fairness of adjudication, and that potential for harm outweighed benefits of public access. State ex rel. Scripps Howard Broadcasting Co. v. Cuyahoga Cty. Court of Common Pleas, Juv. Div. (Ohio, 07-13-1995) 73 Ohio St.3d 19, 652 N.E.2d 179.

Television station was entitled, under Public Records Act, to purchase copy of transcript of contempt proceeding against family services director and attorney arising out of child custody case, notwithstanding contention that release of transcript was prohibited by state law; juvenile court rule restricting access to transcripts did not prevent release of transcript, and that rule was sole basis for refusing to allow purchase of transcript. State ex rel. Scripps Howard Broadcasting Co. v. Cuyahoga Cty. Court of Common Pleas, Juv. Div. (Ohio, 07-13-1995) 73 Ohio St.3d 19, 652 N.E.2d 179.

An indigent parent is entitled to a transcript and counsel on appeal from a judgment permanently terminating his parental rights. State ex rel. Heller v. Miller (Ohio 1980) 61 Ohio St.2d 6, 399 N.E.2d 66, 15 O.O.3d 3.

Requirement that juvenile must make request for recordation of juvenile proceeding is neither burdensome to juvenile nor unconstitutional under due process or equal protection clauses. In re Hannah (Ohio App. 8 Dist., 10-16-1995) 106 Ohio App.3d 766, 667 N.E.2d 76. Constitutional Law ☞ 242.1(4); Constitutional Law ☞ 255(4)

Failure of juvenile to request recordation of juvenile proceeding constitutes waiver. In re Hannah (Ohio App. 8 Dist., 10-16-1995) 106 Ohio App.3d 766, 667 N.E.2d 76. Infants ☞ 203

Juvenile waived his right to recordation of his delinquency proceedings, so as to allow for production of verbatim transcript, by not timely requesting recording. In re Hannah (Ohio App. 8 Dist., 10-16-1995) 106 Ohio App.3d 766, 667 N.E.2d 76. Infants ☞ 243; Infants ☞ 246

An indigent juvenile offender is entitled to a record in a hearing conducted for the purpose of determining whether the juvenile court may waive jurisdiction and bind the offender over to the court of common pleas for criminal prosecution. (Annotation from former RC 2151.26.) State v. Ross (Greene 1970) 23 Ohio App.2d 215, 262 N.E.2d 427, 52 O.O.2d 311. Infants ☞ 68.7(3)

Because the no contact order, prohibiting mother from contacting her child, was continued in a subsequent proceeding, the lack of a complete transcript of initial hearing did not render the order invalid; hearing transcript and the judge's subsequent order continuing the no contact restriction were adequate to show that it was imposed upon proper procedures and evidence that the restriction was in child's best interest. In re F.M. (Ohio App. 8 Dist., Cuyahoga, 08-01-2002) No. 80027, 2002-Ohio-3900, 2002 WL 1767396, Unreported, appeal not allowed 98 Ohio St.3d 1410, 781 N.E.2d 1019, 2003-Ohio-60.

Local rules conditioning right to a transcript upon prepayment of costs are not inconsistent with Juv R 37 where the local rules permit avoidance of costs by filing a poverty affidavit. In re Menich, No. 42727 (8th Dist Ct App, Cuyahoga, 3–26–81).

3. Method of recording

Referee's report/journal entry and supplemental report, stating that juvenile was advised of his right to counsel and he chose to waive this right, were adequate to show juvenile's waiver of his right to counsel, absent request for transcript of admission hearing. In re East (Cuyahoga 1995) 105 Ohio App.3d 221, 663 N.E.2d 983, dismissed, appeal not allowed 74 Ohio St.3d 1482, 657 N.E.2d 1375. Infants ⚏ 246

It is within the trial court's discretion to determine which method of recording shall be used. In re Glenn, No. 35352 (8th Dist Ct App, Cuyahoga, 1–20–77).

4. Public records

Even though an Oklahoma statute provides that juvenile proceedings are to be held in private and records opened only by order of court, the trial court may not enjoin a newspaper from publishing the name or picture of a juvenile charged with murder when the press was in fact present at the hearing with full knowledge of the judge, prosecutor, and defense counsel, and no objections were made to its presence or to the photographing when the child left the courthouse. Oklahoma Pub. Co. v. District Court In and For Oklahoma County (U.S.Okl. 1977) 97 S.Ct. 1045, 430 U.S. 308, 51 L.Ed.2d 355.

Pursuant to Juv R 32(B), 37(B) and RC 2151.14, juvenile court records, the records of social, mental, and physical examinations pursuant to court order, and records of the juvenile court probation department are not public records under RC 149.43. OAG 90–101.

Under RC 1347.08, a juvenile court must permit a juvenile or a duly authorized attorney who represents the juvenile to inspect court records pertaining to the juvenile unless the records are exempted under RC 1347.04(A)(1)(e), 1347.08(C), or 1347.08(E)(2). Under Juv R 37(B), the records may not, however, be put to any public use except in the course of an appeal or as authorized by order of the court. OAG 84–077.

5. Right to counsel

Journal entry with respect to disposition hearing following adjudication of delinquency, which stated that juvenile waived counsel after having been informed by judge of "legal rights, procedures and possible consequences of hearing," did not place waiver affirmatively in record and was therefore insufficient to establish knowing and voluntary waiver of counsel. In re Solis (Ohio App. 8 Dist., 12-22-1997) 124 Ohio App.3d 547, 706 N.E.2d 839. Infants ⚏ 205

Putative father validly waived his right to counsel at paternity hearing, despite the absence of a transcript, where magistrate made handwritten notation that putative father was advised of his right to coun-

sel and blood testing and that he waived those rights, and putative father signed report. Douglas v. Boykin (Ohio App. 12 Dist., 07-07-1997) 121 Ohio App.3d 140, 699 N.E.2d 123. Children Out-of-wedlock ⚏ 57

Transcript of hearing at which putative father waived right to counsel was not mandatory requirement for a valid waiver of counsel in juvenile paternity proceeding, where putative father did not request transcript. Douglas v. Boykin (Ohio App. 12 Dist., 07-07-1997) 121 Ohio App.3d 140, 699 N.E.2d 123. Children Out-of-wedlock ⚏ 57

Failure to request recording device for verbatim transcript in juvenile delinquency proceeding is not per se ineffective assistance of counsel, even when juvenile's liberty is at issue. In re Hannah (Ohio App. 8 Dist., 10-16-1995) 106 Ohio App.3d 766, 667 N.E.2d 76. Infants ⚏ 205

Regardless of trial strategy or decision to waive recording device in juvenile delinquency proceeding, on claim of ineffective assistance of counsel, burden is on juvenile to show that lawyer breached his duty to provide reasonable representation and to show that outcome of case would have been different but for breach. In re Hannah (Ohio App. 8 Dist., 10-16-1995) 106 Ohio App.3d 766, 667 N.E.2d 76. Infants ⚏ 205

A trial court's failure to make a record of an adjudicatory hearing in a stolen car delinquency case in accordance with the mandates of Juv R 37(A) and Juv R 40(D)(2) prevents a finding that an affirmative waiver of the constitutional right to counsel took place, and the trial court magistrate's journal entry, which is the only record of the adjudicatory hearing in question, fails to even minimally satisfy the requirements of Juv R 29 since the magistrate did not check the box indicating whether the juvenile admitted or denied the allegations of the complaint and whether counsel was waived; although the informal detention hearing journal entry sets forth that an express waiver of counsel took place, the journal entry is not adequate evidence of a knowing, voluntary and intelligent waiver of counsel. In re Ward (Ohio App. 8 Dist., Cuyahoga, 06-12-1997) No. 71245, 1997 WL 321492, Unreported.

6. Lack of record, effect

Rule providing that it is appellant's duty to see that the record, including the transcript, is filed with the appellate court does not excuse juvenile court's obligation to provide for the recording of the transcript of delinquency adjudication proceeding. In re A.F. (Ohio App. 8 Dist., Cuyahoga, 03-11-2004) No. 82509, 2004-Ohio-1119, 2004 WL 443096, Unreported. Infants ⚏ 203

Juvenile court's failure to follow requirement to provide record of delinquency adjudication proceeding mandated appellate reversal of delinquency adjudication. In re A.F. (Ohio App. 8 Dist., Cuyahoga, 03-11-2004) No. 82509, 2004-Ohio-1119, 2004 WL 443096, Unreported. Infants ⚏ 246

Guardian ad litem for the children was not prejudiced by the trial court's alleged failure to properly record custody proceedings incident to a dependency action, based on the absence of the record of the in camera interview with the children and significant amounts of inaudible testimony from trial; juvenile court adequately complied with the Juvenile Rules for creation of a record since there was no difficulty in understanding the development of the proceedings regarding custody of the children, the trial judge stated information obtained during the in camera interview with the children in its judgment entry, both parties presented the court with recorded evidence for review, and guardian failed to allege with specificity what evidence or prejudicial errors were contained in the inaudible testimony. In re Mitchell (Ohio App. 11 Dist., Lake, 08-01-2003) No. 2002-L-078, No. 2002-L-079, 2003-Ohio-4102, 2003 WL 21782611, Unreported. Infants ☞ 253

Juvenile court's failure to follow requirement to provide record or termination of parental rights hearing mandated reversal; although court taped hearing, the tape ended in middle of direct examination of mother. In re B.E. (Ohio App. 8 Dist., Cuyahoga, 07-24-2003) No. 81781, 2003-Ohio-3949, 2003 WL 21710762, Unreported. Infants ☞ 246

Mother was not prejudiced, and thus her due process rights were not violated, when the trial court failed to make a record of two hearings, in child dependency proceeding; no evidence was presented at either hearing in which the trial court failed to make a record, and each of the hearings were conducted in order to grant a continuance. In re D.F. (Ohio App. 8 Dist., Cuyahoga, 06-19-2003) No. 81613, 2003-Ohio-3221, 2003 WL 21419537, Unreported. Infants ☞ 203

Trial court made complete record of dispositional hearing, in which county child services agency was awarded permanent custody of children, even though testimony of foster mother of one of children was not recorded, where parents and agency prepared statements of evidence under rule of appellate procedure which allowed for statement of evidence in situations where no report of evidence or proceedings at hearing or trial was made, and trial court settled differences in statements by approving, in its entirety, agency's statement. In re Myers (Ohio App. 4 Dist., Athens, 05-23-2003) No. 02CA50, 2003-Ohio-2776, 2003 WL 21246432, Unreported. Infants ☞ 246

Juvenile court's failure to record adjudicatory and dispositional hearings in delinquency case justified reversal of juvenile's adjudication and disposition. In re Estep (Ohio App. 4 Dist., Meigs, 06-26-2002) No. 01CA2, 2002-Ohio-6141, 2002 WL 31520351, Unreported. Infants ☞ 246

Trial court abused its discretion when it failed to make a record of juvenile's adjudicatory proceedings, as required by juvenile rule. In re Amos (Ohio App. 3 Dist., 09-22-2003) 154 Ohio App.3d 434, 797 N.E.2d 568, 2003-Ohio-5014. Infants ☞ 203

Although proceedings before magistrate, ancillary to delinquency complaint and involving alleged violation of court order, should have been recorded, failure to record did not cause juvenile prejudice, as magistrate's detention order would have expired on its own once court proceeded to disposition on delinquency complaint, and juvenile did not argue that her rights were violated in any respect before the magistrate. In re Smith (Ohio App. 8 Dist., 03-26-2001) 142 Ohio App.3d 16, 753 N.E.2d 930. Infants ☞ 203

Trial court's failure to make record of adjudicatory proceedings in delinquency case, as mandated by rule, warranted reversal and remand for new adjudicatory hearing. In re Collins (Ohio App. 8 Dist., 04-20-1998) 127 Ohio App.3d 278, 712 N.E.2d 798. Infants ☞ 246; Infants ☞ 253; Infants ☞ 254

At the time of a juvenile's "admit" plea where there is no record made of the proceeding there is no record for the judge to review in determining whether the juvenile's motion to withdraw his plea and vacate his sentence should be granted; as a result, a conviction for operating a motor vehicle under the influence of alcohol after underage consumption is vacated with instructions to conduct a new adjudicatory hearing which is properly recorded. In re L.D. (Ohio App. 8 Dist., Cuyahoga, 12-13-2001) No. 78750, 2001 WL 1612114, Unreported.

Juvenile courts must strictly comply with the requirement in amended Juv R 37 and failure to record adjudicatory or dispositional hearings contrary to that rule invalidates a juvenile's plea regardless of whatever information may be contained in the rest of the court's paperwork. Matter of Dikun (Ohio App. 11 Dist., Trumbull, 11-28-1997) No. 96-T-5558, 1997 WL 752630, Unreported.

Complete lack of any record of adjudicatory and dispositional hearings before the magistrate required reversal of juvenile's delinquency adjudication; missing record concerned waiver of counsel and admission to complaint, and lack of record prevented finding that magistrate complied with juvenile procedure rule requiring courts to make every effort to avoid the use of formal court proceedings in cases involving children. In re L.B. (Ohio App. 8 Dist., Cuyahoga, 07-25-2002) No. 79370, No. 79942, 2002-Ohio-3767, 2002 WL 1729905, Unreported.

7. Retention of record; time limitations

Delinquency proceeding would be remanded for limited purpose of findings of fact by juvenile court as to whether juvenile's waiver of his right to trial at the time of his admission to charged offense was knowingly, voluntarily, and intelligently given, where juvenile court made recording of proceeding in compliance with juvenile rule, that recording was subsequently destroyed after period of time prescribed by rule of superintendence had elapsed, and juvenile made no attempt on appeal to reconstruct the record. In re Raypole (Ohio App. 12 Dist., Fayette, 03-10-2003) No. CA2002-01-001, No. CA2002-01-002, 2003-Ohio-1066, 2003 WL 928976, Unreported. Infants ☞ 254

Absence of a recording or transcript of delinquency adjudication did not require a reversal on appeal filed more than three years after that adjudication; court reporter's certificate indicated a recording was made of that proceeding in compliance with juvenile rule, and applicable rule of superintendence did not require retention of that recording for three years. In re Raypole (Ohio App. 12 Dist., Fayette, 03-10-2003) No. CA2002-01-001, No. CA2002-01-002, 2003-Ohio-1066, 2003 WL 928976, Unreported. Infants ☞ 246

Juv R 38   Voluntary surrender of custody

(A) Temporary custody

(1) A person with custody of a child may enter into an agreement with any public or private children services agency giving the agency temporary custody for a period of up to thirty days without the approval of the juvenile court. The agency may request the court to grant a thirty day extension of the original agreement. The court may grant the original extension if it determines the extension to be in the best interest of the child. A case plan shall be filed at the same time the request for extension is filed. At the expiration of the original thirty day extension period, the agency may request the court to grant an additional thirty day extension. The court may grant the additional extension if it determines the extension is in the child's best interest.

The agency shall file an updated case plan at the same time it files the request for additional extension. At the expiration of the additional thirty day extension period, or at the expiration of the original thirty day extension period if no additional thirty day extension was requested, the agency shall either return the child to the custodian or file a complaint requesting temporary or permanent custody and a case plan.

(2) Notwithstanding division (A)(1) of this rule, the agreement may be for a period of sixty days if executed solely for the purpose of obtaining the adoption of a child less than six months of age. The agency may request the court to extend the temporary custody agreement for thirty days. A case plan shall be filed at the same time the request for extension is filed. At the expiration of the thirty day extension, the agency shall either return the child to the child's custodian or file a complaint with the court requesting temporary or permanent custody and a case plan.

(B) Permanent custody

(1) A person with custody of a child may make an agreement with court approval surrendering the child into the permanent custody of a public children service agency or private child placing agency. A public children service agency shall request and a private child placing agency may request the juvenile court of the county in which the child had residence or legal settlement to approve the permanent surrender agreement. The court may approve the agreement if it determines it to be in the best interest of the child. The agency requesting the approval shall file a case plan at the same time it files its request for approval of the permanent surrender agreement.

(2) An agreement for the surrender of permanent custody of a child to a private service agency is not required to be approved by the court if the agreement is executed solely for the purpose of obtaining an adoption of a child who is less than six months of age on the date of the execution of the agreement.

One year after the agreement is entered and every subsequent twelve months after that date, the court shall schedule a review hearing if a final decree of adoption has not been entered for a child who is the subject of an agreement for the surrender of permanent custody.

(Adopted eff. 7–1–94)

Commentary

Staff Notes

1994:

Rule 38 Voluntary Surrender of Custody

Prior to July 1, 1994, this rule was reserved. The 1994 amendment implements the provisions of Revised Code 5103.15 as amended by S.B. 89, regarding the procedure for making voluntary agreements of temporary custody to a public or private agency where extensions are requested.

Pursuant to the above-referenced statute, Juv. R. 38(A) provides that requests for extension of voluntary surrenders of custody must be accompanied by an updated case plan and the court may grant the extension if it determines the extension to be in the best interest of the child. Two such extensions may be granted for up to sixty days. If the agency desires a further extension, a new complaint for temporary or permanent custody must be filed. An agreement for temporary custody may be for sixty days if executed solely for the purpose of obtaining the adoption of a child less than six months of age.

Juv. R. 38(B) sets out procedures for the voluntary surrender of permanent custody. Agreements for permanent custody must have the approval of the juvenile court of the county in which the child resides or has legal settlement. Then, on an annual basis until a final decree of adoption is entered, the court must conduct a review hearing of the agreement.

Juv R 39 Out of county removal hearings

(A) Notice of removal hearing

Upon the filing of a removal action, the court in which the complaint is filed shall immediately contact the court that issued the original dispositional order for information necessary for service of summons and issuance of notice of the removal hearing. The court that issued the original dispositional order shall respond within five days after receiving the request.

Summons shall issue pursuant to Juv. R. 15 and 16.

Notice of the removal hearing shall be sent by first class mail, as evidenced by a certificate of mailing filed with the clerk of court, to the following, not otherwise summoned, at least five days before the hearing:

(1) The court issuing the dispositional order;

(2) The guardian *ad litem* for the child;

(3) Counsel for the child;

(4) The placing entity;

(5) The custodial entity;

(6) The complainant;

(7) The guardian *ad litem* and counsel presently representing the child in the court that issued the original dispositional order;

(8) Any other persons the court determines to be appropriate.

(B) Removal hearing

The removal hearing shall be held not later than thirty days after service of summons is obtained. If, after the removal hearing, the court grants relief in favor of the complainant, the court shall send written notice of such relief to the juvenile court that issued the original dispositional order.

(Adopted eff. 7–1–98)

Commentary

Staff Notes

1998:

Rule 39 Out-of-county removal hearings

The 1998 addition of Juv. R. 39 was intended to establish procedures for removal actions, as defined in Juv. R. 2(EE), which also was added by the 1998 amendments. Pursuant to Juv. R. 15(A), as in other cases within the purview of the Juvenile Rules, a summons must be issued to "the child, the parents, guardian, custodian, and any other persons who appear to the court to be proper or necessary parents." Juv. R. 39(A) includes a list of other entities and persons whose presence at the removal hearing may not be necessary, but who should be aware that the hearing will be conducted. This list includes, but is not limited to, the guardian *ad litem* and counsel for the child from the original proceeding in which the dispositional order was made, resulting in the child's out-of-county foster home placement.

Pursuant to Juv. R. 39(B), the time requirements for the scheduling of the hearing are predicated on service of summons.

Additional 1998 amendments governing removal actions were made to Juv. R. 2(EE), 4(B), 10(A), 11(B), 15(B), and 29(A) and (E).

Library References

OJur 3d: 48, Family Law §1566 et seq.

Juv R 40   Magistrates

(A) Appointment

The court may appoint one or more magistrates. Magistrates first appointed on or after the effective date of this amendment shall be attorneys admitted to practice in Ohio. A magistrate appointed under this rule also may serve as a magistrate under Crim.R. 19. The court shall not appoint as a magistrate any person who has contemporaneous responsibility for working with, or supervising the behavior of, children who are subject to dispositional orders of the ap-pointing court or any other juvenile court.

(B) Compensation

The compensation of the magistrate shall be fixed by the court and no part of the compensation shall be taxed as costs.

(C) Reference and powers

(1) Order of reference.

(a) The court by order may refer any of the following to a magistrate:

(i) pretrial or post-judgment motion or proceeding in any case, except a case involving the determination of a child's status as a serious youthful offender;

(ii) the trial of any case not to be tried to a jury, except the adjudication of a case against an alleged serious youthful offender;

(iii) upon the unanimous written consent of the parties, the trial of any case to be tried to a jury, except the adjudication of a case against an alleged serious youthful offender.

Except as provided in division (C)(1)(a)(iii) of this rule, the effect of a magistrate's order or decision is the same regardless of whether the parties have consented to the order of reference.

(b) An order of reference may be specific to a particular case or proceeding or may refer categories of motions, cases, or proceedings.

(c) The order of reference to a magistrate may do all of the following:

(i) Specify the magistrate's powers;

(ii) Direct the magistrate to report only upon particular issues, perform particular acts, or receive and report evidence only;

(iii) Fix the time and place for beginning and closing the hearings and for the filing of the magistrate's decision or order.

(2) General powers

Subject to the specifications stated in the order of reference, the magistrate shall regulate all proceedings in every hearing as if by the court and do all acts and take all measures necessary or property for the efficient performance of the magistrate's duties under the order. The magistrate may do all of the following:

(a) Issue subpoenas for the attendance of witnesses and the production of evidence;

(b) Rule upon the admissibility of evidence, unless otherwise directed by the order of reference;

(c) Put witnesses under oath and examine them;

(d) Call the parties to the action and examine them under oath.

(e) In cases involving direct or indirect contempt of court, when necessary to obtain the alleged contemnor's presence for hearing, issue an attachment for the alleged contemnor and set bail to secure the alleged contemnor's appearance. In determining bail, the magistrate shall consider the conditions of release prescribed in Crim.R. 46.

(3) Power to enter orders

(a) Pretrial orders. Unless otherwise specified in the order of reference, the magistrate may enter orders effective without judicial approval in pretrial proceedings under Civ.R. 16, in discovery proceedings under Civ.R. 26 to 37, Juv.R. 24 and 25, and in the following situations:

(i) Appointment of an attorney or guardian ad litem pursuant to Juv.R. 4 and 29(B)(4);

(ii) Taking a child into custody pursuant to Juv.R. 6;

(iii) Detention hearings pursuant to Juv.R. 7;

(iv) Temporary orders pursuant to Juv.R. 13;

(v) Extension of temporary orders pursuant to Juv.R. 14;

(vi) Summons and warrants pursuant to Juv.R. 15;

(vii) Preliminary conferences pursuant to Juv.R. 21;

(viii) Continuances pursuant to Juv.R. 23;

(ix) Deposition orders pursuant to Juv.R. 27(B)(3);

(x) Orders for social histories, physical and mental examinations pursuant to Juv.R. 32;

(xi) Other orders as necessary to regulate the proceedings.

(b) Appeal of pretrial orders. Any person may appeal to the court from any order of a magistrate entered under division (C)(3)(a) of this rule by filing a motion to set the order aside, stating the party's objections with particularity. The motion shall be filed no later than ten days after the magistrate's order is entered. The pendency of a motion to set aside does not stay the effectiveness of the magistrate's order unless the magistrate or the court grants a stay.

(c) Contempt in the magistrate's presence. In cases of contempt in the presence of the magistrate, the magistrate may impose an appropriate civil or criminal contempt sanction. Contempt sanctions under division (C)(3)(c) of this rule may be imposed only by a written order that recites the facts and certifies that the magistrate saw or heard the conduct constituting contempt. The contempt order shall be filed and a copy provided by the clerk to the appropriate judge of the court forthwith. The contemnor may by motion obtain immediate review of the magistrate's contempt order by a judge, or the judge or magistrate may set bail pending judicial review.

(d) Other orders. Unless prohibited by the order of reference, magistrates shall continue to be authorized to enter orders when authority to enter orders is specifically conveyed by statute or rule to magistrates or referees.

(e) Form of magistrate's orders. All orders of a magistrate shall be in writing, signed by the magistrate, identified as a magistrate's order in the caption, filed with the clerk, and served on all parties or their attorneys.

(D) Proceedings

(1) All proceedings before the magistrate shall be in accordance with these rules and any applicable statutes, as if before the court.

(2) Except as otherwise provided by law and notwithstanding the provisions of Juv.R. 37, all proceedings before magistrates shall be recorded in accordance with procedures established by the court.

(E) Decisions in referred matters.

Unless specifically required by the order of reference, a magistrate is not required to prepare any report other than the magistrate's decision. Except as to matters on which magistrates are permitted by division (C)(3) of this rule to enter orders without judicial approval, all matters referred to magistrates shall be decided as follows:

(1) *Magistrate's decision.* The magistrate promptly shall conduct all proceedings necessary for decision of referred matters. The magistrate shall then pre-

pare, sign, and file a magistrate's decision of the referred matter with the clerk, who shall serve copies on all parties or their attorneys.

(2) *Findings of fact and conclusions of law.* If any party makes a request for findings of fact and conclusions of law under Civ. R. 52 or if findings and conclusions are otherwise required by law or by the order of reference, the magistrate's decision shall include findings of fact and conclusions of law. If the request under Civ. R. 52 is made after the magistrate's decision is filed, the magistrate shall include the findings of fact and conclusions of law in an amended magistrate's decision. A magistrate's findings of fact and conclusions of law shall indicate conspicuously that a party shall not assign as error on appeal the court's adoption of any finding of fact or conclusion of law unless the party timely and specifically objects to that finding or conclusion as required by Juv. R. 40(E)(3).

(3) *Objections.*

(a) Time for filing. A party may file written objections to a magistrate's decision within fourteen days of the filing of the decision, regardless of whether the court has adopted the decision pursuant to Juv. R. 40(E)(4)(c). If any party timely files objections, any other party also may file objections not later than ten days after the first objections are filed. If a party makes a request for findings of fact and conclusions of law under Civ. R. 52, the time for filing objections begins to run when the magistrate files a decision including findings of fact and conclusions of law.

(b) Form of objections. Objections shall be specific and state with particularity the grounds of objection.

(c) Objections to magistrate's findings of fact. If the parties stipulate in writing that the magistrate's findings of fact shall be final, they may only object to errors of law in the magistrate's decision. Any objection to a finding of fact shall be supported by a transcript of all the evidence submitted to the magistrate relevant to that fact or an affidavit of the evidence if a transcript is not available.

(d) Waiver of right to assign adoption by court as error on appeal. A party shall not assign as error on appeal the court's adoption of any finding of fact or conclusion of law unless the party has objected to that finding or conclusion under this rule.

(4) *Court's action on magistrate's decision.*

(a) When effective. The magistrate's decision shall be effective when adopted by the court as noted in the journal record. The court may adopt the magistrate's decision if no written objections are filed unless it determines that there is an error of law or other defect on the face of the magistrate's decision.

(b) Disposition of objections. The court shall rule on any objections. The court may adopt, reject, or modify the magistrate's decision, hear additional evidence, recommit the matter to the magistrate with instructions, or hear the matter itself. In delinquency, unruly, or juvenile traffic offender cases, the court may hear additional evidence or hear the matter itself only with the consent of the child. The court may refuse to consider additional evidence proffered upon objections unless the objecting party demonstrates that with reasonable diligence the party could not have produced that evidence for the magistrate's consideration.

(c) Permanent and interim orders. The court may adopt a magistrate's decision and enter judgment without waiting for timely objections by the parties, but the filing of timely written objections shall operate as an automatic stay of execution of that judgment until the court disposes of those objections and vacates, modifies, or adheres to the judgment previously entered. The court may make an interim order on the basis of a magistrate's decision without waiting for or ruling on timely objections by the parties where immediate relief is justified. An interim order shall not be subject to the automatic stay caused by the filing of timely objections. An interim order shall not extend more than twenty-eight days from the date of its entry unless, within that time and for good cause shown, the court extends the interim order for an additional twenty-eight days.

(Adopted eff. 7–1–72; amended eff. 7–1–75, 7–1–85, 7–1–92, 7–1–95, 7–1–98, 7–1–01, 7–1–03)

Uncodified Law

2002 H 393, § 3, eff. 7–5–02, reads:

The General Assembly hereby encourages the Supreme Court to amend the Juvenile Rules to make clear that, while a magistrate may not try or sentence a case involving an alleged or adjudicated serious youthful offender, a magistrate may handle ministerial duties in that type of case, including arraignment and setting bail.

Historical and Statutory Notes

Amendment Note: The 7–1–01 amendment inserted "except a case involving the determination of a child's status as a serious youthful offender;" at the end of division (C)(1)(a)(i); and inserted "except the adjudication of a case against an alleged serious youthful offender" at the end of divisions (C)(1)(a)(ii) and (C)(1)(a)(iii).

Amendment Note: The 7–1–98 amendment substituted "Disposition" for "Consideration" in the title of division (E)(4)(b); substituted the first sentence in division (E)(4)(b) for "Except as provided herein, upon consideration of any objections,"; and made other nonsubstantive changes.

Amendment Note: The 7–1–95 amendment substantially rewrote this rule to pertain to magistrates instead of referees; see *Baldwin's Ohio Legislative Service*, 1995, page 7/R–55.

Commentary

Staff Notes

2003:

Juvenile Rule 40(E) Decisions in referred matters

The amendment to this rule is identical to an amendment to Civ. R. 53(E), also effective July 1, 2003.

It was suggested to the Rules Advisory Committee that the waiver rule prescribed by sentence four of former Civ. R. 53(E)(3)(b) [identical to sentence four of former Juv.R. 40(E)(3)(b)] sometimes surprised counsel and *pro se* litigants because they did not expect to be required to object to a finding of fact or conclusion of law in a magistrate's decision in order to assign its adoption by the trial court as error on appeal. A review of relevant appellate decisions seemed to confirm that suggestion.

It was further suggested that counsel or a *pro se* litigant was particularly likely to be surprised by the waiver rule of sentence four of former Civ. R. 53(E)(3)(b) if a trial court, as authorized by sentence two of Civ. R. 53(E)(4)(a), adopted a magistrate's decision prior to expiration of the fourteen days permitted for the filing of objections. See, e.g., *Riolo v. Navin*, 2002 WL 502408, 2002–Ohio–1551, (8th Dist. Ct. App., 4–19–2002).

Since 1995, the potential for surprise posed by the waiver rule may have been exacerbated by the fact that, under the original versions of Juv. R. 40 and Civ. R. 53, a party did not, by failing to file an objection, waive the right to assign as error on appeal the adoption by the trial court of a finding or fact or conclusion of law of a referee. See 30 Ohio St. 3d xlii-xliii (1972) (original version of Juv. R. 40); *Normandy Place Associates v. Beyer*, 2 Ohio St.3d 102, 103 (1982) (syl. 1)(noting absence of waiver rule in original version of Civ. R. 53). As of July 1, 1985, sentence one of Juv. R. 40(E)(6) and sentence one of Civ. R. 53(E)(6) were amended to read "[a] party may not assign as error the court's adoption of a referee's *finding of fact* unless an objection to that finding is contained in that party's written objections to the referee's report" (emphasis added). See 18 Ohio St.2d xxxv (1985)(Juv. R. 40(E)(6)); *State ex rel. Donah v. Windham Exempted Village Sch Dist. Bd. of Ed.*, 69 Ohio St.3d 114, 118 (1994) (confirming that the waiver rule of sentence one of the 1985

version of Civ. R. 53 applied only to findings of fact by referee). The wording of the waiver rule of sentence one of Juv. R. 40(E)(6) was modified slightly effective July 1, 1992. See 64 Ohio St.3d cxlv (1992); *In re McClure*, 1995 WL 423391, No. 7–95–2 (3d Dist. Ct. App., 7–19–95) (applying 1992 version of the waiver rule of sentence one of Juv. R. 40(E)(6)). The present waiver rule, which applies to both findings of fact and conclusions of law, took effect July 1, 1995, and represents a complete reversal of the position of the original Juv. R. 40. See *State ex rel. Booher v. Honda of America Mfg., Inc.*, 88 Ohio St. 3d 52 (2000) (confirming that the waiver rule of sentence four of Civ.R. 53(E)(3)(b), which is identical to the waiver rule of sentence four of Juv. R. 40(E)(3)(b), now applies to conclusions of law as well as to findings of fact by a magistrate).

The amendment thus makes three changes in Juv. R. 40(E), none of which are intended to modify the substantive scope or effect of the waiver rule contained in sentence four of former Juv.R. 40(E)(3)(b) [now division (E)(3)(d)]. First, the amendment retains, but breaks into three appropriately-titled subdivisions, the four sentences which comprised former Juv. R. 40(E)(3)(b). Sentences two and three of former Juv.R. 40(E)(3)(b) are included in a new subdivision (c) entitled "Objections to magistrate's findings of fact." Sentence four of former Juv. R. 40(E)(3)(b), which prescribes the waiver rule, is a new subdivision (d) entitled "Waiver of right to assign adoption by court as error on appeal."

Second, new language is inserted at the beginning of Juv. R. 40(E)(3)(a) to make it more evident that a party may properly file timely objections to a magistrate's decision even if the trial court has previously adopted that decision as permitted by Juv. R. 40(E)(4)(c).

Third, the amendment adds a new sentence to Juv. R. 40(E)(2), which sentence requires that a magistrate who files a decision which includes findings of fact and conclusions of law also provide a conspicuous warning that timely and specific objection as required by Juv. R. 40(E)(3) is necessary to assign as error on appeal adoption by the trial court of any finding of fact or conclusion of law. It is ordinarily assumed that rule language which prescribes a procedural requirement (see, e.g., sentence six of Civ. R. 51(A), which is analogous to the waiver rule of sentence four of Juv. R. 40(E)(3)) constitutes sufficient notice to counsel and to *pro se* litigants of that requirement. The Committee nonetheless concluded that the additional provision requiring that a magistrate's decision that includes findings of fact and conclusions of law call attention of counsel and *pro se* litigants to the waiver rule is justified because, as noted above, the original version of Juv. R. 40 imposed no waiver at all and even the 1985 and 1992 versions imposed waiver only as to findings of fact by referees.

2001:

Rule 40(C) Reference and powers

Divisions (C)(1)(a)(i), (ii), and (iii) were amended to reflect that certain proceedings involving serious youthful offenders shall not be referred to a magistrate, i.e., the hearing on a motion to determine if there is probable cause to prosecute the child as a serious youthful offender, and the adjudication itself, whether to a jury or not. These restrictions recognize the seriousness of the charges and their determination, and are consistent with the restrictions upon the use of magistrates within the Criminal Rules.

Substitute Senate Bill 179, effective January 1, 2002, created the new category of serious youthful offender. Juv. R. 2(KK) was added effective July 1,

2001, defining serious youthful offender as "a child eligible for sentencing as described in sections 2152.11 and 2152.13 of the Revised Code."

1998:

Rule 40(E) Decisions in referred matters

The 1998 amendment was to division (E)(4)(b) of this rule. The amendment was made because some trial judges apparently had avoided ruling upon objections to magistrates' reports since the previous rule appeared to require only "consideration" of the objections. The amendment should clarify that the judge is to rule upon, not just consider, any objections.

An identical amendment was made to division (E)(4)(b) of Civ. R. 53, also effective July 1, 1998.

1995:

Rule 40. Magistrates

Juvenile Rule 40 has been extensively revised. to the extent possible the revisions mirror similar changes in Civ.R. 53 also effective July 1, 1995. For further clarification reference is made to those staff notes.

Rule 40(A) Appointment

Changes the title from referee to magistrate in juvenile court; requires all magistrates of juvenile courts to be attorneys; permits those who are not attorneys and are presently serving as referees (prior to July 1, 1995) to continue to serve as magistrates.

It is intended that this grandfather clause is personal to the non-attorney magistrate and is not extended to the position itself. Subsequent appointment of a non-attorney magistrate who otherwise qualifies under this rule will not affect the status of that non-attorney magistrate.

If otherwise applicable, this rule is intended to apply to "referees" as that term continues to exist in rule and statute.

Rule 40(B) Compensation

Clarifies that the compensation of magistrates shall be fixed by the court; eliminates language that allows compensation to be taxed as costs in certain situations.

Rule 40(C) Reference and Powers

(C)(1) Order of Reference. Division (C)(1)(a)(i) and (ii) set forth the subject matter and types of cases that may be referred to a magistrate by the court pursuant to an order of reference.

Division (C)(1)(a)(iii) adds specific language, consistent with the Court's ruling in *Hartt v. Munobe* (1993), 67 Ohio St.3d 3, that permits magistrates to conduct jury trials and, in order to obviate the consent issue in *Munobe*, requires that consent of the parties must be in writing.

Language is also added, as extracted from Civ.R. 53, which makes it clear that, except in cases under division (c)(1)(a)(iii), the consent of the parties to the order of reference is not required. This is consistent with the existing practice in the court.

Divisions (C)(1)(b) and (c) otherwise leave to the discretion of the court the form and contents of the order of reference and restates existing language in the rule.

(C)(2) General powers. Subpoena language is updated; unnecessary language describing the handling of account cases is deleted. Division (C)(2)(e) incor-

porates language adopted July 1, 1993 in Civ.R. 53 which permits magistrates to issue attachments.

(C)(3) Power to Enter Orders. Division (C)(3)(a) grants to magistrates the power to enter specified orders that are temporary or interlocutory in nature. Due process guarantees to the parties are preserved by allowing any party to file a timely motion to set the order aside and requiring the court itself to address that motion. This expansion of magistrate's power is consistent with similar provisions found elsewhere in rule and statute and is designed to expedite the processing of cases and the time limitations imposed by S.B. 89.

(C)(3)(c) Contempt in the Magistrate's Presence. Provides the magistrate with specific power to impose appropriate contempt sanctions where necessary and addresses conflicting case authority regarding the power of the magistrate to control the courtroom. Safeguards have been provided to assure due process guarantees.

(C)(3)(d) Other Orders. Clarifies that the amended rule is not intended to supersede existing authority which grants to magistrates or referees the power to enter certain orders but is designed to supplement that existing authority. As other rules and statutes continue to carry the term "referee," reference is also made to referees.

Rule 40(D) Proceedings

Prior division (C) is deleted; amended division (D) requires that all proceedings before a magistrate be recorded. If, due to the nature of the facility, the magistrate is not provided with a courtroom separate from chambers, those informal proceedings, such as conferences that would normally take place in chambers, need not be recorded.

Rule 40(E) Decisions in Referred Matters

Eliminates the report-writing requirement unless specifically required by the order of reference; substitutes the requirement that, except in situations in which the magistrate may issue an order, a magistrate issue a written decision, which does not become effective until approved by the court; requires a magistrate to issue findings of fact and conclusions of law in three specific situations: 1) where the order of reference requires them, 2) where otherwise required by law, 3) where findings and conclusions are requested by any party pursuant to Civ.R. 52; assures due process guarantees by retaining the right to file objections; adds to Juv.R. 40 a provision originally found in Civ.R. 53 that allows a party additional time to file counterobjections; and specifies the action to be taken by the court in acting upon a magistrate's decision.

Division (E)(4)(b) contains a new provision that limits the court's power to hear additional evidence or hear the matter itself in certain situations thereby eliminating the double jeopardy issues raised in *Swisher v. Brady* (1978), 438 U.S. 204.

Division (E)(4)(c) addresses the issue of permanent and interim orders. All of these provisions reflect what has been existing practice in many courts in response to increased pressure on the court system to process a burgeoning caseload efficiently and expeditiously. Due process considerations mandate that access to the court via the objection process be retained. Findings and conclusions are restricted to those situations where required by the court or by law or where, in fact, the parties themselves believe findings and conclusions to be necessary. The amendment is designed to facilitate the expeditious resolution of cases while preserving to the parties rights similar to those afforded previously by Juv.R. 40.

1992:

Rule 40(A) Appointment

Masculine references are replaced by gender-neutral language and surplus language is deleted; no substantive change is intended.

Rule 40(B) Powers

This division is completely restructured for clarity, masculine references are replaced by gender-neutral language, and surplus language is deleted; no substantive change is intended.

Rule 40(C) Proceedings

Grammatical changes are made, masculine references are replaced by gender-neutral language, surplus language is deleted, and the style used for rule references is revised. No substantive change is intended.

Rule 40(D) Report

The former reference in division (D)(3) to consent by the parties is deleted because there is no provision in the rule for consent by the parties to an order of reference.

Division (D)(7) was amended to clarify that an interim order shall not extend more than twenty-eight days from the date of its entry; the former rule did not specify when the twenty-eight day period commenced. This amendment makes the rule consistent with the comparable provision in Civ.R. 53(E)(7).

In addition, grammatical changes are made and surplus language is deleted throughout division (D); no substantive change is intended.

Cross References

Referees, Civ R 53
Referees, powers and duties, 2151.16

Library References

Infants ☞206.
Westlaw Topic No. 211.
C.J.S. Infants §§ 63, 68.
Whiteside, Ohio Appellate Practice (2003 Ed.), Text 3.7.
Painter, Ohio Driving Under the Influence Law (2003 Ed.), Text 7.4.
Giannelli & Snyder, Baldwin's Ohio Practice, Evidence § 101.1, 101.5 (2d ed. 2001).
Carlin, Baldwin's Ohio Practice, Merrick–Rippner Probate Law § 3.40, 107.2, 107.41, 107.49, 107.120, 107.179, 107.181 (2003).

Notes of Decisions

Constitutional issues   7
Findings of fact   1
Hearings   9
Invalid reports or judgments   5
Objections to report   2
Procedures   6
Referees, powers and duties   8
Time limitations   3
Transcripts   4

---

1. Findings of fact

Magistrate's findings of fact were sufficient for trial court to make independent analysis and to apply appropriate law in reaching its judgment, and thus trial court did not abuse its discretion when it adopted magistrate's decision, which ordered father to pay $1,167.22 per month in child support to mother of minor child; magistrate had found that father was voluntarily underemployed, that father claimed to earn $5.15 per hour, that father was earning $300,000 to $400,000 annually before parties' separation, that mother had received no child support for child since parties separated, and that father's testimony was incredible and led magistrate to believe that father was attempting to hide income and assets. Howard v. Howard (Ohio App. 6 Dist., Lucas, 10-24-2003) No. L-02-1371, 2003-Ohio-5683, 2003 WL 22417178, Unreported. Child Support ☞ 211

Mother waived challenge to magistrate's finding that change of circumstances warranted change of custody as to nonmarital child, where sole objection raised with trial court was finding that change of custody was in child's best interest. Noonan v. Edson (Ohio App. 12 Dist., Butler, 04-07-2003) No. CA2002-04-088, 2003-Ohio-1767, 2003 WL 1795576, Unreported. Children Out-of-wedlock ☞ 20.11

In child custody matters, litigant must be given opportunity to object to referee's findings of fact. In re Wright (Montgomery 1993) 88 Ohio App.3d 539, 624 N.E.2d 347. Child Custody ☞ 504

Order denying mother's motion to reopen custody cases of her two children, and to recover legal custody of those children from their paternal grandmother, was void due to referee's failure to prepare and file written report detailing findings of fact on which referee's recommendation was based; due to lack of written findings in record, there was no evidence that trial judge made independent analysis, and mother was never given opportunity to object to referee's findings of fact. In re Wright (Montgomery 1993) 88 Ohio App.3d 539, 624 N.E.2d 347. Child Custody ☞ 659

Referee's report must contain sufficient facts for trial court to make independent analysis, and absent sufficient facts to make independent analysis, trial court cannot adopt referee's recommendation. Sharpe v. Sharpe (Lake 1993) 85 Ohio App.3d 638, 620 N.E.2d 916. Reference ☞ 86

The requirement of Juv R 40(D)(1) that the report of the referee set forth his findings in the case is satisfied where a supplemental report provides necessary material lacking in the original. In re Weimer (Cuyahoga 1984) 19 Ohio App.3d 130, 483 N.E.2d 173, 19 O.B.R. 219.

A trial court's failure to make a record of an adjudicatory hearing in a stolen car delinquency case in accordance with the mandates of Juv R 37(A) and Juv R 40(D)(2) prevents a finding that an affirmative waiver of the constitutional right to counsel took place, and the trial court magistrate's journal entry, which is the only record of the adjudicatory hearing in question, fails to even minimally satisfy the requirements of Juv R 29 since the magistrate did not check the box indicating whether the juvenile admitted or denied the allegations of the complaint and whether counsel was waived; although the informal detention hearing journal entry sets forth that an express waiver of counsel took place, the journal entry is not adequate evidence of a knowing, voluntary and intelligent waiver of counsel. In re Ward (Ohio App. 8 Dist., Cuyahoga, 06-12-1997) No. 71245, 1997 WL 321492, Unreported.

Trial court was not precluded from rejecting findings of magistrate that mother did not abandon child, that mother did not relinquish custody of child to child's paternal grandparents, and that mother was able to provide support for child, on grandparents' timely-filed objection to magistrate's decision in proceedings to determine custody of child between mother and paternal grandparents. In re Ratliff (Ohio App. 11 Dist., Portage, 11-29-2002) No. 2001-P-0142, No. 2001-P-0143, 2002-Ohio-6586, 2002 WL 31716783, Unreported. Child Custody ☞ 504

2. Objections to report

Minor's failure to object to magistrate's decision finding minor delinquent and ordering her committed to Department of Youth Services limited scope of appellate review to review for plain error. In re Harper (Ohio App. 2 Dist., Montgomery, 12-12-2003) No. 19948, 2003-Ohio-6666, 2003 WL 22927248, Unreported. Infants ☞ 243

Mother failed to object before trial court to grounds for emergency custody order, removing her child from her home, and thus issue was waived for appeal. In re Lewis (Ohio App. 4 Dist., Athens, 09-25-2003) No. 03CA12, 2003-Ohio-5262, 2003 WL 22267129, Unreported. Infants ☞ 243

After making independent review of magistrate's proposed modification of visitation schedule, juvenile court was free to disagree with magistrate's conclusions and to enter its own order, which it found to be in out-of-wedlock child's best interest. In re Ross (Ohio App. 1 Dist., 08-22-2003) 154 Ohio App.3d 1, 796 N.E.2d 6, 2003-Ohio-4419. Children Out-of-wedlock ☞ 20.4

Mother was not entitled to extraordinary relief in habeas corpus to compel county children services executive director to release her dependent child from its temporary custody, as she had adequate legal remedies in the ordinary course of law to raise her claims; mother could have objected to magistrate's decision, raised issues regarding sufficiency of dependency complaint or constitutionality of child dependency statute in any subsequent hearing in case, or appealed any adverse judgment by the juvenile court. Rammage v. Saros (Ohio 12–13–2002) 2002–Ohio–6669, 2002 WL 31769698.

Mother waived claim that magistrate should not have taken psychologist's testimony in child custody hearing after guardian ad litem withdrew, where objection to magistrate's findings at trial was limited to magistrate's finding that change of custody was in child's best interest. Noonan v. Edson (Ohio App. 12 Dist., Butler, 04-07-2003) No. CA2002-04-088, 2003-Ohio-1767, 2003 WL 1795576, Unreported. Children Out-of-wedlock ☞ 20.11

Father was not entitled to reversal of trial court judgment terminating parental rights and granting permanent custody to county children services board based on time delay in case due to numerous continuances and extensions; services board was not responsible for all continuances, continuances were based on unavailability of key witnesses, father did not object to all continuances, and father did not file objection to the trial court from the magistrate's grant of continuances. In re Hess (Ohio App. 7 Dist., Jefferson, 03-21-2003) No. 02 JE 37, 2003-Ohio-1429, 2003 WL 1465190, Unreported. Infants ☞ 253

Trial court properly dismissed father's objections to magistrate's decision denying his motion for new genetic testing in order to determine paternity since father's objections were not accompanied by an evidentiary transcript; because father's objections were based on the magistrate's failure to take evidence, the trial court needed to have some way of knowing if and why the magistrate failed to do so in order to judge the propriety of the magistrate's actions. Milick v. Ciapala (Ohio App. 7 Dist., Mahoning, 03-19-2003) No. 02 CA 53, 2003-Ohio-1427, 2003 WL

1464400, Unreported. Children Out-of-wedlock ☞ 57

Since mother filed no objections to the magistrate's report modifying father's child support obligation, mother waived, for purposes of appeal, her right to challenge the judgment of the trial court adopting magistrate's report. Dorothy P. v. Leo P. (Ohio App. 6 Dist., Sandusky, 08-30-2002) No. S-01-032, 2002-Ohio-4477, 2002 WL 1998448, Unreported. Child Support ☞ 539

Parents waived right to appeal insufficiency of the evidence claim in termination of parental rights case, where parents failed to object to magistrate's decision regarding termination of parental rights. In re Alyssa C. (Ohio App. 6 Dist., 05-23-2003) 153 Ohio App.3d 10, 790 N.E.2d 803, 2003-Ohio-2673. Infants ☞ 243

While trial court may enter judgment on referee's report without waiting for objections to be filed, it must make independent analysis of referee's report and it has responsibility to critically review and verify to its own satisfaction correctness of report. Sharpe v. Sharpe (Lake 1993) 85 Ohio App.3d 638, 620 N.E.2d 916. Reference ☞ 100(7)

A trial court does not have discretion to overrule the objections and adopt the referee's report without reviewing and considering the transcript where a transcript has been ordered. In re Moorehead (Montgomery 1991) 75 Ohio App.3d 711, 600 N.E.2d 778.

Woman challenging permanent child custody award waived claim that trial court erred in failing to conduct in camera interview of dependent child, where woman failed to file objections when in camera interview was denied. In re Bradford (Ohio App. 10 Dist., Franklin, 08–08–2002) No. 01AP–1151, 2002–Ohio–4013, 2002 WL 1813406, Unreported.

Mother waived her appellate argument that the trial court erred when it determined that the county children's services board was not required to establish that reasonable efforts for reunification of mother and child had been made, in termination of parental rights proceeding, where mother failed to file any written objections to the trial court's decision to grant county's motion for a "reasonable efforts bypass," which excused county from making reasonable efforts to assist mother in reunification due to the prior involuntary termination of mother's parental rights to five of her other children. In re Pittman, No. 20894, 2002-Ohio-2208, 2002 WL 987852 (9th Dist Ct App, 5-08-02).

3. Time limitations

Juvenile court's failure to grant enlargement of time to mother to file objections to magistrate's decision in dependency proceedings did not result in an injustice to mother within meaning of juvenile rule governing enlargement of time to file; mother had a full and fair opportunity to litigate the matters before the magistrate, and failure to file resulted from attorney's ignorance as to filing deadlines. In re Malone (Ohio App. 10 Dist., Franklin, 12-30-2003) No. 03AP-489, 2003-Ohio-7156, 2003 WL 23024377, Unreported. Infants ☞ 204

Juvenile procedure rules, rather than civil procedure rules, governed motion for extension of time to file objections to magistrate's decision in juvenile dependency proceedings. In re Malone (Ohio App. 10 Dist., Franklin, 12-30-2003) No. 03AP-489, 2003-Ohio-7156, 2003 WL 23024377, Unreported. Infants ☞ 204

Mother did not establish an undue delay cognizable in procedendo, relating to magistrate's failure to issue a separate decision in child abuse and dependency proceeding, where the mother's action for extraordinary relief was filed three days after the juvenile court had made its journal entry adjudicating the child as dependent. State ex rel. Nalls v. Russo (Ohio 2002) 96 Ohio St.3d 410, 775 N.E.2d 522, 2002–Ohio–4907.

Father could not appeal juvenile court's adoption of magistrate's decisions granting temporary custody of unruly child to public children services agency, requiring psychological evaluation of child, and requiring anger risk assessment of family members, where father did not object to those decisions in the juvenile court within 14 days of the filing of the decisions. In re Kidd (Ohio App. 11 Dist., Lake, 12-27-2002) No. 2001-L-039, 2002-Ohio-7264, 2002 WL 31886759, Unreported. Infants ☞ 243

The seven day rule of RC 2151.35(B)(3) and Juv R 34(C) can be applied consistently with Juv R 40(D), which (1) mandates the preparation and filing of findings of fact and recommendations by the referee; (2) provides an allowance of fourteen days from the filing of the referee's report for the filing of objections by the parties; and (3) provides for a hearing on the objections; when the dispositional hearing is conducted before a referee, the referee has seven days from the time the case becomes decisional in which to issue his findings of fact and recommendations and at the expiration of the fourteen day period for filing objections, if no objections are filed, the case is decisional and the trial court has seven days to issue its final judgment; however, if objections are filed pursuant to Juv R 40 and a hearing is held, the judge has seven days from the conclusion of the hearing to enter his final judgment. In re Fleming (Lucas 1991) 76 Ohio App.3d 30, 600 N.E.2d 1112.

Juvenile defendant, who had been adjudicated delinquent, waived her right to appeal the findings and conclusions contained in the magistrate's decision, where juvenile defendant failed to file written objections to the magistrate's decision within fourteen days after the filing of that decision. In re Stanford, No. 20921, 2002-Ohio-3755, 2002 WL 1627917 (9th Dist Ct App, Summit, 7-24-02).

4. Transcripts

Unwed mother's claim that the trial court erred in overruling her objection to the magistrate's decision to award the income tax dependency exemption to father because decision was not supported by the evidence was not preserved for appellate review, since mother failed to support her objections with a transcript of proceedings on father's motion to modify child support. Adkins v. Doss (Ohio App. 9 Dist., Medina, 12-31-2003) No. 03CA0046-M, 2003-Ohio-7174, 2003 WL 23094849, Unreported. Children Out-of-wedlock ☞ 73

In reviewing trial court's adoption of magistrate's decision, which ordered father to pay child support to mother of minor child, magistrate's findings of fact would be considered established, because father failed to provide trial court with transcript to support father's contention that magistrate was in error. Howard v. Howard (Ohio App. 6 Dist., Lucas, 10-24-2003) No. L-02-1371, 2003-Ohio-5683, 2003 WL 22417178, Unreported. Child Support ☞ 557(1)

A trial court's refusal to grant a request for a transcript of proceedings concerning a change of child custody from the mother to the father on the mother's objections to the referee's report challenging the weight of the evidence is an abuse of discretion where the court fails to give a substantial reason for its refusal, particularly where the referee's report concerning custody was filed as a journal entry, which is an indicia of "rubber stamping," and the transcript is necessary to resolve manifest weight

questions. In re Swain (Portage 1991) 68 Ohio App.3d 737, 589 N.E.2d 483. Divorce ☞ 150.1(3)

At the time of a juvenile's "admit" plea where there is no record made of the proceeding there is no record for the judge to review in determining whether the juvenile's motion to withdraw his plea and vacate his sentence should be granted; as a result, a conviction for operating a motor vehicle under the influence of alcohol after underage consumption is vacated with instructions to conduct a new adjudicatory hearing which is properly recorded. In re L.D. (Ohio App. 8 Dist., Cuyahoga, 12-13-2001) No. 78750, 2001 WL 1612114, Unreported.

5. Invalid reports or judgments

The magistrate and trial court's failure to comply with the Juvenile Rules for the issuance of a report and the entry of an order in dependency proceedings resulted in a void, and unappealable, judgment; the record did not contain a report with the magistrate's decision. In re D.N. (Ohio App. 8 Dist., Cuyahoga, 03-11-2004) No. 82708, 2004-Ohio-1106, 2004 WL 439965, Unreported. Infants ☞ 246

Referee's report in delinquency proceedings must contain sufficient facts for trial court to make required independent analysis of law and issues; court cannot accept referee's recommendation absent sufficient facts to make independent analysis. In re Montgomery (Ohio App. 8 Dist., 01-21-1997) 117 Ohio App.3d 696, 691 N.E.2d 349, dismissed, appeal not allowed 78 Ohio St.3d 1490, 678 N.E.2d 1228. Infants ☞ 206

Juvenile court erroneously adopted referee's report and proposed journal entry indicating that juvenile knowingly and voluntarily waived counsel and entered admission where there was no indication that referee addressed juvenile personally and determined that he understood nature of allegations and consequences of his admission, that juvenile knowingly and intelligently entered admission, or that he understood nature and ramifications of adjudicatory proceedings before he waived counsel and entered admission; referee's report and proposed journal entry consisted of one page with boilerplate language and check-off boxes to indicate proceedings. In re Montgomery (Ohio App. 8 Dist., 01-21-1997) 117 Ohio App.3d 696, 691 N.E.2d 349, dismissed, appeal not allowed 78 Ohio St.3d 1490, 678 N.E.2d 1228. Infants ☞ 206

Evidence presented at competency hearing and experts' reports did not support finding that mentally retarded juvenile was competent to stand trial; experts' reports and testimony were irreparably muddled with incorrect standards of law and inappropriate judgments pertaining to moral responsibility, and evidence appeared to establish prima facie case that juvenile did not understand nature of proceedings against him and was incapable of assisting in his own defense. In re Williams (Ohio App. 2 Dist., 05-23-1997) 116 Ohio App.3d 237, 687 N.E.2d 507, appeal not allowed 80 Ohio St.3d 1415, 684 N.E.2d 706. Infants ☞ 208

Defendant's appeal from speeding conviction was not moot after defendant paid $25 fine, where juvenile referee's instruction to defendant to pay, coupled with the threat of detention if defendant refused, established that fine was not voluntarily paid. In re Zindle (Summit 1995) 107 Ohio App.3d 342, 668 N.E.2d 969. Infants ☞ 247

It is an abuse of discretion for a trial court to allow a referee to preside over a protracted child support and custody case after he petitioned the court for removal due to bias, and the subsequent order based on the referee's report is improper. In re Reiner

(Cuyahoga 1991) 74 Ohio App.3d 213, 598 N.E.2d 768, dismissed, jurisdictional motion overruled 62 Ohio St.3d 1439, 579 N.E.2d 212.

Juv R 40(D) does not contemplate that a trial court rubber-stamp all reports by referees; thus, a court may, upon consideration of objections properly made, reject a referee's report. In re Bradford (Franklin 1986) 30 Ohio App.3d 87, 506 N.E.2d 925, 30 O.B.R. 185.

Juv R 40(D)(1), which requires copies of juvenile court referee reports to be furnished to the parties, comprehends a supplemental report filed at the request of the court to correct deficiencies in the original; approval of a supplemental report is prejudicial error where a copy of the supplement was not provided to the defending party. In re Weimer (Cuyahoga 1984) 19 Ohio App.3d 130, 483 N.E.2d 173, 19 O.B.R. 219.

A juvenile judge has no authority to commit the trial of a criminal charge against an adult to a referee and any proceedings so committed are null and void. State v. Eddington (Marion 1976) 52 Ohio App.2d 312, 369 N.E.2d 1054, 6 O.O.3d 317. Criminal Law ⬩ 254.1

A decision of the magistrate regarding child support is effective when adopted by the court and a nunc pro tunc order cannot be used to supply the omitted court approval and does not serve to make a child support order effective as of the date of the magistrate's decision; the order of support is ineffective during the period of time between the magistrate's decision and the trial court's signing and approval. No. CT 2001–0032, 2001 WL 950664 (5th Dist Ct App, Muskingum, 8–17–01), State v Tucker.

Where a referee fails to prepare a report upon matters submitted by an order of reference and fails to file such report with the judge and to provide copies to the parties as required under Juv R 40(D)(1), a trial court's denial of a motion to reopen a child custody case and to change custody from a paternal grandmother to the mother is error because a failure to make a referee's report, where a referee is required by statute or rule to make one, will render the ensuing judgment voidable on a timely objection of a party. In re Wright, Nos. 13372+, 1993 WL 257423 (2d Dist Ct App, Montgomery, 7–6–93).

A juvenile court's judgment entered before the filing of a referee's report is invalid. In re Langrehr, No. 2944 (11th Dist Ct App, Trumbull, 11–9–81).

A judgment of the juvenile court in the form of journalized recommendations of the referee is not rendered invalid because it was not immediately signed by the judge. (Annotation from former RC 2151.16.) Allstate Ins. Co. v. Cook (C.A.6 (Ohio) 1963) 324 F.2d 752, 26 O.O.2d 192.

6. Procedures

Grandmother waived for appeal issue of whether her right to discovery was violated in child dependency proceedings, where grandmother made no objection at trial or written objection to magistrate's decision concerning discovery procedure. In re McCann (Ohio App. 12 Dist., Clermont, 01-26-2004) No. CA2003-02-017, 2004-Ohio-283, 2004 WL 111644, Unreported. Infants ⬩ 243

Grandmother waived for appeal issue of whether she was entitled to grant of her motion for new dispositional hearing in child dependency proceedings, where grandmother failed to object to magistrate's denial of her motion. In re McCann (Ohio App. 12 Dist., Clermont, 01-26-2004) No. CA2003-02-017, 2004-Ohio-283, 2004 WL 111644, Unreported. Infants ⬩ 243

Mother, appealing juvenile court's determination that child was a dependent child, waived for appeal irregularities during hearing before magistrate, where mother failed to object. In re Malone (Ohio App. 10 Dist., Franklin, 12-30-2003) No. 03AP-489, 2003-Ohio-7156, 2003 WL 23024377, Unreported. Infants ⬩ 243

Father's failure to object to magistrate's findings or conclusions in proceeding to terminate parental rights and to grant permanent custody of children to family services agency limited review on appeal to whether findings and conclusions adequately supported trial court's decision to grant permanent custody. In re Kincer (Ohio App. 5 Dist., Licking, 11-24-2003) No. 03-CA-43, 2003-Ohio-6356, 2003 WL 22828046, Unreported. Infants ⬩ 243

Trial court's decision not to specifically rule on child support obligor's objection to magistrate's decision, which found obligor to be in contempt for failure to pay child support, did not amount to reversible error regarding county child support enforcement agency's motion to show cause against obligor, since objection lacked specificity and did not state particular grounds, obligor failed to include transcript of magistrate's hearing, and trial court reviewed decision for errors of law and other facial defects. Heifner v. Bess (Ohio App. 5 Dist., Ashland, 11-13-2003) No. 03 COA 013, 2003-Ohio-6047, 2003 WL 22671565, Unreported. Child Support ⬩ 558(4)

Mother could not raise on appeal, from Juvenile Court's adoption of finding of facts and conclusion of law of magistrate in termination of parental rights proceeding, an objection to magistrate's decision, where objection was not raised in lower court. In re K.M. (Ohio App. 9 Dist., Summit, 10-29-2003) No. 21536, 2003-Ohio-5781, 2003 WL 22439756, Unreported. Infants ⬩ 243

Parents failed to preserve argument that there was conflict of interest in dual appointment of children's guardian ad litem as children's attorney when they failed to raise argument when objecting to magistrate's decision to grant permanent custody of children to county services. In re Sessoms (Ohio App. 12 Dist., Butler, 10-06-2003) No. CA2002-11-280, 2003-Ohio-5281, 2003 WL 22283495, Unreported. Infants ⬩ 243

The juvenile court, when referring a matter to a magistrate, is not required to use any specified form of reference, nor is the juvenile court required to journalize an individual order of reference for each issue submitted. State ex rel. Nalls v. Russo (Ohio 2002) 96 Ohio St.3d 410, 775 N.E.2d 522, 2002–Ohio–4907.

Juvenile court's journal entry was sufficient to refer a child abuse and dependency matter to a magistrate; the entry was titled in part an "Order of Reference," it expressly authorized the magistrate to "hear and recommend dispositions on official cases assigned to 'the magistrate' as the Court shall direct," and it directed the magistrate to preside over the child abuse and dependency proceeding. State ex rel. Nalls v. Russo (Ohio 2002) 96 Ohio St.3d 410, 775 N.E.2d 522, 2002–Ohio–4907.

Mother's allegation that juvenile court's journal entry, which was signed by both magistrate and judge and which adjudicated the child as dependent, had failed to comply with the rule requiring the magistrate to prepare a separate decision did not establish that the magistrate and judge lacked jurisdiction over the child abuse and dependency proceeding. State ex rel. Nalls v. Russo (Ohio 2002) 96 Ohio St.3d 410, 775 N.E.2d 522, 2002–Ohio–4907.

The language of the rule regarding the juvenile court's reference of a matter to a magistrate is discretionary rather than mandatory. State ex rel. Nalls v. Russo (Ohio 2002) 96 Ohio St.3d 410, 775 N.E.2d 522, 2002–Ohio–4907.

Court of Appeals would not use abuse-of-discretion standard when reviewing trial court's decision to adopt magistrate's decision committing juvenile, who admitted to offenses of participation in a criminal gang and drug trafficking, to state Department of Youth Services (DYS) rather than releasing juvenile on community control, and review would be limited to errors of law or other defects on face of order, since juvenile failed to file objections to magistrate's decision. In re Harris (Ohio App. 10 Dist., Franklin, 05-15-2003) No. 02AP-1188, 2003-Ohio-2485, 2003 WL 21101271, Unreported. Infants ⇒ 251

Mother was precluded from claiming that trial court erred by considering, in its ruling on magistrate's decision to award permanent custody of her four children to county, additional evidence after the conclusion of testimony in the initial hearing on the matter, where mother herself requested a further hearing so that she could testify. In re Pederson (Ohio App. 10 Dist., Franklin, 04-29-2003) No. 02AP-853, No. 02AP-856, No. 02AP-854, No. 02AP-855, 2003-Ohio-2138, 2003 WL 1962429, Unreported. Infants ⇒ 248.1

Trial court was authorized to hear additional evidence in ruling on mother's objections to magistrate's decision to grant permanent custody of mother's four children to county. In re Pederson (Ohio App. 10 Dist., Franklin, 04-29-2003) No. 02AP-853, No. 02AP-856, No. 02AP-854, No. 02AP-855, 2003-Ohio-2138, 2003 WL 1962429, Unreported. Infants ⇒ 206

Juvenile defendant failed to preserve for appeal any assignment of error challenging the weight and sufficiency of the evidence supporting his adjudication of delinquency; defense trial counsel never provided transcript of the proceedings, which prevented either the trial court or the appellate court from reviewing the factual findings of the magistrate, and moreover, counsel withdrew his objections to the magistrate's decision, affirmatively waiving any objection to factual findings. State v. Hughes (Ohio App. 1 Dist., Hamilton, 02-28-2003) No. C-020035, No. C-020088, 2003-Ohio-890, 2003 WL 554000, Unreported. Infants ⇒ 248.1

Mother waived her appellate argument that the trial court decision adjudication the children dependent was against the manifest weight of the evidence, in child dependency proceeding, where adjudication of dependency was originally made by a magistrate and later adopted by the trial court, and mother failed to object to the magistrate's adjudication. In re C.F. (Ohio App. 9 Dist., Lorain, 11-13-2002) No. 02CA008084, 2002-Ohio-6113, 2002 WL 31513423, Unreported. Infants ⇒ 243

Mother established entitlement to writ of mandamus compelling county child support enforcement agency to stop withholding child support from her wages, where trial court never ruled on mother's timely objections, and order issued by court was an interim order that was not final and appealable. State ex rel. Rangel v. Lucas County Child Support Enforcement Agency (Ohio App. 6 Dist., Lucas, 10-11-2002) No. L-02-1252, 2002-Ohio-5497, 2002 WL 31270279, Unreported. Mandamus ⇒ 105

Magistrate's failure, in dependency proceeding, to satisfy her obligation to determine whether mother was making knowing, intelligent and voluntary admission to facts in complaint was plain error, and mother's failure to object thereto did not waive appellate review of magistrate's failure to comply with

applicable rule. In re Etter (Ohio App. 1 Dist., 06-12-1998) 134 Ohio App.3d 484, 731 N.E.2d 694. Infants ⇒ 243

Failure to draw juvenile court's attention to possible error, by objection or otherwise, when error could have been corrected, results in waiver of issue for purposes of appeal. In re Etter (Ohio App. 1 Dist., 06-12-1998) 134 Ohio App.3d 484, 731 N.E.2d 694. Infants ⇒ 243

Court of Appeals was precluded from considering any portion of the transcript of a magistrate's hearing on juvenile's motion to suppress, as the transcript was not provided to the trial court during earlier proceedings in the matter. In re Dengg (Ohio App. 11 Dist., 03-08-1999) 132 Ohio App.3d 360, 724 N.E.2d 1255. Infants ⇒ 246

Trial court's allowing state witness' mother, a nonparty witness, to communicate extensively out of presence of one of the parties, namely, accused delinquent minor, about referee's findings and recommendations raised questions regarding appearance of unfairness of proceedings and warranted vacation of adjudication of delinquency based upon attempted felonious assault finding and remand for hearing and ruling on objections to initial referee's report and recommendations. In re Ross (Franklin 1995) 107 Ohio App.3d 35, 667 N.E.2d 1012. Infants ⇒ 207; Infants ⇒ 254

Because the no contact order, prohibiting mother from contacting her child, was continued in a subsequent proceeding, the lack of a complete transcript of initial hearing did not render the order invalid; hearing transcript and the judge's subsequent order continuing the no contact restriction were adequate to show that it was imposed upon proper procedures and evidence that the restriction was in child's best interest. In re F.M. (Ohio App. 8 Dist., Cuyahoga, 08-01-2002) No. 80027, 2002-Ohio-3900, 2002 WL 1767396, Unreported, appeal not allowed 98 Ohio St.3d 1410, 781 N.E.2d 1019, 2003-Ohio-60.

A trial court order entry that delineated basis of adjudication of dependency was not required, where neither party made such a request for findings and conclusions of law. In re Ware, No. 19302, 2002-Ohio-4686, 2002 WL 31002612 (2d Dist Ct App, 9-06-02).

Since mother filed no objections to the magistrate's report modifying father's child support obligation, mother waived, for purposes of appeal, her right to challenge the judgment of the trial court adopting magistrate's report. Dorothy P. v. Leo P. (Ohio App. 6 Dist., Sandusky, 08-30-2002) No. S-01-032, 2002-Ohio-4477, 2002 WL 1998448, Unreported.

Notice required by this section to be given to parties must be in writing. (Annotation from former RC 2151.16.) In re Hobson (Franklin 1945) 62 N.E.2d 510, 44 Ohio Law Abs. 85, 44 Ohio Law Abs. 86.

7. Constitutional issues

Neither the magistrate's temporary no contact order, prohibiting mother from contacting her child, nor the judge's continuation of it required written findings of fact, even if mother had requested them, and lack of a decision with findings of fact did not deprive mother of due process; record contained enough facts to conclude that there was adequate basis for the order. In re F.M. (Ohio App. 8 Dist., Cuyahoga, 08-01-2002) No. 80027, 2002-Ohio-3900, 2002 WL 1767396, Unreported, appeal not allowed 98 Ohio St.3d 1410, 781 N.E.2d 1019, 2003-Ohio-60.

A juvenile's double jeopardy protections are violated when the trial court reverses its own judgment entry dismissing the complaint and finding defendant delinquent of rape where the trial court has no remaining jurisdiction to reopen the decision, reverse an acquittal and find defendant delinquent where written objections to the magistrate's report and judgment entry dismissing rape charges against the juvenile are not timely filed within fourteen days. In re Donald Joseph M. (Ohio App. 6 Dist., Sandusky, 09-17-1999) No. S-98-058, 1999 WL 727168, Unreported.

An adjudication of delinquency following the court's initial finding that the state failed to prove beyond a doubt that the minor was guilty of carrying a concealed weapon violates his rights under the Double Jeopardy Clause. In re Phommarath, No. 95APF05-539, 1995 WL 681213 (10th Dist Ct App, Franklin, 11-14-95).

A juvenile is placed in jeopardy at a hearing before a master whose duty is to determine whether he has committed acts that violate a criminal law, and where the potential consequences are stigma and the deprivation of liberty. (Ed. note: Maryland law construed in light of federal constitution.) (See also United States v DiFrancesco, 449 US 117, 101 SCt 426, 66 LEd(2d) 328 (1980).) Swisher v. Brady (U.S.Md. 1978) 98 S.Ct. 2699, 438 U.S. 204, 57 L.Ed.2d 705.

8. Referees, powers and duties

Although proceedings before magistrate, ancillary to delinquency complaint and involving alleged violation of court order, should have been recorded, failure to record did not cause juvenile prejudice, as magistrate's detention order would have expired on its own once court proceeded to disposition on delinquency complaint, and juvenile did not argue that her rights were violated in any respect before the magistrate. In re Smith (Ohio App. 8 Dist., 03-26-2001) 142 Ohio App.3d 16, 753 N.E.2d 930. Infants ☞ 203

While the juvenile court has authority to appoint a referee with power of masters in chancery to hear a case and report his findings and recommendations to the judge, there is no such authority with reference to an investigating counselor, and the action and report of such counselor is ex parte and does not constitute the hearing of "additional testimony" by the judge under such statute. (Annotation from former RC 2151.16.) Dolgin v. Dolgin (Lucas 1965) 1 Ohio App.2d 430, 205 N.E.2d 106, 30 O.O.2d 435.

At present, referees are not required to comply with Gov Jud R IV, which mandates continuing legal education for judges. Both part-time and full-time referees are encouraged to participate in continuing legal education in order to increase their knowledge and understanding of their position as referees and their knowledge of the area of law over which they preside as referee. (Annotation from Gov Jud R IV.) Bd of Commrs on Grievances & Discipline Op 87–041 (9-25-87).

Members of a part-time referee's law firm may not appear before their colleague as referee, but may appear before another judge or referee in the same division. Bd of Commrs on Grievances & Discipline Op 87–036 (9-25-87).

A part-time referee is considered a part-time judge for purposes of the Code of Judicial Conduct and may serve as a member or officer of a local board of education, provided such activity does not reflect adversely upon his impartiality or interfere with the performance of his judicial duties. A part-time referee should not serve as a member or officer of a local board of education if it is likely that said board will be engaged in proceedings that would ordinarily come before him or will be regularly engaged in adversary proceedings in any court. Additionally, a part-time referee should disqualify himself in any case in which his decision could affect any organization which he serves as either an officer or member of its board and he should avoid even the appearance of impropriety in all his activities. (Annotation from Code of Jud Cond Canon 3.) Bd of Commrs on Grievances & Discipline Op 87–032 (6–22–87).

Referees are considered judges for purposes of complying with the Code of Judicial Conduct. In this regard, part-time referees may not practice before the court division on which they serve or before the judge or judges to whom they owe their appointment; however, part-time referees serving the domestic relations division of common pleas court may practice law before other judges in the general, probate, and juvenile divisions of that court so long as they avoid the appearance of impropriety. (Annotation from Code of Jud Cond Canon 2.) (See also Bd of Commrs on Grievances & Discipline Op 87–036 (9–25–87).) Bd of Commrs on Grievances & Discipline Op 87–014 (6–22–87).

9. Hearings

That magistrate in child custody hearing as to nonmarital child took testimony from psychologist after child's guardian ad litem withdrew was not plain error; magistrate continued hearing until after new guardian ad litem was appointed, psychologist's testimony was made available to new guardian ad litem, and guardian ad litem was allowed to call and question psychologist if necessary at subsequent hearing. Noonan v. Edson (Ohio App. 12 Dist., Butler, 04-07-2003) No. CA2002-04-088, 2003-Ohio-1767, 2003 WL 1795576, Unreported. Children Out-of-wedlock ☞ 20.11

An evidentiary hearing before the juvenile court judge after a hearing before a juvenile court referee is not mandatory. In re Stall (Ohio 1973) 36 Ohio St.2d 139, 304 N.E.2d 596, 65 O.O.2d 338.

Rules governing objection to reports of juvenile referee do not require that trial court hold hearing when objections and affidavit about evidence have been filed; further consideration is required, but hearing is within discretion of court. In re Zindle (Summit 1995) 107 Ohio App.3d 342, 668 N.E.2d 969. Infants ☞ 206

The action of a juvenile court in postponing a hearing on a matter submitted to a referee who failed to file findings and recommendations, and in rectifying such deficiency by taking additional testimony and, thereafter, rendering a decision constitutes a substantial compliance with 2151.16. (Annotation from former RC 2151.16.) In re Gutman (Hamilton 1969) 22 Ohio App.2d 125, 259 N.E.2d 128, 51 O.O.2d 252.

Juv R 41 [Reserved]

Juv R 42 Consent to marry

(A) Application where parental consent not required

When a minor desires to contract matrimony and has no parent, guardian, or custodian whose consent to the marriage is required by law, the minor shall file an application under oath in the county where the female resides requesting that the judge of the juvenile court give consent and approbation in the probate court for such marriage.

(B) Contents of application

The application required by division (A) of this rule shall contain all of the following:

(1) The name and address of the person for whom consent is sought;

(2) The age of the person for whom consent is sought;

(3) The reason why consent of a parent is not required;

(4) The name and address, if known, of the parent, where the minor alleges that parental consent is unnecessary because the parent has neglected or abandoned the child for at least one year immediately preceding the application.

(C) Application where female pregnant or delivered of child born out of wedlock

Where a female is pregnant or delivered of a child born out of wedlock and the parents of such child seek to marry even though one or both of them is under the minimum age prescribed by law for persons who may contract marriage, such persons shall file an application under oath in the county where the female resides requesting that the judge of the juvenile court give consent in the probate court to such marriage.

(D) Contents of application

The application required by subdivision (C) shall contain:

(1) The name and address of the person or persons for whom consent is sought;

(2) The age of such person;

(3) An indication of whether the female is pregnant or has already been delivered;

(4) An indication of whether or not any applicant under eighteen years of age is already a ward of the court; and

(5) Any other facts which may assist the court in determining whether to consent to such marriage.

If pregnancy is asserted, a certificate from a physician verifying pregnancy shall be attached to the application. If an illegitimate child has been delivered, the birth certificate of such child shall be attached.

The consent to the granting of the application by each parent whose consent to the marriage is required by law shall be indorsed on the application.

(E) Investigation

Upon receipt of an application under subdivision (C), the court shall set a date and time for hearing thereon at its earliest convenience and shall direct that an inquiry be made as to the circumstances surrounding the applicants.

(F) Notice

If neglect or abandonment is alleged in an application under subdivision (A) and the address of the parent is known, the court shall cause notice of the date and time of hearing to be served upon such parent.

(G) Judgment

If the court finds that the allegations stated in the application are true, and that the granting of the application is in the best interest of the applicants, the court shall grant the consent and shall make the applicant referred to in subdivision (C) a ward of the court.

(H) Certified copy

A certified copy of the judgment entry shall be transmitted to the probate court.

(Adopted eff. 7–1–72; amended eff. 7–1–80, 7–1–94)

Historical and Statutory Notes

Amendment Note: The 7-1-94 amendment made changes to reflect gender-neutral language.

Commentary

Staff Notes

1994:

Rule 42 Consent to Marry

Masculine references in Juv. R. 42 were replaced by gender neutral language and nonsubstantive grammatical revisions were made.

Cross References

Abortion without parental consent, 2151.85

Persons who may marry, 3101.01

Probate court may issue license after juvenile court files consent to marriage, 3101.04

Library References

Marriage ⊗5, 12.1, 18, 19.

Westlaw Topic No. 253.

C.J.S. Marriage §§ 9 to 26, 36.

Carlin, Baldwin's Ohio Practice, Merrick–Rippner Probate Law § 106.20, 106.27 (2003).

Notes of Decisions

Consent 1

Marriage without consent 2

---

1. Consent

A minor youth who has been committed to the youth services department pursuant to RC 2151.355 and 5139.05 and who wishes to get married must first obtain consent, as required by RC 3101.01 and Juv R 42, from one or both parents, from one of the alternative authorities named in RC 3101.01, or from the juvenile court as provided in Juv R 42(A). The youth services department has no authority to either consent or withhold consent to the marriage of a minor committed to its custody. OAG 89–046.

2. Marriage without consent

The marriage of a male person seventeen years of age is void except under the conditions provided for in section. (Annotation from former RC 3101.04.) Carlton v. Carlton (Wood 1945) 76 Ohio App. 338, 64 N.E.2d 428, 32 O.O. 82. Marriage ⟲ 5

Juv R 43 Reference to Ohio Revised Code

A reference in these rules to a section of the Revised Code shall mean the section as amended from time to time including the enactment of additional sections, the numbers of which are subsequent to the section referred to in the rules.

(Adopted eff. 7–1–94)

Commentary

Staff Notes

1994:

Rule 43 Reference to Ohio Revised Code

Juv. R. 43 clarifies that any Revised Code section referred to in these rules shall mean the section as amended from time to time. This provision replicates Civ. R. 81.

Juv R 44 Jurisdiction unaffected

These rules shall not be construed to extend or limit the jurisdiction of the juvenile court.

(Adopted eff. 7–1–72)

Cross References

Scope of rules, exceptions, Juv R 1

Library References

Infants ⟲196.
Westlaw Topic No. 211.
C.J.S. Courts §§ 249 et seq.
C.J.S. Infants §§ 42, 53, 54.

Notes of Decisions

Constitutional issues 2
Jurisdiction 1

---

1. Jurisdiction

Because the Ohio Rules of Juvenile Procedure may not extend or limit the jurisdiction of the juvenile court, a procedural violation has no effect on jurisdictional issues, which are governed by statutory law. Linger v. Weiss (Ohio 1979) 57 Ohio St.2d 97, 386 N.E.2d 1354, 11 O.O.3d 281, certiorari denied 100 S.Ct. 128, 444 U.S. 862, 62 L.Ed.2d 83.

The juvenile court has exclusive original jurisdiction, pursuant to RC 2151.23(A), concerning any child who is alleged in a proper complaint to be neglected, and the court does not lose jurisdiction by failing to adhere to the time limits set forth in Juv R 29(A) and 34(A). Linger v. Weiss (Ohio 1979) 57 Ohio St.2d 97, 386 N.E.2d 1354, 11 O.O.3d 281, certiorari denied 100 S.Ct. 128, 444 U.S. 862, 62 L.Ed.2d 83.

2. Constitutional issues

A procedure which allows a juvenile court master to file written findings of fact with the juvenile court judge who may then make supplemental findings in response to the state's exceptions, the juvenile's exceptions or sua sponte, either on the record or a record supplemented by evidence to which the parties do not object, does not violate the Double Jeopardy Clause. (Ed. note: Maryland law construed in light of federal constitution.) (See also United States v DiFrancesco, 449 US 117, 101 SCt 426, 66 LEd(2d) 328 (1980).) Swisher v. Brady (U.S.Md. 1978) 98 S.Ct. 2699, 438 U.S. 204, 57 L.Ed.2d 705.

Juv R 45 Rules by juvenile courts; procedure not otherwise specified

(A) Local rules

The juvenile court may adopt rules concerning local practice that are not inconsistent with these rules. Local rules shall be adopted only after the court gives appropriate notice and an opportunity for comment. If the court determines that there is an immediate need for a rule, the court may adopt the rule without prior notice and opportunity for comment but promptly shall afford notice and opportunity for comment. Local rules shall be filed with the Supreme Court.

(B) Procedure not otherwise specified

If no procedure is specifically prescribed by these rules or local rule, the court shall proceed in any lawful manner not inconsistent with these rules or local rule.

(Adopted eff. 7–1–72; amended eff. 7–1–94)

Historical and Statutory Notes

Amendment Note: The 7–1–94 amendment added "Rules by juvenile courts;" to the title of the rule; added division (A); designated division (B); and added references to local rules in division (B).

Commentary

Staff Notes

1994:

Rule 45 Rules by Juvenile Courts; Procedure Not Otherwise Specified

Division (A) has been added to permit juvenile courts to develop local rules not inconsistent with the Ohio Rules of Juvenile Procedure. This provision is consistent with similar changes in Civ. R. 83 and App. R. 31.

Library References

Infants ☞191.

Westlaw Topic No. 211.

C.J.S. Infants §§ 42, 53, 54.

Klein & Darling, Baldwin's Ohio Practice, Civil Practice § 24–12 (1997).

Carlin, Baldwin's Ohio Practice, Merrick–Rippner Probate Law § 107.117 (2003).

Notes of Decisions

Constitutional issues 1

---

1. Constitutional issues

The federal courts will abstain from interfering in state proceedings where juveniles seek an injunction against the use of social histories in pre-adjudication instances, although they may hear an issue involving the constitutionality of post-adjudicatory dissemination of the social histories where state law is not clear and the proper factual issues were not decided; the dissemination of social histories compiled by probation officers during juvenile proceedings do not violate a constitutional right to privacy. J. P. v. DeSanti (C.A.6 (Ohio) 1981) 653 F.2d 1080.

Juv R 46   Forms

The forms contained in the Appendix of Forms which the supreme court from time to time may approve are illustrative and not mandatory.

(Adopted eff. 7–1–72)

Juv R 47   Effective date

(A) Effective date of rules

These rules shall take effect on the first day of July, 1972. They govern all proceedings in actions brought after they take effect and also all further proceedings in actions then pending, except to the extent that their application in a particular action pending when the rules take effect would not be feasible or would work injustice, in which event the former procedure applies.

(B) Effective date of amendments

The amendments submitted by the Supreme Court to the general assembly on January 12, 1973, shall take effect on the first day of July, 1973. They govern all proceedings in actions brought after they take effect and also all further proceedings in actions then pending, except to the extent that their application in a particular action pending when the amendments take effect would not be feasible or would work injustice, in which event the former procedure applies.

(C) Effective date of amendments

The amendments submitted by the Supreme Court to the General Assembly on January 10, 1975, and on April 29, 1975, shall take effect on July 1, 1975. They govern all proceedings in actions brought after they take effect and also all further proceedings in actions then pending, except to the extent that their application in a particular action pending when the amendments take effect would not be feasible or would work injustice, in which event the former procedure applies.

(D) Effective date of amendments

The amendments submitted by the Supreme Court to the General Assembly on January 9, 1976 shall take effect on July 1, 1976. They govern all proceedings in actions brought after they take effect and also all further proceedings in actions then pending, except to the extent that their application in a particular action pending when the amendments take effect would not be feasible or would work injustice, in which event the former procedure applies.

(E) Effective date of amendments

The amendments submitted by the Supreme Court to the General Assembly on January 14, 1980, shall take effect on July 1, 1980. They govern all proceedings in actions brought after they take effect and also all further proceedings in actions then pending, except to the extent that their application in a particular action pending when the amendments take effect would not be feasible or would work injustice, in which event the former procedure applies.

(F) Effective date of amendments.

The amendments submitted by the Supreme Court to the General Assembly on December 24, 1984 and January 8, 1985 shall take effect on July 1, 1985. They govern all proceedings in actions brought after they take effect and also all further proceedings in actions then pending, except to the extent that their application in a particular action pending when the amendments take effect would not be feasible or would work injustice, in which event the former procedure applies.

(G) Effective date of amendments

The amendments submitted by the Supreme Court to the General Assembly on January 10, 1991 shall take effect on July 1, 1991. They govern all proceedings in actions brought after they take effect and also all further proceedings in actions then pending, except to the extent that their application in a particular action pending when the amendments take effect would not be feasible or would work injustice, in which event the former procedure applies.

(H) Effective date of amendments

The amendments filed by the Supreme Court with the General Assembly on January 14, 1992 and further filed on April 30, 1992, shall take effect on July 1, 1992. They govern all proceedings in actions brought after they take effect and also all future proceedings in actions then pending, except to the extent that their application in a particular action pending when the amendments take effect would not be feasible or would work injustice, in which event the former procedure applies.

(I) Effective date of amendments

The amendments filed by the Supreme Court with the General Assembly on January 14, 1994 and further revised and filed on April 29, 1994 shall take effect on July 1, 1994. They govern all proceedings in actions brought after they take effect and also all future proceedings in actions then pending, except to the extent that their application in a particular action pending when the amendments take effect would not be feasible or would work injustice, in which event the former procedure applies.

(J) Effective date of amendments

The amendments to Rules 1, 4, and 40 filed by the Supreme court [sic.] with the General Assembly on January 11, 1995 and further revised and filed on April 25, 1995 shall take effect on July 1, 1995. They govern all proceedings in actions brought after they take effect and also all further proceedings in actions then pending, except to the extent that their application in a particular action pending when the amendments take effect would not be feasible or would work injustice, in which event the former procedure applies.

(K) Effective date of amendments

The amendments to Rules 6, 8, 13, 27, 34, 36, and 37 filed by the Supreme Court with the General Assembly on January 5, 1996 and refiled on April 26, 1996 shall take effect on July 1, 1996. They govern all proceedings in actions brought after they take effect and also all further proceedings in actions then pending, except to the extent that their application in a particular action pending when the amendments take effect would not be feasible or would work injustice, in which event the former procedure applies.

(L) Effective date of amendments

The amendments to Rule 30 filed by the Supreme Court with the General Assembly on January 10, 1997 and refiled on April 24, 1997 shall take effect on July 1, 1997. They govern all proceedings in actions brought after they take effect and also all further proceedings in actions then pending, except to the extent that their application in a particular action pending when the amendments take effect would not be feasible or would work injustice, in which event the former procedure applies.

(M) Effective date of amendments

The amendments to rules 2, 4, 10, 11, 15, 16, 29, 39, and 40 filed by the Supreme Court with the General Assembly on January 15, 1998 and further revised and refiled on April 30, 1998 shall take effect on July 1, 1998. They govern all proceedings in actions brought after they take effect and also all further proceedings in actions then pending, except to the extent that their application in a particular action pending when the amendments take effect would not be feasible or would work injustice, in which event the former procedure applies.

(N) Effective date of amendments

The amendments to Juvenile Rules 2, 7, 8, 10, 15, 22, 27, 29, 37, and 40 filed by the Supreme Court with the General Assembly on January 12, 2001, and revised and refiled on April 26, 2001, shall take effect on July 1, 2001. They govern all proceedings in actions brought after they take effect and also all further proceedings in actions then pending, except to the extent that their application in a particular action pending when the amendments take effect would not be feasible or would work injustice, in which event the former procedure applies.

(O) Effective date of amendments

The amendments to Juvenile Rules 2, 10, 15, and 34 filed by the Supreme Court with the General Assembly on January 11, 2002, and refiled on April 18, 2002 shall take effect on July 1, 2002. They govern all proceedings in actions brought after they take effect and also all further proceedings in actions then pending, except to the extent that their application in a particular action pending when the amendments take effect would not be feasible or would work injustice, in which event the former procedure applies.

(P) Effective date of amendments.

The amendments to Juvenile Rule 40 filed by the Supreme Court with the General Assembly on January 9, 2003 and refiled on April 28, 2003, shall take effect on July 1, 2003. They govern all proceedings in actions brought after they take effect and also all further proceedings in actions then pending, except to the extent that their application in a particular action pending when the amendments take effect would not be feasible or would work injustice, in which event the former procedure applies.

(Q) Effective date of amendments

The amendments to Juvenile Rule 29 filed by the Supreme Court with the General Assembly on January 7, 2004 and refiled on April 28, 2004 shall take effect on July 1, 2004. They govern all proceedings in actions brought after they take effect and also all further proceedings in actions then pending, except to the extent that their application in a particular action pending when the amend-

ments take effect would not be feasible or would work injustice, in which event the former procedure applies.

(Adopted eff. 7–1–72; amended eff. 7–1–73, 7–1–75, 7–1–76, 7–1–80, 7–1–85, 7–1–91, 7–1–92, 7–1–94, 7–1–95, 7–1–96, 7–1–97, 7–1–98, 7–1–01, 7–1–02, 7–1–03, 7–1–04)

Historical and Statutory Notes

Amendment Note: The 7–1–04 amendment added division (Q).

Amendment Note: The 7–1–03 amendment added division (P).

Amendment Note: The 7–1–02 amendment added division (O).

Amendment Note: The 7–1–01 amendment added division (N).

Amendment Note: The 7–1–98 amendment added division (M).

Amendment Note: The 7–1–97 amendment added division (L).

Amendment Note: The 7–1–96 amendment added division (K).

Amendment Note: The 7–1–95 amendment added division (J).

Amendment Note: The 7–1–94 amendment added division (I).

Library References

Infants ☞132.

Westlaw Topic No. 211.

C.J.S. Infants §§ 32, 41, 43, 44, 95.

Juv R 48   Title

These rules shall be known as the Ohio Rules of Juvenile Procedure and may be cited as "Juvenile Rules" or "Juv. R. ___."

(Adopted eff. 7–1–72)

OHIO RULES OF EVIDENCE

Publisher's Note: These Rules are published as they appear in the *Ohio Official Reports*.

Publisher's Note: Until 1968, when the Modern Courts Amendment to the Ohio Constitution was adopted, Ohio court procedure was governed entirely by statute and case law. The Modern Courts Amendment required the Supreme Court of Ohio, subject to the approval of the General Assembly, to "prescribe rules governing practice and procedure in all courts of the state." Rules of practice and procedure are the Civil, Criminal, Appellate, and Juvenile Rules, Rules of the Court of Claims, and the Ohio Rules of Evidence. Pursuant to Ohio Constitution Article IV, Section 5(B), such rules "shall not abridge, enlarge, or modify any substantive right," and " [a]ll laws in conflict with such rules shall be of no further force or effect."

Publisher's Note: The Supreme Court Rules Advisory Committee prepared Staff Notes for each of the substantive rule amendments. The Staff Note follows the applicable rule. Although the Supreme Court used the Staff Notes as background for its deliberations, the Staff Notes are not adopted by the Court and are not a part of the rule. Where they interpret the law, describe present conditions, or predict future practices, the Staff Notes represent the views of the Rules Advisory Committee and not necessarily the views of the Supreme Court. Each staff note should be read in light of the language of the rule at the time of its adoption or amendment.

ARTICLE

   I   General Provisions

  II   Judicial Notice

 III   Presumptions

 IV   Relevancy and Its Limits

  V   Privileges

ARTICLE

  VI   Witnesses

 VII   Opinions and Expert Testimony

VIII   Hearsay

 IX   Authentication and Identification

  X   Contents of Writings, Recordings and Photographs

 XI   Miscellaneous Rules

Article I

GENERAL PROVISIONS

Rule

101   Scope of rules: applicability; privileges; exceptions

102   Purpose and construction; supplementary principles

103   Rulings on evidence

104   Preliminary questions

105   Limited admissibility

106   Remainder of or related writings or recorded statements

Cross References

Death; establishing; presumptions, 2105.35

Evid R 101   Scope of rules: applicability; privileges; exceptions

(A) Applicability

These rules govern proceedings in the courts of this state, subject to the exceptions stated in division (C) of this rule.

(B) Privileges

The rule with respect to privileges applies at all stages of all actions, cases, and proceedings conducted under these rules.

(C) Exceptions

These rules (other than with respect to privileges) do not apply in the following situations:

(1) Admissibility determinations. Determinations prerequisite to rulings on the admissibility of evidence when the issue is to be determined by the court under Evid. R. 104.

(2) Grand jury. Proceedings before grand juries.

(3) Miscellaneous criminal proceedings. Proceedings for extradition or rendition of fugitives; sentencing; granting or revoking probation; proceedings with respect to community control sanctions; issuance of warrants for arrest; criminal summonses and search warrants; and proceedings with respect to release on bail or otherwise.

(4) Contempt. Contempt proceedings in which the court may act summarily.

(5) Arbitration. Proceedings for those mandatory arbitrations of civil cases authorized by the rules of superintendence and governed by local rules of court.

(6) Other rules. Proceedings in which other rules prescribed by the Supreme Court govern matters relating to evidence.

(7) Special non-adversary statutory proceedings. Special statutory proceedings of a non-adversary nature in which these rules would by their nature be clearly inapplicable.

(8) Small claims division. Proceedings in the small claims division of a county or municipal court.

(Adopted eff. 7–1–80; amended eff. 7–1–90, 7–1–96, 7–1–99)

Historical and Statutory Notes

Amendment Note: The 7–1–99 amendment inserted "proceedings with respect to community control sanctions;" in division (C)(3).

Amendment Note: The 7–1–96 amendment deleted "and before court-appointed referees and magistrates of this state" after "courts of this state" in division (A).

Commentary

Staff Notes

1999:

(C) Exceptions

The phrase "community control sanctions" was added to division (C)(3) of the rule in accordance with changes resulting from the adoption of Senate Bill 2, effective July 1, 1996, and in order to make the rule conform to current Ohio criminal practice.

1996:

The amendment deleted the rule's reference to proceedings "before court-appointed referees and magistrates." The deleted language was redundant, since proceedings before these judicial officers are "proceedings in the courts of this state." The amendment also harmonized the statement of the rules' applicability with the usage in other rules of practice and procedure, none of which makes specific reference to particular classes of judicial officers before whom proceedings governed by the rules might be conducted. See Civ. R. 1(A), Crim. R. 19A) [sic.], and Juv. R. 1(A). The amendment is intended only as a technical modification and no substantive change is intended.

1980:

Rule 101(A) Applicability

Rule 101(A), the scope rule, is very much like Federal Evidence Rule 101. Rule 101(A) provides in part that "These rules govern proceedings in the courts of this state..." Hence "These rules" may include a proceeding in the Supreme Court, as where the Court hears an action on original jurisdiction based on an extraordinary writ.

The rules also apply to "court-appointed referees." The language "court-appointed" is used because the Supreme Court cannot constitutionally extend its rule-making power to "referees" in the executive department. R.C. 119.09, for example, labels administrative hearing officers in the executive department as "referees." (Editor's Note: Magistrates became subject to the Rules of Evidence as a result of the 1990 amendment.)

Although these rules apply to court-appointed referees, there are exceptions. Thus, Civ. R. 53 may also govern court-appointed referees. Under Civ. R. 53 the court order of reference to the referee can limit the powers of the referee (perhaps with regard to evidentiary matters), and so Civ. R. 53 can prevail over these evidence rules—because Rule 101(C)(6) provides that other Supreme Court rules (like Civ. R. 53) can prevail over these rules as to evidentiary matters.

Moreover, Rule 101(C)(8) states that these rules do not apply to the small claims division of a county or municipal court, presided over by a court-appointed referee pursuant to R.C. 1925.01.

The remaining subdivisions of Rule 101, subdivisions (B) and (C), are similar to the several subdivisions of Federal Evidence Rule 1101. In short, the Ohio Rules Advisory Committee has marked Rule 1101 as "Reserved" and has moved that rule, governing certain exceptions to applicability of the evidence rules, to the first rule, which governs not only scope and applicability of the rules but also the exceptions to applicability. Moving the exceptions to applicability to the first rule, the scope rule, is in keeping with Ohio rule-making tradition. It has been the position of the Supreme Court of Ohio that applicability and exceptions to applicability in a rules package should appear in one rule, the initial rule, rather than be divided among several rules that appear at the beginning and the end of a rules package. For comparison, see Civ. R. 1 and Crim. R. 1 both of which govern not only the scope and applicability of a set of rules but the exceptions of applicability as well.

Rule 101(B) Privileges

This subdivision is Federal Evidence Rule 1101(c). The subdivision provides that privileges apply to all stages of proceedings even though there are exceptions as to the applicability of certain other evidence rules. The language of subdivision (B) is also repeated parenthetically in the first sentence of subdivision (C) just as it is repeated parenthetically in the first sentence of Federal Evidence Rule 1101(d). The double emphasis as to privileges eliminates any doubt as to their applicability.

The application of subdivision (B) may be illustrated by simple example.

Grand jury proceedings are exempted from the Rules of Evidence (Rule 101(C)(2)). Assume that a spouse is called before the grand jury. The prosecutor, aware of the privilege rule's applicability to grand jury proceedings, would be duty bound not to violate the "husband-wife" privilege. Or if he violated his duty, the spouse would be free to invoke the "husband-wife" privilege. As to matters other than privilege, the prosecutor and the grand jury are not bound by the rules of evidence.

Rule 101(C) Exceptions

The introductory sentence states that the rules (other than with respect to privileges) do not apply to the following "situations." The "situations" are set forth as subsections of subdivision (C). The introductory sentence is like Federal Evidence Rule 1101(d) and Uniform Evidence Rule 1101(b).

Rule 101(C)(1) Admissibility Determinations

The subsection states that the court is not bound by the rules of evidence when ruling on a question of admissibility of evidence pursuant to Rule 104(A). In turn Rule 104(A) states, other than with respect to privileges, that a judge is not bound by the rules of evidence when ruling on a question of admissibility. The Federal Advisory Committee's Note to Federal

Evidence Rule 104(a) explains the principles involved thus:

The applicability of a particular rule of evidence often depends upon the existence of a condition. Is the alleged expert a qualified physician? Is a witness whose former testimony is offered unavailable?... In each instance the admissibility of evidence will turn upon the answer to the question of the existence of the condition. Accepted practice, incorporated in the rule, places on the judge the responsibility for these determinations. McCormick § 53 [McCormick § 53 (2d ed. 1972)]; Morgan, Basic Problems of Evidence 45–50 (1962).

To the extent that these inquiries are factual, the judge acts as the trier of fact...

If the question is factual in nature, the judge will of necessity receive evidence pro and con on the issue. The rule provides that the rules of evidence in general do not apply to this process. McCormick § 53, p. 123, n. 8 [McCormick § 53, p. 122, n. 91 (2d ed. 1972)], points out that the authorities are "scattered and inconclusive," and observes:

"Should the exclusionary law of evidence, 'the child of the jury system'... be applied to this hearing before the judge? Sound sense backs the view that it should not, and that the judge should be empowered to hear any relevant evidence, such as affidavits or other reliable hearsay."

Prior Ohio law is not different. 21 O Jur 2d Evidence § 184, 52 OJur 2d Trial § 60, 56 OJur 2d Witnesses § 285.

Rule 101(C)(2) Grand Jury

This subsection is like Federal Evidence Rule 1101(d)(2): rules of evidence do not apply to grand jury proceedings. In the past the rules of evidence have *not* applied to grand juries in Ohio. A federal grand jury may indict on hearsay (*Costello v. United States* (1956), 350 U.S. 359), and there is not any case law in Ohio contrary to the *Costello* position. For discussion of "evidence" in Ohio grand jury proceedings, see 1 Anderson's Ohio Criminal Practice § 14.4.

Rule 101(C)(3) Miscellaneous Criminal Proceedings

This subsection is very similar to Federal Evidence Rule 1101(d)(3) and excludes the rules of evidence from various criminal proceedings.

Extradition and Rendition: Extradition and rendition are excepted from the Ohio Criminal Rules (Crim. R. 1(C)(1)). Extradition is a kind of administrative proceeding rather than a judicial proceeding. See R.C. Ch. 2963. R.C. 2963.09 does provide for a hearing before a judge before extradition may be effected. The judge informs the person of his rights and will give him time to file a habeas corpus. *If* the person files a habeas corpus, the habeas hearing apparently only inquires into the validity of the attempted extradition and does not inquire into the question of guilt or innocence (*Millovich v. Langley* (1953), 68 Ohio Law Abs. 79).

Sentencing and Probation: Sentencing and the granting of probation do not involve the formal rules of evidence. See Crim. R. 32, 32.1, 32.2. See also, 1 Anderson's Ohio Criminal Practice §§ 42.1–43.3. As to revoking probation, Crim. R. 32.3 does require a hearing, but the hearing does not require the application of formal rules of evidence even though the hearing cannot be arbitrary or involve abuse of discretion. See 1 Anderson's Ohio Criminal Practice § 43.4(d).

NOTE: Parole (as distinguished from probation) is an executive function. Revocation of parole now requires a fair hearing with notice, confrontation of witnesses, etc., but the hearing would be conducted by the parole board or some executive department board and not the courts. Constitutional (14th Amend.) standards for a parole revocation are governed by *Morrissey v. Brewer* (1972), 408 U.S. 471. Rules of evidence would not be applicable at a parole hearing before a board or executive authority.

Summonses and arrest and search warrants. A summons or warrant for arrest may be issued on the basis of hearsay. See Crim. R. 4(A). Hence the rules of evidence are not applicable. Search warrants may also be issued on the basis of affidavits and hearsay, and hence the rules of evidence are not applicable. See Crim. R. 41(C).

Bail. The rules of evidence do not apply with respect to release on bail or "otherwise." See Crim. R. 46(I). "Otherwise" with reference to the term "bail" refers to release on a person's own recognizance. See Crim. R. 46.

Rule 101(C)(4) Contempt

This subsection excludes from the rules of evidence those contempt proceedings in which "the court may act summarily." The court may act summarily only when the contempt is committed in the view or hearing of the court, but not when the contempt is committed other than in the actual presence of the court. *In re Neff* (1969), 20 Ohio App.2d 213. In a summary contempt the judge is the "evidence" inasmuch as he had witnessed the contemptuous conduct. Imprisonment for summary contempt is for coercion rather than for punishment (*State v. Granchay* (1965), 1 Ohio App.2d 307). Thus, assume that a person unlawfully hides some assets and then stands in front of the judge and refuses to divulge where the assets are hidden. The judge has witnessed the contempt. He may hold the person in summary contempt and incarcerate him in order to coerce him to purge himself. See *In re Roberts* (1963), 175 Ohio St. 123. In a summary contempt, the person incarcerated "holds the keys to the jail house door."

In the federal system Federal Criminal Rule 42(a) provides for summary contempt. In a summary contempt in the federal system the contempt must have been committed in the presence of the judge, and the judge is his own "evidence." See *United States v. Wilson* (1975), 421 U.S. 309. In Ohio, Crim. R. 42 is marked "Reserved," hence the need for excluding summary contempt from the rules of evidence in this Rule 101(C)(4).

Rule 101(C)(5) Arbitration

The subsection excludes arbitration proceedings authorized by the rules of superintendence and governed by local rules of court from the operation of the rules of evidence. Local rules, such as Cuyahoga County Common Pleas Court Rule 29, governing mandatory arbitration, exclude arbitration from the operation of the rules of evidence. In relevant part, Cuyahoga County Rule 29, Part III, subdivision (F), provides: "A majority of the Board... shall be the judges of the relevancy and materiality of the evidence offered and conformity to legal rules of evidence shall not be necessary." The subdivision further provides for evidence by "affidavit," i.e., hearsay. Of course, if the parties do not agree with the arbitration decision, they may appeal *de novo* pursuant to the rules of superintendence for a formal trial before court and jury.

Rule 101(C)(6) Other Rules

In effect the subsection provides that these rules do not apply to evidentiary matters governed by other rules promulgated by the Supreme Court. Juv. R. 7(F)(3), governing detention hearings, states that the formal rules of evidence are not applicable. Crim. R. 41, governing arrest warrants and search warrants, permits the use of affidavits and hearsay. Other rules permit the use of affidavits on motion (Civ. R. 56 on summary judgment, Civ. R. 65(A) on restraining orders, Crim. R. 47 on motions generally). And so on.

This exclusionary subsection is necessary in order that the Rules of Evidence do not conflict with other rules.

Rule 101(C)(7) Special Non-adversary Statutory Proceedings

The subsection excludes non-adversary special statutory proceedings from the rules of evidence when the rules by their nature would be clearly inapplicable. The "clearly inapplicable" language is borrowed from Civ. R. 1(C).

A special statutory proceeding is one in which special remedial procedure, rather than general procedure, applies. See R.C. 1.12. The Supreme Court can exclude special procedure from the operation of a rules package.

The subsection has excluded only nonadversary statutory proceedings in which the rules would be, by their nature, clearly inapplicable, e.g., a name change pursuant to RC 2717.01. A name change is *ex parte*. To change a name, the court needs only "proof in open court" to effectuate the name change. The formal rules of evidence are by their nature clearly inapplicable to such a judicial proceeding. Ordinarily, the probate of an estate is nonadversary, and the rules of evidence should not be applicable. But if a dispute should arise during the course of the probate proceedings (for example, a will contest, itself a special statutory proceeding governed by R.C. 2107.71–2107.77) the procedure waxes adversary and the rules of evidence should apply.

As for the many "adversary" statutory proceedings, there is every reason to apply the rules of evidence. Commitment of the mentally ill is in effect an adversary special statutory proceeding. R.C. 5122.15 provides for the "informal" conduct of the commitment hearing (to deprive a person of his liberty), although the statute does provide for the cross-examination of witnesses. Recently, *In re Fisher* (1974), 39 Ohio St.2d 71, required counsel to appear at a commitment proceeding. Should the rules of evidence, although the judge sits without a jury, *not* apply? To give a blanket exclusion to special statutory proceedings adversary in nature would leave a substantial gap in the applicability of the Rules of Evidence. And even to exclude adversary statutory proceedings where "the rules would be by their nature clearly inapplicable" would leave a rather debatable gap in the applicability of the rules.

Rule 101(C)(8) Small Claims Division

The subsection excludes small claims proceedings from the rules of evidence although such proceedings are ordinarily adversary in nature. The Evidence Rules Advisory Committee did recognize that R.C. Ch. 1925, governing small claims divisions, does not actually by statute exclude proceedings from the formal rules of evidence although the Chapter does provide for "conciliation procedures" (R.C. 1925.03), and on many occasions referees as "a practical matter" ignore rules of evidence in order to resolve a dispute. Referees obviously require some reliable evidence to prove a claim, but a referee, exercising some discretion, should not deny a layman justice through a formalistic application of the law of evidence. A small claims division is intended as a layman's forum.

Cross References

Acts in contempt of court, 2705.02
Administrative determination of claims by clerk, duties of claimant, defendant, and clerk, evidence, CCR 6
Adult parole authority, Ch 5149
Arbitration, Sup R 15
Bail and suspension of execution of sentence in criminal cases, App R 8
Bail, posting, procedure, Traf R 4
County court proceedings, applicability, 1907.31
Courts, probate, juvenile, necessary parties, 2107.73
Detention, shelter care, hearing, Juv R 7
Dispositional hearing, procedure, Juv R 34
Extradition, Ch 2963
Initial appearance, preliminary hearing in felony cases, procedure, Crim R 5
Injunctions, temporary restraining order, notice, hearing, duration, Civ R 65
Motions, Crim R 47
Pardon, parole, probation, Ch 2967
Penalties and sentencing, Ch 2929
Privileged communications and acts, 2317.02
Proceedings to change name of person, 2717.01
Referees, appointment, powers, duties, Civ R 53; Juv R 40; Traf R 14
Revocation of probation, hearing, counsel, confinement, waiver of counsel, Crim R 32.3
Rules applicable in criminal cases, 2945.41
Rules of evidence and procedure, 2938.15
Search and seizure, warrants, Crim R 41
Sentencing, imposition of, notification of right to appeal, judgment, Crim R 32
Small claims divisions, Ch 1925
State government, adjudication hearing, 119.09
Summary judgment, Civ R 56
Summary punishment for contempt, 2705.01
Venue of will contest, 2107.71
Warrant or summons, issuance, upon complaint, Crim R 4
Warrant or summons upon indictment or information, Crim R 9
Will contests, rules of civil procedure govern, exception, 2107.72

Library References

Courts ⊜85(1), 85(2).

Witnesses ⊜184(1).

Westlaw Topic Nos. 106, 410.

C.J.S. Courts §§ 130, 131.

C.J.S. Witnesses § 252.

OJur 3d: 26, Criminal Law § 1023; 29, Criminal Law § 2251, 2288, 2494; 29A, Criminal Law § 2859, 3088; 33, Decedents' Estates § 1151; 42, Evidence and Witnesses § 10; 64, Jury § 127; 67, Malpractice § 143, 156

Katz & Giannelli, Baldwin's Ohio Practice, Criminal Law § 1.8, 37.13, 39.17, 81.6, 116.9 (1996).

Painter, Ohio Driving Under the Influence Law (2003 Ed.), Text 19.32.

Giannelli & Snyder, Baldwin's Ohio Practice, Evidence § 101.2, 103.6, 1101, 402.8, 410.11, 501.1, 501.6, 601.11, 605.1, 603, 607.4, 802.7 (2d ed. 2001).

Griffin & Katz, Ohio Felony Sentencing Law (2002 Ed.), Text 1.22.

Carlin, Baldwin's Ohio Practice, Merrick–Rippner Probate Law § 39.3, 107.51, 107.72, 107.121, 108.11 (2003).

Evid R 102   Purpose and construction; supplementary principles

The purpose of these rules is to provide procedures for the adjudication of causes to the end that the truth may be ascertained and proceedings justly determined. The principles of the common law of Ohio shall supplement the provisions of these rules, and the rules shall be construed to state the principles of the common law of Ohio unless the rule clearly indicates that a change is intended. These rules shall not supersede substantive statutory provisions.

(Adopted eff. 7–1–80; amended eff. 7–1–96)

Historical and Statutory Notes

Amendment Note: The 7–1–96 amendment rewrote this rule, which prior thereto read:

"The purpose of these rules is to provide procedures for the adjudication of causes to the end that the truth may be ascertained and proceedings justly determined. These rules shall be construed to state the common law of Ohio unless the rule clearly indicates that a change is intended and shall not supersede substantive statutory provisions."

Commentary

Staff Notes

1996:

As originally adopted, Evid. R. 102 referred to the common law of Ohio, but only as a framework for construing the particular rules within the Rules of Evidence. The original text of Rule 102 did not suggest what role, if any, the common law was to have in regard to evidentiary issues as to which the Rules of Evidence were silent.

In the years since Ohio adopted the Rules of Evidence, Ohio has added rules codifying the common law on certain topics that the Rules had not addressed. Thus, for example, prior to the adoption of Evid. R. 616 in 1991, the rules contained no rule governing the impeachment of a witness for bias or interest. See Staff Note (1991), Evid. R. 616. Even after the adoption of Rule 616, other rules of impeachment remained unaddressed. See, e.g., *Ramage v. Central Ohio Emergency Serv., Inc.* (1992), 64 Ohio St.3d 97, 110 (use of learned treatises for impeachment). Similarly, the rules do not expressly address questions regarding the admissibility of expert opinions on certain subjects. See, e.g., *Stinson v. England* (1994), 69 Ohio St.3d 451 (expert opinion on causation is inadmissible unless the opinion is that causation is at least probable).

Omissions such as these occur across the entire body of evidence law. The Rules of Evidence, that is, are not an exhaustive compilation of the rules governing evidence questions, nor are the rules preemptive as to subjects that they do not address. The amendment makes clear in the text of the rule not only that the common law of Ohio provides a framework for construing the content of specific rules, but also that the common law provides the rules of decision as to questions not addressed by specific rules.

In addition, in the portion of the rule that establishes the common law as the basis of interpretation of specific rules, the phrase "common law" was amended to read "principles of the common law." The amendment harmonized the reference with the usage in other rules. See, e.g., Evid. R. 501. In addition, it is intended to acknowledge more clearly the character of the common law as an evolving body of principles and precedents, rather than as a static collection of tightly prescribed rules.

1980:

Rule 102, governing purpose and construction of the evidence rules, differs from Federal Evidence Rule 102.

As originally proposed, Rule 102 was based upon the language of Federal Evidence Rule 102, a rule which provides in relevant part for such construction as "... to secure... promotion of growth and development of the law of evidence to the end that the truth may be ascertained and proceedings justly determined." In *United States v. Batts* (9th Cir. 1977), 558 F.2d 513, the court, relying on the quoted language of Federal Evidence Rule 102, permitted evidence to be admitted pursuant to that rule in spite of a specific provision of Federal Evidence Rule 608(b) prohibiting admission of such evidence. The case has been severely criticized. See, Note, *United States v. Batts: Aberration or Permissible Construction under the Rules of Evidence?*, 9 Toledo L. Rev. 464 (1977–78). Although the *Batts* opinion was withdrawn and later reissued on the basis of a different theory, *United States v. Batts* (1978), 573 F.2d 599, the possibility remains that other courts may rely upon the language of Federal Evidence Rule 102 to exercise a broad discretion to promote "... the growth and development of the law of evidence..." at the expense of specific provisions of particular rules. To avoid the suggestion of such expansive construction, Rule 102 deletes the language "... to secure... promotion of growth and development of the law of evidence..."

The rule states two basic canons of construction. The common law is not modified by statute or rule unless the intent to do so is clearly ascertainable. Secondly, the rule restates the provision of Article IV, Section 5(B), Constitution of Ohio, that the rules of practice and procedure supersede statutes where there is a conflict between the rule and the statute, but the statute to be superseded must relate to procedure and not substance.

Library References

Courts ⊕85(2).

Westlaw Topic No. 106.

C.J.S. Courts § 131.

OJur 3d: 29A, Criminal Law § 2859; 42, Evidence and Witnesses § 10; 59, Insurance § 1353

Am Jur 2d: 29, Evidence § 1; 32B, Federal Rules of Evidence § 12

Painter, Ohio Driving Under the Influence Law (2003 Ed.), Text 13.4.

Giannelli & Snyder, Baldwin's Ohio Practice, Evidence § 404.14, 611.3, 613, 702, 706, 801.25, 801.26, 1101 (2d ed. 2001).

Evid R 103   Rulings on evidence

(A) Effect of erroneous ruling

Error may not be predicated upon a ruling which admits or excludes evidence unless a substantial right of the party is affected, and

(1) Objection. In case the ruling is one admitting evidence, a timely objection or motion to strike appears of record stating

the specific ground of objection, if the specific ground was not apparent from the context; or

(2) Offer of proof. In case the ruling is one excluding evidence, the substance of the evidence was made known to the court by offer or was apparent from the context within which questions were asked. Offer of proof is not necessary if evidence is excluded during cross-examination.

(B) Record of offer and ruling

At the time of making the ruling, the court may add any other or further statement which shows the character of the evidence, the form in which it was offered, the objection made, and the ruling thereon. It may direct the making of an offer in question and answer form.

(C) Hearing of jury

In jury cases, proceedings shall be conducted, to the extent practicable, so as to prevent inadmissible evidence from being suggested to the jury by any means, such as making statements or offers of proof or asking questions in the hearing of the jury.

(D) Plain error

Nothing in this rule precludes taking notice of plain errors affecting substantial rights although they were not brought to the attention of the court.

(Adopted eff. 7–1–80)

Commentary

Staff Notes

1980:

Except for changes in subdivisions (A)(2) and (B), discussed below, Rule 103 follows *verbatim* the language of Federal Evidence Rule 103.

Rule 103(A) Effect of Erroneous Ruling

In effect, Rule 103(A) provides that a case need not be retried for error in the admission or exclusion of evidence (even though there be an objection) unless a substantial right of a party is affected. In short, harmless evidentiary error is not a ground for reversal and retrial. The rule does not purport to define harmless error or that situation in which a substantial right is affected when evidence is erroneously admitted or excluded. The rule merely restates the "substantial right" doctrine of case holdings and reflects the harmless error principle of Crim. R. 52(A): "Any error, defect, irregularity, or variance which does not affect substantial rights shall be disregarded."

The question of harmless and prejudicial error in the admission or exclusion of evidence is applicable to civil cases and significantly applicable to those criminal cases involving constitutional rights. Although standards governing harmless and prejudicial evidentiary error may be found in the case holdings, application of the standards to the factual context of the particular case continues to remain difficult in criminal cases. For example, in *Bumper v. North Carolina* (1968), 391 U.S. 543, defendant was found guilty of rape. During the course of trial an illegally seized rifle, allegedly used by defendant during the course of the rape, was erroneously introduced into evidence. In light of certain facts the majority of the court held the tainted evidence to be prejudicial and reversed whereas the dissent argued vigorously that the error was harmless because there was overwhelming evidence beyond a reasonable doubt to prove that the defendant was guilty of rape.

Federal standards govern harmless and prejudicial error in those cases involving Fourteenth Amendment rights. See, Note, *Harmless Constitutional Error*, 83 Harv. L. Rev. 814 (1970). See also, McCormick § 183 (2d ed. 1972).

Rule 103(A)(1) Objection

Rule 103(A)(1) governs that situation in which evidence is purportedly improperly *admitted* and provides that the person prejudiced by the evidence must object and set forth the specific grounds for his objection unless the grounds for his objection are obvious from the context. The rule does not change traditional law. See, 52 OJur 2d Trial § 81. Rule 103(D), discussed below, governs situations involving "plain error."

Rule 103(A)(2) Offer of Proof

Rule 103(A)(2) governs that situation in which evidence is purportedly improperly *excluded* and provides that the person prejudiced by the exclusion must make offer of proof unless the substance of the evidence sought to be offered is apparent from the context within which questions were asked. The rule does not change traditional practice. See 52 OJur 2d Trial § 84. Upon objection on cross-examination, an offer of proof is dispensed with for the reason that it would be impracticable to speculate on the potential answer.

Rule 103(B) Record of Offer and Ruling

Rule 103(B) provides that a judge may make comments for the record concerning the circumstances surrounding a problem involving admissibility of evidence. The rule varies slightly from its federal counterpart. An introductory phrase has been added which simply states that if the judge makes comments for the record, he should do so "At the time of making the ruling..." In other words, the judge should make his comments while the issue involving admissibility is at hand and not at some later time after the record has been completed.

Rule 103(C) Hearing of Jury

Quite reasonably, Rule 103(C) provides that, where practicable, discussions involving the admissibility of evidence should be conducted in the absence of the jury. It would be quite pointless, for example, to permit the jury to overhear the offer of excluded evidence. The rule is not new to Ohio procedure; judges have always had discretion to conduct hearings regarding admissibility of evidence in the absence of the jury. See 52 OJur 2d Trial § 89. The rule is similar to Rule 104(C).

Rule 103(D) Plain Error

Rule 103(A)(1) provides that a timely objection must be raised in order to exclude evidence, and if objection is not made, error may not be predicated on the admission of the "improper" evidence. On occasion, however, particularly in a criminal trial involving fundamental constitutional rights, the adversary system may break down, perhaps through the inexperience or incompetence of counsel, and highly prejudicial evidence may be introduced into the trial without objection. In that event, pursuant to Rule 103(D), the conviction of the defendant may be reversed on appeal because of "plain error." Thus, in *Payton v. United States* (1955), 222 F. 2d 794, a tainted confession was introduced into evidence without objection. Defendant's conviction was reversed at the appellate level because of "plain error." The plain error principle is not new to Ohio law.

In addition to the plain error principle set forth in Rule 103(D), Crim. R. 52(B), like Federal Criminal Rule 52(B), provides that: "Plain errors or defects affecting substantial rights may be noticed although they were not brought to the attention of the court. Rule 103(D) makes clear that "plain error" applies to admissibility of evidence. Although as in the *Payton* case the "plain error" of Crim. R. 52(B) might apply to admissibility of evidence, it also applies to other "plain error" such as failure to object to prejudicial instructions to the jury.

Cross References

Exceptions to rulings, 2938.09
Exceptions unnecessary, Civ R 46; Crim R 51
Grounds of objection to be stated, 2945.09
Harmless error, Civ R 61
Harmless error, plain error, Crim R 52
Pleadings and motions before trial, defenses and objections, pretrial motions, Crim R 12
Pretrial conference, Crim R 17.1
Pretrial procedure, Civ R 16
Ruling on evidence not ground for new trial unless prejudicial, Crim R 33
Use of depositions in court proceedings, errors and irregularities, Civ R 32

Library References

Appeal and Error ⟊203, 204(1), 205, 206.
Criminal Law ⟊670 to 672, 1036.1(1), 1036.1(9).
Trial ⟊44 to 51.
Westlaw Topic Nos. 30, 110, 388.
C.J.S. Appeal and Error § 202.
C.J.S. Criminal Law §§ 939, 1203 to 1205, 1217.
C.J.S. Trial §§ 73 to 85.
OJur 3d: 4, Appellate Review § 136, 139, 144, 150, 164, 167, 271, 285; 5, Appellate Review § 538; 28, Criminal Law § 2383 to 2385, 2504; 29A, Criminal Law § 3001; 29B, Criminal Law § 3567, 3568, 3569, 3697; 75, Trial § 162 et seq.; 89, Trial § 32 to 34, 155 to 158, 160, 161, 163, 165; 90, Trial § 441
Am Jur 2d: 29, Evidence § 408 to 410, 425, 426
Consideration, in determining facts, of inadmissible hearsay evidence introduced without objection. 79 ALR2d 890
Necessity and sufficiency of renewal of objection to, or offer of, evidence admitted or excluded conditionally. 88 ALR2d 12
Modern status of rules governing legal effect of failure to object to admission of extrinsic evidence violative of parol evidence rule. 81 ALR3d 249
Sufficiency in federal court of motion in limine to preserve for appeal objection to evidence absent contemporary objection at trial. 76 ALR Fed 619
Whiteside, Ohio Appellate Practice (2003 Ed.), Text 1.33, 1.34, 7.3.
Giannelli & Snyder, Baldwin's Ohio Practice, Evidence § 103.7, 104.8, 105.6, 201.8, 404.14, 605.4, 607.5, 614.5, 802.1, 104, 807.15 (2d ed. 2001).

Evid R 104   Preliminary questions

(A) Questions of admissibility generally

Preliminary questions concerning the qualification of a person to be a witness, the existence of a privilege, or the admissibility of evidence shall be determined by the court, subject to the provisions of subdivision (B). In making its determination it is not bound by the rules of evidence except those with respect to privileges.

(B) Relevancy conditioned on fact

When the relevancy of evidence depends upon the fulfillment of a condition of fact, the court shall admit it upon, or subject to, the introduction of evidence sufficient to support a finding of the fulfillment of the condition.

(C) Hearing of jury

Hearings on the admissibility of confessions shall in all cases be conducted out of the hearing of the jury. Hearings on other preliminary matters shall also be conducted out of the hearing of the jury when the interests of justice require.

(D) Testimony by accused

The accused does not, by testifying upon a preliminary matter, subject himself to cross-examination as to other issues in the case.

(E) Weight and credibility

This rule does not limit the right of a party to introduce before the jury evidence relevant to weight or credibility.

(Adopted eff. 7–1–80)

Commentary

Staff Notes

1980:

Rule 104, except for a slight change in subdivision 104(C), is a word for word counterpart of Federal Evidence Rule 104.

Rule 104(A) Questions of Admissibility Generally

Rule 104(A) governs preliminary matters essentially concerning the *competency*, rather than the relevancy, of evidence. The preliminary matters of competency governed by the rule are determined by the court. As a preliminary matter the court determines the qualification of a person to be a witness, i.e., Is the person about to testify as an expert a qualified expert? The court, and not the jury, also determines the existence of a privilege, i.e., Must the witness answer the question at hand or may he invoke the privilege against self–incrimination? The court, as a preliminary matter, also determines the admissibility of evidence, i.e., Is the confession a valid confession or is it contaminated by coercion?

The rule provides that in making a determination on a preliminary matter, the court is not bound by the exclusionary rules of evidence, except that the court is bound by the rules governing privilege.

For an excellent analysis of determination of preliminary matters, see McCormick § 153 (2d ed. 1972). Rule 104(A) does not change prior Ohio practice; see, 52 OJur 2d Trial § 60.

The provisions of Rule 104(A) are modified by Rule 104(B), discussed in the succeeding note, if a question of "conditional relevancy" is involved.

Rule 104(B) Relevancy Conditioned on Fact

Rule 104(B) governs "conditional relevancy", or in terms of the rule, "relevancy" depending upon "the fulfillment of a condition of fact." Conditional relevancy, conditioned upon a fact, is determined by the jury. In contrast, preliminary matters concerning competency, as previously noted, are determined by the court pursuant to Rule 104(A). Rule 104(B) prevents the court from usurping the function of the jury under the guise of determining a preliminary matter of competency. The distinction between the two rules is this: Rule 104(A) deals with *competency* and Rule 104(B) deals with factual *relevancy* or probative value. The distinction may be illustrated by example.

First, Rule 104(B) and determination of conditional relevancy by the jury. In *Coleman v. McIntosh* (1919), 184 Ky. 370, 211 S.W. 872, plaintiff sued defendant for breach of promise to marry. Defendant sought to introduce into evidence an unsigned letter allegedly in the handwriting of plaintiff and relevant to the facts in dispute. Defendant, as a preliminary matter (See Rules 901(A) and 901(B)(2)), authenticated the letter by identifying the handwriting on the basis of prior familiarity. Plaintiff denied that she had written the letter but admitted familiarity with the person to whom the letter was written. On this state of facts, the trial judge refused to admit the letter into evidence. Error. The case involved conditional relevancy and hence a question of fact for the jury to determine; that is, the letter was relevant conditioned upon its genuineness—genuineness being a disputed question of fact to be determined by the jury.

Similarly, it should be noted that Rule 1008, specifically referring to Rule 104, states that there is a question of fact for the jury, rather than a preliminary question for the court, when under certain circumstances secondary evidence (submitted in lieu of an original document) is challenged.

In contrast, the application of Rule 104(A) to determination of a preliminary matter of competency of evidence by the court. In *Potter v. Baker* (1955), 162 Ohio St. 489 [488], plaintiff was knocked unconscious in an auto accident. At some uncertain time after the accident plaintiff regained consciousness and heard a stranger at the scene say, "God, he rushed the light." The trial judge refused to permit the plaintiff to testify as to the quoted statement. It is within the province of the court to determine the admissibility of evidence as a preliminary matter, and the court was correct in finding that in light of the lapse of time, the quoted hearsay utterance did not meet the necessary elements of the spontaneous exclamation exception.

For definitive discussions distinguishing the principles underlying Rule 104(A) and Rule 104(B), see Morgan, *Functions of Judge and Jury in the Determination of Preliminary Questions of Fact*, 43 Harv. L. Rev. 165 (1929). See also McCormick § 53 (2d ed. 1972).

Rule 104(C) Hearing of Jury

The first sentence of Rule 104(C) states that preliminary matters regarding the admissibility of a confession *shall* be conducted out of the hearing of the jury. See *Jackson v. Denno* (1964), 378 U.S. 368. The rule also provides that other preliminary matters should be heard outside the hearing of the jury when the interests of justice require; in short, the judge should exercise his sound discretion.

Unlike its federal counterpart, Rule 104(C) does not provide that a hearing on a preliminary matter should be conducted out of the hearing of the jury "... when the accused is a witness, if he so requests." The principle expressed by the quoted language (which does not appear in the Ohio rule) is governed by the language of the Ohio rule which provides that a hearing on a preliminary matter should be conducted out of the hearing of the jury "when the interests of justice require." Certainly, if an accused is a witness and he requests that the preliminary matter be conducted out of the hearing of the jury, the court should exercise its sound discretion and hear the matter not in the presence of the jury. Indeed, even if the accused does not so request, the court may on its own motion excuse the jury in the "interests of justice."

Rule 104(C), although more specific with regard to confessions, for example, is similar to Rule 103(C).

Rule 104(D) Testimony by Accused

In light of the breadth of cross-examination permitted by Rule 611(B), Rule 104(D), a protective rule, provides that if an accused testifies as to a preliminary matter, he does not subject himself to cross-examination as to other issues in the case.

As noted in the Federal Advisory Committee's Note, "The rule does not address itself to questions of the subsequent use of testimony given by an accused at a hearing on a preliminary matter. See *Walder v. United States* (1954), 347 U.S. 62; *Simmons v. United States* (1968), 380 [390] U.S. 377; *Harris v. New York* (1971), 407 U.S. 222."

Rule 104(E) Weight and Credibility

Rule 104(E) simply provides that if the court determines as a preliminary matter that certain evidence is competent to be admitted, the mere admission of the evidence does not prevent a party from introducing countervailing evidence to the jury that goes to the weight or credibility of the evidence so admitted. Thus, if a court determines that certain evidence may be admitted as an exception to the hearsay rule, an opposing party is free to present evidence that goes to the weight or credibility of that evidence.

Cross References

Pleadings and motions before trial, defenses and objections, pretrial motions, Crim R 12

Library References

Criminal Law ⚎667 to 671.

Trial ⚎43 to 49.

Witnesses ⚎277(1).

Westlaw Topic Nos. 110, 388, 410.

C.J.S. Criminal Law §§ 656, 939, 1145, 1146, 1191, 1201 to 1210.

C.J.S. Trial §§ 72 to 83.

C.J.S. Witnesses §§ 369, 395.

OJur 3d: 29, Criminal Law § 2494, 2501; 42, Evidence and Witnesses § 176; 89, Trial § 77, 78, 80 to 84, 130, 172, 173

Am Jur 2d: 75, Trial § 128 to 132

Modern status of rules as to use of motion in limine or similar preliminary motion to secure exclusion of prejudicial evidence or reference to prejudicial matters. 63 ALR3d 311

Admissibility of hearsay evidence for court's determination, under Rule 104(a) of the Federal Rules of Evidence, of preliminary questions of fact. 39 ALR Fed 720

Katz & Giannelli, Baldwin's Ohio Practice, Criminal Law § 1.8 (1996).

Giannelli & Snyder, Baldwin's Ohio Practice, Evidence § 101.3, 201.8, 404.14, 602.4, 901, 1008, 101, 101.6, 101.7, 104.3, 201.6, 406.6, 408.3, 501.1, 601.4, 607.5, 702.4, 702.5, 706, 702.8, 803.5, 803.9, 803.10, 803.22, 803.27, 807.15, 901.3, 902.1, 1004.3, 1008.3, 103 (2d ed. 2001).

Ohio Personal Injury Practice (2002 Ed.), Text 5.17.

Evid R 105   Limited admissibility

When evidence which is admissible as to one party or for one purpose but not admissible as to another party of [1] for another purpose is admitted, the court, upon request of a party, shall restrict the evidence to its proper scope and instruct the jury accordingly.

(Adopted eff. 7–1–80)

1 So in 62 OS(2d) xxxiv; federal rule reads "or."

Commentary

Staff Notes

1980:

In relevant part, Rule 105, like its federal counterpart, provides that where evidence is admissible as to one party or for one purpose but not admissible as to another party or for another purpose, then the court should give a limiting instruction to the jury to limit the evidence to its proper scope *if* a party requests a limiting instruction. The principle is not new to Ohio law. Thus, in *Agler v. Schine Theatrical Co.* (1938), 59 Ohio App. 68, a sign owned by defendant which had caused plaintiff's injury, was introduced into evidence. The sign so introduced had been changed after the accident. Defendant objected generally to the admission of the evidence but did not request a specific limiting instruction. The sign had been introduced to identify it and not to prove any negligence or to show changes subsequent to the accident. The court upon admitting the evidence did not give an instruction limiting the evidence to a particular purpose. The failure to give a limiting instruction was held not to be in error in the absence of a specific request to limit the scope of admissibility. See also, 21 OJur [2d] Evidence § 188, or McCormick § 59 (2d ed. 1972).

It should be noted that Rule 105 has a very close relationship to Rule 403 which in relevant part provides that evidence otherwise competent may be excluded if to admit the evidence would cause the "danger of unfair prejudice." Thus, if there would be danger of unfair prejudice, evidence ordinarily admissible for a limited purpose should not be admitted even with a limiting instruction. In *Bruton v. United States* (1968), 391 U.S. 121 [123], for example, it was held that the confession of one defendant who does not take the stand but which implicates the other defendant cannot be introduced into evidence in a joint trial even with a limiting instruction which admonishes the jury to consider the confession only in convicting the confessing defendant. The limiting instruction cannot avoid the prejudicing of the non-confessing defendant's constitutional rights. The *Bruton* doctrine is applicable as against the states. See *Harrington v. California* (1969), 395 U.S. 250.

Cross References

Instructing the jury, Crim R 30

Instructions to jury, error, record, objection, cautionary instructions, Civ R 51

Library References

Criminal Law ☞783.

Trial ☞207.

Westlaw Topic Nos. 110, 388.

C.J.S. Trial §§ 270, 311.

OJur 3d: 89, Trial § 32 to 34, 129, 337

Am Jur 2d: 29, Evidence § 262, 263; 75, Trial § 126, 170 to 172

Giannelli & Snyder, Baldwin's Ohio Practice, Evidence § 101.4, 105.5, 106.4, 405.6, 407.6, 408.6, 408.7, 411.4, 609.1, 613.3, 706 (2d ed. 2001).

Evid R 106   Remainder of or related writings or recorded statements

When a writing or recorded statement or part thereof is introduced by a party, an adverse party may require him at that time to introduce any other part or any other writing or recorded statement which is otherwise admissible and which ought in fairness to be considered contemporaneously with it.

(Adopted eff. 7–1–80)

Commentary

Staff Notes

1980:

Rule 106, like Federal Evidence Rule 106, states that when a party introduces a writing or recording, or a part of either, into evidence, the adverse party may require him "at that time" to introduce any other recording or writing, or remainder of the part introduced into evidence, which in fairness places the writing or recording introduced into proper context. The rule is a rule of timing which avoids the need for the adverse party to wait until later to place the writing or recording introduced into proper perspective through cross-examination or rebuttal evidence. The rule merely codifies the better common law tradition. See McCormick § 56 (2d ed. 1972).

The rule is limited to writings and recordings; it does not apply to conversations. Rule 106 is similar to Civ. R. 32(A)(4), which provides that when a part of a deposition is introduced into evidence, "an adverse party may require him to introduce all of it which is relevant to the part introduced."

In contrast to the Federal Rule, Rule 106 explicitly provides that it does not make admissible a writing or a part thereof that is otherwise inadmissible.

Cross References

Depositions, use in court proceedings, partial proffer, Civ R 32; Crim R 15

Library References

Criminal Law ☞396.

Evidence ☞155(1) to 155(11).

Westlaw Topic Nos. 110, 157.

C.J.S. Criminal Law § 758.
C.J.S. Evidence §§ 248 to 250, 501, 502.
OJur 3d: 43, Evidence and Witnesses § 391
Am Jur 2d: 29, Evidence § 839
Requirement, under Rule 106 of Federal Rules of Evidence, that when writing or recorded statement or part thereof is introduced in evidence, another part or another writing or recorded statement must also be introduced in evidence. 75 ALR Fed 892

Giannelli & Snyder, Baldwin's Ohio Practice, Evidence § 410, 410.12, 901.18, 901.19 (2d ed. 2001).

Article II

JUDICIAL NOTICE

Rule
201   Judicial notice of adjudicative facts

Evid R 201   Judicial notice of adjudicative facts

(A) Scope of rule

This rule governs only judicial notice of adjudicative facts; i.e., the facts of the case.

(B) Kinds of facts

A judicially noticed fact must be one not subject to reasonable dispute in that it is either (1) generally known within the territorial jurisdiction of the trial court or (2) capable of accurate and ready determination by resort to sources whose accuracy cannot reasonable[1] be questioned.

(C) When discretionary

A court may take judicial notice, whether requested or not.

(D) When mandatory

A court shall take judicial notice if requested by a party and supplied with the necessary information.

(E) Opportunity to be heard

A party is entitled upon timely request to an opportunity to be heard as to the propriety of taking judicial notice and the tenor of the matter noticed. In the absence of prior notification, the request may be made after judicial notice has been taken.

(F) Time of taking notice

Judicial notice may be taken at any stage of the proceeding.

(G) Instructing jury

In a civil action or proceeding, the court shall instruct the jury to accept as conclusive any fact judicially noticed. In a criminal case, the court shall instruct the jury that it may, but is not required

to, accept as conclusive any fact judicially noticed.

(Adopted eff. 7–1–80)

[1] So in 62 OS(2d) xxxv; federal rule reads "reasonably."

Commentary
Staff Notes

1980:

Rule 201, in its entirety, reflects existing Ohio practice and, except for the added clarifying language to subdivision (A) which is not intended to result in contrary construction, is identical to Federal Evidence Rule 201.

Rule 201(A) Scope of Rule

The addition of the phrase " *i.e.*, the facts of the case" to subdivision (A) is intended as a clarification of the phrase "adjudicative fact" which was not considered as sufficiently self-descriptive. While the "adjudicative fact" phrase has great merit, its history is one of innovation by Prof. K.C. Davis (see McCormick § 328 (2d ed. 1972)) and does not necessarily carry with it an immediately discernible judicial meaning. It is not intended that the Federal Advisory Committee comments describing the term and its implication be any less relevant. See Advisory Committee's Note to Federal Evidence Rule 201(a).

Subdivision (A) limits the operation of the rule to adjudicative facts and does not apply to "legislative facts", i.e., those facts which have relevance to rules of decision or legislative construction and not to the facts necessary to the determination of events in a particular case. An example of "legislative facts" would be the effect of segregation upon children of minority races in determining constitutionality of segregated schools, *Brown v. Board of Education* (1954), 347 U.S. 483.

Given the limitation of application of the rule to adjudicative facts, no amendments or modifications were necessary respecting Civ. R. 44.1 or Crim. R. 27 adopting by reference the provisions of Civil Rule 44.1, relating to notice of foreign law. The rule does not in any way limit the power of a court to take notice of the law of its or another jurisdiction. If a court cannot take judicial notice of relevant law pursuant to Civ. R. 44.1, the rule does not alter that circumstance and the law will be subject to proof in the ordinary course. Likewise, if a law is subject to notice under Civ. R. 44.1, it is not limited in any way by the evidence rule.

Rule 201(B) Kinds of Facts

Subdivision (B) delineates the kind of facts which may be judicially noticed. The formulation in the rule reflects the common law development of the type of facts which may be judicially noticed including prior Ohio law. *Riss & Company v. Bowers* (1961), 114 Ohio App. 429, 444.

There are two categories of facts subject to judicial notice. Rule 201(B)(1) applies to adjudicative facts generally known within the territorial jurisdiction. This category relates to the type of fact that any person would reasonably know or ought to know without prompting within the jurisdiction of the court and includes an infinite variety of data from location of towns within a county to the fact that lawyers as a group enjoy a good reputation in the community. 21 OJur 2d Evidence §§ 16, 18.

A second class of facts subject to judicial notice is provided by Rule 201(B)(2). These are facts capable of accurate and ready determination. There is no need that such facts are also generally known in the community, each of the two classifications being independent of the other. The type of fact contemplated by 201(B)(2) includes scientific, historical and statistical data which can be verified and is beyond reasonable dispute. Such has been the law in Ohio and, again, there is an infinite variety of facts of scientific or historical nature that have been judicially noticed, thereby avoiding the necessity of proof on such issues. See 21 OJur 2d Evidence §§ 51, 63 and 68 for a compendium of such cases in Ohio.

The rule reflects prior Ohio law.

Subdivisions (C), (D), (E), and (F), of the rule reflect preexisting Ohio civil practice and reflect the view that if a court takes judicial notice of an adjudicative fact, no countervailing evidence may be admitted to oppose the fact noticed and the judge instructs the jury to find the fact judicially noticed. McCormick § 334 (2d ed. 1972). Such a view seems justified in light of the provisions of subdivision (E) permitting a hearing on the propriety of the court taking judicial notice of the proposed fact and of the highly restrictive requirements of subdivision (B) that only facts which are not subject to reasonable dispute are subject to judicial notice. The provisions of subdivision (F) authorize the taking of judicial notice at any stage of the proceeding including appeal. See Advisory Committee's Note to Federal Evidence Rule 201(f).

Rule 201(G) Instructing Jury

While this subdivision essentially reflects prior Ohio law, attention is invited to the unique problems of judicial notice of matters going to an element of an offense in criminal cases. In *State v. Bridgeman* (1977), 51 Ohio App.2d 105, the court, in dealing with the necessity to charge on the elements of a crime, whether or not contested by the defendant, established the right of a defendant to have all elements of the case subject to an explicit finding by the jury. The principle would clearly apply to matters subject to judicial notice that go to an element of the defense (Editor's Note: The Staff Note may have meant "offense" rather than "defense.") and the rule does not alter the requirement that the jury find defendant guilty beyond a reasonable doubt as to each element of the offense including any matters of which judicial notice was taken.

Moreover, in *Bridgeman* the court held that such error is plain error and need not be objected to by counsel under Crim. R. 30 and Crim. R. 52(B).

Cross References

Courts, municipal, mayor's, county, appeals, 1901.30
Foreign corporations, evidence, 1703.21
Harmless error, plain error, Crim R 52
Judicial notice of certain law, determination of foreign law, Civ R 44.1
Motion for a directed verdict and judgment notwithstanding the verdict, Civ R 50
Municipal corporations, judicial notice of classification, 703.23
Oath of office, vacancy, appointment, election, additional judges, 1901.10
Pleading a statute, 2941.12
Proof of official record, judicial notice, determination of foreign law, Crim R 27
Records and proceedings of registrar, 4507.25
Summary judgment, Civ R 56

Library References

Criminal Law ⟐304(1) to 304(21).

Evidence ⟐1 to 52.

Westlaw Topic Nos. 110, 157.

C.J.S. Criminal Law §§ 657 to 681.

C.J.S. Evidence §§ 2 to 119.

OJur 3d: 29, Criminal Law § 2753; 29A, Criminal Law § 2877; 42, Evidence and Witnesses § 19 to 94; 59, Insurance § 1354; 60, Insurance § 1666; 61, Intoxicating Liquors § 299

Am Jur 2d: 14, Census § 12; 29, Evidence § 14 to 122

Uniform Judicial Notice of Foreign Law Act. 23 ALR2d 1437

Reception of evidence to contradict or rebut matters judicially noticed. 45 ALR2d 1169

Judicial notice of matters relating to public thoroughfares and parks. 48 ALR2d 1102

Judicial notice of diseases or similar conditions adversely affecting human beings. 72 ALR2d 554

Judicial notice of drivers' reaction time and of stopping distance of motor vehicles traveling at various speeds. 84 ALR2d 979

Judicial notice as to location of street address within particular political subdivision. 86 ALR3d 484

What constitutes "adjudicative facts" within meaning of Rule 201 of Federal Rules of Evidence, concerning judicial notice of adjudicative facts. 35 ALR Fed 440

Effect of Rule 201(g) of the Federal Rules of Evidence, providing for instruction in criminal case that jury need not accept as conclusive fact judicially noticed, on propriety of taking judicial notice on appeal under Rule 201(f). 49 ALR Fed 911

Katz & Giannelli, Baldwin's Ohio Practice, Criminal Law § 56.12 (1996).

Giannelli & Snyder, Baldwin's Ohio Practice, Evidence § 201.4, 201.6, 201.9, 803.52, 901.13 (2d ed. 2001).

Ohio Administrative Law Handbook and Agency Directory, OAC Vol. 17, Text 7.12.

Williams, Ohio Consumer Law (2002 Ed.), Text 11.45.

Article III

PRESUMPTIONS

Rule
301 Presumptions in general in civil actions and proceedings
302 [Reserved]

Evid R 301 Presumptions in general in civil actions and proceedings

In all civil actions and proceedings not otherwise provided for by statute enacted by the General Assembly or by these rules, a presumption imposes on the party against whom it is directed the burden of going forward with evidence to rebut or meet the presumption, but does not shift to such party the burden of proof in the sense of the risk of non-persuasion, which remains throughout the trial upon the party on whom it was originally cast.

(Adopted eff. 7–1–80)

Commentary

Staff Notes

1980:

Rule 301 is a counterpart of Federal Evidence Rule 301. This rule does not change Ohio law relative to the effect of a presumption in civil cases. *Ayers v. Woodard* (1957), 166 Ohio St. 138.

The rule reflects the traditional or orthodox approach known as the Thayer–Wigmore view. It relegates to the role of presumptions in civil cases simply the allocation of burden of production or burden of "going forward" with the evidence. Here, we speak only of a rebuttable presumption since a conclusive presumption is a rule of substantive law and not a rule of evidence. Failure to rebut a presumption with evidence contrary to the fact presumed results in a directed verdict or a required finding by the trier of fact if the basic facts from which the presumption arises are either found or are admitted to exist. However, once a presumption is met with sufficient countervailing evidence, it falls and the presumption serves no further function. If rebutted, the jury is not instructed that a presumption existed.

A presumption, therefore, affects only the burden of going forward with the evidence and is controlled by the trial court's use of directed verdict or instruction to the jury to find the presumed fact if the trier believes the basic facts upon which the presumption arose. The burden of persuasion is not affected and it remains throughout upon the party upon whom it was originally cast.

An example of the function and operation of presumptions under the rule may be illustrated by considering the following hypothetical case.

Y is the owner of a vehicle in which he is riding as a passenger which strikes X's car. X sues Y for negligence and offers evidence, (A), that Y was the owner of the vehicle and was a passenger in the car at the time of the accident. At this point a presumption arises that Y was in control of the automobile, (B). Such a presumption arises as a matter of law. *Lester v. Jurgenson Company* (1968), 400 F.2d 393. Now, if X rests his case and if Y, defendant, produces no evidence that he was not in control of the car (i.e.

non–B), the trial court must instruct the jury that if they find facts, (A), that Y was the owner and was a passenger at the time of the accident, it must find (B), that Y was in control of the car because Y has failed to meet his burden of production.

If, instead, Y introduces evidence that he was not in control of the car, (non–B), because he was asleep at the time, then there has been evidence introduced from which reasonable minds might find non-B and the presumption has been "rebutted" and it falls. The jury would be given no instruction on the subject presumption and the burden of persuasion would remain on the plaintiff X to convince the jury of the element of control (B).

A presumption is to be differentiated from an inference in that the former requires a finding of an ultimate fact as a matter of law unless it is rebutted and an inference merely permits the trier of fact to conclude an ultimate fact, (B), from the existence of basic fact, (A), as a matter of common experience and logic. This is commonly referred to as circumstantial evidence.

Moreover, it should be noted that even if X introduces evidence of (A) (ownership and passenger status) giving rise to the presumption of (B) (control) and Y defendant introduces no evidence of non-B, a directed verdict is not in order because the jury may disbelieve X's evidence of the existence of the basic facts (A) (ownership and passenger status) giving rise to the presumption of (B) (control). A directed verdict is not in order because the jury may disbelieve X's evidence of the existence of the basic facts (A) (ownership and passenger status); therefore, the trial court would have to instruct the jury to find (B) only if they first found (A) to exist.

This view respecting presumptions is thought to avoid the confusion of shifting the burden of persuasion throughout the trial depending on what evidence has been adduced.

However, when a presumption is based upon strong public policy such as the presumption against suicide, it was suggested by Justice Taft that, although the burden of persuasion would not shift, the trial court might be justified in mentioning to the jury that such a presumption exists as a matter of law even if the presumption has been rebutted by the opposing party. *Carson v. Metropolitan Life Insurance Company* (1956), 165 Ohio St. 238. Justice Taft was obviously concerned that the Thayer–Wigmore "bursting the bubble" theory of presumptions did not sufficiently protect the strong public policy respecting suicide and suggested the modification to the general rule accordingly. Nothing in Rule 301 would, by its specific language, preclude similar treatment were the *Carson* situation to arise under the rule. Aside from this rather modest variation, all presumptions are characterized the same by the rule without regard to the underlying policy issue giving rise to the presumption. A presumption arising from mere consideration of accessibility to the evidence such as the presumption that a letter is delivered if properly posted and the presumption of legitimacy arising from strong policy considerations are treated alike under the rules unless modified elsewhere by rule or by statute.

It should be observed that this rule seeks neither to define nor enumerate what presumptions exist. That is a matter of substantive law determined by the legislature or by court decision. McCormick § 343 (2d ed. 1972). There is no rule defining terms such as "burden of proof", "burden of persuasion", or "preponderance". These are left to case law. Nor does the rule apply to presumptions in criminal cases. The function of presumptions in criminal cases is limited by constitutional restrictions of due process. See *State v. Robinson* (1976), 47 Ohio St.2d 103; *State v. Humphries* (1977), 51 Ohio St.2d 95 and *State v. Bridgeman* (1977), 51 Ohio App.2d 105.

Finally, it is noted that the rule does not resolve difficult issues as to sufficiency of evidence necessary to rebut a presumption, the problems inherent in instructing the jury if the presumption is not rebutted, or a number of other difficult problems surrounding the subject. These are left to case law analysis and prior Ohio case law will continue to apply to these peripheral areas. An excellent analysis of the subject is found in Subrin, *Presumptions and Their Treatment Under the Law of Ohio*, 26 Ohio St. L.J. 175 (1965).

Cross References

Air pollution, related determinations by environmental protection agency shall not be used as evidence or create any presumption in civil actions to benefit any person other than the state, 3704.09
Bonds of municipal housing authority conclusively deemed valid in certain instances, 3735.46
Irrebuttable presumption of wrongful imprisonment, 2743.48
Paternity proceedings, presumption as to father and child relationships, 3111.03
Persons presumed to be wholly dependent for their support upon a deceased employee, 4123.59

Presumption of commercial use of weighing or measuring device raised by proof of its existence in commercial setting by person in charge, 1327.59
Presumption of order of death, 2105.21
When presumption of death arises, 2121.01

Library References

Evidence ⊙53 to 89.
Westlaw Topic No. 157.
C.J.S. Common Law § 20.
C.J.S. Evidence §§ 2, 130 to 196, 1341.
OJur 3d: 30, Death § 2; 36, Domicil § 20; 42, Evidence and Witnesses § 96, 115 to 170; 52, Gifts § 39; 52, Guaranty and Suretyship § 223, 253; 56, Injunctions § 168; 59, Insurance § 1355; 60, Insurance § 1668; 61, Intoxicating Liquors § 301; 70, Negligence § 156, 159, 160; 79, Railroads § 400
Am Jur 2d: 29, Evidence § 159 to 166
Comment Note—Effect of presumption as evidence or upon burden of proof, where controverting evidence is introduced. 5 ALR3d 19
Modern status of the rules against basing an inference upon an inference or a presumption upon a presumption. 5 ALR3d 100
Conflict of laws as to presumptions and burden of proof concerning facts of civil case. 35 ALR3d 289
Siegel & Stephen, Ohio Employment Practices Law (2001 Ed.), Text 20.16.
Giannelli & Snyder, Baldwin's Ohio Practice, Evidence § 102.5, 802.5, 803.42 (2d ed. 2001).

Evid R 302   [Reserved]

Article IV

RELEVANCY AND ITS LIMITS

Rule
401 Definition of "relevant evidence"
402 Relevant evidence generally admissible; irrelevant evidence inadmissible
403 Exclusion of relevant evidence on grounds of prejudice, confusion, or undue delay
404 Character evidence not admissible to prove conduct; exceptions; other crimes
405 Methods of proving character
406 Habit; routine practice
407 Subsequent remedial measures
408 Compromise and offers to compromise
409 Payment of medical and similar expenses
410 Inadmissibility of pleas, offers of pleas, and related statements
411 Liability insurance

Evid R 401   Definition of "relevant evidence"

"Relevant evidence" means evidence having any tendency to make the existence of any fact that is of consequence to the determination of the action more probable or less probable than it would be without the evidence.

(Adopted eff. 7–1–80)

Commentary

Staff Notes

1980:

Rule 401 defines relevant evidence and is identical to Federal Evidence Rule 401.

Relevancy is not an inherent characteristic of any item of evidence. When it exists, it is a relationship between an item of evidence and a matter properly provable in the case. Evidence is relevant when it tends as a matter of common experience and logic to prove a matter of consequence. In the rule, "of consequence to the determination" is an expression of materiality. The rule expresses the usual and general concept of relevancy. *Barnett v. State* (1922), 104 Ohio St. 298 and *Whiteman v. State* (1928), 119 Ohio St. 285.

Cross References

Authority of magistrate or judge, 2938.07
Judge to control proceedings during criminal trial, 2945.03

Library References

Criminal Law ⊙338(1).
Evidence ⊙99.

Westlaw Topic Nos. 110, 157.

C.J.S. Criminal Law §§ 710, 712, 714, 725, 823.

C.J.S. Evidence §§ 2 to 5, 197 to 199, 204, 206.

OJur 3d: 29A, Criminal Law § 2909; 31, Decedents' Estates § 376; 42, Evidence and Witnesses § 174; 70, Negligence § 190; 75, Pleading § 483

Am Jur 2d: 29, Evidence § 251 et seq.

Painter, Ohio Driving Under the Influence Law (2003 Ed.), Text 15.14.

Giannelli & Snyder, Baldwin's Ohio Practice, Evidence § 104.6, 106.4, 401.9, 401.11, 402.1, 402.7, 403.1, 403.4, 403.6, 404.6, 404.14, 404.21, 407.4, 407.6, 408.6, 408.7, 411.4, 411.5, 411.6, 702.12, 704.5, 801.4, 802.1, 803.30, 901, 901.25 (2d ed. 2001).

Ohio Personal Injury Practice (2002 Ed.), Text 5.03.

Evid R 402   Relevant evidence generally admissible; irrelevant evidence inadmissible

All relevant evidence is admissible, except as otherwise provided by the Constitution of the United States, by the Constitution of the State of Ohio, by statute enacted by the General Assembly not in conflict with a rule of the Supreme Court of Ohio, by these rules, or by other rules prescribed by the Supreme Court of Ohio. Evidence which is not relevant is not admissible.

(Adopted eff. 7-1-80)

Commentary

Staff Notes

1980:

Rule 402 sets forth the admissibility of relevant evidence. It is a modification of Federal Evidence Rule 402 and restates existing Ohio law.

The essence of the rule is that irrelevant evidence is not admissible and that all relevant evidence is admissible subject to enumerated exceptions.

The exception provided by an Act of Congress has been omitted from the rule. The reference to an Act of Congress does not differentiate between a federal statute which preempts state law and one which does not preempt. If there is preemption, it occurs wholly independently of enumeration in the Ohio rule.

The rule is also modified to remove the inapplicable reference to rules of the Supreme Court of the United States. In its place is the appropriate reference to rules of the Supreme Court of Ohio.

The rule includes an exception for provisions of other rules of the Supreme Court of Ohio. The purpose of the inclusion is to eliminate the potential for conflict between the Rules of Evidence and other rules adopted by the Supreme Court of Ohio.

The rule also contains an exception for the provisions of an enactment of the General Assembly not in conflict with a rule of the Supreme Court. The limitation reflects the provision of Article IV, § 5(B) of the Ohio Constitution relative to the relationship between rules of practice and procedure adopted pursuant to the constitutional provision and the statutes.

Cross References

Accommodation party; oral proof of status, when admissible as against holder in due course, 1303.51

Air pollution, related determinations by environmental protection agency shall not be used as evidence or create any presumption in civil actions to benefit any person other than the state, 3704.09

Driving while intoxicated or drugged, tests, presumptions, 4511.19

Examination and treatment for venereal disease and AIDS, 2907.27

Laboratory report as prima-facie evidence of content, weight and identity of substance, rights of accused, 2925.51

Motor vehicles, aeronautics, watercraft, use of report, 4509.10

Rape, evidence, 2907.02

Sales contract, extrinsic or parol evidence of other agreements, 1302.05

Search warrants, O Const Art I §14

Sexual imposition, 2907.06

Trial for crimes, witness, O Const Art I §10

Written consent to medical procedures, presumption of validity, form, 2317.54

Library References

Criminal Law ⟸337 to 361(4).

Evidence ⟸99 to 117.

Westlaw Topic Nos. 110, 157.

C.J.S. Criminal Law §§ 286, 323, 710 to 748, 799 to 824, 947.

C.J.S. Eminent Domain § 273(6).

C.J.S. Evidence §§ 2 to 6, 197 to 215, 227 to 245, 495 to 507, 768, 769, 783 to 785.

OJur 3d: 29A, Criminal Law § 2908; 42, Evidence and Witnesses § 172; 70, Negligence § 171, 173, 174, 176 to 181, 185 to 187; 75, Pleading § 483, 507; 89, Trial § 32 to 34, 133, 246, 247

Am Jur 2d: 29, Evidence § 251

Admissibility of evidence of absence of other accidents or injuries at place where injury or damage occurred. 10 ALR5th 371

Admissibility of evidence of polygraph test results, or offer or refusal to take test, in action for malicious prosecution. 10 ALR5th 663

Admissibility of evidence in homicide case that victim was threatened by one other than defendant. 11 ALR5th 831

Giannelli & Snyder, Baldwin's Ohio Practice, Evidence § 102.5, 106.4, 401.1, 401.3, 401.4, 403.1, 403.6, 802.1, 901.25 (2d ed. 2001).

Wasil, Waite, & Mastrangelo, Ohio Workers' Compensation Law § 14:132.

Carlin, Baldwin's Ohio Practice, Merrick–Rippner Probate Law § 19.10 (2003).

Evid R 403   Exclusion of relevant evidence on grounds of prejudice, confusion, or undue delay

(A) Exclusion mandatory

Although relevant, evidence is not admissible if its probative value is substantially outweighed by the danger of unfair prejudice, of confusion of the issues, or of misleading the jury.

(B) Exclusion discretionary

Although relevant, evidence may be excluded if its probative value is substantially outweighed by considerations of undue delay, or needless presentation of cumulative evidence.

(Adopted eff. 7–1–80; amended eff. 7–1–96)

Historical and Statutory Notes

Amendment Note: The 7–1–96 amendment substituted "undue delay" for "waste of time" in the title of the rule.

Commentary

Staff Notes

1996:

The amendment modifies the title of the rule to reflect its content. As originally adopted, Evid. R. 403 varied from its federal counterpart by excluding "waste of time" as a separate or independent ground for excluding otherwise relevant and admissible evidence. The title of the Ohio rule, however, was not modified to reflect this difference between the Ohio and federal texts. The amendment substitutes "undue delay" in place of the original title's reference to "waste of time" as a ground of exclusion, so that the title more accurately reflects the content of the Ohio text. The amendment is intended only as a technical correction; no substantive change is intended.

1980:

Rule 403 delineates the first exceptions established by rule to the basic directive of Rule 402 that all relevant evidence is admissible. The rule is essentially the same, in content, as Federal Evidence Rule 403. Except for the omission of a reference to waste of time, the rule is an earlier draft of the federal rule. 51 F.R.D. 345 (1971). The rule represents no significant change in existing Ohio law.

The rule mandates the exclusion of relevant evidence if the court finds that the probative value of the relevant evidence is substantially outweighed by any one of three dangers: unfair prejudice, confusion of the issues, or the misleading of the jury.

Where the court finds that the probative value of relevant evidence is substantially outweighed by considerations of undue delay or needless presentation of cumulative evidence, the court may exclude that relevant evidence but it is not required to do so.

The rule does not refer to waste of time as a basis for exclusion as does Federal Evidence Rule 403. Waste of time is a correlative to undue delay and needless cumulation.

Cross References

Number of witnesses to testify upon character, 2945.57

Library References

Criminal Law ☞338(7).

Evidence ☞146.

Westlaw Topic Nos. 110, 157.

C.J.S. Criminal Law § 711.

C.J.S. Evidence §§ 200, 764.

OJur 3d: 5A, Alternative Dispute Resolution § 86; 27, Criminal Law § 1192; 29A, Criminal Law § 2911, 2913, 2959, 2997, 3072, 3084, 3134; 31, Decedents' Estates § 376; 42, Evidence and Witnesses § 173; 44, Evidence and Witnesses § 924; 67, Malpractice § 143; 89, Trial § 32, 33, 60, 135

Am Jur 2d: 29, Evidence § 256

Modern status of rules as to use of motion in limine or similar preliminary motion to secure exclusion of prejudicial evidence or reference to prejudicial matters. 63 ALR3d 311

Admissibility and prejudicial effect of evidence, in criminal prosecution, of defendant's involvement with witchcraft, satanism, or the like. 18 ALR5th 804

Propriety under Rule 403 of the Federal Rules of Evidence, permitting exclusion of relevant evidence on grounds of prejudice, confusion, or waste of time, of attack on credibility of witness for party. 48 ALR Fed 390

Evidence offered by defendant at federal criminal trial as inadmissible, under Rule 403 of Federal Rules of Evidence, on ground that probative value is substantially outweighed by danger of unfair prejudice, confusion of issues, or misleading the jury. 76 ALR Fed 700

Painter, Ohio Driving Under the Influence Law (2003 Ed.), Text 5.13, 9.4, 15.14.

Giannelli & Snyder, Baldwin's Ohio Practice, Evidence § 101.3, 104.11, 105.3, 401.1, 401.4, 401.11, 402.7, 404.6, 404.7, 404.14, 404.16, 404.18, 404.19, 404.20, 406.1, 406.6, 407.4, 407.6, 407.7, 407.8, 407.9, 408.6, 408.7, 409.4, 411.4, 411.5, 411.6, 607.4, 608.5, 609.2, 609.4, 609.7, 609.8, 609.10, 611.3, 611.6, 613.7, 616.7, 702.9, 703.5, 704.4, 801.4, 105, 409, 609, 801.10, 802.1, 804, 901.1, 901.17, 901.19, 901.22, 901.23, 901.25, 1101, 902.1 (2d ed. 2001).

Adrine & Ruden, Ohio Domestic Violence Law (2002 Ed.), Text 5.11, 5.22, 6.13.

Carlin, Baldwin's Ohio Practice, Merrick–Rippner Probate Law § 19.10 (2003).

Evid R 404   Character evidence not admissible to prove conduct; exceptions; other crimes

(A) Character evidence generally

Evidence of a person's character or a trait of his character is not admissible for the purpose of proving that he acted in conformity therewith on a particular occasion, subject to the following exceptions:

(1) Character of accused. Evidence of a pertinent trait of his character offered by an accused, or by the prosecution to rebut the same is admissible; however, in prosecutions for rape, gross sexual imposition, and prostitution, the exceptions provided by statute enacted by the General Assembly are applicable.

(2) Character of victim. Evidence of a pertinent trait of character of the victim of the crime offered by an accused, or by the prosecution to rebut the same, or evidence of a character trait of peacefulness of the victim offered by the prosecution in a homicide case to rebut evidence that the victim was the first aggressor is admissible; however, in prosecutions for rape, gross sexual imposition, and prostitution, the exceptions provided by statute

enacted by the General Assembly are applicable.

(3) Character of witness. Evidence of the character of a witness on the issue of credibility is admissible as provided in Rules 607, 608, and 609.

(B) Other crimes, wrongs or acts

Evidence of other crimes, wrongs, or acts is not admissible to prove the character of a person in order to show that he acted in conformity therewith. It may, however, be admissible for other purposes, such as proof of motive, opportunity, intent, preparation, plan, knowledge, identity, or absence of mistake or accident.

(Adopted eff. 7–1–80)

Commentary

Staff Notes

1980:

Rule 404 is a slightly modified version of Federal Evidence Rule 404. The modification consists of the addition of limitations upon admissibility of relevant evidence as provided by statute in certain sex offenses. Rule 404 codifies existing Ohio law.

Character or a trait of character may be an element of a crime, a part of a claim, or a part of a defense. When that situation exists, character is an issue. Actions for libel, slander, malicious prosecution, seduction, and assault and battery have been delineated as cases in which character is an issue. *Lakes v. Buckeye State Mutual Insurance Ass'n.* (1959), 110 Ohio App. 115. When character is an issue in the case, it can be proved by any relevant evidence. Rule 404 does not apply to cases where character is an issue.

The second use of character evidence is as circumstantial evidence which gives rise to an inference which tends to establish conduct on a particular occasion. Rule 404 is directed to that usage. It states the basic prohibition on using character evidence to establish conduct on a particular occasion and then sets forth the exceptions to the prohibition.

If character evidence is admissible under the rule, proof of character may be made as provided in Rule 405. If evidence of a witness's character trait of truth and veracity is offered on the issue of credibility, the admissibility is governed by Rules 607, 608, and 609.

Rule 404(A) Character Evidence Generally

Character evidence is generally inadmissible to prove conduct on a particular occasion. Evidence that a defendant is a careless person is not admissible to prove that he was negligent on a particular occasion. *Hatsio v. Red Cab Co.* (1945), 77 Ohio App. 301. Character evidence is relevant in that it tends to prove a material proposition but its prejudicial effect substantially outweighs its probative value and it creates collateral issues. Rule 404(A) restates existing Ohio law.

Rule 404(A)(1) Character of the Accused

The first exception to the general rule of inadmissibility is the limited use of evidence of a character trait of the accused. The basic rule is that the defendant may, at his option, offer evidence of his good character as proof that he did not commit the act charged because such conduct is not in accord with his character. This is often denominated the "mercy defense". If the accused offers evidence of his good character, then and only then, can the prosecution offer evidence of the bad character of the accused. The rule is in accord with existing Ohio law. R.C. 2945.56; *State v. Markowitz* (1941), 138 Ohio St. 106.

Rule 404(A)(1) provides that evidence of the character of the accused, in certain sex offenses, shall be admissible as provided by statute. The purpose of including the provision in the rule is to assure that the rule does not supersede those statutes. R.C. 2907.02(D), rape, and R.C. 2907.05(D), gross sexual imposition, limit evidence of the accused's character trait for promiscuity to specified narrow issues. R.C. 2907.26, rules of evidence in prostitution cases, permits a broader use of character evidence than does the rule.

Rule 404(A)(2) Character of Victim

The character of the victim is seldom relevant evidence in a criminal prosecution. Where self-defense is asserted by the accused, the character of the victim bears directly on the issue of self-defense. The rule accords to existing Ohio law. *McGaw v. State* (1931), 123 Ohio St. 196. Rule 404(A)(2) contains the same provision relative to the sex offenses as does Rule 404(A)(1) and for the same purpose.

Rule 404(A)(3) Character of Witness

A witness's character trait for truth and veracity is always relevant for the purpose of attacking the credibility of the witness. Rule 607 sets forth who may impeach a witness and Rules 608 and 609 provide the methods of proof used in the impeachment of a witness.

Rule 404(B) Other Crimes, Wrongs or Acts

Evidence of other crimes, wrongs or acts of the accused are not admissible to show that the accused committed the crime with which he is now charged. The prosecution may not offer evidence that the accused has perpetrated earlier burglaries to prove that he committed the burglary with which he is now charged. The rule does permit the use of such evidence for other purposes. In a non-exclusive listing, the rule sets forth the purposes of showing motive, opportunity, intent, preparation, plan, knowledge, identity, or absence of mistake or accident.

The rule is in accord with R.C. 2945.59. The statute does not refer specifically to identity, but it has been held that identity was included within the concept of scheme, plan, or system. *State v. Curry* (1975), 43 Ohio St.2d 66. The statute has been held to be subject to narrow construction. *State v. Burson* (1974), 38 Ohio St. 2d 157. Evidence is admissible only when that purpose is inextricably related to the alleged criminal act.

Cross References

Gross sexual imposition, 2907.05
Proof of defendant's motive, 2945.59
Rape evidence, 2907.02
Rules of evidence in prostitution cases, 2907.26

Library References

Criminal Law ⬤376 to 381.
Evidence ⬤106(1) to 106(5), 152.
Witnesses ⬤333 to 362.
Westlaw Topic Nos. 110, 157, 410.
C.J.S. Criminal Law §§ 816 to 824.

C.J.S. Evidence §§ 495 to 507.

C.J.S. Witnesses §§ 464, 480, 490 to 537.

OJur 3d: 27, Criminal Law § 1211; 29A, Criminal
     Law § 2912, 2948, 2951, 2956, 2957, 2959,
     2965 to 2968, 2970, 2977, 2978, 2979, 3133;
     42, Evidence and Witnesses § 206, 207, 227;
     44, Evidence and Witnesses § 922

Am Jur 2d: 29, Evidence § 298 to 351; 30, Evidence
     § 1127

Admissibility of testimony as to general reputation at
     place of employment. 82 ALR3d 525

Admissibility of evidence of subsequent criminal of-
     fenses as affected by proximity as to time and
     place. 92 ALR3d 545

Modern status of admissibility, in forceable rape
     prosecutions, of complainant's general reputa-
     tion for unchastity. 95 ALR3d 1181

Admissibility, under Rule 404(b) of Federal Rules of
     Evidence, of evidence of other crimes, wrongs,
     or acts not similar to offense charged. 97
     ALR3d 1150, 41 ALR Fed 497

Cross-examination of character witness for accused
     with reference to particular acts or crimes—
     modern state rules. 13 ALR4th 796

Admissibility of evidence as to other offense as affect-
     ed by defendant's acquittal of that offense. 25
     ALR4th 934

Admissibility of evidence of pertinent trait under
     Rule 404(a) of the Uniform Rules of Evidence.
     56 ALR4th 402

Impeachment or cross-examination of prosecuting
     witness in sexual offense trial by showing that
     prosecuting witness threatened to make simi-
     lar charges against other persons. 71 ALR4th
     448

Impeachment or cross-examination of prosecuting
     witness in sexual offense trial by showing that
     similar charges were made against other per-
     sons. 71 ALR4th 469

Admissibility of evidence of commission of similar
     crime by one other than accused. 22 ALR5th 1

Admissibility of evidence of prior physical acts of
     spousal abuse committed by defendant ac-
     cused of murdering spouse or former spouse.
     24 ALR5th 465

Admissibility, under Rule 404(b) of the Federal Rules
     of Evidence, of evidence of other crimes,
     wrongs, or acts similar to offense charged to
     show preparation or plan. 47 ALR Fed 781

When is evidence of trait of accused's character
     "pertinent" for purposes of admissibility under
     Rule 404(a)(1) of the Federal Rules of Evi-
     dence. 49 ALR Fed 478

Admissibility of evidence of other crimes, wrongs, or
     acts under Rule 404(b) of Federal Rules of
     Evidence, in civil cases. 64 ALR Fed 648

Admissibility in rape case, under Rule 412 of Federal
     Rules of Evidence, of evidence of victim's past
     sexual behavior. 65 ALR Fed 519

Katz & Giannelli, Baldwin's Ohio Practice, Criminal
     Law § 1.8 (1996).

Painter, Ohio Driving Under the Influence Law (2003
     Ed.), Text 15.12, 19.33.

Giannelli & Snyder, Baldwin's Ohio Practice, Evi-
     dence § 101.3, 405, 102.5, 105.7, 403.4, 403.5,
     405.1, 405.3, 405.4, 405.5, 405.6, 405.7, 609,
     406.3, 406.4, 608.1, 608.3, 608.6, 609.3, 609.5,
     609.6, 609.13, 702.21, 801.16, 803.53, 803.57,
     901.17 (2d ed. 2001).

Adrine & Ruden, Ohio Domestic Violence Law (2002
     Ed.), Text 3.6, 5.22, 8.4, 14.7.

Evid R 405 Methods of proving character

(A) Reputation or opinion

In all cases in which evidence of character or a trait of character of a person is
admissible, proof may be made by testimony as to reputation or by testimony in
the form of an opinion. On cross-examination, inquiry is allowable into relevant
specific instances of conduct.

(B) Specific instances of conduct

In cases in which character or a trait
of character of a person is an essential
element of a charge, claim, or defense,
proof may also be made of specific instances of his conduct.

(Adopted eff. 7–1–80)

Commentary

Staff Notes

1980:

Rule 405 sets forth the methods of proving character and is identical to Federal Evidence Rule 405. It
expands Ohio law by permitting the use of opinion
evidence as to character.

Rule 405(A) Reputation or Opinion

Proof of character or a trait of character may be by
reputation or by opinion whether character is an
issue in the case or is offered as circumstantial
evidence under Rule 404. At common law, proof of
character was only by evidence of reputation. A
witness familiar with the person's reputation in the
community in which he lived could testify as to that
reputation. That is the traditional view to which
Ohio has adhered. *Harper v. Harper* (1833), Wright
283. The witness could not testify as to his opinion
to establish character. *Bucklin v. State* (1851), 20
Ohio 18. With the progression of time the distinction between reputation and opinion has become
blurred in Ohio practice. *Noll v. Wilson* (1934), 47
Ohio App. 134. Under Ohio practice, a witness who
testifies as to reputation of a person's character is
subject to cross-examination as to specific instances
of conduct. *Zeltner v. State* (1899), 13 Ohio C.C.(n.s.)
417. Reputation is essentially a consensus of individual opinions, the general estimation of others.

Rule 405(A) recognizes the impracticality of distinguishing between reputation and opinion and permits testimony as to character in either form.

Rule 405(B) Specific Instances of Conduct

Rule 405(B) permits an additional method of proof
of character, specific instances of conduct, but limits
the method to those cases in which character or a
trait of character is an issue. Such proof may not be
used when character is offered as circumstantial
evidence under Rule 404.

Under existing Ohio practice, evidence of general
reputation rather than evidence of specific acts is
required to establish character when character is in
issue. *Lakes v. Buckeye State Mutual Insurance
Ass'n.* (1959), 110 Ohio App. 115.

Cross References

Gross sexual imposition, 2907.05
Rape evidence, 2907.02
Rules of evidence in prostitution cases, 2907.26

Library References

Criminal Law ☞376 to 380.

Evidence ☞106(1) to 106(5).

Witnesses ☞333 to 359.

Westlaw Topic Nos. 110, 157, 410.

C.J.S. Criminal Law §§ 816 to 824.

C.J.S. Evidence §§ 495 to 507.

C.J.S. Witnesses §§ 464, 480, 490 to 528.

OJur 3d: 29A, Criminal Law § 2951, 2953; 42, Evidence and Witnesses § 229

Am Jur 2d: 29, Evidence § 344 to 351; 81, Witnesses § 503, 504

Admissibility of evidence of accused's good reputation as affected by remoteness of time to which it relates. 87 ALR2d 968

Opinion evidence as to character of accused under Rule 405(a) of Federal Rules of Evidence. 64 ALR Fed 244

Giannelli & Snyder, Baldwin's Ohio Practice, Evidence § 404.1, 404.4, 404.5, 404.6, 404.7, 608.3, 608.8, 609.13, 701.1, 803.53, 608 (2d ed. 2001).

Evid R 406   Habit; routine practice

Evidence of the habit of a person or of the routine practice of an organization, whether corroborated or not and regardless of the presence of eyewitnesses, is relevant to prove that the conduct of the person or organization on a particular occasion was in conformity with the habit or routine practice.

(Adopted eff. 7–1–80)

Commentary

Staff Notes

1980:

The rule is stated in language identical to that of Federal Evidence Rule 406.

Habits of persons and routine practice of organizations are equivalent in concept for the purposes of the rule.

The rule has two objectives. First, it confirms the established principle that habit or routine practice is relevant evidence to prove that conduct on the occasion in issue was in conformity to that habit or routine practice. Secondly, the rule specifies that the relevancy of evidence of habit or of routine practice is not destroyed by the absence of corroboration or by the presence of eyewitnesses.

The rule makes no essential change in Ohio law as it existed prior to the adoption of the Rules of Evidence. Admission of evidence of habit or routine practice involves two major concepts: relevancy and competency. The rule treats relevancy only. The fundamental approach of Ohio courts to the use of evidence of habit was expressed in *Hartman v. Toledo Railways and Light Co.* (1917), 7 Ohio App. 296, where it was said:

Evidence of the habit of a person being circumstantial and secondary in character, its admission is largely within the discretion of the court; and, when there is primary evidence of a fact desired to be proven, there is ordinarily no necessity for resort to secondary evidence to establish the fact; therefore, in the absence of some necessity for the introduction of such evidence to meet some exigency of proof it will be rejected.

In the course of its opinion, p. 303, the court quoted from *Zucker v. Whitridge* (1912), 205 N.Y. 50, as follows:

A question of evidence, to some extent, is a question of sound policy in the administration of the law. Sometimes it is necessary to weigh the probative force of evidence offered, compare it with the practical inconvenience of enforcing a rule to admit it and decide whether, as a matter of good policy, it should be admitted. Uniform conduct under the same circumstances on many prior occasions may be relevant as tending somewhat to show like conduct under like circumstances on the occasion in question. All relevant evidence, however, is not competent.

In the *Hartman* case the court assumed the relevance of the evidence of habit, but held that it was incompetent because the circumstantial evidence of habit could not outweigh the direct evidence from the several eyewitnesses in that case. Whether the disparity between the probative value of the circumstantial evidence of habit and the direct evidence of an eyewitness is so great that it requires the evidence of habit to be declared incompetent is a determination to be made by the court in each case. The absence of an eyewitness or the absence of corroboration has not automatically resulted in the exclusion of evidence of habit in Ohio.

Ohio law had held evidence of habit admissible to show conduct under like circumstances, as where the habits of a brakeman and a conductor in making up a train were each known to the other, and evidence of such habits was admissible on the issue of negligence and the issue of contributory negligence. *Lake Shore & Michigan Southern Railway v. Botefuhr* (1907), 10 Ohio C.C.(n.s.) 281.

Habit is to be distinguished from character. Ohio has made that distinction by admitting evidence of habit to establish the same conduct under like circumstances on the occasion in issue and by excluding evidence of a general disposition toward the conduct in issue. Where the evidence offered was that the plaintiff had experienced earlier narrow escapes at the same rail crossing with the same team of horses, it was held that the evidence was incompetent because it raised collateral issues. It said that negligence cannot be proved by showing habitual negligence. *Baltimore & Ohio Railroad Co. v. Van Horn, Admrx.* (1898), 21 Ohio C.C. 337; *Wheeling & Lake Erie Railway v. Parker, Admr.* (1906), 9 Ohio C.C.(n.s.) 28. These cases treat the offered evidence as evidence of a characteristic negligence rather than as evidence of habit. They are to be contrasted to *Lake Shore & Michigan Railway v. Botefuhr, supra,* which received evidence of habit to establish conduct on the particular occasion. The established conduct is then to be determined as being negligent or not. The cases point up the fact that the line of demarcation between habit and character is not sharply drawn.

Habit is also to be distinguished from custom. Habit applies to individuals and custom applies to industries, vocations, and similar groupings. *Somerby v. Tappan* (1834), Wright 570.

Library References

Criminal Law ☞372(1) to 372(14).

Evidence ☞138, 139.

Westlaw Topic Nos. 110, 157.

C.J.S. Criminal Law § 830.

C.J.S. Evidence §§ 763 to 769, 785.

OJur 3d: 42, Evidence and Witnesses § 234; 59, Insurance § 1380; 69, Mortgages and Deeds of Trust § 543; 70, Negligence § 175, 177 to 179

Am Jur 2d: 29, Evidence § 303

Admissibility of evidence of habit, customary behavior, or reputation as to care of pedestrian on question of his care at time of collision with motor vehicle giving rise to his injury or death. 28 ALR3d 1293

Admissibility of evidence of habit, customary behavior, or reputation as to care of motor vehicle driver or occupant, on question of his care at time of occurrence giving rise to his injury or death. 29 ALR3d 791

Habit or routine practice evidence under Uniform Evidence Rule 406. 64 ALR4th 567

Admissibility of evidence of habit or routine practice under Rule 406, Federal Rules of Evidence. 53 ALR Fed 703

Giannelli & Snyder, Baldwin's Ohio Practice, Evidence § 404.1, 406.5, 901.15 (2d ed. 2001).

Evid R 407 Subsequent remedial measures

When, after an injury or harm allegedly caused by an event, measures are taken which, if taken previously, would have made the injury or harm less likely to occur, evidence of the subsequent measures is not admissible to prove negligence or culpable conduct in connection with the event. This rule does not require the exclusion of evidence of subsequent measures when offered for another purpose, such as proving ownership, control, or feasibility of precautionary measures, if controverted, or impeachment.

(Adopted eff. 7–1–80; amended eff. 7–1–00)

Historical and Statutory Notes

Amendment Note: The 7–1–00 amendment inserted "injury or harm allegedly caused by an" and substituted "injury or harm" for "event" in the first sentence.

Commentary

Staff Notes

2000:

Rule 407 Subsequent remedial measures

In 1997, Federal Rule of Evidence 407 was amended in two respects. The Ohio amendment is based on the first change in the federal rule: the phrase "injury or harm allegedly caused by an" was added to clarify that a repair or remedial measure must take effect after the accident or incident being litigated in order for the rule to apply. A measure that takes effect after purchase but before the accident or incident being litigated is not a subsequent measure. See *Traylor v. Husqvarna Motor* (7th Cir. 1993), 988 F.2d 729, 733 ("The problem with applying Rule 407 was not lack of culpable conduct but the fact that the remedial measures were taken before rather than after the 'event,' which in an accident case the courts have invariably and we think correctly understood to mean the accident."); *Cates v. Sears, Roebuck & Co.* (5th Cir. 1991), 928 F.2d 679, ("The 'event' to which Rule 407 speaks is the accident, not the sale."); *Chase v. General Motors Corp* (4th Cir. 1988), 856 F.2d 17, 21–22.

The second change to the federal rule, which involves strict liability cases, has not been adopted.

1980:

The rule is stated in language identical to that of Federal Evidence Rule 407.

Rule 407 serves to declare a form of relevant evidence to be inadmissible for certain specified purposes as a matter of policy. The Advisory Committee's Note to Federal Evidence Rule 407 points out that the rule rests on two grounds: (1) the subsequent remedial measure is not an admission, and (2) there is a policy of encouraging remedial measures.

The rule does not alter the Ohio law as it had developed prior to the adoption of the Rules of Evidence. The bases for the Ohio position are the same as that expressed in the Advisory Committee's Note. *Rohr, Admr., v. The Scioto Valley Traction Company* (1920), 12 Ohio App. 275.

The rule limits the exclusion of subsequent remedial measures to its being offered on the issues of negligence or culpable conduct. The rule is specific that exclusion is not required when the evidence of subsequent remedial measures is offered for another purpose. Illustrations of other purposes are included in the rule.

The limitation of the rule is in accord with prior Ohio case law. Ohio has recognized that evidence of subsequent remedial measures is admissible on issues other than the negligence of the defendant. The following cases illustrate the other purposes that the courts in Ohio have delineated: control, *East Ohio Gas Co. v. Van Orman* (1931), 41 Ohio App. 56; dangerous condition, site, *Village of Ashtabula v. Bartram* (1888), 3 Ohio C.C. 640; dangerous condition, equipment, *Brewing Co. v. Bauer* (1893), 50 Ohio St. 560; identification of instrument of injury, *Agler v. Schine Theatrical Co., Inc.* (1938), 59 Ohio App. 68; impeachment, *Village of Bond Hill v. Atkinson, Admrx.* (1898), 16 Ohio Cir. Ct. 470, 9 Ohio C.C. Dec. 185; test of the accuracy and weight of opinion, *Massillon Iron & Steel Company v. Weigand* (1912), 15 Ohio C.C.(n.s.) 417; to negate claim that defect was beyond repair (suggested, not held), *Thomas v. Merchants National Bank* (1952), 65 Ohio Law Abs. 353. The illustrations set forth do not constitute an exhaustive list.

Library References

Evidence ⚎140.

Negligence ⚎131.

Products Liability ⚎81.1, 81.5.

Westlaw Topic Nos. 157, 272, 313A.

C.J.S. Negligence §§ 221, 224, 225.

C.J.S. Products Liability §§ 77, 78.

C.J.S. Motor Vehicles § 167(3).

OJur 3d: 42, Evidence and Witnesses § 203, 204; 70, Negligence § 182, 183

Am Jur 2d: 29, Evidence § 275, 628

Admissibility of evidence of precautions taken, or safety measures used, on earlier occasions at place of accident or injury. 59 ALR2d 1379

Admissibility of evidence of repairs, change of conditions, or precautions taken after accident. 64 ALR2d 1296

Admissibility of evidence of repairs, change of conditions, or precautions taken after accident—modern state cases. 15 ALR5th 119

Admissibility of evidence of subsequent remedial measures under Rule 407 of the Federal Rules of Evidence. 50 ALR Fed 935

Katz & Giannelli, Baldwin's Ohio Practice, Criminal Law § 1.8 (1996).

Giannelli & Snyder, Baldwin's Ohio Practice, Evidence § 101.3, 102.5, 105.7, 401.9, 402.7, 407.1, 407.2, 407.3, 407.10, 411, 411.4, 801.17 (2d ed. 2001).

Ohio Personal Injury Practice (2002 Ed.), Text 2.07, 11.06.

Evid R 408   Compromise and offers to compromise

Evidence of (1) furnishing or offering or promising to furnish, or (2) accepting or offering or promising to accept, a valuable consideration in compromising or attempting to compromise a claim which was disputed as to either validity or amount, is not admissible to prove liability for or invalidity of the claim or its amount. Evidence of conduct or statements made in compromise negotiations is likewise not admissible. This rule does not require the exclusion of any evidence otherwise discoverable merely because it is presented in the course of compromise negotiations. This rule also does not require exclusion when the evidence is offered for another purpose, such as proving bias or prejudice of a witness, negativing a contention of undue delay, or proving an effort to obstruct a criminal investigation or prosecution.

(Adopted eff. 7–1–80)

Commentary
Staff Notes

1980:

The rule is stated in language identical to that of Federal Evidence Rule 408.

The first sentence of Rule 408 places a limitation on the admissibility of evidence of an offer to compromise or of a completed compromise. This is a generally accepted position and is based upon two considerations: (1) that the compromise may be based upon considerations other than liability and (2) that compromises of disputes should be encouraged as a matter of policy. Advisory Committee's Note to Federal Evidence Rule 408. As the note points out, the exclusion does not apply when liability for the amount of the claim is not in dispute, that is, it does not apply when the compromise is of an amount admittedly due. Either liability for the claim or the amount of the claim must be in dispute to invoke the exclusion.

The exclusion of the rule is consistent with Ohio law as it existed prior to the adoption of the Rules of Evidence. Evidence of an offer to compromise was incompetent as a fact from which liability might be inferred and was incompetent [sic.] as an admission of such liability. *Shere [Sherer] v. Piper & Yenney* (1875), 26 Ohio St. 476. The evidence was incompetent for reasons of public policy. *Weyant, Admrx. v. McCurdy* (1920), 12 Ohio App. 491.

The second sentence of the rule, "Evidence of conduct or statements made in compromise is likewise not admissible," represents an expansion of the general rule of exclusion. Advisory Committee's Note to Federal Evidence Rule 408.

The second sentence represents a change in Ohio law. It has been held that independent statements of fact material to a cause of action or defense, made by a party, although contemporaneous with negotiations for a compromise were competent evidence as admissions. *Weyant, Admrx. v. McCurdy* (1920), 12 Ohio App. 421; *Kline v. State, ex rel. St. Clair* (1925), 20 Ohio App. 191.

The admissibility of independent fact emerging during settlement negotiations gave rise to a major issue as to whether a particular fact was independent or an integral part of the offer of settlement. It also led to the practice of stating facts in hypothetical or conditional form to avoid admissibility. Advisory Committee's Note to Federal Evidence Rule 408. The technical avoidance of admissibility was a hazard to the uninitiated counsel.

The third sentence of the rule providing that evidence otherwise discoverable is not to be excluded merely because it was presented in the course of settlement negotiations has been included as a safeguard. Without the safeguard, there is the possibility of abuse of the rule by presenting discoverable evidence in the course of settlement negotiations in order to insure its exclusion at trial.

The fourth and final sentence of the rule underscores the thrust of the rule, a rule of exclusion of offers to compromise and of compromises to prove the liability for, or invalidity of, the claim or its amount when either of those matters is at issue. It provides that the exclusion does not apply when the evidence of offer or of compromise is submitted for a purpose other than proving liability for a claim, invalidity of a claim, or the amount of the claim. The enumerated list of other purposes is not exhaustive, being introduced with the phrase "... such as..."

Cross References

Mediation communications privileged, exceptions, 2317.023

Refused offer of judgment may not be filed with court in proceeding to determine costs, Civ R 68

Library References

Evidence ⬿213(1) to 213(5).

Westlaw Topic No. 157.

C.J.S. Evidence §§ 379 to 385.

OJur 3d: 5A, Alternative Dispute Resolution § 86, 158, 163, 164; 27, Criminal Law § 1412; 43, Evidence and Witnesses § 296, 297; 89, Trial § 64, 415

Am Jur 2d: 29, Evidence § 624, 629 to 632

Admissibility of evidence that defendant in negligence action has paid third persons on claims arising from the same transaction or incident as plaintiff's claim. 20 ALR2d 304

Admissibility of evidence of unperformed compromise agreement. 26 ALR2d 858

Admissibility of admissions made in connection with offers or discussions of compromise. 15 ALR3d 13

Evidence involving compromise or offer of compromise as inadmissible under Rule 408 of Federal Rules of Evidence. 72 ALR Fed 592

Katz & Giannelli, Baldwin's Ohio Practice, Criminal Law § 1.8 (1996).

Giannelli & Snyder, Baldwin's Ohio Practice, Evidence § 101.3, 102.5, 105.7, 401.9, 402.7, 408.5, 409, 409.3, 409.4, 410.7, 616.3, 801.17 (2d ed. 2001).

Wasil, Waite, & Mastrangelo, Ohio Workers' Compensation Law § 14:177.

Evid R 409 Payment of medical and similar expenses

Evidence of furnishing or offering or promising to pay medical, hospital, or similar expenses occasioned by an injury is not admissible to prove liability for the injury.

(Adopted eff. 7–1–80)

Commentary

Staff Notes

1980:

The rule is stated in language identical to that of Federal Evidence Rule 409.

The rationale for declaring relevant evidence as to payment of, or offer to pay, medical, hospital or similar expenses inadmissible (incompetent as a matter of policy) is essentially the same as the basis for excluding offers to settle and settlements. An offer to pay medical expenses may be motivated by humanitarian concerns as readily as it may be an admission of liability.

In contrast to Rule 408, Rule 409 does not explicitly state that the evidence of payment of, or offer to pay, medical expenses is admissible for purposes other than the proof of liability. The implication is obvious that such evidence is competent for the purposes of proving issues other than liability or the amount of the claim. Of course, the evidence offered for proof of purposes other than proof of liability must not transgress Rule 403.

As the Advisory Committee's Note to Federal Evidence Rule 408 points out, Rule 409, unlike Rule 408, does not exclude conduct made in extending the offer to pay because they are expected to be incidental and not required to effect the offer or the payment. Because settlement negotiation is not necessary to such an offer, there is no reason to insulate the procedure.

The rule represents no departure from Ohio law as it existed prior to the adoption of the Rules of Evidence. *Quiel v. Wilson* (1940), 34 Ohio Law Abs. 157.

Library References

Damages ⊜59.

Westlaw Topic No. 115.

C.J.S. Damages § 96.

OJur 3d: 43, Evidence and Witnesses § 298
Am Jur 2d: 29, Evidence § 624
Admissibility of evidence showing payment, or offer or promise of payment, of medical, hospital, and similar expenses of injured party by opposing party. 65 ALR3d 932
Giannelli & Snyder, Baldwin's Ohio Practice, Evidence § 401.9, 402.7, 801.17 (2d ed. 2001).

Evid R 410 Inadmissibility of pleas, offers of pleas, and related statements

(A) Except as provided in division (B) of this rule, evidence of the following is not admissible in any civil or criminal proceeding against the defendant who made the plea or who was a participant personally or through counsel in the plea discussions:

(1) a plea of guilty that later was withdrawn;

(2) a plea of no contest or the equivalent plea from another jurisdiction;

(3) a plea of guilty in a violations bureau;

(4) any statement made in the course of any proceedings under Rule 11 of the Rules of Criminal Procedure or equivalent procedure from another jurisdiction regarding the foregoing pleas;

(5) any statement made in the course of plea discussions in which counsel for the prosecuting authority or for the defendant was a participant and that do not result in a plea of guilty or that result in a plea of guilty later withdrawn.

(B) A statement otherwise inadmissible under this rule is admissible in either of the following:

(1) any proceeding in which another statement made in the course of the same plea or plea discussions has been introduced and the statement should, in fairness, be considered contemporaneously with it;

(2) a criminal proceeding for perjury or false statement if the statement was made by the defendant under oath, on the record, and in the presence of counsel.

(Adopted eff. 7–1–80; amended eff. 7–1–91)

Commentary

Staff Notes

1991:

At the time Evid. R. 410 became effective in July 1980, there was "no substantive variation between the Ohio rule and the Federal Rule." Ohio Staff Note (1980). The term "no contest" had replaced the phrase "nolo contendere" used in the federal rule and the phrases "or the equivalent plea from another jurisdiction" and "or a plea of guilty in a violations bureau" had been added to the Ohio rule.

The federal rule, however, was thereafter amended. Several federal cases had read the federal rule broadly to cover some statements made during "plea bargain" discussions between defendants and *law enforcement officers. See United States v. Herman*, 544 F.2d 791, 795–799 (5th Cir. 1977); *United States v. Brooks*, 536 F.2d 1137, 1138–39 (6th Cir. 1976); *United States v. Smith*, 525 F.2d 1017, 1020–22 (10th Cir. 1975). Accordingly, the federal drafters became concerned "that an otherwise voluntary admission to law enforcement officials [might be] rendered inadmissible merely because it was made in the hope of obtaining leniency by a plea." Fed. R. Evid. 410, Advisory Committee Note (1980). Federal Rule 410 now specifies that only plea discussions with the

" *attorney for the prosecuting authority*" are covered by the rule.

The amendment incorporates the same limitation into the Ohio rule. It is intended to clarify an area of ambiguity. The amended rule is designed to protect plea bargaining statements involving attorneys in order to promote the disposition of criminal cases by compromise. Statements made by an accused to the police are not covered by this rationale. Improper inducements by the police may be challenged under the constitutional standards governing the voluntariness of confessions, but may not be excluded under this rule.

Unlike the federal rule, the amendment specifically covers plea bargaining statements made by defense counsel. Such statements are excluded from evidence when made either to the prosecutor or the police.

Two additional changes are effected by the amendment. First, the amendment recognizes an exception in addition to the exception for perjury and false statement prosecutions. This exception applies in "any proceeding in which another statement made in the course of the same plea or plea discussions has been introduced and the statement should, in fairness, be considered contemporaneously with it." This provision is a restatement of the "rule of completeness" found in Evid. R. 106.

Second, the amendment specifically excludes "any statement made in the course of any proceedings under Rule 11 of the Rules of Criminal Procedure or equivalent procedure from another jurisdiction." This provision was added for clarification; the same result would have been reached under the old rule.

1980:

The language of the rule varies from the language of Federal Evidence Rule 410 in minor respects. There is no substantive variation between the Ohio rule and the Federal rule.

The language of Federal Evidence Rule 410 conforms to the language of Fed. Crim. R. 11(e)(6); thus, Federal Evidence Rule 410 begins, "Except as otherwise provided in this paragraph..." The Ohio rule substitutes the word "rule" for the word "paragraph."

Nolo contendere is a plea which is not available in Ohio criminal practice. In its stead, Ohio utilizes the plea of no contest. Crim. R. 11(A). The plea of no contest is available in all offenses.

Rule 410 is not limited to pleas entered in cases pending in Ohio courts. For that reason, the language "or the equivalent plea from another jurisdiction" is included in the rule following the reference to the plea of no contest. Rule 410 thus applies to the plea of no contest entered in Ohio or in another state, to the plea of *nolo contendere* entered in the federal jurisdiction or in another state, and to the equivalent plea, however denominated, entered in another state.

Rule 410 contains a provision which does not appear in the federal rule. It is the plea of guilty in a violations bureau. Violations bureaus are established to receive guilty pleas in certain traffic offenses and guilty pleas to minor misdemeanors. As a matter of policy, the prohibition against utilizing a guilty plea in a violations bureau in any subsequent action has been included. It is intended to encourage the use of the violations bureau in traffic offenses in preference to a time consuming adjudication for the sole purpose of avoiding the use of a guilty plea in a subsequent civil action.

Rule 410 relates to offers and to pleas to the crime charged or any other crime. The latter has reference to any lesser included offense to which the defendant may be permitted to plead or to any offense to which the defendant may offer to plead.

Rule 410 also extends the exclusion to statements made in connection with, and relevant to, the plea or offer. The rationale of the exclusion is essentially the same as that applied to statements made during settlement negotiations which is discussed in the Staff Note to Rule 408. As a curb on loose statements by a defendant in connection with a plea or an offer, the statements can be used in a subsequent prosecution for perjury or false statement provided the statement was made under oath, on the record, and in the presence of counsel. In considering a similar provision in Federal Evidence Rule 410, the U.S. Senate feared that total exclusion would encourage statements contrived to achieve acceptance of a plea. Senate Report 93–1277.

The exclusion of Rule 410 extends only to actions against the person who made the plea or the offer. The plea, the offer or the statement is an admission and operates only against the one who made it.

Rule 410 represents no change in Ohio law in the use of the no contest plea subsequent to the effective date of the Criminal Rules, July 1, 1973. Crim. R. 11(B)(2) provides that neither the plea of no contest nor the admission of the truth of the fact alleged in the charging document, which it represents, may be used against the defendant in any subsequent civil or criminal proceeding. In Ohio practice, the no contest plea has a broader basis than simple avoidance of civil liability by an admission of guilt in a criminal case. Pleas of guilty have long been used in civil cases as an admission. *Freas v. Sullivan* (1936), 130 Ohio St. 486. Crim. R. 12(H) provides that a no contest plea does not preclude, as would a plea of guilty, a defendant from asserting on appeal that the trial court erred in ruling on a pretrial motion. A defendant whose sole issue is one of improper search and seizure may plead no contest and preserve a claim of erroneous ruling on a motion to suppress evidence without the necessity of a trial.

Where the defendant offers a plea of no contest or of guilty and the trial court refuses the plea, the trial court must enter a plea of not guilty, and the refused plea of guilty or of no contest thereafter is not admissible in evidence. Crim. R. 11(G). The bar on admissibility has no express limitation and, presumably, extends to all subsequent civil and criminal proceedings.

As to the admissibility of withdrawn pleas of guilty, Ohio law prior to the adoption of the Rules of Evidence has not been explicit. The general rule is one of non-admissibility, based upon admissibility serving to negate the effect of withdrawal and upon the logic that a plea is annulled if withdrawn. Annot., 86 ALR 2d 326. The issue of possible self-incrimination by use of a withdrawn plea of guilty had not been resolved at the federal or state level prior to the adoption of the Rules of Evidence although the United States Supreme Court had held that evidence of a withdrawn plea of guilty in a federal court was inadmissible on nonconstitutional grounds. *Kercheval v. United States* (1927), 274 U.S. 220.

Cross References

Perjury, 2921.11
Pleas, rights upon plea, effect of guilty or no contest
     pleas, Crim R 11
Withdrawal of guilty plea, Crim R 32.1

Library References

Criminal Law ⊜406(4).
Evidence ⊜207(4).
Westlaw Topic Nos. 110, 157.

C.J.S. Criminal Law §§ 882 to 884.

C.J.S. Evidence §§ 398, 399.

OJur 3d: 5A, Alternative Dispute Resolution § 87; 29, Criminal Law § 2681; 29A, Criminal Law § 3049; 43, Evidence and Witnesses § 325

Am Jur 2d: 29, Evidence § 694

Propriety and prejudicial effect of showing, in criminal case, withdrawn guilty plea. 86 ALR2d 326

Admissibility of defense communications made in connection with plea bargaining. 59 ALR3d 441

Admissibility, in prosecution in another state's jurisdiction, of confession or admission made pursuant to plea bargain with state authorities. 90 ALR4th 1133

When is statement of accused made in connection with plea bargain negotiations so as to render statement inadmissible under Rule 11(e)(6) of the Federal Rules of Criminal Procedure. 60 ALR Fed 854

Giannelli & Snyder, Baldwin's Ohio Practice, Evidence § 106.1, 402.7, 408.1, 408.4, 408.8, 410.11, 801.17, 801.21, 803.55, 1101 (2d ed. 2001).

Adrine & Ruden, Ohio Domestic Violence Law (2002 Ed.), Text 14.12.

Evid R 411   Liability insurance

Evidence that a person was or was not insured against liability is not admissible upon the issue whether he acted negligently or otherwise wrongfully. This rule does not require the exclusion of evidence of insurance against liability when offered for another purpose, such as proof of agency, ownership or control, if controverted, or bias or prejudice of a witness.

(Adopted eff. 7–1–80)

Commentary

Staff Notes

1980:

The rule is stated in language identical to that of Federal Evidence Rule 411 with one exception. The exception is the inclusion of the words "if controverted" which modify purposes other than liability proof. In being explicit, the rule is in conformity to Rule 407 which relates to subsequent remedial measures. The requirement is implicit in the federal rule or is, at least, required under the balancing engendered by Rule 403 of the Federal Rules of Evidence. Rothstein, Understanding the Federal Rules of Evidence, 35. The rationale of the requirement is discussed in the Staff Note to Rule 407.

Rule 411 accords with Ohio practice prior to the adoption of the Rules of Evidence. The general rule of exclusion is stated in *Frank v. Corcoran* (1926), 25 Ohio App. 356. The qualified admission for purposes other than proving negligence is stated in *Kraemer v. Motor Transport Lines* (1937), 56 Ohio App. 427.

Cross References

Discovery of insurance agreements, Civ R 26

Library References

Trial ⟜127.

Westlaw Topic No. 388.

C.J.S. Trial §§ 53, 180.

OJur 3d: 42, Evidence and Witnesses § 252, 253; 89, Trial § 65

Am Jur 2d: 29, Evidence § 404 to 408; 32B, Federal Rules of Evidence § 154 to 157

Privilege of communications or reports between liability or indemnity insurer and insured. 22 ALR2d 659

Admissibility, after enactment of Rule 411, Federal Rules of Evidence, of evidence of liability insurance in negligence actions. 40 ALR Fed 541

Katz & Giannelli, Baldwin's Ohio Practice, Criminal Law § 1.8 (1996).

Giannelli & Snyder, Baldwin's Ohio Practice, Evidence § 101.3, 102.5, 105.7, 402.7, 411.6, 616.3 (2d ed. 2001).

Article V

PRIVILEGES

Rule

501   General rule

Evid R 501   General rule

The privilege of a witness, person, state or political subdivision thereof shall be governed by statute enacted by the General Assembly or by principles of common law as interpreted by the courts of this state in the light of reason and experience.

(Adopted eff. 7–1–80)

Commentary

Staff Notes

1980:

Rule 501 is an adaptation of Federal Evidence Rule 501. It relegates the matter of privileges to determination by statute or case law.

The Federal rule after which the Ohio rule is patterned was adopted by Congress in place of a detailed set of rules respecting privileges proposed by the United States Supreme Court. Congress rejected the proposed rules and adopted a rule essentially removing the matter of privileges from operation of the evidence rules. See 2 Weinstein's Evidence p. 501–2.

Rule 501, like its Federal counterpart, leaves the matter of privileges essentially undisturbed. Statutory and case law pronouncements respecting privileges continue in force by operation of the rule.

Under present statutory provisions the testimonial privileges include: attorney–client, R.C. 2317.02(A); physician–patient, R.C. 2317.02(B); psychologist–patient, R.C. 4732.19; husband–wife, R.C. 2317.02(C); and cleric-penitent, R.C. 2317.02(D).

Other privilege-like statutes clearly remain applicable including the immunity from testifying of broadcasters and newsmen found in R.C. 2739.04 and R.C. 2739.12 respectively. Certain reports required by statute are privileged and will continue to be protected under the rule. See, for example, R.C. 2305.21 and R.C. 2305.24 regarding hospital utilization committee reports and proceedings.

Closely related to the question of privilege is the question of competency of witnesses. Attention is invited to Rule 601 *et seq.* as to this matter.

Parenthetically, it is to be observed that the difficult lines to be drawn between rules of procedure and substantive law so frequently encountered in evidence rules are no more clearly demonstrated than in the area of privileges. In adopting by reference privilege statutes and common law constructions the direct confrontation is avoided.

The rule implicitly adopts the common law precept that no person has a privilege not to testify concerning any matter nor to refuse to produce an object or writing or to prevent another from being a witness or of disclosing information unless otherwise provided by statute or case law. *Ex Parte Frye* (1951), 155 Ohio St. 144.

The privilege rule is to be distinguished from the problems relating to work product of the attorney governed by Civ. R. 26(B)(3). That doctrine enunciated clearly in *Hickman v. Taylor* (1947), 329 U.S. 495, and now incorporated in Civ. R. 26(B)(3) relating to discovery emanates from considerations of concern for case preparation by trial counsel and preservation of the adversary system and is not predicated on the same policies as those relating to privilege.

Problems of considerable magnitude continue with respect to the attorney-client privilege in the case of corporate clients. While R.C. 2317.021 establishes the existence of the privilege to corporate clients, the scope of communication covered by the privilege remains clouded. *In re Tichy* (1954), 161 Ohio St. 104, and *In re Keough* (1949), 151 Ohio St. 307, extend the corporate privilege to certain accident reports prepared in anticipation of litigation. However, much remains in delimiting the privilege in this area. See, for example, *D.I. Chadbourne v. Superior Court*(1964), 60 Cal.2d 723, wherein the court set forth no less than eleven principles governing the limits of the corporate attorney-client privilege. The matter is extensively discussed in *Harper and Row Publisher v. Decker* (1970), 423 F. 2d 487, *affd.* (1971), 400 U.S. 348, relative to the federal attorney-client privilege.

Cross References

Attorney-client privilege, EC 4–4
Availability of public records, 149.43
Client defined, application of attorney-client privilege to dissolve corporation or association, 2317.021
Commercial transactions, pending action, witnesses are not excused from testifying, 1331.13
Competency of witnesses, 2945.42
Compulsory testimony, privilege against prosecution, 5703.34
Confidentiality of records, 5123.89
Confidentiality of review committee proceedings, 2305.251
Court of common pleas to grant transactional immunity, procedure, exceptions, 2945.44
Disclosure of information, 5122.31
Discovery and inspection, disclosure of evidence, by defendant, by prosecuting attorney, Crim R 16
Divorce, annulment and alimony actions, notice of trial, Civ R 75

Duty of certain persons to report believed abuse of mentally retarded adult, immunity, 5123.61
Examination and treatment for venereal disease and AIDS, 2907.27
Failure to report felony or certain suspicious circumstances, 2921.22
False representation or solicitation of authority, 4123.88
General provisions governing discovery, scope of discovery, trial preparation, materials, Civ R 26
Husband-wife privilege inapplicable, 3115.20
Immunity from liability of members of certain professional review organizations, 2305.24
Investigations by attorney general, 1345.06
Motor vehicles, aeronautics, watercraft, use of report, 4509.10
Newspaper reporters not required to reveal source of information, 2739.12
Persons required to report injury or neglect, procedures on receipt of report, 2151.421
Preservation of confidences and secrets of client, DR 4–101
Privileged communications and acts, 2317.02, 4732.19
Prohibition against divulging information, 5715.49
Public utilities commission, hearings, testimony, 4903.08
Records, sealed or expunged, procedures, effects, offense of divulging confidential information, 2151.358
Revelation of news source by broadcasters, 2739.04
Rules of evidence in prostitution cases, 2907.26
Self-incrimination, 3901.23
Survey of public crossings by public utilities commission, classification, priority ratings, additional protective devices, 4907.471
Testimony before committee not to be used in criminal prosecution of witness, exception, 101.44
Testimony of physician in parentage action concerning medical circumstances of mother's pregnancy and condition of child upon birth not privileged, 3111.12
Testimony required, immunity, 3933.02
Trial for crimes, witness, O Const Art I §10

Library References

Witnesses ⚖184(1), 292.
Westlaw Topic No. 410.
C.J.S. Federal Civil Procedure § 521.
C.J.S. Witnesses §§ 252, 430 et seq.
OJur 3d: 23, Courts and Judges § 364; 29A, Criminal Law § 3125; 36, Discovery and Depositions § 5, 30, 33; 44, Evidence and Witnesses § 784; 91, Trusts § 512
Am Jur 2d: 32B, Federal Rules of Evidence § 162; 81, Witnesses § 141 to 302
Right to show in civil case that party or witness refused to testify on same matter under claim of privilege in previous criminal proceeding. 2 ALR2d 1297
Conversations between husband and wife relating to property or business as within rule excluding private communications between them. 4 ALR2d 835
"Communications" within testimonial privilege of confidential communications between husband and wife as including knowledge derived from observation by one spouse of acts of other spouse. 10 ALR2d 1389
Crimes against spouse within exception permitting testimony by one spouse against other in criminal prosecution. 11 ALR2d 646
Party's waiver of privilege as to communications with counsel by taking stand and testifying. 51 ALR2d 521

Persons other than client or attorney affected by, or included within, attorney-client privilege. 96 ALR2d 125

Comment Note—Right of corporation to assert attorney-client privilege. 98 ALR2d 241

Physician-patient privilege: testimony as to communications or observations as to mental condition of patient treated for other condition. 100 ALR2d 648

Applicability of attorney-client privilege to communications with respect to contemplated tortious acts. 2 ALR3d 861

Attorney-client privilege as affected by communications between several attorneys. 9 ALR3d 1420

Attorney-client privilege as affected by its assertion as to communications, or transmission of evidence, relating to crime already committed. 16 ALR3d 1029

Disclosure of name, identity, address, occupation, or business of client as violation of attorney-client privilege. 16 ALR3d 1047

Competency of one spouse to testify against other in prosecution for offense against third party as affected by fact that offense against spouse was involved in same transaction. 36 ALR3d 820

Privilege, in judicial or quasi-judicial proceedings, arising from relationship between psychiatrist or psychologist and patient. 44 ALR3d 24

Applicability of attorney-client privilege to matters relating to drafting of nonexistent or unavailable nontestamentary documents. 55 ALR3d 1322

Competency of one spouse to testify against other in prosecution for offense against child of both or either. 93 ALR3d 1018

Effect, on competency to testify against spouse or on marital communication privilege, of separation or other marital instability short of absolute divorce. 98 ALR3d 1285

Spouse's betrayal or connivance as extending marital communications privilege to testimony of third person. 3 ALR4th 1104

Communication between unmarried couple living together as privileged. 4 ALR4th 422

Applicability of attorney-client privilege to evidence or testimony in subsequent action between parties originally represented contemporaneously by same attorney, with reference to communication to or from one party. 4 ALR4th 765

Existence of spousal privilege where marriage was entered into for purpose of barring testimony. 13 ALR4th 1305

Applicability of attorney-client privilege to communications made in presence of or solely to or by third person. 14 ALR4th 594

Work product privilege as applying to material prepared for terminated litigation or for claim which did not result in litigation. 27 ALR4th 568

Attorney-client privilege as extending to communications relating to contemplated civil fraud. 31 ALR4th 458

Attorney as witness for client in civil proceedings—modern state cases. 35 ALR4th 810

Marital privilege under Rule 501 of Federal Rules of Evidence. 46 ALR Fed 735

Situations in which federal courts are governed by state law privilege under Rule 501 of Federal Rules of Evidence. 48 ALR Fed 259

Psychotherapist-patient privilege under federal common law. 72 ALR Fed 395

"Scholar's privilege" under Rule 501 of Federal Rules of Evidence. 81 ALR Fed 904

Academic peer review privilege in federal court. 85 ALR Fed 691

Giannelli & Snyder, Baldwin's Ohio Practice, Evidence § 101.6, 102, 102.5, 104.3, 402.7, 601, 601.12, 601.16, 601.17, 804.4 (2d ed. 2001).

Ohio Administrative Law Handbook and Agency Directory, OAC Vol. 17, Text 8.12, 8.16.

Article VI

WITNESSES

Rule
601 General rule of competency
602 Lack of personal knowledge
603 Oath or affirmation
604 Interpreters
605 Competency of judge as witness
606 Competency of juror as witness
607 Impeachment
608 Evidence of character and conduct of witness
609 Impeachment by evidence of conviction of crime
610 Religious beliefs or opinions
611 Mode and order of interrogation and presentation
612 Writing used to refresh memory
613 Impeachment by self-contradiction
614 Calling and interrogation of witnesses by court
615 Separation and exclusion of witnesses
616 Methods of impeachment

Evid R 601 General rule of competency

Every person is competent to be a witness except:

(A) Those of unsound mind, and children under ten years of age, who appear incapable of receiving just impressions of the facts and transactions respecting which they are examined, or of relating them truly.

(B) A spouse testifying against the other spouse charged with a crime except when either of the following applies:

(1) a crime against the testifying spouse or a child of either spouse is charged;

(2) the testifying spouse elects to testify.

(C) An officer, while on duty for the exclusive or main purpose of enforcing traffic laws, arresting or assisting in the arrest of a person charged with a traffic violation punishable as a misdemeanor where the officer at the time of the arrest was not using a properly marked motor vehicle as defined by statute or was not wearing a legally distinctive uniform as defined by statute.

(D) A person giving expert testimony on the issue of liability in any claim asserted in any civil action against a physician, podiatrist, or hospital arising out of the diagnosis, care, or treatment of any person by a physician or podiatrist, unless the person testifying is licensed to practice medicine and surgery, osteopathic medicine and surgery, or podiatric medicine and surgery by the state medical board or by the licensing authority of any state, and unless the person devotes at least one-half of his or her professional time to the active clinical practice in his or her field of licensure, or to its instruction in an accredited school. This division shall not prohibit other medical professionals who otherwise are competent to testify under these rules from giving expert testimony on the appropriate standard of care in their own profession in any claim asserted in any civil action against a physician, podiatrist, medical professional, or hospital arising out of the diagnosis, care, or treatment of any person.

(E) As otherwise provided in these rules.

(Adopted eff. 7–1–80; amended eff. 7–1–91)

Commentary

Staff Notes

1991:

Rule 601(A) Children and Mental Incompetents

Evid. R. 601(A) was amended by deleting "and;" from the end of the rule. This is a technical change only.

Rule 601(B) Spouse Testifying

As adopted in 1980, Evid. R. 601(B) provided that a witness was incompetent to testify against his or her spouse in a criminal case unless the charged offense involved a crime against the testifying spouse or the children of either spouse. The rule was based on the policy of protecting the marital relationship from "dissension" and the "natural repugnance" for convicting a defendant upon the testimony of his or her "intimate life partner." 8 J. Wigmore, Evidence 216–17 (McNaughton rev. 1961).

The important issue is who can waive the rule—the defendant or the witness. Under the old rule, the defendant could prevent his or her spouse from testifying. In some situations the policy underlying the rule simply does not apply, but the rule does. For example, if a husband kills his mother-in-law and his wife is a witness, she could be prevented from testifying. This would be true even if they were separated and she desired to testify. Cf. *Locke v. State* (1929), 33 Ohio App. 445, 169 N.E. 833. The amendment

changes this result, by permitting the wife to elect to testify.

This approach is supported by a number of commentators. As McCormick has pointed out: "The privilege has sometimes been defended on the ground that it protects family harmony. But family harmony is nearly always past saving when the spouse is willing to aid the prosecution. The privilege is an archaic survival of a mystical religious dogma and of a way of thinking about the marital relation that is today outmoded." C. McCormick, Evidence 162 (3d ed. 1984). *See also* 8 J. Wigmore, Evidence 221 (McNaughton rev. 1961) ("This marital privilege is the merest anachronism in legal theory and an indefensible obstruction to truth in practice."); Huhn, "Sacred Seal of Secrecy": The Rules of Spousal Incompetency and Marital Privilege in Criminal Cases (1987), 20 Akron L. Rev. 433.

The proposed amendment does not abolish the spousal incompetency rule. The spouse could not be compelled to testify if he or she did not want to testify. In January 1981, the Supreme Court proposed an amendment that would have deleted Evid. R. 601(B). 54 Ohio Bar 175 (1981). This amendment subsequently was withdrawn. 54 Ohio Bar 972 (1981). The current amendment differs from the 1981 proposal. The 1981 proposal would have abolished the spousal incompetency rule in its entirety, thereby permitting the prosecution to force the spouse to testify even when he or she did not wish to testify. The current proposal does not permit the prosecutor to force testimony from an unwilling spouse.

Moreover, the amendment still leaves the defendant with the protection of the confidential communication privilege, which is recognized in R.C. 2317.02(C). and R.C. 2945.42 and governed by Evid. R. 501. This privilege is not affected by Evid. R. 601(B).

Rule 601(D) Medical Experts

Evid. R. 601(D) was amended to prevent the application of the rule in cases in which a physician, podiatrist, hospital, or medical professional is sued as a result of alleged negligence on the part of a nurse or other medical professional. Some cases have held that a nurse is not competent under Evid. R. 601(D) to testify about the standard of nursing care in such a case. *See Harter v. Wadsworth–Rittman* (August 30, 1989), Medina App. No. 1790, unreported, motion to certify record overruled (December 20, 1989), 47 Ohio St.3d 715, 549 N.E.2d 170.

The amendment limits the rule to claims involving care by a physician or podiatrist, and does not prohibit other medical professionals, including nurses, from testifying as to the appropriate standard of professional care in their field.

Also, the requirement that an expert medical witness devote three-fourths of his or her time to active clinical practice or instruction was reduced to at least one-half. The phrase "accredited university" was changed to "accredited school" because some accredited medical schools are not associated with a university.

1980:

Rule 601, of necessity, varies significantly from Federal Evidence Rule 601 which declares all witnesses competent in federal matters, except as otherwise provided in the Federal Rules of Evidence, and also declares that in state matters, the competency of witnesses is to be determined by state law. Rule 601 states the general rule of witness competency for Ohio. In so doing, the rule embodies certain prior Ohio practices and discards others.

One of the purposes of Federal Evidence Rule 601 was to preserve statutes such as the dead man's statute in state matters in those states where such a statute existed. Ohio has chosen to eliminate the exclusion. Rule 601 supersedes R.C. 2317.03, the dead man's statute. By declaring all witnesses to be competent and not providing an exception for the exclusionary provisions of the dead man's statute, a conflict between the rule and the statute is created and the statute is superseded under constitutional provision. Concomitantly, Rule 804(B)(5) provides that the statements formerly excluded by the dead man's statute are exceptions to the hearsay rule. (Editor's Note: This last sentence is incorrect. Rule 601 supersedes the "dead man" statute, thereby permitting the surviving party to testify at trial. Rule 804(B)(5) recognizes a hearsay exception for the *decedent's* statements; these statements were excluded because of the hearsay rule, not the dead man statute.)

R.C. 4733.24 is also superseded by Rule 601. That section conditioned a surveyor's testimony upon his oath, if required, that the chain used conformed to the established standard.

Rule 601(A) Children and Insane Persons

Rule 601(A), in excepting persons of unsound mind and persons under ten years of age who appear incapable of receiving or relating facts properly, restates, *verbatim*, R.C. 2317.01. Ostensibly, a provision relating to civil cases, it also applies in criminal cases. R.C. 2945.41 provides that the rules of evidence in civil causes, where applicable, govern in all criminal causes.

Rule 601(B) Spouse Testifying

R.C. 2945.42 governed the competency of a spouse to testify in a criminal prosecution involving the other spouse and continues to govern the privilege accorded to a spouse. The concepts are to be distinguished. Rule 601 is directed to competency. Rule 501 is directed to privilege and is a general rule serving to maintain R.C. 2945.42 as to privilege. Rule 601(B) modifies R.C. 2945.42 as to competency.

R.C. 2945.42 provided that a spouse could testify in behalf of the other spouse in all criminal prosecutions. That concept is preserved by declaring all persons to be competent witnesses. R.C. 2945.42 provided that a spouse could not testify against the other spouse in a criminal prosecution, but could testify against the other in actions and proceedings, for personal injury of either by the other, bigamy, failure to provide for, neglect of, or cruelty to children under eighteen, twenty-one if mentally or physically handicapped. Additionally, the statute provided that a wife could testify against her husband in a prosecution for felonious assault, aggravated assault, assault, non-support of dependent, or endangering children based upon cruelty to, neglect of, or abandonment of the wife. Rule 601(B) is less restrictive than the statute was under the former practice. The rule establishes the absence of competence in a spouse to testify against the other spouse in a criminal prosecution with the broad exception of any crime against the testifying spouse or any crime against the children of either spouse. No age limit is set for such child, and the language is broad enough to encompass all adult children as well as minors.

Rule 601(B) supersedes R.C. 2945.42 as to spousal competency, but not as to spousal privilege.

Rule 601(C) Traffic Officer

Rule 601(C) restates R.C. 4549.14 and R.C. 4549.16 and preserves the provisions of those statutes.

Rule 601(D) Expert Testimony in Malpractice Cases

Subdivision (D) incorporates into the rule on competency of witnesses the provisions of R.C. 2743.43 with respect to expert testimony on medical liability issues. The application of this subdivision is in accordance with the definition of a "medical claim" as provided in R.C. 2305.11(D)(3).

The rule as adopted supersedes R.C. 2743.43 but does not supersede 2305.11(D)(3) which continues to have a function independent of considerations of competency of witnesses.

Rule 601(E) As Otherwise Provided in These Rules

Rule 605 provides that a judge is not competent to testify in a trial at which he presides. Rule 606(A) provides that a juror is not competent to testify in a trial in which he is serving as a juror. The rule does not exclude an attorney from testifying in a case in which he serves as counsel. Such practice is proscribed by DR5–101(B) and DR5–102 of the Code of Professional Responsibility.

Cross References

Arresting officer as witness, 4549.16
Attorney as witness, withdrawal as counsel, DR 5–102
Cases in which a party shall not testify, 2317.03
Competency of medical witnesses, 2743.43
Competency of witnesses, 2945.42
Confidentiality of review committee proceedings, 2305.251
Conflict of interests, attorney's refusal of employment, DR 5–101
Court, common pleas, competent witnesses, 2317.01
Incompatible roles of advocate and witness, EC 5–9
Incompetency of officer as witness, 4549.14
Privileged communications and acts, 2317.02
Special provisions as to competency of witnesses govern over general provisions, 1.12
Surveyors' chains and testimony, 4733.24
Violator of election laws competent to testify against another offender at trial, hearing, or investigation, 3599.41
Witness, as devisee or legatee, 2107.15

Library References

Witnesses ☞35 to 49.

Westlaw Topic No. 410.

C.J.S. Federal Civil Procedure § 521.

C.J.S. Indians § 6.

C.J.S. Witnesses §§ 49 to 68.

OJur 3d: 27, Criminal Law § 1199, 1202, 1521; 28, Criminal Law § 1981; 29A, Criminal Law § 3046, 3116, 3124, 3126; 30, Death § 159; 31, Decedents' Estates § 329; 32, Decedents' Estates § 1049; 33, Decedents' Estates § 1149, 1259; 36, Discovery and Depositions § 102; 43, Evidence and Witnesses § 415; 44, Evidence and Witnesses § 753, 765, 778, 781, 782; 53, Guardian and Ward § 221; 66, Lost and Destroyed Instruments and Records § 26; 67, Malpractice § 156 to 159, 193; 81, Witnesses § 69; 89, Trial § 32, 33, 79

Am Jur 2d: 29, Evidence § 257

Dead man's statutes as affected by Rule 601 of the Uniform Rules of Evidence and similar state rules. 50 ALR4th 1238

Crimes against spouse within exception permitting testimony by one spouse against other in criminal prosecution—modern state cases. 74 ALR4th 223

Competency of one spouse to testify against other in prosecution for offense against third party as affected by fact that offense against spouse was involved in same transaction. 74 ALR4th 277

Painter, Ohio Driving Under the Influence Law (2003 Ed.), Text 17.6.

Giannelli & Snyder, Baldwin's Ohio Practice, Evidence § 101.6, 102.5, 104.3, 402.7, 501, 501.1, 603, 501.23, 501.24, 601.9, 603.1, 603.3, 616, 616.6, 702.1, 702.5, 702.25, 801.20, 803.4, 803.13, 804, 804.4, 804.25, 807.1, 807.4, 1101 (2d ed. 2001).

Adrine & Ruden, Ohio Domestic Violence Law (2002 Ed.), Text 6.15, 13.6, 15.8.

Ohio Personal Injury Practice (2002 Ed.), Text 2.07, 5.12, 5.17.

Carlin, Baldwin's Ohio Practice, Merrick–Rippner Probate Law § 5.14, 27.9, 56.16, 60.14, 84.35, 107.58 (2003).

Evid R 602   Lack of personal knowledge

A witness may not testify to a matter unless evidence is introduced sufficient to support a finding that he has personal knowledge of the matter. Evidence to prove personal knowledge may, but need not, consist of the testimony of the witness himself. This rule is subject to the provisions of Rule 703, relating to opinion testimony by expert witnesses.

(Adopted eff. 7–1–80)

Commentary
Staff Notes

1980:

Rule 602 is identical to Federal Evidence Rule 602. It conforms with prior Ohio law.

A witness is required to testify from first-hand knowledge which has been acquired by perceiving a fact through one or more of his five senses. Of course, the witness must have had an opportunity to perceive and must have actually perceived. This rule expresses the common law insistence upon the most reliable sources of information. These basic requirements may be furnished by the testimony of the witness himself. Mere mistaken perceptions do not disqualify the witness from testifying based on personal knowledge. Assessment of accuracy of perception is a matter of credibility and not ordinarily one of competence.

This rule does not disqualify a witness who testifies as to a hearsay statement, if the witness has personal knowledge of the making of the statement. In this situation, Rules 801 and 805 would be applicable. This rule would, however, prevent the witness from testifying to the truth of the subject matter of the hearsay statement if he has no personal knowledge of it.

The reference in Rule 602 to Rule 703 is designed to avoid any question of conflict between the two rules, the latter of which permits an expert to express opinions based on facts of which the expert does not have personal knowledge.

Library References
Witnesses ⊗37(1) to 37(6).

Westlaw Topic No. 410.

C.J.S.   Federal Civil Procedure § 521.

C.J.S.   Witnesses §§ 52 to 55.

OJur 3d: 29A, Criminal Law § 3116; 44, Evidence and Witnesses § 765

Am Jur 2d: 81, Witnesses § 75 to 80

Giannelli & Snyder, Baldwin's Ohio Practice, Evidence § 104.6, 402.7, 616, 616.6, 701.3, 701.5, 801.20, 804.18, 901.5 (2d ed. 2001).

Carlin, Baldwin's Ohio Practice, Merrick–Rippner Probate Law § 43.10, 43.15 (2003).

Evid R 603   Oath or affirmation

Before testifying, every witness shall be required to declare that he will testify truthfully, by oath or affirmation administered in a form calculated to awaken his conscience and impress his mind with his duty to do so.

(Adopted eff. 7–1–80)

Commentary
Staff Notes

1980:

Rule 603 is identical to Federal Evidence Rule 603 and conforms to prior Ohio law.

The rule is designed to afford flexibility in dealing with children, persons with mental defects, atheists, members of religions not willing to swear an oath to God, to an extent not otherwise covered in Rule 601.

Oath includes affirmation. R.C. 3.20. An affirmation is simply a solemn undertaking to tell the truth. No special verbal formula is required for either oath or affirmation. R.C. 3.21 and R.C. 2317.30. Perjury by a witness is a crime. R.C. 2921.11.

Rule 603 is not in conflict with Crim. R. 5(B)(3)(b) which provides for an unrepresented defendant to be advised by the court that, as one of his options, he may make an unsworn statement regarding the charge for the purpose of explaining facts in evidence when he moves for discharge for failure of proof at the conclusion of the state's case. Rule 101(C)(6), treating the existence of other rules governing evidence, is an exception to the applicability of the Rules of Evidence.

Cross References
Civil procedure relative to administering of oaths and affirmations applicable to criminal cases, 2945.46

General provisions, form of oath, 3.21

General provisions, oath includes affirmation, 3.20

Oath of witness, 2317.30

Library References
Witnesses ⊗227.

Westlaw Topic No. 410.

C.J.S.   Witnesses § 320.

OJur 3d: 29A, Criminal Law § 3108; 44, Evidence and Witnesses § 849, 850

Am Jur 2d: 81, Witnesses § 86 to 89, 413 to 415

Competency of young child as witness in civil case. 81 ALR2d 386

Witnesses: child competency statutes. 60 ALR4th 369

Giannelli & Snyder, Baldwin's Ohio Practice, Evidence § 601.15, 604.3, 610.1, 802.3 (2d ed. 2001).

Evid R 604   Interpreters

An interpreter is subject to the provisions of these rules relating to qualification as an expert and the administration of an oath or affirmation that he will make a true translation.

(Adopted eff. 7–1–80)

Commentary

Staff Notes

1980:

Rule 604 is identical to Federal Evidence Rule 604 and is in accord with prior Ohio law.

Under prior Ohio law, the qualifications of an interpreter in a court proceeding was a matter within the sound discretion of the court. *Fennen v. State of Ohio* (1903), 1 Ohio C.C. (n.s.) 32. Rule 604 provides that the provisions of the rules relating to qualification of an expert are applicable to interpreters. An expert is one qualified by knowledge, experience, training or education. See Rule 702. Whether a witness qualifies as an expert is a matter for the determination of the court.

Under prior Ohio law, an interpreter was required to take an oath to translate properly to the witness and to the court. R.C. 2311.14(B). Rule 604 restates that requirement.

Cross References

Appointments by court of common pleas, 2301.12
Courts, common pleas, interpreter, 2335.09
Municipal court aides, 1901.33
Use of interpreter in court, 2311.14

Library References

Criminal Law ☞642.
Witnesses ☞230.
Westlaw Topic Nos. 110, 410.
C.J.S. Criminal Law § 1152.
C.J.S. Witnesses § 326.
OJur 3d: 44, Evidence and Witnesses § 763, 769, 849
Am Jur 2d: 81, Witnesses § 100, 413
Disqualification, for bias, of one offered as interpreter of testimony. 6 ALR4th 158
Ineffective assistance of counsel: use or nonuse of interpreter at prosecution of foreign language speaking defendant. 79 ALR4th 1102
Ineffective assistance of counsel: use or nonuse of interpreter at prosecution of hearing-impaired defendant. 86 ALR4th 698

Evid R 605   Competency of judge as witness

The judge presiding at the trial may not testify in that trial as a witness. No objection need be made in order to preserve the point.

(Adopted eff. 7–1–80)

Commentary

Staff Notes

1980:

Rule 605 is identical to Federal Evidence Rule 605. It is consonant with prior Ohio law as set forth in *McCaffrey v. State* (1922), 105 Ohio St. 508, clearly resolving any doubt as to the competency of a judge to testify in the proceedings over which he presides, whether or not objection is raised by either party.

Moreover, the rule is consistent with the requirement of the Code of Judicial Conduct, Canon 3, relating to the duty of a judge to disqualify himself if he has "personal knowledge of disputed evidentiary facts concerning the proceeding." Canon 3C(1)(a). Certainly, the mere presence of a presiding judge on the witness stand in behalf of either party raises serious questions of propriety and due process.

Cross References

Disqualification of judge, assignment of judge, 2701.03

Library References

Appeal and Error ☞203.3.
Criminal Law ☞1036.2.
Witnesses ☞71.
Westlaw Topic Nos. 30, 110, 410.
C.J.S. Appeal and Error § 202.
C.J.S. Witnesses § 105.
OJur 3d: 29A, Criminal Law § 3123; 44, Evidence and Witnesses § 759
Am Jur 2d: 8, Witnesses § 101
Disqualification of judge on ground of being a witness in a case. 22 ALR3d 1198
Judge as witness in cause not on trial before him. 86 ALR3d 633
Giannelli & Snyder, Baldwin's Ohio Practice, Evidence § 601, 601.15, 601.17 (2d ed. 2001).

Evid R 606   Competency of juror as witness

(A) At the trial

A member of the jury may not testify as a witness before that jury in the trial of the case in which he is sitting as a juror. If he is called so to testify, the opposing party shall be afforded an opportunity to object out of the presence of the jury.

(B) Inquiry into validity of verdict or indictment

Upon an inquiry into the validity of a verdict or indictment, a juror may not testify as to any matter or statement occurring during the course of the jury's deliberations or to the effect of anything upon his or any other juror's mind or emotions as influencing him to assent to or dissent from the verdict or indictment or concerning his mental processes in connection therewith. A juror may testify on the question whether extraneous prejudicial information was improperly brought to the jury's attention or whether any outside influence was improperly brought to bear on any juror, only after some outside evidence of that act or event has been presented. However a juror may testify without the presentation of any outside evidence concerning any threat, any bribe, any attempted threat or bribe, or any improprieties of any officer of the court. His affidavit or evidence of any statement by him concerning a matter about which he would be precluded from testifying will not be received for these purposes.

(Adopted eff. 7–1–80)

Commentary

Staff Notes

1980:

Rule 606(A) At the trial

Rule 606(A) is identical to Federal Evidence Rule 606(a).

No prior Ohio case law addresses the question; however, R.C. 2313.42(F) disqualifies for cause a potential juror who has been subpoenaed in good faith as a witness in the case.

The rule makes explicit what has been the practice in Ohio prior to the rules.

Rule 606(B) Inquiry into validity of verdict or indictment

The first sentence of this subdivision is identical to Federal Evidence Rule 606(b). The second and third sentences in the rule are different from the Federal Evidence Rule. The rule conforms to Ohio's *aliunde* rule. *State v. Adams* (1943), 141 Ohio St. 423. The *aliunde* rule requires the introduction of evidence from a competent source other than a juror to impeach a jury verdict. A juror can then testify, but the outside source must first be established. The last sentence of Rule 606(B) is comparable to, although the language is not identical to, the Federal version. The first sentence of the rule characterizes statements by a juror designed to disclose any emotional or mental processes employed by him reaching the jury's decision, whether in oral, written or affidavit form, as inadmissible testimony. This is in accord with Ohio law, as there could be no evidence, *aliunde*, in such circumstances.

The third sentence was designed primarily to conform to the Ohio law pertaining to violation of duty by a court officer. Ohio has held that the *aliunde* rule does not apply where the irregularity is due to the conduct of an officer of the court. *Emmert v. State* (1933), 127 Ohio St. 235; *State v. Adams* (1943), 141 Ohio St. 423.

Included within the coverage of this rule is the situation where a juror has received a threat or offer of a bribe and discloses this solely in the jury room to the other jurors and, unknown to the court, a verdict is reached as the result of these external influences. This constitutes an exception to the requirement that a juror's testimony must be conditioned upon introduction of other evidence.

This provision relates only to matters involving threats or bribes. Affidavits or statements of the juror are within the prohibition of the rule.

Rule 606(B) would have no application where the testimony results from an inquiry not designed to assess the validity of a verdict or indictment, such as information sought to correct a mistake or clerical error pursuant to Civ. R. 60(A). Likewise, this subdivision does not prohibit interrogation of a juror after the return of a verdict.

Cross References

Causes for new trial, 2945.79; Crim R 33

Communication with or investigation of jurors, DR 7–108

Duty of officer in charge of jury, 2315.04

Examination of jurors, causes for challenge, 2313.42, 2945.25

For what cause jury may be discharged, 2945.36

Grand jury, secrecy of proceedings and disclosure, Crim R 6

Trial jurors, challenge for cause, Crim R 24

Library References

Appeal and Error ⚖203.3.

Criminal Law ⚖1036.2.

Witnesses ⚖72, 73.

Westlaw Topic Nos. 30, 110, 410.

C.J.S. Appeal and Error § 202.

C.J.S. Witnesses §§ 107, 108.

OJur 3d: 4, Appellate Review § 255; 29A, Criminal Law § 3179, 3190, 3193, 3214; 44, Evidence and Witnesses § 761; 90, Trial § 494, 495, 497

Am Jur 2d: 29, Evidence § 293; 81, Witnesses § 102

Propriety of jurors asking questions in open court during course of trial. 31 ALR3d 872

Admissibility, in civil case, of juror's affidavit or testimony relating to juror's misconduct outside jury room. 32 ALR3d 1356

Trial jurors as witnesses in same state court or related case. 86 ALR3d 781

Impeachment of verdict by juror's evidence that he was coerced or intimidated by fellow juror. 39 ALR4th 800

Competency of juror as witness, under Rule 606(b) of Federal Rules of Evidence, upon inquiry into validity of verdict or indictment. 65 ALR Fed 835

Giannelli & Snyder, Baldwin's Ohio Practice, Evidence § 601, 601.15, 601.17 (2d ed. 2001).

Evid R 607   Impeachment

(A) Who may impeach

The credibility of a witness may be attacked by any party except that the credibility of a witness may be attacked by the party calling the witness by means of a prior inconsistent statement only upon a showing of surprise and affirmative damage. This exception does not apply to statements admitted pursuant to Evid. R. 801(D)(1)(a), 801(D)(2), or 803.

(B) Impeachment: reasonable basis

A questioner must have a reasonable basis for asking any question pertaining to impeachment that implies the existence of an impeaching fact.

(Adopted eff. 7–1–80; amended eff. 7–1–98)

Historical and Statutory Notes

Amendment Note: The 7–1–98 amendment substituted "Impeachment" for "Who May Impeach" in the title of the Rule; designated division (A) and added the title thereof; added division (B); and made other nonsubstantive changes.

Commentary

Staff Notes

1998:

Rule 607(A) Who may impeach

This paragraph was labeled division (A), a title was added, and the style used for rule references was changed. There was no substantive amendment to this division.

Rule 607(B) Impeachment: reasonable basis

The 1998 amendment added division (B) to the rule.

A party inquiring into specific instances of conduct must have a good faith basis in fact for asking the question. E.g., *State v. Gillard* (1988), 40 Ohio St.3d 226, 231, 533 N.E.2d 272 (" [A] cross-examiner may ask a question if the examiner has a good-faith belief that a factual predicate for the question exists."), cert. denied, 492 U.S. 925, 109 S.Ct. 3263, 106 L.Ed.2d 608 (1989); *Kornreich v. Indus. Fire Ins. Co.* (1936), 132 Ohio St. 78, 88 ("These collateral attacks must be made in good faith...."). This is especially true in criminal cases where the unfair prejudice may be great. See also 1 McCormick, Evidence § 41, at 140 (4th ed. 1992) ("A good faith basis for the inquiry is required."). Professor Graham explains the requirement as follows:

Note that the requirement of a good faith basis applies only when the cross-examiner is effectively asserting in the form of a question the truth of a factual statement included within the question. If the cross-examiner is merely inquiring whether something is or is not true, a good faith basis is not required. Thus the question, "Your glasses were being repaired at the time of the accident, weren't they?" requires a good faith basis, while the question, "Were you wearing your glasses at the time of the accident?" does not.

1 Graham, Handbook of Federal Evidence § 607.2, at 679–80 (4th ed. 1996).

Using the term "reasonable basis," the amendment codifies the good-faith basis-in-fact requirement as recognized at common law. In addition to the Rules of Evidence, the Code of Professional Responsibility imposes requirements on questioning witnesses. See DR 7–106(C).

1980:

This rule is a modification of Federal Evidence Rule 607 and constitutes a departure from prior Ohio law. Under prior law, a party ordinarily could not attack the credibility of his own witness. *State v. Minneker* (1971), 27 Ohio St.2d 155. This principle was referred to as the "voucher rule" and the rule reflected the notion that the party who called a witness presented him as a truthful person. Since parties do not select their witnesses, but must take those persons who have perceived the operative facts, the voucher rule rests on an incorrect assumption.

The court in *Minneker, supra,* applied the voucher rule without real conviction in the premises upon which it rests and alluded to possible statutory modification of this long standing principle rejected in many jurisdictions.

Rule 607 abolishes the general principle, preserving the "voucher rule" in those limited cases in which impeachment by the party calling the witness is predicated upon a prior inconsistent statement unless surprise and affirmative damage can be shown. Otherwise, the party would be entitled to call a known adverse witness simply for the purpose of getting a prior inconsistent statement into evidence by way of impeachment, thus doing indirectly what he could not have done directly.

Requiring a showing of affirmative damage is intended to eliminate an "I don't remember" answer or a neutral answer by the witness as a basis for impeachment by a prior inconsistent statement.

Cross References

Competency of witnesses, 2945.42
Deposition, use at trial or hearing, Crim R 15
Use of depositions in court proceedings, Civ R 32

Library References

Witnesses ☞319 to 326.
Westlaw Topic No. 410.
C.J.S. Witnesses §§ 474 to 480, 536.
OJur 3d: 29A, Criminal Law § 3133 to 3139; 44, Evidence and Witnesses § 730, 904, 913, 922, 923, 932, 934, 942, 943, 947, 969, 974; 89, Trial § 35
Am Jur 2d: 81, Witnesses § 422, 518 to 521, 563 et seq.
Admissibility, in action involving motor vehicle accident, of evidence as to manner in which participant was driving before reaching scene of accident. 46 ALR2d 9
Binding effect, upon party litigant, of testimony of his witnesses at a former trial. 74 ALR2d 521
Admissibility, for purpose of supporting impeached witness, of prior statements by him consistent with his testimony. 75 ALR2d 909
Admissibility of experimental evidence to show visibility or line of vision. 78 ALR2d 152
Necessity and sufficiency of foundation for discrediting evidence showing bias or prejudice of adverse witness. 87 ALR2d 407
Necessity and admissibility of expert testimony as to credibility of witness. 20 ALR3d 684
Cross-examination of witness as to his mental state or condition, to impeach competency or credibility. 44 ALR3d 1203
Cross-examination of character witness for accused with reference to particular acts or crimes— modern state rules. 13 ALR4th 796
Admissibility of affidavit to impeach witness. 14 ALR4th 828
Impeachment of defense witness in criminal case by showing witness' prior silence or failure or refusal to testify. 20 ALR4th 245
Use of plea bargain or grant of immunity as improper vouching for credibility of witness—state cases. 58 ALR4th 1229
Attacking or supporting credibility of witness by evidence in form of opinion or reputation, under Rule 608(a) of Federal Rules of Evidence. 52 ALR Fed 440
Propriety, in federal court action, of attack on witness' credibility by rebuttable evidence pertaining to cross-examination testimony on collateral matters. 60 ALR Fed 8
Use of plea bargain or grant of immunity as improper vouching for credibility of witness in federal cases. 76 ALR Fed 409
Display of physical appearance or characteristic of defendant for purpose of challenging prosecution evidence as "testimony" resulting in waiver of defendant's privilege against self-incrimination. 81 ALR Fed 892
Propriety, under Federal Rule of Evidence 607, of impeachment of party's own witness. 89 ALR Fed 13
Giannelli & Snyder, Baldwin's Ohio Practice, Evidence § 104.11, 404, 405.6, 608.1, 609, 608.5, 609.6, 611.11, 612.4, 613.1, 613.7, 614.3, 616, 616.1, 616.3, 801.12, 1101 (2d ed. 2001).

Carlin, Baldwin's Ohio Practice, Merrick–Rippner Probate Law § 27.9 (2003).

Evid R 608 Evidence of character and conduct of witness

(A) Opinion and reputation evidence of character

The credibility of a witness may be attacked or supported by evidence in the form of opinion or reputation, but subject to these limitations: (1) the evidence may refer only to character for truthfulness or untruthfulness, and (2) evidence of truthful character is admissible only after the character of the witness for truthfulness has been attacked by opinion or reputation evidence or otherwise.

(B) Specific instances of conduct

Specific instances of the conduct of a witness, for the purpose of attacking or supporting the witness's character for truthfulness, other than conviction of crime as provided in Evid. R. 609, may not be proved by extrinsic evidence. They may, however, in the discretion of the court, if clearly probative of truthfulness or untruthfulness, be inquired into on cross-examination of the witness (1) concerning the witness's character for truthfulness or untruthfulness, or (2) concerning the character for truthfulness or untruthfulness of another witness as to which character the witness being cross-examined has testified.

The giving of testimony by any witness, including an accused, does not operate as a waiver of the witness's privilege against self-incrimination when examined with respect to matters that relate only to the witness's character for truthfulness.

(Adopted eff. 7–1–80; amended eff. 7–1–92)

Commentary

Staff Notes

1992:

Rule 608(B) Specific instances of conduct

The amendment substitutes the phrase "character for truthfulness" for the term "credibility." The latter term is too broad and, therefore, may cause confusion.

Evid. R. 608, along with Evid. R. 609 (prior convictions), concerns impeachment by means of character evidence. The rules do not deal with other methods of impeachment, such as bias, which is governed by Evid. R. 616, or prior inconsistent statements, which are governed by Evid. R. 613. Thus, the limitation on the admissibility of extrinsic evidence in Evid. R. 608(B) concerns only specific

acts of conduct reflecting upon untruthful character, and not on "credibility" in general. Extrinsic evidence may be admissible under some other theory of impeachment. Indeed, Evid. R. 616 explicitly provides for the admissibility of extrinsic evidence of bias.

Extrinsic evidence of a prior inconsistent statement is admissible under Evid. R. 613(B), provided a foundation is laid on cross-examination. In addition, extrinsic evidence offered to show contradiction, an impeachment method not specifically covered by any rule, may be admissible under certain circumstances. *State v. Williams* (1984), 16 Ohio App.3d 484, 477 N.E.2d 221 (testimony that rape complainant had engaged in sex with males in the course of prostitution admitted after complainant voluntarily testified that she had not consented to intercourse with defendant because she was a lesbian); G. Joseph & S. Saltzburg, *Evidence in America: The Federal Rules in the States* ch. 42, at 9–10 (1987).

Commentators on the Federal Rules have recognized this problem. See A.B.A. Criminal Justice Section, *Federal Rules of Evidence: A Fresh Review and Evaluation*, 120 F.R.D. 299, 355 (1987) ("The root of the trouble seems to be the Rule's obscure wording. Perhaps foremost of the troubles... is confusion concerning whether wrongdoing offered to show bias... rather than to show credibility-character, is covered by Rule 608(B).") The Federal Rules do not contain a rule on impeachment by bias. Nevertheless, the Supreme Court resolved the issue in *United States v. Abel* (1984), 469 U.S. 45, 105 S.Ct. R. 465, 83 L.Ed.2d 450, holding extrinsic evidence of bias admissible notwithstanding Fed.R.Evid. 608(b).

See also La.Code Evid. art. 608(B) (phrase "character for truthfulness" used in lieu of "credibility").

In addition, masculine references are replaced by gender-neutral language, the style used for rule references is revised, and grammatical changes are made. No substantive change is intended.

1980:

Rule 608(A) Opinion and Reputation Evidence of Character

This subdivision is identical to Federal Evidence Rule 608(a) and modifies prior Ohio law by permitting opinion evidence of truthfulness or untruthfulness of a witness as well as the traditional reputation evidence available under prior Ohio law. *Cowan v. Kenney [Kinney]* (1978) [1878], 33 Ohio St.2d [Ohio St.] 422. This expansion of methods of proving character for truthfulness or untruthfulness parallels the similar provisions respecting methods of proving character in Rule 405(A).

Subdivision (A) further provides, that as to the character trait of a witness, only evidence relating to veracity is admissible. This is consistent with prior Ohio law which prohibited evidence of bad moral character of a witness. *Schueler v. Lynam* (1947), 80 Ohio App. 325.

The rule also conditions evidence of truthful character of a witness upon his character first being attacked by reputation or opinion evidence or otherwise. This represents no departure from prior Ohio law. *Webb v. State* (1876), 29 Ohio St. 351.

Rule 608(B) Specific Instances of Conduct

This subdivision in nearly identical to Federal Evidence Rule 608(b) and reflects prior Ohio law relating to scope of cross-examination. See, for example, *State v. Browning* (1954), 98 Ohio App. 8. It permits cross-examination of a character witness as to specific instances of conduct which may have a clear bearing upon either that witness' truthful character or the basis of his testimony as to the truthful character of the witness about whom the testimony for truthfulness was made. Unlike Federal Evidence Rule 608(b), the rule contains the word "clearly" in the second sentence. The rule requires a high degree of probative value of instances of prior conduct as to truthfulness or untruthfulness of the witness before the court, in the exercise of its discretion, will allow cross-examination as to such prior conduct for purposes of attacking the credibility of the witness.

Except for the provisions of Rule 609 respecting conviction of a crime, collateral or extrinsic evidence of such instances of bad conduct is not admissible. This limitation is also consistent with prior Ohio law. *State v. Cochrane* (1949), 151 Ohio St. 128.

Cross References

Trial for crimes, witness, O Const Art I §10

Library References

Witnesses ⟷333 to 341.

Westlaw Topic No. 410.

C.J.S. Witnesses §§ 491 to 513.

OJur 3d: 25, Criminal Law § 465 to 495; 29A, Criminal Law § 3114, 3129, 3133, 3135, 3136, 3139, 3142, 3146; 44, Evidence and Witnesses § 730, 904, 913, 922, 923, 932, 934, 942, 943, 947, 969, 974; 67, Malpractice § 143; 89, Trial § 35

Am Jur 2d: 81, Witnesses § 422, 518 et seq, 563 to 568, 637

Admissibility, in action involving motor vehicle accident, of evidence as to manner in which participant was driving before reaching scene of accident. 46 ALR2d 9

Binding effect, upon party litigant, of testimony of his witnesses at a former trial. 74 ALR2d 521

Admissibility, for purpose of supporting impeached witness, of prior statements by him consistent with his testimony. 75 ALR2d 909

Admissibility of experimental evidence to show visibility or line of vision. 78 ALR2d 152

Necessity and sufficiency of foundation for discrediting evidence showing bias or prejudice of adverse witness. 87 ALR2d 407

Necessity and admissibility of expert testimony as to credibility of witness. 20 ALR3d 684

Cross-examination of witness as to his mental state or condition, to impeach competency or credibility. 44 ALR3d 1203

Cross-examination of character witness for accused with reference to particular acts or crimes—modern state rules. 13 ALR4th 796

Admissibility of affidavit to impeach witness. 14 ALR4th 828

Impeachment of defense witness in criminal case by showing witness' prior silence or failure or refusal to testify. 20 ALR4th 245

Use of plea bargain or grant of immunity as improper vouching for credibility of witness—state cases. 58 ALR4th 1229

Propriety of questioning expert witness regarding specific incidents or allegations of expert's unprofessional conduct or professional negligence. 11 ALR5th 1

Construction and application of Rule 608(b) of the Federal Rules of Evidence, dealing with use of specific instances of conduct to attack or support credibility. 36 ALR Fed 564

Attacking or supporting credibility of witness by evidence in form of opinion or reputation, under Rule 608(a) of the Federal Rules of Evidence. 52 ALR Fed 440

Display of physical appearance or characteristic of defendant for purpose of challenging prosecution evidence as "testimony" resulting in waiver of defendant's privilege against self-incrimination. 81 ALR Fed 892

Giannelli & Snyder, Baldwin's Ohio Practice, Evidence § 102.3, 404, 403.4, 403.6, 404.7, 404.10, 405.1, 607.1, 607.7, 607.8, 607.9, 609.1, 609.5, 609.6, 609.16, 611.10, 613.1, 616, 613.7, 616.1, 616.5, 701.1, 706.1, 803.53, 806.4, 1101 (2d ed. 2001).

Evid R 609 Impeachment by evidence of conviction of crime

(A) General rule

For the purpose of attacking the credibility of a witness:

(1) subject to Evid. R. 403, evidence that a witness other than the accused has been convicted of a crime is admissible if the crime was punishable by death or imprisonment in excess of one year pursuant to the law under which the witness was convicted.

(2) notwithstanding Evid. R. 403(A), but subject to Evid. R. 403(B), evidence that the accused has been convicted of a crime is admissible if the crime was punishable by death or imprisonment in excess of one year pursuant to the law under which the accused was convicted and if the court determines that the probative value of the evidence outweighs the danger of unfair prejudice, of confusion of the issues, or of misleading the jury.

(3) notwithstanding Evid. R. 403(A), but subject to Evid. R. 403(B), evidence that any witness, including an accused, has been convicted of a crime is admissible if the crime involved dishonesty or false statement, regardless of the punishment and whether based upon state or federal statute or local ordinance.

(B) Time limit.

Evidence of a conviction under this rule is not admissible if a period of more than ten years has elapsed since the date of the conviction or of the release of the witness from the confinement, or the termination of community control sanctions, post-release control, or probation, shock probation, parole, or shock parole imposed for that conviction, whichever is the later date, unless the court determines, in the interests of justice, that the probative value of the conviction supported by specific facts and circumstances substantially outweighs its prejudicial effect. However, evidence of a conviction more than ten years old as calculated herein, is not admissible unless the proponent gives to the adverse party sufficient advance written notice of intent to use such evidence to provide the adverse party with a fair opportunity to contest the use of such evidence.

(C) Effect of pardon, annulment, expungement, or certificate of rehabilitation

Evidence of a conviction is not admissible under this rule if (1) the conviction has been the subject of a pardon, annulment, expungement, certificate of rehabilitation, or other equivalent procedure based on a finding of the rehabilitation of the person convicted, and that person has not been convicted of a subsequent crime which was punishable by death or imprisonment in excess of one year, or (2) the conviction has been the subject of a pardon, annulment, expungement, or other equivalent procedure based on a finding of innocence.

(D) Juvenile adjudications

Evidence of juvenile adjudications is not admissible except as provided by statute enacted by the General Assembly.

(E) Pendency of appeal

The pendency of an appeal therefrom does not render evidence of a conviction inadmissible. Evidence of the pendency of an appeal is admissible.

(F) Methods of proof

When evidence of a witness's conviction of a crime is admissible under this rule, the fact of the conviction may be proved only by the testimony of the witness on direct or cross-examination, or by public record shown to the witness during his or her examination. If the witness denies that he or she is the person to whom the public record refers, the court may permit the introduction of additional evidence tending to establish that the witness is or is not the person to whom the public record refers.

(Adopted eff. 7–1–80; amended eff. 7–1–91, 7–1–03)

Commentary

Staff Notes

2003:

Rule 609(B) Time limit

The amendment added references to "community control sanctions" and "post-release control" in division (B) to reflect the availability of those forms of sanction along with the traditional devices of probation and parole already referred to in the rule. Un-

der the rule as amended, the termination of community control sanctions and post-release control become additional events from which to date the staleness of a conviction under the rule's presumptive exclusion of convictions that are remote in time.

1991:

The amendment makes several changes. One change concerns the trial court's discretion to exclude evidence of prior convictions, and the other change concerns permissible methods of proving prior convictions.

Rule 609(A) Discretion to Exclude

The amended rule clarifies the issue of the trial court's discretion in excluding prior convictions. As adopted in 1980, the Ohio rule differed from its federal counterpart. A clause in Federal Rule 609(a)(1) explicitly authorized the trial court to exclude "felony" convictions; these convictions were admissible only if the "court determines that the probative value of admitting this evidence outweighs its prejudicial effect to the defendant." This clause was deleted from the Ohio rule.

It could have been argued that this deletion meant that Ohio courts did not have the authority to exclude prior felony convictions. In other words, any felony conviction was automatically admissible. Indeed, the rule specified that these convictions "shall be admitted." The Ohio Staff Note (1980), however, suggested otherwise. The Staff Note reads:

In limiting that discretionary grant, Rule 609(A) is directed to greater uniformity in application subject only to the provisions of Rule 403. The removal of the reference to the defendant insures that the application of the rule is not limited to criminal prosecutions.

The Supreme Court addressed the issue in *State v. Wright* (1990), 48 Ohio St.3d 5, 548 N.E.2d 923. The Court wrote: "Evid. R. 609 must be considered in conjunction with Evid. R. 403. The trial judge therefore has broad discretion in determining the extent to which testimony will be admitted under Evid. R. 609."

The amended rule makes clear that Ohio trial judges have discretion to exclude prior convictions. It also specifies how this discretion is to be exercised. Evid. R. 609(A) is divided into three divisions. Division (1) concerns "felony" convictions of witnesses other than the accused (prosecution and defense witnesses in criminal cases and all witnesses in civil cases). The admissibility of these convictions is subject to Evid. R. 403.

Division (A)(2) concerns "felony" convictions of an accused in a criminal case. The risk that a jury would misuse evidence of a prior conviction as evidence of propensity or general character, a use which is prohibited by Evid. R. 404, is far greater when a criminal accused is impeached. *See* C. McCormick, Evidence 99 (3d ed. 1984) ("The sharpest and most prejudicial impact of the practice of impeachment by conviction... is upon... the accused in a criminal case who elects to take the stand.").

Accordingly, admissibility of prior convictions is more readily achieved for witnesses other than the accused. Evid. R. 403 requires that the probative value of the evidence be "substantially" outweighed by unfair prejudice before exclusion is warranted. In other words, Evid. R. 403 is biased in favor of admissibility. This is not the case when the accused is impeached by a prior conviction under Evid. R. 609(A)(2); the unfair prejudice need only outweigh probative value, rather than "substantially" outweigh probative value.

In making this determination the court would consider a number of factors: "(1) the nature of the crime, (2) recency of the prior conviction, (3) similarity between the crime for which there was prior conviction and the crime charged, (4) the importance of defendant's testimony, and (5) the centrality of the credibility issue." C. McCormick, Evidence 94 n. 9 (3d ed. 1984).

Division (A)(3) concerns dishonesty and false statement convictions. Because of the high probative value of these convictions in assessing credibility, they are not subject to exclusion because of unfair prejudice. This rule applies to the accused as well as other witnesses.

The issue raised by Ohio Evid. R. 609 also is raised by the Federal Rule, even though the federal provision explicitly recognized trial judge discretion to exclude evidence of prior convictions. Because the discretionary language in the federal rule referred to balancing the prejudicial effect to the "defendant," the applicability of this clause to civil cases and prosecution witnesses had been questioned. The U.S. Supreme Court in *Green v. Bock Laundry* (1989), 490 U.S. 504, 109 S.Ct. R. 1981, 104 L.Ed.2d 557, ruled that the discretion to exclude convictions under Federal Rule 609(a) did not apply to civil cases or to prosecution witnesses. Moreover, the court ruled that Rule 403 did not apply in this context. An amendment to the federal rule was adopted to change this result.

Rule 609(F) Methods of Proof

The rule as adopted in 1980 specified that convictions admissible under the rule could be "elicited from him [the witness] or established by public record during cross–examination...." The use of the term "cross-examination" was unfortunate. Custom permits counsel to bring out evidence of prior convictions on *direct* examination "for the purpose of lessening the import of these convictions upon the jury." *State v. Peoples* (1971), 28 Ohio App.2d 162, 168, 275 N.E.2d 626. Moreover, impeachment of a witness by proof of a prior conviction during direct examination is permitted under Evid. R. 607, which allows a party to impeach its own witnesses.

The traditional methods of proof are through examination of the witness or by public record. These methods are permissible under division (F).

1980:

Rule 609(A) General Rule

Rule 609(A) is a modified form of Federal Evidence Rule 609(a) and makes a significant modification of prior Ohio law.

Rule 609(A) departs from the federal counterpart in that it limits discretion of the court when evidence of conviction of a crime punishable by death or by more than one year of imprisonment is offered to impeach a witness. The federal rule conditions the introduction of such evidence on the court's determination that the probative value of admission of the evidence outweighs its prejudicial effect upon the defendant. In limiting that discretionary grant, Rule 609(A) is directed to greater uniformity in application subject only to the provisions of Rule 403. The removal of the reference to the defendant insures that the application of the rule is not limited to criminal prosecutions.

Under prior Ohio law, R.C. 2945.42 provided that the conviction of a witness in a criminal prosecution could be shown for the purpose of affecting his credibility. The conviction could be for any crime and was not limited to the common law concept of the *crimen falsi. State v. Murdock* (1961), 172 Ohio St. 221. "Any crime" was held not to extend to convictions of ordinance violations. *State v. Arrington* (1975), 42 Ohio St.2d 114. Although R.C. 2945.42 is stated in terms of criminal prosecutions, an implication that the statute and *Murdock* apply in civil cases appears in *Garland v. Standard Oil Co.* (1963), 119 Ohio App. 291.

Under prior Ohio law, it was well established that the credibility of a witness could be tested by inquiry into collateral offenses with such inquiry limited to those offenses that affected credibility, namely, treason, felony and *crimen falsi. Kornreich v. Industrial Fire Ins. Co.* (1936), 132 Ohio St. 78.

Rule 609(A) modifies prior Ohio law as stated in *Murdock* by limiting the collateral offenses inquiry to crimes punishable by death and crimes punishable by more than one year of imprisonment, and crimes involving dishonesty or false statement irrespective of punishment and extending the inclusion of offenses to ordinance violations. The term felony is not used in the rule because the definition of felony varies among jurisdictions.

Rule 609(A) applies to civil and criminal cases. It supersedes a part of R.C. 2945.42 and negates *Murdock*.

Rule 609(B) Time Limit

This subdivision basically replicates its Federal Evidence Rule counterpart, but calculates the time limit not only from release of confinement, but also from the termination of probation or parole, or shock probation. Beyond the ten year period of time, the court has discretion to admit the conviction with the additional requirement that the proponent provide the adverse party sufficient advance notice in writing of his intent to employ such evidence. Such advance notice permits the adverse party an opportunity to contest the admission of the evidence.

Rule 609(C) Effect of Pardon, Annulment, Expungement or Certification of Rehabilitation

This subdivision is identical to Federal Evidence Rule 609(c) with the exception that the word "expungement" is inserted. Although Ohio does not have the procedure of annulment or rehabilitation, the words were retained because of their availability in other jurisdictions.

R.C. 2953.32 relates to the expungement of the record of a felony conviction at the expiration of three years, or at the conclusion of one year if a misdemeanor. R.C. 2953.32(E) provides that proof of any otherwise admissible prior conviction may be introduced and proved, notwithstanding the fact that for any such prior conviction an order of expungement was previously issued pursuant to R.C. 2953.31 to 2953.36. The rule conflicts with the provision of the statute.

It is to be noted that Rule 609(C) could reduce the time limit provisions of Rule 609(B). If a criminal conviction is annulled, expunged or a certificate of rehabilitation is granted and the provisions of this subdivision apply the time period contemplated by subdivision (B) would not apply, notwithstanding the provisions of R.C. 2953.32(E). *State v. Cox* (1975), 42 Ohio St.2d 200, holds that notwithstanding the provisions of R.C. 2151.358 regarding expungement of juvenile records, confidentiality of juvenile records may not impinge upon the right of a criminal defendant to present relevant evidence pertinent to a material aspect of his defense. Obviously, this holding, predicated upon constitutional considerations, limits the permissible scope of this rule.

Rule 609(D) Juvenile Adjudications

This subdivision differs markedly from the federal rule both in wording and substance. The federal rule makes juvenile adjudications admissible in the discretion of the trial court whereas the Ohio Rule specifically excludes juvenile adjudication as a basis of impeachment unless provided by enactment of the general assembly. The rule preserves legislative prerogatives relating to consequences of juvenile adjudications. R.C. 2151.358 retains effectiveness in cases involving a juvenile. See, for example, R.C. 2151.358(H) pertaining to the use of evidence of a juvenile adjudication in determining appropriate sentencing or probation of the child in a subsequent proceeding.

The holding of *State v. Hale* (1969), 21 Ohio App.2d 207, which permitted the use of juvenile adjudication to rebut claims of good character as a juvenile defendant is not by the precise language of this rule superseded unless the rebuttal evidence is considered as merely a form of impeachment.

Rule 609(E) Pendency of Appeal

This subdivision is identical to Federal Evidence Rule 609(e). It is in accord with prior Ohio law.

Cross References

Competency of witnesses, 2945.42
Degree of offense, charge and verdict, prior convictions, 2945.75
Final release of paroled prisoners, 2967.16
Pardon, commutation, or reprieve, 2967.03
Probation period, 2951.07
Records, sealed or expunged, procedures, effects, offense of divulging confidential information, 2151.358
Sealing of record of first offense, application, hearing, fee, re-examination of sealed record, 2953.32

Library References

Witnesses ⊸337(5) to 337(30), 345(1) to 345(11), 359.

Westlaw Topic No. 410.

C.J.S. Witnesses §§ 503 to 508, 528 et seq.

OJur 3d: 25, Criminal Law § 465; 29A, Criminal Law § 3133, 3134, 3139, 3141, 3142; 44, Evidence and Witnesses § 906, 924 to 929; 89, Trial § 35

Am Jur 2d: 81, Witnesses § 94 to 96, 569 to 586
Pardon as affecting impeachment by proof of conviction of crime. 30 ALR2d 893
Impeachment of witness by showing conviction of contempt. 49 ALR2d 845
Effect of prosecuting attorney asking defense witness other than accused as to prior convictions where he is not prepared to offer documentary proof in event of denial. 3 ALR3d 965
Permissibility of impeaching credibility of witness by showing former conviction, as affected by pendency of appeal from conviction or motion for new trial. 16 ALR3d 726
Use of judgment in prior juvenile court proceeding to impeach credibility of witness. 63 ALR3d 1112
Propriety, on impeaching credibility of witness in civil case by showing former conviction, of questions relating to nature and extent of punishment. 67 ALR3d 761
Right to impeach credibility of accused by showing prior conviction, as affected by remoteness in time of prior offense. 67 ALR3d 824

Use of unrelated traffic offense conviction to impeach general credibility of witness in state civil case. 88 ALR3d 74
Use of unrelated misdemeanor conviction (other than for traffic offense) to impeach general credibility of witness in state civil case. 97 ALR3d 1150
Conviction by court-martial as proper subject of cross-examination for impeachment purposes. 7 ALR4th 468
Right to impeach witness in criminal case by inquiry or evidence as to witness' criminal activity for which witness was arrested or charged, but not convicted—modern state cases. 28 ALR4th 505
Permissibility of impeaching credibility of witness by showing verdict of guilty without judgment of sentence thereon. 28 ALR4th 647
Requirement that defendant in state court testify in order to preserve alleged trial error in rulings on admissibility of prior conviction impeachment evidence under Uniform Rule of Evidence 609, or similar provision or holding—post-Luce cases. 80 ALR4th 1028
Admissibility of evidence of other offense where record has been expunged or erased. 82 ALR4th 913
Construction and application of Rule 609(a) of the Federal Rules of Evidence permitting impeachment of witness by evidence of prior conviction of crime. 39 ALR Fed 570
Construction and application of Rule 609(c) of the Federal Rules of Evidence, providing that evidence of conviction is not admissible to attack credibility of witness if conviction has been subject of pardon, annulment, or other procedure based on finding of rehabilitation or innocence. 42 ALR Fed 942
Construction and application of Rule 609(b) of Federal Rules of Evidence, setting time limit on admissibility of evidence of conviction of crime to attack credibility of witness. 43 ALR Fed 398
Review on appeal, where accused does not testify, of trial court's preliminary ruling that evidence of prior convictions will be admissible under Rule 609 of the Federal Rules of Evidence if accused does testify. 54 ALR Fed 694
Painter, Ohio Driving Under the Influence Law (2003 Ed.), Text 15.12.
Giannelli & Snyder, Baldwin's Ohio Practice, Evidence § 101.3, 102.5, 105.7, 404, 403.4, 404.10, 404.25, 405.1, 405.5, 410.4, 607.1, 607.7, 608, 608.1, 608.4, 609.11, 613.1, 613.7, 616, 616.1, 706.1, 803.57, 806.1, 806.2, 806.5, 1101, 806, 807.14 (2d ed. 2001).
Adrine & Ruden, Ohio Domestic Violence Law (2002 Ed.), Text 14.12.
Carlin, Baldwin's Ohio Practice, Merrick–Rippner Probate Law § 107.114 (2003).

Evid R 610   Religious beliefs or opinions

Evidence of the beliefs or opinions of a witness on matters of religion is not admissible for the purpose of showing that by reason of their nature his credibility is impaired or enhanced.

(Adopted eff. 7–1–80)

Commentary

Staff Notes
1980:

Rule 610 is identical to Federal Evidence Rule 610 and it is consistent with prior Ohio law.

Article I, Section 7, of the Ohio Constitution guarantees religious freedom. One of the specific provisions contained in the section is that no person is incompetent as a witness on account of his religious beliefs.

Although evidence of religious belief or opinion may not be admitted to impair or enhance general credibility, as the Advisory Committee's Note to Federal Evidence Rule 610 states, the rule does not prevent such belief or opinion from being admissible to show interest or bias on the part of the witness.

Library References

Witnesses ☞340(2).

Westlaw Topic No. 410.

C.J.S. Witnesses § 511.

OJur 3d: 44, Evidence and Witnesses § 774, 916, 967

Am Jur 2d: 81, Witnesses § 533

Propriety and prejudicial effect of impeaching witness by reference to religious belief or lack of it. 76 ALR3d 539

Giannelli & Snyder, Baldwin's Ohio Practice, Evidence § 603.1, 607.1, 607.7, 608.1, 613.1, 616.1 (2d ed. 2001).

Carlin, Baldwin's Ohio Practice, Merrick–Rippner Probate Law § 27.9 (2003).

Evid R 611   Mode and order of interrogation and presentation

(A) Control by court

The court shall exercise reasonable control over the mode and order of interrogating witnesses and presenting evidence so as to (1) make the interrogation and presentation effective for the ascertainment of the truth, (2) avoid needless consumption of time, and (3) protect witnesses from harassment or undue embarrassment.

(B) Scope of cross–examination

Cross-examination shall be permitted on all relevant matters and matters affecting credibility.

(C) Leading questions

Leading questions should not be used on the direct examination of a witness except as may be necessary to develop his testimony. Ordinarily leading questions should be permitted on cross-examination. When a party calls a hostile witness, an adverse party, or a witness identified with an adverse party, interrogation may be by leading questions.

(Adopted eff. 7–1–80)

Commentary

Staff Notes

1980:

Rule 611(A) Control of the Court

Rule 611(A) is identical to Federal Evidence Rule 611(a) and conforms to prior Ohio law.

The trial court has discretion in applying and relaxing the general rules for the introduction of testimony according to circumstances to achieve justice. *Ryan [Runyan] v. Price* (1864), 15 Ohio St. 1. The trial court has an active duty to aid in eliciting truth so that the verdict of the jury may approach the ends of justice. *Armour & Co. v. Yoter* (1931), 40 Ohio App. 225. The trial court has discretion to exclude a disparaging course of examination. *Wroe v. State* (1870), 20 Ohio St. 460.

Rule 611(B) Scope of Cross–Examination

Rule 611(B) and Federal Evidence Rule 611(b) stand in diametrical opposition. The federal rule limits the scope of cross-examination to the scope of direct examination with a discretion vested in the trial court to permit additional inquiry as if upon direct examination. In contrast, Rule 611(B) permits cross-examination on all relevant matters and matters affecting credibility. The rule follows the English view and has long been the law of Ohio. *Legg v. Drake* (1853), 1 Ohio St. 286. *Legg* placed a limitation on the basic principle. That limitation was the rule that a party cannot, before the time of opening his case, introduce his grounds for a defense or for affirmative relief through cross-examination of his adversary's witnesses. In a subsequent case, *Bean v. Green* (1878), 33 Ohio St. 444, it was held that the admission of testimony out of time is a question directed to the discretion of the court and although an irregularity, the action of the court permitting the eliciting of evidence in chief on cross-examination did not constitute an abuse of discretion. More recently, in *Cities Service Oil Co. v. Burkett* (1964), 176 Ohio St. 449, it was held that even though the proper time for introduction of evidence in support of a litigant's position was during the introduction of his evidence in chief, testimony adduced on cross-examination within proper limits and tending to establish the litigant's case may be allowed to stand and be considered. The case involved the cross-examination of an agent of a party and was authorized by R.C. 2317.52. In consequence of that authorization to cross-examine, the court stated that there was no sound reason why the trial court, in the exercise of discretion, should not have admitted the testimony elicited on cross-examination. The Ohio rule has the virtue of not requiring the witness to make a later appearance in the cause.

Rule 611(C) Leading Questions

Rule 611(C) is identical to Federal Evidence Rule 611(c) and is in accord with prior Ohio law.

The allowance or refusal of the use of leading questions in the examination of a witness is a matter within the discretion of the trial court. *Evans v. State* (1873), 24 Ohio St. 458. The existence of such discretion is fundamental and well recognized. *State v. Wallen* (1969), 21 Ohio App. 2d 27, 36.

The rule refers to the use of leading questions when the witness being examined is hostile. This accords with prior Ohio law, *State v. Minneker* (1971), 27 Ohio St.2d 155, and the reference to hostility does not foreclose the use of leading questions based on other considerations. Those include surprise, refreshing recollection after memory is exhausted, the handicaps of age, illness, or limited intellect, and preliminary matters.

Cross References

Court, common pleas, trial, procedure, 2315.01
Cross-examination of agents, 2317.52

Examination by deposition or interrogatory, rebuttal, 2317.07

Judge to control proceedings during criminal trial court; authority of magistrate or judge, 2938.07

Order of proceedings of trial, 2938.11, 2945.10

Pleadings and motions, amendments to conform to evidence, Civ R 15

Setting and continuing cases, 2945.02

Will contest, witnesses may be called as upon cross examination, 2107.74

Library References

Witnesses ☞224 to 226, 239 to 244, 268(1) to 269(15), 329 to 330(3).

Westlaw Topic No. 410.

C.J.S. Federal Civil Procedure §§ 522 to 524.

C.J.S. Witnesses §§ 315, 317, 329 to 340, 377 to 397, 483 to 485.

OJur 3d: 29A, Criminal Law § 3128 to 3130, 3132; 44, Evidence and Witnesses § 852, 866, 868 to 871, 881, 882, 896; 89, Trial § 18, 24, 52, 53

Am Jur 2d: 81, Witnesses § 422, 429 to 432, 478 to 480, 509, 510

Cross-examination by leading questions of witness friendly to or biased in favor of cross-examiner. 38 ALR2d 952

Limiting number of noncharacter witnesses in civil case. 5 ALR3d 169

Limiting number of noncharacter witnesses in criminal case. 5 ALR3d 238

Propriety of court's failure or refusal to strike direct testimony of government witness who refuses, on grounds of self-incrimination, to answer questions on cross-examination. 55 ALR Fed 742

Propriety of federal district court's allowance or denial of introduction of surrebuttal evidence in criminal trial. 71 ALR Fed 94

Giannelli & Snyder, Baldwin's Ohio Practice, Evidence § 103.8, 104.9, 106.3, 403.5, 403.8, 607.4, 608.5, 612.4, 614.1, 614.3, 616.3, 616.6, 804.14, 806.3, 901.17, 901.19, 901.22, 901.23, 1002.4, 104, 616 (2d ed. 2001).

Adrine & Ruden, Ohio Domestic Violence Law (2002 Ed.), Text 5.11, 6.13.

Ohio Personal Injury Practice (2002 Ed.), Text 5.03, 10.02.

Carlin, Baldwin's Ohio Practice, Merrick–Rippner Probate Law § 107.72 (2003).

Evid R 612   Writing used to refresh memory

Except as otherwise provided in criminal proceedings by Rule 16(B)(1)(g) and 16(C)(1)(d) of Ohio Rules of Criminal Procedure, if a witness uses a writing to refresh his memory for the purpose of testifying, either: (1) while testifying; or (2) before testifying, if the court in its discretion determines it is necessary in the interests of justice, an adverse party is entitled to have the writing produced at the hearing. He is also entitled to inspect it, to cross-examine the witness thereon, and to introduce in evidence those portions which relate to the testimony of the witness. If it is claimed that the writing contains matters not related to the subject matter of the testimony the court shall examine the writing *in cam-*

era, excise any portions not so related, and order delivery of the remainder to the party entitled thereto. Any portion witheld [sic.] over objections shall be preserved and made available to the appellate court in the event of an appeal. If a writing is not produced or delivered pursuant to order under this rule, the court shall make any order justice requires, except that in criminal cases when the prosecution elects not to comply, the order shall be one striking the testimony or, if the court in its discretion determines that the interests of justice so require, declaring a mistrial.

(Adopted eff. 7–1–80)

Commentary

Staff Notes

1980:

Except for the reference to the Ohio Rules of Criminal Procedure instead of the reference to the Jencks Act, Rule 612 is identical to Federal Evidence Rule 612.

Using a writing to refresh recollection, the subject of Rule 612, is to be distinguished from a past recollection recorded, the subject of Rule 803(5). The distinction has been stated in *State v. Scott* (1972), 31 Ohio St. 2d 1, 5, as follows:

> In the "present recollection refreshed" situation, the witness looks at the memorandum to refresh his memory of the events, but then proceeds to testify upon the basis of his present independent knowledge. However, in the "past recollection recorded" situation, the witness's present recollection is still absent or incomplete, but his present testimony is to the effect that his recollection was complete at the time the memorandum was written, and that such recollection was accurately recorded therein.

It is a long established principle in Ohio law that a witness may refresh his recollection. *Mead v. McGraw* (1869), 19 Ohio St. 55. To be used, a document must actually refresh the witness's recollection. *Lowell [Lovell] v. Wentworth* (1884), 39 Ohio St. 614.

Under prior Ohio law, when a witness used a document to refresh his recollection, the opposing party was entitled to examine the document for use in cross-examination. *State v. Taylor* (1947), 83 Ohio App. 76. The Ohio cases are not specific as to the refreshing of recollection which took place before the giving of testimony.

Rule 612 restates Ohio law in providing that the opposing party has the right to examine a document used to refresh recollection while testifying and to cross-examine on that document. Under prior Ohio law, the propriety in use of the writing to refresh recollection did not determine the admissibility of the record as an independent item of evidence. *Weis v. Weis* (1947), 147 Ohio St. 416, 420.

Rule 612 vests discretion in the court to permit examination of a writing used to refresh recollection before testifying. This provision, together with the basic limitation of the rule which restricts examination to those situations where the writing is used to refresh recollection for the purpose of testifying, serves to avoid the rule being used as an additional method of discovery, particularly as to work product and pretrial preparation.

Rule 612 applies to witnesses and parties and to civil and criminal cases. The exclusion of application to witness statements in criminal proceedings serves to preserve the discovery proceedings of the Criminal Rules.

Cross References

Discovery and inspection, disclosure of evidence, by defendant, by prosecuting attorney, regulation of discovery, Crim R 16
Failure to make discovery, sanctions, Civ R 37
Use of deposition to refresh recollection of deponent as witness, Crim R 15

Library References

Witnesses ☞253 to 257.10.

Westlaw Topic No. 410.

C.J.S. Criminal Law §§ 966 to 971.

C.J.S. Witnesses §§ 357 to 363.

OJur 3d: 25, Criminal Law § 481; 36, Discovery and Depositions § 40; 44, Evidence and Witnesses § 859

Am Jur 2d: 29, Evidence § 866, 877; 81, Witnesses § 440 to 462

Refreshment of recollection by use of memoranda or other writings. 82 ALR2d 473

Use of writing to refresh witness' memory, as governed by Rule 612 of Federal Rules of Evidence. 73 ALR Fed 423

Giannelli & Snyder, Baldwin's Ohio Practice, Evidence § 607.4, 803, 803.22 (2d ed. 2001).

Adrine & Ruden, Ohio Domestic Violence Law (2002 Ed.), Text 13.6, 15.9.

Evid R 613   Impeachment by self-contradiction

(A) Examining witness concerning prior statement

In examining a witness concerning a prior statement made by the witness, whether written or not, the statement need not be shown nor its contents disclosed to the witness at that time, but on request the same shall be shown or disclosed to opposing counsel.

(B) Extrinsic evidence of prior inconsistent statement of witness

Extrinsic evidence of a prior inconsistent statement by a witness is admissible if both of the following apply:

(1) If the statement is offered solely for the purpose of impeaching the witness, the witness is afforded a prior opportunity to explain or deny the statement and the opposite party is afforded an opportunity to interrogate the witness on the statement or the interests of justice otherwise require;

(2) The subject matter of the statement is one of the following:

(a) A fact that is of consequence to the determination of the action other than the credibility of a witness;

(b) A fact that may be shown by extrinsic evidence under Evid. R. 608(A), 609, 616(B) or 706;

(c) A fact that may be shown by extrinsic evidence under the common law of impeachment if not in conflict with the Rules of Evidence.

(C) Prior inconsistent conduct

During examination of a witness, conduct of the witness inconsistent with the witness's testimony may be shown to impeach. If offered for the sole purpose of impeaching the witness's testimony, extrinsic evidence of that prior inconsistent conduct is admissible under the same circumstances as provided for prior inconsistent statements in Evid. R. 613(B)(2).

(Adopted eff. 7–1–80; amended eff. 7–1–98)

Historical and Statutory Notes

Amendment Note: The 7–1–98 amendment rewrote the text of this Rule, which prior thereto read:

"(A) Examining witness concerning prior statement

"In examining a witness concerning a prior statement made by him, whether written or not, the statement need not be shown nor its contents disclosed to him at that time, but on request the same shall be shown or disclosed to opposing counsel.

"(B) Extrinsic evidence of prior inconsistent statement of witness

"Extrinsic evidence of a prior inconsistent statement by a witness is not admissible unless the witness is afforded a prior opportunity to explain or deny the same and the opposite party is afforded an opportunity to interrogate him thereon, or the interests of justice otherwise require. This provision does not apply to admissions of a party-opponent as defined in Rule 801(D)(2)."

Commentary

Staff Notes

1998:

Rule 613 Impeachment by self-contradiction

The amendments codify aspects of the Ohio common law of impeachment concerning prior inconsistent statements and conduct. The title of the rule was changed from "Prior Statements of Witness" to "Impeachment by Self–Contradiction" to more accurately reflect the content of the rule, which deals with prior inconsistent conduct as well as prior inconsistent statements.

Rule 613(A) Examining witness concerning prior statement

Masculine references were made gender-neutral. There was no substantive amendment to this division.

Rule 613(B) Extrinsic evidence of prior inconsistent statement of witness

As adopted in 1980, Rule 613 did not fully specify the circumstances under which extrinsic evidence of a prior inconsistent statement is admissible. Division (B)(1) sets forth the foundational requirement for the admissibility of extrinsic evidence of prior inconsistent statements. There is no substantive change from the 1980 version of the rule. The introductory clause limits the rule to impeachment. Thus, statements that are admissible substantively, such as party admissions or excited utterances, are not governed by this rule, even though they may also have an impeaching effect.

Division (B)(2) sets forth three instances in which extrinsic evidence of a prior inconsistent statement is admissible. Division (B)(2)(a) permits extrinsic evidence if the subject matter of the prior statement is a consequential fact under the substantive law. See Evid. R. 401.

Extrinsic evidence is also admitted if the statement encompasses another method of impeachment that permits the introduction of extrinsic evidence, i.e., bias under Evid. R. 616(A), or the common law. These circumstances track those of impeachment by evidence of specific contradiction as provided in Rule 616(C). See Staff Note, Evid. R. 616(C) (1998).

Rule 613(C) Prior inconsistent conduct

The 1998 amendment added division (C) to this rule. As adopted in 1980, Rule 613 did not provide for impeachment by evidence of prior inconsistent conduct. See Advisory Committee's Note, Fed. Evid. R. 613 ("Under principles of expression unius the rule does not apply to impeachment by evidence of prior inconsistent conduct."). Because no rule prohibits such impeachment, this type of evidence is admissible under Evid. R. 102 if relevant. See 1 McCormick, Evidence § 34, at 113 n. 5 (4th ed. 1992) ("Conduct... evincing a belief inconsistent with the facts asserted on the stand is usable on the same principle."). In a pre-Rules case, the Ohio Supreme Court wrote: "Conduct inconsistent with the testimony of a witness, may be shown as well as former statements thus inconsistent." *Dilcher v. State* (1883), 39 Ohio St. 130, 136 (1883). Accord *Westinghouse Electric Corp v. Dolly Madison Leasing & Furniture Corp.* (1975), 42 Ohio St.2d 122, 132, 326 N.E.2d 651 ("inconsistency in behavior" admissible for impeachment).

In *Westinghouse Electric Corp*, the Court imposed the same foundational requirements for impeachment by prior inconsistent conduct as were required for impeachment by prior inconsistent statements: "an adequate foundation for admission of the film was laid during cross–examination... and the witness was allowed to explain the apparent inconsistency upon redirect." 42 Ohio St.2d at 132.

This division applies to the impeachment of a witness, including a party who testifies. It does not, however, apply to a party's inconsistent conduct that may be introduced on the merits; admissions by the conduct of a party (sometimes known as "implied admissions") may be admissible substantively and are not restricted by this rule. See 1 Giannelli & Snyder, Baldwin's Ohio Practice Evidence § 401.8–.10 (1996) (adverse inferences: spoliation, admissions by conduct, failure to produce evidence or call witnesses).

1980:

Rule 613(A) Examining Witness Concerning Prior Statement

The rule is identical to Federal Evidence Rule 613(a) and represents a departure from prior Ohio law. Ohio has followed the rule established in *Queen Caroline's Case* (1820), 129 Eng. Rep. 976. That rule requires the cross-examiner to show the witness his prior written statement before questioning. The rationale of the decision was fairness. See Stern and Grosh, *A Visit with Queen Caroline: Her Trial and its Rule*, 6 Cap. U. L. Rev. 165 (1977). The rule was abolished by statute in England. Stat. 17 & 18 Vict, c 125, section 25 (1854). The abolition of Queen Caroline's Rule removes an automatic impediment to the cross-examiner. The provision for disclosing the prior statement to opposing counsel preserves the concept of fairness and protects against abuse of the provision.

Rule 613(B) Extrinsic Evidence of Prior Inconsistent Statement of Witness

Prior Ohio law, as a prerequisite to extrinsic proof, required the laying of a foundation in the cross-examination of the witness, the foundation including the time and place of the statement, the person to whom it was made, advising him as to content, and interrogating him as to whether or not such a statement was made. 56 OJur 2d Witnesses § 380. Rule 613(B) preconditions admission of a prior inconsistent statement on the witness' opportunity to explain or deny the same and the opposite party's opportunity to interrogate on the statement. The rule does not do away with the necessity of laying a foundation, a procedure most easily accomplished at the time the witness is cross-examined.

Rule 613(B) differs from the Federal Evidence Rule counterpart in that the witness must be afforded a *prior* opportunity to explain or deny any previous statements, thus making certain that the witness has had such opportunity *before* the extrinsic evidence is admitted.

Cross References

Discovery and inspection, disclosure of evidence, by defendant, by prosecuting attorney, Crim R 16
Use of depositions in court proceedings, Civ R 32

Library References

Witnesses ⬥388(1) to 389.

Westlaw Topic No. 410.

C.J.S. Witnesses §§ 598 to 613.

OJur 3d: 29A, Criminal Law § 3137, 3139, 3142; 44, Evidence and Witnesses § 948

Am Jur 2d: 81, Witnesses § 596 et seq, 638

Admissibility, for purpose of supporting impeached witness, of prior statements by him consistent with his testimony. 75 ALR2d 909

Denial of recollection as inconsistent with prior statement so as to render statement admissible. 99 ALR3d 934

Admissibility of affidavit to impeach witness. 14 ALR4th 828

Use or admissibility of prior inconsistent statements of witness as substantive evidence of facts to which they relate in criminal case—modern state cases. 30 ALR4th 414

Use of prior inconsistent statements for impeachment of testimony of witnesses under Rule 613, Federal Rules of Evidence. 40 ALR Fed 629

Katz & Giannelli, Baldwin's Ohio Practice, Criminal Law § 31.2, 49.15 (1996).

Giannelli & Snyder, Baldwin's Ohio Practice, Evidence § 105.1, 410.10, 607.1, 607.7, 608, 608.1, 608.5, 616, 616.1, 616.7, 801, 801.12, 804.9, 806.7, 901.18, 1101 (2d ed. 2001).

Ohio Personal Injury Practice (2002 Ed.), Text 5.02.

Evid R 614   Calling and interrogation of witnesses by court

(A) Calling by court

The court may, on its own motion or at the suggestion of a party, call witnesses, and all parties are entitled to cross-examine witnesses thus called.

(B) Interrogation by court

The court may interrogate witnesses, in an impartial manner, whether called by itself or by a party.

(C) Objections

Objections to the calling of witnesses by the court or to interrogation by it may be made at the time or at the next available opportunity when the jury is not present.

(Adopted eff. 7–1–80)

Commentary

Staff Notes

1980:

Rule 614 is identical to Federal Evidence Rule 614.

Rule 614(A) Calling by Court

Rule 614(A) conforms to prior Ohio law where it has been well established that the authority to call witnesses is within the inherent power of the court, the court having a fundamental duty to arrive at the truth. 52 OJur 2d Trial § 20.

Rule 614(B) Interrogation by the Court

Rule 614(B) conforms to prior Ohio law. 52 OJur 2d Trial § 20. The rule, however, does not permit the court to interrogate a witness in a manner which conveys the judge's opinion of the witness or his testimony to the jury. *State, ex rel. Wise, v. Chand* (1970), 21 Ohio St.2d 113. The rule explicitly adopts the prior Ohio law by inserting the phrase "in an impartial manner" as a requisite of interrogation by the court. This requirement is merely implicit in Federal Evidence Rule 614(b).

Rule 614(C) Objections

Raising an objection to the calling of a witness by the court or to the court's interrogation of a witness might be misunderstood by the jury and might not be appreciated by the judge in the presence of the jury, thus the provision is made for objection either at the time or at the next available opportunity when the jury is not present.

Library References

Witnesses ⟐246(1) to 246(5).

Westlaw Topic No. 410.

C.J.S. Witnesses §§ 348 to 351.

OJur 3d: 29, Criminal Law § 2674, 3128; 89, Trial § 19 to 22, 32, 33

Am Jur 2d: 81, Witnesses § 3, 359 to 362, 419

Propriety of jurors asking questions in open court during course of trial. 31 ALR3d 872

Manner or extent of trial judge's examination of witnesses in civil cases. 6 ALR4th 951

Calling and interrogation of witness by court under Rule 614 of the Federal Rules of Evidence. 53 ALR Fed 498

Giannelli & Snyder, Baldwin's Ohio Practice, Evidence § 607.4, 611.1, 614.4, 702.7, 901.23 (2d ed. 2001).

Evid R 615   Separation and exclusion of witnesses

(A) Except as provided in division (B) of this rule, at the request of a party the court shall order witnesses excluded so that they cannot hear the testimony of other witnesses, and it may make the order of its own motion. An order directing the "exclusion" or "separation" of witnesses or the like, in general terms without specification of other or additional limitations, is effective only to require the exclusion of witnesses from the hearing during the testimony of other witnesses.

(B) This rule does not authorize exclusion of any of the following persons from the hearing:

(1) a party who is a natural person;

(2) an officer or employee of a party that is not a natural person designated as its representative by its attorney;

(3) a person whose presence is shown by a party to be essential to the presentation of the party's cause;

(4) in a criminal proceeding, a victim of the charged offense to the extent that the victim's presence is authorized by statute enacted by the General Assembly. As used in this rule, "victim" has the same meaning as in the provisions of the Ohio Constitution providing rights for victims of crimes.

(Adopted eff. 7–1–80; amended eff. 7–1–01, 7–1–03)

Historical and Statutory Notes

Amendment Note: The 7–1–01 amendment redesignated former divisions (1) through (3) as new divisions (A) through (C); made changes to reflect gender neutral language and other nonsubstantive changes; and added new division (D).

Commentary

Staff Notes

2003:

Rule 615 Separation and Exclusion of Witnesses

The amendment changed the title of the rule from Exclusion of Witnesses to better reflect its subject matter, divided the rule into divisions to enhance clarity, and made a grammatical correction in new division (B)(2) (former division (B)). No substantive changes were intended by these modifications. Substantively, the amendment established requirements of specificity and notice for orders that regulate communications and contact by or with witnesses during a hearing.

Ohio courts have long exercised authority to order the "separation" of witnesses in order to limit the possibility that the witnesses' testimony might be influenced by the accounts of other witnesses. As originally adopted, Evid. R. 615 followed the federal model in addressing only one kind of separation order, that is, orders excluding witnesses from the courtroom during the testimony of other witnesses. Additional forms of separation were used in Ohio long before adoption of the rule, including, for example, orders limiting out-of-court contact between witnesses, or between witnesses and third-parties. Ohio courts have continued to employ these devices in the years since adoption of the rule. While the rule makes exclusion from the courtroom mandatory on the motion of a party, it is well established that trial courts continue to possess broad and flexible discretion in deciding what additional forms of separation, if any, are appropriate. The breadth of the discretion is reflected in the variety of different separation orders to be found in reported cases and in trial court practice. The variety of separation orders is accompanied by correspondingly diverse views among lawyers and courts (and sometimes among judges in the same court) regarding what additional forms of separation are generally appropriate or ought routinely to be imposed.

In practice, it is most common for trial courts to enter highly abbreviated orders on the subject. Normally a party will move for the "separation" (or "exclusion") of witnesses, and the court will respond with a general statement that the motion is granted. This is usually followed by an announcement to the gallery that prospective witnesses should leave the courtroom and by a statement that the parties are responsible for policing the presence of their own witnesses. Though some courts then orally announce additional limitations on communications to or by witnesses, the far more usual approach is simply to assume that the generic order of "separation" adequately conveys whatever limitations have been imposed.

The brevity of the rule and of most separation orders has led to "confusion about how far the scope of a bald Rule 615 order extends," *United States v. McMahon*, 104 F.3d 638, 648 (4th Cir.1997) (dissenting opinion). Some courts, in Ohio and elsewhere, have suggested that at least some additional forms of separation are implicit even in generally stated orders. This approach, however, entails significant issues of fair warning, since the "implicit" terms of an order may not be revealed to the parties or witnesses until after the putative violation has occurred. That is especially so when the "violation" involves conduct or communications about which there is a great diversity of opinion and practice. (Indeed, even among jurisdictions that follow this approach, there is disagreement as to what additional restrictions are necessarily implied in a generic separation order.) The imposition of sanctions without advance warning that the conduct is sanctionable raises obvious due-process concerns. Moreover, an "implicit-terms" approach is inconsistent with the principle that separation of witnesses beyond exclusion from the courtroom is neither automatic nor a matter of right: if witnesses and parties are bound by implicit additional restrictions whenever exclusion is ordered, then the additional restrictions are in fact automatic and non-discretionary.

The amendment rejects an "implicit-terms" approach and adopts instead the narrower rule employed by several Ohio courts and by what appears to be a majority of other jurisdictions that have addressed the question. Under this rule, generally-stated or "bald" separation orders are effective only to order the exclusion of witnesses from the courtroom during the testimony of other witnesses. *See,* e.g., *State v. Rogers* (Ohio App., 4th Distr., Nov. 15, 2000), unreported, 2000 WL 1728076, at *6–*7, *app. Dism.* (2001), 91 Ohio St. 3d 1471. *See also U.S. v. Rhynes* (4th Cir. 2000), 218 F.3d 310, 321 n. 13 (en banc); *State v. Brown* (Conn. App. 1999), 741 A.2d 321, 325; *In re H.S.H.* (Ill. App. 2001), 751 N.E.2d 1236, 1241–1242. A separation order does not forbid other conduct by witnesses, such as being present during opening statements or discussing the case with other witnesses outside the courtroom. To the extent that a trial court, in the exercise of its discretion, determines to order forms of separation in addition to exclusion, it remains free to do so, but it can do so only by making the additional restrictions explicit and by giving the parties notice of the specific additional restrictions that have been ordered. Notice to the parties is required because, with the exception of contempt, sanctions for violation of the rule tend to have their greatest effect on the parties, rather on the witnesses.

The amendment does not define the standards for ordering forms of separation in addition to exclusion, or the kinds of additional separation that are permissible. Nor does the amendment address the matter of sanctions when a separation order has been violated. These subjects have long been committed to the sound discretion of trial courts to be exercised flexibly within well-established limits. *See, e.g., State v. Smith* (1990), 49 Ohio St.3d 137, 142 (excluding testimony as a sanction is proper only if the party calling the witness "consented to, connived in, [or] procured" the violation, or had knowledge of the witness's disobedience and failed to take affirmative steps to prevent it). The amendment does not change the law on these subjects.

2001:

Rule 615 Exclusion of Witnesses

Divisions (1)–(3) of the previous rule were redesignated as divisions (A)–(C). Clarifying punctuation was inserted immediately before division (A), and in division (C) a masculine reference was replaced with gender-neutral language. No substantive change was intended by either of these amendments.

The substantive amendment added division (D) to the rule recognizing a new category of witnesses who are not subject to an order excluding them from hearing the testimony of other witnesses. In particular, the amended rule permits the victim of an offense to be present at a criminal proceeding regarding the offense to the extent that the victim's presence is authorized by statute enacted by the General Assembly. The right of a victim to be present is limited to those persons who are "victims" within the meaning of the constitutional provisions regarding victims' rights. *See* Ohio Const., Art. I, § 10a. The amendment is designed to harmonize the rule with the provisions of R.C. 2930.09, which permits a victim to be present at any stage of a criminal proceeding conducted on the record (other than a grand jury proceeding) when the defendant is present, "unless the court determines that exclusion of the victim is necessary to protect the defendant's right to a fair trial."

Ordinarily, rules governing witness sequestration would be regarded as "procedural" matters within the meaning of the Modern Courts Amendment, Ohio

Const., Art. IV, § 5(B), so that a rule of practice and procedure (such as Evid. R. 615) would prevail over an inconsistent statute on the same subject (such as R.C. 2930.09). In this instance, however, the statute involves an exercise of the General Assembly's power under the victims' rights provisions of the Ohio Constitution. Ohio Const., Art. I, § 10a. It is at least arguable that legislation enacted under the authority of section 10a is not displaced or rendered ineffective by reason of its inconsistency with a rule of practice and procedure. The amendment is intended to eliminate the conflict between the statute and the rule by deferring to the statutory right of a victim to be present at criminal proceedings. The deference extends only to the right of a *victim* to be present, and only in criminal proceedings. Moreover, whatever the statutory definition of "victim," the rule exempts from sequestration only those persons who are permitted by statute to be present *and* who are "victims" within the meaning of Article I, Section 10a of the Ohio Constitution. These limitations correspond to the extent of the General Assembly's power under the victims' rights provisions of the constitution.

The principal object of witness sequestration orders is to minimize the risk that a witness's testimony will be materially affected by hearing the testimony of other witnesses. Neither the statute nor the amended rule impairs the ability of trial courts to deal effectively with this risk when it exists. Under the statute (as well as under the constitution), the victim's right to be present is limited by the defendant's right to a fair trial. Thus, exclusion of a victim-witness would be permissible in cases in which the trial court is persuaded that the victim-witness's testimony would be altered by reason of the witness's presence during the testimony of other witnesses.

1980:

Rule 615 is identical to Federal Evidence Rule 615. Under prior Ohio law, the separation of witnesses was a matter within the discretion of the trial court. *In re Brown, Weiss and Wohl* (1963), 175 Ohio St. 149. The rule serves to modify the former Ohio law in one regard. Under the rule, a party has a right to the separation of witnesses upon his request.

The enumeration of persons who are not to be excluded from the court room under a separation order is in conformity to prior Ohio law.

Library References

Criminal Law ⊃665(1) to 665(7).

Trial ⊃41(1) to 41(5).

Westlaw Topic Nos. 110, 388.

C.J.S. Contempt § 25.

C.J.S. Criminal Law §§ 1195 to 1199.

C.J.S. Trial §§ 65 to 70.

OJur 3d: 29, Criminal Law § 2658; 89, Trial § 136 to 139

Am Jur 2d: 32B, Federal Rules of Evidence § 348 to 355; 75, Trial § 61 et seq.; 81, Witnesses § 73

Prejudicial effect of improper failure to exclude from courtroom or to sequester or separate state's witnesses in criminal case. 32 ALR2d 358

Exclusion of public during criminal trial. 48 ALR2d 1436

Exclusion from courtroom of expert witnesses during taking of testimony in civil case. 85 ALR2d 478

Effect of witness' violation of order of exclusion. 14 ALR3d 16

Prejudicial effect of improper failure to exclude from courtroom or to sequester or separate witnesses in criminal case. 74 ALR4th 705

Exclusion of witnesses under Rule 615 of the Federal Rules of Evidence. 48 ALR Fed 484

Giannelli & Snyder, Baldwin's Ohio Practice, Evidence § 703.6, 1101 (2d ed. 2001).

Wasil, Waite, & Mastrangelo, Ohio Workers' Compensation Law § 14:167.

Carlin, Baldwin's Ohio Practice, Merrick–Rippner Probate Law § 107.56 (2003).

Evid R 616   Methods of impeachment

In addition to other methods, a witness may be impeached by any of the following methods:

(A) Bias

Bias, prejudice, interest, or any motive to misrepresent may be shown to impeach the witness either by examination of the witness or by extrinsic evidence.

(B) Sensory or mental defect

A defect of capacity, ability, or opportunity to observe, remember, or relate may be shown to impeach the witness either by examination of the witness or by extrinsic evidence.

(C) Specific contradiction

Facts contradicting a witness's testimony may be shown for the purpose of impeaching the witness's testimony. If offered for the sole purpose of impeaching a witness's testimony, extrinsic evidence of contradiction is inadmissible unless the evidence is one of the following:

(1) Permitted by Evid. R. 608(A), 609, 613, 616(A), 616(B), or 706;

(2) Permitted by the common law of impeachment and not in conflict with the Rules of Evidence.

(Adopted eff. 7–1–91; amended eff. 7–1–98)

Historical and Statutory Notes

Amendment Note: The 7–1–98 amendment substituted "Methods of Impeachment" for "Bias of Witness" in the title of the Rule; and rewrote the text of the Rule, which prior thereto read:

"Bias, prejudice, interest, or any motive to misrepresent may be shown to impeach the witness either by examination of the witness or by extrinsic evidence."

Commentary

Staff Notes

1998:

Rule 616 Methods of impeachment

The amendments to this rule codify two common law rules of impeachment, making them more readily accessible for trial use. The prior rule was lettered division (A) but was not otherwise changed by the 1998 amendment; divisions (B)and (C) were added by this amendment. Also, the title of the rule was changed from "Bias of Witness" to "Methods of Impeachment."

Rule 616(B) Sensory or mental defect

The pre-Rules cases permitted inquiry into a witness's capacity to observe, remember, and recall. See *State v. Auerbach* (1923), 108 Ohio St. 96, 98, 140 N.E. 507 ("means of observation"); *Morgan v. State* (1891), 48 Ohio St. 371, 373–74, 27 N.E. 710 (opportunity to observe, "intelligence"); *Lee v. State* (1871), 21 Ohio St. 151, 154 (recollection), and *McAllister v. State* (App. 1932), 13 Ohio Law Abs. 360, 362 (mental condition affects credibility); as well as other factors affecting perception and memory. *Stewart v. State* (1850), 19 Ohio 302, 304 (proper to cross-examine witness on opportunity to observe and to remember).

The post-Rules cases are in accord. The Supreme Court has ruled that a witness's visual impairment is not a ground for incompetency under Evid. R. 601, but rather a factor "relat[ing] to the credibility of the statements made by [the witness]." *Turner v. Turner*(1993), 67 Ohio St.3d 337, 343, 617 N.E.2d 1123. See also *Kenney v. Fealko* (1991), 75 Ohio App.3d 47, 51, 598 N.E.2d 861 ("The Ohio Rules of Evidence do not enumerate the various ways in which the credibility of a witness can properly be attacked.... Under [Evid. R. 611(B)] and the common-law rule, evidence of appellant's state of intoxication was admissible because it was relevant to the issue of her ability to perceive and hence her credibility.").

Division (B) provides for the admissibility of this type of evidence on cross-examination or through extrinsic evidence (i.e., the testimony of other witnesses). This provision does not change Evid. R. 601, which governs the competency of witnesses, or Evid. R. 602, which specifies the firsthand-knowledge requirement.

Rule 616(C) Specific contradiction

There are two distinct methods of impeachment by contradiction. First, self-contradiction involves the use of a witness's own prior inconsistent statements or conduct to contradict the witness's present testimony. Evid. R. 613 governs this type of impeachment.

Second, contradiction may involve the testimony of one witness that conflicts with the testimony of another witness (called "specific contradiction"). The circumstances under which a party may introduce extrinsic evidence of contradiction is typically stated in terms of the so-called "collateral matters" rule. E.g., *Byomin v. Alvis* (1959), 169 Ohio St. 395, 396, 159 N.E.2d 897 (per curiam) ("It is elementary that a witness may not be impeached by evidence that merely contradicts his testimony on a matter that is collateral."); *State v. Cochrane* (1949), 151 Ohio St. 128, 135, 84 N.E.2d 742 ("The cross-examiner is not permitted to introduce rebuttal evidence to contradict the witness on collateral matters.").

The common law rule does not prohibit a party from cross-examining on a "collateral matter." It prohibits only the introduction of extrinsic evidence on the issue. The policy underlying this rule is to "avoid [] the dangers of surprise, jury confusion and wasted time which are the reasons for the rule against impeachment on collateral matters." *State v. Kehn* (1977), 50 Ohio St.2d 11, 17, 361 N.E.2d 1330 (per curiam), cert. denied, 434 U.S. 858, 98 S.Ct. 180, 54 L.Ed.2d 130 (1977).

According to Wigmore, extrinsic evidence of contradiction should be admitted if the evidence would be admissible "for any purpose independently of the contradiction." 3A Wigmore, Evidence § 1003, at

961 (Chadbourn rev. 1970). Explaining this test, McCormick wrote that two types of facts were independently provable: "The first kind are facts that are relevant to the substantive issues in the case". McCormick, Evidence § 47, at 110–11 (3d ed. 1984). Because Rule 616(C) is limited to impeachment, evidence concerning the substantive issues is governed by Rules 401 to 403, not this rule.

The second category are "facts showing bias, interest, conviction of crime, and want of capacity or opportunity for knowledge." Id. In other words, the second category encompasses those methods of impeachment, such as bias, that always permit the introduction of extrinsic evidence. The Ohio Supreme Court appears to have adopted Wigmore's approach in an early case. *Kent v. State* (1884), 42 Ohio St. 426, 431 (Extrinsic evidence is admissible when "the matter offered in contradiction is in any way relevant to the issue, or such as tends to show prejudice or interest."). Evid. R. 616(C)(1) enumerates the rules that fall within this category.

McCormick argued that extrinsic evidence of contradiction should also be admitted in a third situation, one in which such evidence is critical to determining the credibility of a witness's story. He refers to this as "linchpin" evidence: "So we may recognize this third type of allowable contradiction, namely, the contradiction of any part of the witness's account of the background and circumstances of a material transaction, which as a matter of human experience he would not have been mistaken about if his story was true." McCormick, Evidence § 47, at 112 (3d ed. 1984). McCormick provides several examples: *Stephens v. People*, 19 N.Y. 549, 572 (1859) (murder by poisoning with arsenic; defendant's witnesses testified the arsenic was administered to rats in cellar where provisions kept; held proper for state to prove by another witness that no provisions were kept in cellar); *Hartsfield v. Carolina Cas. Ins. Co.*, 451 P.2d 576 (Alaska 1969) (on issue whether insurance cancellation notice was sent to defendant by insurer, defendant denied receipt and also receipt of notices of cancellations of the insurance from two other sources. Evidence of the mailing by the two latter sources was held not collateral). Division (C)(2) of this rule encompasses this category. The phrase "not in conflict with these rules" is intended to ensure that this provision is not used to circumvent the prohibition on the admissibility of extrinsic evidence of specific acts found in Evid. R. 608(B); Evid. R. 608(B) controls.

Extrinsic evidence defined

In the impeachment context, extrinsic evidence means evidence introduced through the testimony of other witnesses. See 1 McCormick, Evidence § 36, at 118 (4th ed. 1992) ("Extrinsic evidence, that is, the production of attacking witnesses... is sharply narrowed for obvious reasons of economy of time and attention."). Accordingly, documentary evidence offered through the witness being impeached is not extrinsic evidence because it typically does not consumed [sic.] much additional time.

1991:

As originally adopted, neither the Ohio nor the Federal Rules contained a rule governing impeachment regarding bias or interest. In *United States v. Abel* (1984), 469 U.S. 45, 105 S.Ct. 465, 83 L.Ed.2d 450, the U.S. Supreme Court held that impeachment of a witness for bias was proper, notwithstanding the lack of a specific rule. According to the Court, "the lesson to be drawn... is that it is permissible to impeach a witness by showing his bias under the Fed. Rules of Evid. just as it was permissible to do so before their adoption." Id. at 51.

Impeachment by bias also is permitted in Ohio. R.C. 2945.42 provides: "No person is disqualified as a witness in a criminal prosecution by reason of his interest in the prosecution as a party or otherwise.... Such interest... may be shown for the purpose of affecting the credibility of such witness." In addition, the Ohio Supreme Court has written: "It is beyond question that a witness' bias and prejudice by virtue of pecuniary interest in the outcome of the proceeding is a matter affecting credibility under Evid. R. 611(B)." *State v. Ferguson* (1983), 5 Ohio St.3d 160, 165, 450 N.E.2d 265. Evid. R. 611(B), however, is the general provision on cross-examination and does not mention explicitly the term bias.

The Rules of Evidence contain a number of impeachment rules (Rules 607, 608, 609, and 613). Because of its importance as a traditional method of impeachment, bias also should be explicitly treated in the Rules of Evidence, as it is in some jurisdictions. *See* Unif. R. Evid. 616; Haw. R. Evid. 609.1; Utah R. Evid. 608(c); Mil. R. Evid. 608(c).

Library References

Witnesses ⬤363(1) to 378.

Westlaw Topic No. 410.

C.J.S. Witnesses §§ 490, 538 to 572.

OJur 3d: 29A, Criminal Law § 3139, 3142, 3144

Giannelli & Snyder, Baldwin's Ohio Practice, Evidence § 102.4, 408.7, 102, 608, 403.6, 410.10, 411.6, 607.1, 607.7, 608.1, 608.5, 608.6, 1101, 609.3, 609.5, 613.1, 613.7, 706.1, 806.4, 613 (2d ed. 2001).

Article VII

OPINIONS AND EXPERT TESTIMONY

Rule

701 Opinion testimony by lay witnesses
702 Testimony by experts
703 Bases of opinion testimony by experts
704 Opinion on ultimate issue
705 Disclosure of facts or data underlying expert opinion
706 Learned treatises for impeachment

Evid R 701 Opinion testimony by lay witnesses

If the witness is not testifying as an expert, his testimony in the form of opinions or inferences is limited to those opinions or inferences which are (1) rationally based on the perception of the witness and (2) helpful to a clear understanding of his testimony or the determination of a fact in issue.

(Adopted eff. 7–1–80)

Commentary

Staff Notes

1980:

The rule is stated in language identical to that of Federal Evidence Rule 701.

It places two limitations upon the admissibility of non-expert opinion evidence. First, the opinions or inferences included in the testimony must be rationally based on the perception of the witness. Second, the opinions or inferences must be helpful to a clear understanding of the testimony or to the determination of a fact in issue.

The rule is in accordance with Ohio law as it has developed prior to the adoption of the Rules of Evidence.

Ohio has long adhered to the general rule that only facts can be given in evidence by a non-expert witness, leaving the necessary and natural deductions from those facts to be made by the jury. The general rule precludes the non-expert witness from testifying as to opinions, inferences, impressions, or conclusions which he draws from the facts he has observed. *Hartford Protection Insurance Co. v. Isaiah C. Harmer* (1853), 2 Ohio St. 452.

Ohio has also long recognized that there is an exception to the general rule which permits a non-expert witness to express his opinion. The exception is made for testimony which is a compound of fact and opinion. *Steamboat Clipper v. Logan* (1849), 18 Ohio 375, 396. A prime example is that of the non-expert witness testifying as to physical condition. The witness is permitted to testify in the form of a conclusion because the primary facts gained from observation and upon which the conclusion is based are too numerous to detail.

In recognizing the exception to the general rule, Ohio has placed it under two limitations, the same two limitations which appear in Rule 701. The first limitation has been expressed as a requirement of an intelligent and reasonable conclusion based upon facts observed. *American Louisiana Pipe Line Co. v. Kennerk* (1957), 103 Ohio App. 133. In delineating the second limitation, earlier Ohio law has not utilized the term helpful. The exception has been described as a rule of necessity, the only efficient proof of fact. *Village of Shelby v. Clagget [Clagett]* (1889), 46 Ohio St. 549. In *Railroad Company v. Schultz* (1885), 43 Ohio St. 270, the court said, at 282:

In matters more within the common observation and experience of men, non-experts may, in cases where it is not practicable to place before the jury all the primary facts upon which they are founded, state their opinions from such facts, where such opinions involve conclusions material to the subject of inquiry.

The Advisory Committee Note to Federal Evidence Rule 701 indicates that "helpful" was chosen because "necessity" had proved to be too elusive and too unadaptable to serve as a standard.

Although Ohio has used "necessity" to describe the basis for admitting non-expert opinion, it has also qualified the term with reference to efficiency of proof and to practicability. It appears that the disparity between Ohio's former concept of necessity and the Federal Rule's concept of helpful is minimal.

Library References

Criminal Law ⬤448(1) to 463.

Evidence ⬤470 to 498.

Westlaw Topic Nos. 110, 157.

C.J.S. Criminal Law §§ 1050 to 1058.

C.J.S. Evidence §§ 509 to 688.

OJur 3d: 29A, Criminal Law § 3088, 3091; 33, Decedents' Estates § 1188; 43, Evidence and Witnesses § 592; 59, Insurance § 1400; 79, Railroads § 404

Am Jur 2d: 31, Expert and Opinion Evidence § 14, 15

Foundation or predicate to permit nonexpert witness to give opinion, in a civil action, as to sanity, mental competency, or mental condition. 40 ALR2d 15

Admissibility of opinion evidence as to point of impact or collision in motor vehicle accident case. 66 ALR2d 1048

Propriety of questioning expert witness regarding specific incidents or allegations of expert's unprofessional conduct or professional negligence. 11 ALR5th 1

Admissibility, in homicide prosecution, of evidence as to tests made to ascertain distance from gun to victim when gun was fired. 11 ALR5th 497

Sufficiency of evidence that witness in criminal case was hypnotized, for purpose of determining admissibility of testimony given under hypnosis or of hypnotically enhanced testimony. 16 ALR5th 841

Construction and application of Rule 701 of Federal Rules of Evidence, providing for opinion testimony by lay witnesses under certain circumstances. 44 ALR Fed 919

Painter, Ohio Driving Under the Influence Law (2003 Ed.), Text 17.7, 17.8.

Giannelli & Snyder, Baldwin's Ohio Practice, Evidence § 406.7, 602.1, 613.5, 704, 704.1, 704.3, 704.4, 801.20, 803.4, 803.13, 804.18, 901.6 (2d ed. 2001).

Adrine & Ruden, Ohio Domestic Violence Law (2002 Ed.), Text 15.8.

Ohio Personal Injury Practice (2002 Ed.), Text 6.04.

Carlin, Baldwin's Ohio Practice, Merrick–Rippner Probate Law § 43.10, 43.15 (2003).

Evid R 702   Testimony by experts

A witness may testify as an expert if all of the following apply:

(A) The witness' testimony either relates to matters beyond the knowledge or experience possessed by lay persons or dispels a misconception common among lay persons;

(B) The witness is qualified as an expert by specialized knowledge, skill, experience, training, or education regarding the subject matter of the testimony;

(C) The witness' testimony is based on reliable scientific, technical, or other specialized information. To the extent that the testimony reports the result of a procedure, test, or experiment, the testimony is reliable only if all of the following apply:

(1) The theory upon which the procedure, test, or experiment is based is objectively verifiable or is validly derived from widely accepted knowledge, facts, or principles;

(2) The design of the procedure, test, or experiment reliably implements the theory;

(3) The particular procedure, test, or experiment was conducted in a way that will yield an accurate result.

(Adopted eff. 7–1–80; amended eff. 7–1–94)

Historical and Statutory Notes

Amendment Note: The 7–1–94 amendment rewrote this rule, which previously read:

"If scientific, technical, or other specialized knowledge will assist the trier of fact to understand the evidence or to determine a fact in issue, a witness qualified as an expert by knowledge, skill, experience, training, or education, may testify thereto in the form of an opinion or otherwise."

Commentary

Staff Notes

1994:

Rule 702 Testimony by Experts

The amendment is intended to clarify the circumstances in which expert testimony is admissible, a subject on which the language of the pre-amendment rule has proved to be uninformative and, at times, misleading. Because the intention is to reflect the Ohio Supreme Court's interpretations of the rule's pre-amendment language, no substantive change from prior law is intended. In particular, there is no intention to change existing Ohio law regarding the reliability of expert testimony.

As originally adopted, Evid. R. 702 employed the same language as is used in the Federal Rules of Evidence to define the admissibility of expert testimony. That language permits a witness with the appropriate expertise to testify as an expert if the testimony "will assist the trier of fact." Evid. R. 702 (1980); F.R.Evid., Rule 702.

The "assist the trier" standard has been the subject of widely varying interpretations in the jurisdictions that have adopted it. In Ohio, however, decisions by the Supreme Court have established that the phrase incorporates two distinct admissibility requirements in addition to the witness's expertise.

First, as at common law, an expert's testimony "assist [s] the trier" only if it relates to a matter "beyond the ken" of the ordinary person. *State v. Koss* (1990), 49 Ohio St.3d 213, 216 (expert testimony is not admissible "when such knowledge is within the ken of the jury"); *State v. Buell* (1980), 22 Ohio St. 3d 124, 131 (expert testimony is admissible if the subject is "sufficiently beyond common experience"), *cert denied*, 479 U.S. 871 (1986); *State v. Thomas* (1981), 66 Ohio St.2d 518, 521 (expert testimony is inadmissible if the subject is not "beyond the ken of the average lay person").

Second, the expert's testimony "assist [s] the trier" only if it meets a threshold standard of reliability, as established either by testimony or by judicial notice. (The trier of fact remains free, of course, to make its own assessment of reliability and to accept or reject the testimony accordingly once it has been admitted.) See *State v. Bresson* (1990), 51 Ohio St.3d 123, 128 (prior case-law establishing reliability of test sufficed to show reliability as a general matter, and test was admissible on a case-specific showing regarding the tester's qualifications and the reliability of the specific test administration); *State v. Williams* (1983), 4

Ohio St.3d 53, 59 (expert testimony as to test was admissible " [i]n view of the unrebutted evidence of reliability of [the test] in general, and of [the witness's] analysis in particular"). See also *State v. Pierce* (1992), 64 Ohio St.3d 490, 494–501 (scientific evidence was admissible where unreliability in specific case was not shown and where balance of probative value and reliability against risk of misleading or confusing the jury did not warrant exclusion).

As to the reliability requirement, the Ohio cases have not adopted a definitive test of the showing required for expert testimony generally. The Ohio cases have, however, clearly rejected the standard of *Frye v. United States* (D.C. Cir. 1923), 293 F. 1013, under which scientific opinions are admissible only if the theory or test in question enjoys "general acceptance" within a relevant scientific community. See *Williams, supra,* 4 Ohio St.3d at 58; *Pierce, supra,* 64 Ohio St.3d at 496. See also *Daubert v. Merrell Dow Pharmaceuticals, Inc.* (1993), __ U.S. __, 113 S.Ct. 2786 (similarly rejecting *Frye* and describing the reliability standard to be employed under the federal counterpart to Evid. R. 702.)

Under Ohio law it is also clear that reliability is properly determined only by reference to the principles and methods employed by the expert witness, without regard to whether the court regards the witness's conclusions themselves as persuasive or correct. See *Pierce, supra,* 64 Ohio St.3d at 498 (emphasizing that unreliability could not be shown by differences in the conclusions of experts, without evidence that the procedures employed were "somehow deficient"). See also *Daubert, supra,* 113 S.Ct. at 2797 (the focus "must be solely on principles and methodology, not on the conclusions they generate").

In view of the interpretation given to the "assist the trier" standard by the Ohio Supreme Court's decisions, the Rule's original language has been at best uninformative, and it appears to have been affirmatively misleading in some cases. It has been unhelpful to courts and attorneys seeking guidance on the admissibility of challenged testimony, often in the midst of trial, because the language itself does not self-evidently convey the specific content that has been given to it by authoritative judicial interpretations.

Moreover, a review of intermediate appellate decisions suggests that the language has been misleading to at least some Ohio lawyers and courts. In particular, in some cases, the parties and the courts have relied on decisions from other jurisdictions that have given a different content to the phrase "assist the trier," and they have as a result mistakenly assumed that Ohio law is in accord with the law of those other jurisdictions.

The amendment is intended to enhance the utility of the rule, and to reduce the occasions for mistaken interpretation, by substituting a codification of the above-noted Supreme Court holdings in place of the vague and misleading "assist the trier" language. Thus, the amended rule expressly states the three existing requirements for the admissibility of expert testimony:

(1) The witness must be qualified to testify by reason of specialized knowledge, skill, experience, training, or education. Evid. R. 702(B), incorporating original Evid. R. 702.

(2) The witness's testimony must relate to matters beyond the knowledge or experience possessed by lay persons, or dispel a misconception common among lay persons. Evid. R. 702(A), codifying *Koss, Buell,* and *Thomas, supra.* (The reference to "dispel [ling] a misconception" is a codification of the specific holding in *Koss, supra,* 49 Ohio St.3d

at 216, that the permissible subject matter of expert testimony includes not only matters beyond common knowledge, but also matters of common but mistaken belief.)

(3) The witness's testimony must have its basis in reliable scientific, technical, or otherwise specialized knowledge. Evid. R. 702(C), codifying *Bresson* and *Williams, supra.* As to evidence regarding a "test, procedure, or experiment," reliability must be shown both as to the test generally (that is, the underlying theory and the implementation of the theory), Evid. R. 702(C)(1) & (2), and as to the specific application. Evid. R. 702(C)(3). See *Bresson, supra; Williams, supra.* See generally 1 P. Giannelli and E. Imwinkelried, Scientific Evidence 1–2 (2d ed. 1993).

Consistently with the intention to do no more than codify existing holdings on the admissibility of expert testimony, the amended rule does not attempt to define the standard of reliability but leaves that to further development through case-law. The amendment also leaves unchanged Ohio's rejection of *Frye* as the exclusive standard of reliability. Similarly, the amendment does not purport to supplant existing case-law as to the acceptable means for showing reliability, whether through judicial notice or testimony. Further, the law remains unchanged that the inquiry as to reliability is appropriately directed, not to the correctness or credibility of the conclusions reached by the expert witness, but to the reliability of the principles and methods used to reach those conclusions.

(While decisions under the federal rules of evidence are frequently inapposite to the interpretation of the Ohio rules, see Evid. R. 102, the federal counterpart to Evid. R. 702 has been interpreted as incorporating a reliability requirement. *Daubert, supra.* To that extent, the United States Supreme Court's discussion of the considerations that may be relevant to a reliability determination may also be helpful in construing the Ohio rule. See *id.,* 113 S.Ct. at 2795–2796.)

Because the amendment is not intended to change existing law, the procedure for challenging and determining the admissibility of expert proofs likewise remains unchanged. As has been true under the original rule, there may be cases where the issues raised by a proffer of expert testimony can be most efficiently resolved by pre-trial hearing, briefing, and argument. In other cases, however, the issues can be resolved as adequately by objection and decision during trial. In either case, these have been, and will continue to be, matters that are determined by the timing of the parties' motions and by the scheduling and supervisory authority of the trial court.

1980:

The rule is stated in language identical to that of Federal Evidence Rule 702.

Rule 702 restates the law of Ohio as to the admissibility of testimony from expert witnesses.

In *Hartford Protection Insurance Co. v. Isaiah C. Harmer* (1853), 2 Ohio St. 452, the general rule that a witness was restricted to facts in his testimony was stated as well as the exception to the general rule in the case of an expert witness. The Court said, at 457:

In everything pertaining to the ordinary and common knowledge of mankind, jurors are supposed to be competent, and, indeed, peculiarly qualified to determine the experienced connection between cause and effect, and to draw the proper conclusion from the facts before them. But they are selected with no view to their knowledge of particular services, trades, and professions, requiring a course of previous study and preparation. As questions connected with these will very often arise, and as the law deprives the jury of no reliable means for ascertaining the truth, it allows them to be aided, in making the proper application, by the opinions of witnesses possessing peculiar skill in those particular departments. But this is only permitted where the nature of the question at issue is such that the jury are incompetent to draw their own conclusions from the facts, without the aid of persons whose skill or knowledge is superior to their own, and such as inexperienced persons are unlikely to prove capable of forming a correct judgment upon, without such assistance. *Fish v. Dodge*, 4 Denio, 311.

The basic principle is restated in *McKay Machine Co. v. Rodman* (1967), 11 Ohio St. 2d 77, where it was held in the first paragraph of the syllabus:

In all proceedings involving matters of a scientific, mechanical, professional or other like nature, requiring special study, experience or observation not within the common knowledge of laymen, expert opinion testimony is admissible to aid the court or the jury in arriving at a correct determination of the litigated issue.

The rule provides that the expert witness may testify as to scientific, technical, or other specialized knowledge in the form of an opinion or otherwise. The Advisory Committee Note to Federal Evidence Rule 702 says that the assumption that experts testify only in the form of opinion is logically unfounded and that the rule recognizes that the expert may give an exposition of relevant principles leaving the trier of the fact to apply the principles to the facts found.

Although Ohio cases discuss expert testimony in terms of opinion and it is normal for the expert to express his opinion, in response to fact he has observed or which he assumes to be true, the absence of an opinion does no violence to Ohio practice. Most expert witnesses provide instruction to the jury in the form of facts and opinion as to the principles involved and upon which the expert opinion is ultimately based. It is not unusual to have a direct conflict in the opinions of experts based upon the same set of facts. The purpose of a jury is to determine the correctness of the divergent opinions. *The Springfield Gas Co. v. Herman* (1933), 46 Ohio App. 309. The jury makes that determination by weighing the testimony, applying the usual test of credibility, finding the presence or absence of facts constituting the hypothesis, and by drawing its own inferences and conclusions from the principles explained.

Cross References

Admissible reports, 2317.36

Appointments by court of common pleas, 2301.12

Award of parental rights and responsibilities, investigation, modification of prior decree, factors determining child's "best interests," child's wishes, 3109.04

Blood tests by court order, 2317.47

Discovery and inspection, Crim R 16

Employment and payment of expert witnesses by board of county commissioners, 307.52

Expert testimony in criminal cases, O Const Art II §39

Fees for experts in parentage actions, 3111.14

Laboratory report as prima-facie evidence of content, weight and identity of substance, rights of accused, 2925.51

Paternity proceedings, expert testimony, 3111.09, 3111.10

Petition to discharge land of dower of insane person, 5305.18

Physical and mental examination of persons, Civ R 35

Plea of not guilty by reason of insanity, procedures, 2945.39

Pre-hearing medical examination, 5122.14

State government, deposit by public agency, appraisal of structures, 163.06

Testimony after verdict to mitigate penalty, reports confidential, 2947.06

Library References

Criminal Law ⟜469 to 481.

Evidence ⟜505 to 546.

Westlaw Topic Nos. 110, 157.

C.J.S. Criminal Law §§ 1059 to 1072.

C.J.S. Evidence §§ 510 to 527, 597 to 688.

OJur 3d: 29A, Criminal Law § 3094, 3097, 3099; 33, Decedents' Estates § 1193; 43, Evidence and Witnesses § 598; 59, Insurance § 1400; 67, Malpractice § 152

Am Jur 2d: 31, Expert and Opinion Evidence § 16 to 18, 26 to 52

Testing qualifications of expert witness, other than handwriting expert, by objective tests or experiments. 78 ALR2d 1281

Necessity and admissibility of expert testimony as to credibility of witness. 20 ALR3d 684

Necessity of expert evidence to support action against hospital for injury to or death of patient. 40 ALR3d 515

Medical malpractice: Necessity and sufficiency of showing of medical witness' familiarity with particular medical or surgical technique involved in suit. 46 ALR3d 275

Admissibility on issue of sanity of expert opinion based partly on medical, psychological, or hospital reports. 55 ALR3d 551

Modern status of rules regarding use of hypothetical questions in eliciting opinion of expert witness. 56 ALR3d 300

Competency of drug addict or user to identify suspect material as narcotic or controlled substance. 95 ALR3d 978

Admissibility and weight of voiceprint evidence. 97 ALR3d 294

Modern status of "locality rule" in malpractice action against physician who is not a specialist. 99 ALR3d 1133

Admissibility and necessity of expert evidence as to standards of practice and negligence in malpractice action against attorney. 14 ALR4th 170

Admissibility of expert or opinion testimony on battered wife or battered woman syndrome. 18 ALR4th 1153

Admissibility of expert or opinion testimony concerning identification of skeletal remains. 18 ALR4th 1294

Admissibility and weight, in criminal case, of expert or scientific evidence respecting characteristics and identification of human hair. 23 ALR4th 1199

Admissibility of expert testimony as to modus operandi of crime—modern cases. 31 ALR4th 798

Admissibility of voice stress evaluation test results or of statements made during test. 47 ALR4th 1202

Right of independent expert to refuse to testify as to expert opinion. 50 ALR4th 680

Propriety of questioning expert witness regarding specific incidents or allegations of expert's unprofessional conduct or professional negligence. 11 ALR5th 1

Admissibility, in homicide prosecution, of evidence as to tests made to ascertain distance from gun to victim when gun was fired. 11 ALR5th 497

Sufficiency of evidence that witness in criminal case was hypnotized, for purpose of determining admissibility of testimony given under hypnosis or of hypnotically enhanced testimony. 16 ALR5th 841

When will expert testimony "assist trier of fact" so as to be admissible at federal trial under Rule 702 of Federal Rules of Evidence. 75 ALR Fed 461

Painter, Ohio Driving Under the Influence Law (2003 Ed.), Text 17.7.

Giannelli & Snyder, Baldwin's Ohio Practice, Evidence § 104.3, 104.11, 601.1, 601.14, 604, 604.3, 701.1, 702.2, 702.3, 702.9, 703.1, 704, 704.1, 704.4, 704.5, 802.1, 803.30, 901.13, 901.25, 1006.3, 1101 (2d ed. 2001).

Adrine & Ruden, Ohio Domestic Violence Law (2002 Ed.), Text 14.16, 15.8, 15.9.

Ohio Personal Injury Practice (2002 Ed.), Text 5.12, 5.16, 5.17.

Meck & Pearlman, Ohio Planning and Zoning Law (2002 Ed.), Text 13.20.

Wasil, Waite, & Mastrangelo, Ohio Workers' Compensation Law § 14:147.

Carlin, Baldwin's Ohio Practice, Merrick–Rippner Probate Law § 12.4, 19.10, 43.10, 43.15 (2003).

Evid R 703   Bases of opinion testimony by experts

The facts or data in the particular case upon which an expert bases an opinion or inference may be those perceived by him or admitted in evidence at the hearing.

(Adopted eff. 7–1–80)

Commentary

Staff Notes

1980:

Rule 703 differs significantly from Federal Evidence Rule 703.

Federal Rule 703 provides for three categories of facts or data upon which an expert may base his opinion. The first category is facts or data perceived by the expert. Those are the facts he observes or the data he collects upon examination or testing. The second category is made up of facts or data known to the expert at the hearing. Normally, the expert is asked to assume the truth of the facts in a hypothesis. The first two categories of the federal rule were recognized in Ohio practice as it existed prior to the Rules of Evidence. The third category is facts or data made known to the expert before the hearing. The federal rule expresses no limitations on the sources of the facts and no limitations upon the methods of making them known. Ohio has not recognized the third category.

Federal Rule 703 also provides the facts or data, however perceived or made known, need not be admissible in evidence if they are of a type reasonably relied upon by experts in that field.

Rule 703 establishes two categories of facts or data. The first is that perceived by the expert which is the same as the first category in the federal rule. The second category is facts or data admitted into evidence at the hearing. The provision diverges sharply from the federal rule.

Rule 703 is in accord with Ohio law. Ohio has held that the hypothesis upon which an expert witness is asked to state his opinion must be based upon facts within the personal knowledge of the witness or upon facts shown by other evidence. *Burens v. Industrial Commission* (1955), 162 Ohio St. 549; *Kraner v. Coastal Tank Lines* (1971), 26 Ohio St.2d 59.

Library References

Criminal Law ⟐486(1) to 486(10).

Evidence ⟐555.1 to 555.10.

Westlaw Topic Nos. 110, 157.

C.J.S.   Criminal Law §§ 1080, 1081.

C.J.S.   Evidence §§ 597 to 616, 639 to 643, 652, 662 to 665, 682, 713.

OJur 3d: 29A, Criminal Law § 3096; 33, Decedents' Estates § 1194; 43, Evidence and Witnesses § 612, 613; 44, Evidence and Witnesses § 765; 59, Insurance § 1400; 67, Malpractice § 30, 160

Am Jur 2d: 31, Expert and Opinion Evidence § 36 et seq.

Consideration by expert witness, in forming his opinion, of impermissible hearsay evidence introduced without objection. 79 ALR2d 919

Admissibility, in criminal prosecution, of expert opinion allegedly stating whether drugs were possessed with intent to distribute—state cases. 83 ALR4th 629

Admissibility of expert opinion stating whether a particular knife was, or could have been, the weapon used in a crime. 83 ALR4th 660

Admissibility of testimony of expert, as to basis of his opinion, to matters otherwise excludible as hearsay—state cases. 89 ALR4th 456

Admissibility, in homicide prosecution, of evidence as to tests made to ascertain distance from gun to victim when gun was fired. 11 ALR5th 497

Sufficiency of evidence that witness in criminal case was hypnotized, for purpose of determining admissibility of testimony given under hypnosis or of hypnotically enhanced testimony. 16 ALR5th 841

What information is of type "reasonably relied upon by experts" within Rule 703, Federal Rules of Evidence, permitting expert opinion based on information not admissible in evidence. 49 ALR Fed 363

Painter, Ohio Driving Under the Influence Law (2003 Ed.), Text 17.5.

Giannelli & Snyder, Baldwin's Ohio Practice, Evidence § 602, 602.1, 702.1, 705.1, 705.3 (2d ed. 2001).

Ohio Personal Injury Practice (2002 Ed.), Text 5.15.

Evid R 704   Opinion on ultimate issue

Testimony in the form of an opinion or inference otherwise admissible is not objectionable solely because it embraces an ultimate issue to be decided by the trier of fact.

(Adopted eff. 7–1–80)

Commentary

Staff Notes

1980:

Rule 704 differs from Federal Evidence Rule 704 in only one regard. The word "solely" has been added after the word "objectionable" to clarify the thrust of the rule. (Editor's Note: Fed R 704 also contains paragraph (b), which was added in 1974.)

The rule does not serve to make opinion evidence on an ultimate issue admissible; it merely provides that opinion evidence on an ultimate issue is not excludable *per se*. The rule must be read in conjunction with Rule 701 and Rule 702, each of which requires that opinion testimony be helpful to, or assist, the trier of the fact in the determination of a factual issue. Opinion testimony on an ultimate issue is admissible if it assists the trier of the fact, otherwise it is not admissible. The competency of the trier of the fact to resolve the factual issue determines whether or not the opinion testimony is of assistance.

The rule is in accordance with Ohio law as it has developed prior to the adoption of the Rules of Evidence.

The general rule in Ohio as to the admissibility of opinion evidence on an ultimate issue was stated in the first two paragraphs of the syllabus in the case of *Shepard [Shepherd] v. Midland Mutual Life Ins. Co.* (1949), 152 Ohio St. 6, as follows:

Although a witness may be qualified to give an opinion concerning a matter upon which opinion evidence may be admissible in and pertinent to the determination of an issue, as a general rule such an opinion, whether expert or otherwise, may not be admitted when it, in effect, answers the very question as to the existence or non-existence of an ultimate fact to be determined by the jury.

Where an ultimate fact to be determined by the jury is one depending upon the interpretation of certain scientific facts which are beyond the experience, knowledge or comprehension of the jury, a witness qualified to speak as to the subject matter involved may express an opinion as to the probability or actuality of a fact pertinent to an issue in the case, and the admission of such opinion in evidence does not constitute an invasion or usurpation of the province or function of the jury, even though such opinion is on the ultimate fact which the jury must determine.

The exception extends to lay opinion testimony as well as to expert opinion testimony. A lay witness may not render an opinion as to the capacity of a testator to make a will, *Runyan v. Price* (1864), 15 Ohio St. 1, but a lay witness may testify as to the capacity to form an intent to dispose of property by a will. *Dunlap, Exr., v. Dunlap* (1913), 89 Ohio St. 28; *Weis v. Weis* (1947), 147 Ohio St. 416. The same example as to capacity is utilized in the Advisory Committee Note to Federal Evidence Rule 704 to illustrate that the effect of the rule is not to admit all opinion on the ultimate issue, but to assure that helpful opinion on the ultimate issue is not automatically excluded.

Library References

OJur 3d: 29A, Criminal Law § 3097; 30, Death § 160; 33, Decedents' Estates § 1190, 1196; 43, Evidence and Witnesses § 597, 603; 59, Insurance § 1400; 79, Railroads § 402

Am Jur 2d: 31, Expert and Opinion Evidence § 22, 23

Giannelli & Snyder, Baldwin's Ohio Practice, Evidence § 613.5, 701.1, 702.23 (2d ed. 2001).

Ohio Personal Injury Practice (2002 Ed.), Text 5.16.

Carlin, Baldwin's Ohio Practice, Merrick–Rippner Probate Law § 38.13, 103.30 (2003).

Evid R 705   Disclosure of facts or data underlying expert opinion

The expert may testify in terms of opinion or inference and give his reasons therefor after disclosure of the underlying facts or data. The disclosure may be in response to a hypothetical question or otherwise.

(Adopted eff. 7–1–80)

Commentary
Staff Notes

1980:

Rule 705 is in direct contrast to Federal Evidence Rule 705.

The federal rule provides that the expert may express his opinion without prior disclosure of the underlying facts or data unless the court requires otherwise. Rule 705 requires disclosure of the underlying facts or data prior to the rendition of the expert's opinion.

The purpose of the federal rule provision is to eliminate the necessity of using a hypothetical question in the direct examination of an expert witness. The federal rule does not eliminate the hypothetical question. If the court requires prior disclosure, the hypothetical question is appropriate. The examiner may use a hypothetical question at his option.

Rule 705 does not require the use of the hypothetical question. Disclosure of the underlying facts or data may be in response to a hypothetical question or otherwise. The rule places no restriction on how the witness learns of the facts admitted into evidence. He could be advised of them by counsel, he could hear them adduced, or they could be stated to him in a hypothetical question. In any event, the witness is required to disclose the underlying facts or data prior to the rendition of his opinion.

The federal rule can result in the disclosure being the burden of the cross-examiner. Under Rule 705, the disclosure is always on direct examination.

Rule 705 varies from prior Ohio practice by making the use of a hypothetical question optional with the examiner. In the former Ohio practice, an expert witness could render an opinion based upon facts within the personal knowledge of the witness or upon facts the witness was asked to assume to be true. When the witness was testifying from personal knowledge of the facts upon which the opinion was based, the personal knowledge was required to be shown. *Williams v. Brown, Exr.*, (1876), 28 Ohio St. 547; *Scott v. Campbell* (1961), 115 Ohio App. 208. If the expert witness was a stranger to the facts, it was necessary for the witness to assume a state of facts, but no assumption was necessary where the witness was personally acquainted with the facts. *Bellefontaine and Indiana Railroad Co. v. Bailey* (1860), 11 Ohio St. 333. When a hypothesis was used, it was incumbent upon the proponent to establish the premises included in the hypothetical question by a preponderance of the evidence. *Haas v. Kundtz* (1916), 94 Ohio St. 238; *Burens v. Industrial Commission* (1955), 162 Ohio St. 549.

Cross References

Discovery of facts known or opinions held expert, Civ R 26

Library References

Criminal Law ⟲486(1) to 486(10).

Evidence ⟲555.1 to 555.10.

Westlaw Topic Nos. 110, 157.

C.J.S. Criminal Law §§ 1080, 1081.

C.J.S. Evidence §§ 597 to 616, 639 to 643, 652, 662 to 665, 682, 713.

OJur 3d: 29A, Criminal Law § 3096; 33, Decedents'
   Estates § 1195; 43, Evidence and Witnesses
   § 612, 613; 59, Insurance § 1400; 67, Malpractice § 160
Am Jur 2d: 31, Expert and Opinion Evidence § 39,
   49, 59
Right of physician, notwithstanding physician-patient
   privilege, to give expert testimony based on
   hypothetical question. 64 ALR2d 1056
Propriety of hypothetical question to expert witness
   on cross-examination. 71 ALR2d 6
Consideration, in determining facts, of inadmissible
   hearsay evidence introduced without objection. 79 ALR2d 890
Competency of general practitioner to testify as expert witness in action against specialist for
   medical malpractice. 31 ALR3d 1163
Medical malpractice: Necessity and sufficiency of
   showing of medical witness' familiarity with
   particular medical or surgical technique involved in suit. 46 ALR3d 275
Admissibility, at criminal prosecution, of expert testimony on reliability of eyewitness testimony. 46
   ALR4th 1047
Giannelli & Snyder, Baldwin's Ohio Practice, Evidence § 702.1, 703.1, 703.5, 705.3 (2d ed.
   2001).
Ohio Personal Injury Practice (2002 Ed.), Text 5.13,
   5.16.

Evid R 706   Learned treatises for impeachment

Statements contained in published
treatises, periodicals, or pamphlets on a
subject of history, medicine, or other science or art are admissible for impeachment if the publication is either of the
following:

(A) Relied upon by an expert witness
in reaching an opinion;

(B) Established as reliable authority
(1) by the testimony or admission of the
witness, (2) by other expert testimony, or
(3) by judicial notice.

If admitted for impeachment, the statements may be read into evidence but
shall not be received as exhibits.

(Adopted eff. 7-1-98)

Commentary

Staff Notes
1998:

Rule 706 Learned treatises for impeachment

The common law rule restricted the use of a
learned treatise to impeachment. See *Hallworth v.
Republic Steel Corp.* (1950), 153 Ohio St. 349, 91
N.E.2d 690 (syllabus, para. 2) ("Medical books or
treatises, even though properly identified and authenticated and shown to be recognized as standard
authorities on the subject to which they relate, are
not admissible in evidence to prove the truth of the
statements therein contained."). When the Rules of
Evidence were adopted in 1980, Ohio rejected Federal Evidence Rule 803(18), which recognizes a hearsay exception for learned treatises. Consequently,
the common law impeachment rule continued, under
Evid. R. 102, as the controlling precedent in Ohio.
See *Ramage v. Cent. Ohio Emergency Serv., Inc.*
(1992), 64 Ohio St.3d. 87, 110, 592 N.E.2d 828 ("In
Ohio, textbooks and other learned treatises are considered hearsay, may not be used as substantive
evidence, and are specially limited to impeachment
purposes only.").

This new Rule of Evidence codifies the common
law rule, making it more readily accessible for trial
use. The syllabus in *Hallworth* referred to treatises
"recognized as standard authorities," *without* requiring reliance by the expert. In a post-Rules case, the
Supreme Court wrote: " [I]n Ohio, a learned treatise
may be used for impeachment purposes to demonstrate that an expert witness is either unaware of the
text or unfamiliar with its contents. Moreover, the
substance of the treatise may be employed only to
impeach the credibility of an expert who has relied
upon the treatise,..., or has acknowledged its authoritative nature." *Stinson v. England* (1994), 69 Ohio
St.3d 451, 458, 633 N.E.2d 532.

A possible expansion of the common law rule concerns the use of judicial notice to establish the treatise as a reliable authority. A court taking judicial
notice of *Gray's Anatomy* illustrates this aspect of
the rule.

The trial court decides under Evid. R. 104(A) if
the treatise is a "reliable authority" and Evid. R.
105 requires a limiting instruction upon request. If
an opposing expert witness refuses to recognize a
treatise as reliable, the judge may permit the impeachment subject to counsel's subsequent laying of
the foundation through its own expert. There is no
need to inform the jury of the trial court's determination.

Library References

OJur 3d: 29A, Criminal Law § 3139 to 3142, 3147;
   43, Evidence and Witnesses § 408 et seq.
Giannelli & Snyder, Baldwin's Ohio Practice, Evidence § 102.4, 607.1, 607.7, 613.7, 803.1,
   803.2, 803.59, 901.24, 1101 (2d ed. 2001).

Article VIII

HEARSAY

Rule	
801	Definitions
802	Hearsay rule
803	Hearsay exceptions; availability of de-clarant immaterial
804	Hearsay exceptions; declarant unavailable

Rule	
805	Hearsay within hearsay
806	Attacking and supporting credibility of declarant
807	Hearsay exceptions; child statements in abuse cases

Evid R 801 Definitions

The following definitions apply under this article:

(A) Statement

A "statement" is (1) an oral or written assertion or (2) nonverbal conduct of a person, if it is intended by him as an assertion.

(B) Declarant

A "declarant" is a person who makes a statement.

(C) Hearsay

"Hearsay" is a statement, other than one made by the declarant while testifying at the trial or hearing, offered in evidence to prove the truth of the matter asserted.

(D) Statements which are not hearsay

A statement is not hearsay if:

(1) Prior statement by witness. The declarant testifies at the trial or hearing and is subject to cross-examination concerning the statement, and the statement is (a) inconsistent with his testimony, and was given under oath subject to cross-examination by the party against whom the statement is offered and subject to the penalty of perjury at a trial, hearing, or other proceeding, or in a deposition, or (b) consistent with his testimony and is offered to rebut an express or implied charge against him of recent fabrication or improper influence or motive, or (c) one of identification of a person soon after perceiving him, if the circumstances demonstrate the reliability of the prior identification.

(2) Admission by party–opponent. The statement is offered against a party and is (a) his own statement, in either his individual or a representative capacity, or (b) a statement of which he has manifested his adoption or belief in its truth, or (c) a statement by a person authorized by him to make a statement concerning the subject, or (d) a statement by his agent or servant concerning a matter within the scope of his agency or employment, made during the existence of the relationship, or (e) a statement by a co-conspirator of a party during the course and in furtherance of the conspiracy upon independent proof of the conspiracy.

(Adopted eff. 7–1–80)

Commentary

Staff Notes

1980:

The ultimate determination of whether statements or conduct are admissible or not for hearsay purposes is substantially the same as prior Ohio law, with two notable exceptions. There are in this rule significant departures as to definition and characterization of statements and conduct as hearsay. There are also important departures from Federal Evidence Rule 801 upon which the Ohio rule is based.

Rule 801(A) Statement

This subdivision defines a "statement" for hearsay purposes as either (1) oral or written assertions or (2) conduct intended as assertive. This definition characterizes the traditional written or oral assertion as subject to hearsay risk. However, not all statements falling within the two enumerated categories are hearsay, or even if hearsay, such statements are not necessarily inadmissible. Whether a statement falling within the purview of 801(A) is hearsay is governed in part by the remaining subdivisions of Rule 801, and whether a statement is admissible, even if hearsay, is governed by Rules 803 and 804.

The second category of assertions falling within the definition of a "statement" is conduct intended as assertive. This definition resolves many difficult problems as to how to characterize conduct having qualities which induce suspicions characteristic of hearsay. The time honored hypothetical serves as an example. Is the fact that the captain of a vessel made X a lookout under a policy that only men of good eyesight are made lookouts evidence that X had good eyesight? Since the relevancy of the captain's conduct depends upon the accuracy of his information, the conduct ends up being no more than the captain stating "X has good eyesight." Is such conduct hearsay? A good many cases found this type of conduct to be hearsay as involving an "implied assertion." The classic case of *Wright v. Doe D'Tatham* (1837), 112 Eng. Rep. 488, is an early example and there are many others. McCormick § 250 (2d ed. 1972). Yet, the courts have not hesitated to classify similar instances of conduct though involving the same implied assertions as nonhearsay. For example, a person fleeing from the scene of a crime is deemed merely relevant evidence tending to establish guilt without consideration of the implied assertion "I am guilty" clearly inherent in the act of fleeing.

The rule solves the difficult problem of drawing lines in such cases by merely rendering conduct not intended by the actor as assertive as not a hearsay statement. If there is not [sic.] intention to communicate by the act, it is not a "statement" for hearsay purposes. The ship captain's conduct would, if otherwise relevant and competent, be admissible as circumstantial evidence of X's eyesight without hearsay risks. The intent of the actor is critical in making the determination as to whether the conduct is assertive.

Rule 801(B) Declarant

This subdivision defines "declarant" as a person who makes a statement defined in Rule 801(A). The definition permits reference to a person who makes statements defined in Rule 801(A) by an identifiable term. The "declarant" is a person who has made such a statement and is used as part of the definition of hearsay in Rule 801(C) and in Rules 803 and 804 relating to hearsay exceptions. The meaning is common to hearsay analysis and represents no departure from prior Ohio law.

Rule 801(C) Hearsay

This subdivision defines hearsay. It is not a departure from prior Ohio law. See 21 OJur 2d Evidence §§283 and 287. Hearsay is limited to statements offered into evidence to prove the truth of the assertion by the declarant not on the witness stand at the time of the declaration. The definition discloses its relative nature. If a statement is not offered to prove its truth but is offered for some other reason such as simply to prove the statement was made, if such fact is relevant, it is not hearsay. Words constituting conduct are not hearsay, e.g., words of a contract, libel, slander, threats and the like.

The terms "statement" and "declarant" as used in this subdivision are defined in subdivisions 801(A) and 801(B) respectively.

Rule 801(D) Statements which are not Hearsay

This subdivision creates new categories of declarations which while constituting "statements" as defined in Rule 801(A), and while falling within the definition of hearsay in Rule 801(C), are not excluded as evidence under the hearsay rule. Such statements as qualify under this subdivision are admissible independent of the hearsay exceptions enumerated in Rule 803 and Rule 804, and are properly characterized as non-hearsay rather than as exceptions to the rule.

There are two categories of statements under this subdivision: first, statements by a witness made at a time prior to his taking the stand and, second, statements by a party opponent or one deemed to be speaking in behalf of a party opponent. The first category includes particular types of declarations by a witness which were characterized as hearsay exceptions or as prior statements subject to use for impeachment or rehabilitative purposes under former Ohio law. The second category constituted admissions under prior Ohio law. The provisions of this subdivision represent some departure from prior Ohio law and from Federal Evidence Rule 801(d) as indicated in the notes following the particular subsections.

Rule 801(D)(1) Prior Statement by Witness

This subsection deals with prior statements of a witness. There are three types of statements by a witness which may qualify as non-hearsay under this subdivision and may be admissible as non-hearsay to prove the matters asserted in such prior statements. The rule does not limit the use of such statements either for impeachment or rehabilitative purposes. The statements may be used as substantive evidence of the matters asserted. The three categories are (a) prior inconsistent statements of a witness if made under oath subject to cross-examination, (b) prior consistent statements offered to rebut charges of recent fabrication or improper motive, and (c) prior identification by a witness.

Rule 801(D)(1)(a) Prior Inconsistent Statements

Under prior Ohio law a prior inconsistent statement, whether or not under oath, was admissible only for impeachment purposes and not for substantive proof of the matter asserted. See Staff Note to Rule 613. Under the Rules, a prior inconsistent statement, whether or not under oath, is still admissible for such impeachment purposes. See Rule 613(B).

Under this subdivision, the prior inconsistent statement of a witness if made under oath at a prior hearing subject to cross-examination, or deposition, and subject to perjury charges is admissible as substantive evidence of the matter asserted. Two aspects of such statements justify the rule. First, there is a high circumstantial guaranty of trustworthiness in that the witness is now on the stand subject to oath, cross-examination and demeanor evaluation and the prior inconsistent statement was also made under oath and was subject to cross-examination. Second, such statement was and continues to be admissible for impeachment purposes under Rule 613, and it is unrealistic to ask the jury to consider such statement to assess the credibility of the witness but not to treat the prior statement as substantive evidence.

The Ohio Rule differs from the Federal counterpart in requiring the added element that the prior inconsistent statement under oath may be admitted under the provision only if it were subject to cross-examination by the party against whom the statement is now offered. Therefore, prior inconsistent statements made, for example, in grand jury proceedings can not be offered as substantive evidence against the criminal defendant under this provision since the grand jury testimony was not subject to cross-examination.

Rule 801(D)(1)(b) Prior Consistent Statements

In this subsection a prior consistent statement, whether or not under oath, may be used as substantive evidence if such prior consistent statement is introduced to refute charges of improper motive or recent fabrication. Under prior Ohio law such evidence was admissible to rehabilitate a witness whose credibility was attacked by such charges. *Miller v. Piqua Transfer and Storage Co.* (1950), 57 Ohio Law Abs. 325.

Rule 613 governs the use of prior inconsistent statements for impeachment purposes but does not govern methods of rehabilitation. Rule 801(D)(1)(b) makes it clear that prior consistent statements may be used to rehabilitate a witness under circumstances authorized under prior Ohio law. Unlike the requirements under Rule 801(D)(1)(a) respecting prior inconsistent statements, if the circumstances arise under which a prior consistent statement may be used to rehabilitate the witness, such statement may be used as substantive proof of the matter asserted without regard to whether the statement was made under oath.

Rule 801(D)(1)(c)

This rule extends the principle recognized in Ohio in *State v. Lancaster* (1971), 25 Ohio St.2d 83. It is identical to Federal Evidence Rule 801(d)(1)(C) except for an added provision for exclusion if the prior identification were made under unreliable circumstances. If a witness has made an identification prior to appearing in court to testify and such identification is the result of the witness having actually perceived the person identified, evidence of such identification is admissible regardless of whether or not the witness can now make an identification. 4 Weinstein's Evidence § 801(d)(1)(C) [01] (1977). The rationale for the rule is that the perception made nearer the event is at least as likely, if not more likely, to be accurate than a subsequent identification in the court room. The added provision requires the trial judge to determine whether the circumstances under which the identification was made demonstrates reliability of the prior identification. This grant of discretion tightens the use of this basis of evidence of identification consistent with constitutional requirements. However, nothing in this rule obviates constitutional requirements relating to line-ups and the like under *Kirby v. Illinois* (1972), 406 U.S. 682.

Rule 801(D)(2) Admission by Party Opponent

This subsection governs statements by a party opponent or by others identified with a party opponent in enumerated relationships. Under prior Ohio law, an admission was characterized as an exception to the hersay [sic.] rule. Some confusion existed as to the proper characterization for statements made by agents, sometimes being characterized as falling within the ubiquitous *res gestae* exception. See *Kimbark v. Timken Roller Bearing Co.* (1926), 115 Ohio St. 161. Also see *Werk v. Martin* (1934), 18 Ohio Law Abs. 81. Aside from the differences in characterization, the determination of admissibility of statements covered by the rule is substantially the same as under prior Ohio law.

Rule 801(D)(2)(a) His Own Statement; Individual or Representative Capacity

This rule is similar to prior Ohio law. *Goz v. Tenney* (1922), 104 Ohio St. 500. It covers statements by a party opponent. The statement need not be against the interest of the declarant at the time made. It is sufficient that the statement be that of a party and that it is offered by the opposing party. A party may not introduce his own statement under this rule. Problems of trustworthiness are not critical in this class of admission since the opposing party controls the decision to introduce the statement and the party declarant will be in court to refute any unfavorable impact of the statement.

Rule 801(D)(2)(b) Adoptive Admissions

This rule is consistent with prior Ohio law. An adoptive admission, or an admission by acquiescence, consists of a statement by a non-party which may be deemed to be that of a party by virtue of the failure of the party to deny the statement. There are obvious risks in attributing a statement of a third person to be that of a party and, in applying the rule, courts have been careful to consider the circumstances under which the utterance is made to insure that the party understood the utterance, that he was free to make a response, and that a reasonable person would have denied the statement. Absent these determinations, a statement of a third person cannot be an admission by acquiescence of a party opponent. See generally McCormick §161 (2d ed. 1972). For a case of adoptive admission applying even in a criminal case see *United States v. Alker* (1958), 255 F. 2d 851.

Rule 801(D)(2)(c) Authorized Statements

A statement authorized by a party is in effect a statement of that party. The rule reflects prior Ohio law. *Garret v. Hanshue* (1895), 53 Ohio St. 482.

Rule 801(D)(2)(d) Vicarious Statements

The statement of a party's agent or employee made in the course of employment concerning matters relating to such employment is admissible against such party. This represents no departure from prior Ohio law although occasionally prior Ohio cases treated the question of admissibility of an agent's statement under principles of *res gastae*. *Western Insurance Co. v. Tobin* (1877), 32 Ohio St. 77. *Cincinnati, H & Ohio Dec. R. Co. v. Klure* (1905), 8 Ohio C.C.(n.s.) 409.

Rule 801(D)(2)(e) Statement of Co–Conspirator

This subsection provides for the admission of a co-conspirator's statement against an accused charged with conspiracy. (Editor's Note: The last statement is misleading. The co-conspirator rule does *not* re-

quire the accused to be "charged with conspiracy.") Such statement must be made during the course and in furtherance of the conspiracy. The rule reflects prior Ohio law. *State v. Carver* (1972), 30 Ohio St.2d 280.

Before a statement of a co-conspirator may be introduced against an accused, the court must first find some independent evidence of a conspiracy. This requirement is specifically mandated by the wording of the rule. Under the Federal Rule, the requirement of independent proof is implicit but not specifically mandated. How much extrinsic evidence is required before a co-conspirator's statement is admitted as an admission by the accused has been subject to differing standards in federal and state treatment of the subject.

Cross References

Conspiracy, 2923.01
Delinquent children, deposition of child sex offense victims, 2152.81
Deposition, Crim R 15
General rules of pleading, effect of failure to deny, Civ R 8
Requests for admission, Civ R 36
Testimony of mentally retarded or developmentally disabled victim, 2945.482
Testimony of mentally retarded or developmentally disabled victim; videotaped testimony, 2945.491
Testimony of previous identification, 2945.55
Trial for crimes, witness, O Const Art I §10
Videotaped preliminary hearing testimony of child victim, 2945.49

Library References

Criminal Law ⟿419(1).

Evidence ⟿314(1).

Westlaw Topic Nos. 110, 157.

C.J.S. Criminal Law §§ 856, 861, 862, 864.

C.J.S. Evidence §§ 259 to 272, 279 to 284, 319.

OJur 3d: 25, Criminal Law § 475; 27, Criminal Law § 1154 to 1200; 29A, Criminal Law § 2995, 2997, 3010, 3021, 3022, 3030, 3034, 3037, 3139; 43, Evidence and Witnesses § 260, 265, 266, 289, 307; 44, Evidence and Witnesses § 946, 976; 59, Insurance § 1387; 61, Intoxicating Liquors § 310; 70, Negligence § 172; 81, Witnesses § 596, 651; 94, Workers' Compensation § 363

Am Jur 2d: 29, Evidence § 493 to 495, 497 to 502

Nonverbal reaction to accusation, other than silence alone, as constituting adopted admission under hearsay rule. 87 ALR3d 706

Denial of recollection as inconsistent with prior statement so as to render statement admissible. 99 ALR3d 934

Admissibility of impeached witness' prior consistent statement—modern state criminal cases. 58 ALR4th 1014

Admissibility of impeached witness' prior consistent statement—modern state civil cases. 59 ALR4th 1000

What is "other proceeding" under Rule 801(d)(1)(A) of the Federal Rules of Evidence, excepting from hearsay rule prior inconsistent statement given "at a trial, hearing, or other proceeding." 37 ALR Fed 855

Admissibility of statement by co-conspirator under Rule 801(d)(2)(E) of the Federal Rules of Evidence. 44 ALR Fed 627

Effect of Rule 801(d)(1)(B) of the Federal Rules of Evidence upon the admissibility of a witness' prior consistent statement. 47 ALR Fed 639

Admissibility of statement under Rule 801(D)(2)(B) of the Federal Rules of Evidence, providing that statement is not hearsay if party-opponent has manifested his adoption or belief in its truth. 48 ALR Fed 721

Admissibility of party's own statement under Rule 801(d)(2)(A) of the Federal Rules of Evidence. 48 ALR Fed 922

Katz & Giannelli, Baldwin's Ohio Practice, Criminal Law § 94.14 (1996).

Painter, Ohio Driving Under the Influence Law (2003 Ed.), Text 13.2.

Giannelli & Snyder, Baldwin's Ohio Practice, Evidence § 104.3, 602, 104.10, 105.1, 105.7, 105.8, 401.9, 501.13, 602.5, 607.2, 607.4, 607.8, 607.9, 612.4, 613.1, 613.3, 613.6, 616.3, 702.11, 802, 802.1, 802.6, 803.1, 803.35, 804.1, 804.9, 804.19, 805.3, 806.1, 807.1, 804, 805, 807, 807.13 (2d ed. 2001).

Adrine & Ruden, Ohio Domestic Violence Law (2002 Ed.), Text 6.14, 7.6, 15.8.

Katz, Ohio Arrest, Search and Seizure (2002 Ed.), Text 26.2.

Carlin, Baldwin's Ohio Practice, Merrick–Rippner Probate Law § 107.38, 107.51 (2003).

Evid R 802   Hearsay rule

Hearsay is not admissible except as otherwise provided by the Constitution of the United States, by the Constitution of the State of Ohio, by statute enacted by the General Assembly not in conflict with a rule of the Supreme Court of Ohio, by these rules, or by other rules prescribed by the Supreme Court of Ohio.

(Adopted eff. 7–1–80)

Commentary

Staff Notes

1980:

This rule is substantially the same as Federal Evidence Rule 802. Differences in wording relate to adjustments in the Ohio rule for state constitutional and statutory references.

The rule reflects prior Ohio law in making hearsay inadmissible except as specifically provided by rule, statute or constitutional provision.

Of course, the forthright statement of the hearsay rule itself masks the complexity of the hearsay area. To discover its real consequence reference must be made to Rule 801 concerning definitional aspects of hearsay, Rule 803 and 804 concerning the exceptions, and Rules 805 and 806 concerning ancillary matters relative to hearsay evidence.

The rule further reflects another area where legislative mandate may be exercised by virtue of the possible impact of this area of evidence law upon substantive issues.

Cross References

Arrest warrant may issue on probable cause found from hearsay; testimony admissible at hearing to suppress evidence, Crim R 4

Business records as evidence, 2317.40

Degree of offense, charge and verdict, prior convictions, 2945.75

Dispositional hearing, procedure, Juv R 34

Laboratory report as prima-facie evidence of content, weight and identity of substance, rights of accused, 2925.51

Official reports admitted as evidence, 2317.42

Proving testimony of absent witness, 2317.06

Suits for delinquent taxes and assessments, procedure, 6115.59

Testimony of deceased or absent witness, 2945.49

Library References

Criminal Law ⟨⟩419(1).

Evidence ⟨⟩314(1).

Westlaw Topic Nos. 110, 157.

C.J.S. Criminal Law §§ 856, 861, 862, 864.

C.J.S. Evidence §§ 259 to 272, 279 to 284, 319.

OJur 3d: 29, Criminal Law § 2996; 43, Evidence and Witnesses § 260; 59, Insurance § 1387; 70, Negligence § 172

Am Jur 2d: 29, Evidence § 493

Written recitals or statements as within rule excluding hearsay. 10 ALR2d 1035

Admissibility, as against hearsay objection, of report of tests or experiments carried out by independent third party. 19 ALR3d 1008

Admissibility of newspaper article as evidence of the truth of the facts stated therein. 55 ALR3d 663

Admissibility of evidence concerning words spoken while declarant was asleep or unconscious. 14 ALR4th 802

Katz & Giannelli, Baldwin's Ohio Practice, Criminal Law § 1.6 (1996).

Giannelli & Snyder, Baldwin's Ohio Practice, Evidence § 102.5, 402.7, 801.1, 801.22, 802.3, 803.1, 803.21, 804.1, 807.1, 901.1, 902.1 (2d ed. 2001).

Carlin, Baldwin's Ohio Practice, Merrick–Rippner Probate Law § 38.13 (2003).

Evid R 803   Hearsay exceptions; availability of declarant immaterial

The following are not excluded by the hearsay rule, even though the declarant is available as a witness:

(1) Present sense impression

A statement describing or explaining an event or condition made while the declarant was perceiving the event or condition, or immediately thereafter unless circumstances indicate lack of trustworthiness.

(2) Excited utterance

A statement relating to a startling event or condition made while the declarant was under the stress of excitement caused by the event or condition.

(3) Then existing, mental, emotional, or physical condition

A statement of the declarant's then existing state of mind, emotion, sensation, or physical condition (such as intent, plan, motive, design, mental feeling, pain, and bodily health), but not including a statement of memory or belief to prove the fact remembered or believed unless it relates to the execution, revocation, identification, or terms of declarant's will.

(4) Statements for purposes of medical diagnosis or treatment

Statements made for purposes of medical diagnosis or treatment and describing medical history, or past or present symptoms, pain, or sensations, or the inception or general character of the cause or external source thereof insofar as reasonably pertinent to diagnosis or treatment.

(5) Recorded recollection

A memorandum or record concerning a matter about which a witness once had knowledge but now has insufficient recollection to enable him to testify fully and accurately, shown by the testimony of the witness to have been made or adopted when the matter was fresh in his memory and to reflect that knowledge correctly. If admitted, the memorandum or record may be read into evidence but may not itself be received as an exhibit unless offered by an adverse party.

(6) Records of regularly conducted activity

A memorandum, report, record, or data compilation, in any form, of acts, events, or conditions, made at or near the time by, or from information transmitted by, a person with knowledge, if kept in the course of a regularly conducted business activity, and if it was the regular practice of that business activity to make the memorandum, report, record, or data compilation, all as shown by the testimony of the custodian or other qualified witness or as provided by Rule 901(B)(10), unless the source of information or the method or circumstances of preparation indicate lack of trustworthiness. The term "business" as used in this paragraph includes business, institution, association, profession, occupation, and calling of every kind, whether or not conducted for profit.

(7) Absence of entry in record kept in accordance with the provisions of paragraph (6)

Evidence that a matter is not included in the memoranda, reports, records, or data compilations, in any form, kept in accordance with the provisions of paragraph (6), to prove the nonoccurrence or nonexistence of the matter, if the matter was of a kind of which a memorandum, report, record, or data compilation was regularly made and preserved, unless the sources of information or other circumstances indicate lack of trustworthiness.

(8) Public records and reports

Records, reports, statements, or data compilations, in any form, of public offices or agencies, setting forth (a) the activities of the office or agency, or (b) matters observed pursuant to duty imposed by law as to which matters there was a duty to report, excluding, however, in criminal cases matters observed by police officers and other law enforcement personnel, unless offered by defendant, unless the sources of information or other circumstances indicate lack of trustworthiness.

(9) Records of vital statistics

Records or data compilations, in any form, of births, fetal deaths, deaths, or marriages, if the report thereof was made to a public office pursuant to requirement of law.

(10) Absence of public record or entry

To prove the absence of a record, report, statement, or data compilation, in any form, or the nonoccurrence or nonexistence of a matter of which a record, report, statement, or data compilation, in any form, was regularly made and preserved by a public office or agency, evidence in the form of a certification in accordance with Rule 901(B)(10) or testimony, that diligent search failed to disclose the record, report, statement, or data compilation, or entry.

(11) Records of religious organizations

Statements of births, marriages, divorces, deaths, legitimacy, ancestry, relationship by blood or marriage, or other similar facts of personal or family history, contained in a regularly kept record of religious organization [1].

(12) Marriage, baptismal, and similar certificates

Statements of fact contained in a certificate that the maker performed a marriage or other ceremony or administered a sacrament, made by a clergyman, public official, or other person authorized by the rules or practices of a religious organization or by law to perform the act certified, and purporting to have been issued at the time of the act or within a reasonable time thereafter.

(13) Family records

Statements of fact concerning personal or family history contained in family Bibles, genealogies, charts, engravings on rings, inscriptions on family portraits, engravings on urns, crypts, or tombstones, or the like.

(14) Records of documents affecting an interest in property

The record of a document purporting to establish or affect an interest in property, as proof of the content of the original recorded document and its execution and delivery by each person by whom it purports to have been executed, if the record is a record of a public office and an applicable statute authorizes the recording of documents of that kind in that office.

(15) Statements in documents affecting an interest in property

A statement contained in a document purporting to establish or affect an interest in property if the matter stated was relevant to the purpose of the document, unless dealings with the property since the document was made have been inconsistent with the truth of the statement or the purport of the document.

(16) Statements in ancient documents

Statements in a document in existence twenty years or more the authenticity of which is established.

(17) Market reports, commercial publications

Market quotations, tabulations, lists, directories, or other published compilations, generally used and relied upon by the public or by persons in particular occupations.

(18) Reputation concerning personal or family history

Reputation among members of his family by blood, adoption, or marriage or among his associates, or in the community, concerning a person's birth, adoption, marriage, divorce, death, legitimacy, relationship by blood, adoption or marriage, ancestry, or other similar fact of his personal or family history.

(19) Reputation concerning boundaries or general history

Reputation in a community, arising before the controversy, as to boundaries of or customs affecting lands in the community, and reputation as to events of general history important to the community or state or nation in which located.

(20) Reputation as to character

Reputation of a person's character among his associates or in the community.

(21) Judgment of previous conviction

Evidence of a final judgment, entered after a trial or upon a plea of guilty (but not upon a plea of no contest or the equivalent plea from another jurisdiction), adjudging a person guilty of a crime punishable by death or imprisonment in excess of one year, to prove any fact essential to sustain the judgment, but not including, when offered by the Government in a criminal prosecution for purposes other than impeachment, judgments against persons other than the accused. The pendency of an appeal may be shown but does not affect admissibility.

(22) Judgment as to personal, family, or general history, or boundaries

Judgments as proof of matters of personal, family or general history, or boundaries, essential to the judgment, if the same would be provable by evidence of reputation.

(Adopted eff. 7–1–80)

¹ So in 62 OS(2d) xlvi; federal rule reads "of a religious organization."

Commentary

Staff Notes

1980:

This rule indicates the exceptions to the hearsay rule in which the unavailability of the declarant is not an element of the particular exception. In establishing exceptions to the hearsay rule there are two aspects that have predominated common law development. These are necessity and a circumstantial guaranty of trustworthiness surrounding the hearsay declaration that tends to assure truthfulness of the hearsay testimony despite the absence of the oath and cross-examination. Rule 803 sets forth those exceptions to the hearsay rule in which necessity is not a critical factor; that is, the hearsay is admissible notwithstanding the fact that the declarant might be readily available to testify and indeed at least as to the recorded recollection exception under Rule 803(5) the declarant must himself be on the witness stand. It might, therefore, be more accurate to characterize the exceptions under this rule as those in which "unavailability" of the declarant is not a requisite.

This rule is similar to Federal Evidence Rule 803, with some significant modification in Rule 803(1) Present sense impression, Rule 803(5) Recorded recollection, Rule 803(6) Records of regularly conducted activity, Rule 803(8) Public records and reports. The rule also eliminates Federal Rule 803(18) Learned treatises, and Rule 803(24) Other exceptions.

The enumerated exceptions reflect those recognized at common law. There is some extension beyond that previously recognized in Ohio. These points are noted in staff notes for the particular exceptions.

Rule 803(1) Present Sense Impression

The present sense impression exception has not been explicitly identified in Ohio. No case has been found expressly adopting the rationale of *Houston Oxygen [Co,] Inc. v. Davis* (1942), 139 Tex. 1, 161

S.W. 2d 474, which introduced the exception to the common law. The exception is, however, part of the older *res gestae* exception to hearsay. Spontaneous exclamations (*res gestae* utterances) are divided into two categories: present sense impression and excited utterance (Rule 803(2)). Present sense impressions are those declarations made by an observer at the time the event is being perceived. The circumstantial guaranty of trustworthiness is derived from the fact that the statement is contemporaneous and there is little risk of faulty recollection, and it is made to another who is capable of verifying the statement at the time it is made. There is no requirement that the statement be made under the influence of an emotion or trauma and it is limited to observations about the event that is taking place. The rule is identical to Federal Evidence Rule 803(1) except for the additional provision that the trial court may exclude such statements if the circumstances under which the statement was made indicate a lack of trustworthiness. The discretion vested in the trial judge is for the purpose of narrowing the availability of this exception.

One of the principal elements of the circumstantial guaranty of trustworthiness of this exception is that the statement was made at a time and under circumstances in which the person to whom the statement was made would be in a position to verify the statement. The provision requiring exclusion if the circumstances do not warrant a high degree of trustworthiness would justify exclusion if, for example, the statement were made by a declarant concerning a perceived event to another by way of a C.B. radio transmission. Other circumstances other than the lack of verification may also taint the trustworthiness of this class of hearsay declaration.

Comparison should be made between the basis of trustworthiness of statements under this exception and those relating to excited utterances under Rule 803(2).

Rule 803(2) Excited Utterances

This exception is identical to Federal Evidence Rule 803(2). Excited utterances have been recognized as an exception to the hearsay rule. *Potter v. Baker* (1955), 162 Ohio St. 488. It is a statement or act incidental to a main fact and explanatory of it, provided it is so connected with the transaction as a whole that the utterance or act is regarded as an expression of the circumstances under which it was made rather than the narrative result of thought. To qualify as an excited utterance consideration must be given to (a) the lapse of time between the event and the declaration, (b) the mental and physical condition of the declarant, (c) the nature of the statement and (d) the influence of intervening circumstances.

This exception derives its guaranty of trustworthiness from the fact that declarant is under such state of emotional shock that his reflective processes have been stilled. Therefore, statements made under these circumstances are not likely to be fabricated. McCormick § 297 (2d ed. 1972).

Rule 803(3) Then Existing Mental, Emotional or Physical Condition

This exception is identical to Federal Evidence Rule 803(3). It is also consistent with prior Ohio law with some expansion of the doctrine particularly as the rule relates to state of mind concerning a testator's will.

Declarations regarding both present state of mind and physical or mental condition were admissible under prior Ohio law. *Wetmore v. Mell* (1852), 1 Ohio St. 26; *Strough v. Industrial Comm.* (1946), 81 Ohio App. 249, *aff'd* 148 Ohio St. 415.

This exception is a restatement of traditional common law exceptions pertaining to bodily and emotional condition, and the state of mind exception announced in the classic *Mutual Life Ins. Co. of New York v. Hillmon* (1892), 145 U.S. 285. Like the common law restrictions, see *Shepard v. U.S.* (1933), 290 U.S. 96, the exception does not include statements of belief of past events by declarant. To include statements of belief about a past event would negate the entire proscription against hearsay evidence.

In one instance, statements of belief by declarant are rendered admissible under this exception. Where the statement is by a testator concerning the execution, revocation, identification or terms of a will, such statement though constituting a belief about a past event is admissible. The declaration in this specific instance is highly trustworthy since it relates so closely to the testator-declarant's affairs, and the general prohibition against statements of belief about past events is unnecessary.

Rule 803(4) Statements for Purposes of Medical Diagnosis or Treatment

This exception is identical to Federal Evidence Rule 803(4).

Statements made by declarant to a physician regarding present and past physical condition are admissible under this exception. The rule, while similar to prior Ohio law, extends the common law doctrine to admit statements made to a physician without regard to the purpose of the examination or need for the patient's history. In *Scott v. Campbell* (1961), 115 Ohio App. 208, the court recognized the exception as it applies to statements made to a treating physician. However, in *Pennsylvania Co. v. Files* (1901), 65 Ohio St. 403, the court set forth the earlier limitation that statements made to a physician in preparation for litigation were not admissible under this common law exception.

The circumstantial guaranty of trustworthiness of this exception is derived from the assumption that a person will be truthful about his physical condition to a physician because of the risk of harmful treatment resulting from untruthful statements.

The rule avoids the necessity of making often artificial distinctions between those medical examinations and diagnosis [sic.] made for purposes of treatment and those made for purposes of trial in cases where both objectives are involved.

The exception is limited to those statements made by the patient which are reasonably pertinent to an accurate diagnosis and should not be a conduit through which matters of no medical significance would be admitted.

Rule 803(5) Recorded Recollection

This exception is sometimes referred to as "past recollection recorded". It is substantially identical to Federal Evidence Rule 803(5) and it reflects pre-existing Ohio law. *State v. Scott* (1972), 31 Ohio St.2d 1.

The exception gathers its circumstantial guaranty of trustworthiness from the fact that the person having made the statement is on the witness stand subject to oath, cross-examination and demeanor evaluation. If the statement was reduced to writing at or near the time of the event and the witness can testify that the writing accurately describes the event that he observed first hand and that it does not now refresh the independent recollection of the witness, it may be admissible as an exception to the hearsay rule. See McCormick § 299 (2d ed. 1972) *et seq.*

Moreover, the *Scott* case, *supra*, also held that this exception to the hearsay rule does not violate the confrontation clause of the U.S. Constitution in criminal cases because the declarant under this exception is, by definition, on the witness stand and is subject to full cross-examination, syllabus 2, *State v. Scott, supra*.

The rule makes explicit the requirement that the foundation for the introduction of the statement under this exception must be made by testimony of the witness himself. The assessment of trustworthiness is thereby focused upon the author and not upon some other person incident to the event.

The exception is to be distinguished from business records in that the writing need not have been prepared by virtue of any business obligation to do so.

This exception is also to be distinguished from the rule relating to refreshing recollection of a witness which involves no hearsay problem at all. It relates to the extent to which a witness may jog his memory by outside aids including a writing. If the writing jogs the memory of the witness then there is no need for the writing to qualify under this exception to the hearsay rule and it does not become evidence. See Rule 612.

Rule 803(6) Record of Regularly Conducted Activity

This rule is identical to Federal Evidence Rule 803(6) with one important modification and it is in substantial conformity with R.C. 2317.40, the Uniform Business Records as Evidence Act, being possibly a bit clearer.

The business records exception derives its circumstantial guaranty of trustworthiness from the fact that records made in the ordinary course of business by employees under an obligation to make such records will be accurate because business cannot, as a matter of course, function without accurate records.

The record keeper, absent self-authenticating provisions must testify that the records are such as are routinely kept as a part of the business and that the entrant (declarant) is under a duty to record the items contained in the record, and that the records are maintained accurately in accordance with a custom or routine.

Of course, there is the necessity to recognize that statements contained in the record either are not themselves hearsay, or if hearsay, that they qualify under some other exception to the hearsay rule. As to the conditions of admissibility of "totem pole" hearsay see Rule 805. The business record can be admitted only to the extent that the business record declarant could have testified if he had been on the witness stand.

Not incorporated into these rules is a problem somewhat pervasive of all hearsay exceptions. The question of admissibility of hearsay evidence in a criminal case has not been dealt with by specific provision except as to public records in Rule 803(8). The confrontation clause of the 6th Amendment raises serious concerns and, at least as to business records, the Ohio Supreme Court has held that R.C. 2317.40 (Business Records Act) does not apply in criminal cases. *State v. Tims* (1967), 9 Ohio St.2d 136. That case involved the use of hospital records in a criminal charge of rape.

More recently the Ohio Supreme Court applied the reasoning of *Tims, supra*, to the records of a probation officer in a hearing to revoke probation where the probation officer did not take the stand to testify concerning the contents of the record. *State v. Mil-*

ler (1975), 42 Ohio St. 2d 102. It is clear that the Supreme Court considers the constitutional requirements of confrontation not limited to hospital records.

Recent U.S. Supreme Court cases have broadened the application of the confrontation clause of the 6th Amendment, and it is not yet known what the permissible limits of hearsay in criminal cases will be when the smoke clears. See *California v. Green* (1970), 399 U.S. 149. These rules do not undertake to unravel these highly intricate constitutional cases and the rules should be applicable in both civil and criminal areas to the extent constitutionally permissible. At least in so doing, hearsay evidence meeting the requirements of the rules would be admissible in a criminal case in behalf of the defendant.

The Federal Evidence Rule was modified in the Ohio version by addition of the phrase "or as provided by Rule 901(B)(10)", following the requirement of testimony by the custodian of the records provision of the rule. This language was added to clearly permit the admission of records which qualify as self-authenticating pursuant to statute such as hospital records under R.C. 2317.422.

The Ohio rule departs from the Federal Evidence rule by deleting "opinions and diagnoses" as admissible under this section. It is not clear how far present Ohio law permits such evidence to be admitted. In *Hytha v. Schwendeman* (1974), 40 Ohio App.2d 478, the Franklin County Court of Appeals set forth seven criteria for a diagnosis to be admissible when contained in a hospital record. The *Hytha* case may retain validity in so far as it may assist in determining the point at which, in medical records, an act, event or condition admissible under the exception becomes an impermissible opinion or diagnosis under the rule.

Rule 803(7) Absence of Entry in Records Kept in Accordance with the Provisions of Paragraph 6

This section is identical to the Federal Evidence Rules and serves the salutary purpose of permitting the negative to be established by the absence of an entry to the same extent that the positive would be established by the existence of an entry. Such may have been implicit in the existing law.

The obvious use of this provision would be to permit, for example, the introduction of a ledger of account not only to show notations of payment but to show lack of payment. If the ledger carries sufficient circumstantial guaranty of trustworthiness to justify its admission to prove the correctness of entries therein, the same logic suggests the accuracy of lack of entries. McCormick § 307 (2d ed. 1972). See also *State v. Colvin* (1969), 19 Ohio St.2d 86, wherein the lack of entry in a public record was held to be admissible on the issue of non-existence of the fact not recorded.

Rule 803(8) Public Records and Reports

The Ohio rule adopts the federal version of the public records exception with three changes:

1. The phrase "unless offered by defendant" was added to subdivision (B) to make it clear that police reports favorable to the defendant could be offered by him in a criminal case. Such exculpatory reports should be available to the defendant since none of the constitutional hazards of confrontation are involved in making such reports admissible on behalf of defendants.

2. "State or political subdivision thereof" is substituted for the term "government". The term "government" has a "federal" connotation and the

substituted phrase is common throughout Ohio law. [Author's Note: The provision to which this paragraph relates was deleted from Rule 803(8) as finally adopted.]

3. Subdivision (C) relating to factual findings in reports resulting from an investigation of a governmental administrative agency or instrumentality was deleted in its entirety because the provisions of subdivision (A) and (B) were deemed adequate to cover admissibiltiy of government reports contemplated by this exception.

With these revisions, the rule permits introduction of public reports subject to the exceptions enumerated. Several Ohio statutory provisions accomplish a similar result. See, for example, R.C. 2317.39 and 2317.42 regarding public records. Also, authorizing public records to be introduced into evidence as an exception to the hearsay rule are numerous Ohio Supreme Court cases including: *Howells v. Limbeck* (1960), 172 Ohio St. 297 (court records); *Carson v. Metropolitan Life Insurance Company* (1951), 156 Ohio St. 104 (records of coroner); and more recently the court held that R.C. 2317.42 authorizes admission of public records as evidence unless the statements contained in the record are themselves hearsay, recognizing the familiar "totempole" hearsay problem. *Westinghouse Electric v. Dolly Madison Leasing & Furniture Corp.* (1975), 42 Ohio St.2d 122.

A similar provision relating to proof of official records is contained in Civ. R. 44(A). This exception does not alter the provisions of Civ. R. 44.

Rule 803(9) Records of Vital Statistics

This exception is in conformity with Federal Rule 803(9) and R.C. 3705.05 relative to birth and death certificates. However, it should be observed that this statute would not, merely by virtue of this subdivision of the hearsay rule, be superseded since the statute also establishes such records as *prima facie* evidence of the facts asserted. *Perry v. Ind. Comm.* (1954), 160 Ohio St. 520.

Rule 803(10) Absence of Public Record or Entry

See comments to Rule 803(7) above. The function of this exception accomplishes the same objective with regard to absence of entry in records.

A similar provision relative to proof of lack of record is found in Civ. R. 44(B) in which the written statement that no record of a specified tenor exists may be admissible to prove that no such record or entry does exist. To the same effect is *State v. Colvin* (1969), 19 Ohio St.2d 86, wherein the court held, construing R.C. 2317.42, that a certification that no record of a license to practice dentistry was found in examining the records of the State Dental Board was admissible to prove no license was issued.

Rule 803(11) Records of Religious Organizations

Rule 803(12) Marriage, Baptismal and Similar Certificates

Rule 803(13) Family Records

These three exceptions are rather long standing common law rules recognized in Ohio for many years. No significant departure from these precedents is involved. McCormick § 322 (2d ed. 1972). Rule 803(11) is a special treatment of a particular kind of business record otherwise covered in Rule 803(6). The Ohio Rules are identical to Federal Evidence Rules 803(11), (12) and (13).

Rule 803(14) Records of Documents Affecting an Interest in Property

This exception covers deeds and other instruments recorded in a public office. It differs from either the business record exception of Rule 803(6) or [the] public record [exception] of Rule 803(8) in that it is not requisite that the document recorded has been prepared in the course of business. This rule relates also to the issue of best evidence in that the copy on record may be admitted to prove the contents and execution of the original. To this extent it is similar to R.C. 5301.43.

R.C. 5301.44, relating to curing defects, provides that a certified copy of such record is "prima facie evidence that such instrument was executed and existed as shown by such record." Rule 803(14) does not supersede this statutory provision.

In essence, all that the rule does is render the hearsay rule inapplicable to records of instruments relating to real property properly recorded as evidence of the facts set forth in the original. *Emmitt v. Lee* (1893), 50 Ohio St. 662.

This rule is identical to Federal Evidence Rule 803(14).

Rule 803(15) Statements in Documents Affecting an Interest in Property

The rule is stated in language identical to that of Federal Evidence Rule 803(15).

Property refers to real and personal property and the document need not be recordable.

The rule is consistent with prior Ohio law. *Garrett v. Hanshue* (1895), 53 Ohio St. 482 (abstract received as evidence of interest); *Walsh v. Barton* (1873), 24 Ohio St. 28 (recent deed as evidence of title in action for specific performance); *Aurilo v. Youngstown* (1959), 84 Ohio L. Abs. 508 (assignment in an action on a contract); *Gager v. Prout* (1891), 48 Ohio St. 89 (estate inventory as evidence of decedent's omissions in a tax return). The statutes also contain examples: R.C. 317.22(B), record of heir's affidavit for county auditor's transfer and indorsement of land or mineral conveyance is *prima facie* evidence in any cause; R.C. 155.02, deed from State of Ohio is *prima facie* evidence of title in any civil action as to certain canal lands; R.C. 315.52, depositions taken by county engineer as to destroyed corners are admissible in causes affecting the title to the land involved.

Rule 803(16) Statements in Ancient Documents

The rule is stated in language identical to that of Federal Evidence Rule 803(16).

The rule modifies prior Ohio law by reducing the period for qualification as an ancient document from thirty years to twenty years. Ohio has followed the common law and utilized the thirty-year period. *Wright v. Hull* (1911), 83 Ohio St. 385.

Rule 803(17) Market Reports, Commercial Publications

The rule is stated in language identical to that of Federal Evidence Rule 803(17).

The rule is in accord with prior Ohio law. It has been held that market reports, weather reports and other reports prepared by skilled persons acquainted with the subject matter are admissible. *Andrews v. State* (1912), 15 Ohio Cir. Ct. (N.S.) 241. In *Pittsburgh C.C. & L.R. Co. v. Sheppard* (1897), 56 Ohio St. 68, it was held that a horses'e [sic.] track record prepared by the Trotting Association was admissible on the issue of value in an action for injury to the horse.

Rule 803(18) Reputation Concerning Personal or Family History

The rule is stated in language identical to that of Federal Evidence Rule 803(19).

The rule is in accord with prior Ohio law. *Stewart v. Welch* (1885), 41 Ohio St. 483 (marriage); *McCune v. Lakin* (1916), 25 Ohio Cir. Ct. (N.S.) 118 (blood relationship); *Harris v. Seabury* (1928), 30 Ohio App. 42 (legitimacy); *Sperry v. Tebbs, Admr.* (1888), 20 Weekly Law Bull. 181 (identity by family history).

Rule 803(19) Reputation Concerning Boundaries or General History

The rule is stated in language identical to that of Federal Evidence Rule 803(20).

The rule is in accord with prior Ohio law. Boundaries, *McCoy's Lessee v. Galloway* (1827), 3 Ohio 283. General history, *Board of Education, City of Wapakoneta v. Unknown Heirs of Aughinbaugh* (1955), 70 Ohio L. Abs. 1.

Rule 803(20) Reputation as to Character

The rule is stated in language identical to that of Federal Evidence Rule 803(21).

The rule is in accord with prior Ohio law which holds that evidence of character or reputation is original evidence. *Upthegrove v. State* (1882), 37 Ohio St. 662.

Rule 803(21) Judgment of Previous Conviction

With one exception, the rule is stated in language identical to that of Federal Evidence Rule 803(22). The modification consists of substituting "no contest or the equivalent plea from another jurisdiction" for "nolo contendere".

The rule makes the judgment of conviction in felony cases either upon conviction or plea of guilty, admissible in subsequent proceedings, civil or criminal, limiting use in criminal cases to impeachment, but permitting use in civil cases to prove any fact essential to sustain the judgment.

The application in criminal cases represents no departure from established Ohio law.

The application in civil cases represents a reversal of Ohio practice. In *State v. Schwartz* (1940), 137 Ohio St. 371, the Court held that a judgment in a criminal case is not admissible as evidence in a subsequent civil case, the criminal case being a bastardy proceeding and the civil case being for non-support. A manslaughter conviction was held to be not admissible in a subsequent action on an insurance policy for unintentional death for the assigned reasons that the parties and the standards of proof were different. *Moorman v. National Casualty Co.* (1947), 49 Ohio L. Abs. 61.

A seldom used statute, R.C. 1.16 provides that anyone injured in person or property by a criminal act may recover full damages in a civil action. No record of conviction, unless it was obtained by confession in open court, can be used in such civil action. The rule is in conflict with R.C. 1.16 and the rule would supersede the statute under the provisions of Article IV, § 5(B), Ohio Constitution.

The Ohio rule applied only to felonies.

Rule 803(22) Judgment as to Personal, Family, or General History, or Boundaries

The rule is stated in language identical to that of Federal Evidence Rule 803(23).

The rule modifies prior Ohio law. In *Marks v. Sigler* (1854), 3 Ohio St. 358, at 361, the court said that judgments were binding on no one except the parties and persons in privity and could not be used as instruments of evidence against strangers to the record. Against strangers, a judgment was only evidence of rendition and not evidence of the facts upon which it was based according to the prior Ohio law. Cases involving boundaries are illustrative: *Cincinnati v. Hosea* (1900), 19 Ohio Cir. Ct. 744; *Niles v. Cedar Point Club* (1898), 85 F. 45.

Cross References

Bank records showing dishonor of instrument admissible, 1303.65

Business records as evidence, 2317.40

Certified copy of record in action to cure defects, 5301.44

Certified copy of record of instrument as evidence, 5301.43

Civil recovery for criminal act, record of conviction as evidence, 2307.60

Copy of record of lost deed to be evidence, 5301.14

Delinquent children, deposition of child sex offense victims, 2152.81

Evidence of marriage, discretion of court, 3105.12

Fetal death certificate, burial permit, 3705.20

Laboratory report as prima-facie evidence of content, weight and identity of substance, rights of accused, 2925.51

Lease of right of way to be recorded, 4961.39

Method of qualification of hospital and certain other records, 2317.422

Minister's license to solemnize marriages, record and license as evidence of authority, 3101.12

Official reports admitted as evidence, 2317.42

Proof of official record, lack of record, Civ R 44

Registration of births, 3705.09

Registration of death, certificate of death, 3705.16

Registration of marriages, divorces, annulments, and dissolutions of marriage, 3705.21

Testimony of mentally retarded or developmentally disabled victim, 2945.482

Testimony of mentally retarded or developmentally disabled victim; videotaped testimony, 2945.491

Videotaped preliminary hearing testimony of child victim, 2945.49

Vital statistics records, issuance of certified copies, 3705.23, 3705.24

Library References

Criminal Law ⬅362 to 368, 419(1) to 421(6), 429(1) to 446.

Evidence ⬅118 to 128, 317 to 324, 325 to 383(12).

Witnesses ⬅ 253.1 to 257.

Westlaw Topic Nos. 110, 157, 410.

C.J.S. Criminal Law §§ 454, 831, 854 to 876, 1025 to 1049.

C.J.S. Evidence §§ 227, 228, 234, 259 to 284, 342 to 363, 813 to 1053.

C.J.S. Municipal Corporations § 447.

C.J.S. Statutes §§ 85, 90, 450 et seq.

C.J.S. Witnesses §§ 357 to 363.

OJur 3d: 25, Criminal Law § 479, 481, 482; 27, Criminal Law § 1154, 1200, 1201, 1202, 1609; 29A, Criminal Law § 2948, 3003, 3006 to 3009, 3012, 3013, 3015, 3056, 3059, 3069, 3139; 30, Death § 1; 31, Decedents' Estates § 376; 33, Decedents' Estates § 1154, 1255; 43, Evidence and Witnesses § 274 to 276, 328 to 330, 334, 397, 400 to 402, 406, 413, 417, 419 to 422, 433, 440 to 442, 471; 59, Insurance § 1387, 1397; 67, Malpractice § 143, 144; 70, Negligence § 172, 184

Am Jur 2d: 29, Evidence § 496 et seq.

Admissibility of sound recordings in evidence. 58 ALR2d 1024

Admissibility of party's book accounts to prove loans or payments by person by or for whom they are kept. 13 ALR3d 284

Admissibility in evidence of sound recording as affected by hearsay and best evidence rules. 58 ALR3d 598

Admissibility under business entry statutes of hospital records in criminal case. 69 ALR3d 22

Admissibility under Uniform Business Records as Evidence Act or similar statute of medical report made by consulting physician to treating physician. 69 ALR3d 104

Admissibility in state court proceedings of police reports as business records. 77 ALR3d 115

Admissibility, under public records exception to hearsay rule, of record kept by public official without express statutory direction or authorization. 80 ALR3d 414

Nonverbal reaction to accusation, other than silence alone, as constituting adoptive admission under hearsay rule. 87 ALR3d 706

Evidence: admissibility of memorandum of telephone conversation. 94 ALR3d 975

Business records: authentication and verification of bills and invoices under Rule 803(6) of the Uniform Rules of Evidence. 1 ALR4th 316

Admissibility in evidence of professional directories. 7 ALR4th 638

Necessity, in criminal prosecution, of independent evidence of principal act to allow admission, under res gestae or excited utterance exception to hearsay rule, of statement made at time of, or subsequent to, principal act. 38 ALR4th 1237

Admissibility of police officer's testimony at state trial relating to motorist's admissions made in or for automobile accident report required by law. 46 ALR4th 291

Uniform Evidence Rule 803(24): the residual hearsay exception. 51 ALR4th 999

Admissibility of school records under hearsay exceptions. 57 ALR4th 1111

Admissibility of evidence of reputation as to land boundaries or customs affecting land, under Rule 803(20) of Uniform Rules of Evidence and similar formulations. 79 ALR4th 1044

Admissibility of police reports under Federal Business Records Act (Federal Rules of Evidence, Rule 803, and predecessor amendments). 31 ALR Fed 457

Admissibility of statement under Rule 803(5) of the Federal Rules of Evidence, providing for recorded-recollection exception to hearsay rule. 35 ALR Fed 605

Construction and application of provision of Rule 803(8)(B), Federal Rules of Evidence, excluding from exception to hearsay rule in criminal cases matters observed by law enforcement officers. 37 ALR Fed 831

When is hearsay statement an "excited utterance" admissible under Rule 803(2) of the Federal Rules of Evidence. 48 ALR Fed 451

Admissibility of statements for purposes of medical diagnosis or treatment as hearsay exception under Rule 803(4) of the Federal Rules of Evidence. 55 ALR Fed 689

Admissibility, over hearsay objection, of police observations and investigative findings offered by government in criminal prosecution, excluded from public records exception to hearsay rule under Rule 803(8)(B) or (C), Federal Rules of Evidence. 56 ALR Fed 168

When is hearsay statement a "present sense impression" admissible under Rule 803(1) of the Federal Rules of Evidence. 60 ALR Fed 524

Admissibility of records other than police reports, under Rule 803(6), Federal Rules of Evidence, providing for business records exception to hearsay rule. 61 ALR Fed 359

Admissibility, under Rule 803(10) of Federal Rules of Evidence, of evidence of absence of public record or entry. 70 ALR Fed 198

Exception to hearsay rule, under Rule 803(3) of Federal Rules of Evidence, with respect to statement of declarant's mental, emotional, or physical condition. 75 ALR Fed 170

Exception to hearsay rule, under Rule 803(11) or Rule 803(12) of Federal Rules of Evidence, with respect to information contained in records of religious organization. 78 ALR Fed 361

Katz & Giannelli, Baldwin's Ohio Practice, Criminal Law § 1.6, 1.8, 115.12 (1996).

Painter, Ohio Driving Under the Influence Law (2003 Ed.), Text 13.2, 13.4, 13.7, 13.8, 13.10.

Giannelli & Snyder, Baldwin's Ohio Practice, Evidence § 101.3, 102.4, 102.5, 104.3, 405.3, 410.4, 601.7, 607.2, 607.4, 607.8, 608.3, 609.15, 612.1, 612.3, 612.4, 613.3, 703.7, 706.2, 801, 801.1, 801.6, 802, 801.11, 801.21, 802.5, 802.6, 804, 802.9, 803.4, 803.8, 803.16, 803.19, 803.21, 803.38, 803.46, 803.49, 804.1, 804.9, 807, 804.14, 805.3, 807.1, 807.3, 612, 901.11, 901.12, 901.16, 901.24, 805, 901, 901.25, 902.3, 902.4, 1002.6, 1002.7, 1005.1, 1006.3 (2d ed. 2001).

Williams, Ohio Consumer Law (2002 Ed.), Text 6.39, 6.40.

Adrine & Ruden, Ohio Domestic Violence Law (2002 Ed.), Text 5.14, 5.15, 5.16, 5.17, 5.18, 5.19, 5.21, 5.23, 6.14, 13.6, 14.12, 15.8, 15.9.

Carlin, Baldwin's Ohio Practice, Merrick–Rippner Probate Law § 107.38, 107.51 (2003).

Evid R 804 Hearsay exceptions; declarant unavailable

(A) Definition of unavailability

"Unavailability as a witness" includes any of the following situations in which the declarant:

(1) is exempted by ruling of the court on the ground of privilege from testifying concerning the subject matter of the declarant's statement;

(2) persists in refusing to testify concerning the subject matter of the declarant's statement despite an order of the court to do so;

(3) testifies to a lack of memory of the subject matter of the declarant's statement;

(4) is unable to be present or to testify at the hearing because of death or then-existing physical or mental illness or infirmity;

(5) is absent from the hearing and the proponent of the declarant's statement has been unable to procure the declarant's attendance (or in the case of a hearsay exception under division (B)(2), (3), or (4) of this rule, the declarant's attendance or testimony) by process or other reasonable means.

A declarant is not unavailable as a witness if the declarant's exemption, refusal, claim of lack of memory, inability, or absence is due to the procurement or wrongdoing of the proponent of the declarant's statement for the purpose of preventing the witness from attending or testifying.

(B) Hearsay exceptions

The following are not excluded by the hearsay rule if the declarant is unavailable as a witness:

(1) Former testimony. Testimony given as a witness at another hearing of the same or a different proceeding, or in a deposition taken in compliance with law in the course of the same or another proceeding, if the party against whom the testimony is now offered, or, in a civil action or proceeding, a predecessor in interest, had an opportunity and similar motive to develop the testimony by direct, cross, or redirect examination. Testimony given at a preliminary hearing must satisfy the right to confrontation and exhibit indicia of reliability.

(2) Statement under belief of impending death. In a prosecution for homicide or in a civil action or proceeding, a statement made by a declarant, while believing that his or her death was imminent, concerning the cause or circumstances of what the declarant believed to be his or her impending death.

(3) Statement against interest. A statement that was at the time of its making so far contrary to the declarant's pecuniary or proprietary interest, or so far tended to subject the declarant to civil or criminal liability, or to render invalid a claim by the declarant against another, that a reasonable person in the declarant's position would not have made the statement unless the declarant believed it to be true. A statement tending to expose the declarant to criminal liability, whether offered to exculpate or inculpate the accused, is not admissible unless corroborating circumstances clearly indicate the trustworthiness of the statement.

(4) Statement of personal or family history. (a) A statement concerning the declarant's own birth, adoption, marriage, divorce, legitimacy, relationship by blood, adoption, or marriage, ancestry, or other similar fact of personal or family history, even though the declarant had no means of acquiring personal knowledge of the matter stated; or (b) a statement concerning the foregoing matters, and death also, of another person, if the declarant was related to the other by blood, adoption, or marriage or was so intimately associated with the other's family as to be likely to have accurate information concerning the matter declared.

(5) Statement by a deceased or incompetent person. The statement was made by a decedent or a mentally incompetent person, where all of the following apply:

(a) the estate or personal representative of the decedent's estate or the guardian or trustee of the incompetent person is a party;

(b) the statement was made before the death or the development of the incompetency;

(c) the statement is offered to rebut testimony by an adverse party on a matter within the knowledge of the decedent or incompetent person.

(6) Forfeiture by wrongdoing. A statement offered against a party if the unavailability of the witness is due to the wrongdoing of the party for the purpose of preventing the witness from attending or testifying. However, a statement is not admissible under this rule unless the proponent has given to each adverse party advance written notice of an intention to introduce the statement sufficient to provide the adverse party a fair opportunity to contest the admissibility of the statement.

(Adopted eff. 7–1–80; amended eff. 7–1–81) [1], 7–1–93, 7–1–01

[1] As originally adopted, Rule 804(B)(1) excluded preliminary hearing testimony from the former testimony exception. *See* 62 OS(2d) xlvii (1980). The exclusion of preliminary hearing testimony, Crim R 5(B), was based upon the Ohio Supreme Court's decision in *State v Roberts,*55 OS(2d) 191, 378 NE(2d) 492 (1978). The Court in *Roberts* held that admitting preliminary hearing testimony in a criminal trial violated the accused's Sixth Amendment right of confrontation. *See also* State v Smith, 58 OS(2d) 344, 390 NE(2d) 778 (1979), vacated, 448 US 902, 100 SCt 3041, 65 LEd(2d) 1132 (1980). Just

days before the Rules of Evidence became effective, the *Roberts* decision was reversed by the U.S. Supreme Court. *See* Ohio v Roberts, 448 US 56, 100 SCt 2531, 65 LEd(2d) 597 (1980). In response, the rule was amended by deleting the clause which exempted preliminary hearing testimony. *See* 53 Ohio Bar 1218 (1980).

Historical and Statutory Notes

Amendment Note: The 7–1–01 amendment deleted "or" from the end of division (A)(4); placed the final sentence of former division (A)(5) as the final separate paragraph of division (A); inserted "all of the following apply" before "(a)" and deleted "and" before "(b)" and "(c)" in division (B)(5); added new division (B)(6); and made other nonsubstantive changes.

Amendment Note: The 7–1–93 amendment substituted "the declarant's" for "his" and "the declarant" for "he" or "him" throughout; inserted "or her" in division (B)(2); and removed references to deaf-mute persons throughout division (B)(5).

Commentary

Staff Notes

2001:

Rule 804(A) Definition of unavailability

The amendment to division (A) of the rule involved clarifying changes in language. In addition, the amendment placed in a separate paragraph what had been in the last sentence of division (A)(5) in order to clarify that the final sentence of the division applies to all of the rule's definitions of "unavailability." No substantive change is intended by these amendments.

Rule 804(B)(6) Forfeiture by wrongdoing

The 2001 amendment added division (B)(6), forfeiture by wrongdoing. This division recognizes a forfeiture rule for hearsay statements that would have been admissible as testimony had the witness been present at trial. It is patterned after the federal rule, which was adopted in 1997. It codifies a principle that has been recognized at common-law in Ohio.

Rationale. The U.S. Supreme Court has recognized the forfeiture doctrine in the context of the right of confrontation. In *Illinois v. Allen*, 397 U.S. 337 (1970), the Court held that while the defendant has the right to be present at his or her trial, the right may be lost where defendant is so disorderly that the trial cannot be continued with his or her presence. Similarly, the Court held in *Taylor v. United States*, 414 U.S. 17 (1973), that defendant's voluntary absence from the courtroom can be construed as a waiver of the defendant's right to confrontation, without a warning from the court. In *Reynolds v. United States*, 98 U.S. 145 (1878), the Court upheld the admissibility of hearsay because the defendant had refused to reveal the declarant's location.

The term "forfeiture" was chosen over alternatives such as "waiver," "waiver by conduct," or "implied" or "constructive waiver" because the rule applies even if the party is not aware of the right of confrontation or the hearsay rule. In other words, the intentional relinquishment of a known right is *not* the standard.

Only a few Ohio cases have addressed the issue, but all have recognized that Ohio's common-law of evidence incorporates a rule of forfeiture similar to the federal rule. See *State v. Kilbane*, 1979 Ohio App. Lexis 10550, Nos. 38428, 38383, 38433 (8th Dist. Ct. App., 4/3/79), at *19; *State v. Liberatore*, 1983 Ohio App. Lexis 13808, No. 46784 (8th Dist. Ct. App. 12/3/83), at *13 ("[T]he evidence in *Steele*

clearly indicated that the defendants had procured the witness' unavailability. The evidence in the instant case is far from clear that defendant procured Mata's 'unavailability'."); *State v. Brown*, 1986 Ohio App. Lexis 6567, No. 50505 (8th Dist. Ct. App. 4/24/86), at *11–12 ("[T]he victim expressed concern that the defendant's brother had threatened her mother and her children. An accused cannot rely on the confrontation clause to preclude extrajudicial evidence from a source which he obstructs.") See also *Steele v. Taylor*, 684 F.2d 1193, 1200–04 (6th Cir. 1982)(federal habeas corpus review of the conviction in *Kilbane*), cert. denied, 460 U.S. 1053 (1983).

Standard. The offering party must show (1) that the party engaged in wrongdoing that resulted in the witness's unavailability, and (2) that one purpose was to cause the witness to be unavailable at trial. See *United States v. Houlihan*, 92 F.3d 1271, 1279 (1st Cir. 1996) ("waiver by homicide") ("[I]t is sufficient in this regard to show that the evildoer was motivated *in part* by a desire to silence the witness; the intent to deprive the prosecution of testimony need not be the actor's *sole* motivation."), cert. denied, 519 U.S. 1118 (1997).

Coverage. As the federal drafters note, "[t]he wrongdoing need not consist of a criminal act. The rule applies to all parties, including the government. It applies to actions taken after the event to prevent a witness from testifying." Fed.R.Evid. 804 advisory committee's note. Thus, the rule does not apply to statements of the victim in a homicide prosecution concerning the homicide, including a felony-murder case.

The Ohio rule does not adopt the word "acquiesce" that is used in the federal rule. This departure from the federal model is intended to exclude from the rule's coverage situations in which, under federal practice, a party's mere inaction has been held to effect a forfeiture. See, e.g. *United States v. Mastrangelo*, 693 F.2d 269, 273–74 (2d Cir. 1982), cert. denied, 467 U.S. 1204 (1984)("Bare knowledge of a plot to kill Bennett and a failure to give warning to appropriate authorities is sufficient to constitute a waiver.") Encouraging a witness to invoke a valid privilege, such as the Fifth Amendment, or the spousal competency rule, Evid. R. 601, does not trigger this rule because such conduct is not wrongdoing. Encouraging a witness to leave the state is wrongdoing in this context because no one has the legal right to refuse to provide testimony in the absence of a privilege or other rule of evidence. The prosecution, however, should not be able to cause a potential defense witness to assert the Fifth Amendment for the sole purpose of making that witness unavailable to the defense and then refuse to immunize that witness's testimony.

The rule extends to potential witnesses. See *United States v. Houlihan*, 92 F.3d 1271, 1279 (1st Cir. 1996) ("Although the reported cases all appear to involve actual witnesses, we can discern no principled reason why the waiver-by-misconduct doctrine should not apply with equal force if a defendant intentionally silences a *potential* witness.") (citation omitted), cert. denied, 519 U.S. 1118 (1997).

The rule governs only the hearsay aspect; the trial court retains authority under Evid. R. 403 to exclude unreliable statements. This is probably also a due process requirement. See generally Comment, The Admission of Hearsay Evidence Where Defendant Misconduct Causes the Unavailability of a Prosecution Witness, 43 Am. U. L. Rev. 995, 1014 (1994) ("The procuring defendant actually acknowledges the reliability of the absent witness' information when he or she endeavors to derail the witness' court appearance-an act the defendant would be less likely to commit if the witness's information is false or untrustworthy.")

The rule does not cover the admissibility of evidence regarding the wrongful act of procuring a witness's unavailability when the evidence is offered as an "implied" admission. Evidence of that character is not hearsay and is governed by the relevance rules. 1 Giannelli & Snyder, Baldwin's Ohio Practice, Evidence Section 401.9 (1996) (admissions by conduct).

Procedures. The trial court decides admissibility under Evid. R. 104(A); the traditional burden of persuasion (preponderance of evidence) rests with the party offering the evidence once an objection is raised. If the evidence is admitted, the court does not explain the basis of its ruling to the jury. This is similar to the procedure used in admitting a co-conspirator statement under Evid. R. 801(D)(2)(c), where the trial judge must decide the existence of a conspiracy as a condition of admissibility but would not inform the jury of this preliminary finding.

The opposing party would, however, have the opportunity to attack the reliability of the statement before the jury, Evid. R. 104(E), and impeach the declarant under Evid. R. 806.

The notice requirement, which is based on Evid. R. 609(B), may trigger an objection by a motion *in limine* and the opportunity for determining admissibility at a hearing outside the jury's presence. See *United States v. Thai*, 29 F.3d 785 (2d Cir. 1994) (unsworn statements made to detective prior to declarant's murder by defendant). ("Prior to admitting such testimony, the district court must hold a hearing in which the government has the burden of proving by a preponderance of the evidence that the defendant was responsible for the witness's absence.")

1993:

Rule 804(A) Definition of unavailability.

The only changes to division (A) are the use of gender neutral language; no substantive change is intended.

Rule 804(B) Hearsay exceptions.

The substantive amendment to this division is in division (B)(5). The amendment to division (B)(5) removes references to "deaf-mutes" as a separate category of incompetent persons whose statements are admissible on behalf of an estate, guardian, or personal representative to rebut certain testimony by adverse parties.

The hearsay exception established by Evid. R. 804(B)(5) is designed to account for the effective abolition of the "Dead Man's Statute" (R.C. 2317.04) by the provisions of Evid. R. 601. The statute prohibited a party from testifying when the adverse party was, among others, "the guardian or trustee of either a deaf and dumb or an insane person." R.C. 2317.04. Under Evid. R. 601, there is no competency bar to a party's testimony in those cases, but if the party does testify, Evid. R. 804(B)(5) permits the guardian or trustee to introduce the statements of the ward in rebuttal.

As originally drafted, Evid.R. 804(B)(5) referred to the same categories of persons subject to guardianship as were referred to in the statute, albeit with some modernization in terminology. In particular, the rule identified "a deaf-mute who is now unable to testify" as a category of declarant-ward distinct from "a mentally incompetent person." As employed in the statute, however, that distinction appears to be no more than a remnant of nineteenth century

guardianship laws, which at one time provided for the guardianship of the "deaf and dumb" separately from provisions for guardians of "idiots" or the "insane." *See* Act of March 9, 1838, Section 17, 36 Ohio Laws 40. To a large extent, provisions of that kind reflected the nineteenth century view that a person who was "deaf and dumb" was probably, if not certainly, mentally incompetent.

The nineteenth century's assumptions about the mental faculties of those with hearing or speech impairments are certainly inaccurate as an empirical matter. In any event, under modern law, the appointment of a guardian for an adult requires a determination that the person is mentally incompetent, and there is no separate provision for the guardianship of incompetent "deaf-mutes." *See* R.C. 2111.02. That being the case, the "deaf-mute" declarants referred to in the rule are necessarily included within the rule's class of "mentally incompetent person [s]": an adult subject to a guardianship is by definition mentally incompetent, without regard to the existence of a "deaf-mute condition."

The identification of a separate class of "deaf-mute" declarants is thus redundant, and it likewise rests on archaic and mistaken views of the effect of hearing and speech impairments on one's mental capacities. The amendment deletes the rule's references to "deaf-mute" declarants in order to eliminate both of these difficulties, and in order to clarify that the rule applies only to statements by declarants who are deceased or mentally incompetent.

1980:

Rule 804 is similar to Federal Evidence Rule 804 with some significant modification in Rule 804(B)(1), Former testimony and Rule 804(B)(3) Statement against interest. The rule eliminates Federal Rule 804(B)(5), Other exceptions. The rule adds a new subsection, Rule 804(B)(5), Statement by a deceased, deaf-mute or incompetent person.

Rule 804(A) Definition of Unavailability

Rule 804(A) provides that certain out-of-court statements may be admitted into evidence as an exception to the hearsay rule if the declarant is "unavailable." The requirement that the declarant be "unavailable" simply indicates, in light of the kind of hearsay exception involved in the rule, that it would be preferable if the declarant would testify and be subject to cross-examination. If the declarant is unavailable, however, then his statement is admitted into evidence on the ground that it is better to admit the evidence as sufficiently trustworthy than not to have any evidence on the issue at all. In short, the hearsay exceptions covered by Rule 804 are "second class" exceptions seemingly less trustworthy than the hearsay exceptions governed by Rule 803. Rule 804 represents the prevailing view in American courts as to "unavailability" of the declarant and the kind of hearsay exceptions governed by the rule. See McCormick § 253 (2d ed. 1972).

Rule 804(A) defines the conditions under which a declarant is deemed to be "unavailable." It becomes readily apparent that unavailability under the rule does not mean that the declarant need be physically absent from the trial; hence under several definitions, although the declarant is present, it is his *testimony* which is "unavailable." There are five conditions set forth in Rule 804(A) under which declarant is deemed to be unavailable.

Pursuant to Rule 804(A)(1) a witness may invoke a privilege—such as the privilege against self-incrimination or the husband-wife privilege—and in that event, the witness is considered unavailable. The court, having ruled that the privilege has been asserted and that the witness is unavailable, may then permit the introduction of that evidence which, pursuant to Rule 804(B), is deemed to be an exception to the hearsay rule. See McCormick § 253 (2d ed. 1972).

Rule 804(A)(2) provides that when a witness refuses to testify, despite all efforts by the court to compel him to do so, he is considered unavailable. The provision extends the earlier rules governing unavailability, but the provision conforms to the modern weight of authority. See McCormick § 253 (2d ed. 1972).

Rule 804(A)(3) states that a witness is unavailable if he suffers from lack of memory. Just as senility or incompetency may cause a loss of memory, so too may a lapse in time between the event and the trial. The provision is less restrictive than some former court holdings. See McCormick § 253 (2d ed. 1972).

Rule 804(A)(4), providing that death, physical infirmity or mental illness renders a witness unavailable, follows long-established tradition. Death presents no problem, but a court will have to use its discretion in deciding that the mental or physical infirmity prohibits testifying. See McCormick § 253 (2d ed. 1972).

Under Rule 804(A)(5) if a witness cannot be compelled to appear or if his residence or existence is unknown, he is unavailable. Reasonable diligence must be exercised to find him or have him appear. Attendance in criminal cases will require stricter compliance. See *Barber v. Page* (1968), 390 U.S. 719; *New York Central RR v. Stevens* (1933), 126 Ohio St. 395; *Bauer v. Pullman Co.* (1968), 15 Ohio App.2d 69. Note that the provision requires—before a witness is deemed to be unavailable because of absence—that an attempt be made to depose him. In short, the witness is unavailable if his attendance *or* "testimony" could not be procured by reasonable means. A deposition is "testimony."

The final sentence of Rule 804(A) provides that a witness will not be deemed unavailable if the proponent of his statement engaged in wrong-doing to prevent the witness from testifying.

Rule 804(B)(1) Former Testimony

Under Rule 804(B)(1) the former testimony of a witness, the witness now being unavailable, may be introduced in evidence as an exception to the hearsay rule. The "testimony" offered in evidence may be testimony given by the witness at another hearing other than at a preliminary hearing in a criminal case, of the same or a different proceeding, or in a deposition. Under the exception, the testimony may be offered either against the party *against* whom it was previously offered or against the party *by* whom it was previously offered, provided that the party against whom the testimony is offered in the trial at hand "had an opportunity and similar motive to develop the testimony by direct, cross or redirect examination." In short, the testimony is trustworthy because there was an opportunity to examine the witness, and cross-examine the witness, in a former proceeding conducted in a context similar to the litigation at hand. This exception specifically excludes testimony at a preliminary hearing because the motives for cross-examination by a defendant may not be coextensive with that at the trial on the merits. [Author's Note: The provision excluding preliminary hearing testimony from the former testimony exception was deleted in 1981.] The rule supersedes R.C. 2317.06 and R.C. 2945.49. The rule is similar to the "former testimony" exception extant in the general law of evidence. See McCormick §254 (2d ed. 1972).

Cf. *State v. Roberts* (1978), 55 Ohio St.2d 191, rev'd. *Ohio v. Roberts*, (1980), [56] U.S. [448], 48 Law Week 4874.

Rule 804(B)(2) Statement Under Belief of Impending Death

Rule 804(B)(2) governs the "dying declaration" exception to the hearsay rule. The traditional exception of the dying declaration has been limited to homicide cases in the criminal area apparently because dying declarations are not among the most reliable forms of hearsay. Homicide is that situation where exceptional need for the evidence is present. See McCormick § 283 (2d ed. 1972). In Ohio the exception had been limited to homicide cases. See 21 OJur 2d Evidence § 341. Rule 804(B)(2) permits the use of the dying declaration in homicide cases in the criminal area *and* permits such use in civil cases as well.

Under the rule, the dying declaration of the deceased victim in criminal homicide cases will continue to be admitted into evidence as an exception to the hearsay rule under the standards set by case holdings. See 27 OJur 2d Homicide §§ 143–148.

Rule 804(B)(2) supersedes such case holdings as *Mitchell v. New York Life Ins. Co.* (1939), 62 Ohio App. 54.

Rule 804(B)(3) Statement Against Interest

Rule 804(B)(3) provides that a declaration against interest may be admitted into evidence as an exception to the hearsay rule. The declarant must of course be unavailable.

The declaration against interest applies to statements of persons other than parties to the action and should be distinguished from statements of parties to the action. The out-of-court statement of a party opponent in the action is an admission, not a declaration against interest. An admission of a party opponent is governed by Rule 801(D)(2) as non-hearsay and does not require the admission to be against the party's "interest" and does not require that the party be "unavailable" before the statement may be admitted.

The rule governing declarations against interest includes declarations against declarant's pecuniary or proprietary interest and also declarations which would subject declarant to civil or criminal liability. The exceptions to the hearsay rule subjecting declarant to civil or criminal liability broaden the traditional law governing declarations against interest and broaden Ohio law as well, the Ohio law having been limited to declarations against pecuniary interest. See *G.M. McKelvey Co. v. General Cas. Co.* (1957), 166 Ohio St. 401. See also McCormick §§276–280 (2d ed 1972).

The admission of evidence involving a declaration against pecuniary interest is illustrated by *Truelsch v. Northwestern Mut. Life Ins. Co.* (1925), 186 Wisc. 239, 202 N.W. 352. Husband, now dead because of suicide, embezzled money from Employer and used some of the money to pay premiums on a life policy, his Wife being beneficiary on the policy. At the suicide scene a letter, addressed to Wife, was found on Husband's body. Among other things the letter said that Husband had used some of the funds embezzled from Employer to pay premiums on the life policy. Wife sued Insurance Company to collect on the policy. Employer sued Insurance Company to collect that amount of embezzled money used to pay premiums. The actions were consolidated. At trial deceased husband's letter was admitted into evidence under the declaration against interest exception to the hearsay rule. Husband was obviously "unavailable" to testify, and his letter, a non-party out-of-court statement, was a declaration against Husband's pecuniary interest and hence admissible as an exception to the hearsay rule.

Rule 804(B)(3), as noted, includes the admissibility of statements which subject the non-party declarant to criminal liability. The rule, in effect, provides that the non-party statement which criminally implicates the non-party may be admitted into evidence *against* a criminal defendant or to *exculpate* a criminal defendant. However, if the non-party statement tends to expose the declarant to criminal liability, whether it is offered to exculpate or inculpate the accused, the statement must be supported by "corroborating circumstances" to "clearly indicate the trustworthiness of the statement." The rule may be made understandable by the following illustrations.

In *People v. Spriggs* (1964), 60 Cal. 2d 868, 389 P. 2d 377, defendant was on trial for possession of heroin. At the time of arrest, defendant's female accomplice, an addict, apparently told a police officer that *she* was the one who possessed the heroin. At trial, the police officer on the stand, would be required—assuming declarant was "unavailable"—to answer the question, "What did she say?" Under the rule, the statement of the unavailable declarant (which would implicate declarant) would have to be supported by "corroborating circumstances." Note that the language is "corroborating circumstances" not "corroborating evidence." Some kind of corroborating circumstances should exist as a condition to admissibility when the statement of the declarant which exposes the declarant to criminal liability is deemed not to be very "trustworthy." Under this rule this is so whether or not the statement tends to inculpate or exculpate the accused. For an excellent analysis of the meaning of "corroborating circumstances" under Federal Evidence Rule 804(b)(3), see *Lowery v. State of Maryland* (1975), 401 F. Supp. 604.

In *Bruton v. United States* (1968), 389 U.S. 818, the Supreme Court held that an out-of-court confession (declaration against penal interest) which implicated the declarant (a co–defendant) could not be used to implicate defendant criminally. One reason for the *Bruton* doctrine is this: a statement (confession) admitting guilt and implicating another person in the same crime, and *made while in custody*, might well be motivated by a desire to curry favor with the authorities and, hence, fail to qualify as being against interest.

Rule 804(B)(4) Statement of Personal or Family History

Rule 804(B)(4) provides that the statement of an unavailable declarant concerning his own family history is admissible as an exception to the hearsay rule even though the declarant had no means of acquiring personal knowledge of the matters stated. The rule also makes admissible declarant's statement concerning another person's family history if the declarant is closely associated with the other person's family. The rule broadens the common law but conforms to the more modern tradition. See McCormick § 322 (2d ed. 1972). The rule is a variation of Rule 803(19), but, as noted above, Rule 804(B)(4) requires that declarant be unavailable.

Rule 804(B)(5) Statement by a Deceased, Deaf-mute, or Incompetent Person

In effect, Rule 601, governing competency of witnesses to testify, supersedes the Dead Man's statute, R.C. 2317.03, which heretofore had prevented an adverse party from testifying against a deceased person, deaf-mute or person now insane who was a "party" to the action by virtue of a representative such as an administrator. Under Rule 601 an adverse party may testify against a deceased person, or deaf-mute or person now insane, provided that such person is a party by representation of an administrator or guardian and provided that in the discretion of the court unfair prejudice would not result pursuant to Rule 403. See the Staff Note for Rule 601.

Because of the modification of the Dead Man's statute by Rule 601, Rule 804(B)(5) permits as an exception to the hearsay rule, testimony on behalf of the deceased person, or deaf-mute, or now insane person to "rebut testimony by an adverse party on a matter which was within the knowledge of the decedent, deaf-mute, or incompetent person." The new exception to the hearsay rule is a fair and necessary adjunct responsive to the modification of the Dead Man's statute. In those jurisdictions in which the Dead Man's statute has been modified or repealed, a rule similar to Rule 804(B)(5) exists. See McCormick § 65 (2d ed. 1972), and Ray, *Dead Man's Statutes*, 24 Ohio St. L. J. 89 (1963).

The Federal Rules of Evidence, not having addressed the Dead Man's statute problem, do not have a rule equivalent to Rule 804(B)(5).

Cross References

Cases in which a party shall not testify, 2317.03
Delinquent children, deposition of child sex offense victims, 2152.81
Deposition in criminal cases, 2945.50; Crim R 15
Proving testimony of absent witness; prisoners, 2317.06
Testimony of mentally retarded or developmentally disabled victim, 2945.482
Testimony of mentally retarded or developmentally disabled victim; videotaped testimony, 2945.491
Use of depositions in court proceedings, Civ R 32
Videotaped preliminary hearing testimony of child victim, 2945.49

Library References

Criminal Law ⟲412(1) to 418.10, 419(4) to 419(6), 421(1), 421(2).
Evidence ⟲272, 275 1/2, 285 to 297, 317(1) to 317(18), 320, 321, 575 to 583.
Westlaw Topic Nos. 110, 157.
C.J.S. Criminal Law §§ 829, 858 to 860, 877 to 885, 892 to 996.
C.J.S. Evidence §§ 228, 259 to 272, 279 to 305, 478 to 495.
OJur 3d: 25, Criminal Law § 477, 481, 991; 27, Criminal Law § 1154, 1200; 29A, Criminal Law § 2994, 2997, 3006, 3010, 3011, 3043, 3046; 30, Death § 1, 148; 31, Decedents' Estates § 1158, 1165, 1167; 43, Evidence and Witnesses § 274, 277, 289, 312 to 314, 333, 356, 357, 363; 52, Gifts § 43, 44, 46; 59, Insurance § 1387; 60, Insurance § 1666; 70, Negligence § 172
Am Jur 2d: 21, Deposition and Discovery § 190, 415; 29, Evidence § 496 et seq., 676, 677, 738 to 746
Admissibility, on issue of child's legitimacy or parentage, of declarations of parents, relatives, or the child, deceased or unavailable. 31 ALR2d 989
Admissibility of dying declaration in civil case. 47 ALR2d 526
Witness' refusal to testify on ground of self-incrimination as justifying reception of evidence of prior statements or admissions. 43 ALR3d 1413
Comment Note—Statements of declarant as sufficiently showing consciousness of impending death to justify admission of dying declaration. 53 ALR3d 785

Comment Note—Sufficiency of showing of consciousness of impending death, by circumstances other than statements of declarant, to justify admission of dying declaration. 53 ALR3d 1196

Admissibility, as against interest, in civil case of declaration of commission of criminal act. 90 ALR3d 1173

Admissibility of former testimony of nonparty witness, present in jurisdiction, who refuses to testify at subsequent trial without making claim of privilege. 92 ALR3d 1138

Admissibility, as against interest, in criminal case of declaration of commission of criminal act. 92 ALR3d 1164

Residual hearsay exception where declarant unavailable: Uniform Evidence Rule 804(b)(5). 75 ALR4th 199

What constitutes statement against interest admissible under Rule 804(b)(3) of the Federal Rules of Evidence. 34 ALR Fed 412

Who is "predecessor in interest" for purposes of Rule 804(b)(1) of the Federal Rules of Evidence. 47 ALR Fed 895

Admissibility of depositions under Federal Evidence Rule 804(b)(1). 84 ALR Fed 668

Katz & Giannelli, Baldwin's Ohio Practice, Criminal Law § 1.6, 1.8 (1996).

Giannelli & Snyder, Baldwin's Ohio Practice, Evidence § 101.3, 102.5, 103.13, 104.3, 801, 601.11, 601.16, 609.15, 801.1, 801.6, 801.17, 802, 801.19, 801.22, 801.28, 802.5, 802.6, 803.1, 803.3, 803.4, 807, 803.51, 805.3, 807.1, 807.3, 1101, 806, 901.18, 601 (2d ed. 2001).

Adrine & Ruden, Ohio Domestic Violence Law (2002 Ed.), Text 5.14, 5.21, 6.14, 7.6.

Carlin, Baldwin's Ohio Practice, Merrick–Rippner Probate Law § 5.14, 38.13, 43.40, 56.16, 60.14, 84.35, 107.51 (2003).

Evid R 805 Hearsay within hearsay

Hearsay included within hearsay is not excluded under the hearsay rule if each part of the combined statements conforms with an exception to the hearsay rule provided in these rules.

(Adopted eff. 7–1–80)

Commentary

Staff Notes

1980:

Rule 805, following the language of Federal Evidence Rule 805, permits the use of "double hearsay" provided that each part of the hearsay chain "conforms with an exception to the hearsay rule." The question of admissibility of "double hearsay" does not often arise, but a few case examples may be found. See McCormick § 313 (2d ed. 1972).

Assume, for example, that a party to the action was admitted to a hospital immediately after the auto accident which is the subject of the present action. At the time of his entry into the hospital he stated among other things to the doctor in the receiving area how the accident occurred. The doctor entered the statement concerning the cause of the accident into the hospital record along with numerous facts concerning the party's personal and medical history. At trial, the party's statement—concerning the cause of the accident contained in the hospital record—can be admitted into evidence against him. *Watts v. Delaware Coach Co.* (1948), 44 Del. 2d 83, 58 A.2d

689. In that case the use of "double hearsay" was involved, although the court did not thoroughly analyze the problem. In effect, the party's statement was admitted for the truth of the matter as an exception to the hearsay rule, i.e., an admission of a party (See Rule 801(D)(2)). And the hospital record containing that statement was admitted as a second exception to the hearsay rule, i.e., a record of regularly conducted activity (business or hospital record) (See Rule 803(6)). The "double hearsay" chain was complete.

Library References

Criminal law ⚖️419(1).

Evidence ⚖️314(1).

Westlaw Topic Nos. 110, 157.

C.J.S. Criminal Law §§ 856, 861, 862, 864.

C.J.S. Evidence §§ 259 to 284, 319.

OJur 3d: 43, Evidence and Witnesses § 274; 59, Insurance § 1387; 70, Negligence § 172

Katz & Giannelli, Baldwin's Ohio Practice, Criminal Law § 1.6 (1996).

Giannelli & Snyder, Baldwin's Ohio Practice, Evidence § 102.5, 602, 602.5, 801.1, 802.1, 802.5, 803, 803.1, 803.19, 803.22, 803.32, 804.1, 807.1 (2d ed. 2001).

Adrine & Ruden, Ohio Domestic Violence Law (2002 Ed.), Text 7.7.

Carlin, Baldwin's Ohio Practice, Merrick–Rippner Probate Law § 5.14, 107.51 (2003).

Evid R 806 Attacking and supporting credibility of declarant

(A) When a hearsay statement, or a statement defined in Evid. R. 801(D)(2), (c), (d), or (e), has been admitted in evidence, the credibility of the declarant may be attacked, and if attacked may be supported, by any evidence that would be admissible for those purposes if declarant had testified as a witness.

(B) Evidence of a statement or conduct by the declarant at any time, inconsistent with the declarant's hearsay statement, is not subject to any requirement that the declarant may have been afforded an opportunity to deny or explain.

(C) Evidence of a declarant's prior conviction is not subject to any requirement that the declarant be shown a public record.

(D) If the party against whom a hearsay statement has been admitted calls the declarant as a witness, the party is entitled to examine the declarant on the statement as if under cross-examination.

(Adopted eff. 7–1–80; amended eff. 7–1–98)

Historical and Statutory Notes

Amendment Note: The 7–1–98 amendment rewrote the text of this Rule, which prior thereto read:

"When a hearsay statement, or a statement defined in Rule 801(D)(2), (c), (d), or (e), has been admitted in evidence, the credibility of the declarant may be attacked, and if attacked may be supported, by any evidence which would be admissible for those purposes if declarant had testified as a witness. Evidence of a statement or conduct by the declarant at any time, inconsistent with his hearsay statement, is not subject to any requirement that he may have been afforded an opportunity to deny or explain. If the party against whom a hearsay statement has been admitted calls the declarant as a witness, the party is entitled to examine him on the statement as if under cross-examination."

Commentary

Staff Notes

1998:

Rule 806 Attacking and supporting credibility of declarant

The content of divisions (A), (B), and (D) was part of the previous rule. These divisions were divided and lettered by the 1998 amendment, masculine references were made gender-neutral, and the style used for rule references was changed; no substantive change is intended.

Division (C) was added by the 1998 amendment. The limitation in Evid. R. 609(F) that the prior conviction be proved by the testimony of the witness or by public record shown to the witness during the examination clearly contemplates the witness's presence at trial; this is in tension with Evid. R. 806, which provides that a hearsay declarant may be impeached "by any evidence which would have been admissible for those purposes if declarant had testified as a witness." In *State v. Hatcher* (1996), 108 Ohio App.3d 628, 671 N.E.2d 572, a witness for the defense at the defendant's first trial was unavailable at the time of defendant's second trial. His testimony from the first trial was admitted into evidence as former testimony under Evid. R. 804(B)(1). The trial court then admitted into evidence certified copies of the declarant's prior felony convictions, which were offered by the prosecution to impeach the witness. The court of appeals noted the "arguable conflict" between Evid. R. 609(F) and Evid. R. 806, but determined that the admission of the certified copies of the witness's prior felony convictions was not error. The amendment clarifies this ambiguity; it does not change the requirements of Evid. R. 609(A) through (E) as applied to hearsay declarants.

1980:

Rule 806, like Federal Evidence Rule 806 in effect states that a hearsay statement admitted into evidence may be impeached on the basis of declarant's inconsistent statements.

The rule provides that declarant's hearsay statement may be impeached by an inconsistent statement made by "the declarant at any time;" hence the impeaching inconsistent statement may be one made by declarant prior to, or subsequent to, his hearsay statement.

Moreover, the rule provides that the hearsay declarant need not have been given "an opportunity to deny or explain" his inconsistent statement; hence it is not necessary to "lay a foundation" before an inconsistent statement is introduced to impeach the hearsay statement. Clearly, under the rule the hearsay statement may be impeached by an inconsistent statement even though the hearsay statement is former testimony introduced into evidence and even though there was no attempt to impeach the hearsay declarant by an inconsistent statement at the time of taking the former testimony.

The rule is consistent with the majority and more modern rule in the United States. See McCormick § 37 (2d ed 1972).

The final sentence of Rule 806 provides that the party against whom the hearsay statement was introduced may call the declarant (assuming that the declarant may be found) in order to examine the declarant as if on cross-examination. The obvious purpose of the provision is to provide an opportunity for clarification of the inconsistent statements. When called on cross-examination, the declarant does not become the witness of the party who calls him.

Library References

Witnesses ⊗333, 363(1), 380(3), 398(1).

Westlaw Topic No. 410.

C.J.S. Witnesses §491 et seq., 538 et seq., 576, 629.

OJur 3d: 43, Evidence and Witnesses § 278; 59, Insurance § 1387; 70, Negligence § 172

Am Jur 2d: 32B, Federal Rules of Evidence § 272, 385 to 428

Giannelli & Snyder, Baldwin's Ohio Practice, Evidence § 607.1, 609.7, 609.15, 613.1, 801.1, 802.1, 803.1, 804.1, 807.1, 1101 (2d ed. 2001).

Evid R 807   Hearsay exceptions; child statements in abuse cases

(A) An out-of-court statement made by a child who is under twelve years of age at the time of trial or hearing describing any sexual act performed by, with, or on the child or describing any act of physical violence directed against the child is not excluded as hearsay under Evid. R. 802 if all of the following apply:

(1) The court finds that the totality of the circumstances surrounding the making of the statement provides particularized guarantees of trustworthiness that make the statement at least as reliable as statements admitted pursuant to Evid. R. 803 and 804. The circumstances must establish that the child was particularly likely to be telling the truth when the statement was made and that the test of cross-examination would add little to the reliability of the statement. In making its determination of the reliability of the statement, the court shall consider all of the circumstances surrounding the making of the statement, including but not limited to spontaneity, the internal consistency of the statement, the mental state of the child, the child's motive or lack of motive to fabricate, the child's use of terminology unexpected of a child of similar age, the means by which the statement was elicited, and the lapse of time between the act and the statement. In making this determination, the court shall not consider whether there is independent proof of the sexual act or act of physical violence.

(2) The child's testimony is not reasonably obtainable by the proponent of the statement.

(3) There is independent proof of the sexual act or act of physical violence.

(4) At least ten days before the trial or hearing, a proponent of the statement has notified all other parties in writing of the content of the statement, the time and place at which the statement was made, the identity of the witness who is to testify about the statement, and the circumstances surrounding the statement that are claimed to indicate its trustworthiness.

(B) The child's testimony is "not reasonably obtainable by the proponent of the statement" under division (A)(2) of this rule only if one or more of the following apply:

(1) The child refuses to testify concerning the subject matter of the statement or claims a lack of memory of the subject matter of the statement after a person trusted by the child, in the presence of the court, urges the child to both describe the acts described by the statement and to testify.

(2) The court finds all of the following:

(a) the child is absent from the trial or hearing;

(b) the proponent of the statement has been unable to procure the child's attendance or testimony by process or other reasonable means despite a good faith effort to do so;

(c) it is probable that the proponent would be unable to procure the child's testimony or attendance if the trial or hearing were delayed for a reasonable time.

(3) The court finds both of the following:

(a) the child is unable to testify at the trial or hearing because of death or then existing physical or mental illness or infirmity;

(b) the illness or infirmity would not improve sufficiently to permit the child to testify if the trial or hearing were delayed for a reasonable time.

The proponent of the statement has not established that the child's testimony or attendance is not reasonably obtainable if the child's refusal, claim of lack of memory, inability, or absence is due to the procurement or wrongdoing of the proponent of the statement for the purpose of preventing the child from attending or testifying.

(C) The court shall make the findings required by this rule on the basis of a hearing conducted outside the presence of the jury and shall make findings of fact, on the record, as to the bases for its ruling.

(Adopted eff. 7–1–91)

Commentary

Staff Notes

1991:

The rule recognizes a hearsay exception for the statements of children in abuse situations. This exception is in addition to the exceptions enumerated in Evid. R. 803 and 804.

Many other jurisdictions have adopted child abuse hearsay exceptions. *See generally* Ringland, They Must Not Speak a Useless Word: The Case for a Children's Hearsay Exception for Ohio (1987), 14 Ohio N.U.L. Rev. 213. The Supreme Court in *State v. Boston* (1989), 46 Ohio St.3d 108, 545 N.E.2d 1220, asked the Rules Advisory Committee to review the subject. *See also* R.C. 2151.35(F).

Evid. R. 807(A) establishes four requirements for admission: (1) the statement must be trustworthy, (2) the child's testimony must be unavailable, (3) independent proof of the act must exist, and (4) the proponent must notify all other parties ten days before trial that such a statement will be offered in evidence. In addition, there are age and subject matter requirements: the child must be under 12 and the statement must relate to an act of sexual abuse or physical violence.

Rule 807(A)(1) Trustworthiness

Evid. R. 807(A)(1) codifies the confrontation requirements specified by the United States Supreme Court in *Idaho v. Wright* (1990), 497 U.S. 805, 110 S.Ct. 3139, 111 L.Ed.2d 638. In *Wright*, the Court ruled a child's statement admitted under a residual hearsay exception violated the Sixth Amendment where there were insufficient particularized guarantees of trustworthiness surrounding the making of the statement.

In determining trustworthiness, the Court adopted a "totality of the circumstances approach" and mentioned a number of factors: spontaneity and consistent repetition, mental state of the child, lack of motive to fabricate, and use of terminology unexpected of a child of similar age. These factors, as well as others, are specified in division (A)(1). The phrase "means by which the statement was elicited" concerns whether the statement was elicited by leading questions or after repeated promptings. Moreover, the time lapse between the act and the statement also is relevant in determining trustworthiness. The list of factors specified is not exhaustive. Additional factors, such as whether the statement was videotaped or whether the parents were involved in divorce or custody proceedings at the time the statement was made, may be relevant.

The last sentence of division (A)(1) provides that independent proof or corroboration of the statement is *not* a permissible factor in determining the trustworthiness of the statement. In *Wright*, the Supreme Court wrote: "the relevant circumstances include only those that surround the making of the statement and that render the declarant particularly worthy of belief." Under this approach, *corroboration* of the statement by independent evidence cannot be used to determine trustworthiness. The independent proof requirement in division (A)(3) is discussed below.

Rule 807(A)(2) and (B) Testimony Not Obtainable

Evid. R. 807(A)(2) requires the court to find that the child's testimony is not reasonably obtainable. Evid. R. 807(B) defines three circumstances that would satisfy this requirement. These circumstances are comparable to the unavailability requirements of Evid. R. 804(A); they have been modified to apply better to a child declarant. For example, a court would not have to specifically *order* the child to testify (as required for an adult under Evid. R. 804(A)(2)), provided the record clearly established a persistent refusal to testify.

In addition, a child who persisted in refusing to testify in a courtroom might be willing to testify via closed circuit television. *See* R.C. 2907.41; *Maryland v. Craig* (1990), 497 U.S. 836, 110 S.Ct. 3157, 111 L.Ed.2d 666. In such a circumstance, the child's testimony would be obtainable, albeit by closed-circuit television, and thus the hearsay statement would not be admissible under this rule.

Rule 807(A)(3) Independent Proof

Although, under division (A)(1) and the *Wright* case, independent proof cannot be used to determine the trustworthiness of a hearsay statement, independent proof is a separate and additional requirement under division (A)(3) that must exist before a statement may be held admissible. This is comparable to the independent proof requirement of the co-conspirator exception, Evid. R. 801(D)(2)(e). The rule thus goes beyond the minimum Confrontation Clause re-

quirements prescribed in *Wright*, as is permitted by *Wright*.

"States are, of course, free, as a matter of state law, to demand corroboration of an unavailable child declarant's statements as well as other indicia of reliability before allowing the statements to be admitted into evidence." *Wright* at 3154 (Kennedy, J., dissenting).

Rule 807(A)(4) Notice

The pre-trial notice requirement is intended to alert opposing parties to the possible use of this exception, which in turn should trigger a request for an out-of-court hearing as required by Evid. R. 807(C).

Rule 807(C) Hearing and Findings

Under Evid. R. 807(C), the admissibility determination must be made in a hearing conducted outside the presence of the jury. In addition, findings of fact supporting the court's ruling must be included in the record.

Library References

Infants ⊝20, 174.

Westlaw Topic No. 211.

C.J.S. Infants §§ 95 to 107, 273, 274.

OJur 3d: 27, Criminal Law § 1202; 29A, Criminal Law § 3012

Giannelli & Snyder, Baldwin's Ohio Practice, Evidence § 104.3, 601.7, 611.3, 801.1, 801.6, 802.6, 802.9, 803.1, 804.1, 807.4, 1101, 807.9, 807.10 (2d ed. 2001).

Adrine & Ruden, Ohio Domestic Violence Law (2002 Ed.), Text 13.6.

Carlin, Baldwin's Ohio Practice, Merrick–Rippner Probate Law § 107.51 (2003).

Article IX

AUTHENTICATION AND IDENTIFICATION

Rule
901 Requirement of authentication or identification
902 Self–authentication
903 Subscribing witness' testimony unnecessary

Evid R 901 Requirement of authentication or identification

(A) General provision

The requirement of authentication or identification as a condition precedent to admissibility is satisfied by evidence sufficient to support a finding that the matter in question is what its proponent claims.

(B) Illustrations

By way of illustration only, and not by way of limitation, the following are examples of authentication or identification conforming with the requirements of this rule:

(1) Testimony of witness with knowledge. Testimony that a matter is what it is claimed to be.

(2) Nonexpert opinion on handwriting. Nonexpert opinion as to the genuineness of handwriting, based upon familiarity not acquired for purposes of the litigation.

(3) Comparison by trier or expert witness. Comparison by the trier of fact or by expert witness with specimens which have been authenticated.

(4) Distinctive characteristics and the like. Appearance, contents, substance, internal patterns, or other distinctive characteristics, taken in conjunction with circumstances.

(5) Voice identification. Identification of a voice, whether heard firsthand or through mechanical or electronic transmission or recording, by opinion based upon hearing the voice at any time under

circumstances connecting it with the alleged speaker.

(6) Telephone conversations. Telephone conversations, by evidence that a call was made to the number assigned at the time by the telephone company to a particular person or business, if (a) in the case of a person, circumstances, including self-identification, show the person answering to be the one called, or (b) in the case of a business, the call was made to a place of business and the conversation related to business reasonably transacted over the telephone.

(7) Public records or reports. Evidence that a writing authorized by law to be recorded or filed and in fact recorded or filed in a public office, or a purported public record, report, statement, or data compilation, in any form, is from the public office where items of this nature are kept.

(8) Ancient documents or data compilation. Evidence that a document or data compilation, in any form, (a) is in such condition as to create no suspicion concerning its authenticity, (b) was in a place where it, if authentic, would likely be, and (c) has been in existence twenty years or more at the time it is offered.

(9) Process or system. Evidence describing a process or system used to produce a result and showing that the process or system produces an accurate result.

(10) Methods provided by statute or rule. Any method of authentication or identification provided by statute enacted by the General Assembly not in conflict with a rule of the Supreme Court of Ohio or by other rules prescribed by the Supreme Court.

(Adopted eff. 7–1–80)

Commentary
Staff Notes
1980:

Rule 901(A) General Provision

If, in the course of everyday affairs, X receives a letter signed by Y, X assumes that Y wrote the letter. From an evidentiary point of view, the common law has not made that assumption. It is a long-standing principle of the common law that most types of demonstrative or physical evidence must be authenticated or identified before such evidence may be deemed to be admissible at trial. Authentication procedure is a form of relevancy; that is, authentication connects the particular evidence sought to be introduced to the issues or persons involved in the trial. To put it another way, authentication or identification lays the foundation for admissibility of particular evidence. McCormick § 218 (2d ed. 1972).

Hence, in litigation between X and Y, if X wishes to introduce into evidence a letter handwritten and signed by Y, X could "authenticate" the letter by direct testimony to the effect that he recognizes the handwriting and signature as that of Y because of previous correspondence between X and Y. McCormick § 221 (2d ed. 1972). In terms of Rule 901(A), the general provisions governing authentication, X would have "authenticated" the letter "as a condition precedent to admissibility... by evidence sufficient to support a finding that the matter in question is what its proponent claims."

Certain evidence, other than physical evidence such as a letter, must also be authenticated or identified, particularly in light of modern communication methods. Thus, X receives a telephone call purportedly from Y. If the telephone call is to be accepted as evidence in a trial, X may "authenticate" or "identify" the voice of Y by preliminarily testifying that he is familiar with the voice of Y as a result of previous conversations with Y. See Rule 901(B)(5).

It should be noted that certain writings, admissible as evidence, need not be authenticated as a condition precedent to admissibility. Such writings, particularly certain public documents, are said to be "self-authenticating." Rule 902 governs admissibility by self-authentication.

Finally, it should be noted that modern pre-trial procedures have made it possible to obviate problems of authentication at trial. A member of the Federal Rules of Evidence Advisory Committee has stated: "... it may be well to remind bench and bar that in any event the problem of authentication or identification should be confronted before actual trial. Whether by interrogatories, depositions, requests for admission or—as is most effective—by confrontation in final pre-trial conference many (if not all) problems of authentication or identification should be isolated and resolved.... In a recent case... the writer had more than 1100 documents admitted in a little over two hours. This was possible because Judge Fullam ordered that counsel should meet *before* the final pre-trial conference to mark all documents and resolve all problems of authenticity or identity. Then at the final pre-trial conference, Judge Fullam resolved those questions of authenticity or identity which counsel could not agree upon. This procedure saved countless trial days of examining, marking and arguing over thousands of sheets of paper." Berger, *Authentication and Identification,* (1974) 33 Fed. Bar J. 79, 79. In Ohio, the same pre-trial authentication procedures are available. Civ. R. 16, governing pre-trial conference, specifically provides in subsection (9) for: "The possibility of obtaining... Admissions into evidence of documents and other exhibits which will avoid unnecessary proof..." Civ. R. 36(A) provides for admission regarding "the genuineness of any documents." Moreover, there is nothing to prevent parties from voluntarily stipulating to the admissibility of evidence otherwise requiring authentication.

But pre-trial procedures, particularly in criminal cases, cannot resolve all authentication of evidence matters. Hence the need for a general rule governing authentication. Rule 901(A), the general provision governing authentication, is based on the principle that the requirement of authenticity or identity is a matter of relevancy conditioned on a preliminary determination of fact. In this respect Rule 901(A) is closely related to Rule 104, which in relevant part governs preliminary questions concerning admissibility of evidence.

In part, Rule 104(A) provides: "Preliminary questions concerning... the admissibility of evidence shall be determined by the court, subject to the provisions of subdivision (B)." In part, Rule 104(B) provides:

"When the relevancy of evidence depends upon the fulfillment of a condition of fact, the court shall admit it upon... the introduction of evidence sufficient to support a finding of the fulfillment of the condition." In short, a party seeking to introduce at trial demonstrative evidence, such as a letter, must authenticate the letter by proper testimony pursuant to Rule 901(A), and the court, pursuant to Rule 104, will determine as a preliminary matter whether the condition of authentication has been satisfied before admitting the letter into evidence. Of course, if the letter is "authenticated" and admitted into evidence, the jury need not be bound by the purported contents of the letter. Thus, the opposing party may present competent evidence that the letter is a forgery. Under such circumstances, the weight to be given to the contents of the letter would be a matter for ultimate determination by the jury. 21 OJur 2d Evidence § 177.

The authentication procedures set forth in the preceding paragraphs do not differ from prior Ohio evidence law. 21 OJur 2d Evidence § 177, § 507, § 527.

It should be noted that authentication of a letter, for example, merely solves a preliminary matter involving admissibility. But the letter, although authentic, may not be admissible in evidence on other grounds. Thus, the letter may have absolutely nothing to do with the issues of the trial at hand and hence may not be admissible for want of relevance pursuant to Rule 401.

Rule 901(A) is the same as Federal Evidence Rule 901(a).

Rule 901(B) Illustrations

Rule 901(B), which follows the wording of Federal Evidence Rule 901(b), sets forth a non-exhaustive list of ten authentication examples. The examples are not a significant departure from prior practice; rather they reflect the general law of Ohio, the several states and the federal system relevant to authentication procedures.

Rule 901(B)(1) Testimony of Witness with Knowledge

The first example permits a witness with knowledge to offer authentication testimony. Thus a person who was present at the signing of a document may offer testimony that he witnessed the ceremony and that the document which is sought to be introduced is "what it is claimed to be." Or a witness having custody of evidence from the time it was seized from the accused to the time of trial may testify that the evidence sought to be introduced is the item which was seized from the accused.

The rule is not new to Ohio. See 21 OJur 2d Evidence § 547.

Rule 901(B)(2) Non-expert Opinion on Handwriting

Pursuant to the second example, a non-expert witness may identify handwriting as a result of his prior familiarity with the writing. The use of such lay testimony, based upon prior familiarity, is conventional procedure. See 21 OJur 2d Evidence §§ 499–500.

Rule 901(B)(3) Comparison by Trier or Expert Witness

It is not necessary, before comparisons may be made between specimens of handwriting, that the person making the comparison be familiar by prior experience with the handwriting in question.

Hence, Rule 901(B)(3) provides that an expert or the jury, as trier of fact, may compare the handwriting in question with a specimen of handwriting which has been authenticated. Ohio cases have followed such procedure. See 21 OJur 2d Evidence § 498, 501.

Comparison between an authenticated specimen or exemplar and a specimen in question is not limited to handwriting. Thus, the trier of fact, with the aid of expert testimony, may be permitted to compare a ballistic missile fired by an expert from a particular gun with the ballistic missile in question. As to ballistic missile identification, see 21 OJur 2d Evidence § 469.

Rule 901(B)(4) Distinctive Characteristics and the Like

Rule 901(B)(4) provides that an item, or even a voice, may be authenticated or identified because of its contents or distinctive characteristics in light of the circumstances involved. A letter or voice over the telephone may be related to a particular person by the very fact that the matters set forth in the letter or the telephone conversation were known peculiarly to a particular person. See McCormick § 255 (2d ed. 1972). Or a telegram might be related to the defendant in light of its contents and the circumstances surrounding its delivery. See 21 OJur 2d Evidence § 562. Or a writing may be related to a particular person by its linguistic patterns and characteristics. See Arens and Meadow, *Psycholinguistics and the Confession Dilemma*, 56 Col. L. Rev. 19 (1956).

Rule 901(B)(5) Voice Identification

A witness may identify a voice and relate it to a particular speaker provided that the witness is familiar with the voice through prior or subsequent opportunity to connect the voice with the speaker. A witness might become familiar with a voice firsthand and later, given the opportunity, be able to connect the voice and the speaker. Thus, a blindfolded kidnap victim, who had a number of conversations with the kidnapper during the course of the crime, might be able later to identify his kidnapper by hearing the kidnapper's voice. The question of voice identification, however, frequently arises in connection with testimony concerning incoming telephone calls. Thus, before a witness offers testimony concerning the substance of a telephone conversation with X, he should first identify the voice as that of X by stating that he is familiar with the voice of X as a result of prior contacts with X. See 21 OJur 2d Evidence § 239, § 253. See also McCormick § 226 (2d ed 1972). And see *In re Roth's Estate* (Probate Court, 1960), 15 Ohio Op. 2d 234 (voice of decedent on electronic recorder authenticated and admitted into evidence).

Rule 901(B)(6) Telephone Conversations

The identification or authentication procedures set forth in Rule 901(B)(6) are most frequently related to outgoing telephone calls.

The first provision of the rule deals with outgoing calls to a person (as distinguished from a business establishment) listed in the telephone directory. Thus if the testifying witness testifies that he dialed a number listed under the name of a particular person, and the person answering the phone identified himself as the person listed in the directory, then the testifying witness may testify as to the contents of the call; that is, "self-identification" (of the person called) is sufficient authentication. The rule codifies the majority rule in the United States. See McCormick § 226 (2d ed. 1972). Of course, the testifying witness may also identify the voice of the recipient of the outgoing call by stating that he recognized the voice on the basis of prior familiarity. See Staff Note to Rule 901(B)(5). Or the testifying witness may identify the voice of the recipient of the outgoing call because only the recipient could have stated matters in the conversation known peculiarly to him. See Staff Note to Rule 901(B)(4).

The second provision of the rule deals with outgoing calls to a business establishment. The testifying witness may authenticate the outgoing call by stating that he dialed the number listed to the business establishment and the conversation related to the business conducted by the establishment. The provision codifies the standard rule in the United States. See McCormick § 226 (2d ed 1972). See also 21 OJur 2d Evidence § 254. And see *Farris v. City of Columbus* (1948), 85 Ohio App. 385.

Rule 901(B)(7) Public Records and Reports

A public record or report, customarily in writing but in any form including a data compilation, may be authenticated by evidence that the record or report is from the public office where it is kept. Such authentication may be by testimony of the person having custody of the record or report in the office where the record or report is kept. Authentication of *copies* of public records has been effected pursuant to Civ. R. 44 and Crim. R. 27, and authentication of *copies* of public reports has been effected pursuant to R.C. 2317.42.

Rule 901(B)(8) Ancient Documents or Data Compilation

Age alone may authenticate or attest to the genuineness of a document; hence the evidentiary term "ancient document rule." Rule 901(B)(8), with two changes, codifies the ancient document rule. First, the rule is extended to data compilations as well as documents. Second, the rule reduces the time in which a document or data compilation will be deemed to be ancient and hence trustworthy from thirty years to twenty years. The time reduction from thirty years to twenty years is consistent with the trend of modern authority. See McCormick § 223 (2d ed. 1972). In Ohio, prior to the adoption of the rule, Ohio followed the thirty-year time limit. See *Wright v. Hull* (1911), 83 Ohio St. 385.

Rule 901(B)(8) does require that the ancient document be in such condition as to create no suspicion concerning its authenticity. And the rule does require that the document have been kept in a place where it would likely be if authentic. Evidence of proper custody or of a proper repository is a common requirement of the ancient document rule. See 21 OJur 2d Evidence §§ 549–550.

Rule 901(B)(9) Process or System

Rule 901(B)(9) provides that the accuracy of the result of a sophisticated process or system may be authenticated by testimony describing the process or system. Thus, in light of the use of computers for modern business record keeping, questions may arise concerning the accuracy of computer results. In conjunction with business records, Rule 803(6), the accuracy of a computer business printout may be authenticated by the testimony of a person having control and direction of the computer system. For authentication of a computer business printout in conjunction with the Nebraska business records act, see the leading case, *Transport Indemnity Co. v. Seib* (1965), 178 Neb. 253, 132 N.W. 2d 871. See also Freed, Computer Print–Outs as Evidence, 16 AmJur. Proof of Facts 273.

Rule 901(B)(9) does not foreclose the taking of judicial notice of the accuracy of the process or system. The introductory clause of Rule 901(B) provides that the examples of authentication set forth are "By way of illustration only, and not by way of limitation...." Hence a court may take judicial notice of the accuracy of a process or system. In a case involving arrest for speeding as a result of radar tracking, the accuracy of the radar system, if not challenged, might be judicially noticed. If challenged, the accuracy of the radar set involved may be authenticated.

Rule 901(B)(10) Methods Provided by Statute or Rule

Methods of authentication may be provided by other rules or statutes. Thus Civ. R. 44 and Crim. R. 27 provide methods for authenticating copies of public records. Civ. R. 30(F) sets forth the method of authenticating depositions. R.C. 2317.422, for example, sets forth the simplified methods for authenticating hospital records.

Cross References

Admissible reports, 2317.36

Pretrial procedure, Civ R 16

Qualification of records of hospital, nursing or rest home, or adult care facility, 2317.422

Library References

Criminal Law ⬤═339, 386, 444 to 447.

Evidence ⬤═102, 148, 188 to 198, 366(1) to 383(12).

Westlaw Topic Nos. 110, 157.

C.J.S. Criminal Law §§ 799, 754, 755, 1025 to 1032, 1044, 1046.

C.J.S. Evidence §§ 3 to 5, 197, 211, 246, 247, 789 to 802, 816 to 839, 870 to 889, 917 to 939, 957 to 964, 976, 982, 983, 992 to 1053.

C.J.S. Witnesses § 25.

OJur 3d: 29A, Criminal Law § 3056, 3058, 3088; 43, Evidence and Witnesses § 456, 462 to 468, 471, 476, 477; 66, Lost and Destroyed Instruments and Records § 2; 89, Trial § 134

Am Jur 2d: 29, Evidence § 774, 849 to 858

Authentication or verification of photograph as basis for introduction into evidence. 9 ALR2d 899

Verification and authentication of slips, tickets, bills, invoices etc., made in regular course of business, under the Uniform Business Records as Evidence Act, or under similar "Model acts." 21 ALR2d 773

Admissibility in evidence of ancient maps and the like. 46 ALR2d 1318

Admissibility in evidence of sample or samples of article or substance of which the quality, condition, or the like is involved in litigation. 95 ALR2d 681

Sufficiency of identification of participants as prerequisite to admissibility of telephone conversation in evidence. 79 ALR3d 79

Admissibility of memorandum of telephone conversations. 94 ALR3d 975

Business records: authentication and verification of bills and invoices under Rule 803(6) of the Uniform Rules of Evidence. 1 ALR4th 316

Cautionary instructions to jury as to reliability of, or factors to be considered in evaluating, voice identification testimony. 17 ALR5th 851

Admissibility in evidence of composite picture or sketch produced by police to identify offender. 23 ALR5th 672

Painter, Ohio Driving Under the Influence Law (2003 Ed.), Text 9.22, 13.9, 13.10.

Giannelli & Snyder, Baldwin's Ohio Practice, Evidence § 102.5, 104.6, 402.7, 701.1, 701.6, 702.4, 702.12, 702.13, 802.1, 802.5, 803.2, 803.27, 803.34, 803.36, 803.42, 803.43, 803.49, 902.1, 104, 902.3, 902.4, 902.5, 803 (2d ed. 2001).

Adrine & Ruden, Ohio Domestic Violence Law (2002 Ed.), Text 5.11, 6.13, 13.6, 15.8.

Carlin, Baldwin's Ohio Practice, Merrick–Rippner Probate Law § 79.24 (2003).

Evid R 902   Self–authentication

Extrinsic evidence of authenticity as a condition precedent to admissibility is not required with respect to the following:

(1) Domestic public documents under seal

A document bearing a seal purporting to be that of the United States, or of any State, district, Commonwealth, territory, or insular possession thereof, or the Panama Canal Zone, or the Trust Territory of the Pacific Islands, or of a political subdivision, department, officer, or agency thereof, and a signature purporting to be an attestation or execution.

(2) Domestic public documents not under seal

A document purporting to bear the signature in his official capacity of an officer or employee of any entity included in paragraph (1) hereof, having no seal, if a public officer having a seal and having official duties in the district or political subdivision of the officer or employee certifies under seal that the signer has the official capacity and that the signature is genuine.

(3) Foreign public documents

A document purporting to be executed or attested in his official capacity by a person authorized by the laws of a foreign country to make the execution or attestation, and accompanied by a final certification as to the genuineness of the signature and official position (a) of the executing or attesting person, or (b) of any foreign official whose certificate of genuineness of signature and official position relates to the execution or attestation or is in a chain of certificates of genuineness of signature and official position relating to the execution or attestation. A final certification may be made by a secretary of embassy or legation, consul general, consul, vice consul, or consular agent of the United States, or a diplomatic or consular official of the foreign country assigned or accredited to the United States. If reasonable opportunity has been given to all parties to investigate the authenticity and accuracy of official documents, the court may, for good cause shown, order that they be treated as presumptively authentic without final certification or permit them to be evidenced by an attested summary with or without final certification.

(4) Certified copies of public records

A copy of an official record or report or entry therein, or of a document authorized by law to be recorded or filed and actually recorded or filed in a public office, including data compilations in any form, certified as correct by the custodian or other person authorized to make the certification, by certificate complying with paragraph (1), (2), or (3) of this rule or complying with any law of a jurisdiction, state or federal, or rule prescribed by the Supreme Court of Ohio.

(5) Official publications.

Books, pamphlets, or other publications purporting to be issued by public authority.

(6) Newspapers and periodicals

Printed materials purporting to be newspapers or periodicals, including notices and advertisements contained therein.

(7) Trade inscriptions and the like

Inscriptions, signs, tags, or labels purporting to have been affixed in the course of business and indicating ownership, control, or origin.

(8) Acknowledged documents

Documents accompanied by a certificate of acknowledgment executed in the manner provided by law by a notary public or other officer authorized by law to take acknowledgments.

(9) Commercial paper and related documents

Commercial paper, signatures thereon, and documents relating thereto to the extent provided by general commercial law.

(10) Presumptions created by law

Any signature, document, or other matter declared by any law of a jurisdiction, state or federal, to be presumptively or prima facie genuine or authentic.

(Adopted eff. 7–1–80)

Commentary

Staff Notes

1980:

Rule 902 follows the language of Federal Evidence Rule 902.

The introductory sentence of Rule 902 states in relevant part, "Extrinsic evidence of authenticity as a condition precedent to admissibility is not required..." for the documents or items set forth in the ten paragraphs of the rule. The meaning is clear: no evidence other than the document or item itself is needed for authentication (for purposes of admissibility) provided that the document or item meets the standards of a particular paragraph of the rule. Although a document may be self-authenticating, the rule does not prevent an opposing party from disputing its authenticity.

Rule 902(1) Domestic Public Documents Under Seal

For purposes of admissibility into evidence, Rule 902(1) provides that a domestic public document attested or executed under the signature of a public officer under seal is self-authenticating. Pursuant to the rule "domestic public document" means a public document of the United States or its territories or of this state or of a sister state.

Rule 902(2) Domestic Public Documents Not Under Seal

The likelihood of a forgery of a public document under seal is minimal, but the possibility of a forgery of a signed public document not under seal is somewhat greater. Rule 902(2) provides that a domestic public document signed by a public official without a seal will be self-authenticating for purposes of admissibility only if the document is certified under seal, by an officer of the same political subdivision having a seal, that the signature on the document is genuine.

Rule 902(3) Foreign Public Documents

Civ. R. 44(A)(2), and Crim. R. 27 by reference to Civ. R. 44(A)(2), have provided for an authentication procedure for copies of foreign official *records*. Rule 902(3) adopts the same procedure and extends the procedure to authentication of originals of foreign public *documents* as distinguished from public records. Hence a foreign public document which follows the authentication procedure of Rule 902(3) is, for purposes of admissibility into evidence, self-authenticating.

In effect, the procedure for authenticating a foreign public document involves a chain of authentication completed by a final authentication of an American official or a foreign official accredited to the United States. Rule 902(3) also provides that the court may deem the foreign public document authentic without a final authentication provided that the parties have had a reasonable opportunity to investigate the authenticity of the document. Finally, Rule 902(3) permits the admission of attested foreign public documents in summary form.

Rule 902(4) Certified Copies of Public Records

Rule 902(4) provides a procedure for self-authentication of copies of certain public documents. The rule applies to copies of official records or reports or entries therein or to recorded documents authorized by law to be recorded or data compilations in any form constituting, for example, a part of an official report. The rule does not apply to unrecorded documents.

The copy of the document governed by the rule should be certified as correct by the custodian of the document or other authorized person, meaning a person authorized to make copies.

In addition, depending upon the particular document governed by the rule, the copy should be accompanied by a certificate "complying with paragraph (1), (2), or (3)" of Rule 902.

The final phrase of Rule 902(4)—"... or complying with any law of a jurisdiction, state or federal, or rule prescribed by the Supreme Court of Ohio"—provides for authentication of copies by other laws or rules or even permits dispensing with authentication by virtue of another rule. Thus a copy of an official report may be certified pursuant to R.C. 2317.42. Or a copy of an official domestic or foreign record may be authenticated by the procedure set forth in Civ. R. 44 or Crim. R. 27. Finally, a copy of a document may be admitted into evidence even though an authentication procedure has been dispensed with. Thus parties may stipulate to the genuineness of a document (or a copy) pursuant to Civ. R. 16(9)(b), or a document (or a copy) may be admitted to be genuine pursuant to Civ. R. 36(A).

For a discussion of Rule 902(4), see 5 Weinstein's Evidence Par. 902(4) [01].

Rule 902(5) Official Publications

Rule 902(5) provides that books, pamphlets or other publications issued by public authority are self-authenticating for purposes of admissibility into evidence. Although the rule is broad in that it does not specify what level of government must authorize the publication, the rule does not differ in kind from prior practice. R.C. 731.42, for example, has long provided in relevant part that printed copies of municipal ordinances, authorized to be printed by the municipality, are admissible into evidence. Civ. R. 44 and Crim. R. 27 have provided that domestic or foreign official records may be evidenced by an official publication thereof.

Rule 902(6) Newspapers and Periodicals

Rule 902(6) provides that printed copies of newspapers and periodicals including notices and advertisements contained therein are self-authenticating for purposes of introduction into evidence. Rule 902(6) is more specific than its federal counterpart through the addition of the words "including notices and advertisements contained therein." Although some courts have accepted copies of newspapers as self-authenticating, other courts have refused to accept advertisements or notices therein as self-authenticating. The likelihood that a newpaper [sic.] will be forged or that someone will go to the expense to place a forged advertisement therein is remote. The Federal Rules Advisory Committee Note infers that Federal Rule 902(6) includes advertisements in newspapers as self-authenticating, but the Federal Rule, unlike Rule 902(6), does not clearly so state. For a discussion of self-authentication of advertisements and notices in newspapers and periodicals, see Comment, *Authentication and the Best Evidence Rule Under the Federal Rules of Evidence*, 16 Wayne L. Rev. 195, 214 (1969).

Rule 902(7) Trade Inscriptions and the Like

Rule 902(7) provides that inscriptions, signs, tags or labels which indicate ownership, control, or origin, and which were affixed in the ordinary course of business, are self-authenticating. In relevant part, the Federal Rules Advisory Committee Note sets forth the common sense rationale of the rule as follows: "Several factors justify dispensing with preliminary proof of genuineness of commercial and mercantile labels and the like. The risk of forgery is minimal. Trademark infringement involves serious penalties. Great efforts are devoted to inducing the public to buy in reliance on brand names, and substantial protection is given them. Hence the fairness of this treatment finds recognition in the cases. *Curtiss Candy Co. v. Johnson*, 163 Miss. 426, 141 So. 762 (1932), Baby Ruth candy bar; *Doyle v. Continental Baking Co.*, 262 Mass. 516, 160 N.E. 325 (1928), loaf of bread; *Weiner v. Mager & Thorne, Inc.*, 167 Misc. 338, 3 N.Y.S. 2d 918 (1938), same."

Rule 902(8) Acknowledged Documents

Pursuant to Rule 902(8) documents accompanied by a certificate of acknowledgment of a notary public or other officer authorized to take acknowledgments are self-authenticating. The rule does not state a new principle of law. In short, the verification by a notary is *prima facie* sufficient that the document is what it purports to be. See *Gambrinus Stock Co. v. Weber* (1885), 41 Ohio St. 689. See also 41 OJur 2d Notaries and Commissioners, §§ 15–16.

Rule 902(9) Commercial Paper and Related Documents

Rule 902(9) provides that pursuant to general commercial law, commercial paper including signatures thereon may be admitted into evidence on the basis self-authentication. The rule finds its source in the Uniform Commercial Code, adopted in Ohio. See R.C. 1301.08 (*prima facie* evidence of genuineness of sundry documents), R.C. 1303.36 (signature admitted unless specifically denied in pleading), and R.C. 1303.65 (presumption of dishonor and notice of dishonor).

Rule 902(10) Presumptions Created by Law

Rule 902(10) provides that a signature or document or other matter may be self-authenticating or presumptively or *prima facie* genuine when a statute so provides. In other words, Rule 902(10) is a catch-all reminder that the examples of self-authentication set forth in Rule 902 are not the only examples of self-authentication. The commercial code statutes, set forth in the Staff Note to Rule 902(9), immediately preceding, are but three of the self-authentication statutes to be found throughout the Revised Code.

Cross References

Adjutant general to be chief of staff, duties, annual report to governor, 5913.01
Banks, building and loan associations, copies of records as evidence, 1125.19
Burden of establishing signatures, defenses, due course, 1303.36
Certificated securities; signatures deemed admitted genuine unless pleadings deny, 1308.04
Certified copy of record of instrument as evidence, 5301.43
Department of transportation, seal, journal, 5501.21
Department seals, specifications, 121.20
Evidence of dishonor, notice of dishonor, 1303.65
Instruments under seal of the superintendent, 3901.06
Labor and industry, official seal, 4121.09
Municipal corporations, bylaws and ordinances as evidence, 731.42
Pretrial procedure, Civ R 16
Prima facie evidence of authenticity of third party documents, 1301.08
Proof of official record, authentication, domestic, Civ R 44
Public utilities, official seal, 4901.03
Records and proceedings of registrar, 4507.25
Records to be public, certified copies as evidence, 313.10

Warrants of pardon and commutation, 2967.06

Library References

Criminal Law ⚬⇒444.
Evidence ⚬⇒366(1) to 381.
Westlaw Topic Nos. 110, 157.
C.J.S. Criminal Law §§ 1025 to 1032, 1044, 1046.
C.J.S. Evidence §§ 870 to 889, 917 to 939, 957 to 964, 976, 982, 983, 992 to 1034.
C.J.S. Witnesses § 25.
OJur 3d: 43, Evidence and Witnesses § 456, 478 to 488; 82, Seals § 9
Am Jur 2d: 29, Evidence § 849
Verification and authentication of slips, tickets, bills, invoices, etc., made in regular course of business, under the Uniform Business Records as Evidence Act, or under similar "Model Acts". 21 ALR2d 773
Proof of public records kept or stored on electronic computing equipment. 71 ALR3d 232
Admissibility of computerized private business records. 7 ALR4th 8
Painter, Ohio Driving Under the Influence Law (2003 Ed.), Text 13.9, 13.10.
Giannelli & Snyder, Baldwin's Ohio Practice, Evidence § 201.12, 402.7, 609.15, 802.5, 803.2, 803.36, 803.42, 803.43, 803.45, 901.1, 901.3, 901.11, 901.14, 1005, 902.3, 902.6, 1005.1, 1005.3 (2d ed. 2001).
Williams, Ohio Consumer Law (2002 Ed.), Text 6.39.
Sowald & Morganstern, Baldwin's Ohio Practice, Domestic Relations Law § 22.8.1 (1997).
Adrine & Ruden, Ohio Domestic Violence Law (2002 Ed.), Text 13.6, 15.8.
White, Ohio Landlord Tenant Law (2003 Ed.), Text 13.15.
Carlin, Baldwin's Ohio Practice, Merrick–Rippner Probate Law § 98.52 (2003).

Evid R 903   Subscribing witness' testimony unnecessary

The testimony of a subscribing witness is not necessary to authenticate a writing unless required by the laws of the jurisdiction whose laws govern the validity of the writing.

(Adopted eff. 7–1–80)

Commentary

Staff Notes

1980:

Rule 903 is the same as Federal Evidence Rule 903.

Under the older common law, in Ohio and elsewhere in the nineteenth century, a document which had been attested to by subscribing witnesses could not be introduced into evidence unless a subscribing witness first authenticated the document by direct testimony at trial. The peculiar rule prevailed, with one exception, even though the document in question was not required by law to be attested to by subscribing witnesses. The exception provided that a document attested to by subscribing witnesses could be authenticated by other means in the event that subscribing witnesses were dead, incapacitated or beyond the court. In later years, in Ohio and elsewhere, the rule was modified to permit authentication of documents, by the person who signed the document for example, without the necessity of first calling a subscribing witness to testify. See 21 OJur

2d Evidence § 546. See also, McCormick § 220 (2d ed. 1972).

Rule 903 simply codifies Ohio case law extant at the time of the adoption of the rule by providing in relevant part that "The testimony of a subscribing witness is not necessary to authenticate a writing...." Hence, under the rule, a writing such as a contract may be authenticated by a person who signed the contract without the necessity of first offering the direct testimony of any subscribing witness.

As an exception, Rule 903 does provide for the testimony of a subscribing witness when "... required by laws of the jurisdiction whose laws govern the validity of the writing." Thus, R.C. 2107.14 and R.C. 2107.18, in conjunction, provide that upon demand of an interested party when a will is sought to be entered for probate, the probate court shall bring in the subscribing witnesses to the will (by subpoena if need be) to determine upon examination and cross-examination whether the execution of the will has complied with the law governing the execution of wills.

It should be noted that when Rule 903 is construed with Rule 902, authenticating testimony of any kind may not be necessary because the document or writing sought to be introduced may be self-authenticating. Thus, pursuant to Rule 902(8), a notarized document is admissible without authenticating testimony.

Cross References

Will proved in certain cases, 2107.16

Library References

Criminal Law ⟷442.

Evidence ⟷374(1) to 374(11).

Westlaw Topic Nos. 110, 157.

C.J.S. Evidence §§ 829 to 833.

OJur 3d: 43, Evidence and Witnesses § 456, 461; 65, Landlord and Tenant § 121; 66, Lost and Destroyed Instruments and Records § 22

Am Jur 2d: 29, Evidence § 850

Giannelli & Snyder, Baldwin's Ohio Practice, Evidence § 901.5 (2d ed. 2001).

Article X

CONTENTS OF WRITINGS, RECORDINGS AND PHOTOGRAPHS

Rule
1001 Definitions
1002 Requirement of original
1003 Admissibility of duplicates
1004 Admissibility of other evidence of contents
1005 Public records
1006 Summaries
1007 Testimony or written admission of party
1008 Functions of court and jury

Evid R 1001　Definitions

For purposes of this article the following definitions are applicable:

(1) Writings and recordings

"Writings" and "recordings" consist of letters, words, or numbers, or their equivalent, set down by handwriting, typewriting, printing, photostating, photographing, magnetic impulse, mechanical or electronic recording, or other forms of date [1] compilation.

(2) Photographs

"Photographs" include still photographs, X-ray films, video tapes, and motion pictures.

(3) Original

An "original" of a writing or recording is the writing or recording itself or any counterpart intended to have the same effect by a person executing or issuing it. An "original" of a photograph includes the negative or any print therefrom. If data are stored in a computer or similar device, any printout or other output readable by sight, shown to reflect the data accurately, is an "original".

(4) Duplicate

A "duplicate" is a counterpart produced by the same impression as the original, or from the same matrix, or by means of photography, including enlargements and miniatures, or by mechanical or electronic re-recording, or by chemical reproduction, or by other equivalent techniques which accurately reproduce the original.

(Adopted eff. 7–1–80)

[1] So in 62 OS(2d) li; federal rule reads "data."

Commentary

Staff Notes

1980:

Article X (Rule 1001 through Rule 1008) is a modern restatement of the "Best Evidence Rule." Rule 1001, relevant to Rule 1002 through Rule 1004, sets forth a series of definitions upon which the succeeding three rules depend. Rule 1001 is a *verbatim* restatement of Federal Evidence Rule 1001.

Paragraph (1) of Rule 1001, recognizing both ancient and modern techniques, defines "writings" and "recordings" in the broadest terms. Hence "words" or "numbers" or their "equivalent" may be "set down" in any form from handwriting to mere impulses in an electronic recording device or mere impulses in the memory bank of a computer.

Paragraph (2) defines "photographs" as including X-ray films, video tapes, and motion pictures as well as traditional "still" photographs.

Paragraph (3) defines what constitutes an "original" of a writing or recording or photograph. The original, pursuant to Rule 1002, is the best evidence. As defined by paragraph (3), the original of a photograph is the negative or any print made therefrom. Recognizing that data, such as words, are stored in a computer, the paragraph defines the original of such data as any printout or other output readable by sight which reflects the data accurately. Importantly, the first sentence of paragraph (3) defines the original of a "writing or recording" as the writing or recording "itself" or as any "counterpart intended to have the same effect by a person executing or issuing it." A counterpart intended to have the effect of an original is a duplicate original and hence, equally with the original, is the best evidence pursuant to Rule 1002. The counterpart concept of the rule represents the more modern view. Thus, a carbon copy of a contract signed by the parties and *intended by the parties* to be a counterpart or duplicate original is admissible as the best evidence without the need to lay a foundation and account for the fact of not producing the original. *International Harvester Co. v. Elfstrom* (1907), 101 Minn. 273, 112 N.W. 252. Or the carbon copy of an unsigned deposit slip *intended by the parties* to be a duplicate original is admissible as the best evidence. *Schroer v. Schroer* (S.Ct. Mo. 1952), 248 S.W.2d 617. The counterpart doctrine of Rule 1001(3) broadens the holding of *Chrismer v. Chrismer* (1956), 103 Ohio App. 23. Although appealing on its facts, the *Chrismer* opinion laid down the broad proposition that the duplicate original carbon of an instrument was secondary evidence and could not be admitted as the best evidence without first laying the foundation accounting for failure to produce the original.

Under Rule 1001(3) a photostat, *intended by the parties* to have the effect of an original, could be a counterpart or duplicate original. But in any event, a photostat also fits the definition of a "duplicate" pursuant to Rule 1001(4). But for exceptional circumstances, a duplicate is admissible as an original pursuant to Rule 1003.

Paragraph (4) of Rule 1001 defines a "duplicate." A duplicate is a counterpart produced by the "same impression" or the "same matrix" as the original. The accurate reproduction of the original may be by photography, chemical reproduction or equivalent techniques. In addition, a duplicate may be reproduced by electronic "re-recording." Hence, a tape recording of a tape recording would be a duplicate. The definition changes the traditional position of the best evidence rule. See *People v. King* (Cal. App. 1950), 255 P. 2d 950, 954 (the traditional rule, holding a disc recording of a tape recording not admissible as in violation of the best evidence rule). Of course, a photostat fits the definition of a "duplicate."

It should be noted that paragraph (4) provides that the duplicate must be an accurate reproduction of the original from the "same impression." In short, the watchwords are accurate reproduction. Hence, a handwritten or retyped version of an original—subject to ready error by virtue of the reproduction method—does not meet the accuracy requirements for a duplicate.

Library References

Criminal Law ☞398(1), 398(2).

Evidence ☞161 to 170.

Westlaw Topic Nos. 110, 157.

C.J.S. Criminal Law §§ 833 to 844.

C.J.S. Evidence §§ 1061 to 1099.

OJur 3d: 29A, Criminal Law § 3050; 43, Evidence and Witnesses § 489, 490; 59, Insurance § 1386; 66, Lost and Destroyed Instruments and Records § 22

Giannelli & Snyder, Baldwin's Ohio Practice, Evidence § 104.6, 803.27, 803.28, 1002.1, 1002.3, 1002.6, 1002.7, 1003.1, 1003.3, 1008.3, 1002, 1003 (2d ed. 2001).

Adrine & Ruden, Ohio Domestic Violence Law (2002 Ed.), Text 15.8.

Evid R 1002   Requirement of original

To prove the content of a writing, recording, or photograph, the original writing, recording, or photograph is required, except as otherwise provided in these rules or by statute enacted by the General Assembly not in conflict with a rule of the Supreme Court of Ohio.

(Adopted eff. 7–1–80)

Commentary

Staff Notes

1980:

Rule 1002, the familiar part of the best evidence rule, requires, with one exception, that the original of a writing, recording or photograph be produced in evidence. The exception provides that the burden of producing an original may be excused by other evidence rules or by statute. Rule 1002 is a counterpart of Federal Evidence Rule 1002.

As a practical matter, the "original" required by Rule 1002 as the best evidence would include a duplicate original or counterpart as defined by Rule 1001(3) and in almost all instances a duplicate as defined by Rule 1001(4), and admissible as the best evidence pursuant to Rule 1003.

The requirement that the original be introduced as the best evidence may be excused by virtue of another evidence rule such as Rule 1005, which permits the use of a copy of a public record as the best evidence, provided that the proper authentication procedure is followed. Random statutes also permit the use of a copy of an original as the best evidence. For example, 44 U.S.C.A. § 399(a) gives the status of an original to photographic copies of an original in the National Archives.

Rule 1002 specifically provides that the original of a writing or photograph or recording is required as the best evidence if the particular writing or photograph or recording is introduced to prove its "content." Thus, if a confession is recorded on tape, the original tape recording would be introducible as the best evidence for its "content." On the other hand, a photograph is seldom introduced to prove the content of the photograph, and hence the best evidence rule is not involved. Customarily, a photograph is authenticated and introduced into evidence, not to prove the content of the photograph, but merely to illuminate the testimony of a witness who by oral testimony is describing what he saw in the scene set forth in the photograph. But on occasion, the photograph may be introduced to prove its content; the photograph itself is the best evidence.

Cross References

Method of qualification of hospital and certain other records, 2317.422

Photographic copies of records admissible as competent evidence, 2317.41

Library References

Criminal Law ☞400(1) to 401.

Evidence ⟐174 to 175.

Westlaw Topic Nos. 110, 157.

C.J.S. Criminal Law §§ 837 to 842.

C.J.S. Evidence §§ 1068 to 1079, 1091, 1102 to 1104, 1114.

OJur 3d: 29A, Criminal Law § 3050, 3051; 43, Evidence and Witnesses § 489, 494; 59, Insurance § 1386; 66, Lost and Destroyed Instruments and Records § 22; 79, Railroads § 409

Am Jur 2d: 29, Evidence § 448

Giannelli & Snyder, Baldwin's Ohio Practice, Evidence § 102.5, 402.7, 802.1, 804.14, 901.1, 901.15, 902.1, 1001, 1001.1, 1001.3, 1008.3 (2d ed. 2001).

Adrine & Ruden, Ohio Domestic Violence Law (2002 Ed.), Text 15.8.

Evid R 1003 Admissibility of duplicates

A duplicate is admissible to the same extent as an original unless (1) a genuine question is raised as to the authenticity of the original or (2) in the circumstances it would be unfair to admit the duplicate in lieu of the original.

(Adopted eff. 7–1–80)

Commentary

Staff Notes

1980:

Rule 1003 is the same as Federal Evidence Rule 1003. With but limited exceptions, the rule treats a "duplicate" as the equivalent of an "original" and hence as the best evidence. In this respect the rule broadens Ohio case law. In *Hine v. [Dayton] Speedway Corp.* (1969), 20 Ohio App.2d 185, the court held a photostatic duplicate of an original document to be admissible as secondary evidence only upon a showing that the original was not available.

The distinction between a duplicate and a duplicate original or counterpart is set forth in Rule 1001(3) and Rule 1001(4) and the accompanying Staff Notes. A duplicate original or counterpart is a copy intended by the parties to be an original whereas a duplicate is merely a copy of the original which reproduces the original by some accurate means such as photostating. The distinction, a narrow one, lies *in the intention of the parties* at the time of execution of the copy. In any event, the duplicate under Rule 1003 is customarily treated as an original.

However, objection may be raised to the introduction of the duplicate as the best evidence, but the objection must be something more than a frivolous objection.

First, pursuant to Rule 1003, a party may object to the introduction of a duplicate if he raises a "genuine question... as to the authenticity of the original." Thus, assume that either the original or the duplicate was corrected or altered after execution and through oversight the counterpart was not corrected. A genuine issue could be raised as to the authenticity of the original or the duplicate.

Second, a party may object to the introduction of a duplicate if it would be "unfair" to admit the duplicate in lieu of the original. Thus, assume that the photostating process fails to reproduce a few important sentences in the duplicate. Upon objection, the court might insist upon production of the original.

Or upon an attempt to introduce a duplicate recording, re-recorded to "bring up" certain suppressed words and eliminate certain distracting noises, the court might deem it fair to produce the original recording for purposes of comparison.

Cross References

Records of superintendent of banks; certified and authenticated copies as evidence, 1125.19

Library References

Criminal Law ⟐403.

Evidence ⟐186(1) to 186(9).

Westlaw Topic Nos. 110, 157.

C.J.S. Criminal Law § 845.

C.J.S. Evidence §§ 1054, 1060, 1065.

OJur 3d: 29A, Criminal Law § 3050; 43, Evidence and Witnesses § 489, 498; 59, Insurance § 1386; 66, Lost and Destroyed Instruments and Records § 22; 79, Railroads § 409

Carbon copies of letters or other written instruments as evidence. 65 ALR2d 342

Photographic representation or photostat of writing as primary or secondary evidence within best evidence rule. 76 ALR2d 1356

Admissibility of duplicates under Rules 1001(4) and 1003 of Federal Rules of Evidence. 72 ALR Fed 732

Painter, Ohio Driving Under the Influence Law (2003 Ed.), Text 13.10.

Giannelli & Snyder, Baldwin's Ohio Practice, Evidence § 1002.1, 1001, 1001.1, 1001.5, 1001.6, 1002, 1002.6, 1002.7, 1004.1, 1005.1, 1006.1, 1007.1, 1008.3 (2d ed. 2001).

Evid R 1004 Admissibility of other evidence of contents

The original is not required, and other evidence of the contents of a writing, recording, or photograph is admissible if:

(1) Originals lost or destroyed

All originals are lost or have been destroyed, unless the proponent lost or destroyed them in bad faith; or

(2) Original not obtainable

No original can be obtained by any available judicial process or procedure; or

(3) Original in possession of opponent

At a time when an original was under the control of the party against whom offered, he was put on notice, by the pleadings or otherwise, that the contents would be subject of proof at the hearing, and he does not produce the original at the hearing; or

(4) Collateral matters

The writing, recording, or photograph is not closely related to a controlling issue.

(Adopted eff. 7–1–80)

Commentary

Staff Notes

1980:

The rule is stated in language identical to that of Federal Evidence Rule 1004.

The rule is in accord with prior Ohio law.

Rule 1004(1) Originals Lost or Destroyed

It has long been the case law of Ohio that any other evidence of content is admissible when the original is lost or destroyed. Deed, *Lessee of Allen v. Parish* (1827), 3 Ohio 107, 121; *Gillmore v. Fitzgerald* (1875), 26 Ohio St. 171; Contract, *Reid v. Sycks* (1875), 27 Ohio St. 285; Note, *Taylor's Administrator v. Colin* (1833), Wright 449; Letter, *Clark v. Longworth* (1833), Wright 189; Corporate record, *State, ex rel. Van Matre v. Buchanan,* (1833), Wright 233; Release, *Hine v. [Dayton] Speedway Corp.* (1969), 20 Ohio App.2d 185. Mutilation is the equivalent of loss. *Fallis v. Griffith* (1833), Wright 303.

Rule 1004(2) Original Not Obtainable

Prior Ohio law treated the original's being out of the jurisdiction as not obtainable. *Fosdick v. Van Horn* (1884), 40 Ohio St. 459.

Rule 1004(3) Original in Possession of Opponent

The necessity for notice to an opponent to produce materials for evidentiary purposes was recognized in prior Ohio law. *Falardeau v. W.H.H. Smith Co.* (1909), 13 Ohio C.C. (n.s.) 268. Formal notice was not required where the nature of the action indicates that the adverse party is to be charged with possession of a written instrument. *Scioto Valley R. Co. v. Cronin* (1882), 38 Ohio St. 122.

Rule 1004(4) Collateral Matters

Particular evidence remains secondary, but admissible, when not related closely to a controlling issue, so long as its admission does not serve to prejudice the adverse party.

Cross References

Photographic copies of records admissible as competent evidence, 2317.41

Library References

Criminal Law ☞400(1) to 401.

Evidence ☞177 to 179(4).

Westlaw Topic Nos. 110, 157.

C.J.S. Criminal Law §§ 837 to 842.

C.J.S. Evidence §§ 1054, 1059, 1065, 1066, 1102 to 1112.

OJur 3d: 29A, Criminal Law § 3050; 43, Evidence and Witnesses § 489, 520 to 523, 526, 528; 59, Insurance § 1386; 66, Lost and Destroyed Instruments and Records § 22; 79, Railroads § 409

Am Jur 2d: 29, Evidence § 451 to 456

Federal Rules of Evidence: Admissibility, pursuant to Rule 1004(1), of other evidence of contents of writing, recording, or photograph, where originals were allegedly lost or destroyed. 83 ALR Fed 554

Giannelli & Snyder, Baldwin's Ohio Practice, Evidence § 403.6, 1001.1, 1002.1, 1002.7, 1003.1, 1005.1, 1006.1, 1007, 1007.1, 1007.3 (2d ed. 2001).

Evid R 1005   Public records

The contents of an official record, or of a document authorized to be recorded or filed and actually recorded or filed, including data compilations in any form if otherwise admissible, may be proved by copy, certified as correct in accordance with Rule 902, Civ. R. 44, Crim. R. 27 or testified to be correct by a witness who has compared it with the original. If a copy which complies with the foregoing cannot be obtained by the exercise of reasonable diligence, then other evidence of the contents may be given.

(Adopted eff. 7–1–80)

Commentary

Staff Notes

1980:

The rule differs from Federal Evidence Rule 1005 in only one regard. The single modification is the addition of a reference to Civ. R. 44 and Crim. R. 27 which relate to the authentication of official records as does Rule 902 which governs self-authentication.

The rule is in accord with prior Ohio law.

The basis of the special treatment for public records is founded upon the necessity to maintain the integrity of such records and the inability to produce them readily by virtue of physical considerations or considerations of inconvenience.

The rule recognizes two methods of authentication. One being the certification set forth in Rule 902, Civ. R. 44, or Crim. R. 27 and the other being the testimony of a witness who has compared the copy to the original record.

In *Lessee of Sheldon v. Coates* (1840), 10 Ohio 278, it was said at 282:

All public documents which cannot be removed from one place to another, may be authenticated by means of a copy, proved on oath to have been examined with the original.

As the Staff Note to Civ. R. 44 points out, that rule did not supersede R.C. 2317.10 and 2317.42 relative to the admissibility of public records described therein. The rule merely established the manner of authentication. Rule 1005 serves to supersede the cited statutes insofar as they provide for the admission of copies of public documents.

Cross References

Certified copy of record of instrument as evidence, 5301.43

Department seals, specifications, 121.20

Evidence of incorporation, articles and proceedings, 1701.92, 1702.53

Execution and evidence of power of attorney, 1337.06

Official reports admitted as evidence, 2317.42

Proof of official record, Civ R 44

Proof of official record, judicial notice, determination of foreign law, Crim R 27

Public record, state government, definition of, 149.43

Library References

Criminal Law ☞400(2), 400(3).

Evidence ☞162(1) to 163.

Westlaw Topic Nos. 110, 157.

C.J.S. Criminal Law §§ 841, 842.

C.J.S. Evidence §§ 1092 to 1100.

OJur 3d: 29A, Criminal Law § 3050; 43, Evidence and Witnesses § 489, 499, 501, 511; 59, Insurance § 1386; 66, Lost and Destroyed Instruments and Records § 22

Am Jur 2d: 29, Evidence § 482 to 484

Painter, Ohio Driving Under the Influence Law (2003 Ed.), Text 13.10.

Giannelli & Snyder, Baldwin's Ohio Practice, Evidence § 609.15, 803.36, 901.11, 902.3, 902.4, 1001.1, 1002.1, 1002.7, 1003.1, 1004.1, 1006.1, 1007.1 (2d ed. 2001).

Evid R 1006   Summaries

The contents of voluminous writings, recordings, or photographs which cannot conveniently be examined in court may be presented in the form of a chart, summary, or calculation. The originals, or duplicates, shall be made available for examination or copying, or both, by other parties at a reasonable time and place. The court may order that they be produced in court.

(Adopted eff. 7–1–80)

Commentary

Staff Notes

1980:

The rule is stated in language identical to that of Federal Evidence Rule 1006.

The rule makes no change in prior Ohio law. As was said in *Heiser Brothers Co. v. Cleveland* (1932), 44 Ohio App. 560, 562:

It has long been the practice to permit experts who have examined voluminous documents, records and accounts to testify as to the net result of their examination.

Cross References

Admissible reports, 2317.36

Library References

Criminal Law ⊕398(2).

Evidence ⊕186(1).

Westlaw Topic Nos. 110, 157.

C.J.S. Criminal Law §§ 843, 844.

C.J.S. Evidence §§ 1054, 1060, 1065.

OJur 3d: 29A, Criminal Law § 3050; 43, Evidence and Witnesses § 489, 509; 59, Insurance § 1386; 66, Lost and Destroyed Instruments and Records § 22

Admissibility of evidence summaries under Uniform Evidence Rule 1006. 59 ALR4th 971

Admissibility of summaries of writings, recordings, or photographs under Rule 1006 of the Federal Rules of Evidence. 50 ALR Fed 319

Giannelli & Snyder, Baldwin's Ohio Practice, Evidence § 703.7, 1001.1, 1002.1, 1002.7, 1003.1, 1004.1, 1005.1, 1007.1 (2d ed. 2001).

Evid R 1007   Testimony or written admission of party

Contents of writings, recordings, or photographs may be proved by the testimony or deposition of the party against whom offered or by his written admission, without accounting for the nonproduction of the original.

(Adopted eff. 7–1–80)

Commentary

Staff Notes

1980:

The rule is stated in language identical to that of Federal Evidence Rule 1007.

The rule adds a concept to prior Ohio law. Ohio has treated the admissions of a party as primary evidence and not as secondary evidence where the admission relates to the contents of a written document. In *State, ex rel. Van Matre* (1833), Wright 233, the admission as to a party's status as a director of a corporation was admissible although the corporate records constituted the best evidence. So, too, the admissions of a party as to being divorced were admissible although the record of the divorce constituted best evidence. *Edgar v. Richardson* (1878), 33 Ohio St. 581.

The rule relates to a party's testimony, his deposition, or his written admission as to the contents of a written instrument. If any one of the three is offered, it is not necessary to account for the absent writing. If the admission of the party is oral rather than in writing, it is admissible if the proponent accounts for the absence of the written instrument under the provisions of Rule 1004.

Library References

Criminal Law ⊕398(1).

Evidence ⊕183.

Westlaw Topic Nos. 110, 157.

C.J.S. Criminal Law §§ 833 to 836.

C.J.S. Evidence §§ 1119 to 1122.

OJur 3d: 29A, Criminal Law § 3050; 43, Evidence and Witnesses § 489, 495; 59, Insurance § 1386; 66, Lost and Destroyed Instruments and Records § 22

Giannelli & Snyder, Baldwin's Ohio Practice, Evidence § 104.6, 801.17, 803.27, 1001.1, 1002.1, 1002.7, 1003.1, 1004.1, 1004.5, 1005.1, 1006.1, 1008.3 (2d ed. 2001).

Evid R 1008   Functions of court and jury

When the admissibility of other evidence of contents of writings, recordings, or photographs under these rules depends upon the fulfillment of a condition of fact, the question whether the condition has been fulfilled is ordinarily for the court to determine in accordance with the provisions of Rule 104. However, when an issue is raised (a) whether the asserted writing ever existed, or (b) whether another writing, recording, or photograph produced at the trial is the original, or (c) whether other evidence of contents correctly reflects the contents, the issue is for the trier of fact to determine as in the case of other issues of fact.

(Adopted eff. 7–1–80)

Commentary

Staff Notes

1980:

The rule is stated in language identical to that of Federal Evidence Rule 1008.

Rule 104 provides that preliminary questions of fact relating to the admissibility of evidence are to be determined by the court. The rule places a limitation on the court's power to make that factual determination. It provides that the factual issue raised by a challenge to secondary evidence on the basis (1) that the original never existed, or (2) that another piece of evidence is the original, or (3) that the secondary evidence is inaccurate in reflecting the contents of the original creates an issue for the trier of the fact. It would seem to follow that the rule has

no effect on the court's general power over fact issues.

The purpose of the rule is to insure that the case is not disposed of by a ruling on the competency and admissibility of secondary evidence under any one of the three defenses enumerated.

The rule serves to place a limitation on the role of the court which has not previously existed in Ohio.

Library References

Criminal Law ⊃736(1).

Trial ⊃138.

Westlaw Topic Nos. 110, 388.

C.J.S. Criminal Law §§ 978, 1290, 1291.

C.J.S. Trial § 207.

OJur 3d: 29A, Criminal Law § 3050; 43, Evidence and Witnesses § 489, 518; 59, Insurance § 1386; 66, Lost and Destroyed Instruments and Records § 22

Giannelli & Snyder, Baldwin's Ohio Practice, Evidence § 1001, 104.6, 1001.1 (2d ed. 2001).

Article XI

MISCELLANEOUS RULES

Rule
1101   [Reserved]
1102   Effective date
1103   Title

Evid R 1101   [Reserved]

Library References

Giannelli & Snyder, Baldwin's Ohio Practice, Evidence § 101 (2d ed. 2001).

Evid R 1102   Effective date

(A) Effective date of rules

These rules shall take effect on the first day of July, 1980. They govern all proceedings in actions brought after they take effect and also all further proceedings in actions then pending, except to the extent that in the opinion of the court their application in a particular action pending when the rules take effect would not be feasible or would work injustice, in which event former evidentiary principles apply.

(B) Effective date of amendments

The amendments submitted by the Supreme Court to the General Assembly on January 14, 1981, and on April 29, 1981, shall take effect on July 1, 1981. They govern all proceedings in actions brought after they take effect and also all further proceedings in actions then pending, except to the extent that their application in a particular action pending when the amendments take effect would not be feasible or would work injustice, in

which event the former procedure applies.

(C) Effective date of amendments

The amendments submitted by the Supreme Court to the General Assembly on January 12, 1990, and further revised and submitted on April 16, 1990, shall take effect on July 1, 1990. They govern all proceedings in actions brought after they take effect and also all further proceedings in actions then pending, except to the extent that their application in a particular action pending when the amendments take effect would not be feasible or would work injustice, in which event the former procedure applies.

(D) Effective date of amendments

The amendments submitted by the Supreme Court to the General Assembly on January 10, 1991 and further revised and submitted on April 29, 1991, shall take effect on July 1, 1991. They govern all proceedings in actions brought after they take effect and also all further proceedings in actions then pending, except to the extent that their application in a particular action pending when the amendments take effect would not be feasible or would work injustice, in which event the former procedure applies.

(E) Effective date of amendments

The amendments filed by the Supreme Court with the General Assembly on January 14, 1992 and further filed on April 30, 1992, shall take effect on July 1, 1992. They govern all proceedings in actions brought after they take effect and also all further proceedings in actions then pending, except to the extent that their application in a particular action pending when the amendments take effect would not be feasible or would work injustice, in which event the former procedure applies.

(F) Effective date of amendments

The amendments submitted by the Supreme Court to the General Assembly on January 8, 1993 and further filed on April 30, 1993 shall take effect on July 1, 1993. They govern all proceedings in actions brought after they take effect and also all further proceedings in actions then pending, except to the extent that their application in a particular action pending when the amendments take effect would not be feasible or would work injustice, in which event the former procedure applies.

(G) Effective date of amendments

The amendments submitted by the Supreme Court to the General Assembly on January 14, 1994 and further filed on April 29, 1994 shall take effect on July 1, 1994. They govern all proceedings in actions brought after they take effect and also all further proceedings in actions then pending, except to the extent that their application in a particular action pending when the amendments take effect would not be feasible or would work injustice, in which event the former procedure applies.

(H) Effective date of amendments

The amendments to Rules 101, 102 and 403 filed by the Supreme Court with the General Assembly on January 5, 1996 and refiled on April 26, 1996 shall take effect on July 1, 1996. They govern all proceedings in actions brought after they take effect and also all further proceedings in actions then pending, except to the extent that their application in a particular action pending when the amendments take effect would not be feasible or would work injustice, in which event the former procedure applies.

(I) Effective date of amendments

The amendments to Rules 607, 613, 616, 706, and 806 filed by the Supreme Court with the General Assembly on January 15, 1998 and further revised and refiled on April 30, 1998 shall take effect

on July 1, 1998. They govern all proceedings in actions brought after they take effect and also all further proceedings in actions then pending, except to the extent that their application in a particular action pending when the amendments take effect would not be feasible or would work injustice, in which event the former procedure applies.

(J) Effective date of amendments

The amendments to Rules 101 and 1102(I) filed by the Supreme Court with the General Assembly on January 13, 1999 shall take effect on July 1, 1999. They govern all proceedings in actions brought after they take effect and also all further proceedings in actions then pending, except to the extent that their application in a particular action pending when the amendments take effect would not be feasible or would work injustice, in which event the former procedure applies.

(K) Effective date of amendments

The amendments to Evidence Rule 407 filed by the Supreme Court with the General Assembly on January 13, 2000 and refiled on April 27, 2000 shall take effect on July 1, 2000. They govern all proceedings in actions brought after they take effect and also all further proceedings in actions then pending, except to the extent that their application in a particular action pending when the amendments take effect would not be feasible or would work injustice, in which event the former procedure applies.

(L) Effective date of amendments

The amendments to Evidence Rules 615 and 804 filed by the Supreme Court with the General Assembly on January 12, 2001, and refiled on April 26, 2001, shall take effect on July 1, 2001. They govern all proceedings in actions brought after they take effect and also all further proceedings in actions then pending, except to the extent that their application in a particular action pending when the amendments take effect would not be feasible or would work injustice, in which event the former procedure applies.

(M) Effective date of amendments.

The amendments to Evidence Rules 609 and 615 filed by the Supreme Court with the General Assembly on January 9, 2003 and refiled on April 28, 2003, shall take effect on July 1, 2003. They govern all proceedings in actions brought after they take effect and also all further proceedings in actions then pending, except to the extent that their application in a particular action pending when the amendments take effect would not be feasible or would work injustice, in which event the former procedure applies.

(Adopted eff. 7–1–80; amended eff. 7–1–81) [1], *7–1–90, 7–1–91, 7–1–92, 7–1–93, 7–1–94, 7–1–96, 7–1–98, 7–1–99, 7–1–00, 7–1–01, 7–1–03*

[1] Subdivision (B) was added in 1981 due to the amendment of Rule 804(B)(1) (former testimony exception to hearsay rule). See footnote to history of Evid R 804.

Historical and Statutory Notes

Amendment Note: The 7–1–01 amendment added division (L).

Amendment Note: The 7–1–00 amendment added division (K).

Amendment Note: The 7–1–99 amendment added division (J).

Amendment Note: The 7–1–98 amendment added division (I).

Amendment Note: The 7–1–96 amendment added division (H).

Amendment Note: The 7–1–94 amendment added division (G).

Amendment Note: The 7–1–93 amendment added division (F).

Commentary

Staff Notes

1999:

Division (I) of this rule, governing rules and amendments that took effect July 1, 1998, was amended to delete an erroneous reference to Rule 611 of the Rules of Evidence. Evid. R. 611 was not amended in 1998 and the reference to it was deleted from division (I).

1980:

Federal Evidence Rule 1102 governs "Amendments" rather than "Effective Date." The effective date for the Federal Rules of Evidence is set forth in the Evidence Rules Enabling Act passed by Congress. Congress's Evidence Rule 1102 sets forth the procedure for amending the federal rules, and in effect provides that amendments will be made pursuant to 28 U.S.C. § 2706.

In Ohio the Constitution (Art. IV, Sec. 5(B)) provides for the date *when* rules made by the Supreme Court will become effective. Rule 1102 merely reflects the Constitution. A similar effective date rule appears in all Ohio rules packages (for example, Civ. R. 86). Rule 1102 will in time also set forth the effective date of amendments of the Rules of Evidence (compare the amendments subdivisions of Civ. R. 86).

Because the Ohio "Effective Date" rule governs matter similar to the federal "Amendments" rule, the Evidence Rules Advisory Committee assigned the same number to the Ohio rule, Rule 1102.

Library References

Courts ⟨key⟩85(3).

Westlaw Topic No. 106.

C.J.S. Courts § 131.

OJur 3d: 29A, Criminal Law § 2859; 42, Evidence and Witnesses § 10

Evid R 1103   Title

These rules shall be known as the Ohio Rules of Evidence and may be cited as "Evidence Rules" or "Evid. R. ___."

(Adopted eff. 7–1–80)

Commentary

Staff Notes

1980:

Rule 1103, like Federal Evidence Rule 1103, is the title rule. A title rule in a Federal rules package does not, however, include an official citation form; hence the sometimes clumsy method of citation for a federal rule—i.e., Rule 16, Federal Rules of Civil Procedure.

Beginning with the Ohio Civil Rules package, the title rule of each rules package contains a citation form for the entire package and a citation form for an individual rule. Thus, "Civil Rules" for the package and "Civ. R. ___" for the individual rule. Rule 1103 carries on the tradition of a simplified, official citation form.

Library References

Courts ⟨key⟩80(2).

Westlaw Topic No. 106.

C.J.S. Courts § 128.

OJur 3d: 42, Evidence and Witnesses § 10

APPENDIX D

Glossary

Act charged — Any act allegedly committed by a child and identified in a complaint, indictment, or information alleging that the child is a delinquent child. RC 2152.02(A).

Adjudicatory hearing — A hearing to determine whether a child is a juvenile traffic offender, delinquent, unruly, neglected, dependent, or abused, or is otherwise within the court's jurisdiction. Juv. R. 2, Juv. R. 29.

Agreement for temporary custody — A voluntary agreement that is authorized by RC 5103.15 and that transfers the temporary custody of a child to a public children services agency or a private child placing agency. RC 2151.011(B)(3); Juv. R. 2.

Bind-over — See **Transfer**.

Category One Offense — Any of the following offenses: aggravated murder, murder, attempted aggravated murder, and attempted murder. RC 2152.02(BB).

Category Two Offense — Any of the following offenses: voluntary manslaughter, kidnapping, rape, felonious sexual penetration, aggravated arson, aggravated robbery, aggravated burglary, and involuntary manslaughter, where the death is a proximate result of the offender's committing or attempting to commit a felony. RC 2152.02(CC).

Child — Under Chapter 2151, a person who is under eighteen years of age, except a juvenile court has jurisdiction over any person adjudicated unruly prior to attaining 18 years until that person attains 21 years. RC 2151.011(B)(5). Under Chapter 2152, a person who is under eighteen years of age with certain exceptions: (1) a person who violates a federal or state law or a municipal ordinance prior to attaining 18 years is deemed a "child" irrespective of that person's age at the time the complaint is filed or the hearing on the complaint is held; (2) a person who, while under 18 years, commits an act that would be a felony if committed by an adult and who is not taken into custody or apprehended for that act until after the person attains 21 years is not a child in relation to that act; (3) a person whose case is transferred for criminal prosecution pursuant to RC 2152.12 is not a child; (4) a person whose case is transferred for criminal prosecution pursuant to RC 2152.12 and who subsequently is convicted of a felony; (5) a person who is adjudicated a delinquent child, has a serious youthful offender dispositional sentence imposed pursuant to RC 2152.13, and whose adult portion of the dispositional sentence is invoked pursuant to RC 2152.14 is not a child. Moreover, the juvenile court retains jurisdiction over a person who is adjudicated a delinquent child or juvenile traffic offender prior to attaining 18 years until the person attains 21 years.

Chronic truant — A child of compulsory school age who is absent without legitimate excuse for absence from the public school the child is supposed to attend for seven or more consecutive school days, 10 or more school days in one school month, or 15 or more school days in a school year. RC 2152.02(D).

Commit — To vest custody as ordered by the court. RC 2151.011(B)(9).

Complaint — The legal document which sets forth the allegations which form the basis for juvenile court jurisdiction. Juv. R. 2(F), Juv. R. 10.

Court proceeding — All action taken by a court from the earlier of (a) the time a complaint is filed or (b) the time a person first appears before an officer of the court until the court relinquishes jurisdiction over the child. Juv. R. 2(G).

Custodian — A person who has legal custody of a child or a public children services agency or private child placing agency that has permanent, temporary, or legal custody of a child. RC 2151.011(B)(11); Juv. R. 2(H).

Detention — The temporary care of children pending court adjudication or disposition, or execution of a court order, in a public or private facility designed to physically restrict movement and activities of children. RC 2151.011(B)(13); Juv. R. 2(K), Juv. R. 7.

Detention hearing — A hearing to determine whether a child shall be held in detention or shelter care prior to or pending execution of a final dispositional order. Juv. R. 2(L), Juv. R. 7(F).

Discovery — A process enabling one party to a court proceeding to gain information from another party. Juv. R. 24.

Dispositional hearing — A hearing to determine what action shall be taken concerning a child who is within the jurisdiction of the court. Juv. R. 2(M), Juv. R. 34.

Ex parte proceeding — A court proceeding done for, or on behalf of, one of the parties. Juv. R. 13.

Expungement — An erasure or destruction of a child's court record. RC 2151.358.

Felony — Any offense specifically classified as a felony, and any offense for which imprisonment of an adult for more than one year may be imposed as a penalty. RC 2901.02(D) and (E); Crim. R. 2(A).

Guardian — A person, association, or corporation that is granted authority by a probate court to exercise parental rights over a child to the extent provided in the court's order and subject to the residual parental rights of the child's parents. RC 2151.011(B)(16); Juv. R. 2(N).

Guardian ad litem — A person appointed to protect the interests of a party in a juvenile court proceeding. RC 2151.281; Juv. R. 2(O), Juv. R. 4(B).

Habitual truant — A child of compulsory school age who is absent without legitimate excuse for absence from the public school the child is supposed to attend for five or more consecutive school days, seven or more school days in one school month, or 12 or more school days in a school year. RC 2151.011(B)(17).

Hearing — Any portion of a juvenile court proceeding before the court, whether summary in nature or by examination of witnesses. Juv. R. 2(Q).

Indigent person — A person who, at the time his need is

determined, is unable by reason of lack of property or income to provide for full payment of legal counsel and all other necessary expenses of representation. Juv. R. 2(R), Juv. R. 4(A).

Juvenile court — A division of the court of common pleas, or a juvenile court separately and independently created, having jurisdiction under RC Chapters 2151 and 2152; RC 2151.011(A)(1); Juv. R. 2(S).

Juvenile judge — A judge of a court having jurisdiction under RC Chapter 2151; RC 2151.011(A)(2); Juv. R. 2(T).

Legal custody — A legal status that vests in the custodian the right to have physical care and control of the child and to determine where and with whom the child shall live, and the right and duty to protect, train, and discipline the child and to provide the child with food, shelter, education, and medical care, all subject to any residual parental rights, privileges, and responsibilities. An individual granted legal custody shall exercise the rights and responsibilities personally unless otherwise authorized by any section of the Revised Code or by the court. RC 2151.011(B)(19); Juv. R. 2(V).

Magistrate — An attorney appointed by a court to conduct proceedings and hearings according to the scope of authority provided by an order of reference. Juv. R. 40.

Mental examination — An examination by a psychiatrist or psychologist. Juv. R. 2(W).

Mental injury — Any behavioral, cognitive, emotional, or mental disorder in a child caused by an act or omission that is described in RC 2919.22 and is committed by the parent or other person responsible for the child's care. RC 2151.011(B)(22).

Mentally retarded person — A person having significantly subaverage general intellectual functioning existing concurrently with deficiencies in adaptive behavior, manifested during the developmental period. RC 5123.01(K); RC 2151.011(B)(23).

Misdemeanor — Any offense specifically classified as a misdemeanor, and any offense for which imprisonment for not more than one year may be imposed as a penalty. RC 2901.02(D) and (F); Crim. R. 2(B).

Party — A child who is the subject of a juvenile court proceeding, his spouse, if any, his parent, or if the parent of a child be himself a child, the parent of such parent and, in appropriate cases, his custodian, guardian or guardian ad litem, the state and any other person specifically designated by the court. Juv. R. 2(Y).

Permanent custody — A legal status that vests in a public children services agency or a private child placing agency all parental rights, duties, and obligations, including the right to consent to adoption, and divests the natural or adoptive parents of all parental rights, privileges, and obligations, including all residual rights and obligations. RC 2151.011(B)(30); Juv. R. 2(Z).

Permanent surrender — The act of a child's parent(s), by a voluntary agreement authorized by RC 5103.15, to transfer the permanent custody of the child to a public children services agency or a private child placing agency. RC 2151.011(B)(31); Juv. R. 2(AA).

Person — An individual, association, corporation, or partnership and the state or any of its political subdivisions, departments, or agencies. Juv. R. 2(BB).

Physical examination — An examination by a physician. Juv. R. 2(CC).

Physically impaired — Having one or more of the following conditions that substantially limit one or more of an individual's major life activities, including self-care, receptive and expressive language, learning, mobility, and self-direction: (a) a substantial impairment of vision, speech, or hearing; (b) a congenital orthopedic impairment; (c) an orthopedic impairment caused by disease, rheumatic fever or any other similar chronic or acute health problem, or amputation or another similar cause. RC 2151.011(B)(33).

Planned permanent living arrangement — A juvenile court order pursuant to which legal custody of a child is given to a public children services agency or private child placing agency without the termination of parental rights, and in which the agency is permitted to make an appropriate placement of the child and enter into a written long-term foster care agreement with a foster care provider or with another person or agency with whom the child is placed. RC 2151.011(B)(36); Juv. R. 2(DD).

Private child-placing agency — Any association, as defined in RC 5103.02, that is certified pursuant to RC 5103.03 to accept temporary, permanent, or legal custody of children for either foster care or adoption. RC 2151.011(A)(3); Juv. R. 2(EE).

Probation — A legal status created by court order following an adjudication that a child is a delinquent child, a juvenile traffic offender, or an unruly child whereby the child is permitted to remain in the parent's, guardian's, or custodian's home subject to supervision, or under the supervision of any agency designated by the court and returned to the court for violation of probation at any time during the period of probation.

Protective supervision — An order of disposition pursuant to which the court permits a child to remain in the custody of the child's parents, guardian, or custodian and stay in the child's home, subject to any conditions and limitations upon the child, the child's parents, guardian, or custodian, or any other person that the court prescribes, including supervision as directed by the court for the protection of the child. RC 2151.011(B)(39).

Public children's services agency — A children services board or a county department of human services that has assumed the administration of the children services function prescribed by RC Chapter 5153. Juv. R. 2(FF).

Removal action — The cause of action first created by RC 2151.55 which applies solely to a child in out-of-county foster home placement who is alleged to be causing a significant and unreasonable disruption to the educational process in the school the child is attending. Juv. R. 2(GG).

Residence or legal settlement of child — The same residence or legal settlement as that of the child's parents, legal guardian, or custodian who stands in the relation of loco parentis. RC 2151.06; Juv. R. 2(HH).

Residual parental rights, privileges, and responsibilities — Those rights, privileges, and responsibilities remaining with the natural parent after the transfer of legal custody of the child, including but not limited to the privilege of reasonable visitation, consent to adoption, the privilege to determine the child's religious affiliation, and the responsibility for support. RC 2151.011(B)(45); Juv. R. 2(II).

Rule of court — A rule promulgated by the Supreme Court or a rule concerning local practice adopted by another court which is not inconsistent with the rules promulgated by the Supreme Court and which rule is filed with the Supreme Court. Juv. R. 2(JJ).

Seal a record — Removal of a child's record from the main court file and securing it in a separate file accessible only to the court and certain persons. RC 2151.358(A).

Secure correctional facility — A facility under the direction of the Department of Youth Services that is designed to physically restrict the movement and activities of children and used for the placement of children after adjudication and disposition. RC 2151.011(B)(48).

Shelter — The temporary care of children in physically unrestricted facilities pending court adjudication or disposition, or execution of a court order. RC 2151.011(B)(50); Juv. R. 2(MM), Juv. R. 7.

Social history — The personal and family history of a child or any other party to a juvenile proceeding which may include the prior record of the person with the juvenile court or any other court. Juv. R. 2(NN), Juv. R. 32.

Subpoena — A document issued by a court commanding the person to whom it is directed to attend and give testimony at a time and place therein specified. Juv. R. 17.

Summons — A document issued by a court requiring the party or person to whom it is directed to appear before the court at the time fixed for hearing. Juv. R. 15.

Temporary custody — Legal custody of a child who is removed from the child's home, which custody may be terminated at any time at the discretion of the court or, if the legal custody is granted in an agreement for temporary custody, by the person who executed the agreement. RC 2151.011(B)(52); Juv. R. 2(OO).

Transfer — The process by which a juvenile court relinquishes jurisdiction and transfers a juvenile case to the criminal courts for prosecution. RC 2152.02(AA); Juv. R. 30.

Unemancipated — A term applicable in RC 2151.85 abortion proceedings to describe a woman who is unmarried and under eighteen years of age who has not entered the armed services of the United States, has not become employed and self-subsisting, or has not otherwise become independent from the care and control of her parent, guardian, or custodian. RC 2151.85(I).

Waiver — See Transfer.

Ward of court — A child over whom the court assumes continuing jurisdiction. Juv. R. 2(QQ).

Table of Laws and Rules

UNITED STATES CONSTITUTION, CODES, AND REGULATIONS

United States Code Annotated

12 U.S.C.A. §	Section No.
3401	14:4
3421	14:4

18 U.S.C.A. §	Section No.
5031	1:2
5032 et seq.	4:3
5042	1:2

28 U.S.C.A. §	Section No.
2254	34:12

42 U.S.C.A. §	Section No.
290dd-2	23:15
627(b)(3)	26:7
671	26:2
672	20:2, 25:14, 27:17
675	20:2, 33:10
5601(A)(12)	19:7
14071	6:1

Public Laws

Pub L No.	Section No.
96-272	1:7

UNITED STATES ACTS

Social Security Act

Act §	Section No.
Title IV-E	27:17

OHIO CONSTITUTION

Art. I §	Section No.
5	23:10
9	19:9
10	14:12, 14:13, 23:11, 23:22, 23:25, 23:27, 23:29, 23:31
10a	22:19, 23:12, 23:17, 25:5
14	14:3, 14:4

Art. I §	Section No.
16	22:19, 23:11

Art. IV §	Section No.
3(B)(2)	34:2
5(B)	22:1, 23:16

OHIO STATUTES

RC	Section No.
1.52	27:18
3.20	16:6
Ch 120	23:3, 23:4, 34:10
120.16(A)	23:3
121.37	15:6
121.38	15:6, 32:2
121.38(B)(1)	15:6
121.38(B)(2)	15:6
149.43 et seq.	35:2
149.43	12:8, 12:10, 21:2
149.43(A)(1)	35:2
149.43(A)(1)(b)	35:2
149.43(A)(1)(c)	35:2
149.43(A)(1)(l)	35:2
305.14	21:2
329.01	9:7
341.11	19:2
1347.04(A)(1)(e)	21:7
1347.08	21:7, 35:2
1347.08(C)	21:7
1347.08(E)(2)	21:7
Ch 2111	16:5
2111.46	16:15
Ch 2151	1:8, 2:3, 14:3, 15:2, 22:4, 32:2, 33:9, 35:4, 36:3
2151.01	1:7, 4:1, 10:3, 15:3
2151.01(A)	4:1, 30:2, 30:6, 30:8
2151.01(B)	30:2, 35:4
2151.01(C)	31:8
2151.02	4:4
2151.02(A)	34:2
2151.02(B)	33:6
2151.03	2:6, 9:2, 9:3, 9:12, 9:16, 16:17, 30:10
2151.03(A)	9:4
2151.03(A)(1)	9:6, 9:9
2151.03(A)(2)	9:6, 9:7
2151.03(A)(3)	9:7
2151.03(A)(4)	9:8
2151.03(A)(5)	9:6, 9:9
2151.03(A)(6)	9:10, 9:15
2151.03(A)(7)	9:11, 9:17
2151.03(B)	9:7
2151.04	9:2, 9:3, 9:12, 10:2, 16:17, 21:6
2151.04(A)	10:3, 10:5, 23:13
2151.04(B)	9:6, 10:4
2151.04(C)	9:8, 10:3, 10:5, 10:6, 16:12
2151.04(D)	9:15, 10:6
2151.05	9:6
2151.06	17:2, 17:4
2151.07	34:2

RC	Section No.
2151.011	2:2, 15:3
2151.011(A)(3)	30:6
2151.011(B)(1)	2:2, 9:6
2151.011(B)(5)	2:2, 30:6
2151.011(B)(5)(e)	22:22
2151.011(B)(6)	32:2
2151.011(B)(6)(a)	28:8
2151.011(B)(6)(b)	2:2
2151.011(B)(6)(c)	2:3, 22:4
2151.011(B)(6)(e)	2:3
2151.011(B)(6)(f)	2:3
2151.011(B)(9)	28:6
2151.011(B)(11)	9:6, 9:11
2151.011(B)(12)	19:2, 19:7
2151.011(B)(13)	33:4
2151.011(B)(15)	30:6
2151.011(B)(16)	9:6, 9:11
2151.011(B)(17)	1:7, 8:4, 30:6, 30:7, 30:13
2151.011(B)(19)	9:10, 9:15, 33:9
2151.011(B)(20)	8:4
2151.011(B)(21)	33:4
2151.011(B)(24)	9:17
2151.011(B)(25)	4:5, 8:4, 9:11
2151.011(B)(26)	9:11, 30:8, 32:2
2151.011(B)(27)	30:13
2151.011(B)(30)	33:4, 33:9
2151.011(B)(34)	27:8
2151.011(B)(35)	30:5
2151.011(B)(41)	30:7
2151.011(B)(42)	19:2
2151.011(B)(44)	19:2
2151.011(B)(46)	4:5, 8:4, 30:6
2151.011(B)(47)	4:5, 8:4
2151.011(B)(48)	28:6
2151.011(C)	9:5, 25:14, 30:10, 31:6
2151.12	15:2
2151.13	15:2, 16:6
2151.13(D)(2)	5:9
2151.14	21:6, 27:8, 35:2
2151.14(A)	27:8
2151.14(C)	32:3
2151.14(D)	21:2, 25:13
2151.16	20:4, 24:1, 24:2
2151.18	15:2
2151.18(A)	35:2
2151.21	18:3, 32:2, 33:8
2151.21(A)(6)	28:4
2151.022	4:4, 4:6, 8:2, 33:2
2151.022(A)	8:1, 8:3, 8:4, 8:7
2151.022(B)	8:1, 8:4, 8:7, 9:7

RC	Section No.
2151.022(C)	8:4, 8:5
2151.022(D)	8:5
2151.022(E)	8:1, 8:7
2151.022(F)	8:1, 8:7
2151.022(G)	8:1, 8:7
2151.23	3:2, 9:7, 9:16, 12:2, 19:7, 27:18, 32:2
2151.23(A)	3:3
2151.23(A)(1)	3:2, 3:3, 9:3, 16:17, 22:4
2151.23(A)(2)	3:3, 16:15, 30:11, 34:4, 34:11
2151.23(A)(3)	9:5, 34:12
2151.23(A)(4)	32:2
2151.23(A)(5)	35:4
2151.23(A)(8)	11:2
2151.23(A)(12)	15:6
2151.23(A)(13)	13:2
2151.23(D)	3:2, 16:15
2151.23(E)	16:15, 34:11
2151.23(F)	16:13, 16:15
2151.23(F)(1)	3:3, 16:15
2151.23(H)	3:3
2151.23(I)	2:3, 22:4
2151.24(A)	5:1
2151.24(B)	5:1
2151.26	1:8, 3:3, 22:1, 22:4, 22:7, 22:9, 22:12, 22:17, 23:9, 27:19
2151.26(A)	22:6, 27:3
2151.26(A)(1)	22:7
2151.26(A)(1)(c)	22:7
2151.26(A)(2)	22:7
2151.26(A)(4)	22:7
2151.26(B)	1:7, 22:1, 22:5, 22:7
2151.26(B)(1)	22:7
2151.26(B)(2)	22:7
2151.26(B)(3)	22:7
2151.26(B)(4)	22:7
2151.26(B)(4)(b)	22:4, 22:7
2151.26(C)(1)	1:7, 22:8
2151.26(D)	22:12
2151.26(E)	3:3
2151.26(F)	22:8, 22:22
2151.27	14:3, 15:2, 16:1, 16:2, 16:4, 16:6, 16:13, 16:14, 16:15, 16:17, 18:4, 31:2
2151.27(A)	16:3, 16:6, 16:7, 16:14, 16:15, 17:2
2151.27(A)(1)	16:10, 16:11, 16:12
2151.27(A)(2)	16:1, 16:8, 16:10, 17:2
2151.27(B)	2:2
2151.27(C)	16:14
2151.27(F)	18:2

RC	Section No.
2151.27(G)	16:13, 31:2
2151.28	18:4, 18:5, 25:4, 25:14, 30:11, 31:2, 31:6
2151.28(A)	23:29
2151.28(A)(1)	19:7, 23:29
2151.28(A)(2)	20:6, 23:29
2151.28(B)	25:14
2151.28(B)(1)	18:2
2151.28(B)(3)	20:6, 25:4
2151.28(C)	18:2, 18:3
2151.28(D)	14:3, 18:3
2151.28(E)	18:3
2151.28(E)(2)	18:3
2151.28(F)	23:3
2151.28(F)(1)	18:3
2151.28(F)(2)	18:3
2151.28(G)	19:6
2151.28(H)	18:5
2151.28(J)	18:3, 18:4, 33:8
2151.29	18:4
2151.031	9:2, 9:7, 9:10, 9:12, 14:3, 19:9, 25:14, 30:10
2151.031(A)	9:13, 16:4, 19:6
2151.31(A)(2)	20:6
2151.31(A)(6)(d)	14:3
2151.031(B)	9:13, 9:14
2151.31(B)(1)	14:3
2151.031(C)	9:15, 19:3, 19:6
2151.31(C)(2)	19:1, 19:6
2151.031(D)	9:10, 9:16, 14:3, 16:4, 20:4, 20:6
2151.031(E)	9:11, 9:17, 20:4, 20:6
2151.31(F)	20:4
2151.32	30:2
2151.33	9:7, 20:2, 25:14, 30:4
2151.33(A)	20:2, 20:3, 32:2
2151.33(B)	20:2
2151.33(B)(2)	32:2
2151.33(B)(2)(a)	30:3
2151.33(B)(2)(b)	30:3
2151.33(C)	20:2
2151.33(D)	20:5, 20:6
2151.33(E)	20:2
2151.33(F)	20:2
2151.34	19:2, 19:7, 27:6, 34:12
2151.35	9:3, 15:2, 23:1, 23:11, 23:23, 23:30, 25:4, 30:11, 33:6, 35:2
2151.35(A)	18:2, 22:19, 23:10, 23:11, 23:13, 23:23, 23:24, 25:4, 25:8, 25:12, 34:9
2151.35(A)(1)	23:32

RC	Section No.
2151.35(A)(2)	35:2
2151.35(B)	31:2
2151.35(B)(1)	20:6, 25:2, 25:4, 34:4
2151.35(B)(2)	25:9
2151.35(B)(2)(a)	25:3
2151.35(B)(2)(b)	25:9
2151.35(B)(2)(c)	25:9, 25:10
2151.35(B)(3)	25:13, 30:3, 30:6, 32:2
2151.35(B)(4)	30:4
2151.35(C)	18:2
2151.35(D)	16:5, 18:2
2151.35(F)	23:16
2151.35(G)	21:4, 23:16, 23:24
2151.35(H)(1)	23:9
2151.36	30:3, 32:2
2151.38	27:3, 33:5
2151.38(A)	2:3, 33:5, 33:9
2151.38(B)	33:5
2151.38(C)	33:5
2151.39	36:2
2151.40	18:2, 35:2
2151.42	30:6, 31:2, 33:11
2151.42(A)	33:4
2151.42(B)	33:4, 33:11
2151.45	36:3
2151.54	36:3
2151.55	13:2, 13:6, 30:13
2151.55(A)	13:2, 13:5
2151.55(B)	13:2
2151.55(C)	13:2
2151.55(D)	13:5, 13:6
2151.55(E)	13:5
2151.56	17:4, 19:2, 29:3, 36:2
2151.61	19:2, 29:3, 36:3
2151.65	27:6, 30:2, 30:3
2151.85	12:2, 12:3, 12:5, 12:6, 12:8, 12:10, 23:3
2151.85(A)	12:3, 12:5, 12:6
2151.85(A)(4)(a)	12:8, 12:9
2151.85(A)(4)(b)	12:8, 12:9
2151.85(B)(1)	12:7, 12:8
2151.85(B)(2)	12:4
2151.85(C)	12:2
2151.85(C)(1)	12:8, 12:9
2151.85(C)(2)	12:8
2151.85(C)(3)(a)	12:8
2151.85(C)(3)(b)	12:8
2151.85(D)	1:8, 12:6, 12:8
2151.85(E)	12:8, 12:10
2151.85(F)	12:8, 35:2
2151.85(G)	12:3, 12:10
2151.85(I)	12:2

RC	Section No.
2151.87	8:2, 8:6
2151.99(B)	14:15
2151.141	21:2, 21:6, 25:13
2151.141(B)(2)(b)	35:2
2151.271	3:2, 5:4, 17:2, 17:4
2151.281	1:8, 23:6
2151.281(A)(2)	23:6
2151.281(B)(1)	23:6
2151.281(B)(2)	23:6
2151.281(C)	23:6
2151.281(G)	23:6
2151.281(G)(4)	3:3
2151.281(H)	23:6
2151.311(A)	19:2
2151.311(A)(2)	19:2
2151.311(C)	19:2
2151.311(C)(1)(a)(i)	19:2
2151.311(C)(1)(a)(ii)	19:2
2151.311(C)(1)(a)(iii)	19:2
2151.311(C)(1)(a)(iv)	19:2
2151.311(C)(1)(b)(i)	19:2
2151.311(C)(1)(b)(ii)	19:2
2151.311(C)(1)(b)(iii)	19:2
2151.311(C)(1)(b)(iv)	19:2
2151.311(C)(2)	19:2
2151.312	19:2, 27:18, 29:3
2151.312(A)	19:2
2151.312(A)(3)	28:6
2151.312(B)	19:2
2151.312(C)	19:2, 22:22
2151.312(C)(1)	19:2
2151.312(C)(2)	19:2, 19:7
2151.312(C)(3)	19:2, 19:7
2151.312(D)	19:2, 27:18
2151.312(F)	19:2
2151.313	14:15, 35:2
2151.313(A)	14:15
2151.313(B)	14:15
2151.313(B)(4)	35:4
2151.314	1:8, 16:4, 19:9, 25:14
2151.314(A)	18:3, 19:4, 19:5, 19:7
2151.314(B)	19:6
2151.314(B)(2)	18:2
2151.314(C)	19:8
2151.314(D)	18:3
2151.331	19:2
2151.352	19:10, 21:2, 21:6, 22:11, 22:15, 23:3, 23:4, 23:5, 23:11, 25:7, 35:2
2151.353	9:3, 10:2, 16:15, 23:30, 25:14, 27:5, 29:2, 30:4, 30:6, 30:10, 30:13, 31:2, 33:5, 33:11

RC	Section No.
2151.353(A)	11:2, 16:5, 16:14, 25:8, 30:4, 33:4
2151.353(A)(1)	30:4
2151.353(A)(2)	30:4, 30:6, 34:4
2151.353(A)(3)	16:14, 30:4, 30:7
2151.353(A)(4) ...	16:5, 25:2, 25:8, 25:12, 27:5, 30:4, 30:8, 30:12, 31:1, 31:8, 31:9, 34:9
2151.353(A)(5)	25:8, 30:4, 30:13
2151.353(A)(6)	30:4
2151.353(B)	16:14, 18:3, 23:5, 27:5
2151.353(C)	30:5, 32:2
2151.353(D)	26:4
2151.353(E)(1)	2:2, 30:6, 32:2, 33:4
2151.353(E)(2)	33:4
2151.353(F)	1:7, 30:6
2151.353(G)	1:7
2151.353(G)(1)	30:5
2151.353(G)(1)(a)	30:5
2151.353(G)(1)(b)	30:5
2151.353(G)(2)	30:5
2151.353(G)(3)	30:5
2151.353(H)	25:14, 34:4
2151.353(I)	30:4
2151.353(J)	30:7, 33:4
2151.354	4:6, 16:15, 29:1
2151.354(A)	11:2, 16:14, 29:3
2151.354(A)(1)	29:2
2151.354(A)(2)	29:2
2151.354(A)(3)	29:2
2151.354(A)(4)	29:2
2151.354(B)	29:4
2151.354(B)(2)	29:4
2151.354(C)(1)	29:5
2151.354(C)(1)(e)	19:2
2151.354(C)(2)	29:5
2151.355	1:7, 4:6, 16:15, 23:9, 27:1, 27:3, 27:18, 27:19, 34:4
2151.355(A)	11:2, 27:3, 27:13, 28:5
2151.355(A)(1)	16:14, 27:3, 27:5
2151.355(A)(2)	27:7, 27:13
2151.355(A)(3)	27:3
2151.355(A)(5)	27:3
2151.355(A)(6)	27:3
2151.355(A)(7)	27:3
2151.355(A)(7)(b)	27:3
2151.355(A)(8)	27:13
2151.355(A)(9)	27:13
2151.355(A)(10)	27:10, 27:13
2151.355(A)(12)	27:10
2151.355(A)(13)	27:10
2151.355(A)(17)	27:8

RC	Section No.
2151.355(A)(25)	19:2, 27:18
2151.355(B)	27:9
2151.355(D)	13:5
2151.355(D)(2)	4:4
2151.355(E)(1)	27:3
2151.355(F)(6)	27:3
2151.355(J)	27:10
2151.355(J)(2)	27:10
2151.356 ...	27:13, 28:2, 28:4, 28:5, 28:10
2151.356(A)(2)	28:8
2151.356(A)(5)	27:13, 28:5
2151.356(B)	28:2
2151.357	19:11, 30:3
2151.358	23:20, 28:10, 35:2, 35:4
2151.358(A)	35:4
2151.358(B)	35:4
2151.358(C)	35:4
2151.358(C)(1)	35:4
2151.358(C)(1)(b)	35:4
2151.358(C)(2)	35:4
2151.358(D)	35:4
2151.358(E)	35:4
2151.358(F)	35:4
2151.358(G)	35:4
2151.358(H)	2:2, 23:20, 35:3
2151.358(I)	35:4
2151.358(J)	35:4
2151.358(K)	35:4
2151.359	30:6, 32:2
2151.411	33:5
2151.411(C)(1)	33:8
2151.412	1:7, 11:4, 25:14, 26:6, 26:7, 30:10, 31:7, 33:10, 34:4
2151.412(A)	26:2
2151.412(A)(1)	26:2
2151.412(A)(2)	26:2, 27:5
2151.412(C)	26:3
2151.412(D)	26:4, 26:6
2151.412(E)(1)	26:4, 33:8
2151.412(E)(2)	26:5, 31:2, 33:10
2151.412(E)(2)(a)	26:5
2151.412(E)(2)(b)	26:5
2151.412(E)(3)	26:5, 31:2, 33:10
2151.412(E)(3)(a)	26:5
2151.412(E)(3)(b)	26:5
2151.412(F)(1)	26:6
2151.412(F)(2)	26:6
2151.412(G)	26:6
2151.412(G)(1)	26:6
2151.412(G)(2)	26:6
2151.412(G)(3)	26:6
2151.412(G)(4)	26:6

RC	Section No.
2151.412(G)(5)	26:6
2151.412(G)(6)	26:6
2151.412(H)	26:6
2151.412(I)	26:6
2151.413	1:7, 16:14, 25:14, 30:6, 31:2
2151.413(A)	31:1
2151.413(B)	31:1
2151.413(C)	31:1
2151.413(D)	31:2
2151.413(D)(1)	30:6, 31:2
2151.413(D)(2)	31:2, 31:6
2151.413(D)(3)(b)	25:14
2151.413(E)	31:2
2151.414	1:7, 23:30, 25:12, 25:14, 30:6, 30:10, 31:4, 31:5, 31:8, 33:10, 33:11, 34:9
2151.414(A)	18:3, 31:8
2151.414(A)(2)	31:2, 31:3
2151.414(B)	30:9, 30:11
2151.414(B)(1)	31:6
2151.414(B)(1)(a)	31:6
2151.414(B)(1)(b)	31:6
2151.414(B)(1)(c)	31:6
2151.414(B)(1)(d)	30:9, 31:6
2151.414(B)(2)	31:6
2151.414(C)	23:6, 30:11, 30:12, 31:6, 31:8
2151.414(D)	30:8, 30:11, 31:6
2151.414(D)(1)	30:11
2151.414(D)(2)	30:11
2151.414(D)(3)	30:11
2151.414(D)(4)	30:11
2151.414(D)(5)	30:11
2151.414(E)	23:13, 30:8, 30:10, 31:6
2151.414(E)(1)	30:10, 31:8
2151.414(E)(2)	30:10
2151.414(E)(3)	30:10
2151.414(E)(4)	30:10
2151.414(E)(5)	30:10
2151.414(E)(6)	30:10
2151.414(E)(7) to (12)	30:11
2151.414(E)(7)(a)	30:10
2151.414(E)(7)(b)	30:10
2151.414(E)(7)(c)	30:10
2151.414(E)(7)(d)	30:10
2151.414(E)(7)(e)	30:10
2151.414(E)(8)	30:10
2151.414(E)(9)	30:10
2151.414(E)(10)	30:10
2151.414(E)(11)	30:10
2151.414(E)(12)	30:10
2151.414(E)(13)	30:10
2151.414(E)(14)	30:10
2151.414(E)(15)	30:10
2151.414(E)(16)	30:10
2151.414(F)	16:5, 18:2, 31:9
2151.415	1:7, 25:14, 30:6, 30:10, 31:4, 33:10, 33:11
2151.415(A)	16:14, 30:6, 30:10
2151.415(A)(1) to (5)	30:6
2151.415(A)(3)	16:14
2151.415(A)(4)	31:9
2151.415(A)(5)	30:13
2151.415(B)	30:6, 33:4
2151.415(C)(1)	23:13, 30:13
2151.415(C)(1)(c)	30:13
2151.415(C)(2)	30:13
2151.415(C)(2)(a)	30:13
2151.415(C)(2)(b)	26:6, 30:13
2151.415(D)	30:6
2151.415(D)(1)	30:6
2151.415(D)(2)	30:6
2151.415(D)(3)	30:6
2151.415(D)(4)	30:6
2151.415(E)	2:2, 33:4
2151.415(F)	31:2, 31:9, 33:4
2151.415(G)	30:13
2151.415(H)	33:10
2151.416	1:7, 33:10
2151.416(A)	33:10
2151.416(B)	33:10
2151.416(C)	33:10
2151.416(D)	33:10
2151.416(E)	33:10
2151.416(G)	33:10
2151.417	1:7, 25:14, 26:5, 33:10, 33:11, 34:4
2151.417(A)	33:11
2151.417(B)	30:6, 33:4
2151.417(C)	16:14, 33:11
2151.417(D)	33:10
2151.417(E)	33:11
2151.417(F)	33:11
2151.417(G)(1)	33:11
2151.417(G)(2)	33:11
2151.417(G)(3)	33:11
2151.417(G)(4)	33:11
2151.417(G)(5)	33:11
2151.417(H)	33:11
2151.417(I)	33:11
2151.417(J)	33:10
2151.417(K)	31:2
2151.417(K)(1)	33:11
2151.417(K)(2)	33:11

RC	Section No.
2151.418	30:6
2151.419	1:7, 19:6, 20:2, 20:4, 25:14, 31:2, 33:11
2151.419(A)	31:8
2151.419(A)(1)	25:14
2151.419(A)(2)	31:2, 31:6, 33:11
2151.419(A)(2)(a) to (e)	25:14
2151.419(A)(2)(a)(i)	25:14
2151.419(A)(2)(a)(ii)	25:14
2151.419(A)(2)(a)(iii)	25:14
2151.419(A)(2)(a)(iv)	25:14
2151.419(A)(2)(a)(v)	25:14
2151.419(A)(2)(b)	25:14
2151.419(A)(2)(c)	25:14
2151.419(A)(2)(d)	25:14
2151.419(A)(2)(e)	25:14
2151.419(A)(3)	25:14, 31:2
2151.419(B)	25:14, 34:4
2151.419(B)(1)	25:14
2151.419(B)(2)	25:14
2151.421	9:7, 9:11, 14:1, 14:16, 14:17, 15:4, 21:2, 23:15, 33:5, 35:3
2151.421(A)	14:17, 21:2
2151.421(B)	14:17, 21:2
2151.421(D)	14:17
2151.421(E)	20:2
2151.421(F)	14:17
2151.421(G)	14:17
2151.421(G)(1)	14:17
2151.421(G)(1)(a)	14:17
2151.421(H)	14:17
2151.421(H)(1)	21:2, 35:2, 35:3
2151.424	18:2, 33:4
2151.424(A)	18:2, 33:4
2151.424(B)	18:2, 33:4
2151.424(C)	18:2, 33:4
2151.3510	27:5
2151.3511	23:16, 23:23
2151.3511(A)(1)	21:4
2151.3511(A)(2)	21:4
2151.3514(A)(1)	30:14
2151.3514(B)	30:14
2151.3514(C)	30:14
2151.3514(D)	30:14
Ch 2152	1:7, 4:1, 7:1, 19:1, 19:6, 27:3, 28:1, 32:2
2152.01	1:7, 5:8, 22:8, 27:3
2152.01(A)	1:7, 4:1
2152.02(A)	22:7
2152.02(AA)	22:1
2152.02(B)	5:5

RC	Section No.
2152.02(BB)	22:7
2152.02(C)	2:3, 22:4
2152.02(C)(3)	2:3, 22:4
2152.02(C)(4)	2:3, 22:22
2152.02(C)(5)	2:3, 22:22
2152.02(C)(6)	2:7
2152.02(CC)	22:7
2152.02(D)	4:5, 8:4
2152.02(F)	4:2, 16:8
2152.02(F)(2)	28:6, 29:3
2152.02(F)(3)	8:6
2152.02(F)(4)	1:7, 4:5, 4:6, 8:4
2152.02(F)(5)	1:7, 4:5, 8:4
2152.02(K)	27:10
2152.02(M)	5:5, 22:7
2152.02(N)	7:2, 16:8
2152.02(U)	27:7
2152.03	2:4, 3:3, 22:4
2152.04	19:1, 19:6
2152.10	4:4, 4:6, 22:1, 22:7, 22:9
2152.10(A)	22:5
2152.10(A)(1)	22:7
2152.10(A)(2)	22:7
2152.10(A)(3)	22:7
2152.10(B)	22:8
2152.11(A)(1)	5:5
2152.11(A)(2)	5:5
2152.11(A)(3)	5:5
2152.11(B)(1)	5:7
2152.11(B)(2)	5:8
2152.011(B)(5)	29:1
2152.11(C)(1)	5:7
2152.11(C)(2)	5:8
2152.11(D)(1)	5:7
2152.11(D)(2)(a)	5:8
2152.11(D)(2)(b)	5:8
2152.11(D)(2)(c)	5:8
2152.11(D)(2)(d)	5:8
2152.11(E)(1)	5:8
2152.11(E)(2)	5:8
2152.11(F)(1)	5:8
2152.11(F)(2)	5:8
2152.11(G)(1)	5:8
2152.12	4:4, 22:1, 22:7, 22:9, 22:12, 22:17
2152.12(A)	2:3, 22:7
2152.12(A)(1)(a)	22:7
2152.12(A)(2)(a)	22:7
2152.12(A)(2)(b)	22:7
2152.12(B)	22:5, 22:8
2152.12(B)(2)	22:6
2152.12(B)(3)	22:8, 22:9, 22:17

RC	Section No.
2152.12(C)	21:6, 22:9, 22:10
2152.12(D)	1:7, 22:8, 32:3
2152.12(E)	1:7, 22:8
2152.12(F)	22:7, 22:8
2152.12(G)	22:12
2152.12(H)	2:4, 3:3, 22:4
2152.12(I)	22:17, 22:22
2152.12(J)	2:3, 22:4
2152.13	14:3, 19:1, 19:6
2152.13(A)(2)	5:3
2152.13(A)(3)	5:3
2152.13(B)	5:3
2152.13(B)(1)	5:3
2152.13(B)(2)	5:3
2152.13(C)	5:3
2152.13(C)(1)	5:9, 23:10, 23:11, 23:29, 23:30
2152.13(C)(2)	5:9, 23:4, 23:7
2152.13(D)(1)	5:3, 5:6, 19:12
2152.13(D)(2)	19:9
2152.13(D)(2)(a)(i)	5:8
2152.13(D)(2)(a)(ii)	5:8
2152.13(D)(2)(a)(iii)	5:8
2152.13(D)(2)(b)	5:8
2152.13(D)(3)	5:13
2152.13(E)(1)	5:7
2152.14	5:9
2152.14(A)(1)	5:10
2152.14(A)(2)	5:10
2152.14(B)	5:10
2152.14(C)	5:10
2152.14(D)	5:11
2152.14(E)(1)	5:11
2152.14(E)(2)	5:12
2152.14(F)	5:12
2152.16	1:7, 4:6, 5:7, 5:8, 27:1, 27:3
2152.16(A)	4:4, 33:9
2152.16(A)(1)(a)	27:3
2152.16(A)(1)(b)	27:3
2152.16(A)(1)(c)	27:3
2152.16(A)(1)(d)	27:3
2152.16(A)(1)(e)	27:3
2152.16(A)(2)	27:4
2152.16(B)	27:4
2152.16(C)	16:8
2152.17	5:8, 27:3
2152.17(A)(1)	27:3
2152.17(A)(2)	27:3
2152.17(A)(3)	27:3
2152.17(B)	27:3
2152.17(C)	4:4, 27:3
2152.17(D)	27:3
2152.17(E)	27:3, 27:18
2152.17(F)	27:3
2152.18(A)	27:3, 27:18
2152.18(B)	27:3
2152.18(C)	25:13
2152.18(C)(1)	27:3, 33:8
2152.18(C)(2)	27:3
2152.18(D)	32:3
2152.18(D)(1)	27:3
2152.18(D)(2)	27:3
2152.18(D)(3)	27:3
2152.18(D)(4)	27:3
2152.18(E)	27:3, 32:3
2152.19	4:6, 5:7, 5:8, 27:19
2152.19(A)	27:2, 27:14, 27:18
2152.19(A)(1)	27:5, 28:6, 29:3
2152.19(A)(2)	27:6
2152.19(A)(3)	19:6, 27:6, 27:7, 27:8, 27:16, 27:18, 29:2, 29:3
2152.19(A)(3)(a)	27:8
2152.19(A)(3)(b)	27:8
2152.19(A)(3)(c)	27:7
2152.19(A)(3)(d)	27:7
2152.19(A)(3)(e)	27:7
2152.19(A)(3)(f)	27:9
2152.19(A)(3)(g)	27:9
2152.19(A)(3)(h)	27:7
2152.19(A)(3)(i)	27:7
2152.19(A)(3)(k)	27:10
2152.19(A)(4)	27:7, 27:17, 28:6, 29:3
2152.19(A)(4)(j)	27:10
2152.19(A)(4)(k)	27:10
2152.19(A)(4)(l)	27:11
2152.19(A)(5)	27:16, 28:6, 29:3
2152.19(A)(6)(a)(i)	27:16
2152.19(A)(6)(a)(ii)	27:16
2152.19(A)(6)(b)	27:16
2152.19(A)(7)	27:18, 32:2
2152.19(A)(8)	16:8, 28:6, 29:3
2152.19(B)	27:8
2152.19(B)(1)	27:11
2152.19(B)(2)	27:9, 27:11
2152.19(C)	15:4, 27:20
2152.19(D)	25:11, 32:3
2152.19(D)(1)	32:3
2152.19(D)(3)	21:7, 21:8, 35:2
2152.19(F)	14:7, 32:2
2152.20	5:8, 27:1, 27:8, 28:3
2152.20(A)(1)	27:12
2152.20(A)(2)	27:15
2152.20(A)(3)	27:8, 27:12, 27:13, 32:3
2152.20(A)(4)(a)	27:15

RC	Section No.
2152.20(A)(4)(b)	27:15
2152.20(B)	27:14
2152.20(B)(1)	27:14
2152.20(B)(2)	27:14
2152.20(B)(3)	27:14
2152.021	14:3, 15:2, 16:1, 16:8, 28:10
2152.021(A)	16:7
2152.21(A)(1) to (5)	28:6
2152.021(A)(1)	16:8, 16:9, 17:2, 28:3
2152.21(A)(2)	28:2, 28:10
2152.21(A)(3)	28:4
2152.21(A)(4)	28:5
2152.21(A)(5)	19:2, 28:6, 28:10
2152.21(A)(5)(b)	28:6
2152.21(A)(5)(i)	28:6
2152.21(A)(6)	19:2, 28:6
2152.21(B)	28:2
2152.21(C)	28:7, 32:3
2152.21(D)	28:10
2152.22(B)(1)	27:4
2152.22(B)(1)(a)	27:4
2152.22(B)(1)(b)	27:4
2152.22(B)(1)(c)	27:4
2152.22(B)(2)	27:4
2152.22(B)(3)	27:4
2152.22(C)(1)	27:4
2152.22(C)(2)	27:4
2152.22(C)(3)	27:4
2152.22(D)	27:4
2152.22(E)	27:4
2152.22(F)	27:4
2152.22(G)	27:4
2152.26	19:2
2152.26(A)(1)(a)	28:10
2152.26(B)	19:2
2152.26(F)	19:2
2152.26(F)(2)	2:7, 19:1, 19:2, 27:18
2152.26(F)(3)	19:1
2152.26(F)(3)(a)	19:2, 19:9
2152.26(F)(3)(b)	19:1, 19:2, 19:9
2152.41	27:6
2152.41(A)	27:6
2152.41(B)	28:6
2152.42(C)	19:11
2152.61(A)	28:11, 32:2
2152.61(B)	28:11, 32:2
2152.61(C)	28:11, 32:2
2152.71	35:2
2152.72	32:3
2152.74	14:8
2152.81	23:17
2152.82	6:1, 6:5, 6:9, 6:10, 6:11

RC	Section No.
2152.82(A)	6:9
2152.82(B)	6:9
2152.82(B)(3)	6:9
2152.82(C)	6:9
2152.82(D)	6:9
2152.83	6:10
2152.83(A)	6:10
2152.83(A)(2)	6:10
2152.83(B)	6:11
2152.83(B)(2)	6:11
2152.83(C)	6:11
2152.83(D)	6:10, 6:11
2152.83(E)	6:12, 6:13
2152.83(F)	6:10, 6:11
2152.83(G)	6:10
2152.84	6:9, 6:10, 6:11, 6:12, 6:13
2152.85	6:1, 6:5, 6:9, 6:10
2152.85(A)	6:13
2152.85(B)	6:13
2152.85(C)	6:13
2152.191	6:1
2153.08	15:2
2153.09	15:2
2153.15	33:2
2153.17	34:2
2301.20	25:12
2307.70	27:13
2317.01	23:18
2317.02	15:4, 23:15
2317.02(B)	23:15
2317.02(G)(1)	23:15
2317.06(B)	18:2
2501.02	34:2, 34:4
2501.02(A)	34:2
2505.02	34:4
2505.073	12:8, 12:10
2505.073(A)	12:10
2505.073(B)	12:8
2512.12(C)	22:10
2705.01	18:3, 33:8
2705.10	18:3, 33:8
2739.04	23:15
2739.12	23:15
2743.51 et seq.	35:2
2743.51	32:3
2743.70	27:8
2743.72	32:3
2901.01(A)(9)	5:5
2901.01(A)(11)(b)	14:10
2901.02(A)	4:4
2901.02(D)	22:8
2901.02(E)	22:8

RC	Section No.
2901.02(G)	4:4
2901.03(A)	22:8
2901.05	23:13
2901.05(D)	23:13
2901.08	4:4, 35:3
2903.01	5:5, 5:7, 5:8, 6:2, 6:16, 22:7, 25:14, 27:3, 30:10
2903.02	5:5, 5:7, 5:8, 6:2, 6:16, 22:7, 25:14, 27:3, 30:10
2903.03	5:5, 22:7, 25:14, 27:3, 30:10
2903.04	5:5, 22:7, 30:10
2903.04(A)	6:2, 27:3
2903.04(D)	28:8
2903.06	7:4, 28:8
2903.07	28:8
2903.08	28:8
2903.11	5:5, 6:2, 25:14, 30:10
2903.12	5:5, 25:14, 30:10
2903.13	5:5, 25:14, 30:10
2903.15	5:5
2903.16	30:10
2903.21	5:5, 30:10
2903.22	5:5
2903.34	30:10
2903.211	5:5, 6:2
2903.322	6:3
2905.01	5:5, 6:2, 6:16, 22:7, 27:3, 30:10
2905.01(A)(1)	6:2, 6:6
2905.01(A)(2)	6:2, 6:6
2905.01(A)(3)	6:2, 6:6
2905.01(A)(4)	6:2
2905.01(A)(5)	6:2, 6:6
2905.02	5:5, 6:2, 30:10
2905.03	30:10
2905.04	6:2, 6:6, 30:10
2905.05	30:10
2905.11	5:5
Ch 2907	2:2, 9:13
2907.01(A)	9:13
2907.01(B)	9:13
2907.01(C)	9:13
2907.01(D)(2)	6:2
2907.01(I)	2:2
2907.02	5:5, 6:2, 6:16, 22:7, 25:14, 27:3, 30:10, 32:3
2907.03	5:5, 6:2, 25:14, 30:10
2907.04	4:4, 25:14, 30:10
2907.05	5:5, 6:2, 25:14, 30:10
2907.05(A)(4)	6:2
2907.06	6:2, 6:3, 25:14, 30:10, 32:3
2907.07	6:2, 30:10
2907.07(C)	4:4

RC	Section No.
2907.08	6:2, 6:3, 30:10
2907.09	30:10
2907.12	6:2, 22:7, 27:3, 30:10, 32:3
2907.21	6:2, 30:10
2907.22	30:10
2907.23	30:10
2907.25	30:10
2907.31	4:4, 30:10
2907.32	30:10
2907.33(A)	4:4
2907.33(B)	8:6
2907.321	4:4, 30:10
2907.321(A)(1)	6:2
2907.321(A)(3)	6:2
2907.322	4:4, 30:10
2907.322(A)(1)	6:2
2907.322(A)(3)	6:2
2907.323	30:10
2907.323(A)(1)	6:2
2907.323(A)(2)	6:2
2909.02	5:5, 22:7, 27:3
2909.03	5:5
2909.05	27:8
2909.06	27:8
2909.07	27:8
2911.01	5:5, 16:8, 22:7, 27:3, 30:10
2911.02	5:5, 30:10
2911.11	5:5, 22:7, 30:10
2911.12	5:5, 30:10
2913.02	4:4
2913.02(B)	4:4
2917.01	5:5
2917.02	5:5
2917.03	5:5
2917.11(B)	27:9, 29:4
2917.31	5:5
2919.12	30:10
2919.12(B)(1)(b)	12:2
2919.22	4:4, 5:5, 9:10, 9:14, 9:15
2919.22(A)	30:10
2919.22(B)(2)	25:14, 30:10
2919.22(B)(3)	9:15
2919.22(B)(5)	6:2
2919.22(C)	30:10
2919.23(A)(1)	4:4
2919.24	4:4, 30:10
2919.25	5:5, 30:10
2919.121(C)	12:2
2921.03	5:5
2921.04	5:5
2921.22(A)	15:4
2921.34	5:5, 27:3

RC	Section No.
2921.34(C)(3)	27:3
2921.331	28:8
Ch 2923	27:8
2923.01	5:5, 27:3
2923.01(H)	23:21
2923.02	5:5, 5:7, 22:7, 27:3
2923.03	5:5, 16:8
2923.03(D)	23:21
2923.11	5:5, 22:7, 27:8
2923.12	22:8, 27:3, 30:10
2923.32	27:14
2923.32(B)	27:14
2923.32(B)(3)	27:18
2923.32(F)	27:14
2923.35(D)(1)(a)	27:14
2923.42	27:14
2923.44	27:14
2923.47	27:14
2923.122	27:11
2923.161	5:5, 30:10
2923.211	27:3
2923.211(A)	4:2, 8:2, 8:6
2925.01	27:9, 27:14, 29:4
2925.02	5:8, 30:10
2925.11(C)(3)	4:4
2925.11(D)	4:4
2925.41	27:14
2925.42	16:7, 27:18
2925.42(A)	27:14
2925.42(B)	27:14
2925.42(B)(1)(a)	27:14
2925.42(B)(1)(b)	27:14
2925.43	27:18
2925.43(E)	27:14
2925.44	27:14
2925.45	27:14
2929.01	27:3
2929.01(Z)	27:7
2929.02(H)	27:7
2929.12(B)	6:12
2929.12(C)	6:12
2929.023	22:22, 27:10
2929.23(A)(3)	27:10
2929.23(E)	27:10
Ch 2930	22:19, 23:12, 23:17, 25:5
2930.02	22:19, 23:12, 23:17, 25:5
2930.05	14:3
2930.05(B)	14:3
2930.09	22:19, 23:12, 23:17, 25:5
2930.14(A)	25:11
2930.14(B)	25:11
2933.41(E)	27:14

RC	Section No.
2933.42	27:18
2933.43	27:14, 27:18
2933.44	27:14
2935.03	14:3
2935.04	14:3
2935.26	14:3
2941.25(A)	27:19
2941.141	27:3
2941.142	27:3
2941.144	27:3
2941.145	27:3
2941.146	27:3
2941.1412(A)	27:3
2945.37	23:7
2945.37(A)	23:7
2945.37(G)	23:7
2945.44	33:8
2945.67	14:2
2945.67(A)	34:8
2945.67(B)	34:10
2945.71	15:3
2945.71(C)	23:29
2945.75	16:8
Ch 2950	6:1
2950.01(B)(1)	6:4
2950.01(B)(2)	6:4
2950.01(D)(1)	6:2, 6:3
2950.01(D)(2)(i)	6:2
2950.01(E)(2)	6:5
2950.01(G)	6:5
2950.01(G)(1)	6:5
2950.01(G)(2)	6:5
2950.01(G)(3)	6:5
2950.01(G)(4)	6:5
2950.01(G)(5)	6:5
2950.01(J)	6:1
2950.01(P)	6:3
2950.01(Q)	6:3
2950.01(S)(1)(b)	6:6
2950.01(S)(1)(b)(iv)	6:6
2950.01(S)(2)	6:6
2950.01(T)	6:7
2950.01(U)(2)	6:8
2950.02	6:3
2950.03	6:9, 6:10
2950.04	6:1, 6:11
2950.04(A)(2)	6:14
2950.04(A)(3)	6:14
2950.04(C)	6:14
2950.05	6:14
2950.06	6:14
2950.07	6:9, 6:10, 6:11, 6:14

RC	Section No.	RC	Section No.
2950.09	6:1, 6:5, 6:9	3113.21	30:3
2950.09(A)	6:5	3113.215	32:2
2950.09(B)	6:5, 6:9, 6:10, 6:11	3113.217	30:3
2950.09(B)(3)	6:11, 6:12	3113.219	30:3
2950.09(C)	6:5, 6:9	3301.121	35:4
2950.09(E)	6:11	3313.20(B)(1)(a)	14:6
2950.09(F)	6:5	3313.20(B)(1)(b)	14:6
2950.10	6:15	3313.48	4:5, 8:4
2950.11(A)	6:15	3313.62	4:5, 8:4
2950.11(B)	6:16	3313.64	30:3
2950.13	6:16	3313.64(C)(2)	27:3
2950.021	6:3	3313.64(I)	27:3
2950.031	6:17	3313.533	29:5
2950.041(A)(2)	6:14	3313.662	35:4
2950.041(C)	6:14	Ch 3321	9:7
2950.081(B)	6:16	3321.01	4:5, 8:4
2950.091	6:1, 6:6, 6:9, 6:10, 6:11, 6:12	3321.04	8:4
2950.091(B)	6:11	3321.04(A)(2)	9:7
2950.091(E)	6:11	3321.38	9:7, 27:16, 29:5
2950.99	6:14	3323.01(A)	32:2
2951.09	33:6	Ch 3331	8:7
2953.08(A)(1)	5:13	3331.01	8:4
2953.08(A)(3)	5:13	Ch 3332	9:7
2953.08(A)(4)	5:13	3716.11	30:10
2953.08(A)(5)	5:13	3793.01	30:14
2953.08(A)(6)	5:13	3793.10	27:9, 28:2, 29:4
2953.31	35:4	Ch 4109	8:7
2963.01 et seq.	36:3	4109.07	8:7
2963.20	36:3	4301.63	4:4
2971.01(G)	6:2	4507.02	28:9
2971.01(L)	6:2	4507.08	27:9, 28:2, 29:4
3105.21(B)	3:2	4507.15	28:2
3107.06	30:8	4507.021	28:10
3107.14	16:15	4507.021(D)(2)(a)	27:9, 28:2, 29:4
3107.14(D)	16:15	4507.021(D)(2)(b)	27:9, 28:2, 29:4
3109.04	3:3, 16:15, 18:2, 25:14, 30:4, 30:7, 34:4	4507.40	28:10
		4507.162	27:9, 28:2, 28:8, 29:4
3109.04(A)	3:2, 16:15	4507.162(A)	28:8, 28:9
3109.04(B)	16:15	4507.162(A)(1)	28:8
3109.04(E)	34:6	4507.162(A)(2)	28:8
3109.06	3:2, 16:15, 34:6	4507.162(C)	28:9
3109.09	27:13, 32:3	4507.162(D)	28:9
3109.10	27:13, 32:3	4509.01	28:10
3109.21	16:15	4509.011	28:10
3109.21(C)	16:13	4509.31	28:10
3109.27	16:13, 31:2	4509.78	28:10
3109.27(A)	16:13	Ch 4511	7:4
3109.27(D)	16:13, 31:2	4511.12	28:8, 28:9
3109.36	16:15	4511.13	28:8, 28:9
3111	23:3	4511.15	28:8, 28:9
3111.13(C)	30:11	4511.19	28:6, 28:8, 28:10
3113.21 to 3113.219	32:2	4511.19(A)	28:2

RC	Section No.
4511.19(B)	28:2
4511.20	28:8, 28:9
4511.21	28:8
4511.22	28:8
4511.23	28:8, 28:9
4511.25	28:8, 28:9
4511.26	28:9
4511.48	28:8, 28:9
4511.57	28:8, 28:9
4511.65	28:8, 28:9
4511.75	28:8, 28:9
4511.99	28:10
4511.191	28:8
4511.192	28:8
4511.201	28:8
4511.202	28:8
4513.99	28:7
4513.99(F)	28:7
4513.99(G)	28:7
4513.263	28:7
4513.263(B)(1)	28:7
4513.263(B)(2)	28:7
4513.263(B)(3)	28:7
4549.02	28:8
4549.03	28:8
4549.021	28:8
4732.19	23:15
Ch 4757	23:15
5101.141	27:17
5103.02	33:10
5103.03	30:6, 33:10
5103.10	27:5
5103.15	1:7, 23:6, 30:8
5103.15(A)(1)	11:3
5103.15(A)(2)	11:4
5103.15(A)(3)	11:4
5103.15(B)(1)	11:5
5103.15(B)(2)	11:5
5103.16	9:9
5103.17	9:9
5103.20	36:2
5103.151	1:7
5103.153	26:2
5120.162	19:2
5123.01(K)	33:4
5123.01(N)	33:4
Ch 5139	33:9

RC	Section No.
5139.01(A)(2)	33:9
5139.01(A)(3)	27:3, 33:9
5139.01(A)(21)	33:9
5139.01(A)(25)	33:9
5139.01(A)(26)	33:9
5139.04	27:3
5139.05(A)	27:3
5139.05(A)(1)	27:3
5139.05(A)(2)	27:3
5139.05(A)(3)	27:3
5139.05(A)(4)	27:3
5139.05(B)	27:4, 33:9
5139.05(D)	35:2
5139.06(C)(2)	19:2
5139.34	1:7, 15:3, 27:8
5139.34(A)	15:3
5139.34(B)(1)	15:3
5139.34(B)(2)	15:3
5139.39	27:8
5139.43(C)(2)(a)	15:3
5139.43(C)(3)(a)	15:3
5139.51	27:4, 33:9
5139.52	27:4, 33:9
5139.54	27:4
5139.281	27:6
5153.16(A)(2)	19:7
5153.16(A)(7)	20:2
5153.17	21:2, 23:15, 35:2

RC II	Section No.
2151.56	36:3

RC IV	Section No.
2151.56	36:2

RC IX	Section No.
2151.56	36:2

RC V	Section No.
2151.56	36:2, 36:3

RC VI	Section No.
2151.56	36:2

RC VII	Section No.
2151.56	36:2

RC VIII	Section No.
2151.56	36:2

OHIO COURT RULES

Ohio Rules of Appellate Procedure

Rule	Section No.	Rule	Section No.
4(A)	34:5	7(C)	34:6, 34:8
4(B)	34:8	9	34:9
7	34:2	9(C)	22:18, 25:12
7(A)	34:6, 34:7	12(B)	34:11
7(B)	34:7	12(C)	34:11

Ohio Rules of Civil Procedure

Rule	Section No.	Rule	Section No.
2(Y)	23:3	16	24:4
4(A)	18:4, 23:5	24	23:6
4(C)	18:4	26 to 37	24:4
4(D)	18:4, 18:5	29(E)	25:8
4.1	18:4	29(E)(4)	25:8
4.1(1)	18:4	29(F)	25:8
4.1(2)	18:4	30(C)	22:9, 22:10
4.1(3)	18:4	41(A)(1)	25:4
4.2	18:4	50(B)	34:5
4.2(2)	18:2	52	24:7, 24:8
4.3	18:4	53	24:1, 34:4
4.4	18:4	58(B)	34:5
4.4(A)(2)	18:4	59	34:5
4.5	18:4	60	33:2
4.6	18:4	60(B)	22:22, 33:2, 34:11
5(B)	21:3		

Ohio Rules of Criminal Procedure

Rule	Section No.	Rule	Section No.
3	16:8	16	21:2, 21:3, 22:15
4	14:3	16(B)	21:2, 21:3
7	5:9	16(B)(1)(f)	21:2
7(D)	16:16	19	24:2
11	23:8, 23:9	29	2:5, 23:13
11(C)(2)	23:9	31(C)	16:16
12(H)	23:8	46	22:22, 24:5
12(J)	34:8	52(A)	35:3

Ohio Rules of Evidence

Rule	Section No.	Rule	Section No.
101	22:13, 23:14	702	23:19
101(A)	25:9	703	23:19
101(C)	23:14	704	23:19
101(C)(6)	22:13, 25:9	801	22:13, 23:16
102	35:3	801(D)(2)	23:16
104	25:9	802	25:9
401	25:9	803	23:16
402	25:9, 35:3	803(2)	23:16
404(B)	23:20	803(4)	23:16
408	15:4	803(6)	23:16
501	23:15	803(8)	23:16
601	25:9	804	23:16
601(A)	23:18	804(A)	23:16
602	25:9	805	23:16
609	23:20	807	23:16, 23:25
609(D)	23:20, 35:3	902	23:16
611(B)	25:9	1005	23:16
615	23:17		

Ohio Rules of Juvenile Procedure

Rule	Section No.	Rule	Section No.
1	1:8	2(OO)	30:6
1(B)	15:3	2(R)	22:11
1(B)(3)	32:3	2(V)	30:6, 30:7, 30:13, 33:9
1(C)(1)	34:5	2(X)	17:4
1(C)(6)	12:6	2(Y)	2:2, 15:2, 16:5, 17:4, 18:2, 23:17, 32:2, 34:3
2	22:13, 23:3		
2(22)	3:3	2(Z)	30:8, 33:9
2(AA)	11:2	3	14:10, 18:5, 22:4, 22:9, 22:11, 23:4
2(B)	23:1, 31:4, 31:5, 33:6	4	23:3, 23:5, 24:4
2(BB)	16:2	4(A)	15:2, 18:3, 22:11, 23:3, 23:5
2(C)	11:2	4(B)	1:8, 23:6, 30:12
2(D)	2:2	4(B)(2)	23:6
2(DD)	30:13	4(B)(7)	13:2
2(EE)	30:6	4(C)	23:6
2(F)	16:1	4(C)(2)	23:6
2(FF)	30:6	4(E)	18:2
2(G)	15:2	4(G)	32:2
2(GG)	13:2, 23:6, 23:13	6	14:3, 19:6, 23:3, 24:4
2(H)	16:5	6(A)(3)(g)	14:3
2(II)	30:7	6(B)	14:3, 20:4
2(J)	19:2	7	1:8, 19:1, 19:6, 19:7, 19:9, 24:4, 33:3
2(JJ)	19:2	7(A)	14:9, 19:3, 19:6
2(K)	19:2, 19:7	7(A)(1)(b)	19:1, 19:6
2(L)	19:5	7(A)(5)	19:1, 19:6
2(LL)	5:6	7(B)	14:3
2(M)	25:2	7(B)(1)	19:2
2(MM)	19:7	7(B)(2)	19:2
2(N)	16:5, 23:6	7(C)	19:3
2(NN)	35:2	7(D)	19:3

Rule	Section No.
7(E)(1)	19:3
7(E)(2)	19:3, 19:10
7(E)(3)	19:3
7(E)(3)(b)	19:10
7(F)	1:8
7(F)(1)	19:4, 19:5, 19:7
7(F)(2)	19:4
7(F)(3)	19:5, 19:6
7(G)	19:4, 19:8, 34:12
7(H)	19:2
7(I)	19:11, 21:6
7(J)	19:10
9	2:6
9(A)	15:2, 15:3, 15:4
9(B)	15:2, 15:3
10	15:2, 16:1, 16:6, 16:8
10(A)	13:2, 13:3, 16:1, 16:2, 16:8, 16:10, 16:15, 17:2
10(B)	16:3, 16:5, 16:8, 16:14
10(B)(1)	16:7, 16:8, 16:9, 16:10, 16:11, 16:12, 16:14, 16:15
10(B)(2)	16:5
10(B)(3)	16:6
10(C)	16:2, 16:6, 16:9
10(D)	16:14
10(F)	16:14
11	16:15
11(A)	17:4
11(B)	13:2, 13:3, 17:2, 17:4
11(C)	17:4
11(D)	17:4
13	19:11, 20:2, 20:6, 21:6, 24:4, 34:4
13(A)	9:7, 20:2
13(B)	20:2
13(B)(2)	20:2
13(B)(3)	20:6
13(B)(5)	20:6
13(C)	20:3
13(D)	20:5
13(E)	20:5
13(F)	20:4
14	24:4
14(A)	30:6
14(B)	30:6
14(C)	33:4
15	1:8, 13:4, 24:4
15(A)	1:8, 18:2, 18:3
15(B)	18:3
15(B)(2)	18:3
15(B)(3)	23:3
15(B)(4)	33:8
15(B)(8)	13:2, 13:4

Rule	Section No.
15(B)(9)	18:3
15(C)	18:3, 33:8
15(D)	14:3
16	1:8, 13:4
16(A)	18:2, 18:4, 18:5
17	18:4, 21:5
17(D)	21:5
17(F)	33:8
17(G)	21:5
18(A)	19:7
18(B)	19:7
18(C)	33:2
19	33:2
20(A)	21:3
20(B)	21:3
20(C)	21:3
21	24:4
22	2:5, 16:16
22(A)	16:14, 16:16
22(B)	16:16
22(D)	2:5, 16:17
22(D)(2)	34:12
22(D)(3)	14:2, 23:14
22(D)(4)	21:3, 22:15
22(D)(5)	5:3
22(E)	5:3, 16:17, 21:3
22(F)	14:2, 23:31, 34:6, 34:8, 34:11
23	24:4
24 to 25	24:4
24	15:2, 21:2, 21:3, 21:6, 22:15, 35:2
24(A)	21:2, 21:3
24(A)(1)	21:2
24(A)(2)	21:2
24(A)(3)	21:2, 21:3
24(A)(6)	21:2
24(B)	21:3, 22:15
24(C)	21:3
25	21:4, 33:8
27	1:8, 18:2, 19:12, 23:11, 23:23, 35:2
27(A)	22:19, 23:10, 23:11, 23:23, 23:24, 25:5, 25:6
27(A)(1)	5:6
27(A)(2)	23:32
27(A)(3)	5:6
27(B)	23:24
27(B)(1)	19:6, 25:14
27(B)(2)	23:18
27(B)(3)	21:4, 24:4
27(C)	23:24
29	1:8, 5:3, 20:2, 22:15, 23:1, 23:8, 23:9, 23:29, 28:8, 33:6
29(A)	1:8, 13:2, 13:5, 18:4, 19:7, 20:6, 23:29, 34:12

Rule	Section No.
29(B)	23:9, 23:27, 25:7
29(B)(3)	23:3, 23:4
29(B)(4)	23:3, 24:4
29(B)(5)	23:24, 23:27, 23:30
29(C)	1:8, 23:8, 23:9
29(D)	23:4, 23:6, 23:8, 23:9
29(D)(1)	23:9
29(D)(2)	23:8, 23:9
29(E)	23:13
29(E)(1)	18:2
29(E)(2)	23:17
29(E)(4)	13:2, 13:5, 23:13, 25:2, 25:8, 30:11, 33:6
29(F)	1:8, 5:3, 17:4
29(F)(2)	23:1
29(F)(2)(a)	25:4
29(F)(2)(b)	25:4, 34:4
29(F)(2)(d)	8:6, 25:4, 27:2
30	1:8, 19:7, 21:6, 22:1, 22:5, 22:8, 22:9, 22:11, 22:19, 27:19, 34:12
30(A)	2:3, 22:8
30(B)	22:7
30(C)	22:8
30(C)(2)	32:3
30(D)	22:12
30(E)	22:17, 22:21
30(F)	22:8, 22:10
30(G)	22:17
30(H)	22:17, 22:22
32	21:6, 23:28, 24:4, 25:9, 35:4
32(A)	21:6
32(A)(2)	22:8, 22:13
32(A)(4)	23:7
32(B)	21:6, 23:16, 35:2
32(C)	21:6, 22:15, 25:10, 35:2
34	20:2, 23:1, 25:2, 25:4, 34:4
34(A)	1:8, 23:1, 25:4, 27:9, 28:2, 29:4
34(B)(1)	25:3
34(B)(2)	25:9
34(B)(3)	25:9, 25:10
34(C)	25:13, 27:8, 30:3, 32:2, 33:6
34(D)	30:4
34(D)(1)	30:4
34(D)(2)	30:4, 30:6
34(D)(3)	30:4
34(D)(4)	30:4
34(D)(5)	30:4, 30:13
34(E)	30:5
34(F)	26:3, 26:4
34(G)	33:4
34(H)	32:2
34(I)	25:2, 25:9, 31:4, 31:5
34(J)	25:7
35(A)	29:3, 33:2
35(B)	29:3, 33:6, 33:7
35(C)	33:3
36(A)	33:4, 33:11
36(C)	33:10
36(C)(1)	33:11
36(C)(2)	33:11
36(C)(3)	33:11
36(C)(4)	33:11
37	22:18, 23:30, 25:12
37(A)	22:18, 23:30, 25:12, 34:9
37(B)	23:11, 34:9, 35:2
38(A)(1)	11:3, 11:4
38(A)(2)	11:4
38(B)(1)	11:5
38(B)(2)	11:5, 33:11
39	13:2, 23:6, 23:13
39(A)	13:4
39(B)	13:2, 13:5
40	20:4, 23:3, 24:1, 24:2, 24:9, 34:4
40(A)	24:2
40(C)(1)	5:1, 5:3, 5:6, 24:3
40(C)(1)(a)(iii)	24:3
40(C)(2)	24:5
40(C)(3)(a)	24:4
40(C)(3)(b)	24:4
40(C)(3)(c)	24:4
40(C)(3)(d)	24:1
40(C)(3)(e)	24:4
40(D)	24:6
40(D)(2)	24:9
40(D)(5)	23:31
40(D)(6)	24:9, 34:4
40(D)(7)	23:31
40(E)(1)	24:7
40(E)(2)	24:7
40(E)(3)(a)	24:8
40(E)(3)(b)	24:8, 34:4
40(E)(3)(c)	24:8
40(E)(3)(d)	24:8
40(E)(4)(a)	24:9
40(E)(4)(b)	24:9
40(E)(4)(c)	24:9
44	1:8, 19:7, 22:1, 25:4
47(A)	1:8

Rules of Superintendence for the Courts of Ohio

Rule	Section No.	Rule	Section No.
15	15:5	23(I)	12:7
15(B)	15:5	24	12:2
15(B)(1)	15:5	25(A)	12:10
16	15:4	25(B)(1)	12:10
23(A)	12:3, 12:8, 12:10	25(B)(2)	12:10
23(B)	12:4	25(B)(3)	12:10
23(C)	12:4	25(B)(4)	12:10
23(D)	12:7, 12:8	25(C)	12:10
23(E)	12:8	25(D)	12:10
23(F)(1)	12:10	25(E)	12:10
23(F)(2)	12:10	25(F)	12:10
23(G)	12:10	25(G)	12:10
23(H)	12:6, 12:8	26.03(H)	35:2

Rules of Supreme Court

Section No.	Section No.
2(F)	30:6

Ohio Code of Professional Responsibility

Rule	Section No.
DR 2-110(C)(1)(d)	23:3

IDAHO STATUTES

Stat. Ann.	Section No.
9-203(7)	23:15

ILLINOIS SESSION LAW

Ill. Laws.	Section No.
131	22:1

NEW JERSEY STATUTES

Stat. Ann.	Section No.
2C:7-1 et seq.	6:1

TENNESSEE STATUTES

Stat. Ann.	Section No.
37-1-134(f)	23:28

WYOMING STATUTES

Stat. Ann. §	Section No.
14-6-237(f)	23:28

Table of Cases

A

A., In re, 65 Misc. 2d 1034, 319 N.Y.S.2d 691 (Fam. Ct. 1971)—23:28

A and M, Application of, 61 A.D.2d 426, 403 N.Y.S.2d 375, 6 A.L.R.4th 532 (4th Dep't 1978)—23:15

Ackerman v. Lucas County Children Services Bd., 49 Ohio App. 3d 14, 550 N.E.2d 549 (6th Dist. Lucas County 1989)—17:2

Adam, In re, 120 Ohio App. 3d 364, 697 N.E.2d 1100, 127 Ed. Law Rep. 1029 (11th Dist. Lake County 1997)—14:6

Adams, In re, 2003-Ohio-4112, 2003 WL 21783682 (Ohio Ct. App. 7th Dist. Mahoning County)—23:9

Adams, In re, 2003-Ohio-4112, at ¶ 33, 2004 WL 21783682 (Ohio Ct. App 7th Dist. Mahoning County)—23:7

Adams, In re, 2003-Ohio-4112, at ¶ 5, 2003 WL 21783682 (Ohio Ct. App. 7th Dist. Mahoning County 2003)—24:9

Addison, Matter of, 1996 WL 732440 (Ohio Ct. App. 8th Dist. Cuyahoga County 1996)—30:11

Adkins Children, In re, 1990 WL 95043 (Ohio Ct. App. 12th Dist. Butler County 1990)—23:10

Adkins Children, Matter of, 1992 WL 56768 (Ohio Ct. App. 12th Dist. Butler County 1992)—31:9

Adoption of Nowowiejski, Matter of, 1990 WL 187377 (Ohio Ct. App. 6th Dist. Lucas County 1990)—3:3, 23:6

Agler, In re, 19 Ohio St. 2d 70, 48 Ohio Op. 2d 85, 249 N.E.2d 808 (1969)—1:7, 23:3, 23:10, 23:13, 23:14, 23:27

Agosto, In re, 553 F. Supp. 1298, 12 Fed. R. Evid. Serv. 639 (D. Nev. 1983)—23:15

Agosto, In re, 85 Ohio App. 3d 188, 619 N.E.2d 475 (8th Dist. Cuyahoga County 1993)—14:3

A Juvenile, Appeal of, 61 Ohio App. 2d 235, 15 Ohio Op. 3d 400, 401 N.E.2d 937 (11th Dist. Lake County 1978)—23:5

A Juvenile, State ex rel. v. Hoose, 43 Ohio App. 3d 109, 539 N.E.2d 704 (11th Dist. Lake County 1988)—22:10, 22:14

Ake v. Oklahoma, 470 U.S. 68, 105 S. Ct. 1087, 84 L. Ed. 2d 53 (1985)—22:10, 23:19

Akron Center for Reproductive Health v. Rosen, 633 F. Supp. 1123 (N.D. Ohio 1986)—12:2

Akron Center for Reproductive Health v. Slaby, 854 F.2d 852 (6th Cir. 1988)—12:2

Alderman v. U.S., 394 U.S. 165, 89 S. Ct. 961, 22 L. Ed. 2d 176 (1969)—14:2

Alexander, Matter of, 1997 WL 799517 (Ohio Ct. App. 11th Dist. Trumbull County 1997)—30:11

Alexander, No. H-82-23 (6th Dist. Ct. App., Huron, 12-28-82), In re—34:9

Allen, In re, 2002-Ohio-5555, 2002 WL 31312392 (Ohio Ct. App. 5th Dist. Delaware County 2002)—30:7

Allstate Ins. Co. v. Cook, 324 F.2d 752, 26 Ohio Op. 2d 192 (6th Cir. 1963)—35:3

Alonzo B., In re, 1999 WL 63649 (Ohio Ct. App. 6th Dist. Erie County 1999)—27:13, 34:4

Alyssa C., In re, 153 Ohio App. 3d 10, 2003-Ohio-2673, 790 N.E.2d 803 (6th Dist. Lucas County 2003)—23:3

A.M., In re, 139 Ohio App. 3d 303, 743 N.E.2d 937 (8th Dist. Cuyahoga County 2000)—22:15

Amanda W., In re, 124 Ohio App. 3d 136, 705 N.E.2d 724 (6th Dist. Lucas County 1997)—23:27, 26:6, 31:8

Amos, In re, 154 Ohio App. 3d 434, 2003-Ohio-5014, 797 N.E.2d 568 (3d Dist. Crawford County 2003)—23:3, 23:9, 23:30

Anders v. State of Cal., 386 U.S. 738, 87 S. Ct. 1396, 18 L. Ed. 2d 493 (1967)—34:10

Anderson, In re, 92 Ohio St. 3d 63, 2001-Ohio-131, 748 N.E.2d 67 (2001)—34:5

Anderson v. Charles, 447 U.S. 404, 100 S. Ct. 2180, 65 L. Ed. 2d 222 (1980)—14:10

Anderson, No. 02CA38 (4th Dist. Athens County 2002), In re—23:6

Andresen v. Maryland, 427 U.S. 463, 96 S. Ct. 2737, 49 L. Ed. 2d 627 (1976)—14:4

Angle v. Children's Services Division, Holmes County Welfare Dept., 63 Ohio St. 2d 227, 17 Ohio Op. 3d 140, 407 N.E.2d 524 (1980)—11:6

Anonymous, Juvenile Court No. 6358-4, In re, 14 Ariz. App. 466, 484 P.2d 235 (Div. 2 1971)—22:13

Anteau, In re, 67 Ohio App. 117, 21 Ohio Op. 129, 36 N.E.2d 47 (6th Dist. Lucas County 1941)—16:7

Anthony M., Matter of, 1995 WL 96786 (Ohio Ct. App. 6th Dist. Lucas County 1995)—33:7

Anthony P., Matter of, 104 Misc. 2d 1024, 430 N.Y.S.2d 479 (Fam. Ct. 1980)—23:29

Antonio M., Matter of, 1997 WL 525092 (Ohio Ct. App. 6th Dist. Lucas County 1997)—25:9

Appeal in Maricopa County Juvenile Action Numbers JV-512600 and JV-512797, Matter of, 187 Ariz. 419, 930 P.2d 496 (Ct. App. Div. 1 1996)—14:8

Appeal No. 544 September Term, 1974 from Circuit Court for Cecil County Sitting as a Juvenile Court, In re, 25 Md. App. 26, 332 A.2d 680 (1975)—23:9

Appeal No. 245 (75) from Circuit Court for Kent County, In re, 29 Md. App. 131, 349 A.2d 434 (1975)—14:9, 14:10

Argersinger v. Hamlin, 407 U.S. 25, 92 S. Ct. 2006, 32 L. Ed. 2d 530 (1972)—22:11

Aristotle R., In re, 2004-Ohio-217, 2004 WL 88588 (Ohio Ct. App. 6th Dist. Sandusky County)—23:15

Arizona v. Fulminante, 499 U.S. 279, 111 S. Ct. 1246, 113 L. Ed. 2d 302 (1991)—14:9

Arizona v. Hicks, 480 U.S. 321, 107 S. Ct. 1149, 94 L. Ed. 2d 347 (1987)—14:4

Arizona v. Mauro, 481 U.S. 520, 107 S. Ct. 1931, 95 L. Ed. 2d 458 (1987)—14:10

Arizona v. Roberson, 486 U.S. 675, 108 S. Ct. 2093, 100 L. Ed. 2d 704 (1988)—14:10

Artler, No. 34723 (8th Dist. Ct. App., Cuyahoga, 7-15-76), In re—9:7

Arvin, In re, 1990 WL 37783 (Ohio Ct. App. 1st Dist. Hamilton County 1990)—30:10

Asberry, State ex rel. v. Payne, 82 Ohio St. 3d 44, 1998-Ohio-596, 693 N.E.2d 794 (1998)—23:3

Atkinson v. Grumman Ohio Corp., 37 Ohio St. 3d 80, 523 N.E.2d 851 (1988)—25:13

Atwater v. City of Lago Vista, 532 U.S. 318, 121 S. Ct. 1536, 149 L. Ed. 2d 549 (2001)—14:3

Atwell, Nos. 40667, 40719 (8th Dist. Ct. App., Cuyahoga, 1-17-80), In re—2:5, 23:7

Auterson, 1982 WL 6000 (Ohio Ct. App. 12th Dist. Clermont County 1982)—2:5

Awkal, In re, 95 Ohio App. 3d 309, 642 N.E.2d 424 (8th Dist. Cuyahoga County 1994)—23:13, 23:19, 30:2, 30:8, 30:11, 31:6

B

Babbs, In re, 2004-Ohio-583, 2004 WL 249608 (Ohio Ct. App. 10th Dist. Franklin County 2004)—31:4

Baby Boy Blackshear, In re, 90 Ohio St. 3d 197, 2000-Ohio-173, 736 N.E.2d 462 (2000)—9:7, 9:16

Baby Boy Puckett, In re, 1996 WL 174607 (Ohio Ct. App. 12th Dist. Butler County 1996)—31:8

Baby Girl Baxter, In re, 17 Ohio St. 3d 229, 479 N.E.2d 257 (1985)—23:6, 23:14, 25:2, 31:8

Baby Girl Doe, In re, 149 Ohio App. 3d 717, 2002-Ohio-4470, 778 N.E.2d 1053 (6th Dist. Lucas County 2002)—23:5, 23:19, 30:10

Baby Girl S., In re, 32 Ohio Misc. 217, 61 Ohio Op. 2d 439, 290 N.E.2d 925 (C.P. 1972)—9:3, 10:5, 30:11

Bacorn, In re, 116 Ohio App. 3d 489, 688 N.E.2d 575 (11th Dist. Portage County 1996)—23:13, 30:13

Bacorn, Matter of, 1996 WL 762005 (Ohio Ct. App. 11th Dist. Portage County 1996)—30:11, 30:12

Bailey, In re, 150 Ohio App. 3d 664, 2002-Ohio-6792, 782 N.E.2d 1177 (2d Dist. Montgomery County 2002)—23:7

Bailey, In re, 98 Ohio St. 3d 309, 2003-Ohio-859, 784 N.E.2d 109 (2003)—34:12

Baker, 1982 WL 6832 (Ohio Ct. App. 3d Dist. Hardin County 1982)—16:12, 16:17

Baker, In re, 18 Ohio App. 2d 276, 47 Ohio Op. 2d 411, 248 N.E.2d 620 (4th Dist. Hocking County 1969)—4:4, 14:2, 23:14

Balazy, In re, 1993 WL 164790 (Ohio Ct. App. 9th Dist. Lorain County 1993)—26:6

Baldridge, Matter of, 1991 WL 96335 (Ohio Ct. App. 10th Dist. Franklin County 1991)—31:8

Ball, In re, 2003-Ohio-395, 2003 WL 193519 (3rd Dist. Allen County 2003)—2:5

Baltimore City Dept. of Social Services v. Bouknight, 493 U.S. 549, 110 S. Ct. 900, 107 L. Ed. 2d 992, 29 Fed. R. Evid. Serv. 273 (1990)—1:4, 14:16

Barber, In re, 1993 WL 285902 (Ohio Ct. App. 11th Dist. Lake County 1993)—14:10

Barcelo, Matter of, 1998 WL 553165 (Ohio Ct. App. 11th Dist. Geauga County 1998)—30:7

Barger, In re, 1996 WL 647631 (Ohio Ct. App. 2d Dist. Montgomery County 1996)—9:12, 21:2

Barker v. Wingo, 407 U.S. 514, 92 S. Ct. 2182, 33 L. Ed. 2d 101 (1972)—23:29

Barnebey v. Zschach, 71 Ohio St. 3d 588, 646 N.E.2d 162 (1995)—34:12

Barnett, Matter of, 1990 WL 85131 (Ohio Ct. App. 6th Dist. Sandusky County 1990)—31:6

Barnhouse, In re, 1996 WL 39650 (Ohio Ct. App. 10th Dist. Franklin County 1996)—27:3, 33:6

Barzak, In re, 24 Ohio App. 3d 180, 493 N.E.2d 1011 (11th Dist. Trumbull County 1985)—10:5, 21:2, 23:6, 23:15, 23:16

Baumgartner, In re, 50 Ohio App. 2d 37, 4 Ohio Op. 3d 22, 361 N.E.2d 501 (10th Dist. Franklin County 1976)—30:11

Bays, In re, 2003-Ohio-1256, 2003 WL 1193787 (Ohio Ct. App. 2d Dist. Greene County 2003)—23:4

Beasley, In re, 1993 WL 468401 (Ohio Ct. App. 9th Dist. Summit County 1993)—26:4

Beatty v. Riegel, 115 Ohio App. 448, 21 Ohio Op. 2d 71, 185 N.E.2d 555 (2d Dist. Montgomery County 1961)—35:3

Becker, In re, 39 Ohio St. 2d 84, 68 Ohio Op. 2d 50, 314 N.E.2d 158 (1974)—22:23, 34:2, 34:4, 34:8

Beckett, In re, 1992 WL 29233 (Ohio Ct. App. 12th Dist. Butler County 1992)—32:2

Beckwith v. U.S., 425 U.S. 341, 96 S. Ct. 1612, 48 L. Ed. 2d 1 (1976)—14:10

Beechler, In re, 115 Ohio App. 3d 567, 685 N.E.2d 1257 (4th Dist. Ross County 1996)—23:9

Beeman, In re, 1996 WL 494877 (Ohio Ct. App. 11th Dist. Lake County 1996)—16:16

Belanger, In re, 2002-Ohio-4956, 2002 WL 31107545 (Ohio Ct. App. 11th Dist. Ashtabula County 2002)—30:12, 31:6

Belden/Haywood Children, In re, 1995 WL 347924 (Ohio Ct. App. 5th Dist. Stark County 1995)—30:8

Belk, In re, 97 Ohio App. 114, 55 Ohio Op. 330, 123 N.E.2d 757 (3d Dist. Crawford County 1954)—17:2

Benjamin L., In re, 92 N.Y.2d 660, 685 N.Y.S.2d 400, 708 N.E.2d 156 (1999)—23:29

Benn, In re, 18 Ohio App. 2d 97, 47 Ohio Op. 2d 170, 247 N.E.2d 335 (8th Dist. Cuyahoga County 1969)—23:10

Bennett, In re, 134 Ohio App. 3d 699, 731 N.E.2d 1226 (12th Dist. Brown County 1999)—23:19

Bennett, In re, 1995 WL 675968 (Ohio Ct. App. 1st Dist. Hamilton County 1995)—31:9, 33:4

Bennett, In re, 1997 WL 321149 (Ohio Ct. App. 8th Dist. Cuyahoga County 1997)—33:6

Bennett, No. CA 78-35 (5th Dist. Ct. App., Muskingum, 4-25-79), In re—9:3

Benton v. Maryland, 395 U.S. 784, 89 S. Ct. 2056, 23 L. Ed. 2d 707 (1969)—23:31

Berkemer v. McCarty, 468 U.S. 420, 104 S. Ct. 3138, 82 L. Ed. 2d 317 (1984)—14:10

Bernstein, Nos. 33531, 33532 (8th Dist. Ct. App., Cuyahoga, 1-2-75), In re—7:2, 16:6, 21:3

B.G., In re, 2003-Ohio-3256, 2003 WL 21434172 (Ohio Ct. App. 8th Dist. Cuyahoga County 2003)—31:5

Bibb, In re, 70 Ohio App. 2d 117, 24 Ohio Op. 3d 159, 435 N.E.2d 96 (1st Dist. Hamilton County 1980)—10:2, 10:4, 23:13, 25:2, 34:12

Billman, In re, 92 Ohio App. 3d 279, 634 N.E.2d 1050 (8th Dist. Cuyahoga County 1993)—23:27

Birch v. Birch, 11 Ohio St. 3d 85, 463 N.E.2d 1254 (1984)—16:15

Bishop, In re, 36 Ohio App. 3d 123, 521 N.E.2d 838 (5th Dist. Ashland County 1987)—9:3, 10:2, 10:5, 23:13

Bishop v. State, 265 Ga. 821, 462 S.E.2d 716 (1995)—22:3

Black, No. C-800021 (1st Dist. Ct. App., Hamilton, 1-28-81), In re—25:2

Black, No. 40247 (8th Dist. Ct. App., Cuyahoga, 1-25-80), In re—23:18

Blakey, In re, 65 Ohio App. 3d 341, 583 N.E.2d 1343 (10th Dist. Franklin County 1989)—18:2, 34:3

Bleier v. Crouse, 13 Ohio App. 69, 1920 WL 515 (1st Dist. Hamilton County 1920)—1:6, 18:2

Board of Educ. v. Day, 30 Ohio Misc. 2d 25, 506 N.E.2d 1239, 39 Ed. Law Rep. 271 (C.P. 1986)—30:3

Board of Education v. Earls, 536 U.S. 822, 122 S. Ct. 2559, 153 L. Ed. 2d 735 (2002)—1:4, 14:6

Boehmke, In re, 44 Ohio App. 3d 125, 541 N.E.2d 630 (8th Dist. Cuyahoga County 1988)—34:4

Bolden, In re, 37 Ohio App. 2d 7, 66 Ohio Op. 2d 26, 306 N.E.2d 166 (3d Dist. Allen County 1973)—23:4, 25:4, 27:18, 27:19, 34:4

Boling v. Romer, 101 F.3d 1336 (10th Cir. 1996)—14:8

Bolser, Matter of, 1996 WL 761216 (Ohio Ct. App. 11th Dist. Geauga County 1996)—21:2

Booker, In re, 133 Ohio App. 3d 387, 728 N.E.2d 405 (1st Dist. Hamilton County 1999)—34:10

Bowen, Matter of, 1987 WL 13696 (Ohio Ct. App. 6th Dist. Wood County 1987)—17:2

Bowman, In re, 101 Ohio App. 3d 599, 656 N.E.2d 355 (9th Dist. Summit County 1995)—18:2, 20:2, 33:4

Bowman, Matter of, 1992 WL 238457 (Ohio Ct. App. 5th Dist. Stark County 1992)—18:4

Bowman, No. 79AP-798 (10th Dist. Ct. App., Franklin, 6-26-80), In re—10:3, 25:2, 30:11

Boyer v. Boyer, 46 Ohio St. 2d 83, 75 Ohio Op. 2d 156, 346 N.E.2d 286 (1976)—16:15

Boyer, No. 34724 (8th Dist. Ct. App., Cuyahoga, 12-31-75), In re—4:6, 33:6

B.P., In re, 2002-Ohio-6318, 2002 WL 31619047 (Ohio Ct. App. 8th Dist. Cuyahoga County 2002)—23:3

Bradford, In re, 30 Ohio App. 3d 87, 506 N.E.2d 925 (10th Dist. Franklin County 1986)—24:9

Brakora v. Haudenschield, 1995 WL 695089 (Ohio Ct. App. 3d Dist. Hardin County 1995)—17:4

Breed v. Jones, 421 U.S. 519, 95 S. Ct. 1779, 44 L. Ed. 2d 346 (1975)—1:4, 22:3, 22:24, 23:2, 23:31

Bremmer, Matter of, 1993 WL 95556 (Ohio Ct. App. 8th Dist. Cuyahoga County 1993)—27:3, 27:18

Brent, No. 35400 (8th Dist. Ct. App., Cuyahoga, 2-17-77), In re—14:5

Bretz, Matter of, 1990 WL 210753 (Ohio Ct. App. 5th Dist. Holmes County 1990)—9:15

Brewer, Matter of, 1996 WL 65939 (Ohio Ct. App. 7th Dist. Belmont County 1996)—31:8

Brewer v. Williams, 430 U.S. 387, 97 S. Ct. 1232, 51 L. Ed. 2d 424 (1977)—14:11, 14:13

Bridges, Matter of, 1986 WL 7109 (Ohio Ct. App. 6th Dist. Lucas County 1986)—16:6, 16:17

Brinegar v. U.S., 338 U.S. 160, 69 S. Ct. 1302, 93 L. Ed. 1879 (1949)—14:4

Brittany and Marcus B., Matter of, 1996 WL 11135 (Ohio Ct. App. 6th Dist. Wood County 1996)—16:14, 30:11, 31:8, 33:10

Brock Children, Matter of, 1995 WL 495414 (Ohio Ct. App. 5th Dist. Stark County 1995)—30:6

Brodbeck, In re, 97 Ohio App. 3d 652, 647 N.E.2d 240 (3d Dist. Mercer County 1994)—10:5, 23:5, 23:13, 30:10, 30:13, 31:6

Brodie v. Summit County Children Services Bd., 51 Ohio St. 3d 112, 554 N.E.2d 1301 (1990)—14:17

Brofford, In re, 83 Ohio App. 3d 869, 615 N.E.2d 1120 (10th Dist. Franklin County 1992)—1:8, 16:2, 25:2, 31:4, 31:5, 31:8

Brookhart v. Janis, 384 U.S. 1, 86 S. Ct. 1245, 16 L. Ed. 2d 314 (1966)—23:26

Brooks, In re, 112 Ohio App. 3d 54, 677 N.E.2d 1229 (9th Dist. Summit County 1996)—23:9

Brown, In re, 183 N.W.2d 731 (Iowa 1971)—22:16

Brown, In re, 1986 WL 13385 (Ohio Ct. App. 1st Dist. Hamilton County 1986)—23:19, 31:5

Brown, In re, 43 Ohio App. 3d 212, 540 N.E.2d 317 (1st Dist. Hamilton County 1988)—32:2

Brown, In re, 60 Ohio App. 3d 136, 573 N.E.2d 1217 (1st Dist. Hamilton County 1989)—10:4, 23:19, 31:8, 34:9

Brown, In re, 96 Ohio App. 3d 306, 644 N.E.2d 1117 (2d Dist. Montgomery County 1994)—25:4

Brown, In re, 98 Ohio App. 3d 337, 648 N.E.2d 576 (3d Dist. Marion County 1994)—18:2, 30:8, 30:10, 30:12, 31:8

Brown v. Illinois, 422 U.S. 590, 95 S. Ct. 2254, 45 L. Ed. 2d 416 (1975)—14:2, 14:9

Brown v. Miami County Children's Service Bd., 1991 WL 47530 (Ohio Ct. App. 2d Dist. Miami County 1991)—18:2

Brown v. Ohio, 432 U.S. 161, 97 S. Ct. 2221, 53 L. Ed. 2d 187 (1977)—23:31

Brown Chilren, Matter of, 1995 WL 347821 (Ohio Ct. App. 5th Dist. Stark County 1995)—26:6

Brown, No. 3-CA-79 (5th Dist. Ct. App., Fairfield, 7-20-79), In re—16:12, 18:4, 18:5, 25:2

Brown, No. 34450 (8th Dist. Ct. App., Cuyahoga, 1-8-76), In re—34:11

Bruggeman, State ex rel. v. Auglaize Cty. Court of Common Pleas, 87 Ohio St. 3d 257, 1999-Ohio-52, 719 N.E.2d 543 (1999)—34:12

Bryan v. Superior Court, 7 Cal. 3d 575, 102 Cal. Rptr. 831, 498 P.2d 1079 (1972)—22:14

Bryant, 1982 WL 6001 (Ohio Ct. App. 12th Dist. Butler County 1982)—10:5, 16:17, 18:3, 25:2

B.S., In re, 103 Ohio Misc. 2d 34, 725 N.E.2d 362 (C.P. 1998)—22:6, 22:7

B.S., In re, 205 Ariz. 611, 74 P.3d 285 (Ct. App. Div. 1 2003)—12:2

Buffington, In re, 89 Ohio App. 3d 814, 627 N.E.2d 1013 (6th Dist. Huron County 1993)—33:8

Bullard, In re, 22 N.C. App. 245, 206 S.E.2d 305 (1974)—22:3

Bumper v. North Carolina, 391 U.S. 543, 88 S. Ct. 1788, 20 L. Ed. 2d 797 (1968)—14:5

Burchett, State ex rel. v. Juvenile Court for Scioto County, 28 Ohio Op. 2d 116, 92 Ohio L. Abs. 357, 194 N.E.2d 912 (Ct. App. 4th Dist. Scioto County 1962)—17:2

Burchfield, In re, 51 Ohio App. 3d 148, 555 N.E.2d 325 (4th Dist. Athens County 1988)—10:2, 21:4

Burdeau v. McDowell, 256 U.S. 465, 41 S. Ct. 574, 65 L. Ed. 1048, 13 A.L.R. 1159 (1921)—14:4

Burgess, In re, 13 Ohio App. 3d 374, 469 N.E.2d 967 (12th Dist. Preble County 1984)—4:2, 16:8, 16:16

Burgess, No. 3053 (9th Dist. Ct. App., Lorain, 11-5-80), In re—8:2

Burich, State ex rel. v. Ferreri, No. 69218 (8th Dist. Ct. App., Cuyahoga, 9-1-95)—3:3, 33:4

Burkhart, In re, 15 Ohio Misc. 170, 44 Ohio Op. 2d 329, 239 N.E.2d 772 (Juv. Ct. 1968)—9:3, 10:3

Burrell, In re, 58 Ohio St. 2d 37, 12 Ohio Op. 3d 43, 388 N.E.2d 738 (1979)—9:6, 10:3

Burton, In re, 1997 WL 473099 (Ohio Ct. App. 8th Dist. Cuyahoga County 1997)—25:7, 27:8, 33:6

Burton S., In re, 136 Ohio App. 3d 386, 736 N.E.2d 928 (6th Dist. Ottawa County 1999)—2:5, 23:19

Butcher, Matter of, 1991 WL 62145 (Ohio Ct. App. 4th Dist. Athens County 1991)—30:4, 30:10, 30:11, 31:8

Butkus, Matter of, 1997 WL 401527 (Ohio Ct. App. 12th Dist. Warren County 1997)—31:9

Butler, State ex rel. v. Demis, 66 Ohio St. 2d 123, 20 Ohio Op. 3d 121, 420 N.E.2d 116 (1981)—23:3

Butt, In re, 20 Ohio Misc. 2d 15, 486 N.E.2d 255 (C.P. 1984)—34:12

Byerly, Matter of, 1998 WL 684178 (Ohio Ct. App. 11th Dist. Portage County 1998)—18:2

Byrd, In re, 66 Ohio St. 2d 334, 20 Ohio Op. 3d 309, 421 N.E.2d 1284 (1981)—16:15, 30:11

C

C., In re, 61 Ohio Misc. 2d 610, 580 N.E.2d 1182 (C.P. 1991)—2:3, 22:5

Caldwell, In re, 76 Ohio St. 3d 156, 1996-Ohio-410, 666 N.E.2d 1367 (1996)—27:3

Caldwell, No. 420 (7th Dist. Ct. App., Carroll, 12-13-79), In re—20:6

California v. Acevedo, 500 U.S. 565, 111 S. Ct. 1982, 114 L. Ed. 2d 619 (1991)—14:4

California v. Beheler, 463 U.S. 1121, 103 S. Ct. 3517, 77 L. Ed. 2d 1275 (1983)—14:10

California v. Ciraolo, 476 U.S. 207, 106 S. Ct. 1809, 90 L. Ed. 2d 210 (1986)—14:4

California v. Green, 399 U.S. 149, 90 S. Ct. 1930, 26 L. Ed. 2d 489 (1970)—23:25

California v. Greenwood, 486 U.S. 35, 108 S. Ct. 1625, 100 L. Ed. 2d 30 (1988)—14:4

California v. Prysock, 453 U.S. 355, 101 S. Ct. 2806, 69 L. Ed. 2d 696 (1981)—14:10

Campbell, In re, 138 Ohio App. 3d 786, 742 N.E.2d 663 (10th Dist. Franklin County 2000)—30:8, 30:10, 30:11

Campbell, In re, 13 Ohio App. 3d 34, 468 N.E.2d 93 (12th Dist. Butler County 1983)—10:5

Campbell, Matter of, 1997 WL 401546 (Ohio Ct. App. 11th Dist. Lake County 1997)—2:2

Cannon, Matter of, 1990 WL 237462 (Ohio Ct. App. 5th Dist. Stark County 1990)—30:10, 31:8

Cantwell v. State of Connecticut, 310 U.S. 296, 60 S. Ct. 900, 84 L. Ed. 1213, 128 A.L.R. 1352 (1940)—9:7

Caplinger, In re, 2002-Ohio-3087, 2002 WL 1343653 (Ohio Ct. App. 5th Dist. Muskingham County 2002)—27:3

Carl, In re, 1995 WL 363820 (Ohio Ct. App. 8th Dist. Cuyahoga County 1995)—30:12

Carlos B., Matter of, 86 Misc. 2d 160, 382 N.Y.S.2d 655 (City Fam. Ct. 1976)—14:13

Carlos O., In re, 96 Ohio App. 3d 252, 644 N.E.2d 1084 (6th Dist. Wood County 1994)—4:4, 19:7, 23:29

Carl T., In re, 1 Cal. App. 3d 344, 81 Cal. Rptr. 655 (2d Dist. 1969)—14:13, 14:14

Carolyn Wheat, Matter of, 1996 WL 695664 (Ohio Ct. App. 8th Dist. Cuyahoga County 1996)—34:4

Carpenter, In re, 31 Ohio App. 2d 184, 60 Ohio Op. 2d 287, 287 N.E.2d 399 (10th Dist. Franklin County 1972)—8:6

Carpenter, In re Custody of, 41 Ohio App. 3d 182, 534 N.E.2d 1216 (2d Dist. Greene County 1987)—16:15

Carroll, In re, 124 Ohio App. 3d 51, 705 N.E.2d 402 (2d Dist. Greene County 1997)—30:5

Carter, In re, 123 Ohio App. 3d 532, 704 N.E.2d 625 (4th Dist. Pickaway County 1997)—23:16, 23:31

Carter, In re, 1996 WL 103778 (Ohio Ct. App. 12th Dist. Butler County 1996)—15:2

Carter, No. 78-16 (6th Dist. Ct. App., Wood, 1-26-79), In re—16:15

Caruso, Matter of, 1991 WL 82985 (Ohio Ct. App. 6th Dist. Lucas County 1991)—33:6

Cason v. Cook, 810 F.2d 188, 37 Ed. Law Rep. 473 (8th Cir. 1987)—14:6

Cass, Matter of, 1995 WL 631650 (Ohio Ct. App. 12th Dist. Preble County 1995)—25:4, 25:14

Catherine M., Matter of, 1995 WL 326354 (Ohio Ct. App. 6th Dist. Lucas County 1995)—30:10, 30:11

Cavanaugh v. Sealey, 1997 WL 25521 (Ohio Ct. App. 8th Dist. Cuyahoga County 1997)—34:4

C.F., In re, 2003-Ohio-3260, 2003 WL 21434769 (Ohio Ct. App. 8th Dist. Cuyahoga County 2003)—30:7, 30:11

Chambers, Matter of, 116 Ohio App. 3d 312, 688 N.E.2d 25 (3d Dist. Logan County 1996)—23:8

Chambers v. Maroney, 399 U.S. 42, 90 S. Ct. 1975, 26 L. Ed. 2d 419 (1970)—14:4

Chapa, Matter of, 1996 WL 156743 (Ohio Ct. App. 3d Dist. Hancock County 1996)—28:10

Chapman, Matter of, 1998 WL 258418 (Ohio Ct. App. 11th Dist. Ashtabula County 1998)—25:4

Chavis, Matter of, 31 N.C. App. 579, 230 S.E.2d 198 (1976)—23:9

Cheesman, Matter of, 1993 WL 437666 (Ohio Ct. App. 12th Dist. Butler County 1993)—3:3

Children's Home of Marion County v. Fetter, 90 Ohio St. 110, 106 N.E. 761 (1914)—3:2, 30:11, 34:12

Children's Hospital of Akron v. Johnson, 68 Ohio App. 2d 17, 22 Ohio Op. 3d 11, 426 N.E.2d 515 (9th Dist. Summit County 1980)—32:2

Chimel v. California, 395 U.S. 752, 89 S. Ct. 2034, 23 L. Ed. 2d 685 (1969)—14:4

Christman v. Washington Court House [School Dist.], 30 Ohio App. 3d 228, 507 N.E.2d 384, 39 Ed. Law Rep. 283 (12th Dist. Fayette County 1986)—30:3

Christopher, In re, 54 Ohio App. 2d 137, 8 Ohio Op. 3d 271, 376 N.E.2d 603 (5th Dist. Morrow County 1977)—23:6, 30:11, 31:7, 33:4

Church, Matter of, 1983 WL 3182 (Ohio Ct. App. 4th Dist. Lawrence County 1983)—23:3, 23:6

Cincinnati House of Refuge v. Ryan, 37 Ohio St. 197, 1881 WL 85 (1881)—1:6

Clark, In re, 141 Ohio App. 3d 55, 2001-Ohio-4126, 749 N.E.2d 833 (8th Dist. Cuyahoga County 2001)—23:9

Clark, In re, 21 Ohio Op. 2d 86, 90 Ohio L. Abs. 21, 185 N.E.2d 128 (C.P. 1962)—9:7, 20:3

Clark, Matter of, 1995 WL 153010 (Ohio Ct. App. 7th Dist. Harrison County 1995)—26:6, 30:11

Clark v. Bayer, 32 Ohio St. 299, 1877 WL 120 (1877)—30:11

Clark v. Clark, 114 Ohio App. 3d 558, 683 N.E.2d 800 (12th Dist. Butler County 1996)—9:15

Clark, State ex rel. v. Allaman, 154 Ohio St. 296, 43 Ohio Op. 190, 95 N.E.2d 753 (1950)—16:15, 16:17

Clemens, In re, 2002-Ohio-3370, 2002 WL 1401663 (Ohio Ct. App. 11th Dist. Geauga County 2002)—24:8

Clemens, In re, 2002-Ohio-3370, 2002 WL 1401663 (Ohio Ct. App. 11th Dist. Lake County 2002)—14:2

Clermont Cty. Dept. of Human Serv., State ex rel. v. Walsson, 108 Ohio App. 3d 125, 670 N.E.2d 287 (12th Dist. Clermont County 1995)—3:3

Cleveland Surgi-Center, Inc. v. Jones, 2 F.3d 686 (6th Cir. 1993)—12:10

Cloud, In re, 1997 WL 264264 (Ohio Ct. App. 12th Dist. Butler County 1997)—16:15, 30:4

C.M., In re, 2004-Ohio-1927, 2004 WL 829937 (Ohio Ct. App. 12th Dist. Butler County 2004)—27:3

Cobb, Matter of, 1996 WL 65840 (Ohio Ct. App. 8th Dist. Cuyahoga County 1996)—23:5

Cody, State ex rel. v. Toner, 8 Ohio St. 3d 22, 456 N.E.2d 813 (1983)—23:3

Coffey, Matter of, 1991 WL 57153 (Ohio Ct. App. 5th Dist. Tuscarawas County 1991)—30:4

Coffey, Matter of, 1998 WL 24341 (Ohio Ct. App. 12th Dist. Madison County 1998)—30:7

Cole v. State of Ark., 333 U.S. 196, 68 S. Ct. 514, 92 L. Ed. 644 (1948)—22:12

Coles, Matter of, 1994 WL 237974 (Ohio Ct. App. 11th Dist. Trumbull County 1994)—30:10

Collier, No. 8AP-825 (10th Dist. Ct. App., Franklin, 6-4-81), In re—9:12

Collier, No. 39343 (8th Dist. Ct. App., Cuyahoga, 12-13-79), In re—30:11

Collins, In re, 127 Ohio App. 3d 278, 712 N.E.2d 798 (8th Dist. Cuyahoga County 1998)—23:30, 25:12

Collins, In re, 1995 WL 688792 (Ohio Ct. App. 9th Dist. Summit County 1995)—10:3, 10:5

Collins, In re, 20 Ohio App. 2d 319, 49 Ohio Op. 2d 448, 253 N.E.2d 824 (8th Dist. Cuyahoga County 1969)—23:4, 23:27

Collins, Matter of, 1990 WL 36309 (Ohio Ct. App. 11th Dist. Lake County 1990)—31:4, 31:6

Colorado v. Bertine, 479 U.S. 367, 107 S. Ct. 738, 93 L. Ed. 2d 739 (1987)—14:4

Colorado v. Connelly, 479 U.S. 157, 107 S. Ct. 515, 93 L. Ed. 2d 473 (1986)—14:9

Colorado v. Spring, 479 U.S. 564, 107 S. Ct. 851, 93 L. Ed. 2d 954 (1987)—14:10

Com. v. Dingfelt, 227 Pa. Super. 380, 323 A.2d 145 (1974)—14:6

Com. v. Durham, 255 Pa. Super. 539, 389 A.2d 108 (1978)—2:6

Com. v. Ransom, 446 Pa. 457, 288 A.2d 762 (1972)—22:14

Com. v. Wayne W., 414 Mass. 218, 606 N.E.2d 1323 (1993)—22:3

Commonwealth v. Fisher, 213 Pa. 48, 62 A. 198 (1905)—1:2

Conley/Wilt Children, In re, 1998 WL 72266 (Ohio Ct. App. 2d Dist. Clark County 1998)—25:14

Connecticut v. Barrett, 479 U.S. 523, 107 S. Ct. 828, 93 L. Ed. 2d 920 (1987)—
14:10

Cook, Matter of, 1990 WL 157225 (Ohio Ct. App. 2d Dist. Clark County
1990)—30:10

Cook, Matter of, 1998 WL 719524 (Ohio Ct. App. 3d Dist. Hancock County
1998)—34:3

Cook v. Court of Common Pleas of Marion County, 28 Ohio App. 3d 82, 502
N.E.2d 245 (3d Dist. Marion County 1986)—16:13

Coolidge v. New Hampshire, 403 U.S. 443, 91 S. Ct. 2022, 29 L. Ed. 2d 564
(1971)—14:4

Cooper v. Oklahoma, 517 U.S. 348, 116 S. Ct. 1373, 134 L. Ed. 2d 498
(1996)—23:7

Cope v. Campbell, 175 Ohio St. 475, 26 Ohio Op. 2d 88, 196 N.E.2d 457
(1964)—1:6, 23:10

Corcoran, In re, 68 Ohio App. 3d 213, 587 N.E.2d 957 (11th Dist. Geauga
County 1990)—15:2, 23:29, 34:9

Cordell v. Cordell, 1992 WL 67629 (Ohio Ct. App. 8th Dist. Cuyahoga County
1992)—30:12

Corey, In re, 145 Ohio St. 413, 31 Ohio Op. 35, 61 N.E.2d 892 (1945)—18:2,
34:12

Cornell, In re, 2003-Ohio-5007, at ¶ 28, 2003 WL 22171435 (Ohio Ct. App.
11th Dist. Portage County 2003)—30:11

Corona, 1981 WL 4502 (Ohio Ct. App. 8th Dist. Cuyahoga County 1981)—
1:8, 16:8, 16:17, 27:18

Corry M., In re, 134 Ohio App. 3d 274, 730 N.E.2d 1047 (11th Dist. Lake
County 1999)—23:16

Cory Y., Matter of, 1995 WL 612929 (Ohio Ct. App. 6th Dist. Lucas County
1995)—19:6

Cottrill, Matter of, 1998 WL 377675 (Ohio Ct. App. 4th Dist. Ross County
1998)—33:6

Coulter, 1981 WL 9749 (Ohio Ct. App. 1st Dist. Hamilton County 1981)—
16:14, 30:11

Covin, In re, 8 Ohio App. 3d 139, 456 N.E.2d 520 (1st Dist. Hamilton County
1982)—16:14, 30:12

Cowling, In re, 72 Ohio App. 3d 499, 595 N.E.2d 470 (9th Dist. Summit
County 1991)—18:4

Cox, In re, 36 Ohio App. 2d 65, 65 Ohio Op. 2d 51, 301 N.E.2d 907 (7th Dist.
Mahoning County 1973)—2:3, 27:18, 33:9

Cox, Matter of, 1986 WL 7900 (Ohio Ct. App. 4th Dist. Highland County
1986)—16:14, 18:3

Cox v. Court of Common Pleas of Franklin County, Div. of Domestic Relations, Juvenile Branch, 42 Ohio App. 3d 171, 537 N.E.2d 721 (10th Dist.
Franklin County 1988)—2:2, 9:7, 32:2

Cox v. Turley, 506 F.2d 1347 (6th Cir. 1974)—19:2

Cox v. U. S., 473 F.2d 334 (4th Cir. 1973)—22:3

Coy, In re, 67 Ohio St. 3d 215, 1993-Ohio-202, 616 N.E.2d 1105 (1993)—1:8,
23:16

Coy v. Iowa, 487 U.S. 1012, 108 S. Ct. 2798, 101 L. Ed. 2d 857, 25 Fed. R.
Evid. Serv. 865 (1988)—23:23

C.R., In re, 2004-Ohio-131, 2004 WL 63623 (Ohio Ct. App. 8th Dist. Cuyahoga
County 2004)—30:13

Cradle v. Peyton, 208 Va. 243, 156 S.E.2d 874 (1967)—22:3

Crager, In re, 2003-Ohio-5548, 2003 WL 22386961 (Ohio Ct. App. 4th Dist.
Lawrence County 2003)—30:10

Cramer, Matter of, 1998 WL 430544 (Ohio Ct. App. 5th Dist. Licking County 1998)—25:14

Crandell v. State, 1975 OK CR 127, 539 P.2d 398 (Okla. Crim. App. 1975)—22:12

Crawford, In re, 1999 WL 100377 (Ohio Ct. App. 5th Dist. Stark County 1999)—9:7

Crawford v. Washington, 124 S. Ct. 1354, 158 L. Ed. 2d 177, 63 Fed. R. Evid. Serv. 1077 (U.S. 2004)—23:25

Creek, In re, 243 A.2d 49 (D.C. 1968)—14:10

Cremeans, Matter of, 1992 WL 47278 (Ohio Ct. App. 8th Dist. Cuyahoga County 1992)—16:14, 26:6, 30:13

Criswell v. Brentwood Hosp., 49 Ohio App. 3d 163, 551 N.E.2d 1315 (8th Dist. Cuyahoga County 1989)—14:17

Crose, Matter of, 1982 WL 3824 (Ohio Ct. App. 2d Dist. Darke County 1982)—16:14, 16:17, 23:16, 25:9, 25:10

Cross, In re, 96 Ohio St. 3d 328, 2002-Ohio-4183, 774 N.E.2d 258 (2002)—27:8, 33:7

Crowe, In re, 1987 WL 7053 (Ohio Ct. App. 2d Dist. Montgomery County 1987)—4:2

C. T. F., In Interest of, 316 N.W.2d 865 (Iowa 1982)—23:29

Cummings, Matter of, 1989 WL 104753 (Ohio Ct. App. 5th Dist. Guernsey County 1989)—26:2

Cundiff, In re, 1995 WL 768599 (Ohio Ct. App. 5th Dist. Stark County 1995)—26:6

Cunningham, In re, 59 Ohio St. 2d 100, 13 Ohio Op. 3d 78, 391 N.E.2d 1034 (1979)—9:2, 25:2, 30:2, 30:8, 30:11

Curley/Brown Children, In re, 1993 WL 473832 (Ohio Ct. App. 9th Dist. Summit County 1993)—23:5, 23:12

Curry, In re, 2004-Ohio-750, at ¶ 46, 2004 WL 307476 (Ohio Ct. App. 4th Dist. Washington County)—23:6

Cuyahoga Cty. Dept. of Children & Family Serv., State ex rel. v. Ferreri, 96 Ohio App. 3d 660, 645 N.E.2d 837 (8th Dist. Cuyahoga County 1994)—3:3

Cuyler v. Sullivan, 446 U.S. 335, 100 S. Ct. 1708, 64 L. Ed. 2d 333 (1980)—23:5

C.W., In re, 2004-Ohio-1987, at ¶ 17, 2004 WL 840124 (Ohio Ct. App. 9th Dist. Summit County 2004), motion to certify allowed, 102 Ohio St. 3d 1481, 2004-Ohio-3069 (2004)—30:9

D

D., In re, 36 A.D.2d 970, 321 N.Y.S.2d 510 (2d Dep't 1971)—23:13

Dague, Matter of, 1987 WL 19093 (Ohio Ct. App. 5th Dist. Delaware County 1987)—32:2

Dake, In re, 87 Ohio L. Abs. 483, 180 N.E.2d 646 (Juv. Ct. 1961)—10:3

Dalton, In re, 115 Ohio App. 3d 794, 686 N.E.2d 345 (7th Dist. Belmont County 1996)—4:4

Dandoy, State ex rel. v. Superior Court In and For Pima County, 127 Ariz. 184, 619 P.2d 12 (1980)—23:7

Daniel E., In re, 122 Ohio App. 3d 139, 701 N.E.2d 408 (6th Dist. Sandusky County 1997)—23:28

Daniel T., In re, 446 A.2d 1042 (R.I. 1982)—14:13, 14:14

Darling, In re, 2003-Ohio-7184, 2003 WL 23094930 (Ohio Ct. App. 9th Dist. Wayne County 2003)—10:6

Darnell, In re, 173 Ohio St. 335, 19 Ohio Op. 2d 269, 182 N.E.2d 321 (1962)—1:6, 23:10

Darst, In re, 117 Ohio App. 374, 24 Ohio Op. 2d 144, 192 N.E.2d 287 (10th Dist. Franklin County 1963)—9:3, 10:2, 10:3, 25:2

Daudt, In re, 1986 WL 9630 (Ohio Ct. App. 12th Dist. Butler County 1986)—27:13, 32:2

Daudt v. Daudt, 1987 WL 13715 (Ohio Ct. App. 12th Dist. Butler County 1987)—27:13

Davis, In re, 22 Ohio Op. 2d 108, 87 Ohio L. Abs. 222, 179 N.E.2d 198 (Juv. Ct. 1961)—2:2, 17:4

Davis, In re, 84 Ohio St. 3d 520, 1999-Ohio-419, 705 N.E.2d 1219 (1999)—25:13

Davis, Matter of, 1984 WL 5666 (Ohio Ct. App. 4th Dist. Hocking County 1984)—30:10

Davis v. Alaska, 415 U.S. 308, 94 S. Ct. 1105, 39 L. Ed. 2d 347 (1974)—1:4, 23:24, 35:3

Davis v. Smith, 1993 WL 277536 (Ohio Ct. App. 9th Dist. Summit County 1993)—31:5

Davis v. State, 297 So. 2d 289 (Fla. 1974)—22:3

Day, No. 669 (11th Dist. Ct. App., Geauga, 8-23-76), In re—27:18

D.B., In re, 2003-Ohio-3521, 2003 WL 21511310 (Ohio Ct. App. 8th Dist. Cuyahoga County 2003)—30:13

Deanna B., Matter of, 1995 WL 112895 (Ohio Ct. App. 6th Dist. Lucas County 1995)—31:9

Deborah C., In re, 30 Cal. 3d 125, 177 Cal. Rptr. 852, 635 P.2d 446 (1981)—14:10

Decker, In re, 20 Ohio App. 3d 203, 485 N.E.2d 751 (3d Dist. Van Wert County 1984)—23:15

Decker, In re, 28 Ohio N.P. (n.s.) 433, 1930 WL 2382 (Juv. Ct. 1930)—16:7

Deehan, Matter of, 1995 WL 560870 (Ohio Ct. App. 10th Dist. Franklin County 1995)—25:9, 33:11

DeGeronimo, No. 40089 (8th Dist. Ct. App., Cuyahoga, 6-28-79), In re—2:2, 4:2, 27:8, 33:5

Dengg, In re, 132 Ohio App. 3d 360, 724 N.E.2d 1255 (11th Dist. Portage County 1999)—14:6

Dettweiler, In re, 1993 WL 471405 (Ohio Ct. App. 5th Dist. Stark County 1993)—31:8

Devlin, In re, 78 Ohio App. 3d 543, 605 N.E.2d 467 (10th Dist. Franklin County 1992)—34:4

D.G., In re, 91 Ohio Misc. 2d 226, 698 N.E.2d 533 (C.P. 1998)—23:7

D.H., In re, 2003-Ohio-6478, 2003 WL 22861922 (Ohio Ct. App. 8th Dist. Cuyahoga County 2003)—18:2, 34:4

Diane P., Matter of, 110 A.D.2d 354, 494 N.Y.S.2d 881 (2d Dep't 1985)—14:2

Dickerson, 1982 WL 3447 (Ohio Ct. App. 4th Dist. Lawrence County 1982)—9:5

Dickerson v. U.S., 530 U.S. 428, 120 S. Ct. 2326, 147 L. Ed. 2d 405 (2000)—14:10

Diebler v. State, 43 Ohio App. 350, 13 Ohio L. Abs. 20, 183 N.E. 84 (5th Dist. Richland County 1932)—16:16

Dillen, Matter of, 1990 WL 42303 (Ohio Ct. App. 4th Dist. Hocking County 1990)—30:10

Dillon, 1981 WL 2676 (Ohio Ct. App. 4th Dist. Lawrence County 1981)—10:3

Dillon, 1981 WL 4218 (Ohio Ct. App. 9th Dist. Wayne County 1981)—9:12

Dispatch Printing Co., State ex rel. v. Lias, 68 Ohio St. 3d 497, 1994-Ohio-335, 628 N.E.2d 1368 (1994)—23:11, 33:8, 34:4

Dispatch Printing Co., State ex rel. v. Louden, 91 Ohio St. 3d 61, 2001-Ohio-268, 741 N.E.2d 517 (2001)—19:12

Disqualification of Floyd, In re, 101 Ohio St. 3d 1215, 2003-Ohio-7354, 803 N.E.2d 816 (2003)—23:28

Disqualification of Ruben, In re, 77 Ohio St. 3d 1232, 674 N.E.2d 348 (1995)—22:20

Dixon, Matter of, 1991 WL 325657 (Ohio Ct. App. 6th Dist. Lucas County 1991)—26:6, 31:7

Dixon, Matter of, 1992 WL 277966 (Ohio Ct. App. 6th Dist. Erie County 1992)—25:4, 30:10

D.N., In re, 2004-Ohio-1106, 2004 WL 439965 (Ohio Ct. App. 8th Dist. Cuyahoga County 2004)—24:9

D.N., In re, 2004-Ohio-1106, at ¶ 15, 2004 WL 439965 (Ohio Ct. App. 8th Dist. Cuyahoga County 2004)—24:9

Doe, Complaint of, 1998 WL 400769 (Ohio Ct. App. 10th Dist. Franklin County 1998)—12:9

Doe, In Interest of, 54 Haw. 647, 513 P.2d 1385 (1973)—8:6

Doe, In re, 167 N.E.2d 396 (Ohio Juv. Ct. 1956)—30:2

Doe, In re, 1991 WL 96269 (Ohio Ct. App. 2d Dist. Montgomery County 1991)—12:9

Doe, In re, 57 Ohio Misc. 2d 20, 565 N.E.2d 891 (C.P. 1990)—1:8

Doe, In re, 86 N.M. 37, 519 P.2d 133 (Ct. App. 1974)—22:16

Doe, In re Petition of, 2003-Ohio-6509, 2003 WL 22871690 (Ohio Ct. App. 10th Dist. Franklin County 2003)—12:9

Doe, Matter of, 1993 WL 355692 (Ohio Ct. App. 6th Dist. Lucas County 1993)—23:6

Doe, Matter of, 1993 WL 541121 (Ohio Ct. App. 6th Dist. Lucas County 1993)—25:13

Doe v. Roman, 2002-Ohio-6671, 2002 WL 31732468 (Ohio Ct. App. 5th Dist. Tuscarawas County 2002)—14:17

Doe, State ex rel. v. Tracy, 51 Ohio App. 3d 198, 555 N.E.2d 674 (12th Dist. Warren County 1988)—22:10

Doe Children, In re, 93 Ohio App. 3d 134, 637 N.E.2d 977 (6th Dist. Lucas County 1994)—3:2, 23:13, 30:10, 33:4

Doggett v. U.S., 505 U.S. 647, 112 S. Ct. 2686, 120 L. Ed. 2d 520 (1992)—23:29

Domineck, Matter of, 1990 WL 170674 (Ohio Ct. App. 12th Dist. Butler County 1990)—34:5

Donald L. v. Superior Court, 7 Cal. 3d 592, 102 Cal. Rptr. 850, 498 P.2d 1098 (1972)—22:3, 22:21

Donaldson, In re, 269 Cal. App. 2d 509, 75 Cal. Rptr. 220 (3d Dist. 1969)—14:6

Don B., In re, 2003-Ohio-1400, 2003 WL 1448059 (Ohio Ct. App. 6th Dist. Huron County 2003)—17:4

Doss, In re, 65 Ohio Misc. 2d 8, 640 N.E.2d 618 (C.P. 1994)—21:3, 22:15, 22:24

Douglas, In re, 11 Ohio Op. 2d 340, 82 Ohio L. Abs. 170, 164 N.E.2d 475 (Juv. Ct. 1959)—9:6, 10:2, 15:2, 20:2

Douglas v. Boykin, 121 Ohio App. 3d 140, 699 N.E.2d 123 (12th Dist. Butler County 1997)—23:3, 23:4

Dowell, Matter of, 1992 WL 200887 (Ohio Ct. App. 6th Dist. Lucas County 1992)—31:7

Doyle, In re, 122 Ohio App. 3d 767, 702 N.E.2d 970 (2d Dist. 1997)—23:3, 23:4, 23:9

Doyle v. Ohio, 426 U.S. 610, 96 S. Ct. 2240, 49 L. Ed. 2d 91 (1976)—14:10

D.R., In re, 153 Ohio App. 3d 156, 2003-Ohio-2852, 792 N.E.2d 203 (9th Dist. Summit County 2003)—30:7

D.R., In re, 63 Ohio Misc. 2d 273, 624 N.E.2d 1120 (C.P. 1993)—22:19, 25:5

Draper v. State of Wash., 372 U.S. 487, 83 S. Ct. 774, 9 L. Ed. 2d 899 (1963)—25:12

Draper v. U.S., 358 U.S. 307, 79 S. Ct. 329, 3 L. Ed. 2d 327 (1959)—14:4

Driscoll, State ex rel. v. Hunter, 1998 WL 102477 (Ohio Ct. App. 8th Dist. Cuyahoga County 1998)—34:12

Drope v. Missouri, 420 U.S. 162, 95 S. Ct. 896, 43 L. Ed. 2d 103 (1975)—23:7

Drushal v. Drushal, 1983 WL 4058 (Ohio Ct. App. 9th Dist. Summit County 1983)—30:10

Duckworth v. Eagan, 492 U.S. 195, 109 S. Ct. 2875, 106 L. Ed. 2d 166 (1989)—14:10

Duffy, In re, 591 S.E.2d 598 (N.C. Ct. App. 2004)—9:8

Duganitz, State ex rel. v. Court, 23 Ohio Op. 3d 572 (Ct. App. 8th Dist. Cuyahoga County 1981)—22:8

Dukes, In re, 81 Ohio App. 3d 145, 610 N.E.2d 513 (9th Dist. Summit County 1991)—16:12, 23:16

Dulaney, In re, 1998 WL 310746 (Ohio Ct. App. 2d Dist. Montgomery County 1998)—35:4

Dunaway v. New York, 442 U.S. 200, 99 S. Ct. 2248, 60 L. Ed. 2d 824 (1979)—14:3, 14:9

Duncan, In re, 62 Ohio L. Abs. 173, 107 N.E.2d 256 (Ct. App. 2d Dist. Preble County 1951)—9:9, 16:7

Duncan, Matter of, 1993 WL 257269 (Ohio Ct. App. 12th Dist. Preble County 1993)—10:2, 34:4

Duncan v. State of La., 391 U.S. 145, 88 S. Ct. 1444, 20 L. Ed. 2d 491 (1968)—23:10

Duncan/Walker Children, Matter of, 109 Ohio App. 3d 841, 673 N.E.2d 217 (5th Dist. Stark County 1996)—16:14, 23:6, 30:12, 31:5

Duncan/Walker Children, Matter of, 1995 WL 434114 (Ohio Ct. App. 5th Dist. Stark County 1995)—25:14

Dunham/Lewers Children, In re, 1995 WL 434172 (Ohio Ct. App. 5th Dist. Stark County 1995)—30:5

Dunlop, Matter of, 1984 WL 14171 (Ohio Ct. App. 8th Dist. Cuyahoga County 1984)—14:9

Dunn, In re, 102 Ohio App. 3d 217, 656 N.E.2d 1341 (3d Dist. Marion County 1995)—11:6

Durham, In re, 1998 WL 635107 (Ohio Ct. App. 10th Dist. Franklin County 1998)—27:19

Dusky v. U.S., 362 U.S. 402, 80 S. Ct. 788, 4 L. Ed. 2d 824 (1960)—23:7

Dutton v. Evans, 400 U.S. 74, 91 S. Ct. 210, 27 L. Ed. 2d 213 (1970)—23:25

Dych, Matter of, 1990 WL 79028 (Ohio Ct. App. 5th Dist. Guernsey County 1990)—3:2

Dye, In re, 1995 WL 231214 (Ohio Ct. App. 9th Dist. Summit County 1995)—26:6, 30:11

E

East, In re, 105 Ohio App. 3d 221, 663 N.E.2d 983 (8th Dist. Cuyahoga County 1995)—23:4

East, In re, 32 Ohio Misc. 65, 61 Ohio Op. 2d 38, 61 Ohio Op. 2d 108, 288 N.E.2d 343 (C.P. 1972)—10:2, 10:3, 10:5

Easterday, State ex rel. v. Zieba, 58 Ohio St. 3d 251, 569 N.E.2d 1028 (1991)—3:2

Eastlake, City of v. Ruggiero, 7 Ohio App. 2d 212, 36 Ohio Op. 2d 345, 220 N.E.2d 126 (7th Dist. Lake County 1966)—8:6

Edgerson, In re, 144 Ohio App.3d 113, 2001-Ohio-4237, 759 N.E.2d 806 (8th Dist. Cuyahoga County 2001)—34:9

Edwards, In re, 117 Ohio App. 3d 108, 690 N.E.2d 22 (8th Dist. Cuyahoga County 1996)—33:6

Edwards v. Arizona, 451 U.S. 477, 101 S. Ct. 1880, 68 L. Ed. 2d 378 (1981)—14:10, 14:11, 14:13

Efaw, Matter of, 1998 WL 224905 (Ohio Ct. App. 4th Dist. Athens County 1998)—31:8

Egbert Children, In re, 99 Ohio App. 3d 492, 651 N.E.2d 38 (12th Dist. Butler County 1994)—23:19, 30:10

Elliott, In re, 2004-Ohio-388, 2004 WL 187413 (Ohio Ct. App. 7th Dist. Jefferson County 2004)—31:5

Elliott, In re, 87 Ohio App. 3d 816, 623 N.E.2d 217 (12th Dist. Fayette County 1993)—7:4, 16:7, 16:16

Elliott, Matter of, 1993 WL 268846 (Ohio Ct. App. 4th Dist. Lawrence County 1993)—18:2, 23:12

Elmer v. Lucas County Children Services Bd., 36 Ohio App. 3d 241, 523 N.E.2d 540 (6th Dist. Lucas County 1987)—31:8

Emery, In re, 2003-Ohio-2206, 2003 WL 2003811 (Ohio Ct. App. 4th Dist. Lawrence County 2003)—23:6

Emery, In re, 2003-Ohio-2206, at ¶ 21, 2004 WL 2003811 (Ohio Ct. App. 4th Dist. Lawrence County)—23:6

Endsley v. Endsley, 89 Ohio App. 3d 306, 624 N.E.2d 270 (9th Dist. Wayne County 1993)—30:6

Eng, In re, 1992 WL 348184 (Ohio Ct. App. 2d Dist. Montgomery County 1992)—3:3

Enochs, Matter of, 1997 WL 117207 (Ohio Ct. App. 5th Dist. Stark County 1997)—18:2

Eplin, Matter of, 1995 WL 495451 (Ohio Ct. App. 5th Dist. Stark County 1995)—23:6, 23:24, 23:27, 30:12

Eppinger, Matter of, 1994 WL 55786 (Ohio Ct. App. 8th Dist. Cuyahoga County 1994)—30:12

Erica, In re, 65 Ohio Misc. 2d 17, 640 N.E.2d 623 (C.P. 1994)—26:6

Eric W., In re, 113 Ohio App. 3d 367, 680 N.E.2d 1275 (6th Dist. Erie County 1996)—28:2

Estelle v. Smith, 451 U.S. 454, 101 S. Ct. 1866, 68 L. Ed. 2d 359 (1981)—14:11

Etchell, Matter of, 1987 WL 10613 (Ohio Ct. App. 8th Dist. Cuyahoga County 1987)—35:2

Etter, In re, 134 Ohio App. 3d 484, 731 N.E.2d 694 (1st Dist. Hamilton County 1998)—23:6

Evans, Matter of, 1987 WL 26739 (Ohio Ct. App. 2d Dist. Miami County 1987)—21:2

Everhart, In re, 1996 WL 724774 (Ohio Ct. App. 9th Dist. Summit County 1996)—31:8

Ezell v. Manual, 1990 WL 746729 (Ohio Ct. App. 8th Dist. Cuyahoga County 1990)—19:7, 34:12

F

Fambro, In re, 1997 WL 165427 (Ohio Ct. App. 2d Dist. Clark County 1997)—25:7

Farace, Matter of, 1997 WL 802819 (Ohio Ct. App. 4th Dist. Scioto County 1997)—16:14, 30:7

Fare v. Michael C., 442 U.S. 707, 99 S. Ct. 2560, 61 L. Ed. 2d 197 (1979)—1:4, 14:10

Faretta v. California, 422 U.S. 806, 95 S. Ct. 2525, 45 L. Ed. 2d 562 (1975)—
23:4

Farinacci, No. 37973 (8th Dist. Ct. App., Cuyahoga, 11-30-78), In re—7:2,
16:9, 28:10

Farley v. Farley, 85 Ohio App. 3d 113, 619 N.E.2d 427 (5th Dist. Licking
County 1992)—31:9

Farrar, Matter of, 1995 WL 495471 (Ohio Ct. App. 5th Dist. Guernsey County
1995)—30:6

Fassinger, In re, 42 Ohio St. 2d 505, 71 Ohio Op. 2d 503, 330 N.E.2d 431
(1975)—16:14

Fassinger, In re, 43 Ohio App. 2d 89, 72 Ohio Op. 2d 292, 334 N.E.2d 5 (8th
Dist. Cuyahoga County 1974)—16:14, 18:3, 23:13

Fee, Matter of, 1993 WL 541133 (Ohio Ct. App. 6th Dist. Erie County 1993)—
27:3

Feiler, No. C-780549 (1st Dist. Ct. App., Hamilton, 10-17-79), In re—10:3,
25:2

Feke, No. 42242 (8th Dist. Ct. App., Cuyahoga, 3-12-81), In re—10:4

Feldman, No. 34223 (8th Dist. Ct. App., Cuyahoga, 12-23-75), In re—9:3,
10:3, 25:2

Fellers v. U.S., 124 S. Ct. 1019, 157 L. Ed. 2d 1016 (U.S. 2004)—14:11

Felton, In re, 124 Ohio App. 3d 500, 706 N.E.2d 809 (3d Dist. Auglaize County
1997)—16:16

Ferguson v. City of Charleston, 532 U.S. 67, 121 S. Ct. 1281, 149 L. Ed. 2d
205 (2001)—1:4, 14:16

Ferrell, Matter of, 1990 WL 42275 (Ohio Ct. App. 4th Dist. Gallia County
1990)—9:5, 26:2, 31:8

Fetters, In re, 110 Ohio App. 3d 483, 674 N.E.2d 766 (12th Dist. Preble
County 1996)—16:7, 16:8, 34:4

Fetters, Matter of, 1998 WL 102997 (Ohio Ct. App. 12th Dist. Preble County
1998)—30:3

Fields, 1982 WL 6650 (Ohio Ct. App. 6th Dist. Williams County 1982)—31:6

Finlaw, In re, 69 Ohio App. 3d 474, 590 N.E.2d 1340 (2d Dist. Greene County
1990)—28:2

Fitzgerald, In re, 1998 WL 46767 (Ohio Ct. App. 9th Dist. Summit County
1998)—18:2, 18:4

Flanagan, Matter of, 1998 WL 195866 (Ohio Ct. App. 3d Dist. Seneca County
1998)—25:14

Fleming, In re, 76 Ohio App. 3d 30, 600 N.E.2d 1112 (6th Dist. Lucas County
1991)—1:8, 25:13

Fleming, Matter of, 1993 WL 277186 (Ohio Ct. App. 8th Dist. Cuyahoga
County 1993)—16:14, 25:9, 30:6, 30:7

Flemming, No. 83-5591-09 (Ct. of Claims 1983), In re—35:2

Fletcher v. Weir, 455 U.S. 603, 102 S. Ct. 1309, 71 L. Ed. 2d 490 (1982)—
14:10

Florida v. Jimeno, 500 U.S. 248, 111 S. Ct. 1801, 114 L. Ed. 2d 297 (1991)—
14:5

Florida v. Meyers, 466 U.S. 380, 104 S. Ct. 1852, 80 L. Ed. 2d 381 (1984)—
14:4

Florida v. Riley, 488 U.S. 445, 109 S. Ct. 693, 102 L. Ed. 2d 835 (1989)—14:4

Florida v. Wells, 495 U.S. 1, 110 S. Ct. 1632, 109 L. Ed. 2d 1 (1990)—14:4

Flynn, In re, 101 Ohio App. 3d 778, 656 N.E.2d 737 (8th Dist. Cuyahoga
County 1995)—23:9, 34:4

Flynn, Matter of, 1983 WL 3457 (Ohio Ct. App. 10th Dist. Franklin County
1983)—16:7

F.M., In re, 2002-Ohio-3900, 2002 WL 1767396 (Ohio Ct. App. 8th Dist. Cuyahoga County 2002)—20:2

Forrest, In re, 1996 WL 434180 (Ohio Ct. App. 10th Dist. Franklin County 1996)—31:8

Fortini, State ex rel. v. Hoffman, 12 Ohio App. 341, 1920 WL 502 (1st Dist. Hamilton County 1920)—1:6

Fortney v. Hines, 1990 WL 173358 (Ohio Ct. App. 5th Dist. Tuscarawas County 1990)—23:3

Fotiou Children, In re, 1991 WL 3213 (Ohio Ct. App. 12th Dist. Madison County 1991)—30:11, 30:12, 31:8

Foust, In re, 57 Ohio App. 3d 149, 567 N.E.2d 1042 (3d Dist. Crawford County 1989)—31:4, 31:5

Fox, In re, 60 Ohio Misc. 31, 14 Ohio Op. 3d 80, 395 N.E.2d 918 (C.P. 1979)—7:4

Franklin, In re, 1997 WL 624844 (Ohio Ct. App. 2d Dist. Clark County 1997)—23:4

Franklin, In re, 88 Ohio App. 3d 277, 623 N.E.2d 720 (3d Dist. Marion County 1993)—18:2

Fraser, Matter of, 1992 WL 238498 (Ohio Ct. App. 5th Dist. Stark County 1992)—18:4

Frazer, State ex rel. v. Administrator/Director, Juvenile Court Detention Home, 107 Ohio App. 3d 245, 668 N.E.2d 546 (8th Dist. Cuyahoga County 1995)—19:2, 34:12

Frederick, In re, 63 Ohio Misc. 2d 229, 622 N.E.2d 762 (C.P. 1993)—15:2, 16:16

Frenz, In re, 2003-Ohio-3653, 2003 WL 21545125 (Ohio Ct. App. 5th Dist. Tuscarawas County 2003)—17:4

Fries, Matter of, 1997 WL 428649 (Ohio Ct. App. 8th Dist. Cuyahoga County 1997)—33:6

Frinzl, In re, 152 Ohio St. 164, 39 Ohio Op. 456, 87 N.E.2d 583 (1949)—18:5, 33:2, 34:12

Fryerson, State ex rel. v. Tate, 84 Ohio St. 3d 481, 1999-Ohio-465, 705 N.E.2d 353 (1999)—22:4, 34:12

Fudge, In re, 59 Ohio App. 2d 129, 13 Ohio Op. 3d 176, 392 N.E.2d 1262 (2d Dist. Clark County 1977)—2:5

Fuhrman, No. 91-0206 (1st Dist. Ct. App., Hamilton, 11-22-91), In re—35:2

Fulk, In re, 132 Ohio App. 3d 470, 1999-Ohio-840, 725 N.E.2d 357 (3d Dist. Crawford County 1999)—23:9

Fulton, Matter of, 1992 WL 238898 (Ohio Ct. App. 4th Dist. Athens County 1992)—26:2

Fulwood v. Stone, 394 F.2d 939 (D.C. Cir. 1967)—19:9

Fusik, No. 41569 (8th Dist. Ct. App., Cuyahoga, 6-12-80), In re—24:9, 25:4

Fyffe, State ex rel. v. Pierce, 40 Ohio St. 3d 8, 531 N.E.2d 673 (1988)—22:19, 23:11

G

Gage, Matter of, 49 Or. App. 599, 624 P.2d 1076 (1980)—14:10

Gall, Matter of, 1986 WL 7100 (Ohio Ct. App. 3d Dist. Paulding County 1986)—16:11

Gallagher v. Gallagher, 115 Ohio App. 453, 21 Ohio Op. 2d 74, 185 N.E.2d 571 (3d Dist. Henry County 1962)—9:5

Gallegos v. Colorado, 370 U.S. 49, 82 S. Ct. 1209, 8 L. Ed. 2d 325, 87 A.L.R.2d 614 (1962)—1:3, 14:9

Galloway, In re, 77 Ohio App. 3d 61, 601 N.E.2d 83 (6th Dist. Lucas County 1991)—25:13

Gamble v. Dotson, 1991 WL 57229 (Ohio Ct. App. 9th Dist. Lorain County 1991)—16:15, 25:14

Gandarilla, No. 89JU-05-3985 (Juv., Franklin, 11-15-89), In re—25:4

Gannett Co., Inc. v. DePasquale, 443 U.S. 368, 99 S. Ct. 2898, 61 L. Ed. 2d 608 (1979)—23:11

Gantt, Matter of, 61 Ohio App. 2d 44, 15 Ohio Op. 3d 67, 398 N.E.2d 800 (6th Dist. Wood County 1978)—23:26

Garabrandt v. Lucas County Children Services Bd., 47 Ohio App. 3d 119, 547 N.E.2d 997 (6th Dist. Lucas County 1988)—18:2, 26:7

Garcia, Matter of, 1993 WL 390100 (Ohio Ct. App. 6th Dist. Wood County 1993)—18:5

Garrison v. Jennings, 1974 OK CR 216, 529 P.2d 536 (Okla. Crim. App. 1974)—23:31

Garth D., In re, 55 Cal. App. 3d 986, 127 Cal. Rptr. 881 (4th Dist. 1976)—14:9

Gary M., Matter of, 1998 WL 336904 (Ohio Ct. App. 6th Dist. Lucas County 1998)—30:11

Gaskins v. Shiplevy, 74 Ohio St. 3d 149, 1995-Ohio-262, 656 N.E.2d 1282 (1995)—22:4

Gaskins v. Shiplevy, 76 Ohio St. 3d 380, 1996-Ohio-387, 667 N.E.2d 1194 (1996)—22:4

Gault, Application of, 387 U.S. 1, 87 S. Ct. 1428, 18 L. Ed. 2d 527 (1967)—1:4, 14:3, 16:7, 18:2, 19:9, 22:3, 22:11, 22:12, 22:14, 23:2, 23:3, 23:4, 23:22, 23:27, 23:30, 34:9

Gebell v. Dollison, 57 Ohio App. 2d 198, 9 Ohio Op. 3d 23, 11 Ohio Op. 3d 187, 386 N.E.2d 845 (1st Dist. Clermont County 1978)—28:10

Geboy v. Gray, 471 F.2d 575 (7th Cir. 1973)—22:3, 22:11, 22:12

Gentry, Matter of, 1990 WL 12115 (Ohio Ct. App. 5th Dist. Licking County 1990)—25:14

George, Matter of, 1995 WL 399137 (Ohio Ct. App. 12th Dist. Brown County 1995)—25:4

Gersper v. Ashtabula County Children Services Bd., 59 Ohio St. 3d 127, 570 N.E.2d 1120 (1991)—14:17

Gerstein v. Pugh, 420 U.S. 103, 95 S. Ct. 854, 43 L. Ed. 2d 54, 19 Fed. R. Serv. 2d 1499 (1975)—14:3

Gibson, In re, 1994 WL 520842 (Ohio Ct. App. 8th Dist. Cuyahoga County 1994)—25:4

Gibson, In re, 61 Ohio St. 3d 168, 573 N.E.2d 1074 (1991)—30:4

Gibson, No. 78AP-856 (10th Dist. Ct. App., Franklin, 7-19-79), In re—30:8

Gideon v. Wainwright, 372 U.S. 335, 83 S. Ct. 792, 9 L. Ed. 2d 799, 93 A.L.R.2d 733 (1963)—14:13, 22:11

Giffin, Matter of, 1997 WL 691473 (Ohio Ct. App. 4th Dist. Athens County 1997)—34:3

Gilbert, In re, 1987 WL 17709 (Ohio Ct. App. 12th Dist. Butler County 1987)—21:3

Gilbert, In re, 45 Ohio App. 2d 308, 74 Ohio Op. 2d 480, 345 N.E.2d 79 (9th Dist. Summit County 1974)—23:31, 34:8

Gilbert, Matter of, 1990 WL 25084 (Ohio Ct. App. 3d Dist. Marion County 1990)—25:9, 30:10, 30:12

Gilbert, Matter of, 1996 WL 435426 (Ohio Ct. App. 12th Dist. Butler County 1996)—26:6, 30:11

Gilbert v. California, 388 U.S. 263, 87 S. Ct. 1951, 18 L. Ed. 2d 1178 (1967)—14:12, 14:13

Gillespie, In re, 150 Ohio App. 3d 502, 2002-Ohio-7025, 782 N.E.2d 140 (10th Dist. Franklin County 2002)—3:3, 19:9

Gishwiler v. Dodez, 4 Ohio St. 615, 1855 WL 28 (1855)—30:11

Gladys R., In re, 1 Cal. 3d 855, 83 Cal. Rptr. 671, 464 P.2d 127 (1970)—2:6

Glenn, In re, 139 Ohio App. 3d 105, 742 N.E.2d 1210 (8th Dist. Cuyahoga County 2000)—23:5, 30:10

Glenn, No. 35352 (8th Dist. Ct. App., Cuyahoga, 1-20-77), In re—23:30

Globe Newspaper Co. v. Superior Court for Norfolk County, 457 U.S. 596, 102 S. Ct. 2613, 73 L. Ed. 2d 248 (1982)—23:11

G. M. K. v. State, 312 So. 2d 538 (Fla. Dist. Ct. App. 2d Dist. 1975)—23:9

Godinez v. Moran, 509 U.S. 389, 113 S. Ct. 2680, 125 L. Ed. 2d 321 (1993)—23:4, 23:7, 23:9

Goff, In re, 2003-Ohio-6768, 2003 WL 22952808 (Ohio Ct. App. 11th Dist. Portage County 2003)—18:2

Goins, In re, 137 Ohio App. 3d 158, 738 N.E.2d 385 (12th Dist. Clinton County 1999)—14:10

Goldberg v. Kelly, 397 U.S. 254, 90 S. Ct. 1011, 25 L. Ed. 2d 287 (1970)—23:22

Good, In re, 118 Ohio App. 3d 371, 692 N.E.2d 1072 (12th Dist. Butler County 1997)—1:6, 16:8

Goodwin, Matter of, 1998 WL 517688 (Ohio Ct. App. 5th Dist. Licking County 1998)—31:3

Gordon, In re, 2002-Ohio-4959, 2002 WL 31107543 (Ohio Ct. App. 11th Dist. Trumbull County 2002)—26:6

Gordon, Matter of, 1990 WL 138358 (Ohio Ct. App. 12th Dist. Madison County 1990)—30:11

Gordon, Matter of, 1996 WL 434122 (Ohio Ct. App. 4th Dist. Gallia County 1996)—30:11

Goshorn, In re, 82 Ohio L. Abs. 599, 167 N.E.2d 148 (Juv. Ct. 1959)—17:2

Graham, In re, 147 Ohio App. 3d 452, 2002-Ohio-2407, 770 N.E.2d 1123 (7th Dist. Mahoning County 2002)—22:4, 22:7, 23:9

Graham, In re, 2002-Ohio-6615, 2002 WL 31718885 (Ohio Ct. App. 7th Dist. Mahoning County 2002)—27:15

Grand Jury Proceedings of John Doe v. U.S., 842 F.2d 244, 25 Fed. R. Evid. Serv. 1081 (10th Cir. 1988)—23:15

Graybill/Rowe Children, In re, 77 Ohio St. 3d 373, 1997-Ohio-267, 674 N.E.2d 676 (1997)—30:6

Greaser, In re, 1995 WL 767983 (Ohio Ct. App. 5th Dist. Stark County 1995)—3:3

Green, In re, 18 Ohio App. 3d 43, 480 N.E.2d 492 (2d Dist. Montgomery County 1984)—21:6, 23:13, 23:19

Green, In re, 4 Ohio App. 3d 196, 447 N.E.2d 129 (10th Dist. Franklin County 1982)—23:8, 23:9

Green, Matter of, 1990 WL 190134 (Ohio Ct. App. 10th Dist. Franklin County 1990)—34:4

Greene, Matter of, 1992 WL 341385 (Ohio Ct. App. 10th Dist. Franklin County 1992)—31:5

Gregory v. Flowers, 32 Ohio St. 2d 48, 61 Ohio Op. 2d 295, 290 N.E.2d 181 (1972)—1:8

Griffin, In re, 1996 WL 547921 (Ohio Ct. App. 3d Dist. Union County 1996)—33:6

Griffin v. California, 380 U.S. 609, 85 S. Ct. 1229, 14 L. Ed. 2d 106 (1965)—22:14, 23:27

Griffin v. Illinois, 351 U.S. 12, 76 S. Ct. 585, 100 L. Ed. 891, 55 A.L.R.2d 1055 (1956)—23:30

Grimes, In re, 147 Ohio App. 3d 192, 2002-Ohio-1547, 769 N.E.2d 420 (7th Dist. Monroe County 2002)—23:7

Grimes, Matter of, 1988 WL 80498 (Ohio Ct. App. 3d Dist. Logan County 1988)—31:4

Grimm, Matter of, 1993 WL 544362 (Ohio Ct. App. 5th Dist. Tuscarawas County 1993)—25:4

Groh v. Ramirez, 124 S. Ct. 1284, 157 L. Ed. 2d 1068 (U.S. 2004)—14:4

Grubbs, 1982 WL 5285 (Ohio Ct. App. 8th Dist. Cuyahoga County 1982)—10:3, 34:11

Guggenheim, People ex rel. v. Mucci, 77 Misc. 2d 41, 352 N.Y.S.2d 561 (Sup 1974)—22:13

Gustafson v. Florida, 414 U.S. 260, 94 S. Ct. 488, 38 L. Ed. 2d 456 (1973)—14:4

Guthrie, No. CA 6383 (2d Dist. Ct. App., Montgomery, 2-22-80), In re—9:3, 25:2, 25:9

Gutman, In re, 22 Ohio App. 2d 125, 51 Ohio Op. 2d 252, 259 N.E.2d 128 (1st Dist. Hamilton County 1969)—10:3, 10:5, 30:2

Guy, In re, 1997 WL 133527 (Ohio Ct. App. 12th Dist. Butler County 1997)—33:6

H

H------, In re, 24 Ohio Op. 2d 334, 92 Ohio L. Abs. 436, 192 N.E.2d 683 (Juv. Ct. 1963)—9:3, 10:3, 10:4

H., In re, 37 Ohio Misc. 123, 66 Ohio Op. 2d 178, 66 Ohio Op. 2d 368, 305 N.E.2d 815 (C.P. 1973)—9:6

H., In re, 71 Misc. 2d 1042, 337 N.Y.S.2d 118 (Fam. Ct. 1972)—15:2

Haas, In re, 45 Ohio App. 2d 187, 74 Ohio Op. 2d 231, 341 N.E.2d 638 (5th Dist. Stark County 1975)—25:7

Hadsell, No. 41004 (8th Dist. Ct. App., Cuyahoga, 6-19-80), In re—10:4, 16:14, 30:11

Hairston, In re, 1996 WL 465249 (Ohio Ct. App. 10th Dist. Franklin County 1996)—23:9, 25:7

Hale, Matter of, 1986 WL 4925 (Ohio Ct. App. 6th Dist. Wood County 1986)—27:6

Haley v. State of Ohio, 332 U.S. 596, 68 S. Ct. 302, 92 L. Ed. 224 (1948)—1:3, 14:9

Hall, In re, 65 Ohio App. 3d 88, 582 N.E.2d 1055 (10th Dist. Franklin County 1989)—27:13, 30:11

Hall, Matter of, 1991 WL 44356 (Ohio Ct. App. 12th Dist. Preble County 1991)—33:6

Hamil, In re, 69 Ohio St. 2d 97, 23 Ohio Op. 3d 151, 431 N.E.2d 317 (1982)—32:2

Hampton, In re, 24 Ohio App. 2d 69, 53 Ohio Op. 2d 192, 263 N.E.2d 910 (8th Dist. Cuyahoga County 1970)—23:31, 34:4

Handelsman v. Handelsman, 108 Ohio App. 30, 9 Ohio Op. 2d 101, 160 N.E.2d 543 (7th Dist. Columbiana County 1958)—3:2

Hannah, In re, 106 Ohio App. 3d 766, 667 N.E.2d 76 (8th Dist. Cuyahoga County 1995)—23:5, 23:30

Hansen v. State, 904 P.2d 811 (Wyo. 1995)—22:3

Hardesty v. Hardesty, 16 Ohio App. 3d 56, 474 N.E.2d 368 (10th Dist. Franklin County 1984)—3:2

Harding, In re, 1995 WL 28993 (Ohio Ct. App. 9th Dist. Summit County 1995)—18:2

Harding, Matter of, 1993 WL 7914 (Ohio Ct. App. 8th Dist. Cuyahoga County 1993)—30:10

Hare, Matter of, 1998 WL 118039 (Ohio Ct. App. 4th Dist. Scioto County 1998)—30:6, 31:3

Harman, In re, 63 Ohio Misc. 2d 529, 635 N.E.2d 96 (C.P. 1994)—27:14, 27:18

Harper, In re, 2003-Ohio-6666, 2003 WL 22927248 (Ohio Ct. App. 2d Dist. Montgomery County 2003)—24:8

Harris, In Interest of, 218 Kan. 625, 544 P.2d 1403 (1976)—22:13

Harris, In re, 104 Ohio App. 3d 324, 662 N.E.2d 34 (2d Dist. Montgomery County 1995)—23:9

Harris, Matter of, 1995 WL 472917 (Ohio Ct. App. 8th Dist. Cuyahoga County 1995)—30:6, 33:4

Harris v. Alvis, 61 Ohio L. Abs. 311, 104 N.E.2d 182 (Ct. App. 2d Dist. Franklin County 1950)—2:4

Harris v. New York, 401 U.S. 222, 91 S. Ct. 643, 28 L. Ed. 2d 1 (1971)—14:9, 14:10

Harris, State ex rel. v. Anderson, 76 Ohio St. 3d 193, 1996-Ohio-412, 667 N.E.2d 1 (1996)—3:3, 22:4

Harrison, In re Guardianship of, 60 Ohio App. 3d 19, 572 N.E.2d 855 (1st Dist. Hamilton County 1989)—3:3

Harshey, In re, 40 Ohio App. 2d 157, 69 Ohio Op. 2d 165, 318 N.E.2d 544, 83 A.L.R.3d 815 (8th Dist. Cuyahoga County 1974)—9:9

Hart, Matter of, 1993 WL 69694 (Ohio Ct. App. 3d Dist. Marion County 1993)—30:12, 31:8

Hart, Matter of, 1998 WL 183863 (Ohio Ct. App. 8th Dist. Cuyahoga County 1998)—25:4

Hartman, In re, 2 Ohio St. 3d 154, 443 N.E.2d 516 (1983)—34:2

Hartney, In re, 1996 WL 137432 (Ohio Ct. App. 9th Dist. Summit County 1996)—31:6

Hartshorne v. Hartshorne, 89 Ohio L. Abs. 243, 185 N.E.2d 329 (Ct. App. 7th Dist. Columbiana County 1959)—3:2, 16:15

Harvey, In re, 222 Pa. Super. 222, 295 A.2d 93 (1972)—14:3

Haslam v. Haslam, 1981 WL 4801 (Ohio Ct. App. 7th Dist. Monroe County 1981)—16:15

Hatfield, In re, 2003-Ohio-5404, 2003 WL 22318010 (Ohio Ct. App. 4th Dist. Lawrence County 2003)—27:13

Haubeil, In re, 2002-Ohio-4095, 2002 WL 1823001 (Ohio Ct. App. 4th Dist. Ross County 2002)—14:10

Hay, In re, 1995 WL 324046 (Ohio Ct. App. 4th Dist. Lawrence County 1995)—9:3

Hayes, In re, 2002-Ohio-2446, 2002 WL 819216 (Ohio Ct. App. 5th Dist. Tuscarawas County 2002)—23:3

Hayes, In re, 29 Ohio App. 3d 162, 504 N.E.2d 491 (10th Dist. Franklin County 1986)—4:4, 23:20, 35:3

Hayes, In re, 62 Ohio App. 289, 16 Ohio Op. 10, 30 Ohio L. Abs. 568, 23 N.E.2d 956 (2d Dist. Franklin County 1939)—9:6, 10:3, 16:7

Hayes v. Municipal Court of Oklahoma City, 1971 OK CR 274, 487 P.2d 974 (Okla. Crim. App. 1971)—8:6

Haziel v. U. S., 404 F.2d 1275 (D.C. Cir. 1968)—22:11

Heater, In re, 1997 WL 117136 (Ohio Ct. App. 5th Dist. Stark County 1997)—17:3

Hederson, In re, 30 Ohio App. 3d 187, 507 N.E.2d 418 (9th Dist. Summit County 1986)—30:10

Height, In re, 47 Ohio App. 2d 203, 1 Ohio Op. 3d 279, 353 N.E.2d 887 (3d Dist. Van Wert County 1975)—16:15, 23:6

Heightland, No. 989 (4th Dist. Ct. App., Athens, 2-18-80), In re—10:3

Heising, Matter of, 29 Or. App. 903, 565 P.2d 1105 (1977)—22:17

Heist, In re, 11 Ohio Op. 537, 27 Ohio L. Abs. 1, 3 Ohio Supp. 259 (Juv. Ct. 1938)—1:6

Heller, State ex rel. v. Miller, 61 Ohio St. 2d 6, 15 Ohio Op. 3d 3, 399 N.E.2d 66 (1980)—9:2, 23:3, 23:30, 30:2, 34:9, 34:10

Hemphill v. Johnson, 31 Ohio App. 2d 241, 60 Ohio Op. 2d 404, 287 N.E.2d 828 (2d Dist. Montgomery County 1972)—2:4

Henderson, In re, 1997 WL 752633 (Ohio Ct. App. 11th Dist. Lake County 1997)—21:2

Henderson, In re, 2002-Ohio-2575, 2002 WL 1160073 (Ohio Ct. App. 12th Dist. Butler County 2002)—27:3

Hendrickson, In re, 114 Ohio App. 3d 290, 683 N.E.2d 76 (2d Dist. Greene County 1996)—23:9

Hennessey, In re, 146 Ohio App. 3d 743, 2001-Ohio-2267, 768 N.E.2d 663 (3d Dist. Mercer County 2001)—2:2, 19:2, 27:6, 27:18

Henry, State ex rel. v. Grossmann, 5 Ohio St. 3d 235, 450 N.E.2d 1156 (1983)—34:9

Hensley, In re, 1993 WL 119959 (Ohio Ct. App. 12th Dist. Butler County 1993)—30:11, 31:7

Herring, In re, 1996 WL 385611 (Ohio Ct. App. 9th Dist. Summit County 1996)—33:6

Hess, In re, 2003-Ohio-1429, 2003 WL 1465190 (Ohio Ct. App. 7th Dist. Jefferson County 2003)—31:5

Hester, In re, 1 Ohio App. 3d 24, 437 N.E.2d 1218 (10th Dist. Franklin County 1981)—14:2, 34:8

Hester, In re, 3 Ohio App. 3d 458, 446 N.E.2d 202 (10th Dist. Franklin County 1982)—21:3, 23:29, 34:11

Hester v. U.S., 265 U.S. 57, 44 S. Ct. 445, 68 L. Ed. 898 (1924)—14:4

Heston, In re, 129 Ohio App. 3d 825, 719 N.E.2d 93 (1st Dist. Hamilton County 1998)—23:5, 23:16

Heth, State ex rel. v. Moloney, 126 Ohio St. 526, 186 N.E. 362 (1933)—2:2

Hiatt, In re, 86 Ohio App. 3d 716, 621 N.E.2d 1222 (4th Dist. Adams County 1993)—26:6, 30:10, 30:12, 31:6

Hicks, No. H-78-7 (6th Dist. Ct. App., Huron, 11-17-78), In re—21:2

Higby, In re, 81 Ohio App. 3d 466, 611 N.E.2d 403 (9th Dist. Wayne County 1992)—30:10, 31:6

Hill, Matter of, 1993 WL 291068 (Ohio Ct. App. 3d Dist. Union County 1993)—27:19

Hinko, In re, 84 Ohio App. 3d 89, 616 N.E.2d 515 (8th Dist. Cuyahoga County 1992)—2:2, 23:4, 27:6, 32:2

Hitchcock, In re, 120 Ohio App. 3d 88, 696 N.E.2d 1090 (8th Dist. Cuyahoga County 1996)—18:2, 30:7, 31:9, 33:4, 34:3

Hitchcock, In re, 81 Ohio St. 3d 1222, 2000-Ohio-436, 689 N.E.2d 43 (1998)—23:30

Hitchcock, State ex rel. v. Cuyahoga Cty. Court of Common Pleas, Probate Div., 97 Ohio App. 3d 600, 647 N.E.2d 208 (8th Dist. Cuyahoga County 1994)—3:3, 33:4

Hobson, In re, 44 Ohio L. Abs. 85, 44 Ohio L. Abs. 86, 62 N.E.2d 510 (Ct. App. 2d Dist. [sic] Franklin County 1945)—10:3, 23:9, 24:7

Hodge/Burchett Children, In re, 1995 WL 470540 (Ohio Ct. App. 12th Dist. Butler County 1995)—30:10

Hodgkin, Matter of, 1990 WL 235496 (Ohio Ct. App. 12th Dist. Preble County 1990)—25:2

Hoff v. Hoff, 1993 WL 280455 (Ohio Ct. App. 9th Dist. Wayne County 1993)—30:10, 30:11, 31:6

Hoffman, In re, 97 Ohio St. 3d 92, 2002-Ohio-5368, 776 N.E.2d 485 (2002)—30:12

Hogan, Matter of, 1990 WL 178092 (Ohio Ct. App. 6th Dist. Lucas County 1990)—25:9, 25:14, 30:3, 30:12

Holcomb, In re, 147 Ohio App. 3d 31, 2002-Ohio-2042, 768 N.E.2d 722 (8th Dist. Cuyahoga County 2002)—23:9

Holcomb, In re Adoption of, 18 Ohio St. 3d 361, 481 N.E.2d 613 (1985)—23:13

Holcomb, No. 39694 (8th Dist. Ct. App., Cuyahoga, 10-4-79), In re—9:12, 10:3, 16:14, 25:12, 30:11, 30:12

Holewinski, Matter of, 1993 WL 155636 (Ohio Ct. App. 6th Dist. Lucas County 1993)—18:2, 25:9

Holley, In re, 107 R.I. 615, 268 A.2d 723 (1970)—14:13

Holley v. Higgins, 86 Ohio App. 3d 240, 620 N.E.2d 251 (10th Dist. Franklin County 1993)—23:3

Holloway, In re, 1997 WL 102016 (Ohio Ct. App. 2d Dist. Montgomery County 1997)—30:12

Holloway v. Arkansas, 435 U.S. 475, 98 S. Ct. 1173, 55 L. Ed. 2d 426 (1978)—23:5

Holloway v. Clermont County Dept. of Human Services, 80 Ohio St. 3d 128, 1997-Ohio-131, 684 N.E.2d 1217 (1997)—30:6, 34:12

Holmes, In re, 70 Ohio App. 2d 75, 24 Ohio Op. 3d 93, 434 N.E.2d 747 (1st Dist. Hamilton County 1980)—27:13, 34:4

Holtgreven, Matter of, 1995 WL 368841 (Ohio Ct. App. 3d Dist. Hancock County 1995)—25:7

Hommes, Matter of, 1996 WL 760920 (Ohio Ct. App. 11th Dist. Ashtabula County 1996)—30:11, 30:12

Honeycutt, Matter of, 1998 WL 124518 (Ohio Ct. App. 7th Dist. Belmont County 1998)—31:8

Hood v. Hood, 1991 WL 123045 (Ohio Ct. App. 9th Dist. Summit County 1991)—9:3, 25:3, 25:4

Hoodlet, In re, 72 Ohio App. 3d 115, 593 N.E.2d 478 (4th Dist. Athens County 1991)—18:2, 27:18, 30:3, 32:2

Hopkins, In re, 78 Ohio App. 3d 92, 603 N.E.2d 1138 (4th Dist. Hocking County 1992)—31:4, 31:5

Horton, Matter of, 1985 WL 4585 (Ohio Ct. App. 10th Dist. Franklin County 1985)—4:4

Horton v. California, 496 U.S. 128, 110 S. Ct. 2301, 110 L. Ed. 2d 112 (1990)—14:4

House, In re, 1992 WL 35038 (Ohio Ct. App. 12th Dist. Butler County 1992)—23:24

Houston, In re, 1998 WL 827608 (Ohio Ct. App. 8th Dist. Cuyahoga County 1998)—27:3

Howard, In re, 119 Ohio App. 3d 201, 695 N.E.2d 1 (1st Dist. Hamilton County 1997)—23:6

Howard, In re, 119 Ohio App. 3d 33, 694 N.E.2d 488 (12th Dist. Butler County 1997)—14:10, 23:23

Howard, In re, 150 Ohio App. 3d 1, 2002-Ohio-6004, 778 N.E.2d 1106 (7th Dist. Mahoning County 2002)—33:9

Howard, In re, 31 Ohio App. 3d 1, 508 N.E.2d 190 (1st Dist. Hamilton County 1987)—14:3, 14:14, 16:8

Howard v. Catholic Social Serv. of Cuyahoga Cty., Inc., 70 Ohio St. 3d 141, 1994-Ohio-219, 637 N.E.2d 890 (1994)—34:4, 34:11, 34:12

Howard, State ex rel. v. Ferreri, 70 Ohio St. 3d 587, 1994-Ohio-234, 639 N.E.2d 1189 (1994)—23:30, 34:9, 35:2

Howard, State ex rel. v. Ferreri, No. 66559 (8th Dist. Ct. App., Cuyahoga, 2-10-94)—25:4

Howell, In re Adoption of, 77 Ohio App. 3d 80, 601 N.E.2d 92 (4th Dist. Lawrence County 1991)—23:6

Howell, No. 79-CA-16 (5th Dist. Ct. App., Coshocton, 1-31-80), In re—10:3, 25:4

Howser v. Ashtabula County Children's Services Board, 1983 WL 6096 (Ohio Ct. App. 11th Dist. Ashtabula County 1983)—16:1

Hua, In re, 62 Ohio St. 2d 227, 16 Ohio Op. 3d 270, 405 N.E.2d 255 (1980)—30:11

Huber, In re, 1995 WL 765940 (Ohio Ct. App. 2d Dist. Montgomery County 1995)—30:12

Hudson v. Palmer, 468 U.S. 517, 104 S. Ct. 3194, 82 L. Ed. 2d 393 (1984)—14:4

Hughes, Matter of, 1990 WL 7970 (Ohio Ct. App. 3d Dist. Logan County 1990)—31:4

Hughes v. Scaffide, 58 Ohio St. 2d 88, 12 Ohio Op. 3d 92, 388 N.E.2d 1233 (1979)—9:2, 9:5

Hughes v. State, 653 A.2d 241 (Del. 1994)—22:3

Hughley, In re, 1998 WL 57380 (Ohio Ct. App. 1st Dist. Hamilton County 1998)—27:3

Hulsey, Matter of, 1995 WL 544019 (Ohio Ct. App. 4th Dist. Adams County 1995)—25:14

Hunt, In re, 46 Ohio St. 2d 378, 75 Ohio Op. 2d 450, 348 N.E.2d 727 (1976)—16:12, 16:17, 34:12

Hunter, In re, 99 Ohio Misc. 2d 107, 716 N.E.2d 802 (C.P. 1999)—22:15

Hurlow, Matter of, 1997 WL 701328 (Ohio Ct. App. 4th Dist. Gallia County 1997)—31:8, 34:4, 34:11

Hurlow, Matter of, 1998 WL 655414 (Ohio Ct. App. 4th Dist. Gallia County 1998)—30:11

Husk, In re, 2002-Ohio-4000, 2002 WL 1803698 (Ohio Ct. App. 4th Dist. Washington County 2002)—23:4

Hutchison, 1982 WL 3455 (Ohio Ct. App. 4th Dist. Lawrence County 1982)—16:14, 16:17, 18:3

Huxley v. Huxley, 1984 WL 6176 (Ohio Ct. App. 9th Dist. Wayne County 1984)—3:3

Hyrb, No. 36910 (8th Dist. Ct. App., Cuyahoga, 12-1-77), In re—10:3

I

Illinois v. Allen, 397 U.S. 337, 90 S. Ct. 1057, 25 L. Ed. 2d 353 (1970)—23:12, 23:23, 23:26

Illinois v. Gates, 462 U.S. 213, 103 S. Ct. 2317, 76 L. Ed. 2d 527 (1983)—14:4

Illinois v. Lafayette, 462 U.S. 640, 103 S. Ct. 2605, 77 L. Ed. 2d 65 (1983)—14:4

Illinois v. Perkins, 496 U.S. 292, 110 S. Ct. 2394, 110 L. Ed. 2d 243 (1990)—14:11

Illinois v. Rodriguez, 497 U.S. 177, 110 S. Ct. 2793, 111 L. Ed. 2d 148 (1990)—14:5

Illinois v. Vitale, 447 U.S. 410, 100 S. Ct. 2260, 65 L. Ed. 2d 228 (1980)—1:4, 23:2, 23:31

Infant Boy Reed, Matter of, 1990 WL 187177 (Ohio Ct. App. 7th Dist. Columbiana County 1990)—16:13

Infant Female Luallen, In re, 27 Ohio App. 3d 29, 499 N.E.2d 358 (1st Dist. Hamilton County 1985)—10:5, 18:2

Inge v. Slayton, 395 F. Supp. 560 (E.D. Va. 1975)—22:3, 22:11

In Koogle, 1983 WL 2461 (Ohio Ct. App. 2d Dist. Greene County 1983)—
    18:2, 32:2

In Matter of Ackert, 1996 WL 72617 (Ohio Ct. App. 5th Dist. Holmes County
    1996)—26:3, 30:12

In Matter of Bailey D., 1998 WL 196287 (Ohio Ct. App. 6th Dist. Lucas
    County 1998)—25:4

In Matter of Barr, 1996 WL 608465 (Ohio Ct. App. 5th Dist. Stark County
    1996)—16:16

In Matter of Black, 1997 WL 567924 (Ohio Ct. App. 3d Dist. Defiance County
    1997)—30:4, 30:7

In Matter of Bowers, 1998 WL 46360 (Ohio Ct. App. 2d Dist. Greene County
    1998)—2:6

In Matter of Brandon M., 1998 WL 196288 (Ohio Ct. App. 6th Dist. Lucas
    County 1998)—30:12

In Matter of Brown, 1998 WL 430028 (Ohio Ct. App. 5th Dist. Richland
    County 1998)—28:5, 34:4

In Matter of Buchanan, 1997 WL 451472 (Ohio Ct. App. 2d Dist. Clark
    County 1997)—30:13

In Matter of Bundy, 1981 WL 6034 (Ohio Ct. App. 4th Dist. Lawrence County
    1981)—16:17

In Matter of Bunting Children, 1995 WL 507604 (Ohio Ct. App. 5th Dist.
    Stark County 1995)—30:6

In Matter of Burrows, 17 A.D.D. 379 (Ohio Ct. App. 4th Dist. Athens County
    1996)—30:12, 31:7

In Matter of Butler, 1996 WL 132238 (Ohio Ct. App. 5th Dist. Stark County
    1996)—26:6

In Matter of Buzzard, 1995 WL 739890 (Ohio Ct. App. 10th Dist. Franklin
    County 1995)—16:14, 30:12

In Matter of Cantrell, 1996 WL 363816 (Ohio Ct. App. 5th Dist. Licking
    County 1996)—17:4

In Matter of Caputo, 1998 WL 170205 (Ohio Ct. App. 12th Dist. Butler
    County 1998)—34:4, 34:5

In Matter of Carroll, 1996 WL 535302 (Ohio Ct. App. 2d Dist. Greene County
    1996)—9:7

In Matter of Christopher B., 1997 WL 379631 (Ohio Ct. App. 6th Dist. Lucas
    County 1997)—30:12, 34:5

In Matter of Ciara B., 1998 WL 355869 (Ohio Ct. App. 6th Dist. Lucas County
    1998)—18:2, 34:3

In Matter of Cooperman, 1995 WL 23162 (Ohio Ct. App. 8th Dist. Cuyahoga
    County 1995)—30:8, 30:10

In Matter of Copeland, 1995 WL 453422 (Ohio Ct. App. 11th Dist. Ashtabula
    County 1995)—25:7, 27:3

In Matter of Crenshaw, 1997 WL 219118 (Ohio Ct. App. 5th Dist. Stark
    County 1997)—16:14, 30:4, 30:6, 30:13, 31:7

In Matter of Crosten, 1996 WL 130937 (Ohio Ct. App. 4th Dist. Athens
    County 1996)—31:8

In Matter of Davis, 1995 WL 723155 (Ohio Ct. App. 3d Dist. Marion County
    1995)—25:2

In Matter of Davis, 1996 WL 752861 (Ohio Ct. App. 5th Dist. Stark County
    1996)—25:4

In Matter of Davon B., 1997 WL 243574 (Ohio Ct. App. 6th Dist. Lucas
    County 1997)—25:9

In Matter of Dingess, 1997 WL 282191 (Ohio Ct. App. 4th Dist. Scioto County
    1997)—18:2

In Matter of Dodson, 1996 WL 98730 (Ohio Ct. App. 3d Dist. Shelby County 1996)—9:12, 30:4, 30:5

In Matter Of: Escue, 1981 WL 5930 (Ohio Ct. App. 4th Dist. Lawrence County 1981)—10:3, 16:14, 30:2

In Matter of Evener, 1981 WL 6031 (Ohio Ct. App. 4th Dist. Athens County 1981)—16:14

In Matter of Gipson, 1997 WL 665741 (Ohio Ct. App. 3d Dist. Hardin County 1997)—31:8

In Matter of Greenwalt, 1993 WL 116111 (Ohio Ct. App. 5th Dist. Tuscarawas County 1993)—31:8

In Matter of Greer, 1996 WL 753162 (Ohio Ct. App. 5th Dist. Guernsey County 1996)—30:6

In Matter of Hainline, 1995 WL 9402 (Ohio Ct. App. 3d Dist. Van Wert County 1995)—25:14

In Matter of Hattery, 1986 WL 9657 (Ohio Ct. App. 3d Dist. Marion County 1986)—31:4

In Matter of Hendricks, 1996 WL 202856 (Ohio Ct. App. 11th Dist. Ashtabula County 1996)—25:7, 30:10

In Matter of Heyman, 1996 WL 465238 (Ohio Ct. App. 10th Dist. Franklin County 1996)—30:11

In Matter of Hill, 1997 WL 473098 (Ohio Ct. App. 8th Dist. Cuyahoga County 1997)—34:4

In Matter of Hoeflick, 1995 WL 495829 (Ohio Ct. App. 5th Dist. Licking County 1995)—30:12

In Matter of Jane Doe, 1990 WL 640269 (Ohio Ct. App. 8th Dist. Cuyahoga County 1990)—12:9, 34:6

In Matter of Johnson, 1995 WL 229118 (Ohio Ct. App. 8th Dist. Cuyahoga County 1995)—25:4

In Matter of Jones, 1996 WL 724757 (Ohio Ct. App. 9th Dist. Lorain County 1996)—25:4

In Matter of Keck, 1997 WL 473097 (Ohio Ct. App. 8th Dist. Cuyahoga County 1997)—23:9

In Matter of Keller, 1994 WL 695338 (Ohio Ct. App. 8th Dist. Cuyahoga County 1994)—25:4, 30:6

In Matter of Kelly, 1995 WL 656944 (Ohio Ct. App. 10th Dist. Franklin County 1995)—27:3, 27:18, 33:6

In Matter of Kennedy, 1995 WL 495816 (Ohio Ct. App. 5th Dist. Guernsey County 1995)—25:9

In Matter of King, 1996 WL 368236 (Ohio Ct. App. 3d Dist. Auglaize County 1996)—32:2

In Matter of Kirksey Children, 1996 WL 74086 (Ohio Ct. App. 5th Dist. Stark County 1996)—30:6

In Matter of Knotts, 1997 WL 38084 (Ohio Ct. App. 3d Dist. Mercer County 1997)—30:6, 31:7

In Matter of Kost, 1994 WL 24374 (Ohio Ct. App. 10th Dist. Franklin County 1994)—33:4

In Matter of Lawson/Reid Children, 1997 WL 189379 (Ohio Ct. App. 2d Dist. Clark County 1997)—25:14, 30:12, 31:8

In Matter of Lewis, 1997 WL 217573 (Ohio Ct. App. 4th Dist. Athens County 1997)—30:6

In Matter of Lloyd, 1997 WL 115886 (Ohio Ct. App. 5th Dist. Richland County 1997)—23:7

In Matter of Marrs, 1998 WL 896669 (Ohio Ct. App. 2d Dist. Clark County 1998)—30:10

In Matter of Marshall, 1996 WL 648742 (Ohio Ct. App. 11th Dist. Geauga County 1996)—31:8

In Matter of Matis, 1995 WL 314683 (Ohio Ct. App. 9th Dist. Summit County 1995)—18:2, 30:10

In Matter of McKenzie, 1995 WL 608285 (Ohio Ct. App. 9th Dist. Wayne County 1995)—31:8

In Matter of McKinley, 1998 WL 355874 (Ohio Ct. App. 7th Dist. Belmont County 1998)—27:18

In Matter of Mills, 1996 WL 132286 (Ohio Ct. App. 5th Dist. Licking County 1996)—30:10, 30:11

In Matter of Myer, 1981 WL 6316 (Ohio Ct. App. 5th Dist. Delaware County 1981)—23:6

In Matter of N.B., 1996 WL 174546 (Ohio Ct. App. 12th Dist. Butler County 1996)—21:5, 25:4

In Matter of Neighbors, 1993 WL 564218 (Ohio Ct. App. 5th Dist. Richland County 1993)—23:14, 25:2

In Matter of Nelson, 1996 WL 200618 (Ohio Ct. App. 11th Dist. Geauga County 1996)—18:2, 31:9, 34:3

In Matter of Nelson, 1999 WL 4273 (Ohio Ct. App. 5th Dist. Stark County 1998)—30:12

In Matter of Parker, 1981 WL 6774 (Ohio Ct. App. 3d Dist. Van Wert County 1981)—9:3, 10:3, 16:12, 25:2, 34:11

In Matter of Price, 1997 WL 126833 (Ohio Ct. App. 3d Dist. Marion County 1997)—10:2, 25:4

In Matter of Pritt, 1996 WL 132250 (Ohio Ct. App. 5th Dist. Stark County 1996)—25:4

In Matter of Reid, 1998 WL 409115 (Ohio Ct. App. 3d Dist. Paulding County 1998)—30:11

In Matter of Rhodes, 1997 WL 143942 (Ohio Ct. App. 10th Dist. Franklin County 1997)—16:8, 16:17

In Matter of Ritter, 1996 WL 635798 (Ohio Ct. App. 11th Dist. Trumbull County 1996)—31:5

In Matter of Rivera, 1996 WL 476448 (Ohio Ct. App. 8th Dist. Cuyahoga County 1996)—16:12

In Matter of Robinson, 1997 WL 599156 (Ohio Ct. App. 4th Dist. Scioto County 1997)—30:10

In Matter of Rundio, 1993 WL 379512 (Ohio Ct. App. 4th Dist. Pickaway County 1993)—18:2, 30:2, 34:3

In Matter of Rushing, 1981 WL 6066 (Ohio Ct. App. 4th Dist. Lawrence County 1981)—23:3

In Matter of Seven A. Children, 1995 WL 557329 (Ohio Ct. App. 6th Dist. Fulton County 1995)—26:6, 30:11

In Matter of Shawn W., 1996 WL 549223 (Ohio Ct. App. 6th Dist. Lucas County 1996)—30:8, 30:10

In Matter of Short, 1981 WL 6049 (Ohio Ct. App. 4th Dist. Lawrence County 1981)—34:4

In Matter Of: Skeens, 1982 WL 3994 (Ohio Ct. App. 10th Dist. Franklin County 1982)—27:19

In Matter of Spaulding, 1993 WL 115934 (Ohio Ct. App. 6th Dist. Lucas County 1993)—23:6, 25:9, 33:4

In Matter of Stamper, 1997 WL 722784 (Ohio Ct. App. 3d Dist. Union County 1997)—30:13

In Matter of Stewart, 1996 WL 703406 (Ohio Ct. App. 11th Dist. Portage County 1996)—10:5, 31:8

In Matter of Surfer, 1998 WL 231012 (Ohio Ct. App. 10th Dist. Franklin County 1998)—10:6

In Matter of Taeovonni, 1995 WL 495564 (Ohio Ct. App. 5th Dist. Tuscarawas County 1995)—25:4

In Matter of Thomas, 1995 WL 363895 (Ohio Ct. App. 8th Dist. Cuyahoga County 1995)—33:2

In Matter Of: Tovar, 1984 WL 5678 (Ohio Ct. App. 4th Dist. Lawrence County 1984)—18:2

In Matter of Trent, 1988 WL 36361 (Ohio Ct. App. 4th Dist. Ross County 1988)—16:13

In Matter of Velentine, 1995 WL 498958 (Ohio Ct. App. 5th Dist. Coshocton County 1995)—25:4

In Matter of Voshel, 1995 WL 256186 (Ohio Ct. App. 9th Dist. Wayne County 1995)—18:2

In Matter of Webb, 1995 WL 499007 (Ohio Ct. App. 5th Dist. Stark County 1995)—30:12

In Matter of Webster Children, 1996 WL 132234 (Ohio Ct. App. 5th Dist. Stark County 1996)—33:8

In Matter of Wilson Children, 1996 WL 363434 (Ohio Ct. App. 5th Dist. Stark County 1996)—26:4

In Matter of Yearian, 1996 WL 589264 (Ohio Ct. App. 11th Dist. Portage County 1996)—18:2

In Re Coe, 1983 WL 5648 (Ohio Ct. App. 5th Dist. Stark County 1983)—16:13

In Re: Davis, 1982 WL 2959 (Ohio Ct. App. 5th Dist. Tuscarawas County 1982)—16:8

In Re: Hunter, 1984 WL 5445 (Ohio Ct. App. 8th Dist. Cuyahoga County 1984)—21:2

In Re: Johnson, 1983 WL 2516 (Ohio Ct. App. 2d Dist. Montgomery County 1983)—23:7

In Re King, 1981 WL 4228 (Ohio Ct. App. 9th Dist. Summit County 1981)—18:3

In Re: Martin, 1981 WL 6463 (Ohio Ct. App. 5th Dist. Ashland County 1981)—28:10

In Re: Michelee Blankenship v. Collmar, 1981 WL 3920 (Ohio Ct. App. 9th Dist. Summit County 1981)—16:14

In Re Miller, 1984 WL 7022 (Ohio Ct. App. 1st Dist. Hamilton County 1984)—18:2, 31:8

In Re P. C., 2004-Ohio-1230, 2004 WL 509368 (Ohio Ct. App. 9th Dist. Summit County 2004)—30:11

In Re Ridenour, 2004-Ohio-1958, at ¶ 47, 2004 WL 834579 (Ohio Ct. App. 11th Dist. Lake County)—23:6

In Re: Spears, 1984 WL 5682 (Ohio Ct. App. 4th Dist. Athens County 1984)—16:12, 18:2

In Re: Vaughn, 1987 WL 18479 (Ohio Ct. App. 8th Dist. Cuyahoga County 1987)—32:2

In the Interest of Way, 319 So. 2d 651 (Miss. 1975)—23:21

In the Matter Bell, 1981 WL 6690 (Ohio Ct. App. 3d Dist. Shelby County 1981)—16:14, 18:2

In the Matter Finley, 1984 WL 6377 (Ohio Ct. App. 8th Dist. Cuyahoga County 1984)—14:14

In the Matter Hawkins, 1981 WL 6687 (Ohio Ct. App. 3d Dist. Marion County 1981)—10:3

In the Matter of Anonymous, 2003 WL 23325701 (Ala. Ct. Civil App.)—12:2

In the Matter of Banks Griggs v. Griggs Banks Jones, 1981 WL 5593 (Ohio Ct. App. 6th Dist. Lucas County 1981)—16:14, 18:3, 23:9, 30:11

In the Matter Of: Crisp, 1981 WL 2983 (Ohio Ct. App. 10th Dist. Franklin County 1981)—10:3

In the Matter Of: Daniels, 1981 WL 3907 (Ohio Ct. App. 9th Dist. Summit County 1981)—16:17

In the Matter Of: Dolibor, 1981 WL 5953 (Ohio Ct. App. 4th Dist. Ross County 1981)—16:16

In the Matter Of: Espy, 1982 WL 2490 (Ohio Ct. App. 8th Dist. Cuyahoga County 1982)—30:10, 30:11, 31:7

In the Matter of Ewing, 1983 WL 4671 (Ohio Ct. App. 8th Dist. Cuyahoga County 1983)—34:11

In the Matter Of: Foos, 1985 WL 7370 (Ohio Ct. App. 3d Dist. Marion County 1985)—30:10

In the Matter of Hawkins, 1983 WL 4091 (Ohio Ct. App. 9th Dist. Lorain County 1983)—14:9, 14:10, 23:15

In the Matter Of: Hollins, 1983 WL 5102 (Ohio Ct. App. 5th Dist. Guernsey County 1983)—30:12

In the Matter Of: Kahan, 1982 WL 6596 (Ohio Ct. App. 6th Dist. Lucas County 1982)—23:8

In the Matter of Kuhn, 1982 WL 3392 (Ohio Ct. App. 4th Dist. Pickaway County 1982)—9:7, 10:2

In the Matter of Lenard, 1984 WL 4275 (Ohio Ct. App. 4th Dist. Athens County 1984)—30:8

In the Matter Of: Lewis, 1982 WL 3527 (Ohio Ct. App. 4th Dist. Lawrence County 1982)—16:14

In the Matter Of: Lucas, 1982 WL 3444 (Ohio Ct. App. 4th Dist. Lawrence County 1982)—30:10

In the Matter of Nicholson, 1983 WL 3291 (Ohio Ct. App. 4th Dist. Hocking County 1983)—9:7

In the Matter of Pollard, 1981 WL 4690 (Ohio Ct. App. 8th Dist. Cuyahoga County 1981)—4:4

In the Matter of Price, 1981 WL 4645 (Ohio Ct. App. 8th Dist. Cuyahoga County 1981)—10:5, 19:7

In the Matter of Quillen, 1981 WL 5841 (Ohio Ct. App. 6th Dist. Huron County 1981)—8:3

In the Matter Of: Skaggs, 1981 WL 5904 (Ohio Ct. App. 4th Dist. Scioto County 1981)—25:2, 31:7

In the Matter Of: Stewart, 1985 WL 7212 (Ohio Ct. App. 5th Dist. Licking County 1985)—31:8

In the Matter Of: Strowbridge, 1982 WL 3565 (Ohio Ct. App. 4th Dist. Lawrence County 1982)—16:14, 23:6

In the Matter of Thomas, 1983 WL 4689 (Ohio Ct. App. 8th Dist. Cuyahoga County 1983)—14:3

In the Matter Of: Wellinger, 1983 WL 2645 (Ohio Ct. App. 8th Dist. Cuyahoga County 1983)—30:10, 30:11, 31:7

In the Matter Of: Wiseman, 1981 WL 6404 (Ohio Ct. App. 5th Dist. Licking County 1981)—10:3

In the Matter of Wurtzel, 1984 WL 4268 (Ohio Ct. App. 4th Dist. Pickaway County 1984)—31:8

Iowa v. Tovar, 124 S. Ct. 1379, 158 L. Ed. 2d 209 (U.S. 2004)—23:9

Ironton, City of v. Bundy, 98 Ohio App. 416, 57 Ohio Op. 451, 129 N.E.2d 831 (4th Dist. Lawrence County 1954)—16:16

Isiah B., In Interest of, 176 Wis. 2d 639, 500 N.W.2d 637, 83 Ed. Law Rep. 419 (1993)—14:6

Ison, In re, 47 Ohio App. 3d 103, 547 N.E.2d 420 (9th Dist. Wayne County 1989)—30:10

J

Jackson, In re, 21 Ohio St. 2d 215, 50 Ohio Op. 2d 447, 257 N.E.2d 74 (1970)—22:14, 22:24

Jackson, In re, 46 Mich. App. 764, 208 N.W.2d 526 (1973)—14:3

Jackson v. State, 17 Md. App. 167, 300 A.2d 430 (1973)—14:13

Jacobs, In re, 148 Ohio App. 3d 173, 2002-Ohio-2844, 772 N.E.2d 671 (3d Dist. Seneca County 2002)—27:13, 28:5

Jacquawn J., Matter of, 1997 WL 458038 (Ohio Ct. App. 6th Dist. Sandusky County 1997)—18:2

Jahnke v. State, 692 P.2d 911 (Wyo. 1984)—22:3

James v. Child Welfare Bd., 9 Ohio App. 2d 299, 38 Ohio Op. 2d 347, 224 N.E.2d 358 (9th Dist. Summit County 1967)—3:3

James v. Cox, 323 F. Supp. 15 (E.D. Va. 1971)—22:11, 22:12

James D., In re, 43 Cal. 3d 903, 239 Cal. Rptr. 663, 741 P.2d 161, 41 Ed. Law Rep. 722 (1987)—14:3

James J., Matter of, 1995 WL 283884 (Ohio Ct. App. 6th Dist. Huron County 1995)—25:5

James, No. 30608 (8th Dist. Ct. App., Cuyahoga, 2-3-72), In re—16:16

Jandrew, Matter of, 1997 WL 802848 (Ohio Ct. App. 4th Dist. Washington County 1997)—9:15, 10:5

Jane Doe, In re, 135 Ohio App. 3d 719, 735 N.E.2d 504 (4th Dist. Scioto County 1999)—12:7

Jane Doe, In re Complaint of, 134 Ohio App. 3d 569, 731 N.E.2d 751 (4th Dist. Athens County 1999)—12:9

Jane Doe, In re Complaint of, 83 Ohio App. 3d 904, 615 N.E.2d 1142 (10th Dist. Franklin County 1992)—12:9

Jane Doe, In re Complaint of, 83 Ohio App. 3d 98, 613 N.E.2d 1112 (10th Dist. Franklin County 1993)—12:9

Jane Doe, In re Complaint of, 96 Ohio App. 3d 435, 645 N.E.2d 134 (10th Dist. Franklin County 1994)—12:9

Jane Doe 93-1, No. 66355 (8th Dist. Ct. App., Cuyahoga, 11-1-93), In re—12:9

Jane Doe 1, In re, 57 Ohio St. 3d 135, 566 N.E.2d 1181 (1991)—12:9

Jane Doe 01-01, In re, 141 Ohio App. 3d 20, 749 N.E.2d 807 (8th Dist. Cuyahoga County 2001)—12:4, 12:9

Janie M., In re, 131 Ohio App. 3d 637, 723 N.E.2d 191 (6th Dist. Lucas County 1999)—23:3, 23:6

Januszewski, Ex parte, 196 F. 123 (C.C.S.D. Ohio 1911)—1:6, 23:10

Jasmine V., Matter of, 1997 WL 440921 (Ohio Ct. App. 6th Dist. Williams County 1997)—27:3

Jason R., In re, 77 Ohio Misc. 2d 37, 666 N.E.2d 666 (C.P. 1995)—23:23, 25:5

Jasper, Matter of, 1998 WL 729234 (Ohio Ct. App. 12th Dist. Warren County 1998)—31:9

J.B., In re, 71 Ohio Misc. 2d 63, 654 N.E.2d 216 (C.P. 1995)—2:3, 22:5, 33:5

J.D., In re, 2004-Ohio-358, 2004 WL 170338 (Ohio Ct. App. 8th Dist. Cuyahoga County 2004)—31:5

Jeffrey C., In re, 81 Misc. 2d 651, 366 N.Y.S.2d 826 (Fam. Ct. 1975)—23:7

Jehovah's Witnesses in State of Wash. v. King County Hospital Unit No. 1 (Harborview), 278 F. Supp. 488 (W.D. Wash. 1967)—9:7

Jenkins, In re, 101 Ohio App. 3d 177, 655 N.E.2d 238 (12th Dist. Butler County 1995)—23:9

Jenkins v. Anderson, 447 U.S. 231, 100 S. Ct. 2124, 65 L. Ed. 2d 86 (1980)—
14:10

Jennifer L., Matter of, 1998 WL 230808 (Ohio Ct. App. 6th Dist. Lucas
County 1998)—18:2, 30:12

Jennings, Matter of, 1993 WL 99444 (Ohio Ct. App. 3d Dist. Allen County
1993)—30:10

Jensen, Matter of, 54 Or. App. 1, 633 P.2d 1302 (1981)—9:7

Jeroncic, Matter of, 1991 WL 127255 (Ohio Ct. App. 8th Dist. Cuyahoga
County 1991)—31:6, 31:8

Jesse McM., In re, 105 Cal. App. 3d 187, 164 Cal. Rptr. 199 (1st Dist. 1980)—
23:11

Jessica M. B., In re, 2004-Ohio-1040, 2004 WL 413307 (Ohio Ct. App. 6th
Dist. Ottawa County 2004)—25:4

J. F., In re, 17 Ohio Misc. 40, 46 Ohio Op. 2d 49, 242 N.E.2d 604 (Juv. Ct.
1968)—33:5

J. H., In re, 2003-Ohio-5611, 2003 WL 22399693 (Ohio Ct. App. 9th Dist.
Summit County 2003)—30:11

J.J., In re, 2004-Ohio-1429, 2004 WL 574135 (Ohio Ct. App. 9th Dist. Summit County)—23:9

J.J., In re, 64 Ohio App. 3d 806, 582 N.E.2d 1138 (12th Dist. Butler County
1990)—10:5, 30:4, 32:2

J. M., State ex rel. v. Taylor, 166 W. Va. 511, 276 S.E.2d 199, 25 A.L.R.4th
1063 (1981)—23:4, 23:9

J.O., In re, 2004-Ohio-2121, 2004 WL 894571 (Ohio Ct. App. 9th Dist. Wayne
County 2004)—30:11

Joanne M., In re, 103 Ohio App. 3d 447, 659 N.E.2d 864 (6th Dist. Lucas
County 1995)—23:11

Joey O., Matter of, 1997 WL 785621 (Ohio Ct. App. 6th Dist. Lucas County
1997)—27:3, 27:18, 32:2

Johnson, 1982 WL 8498 (Ohio Ct. App. 1st Dist. Hamilton County 1982)—
25:2

Johnson, In re, 106 Ohio App. 3d 38, 665 N.E.2d 247 (1st Dist. Hamilton
County 1995)—2:4, 23:4, 23:6, 23:27, 25:3, 25:7

Johnson, In re, 1987 WL 16145 (Ohio Ct. App. 5th Dist. Licking County
1987)—18:2

Johnson, In re, 1991 WL 123047 (Ohio Ct. App. 9th Dist. Lorain County
1991)—30:11

Johnson, In re, 2003-Ohio-3278, at ¶ 12, 2004 WL 21446385 (Ohio Ct. App.
7th Dist. Columbiana County)—23:6

Johnson, In re, 61 Ohio App. 3d 544, 573 N.E.2d 184 (8th Dist. Cuyahoga
County 1989)—21:2, 21:3, 23:20, 35:3

Johnson, Matter of, 1995 WL 146064 (Ohio Ct. App. 4th Dist. Ross County
1995)—26:2

Johnson, Matter of, 1995 WL 21690 (Ohio Ct. App. 9th Dist. Lorain County
1995)—34:4

Johnson v. City of Opelousas, 488 F. Supp. 433 (W.D. La. 1980)—8:6

Johnson v. Timmerman-Cooper, 93 Ohio St. 3d 614, 2001-Ohio-1803, 757
N.E.2d 1153 (2001)—22:4

Johnson v. Trumbull County Children Services Bd., 1990 WL 162587 (Ohio
Ct. App. 11th Dist. Trumbull County 1990)—26:6, 31:8

Johnson v. Zerbst, 304 U.S. 458, 58 S. Ct. 1019, 82 L. Ed. 1461, 146 A.L.R.
357 (1938)—14:13, 22:11

Johnston, In re, 142 Ohio App. 3d 314, 755 N.E.2d 457 (11th Dist. Ashtabula
County 2001)—23:4

Joiner, In re, 2004-Ohio-1158, 2004 WL 473260 (Ohio Ct. App. 11th Dist. Ashtabula County 2004)—30:11

Jones, In re, 114 Ohio App. 319, 19 Ohio Op. 2d 286, 182 N.E.2d 631 (3d Dist. Allen County 1961)—14:3

Jones, In re, 29 Ohio App. 3d 176, 504 N.E.2d 719 (8th Dist. Cuyahoga County 1985)—26:6, 31:4

Jones, In re, 33 Ohio Op. 331, 46 Ohio L. Abs. 132, 68 N.E.2d 97 (Juv. Ct. 1946)—3:3

Jones, In re, 46 Ill. 2d 506, 263 N.E.2d 863 (1970)—23:11

Jones, Matter of, 1991 WL 273988 (Ohio Ct. App. 7th Dist. Mahoning County 1991)—25:14

Jones v. Lucas County Children Services Bd., 46 Ohio App. 3d 85, 546 N.E.2d 471 (6th Dist. Lucas County 1988)—23:5

Jones v. Murray, 962 F.2d 302 (4th Cir. 1992)—14:8

Jones v. State, 1982 OK CR 196, 654 P.2d 1080 (Okla. Crim. App. 1982)—22:3

Joseph S., In re, 1996 WL 185160 (Ohio Ct. App. 6th Dist. Lucas County 1996)—27:3

Joshua S., In re, 1996 WL 256596 (Ohio Ct. App. 6th Dist. Erie County 1996)—27:13, 27:18, 32:2

J. P., In re, 32 Ohio Misc. 5, 61 Ohio Op. 2d 24, 287 N.E.2d 926 (C.P. 1972)—4:4

J. P. v. DeSanti, 653 F.2d 1080 (6th Cir. 1981)—21:6, 35:2

J.P. v. DeSanti, No. C78-697 (N.D. Ohio, 12-18-78)—21:6

J. R. M., In Interest of, 487 S.W.2d 502 (Mo. 1972)—14:4

J. S., In re, 140 Vt. 458, 438 A.2d 1125 (1981)—23:11

Juniper, 1982 WL 4229 (Ohio Ct. App. 10th Dist. Franklin County 1982)—23:8

Justice, In re, 59 Ohio App. 2d 78, 13 Ohio Op. 3d 139, 392 N.E.2d 897 (1st Dist. Clinton County 1978)—9:3, 10:4, 10:5, 30:11, 31:7

Juvenile Dept. of Coos County, State ex rel. v. Welch, 12 Or. App. 400, 501 P.2d 991 (1972)—23:9

Juvenile Dept. of Coos County and Children's Services Div., State ex rel. v. Clements, 95 Or. App. 640, 770 P.2d 937 (1989)—23:9

Juvenile Dept. of Klamath County, State ex rel. v. Reynolds, 317 Or. 560, 857 P.2d 842 (1993)—23:10

J.W., In re, 85 Ohio Misc. 2d 1, 682 N.E.2d 1109 (C.P. 1997)—14:10

K

K., In re, 31 Ohio Misc. 218, 60 Ohio Op. 2d 134, 60 Ohio Op. 2d 388, 282 N.E.2d 370 (Juv. Ct. 1969)—11:6

Kasler, Matter of, 1991 WL 100360 (Ohio Ct. App. 4th Dist. Athens County 1991)—9:3, 10:2, 10:4, 10:5, 30:10, 31:6

Katz v. U.S., 389 U.S. 347, 88 S. Ct. 507, 19 L. Ed. 2d 576 (1967)—14:4

Kaupp v. Texas, 538 U.S. 626, 123 S. Ct. 1843, 155 L. Ed. 2d 814 (2003)—14:3

Keener v. Taylor, 640 F.2d 839, 22 Ohio Op. 3d 248 (6th Cir. 1981)—22:24

Kelly, In re, 1999 WL 132862 (Ohio Ct. App. 10th Dist. Franklin County 1999)—3:3, 19:9

Keltner, Matter of, 1995 WL 22722 (Ohio Ct. App. 12th Dist. Butler County 1995)—30:10

Kemplen v. State of Md., 428 F.2d 169 (4th Cir. 1970)—1:4, 22:1, 22:3, 22:11, 22:12, 22:23

Kemp, No. 41320 (8th Dist. Ct. App., Cuyahoga, 6-26-80), In re—10:4, 16:14, 25:2

Kennedy, In re, 94 Ohio App. 3d 414, 640 N.E.2d 1176 (3d Dist. Marion County 1994)—3:3

Kent v. U.S., 383 U.S. 541, 86 S. Ct. 1045, 16 L. Ed. 2d 84 (1966)—1:4, 19:9, 22:3, 22:9, 22:11, 22:23, 33:5

Kent v. U. S., 401 F.2d 408 (D.C. Cir. 1968)—1:4, 22:23

Kentucky v. Stincer, 482 U.S. 730, 107 S. Ct. 2658, 96 L. Ed. 2d 631, 22 Fed. R. Evid. Serv. 1164 (1987)—23:18

Kessler, In re, 90 Ohio App. 3d 231, 628 N.E.2d 153 (6th Dist. Huron County 1993)—29:2, 32:2, 33:4, 34:6

K.G., In re, 89 Ohio Misc. 2d 16, 693 N.E.2d 1186 (C.P. 1997)—22:25

Kheirkhah, In re, 2004-Ohio-521, at ¶ 17, 2004 WL 231495 (Ohio Ct. App. 11th Dist. Lake County)—23:6

Kidd, In re, 2002-Ohio-7264, 2002 WL 31886759 (Ohio Ct. App. 11th Dist. Lake County 2002)—29:2

Kidd, No. 34295 (8th Dist. Ct. App., Cuyahoga, 11-26-75), In re—9:3

Kilgallion v. Children's Hosp. Medical Center, 1987 WL 9742 (Ohio Ct. App. 1st Dist. Hamilton County 1987)—9:7

Killitz, Matter of, 59 Or. App. 720, 651 P.2d 1382 (1982)—14:10

Kimble, In re, 114 Ohio App. 3d 136, 682 N.E.2d 1066 (3d Dist. Crawford County 1996)—23:4, 23:9

Kinstle, Matter of, 1998 WL 148075 (Ohio Ct. App. 3d Dist. Logan County 1998)—34:4

Kirby, In re, 101 Ohio St. 3d 312, 2004-Ohio-970, 804 N.E.2d 476 (2004)—23:9

Kirby v. Illinois, 406 U.S. 682, 92 S. Ct. 1877, 32 L. Ed. 2d 411 (1972)—14:13, 14:14

K.J.F., In re, 2004-Ohio-263, 2004 WL 102847 (Ohio Ct. App. 2d Dist. Clark County)—23:6

Kleich Children, In re, 77 Ohio St. 3d 373, 1997-Ohio-266, 674 N.E.2d 676 (1997)—30:6

Klopfer v. State of N. C., 386 U.S. 213, 87 S. Ct. 988, 18 L. Ed. 2d 1 (1967)—23:29

K.M., In re, 2003-Ohio-5781, at ¶ 4, 2003 WL 22439756 (Ohio Ct. App. 9th Dist. Summit County 2003)—24:8

K. M. S. v. State, 129 Ga. App. 683, 200 S.E.2d 916 (1973)—2:6

Knight, In re, 135 Ohio App. 3d 172, 733 N.E.2d 303 (8th Dist. Cuyahoga County 1999)—23:27

Knipp, Matter of, 1983 WL 3161 (Ohio Ct. App. 4th Dist. Scioto County 1983)—23:16

Knipper, In re, 39 Ohio App. 3d 35, 528 N.E.2d 1319 (1st Dist. Hamilton County 1987)—3:3

Knisley, Matter of, 1998 WL 372703 (Ohio Ct. App. 4th Dist. Ross County 1998)—16:15, 25:14

Knott v. Langlois, 102 R.I. 517, 231 A.2d 767 (1967)—22:17

Knotts, In re, 109 Ohio App. 3d 267, 671 N.E.2d 1357 (3d Dist. Mercer County 1996)—23:13, 25:2, 31:5

Konneker, In re, 30 Ohio App. 502, 7 Ohio L. Abs. 137, 165 N.E. 850 (9th Dist. Summit County 1929)—10:3

Kovalak v. Kovalak, 1998 WL 456506 (Ohio Ct. App. 8th Dist. Cuyahoga County 1998)—3:3

K.P., In re, 2004-Ohio-1448, 2004 WL 583867 (Ohio Ct. App. 8th Dist. Cuyahoga County)—23:6

Krause v. State, 31 Ohio St. 2d 132, 60 Ohio Op. 2d 100, 285 N.E.2d 736 (1972)—1:8

Krechting, In re, 108 Ohio App. 3d 435, 670 N.E.2d 1081 (12th Dist. Clermont County 1996)—32:2

Kriak, In re, 30 Ohio App. 3d 83, 506 N.E.2d 556 (9th Dist. Medina County 1986)—23:3

Kronjaeger, In re, 166 Ohio St. 172, 1 Ohio Op. 2d 459, 140 N.E.2d 773 (1957)—9:3, 9:5, 9:9, 10:2

Kuchinsky, No. 41944 (8th Dist. Ct. App., Cuyahoga, 10-23-80), In re—7:4

Kuhlmann v. Wilson, 477 U.S. 436, 106 S. Ct. 2616, 91 L. Ed. 2d 364 (1986)—14:11

Kutzli, In re, 71 Ohio App. 3d 843, 595 N.E.2d 1026 (3d Dist. Paulding County 1991)—25:4, 25:14

Kuzel, Matter of, 1993 WL 93331 (Ohio Ct. App. 3d Dist. Allen County 1993)—23:5

K.W., In re, 73 Ohio Misc. 2d 20, 657 N.E.2d 611 (C.P. 1995)—22:24

Kwok T. v. Mauriello (In Matter of Kwok T.), 43 N.Y.2d 213, 401 N.Y.S.2d 52, 371 N.E.2d 814 (1977)—14:4

Kyllo v. U.S., 533 U.S. 27, 121 S. Ct. 2038, 150 L. Ed. 2d 94 (2001)—14:4

L

L., In re, 12 Ohio Misc. 251, 41 Ohio Op. 2d 341, 231 N.E.2d 253 (Juv. Ct. 1967)—3:3

L---, In re, 25 Ohio Op. 2d 369, 92 Ohio L. Abs. 475, 194 N.E.2d 797 (Juv. Ct. 1963)—14:3

L., In re, 29 A.D.2d 182, 287 N.Y.S.2d 218 (2d Dep't 1968)—14:10

L., Matter of, 24 Or. App. 257, 546 P.2d 153 (1976)—23:11

Lacey v. Laird, 166 Ohio St. 12, 1 Ohio Op. 2d 158, 139 N.E.2d 25 (1956)—9:7

Lake Cty. Dept. of Human Serv. v. Adams, 82 Ohio App. 3d 494, 612 N.E.2d 766 (11th Dist. Lake County 1992)—3:3

Lamar L., Matter of, 1995 WL 112903 (Ohio Ct. App. 6th Dist. Lucas County 1995)—25:9

Lamb v. Brown, 456 F.2d 18 (10th Cir. 1972)—22:3

Lambert, In re, 63 Ohio App. 3d 121, 577 N.E.2d 1184 (4th Dist. Lawrence County 1989)—27:13, 27:18

Lambert v. Wicklund, 520 U.S. 292, 117 S. Ct. 1169, 137 L. Ed. 2d 464 (1997)—12:2

Lamier, State ex rel. v. Lamier, 105 Ohio App. 3d 797, 664 N.E.2d 1384 (8th Dist. Cuyahoga County 1995)—1:8, 16:2

Langrehr, 1981 WL 4294 (Ohio Ct. App. 11th Dist. Trumbull County 1981)—23:8

Langston, In re, 119 Ohio App. 3d 1, 694 N.E.2d 468 (5th Dist. Stark County 1997)—22:1, 34:4, 34:8

Lannom, Matter of, 1997 WL 761323 (Ohio Ct. App. 2d Dist. Clark County 1997)—25:2

Lapp v. Ohio Bureau of Motor Vehicles, No. 1128 (5th Dist. Ct. App., Muskingum, 9-25-75)—28:10

Laquatra, Matter of, 1998 WL 23841 (Ohio Ct. App. 8th Dist. Cuyahoga County 1998)—16:8, 27:3, 27:18

Larson's Welfare, In re, 254 N.W.2d 388 (Minn. 1977)—14:10

Lassiter v. Department of Social Services of Durham County, N. C., 452 U.S. 18, 101 S. Ct. 2153, 68 L. Ed. 2d 640 (1981)—1:4, 9:2, 23:2, 23:3, 34:10

Lawson, In re, 98 Ohio App. 3d 456, 648 N.E.2d 889 (10th Dist. Franklin County 1994)—18:2, 21:6, 25:4, 25:10, 27:6

L.D., In re, 63 Ohio Misc. 2d 303, 626 N.E.2d 709 (C.P. 1993)—16:16

Leach v. State, 428 S.W.2d 817 (Tex. Civ. App. Houston 14th Dist. 1968)—
    14:10

Lee, In re, 145 Ohio App. 3d 167, 762 N.E.2d 396 (8th Dist. Cuyahoga County
    2001)—23:31

Lee, In re, 1996 WL 665058 (Ohio Ct. App. 4th Dist. Athens County 1996)—
    26:6

Lee, No. CA-2856 (5th Dist. Ct. App., Licking, 11-1-82), In re—10:3, 16:17

Lefkowitz v. Turley, 414 U.S. 70, 94 S. Ct. 316, 38 L. Ed. 2d 274 (1973)—
    22:14, 23:27

Leftwich, In re, 1997 WL 202247 (Ohio Ct. App. 10th Dist. Franklin County
    1997)—9:10

Legg, In re, 68 Ohio Misc. 2d 1, 646 N.E.2d 266 (C.P. 1993)—23:16

Lehman v. Lycoming County Children's Services Agency, 458 U.S. 502, 102
    S. Ct. 3231, 73 L. Ed. 2d 928 (1982)—34:12

Leis, State ex rel. v. Black, 45 Ohio App. 2d 191, 74 Ohio Op. 2d 270, 341
    N.E.2d 853 (1st Dist. Hamilton County 1975)—2:4, 3:3

Leonard, In re, 1997 WL 208137 (Ohio Ct. App. 12th Dist. Butler County
    1997)—30:11

Leonard v. Licker, 3 Ohio App. 377, 26 Ohio C.D. 427, 1914 WL 1176 (5th
    Dist. Richland County 1914)—1:6

Leonhardt, In re, 62 Ohio Misc. 2d 783, 610 N.E.2d 1238 (C.P. 1993)—23:9

Lesher v. Lavrich, 632 F. Supp. 77 (N.D. Ohio 1984)—26:7

Lester, In re v. Lester, 1993 WL 392122 (Ohio Ct. App. 9th Dist. Summit
    County 1993)—16:12

Leu, Matter of, 1993 WL 134004 (Ohio Ct. App. 6th Dist. Wood County
    1993)—9:12

Leveck, In re, 2003-Ohio-1269, 2003 WL 1205082 (Ohio Ct. App. 3d Dist.
    Hancock County 2003)—25:14

Leverett, Matter of, 1998 WL 141192 (Ohio Ct. App. 8th Dist. Cuyahoga
    County 1998)—26:6, 30:7

Lewandowski, Matter of, 1986 WL 9211 (Ohio Ct. App. 7th Dist. Columbiana
    County 1986)—16:6

Lewis, Matter of, 1992 WL 150202 (Ohio Ct. App. 7th Dist. Mahoning County
    1992)—30:10

Lewis v. Reed, 117 Ohio St. 152, 5 Ohio L. Abs. 420, 157 N.E. 897 (1927)—
    18:2, 34:12

Lewis v. U.S., 146 U.S. 370, 13 S. Ct. 136, 36 L. Ed. 1011 (1892)—23:23

Lexington Herald Leader Co., Inc. v. Tackett, 601 S.W.2d 905 (Ky. 1980)—
    23:11

Likens, Matter of, 1986 WL 11910 (Ohio Ct. App. 2d Dist. Greene County
    1986)—3:3, 10:5, 16:16, 26:2

Linda M., Matter of, 1998 WL 200161 (Ohio Ct. App. 6th Dist. Lucas County
    1998)—30:10

Lindon v. Lindon, 1989 WL 155730 (Ohio Ct. App. 5th Dist. Tuscarawas
    County 1989)—3:2

Lindsay, In re, 1991 WL 131494 (Ohio Ct. App. 9th Dist. Summit County
    1991)—30:11

Lindsay v. Lindsay, 257 Ill. 328, 100 N.E. 892 (1913)—1:2

Linger v. Weiss, 57 Ohio St. 2d 97, 11 Ohio Op. 3d 281, 386 N.E.2d 1354
    (1979)—1:8, 19:4, 19:7, 20:6, 23:29, 25:4, 34:12

Linger, No. CA-2556 (5th Dist. Ct. App., Licking, 7-12-79), In re—9:3, 20:6

Lionel F., Matter of, 76 N.Y.2d 747, 559 N.Y.S.2d 228, 558 N.E.2d 30 (1990)—
    23:31

Lippitt, No. 38421 (8th Dist. Ct. App., Cuyahoga, 3-9-78), In re—3:2, 9:7,
    34:9

Livingston, Matter of, 1981 WL 2722 (Ohio Ct. App. 2d Dist. Clark County 1981)—10:4

Lomeli, In re, 106 Ohio App. 3d 242, 665 N.E.2d 765 (3d Dist. Putnam County 1995)—4:4

Long, Matter of, 1993 WL 329975 (Ohio Ct. App. 12th Dist. Brown County 1993)—31:6

Lorain County Children Services v. Murray, 1996 WL 15843 (Ohio Ct. App. 9th Dist. Lorain County 1996)—18:5

Lorain County Children Services v. Simmons, 1990 WL 121102 (Ohio Ct. App. 9th Dist. Lorain County 1990)—30:10

Lovejoy, In re, 1998 WL 114400 (Ohio Ct. App. 9th Dist. Lorain County 1998)—25:9

Lowry v. Lowry, 48 Ohio App. 3d 184, 549 N.E.2d 176 (4th Dist. Ross County 1988)—23:3, 23:12, 23:17

Lozano, In re, 66 Ohio App. 3d 583, 585 N.E.2d 889 (8th Dist. Cuyahoga County 1990)—32:2

Lucas, In re, 29 Ohio App. 3d 165, 504 N.E.2d 472 (3d Dist. Putnam County 1985)—23:16

Luchene v. Wagner, 12 Ohio St. 3d 37, 465 N.E.2d 395 (1984)—34:12

Ludy v. Ludy, 84 Ohio App. 195, 39 Ohio Op. 241, 53 Ohio L. Abs. 47, 82 N.E.2d 775 (2d Dist. Franklin County 1948)—10:3, 16:14

Lugo, Matter of, 1991 WL 106085 (Ohio Ct. App. 6th Dist. Wood County 1991)—27:19

Luke, Matter of, 1984 WL 2667 (Ohio Ct. App. 5th Dist. Coshocton County 1984)—10:5, 30:11, 31:7, 33:2

Lyons, Matter of, 1987 WL 15482 (Ohio Ct. App. 4th Dist. Ross County 1987)—31:4

M

M., In re, 65 Ohio Misc. 7, 18 Ohio Op. 3d 283, 19 Ohio Op. 3d 112, 416 N.E.2d 669 (C.P. 1979)—30:8, 31:7

M., In re, 70 Cal. 2d 444, 75 Cal. Rptr. 1, 450 P.2d 296 (1969)—14:10

Mack, In re, 148 Ohio App. 3d 626, 2002-Ohio-4161, 774 N.E.2d 1243 (3d Dist. Crawford County 2002)—23:16, 25:9

Mack, In re, 22 Ohio App. 2d 201, 51 Ohio Op. 2d 400, 260 N.E.2d 619 (1st Dist. Hamilton County 1970)—22:3

MacPherson, No. 34106 (8th Dist. Ct. App., Cuyahoga, 4-3-75), In re—9:7, 17:2, 34:11

Madison v. Jameson, 1997 WL 416319 (Ohio Ct. App. 9th Dist. Summit County 1997)—30:11

Mahley, In re, 2004-Ohio-1772, 2004 WL 740003 (Ohio Ct. App. 5th Dist. Guernsey County 2004)—30:2

Maine v. Moulton, 474 U.S. 159, 106 S. Ct. 477, 88 L. Ed. 2d 481 (1985)—14:11

Makuch, In re, 101 Ohio App. 3d 45, 654 N.E.2d 1331 (9th Dist. Lorain County 1995)—23:13, 31:6

Malloy v. Hogan, 378 U.S. 1, 84 S. Ct. 1489, 12 L. Ed. 2d 653 (1964)—14:12, 23:27

Malone v. State, 130 Ohio St. 443, 5 Ohio Op. 59, 200 N.E. 473 (1936)—1:6, 35:3

Mancino v. City of Lakewood, 36 Ohio App. 3d 219, 523 N.E.2d 332 (8th Dist. Cuyahoga County 1987)—18:2

Mann v. Gray, 622 F. Supp. 1225 (N.D. Ohio 1985)—35:3

Manson v. Brathwaite, 432 U.S. 98, 97 S. Ct. 2243, 53 L. Ed. 2d 140 (1977)—14:14

Manuel, In re, 1997 WL 761311 (Ohio Ct. App. 2d Dist. Montgomery County 1997)—35:4

Marich v. Knox County Dept. of Human Services/Children Services Unit, 45 Ohio St. 3d 163, 543 N.E.2d 776 (1989)—11:6, 34:12

Mark H., In re, 1999 WL 253163 (Ohio Ct. App. 6th Dist. Lucas County 1999)—30:10, 31:8

Mark J., Matter of, 96 Misc. 2d 733, 412 N.Y.S.2d 549 (Fam. Ct. 1979)—14:14

Marsh, In re, 40 Ill. 2d 53, 237 N.E.2d 529 (1968)—14:4

Marshall, Matter of, 1987 WL 19029 (Ohio Ct. App. 3d Dist. Putnam County 1987)—9:12

Martin v. Ohio, 480 U.S. 228, 107 S. Ct. 1098, 94 L. Ed. 2d 267 (1987)—23:13

Mary B., In re, 20 Cal. App. 3d 816, 98 Cal. Rptr. 178 (3d Dist. 1971)—23:9

Mary Beth v. Howard, 1995 WL 601110 (Ohio Ct. App. 8th Dist. Cuyahoga County 1995)—9:3, 10:5, 20:2, 25:14, 26:7

Mary Beth, Matter of v. Timothy H., 1995 WL 250236 (Ohio Ct. App. 8th Dist. Cuyahoga County 1995)—34:4

Maryland v. Craig, 497 U.S. 836, 110 S. Ct. 3157, 111 L. Ed. 2d 666, 30 Fed. R. Evid. Serv. 1 (1990)—23:23

Maryland v. Garrison, 480 U.S. 79, 107 S. Ct. 1013, 94 L. Ed. 2d 72 (1987)—14:4

Maryland v. Pringle, 124 S. Ct. 795, 157 L. Ed. 2d 769 (U.S. 2003)—14:3, 14:4

Mason, In re, 1997 WL 803083 (Ohio Ct. App. 9th Dist. Summit County 1997)—27:11, 33:5

Massachusetts v. Sheppard, 468 U.S. 981, 104 S. Ct. 3424, 82 L. Ed. 2d 737 (1984)—14:2

Massachusetts v. Upton, 466 U.S. 727, 104 S. Ct. 2085, 80 L. Ed. 2d 721 (1984)—14:4

Massengill, In re, 76 Ohio App. 3d 220, 601 N.E.2d 206 (6th Dist. Lucas County 1991)—10:5, 18:2, 30:8

Massiah v. U.S., 377 U.S. 201, 84 S. Ct. 1199, 12 L. Ed. 2d 246 (1964)—14:11

Massie, No. 477 (4th Dist. Ct. App., Jackson, 3-30-84), In re—16:14

Masters, In re, 165 Ohio St. 503, 60 Ohio Op. 474, 137 N.E.2d 752 (1956)—9:5, 9:6, 34:4

Mastin, Nat'l Disability Law Rep. 1 Disability Law Rep.", Matter of, 1997 WL 795809 (Ohio Ct. App. 9th Dist. Lorain County 1997)—30:11, 31:7

Mathe, Matter of, 1985 WL 4436 (Ohio Ct. App. 11th Dist. Ashtabula County 1985)—26:2

Mathews v. Eldridge, 424 U.S. 319, 96 S. Ct. 893, 47 L. Ed. 2d 18 (1976)—18:2

Matter of Ferguson, The, 1983 WL 2929 (Ohio Ct. App. 8th Dist. Cuyahoga County 1983)—31:7

Matter Of: Hester, 1981 WL 3170 (Ohio Ct. App. 10th Dist. Franklin County 1981)—19:7

Matter Of: Wayne, 1981 WL 3452 (Ohio Ct. App. 10th Dist. Franklin County 1981)—30:11

Maydock, In re, 1997 WL 117081 (Ohio Ct. App. 5th Dist. Stark County 1997)—18:2

Mayer v. City of Chicago, 404 U.S. 189, 92 S. Ct. 410, 30 L. Ed. 2d 372 (1971)—23:30

Mayle, Matter of, 1991 WL 100527 (Ohio Ct. App. 5th Dist. Stark County 1991)—30:10

M.B., In re, 2004-Ohio-597, 2004 WL 239924 (Ohio Ct. App. 9th Dist. Summit County 2004)—30:11

McCall, No. 42420 (8th Dist. Ct. App., Cuyahoga, 3-5-81), In re—10:3, 10:4

McCarthy v. U.S., 394 U.S. 459, 89 S. Ct. 1166, 22 L. Ed. 2d 418 (1969)—23:9

McCarthy, No. 38243 (8th Dist. Ct. App., Cuyahoga, 4-20-78), In re—10:3, 10:5

McCourt, In re, 1987 WL 15812 (Ohio Ct. App. 9th Dist. Medina County 1987)—2:5

McCourt, Matter of, 1993 WL 327677 (Ohio Ct. App. 7th Dist. Belmont County 1993)—2:3, 22:5, 27:8

McCoy, In re, 138 Ohio App. 3d 774, 742 N.E.2d 247 (2d Dist. Greene County 2000)—23:13

McCoy, Matter of, 1993 WL 534660 (Ohio Ct. App. 12th Dist. Fayette County 1993)—14:10

McCrary, In re, 75 Ohio App. 3d 601, 600 N.E.2d 347 (12th Dist. Madison County 1991)—23:13, 30:10

McCune/Warnken Children, In re, 2004-Ohio-293, 2004 WL 113483 (Ohio Ct. App. 5th Dist. Stark County 2004)—30:12

McCurdy, Matter of, 1993 WL 544430 (Ohio Ct. App. 5th Dist. Morrow County 1993)—18:2

McCutchen, Matter of, 1991 WL 34881 (Ohio Ct. App. 5th Dist. Knox County 1991)—30:12, 31:2, 31:5, 31:8

McDaniel, Matter of, 1993 WL 33308 (Ohio Ct. App. 4th Dist. Adams County 1993)—16:14, 30:6, 30:10, 30:11, 30:13, 31:4, 31:8

McDermitt, In re Adoption of, 63 Ohio St. 2d 301, 17 Ohio Op. 3d 195, 408 N.E.2d 680 (1980)—16:17

McDonough v. Widnall, 891 F. Supp. 1439 (D. Colo. 1995)—14:4

McFadden v. Kendall, 81 Ohio App. 107, 36 Ohio Op. 414, 77 N.E.2d 625 (3d Dist. Auglaize County 1946)—3:3

McGinty, Matter of, 1992 WL 67580 (Ohio Ct. App. 8th Dist. Cuyahoga County 1992)—18:2

McKeiver v. Pennsylvania, 403 U.S. 528, 91 S. Ct. 1976, 29 L. Ed. 2d 647 (1971)—1:4, 23:2, 23:3, 23:10, 23:11

McKelvin, In re, 258 A.2d 452 (D.C. 1969)—14:13

McKenzie, In re, 102 Ohio App. 3d 275, 656 N.E.2d 1377 (8th Dist. Cuyahoga County 1995)—23:9

McKeown v. McKeown, 1991 WL 149718 (Ohio Ct. App. 9th Dist. Summit County 1991)—31:8

McKinney v. McClure, 102 Ohio App. 3d 165, 656 N.E.2d 1310 (12th Dist. Butler County 1995)—23:3

McKune v. Lile, 536 U.S. 24, 122 S. Ct. 2017, 153 L. Ed.2d 47 (2002)—23:27

McMann v. Richardson, 397 U.S. 759, 90 S. Ct. 1441, 25 L. Ed. 2d 763 (1970)—23:5

McNeal v. Miami County Childrens Services Bd., 1991 WL 19395 (Ohio Ct. App. 2d Dist. Miami County 1991)—30:6

McNeal v. Miami Cty. Children's Services Bd., 64 Ohio St. 3d 208, 594 N.E.2d 587 (1992)—34:12

McWhorter, In re, 1994 WL 673098 (Ohio Ct. App. 12th Dist. Butler County 1994)—23:7

M.D., In re, 38 Ohio St. 3d 149, 527 N.E.2d 286 (1988)—2:6, 15:2

Meacham, In re, 1990 WL 200335 (Ohio Ct. App. 5th Dist. Stark County 1990)—18:2

Medina v. California, 505 U.S. 437, 112 S. Ct. 2572, 120 L. Ed. 2d 353 (1992)—23:7

Medina, City of v. Coles, 1987 WL 14424 (Ohio Ct. App. 9th Dist. Medina County 1987)—16:9

Mellott v. Alvis, 109 Ohio App. 486, 12 Ohio Op. 2d 23, 81 Ohio L. Abs. 532, 162 N.E.2d 623 (10th Dist. Franklin County 1959)—2:4

Meng, State ex rel. v. Todaro, 161 Ohio St. 348, 53 Ohio Op. 252, 119 N.E.2d 281 (1954)—2:2

Menich, No. 42727 (8th Dist. Ct. App., Cuyahoga, 3-26-81), In re—23:30

Mercer v. State, 450 S.W.2d 715 (Tex. Civ. App. Austin 1970)—14:6

Mesko, Matter of, 1997 WL 205279 (Ohio Ct. App. 7th Dist. Belmont County 1997)—30:11, 30:12

Messner, In re, 19 Ohio App. 2d 33, 48 Ohio Op. 2d 31, 249 N.E.2d 532 (6th Dist. Huron County 1969)—36:3

Meyer, In re, 98 Ohio App. 3d 189, 648 N.E.2d 52 (3d Dist. Defiance County 1994)—17:2, 17:4, 23:13, 30:10, 31:8

Michael, In re, 119 Ohio App. 3d 112, 694 N.E.2d 538 (2d Dist. Montgomery County 1997)—23:14, 23:16

Michael D., In re, 1995 WL 584516 (Ohio Ct. App. 4th Dist. Jackson County 1995)—31:4

Michael P., Matter of, 50 A.D.2d 598, 375 N.Y.S.2d 153 (2d Dep't 1975)—14:10

Micheal Legg, In re, 2002-Ohio-4582, 2002 WL 2027290 (Ohio Ct. App. 8th Dist. Cuyahoga County 2002)—23:6

Michigan v. Jackson, 475 U.S. 625, 106 S. Ct. 1404, 89 L. Ed. 2d 631 (1986)—14:11

Michigan v. Mosley, 423 U.S. 96, 96 S. Ct. 321, 46 L. Ed. 2d 313 (1975)—14:10

Milgrim, In re, 2001 WL 112123 (Ohio Ct. App. 8th Dist. Cuyahoga County 2001)—23:29

Mill v. Brown, 31 Utah 473, 88 P. 609 (1907)—1:2

Miller, In re, 119 Ohio App. 3d 52, 694 N.E.2d 500 (2d Dist. Clark County 1997)—23:4, 23:6, 23:9

Miller, In re, 12 Ohio St. 3d 40, 465 N.E.2d 397 (1984)—23:3

Miller, In re, 2002-Ohio-3360, 2002 WL 1400544 (Ohio Ct. App. 11th Dist. Ashtabula County 2002)—19:7

Miller, In re, 33 Ohio App. 3d 224, 515 N.E.2d 635 (8th Dist. Cuyahoga County 1986)—3:3, 18:4, 33:2

Miller, In re, 61 Ohio St. 2d 184, 15 Ohio Op. 3d 211, 399 N.E.2d 1262 (1980)—11:6

Miller, In re, 82 Ohio App. 3d 81, 611 N.E.2d 451 (6th Dist. Lucas County 1992)—27:8

Miller v. Fenton, 474 U.S. 104, 106 S. Ct. 445, 88 L. Ed. 2d 405 (1985)—14:9

Miller v. Quatsoe, 332 F. Supp. 1269 (E.D. Wis. 1971)—22:12

Miller, No. 96AP09075 (5th Dist. Ct. App., Tuscarawas, 5-23-97), In re—16:13

Miller, Nos. 77-11-171 to 77-11-174 (Juv., Carroll 1978), In re—9:7

Mills, In re, 1997 WL 576384 (Ohio Ct. App. 9th Dist. Summit County 1997)—31:8

Mills, In re, 2002-Ohio-2503, 2002 WL 925270 (Ohio Ct. App. 5th Dist. Ashland County 2002)—27:3

Mincey v. Arizona, 437 U.S. 385, 98 S. Ct. 2408, 57 L. Ed. 2d 290 (1978)—14:9, 14:10

Minnesota v. Murphy, 465 U.S. 420, 104 S. Ct. 1136, 79 L. Ed. 2d 409 (1984)—14:10

Minnesota v. Olson, 495 U.S. 91, 110 S. Ct. 1684, 109 L. Ed. 2d 85 (1990)—14:4

Minnick v. Mississippi, 498 U.S. 146, 111 S. Ct. 486, 112 L. Ed. 2d 489 (1990)—14:10

Minor Boy v. State, 91 Nev. 456, 537 P.2d 477 (1975)—14:3

Minton, In re, 112 Ohio App. 361, 16 Ohio Op. 2d 283, 176 N.E.2d 252 (2d Dist. Darke County 1960)—9:3

Miranda v. Arizona, 384 U.S. 436, 86 S. Ct. 1602, 16 L. Ed. 2d 694, 10 A.L.R.3d 974 (1966)—1:4, 14:9, 14:10

Mitchell, In re, 93 Ohio App. 3d 153, 637 N.E.2d 989 (8th Dist. Cuyahoga County 1994)—34:4

M.L.B. v. S.L.J., 519 U.S. 102, 117 S. Ct. 555, 136 L. Ed. 2d 473 (1996)—1:4, 9:2, 23:2, 34:9

M.L.R., In re, 150 Ohio App. 3d 39, 2002-Ohio-5958, 779 N.E.2d 772 (8th Dist. Cuyahoga County 2002)—23:3

Mobley v. Allaman, 89 Ohio L. Abs. 473, 184 N.E.2d 707 (Prob. Ct. 1961)—18:5

Mojica, In re, 107 Ohio App. 3d 461, 669 N.E.2d 35 (8th Dist. Cuyahoga County 1995)—14:2, 34:8

Moloney, In re, 24 Ohio St. 3d 22, 492 N.E.2d 805 (1986)—26:4

Montasser, Matter of, 1992 WL 348236 (Ohio Ct. App. 6th Dist. Lucas County 1992)—18:4

Montgomery, In re, 117 Ohio App. 3d 696, 691 N.E.2d 349 (8th Dist. Cuyahoga County 1997)—23:4, 23:9

Montgomery County Children Services Board v. Kiszka, 1983 WL 2483 (Ohio Ct. App. 2d Dist. Montgomery County 1983)—30:11, 31:6

Moore, In re, 153 Ohio App. 3d 641, 2003-Ohio-4250, 795 N.E.2d 149 (3d Dist. Hardin County 2003)—23:3, 23:5

Moore, In re, 153 Ohio App. 3d 641, 2003-Ohio-4250, at ¶ 15, 795 N.E.2d 149 (3d Dist. Hardin County 2003)—18:3

Moore, In re, 1995 WL 338489 (Ohio Ct. App. 9th Dist. Summit County 1995)—31:8

Moore, Matter of, 1993 WL 172263 (Ohio Ct. App. 6th Dist. Lucas County 1993)—31:7

Moore v. Illinois, 434 U.S. 220, 98 S. Ct. 458, 54 L. Ed. 2d 424 (1977)—14:13

Moore v. Moore, 1991 WL 13905 (Ohio Ct. App. 4th Dist. Gallia County 1991)—25:2

Moorehead, In re, 75 Ohio App. 3d 711, 600 N.E.2d 778 (2d Dist. Montgomery County 1991)—24:9

Moore, No. CA291 (12th Dist. Ct. App., Preble, 5-20-81), In re—16:17, 25:2

Morales, No. 33919 (8th Dist. Ct. App., Cuyahoga, 4-24-75), In re—34:2, 34:4

Moran, In re, 1994 WL 123683 (Ohio Ct. App. 1st Dist. Hamilton County 1994)—3:3, 23:6

Moran v. Burbine, 475 U.S. 412, 106 S. Ct. 1135, 89 L. Ed. 2d 410 (1986)—14:10

Morgan, In re, 2003-Ohio-2543, 2003 WL 21135298 (Ohio Ct. App. 12th Dist. Butler County)—23:9

Morris, In re, 1991 WL 96271 (Ohio Ct. App. 2d Dist. Montgomery County 1991)—30:8

Morris, In re, 2002-Ohio-5881, 2002 WL 31414557 (Ohio Ct. App. 12th Dist. Butler County 2002)—23:17

Morris, In re, 29 Ohio Misc. 71, 58 Ohio Op. 2d 126, 278 N.E.2d 701 (C.P. 1971)—14:4

Morris v. Lucas County Children Services Bd., 49 Ohio App. 3d 86, 550 N.E.2d 980 (6th Dist. Lucas County 1989)—34:10

Morrison v. Morrison, 45 Ohio App. 2d 299, 74 Ohio Op. 2d 441, 344 N.E.2d 144 (9th Dist. Summit County 1973)—20:2, 34:4

Morrissey v. Brewer, 408 U.S. 471, 92 S. Ct. 2593, 33 L. Ed. 2d 484 (1972)—22:12, 23:22

Moses, Matter of, 1992 WL 32117 (Ohio Ct. App. 6th Dist. Lucas County 1992)—25:13, 25:14

Moss v. Weaver, 383 F. Supp. 130 (S.D. Fla. 1974)—19:6

Motill, 1981 WL 4586 (Ohio Ct. App. 8th Dist. Cuyahoga County 1981)—34:4, 34:5

Motley, In re, 110 Ohio App. 3d 641, 674 N.E.2d 1268 (9th Dist. Summit County 1996)—33:6

Motter, In re, 1998 WL 314362 (Ohio Ct. App. 12th Dist. Butler County 1998)—30:7

Mourey, In re, 2003-Ohio-1870, 2003 WL 1869911 (Ohio Ct. App. 4th Dist. Athens County 2003)—30:11

Muldrew, In re, 2002-Ohio-7288, 2002 WL 31888158 (Ohio Ct. App. 2d Dist. Montgomery County 2002)—30:13

Muldrew, In re, 2004-Ohio-2044, 2004 WL 870427 (Ohio Ct. App. 2d Dist. Montgomery County 2004)—30:9

Mull, Matter of, 1997 WL 155412 (Ohio Ct. App. 3d Dist. Seneca County 1997)—25:14

Mullaney v. Wilbur, 421 U.S. 684, 95 S. Ct. 1881, 44 L. Ed. 2d 508 (1975)—23:13

Mullenax, In re, 108 Ohio App. 3d 271, 670 N.E.2d 551 (9th Dist. Lorain County 1996)—18:2, 18:4

Mundy, Matter of, 1998 WL 60502 (Ohio Ct. App. 12th Dist. Preble County 1998)—32:2

Murchison, In re, 349 U.S. 133, 75 S. Ct. 623, 99 L. Ed. 942 (1955)—23:28

Murphy v. Plain Dealer Pub. Co., 19 Media L. Rep. (BNA) 1556, 1991 WL 337361 (N.D. Ohio 1991)—35:2

Murray, In re, 52 Ohio St. 3d 155, 556 N.E.2d 1169 (1990)—34:4

Murray v. U.S., 487 U.S. 533, 108 S. Ct. 2529, 101 L. Ed. 2d 472 (1988)—14:2

M.W., In re, 2004-Ohio-438, 2004 WL 199962 (Ohio Ct. App. 9th Dist. Lorain County)—23:13

M. W., In re, 2004-Ohio-438, 2004 WL 199962 (Ohio Ct. App. 9th Dist. Lorain County 2004)—30:10

Myers, In re, 2004-Ohio-539, at ¶ 8, 2004 WL 231796 (Ohio Ct. App. 3d Dist. Seneca County)—23:28

Myers, In re, 2004-Ohio-539, at ¶ 8, 2004 WL 231796 (Ohio Ct. App. 3d Dist. Seneca County 2004)—24:5

Myers, Matter of, 1986 WL 3917 (Ohio Ct. App. 5th Dist. Delaware County 1986)—34:4

N

Nace, State ex rel. v. Johnston, 1984 WL 3476 (Ohio Ct. App. 4th Dist. Hocking County 1984)—32:2

Nagle, State ex rel. v. Olin, 64 Ohio St. 2d 341, 18 Ohio Op. 3d 503, 415 N.E.2d 279 (1980)—9:7

Nalls, State ex rel. v. Russo, 96 Ohio St.3d 410, 2002-Ohio-4907, 775 N.E.2d 522 (2002)—24:3

Nance, No. 1452 (4th Dist. Ct. App., Lawrence, 10-16-80), In re—16:17

Nardone v. U.S., 308 U.S. 338, 60 S. Ct. 266, 84 L. Ed. 307 (1939)—14:2

Nation, In re, 61 Ohio App. 3d 763, 573 N.E.2d 1155 (3d Dist. Shelby County 1989)—23:4, 23:6, 23:9

National Treasury Employees Union v. Von Raab, 489 U.S. 656, 109 S. Ct. 1384, 103 L. Ed. 2d 685 (1989)—1:4, 14:6

N.B., In re, 2003-Ohio-3656, 2003 WL 21545142 (Ohio Ct. App. 8th Dist. Cuyahoga County 2003)—30:6

N.B., In re, 2004-Ohio-859, at ¶ 2, 2004 WL 350947 (Ohio Ct. App. 8th Dist. Cuyahoga County 2004)—34:4

Neff, No. 1-78-9 (3d Dist. Ct. App., Allen, 6-14-78), In re—16:12, 16:14, 34:3, 34:11

Neil v. Biggers, 409 U.S. 188, 93 S. Ct. 375, 34 L. Ed. 2d 401 (1972)—14:14

Nelson, In re, 2004-Ohio-268, 2004 WL 103021 (Ohio Ct. App. 2d Dist. Montgomery County 2004)—25:14

Nelson v. State, 120 Wash. App. 470, 85 P.3d 912 (Div. 1 2003)—35:4

Neuenschwander v. Wayne Cty. Children Serv. Bd., 92 Ohio App. 3d 767, 637 N.E.2d 102 (9th Dist. Wayne County 1994)—14:17

New Jersey v. T.L.O., 469 U.S. 325, 105 S. Ct. 733, 83 L. Ed. 2d 720, 21 Ed. Law Rep. 1122 (1985)—1:4, 14:4, 14:6

News Herald, State ex rel. v. Ottawa Cty. Court of Common Pleas, Juv. Div., 77 Ohio St. 3d 40, 1996-Ohio-354, 671 N.E.2d 5 (1996)—22:19, 23:11

Newton, In re, 12 Ohio App. 2d 191, 41 Ohio Op. 2d 290, 231 N.E.2d 880 (1st Dist. Hamilton County 1967)—33:8

New York v. Belton, 453 U.S. 454, 101 S. Ct. 2860, 69 L. Ed. 2d 768 (1981)—14:4

New York v. Quarles, 467 U.S. 649, 104 S. Ct. 2626, 81 L. Ed. 2d 550 (1984)—14:10

N.H., In re, 63 Ohio Misc. 2d 285, 626 N.E.2d 697 (C.P. 1992)—22:19, 25:5

Nicholson, In re, 132 Ohio App. 3d 303, 724 N.E.2d 1217 (8th Dist. Cuyahoga County 1999)—14:8, 23:9

Nickerson, No. 58639 (8th Dist. Ct. App., Cuyahoga, 6-4-90), In re—17:3

Nix v. Williams, 467 U.S. 431, 104 S. Ct. 2501, 81 L. Ed. 2d 377 (1984)—14:2

Noble's Welfare, In re, 15 Wash. App. 51, 547 P.2d 880 (Div. 1 1976)—14:10

Noe, In re, 1997 WL 411594 (Ohio Ct. App. 12th Dist. Butler County 1997)—31:8

Nolte v. Nolte, 60 Ohio App. 2d 227, 14 Ohio Op. 3d 215, 396 N.E.2d 807 (8th Dist. Cuyahoga County 1978)—24:7

Norlin, Matter of, 1990 WL 209855 (Ohio Ct. App. 8th Dist. Cuyahoga County 1990)—14:10

Normandy Place Associates v. Beyer, 2 Ohio St. 3d 102, 443 N.E.2d 161 (1982)—34:4

Norris Children, In re, 77 Ohio St. 3d 374, 1997-Ohio-30, 674 N.E.2d 677 (1997)—30:6

North Carolina v. Alford, 400 U.S. 25, 91 S. Ct. 160, 27 L. Ed. 2d 162 (1970)—23:9

North Carolina v. Butler, 441 U.S. 369, 99 S. Ct. 1755, 60 L. Ed. 2d 286 (1979)—14:10

North Carolina v. Pearce, 395 U.S. 711, 89 S. Ct. 2072, 23 L. Ed. 2d 656 (1969)—23:31

Northern Columbiana County Community Hosp. Ass'n v. Department of Youth Services, 38 Ohio St. 3d 102, 526 N.E.2d 802 (1988)—27:3

Norton, Matter of, 1990 WL 187073 (Ohio Ct. App. 5th Dist. Stark County 1990)—30:10

Nowak, In re, 133 Ohio App. 3d 396, 728 N.E.2d 411 (11th Dist. Geauga County 1999)—33:6, 33:8

N.S., In re, 2004 WL 254215 (Tex. App. Waco 2004)—23:7

Nunn, In re, 1995 WL 768544 (Ohio Ct. App. 5th Dist. Morgan County 1995)—25:10

O

O---, In re, 28 Ohio Op. 2d 165, 95 Ohio L. Abs. 101, 199 N.E.2d 765 (Juv. Ct. 1964)—9:5, 9:9, 16:15

O'Donnell v. Franklin County Children Services, Starr Commonwealth Corporation, 1981 WL 3734 (Ohio Ct. App. 10th Dist. Franklin County 1981)—3:2

Ohio v. Akron Center for Reproductive Health, 497 U.S. 502, 110 S. Ct. 2972, 111 L. Ed. 2d 405 (1990)—12:2

Ohio v. Roberts, 448 U.S. 56, 100 S. Ct. 2531, 65 L. Ed. 2d 597, 7 Fed. R. Evid. Serv. 1 (1980)—23:25

Ohio, State of v. Bortree, 1982 WL 6755 (Ohio Ct. App. 3d Dist. Logan County 1982)—14:5

Ohio, State of v. Hull, 1981 WL 5992 (Ohio Ct. App. 4th Dist. Athens County 1981)—14:10

Oklahoma Pub. Co. v. District Court In and For Oklahoma County, 430 U.S. 308, 97 S. Ct. 1045, 51 L. Ed. 2d 355 (1977)—1:4

Olah, In re, 142 Ohio App. 3d 176, 754 N.E.2d 1271 (9th Dist. Lorain County 2000)—25:4

Oliver, In re, 333 U.S. 257, 68 S. Ct. 499, 92 L. Ed. 682 (1948)—22:12, 23:11, 23:23

Oliver v. U.S., 466 U.S. 170, 104 S. Ct. 1735, 80 L. Ed. 2d 214 (1984)—14:4

Omosun Children, In re, 106 Ohio App. 3d 813, 667 N.E.2d 431 (11th Dist. Trumbull County 1995)—23:29, 25:13, 30:12

Onion, In re, 128 Ohio App. 3d 498, 715 N.E.2d 604 (11th Dist. Ashtabula County 1998)—23:9

Order Requiring Fingerprinting of a Juvenile, In re, 42 Ohio St. 3d 124, 537 N.E.2d 1286 (1989)—14:4, 14:15

Oregon v. Bradshaw, 462 U.S. 1039, 103 S. Ct. 2830, 77 L. Ed. 2d 405 (1983)—14:10

Oregon v. Hass, 420 U.S. 714, 95 S. Ct. 1215, 43 L. Ed. 2d 570 (1975)—14:10

Oregon v. Mathiason, 429 U.S. 492, 97 S. Ct. 711, 50 L. Ed. 2d 714 (1977)—14:10

Oregonian Pub. Co., State ex rel. v. Deiz, 289 Or. 277, 613 P.2d 23 (1980)—23:11

Orwell, In re, 1993 WL 531958 (Ohio Ct. App. 2d Dist. Montgomery County 1993)—30:7

Orwell v. Orwell, 1990 WL 157170 (Ohio Ct. App. 2d Dist. Montgomery County 1990)—30:10, 31:7

Osborn, No. CA 1744 (5th Dist. Ct. App., Richland, 1-16-79), In re—16:7, 16:14, 18:3, 18:4

Osman, In re, 109 Ohio App. 3d 731, 672 N.E.2d 1114 (11th Dist. Portage County 1996)—8:6, 23:13, 29:3

Overbay, In re, 1997 WL 89160 (Ohio Ct. App. 12th Dist. Butler County 1997)—10:6, 30:2

Oviedo v. Jago, 809 F.2d 326 (6th Cir. 1987)—22:3

Owen, In re, 1990 WL 187084 (Ohio Ct. App. 5th Dist. Stark County 1990)—18:4

Owens, In re, 1986 WL 14515 (Ohio Ct. App. 8th Dist. Cuyahoga County 1986)—31:4

Owens, In re, 1995 WL 617630 (Ohio Ct. App. 5th Dist. Stark County 1995)—10:2

P

Pachin, In re, 50 Ohio App. 3d 44, 552 N.E.2d 655 (2d Dist. Montgomery County 1988)—19:5, 30:8

Palmer, In re, 12 Ohio St. 3d 194, 465 N.E.2d 1312 (1984)—16:13, 30:8, 31:2

Palmer, Matter of, 1983 WL 6408 (Ohio Ct. App. 5th Dist. Stark County 1983)—18:2

Palmore v. Sidoti, 466 U.S. 429, 104 S. Ct. 1879, 80 L. Ed. 2d 421 (1984)—9:6

Parish, Matter of, 1990 WL 68912 (Ohio Ct. App. 6th Dist. Lucas County 1990)—25:2

Parker, In re, 7 Ohio App. 3d 38, 453 N.E.2d 1285 (6th Dist. Lucas County 1982)—32:2

Parks, Matter of, 1990 WL 121866 (Ohio Ct. App. 6th Dist. Lucas County 1990)—31:8

Parsons, In re, 1996 WL 285370 (Ohio Ct. App. 9th Dist. Lorain County 1996)—18:2

Pasqualone v. Pasqualone, 63 Ohio St. 2d 96, 17 Ohio Op. 3d 58, 406 N.E.2d 1121 (1980)—16:13

Pate v. Robinson, 383 U.S. 375, 86 S. Ct. 836, 15 L. Ed. 2d 815 (1966)—23:7

Patterson, In re, 134 Ohio App. 3d 119, 730 N.E.2d 439 (9th Dist. Summit County 1999)—30:11

Patterson, In re, 16 Ohio App. 3d 214, 475 N.E.2d 160 (12th Dist. Madison County 1984)—26:2, 33:4, 34:4

Patterson, Matter of, 1990 WL 41693 (Ohio Ct. App. 5th Dist. Coshocton County 1990)—10:5

Patterson v. Illinois, 487 U.S. 285, 108 S. Ct. 2389, 101 L. Ed. 2d 261 (1988)—14:11

Patterson v. New York, 432 U.S. 197, 97 S. Ct. 2319, 53 L. Ed. 2d 281 (1977)—23:13

Paul T., In re, 15 Cal. App. 3d 886, 93 Cal. Rptr. 510 (1st Dist. 1971)—14:10

Payton v. New York, 445 U.S. 573, 100 S. Ct. 1371, 63 L. Ed. 2d 639 (1980)—14:4

Pead, No. 79AP-906 (10th Dist. Ct. App., Franklin, 6-10-80), In re—30:6

Peaks, State ex rel. v. Allaman, 51 Ohio Op. 321, 66 Ohio L. Abs. 403, 115 N.E.2d 849 (Ct. App. 2d Dist. Montgomery County 1952)—1:6, 19:9

Pegan v. Crawmer, 76 Ohio St. 3d 97, 1996-Ohio-419, 666 N.E.2d 1091 (1996)—34:12

Peggy L., In re, 1995 WL 803443 (Ohio Ct. App. 6th Dist. Lucas County 1995)—27:3, 33:6

Pendleton v. State, 1990 WL 104964 (Ohio Ct. App. 8th Dist. Cuyahoga County 1990)—23:5

Pennington, In re, 150 Ohio App. 3d 205, 2002-Ohio-6381, 779 N.E.2d 1093 (2d Dist. Montgomery County 2002)—16:16

Pennsylvania v. Bruder, 488 U.S. 9, 109 S. Ct. 205, 102 L. Ed. 2d 172 (1988)—14:10

Pennsylvania v. Ritchie, 480 U.S. 39, 107 S. Ct. 989, 94 L. Ed. 2d 40, 22 Fed. R. Evid. Serv. 1 (1987)—21:2

People v. Cauley, 32 P.3d 602 (Colo. Ct. App. 2001)—23:19

People v. Chambers, 66 Ill. 2d 36, 4 Ill. Dec. 308, 360 N.E.2d 55 (1976)—8:6

People v. Estergard, 169 Colo. 445, 457 P.2d 698 (1969)—9:7

People v. Fields, 388 Mich. 66, 199 N.W.2d 217 (1972)—22:3

People v. Fitzgerald, 101 Misc. 2d 712, 422 N.Y.S.2d 309 (County Ct. 1979)—23:15

People v. Fleming, 134 Ill. App. 3d 562, 89 Ill. Dec. 478, 480 N.E.2d 1221 (1st Dist. 1985)—14:11

People v. Flowers, 23 Mich. App. 523, 179 N.W.2d 56 (1970)—14:5

People v. Hana, 443 Mich. 202, 504 N.W.2d 166 (1993)—22:13

People v. J.S., 103 Ill. 2d 395, 83 Ill. Dec. 156, 469 N.E.2d 1090 (1984)—22:3

People v. Macias, 16 Cal. 4th 739, 66 Cal. Rptr. 2d 659, 941 P.2d 838 (1997)—22:14

People v. Overton, 20 N.Y.2d 360, 283 N.Y.S.2d 22, 229 N.E.2d 596 (1967)—14:6

People v. P.H., 145 Ill. 2d 209, 164 Ill. Dec. 137, 582 N.E.2d 700 (1991)—22:3

People v. Stewart, 63 Misc. 2d 601, 313 N.Y.S.2d 253 (City Crim. Ct. 1970)—14:6

People v. Thorpe, 641 P.2d 935 (Colo. 1982)—22:3

People in Interest of T.M., 742 P.2d 905 (Colo. 1987)—23:10

Perales, In re, 52 Ohio St. 2d 89, 6 Ohio Op. 3d 293, 369 N.E.2d 1047 (1977)—9:2, 9:5, 16:15, 30:2, 30:8, 30:11

Pethel, No. 79CA25 (4th Dist. Ct. App., Washington, 11-9-81), In re—16:14

Pettry v. McGinty, 60 Ohio St. 2d 92, 14 Ohio Op. 3d 331, 397 N.E.2d 1190 (1979)—34:12

Pharr, Ex parte, 10 Ohio App. 395, 1919 WL 870 (1st Dist. Hamilton County 1919)—2:4

Phillips, In re, 1998 WL 177556 (Ohio Ct. App. 2d Dist. Montgomery County 1998)—30:6

Phillips, In re, 2003-Ohio-5107, 2003 WL 22227364 (Ohio Ct. App. 12th Dist. Butler County 2003)—34:11

Phillips, In re, 2003-Ohio-5107, at ¶ 6, 2003 WL 22227364 (Ohio Ct. App. 12th Dist. Butler County 2003)—34:3

Philpot v. Williams, 8 Ohio App. 3d 241, 456 N.E.2d 1315 (1st Dist. Hamilton County 1983)—23:18

Philpott, No. 41186 (8th Dist. Ct. App., Cuyahoga, 6-5-80), In re—10:3, 10:4, 31:7

Phommarath, Matter of, 1995 WL 681213 (Ohio Ct. App. 10th Dist. Franklin County 1995)—23:31, 24:9

Piazza, In re, 7 Ohio St. 2d 102, 36 Ohio Op. 2d 84, 218 N.E.2d 459 (1966)—34:12

Pickett, In re, 1993 WL 386259 (Ohio Ct. App. 12th Dist. Butler County 1993)—30:10

Pieper Children, In re, 74 Ohio App. 3d 714, 600 N.E.2d 317 (12th Dist. Preble County 1991)—9:6, 10:2, 16:12, 25:2, 30:8

Pieper Children, In re, 85 Ohio App. 3d 318, 619 N.E.2d 1059 (12th Dist. Preble County 1993)—10:5, 10:6, 23:13, 25:14, 32:2

Piland v. Clark County Juvenile Court Services, 85 Nev. 489, 457 P.2d 523 (1969)—23:29

Pima County, Juvenile Action, No. 63212-2, Matter of, 129 Ariz. 371, 631 P.2d 526 (1981)—23:31

Pitts, In re, 38 Ohio App. 3d 1, 525 N.E.2d 814 (5th Dist. Knox County 1987)—9:12, 9:13, 9:14, 9:15, 25:2

Plain Dealer Publishing Co., State ex rel. v. Geauga Cty. Court of Common Pleas, Juv. Div., 90 Ohio St. 3d 79, 2000-Ohio-35, 734 N.E.2d 1214 (2000)—19:12, 22:19, 23:11

Planned Parenthood of Northern New England v. Heed, 296 F. Supp. 2d 59, 2003 DNH 222 (D.N.H. 2003)—12:2

Plumley, In re, 2004-Ohio-1161, 2004 WL 458310 (Ohio Ct. App. 11th Dist. Portage County 2004)—11:6

Pointer v. Texas, 380 U.S. 400, 85 S. Ct. 1065, 13 L. Ed. 2d 923 (1965)—23:22

Poling, In re, 64 Ohio St. 3d 211, 1992-Ohio-144, 594 N.E.2d 589 (1992)—3:3, 16:15, 30:4, 30:7

Pollard, In re, 1981 WL 4690 (Ohio Ct. App. 8th Dist. Cuyahoga County 1981)—16:16

Poole v. Cuyahoga County Dept. of Human Services, 1993 WL 35586 (Ohio Ct. App. 8th Dist. Cuyahoga County 1993)—31:4

Popovich, Matter of, 1993 WL 19619 (Ohio Ct. App. 7th Dist. Belmont County 1993)—4:4, 8:2

Port v. Heard, 764 F.2d 423 (5th Cir. 1985)—23:15

Portzer v. Cuyahoga County Dept. of Human Services, 1995 WL 350096 (Ohio Ct. App. 8th Dist. Cuyahoga County 1995)—20:6

Poth, In re, 2 Ohio App. 3d 361, 442 N.E.2d 105 (6th Dist. Huron County 1981)—33:8

Poth, Matter of, 1982 WL 9371 (Ohio Ct. App. 6th Dist. Huron County 1982)—9:3, 10:3, 17:2, 30:11

Potter, In Interest of, 237 N.W.2d 461 (Iowa 1976)—23:13

Powell v. Hocker, 453 F.2d 652 (9th Cir. 1971)—22:3

Prescott v. State, 19 Ohio St. 184, 1869 WL 42 (1869)—1:6, 23:10

Press-Enterprise Co. v. Superior Court of California for Riverside County, 478 U.S. 1, 106 S. Ct. 2735, 92 L. Ed. 2d 1 (1986)—23:11

Press-Enterprise Co. v. Superior Court of California, Riverside County, 464 U.S. 501, 104 S. Ct. 819, 78 L. Ed. 2d 629 (1984)—23:11

Preston, Matter of, 1993 WL 35682 (Ohio Ct. App. 5th Dist. Richland County 1993)—8:5

Pribanic, Matter of, 1991 WL 3813 (Ohio Ct. App. 6th Dist. Erie County 1991)—16:8

Price, Matter of, 1993 WL 76957 (Ohio Ct. App. 2d Dist. Greene County 1993)—30:8, 31:8

Price, Matter of, 1994 WL 245663 (Ohio Ct. App. 8th Dist. Cuyahoga County 1994)—34:4

Prince v. Massachusetts, 321 U.S. 158, 64 S. Ct. 438, 88 L. Ed. 645 (1944)—9:7

Priser, In re, 2004-Ohio-1315, 2004 WL 541124 (Ohio Ct. App. 2d Dist. Montgomery County)—23:19

Province, Ex parte, 127 Ohio St. 333, 188 N.E. 550 (1933)—18:5

Pryor, In re, 86 Ohio App. 3d 327, 620 N.E.2d 973 (4th Dist. Athens County 1993)—16:15, 23:6, 30:2, 30:4, 30:7

Q

Queen, Matter of, 1993 WL 285943 (Ohio Ct. App. 4th Dist. Pickaway County 1993)—30:10

Quilloin v. Walcott, 434 U.S. 246, 98 S. Ct. 549, 54 L. Ed. 2d 511 (1978)—18:2

Qutb v. Strauss, 11 F.3d 488 (5th Cir. 1993)—8:6

R

R. A. H., In re, 314 A.2d 133 (D.C. 1974)—14:10

Rakas v. Illinois, 439 U.S. 128, 99 S. Ct. 421, 58 L. Ed. 2d 387 (1978)—14:2

Raleigh Fitkin-Paul Morgan Memorial Hospital and Ann May Memorial Foundation in Town of Neptune v. Anderson, 42 N.J. 421, 201 A.2d 537 (1964)—9:7

Rammage v. Saros, 97 Ohio St. 3d 430, 2002-Ohio-6669, 780 N.E.2d 278 (2002)—34:12

Ramona R. v. Superior Court, 37 Cal. 3d 802, 210 Cal. Rptr. 204, 693 P.2d 789 (1985)—22:14

Ramsey Children, In re, 102 Ohio App. 3d 168, 656 N.E.2d 1311 (5th Dist. Stark County 1995)—23:4, 25:9

Ramsey Children, In re, 1993 WL 500464 (Ohio Ct. App. 5th Dist. Stark County 1993)—18:2

Ranker, Matter of, 1996 WL 761159 (Ohio Ct. App. 11th Dist. Portage County 1996)—30:10

Rarey v. Schmidt, 115 Ohio St. 518, 5 Ohio L. Abs. 12, 154 N.E. 914 (1926)—18:2, 34:12

Rawlings v. Kentucky, 448 U.S. 98, 100 S. Ct. 2556, 65 L. Ed. 2d 633 (1980)—14:2

Raypole, In re, 2003-Ohio-1066, 2003 WL 928976 (Ohio Ct. App. 12th Dist. Fayette County 2003)—19:2

R.D.S.M. v. Intake Officer, 565 P.2d 855 (Alaska 1977)—23:29

Reed, No. CA 1325 (5th Dist. Ct. App., Tuscarawas, 7-24-79), In re—16:7, 16:12, 18:3

Reese, In re, 4 Ohio App. 3d 59, 446 N.E.2d 482 (10th Dist. Franklin County 1982)—9:5, 9:6

Reeves v. Warden, Md. Penitentiary, 346 F.2d 915 (4th Cir. 1965)—14:5

Reigle, Matter of, 1993 WL 451203 (Ohio Ct. App. 3d Dist. Hancock County 1993)—18:2

R. E. M. v. State, 532 S.W.2d 645 (Tex. Civ. App. San Antonio 1975)—22:14

Renfro, State ex rel. v. Cuyahoga County Dept. of Human Services, 54 Ohio St. 3d 25, 560 N.E.2d 230 (1990)—21:2, 35:2

Reynolds, In re, 1996 WL 379343 (Ohio Ct. App. 12th Dist. Madison County 1996)—4:4, 33:6

Reynolds, Matter of, 1993 WL 220253 (Ohio Ct. App. 12th Dist. Butler County 1993)—30:10

Reynolds v. Goll, 75 Ohio St. 3d 121, 1996-Ohio-153, 661 N.E.2d 1008 (1996)—30:11

Reynolds v. Goll, 80 Ohio App. 3d 494, 609 N.E.2d 1276 (9th Dist. Lorain County 1992)—3:2

Reynolds v. Ross County Children's Services Agency, 1981 WL 6057 (Ohio Ct. App. 4th Dist. Ross County 1981)—34:12

Reynolds v. Ross County Children's Services Agency, 5 Ohio St. 3d 27, 448 N.E.2d 816 (1983)—18:3, 30:11

Rhode Island v. Innis, 446 U.S. 291, 100 S. Ct. 1682, 64 L. Ed. 2d 297 (1980)—14:10, 14:11

Rice, In re Interest of, 204 Neb. 732, 285 N.W.2d 223 (1979)—9:7

Rich v. Erie Cty. Dept. of Human Resources, 106 Ohio App. 3d 88, 665 N.E.2d 278 (6th Dist. Erie County 1995)—16:3

Richard Carl S., Matter of, 1998 WL 667044 (Ohio Ct. App. 6th Dist. Sandusky County 1998)—26:6

Richard, Laqueeda, Shennell & Dominique, In re, 1994 WL 702071 (Ohio Ct. App. 2d Dist. Montgomery County 1994)—30:11

Richardson, In re, 2004-Ohio-2170, at ¶ 20, 2004 WL 911316 (Ohio Ct. App. 5th Dist. Guernsey County 2004)—30:10

Richmond Newspapers, Inc. v. Virginia, 448 U.S. 555, 100 S. Ct. 2814, 65 L. Ed. 2d 973 (1980)—23:11

Riddle, In re, 79 Ohio St. 3d 259, 1997-Ohio-391, 680 N.E.2d 1227 (1997)—9:6, 10:2, 10:3

Rinehart, In re, 10 Ohio App. 3d 318, 462 N.E.2d 448 (4th Dist. Ross County 1983)—27:12, 27:18, 33:8

Ringo, In re, 2002-Ohio-1218, 2002 WL 418968 (Ohio Ct. App. 3d Dist. Crawford County 2002)—27:3

Rise v. State of Or., 59 F.3d 1556 (9th Cir. 1995)—14:8

Risner v. Com., 508 S.W.2d 775 (Ky. 1974)—22:17

Rivas, In re, 2002-Ohio-3747, 2002 WL 1626663 (Ohio Ct. App. 9th Dist. Lorain County 2002)—10:6

Rivera v. Morris, 1992 WL 877341 (Ohio Ct. App. 8th Dist. 1992)—19:7, 34:12

Riverside, County of v. McLaughlin, 500 U.S. 44, 111 S. Ct. 1661, 114 L. Ed. 2d 49 (1991)—14:3

R. K., In re, 2004-Ohio-439, 2004 WL 200002 (Ohio Ct. App. 9th Dist. Lorain County 2004)—30:11

R. L. K., In Interest of, 67 Ill. App. 3d 451, 23 Ill. Dec. 737, 384 N.E.2d 531 (4th Dist. 1978)—23:31

RLR v. State, 487 P.2d 27 (Alaska 1971)—23:10, 23:11, 23:23

Robert O., Matter of, 109 Misc. 2d 238, 439 N.Y.S.2d 994 (Fam. Ct. 1981)—14:10

Robert S., In re, 98 Ohio App. 3d 84, 647 N.E.2d 869 (6th Dist. Huron County 1994)—23:16

Roberts, No. 34232 (8th Dist. Ct. App., Cuyahoga, 11-13-75), In re—23:30

Robert T., In re, 8 Cal. App. 3d 990, 88 Cal. Rptr. 37 (1st Dist. 1970)—14:5

Robinson, In re, 2004-Ohio-376, 2004 WL 177720 (Ohio Ct. App. 5th Dist. Stark County 2004)—30:11

Robinson v. Robinson, 19 Ohio App. 3d 323, 484 N.E.2d 710 (10th Dist. Franklin County 1984)—34:4

Rockey v. 84 Lumber Co., 66 Ohio St. 3d 221, 1993-Ohio-174, 611 N.E.2d 789 (1993)—1:8

Rodgers, In re, 138 Ohio App. 3d 510, 741 N.E.2d 901 (12th Dist. Preble County 2000)—30:10

Rodgers, In re, 1990 WL 187334 (Ohio Ct. App. 6th Dist. Lucas County 1990)—25:4

Roe v. Wade, 410 U.S. 113, 93 S. Ct. 705, 35 L. Ed. 2d 147 (1973)—9:14

Rogers, In re, 124 Ohio App. 3d 392, 706 N.E.2d 390 (9th Dist. Summit County 1997)—23:9

Rogers, Matter of, 1989 WL 98423 (Ohio Ct. App. 3d Dist. Putnam County 1989)—9:15

Ronald B., Matter of, 61 A.D.2d 204, 401 N.Y.S.2d 544 (2d Dep't 1978)—14:3

Ronny, In re, 40 Misc. 2d 194, 242 N.Y.S.2d 844 (Fam. Ct. 1963)—14:5

Rose, Matter of, 1992 WL 110289 (Ohio Ct. App. 8th Dist. Cuyahoga County 1992)—18:2

Ross, In re, 107 Ohio App. 3d 35, 667 N.E.2d 1012 (10th Dist. Franklin County 1995)—18:2, 24:8

Rossantelli Children, In re, 2002-Ohio-2525, 2002 WL 999301 (Ohio Ct. App. 5th Dist. Delaware County 2002)—23:16

Rough, In re, 1989 WL 11513 (Ohio Ct. App. 12th Dist. Butler County 1989)—16:8

Roux, In re, 1998 WL 551990 (Ohio Ct. App. 7th Dist. Noble County 1998)—27:3

Rowe, Matter of, 1998 WL 65460 (Ohio Ct. App. 4th Dist. Scioto County 1998)—25:14, 31:8

Royal, In re, 132 Ohio App. 3d 496, 725 N.E.2d 685 (7th Dist. Mahoning County 1999)—23:4, 33:6

Rozic, Matter of, 1994 WL 393709 (Ohio Ct. App. 8th Dist. Cuyahoga County 1994)—19:6

RS, In re, 2003-Ohio-1594, 2003 WL 1689595 (Ohio Ct. App. 9th Dist. Summit County 2003)—10:5

Ruiz, In re, 27 Ohio Misc. 2d 31, 500 N.E.2d 935 (C.P. 1986)—2:2, 9:7, 9:14, 10:5

Rule, In re, 1 Ohio App. 2d 57, 30 Ohio Op. 2d 76, 203 N.E.2d 501 (3d Dist. Crawford County 1963)—18:2, 34:3, 34:4

Rulison, 1981 WL 4326 (Ohio Ct. App. 11th Dist. Lake County 1981)—8:2

Runyon, Matter of, 1993 WL 79291 (Ohio Ct. App. 4th Dist. Highland County 1993)—30:10

Russell, In re, 12 Ohio St. 3d 304, 466 N.E.2d 553 (1984)—4:4

Russell v. Parratt, 543 F.2d 1214 (8th Cir. 1976)—22:3

Rutherford, In re, 1991 WL 65113 (Ohio Ct. App. 9th Dist. Summit County 1991)—16:12

R.W., In re, 2003-Ohio-401, 2003 WL 194771 (Ohio Ct. App. 8th Dist. Cuyahoga County 2003)—25:5

R. W. v. State, 135 Ga. App. 668, 218 S.E.2d 674 (1975)—14:10

R.W.J., In re, 155 Ohio App. 3d 52, 2003-Ohio-5407, 798 N.E.2d 1206 (2d Dist. Clark County 2003)—27:3

R.W.T. v. Dalton, 712 F.2d 1225 (8th Cir. 1983)—19:6

S

S., In re, 102 Ohio App. 3d 338, 657 N.E.2d 307 (6th Dist. Lucas County 1995)—23:14, 23:24

S., In re, 36 A.D.2d 642, 319 N.Y.S.2d 752 (2d Dep't 1971)—14:3

S, In re, 73 Misc. 2d 187, 341 N.Y.S.2d 11 (Fam. Ct. 1973)—15:2

Sabrina J. v. Robbin C., 2002-Ohio-2691, 2002 WL 1303148 (Ohio Ct. App. 6th Dist. Lucas County 2002)—23:3

Sadiku, In re, 139 Ohio App. 3d 263, 743 N.E.2d 507 (9th Dist. Summit County 2000)—25:9, 25:10

Salsgiver, In re, 2003-Ohio-1203, 2003 WL 1193789 (Ohio Ct. App. 11th Dist. Geauga County 2003)—30:12

Salsgiver, In re, 2003-Ohio-1206, 2003 WL 1193784 (Ohio Ct. App. 8th Dist. Cuyahoga County 2003)—23:6

Sanders, In re, 72 Ohio App. 3d 655, 595 N.E.2d 974 (8th Dist. Cuyahoga County 1991)—27:3, 27:18, 32:2

Sanders v. Coman, 864 F. Supp. 496 (E.D. N.C. 1994)—14:8

Santobello v. New York, 404 U.S. 257, 92 S. Ct. 495, 30 L. Ed. 2d 427 (1971)—23:9

Santosky v. Kramer, 455 U.S. 745, 102 S. Ct. 1388, 71 L. Ed. 2d 599 (1982)—1:4, 9:2, 23:2, 23:13, 31:6

Sappington, In re, 123 Ohio App. 3d 448, 704 N.E.2d 339 (2d Dist. Montgomery County 1997)—23:6

Schall v. Martin, 467 U.S. 253, 104 S. Ct. 2403, 81 L. Ed. 2d 207 (1984)—1:4, 19:6

Schmerber v. California, 384 U.S. 757, 86 S. Ct. 1826, 16 L. Ed. 2d 908 (1966)—14:12

Schmidt, In re, 25 Ohio St. 3d 331, 496 N.E.2d 952 (1986)—18:2, 23:13, 31:6

Schneckloth v. Bustamonte, 412 U.S. 218, 93 S. Ct. 2041, 36 L. Ed. 2d 854 (1973)—14:5

Schoeppner's Adoption, In re, 46 Ohio St. 2d 21, 75 Ohio Op. 2d 12, 345 N.E.2d 608 (1976)—9:6

Schroder, Matter of, 1988 WL 100632 (Ohio Ct. App. 12th Dist. Brown County 1988)—21:3

Schuerman, In re, 74 Ohio App. 3d 528, 599 N.E.2d 728 (3d Dist. Paulding County 1991)—9:15, 10:6

Schulte, Matter of, 1993 WL 195853 (Ohio Ct. App. 6th Dist. Lucas County 1993)—3:3

Schulte v. Schulte, 71 Ohio St. 3d 41, 1994-Ohio-459, 641 N.E.2d 719 (1994)—23:18

Scott, In re, 1995 WL 476200 (Ohio Ct. App. 12th Dist. Butler County 1995)—25:4

Scott v. Illinois, 440 U.S. 367, 99 S. Ct. 1158, 59 L. Ed. 2d 383 (1979)—22:11

Scott K., In re, 24 Cal. 3d 395, 155 Cal. Rptr. 671, 595 P.2d 105 (1979)—14:5

Scripps Howard Broadcasting Co., State ex rel. v. Cuyahoga Cty. Court of

Common Pleas, Juv. Div., 73 Ohio St. 3d 19, 652 N.E.2d 179 (1995)— 23:11, 34:9, 35:2

Searcy, Matter of, 1992 WL 62189 (Ohio Ct. App. 8th Dist. Cuyahoga County 1992)—30:12

Seattle, City of v. Pullman, 82 Wash. 2d 794, 514 P.2d 1059 (1973)—8:6

Segura v. U.S., 468 U.S. 796, 104 S. Ct. 3380, 82 L. Ed. 2d 599 (1984)—14:2

Sekulich, In re, 65 Ohio St. 2d 13, 19 Ohio Op. 3d 192, 417 N.E.2d 1014 (1981)—17:4, 27:12, 27:19, 34:4

Sellers, In re, 1998 WL 654119 (Ohio Ct. App. 1st Dist. Hamilton County 1998)—30:12

Serfass v. U.S., 420 U.S. 377, 95 S. Ct. 1055, 43 L. Ed. 2d 265 (1975)—23:31

Seven Hills, City of v. Gossick, 1984 WL 3582 (Ohio Ct. App. 8th Dist. Cuyahoga County 1984)—19:7

Seymore, In re, 1999 WL 247775 (Ohio Ct. App. 9th Dist. Lorain County 1999)—18:2

Seymour, Matter of, 1993 WL 49263 (Ohio Ct. App. 4th Dist. Hocking County 1993)—25:9, 30:11

Shackelford, In re, 1990 WL 68954 (Ohio Ct. App. 2d Dist. Montgomery County 1990)—16:14, 18:2, 18:4, 30:13

Shadwick v. City of Tampa, 407 U.S. 345, 92 S. Ct. 2119, 32 L. Ed. 2d 783 (1972)—14:4

Shaeffer Children, In re, 85 Ohio App. 3d 683, 621 N.E.2d 426 (3d Dist. Van Wert County 1993)—18:3, 18:5, 23:6, 23:19, 30:2, 30:11, 30:12, 31:5, 34:4, 34:5

Shahan, Matter of, 1997 WL 374517 (Ohio Ct. App. 4th Dist. Hocking County 1997)—30:10

Shampine, In re, 1991 WL 232156 (Ohio Ct. App. 8th Dist. Cuyahoga County 1991)—25:3

Shanequa H., In re, 109 Ohio App. 3d 142, 671 N.E.2d 1113 (6th Dist. Lucas County 1996)—30:10

Sharp, Ex parte, 15 Idaho 120, 96 P. 563 (1908)—1:2

Sharpe v. Sharpe, 85 Ohio App. 3d 638, 620 N.E.2d 916 (11th Dist. Lake County 1993)—21:2, 24:9

Shawnta J., In re, 1998 WL 161101 (Ohio Ct. App. 6th Dist. Lucas County 1998)—30:10

Sheila O. v. Superior Court, 125 Cal. App. 3d 812, 178 Cal. Rptr. 418 (1st Dist. 1981)—22:14

Shiflett v. Korp, 1990 WL 139741 (Ohio Ct. App. 8th Dist. Cuyahoga County 1990)—30:12

Shott, In re, 75 Ohio App. 3d 270, 599 N.E.2d 363 (12th Dist. Warren County 1991)—30:6, 32:2

Shuman, Matter of, 1997 WL 33298 (Ohio Ct. App. 9th Dist. Lorain County 1997)—34:4

Silvia, In re, 1993 WL 464606 (Ohio Ct. App. 10th Dist. Franklin County 1993)—31:8

Simmons, In re, 24 N.C. App. 28, 210 S.E.2d 84 (1974)—14:10

Simmons v. U.S., 390 U.S. 377, 88 S. Ct. 967, 19 L. Ed. 2d 1247 (1968)— 14:14, 22:14

Simon, No. CA1011 (2d Dist. Ct. App., Darke, 10-15-80), In re—25:10

Simons, In re, 118 Ohio App. 3d 622, 693 N.E.2d 1111 (2d Dist. Montgomery County 1997)—23:28

Sims, In re, 13 Ohio App. 3d 37, 468 N.E.2d 111 (12th Dist. Preble County 1983)—9:3, 9:6, 16:12, 23:9, 23:16

Sims v. Engle, 619 F.2d 598 (6th Cir. 1980)—22:24

Siniard, No. C-78-063 (6th Dist. Ct. App., Lucas, 2-9-79), In re—9:3, 9:8, 19:7, 34:4

Sink v. Auglaize County Welfare Dep't, No. 2-80-15 (3d Dist. Ct. App., Auglaize, 4-15-80)—34:12

Sisinger, In re Marriage of, 5 Ohio App. 3d 28, 448 N.E.2d 842 (10th Dist. Franklin County 1982)—34:4

Sitgraves, No. 71862 (8th Dist. Ct. App., Cuyahoga, 11-26-97), In re—18:2, 18:4

Sizemore v. Smith, 6 Ohio St. 3d 330, 453 N.E.2d 632 (1983)—18:4

Skeen, In re, 71 Ohio St. 3d 1411, 641 N.E.2d 1110 (1994)—9:10

Skinner v. Railway Labor Executives' Ass'n, 489 U.S. 602, 109 S. Ct. 1402, 103 L. Ed. 2d 639 (1989)—1:4, 14:6

Small, In re, 114 Ohio App. 248, 19 Ohio Op. 2d 128, 181 N.E.2d 503 (2d Dist. Darke County 1960)—3:2

Smalley, In re, 62 Ohio App. 3d 435, 575 N.E.2d 1198 (8th Dist. Cuyahoga County 1989)—14:3, 14:10

Smart, In re, 21 Ohio App. 3d 31, 486 N.E.2d 147 (10th Dist. Franklin County 1984)—23:16, 25:2, 30:8

Smith, In re, 142 Ohio App. 3d 16, 753 N.E.2d 930 (8th Dist. Cuyahoga County 2001)—16:16, 18:3, 23:4, 23:6

Smith, In re, 1995 WL 348431 (Ohio Ct. App. 12th Dist. Butler County 1995)—26:5

Smith, In re, 1995 WL 89455 (Ohio Ct. App. 9th Dist. Summit County 1995)—18:2

Smith, In re, 2003-Ohio-800, 2003 WL 470198 (Ohio Ct. App. 11th Dist. Ashtabula County 2003)—31:6

Smith, In re, 32 Ohio App. 3d 82, 513 N.E.2d 1387 (12th Dist. Butler County 1986)—27:3

Smith, In re, 61 Ohio App. 3d 788, 573 N.E.2d 1170 (6th Dist. Lucas County 1989)—34:4

Smith, In re, 64 Ohio App. 3d 773, 582 N.E.2d 1117 (6th Dist. Lucas County 1990)—17:2, 17:4, 18:5

Smith, In re, 77 Ohio App. 3d 1, 601 N.E.2d 45 (6th Dist. Ottawa County 1991)—23:6, 25:9, 30:8, 34:3

Smith, In re, 7 Ohio App. 3d 75, 454 N.E.2d 171 (2d Dist. Greene County 1982)—23:15

Smith, In re, 80 Ohio App. 3d 502, 609 N.E.2d 1281 (1st Dist. Hamilton County 1992)—2:6, 15:2

Smith, Matter of, 1991 WL 325699 (Ohio Ct. App. 6th Dist. Ottawa County 1991)—34:12

Smith v. Daily Mail Pub. Co., 443 U.S. 97, 99 S. Ct. 2667, 61 L. Ed. 2d 399 (1979)—1:4

Smith v. Grossmann, 6 O.B.R. 83 (S.D. Ohio 1982)—23:2

Smith v. Maryland, 442 U.S. 735, 99 S. Ct. 2577, 61 L. Ed. 2d 220 (1979)—14:4

Smith v. Privette & State, 13 Ohio L. Abs. 291, 1932 WL 1836 (Ct. App. 2d Dist. Franklin County 1932)—10:3, 16:7

Smith v. State of Illinois, 390 U.S. 129, 88 S. Ct. 748, 19 L. Ed. 2d 956 (1968)—23:24

Smith Children, Matter of, 1990 WL 70926 (Ohio Ct. App. 12th Dist. Warren County 1990)—16:14, 24:9, 30:6, 30:13, 34:4

Snider, In re, 14 Ohio App. 3d 353, 471 N.E.2d 516 (3d Dist. Defiance County 1984)—16:15, 18:3

Snitzky, In re, 73 Ohio Misc. 2d 52, 657 N.E.2d 1379 (C.P. 1995)—22:17

Snook, Matter of, 1992 WL 98879 (Ohio Ct. App. 3d Dist. Seneca County 1992)—31:6

Soboslay, Matter of, 1986 WL 12865 (Ohio Ct. App. 8th Dist. Cuyahoga County 1986)—34:3

Solarz, No. 42275 (8th Dist. Ct. App., Cuyahoga, 11-6-80), In re—9:3, 10:3, 34:11

Solis, In re, 124 Ohio App. 3d 547, 706 N.E.2d 839 (8th Dist. Cuyahoga County 1997)—25:12

Sonnenberg v. State, 40 Ohio App. 475, 10 Ohio L. Abs. 271, 178 N.E. 855 (2d Dist. Franklin County 1931)—10:3

Sopher, In re, 1986 WL 2354 (Ohio Ct. App. 8th Dist. Cuyahoga County 1986)—33:4

Sopko v. Maxwell, 3 Ohio St. 2d 123, 32 Ohio Op. 2d 99, 209 N.E.2d 201 (1965)—16:3

Sours, Matter of, 1988 WL 81057 (Ohio Ct. App. 3d Dist. Hancock County 1988)—18:2

South Dakota v. Opperman, 428 U.S. 364, 96 S. Ct. 3092, 49 L. Ed. 2d 1000 (1976)—14:4

Sparto, State ex rel. v. Williams, 86 Ohio App. 377, 41 Ohio Op. 474, 55 Ohio L. Abs. 341, 86 N.E.2d 501 (2d Dist. Darke County 1949)—16:15

Speck v. Auger, 558 F.2d 394 (8th Cir. 1977)—22:3

Spencer, In re, 288 Minn. 119, 179 N.W.2d 95 (1970)—14:13

Spillman, In re, 2003-Ohio-713, 2003 WL 352477 (Ohio Ct. App. 12th Dist. Clinton County 2003)—30:12

Spitler, State ex rel. v. Seiber, 16 Ohio St. 2d 117, 45 Ohio Op. 2d 463, 243 N.E.2d 65 (1968)—34:12

Spradlin, In re, 140 Ohio App. 3d 402, 2000-Ohio-2003, 747 N.E.2d 877 (4th Dist. Highland County 2000)—23:6

Sprague, In re, 113 Ohio App. 3d 274, 680 N.E.2d 1041 (12th Dist. Butler County 1996)—18:2

Spurlock Children, In re, 1992 WL 12778 (Ohio Ct. App. 12th Dist. Butler County 1992)—31:8

Squires v. Squires, 12 Ohio App. 3d 138, 468 N.E.2d 73 (12th Dist. Preble County 1983)—17:4

Stacey S., In re, 136 Ohio App. 3d 503, 1999-Ohio-989, 737 N.E.2d 92 (6th Dist. Lucas County 1999)—23:3, 23:6, 23:27, 30:10

Stackhouse, In re, 1991 WL 37940 (Ohio Ct. App. 4th Dist. Athens County 1991)—18:2

Stall, In re, 36 Ohio St. 2d 139, 65 Ohio Op. 2d 338, 304 N.E.2d 596 (1973)—24:9

Stanley, In re, 1993 WL 512502 (Ohio Ct. App. 10th Dist. Franklin County 1993)—23:19, 25:9, 30:10, 31:7, 31:8

Stanley v. Illinois, 405 U.S. 645, 92 S. Ct. 1208, 31 L. Ed. 2d 551 (1972)—18:2, 30:8

Stantz, Matter of, 1991 WL 249431 (Ohio Ct. App. 5th Dist. Stark County 1991)—31:8

Stapleton, Matter of, 1991 WL 110217 (Ohio Ct. App. 4th Dist. Scioto County 1991)—30:10

Starkey, In re, 150 Ohio App. 3d 612, 2002-Ohio-6892, 782 N.E.2d 665 (7th Dist. Mahoning County 2002)—18:2, 18:4

Starkey, In re, 1996 WL 148656 (Ohio Ct. App. 9th Dist. Summit County 1996)—31:5

State v. Adams, 69 Ohio St. 2d 120, 23 Ohio Op. 3d 164, 431 N.E.2d 326 (1982)—22:1, 22:2, 22:3, 22:8, 22:22

State v. Agee, 86 Ohio St. 3d 1489, 716 N.E.2d 721 (1999)—22:1

State v. Aller, 82 Ohio App. 3d 9, 610 N.E.2d 1170 (6th Dist. Lucas County 1992)—8:5, 16:16

State v. Angel C., 245 Conn. 93, 715 A.2d 652 (1998)—22:3

State v. Bare, 153 Ohio App. 3d 193, 2003-Ohio-3062, 792 N.E.2d 732 (2d Dist. Champaign County 2003)—4:4

State v. Bayless, 1995 WL 328029 (Ohio Ct. App. 3d Dist. Crawford County 1995)—35:3

State v. Behl, 547 N.W.2d 382 (Minn. Ct. App. 1996)—22:3

State v. Bell, 48 Ohio St. 2d 270, 2 Ohio Op. 3d 427, 358 N.E.2d 556 (1976)—14:10

State v. Berard, 121 R.I. 551, 401 A.2d 448 (1979)—22:3

State v. Bickerstaff, 10 Ohio St. 3d 62, 461 N.E.2d 892 (1984)—22:22, 23:29

State v. Biedenharn, 19 Ohio App. 2d 204, 48 Ohio Op. 2d 338, 250 N.E.2d 778 (1st Dist. Hamilton County 1969)—16:3

State v. Black, 54 Ohio St. 2d 304, 8 Ohio Op. 3d 296, 376 N.E.2d 948 (1978)—23:21

State v. Blogna, 60 Ohio App. 3d 141, 573 N.E.2d 1223 (5th Dist. Stark County 1990)—35:3

State v. Bobo, 65 Ohio App. 3d 685, 585 N.E.2d 429 (8th Dist. Cuyahoga County 1989)—14:10

State v. Bolan, 27 Ohio St. 2d 15, 56 Ohio Op. 2d 8, 271 N.E.2d 839 (1971)—14:10

State v. Boston, 46 Ohio St. 3d 108, 545 N.E.2d 1220 (1989)—23:16, 23:19

State v. Brewster, 1 Ohio Op.3d 372 (App., Franklin 1976)—35:3

State v. Brown, 1987 WL 18253 (Ohio Ct. App. 8th Dist. Cuyahoga County 1987)—22:3

State v. Buchholz, 11 Ohio St. 3d 24, 462 N.E.2d 1222 (1984)—14:10

State v. Burgun, 49 Ohio App. 2d 112, 3 Ohio Op. 3d 177, 359 N.E.2d 1018 (8th Dist. Cuyahoga County 1976)—16:8

State v. Butler, 11 Supp. 18, 38 Ohio Law Abs. 211 (Juv., Tuscarawas 1943)—4:4

State v. Carder, 9 Ohio St. 2d 1, 38 Ohio Op. 2d 1, 222 N.E.2d 620 (1966)—14:5, 14:15

State v. Carey, 107 Ohio App. 149, 8 Ohio Op. 2d 49, 157 N.E.2d 381 (2d Dist. Miami County 1958)—23:18

State v. Carmichael, 35 Ohio St. 2d 1, 64 Ohio Op. 2d 1, 298 N.E.2d 568 (1973)—22:8, 22:9, 22:13, 22:16, 23:14

State v. Carmichael, 35 Ohio St. 2d 1 syl. 1, 64 Ohio Op. 2d 1, 298 N.E.2d 568 (1973)—22:8

State v. Carter, 27 Ohio St. 2d 135, 56 Ohio Op. 2d 75, 272 N.E.2d 119 (1971)—22:8, 22:24

State v. Casalicchio, 58 Ohio St. 3d 178, 569 N.E.2d 916 (1991)—27:14

State v. Chapin, 67 Ohio St. 2d 437, 21 Ohio Op. 3d 273, 424 N.E.2d 317 (1981)—23:7

State v. Chrisman, 9 Ohio St. 2d 27, 38 Ohio Op. 2d 16, 222 N.E.2d 649 (1966)—16:16

State v. Clark, 71 Ohio St. 3d 466, 1994-Ohio-43, 644 N.E.2d 331 (1994)—23:18

State v. Clark, 84 Ohio App. 3d 789, 618 N.E.2d 257 (5th Dist. Stark County 1993)—2:2

State v. Cole, 1983 WL 4463 (Ohio Ct. App. 12th Dist. Butler County 1983)—22:13

State v. Cole, 1995 WL 753956 (Ohio Ct. App. 8th Dist. Cuyahoga County 1995)—35:3

State v. Compton, 304 N.J. Super. 477, 701 A.2d 468 (App. Div. 1997)—23:19

State v. Cook, 83 Ohio St. 3d 404, 1998-Ohio-291, 700 N.E.2d 570 (1998)—
6:1, 6:2

State v. Corrado, 1993 WL 76234 (Ohio Ct. App. 11th Dist. Lake County
1993)—27:18

State v. Cowans, 10 Ohio St. 2d 96, 39 Ohio Op. 2d 97, 227 N.E.2d 201
(1967)—14:11

State v. Cox, 42 Ohio St. 2d 200, 71 Ohio Op. 2d 186, 327 N.E.2d 639 (1975)—
35:3

State v. Crowell, No. 42457 (8th Dist. Ct. App., Cuyahoga, 3-19-81)—7:4

State v. Crumedy, 1997 WL 37790 (Ohio Ct. App. 8th Dist. Cuyahoga County
1997)—21:2

State v. Cunningham, No. 31563 (8th Dist. Ct. App., Cuyahoga, 11-9-72)—2:5

State v. Cutlip, 2004-Ohio-2120, 2004 WL 895980 (Ohio Ct. App. 9th Dist.
Medina County 2004)—23:25

State v. D'Ambrosio, 67 Ohio St. 3d 185, 1993-Ohio-170, 616 N.E.2d 909
(1993)—23:28

State v. Davis, 1997 WL 605193 (Ohio Ct. App. 2d Dist. Clark County 1997)—
22:7

State v. Davis, 56 Ohio St. 2d 51, 10 Ohio Op. 3d 87, 381 N.E.2d 641 (1978)—
14:4, 14:5, 14:15

State v. DeLong, 456 A.2d 877 (Me. 1983)—23:15

State v. Dever, 64 Ohio St. 3d 401, 1992-Ohio-41, 596 N.E.2d 436 (1992)—
23:16

State v. D.H., 340 So. 2d 1163 (Fla. 1976)—2:6

State v. Dickens, 1987 WL 17928 (Ohio Ct. App. 9th Dist. Summit County
1987)—22:8

State v. Douglas, 20 Ohio St. 3d 34, 485 N.E.2d 711 (1985)—1:8, 22:1, 22:2,
22:8, 22:17

State v. Doyle, 1991 WL 286149 (Ohio Ct. App. 3d Dist. Allen County 1991)—
22:6

State v. Duncan, 53 Ohio St. 2d 215, 7 Ohio Op. 3d 380, 373 N.E.2d 1234
(1978)—23:16

State v. Dunham, 154 Ohio St. 63, 42 Ohio Op. 133, 93 N.E.2d 286 (1950)—
9:7

State v. Durfee, 322 N.W.2d 778 (Minn. 1982)—23:19

State v. Earich, 19 Ohio Op. 2d 39, 86 Ohio L. Abs. 90, 176 N.E.2d 191 (Juv.
Ct. 1961)—9:7

State v. Eastham, 39 Ohio St. 3d 307, 530 N.E.2d 409 (1988)—23:23

State v. Eddington, 52 Ohio App. 2d 312, 6 Ohio Op. 3d 317, 369 N.E.2d
1054 (3d Dist. Marion County 1976)—24:1

State v. Edwards, 49 Ohio St. 2d 31, 3 Ohio Op. 3d 18, 358 N.E.2d 1051
(1976)—23:21

State v. Eppinger, No. 30798 (8th Dist. Ct. App., Cuyahoga, 12-9-71)—23:20,
34:9, 35:3

State v. Eubank, 60 Ohio St. 2d 183, 14 Ohio Op. 3d 416, 398 N.E.2d 567
(1979)—23:14

State v. Evans, 144 Ohio App. 3d 539, 760 N.E.2d 909 (1st Dist. Hamilton
County 2001)—14:9, 14:10, 23:27

State v. Faulkner, 102 Ohio App. 3d 602, 657 N.E.2d 602 (3d Dist. Marion
County 1995)—27:3

State v. Felty, 2 Ohio App. 3d 62, 440 N.E.2d 803 (1st Dist. Hamilton County
1981)—34:8

State v. Fowler, 27 Ohio App. 3d 149, 500 N.E.2d 390 (8th Dist. Cuyahoga
County 1985)—23:16

State v. Fox, 1998 WL 525577 (Ohio Ct. App. 5th Dist. Stark County 1998)—35:3

State v. Frazier, 61 Ohio St. 3d 247, 574 N.E.2d 483 (1991)—23:18

State v. Fred Podeyn, 1996 WL 20873 (Ohio Ct. App. 6th Dist. Huron County 1996)—35:3

State v. Fullmer, 76 Ohio App. 335, 32 Ohio Op. 53, 43 Ohio L. Abs. 193, 62 N.E.2d 268 (2d Dist. Montgomery County 1945)—34:7

State v. Gaida, No. 30423 (8th Dist. Ct. App., Cuyahoga, 3-2-72)—2:5, 7:4, 16:16

State v. Gibbs, 94 Idaho 908, 500 P.2d 209 (1972)—22:3, 22:12

State v. Gilroy, 1995 WL 243440 (Ohio Ct. App. 3d Dist. Auglaize County 1995)—35:3

State v. Golphin, 1996 WL 673975 (Ohio Ct. App. 8th Dist. Cuyahoga County 1996)—22:4

State v. Golphin, 78 Ohio St. 3d 1441, 676 N.E.2d 1187 (1997)—3:3

State v. Golphin, 81 Ohio St. 3d 543, 1998-Ohio-336, 692 N.E.2d 608 (1998)—22:4

State v. Grady, 3 Ohio App. 3d 174, 444 N.E.2d 51 (8th Dist. Cuyahoga County 1981)—27:18

State v. Griffin, 93 Ohio App. 299, 51 Ohio Op. 47, 63 Ohio L. Abs. 122, 106 N.E.2d 668 (2d Dist. Champaign County 1952)—10:2

State v. Hale, 21 Ohio App. 2d 207, 50 Ohio Op. 2d 340, 256 N.E.2d 239 (10th Dist. Franklin County 1969)—35:3

State v. Hall, 57 Ohio App. 3d 144, 567 N.E.2d 305 (8th Dist. Cuyahoga County 1989)—35:3

State v. Hanning, 89 Ohio St. 3d 86, 2000-Ohio-436, 728 N.E.2d 1059 (2000)—1:6, 22:7, 22:8

State v. Harris, 1981 WL 3505 (Ohio Ct. App. 10th Dist. Franklin County 1981)—22:18

State v. Harris, 48 Ohio St. 2d 351, 2 Ohio Op. 3d 472, 359 N.E.2d 67 (1976)—14:10

State v. Hawkins, 1998 WL 134321 (Ohio Ct. App. 10th Dist. Franklin County 1998)—35:3

State v. Hawkins, 66 Ohio St. 3d 339, 612 N.E.2d 1227 (1993)—35:3

State v. Henry, 78 N.M. 573, 434 P.2d 692 (1967)—23:29

State v. Hershberger, 83 Ohio L. Abs. 62, 168 N.E.2d 13 (Ct. App. 9th Dist. Wayne County 1959)—33:8

State v. Hill, No. 76AP-504 (10th Dist. Ct. App., Franklin, 12-28-76)—16:8

State v. Holland, 346 N.W.2d 302 (S.D. 1984)—23:19

State v. Holt, 132 Ohio App. 3d 601, 725 N.E.2d 1155 (1st Dist. Hamilton County 1997)—14:10

State v. Holt, 17 Ohio St. 2d 81, 46 Ohio Op. 2d 408, 246 N.E.2d 365 (1969)—23:18

State v. Homer, 78 Ohio App. 3d 477, 605 N.E.2d 426 (11th Dist. Geauga County 1992)—2:2

State v. Hopfer, 112 Ohio App. 3d 521, 679 N.E.2d 321 (2d Dist. Montgomery County 1996)—14:10, 22:8, 22:22

State v. Houston, 70 Ohio App. 3d 152, 590 N.E.2d 839 (6th Dist. Lucas County 1990)—22:8, 22:23

State v. Hunt, 2 Ariz. App. 6, 406 P.2d 208 (1965)—14:3

State v. Hurt, 30 Ohio St. 2d 86, 59 Ohio Op. 2d 106, 282 N.E.2d 578 (1972)—14:13

State v. Ivey, 98 Ohio App. 3d 249, 648 N.E.2d 519 (8th Dist. Cuyahoga County 1994)—9:15

State v. Jackson, 90 Ohio L. Abs. 577, 190 N.E.2d 38 (Ct. App. 10th Dist. Franklin County 1960)—16:16

State v. James, 106 Ohio App. 3d 686, 666 N.E.2d 1185 (9th Dist. Summit County 1995)—27:3

State v. Johnson, 1996 WL 355288 (Ohio Ct. App. 8th Dist. Cuyahoga County 1996)—19:2

State v. Jones, 53 Ohio App. 2d 308, 7 Ohio Op. 3d 391, 373 N.E.2d 1272 (9th Dist. Summit County 1977)—14:10

State v. Jones, 88 Ohio St. 3d 430, 2000-Ohio-374, 727 N.E.2d 886 (2000)—14:3

State v. Joseph T., 175 W. Va. 598, 336 S.E.2d 728, 28 Ed. Law Rep. 1169 (1985)—14:6

State v. Kaiser, 56 Ohio St. 2d 27, 10 Ohio Op. 3d 74, 381 N.E.2d 632 (1978)—14:14

State v. Kassow, 28 Ohio St. 2d 141, 57 Ohio Op. 2d 390, 277 N.E.2d 435 (1971)—14:9

State v. Kelly, 154 Ohio App. 3d 285, 2003-Ohio-4783, 797 N.E.2d 104 (9th Dist. Medina County 2003)—35:3

State v. Kimbler, No. 77AP-127 (10th Dist. Ct. App., Franklin, 9-20-77)—3:3

State v. King, 10 Ohio App. 3d 161, 460 N.E.2d 1383 (1st Dist. Hamilton County 1983)—23:21

State v. Kiraly, 56 Ohio App. 2d 37, 10 Ohio Op. 3d 53, 381 N.E.2d 649 (8th Dist. Cuyahoga County 1977)—14:13

State v. Kittle, 2003-Ohio-3097, 2003 WL 21385035 (Ohio Ct. App. 6th Dist. Lucas County 2003)—23:18

State v. Klingenberger, 113 Ohio St. 418, 3 Ohio L. Abs. 675, 149 N.E. 395 (1925)—2:4, 3:3, 22:22

State v. Koballa, 2003-Ohio-3535, 2003 WL 21513041 (Ohio Ct. App. 8th Dist. Cuyahoga County 2003)—35:3

State v. Konicek, 16 Ohio App. 3d 17, 474 N.E.2d 363 (8th Dist. Cuyahoga County 1984)—7:4

State v. Kunkleman, No. L-79-156 (6th Dist. Ct. App., Lucas, 4-25-80)—16:16

State v. Lathan, 30 Ohio St. 2d 92, 59 Ohio Op. 2d 109, 282 N.E.2d 574 (1972)—14:13

State v. Lee, 1983 WL 5753 (Ohio Ct. App. 8th Dist. Cuyahoga County 1983)—4:4, 21:3

State v. Lee, 9 Ohio App. 3d 282, 459 N.E.2d 910 (9th Dist. Summit County 1983)—23:18

State v. Lewis, 4 Ohio App. 3d 275, 448 N.E.2d 487 (3d Dist. Union County 1982)—23:18

State v. Lipker, 16 Ohio App. 2d 21, 45 Ohio Op. 2d 34, 241 N.E.2d 171 (4th Dist. Lawrence County 1968)—14:10

State v. Loines, 20 Ohio App. 3d 69, 484 N.E.2d 727 (8th Dist. Cuyahoga County 1984)—16:8

State v. Long, 7 Ohio App. 3d 248, 455 N.E.2d 534 (10th Dist. Franklin County 1983)—7:4

State v. Lopez, 112 Ohio App. 3d 659, 679 N.E.2d 1155 (9th Dist. Lorain County 1996)—22:8

State v. Lopez, 306 S.C. 362, 412 S.E.2d 390 (1991)—23:19

State v. Lowder, 79 Ohio App. 237, 34 Ohio Op. 568, 72 N.E.2d 785 (5th Dist. Stark County 1946)—35:3

State v. Lowe, 1995 WL 470543 (Ohio Ct. App. 12th Dist. Fayette County 1995)—35:4

State v. Loyd, 297 Minn. 442, 212 N.W.2d 671 (1973)—14:10

State v. Lukens, 66 Ohio App. 3d 794, 586 N.E.2d 1099 (10th Dist. Franklin County 1990)—8:5, 35:3

State v. Madison, 64 Ohio St. 2d 322, 18 Ohio Op. 3d 491, 415 N.E.2d 272 (1980)—14:14

State v. Majoros, No. 42062 (8th Dist. Ct. App., Cuyahoga, 11-13-80)—4:4

State v. Mann, 1982 WL 5770 (Ohio Ct. App. 11th Dist. Ashtabula County 1982)—35:3

State v. Mardis, 134 Ohio App. 3d 6, 729 N.E.2d 1272 (10th Dist. Franklin County 1999)—14:10

State v. Marinski, 139 Ohio St. 559, 23 Ohio Op. 50, 41 N.E.2d 387 (1942)—35:3

State v. Marks, 1987 WL 6763 (Ohio Ct. App. 4th Dist. Athens County 1987)—35:3

State v. Martinez, 276 Kan. 527, 78 P.3d 769 (2003)—14:8

State v. Matha, 107 Ohio App. 3d 756, 669 N.E.2d 504 (9th Dist. Lorain County 1995)—23:13, 27:19

State v. Maupin, 42 Ohio St. 2d 473, 71 Ohio Op. 2d 485, 330 N.E.2d 708 (1975)—23:19

State v. McCallister, 1987 WL 27857 (Ohio Ct. App. 5th Dist. Stark County 1987)—33:9

State v. McClary, 207 Conn. 233, 541 A.2d 96 (1988)—23:19

State v. McDonald, 1990 WL 78593 (Ohio Ct. App. 2d Dist. Montgomery County 1990)—22:13, 22:17

State v. McGuire, 1987 WL 31129 (Ohio Ct. App. 11th Dist. Lake County 1987)—35:3

State v. McMillan, 62 Ohio App. 3d 565, 577 N.E.2d 91 (9th Dist. Lorain County 1989)—23:18

State v. Mendenhall, 21 Ohio App. 2d 135, 50 Ohio Op. 2d 227, 255 N.E.2d 307 (11th Dist. Lake County 1969)—2:5

State v. Metz, 1997 WL 305220 (Ohio Ct. App. 4th Dist. Washington County 1997)—21:2, 21:3

State v. Miller, No. 33127 (8th Dist. Ct. App., Cuyahoga, 1-23-75)—23:9

State v. Mohi, 901 P.2d 991 (Utah 1995)—22:3

State v. Moody, 55 Ohio St. 2d 64, 9 Ohio Op. 3d 71, 377 N.E.2d 1008 (1978)—14:14

State v. Moreland, 50 Ohio St. 3d 58, 552 N.E.2d 894 (1990)—23:18, 23:19

State v. Morris, 42 Ohio St. 2d 307, 71 Ohio Op. 2d 294, 329 N.E.2d 85 (1975)—14:4

State v. Moyers, 137 Ohio App. 3d 130, 2000-Ohio-1669, 738 N.E.2d 90 (3d Dist. Seneca County 2000)—6:2

State v. Mullins, 34 Ohio App. 3d 192, 517 N.E.2d 945 (5th Dist. Fairfield County 1986)—23:21

State v. Neguse, 71 Ohio App. 3d 596, 594 N.E.2d 1116 (10th Dist. Franklin County 1991)—2:4, 3:3

State v. Neiderhelman, 1995 WL 550030 (Ohio Ct. App. 12th Dist. Clermont County 1995)—35:3

State v. Newton, 1983 WL 6836 (Ohio Ct. App. 6th Dist. Fulton County 1983)—1:8, 19:7, 22:9, 22:17, 23:29

State v. Newton, 1991 WL 3214 (Ohio Ct. App. 12th Dist. Warren County 1991)—35:3

State v. Olivas, 122 Wash. 2d 73, 856 P.2d 1076 (1993)—14:8

State v. Osborne, 50 Ohio St. 2d 211, 4 Ohio Op. 3d 406, 364 N.E.2d 216 (1977)—14:10

State v. Ostrowski, 30 Ohio St. 2d 34, 59 Ohio Op. 2d 62, 282 N.E.2d 359 (1972)—14:12, 23:10, 23:11

State v. Ostrowski, 30 Ohio St. 2d 34, 59 Ohio Op. 2d 62, 282 N.E.2d 359 (1972)—23:17

State v. Oviedo, 5 Ohio App. 3d 168, 450 N.E.2d 700 (6th Dist. Wood County 1982)—22:17

State v. Parks, 51 Ohio App. 3d 194, 555 N.E.2d 671 (2d Dist. Montgomery County 1988)—18:2, 22:8, 22:12, 22:13

State v. Payne, 118 Ohio App. 3d 699, 693 N.E.2d 1159 (3d Dist. Seneca County 1997)—22:3, 22:20, 22:24

State v. Payne, 1982 WL 3487 (Ohio Ct. App. 4th Dist. Pickaway County 1982)—17:4

State v. Penrod, 62 Ohio App. 3d 720, 577 N.E.2d 424 (9th Dist. Summit County 1989)—22:24, 23:31

State v. Perricone, 37 N.J. 463, 181 A.2d 751 (1962)—9:7

State v. Perry, 14 Ohio St. 2d 256, 43 Ohio Op. 2d 434, 237 N.E.2d 891 (1968)—14:10

State v. Peterson, 9 Ohio Misc. 154, 38 Ohio Op. 2d 220, 38 Ohio Op. 2d 245, 223 N.E.2d 838 (Mun. Ct. 1966)—2:4

State v. Pratt, 1997 WL 666788 (Ohio Ct. App. 9th Dist. Summit County 1997)—35:3

State v. Ralston, 67 Ohio App. 2d 81, 21 Ohio Op. 3d 403, 425 N.E.2d 916 (1st Dist. Clermont County 1979)—23:21

State v. Reddick, 113 Ohio App. 3d 788, 682 N.E.2d 38 (9th Dist. Lorain County 1996)—22:24

State v. Reed, 54 Ohio App. 2d 193, 8 Ohio Op. 3d 333, 376 N.E.2d 609 (5th Dist. Coshocton County 1977)—23:29

State v. Reyes-Cairo, 1997 WL 256670 (Ohio Ct. App. 6th Dist. Lucas County 1997)—35:3

State v. Reynolds, 80 Ohio St. 3d 670, 1998-Ohio-171, 687 N.E.2d 1358 (1998)—14:5

State v. R.G.D., 108 N.J. 1, 527 A.2d 834 (1987)—22:10

State v. Rice, 1990 WL 97687 (Ohio Ct. App. 6th Dist. Lucas County 1990)—28:2, 28:10

State v. Riggins, 68 Ohio App. 2d 1, 22 Ohio Op. 3d 1, 426 N.E.2d 504 (8th Dist. Cuyahoga County 1980)—22:3, 22:4, 22:13, 22:18, 22:22

State v. Robinson, 1983 WL 5630 (Ohio Ct. App. 8th Dist. Cuyahoga County 1983)—23:29

State v. Robinson, 98 Ohio App. 3d 560, 649 N.E.2d 18 (8th Dist. Cuyahoga County 1994)—35:3

State v. Ross, 23 Ohio App. 2d 215, 52 Ohio Op. 2d 311, 262 N.E.2d 427 (2d Dist. Greene County 1970)—22:18, 23:30

State v. Said, 71 Ohio St. 3d 473, 1994-Ohio-402, 644 N.E.2d 337 (1994)—23:18

State v. Salmon, 1981 WL 4980 (Ohio Ct. App. 8th Dist. Cuyahoga County 1981)—22:24

State v. Schaaf, 109 Wash. 2d 1, 743 P.2d 240 (1987)—23:10

State v. Schmidt, 29 Ohio St. 3d 32, 505 N.E.2d 627, 38 Ed. Law Rep. 1137 (1987)—9:7

State v. Self, 56 Ohio St. 3d 73, 564 N.E.2d 446 (1990)—23:16

State v. Shardell, 107 Ohio App. 338, 8 Ohio Op. 2d 262, 79 Ohio L. Abs. 534, 153 N.E.2d 510 (8th Dist. Cuyahoga County 1958)—1:6, 23:13, 23:14, 23:27

State v. Sheardon, 31 Ohio St. 2d 20, 60 Ohio Op. 2d 11, 285 N.E.2d 335 (1972)—14:13

State v. Shedrick, 59 Ohio St. 3d 146, 572 N.E.2d 59 (1991)—35:3

State v. Shedrick, 61 Ohio St. 3d 331, 574 N.E.2d 1065 (1991)—23:20, 35:3

State v. Sherow, 101 Ohio App. 169, 1 Ohio Op. 2d 100, 138 N.E.2d 444 (4th Dist. Gallia County 1956)—35:2

State v. Simpson, 148 Ohio App. 3d 221, 2002-Ohio-3077, 772 N.E.2d 707 (5th Dist. Licking County 2002)—22:7

State v. Sims, 3 Ohio App. 3d 321, 445 N.E.2d 235 (8th Dist. Cuyahoga County 1981)—14:10

State v. Smagula, 117 N.H. 663, 377 A.2d 608 (1977)—22:3

State v. Smith, 29 Ohio App. 3d 194, 504 N.E.2d 1121 (8th Dist. Cuyahoga County 1985)—22:8

State v. Soke, 1993 WL 266951 (Ohio Ct. App. 8th Dist. Cuyahoga County 1993)—2:4, 22:9

State v. Spencer, 1995 WL 363961 (Ohio Ct. App. 8th Dist. Cuyahoga County 1995)—19:2

State v. Steele, 8 Ohio App. 3d 137, 456 N.E.2d 513 (10th Dist. Franklin County 1982)—22:22, 23:29

State v. Stein, 203 Kan. 638, 456 P.2d 1 (1969)—14:6

State v. Steinhauer, 216 So. 2d 214 (Fla. 1968)—22:3

State v. Storch, 66 Ohio St. 3d 280, 1993-Ohio-38, 612 N.E.2d 305 (1993)—23:16, 23:25

State v. Stricklen, 63 Ohio St. 2d 47, 17 Ohio Op. 3d 29, 406 N.E.2d 1110 (1980)—14:13

State v. Strodes, 42 Ohio App. 2d 8, 71 Ohio Op. 2d 49, 325 N.E.2d 899 (2d Dist. Clark County 1974)—14:13

State v. Taylor, 26 Ohio App. 3d 69, 498 N.E.2d 211 (3d Dist. Auglaize County 1985)—3:3, 22:3, 22:4, 22:12

State v. Taylor, 66 Ohio St. 3d 295, 612 N.E.2d 316 (1993)—23:16

State v. Tilley, 1993 WL 385318 (Ohio Ct. App. 5th Dist. Stark County 1993)—22:8

State v. Tillman, 66 Ohio App. 3d 464, 585 N.E.2d 550 (9th Dist. Lorain County 1990)—2:4, 3:3

State v. Trapp, 52 Ohio App. 2d 189, 6 Ohio Op. 3d 175, 368 N.E.2d 1278 (1st Dist. Hamilton County 1977)—22:22, 23:29

State v. Turner, No. 39951 (8th Dist. Ct. App., Cuyahoga, 5-3-79)—22:24

State v. Uhler, 80 Ohio App. 3d 113, 608 N.E.2d 1091 (9th Dist. Wayne County 1992)—23:16

State v. Villagomez, 44 Ohio App. 2d 209, 73 Ohio Op. 2d 215, 337 N.E.2d 167 (3d Dist. Defiance County 1974)—16:3

State v. Wagner, 30 Ohio App. 3d 261, 508 N.E.2d 164 (8th Dist. Cuyahoga County 1986)—23:16

State v. Wallace, 37 Ohio St. 3d 87, 524 N.E.2d 466 (1988)—23:16

State v. Walls, 96 Ohio St. 3d 437, 2002-Ohio-5059, 775 N.E.2d 829 (2002)—2:3, 22:4

State v. Watson, 47 Ohio St. 3d 93, 547 N.E.2d 1181 (1989)—22:1, 22:8, 22:13

State v. Weber, 19 Ohio App. 3d 214, 484 N.E.2d 207 (1st Dist. Hamilton County 1984)—35:4

State v. West, 134 Ohio App. 3d 45, 730 N.E.2d 388 (1st Dist. Hamilton County 1999)—6:4

State v. Whatley, 320 So. 2d 123 (La. 1975)—14:10

State v. Whisenant, 127 Ohio App. 3d 75, 711 N.E.2d 1016 (11th Dist. Portage County 1998)—14:2, 14:10, 22:1, 22:6, 22:8, 22:10, 22:22, 22:26

State v. Whisner, 47 Ohio St. 2d 181, 1 Ohio Op. 3d 105, 351 N.E.2d 750 (1976)—9:7

State v. White, 15 Ohio St. 2d 146, 44 Ohio Op. 2d 132, 239 N.E.2d 65 (1968)—23:14

State v. White, 6 Ohio App. 3d 1, 451 N.E.2d 533 (8th Dist. Cuyahoga County 1982)—35:3

State v. Whiteside, 6 Ohio App. 3d 30, 452 N.E.2d 332 (3d Dist. Allen County 1982)—22:22, 22:23

State v. Wilcox, 26 Ohio N.P. (n.s.) 343, 1926 WL 2503 (Juv. Ct. 1926)—2:2

State v. Williams, 16 Ohio App. 3d 484, 477 N.E.2d 221 (1st Dist. Hamilton County 1984)—35:3

State v. Williams, 51 Ohio St. 2d 112, 5 Ohio Op. 3d 98, 364 N.E.2d 1364 (1977)—16:17

State v. Willman, 77 Ohio App. 3d 344, 602 N.E.2d 323 (1st Dist. Hamilton County 1991)—35:3

State v. Wilson, 156 Ohio St. 525, 46 Ohio Op. 437, 103 N.E.2d 552, 30 A.L.R.2d 763 (1952)—23:18

State v. Wilson, 73 Ohio St. 3d 40, 1995-Ohio-217, 652 N.E.2d 196 (1995)—2:4, 3:3, 22:1, 22:4

State v. Wilson, 73 Ohio St. 3d 40, syl., para. 1, 1995-Ohio-217, 652 N.E.2d 196 (1995)—22:4

State v. Wingerd, 40 Ohio App. 2d 236, 69 Ohio Op. 2d 217, 318 N.E.2d 866 (4th Dist. Athens County 1974)—14:6

State v. Workman, 14 Ohio App. 3d 385, 471 N.E.2d 853 (8th Dist. Cuyahoga County 1984)—21:2, 23:18

State v. Wylie, 1983 WL 5631 (Ohio Ct. App. 8th Dist. Cuyahoga County 1983)—34:4

State v. Yoss, 10 Ohio App. 2d 47, 39 Ohio Op. 2d 81, 225 N.E.2d 275 (7th Dist. Carroll County 1967)—22:16

State v. Young, 234 Ga. 488, 216 S.E.2d 586 (1975)—14:6

State v. Young, 44 Ohio App. 2d 387, 73 Ohio Op. 2d 462, 339 N.E.2d 668 (10th Dist. Franklin County 1975)—22:22, 23:29

State, ex rel. Duganitz v. Court of Common Pleas of Cuyahoga County, 69 Ohio St. 2d 270, 23 Ohio Op. 3d 267, 432 N.E.2d 163 (1982)—27:19

State in Interest of Aaron, In re, 266 So. 2d 726 (La. Ct. App. 3d Cir. 1972)—23:30

State in Interest of Carlo, In re, 48 N.J. 224, 225 A.2d 110 (1966)—14:9

State In Interest of Causey, 363 So. 2d 472 (La. 1978)—23:7

State in Interest of D.A.M., In re, 132 N.J. Super. 192, 333 A.2d 270 (App. Div. 1975)—23:27

State in Interest of H. M. T., 159 N.J. Super. 104, 387 A.2d 368 (App. Div. 1978)—23:29

State in Interest of Hunter, 387 So. 2d 1086 (La. 1980)—22:3

State In Interest of W. J., In re, 116 N.J. Super. 462, 282 A.2d 770 (App. Div. 1971)—23:21

Staten, In re, 1998 WL 735949 (Ohio Ct. App. 2d Dist. Montgomery County 1998)—30:11

Steagald v. U.S., 451 U.S. 204, 101 S. Ct. 1642, 68 L. Ed. 2d 38 (1981)—14:4

Steele v. U.S., 267 U.S. 498, 45 S. Ct. 414, 69 L. Ed. 757 (1925)—14:4

Steinhauer v. State, 206 So. 2d 25 (Fla. Dist. Ct. App. 3d Dist. 1967)—22:11

Stertzbach, Matter of, 1990 WL 52454 (Ohio Ct. App. 5th Dist. Stark County 1990)—25:9

Stevens, In re, 1993 WL 265130 (Ohio Ct. App. 2d Dist. Montgomery County 1993)—10:6, 25:14, 26:2, 26:4, 30:10, 31:7, 31:8

Stillman, In re, 155 Ohio App. 3d 333, 2003-Ohio-6228, 801 N.E.2d 475 (11th Dist. Ashtabula County 2003)—30:11

Stoffer, Matter of, 1995 WL 347906 (Ohio Ct. App. 5th Dist. Stark County 1995)—16:14

Stone, In re, 2003-Ohio-3071, 2003 WL 21373156 (Ohio Ct. App. 12th Dist. Clinton County 2003)—23:7

Stoutzenberger, In Interest of, 235 Pa. Super. 500, 344 A.2d 668 (1975)—14:13

Stovall v. Denno, 388 U.S. 293, 87 S. Ct. 1967, 18 L. Ed. 2d 1199 (1967)—14:14

Stover, Custody of, 1993 WL 385313 (Ohio Ct. App. 5th Dist. Guernsey County 1993)—23:3

Strickland, Matter of, 1987 WL 13057 (Ohio Ct. App. 12th Dist. Warren County 1987)—21:2

Strickland v. Washington, 466 U.S. 668, 104 S. Ct. 2052, 80 L. Ed. 2d 674 (1984)—22:11, 23:5

Strothers, State ex rel. v. Colon, 1999 WL 125847 (Ohio Ct. App. 8th Dist. Cuyahoga County 1999)—33:10

Strothers, State ex rel. v. Wertheim, 80 Ohio St. 3d 155, 1997-Ohio-349, 684 N.E.2d 1239 (1997)—14:17

Strunk v. U.S., 412 U.S. 434, 93 S. Ct. 2260, 37 L. Ed. 2d 56 (1973)—23:29

St. Thomas Medical Center v. Morgan, 1984 WL 5207 (Ohio Ct. App. 9th Dist. Summit County 1984)—32:2

Sullivan, Matter of, 1992 WL 42813 (Ohio Ct. App. 3d Dist. Seneca County 1992)—16:14

Sullivan, Nos. 79 AP-893, 79 AP-894 (10th Dist. Ct. App., Franklin, 12-16-80), In re—9:7, 10:3, 16:7

Summers v. State, 248 Ind. 551, 230 N.E.2d 320 (1967)—22:16, 22:17

Surdel v. MetroHealth Med. Ctr., 135 Ohio App. 3d 141, 733 N.E.2d 281 (8th Dist. Cuyahoga County 1999)—14:17

Swackhammer, Matter of, 1986 WL 13411 (Ohio Ct. App. 4th Dist. Ross County 1986)—16:8

Swain, In re, 68 Ohio App. 3d 737, 589 N.E.2d 483 (11th Dist. Portage County 1991)—24:9

Sweat, Matter of, 1987 WL 13054 (Ohio Ct. App. 12th Dist. Warren County 1987)—10:5

Swisher, In re, 1997 WL 164311 (Ohio Ct. App. 9th Dist. Summit County 1997)—31:8

Swisher v. Brady, 438 U.S. 204, 98 S. Ct. 2699, 57 L. Ed. 2d 705, 25 Fed. R. Serv. 2d 1463 (1978)—1:4, 23:2, 23:31, 24:9

S. W. T.'s Welfare, Matter of, 277 N.W.2d 507 (Minn. 1979)—23:7

Szabat, No. 94-P-0049 (11th Dist. Ct. App., Portage, 9-1-95), In re—30:10

Szymczak, Matter of, 1998 WL 414924 (Ohio Ct. App. 8th Dist. Cuyahoga County 1998)—34:4

T

Taceia R., Matter of, 1996 WL 71003 (Ohio Ct. App. 6th Dist. Lucas County 1996)—26:6

Tackett, Matter of, 1990 WL 34369 (Ohio Ct. App. 4th Dist. Adams County 1990)—30:11, 30:12

Tague v. Louisiana, 444 U.S. 469, 100 S. Ct. 652, 62 L. Ed. 2d 622 (1980)—14:10

Tailford, In re, 95 Ohio St. 411, 116 N.E. 1086 (1917)—1:6

Tanker, In re, 142 Ohio App. 3d 159, 754 N.E.2d 813 (8th Dist. Cuyahoga County 2001)—30:13

Tate v. State, 864 So. 2d 44 (Fla. Dist. Ct. App. 4th Dist. 2003)—23:7

Taylor, In re, 1995 WL 134754 (Ohio Ct. App. 9th Dist. Lorain County 1995)—27:19

Taylor, Matter of, 1990 WL 193601 (Ohio Ct. App. 4th Dist. Scioto County 1990)—26:6

Taylor, Matter of, 1995 WL 497614 (Ohio Ct. App. 5th Dist. Coshocton County 1995)—30:12, 31:4, 31:5

Taylor v. Alabama, 457 U.S. 687, 102 S. Ct. 2664, 73 L. Ed. 2d 314 (1982)—14:9

Taylor v. U.S., 414 U.S. 17, 94 S. Ct. 194, 38 L. Ed. 2d 174 (1973)—23:23, 23:26

T.B., No. K97-1055 (5th Dist. Ct. App., Licking, 1-26-98), In re—13:6

T.C., In re, 140 Ohio App. 3d 409, 2000-Ohio-1769, 747 N.E.2d 881 (3d Dist. Allen County 2000)—23:3, 23:5

Terrance P., In re, 124 Ohio App. 3d 487, 706 N.E.2d 801 (6th Dist. Lucas County 1997)—34:11

Terrance P., In re, 129 Ohio App. 3d 418, 717 N.E.2d 1160 (6th Dist. Lucas County 1998)—23:5, 23:9

Terry v. Ohio, 392 U.S. 1, 88 S. Ct. 1868, 20 L. Ed. 2d 889 (1968)—14:3

Terry H., In re, 1 O.B.R. 377 (C.P., Cuyahoga 1982)—22:21, 23:28

Terry W., In re, 59 Cal. App. 3d 745, 130 Cal. Rptr. 913 (2d Dist. 1976)—23:15

Texas v. Brown, 460 U.S. 730, 103 S. Ct. 1535, 75 L. Ed. 2d 502 (1983)—14:4

The Cincinnati Post, State ex rel. v. Second Dist. Court of Appeals, 65 Ohio St. 3d 378, 604 N.E.2d 153 (1992)—12:8, 12:10

Theodore F., In re, 47 A.D.2d 945, 367 N.Y.S.2d 103 (2d Dep't 1975)—23:9

Therklidsen, In re, 54 Ohio App. 2d 195, 8 Ohio Op. 3d 335, 376 N.E.2d 970 (10th Dist. Franklin County 1977)—1:8, 19:7, 23:29

Thomas, In re, 1993 WL 141597 (Ohio Ct. App. 9th Dist. Summit County 1993)—18:2

Thomas, No. 15813 (9th Dist. Ct. App., Summit, 3-10-93), In re—26:4

Thomas, Nos. 39494, 39495 (8th Dist. Ct. App., Cuyahoga, 7-19-79), In re—9:6, 10:2, 16:7

Thompson, Matter of, 1990 WL 34242 (Ohio Ct. App. 4th Dist. Jackson County 1990)—18:2

Thompson, State ex rel. v. Murray, 1984 WL 3422 (Ohio Ct. App. 12th Dist. Madison County 1984)—3:2

Thrasher v. Thrasher, 3 Ohio App. 3d 210, 444 N.E.2d 431 (9th Dist. Summit County 1981)—16:15, 30:11

Three Juveniles v. Com., 390 Mass. 357, 455 N.E.2d 1203 (1983)—23:15

Tikyra A., In re, 103 Ohio App. 3d 452, 659 N.E.2d 867 (6th Dist. Huron County 1995)—10:2, 10:3, 23:13

Tilton, In re, 161 Ohio St. 571, 53 Ohio Op. 427, 120 N.E.2d 445 (1954)—9:9, 30:11

Timberlake, In re, 2003-Ohio-1183, 2003 WL 1094078 (Ohio Ct. App. 10th Dist. Franklin County 2003)—26:2, 33:11

Tingley v. Williams County Department of Human Services, 1993 WL 313710 (Ohio Ct. App. 6th Dist. Williams County 1993)—3:2, 27:13, 32:2

Tingley v. Williams Cty. Dept. of Human Serv., 100 Ohio App. 3d 385, 654 N.E.2d 148 (6th Dist. Williams County 1995)—27:13, 32:2

Tirado, Matter of, 1998 WL 30097 (Ohio Ct. App. 7th Dist. Mahoning County 1998)—31:8

T.K., In re, 2003-Ohio-2634, 2003 WL 21185949 (Ohio Ct. App. 9th Dist. Wayne County 2003)—30:10

T.L.K., In re, 2 Ohio Op.3d 324 (C.P., Ross 1976)—23:29

Tobin, Matter of, 1995 WL 495305 (Ohio Ct. App. 5th Dist. Licking County 1995)—28:4

Toler, 1983 WL 4356 (Ohio Ct. App. 12th Dist. Preble County 1983)—14:10, 23:21

Tony C., In re, 21 Cal. 3d 888, 148 Cal. Rptr. 366, 582 P.2d 957 (1978)—14:3

Torok, In re, 161 Ohio St. 585, 53 Ohio Op. 433, 120 N.E.2d 307 (1954)—30:11

Torres, State ex rel. v. Simmons, 68 Ohio St. 2d 118, 22 Ohio Op. 3d 340, 428 N.E.2d 862 (1981)—22:23

T.R., In re, 52 Ohio St. 3d 6, 556 N.E.2d 439 (1990)—1:6, 22:19, 23:11, 25:5

Travis, In re, 110 Ohio App. 3d 684, 675 N.E.2d 36 (10th Dist. Franklin County 1996)—14:10

Travis Children, In re, 80 Ohio App. 3d 620, 609 N.E.2d 1356 (5th Dist. Stark County 1992)—23:5, 30:6, 34:3

Trizzino, No. 40982 (8th Dist. Ct. App., Cuyahoga, 1-31-80), In re—10:3, 16:12, 18:3

Trumbull County Children Services Bd., In re, 32 Ohio Misc. 2d 11, 513 N.E.2d 360 (C.P. 1986)—21:2

Tsesmilles, In re, 24 Ohio App. 2d 153, 53 Ohio Op. 2d 363, 265 N.E.2d 308 (7th Dist. Columbiana County 1970)—23:10, 23:14

Tucker, In Interest of, 20 Ill. App. 3d 377, 314 N.E.2d 276 (1st Dist. 1974)—14:3

Turner, In re, 12 Ohio Misc. 171, 41 Ohio Op. 2d 264, 231 N.E.2d 502 (C.P. 1967)—9:3, 10:3, 10:5

Turner, In re, 77 Ohio St. 3d 375, 674 N.E.2d 677 (1997)—30:6

Turner, State ex rel. v. Albin, 118 Ohio St. 527, 6 Ohio L. Abs. 341, 161 N.E. 792 (1928)—18:3, 33:8

U

Uehlein, Matter of v. Fuller, 1993 WL 129333 (Ohio Ct. App. 9th Dist. Lorain County 1993)—30:10

Unborn Child Copeland, No. 7910111 (Juv., Cuyahoga, 6-9-79), In re—9:7

Union County Child Welfare Bd. v. Parker, 7 Ohio App. 2d 79, 36 Ohio Op. 2d 162, 218 N.E.2d 757 (3d Dist. Union County 1964)—16:15, 16:17, 18:5

Urbasek, In re, 38 Ill. 2d 535, 232 N.E.2d 716 (1967)—1:4

U.S. v. Ash, 413 U.S. 300, 93 S. Ct. 2568, 37 L. Ed. 2d 619 (1973)—14:13

U.S. v. Bland, 472 F.2d 1329 (D.C. Cir. 1972)—22:3

U.S. v. Bowers, 660 F.2d 527, 9 Fed. R. Evid. Serv. 387 (5th Cir. 1981)—23:19

U.S. v. Dionisio, 410 U.S. 1, 93 S. Ct. 764, 35 L. Ed. 2d 67 (1973)—14:4, 14:12

U.S. v. Dunn, 480 U.S. 294, 107 S. Ct. 1134, 94 L. Ed. 2d 326 (1987)—14:4

U.S. v. Euge, 444 U.S. 707, 100 S. Ct. 874, 63 L. Ed. 2d 141 (1980)—14:12

U.S. v. Henry, 447 U.S. 264, 100 S. Ct. 2183, 65 L. Ed. 2d 115 (1980)—14:11

U.S. v. Ismail, 756 F.2d 1253, 17 Fed. R. Evid. Serv. 1450 (6th Cir. 1985)—23:15

U.S. v. Jacobsen, 466 U.S. 109, 104 S. Ct. 1652, 80 L. Ed. 2d 85 (1984)—14:4

U.S. v. James Daniel Good Real Property, 510 U.S. 43, 114 S. Ct. 492, 126 L. Ed. 2d 490 (1993)—22:12

U.S. v. Karo, 468 U.S. 705, 104 S. Ct. 3296, 82 L. Ed. 2d 530 (1984)—14:4

U.S. v. Kimler, 335 F.3d 1132, 61 Fed. R. Evid. Serv. 1024 (10th Cir. 2003)—14:8

U.S. v. Knotts, 460 U.S. 276, 103 S. Ct. 1081, 75 L. Ed. 2d 55 (1983)—14:4

U.S. v. Leon, 468 U.S. 897, 104 S. Ct. 3405, 82 L. Ed. 2d 677 (1984)—14:2

U.S. v. Mara, 410 U.S. 19, 93 S. Ct. 774, 35 L. Ed. 2d 99 (1973)—14:4, 14:12

U.S. v. Miller, 425 U.S. 435, 96 S. Ct. 1619, 48 L. Ed. 2d 71 (1976)—14:4

U.S. v. Place, 462 U.S. 696, 103 S. Ct. 2637, 77 L. Ed. 2d 110 (1983)—14:4

U.S. v. Quinones, 516 F.2d 1309 (1st Cir. 1975)—22:3

U.S. v. Ramsey, 367 F. Supp. 1307 (W.D. Mo. 1973)—14:9

U.S. v. Reynard, 220 F. Supp. 2d 1142 (S.D. Cal. 2002)—14:8

U.S. v. Robinson, 414 U.S. 218, 94 S. Ct. 467, 38 L. Ed. 2d 427 (1973)—14:4

U.S. v. Robinson, 485 U.S. 25, 108 S. Ct. 864, 99 L. Ed. 2d 23 (1988)—22:14, 23:27

U.S. v. Ross, 456 U.S. 798, 102 S. Ct. 2157, 72 L. Ed. 2d 572 (1982)—14:4

U.S. v. Santana, 427 U.S. 38, 96 S. Ct. 2406, 49 L. Ed. 2d 300 (1976)—14:4

U.S. v. Scott, 437 U.S. 82, 98 S. Ct. 2187, 57 L. Ed. 2d 65 (1978)—23:31

U.S. v. Sczubelek, 255 F. Supp. 2d 315 (D. Del. 2003)—14:8

U.S. v. Wade, 388 U.S. 218, 87 S. Ct. 1926, 18 L. Ed. 2d 1149 (1967)—14:12, 14:13

U.S. v. Watson, 423 U.S. 411, 96 S. Ct. 820, 46 L. Ed. 2d 598 (1976)—14:3

U.S. v. White, 401 U.S. 745, 91 S. Ct. 1122, 28 L. Ed. 2d 453 (1971)—14:4

U.S. v. Whitfield, 747 F. Supp. 807 (D.D.C. 1990)—14:5

U.S. v. Williams, 459 F.2d 903 (2d Cir. 1972)—22:8

U.S. v. Wright, 564 F.2d 785, 2 Fed. R. Evid. Serv. 189, 48 A.L.R. Fed. 119 (8th Cir. 1977)—14:5

U. S. ex rel. Turner v. Rundle, 438 F.2d 839 (3d Cir. 1971)—22:3, 22:12, 22:23

V

V. v. City of New York, 407 U.S. 203, 92 S. Ct. 1951, 32 L. Ed. 2d 659 (1972)—23:13

Vandale, Matter of, 1993 WL 235599 (Ohio Ct. App. 4th Dist. Washington County 1993)—18:2, 23:12

Vanderlaan, State ex rel. v. Pollex, 96 Ohio App. 3d 235, 644 N.E.2d 1073 (6th Dist. Wood County 1994)—18:2, 23:12

Vanek, Matter of, 1995 WL 787429 (Ohio Ct. App. 11th Dist. Ashtabula County 1995)—16:8

VanGundy, Matter of, 1998 WL 181644 (Ohio Ct. App. 4th Dist. Ross County 1998)—31:8

Vaughn, In re, 1990 WL 116936 (Ohio Ct. App. 12th Dist. Butler County 1990)—21:4, 23:17, 27:3

Vega v. Bell, 47 N.Y.2d 543, 419 N.Y.S.2d 454, 393 N.E.2d 450 (1979)—22:3

Vernonia School Dist. 47J v. Acton, 515 U.S. 646, 115 S. Ct. 2386, 132 L. Ed. 2d 564, 101 Ed. Law Rep. 37 (1995)—1:4, 14:6

Veselich, In re, 22 Ohio App. 528, 5 Ohio L. Abs. 277, 154 N.E. 55 (8th Dist. Cuyahoga County 1926)—18:4

Vickers Children, In re, 14 Ohio App. 3d 201, 470 N.E.2d 438 (12th Dist. Butler County 1983)—1:8, 23:16, 25:2

V. S., In re, 2003-Ohio-5612, 2003 WL 22399705 (Ohio Ct. App. 9th Dist. Lorain County 2003)—30:10

W

W., In re, 19 N.Y.2d 55, 277 N.Y.S.2d 675, 224 N.E.2d 102 (1966)—1:3

Wadsworth, Matter of, 1991 WL 147748 (Ohio Ct. App. 5th Dist. Tuscarawas County 1991)—31:8

W.A.F., Matter of, 573 A.2d 1264 (D.C. 1990)—23:7

Walker, In re, 282 N.C. 28, 191 S.E.2d 702 (1972)—23:3

Wall, In re, 60 Ohio App. 3d 6, 572 N.E.2d 248 (9th Dist. Wayne County 1989)—23:13

Wallace, People ex rel. v. Labrenz, 411 Ill. 618, 104 N.E.2d 769, 30 A.L.R.2d 1132 (1952)—9:7

Waller v. Georgia, 467 U.S. 39, 104 S. Ct. 2210, 81 L. Ed. 2d 31 (1984)—23:11

Walter v. U.S., 447 U.S. 649, 100 S. Ct. 2395, 65 L. Ed. 2d 410 (1980)—14:4

Walters v. The Enrichment Ctr. of Wishing Well, Inc., 133 Ohio App. 3d 66, 726 N.E.2d 1058 (8th Dist. Cuyahoga County 1999)—14:17

Ward, In re, 1997 WL 321492 (Ohio Ct. App. 8th Dist. Cuyahoga County 1997)—23:4

Ward, In re, 75 Ohio App. 3d 377, 599 N.E.2d 431 (3d Dist. Defiance County 1992)—10:4, 30:6

Warden, Md. Penitentiary v. Hayden, 387 U.S. 294, 87 S. Ct. 1642, 18 L. Ed. 2d 782 (1967)—14:4

Ware, No. 40983 (8th Dist. Ct. App., Cuyahoga, 7-17-80), In re—10:5, 18:2

Washburn, In re, 70 Ohio App. 3d 178, 590 N.E.2d 855 (3d Dist. Wyandot County 1990)—23:29

Washington, In re, 143 Ohio App. 3d 576, 758 N.E.2d 724 (8th Dist. Cuyahoga County 2001)—23:16

Washington, In re, 1996 WL 631105 (Ohio Ct. App. 8th Dist. Cuyahoga County 1996)—21:3

Washington, In re, 75 Ohio St. 3d 390, 1996-Ohio-186, 662 N.E.2d 346 (1996)—2:6

Watkins, In re v. Harris, 1995 WL 513118 (Ohio Ct. App. 9th Dist. Summit County 1995)—31:8

Watkins, No. 42409 (8th Dist. Ct. App., Cuyahoga, 1-22-81), In re—27:13, 27:18, 32:2

Watson, Application of, 31 Ohio St. 3d 220, 509 N.E.2d 1240 (1987)—35:4

Watson, In re, 47 Ohio St. 3d 86, 548 N.E.2d 210 (1989)—14:10, 23:14

Watts, In re, 1995 WL 592249 (Ohio Ct. App. 9th Dist. Summit County 1995)—30:12

Watts v. Cuyahoga County Welfare Dep't, No. 40584 (8th Dist. Ct. App., Cuyahoga, 6-12-80)—9:15

Wayne, 1981 WL 3652 (Ohio Ct. App. 10th Dist. Franklin County 1981)—20:2, 31:7, 34:11

Weaver, In re, 79 Ohio App. 3d 59, 606 N.E.2d 1011 (12th Dist. Butler County 1992)—30:10, 31:8

Webb, In re, 64 Ohio App. 3d 280, 581 N.E.2d 570 (1st Dist. Hamilton County 1989)—23:19, 31:7

Weber, In re, 61 Ohio App. 3d 636, 573 N.E.2d 730 (8th Dist. Cuyahoga County 1989)—27:8, 28:2, 28:4

Weeks, Matter of, 1991 WL 12147 (Ohio Ct. App. 12th Dist. Clermont County 1991)—9:10, 9:15

Weimer, In re, 19 Ohio App. 3d 130, 483 N.E.2d 173 (8th Dist. Cuyahoga County 1984)—24:7

Wells, In re, 2004-Ohio-1572, at ¶ 19, 2004 WL 1152844 (Ohio Ct. App. 7th Dist. Belmont County 2004)—34:5

Welsh v. Wisconsin, 466 U.S. 740, 104 S. Ct. 2091, 80 L. Ed. 2d 732 (1984)—14:4

West, In re, 128 Ohio App. 3d 356, 714 N.E.2d 988 (8th Dist. Cuyahoga County 1998)—23:9

West v. U.S., 399 F.2d 467 (5th Cir. 1968)—14:10

Whaley, In re, 86 Ohio App. 3d 304, 620 N.E.2d 954 (4th Dist. Athens County 1993)—3:2

White, In re, 1999 WL 43321 (Ohio Ct. App. 8th Dist. Cuyahoga County 1999)—25:4

Whiteman, Matter of, 2 A.D.D. 386 (Ohio Ct. App. 6th Dist. Williams County 1993)—9:3, 10:2, 25:2, 30:4, 30:10, 31:7

White, No. 40971 (8th Dist. Ct. App., Cuyahoga, 7-31-80), In re—4:4, 14:9

Whitmer, No. 28098 (8th Dist. Ct. App., Cuyahoga, 6-2-67), In re—9:9

Whittington, In re, 17 Ohio App. 2d 164, 46 Ohio Op. 2d 237, 245 N.E.2d 364 (5th Dist. Fairfield County 1969)—34:4

Wieland, In re, 89 Ohio St. 3d 535, 2000-Ohio-233, 733 N.E.2d 1127 (2000)—23:15

Wilkinson, In re, 1996 WL 132196 (Ohio Ct. App. 2d Dist. Montgomery County 1996)—34:4

Williams, In re, 101 Ohio St. 3d 398, 2004-Ohio-1500, 805 N.E.2d 1110 (2004)—23:3, 23:6

Williams, In re, 111 Ohio App. 3d 120, 675 N.E.2d 1254 (10th Dist. Franklin County 1996)—22:22, 34:4

Williams, In re, 116 Ohio App. 3d 237, 687 N.E.2d 507 (2d Dist. Montgomery County 1997)—23:7

Williams, In re, 2004-Ohio-678, at ¶ 13, 2004 WL 285560 (Ohio Ct. App. 10th Dist. Franklin County)—23:3

Williams, In re, 31 Ohio App. 3d 241, 510 N.E.2d 832 (10th Dist. Franklin County 1986)—4:4, 23:31

William S., In re, 75 Ohio St. 3d 95, 1996-Ohio-182, 661 N.E.2d 738 (1996)—23:13, 30:10

Williams, In re, 7 Ohio App. 3d 324, 455 N.E.2d 1027 (1st Dist. Hamilton County 1982)—30:4, 30:8

Williams, Matter of, 1995 WL 380063 (Ohio Ct. App. 3d Dist. Allen County 1995)—34:4

Williams, Matter of, 1997 WL 317534 (Ohio Ct. App. 10th Dist. Franklin County 1997)—18:2

Williams v. Williams, 44 Ohio St. 2d 28, 73 Ohio Op. 2d 121, 336 N.E.2d 426 (1975)—20:5

Williams, State ex rel. v. Court of Common Pleas of Lucas County, 42 Ohio St. 2d 433, 71 Ohio Op. 2d 410, 329 N.E.2d 680 (1975)—22:22, 23:29

Williams County Department of Social Services v. Gilman, 1982 WL 6438 (Ohio Ct. App. 6th Dist. Williams County 1982)—23:5

Williams, No. 37370 (8th Dist. Ct. App., Cuyahoga, 4-27-78), In re—10:3, 10:5

Willis, Matter of, 1981 WL 6749 (Ohio Ct. App. 3d Dist. Henry County 1981)—16:12

Willmann, In re, 24 Ohio App. 3d 191, 493 N.E.2d 1380 (1st Dist. Hamilton County 1986)—10:5, 25:8

Wilson, In re, 21 Ohio App. 3d 36, 486 N.E.2d 152 (6th Dist. Huron County 1984)—18:4

Wilson, Matter of, 1981 WL 6717 (Ohio Ct. App. 3d Dist. Paulding County 1981)—23:4

Wilson v. State, 370 Md. 191, 803 A.2d 1034 (2002)—23:19

Wilson v. U.S., 221 U.S. 361, 31 S. Ct. 538, 55 L. Ed. 771 (1911)—1:4, 14:16

Wilson, State ex rel. v. Bambrick, 156 W. Va. 703, 195 S.E.2d 721 (1973)—23:3

Wilson Children, Matter of, 1995 WL 156326 (Ohio Ct. App. 5th Dist. Stark County 1995)—9:15

Winegardner, Matter of, 1995 WL 657113 (Ohio Ct. App. 3d Dist. Hardin County 1995)—30:11

Wingo, In re, 143 Ohio App. 3d 652, 2001-Ohio-2477, 758 N.E.2d 780 (4th Dist. Ross County 2001)—23:5

Winship, In re, 397 U.S. 358, 90 S. Ct. 1068, 25 L. Ed. 2d 368 (1970)—1:4, 22:9, 23:2, 23:13

Winstead, In re, 67 Ohio App. 2d 111, 21 Ohio Op. 3d 422, 425 N.E.2d 943 (9th Dist. Summit County 1980)—23:15

Wisconsin v. Yoder, 406 U.S. 205, 92 S. Ct. 1526, 32 L. Ed. 2d 15 (1972)—9:7

Wise, In re, 96 Ohio App. 3d 619, 645 N.E.2d 812 (9th Dist. Wayne County 1994)—23:5

Wolff v. McDonnell, 418 U.S. 539, 94 S. Ct. 2963, 41 L. Ed. 2d 935 (1974)—22:12, 22:16

Wood, Matter of, 1986 WL 4947 (Ohio Ct. App. 3d Dist. Marion County 1986)—27:19

Wood, Matter of, 236 Mont. 118, 768 P.2d 1370 (1989)—22:3

Woodard v. Wainwright, 556 F.2d 781 (5th Cir. 1977)—22:3

Woods, Matter of, 1993 WL 19546 (Ohio Ct. App. 8th Dist. Cuyahoga County 1993)—30:8

Woodson, In re, 98 Ohio App. 3d 678, 649 N.E.2d 320 (10th Dist. Franklin County 1994)—27:3

Workman, Matter of, 1993 WL 222843 (Ohio Ct. App. 5th Dist. Tuscarawas County 1993)—23:16, 31:5

Workman, Matter of, 1993 WL 33316 (Ohio Ct. App. 4th Dist. Jackson County 1993)—31:8

Workman v. Cardwell, 338 F. Supp. 893, 31 Ohio Misc. 99, 60 Ohio Op. 2d 187, 60 Ohio Op. 2d 250 (N.D. Ohio 1972)—35:3

Wright, In re, 1996 WL 397143 (Ohio Ct. App. 9th Dist. Lorain County 1996)—30:2

Wright, In re, 88 Ohio App. 3d 539, 624 N.E.2d 347 (2d Dist. Montgomery County 1993)—23:30

Writ of Habeas Corpus for Baker, In re, 116 Ohio App. 3d 580, 688 N.E.2d 1068 (10th Dist. Franklin County 1996)—22:23

Wyman v. James, 400 U.S. 309, 91 S. Ct. 381, 27 L. Ed. 2d 408 (1971)—14:16

Wyrick v. Fields, 459 U.S. 42, 103 S. Ct. 394, 74 L. Ed. 2d 214 (1982)—14:10

Wyrock, No. 41827 (8th Dist. Ct. App., Cuyahoga, 10-23-80), In re—21:3, 23:20, 35:3

Wyrock, No. 41305 (8th Dist. Ct. App., Cuyahoga, 6-5-80), In re—23:30

Y

Yarborough v. Alvarado, 124 S. Ct. 2140 (U.S. 2004)—1:4, 14:10

York, In re, 142 Ohio App. 3d 524, 756 N.E.2d 191 (8th Dist. Cuyahoga County 2001)—23:7

Young, In re, 58 Ohio St. 2d 90, 12 Ohio Op. 3d 93, 388 N.E.2d 1235 (1979)—30:11

Young v. Young, 1987 WL 5501 (Ohio Ct. App. 12th Dist. Clermont County 1987)—9:3

Young Children, In re, 76 Ohio St. 3d 632, 1996-Ohio-45, 669 N.E.2d 1140 (1996)—30:6

Young Children, Matter of, 1995 WL 434274 (Ohio Ct. App. 5th Dist. Stark County 1995)—30:6

Z

Zacek v. Zacek, 11 Ohio App. 3d 91, 463 N.E.2d 391 (10th Dist. Franklin County 1983)—34:4

Zakov, In re, 107 Ohio App. 3d 716, 669 N.E.2d 344 (11th Dist. Geauga County 1995)—24:9, 34:4

Zeiser, In re, 133 Ohio App. 3d 338, 728 N.E.2d 10 (11th Dist. Lake County 1999)—9:6

Zerick, In re, 57 Ohio Op. 331, 74 Ohio L. Abs. 525, 129 N.E.2d 661 (Juv. Ct. 1955)—10:3

Zhang, In re, 135 Ohio App. 3d 350, 734 N.E.2d 379 (8th Dist. Cuyahoga County 1999)—18:2, 23:3, 23:6

Zindle, In re, 107 Ohio App. 3d 342, 668 N.E.2d 969 (9th Dist. Summit County 1995)—24:5, 24:9

INDEX

ORC	Ohio Revised Code
Evid. R	Rules of Evidence
Juv. R	Rules of Juvenile Procedure
T	Text

Cross references to another main heading are in CAPITAL LETTERS.

ABANDONMENT

Children. See DEPENDENT AND NEGLECTED CHILDREN

ABORTION

Appeal
    Dismissal of complaint, **T 12:10**
    Fees and costs, **ORC 2151.85(H)**
    Forms, **ORC 2151.85(G)**
Attorney, appointment for minor female, **T 12:4**
Complaint for, **ORC 2151.85**
    Appeals, **ORC 2151.85(E)**
        Dismissal of complaint, **T 12:10**
        Fees and costs, **ORC 2151.85(H)**
        Forms, **ORC 2151.85(G)**
    Confidentiality of records, **ORC 2151.85(F)**
    Fees and costs, **ORC 2151.85(H)**
    Filing, **ORC 2151.85(A)**
    Forms, **ORC 2151.85(G)**
    Hearings, **ORC 2151.85(B)**
    Unemancipated, defined, **ORC 2151.85(I)**
Guardian ad litem, appointment for minor female, **T 12:4**
Parental consent
    Complaint for abortion without, **ORC 2151.85, T 12:9**
Parental notification, **T 12, T 12:6**
    Abortion, of, **T 12:9**
    Abuse, child, affecting, **T 12:2**
    Appeal, **T 12:10**
    Complaint, **T 12:3**
    Hearing, **T 12:8**
        Scheduling, **T 12:7**
    Jurisdiction, **T 12:2**
    Not allowed, **ORC 2151.85(C), 2151.85(D)**
    Summons, **T 12:6**
    Venue, **T 12:5**

ABUSE OF CHILDREN

See CHILD ABUSE

ACCIDENTS

Character evidence, as, **Evid. R 404**

ACCOMPLICES

See also AIDING AND ABETTING
Testimony by, corroboration requirement, **T 23:21**

ACTIONS

See also particular subject concerned
Appeals. See APPEALS

ACTIONS—*continued*

Contempt of court. See CONTEMPT
Continuances. See CONTINUANCES
Delinquents, concerning. See DELINQUENCY
Dismissal. See DISMISSAL OF ACTIONS
Evidence rules, applicability, **Evid. R 101**
Hearings. See HEARINGS
Parties to. See PARTIES TO ACTIONS
Permanent custody. See PERMANENT CUSTODY
Witnesses. See WITNESSES AND TESTIMONY

ADJUDICATORY HEARINGS

Generally, **Juv. R 29, ORC 2151.35 to 2151.353, T 23**
Access rights, applicability, **T 23:11**
Admissions. See also GUILTY PLEAS
    Acceptance, **Juv. R 29(D), T 23:9**
    Entry, **Juv. R 29(C), T 23:8**
Advisement and findings, **Juv. R 29(B)**
Amendment
    Complaint, **T 16:16**
    Pleading, **Juv. R 22(B)**
Attorney, **Juv. R 29(B)**
Best interests of child, consideration in dependency determination, **T 25:2**
Bifurcation from dispositional hearing, **T 23:1**
Competency of witnesses. See COMPETENCY OF WITNESSES
Competency to stand trial. See COMPETENCY TO STAND TRIAL
Complaint, amendment of, **T 16:16**
Confrontation rights. See CONFRONTATION RIGHTS
Continuances, **T 19:7**
    Evaluations, for, **T 23:29**
    Obtaining counsel, for, **T 23:29**
    Service of process, to allow, **T 23:29**
Cross-examinations, **T 23:24**
Definition, **Juv. R 2(B)**
Denials
    Entry, **Juv. R 29(C), T 23:8**
    Procedure following, **Juv. R 29(E)**
Detention prior to. See DETENTION AND DETENTION HOMES
Determination of issues, **Juv. R 29(F), ORC 2151.28(B), 2151.353(A)**

ADJUDICATORY HEARINGS—*continued*
Dispositional hearings following. See
    DISPOSITIONAL HEARINGS
Double jeopardy. See DOUBLE JEOPARDY
Due process requirements, **T 23:2**
Entry of adjudication, **Juv. R 29(F)**
Evidence. See EVIDENCE
Evidence rules applicable, **T 23:14**
Exclusion of general public, **Juv. R 27(A), ORC
    2151.35(A), T 23:11**
Expungement of records, **T 35:4**
General public, exclusion of, **Juv. R 27(A), ORC
    2151.35(A), T 23:11**
Guardians ad litem. See GUARDIANS AD LITEM
Guilty pleas. See GUILTY PLEAS
Hearsay, admissibility, **T 23:16**
Judges. See also JUDGES
    Transfer hearing judge as, **T 22:21, T 23:28**
Jury trials. See JURY TRIALS
Location, **Juv. R 11(C), ORC 2151.271, T 17:4**
Magistrates. See MAGISTRATES
Mental competency. See COMPETENCY TO
    STAND TRIAL
Notice, **ORC 2151.35(C)**
    Charges, of, **T 1:4**
Objections
    Separate hearings for adjudication and disposi-
        tion not held, failure to object waives error, **T
        25:2**
    Time for filing, **T 16:17**
Ohio rules of evidence applicable, **T 23:14**
Pleadings, amendment of, **Juv. R 22(B)**
Pleas. See PLEAS, generally
Prehearing motions, **Juv. R 22(D)**
    Time for filing, **T 16:17**
Prior juvenile record, admissibility, **T 35:2, T 35:3**
Private nature of proceedings, **Juv. R 27(A), T 23:11**
Privileged communications, **T 23:14**
    See also PRIVILEGED INFORMATION.
Public trials, **Juv. R 27(A)**
    IJA-ABA standards providing for, **T 23:11**
    Jurisdictions permitting, **T 23:11**
Reasonable doubt standard of proof, **T 23:1, T 23:13**
Removal of child from home, reasonable efforts to
    prevent, **T 25:14**
Removal of unruly nonresident children residing in
    foster homes, actions by school superintendents
    for, **Juv. R 29(A), Juv. R 39, T 13:5**
Right to be present, **T 23:12**
Right to counsel, **Juv. R 29(B), T 1:4, T 23:2, T 23:3**
    See also RIGHT TO COUNSEL, generally.
Scheduling, **ORC 2151.35(E)**
Self-incrimination. See SELF-INCRIMINATION
Separate hearing for disposition not held, effect, **T
    25:2**
Serious youthful offender, **T 5:6**
Shelter care determination, **ORC 2151.28(B)**
Social histories inadmissible, **T 23:16**
Speedy trial, **Juv. R 29(A), ORC 2151.28(A), T
    19:7, T 23:31**
    See also SPEEDY TRIAL, generally.
Statements of children, admissibility, **ORC
    2151.35(F)**
Testimony from transfer hearing inadmissible, **T
    22:14**
Time requirements, **T 23:31**
Transcripts. See TRANSCRIPTS

ADJUDICATORY HEARINGS—*continued*
Transfer of case
    Another county, to, **T 17:4**
    Criminal proceedings, for; double jeopardy, **T
        22:24**
Trial, analogous to, **T 23:1**
Truancy, **T 23:32**
Venue, **T 17:4**
Witnesses. See COMPETENCY OF WITNESSES;
    WITNESSES AND TESTIMONY

ADMINISTRATIVE AGENCIES
Records and reports, hearsay exceptions, **Evid. R
    803(8), Evid. R 803(10)**

ADMINISTRATIVE REVIEW
Case plans. See CASE PLANS
Dispositional hearings as substitute for, **ORC
    2151.415(H)**
Foster care, **T 33:10**
Juvenile court hearing as substitute for, **ORC
    2151.417(I)**

ADMISSIBILITY OF EVIDENCE
Generally, **Evid. R 609**
Annulments of convictions, **Evid. R 609**
Authentication, **Evid. R 901 to Evid. R 903**
Certificates of rehabilitation, **Evid. R 609**
Character evidence, **Evid. R 404 to Evid. R 406**
Compromise offers, **Evid. R 408**
Confessions, **T 14:9**
    Hearings on, **Evid. R 104**
Conviction, evidence of, **Evid. R 609**
Determinations, **Evid. R 101, Evid. R 104**
Developmentally disabled or mentally retarded
    victim, testimony of, **ORC 2152.821**
Disposition, concerning; admissibility at adjudicatory
    hearing, **T 25:9**
Dispositional hearings, **T 25:9**
Diversion programs, statements made during
    participation, **T 15:3**
Duplicate photographs, writings, or recordings, **Evid.
    R 1003**
Expungement of records, **Evid. R 609**
Guilty pleas, **Evid. R 410**
Hearsay, **Evid. R 802, T 23:16**
Insurance policies, **Evid. R 411**
Irrelevant evidence, **Evid. R 402**
Juvenile proceedings, **Evid. R 609**
Limited purpose, **Evid. R 105**
Medical bills, offer to pay as proof of liability, **Evid.
    R 409**
Mentally retarded or developmentally disabled
    victim, testimony of, **ORC 2152.821**
Negligence, proving; remedial measures, **Evid. R 407**
No contest pleas, **Evid. R 410**
Ownership of property, proving, **Evid. R 407**
Pardons, **Evid. R 609**
Partial statements or writings, **Evid. R 106**
Pendency of appeal as evidence, **Evid. R 609**
Pleas, **Evid. R 410**
Preliminary questions, **Evid. R 104**
Public records, **Evid. R 1005**
Records of prior juvenile proceedings, admissibility,
    T 35:2, T 35:3
Rehabilitation certificates, **Evid. R 609**
Related statements or writings, **Evid. R 106**

ADMISSIBILITY OF EVIDENCE
—continued

Religious beliefs, **Evid. R 610**

Remedial measures, subsequent, **Evid. R 407**

Rulings on, objection, **Evid. R 103**

Subsequent remedial measures, **Evid. R 407**

Witnesses
> Convictions, **Evid. R 609**
> Inconsistent statements, **Evid. R 613**
> Mentally retarded or developmentally disabled victim, **ORC 2152.821**

ADMISSIONS

Generally, **Evid. R 801(D)**

See also GUILTY PLEAS.

Adjudicatory hearings, **Juv. R 29(C), Juv. R 29(D), T 23:8, T 23:9**

Examination by court, **T 23:9**

Special precautions to safeguard rights, **T 23:9**

Voluntarily and intelligently made, **T 23:9**

ADOLESCENTS

See JUVENILES

ADOPTION

Adult case dispositional hearing notice, **ORC 2151.424**

Case plans, seeking and preparing child for adoption, **ORC 2151.413(D)**

Certification of case to juvenile court following dismissal of petition
> Complaint for custody, not considered to be, **T 16:15**

Criminal records check of prospective parents, **ORC 2151.86**

Declarants, hearsay exception, **Evid. R 804(B)(4)**

Nonresident children, placement, **ORC 2151.39**

Notice of adult case dispositional hearing, **ORC 2151.424**

Parents, prospective
> Adult case dispositional hearing notice, **ORC 2151.424**
> Criminal records check, **ORC 2151.86**
> Summons issuance, **T 18:2**

Records and reports
> Criminal records check of prospective parents, **ORC 2151.86**

Summons issuance to prospective parents, **T 18:2**

Unlawful placement, neglect finding due to, **T 9:9**

Withdrawal of consent to adoption not considered neglect of child, **T 9:5**

ADOPTION ASSISTANCE AND CHILD WELFARE ACT OF 1980

State compliance with federal law, **T 1:7**

ADULT CASES

Appeals, **ORC 2151.52**

Bonds for suspended sentences, **ORC 2151.50**

Charges, **ORC 2151.43**

Complaints, **ORC 2151.44**

Hearing charges, **Juv. R 27(A)**
> Notice, **ORC 2151.424**

Jurisdiction, **ORC 2151.23(A), 2151.23(B)**

Jury trials, **ORC 2151.47**

Notice of dispositional hearings, **ORC 2151.424**

Prison, confinement in, **T 27:18**

Suspension of sentence, **ORC 2151.49**

AFFIDAVITS

Continuing jurisdiction, filing in support of motion to invoke, **T 33:2**

Service of process, **Juv. R 18(D)**
> Publication, by; filing with court, **T 18:4**

AFFIRMATIONS

See OATHS AND AFFIRMATIONS

AFFIRMATIVE DEFENSES

Burden of proof, **T 23:13**

Insanity defense, availability in juvenile court proceedings, **T 23:8**

AGE JURISDICTION

See JURISDICTIONAL AGE

AGED PERSONS

Victims of crime. See VICTIMS OF CRIME, at Age 65 or over

AGGRAVATED MURDER

Juvenile delinquency adjudication deemed conviction, **ORC 2151.355(G)**

AGGRAVATED VEHICULAR HOMICIDE

Minor committing, prosecution as delinquent, **T 7:4**

AIDING AND ABETTING

Commitment, aiding escape from, **ORC 2151.99(A), 2151.422 to 2151.54**

Delinquency, **ORC 2151.99(A)**

ALCOHOL OR DRUG TESTING AND TREATMENT

Abused, neglected, or dependent children, **ORC 2151.914(A), 2151.3514, T 30:10**

Adequate parental care, **ORC 2151.914(A)**

Athletes, high school, **T 14:6**

Certified program requirements, **ORC 2151.3514**

Delinquency, **ORC 2151.354(B), 2152.74**

Delinquency dispositions, **ORC 2152.19, T 27:9**

Orders requiring testing and treatment, **ORC 2151.3514**

Parents of neglected, abused, or dependent children, **ORC 2151.914(A), 2151.3514, T 30:10**

Protective supervision, **ORC 2151.3514(B)**

Temporary custody, **ORC 2151.3514**

Unruly children, **ORC 2151.354(B)**

Urinalysis
> Athletes, high school, **T 14:6**
> Delinquency, **ORC 2152.74**

ALCOHOLIC BEVERAGES

Possession or purchase by minor as delinquent act, **T 4:4**

ALIMONY

See SPOUSAL SUPPORT

ALIUNDE RULE

Generally, **Evid. R 606**

ALLOCATION OF PARENTAL RIGHTS AND RESPONSIBILITIES

See also CUSTODY OF CHILDREN, INSTITUTIONAL; PERMANENT CUSTODY; TEMPORARY CUSTODY

Certification of cases to juvenile court, **ORC 2151.23(C) to 2151.23(F), T 3:2**

ALLOCATION OF PARENTAL RIGHTS AND RESPONSIBILITIES—*continued*

Definitions, **Juv. R 2**

Investigative reports, **Juv. R 32(D)**

Mediation, use of, **T 15:4**

Permanent. See PERMANENT CUSTODY

Temporary. See TEMPORARY CUSTODY

Voluntary surrender

    Permanent custody, **Juv. R 38(B)**

    Temporary custody, **Juv. R 38(A)**

ALTERNATIVE DISPUTE RESOLUTION

Arbitration, **T 15:5**

Family & Child First Council, **T 15:6**

Mediation, **T 15:4**

AMENDMENTS OF PLEADINGS

Generally, **Juv. R 22(B), T 16:16**

ANCIENT DOCUMENTS

Authentication, **Evid. R 901**

Hearsay exception, **Evid. R 803(16)**

ANNUAL REPORTS OF JUVENILE COURTS

Generally, **ORC 2152.71(D)**

ANNULMENT OF MARRIAGE

Juvenile procedure rules, applicability, **Juv. R 1(C)**

ANSWERS

See COMPLAINTS

APPEALS

Generally, **T 34**

Abortion, complaint for in juvenile court

    Dismissal of complaint, **T 12:10**

    Fees and costs, **ORC 2151.85(H)**

    Forms, **ORC 2151.85(G)**

    Right to, **ORC 2151.85(E)**

Administrative review. See ADMINISTRATIVE REVIEW

Adult cases, **ORC 2151.52**

Affirming juvenile court ruling, **T 34:11**

Age of majority reached while appeal pending, effect on court's jurisdiction, **T 33:4, T 33:5**

    Transfer of case for criminal proceedings, appeal from, **T 22:24**

Appropriations for, **ORC 2151.10**

Bonds, **T 34:7**

Complaints

    Delinquency complaints, dismissal of; appeal, **T 34:8**

    Appointment of attorney for indigent party, **T 34:10**

    Double jeopardy, **T 23:31**

    Refusal to file, **T 15:2**

Detention hearings, **T 19:5**

Dismissal of complaint for abortion, **T 12:10**

Dismissal of delinquency complaint, appeal by state, **T 34:8**

    Appointment of attorney for indigent party, **T 34:10**

    Double jeopardy, **T 23:31**

Disposition, case remanded for; time for hearing, **T 34:11**

Dispositional hearings, advising parties of rights, **T 25:4**

Error in juvenile court judgment, reversal due to, **T 34:11**

APPEALS—*continued*

Failure to raise issue at trial, effect, **T 16:17**

Final orders. See FINAL ORDERS

Habeas corpus as alternative to, **T 34:12**

Intake decisions, **T 15:2**

Judgment notwithstanding verdict motion suspends time for filing notice of appeal, **T 34:5**

Jurisdiction, **T 34**

Juvenile procedure rules, applicability, **Juv. R 1(C)**

Modification of juvenile court order, **T 34:11**

New trial motion suspending time for filing notice of appeal, **T 34:5**

Nonjurisdictional issues, failure to raise at trial, **T 16:17**

Notice

    Amendment to include certification by prosecutor, **T 34:8**

    Suppression of evidence, appeal from, **T 34:8**

    Time for filing, **T 34:5, T 34:8**

Pendency of

    Evidence, as, **Evid. R 609**

    Hearsay exceptions, **Evid. R 803(21)**

Precedence of cases, **T 34:6**

    Suppression of evidence, appeal from, **T 34:8**

Prosecutors, standing, **T 34:3**

Reconsideration motion, effect on time for filing notice of appeal, **T 34:5**

Rehearing, motion for; effect on time for filing notice of appeal, **T 34:5**

Release of child pending, **T 34:6**

Reversal or remand of juvenile court's judgment, **T 34:11**

Right to, **Juv. R 34(J)**

Right to counsel, **T 34:10**

Serious youthful offender, **T 5:13**

Standing, **T 34:3**

State, by, **T 34:8**

    Double jeopardy, **T 23:31**

Stay pending appeal, **T 34:6**

Supersedeas bonds, **T 34:7**

Suppression of evidence, from, **Juv. R 22(D) to Juv. R 22(F), T 14:2, T 23:31**

    Appointment of attorney for indigent party, **T 34:10**

    Certification by prosecutor, **Juv. R 22(F), T 34:6, T 34:11**

    Prosecution following unsuccessful appeal, **T 34:8, T 34:11**

    Release of child from detention or shelter care pending appeal, **Juv. R 22(F), T 34:6**

    Speedy trial considerations, **Juv. R 22(F), T 34:8, T 34:11**

Suspension of time for filing notice of appeal, **T 34:5**

Time for filing notice of appeal, **T 34:5**

Transcripts, right to, **T 34:9**

Transfer of jurisdiction, from, **T 34**

    Conviction required for, **T 22:23**

    Age of majority attained prior to appeal, effect, **T 22:23**

    Guilty plea does not waive, **T 22:22**

Weight of evidence, juvenile court order against; reversal, **T 34:11**

APPEARANCE

Attorneys, **Juv. R 4(D)**

Juvenile, **ORC 2151.28(E), 2151.311**

    Excusing attention, **ORC 2151.35(A)**

    Taking into custody to ensure, **ORC 2151.31, T 14:3**

APPEARANCE—*continued*
Summons, **Juv. R 16(A)**, **ORC 2151.28**

APPROPRIATIONS
Detention homes, **ORC 2151.10, 2152.41**
Family foster homes, **ORC 2151.331**
Juvenile courts, **ORC 2151.10**
Youth services department, to, **T 15:3**

ARBITRATION AND AWARD
Alternative dispute resolution, **T 15:5**
Evidence rules, exemptions, **Evid. R 101**

ARRESTS
Generally, **ORC 2151.14, 2151.27, 2152.03**
Authority to make, **ORC 2151.31, T 14:3**
Child abuse offenders, **ORC 2151.43**
Children, **Juv. R 6**
Citizens' arrests, **T 14:3**
Contempt, parents' failure to provide child support, **ORC 2151.43**
Detention subsequent to. See DETENTION AND DETENTION HOMES
Disposition of minor in custody, **T 14:3**
Electronically monitored house arrest, **ORC 2151.355(J), ORC 2152.19, T 27:10**
Expungement of records, **T 35:4**
Felony cases, **T 14:3**
Fingerprinting minor, consent of juvenile court, **ORC 2151.313, T 14:15**
Invalid, effect on subsequent prosecution, **T 14:3**
Misdemeanor cases, **T 14:3**
Photographing minor, consent of juvenile court, **ORC 2151.313, T 14:15**
Private residence, in; search warrant required, **T 14:4**
Probable cause, **T 14:3**
Probation officers, by, **ORC 2151.14**
Records, expungement, **T 35:4**
Statistical data, **T 35:4**
Warrantless, **ORC 2151.14, T 14:3**
Warrants for, **T 14:3**
    Evidence rules, applicability, **Evid. R 101**

ASSAULT AND BATTERY
Minor committing, parental liability, **ORC 2151.355(G), T 32:2**

ASSESSMENTS, SPECIAL
Detention homes, funding, **ORC 2152.43**
Juvenile rehabilitation facilities, to support, **ORC 2151.66, 2151.78**

ATTORNEY GENERAL
Federal law violation by juvenile, certification of cases for prosecution in federal district court, **T 4:3**
Juvenile court records of delinquent child, obtaining for reparation of victims of crimes, **T 35:2**

ATTORNEY-CLIENT PRIVILEGE
Child abuse, applicability to reports of, **ORC 2151.421(A)**
Neglected children, applicability to reports of, **ORC 2151.421(A)**

ATTORNEYS
See also RIGHT TO COUNSEL
Adjudicatory hearing, **Juv. R 29(B)**
Appointment
    Minor female seeking abortion, for, **T 12:4**

ATTORNEYS—*continued*
Child abuse to be reported by, **ORC 2151.99(B), 2151.421(A)**
Conflict of interest, guardian ad litem as ward's attorney, **Juv. R 4(C)**
Court appointment, **Juv. R 4(A)**
    Fees, **Juv. R 4(G)**
    Indigent persons. See INDIGENT PERSONS, at Attorney appointed for
Court employee appointed to assist indigent persons in obtaining, **ORC 2151.314(D)**
Detention hearing, **Juv. R 7(F)**
Fees
    Court-appointed counsel, **Juv. R 4(G)**
Guardian ad litem as, **Juv. R 4(C)**, **ORC 2151.281(H), T 23:6**
    Conflict of interest, **T 23:6**
    Withdrawal of counsel, **T 23:6**
Indigents, for. See INDIGENT PERSONS
Ineffective assistance of counsel. See INEFFECTIVE ASSISTANCE OF COUNSEL
Inspection of records by, **T 35:2**
Magistrates required to be, **T 24:2**
Prosecuting. See PROSECUTORS
Removal hearings out of county, **Juv. R 39**
Right to. See RIGHT TO COUNSEL
Runaway consenting to return, guardian's signature required, **T 36:2**
Service of process on, **Juv. R 20(B)**
Termination of parental rights, **ORC 2151.353(B), T 34:10**
Waiver of right to, **Juv. R 3**
Withdrawal from juvenile proceedings, **Juv. R 4(F)**

AUDITORS, COUNTY
Juvenile rehabilitation facilities, powers and duties, **ORC 2151.79**

AUTHENTICATION OF EVIDENCE
Generally, **Evid. R 901 to Evid. R 903**
Acknowledged documents, **Evid. R 902**
Ancient documents, **Evid. R 901**
Commercial paper, **Evid. R 902**
Comparison of authenticated specimens, **Evid. R 901**
Congressional acts, presumptions under, **Evid. R 902**
Expert witness comparing authenticated specimens, **Evid. R 901**
Foreign public documents, **Evid. R 902**
Handwriting, nonexpert opinion, **Evid. R 901**
Illustrations, **Evid. R 901**
Methods provided by statute or rule, **Evid. R 901**
Newspapers, **Evid. R 902**
Official publications, **Evid. R 902**
Periodicals, **Evid. R 902**
Public records, **Evid. R 901, Evid. R 902**
Requirement, **Evid. R 901**
Seal, domestic public documents under, **Evid. R 902**
Self-authentication, **Evid. R 902**
Subscribing witness' testimony, **Evid. R 903**
Telephone conversations, **Evid. R 901**
Trade inscriptions, **Evid. R 902**
Voice identification, **Evid. R 901**

AUTOMOBILES
See MOTOR VEHICLES

BAIL

Adult offenders, juvenile proceedings, **T 22:25**
Criminal prosecution as adult
    Binding over, **T 22:25**
    Delinquency cases, **T 19:9**
Delinquency cases, **T 19:9**
    Denial, **T 34:6**
Evidence rules, applicability, **Evid. R 101**
Recognizance
    Juvenile delinquent
        Transfer from juvenile court, **ORC 2152.12(F)**
    Juvenile on probation, parent required to post, **T 32:2**
Transfer for criminal prosecution, **ORC 2152:12(F), T 22:25**
Unruly children, **T 19:9**

BAILIFFS

Generally, **ORC 2151.13**

BANK RECORDS

Warrantless searches, **T 14:4**

BAPTISMAL CERTIFICATES

Hearsay exceptions, **Evid. R 803(12)**

BATTERED CHILDREN

See CHILD ABUSE

BEST EVIDENCE RULE

Generally, **Evid. R 1001**

BEST INTERESTS OF CHILD

Abortion notification of parents, **T 12:2**
Dependency determination, **ORC 2151.414, T 25:2**
Dispositional hearings, **ORC 2151.415(B), T 25:2**
    Modification of orders, **T 33:4**
Diversion programs, **T 15:3**
Guardians ad litem, protection of, **T 23:6**
Permanent custody standard, **ORC 2151.414(A), 2151.414(D)**

BIBLES

Hearsay exceptions, when containing family history, **Evid. R 803(13)**

BINDING OVER

See TRANSFER FOR CRIMINAL PROSECUTION

BIRTH

Declarants, hearsay exceptions, **Evid. R 804(B)(4)**
Records, hearsay exceptions, **Evid. R 803(9)**

BONDS, SURETY

Adult offenders, suspended sentences, **ORC 2151.50**
Appeals. See APPEALS
Forfeiture, adult offenders tried in juvenile courts, **ORC 2151.50**
Juvenile court personnel, **ORC 2151.13**
    Judges acting as clerks, **ORC 2151.12**
Juvenile rehabilitation facility superintendent, **ORC 2151.70**
Probation officers, juvenile courts, **ORC 2151.13**

BOUNDARIES

Hearsay exceptions, **Evid. R 803(19)**

BRIEFS

Continuing jurisdiction, motion to invoke supported by brief, **T 33:2**

BUSINESS RECORDS

Hearsay exceptions, **Evid. R 803(6)**
    Medical and hospital records as, **T 23:16**

CAMPS AND CAMPING

Juvenile rehabilitation, **ORC 2151.65 to 2151.84**
    See also REHABILITATION.

CARS

See MOTOR VEHICLES

CASE PLANS

Generally, **ORC 2151.412, T 26**
Abuse, neglect or dependency cases, notice, **T 18:3, T 19:5**
Abused children, **T 26:2**
    Temporary custody
        Mandatory counseling for parents, **ORC 2151.412(H)**
        Supportive services, participation in by parents, **ORC 2151.412(H)**
Administrative review, **ORC 2151.416**
    Approval by court, **T 33:11**
    Meetings, **ORC 2151.416(C)**
    Modification by court, **T 33:11**
    Panel for review, **T 33:10**
    Reports, **ORC 2151.416(D), 2151.416(H)**
    Review panel, **ORC 2151.416(B)**
    Revised plans, **ORC 2151.416(E), T 33:10**
    Rules, **ORC 2151.416(F)**
    Scope, **T 33:10**
    Semiannual, **ORC 2151.416(A), T 33:10**
        Court, by, **T 33:10**
        Meetings, **T 33:10**
        Reports, **T 33:10**
        Review panel, **T 33:10**
        Revisions, **T 33:10**
        Scope, **T 33:10**
    Termination of custody upon, **ORC 2151.416(G)**
Adoption, seeking and preparing child for, **ORC 2151.413(D)**
Agreement between parties, attempt to obtain, **ORC 2151.412(D)**
Approval by court, **T 26:4**
    Changes, **T 26:5**
Changes, **T 26:5**
    Hearings on, **ORC 2151.416(E)**
Children services agencies, by, **T 26:2**
Dependency and neglect, **T 26:2**
    Notice of case plan, **T 18:3, T 19:5**
    Temporary custody
        Mandatory counseling for parents, **ORC 2151.412(H)**
        Supportive services, participation in by parents, **ORC 2151.412(H)**
Development, priorities, **ORC 2151.412(G)**
Due process considerations, **T 26:7**
Failure to implement
    Children services agencies, effect on motion for permanent custody, **ORC 2151.414(C)**
    Permanent custody motion, effect on, **T 31:8**
Filing, **ORC 2151.412(C)**
Foster care, **T 26:2**
Goals, **T 26:6**
    Rules, **ORC 2151.412(F)**
    Temporary custody, **ORC 2151.412(F)**

CASE PLANS—*continued*

Hearings for revision of plans, **ORC 2151.416(E)**

Journalization, **ORC 2151.353(D), 2151.412(D), 2151.412(E), 2151.417(F), T 26:4, T 33:11**

Maintenance, **ORC 2151.412(A), T 26:2**

Modification

    Threat of immediate harm to child

        Approval of court, when required, **ORC 2151.412(E)**

Neglected children. See Dependency and neglect, this heading

Permanent custody, **T 26:2**

Planned permanent living arrangements, **T 26:2**

Preparation, **ORC 2151.412(A), T 26:2**

Priorities, **T 26:6**

Private child placing agency, applicability of provisions to, **ORC 2151.412(A)**

Protective supervision, **T 26:2**

Review hearings, **ORC 2151.417(A)**

    Approval of plan, **ORC 2151.417(F)**

    Modification of plan, **ORC 2151.417(F)**

    Revised plans, **ORC 2151.417(D)**

Revised

    Review hearings, **ORC 2151.417(D)**

Rules, **ORC 2151.412(B)**

Summons to contain, **T 18:3**

Temporary custody, **T 26:2**

    Abused or neglected children

        Mandatory counseling for parents, **ORC 2151.412(H)**

        Supportive services, participation in by parents, **ORC 2151.412(H)**

    Agreements, extension of, **T 11:4**

    Extension

        Reports on progress of plans, **ORC 2151.415(D)**

    Goals, **ORC 2151.412(F)**

Time for filing, **T 26:3**

CASE RECORDS

Temporary custody, statement that placement consistent with best interests and welfare of child, **ORC 2151.33(F)**

CASHBOOKS

Juvenile courts to maintain, **ORC 2152.71(A), T 35:2**

CEMETERIES

Inscriptions on gravestones and monuments, hearsay exceptions, **Evid. R 803(13)**

CERTIFICATION HEARINGS

See TRANSFER FOR CRIMINAL PROSECUTION

CERTIFICATION OF CASES TO JUVENILE COURTS

Generally, **ORC 2151.23(C) to 2151.23(F), 2152.03, T 3:2, T 16:15**

Certification as complaint, **Juv. R 10(A), T 16:15**

Supplementing, **T 16:15**

CHARACTER EVIDENCE

Generally, **Evid. R 404 to Evid. R 406**

Defendants, **Evid. R 404**

Habits and customs, **Evid. R 406**

Hearsay, **Evid. R 803(20)**

Methods of proving, **Evid. R 405**

Plaintiff, **Evid. R 404**

Routine practices, **Evid. R 406**

Victims of crime, **Evid. R 404**

CHARACTER EVIDENCE—*continued*

Witnesses, **Evid. R 404**

    Impeachment purposes, for, **Evid. R 608**

CHILD ABUSE

Generally, **ORC 2151.031, 2151.421 to 2151.54, T 9:12**

See also DEPENDENT AND NEGLECTED CHILDREN.

Abortion notification of parents affected by, **T 12:2**

Abuse or neglect, danger of; detention due to, **T 14:3**

Abuser, removal from child's home, **ORC 2151.353(A), T 30, Juv. R 29(E), ORC 2151.35**

Adjudicatory hearing, **Juv. R 29(E), ORC 2151.35**

Alcohol or drug addiction testing and treatment, **ORC 2151.914(A), 2151.3514, T 30:10**

Appeals, **T 34**

Attendance of child at dispositional hearing, **T 25:5**

Attorney representing interests of child, **Juv. R 4(A), T 23:6**

Case plans. See CASE PLANS

Charges, **ORC 2151.43**

Clear and convincing evidence standard of proof, **T 23:13**

Commitment to custody of children services agency, **ORC 2151.353(A)**

    See also PERMANENT CUSTODY; TEMPORARY CUSTODY.

Competency of children as witnesses, **Juv. R 27(B)**

Complaints, **Juv. R 10(A), ORC 2151.27(A), 2151.27(C), 2151.44, T 14**

    Basis for, **T 16:3**

    Best interests of child as sole allegation, insufficient, **T 16:14**

    Dismissal, **ORC 2151.35, 2151.35(A)**

    Foster care, **T 16:14**

    Oath requirement, **T 16:6**

    Permanent custody, **T 16:14**

    Planned permanent living arrangement, prayer for, **T 16:14**

    Sufficiency, **T 16:7**

    Temporary custody, **T 16:14**

    Temporary orders, **Juv. R 13(B)**

    Time for filing, **T 16:4**

Constitutional issues, **T 14:16**

Continuing jurisdiction

    Duration, **T 33:4**

    Termination, **T 33:4**

Conviction of offense not required for abuse finding, **ORC 2151.031, T 9:12**

Corporal punishment, abuse determination, **T 9:12**

Court supervision of parental custody as disposition, **ORC 2151.353(A)**

Court taking custody of child, **Juv. R 6, ORC 2151.31**

    Hearings, **Juv. R 27(B)**

Custody of child, **Juv. R 6, ORC 2151.31**

Danger of abuse or neglect, detention due to, **T 14:3**

Death of child, abuse determination, **ORC 2151.031(C), T 9:12**

Definition, **Juv. R 2(A), ORC 2151.031, T 9:12**

Depositions

    Testimony taken by, **ORC 2151.35(G)**

    Victims, of, **Juv. R 27(B)**

Detention, **T 19:2**

    Separation from adults, **ORC 2152.26(D)**

Discipline, abuse determination, **T 9:12**

Discovery of records concerning, **T 21:2**

CHILD ABUSE—*continued*
Dispositional hearings, **Juv. R 34(A), ORC 2151.353**
  Case plans, **Juv. R 34(F)**
    Review, **Juv. R 36**
  Orders, **Juv. R 34(D)**
    Review, **Juv. R 36**
  Review hearings, **Juv. R 36, T 33:11**
Drug abuse by parent
  Pregnancy, **T 9:14, T 9:16**
  Treatment, mandatory, **T 30:10**
Emergency medical or surgical care, **Juv. R 13, ORC 2151.33**
Endangering children, **ORC 2151.031(B), T 9:14**
Excited utterance, hearsay exception, **T 23:16**
Explanation given at variance with injury as evidence of abuse, **ORC 2151.031(C), T 9:15**
Faith healing instead of medical treatment of sick child, exemption, **ORC 2151.421(H), T 9:6**
Final orders, **T 34:4**
Finding of fault on part of parent, guardian, or custodian, **T 9:12**
Foster care. See DEPENDENT AND NEGLECTED CHILDREN, at Planned permanent living
Guardian ad litem, appointment, **Juv. R 13(B), ORC 2151.281, 2151.281(B), T 23:6**
Health insurance coverage, **ORC 2151.33**
Hearings, **Juv. R 27(B)**
  Dispositional hearings, **Juv. R 34(A)**
    Case plans, **Juv. R 34(F), Juv. R 36**
    Orders, **Juv. R 34(D), Juv. R 36**
  Foster parents' notice, **T 33:4**
  Modification hearing, **T 33:4**
Hearsay exception for statements of child, **T 23:16**
Intake. See INTAKE, generally
Investigation, **ORC 2151.141**
Jurisdiction, **ORC 2151.23(A)**
Legal custody, **T 30:7**
Mandatory disposition to drug treatment, **T 30:10**
Medical or surgical care, emergency order, **Juv. R 13, ORC 2151.33**
Medical statements, hearsay exception, **T 23:16**
Mental injury, **T 9:15, T 9:16**
  Inflicted by other than accidental means as constituting, **ORC 2151.031(C), 2151.031(D)**
Minor witnesses, determining competency of, **T 23:18**
Modification hearing, **T 33:4**
Nonaccidental injuries as evidence of abuse, **T 9:15**
Nonparent abusing child, effect on abuse determination, **T 9:12**
Orders
  Dispositional, **Juv. R 34(D)**
    Case plans, **Juv. R 34(F), Juv. R 36**
    Review, **Juv. R 36**
  Temporary, **Juv. R 13(B)**
    Modification, **Juv. R 34(G)**
Out-of-home care abuse, **T 9:17**
  Defined, **ORC 2151.011(B), 2151.031(E)**
Parent, abuser required to be, **T 9:16**
Penalties, **ORC 2151.99(A)**
Permanent custody, **T 30:8 to T 30:12**
  See also PERMANENT CUSTODY, generally.
Physical injury, **T 9:15, T 9:16**
Physician-patient privilege inapplicable, **T 23:15**
Planned permanent living arrangements, **T 16:14, T 30:13**
Prenatal conduct of mother, **T 9:14, T 9:16**
Professionals required to report abuse, **T 14:17**
Protective supervision, **T 30:5**

CHILD ABUSE—*continued*
Registries, central, **ORC 2151.421(F)**
Removal of abuser from child's home, **ORC 2151.353(A), T 30**
Removal of children from home, reasonable efforts to prevent, **T 25:14**
Reporting requirements, **ORC 2151.421, T 14:17, T 16:2**
  Attorney-client privilege, applicability, **ORC 2151.421(A)**
  Failure to report, civil action by guardian for, **T 23:6**
  Homeless or domestic violence shelters, children living in, **ORC 2151.422**
  Penalties for violations, **ORC 2151.99(B)**
  Physician-patient privilege, applicability, **ORC 2151.421(A)**
Self-incrimination privilege, **T 23:27**
Sexual abuse. See SEXUAL ABUSE
Shelter care. See SHELTER CARE
Siblings of abused children, grounds for dependency determination, **ORC 2151.04(D)**
Social history, court report, **Juv. R 32**
Statements of children, admissibility, **ORC 2151.35(F)**
Stay pending appeal, **T 34:6**
Summons of child, **T 18:2**
Supervised custody as disposition, **ORC 2151.353(A)**
Support of abused children by juvenile court, **ORC 2151.10**
Temporary custody, **T 30:6**
  See also TEMPORARY CUSTODY.
Temporary orders, **Juv. R 13(B)**
  Modification, **Juv. R 34(G)**
Termination of parental rights. See PERMANENT CUSTODY
Testimony of children
  Hearsay rule, exception, **Evid. R 807**
Unfit parents, **ORC 2151.05**
Venue, **T 17:4**
Witnesses, determining competency of, **T 23:18**

CHILD CARE AGENCIES
See CHILDREN SERVICES AGENCIES

CHILD SUPPORT
Actions
  Juvenile courts, **ORC 2151.231**
  Parentage action, conversion into, **ORC 2151.231, 2151.232**
Adjudicatory hearing, **Juv. R 29(E)**
Commitment for rehabilitation or protection, **ORC 2151.36**
Complaint, **Juv. R 10(A)**
Foster care facilities, in, **ORC 2152.41**
Jurisdiction, **ORC 2151.23(A), 2151.23(B), 2151.23(D), 2151.23(G)**
Juvenile courts
  Actions for orders, **ORC 2151.231, 2151.232**
Nonsupport, charges filed, **ORC 2151.43**
Orders
  Actions in juvenile courts, **ORC 2151.231**
Payment for care, support, maintenance, and education of child, **ORC 2151.361**
Social history or examination of child, **Juv. R 32**
Temporary orders regarding, **ORC 2151.33(B)**
Uniform reciprocal enforcement of support act, juvenile court jurisdiction, **ORC 2151.23(B)**

CHILDREN
See JUVENILES

CHILDREN SERVICES AGENCIES
Abuse in out-of-home care, **T 9:17**
Adult case dispositional hearing notice, **ORC 2151.42**
Case plans. See CASE PLANS, generally
Child abuse reporting, duties, **ORC 2151.99(B), 2151.421(F), T 16:2**
 Children living in homeless or domestic violence shelters, **ORC 2151.422**
Complaints, filing, **T 16:2**
Custody, termination of, **T 33:10**
Dispositional orders
 Extension, motion for, **ORC 2151.353(G)**
 Hearing notice, adult cases, **ORC 2151.424**
 Modification, motions, **ORC 2151.353(E)**
 Motions for, **ORC 2151.415(A)**
 Termination, motions, **ORC 2151.353(E)**
Foster care, placement of children in
 Factors to consider, **ORC 2151.415(C)**
 Removal from residential placement, **ORC 2151.415(G)**
Intersystem services to children cluster, local
 Dispute resolution, **T 15:6**
Motions for temporary custody of child
 Temporary shelter care placement, following, **ORC 2151.33(C)**
Neglect in out-of-home care, **T 9:11**
Nonresidents, placements, **ORC 2151.39**
Payment for care, support, maintenance, and education of child, **ORC 2151.361**
Permanent custody, **ORC 2151.353, 2151.413, 2151.414**
 See also PERMANENT CUSTODY, generally.
 Agreement, **T 11:5**
 Failure to implement case plan, effect on, **ORC 2151.414(C)**
 Parents ceasing to be parties to action, **ORC 2151.35(D), T 18:2**
Placement of child by parent not considered abandonment, **T 9:5**
Removal of child from home, reasonable efforts to prevent, **T 25:14**
 Determination by court, **ORC 2151.419(A)**
 Findings of fact by court, **ORC 2151.419(B)**
Temporary custody, **ORC 2151.353**
 See also TEMPORARY CUSTODY, generally.
 Agreements, **T 11:3**
  Case plan, filing of, **T 11:4**
  Extension, **T 11:4**
 Dispositional orders, motions for, **ORC 2151.415(A)**
 Extension, **ORC 2151.415(D)**
 Motion for following temporary shelter care placement, **ORC 2151.33(C)**
 Payment for care, support, maintenance, and education of child, **ORC 2151.361**
 Pending outcome of adjudicatory and dispositional hearings, **T 20:5**
Termination of custody, **T 33:10**
Voluntary placement of child, **T 19:7**

CIGARETTES
Prohibitions relating to cigarettes and tobacco products, **ORC 2151.87**

CITIZENS' ARRESTS
Generally, **T 14:3**

CIVIL SERVICE
Juvenile rehabilitation facility employees, **ORC 2151.70**

CLERKS OF COURTS
Computerization of offices, costs applied to, **ORC 2151.541**
Deputy clerks administering oaths, **T 16:6**
Records, **ORC 2151.12**
 Juvenile delinquency complaint, when victim 65 or older or disabled, **ORC 2152.71(B), 2152.71(C)**

CLOSED-CIRCUIT TELEVISION
Sex offense victims, minor, testimony of, **Juv. R 37, ORC 2151.351, T 23:16, T 23:23**

COMMERCIAL PAPER
Authentication, **Evid. R 902**

COMMITMENT OF CHILDREN
Delinquency. See DELINQUENCY

COMMUNICABLE DISEASES
Sex offenses committed by minor, notice to victim of communicable diseases, **ORC 2151.14(C)**

COMMUNITY RESOURCES
See DIVERSION PROGRAMS

COMMUNITY SERVICE
Delinquency case
 Other dispositions, **ORC 2152.19, T 27:7**
 Restitution ordered, **T 27:13**

COMPENSATION
Detention home employees, **ORC 2152.41**
Guardians ad litem, **Juv. R 4(G), ORC 2151.281(D)**
Juvenile court employees, **ORC 2151.13**
 Detention home employees, **ORC 2152.41**
Juvenile rehabilitation facilities
 Boards of trustees, **ORC 2151.69, 2151.80**
 Employees, **ORC 2151.70**
 Superintendent, **ORC 2151.70**

COMPETENCY OF WITNESSES
Age ten or under, standards, **T 23:18**
Child abuse victim, **Juv. R 27(B)**
Dependent or neglected child, **Juv. R 27(B)**
Expert testimony admissible to prove, **T 23:18**
Judges, **Evid. R 605**
Jurors, **Evid. R 606**
Minors, court's discretion, **T 23:18**
Voir dire examination of minor witnesses, **T 23:18**

COMPETENCY TO STAND TRIAL
Insanity distinguished, **T 23:7**
Mental examination ordered by court where competency at issue, **T 23:7**
Preponderance of evidence standard of proof inapplicable to juvenile proceedings, **T 23:7**

COMPLAINTS
Generally, **T 16**
Abortion for minor without parental consent, **ORC 2151.85**
 Appeals, **ORC 2151.85(E)**
 Fees and costs, **ORC 2151.85(H)**
 Filing, **ORC 2151.85(A)**
 Forms, **ORC 2151.85(G)**
 Hearings, **ORC 2151.85(B)**

COMPLAINTS—*continued*

Abused children, **Juv. R 10(A), ORC 2151.44, T 16:2**
 Dependency complaints, **T 16:11**
 Dismissal, **ORC 2151.35(A)**
 Foster care, **T 16:14**
 Neglect and abuse complaints, **T 16:11**
 Permanent custody, **T 16:14**
 Planned permanent living arrangement, **T 16:14**
 Sufficiency of complaint, **T 16:7**
 Temporary custody, **T 16:14**
 Time for filing, **T 16:4**
 Unruly complaints, **T 16:10**
Adults, against; for child abuse or contributing to delinquency, **ORC 2151.44**
Age of majority, filing after juvenile attains; jurisdiction of juvenile court, **T 2:2**
Allegations required, **T 16:7**
Amendment, **Juv. R 22(B), T 16:16**
Answers, **Juv. R 22(C) to Juv. R 22(E)**
 Defect in complaint, objection raised by answer, **T 16:17**
Appeal from refusal to file, **T 15:2**
Best interests of child as sole allegation, insufficient, **T 16:14**
Certification of cases, **Juv. R 10(A), T 16:15**
Child abuse, **ORC 2151.27(A), 2151.27(B)**
 See also Abused children, this heading.
 Dismissal, **ORC 2151.35**
Child care agency filing, **T 16:2**
Complainant compelling filing, **T 15:2**
Contents, **Juv. R 10(B), T 16:7**
Continuing jurisdiction invoked by filing, **T 33:2**
Crime charged, amendment, **T 16:16**
Custody of child, **Juv. R 10(A), Juv. R 10(D), Juv. R 10(G)**
 Institutional, **ORC 2151.27(A)**
Defects, **Juv. R 22(D)**
 Habeas corpus not proper remedy to challenge, **T 34:12**
 Objections based on, **Juv. R 22(D), T 16:17**
Definition, **Juv. R 2(E)**
Delinquent child. See DELINQUENCY
Dependency and neglect, **Juv. R 10, ORC 2151.27(A), T 16:11, T 16:12**
 Amendment to include additional child, **T 16:16**
 Child care agency, filing by required, **T 16:2**
 Dispositional orders, **T 16:14**
 Foster care, **T 16:14**
 Permanent custody, **T 16:14**
 Sufficiency of complaint, **T 16:7**
 Supplemental complaint filed with certification, **T 16:15**
 Temporary custody, **T 16:14**
 Time for filing, **T 16:4**
Detention
 Filing following, time limits, **T 19:7**
 Hearings, **ORC 2151.314(A)**
 Time for filing, **T 16:4**
Dismissal, **ORC 2151.35(A)**
 Age jurisdiction, failure to establish, **T 2:5**
 Dispositional hearing, failure to timely hold, **ORC 2151.35(B)**
 Expungement of records, **T 35:4**
Elements of crime required, **T 16:7**
Eligibility to file, **T 16:2**
Failure to file, **T 16:14**
Filing, **Juv. R 10(A)**
 Age of majority, filing after attaining; juvenile court jurisdiction, **T 2:2**
 Complainant compelling, **T 15:2**

COMPLAINTS—*continued*

Filing—*continued*
 Eligibility to file, **T 16:2**
 Failure to file, hearing not permitted, **T 16:2**
 Place of, **T 17:2**
 Screening information prior to, **Juv. R 9(B)**
Firearm specification, imposition of additional term of commitment of delinquent, **T 16:8, T 27:3**
Form, **Juv. R 10(B), T 16:6**
Habeas corpus, **Juv. R 10(G)**
Indictment contrasted, **T 1:6**
Intake, decision to file complaint made during, **T 15:2**
Jurisdictional defects, **T 16:17**
Juvenile traffic offenders. See TRAFFIC OFFENDERS, JUVENILE
Liberal construction, **T 1:6**
Long term foster care, for, **Juv. R 10(F)**
Names and addresses required in, **T 16:8**
Neglect. See Dependency and neglect, this heading
Notice to parent of category of complaint, sufficiency, **T 16:7**
Oath or affirmation required with filing, **T 16:6**
 Exceptions, **T 16:6**
Objections due to defects, **Juv. R 22(D), T 16:17**
Parent, guardian, or custodian; name and address included in complaint, **T 16:8**
Permanent custody. See PERMANENT CUSTODY
Personal knowledge of facts not required for filing, **T 16:2**
Planned permanent living arrangements, **T 16:14**
Probation violation by unruly child, original disposition order reviewed, **T 29:3**
Screening information prior to filing complaint, **Juv. R 9(B), T 15:2**
Service of process, **ORC 2151.28**
 Publication, by; when name or address of parent unknown, **T 16:8**
Sex offenders, petitions for reclassification or declassification, **T 6:13**
Shelter care
 Time for filing, **T 16:4, T 19:7**
Specific facts required, **T 16:8**
 Failure to include, timeliness of objections, **T 16:17**
Specific grounds required, **T 16:14**
Standing to file, **T 16:2**
Statistical record maintained by clerk of court, **ORC 2152.71(B), 2152.71(C)**
Statute or ordinance violated, designation, **T 16:7**
Sufficiency, **T 16:7, T 16:14**
 Objections, timeliness, **Juv. R 22(D), T 16:17**
Summons, copy of complaint to accompany, **T 18:3**
Supplemental complaint filed with certification, **T 16:15**
Temporary custody, **T 16:14**
Time for filing, **T 16:4**
Traffic offenders, juvenile. See TRAFFIC OFFENDERS, JUVENILE
Transfer of cases, **Juv. R 10(A), T 16:15**
Type of case, designation required, **T 16:7**
Uniform traffic ticket as, **Juv. R 10(C), T 16:2, T 16:7, T 16:9**
Unruly child, **Juv. R 10(A), ORC 2151.27(A), 2151.27(B), T 16**
Unruly complaints, **T 16:10**
Verification of amendment, **T 16:16**
Victim of delinquent 65 or older or disabled, record, **ORC 2152.71(B), 2152.71(C)**

COMPLAINTS—*continued*
Withdrawal, expungement of records, **ORC 2151.358(F)**, **T 35:4**

COMPUTERS
Juvenile courts
Computerization, costs applied to, **ORC 2151.541**

CONCLUSIONS OF LAW
Generally, **Juv. R 29(F)**, **ORC 2151.353(A)**

CONFESSIONS
Admissibility, **Evid. R 104**, **T 14:9**
Admissions. See also ADMISSIONS
Miranda rights. See also MIRANDA RIGHTS, generally
Request for probation officer not sufficient to invoke, **T 1:4**
Voluntariness, **T 14:9**

CONFIDENTIAL INFORMATION
See PRIVILEGED INFORMATION

CONFLICT OF INTEREST
Guardian ad litem as ward's attorney, **Juv. R 4(C)**, **T 23:6**

CONFRONTATION RIGHTS
Generally, **Evid. R 801**
Adjudicatory hearings, **T 1:4**, **T 23:2**, **T 23:22 to T 23:26**
Cross-examinations. See CROSS-EXAMINATIONS
Defendant's right to be present during proceedings, **T 23:23**
Delinquent child, inquiry into previous adjudication of confederate delinquent, **T 35:2**
Face-to-face confrontation, rights to, **T 23:23**
Neglect and dependency cases, applicability, **T 23:27**
Sex crimes against minors, **T 23:23**
Transfer of case for criminal proceedings, **T 22:13**
Waiver
Conduct, by, **T 23:26**
Knowledge and understanding of effect required, **T 23:26**

CONSPIRACY
Co-conspirator exception, **Evid. R 801**

CONSTABLES
Service of process by, **ORC 2151.14**

CONSTITUTIONALITY
Curfews, **T 8:6**
DNA databases, **T 14:8**
Removal of unruly nonresident children residing in foster homes, actions by school superintendents for, **T 13:6**
Self-incrimination. See SELF-INCRIMINATION
Sex offense victims, minor, testimony by closed-circuit television, **T 23:23**
Transfer to criminal court, mandatory, **T 22:1**, **T 22:3, 21:3**

CONTEMPT
Generally, **ORC 2151.21**
Appropriations, insufficient, **ORC 2151.10**
Deposition, failure to answer, **T 33:8**
Discovery, noncompliance, **Juv. R 17(F)**

CONTEMPT—*continued*
Employer penalizing witness for court attendance, **ORC 2151.211**
Evidence rules, applicability, **Evid. R 101**
Failure to answer service, **ORC 2151.28(J)**
Hearings, **T 33:8**
Jurisdiction, **T 33:8**
Magistrate hearing, failure of witness to appear, **Juv. R 40(C)**
Notice, **T 33:8**
Parent ordered to bring child to hearing, failure to comply, **T 33:8**
Reimbursement for emergency medical or surgical treatment, failure, **ORC 2151.33**
Subpoena, noncompliance, **T 33:8**
Summons, failure to obey, **T 33:8**

CONTINUANCES
Generally, **Juv. R 23**, **ORC 2151.22**
Adjudicatory hearings, **Juv. R 29(A)**, **T 19:7**, **T 23:31**
Discovery, failure to comply, **Juv. R 24(C)**
Dispositional hearings, **Juv. R 34(A)**, **ORC 2151.35(A), 2151.35(B)**, **T 25:4**

CONTINUING JURISDICTION
See JURISDICTION

CONTRIBUTING TO DELINQUENCY
See DELINQUENCY

CONVICTIONS
Hearsay exception, **Evid. R 803(21)**
Impeachment of evidence, **Evid. R 609**
Judgment, hearsay exception, **Evid. R 803(21)**
Permanent custody affected by, **T 30:10**

CORONERS
Child abuse, reporting, **ORC 2151.99(B)**, **2151.421(A)**

CORPORAL PUNISHMENT
Abuse determination, **T 9:12**

CORROBORATIVE EVIDENCE
Accomplice's testimony requiring, **T 23:21**

CORRUPT ACTIVITY
Juvenile delinquents, criminal forfeiture, **ORC 2151.355(B)**

CORRUPTION OF MINOR
Adult prosecuted for. See ADULT CASES, generally
Juvenile cannot be charged with, **T 4:4**

COSTS
Generally, see FEES AND COSTS
Court costs. See COURT COSTS

COUNSELING SERVICES
Temporary order requiring party to attend, **ORC 2151.33(B)**

COUNTIES
Appropriations
Detention homes, **ORC 2152.41**
Family foster homes, **ORC 2151.331**
Juvenile courts, to, **ORC 2151.10**

COUNTIES—*continued*

Appropriations—*continued*

    Juveniles, for

        Committed by court, support and mainte-
nance, **ORC 2151.36**

        Rehabilitation facilities, **ORC 2151.77**

Assessments for juvenile rehabilitation facilities,
ORC 2151.66, 2151.78

Auditors. See AUDITORS, COUNTY

Children, local intersystem services cluster for

    Dispute resolution, **T 15:6**

Commissioners. See COUNTY COMMISSIONERS

Extradition costs, payment, **T 36:3**

Family and children first councils

    Dispute resolution, **T 15:6**

Intersystem services to children cluster, local

    Dispute resolution, **T 15:6**

Juvenile court

    Cooperation with, **ORC 2151.40**

    Reimbursement, **ORC 2151.36**

Juvenile rehabilitation facilities, **ORC 2151.65 to
2151.84**

    See also REHABILITATION.

COUNTY COMMISSIONERS

Detention homes, powers

    Trustees

        Appointment, **ORC 2152.44**

        Removal, **ORC 2151.349**

Family foster homes

    Powers and duties, **ORC 2151.331**

COUNTY COURTS

Child brought before, transfer to juvenile court, **ORC
2152.03**

COURT COSTS

Generally, **ORC 2151.54**

Abortion, complaint for in juvenile court, **ORC
2151.85(H)**

    Appeals, **ORC 2151.85(H)**

Counties, reimbursement by, **ORC 2151.36**

Custody investigation, **Juv. R 32(D)**

Service of process, **ORC 2151.19**

Witness, **ORC 2151.28(J)**

COURTHOUSES

Generally, **ORC 2151.09**

COURTS

See particular court by name

Contempt. See CONTEMPT

Costs. See COURT COSTS

Federal. See FEDERAL COURTS

Juvenile courts. See JUVENILE COURTS

COURTS OF APPEALS

See also APPEALS

Docket priority, actions concerning juvenile court

    appropriations, **ORC 2151.10**

Jurisdiction, **T 34:2**

COURTS OF COMMON PLEAS

Child brought before, transfer to juvenile court, **ORC
2152.03**

Clerks as juvenile court clerks, **ORC 2151.12**

Judges, assignment to juvenile courts, **ORC 2151.07**

CRIME VICTIMS

See VICTIMS OF CRIME

CRIMES AND OFFENSES

See also particular subject concerned

Adoptive parents, disqualification, **ORC 2151.86**

Detention home employees, disqualification, **ORC
2151.86**

Felonies. See FELONIES

Gang activity, mandatory commitment, **T 27:3**

Sex offenses. See SEX OFFENDERS

CRIMINAL DAMAGING

Restitution as probation condition, **T 27:13**

CRIMINAL FORFEITURE

Generally, **T 27:14**

CRIMINAL GANG ACTIVITY

Mandatory commitment, **T 27:3**

**CRIMINAL IDENTIFICATION AND
INVESTIGATIONS BUREAU**

Criminal records check

    Adoptive and foster parents, prospective, **ORC
2151.86**

Records and reports

    Weekly report from juvenile courts, **ORC
2152.71(A)**

CRIMINAL MISCHIEF

Restitution as probation condition, **T 27:14**

CRIMINAL PROSECUTIONS

Concurrent jurisdiction, **T 3:3**

Confidential information divulged, **T 35:4**

Evidence rules, applicability, **Evid. R 101**

Juveniles. See TRANSFER FOR CRIMINAL PROS-
ECUTION

Obstruction, evidence of compromise to prove, **Evid.
R 408**

CROSS-EXAMINATIONS

Generally, **Juv. R 34(B)**

Adjudicatory hearings, **T 23:24**

Confidentiality not to limit right to cross-examine

    witness, **T 23:24**

Dispositional hearings, **Juv. R 34(B), T 25:9**

Expert witnesses, **Evid. R 705**

Leading questions, **Evid. R 611(B)**

Prior juvenile record, concerning, **T 35:2**

Right to cross-examine overrides confidentiality of

    juvenile records, **T 23:24**

Scope, **Evid. R 611**

CRYPTS

Inscriptions, hearsay exceptions, **Evid. R 803(13)**

CURFEWS

Constitutionality, **T 8:6**

Delinquency dispositions, **ORC 2152.19, T 27:7**

Exceptions, **T 8:6**

Unruly child, determination as due to violation, **T 8:6**

CUSTODIAL INTERROGATION

Generally, **T 14:10**

CUSTODY OF CHILDREN, DOMESTIC

See ALLOCATION OF PARENTAL RIGHTS AND
RESPONSIBILITIES

CUSTODY OF CHILDREN, INSTITUTIONAL

Administrative review, **T 33:10**

Complaints, **ORC 2151.27(A)**
    Long term foster care, for, **Juv. R 10(F)**

Court custody, **T 27:17**

Delinquent child, **T 27:17**

Detention
    Family foster homes, in, **ORC 2151.331**

Discharge
    Early release, **ORC 2151.38(A), 2151.38(B)**
    Institution or agency applying for, **ORC 2151.38(B)**
    Minimum term of institutionalization, **ORC 2151.38(A), 2151.38(B)**
    Multiple offenses, consecutive terms, **ORC 2151.38(B)**

Foster care, reimbursement of juvenile courts for costs, **ORC 2151.152**

Long term foster care, complaints for, **Juv. R 10(F)**

Modification of orders, **ORC 2151.42**

Notice
    Release of child, to committing court, **ORC 2151.38(B), 2151.38(C)**

Orders
    Modification
        Termination of parental rights, **ORC 2151.42(A)**

Out-of-home care defined, **ORC 2151.011(B)**

Permanent custody. See PERMANENT CUSTODY

Placement
    Correctional facilities, **ORC 2151.23(H)**
    Dispositional orders, notice, **ORC 2151.3510**

Rehabilitation facilities
    Criminal records check of employees, **ORC 2151.86**

Removal of child from placement with parents
    Ex parte proceeding, **ORC 2151.31(D)**
    Temporary order, **ORC 2151.33(B)**

Temporary custody. See TEMPORARY CUSTODY

Temporary orders
    Extension, **Juv. R 14(B)**
    Modification, **Juv. R 14(C)**
    Termination, **Juv. R 14(A)**

CUSTOMS

Evidence of, **Evid. R 406**

CUYAHOGA COUNTY JUVENILE COURT

Generally, **ORC 2151.07, T 1:6**

DAMAGES

See also RESTITUTION

Parental liability for acts of child, **ORC 2151.355(G), 2151.411, T 27:13, T 32:2**

DATA PROCESSING

DNA databases, **T 14:8**

Evidence generated by, defined, **Evid. R 1001**

Sex offenders
    Internet dissemination of juvenile registrants, **T 6:16**

DAY CARE

Provider defined, **ORC 2151.011(B)**

DAY CARE CENTERS

Employees
    Crimes disqualifying applicants, **ORC 2151.86**

DAY CARE CENTERS—*continued*

Employees—*continued*
    Reporting of child abuse, **ORC 2151.99(B), 2151.421(A)**

DAY REPORTING

Delinquent child dispositions, **ORC 2152.19, T 27:7**

DEAD MAN'S STATUTE

Generally, **Evid. R 601**

DEATH

Abused child, determination, **T 9:12**

Dying declaration, hearsay exception, **Evid. R 804(B)(2)**

Records, hearsay exception, **Evid. R 803(9)**

DECLARANTS

Defined, **Evid. R 801**

Unavailable, **Evid. R 804**

DECLARATIONS AGAINST INTEREST

Generally, **Evid. R 804(B)(3)**

DEFENDANTS

Character evidence, admissibility, **Evid. R 404**

Competency. See COMPETENCY TO STAND TRIAL

Confessions. See CONFESSIONS

Confrontation rights. See CONFRONTATION RIGHTS

Delinquency adjudications, admissibility, **Evid. R 609**

Hearsay, **Evid. R 801**

Identification. See IDENTIFICATION

Juveniles, transfer for criminal prosecution. See TRANSFER FOR CRIMINAL PROSECUTION

Self-incrimination, **Evid. R 608**

Statements by, **Evid. R 801**

Witness, as; preliminary matter, cross-examination limitations, **Evid. R 104**

Writings, **Evid. R 1001**

DEFENSES

Generally, **Juv. R 22(C), Juv. R 22(D)**

Affirmative, burden of proof, **T 23:13**

Common law infancy defense, **T 2:6**

Defect in complaint or indictment, **Juv. R 22(D)**

Denials, adjudicatory hearings, **Juv. R 29(C), Juv. R 29(E)**

Insanity defense, availability in juvenile court proceedings, **T 23:8**

Prehearing motions, **Juv. R 22(D), Juv. R 22(E)**

DEFINITIONS

Abandoned children, **T 9:4**

Abused child, **Juv. R 2(A), ORC 2151.031, T 9:12**

Act charged, **ORC 2152.02(A)**

Adjudicatory hearing, **Juv. R 2(B), T 23:1**

Agreement for temporary custody, **Juv. R 2(C)**

Child, **Juv. R 2(D), T 2:2**
    Abused, **Juv. R 2(A), ORC 2151.031, T 9:12**
    Delinquent, **Juv. R 2(H), ORC 2152.02(F), T 4:2**
    Juvenile traffic offender, **Juv. R 2(S)**
    Neglected, **Juv. R 2(W)**
    Unruly, **Juv. R 2(LL)**

Child abuse, **Juv. R 2(A), ORC 2151.031, T 9:12**

Child-victim oriented offender, **T 6:6**

DEFINITIONS—*continued*

Child-victim predator, **T 6:8**

Chronic truant, **ORC 2152.02(D)**

Cigarette, **ORC 2151.87(A)**

Clear and convincing evidence, **T 23:13**

Complaint, **Juv. R 2(E)**

Court rule, **Juv. R 2(HH)**

Custodian, **ORC 2151.011(B)**

Custodian of child, **Juv. R 2(G)**

Day care provider, **ORC 2151.011(B)**

Declarants, **Evid. R 801**

Delinquent child, **ORC 2152.02(F)**

Delinquent children, **Juv. R 2(H), T 4:2**

Dependent children, **ORC 2151.04, T 10:2**

Detention of child, **Juv. R 2(J)**

Discretionary serious youthful offender, **ORC 2152.02(G)**

Dispositional hearing, **Juv. R 2(L)**

Drug abuse offense, **ORC 2152.02(J)**

Duplicate, **Evid. R 1001**

Economic loss, **ORC 2152.02(L)**

Electronic monitoring device, **ORC 2152.02(K)**

Firearm, **ORC 2152.02(M)**

Guardian, **Juv. R 2(M), ORC 2151.011(B)**

Guardian ad litem, **Juv. R 2(N), T 23:6**

Habitual child-victim oriented offender, **T 6:7**

Habitual sex offender, **T 6:3**

Hearing, **Juv. R 2(O)**

Hearsay, **Evid. R 801**

Independent living services, **ORC 2151.81(A)**

Indigent person, **Juv. R 2(P)**

Intake, **T 15:2**

Juvenile courts, **ORC 2151.011 to 2151.06**

Juvenile delinquents, **T 4:2**

Juvenile proceeding, **Juv. R 2**

Juvenile traffic offender, **Juv. R 2(S), ORC 2152.02(N), T 7:2**

Mental examination, **Juv. R 2(V)**

Mental illness, **ORC 2151.011(B)**

Mentally retarded or developmentally disabled victim, **ORC 2152.821(A)**

Neglected children, **Juv. R 2(W), ORC 2151.03, T 9:4**

Original writings or recordings, **Evid. R 1001**

Physical examination, **Juv. R 2(BB)**

Private child placing agency, **ORC 2151.011(A)**

Probation, **T 27:8**

Relevant evidence, **Evid. R 401**

Rule of court, **Juv. R 2(HH)**

Sexual abuse, **T 9:12**

Sexual predator, **T 6:4**

Sexually oriented offender, **T 6:2**

Sexually oriented offense, **ORC 2152.02(Y)**

Shelter care, **Juv. R 2(II)**

Tobacco product, **ORC 2151.87(A)**

Traffic offender, juvenile, **T 7:2**

Unemancipated, **ORC 2151.85(I)**

Unruly children, **Juv. R 2(LL), ORC 2151.022, T 8:2**

Ward of court, **Juv. R 2(MM)**

Young adult, **ORC 2151.81(B)**

Youth smoking education program, **ORC 2151.87(A)**

DELINQUENCY

Abuse, neglect or dependency investigation, **ORC 2151.141**

Adjudication, **ORC 2151.355**
    Pupils permanently excluded from schools, retention of records by school boards, **ORC 2151.358(K)**
    School boards, notification of, **ORC 2151.355(K)**
    Transfer of jurisdiction after precluded by double jeopardy, **T 22:24**

Adjudicatory hearings. See ADJUDICATORY HEARINGS

Adult criminal court, transfer to, **T 4:7**

Adult facility, confinement in, **T 27:18**

Adult sentence, imposition
    Electronically monitored house detention, **T 27:10**

Age of majority reached prior to disposition of case
    Electronically monitored house detention, **T 27:10**

Aggravated felonies committed by juveniles. See Felonies committed by juveniles, this heading

Alcohol
    Possession or purchase by minor regarded as delinquency, **T 4:4**
    Treatment program as disposition, **ORC 2152.19, T 27:9**

Amenability to rehabilitation, determination, **ORC 2152.12(C)**

Appeals, **T 34**
    See also APPEALS, generally.

Apprehension, **ORC 2151.14, 2151.31, 2152.03**

Bail, **T 19:9**

Bond posted by parents, **T 32:2**

Burden of proof, reasonable doubt standard, **T 1:4**

Case history, **ORC 2152.41**

Catch all provision, **T 27:18**

Commitment of children, **ORC 2151.355**
    Discharge
        Minimum term of institutionalization, **ORC 2151.38(A), 2151.38(B)**
        Multiple offenses, consecutive terms, **ORC 2151.38(B)**
    Early release, **ORC 2151.38(A), 2151.38(B)**
    Firearm specification, imposition of additional term, **T 16:8, T 27:3**
    Gang activity, mandatory commitment for, **T 27:3**
    House detention, electronically monitored, **ORC 2152.19, T 27:10**
    Suspended commitment order, reinstatement of, **T 33:7**
    Youth services department, institutionalization
        Early release, **ORC 2151.38(A), 2151.38(B)**

Community service
    Other dispositions, **ORC 2152.19, T 27:7**
    Restitution, **T 27:13**

Complaints, **Juv. R 10(A), ORC 2151.27, T 16**
    See also COMPLAINTS, generally.
    Amendment, **T 16:16**
        Statute or ordinance violated, designation, **T 16:7**
    Dismissal, state appealing, **T 34:8**
    Firearm specification, imposition of additional term of commitment, **T 16:8, T 27:3**
    School boards, notification of, **ORC 2151.27(F)**
    Statistical record maintained by clerk of court, **ORC 2152.71(B), 2152.71(C)**
    Sufficiency, **T 16:7**

DELINQUENCY—*continued*

Complaints—*continued*
> Victim of delinquent 65 or older or disabled, **ORC 2152.71(C)**
> Record, **2151.27(D), ORC 2152.71(B)**

Concealed or misrepresented age, prosecution in juvenile court waived, **T 2:4**

Contributing to, **ORC 2151.99(A), 2151.422 to 2151.54**
> Charges, **ORC 2151.43**
> Complaints, **ORC 2151.44**
> Delinquency charge resulting from, **T 4:4**
> Marriage of minor, effect, **T 2:2**

Corrupt activity, criminal forfeiture, **ORC 2151.355(B)**

Costs and reimbursements, **T 27:15**

Court custody, **T 27:17**

Court order, violation as delinquent act, **T 4:6**

Court records
> Attorney general obtaining for reparation of victims of crimes, **T 35:2**

Crimes applicable only to adults not regarded as delinquency, **T 4:4**

Criminal damaging or criminal mischief, restitution as disposition of case, **T 27:13**

Criminal prosecution, **ORC 2152.12**
> See also TRANSFER FOR CRIMINAL PROSECUTION.
> Category one and two offenses, **ORC 2152.12(B)**
>> Repeat offenders, **ORC 2152.12(C)**
> Firearm, offense committed with, factor to consider, **ORC 2152.12(B), 2152.12(C)**
> Violent crime, factor to consider, **ORC 2152.12(C)**

Curfew as disposition, **ORC 2152.19, T 27:7**

Custody of child, **ORC 2152.19, T 27:17**

Day reporting, **ORC 2152.19, T 27:7**

Defined, **Juv. R 2(H), T 4:2**

Detention. See DETENTION AND DETENTION HOMES

Dismissal of complaint, state appealing, **T 34:8**

Disposition by court, other, **ORC 2152.19, T 27:18**

Dispositional hearings. See DISPOSITIONAL HEARINGS, generally

Dispositional orders. See JUVENILE COURTS

Diversion programs, **T 15:3**
> See also DIVERSION PROGRAMS, generally.

DNA testing, **ORC 2152.74**

Double jeopardy, applicability, **T 1:4, T 22:24**
> Suspended commitment order, reinstatement of, **T 33:7**

Drivers' licenses, suspension or revocation, **ORC 2152.19, T 27:11**
> Probationary operator's license, **ORC 2151.355(C)**
> Temporary instruction permit, **ORC 2151.355(C)**

Drug dispositions, **ORC 2152.19, T 27:9**

Drug possession regarded as, **T 4:4**

Drug testing
> Urinalysis, by, **ORC 2152.74**

Educational dispositions, **ORC 2152.19, T 27:3**

Electronically monitored house detention, **ORC 2151.355(J), ORC 2152.19, T 27:10**

Employment as disposition, **T 27:7**

Endangering children, delinquency charge resulting from, **T 4:4**

DELINQUENCY—*continued*

Enhancement of offense, use of prior adjudication for, **T 35:2**

Expenses for care, funding from juvenile courts, **ORC 2151.10**

Expungement of records, **ORC 2151.358, T 35:4**
> Fingerprints and photographs, **ORC 2151.313**

Extradition, **T 36:3**

Federal district court, prosecution in, **T 4:3**

Federal penal law, **T 4:3**

Felonies committed by juveniles
> Disposition distinctions from misdemeanors, **T 4:4**
> Fingerprints, **ORC 2151.313, T 14:15**
> Photographs, **ORC 2151.313, T 14:15**
> Transfer to adult court, **Juv. R 30**
>> See also TRANSFER FOR CRIMINAL PROSECUTION.
> Youth services department, institutionalization, **ORC 2151.355(A), T 27:3**

Females, trials, **ORC 2151.16**

Final order, delinquency finding as, **T 34:4**

Fines, **T 27:12**

Fingerprints, **ORC 2151.99(C), 2151.313, T 35:4**

Firearm specification, imposition of additional term, **T 16:8, T 27:3**

Foreign jurisdiction, juvenile domiciled in, criminal prosecution, **ORC 2152.12(C)**

Foreign state, adjudication in, **T 36:2**

Foster care
> Placement effect, **T 32:3**
> Violent character warning, **ORC 2152.72**

Foster care placement effect, **T 32:3**

Gang activity, **T 27:3**
> Mandatory commitment, **T 27:3**

Genetic testing, **ORC 2152.74**

Guardian ad litem, appointment, **ORC 2151.281, 2151.281(A)**

Handicapped child
> Educational program for, court-ordered, **T 27:18**

Hearings. See HEARINGS, generally

High school diploma program as disposition, **ORC 2152.19**

House detention, electronically monitored, **ORC 2151.355(J), ORC 2152.19, T 27:10**

Imprisonment
> Failure to pay fines or costs, due to, **T 27:12**

Infancy as defense, **T 2:2**

Institutionalization
> Commitment to youth services department
>> Early release, **ORC 2151.38(B)**
>> Discharge
>>> Minimum term, **ORC 2151.38(A), 2151.38(B)**
>>> Multiple offenses, consecutive terms, **ORC 2151.38(B)**

Intake, **T 15:2**
> See also INTAKE, generally.

Intensive supervision disposition, **ORC 2152.19, T 27:7**

Interference with custody, delinquency charges resulting from, **T 4:4**

Interstate agreements, **ORC 2151.56 to 2151.61, T 36:2**
> Jurisdiction of juvenile courts, **ORC 2151.23(A)**

Jail confinement, **Juv. R 7(H), ORC 2151.34, ORC 2152.26(C), T 19:2, T 27:17**

Jurisdiction, **ORC 2151.23(A), T 2, T 3:2, T 4**

Jury trials, right to inapplicable, **T 1:4**

DELINQUENCY—*continued*

Labor performed for victim as restitution, **T 27:13**

Law violation as delinquent act, **T 4:4**

Married minor, **T 2:2**

Maximum term of commitment, **T 27:3**

Mediation with victim as disposition, **T 27:20**

Medical and mental examinations, **ORC 2151.53, ORC 2152.12(C)**

Medical records, youth services department to receive upon commitment of child, **T 27:3**

Minimum period of commitment, **T 27:3**

Misdemeanors
  Disposition distinguished from delinquent felons, **T 4:4**
  Minor committing, delinquency determination, **T 4:4**

Mistaken belief as to age, transfer from adult court to juvenile court, **T 2:4**

Monitored house detention, **ORC 2151.355(J), ORC 2152.19, T 27:10**

Motor vehicle registration, revocation, **T 27:11**

Multiple dispositions, **T 27:19**

Murders committed by juveniles
  Commitment to youth services department, **ORC 2151.355(A)**
  Transfer to adult court, **Juv. R 30**
    See also TRANSFER FOR CRIMINAL PROSECUTION.
  Transfer to criminal court for subsequent offense mandatory, **T 22:5**

Not guilty child, expungement of records, **ORC 2151.358, T 35:4**

Obscenity offenses, delinquency charges resulting from, **T 4:4**

Offense of violence, commitment of child considered due to, **T 32:2**

Ohio penal law, **T 4:4**

Out-of-state placement, interstate agreements concerning, **T 36:2**

Parental liability, **ORC 2151.355(G), 2151.411**

Persons in need of supervision distinguished, **T 1:3**

Persons over age twenty-one, **T 36:2**

Photographs, **ORC 2151.99(C), 2151.313, T 35:4**

Plural findings, **T 27:19**

Prevention programs. See DIVERSION PROGRAMS

Prior adjudications
  Confederate delinquent, inquiry into, **T 35:2**
  Conviction, as; misdemeanor elevated to felony, **T 4:4**
  Theft adjudication as element, proof beyond reasonable doubt, **T 4:4**

Prior delinquency conviction, effect on degree of offense for current delinquent act, **T 16:8**

Probation, **ORC 2151.355(A), 2151.356(A), ORC 2152.19, T 4:4, T 27:8**
  See also PROBATION, generally.
  Searches authorized, **ORC 2151.355(L)**
  Weapons or dangerous ordnance, possession prohibited, **ORC 2151.355(A)**

Psychological profile provided to foster caregivers, **ORC 2152.72**

Reasonable doubt standard of proof, **T 1:4, T 23:13**

Recognizance
  Parent to enter into, **T 32:2**
  Transfer of case from juvenile court, **ORC 2152.12(F)**

Records and reports
  Annual report by juvenile court, **ORC 2152.71(D)**

DELINQUENCY—*continued*

Records and reports—*continued*
  Copies, providing, **ORC 2151.14(D), 2151.141**
  Expungement of records, **ORC 2151.358**
    Fingerprints and photographs, **ORC 2151.313**
  Physical and mental examinations, **ORC 2151.53**
  Pupils permanently excluded from schools, retention of records by school boards, **ORC 2151.358(K)**
  Sealing of records, **ORC 2151.358**
    Fingerprints and photographs, **ORC 2151.313**
  Social histories. See SOCIAL HISTORIES

Rehabilitation, **ORC 2151.65 to 2151.84**
  See also REHABILITATION.

Reimbursements, **T 27:15**

Release from commitment
  Jurisdiction, **T 33:9**
  School transcript provided to child's prior school, **ORC 2151.355(F), T 27:3**
  Youth services department, from. See YOUTH SERVICES DEPARTMENT

Removal of child from home, reasonable efforts to prevent, **T 25:14**

Repair of damaged property as restitution, **T 27:13**

Repeat offender
  Bond posted by parents, forfeiture, **T 32:2**
  Category one and two offenses, transfer to adult court, **ORC 2152.12(C)**

Restitution by, **ORC 2151.355(A), ORC 2152.20, T 27:13**
  Complaints resulting in, statistical record, **ORC 2152.71(B)**

School transcripts, provision to youth services department upon commitment, **ORC 2151.355(F), T 27:3**

Sealing of records, **ORC 2151.358, T 35:4**
  Fingerprints and photographs, **ORC 2151.313**

Searches authorized, **ORC 2151.355(L)**

Serious youthful offender. See SERIOUS YOUTHFUL OFFENDER

Sex offenses
  Indefinite term, **ORC 2151.355(A)**

Sex offenses. See SEX OFFENDERS

Sexually oriented material, pandering
  Delinquency charges resulting from, **T 4:4**

Shelter care, **T 19**
  See also SHELTER CARE, generally.

Silence, advising parties of rights prior to detention hearing, **T 19:5**

Social histories. See SOCIAL HISTORIES

Statute violated, providing to youth services department upon commitment, **ORC 2151.38(C), 2151.38(D)**

Stay pending appeal, **T 34:6**

Summons, **T 18**
  See also SUMMONS, generally.

Temporary custody as disposition of case, **ORC 2151.355(A), T 27:3**

Theft offenses, restitution as probation condition, **ORC 2151.355(A), T 27:13**

Traffic offenders. See also TRAFFIC OFFENDERS, JUVENILE
  Delinquent act, traffic offense as, **ORC 2151.356(A), T 7:4**

Transfer to adult criminal court, **ORC 2152.10 et seq., T 4:7**

Truancy dispositions, **T 4:5, T 27:16**

Unfit parents, **ORC 2151.05**

DELINQUENCY—*continued*

Unruly child, disposition as delinquent, **ORC 2151.354(A), T 29:3**

Venue. See VENUE, generally

Victim impact statement, **ORC 2151.355(H), ORC 2152.19**

Victim reconciliation as disposition, **T 27:20**

Violation of court order or law as delinquent act, **T 4:6**

Violent character warning, **ORC 2152.72**

Warrant against, **Juv. R 15(E)**

Witness at proceeding, penalization by employer prohibited, **ORC 2151.211**

Youth services department, powers and duties. See YOUTH SERVICES DEPARTMENT

DENIALS

Adjudicatory hearings, **Juv. R 29(C), Juv. R 29(E), T 23:8**

DENTISTS

Child abuse to be reported, **ORC 2151.99(B), 2151.421(A)**

DEPARTMENTS, STATE

Job and Family Services (formerly Human Services). See JOB AND FAMILY SERVICES

Youth services. See YOUTH SERVICES DEPARTMENT

DEPENDENT AND NEGLECTED CHILDREN

See also CHILD ABUSE

Abandoned children
   Defined, **T 9:4**
      Illegal placement of child distinguished from, **T 9:9**
      Neglect, defined as, **ORC 2151.03, T 9:4**
      Permanent custody. See PERMANENT CUSTODY, generally
      Presumption of abandonment, **T 9:5**

Abuse or neglect, danger of; detention due to, **T 14:3**

Abuser, removal from child's home, **ORC 2151.353(A)**

Address of child, inclusion in pleadings, **T 16:13**

Adjudicatory hearings, **ORC 2151.35**
      Findings
         Danger to child and underlying family problems, **ORC 2151.28**

Alcohol or drug addiction testing and treatment, **ORC 2151.914(A), 2151.3514, T 30:10**

Alternative dispositions, **T 30:4**

Appeals, **T 34**
      See also APPEALS, generally.

Case plans, **T 26:2**

Child's attendance at dispositional hearing, **T 25:5**

Clear and convincing evidence standard of proof, **T 23:13**

Cocaine use, prenatal, **T 9:7**

Commitment to children services agency, **ORC 2151.353(A)**
      See also PERMANENT CUSTODY; TEMPORARY CUSTODY.

Complaints. See COMPLAINTS, at Dependency and neglect

Constitutional issues, **T 14:16**

Continuing jurisdiction
      Duration, **T 33:4**
      Termination, **T 33:4**

Costs of dispositions, **T 30:3**

DEPENDENT AND NEGLECTED CHILDREN—*continued*

Custodians of child, inclusion in pleadings, **T 16:13**

Danger of abuse or neglect, detention due to, **T 14:3**

Definitions, **ORC 2151.03, 2151.04, 2151.05, T 9:4, T 10:2**

Dependent children
   Abused or neglected siblings, **ORC 2151.04(D), T 10:2, T 10:6**
   Adequate parental care lacking, **ORC 2151.04, 2151.05**
   Adjudicatory hearings, **ORC 2151.35**
   Adultery as grounds for finding, **T 10:3**
   Apprehension
      Jurisdiction, **ORC 2151.23(A)**
   Best interests of, determination, **ORC 2151.414**
   Cohabitation as sole factor to establish dependency, **T 10:3**
   Complaints, **ORC 2151.27**
   Conditions or environment, factor in determination, **ORC 2151.04(C)**
   Court supervision of parental custody as disposition, **ORC 2151.353(A)**
   Criminal conduct of parent, factor in dependency determination, **T 10:5**
   Danger of abuse or neglect, **T 10:6**
   Definition, **ORC 2151.04, 2151.05, T 10:2**
   Delinquency adjudication of parent, factor in dependency determination of child, **T 10:5**
   Dependency proceedings, waiver of constitutional rights, **T 23:9**
   Destitute children as, **ORC 2151.04(A), T 10:2**
   Determination as, **ORC 2151.414**
   Detrimental effect of returning child to parents, factor in dependency determination, **T 10:5**
   Disposition, **ORC 2151.353(A)**
   Divorce as sole factor to establish dependency, **T 10:3**
   Expenses for care, funding by juvenile courts, **ORC 2151.10**
   Failure to cooperate with welfare department as grounds, **T 10:3**
   Fault of parent not required, **T 10:2**
   Financial instability of parents as factor, **T 10:3**
   Foster care removal detrimental, factor in dependency determination, **T 10:4, T 10:5**
   Health of parent, factor in determination, **T 10:4**
   Homeless children as, **ORC 2151.04(A), T 10:2, T 10:3**
   Hospitalization of parent as factor in determination, **T 10:4**
   Illegal marriage of parents as sole factor to establish dependency, **T 10:3**
   Illegitimacy as sole factor to establish dependency, **T 10:3**
   Immaturity of parent as factor, **T 10:3**
   Imprisonment of parent as sole factor to establish dependency, **T 10:3**
   Jurisdiction, **T 10**
      See also JURISDICTION.
   Lack of parental care as grounds, **T 10:3**
   Mental condition of parent, factor in determination, **ORC 2151.04(B), T 10:4**
   Mere unhappiness of child insufficient, **T 10:5**
   Minor parent, insufficient for dependency finding, **T 10:3**
   Neglected children distinguished from, **T 10:2**
   Newborn child, dependency determination, **T 10:5**
   Orphans placed with relatives, dependency determination, **T 10:4**
   Permanent custody. See PERMANENT CUSTODY, generally
   Physical or psychological condition of parent,

**DEPENDENT AND NEGLECTED
  CHILDREN**—*continued*
Dependent children—*continued*
    factor in determination, **ORC 2151.04(B), T 10:4**
    Poverty of mother not sufficient for finding of dependency, **T 10:5**
    Public funds, support by as factor in determination, **T 10:3**
    Relatives, placement with; factor in dependency determination, **T 10:3**
    Termination of parental rights. See PERMANENT CUSTODY
Detention, **T 19:2**
    Juvenile delinquents, **ORC 2152.26(A)**
    Separation from adults, **ORC 2152.26(D)**
    Temporary, **ORC 2151.33**
Determination as, **ORC 2151.414, T 10**
Discovery of records concerning, **T 21:2**
Disposition, **ORC 2151.353**
    See also DISPOSITIONAL HEARINGS, generally.
    Review hearings, **T 33:11**
Expert witnesses, use of in proceedings, **T 23:19**
Faith healing not regarded as medical neglect, **ORC 2151.03, 2151.421(H)**
Final orders, **T 34:4**
Foster care, **ORC 2151.353(A), T 30:13**
Foster parents' notice of hearing, **T 33:4**
Guardians ad litem, appointment, **ORC 2151.281, T 23:6**
Hearings
    Foster parents, notice to, **T 33:4**
    Modification hearing, **T 33:4**
    Required, **T 20:4**
Hearsay exception for statements of child, **T 23:16**
Heroin use, prenatal, **T 9:7**
Holding of child for processing purposes
    Adult jail, in, **ORC 2151.311(C)**
Homeless children regarded as dependent, **T 10:2, T 10:3**
Illegal placement as grounds for neglect finding, **T 9:9**
Illness or injury, detention due to, **ORC 2151.31, T 14:3**
    Emergency medical or surgical treatment, **Juv. R 13(C), ORC 2151.33**
Imprisonment of parent as grounds for neglect finding, **T 9:6**
Intake, **T 15:2**
    See also INTAKE, generally.
Jails, **Juv. R 7(H), ORC 2152.26**
Jurisdiction, **T 9, T 10**
    See also JURISDICTION.
Law enforcement officer, by, **ORC 2151.31**
Legal custody, **T 30:7**
Limitations, **T 1:3**
Mandatory drug or alcohol treatment for parent, **T 30:10**
Medical examination of child, **T 19:11**
Medical neglect, **ORC 2151.03, T 9:7**
Medical or surgical services, **Juv. R 13(C), ORC 2151.33, 2152.41, T 19:11**
Mental health services required, **T 19:11**
Mental illness of parent
    Confinement in mental hospital as grounds for neglect finding, **T 9:6**
    Dependency finding, grounds for, **T 10:4**
Mental injury as neglect, **T 9:10**

**DEPENDENT AND NEGLECTED
  CHILDREN**—*continued*
Minor witnesses, determining competency of, **T 23:18**
Modification hearing, **T 33:4**
Neglected children
    Abandonment as grounds for finding, **ORC 2151.03, T 9:5**
        Illegal placement distinguished from, **T 9:9**
    Adequate parental care lacking, **ORC 2151.03, 2151.05, T 9:6**
    Adjudicatory hearings, **ORC 2151.35**
    Adoption placement unauthorized, grounds for neglect finding, **T 9:9**
    Apprehension, **ORC 2151.14, 2151.31, 2152.03**
    Best interests of, determination, **ORC 2151.414**
    Cocaine use, prenatal, **T 9:7**
    Cohabitation of parent, effect on neglect finding, **T 9:6**
    Complaints, **ORC 2151.27**
    Confinement, **T 19:2**
    Contributing to, **ORC 2151.99(A), 2151.422 to 2151.54**
    Court supervision of parental custody as disposition, **ORC 2151.353(A)**
    Definitions, **ORC 2151.03, T 9:4**
    Dependent children distinguished from, **T 10:2**
    Determination as, **ORC 2151.414**
    Detrimental impact of improper care, proof of required, **T 9:6**
    Disposition, **ORC 2151.353**
    Educational neglect, **ORC 2151.03, T 9:7**
    Failure to thrive, **T 9:7**
    Faith healing instead of medical treatment, exemption, **ORC 2151.421(H)**
    Fault of parents as grounds for finding, **ORC 2151.03, T 9:6**
    Guardian ad litem appointed for, **ORC 2151.281, T 23:6**
    Habits of parents as grounds for finding, **ORC 2151.03, T 9:6**
    Heroin use, prenatal, **T 9:7**
    Illegal placement as grounds for finding, **ORC 2151.03, T 9:9**
    Imprisonment of parent as grounds for neglect finding, **T 9:6**
    Interracial marriage of parent, effect on neglect finding, **T 9:6**
    Interstate agreements, **ORC 2151.56 to 2151.61**
    Jurisdiction. See JURISDICTION, at Dependent and neglected children
    Medical neglect, **ORC 2151.03, T 9:7**
    Mental illness of parent, confinement in mental hospital as grounds for neglect finding, **T 9:6**
    Mental injury, **T 9:10**
    Out-of-home care, **T 9:11**
        Defined, **ORC 2151.011(B)**
    Permanent custody. See PERMANENT CUSTODY, generally
    Physical or mental injury, **T 9:10**
    Physician-patient privilege inapplicable, **T 23:15**
    Pregnant woman refusing treatment for unborn child, court ordering treatment, **T 9:7**
    Rehabilitation facilities, **ORC 2151.65 to 2151.84**
    Relatives, placement with
        Abandonment, not considered to be, **T 9:5**
        Illegal placements, **T 9:9**
        Temporary placement, insufficient grounds for neglect finding, **T 9:6**
    Religious grounds
        Failure to send child to school based on, **T 9:7**
        Medical treatment refusal based on, neglect determination, **ORC 2151.421(H), T 9:7**
    Siblings of, as grounds for dependency determi-

DEPENDENT AND NEGLECTED CHILDREN—*continued*

Neglected children—*continued*
    nation, **ORC 2151.04(D)**
    Special needs of child, failure to provide for, **ORC 2151.03, T 9:8**
    Spiritual treatment not regarded as medical neglect, **ORC 2151.03, 2151.421(H), T 9:7**
    Subsistence, failure to provide, **ORC 2151.03, T 9:7**
    Supervision, failure to provide, **T 9:11**
    Support by juvenile court, **ORC 2151.10**
    Termination of parental rights. See PERMANENT CUSTODY

Newborn child, dependency determination, **T 10:5**

Notice to parent of child's admission, **Juv. R 7(C), Juv. R 7(E), ORC 2151.311(A), T 19:3**

Orphans. See also ORPHANS
    Dependency determination, **T 10:4**

Out-of-home care neglect, **T 9:11**

Parents, right of child to contact, **T 19:10**
    Advising child of rights upon admission, **Juv. R 7(E), T 19:3**

Permanent custody, **T 30:8 to T 30:12**
    See also PERMANENT CUSTODY.

Physical examination of child, **Juv. R 7(I)**

Physical or mental injury due to parental omissions, **T 9:10**

Placement of children, **Juv. R 7(A), Juv. R 7(B), ORC 2152.26(A), T 19:2**
    Detention
        Juvenile delinquents, **ORC 2151.355(A)**
        Temporary, **ORC 2151.33**
    Shelter care
        Probable cause hearings, **Juv. R 13(F)**

Planned permanent living arrangement
    Generally, **ORC 2151.353(A)**
    Case plan requirement, **T 26:2**
    Complaint prayer for, **T 16:14**
    Definition, **T 30:13**
    Disposition of abused, neglected, or dependent children, **T 30:13**
    Notice of hearing, **T 33:4**
    Requirements, generally, **T 30:13**

Probation revocation hearing pending, **Juv. R 35(C)**

Protection of child, detention due to, **ORC 2151.31, T 14:3**

Protective supervision, **T 30:5**

Provision of care and subsistence for child, **T 9:11**

Recreational activities required, **T 19:10**

Rehearings, **Juv. R 7(G), ORC 2151.314, T 19:5**

Release of child, **Juv. R 7, ORC 2151.311(A), 2151.314, T 19:3**
    Detention hearings, standards for determination, **T 19:5**
    Parents, to; as priority, **T 19:2**

Removal of abuser from child's home, **ORC 2151.353(A)**

Removal of children from home, reasonable efforts to prevent, **T 25:14**

Reporting, **ORC 2151.421, T 16:2**
    Attorney-client privilege, applicability, **ORC 2151.421(A)**
    Physician-patient privilege, applicability, **ORC 2151.421(A)**

Reports, **Juv. R 7(E), ORC 2151.37, 2151.40**
    Admission, for, **Juv. R 7(C), Juv. R 7(E), T 19:3**
    Hearings, evidence, **T 19:5**

Reversal of dependency or neglect finding, **T 34:11**

DEPENDENT AND NEGLECTED CHILDREN—*continued*

Right to counsel, **Juv. R 7(E), Juv. R 7(J), T 19:3, T 19:5**

Rights of child, **Juv. R 7(E), Juv. R 7(J), T 19:10**
    Advising of, **T 19:3**

Runaways, **Juv. R 6(A), ORC 2151.31, T 14:3**

Schooling costs of children, **ORC 2151.357**

Securities issue to finance, **ORC 2151.655**

Separation from adults, **Juv. R 7(H), ORC 2151.34, ORC 2152.26(D), T 19:2**

Shelter care distinguished from, **T 19:2**
    See also SHELTER CARE.

Special needs of child, failure to provide for, **T 9:8**

Spiritual medical treatment not regarded as medical neglect, **ORC 2151.421(H), T 9:7**

Statement of reasons for failure to release, **Juv. R 7(C), ORC 2151.31, T 19:3**

Statements of children, admissibility, **ORC 2151.35(F)**

Stay pending appeal, **T 34:6**

Summons, **T 18**
    See also SUMMONS, generally.
    Immediate detention, for, **ORC 2151.28(G)**

Supervised custody as disposition, **ORC 2151.353(A)**

Supervision, failure to provide, **T 9:11**

Telephone rights, **Juv. R 7(J), T 19:10**

Temporary custody, **T 30:6**
    See also TEMPORARY CUSTODY, generally.

Temporary orders, **ORC 2151.33(B)**

Termination of parental rights. See PERMANENT CUSTODY

Time limits, **ORC 2152.41, T 19:7, T 23:31**

Time of neglect or dependency, establishment, **T 9:3**

Traffic offenders, **ORC 2152.41**
    Commitment, **T 28:6**

Unavailable, confinement in jail permitted, **T 19:2**

Unborn child, medical treatment refused by mother; neglect determination, **T 9:7**

Unruly children, time limits on confinement, **T 19:7**

Venue. See VENUE, generally

Visitation, **Juv. R 7(J), T 19:3, T 19:10**

Witnesses, determining competency of, **T 23:18**

DEPOSITIONS

Generally, **Juv. R 25**

Abused child, testimony taken by, **ORC 2151.35(G), T 21:4**

Child abuse victims, **Juv. R 27(B)**

Contempt for failure to answer, **T 33:8**

Juvenile proceedings, **Juv. R 17(A)**

Minor sex offense victims, videotaped, **ORC 2151.3511**

Place of taking
    Juvenile proceeding, **Juv. R 17(A)**

Sex offenses, minor victims, **T 23:16**

Subpoenas
    Juvenile proceeding, **Juv. R 17(A)**

Testimony of abused child, **T 21:4**

Videotaped
    Sex offenses, minor victims, **ORC 2151.3511, T 23:16**

DESTRUCTION OF PROPERTY

Restitution. See RESTITUTION

DETENTION AND DETENTION HOMES

Generally, **Juv. R 13, T 19:1 et seq:**

DETENTION AND DETENTION HOMES
—continued
Abuse or neglect of sibling, detention due to, **T 14:3**

Abused children, confinement in, **T 19:2**

Adjudicatory hearings, time limits when child confined in detention home, **Juv. R 29(A), T 19:7**

Admissions, **Juv. R 7(C) to Juv. R 7(E), ORC 2151.311(A), T 19:3**

Adults, separation from, **Juv. R 7(H), ORC 2151.311(C), 2151.312, 2151.355(A), T 19:2**

Appeals of decisions, **T 19:5**

Appropriations, **ORC 2151.10**

Arrests. See also ARRESTS
    Not considered to be detention, **ORC 2151.31(B)**

Attorneys, right to, **Juv. R 7(E), Juv. R 7(J), T 19:3, T 19:10**

Child labor law violations, detention due to, **T 14:3**

Commitment of traffic offenders, **T 28:6**

Continuing jurisdiction proceedings pending, detention of child during, **T 33:3**

Court appearance, detention to ensure, **ORC 2151.31, T 14:3**

Court officer, detention by, **ORC 2151.31**

Court order for detention, **ORC 2151.31, T 14:3**

Criminal prosecution, case transferred for, **ORC 2152.26**

Danger of abuse or neglect, detention due to, **T 14:3**

Dependent and neglected children, confinement in, **T 19:2**

Disposition of delinquency cases to, **T 27:4**

Due process considerations, **T 1:4**

Education of children placed in, **ORC 2152.41, T 19:11**
    Costs, **ORC 2151.357, T 19:11**

Electronically monitored house arrest, **ORC 2151.355(J), T 27:10**

Emergency medical or surgical treatment, **Juv. R 13(C), ORC 2151.33**

Employees, **ORC 2152.41**
    Compensation, **ORC 2152.41**
    Criminal records check, **ORC 2151.86**

Endangering others or self, detention due to, **ORC 2151.31, T 14:3**

Evidence at detention hearings, **T 19:5**

Ex parte proceedings, **Juv. R 13(D)**

Family foster homes, **ORC 2151.331**

Fingerprinting and photographing minor, **ORC 2151.311(D)**

Foster homes, **ORC 2152.26(A)**

Grounds for detention, **Juv. R 7, ORC 2151.28(G), 2151.31, T 19:8**

Hearings. See DETENTION HEARINGS

Motions for release, **T 19:8**

Notice of hearing, **T 19:3**

Placement in
    Probable cause hearings, shelter care, **Juv. R 6(B)**

DETENTION HEARINGS
Generally, **Juv. R 7(F), Juv. R 27(B), ORC 2151.314, T 19:5**

Closure of hearing, **T 19:12**

Findings of fact, **T 19:5**

Rehearing, **Juv. R 7(G), ORC 2151.314**

Shelter care, determination of need for, **T 19:5**

Temporary custodian, appointment of, **T 19:5**

Time limits, **T 19:7**

DISABLED PERSONS
Victims of crime, **ORC 2151.355(A), 2151.355(E), T 32:3**

DISCLOSURE
Witnesses' statements, to opposing counsel, **Evid. R 613**

DISCOVERY
Caseworker's reports, **T 21:2**

Child abuse reports, **T 21:2**

Commencement, **Juv. R 24(A)**

Contempt, **Juv. R 17(F)**

Court records, **T 21:7**

Denial of discovery, **T 21:2**

Deposition of abused child, **T 21:4**

Failure to comply, **Juv. R 24(C)**

Inspection of reports, **T 21:7**

Juvenile proceedings
    Subpoenas, **Juv. R 17(A), Juv. R 17(E)**
    Transfer for criminal prosecution, **T 22:15**

Limitations, **Juv. R 24(B), T 21:2**

Medical reports, **T 21:6, T 22:15**

Motions for
    Failure to file, **T 21:2**
    Hearing, **Juv. R 22(D)**
    Time requirements, **T 21:2**

Oral statements, **T 21:2**

Order granting, **Juv. R 24(B), T 21:2**

Police reports, **T 21:2**

Privileged information, **Juv. R 24(B)**

Production of documents, **Juv. R 24(A)**
    Subpoenas, **Juv. R 17(A), Juv. R 17(E)**
    Sanctions, failure to obey, **Juv. R 17(F)**

Protective orders, limiting, **Juv. R 24(B), ORC 2151.31(F)**

Reciprocal, **Juv. R 24(B)**

Requests for, **T 21:2**

Restrictions, **Juv. R 24(B)**

Sanctions, **Juv. R 24(B), T 21:3**
    Subpoenas, failure to obey, **Juv. R 17(F)**

Service of request upon opposing party, **T 21:3**

Social history, **T 21:6**

Social worker's reports, **T 21:2**

Subpoenas, **T 21:5**
    Production of documents, **Juv. R 17(A), Juv. R 17(E)**
    Sanctions, failure to obey, **Juv. R 17(F)**

Transfer for criminal prosecution, **T 22:15**

Updating information, **T 21:2**

Victim impact statements, **T 21:8**

Witnesses' names and addresses, **T 21:2**

Written statements, **T 21:2**

DISMISSAL OF ACTIONS
Adjudicatory hearing, **Juv. R 29(F), ORC 2151.35(A)**
    Failure to comply with time limits, **T 19:7, T 23:31**

Appeal by state, **T 34:8**
    Appointment of attorney for indigent parties, **T 34:10**

Expungement of records following, **T 35:4**

Juvenile proceedings, **ORC 2151.35**

Motion for, **Juv. R 22(A)**

Speedy trial, failure to hold, **T 23:31**

DISPOSITIONAL HEARINGS

Generally, **Juv. R 34, ORC 2151.35, 2151.352 to 2151.357, T 25**

Abused children, **ORC 2151.353**
    Alternatives, **T 30:4**
    Child's attendance, **T 25:5**
    Costs of dispositions, **T 30:3**

Adjournment of proceedings, **Juv. R 27(A), T 25:4**

Administrative review, substitute for, **ORC 2151.415(H)**

Admissibility of evidence, **ORC 2151.35(B), T 25:9**

Amendment of orders, **ORC 2151.417(B)**

Appeals
    Advising parties of rights, **T 25:4**
    Remand for disposition, time for, **Juv. R 34(J), T 34:11**

Best interests of child, consideration, **ORC 2151.415(B), T 25:2**

Bifurcated hearing, **T 25:2**

Bifurcation, **Juv. R 34(J)**

Burden of proof
    Preponderance of evidence, **T 25:8**

Case plans, **Juv. R 34(F)**
    Journalization of, **ORC 2151.353(D)**
    Review, **Juv. R 36**

Children's services boards, commitment of child to, **ORC 2151.353**

Child's attendance, **T 25:5**

Commitment of child
    Permanent custody, **ORC 2151.353**
    Temporary custody, **ORC 2151.353**

Conducting, **ORC 2151.35(B)**

Continuances, **ORC 2151.35(A), 2151.35(B), 2151.352, T 25:3**

Costs, **T 30:3**

Cross-examinations, **T 25:9**
    Expert witnesses, **ORC 2151.35(B)**

Definition, **Juv. R 2(L)**

Delay between adjudication and disposition, effect, **T 25:4**

Delinquent children, **ORC 2151.355, T 27**

Dependent and neglected children, **ORC 2151.353**
    Child's attendance at hearing, **T 25:5**
    Dependency or neglect finding required prior to disposition, **T 25:2**

Evidence, **Juv. R 34(B), T 25:9**

Ex parte proceedings
    Temporary orders, **ORC 2151.33(D)**

Exclusion of public, **Juv. R 27(A), ORC 2151.35, 2151.35(A), T 25:5**

Expungement of records, advising child of rights, **Juv. R 34(J), T 25:7**

Failure to timely hold, dismissal of complaint without prejudice, **ORC 2151.35(B)**

Final orders, disposition of case as requirement, **T 34:4**

Foster care, **T 30:13**
    Placement of children in, **ORC 2151.415(C)**
    Temporary custody granted for placement, **ORC 2151.353**

Guardian, placing child with, **ORC 2151.353**

Human service departments, commitment of child to, **ORC 2151.353**

Informal proceedings, **Juv. R 27(A), T 25:6**

Judges, retention of adjudicatory hearing judge, **Juv. R 34(B), T 25:3**

Judgment, **Juv. R 34(C), T 25:13**

DISPOSITIONAL HEARINGS—*continued*

Juvenile sex offender registrant, **ORC 2152.83, ORC 2152.84**

Legal custody, **T 30:7**

Medical and mental examinations, inspection of records, **T 25:10**

Modification of orders, **ORC 2151.42, 2151.415(F)**
    Best interests of child, consideration, **T 33:4**
    Children services agencies, motions for, **ORC 2151.353(E)**
    Jurisdiction, **T 33:4**
    Permanent custody, **T 30:8 to T 30:12**

Motions, **ORC 2151.415(A)**

Neglected children. See Dependent and neglected children, this heading

Notice, **ORC 2151.35(C)**

Oath requirement, **T 25:9**

Orders, **ORC 2151.35(B), 2151.415(B)**
    Abused children, **Juv. R 34(D)**
    Review, **Juv. R 36**
    Modification, **ORC 2151.42**

Parents, placing child with, **ORC 2151.353**

Permanent custody. See PERMANENT CUSTODY

Preponderance of evidence, **T 25:9**

Probation violation, disposition of case following, **T 33:6**

Procedendo writ, remedy for delay between adjudication and disposition, **T 25:13**

Procedure, **ORC 2151.35(B)**

Protective supervision, **T 30:5**
    Contact between parent and child, order preventing, **ORC 2151.353(C)**
    Restrictions on persons, **ORC 2151.353(C)**
    Termination, **ORC 2151.353(G)**
    Vacation of home by parent, order requiring, **ORC 2151.353(C)**

Public, exclusion from proceedings, **Juv. R 27(A), ORC 2151.35(A), T 25:5**

Relatives, commitment to temporary custody of, **ORC 2151.353(A)**

Removal of child from home, **ORC 2151.353(H)**
    Reasonable efforts to prevent, **T 25:14**
    Determination, **ORC 2151.419(A)**
    Findings of fact, **ORC 2151.419(B)**

Rescheduling, **T 25:4**

Restraining order, **Juv. R 34(H)**

Retention of jurisdiction by court, **ORC 2151.353(E), 2151.415(E)**

Review hearings, **ORC 2151.417(A), 2151.417(C), T 33:11**
    Citizens review board, **T 33:11**
    Notice, **ORC 2151.417(E), T 33:11**
    Referees, **T 33:11**
    Revised case plans, **ORC 2151.417(D)**
    Scope, **T 33:11**

Right to counsel, **ORC 2151.352**

Rights, advisement of, **Juv. R 34(J), ORC 2151.33(D)**

Rules of evidence, applicability, **Evid. R 101, T 25:9**

Scheduling, **Juv. R 34(A), ORC 2151.35(E)**

School district, determination, **Juv. R 34(C), ORC 2151.357**

Separate hearing for adjudication not held, effect, **T 25:2**

Social histories, cross-examinations, **Juv. R 34(B)**

Statements of children, admissibility, **ORC 2151.35(F)**

Supervision of placement by court, **ORC 2151.353(A)**

DISPOSITIONAL HEARINGS—*continued*
Temporary custody, **T 30:6**
   Children services agencies, motions for
      dispositional orders, **ORC 2151.415(B)**
   Commitment of child to, **ORC 2151.353**
   Extension, **ORC 2151.415(D)**
   Termination, **ORC 2151.353(F)**
Temporary ex parte orders, **ORC 2151.33(D)**
Termination of orders, **ORC 2151.415(F)**
   Best interests of child, consideration, **T 33:4**
   Children services agencies, motions for, **ORC
      2151.353(E)**
   Jurisdiction, **T 33:4**
Time for holding, **Juv. R 29(F)**, **ORC 2151.35(B)**, **T
   25:4**
Traffic offender, **ORC 2151.356(A)**, **T 27**
Transcripts, **ORC 2151.35(A)**, **T 23:30**, **T 25:12**
Unruly child, **ORC 2151.354(A)**, **T 29:3**
Victim impact statement, **T 25:11**

**DISPUTE RESOLUTION AND CONFLICT
   MANAGEMENT**
Arbitration, **T 15:5**
Family and children first councils, **T 15:6**
Mediation, **T 15:4**

DISTRICT COURTS, UNITED STATES
Juveniles, prosecution in, **T 4:3**

DISTRICT DETENTION HOMES
See also DETENTION AND DETENTION HOMES,
   generally.

DIVERSION PROGRAMS
Admission of allegations not required for eligibility,
   T 15:3
Agencies
   Operated by, **T 15:3**
   Participation with court in programs, **ORC
      2152.73**, **T 15:3**
Appropriateness, factors in determination, **T 15:3**
Arbitration, **T 15:5**
Best interests of child, consideration, **T 15:3**
Court action, as option to, **T 15:3**
Court operated, **T 15:3**
Due process considerations, **T 15:3**
Eligibility, **T 15:3**
Funding, **T 15:3**
Guidelines, **T 15:3**
Intake, consideration of diversion as option, **T 15:2**
Misuse, **T 15:3**
Prior court record, child inappropriate for participa-
   tion in program, **T 15:3**
Right to counsel, **T 15:3**
Statements made during participation inadmissible in
   subsequent court proceedings, **T 15:3**
Violation of terms, effect, **T 15:3**

DIVORCE
Declarants, hearsay exception, **Evid. R 804(B)(4)**
Juvenile procedure rules, applicability, **Juv. R 1(C)**

DNA DATABASES
Generally, **T 14:8**

DNA TESTING
Generally, **ORC 2152.74**

DOCKETS
Generally, **ORC 2152.71(A)**, **T 35:2**

DOCUMENTARY EVIDENCE
Generally, **Evid. R 1001 to Evid. R 1008**
Absent, proving; hearsay exception, **Evid. R 803(7)**,
   Evid. R 803(10)
Best evidence rule, **Evid. R 1001**
Copies, admissibility, **Evid. R 1003**
Dispositional hearings, admissibility during, **T 25:13**
Insurance policies, **Evid. R 411**
Introduction, **Evid. R 106**
Lost or destroyed, **Evid. R 1004**
Subpoenas for production, **Juv. R 17(A)**, **Juv. R
   17(E)**
Summaries, **Evid. R 1006**

DOMESTIC RELATIONS COURTS
Certification of cases to juvenile courts, **T 3:2**, **T
   16:15**
Custody of children
   Jurisdiction, **T 3:2**
Judges
   Juvenile court clerks, as, **ORC 2151.12**
Jurisdiction
   Custody of children, **T 3:2**

DOMESTIC VIOLENCE
Child abuse. See CHILD ABUSE
Sexual abuse of children. See SEXUAL ABUSE
Shelters for victims
   Child abuse reporting, **ORC 2151.422**

DOUBLE JEOPARDY
Adjudicatory hearings, **T 23:2**, **T 23:31**
Appeal by state following dismissal of delinquency
   complaint, **T 23:31**, **T 34:8**
Applicability to juvenile proceedings, **T 1:4**
Delinquency adjudication bars transfer for criminal
   proceedings, **T 22:24**, **T 23:31**
Juvenile traffic offender and delinquency charges aris-
   ing from same act, **T 7:4**, **T 23:31**
Mistrial, retrial following, **T 23:31**
Status offender and delinquency charges arising from
   same act, **T 23:31**
Suspended commitment orders, reinstatement of, **T
   33:7**
Transfer of case
   Criminal proceedings, for; applicability, **T
      22:24**, **T 23:31**
   Juvenile court, to; jeopardy not attaching, **T 2:4**

DRIVERS' LICENSES
Minors
   Delinquent
      Suspension or revocation, **ORC 2151.355(D)**
Occupational driving privileges, **T 28:9**
Probationary operator's license
   Suspension or revocation
      Juvenile delinquents, **ORC 2151.355(C)**
      Juvenile traffic offenders, **ORC 2151.356(B)**
      Unruly children, **ORC 2151.354(B)**
Suspension or revocation, **ORC 2151.354 to
   2151.356**
   Delinquent child, **ORC 2151.355(C)**,
      2151.355(D), **T 27:11**
      Probationary operator's license, **T 27:11**
      Temporary instruction permit, **T 27:11**
   Drivers' intervention program, **T 27:11**, **T 29:4**

DRIVERS' LICENSES—*continued*
Suspension or revocation—*continued*
Juvenile traffic offenders, **ORC 2151.356(B), T 28:2**
Probationary operator's license, **T 28:8**
Occupational driving privileges, **T 28:9**
Unruly child, **ORC 2151.354(B), T 29:4**
Probationary operator's license, **T 29:4**
Temporary instruction permit, **T 29:4**
Temporary instruction permit
Suspension or revocation
Juvenile delinquents, **ORC 2151.355(C)**
Juvenile traffic offenders, **ORC 2151.356(B)**
Unruly children, **ORC 2151.354(B)**

DRUG ABUSE
Felony offense
Forfeiture of property, **T 27:14**
Parents' drug use
Adequate parental care determination effect, **ORC 2151.414(E)**
Neglect, prenatal drug use as, **T 9:7**
Treatment and testing. *See* ALCOHOL OR DRUG TESTING AND TREATMENT

DRUG POSSESSION
Minor, by; effect on delinquency determination, **T 4:4**

DUE PROCESS
Adjudicatory hearings, **T 23:2**
Case plans, **T 26:7**
Confessions, voluntariness, **T 14:9**
Confrontation rights, transfer hearings, **T 22:13**
Contempt proceedings, **T 33:8**
Disposition, case remanded for; hearing not denial of due process, **T 34:11**
Diversion programs, considerations, **T 15:3**
Identification procedures, **T 14:14**
Permanent custody action
Summons, failure to explain effects of permanent custody order as due process issue, **T 18:3**
Transfer of case for criminal proceedings, **T 1:4**
Confrontation rights, **T 22:13**
Unruly children, applicability to proceedings, **T 23:2**

DYING DECLARATIONS
Generally, **Evid. R 804(B)(2)**

EDUCATION
See SCHOOLS AND SCHOOL DISTRICTS

EDUCATION, LOCAL BOARDS
Delinquency adjudications, notification of, **ORC 2151.355(K)**
Delinquency complaints, notification of, **ORC 2151.27(F)**
Juvenile rehabilitation facilities, agreements with, **ORC 2151.653**
Removal of unruly nonresident children residing in foster homes, actions by school superintendents for, **T 13**
Constitutionality, **T 13:6**
Hearings, **Juv. R 29(A), Juv. R 39, T 13:5**
Jurisdiction, **ORC 2151.23(A), T 13:2**
Notice, **Juv. R 39(A), T 13:4**
Summons, **Juv. R 15(B), Juv. R 39(A), T 13:4**
Transfer of action, **Juv. R 11(B), T 13:3**
Venue, **Juv. R 10(A), T 13:3**

EDUCATIONAL NEGLECT
Generally, **T 9:7**

ELECTRONIC SURVEILLANCE
Privacy expectation, **T 14:4**

ELECTRONIC TRANSMISSION
Pleadings and motions, **Juv. R 8**

ELECTRONICALLY MONITORED HOUSE DETENTION
Arrests, **ORC 2151.355(J)**
Defined, **ORC 2152.02(K)**
Disposition, **ORC 2152.19(A)(3), T 27:10**

EMERGENCY MEDICAL SERVICES
Child, for, **Juv. R 13(C), Juv. R 13(G), ORC 2151.33, T 9:6**

EMOTIONAL ABUSE OR TRAUMA
Definition, **ORC 2151.031(C), 2151.031(D)**
Sex crime victims, minor, testimony by, **T 23:23**
Witness to sex crime, minor, **T 23:23**

EMPLOYER AND EMPLOYEE
Delinquency disposition, employment as, **T 27:7**
Expunged records, questions concerning prohibited, **ORC 2151.358(I), T 35:4**
Minor employed illegally, effect on unruly child determination, **T 8:7**
Witness at juvenile proceeding, employee as; penalization by employer prohibited, **ORC 2151.211**

ENDANGERING CHILDREN
Child abuse, as, **T 9:12**
Delinquency charge resulting from, **T 4:4**

ERRORS, PLAIN
Generally, **Evid. R 103**

ESCAPE
Extradition, **T 36:3**
Interstate agreements for return of escapees, **T 36:2**

EVIDENCE
Admissibility. *See* ADMISSIBILITY OF EVIDENCE
Adoptive parents, prospective, having right to present, **T 18:2**
Authentication. *See* AUTHENTICATION OF EVIDENCE
Best evidence rule, **Evid. R 1001**
Character evidence. *See* CHARACTER EVIDENCE
Clear and convincing evidence, defined, **T 23:13**
Detention hearings, **Juv. R 7(F), T 19:5**
Discovery. *See* DISCOVERY
Dispositional hearing, **Juv. R 34(B)**
Documentary. *See* DOCUMENTARY EVIDENCE
Expert witnesses. *See* EXPERT WITNESSES
Failure of mother to produce son
Application of 5th amendment privilege, **T 14:16**
Foster parents having right to present, at hearings, **ORC 2151.424, T 18:2**
Hearsay. *See* HEARSAY
Insurance policies, **Evid. R 411**
Irrelevant, inadmissibility, **Evid. R 402**
Liability, proving, **Evid. R 408, Evid. R 409**
Negligence, proving, **Evid. R 407, Evid. R 411**
Permanent custody proceedings, **T 31:5**

EVIDENCE—*continued*
Photographs. See PHOTOGRAPHS
Pleas, inadmissibility, **Evid. R 410**
Production of documents, **Juv. R 17(A), Juv. R 17(E)**
Relevancy. See RELEVANCY OF EVIDENCE
Reputation. See REPUTATION
Rules, **Evid. R 101 to Evid. R 1103**
    Adjudicatory hearings, applicability, **T 23:14**
    Applicability, **Evid. R 101**
    Citation, **Evid. R 1103**
    Construction, **Evid. R 102**
    Dispositional hearings, applicability, **T 25:9**
    Effective date, **Evid. R 1102**
    Exceptions, **Evid. R 101**
    Purpose, **Evid. R 102**
    Scope, **Evid. R 101**
    Supplementary principles, **Evid. R 102**
    Transfer hearings, applicability, **T 22:13**
Rulings on, **Evid. R 103**
Search warrants to obtain. See SEARCH WARRANTS
Seizure. See SEARCH AND SEIZURE
Social histories as. See SOCIAL HISTORIES
Suppression. See SUPPRESSION OF EVIDENCE
Transcripts. See TRANSCRIPTS
Transfer of case for criminal proceedings
    Evidence rules, applicability, **T 22:13**
    Right to present evidence, **T 22:16**
Witnesses. See WITNESSES AND TESTIMONY

EX PARTE PROCEEDINGS
Generally, **Juv. R 13(D)**
Removal of child, authorizing, **ORC 2151.31(D)**
Temporary orders, **ORC 2151.33(D)**

EXCITED UTTERANCES
Generally, **Evid. R 803(2)**
Abused children, **T 23:16**

EXCLUSIONARY RULE
See also SUPPRESSION OF EVIDENCE
Derivative evidence doctrine, **T 14:2**
Good faith exception, **T 14:2**

EXECUTION OF JUDGMENT
Adult cases tried in juvenile courts, **ORC 2151.50**
Stay
    Magistrate's decision, filing of objections to Juvenile court, **Juv. R 40(E)**
Support of juveniles committed in juvenile proceedings, **ORC 2151.36**

EXPERT WITNESSES
Generally, **Evid. R 702 to Evid. R 705**
Authentication, **Evid. R 901**
Basis of testimony, **Evid. R 703**
Competency of witness, to prove, **T 23:18**
Cross-examination, disclosing facts behind opinion, **Evid. R 705**
Dependency and neglect cases, **T 23:19**
Due process right to, **T 23:19**
Facts, disclosure, **Evid. R 705**
Hypothetical questions, **T 23:19**
Interpreters as, **Evid. R 604**
Objections to testimony, **Evid. R 704**
Personal observations as basis for opinion, **T 23:19**
Qualifications for, **T 23:19**

EXPERT WITNESSES—*continued*
Ultimate issues, opinion concerning admissible, **T 23:19**

EXPUNGEMENT OF RECORDS
Generally, **ORC 2151.313(B), 2151.358, T 35:4**
Admissibility as evidence, **Evid. R 609**
Dismissal of complaint, following, **ORC 2151.358(F), T 35:4**
Dispositional hearing, advising child of rights, **Juv. R 34(J), T 25:13**
Effect, **T 35:4**
Fingerprints, **ORC 2151.313**
Impeachment of evidence, **Evid. R 609**
Index references deleted, **T 35:4**
Not guilty determination, **T 35:4**
Photographs, **ORC 2151.313**
Traffic offenders, juvenile, **T 35:4**
Violations, **ORC 2151.99(C), 2151.358, T 35:4**
Withdrawal of complaint, following, **T 35:4**

EXTRADITION
Generally, **T 36:3**
Hearings, **T 36:3**

FACSIMILE TRANSMISSION
Pleadings and motions, **Juv. R 8**

FAIR TRIALS
See DUE PROCESS

FAITH HEALING
Children, of, **ORC 2151.03, 2151.421(H)**

FALSE ARREST
Records to be delivered to court when right to bring action not waived, **T 35:4**

FAMILY AND CHILDREN FIRST CABINET COUNCIL
Dispute resolution, **T 15:6**

FEDERAL COURTS
District courts, prosecution of juveniles in, **T 4:3**
Juvenile Justice and Delinquency Prevention Act of 1974 governing, **T 1:2**
Supreme court cases, **T 1:4**

FEES AND COSTS
See also particular subject concerned
Abortion, complaint for in juvenile court, **ORC 2151.85(H)**
    Appeals, **ORC 2151.85(H)**
Court costs. See COURT COSTS
Criminal records check, **ORC 2151.86**
Delinquency cases, **T 27:15**
Extradition, **T 36:3**
Subpoenas, **Juv. R 17(B)**
Transportation costs, return of runaway or escapee to former state, **T 35:2**

FELONIES
See also particular subject concerned
Arrests, authority to make, **T 14:3**
Dispositional orders, felony specification, **ORC 2152.17**
Minor committing. See DELINQUENCY
Miranda rights, **T 14:10**
Permanent custody affected by conviction, **T 30:10**

FELONIES—*continued*
Prior conviction elevating crime to, delinquency adjudication as conviction, **T 4:4**
Transfer to adult court. See TRANSFER FOR CRIMINAL PROSECUTION

FELONIOUS SEXUAL PENETRATION
Juvenile delinquency adjudication deemed conviction, **ORC 2151.355(G)**

FEMALES
Pregnant, consent of juvenile court for marriage, **Juv. R 42**
Trials, female referee appointed for female defendant, **ORC 2151.16**

FINAL ORDERS
Appeals from, **T 34:2**
Custody orders, **T 20:5, T 34:4**
Delinquency finding as, **T 34:4**
Disposition of case required, **T 34:4**
Magistrates' reports
  Failure to file findings of fact, effect on determination of judgment as final order, **T 34:4**
  Objections to, requirement for appeal, **T 34:4**
Temporary custody orders, **T 20:5, T 34:4**
Transfer of case for criminal prosecution, **T 22:23, T 34:2, T 34:4**

FINANCIAL RESPONSIBILITY, MOTOR VEHICLE
Juvenile traffic offenders, **T 28:3**

FINDINGS OF FACT AND CONCLUSIONS OF LAW
Generally, **Juv. R 29(F), ORC 2151.35(A), 2151.353(A)**
Detention hearings, **T 19:5**
Judicial notice, **Evid. R 201**
Juvenile court
  Magistrate's report, **Juv. R 40(E)**
Magistrates, by
  Juvenile courts, **Juv. R 40(E)**
Permanent custody requirements, **T 30:12, T 31:6**
Removal of child from home, reasonable efforts to prevent, **T 25:14**
Shelter care hearings, **T 19:5**
Temporary orders, written findings required, **ORC 2151.33(C)**
Transfer for criminal prosecution, amenability to rehabilitation
  Not required, **T 22:8, T 22:17**

FINES AND FORFEITURES
Corrupt activity, **ORC 2151.355(B)**
Criminal forfeiture, **T 27:14**
Delinquency cases, **ORC 2151.355(A), T 27:14**
Traffic offenders, **ORC 2151.356(A), T 28:3**

FINGERPRINTS
Generally, **ORC 2151.311(D), 2151.313**
Arrest of minor, exception, **T 14:15**
Due process not violated by, **T 14:12**
Expungement of record, destruction, **T 35:4**
Felony exception, **T 14:15**
Retention, **T 14:15**
Violations, **ORC 2151.99(C)**

FIREARMS
See WEAPONS

FIRSTHAND KNOWLEDGE RULE
Generally, **Evid. R 602**

FOOD WITHHOLDING
Permanent custody affected by, **T 30:10**

FOREIGN COUNTRIES
Juvenile delinquents domiciled in, criminal prosecution, **ORC 2152.12(C)**

FOREIGN STATES
Juvenile delinquents domiciled in, criminal prosecution, **ORC 2152.12(C)**

FORESTRY CAMPS
Juveniles, for, **ORC 2151.65 to 2151.84**
  See also REHABILITATION, generally.

FORMS
Generally, **Juv. R 46**
Abortion, complaint for in juvenile court, **ORC 2151.85(G)**
  Appeals, **ORC 2151.85(G)**
Complaint, **Juv. R 10(B)**
Medical information, **ORC 2151.3529, ORC 2151.3530**
Subpoenas, **Juv. R 17(A)**
Summons, **Juv. R 15(B)**
Warrant against child, **Juv. R 15(E)**

FOSTER CARE
Abused children. See DEPENDENT AND NEGLECTED CHILDREN, at Planned permanent living
Administrative review, **T 33:10**
Adult cases, notice of dispositional hearings, **ORC 2151.424**
Case plans, **ORC 2151.412(A), T 26:2, T 33:10**
Children services agencies
  Placement, factors to consider, **ORC 2151.415(C)**
  Removal of child from residential placement, **ORC 2151.415(G)**
Complaints, **T 16:14**
Costs of, juvenile courts reimbursed for, **ORC 2151.152**
Dangerous propensities, warning foster home of, **ORC 2152.72**
Delinquency affecting placement, **T 32:3**
  Disclosure of dangerous character, **ORC 2152.72**
  Psychological profile, **ORC 2152.72**
Dependent children. See DEPENDENT AND NEGLECTED CHILDREN, at Planned permanent living
Detention, foster home as place of, **ORC 2151.331, ORC 2152.26(A)**
Drift, prevention, **T 1:7**
Funding, **ORC 2152.41, T 15:3**
Hearing notice, **T 33:4**
  Adult cases, **ORC 2151.424**
Juvenile courts. See JUVENILE COURTS
Juvenile facilities
  Detention, as place of, **ORC 2151.331**
Long term care
  Abused, dependent, and neglected children. See DEPENDENT AND NEGLECTED CHIL-

FOSTER CARE—*continued*
Long term care—*continued*
DREN, at Planned permanent living
Complaints for, **Juv. R 10(F)**
Neglected children. See DEPENDENT AND NEGLECTED CHILDREN, at Planned permanent living
Nonresident children, **ORC 2151.39, 2151.55**
Removal of unruly nonresident children residing in foster homes, actions by school superintendents for, **T 13**
Constitutionality, **T 13:6**
Hearings, **Juv. R 29(A), Juv. R 39, T 13:5**
Jurisdiction, **ORC 2151.23(A), T 13:2**
Notice, **Juv. R 39(A), T 13:4**
Summons, **Juv. R 15(B), Juv. R 39(A), T 13:4**
Transfer of action, **Juv. R 11(B), T 13:3**
Venue, **Juv. R 10(A), T 13:3**
Parents, prospective
Criminal records check, **ORC 2151.86**
Delinquency finding delay to protect, **T 32:3**
Parties to actions, foster parents as, **T 18:2**
Permanent custody motion, effect on, **T 31:7**
Placement of children in, **ORC 2151.415(C), T 19:2**
Factors to consider, **ORC 2151.415(C)**
Removal of unruly nonresident children residing in foster homes, actions by school superintendents for, **T 13**
Constitutionality, **T 13:6**
Hearings, **Juv. R 29(A), Juv. R 39, T 13:5**
Jurisdiction, **ORC 2151.23(A), T 13:2**
Notice, **Juv. R 39(A), T 13:4**
Summons, **Juv. R 15(B), Juv. R 39(A), T 13:4**
Transfer of action, **Juv. R 11(B), T 13:3**
Venue, **Juv. R 10(A), T 13:3**
Temporary, **ORC 2152.41**
Youth services department. See Youth services department placing child in, this heading
Psychological profile of delinquent, **ORC 2152.72**
Removal of child from residential placement, **ORC 2151.415(G)**
Detrimental effect, factor in dependency determination, **T 10:4, T 10:5**
Nonresident child, action by school superintendent for removal of, **T 13**
Constitutionality, **T 13:6**
Hearings, **Juv. R 29(A), Juv. R 39, T 13:5**
Jurisdiction, **ORC 2151.23(A), T 13:2**
Notice, **Juv. R 39(A), T 13:4**
Summons, **Juv. R 15(B), Juv. R 39(A), T 13:4**
Transfer of action, **Juv. R 11(B), T 13:3**
Venue, **Juv. R 10(A), T 13:3**
Residential use of property, foster homes considered for zoning purposes, **ORC 2151.418**
Right to counsel during proceedings, **ORC 2151.353(B)**
Summons
Explaining effect of foster care, **T 18:3**
Foster parents, **Juv. R 15.2**
Removal of unruly nonresident children residing in foster homes, **Juv. R 15(B)**
Temporary custody, commitment of child as disposition of case, **ORC 2152.41**
Warning of delinquent's violent character, **ORC 2152.72**
Youth services department placing child in
Early release, following, **T 33:9**
Funding, **T 15:3**
Minimum time for commitment served, following, **T 33:9**

FOSTER CARE—*continued*
Zoning, foster homes considered residential use of property for purposes of, **ORC 2151.418**

FOSTER HOMES
Defined, **ORC 2151.011**
Juvenile delinquents
Disclosure of status, **ORC 2152.72**
Psychological examinations, **ORC 2152.72**
Private child placing agencies
Juvenile delinquents, placement, **ORC 2152.72**

FRAUD
Modification or vacation of judgment due to, **T 33:2**

FREEDOM OF PRESS
Newspaper publishing name of alleged juvenile offender, **T 1:4**

FRUIT OF THE POISONOUS TREE
Generally, **T 14:2**

GAG ORDERS
Public trials, **T 23:11**

GANG ACTIVITY
Mandatory commitment, **T 27:3**

GENETIC TESTING
DNA testing, delinquents, **ORC 2152.74**

GIFTS AND GRANTS
Delinquency prevention, for, **ORC 2152.73**
Juvenile courts, to, **ORC 2152.73**
Juvenile rehabilitation facilities, to, **ORC 2151.67**

GRAND JURIES
Evidence rules, applicability, **Evid. R 101**
Juvenile proceedings with adult defendants transferred to, **ORC 2151.43**
Juveniles tried as adults, indictments not limited to charges filed in juvenile court, **T 22:22**
Serious youthful offender status, **T 5:5**

GRANDPARENTS
Parties to actions, **T 18:2**

GROUP HOMES
Youth services department placing child in, **T 33:9**

GUARDIANS AD LITEM
Abortion
Minor female seeking abortion, **T 12:4**
Parental consent, without, **ORC 2151.85(B)**
Abused children, appointment for, **T 23:6**
Appointment, **Juv. R 4(B), ORC 2151.32, 2151.281, T 23:6**
Abortion, **T 12:4**
Child abuse cases, **Juv. R 13(B)**
Volunteer, of, **ORC 2151.281(J)**
Attorney serving as, **Juv. R 4(C), T 23:6**
Conflict of interest, **T 23:6**
Withdrawal of counsel, **T 23:6**
Best interests of child, protection of, **T 23:6**
Compensation, **Juv. R 4(G), ORC 2151.281(D)**
Counsel, as, **Juv. R 4(C), ORC 2151.281(H)**
Definition, **Juv. R 2(N)**
Delinquent or unruly juveniles, **ORC 2151.281**
Discharge, **ORC 2151.281(D)**
Duties, **ORC 2151.281(J)**

GUARDIANS AD LITEM—*continued*

Faithful discharge of duties, **ORC 2151.281(D)**

Mentally incompetent parent, appointment for, **ORC 2151.281(C)**

Minor parent, appointment for, **ORC 2151.281(C)**

Neglected children, appointment for, **ORC 2151.281, T 23:6**

Notice to, **Juv. R 4(E)**

Parent-child conflicts, **T 23:6**

Permanent custody, hearing on motion for
　Report, filing of, **ORC 2151.414(C)**

Removal cases, **Juv. R 39, T 23:6**

Runaway consenting to return, guardian's signature required, **T 36:2**

Shelter care, motions for release from, **T 19:5**

Summons issued to, **T 18:2**

System established in New York, **T 1:3**

Temporary or permanent custody agreements, appointment in cases involving, **ORC 2151.281(G)**

Training by Job and Family Services, **ORC 2151.281(J)**

Withdrawal, **Juv. R 4(F)**

GUARDIANSHIP

Actions by guardian
　Child support orders in juvenile courts, for, **ORC 2151.231**

Ad litem. See GUARDIANS AD LITEM

Appointment, **ORC 2151.32**

Definitions, **Juv. R 2(M)**

Juvenile courts, restraining order on guardian, **ORC 2151.359**

Minors
　Child support, actions for orders in juvenile courts, **ORC 2151.231**

Parental care, defined, **ORC 2151.05**

Summons, issuance to, **ORC 2151.28, T 18:2**

Support and maintenance of ward after commitment of ward, **ORC 2151.36**

Unfit guardians, **ORC 2151.05**

GUILTY PLEAS

Acceptance by court, requirements, **T 23:9**

Admissibility as evidence, **Evid. R 410**

Consequences, informing accused of
　Juvenile offenders tried as adults, **ORC 2151.35**

Effect, **T 23:9**

Juvenile offenders tried as adults
　Appeal not waived by guilty plea, **T 22:22**
　Consequences, informing accused of, **ORC 2151.35**

Knowledge and understanding of effect required, **T 23:8**

Perjury proceedings, admissibility, **Evid. R 410**

Permanent custody affected by, **T 30:10**

Voluntariness, **T 23:9**

GUNS

See WEAPONS, at Firearms

HABEAS CORPUS

Generally, **T 34:12**

Adequate remedy at law lacking, **T 34:12**

Complaint, **Juv. R 10(G)**
　Defects, as challenge to, **T 34:12**

Custody of child, **Juv. R 10(A), Juv. R 10(G)**
　Investigation, **Juv. R 32(D)**
　Jurisdiction of juvenile court, **ORC 2151.23(A)**

HABEAS CORPUS—*continued*

Imprisoned parent not served with summons, challenging permanent custody order, **T 34:12**

Jurisdiction
　Federal, **T 34:12**
　Juvenile court, **ORC 2151.23(A)**

Release of child from institution, use for, **T 34:12**

Right to counsel, use to enforce, **T 34:12**

HABITS

Evidence of, **Evid. R 406**

HAMILTON COUNTY JUVENILE COURT

Generally, **ORC 2151.07, 2151.08**

HANDICAPPED PERSONS

Victims of crime, **ORC 2151.355(A), 2151.355(E), T 32:3**
　Juvenile delinquency
　　Disposition of case, **ORC 2152.12(C)**

HARMLESS ERRORS

Generally, **Evid. R 103**

HEALTH AND HOSPITALIZATION INSURANCE

Abused children, **ORC 2151.33(B)**

Child
　Abused, neglected, or dependent, **ORC 2151.33(B)**

Court ordered coverage for child, **T 30**

Dependents, coverage
　Children, abused, neglected, or dependent, **ORC 2151.33(B)**

HEARINGS

Generally, **Juv. R 27(A)**

See also TRIALS.

Abortion
　Complaint for in juvenile court, **ORC 2151.85(B)**
　Parental notification, **T 12:8**
　Scheduling, **T 12:7**

Adjudicatory. See ADJUDICATORY HEARINGS

Adoptive parents having right to present evidence, **T 18:2**

Adults, charges against, **Juv. R 27(A), ORC 2151.43**

Appropriations, **ORC 2151.10**

Attorneys. See ATTORNEYS; RIGHT TO COUNSEL

Bifurcated procedure, **T 1:3, T 23:1, T 25:2**
　See also ADJUDICATORY HEARINGS; DISPOSITIONAL HEARINGS.

Child abuse. See CHILD ABUSE

Contempt proceedings, **T 33:8**

Continuing jurisdiction invoked by filing new complaint, **T 33:2**

Criminal prosecution of juvenile, determination. See TRANSFER FOR CRIMINAL PROSECUTION

Definition, **Juv. R 2(O)**

Detention hearings. See DETENTION HEARINGS

Discovery motion, on, **Juv. R 22(D)**

Dispositional. See DISPOSITIONAL HEARINGS

Early release from youth services department custody, **ORC 2151.38(B), T 33:9**

Ex parte orders, **T 20:4**
　Removal of child, authorizing, **ORC 2151.31(E)**

HEARINGS—*continued*

Exclusion from, **Juv. R 27(A)**
  General public, **T 22:19**
Expungement of records, **ORC 2151.358(D)**
Extradition, **T 36:3**
Foster parents having right to present evidence, **T 18:2**
Gag orders, **T 22:19**
Magistrates, before, **T 24:4**
Notice, generally. See NOTICE
Parents' right to attend, **ORC 2151.352**
Permanent custody. See PERMANENT CUSTODY, generally
Placement of child prior to. See DETENTION AND DETENTION HOMES
Probation revocation, **T 33:6**
Proposed actions, **Juv. R 13(E)**
Public, exclusion of, **T 22:19**
Recording. See TRANSCRIPTS
Release of child from youth services department institution, **ORC 2151.38(A), 2151.38(B)**
  Violation of terms of release, **T 33:9**
Removal of child from placement with parents
  Ex parte order, **ORC 2151.31**
  Out of county hearings, **Juv. R 39**
Removal of unruly nonresident children
  Foster homes, **Juv. R 29(A)**
  Hearings, **Juv. R 39**
  School superintendents' actions, **T 13:5**
Restitution, hearing on existence of damages and amount of restitution, **T 27:13**
Restraining orders on parents, **ORC 2151.359, T 32:2**
Revocation of probation, **Juv. R 35(B)**
Right to counsel. See RIGHT TO COUNSEL
Runaways, holding in custody while awaiting requisition, **T 36:2**
Scheduling, **ORC 2151.35(E)**
Sealing of records. See SEALING OF RECORDS
Separation of children and adults, **Juv. R 27(A), ORC 2151.24**
Sex offenders, dispositional completion hearing, **T 6:12**
Subpoenas for attendance, **Juv. R 17(A)**
Summons to appear, **Juv. R 15, Juv. R 16(A), ORC 2151.28**
Temporary care orders, **T 20:2**
Temporary orders, **Juv. R 13(E), ORC 2151.33**
  Ex parte orders, **ORC 2151.33(D)**
Transcripts. See TRANSCRIPTS
Transfer of jurisdiction. See TRANSFER FOR CRIMINAL PROSECUTION
Venue. See VENUE
Victims, **T 22:19**
Violations by child released from youth services department institution, **ORC 2151.38(B), 2151.38(C)**
Waiver of rights, **Juv. R 3**
Youth services department, **T 33:9**

HEARSAY

Generally, **Evid. R 801 to Evid. R 806**
Absence of document, proving, **Evid. R 803(7), Evid. R 803(10)**
Abused children, admissibility of statements, **ORC 2151.35(F)**
Adjudicatory hearings, admissibility, **T 23:16**
Ancient documents, exception, **Evid. R 803(16)**

HEARSAY—*continued*

Baptismal certificates, exception, **Evid. R 803(12)**
Birth records, exception, **Evid. R 803(9)**
Boundaries, reputation of; exception, **Evid. R 803(19)**
Business records, exception, **Evid. R 803(6)**
  Hospital and medical records as, **T 23:16**
Character evidence, **Evid. R 803(20)**
Child abuse, statements by victims, **Evid. R 807**
Co-conspirators, statements of, **T 23:25**
Commercial publications, exception, **Evid. R 803(17)**
Confrontation rights, considerations, **T 23:25**
Convictions, final judgments; exception, **Evid. R 803(21)**
Crypts, inscriptions; exception, **Evid. R 803(13)**
Death records, exception, **Evid. R 803(9)**
Decedent's statement, exception, **Evid. R 804(B)(5)**
Definition, **Evid. R 801**
Dependent children, admissibility of statements, **ORC 2151.35(F)**
Dispositional hearings, admissibility, **T 25:9**
Dying declarations, **Evid. R 804(B)(2)**
Emotional condition, exception, **Evid. R 803(3)**
Exceptions, **Evid. R 803, Evid. R 804**
  Child statements in abuse cases, **Evid. R 807**
Excited utterance, exception, **Evid. R 803(2)**
  Abused children, **T 23:16**
Family history records or statements, exceptions, **Evid. R 803(13), Evid. R 804(B)(4)**
Genealogies, exception, **Evid. R 803(13)**
Judgments, exception, **Evid. R 803(21), Evid. R 803(22)**
Learned treatises for impeachment, **Evid. R 706**
Market reports, exception, **Evid. R 803(17)**
Marriage certificates, exception, **Evid. R 803(9), Evid. R 803(12)**
Medical statements, exception, **Evid. R 803(4)**
  Abused children, **T 23:16**
Memorandum, exception, **Evid. R 803(5) to Evid. R 803(7)**
Mental condition, exception, **Evid. R 803(3)**
Mentally incompetent person's statement, exception, **Evid. R 804(B)(5)**
Motives, exceptions, **Evid. R 803(3)**
Neglected children, admissibility of statements, **ORC 2151.35(F)**
Pain, statements about; exception, **Evid. R 803(3), Evid. R 803(4)**
Pecuniary interest of declarant, statement exception, **Evid. R 804(B)(3)**
Pendency of appeal, exception, **Evid. R 803(21)**
Periodicals, exception, **Evid. R 803(17)**
Personal history statement, exception, **Evid. R 804(B)(4)**
Physical condition, exception, **Evid. R 803(3)**
Present sense impression, exception, **Evid. R 803(1)**
Property ownership
  Records affecting, exception, **Evid. R 803(14)**
  Statements affecting, exception, **Evid. R 803(15)**
Proprietary interest of declarant, statement exception, **Evid. R 804(B)(3)**
Public records exception, **Evid. R 803(8), Evid. R 803(10), T 23:16**
Records, exceptions, **Evid. R 803(4) to Evid. R 803(18)**
Reliability requirement, **T 23:25**
Religious organizations' records, **Evid. R 803(11)**

HEARSAY—*continued*
Reputation, exception, **Evid. R 803(18) to Evid. R 803(20)**
Rule, **Evid. R 802**
Search, probable cause based on, **T 14:4**
Secondhand hearsay, **Evid. R 805**
Sexual offenses against minors, statements of victims, **Evid. R 807**
Tombstone inscriptions, exception, **Evid. R 803(13)**
Transfer hearings, admissibility, **T 22:13**
Unavailability of witness requirement, **T 23:25**
Vital statistics, exception, **Evid. R 803(9)**

HOLIDAYS
Time computation, effect on, **Juv. R 18(A)**

HOME
Temporary order for party to vacate, **ORC 2151.33(B)**

HOMELESS PERSONS
Shelters, reporting of child abuse, **ORC 2151.422**

HOMICIDE
Dying declaration, hearsay exception, **Evid. R 804(B)(2)**

HOSPITALS
Bills, offer to pay as proof of liability, **Evid. R 409**
Children, for
    Criminal records check of employees, **ORC 2151.86**
Records and reports, hearsay exceptions, **Evid. R 803(4)**

HOT PURSUIT DOCTRINE
Generally, **T 14:4**

HOUSE DETENTION
Arrests, **ORC 2151.355(J)**
Disposition, **T 27:10**

HUSBAND AND WIFE
See also MARRIAGE
Witnesses, in actions involving spouse, **Evid. R 501, Evid. R 601**

IDENTIFICATION
Generally, **T 14:12**
Blood specimens, **T 14:12**
Due process requirements, **T 14:14**
Fingerprints. See FINGERPRINTS
Handwriting exemplars, **T 14:12**
In-court, independent source, **T 14:13**
Line-ups, **T 14:12**
    Right to counsel, **T 14:13**
Photographs. See PHOTOGRAPHS AND PHOTOGRAPHIC DISPLAYS
Prior, **Evid. R 801(D)**
Right to counsel, **T 14:13**
Self-incrimination, privilege against inapplicable, **T 14:12**
Suggestive procedures, effect, **T 14:14**
Telephone conversations, **Evid. R 901**
Voice, **Evid. R 901, T 14:12**

ILLEGITIMATE CHILDREN
Minor delivered of, marriage application, **Juv. R 42(C) to Juv. R 42(E)**

ILLEGITIMATE CHILDREN—*continued*
Parties to actions concerning, **T 18:2**

ILLINOIS JUVENILE COURT ACT OF 1899
Generally, **T 1:2**

IMMORAL LIFESTYLE
Inadequate parental care, **T 9:6**

IMMUNITY FROM PROSECUTION
Child abuse, persons reporting, **ORC 2151.421**
Juvenile court's power to grant, **T 33:6**

IMPEACHMENT
Basis for, **Evid. R 607**
Interest, by, **Evid. R 616**
Juvenile court records used for, **T 1:4, T 23:20, T 35:2, T 35:3**
Learned treatises for purposes of, **Evid. R 706**
Methods of, **Evid. R 616**
Miranda rights violated, admissibility of statements, **T 14:10**
Motive to misrepresent, by, **Evid. R 616**
Perjury, **Evid. R 609**
Prejudice, by, **Evid. R 616**
Sensory or mental defect, by, **Evid. R 616**
Silence of defendant, by, **T 14:10**
Specific contradiction, by, **Evid. R 616**
Treatises, use of, **Evid. R 706**
Witnesses, **Evid. R 607 to Evid. R 610**
    Convicted of crime, **Evid. R 609**

IMPLIED ASSERTIONS
Generally, **Evid. R 801**

IMPORTUNING
Juvenile cannot be charged with, **T 4:4**

IMPRESSIONS, PRESENT SENSE
Generally, **Evid. R 803(1)**

IMPRISONMENT
See PRISONERS

INDEPENDENT LIVING SERVICES
Generally, **ORC 2151.82**
Defined, **ORC 2151.81(A)**
Joint agreement for provision of services, **ORC 2151.83**
Model agreements, **ORC 2151.84**

INDICTMENT OR INFORMATION
Complaint in juvenile court compared, **T 1:6**
Juveniles tried as adults, grand jury not limited to charges filed in juvenile court, **T 22:22**

INDIGENT PERSONS
Attorney appointed for, **Juv. R 4(A), Juv. R 15(B), Juv. R 29(B), ORC 2151.28, 2151.28(F)**
    Adjudicatory hearings, **Juv. R 29(B), T 23:3**
    Appeals, **T 34:10**
    Compensation, **Juv. R 4(G)**
    Detention hearings, **T 19:5**
    Detention homes and shelter care, advising of following admission, **T 19:3**
    Habeas corpus used to enforce rights, **T 34:12**
    Juvenile court employee to assist in obtaining, **ORC 2151.314(D)**

INDIGENT PERSONS—*continued*
Attorney appointed for—*continued*
Juveniles tried as adults, transfer hearings, **T 22:11**
Permanent custody proceedings, **ORC 2151.353(B), 2151.414(A), T 1:4, T 23:2, T 23:3, T 34:10**
Probation revocation hearing, **T 33:6**
Summons, statement concerning rights included in, **ORC 2151.28, 2151.28(F), T 18:3**
Waiver of right to attorney, effect, **T 23:4**
Child as, grounds for dependency finding, **ORC 2151.04(A), T 10:2, T 10:3**
Definition, **Juv. R 2(P)**
Transcripts provided to, **T 23:30, T 34:9**
Transfer of case for criminal proceedings, **T 22:18**
Waiver of right to attorney, **T 23:4**

INEFFECTIVE ASSISTANCE OF COUNSEL
Conflicts of interest, **T 23:5**
Objective standard of reasonableness, failure to meet as, **T 23:5**

INJUNCTIVE RELIEF
Restraining orders, **Juv. R 34(H)**
Parents, issued against, **ORC 2151.359, T 32:2**

INSURANCE
Evidence of policies, admissibility, **Evid. R 411**
Health
Court ordered coverage for child, **T 30**

INTAKE
Abuse of discretion, **T 15:3**
Appeals of decisions, **T 15:2**
Complaints; filing, determination, **T 15:2**
Defined, **T 15:2**
Informal court proceedings, consideration as option, **Juv. R 9(A), T 15:2**
Mediation, consideration as option, **T 15:2**
Referrals made during, determination, **T 15:2**
Right to counsel, **T 15:2**
Screening case prior to filing complaint, **Juv. R 9(B), T 15:2**
Sufficient facts for filing complaint, determination, **T 15:2**

INTENSIVE SUPERVISION
Delinquency dispositions, **T 27:7**

INTERFERENCE WITH CUSTODY
Delinquency charges resulting from, **T 4:4**

INTERNET
Sex offenders
Internet dissemination of juvenile registrants, **T 6:16**

INTERPRETERS
Generally, **Evid. R 604**

INTERSTATE AGREEMENTS
Generally, **ORC 2151.56 to 2151.61, T 36**
Jurisdiction of juvenile courts, **ORC 2151.23(A)**

INVESTIGATIONS
Child abuse allegations, **T 14:17**
Custody, **Juv. R 32(D)**

INVESTIGATIONS—*continued*
Parental consent to search, **T 14:5**
Reports of child abuse, **T 14:17**
Transfer for criminal prosecution, **Juv. R 30(C)**

INVOLUNTARY MANSLAUGHTER
Juvenile delinquency adjudication deemed conviction, **ORC 2151.355(G)**

JAILS
See also PRISONERS
Detention of minors in, **Juv. R 7(H), ORC 2151.34, ORC 2152.26(C)**
Electronically monitored house detention, **T 27:10**
Interstate compact states, policy concerning, **T 36:2**
Separation from adults, **T 19:2, T 27:18**
Warrantless search of cells, **T 14:4**

JEOPARDY
See DOUBLE JEOPARDY

JOB AND FAMILY SERVICES, COUNTY
Child abuse
Filing of charges by, **ORC 2151.43**
Reporting, **ORC 2151.421(F), T 16:2**
Child support, actions to collect, **ORC 2151.43**
Contributing to delinquency of juveniles, filing of charges by, **ORC 2151.43**
Custody of children
Permanent, **ORC 2151.353**
See also PERMANENT CUSTODY, generally.
Temporary, **ORC 2151.353**
See also TEMPORARY CUSTODY, generally.
Records, admissibility of evidence, **T 23:16**
Reports from institutions, **ORC 2151.37**
Support of minors, payments to, **ORC 2151.49**

JOB AND FAMILY SERVICES, STATE
Case plans
Administrative review
Reports, **ORC 2151.416(H)**
Rules, **ORC 2151.416(F)**
Goals
Rules, **ORC 2151.412(F)**
Rules, **ORC 2151.412(B)**
Child abuse registry, **ORC 2151.99(B), 2151.421(F)**
Custody of children
Permanent, **ORC 2151.353**
See also PERMANENT CUSTODY, generally.
Placement of nonresidents, supervision, **ORC 2151.39**
Return of nonresidents to county of residence, **ORC 2151.36**
Temporary, **ORC 2151.353**
See also TEMPORARY CUSTODY, generally.
Foster care
Juvenile courts, reimbursed for costs, **ORC 2151.152**
Guardians ad litem, training, **ORC 2151.281(J)**
Medical information forms
Distribution, **ORC 2151.3530**
Written materials, **ORC 2151.3529**
Records and reports
Case plans, administrative review, **ORC 2151.416(H)**
Institutions, from, **ORC 2151.37**

JOB AND FAMILY SERVICES, STATE
—*continued*

Records and reports—*continued*
Medical information forms
Distribution, **ORC 2151.3530**
Written materials, **ORC 2151.3529**
Rulemaking powers
Case plans, **ORC 2151.412(B)**
Goals, **ORC 2151.412(F)**

JOURNALS

Juvenile courts to maintain, **T 35:2**

JUDGES

Adjudicatory hearings, transfer hearing judge presiding, **T 22:21, T 23:28**
Assignment, **ORC 2151.07**
Bond when acting as clerk, **ORC 2151.12**
Clerk, as, **ORC 2151.12**
Compensation, **ORC 2151.13**
Competency as witnesses, **Evid. R 605**
Defined, **ORC 2151.011**
Dispositional hearings, retention of adjudicatory hearing judge, **Juv. R 34(B), T 25:3**
Expenses, **ORC 2151.13**
Hamilton county, **ORC 2151.08**
Impartiality, **T 22:20, T 23:28**
Transfer hearing
Bias as resulting from fact disclosure in, **T 23:28**
Disqualification upon retention of juvenile court jurisdiction, **T 22:21, T 23:28**
Wise and merciful father, as, **T 1:2**
Witness, as; competency, **Evid. R 605**

JUDGMENT ENTRIES

Dispositional hearings, **Juv. R 34(C)**
School attended by child, commitment order sent to, **T 27:3**

JUDGMENT NOTWITHSTANDING VERDICT

Appeals, time for filing notice suspended by motion, **T 34:5**

JUDGMENTS

Civil disabilities not imposed on juvenile by, **T 35:2**
Convictions, prior; hearsay exception, **Evid. R 803(21)**
Dispositional hearing
Entry following, **Juv. R 34(C)**
Time requirements, **ORC 2151.35(B)**
Entries. See JUDGMENT ENTRIES
Execution. See EXECUTION OF JUDGMENT
Hearsay exception, **Evid. R 803(21), Evid. R 803(22)**
Modification grounds, **T 33:2**
Vacating. See VACATION OF JUDGMENTS

JUDICIAL NOTICE

Adjudicative facts, **Evid. R 201**

JURISDICTION

Generally, **Juv. R 44, ORC 2151.07, 2151.23**
Abused and neglected children, **T 9**
Abused children, **ORC 2151.23(A), T 9:12**
Age jurisdiction. See JURISDICTIONAL AGE
Adult cases, **ORC 2151.23**
Age jurisdiction, **T 2**
See also JURISDICTIONAL AGE.

JURISDICTION—*continued*

Appeals, **T 34:2**
Age twenty-one reached while appeal pending, effect, **T 33:4, T 33:5**
Certification of cases to juvenile court, **ORC 2151.23(C) to 2151.23(F), 2152.03, T 3:2, T 16:15**
Jurisdiction continuing and exclusive, **T 3:2**
Child, defined, **T 2:2**
Child support, **ORC 2151.23(A)**
Complaints
Continuing jurisdiction invoked by filing, **T 33:2**
Filed after child reaches age eighteen, juvenile court jurisdiction, **T 2:2**
Concurrent jurisdiction, **T 3:3**
Contempt, **ORC 2151.21, T 33:8**
Continuing, **Juv. R 35(A), T 3:2, T 33**
Duration, **T 33:4**
Termination, **T 33:4**
Criminal capacity, minimum age, **T 2:2**
Criminal prosecution
Concurrent jurisdiction, **T 3:3**
Transfer of jurisdiction. See TRANSFER FOR CRIMINAL PROSECUTION
Custody action, **ORC 2151.23**
Domestic relations courts, **T 3:2, T 3:3**
Juvenile court not exercising, **T 3:2, T 3:3**
Permanent custody proceeding, **T 33:4, T 33:5**
Probate courts, **T 3:2, T 3:3**
Delinquent children, **T 3:2, T 3:3, T 4**
Age jurisdiction, **T 2**
Dependent and neglected children, **ORC 2151.23(A)**
Abandonment, **T 9:5**
Age jurisdiction, **T 2**
Drug use, prenatal, **T 9:7**
Exclusive original jurisdiction of juvenile court, **T 3:2**
Mental injury, **T 9:10**
Notice of intention to apprehend, **ORC 2151.23(A)**
Time of dependency or neglect, establishing, **T 9:3**
Detention homes, child placed in pending continuing jurisdiction proceedings, **T 33:3**
Domestic relations courts
Certification of jurisdiction to juvenile court, **T 3:2, T 16:15**
Custody of children, **T 3:2, T 3:3**
Double jeopardy
Transfer of cases to juvenile court, **T 2:4**
Early release of child from youth services department custody, **T 33:9**
Exclusive and continuing when cases certified to juvenile court, **T 3:2**
Extradition, **T 36:3**
Federal law violation, procedure for prosecution, **T 4:3**
Foster homes, actions by school superintendents for removal of unruly nonresident children residing in, **ORC 2151.23(A), T 13:2**
Grounds for invoking continuing jurisdiction, inclusion in motion, **T 33:2**
Habeas corpus, **ORC 2151.23(A), T 34:12**
Infancy as defense to delinquency, **T 2:2**
Juvenile justice project recommendations, **T 1:5**
Lack of jurisdiction as grounds for modification or vacation of judgment, **T 33:2**
Marital status of child, effect, **T 2:2**
Marriage of juveniles, **ORC 2151.23(A)**
Mentally ill child, hospitalization, **ORC 2151.23(A)**
Minimum age, **T 2:2**

JURISDICTION—*continued*

Misrepresentation of age, effect, **T 2:4**

Modification of judgment due to lack of jurisdiction, **T 33:2**

Neglected children. See Dependent and neglected children, this heading

Objections to
Failure to make prior to hearing, **T 2:5**
Timeliness, **T 16:17**

Offense committed before age of eighteen, jurisdiction over adult, **T 33:5**

Parental liability for acts of child, **ORC 2151.355(G), 2151.411, T 27:13, T 32:2**

Parents, over
Counsel costs, liability for, **T 32:2**
Medical expenses of child, liability for, **T 32:2**
Orders regarding, **T 32:2**
Urinalysis of drug abusing parent, **T 32:2**

Parole violation, concurrent jurisdiction, **T 3:3**

Paternity proceedings, **ORC 2151.23(B)**

Permanent custody, **ORC 2151.23(A)**
Agreements, **ORC 2151.23(A), T 11:2**
Termination of court's jurisdiction upon commitment of child, **T 33:5, T 33:9**

Probate courts
Custody of children, **T 3:2, T 3:3**

Probation revocation, **T 33:6**

Prosecution, burden to establish age jurisdiction, **T 2:5**

Release of child from commitment, **T 33:9**

Relief sought, inclusion in motion to invoke continuing jurisdiction, **T 33:2**

Relinquishment for criminal prosecution. See TRANSFER FOR CRIMINAL PROSECUTION, generally

Restitution ordered by court, **T 32:2**

Retention by juvenile court, **T 3:2**
Adjudicatory hearing, **T 22:21**
Dispositional hearing, **ORC 2151.353(E), 2151.415(E)**
Disqualification of transfer hearing judge, **T 22:21**

Stipulation of juvenile's age, sufficient to establish age jurisdiction, **T 2:5**

Subject matter jurisdiction, **T 3**

Summons, effect of failure to issue, **T 18:2**

Support and maintenance action, **ORC 2151.23(B), 2151.23(D)**

Temporary custody agreements, **ORC 2151.23(A), T 11:2**

Termination, **ORC 2151.38(A), T 33:4, T 33:5**
Transfer for criminal prosecution. See TRANSFER FOR CRIMINAL PROSECUTION

Terms of court; expiration, effect on continuing jurisdiction, **T 33:2**

Time limits for adjudicatory hearings, effect of failure to comply, **T 19:7**

Traffic offenders, juvenile, **T 7:3**
Age jurisdiction, **T 2**
Exclusive original jurisdiction of juvenile court, **T 3:2**

Transfer for criminal prosecution. See TRANSFER FOR CRIMINAL PROSECUTION

Transfer of case
Another county, to. See TRANSFER TO ANOTHER COUNTY
Criminal prosecution, for. See TRANSFER FOR CRIMINAL PROSECUTION
Domestic relations court, to, **T 3:2**

JURISDICTION—*continued*

Twenty-one years of age, termination of jurisdiction upon child reaching, **ORC 2151.38(A), T 33:4, T 33:5**

Unborn child as victim of crime, **T 2:2**

Unruly children, **T 8**
Age jurisdiction, **T 2**

Vacation of judgment due to lack of jurisdiction, **T 33:2**

Venue. See VENUE

Waiver, **T 2:3**

Youth services department, commitment of child to
Release of child, **T 33:9**
Termination of court's jurisdiction, **T 33:4, T 33:5, T 33:9**

JURISDICTIONAL AGE

Generally, **T 2**

Age of majority reached prior to being apprehended, effect, **T 2:3**

Age of majority reached prior to disposition of case, treatment of child as adult
Electronically monitored house detention, **T 27:10**

Appeal from adjudication, child reaching twenty-one years of age during; effect, **T 33:4, T 33:5**

Common law infancy defense, **T 2:6**

Concealed or misrepresented age, prosecution in juvenile court waived, **T 2:4**

Concurrent jurisdiction, **T 3:3**

Dismissal of complaint, failure to establish age jurisdiction, **T 2:5**

Fourteen or older at time of offense, **T 22:5**

Marital status of child, effect, **T 2:2**

Minimum age for criminal capacity, **T 2:2**

Mistaken belief as to age, **T 2:4**

Prosecution's burden to establish age jurisdiction, **T 2:5**

Transfer of case for criminal proceedings, **T 22:5**
Appeals, age of majority attained prior to; effect, **T 22:23**
Murder or attempted murder, child previously adjudicated delinquent for; mandatory transfer, **T 22:5**

Twenty-one years of age, termination of jurisdiction when child reaches, **ORC 2151.38(A), T 33:4, T 33:5**

JURY TRIALS

Adults, juvenile court proceedings against, **ORC 2151.47**

Competency of juror, objections, **Evid. R 606**

Desirability of providing, **T 23:10**

Duty of jurors, **Evid. R 1008**

IJA-ABA standards providing for, **T 23:10**

Instructions to jurors
Judicial notice, **Evid. R 201**
Limited admissibility, **Evid. R 105**

Juvenile courts, **ORC 2151.35**

Right to, inapplicable to juvenile proceedings, **ORC 2151.35(A), T 1:4, T 23:2, T 23:10**

Witnesses, jurors' competency as, **Evid. R 606**

JUVENILE COURTS

Generally, **Juv. R 1 to Juv. R 48, ORC 2152.01**
See also particular subject concerned.

Abortion, complaint for by minor, **ORC 2151.85**
Appeals, **ORC 2151.85(E)**
Filing, **ORC 2151.85(A)**

JUVENILE COURTS—*continued*

Abortion, complaint for by minor—*continued*
    Hearings, **ORC 2151.85(B)**

Abused children, powers and duties. See CHILD ABUSE

Action to be avoided, **Juv. R 9(A), T 15:2**

Actions for child support orders, **ORC 2151.231, 2151.232**

Adjudicatory hearings, **ORC 2151.35**
    See also ADJUDICATORY HEARINGS.
    Attorneys, **ORC 2151.28**
        Summons, statement concerning rights to be included, **ORC 2151.28**
        Dependent child determination, **ORC 2151.28**

Adult cases in. See ADULT CASES

Alternative dispute resolution, **T 15:4**

Appeals. See APPEALS

Appearance
    Attorney, **Juv. R 4(D)**
    Excusing attention, **ORC 2151.35**
    Subpoena for, **Juv. R 17(A)**

Appropriations, **ORC 2151.10**

Attendance of juvenile, **ORC 2151.35**

Attorneys representing parties
    Appearance, **Juv. R 4(D)**
    Appointment by court, **Juv. R 4(A)**
        Compensation, **Juv. R 4(G)**
    Withdrawal, **Juv. R 4(F)**

Bailiffs, **ORC 2151.13**

Bifurcated hearings, **T 25:2**
    See also ADJUDICATORY HEARINGS; DISPOSITIONAL HEARINGS.

Buildings and facilities, **ORC 2151.09**

Case plan, journalization of, **ORC 2151.353(D)**

Cashbooks, **ORC 2152.71(A), T 35:2**

Certification of cases to. See also CERTIFICATION OF CASES TO JUVENILE COURTS
    Complaint, as, **Juv. R 10(A), T 16:15**

Child support
    Action for orders, **ORC 2151.231**

Cigarettes, prohibitions relating to cigarettes and tobacco products, **ORC 2151.87(D)(F)**

Civil court, as, **T 1:2**

Clerks, **ORC 2151.12**
    See also CLERKS OF COURTS.

Complaints, **ORC 2151.27**
    See also COMPLAINTS.
    Child eighteen years of age or older, against; effect, **ORC 2151.27(B)**
    Dependency and neglect, **ORC 2151.27(A), 2151.27(C)**
    Dismissal, **ORC 2151.35**
    Filing
        Place of, **ORC 2151.27**
    School boards, notification of, **ORC 2151.27(F)**
    Unruly children, **ORC 2151.27**
    Victim of delinquent 65 or older or disabled, records, **ORC 2151.27(D)**

Computerization, costs applied to, **ORC 2151.541**

Concurrent jurisdiction, **T 3:3**

Contempt. See CONTEMPT

Continuances. See CONTINUANCES

Continuing jurisdiction, **Juv. R 35(A), T 33:2**

Cooperation of private and public agencies, **ORC 2151.40**

Courthouse building and sites, **ORC 2151.09, 2151.24**

Creation, **ORC 2151.07**

JUVENILE COURTS—*continued*

Criminal identification records
    Weekly report to criminal identification and investigation bureau, **ORC 2152.71(A)**

Custody of children, powers and duties
    Grounds for taking custody, **Juv. R 6(A)**
    Hearings, **Juv. R 27(B)**

Cuyahoga county, **ORC 2151.07, T 1:6**

Definitions, **Juv. R 2**

Delinquency proceedings. See DELINQUENCY

Dependent children, powers and duties. See DEPENDENT AND NEGLECTED CHILDREN

Depositions, **Juv. R 17(A)**
    See also DEPOSITIONS.

Detention hearings
    Definition, **Juv. R 2(K)**

Development
    1925-1966, **T 1:3**
    Early history, **T 1:2**
    Future directions, **T 1:5**
    Ohio, **T 1:6**
    Philosophy, **T 1:2**
    Supreme court cases affecting, **T 1:4**

Developmentally disabled or mentally retarded victim, **ORC 2152.821**

Discovery. See DISCOVERY

Dismissal of actions, **ORC 2151.35**
    See also DISMISSAL OF ACTIONS.

Dispositional hearings. See DISPOSITIONAL HEARINGS

Dispositional orders, **ORC 2151.35(B), ORC 2152.01, T 27:3 et seq:**
    Commitment of delinquent children to custody of youth services department, **ORC 2152.16**
    Community control sanctions, **ORC 2152.19(A)**
    Day reporting, **ORC 2152.19(A)**
    Discretionary transfer, **ORC 2152.10**
    Electronic monitoring, **ORC 2152.19(A)(3)**
    Enhanced acts, more restrictive dispositions for commission of, **ORC 2152.11**
    Felony specification, **ORC 2152.17**
    Fines, **ORC 2152.20**
    Hearing, juvenile sex offender registrant, **ORC 2152.83, ORC 2152.84**
    Invoking adult portion of sentence, **ORC 2152.14**
    Juvenile sex offender registrant, **ORC 2152.82 et seq.**
    Mandatory transfer, **ORC 2152.10**
    Notice, **ORC 2151.3510, ORC 2152.18**
    Petitioning of judge by juvenile sex offender registrant, **ORC 2152.85**
    Place and duration of institutionalization, **ORC 2152.18**
    Probation, **ORC 2152.19**
    Records, **ORC 2152.18**
    Restitution, **ORC 2152.20**
    Serious youthful offender, **ORC 2152.13**
    Temporary custody, **ORC 2152.19**
    Terrorism, recovery of costs where offense constitutes act of, **ORC 2152.201**
    Traffic offender, **ORC 2151.356, ORC 2152.21**

Diversion programs. See DIVERSION PROGRAMS

Dockets, **ORC 2152.71(A), T 35:2**

Domestic relations court judges serving as clerks in, **ORC 2151.12**

Electronic transmission, filing by, **Juv. R 8**

Employees, **ORC 2151.13**
    Rules, **ORC 2151.17**

Evidence. See ADMISSIBILITY OF EVIDENCE; EVIDENCE

JUVENILE COURTS—*continued*

Ex parte proceedings, **Juv. R 13(D), T 20:4**
  Removal of child, authorizing, **ORC 2151.31(D)**

Examination of child
  Definitions, **Juv. R 2(BB), Juv. R 2(V)**
  Transfer for criminal prosecution, **ORC 2152.12**
    Category one and two offenses, **ORC 2152.12(B)**

Expenses, **ORC 2151.10**

Expungement of records. See EXPUNGEMENT OF RECORDS

Fees and costs
  Assessment, **Juv. R 4(G)**
  Computerization, for, **ORC 2151.541**
  Witness, **Juv. R 17(B), Juv. R 17(C)**

Filing by facsimile transmission, **Juv. R 8**

Final orders. See FINAL ORDERS

Findings of fact, **ORC 2151.35**

Forms
  Subpoena, **Juv. R 17(A)**

Foster care
  Court reimbursed for costs, **ORC 2151.152**
  Placement of children in, **ORC 2151.415(C)**
  Removal of unruly nonresident children residing
    in foster homes, actions by school
    superintendents for, **T 13**
  Constitutionality, **T 13:6**
  Hearings, **Juv. R 29(A), Juv. R 39, T 13:5**
  Jurisdiction, **ORC 2151.23(A), T 13:2**
  Notice, **Juv. R 39(A), T 13:4**
  Summons, **Juv. R 15(B), Juv. R 39(A), T 13:4**
  Transfer of action, **Juv. R 11(B), T 13:3**
  Venue, **Juv. R 10(A), T 13:3**

Future directions, **T 1:5**

Guardians ad litem
  Abortion without parental consent complaint, **ORC 2151.85**
  Appointment, **Juv. R 4(B)**

Hamilton County, **ORC 2151.07, 2151.08**

Hearings. See also HEARINGS, generally
  Adjudicatory. See ADJUDICATORY HEARINGS
  Custody of children, court taking, **Juv. R 27(B)**
  Definition, **Juv. R 2(O)**
  Dispositional. See DISPOSITIONAL HEARINGS
  Early release from youth services department
    custody, **ORC 2151.38(B), 2151.38(C)**
  Release of child from youth services department
    institution, **ORC 2151.38(A), 2151.38(A) to 2151.38(C), 2151.38(B)**
  Removal of unruly nonresident children residing
    in foster homes, actions by school
    superintendents for, **Juv. R 29(A), Juv. R 39, T 13:5**
  Subpoena for attendance, **Juv. R 17(A)**
  Transfer. See TRANSFER FOR CRIMINAL PROSECUTION
  Violations by child released from youth services
    department institution, **ORC 2151.38(B), 2151.38(C), 2151.38(D)**

History and philosophy, **T 1**

Illinois Juvenile Court Act of 1899, **T 1:2**

Indigent persons
  Counsel appointed for, **Juv. R 4(A)**
  Compensation, **Juv. R 4(G)**
  Definition, **Juv. R 2(P)**

Informal proceedings, **T 15:2**

Intake. See INTAKE

Job and Family Services, state, reimbursement of
  courts for foster care costs, **ORC 2151.152**

JUVENILE COURTS—*continued*

Journals, **ORC 2152.71(A), T 35:2**

Judges. See JUDGES

Judgments. See JUDGMENTS

Jurisdiction. See JURISDICTION

Jury trials
  Not held, **ORC 2151.35**

Juvenile court movement, **T 1:2**

Juvenile sex offender registrant, **ORC 2152.82 et seq.**

Long term foster care, complaints for, **Juv. R 10(F)**

Magistrate's decision, adoption by, **T 24:9**

Mentally retarded or developmentally disabled
  victim, testimony, **ORC 2152.821**

Motions. See MOTIONS

Multiple dispositions, **T 27:19**

Neglected children, powers and duties. See DEPENDENT AND NEGLECTED CHILDREN

Notice. See NOTICE

Ohio, development in, **T 1:6**

Orders
  Bindover, **ORC 2152.12**
    Category one and two offenses, **ORC 2152.12(B)**
  Case plans, **Juv. R 34(F)**
    Review, **Juv. R 36**
  Dispositional, notice, **ORC 2151.3510**
  Dispositional orders, abused children, **Juv. R 34(D)**
    Review, **Juv. R 36**
  Protective supervision, for, **Juv. R 34(E)**
  Temporary
    Modification, **Juv. R 34(G)**

Parens patriae doctrine, **T 1:2, T 1:4, T 1:6**

Parties to actions
  Definition, **Juv. R 2(X)**

Permanent custody awards by. See PERMANENT CUSTODY

Philosophy, **T 1:2**

Pleadings
  Filing by facsimile transmission, **Juv. R 8**

Prevention of delinquency, participation, **ORC 2152.73, T 15:3**

Purpose, **ORC 2151.01**

Quasi-criminal nature, **T 1:3**

Records and reports, **ORC 2151.12**
  See also RECORDS AND REPORTS.

Relief from judgment. See VACATION OF JUDGMENTS

Relinquishment of juvenile court control, **ORC 2152.22**

Removal of child from home, **ORC 2151.353(H)**

Review hearings, **ORC 2151.417, T 33:11**
  Administrative review, substitute for, **ORC 2151.417(I)**
  Citizens review board, **ORC 2151.417(G)**
  Magistrates, **ORC 2151.417(G)**
  Notice, **ORC 2151.417(E)**
  Orders, **ORC 2151.417(F)**
    Publication, **ORC 2151.417(H)**
  Publication of orders, **ORC 2151.417(H)**
  Revised case plans, **ORC 2151.417(D)**
  Scheduling, **ORC 2151.417(C)**

Rights of children
  Attorney representing, **Juv. R 4(A)**

Rules of procedure. See JUVENILE RULES OF PROCEDURE

Screening cases prior to filing complaint, **Juv. R 9(B), T 15:2**

Seal, **ORC 2151.20**

JUVENILE COURTS—*continued*

Sealing of records. See SEALING OF RECORDS

Service of process. See SERVICE OF PROCESS

Sessions, **ORC 2151.22**

Social history of children
Definition, **Juv. R 2(JJ)**

Subpoenas, **Juv. R 17**
Discovery, **Juv. R 17(A), Juv. R 17(E)**
Hearings, attendance, **Juv. R 17(A)**
Privileged information, **Juv. R 17(G)**
Protection, **Juv. R 17(D)**
Service, **Juv. R 17(C)**

Temporary care orders, **T 20:2**

Temporary orders, **Juv. R 13, ORC 2151.33**
Modification, **Juv. R 34(G)**

Terms of courts, **Juv. R 18(C), ORC 2151.22**
Expiration, effect on continuing jurisdiction, **T 33:2**

Terrorism, recovery of costs where offense constitutes act of, **ORC 2152.201**

Tobacco products, prohibitions relating to cigarettes and tobacco products, **ORC 2151.87(D)(F)**

Traffic offenders, powers and duties. See TRAFFIC OFFENDERS, JUVENILE

Transcripts, **ORC 2151.35**
See also TRANSCRIPTS.

Transfer of case
Another county, to. See TRANSFER TO ANOTHER COUNTY
Criminal prosecution, for. See TRANSFER FOR CRIMINAL PROSECUTION
Municipal, county, or common pleas court; from, **ORC 2152.03**

Unruly children, powers and duties. See UNRULY CHILDREN

Vacation of judgment. See VACATION OF JUDGMENTS

Videotaped testimony, minor sex offense victims, **ORC 2151.3511**

Witnesses
Fees and costs, **Juv. R 17(B), Juv. R 17(C)**
Mentally retarded or developmentally disabled victim, **ORC 2152.821**
Videotape recordings, minor sex offense victims, **ORC 2151.3511**

JUVENILE DELINQUENTS

See DELINQUENCY

JUVENILE JUSTICE AND DELINQUENCY PREVENTION ACT OF 1974

Generally, **T 1:2**

JUVENILE JUSTICE PROJECT

Generally, **T 1:5**

JUVENILE RULES OF PROCEDURE

Generally, **Juv. R 1 to Juv. R 48, ORC 2151.17, T 1:8**

Applicability, **Juv. R 1(A)**

Conflicts within, **T 1:8**

Construction, **Juv. R 1(B)**

Definition, **Juv. R 2(HH)**

Effective date, **Juv. R 47**

Exceptions, **Juv. R 1(C)**

Jurisdiction, effect on, **Juv. R 44**

Local rules, adoption, **Juv. R 45(A)**

Procedure not specified, **Juv. R 45(B)**

JUVENILE RULES OF PROCEDURE
—*continued*

Revised code references, **Juv. R 43**

Title, **Juv. R 48**

JUVENILE SEX OFFENDER REGISTRANT

See SEX OFFENDERS

JUVENILE TRAFFIC OFFENDERS

See TRAFFIC OFFENDERS, JUVENILE

JUVENILES

See also particular subject concerned

Abortion, complaint for
Parental consent, without, **ORC 2151.85**
Appeals, **ORC 2151.85(E)**
Confidentiality of records, **ORC 2151.85(F)**
Unemancipated, defined, **ORC 2151.85(I)**

Abused. See CHILD ABUSE

Adjudication. See ADJUDICATORY HEARINGS

Adoption. See ADOPTION

Alternative diversion programs, **ORC 2151.331**

Corrupting. See CORRUPTION OF MINOR

Criminal prosecution. See TRANSFER FOR CRIMINAL PROSECUTION

Delinquent. See DELINQUENCY

Dependent. See DEPENDENT AND NEGLECTED CHILDREN

Detention. See DETENTION AND DETENTION HOMES

Disposition. See DISPOSITIONAL HEARINGS

Diversion programs. See DIVERSION PROGRAMS

Foster care. See FOSTER CARE

Intake. See INTAKE

Interference with custody, delinquency charges resulting from, **T 4:4**

Neglected. See DEPENDENT AND NEGLECTED CHILDREN

Orphans. See ORPHANS

Parent as, appointment of guardian ad litem, **ORC 2151.281(C)**

Parole. See PAROLE

Prisoners, as. See PRISONERS, at Children as

Probation. See PROBATION

Rehabilitation. See REHABILITATION

Right to counsel. See RIGHT TO COUNSEL

Runaways. See RUNAWAYS

Serious youthful offender. See SERIOUS YOUTHFUL OFFENDER

Sex offenses committed by, notice to victims of communicable diseases, **ORC 2151.14(C)**

Social histories. See SOCIAL HISTORIES

Support. See CHILD SUPPORT

Temporary custody. See TEMPORARY CUSTODY

Termination of parental rights. See PERMANENT CUSTODY

Traffic offenders. See TRAFFIC OFFENDERS, JUVENILE

Unruly. See UNRULY CHILDREN

Witnesses, as
Child abuse, exception to hearsay rule, **Evid. R 807**
Competency, **Evid. R 601**

LAWYERS

See ATTORNEYS; RIGHT TO COUNSEL

LEADING QUESTIONS
Generally, **Evid. R 611(B)**

LEARNED TREATISES
Impeachment of witness, **Evid. R 706**

LEGACIES AND DEVISES
Juvenile courts, to, **ORC 2152.73**
Juvenile rehabilitation facilities, to, **ORC 2151.67**

LEGAL CUSTODY
Generally, **T 30:7**
Definition, **T 33:9**
Youth services department obtaining. See YOUTH SERVICES DEPARTMENT, generally

LEGITIMACY OF BIRTH
Declarant, hearsay exception, **Evid. R 804(B)(4)**

LICENSES AND PERMITS
Drivers' licenses. See DRIVERS' LICENSES

LONG-TERM FOSTER CARE
See FOSTER CARE

LOST INSTRUMENTS AND RECORDS
Evidence, **Evid. R 1004**

MAGISTRATES
Generally, **T 24**
Appointment, **Juv. R 40(A)**
Attorneys as, **T 24:2**
Decision by, **Juv. R 40(E)**
    Adoption by juvenile court, **T 24:9**
    Time for filing, **T 24:7**
Duties, **Juv. R 40(B), T 24:3**
Findings of fact by, **Juv. R 40(E)**
Hearings, **T 24:4**
Order of reference, **Juv. R 40(E), T 24:3**
Powers, **Juv. R 40(B), T 24:4**
Pretrial orders, **T 24:5**
Proceedings before, **Juv. R 40(C)**
    Recording of, **Juv. R 40(D), T 24:6**
Qualifications, **T 24:2**
Recording of proceedings, **Juv. R 40(D), T 24:6**
Reports. See MAGISTRATES' REPORTS

MAGISTRATES' REPORTS
Findings of fact
    Not filed, effect on determination of judgment as final order, **T 34:4**
Objections, **T 24:8, T 24:9**
    Filing not required for appeal, **T 34:4**

MALICIOUS PROSECUTION
Records to be delivered to court when right to bring action not waived, **T 35:4**

MANDATORY REPORTING ACT
Generally, **ORC 2151.421**

MANDATORY TRANSFER TO CRIMINAL COURT
Constitutionality, **T 22:1, 21:3**

MARRIAGE
Certificate, hearsay exceptions, **Evid. R 803(9), Evid. R 803(12)**

MARRIAGE—continued
Consent to minor's marriage, **Juv. R 42, ORC 2151.23(A)**
    Marriage without consent, **ORC 2151.022(D), T 8:7**
Declarants, hearsay exceptions, **Evid. R 804(B)(4)**
Unruly child, determination due to marriage without consent, **T 8:7**

MEDIATION
Generally, **T 15:4**
Delinquency disposition, **T 27:20**
Intake, consideration of mediation as option, **T 15:2**

MEDICAL AND MENTAL EXAMINATIONS
Competency to stand trial, mental examination to determine, **T 23:7**
Court ordering, **Juv. R 32, 2151.53, ORC 2152.12**
    Physician-patient or psychologist-patient privilege inapplicable, **T 23:15**
Definition, **Juv. R 2(BB), Juv. R 2(V)**
Delinquent's psychological profile disclosed to foster parents, **ORC 2152.72**
Detention or shelter care, child in, **Juv. R 7(I), T 19:11**
Discovery, **T 21:6**
Foster caregiver, psychological profile of delinquent provided to, **ORC 2152.72**
Records and reports
    Discovery, **T 22:15**
    Foster caregiver disclosures, **ORC 2152.72**
    Hearsay exceptions, **Evid. R 803(4)**
    Inspection prior to dispositional hearing, **T 25:10**
    Youth services department receiving upon commitment of child, **T 27:3**
Self-incrimination privilege, **T 22:14**
Serious youthful offender, mental competency procedure, **T 5:5**
Transfer for criminal prosecution, **Juv. R 30(C), ORC 2152.12, T 22:10**
    Waiver, **Juv. R 30(F)**
Waiver, **Juv. R 30(F), ORC 2152.12(C), T 22:10**

MEDICAL TREATMENT
Alcohol or drug programs. See ALCOHOL OR DRUG TESTING AND TREATMENT
Emergency orders for, **Juv. R 13, ORC 2151.33, T 9:7, T 20:3**
Failure to obtain for child, medical neglect, **ORC 2151.03, T 9:7**
Permanent custody, matters precluding, **T 30:5**

MENTAL EXAMINATIONS
See MEDICAL AND MENTAL EXAMINATIONS

MENTAL ILLNESS
Costs of private psychiatric care of delinquent child, **T 32:2**
Examinations. See MEDICAL AND MENTAL EXAMINATIONS
Hearings on hospitalization, applicability of juvenile procedure rules, **Juv. R 1(C)**
Hearsay exception of statement, **Evid. R 804(B)(5)**
Jurisdiction, **ORC 2151.23(A)**
Parent, of
    Adequate parental care lacking, factor in determination, **ORC 2151.414(E)**
    Dependent child finding, grounds for, **T 10:4**
    Neglected child finding, grounds for, **T 9:6**

MENTAL INJURY

Neglect of children, **T 9:10**

MENTALLY RETARDED AND DEVELOPMENTALLY DISABLED PERSONS

Hearings on institutionalization, applicability of juvenile procedure rules, **Juv. R 1(C)**

Hearsay exception of statement, **Evid. R 804(B)(5)**

Jurisdiction, **ORC 2151.23(A)**

Miranda rights, waiver, **T 14:10**

Testimony of, **ORC 2152.821**

MINORS

See JUVENILES

MIRANDA RIGHTS

Generally, **T 14:10**

Attorney

Presence of prior to juvenile's waiver of rights, **T 14:10**

Request for made, effect on subsequent interrogation, **T 14:10**

Confession, request for probation officer insufficient for suppression, **T 1:4**

Court's duty to inform unrepresented parties, of, **T 23:27**

Custodial interrogations, **T 14:10**

Felony cases, **T 14:10**

Juvenile proceedings, applicability, **T 14:10**

Mentally retarded and developmentally disabled persons, waiver of rights, **T 14:10**

Misdemeanor cases, **T 14:10**

Parent's presence prior to juvenile's waiver of rights, **T 14:10**

Private citizens, statements to not protected, **T 14:10**

Public safety exception, **T 14:10**

Special education students, waiver of rights, **T 14:10**

Statements obtained in violation of, admissible for impeachment purposes, **T 14:9**, **T 14:10**

Totality of the circumstances to determine validity of waiver, **T 14:10**

Voluntary statements to police, burden of proof, **T 14:10**

Waiver

Burden of proof, **T 14:10**

Special education students, **T 14:10**

Totality of circumstances standard, **T 14:10**

Waiver of right to counsel, as, **T 14:11**

MISDEMEANORS

Arrests, authority to make, **T 14:3**

Delinquency adjudication as conviction elevating crime from misdemeanor to felony, **T 4:4**

Minor committing

Delinquency, as, **T 4:4**

Distinctions in disposition from delinquent felons, **T 4:4**

Miranda rights, **T 14:10**

MISREPRESENTATION

See FRAUD

MOTIONS

Generally, **Juv. R 19**

Continuing jurisdiction, **Juv. R 35(A)**, **T 33:2**

Custody of children, for permanent custody by children services agency, **ORC 2151.413, 2151.414**

MOTIONS—*continued*

Early release of child from youth services department custody, **T 33:9**

Electronic transmission, **Juv. R 8**

Extension of time to make, **Juv. R 18(B)**, **Juv. R 22(E)**

Filing

Facsimile transmission, by, **Juv. R 8**

Jurisdiction, continuing, **Juv. R 35(A)**, **T 33:2**

New trial motion, effect on time for filing notice of appeal, **T 34:8**

Permanent custody. See PERMANENT CUSTODY

Prehearing, **Juv. R 22(D)**, **Juv. R 22(E)**

Time for filing, **T 16:17**

Reconsideration motion, effect on time for filing notice of appeal, **T 34:5**

Rehearing motion, effect on time for filing notice of appeal, **T 34:5**

Service of process, **Juv. R 18(D)**

Specificity, **Juv. R 19**

Time for making, **Juv. R 18(D)**

Extensions, **Juv. R 18(B)**, **Juv. R 22(E)**

Unruly children, review of original disposition order when amenability to treatment lacking, **T 29:3**

MOTIVES

Evidence of other crimes proving, **Evid. R 404**

Hearsay exceptions, **Evid. R 803(3)**

Proof, **Evid. R 404**

MOTOR VEHICLES

Searching

Arrest, incident to, **T 14:4**

Inventory searches, **T 14:4**

Investigatory stops, **T 14:4**

Privacy expectation, **T 14:4**

Suspension or revocation of registration

Delinquent child, **T 27:11**

Traffic offenders, **T 28:2**

Unruly child, disposition of case, **T 29:4**

MUNICIPAL CORPORATIONS

Cooperation with juvenile courts, **ORC 2151.40**

MUNICIPAL COURTS

Child brought before, transfer to juvenile court, **ORC 2152.03**

MURDER

Juvenile delinquency adjudication deemed conviction, **ORC 2151.355(G)**

Minor committing. See DELINQUENCY, at Felonies committed by juveniles

Transfer of minors to adult court. See TRANSFER FOR CRIMINAL PROSECUTION, generally

NAMES

Newspaper publishing name of alleged juvenile offender, **T 1:4**

NEGLECTED CHILDREN

See DEPENDENT AND NEGLECTED CHILDREN

NEGLIGENCE

Remedial measures, admissibility, **Evid. R 407**

NEW TRIALS

Appeals, time for filing notice suspended by motion, **T 34:5**

NEWBORNS

Dependency determination, **T 10:5**

NEWSPAPERS

Authentication, **Evid. R 902**
Name of alleged juvenile offender, publication, **T 1:4**
Notice. See NOTICE

NO CONTEST PLEAS

Admissibility as evidence, **Evid. R 410**
Adult cases, effect, **T 23:8**
Consequences, informing accused of
    Juvenile offenders tried as adults, **ORC 2151.35**
Inapplicable to juvenile proceedings, **T 23:8**
Juvenile offenders tried as adults
    Consequences, informing accused of, **ORC 2151.35**
Perjury proceedings, admissibility as evidence, **Evid. R 410**

NONRESIDENTS

Juvenile rehabilitation facilities, admittance to, **ORC 2151.654**
Placement, **ORC 2151.39, 2151.654**

NOT GUILTY PLEAS

Generally, **T 23:8**

NOTICE

See also particular subject concerned
Abortion, notification of parents, **T 12, T 12:10**
    Abuse of child affecting notice, **T 12:2**
    Complaint, **T 12:3**
    Summons, **T 12:6**
    Venue, **T 12:5**
Adjudicatory hearings, **Juv. R 29(B), ORC 2151.35(C)**
    Charges, of, **T 1:4**
Appeals. See APPEALS
Attorneys of record, juvenile proceedings, **Juv. R 4(D)**
Case plan
    Abuse, neglect or dependency case, **T 18:3, T 19:5**
Contempt proceedings, **T 33:8**
Continuing jurisdiction, **Juv. R 35(A), T 33:2**
Criminal prosecutions
    Delinquents, **ORC 2152.12(D)**
Delinquency adjudication, notification of school boards, **ORC 2151.355(K)**
Delinquency complaints, notification of school boards, **ORC 2151.27(F)**
Detention of child, **Juv. R 7(C), Juv. R 7(E), ORC 2151.311(A)**
    Hearing, **Juv. R 7(F), ORC 2151.314, T 19:5**
Dispositional hearings, **ORC 2151.35(C)**
    Review hearings, **ORC 2151.417(E)**
Dispositional orders, **ORC 2151.3510, ORC 2152.18**
Ex parte orders, following, **T 20:5**
Expungement of records, **ORC 2151.358(G), T 35:4**
Guardians ad litem, to, **Juv. R 4(E)**
Judge's decision on referee's recommendations, **ORC 2151.16**
Jurisdiction, continuing, **Juv. R 35(A), T 33:2**
Juvenile sex offender registrant. See SEX OFFENDERS
Parental notification of abortion, **T 12, T 12:8, T 12:10**
    Complaint, **T 12:3**

NOTICE—continued

Parental notification of abortion—*continued*
    Hearing, scheduling of, **T 12:7**
    Summons, **T 12:6**
    Venue, **T 12:5**
Permanent custody proceedings, **ORC 2151.414**
Probation violations, **T 33:6**
Proceeding without, **Juv. R 13(D)**
Proposed actions, **Juv. R 13(E)**
Release of child, to committing court, **ORC 2151.38(C), 2151.358(B), T 33:9**
Removal hearings, out of county, **Juv. R 39**
Removal of unruly nonresident children residing in foster homes, actions by school superintendents for, **Juv. R 39(A), T 13:4**
Restraining orders, **ORC 2151.359, T 32:2**
Review hearings, **T 33:11**
Right to counsel, **ORC 2151.314(A)**
    Notice for temporary order to contain statement concerning, **ORC 2151.33(C)**
Sealing of records, **ORC 2151.358(C), 2151.358(G), T 35:4**
Sex offenders. See SEX OFFENDERS
Sex offenses committed by minor, notice to victim of communicable diseases, **ORC 2151.14(C)**
Summons. See SUMMONS
Temporary or emergency orders, **Juv. R 7(E), T 20:5**
    Ex parte orders, **ORC 2151.33(D)**
Termination of youth services department custody, **T 33:9**
Transfer for criminal prosecution, hearing, **Juv. R 30(C), Juv. R 30(D), ORC 2152.12(D), T 22:12**
Unruly child, motion to review original disposition order when child not amenable to treatment, **T 29:3**
Youth services department, termination of custody, **T 33:9**

NURSES

Child abuse to be reported, **ORC 2151.99(B), 2151.421(A)**

OATHS AND AFFIRMATIONS

Complaints, required with filing, **T 16:6**
    Exceptions, **T 16:6**
Dispositional hearings, **T 25:9**
Interpreters, **Evid. R 604**
Witnesses, **Evid. R 603**

OBJECTIONS

Bifurcated hearings for adjudication and disposition not held, failure to object waives error, **T 25:2**
Court calling and interrogating witnesses, **Evid. R 614**
Expert witnesses' testimony, **Evid. R 704**
Judge as witness, **Evid. R 605**
Juror as witness, **Evid. R 606**
Records, appearing on, **Evid. R 103**
Refreshing memory, **Evid. R 612**
Rulings on, errors, **Evid. R 103**

OBSCENITY

Offenses of
    Delinquency charge resulting from, **T 4:4**
    Unruly child determination resulting from, **T 4:4**

OFFERS

Proof, of, **Evid. R 103**

OFFICES

Privacy expectation, **T 14:4**

OHIO CONSTITUTION

Modern courts amendment, **T 1:7**

OHIO SUPREME COURT

Rulemaking authority, **T 1:7**

OPEN FIELD DOCTRINE

Generally, **T 14:4**

OPINION TESTIMONY

Dispositional hearings, admissibility of evidence, **T 25:9**

Lay testimony, **Evid. R 701**

Ultimate issue prohibition, **Evid. R 704**

ORIGINAL EVIDENCE RULE

Generally, **Evid. R 1001**

ORPHANS

Dependency determination, **T 10:4**

Permanent custody, **ORC 2151.414**
  See also PERMANENT CUSTODY, generally.

Temporary custody. See TEMPORARY CUSTODY, generally

PARDONS

Admissibility, **Evid. R 609**

Impeachment of evidence, **Evid. R 609**

PARENS PATRIAE DOCTRINE

Generally, **T 1:2, T 1:4, T 1:6**

PARENT AND CHILD

Adequate parental care, defined, **ORC 2151.011**

Drug or alcohol treatment of abusive parents, **T 30:10**

Guardian ad litem in parent-child conflicts, **T 23:6**

Residual rights, defined, **ORC 2151.011**

PARENTAGE ACTIONS

Acknowledgment of paternity
  Child support actions subsequent to filing of, **ORC 2151.232**
  Rescission, **ORC 2151.232**

Child support
  Action for converted into, **ORC 2151.232**

PARENTAL RIGHTS, TERMINATION

See PERMANENT CUSTODY

PARENT-CHILD PRIVILEGE

Applicability, **T 23:15**

PAROLE

Concurrent jurisdiction, **T 3:3**

Interstate compacts concerning, **T 36:2**

Residence by parolee in other state, **T 36:2**

Youth services department releasing child on, **ORC 2151.38**

PARTIES TO ACTIONS

Generally, **ORC 2151.28**

Additional parties, who are, **ORC 2151.424, T 18:2**

Adoptive parents, prospective, as, **ORC 2151.424, T 18:2**

Appeals, standing to bring, **T 34:3**

Child in custody of child services agency, effect, **T 18:2**

PARTIES TO ACTIONS—*continued*

Children committed to permanent custody of children services agency, parents ceasing to be, **ORC 2151.35(D)**

Counseling services, temporary orders, **ORC 2151.33(B)**

Defined, **Juv. R 2(X), T 18:2**

Foster parents as, **T 18:2**

Grandparents, **T 18:2**

Home, temporary order to vacate, **ORC 2151.33(B)**

Illegitimate child, proceedings concerning; putative father as party, **T 18:2**

Juvenile proceedings
  Assistance of counsel, **Juv. R 4(A)**
  Definition, **Juv. R 2(X)**
  Right to counsel, **ORC 2151.28**

Mental examinations, **Juv. R 32, ORC 2151.53**

Noncustodial parent, **T 18:2**

Parents, **T 16:5, T 18:2, T 23:17**
  Adoptive parents, prospective, **ORC 2151.424, T 18:2**
  Foster Parents, **ORC 2151.424, T 18:2**
  Permanent custody granted to children services agency, **ORC 2151.414(F), T 18:5, T 31:9**

Permanent custody granted to children services agency, parents ceasing to be, **ORC 2151.414(F), T 18:5, T 31:9**

Physical examinations, **Juv. R 32**

Prosecuting attorney, **T 18:2**

Putative father, **T 18:2**

Relative of child as temporary custodian not considered to be, **ORC 2151.314(B)**

Residence of child, temporary order for party to vacate, **ORC 2151.33(B)**

Right to counsel, **ORC 2151.28(F)**
  Notice, **ORC 2151.314(A)**

Standing to bring appeals, **T 34:3**

Summons. See SUMMONS

PAST RECOLLECTION RECORDED

Generally, **Evid. R 803(5)**

PAT-DOWN SEARCH

Reasonable suspicion standard, **T 14:3**

PATERNITY PROCEEDINGS

Jurisdiction, **ORC 2151.23(B)**

Juvenile procedure rules, applicability, **Juv. R 1(C)**

PERJURY

Impeachment of witness for prior, **Evid. R 609**

Pleas admissible as evidence, **Evid. R 410**

PERMANENT CUSTODY

Abandoned children
  Inability to locate parents, determination required for custody award, **ORC 2151.413(B)**
  Preclusion of permanent custody, **T 30:9**

Abused children, **ORC 2151.353, T 30:8 to T 30:12**

Address of child, inclusion in pleadings, **T 16:13**

Adequate parental care lacking
  Definition, **T 9:6**
  Determination, **ORC 2151.353(A)**

Adjudicatory hearing, **ORC 2151.35, 2151.35(A)**
  Neglectful conditions to exist at time of, **T 9:3**
  Right of parents to be present, **T 23:12**

Agreements, **T 11**
  Children services agencies, **T 11:5**
  Court approval required, **T 11:5**

PERMANENT CUSTODY—*continued*
Agreements—*continued*
Guardian ad litem
Appointment in cases involving, **ORC 2151.281(G)**
Jurisdiction, **T 11:2**
Parental revocation, **T 11:6**
Alcoholism of parent, factor in determining lack of adequate parental care, **ORC 2151.414(E)**
Appeals, **T 34:2, T 34:4**
Best interests of child, determination, **ORC 2151.414, 2151.414(A)**
Adoption, probability of, **ORC 2151.414(D)**
Custodial history of child, **ORC 2151.414(D)**
Factors to consider, **ORC 2151.414(D)**
Interaction of child with parents, siblings, relatives, and others, **ORC 2151.414(D)**
Modification of orders, **ORC 2151.42(B)**
Need for permanent placement, **ORC 2151.414(D)**
Wishes of child, **ORC 2151.414(D)**
Burden of proof, **ORC 2151.414(B), T 1:4**
Case plans, **ORC 2151.412(A), T 26:2**
Adoption, seeking and preparing child for, **ORC 2151.413(D)**
Children placed in long term foster care, **ORC 2151.413(C)**
Children services agencies
Commitment of child to, **ORC 2151.414**
Failure to implement case plan, effect on, **ORC 2151.414(C)**
Parents ceasing to be parties to action, **T 18:2**
Termination, **T 33:10**
Child's wishes, effect, **ORC 2151.414(D)**
Clear and convincing evidence standard, **ORC 2151.414(B), 2151.414(E), T 1:4, T 23:2, T 23:13**
Complaints, **Juv. R 10, ORC 2151.27(C), T 16:14**
Objections to defects, timeliness, **T 16:17**
Statement that permanent custody sought, **Juv. R 10(D)**
Continuing inadequate care likely, factor, **ORC 2151.414(E)**
Counsel appointed for parents, **ORC 2151.353(B), 2151.414(A), T 1:4, T 23:2, T 23:3, T 34:10**
Custodians of child, inclusion in pleadings, **T 16:13**
Delinquent children, disposition of cases, **T 27:17**
Dependent children, **T 30:8 to T 30:12**
Dispositional hearings. See DISPOSITIONAL HEARINGS, generally
Effect of award
Explanation of contained in notice of proceedings, **ORC 2151.414(A)**
Effect on parents not to be considered, **ORC 2151.414(C)**
Emotional disorders of parent, factor in determining lack of adequate parental care, **ORC 2151.414(E)**
Emotional neglect of child as factor in determining lack of adequate parental care, **ORC 2151.414(E)**
Evidence, **T 31:5**
Failure to support, visit, or communicate with child; factor in determining lack of adequate parental care, **ORC 2151.414(E)**
Felony conviction of parent, **T 30:10**
Final orders, **T 34:4**
Findings of fact and conclusions of law, **ORC 2151.414(C)**
Grounds, **ORC 2151.414**
Hearing on motion, **ORC 2151.414**
Guardian ad litem's report, **ORC 2151.414(C)**
Inability to locate parents of abandoned child, show-

PERMANENT CUSTODY—*continued*
ing of required, **ORC 2151.413(B)**
Incarceration of parent, factor in determining lack of adequate parental care, **ORC 2151.414(E)**
Indigent persons
Attorney appointed for, **ORC 2151.353(B), 2151.414(A), T 1:4, T 23:2, T 23:3, T 34:10**
Transcripts provided to, **T 23:30, T 34:9**
Initial dependency, neglect, or abuse proceedings; request made at, **ORC 2151.353**
Investigation upon filing of complaint, **Juv. R 32(D)**
Job and Family Services, state or county; commitment of child to, **ORC 2151.353**
Jurisdiction, **ORC 2151.23(A)**
Agreements, **T 11:2**
Termination upon commitment of child, **T 33:4, T 33:5, T 33:9**
Juvenile proceedings subsequent to permanent custody order, names and addresses of parents not required on complaint, **T 16:8**
Medical treatment withholding, **T 30:10**
Mental illness of parent, factor in determining lack of adequate parental care, **ORC 2151.414(E)**
Mental neglect of child as factor in determining lack of adequate parental care, **ORC 2151.414(E)**
Modification of order, **ORC 2151.42(B)**
Motions for, **ORC 2151.413, T 31**
Generally, **T 31:1 et seq:**
Case plan requirements, **T 31:2, T 31:8**
Circumstances permitting, **T 31:2**
Documentation, **T 31:2**
Filing, **T 31:2**
Foster parents as psychological parents, **T 31:7**
Hearing on, **ORC 2151.414, T 31:3, T 31:4**
Guardian ad litem's report, **ORC 2151.414(C)**
Prerequisites, **T 31:2**
Temporary custody for a year or more, **T 31:2**
Time requirements, **T 31:3**
Neglected children, **T 30:8 to T 30:12**
Factor in determining lack of adequate parental care, **ORC 2151.414(E)**
Nonplacement finding, mandatory, **T 30:9**
Notice, **ORC 2151.414(A)**
Order, modification, **ORC 2151.42**
Orphans, **ORC 2151.413**
Parents ceasing to be parties to action, **ORC 2151.414(F), T 31:9**
Parties to action, parents ceasing to be, **ORC 2151.414(F), T 31:9**
Preference of child, consideration, **ORC 2151.414(D)**
Rehabilitation of parents, **T 30:10**
Relationship between parent and child, factor in determining best interests of child, **ORC 2151.414(A)**
Relatives
Unavailable to take custody of orphaned child
Determination required, **ORC 2151.413**
Religion of child, effect, **ORC 2151.32, T 25:14**
Requirements, generally, **T 30:9**
Reversal of order, effect, **T 34:11**
Review hearings, **T 33:11**
Orders, **ORC 2151.417(F)**
Right to counsel during proceedings, **ORC 2151.353(B), 2151.414(A), T 1:4, T 23:2, T 23:3, T 34:10**
Schooling costs, **ORC 2151.357**
Service of process
Explanation of effect to be included, **T 18:4**
Waiver, **T 18:5**

PERMANENT CUSTODY—*continued*

Sexual abuse of child affecting, **ORC 2151.414(E), T 30:10**

Standard of evidence, **T 31:5**

Stepparent, standing to appeal, **T 34:3**

Suitability of parent, determination, **ORC 2151.353, 2151.414(E)**

Summons, explanation of effect to be included, **ORC 2151.28(D), 2151.28(I), 2151.353(B), T 18:3**

Temporary custody
> Motion for permanent custody following, **ORC 2151.353**
> Year or more, **T 31:2**

Termination, **ORC 2151.38(A)**

Transcripts of hearings, **ORC 2151.35, 2151.35(A), T 23:30, T 25:12, T 34:9**

Unsuitability of parent, determination, **ORC 2151.353, 2151.414(E)**

PERSONAL PROPERTY

Statements or records affecting ownership, hearsay exceptions, **Evid. R 803(14), Evid. R 803(15)**

PERSONS IN NEED OF SUPERVISION STATUS

Generally, **T 1:3**

PHOTOGRAPHS AND PHOTOGRAPHIC DISPLAYS

Generally, **ORC 2151.311(D)**

Abused children, **ORC 2151.421(C)**

Admissibility, **Evid. R 1001 et seq.**

Arrest of minor, exception to consent requirements, **ORC 2151.313(A), T 14:15**

Consent of juvenile court, **T 14:15**

Consent of juvenile court required, **ORC 2151.313(A)**

Definitions, **Evid. R 1001**

Discovery, **Juv. R 24(A)**

Due process not violated by, **T 14:12**

Duplicate, admissibility, **Evid. R 1003**

Expungement, **ORC 2151.313, T 35:4**

Felony exception to consent requirements, **ORC 2151.313(A), T 14:15**

Original, **Evid. R 1002**
> Lost or destroyed, **Evid. R 1004**

Retention, **ORC 2151.313, T 14:15**

Right to counsel inapplicable, **T 14:13**

Suggestive and unnecessary procedure, **T 14:14**

Totality of circumstances standard, **T 14:14**

Violations, **ORC 2151.99(C), 2151.313**

PHYSICAL EXAMINATIONS

See MEDICAL AND MENTAL EXAMINATIONS

PHYSICIAN-PATIENT PRIVILEGE

See PRIVILEGED INFORMATION

PHYSICIANS

Child abuse to be reported by, **ORC 2151.99(B), 2151.421(A)**

Emergency treatment of child, **Juv. R 13(C), Juv. R 13(G), ORC 2151.33**

Physician-patient privilege. See PRIVILEGED INFORMATION

PINS

Generally, **T 1:3**

PLAIN ERRORS

Generally, **Evid. R 103**

PLAIN VIEW DOCTRINE

Generally, **T 14:4**

PLAINTIFFS

Character evidence, admissibility, **Evid. R 404**

PLANNED PERMANENT LIVING ARRANGEMENT

Dependent children. See DEPENDENT OR NEGLECTED CHILDREN

PLEADINGS

Generally, **Juv. R 22**

See also COMPLAINTS.

Electronic transmission, **Juv. R 8**

Filing
> Facsimile transmission, by, **Juv. R 8**

Service of process, **Juv. R 20**

PLEAS

Admissibility, **Evid. R 410**
> Perjury proceedings, **Evid. R 410**

Guilty pleas, **T 23:8**
> See also GUILTY PLEAS.

Inadmissibility, **Evid. R 410**

Insanity defense, availability in juvenile court proceedings, **T 23:8**

No contest pleas
> Adult cases, effect, **T 23:8**
> Inapplicable in juvenile proceedings, **T 23:8**

Not guilty pleas, **T 23:8**

Withdrawal of guilty or no contest plea, admissibility, **Evid. R 410**

POLICE

Investigations, **T 14**
> See also particular subject concerned.

Reports
> Discovery, **T 21:2**
> Public records, as, **T 23:16**

Witness, as; competency, **Evid. R 601**

POOR PERSONS

See INDIGENT PERSONS

PREGNANCY

Abortion. See ABORTION

Minor, marriage application, **Juv. R 42(C) to Juv. R 42(E)**

PREHEARING CONFERENCES

Generally, **Juv. R 21**

PREJUDICE

Evidence excluded on grounds of, **Evid. R 403**

Impeachment, **Evid. R 616**

Jurors, testifying as to, **Evid. R 606**

Witnesses, evidence of compromise to prove, **Evid. R 408**

PRELIMINARY CONFERENCES

Generally, **Juv. R 21**

PRELIMINARY HEARINGS

Juvenile committing felony, determination of existence of probable cause, **Juv. R 30(A), T 22:8**

PRELIMINARY HEARINGS—*continued*
Mandatory
    Hearings, **T 22:7**
Serious youthful offender, **T 5:3**
Testimony, **Evid. R 804(B)(1)**

PRESENT SENSE IMPRESSIONS
Generally, **Evid. R 803(1)**

PRESUMPTIONS
Abandonment, for purpose of neglected and abused
    child jurisdiction, **Evid. R 301**
Civil actions, **Evid. R 301**
Right to counsel, waiver, **T 23:4**

PRETRIAL ORDERS
Appeal from magistrate's order, **T 24:5**
Magistrates, by, **T 24:5**

PREVENTIVE DETENTION
See DETENTION AND DETENTION HOMES

PRIOR CONVICTIONS
Delinquency adjudication as conviction to elevate
    misdemeanor to felony, **T 4:4**
Juvenile record, admissibility, **T 1:4, T 23:20, T
    35:2, T 35:3**

PRIOR STATEMENTS
Consistent, **Evid. R 801(D)**
Inconsistent, **Evid. R 613, Evid. R 801(D)**

PRIOR TESTIMONY
Generally, **Evid. R 804(B)(1)**

PRISONERS
Children as, **ORC 2151.34, ORC 2152.26(C)**
    Credit for upon transfer of case for criminal
        proceedings, **T 22:22**
    Separation from adults, **ORC 2152.26(D), T
        19:2, T 27:18**
    Traffic offenders, **ORC 2152.26, T 28:6**
Jail. See JAILS
Parent as
    Appearance of parent at hearings, **T 18:2**
    Dependent child finding, grounds for, **T 10:3**
    Failure to serve summons, habeas corpus to chal-
        lenge permanent custody order, **T 34:12**
    Lack of adequate parental care, factor in deter-
        mination of, **ORC 2151.414(E)**
    Neglected child finding, grounds for, **T 9:6**
    Summons, issuance to, **T 18:2**
Parole. See PAROLE

PRIVACY EXPECTATION
Generally, **T 14:4**

PRIVATE CHILD PLACING AGENCIES
Case plans by, **ORC 2151.412(A)**
Motion for temporary custody of child
    Temporary shelter care placement, following,
        ORC 2151.33(C)

PRIVILEGED INFORMATION
Abortion without parental consent records, **ORC
    2151.85(F)**
Child abuse reports, **ORC 2151.99(B), 2151.421(I),
    T 14:17**
Divulging, criminal prosecutions, **T 35:4**
Juvenile court records, **T 1:2, T 35:2**
Names of alleged juvenile offenders, **T 1:4**

PRIVILEGED INFORMATION—*continued*
Parent-child privilege, applicability, **T 23:15**
Physician-patient privilege
    Child abuse cases, inapplicable, **ORC
        2151.421(A), T 23:15**
    Court ordered examinations, inapplicable to, **T
        23:15**
    Neglected children cases, inapplicable, **ORC
        2151.421(A), T 23:15**
Prior convictions, admissibility for impeachment
    purposes, **T 1:4**
Probation records, **ORC 2151.14, T 27:8, T 35:2**
Protective orders limiting discovery, **Juv. R 24(B)**
Psychologist-client privilege
    Court ordered examinations, inapplicable, **T
        23:15**
Records and reports of juvenile court, **T 1:2, T 35:2**
Social history, **T 35:2**
Subpoenaed information
    Withholding, **Juv. R 17(G)**
Welfare records, **T 23:15**

PRIVILEGES AND IMMUNITIES
Generally, **Evid. R 501**

PROBATE COURTS
Adoption petition dismissal, certification of case fol-
    lowing not considered complaint for custody, **T
    16:15**
Concurrent jurisdiction, **T 3:3**
Custody of children
    Jurisdiction, **T 3:2, T 3:3**
Fees and costs, jury trials, **ORC 2151.47**
Judges
    Assignment to juvenile court, **ORC 2151.07**
    Liability for employees, **ORC 2151.13**
    Witness, as; competency, **Evid. R 605**
Jurisdiction
    Concurrent, **T 3:3**
    Custody of children, **T 3:2, T 3:3**

PROBATION
Burden of proof, revocation of probation, **T 33:6**
Commitment order, imposition of probation upon
    suspension of, **T 33:7**
Complaint for violation, review of unruly child's
    original disposition order following, **T 29:3**
Confidential nature of records, **T 27:8**
Contracts between juvenile courts and agencies, **ORC
    2151.151**
County departments, powers and duties, **ORC
    2151.15**
Defined, **T 27:8**
Delinquents, **ORC 2151.356(A), T 27:8**
    Weapons and dangerous ordnance, possession
        prohibited, **ORC 2151.355(A)**
Department powers and duties, **ORC 2151.14**
Detention pending revocation, **Juv. R 35**
Disposition of case following probation violation, **T
    33:6**
Disposition order, **ORC 2152.19**
Failure to exercise parental control, effect, **T 32:2**
Hearings on revocation of probation, **T 33:6**
Interstate compact on juveniles, **ORC 2151.56 to
    2151.61, T 36:2**
Jurisdiction, **T 33:6**
Juveniles
    Defined, **ORC 2151.011**
    Search and seizure, **ORC 2151.355(L)**

PROBATION—*continued*

Notice of violations, **Juv. R 35(B), T 33:6**

Officers, **ORC 2151.13 to 2151.15, T 27:8**
    Appointment, **ORC 2151.13**
    Arrest powers, **ORC 2151.14**
    Assistance of law enforcement officers, **ORC 2151.14**
    County department of probation, **ORC 2151.15**
    Searches by, **T 14:7**

Recognizance bond, parents required to post, **T 32:2**

Records and reports, **ORC 2151.14, T 27:8**
    Confidentiality, **T 35:2, T 35:3**
    Copies, providing, **ORC 2151.14(D), 2151.141**

Repeat delinquent act, forfeiture of recognizance bond posted by parents, **T 32:2**

Residence by probationer in other state, **T 36:2**

Restitution as condition of probation
    Delinquent children, **T 27:8**

Revocation, **Juv. R 35(B), Juv. R 35(C), T 33:6**

Right to counsel, revocation hearing, **Juv. R 35(B), T 33:6**

Services, juvenile judges contracting for, **ORC 2151.151**

Statement of conditions, **Juv. R 34(C)**

Suspension of commitment order, imposition of probation upon, **T 33:7**

Traffic offenders, juvenile, **ORC 2151.356(A), T 28:4**

Unruly children, **ORC 2151.354(A), T 29:3**

Violations, **T 27:8**
    Disposition of case, **T 33:6**
    Recognizance bond posted by parents, forfeiture, **T 32:2**
    Review of unruly child's original disposition order due to, **T 29:3**
    Revocation of probation due to, **T 33:6**
    Delinquency, as, **T 4:4**

Warrantless searches of delinquent child on probation, **T 14:7**

Written statement of conditions required, **T 27:8**

Youth services department supervision after release from, **T 27:8**

PROBATION DEPARTMENTS, COUNTY

Generally, **ORC 2151.15**

PROBATION DEPARTMENTS, JUVENILE COURTS

Generally, **ORC 2151.14, T 27:8**

PROCEDENDO

Dispositional hearing, untimely delay following adjudication; remedy, **T 25:13**

PROCESS, SERVICE OF

See SERVICE OF PROCESS

PROHIBITION WRITS

Transfer of case for criminal prosecution, inapplicable to, **T 22:23**

PROSECUTORS

Cooperation with juvenile courts, **ORC 2151.40**

Party to action, as, **T 18:2**

PROTECTIVE ORDERS

Discovery procedure, **Juv. R 24(B), ORC 2151.31(F)**

PSYCHOLOGICAL EXAMINATIONS

See MEDICAL AND MENTAL EXAMINATIONS

PSYCHOLOGISTS

Child abuse, reporting, **ORC 2151.99(B), 2151.421(A)**

PUBLIC CHILDREN SERVICES AGENCIES

See CHILDREN SERVICES AGENCIES

PUBLIC DEFENDERS

Juvenile proceedings, duties, **ORC 2151.28(F), 2151.314, 2151.352**

PUBLIC SAFETY EXCEPTION

Generally, **T 14:10**

PUBLICATIONS

See also RECORDS AND REPORTS

Authentication, **Evid. R 902**

Hearsay exceptions, **Evid. R 803(17)**

QUESTIONS OF LAW

Appeals on, **ORC 2151.52**

RAP SHEET

Foster caregivers, providing to, **ORC 2152.72**

RAPE

Age jurisdiction, **T 2:2**

Juvenile delinquency adjudication deemed conviction, **ORC 2151.355(G)**

REAL PROPERTY

Statements or records affecting ownership, hearsay exceptions, **Evid. R 803(14), Evid. R 803(15)**

RECIPROCITY

Juvenile rehabilitation facilities, admittance to, **ORC 2151.654**

RECORDS AND REPORTS

See also particular subject concerned

Ancient documents
    Authentication, **Evid. R 901**
    Hearsay exception, **Evid. R 803(16)**

Annual report of juvenile court, **ORC 2152.71(D)**

Arrest records, expungement, **ORC 2151.313, 2151.358, T 35:4**

Attorney's access, **ORC 2151.352**

Authentication. See AUTHENTICATION OF EVIDENCE

Bank records, warrantless searches, **T 14:4**

Cases, maintenance, **ORC 2152.71**

Certified copies
    Providing, **ORC 2151.14(D), 2151.141**
    Self-authenticating records, **T 23:16**

Child abuse, **ORC 2151.421, T 16:2**

Clerk's powers, **ORC 2151.12**

Complaints, statistical records, **ORC 2152.71(B)**

Confidentiality, **ORC 2151.14, T 1:2, T 35:2, T 35:3**
    Exception, **ORC 2151.14(C)**

Copying
    Admissibility of copies, **Evid. R 1003**
    Certified copies, self-authenticating records, **T 23:16**
    Definitions, **Evid. R 1001**

Custody
    Investigation, **Juv. R 32(D)**
    Permanent custody proceeding, transcript, **ORC 2151.35(A), T 23:30, T 25:12, T 34:9**

Day reporting, delinquent child disposition, **T 27:7**

RECORDS AND REPORTS—*continued*
Definition, **Evid. R 1001**
Denial of inspection, **T 35:2**
Destruction of fingerprints and photographs, **ORC 2151.313**
Disclosure, **Evid. R 106**
Documentary evidence. See DOCUMENTARY EVIDENCE
Expungement. See EXPUNGEMENT OF RECORDS
Hearings, **ORC 2151.35**
    Transcripts, **ORC 2151.35(A)**
Informal court proceedings, **T 15:2**
Inspection of records, **T 35:2**
    Sealed records, **T 35:4**
Institutions, **ORC 2151.37**
    Providing records to court upon release of child, **ORC 2151.355(F), T 27:4**
Investigative reports, public inspection, **Juv. R 32(C)**
Job and Family Services, county
    admissibility of evidence, **T 23:16**
Job and Family Services, state
    Case plans, administrative review, **ORC 2151.416(H)**
    Institutions, from, **ORC 2151.37**
    Medical information forms
        Distribution, **ORC 2151.3530**
        Written materials, **ORC 2151.3529**
Juvenile courts, **ORC 2151.12, 2152.71, T 35**
    Dispositional orders, **ORC 2152.18**
    Informal court proceedings, **T 15:2**
    Prior convictions, admissibility for impeachment purposes, **T 23:20**
    Statistical record maintained by clerk of court, **ORC 2152.71(C)**
Limitation of inspection of records, **T 35:2**
Magistrate's decisions, **Juv. R 40(E)**
Medical records. See MEDICAL AND MENTAL EXAMINATIONS
Original, **Evid. R 1001, Evid. R 1002**
    Lost or destroyed, **Evid. R 1004**
Permanent custody proceedings, **ORC 2151.35(A), T 23:30, T 25:13, T 34:9**
Permanent exclusion of pupils from school
    Retention of records notwithstanding sealing order, **ORC 2151.358(K)**
Police records
    Admissibility of evidence, **T 23:16**
    Discovery, **T 21:2**
Prior convictions admissible for impeachment purposes, **T 23:20**
Probation, **ORC 2151.14, T 27:8**
    Confidentiality, **T 35:2**
Public, **T 35:2**
    Admissibility of copies, **Evid. R 1005**
    Hearsay exceptions, **Evid. R 803(8), Evid. R 803(10), T 23:16**
Referees' reports. See MAGISTRATES' REPORTS
Release of child from youth services department commitment, **T 33:9**
School records. See SCHOOLS AND SCHOOL DISTRICTS
Sealing. See SEALING OF RECORDS
Self-authenticating records, certified copies admissible, **T 23:16**
Shelter care
    Admission, for, **T 19:3**
    Evidence at detention hearings, **T 19:5**
Social histories. See SOCIAL HISTORIES
Summons, **ORC 2151.19, 2151.28**

RECORDS AND REPORTS—*continued*
Transcripts. See TRANSCRIPTS
Transfer of case, **Juv. R 11(D), ORC 2151.271, T 17:4**
Violations, **ORC 2151.99(C), 2151.358(J)**
Youth services department. See YOUTH SERVICES DEPARTMENT

REFEREES
Generally, see MAGISTRATES
Reports. See MAGISTRATES' REPORTS

REFRESHING RECOLLECTION
Generally, **Evid. R 612**

REGISTRATION
Juvenile sex offender registrant. See SEX OFFENDERS

REHABILITATION
Generally, **ORC 2151.65 to 2151.84**
Accounts and accounting by facilities, **ORC 2151.75, 2151.79**
Acquisition of facilities, **ORC 2151.65**
Admissions, **ORC 2151.65**
    Delinquent children, **T 27:3**
    Determination by court, **ORC 2151.65**
    Nonresident juveniles, **ORC 2151.654**
Age of victim
    Duration of commitment affected by, **T 27:3**
Amenability to, determination, **ORC 2152.12(C)**
Appraisal of facilities, **ORC 2151.77**
Boards of trustees, **ORC 2151.68 to 2151.75**
Certificate of, admissibility as evidence, **Evid. R 609**
County auditor, powers and duties, **ORC 2151.79**
Degree of violation, duration of commitment affected by, **T 27:3**
Detention homes. See DETENTION AND DETENTION HOMES
Districts, **ORC 2151.65 to 2151.84**
Duration of commitment, delinquent child, **T 27:3**
Education, cost, **ORC 2151.357**
Eligibility, **ORC 2152.12(C)**
Escape from, interstate agreement for return, **T 36:2**
Expenses of committed child, parents ordered to pay, **T 32:2**
Extradition of escapees, **T 36:3**
Financing facilities, **ORC 2151.66, 2151.77, 2151.651**
    Gifts and bequests, **ORC 2151.67**
    Youth services department, from, **ORC 2151.651**
Firearm, use of in committing crime
    Duration of commitment affected by, **T 27:3**
Gifts and bequests for, **ORC 2151.67**
Independent living services
    Generally, **ORC 2151.82**
    Defined, **ORC 2151.81(A)**
    Joint agreement for provision of services, **ORC 2151.83**
    Model agreements, **ORC 2151.84**
Management of facilities, **ORC 2151.71**
Out-of-state placements, interstate agreements concerning, **T 36:2**
Permanent custody requirements of parents, **T 30:10**
Programs, **ORC 2151.653**
School boards, agreements, **ORC 2151.653**
School district of child, determination, **ORC 2151.37**
Sealing of records, **T 35:4**

REHABILITATION—*continued*

Site of facility, selection, **ORC 2151.76**

Superintendents of facilities, **ORC 2151.70**

Taxes to support, **ORC 2151.66, 2151.78**

Teachers, **ORC 2151.653**

Temporary custody of delinquent child as disposition of case, **T 27:3**

Termination of commitment, **ORC 2151.65**

Transfer of child, **ORC 2151.65**

Trustees of facilities, **ORC 2151.68 to 2151.75**
Expenses, **ORC 2151.80**

Withdrawal from districts, **ORC 2151.78**

Youth services department providing. See YOUTH SERVICES DEPARTMENT

RELATIVES

Custody proceedings, consideration. See PERMANENT CUSTODY, at Relatives

RELEASE OF CHILD

Criminal prosecution, for, **Juv. R 30(H), T 22:22**

Parent or guardian, to, **Juv. R 7(B), Juv. R 7(D), Juv. R 7(F), ORC 2151.311, 2151.314**

Youth services department commitment, from. See YOUTH SERVICES DEPARTMENT

RELEVANCY OF EVIDENCE

Generally, **Evid. R 401 to Evid. R 411**

Admissible evidence, **Evid. R 402**

Conditioned on fact, preliminary questions, **Evid. R 104**

Definition, **Evid. R 401**

Exclusion of evidence, **Evid. R 403**

RELIEF FROM JUDGMENTS

See VACATION OF JUDGMENTS

RELIGION

Admissibility as evidence, **Evid. R 610**

Custody or placement of children, consideration, **ORC 2151.32, T 25:14**

Failure to send child to school due to religious beliefs, effect on neglect determination, **T 9:7**

Faith healing of children, **ORC 2151.421(H)**

RELIGIOUS ORGANIZATIONS

Records, hearsay exceptions, **Evid. R 803(11)**

REPAIR RULE

Generally, **Evid. R 407**

REPEAT OFFENDERS

Juvenile delinquents
Category one and two offenses, transfer to adult court, **ORC 2152.12(C)**

REPORTS

See RECORDS AND REPORTS

REPUTATION

Family history, hearsay exceptions, **Evid. R 801(18), Evid. R 803(13)**

Hearsay exceptions, **Evid. R 803(18) to Evid. R 803(20)**

RES GESTAE

Generally, **Evid. R 803(1)**

RESIDENCY REQUIREMENTS

Minor's residence
Change of, transfer of case to another county, **ORC 2151.271**
Defined, **ORC 2151.06**

Sex offenders
Address changes, registration requirements, **T 6:14**
Residence limitation, residence near school, **T 6:17**

RESTITUTION

Aged person as victim of crime, **T 27:13**

Community service, **T 27:7**

Disposition of case, **ORC 2152.20, T 27:8**

Hearing on existence of damages and amount of restitution, **T 27:13**

Labor performed for victim, **T 27:8**

Notice to victims of eligibility for, **T 32:3**

Parental liability for acts of child, **ORC 2151.355(G), 2151.411, T 27:13, T 32:2**

Probation condition, **T 27:8**

Repair of damaged property, **T 27:8**

Traffic offenders, juvenile, **T 28:5**

RESTRAINING ORDERS

See INJUNCTIVE RELIEF

REVIEW

Administrative review. See ADMINISTRATIVE REVIEW

Appeal. See APPEALS

RIGHT TO COUNSEL

Generally, **ORC 2151.28(F), 2151.352**

Adjudicatory hearings, **Juv. R 29(B), T 1:4, T 23:2, T 23:3**

Adversary proceedings, commencement triggering, **T 14:11**

Appeals, **T 34:10**

Custodial interrogations, during, **T 14:11**

Detention hearings, **Juv. R 7(F), ORC 2151.314, T 19:5**

Detention homes, advising child upon admission, **T 19:3, T 19:10**

Dispositional hearings, **ORC 2151.352**

Diversion programs, **T 15:3**

Effective assistance included, **T 22:11, T 23:5**

Identification procedures, **T 14:13**

Indigent persons. See INDIGENT PERSONS

Intake, during, **T 15:2**

Judge's duty to inform unrepresented parties of, **T 23:3**

Juvenile proceedings, **Juv. R 4(A)**

Notice, **ORC 2151.314(A)**

Permanent custody proceedings, **ORC 2151.353(B), 2151.414(A), T 1:4, T 23:2, T 23:3, T 34:10**

Presumption against waiver, **T 23:4**

Probation revocation hearing, **T 33:6**

Removal of child from placement with parents, hearing concerning, **T 23:3**

Summons, statement concerning rights included in, **ORC 2151.28(F), T 18:3, T 23:3**

Temporary orders, notice to contain statement concerning, **ORC 2151.33(C)**

Transfer of case for criminal proceedings, **T 22:11**

RIGHT TO COUNSEL—continued

Waiver, **Juv. R 3, T 23:4**
    Burden of proof, **T 14:11**
        Identification procedures, **T 14:13**
    Child, by; advice of counsel required, **T 23:4**
    Court's duty to inform unrepresented party of
        right to silence, **T 23:27**
    IJA-ABA standards prohibiting, **T 23:4**
    Indigent persons, **T 23:4**
    Knowledge and understanding of effect required,
        T 23:4
    Presumption against waiver, **T 23:4**
    Strong presumption against finding of, **T 23:4**
    Transfer for criminal prosecution, **T 22:11**
    Waiver of Miranda rights as, **T 14:11**

RULE OF COMPLETENESS

Generally, **Evid. R 106**

RULES OF COURTS

Construction
    Evidence rules, **Evid. R 102**
    Juvenile procedure rules, **Juv. R 1(B)**
Definition, **Juv. R 2(HH)**
Evidence rules, **Evid. R 101 to Evid. R 1103**
    See also EVIDENCE; particular subject
        concerned.
Juvenile rules, **Juv. R 1 to Juv. R 48**
    See also particular subject concerned.

RUNAWAYS

Generally, **T 8:3**
See also UNRULY CHILDREN, generally.
Apprehension and custody, **ORC 2151.31, T 14:3**
Consent to return, **T 36:2**
Court taking custody, **Juv. R 6(A), ORC 2151.31**
Detention, **ORC 2151.31**
Interstate agreement on, **ORC 2151.56 to 2151.61, T
    36:2**
Rehabilitation facilities, **ORC 2151.65 to 2151.84**
    See also REHABILITATION, for general provi-
        sions.

SALARIES

See COMPENSATION

SANCTIONS

Subpoenas, failure to obey, **Juv. R 17(F)**

SCHOOL BOARDS

Juvenile rehabilitation facilities, agreements with,
    ORC 2151.653

SCHOOLS AND SCHOOL DISTRICTS

Attendance, defined, **ORC 2151.022(B)**
Commitment of child to youth services department
    Journal entry sent to child's school, **ORC
        2151.355(F), T 27:3**
    Transcripts to department, **ORC 2151.355(F), T
        27:3**
Delinquents, educational programs for, **ORC
    2152.19, T 27:7**
Dispositional hearing, determination of child's school
    district for payment of education costs, **Juv. R
    34(C)**
Failure to send child to school as neglect, **T 9:7**
Foster homes, actions by school superintendents for
    removal of unruly nonresident children residing in,
    T 13
    Constitutionality, **T 13:6**
    Hearings, **Juv. R 29(A), Juv. R 39, T 13:5**

SCHOOLS AND SCHOOL DISTRICTS
—continued

Foster homes, actions by school superintendents for
    removal of unruly nonresident children residing in
    —continued
    Jurisdiction, **ORC 2151.23(A), T 13:2**
    Notice, **Juv. R 39(A), T 13:4**
    Summons, **Juv. R 15(B), Juv. R 39(A), T 13:4**
    Transfer of action, **Juv. R 11(B), T 13:3**
    Venue, **Juv. R 10(A), T 13:3**
Institutionalized children, schooling costs, **ORC
    2151.357**
Journal entry ordering commitment sent to child's
    school, **ORC 2151.355(F)**
Locker search, **T 14:6**
Permanent exclusion of pupils
    Reports of violations for which pupils subject to
        Retention of records notwithstanding sealing
            order, **ORC 2151.358(K)**
Records and reports
    Admissibility of evidence, **T 23:16**
    Permanent exclusion of pupils
        Retention of records notwithstanding sealing
            order, **ORC 2151.358(K)**
    Public records exception to hearsay rule, **T
        23:16**
    Youth services department, to, **ORC
        2151.355(F), T 27:3**
Rehabilitation facilities, **ORC 2151.65 to 2151.84**
    See also REHABILITATION, generally.
Religious grounds for failure to send child to school,
    effect on neglect finding, **T 9:7**
Search and seizure, **T 14:6**
    Constitutionality, **T 1:4**
    Reasonable suspicion standard, **T 14:6**
    Student lockers, consent by school officials, **T
        14:6**
    Urinalysis drug testing of high school athletes, **T
        14:6**
Sex offenders
    Residence limitation, residence near school, **T
        6:17**
Teachers. See TEACHERS
Transcripts to youth services department, **ORC
    2151.355(F), T 27:3**
Truancy
    Delinquency, **T 4:5**
    Effect on unruly child determination, **T 8:4**
Weapons
    Illegal conveyance or possession of on school
        premises
        Drivers' licenses, suspension or revocation,
            ORC 2151.355(D)

SEALING OF RECORDS

Generally, **ORC 2151.358, T 35:4**
Divulging confidential information, criminal prosecu-
    tion, **ORC 2151.99(C), T 35:4**
Fingerprints and photographs, **ORC 2151.313**
Permanent exclusion of pupils; retention of records
    notwithstanding sealing order, **ORC 2151.358(K)**

SEALS

Juvenile courts, **ORC 2151.20**

SEARCH AND SEIZURE

Consent by parent to search, **T 14:5**
Constitutional safeguards, application to juvenile
    cases, **T 14:4**
DNA databases, **T 14:8**
Governmental searches, **T 14:4**

SEARCH AND SEIZURE—continued

Juvenile delinquents placed on probation, **ORC 2151.355(L)**

Motor vehicles. See MOTOR VEHICLES

Ownership affecting consent by parent, **T 14:5**

Parent's consent to search, **T 14:5**

Pat-down search. See PAT-DOWN SEARCH

Private citizen searches not protected, **T 14:4**

School searches, **T 1:4, 11:7**

Warrantless searches. See WARRANTLESS SEARCHES

Warrants. See SEARCH WARRANTS

SEARCH WARRANTS

Arrest in private residence, to effect, **T 14:4**

Contents, requirements, **T 14:4**

Evidence, for; applicability of rules of evidence, **Evid. R 101**

Hearsay, probable cause based on, **T 14:4**

Informant's statement, issuance upon, **T 14:4**

Issuance, **T 14:4**

Magistrate issuing, **T 14:4**

Probable cause, **T 14:4**

Totality of circumstances standard to determine probable cause, **T 14:4**

SEAT BELTS

Juveniles, violations of law, **T 28:7**

SECURITIES, PUBLIC

Detention homes, to finance, **ORC 2151.655**

SELF-INCRIMINATION

Generally, **Evid. R 608, T 1:3**

Adjudicatory hearings, **T 1:4, T 23:2, T 23:27**
    Identification procedures, privilege against inapplicable, **T 14:12**

Court's duty to inform unrepresented parties of, **T 23:27**

Neglect and dependency cases, applicability to, **T 23:27**

Parents unable to waive child's privilege against, **T 23:27**

Testimony, waiver by, **T 23:27**

Transfer hearing, testimony inadmissible at criminal proceeding, **T 22:14**

SENSE IMPRESSIONS

Generally, **Evid. R 803(1)**

SENTENCES

Blended sentences, serious youthful offender, **T 5:2**

Juveniles tried as adults, credit for time in juvenile custody, **T 22:22**

Suspension, adult cases tried in juvenile courts, **ORC 2151.49, 2151.50**

SERIOUS YOUTHFUL OFFENDER

Generally, **T 4:7, T 5:1**

Adjudicatory hearing, **T 5:6**

Adult sentences, **T 5:10 to T 5:12**

Appeals, **T 5:13**

Bail, procedural rights, **T 5:9**

Blended sentences, **T 5:2**

Defined, **ORC 2152.02(X)**

Discretionary SYO status, **ORC 2152.02(H), T 5:8**

Dispositional orders, **ORC 2152.13**

Enhancements, **T 5:5**

SERIOUS YOUTHFUL OFFENDER —continued

Grand jury indictment, procedural rights, **T 5:9**

Hearing, invoking adult sentence, **T 5:11**

Invoking adult sentences, **T 5:10 to T 5:12**

Mandatory SYO status, **T 5:7**

Mental competency procedure, **T 5:9**

Preliminary hearing, **T 5:3**

Procedural rights, **T 5:9**

Speedy trial, procedural rights, **T 5:9**

Subsequent procedures, **T 5:12**

Venue, **T 5:4**

SERVICE OF PROCESS

Generally, **Juv. R 16, Juv. R 20**

Affidavits
    Publication, by, **T 18:4**
    Time, **Juv. R 18(D)**

Appearance at hearing as waiver, **T 18:5**

Attorneys, on, **Juv. R 20(B)**

Certification of type of service required, **T 18:4**

Certified mail, by, **Juv. R 16(A), Juv. R 18(E), ORC 2151.28, 2151.29, T 18:4**

Civil rules of procedure governing, **T 18:4**

Clerks of courts, by, **ORC 2151.14**

Constables, by, **ORC 2151.14**

Electronic transmission, **Juv. R 8**

Methods, **Juv. R 16(A), ORC 2151.14, 2151.29, T 18:4**

Motions, time for, **Juv. R 18(D)**

Nonresidents, on, **Juv. R 16(A), ORC 2151.29**

Permanent custody
    Explanation of effect to be included, **ORC 2151.414(A), T 18:4**
    Waiver of service, **T 18:5**

Personal service, **Juv. R 16(A), T 18:4**

Probation officer, by, **ORC 2151.14**

Proof of service, **Juv. R 20(C)**
    Publication affidavit, **Juv. R 16(A)**

Publication, by, **Juv. R 16(A), ORC 2151.29, T 18:4**
    Affidavits filed with court, **T 18:4**
    Hearing, time for stated in publication, **T 18:4**
    Name or address of parent unknown, **T 16:8**
    Reasonable diligence to locate party, **T 18:4**

Residence service, **Juv. R 16(A), ORC 2151.29, T 18:4**

Sixteen years old, child younger than, **T 18:4**

Stipulation, waiver by, **T 18:5**

Subpoenas, **Juv. R 17(C), ORC 2151.28(J)**

Summons. See SUMMONS

Time requirements, **Juv. R 18(D)**

Waiver, **T 18:5**

Warrant for custody of child, **Juv. R 16(B)**

SETTLEMENTS

Offers as evidence, **Evid. R 408**

SEX OFFENDERS

Generally, **ORC 2152.82 et seq., T 6:1**

Address changes, registration requirements, **T 6:14**

Application of certain sections of revised code, **ORC 2152.191**

Child adjudicated as child delinquent for committing a sexually oriented offense, **ORC 2152.811**

Child-victim oriented offender, defined, **T 6:6**

Child-victim predator, defined, **T 6:8**

SEX OFFENDERS—*continued*

Communicable diseases, notice to victim of, **ORC 2151.14(C)**

Community notification requirements, **T 6:15**

Definitions, **ORC 2152.02(Y), T 6:2 to T 6:8**

Dispositional completion hearing, **T 6:12**

Dissemination via Internet of juvenile registrants, **T 6:16**

Effect of redesignation of offense on existing order, **ORC 2152.851**

Habitual child-victim oriented offender, defined, **T 6:7**

Habitual sex offender, defined, **T 6:3**

Internet dissemination of juvenile registrants, **T 6:16**

Juvenile delinquents
    Child adjudicated as for committing a sexually oriented offense, **ORC 2152.811**
    Indefinite term, **ORC 2151.355(A)**

Juvenile sex offender registrant
    Discretionary classification, **T 6:11**
    Dispositional order, **ORC 2152.82, ORC 2152.83**
    Hearing, **ORC 2152.83, ORC 2152.84**
    Mandatory classification, **T 6:10**
    Petitioning of judge by, **ORC 2152.85, T 6:13**
    Redesignation of offense on existing order, effect of, **ORC 2152.851**
    Repeat offender classification, **T 6:9**

Minor victims
    Deposition testimony, **T 23:16**
    Testimony of, **Juv. R 37, ORC 22:23, ORC 2151:351, T 23:16, T 23:23**

Notice to victim of communicable diseases, **ORC 2151.14(C)**

Notification requirements, **T 6:15**

Petitioning of judge by juvenile sex offender registrant, **ORC 2152.85, T 6:13**

Redesignation of offense on existing order, effect of, **ORC 2152.851**

Registration requirements, **T 6:14**

Residence limitation, residence near school, **T 6:17**

Sexual predator, defined, **T 6:4**

Sexually oriented offender, defined, **T 6:2**

Sexually oriented offense, defined, **ORC 2152.02(Y)**

Victims
    Crime witnesses, minor, as victims, **T 23:23**
    Deposition testimony, **T 23:16**
    Disposition of, **ORC 2152.81**
    Minor victims
        Deposition testimony, **T 23:16**
        Testimony of, **Juv. R 37, ORC 22:23, ORC 2151:351, T 23:16, T 23:23**

SEXUAL ABUSE

Abused child finding, basis for, **ORC 2151.031(A), T 9:13**

Adequate parental care lacking, factor in determination, **ORC 2151.414(E)**

Confrontation rights
    Face-to-face confrontation, right to, **T 23:23**

Definition, **T 9:13**

Deposition testimony, **T 23:16**
    Videotaped, **ORC 2151.3511**

Permanent custody. See PERMANENT CUSTODY, generally

Testimony, exception to hearsay rule, **Evid. R 807**

SEXUALLY ORIENTED MATERIAL

Pandering
    Delinquency charge resulting from, **T 4:4**

SHELTER CARE

Generally, **Juv. R 7, ORC 2151.31, 2151.311**

See also DETENTION AND DETENTION HOMES, for general provisions.

Adjudicatory hearing to determine placement, **ORC 2151.28(B)**

Complaints
    Time for filing, **T 16:4**

Court order for shelter care, **ORC 2151.31(C)**

Defined, **ORC 2151.011**

Definitions, **Juv. R 2(II), Juv. R 2(J), Juv. R 2(K)**

Detention homes distinguished from, **T 19:2**

Hearings, **ORC 2151.314**
    Definition, **Juv. R 2(K)**
    Determination of need for, **T 19:5**
    Findings of fact, **T 19:5**
    Motions for release, on, **T 19:5**
    Removal of child from home, reasonable effort to prevent, **T 25:14**
    Required, **T 20:4**
    Shelter care placement
        Probable cause for, **Juv. R 6(B), Juv. R 13(B), Juv. R 13(F)**
    Temporary custodian, appointment of, **T 19:5**

Motion for release from, **ORC 2151.314(B)**

Placement in
    Probable cause hearings, shelter care, **Juv. R 13(B)**

Release of child, **ORC 2151.314(B)**
    Motion for, **ORC 2151.314(B), T 19:5**

Temporary placement, **ORC 2151.33(B)**
    Motion for temporary custody following, **ORC 2151.33(C)**

SILENCE

Detention hearings, advising parties of rights prior to, **T 19:5**

Impeachment purposes, admissibility, **T 14:10**

Inadmissible as evidence of guilt, **T 23:27**

Right to, **T 1:3, T 22:14**
    Court's duty to inform unrepresented parties of, **T 23:27**

SIMILAR ACTS

Generally, **Evid. R 404**

SMALL CLAIMS COURTS

Evidence rules, exemption, **Evid. R 101**

SOCIAL HISTORIES

Abused children, **Juv. R 32(A)**

Adjudicatory hearings, admissibility, **Juv. R 32(B), T 23:16**

Commitment to youth services department, effect, **ORC 2151.355(F)**

Confidentiality, **T 35:2**

Cross-examination, **Juv. R 34(B)**

Definitions, **Juv. R 2(JJ)**

Dependent children, **Juv. R 32(A)**

Inspection, **Juv. R 32(C), T 21:6, T 22:15, T 25:10, T 35:2**

Limitations on use, **Juv. R 32(B)**

Neglected children, **Juv. R 32(A)**

Supplementing, **T 25:10**

Transfer of case for criminal proceeding, **Juv. R 32(A)**
    Access to, **T 22:15**
    Admissibility as evidence, **T 22:13**

SOCIAL HISTORIES—*continued*

Transfer of case to another county, **Juv. R 11(D)**, **ORC 2151.271**

Youth services department receiving upon commitment of child, **ORC 2151.355(F)**, **T 27:3**

SPECIAL ASSESSMENTS

See ASSESSMENTS, SPECIAL

SPEECH PATHOLOGISTS

Child abuse, reporting, **ORC 2151.99(B)**, **2151.421(A)**

SPEEDING TICKETS

Generally, **T 16:9**

SPEEDY TRIAL

Adjudicatory hearing, **Juv. R 29(A)**, **ORC 2151.28(A)**, **T 23:31**

Appeal by state from suppression of evidence, certification made in bad faith, **T 34:11**

Continuances, good cause, **T 23:31**

Detention, **Juv. R 7(F)**, **T 19:7**, **T 23:31**

Dismissal for failure to comply, **T 23:31**

Juveniles tried as adults, **T 23:31**
     Time tolls from date juvenile court relinquishes jurisdiction, **T 22:22**

Shelter care, **Juv. R 7(F)**, **T 19:7**, **T 23:31**

SPONTANEOUS EXCLAMATIONS

Generally, **Evid. R 803(2)**

SPOUSAL SUPPORT

Juvenile procedure rules, applicability, **Juv. R 1(C)**

Modification of award, juvenile court's jurisdiction, **ORC 2151.23(C)**

STANDARD JUVENILE COURT ACT

Generally, **T 1:6**

STANDING

See also PARTIES TO ACTIONS, generally

Appeals, **T 34:3**

Complaints, filing, **T 16:2**

Suppression of evidence, motion for, **T 14:2**

STATE AID

See APPROPRIATIONS

STATE DEPARTMENTS

Job and Family Services. See JOB AND FAMILY SERVICES, STATE

Youth services. See YOUTH SERVICES DEPARTMENT

STATE OF MIND

Generally, **Evid. R 803(3)**

STATUTES

Juvenile rules referring to, **Juv. R 43**

STAY OF EXECUTION

Generally, **T 34:6**

STOP AND FRISK

See PAT-DOWN SEARCH

SUBPOENAS

Generally, **Juv. R 17**, **ORC 2151.28(J)**

Contempt for noncompliance, **Juv. R 17(F)**, **T 33:8**

Contents, **Juv. R 17(A)**

SUBPOENAS—*continued*

Costs, **ORC 2151.19**
     Juvenile proceeding, **Juv. R 17(B)**

Depositions, for, **Juv. R 17(A)**

Discovery by, **T 21:5**

Failure to obey, **Juv. R 17(F)**

Format, **Juv. R 17(A)**

Hearings, for
     Juvenile proceeding, **Juv. R 17(A)**

Issuance, **Juv. R 17(A)**

Privileged information
     Withholding, **Juv. R 17(G)**

Records and reports, **Juv. R 17(A)**, **Juv. R 17(E)**

Responses, duties, **Juv. R 17(E)**

Sanctions, failure to obey, **Juv. R 17(F)**

Service, **Juv. R 17(C)**

Witnesses, **ORC 2151.28(J)**
     Attendance, **Juv. R 17(A)**
     Protection, **Juv. R 17(D)**
     Refusal to testify, **Juv. R 17(F)**

SUBPOENAS DUCES TECUM

Generally, **Juv. R 17(A)**, **Juv. R 17(E)**

SUMMONS

Generally, **Juv. R 15**, **ORC 2151.19, 2151.28**

Abortion, parental notification, **T 12:6**

Adoptive parents, prospective, **T 18:2**

Attorney, right to inclusion of statement concerning, **T 18:3**

Case plan, statement in summons, **T 18:3**

Child, issuance to, **ORC 2151.28(C)**, **T 18:2**
     Custody taken after service, **ORC 2151.28(G)**

Child abuse proceedings, **ORC 2151.28(A)**, **T 18:2**

Complaint
     Copy to accompany summons, **T 18:3**
     Summary statement of contained in summons, **T 18:3**

Contempt for failure to appear, **ORC 2151.28(J)**, **T 33:8**

Contents, **ORC 2151.28**, **T 18:3**

Costs, **ORC 2151.19**

Custodian, issuance to, **ORC 2151.28(C)**, **T 18:2**

Dependency and neglect proceedings, **ORC 2151.28(A)**, **T 18:2**

Endorsement with order for personal appearance, **ORC 2151.28(E)**, **T 18:3**

Failure to issue, effect on jurisdiction, **T 18:2**

Form, **Juv. R 15(A)**, **T 18:3**

Foster care, **T 18:2**
     Explaining effect of foster care, **T 18:3**
     Removal of unruly nonresident children, **Juv. R 15(B)**

Foster parent as party, **T 18:2**

Guardian, issuance to, **ORC 2151.28(A)**, **T 18:2**

Illegitimate child, proceedings concerning; issuance of summons to putative father, **T 18:2**

Incarcerated parent, **T 18:2**

Name of person with whom child resides, inclusion in, **T 18:3**

Noncustodial parent, issuance to, **T 18:2**

Parent, issuance to, **ORC 2151.28(C)**, **T 18:2**
     Foster parent as party, **T 18:2**
     Order to bring child to hearing, contempt for failure to comply, **T 33:8**
     Parent under eighteen years old, requirement, **ORC 2151.281(F)**

Permanent custody action, requirements, **ORC**

SUMMONS—*continued*

Parent, issuance to—*continued*
    2151.28(C), 2151.28(I), **T 18:3**
    Prospective adoptive parents, **T 18:2**

Parties required to receive, **ORC 2151.28(C)**, **T 18:2**

Permanent custody, explanation of effect required, **ORC 2151.28(D), 2151.28(I), T 18:3**

Prospective adoptive parents, **T 18:2**

Putative father, issuance to, **T 18:2**

Removal of unruly nonresident children residing in foster homes, actions by school superintendents for, **Juv. R 15(B), Juv. R 39(A), T 13:4**

Right to counsel, statement concerning included in, **ORC 2151.28, 2151.28(F), T 23:3**

Service, **Juv. R 16(A), ORC 2151.19, 2151.28, 2151.29, T 18:4**
    See also SERVICE OF PROCESS, generally.

Statute or ordinance violated, inclusion, **T 18:3**

Temporary custody; explanation of effect required, **ORC 2151.353(B), T 18:3**

Waiver, **ORC 2151.28(H)**

SUPERSEDEAS BONDS

Appeals, **T 34:7**

SUPPORT

See CHILD SUPPORT

SUPPRESSION OF EVIDENCE

Independent source for obtaining evidence, exception, **T 14:2**

Inevitable discovery rule, **T 14:2**

Motion granted, appeal by state, **Juv. R 22(D) to Juv. R 22(F), T 14:2, T 23:31**
    Appointment of attorney for indigent party, **T 34:10**
    Certification by prosecutor, **Juv. R 22(F), T 34:8**
    Prosecution following unsuccessful appeal, **T 34:8, T 34:11**
    Release of child from detention or shelter care pending appeal, **Juv. R 22(F), T 34:6**
    Speedy trial considerations, **Juv. R 22(F), T 34:8, T 34:11**

Standing, **T 14:2**

Taint diminished by intervening events, **T 14:2**

SUPREME COURT, STATE

Assignment of judges to juvenile courts, **ORC 2151.07**

Rulemaking powers for juvenile courts, **ORC 2151.17**

SUPREME COURT, UNITED STATES

Juvenile cases, **T 1:4**

SURETY BONDS

See BONDS, SURETY

SURGICAL TREATMENT

See MEDICAL TREATMENT

TAPE RECORDINGS

Evidence, as, **Evid. R 106**

TEACHERS

Child abuse, reporting, **ORC 2151.99(B), 2151.421(A)**

Juvenile rehabilitation facilities, **ORC 2151.653**

TEMPORARY CUSTODY

Abandoned children, **ORC 2151.413(B)**

TEMPORARY CUSTODY—*continued*

Abused children, **T 30:6**

Agreements, **T 11**
    Children services agencies, **T 11:3**
        Case plan, filing of, **T 11:4**
        Extension, **T 11:4**
    Extension, **T 11:4**
    Guardian ad litem, appointment in cases involving, **ORC 2151.281(G)**
    Jurisdiction, **ORC 2151.23(A), T 11:2**
    Payment for care, support, maintenance, and education of child, **ORC 2151.361**
    Without court approval, **T 11:3**

Alcohol treatment for parent, **ORC 2151.3514(B)**

Best interests of child, written findings of fact regarding, **ORC 2151.33(E)**

Case plans, **ORC 2151.412(A), T 26:2**
    Abused or neglected children
        Mandatory counseling for parents, **ORC 2151.412(H)**
        Supportive services, participation in by parents, **ORC 2151.412(H)**
    Goals, **ORC 2151.412(F)**

Children services agencies
    Commitment to as disposition of case, **ORC 2151.353(A)**
    Dispositional orders, motions for, **ORC 2151.415(A)**
    Pending outcome of adjudicatory and dispositional hearings, **T 20:5**
    Termination, **T 33:10**

Commitment of child to, **ORC 2151.353(A)**

Complaint, **Juv. R 10(E), T 16:14**

Continuing jurisdiction
    Duration, **T 33:4**
    Termination, **T 33:4**

Delinquency, disposition of case, **ORC 2151.355(A), T 27:3**

Dependent children, **T 30:6**

Dispositional orders, motions for, **ORC 2151.415(A), ORC 2152.19**

Drug treatment for parent, **ORC 2151.3514(B)**

Extension, **ORC 2151.415(D)**

Family-like setting, placement consistent with, **ORC 2151.33(F)**

Final order, **T 20:5, T 34:4**

Inadequate parental care, **T 9:6**

Job and Family Services, county or state; commitment of child as disposition of case, **ORC 2151.353**

Jurisdiction
    Agreements, **T 11:2**

Juvenile proceedings subsequent to temporary custody order, names and addresses of parents to be included on complaint, **T 16:8**

Motion for
    Temporary shelter care placement, following, **ORC 2151.33(C)**

Neglected children, **T 30:6**

Payment for care, support, maintenance, and education of child, **ORC 2151.361**

Permanent custody motion filed following award
    See also PERMANENT CUSTODY, generally.

Permanent custody motions, **ORC 2151.413(A), T 31:2**

Rehabilitation of family
    Annual report of agency efforts, **T 1:6**

Review hearings, **T 33:11**
    Orders, **ORC 2151.417(F)**

Right to counsel, **ORC 2151.353(B)**

TEMPORARY CUSTODY—*continued*

Summons, explanation of effect to be included, **ORC 2151.353(B), T 18:3**

Sunset date, **T 30:6**

Temporary orders, **ORC 2151.33(B)**

Termination, **ORC 2151.353(F)**

TEMPORARY ORDERS

Generally, **Juv. R 13, ORC 2151.33, T 20**

Ex parte proceedings, **ORC 2151.33(D)**

Hearings, **ORC 2151.33(D)**

Notice

    Ex parte proceedings, **ORC 2151.33(D)**

    Right to counsel, to contain statement concerning, **ORC 2151.33(C)**

Time limitations, **T 20:6**

Types of orders, **T 20:2**

Written findings of fact required, **ORC 2151.33(C)**

TERMINATION OF PARENTAL RIGHTS

See PERMANENT CUSTODY

TERRORISM

Dispositional orders, recovery of costs where offense constitutes act of terrorism, **ORC 2152.201**

TESTIMONY

See WITNESSES AND TESTIMONY

THEFT

Minor committing

    Parental liability, **T 32:2**

    Restitution as probation condition, **T 27:8**

Prior adjudication as element of delinquency, proof beyond reasonable doubt, **T 4:4**

TIME

Generally, **Juv. R 18**

Abandonment presumption, **T 9:3**

Computation, **Juv. R 18(A)**

Extension, **Juv. R 18(B), Juv. R 22(E)**

    Service by mail, after, **Juv. R 18(E)**

Speedy trial. See SPEEDY TRIAL

Term of court, effect of expiration, **Juv. R 18(C)**

TOBACCO PRODUCTS

Prohibitions relating to cigarettes and tobacco products, **ORC 2151.87**

TOMBSTONES

Inscriptions, hearsay exceptions, **Evid. R 803(13)**

TOWNSHIPS

Cooperation with juvenile courts, **ORC 2151.40**

TRAFFIC OFFENDERS, JUVENILE

Generally, **T 7**

Abuse, neglect or dependency investigation, **ORC 2151.141**

Adjudicatory hearing, **Juv. R 29(E), ORC 2151.35(A)**

Aggravated vehicular homicide, prosecution as delinquent, **T 7:4**

Appeals, **T 34:2**

Commitment of child, **T 28:6**

Community control, **T 28:11**

Complaints, **Juv. R 10, ORC 2151.27(A), 2151.27(B)**

    Oath not required, **T 16:6**

TRAFFIC OFFENDERS, JUVENILE —*continued*

Complaints—*continued*

    Statute or ordinance violated, designation, **T 16:7**

    Ticket as, **Juv. R 10(C), T 16:2, T 16:8**

Conflicts between juvenile rules of procedure and traffic rules, **T 1:8**

Court costs, **ORC 2151.54**

Court order, failure to comply; effect, **T 27**

Death resulting from juvenile's driving, determination as delinquency or traffic offense, **T 7:4**

Definition, **Juv. R 2(S), T 7:2**

Delinquency, determination of act as, **ORC 2151.356(A), T 7:4**

Detention, **ORC 2152.41, T 19**

    See also DETENTION AND DETENTION HOMES, generally.

Discharge, notice to committing court, **ORC 2151.358(B)**

Dismissal of action or complaint, **ORC 2151.35**

Disposition, **ORC 2151.356, ORC 2152.21**

Dockets, **ORC 2152.71(A), T 35:2**

Drivers' licenses

    Suspension or revocation, **ORC 2151.356(A), T 28:2**

    Probationary operator's license, **ORC 2151.356(B), T 28:8**

    Temporary instruction permit, **ORC 2151.356(B)**

Emergency medical care, **ORC 2151.33**

Expungement of records, **T 35:4**

Financial responsibility act, applicability, **T 28:3**

Fines, **T 28:3**

Foster homes as place of detention, **ORC 2151.331**

Intake. See INTAKE, generally

Jail commitment, **T 28:6**

Jurisdiction. See JURISDICTION

Juvenile Traffic Violations Bureau, **T 7:3**

Motor vehicle registration, suspension or revocation, **T 28:2**

Moving violations, **T 27**

Parental orders, **T 28:11**

Probation, **ORC 2151.356(A), T 28:4**

Probationary license, revocation, **T 28:8**

Reasonable doubt standard of proof, **T 23:13**

Records and reports

    Copies, providing, **ORC 2151.14(D), 2151.141**

Restitution ordered as disposition of case, **T 28:5**

Seat belt law, violations, **T 28:7**

Shelter care, **T 19**

    See also DETENTION AND DETENTION HOMES.

Speeding ticket, **T 16:9**

Speedy trial, **T 23:29**

Summons, **T 18**

    See also SUMMONS, generally.

Tickets

    Complaint as, **Juv. R 10(C), T 16:2, T 16:8**

    Contents, **T 16:7**

Vehicular homicide, prosecution as delinquent, **T 7:4**

Venue, **T 17:2, T 17:4**

Warrant, **Juv. R 15(E)**

TRANSCRIPTS

Adjudicatory hearings, **T 23:30**

Custody actions

    Institutional proceedings, **ORC 2151.35**

TRANSCRIPTS—*continued*

Dispositional hearings, **T 25:12**

Indigent persons, provision to, **T 23:30, T 34:9**
    Transfer of case for criminal proceedings, **T 22:18**

Juvenile proceedings, **ORC 2151.35**

Permanent custody proceedings, **ORC 2151.35, 2151.35(A), T 23:30, T 34:9**

Request for, **Juv. R 37(A), ORC 2151.35**

Restrictions, **Juv. R 37(B)**

Right to, **T 23:30, T 34:9**
    Transfer of case for criminal proceedings, **T 22:18**

Sua sponte motion, **Juv. R 37(A)**

Transfer of case for criminal proceedings, right to transcript, **T 22:18**

Use, **Juv. R 37(B), T 34:9**

TRANSFER FOR CRIMINAL PROSECUTION

Generally, **Juv. R 30, T 22**

Access to reports and discovery, **T 22:15**

Admissibility of evidence, **ORC 2151.358(H)**

Adult criminal court, transfer to, **T 4:7**

Age
    Factor in determining amenability to rehabilitation, **T 22:8**
    Fourteen or older at time of offense, **T 22:5**

Amenability to rehabilitation, **T 22:8**
    Attorney's duty to show, **T 22:11**
    Criminal court cannot consider after transfer made, **T 22:22**
    Factors to consider, **T 22:8, T 22:17**
    Findings of fact not required, **T 22:8, T 22:17**
    Hearing to determine, **T 22:8**
    Standard of proof, **T 22:12**

Appeals, **T 34**
    Age of majority attained prior to appeal, effect, **T 22:23**
    Conviction required, **T 22:23**
    Waiver not made by subsequent guilty plea, **T 22:22**

Bail, **T 22:25**

Child, defined
    Subsequent offenses, for purposes of, **T 2:3**

Complaints resulting in, statistical record, **ORC 2152.71(B)**

Completion of transfer, effect, **T 22:22**

Confrontation rights, **T 22:13**

Constitutionality, **T 22:1, 21:3**

Convicted offenders previously transferred, automatic criminal prosecution, **T 22:22**

Criteria for mandatory transfer, **T 22:6**

Delinquency adjudication precludes transfer, double jeopardy, **T 22:24, T 23:31**

Detention of child, **T 19:2, T 22:22**
    See also DETENTION AND DETENTION HOMES, generally.

Discovery rules, applicability, **T 22:15**

Discretionary, **Juv. R 30(C), T 22:8**
    Hearings, **T 22:8**
    Investigations, **T 22:8**
    Statutory factors, **T 22:8**

Dispositional orders. See JUVENILE COURTS

Double jeopardy, delinquency adjudication already made, **T 22:24, T 23:31**

Due process requirements, **T 1:4**

Effective assistance of counsel required, **T 22:11**

TRANSFER FOR CRIMINAL PROSECUTION—*continued*

Eligibility for
    Age
        Fourteen or older, **T 22:5**
        Time of offense controls, **T 22:5**
    Amenability to rehabilitation. See Amenability to rehabilitation, this heading
    Felony offenses, **T 22:8**
    IJA-ABA standards, **T 22:8**
    Mandatory transfer, **T 22:6**
    Public safety considerations, **T 22:8**

Evidence
    Admissibility, **ORC 2151.358(H)**
    Hearsay, admissibility, **T 22:13**
    Mental examinations, **Juv. R 30(C), T 22:10**
    Right to present, **T 22:16**
    Rules, applicability, **T 22:13**
    Social history admissible, **T 22:13**

Family environment, factor in determining amenability to rehabilitation, **T 22:8**

Felonies other than those subject of transfer hearing, effect, **T 22:22**

Fine imposed in juvenile court, transfer after, **T 27:12**

Future prosecutions, effect, **T 22:22**

Grand jury indictments not limited to charges filed in juvenile court, **T 22:22**

Guilty pleas in criminal proceedings, appeal from transfer decision not waived by, **T 22:22**

Hearings, **Juv. R 30(E), T 22:3, T 22:9**
    Attorney's duties, **T 22:11**
    Evidence. See Evidence, this heading
    Judge disqualification, **T 22:21, T 23:28**
    Notice, requirements, **Juv. R 30(D), T 22:12**
    Preliminary hearing, probable cause determination, **Juv. R 30(A), T 22:8**
    Right to counsel, **T 22:11**
    Self-incrimination privilege, testimony from transfer hearing inadmissible at criminal proceeding, **T 22:14**
    Transcript, right to, **T 22:18**

Hearsay, admissibility, **T 22:13**

IJA-ABA standards, **T 22:8**

Impartial judge, **T 22:20**

Improper transfer, effect, **T 22:4**

Indigent minors
    Appointment of counsel, **T 22:11**
    Transcript, right to, **T 22:18**

Investigation, **Juv. R 30(C)**

Jurisdiction of courts, **T 22:4**

Jurisdiction of juvenile courts, **Juv. R 30(E)**
    Transfer hearing judge as adjudicatory hearing judge, **T 22:21**
    Waiver, **T 2:3**

Juvenile court judges, survey of factors considered, **T 22:8**

Juvenile procedure rules, applicability, **Juv. R 1(C)**

Juvenile record
    Admissibility, **T 35:2, T 35:3**
    Factor in determining amenability to rehabilitation, **T 22:8**

Mandatory, **Juv. R 30(B), T 22:7**
    Eligibility for, **T 22:6**
    Hearings, **T 22:7**
    Investigations, **T 22:7**

Medical and mental examinations
    Waiver, **Juv. R 30(F)**

Medical reports, access, **T 22:15**

Mental and physical health, factor in determining amenability to rehabilitation, **T 22:8**

Mental examinations, **Juv. R 30(C), T 22:10**

TRANSFER FOR CRIMINAL PROSECUTION—*continued*

Motion to suppress, **T 22:26**

Murder committed by juvenile
Previously adjudicated delinquent, mandatory transfer, **T 22:7**

Notice of transfer hearing, requirements, **Juv. R 30, T 22:12**

Order of transfer, **Juv. R 30(G)**
Not final appealable order, **T 34:2, T 34:4**

Preliminary hearing, probable cause determination, **Juv. R 30(A), T 22:8**

Previous efforts to treat or rehabilitate, factor in determining amenability to rehabilitation, **T 22:8**

Probable cause requirements, **Juv. R 30(A), T 22:6**
Preliminary hearing, **Juv. R 30(A), T 22:8**

Public safety
Considerations, **T 22:8**
Standard of proof, **T 22:9**

Purpose
Right to counsel, **T 22:2**

Rationale, **T 22:2**

Records and reports, access, **T 22:15**
Juvenile record. See Juvenile record, this heading
Social histories. See Social histories, this heading

Release terms and conditions, **Juv. R 30(H), T 22:22**

Right to counsel, **T 22:11**

Safety of the community, effect, **T 22:8**

School record, factor in determining amenability to rehabilitation, **T 22:8**

Self-incrimination privilege, testimony from transfer hearing inadmissible at criminal proceeding, **T 22:14**

Sentences, credit for time in juvenile custody, **T 22:22**

Seriousness of offense, effect, **T 22:8**

Social histories, **T 22:8**
Access to, **T 22:15**
Transfer hearing, admissibility, **T 22:13**

Speedy trial, **T 23:29**
Right to attaches date juvenile court relinquishes jurisdiction, **T 22:22**

Standard of proof for transfer, **T 22:9**

Statement of reasons
Specificity requirements, **T 22:17**

Status of offender as child after conviction, **T 2:3**

Statutory factors, **T 22:8**

Subsequent conviction
Status of offender as child, **T 2:3**

Transcripts, right to, **T 22:18, T 23:30**

Transfer hearings. See Hearings, this heading

Venue, **T 17:4**

Victim's status, consideration in transfer decision, **T 22:8, T 32:3**

Waiver, **T 22:9**
Counsel, **T 22:11**
Examinations, **Juv. R 30(F)**

TRANSFER FROM MUNICIPAL, COUNTY, OR COMMON PLEAS COURT

Generally, **ORC 2152.03**

TRANSFER TO ANOTHER COUNTY

Generally, **Juv. R 11, ORC 2151.271, T 17:4**

Certification as complaint, **Juv. R 10(A), T 16:15**

Fine imposition, subsequent to, **T 27:12**

TRANSFER TO ANOTHER COUNTY
—*continued*

Removal of unruly nonresident children residing in foster homes, actions by school superintendents for, **Juv. R 11(B), T 13:3**

TRANSPORTATION COSTS

Generally, **ORC 2151.54**

TREATISES

Impeachment of witness, **Evid. R 706**

TRIALS

Jury trials. See JURY TRIALS

Preliminary questions, **Evid. R 104**

Transfer of jurisdiction for criminal prosecutions. See TRANSFER FOR CRIMINAL PROSECUTION

TRUANCY

Adjudicatory hearing, **T 23:32**

Chronic truant, defined, **ORC 2152.02(D)**

Complaint, **T 16:1**

Delinquent child dispositions, **T 27:16**

Unruly children, **ORC 2151.022(B), T 4:5, T 8:4, T 16:1, T 29:5**

TRUSTEES

Juvenile rehabilitation facilities, **ORC 2151.68 to 2151.75**

ULTIMATE ISSUE PROHIBITION

Generally, **Evid. R 704**

UNBORN CHILDREN

Pregnant woman refusing treatment resulting in court-ordered treatment, **T 9:7**

UNIFORM EXTRADITION ACT

Generally, **T 36:3**

UNIFORM RECIPROCAL ENFORCEMENT OF SUPPORT ACT

Juvenile court jurisdiction, **ORC 2151.23(B)**

UNRULY CHILDREN

Generally, **T 29**

Adjudicatory hearing, **Juv. R 29(E), ORC 2151.35(A)**

Alternative diversion programs, **ORC 2151.331**

Amenability to rehabilitation under unruly disposition lacking, disposition as delinquent, **ORC 2151.354(A), T 29:3**

Appeals, **T 34:2**

Apprehension, **ORC 2151.14, 2151.31, 2152.03**

Bail, **T 19:9**

Child labor laws, violation, **ORC 2151.022, T 8:7**

Commitment to custody of court, **ORC 2151.354(A)**

Complaints, **Juv. R 10(A), ORC 2151.27(A), 2151.27(B), T 16**

Contributing to, **ORC 2151.99(A), 2151.422 to 2151.54**

Court order violation by, review of original disposition order due to, **T 29:3**

Criminal associates, **ORC 2151.022(E), T 8:7**

Curfew violations, **T 8:6**

Custodian, failure to obey, **ORC 2151.022(A), T 8:2**

Definitions, **Juv. R 2(LL), ORC 2151.022, T 8:2**

Delinquent, disposition of child as, **ORC 2151.354(A), T 29:3**

UNRULY CHILDREN—*continued*
Deporting, **ORC 2151.022(C)**
Deportment, **T 8:2**
Detention homes, **T 19**
    See also DETENTION AND DETENTION
        HOMES, generally.
Disobedience, habitual, **ORC 2151.022(A), T 8:2**
Disposition, **ORC 2151.354(A), T 29, T 29:3**
    See also DISPOSITIONAL HEARINGS, gener-
        ally.
Disreputable places, frequenting, **ORC 2151.022(E),
    T 8:7**
Diversion programs. See DIVERSION PROGRAMS,
    generally
Drivers' licenses, suspension or revocation, **ORC
    2151.354(A), T 29:4**
    Probationary operator's license, **ORC
        2151.354(B), T 29:4**
    Temporary instruction permit, **ORC
        2151.354(B), T 29:4**
Drug or alcohol abuse counseling program, court-
    ordered participation in, **ORC 2151.354(B)**
Due process, applicability to proceedings, **T 23:2**
Employment in violation of law, **ORC 2151.022(F),
    T 8:7**
Endangering others, **ORC 2151.022(C), T 8:5**
Expungement of records. See EXPUNGEMENT OF
    RECORDS, generally
Failure to obey parents or guardian, **ORC
    2151.022(A), T 8:2**
Fingerprints. See FINGERPRINTS
Foster homes as place of detention, **ORC 2151.331**
Guardian, failure to obey, **ORC 2151.022(A), T 8:2**
Guardian ad litem, appointment, **ORC 2151.281,
    2151.281(A)**
Injuring others, **ORC 2151.022(C), T 8:5**
Intake. See INTAKE, generally
Interstate agreements, **ORC 2151.56 to 2151.61, T
    36:2**
Jurisdiction. See JURISDICTION
Law applicable to children, violation, **ORC
    2151.022(G), T 8:2**
Marriage without parental consent, **ORC
    2151.022(D), T 8:7**
Motion to review original disposition order, **T 29:3**
Motor vehicle registration, suspension or revocation,
    T 29:4
Not guilty determination, expungement of records,
    ORC 2151.358, T 35:4
Notice, motion to review original disposition order
    when child not amenable to treatment, **T 29:3**
Parents, failure to obey, **ORC 2151.022(A), T 8:2**
Pattern of misconduct required for finding, **T 8:3**
Photographs. See PHOTOGRAPHS
Probation, **ORC 2151.354(A), T 29:3**
    See also PROBATION, generally.
    Revocation, jurisdiction, **T 33:6**
    Violations regarded as delinquency, **T 4:4**
Reasonable doubt standard of proof, **T 23:13**
Removal of child from home, reasonable efforts to
    prevent, **T 25:14**
Review of original disposition order, motion for, **T
    29:3**
Sealing of records. See SEALING OF RECORDS
Sexual promiscuity, **ORC 2151.022(C)**
Shelter care, **T 19**
    See also DETENTION AND DETENTION
        HOMES, generally.

UNRULY CHILDREN—*continued*
Stay pending appeal, **T 34:6**
Summons, **T 18**
    See also SUMMONS, generally.
Teachers, failure to obey, **ORC 2151.022(A), T 8:2**
Treatment, child not amenable to; disposition as
    delinquent, **ORC 2151.354(A), T 29:3**
Truancy, **ORC 2151.022(B), T 4:5, T 8:4**
Truancy cases, **T 29:5**
Youth services department, commitment to not
    permitted, **T 29:2**

URINALYSIS
Drug testing of high school athletes, **T 14:6**

UTTERANCES, EXCITED
Generally, **Evid. R 803(2)**

VACATION OF JUDGMENTS
Fraud as grounds, **T 33:2**
Grounds, **T 33:2**
Jurisdiction lacking as grounds, **T 33:2**
Misrepresentation as grounds, **T 33:2**

VANDALISM
Parental liability, **T 32:2**

VEHICULAR HOMICIDE
Minor committing, prosecution as delinquent, **T 7:4**

VENUE
Abortion proceedings, **T 12:5**
Adjudicatory hearings, **T 17:4**
    Transfer of cases, **Juv. R 11, T 17:4**
Change of, **ORC 2151.271, T 17:4**
County of behavior's occurrence, **T 17:2**
Criminal prosecution, transfer of case for, **T 17:4**
    See also TRANSFER FOR CRIMINAL PROSE-
        CUTION, generally.
Disposition following adjudicatory hearing, transfer
    of case for, **T 17:4**
Fine, imposition; transfer following not permitted, **T
    17:4**
Juvenile proceedings, **ORC 2151.27(A)**
Move by parents or child, effect, **T 17:2**
    Change of venue following, **T 17:4**
Prejudicial error, proof of venue, **T 17:3**
Proceedings pending in other juvenile court, transfer
    to court of child's residence, **Juv. R 11(B), T 17:4**
Proof of venue, **T 17:3**
Records to accompany transfer of case, **Juv. R 11(D),
    T 17:4**
Removal of unruly nonresident children residing in
    foster homes, actions by school superintendents
    for, **Juv. R 10(A), T 13:3**
Residence of child, **Juv. R 11, T 17:2**
    Change in, transfer of case due to, **T 17:4**
Serious youthful offender, **T 5:4**
Transfer, **ORC 2151.271, T 17:4**
    See also TRANSFER TO ANOTHER
        COUNTY.

VERDICTS
Impeachment, testimony by jurors, **Evid. R 606**

VICTIMS OF CRIME
Age five or under
    Effect in cases of juvenile delinquents,
        2151.355(E), ORC 2152.12(C)

VICTIMS OF CRIME—*continued*

Age 65 or over
    Restitution ordered for, **ORC 2151.355(A), T 27:13**

Character evidence, admissibility, **Evid. R 404**

Developmentally disabled or mentally retarded victim, testimony of, **ORC 2152.821**

Handicapped persons, effect in juvenile delinquency cases, **2151.355(A), 2151.355(E), ORC 2152.12(C), T 32:3**

Impact statements, **ORC 2151.355(H), T 21:8, T 25:11**

Juvenile court records of delinquent child, attorney general obtaining, **T 35:2**

Juvenile delinquents committing crimes, **ORC 2152.12(C)**

Mediation with, as delinquency disposition, **T 27:20**

Mentally retarded or developmentally disabled victim, testimony of, **ORC 2152.821**

Notice, entitlement to restitution, **ORC 2151.355(G), T 32:3**

Physical harm
    Juvenile delinquents committing crimes, **ORC 2152.12(C)**

Reconciliation with, as delinquency disposition, **T 27:20**

Restitution, **ORC 2151.355(A), T 27:13, T 32:3**

Right to be present at proceedings, **ORC 2930.09**

Separation of witnesses, **T 23:17**

Sex crime witnesses, minor, as victims, **T 23:23**

Sex offense victims
    Crime witnesses, minor, as victims, **T 23:23**
    Disposition of, **ORC 2152.81**
    Minor victims
        Deposition testimony, **T 23:16**
        Testimony of, **Juv. R 37, ORC 22:23, ORC 2151:351, T 23:16, T 23:23**

Statement before disposition, **ORC 2930.14(A) et seq.**

Unborn children, jurisdiction, **T 2:2**

Witnesses, mentally retarded or developmentally disabled victim, **ORC 2152.821**

VIDEOTAPE RECORDING

Depositions
    Sex offenses, minor victims, **T 23:16**

Juvenile proceedings, **Juv. R 37**
    Minor sex offense victims, **ORC 2151.3511**

Minor sex offense victims
    Juvenile proceedings, **ORC 2151.3511**

Sex offense victims, minor, testimony of, **Juv. R 37, 22:23, ORC 2151:351, T 23:16, T 23:23**

VIOLENT CHARACTER OF DELINQUENTS

Foster caregiver disclosure, **ORC 2152.72**

VISITATION RIGHTS

Detention or shelter facilities, **Juv. R 7(J), T 19:3, T 19:10**

Temporary orders, **ORC 2151.33(B)**

VITAL STATISTICS

Hearsay exceptions, **Evid. R 803(9)**

VOIR DIRE

Minor witnesses, determining competency of, **T 23:18**

VOUCHER RULE

Generally, **Evid. R 607**

WAGES

See COMPENSATION

WAIVER

Examination of child, **Juv. R 30(F)**

Investigation of child, **T 22:9**

Rights of child, **Juv. R 3**
    Counsel. See RIGHT TO COUNSEL

Service of process, **T 18:5**

Transfer of child for criminal prosecution, **T 22:9**

WAIVER HEARINGS

See TRANSFER FOR CRIMINAL PROSECUTION

WARRANTLESS SEARCHES

Aerial surveillance, **T 14:4**

Arrest, incident to, **T 14:4**

Bank records, **T 14:4**

Caseworker, home visits by, **T 14:16**

Consent
    Authority to provide, **T 14:5**
    Parent, by, **T 14:5**
    School officials, by, **T 14:6**
    Voluntariness, **T 14:5**

DNA databases, **T 14:8**

Electronic surveillance, privacy expectation, **T 14:4**

Home visits by caseworker, applicability, **T 14:16**

Hot pursuit doctrine, **T 14:4**

Incident to arrest, **T 14:4**

Jail cells, **T 14:4**

Lockers, **T 14:6**

Motor vehicles. See MOTOR VEHICLES

Offices, privacy expectation, **T 14:4**

Open field exception, **T 14:4**

Ownership affecting parent's consent, **T 14:5**

Plain view doctrine, **T 14:4**

Privacy expectation, **T 14:4**

Probation officers, by, **T 14:7**

Residence, privacy expectation, **T 14:4**

School searches, **T 14:6**

Trash, searches of, **T 14:4**

WARRANTS

Arrests, **T 14:3**
    Evidence rules, applicability, **Evid. R 101**

Costs, **ORC 2151.19**

Custody of child, court taking, **Juv. R 15(D), Juv. R 15(E), Juv. R 16(B), ORC 2151.30, 2151.311(B), T 14:3**

Search warrants. See SEARCH WARRANTS

WAYWARD CHILDREN

See UNRULY CHILDREN

WEAPONS

Dangerous ordnances
    School premises, illegal conveyance or possession on
        Drivers' licenses, suspension or revocation, **ORC 2151.355(D)**

Firearms
    Commitment, additional, **T 16:8, T 27:3**
    Defined, **ORC 2152.02**

WEAPONS—*continued*
Firearms—*continued*
    Juvenile delinquents, possession, **ORC 2151.355(A)**
        Firearms specification, imposition of additional term of commitment, **T 16:8, T 27:3**
    School premises, illegal conveyance or possession on
        Drivers' licenses, suspension or revocation, **ORC 2151.355(D)**
Possession
    School premises, illegal conveyance or possession on
        Drivers' licenses, suspension or revocation, **ORC 2151.355(D)**
School premises
    Illegal conveyance or possession on
        Drivers' licenses, suspension or revocation, **ORC 2151.355(D)**
Serious youthful offender status, **T 5:5**

WELFARE DEPARTMENTS
See JOB AND FAMILY SERVICES, COUNTY
See JOB AND FAMILY SERVICES, STATE

WITNESSES AND TESTIMONY
Generally, **Juv. R 29(E), ORC 2151.28(J)**
Accomplice's testimony, corroboration requirement, **T 23:21**
Authentication, **Evid. R 901**
Calling by court, **Evid. R 614**
Child abuse victims, competency, **Juv. R 27(B)**
Competency. See COMPETENCY OF WITNESSES
Conduct of witness, **Evid. R 608**
Contempt. See CONTEMPT, generally
Convicted of crime, credibility as witness, **Evid. R 609**
Corroboration of accomplice's testimony required, **T 23:21**
Credibility of witness, **Evid. R 607 to Evid. R 610**
    Conviction of crime, **Evid. R 609**
    Hearsay declarant, **Evid. R 806**
Declarations against interest, concerning, **Evid. R 804(B)(3)**
Defendant as witness
    Preliminary matters, cross-examination limitations, **Evid. R 104**
Dependent or neglected children, competency, **Juv. R 27(B)**
Developmentally disabled or mentally retarded victim, **ORC 2152.821**
Examination, **Evid. R 611 to Evid. R 615**
    Court, by, **Evid. R 614**
Exclusion, **Evid. R 615**
Expert witnesses. See EXPERT WITNESSES
Expunged records, questions concerning, **ORC 2151.358(I)**
Failure to appear or answer, **Evid. R 804(A)(2), Evid. R 804(A)(5), ORC 2151.28(J), T 33:8**
Fees and costs, **Juv. R 17(C), ORC 2151.28(J)**
    Party unable to pay, **Juv. R 17(B)**
Former testimony, hearsay exception, **Evid. R 804(B)(1)**
Impeachment, **Evid. R 607 to Evid. R 610**
    See also IMPEACHMENT.
    Convicted of crime, **Evid. R 609**
    Learned treatises, **Evid. R 706**
Interpreters as witnesses, **Evid. R 604**
Judge as witness, competency, **Evid. R 605**

WITNESSES AND TESTIMONY —*continued*
Juror as witness, competency, **Evid. R 606**
Lay opinion testimony, **Evid. R 701**
    Ultimate issue prohibition, **Evid. R 704**
Magistrate, before, **Juv. R 40(C)**
Mentally retarded or developmentally disabled victim, **ORC 2152.821**
Minors as witnesses, **Evid. R 807**
    Competency, **Evid. R 601, Juv. R 27(B)**
Oaths, **Evid. R 603**
Opinion testimony. See OPINION TESTIMONY
Penalization by employer prohibited, **ORC 2151.211**
Personal knowledge of subject matter, **Evid. R 602**
Preliminary hearings, **Evid. R 804(B)(1)**
Preliminary questions, **Evid. R 104**
Prior inconsistent conduct, **Evid. R 613**
Prior statements, **Evid. R 613**
Prior testimony, hearsay exception, **Evid. R 804(B)(1)**
Privileges, **Evid. R 501**
Qualifications, **Evid. R 104**
Refreshing recollection, **Evid. R 612**
Self-incrimination. See SELF-INCRIMINATION
Separation of witnesses, **Juv. R 29(E), T 23:17**
    Parents as parties to juvenile proceedings, exception, **T 23:17**
Sequestration, **Evid. R 615**
Sex crime witnesses, minor, as victims, **T 23:23**
Sex offense victims, minor, testimony of, **Juv. R 37, ORC 2151:351, T 23:16, T 23:23**
Transfer hearing testimony inadmissible at criminal proceeding or adjudicatory hearing, **T 22:14**
Unavailable witnesses, **Evid. R 804(A)**
Victims, separation of witnesses, **T 23:17**
Writings used to refresh memory, **Evid. R 612**
Written, **Evid. R 1007**

WRITINGS
Generally, **Evid. R 1001 to Evid. R 1007**
Definitions, **Evid. R 1001**
Disclosure, **Evid. R 106**
Duplicate, admissibility, **Evid. R 1003**
Original, **Evid. R 1002**
    Defined, **Evid. R 1001**
    Lost or destroyed, **Evid. R 1004**
Witnesses using to refresh memory, **Evid. R 612**

WRITS OF PROHIBITION
See PROHIBITION WRITS

YOUTH SERVICES DEPARTMENT
Generally, **ORC 2151.38, 2151.355, T 1:6, T 27:3**
Appropriations to, **T 15:3**
Certification to committing court of child's release from custody, **T 33:9**
Child's motion for early release, **ORC 2151.38(B), T 33:9**
Cigarettes, prohibitions relating to cigarettes and tobacco products, **ORC 2151.87**
Commitment of child to, **ORC 2151.355(A)**
    Consecutive commitments, **T 27:3**
    Credit for jail time served, **T 27:3**
    Discharge
        Minimum term of institutionalization, **ORC 2151.38(B)**
        Multiple offenses, consecutive terms, **ORC 2151.38(B)**

YOUTH SERVICES DEPARTMENT
—continued
Commitment of child to—*continued*
    Dispositional orders, **ORC 2152.16**
    Early release, **ORC 2151.38(B), T 33:9**
    Juveniles guilty of felonies or murders, **ORC 2151.355(A)**
        Early release, **ORC 2151.38(B)**
    Minimum period, **ORC 2151.38(A), 2151.38(B)**
    Suspended commitment orders, reinstatement of, **T 33:7**
    Termination of commitment, **ORC 2151.38(A)**
    Termination of court's jurisdiction, **ORC 2151.38(A), T 33:5, T 33:9**
Degree of violation
    Duration of commitment affected by, **ORC 2151.355(A), T 27:3**
    Providing to department upon commitment of child, **ORC 2151.38(C), T 27:3**
Dispositional orders
    Commitment of delinquent children to custody of youth services department, **ORC 2152.16**
Early release, **ORC 2151.38(B), T 33:9**
Effect of commitment to, **T 33:9**
Felony committed by juvenile, institutionalization due to, **ORC 2151.355(A), T 27:3**
    Early release, **ORC 2151.38(A), 2151.38(B)**
Foster care placement of children
    Early release, following, **ORC 2151.38(B), T 33:9**
    Funding, **T 15:3**
    Minimum time for commitment served, following, **ORC 2151.38(C), T 33:9**
Funding of programs, **T 15:3**
Hearings on release, **ORC 2151.38(B), 2151.38(C), T 33:9**
    Request for early release, **ORC 2151.38(C)**
Institutions, reporting requirements, **ORC 2151.37, 2151.40, 2151.355(F), T 27:3**
    Specific institution not designated by committing court, **ORC 2151.355(F), T 27:3**
Judicial release, **T 33:9**
Juvenile rehabilitation facilities, **ORC 2151.651**
Medical records, receiving upon commitment of child, **ORC 2151.355(F), T 27:3**
Medical release, **T 33:9**
Minimum period of commitment, **ORC 2151.38(A), 2151.38(B), T 33:9**
Notice to committing court termination of department custody, **ORC 2151.38(C), 2151.358(B), T 33:9**
Parents, release of child to, **ORC 2151.38(A) to 2151.38(C), T 33:9**
    Minimum time for commitment served, following, **ORC 2151.38(C)**
Parole, releasing child on
    Early release, following, **ORC 2151.38(B)**
    Minimum time for commitment served, following, **ORC 2151.38(C)**
Probation, supervision of child released from, **T 27:8**
Records and reports
    Institutional record of child, to juvenile court, **ORC 2151.37, 2151.40, 2151.355(F), T 27:3**
    Medical records, department to receive upon commitment of child, **ORC 2151.355(F), T 27:3**
    Progress reports on children released from custody, **ORC 2151.38(E), 2151.38(F)**
    Rehabilitation plan of children released from custody, **ORC 2151.38(C) to 2151.38(E), T 33:9**
    Release of child, reports to committing court, **T 33:9**

YOUTH SERVICES DEPARTMENT
—continued
Records and reports—*continued*
    School transcript of released child, **ORC 2151.355(F)**
Refusal to accept committed child, prohibition, **ORC 2151.355(F)**
Rehabilitation plan prior to release of children from institutions, **ORC 2151.38(C), 2151.38(D), T 33:9**
Release authority
    Defined, **ORC 2151.38(G)**
    Judicial release, hearings on, **ORC 2151.38(B)**
    Request for early release
        Hearings, **ORC 2151.38(C)**
    Terms and conditions of release, **ORC 2151.38(B)**
        Copy to court in child's new locale, **ORC 2151.38(B)**
Release of children, **ORC 2151.38(A) to 2151.38(C), T 33:9**
    Early release, **ORC 2151.38(B), T 33:9**
        Juveniles guilty of felonies or murder, **ORC 2151.38(B)**
    Juvenile court hearing, **ORC 2151.38(B), 2151.38(C), T 33:9**
    Minimum term of institutionalization, **ORC 2151.38(A), 2151.38(B)**
    Multiple offenses, consecutive terms, **ORC 2151.38(B)**
    Notice to committing court, **ORC 2151.38(B), 2151.38(C), 2151.358(B), T 33:9**
    Rehabilitation plan, **ORC 2151.38(C) to 2151.38(E), T 33:9**
    School transcript, transmittal to juvenile court and school, **ORC 2151.355(F), T 27:3**
    Sealing of records, **T 35:4**
    Violation of terms of release, **ORC 2151.38(B) to 2151.38(D), T 33:9**
Return to custody due to violation of terms of release, **ORC 2151.38(B) to 2151.38(D), T 33:9**
School attended by child
    Judgment entry ordering commitment sent to school, **ORC 2151.355(F), T 27:3**
    Release of child from commitment, updated transcript provided to child's prior school, **ORC 2151.355(F), T 27:3**
    Transcripts provided to department upon commitment of child, **ORC 2151.355(F), T 27:3**
Sealing of records, **T 35:4**
Statute violated by delinquent child, providing to department upon commitment of child, **ORC 2151.38(C), T 27:3**
Sua sponte motion for early release of child, **ORC 2151.38(B), T 33:9**
Supervised release
    Defined, **ORC 2151.38(G)**
Tobacco products, prohibitions relating to cigarettes and tobacco products, **ORC 2151.87**
Treatment plan for child pursuant to release, **ORC 2151.38(B), 2151.38(C), 2151.38(E), T 33:9**
Unruly children, commitment not permitted, **T 29:2**
Violation of terms of release, **ORC 2151.38(B) to 2151.38(D), T 33:9**
Youth smoking education program
    Prohibitions relating to cigarettes and tobacco products, **ORC 2151.87**

YOUTH SMOKING EDUCATION PROGRAM

Prohibitions relating to cigarettes and tobacco products, **ORC 2151.87**

YOUTHS
See JUVENILES

ZONING
Foster homes
    Residential use of property, considered, **ORC**
    2151.418